Encyclopedia of

HISTORIANS

AND

HISTORICAL WRITING

Volume I

Encyclopedia of

HISTORIANS

AND

HISTORICAL WRITING

Volume 1
A–L

Editor
KELLY BOYD

FITZROY DEARBORN PUBLISHERS
LONDON   CHICAGO

British Library Cataloguing in Publication Data
Encyclopedia of historians and historical writing
　　1. Historians – Encyclopedias
　　I. Boyd, Kelly
　　907.2′02

ISBN 1–884964–33–8

Library of Congress Cataloging in Publication Data is available.

First published in the USA and UK 1999

Typeset by The Florence Group, Stoodleigh, Devon
Printed by Vail-Ballou Press, Binghamton, New York

Cover design by Philip Lewis

CONTENTS

EDITOR'S NOTE

The *Encyclopedia of Historians and Historical Writing* provides a guide to influential historians and historical debates since the writing of history began. It is distinctive because it goes beyond the Western historical canon to include writers from other cultures and traditions. The selection of historians and topics was achieved with the help of the distinguished group of Advisers (listed on page xi) who enabled me to construct a list of entries. Contributors were also generous with their suggestions.

The volume contains three types of essays. First, essays on *individual historians* assess their scholarly achievements and place their writings in the context of historiographical developments and debates. Accompanying each essay is a brief biographical sketch, a list of principal writings, and suggestions for further reading about the historian's work. These are not exhaustive lists, but are meant to provide further opportunities for exploration by the reader. The individuals chosen were, as a rule, born no later than 1945. This admittedly arbitrary date was selected in order to focus the volume on the work of scholars who, at the time the list was constructed, had reached the age of 50 and had produced a substantial body of significant work. Many scholars born after 1945 merit inclusion, but they will have to wait for the next edition. Also included are a number of non-historians whose work has greatly influenced historical writing, for example Clifford Geertz and Jürgen Habermas.

A second category of essays focuses on *nations* or *geographical regions*. These articles provide a survey of the debates around historiographical questions within national histories. Some nations – for example Britain, France, Germany, Russia, and the United States – receive multiple entries to reflect their extended historical traditions. Other areas of the world are treated sometimes as regions (Southeast Asia, Latin America, Central Europe, Pacific/Oceanic, Indian Ocean) and sometimes as distinct nations (Brazil, Cuba, Australia, Japan). China is represented by two types of essay. One offers a consideration of the rich tradition of historical writing in China since ancient times, while the other examines the historiographical debates that have engaged later historians of the Chinese past. There are also essays on the development of historical thinking in medieval, Renaissance, and Enlightenment Europe. Each essay is accompanied by an extensive bibliography which, although accenting English-language contributions, also includes important works in other languages.

The final category includes *topical* essays. These in turn take three forms. One set of essays focuses on the various historical subdisciplines, such as social or agricultural history, and traces their emergence and distinctive features. A second set examines methods that shape historical writing, such as prosopography, or, in a different vein, the use of computers. A third introduces the reader to some of the most-studied historical debates, for example on the Industrial Revolution or slavery. Where appropriate, contributors move beyond the boundaries of individual nations and cultures. The accompanying bibliographies contain information that helps to widen access to these topics.

All entries include bibliographical material. In the Principal Writings list in each entry on an individual historian, titles are given in the language (and with the date) of first publication, followed by the title and date of first publication in English. Later translations are noted if there was a major revision, but the publishing history of individual volumes is not the focus of this encyclopedia. The Further Reading sections have a similar format, with fuller publication details. The Further Reading lists were, as a rule, provided by the contributor. In both sections, if there is no published English-language translation, a literal translation is given.

The entries are arranged alphabetically. Where there are several entries sharing the same general heading (e.g., China), the suborder is chronological. For ease of use there are several other reference aids. There is a Thematic List at the beginning of both volumes to identify different categories, for example, historians of France. There is also a Chronological List of historians to help indicate different generations of writers. There are two indexes. The Title Index (page 1357) is meant for use with entries on individual historians, and allows readers to find an author via a title. The Further Reading Index (page 1411) is arranged by author and allows the reader to identify the different entries that place in context a great number of works by a great many historians. This is especially useful for tracing the work of historians who do not have an individual entry. For example, Lyndal Roper's work is cited in the bibliographies of both the entry on the Reformation and that on Sexuality; consulting these entries shows the context in which she works. Finally, most entries have a *See also* list that points the reader to other entries in which a historian or topic is discussed.

This project was originally envisaged as a 1-volume encyclopedia, but the vibrancy of historical writing demanded more space. There is, of course, more to say, but two volumes should keep readers occupied for some time. This work is not designed for the specialist – though I hope specialists will find useful material here – but for the informed reader who wants to know more about how to approach particular writers or topics. From Herodotus to Simon Schama, from Archaeology to Technology, from the Marxist Interpretation to Postmodernism, the *Encyclopedia of Historians and Historical Writing* is a guide to the discipline on the eve of the third millennium.

Acknowledgments

These volumes would not have been possible without the help of several individuals and institutions. First, there were the advisers, who engaged with my suggestions for entries, proposed improvements, recommended appropriate contributors, and sometimes took on entries themselves. In addition, there are almost 400 contributors, many of whom I feel I have come to know well, at least via e-mail. They responded to my queries and criticisms with grace and alacrity and offered suggestions and support throughout the gestation of the project. Of the contributors I would particularly like to thank Priscilla Roberts, who responded to my requests for yet another essay too many times to count.

Second, I would like to thank my friends and colleagues at the Institute of Historical Research, University of London and at Middlesex University who, in the early stages, indulged me in endless conversations about who and what to include, and, in later stages, allowed me to persuade them to become contributors, or simply offered ongoing moral support as the project drew to a close. They include Michael Armstrong, Meg Arnot, Richard Baxell, Stuart Carroll, Anna Davin, Anne Goldgar, Tim Hitchcock, Caroline Johns, Vivien Miller, Martine Morris, Gareth Prosser, Heather Shore, John Styles, Keith Surridge, Cornelie Usborne, Amanda Vickery, Tim Wales, and Glen Wilkinson. I am particularly grateful to the staffs of the Institute of Historical Research and the Senate House Library of the University of London who provided me with the facilities for much of the research for the biographical and bibliographical portions of the book. The policy of the Institute of Historical Research of opening on Saturday and most holidays was immensely helpful.

Third, I would like to thank Daniel Kirkpatrick at Fitzroy Dearborn. His continuing patience, good sense, and, most importantly, his encouraging me to develop the encyclopedia beyond its initial remit kept me going. He has made the editing of this volume an intellectually stimulating and a genuinely enjoyable experience. I am particularly grateful for the space he gave me during much of the project and the intense attention he lavished on it in the final stages. I must also acknowledge the help I received from others at the press over the years, particularly Mark Hawkins-Dady, Lesley Henderson, and Carol Jones, but also those who were dragooned into working on the mammoth indexes. Delia Gaze, Jackie Griffin, Jane Samson, and Heather Shore also worked on the project as, variously, proofreaders, research assistants, and list constructors.

Finally, I must thank my husband, Rohan McWilliam. The project excited him from the beginning and he never tired of discussing the opportunities implicit in it. When my energy flagged, he rejuvenated it. When contributors dropped out, he graciously agreed to write one more essay, despite his own publishing commitments. Most importantly, he kept me intellectually engaged. I can never repay this debt.

KELLY BOYD
Middlesex University, 1999

ADVISERS

David Arnold
T.H. Barrett
Carl Berger
Paul Buhle
Richard W. Bulliet
R.J. Crampton
Geoff Eley
J.H. Elliott
Donna J. Guy
John Hirst

Nicholas Jardine
James M. McPherson
P.J. Marshall
Ali A. Mazrui
Janet L. Nelson
Richard Pipes
Terence O. Ranger
Anthony Reid
F.W. Walbank

CONTRIBUTORS

Andrew J. Abalahin
Phillip C. Adamo
David Allan
Michael Almond-Welton
Edward A. Alpers
David Arnold
Margaret L. Arnot
William Ashworth
Brenda Assael
Samira Ali Atallah
Raphaela Averkorn

Virginia R. Bainbridge
János M. Bak
Oscar Julian Bardeci
John W. Barker
Robert E. Barnett
T.H. Barrett
Jonathan Barry
Paul Barton-Kriese

Robert P. Batchelor
Gábor Bátonyi
Richard Baxell
Jonathan Beecher
Charlotte Behr
Maxine Berg
Christopher Berkeley
Theodore Binnema
Jeremy Black
Lee Blackwood
Vivian Blaxell
Laurie Robyn Blumberg
Stuart Blyth
Lori Lyn Bogle
Geoffrey Bolton
Dain Borges
Hugh Bowden
Kelly Boyd
James M. Boyden
Clara Brakel-Papenhuyzen

Yuri Bregel
Ernst Breisach
Michael Brett
Ralf Bröer
Marilynne Bromley
Kenneth D. Brown
Daniel Brownstein
Gary S. Bruce
Jon L. Brudvig
Gayle K. Brunelle
Maurice P. Brungardt
Glenn E. Bugos
Paul Buhle
Michael Burns
David T. Burrell
Annarita Buttafuoco

I.A. Caldwell
Jean Calmard
Kenneth R. Calvert
Marybeth Carlson
Catherine Carmichael
Gennaro Carotenuto
Stuart Carroll
Dipesh Chakrabarty
Kathleen Egan Chamberlain
Chun-shu Chang
Stephen K. Chenault
Yeong-han Cheong
Yŏng-ho Choe
John Chryssavgis
Emily Clark
Inga Clendinnen
Cecil H. Clough
Ken Coates
Adam Cobb
Alvin P. Cohen
Roger Collins
Kathleen Comerford
Demetrios J. Constantelos
Lauren Coodley
Hera Cook
Timothy P. Coon
Douglas Cremer
Brian Crim
Geoff Cunfer
Patrick Curry

Ubiratan D'Ambrosio
Belinda Davis
Dennis A. Deslippe
John A. Dickinson
Gerald Diesener
Frank Dikötter
Roy Palmer Domenico
Mark Richard Dorsett
Richard Drake
Lincoln A. Draper
Erika Dreifus
Seymour Drescher

John Dunne
Eric R. Dursteler
Carl Dyke

Nancy Pippen Eckerman
Anthony O. Edmonds
Elizabeth B. Elliot-Meisel
Linda Eikmeier Endersby
Amy Louise Erickson
Maria Elina Estebanez
J.A.S. Evans
Jennifer V. Evans
Philip Evanson
Nicholas Everett

Toyin Falola
Lee A. Farrow
Susan Fast
Silvia Figueirôa
Annette Finley-Croswhite
James Fisher
Michael H. Fisher
Brian H. Fletcher
John F. Flynn
Robert F. Forrest
John Bellamy Foster
Robert Wallace Foster
Billy Frank
James E. Franklin
James Friguglietti
Richard Frucht
Patrick J. Furlong

Nancy Gallagher
Kathleen E. Garay
Anna Geifman
Gene George
Daniel M. German
Peter Ghosh
Peter Gibbons
Sheridan Gilley
Stephen D. Girvin
Thomas F. Glick
Brian Gobbett
Jacqueline Goggin
Robert Goodrich
Piotr Górecki
Eliga H. Gould
Dmitry A. Goutnov
Jeanine Graham
Jonathan A. Grant
Christopher Gray
Jay D. Green
Ronald J. Grele
Rita Gudermann
Hugh L. Guilderson

John Haag
Bertil Häggman
H. Hazel Hahn

Drew Philip Halevy
Stephen Gilroy Hall
Christine S. Hallas
Rick Halpern
G.M. Hamburg
Milan Hauner
Michael Haynes
J.S.W. Helt
A.C. Hepburn
Arne Hessenbruch
Martin Hewitt
Tim Hitchcock
Daniel L. Hoffman
Sandie Holguín
Peter C. Holloran
Roger Hood
John Hooper
Fred Hoover
Mark J. Hudson
Pat Hudson
Patrick H. Hutton

Juliet Graver Istrabadi

Louise Ainsley Jackson
Margaret D. Jacobs
Dominic Janes
Kyle Jantzen
Jennifer W. Jay
M.A. Jazayery
Madeleine Jeay
Keith Jenkins
Lionel Jensen
William T. Johnson
Robert D. Johnston
Colin Jones
Davis D. Joyce

Thomas E. Kaiser
Aristotle A. Kallis
Simon Katzenellenbogen
Nikki R. Keddie
Sean Kelsey
Helen King
Dennis B. Klein
Louis A. Knafla
Franklin W. Knight
Dorothy Ko
Martin Kramer

Robert A. LaFleur
Andrew Lambert
Peter A. Lambert
Michelle A. Laughran
Ross Laurie
David D. Lee
Gary P. Leupp
Anthony Levi
Ernest A. LeVos
Gwynne Lewis

Li Tana
Helen Liebel-Weckowicz
Felice Lifshitz
Craig A. Lockard
Chris Lorenz
Lucas J. Luchilo
Erik A. Lund

Ian McBride
Lawrence W. McBride
Joseph M. McCarthy
Jennifer Davis McDaid
Ken McPherson
Rohan McWilliam
Joseph Maiolo
Iskandar Mansour
P.J. Marshall
Geoffrey H. Martin
R.N.D. Martin
Herbert W. Mason
Saho Matsumoto
Allan Megill
David A. Meier
Martin R. Menke
Sharon D. Michalove
Francine Michaud
Dean Miller
Joseph C. Miller
James Millhorn
Matthew A. Minichillo
R. Scott Moore
John Moorhead
Seán Farrell Moran
Gwenda Morgan
Martine Bondois Morris
William Morrison
John A. Moses
J. Todd Moye
James M. Murray

Caryn E. Neumann
Helen J. Nicholson
Myron C. Noonkester

Michael L. Oberg
Robert Olson
David Ortiz, Jr.

Donald R. Palm
Bryan D. Palmer
Rekha Pande
Peter J. Parish
Inderjeet Parmar
Robert Pascoe
Joseph F. Patrouch
Frederik J.G. Pedersen
Douglas Peers
William A. Pelz
Carlos Pérez
John R. Perry

Matt Perry
Indira Viswanathan Peterson
Gregory M. Pfitzer
Christopher Phelps
Daniel J. Philippon
Keith H. Pickus
Katherine Pinnock
Dmitri Polikanov
Joy Porter
Gareth Prosser

Karen Racine
John Radzilowski
Ruggero Ranieri
David Reher
John G. Reid
Chad Reimer
Thomas Reimer
Thomas D. Reins
David Reisman
Timothy Reuter
Lucy Riall
Paul John Rich
Eric Richards
Peter G. Riddell
Ronald T. Ridley
Edward J. Rielly
Andrew Rippin
Harry Ritter
Cristina Rivera-Garza
Priscilla M. Roberts
Kristen D. Robinson
Adam W. Rome
Tom I. Romero II
W.D. Rubinstein
Ronald Rudin
Guido Ruggiero
Peter Rushton

Jennifer E. Salahub
Janos Salamon
Frank A. Salamone
Gloria Ibrahim Saliba
Joyce E. Salisbury
Jane Samson
Thomas Sanders
Christopher Saunders
Birgit Sawyer
Thomas Schlich
Frank Schuurmans
Bill Schwarz
Jutta Schwarzkopf
Joanne Scott
Tom Scott
Christopher MacGregor Scribner
John Seed
Sara Ann Sewell
Pamela Sharpe
Kathleen Sheldon
Todd David Shepard

Susan Shifrin
Charles Shively
Margaret Shkimba
Mona L. Siegel
Tom Sjöblom
Russell C. Smandych
John David Smith
Alvin Y. So
Richard J. Soderlund
Robert Fairbairn Southard
Daniela Spenser
David B. Starr
Amy Stevens
Raymond G. Stokes
Dennis Stoutenburg
Carl Strikwerda
K.J. Stringer
Benedikt Stuchtey
Gavin A. Sundwall
Keith Surridge
Guillaume de Syon
Tamás Szmrecsányi

De-min Tao
H. Micheal Tarver
Elizabeth A. Ten Dyke
Jack Ray Thomas
Bruce Thompson
Joel E. Tishken
John Tonkin
Francesca Trivellato
Kathleen Troup
Brett Troyan

Cornelie Usborne

Wray Vamplew
Elizabeth T. Van Beek
Jonathan F. Vance
Ruud van Dijk
Kevern J. Verney
Angela Vietto

William T. Walker
Carl Watkins
David Robin Watson
Deirdre Chase Weaver
Diana Webb
Gregory Weeks
Jessica Weiss
John D. Windhausen
Edward M. Wise
Ronald G. Witt
Don J. Wyatt

Xiao-bin Ji

Edwin M. Yamauchi
Ying-shih Yu

Matthias Zimmer

ALPHABETICAL
LIST OF ENTRIES

THEMATIC LIST

Entries by Category

REGIONS AND PERIODS

Africa
Ancient World
Asia
    1) China
    2) India
    3) Japan and Korea
    4) Middle East
    5) Southeast Asia and Australasia
Byzantium
Europe
    1) Medieval
    2) Early Modern and Modern
    3) Britain

    4) Eastern and Central
    5) France
    6) Germany
    7) Ireland
    8) Italy
    9) Low Countries
    10) Russia and Central Asia
    11) Scandinavia
    12) Spain and Portugal
North and South America
    1) Canada
    2) Latin America
    3) United States

TOPICS

Art History
Cultural History
Demographic History
Diplomatic History
Economic History
Intellectual History
Jewish History
Legal History

Military History
Periods, Themes, Branches of History
Political History
Religion
Science, Medicine, Technology, and Ecology
Social History
Theories and Theorists
Women's and Gender History

REGIONS AND PERIODS

Africa

Afigbo, A.E.
Africa entries
African Diaspora
Ajayi, Jacob F. Ade
Ayandele, Emmanuel Ayankami
Bernal, Martin
Boahen, A. Adu
Coquery-Vidrovitch, Catherine
Davidson, Basil
Diop, Cheikh Anta

Egypt: since the 7th Century CE
Feierman, Steven
Gallagher, John
Gsell, Stéphane
Hargreaves, John D.
Iliffe, John
Julien, Charles-André
Laroui, Abdallah
Lovejoy, Paul E.
Marks, Shula

Mazrui, Ali A.
Ogot, Bethwell A.
Oliver, Roland
Ranger, Terence O.
Rodney, Walter
South Africa
Thompson, Leonard
Vansina, Jan

Ancient World

Ammianus Marcellinus
Bauer, Walter
Beloch, Karl Julius
Bernal, Martin
Breasted, James Henry
Brown, Peter
Caesar, Julius
Cassiodorus
Cassius Dio
Daube, David
Diodorus Siculus
Dionysius of Halicarnassus
Droysen, J.G.
Egypt: Ancient
Eusebius of Caesarea

Finley, M.I.
Fustel de Coulanges, Numa
Gibbon, Edward
Greece: Ancient
Herodotus
Jones, A.H.M.
Josephus
Livy
Meyer, Eduard
Momigliano, Arnaldo
Mommsen, Theodor
Near East: Ancient
Niebuhr, B.G.
Plutarch
Polybius

Roman Empire
Rostovtzeff, M.I.
Sallust
Sanctis, Gaetano de
Scriptores Historiae Augustae
Suetonius
Syme, Ronald
Tacitus
Thucydides
Velleius Paterculus
Vernant, Jean-Pierre
Watson, Alan
Wilamowitz-Möllendorff, Ulrich von
Xenophon

Asia : 1) China

Ban Gu
Chen Yinke
China entries
China: Historical Writing entries
Eberhard, Wolfram
Fairbank, John K.
Gu Jiegang

Kong-zi
Liang Qichao
Liu Zhiji
Ma Huan
Maspero, Henri
Mongol Empire
Naitō Torajirō

Needham, Joseph
Pelliot, Paul
Sima Guang
Sima Qian
Spence, Jonathan D.
Wang Fuzhi
Zhang Xuecheng

Asia: 2) India

Bīrūnī, Abū Rayhān al-
Chaudhuri, K.N.
Dutt, R.C.

Eaton, Richard Maxwell
Gopal, Sarvepalli
Guha, Ranajit

India: since 1750
Kosambi, D.D.
Thapar, Romila

Asia: 3) Japan and Korea

Arai Hakuseki
Boxer, C.R.
Gunki monogatari
Hayashi School
Japan

Japanese Chronicles
Kitabatake Chikafusa
Korea
Maruyama Masao
Mito School

Niida Noboru
Otsuka Hisao
Shigeno Yasutsugu
Shiratori Kurakichi

Asia: 4) Middle East

Bartol'd, Vasilii Vladimirovich
Browne, Edward G.
Byzantium
Cahen, Claude
Eberhard, Wolfram
Hodgson, Marshall G.S.
Hourani, Albert
Ibn al-Athīr, 'Izz al-Dīn
Ibn Khaldūn

Inalcık, Halil
Iran:: since 1500
Issawi, Charles P.
Kasravi, Ahmad
Kedourie, Elie
Köprülü, M.F.
Lewis, Bernard
Massignon, Louis
Middle East: Medieval

Naima, Mustafa
Near East: Ancient
Ottoman Empire
Rashīd al-Dīn, Fazlallah
Rodinson, Maxime
Said, Edward
Watt, W. Montgomery
Zaydān, Jurjī

Asia: 5) Southeast Asia and Australasia

Ali Haji, Raja
Anderson, Benedict
Australia
Babad
Beaglehole, John C.
Bean, C.E.W.
Blainey, Geoffrey
Bugis and Makasar Chronicles
Clark, Manning

Dening, Greg
Furnivall, J.S.
Grimshaw, Patricia
Ileto, Reynaldo Clemeña
Indian Ocean Region
Lake, Marilyn
Le Quy Don
Malay Annals
New Zealand

Pacific/Oceanic History
Ranggawarsita, Raden Ngabei
Raniri, Nur ud-Din ar-
Scott, James C.
Southeast Asia
Vietnam
Vietnamese Chronicles
Wood, G.A.
Yamin, Muhammad

Byzantium

Brown, Peter
Bury, J.B.
Byzantium
Cameron, Averil

Kazhdan, A.P.
Komnene, Anna
Obolensky, Dimitri
Ostrogorsky, George

Procopius
Psellos, Michael
Runciman, Steven
Vasiliev, A.A.

Europe: 1) Medieval

Anglo-Saxon Chronicle
Annales regni Francorum
Barraclough, Geoffrey
Bede
Bloch, Marc
Bolland, Jean
Burns, Robert Ignatius
Byzantium
Cam, Helen
Camden, William
Castro, Américo
Cheney, C.R.
Crusades
Delisle, Léopold
Duby, Georges
Einhard
Froissart, Jean
Ganshof, F.L.
Giesebrecht, Wilhelm von
Gilson, Etienne
Gregory of Tours
Guichard, Pierre
Gurevich, Aron

Haller, Johannes
Haskins, Charles Homer
Hilton, Rodney
Holy Roman Empire
Hughes, Kathleen
Huizinga, Johan
Janssen, Johannes
Kantorowicz, Ernst H.
Knowles, David
Krusch, Bruno
Lea, Henry Charles
Lévi-Provençal, Evariste
Levison, Wilhelm
Leyser, Karl
Lopez, Roberto S.
Mabillon, Jean
Maitland, F.W.
Medieval Chronicles
Medieval Historical Writing
Muratori, L.A.
Orderic Vitalis
Otto of Freising
Paris, Matthew

Pirenne, Henri
Postan, M.M.
Power, Eileen
Roger of Wendover
Rörig, Fritz
Salvemini, Gaetano
Savigny, Friedrich Karl von
Saxo Grammaticus
Schramm, Percy Ernst
Snorri Sturluson
Southern, R.W.
Switzerland
Thietmar
Thorne, Samuel E.
Ullmann, Walter
Vernadsky, George
Villani, Giovanni
Waitz, Georg
White, Lynn, Jr.
Widukind of Corvey
William of Malmesbury
William of Tyre

Europe: 2) Early Modern and Modern

Blum, Jerome
Boxer, C.R.
Braudel, Fernand
Brenner, Robert
Broué, Pierre
Burckhardt, Jacob
Burke, Peter
Carr, E.H.
Chartier, Roger
Cipolla, Carlo M.
Darnton, Robert
Davies, Norman
Davies, R.W.
Davis, Natalie Zemon
Delbrück, Hans
Delumeau, Jean
Deutscher, Isaac
de Vries, Jan
Dickens, A.G.
Elliott, J.H.
Enlightenment Historical Writing
Europe: Modern

European Expansion
Froude, J.A.
Fruin, Robert
Gallagher, John
Gay, Peter
Geyl, Pieter
Gilbert, Felix
Ginzburg, Carlo
Giovio, Paolo
Greece: Modern
Guicciardini, Francesco
Hobsbawm, E.J.
Howard, Michael
Hufton, Olwen H.
Hunt, Lynn
Joll, James
Kelly-Gadol, Joan
Kennedy, Paul M.
Kristeller, Paul Oskar
Machiavelli, Niccolò
McNeill, William H.
Mahan, Alfred Thayer

Marrus, Michael R.
Mattingly, Garrett
Mayer, Arno J.
Mosse, George L.
Motley, John Lothrop
Parker, Geoffrey
Raynal, Guillaume-Thomas
Renaissance Historical Writing
Robinson, James Harvey
Rostow, W.W.
Schama, Simon
Schorske, Carl E.
Scott, Joan Wallach
Scribner, R.W.
Switzerland
Thorne, Samuel E.
Ullman, Berthold L.
Venturi, Franco
Vergil, Polydore
Wallerstein, Immanuel
Wedgwood, C.V.
Yates, Frances A.

Europe: 3) Britain

Acton, Lord
Anderson, Perry
Anglo-Saxon Chronicle
Bede
Briggs, Asa
Britain entries
British Empire
Buckle, Henry Thomas
Butterfield, Herbert
Cam, Helen
Camden, William
Carlyle, Thomas
Carr, E.H.
Chadwick, Owen
Cheney, C.R.
Clapham, J.H.
Clark, Alice
Cole, G.D.H.
Davidoff, Leonore
Dickens, A.G.
Dyos, H.J.
Elton, G.R.
Engels, Friedrich
Foxe, John
Froude, J.A.
Gallagher, John
Gardiner, Samuel Rawson
Habakkuk, H.J.

Halévy, Elie
Hammond, J.L. and Barbara
Hexter, J.H.
Hill, Christopher
Hilton, Rodney
Hobsbawm, E.J.
Holdsworth, W.S.
Holinshed, Raphael
Howard, Michael
Hughes, Kathleen
Hume, David
Jones, Gareth Stedman
Knowles, David
Landes, David
Macaulay, Thomas Babington
Maitland, F.W.
Milsom, S.F.C.
Namier, Lewis
Paris, Matthew
Pinchbeck, Ivy
Plucknett, T.F.T.
Plumb, J.H.
Pocock, J.G.A.
Radzinowicz, Leon
Roger of Wendover
Rostow, W.W.
Rowbotham, Sheila
Russell, Conrad

Samuel, Raphael
Scotland
Seeley, J.R.
Selden, John
Skinner, Quentin
Southern, R.W.
Stenton, F.M.
Stone, Lawrence
Stubbs, William
Tawney, R.H.
Taylor, A.J.P.
Thirsk, Joan
Thomas, Keith
Thompson, E.P.
Thompson, F.M.L.
Thorne, Samuel E.
Trevelyan, G.M.
Trevor-Roper, Hugh
Vergil, Polydore
Walkowitz, Judith R.
Webb, Beatrice and Sidney
Wedgwood, C.V.
William of Malmesbury
Williams, Raymond
Wilson, Charles H.
Wrigley, E.A.

Europe: 4) Eastern and Central

Austro-Hungarian Empire
The Balkans
Barkan, Ömer Lütfi
Blum, Jerome
Brunner, Otto
Central Europe
Davies, Norman
East Central Europe
Fügedi, Erik

Halecki, Oskar
Jelavich, Barbara and Charles
Kołakowski, Leszek
Kula, Witold
Lelewel, Joachim
Macartney, C.A.
Marczali, Henrik
Palacký, František
Pekař, Josef

Poland entries
Polanyi, Karl
Rothschild, Joseph
Seton-Watson, Hugh
Seton-Watson, R.W.
Srbik, Heinrich von
Stavrianos, Leften Stavros
Sugar, Peter F.
Szekfű, Gyula

Europe: 5) France

Annales regni Francorum
Ariès, Philippe
Bloch, Marc
Bodin, Jean
Chartier, Roger
Cobb, Richard
Cobban, Alfred
Corbin, Alain
Darnton, Robert
Davis, Natalie Zemon
Delisle, Léopold
Delumeau, Jean
Duby, Georges
Einhard
Febvre, Lucien
Foucault, Michel
France entries

Froissart, Jean
Furet, Francois
Fustel de Coulanges, Numa
Gilson, Etienne
Godechot, Jacques Léon
Gregory of Tours
Guizot, François
Henry, Louis
Hufton, Olwen H.
Hunt, Lynn
Labrousse, Ernest
Lavisse, Ernest
Lefebvre, Georges
Le Roy Ladurie, Emmanuel
Marrus, Michael R.
Mathiez, Albert
Michelet, Jules

Mousnier, Roland
Ozouf, Mona
Renouvin, Pierre
Rudé, George
Scott, Joan Wallach
Seignobos, Charles
Simiand, François
Soboul, Albert
Thierry, Augustin
Tilly, Charles
Tilly, Louise A.
Tocqueville, Alexis de
Voltaire
Vovelle, Michel
Weber, Eugen
Zeldin, Theodore

Europe: 6) Germany

Barraclough, Geoffrey
Bock, Gisela
Bracher, Karl Dietrich
Broszat, Martin
Conze, Werner
Delbrück, Hans
Dopsch, Alfons
Droysen , J.G.
Engels, Friedrich
Ennen, Edith
Fischer, Fritz
Gall, Lothar
Gatterer, Johann Christoph
Germany entries
Giesebrecht, Wilhelm von
Haller, Johannes
Hartung, Fritz
Hausen, Karin
Hillgruber, Andreas

Hintze, Otto
Janssen, Johannes
Joll, James
Kehr, Eckart
Kocka, Jürgen
Koonz, Claudia
Koselleck, Reinhart
Krusch, Bruno
Kuczynski, Jürgen
Lamprecht, Karl
Levison, Wilhelm
Lüdtke, Alf
Mason, Tim
Meinecke, Friedrich
Miller, Susanne
Mommsen, Hans
Mommsen, Wolfgang J.
Mosse, George L.
Niethammer, Lutz

Otto of Freising
Ranke, Leopold von
Ritter, Gerhard A.
Rörig, Fritz
Rosenberg, Arthur
Rosenberg, Hans
Schieder, Theodor
Schnabel, Franz
Schramm, Percy Ernst
Scribner, R.W.
Sudhoff, Karl
Sybel, Heinrich von
Thietmar
Treitschke, Heinrich von
Vagts, Alfred
Waitz, Georg
Weber, Hermann
Wehler, Hans-Ulrich
Widukind of Corvey

Europe: 7) Ireland

Froude, J.A.
Green, Alice Stopford

Ireland
Lecky, W.E.H.

Lyons, F.S.L.
Moody, T.W.

Europe: 8) Italy

Baron, Hans
Cantimori, Delio
Chabod, Federico
Cipolla, Carlo M.
Croce, Benedetto
De Felice, Renzo
De Sanctis, Francesco
Garin, Eugenio
Giannone, Pietro
Gilbert, Felix
Ginzburg, Carlo

Giovio, Paolo
Gramsci, Antonio
Guicciardini, Francesco
Italy entries
Kelly-Gadol, Joan
Machiavelli, Niccolò
Mack Smith, Denis
Manzoni, Alessandro
Martines, Lauro
Momigliano, Arnaldo
Pieri, Piero

Pieroni Bortolotti, Franca
Portelli, Alessandro
Procacci, Giuliano
Renaissance Historical Writing
Romeo, Rosario
Salvemini, Gaetano
Sarpi, Paolo
Spriano, Paolo
Ullman, Berthold L.
Villani, Giovanni
Villari, Pasquale

Europe: 9) Low Countries

de Vries, Jan
Fruin, Robert
Geyl, Pieter

Low Countries
Motley, John Lothrop
Parker, Geoffrey

Pirenne, Henri
Schama, Simon

Europe: 10) Russia and Central Asia

Bartol'd, Vasilii Vladimirovich
Blum, Jerome
Carr, E.H.
Central Asia
Davies, R.W.
Deutscher, Isaac
Karamzin, N.M.

Kliuchevskii, V.O.
Lewin, Moshe
Medvedev, Roy
Miliukov, Pavel
Pipes, Richard
Platonov, S.F.
Poliakov, Léon

Raeff, Marc
Russia entries
Solov'ev, Sergei
Vasiliev, A.A.
Vernadsky, George
Vinogradoff, Paul
Zaionchkovskii, P.A.

Europe: 11) Scandinavia

Gurevich, Aron
Heckscher, Eli F.

Saxo Grammaticus
Snorri Sturluson

Sweden

Europe: 12) Spain and Portugal

Boxer, C.R.
Braudel, Fernand
Burns, Robert Ignatius
Carr, Raymond
Domínguez Ortiz, Antonio

Elliott, J.H.
Guichard, Pierre
Lea, Henry Charles
Lévi-Provençal, Evariste
Maravall, José Antonio

Menéndez Pidal, Ramón
Parker, Geoffrey
Sánchez-Albornoz, Claudio
Spain entries
Thomas, Hugh

North and South America: 1) Canada

Canada
Creighton, Donald Grant
Eccles, W.J.
Frégault, Guy

Groulx, Lionel
Innis, Harold A.
Lower, A.R.M.
Morton, W.L.

Ormsby, Margaret A.
Ouellet, Fernand
Séguin, Maurice
Trigger, Bruce G.

North and South America: 2) Latin America

Argentina
Basadre, Jorge
Bolton, Herbert E.
Borah, Woodrow
Boxer, C.R.
Brazil
Castro, Américo
Central America
Chevalier, François
Cosío Villegas, Daniel
Cuba
Díaz del Castillo, Bernal
Freyre, Gilberto
Garcilaso de la Vega
Germani, Gino

Gibson, Charles
Góngora, Mario
González Casanova, Pablo
Halperín-Donghi, Tulio
Hanke, Lewis
Holanda, S.B. de
Las Casas, Bartolomé de
Latin America entries
Lavrin, Asunción
León-Portilla, Miguel
Levene, Ricardo
Mexico
Mitre, Bartolomé
Moreno Fraginals, Manuel
O'Gorman, Edmundo

Ortiz, Fernando
Pérez, Louis A., Jr.
Prado Júnior, Caio
Prebisch, Raúl
Prescott, William H.
Raynal, Guillaume-Thomas
Rock, David
Rodrigues, José Honório
Romero, José Luis
Scobie, James R.
Stein, Stanley J.
Tannenbaum, Frank
Varnhagen, Francisco Adolfo de
Williams, Eric

North and South America: 3) United States

Adams, Henry
African American History
African Diaspora
Ambrose, Stephen E.
Andrews, Charles McLean
Axtell, James
Bailyn, Bernard
Bancroft, George
Beard, Charles A. and Mary Ritter Beard
Becker, Carl L.
Boorstin, Daniel J.
Chandler, Alfred D., Jr.
Commager, Henry Steele
Commons, John R.
Cott, Nancy F.
Crosby, Alfred W., Jr.
Curti, Merle
Curtin, Philip D.
Davis, David Brion
Debo, Angie
Degler, Carl N.
Du Bois, W.E.B.
Dunning, William A.
Elkins, Stanley
Fogel, Robert William
Foner, Eric
Foner, Philip S.
Franklin, John Hope
Genovese, Eugene D.
Goldman, Eric
Gordon, Linda
Greene, Jack P.

Gutman, Herbert G.
Handlin, Oscar
Hartz, Louis
Hine, Darlene Clark
Hofstadter, Richard
Horwitz, Morton J.
Hughes, Thomas P.
Jensen, Merrill
Jordan, Winthrop D.
Kerber, Linda K.
Kessler-Harris, Alice
Kolko, Gabriel
LaFeber, Walter
Lasch, Christopher
Lerner, Gerda
Leuchtenburg, William
Levine, Lawrence W.
Lewis, David Levering
Link, Arthur S.
Litwack, Leon F.
Mahan, Alfred Thayer
Malin, James C.
Meier, August
Merchant, Carolyn
Miller, Perry
Montgomery, David
Morgan, Edmund S.
Morison, Samuel Eliot
Mumford, Louis
Nash, Gary B.
Nevins, Allan
Osgood, Herbert Levi

Owsley, Frank Lawrence
Painter, Nell Irvin
Parkman, Francis
Parrington, Vernon Louis
Pessen, Edward
Phillips, Ulrich Bonnell
Potter, David M.
Prucha, Francis Paul
Quinn, David B.
Schlesinger, Arthur M., Jr.
Scott, Anne Firor
Semple, Ellen Churchill
Smith, Henry Nash
Smith, Merritt Roe
Smith-Rosenberg, Carroll
Spruill, Julia Cherry
Stampp, Kenneth M.
Takaki, Ron
Tocqueville, Alexis de
Turner, Frederic Jackson
Ulrich, Laurel Thatcher
United States entries
United States: Historical Writing, 20th Century
Wiebe, Robert H.
Williams, William Appleman
Wood, Gordon S.
Woodson, Carter G.
Woodward, C. Vann
Worster, Donald
Zinn, Howard

TOPICS

Art History

Art History
Burckhardt, Jacob
Gombrich, E.H.

Huizinga, Johan
Panofsky, Erwin
Pevsner, Nikolaus

Schama, Simon
Winckelmann, J.J.

Cultural History

Anthropology, Historical
Art History
The Body
Bourdieu, Pierre
Braudel, Fernand
Burckhardt, Jacob
Burke, Peter
Chartier, Roger
Chevalier, François
China: Modern
Consumerism and Consumption
Corbin, Alain
Cultural History
Darnton, Robert
Davis, David Brion

Davis, Natalie Zemon
Europe: Modern
Freyre, Gilberto
Garin, Eugenio
Gay, Peter
Ginzburg, Carlo
Hanke, Lewis
Herder, J.G.
Huizinga, Johan
Hunt, Lynn
Intellectual History
Köprülü, M.F.
Lamprecht, Karl
Mentalities, History of
Miliukov, Pavel

Mosse, George L.
Mumford, Lewis
Ozouf, Mona
Ranger, Terence O.
Schorske, Carl E.
Soboul, Albert
Theatre
Thomas, Keith
Thompson, E.P.
Vico, Giambattista
Vovelle, Michel
Williams, Raymond
Zeldin, Theodore

Demographic History

Annales School
Cambridge Group
Cipolla, Carlo M.

Demography
de Vries, Jan
Henry, Louis

Migration
Wrigley, E.A.

Diplomatic History

Ambrose, Stephen E.
Annales regni francorum
Butterfield, Herbert
Carr, E.H.
Chabod, Federico
Diplomatic History
Droysen, J.G.
Elliott, J.H.
Europe: Modern

Fischer, Fritz
Gilbert, Felix
Intelligence and Espionage
Jelavich, Barbara and Charles
Kedourie, Elie
Kennedy, Paul M.
Kolko, Gabriel
LaFeber, Walter
Mattingly, Garrett

Mayer, Arno J.
Motley, John Lothrop
Ranke, Leopold von
Renouvin, Pierre
Rodrigues, José Honório
Taylor, A.J.P.
Vagts, Alfred
Williams, William Appleman

Economic History

Beard, Charles A. and Mary Ritter Beard
Business History
Cardoso, Fernando Henrique
Cipolla, Carlo M.
Cole, G.D.H.
Economic History

Hammond, J.L. and Barbara
Hill, Christopher
Hilton, Rodney
Hobsbawm, E.J.
Industrial Revolution
Otsuka Hisao

Polanyi, Karl
Postan, M.M.
Power, Eileen
Tawney, R.H.
Thompson, E.P.
Vinogradoff, Paul

Intellectual History

Berlin, Isaiah
Dilthey, Wilhelm
Foucault, Michel
Intellectual History

Lovejoy, Arthur O.
Meinecke, Friedrich
Pocock, J.G.A.
Skinner, Quentin

Weber, Max
White, Hayden V.

Jewish History

Baron, Salo Wittmayer
Braham, Randolph L.
Dubnov, Simon
Goitein, S.D.

Graetz, Heinrich
Hilberg, Raul
Holocaust
Jewish History

Josephus
Katz, Jacob
Marrus, Michael R.

Legal History

Bodin, Jean
Daube, David
Góngora, Mario
Hargreaves, John D.
Holdsworth, W.S.
Horwitz, Morton J.

Legal History
Maitland, F.W.
Milsom, S.F.C.
Plucknett, T.F.T.
Radzinowicz, Leon
Savigny, Friedrich Karl von

Simpson, A.W.B.
Sinclair, Keith
Vinogradoff, Paul
Watson, Alan

Military History

Delbrück, Hans
Howard, Michael
Keegan, John
Kennedy, Paul M.
Mahan, Alfred Thayer

Mattingly, Garrett
Military History
Napoleonic Wars
Naval History
Pieri, Piero

Schramm, Percy Ernst
Thorne, Samuel E.
Vagts, Alfred

Periods, Themes, Branches of History

African American History
African Diaspora
Agrarian History
America: Pre-Columbian
Archaeology
Art History
Astrology
The Body
Business History
Childhood
Comparative History
Computers and Computing, History of
Computing and History
Consumerism and Consumption
Counter-Reformation
Crime and Deviance
Crusades
Cultural History
Demography
Design History
Diplomatic History
Documentary Film
Dress
Eastern Orthodoxy
Ecclesiastical History
Ecology
Economic History
Environmental History
Ethnicity
Ethnohistory
European Expansion
The Family
Feminism

Feudalism
Film
Frontiers
Gender
Historical Geography
Historical Maps and Atlases
Historiology
History Workshop
Holocaust
Homosexuality
Imperialism
Indian Ocean Region
Indigenous Peoples
Industrial Revolution
Intellectual History
Intelligence and Espionage
Islamic Nations and Cultures
Labor History
Legal History
Leisure
Literature and History
Local History
Maritime History
Marriage
Marxist Interpretation of History
Masculinity
Media
Medicine, History of
Memory
Mentalities, History of
Metahistory
Migration
Military History

Musicology
Napoleonic Wars
Nationalism
Native American History
Natural Sciences, Historical
Naval History
Oral History
Orientalism
Orthodoxy, Eastern
Pacific/Oceanic History
Philosophy of History
Political and Constitutional History
Popular History
Prehistory
Prosopography
Protestantism
Quantitative Method
The Reformation
Religion
Religions, Comparative History of
Rhetoric and History
Science, History of
Sexuality
Slavery entries
Social History
Sociology and History
Sport, History of
The State
Theatre
Urban History
World History
World War I
World War II

Political History

Althusser, Louis
Beard, Charles A. and Mary Ritter Beard
Elton, G.R.
Foner, Eric
Furet, François
Genovese, Eugene D.
Guizot, François
Jones, Gareth Stedman
Hartz, Louis

Hofstadter, Richard
Legal History
Leuchtenburg, William
Macaulay, Thomas Babington
Maitland, F.W.
Namier, Lewis
Pocock, J.G.A.
Political and Constitutional History
Russell, Conrad

Schama, Simon
Schlesinger, Arthur M., Jr.
Seeley, J.R.
Skinner, Quentin
The State
Stubbs, William
Trevelyan, G.M.

Religion

Bauer, Walter
Bolland, Jean
Brown, Peter
Bultmann, Rudolf
Catholicism/Catholic Church
Chadwick, Owen
Cheney, C.R.
Christianity
Counter-Reformation

Delumeau, Jean
Dickens, A.G.
Eastern Orthodoxy
Foxe, John
Janssen, Johannes
Lea, Henry Charles
Mansi, Giovanni Domenico
Pagels, Elaine
Protestantism

Ranke, Leopold von
The Reformation
Religion
Religions, Comparative
Sarpi, Paolo
Troeltsch, Ernst
Ullmann, Walter
Wellhausen, Julius

Science, Medicine, Technology, and Ecology

Crosby, Alfred W., Jr.
Dilthey, Wilhelm
Duhem, Pierre
Fleck, Ludwig
Garin, Eugenio
Heilbron, J.L.
Hughes, Thomas P.
Kuhn, Thomas S.
Mach, Ernst
Malin, James C.

Medicine, History of
Merchant, Carolyn
Merton, Robert K.
Mumford, Lewis
Needham, Joseph
Rosenberg, Charles E.
Sarton, George
Sauer, Carl O.
Science, History of
Semple, Ellen Churchill

Sigerist, Henry E.
Smith, Merritt Roe
Sudhoff, Karl
Technology
Temkin, Owsei
Trigger, Bruce G.
Vico, Giambattista
Whewell, William
White, Lynn, Jr.
Worster, Donald

Social History

Althusser, Louis
Annales School
Bloch, Marc
Braudel, Fernand
Cobb, Richard
Cole, G.D.H.
Conze, Werner
Corbin, Alain
Gutman, Herbert G.
Hammond, J.L. and Barbara
Hill, Christopher
Hilton, Rodney
History Workshop

Hobsbawm, E.J.
Hunt, Lynn
Lamprecht, Karl
Lefebvre, Georges
Marx, Karl
Marxist Interpretation of History
Mathiez, Albert
Montgomery, David
Pinchbeck, Ivy
Plumb, J.H.
Power, Eileen
Scott, Joan Wallach
Seignobos, Charles

Simiand, François
Soboul, Albert
Social History
Tawney, R.H.
Thomas, Keith
Thompson, E.P.
Thompson, F.M.L.
Tilly, Charles
Trevelyan, G.M.
Webb, Beatrice and Sidney
Weber, Max

Theories and Theorists

Althusser, Louis
Anderson, Benedict
Anderson, Perry
Annales School
Anthropology, Historical
Ariès, Philippe
Barraclough, Geoffrey
Begriffsgeschichte
Berlin, Isaiah
Bernal, Martin
Bloch, Marc
Bodin, Jean
Bourdieu, Pierre
Braudel, Fernand
Buckle, Henry Thomas
Burckhardt, Jacob
Butterfield, Herbert
Cambridge Group
Cardoso, Fernando Henrique
Carlyle, Thomas
Carr, E.H.
Cassirer, Ernst
Chandler, Alfred D., Jr.
Chartier, Roger
Cipolla, Carlo M.
Collingwood, R.G.

Comte, Auguste
Croce, Benedetto
Dening, Greg
Dilthey, Wilhelm
Engels, Friedrich
Erikson, Erik H.
Foucault, Michel
Freud, Sigmund
Gatterer, Johann Christoph
Gay, Peter
Geertz, Clifford
Gramsci, Antonio
Habermas, Jürgen
Hegel, G.W.F.
Henry, Louis
Herder, J.G
History from Below
James, C.L.R.
Kiernan, V.G.
Kong-zi
Lovejoy, Arthur O.
McLuhan, Marshall
Marx, Karl
Montesquieu
Moore, Barrington, Jr.
Nietzsche, Friedrich

Popper, Karl
Postcolonialism
Postmodernism
Ranke, Leopold von
Rhetoric and History
Said, Edward W.
Schlözer, August Ludwig von
Schorske, Carl E.
Scott, James C.
Simiand, François
Spengler, Oswald
Subaltern Studies
Tilly, Charles
Todorov, Tsvetan
Toynbee, Arnold J.
Turner, Victor
Universal History
Villari, Pasquale
Voltaire
Vovelle, Michel
Weber, Max
Whig Interpretation of History
White, Hayden V.
Williams, Raymond

Women's and Gender History

Bock, Gisela
Clark, Alice
Cott, Nancy F.
Davidoff, Leonore
Davis, Natalie Zemon
Gordon, Linda
Grimshaw, Patricia
Hausen, Karin
Hine, Darlene Clark
Hufton, Olwen H.

Kelly-Gadol, Joan
Kerber, Linda K.
Kessler-Harris, Alice
Koonz, Claudia
Lake, Marilyn
Lavrin, Asunción
Lerner, Gerda
Painter, Nell Irvin
Pieroni Bortolotti, Franca
Pinchbeck, Ivy

Rowbotham, Sheila
Scott, Anne Firor
Scott, Joan Wallach
Smith-Rosenberg, Carroll
Spruill, Julia Cherry
Tilly, Louise A.
Ulrich, Laurel Thatcher
Walkowitz, Judith R.
Women's History entries

CHRONOLOGICAL LIST
OF HISTORIANS

551–479 BCE	Kong-zi [Confucius]
c.484–after 424 BCE	Herodotus
c.460/455–c.399 BCE	Thucydides
c.428–c.354 BCE	Xenophon
c.200–c.118 BCE	Polybius
c.145–c.87 BCE	Sima Qian
c.104–c.20 BCE	Diodorus Siculus
100–44 BCE	Julius Caesar
86–35 BCE	Sallust
c.60–after 7 BCE	Dionysius of Halicarnassus
59 BCE–c.17 CE	Livy
c.20/19 BCE–after 30 CE	Velleius Paterculus
c.32–92 CE	Ban Gu
37/8–c.94 CE	Josephus
before 50–after 120 CE	Plutarch
c.56–after 118 CE	Tacitus
c.70–c.140 CE	Suetonius
c.150–235 CE	Cassius Dio
c.265–339 CE	Eusebius of Caesarea
c.330–c.395 CE	Ammianus Marcellinus
c.487–c.585	Cassiodorus
c.500–after 542	Procopius
538/9–594/5	Gregory of Tours
661–721	Liu Zhiji
c.672/3–735	Bede
c.770–840	Einhard
c.925–after 973	Widukind of Corvey
973–c.1050	Abū Rayhān al-Bīrūnī
975–1018	Thietmar, bishop of Merseburg
1018–after 1081	Michael Psellos
1019–1086	Sima Guang
1075–1142/3	Orderic Vitalis
1083–c.1153/4	Anna Komnene
c.1090–c.1143	William of Malmesbury
c.1114–1158	Otto of Freising
c.1130–1186	William of Tyre
1160–1233	ʿIzz al-Dīn Ibn al-Athīr
1178/9–1241	Snorri Sturluson
fl.1185–1208	Saxo Grammaticus
c.1200–c.1259	Matthew Paris
d. 1236	Roger of Wendover
1247–1318	Fazlallah Rashīd al-Dīn
1276–1348	Giovanni Villani
1293–1354	Kitabatake Chikafusa
1332–1406	Ibn Khaldūn
c.1337–after 1404	Jean Froissart
fl.1413–33	Ma Huan
1469–1527	Niccolò Machiavelli
1470(?)–1555(?)	Polydore Vergil
1474–1566	Bartolomé de Las Casas
1483–1540	Francesco Guicciardini
c.1486–1552	Paolo Giovio
c.1492–1584	Bernal Díaz del Castillo
1516–1587	John Foxe
1529/30–1596	Jean Bodin
1539–1616	Garcilaso de la Vega
1551–1623	William Camden
1552–1623	Paolo Sarpi
fl.1560–80	Raphael Holinshed
1584–1654	John Selden
1596–1665	Jean Bolland
1619–1692	Wang Fuzhi
1632–1707	Jean Mabillon
1655–1716	Mustafa Naima
1657–1725	Arai Hakuseki
d. 1658	Nur ud-Din ar-Raniri
1668–1744	Giambattista Vico
1672–1750	L.A. Muratori
1676–1748	Pietro Giannone
1689–1755	Montesquieu
1692–1769	Giovanni Domenico Mansi
1694–1778	Voltaire
1711–1776	David Hume
1713–1796	Guillaume-Thomas Raynal
1717–1768	J.J. Winckelmann
c.1726–c.1784	Le Quy Don
1729–1799	Johann Christoph Gatterer
1735–1809	August Ludwig von Schlözer
1737–1794	Edward Gibbon
1738–1801	Zhang Xuecheng
1744–1803	J.G. Herder
1766–1826	N.M. Karamzin
1770–1831	G.W.F. Hegel
1776–1831	B.G. Niebuhr

1779–1861	Friedrich Karl von Savigny	1853–1938	Karl Sudhoff
1785–1873	Alessandro Manzoni	1854–1929	Karl Julius Beloch
1786–1861	Joachim Lelewel	1854–1942	Charles Seignobos
1787–1874	François Guizot	1854–1925	Paul Vinogradoff
1794–1866	William Whewell	1855–1930	Eduard Meyer
1795–1881	Thomas Carlyle	1855–1918	Herbert Levi Osgood
1795–1886	Leopold von Ranke	1856–1939	Sigmund Freud
1795–1856	Augustin Thierry	1856–1915	Karl Lamprecht
1796–1859	William H. Prescott	1856–1940	Henrik Marczali
1798–1857	Auguste Comte	1857–1922	William A. Dunning
1798–1874	Jules Michelet	1857–1940	Bruno Krusch
1798–1876	František Palacký	1858–1943	Beatrice Webb
1800–1891	George Bancroft	1859–1943	Pavel Miliukov
1800–1859	Thomas Babington Macaulay	1859–1947	Sidney Webb
1802–1873	Raden Ngabei Ranggawarsita	1860–1941	Simon Dubnov
1805–1859	Alexis de Tocqueville	1860–1933	S.F. Platonov
1808–1884	J.G. Droysen	1861–1927	J.B. Bury
c.1809–c.1870	Raja Ali Haji	1861–1916	Pierre Duhem
1813–1886	Georg Waitz	1861–1940	Otto Hintze
1814–1889	Wilhelm von Giesebrecht	1861–1932	Frederick Jackson Turner
1814–1877	John Lothrop Motley	1861–1914	Jurjī Zaydān
1816–1878	Francisco Adolfo de Varnhagen	1862–1926	Edward G. Browne
1817–1883	Francesco De Sanctis	1862–1945	John R. Commons
1817–1891	Heinrich Graetz	1862–1954	Friedrich Meinecke
1817–1903	Theodor Mommsen	1862–1935	Henri Pirenne
1817–1895	Heinrich von Sybel	1863–1943	Charles McLean Andrews
1818–1897	Jacob Burckhardt	1863–1936	James Harvey Robinson
1818–1894	J.A. Froude	1863–1932	Ellen Churchill Semple
1818–1883	Karl Marx	1864–1932	Stéphane Gsell
1820–1895	Friedrich Engels	1864–1920	Max Weber
1820–1879	S.M. Solov'ev	1865–1935	James Henry Breasted
1821–1862	Henry Thomas Buckle	1865–1947	Johannes Haller
1821–1906	Bartolomé Mitre	1865–1942	Shiratori Kurakichi
1823–1899	Robert Fruin	1865–1923	Ernst Troeltsch
1823–1893	Francis Parkman	1865–1928	G.A. Wood
1825–1909	Henry Charles Lea	1866–1952	Benedetto Croce
1825–1901	William Stubbs	1866–1934	Naitō Torajirō
1826–1910	Léopold Delisle	1867–1953	A.A. Vasiliev
1827–1917	Pasquale Villari	1868–1953	Alfons Dopsch
1827–1910	Shigeno Yasutsugu	1868–1963	W.E.B. Du Bois
1829–1902	Samuel Rawson Gardiner	1869–1930	Vasilii Vladimirovich Bartol'd
1829–1891	Johannes Janssen	1869–1968	Ramón Menéndez Pidal
1830–1889	Numa Fustel de Coulanges	1870–1953	Herbert E. Bolton
1833–1911	Wilhelm Dilthey	1870–1937	Elie Halévy
1834–1902	Lord Acton	1870–1937	Charles Homer Haskins
1834–1895	J.R. Seeley	1870–1937	Josef Pekař
1834–1896	Heinrich von Treitschke	1870–1952	M.I. Rostovtzeff
1838–1918	Henry Adams	1870–1957	Gaetano de Sanctis
1838–1903	W.E.H. Lecky	1871–1944	W.S. Holdsworth
1838–1916	Ernst Mach	1871–1929	Vernon Louis Parrington
1840–1914	Alfred Thayer Mahan	1872–1949	J.L. Hammond
1841–1911	V.O. Kliuchevskii	1872–1945	Johan Huizinga
1842–1922	Ernest Lavisse	1873–1945	Carl L. Becker
1844–1900	Friedrich Nietzsche	1873–1946	J.H. Clapham
1844–1918	Julius Wellhausen	1873–1961	Barbara Hammond
1847–1929	Alice Stopford Green	1873–1929	Liang Qichao
1848–1929	Hans Delbrück	1873–1962	Arthur O. Lovejoy
1848–1909	R.C. Dutt	1873–1957	Gaetano Salvemini
1848–1931	Ulrich von Wilamovitz-Möllendorff	1873–1935	François Simiand
1850–1906	F.W. Maitland	1874–1948	Charles A. Beard

1874–1945	Ernst Cassirer	1892–1982	E.H. Carr
1874–1934	Alice Clark	1892–1968	Erwin Panofsky
1874–1959	Georges Lefebvre	1892–1986	Alfred Vagts
1874–1932	Albert Mathiez	1893–1980	Gu Jiegang
1875–1950	Carter G. Woodson	1893–1979	James C. Malin
1876–1958	Mary Ritter Beard	1893–1974	Piero Pieri
1876–1947	Wilhelm Levison	1893–1974	Pierre Renouvin
1876–1962	G.M. Trevelyan	1893–1984	Claudio Sánchez-Albornoz
1877–1960	Walter Bauer	1893–1969	Frank Tannenbaum
1877–1934	Ulrich Bonnell Phillips	1894–1952	Harold A. Innis
1878–1956	Lucien Febvre	1894–1956	Evariste Lévi-Provençal
1878–1960	J.S. Furnivall	1894–1970	Percy Ernst Schramm
1878–1967	Lionel Groulx	1895–1989	Salo Wittmayer Baron
1878–1945	Paul Pelliot	1895–1980	F.L. Ganshof
1878–1951	Heinrich von Srbik	1895–1963	Ernst H. Kantorowicz
1879–1968	C.E.W. Bean	1895–1988	Ernest Labrousse
1879–1952	Eli F. Heckscher	1895–1978	C.A. Macartney
1879–1951	R.W. Seton-Watson	1895–1990	Lewis Mumford
1880–1971	Lawrence Henry Gipson	1896–1961	Ludwig Fleck
1880–1936	Oswald Spengler	1896–1974	David Knowles
1880–1967	F.M. Stenton	1897–1996	Merle Curti
1880–1962	R.H. Tawney	1897–1965	T.F.T. Plucknett
1881–1969	Fernando Ortiz	1898–1982	Otto Brunner
1882–1952	Fritz Rörig	1898–1976	Daniel Cosío Villegas
1882–1965	Berthold L. Ullman	1898–1982	Ivy Pinchbeck
1883–1967	Fritz Hartung	1899–1981	M.M. Postan
1883–1945	Henri Maspero	1899–1986	Julia Cherry Spruill
1883–1962	Louis Massignon	1899–1981	Frances A. Yates
1883–1955	Gyula Szekfű	1900–1988	Hans Baron
1884–1976	Rudolf Bultmann	1900–1979	Herbert Butterfield
1884–1978	Etienne Gilson	1900–1987	Gilberto Freyre
1884–1956	George Sarton	1900–1980	S.D. Goitein
1885–1968	Helen Cam	1900–1962	Garrett Mattingly
1885–1972	Américo Castro	1900–1995	Joseph Needham
1885–1959	Ricardo Levene	1901–1971	John C. Beaglehole
1886–1944	Marc Bloch	1901–1960	Federico Chabod
1886–1964	Karl Polanyi	1901–1968	Alfred Cobban
1887–1966	Pieter Geyl	1901–1989	C.L.R. James
1887–1976	Samuel Eliot Morison	1901–1986	Raúl Prebisch
1887–1966	Franz Schnabel	1902–1985	Fernand Braudel
1887–1973	George Vernadsky	1902–1998	Henry Steele Commager
1888–1960	Lewis Namier	1902–1979	Donald Grant Creighton
1888–1967	Gerhard A. Ritter	1902–1994	Erik H. Erikson
1889–1959	G.D.H. Cole	1902–1982	S.B. de Holanda
1889–1943	R.G. Collingwood	1902–1933	Eckart Kehr
1889–1988	A.R.M. Lower	1902–1976	George Ostrogorsky
1889–1940	Eileen Power	1902–1983	Nikolaus Pevsner
1889–1943	Arthur Rosenberg	1902–1994	Karl Popper
1889–1975	Carl O. Sauer	1902–	Owsei Temkin
1889–1975	Arnold J. Toynbee	1903–1980	Jorge Basadre
1890–1988	Angie Debo	1903–	Steven Runciman
1890–1946	Ahmad Kasravi	1903–1989	Ronald Syme
1890–1966	M.F. Köprülü	1903–1962	Muhammad Yamin
1890–1971	Allan Nevins	1904–	C.R. Boxer
1890–1956	Frank Lawrence Owsley	1904–1966	Delio Cantimori
1890–1969	Chen Yinke	1904–1970	A.H.M. Jones
1891–1937	Antonio Gramsci	1904–	Jacob Katz
1891–1973	Oskar Halecki	1904–1997	Jürgen Kuczynski
1891–1989	Charles-André Julien	1904–1966	Niida Noboru
1891–1957	Henry E. Sigerist	1904–1988	Hans Rosenberg

1904–1983	P.A. Zaionchkovskii	1912–	R.W. Southern
1905(?)–1979	Ömer Lütfi Barkan	1912–	Kenneth M. Stampp
1905–1991	Felix Gilbert	1913–1993	Jerome Blum
1905–1993	Lewis Hanke	1913–	V.G. Kiernan
1905–1980	Merrill Jensen	1913–	Barrington Moore, Jr.
1905–	Paul Oskar Kristeller	1913–1987	José Honório Rodrigues
1905–1963	Perry Miller	1913–	Leften Stavros Stavrianos
1906–1987	C.R. Cheney	1914–1984	Philippe Ariès
1906–1995	Edmundo O'Gorman	1914–	Daniel J. Boorstin
1906–	Leon Radzinowicz	1914–	François Chevalier
1906–1986	Henry Nash Smith	1914–	Basil Davidson
1906–1990	A.J.P. Taylor	1914–1996	Maruyama Masao
1907–1967	Isaac Deutscher	1914–1982	Albert Soboul
1907–	Edith Ennen	1914–	Hugh Trevor-Roper
1907–1991	John K. Fairbank	1914–	Franco Venturi
1907–1989	Jacques Léon Godechot	1914–	Jean-Pierre Vernant
1907–1966	D.D. Kosambi	1914–1991	Charles H. Wilson
1907–1984	T.W. Moody	1915–1991	Manning Clark
1907–1993	Roland Mousnier	1915–	John Hope Franklin
1907–1996	Otsuka Hisao	1915–	Eric Goldman
1907–1990	Caio Prado Júnior	1915–1989	Mario Góngora
1907–	Samuel E. Thorne	1915–1985	H.J. Habakkuk
1907–1987	Lynn White, Jr.	1915–	Oscar Handlin
1908–1984	Geoffrey Barraclough	1915–	Albert Hourani
1908–	Fritz Fischer	1915–1993	Susanne Miller
1908–1987	Arnaldo Momigliano	1915–	Maxime Rodinson
1908–1980	W.L. Morton	1915–	Carl E. Schorske
1908–1984	Theodor Schieder	1916–	Owen Chadwick
1908–	C. Vann Woodward	1916–1993	Erik Fügedi
1909–1997	Isaiah Berlin	1916–	Rodney Hilton
1909–1991	Claude Cahen	1916–1970	Richard Hofstadter
1909–	David Daube	1916–	Halil Inalcık
1909–	Antonio Domínguez Ortiz	1916–	Charles P. Issawi
1909–1989	Wolfram Eberhard	1916–1988	Witold Kula
1909–	Eugenio Garin	1916–	Bernard Lewis
1909–	E.H. Gombrich	1916–	Edmund S. Morgan
1909–1996	Margaret A. Ormsby	1916–	W.W. Rostow
1909–	David B. Quinn	1916–1984	Hugh Seton-Watson
1909–1977	José Luis Romero	1916–	Leonard Thompson
1909–	W. Montgomery Watt	1917–1996	Richard Cobb
1910–1986	Werner Conze	1917–	W.J. Eccles
1910–	A.G. Dickens	1917–	E.J. Hobsbawm
1910–1994	Philip S. Foner	1917–	William H. McNeill
1910–1996	J.H. Hexter	1917–	Arthur M. Schlesinger, Jr.
1910–1986	Robert S. Lopez	1918–1990	Louis Althusser
1910–	Robert K. Merton	1918–	Alfred D. Chandler, Jr.
1910–1997	Léon Poliakov	1918–1977	Guy Frégault
1910–1971	David M. Potter	1918–1994	James Joll
1910–1993	George Rudé	1918–	George L. Mosse
1910–1983	Walter Ullmann	1918–	Dimitri Obolensky
1910–1997	C.V. Wedgwood	1918–1984	Maurice Séguin
1911–1979	Gino Germani	1919–	Raymond Carr
1911–1991	Louis Henry	1919–1996	Georges Duby
1911–1980	Marshall McLuhan	1919–1980	John Gallagher
1911–1986	José Antonio Maravall	1919–1986	Louis Hartz
1911–	J.H. Plumb	1919–	Lawrence Stone
1911–1981	Eric Williams	1919–	Peter F. Sugar
1912–	Woodrow Borah	1920–1985	Charles Gibson
1912–1986	M.I. Finley	1920–	Gerda Lerner
1912–	Christopher Hill	1920–1992	Karl Leyser

1920–	Arthur S. Link	1926–1989	Martin Broszat
1920–	Denis Mack Smith	1926–	Robert William Fogel
1920–	Manuel Moreno Fraginals	1926–1984	Michel Foucault
1920–1992	Edward Pessen	1926–	Clifford Geertz
1920–	Stanley J. Stein	1926–	Tulio Halperín-Donghi
1920–1983	Victor Turner	1926–	Raul Hilberg
1921–	Asa Briggs	1926–1977	Kathleen Hughes
1921–	Robert Ignatius Burns	1926–1992	Elie Kedourie
1921–	Carl N. Degler	1926–	Miguel León-Portilla
1921–1978	H.J. Dyos	1926–	Arno J. Mayer
1921–1994	G.R. Elton	1926–	Fernand Ouellet
1921–	Moshe Lewin	1926–	Giuliano Procacci
1921–	Francis Paul Prucha	1927–	David Brion Davis
1921–	Anne Firor Scott	1927–1997	François Furet
1921–1990	William Appleman Williams	1927–	Leszek Kołakowski
1921–1988	Raymond Williams	1927–	Lauro Martines
1922–	Bernard Bailyn	1927–	David Montgomery
1922–	Karl Dietrich Bracher	1928–	Natalie Zemon Davis
1922–	Randolph L. Braham	1928–1985	Herbert G. Gutman
1922–	Carlo M. Cipolla	1928–1982	Joan Kelly-Gadol
1922–	Philip D. Curtin	1928–	Hermann Weber
1922–	Pablo González Casanova	1928–	Hayden V. White
1922–	Ranajit Guha	1929–	Jacob F. Ade Ajayi
1922–1968	Marshall G.S. Hodgson	1929–1996	Renzo De Felice
1922–	Michael Howard	1929–	Jürgen Habermas
1922–	Charles Jelavich	1929–	Emmanuel Le Roy Ladurie
1922–1997	A.P. Kazhdan	1929–	Leon F. Litwack
1922–1996	Thomas S. Kuhn	1929–	Bethwell A. Ogot
1922–	William E. Leuchtenburg	1929–	Terence O. Ranger
1922–1993	Keith Sinclair	1929–1981	James R. Scobie
1922–	Joan Thirsk	1929–	Charles Tilly
1922–	Howard Zinn	1929–	Jan Vansina
1923–	Jean Delumeau	1930–	Geoffrey Blainey
1923–1985	Cheikh Anta Diop	1930–	Pierre Bourdieu
1923–	Peter Gay	1930–	J.H. Elliott
1923–	Sarvepalli Gopal	1930–	Eugene D. Genovese
1923–	Thomas P. Hughes	1930–	Hans Mommsen
1923–1995	Barbara Jelavich	1930–	Wolfgang J. Mommsen
1923	Reinhart Koselleck	1930–	Louise A. Tilly
1923–1983	F.S.L. Lyons	1930–	Immanuel Wallerstein
1923–	August Meier	1930–	Robert H. Wiebe
1923–	S.F.C. Milsom	c.1930s	Asunción Lavrin
1923–	Roland Oliver	c.1930s	Mona Ozouf
1923–	Richard Pipes	1931–	Fernando Henrique Cardoso
1923–	Marc Raeff	1931–	Alfred W. Crosby, Jr.
1924–	Aron Gurevich	1931–	Greg Dening
1924–	John D. Hargreaves	1931–	Jack P. Greene
1924–	David S. Landes	1931–	Winthrop D. Jordan
1924–	J.G.A. Pocock	1931–	Joseph Rothschild
1924–1987	Rosario Romeo	1931–	A.W.B. Simpson
1924–1993	E.P. Thompson	1931–	Romila Thapar
1925–	R.W. Davies	1931–	Hugh Thomas
1925–	Stanley Elkins	1931–	Hans-Ulrich Wehler
1925–1989	Andreas Hillgruber	1931–	E.A. Wrigley
1925–	Roy Medvedev	1932–	A. Adu Boahen
1925–1985	Franca Pieroni Bortolotti	1932–	Leonore Davidoff
1925–1988	Paolo Spriano	1932–	Gabriel Kolko
1925–	F.M.L. Thompson	1932–1994	Christopher Lasch
1925–	Eugen Weber	1933–	Walter LaFeber
1926–	Pierre Broué	1933–	Abdallah Laroui

1933–	Lawrence W. Levine	1939–	Lutz Niethammer
1933–	Ali A. Mazrui	1939–	Ronald Takaki
1933–	Gary B. Nash	1939–	Tsvetan Todorov
1933–	Keith Thomas	1940–	Averil Cameron
1933–	Michel Vovelle	1940–	Richard Maxwell Eaton
1933–	Alan Watson	1940–	Steven Feierman
1933–	Gordon S. Wood	1940–	Linda Gordon
1933–	Theodore Zeldin	1940–	Linda K. Kerber
1934–	K.N. Chaudhuri	1940–1990	Tim Mason
1934–	J.L. Heilbron	1940–	Quentin Skinner
1934–	John Keegan	1940–	Merritt Roe Smith
1934–1996	Raphael Samuel	c.1940s	Claudia Koonz
1935–	Peter Brown	1941–	James Axtell
1935–	Catherine Coquery-Vidrovitch	1941–	Alice Kessler-Harris
1935–	Edward W. Said	1941–	Jürgen Kocka
1936–	Stephen E. Ambrose	1941–	Michael R. Marrus
1936–	Benedict Anderson	1941–	Joan Wallach Scott
1936–	Emmanuel Ayankami Ayandele	1941–1998	R.W. Scribner
1936–	Alain Corbin	1941–	Donald Worster
1936–	Lothar Gall	1942–	Gisela Bock
1936–	David Levering Lewis	1942–	Gareth Stedman Jones
1936–	Shula Marks	1942–	Nell Irvin Painter
1936–	Carolyn Merchant	1942–	Alessandro Portelli
1936–	Charles E. Rosenberg	1942–1980	Walter Rodney
1936–	James C. Scott	1943–	Robert Brenner
1936–	Carroll Smith-Rosenberg	1943–	Jan de Vries
1936–	Jonathan D. Spence	1943–	Eric Foner
1937–	A.E. Afigbo	1943–	Paul E. Lovejoy
1937–	Martin Bernal	1943–	Alf Lüdtke
1937–	Peter Burke	1943–	Elaine Pagels
1937–	Conrad Russell	1943–	Geoffrey Parker
1937–	Bruce G. Trigger	1943–	Louis A. Pérez, Jr.
1938–	Perry Anderson	1943–	Sheila Rowbotham
1938–	Patricia Grimshaw	1945–	Roger Chartier
1938–	Karin Hausen	1945–	Nancy F. Cott
1938–	Morton J. Horwitz	1945–	Lynn Hunt
1938–	Olwen H. Hufton	1945–	Paul M. Kennedy
1938–	Laurel Thatcher Ulrich	1945–	David Rock
1939–	Robert Darnton	1945–	Simon Schama
1939–	Norman Davies	1945–	Judith R. Walkowitz
1939–	Carlo Ginzburg	1946–	Reynaldo Clemeña Ileto
1939–	Pierre Guichard	1947–	Darlene Clark Hine
1939–	John Iliffe	1949–	Marilyn Lake

INTRODUCTION

Rethinking History?

The writing of history has undergone a transformation in the past forty years. New historical methods, questions, sources, and topics have altered not only the public's perception of history, but the way the profession examines itself. From a discipline mainly concerned with affairs of state, it has moved to one where the common man and woman are probed for their recollections of how they lived their everyday lives. Historians now touch on everything from the sacred to the mundane. The present book reflects this metamorphosis of the subject.

A volume published on historians and historical writing forty years ago would have had three notable features. First, it would have been dominated by the men who have recorded and analyzed the past. Whether they were chroniclers or interpreters of the past, men dominated the ranks of historical writers. Second, with one or two exceptions these men would all have been part of a tradition that focused on Western civilization, initially centered on the classical world, but later shifting to the places where Europeans had made some inroads. An entry or two might have been reserved for the great historians of the Islamic world or China, but the ranks would have overflowed with Europeans and North Americans. Finally, most of the writers would have been practitioners of political or diplomatic history. History (and its sister art, biography) was seen to be the story of nations and nation building. The most prominent practitioners wrote about kings and presidents, parliaments and political movements. Those who focused on other aspects had their work qualified in its description as, for example, "economic" or "intellectual" history.[1]

An encyclopedia today that limited itself to mostly male historians of European or American politics would be doing a disservice to the reader who wished to understand how history is now studied. That women have infiltrated the ranks of historians in greater numbers is only the smallest part of this story. More significant is the expansion of the historical imagination. New techniques and approaches have placed history at the center of efforts to understand the complexities of the modern world by delving more deeply into the global past. The expansion of higher education around the world has encouraged this phenomenon by formalizing the study of once "exotic" cultures that had been the preserve of anthropologists and archaeologists. New ways of interrogating sources have allowed historians to recover the past in regions once thought to be lost forever to history because their cultures were preliterate. All of these developments we have tried to reflect in the *Encyclopedia of Historians and Historical Writing*.

This *Encyclopedia* is a compendium of the practice of history. It seeks to acquaint readers with the varieties of historical writing that have developed since the ancient world through a consideration of both individual historians and their subjects. This essay provides an overview of some of the trends that have emerged. It offers a brief and general account that traces the development of historical writing and then an assessment of how the discipline stands at the beginning of the third millennium in a world obsessed with the present moment.

* * *

History has a history. The earliest historians whose individual works have survived, such as **Herodotus** (*c*.484–after 424 BCE) and **Thucydides** (460/455–*c*.399 BCE), focused on military exploits. They wished to recount the military campaigns of their society, and were historians because they were concerned for the authenticity of their accounts. Herodotus tried to compare different sources about a battle, and both he and Thucydides strove to place the wars they discussed in their proper historical context. They asked the basic historical question: why did events happen when they did? These men traced the answer to a variety of causative factors, and their analysis of both the antecedents and outcomes of the wars made them forerunners of the modern historical discipline. In China, too, similar questions were asked. China's ruling houses had a tradition of recording important events under each emperor, but the rare individual who wished to offer a wider interpretation might, like **Sima Qian** (*c*.145–*c*.87 BCE), be forced to become a eunuch in order to retain access to the sources he needed. Sima Qian's *Shiji* (*Historical Records*) was to be a comprehensive history of China, but it also sought to draw out moral lessons for its readers. It is the template for most histories that followed in China and the surrounding areas. The dissatisfaction of **Ban Gu** (*c*.32–92 CE) with Sima Qian's account drove him to write the first dynastic history of China, which enlarged on the critical techniques his predecessor had developed. Clearly, historical writing was developing simultaneously in East and West.

During the Middle Ages, historians faithfully recorded events and, as monks, often focused on the concerns of the church. The *Historia ecclesiastica gentis Anglorum* (Ecclesiastical History of the English People, 731) of **Bede** (*c*.672/3–735) is a good example of this. The biography of Charlemagne by **Einhard** (*c*.770–840) broke new ground in dealing with a secular rather than a religious figure. Elsewhere, historians of Byzantium such as **Michael Psellos** (1018–after 1081) and **Anna Komnene** (1083–*c*.1153/4) offered dynastic histories that did not simply focus on theological explanations, while the Islamic historian **Ibn Khaldūn** (1332–1406) explored the possibilities of universal history.

It was the Renaissance that fostered a new way of looking at the past. Although still concerned mostly with politics and kings, the analysis shifted more and more to the question of historical causation. Biographies began to move beyond the hagiographic, seeking an understanding of the complexities of man (and I do mean man) as a historical actor. There was also a small but growing public interested in works of history. Renaissance humanist writers such as **Machiavelli** (1469–1527) and **Guicciardini** (1483–1540) wished to make a break with the descriptive chronicles that had come to be accepted as historical writing during the medieval period. Instead, they harked back to ancient writers such as **Livy** (59 BCE–*c*.17 CE) and to the explanation of events. History was then seen as something that should be written in service to the state, often commissioned by a noble patron. Thus the attempt by historians to interpret the past did not always make them popular, and Guicciardini was under constant surveillance by the civil authorities as he wrote his history of Italy.

The 18th-century Enlightenment equipped history with the values of skepticism and empiricism and the need for a more rigorous analysis of change over time. This was true of **David Hume**'s *History of England* (1754–62) and of what must be the most influential of histories written before the 19th century: **Edward Gibbon**'s *The History of the Decline and Fall of the Roman Empire* (1776–88). His multivolume masterpiece contained not only a strong narrative backbone, but an analytical framework that strove to explain the evolution of the human condition. The complex historical questions posed by Gibbon set the stage for a revolution in historical research during the 19th century.

If history had been primarily a form of literature up to this time, the modern discipline of history was characterized by an emphasis on precision. The researches of **Leopold von Ranke** (1795–1886) ushered in a new period when scientific methods were increasingly imposed by historians on themselves. Ranke's innovation was in his use of sources. He traveled from archive to archive, then still controlled by the ruling houses, families, and religious bodies that had created them. He searched for tangible proof of what had happened in the past, trying to establish undisputed or at least rigorously tested facts. He and his fellow positivists dominated 19th-century historical writing, and scholars became used to sifting through European archives and employing a scientific approach. Most were still concerned with high political history. Ranke's work ranged from a study of the popes to a universal history placing all of his broad-ranging research into perspective. His younger American contemporary **Henry Charles Lea** (1825–1909) also benefited from the reorganization and opening of archives, and spent his life working on the first authoritative account of the Inquisition. Nineteenth-century historians for the most part belonged to a great narrative tradition enriched by a wide range of new sources. No longer reliant on official accounts, hazy memoirs, and earlier chronicles, they also became central interpreters of the present by examining the past.

Historical works inevitably mediated the politics and culture of their time. In the 19th century, a period characterized by the spread of nationalism, historians increasingly found a role in making sense of the nation and providing it with a past. The histories of the United States by **George Bancroft** (1800–1891) sought to give the new nation a stronger identity. **François Guizot** (1787–1874) and **Augustin Thierry** (1795–1856) in France and **Lord Acton** (1834–1902) in Britain wrote works arguing that ideas of liberty were crucial for historical development. The need to account for the growth of liberty and progress gave rise to the **Whig interpretation of history**. In the century of Ranke, **Thomas Babington Macaulay** (1800–1859), and **Jacob Burckhardt** (1818–1897), history was established both as an academic discipline and as an essential component of the educated person.

By the beginning of the 20th century most modern states were firmly established and the desire to bolster them by creating cozy historical narratives about the nation no longer seemed quite so necessary. In keeping with the widespread critique of modern society, historians began to look beyond the ideologies of state-building to ask if they had considered all the reasons for historical change. Take for example the American historian **Charles A. Beard** (1874–1948). Rather than accepting that the foundation of the United States had been a straightforward question of the clash of political ideas, he asked what was in it for the Founding Fathers of the American Constitution. He argued that these elites had a noticeable financial stake in independence from Britain. Whether or not he was right in his analysis, Beard forced historians to construct new questions and analytical frameworks for their investigations. Other historians raised questions about sectors of society that had often been overlooked. **W.E.B. Du Bois** (1868–1963) offered an early study of African Americans and their place in US history. In the first few decades of the 20th century historical orthodoxies were repeatedly challenged, but the older tradition of empirical, narrative history steadfastly held its ground.

Since World War II that situation has changed. Historians have increasingly engaged with theory – analytical frameworks from other disciplines – as a way to enrich their explanations of the past. Perhaps more importantly, the dominant emphasis on high politics has receded and today there is very little of the past that does not serve as grist for some researcher's mill.[2] These postwar changes have not been, however, just the result of the satisfactory answering of earlier questions and the belief that there was nothing useful remaining to be said. Instead, new questions and methods emerged at a particular historical moment that might be loosely characterized as the creation of a new global intellectual culture. It came at the culmination of several centuries of transcontinental and transoceanic migration, when cultures were coming into contact more frequently and more people were being encouraged to increase their understanding of the past as well as the present. These factors combined to energize and transform historical writing as well as other scholarly disciplines. The spread of higher education across the world in turn produced a larger number of people entering the historical profession, although popular historians such as the Americans Barbara Tuchman and Bruce Catton succeeded in researching and writing outside the academy and reaching an audience that most academics could not begin to touch.

Although in the late 20th century it is clear that global communications have never been so good, it is not in this sense that I speak of the creation of a global intellectual culture emerging in the wake of World War II. Rather it is that the turmoil of the 1920s and 1930s caused the movement of scores of intellectuals around the globe. This, of course, was not unique to historical studies, but the discipline benefited from it. The migrants sometimes carried with them different notions of historical study, and also a rich body of knowledge about their home cultures. They did not always have an immediate effect on the groups of scholars who took them in, but enriched the lives of graduate students and younger scholars eager to unravel the complexities of both the modern world and the ancient. Sometimes dissidents in their own countries, but more often victims of state ideologies that excluded them, these men and women were anxious to continue their research, but also to educate a new audience, and, most importantly, to explain their betrayal by their home countries. Historians who fled from fascism, such as **Arnaldo Momigliano** (1908–1987), gently led their new colleagues to an understanding of the irrationality of the system they had just rejected.

This irrationality was a major stimulus to the development of new methods of understanding the past. Although underlying prejudices were sometimes explored in political and diplomatic history, the emphasis on archival sources meant that some factors behind historical change had been little studied. It became necessary to understand the structure of belief systems in the past. Perhaps most crucially, history had mostly been about elites, great men and the way in which they shaped their societies. One of the first significant changes to historical study was the broadening of the subjects covered. In other words, the period saw the emergence of the most influential branch of history in the 20th century: **social history**. Social history generated an approach known as **history from below** (also known as "bottom-up" history or the history of everyday life). The common man and woman had been examined before, for example in the study of English workers and the Industrial Revolution by **J.L. and Barbara Hammond** (1872–1949; 1873–1961), but now their struggles moved center stage, as in the work of **Alf Lüdtke** (1943–) on *Altagsgeschichte* (the history of everyday life). The history of society at first focused on the lives of workers, but soon every aspect of society came under its purview, from the study of Brazilian slavery to the English middle-classes.[3] Social history seeks to understand how groups find a voice and how structures shape people's lives. From a focus on class, it has more recently embraced questions of race and gender to broaden readers' understanding of a range of cultures.

Underpinning the new social history was the growing influence of Marxist theory on the academy. It was not necessary to be a Marxist in order to be a social historian but Marxism was frequently responsible for setting the terms of the debates. The ideas of **Karl Marx** (1818–1883) about modern capitalist society were anchored in historical study, and the 20th century witnessed the swelling ranks of scholars impatient to utilize his ideas to examine a broad range of historical moments. Undoubtedly the most influential of the new historians working in the Marxist tradition was **E.P. Thompson** (1924–1993), whose *The Making of the English Working Class* (1963) inspired researchers around the world. Thompson's left-wing politics drew him towards the history of the common people whom he successfully endowed with agency. Whereas proponents of Marx's theories often cast workers as the unwitting dupes of the dominant class, Thompson argued that by the early 19th century in Britain these people lived, worked, and struggled to challenge their subordinate role in society. Thompson's magisterial work had its critics, but it had far more admirers who extracted from it a dignity for men and women often portrayed earlier as faceless and powerless. Scholars from many countries established the reality of conflict where it had been denied before. Perhaps this is best seen in the development of **subaltern studies**, which specifically scrutinizes the relationships between colonizers and colonized. Subaltern studies arose in the wake of the independence movements of the postwar period and examined often dispossessed, colonized groups after many years of Western depictions of them as either childlike or cunning.

The **Marxist interpretation** was one of many approaches that helped to enrich historical debate. Other influences came from parallel academic disciplines, especially those that had emerged during the previous hundred years. **Anthropology** and **sociology** were major contributors to social history. Both offered new and rigorous systems for examining society.[4] Sociology helped in the effort to understand social divisions, whether between classes in the modern world or orders in the medieval. It enabled historians to think about how different groups dealt with one another and how these dynamics affected other things in society. Anthropology, particularly cultural anthropology, assisted in the struggle to understand the symbolic relationships of the past. What was the meaning of the gift in early modern Europe? How did protestors use symbolic objects in riots to make their hostility clear? **Robert Darnton** (1939–) brilliantly knitted these disciplines together in his essay on the "Great Cat Massacre."[5] He employed the (to modern eyes) bizarre murder of some cats by a group of disgruntled artisans in late 18th-century Paris as a way of opening up a culture and exploring its otherness. Anthropology was also employed in studies of the family, of ritual, and in a range of other areas. The essay by **Terence O. Ranger** (1929–) in *The Invention of Tradition* (1983) illustrated this for African as well as European culture.[6] The theories of **Freud** (1856–1939) and other psychoanalysts were similarly employed by historians, although perhaps to less effect.[7]

Many of the historians and historical approaches discussed above and below owed a great deal to the most influential school of historical thought to arise in the 20th century. The **Annales school** emerged in the first half of the century in France and was centered on the academic journal *Annales*. Social and economic history were knitted together in the first half of the century in the writings of the medievalist **Marc Bloch** (1886–1944) on **feudalism** and the work of **Lucien Febvre** (1878–1956) on **mentalities**. Both were founders of the journal *Annales* and both broke with earlier analytical modes to focus on what might be characterized as broader questions of historical interest. Bloch examined feudalism from the viewpoint of the peasant as well as the lord, while Febvre's work helped to establish the importance of the irrational as well as the rational as a historical force. This work expanded in the second half of the 20th century, and might be said to have culminated in *La Méditerranée et le monde méditerranéen à l'époque de Philippe II* (1949; *The Mediterranean and the Mediterranean World in the Age of Philip II*, 1972–73) by **Fernand Braudel** (1902–1985). His work focused on *la longue durée*, that is, change over a long period of time, but it also reached beyond conventional boundaries to examine the inter-relatedness of regions. He demonstrated that historians must move beyond national borders in order to understand the past.

Economic theories also had a great impact on historiography. In the postwar period there were increasing numbers of scholars who wanted to focus on the problem of why some societies had thrived and others had not. Implicit was a question about how actively rich nations had worked to impede the advance of poorer ones. For example, "dependency theory" offered an explanatory mode that pinned much of the blame on the active efforts of industrialized nations to maintain their dominance. **Fernando Henrique Cardoso** (1931–) and Enzo Faletto's *Dependencia y desarrollo en América Latina* (1969; *Dependency and Development in Latin America*, 1979) explored this idea in the context of Latin America. Although dependency theory emerged as an explanation for 20th-century phenomena, historians raided the idea to think about the past. Maurice P. Brungardt's essay in the *Encyclopedia*, **Latin America: National**, traces the use of this theory in the historiography. He demonstrates that the historians did not always agree with the theorists, but historians were crucial in testing economic theories outside the scene of their creation.

Economic and social history were entwined from early in the century, but they increasingly went their own ways. Very much a discipline in its own right, **economic history** has employed quantification and economic theory to explore specific questions about the past. Economic historians might deal with questions of finance, trade cycles, entrepreneurship, or the development of systems of accounting. In economic history are also found the roots of modern-day business history. Economic historians also delve into larger questions, as in the work of **Immanuel Wallerstein** (1930–) on the "modern world-system." Financial systems, the movement of money, and the inter-relatedness of different economies continue to spark debate among economic historians.

The Cinderella discipline of the profession has been **cultural history**, an area that was originally part of intellectual history.[8] Cultural history seeks to explain the ways in which different cultures work and evolve. This is a rather broad definition, so it can encompass historians of religion, gender, leisure, entrepreneurship, or just about any subject as long as it explores the way cultural practices developed. As Bill Schwarz's essay in this volume suggests, cultural history had its roots in the study of "high culture," but it has now broadened its scope to the study of **mentalities** or the way cultures formulate their beliefs. Thus, **Natalie Zemon Davis'** (1928–) study of the imposter Martin Guerre revealed the problems of religion, gender, and power in early modern France. **Emmanuel Le Roy Ladurie's** (1929–) *Montaillou* (1975) combined theory and intensive archival research to create the world of a medieval French village. Both are works of social as well as cultural history. [9]

Intellectual history, on the other hand, can in some ways be seen as a branch of philosophy, as it initially focused on great thinkers and the evolution of their ideas. More recently, it has been joined by the "history of ideas," which traces how an idea develops over time. Ideas in this sense are imbedded in a specific culture, and thus can be explored for their meaning. The separation between historians and philosophers comes in the former's intense interest in the context of the idea and how the surrounding society contributed to an idea's transformation.

What is clear is that although historians have increasingly employed theories from a broad range of disciplines they have also clung to the use of evidence in their exploration of the past. But the areas that counted as evidence also expanded in these years.

Where before high politics had demanded a consideration of the correspondence between ministers and ministries, now historians were eager to explore arrest reports, postmortems, and parish records. They mapped out localities by using earlier maps and utilized census records to trace small movements of population. **Demographic history** originated in France under **Louis Henry** (1911–1991); later the **Cambridge Group** formulated new questions about family size and personal space. The use of Inquisition records by **Carlo Ginzburg** (1939–) not only told us about religious belief in the 16th century but about the universe of the subject.[10] **Oral history** also expanded beyond informal remembrances to a theorized methodology; it has been employed to explore the lives of both elites and peasants. **African American history** was similarly transformed by the employment of folk-tales and songs as well as plantation records. The use of sources once rejected as unworthy was combined with those often lightly examined to produce a richer understanding of the "peculiar institution" of slavery in the United States.

This broadening of the definition of evidence was part of the expansion of study of marginal groups that was a characteristic of the 1960s and 1970s. In America, the civil rights movement sparked a new interest in what might best be characterized as non-elite groups. Black history began to emerge, first focusing on the world of the African American slave in a range of works (see the entry on **Slavery: Modern**), but eventually reaching out to a fuller treatment of the **African diaspora**. Many would have initially argued that the sources were not available to study this topic, but they were proven wrong. Similarly, **women's history** emerged at the same time, with similar worries about a lack of sources.[11] For historians used to exploring archives for evidence, both groups presented challenges, and women's history in particular has established that historical sources about the female sex can be found in a range of materials.

As empirical studies grew, race, class, and gender were postulated as historical forces that shaped both lived experience and state policy. Class had long been seen as an important factor in understanding the past. Race moved from a focus on specific groups to a consideration of how skin color and scientific categories were exploited to maintain white dominance. *Orientalism* (1978) by Edward W. Said (1935–) elegantly demonstrated this. More recent studies have begun to explore whiteness as a historical category.[12] **Gender** history extends the investigations that feminist historians initiated by reminding us that men as well as women have had a gendered historical experience. Thus, gender history incorporates the insights provided by women's history and the history of **masculinity** to explore the way attitudes toward gender have shaped lives. This goes beyond questions of women's political enfranchisement to histories of state formation, such as Theda Skocpol's work on the welfare benefits provided for American Civil War veterans and the gendered assumptions implicit therein.[13]

If the types of empirical evidence to be used and the range of theories to be consulted expanded, there was at the same time a constant debate about how sources should be interpreted. From Ranke onwards many historians subscribed to a notion that reading a source was a matter of some skill, but that the sources themselves were relatively uncomplicated. Twentieth-century historians have questioned this in two ways. First, there has been the emphasis on the historian and on how his or her concerns can affect the way evidence is read. **Carl L. Becker** (1873–1945) raised this issue most influentially in his essay "Everyman His Own Historian" (1931), which argued that historians were not neutral readers of texts. Instead they brought with them their own concerns and they interpreted the past through the lens of the present. For Becker, most historians came to their subjects because of some present-day concern. History therefore was not necessarily an objective pursuit and was caught up in the great 20th-century belief: relativism. Relativism provided an explanation for why different generations of historians could examine the same events and documents and develop different interpretations. History depended on the historian's point of view. This position was most influentially expressed by E.H. Carr (1892–1982) in *What Is History?* (1961).

Relativism places an emphasis on the problem of the historian as interpreter, but the influence of literary tools of analysis has led to a theoretical debate that has been exercising philosophers of history for the past twenty years. This shifts the problem of analysis from the reader to the text that is being read. **Postmodernism** refers to a cluster of ideas that reject the possibility that a text is a transparent piece of evidence which historians can employ to elucidate the past. Instead texts become slippery objects.[14] Postmodernism came into its own in the era of the collapse of the grand narratives that had previously underpinned the modern study of history. The disintegration of Marxist orthodoxies (which had already been in train before the fall of the Berlin Wall in 1989) inspired discussion of whether categories such as class had any usefulness any longer. Postmodernists, to put it simply, argue that we can never really recover the facts about an event; all that is available to us are a series of discourses from the past. As Keith Jenkins notes in his essay in this encyclopedia: "This is not to deny the actuality of the world (or of worlds past) but is simply to say that it is human discourse that appropriates it and gives it all the meanings it can be said to have." The most important figure in postmodernist history is probably **Hayden V. White** (1928–) whose work on texts led him to characterize historical analysis as **metahistory**. Metahistory implies that any representation of historical reality needs severe questioning. Postmodernism is a difficult proposition for most conventional historians because at its most extreme it appears to deny that the past can ever be really known. We do not possess the past, only a series of discourses that have been left behind. For this reason, postmodernism was one of the most problematic theories to be reckoned with in the late 20th century.[15]

Historiography is the blanket term for thinking about methods of historical research, and all of the movements and methods discussed above have their advocates and detractors. In fact, the late 20th century has seen the historical profession turn far more reflexive about what it does and the way it does it. General readers are often unaware of the contentiousness of the historical method employed by the historian they are reading. Perhaps this is unsurprising, as most general readers are often unconsciously conservative in their historical tastes. They still like a good narrative and most would consider the debates over how a text can or cannot be read as self-indulgent. This is not to say that the general reader has not been exposed to many of the new trends of history in this century. **Military history** itself, one of the most enduring of genres, has been energized by new research into the experience of the common soldier as well as fresh treatments of the role of technology in war, to name just two aspects.[16] But these debates continue to rage within the historical profession around the world.

As the new millennium begins where does the writing of history stand? One of the great merits of history is that it remains accessible to the general reader. From 1935 to 1967, many American homes bought Will and Ariel Durant's *Story of Civilization* series.[17] Popular history continues in books (particularly biographies) but it also has found a niche on television. Jeremy Isaacs' *The World at War* (1973) or Ken Burns' series *The Civil War* (1990) were triumphs of the documentary genre that found a popular audience. One of the publishing surprises of 1998 was the rise in sales of **Howard Zinn**'s *A People's History of the United States* (1980; revised 1995), after a brief mention by the character played by Matt Damon in the film *Good Will Hunting*. The film was not about history, but Damon made it seem a sexy topic to read about.

History is clearly far from dead. The expansion of topics of interest confirms this, but so does the continuing interest of the general public in interpretations of the past. Sometimes these interpretations have a political edge; for example, *The Rise and Fall of the Great Powers: Economic Change and Military Conflict from 1500 to 2000* (1987) by Paul M. Kennedy (1945–) sparked a widely followed debate about the possible decline of US power.

Where does this leave historical writing? Academic historians remain committed to their discipline even if they differ about what that discipline exactly is. They revel in the complexity and the opportunity to seek out new areas for study. They persist in stressing that people in the past experienced material realities from day to day, and they valorize rigorous attempts to uncover the past and to try to understand it. They use theory to help them to understand the possibilities of interpretation rather than to substitute for the necessarily painstaking research required of them. They struggle to write for the general reader. Historical writing remains dynamic at the start of the third millennium.

KELLY BOYD

Notes

1. For useful overviews of the history of history, see Ernst Breisach, *Historiography: Ancient, Medieval and Modern* (Chicago: University of Chicago Press, 1983, 1994); Michael Bentley, ed., *Companion to Historiography* (London: Routledge, 1997). **Bold** in the text indicates the Encyclopedia contains an entry on this person or topic.

2. A list of recent research on unexpected topics might include David Yosifon and Peter N. Stearns, "The Rise and Fall of American Posture," *American Historical Review* 103 (1998), 1057–95; Marybeth Hamilton, "Sexual Politics and African-American Music; or, Placing Little Richard in Context," *History Workshop Journal* 46 (1998), 161–76; Chris Wickham, "Gossip and Resistance among the Medieval Peasantry," *Past and Present* 160 (1998), 3–24.

3. Gilberto Freyre, *Casa-grande e senzala: formação da família brasileira sob o regime de economia patriarcal* (Rio de Janeiro: Maia & Schmidt, 1933); in English as *The Masters and the Slaves: A Study in the Development of Brazilian Civilization* (New York: Knopf, 1946, London: Secker and Warburg, 1947); Leonore Davidoff and Catherine Hall, *Family Fortunes: Men and Women of the English Middle Class, 1780–1850* (London: Hutchinson, and Chicago: University of Chicago Press, 1987).

4. Early discussions of their usefulness are found in Keith Thomas, "History and Anthropology," *Past and Present* 24 (1963), 3–24; Peter Burke, *Sociology and History* (London and Boston: Allen and Unwin, 1980); and Philip Abrams, *Historical Sociology* (Ithaca, NY: Cornell University Press, and Shepton Mallet, Somerset: Open University Press, 1982).

5. Robert Darnton, "Workers Revolt: The Great Cat Massacre of the rue Saint Séverin," in his *The Great Cat Massacre and Other Episodes in French Cultural History* (New York: Basic Books, and London: Allen Lane, 1984), 74–104.

6. "The Invention of Tradition in Colonial Africa," in Eric J. Hobsbawm and Terence O. Ranger, eds., *The Invention of Tradition* (Cambridge and New York: Cambridge University Press, 1983).

7. A good introduction to Freud is found in Peter Gay, *Freud for Historians* (New York: Oxford University Press, 1985). Graham Dawson, *Soldier Heroes: British Adventure, Empire, and the Imaginings of Masculinities* (London and New York: Routledge, 1994) uses Melanie Klein's work to advantage.

8. Lynn Hunt, ed., *The New Cultural History* (Berkeley: University of California Press, 1989).

9. Natalie Zemon Davis, *The Return of Martin Guerre* (Cambridge, MA: Harvard University Press, 1983); Emmanuel Le Roy Ladurie, *Montaillou: village occitan de 1294 à 1324* (Paris: Gallimard, 1975), in English as *Montaillou: The Promised Land of Error* (New York: Braziller, 1978) and as *Montaillou: Cathars and Catholics in a French Village, 1294–1324* (London: Scolar Press, 1978).

10. Carlo Ginzburg, *Il formaggio e i vermi: il cosmo di un mugnaio del '500* (Turin: Einaudi, 1976); in English as *The Cheese and the Worms: The Cosmos of a Sixteenth-Century Miller* (Baltimore: Johns Hopkins University Press, and London: Routledge, 1980).

11. See, for example, Gerda Lerner, *The Majority Finds Its Past: Placing Women in History* (New York: Oxford University Press, 1979); Michelle Perrot, ed., *Une Histoire des femmes*

est-elle possible? (Paris: Rivage, 1984); in English as *Writing Women's History* (Oxford and Cambridge, MA: Blackwell, 1992); and Joan Wallach Scott, *Gender and the Politics of History* (New York: Columbia University Press, 1988).

12. David Roediger, *Towards the Abolition of Whiteness: Essays on Race, Politics and Working Class History* (London and New York: Verso, 1994); Catherine Hall, *White, Male and Middle Class: Explorations in Feminism and History* (Cambridge: Polity Press, 1992); Vron Ware, *Beyond the Pale: White Women, Racism and History* (London: Verso, 1992).

13. Theda Skocpol, *Protecting Soldiers and Mothers: The Political Origins of Social Policy in the United States* (Cambridge, MA: Harvard University Press, 1992).

14. See the debates in Keith Jenkins, ed., *The Postmodern History Reader* (London and New York: Routledge, 1997).

15. See Richard J. Evans' critique of postmodernism, In *Defence of History* (London: Granta Books, 1997).

16. See, for example, John Keegan, *The Face of Battle* (London: Cape, and New York: Viking, 1976); and Joanna Bourke, *Dismembering the Male: Men's Bodies, Britain and the Great War* (Chicago: University of Chicago Press, and London: Reaktion, 1996) for some of these new developments.

17. See Joan Shelley Rubin, *The Making of Middle-brow Culture* (Chapel Hill: University of North Carolina Press, 1992), chapter 5.

A

Acton, Lord 1834–1902
British historian

Lord Acton has attracted many detailed studies of his life and scholarship, yet his reputation and legacy are curious. He is remembered today as an exponent of scientific methods in history and as a scholar, devoted to the study of liberty, whose best known epigram is "power tends to corrupt and absolute power corrupts absolutely." He is also notorious for having risen to the heights of the historical profession without actually writing a book; the only work published in book form during his lifetime was his inaugural lecture when he became Regius professor of history at Cambridge. In fact, Acton was a far more complex figure than his modern reputation suggests.

Most of Acton's life was spent outside the academy. He was born into the aristocracy and was able to become an independent scholar. The key to Acton's life and work was his Roman Catholic faith. A precocious learner, he opted at the age of 16 to study in Munich under the tutelage of the scholar and priest Johann Ignaz von Döllinger, who became his mentor. It was Döllinger who introduced the young John Dalberg Acton (later Lord Acton) to church history, which would become one of the chief subjects of his scholarship. He also absorbed from his tutor the new German historical methods (the scientific focus on primary sources associated with Ranke) that he was to propagate in Britain. He made extensive trips to archives around Europe, where his ability to speak many languages was put to good use. He also began to collect books and manuscripts; his library eventually extended to some 60,000 volumes.

Despite his reputation, Acton was in fact immensely productive as a historian. Rather than books, his output took the form of articles, reviews, and lectures (many of which were posthumously collected and published by his admirers). All his work was characterized by deep learning and exposure to the relevant archival materials. For the most part he concentrated on modern history, which he defined in 1895 as the history of the previous 400 years.

His essays focused on topics in British and European history from the Reformation and Counter-Reformation to the French Revolution. He was particularly interested in the political role of the papacy. Acton was also a leading reviewer of other scholars and many of his essays were historiographical, such as his article on German schools of history that appeared in the first issue of the *English Historical Review* in 1886.

Ironically, he is best known for the work he never wrote, a projected history of liberty, which occupied his thoughts but was never brought to fruition. He was a strong believer in the impact of ideas (and especially religious ideas) in different historical periods. Acton's research in archives persuaded him of the importance of impartiality, which is why he has become known as a defender of scientific history. Yet he also believed that historians could pass judgment on events and people in the past once they had mastered the evidence. For Acton there were universal moral absolutes that could be discerned throughout history and which the historian had to express. As his editors Figgis and Laurence wrote in 1907: "he was eminently a Victorian in his confidence that he was right." It is not, however, correct to describe Acton as a Whig historian. He disliked the use of history to satisfy modern political purposes.

Much of Acton's early work took the form of apologetics for Roman Catholicism; he was close to John Henry Newman at one point. Inspired by Döllinger, he attempted to construct a liberal Catholicism in Britain that recognized the importance of the individual right of conscience. He opposed the growing ultramontanism of the church in Europe and many of the temporal claims of the pope which culminated in the declaration of papal infallibility in 1870 and which Acton did his best to resist. He once claimed to belong to the soul rather than the body of the church. Many of his historical articles were published in Catholic periodicals such as the *Rambler* and the *Home and Foreign Review*, which he variously owned and edited. By temperament, Acton was conservative, an admirer of Burke with an abhorrence of revolution. He feared the tyranny of the majority and disliked the secular nature of Victorian utilitarianism, including the ideas of liberal figures such as John Stuart Mill. Acton's liberalism (apparent in his writings) took the form of opposition to any form of absolutism. Thus he sympathized with the principle of states' rights in the United States (a country he visited in 1853) and supported the Confederacy during the Civil War, even defending slavery. Acton's liberalism was also evident in his support of Irish home rule in 1886. Yet his was a particular kind of liberalism. Although he supported the rights of the individual, he also believed that society had to move toward a greater spiritual unity.

Acton helped to launch the *English Historical Review* in 1886, which became the flagship journal of the historical profession; and as Regius professor of history at Cambridge, he inspired the *Cambridge Modern History*. Although he wrote nothing for it (he died while it was in progress), he established the structure of the project, which promised an impartial account of modern events. Setting "ultimate history" as a goal to which historians should aspire even if it could not be achieved, he informed contributors that "our Waterloo must be one that satisfies French and English, German and Dutch alike." Thus Acton has come down to us as a defender of an objectivity in which the historian's character should not interfere with the compilation of historical facts. Yet it is the paradoxical attachment to impartiality and interpretation in Acton that has drawn modern historians such as Herbert Butterfield, Owen Chadwick, Gertude Himmelfarb, and Hugh Tulloch to investigate the complexities of this pillar of the historical world in Victorian Britain.

ROHAN MCWILLIAM

See also Catholicism; Clapham; Europe: Modern; Halecki; Reformation; Sarpi; Universal

Biography

John Emerich Edward Dalberg Acton, 1st Baron Acton. Born Naples, Italy, 10 January 1834. Studied with Cardinal Wiseman at the Roman Catholic College at Oscott, 1843–47; then briefly with Dr. Logan in Edinburgh, 1847–48; and finally with Johann Ignaz von Döllinger in Munich, 1848–54. Traveled extensively in Europe and the US, 1855–59, then settled in England. Member of Parliament for Carlow, 1859–65, and Bridgnorth, 1865–66. Regius professor, Cambridge University, 1895–1902. Married Countess Marie Arco-Valley, 1865 (1 son, 3 daughters). Created 1st Baron Acton of Aldenham, 1869. Died Tegernsee, Bavaria, 19 June 1902.

Principal Writings

A Lecture on the Study of History, 1895
Lectures on Modern History, edited by John Neville Figgis and Reginald Vere Laurence, 1906
Historical Essays and Studies, edited by John Figgis and Reginald Vere Laurence, 1907
The History of Freedom and Other Essays, edited by John Neville Figgis and Reginald Vere Laurence, 1907
Lectures on the French Revolution, edited by John Neville Figgis and Reginald Vere Laurence, 1910
Essays on Freedom and Power, edited by Gertrude Himmelfarb, 1948
Essays on Church and State, edited by Douglas Woodruff, 1952

Further Reading
Butterfield, Herbert, *Lord Acton*, London: Historical Association 1948
Butterfield, Herbert, *Man on His Past: The Study of the History of Historical Scholarship*, Cambridge: Cambridge University Press, 1955; Boston: Beacon Press, 1960
Chadwick, Owen, *Acton and History*, Cambridge and New York: Cambridge University Press, 1998
Fasnacht, George Eugene, *Acton's Political Philosophy: An Analysis*, London: Hollis and Carter, 1952
Himmelfarb, Gertrude, *Lord Acton: A Study in Conscience and Politics*, London: Routledge, 1952; Chicago: University of Chicago Press, 1953
Kochan, Lionel, *Acton on History*, London: Deutsch, 1954
Mathew, David, *Lord Acton and His Times*, London: Eyre and Spottiswoode, and Tuscaloosa: University of Alabama Press, 1968
Schuettinger, R.L., *Lord Acton, Historian of Liberty*, La Salle, IL: Open Court, 1976
Tulloch, Hugh, *Acton*, London: Weidenfeld and Nicolson, and New York: St. Martin's Press, 1988
Watson, George, *Lord Acton's History of Liberty: A Study of His Library, with an Edited Text of His History of Liberty Notes*, London: Scolar Press, 1994

Adams, Henry 1838–1918
US historian

Henry Adams is a singular presence in American history and historiography. His uniqueness stems from the lack of a clearly discernible boundary between Adams the historian and Adams the historical subject; both aspects have had lasting influences on American historiography. This confusion between author and subject becomes evident when we remember that Adams considered his "autobiography," *The Education of Henry Adams* (privately printed, 1907; 1918) to be a sequel to his best-known work on medieval history, *Mont-Saint-Michel and Chartres* (privately printed 1904; 1913).

That Adams would write history was practically foreordained; that he would become a historian was unexpected, most of all to himself. For the Adams family, writing history was what one did after one *made* history. Adams' ancestors had served alongside Jefferson and Franklin in the Continental Congress and in diplomatic corps at the great courts of Europe; no less was expected from Henry. That doing and writing history was a family inheritance was clear to him from childhood, when he helped proofread his grandfather's papers which his father was editing for publication.

Henry Adams never made history, at least not in the way he and his family expected. The time when the well-educated sons of the best families were presumed political timber had passed by the time Adams reached his maturity, and he did not have the temperament to engage in the jangling, jostling arena of Gilded Age politics. This failure to "hitch" his career to "the family go-cart" (in his words) had a profound effect both on Adams' writing and his impact on subsequent historiography.

Adams slipped into writing history haphazardly. After graduation from Harvard College in 1858, he went to the University of Berlin to study law. That plan did not last long, as his knowledge of German was inadequate to the task. He tried his hand at freelance journalism, travelling around Europe and sending his reports back to American newspapers. By 1860, he had returned to the United States to become his father's private secretary. Charles Francis Adams had just been elected to Congress, and Henry therefore had a front-row view in Washington of the "Great Secession Winter" (as he called it in one of his articles) of 1860–61.

When Lincoln appointed the elder Adams Ambassador to Great Britain, Henry accompanied him to London, continuing both his service as secretary and his journalistic career. By the time his father left the post in 1868, Henry had written a number of newspaper and journal articles, mainly on politics and finance, but he also published his first historical essays. Adams did not view these essays any differently from his other writing; he was seeking to establish his intellectual reputation, not to become an historian. Yet in 1868, Henry Adams found himself at 30 years old without any clear career path. While he had some modest success in journalism, it did not seem a distinguished enough career choice for an Adams. Nor was journalism a stepping stone to a political career, as he may have thought ten years earlier. The greed and corruption of Gilded Age America so repelled Adams that a life toadying to Robber Barons for money and *hoi polloi* for votes now seemed out of the question.

With these options closed off Adams accepted an assistant professorship to teach medieval history at Harvard College, along with which he would become editor of the *North American Review*, a journal he hoped to turn into an organ for political reform. He had few formal qualifications to teach medieval history, but in the years before professionalization and the impact of German scholarship on American higher education, neither did anyone else. Harvard President Charles Eliot chose Adams, in part, because of his exposure to the German seminar system, meager as it was. Despite his lack of preparation to teach the Middle Ages – Adams claimed always to be just a lesson ahead of the students – he succeeded in establishing the first graduate seminars based on the German model and set high standards for scholarship. He demanded students base their work solidly on documentary evidence. In this, Adams was on the leading edge of the historical practice of the day. His approach was close to that of the much more professionalized Herbert Baxter Adams, who began teaching graduate seminars in history at Johns Hopkins University by the end of the decade. Like Herbert Baxter Adams, Henry Adams viewed history as past politics. His seminars and writings emphasized medieval secular and church politics, the law and constitutionalism.

By the time Adams left Harvard for Washington in 1877, he had already turned his attention to the history of the early American republic, which would become his main historical concern for the next decade and a half. He had already begun teaching American history during his last few semesters at Harvard, and edited *Documents Relating to New England Federalism, 1800–1815* (1877), which defended his grandfather John Quincy Adams' anti-federalist views. Given unrestricted access to the papers of Albert Gallatin, Jefferson's treasury secretary, Adams produced an admiring biography in 1879.

His appetite thus whetted, Adams threw himself entirely into his *magnum opus*, the nine-volume *The History of the United States during the Administrations of Jefferson and Madison* (1889–91). It was a magisterial achievement, admired both for its graceful and subtle literary style and its unparalleled historical research. Adams immersed himself in state documents, not only in the United States, but in London, Paris, and Madrid as well. While a number of Adams' judgments have been challenged by subsequent historians (for example, modern historians have a higher opinion of Madison's abilities than Adams did), the work remains a masterpiece.

The significance of the *History*, however, goes beyond Adams' interpretation of the early American republic. Adams' goal was nothing less than the construction of history as a true science. "Scientific history," of course, was the siren call of an entire generation of scholars who were importing German scholarship and pedagogy to the new graduate schools of late 19th-century America. Influenced especially by Leopold von Ranke, however, their idea of scientific history was more limited than what Adams was striving for. Their method was scientific in that it emphasized empiricism; the historian's

version of direct laboratory observation was intimate familiarity with all the relevant documents. Beyond that, scientific historians shared with the physicist and chemist faith that careful observation (or close reading of documents) would lead to true knowledge of nature (or *wie es eigentlich gewesen ist*).

To understand Adams' more expansive view of scientific history, consideration must be given to the two major works he wrote after 1900, *Mont-Saint-Michel* and *The Education*. Neither book is a history in any conventional sense; one is more likely to find them read today for their literary merit than the historical information they impart. Meditative and quasi-novelistic, the two taken together present a complex and subtle interpretation that weaves together the High Middle Ages, the changes wrought by industrial capitalism, and the philosophy of history.

For Adams, to be truly scientific, historians had to reveal laws of social and political development, just as Darwin had revealed the laws of natural selection in biology. To be sure, Adams was not the only 19th-century intellectual to think along these lines, but his thinking developed eccentrically, relatively unaffected by Marx (Adams could accept neither his materialism nor his socialist conclusions) or Comte (whose periodization of history Adams accepted as descriptive but insufficient as scientific explanation). Inspired by the new developments in electricity and radioactivity, Adams settled on energy, or "force" as the prime mover in history.

The contrasting subtitles Adams applied to the two books points to the role force played in history: *Mont-Saint-Michel* was "a study of 13th-century unity," while *The Education* was "a study of 20th-century multiplicity." Adams argued that the historical forces of the 13th century produced a unified worldview, exemplified by Aquinas' *Summa Theologica*, the glorious architecture of Mont-Saint-Michel Abbey and Chartres Cathedral, and most of all, the cult of the Virgin Mary. History since the rebuilding of Chartres, was, for Adams, the disintegration of this synthesis into the multiplicity and chaos of modern life. As the Virgin was the symbol of unity, so the electrical generator (known as a dynamo in Adams' day) was the symbol of multiplicity. In the most moving passage in *The Education*, Adams wanders through a display of machines at the Paris Exhibition of 1900 with, in his words, "his historical neck broken by the sudden irruption of forces totally new."

Today's social scientists, if they read Adams at all, would certainly find his modernization theory unsatisfactory. American historians and literary critics (as opposed to medievalists), however, find in Adams an intellectual odyssey of the first rank. For example, Henry Steele Commager argued that Adams is more significant as a symbol than for his historical writing: "Adams illuminates . . . the course of American history."

What it is exactly that Adams illuminates is the source of some confusion. The traditional interpretation viewed him as a member of a misplaced elite – a dyspeptic Mugwump reformer, or a thoughtful intellect who sought to return republican virtues to governing, depending on whether or not the author liked Adams. A revisionist view places him in the forefront of antimodernism, railing against the dehumanization of modern society. Regardless whether Adams fits either of these wardrobes, he will continue to engage generations of readers with his omnivorous intellect and an incomparable literary style that raises irony to an art form.

CHRISTOPHER BERKELEY

See also Social; Williams, W.

Biography
Henry Brooks Adams. Born 16 February 1838, grandson and great-grandson of US presidents. Received BA, Harvard College, 1858; attended seminars at University of Berlin, 1858. Served as private secretary to his father, Charles Francis Adams, while he served in Congress, 1859–60, and when he was appointed ambassador to the Court of St. James's, 1861–68. Assistant professor of medieval history, Harvard University, and editor, *North American Review*, 1870–77. Married Marian Hooper, 1872 (she committed suicide, 1885). Moved to Washington, DC, 1877. President, American Historical Association, 1894. Died Washington, 27 March 1918.

Principal Writings
With Charles Francis Adams, Jr., *Chapters of Erie and Other Essays*, 1871
Editor, *Essays in Anglo-Saxon Law*, 1876
Editor, *Documents Relating to New England Federalism, 1800–1815*, 1877
The Life of Albert Gallatin, 1879
John Randolph, 1882
The History of the United States during the Administrations of Jefferson and Madison, 9 vols., 1889–91; abridged as *The Formative Years: A History of the United States during the Administrations of Jefferson and Madison*, 2 vols., 1947
Mont-Saint-Michel and Chartres, 1904
The Education of Henry Adams, 1907
The Degradation of the Democratic Dogma, 1919

Further Reading
Burich, Keith R., "Henry Adams, the Second Law of Thermodynamics, and the Course of History," *Journal of the History of Ideas* 48 (1987), 467–82
Burich, Keith R., "'Our power is always running ahead of our mind': Henry Adams's Phases of History," *New England Quarterly* 62 (1989), 163–86
Hall, Donald, "Henry Adams's History," *Sewanee Review* 95 (1987), 518–25
Jordy, William H., *Henry Adams, Scientific Historian*, New Haven: Yale University Press, 1952
Lears, T.J. Jackson, "In Defense of Henry Adams," *Wilson Quarterly* 7/4 (1983), 82–93
Levenson, Jacob Clavner, *The Mind and Art of Henry Adams* Boston: Houghton Mifflin, 1957
Levenson, Jacob Clavner et al., eds., *The Letters of Henry Adams*, 6 vols., Cambridge, MA: Harvard University Press, 1982–88
Samuels, Ernest, *The Life of Henry Adams*, 3 vols., Cambridge, MA: Harvard University Press, 1948–64; abridged as *Henry Adams*, 1989
Stevenson, Elizabeth, *Henry Adams: A Biography*, New York: Macmillan, 1956

Afigbo, A.E. 1937–
Nigerian historian

A.E. Afigbo has written about the history of his own Igbo area of Nigeria. His major concern has been to establish the origins of its modern history through establishing its pre-European history, attempting to sort out its "authentic" trajectory of development from European-imposed practices. His basic thesis has been that European colonialism distorted both authentic African development and the manner in which African practices were presented to the world.

His book *The Warrant Chiefs* (1972) clearly spelled out his perspective. In it Afigbo provided a carefully reasoned presentation of how British preconceptions regarding development forced a system of rule on the Igbo in conformity with those preconceptions. Indirect rule had been developed in India and transplanted to northern Nigeria by F.J.D. Lugard. It was an idea that fit the 19th century's evolutionary schemes of unilineal cultural evolution, placing peoples and forms of government into a set hierarchical pattern.

In *The Making of Modern Africa* (1986), Afigbo and others developed these themes on a broader canvas. They examined the consequences of colonial ideology and policy in light of their influence on more current developments. The goal of the work was to illuminate the African present through providing a historical depth that allowed a logical understanding of the situation. Thus, rather than seeing individual events as isolated, illogical outbursts, the student is able to note their historical antecedents and place them in context.

Afigbo has also been concerned with the response Nigerian historians have made to colonial versions of history. In his article "Of Origins and Colonial Order" (1994), he noted that various re-estimates of the hypotheses have led to advances in Nigerian historical thinking and methodology. Afigbo argued that responses to the "Hamitic hypothesis" (that everything of value found in Africa ultimately derived from the Hamites – supposedly members of the Caucasian race) have had great influence in the development of Nigerian nationalism as well as rivalries between communities. It also had an impact on the development of Christian identities in Nigeria.

Afigbo's interest in the development of Christianity in Nigeria and its relationship to the origins of Nigerian nationalism has been an abiding one during his career. His 1994 article on Dandeson Coates Crowther addressed the role that Crowther, a Sierra Leonian, played in that process. Crowther came to Nigeria as archdeacon of the Niger Delta pastorate. The pastorate was a force for self-government within the mission movement. It fought for the independence of Africans within the Christian movement and against the domination of European missionaries.

Afigbo has become increasingly concerned with the oppression of African women, as his 1992 valedictory address, "Of Men and War, Women and History," demonstrated. In 1993 he developed his ideas further in his response to an article by Ali Mazrui. Afigbo agreed that Mazrui was correct in supporting the empowerment of women, but felt that he was incorrect in making distinctions among types of sexism because all sexism is wrong. Moreover, Afigbo held that Mazrui displayed a great ignorance of indigenous African cultures, which led him to serious misinterpretations of reality.

In sum, Afigbo has been concerned with the issue of identity throughout his distinguished career. Specifically, he has been involved with the manner in which colonialism and its institutions have influenced the development of identity. The role of the Church in the process of independence and the emergence of national identity has figured prominently in his work. His recent writings have centered on the role of women in Nigerian history and the need for their empowerment in Nigerian public life.

FRANK A. SALAMONE

Biography

Adiele Eberechukwu Afigbo. Born Ihube, Okigwe, Imo State, Nigeria, 22 November 1937. Educated at Methodist Central School, Ihube, 1944–51; St. Augustine's Grammar School, Nkwerre, Orlu, 1952–56; University College, Ibadan, 1958–61; University of Ibadan, 1962–64, BA, PhD. Lecturer, University of Ibadan, 1964–65; taught at University of Nigeria, Nsukka (rising to professor), 1966–92. Appointed commissioner for education, Imo State, 1984. Married Ezihe Onukafo Nnochir, 1966 (2 sons, 2 daughters).

Principal Writings

The Warrant Chiefs: Indirect Rule in Southeastern Nigeria, 1891–1929, 1972

Ropes of Sand: Studies in Igbo History and Culture, 1981

With others, *The Making of Modern Africa*, 2 vols., 1986

The Igbo and Their Neighbours: Inter-group Relations in Southeastern Nigeria to 1953, 1987

"Beyond Hearsay and Academic Journalism: The Black Woman and Ali Mazrui," *Research in African Literatures* 24 (1993), 105–11

"Dandeson Coates Crowther and the Niger Delta Pastorate: Blazing Torch or Flickering Flame?" *International Bulletin of Missionary Research* 18 (1994), 166–70

"Of Origins and Colonial Order: Southern Nigerian Historians and the 'Hamitic Hypothesis' c.1870–1970," *Journal of African History* 35 (1994), 427–55

Africa: Central

The historiography of Central Africa remains the most stunted of all the regions of Africa. This is due to a number of factors which vary from nation to nation, but some overall generalities can be made. First, with the exception of the Portuguese in the Kongo kingdom and European competition in the Gabon estuary, European interest, exploration, and conquest came relatively late to Central Africa with the result that the region was relegated to administrative and intellectual backwaters. Second, Central Africa endured the most paternalistic colonial powers of Africa, the Portuguese and Belgians. Whatever one's ideological perspective regarding colonialism might be, it is difficult to deny that fewer attempts to reconstruct the past were made in the Belgian and Portuguese colonies, compared with the British, French, and German colonies. To this end, colonial documents are much shallower for parts of Central Africa than they are for elsewhere on the continent. Third, acidic soils, high humidity, and heavy rainfall hamper the preservation and excavation of archaeological evidence and interfere with the preservation of written or printed material. Finally, infrastructural problems with training, transportation, and health access of many contemporary Central African states dampen research efforts for both domestic and foreign scholars.

Central African historiography is also heavily plagued by imbalance in regional representation, with works on the savanna and coastal regions vastly outnumbering those on the forest and inland areas. In addition, most major works have tended to be written by Western Europeans and North Americans and the development of a large group of indigenous Central African historians is still underway. Some places, such as Lovanium University in Kinshasa and the Université Libre du Congo in Lubumbashi, have developed strong history departments. The growth of Central African historiography shares many commonalities with West and East African historiography, but has also made numerous independent contributions to African historiography generally, as evidenced below.

The emergence of modern Central African historiography can be traced to the middle of the 20th century amid the rumblings of decolonization. While works of history were certainly written before the end of World War II, these writings were simply the story of Europeans in Africa, such as Henry M. Stanley's *Through the Dark Continent* (1878) or Albert Schweitzer's *Zwischen wasser und Urwald* (1923; *On the Edge of the Primeval Forest*, 1923). But, with the growth of anti-colonial sentiments throughout the region from 1945 to 1960, demands for intellectual freedom accompanied the calls for political freedom.

In order to counter the pre-existing Eurocentric works, the early Africanist historians focused on the accomplishments and achievements of great African kingdoms. By focusing on the great kingdoms, these early writers were attempting to validate the claim that African history was the same as any other history and equally worthy of study. Among these pioneering works was Jan Vansina's *Kingdoms of the Savanna* (1966) which, despite its age, still stands up remarkably well. In it, Vansina described the precolonial history of the kingdoms of the southern savanna belt stretching from northern Angola to eastern Zambia. Little emphasis is given to non-centralized polities, the forest region, and social and cultural events. The last point is one which is a perennial issue in early Central African historiography – that is, an overemphasis on political history and organization. But the reverse was true of Zairian scholarship, which favored social history and has only recently produced political histories. Another work of this nature was Basil Davidson's *A History of East and Central Africa to the Late 19th Century* (1969); Davidson was well known for his radically-based scholarship. This work also advanced the greatness of Africa's precolonial past. This period of scholarship favored precolonial studies because they were uniquely African and could easily be used to assert Africa's place in world history, while minimizing the discussion of Europe. Yet, interest in political histories has not disappeared and can be found in studies such as Joseph Vogel's *Great Zimbabwe* (1994).

Once works like the above had made a place for African history in the historical discipline, scholars felt the need to counter many of the pre-existing Eurocentric histories. The primary target for demolition was the myth that Africans welcomed the colonialism of the "superior" Europeans. Numerous studies appeared demonstrating the elaborate and creative ways in which Africans resisted foreign intrusion by the Europeans. The precursor in this subfield was Terence O. Ranger's study of resistance in Zimbabwe, entitled *Revolt in Southern Rhodesia, 1896–97* (1967). Ranger's study was particularly interesting in that it dealt with religion as well as resistance. Ranger's book sparked studies of resistance, not just concerning Central Africa, but pertaining to every region of the continent. While much of his argument has since been abandoned, the work still stands as a classic in African history. These studies, while still favoring coastal and savanna peoples, were less politically motivated and took account of social, cultural, and religious agency.

By the 1970s, Central African history began to push itself in innovative directions. Religion became a fruitful means of investigation with studies such as Ranger's edited work *The*

Historical Study of African Religion (1972), which continued to stress the role of religion in resistance. Mention must also be made of Victor Turner's classic studies of the Ndembu of Zambia, *Forest of Symbols* (1967) and *The Ritual Process* (1969). Both still stand as classics in religious studies regardless of one's geographical focus. Another seminal work is Luc de Heusch's *Le roi ivre* (The Ivory King, 1972), a mythical analysis of southern savanna states in a Levi-Straussian tradition. One could easily make the claim that religion may be the most valuable contribution scholars of Central Africa have made to African historiography generally. This trend continues with innovative works such as Hugo F. Hinfelaar's *Bemba-Speaking Women of Zambia in a Century of Religious Change, 1892–1992* (1994) which investigated religion and gender across social, economic, and political axes in explaining the decline of the house-cult and the religious subjugation of the Bemba-speaking women.

Economics also became a preoccupation in Central African historiography with studies such as Phyllis Martin's *External Trade of the Loango Coast, 1576–1870* (1972), William J. Barber's *Economy of British Central Africa* (1961), and Samir Amin and Catherine Coquery-Vidrovitch's *Histoire économique du Congo, 1880–1968* (The Economic History of the Congo, 1969). Most economic histories, these being no exception, focus on the more recent past. This is largely due to the large amount of material relating to economic matters generated after European contact and the greater difficulty in reconstructing economic history from oral tradition. Most economic-based studies examined the changing nature of African life and economic structure with the injection of European trade and contact. The effects were often the most profound among coastal peoples, but as these scholars demonstrated, the introduction of European economic systems had wide and profound consequences. Recent works such as William J. Samarin's *The Black Man's Burden* (1989) and Piet Konings' *Labour Resistance in Cameroon* (1993) illustrate that economic history will continue to be a fruitful means of investigation for Central African history.

Huge amounts of quantitative and statistical data can be found in colonial records, yet the documents have not spawned the number of studies that they warrant. An early study based on quantitative materials was Bruce Fetter's *The Creation of Elisabethville, 1910–1940* (1976), which dealt with the establishment of one of the largest cities of Central Africa. Fetter has also published two works of demography, *Colonial Rule and Regional Imbalance in Central Africa* (1983) and an edited work entitled *Demography from Scanty Evidence* (1990). Both dealt with the changing nature of demography, migration, and mortality during the colonial era. While Fetter's method has been attacked, he provided a valuable pan-disciplinary lesson to Central African historians – that there are massive amounts of data waiting to be analyzed and traditional methods of historical analysis will not suffice in their investigation. Until they are exploited, our potential picture of Central African history will be incomplete.

Central Africa was the last region of Africa to have its general history written. While A.J. Wills wrote *An Introduction to the History of Central Africa* in 1964, it was essentially the history of Europe in Africa, engrossed with conquest and occupation. The fairly recent 2-volume edited work from David Birmingham and Phyllis Martin, *History of Central Africa*, first appeared in 1983 and has gone through three impressions, most recently in 1990. This is a full two decades after the publication of the *Oxford History of East Africa* in 1963. *History of Central Africa* is more fully geographically representative in that the forest zones and north-central savanna are discussed. Yet, the works are also heavily weighted in favor of political economy (especially vol. 2) at the expense of culture, society, and religion. To the editor's credit, many of the essays concern Lusophone Africa, a region which has been difficult to study given the lateness of the independence of Angola and Mozambique and the volatility of their political systems until quite recently. While Birmingham and Martin's efforts were definitely steps in the right direction, we still await a genuinely comprehensive general history of Central Africa.

The creativity of Central African historiography is far from over. Some recent works indicate that historical methodology is not stagnant for Central Africanists. For instance, Jan Vansina, ever the pioneer, published *Paths in the Rainforest* (1990) utilizing historical linguistics to trace the history of the millennia-old political tradition of Equatorial Africa. The region also finally has a reader of precolonial documents entitled *Readings in Precolonial Central Africa* (1995) from Théophile Obenga, a most useful addition to the teaching of Central African history. Phyllis Martin's *Leisure and Society in Colonial Brazzaville* (1995), was a social history of the highest order. So, while many aspects of Central African history remain neglected, such as environment, demography, urbanization, and medicine, the field is not undynamic. The newness of Central African historiography ensures that it will be some time before scholars of the region run out of fresh ideas.

TOYIN FALOLA and JOEL E. TISHKEN

See also Coquery-Vidrovitch; Davidson; Ranger; Turner, V.; Vansina

Further Reading

Amin, Samir, and Catherine Coquery-Vidrovitch, *Histoire économique du Congo, 1880–1968: du Congo français à l'union douanière et économique d'Afrique Centrale* (The Economic History of the Congo, 1880–1968: From the French Congo to the Economic and Customs Union of Central Africa), Dakar: IFAN, 1969

Barber, William J., *Economy of British Central Africa: A Case Study of Economic Development in a Dualistic Society*, Stanford, CA: Stanford University Press, 1961

Bawele, Mumbanza mwa, and Sabakinu Kivilu, "Historical Research in Zaire: Present Status and Future Perspectives," in Bogumil Jewsiewicki and David Newbury eds., *African Historiographies: What History for Which Africa?*, Beverly Hills, CA: Sage, 1986

Bawele, Mumbanza mwa, "L'Evolution de l'historiographie en Afrique Centrale: le cas du Zaire" (The Evolution of the Historiography of Central Africa: The Case of Zaire), *Storia della Storiografia* 19 (1991), 89–110

Bayle des Hermens, R. de, "The Prehistory of Central Africa, Part 1," in *UNESCO General History of Africa*, vol. 1, London: Heinemann, and Berkeley: University of California Press, 1981

Birmingham, David, and Phyllis Martin, eds., *History of Central Africa*, 2 vols., London: Longman, 1983

Davidson, Basil, *East and Central Africa to the Late Nineteenth Century*, London: Longman, 1967; revised as *A History of East and Central Africa to the Late Nineteenth Century*, Garden City, NY: Anchor, 1969

Fetter, Bruce, *The Creation of Elisabethville, 1910–1940*, Stanford,

CA: Hoover Institution Press, 1976

Fetter, Bruce, *Colonial Rule and Regional Imbalance in Central Africa*, Boulder, CO: Westview, 1983

Fetter, Bruce, ed., *Demography from Scanty Evidence: Central Africa in the Colonial Era*, Boulder, CO: Rienner, 1990

Heusch, Luc de, *Le roi ivre, ou, l'origine de l'état: mythes et rites bantous* (The Ivory King; or, The Origin of the State), Paris: Gallimard, 1972

Hinfelaar, Hugo F., *Bemba-Speaking Women of Zambia in a Century of Religious Change, 1892–1992*, Leiden and New York: Brill, 1994

Konings, Piet, *Labour Resistance in Cameroon: Managerial Strategies and Labour Resistance in the Agro-Industrial Plantations of the Cameroon Development Corporation*, London: Currey, 1993

McCracken, John, "Central African History" [review article], *Journal of African History* 26 (1985), 241–48

Martin, Phyllis, *External Trade of the Loango Coast, 1576–1870: The Effects of Changing Commercial Relations in the Vili Kingdom of Loango*, Oxford: Oxford University Press, 1972

Martin, Phyllis, *Leisure and Society in Colonial Brazzaville*, New York and Cambridge: Cambridge University Press, 1995

Obenga, Théophile, ed., *Afrique Centrale pré-colonial: documents d'histoire vivante*, Paris: Présence Africaine, 1974; in English as *Readings in Precolonial Central Africa: Texts and Documents*, London: Karnak, 1995

Oliver, Roland et al., eds., *History of East Africa*, 3 vols., Oxford: Oxford University Press, 1963–76

Ranger, Terence O., *Revolt in Southern Rhodesia, 1896–97: A Study of African Resistance*, London: Heinemann, and Evanston, IL: Northwestern University Press, 1967

Ranger, Terence O., and Isaria N. Kimambo, eds., *The Historical Study of African Religion: With Special Reference to East and Central Africa*, London: Heinemann, and Berkeley: University of California Press, 1972

Samarin, William J., *The Black Man's Burden: African Colonial Labor on the Congo and Ubangi Rivers, 1880–1900*, Boulder, CO: Westview Press, 1989

Schweitzer, Albert, *Zwischen Wasser und Urwald: Erlebnisse und Beobachtungen eines Arztes im Urwalde Äquatorial Afrikas*, Bern: Haupt, 1923; in English as *On the Edge of the Primeval Forest: Experiences and Observations of a Doctor in Equatorial Africa*, London: Black, 1923; New York: Macmillan, 1931

Stanley, Henry M., *Through the Dark Continent*, 2 vols., New York: Harper, and London: Sampson Low, 1878

Thornton, John, "Pre-Colonial Central African History" [review article], *Canadian Journal of African Studies* 16 (1982), 631–33

Turner, Victor, *The Forest of Symbols: Aspects of Ndembu Ritual*, Ithaca, NY: Cornell University Press, 1967

Turner, Victor, *The Ritual Process: Structure and Anti-Structure*, Chicago: Aldine Press, and London: Routledge, 1969

Vansina, Jan, *Kingdoms of the Savanna*, Madison: University of Wisconsin Press, 1966

Vansina, Jan, *Paths in the Rainforests: Toward a History of Political Tradition in Equatorial Africa*, Madison: University of Wisconsin Press, 1990

Vogel, Joseph, *Great Zimbabwe: The Iron Age in South Central Africa*, New York: Garland, 1994

Wills, Alfred John, *An Introduction to the History of Central Africa*, New York and London: Oxford University Press, 1964

Africa: Eastern and Southern

In many ways, it is artificial to combine the historiographies of Eastern and Southern Africa. Yet, they also share a number of historiographical commonalities. Some of these commonalities are unique to these regions and others they share with the rest of the continent. Of relevance to both regions are the themes of German colonialism, white settlers, resistance to imperialism, South Asian immigration, and decolonization/independence movements. As the nation of South Africa already has an entry in this volume that closely examines the Apartheid state and Afrikaner scholarship, this entry will not discuss white South Africa in much detail.

One could place the beginnings of the historiography of these regions in the late 19th and early 20th centuries with the emergence of a literate indigenous elite who recorded the history of their peoples and regions. The fact that they were not professionally trained historians has led many to refer to these early writers as chroniclers. In the interests of space, this article will adhere to traditional historiographical interpretations that trace the emergence of a historiography to the 1960s with the first professionally trained historians of African history. Discussion of these early chroniclers/historians can be found in John Rowe's article "Progress and a Sense of Identity: African Historiography in East Africa" (1977).

While Eastern and Southern Africa were not the only parts of Africa to experience German colonialism, Tanganyika and Namibia bore the brunt of the German policy of genocide. Large portions of Namibia and southwestern Tanzania remain sparsely populated to this day because of German methods of "pacification." Works such as John Iliffe's *Tanganyika under German Rule, 1905–1912* (1969) and Kaire Mbuende's *Namibia, the Broken Shield* (1986) are important for their discussion of German brutality. Mbuende examined the German seizure of African cattle and land, African resistance to such attempts, and the slaughter of large numbers of Herero and Nama as a result.

Africans of Tanganyika also resisted German intrusion. This resistance gave birth to one of the most famous, as well as largest, resistance movements in African colonial history, the Maji Maji. G.C.K. Gwassa's study *Kumbukumbu za vita vya Maji Maji* (Records of the Maji Maji Rising, 1967) examined the role of the prophet Kinjinkitile in mobilizing numerous Tanganyikan peoples against the Germans. The rebellion earned its name from the KiSwahili word for water (*maji*) as the movement formed around the distribution of medicines that would turn German bullets to water. While Germany by no means possessed a monopoly on colonial brutalities, scholars of East and Southern Africa have done well to remind us of the particularly fierce pattern of German colonialism.

Large numbers of white settlers established themselves throughout Eastern and Southern Africa. South Africa is the most notable and well-known preserve of white settlement, but European settlers could also be found in Namibia, Zimbabwe, and Kenya and in smaller numbers throughout both regions. Africans were displaced, and their land, usually the most fertile land, was confiscated by Europeans. Some "scholarship" turned up which justified land appropriation. Even as recently as 1953 works like Elspeth Huxley's *White Man's Country* argued that because Africans had not transformed every acre and had possessed a different notion of land ownership, they were not fit to control the best land in Africa. To counter arguments such as these, other scholarship began to appear in the late 1960s arguing that European claims to land were unfounded and unethically based. Africans hardly sat still while their ancestral lands were appropriated. The rest of the world had heard little of African resistance to land confiscation not because Africans did not attempt to halt European advancement, but because of the silencing of African voices. A noteworthy work in this regard was *Le mouvement "Mau Mau"* (The Mau Mau Movement, 1971) from Robert Buijtenhuijs; it investigated the Mau Mau insurgency of 1953–54 when displaced Kikuyu rose against the white government of Kenya. Much of this scholarship has, understandably, been quite politically charged. Much of the literature from the perspective of white settlers was nothing short of racist. The heyday of studies of white settlership was in the 1960s. Since that time most discussion of white settlership has been absorbed into discussions of decolonization.

Allied with the issue of white settlership has been the notion of resistance in general. Like other regions of Africa, East and Southern Africa witnessed a tremendous growth of studies of African resistance to colonialism beginning in the 1960s. These scholars were attempting to illustrate the varied ways in which Africans tried to thwart European encroachment, rather than welcome it, which had been the colonial myth. George Shepperson and Thomas Price in *Independent African* (1958) investigated the complex religious and military resistance of John Chilembwe and his Providence Industrial Mission in southern Malawi. While the movement was rather short-lived, Chilembwe, like other resistance leaders, has remained an important cultural icon to contemporary Africans. Allen Isaacman discussed the many-faceted responses that occurred in the Zambesi valley in *The Tradition of Resistance in Mozambique* (1976). The sorts of works one may find in this genre of resistance are as varied as were the forms of resistance. Whether the responses were military, religious, social, diplomatic, or as was most often the case, a combination thereof, resistance has been a fruitful means of investigation. Some more recent scholarship has begun to indicate that resistance often came in much more subtle and complex forms. Jean Comaroff's book *Body of Power, Spirit of Resistance* (1985) illustrated the ways in which the Tshidi of South Africa and Botswana used clothing, color, and symbols as a means of resistance.

Other works dealt with resistance against racist regimes once colonialism was entrenched. Literature on the nation of South Africa has been especially productive in this regard. Cherryl Walker looked at the role of gender in resistance and political organizing in *Women and Resistance in South Africa* (1982). Much of this literature is also concerned with radical politics. *I Write What I Like* (1978), for instance, discussed the life and death of Steve Biko, the formation of the Black Consciousness movement, and student political activism against the Apartheid regime. As Lyn Graybill's recent work *Religion and Resistance Politics in South Africa* (1995) indicated, resistance is not a theme that has exhausted its relevance for Eastern and Southern African history.

These regions are unique for their large South Asian populations. As occurred in several other parts of the world, such as Trinidad and Fiji, South Asians were used as indentured laborers in Africa. J.S. Mangat's pioneering work *A History of Asians in East Africa c.1886 to 1945* (1969) investigated the role of South Asian laborers in Kenya, Uganda, and Tanganyika, especially in railroad construction. Much of the scholarship on Asians in Africa has been concerned with economics, as the fairly recent work of Robert Gregory, *South*

Asians in East Africa (1993), demonstrated. Works on Asians in Africa that looked at the Asian experience in Africa more holistically would be a welcome addition to the field.

Perhaps no theme has spurred as many works as that of decolonization. This was due to a number of factors. The unwillingness of Portugal to relinquish its colonies led to long and bloody anti-colonial civil wars in Angola and Mozambique. The civil wars in both nations, even as recently as the 1990s, were residual effects of the decolonization process. David Birmingham's *Frontline Nationalism in Angola and Mozambique* (1992) explored the civil wars in these two former Portuguese colonies. Second, the strong entrenchment of racist states like Southern Rhodesia and South Africa and the neo-colonial dominance of South Africa over Namibia created tense and bitter struggles of Africans against these regimes. Terence Ranger analyzed the decolonization process as manifested through Mau Mau, FRELIMO, and guerrilla war in Zimbabwe in *Peasant Consciousness and Guerrilla War in Zimbabwe* (1985). It was his contention that decolonization was aided by the support and civil disobedience of the general population and was not due just to the efforts of radical political and paramilitary groups. Lastly, East Africa also housed one of the most famous independence era leaders, Jomo Kenyatta. George Delf's 1961 biography of Kenyatta traced the political leader's evolution from his traditional background to left-wing political activist to campaigner for independence. The edited work of B.A. Ogot and W.R. Ochieng, *Decolonization and Independence in Kenya, 1940–93* (1995), illustrated the importance that decolonization continues to have to Africans despite the unfulfilled promises of the independence era.

South and East African historiography has made a number of important contributions to African studies in general, but mention must be made of two areas in which it has been especially productive. South African historiography has led the way in studies of labor history. Bill Freund's *The African Worker* (1988) is often seen as the finest example of this genre of scholarship. Given the obvious connections labor had with trade unions, radical politics, and resistance, it should not be difficult to understand why labor was an important means of analysis in Southern African history. East African historiography has increased awareness of the importance of the environment in African history through its pioneering works in ecological history. The 1970s witnessed an outpouring of significant works like Helge Kjekshus's *Ecology Control and Economic Development in East African History* (1977) and *Ecology and History in East Africa* (1979) edited by B.A. Ogot. Works on ecological history have not disappeared, but they have not reached the volume of the 1970s.

A couple of shortcomings can be identified in the historiographies of these regions. First, South Africa the nation was too often equated with South Africa the region. The historiographies of nations like Namibia, Botswana, and Malawi are relatively shallow and in complete imbalance with that of South Africa. One can claim that population, economic power, and the like justified this, but the fact remains that we know little of the Namibian past. Second, East African historiography was also plagued by geographic imbalance. The Swahili Coast was heavily favored in research over the inland areas. The Great Lakes region was an important one in African history yet we know little about its history (human evolution aside) when compared with other areas. Lastly, due to the legacy of the settler colony and racist regime, political economy was the focus of a vast majority of studies. Hopefully, the historiographies of these regions will begin to address these imbalances in the coming decades.

TOYIN FALOLA and JOEL E. TISHKEN

See also Iliffe; Ogot; Ranger

Further Reading

Baumhögger, Goswin, "Die Geschichte Ostafrikas im Spiegel der Neueren Literatur" (The History of Africa as Depicted in Contemporary Literature), *Geschichte in Wissenschaft und Unterricht* 22 (1971), 678–704; 22 (1971), 747–68

Beinart, William, "Political and Collective Violence in Southern African Historiography," *Journal of Southern African Studies* 18:3 (1992), 456–86

Biko, Steve, *I Write What I Like: A Selection of His Writing*, edited with a personal memoir by Aelred Stubbs, London: Bowerdean, 1978; New York: Harper, 1979

Birmingham, David, *Frontline Nationalism in Angola and Mozambique*, Trenton, NJ, and London: Africa World Press, 1992

Bozzoli, Belinda, and Peter Delius, "Radical History and South African Society," *Radical History Review* 46 (1990), 13–45

Buijtenhuijs, Robert, *Le mouvement "Mau Mau": Une révolte paysanne et anti-coloniale en Afrique noire* (The Mau Mau Movement: A Peasant and Anti-Colonial Revolt in Sub-Saharan Africa), The Hague: Mouton, 1971

Chanaiwa, David, "Historiographical Traditions of Southern Africa," *Journal of Southern African Affairs* 3 (1978), 175–93

Comaroff, Jean, *Body of Power, Spirit of Resistance: The Culture and History of a South African People*, Chicago: University of Chicago Press, 1985

Delf, George, *Jomo Kenyatta: Toward Truth about "The Light of Kenya,"* London: Gollancz, and Garden City, NY: Doubleday, 1961

Freund, Bill, *The African Worker*, Cambridge and New York: Cambridge University Press, 1988

Gatheru Wanjohi, N., "Historical Scholarship in the East African Context," *International Social Science Journal* 33 (1981), 667–74

Graybill, Lyn S., *Religion and Resistance Politics in South Africa*, Westport, CT: Praeger, 1995

Gregory, Robert, *South Asians in East Africa: An Economic and Social History, 1890–1980*, Boulder, CO: Westview Press, 1993

Gwassa, G.C.K., *Kumbukumbu za vita vya Maji Maji*, 1967; edited by John Iliffe as *Records of the Maji Maji Rising*, Nairobi: East African Publishing House, 1967

Herzog, Jürgen, "Ökologie als Thema der Geschichte? Kritisches und Nachdenkliches zur Afrika-Historiographie" (Ecology as a Historial Theme: Critical Thoughts and Reflections on African Historiography), *Asien, Afrika, Lateinamerika* 16 (1988), 288–96

Huxley, Elspeth, *White Man's Country: Lord Delamere and the Making of Kenya*, 2 vols., London: Macmillan, 1953; New York: Praeger, 1968

Iliffe, John, *Tanganyika under German Rule, 1905–1912*, Cambridge: Cambridge University Press, 1969

Ingham, Kenneth, "Some Reflections on East African Historiography," *Historia* 21:2 (1976), 38–42

Isaacman, Allen, and Barbara Isaacman, *The Tradition of Resistance in Mozambique: The Zambesi Valley, 1850–1921*, Berkeley: University of California Press, and London: Heinemann, 1976

Kjekshus, Helge, *Ecology Control and Economic Development in East African History: The Case of Tanganyika, 1850–1950*, Berkeley: University of California Press, 1977; revised with new introduction, London: Currey, and Athens: Ohio University Press, 1996

Mangat, J.S., *A History of Asians in East Africa, c.1886 to 1945*, Oxford: Oxford University Press, 1969

Mbuende, Kaire, *Namibia, the Broken Shield: Anatomy of Imperialism and Revolution*, Malmö: Liber, 1986

Ogot, Bethwell A., ed., *Ecology and History in East Africa: Proceedings of the 1975 Conference of the Historical Association of Kenya*, Nairobi: Kenya Literature Bureau, 1979

Ogot, Bethwell A., and W.R. Ochieng, eds., *Decolonization and Independence in Kenya, 1940–93*, London: Currey, and Athens: Ohio University Press, 1995

Peterson, Christian, "The South African Agrarian Transformation, 1880–1920: A Historiographical Overview," *Ufahamu* 21 (1993), 110–19

Ranger, Terence O., *Peasant Consciousness and Guerrilla War in Zimbabwe: A Comparative Study*, London: Currey, and Berkeley: University of California Press, 1985

Rowe, John, "Progress and a Sense of Identity: African Historiography in East Africa," *Kenya Historical Review* 5 (1977), 23–34

Schoenbrun, David, "A Past Whose Time has Come: Historical Context and East Africa's Great Lakes," *History and Theory* 32 (1993), 32–56

Shepperson, George, and Thomas Price, *Independent African: John Chilembwe and the Origins, Setting and Significance of the Nyasaland Native Rising of 1915*, Edinburgh: Edinburgh University Press, 1958

Smith, Iain R., "The Revolution in South African Historiography," *History Today* 38 (February 1988), 8–10

Walker, Cherryl, *Women and Resistance in South Africa*, London: Onyx, 1982; New York: Monthly Review Press, 1991

Africa: North and the Horn

This region corresponds to the part of the continent known to the Greeks and Romans, either because, like Egypt and North Africa, it had long formed part of the Mediterranean world, or because, like Azania on the East African coast, it had been reached from the Mediterranean via the Nile and the Red Sea. The written records of antiquity begin with the ancient Egyptians, and end with the accounts of the region in Greek and Latin, including the references in the Bible. These are important because of the information they provide, the concepts they represent, and finally, because they were the starting point for modern European study of the continent. The interval was filled by the very different tradition of the Arabic and Islamic world. Arabic geography was based on Ptolemy, and extended the picture of the continent sketched by the Greeks and Romans, without advancing the frontier of knowledge further south than the Western and Central Sudan. Arabic writers, on the other hand, were cut off by language from the historical literature of Greece and Rome, and concentrated on their own history in Africa north of the Sahara from the 7th century onwards. Written from an Islamic point of view, this remained substantially unknown to post-classical Europe before the 17th and 18th centuries. The information it provided about a region of which Europeans had little direct knowledge from the end of antiquity to the Renaissance had then to be matched with the Greek and Latin material upon which European scholarship was primarily based. In the 19th century the combination became the starting point for the historical study of Africa as a whole.

For more than two thousand years, the Pharaonic kingdom of Egypt recorded itself as the center of a world embracing the Sahara, the Nile as far as Khartoum, and the Red Sea. To this perception of the desert, the river, and the sea, Herodotus and his Greek and Roman successors added the mountains of the Atlas, encompassing the whole within a world centered upon the Mediterranean. Within that world, Egypt was recognized as the home of an incredibly ancient civilization, whose myth of Isis and Osiris spread throughout the Roman empire, but whose subjection to that empire doomed its civilization to the past. The Sahara, on the other hand, beyond which lived the Ethiopians or "burnt faces," was a desert land without a history of its own. The Mediterranean coast, and the mountains of Atlas, came alive only in so far as they were colonized by Greeks, Carthaginians, and Romans, and eventually civilized in the Roman manner. Beyond the Roman frontier in North Africa, from Sale on the Atlantic to Tripoli and Cyrenaica, the barbarian or "Berber" tribal population existed largely as troublemakers. To the south of Aswan the kingdoms and peoples of Meroe on the Nile; Axum on the Red Sea; and Azania on the East African coast, were barbarians with whom to trade.

The Roman frontier across northern Africa made a political distinction between civilization and barbarism. This distinction changed in the 5th century CE when the Roman empire broke up, but civilization was equated with Christianity, and spread to include the kingdoms of the Nilotic Sudan and Ethiopia. In the 7th century the political distinction reappeared with the Arab conquests, which reunited Egypt and North Africa in the Arab empire, where Islam took the place of Christianity as the dominant religion. Islam, however, like Christianity, spread far beyond its borders, thanks to the development of trade through the Red Sea with the Horn and East Africa, and for the first time by camel across the Sahara to the central and western Sudan. This trade with tropical Africa in slaves, gold, and ivory, integrated the northern and eastern regions of the continent into the Islamic world of the Mediterranean and Middle East.

In the process, the ethnic pattern changed. With Mecca now the center of the world, the population of the region by the offspring of Noah included the Berbers of North Africa and the Sahara, "barbarians" now classified as a race. Meanwhile the subject Christian population of Egypt was turned by its religion into another nation called the Qibt or Copts, that is, "Egyptians." To the south, the "black" peoples of antiquity became the Habash or "Abyssinians"; the Nuba or Nubians; and the Sudan or "Blacks." The picture, however, was progressively modified by the prestige of Arab ancestry and the immigration into Africa of Arab bedouin. As a result, a process of Arabization as well as Islamicization extended right across the region. By the 15th century the Copts had become a small minority in Muslim Arab Egypt, while the Christian Nubians had disappeared, leaving only the Christian Ethiopians in opposition to the Muslim Somalis of the Horn. To the west of the Nile, the Muslim Berbers succumbed from the 11th century onwards to the attraction of Arab ancestry and the spread of spoken Arabic, to the point at which Berber speakers are now a minority in North Africa and the Sahara. To the south of the desert, Islamicization meanwhile produced self-consciously Islamic peoples like the Hausa.

These changes were expressed in terms of fictitious genealogies and legendary migrations out of Arabia: see for example, Norris's *Saharan Myth and Saga* (1972) and Brett and Fentress' *The Berbers* (1996). The outstanding overview was that of Ibn Khaldūn at the end of the 14th century, whose history of the world, revolved around the Berbers in the west and the Arabs in the east. As discussed in Ibn Khaldūn's Introduction or *Muqaddimah*, their deeds were made possible by the primitive virtues of nomadic peoples, an observation which so far as the Sahara and the Horn are concerned reflected the introduction of the camel from Arabia as a pastoral animal in the later centuries of the ancient world. Ibn Khaldūn's views, discussed by Brett in "The Way of the Nomad" (1995), were taken up by European readers in the 19th century as a key to the history and society of the region.

The development of relations between western Europe and these lands in the later Middle Ages had been cut short by warfare in the 16th century between the Habsburgs and Ottomans, which brought the Turks to the borders of Morocco. At a time when Europeans had found their way round the continent as a whole, they were left in ignorance of northern Africa, relying on the early 16th-century account by the Moroccan Leo Africanus, which was rapidly translated into Italian, French, and English. Leo's *History and Description of Africa* (written 1526, in English 1600) was a final version of the medieval account of Africa by Arab geographers and travellers, both informative and misleading, as the maps which Ortelius based upon it show. By the 18th century, however, European residents in Egypt and North Africa like Thomas Shaw, were making their own observations, comparing these with their own sources, the Bible on the one hand, the classical authors on the other. At the beginning of the 19th century, E.W. Bovill has noted, these observations expanded into an enormous new literature with the French *Description de l'Egypte*, commissioned by Napoleon in 1798–1801, and the British and French exploration of the Sahara. The discovery of ancient as well as Muslim Egypt was then matched by the discovery of Muslim states and peoples to the south of the Sahara, establishing a connection between the Mediterranean coast and that of West Africa. A similar connection was made with the Christian kingdom of Ethiopia, discovered by the Portuguese in the 16th century, and visited by James Bruce at the end of the 18th.

The outcome in terms of historical perception was contradictory. The conquest of all but Ethiopia by Britain, France, Italy, and Spain between 1830 and 1912, promoted a view of Islam as a backward religion and the Arabs as a backward race in need of European rule, which in the case of French North Africa was supposed to restore the country to the European civilization it had enjoyed under the Romans. On the other hand, as Seligman's *Races of Africa* (1930) and MacGaffey's "Concepts of Race" (1966) have shown, the view of black Africans as an inferior race, which the Atlantic slave trade had encouraged, was combined with the new knowledge of ancient Egypt and Muslim and Christian Africa to suggest that what civilization there was in "the Dark Continent" was the result of successive invasions of Africa by "white" peoples from Asia and Europe. In this so-called "Hamitic hypothesis," the north and northeastern part of the continent known to the Greeks and Romans and thus to western Europe, became the homeland of basically "white" peoples – ancient Egyptians, Berbers, Ethiopian Semites, Somalis, Arabs, Fulanis, and so on, who had given the whole of Africa its history prior to the arrival of the modern Europeans.

In this postcolonial age, the Hamitic hypothesis has quite rightly been abandoned for the racial nonsense it is. It leaves its trace, however, in the notion of a White as distinct from a Black Africa, including the Sudan, Ethiopia, and the Horn, as in Julien's *Histoire de l'Afrique blanche* (History of White Africa, 1966). Meanwhile in Diop's *The African Origin of Civilization* (1974) and Martin Bernal's *Black Athena* (1987), it has been inverted by the contention that the ancient Egyptians were not only black, but the creators of "white" Greek civilization. Race aside, the position is in fact reversed in the sense that the north and northeast is now studied from an African as well as a classical and Islamic point of view, as part of the common history of the continent and its native peoples. For this reason the region is best covered by general histories of Africa, culminating in the multivolume *Cambridge History of Africa* (edited by Fage and Oliver, 1975–86) and the UNESCO *General History of Africa* (1981–93). These represent most of the authors at present at work on North Africa, the Nile valley, Ethiopia and the Horn, with appropriate bibliographies.

MICHAEL BRETT

See also Bernal; Curtin; Diop; Ibn Khaldūn; Iliffe; Julien; Laroui; Oliver

Further Reading

Bernal, Martin, *Black Athena: The Afroasiatic Roots of Classical Civilization*, 2 vols. to date, London: Free Association Press, and New Brunswick, NJ: Rutgers University Press, 1987–91

Bovill, E.W., *The Golden Trade of the Moors*, London and New York: Oxford University Press, 1958; revised 1968

Brett, Michael, "The Way of the Nomad," *Bulletin of the School of Oriental and African Studies*, 58 (1995), 251–69

Brett, Michael, and Elizabeth Fentress, *The Berbers*, Oxford and Cambridge, MA: Blackwell, 1996

Bruce, James, *Travels to Discover the Source of the Nile*, 5 vols., Edinburgh and London: Robinson, 1790; enlarged and revised to 8 vols., 1804

Curtin, Philip D. *et al.*, *African History*, Boston: Little Brown, 1978; revised London and New York: Longman, 1992

Diop, Cheikh Anta, *Antériorité des civilisations nègres: mythe ou vérité historique?*, Paris: Présence africaine, 1967; in English as *The African Origin of Civilization: Myth or Reality*, New York: Lawrence Hill, 1974

Fage, John Donnelly, and Roland Oliver, eds., *The Cambridge History of Africa*, 8 vols., Cambridge and New York: Cambridge University Press, 1975–86

Fage, John Donnelly, *A History of Africa*, New York: Knopf, 1978; 3rd edition, London and New York: Routledge, 1995

Ibn Khaldūn, *Muqaddima*, written 1375–78; in English as *The Muqaddimah: An Introduction to History*, 2nd edition, Princeton: Princeton University Press, 1967, London: Routledge/Secker and Warburg, 1978

Iliffe, John, *Africans: The History of a Continent*, Cambridge and New York: Cambridge University Press, 1995

Julien, Charles-André, *Histoire de l'Afrique blanche, des origines à 1945* (A History of White Africa from its Origins to 1945), Paris: Presses Universitaires de France, 1966

Leo Africanus, *History and Description of Africa*, written 1526; in English 1600; 3 vols., London: Hakluyt Society, 1896

MacGaffey, Wyatt, "Concepts of Race in the Historiography of Northeast Africa," *Journal of African History* 7 (1966), 1–17

Norris, H.T., *Saharan Myth and Saga*, Oxford: Clarendon Press, 1972

Oliver, Roland, and John Donnelly Fage, *A Short History of Africa*, London and Baltimore: Penguin, 1962; 6th edition 1986

Oliver, Roland, *The African Experience*, London: Weidenfeld and Nicolson, 1991; New York: Icon, 1992

Seligman, Charles Gabriel, *Races of Africa*, London: Butterworth, 1930; 3rd edition, Oxford and New York: Oxford University Press, 1957

Shaw, Thomas, *Travels or Observations Relating to Several Parts of Barbary and the Levant*, Oxford, 1738

UNESCO International Scientific Committee, *General History of Africa*, 8 vols., London: Heinemann, and Berkeley: University of California Press, 1981–93

Africa: West

The basic argument throughout much of pre-colonial African history is whether migrations from "more developed" areas influenced indigenous African, including West African, developments. Often these arguments begin with discussions regarding the significance of climate and ecology on the course of West Africa's history. Those who argue against indigenous development of African civilization and of the agricultural innovation to support it point to its tropical climate. Of Africa's 11,000,000 square miles 9,000,000 are in the tropics, including the entire region of West Africa. West Africa, in fact, is in the Inter Tropical Climate zone (ITC), an area marked by low pressure air and periods of regionally high rainfall. The rainfall, however, while heavy at times is erratic. The erratic nature of the rainfall not only leads to the leaching of soil, but also to limits on agriculture and, consequently, on population. There are variations in the climate and ecological zones of West Africa. The areas of Zaire and the Guinea Coast, for examples, are marked by tropical rain forests. The continental uplift of other areas is marked by regional basins, such as those found in the Niger River area. These basins favor navigable rivers, but precipitous falls hinder the penetration of the interior, having a great effect on the course of African history.

Ajayi and Crowder's *Historical Atlas of Africa* (1985) is excellent in addressing the role of geography in African history. Work on African agriculture has been extensive and the 1984 volume edited by Clark and Brandt outlines the major developments. Greenberg's classic on linguistics, *The Languages of Africa* (1963), still remains the benchmark for such studies, for it addresses the dispute regarding the role of migrations in African history. Greenberg used linguistic evidence to trace the path of African migrations and argued strongly against the "Hamitic hypothesis" that dominated so much colonial thought on Africa, stressing that all developments came from the "Hamitic" peoples from the east. Current archaeological evidence argues strongly for the fact West Africa was one of the areas in which indigenous farming developed. It indicates a long period of development, rather than a revolutionary leap resulting from outside introduction of crops.

Similar arguments regarding indigenous development versus outside influence have raged regarding the Savannah Empires and Forest Kingdoms. Certainly, climate changes affected the development of the Savannah Kingdoms and Empires and offer a clue regarding their development. Essential information on the early kingdoms and debates regarding their origins and development are found in the primary writings of Leo Africanus, Ibn Battuta and other Arab travellers. Bovill's *Golden Trade of the Moors* (1958), although somewhat dated, is still quite readable if corrected with later works such as Ajayi and Crowder's *History of West Africa* (1971–74), and the appropriate volumes of *The Cambridge History of Africa*. Ajayi and Crowder provided an important overview to the Islamic rule of West Africa. More detailed specialized work can be found in Last's *The Sokoto Caliphate* (1967). Hodgkin's *Nigerian Perspectives* (1960) furnished an interesting introduction to the important travel writing that supplies so much insight into the Islamic jihads.

Although geographical conditions generally provided protection and isolation for the peoples of the coastal area from the Senegambia region to Cameroon, there were exceptions. Certainly, the similarities in customs and language suggest a common origin and long isolation from outside influences. Benin, the Ashanti, Dahomey, the Wolof, and the Serer states supply exceptions to the theme of isolated and protected peoples. These centralized governments certainly had intense contact with their neighbors, resulting in warfare, trade, and religious borrowing. In addition, there were essential developments among the so-called stateless peoples, such as the Igbo and Tiv, exhibiting their own political and artistic genius.

The history of the forest zone is marked by a constant search for a balance of power in the face of outside attacks from the savannah region, especially in the 19th-century period of jihads. Islam also provided stability and a means for adapting outside influences while regulating trade and developing governmental institutions. It provided a means for uniting related people into larger wholes. Nonetheless, it did not penetrate to the mass of people, and even today the Yoruba take care to hedge their bets by having various members of their families follow different religions.

The Renaissance and Reformation in Europe unleashed a power that drove Europeans to the ends of the world in pursuit of money and adventure. As capitalism in its mercantilistic form emerged as the dominant economic and political paradigm, the Atlantic nations began their trade expansion. That expansion made its first mark along the west coast of Africa.

Once again the basic debate is between those who provide a Eurocentric African history and those scholars who seek either an Afrocentric or dialogic view of the interaction between European and African peoples, histories, cultures, and societies. Jan Vansina has long sought to present a dynamic image of African response and activism to the coming of European powers. Much of the debate has focused on the significance of the African slave trade and the works of Philip Curtin, Paul Lovejoy, J.E. Inikori, and David Henige have reflected and contributed to these debates. There has also been a discussion regarding the missionary influence in West Africa. These debates are complicated, but tend to focus on the degree of African response to European influence in religion, culture, politics, and society. There is an increasing understanding of the manner in which Africans helped to shape their own destinies. It is rather naive to picture Africans as passive observers in the major events that took place over five centuries of contact.

The debate over the African responses to European power often revolves on the question of the merits of direct and indirect rule. Crowder's *West Africa under Colonial Rule* (1968) depicted the colonial period in general and Senegal's experience in particular. Johnson's *The History of the Yorubas* (1921) also treated the situation in Senegal and the coming of Black power. Hollis Lynch contributed an example of a pan-African leader in his work on Edward Wilmot Blyden. Studies of particular movements to independence include J.H. Kopytoff on Nigeria; Christopher Fyfe on Sierra Leone; David Kimble on the Gold Coast; and Samuel Johnson, S.O. Biobaku, Michael Crowder, and Elizabeth Isichei on various areas of Nigeria.

Gifford and Louis' *The Transfer of Power in Africa* (1982) and *Decolonization and African Independence* (1988) focused on the end of colonialism and the rise of nationalism in Africa. Hodgkin's *Nationalism in Colonial Africa* (1956) and *African Political Parties* (1961) provide a general overview of the independence period. The literature on African one-party states and on Africa's political parties in general is quite wide, including works from Gwendolyn Carter, James S. Coleman (alone and with Carl G. Rosberg), Dennis Austin, and Richard L. Sklar. Autobiographies serve to illustrate the interaction between individual leaders and great events. Most notable are those by Kwame Nkrumah, Obafemi Awolowo, and Ahmadu Bello.

The spread of Islam was one way in which Africans responded to the spread of European influence in West Africa. In general these were countermovements by the Fulani against European hegemony. Usman dan Fodio, Seku Ahmadu, Al-Kanemi, and other Fulani began to purify their religion as a means for organizing the faithful against the infidel invaders. Again, arguments regarding the origin of the Fulani, the indigenous nature of West African Islam, and other aspects of the debate regarding the originality of West African peoples is found in discussions of West African Islam.

Some have used post-independence movements as "proof" of African inferiority and dependence on the outside world. West Africa has had major setbacks in its economic and political developments. Nigeria, for example, has spent most of the period in its post-independence period engaged in civil war or under ever-more repressive military rule. Liberia's civil war has also proved increasingly bloody and convoluted.

The economic consequences of West Africa's instability have proved significant. There has been a growing division between rich and poor over the years. There have, however, been some hopeful signs. The recovery of Ghana and the promise of democratic reform by Jerry Rawlings hold out some promise. The peaceful transition of power in Senghor's Senegal and in other countries shows that democratic traditions are not dead.

The overall issue in West African historical debates has centered on the issue of "invention versus diffusion." At every phase of its historical periodization there have been those who have stressed the dependent nature of West Africa and its borrowing of institutions from others, whether they are Hamites, Arabs, or Europeans. Fortunately, there have also been those who have stressed the interactive nature of cultural change and the originality of much of West African culture and history and the manner in which even borrowed elements are integrated within existing cultural institutions. The trend today is to examine the dialogic nature of West African history, stressing the active role that West Africans have played in their destiny.

FRANK A. SALAMONE

See also Ajayi; Boahen; Curtin; Lovejoy; Rodney; Vansina

Further Reading

Ajayi, J. F. Ade, *Christian Missions in Nigeria, 1841–1891*, London: Longman, and Evanston, IL: Northwestern University Press, 1965

Ajayi, J. F. Ade, and Michael Crowder, eds., *A History of West Africa*, 2 vols., London: Longman, 1971–74; New York: Columbia University Press, 1972–74

Ajayi, J. F. Ade, and Michael Crowder, eds., *Historical Atlas of Africa*, Cambridge and New York: Cambridge University Press, 1985

Akinjogbin, I.A., *Dahomey and Its Neighbors, 1708–1815*, Cambridge: Cambridge University Press, 1967

Alagoa, Ebiegberi Joe, *The Small Brave City State: A History of Nembe-Brass in the Niger Delta*, Ibadan: Ibadan University Press, 1964

Anstey, Roger, *The Atlantic Slave Trade and British Abolition, 1760–1810*, London: Macmillan, and Atlantic Highlands, NJ: Humanities Press, 1975

Asiwaju, A.I., *Western Yorubaland under European Rule, 1889–1945: A Comparative Analysis of French and British Colonialism*, London: Longman, 1976

Atanda, J. A., *The New Oyo Empire: Indirect Rule and Change in Western Nigeria, 1894–1934*, London: Longman, 1973

Austin, Dennis, *Politics in Ghana*, London and New York: Oxford University Press, 1964

Awolowo, Obafemi, *Awo: The Autobiography of Chief Obafemi Awolowo*, Cambridge and New York: Cambridge University Press, 1962

Azarya, Victor, *Aristocrats Facing Change: The Fulbe in Guinea, Nigeria, and Cameroon*, Chicago: University of Chicago Press, 1978

Ba, Amadou Hampata, "Out of the Land of Shadows," *UNESCO Courier* (May 1990), 22–25

Bello, Ahmadu, *My Life*, Cambridge: Cambridge University Press, 1962

Biobaku, Saburi Oladeni, *The Egba and Their Neighbors, 1842–1872*, Oxford: Oxford University Press, 1957

Bovill, E.W., *The Golden Trade of the Moors*, London and New York: Oxford University Press, 1958; revised 1968

Brooks, George E., "A Provisional Historical Schema for Western Africa Based on Seven Climate Periods (c. 9000 BC to the Nineteenth Century)," *Cahiers d'Etudes Africaines* 26 (1986), 101–02

Brooks, George E., "Ecological Perspectives on Mande Population Movements, Commercial Networks, and Settlement Patterns from the Atlantic Wet Phase (c.5500–2500 BC to the Present)," *History in Africa* 16 (1989), 23–40

Carter, Gwendolen, *Independence for Africa*, New York: Praeger, 1960; London: Thames and Hudson, 1961

Carter, Gwendolen, ed., *African One Party States*, Ithaca, NY: Cornell University Press, 1962

Carter, Gwendolen, ed., *National Unity and Regionalism in Eight South African States: Nigeria, Niger, the Congo, Gabon, Central African Republic, Chad, Uganda, Ethiopia*, Ithaca, NY: Cornell University Press, and London: Oxford University Press, 1966

Clark, J. Desmond, ed., *The Cambridge History of Africa*, vol. 1: *From Earliest Times to c.500 BC*, Cambridge: Cambridge University Press, 1982

Clark, J. Desmond, and Steven A. Brandt, eds., *From Hunters to Farmers: The Causes and Consequences of Food Production in Africa*, Berkeley: University of California Press, 1984

Coleman, James Smoot, *Nigeria: Background to Nationalism*, London: Cambridge University Press, and Berkeley: University of California Press, 1958

Coleman, James Smoot, and Carl G. Rosberg, Jr., eds., *Political Parties and National Integration in Tropical Africa*, Berkeley: University of California Press, 1964

Crowder, Michael, *Senegal: A Study in French Assimilation Policy*, Oxford and New York: Oxford University Press, 1962; revised London: Methuen, 1967

Crowder, Michael, *The Story of Nigeria*, London: Faber, 1962; revised 1978

Crowder, Michael, *West Africa under Colonial Rule*, London: Hutchinson, and Evanston, IL: Northwestern University Press, 1968

Crowder, Michael, ed., *West African Resistance: The Military Response to Colonial Occupation*, London: Hutchinson, 1971

Crowder, Michael, ed., *The Cambridge History of Africa*, vol. 8: *From c.1940 to c.1975*, Cambridge: Cambridge University Press, 1984

Curtin, Philip D., *The Atlantic Slave Trade: A Census*, Madison: University of Wisconsin Press, 1969

Daaku, Kwame Yeboah, *Trade and Politics on the Gold Coast, 1600–1720: A Study of the African Reaction to European Trade*, Oxford: Oxford University Press, 1970

Dike, Kenneth Onwuka, *Trade and Politics in the Niger Delta, 1830–1885: An Introduction to the Economic and Political History of Nigeria*, Oxford: Oxford University Press, 1956

Egharevba, Jacob R., *A Short History of Benin*, Lagos: Church Missionary Society Bookshop, 1936; revised 1953

Fage, John Donnelly, "Slaves and Societies in West Africa, c.1445–c.1700," *Journal of African History* 21 (1980), 289–310

Forde, Daryll, and Phyllis Kaberry, eds., *West African Kingdoms in the Nineteenth Century*, Oxford: Oxford University Press, 1967

Fyfe, Christopher, *A History of Sierra Leone*, London: Oxford University Press, 1962

Gailey, Harry, *A History of the Gambia*, London: Routledge, 1964

Gifford, Prosser, and William Roger Louis, eds., *France and Britain in Africa: Imperial Rivalry and Colonial Rule*, New Haven: Yale University Press, 1971

Gifford, Prosser, and William Roger Louis, eds., *The Transfer of Power in Africa: Decolonization, 1940–1960*, New Haven: Yale University Press, 1982

Gifford, Prosser, and William Roger Louis, eds., *Decolonization and African Independence: The Transfers of Power, 1960–1980*, New Haven: Yale University Press, 1988

Greenberg, Joseph, *The Languages of Africa*, Bloomington: Indiana University Press, 1963; 3rd edition, 1970

Henige, David, "Measuring the Immeasurable: The Atlantic Slave Trade, West African Population, and the Pyrrhonion Critic," *Journal of African History* 27 (1986), 195–313

Herskovits, Melville, *Dahomey: An Ancient African Kingdom*, 2 vols., New York: Augustin, 1938; reprinted 1967

Hodgkin, Thomas, *Nationalism in Colonial Africa*, London: Muller, 1956; New York: New York University Press, 1957

Hodgkin, Thomas, *Nigerian Perspectives*, London: Oxford University Press, 1960

Hodgkin, Thomas, *African Political Parties*, Harmondsworth: Penguin, 1961; Gloucester, MA: Peter Smith, 1971

Ibn Battuta, *Travels of Ibn Battuta, AD 1325–1354*, edited and translated by H.A.R. Gibb, 4 vols., Cambridge: Cambridge University Press for the Hakluyt Society, 1958–71

Ikime, Obaro, *Niger Delta Rivalry: Itsekiri-Urhobo Relations and the European Presence, 1884–1936*, London: Longman, and New York: Humanities Press, 1969

Inikori, J.E., ed., *Forced Migration: The Impact of the Export Slave Trade on African Societies*, London: Hutchinson, 1982

Isichei, Elizabeth, *History of Nigeria*, London and New York: Longman, 1983

Johnson, Samuel, *The History of the Yorubas from the Earliest Times to the Beginning of the Protectorate*, Lagos: C.M.S., and London: Routledge, 1921; Westport, CT: Negro University Press, 1970

Jones, G.I., *The Trading States of the Oil Rivers: A Study of Political Development in Eastern Nigeria*, London: Oxford University Press, 1963

July, Robert W., *Precolonial Africa: An Economic and Social History*, New York: Scribner, 1975

Kimble, David, *A Political History of Ghana, 1850–1928: The Rise of Gold Coast Nationalism*, Oxford: Oxford University Press, 1963

Kirk-Greene, Anthony Hamilton Millard, *Crisis and Conflict in Nigeria: A Documentary Sourcebook*, 2 vols., London: Oxford University Press, 1971

Kopytoff, Jean Heskovits, *A Preface to Modern Nigeria: The "Sierra Leonians" in Yoruba, 1830–1890*, Madison: University of Wisconsin Press, 1965

Last, Murray, *The Sokoto Caliphate*, New York: Humanities Press, and London: Longman, 1967

Law, Robin, *The Oyo Empire, c.1600–c.1836: A West African Imperialism in the Era of the Atlantic Slave Trade*, Oxford: Oxford University Press, 1977

Louis, William Roger, "The Berlin Conference," in Prosser Gifford and William Roger Louis, eds., *France and Britain in Africa: Imperial Rivalry and Colonial Rule*, New Haven: Yale University Press, 1971

Louis, William Roger, ed., *Imperialism: The Robinson and Gallagher Controversy*, New York: New Viewpoints, 1976

Lovejoy, Paul E., *Caravans of Kola: The Hausa Kola Trade, 1700–1900*, Zaria: Ahmadu Bello University Press, 1980

Lovejoy, Paul E., ed., *The Ideology of Slavery in Africa*, Beverly Hills, CA: Sage, 1981

Lovejoy, Paul E., *Transformations in Slavery: A History of Slavery in Africa*, Cambridge and New York: Cambridge University Press, 1983

Lovejoy, Paul E., ed., *Africans in Bondage: Studies in Slavery and the Slave Trade: Essays in Honor of Philip D. Curtin on the Occasion of the Twenty-Fifth Anniversary of African Studies at the University of Wisconsin*, Madison: University of Wisconsin Press, 1986

Lovejoy, Paul E., *Salt of the Desert Sun: A History of Salt Production and Trade in the Central Sudan*, Cambridge: Cambridge University Press, 1986

Lovejoy, Paul E., *Concubinage and the Status of Women in Early Colonial Northern Nigeria*, Johannesburg: University of the Witwatersrand African Studies Institute, 1988

Lovejoy, Paul E., "The Impact of the Atlantic Slave Trade on Africa: A Review of the Literature," *Journal of African History* 30 (1989), 365–94

Lovejoy, Paul E., "Revolutionary Mahdism and Resistance to Colonial Rule in the Sokoto Caliphate, 1905–06," *Journal of African History* 31 (1990), 217–44

Lovejoy, Paul E., and Jan S. Hogendorn, *Slow Death for Slavery: The Course of Abolition in Northern Nigeria, 1897–1936*, Cambridge: Cambridge University Press, 1993

Lovejoy, Paul E., and A.S. Kanya-Forstner, eds., *Slavery and Its Abolition in French West Africa: The Official Papers of G. Poulet, E. Roume, and G. Deherme*, Madison: University of Wisconsin Press, 1994

Lovejoy, Paul E., "British Abolition and Its Impact on Slave Prices along the Atlantic Coast of Africa, 1783–1850," *Journal of Economic History* 55 (1995), 98–119

Lynch, Hollis R., *Edward Wilmot Blyden*, London and New York: Oxford University Press, 1967

Newbury, Colin Walter, *The Western Slave Coast and Its Rulers: European Trade and Administration among the Yoruba and Adja-Speaking People of South-Western Nigeria, Southern Dahomey and Togo*, Oxford: Oxford University Press, 1961

Nkrumah, Kwame, *Ghana*, Edinburgh and New York: Nelson, 1959

Oliver, Roland, *Sir Harry Johnston and the Scramble for Africa*, London: Chatto and Windus, 1957; New York: St. Martin's Press, 1958

Rattray, Robert Sutherland, *Ashanti*, Oxford: Clarendon Press, 1923; reprinted 1969

Rattray, Robert Sutherland, *Ashanti Law and Constitution*, London: Oxford University Press, 1929; reprinted 1969

Rodney, Walter, *A History of the Upper Guinea Coast, 1545–1800*, Oxford: Oxford University Press, and New York: Monthly Review Press, 1970

Rotberg, Robert I. and Ali A. Mazrui, eds., *Protest and Power in Black Africa*, New York: Oxford University Press, 1970

Ryder, Alan Frederick Charles, *Benin and the Europeans, 1485–1897*, New York: Humanities Press, 1969

Sklar, Richard L., *Nigerian Political Parties: Power in an Emergent African Nation*, Princeton: Princeton University Press, 1963

Vansina, Jan, *Kingdoms of the Savanna*, Madison: University of Wisconsin Press, 1966

Wilks, Ivor, *Asante in the Nineteenth Century: The Structure and Evolution of a Political Order*, Cambridge and New York: Cambridge University Press, 1975

Wolfson, Freda, *Pageant of Ghana*, London: Oxford University Press, 1958

African American History

Historical debate on colonial slavery has centered on explaining the origins and development of wholesale black servitude after the first black Africans arrived in North America at Jamestown, Virginia in 1619. Winthrop Jordan, in *White over Black* (1968), showed the evolution of negative racial attitudes towards blacks in 18th-century America, examining why black Africans, rather than white indentured servants or Native Americans, were condemned to bondage for life. David Brion Davis's two works on the problem of slavery in western culture and in the age of revolution, have provided the most authoritative attempt to account for the entrenchment of black slavery in the southern colonies at a time when the philosophical justifications for slavery appeared to be dying out in western society, and were in striking contrast to the libertarian values of the American Revolution, 1776–87.

Research into African American history has always been a controversial area because of its often highly charged racial and political connotations. This is no more true than in the study of antebellum slavery. Abolitionist accounts like Harriet Beecher Stowe's *Uncle Tom's Cabin* (1851), sought to portray the physical brutality, immorality, and economic shortcomings of the "Peculiar Institution." Such proselytizing works often generated equally partisan writings by southern pro-slavery apologists.

Two important early 20th-century works were Ulrich Bonnell Phillips' *American Negro Slavery* (1918) and *Life and Labor in the Old South* (1929). Phillips, himself descended from a southern slaveowning family, argued that slavery was economically unprofitable by the 1850s but was retained by antebellum planters as a means of social control and to provide a "civilizing school" for black slaves.

Autobiographies of runaway slaves constitute the most important written records by African Americans themselves. Foremost of these is Frederick Douglass' *Narrative* (1845). More generally, slave illiteracy rates of 90 to 95 per cent have posed a major challenge to historians in unearthing black testimony. In the absence of written evidence, attention has been paid to the study of oral source material. Particularly important are the Works Progress Administration (WPA) narratives, comprised of interviews with former slaves under New Deal initiatives during the 1930s. Slave folk tales, such as the Brer

Rabbit stories, first published by the southern white journalist Joel Chandler Harris as *The Songs and Sayings of Uncle Remus* (1880), have also received close attention. A detailed analysis of the sociological significance of slave folklore is Lawrence Levine's *Black Culture and Black Consciousness* (1977).

The starting point for modern debate on slave life was Stanley Elkins' *Slavery: A Problem in American Institutional and Intellectual Life* (1959). Elkins focused less on the physical hardships of slavery than on its psychological impact. In a controversial thesis he compared antebellum slavery to the Nazi concentration camps of World War II, and suggested that African American slaves were mentally "infantilized" by the severe, authoritarian regimes on southern plantations. This hypothesis was vigorously challenged in subsequent works such as John Blassingame's *The Slave Community* (1972), George Rawick's *From Sundown to Sunup* (1972), and Herbert Gutman's *The Black Family in Slavery and Freedom* (1976). Applying Gramsci's concept of "oppressive hegemony" to the institution of slavery, Eugene Genovese in *Roll, Jordan, Roll* (1974) viewed slave life as a blend of accommodationism and resistance. Slaves sought both to play on, and adapt to, the paternalistic feelings of planters in order to ameliorate the harshness of day to day slave life. Since the early 1970s research has centered on the means by which slaves resisted the process of infantilization through the perpetuation of a dynamic African American culture.

The economics of antebellum slavery has had considerable analysis. Despite the claims of 19th-century abolitionists to the contrary, most present day historians accept that slavery was an economically viable institution down to the outbreak of the Civil War in 1861. Recent debate has concentrated on the contentious claims made in Robert W. Fogel and Stanley Engerman's *Time on the Cross* (1974). Using econometric analysis, Fogel and Engerman concluded that southern slave agricultural production, relying on a combination of positive incentives and gang labor techniques, was actually 35 per cent more efficient than northern free farm labor. *Reckoning with Slavery* (1976) by Paul David *et al.*, showed the deep misgivings of many historians as to both the methodology and findings of Fogel and Engerman's work. In a different vein Genovese's *The Political Economy of Slavery* (1965), highlighted the political and labor problems that would have been implicit in any attempt to make widespread use of slave labor in non-agricultural occupations, in particular industry and manufacturing.

Early academic research on the African American experience during the Civil War and Reconstruction was dominated by the turn of the century historian William A. Dunning. Reflecting the racial conservatism of his era, Dunning's *Reconstruction* (1907), portrayed the period as one of national shame and humiliation. The south was placed under the domination and misrule of corrupt northern "Carpetbagger" politicians, their southern white allies, the "Scalawags," and illiterate freed slaves. This view was reinforced by numerous state studies carried out by Dunning's research students. With some notable exceptions, not least W.E.B. Du Bois' *Black Reconstruction* (1935), the Dunning school remained dominant until World War II.

In the 1950s, changing racial attitudes, marked by the awakening of the civil rights movement, saw a new generation of historians, the "Revisionists," cast doubt on the Dunning interpretation. John Hope Franklin's *Reconstruction: After the Civil War* (1961), and Kenneth M. Stampp's *The Era of Reconstruction* (1965), showed the positive achievements of the 1860s and 1870s, for example the modernizing of state constitutions and the introduction of public school systems in the South. The lurid images of political corruption and economic ruin evoked by Dunning were seen to be exaggerated.

Since the 1970s Reconstruction historiography has been dominated by "Post Revisionist" or "Radical Revisionist" historians. Important "Post Revisionist" works include Leon Litwack's *Been in the Storm So Long* (1979), and Eric Foner's *Reconstruction* (1988). Their accounts dismissed the views of Dunning as dated and discredited. Instead, they stressed the extent to which the planter class, the "Bourbon Aristocracy," retained social, economic, and political power in the South after the Civil War. The system of sharecropping, and the failure of Republican state and congressional leaders to provide freed slaves with an effective means of achieving independent landownership, have been seen as condemning southern blacks to a position of extreme poverty and serfdom well into the 20th century.

Among the lowest points in African American history since emancipation was the Supreme Court's "separate but equal" ruling in *Plessy v. Ferguson* in 1896, which provided constitutional approval for racial segregation. Discussion on the origins of segregation has focused on the work of C. Vann Woodward and Joel Williamson. Woodward's *The Strange Career of Jim Crow* (1955), saw the *Plessy* decision as a major departure in the pattern of southern race relations. Williamson's *The Crucible of Race* (1984) viewed the ruling as rather providing *de jure* authority for the *de facto* segregation that he believed was already endemic in the South by the 1890s.

From 1895 to 1915 the most important African American leader was the conservative accommodationist Booker T. Washington. Washington's philosophy was most clearly outlined in his autobiography *Up from Slavery* (1901), in which he urged southern blacks to concentrate first on economic and moral improvement, rather than the struggle for civil and political rights. He also championed the then fashionable idea of "industrial education," placing emphasis on the learning of trades and practical skills as opposed to traditional academic subjects.

Dating back to the slave narratives of the 19th century there had been a tendency for the study of African American history to focus on biographical and autobiographical works on the major black civil rights spokesmen of their era. This has been the case both in respect to Washington and the black nationalist leader of the 1920s, Marcus Garvey. Easily the most significant research on Washington's life has been two works by Louis Harlan, *The Making of a Black Leader, 1856-1901* (1972) and *The Wizard of Tuskegee, 1901-1915* (1983). Harlan also jointly edited a 14-volume collection of Washington's writings and correspondence, *The Booker T. Washington Papers* (1972-89). An important, and balanced, modern study of Garvey and Garveyism is Judith Stein's *The World of Marcus Garvey* (1986). Robert Hill is the editor of a projected 10-volume collection of primary source material, *The Marcus Garvey and Universal Negro Association Papers* which has been in the process of publication since 1983. Eight volumes have thus far appeared in print.

A leading opponent of both Washington and Garvey was the northern-born black spokesman W.E.B. Du Bois. The erudite Du Bois was the author of many major academic and autobiographical works that are central to the understanding of African American history. During his long life, 1868–1963, he variously took on the roles of civil rights campaigner, journalist, author, academic, and political activist, but failed to develop any mass following. However, since his death Du Bois has received widespread recognition from both historians and African Americans. He is seen as a major intellectual influence on black protest within the United States in the 1960s, and the successful challenges to European colonialism by black Africans since 1945.

World War I ushered in a period of important social and economic change in African American life. Between 1915 and 1925 some 1,250,000 blacks migrated from the agricultural South to seek industrial employment in the cities of the North. This "Great Migration" has received much detailed investigation by historians such as James Grossman, Carole Marks, and Joe William Trotter, who have sought to understand its causes and impact upon African American society. Reflecting a trend in recent thought Marks, in *Farewell, We're Good and Gone* (1989), concluded that the real beneficiaries of the migration were northern factory employers. For black migrants themselves the experience, at least in the short to medium term, was at best a zero sum game, trading one set of problems in the South for other, no less serious, difficulties in the North.

Alex Haley's *The Autobiography of Malcolm X* (1965), and E.U. Essien Udom's *Black Nationalism* (1962), are key works in understanding the development of black nationalist thought during the 1950s and 1960s. In respect to Malcolm X himself there has been a tendency by historians to engage in a psychological analysis of their subject, most notably Eugene Wolfenstein's *The Victims of Democracy* (1981), and Bruce Perry's *Malcolm* (1991). Bobby Seale's *Seize the Time* (1968), and Stokely Carmichael and Charles Hamilton's *Black Power* (1967), are important first-hand accounts by the younger generation of Black Power radicals influenced by the legacy of Malcolm X's teachings in the late 1960s and early 1970s.

Martin Luther King, Jr., and the mainstream civil rights movement during the 1950s and 1960s, have predictably been the focus of extensive research. Most significant of the many biographical studies on King is David Garrow's *Bearing the Cross* (1986). Garrow saw King's religious faith, and the conviction that he was the instrument of divine will, as the main sources of inspiration in King's life and career. Clayborne Carson is at present editor of a major project to publish the personal papers and writings of King.

Despite, or perhaps in part because of, the proliferation of works on King, a recent trend has been for academic researchers to turn to the study of the civil rights movement at local, grass roots level. This is reflected in Adam Fairclough's *Race and Democracy* (1995), and Aldon Morris' *The Origins of the Civil Rights Movement* (1984).

There is also a growing interest in earlier civil rights leadership, and the changes in African American society during the 1930s and 1940s, that facilitated the emergence of the civil rights movement during the mid-1950s. In this vein, the life and career of one of the elder statesmen of civil rights protest

has been given greater prominence in Paula Pfeffer's *A. Philip Randolph* (1990). The general experience of blacks during the New Deal and World War II has received sound coverage in John Kirby's *Black Americans in the Roosevelt Era* (1980), Harvard Sitkoff's *A New Deal for Blacks* (1978), and Neil Wynn's *The Afro-American and the Second World War* (1976). However, no reference to these years would be complete without mention of Gunnar Myrdal's *An American Dilemma* (1944). A detailed sociological investigation of black life in the United States, Myrdal's work has exerted a profound influence on the research of 20th-century African American history.

Until the 1940s African American history was in many respects regarded as a fringe area of academic research. Early postwar scholars in the field were often motivated more by idealism, and the desire to campaign for an end to segregation and racial discrimination, than career ambitions. Historians such as Eugene Genovese, Leon Litwack, and August Meier thus combined scholarly activity with grass roots participation in the civil rights protests of the 1950s and 1960s. By the 1980s and 1990s African American history had achieved clear recognition as a mainstream area of academic study. Leading researchers in the subject now receive the scholarly acclaim that their work deserves. Paradoxically, growing pessimism over recent developments in US race relations, and greater appreciation of the limitations of the civil rights movement have resulted in a sense of disillusionment with the radical and liberal ideals that inspired this historiographical revolution. Present day historians, while highlighting with great clarity the many injustices in the past treatment of African Americans in US society, have, as yet, been unable to signpost a way forward to the future that might provide an effective solution to this unfortunate historical legacy.

KEVERN J. VERNEY

See also Davis, D.; Du Bois; Dunning; Elkins; Fogel; Franklin; Genovese; Gutman; Hine; Levine; Lewis, D.; Litwack; Meier; Phillips; Stampp; Woodson; Woodward

Further Reading

Blassingame, John, *The Slave Community: Plantation Life in the Antebellum South*, New York: Oxford University Press, 1972; revised 1979

Burson, George S., Jr., "The Second Reconstruction: A Historiographical Essay on Recent Works," *Journal of Negro History* 59 (1974), 322–36

Carmichael, Stokely [Kwame Tore] and Charles V. Hamilton, *Black Power: The Politics of Liberation in America*, New York: Random House, 1967; London: Cape, 1968

Carson, Clayborne, general editor, *The Martin Luther King Papers*, 2 vols. to date, Berkeley: University of California Press, 1992–

Cronon, E. David, *Black Moses: The Story of Marcus Garvey and the Universal Negro Improvement Association*, Madison: University of Wisconsin Press, 1955

David, Paul, Herbert G. Gutman, Richard Sutch, Peter Temin, and Gavin Wright, *Reckoning with Slavery: A Critical Study in the Quantitative History of American Negro Slavery*, New York: Oxford University Press, 1976

Davis, David Brion, *The Problem of Slavery in Western Culture*, Ithaca, NY: Cornell University Press, 1966; revised 1988

Davis, David Brion, *The Problem of Slavery in the Age of Revolution, 1770–1823*, Ithaca, NY: Cornell University Press, 1975

Douglass, Frederick, *Narrative of the Life of Frederick Douglass, an American Slave*, n.p.: Anti-Slavery Office, 1845

Du Bois, W.E.B., *Souls of Black Folk: Essays and Sketches*, Chicago: McClurg, 1903; London: Constable, 1905

Du Bois, W.E.B., *Black Reconstruction*, New York: Harcourt Brace, 1935; as *Black Reconstruction in America*, Cleveland: World, 1964, London: Cass, 1966, reprinted New York: Atheneum, 1992

Dunning, William A., *Reconstruction: Political and Economic, 1865–1877*, New York: Harper, 1907

Elkins, Stanley, *Slavery: A Problem in American Institutional and Intellectual Life*, Chicago: University of Chicago Press, 1959; 3rd edition 1976

Ellison, Mary, *The Black Experience: American Blacks since 1865*, New York: Barnes and Noble, and London: Batsford, 1974

Fairclough, Adam, *Race and Democracy: The Civil Rights Struggle in Louisiana, 1915–1972*, Athens: University of Georgia Press, 1995

Fogel, Robert William, and Stanley Engerman, *Time on the Cross: The Economics of American Negro Slavery*, 2 vols., Boston: Little Brown, and London: Wildwood, 1974

Foner, Eric, *Reconstruction: America's Unfinished Revolution, 1863–1877*, New York: Harper, 1988; abridged as *A Short History of Reconstruction*, 1990

Franklin, John Hope, *From Slavery to Freedom: A History of American Negroes*, New York: Knopf, 1947; revised, with Alfred A. Moss, Jr., as *From Slavery to Freedom: A History of African Americans*, 7th edition, New York: McGraw Hill, 1994

Franklin, John Hope, *Reconstruction: After the Civil War*, Chicago: University of Chicago Press, 1961; 2nd edition 1994

Franklin, John Hope, and August Meier, eds., *Black Leaders of the Twentieth Century*, Urbana: University of Illinois Press, 1982

Franklin, John Hope, *Race and History: Selected Essays, 1938–1988*, Baton Rouge: Louisiana State University Press, 1989

Garrow, David, *Bearing the Cross: Martin Luther King, Jr., and the Southern Christian Leadership Conference*, New York: Morrow, 1986; London: Cape, 1988

Genovese, Eugene D., *The Political Economy of Slavery: Studies in the Economy and Society of the Slave South*, New York: Pantheon, 1965; London: MacGibbon and Kee, 1968

Genovese, Eugene D., *Roll, Jordan, Roll: The World the Slaves Made*, New York: Pantheon, 1974; London: Deutsch, 1975

Gutman, Herbert G., *Slavery and the Numbers Game: A Critique of Time on the Cross*, Urbana: University of Illinois Press, 1975

Gutman, Herbert G., *The Black Family in Slavery and Freedom, 1750–1925*, New York: Pantheon, and Oxford: Blackwell, 1976

Haley, Alex, *The Autobiography of Malcolm X*, New York: Grove, 1965; London: Hutchinson, 1968

Harlan, Louis, *Booker T. Washington: The Making of a Black Leader, 1856–1901*, Oxford and New York: Oxford University Press, 1972

Harlan, Louis, ed., *The Booker T. Washington Papers*, 14 vols., Urbana: University of Illinois Press, 1972–89

Harlan, Louis, *Booker T. Washington: The Wizard of Tuskegee, 1901–1915*, Oxford and New York: Oxford University Press, 1983

Hill, Robert A., ed., *The Marcus Garvey and Universal Negro Improvement Association Papers*, 8 vols. to date, Berkeley: University of California Press, 1983–

Hine, Darlene Clark, ed., *The State of Afro-American History: Past, Present, and Future*, Baton Rouge: Louisiana State University Press, 1986

Jordan, Winthrop D., *White over Black: American Attitudes toward the Negro, 1550–1812*, Chapel Hill: University of North Carolina Press, 1968; abridged as *The White Man's Burden: Historical Origins of Racism in the United States*, New York: Oxford University Press, 1974

Kirby, John B., "An Uncertain Context: America and Black Americans in the Twentieth Century," *Journal of Southern History* 46 (1980), 571–86

Kirby, John B., *Black Americans in the Roosevelt Era: Liberalism and Race*, Knoxville: University of Tennessee Press, 1980

Lane, Ann J., ed., *The Debate over Slavery: Stanley Elkins and His Critics*, Urbana: University of Illinois Press, 1971

Levine, Lawrence W., *Black Culture and Black Consciousness: Afro-American Folk Thought from Slavery to Freedom*, Oxford and New York: Oxford University Press, 1977

Lewis, David Levering, *W.E.B. Du Bois: Biography of a Race, 1868–1919*, New York: Holt, 1993

Litwack, Leon F., *Been in the Storm So Long: The Aftermath of Slavery*, New York: Knopf, 1979; London: Athlone Press, 1980

Marable, Manning, *Race, Reform, and Rebellion: The Second Reconstruction in Black America, 1945–1990*, Jackson: University Press of Mississippi, and London: Macmillan, 1984

Marable, Manning, *W.E.B. Du Bois: Black Radical Democrat*, Boston: Twayne, 1986

Marks, Carole, *Farewell, We're Good and Gone: The Great Black Migration*, Bloomington: Indiana University Press, 1989

Meier, August, *Negro Thought in America, 1880–1915: Racial Ideologies in the Age of Booker T. Washington*, Ann Arbor: University of Michigan Press, 1963

Meier, August, and Elliott M. Rudwick, *Black History and the Historical Profession, 1915–1980*, Urbana: University of Illinois Press, 1986

Morris, Aldon, *The Origins of the Civil Rights Movement*, New York: Free Press, and London: Collier Macmillan, 1984

Myrdal, Gunnar, *An American Dilemma: The Negro Problem and Modern Democracy*, 2 vols., New York: Harper, 1944

Perry, Bruce, *Malcolm: The Life of a Man Who Changed America*, Barrytown, NY: Station Hill, 1991

Pfeffer, Paula, *A. Philip Randolph: Pioneer of the Civil Rights Movement*, Baton Rouge: Louisiana State University Press, 1990

Phillips, Ulrich Bonnell, *American Negro Slavery: A Survey of the Supply, Employment, and Control of Negro Labor as Determined by the Plantation Regime*, New York: Appleton, 1918; reprinted Baton Rouge: Louisiana State University Press, 1966

Phillips, Ulrich Bonnell, *Life and Labor in the Old South*, Boston: Little Brown, 1929

Phillips, Ulrich Bonnell, *The Slave Economy of the Old South: Selected Essays in Economic and Social History*, edited by Eugene D. Genovese, Baton Rouge: Louisiana State University Press, 1968

Pinkney, Alphonso, *Red, Black and Green: Black Nationalism in the United States*, Cambridge and New York: Cambridge University Press, 1976

Rawick, George, *From Sundown to Sunup: The Making of the Black Community*, Westport, CT: Greenwood Press, 1972

Seale, Bobby, *Seize the Time: The Story of the Black Panther Party and Huey P. Newton*, New York: Random House, 1968; London: Hutchinson, 1970

Sitkoff, Harvard, *A New Deal for Blacks: The Emergence of Civil Rights as a National Issue*, Oxford and New York: Oxford University Press, 1978

Stampp, Kenneth M., *The Era of Reconstruction, 1865–1877*, New York: Knopf, and London: Eyre and Spottiswoode, 1965

Starobin, Robert, "The Negro: A Central Theme in American History," *Journal of Contemporary History* 3 (1968), 37–53

Stein, Judith, *The World of Marcus Garvey: Race and Class in Modern Society*, Baton Rouge: Louisiana State University Press, 1986

Trotter, Joe William, Jr., ed., *The Great Migration in Historical Perspective: New Dimensions of Race, Class, and Gender*, Bloomington: Indiana University Press, 1991

Udom, Essien Udosen Essien, *Black Nationalism: The Rise of the Black Muslims*, Chicago: University of Chicago Press, 1962; Harmondsworth: Penguin, 1966

Washington, Booker T., *Up from Slavery*, New York: Doubleday Page, and London: Fisher Unwin, 1901

White, John, *Black Leadership in America*, London and New York: Longman, 1985; revised 1990

Williamson, Joel, *The Crucible of Race: Black–White Relations in the American South since Emancipation*, New York: Oxford University Press, 1984; abridged as *A Rage for Order*, 1986

Wolfenstein, Eugene, *The Victims of Democracy: Malcolm X and the Black Revolution*, Berkeley: University of California Press, 1981; London: Free Association Press, 1989

Woodward, C. Vann, *The Strange Career of Jim Crow*, New York: Oxford University Press, 1955; 3rd edition 1974

Wynn, Neil, *The Afro-American and the Second World War*, London: Elek, and New York: Holmes and Meier, 1976; revised 1993

African Diaspora

Melville Herskovits' works can be taken as a starting point of academic studies of the African diaspora. Inspired by such works as Carter Woodson's *The African Background Outlined* (1936) and W.E.B. Du Bois' *Black Folk, Then and Now* (1939), he began studying African Americans in the United States and expanded his work to include Africa and the Caribbean. He was concerned, among other things, with the "survivals" of African beliefs and practices among those peoples who had been removed from Africa and transplanted elsewhere.

His debates with the African American sociologist E. Franklin Frazier provide the irony of a Jewish American arguing for the importance of African culture to the African American while an African American disputes the survival of any important elements in the African American population. Indeed, Frazier believed that stressing African ties was dangerous to the progress of his people.

Certainly, the atmosphere has changed appreciably since Herskovits' trail blazing writings. In fact, Herskovits himself noted these changes between his original publication of *The Myth of the Negro Past* in 1941 and its paperback publication in 1958. Among others, Roger Bastide's *Les Amériques noires: les civilisations africaines dans le nouveau monde* (1967; *African Civilisations in the New World*, 1971) owes a great deal to Herskovits' *The Myth of the Negro Past*. Nevertheless, Bastide is quick to note the dangers of Herskovits' position, arguing that in his notion of "reinterpretation" Herskovits sees the African American as unable to be assimilated into American culture, for the African American would always interpret the past in African terms.

However, Bastide noted that Frazier's position, while understandable, also ignored the African roots of African American culture through denying any survival of African culture. Moreover, as Bastide noted, seeking to have African Americans totally absorbed into the mainstream on Euro-American terms is a betrayal of that community. Despite its dangers, therefore, Herskovits' position is the foundation of the modern movement termed negritude which began in Haiti and has been so influential on such causes as the Black Power movement and cultural diversity.

Certainly, there have been a plethora of studies examining the connection between Africa and various areas where members of the diaspora have settled. Major emphasis, however, has been on the United States and the Caribbean. These studies have covered general overviews (Harris and Segal); the role of pan-Africanism in the diaspora (Walters); artistic connections (Salamone and Weinstein); religion (Gray and Evans); women (Terborg-Penn, and James and Farmer); myth (Wilentz); and architectural similarities.

In general, these studies have followed two broad paths. One set has focused on actual historical connections, painstakingly established through archaeological and other historical comparative methods. The other set of studies has concentrated on the symbolic meaning of Africa to African Americans and Afro-Caribbeans. Both studies have served important functions and have influenced each other. Moreover, Herskovits anticipated both of these paths in the preface and introduction to *The Myth of the Negro Past*. As he noted in the preface "Problems in Negro research attacked with out an assessment of historic depth, and a willingness to regard the historical past of an entire people as the equivalent of its written history, can clearly be seen to have made for confusion and error in interpretation, and misdirected judgment in evaluating practical ends."

In the book's introduction, Herskovits argued that the result of believing that the African American has no past and that African culture is not worth much in any case had deeper implications: "The myth of the Negro past is one of the principal supports of race prejudice in this country. Unrecognized in its efficacy, it rationalizes discrimination in every day contact between Negroes and whites, influences the shaping of policy where Negroes are concerned, and affects the trends of research by scholars whose theoretical approach, methods, and systems of thought presented to students are in harmony with it."

Therefore, for Herskovits and those who have come after him, studies concerning the African diaspora are not simply about historical connections. They are also about the way in which these affinities have an impact on the relationships between people; that is, they explore the meanings that are attached to these connections and the manner in which they alter and affect human social interactions. Herskovits, in fact, was quite aware of the political nature of his work and the manner in which it could and did in a few short years begin to affect American racial and ethnic relationships. It has led to a significant amount of additional research and certainly has affected the manner in which research, theory, methods, and teaching has evolved.

FRANK A. SALAMONE

See also Du Bois; Woodson

Further Reading

Aguessy, Honorat, *Cultures vodoun: Manifestations, migrations, métamorphoses (Afrique, Caraibes, Amériques)* (Voodoo Cultures: Manifestations, Migrations, Metamorphoses in Africa, the Caribbean and the Americas), Benin: Institut de Développement et d'Echange Endogènes, 1992(?)

"Architecture from the Diaspora." *American Visions* 8 (1993), 11–12

Azevedo, Mario, ed., *Africana Studies: A Survey of Africa and the African Diaspora*, Durham, NC: Carolina Academic Press, 1993

Bastide, Roger, *Les Amériques noires: les civilisations africaines dans le nouveau monde*, Paris: Payot, 1967, 3rd edition Paris: L'Harmattan, 1996; in English as *African Civilisations in the New World*, London: Hurst, and New York: Harper, 1971

Conniff, Michael, and Thomas J. Davis, eds., *Africans in the Americas: A History of the Black Diaspora*, New York: St. Martin's Press, 1994

Du Bois, W.E.B., *Black Folk, Then and Now: An Essay in the History and Sociology of the Negro Race*, New York: Holt, 1939

Evans, Bernadette, "Suffering and the African Diaspora," *Journal of Women and Religion* 9/10 (1990–91), 63–71

Frazier, Edward Franklin, *The Negro Family in the United States*, Chicago: University of Chicago Press, 1939

Frazier, Edward Franklin, *The Black Bourgeoisie*, Glencoe, IL: Free Press, 1957

Gray, John, *Àshe, Traditional Religion, and Healing in Sub-Saharan Africa and the Diaspora: A Classified International Bibliography*, Westport, CT: Greenwood Press, 1989

Harris, Joseph E., *Global Dimensions of the African Diaspora*, Washington, DC: Howard University Press, 1982

Herskovits, Melville, *The Myth of the Negro Past*, New York: Harper, 1941; reprinted Boston: Beacon Press, 1958

James, Joy, and Ruth Farmer, eds., *Spirit, Space, and Survival: African American Women in (White) Academe*, New York: Routledge, 1993

Kilson, Martin L., and Robert I. Rotberg, eds., *The African Diaspora: Interpretive Essays*, Cambridge, MA: Harvard University Press, 1976

Lemelle, Sidney J. and Robin D.G. Kelley, eds., *Imagining Home: Class, Culture, and Nationalism in the African Diaspora*, London and New York: Verso, 1994

Salamone, Frank A., ed., *Art and Culture in Nigeria and the Diaspora*, Williamsburg, VA: College of William and Mary, 1991

Segal, Ronald, *The Black Diaspora*, London: Faber, and New York: Farrar Straus, 1995

Terborg-Penn, Rosalyn, Sharon Harley, and A. B. Rushing, eds., *Women in Africa and the African Diaspora*, Washington, DC: Howard University Press, 1987

Walters, Ronald W., *Pan-Africanism in the African Diaspora: An Analysis of Modern Afrocentric Political Movements*, Detroit: Wayne State University Press, 1993

Weinstein, Norman, *A Night in Tunisia: Imaginings of Africa in Jazz*, Metuchen, NJ: Scarecrow Press, 1992

Wilentz, Gay, "If You Surrender to the Air: Folk Legends of Flight and Resistance in African American Literature," *Melus* 16 (1989), 21–32

Woodson, Carter G., *The African Background Outlined; or, Handbook for the Study of the Negro*, Washington, DC: Association for the Study of Negro Life and History, 1936

Agrarian History

Over the course of the past ten millennia, the human experience has primarily been a rural experience. Most people were peasants or farmers. Even those few who were not agriculturists have been deeply effected by rural life and its rhythms and ways. Most of the world's languages are thickly seeded with rural words, terms, phrases, maxims, and proverbs. English, for example, contains more than 75 words or terms to describe rural people. Despite this, historians have paid relatively little attention to the rural world. Part of the reason has to do with the lack of status experienced by most rural dwellers in most historical periods. Indeed, many of the words used to describe peasants have negative connotations. In English, this includes words such as "villain" (from Old French), and words borrowed from other languages, including "pariah" (from Tamil) and "peon" (from Spanish).

The first to become interested in the peasant masses were the people collecting folk songs and tales in the late 18th and early 19th centuries. This activity, first evident in western Europe but soon overspreading the whole continent, often had a distinctly nationalistic character. Collectors like the brothers Grimm went out to discover the "true *Volk*," those uncorrupted country dwellers amongst whom the real values of a people lay. In his studies of poetry in the 1770s, German writer J.G. Herder (1744–1803), for example, put forward the belief that those whom the elites called savages "are often more moral than we are." In eastern Europe, among many largely peasant peoples, small groups of educated elites created grammars and dictionaries of languages long-ignored by the wealthy and powerful. Such books were often the first steps in the rise of a mass national consciousness.

If the prehistory of rural studies drew heavily on the nostalgia of Romantics, it also owed much to the mania for scientific description so characteristic of the Enlightenment. Mapmakers, local archaeologists, and history buffs turned a discerning if sometimes amateur eye to the world around them. Educated rural gentry and gentleman farmers like America's Thomas Jefferson (1743–1826) often provided the first descriptions of the countryside and its monuments and landmarks. By the mid-19th century, the more systematic science of agronomy, pioneered by the German Justus Liebig (1803–73), had begun to offer detailed descriptions of farming practices. These descriptions emphasized geology and farming styles, but also included a fair amount of history. In the United States, by mid-century, many states had formed agricultural societies, often funded by wealthier farmers, which began to compile information on farming and husbandry.

Yet another important influence in agrarian history was the discovery of ancient agriculture in the Middle East and the Neolithic agricultural revolution. This stemmed in good measure from archaeological finds in Egypt, Mesopotamia, Palestine, and elsewhere in the late 19th and early 20th centuries.

The development of a scientific history of European peasantry – focusing mainly on the pre-modern era – also dates to the late 19th and early 20th centuries. In France there was the pioneering work of Fustel de Coulanges (1830–89), and in Britain F.W. Maitland's (1850–1906) work with the Domesday book was also important.

Despite the influence of scientific methodology, the study of country people as possessors of unique and special values continued to be an important theme in late 19th-century agrarian histories. Nowhere was this more true than in the United States, whose deepest national myths revolved around the Jeffersonian ideal of the yeoman farmer. By the end of the 19th century, this ideal seemed under increasing threat due to industrialization, urbanization, and an influx of seemingly unassimilable foreign immigrants. Responding to this concern, historian Frederick Jackson Turner (1861–1932) put forward his famous "frontier thesis" in 1892, which posited, among other things, that the American frontier was the true incubator of democracy, in contrast to the city with its emerging mass culture, its industry, and its new immigrant inhabitants. Although Turner's ideas continue to be debated, their influence on succeeding generations of American historians has been of paramount importance. Turner's work also stimulated scholarly interest in preserving and explaining America's rural experience, an experience that seemed to be under siege. By 1920, over the half the nation's population lived in urban areas, and farmers seemed to be an increasingly marginalized group, a feeling that has remained constant in the United States.

By 1927, a group of American scholars launched the journal *Agricultural History*. Following on this development, a number of comprehensive histories of American agriculture appeared, which were followed by John D. Hicks' *The Populist Revolt* (1931), which examined the history of the nation's most extensive agrarian protest movement. Hicks' book, appearing as it did during the Great Depression, was sympathetic to the Populists, viewing them as a protest movement with legitimate grievances. Later scholars, however, portrayed the Populists as narrow and bigoted. The issues raised by Populism continued to generate a mass of literature in the decades following World War II. The other major focus of US agricultural historians since the 1920s has been slavery and the slave economy in the rural South, and the changes wrought on the South in the years following the US Civil War. Writing on slavery – so intertwined with America's painful internal debate over racial equality – has often generated heated debate.

Meanwhile, in Europe, and especially in France, the emergence of a new history around the journal *Annales: Economies, Sociétés, Civilisations*, founded by Lucien Febvre (1878–1956) and Marc Bloch (1886–1944) in 1929, had a great impact on the study of the rural past. Bloch's work on medieval France and its peasantry had a most profound effect on rural studies and history as a discipline. Bloch was able to combine detailed local knowledge with methodological sophistication; he furthered his historical understanding with interdisciplinary studies in agronomy, cartography, archaeology, and folklore; and he mastered the art of comparative history. The *Annales* school opened up new territory for rural historians. Although Bloch did not survive World War II, his legacy and that of his colleagues can still be felt throughout the discipline, and is evident in the rich literature on rural France.

In his classic, *Les Paysans de Languedoc* (1966; *The Peasants of Languedoc*, 1974), Emmanuel Le Roy Ladurie built on Bloch's work by attempting a "total history" of a French rural province, from the late Middle Ages through the beginning of the 19th century. Using tax rolls as his major source, Ladurie illustrated the problems of an agrarian peasant society unable to overcome Malthus' law and maintain a long-term balance between population and food production. Chronologically, the first phase of his history explored the preconditions for growth that resulted from the demographic collapse of the late Middle Ages. The next phase was a period of growth, followed by a period of maturity after 1600, and finally a recession which set back the peasants once again. Although the basis of Le Roy Ladurie's book was economic, he broadened his scope to consider the social and psychological dimensions of his subject, paying special attention to the outbreaks of peasant unrest that accompanied what he described as the "Great Agrarian Cycle." Another notable work by Le Roy Ladurie was *Montaillou* (1975), in which he used detailed inquisition records to present an intimate portrait of the mentalité and lifestyle of peasants in a southern French village.

The importance of the peasant had also been noted in more recent periods. As modern industrial states mobilized peasant conscripts for war, factory work, or food production, they also sought to assimilate peasants' diverse, local cultures, dialects, and attitudes into the mainstream of the nation-state. This phenomenon was the subject of Eugen Weber's important *Peasants into Frenchmen* (1976).

The encounter of the peasant world with the world of industrial capitalism has been the starting point for many studies with a rural-history theme. This subject has been of great interest to historians as well as to social scientists, particularly sociologists. One study that has influenced both history and sociology is William Thomas and Florian Znaniecki's *The Polish Peasant in Europe and America* (1918–20). The authors' study of Polish peasant letters seemed to indicate that under the impact of modern ways, peasants were becoming "socially disorganized" – that is, their previous modes of social organization were crumbling and they were struggling to find new modes. This led to an increase in social deviance and a breakdown of the family, among other things. Thomas and Znaniecki's work marked the ascendancy of modernization theory, which posited that peasants were absorbed into the modern, industrial world (very often becoming members of the industrial proletariat) by a linear, unidirectional process called modernization. This model of social change proved enormously influential among historians studying the peasantry, as well as among those who examined the migration of peasant laborers to the new industrial centers of Europe and North America. Modernization theory remained important for historians until the 1980s, but even after that its influence could still be detected among historians who tended to view the processes by which peasants and their descendants become workers and, adopt and maintain ethnic identities as an immutable, linear process.

Since modernization theory did attempt to describe real and important changes, albeit in a simplified and imperfect fashion, its gradual demise has left many historians searching for new models. Perhaps the most coherent answer to modernization theory has come from Ewa Morawska, who adopted a threefold explanation of change in the world of the East Central European peasants. First, peasants become increasingly open to new experiences and aware of new options in the world beyond the village. Second, they begin to see the possibility of advancing their own goals – however limited those goals may seem – instead of being completely dominated by powerful external forces. Third, peasants begin to accept "quantitative bases for acquiring and distributing rewards" which leads to the belief that the material world is expandable. One important aspect of this approach is that it allows historians to think of peasants as legitimate historical actors rather than as objects buffeted to and fro by large, impersonal forces.

Since the 1970s the history of immigration has reflected an increasing interest in the peasant origin of immigrants. Some authors have attempted to follow immigrant communities from their villages of origin to their new homes on another continent away. For some immigrants, particularly those from Scandinavia, this migration was a rural-to-rural one. Robert Östergren, for example, has written on how a Swedish rural community transplanted itself to the New World (1988). These immigrants quickly adopted American styles of farming, but preserved folkways, culture, religion, and even dialect intact. Jon Gjerde carried out a similar study on Norwegians.

Even if immigrants' destinations were cities rather than countrysides, rural history has proved useful in understanding their adaptation, and the ways in which they developed identities. In the 1970s, researchers began to rediscover ethnic groups in major North American cities that seemed to have retained characteristics of their rural ancestry. The idea of "peasant villages" in urban neighborhoods proved appealing and was an important step forward in understanding the urban experience (at least in North America) even though this notion has been modified by the realization that peasant immigrants were not simply preserving the old village intact, but consciously forming hybrid ethnic cultures composed of both new and old elements.

Agricultural history has been enriched by interdisciplinary efforts. For example, anthropologist Sidney Mintz has written on the history of sugar. His work touches on the complex interactions of crops and market, producers and consumers, as well as on topics such as slavery, diet, and colonialism. Joseph A. Amato's work on the Jerusalem artichoke examined the question of how plants become crops, and the hysteria that can attend new crop development. William Cronon's *Nature's Metropolis* (1991) dealt with the rapid expansion of commercial farming and its relationship to the development of major market centers like Chicago. John Hudson combined geography and history to explore the role of railroads in the settlement of the North American Great Plains (1985).

Since World War II, American agricultural history has largely been focused on the history of farm protest and radical movements, and the history of the southern farm economy before and after slavery. American agricultural historians have also worked on the nature of the frontier, in a continuing dialogue with Turner's "frontier thesis," as well as on the changes in the economics of farming and the role of the government therein.

Historians have continued to argue over the nature and origins of the American Populist movement. There has been much debate over whether Populists had legitimate grievances and viable solutions to rural problems or whether they were simply narrow-minded bumpkins upset by changes they little understood. These divergent positions probably said as much about historians' attitudes toward the countryside as they did about who the Populists were. Recent studies on this subject have tended to focus on Populism at the state and local level, adding greater detail to the overall picture. Likewise, as studies of the slave economy in American South have long focused on the question of whether it was a viable system or not, recent, more specialized studies have appeared to add new levels of complexity to the question. Historians such as Joan Jensen have focused on the long-neglected role of women in America agriculture (1986).

In the early 1980s, Robert Swierenga called for a "new rural history" that would prove to be the equal counterpart to urban history. His call has been partially realized by historians who have focused developed new lines of inquiry relating to the environment, ethnicity, and gender, while incorporating the best work from related natural and social sciences. Yet the traditional foci remain, and aside from sociology and agronomy, there is but one small history-oriented rural studies program in the US (at Southwest State University in Minnesota). For Europe, work on the peasantry, as begun by the *Annales* historians, has continued, although specialization has been some less pronounced. The issue of peasant migration to urban centers on several continents has attracted considerable attention from scholars throughout the world and will continue to do so in the years to come.

JOHN RADZILOWSKI

See also Annales School; Bloch; Blum; Brenner; Davis, N.; Febvre; Fogel; Hobsbawm; Le Roy Ladurie; Maitland; Rudé; Turner, F.; Weber, E.

Further Reading

Aitken, Hugh G.H., ed., *Did Slavery Pay? Readings in the Economics of Black Slavery in the United States*, Boston: Houghton Mifflin, 1971

Amato, Joseph A., *Countryside, A Mirror of Ourselves: Essays about Calling Farmers' Names, Peasants Living in the City, and Other Rural Gleanings*, Marshall, MN: Amati Venti, 1982

Amato, Joseph A., *The Great Jerusalem Artichoke Circus: The Buying and Selling of the Rural American Dream*, Minneapolis: University of Minnesota Press, 1993

Arensberg, Conrad, *The Irish Countryman: An Anthropological Study*, New York: Macmillan, 1937

Billington, Ray Allen, *Frederick Jackson Turner: Historian, Scholar, Teacher*, New York: Oxford University Press, 1973

Bloch, Marc, *L'Ile de France: les pays autour de Paris*, Paris: Cerf, 1913; in English as *The Ile-de-France: The Country around Paris*, Ithaca, NY: Cornell University Press, and London: Routledge, 1971

Bloch, Marc, *Les Caractères originaux de l'histoire rurale française*, Cambridge, MA: Harvard University Press, 1931; in English as *French Rural History: An Essay on Its Basic Characteristics*, Berkeley: University of California Press, 1966

Bloch, Marc, *La Société feodale*, 2 vols., Paris: Michel, 1939–40; in English as *Feudal Society*, 2 vols., Chicago: University of Chicago Press, and London: Routledge, 1961

Blum, Jerome, *The European Peasantry from the Fifteenth to the Nineteenth Century*, Washington, DC: Service Center for Teachers of History, 1960

Burke, Peter, *Popular Culture in Early Modern Europe*, London: Temple Smith, and New York: New York University Press, 1978

Byrnes, Robert F., ed., *Communal Families in the Balkans: The Zadruga: Essays by Philip E. Mosely and Essays in His Honor*, Notre Dame, IN: University of Notre Dame Press, 1976

Cochrane, Willard W., *The Development of American Agriculture: A Historical Analysis*, Minneapolis: University of Minnesota Press, 1979

Conzen, Kathleen Neils, *Making Their Own America: Assimilation Theory and the German Peasant Pioneer*, New York: Berg, 1990

Coulton, George Gordon, *The Medieval Village*, Cambridge: Cambridge University Press, 1925; reprinted as *Medieval Village, Manor, and Monastery*, New York: Harper, 1962

Critchfield, Richard, *Villages*, Garden City, NY: Anchor Press, 1981

Cronon, William, "Revisiting the Vanishing Frontier: The Legacy of Frederick Jackson Turner," *Western Historical Quarterly* 18 (1987), 157–76

Cronon, William, *Nature's Metropolis: Chicago and the Great West*, New York: Norton, 1991

Danbom, David B., *Born in the Country: A History of Rural America*, Baltimore: Johns Hopkins University Press, 1995

Davis, James C., *Rise from Want: A Peasant Family in the Machine Age*, Philadelphia: University of Pennsylvania Press, 1986

Davis, Natalie Zemon, *The Return of Martin Guerre*, Cambridge, MA: Harvard University Press, 1983

Eklof, Ben and Stephen P. Frank, ed., *The World of the Russian Peasant: Post-Emancipation Culture and Society*, Boston: Unwin Hyman, 1990

Evans, Richard J. and W. R. Lee, eds., *The German Peasantry: Conflict and Community in Rural Society from the Eighteenth to the Twentieth Centuries*, New York: St. Martin's Press, and London: Croom Helm, 1986

Fite, Gilbert C., *The Farmers' Frontier, 1865–1900*, New York: Holt Rinehart, 1966

Fite, Gilbert C., *American Farmers: The New Minority*, Bloomington: Indiana University Press, 1981

Fogel, Robert William, and Stanley L. Engerman, *Time on the Cross: The Economics of American Negro Slavery*, 2 vols., Boston: Little Brown, and London: Wildwood, 1974

Fukutake, Tadashi, *Nihon noson shakairon*, Tokyo: Shuppankai, 1964; in English as *Japanese Rural Society*, Ithaca, NY: Cornell University Press, 1967

Gjerde, Jon, *From Peasants to Farmers: The Migration from Balestrand, Norway, to the Upper Middle West*, Cambridge and New York: Cambridge University Press, 1985

Gross, Feliks, *Il Paese: Values and Social Change in an Italian Village*, New York: New York University Press, 1973

Guillaumin, Emile, *La Vie d'un simple (mémoires d'un métayer)*, Paris: Stock, 1904; in English as *The Life of a Simple Man*, London: Selwyn and Blount, 1919; revised Hanover, NH: University Presses of New England, and London: Sinclair Brown, 1983

Hahn, Steven, and Jonathan Prude, eds., *The Countryside in the Age of Capitalist Transformation: Essays in the Social History of Rural America*, Chapel Hill: University of North Carolina Press, 1985

Hicks, John D., *The Populist Revolt*, Minneapolis: University of Minnesota Press, 1931

Hobsbawm, Eric J., and George Rudé, *Captain Swing: A Social History of the Great English Agricultural Uprising of 1830*, New York: Pantheon, 1968; London: Lawrence and Wishart, 1969

Homans, George C., *English Villagers of the Thirteenth Century*, Cambridge, MA: Harvard University Press, 1941

Hudson, John C., *Plains Country Towns*, Minneapolis: University of Minnesota Press, 1985

Jensen, Joan M., *Loosening the Bonds: Mid-Atlantic Farm Women, 1750–1850*, New Haven: Yale University Press, 1986

Le Roy Ladurie, Emmanuel, *Les Paysans de Languedoc*, 2 vols., Paris: Mouton, 1966; in English as *The Peasants of Languedoc*, Urbana: University of Illinois Press, 1974

Le Roy Ladurie, Emmanuel, *Montaillou, village occitan de 1294 à 1324*, Paris: Gallimard, 1975; in English as *Montaillou: The Promised Land of Error*, New York: Braziller, 1978, and as *Montaillou: Cathars and Catholics in a French Village, 1294–1324*, London: Scolar Press, 1978

Luebke, Frederick C., ed., *Ethnicity on the Great Plains*, Lincoln: University of Nebraska Press, 1980

Maitland, F.W., *Domesday Book and Beyond: Three Essays in the Early History of England*, Cambridge: Cambridge University Press, 1897

Mintz, Sidney W., *Sweetness and Power: The Place of Sugar in Modern History*, New York: Viking, and London: Sifton, 1985

Mintz, Sidney W., *Crops and Human Culture*, Marshall, MN: Southwest State University, 1994

Morawska, Ewa, *For Bread with Butter: The Life Worlds of East Central Europeans in Johnstown, Pennsylvania, 1890–1940*, Cambridge and New York: Cambridge University Press, 1985

Ostergren, Robert C., *A Community Transplanted: The Trans-Atlantic Experience of a Swedish Immigrant Settlement in the Upper Middle West, 1835–1915*, Madison: University of Wisconsin Press, 1988

Rothstein, Morton, *Writing American Agricultural History*, Marshall, MN: Southwest State University, 1996

Saloutos, Theodore, *The American Farmer and the New Deal*, Ames: Iowa State University Press, 1982

Struever, Stuart, ed., *Prehistoric Agriculture*, Garden City, NY: Natural History Press, 1971

Swierenga, Robert P., "The Dutch Transplanting in the Upper Middle West," Marshall, MN: Southwest State University, 1991

Thomas, William I., and Florian Znaniecki, *The Polish Peasant in Europe and America*, 5 vols., Boston: Badger, 1918–20, London: Constable, 1958; edited and abridged by Eli Zaretsky, Urbana: University of Illinois Press, 1984

Toch, Michael, "Lords and Peasants: A Reappraisal of Medieval Economic Relationships," *Journal of European Economic History* 15 (1986), 163–82

Vucinich, Wayne S., ed., *The Peasant in Nineteenth-Century Russia*, Stanford, CA: Stanford University Press, 1968

Weber, Eugen, *Peasants into Frenchmen: The Modernization of Rural France, 1870–1914*, Stanford, CA: Stanford University Press, and London: Chatto and Windus, 1976

Winner, Irene, *A Slovenian Village: Zerovnica*. Providence, RI: Brown University Press, 1971

Wrightson, Keith and David Levine, *Poverty and Piety in an English Village: Terling, 1525–1700*, New York: Academic Press, 1979; revised Oxford and New York: Oxford University Press, 1995

Ajayi, Jacob F. Ade 1929–
Nigerian historian

Combining exemplary scholarship and teaching with an equally outstanding record of university and professional service, Jacob Ade Ajayi has made a pioneering contribution to the progress and success of African history worldwide. Ajayi was a foundation student at the University College of Ibadan in 1948, and his academic career encompasses the entire postwar era and the dramatic transformations that have marked what is now almost half a century. He completed his academic training at the University of London, receiving his PhD and returning home to join the staff of the Department of History at Ibadan in 1958, just two years before Nigerian independence. His research and writing focused then, as it has ever since, on the nature and forces of change in 19th- and 20th-century Africa, with special attention to aspects of continuity in the African experience and the dialectic between external and internal elements in that dynamic process. In particular, Ajayi's work is characterized by attention to African agency and his keen sense of the durability of African values, however they might accommodate external influences, during these two centuries of extremely rapid and profound transformation. In Ajayi's hands, Africans are presented as real, living human beings who are faced with difficult choices and must draw upon their individual and cultural resources to survive. His scholarship makes the reader keenly aware of both the adaptability of African society and its very resilience. He first sounded these themes in "The Continuity of African Institutions under Colonialism," a paper given at the International Congress of African Historians held at University College, Dar es Salaam, in October 1965, in which he especially focused on what he termed "the politics of survival." Emphasizing what one scholar calls Ajayi's recognition of "the ambiguities of historical change," his scholarship has been marked by its excellence and its durability. Apart from his many scholarly articles and his pathbreaking *Christian Missions in Nigeria, 1841–1891*, which inaugurated the Ibadan History series in 1965, it is noteworthy that Ajayi's major scholarly contributions have been collaborative. To some extent this judicious deployment of his energies reflects the administrative demands that began to occupy an increasing proportion of his time at Ibadan, not to mention his many important international professional commitments. No less significantly, however, it also reflects his abiding commitment to the creation and nurturing of a community of scholars based at Ibadan, which has remained his home university throughout his career. One, but only one, aspect of this community is what we have come to know as the Ibadan School of history and the Ibadan history series of which Ajayi has been general editor since 1970.

More broadly conceived, as in his teaching and mentoring, Ajayi should be regarded as a leader among senior historians of Africa in collaborative, critical scholarship on Africa.

Here we should let his students speak for themselves. According to one, "Ajayi stimulates his students to question stereotypes and to be original in interpretation. He welcomes criticisms of his own ideas and responds to such criticisms in the best traditions of historical scholarship." Another notes that "Ajayi consciously taught his students to be courageously critical. For this particular element of training he gladly allowed his students to use him as their punching bag. He made his students feel comfortable to criticize his own works right in front of him and to argue and disagree with him in his tutorials." A third attributes his lasting impact on the Nigerian academic community to "his incomparable ability as a teacher and a guide." Not only does Ajayi belong "to the pioneer generation of dedicated scholars who effected a kind of academic revolution that has resulted in winning acceptability and respectability for African History in the academic world," as one of these former students writes, but, "as a scholar with a mission to make academic African history relevant to the lives of the mass of African peoples," to quote another, he also contributed mightily to achieving that goal. No wonder, then, that "The Ibadan department of history has produced more good history than any other department in Africa," observes a North American colleague, and that, in the words of a British historian of West Africa, "within Africa, Nigeria occupies a special place in the field of Africanist scholarship, as one of the earliest countries to develop a tradition of indigenous academic scholarship; and also as a place where, despite the adverse financial and other conditions faced by University scholars in recent years, the study of Africa has continued to flourish, so that, whatever may be the case with other countries, the history of Nigeria continues to be written principally by Nigerian scholars." Perhaps, as one of his former students writes, for these collective achievements "no single individual would be given, or lay claim to, sole credit," but there is no other scholar whose leadership and practice so uniquely exemplifies their enduring qualities. In recognition of his singular scholarly achievement, in 1993 the African Studies Association of the United States recognized Ajayi with its Distinguished Africanist Award, the first African scholar so honored.

EDWARD A. ALPERS

See also Africa: West

Biography

Jacob Festus Ade Ajayi. Born Ikole-Ekiti, Ondo State, Nigeria, 26 May 1929. Educated locally at St. Paul's School, 1934–39; Christ's School, 1940; Igbobi College, Lagos, 1941–48; Hughes College, Yaba, 1947; University College, Ibadan, 1949–51; University of Leicester, England, 1952–55, BA; University College, London, 1955–58, PhD. Taught at University College, Ibadan, 1958–72 (rising to professor), and 1978–89. Vice-chancellor, University of Lagos, 1972–78. Married Christiana Aduke Martins, 1956 (4 daughters, 1 son).

Principal Writings

With Robert S. Smith, *Yoruba Warfare in the Nineteenth Century*, 1964

Editor with Ian Espie, *A Thousand Years of West African History*, 1965
Christian Missions in Nigeria, 1841–1891: The Making of a New Elite, 1965
"The Continuity of African Institutions under Colonialism," in Terence O. Ranger, ed., *Emerging Themes of African History: Proceedings of the International Congress of African Historians*, 1968
Editor with Michael Crowder, *A History of West Africa*, 2 vols., 1971–74
Editor with Michael Crowder, *Historical Atlas of Africa*, 1985
Editor, *Africa in the Nineteenth Century until the 1880s*, 1989 [UNESCO General History of Africa, vol. 6]
Editor, *People and Empires in African History: Essays in Memory of Michael Crowder*, 1992
The African Experience with Higher Education, 1996

Further Reading

Falola, Toyin, ed., *African Historiography: Essays in Honour of Jacob Ade Ajayi*, London: Longman, 1993

Ali Haji, Raja *c.*1809–*c.*1870
Malay/Bugis writer

Raja Ali Haji was one of the greatest Malay writers of the 19th century. He belonged to the Malay-Bugis royal house of Riau and underwent a broad education, which was to equip him to make a significant contribution to various areas of learning. His fame as a scholar spread throughout the region, and by the age of 32 he had assumed significant responsibilities in acting as joint regent and ruling Lingga for the young sultan Mahmud. However he is remembered not as an administrator, but rather as a writer and thinker.

Raja Ali Haji is best known for his historical writings, which center upon the works *Tuhfat al-Nafis* (The Precious Gift, completed late 1860s) and *Silsilah Melayu dan Bugis* (The History of the Malay and Buginese People, completed 1865). The former of these is his greatest work and represents a synthesis of various sources.

Raja Ali Haji completed the *Tuhfat al-Nafis* during a period when the Malay world was in great flux. Rivalries and conflicts were evident between the Bugis, their Malay hosts, and the Dutch colonial authorities. Raja Ali Haji's purposes in drawing up the *Tuhfat al-Nafis* were several; he was concerned not only to record the history of the Johor empire's relationship with the Bugis, the other Malay states, and the Dutch, but he also wrote for a didactic purpose, to enable contemporary readers to learn lessons from the past.

His approach to historiography represented a revolutionary new stage for the Malay world. He was not satisfied merely to glorify past rulers, as had been the case with the earlier Malay historical classics such as the *Sejarah Melayu* (Malay Annals), but he demonstrated a sensitivity to new worldviews and the issues raised by changing times. He diverged from early Malay historians in other ways, such as his concern for chronology and the relationship between an event and the time that it occurred, which he showed by regularly providing the dates of the events in question. Moreover, he acknowledged an acceptance of modern historical methods by clearly identifying his sources throughout his historical works.

In his historical writing Raja Ali Haji was no longer preoccupied with propounding the view of Malay rulers' divine right to rule, as had been the case with earlier historical writing; rather his was the more critical worldview necessary to support his quest for historical objectivity. Though he consciously presented his historical accounts through the lenses of his own Bugis identity, his works were much more than mere products of Bugis historical apologetics. Another unique aspect of the *Tuhfat al-Nafis* was that in recording over 200 years of history and covering the entire Malay world in its scope, it added a new dimension to Malay historiography.

The diverse skills of Raja Ali Haji are reflected in the scope of his writings, which cover fields as varied as theology, law, history, grammar, poetry, and statecraft. In addition to the two historical works mentioned above, his principal writings include two works on grammar – the *Bustan al-Katibin* (Garden of Writers, 1857) and the uncompleted *Kitab Pengetahuan Bahasa* (Book of Malay Language) – two works on statecraft – *Intizam Waza'if al-Malik* (Systematic Arrangement of the Duties of Ruler, 1857) and *Thamarat al-Mahammah* (Benefits of Religious Duties, 1857) – as well as a range of poetic works written separately or embedded within his other writings.

Raja Ali Haji was an arch-conservative in his views. In his writings he called on individuals to follow the ways of their ancestors in order to arrest social decay, and portrayed the society of the prophet Muhammad as an ideal to which individuals should strive. He called for adherence to God's laws, serious study of religious literature, and obedience to established scholarship. He called for the conduct of the state to be based on social harmony in the name of God, and attributed the decline of Riau to the failure of people – both rulers and subjects – to follow the teachings of the Prophet.

PETER G. RIDDELL

See also Malay Annals

Biography

Raja Ali al-Haji Riau. Born Selangor, c.1809. Widely traveled as a young man; completed his father's history of the Buginese people of the Malay world. Also served as ruler of Riau, and joint regent of Lingga, c.1837–57. Two daughters and a son were also historians. Died c.1870.

Principal Writings

Silsilah Melayu dan Bugis (The History of the Malay and Buginese People), completed 1865; reprinted 1984

Tuhfat al-Nafis, completed late 1860s; in English as *The Precious Gift* (Tuhfat al-Nafis), 1982

Further Reading

Andaya, Barbara Watson, and Virginia Matheson, "Islamic Thought and Malay Tradition: The Writings of Raja Ali Haji of Riau (c.1809–c.1870)," in Anthony Reid and David G. Marr, eds., *Perceptions of the Past in Southeast Asia*, Singapore: Heinemann, 1979

Beardow, T., "Sources Used in the Compilation of the Silsilah Melayu dan Bugis," *Review of Indonesian and Malayan Affairs* 20 (1986), 118–35

Iskandar, Teuku, "Raja Ali Haji, Tokoh dari Pusat Kebudayaan Johor-Riau," *Dewan Bahasa*, December 1964

Matheson, Virginia, "The Tuhfat al-Nafis: Structure and Sources," *Bijdragen tot Taal-, Land- en Volkenkunde* 128 (1971), 379–90

Matheson, Virginia, "Question Arising from a Nineteenth Century Riau Syair," *Review of Indonesian and Malayan Affairs* 17 (1983), 1–61

Maxwell, W.E., "Raja Haji," *Journal of the Straits Branch of the Royal Asiatic Society* 22 (1890), 173–224

Noorduyn, J., "The Bugis Genealogy of the Raja Muda Family of Riau-Johor," *Journal of the Malay Branch of the Royal Asiatic Society* 61/2 (1988), 63–92

Osman, M.T. "Raja Ali Haji of Riau: A Figure of Transition or the Last of the Classical Pujanggas?" in S.M.N. Al-Attas ed., *Bahasa Kesustraan Dan Kebudayaan Melayu: Essei-essei penghormatan kepada Pendita Za'ba*, Kuala Lumpur: Kementerian Kebudayaan, Belia dan Sukan Malaysia, 1976

Sham, A. H., *Puisi-Puisi Raja Ali Haji*, Kuala Lumpur: Dewan Bahasa dan Pustaka, 1993

Winstedt, Richard O., "A History of Johor (1365–1895)," *Journal of the Malay Branch of the Royal Asiatic Society* 10/3 (1932)

Winstedt, Richard O., *A History of Classical Malay Literature*, Kuala Lumpur: Oxford University Press, 1939; revised by Y.A. Talib, 1991

Althusser, Louis 1918–1990

French (Algerian-born) philosopher

Louis Althusser shot to prominence in France in 1965 with two difficult but innovatory books of Marxist theory: *Pour Marx* (*For Marx*, 1969), and *Lire le Capital* (*Reading "Capital,"* 1970). His work was introduced to an English-speaking readership in 1966 in a lengthy review by Eric J. Hobsbawm in the *Times Literary Supplement*. In the following year "Contradiction and Overdetermination" (from *For Marx*) appeared, with a commendatory preface, in the pages of *New Left Review*. The two books had an international impact. During the late 1960s and the first half of the 1970s various forms of Althusserian structuralist Marxism inspired new work and sparked off debates across the whole field of the human sciences. In anthropology, literary studies, feminist theory, art history, film studies, and especially cultural studies, a stream of publications, conferences, and debates testified to the potential of some of Althusser's conceptual innovations. Whatever his intentions as a Communist, his influence was not in the direction of reaffirming tired Leninist orthodoxies. Quite the contrary: he stimulated a radical questioning of a whole series of central assumptions of the intellectual left in France and elsewhere.

In the 1960s Althusser elaborated a highly sophisticated and complex philosophy – a theory of theoretical practice. Positing a radical break between ideology and science, an "epistemological break" that could be pinpointed in the development of Marx's own writing in 1844–45, Althusser directed attention to the concepts of the later works, above all, *Capital*. The early writings of Marx, he argued, were no more than an inversion of the idealism of Hegel and were thus incapable of grasping the complexity of the historical process. But the later works of Marx constituted a quite distinct problematic and a set of concepts – social formation, forces and relations of production, determination in the last instance, relative autonomy of the superstructures, and so on – which for the first time constituted the basis for a science of history. Preoccupied with developing this positive science and polemicizing against opponents,

Marx never found the time to think about his innovations in a systematic philosophical form. Althusser's self-appointed task was to elucidate the Marxist philosophy implicit within this emergent science and filter out some of the ideological pollutants that still lingered.

Althusser's attempt to think through the philosophical implications of Marx's conceptual innovations from *The German Ideology* to *Capital* was ambitious and often suggestive. The de-centering of totality and the concept of differential temporality were particularly important for his critical project. Historical time, Althusser argued, is always multilinear. There is no evolutionary movement of all the elements of the totality – say, for instance, the economic, the social, the political, and the ideological – such that they are all aligned in what he termed an "essential section." The totality does not constitute an "expressive totality" in which the whole can be read in each of its parts. These arguments in *Reading Capital* pose some significant questions for historical work, as Pierre Vilar conceded in what is perhaps the most searching critical account of Althusser by a historian.

Althusser's careful periodization of Marx's work, whatever questions it might raise about the devaluation of the early writings, did draw attention to the need to place specific texts within a precise intellectual history. Following on from this, he emphasized the need to read Marx closely and critically. In Western Marxism there was a tendency to appropriate elements of Marx arbitrarily and superficially. Althusser in this way played a valuable pedagogic role. His wholesale assault on Western Marxism was, however, excessive and in places disingenuous. Sartre's *Search for a Method* (1960, translated 1963), for instance, had already made some of the criticisms of a reductionist Marxism which Althusser was to announce a few years later as his own. The attack on those who corrupted Marxism with alien imports from Hegel, phenomenology, existentialism, or whatever, is somewhat weakened by Althusser's own extensive borrowings from such non-Marxist theorists as Baruch Spinoza, Gaston Bachelard, Jacques Lacan, and Sigmund Freud. And yet the essential point remained, that the implications for concrete historical research of the works of the mature Marx had not been very thoroughly pursued. Althusser's work was a part of a shift in this direction in the later 1960s and contributed significantly to work in, for instance, French anthropology (see Kahn and Llobera) and in the history of precapitalist societies (Hindess and Hirst). Althusser's influence, as Perry Anderson noted in *Arguments within English Marxism* (1980), "has proved remarkably productive – generating an impressively wide range of works dealing with the real world, both past and present."

In "Contradiction and Overdetermination" and "Ideology and Ideological State Apparatuses" (from *Lenin and Philosophy*) Althusser himself produced two important essays which did productively combine theoretical argument and at least the beginnings of concrete analysis of concrete situations. Concepts elaborated in these essays – overdetermination, ideological state apparatus, interpellation – were eagerly appropriated. His brilliant formulation of ideology as "the imaginary relationship of individuals to their real conditions of existence" has been especially influential. However, despite immense claims for the refurbished historical materialism that was to emerge from Althusser's project, it seemed to fizzle out in his own work.

His attempts to meet some of his critics' points – and especially the simplifications of the science–ideology distinction – led in the late 1960s to a redefinition of philosophy as a theoretical intervention within politics and a political intervention within theory. This formulation of an imaginary space led to nowhere very much, and his writing became increasingly fragmentary and sporadic. Althusser's influence faded rapidly from the mid-1970s: the political collapse of the left intelligentsia in Paris and the personal tragedy of the Althussers were contributory. So too was the way in which Althusser's critical readings of Marx served, for many, as a bridge not into concrete political and historical analysis but out of Marxism altogether and into the increasingly ascendant work of Lacan, Jacques Derrida, and Michel Foucault. By the time of his death in 1990 his most important writing was already 20 or more years behind him. Having said that, the recent publication in France of two substantial volumes of Althusser's *Ecrits philosophiques et politiques* (1994; *The Spectre of Hegel*, 1997), and the future publication of manuscript material, promise to provide new and unexpected critical perspectives on his thought. As the polemics and enthusiasms of the late 1960s and 1970s fade irretrievably into the past, Althusser is taking his place alongside Sartre, Merleau-Ponty, Foucault, and Derrida as one of the major figures in the remarkable explosion of French critical theory after 1945.

JOHN SEED

See also Anderson, P.; Foucault; Garin; Hegel; History from Below; History Workshop; Hobsbawm; Marks; Marxist Interpretation; Montesquieu; Political; Social; South Africa; Thompson, E.

Biography
Born Birmandreis, near Algiers, 16 October 1918, son of a bank manager. Passed entrance examination, Ecole Normale Supérieure, July 1939, but was called up for army service two months later; captured in Brittany, June 1940, and held in German prisoner-of-war camp, 1940–45. Returned to the Ecole Normal Supérieure, received degree, 1948, and taught there, 1948–80. Joined French Communist party, 1948. From 1947 suffered increasing periods of mental illness and spells of hospitalization, culminating (November 1980) in his killing of Hélène Rytmann Legotier, his wife (married 1976; had lived with her since 1940s). Released from psychiatric confinement, 1983; withdrew from political and intellectual activity. Died Paris, 22 October 1990.

Principal Writings
Montesquieu: la politique et l'histoire, 1959; in English in *Politics and History*, 1972
With Etienne Balibar et al., *Lire le Capital*, 2 vols., 1965; abridged edition (by Althusser and Balibar only) in English as *Reading "Capital,"* 1970
Pour Marx, 1965; in English as *For Marx*, 1969
Lénine et la philosophie, 1969, revised edition, 1972; in English as *Lenin and Philosophy*, 1971
Politics and History: Montesquieu, Rousseau, Hegel and Marx, 1972
Essays in Self-Criticism, 1976
Philosophy and the Spontaneous Philosophy of the Scientists and Other Essays, 1990
L'Avenir dure longtemps, suivi de Les Faits, 1992; in English as *The Future Lasts a Long Time, and The Facts*, 1993
Ecrits philosophiques et politiques, 2 vols., 1994; in English as *The Spectre of Hegel: Early Writings*, 1997

Further Reading

Anderson, Perry, *Arguments within English Marxism*, London: Verso, 1980

Benton, Ted, *The Rise and Fall of Structural Marxism: Althusser and His Influence*, London: Macmillan, and New York: St. Martin's Press, 1984

Clarke, Simon *et al.*, *One-Dimensional Marxism: Althusser and the Politics of Culture*, London: Allison and Busby, and New York: Schocken, 1980

Elliott, Gregory, *Althusser: The Detour of Theory*, London: Verso, 1987

Elliott, Gregory, ed., *Althusser: A Critical Reader*, Oxford and Cambridge, MA: Blackwell, 1994

Hindess, Barry, and Paul Q. Hirst, *Pre-Capitalist Modes of Production*, London: Routledge, 1975

Hobsbawm, Eric J., "The Structure of *Capital*" (1966) in Gregory Elliott, ed., *Althusser: A Critical Reader*, Oxford and Cambridge, MA: Blackwell, 1994

Kahn, Joel S., and Josep Llobera, *The Anthropology of Pre-Capitalist Societies*, London: Macmillan 1981

Kaplan, E. Ann, and Michael Sprinker, eds., *The Althusserian Legacy*, London: Verso, 1993

Lezra, Jacques, ed., *Depositions: Althusser, Balibar, Macherey, and the Labor of Reading*, New Haven: Yale University Press, 1995

Thompson, E.P., *The Poverty of Theory and Other Essays*, London: Merlin Press, and New York: Monthly Review Press, 1978

Vilar, Pierre, "Marxist History, a History in the Making: Dialogue with Althusser," *New Left Review* 80 (July/August 1973), 61–106; also in Gregory Elliott, ed., *Althusser: A Critical Reader*, Oxford and Cambridge, MA: Blackwell, 1994

Ambrose, Stephen E. 1936–

US biographer and military/diplomatic historian

One of the most prolific historians in the United States today, Ambrose has written or edited 24 books and more than 100 articles. His area of expertise is difficult to describe since he writes at the intersection of military history, historical biography, and the history of international relations, with a special interest in biography. Nor does his work examine a particular period, as he publishes on topics ranging from the Jeffersonian era in the United States to Richard Nixon. Moreover, his work does not fit easily into the usual historiographical categories informing the history of foreign relations – realist, revisionist, or postrevisionist. For the past two decades, however, there has been one consistent pattern in his work: by and large he has tried to appeal to a general audience rather than simply write for his fellow historians. Ambrose is the historian as public intellectual.

Ambrose began his career as a military historian/biographer of the Civil War period, with his first three books dealing with a Union soldier in the South; Lincoln's Chief of Staff, Henry W. Halleck; and the Civil War military theorist Emory Upton.

In the mid-1960s, Ambrose developed a powerful scholarly fascination with President Dwight Eisenhower, serving as an assistant editor of volumes 1–5 of the Eisenhower papers. Three years later he published a substantial biographical study of Eisenhower and World War II. His interest in Eisenhower culminated with the publication of perhaps his most important work, a massive 2-volume biography. These works put Ambrose in the forefront of Eisenhower revisionism – an attempt by scholars such as Robert Divine, Fred Greenstein, and Ambrose

to paint Eisenhower, especially as president, in a positive light. For Ambrose, Eisenhower was "firm, fair, objective, dignified." In fact, "he was everything most Americans wanted in a President."

Ambrose is considerably more critical of Richard Nixon in his 3-volume biography of Eisenhower's vice president. Although he admits to having "a grudging respect and then a genuine admiration" for Nixon, he nonetheless concluded that Nixon "had broken the law [during Watergate] . . . and . . . deserved to be repudiated by the American people." Nixon simply was not the man or president that Eisenhower was.

Although these multivolume biographies sold well, Ambrose's most widespread impact, at least on undergraduate students, has come in his interpretive textbook, *Rise to Globalism* (1971), which is currently in its 7th edition and 29th printing. Ambrose wrote a masterful narrative synthesis of foreign policy during World War II and the Cold War. According to historian Ronald Steel, the work is "a splendid example of the impact of revisionist analysis on the reinterpretation of American wartime and postwar diplomacy." Like revisionists, Ambrose suggested that United States policy was at least partly responsible for the beginning and continuation of the Cold War, although he certainly did not see the Soviets as benign innocents. With the collapse of communism, Ambrose has become increasingly uncritical of Truman's containment policy, however. In a 1991/92 article in *Foreign Affairs*, for example, he argued that "the Truman Doctrine won its great victory [with] the retreat of communism." In a sense, he seems to be moving into the postrevisionist camp.

Ambrose's most recent works further illustrate his wide-ranging interests. His 1994 book on D-Day was a lovingly and painstakingly detailed account of the landing and battle, based on 1,200 interviews with participants. His latest study, *Undaunted Courage* (1996), dealt with Lewis and Clark's expedition, an event almost a century and a half before D-Day. In it Ambrose maintained his fierce commitment to telling an exciting tale. Both works are celebratory narratives aimed at the educated general public.

Stephen Ambrose is, ultimately, a teller of stories. This is not to say that he eschews analysis and avoids theory. But in the final reckoning he wants to make history live for the public through the people of the past – the "great" and powerful ones like Eisenhower and Nixon and the ordinary ones like a Wisconsin boy in Dixie or a young soldier on Omaha Beach.

ANTHONY O. EDMONDS

See also United States: 20th Century

Biography

Born Decatur, Illinois, 10 January 1936. Received BA, University of Wisconsin, 1957, PhD 1963; MA, Louisiana State University, 1958. Taught at Louisiana State University, 1960–64; Johns Hopkins University, 1964–69; Naval War College, 1969–70; and Kansas State University, 1970–71; professor, University of New Orleans, from 1971.

Principal Writings

Editor, *Wisconsin Boy in Dixie*, 1961
Halleck: Lincoln's Chief of Staff, 1962
Upton and the Army, 1964
Assistant editor, *The Papers of Dwight David Eisenhower*, vols. 1–5, 1967

The Supreme Commander: The War Years of General Dwight D. Eisenhower, 1970
Rise to Globalism: American Foreign Policy since 1938, 1971
Eisenhower, 2 vols., 1983–84
Nixon, 3 vols., 1987–91
"The Presidency and Foreign Policy," *Foreign Affairs* 70 (Winter 1991/92), 120–37
D-Day, June 6, 1944: The Climactic Battle of World War II, 1994
Undaunted Courage: Meriwether Lewis, Thomas Jefferson, and the Opening of the American West, 1996
The Victors: Eisenhower and His Boys, 1998

America: Pre-Columbian

The European landfall in the Americas coincided with the Renaissance fascination with antiquities and the emergence of archaeology. Europeans endlessly speculated about native origins and functions of New World antiquities. By the end of the 20th century, the study of pre-Columbian America had grown increasingly interdisciplinary and was claiming scientific status.

Willey and Sabloff in *A History of American Archaeology* (1974) call the years to 1840 the Speculative period. Explorers, soldiers, priests, traders, travelers, and colonial administrators described ancient monuments and linked the remains (and sometimes the native inhabitants) to imagined peoples, like the survivors of Atlantis, a lost white race, or some biblical group. Thomas Jefferson's 1780 excavation of a Virginia mound is well known as the first controlled excavation in the Americas, but his conclusion that the Indians had built them would not become accepted for another century.

The first scientific work appeared in the Classificatory-Descriptive period, spanning 1840–1914. Systematic artifact typologies and attempts at explaining mound functions emerged in the 1840s with Stephens' *Incidents of Travel* series (1841; 1843), which mapped state-satellite relationships, suggesting early complex societies in Central America. Squier and Davis' *Ancient Monuments of the Mississippi Valley* (1848) surveyed, excavated, and cataloged mound types, but doubted that North American natives had built them. These men were private individuals driven by curiosity. Until the emergence of universities and endowed institutions around 1900, such types dominated American archaeology.

After its founding in 1846, the Smithsonian Institution provided the only consistent public support for archaeology. Cyrus Thomas of the Institution's Bureau of Ethnology and Frederic Putnam of Harvard University's Peabody Museum were the leaders in excavation, creating typologies, professionalizing archaeology, and proving the antiquity of man in the Americas. Thomas' *Report on the Mound Explorations of the Bureau of Ethnology* (1894) demolished the moundbuilder race myth. Putnam led excavations in the Ohio Valley and helped establish anthropology departments and museums in the United States.

Archaeology did not begin to abandon scientific racism until after World War I. Daniel Wilson's suggestion in *Prehistoric Man* (1862) that classical Meso-American civilizations were comparable to ancient Egypt and Mesopotamia was unpopular in an age of American manifest destiny. The period's central weakness was a conviction in the primitiveness of American natives, which denied significant culture change and chronological depth. As a result, scholars of American prehistory studied static culture areas, like those outlined by W. H. Holmes in "Areas of American Culture Characterization . . ." (1914). If culture change was identified, it was attributed to migration.

Archaeologists between 1914 and 1960, called the Classificatory-Historical period, used cultural categories to develop regional sequences, rejecting cultural stasis. Manuel Gamio produced the first controlled stratigraphic work from his 1911–13 excavations in the Valley of Mexico. His *La Población del Valle de Teotihuacan* (The Population of the Valley of Teotihuacan, 1922) provided the first regional chronology for the Americas. McKern's "Midwestern Taxonomic Method" (1939) synthesized eastern North American prehistory, attributing cultural change to local development, rather than migration. Occasionally, regional studies revolved around specific issues. Gordon Willey initiated settlement archaeology with *Prehistoric Settlement Patterns in the Viru Valley* (1953), which studied settlement as a reflection of ecological-technological interactions and sociopolitical organization.

Dissenters, however, argued for more attention to chronology. W.W. Taylor's *A Study of Archaeology* (1948) criticized identifying cultures by cataloging traits at the expense of chronology, regional comparisons, and culture change. Meanwhile, scientific advances were being applied to archaeology, facilitating the search for chronology. Able to identify native cultures in time, archaeologists could then identify how they changed. Radiocarbon dating, widespread by the 1950s, was one of several new dating techniques, including dendrochronology and obsidian hydration.

Many older archaeologists warily accepted the marriage of science and archaeology, but not graduate students educated in the 1950s. The most prolific was Lewis Binford, whose "Archaeology as Anthropology" (1962), became the manifesto of the "New Archaeology," inaugurating the modern Explanatory period. Influenced by the neo-evolutionary theories of social anthropologists and enthusiastically interdisciplinary, New Archaeologists were convinced that every interaction left some material trace. J.J.F. Deetz found that *The Dynamics of Stylistic Change in Arikara Ceramics* (1965) revealed a shift from matrilocality to patrilocality based on patterned distribution of pot shards. This philosophy of archaeology, based on a positivist view of science, seeks laws of cultural dynamics (or processes), usually attributing social change to environment and technology. Wedding science to archaeology has produced several subdisciplines, such as paleoethnoarchaeology and zooarchaeology, and numerous studies on the natural environment, diet, disease, technology, and village organization. Robert Adams, in *The Evolution of Urban Society* (1966), argued that a series of interrelated environmental-technological adaptations resulted in historical watersheds producing urban states.

Attempts to find laws of cultural processes evolved into widespread interest in theory by the 1970s. Lewis Binford initiated "middle range theory," explained in *For Theory Building in Archaeology* (1977) as correlating material culture to group behavior by studying how static traits relate to a dynamic cultural system expressed in physical remains in observable simple societies, thereby explaining conditions shaping a site's distribution of artifacts. Much theorizing assessed the impact of population change. According to Kent Flannery in "The Cultural Evolution of Civilizations" (1972), population growth created social and environmental pressures, forcing societies to a historical threshold and providing the impetus for complex societies. M.N. Cohen, refuting the traditional view that plant domestication permitted larger populations with evidence from Peru, adopted "population-growth determinism" in "Population Presence and the Origins of Agriculture" (1977) to argue that greater demands on resources force societies to find new means of production.

The New Archaeologists have not gone unchallenged. By the mid-1980s, postprocessualists questioned positivism and the belief that human populations were materially oriented. Ian Hodder's *Reading the Past* (1986) accepted processualism only as it explains human populations as biological entities. Ideology leaves no material trace, and processualists regarded ideas as tangential to cultural evolution. Processualists also ignored gender, but Christine Hastorf shows in "Gender, Space, and Food in Prehistory" (1991) that diet differentiation indicates the sexual division of labor in pre-Inca Peru.

Most recent work reveals a balance between processualism and postprocessualism. Bruce Trigger (1991) suggested that recovering prehistoric mentalities requires fusing historical and archaeological sources by considering "internal constraints" (ideology, ethnicity, religion) and "external constraints" (ecology and technology).

JAMES FISHER

See also Archaeology; Prehistory; Trigger

Further Reading

Adams, Robert McCormick, *The Evolution of Urban Society: Early Mesopotamia and Prehispanic Mexico*, Chicago: Aldine, and London: Weidenfeld and Nicolson, 1966
Bacus, Elisabeth A. *et al.*, *A Gendered Past: A Critical Bibliography of Gender in Archaeology*, Ann Arbor: University of Michigan Museum of Anthropology, Technical Report 25, 1993
Binford, Lewis R., *An Archaeological Perspective*, New York: Seminar Press, 1972 (includes a reprint of "Archaeology as Anthropology")
Binford, Lewis R., ed., *For Theory Building in Archaeology: Essays on Found Remains, Aquatic Resources, Spatial Analysis, and Systemic Modelling*, New York: Academic Press, 1977
Binford, Lewis R., and Jeremy Sabloff, "Paradigms, Systematics, and Archaeology," *Journal of Anthropological Research* 38 (1982), 137–53
Cohen, M.N., "Population Presence and the Origins of Agriculture: An Archaeological Example from the Coast of Peru," in Charles A. Reed, ed., *Origins of Agriculture*, The Hague: Mouton, 1977
Deetz, James J.F., *The Dynamics of Stylistic Change in Arikara Ceramics*, Urbana: University of Illinois Press, 1965
Flannery, Kent V., "The Cultural Evolution of Civilizations," *Annual Review of Ecology and Systematics* 3 (1972), 399–426
Gamio, Manuel, *La Población del Valle de Teotihuacan* (The Population of the Valley of the Teotihuacan), 3 vols., Mexico City: Secretaria de Fomento, 1922
Gladwin, Winifred and Harold S. Gladwin, *A Method for the Designation of Cultures and Their Variations*, Globe, AZ: Medallion Papers, no. 15, 1930
Griffin, James B., *The Fort Ancient Aspect: Its Cultural and Chronological Position in Mississippi Valley Archaeology*, Ann Arbor: University of Michigan Press, 1943
Griffin, James B., "The Pursuit of Archaeology in the United States," *American Anthropologist* 61 (1959), 379–88

Griffin, James B., "Eastern North American Archaeology: A Summary," *Science*, 156 (1967), 175–91
Hammond, Norman, "Lords of the Jungle: A Prosopography of Maya Archaeology," in Richard M. Leventhal and Alan L. Kolata, eds., *Civilization in the Ancient Americas: Essays in Honor of Gordon R. Willey*, Cambridge, MA: Peabody Museum of Archaeology and Ethnology, 1983
Hastorf, Christine A., "Gender, Space, and Food in Prehistory," in J.M. Gero and M.W. Conkey, eds., *Engendering Archaeology: Women and Prehistory*, Oxford and Cambridge, MA: Blackwell, 1991
Hinsley, Curtis M., Jr., *Savages and Scientists: The Smithsonian Institution and the Development of American Anthropology, 1846–1910*, Washington, DC: Smithsonian Institution Press, 1981
Hodder, Ian, *Reading the Past: Current Approaches to Interpretation in Archaeology*, Cambridge and New York: Cambridge University Press, 1986
Holmes, W.H., "Areas of American Culture Characterization Tentatively Outlined as an Aid in the Study of Antiquities," *American Anthropologist* 16 (1914), 413–46
Kennedy, Roger G., *Hidden Cities: The Discovery and Loss of Ancient North American Civilization*, New York: Free Press, 1994
Kidder, Alfred V., *Introduction to the Study of Southwestern Archaeology, with a Preliminary Account of the Excavation of the Pecos*, New Haven: Yale University Press, 1924
Leone, Mark P., "Some Opinions about Recovering Mind," *American Antiquity* 47 (1982), 742–60
Lightfoot, Kent G., "Culture Contact Studies: Redefining the Relationship Between Prehistoric and Historical Archaeology," *American Antiquity* 60 (1995), 199–217
McKern, W.C., "The Midwestern Taxonomic Method as an Aid to Archaeological Culture Study," *American Antiquity* 4 (1939), 301–13
Meltzer, David J., Don D. Fowler, and Jeremy A. Sabloff, eds., *American Archaeology, Past and Future: A Celebration of the Society for American Archaeology, 1935–1985*, Washington, DC: Smithsonian Institution Press, 1986
Plog, Fred, *The Study of Prehistoric Change*, New York: Academic Press, 1974
Silverberg, Robert, *Mound Builders of Ancient America: The Archaeology of a Myth*, Greenwich, CT: New York Graphic Society, 1968
Spielmann, Katherine A. (guest editor, special issue) "The Archaeology of Gender in the American Southwest," *Journal of Anthropological Research* 51 (1995)
Squier, Ephraim G., and Edwin Hamilton Davis, *Ancient Monuments of the Mississippi Valley*, Washington, DC: Smithsonian Institution, 1848
Stephens, John L., *Incidents of Travel in Central America, Chiapas, and Yucatan*, 2 vols., New York: Harper, and London: Murray, 1841
Stephens, John L., *Incidents of Travel in Yucatan*, 2 vols., New York: Harper, and London: Murray, 1843
Taylor, Walter Willard, *A Study of Archaeology*, Menasha, WI: American Anthropological Association, 1948
Thomas, Cyrus, *Report on the Mound Excavations of the Bureau of Ethnology*, 12th Annual Report of the Bureau of American Ethnology, Washington, DC: Smithsonian Institution, 1894; reprinted 1985
Trigger, Bruce G., *Time and Traditions: Essays in Archaeological Interpretation*, New York: Columbia University Press, and Edinburgh: Edinburgh University Press, 1978
Trigger, Bruce G., "Archaeology and the Image of the American Indian," *American Antiquity* 45 (1980), 662–76
Trigger, Bruce G., *A History of Archaeological Thought*, Cambridge and New York: Cambridge University Press, 1989
Trigger, Bruce G., "Constraint and Freedom: A New Synthesis for Archaeological Explanation," *American Anthropologist* 93 (1991), 551–69

Willey, Gordon R., *Prehistoric Settlement Patterns in the Viru Valley, Peru*, Washington, DC: Bureau of American Ethnology, Bulletin 155, 1953

Willey, Gordon R., and Philip Phillips, *Method and Theory in American Archaeology*, Chicago: University of Chicago Press, 1958

Willey, Gordon R., *An Introduction to American Archaeology*, 2 vols., Englewood Cliffs, NJ: Prentice Hall, 1967–71

Willey, Gordon R., and Jeremy A. Sabloff, *A History of American Archaeology*, San Francisco: W.H. Freeman, and London: Thames and Hudson, 1974

Wilson, Daniel, *Prehistoric Man: Researches into the Origins of Civilization in the Old and New World*, London: Macmillan, 1862

Ammianus Marcellinus *c.330–c.395* CE

Roman historian

Ammianus Marcellinus wrote his *Res gestae* (Accomplished Deeds or *History*) in Rome *c.*390. In 31 books, it was the most significant historiographical work written in Latin since the writings of Tacitus. The books that came down to us (books 14–31) covered contemporary history from 353 till the battle at Adrianopolis in 378. The lost books (books 1–13) recorded the 250 years from the principate of the emperor Nerva (96–98) onwards. The *History* forms the most important narrative source for the political, military and administrative history of these 25 years. It also provides valuable information on social conditions in the Roman empire, in the Near East, the Balkans and among the Germanic peoples. It is a work composed in the tradition of ancient historiography, with numerous digressions on geography, ethnography or natural phenomena. The character studies for which Ammianus is famous added a human dimension to his writing.

Ammianus used his work for autobiographical remarks which are almost the only source for our knowledge about him. We gain a broad outline of his life, especially his years as an officer in the Roman army, when he participated in some of the campaigns he later recorded in his work. Neither the date of his birth nor of his death is known. He came from a well-to-do Greek family, as he mentioned himself (19.8.6 and 31.16.9) and could have been born around 330. It is commonly assumed that his home town was Antioch in Syria, but despite frequent references to this town he does not indicate that he came from here. The assumption is based on the identification of the recipient of a letter (no.1063) from the orator Libanios to a man called Marcellinus with the historian but this interpretation has been challenged by Bowersock. Ammianus served in the elite corps of the *protectores domestici* and in 353 he belonged to the staff of Ursicinus, commander of the Oriental army in Mesopotamia. Because of his active military career Ammianus was one of the few ancient historians with a deep understanding of military operations and the ability to describe battles, weapons, and strategies precisely. He accompanied Ursicinus to Gaul when he was sent there to quell a provincial rebellion. The stay in Gaul allowed Ammianus to study the people and geography, information he used for a long digression on Gaul (15. 9–11), but also to meet Julian, the later emperor, whom he admired. He then followed Ursicinus to Mesopotamia and took part in the Persian offensive in 359, in which the Persians besieged Amida and captured it. Ammianus' account of details of the campaign (18.4–19, and 8) and his personal involvement in the events is partly written like a novel. Four years later he joined in the Persian campaign of the emperor Julian and gave a lively eyewitness account of the successful advance into Persia, the retreat and the death of Julian and the difficult return of the army under heavy losses. Ammianus felt that the peace treaty which emperor Jovian concluded with the Persians was shameful and this seemed to have been the reason why he retired from the army. Because he was no longer actively involved in the major events of his time, we are less well informed about his life from his narrative. He lived for some time in Antioch and travelled in Greece and Egypt. The country, the Nile, the pyramids and the crocodile are described in a digression (22.15–16). Sometime after 378 he settled in Rome. He liked the city but he disliked the inhabitants intensely and in two famous digressions (14.6 and 28.4) he painted a scathing picture of the customs of the Roman upper and lower classes. The latest contemporary allusion in his work was to the consulship of Neoterius in the year 390. He praised the Serapeum in Alexandria but made no mention of its destruction, suggesting that he completed his work before this event in 392.

Ammianus endeavored to write with as much truth, accuracy and impartiality as he could (introduction to book 15). The second introduction at the beginning of book 26 does not necessarily mean that Ammianus had published the earlier books already and decided to restart. There was no obvious break in his narrative and it could be that he wanted to explain his concerns about writing contemporary history and to emphasize the necessity to concentrate only on the events which really mattered (Matthews 1989). Likewise he alerted his readers to a change in his approach (26.5.15). Whereas he recorded the history until Julian's death in an annalistic fashion according to the emperors, he described later events in their geographical context. For the lost books Ammianus must have relied on literary sources, such as Herodian. For his contemporary history he used primarily his own experiences, interviews with eyewitnesses, and official documents. His acquaintance with leading personalities at the court, in the provinces and in Rome proved to be useful too.

Ammianus' religious ideas were deistic; he frequently referred to a supreme power and believed in divination and astrology. He had a liberal attitude to other religions and treated the Christian religion respectfully. Despite the catastrophes he witnessed in his lifetime, the loss of the eastern provinces, barbarian attacks, and the disaster at Adrianopolis which led to permanent Gothic settlement on imperial soil, he believed in the everlasting greatness of Rome (31.5.11). The Greek Ammianus wrote in Latin, the language of Rome, the empire with which he identified himself. His language was somewhat artificial and cluttered and he demonstrated continuously his broad literary education. He wrote in a rhetorical and dramatic style fashionable at his time.

If the letter of Libanios mentioned above was in fact written to Ammianus Marcellinus his work must have been quite successful in the literary circles of Rome, because the recipient was congratulated on the success of his public readings. There is no further evidence that his *History* was popular because very few contemporary or later authors seemed to have known it or quoted from it. Ammianus was not read in the Middle Ages either and the work survived in two manuscripts from the monasteries of Fulda (9th century, Vaticanus lat. 1873) and Hersfeld (only fragments Kassel Philol. 2027). It was first published in 1474 by Angelus Sabinus and since Gibbon's *Decline and Fall of the Roman Empire*, the *History* was gradually rediscovered. In the last 30 years an increasing number of studies have been dedicated to many different aspects of Ammianus' work.

CHARLOTTE BEHR

See also Roman; Scriptores; Syme

Biography
Born Antioch, Syria, *c*.330. Served in elite military corps of *protectores domestici*, as personal aide to general Ursicinus, in the Asia campaigns, 354–60; took part in emperor Julian's campaign in Persia, 363; after Julian's death, left army to travel before settling in Rome. Died Rome, *c*.395.

Principal Writings
Res gestae, *c*.390; in English as *The Later Roman Empire*, AD 354–378, translated by Walter Hamilton, 1986
Works (Loeb edition), translated by J.C. Rolfe, 3 vols., 1935–39

Further Reading
Austin, N.J.E., *Ammianus on Warfare: An Investigation into Ammianus' Military Knowledge*, Brussels: Latomus, 1979
Blockley, Roger C., *Ammianus Marcellinus. A Study of His Historiography and Political Thought*, Brussels: Latomus, 1975
Bowersock, Glen Warren, "Review of John F. Matthews, *The Roman Empire of Ammianus*," *Journal of Roman Studies* 80 (1990), 244–50
Camus, Pierre-Marie, *Ammien Marcellin: Témoin des courants culturels et religieux à la fin du IVe siècle* (Ammianus Marcellinus: Witness of Cultural and Religious Trends at the End of the 4th Century), Paris: Belles Lettres, 1967
Crump, Gary A., *Ammianus Marcellinus as a Military Historian*, Wiesbaden: Steiner, 1975
Demandt, Alexander, *Zeitkritik und Geschichtsbild im Werk Ammians* (Comments on Contemporary Issues and the Conception of History in the Writings of Ammianus), Bonn: Habelt, 1965
Elliott, Thomas G., *Ammianus Marcellinus in Fourth-Century History*, Sarasota, FL: Stevens, 1983
Jonge, Pieter de, *Philological and Historical Commentary on Ammianus Marcellinus*, vols.14–19, Groningen: Wolters, 1935–82; continued by J. den Boeft, Daniél van Hengst, H. C. Teitler and J. W. Drijvers, Groningen: Egbert Forsten, vols. 20–22, 1987–95
Matthews, John F., "Ammianus Marcellinus," in T. James Luce, ed., *Ancient Writers: Greece and Rome*, 2 vols., New York: Scribner, 1982
Matthews, John F., *The Roman Empire of Ammianus*, London: Duckworth, and Baltimore: Johns Hopkins University Press, 1989
Rike, R.L., *Apex Omnium: Religion in the Res Gestae of Ammianus*, Berkeley: University of California Press, 1987
Sabbah, Guy, *La méthode d'Ammien Marcellin: Recherches sur la construction du discours historique dans les Res Gestae* (The Method of Ammianus Marcellinus: Research into the Construction of Historical Discourse in the Res Gestae), Paris: Belles Lettres, 1978
Syme, Ronald, *Ammianus and the Historia Augusta*, Oxford: Oxford University Press, 1968
Thompson, E.A., *The Historical Work of Ammianus Marcellinus*, Cambridge: Cambridge University Press, 1947

Anderson, Benedict 1936–
British historian of Southeast Asia

Benedict Anderson has distinguished himself in the study of Southeast Asia and has also become well known to a broader audience as a theorist of nationalism. From his detailed study of the Javanese revolution in 1944–46 to his comparative, global examination of the history of nationalism, Anderson has always been engaged with the idea of "nation-ness," although his attitude toward nationalism has clearly evolved. His work has traced both the history and the structure of nationalism, providing a theoretical framework that cannot be ignored by anyone wishing to understand this phenomena or to study it further.

A student at Cornell under the mentorship of George Kahin, founder of the Cornell Modern Indonesia Project, Anderson lived in Indonesia during the early 1960s while conducting his doctoral research. His dissertation was published as *Java in a Time of Revolution* (1972), a highly detailed study of the move toward independence in 1944–46 and the role of youth in that movement. Another product of Anderson's work on Indonesia was the Cornell paper he co-authored on the 1965 coup, which questioned the military government's legitimacy. As a result of this work, Anderson was eventually banned from Indonesia, and turned his attention to Thailand.

In reflecting on the course of his career in the introduction to *Language and Power* (1990), Anderson attributed his sympathy with nationalist movements in Southeast Asia to "an inverted Orientalism." His exile and subsequent study of Siam forced him to begin to think comparatively, "against the friendly Orientalist grain." His exile also led him to a new concentration on documents, especially Indonesian literature. Combined with the influence of his brother Perry Anderson and others in the circle of the *New Left Review*, these changes led Anderson to write his much-read and often-cited *Imagined Communities* (1983).

Imagined Communities begins with the premise that nationality and nationalism are "cultural artifacts" and goes on to analyze the origins, growth, and structure of these ideas. The nation is defined by four key attributes: It is an imagined political community that is both inherently limited and sovereign. The nation is imagined because it is not a face-to-face society; since most members of a nation will never know each other, they can only constitute a community by imagining their connection. It is limited because it has boundaries beyond which lie other nations, and sovereign because the concept developed as the Enlightenment was challenging the legitimacy of the sovereign monarch. And finally, the nation is a community because, despite real inequalities, the nation is imagined as a "horizontal comradeship."

The nation thus defined developed in the 18th century; its roots lay in religious communities and dynastic realms, which it displaced. A key reason for this change is the modern shift in apprehension of time. The shift was from the medieval analogical mind, which perceived the present as foreordained, and the past and the future as simultaneous, to the new, more secular conception of time that perceived history as an endless chain of cause and effect. While this shift has been amply documented elsewhere, Anderson masterfully draws the connection between this shift in perception and the rise of print culture, especially the novel and the newspaper, which he argued represented the type of community that is the nation.

Perhaps the most important contribution of *Imagined Communities* was Anderson's argument that the origins of nationalism were in the New World, not the European nationalist movements after 1820, which he called "second wave." It was the creole communities of the Americas, he argued, that developed conceptions of their "nation-ness" first. The administrative structures developed through the imperialist system actually helped to create the perception of a "fatherland" in those colonial areas. Struggles for independence in the Americas then served as models for the European movements, but the "last wave" of nationalism in the late 19th and 20th centuries has become official nationalism, which is harnessed to serve the interest of the state.

In more recent works, Anderson has returned to a focus on Indonesia and Siam, often with an interpretive or literary approach to cultural issues. It remains to be seen to what extent he may yet return to the comparative theorizing of *Imagined Communities*, but it is clear that he has already established a formidable theoretic explication of nationalism that has left a permanent mark on thinking on this subject, and with which future theorists will have to contend.

ANGELA VIETTO

See also Ethnicity; Media; Memory; Nationalism; Postcolonialism; Southeast Asia; World

Biography
Benedict Richard O'Gorman Anderson. Born Kunming, Yunnan, China, 26 August 1936, of English parents. Received BA in classics, Cambridge University, 1957; PhD in political science, Cornell University, 1967. Taught (rising to professor) at Cornell University from 1967.

Principal Writings
Some Aspects of Indonesian Politics under the Japanese Occupation, 1944–45, 1961
Mythology and the Tolerance of the Javanese, 1965
Java in a Time of Revolution: Occupation and Resistance, 1944–1946, 1972
Editor, *Religion and Social Ethos in Indonesia,* 1977
Editor with Audrey Kahin, *Interpreting Indonesian Politics: Thirteen Contributions to the Debate,* 1982
Imagined Communities: Reflections on the Origin and Spread of Nationalism, 1983
Language and Power: Exploring Political Cultures in Indonesia, 1990

Further Reading
Hadiz, Vedi R., *Politik, budaya, dan perubahan sosial: Ben Anderson dalam studi politik Indonesia,* Jakarta: Penerbit PT Gramedia, 1992

Anderson, Perry 1938–
British historian and social theorist

Perry Anderson's sizeable and wide-ranging oeuvre does not fit comfortably into any academic specialism. He is the author of books on the social and political history of the classical world, on absolutism in early modern Europe, on the intellectual history of 20th-century Marxism, and on the work of E.P. Thompson. His numerous essays have intervened in almost every area of the human sciences and have engaged critically with a series of post-1945 intellectual figures, ranging from Fernand Braudel to Isaiah Berlin, from Carlo Ginzburg to Ernest Gellner. Anderson has been variously historian, historical sociologist, political theorist, leading English Marxist of his generation, and, for more than two decades from 1962, editor of *New Left Review*. His work has always been characterized by its cold elegance of style and its unusual fusion of the high theory of European Marxist provenance (notably Jean-Paul Sartre, Antonio Gramsci, and Louis Althusser) and an idiom of logical argument, historical specificity, and empirical evidence.

"Origins of the Present Crisis" (1964) was his first essay to make a significant impact. Challenging orthodoxies of both right and left, it was a vigorous indictment of British traditionalism. The stultifying conservatism of Britain at the end of 13 years of Tory government was traced back to a premature and incomplete bourgeois revolution in the 17th century and the subsequent incorporation of a supine industrial bourgeoisie in the 19th. Provoking the ire of E.P. Thompson, who replied in "The Peculiarities of the English," "Origins" initiated a seminal debate for a number of younger historians in the 1970s and has continued to feed into debate on the historical causes of Britain's long-term economic decline (see especially Geoff Ingham's *Capitalism Divided?*, 1984). Some of the themes of "Origins" were followed up by Anderson five years later in another remarkable essay, again demonstrating the influence of Gramsci, "Components of the National Culture" (1968). This anatomized the parochial conservatism of British intellectual life and provided a series of brilliant and acerbic short surveys of the major disciplines within the humanities and social sciences. These two essays and some later reworkings of the same issues are included in *English Questions* (1992).

At the end of the 1960s Anderson turned to larger questions, though still within a Gramscian framework. Seeking to explain differences of state formation across Europe, both East and West, his project was nothing less than a comparative history of the complex and uneven development of state forms from the classical world to the present. The first volume, *Passages from Antiquity to Feudalism* (1974), stressed the unique origins of Western European capitalism. It was a particular synthesis of classical antiquity and the institutions of the Germanic peoples who had overthrown Roman hegemony that formed European feudalism. And this unique formation, in turn, provided the basis for the transition to capitalism. The much larger second volume, *Lineages of the Absolutist State* (1974), is concerned with the character of the early modern state in the transition from feudalism to capitalism and in particular the contrast between Eastern and Western types of absolutism. Out of this temporally-elongated conjuncture there emerged the distinctive characteristics of modern European states and some of the continent's central divisions, which subsequent developments in the 19th and 20th centuries simply ratified.

Two further volumes have been promised: the first dealing with "the chain of the great bourgeois revolutions, from the Revolt of the Netherlands to the Unification of Germany"; and a second examining the states of contemporary Europe. Some important work arising out of this continuing project has been published in the intervening years (see especially "The Antinomies of Antonio Gramsci" and "The Notion of Bourgeois Revolution" in *English Questions*). However the crisis of Marxism in Western Europe (and especially in Paris) from the mid-1970s diverted Anderson's focus for a number of years. *Considerations on Western Marxism* (1976) provided a lucid overview of the evolution of Western Marxism over the preceding fifty years, optimistically tracing out a shift in the 1970s away from a concentration on philosophy and high culture and toward questions of political power and socioeconomic transformation. *Arguments Within English Marxism* (1980) attempted to moderate the rage of E.P. Thompson's *The Poverty of Theory* (1978) – an unmeasured assault on Marxist theory in its Althusserian form. Here Anderson was generous in his concessions to Thompson, but uncompromising in his defence of theory and the value of European Marxisms. He made a number of incisive criticisms of Thompson's historical writing. He also judiciously corrected several errors and distortions in *The Poverty of Theory*. Three years later Anderson's Wellek Library lectures – *In the Tracks of Historical Materialism* (1983) – contrasted the rapid growth of Marxian influence in the Anglo-American academy during the 1970s with its sudden collapse in Italy and France and offered some incisive criticisms of poststructuralism. These three interventions provide crisp and coherent surveys of sometimes bewilderingly complex debates.

Anderson's work over three decades has been consistent in its commitment to a critical appropriation of European Marxist theories, and in its precise purpose: to develop historical and political explanations. This has not been confined to his own writings. Under his direction *New Left Review* and New Left Books (now Verso) have been of decisive importance in diffusing within the English-speaking world the otherwise unavailable work of a whole series of European theorists of Marxist provenance – Sartre, Althusser, Bloch, Poulantzas, Adorno, Benjamin, among many others.

JOHN SEED

See also Althusser; Brenner; Gramsci; Jones, G.; Marxist Interpretation; Mayer; State; Thompson, E.; Tilly, C.; Whig

Biography
Born London, 1938. Educated at Eton College and Oxford University. Editor, *New Left Review*, 1962–82. Taught at Cornell University; New School of Social Research, New York; University of California, Los Angeles; and London School of Economics.

Principal Writings
"Origins of the Present Crisis," *New Left Review* 23 (1964), 26–54
Towards Socialism, 1965
"Components of the National Culture," *New Left Review* 50 (1968), 3–58
Lineages of the Absolutist State, 1974
Passages from Antiquity to Feudalism, 1974
Considerations on Western Marxism, 1976
"The Antinomies of Antonio Gramsci," *New Left Review* 100 (November 1976–January 1977), 5–80
Arguments within English Marxism, 1980

In the Tracks of Historical Materialism: The Wellek Library Lectures, 1983
English Questions, 1992
A Zone of Engagement, 1992

Further Reading
Fulbrook, Mary, and Theda Skocpol, "Destined Pathways: The Historical Sociology of Perry Anderson," in Theda Skocpol, ed., *Vision and Method in Historical Sociology*, Cambridge and New York: Cambridge University Press, 1984
Ingham, Geoffrey, *Capitalism Divided? The City and Industry in British Social Development*, London: Macmillan, and New York: Schocken, 1984
Johnson, Richard, "Barrington Moore, Perry Anderson and English Social Development," *Working Papers in Cultural Studies* 9 (1976), 7–28
Porter, R., and C.R. Whittaker, "States and Estates," *Social History* 3 (1976), 367–76
Runciman, W.G., "Comparative Sociology or Narrative History: A Note on the Methodology of Perry Anderson," *European Journal of Sociology* 21 (1980), 162–78
Thomas, Keith, "Jumbo History," *New York Review of Books* (17 April 1975), 26–28
Thompson, E.P., *The Poverty of Theory and Other Essays*, London: Merlin Press, and New York: Monthly Review Press, 1978

Andrews, Charles McLean 1863–1943
US historian of colonial America

The irony of Charles McLean Andrews, the man who at the least reoriented or at the most invented the study of colonial America, was that he wrote little on the period which he demanded that scholars take greater interest: the years 1690 to 1750. Andrews had two crusading goals. First, he strove to rescue the colonial period from patriotic and filiopietistic amateur historians who favored rhetorical flourish over documentable fact. Historians such as George Bancroft wrote nationalistic histories scantly touching on the colonial period. As a result, American history, to judge by their works, began with the American Revolution, the formative event of the nation.

Second, Andrews rebuked the exceptionalism and related geographical parochialism that pervaded American historiography. Historians, he maintained, must view early America as part of the British empire, and set that within its European context. Here Andrews lived up to his own demands. He researched indefatigably in British archives, wrote on medieval and early modern England and the West Indies, and declared that the American Revolution "is a colonial and not an American problem." As he wrote in *The Colonial Background of the American Revolution* (1924; revised 1931), his most often reprinted work, the United States emerged as a product of a long-term British expansion, "after one hundred and seventy-five years of membership in the British family; and it is in light of such association, therefore, that the colonial period of our history must be approached and, in the first instance, judged."

Andrews was part of the second generation of scientific historians emerging in America at the end of the 19th century. They aimed to study the past "as it was," keeping contemporaneous sentiments to the fore, while suppressing contemporary ones. Likewise, Andrews demanded an objective view, an historical vision that required colonialists to stand astride the Atlantic, one eye on Britain, the other on the colonies. The colonial relationship had always been two-sided, and Andrews' aim was to place the colonies within the empire. In Andrews' view, the colonists were Englishmen transplanted, not Americans in the making.

Because he was preoccupied with the British empire, Andrews has been misleadingly labeled the founder of the "imperial school" of early American historiography. His province, however, was not biographies of administrators or the history of administrative policies. Andrews focused on "the development and interrelation of ideas and institutions," which he believed to be at the center of proper historical research. Royal charters, proprietorships, colonial land policy, and commerce drew most of his attention. Of his 4-volume *The Colonial Period of American History* (1934–38), the first three covered the creation of British colonial charters and development of colonial assemblies. Only the final volume covered his cherished dark ages of early America, the years 1690 to 1750.

Few present-day historians of early America would disagree with Andrews' insistence on treating British North America as part of a large empire that was affected by events in England as well as in the Caribbean. Few would still consider the years 1690 to 1750 as a historiographical desert. Nonetheless, even fewer follow Andrews' institutionally-oriented vision. He can be criticized for ignoring all but political institutions. He neglected ecclesiastical organizations, slavery as a legal institution, women's legal position, and local social institutions, such as militias and educational establishments. Most ironically, the historian who tried to free early America from its provincialism never overcame his own nationalistic assumptions. Andrews' colonial America was British, and while he chided his predecessors for ignoring the West Indies, he ignored New Spain, New France, and non-English immigrants. For his conviction that ideas were important, they play a negligible role in his histories. Puritanism is an outmoded system of thought; revolutionary ideologies are marginalized. Even the revolution becomes nearly a non-event, brought about by a centralizing imperial system unaware of colonial conditions and by colonists used to self-government.

In his time, Andrews came under attack from social historians who saw every event in terms of class conflict, especially the revolution. Even in a book on 18th-century folkways, he had slighted patterns of social interaction and thought in favor of minutiae and oddities, giving little attention to broader themes. These new historians, however, usually affected by the Progressive movement and relativism, abandoned Andrews' objective approach and embraced writing histories that were relevant to contemporaries. Other historians turned their research to ideas, such as Puritanism, the frontier, nature, liberalism, and democracy, or looked to the unique environment in hopes of finding a quintessential Americanness. Whereas Andrews found colonial America across the ocean in British archives, the next two generations of colonial historians would confine themselves to mainland American sources. By publishing little or nothing, even most of his graduate students failed to propagate his views. By 1960, it seemed as though Andrews' research agenda and institutional paradigm was all but abandoned.

Historians rarely prove to be prophets, but Andrews may be the exception. He once predicted: "if my name lives, it is because I was the author of [the] Guides." The guides to which he referred were the *Guide to the Manuscript Materials for the History of the United States to 1783, in the British Museum, in Minor London Archives, and in the Libraries of Oxford and Cambridge* (1908) and *Guide to the Materials for American History, to 1783, in the Public Record Office of Great Britain* (1912–14). These invaluable research guides, undertaken to direct researchers to the evolution of the British administrative system, have provided the basis for the renewed interest since the early 1960s in British imperial policy, the island colonies, and transatlantic political, religious, and trade networks. This recent work, hardly coherent enough to be considered a school itself, but often owing to Andrews' outlining of essential British sources, has helped restore an Atlantic perspective to the study of colonial America.

JAMES FISHER

See also Gipson; United States: Colonial

Biography

Born Wethersfield, Connecticut, 22 February 1863. Received BA, Trinity College, Hartford, Connecticut, 1884; high school principal, West Hartford, Connecticut, 1884–86; studied with Herbert Baxter Adams, Johns Hopkins University, PhD 1889. Taught at Bryn Mawr College, 1889–1907; Johns Hopkins University, 1907–10; and Yale University, 1910–33. Married Evangeline Holcombe Walker, 1895 (1 son, 1 daughter). Died East Dover, Connecticut, 9 September 1943.

Principal Writings

"American Colonial History, 1690–1750," *American Historical Association Annual Report*, 1898

Colonial Self-Government, 1652–1689, 1904

Guide to the Manuscript Materials for the History of the United States to 1783, in the British Museum, in Minor London Archives, and in the Libraries of Oxford and Cambridge, 1908

Guide to the Materials for American History, to 1783, in the Public Record Office of Great Britain, 2 vols., 1912–14

Colonial Folkways: A Chronicle of American Life in the Reign of the Georges, 1919

The Colonial Background of the American Revolution: Four Essays in American Colonial History, 1924; revised 1931

"These Forty Years," *American Historical Review* 30 (1925), 225–50

"American Revolution: An Interpretation," *American Historical Review* 31 (1926), 219–32

The Colonial Period of American History, 4 vols., 1934–38

"On the Writing of Colonial History," *William and Mary Quarterly* 3rd series, 1 (1944), 27–48

Further Reading

Eisenstadt, Abraham Seldin, *Charles McLean Andrews: A Study in American Historical Writing*, New York: Columbia University Press, 1956

Gipson, Lawrence Henry, "Charles McLean Andrews and the Reorientation of the Study of American Colonial History," *Pennsylvania Magazine of History and Biography* 59 (1935), 209–22

Johnson, Richard R., "Charles McLean Andrews and the Invention of American Colonial History," *William and Mary Quarterly* 3rd series, 43 (1986), 519–41

Kross, Jessica, "Charles McLean Andrews," in Clyde N. Wilson, ed., *Twentieth-Century American Historians*, Detroit: Gale, 1983 [*Dictionary of Literary Biography*, vol. 17]

Labaree, Leonard W., "Charles McLean Andrews: Historian, 1863–1943," *William and Mary Quarterly* 3rd series, 1 (1944), 3–14

Pierson, G.W. *et al.*, "Charles McLean Andrews: A Bibliography," *William and Mary Quarterly* 3rd series, 1 (1944), 15–26

Riggs, John, "Charles McLean Andrews and the British Archives," MA thesis, Yale University, 1949

Savelle, Max, "The Imperial School of American Colonial Historians," *Indiana Magazine of History* 45 (1949), 123–44

Anglo-Saxon Chronicle

The Anglo-Saxon Chronicle, as it is usually called, consists of seven surviving chronicles from the Middle Ages that record events from year to year, in most of the manuscripts from the beginning of the Christian era to about the time of the Norman invasion. Although one must be cautious regarding the historical reliability of the recorded events, especially for earlier entries, the importance of the *Chronicle* can hardly be overstated.

The Anglo-Saxon Chronicle, written in English, is not only the earliest continuous history in English (or in any western vernacular) but also a treasure trove of information about England from the beginning of the Anglo-Saxon period through the middle of the 12th century. The disruptions attendant upon William the Conqueror's invasion of England in 1066 brought to an end those chronicles that were still being written. Monks at Peterborough, however, worked from 1121 until 1154 to reconstruct and extend their chronicle from a borrowed Canterbury manuscript, apparently to substantiate ownership claims after a fire destroyed much of their monastery in 1116.

How the *Chronicle* came about has been the subject of much speculation, especially regarding the possible role of Alfred the Great (849–99). No evidence exists to prove that Alfred ordered its creation, but the educational and historical climate that he fostered may have inspired the *Chronicle* even if he had no direct involvement. The *Chronicle* certainly began shortly after 890 during Alfred's reign when earlier chronicles, sometimes written on Easter tables, were synthesized at Winchester, the Wessex capital, into a prototype that was circulated to a variety of monasteries throughout the kingdom. This original was copied and supplemented with subsequent notices from Wessex as well as with items of local significance.

Despite the common origin, some of the chronicles possess distinguishing characteristics that make them especially interesting to later students of the Middle Ages. The Peterborough manuscript, for example, runs longer than any of the others (until 1153), while the Parker Chronicle and one of the two Abingdon Chronicles begin earlier, with entries dating back to 60 BCE rather than to Christ's birth in AD 1. The Parker Chronicle is unique in that it demonstrates the writing of at least 13 scribes who were recording history as it occurred, in contrast to the other manuscripts, which are copies made no earlier than the 10th century and therefore lack the diversity of handwriting and the sense of immediacy conveyed by the Parker Chronicle.

At a time when historical writings usually were in Latin, the choice of English for the *Chronicle* demonstrates the widespread unfamiliarity with Latin, even in the monasteries, that Alfred laments in his preface to St. Gregory's *Pastoral Care*. While the choice of English may have sprung from necessity, it helped to establish English as a written language suitable for recording the history of the nation. Alfred's effort to establish schools for the sons of the important men of his kingdom seems not to have taken firm root, for his death was soon followed by another collapse of learning that lasted until Edgar's reign approximately sixty years later. Nonetheless, Alfred's establishment of English, ironically made possible by the decline of classical learning, was permanent, and the *Anglo-Saxon Chronicle* played a major role in the rise of English as a language for historical, literary, and scholarly writing.

The *Chronicle*, however, should not be viewed as a history in the modern sense of that term. The chroniclers and copyists had little interest in synthesizing and interpreting. As Charles Plummer, perhaps the scholar most responsible for helping the modern world to understand and appreciate the importance of *The Anglo-Saxon Chronicle*, pointed out in the second volume of *Two of the Saxon Chronicles Parallel* (1892–99), the purpose of the *Chronicles* "was to *characterize* the receding series of years, each by a mark and sign of its own, so that the years might not be confused in the retrospect of those who had lived and acted in them." Plummer added that the brief annual references "present merely a name or two, as of a battlefield and a victor, but to the men of the day they suggested a thousand particulars, which they in their comrade-life were in the habit of recollecting and putting together. That which to us seems a lean and barren sentence, was to them the text for a winter evening's entertainment."

As an individual living near the end of the 20th century might recall a myriad of events by a simple reference to the Tet Offensive in 1968 – memories of both the Vietnam War and other events of that year, such as the assassinations of Martin Luther King and Robert Kennedy – so a statement, however brief, after a particular year in the 10th century would summon memories of that event and, through association, recollections of other events from the same year. One sentence is allotted to the slaying of Bryhtnoth at Maldon in 991, an encounter described in detail in one of the greatest poems of the Anglo-Saxon period, but that one sentence would be sufficient to bring the context and effects of the battle back into view – and to stimulate a long evening's conversation.

Modern readers can locate a wide range of topics in the *Chronicle*, among them the arrival of the Angles, Saxons, and Jutes in 449; the precarious state of Christianity immediately following the death of Æthelberht in 616; fire-breathing dragons in the sky over Northumbria in 793, followed by a famine and the arrival of church-destroying marauders; Alfred's nine battles against the Danes in 871 and his peace accord with Guthrum in 878; Cnut's accession to the kingdom of all of England in 1017; and William's invasion in 1066. The historian, sociologist, literary scholar, or linguist can revel in the wealth that constitutes *The Anglo-Saxon Chronicle*; but so can the general reader who simply opens the *Chronicle* in translation and reads and imagines.

EDWARD J. RIELLY

Further Reading

Asser, John, *De Rebus gestis Aelfredi*, completed 893; in English as *Asser's Life of King Alfred*, Boston: Ginn, 1906

Bately, Janet, ed., *The Anglo-Saxon Chronicle: Texts and Textual Relationships*, Reading, Berkshire: University of Reading, 1991

Borgmann, Ulrike, *Von Lindisfarne bis Hastings: Kampf und Kriegskunst in der angelsächsischen Chronik* (From Lindisfarne to Hastings: Battle and Warfare in the Art of the Anglo-Saxon Chronicle), Trier: Wissenschaftlicher Verlag Trier, 1993

Clark, Cecily, ed., *The Peterborough Chronicle, 1070–1154*, London: Oxford University Press, 1958

Dumville, David, and Simon Keynes, eds., *The Anglo-Saxon Chronicle: A Collaborative Edition*, Cambridge: Brewer, 1983–

Garmonsway, George Norman, trans., *The Anglo-Saxon Chronicle*, London: Dent, and New York: Dutton, 1953

Hocutt, Gregory D., *Narrative Style in the Peterborough Chronicles for 753 and 1137*, 1985

Lutz, Angelika, *Die Version G der Angelsächsischen Chronik: Rekonstruktion und Edition* (Version G of the Anglo-Saxon Chronicle: Reconstruction and Editing), Munich: Fink, 1981

Plummer, Charles, ed., *Two of the Saxon Chronicles Parallel (787–1001 AD)*, 2 vols., Oxford: Clarendon Press, 1892–99

Rositzke, Harry August, trans., *The Peterborough Chronicle*, New York: Columbia University Press, 1951

Shannon, Ann, *A Descriptive Syntax of the Parker Manuscript of the Anglo-Saxon Chronicle from 734 to 891*, The Hague: Mouton, 1964

Shores, David L., *A Descriptive Syntax of the Peterborough Chronicle from 1122 to 1154*, The Hague: Mouton, 1971

Smith, Albert Hugh, ed., *The Parker Chronicle*, London: Methuen, 1935

Whitelock, Dorothy, with David C. Douglas and Susie I. Tucker, eds., *The Anglo-Saxon Chronicle: A Revised Translation*, London: Eyre and Spottiswoode, and New Brunswick, NJ: Rutgers University Press, 1961

Annales regni Francorum

The *Annales regni Francorum* (ARF; Royal Frankish Annals) are the most important source for the political and military history of the Frankish kingdom from the death of Charles Martel in 741 until 829. It is most likely that the earliest part of the ARF was compiled and edited between 787 and 793, but it is still debated how and by whom. After 793 there were annual entries but no names of the writer or writers are known. The annual texts became longer and more detailed. The entries were extremely well informed, the language showed good inside knowledge and diplomatic and legal terminology was used. This has led to the assumption that the ARF were produced at, or close to, the royal court, possibly even instigated by Charlemagne himself. The official character of the text is further supported by significant omissions and the bias of some reports. For instance, the death of Louis the Pious' nephew, Bernard, was not mentioned in the entry of 818, the year he was punished by blinding for his participation in a revolt. In the last part of the ARF (years 808–829) a change of writers is obvious at the end of the year 820. The annals end abruptly in 829 without any explicit reason, suggesting that Hilduin, abbot of St. Denis could have been the author of the entries from 821 onwards. He was archchaplain at the royal court from 818 and was forced to leave the court in 830 because of his resistance to the empress Judith.

Despite the fact that annals were a form of historiography known in antiquity, the origins of the early medieval annals were distinct. It is hypothetical but very probable, as Ganshof has shown in his 1970 article, that year-by-year entries were first made into Easter Tables. In Easter Tables the calculated dates of Easter were given for many years. They were first compiled in Anglo-Saxon England. In Northumbrian monasteries and in Canterbury monks started to note events about the monastery which were considered worth remembering and later entered also general political occurrences into the margins each year. It is likely that Easter Tables with this kind of annotation were used by Anglo-Saxon missionaries on the Continent in the 8th century, and that they were exchanged between Frankish monasteries, becoming successful as a kind of aide-memoire more than historical works. The marginal entries gradually became longer until they were no longer written in the margins but on an additional page, forming the so-called minor annals. These were used to compile the major annals like the ARF which developed in a new environment fulfilling different purposes. The ARF were an instrument of the Carolingian court used to publicize military and diplomatic successes. This is shown in the extensive reporting of successful campaigns, of foreign delegations received by the king expressing their submission under Carolingian power, and of the diplomatic exchanging of gifts. There is, however, no evidence that Charlemagne or Louis the Pious supervised or influenced the writing of the ARF directly.

The ARF have come down to us in numerous manuscripts. The oldest manuscript is from the monastery of Lorsch, which is why these annals were known originally as Annales Laurissenses maiores. Only when Leopold von Ranke argued in 1854 that they were part of the official Carolingian historiography did they become commonly known as ARF. Friedrich Kurze who edited the ARF for the *Monumenta Germaniae Historica* series in 1895 distinguished five groups of manuscripts. The manuscripts of group E are citing a substantially revised version of the Annals up to the entry of the year 812. This revision included not only polished language, demonstrating the effects of the Carolingian Renaissance, but also further information from other sources, sometimes with a contradicting or differing viewpoint of the events. For instance, the extent of the military and political crisis in the year 778, when not only the Saxons rebelled under Widukind, but also the Frankish army was defeated in the Pyrenees, was only mentioned in the later version. Similarly the problems of the year 793, when the Saxons rebelled again and the Saracens crossed the Pyrenees and defeated a Frankish contingent in southern France, were only referred to in the later version. This revision was done in the years after Charles' death in 814. The assumption that Einhart was the editor of this revision (which was based on stylistic similarities between the revised ARF and the *Vita Caroli*) has now been rejected. It is likely, however, that Einhart knew this later version of the ARF when he wrote the *Vita Caroli* (The Life of Charlemagne).

The ARF were continued in the *Annales Bertiniani*, which recorded from 843 onwards the history of the west Frankish kingdom until the late 9th century; the *Annales Fuldenses* recorded the history of the east Frankish kingdom from 838 till 901. The *Annales Xantenses* had a more regional character and focused on the middle kingdom.

CHARLOTTE BEHR

Editions

Annales regni Francorum, edited by Friedrich Kurze, Hannover: Hahn, 1895, reprinted 1909, 1950; revised as *Annales qui dicuntur Einhardi*, edited by Friedrich Kurze, Hannover: Weidmann, 1895; in English as *Carolingian Chronicles*, edited by Bernhard Walter Scholz, Ann Arbor: University of Michigan Press, 1970

Further Reading

Fichtenau, Heinrich, "Karl der Grosse und das Kaisertum" (Charlemagne and the Empire), *Mitteilungen des Instituts für Österreichische Geschichtsforschung* 61 (1953), 257–334

Ganshof, F.L., "L'Historiographie dans la monarchie franque sous les Mérovingiens et les Carolingiens" (The Historiography of the Frankish Monarchy under the Merovingians and Carolingians), *La storiografia altomedievale* (Settimane di studio del Centro italiano di studi sull'alto medioevo) 17, vol. 2, Spoleto 1970

Hoffmann, Hartmut, *Untersuchungen zur karolingischen Annalistik* (Research on the Writing of Carolingian Annals), Bonn: Röhrscheid, 1958

Innes, Matthew, and Rosamond McKitterick, "The Writing of History," in Rosamond McKitterick, ed., *Carolingian Culture: Emulation and Innovation*, Cambridge: Cambridge University Press, 1994

Levinson, Wilhelm, and Heinz Löwe, eds., *Deutschlands Geschichtsquellen im Mittelalter: Vorzeit und Karolinger* (Germany's Historical Sources of the Middle Ages: Antiquity and the Carolingians), Weimar, 1952–73 [revision of Wilhelm Wattenbach's edition]

McCormick, Michael, *Les Annales du haut Moyen Age* (Annals of the Early Middle Ages), Turnhout: Brepols, 1975

McKitterick, Rosamond, *The Frankish Kingdoms under the Carolingians, 751–987*, London: Longman, 1983

Poole, Reginald Lane, *Chronicles and Annals: A Brief Outline of Their Origin and Growth*, Oxford: Oxford University Press, 1926

Annales School

According to historian Traian Stoianovich, "No other group of twentieth-century scholars in any country has made a more valuable contribution to historiography and the historical method than the Annales School." For H. Stuart Hughes the *Annales* represented "The single most important forum for the revitalization of historical studies in the Western World." Such fulsome praise has been contested, particularly by Anglo-Saxon empiricist and many *marxisant* historians, but there can surely be no doubt that, since the first appearance of its journal in 1929 (the *Annales d'histoire économique et sociale* as it was first called), *Annalisme* has played a decisive role in dictating the agenda of 20th-century historical writing.

The founders of the school – Lucien Febvre and Marc Bloch – were neopositivists, influenced by Auguste Comte and the more influential sociologist Emile Durkheim, as well as by the socioeconomic historians François Simiand and Ernest Labrousse. They laid the early foundations and methodological parameters of the school. Febvre, in particular, left the Anglo-Saxon, archivally-based territory of the historian, with its emphasis on the politics and diplomacy of Great Men and Great Powers, for the more exotic, and human, fields of Love, Sex, and Death. In *Le Problème de l'incroyance au XVIe siècle* (1942; *The Problem of Unbelief in the Sixteenth Century*, 1982), Febvre marched boldly into the fields of literature and psychology in order to establish the *mentalité* of the age. Henceforward, *l'histoire des mentalités* and Annaliste history would be coterminous. However, for the Annales school, the "science of Man" would be, above all, a human science. As Febvre explained in his inaugural lecture in the Collège de France: "We seek history as a human science, and therefore constituted on facts, yes, but, human facts. Written sources, yes, but we deal in human written sources." Marc Bloch preferred the *social* interpretation of history: his classic 2-volume work, *La Société féodale* (1939–40; *Feudal Society*, 1961) dealt less with the juridical than with the social relations which bound feudal society together, although part 2 of the first volume, with its emphasis on the environment and "mental climate," bore witness to the influence of Febvre while heralding Braudel's great works. It has been argued (by Georges Duby, for example) that Febvre and Bloch's 20th-century historical reworking of the Enlightenment project only assumed international status with the arrival of Fernand Braudel and the intellectual Cold War between the West and the Soviet Union after 1945. Not that *Annalisme* under Braudel should be dismissed simply as the most effective intellectual riposte to the hegemony of the marxist historical method. For one thing, its insistence on long time-spans, "material" history, *structures* and *conjonctures*, seemed to many like historical materialism without the class struggle; for another, its disciples were too ideologically diverse to be described, collectively, as "anti-Marxist" (Bloch's great hero was the socialist Jean Jaurès, while the Marxist historian E.P. Thompson was a contributor to the *Annales: Economies, Sociétés, Civilisations* as it was renamed after 1946). Immanuel Wallerstein, influenced both by Marx's historical materialism and by Fernand Braudel, is close to the mark when he wrote that "the Annales had an intellectual world-view that seemed to express resistance to both Anglo-Saxon intellectual hegemony and sclerotic official Marxism simultaneously." And Fernand Braudel was a "world historian," both in his approach to the writing of history and the recognition his history received. With the prestige of the journal behind him, and supported by the institutions of the Collège de France and the Ecole des Hautes Etudes en Sciences Sociales, Braudel – with a little financial help from his American friends – set about the task of extending the influence of the Annales school worldwide. From 1963 to his death in 1985, he directed its activities from the Maison des Sciences de l'Homme, a pretentious, but revealing name.

The original Maison which Febvre, Bloch, and Braudel had inhabited, and to which other leading historians like François Furet, Emmanuel Le Roy Ladurie, and Jacques Revel have since built extensions, was constructed upon four main pillars – geography, demography, sociology, and economics. If Febvre and Bloch drew primarily upon sociology, economic history, literature, and psychology, *Braudeliens* tapped into another rich vein of the French historical tradition – geography. In his insistence that mountains, as much as money, maketh Man, as well as in his relativism, Braudel placed the Annales school firmly in the tradition which extends from Montesquieu in the mid-18th century to Vidal de la Blache at the end of the 19th. In addition to a proper concern for geography, a rapid survey of articles published in the *Annales: E.S.C.* will immediately establish the importance of demographic studies to the *annaliste* historian. Here again, he/she could draw upon the pioneering work of French demographers like Louis Henry and his followers, work which inspired Peter Laslett and the creation of the Cambridge Population Group. In recent years, "culture," even political history, and the study of elites, have found a place between the covers of the house journal, thus placating, in some measure, early critics such as Tony Judt. In addition, there was a move in the 1980s to shift the chronological focus from pre-1789 to post-1789 topics.

Given the fall of communism, *vieux-style*, and the not unrelated rise of "post-modernism," is *annalisme* on the wane? Peter Burke, an early British disciple, thinks that it might be.

However, news of its death would be premature. The founders and leading disciples of the school were both too variegated and too steeped in the French historical and intellectual tradition for contemporary political events to dictate its demise. There is also the fact that, as this contribution has noted, whatever the *annaliste* historian has done in particular fields of research, other historians have done as well, or even better. Nonetheless, it would be difficult to argue against Burke's general conclusion that "the outstanding achievement of the Annales group, over all three generations, has been the reclaiming of vast areas for the historian. The group has extended the territory of the historian to unexpected areas of human behaviour and to social groups neglected by traditional historians ... The discipline will never be the same again."

GWYNNE LEWIS

See also Agrarian; Anthropology; Barkan; Bloch; Boorstin; Braudel; Burke; Cahen; Canada; Chabod; Chartier; Chevalier; Consumerism; Cultural; Demography; Diplomatic; Duby; Economic; Environmental; Europe: Modern; Febvre; France: to 1000; France: 1000–1450; France: 1450–1789; Frontiers; Fügedi; Furet; Ganshof; Góngora; Halperín-Donghi; Hilton; History from Below; Historical Geography; History Workshop; Holanda; Hunt; Inalcık; Kedourie; Kula; Labrousse; Lefebvre; Legal; Le Roy Ladurie; Lewis, B.; Local; McNeill; Mentalities; Needham; Parker; Pirenne; Poland: to the 18th Century; Poland: since the 18th Century; Poliakov; Renouvin; Sanchéz-Albornoz; Soboul; Social; Spain: to 1450; Spain: Imperial; Spain: Modern; Wallerstein; Weber, E.; World; Zeldin

Further Reading

Aymard, M., "The *Annales* and French Historiography (1929–1972)," *Journal of European Economic History* 1 (1972), 491–511

Bloch, Marc, *Apologie pour l'histoire, ou, métier d'historien*, Paris: Colin, 1949; in English as *The Historian's Craft*, New York: Knopf, 1953, Manchester: Manchester University Press, 1954

Bloch, Marc, *La Société féodale*, 2 vols., Paris: Michel, 1939–40; in English as *Feudal Society*, 2 vols., Chicago: University of Chicago Press, and London: Routledge, 1961

Braudel, Fernand, "Lucien Febvre, 1878–1956," *Annales: ESC* 11 (1956), 289–91

Burguière, André, "Histoire d'une histoire: la naissance des *Annales*," *Annales: ESC* 34 (1979), 1344–59

Burguière, André, "The Fate of the History of *Mentalités* in the *Annales*," *Comparative Studies in Society and History* 24 (1982), 424–37

Burke, Peter *The French Historical Revolution: The Annales School, 1929–89*, Cambridge: Polity Press, and Stanford, CA: Stanford University Press, 1990

Carrard, Philippe, *Poetics of the New History: French Historical Discourse from Braudel to Chartier*, Baltimore: John Hopkins University Press, 1992

Clark, Stuart, "The Annales Historians," in Quentin Skinner, ed., *The Return of Grand Theory in the Human Sciences*, Cambridge and New York: Cambridge University Press, 1985

Duby, Georges, *L'Histoire continue*, Paris: Jacob, 1991; in English as *History Continues*, Chicago: University of Chicago Press, 1994

Febvre, Lucien, *Le Problème de l'incroyance au XVIe siècle: la religion de Rabelais*, Paris: Michel, 1942; in English as *The Problem of Unbelief in the Sixteenth Century: The Religion of Rabelais*, Cambridge, MA: Harvard University Press, 1982

Febvre, Lucien, "De la *Revue de synthèse historique* aux *Annales*" (From the *Revue de synthèse historique* to the *Annales*), *Annales: ESC* 7 (1952), 289–92

Fink, Carole, *Marc Bloch: A Life in History*, Cambridge and New York: Cambridge University Press, 1989

Fox-Genovese, Elizabeth, "The Political Crisis of Social History," *Journal of Social History* 10 (1976), 205–20

Furet, François, "Beyond the Annales," *Journal of Modern History* 55 (1983), 389–410

Hughes, H. Stuart, *The Obstructed Path: French Social Thought in the Years of Desperation, 1930–1960*, New York: Harper, 1968

Iggers, George G., "The Annales Tradition," in his *New Directions in European Historiography*, Middletown, CT: Wesleyan University Press, 1975, revised 1985; London: Methuen, 1985

Judt, Tony, "A Clown in Regal Purple: Social History and the Historian," *History Workshop Journal* 7 (1979), 66–94

Keylor, William R., *Academy and Community: The Foundation of the French Historical Profession*, Cambridge, MA: Harvard University Press, 1975

Le Roy Ladurie, Emmanuel, *Le Territoire de l'historien*, 2 vols., Paris: Gallimard, 1973–78; selections in English as *The Territory of the Historian*, Brighton: Harvester Press, and Chicago: University of Chicago Press, 1979, and as *The Mind and Method of the Historian*, 1981

Revel, Jacques, "Histoire et sciences sociales: Les paradigmes des *Annales*," *Annales: ESC* 34 (1979), 1360–76

Sewell, William H., Jr., "Marc Bloch and the Logic of Comparative History," *History and Theory* 6 (1967), 208–18

Stoianovich, Traian, *French Historical Method: The Annales Paradigm*, Ithaca, NY: Cornell University Press, 1976

Stone, Lawrence, "The Revival of Narrative: Reflections on a New Old History," *Past and Present* 85 (1979), 3–24

Wallerstein, Immanuel, "Beyond *Annales*?", *Radical History Review* 49 (1991), 7–16

Anthropology, Historical

Historical anthropology is one of the most fruitful areas of interdisciplinary collaboration in the social sciences. In recent decades many historians, dissatisfied with the paradigms governing their research, have turned to anthropology for new topics for investigation, methods of inquiry, and interpretive strategies.

Anthropology has appealed to historians in part because it appears to be primarily concerned with the ethnographic study of "simple" societies whose structures turn on relations of kinship, and which are culturally homogeneous. However, since the end of World War II anthropologists have become highly critical of research following this model, which was often inspired by the structural-functionalism of A.R. Radcliffe-Brown and Bronisław Malinowski. As Bernard Cohn and John and Jean Comaroff have observed, studies in which societies were represented in this way were often partial, biased, and unwitting handmaidens to the domination of non-Western peoples by Europeans and Americans.

New theoretical perspectives in anthropology are reflected in the exemplary work of Sidney Mintz, Jay O'Brien and William Roseberry, Marshall Sahlins, Jane and Peter Schneider, and Eric Wolf, who have situated culture in historical contexts and undertaken longitudinal studies. They have examined complex societies, cultural consequences of the expansion of global capitalism, and struggles implicating class, ethnicity, gender, and race.

Thus, just as historians began to incorporate anthropology into their work, anthropologists have turned to history. Despite this irony, in *The Historical Anthropology of Early Modern Italy* (1987) Peter Burke contrasted historical anthropology with social history, emphasizing the fact that the former tends to be qualitative rather than quantitative. Its units of analysis are often small communities rather than large populations; its goal is to interpret the past rather than to provide narrative explanations of change, and it often focuses on symbolic dimensions of culture.

Certain trends stand out in the turn to anthropology by historians. These include a shift away from political and heroic history initiated by members of the Annales school in France after 1929. In the 1960s E.P. Thompson led a challenge to orthodox Marxist theory by making the concept of culture central to his work. In the following decade research on popular behavior, including witchcraft and uprisings, and family and kinship, similarly brought anthropology to history.

In the 1980s symbolism and language received considerable attention while, at the same time, historians who were seeking to overcome the theoretical dichotomies of structure and agency, or objectivity and subjectivity, gained inspiration from anthropology. More recently, historical aspects of social memory have been the focus of numerous studies. The balance of this essay will offer a brief discussion of these trends.

The Annales school, so-called after the journal of the same name founded in 1929 by Marc Bloch and Lucien Febvre, is often credited with inspiring the initial interchange between historians and anthropologists. While the Annales school is characterized by considerable diversity, it did encourage generations of historians, including the prominent Fernand Braudel, Jacques Le Goff, Emmanuel Le Roy Ladurie, and Pierre Nora, to shift their attention from political events and heroic individuals to long-term trends, regional and community studies, and the daily lives of ordinary people. In seeking to understand these, historians often referred to the work of Emile Durkheim on social organization, Clifford Geertz on interpretation, Arnold van Gennep on rites of passage, Lucien Lévy-Bruhl on *mentalités*, Marcel Mauss on exchange, and Victor Turner on ritual.

Research on *mentalités*, or unconsciously held, socially shared, cognitive frameworks that predispose members of a given community to interpret and act in the world in culturally patterned ways, emerged from the Annales school. Historians of *mentalités* sought to capture and analyze what they viewed as durable sets of beliefs characteristic of particular social formations, for example, feudalism.

In "Mentalities: A History of Ambiguities," Jacques Le Goff observed that the concept of *mentalités* was important to history as it raised the problem of the "power of human consciousness and understanding to influence the course of history." As collective phenomena, *mentalités* can simultaneously resist change and play a crucial role in social transformation. Le Goff also pointed out that just as *mentalités* can unify a society, they can also coincide with social divisions.

Carlo Ginzburg made a similar point in *Il formaggio e il vermi* (1976; *The Cheese and the Worms*, 1980) when he noted that the idea of *mentalités* is a basis for the premise that not only elites, but also "common people," possess coherent worldviews, and that their beliefs are worthy of investigation. Ginzburg's study explored the ideas of an ordinary man, a miller, who was prosecuted by the 16th-century Italian Counter-Reformation Inquisition. In this way Ginzburg expanded the study of *mentalités* to include the exercise of power and domination in society.

The desire to study the culture of daily life required that historians do more than rely on traditional documentary sources for their contents. They attempted to decode the social and ideological significance of documents as well, and made use of evidence previously overlooked by their colleagues. Parish registers, records of wages and food prices, trial testimony, diaries, pamphlets, personal correspondence, material culture, contemporary descriptions of body language and the social use of space, sermons, medical records, folk customs, and oral narrative (when researching the recent past) all have become rich sources for historical anthropology.

In the 1960s Marxist historians turned to new kinds of source materials for their work. Yet their research was motivated by concerns quite different from those of the Annales school. E.P. Thompson challenged the orthodox Marxist approach to human behavior in which actors are seen as motivated in the first instance by economics, and only secondarily by culture or ideology. In *The Making of the English Working Class* (1963) he saw the formation of class consciousness and, therefore, class identity, as necessarily mediated by elements of culture including traditions and value systems, and as influenced by technological and social change. Inspired by feminist theory, Anna Clark, author of *The Struggle for the Breeches* (1995), reappraised Thompson and included consideration of the social construction of gender in her analysis of late 18th- and early 19th-century British working-class politics.

The publication of Peter Laslett's *The World We Have Lost* (1965, 1984) heralded the desire of historians to describe patterns of kinship, often in peasant society, and understand their significance with respect to other social structures, relationships, and processes including production and exchange, and the emergence of regional variation. The work of anthropologist Jack Goody has been a significant influence on these projects. *Interest and Emotion* (1984), edited by Hans Medick and David Sabean, benefited from a sophisticated exchange between historians and anthropologists in which kinship was viewed as revealing not only social structure but also culturally constituted subjective states.

Connections between objective and subjective elements of culture, often with an explicit focus on the production and manipulation of symbolic codes, including language, have received attention in the work of Leora Auslander, Roger Chartier, Natalie Zemon Davis, Lynn Hunt, Alan Macfarlane, and Ulinka Rublack. The scope of research undertaken in these studies has been vast and has included analyses of style and social class in modern France; the behavior of crowds in 16th-century France; politics and culture in the French Revolution; capitalism, identity, and culture in 16th- to 18th-century Britain; and gender, the body, and normative behavior in early modern Germany.

Historians have also applied anthropological strategies to the study of non-European cultures. In *Clio in Oceania* (1991), edited by Aletta Biersack, historians and anthropologists collaborated in the study of concepts and practices of history in the Pacific. Phillip C.C. Huang and Robert Marks have explored peasant society and revolution in China.

Memory is an object of historical interest in the work of Mary Carruthers, John R. Gillis, Eric Hobsbawm and Terence Ranger, Jacques Le Goff, Pierre Nora, Luisa Passerini, and Henry Rousso. These authors have written on mnemonic technology in medieval Europe; the uses of tradition and commemorative ritual; the relationship between historical change and the growth of institutions of memory (museums and archives) in the 20th century; and the recollection and repression of memories of fascism in Italy and the Vichy regime in France.

Studies in anthropological history have been criticized for being anecdotal and too specific to contribute to general historical knowledge. The contingency of interpretive perspectives has raised questions about the validity of conclusions that might be drawn from such studies, and questions have been raised about the applicability of modern categories (such as "society") to premodern times.

The German historian Alf Lüdtke, a proponent of *Alltagsgeschichte*, or the history of everyday life, has had to defend his work against such charges. Specifically, in the introduction to *The History of Everyday Life* (1995), he noted that *Alltagsgeschichte* has been accused of being concerned solely with historical "tinsel and trivia" and producing little more than a "sentimental celebration" of ordinary people. The German case is exceptional as Lüdtke and others have been accused of exculpating Germans for their acquiescence to Nazism by failing to focus on historical data that could be used to ask hard questions about the responsibility individuals bore for the state's crimes. Nonetheless, Lüdtke's response bears on criticisms of historical anthropology in general.

Specifically, Lüdtke argued that the history of everyday life provides concrete evidence of the connections between life circumstances and subjectivity through which patterns of domination and hegemony intercede. Thus, this approach to the past enhances our understanding of the reasons why, and the practices through which, people acquiesce in – or resist – certain political, economic, and cultural orders.

While not all anthropological historians take a political approach in their work, Lüdtke's defense of *Alltagsgeschichte* does point to important reasons for undertaking historical anthropology. Other reasons include giving voice to previously mute historical subjects, exploring particular expressions of general trends and, ultimately, through the study of historical others, better understanding ourselves.

ELIZABETH A. TEN DYKE

See also Axtell; Bloch; Bolton; Burke; Castro; Consumerism; Corbin; Crime; Cultural; Darnton; Davis, N., Dening; Design; Ethnicity; Finley; Geertz; Guichard; Gurevich; Ileto; Legal; Le Roy Ladurie; Lüdtke; Mexico; Native American; Scribner; Trigger; Turner, V.; World

Further Reading

Auslander, Leora, *Taste and Power: Furnishing Modern France*, Berkeley: University of California Press, 1996

Biersack, Aletta, ed., *Clio in Oceania: Toward a Historical Anthropology*, Washington, DC: Smithsonian Institution Press, 1991

Bloch, Marc, *La Société féodale*, 2 vols., Paris: Michel, 1939–40; in English as *Feudal Society*, Chicago: University of Chicago Press, and London: Routledge, 1961

Braudel, Fernand, *La Méditerranée et le monde méditerranéen à l'époque de Philippe II*, 2 vols., Paris: Colin, 1949, revised 1966; in English as *The Mediterranean and the Mediterranean World in the Age of Philip II*, 2 vols., London: Collins, and New York: Harper, 1972–73

Burke, Peter, *The Historical Anthropology of Early Modern Italy: Essays on Perception and Communication*, Cambridge and New York: Cambridge University Press, 1987

Carruthers, Mary, *The Book of Memory: A Study of Memory in Medieval Culture*, Cambridge and New York: Cambridge University Press, 1990

Chartier, Roger, *Cultural History: Between Practices and Representations*, Cambridge: Polity Press, and Ithaca, NY: Cornell University Press, 1988

Clark, Anna, *The Struggle for the Breeches: Gender and the Making of the British Working Class*, Berkeley: University of California Press, and London: Rivers Oram, 1995

Cohn, Bernard, *An Anthropologist among the Historians and Other Essays*, Delhi and New York: Oxford University Press, 1988

Comaroff, John, and Jean Comaroff, *Ethnography and the Historical Imagination*, Boulder, CO: Westview Press, 1992

Darnton, Robert, *The Great Cat Massacre and Other Episodes in French Cultural History*, New York: Basic Books, and London: Allen Lane, 1984

Davis, Natalie Zemon, *Society and Culture in Early Modern France: Eight Essays*, Stanford, CA: Stanford University Press, and London: Duckworth, 1975

Davis, Natalie Zemon, "Anthropology and History in the 1980s: The Possibilities of the Past," *Journal of Interdisciplinary History* 12 (1981), 267–75

Durkheim, Emile, *Readings from Emile Durkheim*, edited by Kenneth Thompson, London: Tavistock, 1985

Geertz, Clifford, *The Interpretation of Cultures: Selected Essays*, New York: Basic Books, 1973; London: Hutchinson, 1975

Gennep, Arnold van, *Les Rites de passage*, Paris: Nourry, 1909; in English as *The Rites of Passage*, Chicago: University of Chicago Press, and London: Routledge, 1960

Gillis, John R., ed., *Commemorations: The Politics of National Identity*, Princeton: Princeton University Press, 1994

Ginzburg, Carlo, *Il formaggio e i vermi: il cosmo di un mugnaio del '500*, Turin: Einaudi, 1976; in English as *The Cheese and the Worms: The Cosmos of a Sixteenth-Century Miller*, Baltimore: Johns Hopkins University Press, and London: Routledge, 1980

Goody, Jack, Joan Thirsk, and E.P. Thompson, eds., *Family and Inheritance: Rural Society in Western Europe, 1200–1800*, Cambridge: Cambridge University Press, 1976

Goody, Jack, *The Oriental, the Ancient and the Primitive: Systems of Marriage and the Family in the Pre-Industrial Societies of Eurasia*, Cambridge and New York: Cambridge University Press, 1990

Hobsbawm, Eric J., and Terence O. Ranger, eds., *The Invention of Tradition*, Cambridge and New York: Cambridge University Press, 1983

Huang, Philip C.C., *The Peasant Economy and Social Change in North China*, Stanford, CA: Stanford University Press, 1985

Hunt, Lynn, *Politics, Culture, and Class in the French Revolution*, Berkeley: University of California Press, 1984; London: Methuen, 1986

Laslett, Peter, *The World We Have Lost*, London: Methuen, 1965, New York: Scribner, 1966; revised 1984

Le Goff, Jacques, "Mentalities: A History of Ambiguities," in Jacques Le Goff and Pierre Nora, eds., *Constructing the Past: Essays in Historical Methodology*, Cambridge and New York: Cambridge University Press, 1985

Le Goff, Jacques, *Storia e memoria*, Turin: Einaudi, 1986; in English as *History and Memory*, New York: Columbia University Press, 1992

Le Roy Ladurie, Emmanuel, *Le Carnaval de Romans: de la Chandeleur au mercredi des Cendres, 1579–1580*, Paris: Gallimard, 1979; in English as *Carnival in Romans*, New York: Braziller, 1979, London: Scolar Press, 1980

Le Roy Ladurie, Emmanuel, *Montaillou, village occitan de 1294 à 1324*, Paris: Gallimard, 1975; in English as *Montaillou: The Promised Land of Error*, New York: Braziller, 1978, and as *Montaillou: Cathars and Catholics in a French Village, 1294–1324*, London: Scolar Press, 1978

Lévy-Bruhl, Lucien, *La Mentalité primitive: le monde mythique des Australiens et des Papous*, Paris: Alcan, 1922; in English as *Primitive Mentality*, New York: Macmillan, and London: Allen and Unwin, 1923

Lüdtke, Alf, "Introduction: What Is the History of Everyday Life and Who Are Its Practitioners," in Alf Lüdtke, ed., *The History of Everyday Life: Reconstructing Historical Experiences and Ways of Life*, Princeton: Princeton University Press, 1995

Macfarlane, Alan, *The Origins of English Individualism: The Family, Property and Social Transmission*, Oxford: Blackwell, 1978; New York: Cambridge University Press, 1979

Macfarlane, Alan, *The Culture of Capitalism*, Oxford and New York: Blackwell, 1987

Malinowski, Bronisław, *The Early Writings of Bronisław Malinowski*, Cambridge and New York: Cambridge University Press, 1993

Marks, Robert, *Rural Revolution in South China: Peasants and the Making of History in Haifeng County, 1570–1930*, Madison: University of Wisconsin Press, 1984

Mauss, Marcel, *Essai sur le don: forme et raison de l'échange dans les sociétés archaïques*, Paris: Alcan, 1925; in English as *The Gift: Forms and Functions of Exchange in Archaic Societies*, Glencoe, IL: Free Press, and London: Cohen and West, 1954; revised as *The Gift: The Form and Reason for Exchange in Archaic Societies*, New York: Norton, and London: Routledge, 1990

Medick, Hans, and David Warren Sabean, eds., *Interest and Emotion: Essays on the Study of Family and Kinship*, Cambridge and New York: Cambridge University Press, 1984

Medick, Hans, "'Missionaries in a Row Boat': Ethnological Ways of Knowing as a Challenge to Social History," *Comparative Studies in Society and History* 29 (1987), 76–98

Mintz, Sidney W., *Sweetness and Power: The Place of Sugar in Modern History*, New York: Viking, and London: Sifton, 1985

Nora, Pierre, ed., *Les Lieux de mémoire*, 3 vols., Paris: Gallimard, 1984–92; abridged in English as *Realms of Memory: Rethinking the French Past*, 2 vols., New York: Columbia University Press, 1996–97

O'Brien, Jay, and William Roseberry, *Golden Ages, Dark Ages: Imagining the Past in Anthropology and History*, Berkeley: University of California Press, 1991

Passerini, Luisa, *Torino operaia e fascismo: una storia orale*, Rome: Laterza, 1984; in English as *Fascism in Popular Memory: The Cultural Experience of the Turin Working Class*, Cambridge and New York: Cambridge University Press, 1987

Radcliffe-Brown, Alfred Reginald, *Structure and Function in Primitive Society: Essays and Addresses*, Glencoe, IL: Free Press, and London: Cohen and West, 1952

Rousso, Henry, *Le Syndrome de Vichy, 1944–1980*, Paris: Seuil, 1987; in English as *The Vichy Syndrome: History and Memory in France since 1944*, Cambridge, MA: Harvard University Press, 1991

Rublack, Ulinka, "Pregnancy, Childbirth and the Female Body in Early Modern Germany," *Past and Present* 150 (1996), 84–110

Sabean, David Warren, *Power in the Blood: Popular Culture and Village Discourse in Early Modern Germany*, Cambridge and New York: Cambridge University Press, 1984

Sabean, David Warren, *Property, Production and Family in Neckarhausen, 1700–1870*, Cambridge and New York: Cambridge University Press, 1990

Sahlins, Marshall, *Islands of History*, Chicago: University of Chicago Press, and London: Tavistock, 1995

Schneider, Jane C., and Peter T. Schneider, *Festival of the Poor: Fertility Decline and the Ideology of Class in Sicily, 1860–1980*, Tucson: University of Arizona Press, 1996

Segalen, Martine, *Sociologie de la famille*, Paris: Colin, 1981; in English as *Historical Anthropology of the Family*, Cambridge and New York: Cambridge University Press, 1986

Thomas, Keith, *Religion and the Decline of Magic: Studies in Popular Beliefs in Sixteenth- and Seventeenth-Century England*, London: Weidenfeld and Nicolson, and New York: Scribner, 1971

Thompson, E.P., *The Making of the English Working Class*, London: Gollancz, 1963; New York: Pantheon, 1964

Turner, Victor, *The Ritual Process: Structure and Anti-Structure*, Chicago: Aldine Press, and London: Routledge, 1969

Wolf, Eric R., *Peasants*, Englewood Cliffs, NJ: Prentice Hall, 1966

Wolf, Eric R., *Europe and the People Without History*, Berkeley: University of California Press, 1982

Arai Hakuseki 1657–1725

Japanese Confucian scholar, poet, and historian

Arai Hakuseki was retained as a tutor by Ienobu from 1693, when the future Tokugawa shogun ruled as daimyo of Kōfu (modern Yamanashi Prefecture). After Ienobu's succession as national ruler, Hakuseki influenced shogunal policy in such areas as foreign relations, foreign trade, and currency reform. He sought to recast the role of shogun as "national king" (kokuō), equal in status to the sovereign of Korea, the only country with which Japan had formal diplomatic relations. He attempted to limit the outflow of silver by further curbing the already limited trade contacts with the outside world, and to improve shogunate finances by withdrawing debased coins from circulation. He left official service with the death of Ietsugu in 1716.

Arai's historical writings include *Hankanpu* (Genealogies of the Shogunate's Protectors, 1702), *Tokushi yoron* (1724; *Lessons from History*, 1982), *Koshitsū* (Survey of Ancient History, 1716), and a lost work, *Shigi* (Historical Doubts). The first of these, commissioned by Ineobu and constituting 13 volumes, established the historical relationship between 337 daimyo families and the Tokugawa ruling family from 1600 to 1680. While fulfilling this political purpose, it is considered to be a work of objective scholarship, replete with genealogical tables and individual biographies.

Tokushi yoron, Hakuseki's masterpiece, is a general political history of Japan, written for the edification of Ienobu and future Tokugawa shoguns. Modelled upon the *Zizhi tongjian* (Comprehensive Mirror for Aid in Government) of the Chinese scholar Sima Guang (1019–86), it combined factual narrative with commentary. It also drew upon the 14th-century Japanese work *Jinnō Shōtōki* (written *c.*1339; *A Chronicle of Divine Sovereigns*, 1980) by Kitabatake Chikafusa, for factual information, reflecting this work's thematic organization. Hakuseki also shares Kitabatake's concern with periodization. However while the 14th-century scholar's periodization scheme highlights changes in the conduct of imperial succession, Hakuseki's work pioneered in emphasizing major changes in the locus of actual political power. In this it reflected his own involvement in practical administration.

In *Tokushi yoron*, Hakuseki divided the history of Japan from 858 to 1709 into nine civil, and five military periods. These overlap from 1192 to 1392, when, in Hakuseki's view, the hereditary military class (*bushi* or *samurai*) was still struggling to gain the upper hand over the court aristocracy (*kuge*) and attain national hegemony. In most cases the periods begin with a genuine change in the nature of power. Thus, for example, where Kitabatake divided the ancient and medieval periods at 884, when for the first time someone other than a member of the imperial family decided the issue of imperial succession, Hakuseki ended the period of direct imperial rule at 858, when for the first time a person of non-imperial blood, the noble Fujiwara Yoshifusa, became regent and wielded real administrative power.

The eight subsequent periods of civil rule in Hakuseki's scheme began with the first instance of a Fujiwara regent deposing a reigning emperor (884); the establishment of a permanent hereditary Fujiwara regency (967); reestablishment of direct imperial rule (1068); the emergence of rule by In or Abdicated Emperors (1086); the founding of the first (Kamakura) shogunate (1192); the assertion of full shogunal control over the Kyoto court (1219); imperial restoration (1333); and the destruction of the court's power (1336).

Overlapping these periods, Hakuseki posited the following periods in the history of military administration: the foundation of the Kamakura shogunate (1192); the shogunate's partial loss of power to military vassals (1219); the second (Muromachi or Ashikaga) shogunate (1338); the period of warlord rule (1573); and the third (Edo or Tokugawa) shogunate (1603). This periodization system resembles that applied to Japanese history by modern scholars.

Hakuseki wrote that, "History is to narrate events in accordance with the facts and show men the lessons thereof." Throughout his writings, he manifested a rationalistic concern with questions of causality. In discussing the origins of the hereditary military class, for example, he broke with earlier mystical or moralistic explanations, emphasizing instead the rebellion of Fujiwara Masakado in 939. The significance of this first large-scale samurai rebellion against the court had been largely ignored by earlier writers.

The rationalism of Hakuseki's *Koshitsū* is also striking; in surveying the ancient period, he broke with the mythological accounts still credited and repeated by the Hayashi and Mito schools. "The gods" in the chronicles, he categorically asserted, "were men." To get at the truth of ancient history, he averred, one must study Korean and other accounts, critically comparing them with Japan's own records.

As a Confucian scholar, however, Hakuseki accepted certain fundamental assumptions about the nature of historical change which may have limited his rationalistic approach. *Tokushi yoron* began as a series of lectures for Ienobu, designed to influence his administration; in the Chinese tradition, Hakuseki used the historical record to adduce moral and practical lessons for the present. He also used that record to legitimize the regime which employed him, and may have indulged in a selective discussion of the actions of past Tokugawa rulers.

Like earlier writers, Hakuseki applied a modified version of the Mandate of Heaven theory to Japanese history, which recognizes the ongoing legitimacy of a single imperial line, but attributed shifts in actual power to the moral failings of those who wield it. Thus real power passed to Fujiwara regents from emperors due to the latters' inability to cope with social change; thereafter, the incompetence of the regency, then *In*, produces a power vacuum inevitably leading to military rule. This succession of administrations was, in Hakuseki's view, engineered by Heaven, and legitimized by the fact that the Minamoto, Ashikaga, and Tokugawa shoguns were all descended from the line of an emperor (Seiwa, reigned 859–76).

GARY P. LEUPP

See also Japan

Biography
Born Edo (now Tokyo), 24 March 1657, son of a masterless samurai. Served a minor feudal lord, 1683–85; joined school of Confucian scholar Kinoshita Jun'an; in 1693 became tutor to Tokugawa Tsunatoyo, lord of Kōfu and nephew of the childless shogun, who succeeded as sixth Tokugawa shogun, Ienobu; policy adviser to Ienobu, 1709–13, and Ietsugu, 1713–16. Retired to write, 1716–25. Died Edo, 29 June 1725.

Principal Writings
Hankanpu (Genealogies of the Shogunate's Protectors), 13 vols., 1702
Seiyō kibun (Notes on What I Heard about the West [Europe] – his account of the interrogation of the captured Italian Catholic missionary Giovanni Sidotti), 1709
Koshitsū (Survey of Ancient History), 1716
Oritaku shiba no ki, *c.*1716; in English as *Told Round a Brushwood Fire: The Autobiography of Arai Hakuseki*, 1980 [autobiography]
Tokushi yoron, 1724; in English as *Lessons from History*, 1982

Further Reading
Blacker, Carmen, "Japanese Historical Writing in the Tokugawa Period," in William G. Beasley and Edwin G. Pulleyblank, eds., *Historians of China and Japan*, London: Oxford University Press, 1961
Kemper, Ulrich, *Arai Hakuseki und seine Geschichtsauffassung* (Arai Hakuseki and his Interpretation of History), Wiesbaden: Harrassowitz, 1967
Nakai, Kate Wildman, *Shogunal Politics: Arai Hakuseki and the Premises of Tokugawa Rule*, Cambridge, MA: Harvard University, Council on East Asian Studies, 1988
Nakai, Kate Wildman, "Tokugawa Confucian Historiography: The Hayashi, the Early Mito School, and Arai Hakuseki," in Peter Nosco, ed., *Confucianism and Tokugawa Culture*, Princeton: Princeton University Press, 1984

Archaeology

As Andrew L. Christenson explained in *Tracing Archaeology's Past* (1989), "Writing the history of archaeology is not possible unless evidence remains for historians to interpret." While the history of archaeology popularly begins with the record of an ancient king's gift to his daughter, it presently involves a highly technical and cooperative effort. Today's archaeologist must integrate proposition formulation with proposition testing.

Technically speaking, until the Italian merchant, Cyriacus of Ancona, also known as Ciriaco de' Pizzicolli, systematically studied antiquity's evidences in the early 15th century, historical archaeology did not exist. Much earlier, Nabonidus, the last Babylonian king (555–538 BCE), had excavated the city of Ur in search of the 2500-year-old Sumerian civilization. According to literary sources, his daughter Belshalti-Nanner, sister of Belshazzar, displayed these artifacts in a special room. Thus began the non-historical, non-comfirmable testimony of archaeology. At this early stage of prehistory, looters, grave robbers, and mercenaries sought hidden treasures and destroyed contextual evidence in the process, rendering impossible the scientific validation of data which could reconstruct past human behavior.

In classical antiquity, Herodotus' ethnographical descriptions bordered anthropological observances but the Greeks failed to approach a historical recording of archaeology. As E.D. Phillips observed in "The Greek Vision of Prehistory," (1964), "[while] they did occasionally make discoveries of archaeological interest and even drew correct conclusions . . . such discoveries were accidental and never made in deliberate search for knowledge of former ages." Other Greek travellers, from Hecataeus of Miletus to Posidonius, chronicled the lifestyles of barbarians they encountered, rationally considering their primitive forerunners albeit in a disorganized and inconsistent manner. Roman "investigations" of antiquity amounted to a systematic looting of the riches of the past. All speculations of the past were devoid of modern archaeological concerns.

In search of relics medieval Europeans plundered ancient sites of which tumuli and megaliths were the most popular. Only the Bible was thought to contain accurate knowledge of the past. For this reason, interpretation of archaeological data was unfairly biased if exercised at all. As northern Italy emerged from waning feudalism, it sought justification for its development by calling on historical precedents from antiquity. The glorious past was emulated by Renaissance scholars. Material as well as literary evidences of the past became increasingly important. Petrarch (1304–74), identified by many as the "father of humanism," considered the study, understanding, and imitation of the past as an essential prerequisite for modelling the ideal of perfection. Influence on his peers led to the first codification of archaeological monuments based on human observation.

Ciriaco de' Pizzicolli (1391–c.1450) studied public inscriptions of ancient monuments across the eastern Mediterranean for a quarter of a century. His systematic gathering and recording of coins, books, and art pieces as well as his drawings of monuments and collection of inscriptions inaugurated the modern era of historical archaeology. The Florentine Cosimo I de' Medici first collected statuary, gems, and specie. From the close of the 15th century, popes like Pius II subventioned entrepreneurs to restore buildings of antiquity situated in the papal states, or like Sixtus IV prohibited exportation of antiquities, while others, like Alexander II, displayed their collections publicly.

Europeans made historical inquiry about the identity of the inhabitants of North and South America, inaugurating attention to potential genealogical connection between these peoples and Tartars, Israelites, Iberians, Carthaginians, and others. This New World archaeology flourished between the 16th and 18th centuries.

However, the center of archaeological investigation remained in Europe proper. In Wales and England, John Leland (1503–52), serving as the King's Antiquary from age thirty, emphasized on-site, topographical investigation of extant prehistory as well as accumulation of lists of present-day genealogies and place-names. He also salvaged books from monastic libraries on the verge of dissolution. In Italy, especially at Palestrina and Tivoli, Andrea Palladio, and Pirro Ligorio surveyed Roman prehistory.

William Camden (1551–1623) produced the first publication of British antiquities in 1586, entitled *Britannia*, which survived as a classical reference tool well into the 19th century. This work provided for the history of archaeology the introduction of the study of what is now termed "crop marks" long before aerial photography was developed. Following this, the investigation of megaliths was advanced by the excavation of Carnac by de Robien (1698–1750). In the 18th and 19th centuries, the term antiquarian, which originally applied to anyone who undertook the task of collecting antiquities from speculating sites, came to identify those who sought to immortalize the past rather than merely to realize economic gain. The field archaeology of William Stukeley (1687–1765) and William Borlase (1695–1772) advanced interpretation of the past beyond reconstruction of antiquity via inaccurate interpretation of the accounts available in classical literature, bringing to a close the era of protoarchaeology based on written sources while ushering in the era of archaeology which gathered description and analysis through firsthand study of the monuments. Christian Jürgensen Thomsen (1788–1865) refined classification of collections of antiquities according to materials used to make tools and weapons, based on Lucretius' Three Age model, establishing the Stone, Bronze, and Iron ages.

In the mid-1850s, Jacques Boucher de Perthes and Hugh Falconer shifted the interest to paleoarchaeology with their interpretation of flint implements discovered in gravel pits with the bones of extinct animals to prove the existence of ancient human life. Charles Darwin (1809–82) and Sir Charles Lyell (1797–1875) produced the first measurable rule for doing modern archaeology in the domain of the natural sciences, a direction that was further developed by the unilinear evolutionary archaeological approaches of Lewis Henry Morgan in his study of the Iroquois, Edward Tylor in his studies on the superiority of European civilization, and Herbert Spencer in his apology for colonialism. Ethnologists Friedrich Ratzel (1844–1941) and Franz Boas (1858–1942)) displaced cultural evolutionism with liberal relativism. Neo-evolutionism was advanced by Leslie White (1900–72) and Julian Steward (1902–75) through the discipline of cultural ecology. White's "basic law of evolution" (Culture = Energy × Technology; $C = E \times T$) championed his concept of General Evolution. Steward applied the notion of "settlement archaeology" which understood household residence to be a product of interactions between the environment and culture. Technological advancements increasingly altered the direction of archaeology through the use of aerial photography, heavy machinery, metal detectors, computer electronics, radiocarbon dating, and more recent developments. In what is now considered a classic article, "The Revolution in Archaeology," (1971), Paul S. Martin likened the changes in the history of archaeology that followed to a religious conversion.

"New Archaeology," the processual movement of the mid-1960s and 1970s, led by Lewis R. Binford and David L. Clarke, promised a revolution that, in reaction, led to historical analyses of the component parts of archaeological studies. Ian Hodder's idea of a "Contextual Archaeology," which is postprocessual, admitted that group relation studies in Binford's new archaeology could disguise social relations as easily as reflect them. Modern archaeological movements have applied differing methodologies and approaches to the discipline including Text-aided Archaeology (Classical, Egyptology, Assyriology) and Prehistoric Archaeology (Antiquarian, Scandinavian-style, Paleolithic-Evolutionary, Culture-Historical, Functional, Processual, and Postprocessual).

Although archaeology will always be limited because the human behavior of antiquity cannot be observed firsthand, the marriage of evolutionism to historicism has ensured that archaeological conclusions will not be diminished, at least in the near future, by external beliefs and societal codes. Instead, it will continue to trace scientifically the development of human behavior from the past, contributing to a balanced understanding of the present.

DENNIS STOUTENBURG

See also America: Pre-Columbian; Prehistory

Further Reading

Aubrey, John, Monumenta Britannica, 1665–93

Binford, Lewis R., Bones: Ancient Men and Modern Myths, London and New York: Academic Press, 1981

Binford, Sally R., and Lewis R. Binford, eds., New Perspectives in Archaeology, Chicago: Aldine, 1968

Borlase, William, Antiquities of Cornwall, London, 1754

Botta, Paul-Emile, Monument du Nenive (Nineveh's Monuments), 5 vols., Paris: Imprimerie Nationale, 1849–50

Brunhouse, Robert Levere, In Search of the Maya: The First Archaeologists, Albuquerque: University of New Mexico Press, 1973

Camden, William, Britannia, London: Newbury, 1586; in English 1610

Carter, Howard, The Tomb of Tutankhamen, 3 vols., London and New York: Cassell, 1923–33; reprinted 1972

Ceram, C.W. [pseudonym of K.W. Marek], Der erste Amerikaner: Das Rätsel des vor-kolumbischen Indianers, Hamburg: Rowohlt, 1972; in English as The First American: A Story of North American Archeology, New York: Harcourt Brace, 1971

Chang, Kwang-chih, The Archaeology of Ancient China, New Haven: Yale University Press, 1963; revised 1977

Chaplin, Raymond Edwin, The Study of Animal Bones from Archaeological Sites, London and New York: Seminar Press, 1971

Childe, Vere Gordon, Dawn of European Civilization, London: Kegan Paul Trench Trübner, and New York: Knopf, 1925; revised 1939, 1947, 1950, 1957

Childe, Vere Gordon, Danube in Prehistory, Oxford: Oxford University Press, 1929; reprinted New York: AMS Press, 1976

Childe, Vere Gordon, Social Evolution, New York: Schuman, 1951; London: Watts, 1952

Christenson, Andrew L., ed., Tracing Archaeology's Past: The Historiography of Archaeology, Carbondale: Southern Illinois University Press, 1989

Clarke, David L., Analytical Archaeology, London: Methuen, 1968; revised London: Methuen, and New York: Columbia University Press, 1978

Daniel, Glyn, ed., Towards a History of Archaeology, London: Thames and Hudson, 1981

Darwin, Charles, Journal of Researches into the Geology and Natural History of the Various Countries Visited by HMS Beagle, under the Command of Captain Fitzroy, RN, from 1832 to 1836, London: Colbourn, 1839; revised 1839; reprinted as The Voyage of the Beagle, 1905

Darwin, Charles, On the Origin of Species by Means of Natural Selection; or, The Preservation of Favoured Races in the Struggle for Life, London: Murray, 1859, New York: Appleton, 1860; 6 revisions, 1860–76

Darwin, Charles, The Descent of Man, and Selection in Relation to Sex, 2 vols., London: Murray, and New York: Appleton, 1871

Davis, Joseph B., and John Thurman, Crania Britannica: Delineations and Descriptions of the Skulls of the Aboriginal and Early Inhabitants of the British Isles, 2 vols., London: privately printed, 1865

Dymond, D.P., Archaeology and History: A Plea for Reconciliation, London: Thames and Hudson, 1974

Gould, Richard A., Living Archaeology, Cambridge and New York: Cambridge University Press, 1980

Hodder, Ian, Reading the Past: Current Approaches to Interpretation in Archaeology, Cambridge and New York: Cambridge University Press, 1986

Hudson, Kenneth, A Social History of Archaeology: The British Experience, London: Macmillan, 1981

Klindt-Jensen, Ole, A History of Scandinavian Archaeology, London: Thames and Hudson, 1975

Laming-Emperaire, Annette, Origines de l'archéologie préhistorique en France, des superstitions médiévales à la découverte de l'homme fossile (Origins of Prehistoric Archaeology in France: Medieval Beliefs and the Discovery of Human Fossils), Paris: Picard, 1964

Lartet, Edouard, and Henry Christy, Reliquiae Aquitanicae, Being Contributions to the Archaeology and Paleontology of Périgord and Adjoining Provinces of Southern France, London: Williams and Norgate, 1865–75

Layard, Austen Henry, Nineveh and Its Remains, 2 vols., London: Murray, 1849; New York: Putnam, 1850

Leakey, Mary, Disclosing the Past: An Autobiography, Garden City, NY: Doubleday, and London: Weidenfeld and Nicolson, 1984

Leone, Mark P., ed., Contemporary Archaeology: A Guide to Theory and Contributions, Carbondale, IL: Southern Illinois University Press, 1972

Levine, Philippa, The Amateur and the Professional: Antiquarians, Historians, and Archaeologists in Victorian England, 1838–1886, Cambridge and New York: Cambridge University Press, 1986

Lloyd, Seton H., Foundations in the Dust: A Story of Mesopotamian Exploration, Oxford and New York: Oxford University Press, 1947; revised London: Thames and Hudson, 1980

Lubbock, John, Pre-historic Times, as Illustrated by Ancient Remains, and the Manners and Customs of Modern Savages, London: Williams and Norgate, 1865; New York: Appleton, 1872

Lubbock, John, The Origin of Civilisation and the Primitive Condition of Man: Mental and Social Conditions of Savages, London: Longman, 1870; New York: Appleton, 1871

MacNeish, Richard S., The Science of Archaeology?, North Scituate, MA: Duxbury Press, 1978

Martin, Paul S., "The Revolution in Archaeology," American Antiquity 36 (1971), 1–8

Meltzer, David J., Don D. Fowler, and Jeremy A. Sabloff, eds., American Archaeology, Past and Future: A Celebration of the Society for American Archaeology 1935–1985, Washington, DC: Smithsonian Institution Press, 1986

Michels, Joseph W., Dating Methods in Archaeology, New York: Seminar Press, 1973

Montfaucon, Bernard de, *L'Antiquité expliquée et représentée en figures*, 5 vols. in 10, Paris: Delaulne, 1719–24; in English as *Antiquity Explained, and Represented in Sculpture*, London: Tonson and Watts, 1721–22; reprinted in 2 vols., New York: Garland, 1976

Nilsson, Sven, *Skandinaviska Nordens Ur-invånare*, 2 vols., Lund: Berlingska, 1838–43

Petrie, William Matthews Flinders, *Methods and Aims in Archaeology*, London and New York: Macmillan, 1904; reprinted 1972

Phillips, E.D., "The Greek Vision of Prehistory," *Antiquity* 38 (1964), 171–78

Redman, Charles L., ed., *Research and Theory in Current Anthropology*, New York: Wiley, 1973

Renfrew, Colin, *Before Civilization: The Radiocarbon Revolution and Prehistoric Europe*, London: Cape, and New York: Knopf, 1973

Schliemann, Heinrich, *Ilios: Stadt und Land der Trojaner*, Leipzig: Brookhaus, 1881; in English as *Ilios: The City and Country of the Trojans*, London: Murray, 1880, New York: Harper, 1881; reprinted 1981

Semenov, Sergei Aristarkhovich, *Pervobytnaia teknika: Opyt izucheniia drevneishikh orudsii i izdelii po sledam roboty*, Moscow: Izd-vo Akademii nauk SSR, 1957; in English as *Prehistoric Technology: An Experimental Study of the Oldest Tools and Artefacts from Times of Manufacture and Wear*, London: Cory Adams and Mackay, and New York: Barnes and Noble, 1964

Service, Elman R., *Primitive Social Organization: An Evolutionary Perspective*, New York: Random House, 1962

South, Stanley A., *Method and Theory in Historical Archaeology*, New York: Academic Press, 1977

Stukeley, William, *Itinerarium curiosum; or, An Account of the Antiquitys and Remarkable Curiositys in Nature or Art, Observ'd in Travels Thro' Great Britain*, London, 1724; revised 1776

Thomsen, Christian Jürgensen, *Ledetraad til Nordisk Oldkyndighed* (A Guide to Northern Antiquities), Copenhagen: Møllers, 1836

Trigger, Bruce G., *Beyond History: The Methods of Prehistory*, New York: Holt Rinehart, 1968

Tylor, Edward, *Anthropology: An Introduction to the Study of Man and Civilization*, London: Macmillan, and New York: Appleton, 1881

Watson, Patty Jo, Steven A. LeBlanc, and Charles L. Redman, *Explanation in Archaeology: An Explicitly Scientific Approach*, New York: Columbia University Press, 1971

Winckelmann, J.J., *Geschichte der Kunst des Altertums*, Dresden: Walterischen, 1764; in English as *The History of Ancient Art*, 4 vols., Boston: Osgood, 1849–73

Worsaae, Jens Jakob Asmussen, *Danmarks Oldtid* (Ancient Denmark), Copenhagen: Klein, 1842

Argentina

Argentina, one of the strongest Latin American countries in terms of economic development, has been shaped by its colonial past in innumerable ways. Once a backwater of the Spanish empire, it flourished in the late 17th and 18th centuries. A leading proponent of independence during the early 19th century, it suffered economic stagnation and political turmoil until the export sector contributed to its entry into world economy and to unparalleled economic growth and prosperity. The liberal dream of unending economic progress soon shattered with the depression of the 1930s and the emergence of authoritarian regimes. Subsequently, the military regimes of the 1960s, 1970s, and early 1980s tarnished Argentina's image abroad with its

desaparecidos (disappeared ones), economic decline, debt, and the foolhardy military adventure of the Falklands War. After that humiliation, authoritarianism gave way to greater democracy and economic liberalization during the remainder of the 1980s and 1990s. How have historians approached the complex texture of Argentina's history? Investigating the lost opportunities of a country with so much potential for economic growth and democracy, scholars have written extensively on the various questions surrounding that nation's ideological, political, social, and economic developments.

The roots of Argentina's political and economic problems stem from the colonial inheritance of Spanish rule, which it shared with the other Spanish American nations. Argentina's early colonial history has not been adequately studied because of its frontier status. On the frontier, the mission played an important role as the first stage of capitalist penetration into the territories of precapitalist peoples and cultures, and their subsequent incorporation into an emerging world market. Magnus Mörner's pioneering monograph *The Political and Economic Activities of the Jesuits in the La Plata Region* (1953) examined the role of the Jesuits in establishing a mission system during the early phase of colonization, up to 1700. Nicholas P. Cushner, expanding on this earlier work, studied the Jesuits' mission economy in *Jesuit Ranches and the Agrarian Development of Colonial Argentina, 1650–1767* (1983). His investigation provided a detailed analysis of the workings of the mission commercial enterprise before the establishment by the Spanish Bourbons of the viceroyalty of the Rio de la Plata in 1776.

The creation of the viceroyalty signified the growing importance of this peripheral region to the Spanish imperial system. Contraband trade and Portuguese incursions into the Rio de La Plata influenced Bourbon policy in creating a more substantial Spanish presence for defensive purposes. Modeled on French administrative organization, the Bourbons established the intendant system in their new viceroyalty as a means to centralize authority. John Lynch's fundamental work *Spanish Colonial Administration, 1782–1810* (1958) supplied a critical understanding of this reform's impact on the political and economic structures of the region. The Bourbon reforms stimulated economic development during the 18th century, contributing to the emerging status of Buenos Aires as an entrepôt for imports and exports.

James R. Scobie emphasized the importance of the rise of Buenos Aires as an explanatory tool for an understanding of Argentine history in *Argentina: A City and a Nation* (1964). The city became the center of government and commerce during the 18th century. Susan Migden Socolow, an astute historian of the colonial merchant and government elites of Buenos Aires, explored the impact of Bourbon bureaucratic modernization in *The Bureaucrats of Buenos Aires, 1769–1810* (1987). An earlier study by Socolow, *The Merchants of Buenos Aires, 1778–1810* (1978), focused on the important and influential group of merchants that benefited from Bourbon commercial policy. Most research has been on the large import merchants of the capital, although Jay Kinsbruner's comparative study, *Petty Capitalism in Spanish America* (1987), remains unique in its concentration on a lesser known group of retail grocers in Buenos Aires and other Spanish colonial cities from 1750 to 1850.

As a result of this tremendous economic growth, Buenos Aires would be one of the first cities to struggle for independence from Spain and its odious monopolistic commercial policies. The commercial disruption caused by Spain's embroilment in the European wars of the Napoleonic era influenced the merchant elite's desire for independence. Most works have concentrated on Buenos Aires, but the pre-eminent scholar of Argentine history, Tulio Halperín-Donghi, in his masterful work *Politics, Economics, and Society in Argentina in the Revolutionary Period* (1975), provided a detailed social and political history that analyzed not only the events in the capital but also in the provinces. A consummate historian, Halperín-Donghi demonstrated a superb command of provincial history as he elucidated this critical period of transition from colony to nation.

During the first half of the 19th century, *caudillo* politics dominated the life of the new republic as the interior provinces struggled against the encroaching hegemony of Buenos Aires. The breakdown of the colonial state caused divisions between the interior provinces and capital as Buenos Aires sought to implement liberal political and economic reforms that were supported by creole merchants and professionals in the wake of independence. The interior provinces and conservative governments reacted against these innovations, as attested by David Bushnell's examination of the period's liberal legislation in *Reform and Reaction in the Platine Provinces, 1810–1852* (1983). The author surveyed not only the resistance of a sector of Buenos Aires society against this modernization by law but also the reaction of the traditional *caudillos* and their followers in the interior. The provinces put their hope in the quintessential *caudillo* of 19th-century Argentina, Juan Manuel de Rosas, who dominated Argentina's political, social, and economic life from 1835 to 1852. In the first English-language treatment of Rosas, John Lynch analyzed the career of one of the most polemical figures in Argentine historiography in *Argentine Dictator: Juan Manuel de Rosas, 1829–1852* (1981). Earlier biographers concentrated on the dominant liberal figures of the period, Domingo Faustino Sarmiento and Bartolomé Mitre, both future presidents who were opposed to Rosas. Allison Williams Bunkley's *The Life of Sarmiento* (1952) and William Jeffrey's *Mitre and Argentina* (1952) were sympathetic treatments of these liberal statesmen and nation-builders. Intellectual historians have investigated the traditional and liberal ideas that contributed to the century's political strife. An early work by José Luis Romero, *Las ideas políticas en Argentina* (1946; *A History of Argentine Political Thought*, 1963), was a general survey of the history of political ideas from the colonial period to the 1940s written from a 20th-century liberal perspective. On the other hand, Nicolas Shumway's *The Invention of Argentina* (1991) concentrated exclusively on the period from 1808 to 1880 and the guiding national myths that contributed to the creation of an Argentine nationality based on exclusion.

Economic historians have also fastened on the finances and economic growth of the early 19th century and their relationship to political instability. An early attempt to bring some economic understanding to the seeming political chaos of the early republic was Miron Burgin's *The Economic Aspects of Argentine Federalism, 1820–1852* (1946), which analyzed not only Rosas' economic policies, but the constraints and

possibilities open to him. Focusing on Argentina's phenomenal economic growth from 1880 to 1930, economic historians have largely ignored the history of exports prior to this golden age. Hilda Sábato's *Agrarian Capitalism and the World Market* (1990) examined the early phase of Argentina's economic growth based on wool exports. Another work on early economic development is Jonathan C. Brown's *A Socioeconomic History of Argentina, 1776–1860* (1979), which carried a deceptive title since it is, in actuality, an investigation of the relationship between the growth of trade in Buenos Aires and the development of agribusiness in the surrounding province. Douglas Friedman also studied this early period in *The State and Underdevelopment in Spanish America* (1984), a perceptive comparative study that argued against dependency theory by exploring the internal factors that contributed to the growth of the export sector and, subsequently, "dependence." He concluded that it was the need to achieve internal political stability through access to economic resources that led to the decision to concentrate on exports, the only source of revenues.

No examination of Argentine economic history can ignore the important role of Britain and the British merchant in the 19th century. Henry S. Ferns, utilizing the archives of the British Foreign Office, appraised the political, economic, and financial relationship between the two nations in *Britain and Argentina in the Nineteenth Century* (1960). More recently, Vera Blinn Reber, through exhaustive research in British and Argentine archives, investigated 19th-century Argentina's integration into the world market by looking at British commercial houses in *British Mercantile Houses in Buenos Aires, 1810–1880* (1979). Besides studying these institutions, she also provided a portrait of the British community in Buenos Aires.

During the latter half of the 19th century, Argentina's export economy contributed to some degree of political stability. The nation's world market integration depended on the development of a viable infrastructure that would link the provinces and their agricultural exports to the ports of Buenos Aires. British capital invested heavily during the 19th century in the creation of Argentina's railroads, which many scholars have seen as symbolic of the nation's economic dependence. Two studies, Colin M. Lewis' *British Railways in Argentina, 1857–1914* (1983) and Winthrop R. Wright's *British-Owned Railways in Argentina* (1974), explored the impact of British investments on Argentina's economic development. Based on British archival research, Lewis' study counteracted arguments made by Argentina's economic nationalists who condemned the railroads as a guise for British imperialism. He appeared to be responding to Wright's earlier investigation that analyzed the rise of economic nationalism and Peronismo as a response to the undue influence of British interests on Argentina's economy. Overall, Lewis, apparently influenced by the economic historian D.C.M. Platt, concluded that these investments were beneficial to Argentina.

The railroads contributed to the development of the provinces and the production of agricultural exports on the pampas. Scobie's *Revolution on the Pampas* (1964) examined the crucial period of world market integration at the end of the 19th century. Other scholars have followed Scobie's lead by concentrating on Argentina's agricultural history. *The Agricultural Development of Argentina* (1969), by Darrell F. Fienup, Russell H. Brannon, and Frank A. Fender, was a general review of that history with policy recommendations. Using a social science methodology, Peter H. Smith scrutinized how the beef industry interests affected the nation's political life up to 1946 in *Politics and Beef in Argentina* (1969). Carl E. Solberg provided a comparative framework to answer why Canadian wheat became more productive than Argentina's in *The Prairies and the Pampas* (1987). His approach contemplated the role of state intervention, or the lack of it, in the divergent outcomes of these two nations.

A few historians have focused at the regional level on late 19th- and early 20th-century Argentina's phenomenal economic growth. Many of these projects were also works of social and urban history. To complement his work on the pampas, Scobie concentrated on Buenos Aires during this period in *Buenos Aires* (1974), in which he argued that the commercial-bureaucratic nature of the city contributed to its development as a hub for the nation. Scobie also worked on an analysis of the export era's effect on three provincial capitals: Corrientes, Salta, and Mendoza. His *Secondary Cities of Argentina* (1988), a work of regional and urban history, investigated how demographic and social factors could account for differential economic growth. Donna J. Guy's research on the domestic market for sugar during the export era, *Argentine Sugar Politics* (1980), focused on the divisions among the elites associated with exports and those involved with domestic production. During this period, the arrival of thousands of European immigrants contributed to economic development in Buenos Aires and the interior. By exploring one of the most important interior cities, Córdoba, Mark D. Szuchman revealed this population's social mobility in *Mobility and Integration in Urban Argentina* (1980), an urban and social history.

Social historians of 19th-century Argentina have contributed to our understanding of various facets of the social life of neglected groups. One group that has not received sufficient attention from historians is the black population, which comprised approximately a third of Buenos Aires' population by the end of the colonial period. George Reid Andrews' *The Afro-Argentines of Buenos Aires, 1800–1900* (1980) filled in this lacuna in our historical knowledge by examining the "disappearance" of the city's black community. He demonstrated that blacks played a significant role in the War of Independence and the subsequent *caudillo* politics of the 19th century. Although officially "extinct" by the end of the century, the black community continued to maintain a vibrant urban life into the 1880s and 1890s. Also suffering official misinterpretation is the figure of the gaucho, who, with the onslaught of modernization on the pampas, was soon relegated to the status of vagrant and social outcast. The export era transformed the life of the gaucho who became a peon on the large *estancias* (ranches) of the nation's landed elite. Richard W. Slatta studied this transformation of the gaucho from free man to hired hand and literary myth in *Gauchos and the Vanishing Frontier* (1983).

The influx of European immigrants to the pampas also circumscribed the gaucho's life. Immigrant history is well represented in numerous studies of the various European groups that came searching for work in the pampas and Buenos Aires. Ezequiel Gallo examined the participation of Swiss and German immigrants in the agrarian unrest that swept Santa Fe province during Argentina's golden age in *Farmers in Revolt*

(1976). Ronald C. Newton's *German Buenos Aires* (1977) was a close analysis of how the city's German community began the 20th century with ethnic solidarity, but later became riven with class and political divisions. Jewish immigrants also received the attention of scholars during the last two decades. Robert Weisbrot researched the internal organization of Argentina's Jewish community in *The Jews of Argentina* (1979). Another work on the Jewish diaspora to Argentina is *From Pale to Pampa* (1982), by Eugene F. Sofer, which looked exclusively at the Eastern European Jews who settled in Buenos Aires. The reception of these foreign immigrants and the rise of nationalism was examined by Carl E. Solberg in *Immigration and Nationalism* (1970), a comparative analysis based on the writings of Argentine and Chilean intellectuals as well as newspapers and journals of the period. One lasting legacy of the immigrant experience on world popular culture has been the tango. Simon Collier's *The Life, Music, and Times of Carlos Gardel* (1986), about the famous tango dancer and Argentine national icon, is much more than a biography; it is also a cultural history about the role of the tango in the lives of immigrants.

Historians of the family and gender have investigated other aspects of Argentina's 19th-century social history. Mark D. Szuchman studied the relationship between the family, education, and the state during the period of *caudillo* politics under Rosas in *Order, Family, and Community in Buenos Aires, 1810–1860* (1988). He concluded that Rosas brought relative stability to Buenos Aires for the lower classes. Public education, reflecting authoritarian values, played an important role in undermining former attachments to family and neighborhood, while emphasizing loyalty to the state. The role of prostitution in defining work, family, class, and citizenship in late 19th- and early 20th-century Buenos Aires was treated in Donna J. Guy's *Sex and Danger in Buenos Aires* (1991). She argued that the upper and middle classes feared the underworld that the prostitutes inhabited. Some of this fear sprang from the large number of immigrants involved in prostitution. The call for social control was intertwined with the idea that prostitution was subverting the traditional norms of the family, society, and nation.

Peronismo dominated the political landscape of the latter half of the 20th century in Argentina. In order to gain an understanding of the roots of this phenomena, political historians have researched the period prior to the rise of the movement. Early 20th-century Argentina saw the rise of numerous political parties supported by the new interest groups called into existence by export-led growth, the emerging middle classes, and working-class and immigrant groups. One of the most important political parties of this period was the Radical party, which ruled Argentina from 1914 to 1930. David Rock's *Politics in Argentina, 1890–1930* (1975) was a perceptive analysis of this party's triumph and defeat. This study investigated how the export sector, based on landed interests, founded a socioeconomic structure that could not accommodate the divergent class interests created by economic growth. The Radical party, supported by the urban middle class, soon lost this constituency when it could not fulfill its promises of reform. The rising working-class movement proved another challenge to Radical party politics. Richard J. Walter provided a narrative history of Argentina's Socialist party in *The Socialist*

Party of Argentina, 1890–1930 (1977), which explored the role of the party on a national level. These challenges to the traditional political, social, and economic structures, especially the *Semana Trágica* (Tragic Week) of January 1919, caused a reaction by Argentina's conservative forces, embodied in the Argentine Patriotic League. Sandra McGee Deutsch's *Counterrevolution in Argentina, 1900–1932* (1986) concentrated on the league's role in Argentina's politics from 1919 to 1923. Richard J. Walter examined this turbulent period on a regional level in *The Province of Buenos Aires and Argentine Politics, 1912–1943* (1985), which surveyed the conflict between the province and the federal government as well as that of the Conservative and Radical parties for control of the province. Using a comparative methodology, Karen L. Remmer probed the competitive party systems of Argentina and Chile and the subsequent implementation of social legislation in *Party Competition in Argentina and Chile* (1984). She concluded that Chile's elitist political system hindered viable social legislation while Argentina's political elites had to respond to the nation's divergent interests by passing significant social legislation. Peter H. Smith applied a statistical methodology to gain an understanding of the early and mid-20th-century political history of Argentina in *Argentina and the Failure of Democracy* (1974), which concentrated on a computer analysis of the Chamber of Deputies during the years under review. He also examined the various political parties of the early 20th century and the rise of Peronismo from its populist roots in the 1940s to its nominal demise in the 1950s when it became bureaucratic and authoritarian in nature.

There have been numerous interpretations of Peronismo by historians in a variety of fields since the emergence of the movement in the 1940s. This fascination persisted as the influence of Peronismo continued to resonate in the political life of the country. Seeking to understand Argentina by understanding Juan Domingo Perón, one of the many populist leaders that emerged in Latin America in the 1930s and 1940s, historians have focused on biography for a glimpse of this controversial figure who led the destiny of his nation along with his wife, Evita. Three representative biographies were Robert J. Alexander's *Juan Domingo Perón* (1979), Joseph A. Page's *Perón: A Biography* (1983), and Robert D. Crassweller's *Perón and the Enigma of Argentina* (1987). Alexander's work strove for objectivity in the face of conflicting interpretations of this populist leader's life and influence on Argentina's political and economic life. On the other hand, some have characterized Page's biography as revisionist in nature. This comprehensive work, which covers Perón's life from birth to death, scrutinized the varying interpretations surrounding his major decisions. Crassweller's book was a much more ambitious study that focused on cultural and psychological factors for an explanation of Perón and Peronismo. The subject of musicals and movies, Perón's wife, Evita, has also received her share of attention by historians. *Eva Perón* (1980), by Nicholas Fraser and Marysa Navarro, was a standard biography that related Evita's life in a straightforward, objective manner. Julie M. Taylor's *Eva Perón: The Myths of a Woman* (1979) was a unique exploration of the three myths about Evita as the Lady of Hope, the Black Myth, and Revolutionary Eva. She used an anthropological methodology to understand the symbol of Evita and its perception by various sectors of Argentine society.

Historians captivated by Peronismo have also produced general histories from a variety of perspectives. Early works on Argentina under Perón are George I. Blanksten's *Perón's Argentina* (1953), which focused on Perón's first administration, and Arthur P. Whitaker's *Argentine Upheaval* (1956), an account of the 1955 and 1956 events that led to the collapse of Perón's regime. In search of its foundations, scholars have focused their attention on one of the pillars of Peronismo, labor. This labor history situated the movement's rise with the rapid industrial growth of the early 20th century and the emergence of a strong working class that challenged the nation's traditional structures. David Tamarin analyzed the unionization of the working class during the Depression and its transformation into an organized political force in *The Argentine Labor Movement, 1930–1945* (1985). The author also explored labor's relationship to the military government of 1943 to 1945.

Joel Horowitz's empirical study, *Argentine Unions, the State, and the Rise of Perón, 1930–1945* (1990) investigated similar terrain, but concentrated on the period of the *Concordancia* from 1932 to 1943. By studying the period's union periodicals and other important sources, such as interviews with union leaders, he surveyed not only the links between the unions and the state, but also how Perón mobilized labor for his ultimate victory in 1945. Daniel James' research observed the effect of the legacy of Peronismo on the working class during the period from 1955 to 1973 in *Resistance and Integration* (1988). This legacy is one of ambivalence and contradictory aims as Peronismo could accommodate the visions of a left utopia or an authoritarian present.

Perón's fall did not diminish his influence or that of his movement on the political, social, and economic struggles of 20th-century Argentina. The traditional political elites had to respond to Peronismo's attraction to the nation's masses. Lars Schoultz's *The Populist Challenge* (1983) investigated the political hangover of Peronismo on Argentina's body politic and concluded that its legacy, as well as the liberal response, will continue to haunt the nation into the future. Others have also studied the question of the legacy of Peronismo on events of the 1960s and 1970s. One group that had an abiding impact on the Argentina of these decades was the Montoneros, a leftist urban guerrilla group. Richard Gillespie's *Soldiers of Perón* (1983) was a definitive study of this group, which made use of many interviews with leaders of the movement as well as internal documents for an understanding of their ideology and basis for actions. Donald C. Hodges also studied the Montoneros, as well as other revolutionary groups, in *Argentina, 1943–1987: The National Revolution and Resistance* (revised 1988), an analysis of how revolutionary groups have had an impact on Argentine politics since World War II. Both Gillespie and Hodges are sympathetic to the Montoneros and the social revolution promised under the inspiration of the leftist ideas implicit in Peronismo.

The military, Peronismo's other pillar, has received some attention from historians as they have sought to understand that institution's role in the political life of the country. Robert A. Potash has written an excellent 3-volume study of the army since 1928 which examined the role of the army and the motivation of individual officers in the major political events of the period. Potash concluded that it was not lust for power that led to the military's intervention, but the civil sector's failure to unite to defend constitutional government. Another treatment of the military is Marvin Goldwert's *Democracy, Militarism, and Nationalism in Argentina, 1930–1966* (1972), which, instead of exploring personal motivations and ties between officers as Potash had, dissected the ideology of the officers. He divided the ideology of nationalism into two distinct currents, a liberal nationalism and an integral nationalism, and situated the origins of liberal nationalism with Sarmiento and Mitre, while associating integral nationalism with Rosas. For Goldwert, these two contradictory currents influenced the decisions and actions of Argentina's military officers.

Economic historians have also tackled the thorny history of 20th-century Argentina. An early general overview of Argentina's economy is *La economía argentina* (1963; *The Argentine Economy*, 1967), written by the former cabinet minister Aldo Ferrer. An introduction to the nation's 20th-century economic history is Laura Randall's *An Economic History of Argentina in the Twentieth Century* (1978), which countered the dependency analysis of Argentine history by relying on an econometric methodology. William C. Smith provided an overview of the late 20th century in *Authoritarianism and the Crisis of the Argentine Political Economy* (1989), which investigated the political economy of Argentina during the period of authoritarian rule in the 1960s, 1970s, and early 1980s. A specialized study of a particular industry is Carl E. Solberg's *Oil and Nationalism in Argentina* (1979), which examined the relationship between the oil industry and the rise of economic nationalism.

During the 20th century the United States supplanted Britain as the dominant force in Latin America. The decline of Britain's influence over Argentina's export sector was traced by Roger Gravil, *The Anglo-Argentine Connection, 1900–1939* (1985), which explored the issues surrounding the impact of this relationship by focusing on trade. Some have argued that the British exploited the Argentine economy and contributed to the nation's underdevelopment. Others have explained Argentina's economic decline as a result of Perón's policies regarding British investment in the economy. The relationship between the United States and Argentina has always been a stormy one. An initial diplomatic history of relations between the two nations was Harold F. Peterson's *Argentina and the United States, 1810–1960* (1964), which examined the emergence of the conflict between the two nations. Joseph S. Tulchin surveyed the development of this antagonism in *Argentina and the United States* (1990), which concluded that it was the similarities of moralism, messianism, and exceptionalism that have kept the US and Argentina apart. The fragile ties between the two nations were sorely tested during World War II as a result of the German influence on the nation's military leaders. Ronald C. Newton explored the supposed threat in *The "Nazi Menace" in Argentina, 1931–1947* (1992); he lambasted US reaction and contrasted it with British diplomacy during this crucial period. Newton also studied the Nazi agents and their influence on Argentina's German community. Taking a comparative approach, Michael J. Francis' *The Limits of Hegemony* (1977) examined Argentina and Chile and how the relationship of the elite of each nation to the US determined its foreign policy. More specifically, Randall Bennett Woods investigated the emergence of US policy toward Argentina during the war as it took shape in the corridors of the US State Department

in *The Roosevelt Foreign Press Policy Establishment and the "Good Neighbor"* (1979).

In 1982, the British defeated Argentina in the Falklands War, which led to the subsequent discredit of the military regimes of the 1960s, 1970s, and early 1980s. Humiliated, the military stepped down from power and allowed democracy to return to the country. David Rock's excellent study of Argentina history provided a sweeping analysis of how the tributary colonial institutions shaped contemporary Argentina's political, social, and economic life. His interpretation ended with the arrival of democracy under the administration of the Radical party candidate Raul Alfonsín. Since 1989, Carlos Sadl Menem, a Perónist, has ruled the destiny of his country by instituting a neoliberal economic program in order to create a free-market economy. His policies have created havoc within the Perónist party as pro- and anti-Menem wings developed. Argentina's future is uncertain as it attempts to modernize its political, social, and economic structures in the late 20th century.

CARLOS PÉREZ

See also Germani; Halperín-Donghi; Latin America: National; Lavrin; Levene; Mitre; Prebisch; Rock; Romero; Scobie; Women's History: Latin America

Further Reading

Alexander, Robert Jackson, *Juan Domingo Perón*, Boulder, CO: Westview Press, 1979

Andrews, George Reid, *The Afro-Argentines of Buenos Aires, 1800–1900*, Madison: University of Wisconsin Press, 1980

Baily, Samuel L., *Labor, Nationalism, and Politics in Argentina*, New Brunswick, NJ: Rutgers University Press, 1967

Barager, Joseph R., "The Historiography of the Rio de la Plata Area since 1830," *Hispanic American Historical Review* 39 (1959), 588–642

Blanksten, George I., *Perón's Argentina*, Chicago: University of Chicago Press, 1953

Bouvard, Marguerite Guzman, *Revolutionizing Motherhood: The Mothers of the Plaza de Mayo*, Wilmington, DE: Scholarly Resources, 1994

Brown, Jonathan C., *A Socioeconomic History of Argentina, 1776–1860*, Cambridge and New York: Cambridge University Press, 1979

Brown, Jonathan C., "The Bondage of Old Habits in Nineteenth-Century Argentina," *Latin American Research Review* 21 (1986), 3–31

Bunkley, Allison Williams, *The Life of Sarmiento*, Princeton: Princeton University Press, 1952; reprinted New York: Greenwood Press, 1969

Burgin, Miron, *The Economic Aspects of Argentine Federalism, 1820–1852*, Cambridge, MA: Harvard University Press, 1946; reprinted New York: Russell, 1971

Bushnell, David, *Reform and Reaction in the Platine Provinces, 1810–1852*, Gainesville: University Presses of Florida, 1983

Calvert, Susan, and Peter Calvert, *Argentina: Political Culture and Instability*, Pittsburgh: University of Pittsburgh Press, and Basingstoke: Macmillan, 1989

Ciria, Alberto, *Partidos y poder en la Argentina moderna*, Buenos Aires: Alvarez, 1964; in English as *Parties and Power in Modern Argentina, 1930–1946*, Albany: State University of New York Press, 1974

Collier, Simon, *The Life, Music, and Times of Carlos Gardel*, Pittsburgh: University of Pittsburgh Press, 1986

Crassweller, Robert D., *Perón and the Enigma of Argentina*, New York: Norton, 1987

Cushner, Nicholas P., *Jesuit Ranches and the Agrarian Development of Colonial Argentina, 1650–1767*, Albany: State University of New York Press, 1983

Denis, Pierre, *La République argentine: la mise en valeur du pays*, Paris: Colin, 1920; in English as *The Argentine Republic: Its Development and Progress*, London: Unwin, and New York: Scribner, 1922

Deutsch, Sandra McGee, *Counterrevolution in Argentina, 1900–1932: The Argentine Patriotic League*, Lincoln: University of Nebraska Press, 1986

Ferns, Henry Stanley, *Britain and Argentina in the Nineteenth Century*, Oxford: Clarendon Press, 1960; New York: Arno, 1977

Ferrer, Aldo, *La economía argentina: las etapas de su desarrollo y problemas actuales*, Mexico City: Fondo de Cultura Economica, 1963; in English as *The Argentine Economy*, Berkeley: University of California Press, 1967

Fienup, Darrell F., Russell H. Brannon, and Frank A. Fender, *The Agricultural Development of Argentina: A Policy and Development Perspective*, New York: Praeger, 1969

Francis, Michael J., *The Limits of Hegemony: United States Relations with Argentina and Chile during World War II*, Notre Dame, IN: University of Notre Dame Press, 1977

Fraser, Nicholas, and Marysa Navarro, *Eva Perón*, London: Deutsch, 1980; New York: Norton, 1981

Friedman, Douglas, *The State and Underdevelopment in Spanish America: The Political Roots of Dependency in Peru and Argentina*, Boulder, CO: Westview Press, 1984

Gallo, Ezequiel, *Farmers in Revolt: The Revolution of 1893 in the Province of Santa Fe, Argentina*, London: University of London Institute of Latin American Studies, 1976

Gavshon, Arthur L., and Desmond Rice, *The Sinking of the "Belgrano,"* London: Secker and Warburg, 1983

Gillespie, Richard, *Soldiers of Perón: Argentina's Montoneros*, Oxford and New York: Oxford University Press, 1983

Goldwert, Marvin, *Democracy, Militarism, and Nationalism in Argentina, 1930–1966: An Interpretation*, Austin: University of Texas Press, 1972

Gravil, Roger, *The Anglo-Argentine Connection, 1900–1939*, Boulder, CO: Westview Press, 1985

Guy, Donna J., *Argentine Sugar Politics: Tucumán and the Generation of Eighty*, Tempe: Arizona State University Center for Latin American Studies, 1980

Guy, Donna J., *Sex and Danger in Buenos Aires: Prostitution, Family, and Nation in Argentina*, Lincoln: University of Nebraska Press, 1991

Halperín-Donghi, Tulio, *Politics, Economics, and Society in Argentina in the Revolutionary Period*, Cambridge and New York: Cambridge University Press, 1975

Hodges, Donald C., *Argentina, 1943–1976: The National Revolution and Resistance*, Albuquerque: University of New Mexico Press, 1976; revised (with dates 1943–1987) 1988

Horowitz, Joel, *Argentine Unions, the State, and the Rise of Perón, 1930–1945*, Berkeley: University of California Institute of International Studies, 1990

James, Daniel, *Resistance and Integration: Peronismo and the Argentine Working Class, 1946–1976*, Cambridge and New York: Cambridge University Press, 1988

Jeffrey, William, *Mitre and Argentina*, New York: Library Publishers, 1952

Kinsbruner, Jay, *Petty Capitalism in Spanish America: The Pulperos of Puebla, Mexico City, Caracas, and Buenos Aires*, Boulder, CO: Westview Press, 1987

Leonard, V.W., *Politicians, Pupils, and Priests: Argentine Education since 1943*, New York: Lang, 1989

Lewis, Colin M., *British Railways in Argentina, 1857–1914: A Case Study of Foreign Investment*, London: Athlone Press, and Atlantic Highlands, NJ: Humanities Press, 1983

Lewis, Paul H., *The Crisis of Argentine Capitalism*, Chapel Hill: University of North Carolina Press, 1990

Luis de Imaz, José, *Los que mandan*, Buenos Aires: Editorial Universitaria de Buenos Aires, 1964; in English as *Los que mandan (Those Who Rule)*, Notre Dame, IN: University of Notre Dame Press, 1977

Lynch, John, *Spanish Colonial Administration, 1782–1810: The Intendant System in the Viceroyalty of the Río de la Plata*, London: Athlone Press, 1958; New York: Greenwood Press, 1969

Lynch, John, *Argentine Dictator: Juan Manuel de Rosas, 1829–1852*, Oxford and New York: Oxford University Press, 1981

McGann, Thomas Francis, *Argentina, the United States, and the Inter-American System, 1880–1914*, Cambridge, MA: Harvard University Press, 1957

Mörner, Magnus, *The Political and Economic Activities of the Jesuits in the La Plata Region*, Stockholm: Institute of Ibero-American Studies, 1953

Munck, Ronaldo, *Argentina, from Anarchism to Peronismo: Workers, Unions, and Politics, 1855–1985*, London: Zed Press, 1987

Newton, Ronald C., *German Buenos Aires, 1900–1933: Social Change and Cultural Crisis*, Austin: University of Texas Press, 1977

Newton, Ronald C., *The "Nazi Menace" in Argentina, 1931–1947*, Stanford, CA: Stanford University Press, 1992

O'Donnell, Guillermo, *1966–1793, el estado burocrático autoritario: triunfos, derrotas y crisis*, Buenos Aires: Editorial de Belgrano, 1982; in English as *Bureaucratic Authoritarianism: Argentina, 1966–1973, in Comparative Perspective*, Berkeley: University of California Press, 1988

Page, Joseph A., *Perón: A Biography*, New York: Random House, 1983

Peterson, Harold F., *Argentina and the United States, 1810–1960*, Albany: State University of New York Press, 1964

Potash, Robert A., *The Army and Politics in Argentina*, 3 vols., Stanford, CA: Stanford University Press, 1969–96

Randall, Laura, *An Economic History of Argentina in the Twentieth Century*, New York: Columbia University Press, 1978

Reber, Vera Blinn, *British Mercantile Houses in Buenos Aires, 1810–1880*, Cambridge, MA: Harvard University Press, 1979

Remmer, Karen L., *Party Competition in Argentina and Chile: Political Recruitment and Public Policy, 1890–1930*, Lincoln: University of Nebraska Press, 1984

Rennie, Ysabel F., *The Argentine Republic*, New York: Macmillan, 1945; reprinted Westport, CT: Greenwood Press, 1975

Rock, David, *Politics in Argentina, 1890–1930: The Rise and Fall of Radicalism*, Cambridge and New York: Cambridge University Press, 1975

Rock, David, *Argentina, 1516–1982: From Spanish Colonization to Alfonsín*, Berkeley: University of California Press, 1985; revised 1987

Romero, José Luis, *Las ideas políticas en Argentina*, Mexico City: Fondo de Cultura Economica, 1946; in English as *A History of Argentine Political Thought*, Stanford, CA: Stanford University Press, 1963

Sábato, Hilda, *Agrarian Capitalism and the World Market: Buenos Aires in the Pastoral Age, 1840–1890*, Albuquerque: University of New Mexico Press, 1990

Schoultz, Lars, *The Populist Challenge: Argentine Electoral Behavior in the Postwar Era*, Chapel Hill: University of North Carolina Press, 1983

Scobie, James R., *Argentina: A City and a Nation*, New York: Oxford University Press, 1964; revised 1971

Scobie, James R., *Revolution on the Pampas: A Social History of Argentine Wheat, 1860–1910*, Austin: University of Texas Press, 1964

Scobie, James R., *Buenos Aires: Plaza to Suburb, 1870–1910*, New York: Oxford University Press, 1974

Scobie, James R., *Secondary Cities of Argentina: The Social History of Corrientes, Salta, and Mendoza, 1850–1910*, edited by Samuel L. Baily, Stanford, CA: Stanford University Press, 1988

Shumway, Nicolas, *The Invention of Argentina*, Berkeley: University of California Press, 1991

Slatta, Richard W., *Gauchos and the Vanishing Frontier*, Lincoln: University of Nebraska Press, 1983

Smith, Peter H., *Politics and Beef in Argentina: Patterns of Conflict and Change*, New York: Columbia University Press, 1969

Smith, Peter H., *Argentina and the Failure of Democracy: Conflict among Political Elites, 1904–1955*, Madison: University of Wisconsin Press, 1974

Smith, William C., *Authoritarianism and the Crisis of the Argentine Political Economy*, Stanford, CA: Stanford University Press, 1989

Socolow, Susan Migden, *The Merchants of Buenos Aires, 1778–1810: Family and Commerce*, Cambridge and New York: Cambridge University Press, 1978

Socolow, Susan Migden, "Recent Historiography of the Rio de la Plata: Colonial and Early National Periods," *Hispanic American Historical Review* 64 (1984), 105–20

Socolow, Susan Migden, *The Bureaucrats of Buenos Aires, 1769–1810: amor al real servicio*, Durham, NC: Duke University Press, 1987

Sofer, Eugene F., *From Pale to Pampa: A Social History of the Jews of Buenos Aires*, New York: Holmes and Meier, 1982

Solberg, Carl E., *Immigration and Nationalism: Argentina and Chile, 1890–1914*, Austin: University of Texas Press for Institute of Latin American Studies, 1970

Solberg, Carl E., *Oil and Nationalism in Argentina: A History*, Stanford, CA: Stanford University Press, 1979

Solberg, Carl E., *The Prairies and the Pampas: Agrarian Policy in Canada and Argentina, 1880–1930*, Stanford, CA: Stanford University Press, 1987

Szuchman, Mark D., *Mobility and Integration in Urban Argentina: Córdoba in the Liberal Era*, Austin: University of Texas Press, 1980

Szuchman, Mark D., *Order, Family, and Community in Buenos Aires, 1810–1860*, Stanford, CA: Stanford University Press, 1988

Tamarin, David, *The Argentine Labor Movement, 1930–1945: A Study in the Origins of Peronismo*, Albuquerque: University of New Mexico Press, 1985

Taylor, Carl C., *Rural Life in Argentina*, Baton Rouge: Louisiana State University Press, 1948

Taylor, Julie M., *Eva Perón: The Myths of a Woman*, Chicago: University of Chicago Press, 1979

Tulchin, Joseph S., *Argentina and the United States: A Conflicted Relationship*, Boston: Twayne, 1990

Waisman, Carlos H., *Reversal of Development in Argentina: Postwar Counterrevolutionary Policies and Their Structural Consequences*, Princeton: Princeton University Press, 1987

Walter, Richard J., *Student Politics in Argentina: The University Reform and Its Effects, 1918–1964*, New York: Basic Books, 1968

Walter, Richard J., *The Socialist Party of Argentina, 1890–1930*, Austin: University of Texas Press for Institute of Latin American Studies, 1977

Walter, Richard J., *The Province of Buenos Aires and Argentine Politics, 1912–1943*, Cambridge and New York: Cambridge University Press, 1985

Weisbrot, Robert, *The Jews of Argentina: From the Inquisition to Perón*, Philadelphia: Jewish Publication Society of America, 1979

Whitaker, Arthur Preston, *Argentine Upheaval: Perón's Fall and the New Regime*, London: Atlantic Press, and New York: Praeger, 1956

Woods, Randall Bennett, *The Roosevelt Foreign Press Policy Establishment and the "Good Neighbor": The United States and Argentina, 1941–1945*, Lawrence: Regents Press of Kansas, 1979

Wright, Winthrop R., *British-Owned Railways in Argentina: Their Effect on Economic Nationalism, 1854–1948*, Austin: University of Texas Press for Institute of Latin American Studies, 1974

Wynia, Gary W., *Argentina in the Postwar Era: Politics and Economic Policy Making in a Divided Society*, Albuquerque: University of New Mexico Press, 1978

Ariès, Philippe 1914–1984
French social historian

One of the pioneers of the *mentalité* approach to social life in the past, Ariès produced works of bold interpretation based on a novel use of literary and iconographic sources. He was among the first to study the social status and artistic images of children, and the changing meaning of death, in western society. It is a tribute to his originality that all subsequent historians acknowledge his inventiveness in establishing these topics for discussion, even though he never held a professional post in history, and disarmed much criticism by describing himself as merely a "Sunday historian."

Ariès was originally trained in demographic history using orthodox statistical techniques. It was because he recognized the historically specific nature of demographic regimes that he came to study the problem of changing attitudes to children. Accompanying the great structural and economic changes in family life during modernization, he deduced, there must have been an equally profound alteration in the "idea" of family life and in the concept of childhood. By the 19th century, the child was the center of both family life and public concern. How had this developed, and was it really a radical change from previous periods? Ariès explored the social images of, and ideas about, children from the Middle Ages to the present in *L'Enfant et la vie familiale sous l'Ancien Régime* (1960; *Centuries of Childhood*, 1962), proposing a model of the changing social idea of childhood before industrialization. On the basis particularly of pictorial evidence, he concluded that the Middle Ages had no concept of the child: whatever the private relationships between parents and children, there was no *social* recognition of the particular nature of childhood. Someone too young to take part in social life did not count. Only when they stepped from the domestic setting straight into the adult world, at the early age of about seven years old, dressed like little adults, were children noticed. Their involvement in adult affairs, by training just after infancy for their future role in life, meant that there was no period of general education between infancy and adulthood. In the 16th century, by contrast, children were *discovered*, initially with indulgence (which Ariès called "coddling"), then with increasing anxiety and careful discipline. Forms of controlled schooling developed, inspired by a burgeoning middle-class educational literature. The baby (the French even borrowed the English word) was distinguished from the child, who, dressed differently from adults and contained in schools, was segregated both symbolically and actually from both the home and the larger adult world. This constraint was, from the 17th century onward, continually extended among the middle class, so that by the 19th century adulthood was delayed even further.

Ariès admitted to some problems and omissions in his model: it was far from universal. Women were given virtually no education until the 19th century, and child labor was so common among the poor that children continued to enter the adult world early. Even when children were sent to school, they were divided on class lines in the length and form of their education. Moreover, by concentrating on the level of the "social," he left his critics to focus on the reality of private relationships, which do not appear to have been characterized by parental attitudes of mistrust and authoritarian control. Yet the striking image of the modern child in limbo between home and work, programmed through an increasingly lengthy education, had been established by Ariès' study.

His work on death was equally dramatic and sweeping. From a medieval period characterized by the omnipresence of death, when people were prepared by ritual remedies for the inevitable, western society has developed a unique inability to cope with mortality. In the early modern period individuals were responsible for making a "good" death, reconciling themselves both to God and the living, a process in which the deathbed speeches of the dying person, rather than the ritual ceremonies of the bereaved, became central. By contrast, death in the 18th and 19th centuries became an enemy: the focus switched to mourning the death of the *other*, bitterly resented because, with gradually improving medical knowledge, it was seen as avoidable and unnecessary. The graveyard, with its increasingly elaborate memorials, became a scene of sentimental remembrance. In the modern period, death became invisible, institutionalized and technologically controlled. Society became unable to relate to something monopolized and controlled by medical experts.

In both his most famous works, the healthier, longer-living people of modern society were portrayed as uneasy with themselves and others. Care for children as a distinct group was accompanied by segregation, discrimination and mistrust. The physical conquest of death left people unable to deal with it emotionally. Like other revisionist historians (Foucault for example), although from a very different political tradition of Catholic nostalgia, Ariès tried to show that progress at one level brought losses and drawbacks at others. His works are now subject to much more careful empirical evaluation than was possible at their publication. Much of the detailed characterizations seem overdone, and the periodization far too sweeping. Yet historians regularly review Ariès' contributions because they are the starting point of their own.

PETER RUSHTON

See also Childhood; Europe: Modern; Family; Mentalities; Sexuality; Vovelle

Biography

Born Blois, 21 July 1914. Schooled as a historian, but failed his agrégation. Director of publications and documentation, Institut Français de Recherches Fruitières Outre Mer, a society trading in tropical fruit, 1943–79; proofreader, later director, Plon publishers; director, Ecole des Hautes Etudes en Science Sociales, 1978–84. Died Toulouse, 8 February 1984.

Principal Writings

Histoire des populations françaises et de leurs attitudes devant la vie depuis le XVIIIe siècle (A History of the French Population and Their Attitudes Towards Life before the 18th Century), 1948; revised and expanded 1971

L'Enfant et la vie familiale sous l'Ancien Régime, 1960; in English as *Centuries of Childhood: A Social History of Family Life*, 1962

Essais sur l'histoire de la mort en Occident du Moyen-Age à nos jours, 1975; in English as *Western Attitudes Toward Death: From the Middle Ages to the Present*, 1974

L'Homme devant la mort, 1977; in English as *The Hour of Our Death*, 1980

Editor with André Bejin, *Sexualités occidentales*, 1982; in English as *Western Sexuality: Practice and Precept in Past and Present Times*, 1985

Images de l'homme devant la mort, 1983; in English as *Images of Man and Death*, 1985

Editor with Georges Duby, *Histoire de la vie privée*, 5 vols., 1985–87; in English as *A History of Private Life*, 5 vols., 1987–91

Essais de mémoire, 1943-1983, 1993

Further Reading

Burton, Anthony, "Looking Forward from Ariès? Pictorial and Material Evidence for the History of Childhood and Family Life," *Continuity and Change* 4 (1989), 203–29

Gittings, Clare, *Death, Burial and the Individual in Early Modern England*, London: Croom Helm, 1984

Hanawalt, Barbara A., *The Ties That Bound: Peasant Families in Medieval England*, Oxford and New York: Oxford University Press, 1986

Hanawalt, Barbara A., "Historical Descriptions and Prescriptions for Adolescence," *Journal of Family History* 17 (1992), 341–51

Houlbrooke, Ralph, ed., *Death, Ritual and Bereavement*, London: Routledge, 1989

Hutton, Patrick H., and Robert I. Wiener, "Philippe Ariès: Traditionalism as a Vision of History," *Proceedings of the Annual Meeting of the Western Society for French History* 15 (1988), 388–97

Hutton, Patrick H., "The Problem of Memory in the Historical Writings of Philippe Ariès," *History and Memory* 4 (1992), 95–122

Johansson, Sheila Ryan, "Centuries of Childhood/Centuries of Parenting: Philippe Ariès and the Modernization of Privileged Infancy," *Journal of Family History* 12 (1987), 343–65

Morel, Marie-France, "Reflections on Some Recent French Literature on the History of Childhood," *Continuity and Change* 4 (1989), 323–37

Pollock, Linda, *Forgotten Children: Parent–Child Relations from 1500 to 1900*, Cambridge and New York: Cambridge University Press, 1983

Vann, Richard T., "The Youth of Centuries of Childhood," *History and Theory* 21 (1982), 279–97

Wilson, Adrian, "The Infancy of the History of Childhood: An Appraisal of Philippe Ariès," *History and Theory* 19 (1980), 132–53

Art History

The study of art history has proceeded in much the same way as the study of history itself. Like historians, art historians have always struggled to balance the acts of individuals against the larger movements of society and/or nature. Some philosophies lean towards one extreme, some the other; most attempt to take both into account. The difference between the two disciplines is obvious only in terms of the word "art," and yet "art" as an entity is central to a deeper distinction. Historians focus on understanding the process and progress of historical events; the tools, i.e. documents, which they use to achieve that end remain tools, often interchangeable and relatively insignificant in themselves. Although some art historians follow historians closely and use art objects merely as documents to explain historical process, art history on the whole consciously places the nature of art at the core of its approach. Questions concerning the somewhat mysterious relationship between art and its maker(s), and questions about creativity itself, must be dealt with before the historical process can be addressed.

Art has been produced for millennia; however, the desire to understand the relationship between various art objects within an historical context – a history of art – is a relatively modern phenomenon. An interest in collecting and cataloging art has been around for a much longer time (Pausanias and Pliny provide examples from the first centuries CE), but catalogues and commentaries about art do not represent art historical thought. They are often impressive and invaluable efforts, but in terms of art history they are generally significant in that they provide information – important raw material.

Giorgio Vasari (1511–74) worked very much within the mindset of a collector, but his *Le vite de' più eccellenti architetti, pittori et scultori italani* (1550, revised 1568; *The Lives of the Most Eminent Painters, Sculptors, and Architects*, 1912–15) provided new ideas as well; he is, therefore, often considered to be the first art historian. He "collected" information concerning the lives of Renaissance artists (contemporary artists to him), and his book is largely a compilation of biographies. He was, however, interested in "investigating into the causes and roots of things," and he arranged his biographies in terms of the infancy, adolescence, and maturity of art. In so doing, Vasari noted the connection between Michelangelo's work and the learning process that proceeded him, and set the stage for art history.

It was J.J. Winckelmann (1717–68) who perceived the first fully defined model for identifying stylistic development. Although his focus in *Geschichte der Kunst des Altertums* (1764; *The History of Ancient Art*, 1849–73) centered on Greek art, his principal objective was a search for "the essential nature of art." He analyzed original works of art directly and organized the stylistic variations that he found into a sequence of various periods that are related to each other in the same way that periods in the life of a biological organism are related to each other: birth, development, maturity, and decay. This model established art history as a "scientific" pursuit, not only because of its overt biological overtones, but because of the analytical method that he pursued.

Gottfried Semper (1803–79) followed Winckelmann in pursuing scientific models. He took the biological parallel a step further and adapted the history of art to evolutionary theory. Art was to Semper what a biological organism was to Darwin – its history forms a continuous, linear process of development from simple to complex towards a single goal. Like nature, art utilizes only a few basic types, modifying them as time progresses. According to Semper, changes in style, as represented by the variously modified types, are brought about by material and technical innovations. Many art historians have rightly criticized this theory for placing the impetus of artistic creation outside of art itself, yet Semper's recognition that art is influenced by the specific properties of the medium and method with which it is produced is certainly valid. Moreover, Semper's approach was a significant departure from Winckelmann who looked to various socio-political circumstances for explanations of stylistic change. Semper directed attention to the artistic process, if not to artistic creativity itself.

Semper and a growing number of other first generation art historians were interested in the problem of establishing an overall structure for art history. At the same time another group of scholars were approaching art history from a different angle. Connoisseurship is a branch of art history that can also trace its ancestry back to Winckelmann, at least in terms of Winckelmann's insistence on analyzing original artwork. Connoisseurs concentrate almost exclusively on individual works of art and are concerned only with determining the authentic "identity" of those works (i.e. artist, date, provenance); they are not interested in dealing with art history as a sweeping construct, nor are they particularly concerned with its development(s).

Bernard Berenson (1865–1959) ranks as one of the best known connoisseur-scholars. Focusing on the 14th and 15th centuries in Italy, he dealt exclusively with the single medium of painting, recognizing, as do almost all modern art historians, that significant changes can occur in style without significant changes in material and techniques (though it is true that such changes are often parallel). However, like Semper, Berenson was attracted by the "scientific" approach to art history (used here in its broadest sense). He held that connoisseurship "proceeds as scientific research always does, by the isolation of the characteristics of the known and their confrontation with the unknown." Expanding upon the pioneering efforts of Giovanni Morelli (1816–91), Berenson held that the hand of a specific artist can be identified in a work of art by the comparison of minute details in that work with those same aspects evident in a work undoubtedly proven to be by the same artist. He focused on unnecessary details, such as ears, hands, and drapery folds, because they tended to be unconsciously executed, and were more likely to be a stereotypical, and therefore unchanging, aspect of the artist's work. Berenson utilized documentary information, but if forced to choose between archival sources and morphological analysis, he put more trust in the latter. He went even further, stating that the "essential equipment" of an experienced connoisseur was a sense of quality, not any methodological system.

Connoisseurship – particularly when practiced with this carefully cultivated "sense of quality" – has produced remarkable results for the history of art. Berenson himself identified many Italian paintings. Sir John Beazley is another notable example: he identified hundreds of previously unknown ancient Greek vase painters solely through his study of pottery fragments scattered in museums around the world. Even in less gifted hands, connoisseurship remains important to art history because it calls attention to the necessity of looking very closely at the work of art itself.

Connoisseurship's basic premises were quickly adopted by almost all historians, but it remained a peripheral movement nevertheless. Most continued to be fascinated with the larger question of the development of style. The writings of G.W.F. Hegel (1770–1831) provided a methodological vision that had significant influence on the development of art history as a discipline. Hegel was not devoted to art specifically, but his overall philosophy included art, identifying it, along with religion and philosophy, as a manifestation of the "Absolute Infinite Spirit." His major contribution was the construction of a dialectic system – a force that propels all aspects of the world to constant movement through struggle. This repeating model of thesis-antithesis-synthesis was seized upon by many historians as a means by which to explain stylistic change.

In his famous *Kunstgeschichtliche Grundbegriffe* (1915; *Principles of Art History*, 1932), Heinrich Wölfflin (1864–1945) developed an important art historical model that was Hegelian in terms of its dialectical basis. Like the connoisseurs, Wölfflin developed a system of morphological analysis, but with his analysis he endeavored to demonstrate fundamental differences between period styles and national styles of a given period. He created five pairs of polar concepts, called *Grundbegriffe*, which he applied to the Renaissance (described by linear, planer, closed, composite, and clear) and the Baroque (represented by the opposite pole: painterly, recessional, open, fused, and relatively unclear). He claimed that the history of art shifted continually between these two very different modes of vision; that, though opposed, these two modes of vision are of equal value; and that the development from one to the other is internal, logical, and can't be reversed (i.e. the Baroque could not exist without the Renaissance preceding it). He refused to venture beyond the statement that change is intrinsic to the system and that movement between the two closed poles is somehow self-activated. The rigidity of his system is criticized: it is not applicable to other periods, nor does it take into account the possibility that his dialectical characteristics could exist simultaneously in a period, or even in a specific work of art. Even the Renaissance and Baroque periods were not as homogenous as he suggested; for instance, he totally overlooked Mannerism. His morphological, comparative approach, however, is still utilized; furthermore, it provided a descriptive terminology that still forms the basis for discussions of style, however diverse the respective examples may be.

Like Wölfflin, Alois Riegl (1858–1905) studied form, drawing attention away from the value judgments that permeated art history. "Major" and "minor" arts were dealt with on the same level. Phases of art previously seen as periods of decline, such as Late Antique and Baroque, were seen by Riegl as an integral part of a continuous development, one style growing from the one before it and leading to the next. Riegl's theory can be seen as a marriage between Semper's evolutionary approach and Wölfflin's cyclical approach. Polar concepts were used to describe changes in style; for Riegl, changes could be encapsulated in terms of "haptic" and "optic." Style moves organically from one pole to the other and back again, infusing the "linear" progression of art history with a spiral twist. The similarity of Riegl's theory to Semper's theory ends abruptly with their common evolutionary model; Riegl developed his concept of *Kunstwollen* as a direct antithesis to Semper's view of materialistic and technological causation. *Kunstwollen* is both his greatest achievement and his most criticized fault. With *Kunstwollen*, Riegl argued that the impetus of art was not to be found in external forces, not in materials, techniques, or even nature, but rather in art itself. He placed art firmly within the realm of artistic creativity, but simultaneously stripped the individual artist of personal power over creativity by implying that *Kunstwollen* is an autonomous, almost supernatural force drawn from a shared national identity that necessarily governs the work of all artists. Nevertheless, although *Kunstwollen* remains confusing and almost universally rejected due to its vagaries, Riegl's detailed analysis of style and his attempt to place formal characteristics of style in relationship with other styles and a larger sociohistorical scope continues to serve as an extremely influential art historical model.

Questions prompted by Riegl's work led art historians to consider more closely the role of culture in art history. Max Dvorak (1874–1921) looked to literature, philosophy, science, and economics for parallels, not causes, of stylistic changes in art. His theory states that all human endeavor is caused by a spiritual outlook; for instance, the art and philosophy of a given period were both derived from, and then became "symptomatic" of, this spiritual and ideological force, *Geistesgeschichte*.

Erwin Panofsky (1892–1968) also believed in an intrinsic link between art and culture, although he did not share Dvorak's (or Hegel's) sense of an overwhelming, all-powerful spirit-of-the-age. He simply held that cultural history could shed light on art history and visa versa. His methodology began with basic formal analysis, proceeded to identify and analyze subject matter, and then, through the comparative use of documentation, grew to embrace the aspects of cultural history. According to Panofsky, an image can depict one thing, represent another, and still express aspects of "something else." The study of an art work as a "symptom" of "symbolic value" on this third level is called iconology. In spite of the fact that iconological approaches present dangers – for example, when to stop searching for hidden meaning, perhaps finding it where it does not exist – iconology is valuable because it acknowledges that art is not created in a vacuum and that stylistic changes are tied to cultural roots, consciously or unconsciously.

The issue of consciousness, in turn, became significant throughout the scholarly world. Psychology and psychoanalysis raised many questions that affected all studies of human actions. Sigmund Freud (1856–1939) was not an art historian, but he dealt with art directly in some of his writings and he exerted great influence on a great many disciplines including art history. One of his books focused on a single passage in Leonardo da Vinci's notebooks, highlighting its importance as Leonardo's only reference to his childhood. He proceeded to psychoanalyze the sexual implications of this memory combining it with biographical information of Leonardo's early life. He then discussed how this psychological influence manifested itself in Leonardo's art, holding that it is specifically revealed by compositional innovations in his painting of the Virgin and Child with St. Anne, and in the smile of both the Virgin and the Mona Lisa. Critics point to the unreasonable amount of weight placed on one brief, vague comment and note that Freud overlooked the possibility that formal, sociological, and cultural factors could explain Leonardo's innovations equally well and probably even more successfully. The critics themselves, however, failed in a similar way; they overlooked the possibility that psychological factors can indeed influence artistic innovations. The suggestion of this possibility, even if it was overstated, is Freud's contribution to the history of art. A number of art historians, notably Ernst Kris (1900–1957), have pursued his ideas.

Oddly enough, psychology can have an effect similar to Riegl's *Kunstwollen*; it puts artistic creativity in the hands of the artist, then takes it away, not by giving it to external forces in general, but to external forces acting on the psyche of the artist. Ernst Gombrich (1909–) is one who attempted to reconcile the psychological influences on an artist with the personal freedom of artistic expression; he also sought a reconciliation of psychology in general with formal analysis. Central to his theory is the belief that all art, even representational art, remains basically conceptual. Gombrich's theory of making and matching is also described as a system of schemata and corrections. Schemata are conceptual images caused and perpetuated by tradition. Art can exist as schemata alone, but a constant willingness to change, correct, and revise also exists, so schemata can also serve as the starting point from which an individual artist builds. Tradition then adapts to incorporate individual innovations, thus creating a continuous, but not necessarily linear, process. Gombrich maintained that the effect of psychology on an artist causes him to reconsider his perception of nature by comparing it to nature, thereby altering his view and modifying his use of formal elements in making schemata. Components of style, however, always remain formal and should be explained in empirical terms.

If psychology provided one way of looking at the relationship between the world and the art produced within it, other modern social philosophies and movements provided other ways. Marxist philosophy, for instance, made a clear mark on the history of art, particularly in the work of Frederick Antal (1887–1954). Antal held that art works can be explained by political, economic, and social factors. He utilized the now familiar concept of antithetical polarities to describe a dichotomy of styles; however, his distinctions were not based on formal aspects but on the class which produced the work of art, claiming that the acceptance of a particular art work by a particular class proves that it was produced for that class. Style is defined as being either "rational" or "irrational." "Rational" art is connected to the emergence of a progressive trend which strives to bring upper and lower classes together (it is usually produced by an active middle class), while "irrational" art (i.e. emotional, sentimental, mystical art) reflected an attitude that accepted the division of classes.

Even without an overtly Marxist point of view, social history on the whole was increasingly incorporated into art history. Studies on patronage, church history, and political issues in relation to art and artists had long been part of the art historical tradition; in the 20th century, however, many scholars looked to social factors to explain (or at least parallel) the progress of art itself. Arnold Hauser provided the most ambitious presentation of this idea in his multivolume *A Social History of Art* (1951).

Social causes can only rarely be proven to influence the formal elements of art, so social art historians usually stress content. The examination of iconography in light of political, economic, and social events as well as literature and science, can, to a certain extent, be considered along the same lines as iconology and should be valued for the same reasons. Yet, these theories tend to reintroduce a system of value judgment to art history that does not derive from the work of art itself. In iconology, formal aspects of style and external forces maintain a reciprocal relationship, whereas social theories often reduce style to a mere reflection of an outer impulse. The connection between social issues and art, however, has been clearly drawn and remains a significant part of art historical thought.

Art history today is very much the sum total of its own history. All the ideas that have been utilized in the search for an overarching structure for art history are still at the core of art historical studies. All ideas, in spite of their frequently conflicting natures, serve to enrich the discipline. There is,

however, less of an overt effort to establish an overarching structure as there has been in the past. Overall perspectives from which one can view art history are currently more popular. Following the examples of the psychological and the social approaches that were developed earlier in the century, philosophical concepts such as deconstructionism and semiotics, and social concepts such as feminism and multiculturalism have now taken root. The many fields of study in non-western art history have also grown significantly in recent years. A parallel historiography for non-western art is being developed and will, no doubt, add a new direction to the established tradition that has largely (but not exclusively) concentrated on western art.

JULIET GRAVER ISTRABADI

See also Burckhardt; Design; Gombrich; Panofsky; Pevsner; Schama; Winckelmann

Further Reading

Antal, Frederick, *Classicism and Romanticism, with Other Studies in Art History*, New York: Basic Books, and London: Routledge, 1966

Berenson, Bernard, "Rudiments of Connoisseurship," in his *The Study and Criticism of Italian Art*, London: Bell, 1902; republished as *Rudiments of Connoisseurship*, New York: Schocken, 1962

Carrier, David, *Principles of Art History Writing*, University Park: Pennsylvania State University Press, 1991

Dvorak, Max, *Idealismus und Naturalismus in der gotischen Skulptur und Malerei*, Munich: Oldenbourg, 1918; in English as *Idealism and Naturalism in Gothic Art*, Notre Dame, IN: University of Notre Dame Press, 1967

Focillon, Henri, *Vies des formes*, Paris: Alcan, 1934; in English as *The Life of Forms in Art*, New Haven: Yale University Press, and London: Oxford University Press, 1942

Freud, Sigmund, *Eine Kindheitserinnerung des Leonardo da Vinci*, Leipzig: Deuticke, 1910; in English as *Leonardo da Vinci: A Psychosexual Study of Infantile Reminiscence*, New York: Moffat Yard, 1916, London: Kegan Paul, 1922

Gombrich, E.H., "Meditations on a Hobby Horse; or, Roots of Artistic Forms," in Lancelot Whyte, ed., *Aspects of Form: A Symposium on Form in Nature and Art*, New York: Pelligrini and Cudahy, and London: Lund Humphries, 1951; republished in *Meditations on a Hobby Horse, and Other Essays on the Theory of Art*, London: Phaidon, 1963

Gombrich, E.H., *Art and Illusion: A Study in the Psychology of Pictorial Representation*, London: Phaidon, and New York: Pantheon, 1960

Gombrich, E.H., "Style," in David L. Sills, ed., *International Encyclopedia of the Social Sciences*, 19 vols., New York: Macmillan, 1968–91, 15:353–60

Hauser, Arnold, *Sozialgeschichte der Kunst und Literatur*, 2 vols., Munich: Beck, 1953; in English as *A Social History of Art*, 2 vols., London: Routledge, 1951, and 4 vols., New York: Vintage, 1951

Hauser, Arnold, *Philosophie der Kunstgeschichte*, Munich: Beck, 1958; in English as *The Philosophy of Art History*, New York: Knopf, and London: Routledge, 1959

Kleinbauer, W. Eugene, *Modern Perspectives in Western Art History: An Anthology of Twentieth-Century Writings on the Visual Arts*, New York: Holt Rinehart, 1971

Klingender, Francis D., *Marxism and Modern Art: An Approach to Social Realism*, London: Lawrence and Wishart, 1943; New York: International 1945

Kris, Ernst, *Psychoanalytic Explorations in Art*, New York: International University Press, and London: Allen and Unwin, 1953

Kubler, George, *The Shape of Time: Remarks on the History of Things*, New Haven: Yale University Press, 1962

Minor, Vernon Hyde, *Art History's History*, Englewood Cliffs, NJ: Prentice Hall, 1994

Morelli, Giovanni, *Kunst-kritische Studien über italienische Malerei*, 3 vols., Leipzig: Brockhaus, 1890–93; in English as *Italian Painters: Critical Studies of Their Works*, 2 vols., London: Murray, 1892–93

Pächt, Otto, "Art Historians and Art Critics, 6: Alois Riegl," *Burlington Magazine* (May 1963), 188–93

Panofsky, Erwin, *Studies in Iconology: Humanistic Themes in the Art of the Renaissance*, New York: Oxford University Press, 1939

Panofsky, Erwin, *Meaning in the Visual Arts*, Garden City, NY: Doubleday, 1955

Podro, Michael, *The Critical Historians of Art*, New Haven: Yale University Press, 1982

Preziosi, Donald, *Rethinking Art History: Meditations on a Coy Science*, New Haven: Yale University Press, 1989

Riegl, Alois, *Stilfragen: Grundlegungen zu einer Geschichte der Ornamentik* (Questions of Style: Foundations for a History of Decorative Art), Berlin: Siemans, 1893

Riegl, Alois, *Die spät-römische Kunst-Industrie* (The Late Roman Art Industry), 2 vols., Vienna: K.K. Hof- und Staatsdruckerei, 1901

Riegl, Alois, *Die Entstehung der Barock-kunst in Rom* (The Origin of Baroque Art in Rome), Vienna: Schroll, 1908

Roskill, Mark, *What is Art History?*, New York: Harper, and London: Thames and Hudson, 1976

Semper, Gottfried, *Der Stil in den technischen und tektonischen Künsten; oder, Praktische Aesthetik: Ein Handbuch für Techniker, Künstler und Kunstfreunde* (Style in the Technical and Tectonic Arts: A Handbook for Technicians, Artists, and Art Lovers), 2 vols., Frankfurt: Verlag für Kunst und Wissenschaft, 1860–63

Shapiro, Meyer, "Style," in Morris Philipson, ed., *Anthropology Today*, Chicago: University of Chicago Press, 1953

Shapiro, Meyer, "Leonardo and Freud: An Art-Historical Study," *Journal of the History of Ideas* 17 (1956), 147–78

Vasari, Giorgio, *Le vite de' più eccellenti architetti, pittori et scultori italani*, 3 vols., Florence: H. Torrentino, 1550, revised 1568; in English as *Lives of the Most Eminent Painters, Sculptors and Architects*, 10 vols., London: Macmillan–Medici Society, 1912–15, reprinted New York: AMS, 1976

Winckelmann, J.J., *Geschichte der Kunst des Altertums*, Dresden: Walterischen, 1764; in English as *The History of Ancient Art*, 4 vols., Boston: Osgood, 1849–73

Wölfflin, Heinrich, *Der Klassische Kunst: Eine Einführung in die italienische Renaissance*, Munich: Bruckmann, 1899; in English as *Classic Art: An Introduction to the Italian Renaissance*, London and New York: Phaidon, 1952

Wölfflin, Heinrich, *Kunstgeschichtliche Grundbegriffe: Das Problem der Stilentwicklung in der neueren Kunst*, Munich: Bruckmann, 1915; in English as *Principles of Art History: The Problem of the Development of Style in Later Art*, New York: Holt, and London: Bell, 1932

Wollheim, Richard, "Giovanni Morelli and the Origins of Scientific Connoisseurship," in his *On Art and the Mind*, Cambridge, MA: Harvard University Press, and London: Allen Lane, 1974

Astrology

This discussion is necessarily both brief and summary, and mainly concerns the literature in English. Astrology is the practice of relating the heavenly bodies to lives and events on earth, and the tradition that has thus been generated. Within that tradition there are many different ways of doing so, and rationales – from highly technical (but impassioned) arguments for one way of dividing up space into "houses" as against others, to larger conceptual questions such as whether the stars should be construed as signs or actual causes. A broad initial definition is best, however, so as not to miss out too much.

There are three good reasons to study the history of astrology. First is its distinctiveness as a form of knowledge whose basic concepts and practices have lasted an extraordinarily long time – since their origins in roughly 2000 BCE, in Mesopotamia – interacted with a wide array of other traditions – notably Platonism and neo-Platonism, Aristotelianism, Christianity (especially Thomism, but also the antagonism of Augustine and the Protestant Reformation), humanism, magic (initially Hermetic), and occultism, and modern science – and succeeded in adapting to such a variety of often distinctly hostile social and intellectual conditions.

Second, between about 1300 and 1700, astrology was a relatively integral part of European society and culture. And third, even as a relatively marginal pursuit after around 1700, it continued to be attacked in ways that are very revealing about the attackers. The latter have principally featured the Christian church (since its origins), natural philosophers and scientists (mostly since the mid-17th century), and literati and professional intellectuals (beginning in the 18th century). Mistaking polemical assertion for historical fact has often resulted in perennially and laughably exaggerated reports of the "death" of astrology by some historians, especially historians of science, who ought to have known better.

There are also at least two reasons why its historiography is difficult, and as challenging as it is rewarding. One is the weight of mainstream intellectual opinion against it – something whose origins lie precisely in the history being studied, but which is frequently restimulated by astrology's continued existence, and makes the resort to "Whiggish" anachronism a constant temptation. Another problem is that astrology once frequently united disciplines long since sundered, and in some cases suppressed, and whose fragmentation modern academies have inherited: astronomy, natural philosophy, medicine, natural magic, religious prophecy, divination, and what is now psychology and sociology. The temptation therefore is to doubt that such a now-fabulous beast ever existed.

These problems have more or less defined the historiography of astrology, which I shall illustrate using three different examples. Respecting the history of Greek astrology, the historian of science George Sarton's early work was badly marred by his open contempt for the astrologers he was studying (based, it would seem, in his feelings about their modern heirs). This included his eagerness to salvage ancient "astronomy" but jettison the "astrology" from which it was inseparable; in this Sarton was unfortunately typical of historians of science until about the 1980s. (He was memorably taken to task in 1951 by Otto Neugebauer in a short paper, "The Study of Wretched Subjects." For a contrasting approach to the same subject-matter that successfully avoided anachronism, see the work of G.E.R. Lloyd, who pointed out that the explanandum is not "the victory of rationality over magic: there was no such victory: but rather how the criticism of magic got some purchase." Tamsyn Barton has followed up and developed this lead in her recent work on Greek astrology.

Another revealing case-study is the historiography of Hermetic and neo-Platonic astrology which was stimulated by the work of D.P. Walker and Frances Yates, in particular her *Giordano Bruno and the Hermetic Tradition* (1964). It is true that Yates sometimes overstated her case; on the other hand, that was arguably necessary after decades of scholarship which massively ignored and/or misrepresented this important and fascinating area, one which – even at the Warburg Institute where she worked, and whose founders Warburg and Saxl were responsible for pioneering studies such as *Saturn and Melancholy* (1964) – was, both then and since, often apparently regarded as embarrassing and somewhat disreputable. Only as a result of her labors, however, has a relatively balanced and full assessment of magic, including magical astrology and astrological magic, become possible.

My third example concerns early modern astrology in England, when it attained extraordinary importance in 1640–1700. Keith Thomas' *Religion and the Decline of Magic* (1971) has been highly influential in Britain, but his account is somewhat skewed contextually by anachronistically asking the wrong question – why did "so many otherwise intelligent people" believe in astrology? – instead of: why did so many people stop believing in it, who exactly did, and why? These are the questions that Patrick Curry's *Prophecy and Power* (1989) sets out to answer instead. For another very different book that tries to do the same, see Ann Geneva's *Astrology and the Seventeenth-Century Mind* (1995). Geneva's approach is "internalist" and closely textual, whereas Curry's is "externalistic" and broadly sociological; yet their common commitment to a history that takes the beliefs and practices of its historical subjects seriously, in their own terms, shows that divide is not fundamental.

Finally, there is a recent and encouraging tendency for scholars to become more familiar with the actual practices of astrologers in order to write better histories, and astrologers themselves to become involved in and/or produce more scholarly studies of their subject. An example of the former is the recent edition of Abu Ma'Shar's *Abbreviation of the Introduction to Astrology* (1994) by Charles Burnett *et al.*; of the latter, the translations of Greek, Latin, and Arabic texts by Project Hindsight in the US, and the editions of Lilly, Gadbury and others by Regulus Press in England.

PATRICK CURRY

See also Garin; Thomas, K.

Further Reading

Allen, Don Cameron, *The Star-Crossed Renaissance: The Quarrel about Astrology and Its Influence in England*, Durham, NC: Duke University Press, 1941; London: Cass, 1967
Baigent, Michael, *From the Omens of Babylon: Astrology and Ancient Mesopotamia*, London: Penguin, 1994
Barton, Tamsyn, *Ancient Astrology*, London and New York: Routledge, 1994
Barton, Tamsyn, *Power and Knowledge: Astrology, Physionomics, and Medicine under the Roman Empire*, Ann Arbor: University of Michigan Press, 1994
Boll, Franz, *Sternglaube und Sterndeutung: Die Geschichte und das Wesen der Astrologie* (Belief in the Stars and Reading the Stars: The History and Nature of Astrology), Leipzig: Teubner, 1918
Bouché-Leclercq, Auguste, *L'Astrologie Grecque* (Greek Astrology), Paris: Leroux, 1899
Burnett, Charles, ed., *Adelard of Bath: An English Scientist and Arabist of the Early Twelfth Century*, London: Warburg Institute, 1987
Butler, Jon, "Magic, Astrology, and the Early American Religious Heritage, 1600–1760," *American Historical Review* 84 (1979), 317–46

Campion, Nicholas, *The Great Year: Astrology, Millenarianism, and History in the Western Tradition*, New York: Arkana, 1994
Capp, Bernard, *Astrology and the Popular Press: English Almanacs, 1500–1800*, London: Faber, 1979
Carey, Hilary, *Courting Disaster: Astrology at the English Court and University in the Later Middle Ages*, London: Macmillan, and New York: St. Martin's Press, 1992
Caroti, Stefano, *La critica contra l'astrologia di Nicole Oresme e la sua influenza nel medioevo e nel Rinascimento* (Nicole Oresme's Critique of Astrology and Its Influence in the Middle Ages and the Renaissance), Rome: Lincei, 1979
Cumont, Franz, *Astrology and Religion among the Greeks and Romans*, London and New York: Putnam, 1912
Curry, Patrick, ed., *Astrology, Science and Society: Historical Essays*, Woodbridge, Suffolk: Boydell, 1987
Curry, Patrick, *Prophecy and Power: Astrology in Early Modern England*, Cambridge: Polity Press, and Princeton: Princeton University Press, 1989
Curry, Patrick, *A Confusion of Prophets: Victorian and Edwardian Astrology*, London: Collins and Brown, 1992
Ernst, Germana, *Religione, ragione e natura ricerche su Tommaso Campanella e il tardo Rinasciamento* (Religion, Reason, and Nature: Research on Tommaso Campanella and the Late Renaissance), Milan: Angeli, 1991
Federici-Vescovini, Graziella, *Astrologia escienza: La crisi dell'aristotelismo sul cadre de Trecento e Biagio Pelacani da Parma* (Astrology and Science: The Crisis of Aristotelianism in the 14th Century and Biagio Pelacani of Parma), Florence: Vallecchi, 1979
Festugière, André Jean, *La Révélation d'Hermès Trimégiste* (The Revelation of Hermes Trismegistus), 4 vols., Paris: Lecoffre, 1949–54
Field, J.V., "A Lutheran Astrologer: Johannes Kepler," *Archive for History of the Exact Sciences* 31 (1984), 189–272
Garin, Eugenio, *Lo zodiaco della vita: la polemica sull'astrolgia dal Trecento al Cinquecento*, Rome: Laterza, 1976; in English as *Astrology in the Renaissance: The Zodiac of Life*, London: Routledge, 1983
Geneva, Ann, *Astrology and the Seventeenth-Century Mind: William Lilly and the Language of the Stars*, Manchester: Manchester University Press, 1995
Godwin, Joscelyn, *The Theosophical Enlightenment*, Albany: State University of New York Press, 1994
Gundel, Wilhelm and Hans Georg Gundel, *Astrologumena: Die astrologische Literatur in der Antike und ihre Geschichte* (Astrologeumena: Astrological Literature in Antiquity and Its History), Wiesbaden: Steiner, 1966
Halbronn, Jacques, *Le Monde Juif et l'Astrologie: Histoire d'un vieux couple* (The Jewish World and Astrology: The History of an Old Couple), Milan: Archae, 1979
Howe, Ellic, *Urania's Children: The Strange World of the Astrologers*, London: Kimber, 1967; reprinted as *Astrology and the Third Reich*, 1984
Hübner, Wolfgang, *Die Eigenschaften der Tierkreiszeichen in der Antike: Ihre Darstellung und Verwendung unter besonderer Berücksichtigung des Manilius* (The Attributes of the Zodiac in Antiquity: Uses and Portrayals, with Special Reference to Manilius), Wiesbaden: Steiner, 1982
Kitson, Annabella, ed., *History and Astrology: Clio and Urania Confer*, London: Unwin, 1989
Knappich, Wilhelm, *Geschichte der Astrologie* (The History of Astrology), Frankfurt: Klostermann, 1967
Labrousse, Elisabeth, *L'entrée de Saturne au lion (l'éclipse de soleil du 12 août 1654)* (The Entrance of Saturn into Leo: The Eclipse of the Sun of 12 August 1654), The Hague: Nijhoff, 1974
Lemay, Richard, *Joseph, Abu Mashar and Latin Aristotelianism in the Twelfth Century: The Recovery of Aristotle's Natural Philosophy Through Arabic Astrology*, Beirut: American University of Beirut, 1962

Leventhal, Herbert, *In the Shadow of the Enlightenment: Occultism and Renaissance Sciences in Eighteenth-Century America*, New York: New York University Press, 1976

Lilly, William, *Christian Astrology*, 1651; reprinted London: Regulus, 1985

Lindsay, Jack, *The Origins of Astrology*, London: Muller, and New York: Barnes and Noble, 1971

Lipton, Joshua, *The Rational Evaluation of Astrology in the Period of Arabo-Latin Translation, c.1126–1187 AD*, Berkeley: University of California Press, 1978

Lloyd, Geoffrey Ernest Richard, *Magic, Reason and Experience: Studies in the Origins and Development of Greek Science*, Cambridge and New York: Cambridge University Press, 1979

Long, A.A., "Astrology: Arguments *pro* and *contra*," in Jonathan Barnes *et al.*, eds., *Science and Speculation: Studies in Hellenistic Theory and Practice*, Cambridge and New York: Cambridge University Press, 1982

Ma'Shar, Abu, *Abbreviation of the Introduction to Astrology*, edited by Charles Burnett, Keiji Yamamoto, and Michio Yano, Leiden and New York: Brill, 1994

Müller-Jahncke, Wolf-Dieter, *Astrologisch-Magische Theorie und Praxis in der Heilkunde der frühen Neuzeit* (Astrological-Magical Theory and Practice in the Healing Arts of the Early Renaissance), Stuttgart: Steiner, 1985

Neugebauer, Otto, *The Exact Sciences in Antiquity*, Copenhagen: Munksgaard, 1951; Princeton: Princeton University Press, 1952

Neugebauer, Otto, "The Study of Wretched Subjects," *Isis* 42 (1951), 111

North, John D., "Astrology and the Fortunes of Churches," *Centaurus* 24 (1980), 181–211

North, John D., *Horoscopes and History*, London: Warburg Institute, 1986

Ptolemy, *Tetrabiblos*, edited by Frank E. Robbins, Cambridge, MA: Harvard University Press, 1940

Saxl, Fritz, Raymond Klibansky, and Erwin Panofsky, *Saturn and Melancholy: Studies in the History of Natural Philosophy, Religion and Art*, London: Nelson, and New York: Basic Books, 1964

Simon, Gérard, *Kepler: astronome, astrologue* (Kepler: Astronomer, Astrologer), Paris: Gallimard, 1979

Tester, Jim, *A History of Western Astrology*, Woodbridge, Suffolk: Boydell, 1987

Thomas, Keith, *Religion and the Decline of Magic: Studies in Popular Beliefs in Sixteenth- and Seventeenth-Century England*, London: Weidenfeld and Nicolson, and New York: Scribner, 1971

Thorndike, Lynn, *A History of Magic and Experimental Science*, 8 vols., New York: Macmillan, 1923–58

Walker, Daniel Pickering, *Spiritual and Demonic Magic from Ficino to Campanella*, London: Warburg Institute, 1958; Notre Dame, IN: University of Notre Dame Press, 1975

Webster, Charles, *From Paracelsus to Newton: Magic and the Making of Modern Science*, Cambridge and New York: Cambridge University Press, 1982

Yates, Frances A., *Giordano Bruno and the Hermetic Tradition*, Chicago: University of Chicago Press, and London: Routledge, 1964

Zambelli, Paola, ed., *"Astrologi hallucinati": Stars and the End of the World in Luther's Time*, Berlin and New York: de Gruyter, 1986

Zambelli, Paola, *The Speculum Astronomie and Its Enigma: Astrology, Theology, and Science in Albertus Magnus and His Contemporaries*, Dordrecht and Boston: Kluwer, 1992

Australia

The modern history of the island continent is an interesting example of British expansion, a case study in the dispossession of an indigenous people, a frontier society worthy of contrast with the American West and Argentina, a good instance of a traditional masculinist culture, a rich theater for working-class culture and politics, and a textbook example of a modern multicultural society. It is also, curiously, a nation which decolonized without a war of independence, and achieved democracy without popular insurrection. It has a rich historiographical tradition based on its public universities and its large reading public. Despite the tiny size of its population, Australian scholars contribute 2 per cent of the world's new knowledge each year, including historical knowledge.

In the colonial period there had been several significant histories documenting the early settlements, mainly for the benefit of British readers. After the federation of the six colonies in 1901, the first major modern work was the multivolume history of Australia's involvement in World War I, edited by a journalist turned professional historian, C.E.W. Bean. Bean used his experience as a war correspondent to good effect, describing the conflict from the common soldier's point of view, and he found himself in some demand advising other war historians around the English-speaking world. The set of twelve red-spined volumes sold well throughout Australia, forming a valuable reference collection in a nation which had lost 60,000 of a population of only five million. The other two popular historians of the period were the academic Sir Keith Hancock, whose *Australia* (1930) remained a key interpretive text for half a century, and the left-wing populist Brian Fitzpatrick. Fitzpatrick argued that British capital had dominated Australian history and that "the people" had been thwarted in their attempts to own their own land.

After World War II the variety and depth of Australian history increased quickly. The number of universities and their student population increased dramatically in the postwar period. Melbourne's traditionally strong History department was joined by new sister departments in other parts of Australia. Manning Clark was appointed to the first chair in Australian history, at the Australian National University (then Canberra University College) in 1949 and began the work on his epic six-volume *History of Australia* (1962–87). Clark was the first to take seriously the content of the ideas which constituted debates about the nation's identity. Left-wing critics accused him of not understanding materialist history; the much larger number of right-wing adversaries were enraged by his iconoclasm. Clark's protégés include Michael Roe. Roe's *Quest for Authority* (1965) remains a basic text for understanding the ideological options available to colonists in the middle of the 19th century. The leading postwar conservatives included J.M. Ward, who specialized in imperial history, and Douglas Pike, who began the massive collaborative project, the *Australian Dictionary of Biography* (ADB; 1966–). The ADB is an excellent biographical compilation, with a subtle mix of prominent people and representatives of the *hoi polloi*.

Fitzpatrick's work continued to remain influential. Although Fitzpatrick never obtained an academic post, he inspired a school of radical nationalists to whom the label Old Left was later attached. Central to this group were Ian Turner, a charismatic and versatile labor historian, Robin Gollan, who wrote the classic text *Radical and Working-Class Politics* (1960), an account of the mobilization of labor in the period from 1850 to 1910, and Russel Ward, whose book *The Australian Legend* (1958) is an Australian variant of the Frederick Jackson Turner "frontier" thesis. Ward argued that the distinctively Australian traits of the "larrikin" came from the experiences of the 19th-century bush workers. On the edges of the Old Left group were the art historian Bernard Smith and the social-cultural historian Geoffrey Serle.

The 1960s saw the emergence of new professional historians whose work was less pointedly partisan. In *Men of Yesterday* (1961), Margaret Kiddle painted a glorious picture of the "squattocracy," or landed gentry, who settled in western Victoria. Quantitative method made its appearance in the work of the economic historian N.G. Butlin, who challenged the earlier work of Fitzpatrick, and also in the statistical analysis of the convict population produced by Lloyd Robson (*The Convict Settlers of Australia*, 1965). Robson showed that earlier images of the convicts as innocent victims of a brutal process could not be sustained by the facts. Geoffrey Blainey had freelanced during the 1950s but took up an academic appointment and wrote the bestselling *The Tyranny of Distance* (1966), a phrase which entered the lexicon of Australian leaders and became a standard way of thinking about the country's problems. After Keith Hancock returned from Oxford to Australia his best work was a remarkable vignette of environmental history, *Discovering Monaro* (1972). In 1974 two fine reworkings of well-traveled ground appeared: Bill Gammage's account World War I soldiers, *The Broken Years*, and a new version of the colonial period by Ken Inglis. In *The Australian Colonists*, Inglis had a keen eye for the emergence of peculiarly Australian customs and traditions.

The period from 1975 to 1988 saw fundamental realignments in the national historiography. The position of the Left changed, with the emergence of the young Turks who made up the Australian New Left. At the University of Melbourne, Stuart Macintyre produced *Winners and Losers* (1985), a reassessment of the sources of progress in the Australian polity. R.W. Connell and T.H. Irving restated the theory of social class in their 1980 work, *Class Structure in Australian History*, while Humphrey McQueen questioned the radical credentials of the Labour Party in his contentious book *A New Britannia* (1970, revised 1975), and Tim Rowse examined the role of liberal intellectuals typified by Hancock.

Alongside these developments emerged a strong school of feminist historians, led by Anne Summers, Beverley Kingston, and Miriam Dixson, all of whom produced major critiques of masculine culture in Australia in the same year, 1975. These historians argued that women's place in the national history had been ignored, and that new frameworks of explanation had to be built. Dixson was interested in the role of women in fashioning a national identity, and took issue particularly with her colleague at the University of New England, Russel Ward, whose "Australian Legend" now seemed narrowly masculinist. Summers contended that men could understand women only in the old dualism of Magdelene or Madonna. Until women could be seen outside this duality their prospects were limited. Kingston opened up the sphere of women's work, including unpaid housework, as a proper subject for historians. These early statements were succeeded by numerous feminist historians, typified by Drusilla Modjeska and Kerreen Reiger, who reexamined traditional topics with the women's question in view.

Many traditional topics were being reworked in this period. British historian George Rudé analyzed the minority of convicts transported for political reasons, while Robert Hughes, based in New York, wrote a wonderful summary of the convict experience in *The Fatal Shore* (1987). Paul Carter's *The Road to Botany Bay* (1987) was an exploration of the mental maps of the early settlers. John Hirst offered a fresh and imaginative vision of early New South Wales in *Convict Society and Its Enemies* (1983), Graeme Davidson told the urban story of Melbourne, while John Merritt retold the history of a major trade union from within to produce insights which had not been observed by traditional labor historians. As a corrective to excessive nationalism, Alan Atkinson in *Camden* (1988) demonstrated how very English this early settlement had been. John McQuilton argued that Ned Kelly should be seen as a "social bandit" rather than an unprincipled criminal, while the frontier story of Victoria's Gippsland region was explained by Don Watson as a chapter in Scottish migration. Tom Stannage rewrote the history of Perth (Western Australia) as a story of flawed success, while Janet McCalman used oral history methods to great effect in *Struggletown* (1984), the story of the inner working-class suburb of Richmond, Victoria. Oral history had been a long time in winning acceptance among Australian historians, who were obsessively wedded to the printed document, so McCalman's achievement was all the finer within that context. Gavin Souter examined the symbols and ceremonies of the new Commonwealth in its infant years, while excellent biographies of key leaders were produced by A.W. Martin (colonial politician Sir Henry Parkes), John Rickard (reformist judge H.B. Higgins) and Warren Osmond (policymaker Frederic Eggleston). Biographies in Australia had for the most part been innocent of psychological depth: these historians opened new opportunities for the craft of biography. Lloyd Robson applied his quantitative methodology to World War I soldiers, and Michael McKernan looked more critically at the home front during that war. Raymond Evans undertook a regional study of the effects of the war on Queensland, emphasizing the strong political connotations of domestic conflicts.

Perhaps the most remarkable revisionism of this period, however, was the sudden and dramatic attention paid to Aboriginal history, previously an arcane and specialized field. The leading prehistorian, D.J. Mulvaney, produced an archaeological overview in 1975, while Kenneth Maddock prepared a fresh anthropological version. Lyndall Ryan issued an excellent reconstruction of traditional Aboriginal life in the island colony of Tasmania. But the turning point came with the book by Henry Reynolds, *The Other Side of the Frontier* (1981), which described the impact of British settlement from the receiving end. Reynolds continued to produce fresh books on this theme, and brought a new level of sophistication to the debate. Then well-established historians joined in. Blainey popularized much of the technical research in his *Triumph of the Nomads* (1975), which countered the public view of nomadism as a defensive strategy and showed that "primitive" people were adaptive and versatile. Butlin, the eminent economic historian, used ecological evidence to argue that the carrying capacity of the continent was much greater than the traditional estimate of 300,000 indigenes would suggest, and asserted that it must be inferred that British settlement was far more destructive than usually imagined. Ann McGrath showed that Aborigines had adapted well to the opportunities of working with cattle in the Northern Territory, and had claimed the new industry as their own. Still there were very few Aboriginal historians writing their own version, a fact which made *Reading the Country* (1984) particularly welcome. This book was a joint effort between an Aboriginal stockman and two outsiders (Paddy Roe, with Krim Benterrak, and Stephen Muecke) recounting the oral tradition of his land, the area around Broome, Western Australia.

The bicentennial celebrations of 1988 stimulated several new synthetic works, some of which drew on the newer historiographical trends. The Crowley series contained five snapshot accounts of the national history at fifty-year intervals (1838, 1888, etc.) which had the virtue of focusing collaborative attention to social themes to an extent which had not occurred before. Other projects of 1988 included the series edited for Oxford University Press by Geoffrey Bolton, the social history series edited by Verity Burgmann and Jenny Lee, and the ethnic encyclopedia assembled by James Jupp. Professional history had achieved a level of recognition unimaginable even twenty years earlier. Australian history was taught at 34 of the nation's 36 universities, and, although its popularity among school-leavers had reached a plateau, it was a well-established field. The standard of teaching was high, and there were better books available than before, as much of the quality of scholarship had improved.

The 1990s registered a new confidence that history could contribute very directly to national debates and policy issues. The New South Wales premier created a History Council to provide historical advice to all government agencies. As the centenary of the Australian Constitution neared, several works examined the context which had surrounded federation in 1901. Macintyre in *A Colonial Liberalism* (1991) treated three key players in defining Australian citizenship – George Highbotham, David Syme and Charles Pearson – while Alastair Davidson wrote the first general history of the Australian State, a major if unobtrusive element of the national history. A feminist account of this nation-building was offered by the team comprising Patricia Grimshaw, Marilyn Lake, Ann McGrath and Marian Quartly. Important new statements in Australian intellectual history were made by Joy Damousi in *Women Come Rally* (1994), and by John McLaren describing the politics of Australian literature in the Cold War. Historians were annexing new territories, including ecological history (Stephen Pyne's account of fire), sports history (Robert Pascoe's social history of Australian Rules football), and a critique of Harry Braverman in the history of women's work (Raelene Frances). The history of Australia's minority cultures was well represented by the overview of Italian immigration and settlement edited by Stephen Castles. Finally, a magnificent study of Irish emigration to Australia, *Oceans of Consolation* (1994), was edited by David Fitzpatrick (son of Brian) while based in Dublin. This book wove the personal letters of a dozen or so families into the broader story of migration. It was typical of the new maturity in Australian historiography: well-crafted, sophisticated in its theorizing, and written for an international audience.

ROBERT PASCOE

See also Bean; Blainey; Britain: British Empire; Clark, M.; Dening; Ethnicity; Grimshaw; Indian Ocean; Lake; Legal; Maritime; Popular; Prehistory; Sport; Women's History: Australia; Wood, G.A.; World War I; World War II

Further Reading

Atkinson, Alan, *Camden*, Melbourne and New York: Oxford University Press, 1988

Bean, C.E.W., editor, *The Official History of Australia in the War of 1914–18*, 12 vols., Sydney: Angus and Robertson, 1921–42; abridged as *Anzac to Amiens*, 1946

Benterrak, Krim, Stephen Muecke, and Paddy Roe, *Reading the Country: Introduction to Nomadology*, Fremantle: Fremantle Arts Centre Press, 1984

Blainey, Geoffrey, *The Tyranny of Distance: How Distance Shaped Australia's History*, Melbourne: Sun, 1966, London: Macmillan, and New York: St. Martin's Press, 1968; revised 1982

Blainey, Geoffrey, *Triumph of the Nomads: A History of Ancient Australia*, Melbourne: Macmillan, 1975; Woodstock, NY: Overlook, and London: Macmillan, 1976; revised 1982

Bolton, Geoffrey, general editor, *The Oxford History of Australia*, 5 vols., Melbourne and New York: Oxford University Press, 1986–92

Burgmann, Verity, and Jenny Lee, eds., *A People's History of Australia since 1788*, 4 vols., Melbourne: McPhee Gribble, and New York: Penguin, 1988

Butlin, Noel George, *Investment in Australian Economic Development, 1861–1900*, Cambridge: Cambridge University Press, 1964

Butlin, Noel George, *Our Original Aggression: Aboriginal Populations of Southeastern Australia, 1788–1850*, Sydney and Boston: Allen and Unwin, 1983

Carter, Paul, *The Road to Botany Bay: An Essay in Spatial History*, London: Faber, 1987; New York: Knopf, 1988

Castles, Stephen *et al.*, eds., *Australia's Italians: Culture and Community in a Changing Society*, Sydney: Allen and Unwin, 1992

Clark, Manning, *A History of Australia*, 6 vols., Melbourne: Melbourne University Press, and New York and London: Cambridge University Press, 1962–87

Connell, Robert W., and T.H. Irving, *Class Structure in Australian History: Documents, Narrative, and Argument*, Melbourne: Longman Cheshire, 1980

Crowley, Frank K. *et al.*, general editors, *Australians: A Historical Library*, 11 vols., Sydney: Fairfax Syme and Weldon, and Cambridge: Cambridge University Press, 1987

Damousi, Joy, *Women Come Rally: Socialism, Communism and Gender in Australia, 1890–1955*, Melbourne and New York: Oxford University Press, 1994

Davidson, Alastair, *The Invisible State: The Formation of the Australian State, 1788–1901*, Cambridge and New York: Cambridge University Press, 1991

Davison, Graeme, *The Rise and Fall of Marvellous Melbourne*, Melbourne: Melbourne University Press, 1978

Dixson, Miriam, *The Real Matilda: Woman and Identity in Australia, 1788–1975*, Ringwood: Penguin, 1976; revised 1984

Evans, Raymond, *Loyalty and Disloyalty: Social Conflict on the Queensland Homefront, 1914–1918*, Sydney and Boston: Allen and Unwin, 1987

Fitzpatrick, Brian, *The British Empire in Australia: An Economic History, 1834–1939*, Melbourne: Melbourne University Press, and Oxford: Oxford University Press, 1941; revised 1949

Fitzpatrick, David, ed., *Oceans of Consolation: Personal Accounts of Irish Migration to Australia*, Ithaca, NY: Cornell University Press, 1994

Frances, Raelene, *The Politics of Work: Gender and Labour in Victoria, 1880–1939*, Melbourne, Cambridge and New York: Cambridge University Press, 1993

Gammage, Bill, *The Broken Years: Australian Soldiers in the Great War*, Canberra: Australian National University Press, 1974; New York: Penguin, 1975

Gollan, Robin, *Radical and Working-Class Politics: A Study of Eastern Australia, 1850–1910*, 1960, reprinted Melbourne: Melbourne University Press, 1976

Grimshaw, Patricia, Marilyn Lake, Ann McGrath and Marian Quartly, *Creating a Nation*, Melbourne: McPhee Gribble, and New York: Viking, 1994

Hancock, W.K., *Australia*, London: Benn, and New York: Scribner, 1930; reprinted 1960

Hancock, W.K., *Discovering Monaro: A Study of Man's Impact on His Environment*, Cambridge: Cambridge University Press, 1972

Hirst, John Bradley, *Convict Society and Its Enemies: A History of Early New South Wales*, Sydney and Boston: Allen and Unwin, 1983

Hughes, Robert, *The Fatal Shore: A History of the Transportation of Convicts to Australia, 1787–1868*, New York: Knopf, and London: Collins, 1987

Inglis, Kenneth, *The Australian Colonists: An Exploration of Australian Social History, 1788–1870*, Melbourne: Melbourne University Press, 1974

Jupp, James, general editor, *The Australian People: An Encyclopedia of the Nation, Its People, and Their Origins*, Sydney: Angus and Robertson, 1988

Kiddle, Margaret, *Men of Yesterday: A Social History of the Western District of Victoria, 1834–90*, Melbourne: Melbourne University Press, 1961

Kingston, Beverley, *My Wife, My Daughter and Poor Mary Ann: Women and Work in Australia*, Melbourne: Nelson, 1975

McCalman, Janet, *Struggletown: Public and Private Life in Richmond, 1900–65*, Melbourne: Melbourne University Press, 1984

McGrath, Ann, *"Born in the Cattle": Aborigines in the Cattle Country*, Sydney and Boston: Allen and Unwin, 1987

Macintyre, Stuart, *Winners and Losers: The Pursuit of Social Justice in Australian History*, Sydney and Boston: Allen and Unwin, 1985

Macintyre, Stuart, *A Colonial Liberalism: The Lost World of Three Victorian Visionaries*, Melbourne, New York, and Oxford: Oxford University Press, 1991

McKernan, Michael, *The Australian People and the Great War*, Melbourne and Cambridge: Nelson, 1980

McLaren, John, *Writing in Hope and Fear: Literature as Politics in Postwar Australia*, Melbourne and Cambridge: Cambridge University Press, 1996

McQueen, Humphrey, *A New Britannia: An Argument Concerning the Social Origins of Australian Radicalism and Nationalism*, Melbourne: Penguin, 1970; revised 1975

McQuilton, John, *The Kelly Outbreak, 1878–1880: The Geographical Dimension of Social Banditry*, Melbourne: Melbourne University Press, 1979

Maddock, Kenneth, *The Australian Aborigines: A Portrait of Their Society*, London: Allen Lane, 1973

Martin, Allan William, *Henry Parkes: A Biography*, Melbourne: Melbourne University Press, 1964

Merritt, John, *The Making of the AWU*, Melbourne and New York: Oxford University Press, 1986

Modjeska, Drusilla, *Exiles at Home: Australian Women Writers, 1925–1945*, London: Sirius, 1981

Molony, John, *The Penguin History of Australia*, New York: Viking, and London: Penguin, 1988

Mulvaney, Derek John, *The Prehistory of Australia*, London: Thames and Hudson, and New York: Praeger, 1969; revised 1975

Osmond, Warren, *Frederic Eggleston: An Intellectual in Australian Politics*, Sydney and Boston: Allen and Unwin, 1985

Pascoe, Rob, *The Winter Game: The Complete History of Australian Football*, Melbourne: Heinemann, 1995

Pike, Douglas, Bede Nairn, Geoffrey Serle, and John Ritchie, general editors, *Australian Dictionary of Biography*, 13 vols to date, Melbourne, London, and New York: Melbourne University Press, 1966–

Pyne, Stephen J., *Burning Bush: A Fire History of Australia*, New York: Holt, 1991; Sydney: Allen and Unwin, 1992

Reiger, Kerreen, *The Disenchantment of the Home: Modernizing the Australian Family, 1880–1940*, Melbourne and New York: Oxford University Press, 1985

Reynolds, Henry, *The Other Side of the Frontier: Aboriginal Resistance to the European Invasion of Australia*, Ringwood and Harmondsworth: Penguin, 1981

Rickard, John D., *H.B. Higgins: The Rebel as Judge*, Sydney and London: Allen and Unwin, 1984

Robson, Leslie Lloyd, *The Convict Settlers of Australia: An Enquiry into the Origin and Characteristics of the Convicts Transported to New South Wales and Van Diemen's Land, 1787–1852*, Melbourne: Melbourne University Press, and New York: Cambridge University Press, 1965

Robson, Leslie Lloyd, *The First AIF: A Study of Its Recruitment, 1914–18*, Melbourne: Melbourne University Press, 1970

Roe, Michael, *Quest for Authority in Eastern Australia, 1835–1851*, Melbourne: Melbourne University Press, 1965

Rowse, Tim, *Australian Liberalism and National Character*, Melbourne: Kibble, 1978

Rudé, George, *Protest and Punishment: The Story of the Social and Political Protestors Transported to Australia, 1788–1868*, Oxford and New York: Oxford University Press, 1978

Ryan, Lyndall, *The Aboriginal Tasmanians*, Vancouver: University of British Columbia Press, 1981

Serle, Geoffrey, *The Golden Age: A History of the Colony of Victoria, 1851–1861*, Melbourne: Melbourne University Press, 1963

Smith, Bernard, *Australian Painting, 1788–1970*, Melbourne and New York: Oxford University Press, 1971

Souter, Gavin, *Lion and Kangaroo: The Initiation of Australia, 1901–19*, Sydney: Collins, 1976

Stannage, Tom, *The People of Perth: A Social History of Western Australia's Capital City*, Perth: Perth City Council, 1979

Summers, Anne, *Damned Whores and God's Police: The Colonization of Women in Australia*, Melbourne: Penguin, and London: Allen Lane, 1975

Turner, Ian, *Industrial Labour and Politics: The Dynamics of the Labour Movement in Eastern Australia, 1900–1921*, Canberra: Australian National University Press, 1965

Ward, John M., *Earl Grey and the Australian Colonies, 1846–1957*, Melbourne: Melbourne University Press, 1958

Ward, Russel, *The Australian Legend*, Melbourne and New York: Oxford University Press, 1958

Watson, Don, *Caledonia Australis: Scottish Highlanders on the Frontier of Australia*, Sydney: Collins, 1984

Austro-Hungarian Empire

The study of the Austrian/Austro-Hungarian empire has experienced tremendous growth in the past half century. Often relegated to a trivial role, the multinational empire was rarely treated seriously by historians outside the Austrian Republic itself. After World War I, however, an ever-growing interest, particularly in the United States, in the development of 19th-century Austria, led to a virtual explosion in Austrian historiography. Historians have come to view the empire as an extremely important and integral part of the European continent, a part which played a much greater role in the development of Central Europe than was before realized or recognized. Furthermore, in light of events in southern Europe after the collapse of the Yugoslav state in 1989, an intense historical focus has been placed on the empire's social makeup and origins, its subsequent political and cultural development, and the reasons for the final collapse in 1918.

A study of the Austrian/Austro-Hungarian empire is impossible without a serious discussion of the ruling house of Habsburg. From its earliest origins the Austrian empire was a creation of the Habsburg family's desire to remain a powerful influence in the social fabric of post-Napoleonic Europe. Even after the Ausgleich of 1867 which formally altered the status of the Austrian empire into a dual monarchy, reviving the ancient kingdom of Hungary and thereby creating the Austro-Hungarian monarchy, the Habsburg family still reigned over a wide territory and a vast assortment of nationalities and religions. Subsequently, many of the early histories of the Austrian empire carried with them an extreme bias against the Habsburg family and the aristocratic heritage which it represented. These early perceptions were reinforced by the large Slavic influence on Western perceptions of the empire. During the 1920s and 1930s little hard and reliable data was available for the Austrian historian aside from accounts written by immigrants and dissidents who often displayed obvious biases. The empire was portrayed quite negatively as in Henry Wickham Steed's *The Hapsburg Monarchy* (1913), which saw the fall of the empire as being an essential step toward the growth of peace and stability in Europe. The Austrian empire was viewed as an antiquated state which suffered existence only at the hands of the other European great powers. In this vein the monarchy was often slandered and the many nationalities portrayed as oppressed peoples suffering under the yoke of tyranny. Typical of this era was Oszkar Jaszi's *The Dissolution of the Habsburg Monarchy* (1929). Jaszi contended that the Austrian empire was an oppressive state responsible for the retardation of Balkan national aspirations. Samuel Harrison Thomson, however, writing in the same period, signaled a change in Austrian studies. His major contribution, *Czechoslovakia in European History* (1943), contained a decided pro-Czech stance, but only in so far as they had legitimate demands for equal treatment by the Austrian government. Overall, Thomson dealt with the Austrian and Habsburg rulers objectively. Despite many lingering prejudices, these earlier studies served Austrian historiography by focusing scholarly attention on the Austrian empire and elevating its role in history.

Only after World War II did historians begin to view the monarchy in a more objective light. A new generation of historians from Austria, Britain, and the United States began working with original material released after the revolution of 1918. Writing much of their material in a vacuum, scholars such as Hans Kohn, Arthur J. May, and Robert Kann began to lead the field in Austrian, and to some degree, Central European studies. Hans Kohn's most famous book, *The Habsburg Empire, 1804–1918* (1961), served as a broad social, political history of the empire from the crowning of the emperor in 1804 to the revolution of 1918. Another important work by Kohn in which he examined the empire's diverse nationalities is *Pan-Slavism: Its History and Ideology* (1953). A more definitive work and one still widely regarded as the most comprehensive and important study in English, is Arthur J. May's *The Hapsburg Monarchy, 1867–1914* (1951). Although May's study discusses only the latter half of the empire, from the *Ausgleich* (compromise) with Hungary in 1867, the work is a highly valuable presentation of the political, economic, social, legal, and national development

of the region under Habsburg suzerainty. May followed up this important study with a later work, *The Passing of the Hapsburg Monarchy* (1966) in which he traced the final years of the empire in greater detail.

It was left to the work of Robert A. Kann, however, to dominate the field of Austrian history for the next thirty years. Kann was born in Austria, but moved to the United States where he taught history at Rutgers University. Kann wrote the comprehensive study, *A History of the Habsburg Empire, 1526–1918* (1974) as a textbook. The work was massive in its scope and Kann discussed the vast array of people and events which characterized the era in fields as varying as politics, music, philosophy, and science. Though the work is not an in-depth analysis of the period it does come to grips with the many complexities of the Habsburg/Austrian era. Kann's other works include *The Multinational Empire* (1950), wherein he examined the many ethnic and religious groups which lived under the empire's umbrella, and *The Habsburg Monarchy* (1957), which examined the successes and failures of the Austrian empire in creating a cohesive nation-state. These broad analyses produced by Kann are readily approachable and are a testament to Kann's command of the era; however, the student must turn elsewhere in order to gain a more detailed account of Austrian history.

Austrian imperial diplomatic history has not suffered for lack of attention. Worth mentioning are Enno Kraehe's *Metternich's German Policy* (1963) and Paul Schroeder's *Metternich's Diplomacy at Its Zenith* (1962). Both works are even-handed, diplomatic treatments of the early years of the Austrian empire and the intrigues of Prince Metternich. Schroeder's is particularly instructive in that he portrays the diplomatic maneuvering as seen at the time. Barbara Jelavich produced a brilliant work on the role of the Austrian empire within the European framework, *The Habsburg Empire in European Affairs, 1814–1918* (1969). Jelavich traced the foreign relations of the empire from the time of Metternich until the outbreak of World War I, emphasizing the importance the empire played in the subsequent development of Europe. R. John Rath's *The Viennese Revolution of 1848* (1957) is a well-written account of the politics of the revolution, a subject often overlooked by European historians. More recently, an excellent political study has been produced by F.R. Bridge, *The Habsburg Monarchy among the Great Powers, 1815–1918* (1990). Bridge examined the collapse of the Austrian position in Italy and Germany and emphasized the overwhelming political importance of the Balkan peninsula as the sole remaining sphere of expansion for the Austrian monarchy. He further stressed the role this played toward the outbreak of World War I. John W. Boyer in *Political Radicalism in Late Imperial Vienna: Origins of the Christian Social Movement, 1848–1897* (1981) examined the rapid rise of the Christian Socialist party in Vienna under the leadership of Karl Leuger and the decline of liberalism in the tumultuous political atmosphere of turn-of-the-century Vienna. Boyer continued this important examination of the Viennese political scene in *Culture and Political Crises in Vienna* (1995).

The area of military studies has long suffered neglect, the most influential work being that of Gordon A. Craig, *The Battle of Königgrätz* (1964). Craig went to great efforts to convey an impartial account of the Austro-Prussian war, and brought into serious question the common belief of a complete

Austrian military defeat. István Deák conducted a sociological study of the Austrian army. Though not actually a military history Deak has produced a fascinating study of the Austrian Officer Corps, its reliance upon an aristocratic heritage, the complex role of nationality and religion in its makeup, and its role in the society of the Austro-Hungarian empire in *Beyond Nationalism* (1990).

Jerome Blum's *Noble Landowners and Agriculture in Austria, 1815–1848* (1948) proved to be an important pioneering work in the economic history of the empire. For a more comprehensive study, however, the more recent work by David Good, *The Economic Rise of the Habsburg Empire, 1750–1914* (1984), provided a clear analysis of the economic strengths and weaknesses of the empire from its outset to its demise.

An important milestone in Austrian cultural history was established by Carl E. Schorske when a collection of previously published articles was brought into the mainstream with the book, *Fin-de-Siècle Vienna* (1979). Schorske examined turn-of-the-century Vienna, and the intellectual roots of the modernist era as seen in the fields of politics, literature, architecture, psychology, and art. Schorske artfully followed the evolutionary development of the era. The liberal bourgeoisie's internal struggle with democracy, as seen in the literature of some of the eras most important personages, through the rise of the masses under Karl Leuger and the redevelopment of Vienna into a modern city, and finally to the explosion of the modernist movement with the birth of expressionism. A student of Schorske's, William J. McGrath, has produced a similar study of the closely interwoven art and politics of fin-de-siècle Vienna in *Dionysian Art and Populist Politics in Austria* (1974). William M. Johnston offers an equally insightful work in *The Austrian Mind* (1972). Johnston conducted a close examination of the Austrian psyche as it developed through art and literature throughout the imperial period and beyond. He explored the intellectuals' fascination with death, decadence, and the collapse of the empire.

More recent studies have produced a number of important works in the field of social history. J. Robert Wegs in *Growing Up Working Class* (1989) is only one of several approaching the era from a grass roots level. Developments in the relatively new field of psychohistory have benefited the growing spectrum of Austrian studies. Peter Lowenberg's *Decoding the Past* (1983) psychoanalyzed several prominent Viennese. The political era is observed from this fresh perspective in *The Austro-Marxists, 1830–1918* (1985) by Mark E. Blum.

Recent years have witnessed a virtual explosion of analytical studies of the Austrian/Austro-Hungarian empire. From barely a few score works available in English at the turn of the century to virtually hundreds of published books, and several thousand articles, dealing with almost of every facet of the Austrian empire. The *Austrian History Yearbook* is a professional historical journal dedicated to the further study of Austrian and Habsburg history specifically, and Central European history in general and is a valuable edition to the ever growing host of Austrian historical studies.

STEPHEN K. CHENAULT

See also Balkans; Blum; Brunner; Central Europe; Germany: 1450–1800; Jelavich; Macartney; Marczali; Palacký; Pekař; Schorske; Seton-Watson, H.; Seton-Watson, R.; Srbik; Sugar; Szekfű; Taylor

Further Reading

Blum, Jerome, *Noble Landowners and Agriculture in Austria, 1815–1848: A Study in the Origins of the Peasant Emancipation of 1848*, Baltimore: Johns Hopkins Press, 1948

Blum, Mark E., *The Austro-Marxists, 1830–1918: A Psychobiographical Study*, Lexington: University of Kentucky Press, 1985

Boyer, John W., *Political Radicalism in Late Imperial Vienna: Origins of the Christian Social Movement, 1848 to 1897*, Chicago: University of Chicago Press, 1981

Boyer, John W., *Culture and Political Crises in Vienna: Christian Socialism in Power, 1897–1918*, Chicago: University of Chicago Press, 1995

Bridge, F.R., *The Habsburg Monarchy among the Great Powers, 1815–1918*, New York: Berg, 1990

Cohen, Gary, *The Politics of Ethnic Survival: Germans in Prague, 1861–1914*, Princeton: Princeton University Press, 1981

Craig, Gordon A., *The Battle of Königgrätz: Prussia's Victory over Austria*, Philadelphia: Lippincott, 1964; London: Weidenfeld and Nicolson, 1965

Deák, István, *Beyond Nationalism: A Social and Political History of the Habsburg Officer Corps, 1848–1918*, New York: Oxford University Press, 1990

Good, David, *The Economic Rise of the Habsburg Empire, 1750–1914*, Berkeley: University of California Press, 1984

Jaszi, Oszkar, *The Dissolution of the Habsburg Monarchy*, Chicago: University of Chicago Press, 1929

Jelavich, Barbara, *The Habsburg Empire in European Affairs, 1814–1918*, Chicago: Rand McNally, 1969

Johnston, William M., *The Austrian Mind: An Intellectual and Social History, 1848–1938*, Berkeley: University of California Press, 1972

Kann, Robert A., *The Multinational Empire: Nationalism and National Reform in the Habsburg Monarchy, 1848–1918*, 2 vols., New York: Columbia University Press, 1950

Kann, Robert A., *The Habsburg Monarchy: A Study in Integration and Disintegration*, New York: Praeger, 1957

Kann, Robert A., *A History of the Habsburg Empire, 1526–1918*, Berkeley: University of California Press, 1974

Kohn, Hans, *Pan-Slavism: Its History and Ideology*, Notre Dame, IN: University of Notre Dame Press, 1953

Kohn, Hans, *The Habsburg Empire, 1804–1918*, Princeton: Van Nostrand, 1961

Kraehe, Enno, *Metternich's German Policy*, 2 vols., Princeton: Princeton University Press, 1963

Lowenberg, Peter, *Decoding the Past: The Psychohistorical Approach*, New York: Knopf, 1983

Macartney, C.A., *The Habsburg Empire, 1790–1918*, London: Weidenfeld and Nicolson, 1968, New York: Macmillan, 1969; revised abridgement as *The House of Austria: The Later Phase, 1790–1918*, Edinburgh University Press, 1978

McGrath, William J., *Dionysian Art and Populist Politics in Austria*, New Haven: Yale University Press, 1974

May, Arthur J., *The Hapsburg Monarchy, 1867–1914*, Cambridge, MA: Harvard University Press, 1951

May, Arthur J., *The Passing of the Hapsburg Monarchy, 1914–1918*, Philadelphia: University of Pennsylvania Press, 1966

Rath, Reuben John, *The Viennese Revolution of 1848*, Austin: University of Texas Press, 1957

Schorske, Carl E., *Fin-de-Siècle Vienna: Politics and Culture*, New York: Knopf, 1979; London: Weidenfeld and Nicolson, 1980

Schroeder, Paul W., *Metternich's Diplomacy at Its Zenith, 1820–1823*, Austin: University of Texas Press, 1962

Shedel, James, *Art and Society: The New Art Movement in Vienna, 1897–1914*, Palo Alto, CA: Society for the Promotion of Science and Scholarship, 1981

Steed, Henry Wickham, *The Hapsburg Monarchy*, London: Constable, and New York: Scribner, 1913

Taylor, A.J.P., *The Habsburg Monarchy, 1815–1918: A History of the Austrian Empire and Austria-Hungary*, London: Macmillan, 1941; revised [with dates *1809–1918*], London: Hamish Hamilton, 1948, New York: Harper, 1965

Thomson, Samuel Harrison, *Czechoslovakia in European History*, Princeton: Princeton University Press, 1943

Wegs, J. Robert, *Growing Up Working Class: Continuity and Change among Viennese Youth, 1890–1938*, University Park: Pennsylvania State University Press, 1989

Axtell, James 1941–

US colonial and ethnohistorian

The American "frontier" is no longer what it used to be. As the term was applied by generations of American historians, most famously Frederick Jackson Turner, the frontier was an imaginary line drawn across successive western boundaries separating primitive savages from advanced Western civilization, a line marking the chasm between two antagonistic cultures. The frontier that was so historically creative for Turner has assumed its own dynamic character in the hands of James Axtell and nearly two generations of ethnohistorians. "Wherever diverse cultures came together, whether for trade, war, or love," Axtell wrote in a 1978 review essay, "there was the frontier." Frontiers have become contact arenas in which multiple autonomous societies take part in mutual culture exchange on roughly egalitarian terms. Once one group established its hegemony and the other(s)' ability to control its own destiny was compromised, the frontier disappeared. The very concept once used to explain the emergence of Anglo-American democracy, now explains America's multi-ethnic origins.

Working from this new, multifocal frontier, Axtell has been among the foremost writers restoring Native Americans to their central role in early American history. In his published collections of essays and in the first volume of his projected trilogy on the cultural origins of North America, *The Invasion Within* (1985), he has persistently and rightly insisted that the Indians were the primary determinants of events in early America. Given their importance, it is imperative for historians to understand the motivations of Indians on their own terms.

Understanding Indian motivations involved a huge methodological problem: How to study groups which left little or no written records? To resolve this dilemma, Axtell, and most other historians of American Indians, have developed ethnohistory, a hybrid discipline using anthropological methods to interpret historical sources. Archaeology, linguistics, cultural anthropology and ethnography help filter out the biases in the written accounts left by European observers of colonized societies. Axtell wrote in *The European and the Indian* (1981): "ethnohistory is essentially the use of historical and ethnological methods and materials to gain knowledge of the nature and causes of sociocultural change." In short, ethnohistory allows its practitioner to recapture some of the logic of and changes in nonliterate societies. Assessing cultural change incorporates a second focus of Axtell's work; he covers long periods of time to measure the change so important to the undertaking. *The Invasion Within* spans just under three hundred years.

The central theme of Axtell's work has been the mutual transculturation of Indians and Europeans. Unlike Francis Jennings

in *The Invasion of America* (1975), and others, who, whether chauvinistically or not, claim that Euroamerican culture left Indian societies broken, Axtell sees creative adaptations. This is most often and effectively pursued, according to Axtell, through pedagogical programs – the methods by which people are socialized. As a result, his work to date has focused on the invasion within, that is, English and French efforts to turn Indians into Europeans and Indian efforts to turn Indians into Europeans. If the number of converts and depth of socialization are fair indicators of conversions, the Indians were the most successful at incorporating aliens into their societies. Beyond an individual level, Indians shaped European society and vice versa in myriad ways. In many situations, Europeans depended upon Indians for food, tobacco, labor, transportation, military allies, and sexual partners. On the other hand, the European impact on Indian cultures brought superior technology, alcohol, and deadly viruses, all of which gradually undermined Indian autonomy by fostering dependence, breeding heightened violence, and undermining subsistence, production, confidence, and family and village life. It also produced native converts to Euroamerican societies. Axtell would remind us, however, that this change was slow and initiated by natives on their own terms. That various natives would lose their sovereignty was hardly inevitable early in their relations with Europeans.

Unlike most historians, Axtell cannot be labeled an archive-bound historian; in part, the interdisciplinary nature of ethnohistory and politicization of Indian affairs forces its adherents into a marriage of public and academic life. He has drawn upon artifacts housed in museums across northeastern America and helped create Native American exhibits, served as an expert witness in land compensation cases involving the Mashpee Indians of Long Island, lectured before many nonacademic audiences on the legacy of Indian-European interaction, and repeatedly addressed moral issues inherent in writing histories of frontiers.

For all his historical imagination, Axtell still remains somewhat bound by the limits of cultural anthropology. He allows for little variation among cultural groups which are themselves too broadly defined and tends to homogenize ethnic minds, especially Indian ones. For example, he maintains the ethnographic interpretive category "Eastern Woodland culture area" to explain roughly similar native beliefs and values despite the diversity of native languages, religions, social organizations, and ecologies.

His jargon-free and witty prose has made his work accessible for historians and lay people. That he has already produced three collections of mostly previously published essays and is frequently sought to speak before nonacademic audiences testifies to his popularity. Whether he (and other ethnohistorians) influence the larger profession and future syntheses of early American history, however, remains to be seen.

JAMES FISHER

See also Ethnohistory; Indigenous; Native American

Biography

James Lewis Axtell. Born Endicott, New York, 20 December 1941. Received BA, Yale University, 1963; PhD, Cambridge University,

1967. Taught at Yale University, 1966–72; Sarah Lawrence College, 1972–75; Northwestern University, 1977–78; and College of William and Mary, from 1978. Married Susan Carol Hallas, 1963 (2 sons).

Principal Writings

The School Upon a Hill: Education and Society in Colonial New England, 1974

"The Ethnohistory of Early America: A Review Essay," *William and Mary Quarterly* 3rd series, 35 (1978), 110–44

With James Ronda, *Indian Missions: A Critical Bibliography*, 1978

The European and the Indian: Essays in the Ethnohistory of Colonial North America, 1981

Editor, *Indian Peoples of Eastern America: A Documentary History of the Sexes*, 1981

The Invasion Within: The Contest of Cultures in Colonial North America, 1985

After Columbus: Essays in the Ethnohistory of Colonial North America, 1988

Beyond 1492: Encounters in Colonial North America, 1992

The Indians' New South, 1997

Further Reading

Baerreis, David A., Richard M. Dorson, Fred Eggan, John C. Ewers, Eleanor Leacock, Nancy O. Lurie, Wilcomb E. Washburn, "Symposium on the Concept of Ethnohistory," *Ethnohistory* 8 (1961), 1–92

Edmunds, R. David, "Native Americans, New Voices: American Indian History, 1895–1995," *American Historical Review* 100 (1995), 717–40

Fenton, William, "Ethnohistory and Its Problems," *Ethnohistory* 9 (1962), 1–23

Jennings, Francis, *The Invasion of America: Indians, Colonialism, and the Cant of Conquest*, Chapel Hill: University of North Carolina Press, 1975

Kupperman, Karen O., "Ethnohistory: Theory and Practice," *Reviews in American History* 10 (1982), 331–34

Lamar, Howard R., and Leonard Thompson, eds., *The Frontier in History: North America and Southern Africa Compared*, New Haven: Yale University Press, 1981

Martin, Calvin, "Ethnohistory: A Better Way to Write Indian History," *Western Historical Quarterly* 9 (1978), 41–56

Merrell, James H., "Some Thoughts on Colonial Historians and American Indians," *William and Mary Quarterly* 3rd series, 46 (1989), 94–119

Sturtevant, William C., "Anthropology, History, and Ethnohistory," *Ethnohistory* 13 (1966), 1–51

Trigger, Bruce G., "Sixteenth Century Ontario: History, Ethnohistory, and Archaeology," *Ontario History* 71 (1979), 205–22

Young, Mary E., "The Dark and Bloody but Endlessly Inventive Middle Ground of Indian Frontier Historiography," *Journal of the Early Republic* 13 (1993), 193–205

Ayandele, Emmanuel Ayankami 1936–

Nigerian historian

E.A. Ayandele has specialized in writing about the missionary impact in Nigeria, especially in western Nigeria among the Yoruba. Moreover, he has concentrated on the work of indige-

nous African missionaries, especially Bishop James Johnson whose work he so brilliantly discusses in *Holy Johnson* (1970). It is Ayandele's contention that the earlier missionaries were on their way toward creating a more truly indigenous and independent church. Bishop Johnson, a Sierra Leonian, had great missionary success. The Church Mission Society, basically a Church of England organization, however, fell victim to the developmentalist philosophy of the times that stated that Africans were not yet ready to assume leadership positions and must be followers and not leaders, ignoring the reality before them. Therefore, European missionaries began to assume greater leadership positions within the churches in Africa. Although Johnson himself never left the Anglicans, his experiences inspired others to secede from mission churches. Ayandele traces the growth of independent African churches to the increasing discrimination within the European dominated missionary societies. These African churches became an incubator of African nationalism, basically appealing to the westernized elite. These African churches stood out in the colonial context, for they were run by indigenous Africans and provided experience with self-rule unique in the colonial situation.

Johnson and other indigenous leaders became early nationalists, working to unite linguistic units into cohesive peoples and a geographical expression into a country. This nationalistic use of Christianity is an important aspect of its history in Africa that has often been overlooked. One of Ayandele's important contributions has been to highlight its significance within the history of Nigeria, and, by extension, Africa itself. This perspective also alerts the student to the active role of peoples colonized within their own history, and, therefore, their own creative power in shaping historical events.

FRANK A. SALAMONE

Biography

Born Ogbomosho, Oyo State, Nigeria, 12 October 1936. Educated at Baptist Boys' High School, Oyo, 1948–53; Nigerian College of Arts, Sciences and Technology, Ibadan, 1954–56; University College, Ibadan, 1956–61; King's College, University of London, 1961–63, BA, PhD. Taught history, University of Ibadan, 1963–75 (rising to professor, then principal); acting vice-chancellor, University of Calabar, 1975–80, then vice-chancellor, 1980–81. Married Margaret Oyebimpe Adeshima, 1975 (2 sons).

Principal Writings

The Missionary Impact on Modern Nigeria, 1842–1914: A Political and Social Analysis, 1966

Holy Johnson: Pioneer of African Nationalism, 1836–1917, 1970

A Visionary of the African Church: Mojola Agbebi, 1860–1917, 1971

African Exploration and Human Understanding, 1972

The Educated Elite of the Nigerian Society, 1974

African Historical Studies, 1979

Nigerian Historical Studies, 1979

"Joseph Christopher Okwudile Anene, 1918–1968," in Boniface I. Obichere, ed., *Studies in Southern African History*, 1982

The Ijebu of Yorubaland, 1850–1950: Politics, Economy, and Society, 1992

B

Babad

The usual translation of the Javanese term *babad* as "chronicle" or "history book" is somewhat misleading, as most Javanese and Balinese *babad* texts are neither "a chronological record of events," nor do they give very accurate accounts of historical happenings arranged in chronological order. While according to Javanese dictionaries the relationship with the verb *mbabad*, "to make a clearing in the forest," is questionable, Brakel and Moreh suggest it is possible that the Javanese term *babad* derives from an Arabic word meaning "chapter of a book," or "scene of a (shadow) play." This second derivation agrees with the view proposed by Brandes first and followed by Pigeaud, that the Javanese genre of *babad* texts comprising historical writings mixed with myths and legends from various sources (often in metrical verse, sometimes in prose) developed from 17th- and 18th-century *Serat Kandha* (books of stories). These universal histories or compendiums of mythology, first composed by scholars of the Islamic Pasisir culture in the north coast districts of Java, were and still are used as sources by professional storytellers and by performers of the shadow puppet theater (*wayang purwa*).

According to Brandes, the term *babad* followed by the name of a realm, such as *Babad Demak*, should not be considered as a book title but merely indicative of which period and realm the contents deal with. Brandes also emphasized the literary function of these texts and pointed at the interaction between written and oral traditions, including the shadowplay, thereby explaining the structure and the often mythical contents, as well as the many variant versions of Javanese historical texts. The Javanese scholar Djajadiningrat confirmed Brandes' view and characterized Javanese historiography as medieval, illustrating this with many examples.

As Javanese history books called *babad* or *sejarah* were usually composed for a ruling noble family, they contain genealogy and history seen from the dynasty's point of view. Thus, stories dealing with the end of the Hindu-Buddhist kingdoms in East Java and the rise of Islamic kingdoms on the north coast of Java as told in *Serat Kandha* and *babad* do not give unbiased accounts of these events and therefore according to Ricklefs their historical significance "is not to be found in their value as sources on the fall of Majapahit, but rather as documents revealing how Javanese courts saw their own past and their own place and significance in Javanese history."

Apart from historical data in royal charters, the earliest writings on political and dynastic history from the pre-Islamic era in Java were composed in the East Javanese 14th–15th centuries kingdom of Majapahit, following the Chinese invasion into East Java. The famous *Desawarnana* (Description of Districts), a literary work written by a high Buddhist official for king Hayam Wuruk, contains a chronicle of events at the Majapahit court between 1353 and 1364. More historically relevant information is found in the *Pararaton* (Book of Kings) which gives an account in Old Javanese prose of the 1293 war with the Chinese invaders, the founding of the Majapahit kingdom, and the reign of king Hayam Wuruk, followed by a brief survey of subsequent kings until 1389. One reason why this work is considered as a prototype of the *babad* genre of the following Islamic period is that its initial chapters likewise relate the mythical origin of the Majapahit dynasty. Moreover, the dating of important events in the *Pararaton* is often by means of a chronogram (*sengkala*), similar to the lists of chronograms referring to important historical events (*babad sengkala*) composed at the Islamic courts, which were used by Javanese authors of court histories. In 1965 Berg suggested a parallel between the founding of the Islamic realm of Mataram and the founding of Hindu-Buddhist realm of Majapahit, because the expression *Babad Tanah Jawi* (Chronicle of the Land of Jawa), the name of the famous history books of the Central Javanese kingdoms, occurs in the *Pararaton*, but his theory has found little support.

Pigeaud made a distinction between the main *babad* written at the courts of the Central Javanese rulers, and local histories of noblemen which were written mainly to prove the rights to rule of a particular noble family in Java or Bali, by producing genealogical trees going back to Majapahit times or before. So far, scholarly attention has focused mainly on the various *Babad Tanah Jawi* texts composed by poets in service of the Javanese rulers of Surakarta and Yogyakarta during the 18th and 19th centuries. Local *babad* as well as genealogies and tales of Islamic saints recorded in historical books from the early Islamic period on were incorporated into the court *babad*, but are as yet insufficiently known.

From the end of the 19th century, when European scholars started serious study of Javanese history, the reliability of the historical information in *babad* texts has been questioned. Gradually a scholarly method developed according to which evidence from Indonesian historical texts was accepted only if it could be verified from other independent – Indonesian as well as foreign – sources. However, in the course of the 20th century an anthropological interest developed in the "non-historical" elements of Javanese historical texts, including social structure and religious systems. Again, in a reaction to Berg's 1938 article on Javanese historiography, Drewes warned against the tendency to neglect historiographical material in Javanese historical texts by pointing out that these often contained useful and reliable historical evidence, especially when the author described events and situations which he had personally witnessed. Brakel's conclusion that: "ultimately, the historical 'reliability' of a text will largely depend on the character, the structure and the function of that text," reflects a growing awareness that Javanese historical texts need to be studied and evaluated within their own cultural context.

CLARA BRAKEL-PAPENHUYZEN

See also Ranggawarsita; Southeast Asia

Further Reading

Berg, C.C., "Javaansche geschiedschrijving" (Javanese Historiography), in Frederick Willem Stapel, ed., *Geschiedenis van Nederlandsch-Indié*, vol. 2, Amsterdam: van de Vondel, 1938

Berg, C.C., "Twee nieuwe publicaties betreffende de geschiedenis en geschiedschrijving van Mataram" (Two New Publications on the History and Historiography of Mataram), *Indonesie* 8 (1955), 97–128

Berg, C.C., "Babad en babad-studie" (Babad and the Study of Babad), *Indonesie* 10 (1957), 68–84

Berg, C.C., "The Javanese Picture of the Past," in Mohammad Ali Soedjatmoko, G.J. Resink, and George McTurnan Kahin, eds., *An Introduction to Indonesian Historiography*, Ithaca, NY: Cornell University Press, 1965

Brakel, L.F., "*Dichtung und Wahrheit*: Some Notes on the Development of the Study of Indonesian Historiography," *Archipel* 20 (1980), 35–44

Brakel, Clara, and Shmuel Moreh, "Reflections on the Term *baba*: From Medieval Arabic Plays to Contemporary Javanese Masked Theater," *Edebiyat* 7 (1996), 21–39

Brandes, Jan Laurens Andries, *Pararaton (Ken Arok) of het boek der koningen van Tumapel en van Majapahit* (Paraton [Ken Arok] or the Book of the Kings of Tumapel and of Majapahit), Batavia: Albrecht, and The Hague: Nijhoff, 1920

Carey, Peter B.R., *Babad Dipanagara: An Account of the Outbreak of the Java War (1825–30)*, Kuala Lumpur: Malaysian Branch of the Royal Asiatic Society, 1981

Creese, H.M., "Balinese Babad as Historical Sources: A Reinterpretation of the Fall of Gelgel," *Bijdragen Koninklijk Instituut voor Taal-, Land- en Volkenkunde* 147/2-3, 236–60

Day, John Anthony, "*Babad Kandha, Babad Kraton*, and Variation in Modern Javanese Literature," *Bijdragen Koninklijk Instituut v. Taal-, Land- en Volkenkunde* 134 (1978), 433–50

Djajadiningrat, Hoesein, *Critische beschouwing van de Sadjarah Banten: Bijdrage ter kenschetsing van de Javaansche geschiedschrijving* (Critical Reflection on the Sadjarah Banten: A Contribution to the Characterization of Javanese Historiography), Haarlem: Enschede, 1913

Drewes, G.W.J., "Over werkelijke en vermeende Geschiedschrijving in de Nieuwjavaansche litteratuur" (On Real and Supposed Historiography in Modern Javanese Literature), *Djawa* 19 (1939), 244–257

Fox, James J., "Sunan Kalijaga and the Rise of Mataram: A Reading of the *Babad Tanah Jawi* as a Genealogical Narrative," in Peter G. Riddell and Tony Street, eds., *Islam: Essays on Scripture, Thought and Society: A Festschrift in Honour of Anthony H. Johns*, Leiden: Brill, 1997

Graaf, H.J. de, "De historische betrouwbaarheid der Javaansche overlevering" (The Historical Reliability of the Javanese Tradition), *Bijdragen Koninklijk Instituut voor Taal-, Land- en Volkenkunde* 112 (1956), 55–73

Kartodirdjo, Sartono, ed., *Profiles of Malay Culture: Historiography, Religion and Politics*, Jakarta: Ministry of Education and Culture, 1976

Krom, Nicolas Johannes, *Hindoe-Javaansche geschiedenis* (Hindu-Javanese History), The Hague: Nijhoff, 1926; revised 1931

Olthof, W.L., ed. and trans., *Babad Tanah Djawi in proza: Javaansche geschiedenis* (Babad Tanah Djawi in Prose: Javanese History), 2 vols., The Hague: Nijhoff, 1941

Pigeaud, Theodore Gauthier Thomas, *Literature of Java*, 3 vols., The Hague: Nijhoff, 1967–70

Ras, Johannes Jacobus, "The Babad Tanah Jawi and Its Reliability: Questions of Content, Structure and Function" and "The Genesis of the Babad Tanah Jawi: Origin and Function of the Javanese Court Chronicle," in his *The Shadow of the Ivory Tree: Language, Literature and History in Nusantara*, Leiden: Vakgroep Talen en Culturen van Zuidoost-Azie en Oceanie, Rijksuniversiteit te Leiden, 1992

Ricklefs, Merle Calvin, "A Consideration of Three Versions of the Babad Tanah Djawi," *Bulletin School of Oriental and African Studies* 35 (1972), 285–96

Ricklefs, Merle Calvin, *Jogjakarta under Sultan Mangkubumi, 1749–1792: A History of the Division of Java*, London: Oxford University Press, 1974

Ricklefs, Merle Calvin, *Modern Javanese Historical Tradition: A Study of an Original Kartasura Chronicle and Related Materials*, London: School of Oriental and African Studies, 1978

Ricklefs, Merle Calvin, "The Evolution of the *Babad Tanah Jawi* Texts," *Bijdragen Koninklijk Instituut voor Taal-, Land- en Volkenkunde* 135 (1979), 443–54

Ricklefs, Merle Calvin, *A History of Modern Indonesia, c.1300 to the Present*, London: Macmillan, and Bloomington: Indiana University Press, 1981; 2nd edition Macmillan, and Stanford, CA: Stanford University Press, 1993

Robson, Stuart O., *Deśawarnana (Nāgarakrtāgama)* (Description of Districts), Leiden: KITLV Press, 1995

Rubinstein, R., "The Brahmana According to Their Babad," in Hildred Geertz, ed., *State and Society in Bali: Historical, Textual and Anthropological Approaches*, The Hague: Nijhoff, 1991

Soedjatmoko, Mohammad Ali, G. J. Resink, George McTurnan Kahin, eds., *An Introduction to Indonesian Historiography*, Ithaca, NY: Cornell University Press, 1965

Uhlenbeck, E.M., *A Critical Survey of Studies on the Languages of Java and Madura*, The Hague: Nijhoff, 1964

Worsley, P.J., *Babad Buleleng: A Balinese Dynastic Genealogy*, The Hague: Nijhoff, 1972

Bailyn, Bernard 1922–
US historian

As one of his students, Gordon Wood, put it in 1991, "few if any American historians in the modern era of professional history-writing have dominated their particular subject of specialization to the degree that Bailyn has dominated early American history in the past thirty years."

Bernard Bailyn's studies of the American colonies and the coming of the revolution center on issues of culture change – the ways in which transplanting European culture created a new and distinct society. In his work four general areas emerge: he has analyzed the importance of the specific conditions of settlement; the formation of provincial ("creole") elites; the habits and routines of colonial social and political life; and the growth of new ideological assumptions regarding politics and authority. In all of these studies, he has noted the growing distance between imperial political and social institutions, and the role and understanding of those institutions in colonial America. The central and most influential of his works is *The Ideological Origins of the American Revolution* (1967).

Although he is often described as an intellectual historian, and the emphasis on ideas in *The Ideological Origins* would seem evidence for this, Bailyn is better understood as a historian of society, or as a social historian in the broadest sense. His early work on New England merchants and "Politics and Social Structure in Virginia" (1959), described the formation of the habits and practices of creole elites – merchants in the northern colonies and planters in the Chesapeake. That work, along with *Education in the Forming of American Society* (1960), showed the adoption of modes of life and thought that went with the creation of new societies, based on European culture, but formed in a very different physical and social environment. Two major books, *The Origins of American Politics* (1968) and *The Ideological Origins of the American Revolution*, extended this description to explain the growing distance between imperial assumptions and colonial experience in both the practice and the theory of colonial politics. The analysis of the social and ideological roots of the revolution was essentially completed in the biography, *The Ordeal of Thomas Hutchinson* (1974), in which were shown the profound differences between loyalist and colonial attitudes, and the attendant misunderstandings, especially in the contrast between the elite figures of John Adams and Hutchinson. Adams' resentments are understood as an outgrowth of conflicting assumptions about the foundations of authority: Hutchinson came from a world of tightly structured social hierarchies, while Adams lived in a more fluid social, economic, and political culture.

Ideology, for Bailyn, provides the key to understanding those differences, defined as that which serves to mediate between society and intellect. A prominent concern throughout is with the ideology of authority, and how that ideology changed, from one of assumed deference and hierarchy to one in which "authority was questioned before it was obeyed" ("The Central Themes of the American Revolution" [1973]). This particular emphasis appears in his work in an edited volume of previously unpublished political pamphlets (*Pamphlets of the Revolution* [1965]). There he discovered the deep influences of back bench or "radical Whig" ideas (commonly thought of as "Republican") on American political understanding. But the degree of that influence was comprehensible only with the background of political habits that Bailyn described in *Origins of American Politics*. Thus his three books of the mid-1960s explained how the different political, and social lives of Americans had led them to interpret British political writings very differently from those who lived in the British homeland.

Bailyn's writing grows in large part from the influence of his mentor, Oscar Handlin, and in reaction to the earlier Progressive historians (particularly Beard) and the later neo-Progressives. From Handlin came the sense of "the constructed nature of both personality and society," which extended in Bailyn's work to the view that politics "is best understood as society operating upon government." Those notions provided the basis of Bailyn's understanding of politics and change.

The Progressives had argued that revolutionary rhetoric taken at face value disguised the crucial role of class conflict in creating the revolution. Bailyn's early work in turn provided a critique of class theory as applied to the colonial period. But he was especially conscious of the Progressive critiques of earlier writing as he developed his argument for the role of ideology. To stave off such dismissals, he accumulated the evidence to show that the differences between America and Britain were deep-rooted in the colonial society, a pattern developing long before the events of the 1760s, and a social pattern that gave specific meaning to ideological interpretations. Thus his argument comes to look much like that of Tocqueville's for the French Revolution, although Bailyn has generally argued that the Revolution had less to do with modernization than environmental difference.

Bailyn's Harvard University graduate students (more than sixty by 1991) have gone a variety of directions. Some, like Gordon Wood, have followed his lead (Wood has elaborated on Bailyn's republican synthesis to reconstruct and recover an entirely new range of meanings from the constitutional experiments that followed the revolution); while others, such as James Henretta, have become influential in challenging Bailyn's synthesis.

The strongest critiques of Bailyn's work come from scholars who emphasize the differences among the American colonists, as well as the role of economic forces, thus tending to undermine the sense of a fundamental shared culture and especially a shared motivation to revolt. Works by Edward Countryman (*The American Revolution*, 1985) and Jack P. Greene (*Pursuits of Happiness*, 1988) have challenged Bailyn on the basis of the many local studies that appeared as part of the new social history, which began in the late 1960s.

Bailyn has continued his exploration of colonial history by launching a new study of immigration (*The Peopling of British North America* [1986], *Voyagers to the West* [1986]), which seems to fit his earlier studies in two ways: he describes a population frustrated by encounters with the British structures of authority and privilege, and he describes a British government unable to recognize or begin to cope with the nature of those complaints.

Bailyn's books and articles build a formidable case for cultural change. He has contributed significantly to the literature on Republicanism and has expanded the ways in which historians study the roles of ideas and ideology in relation to the modes of everyday life. In these ways he has influenced historical practice and the understanding of early American history.

DONALD R. PALM

See also Ethnicity; Migration; Miller, P.; Quinn; United States: Colonial; United States: 19th Century; Wood, Gordon

Biography

Born Hartford, Connecticut, 10 September 1922. Received BA, Williams College, 1945, MA, Harvard University, 1947, PhD 1953. Served in Army Security Service and Army Signal Corps, World War II. Taught (rising to professor), Harvard University, 1954–93 (emeritus). Married Lotte Lazarsfeld, 1952 (3 sons).

Principal Writings

The New England Merchants in the Seventeenth Century, 1955
"Politics and Social Structure in Virginia," in James M. Smith, ed., *Seventeenth-Century America*, Chapel Hill: University of North Carolina Press, 1959

Education in the Forming of American Society: Needs and Opportunities for Study, 1960

Pamphlets of the American Revolution, 1965

The Ideological Origins of the American Revolution, 1967; revised 1992

The Origins of American Politics, 1968

"The Central Themes of the American Revolution: An Interpretation," in Stephen G. Kurtz and James H. Hutson, eds., *Essays on the American Revolution*, Chapel Hill: University of North Carolina Press, 1973

The Ordeal of Thomas Hutchinson, 1974

With others, *The Great Republic: A History of the American People*, 1977; 4th edition 1992

The Peopling of British North America: An Introduction, 1986

Voyagers to the West: A Passage in the Peopling of America on the Eve of the Revolution, 1986

Faces of Revolution: Personalities and Themes in the Struggle for American Independence, 1990

Editor with Philip D. Morgan, *Strangers within the Realm: Cultural Margins of the First British Empire*, 1991

On the Teaching and Writing of History: Responses to a Series of Questions, 1994

Further Reading

Henretta, James A., Michael G. Kammen, and Stanley N. Katz, eds., *The Transformation of Early American History: Society, Authority, and Ideology*, New York: Knopf, 1991

Shalhope, Robert E., "Toward a Republican Synthesis: The Emergence of an Understanding of Republicanism in American Historiography," *William and Mary Quarterly* 29 (1972), 49–80

Shalhope, Robert E., "Republicanism and Early American Historiography," *William and Mary Quarterly* 39 (1982), 334–56

The Balkans

The term Balkans describes an area of geographic and ethnic diversity that consists of modern-day Romania, Bulgaria, Albania, Greece, Macedonia, Yugoslavia, Croatia, Bosnia, and Slovenia. Objectivity has repeatedly eluded Balkan history because most prominent pre-World War II Balkan historians were also politicians, and, especially under communist regimes, many historians worked in state research institutes dedicated primarily to promoting their government's policies. The arduous struggles that Balkan people waged for their freedom against the Ottoman and Habsburg empires have also focused most Balkan historians on the study of only their own nations.

Influenced by West European rationalism, a few 17th- and 18th-century Balkan intellectuals, seeking a better understanding of their national identities, substituted well-documented and analytical histories for chronicles. In the process they uncovered some of the enduring problems of Balkan history. Mavro Orbini (mid-16th century–1611), a Croat, introduced the question of national origins when he theorized that the Slavs were autochthonous to the Balkans, but another Croat, Ivan Lucius (1604–79), proved that they did not arrive until the 6th century CE. The earliest Romanian historians, Miron Costin (?1633–91), Constantin Cantacuzino (?1640–1716), and Dimitrie Cantemir (1673–1723), concluded that Romanians were Latins, not Slavs, because they originated during the Daco-Roman era (c. 50 BCE–273 CE) and never left their homeland. Orbini also introduced the issue of pan-Slavism by stressing the common ethnicity of the South Slavs (Croats, Serbs, and Slovenes). However, a fellow

Croat, Ritter Pavao Vitezović (1652–1713), identified all the South Slavs with the Croats. Early Serbian historians, such as Count Djordje Branković (1645–1711) and Jovan Rajić (1726–1801), maintained that the Serbs had a separate national identity, although Rajić included them among the South Slavs. Additionally, he broadened the pan-Slavic concept by closely connecting the South Slavs with the Russians. The first Bulgarian historian, Paissi Hilendarski (?1722/23–?1773/98), also believed that all Slavs were related, the ties between the Bulgarians and the Russians being especially close.

During the 19th century many Balkan historians studied at German or Austrian universities where they learned German methods for critically analyzing documents. Several of them, such as the Bulgarian Iordan Ivanov (1872–1947), the Serbian Mihailo Gavrilović (1868–1924), the Croatian Ivan Sakcinski Kukuljević (1816–89), the Greeks Spyridon Lambros (1851–1919) and Konstantinos Sathas (1842–1914), and the Romanians Ioan Bogdan (1864–1919) and Nicolae Iorga (1871–1940), also scoured Europe for documents and published what they found. Furthermore, scholars from Romania, such as Alexandru Odobescu (1834–95), Vasile Parvân (1882–1927), Constantin Daicoviciu (1898–1973), and Ion Nestor (1905–74), and from Bulgaria like Krastiu Miyatev (1892–1966) and Vassil Zlatarski (1866–1935), introduced archaeology to augment the scanty written evidence for ancient and medieval Balkan history.

The steady decline of the Ottoman empire and the influence of German nationalism prompted 19th-century Balkan historians to intensify their predecessors' stress on national political history. By 1914 all the Balkan peoples under Ottoman domination had obtained their independence, while the Croats, Bosnians, and Slovenes remained subjects of Austria-Hungary. Serbian and Croatian historians continued to debate the South Slav issue, with scholars from both nations advocating the establishment of Yugoslavia, but without clarifying how they would apportion political power among themselves.

Balkan peoples based their claims for independence or political rights on nationality, and history helped to prove that each group met the requirements for nationhood. Theorists included literary culture as a major determinant of nationhood, so Balkan historians such as the Serbian Stojan Novaković (1842–1915), who had heretofore concentrated on political history, began exploring literary topics. As a result cultural history became a favorite theme for future Balkan historical research.

Another determinant of nationhood was independence. Every Balkan ethnic group except the Slovenes had established a kingdom at some time during the Middle Ages. For nationalistic reasons, Lambros, Novaković, the Croatian Tadija Smičiklas (1843–1914), the Romanian Alexandru D. Xenopol (1847–1920), and the Bulgarian Marin Drinov (1838–1906) stressed the ancient and medieval eras and hurried through the intervening centuries to their modern movements for national liberation. Novaković's publications on Balkan medieval history included research on the boundaries of the Serbian kingdom. Historical geography had practical applications for the pre-1914 territorial squabbles between Serbia, Bulgaria, and Greece because each justified their modern territorial claims on the areas occupied by their medieval kingdoms. Unfortunately, these boundaries often overlapped.

The previously broached question of national origins became a defense against this "kingdom formula" when state formation was subordinated to length of residence. For example, Greece's most outstanding 19th-century historian, Konstantinos Paparregopoulos (1815–91) argued that neither the Slavs nor the Albanians had replaced the ancient Greeks, but that the Greeks had continuously occupied their homeland since antiquity, and served as a source for Eastern European culture. The Albanians justified their ambitions for independence and land by identifying themselves with the ancient Illyrians. The Romanians used their Daco-Roman theory to demand Transylvania from Hungary.

Between 1919 and 1939 these time-honored practices culminated with some excellent political histories, such as those of Constantin C. Giurescu (1901–77) and Iorga for Romania, and Mikhail D. Dimitrov (1881–1966) and Dimiter T. Strashimirov (1868–1939) for Bulgaria. Historians also researched economic, social, and new cultural topics that enriched Balkan history. Prominent among them are: the Romanian David Prodan (1902–92) on social history; the Bulgarian Zhak Natan (1902–74) on economic history; and the Greek Yanis Kordatos (1891–1961), who created a major controversy by attacking the continuity of the Greek nation using Marxist theory.

The communist regimes that seized power in every Balkan country except Greece after 1945 forced historians to revise their national histories with Marxism-Leninism. Although most of this political history is useless, a few scholars, such as the Romanian Alexandru Duțu, wrote erudite social, economic, and cultural histories on less ideologically sensitive medieval, Ottoman, and pre-communist economic topics. Valuable research guides and new collections of documents also appeared during these years. Communism, by attracting attention to the Balkans, stimulated Western interest in its history, resulting in the formation of a large community of historians; many have been Balkan émigrés, who have published penetrating analyses on all aspects of Balkan history. These scholars include: Stephen Fischer-Galati and Keith Hitchins on Romania; John D. Bell and Maria Todorova on Bulgaria; Richard Clogg and Steven Runciman on Greece; Bernd Fischer and Nicholas Pano on Albania; and Gale Stokes, Ivo Banac, and David MacKenzie on Yugoslavia. Beginning with R.W. Seton-Watson earlier in the 20th century a number of Western historians, including Hugh Seton-Watson, M.S. Anderson, Robert Wolff, Joseph Rothschild, Leften Stavrianos, Peter Sugar, Barbara Jelavich, John V.A. Fine, Jr., James F. Brown, John Lampe, Marvin Jackson, and the Yugoslav Traian Stoianovich, have broken the limitations of Balkan national history by writing integrated histories on various subjects. Since 1989 Balkan historians have themselves displayed greater interest in their relationships with Europe and the world than ever before, which may make their studies more diverse in the future.

Robert F. Forrest

See also Austro-Hungarian; Barkan; Central Europe; East Central Europe; Fischer; Greece: Modern; Halecki; Inalcık; Jelavich; Obolensky; Ottoman; Seton-Watson, R.; Stavrianos; Sugar

Further Reading

Anderson, Matthew Smith, *The Eastern Question, 1774–1923: A Study in International Relations*, London: Macmillan, and New York: St. Martin's Press, 1966

Banac, Ivo, *The National Question in Yugoslavia: Origins, History, Politics*, Ithaca, NY: Cornell University Press, 1984

Bell, John D., *The Bulgarian Communist Party from Blagoev to Zhivkov*, Stanford, CA: Hoover Institution Press, 1986

Berend, Tibor Iván, and György Ránki, *East Central Europe in the Nineteenth and Twentieth Centuries*, Budapest: Akadémiai Kiadó, 1977

Bogdan, Ioan, *Cronici inedite atingătoare de istoria romînilor* (Unpublished Chronicles Touching on Romanian History), Bucharest: Socecŭ, 1895

Branković, Djordje, *Slaveno-Serbske Hronike* (Slavo-Serbian Chronicles), 5 manuscript vols., *c.*1700, never published

Brown, James F., *Hopes and Shadows: Eastern Europe after Communism*, Durham, NC: Duke University Press, and London: Longman, 1994

Cantacuzino, Constantin, *Istoria Țării Românești* (History of Wallachia) [unfinished], *c.*1700; first published 1858, reprinted Bucharest: Editora Academici Romane, 1991

Cantemir, Dimitrie, *Hronicul vechimii romano-moldo-vlahilor* (Chronicle of the Antiquity of the Romano-Moldavians and Wallachians), written 1719–22; published 1835–36, reprinted Bucharest: Albatros, 1981

Clogg, Richard, *A Concise History of Greece*, Cambridge and New York: Cambridge University Press, 1991

Costin, Miron, *Letopisetul Țării Moldovei* (Chronicle of Moldavia), 1675; reprinted Bucharest: Minowa, 1979

Daicoviciu, Constantin, *La Transylvanie dans l'antiquité* (Transylvania in Antiquity), Bucharest, 1945

Dimitrov, Mikhail D., *Poiava razvitie i ideologiia na fashizma v Bulgarii* (Appearance, Development, and Ideology of Fascism in Bulgaria), 1947

Drinov, Marin, *Zaselenie balkanskogo poluostrova slavianami* (The Settlement of the Balkan Peninsula by the Slavs), 1872

Dutu, Alexandru, *Les Livres de sagesse dans la culture Roumaine*, Bucharest, 1971

Fine, John Van Antwerp, Jr., *The Early Medieval Balkans: A Critical Survey from the Sixth to the Late Twelfth Century*, Ann Arbor: University of Michigan Press, 1983

Fine, John Van Antwerp, Jr., *The Late Medieval Balkans: A Critical Survey from the late Twelfth Century to the Ottoman Conquest*, Ann Arbor: University of Michigan Press, 1987

Fischer, Bernd Jürgen, *King Zog and the Struggle for Stability in Albania*, New York: Columbia University Press, 1984

Fischer-Galati, Stephen, *Twentieth-Century Romania*, New York: Columbia University Press, 1970; revised 1991

Gavrilović, Mihailo, *Ispisi iz pariskih arhiva: gradja za istoriju prvog srpskog ustanka* (Transcripts from Parisian Archives: Sources for the History of the First Serbian Uprising), Belgrade: Srpska Kraljevska Akademija, 1904

Giurescu, Constantin C., *The Making of the Romanian People and Language*, Bucharest: Meridiane, 1972

Hilendarski, Paissi, *Tsarstvennik ili istoriia bolgarskaia* (A Book of Kings or a History of Bulgaria), written 1762; published 1844

Hitchins, Keith, *Rumania, 1866–1947*, Oxford and New York: Oxford University Press, 1994

Horecky, Paul L., ed., *Southeastern Europe: A Guide to Basic Publications*, Chicago: University of Chicago Press, 1969

Iorga, Nicolae, *Studii și documentente cu privire la istoria romînilor* (Studies and Documents Concerning the History of the Romanians), 31 vols., 1901–16

Iorga, Nicolae, *Histoire des Roumains et de la romanité orientale* (A History of the Romanians and of the Latin East), 10 vols., 1937–45; partially translated as *A History of Roumania: Land, People, Civilisation*, London: Unwin, 1925, reprinted New York: AMS, 1970

Ivanov, Iordan, *Bogomilski knigi i legendi* (Bogomil Books and Legends), Sofia: Pridvorna Pechatnitsa, 1925; reprinted 1970

Jackson, Marvin R., and John R. Lampe, *Balkan Economic History, 1550–1950: From Imperial Borderlands to Developing Nations*, Bloomington: Indiana University Press, 1982

Jelavich, Barbara, *Russia and the Greek Revolution of 1843*, Munich: Oldenbourg, 1966

Jelavich, Barbara, *History of the Balkans*, 2 vols., Cambridge and New York: Cambridge University Press, 1983

Kaser, Michael C., general editor, *The Economic History of Eastern Europe, 1919–1975*, 3 vols. to date, Oxford and New York: Oxford University Press, 1985–86

Kordatos, Yanis, *Historia tes neoteros Helladas* (History of Modern Greece), 5 vols., Athens: Ekdoses, 1957–58

Kukuljević, Ivan Sakcinski, ed., *Arhiv za povestnicu jugoslavensku* (Archive for Yugoslav History), 12 vols., 1851–75 [periodical]

Lambros [Lampros], Spyridon, *Historia tes Hellados*, 6 vols. in 5, Athens: Karolo Bek, 1886–88

Lucius, Ivan [Giovanni Lucio], *De regno Dalmatiae et Croatiae* (The Kingdom of Dalmatia and Croatia), 6 vols., Venice: Curti, 1666; reprinted Bologna: Forni, 1977

MacKenzie, David, *The Serbs and Russian Pan-Slavism, 1875–1878*, Ithaca, NY: Cornell University Press, 1967

Miyatev, Krastiu [Krustiu Miiyatev], *Dekorativnata zhipopis' na sofiiskiia nekropol* (The Decorative System of Bulgarian Murals), Sofia: Pridvorna Pechatnitsa, 1925

Natan, Zhak [Jacques P. Nathan], *Ikonomicheska istoriia na bulgariia* (Economic History of Bulgaria), 2 vols., Sofia: Pechatnitsa Rakovski, 1938

Nestor, Ion, *Der Stand der Vorgeschichtsforschung in Rumänien* (The State of Prehistoric Research in Romania), 1933

Novaković, Stojan, *Srbi i Turci XIV i XV veka* (The Serbs and the Turks in the 14th and the 15th Centuries), Belgrade: Drizavnoj, 1893; reprinted Belgrade: Kultura, 1960

Odobescu, Alexandru, *La Trésor de pétrossa* (The Treasure of Pietroasa), Paris: Rothschild, 1889–1900; reprinted in *Opere*, vol.4, Bucharest, 1976

Okey, Robin, *Eastern Europe, 1740–1980: Feudalism to Communism*, Minneapolis: University of Minnesota Press, and London: Hutchinson, 1982; revised 1986

Orbini, Mavro, *Il regno degli Slavi* (The Kingdom of Slavs), Pesh: Concordia, 1601; reprinted Munich: Sagner, 1985

Pano, Nicholas, *The People's Republic of Albania*, Baltimore: Johns Hopkins University Press, 1968

Paparregopoulos, Konstantinos, *Historia tou hellenikou ethnous* (History of the Greek People), 6 vols., Athens: Passaree, 1860–77; abridged in French as *Histoire de la civilisation hellénique*, Paris: Hachette, 1878

Parvân, Vasile, *Inceputurile vieții romane la gurile Dunării* (The Beginnings of Roman Life at the Mouth of the Danube), Bucharest: Cultura National, 1923

Prodan, David, *Supplex libellus valachorum; or, The Political Struggle of the Romanians in Transylvania during the Eighteenth Century*, Bucharest: Publishing House of the Academy of the Socialist Republic of Romania, 1971

Rajić, Jovan, *Istoria raznih slavenskih narodov naipače Bolgar, Horvatov i Serbov* (The History of Various Slavic Peoples Especially Bulgars, Croats, and Serbs), 4 vols., 1794–95

Rothschild, Joseph, *Return to Diversity: A Political History of East Central Europe since World War II*, Oxford and New York: Oxford University Press, 1989; revised 1993

Runciman, Steven, *The Great Church in Captivity: A Study of the Patriarchate of Constantinople from the Eve of the Turkish Conquest to the Greek War of Independence*, Cambridge: Cambridge University Press, 1968

Sathas, Konstantinos, *Mnemeia Hellenikes historias: Documents inédits relatifs à l'histoire de la Grèce au Moyen Age* (Unpublished Greek Documents Relating to the History from the Classical Era to the Middle Ages), 9 vols., Paris: Maisonneuve, 1880–90

Seton-Watson, Hugh, *The East European Revolution*, London: Methuen, 1950; 3rd edition New York: Praeger, and London: Methuen, 1956

Seton-Watson, R.W., *The Southern Slav Question and the Habsburg Monarchy*, London: Constable, 1911; reprinted New York: Fertig, 1969

Smičiklas, Tadija, *Poviest hrvatska* (Croatian History), 2 vols., Zagreb: Naklada Matice hrvatske, 1879–82

Stavrianos, Leften Stavros, *The Balkans since 1453*, New York: Rinehart, 1958

Stoianovich, Traian, *Balkan Worlds: The First and Last Europe*, Armonk, NY: Sharpe, 1994

Stokes, Gale, *Politics as Development: The Emergence of Political Parties in Nineteenth-Century Serbia*, Durham, NC: Duke University Press, 1990

Strashimirov, Dimiter T., *Istoriya na aprilskoto vastanie* (A History of the April Uprising), 3 vols., Plovdiv: Plovdivskata Okruzhna Postoianna Komisiia, 1907

Sugar, Peter F., *Southeastern Europe under Ottoman Rule, 1354–1804*, Seattle: University of Washington Press, 1977

Todorov, Nikolai, *The Balkan City, 1400–1900*, Seattle: University of Washington Press, 1983 [Russian original]

Todorova, Maria N., *Balkan Family Structure and the European Pattern: Demographic Developments in Ottoman Bulgaria*, Washington, DC: American University Press, 1993

Vitezović, Ritter Pavao, *Die Ehre des Herzogthums Krain* (The Honor of the Duchy Croatia), 1689

Wolff, Robert L., *The Balkans in Our Time*, Cambridge, MA: Harvard University Press, 1956; revised 1974

Xenopol, Alexandru D., *Istoria românilor din Dacia Traiană* (The History of the Romanians in Trajan Dacia), 6 vols., Iassi: Goldner, 1888–93

Zlatarski, Vassil, *Istoria na balgarskata darjava* (History of the Bulgarian State), 4 vols., Sofia: Dŭrzh, 1918–40

Ban Gu [Pan Ku] 32–92 CE

Chinese historian

Ban Gu is best known as the principal author of *Han shu* (History of the Han). As the first dynastic history of China, *Han shu* defined the standard format for later dynastic histories. Moreover, since most of the sources Ban Gu used have been lost, *Han shu* now serves as one of the most important sources for the study of the history of the Former Han (206–8 BCE).

In his historical scholarship, Ban Gu was inspired by his father Ban Biao (3–54 CE). The latter was dissatisfied by the parts of Sima Qian's (c.145–c.87 BCE) *Shiji* (Historical Records) that dealt with the history of the Han dynasty. To develop a good history of the Former Han, Ban Biao wrote several dozen chapters of his own work. The chapters are now lost, but parts of them were incorporated into *Han shu* by Ban Gu.

Although the *Han shu* project grew out of an initial dissatisfaction with *Shiji*, Ban Gu's work was still very much influenced by Sima Qian's. Like Sima Qian, Ban Gu was able to take advantage of source materials in the imperial archives in composing his historical work. In the presentation of the history of the earlier parts of the Former Han history, Ban Gu frequently adopted the accounts written by Sima Qian, although Ban Gu often also added his own selections of extra information. *Han shu*'s one hundred chapters are divided into four categories: imperial annals, tables of important persons and institutions, treatises on specialized subjects, and "biographies" (which included the lives of important individuals and accounts of foreign peoples). This general division of chapters is very similar to that of *Shiji*, except for the fact that *Han shu* does not contain a separate group of chapters on "hereditary families."

In spite of the similarities between the two works, *Han shu* is much more than an imitation of *Shi ji*. *Han shu* differs from the earlier work on several accounts. First, as a dynastic history, *Han shu* was written to cover the history of the Former Han. *Shiji*, on the other hand, was written as a comprehensive history covering all periods from the early legendary emperors to Sima Qian's own time. Second, within the larger format of presentation adapted from Sima Qian, Ban Gu added a few innovations. He added a new kind of table on the evolution of institutional structure of government and the occupants of important official positions under the Former Han. He also added three new kinds of treatise: on the development of penal law, on administrative geography and on the extant literature (in the broad sense, including works on philosophy, history, and other subjects). Ban Gu was also different from Sima Qian in philosophical outlook. He has generally been considered by later scholars to be a Confucian, whereas Sima Qian has not.

Han shu is not only the first dynastic history of China, but Chinese scholars have also considered it to be one of the best written. With few exceptions, most of the later dynastic histories were written according to the "annals + tables + treatises + biographies" structure used in *Han shu*.

Ban Gu did not complete the treatise on astronomy and the eight tables in his lifetime. His sister Ban Zhao (?48–116 CE) and Ma Xu finished these parts after Ban Gu's death. Ma Xu's exact dates are not clear, but we do know that he was still active in 141.

For the beginner, the most helpful English-language introduction to *Han shu* is A.F.P. Hulsewé's essay on this work in *Early Chinese Texts* (1993). The essay provides much of the information presented here and gives much further information on the transmission of the text as well as important editions and secondary scholarship.

XIAO-BIN JI

See also China: Early and Middle Imperial; China: Early and Middle Imperial, Historical Writing

Biography
Born Shanxi, 32 CE. Educated at higher imperial academy, Loyang. Imperial librarian; emperor's attendant in charge of secretarial affairs. Died Loyang, Henan, 92 CE.

Principal Writings
Han shu (History of the Han), 100 vols., completed 80s CE; partially translated in: Homer H. Dubs, *The History of the Former Han Dynasty*, 3 vols., 1937–48; Clyde Bailey Sargent, *Wang Mang*, 1947; Nancy Lee Swann, *Food and Money in Ancient China*, 1950; Burton Watson, *Courtier and Commoner in Ancient China*, 1974; Anthony Francis Paulus Hulsewé, *China in Central Asia: The Early Stage, 125 BC–AD 23*, 1979; David R. Knechtges, *The Han shu Biography of Yang Xiong (53 BC–AD 18)*, 1982
Pai hu t'ung, written 79 CE; translated as *Po Hu T'ung: The Comprehensive Discussions in the White Tiger Hall*, 2 vols., 1949–52

Further Reading
Beilenstein, Hans A.A., "The Restoration of the Han Dynasty," *Bulletin of the Museum of Far Eastern Antiquities* [Stockholm] 21 (1954)
Chen Zhi [Chen Chih], *Han shu xin zheng* (New Evidential Studies on *Han shu*), Tianjin: Renmin, 1959; reprinted 1979
Dubs, Homer H., "The Reliability of Chinese Histories," *Far Eastern Quarterly* 6 (1946–47), 23–43
Hulsewé, Anthony F.P., "Notes on the Historiography of the Han Period," in William G. Beasley and Edwin G. Pulleyblank, eds., *Historians of China and Japan*, London: Oxford University Press, 1961
Hulsewé, Anthony F.P., "Han shu," in Michael Loewe, ed., *Early Chinese Texts: A Bibliographical Guide*, Berkeley, CA: Institute of East Asian Studies, 1993
Sargent, Clyde B., "Subsidized History: Pan Ku and the Historical Records of the Former Han Dynasty," *Far Eastern Quarterly* 3 (1943–44), 119–43
van der Sprenkel, O.B., *Pan Piao, Pan Ku, and the Han History*, Occasional Paper 3, Canberra: Australian University Centre of Oriental Studies, 1964
Wang Xianqian [Wang Hsien Chien], *Han shu bu zhu* (Supplementary Notes on *Han shu*), 2 vols., 1900; reprinted Beijing: Zhonghua, 1983
Yang Shuda [Yang Shu ta], *Han shu kui guan* (Investigations into *Han shu*), Beijing: Kexue, 1955

Bancroft, George 1800–1891
US historian

The author of sweeping, highly romanticized sagas of American history, George Bancroft was a pioneer historian, and his significance lies in this role. He was the first to unearth and examine documents from America's initial century, the one to whom later scholars turned for sources. Moreover, he wrote at a time when transcendentalism, literary romanticism, nationalism, and reform were the dominant intellectual streams of thought, and was, therefore, one of the first to espouse American exceptionalism and divine purpose.

A child prodigy, Bancroft graduated from Harvard in 1817 at the age of 17. He studied theology at Göttingen University in Germany, but rejected the ministry as a profession almost immediately. His inclination to teach was similarly overshadowed by a desire to pursue his own interests, not simply to instruct others. Thus, Bancroft became active in the Democratic party, and was largely responsible for uniting Boston's short-lived Workingmen's party and Anti-Masons with Jacksonian Democrats in the 1836 election.

For his party leadership in Massachusetts, Bancroft was rewarded with a cabinet position by president James K. Polk. Appointed secretary of the Navy in 1845, he became embroiled in negotiations with Mexico for Texas independence and sent John Frémont to the West Coast, an exploratory mission that ended in the infamous Bear Flag rebellion. While Bancroft ruled Boston and then ran the Navy from Washington, he also wrote literary criticism and started his multivolume *History of the United States from the Discovery of the American Continent* (1834–74), which he would not complete until into his retirement.

Bancroft's version of the past was relatively simple. He traced great individuals as they advanced through time. His theory was that history unveiled the record of a divine plan. God, he believed, was visible in history, and providence guided the affairs of men and nations. Progress, therefore, was part of this larger plan, and seen most vividly in the saga of the New World. Mankind was intended by God to progress toward a future state where truth, justice, beauty, and morality would guide and raise it further.

Bancroft's focus was great men and events, and all others faded into the background, unknown and unimportant. A true Jeffersonian in philosophy, he adhered to the theory of racial and national evolution; each race and every nation progressed through stages. The Anglo-Saxon race, of course, was superior, yet he absolutely believed in mankind's goodness. Thus, Bancroft held the conviction that God had placed reason, kindness, love, and beauty within the reach of all, and other races would eventually catch up. Indigenous Americans were, he claimed, feeble barbarians, who desperately needed the hand of white Europeans to guide them toward improvement, and the main reason for the nation's agricultural blessings was the Native Americans' inability to use the land. Having lain dormant for centuries, the land was ready to produce if only Europeans developed it.

Although he generally called himself a Jacksonian Democrat, Bancroft is probably more accurately termed a Jeffersonian Republican operating within the scope of Jacksonian Democracy. He considered big questions, and his thoughts frequently turned to ideas like the evolution of freedom and democracy throughout history or sovereignty of the people and their right to use it freely. Liberty, he believed, made America the hope of the world. Nevertheless, Bancroft feared that unrestricted democracy could lead to mob rule as did Tocqueville, and he disliked the rabble that he felt characterized president Jackson's administration. He favored unionism, national expansion, and generally agreed with Jackson's views on the national bank, but an aristocrat at heart, he tended to adhere more strongly to Jeffersonian principles.

Bancroft's lengthy histories often read like novels. His style was flowery and extravagant, and although his scholarship was seldom disputed, Bancroft was not above altering information in favor of drama. In short, he liked heroes without warts, and one critic accused him of writing about the US as if he were writing the history of the Kingdom of Heaven. Bancroft's research, however, incorporated a range of sources including literature and philosophy, and his writings centered on historical questions such as the clash of good and evil in history or the power of fate in men and nations. His history displayed the overwhelming optimism so evident of America's Golden Age and the absolute conviction that American political, economic, and cultural opportunities were exceptional in the history of the world. Whether writing about the creation of the Constitution or exploration, God's hand was clearly in the picture.

As the romanticism of America's antebellum period waned and the combined forces of industrialization and urbanization took hold after the Civil War, Bancroft was criticized more and more for his tendency to neglect accuracy for drama and for his out-of-date style. His brand of history began to be replaced by a slightly more pessimistic tone that prided itself on pithy accuracy.

Still, Bancroft's place in American history is secure despite his lack of professional training and the demise of American exceptionalism after 1893. Bancroft discovered, collected, and pored over documents and manuscripts from colonial and revolutionary America. He unearthed Jacksonian era sources that would prove invaluable to later historians, and he operated without monographic material available to fall back upon. In other words, Bancroft was in the enviable position of being the first to use many of the primary historical documents of the United States. He recorded much of the factual information that later historians would turn to in their attempts to reinterpret American history. He wrote history that an eager public wanted to read, thus making his the first peoples' historians as well. Finally, in his unbridled nationalistic defense of the US as God's City upon a Hill, he challenged those who followed to formulate new interpretations of big events and American heroes.

KATHLEEN EGAN CHAMBERLAIN

See also Andrews; Gipson; Nationalism; Schlesinger; United States: 19th Century

Biography

Born Worcester, Massachusetts, 30 October 1800, son of a clergyman. Studied at Phillips Exeter Academy; Harvard University, BA 1817; Göttingen University, PhD 1820. Taught at Harvard University, 1822–23; established Round Hill School, Northampton, Massachusetts, 1823–31. Collector of the Port of Boston and Democratic party chair, 1836–45; secretary of the Navy, 1845–46; minister plenipotentiary to England, 1846–49; minister to Court of Prussia, 1867–73. Presented eulogies for Andrew Jackson, Washington, DC, June 1845, and Abraham Lincoln, New York City, 1866. Retired from public service, 1873; wrote history throughout his retirement. Married 1) Sarah Dwight, 1827 (died 1837; 1 daughter, 2 sons); 2) Mrs. Elizabeth Bliss, née Davis, 1838 (1 daughter). Died Washington, DC, 17 January 1891.

Principal Writings

History of the United States from the Discovery of the American Continent, 10 vols., 1834–74

History of the Colonization of the United States, 3 vols., 1837–40

An Oration Delivered at the Commemoration in Washington of the Death of Andrew Jackson, 1845

Memorial Address on the Life and Character of Abraham Lincoln, 1866

History of the Formation of the Constitution of the United States of America, 2 vols., 1882

"The Relations Between Hamilton and Washington," *American Antiquarian Society, Proceedings of the Council*, by the Council, new series 3, 1884

Martin Van Buren to the End of His Public Career, 1889

The History of the Battle of Lake Erie and Miscellaneous Papers, edited by Oliver Dyer, 1891

Further Reading

Dawes, N.H., and F.T. Nichols, "Revaluing Bancroft," *New England Quarterly* 6 (1933), 278–93

Levin, David, *History as Romantic Art: Bancroft, Prescott, Motley, and Parkman*, Stanford, CA: Stanford University Press, 1959

Nye, Russel Blaine, *George Bancroft: Brahmin Rebel*, New York: Knopf, 1944

Barkan, Ömer Lütfi 1905(?)–1979
Turkish economic and legal historian

With the exception of Halil Inalcık, Ö.L. Barkan is the most widely respected economic and demographic historian of the 15th- and 16th-century Ottoman empire. He is prominent as the first historian to exploit and use widely the records and documents in the Ottoman archives, especially the Prime Ministers' Archives in Istanbul. He and his students established a new school of Ottoman historical studies and methodology, primarily archivally based, that continues to influence contemporary Ottoman studies in Turkey and in many other countries. Barkan was influenced by his studies in Strasbourg during the early 1930s and by the work of Lucien Febvre and the Annales school, although his work neither imitated nor confirmed the Annales school approach. His approach differed from the Braudelian school in that he did not emphasize the parallels and common dimensions of Ottoman and European history in the early modern period, but rather argued that the Ottoman empire was truly its own creation. This view is presently contested by many Ottoman historians.

Barkan focused on the historical, judicial and statutory laws concerning the peasants of the 15th and 16th centuries. He contended there was no feudalism in the empire comparable to European feudalism as posited by the Annales school, especially by Marc Bloch, or the Turkish historian Mübeccel Kıral. Furthermore, Barkan, along with Halil Inalcık, rejected the Marxist theory that the Asiatic mode of production was applicable to the Ottoman empire as Sencer Divitçioğlu and other Turkish Marxist historians had suggested. This stance allowed Barkan and Inalcık to diminish the Marxist influence on Ottoman studies and, consequently, also on the study of modern Turkish history.

Many of Barkan's early works were studies of documents dealing with the legal status of peasants. Beginning in 1942–43, he began to publish agrarian and landed estate law codices that had been in force in various parts of the empire, especially the Balkans. This was the first time that such research had been done. During the 1940s and 1950s, Barkan published numerous substantial works on imperial methods of colonizing and settling conquered lands, especially in the Balkans, on demographic changes in the cities, and on methods of provisioning them. These studies laid the basis for the first detailed and accurate account of how the empire had expanded. This, in turn, meant explanations of circumstances of how the conquered lands were Turkicized and Islamized, especially in the Balkans, and to what extent. These were and still are extremely contentious issues.

Barkan produced several major studies on the demography of the empire, especially of the European provinces of the empire. On this topic he entered into a dispute with Fernand Braudel who put the population of the empire at the end of the 16th century at 22 million whereas Barkan suggested 30–35 million. The latter figure is today thought to be too high. Barkan published some of his work on demography in French and English, which enhanced his reputation in Europe and the United States. His works were little read and circulated among European medievalists and early modernists who did not read Turkish. None of his major works has been translated, and thus have not had as much recognition or as much influence on early modern European history and the history of the Mediterranean as they might have.

Barkan also had an interest in the effects that the European price revolution and the Atlantic economy had on the fluctuation of prices in the Ottoman empire. He concluded that the price revolution had major negative effects on the empire, and had facilitated its incorporation in the world economy of the 16th century.

Barkan's entire corpus of work has recently come under attack, especially in Turkey and notably by Halil Berktay, who, in *New Approaches to State and Peasant* (1992), accused Barkan of "document fetishism" and "state fetishism" and claimed that his publications, especially the earlier ones, reflected the bias of his strong Turkish nationalism and preference for state authoritarianism. Berktay argued that such ideological stances prevented Barkan from comprehending the role that class played in history and prevented him from understanding the common dimensions of Ottoman and other histories, especially European feudalism. Berktay criticized Barkan's work as lacking analytical rigor, adequate methodology, and historical detachment.

In spite of recent criticism of his methodology, his theories, and the influence of ideology on his work, the bulk of Barkan's output will continue to play an influential role in Ottoman studies. His work supplies an indispensable corpus of documents and materials that seem unlikely to be paralleled in the future. Whether his findings are accepted or rejected, his works remain pivotal to the study of 15th- and 16th-century Ottoman history.

ROBERT OLSON

See also Ottoman

Biography
Born Edirne, 1905(?). Studied at University of Istanbul; Superior Normal School, BA 1927; University of Strasbourg, 1931. Taught at History Institute, University of Istanbul, 1933–37; then moved to the newly created Faculty of Economics (rising to professor), where he remained until his retirement. Founded Institute of Economic History, 1950; appointed professor ordinarius, 1957. Died 23 August 1979.

Principal Writings
"Osmanlı Imparatorluğunda bir iskân ve kolonizasyon methodu olarak vakıflar ve temlikler" (The Religious Foundations and Landed Estates as Methods of Colonialization and Settlement in the Ottoman Empire), *Vakıflar Dergisi* 2 (1942), 279–353 [224 documents]

XV. ve XVI. asırlarda Osmanlı imparatorluğunda ziraî ekonominin hukukî ve malî esasları (Judicial and Financial Principles of the Agriculture Economy of the Ottoman Empire in the 15th and 16th Centuries), Istanbul, 1943

"Osmanlı imparatorluğunda bir iskân ve kolonizasyon methodu olarak sürgünler" (Deportations as a Method of Settlement and Colonization in the Ottoman Empire), *Iktisat Facültesi Mecmuası* 11 (1946–50), 524–69; 13 (1951–52), 58–79; 15 (1953–54), 209–329

"Quelques observations sur l'organisation économique et sociale de villes Ottomans des XVIe et XVIIe siècles" (Some Observations on the Economic and Social Organization of Ottoman Cities in the 16th and 17th centuries), *Recueil Société Jean Bodin pour l'histoire comparative des institutions: la ville*, 1955, 289–311

"1079–1080 (1669–1670) mâlî yılına âit bir Osmanlı bütçesi ekleri" (An Ottoman Budget for the Financial Year 1079–1080 (1669–1670) and Annexes), *Iktisat Facültesi Mecmuası* 17 (1955–56), 225–303

"1070–1071 (1660–1661) tarihli Osmanlı bütçesi ve bir mukayese" (The Ottoman Budget Dated 1070–1071 (1660–1661) and a Comparison), *Iktisat Facültesi Mecmuası* 17 (1955–56), 304–47

"Essai sur les données statistiques des registres de recensement dans l'Empire Ottoman aux XVe et XVIe siècles" (Essay on the Statistical Data of the Population Registers of the Ottoman Empire in the 15th and 16th centuries), *Journal of the Economic and Social History of the Orient* 1 (1957), 9–36

"894 (1488–1489) yılı cizyesinin tahsılatına âit muhasebe bilânçoları" (The Book-Keeping Balances of the *Cizye* Tax for the Year 894), *Belgeler* 1 (1964), 1–17

"Edirne askerî kassâmı na âit tereke defterleri, 1545–1659" (The Inheritance Register of the Edirne Military Kassam [adjuster of inheritance shares], 1545–1659), *Belgeler* 3 (1966), 1–479

"XVI. asrın ikinci yarısında Türkiye'de fiyat hareketleri" (The Fluctuation of Prices in Turkey in the Second Half of the 16th Century), *Belleten* 34 (1970), 557–607

With Ekrem Hakkı Ayverdi, *Istanbul vakıfları tahrir defteri 953/1456 tarihli* (Register of the Transactions of the Charitable Foundations of Istanbul for the Year 963/1456), Istanbul, 1970

"Timar" (Landed Estates), *Islâm Ansiklopedisi* (Encyclopedia of Islam) fascicules 123 and 124 (1972), 286–333

Süleymaniye cami ve imareti inşaatı, 1550–1557 (The Construction of Süleymaniye Mosque and Its Charitable Complex, 1550–1557), 2 vols., Ankara, 1972

"The Price Revolution of the 16th century: A Turning Point in the Economic History of the Near East," *International Journal of Middle East Studies* 6/1 (1975), 3–28

Türkiye'de toprak meselesi (The Land Question in Turkey), Istanbul, 1980

With Enver Meriç, *Hudavendigâr (Bursa) livâsı sayım defterleri* (The Population Registers of the Province of Bursa), Ankara, 1988

Further Reading

Bacqué-Grammont, Jean-Louis, and Paul Dumont, editors, *Contribution à l'historie économique et social de l'empire Ottoman* (Contributions to the Social and Economic History of the Ottoman Empire), Leuven: Peeters, 1983

Berktay, Halil, and Suraiya Faroqhi, editors, *New Approaches to State and Peasant in Ottoman History*, London: Cass, 1992

Inalcık, Halil, with Donald Quataert, *An Economic and Social History of the Ottoman Empire, 1300–1914*, Cambridge and New York: Cambridge University Press, 1994

"Mémorial Omer Lütfi Barkan" (Memorial to Ömer Lütfi Barkan), *Paris Bibliothèque de l'institut Français d'études Anatoliennes d'Istanbul* 23 (1980), vii–ix

"Ord. Prof. Ömer Lütfi Barkan'a armağanı" [Festschrift], *Iktisat Facültesi Mecmuası* 41 (1982/83), 1–38

Şakiroğlu, Mahmut Hasan, "Ord. Prof. Ömer Lütfi Barkan" [complete bibliography], *Belleten* [Turkey] 44 (1980), 153–77

Baron, Hans 1900–1988

US (German born) historian of the Renaissance

One of many German Jewish scholars to emigrate to the United States in the years just preceding World War II, Baron revolutionized the study of early Italian Renaissance humanism across a wide range of fields. His *The Crisis of the Early Italian Renaissance* (1955) is one of the major works on the Italian Renaissance written in this century and certainly the most controversial. The product of decades of research and numerous specialized articles, the book imposed a broad interpretive framework on Italian humanism, endeavoring to relate intellectual change to political and sociological development. In place of the relatively vague evolutionary approach to humanism characteristic of pre-World War II scholarship, Baron sharply contrasted Trecento with Quattrocento humanism, explaining the passage from the first to the second as the result of a crisis. He buttressed his thesis with substantial documentation from literary sources, many of them hitherto neglected.

Baron characterized Petrarch and his immediate 14th-century disciples as envisaging humanistic studies within a Christian context which privileged the contemplative life and political quietism over the active life of the citizen. In the early years of the 15th century, however, he identified a new humanism stressing the importance of civic life and political participation. This new movement Baron called "civic humanism" and saw it as beginning in Florence. In Baron's view the titanic struggle between republican Florence and Giangaleazzo Visconti from 1389 to 1402, which nearly ended in the destruction of the Florentine republic, made Florentine humanists realize the value of their civic culture and led to a sudden change in attitude. The earliest manifestation of this new position, Leonardo Bruni's *Laudatio urbis florentinae* (1403/4), marked the beginning of a republican interpretation of history and politics which, diffused over the Alps in the 16th century, served as the core of the republican tradition in Western European culture down to the 19th century. Furthermore, the humanists' new positive assessment of the lay life, together with their justification of wealth, laid a theoretical foundation for the modern secular view of society.

Immediately inciting controversy by its description of Florence's government as republican, *The Crisis* inspired dozens of young scholars, many of them American, to turn to the Florentine archives in search of a better understanding of Florentine institutional and social history in the Renaissance. Other researchers investigated pre-1400 appearances of republican thought in Western Europe and tested the political character of other Italian city-state regimes against the Florentine example. In *The Articulate Citizen and the English Renaissance* (1965) Arthur Ferguson utilized Baron's concept of "civic humanism" for a study of 16th-century English political thought and J.G.A. Pocock's *The Machiavellian Moment: Florentine Political Thought and the Atlantic Republican Tradition* (1975) did the same in its wide-ranging study of European republicanism down to modern times.

Closely tied to the central themes of *The Crisis*, Baron's subsequent writings on Machiavelli significantly altered our conception of Machiavelli's intellectual development and the character of his thought. His now widely accepted dating of the *Prince* as prior to the *Discourses* suggested an evolution of Machiavelli's ideas from the largely amoral position of the first work to the republican convictions of the second. Baron's later contributions to Petrarch studies, however, have been less important. Committed to the assumption that a close reading of Petrarch's texts against a background of the biography would allow scholars to demonstrate the precise evolution of Petrarch's thought, his work largely overlooked the rhetorical element so prominent in the humanist's writings.

This tendency to discount the literary/rhetoric dimension of humanist thought, together with his need to find a simplistic ethical purity in the civic humanists and his pursuit of certitude for conclusions which can only be probable at best, constitute generally recognized shortcomings in Baron's work. Nonetheless, Baron's basic distinctions between 14th- and 15th-century Italian humanism continue to dominate the interpretation of the movement in these centuries.

RONALD G. WITT

See also Italy: Renaissance; Renaissance Historical Writing; Ullman

Biography

Born Berlin, 22 June 1900, to a Jewish family. Received PhD, University of Berlin, 1922. Notgemeinschaft der deutschen Wissenschaft fellow, Italy, 1925–27; lecturer in medieval and modern history, University of Berlin, 1929–33; emigrated, first to England, 1937, then to US, 1938; taught at Queen's College, 1939–42; member, Institute for Advanced Study, Princeton, 1944–48; research fellow, Newberry Library, from 1949. Married Edith Fanny Alexander (2 children). Died 26 November 1988.

Principal Writings

Calvins Staatsanschauung und das konfessionelle Zeitalter (Calvin's Conception of the State and the Age of Confessions), 1924

Leonardo Bruni Aretino: Humanistisch-philosophische Schriften mit einer Chronologie seiner Werke und Briefe (Leonardo Bruni Aretino: Humanistic and Philosophical Writings with a Chronology of his Works and Letters), 1928; reprinted 1969

The Crisis of the Early Italian Renaissance: Civic Humanism and Republican Life in an Age of Classicism and Tyranny, 2 vols., 1955; revised in 1 vol., 1966

Humanistic and Political Literature in Florence and Venice at the Beginning of the Renaissance: Studies in Criticism and Chronology, 1955

From Petrarch to Bruni: Studies in Humanistic and Political Literature, 1968

Petrarch's Secretum: Its Making and Its Meaning, 1985

In Search of Florentine Civic Humanism: Essays on the Transition from Medieval to Modern Thought, 2 vols., 1988

Further Reading

"AHR Forum: Hans Baron's Renaissance Humanism," *American Historical Review*, 101 (1996), 107–44

Fubini, Riccardo, "Renaissance Historian: The Career of Hans Baron," *Journal of Modern History* 64 (1992), 541–74

Molho, Anthony, and John Tedeschi, eds., *Renaissance: Studies in Honor of Hans Baron*, Florence: Sansoni, 1970; DeKalb: Northern Illinois University Press, 1971

Rabil, Albert, "The Significance of 'Civic Humanism' in the Interpretation of the Italian Renaissance," in Albert Rabil, ed., *Renaissance Humanism: Foundations, Forms, and Legacy*, 3 vols., Philadelphia: University of Pennsylvania Press, 1988

Baron, Salo Wittmayer 1895–1989

Austrian Jewish historian

Salo Wittmayer Baron rightly understood himself to be in the succession of the synthesizing Jewish historians Isaac Marcus Jost and Heinrich Graetz – about both of whom he wrote with critical admiration – as well as his older contemporary Simon Dubnow. Baron's evident affinity for his predecessors sprang less from a desire to match his with their already great reputations than from a fine historiographic selfconsciousness that he also displayed in his insightful essays on the Renaissance Jewish historian Azariah de Rossi and his reflective essays on the present tasks of Jewish historiography. Baron's education in Europe gave him the several areas of expertise that served him so well in America as a generalist historian of the Jews.

His wealthy family from Tarnow in Galicia could send him both to a yeshiva and a gymnasium, while engaging a private tutor for him at home. He studied first at the University of Kraców in Galicia and, from the summer of 1914, in Vienna. There he studied at the rabbinical Israelitisch-Theologischen Lehranstalt and at the University of Vienna where, by 1923, he earned degrees in history, political science, and law. He had begun publishing articles in the Hebrew press while still a teenager, but his first historical publications – notably his thoughtful 1918 comparison of the Jewish historian Heinrich Graetz (1817–91) with Leopold von Ranke (1795–1886) – date from his Vienna period.

Baron's scholarly career in America began in 1926 when the American Reform leader Stephen Wise, who had established the Jewish Institute of Religion because of his dissatisfaction with rabbinical education at the Hebrew Union College in Cincinnati, Ohio, appointed Baron the Institute's librarian. From this position he was appointed in 1929 to a new professorship in Jewish history, endowed by Linda Miller, at Columbia University. This remained Baron's professional seat until his retirement in 1963. The English-language publication that gave him the needed reputation for the Columbia appointment was his famous "Ghetto and Emancipation: Shall We Revise the Traditional View?," which appeared in the *Menorah Journal* in 1928. The "traditional view," which Baron faulted with the now famous term the "lachrymose tradition," held that ghetto Jews had been uniformly miserable until, during late 18th-century emancipation, progress set in. No doubt mindful of the catastrophes of World War I and subsequent pogroms, Baron was skeptical about post-Emancipation progress. At the same time, however, he also doubted that their earlier history in Europe had been so unhappy: he demonstrated that ghetto Jews had often enjoyed a measure of autonomy and had therefore been the subjects of their own history rather than mere objects of persecution.

These insights informed his 1931 Schermerhorn lectures at Columbia in which Baron first stated his thesis that Jewish religious and social history had simultaneously to be studied as the interactive processes that they were. His interest in Jewish social history followed from his admiration for Dubnow, but he also insisted that it was Jewish religion that gave and had given exilic Jews the power to survive and act for themselves. In the Jewish political terms of his time, that is, Baron esteemed the history of Judaism as a religion and of Jews as a people among peoples, whether in diaspora or in their homeland. In this, as in all his work, Baron also worried that Jewish religious and secularist scholarship would follow diverging paths. With these thoughts in mind, as the title he chose implied, Baron wrote the first edition of his celebrated *A Social and Religious History of the Jews* (1937). Despite the initial anxieties of Columbia University Press, this highly readable work received warm reviews and sold very well (especially the less expensive Jewish Publication Society edition). Baron also wrote in pained awareness of the increasingly bad situation in which Europe's Jews found themselves and, in his epilogue, he stated explicitly that historical "interpretation and reinterpretation" are needed as a guide to present action.

After World War II, Baron greatly expanded the *Social and Religious History* with his never 2nd edition (18 volumes; 1952–83). Its early volumes, especially those dealing with Jewish religious and intellectual history in late antiquity and the early Middle Ages, are awesome in synthetic power, graceful in language, and – though necessarily heavily dependent on secondary sources – often original in their conclusions. Unlike Graetz, he did not blame the church for the persecutions as much as he did incipient nationalism. Similarly, he explained medieval migrations of Jews less as a response to persecutions than as peaceable choices to go where life seemed better. The later volumes, however, are less successful because of a faulty sense of proportion: Baron spent six volumes in providing social and political context for a religious and intellectual account of modernity that, despite his longevity, he did not live to provide.

In the meantime, Baron completed other major works, notably *The Jewish Community* (1942–48) and *The Russian Jew under Tsars and Soviets* (1964). His basic notion for *The Jewish Community* was already in mind when he prepared the *Social and Religious History*, namely that Jewish communal organization had taken the place of the nonexisting Jewish state. He dated this development to the deuteronomic revolution under Josiah, in whose course collective gatherings of Jews replaced the sanctuary as a center of Jewish experience. This meant, further, that the essence of Jewish community had always been ethical and intellectual, despite the more or less political tasks that community institutions had necessarily played. Consequently, Baron did not join Dubnow in his demands for Jewish autonomism in Eastern Europe, despite his admiration for Dubnow's social approach to history. Though occasionally faulted by reviewers for claiming more certitude than evidence allowed, *The Jewish Community* – like the *Social and Religious History* – has remained a standard work despite its known flaws and the progress of later research.

ROBERT FAIRBAIRN SOUTHARD

See also Dubnow; Jewish

Biography

Born Tarnow, Austria, 26 May 1895. Educated at Israelitisch-Theologischen Lehranstalt; PhD, University of Vienna, 1917, PolScD 1922, JD 1923. Ordained rabbi, 1920. Taught at Jüdisches Pädagogium, Vienna, 1919–26; then, after moving to the US, at Jewish Institute of Religion, 1926–30: librarian, 1927–30; professor of Jewish history, Columbia University, 1930–63 (emeritus); director, Center for Israel and Jewish Studies, 1950–68. Knight, Order of Merit, Italy, 1972. Married Jeannette G. Meisel, 1934 (2 daughters). Died New York City, 25 November 1989.

Principal Writings

"Ghetto and Emancipation: Shall We Revise the Traditional View?" *Menorah Journal* 14 (1928), 515–26

A Social and Religious History of the Jews, 3 vols., 1937; revised in 18 vols., 1952–83

The Jewish Community: Its History and Structure to the American Revolution, 3 vols., 1942–48

The Jews of the United States, 1790–1840: A Documentary History, 1963

History and Jewish Historians: Essays and Addresses, 1964
The Russian Jew under Tsars and Soviets, 1964; revised 1976
Ancient and Medieval Jewish History: Essays, edited and with a foreword by Leon A. Feldman, 1972
The Contemporary Relevance of History: A Study in Approaches and Methods, 1986

Further Reading

Baron, Jeannette Meisel, "A Bibliography of the Printed Writings of Salo Wittmayer Baron," in *Salo Wittmayer Baron Jubilee Volume: On the Occasion of His Eightieth Birthday*, 3 vols., Jerusalem: American Academy for Jewish Research, and New York: Columbia University Press, 1974

Feldman, Louis H., Robert Chazan, and Ismar Schorsch, on Baron, *AJS Review* 18 (1993), 1–50

Liberles, Robert, *Salo Wittmayer Baron: Architect of Jewish History*, New York: New York University Press, 1995

Barraclough, Geoffrey 1908–1984
British medievalist and international historian

As an anglophone medieval historian during the 1930s, Geoffrey Barraclough was distinguished by the fact that he had mastered the German language, German historical literature, and Germanic *Geschichtswissenschaft* (historical science). He discovered a number of important manuscript sources which he declined to utilize fully; instead, Barraclough's mission became to publicize for anglophone audiences the official German perspective on the history of the German-speaking lands. He drew upon his friendships with German academics to produce, in 1938, a collection containing English translations of articles by the leading medieval historians of the Nazi Third Reich (*Medieval Germany, 911–1250*). The studies highlighted various medieval factors which were said to account for Germany's *Sonderweg* (special path) among modern European nations, particularly the frustrated desires of the *Volk* (folk) for a unified nation-state. However, it was Barraclough's own statements of the official 1930s German perspective which would become the most influential treatments of medieval German history available to anglophone audiences. His three post-World War II studies, *The Origins of Modern Germany*, and *Factors in German History* (both 1946) and *The Medieval Empire* (1950), were written to explicate for the widest possible audience the long-term historical causes – such as the "meddling" (from the 11th century onwards) of the Roman Catholic church in the affairs of the medieval German empire – which Barraclough claimed had led to the foundation of the modern Third Reich, as well as to argue explicitly for the establishment of a strong ethnic German state.

Within a few years, however, Barraclough began to ponder seriously the events of 1939–45 and the role of historians in them. In *Factors in German History* (1946) he had asserted, "No feature of German history is more remarkable than the persistence through the centuries of a sense of unity, reaching back in unbroken continuity to the tenth century." By 1963 he described longings for an imagined medieval unity as "in large degree a fiction, conjured up by the overheated romantic," and "unity" he now understood as a smokescreen to conceal plans for hegemony. He recoiled from the European tradition of historical scholarship in service to modern political units, explicitly rejecting the idea that history had any relevance for current situations: "the validity, or otherwise, of the ideal of European integration is neither strengthened nor weakened by a consideration of past precedents." The 19th-century Germanic historiographical paradigm, oriented around disembodied ideas and ethnic nation-states, had not only facilitated the conflagrations of the 20th century, but had prevented historians from recognizing important 20th-century developments, such as the rise of the Soviet Union. Barraclough's reaction against the idealist position was complete, as he increasingly emphasized the constructed, contingent nature of all historical institutions and ideas. His 1968 survey *The Medieval Papacy*, describing how the various rulers of the Roman church were historically-enmeshed individuals constantly altering their policies in the face of changing circumstances, is still widely considered the standard introduction to the subject in English; the volume provoked unrepentant idealist Walter Ullmann's widely-read counter-survey: *A Short History of the Papacy* (1972).

From the mid-1950s onward, Barraclough neglected empirical scholarship in favor of synthesizing secondary historical literature. He aimed to foster an enlightened understanding of the multiple and diverse human cultures of the globe. His first synthetic effort, *An Introduction to Contemporary History* (1964), remains his most widely read book. "The European age ... is over," he wrote, "and with it the predominance of the old European scale of values." Methodologically speaking, he promoted a new approach to the science of history: to replace the philological analysis of archival materials favored by 19th-century European *Geschichtswissenschaft* with a cliometric version of history as a 20th-century social science. Barraclough held a series of teaching posts, particularly at Oxford University, but gave less attention to graduate students than to the general public; for instance, he was invited in 1974 to explain world history on a Japanese TV series.

By the 1970s, Barraclough was attacking Eurocentric visions of historical development and by 1979 the entire paradigm of "Western Civilization" as obfuscatory perversions of history. He rarely, if ever, cited any sources in his discussions. In 1971, Barraclough even attacked the idea of learning foreign languages because the mastery of languages could lead to antiquarianism and obstruct the mastery of global history. In 1976, Barraclough presented his own decision to study medieval history as a fall-back plan, adopted after he had failed to profit as a salesman of essential oils. Not a trace remained of the devotee of germanophone *Geschichtswissenschaft* who had, in 1934, placed the European Middle Ages at the explanatory center of 20th-century political conflicts and whose claim to fame was that he understood the Germans.

Barraclough spent several decades running away from his own mid-century incarnation, becoming the consummate publicist of a new vision of history, although making no original scholarly contributions. After the atrocities of the 20th century, he felt it was no longer possible "for any sensitive person to view the course of history with the old complacency," yet at the same time he recognized that conservatism was the "characteristic occupational malady" of the historian. He saw in the example of the social sciences a possibility of breaking with the mythological roots of history, which had doomed the discipline to support existing regimes no matter how morally repugnant. That World History, the social science paradigm, and other novelties were lauded by an eminent refugee from that most traditional of historical fields, namely medieval European history, helped legitimate the widespread calls for change in the discipline of history, most of which – unlike Barraclough's – came from less lofty academic institutions.

FELICE LIFSHITZ

See also Germany: to 1450; Holy Roman Empire; Ullmann; World

Biography

Born Bradford, Yorkshire, 10 May 1908, son of a wool merchant. Educated at Bootham School, York, 1921–24; Bradford Grammar School, 1924–25; Oriel College, Oxford, BA, 1929; University of Munich. During World War II called to the Foreign Office before serving in the Royal Air Force Voluntary Reserve, 1942–45. Fellow, Merton College, Oxford, 1934–36; taught at St. John's College, Cambridge, 1936–39; rose to professor, University of Liverpool, 1945–56; University of London, 1956–62; University of California, 1965–68; Brandeis University, 1968–70; Oxford University, 1970–73; fellow, All Souls College, Oxford, 1970–73. Married 1) Marjorie Gardner, 1929 (marriage dissolved; 1 son); 2) Diana Russell-Clarke, 1945 (marriage dissolved; 2 sons); 3) Gwendolyn Lambert. Died Burford, England, 26 December 1984.

Principal Writings

Papal Provisions: Aspects of Church History, Constitutional, Legal and Administrative in the Later Middle Ages, 1934
Public Notaries and the Papal Curia: A Calendar and a Study of a "Formularium Notariorum Curie" from the Early Years of the Fourteenth Century, 1934
"Un document inédit sur la soustraction d'obédience de 1398" (An Unpublished Document Concerning the Retraction of Obedience of 1398), *Revue d'Histoire Ecclésiastique* 30 (1934), 101–15
Editor and translator, *Mediaeval Germany, 911–1250: Essays by German Historians*, 2 vols., 1938
Factors in German History, 1946
The Origins of Modern Germany, 1946; revised 1947
The Medieval Empire: Idea and Reality, 1950
History in a Changing World, 1957
European Unity in Thought and Action, 1963
An Introduction to Contemporary History, 1964
The Medieval Papacy, 1968
"Contemporary World History," in Norman Cantor, ed., *Perspectives on the European Past: Conversations with Historians*, 1971
Management in a Changing Economy (AMA survey report), 1976
Main Trends in History, 1979
Turning Points in World History, 1979
Editor, *The Christian World: A Social and Cultural History*, 1981
From Agadir to Armageddon: Anatomy of a Crisis, 1982
Editor, *The Times Atlas of World History*, 1984

Further Reading

Dewar, Kenneth C., "Geoffrey Barraclough: From Historicism to Historical Science," *Historian* 56 (1994), 449–64

Bartol'd, Vasilii Vladimirovich

[Wilhelm Barthold], 1869–1930
Russian Orientalist

Bartol'd was a prolific scholar: the total number of his published works is 684. His interest was the history of Central Asia, primarily in Islamic times. In this field Bartol'd had few predecessors, and those almost exclusively Russian scholars of the 19th century. When he began his scholarly career the history of Central Asia was still very little known, and the development of this field fell upon him. He studied a great number of primary sources in Persian, Arabic, and Turkic, many of which he discovered in manuscript collections in Central Asia, Russia, Europe, and Turkey; he devoted numerous works to the description, analysis, and publication of these sources. In studying the history of Central Asia, he saw as his main task to apply to this area "the same laws of historical evolution which had been established for the history of Europe." In his general historical views, he was particularly close to the German positivist historiography of the end of the 19th century. He saw the process of world history as one of gradual rapprochement of individual peoples ("societies") as a result of the expansion of advanced culture upon an ever vaster region, accompanied by the shift of world centers of more advanced culture themselves; accordingly, "the main content of history of any given country is the degree to which it is participating in world cultural intercourse." The expansion of culture, and of cultural influences from some people to others, according to Bartol'd, was connected with the development of international trade, the centers of which were cities and the routes of which were the main avenues for the transmission of culture.

Bartol'd himself did not devote any special work to expounding his general theoretical views, which can be established mainly from remarks scattered through numerous works on specific historical problems. His works are distinguished more by historical analysis than by synthesis; they are full of new facts (often with attention to minute details), which he was the first to extract from the sources. During the Soviet period, Bartol'd rejected the growing demands for ideological conformity and the Marxist interpretation of history and retained his theoretical views and the approach to the study of Central Asia and Iran until the end of his life. Most works of Bartol'd retain their scholarly value, especially due to the wealth of factual material that he introduced and analyzed for the first time. Among his works, the monumental *Turkestan v epokhu mongol'skogo nashestviia* (1898–1900; *Turkestan Down to the Mongol Invasion*, 1928) exerted the most profound influence on all the later study of the medieval history of Central Asia, and is still a solid foundation and a point of reference for studies of this period. No less important for the modern scholarship are his works dealing with the study of primary sources. His works on the Timurid period of Central Asian history have also become a basis for all subsequent research. His contributions to the historical geography of Central Asia and Iran also remain of great importance, especially those dealing with the study of the history of irrigation and the Amu Darya question, although his views on the latter were disputed by some Russian archaeologists. His outline histories of the Turkic peoples of Central Asia, especially the Turkmens and Kirghiz, are still indispensable, despite the publication of separate histories of each Central Asian republic (which heavily depended on Bartol'd's works for the medieval period). His collected works (*Sochineniia*) published in ten volumes in 1963–77 include almost all of his works. About forty works have been translated into European languages, and new translations continue to appear; 18 articles in journals and collective volumes and 247 articles in *The Encyclopaedia of Islam* were written in German by Bartol'd himself. Bartol'd's body of work laid a firm foundation for all modern study of Central Asia.

YURI BREGEL

See also Mongol

Biography

Born St. Petersburg, 1869, of German descent. Studied Arabic, Persian, and Turkish languages, University of St. Petersburg, 1887–91, before joining faculty, 1896. Member, Russian Academy of Sciences, 1910–30; director, Institute of Turkic Studies, 1917–30; head, Collegium of Orientalists; deputy chairman, Central Asian Department, Academy of Material Culture. Died Leningrad (St. Petersburg), 1930.

Principal Writings

Turkestan v epokhu mongol'skogo nashestviia, 2 vols., 1898–1900; vol. 2 in English revised as *Turkestan Down to the Mongol Invasion*, 1928; revised with additional chapter, 1968

Svedeniia ob Aral'skom more i nizov'iakh Amu-dar'i s drevneishikh vremen do XVII veka (Data on the Aral Sea and the Lower Reaches of the Amu Darya from the Earliest Times to the 17th century), 1902

Istoriko-geograficheskii obzor Irana, 1903; in English as *An Historical Geography of Iran*, 1984

Istoriia izucheniia vostoka v Evrope i v Rossii (History of the Study of the East in Europe and in Russia), 1911

K istorii orosheniia Turkestana (To the History of the Irrigation of Turkestan), 1914

Islam, 1918

Kul'tura musul'manstva, 1918; in English as *Mussulman Culture*, 1934

Ulugbek i ego vremia, 1918; in English in *Four Studies on the History of Central Asia*, vol. 2, 1958

Dvenadtsat' lektsii po istorii turetskikh narodov Srednei Azii (Twelve Lectures on the History of the Turkic Peoples of Central Asia), 1927

Istoriia kul'turnoi zhizni Turkestana (History of the Cultural Life of Turkestan), 1927

Kirgizy: istoricheskii ocherk (The Kirghiz: Historical Outline), 1927

Mir-Ali-Shir i politicheskaia zhizn', 1928; in English in *Four Studies on the History of Central Asia*, vol. 3, 1962

Ocherk istorii turkmenskogo naroda, 1929; in English in *Four Studies on the History of Central Asia*, vol. 3, 1962

Sochineniia (Collected Works), 10 vols., 1963–77

Further Reading

Bosworth, Clifford Edmund, editor's introduction in Barthold, *An Historical Geography of Iran*, Princeton: Princeton University Press, 1984

Bregel, Yuri, "The Bibliography of Barthold's Works and the Soviet Censorship," *Survey* 24/3 (1979), 91–107

Bregel, Yuri, "Barthold and Modern Oriental Studies," *International Journal of Middle East Studies* 12 (1980), 385–403

Inayatullah, Dr., "V.V. Barthold: His Life and Works (1869–1930)," *Journal of the Pakistan Historical Society* 9 (1961), 81–86

Minorsky, Vladimir, translator's foreword in Barthold, *Four Studies on the History of Central Asia*, vol. 1, Leiden: Brill, 1956

Stewart, F. Henderson, "A Classic of Central Asian History: Barthold's *Turkestan* in Russian and English," *Asian Affairs* 57 (1970), 47–51

Umniakov, Ivan Ivanovich, *Annotirovannaia bibliografiia trudov akademika V.V. Bartol'da* (Bibliography of Bartol'd's Works and Works on Bartol'd), Moscow: Glavnaia redaktsiia vostochnoi lit-ry, 1976; also includes Nataliia Nikolaevna Tumanovich, *Opisanie arkhiva akademika V.V. Bartol'da* (An Inventory of Bartol'd's Archive)

Basadre, Jorge 1903–1980
Peruvian historian

Jorge Basadre is widely recognized as the leading Peruvian historian of the 20th century. His high reputation is based on a vast output of important books, articles, essays, and prefaces written during more than fifty years of research and advocacy from 1929 until his death in 1980. Three titles deserve special mention. *Meditaciones sobre el destino histórico del Perú* (Meditations on the Historical Destiny of Peru, 1947) is a major essay on Peruvian identity in which Basadre argued the case for Peru's destiny as a *mestizo* and bilingual nation. His *Introducción a las bases documentales para la historia de la República del Perú con algunas refleciones* (Introduction to the Documentary Sources for the History of the Republic of Peru with Some Reflections, 1971) remains an indispensable guide to sources for Peruvian history since independence. Finally, his multivolume *Historia de la República del Perú* (History of the Republic of Peru, 1939) may be the finest history of any Latin American nation written by a single individual. It represents a last, brilliant example of the *Historia general* or "general history" genre that presumes mastery of political, economic, social, and cultural history, and that flourished before the rise of the monograph and other works of more specialized scholarship.

Jorge Basadre was born in 1903 and grew up in Tacna in southern Peru during the Chilean occupation following the 1879–83 War of the Pacific between Chile, Bolivia, and Peru. He came from a merchant immigrant family on his mother's side, and on his father's side from a family of long-established landowners. Basadre emphasized that Tacna had always been a province of small landowners and did not suffer the oppression of the large estate. He had no early memories of class conflict due to the solidarity that existed between all classes resisting the Chilean occupation.

In 1919 Basadre was sent to study at the University of San Marcos in Lima. In 1928 he completed a thesis in history on the early Peruvian republic which led almost immediately to a faculty appointment at San Marcos in Peruvian history. From 1932 to 1935 he undertook research in Spain where he worked alongside Silvio Zavala, Ángel Rosenblatt, and Américo Castro. During the 1950s, he served on the UNESCO commission for the history of humanity. UNESCO work brought him into contact with leading French historians, and Basadre was able to invite Fernand Braudel to Lima at a time when Braudel's work was unknown in Peru. The introductions to different editions of the *Historia de la República del Perú* attest to Basadre's knowledge of historical writing, ancient and modern, and to his determination to keep up with changes in historical methodology and conceptualization while devoting his best efforts to a panoramic study of the achievements and failures – some truly catastrophic – of republic of Peru.

Historia de la República del Perú is a wide-ranging work of synthesis and analysis that extends from the era of independence in the 1820s to a period of national turmoil and conflict in the early 1930s. Throughout this work – which reached 17 volumes by the time of the 6th edition of 1968 – Basadre sought to discover themes in Peruvian history, and to identify the aspirations of the Peruvian people. Among the themes are a tremendous and continual struggle for power which included military coups (especially in 1914, 1919, and 1930), civilian insurrections (principally 1855, 1872, and 1895), and numerous *montonero* rebellions, barracks revolts, and politically inspired assassinations. At the same time, definite republican ideas such as the written constitution, a strong executive and equally strong congress, the non-re-election of chief executives, and freedom of the press were generally honored from the 1820s until 1920. Army revolts and other rebellions occurred frequently enough to be commonplace, but the episodes of dictatorship were brief and quickly followed by amnesties and a return to republican forms. Adding up a balance sheet, Basadre found much promise in the political life of the Peruvian republic, at least until 1919.

In 1919, former President Augusto B. Leguía seized power, and gradually established a police state. During eleven years from 1919 to 1930 Leguía ended the independence of congress, strictly limited freedom of the press, jailed or exiled opponents, and established a veritable personality cult while presiding three times over his own re-election. An aura of progress was provided by foreign loans used to pay for internal improvements. Leguía's dictatorship established unwise and unwanted deviations from republican norms. The regime adopted the position that the Peruvian people should be economically active, and the government undertook a program of public works. It also asserted that there was no need for politics, and Basadre concluded that Leguía's dictatorship destroyed the republican institutions of Peru. Only the Army remained intact, although the seeds of Peru's first mass-based political party, the *Alianza Popular Revolucionaria Americana* (American Popular Revolutionary Alliance or APRA), had been planted. In 1930, as the effects of the oncoming world depression began to be felt, a provincial barracks revolt easily led to Leguía's ouster. The 1930 revolution in turn paved the way for a conflict between the Army and APRA which turned into a virtual civil war between late 1931 and 1933. Among the victims were military hero and Peruvian president Luis M. Sánchez Cerro, who was assassinated, and APRA, which remained proscribed or under watchful Army vigilance for more than a generation. The *Aprista* massacre of captive officers and soldiers in the northern coastal city of Trujillo in 1932, and the Army reprisals, may have been the worst crimes committed during the republic up to that time. They were more damaging to Peru than the defeat by Chile in the War of the Pacific. The events of 1932 made Peruvians enemies of each other in ways previously unknown, whereas the war had united Peruvians against the Chilean invader.

Basadre's compelling political history recognized the realities of social class. The weaknesses of Peru until the 1930s flowed from an oligarchical ruling class that thwarted the aspirations of Peru's industrial entrepreneurs, the middle class, the urban working class, and most of all, the indigenous American masses. The final volumes of the *Historia de la República del Perú* suggest that Basadre agreed with the APRA formula that an alliance of the indigenous people, urban workers, middle-class intellectuals, and progressive national entrepreneurs was the best way to contest the power of the oligarchy and imperialism.

In 1968, Basadre prepared a 6th edition of his epochal history, and surveyed certain transformations that had overtaken Peru. The great work now stood as a sort of "prehistory" to a still-unfolding post-1930 era of accelerating social and economic change. He concluded that, as during earlier times, an immense task remained for the nation, and that the promises of the republic remained unfulfilled.

PHILIP EVANSON

See also Latin America: National

Biography

Born Tacna, 12 February 1903. Educated at Colegio Alemán, Lima; DLitt, University of San Marcos, Lima, 1928, BLaw 1931, DLaw 1936. Taught at University of San Marco, 1928–80. Died Lima, 29 June 1980.

Principal Writings

La iniciación de la república: contribución al estudio de la evolución política y social del Perú (The Beginning of the Republic: Contribution to the Study of the Social and Political Evolution of Peru), 2 vols., 1929

La multitud, la ciudad y el campo en la historia de Perú (The Crowd, the City, and the Countryside in Peruvian History), 1929

Perú, problema y posibilidad: ensayo de una síntesis de la evolución histórico del Perú (Peru, Problem and Possibility: A Synthesis of the Historical Evolution of Peru), 1931

Historia del derecho peruano (The History of Peruvian Law), 1937

Historia de la República del Perú (History of the Republic of Peru), 2 vols., 1939; 7th edition, 17 vols., 1983

El Conde de Lemos y su tiempo (The Count of Lemos and His Time), 1945; revised 1948

Los fundamentos de la historia del derecho (Fundamentals of the History of Law), 1947

Meditaciones sobre el destino histórico del Perú (Meditations on the Historical Destiny of Peru), 1947

Chile, Perú y Bolivia independientes (The Independence of Chile, Peru, and Bolivia), 1948

La promesa de la vida peruana y otros ensayos (The Promise of Peruvian Life and Other Essays), 1958

Infancia en Tacna (A Childhood in Tacna), 1959

En la Biblioteca Nacional: ante el problema de las "elites" (In the National Library: Facing the Problem of the "Elites"), 1968

Introducción a las bases documentales para la historia de la República del Perú con algunas reflexiones (Introduction to the Documentary Sources for the History of the Republic of Peru with Some Reflections), 2 vols., 1971

La vida y la historia: ensayos sobre personas, lugares y problemas (Life and History: Essays on People, Places, and Problems), 1975

Elecciones y centralismo en el Perú: apuntes para um esquema histórico (Elections and Centralism in Peru: Suggestions for a History), 1980

Further Reading

Pacheco Velez, César, "Jorge Basadre," *Revista de Historia América* 92 (1982), 195–213

Bauer, Walter 1877–1960

German theologian and lexicographer

Although Walter Bauer is perhaps more widely known for his lexicon of the New Testament and other early Christian literature, his continuing importance in historiography derives primarily from his analysis of the character and nature of Christianity in various geographic locations in the 2nd and early 3rd centuries. His work in this area was first published in 1934 as *Rechtgläubigkeit und Ketzerei im ältesten Christentum*, subsequently reprinted with minor additions and corrections, and two supplementary essays in 1964, and finally translated into English and published as *Orthodoxy and Heresy in Earliest Christianity* in 1971. It details what has come to be known as the "Bauer thesis" on the origins and forms of early Christianity, arguing in essence for the primacy of "heresy" in many areas.

Even though the original German work received relatively little attention, no serious study of early Christianity today could ignore Bauer's book. In fact, it would be almost impossible to overstate its significance. It has been described as "seminal" by R.A. Markus: as "one of the most influential monographs on Christian origins to appear in this century" by Gary Burke; as "epochal" by James M. Robinson; and as "ingenious" by Helmut Koester. Critics have been almost as outspoken. The English edition contains a helpful appendix with a list and brief summaries of reviews including several by opponents of the thesis. Many more responses have appeared since 1971 and it would be fair to say that Bauer's views remain controversial.

So what did Bauer propose? He first challenged the traditional view (usually linked with the church historian Eusebius) that "orthodoxy" in Christianity connoted the original belief held by the majority and that "heresy" involved deviation from correct Christian teaching held only by a minority in the first two centuries CE. He then sought to prove that what was termed "heresy" by the church in the late 2nd century and following was actually the earliest or strongest form of Christianity in many regions. Finally, he argued that it was only as the emerging catholic church, especially at Rome, imposed its brand of Christianity by using a variety of authoritarian techniques, that its "orthodoxy" triumphed in the later centuries.

Specifically, Bauer analyzed developments in Edessa, Egypt (especially Alexandria), Asia Minor (primarily Smyrna), Macedonia, and Rome in the early 2nd century. He concluded, among other things, that Christianity in Edessa was established by Marcion, Bar Daisan, and Mani, all "heretics" according to Eusebius and other catholic fathers. In a similar way, he believed that heretical groups (gnostics or at least docetics) were predominant in Asia Minor, based on the letters of Ignatius. Finally, he held that Alexandrian Christianity was so diverse that no real distinction existed among Christian groups there until the Alexandrian bishops began to prescribe orthodox beliefs and practices in the early 3rd century. For example, one of the many items used by Bauer to illustrate Alexandrian diversity involved a story told by Eusebius about the church father Origen, who, as a young man was given shelter by a Christian woman in Alexandria. Bauer found significance in the fact that not only did the woman allow the young Origen to live in her house along with a famous heretic named Paul, but that she treated the heretic "like her son." Moreover, since according to Eusebius, the man was merely one "among a number of heretics" living in Alexandria at that time, Bauer was able to infer that "heresy" and orthodoxy (represented by Origen) freely mingled at the end of the 2nd century.

Bauer deliberately did not include developments in the 1st century and excluded most New Testament material. He believed that if his reconstruction was correct for the 2nd century, it would also prove true for the 1st. James Dunn's 1977 study did much to extend, or at least reinforce, Bauer's view of Christianity in the 1st century, although it too remains controversial. Many of Bauer's theories are based on the religious historiography of F.C. Baur (1762–1860), and Adolf Harnack (1851–1930). Their influence is especially clear in Bauer's challenge to the Eusebian view of church history and his recognition of great diversity among early Christians. In fact, those two points, along with his reconstruction of the origins of Christianity in Edessa, remain his most widely accepted ideas today.

In other areas, Bauer's views have been less influential. His failure to provide a comprehensive definition of "orthodoxy" and "heresy," his frequent and admitted use of arguments from silence, his excessive distrust of patristic writings coupled with a relatively uncritical acceptance of the veracity (and legitimacy) of the heretics, and his unfamiliarity or unconcern for sociological theories regarding group "self-definition" have all been criticized by reviewers. Nevertheless, even the most convincing critics of parts of the Bauer thesis, such as James McCue, recognize that his work remains a great piece of scholarship. In fact, as Robert Wilken aptly noted, Bauer actually created "a new paradigm" for all subsequent investigations in early church history.

DANIEL L. HOFFMAN

See also Eusebius

Biography

Born Königsberg, Prussia, 8 August 1877. Studied in Marburg, Berlin, and Strasbourg, receiving the Habilitation, 1903. Taught theology, University of Breslau, 1913–16; taught New Testament (rising to professor), University of Göttingen, 1916–46. Died Göttingen, 17 November 1960.

Principal Writings

Das Leben Jesu im Zeitalter der neutestamentlichen Apokryphen (The Life of Jesus in the Age of the New Testament Apocrypha), 1909

Rechtgläubigkeit und Ketzerei im ältesten Christentum, 1934, revised 1964; in English as *Orthodoxy and Heresy in Earliest Christianity*, 1971

Griechisch-deutsches Wörterbuch zu den Schriften des Neuen Testaments und der übrigen urchristlichen Literatur, 1937; in English as *A Greek-English Lexicon of the New Testament, and Other Early Christian Literature*, 1957

Further Reading

Burke, Gary T., "Walter Bauer and Celsus: The Shape of Late Second-Century Christianity," *Second Century* 4 (1984), 1–7

Desjardins, Michel, "Bauer and Beyond: On Recent Scholarly Discussions of *aipesis* [heresy] in the Early Christian Era," *Second Century* 8 (1991), 65–82

Dunn, James, *Unity and Diversity in the New Testament: An Enquiry into the Character of Earliest Christianity*, London: SCM Press, and Philadelphia: Westminster Press, 1977

Heron, Alisdair I.C., "The Interpretation of 1 Clement in Walter Bauer's *Rechtgläubigkeit und Ketzerei im ältesten Christentum*," *Ekklesiastikos Pharos* 55 (1973), 517–45

McCue, James, "Orthodoxy and Heresy: Walter Bauer and the Valentinians," *Vigiliae Christianae* 33 (1979), 118–30

Markus, R.A., Review of *Orthodoxy and Heresy in Earliest Christianity*, by Bauer, *New Blackfriars* 54 (1973), 283

Markus, R.A., "The Problem of Self-Definition: From Sect to Church," in E.P. Sanders, ed., *Jewish and Christian Self-Definition*, Philadelphia: Fortress Press, 1980

Marshall, I. Howard, "Orthodoxy and Heresy in Earlier Christianity," *Themelios* 2 (1976), 5–14

Norris, Frederick W., "Ignatius, Polycarp, and 1 Clement: Walter Bauer Reconsidered," *Vigiliae Christianae* 30 (1976), 23–44

Reidel, Walter, "'Vom andern und vom selbst': Walter Bauers Biographien" ('Of others and of self': Walter Bauer's biographies), *Zeitschrift der Gesellschaft für Kanada-Studien* [West Germany] 9 (1989), 83–96

Robinson, James McConkey, and Helmut Koester, *Trajectories through Early Christianity*, Philadelphia: Fortress Press, 1971

Robinson, Thomas A., *The Bauer Thesis Examined: The Geography of Heresy in the Early Christian Church*, Lewiston, ME: Mellen, 1988

Turner, Henry Ernest William, *The Pattern of Christian Truth: A Study in the Relations Between Orthodoxy and Heresy in the Early Church*, London: Mowbray, 1954; New York: AMS Press, 1978

Wilken, Robert L., "Diversity and Unity in Early Christianity," *Second Century* (1981), 101–10

Beaglehole, John C. 1901–1971

New Zealand historian of Pacific exploration

After completing his early studies at Victoria University College, Wellington, John Beaglehole proceeded in 1926 to London where his doctoral research was supervised by A. P. Newton. In London he also met R. H. Tawney and Harold J. Laski, and was influenced by their radical ideas. He returned to New Zealand with some reluctance. As a consequence of defending academic freedom on an occasion when it seemed to be under threat, he not only had his temporary lectureship at Auckland University College terminated by the authorities, but was passed over for chairs in history at both Auckland and Wellington before being offered a lectureship at the latter college.

Such experiences confirmed rather than moderated Beaglehole's beliefs about the role and place of an intellectual in modern society, and these attitudes were displayed in several of his historical works. Unlike most other short histories of New Zealand, his *New Zealand: A Short History* (1936) devoted more space to the 20th century than the 19th, and he highlighted the follies of governments before and during the depression of the 1930s. *The University of New Zealand* (1937) critically considered intellectual maturity as well as institutional growth in a colonial society; and *Victoria University College* (1949) included the sorry tale of how during World War I the German-born Professor of Modern Languages was, over the protests of the college's staff and governing body, removed from his post by government legislation. "Depressing as is this story of defeat," Beaglehole commented of the episode, "there is nothing in the college's record of which its men and women have the right to feel more proud."

Beaglehole wrote *The Discovery of New Zealand* (1939) as one of the centennial surveys, and was for several years thereafter a historical adviser to the Department of Internal Affairs, helping to shape that government department's extensive and significant program of historical publications. He saw these projects as crucial to the development of a New Zealand scholarly tradition, a matter he discussed in his 1954 lecture, *The New Zealand Scholar*. The title echoed Ralph Waldo Emerson's famous address of 1837, "The American Scholar," which heralded the period when "the American mind became adult." Beaglehole looked forward to an equivalent "intellectual declaration of independence" in New Zealand. He himself moved easily and regularly between London and New Zealand, between metropolis and "province," rather like the subject of his later scholarly endeavors.

In the early 1930s Beaglehole had been asked to contribute a volume on European exploration of the Pacific to a "Pioneer Histories" series. *The Exploration of the Pacific* (1934) was well received both for its scholarship and its style. Beginning with Magellan, it provided a dramatic narrative of several voyages, ending with James Cook, of whom Beaglehole noted: "The study of Cook is the illumination of all discovery." The illumination of Cook was eventually to become Beaglehole's scholarly preoccupation: his magisterial biography, *The Life of Captain James Cook*, completed in 1971, was published posthumously in 1974. Beaglehole's Cook is a rational if sometimes irascible man, a humane and heroic navigator whose writing skills developed alongside his scientific achievements. Beaglehole had written in 1934 that there could be no "final" history without "the story from the native viewpoint as well as the European"; and though in the *Life* he gave careful attention to the indigenous peoples and their cultures, Cook's activities and accomplishments remain dominant. More recently, scholars have viewed Cook from perspectives other than exploration, and have found him in certain respects more problematical and the enterprise on which he was engaged less admirable than did Beaglehole.

Before writing the *Life*, Beaglehole spent some twenty years preparing authoritative editions of Cook's journals for all three of his Pacific voyages. *The Journals of Captain James Cook on His Voyages of Discovery* were published between 1955 and 1967; Beaglehole's edition of *The Endeavour Journal of Joseph Banks* (1962), with an essay on "The Young Banks," was a necessary complement to Cook's record of his first Pacific voyage. Annotated in great detail, and including weighty introductory essays on the scientific and intellectual background, the nature and course of each voyage, and the editor's resolution of textual intricacies, these volumes are Beaglehole's finest accomplishment: they provided reliable texts for the rapidly growing numbers of Pacific scholars, and they stimulated a great deal of further research.

As his own country's scholarly tradition was slight, Beaglehole was, in a local perspective, important as the first New Zealand historian to develop an international reputation, and through both his teaching and personal example he encouraged New Zealanders to cherish and nourish intellectual life. Several of Beaglehole's students became notable historians, some in Pacific history, others in New Zealand history. All of them shared his passion for good writing, his respect for documentary sources, and his concern for what he described as "technical accomplishment, for professional standards, even to the point of pedantry." In the wider historiographical framework, he made a

major contribution to the history of European exploration and 18th-century European intellectual life.

PETER GIBBONS

See also New Zealand

Biography

John Cawte Beaglehole. Born Wellington, 13 June 1901. Educated at Wellington College; Victoria University College, MA 1924; University of London, PhD 1929. Taught at Victoria University College, 1924–26; then held a postgraduate traveling scholarship, 1926–29; tutor/organizer, Workers' Educational Association, 1930–31; taught at Auckland University College, 1932; odd jobs, 1933–35; taught at Victoria University College, 1936–63; professor of British Commonwealth history, Victoria University of Wellington, 1963–66 (emeritus). Married Elsie Mary Holmes, 1930 (3 sons). Died Wellington, 10 October 1971.

Principal Writings

The Exploration of the Pacific, 1934
New Zealand: A Short History, 1936
The University of New Zealand: An Historical Study, 1937
The Discovery of New Zealand, 1939
Victoria University College: An Essay Towards a History, 1949
Editor, *The Journals of Captain James Cook on His Voyages of Discovery*, 4 vols. in 5, 1955–67
Editor, *The Endeavour Journal of Joseph Banks*, 2 vols., 1962
The Life of Captain James Cook, 1974

Further Reading

Beaglehole, T.H., "'Home'? J.C. Beaglehole in London, 1926–1929," *Turnbull Library Record* 14 (1981), 69–82
Munz, Peter, "A Personal Memoir," in Peter Munz, ed., *The Feel of Truth: Essays in New Zealand and Pacific History Presented to F.L.W. Wood and J.C. Beaglehole*, Wellington: Reed, 1969, 11–24

Bean, C.E.W. 1879–1968
Australian military historian

C.E.W. Bean is Australia's best known and most influential military historian. Technically he ranks among the so-called amateur historians who made such an important contribution to Australian historiography. At Oxford University he read classics and after graduating turned to law before entering journalism. He thus spent his career outside the ranks of professional historians who gradually found places on the staffs of Australian universities after 1891. Yet what Bean lacked in university training he compensated for in other ways. A gifted writer, he had a natural capacity for handling original sources and for blending analytical skill with narrative power. He wrote with poise and balance, but he also had a point of view that gave his work wider significance.

By birth and background Bean belonged to the Anglo-Saxon element in Australian society which predominated until after World War II. Born in New South Wales of English parents, he was mainly educated in England, but in 1904 returned to Australia. He relished the English heritage, but admired the way in which it had been reshaped by Australian conditions. This was made evident in his early writings, notably *On the Wool*

Track (1910) and *The Dreadnought of the Darling* (1911), both originally produced as articles while he was a journalist with the Sydney *Morning Herald*. Written in a colorful, perceptive style, the two books brought the inland and its people to life and revealed Bean's attachment to both. The bush dwellers drew strength from their British heritage, but they also possessed a pioneering spirit that had died in England. Hardship made them tough and resilient and they had turned their backs on the obsequiousness that in England was produced by the class system. They treated people on their merits and displayed a spirit of "mateship" which Bean admired. Indeed, he saw the men of the bush as the real Australians, far superior to city dwellers. As with most contemporaries he showed little interest in the Aboriginal people and until the early 1940s strongly supported the White Australia policy.

Bean had long possessed an interest in military history that he derived from his father and his experiences at school and university. When war began in 1914 he was appointed official war correspondent after winning a ballot conducted by the Australian Journalists Association. Over the next four years he accompanied Australian troops to Gallipoli and France, gaining front-line experience. His despatches appeared in the Australian press and he produced other writings including *The Anzac Book* (1916), *Letters from France* (1917), and *In Your Hands, Australians* (1918). The government planned a full-scale history of Australia's military involvement and Bean from the outset began collecting material. At the end of the war funds were provided for the project and Bean edited a 12-volume work, of which he wrote six, all dealing with military operations. In 1946 he produced an abridgment under the title *Anzac to Amiens*.

Unlike his British counterparts, whose Official History was censored and written from the standpoint of those in command, Bean had a free hand. He emphasized the experiences of the troops and based his writing not only on official sources but on personal experiences, interviews, and eyewitness accounts. Research was carefully planned and meticulously conducted. Bean had a grasp of military tactics, an understanding of logistical problems and a detailed knowledge of the terrain. All this gave life, feeling and depth to a free-flowing narrative intended not for the expert, but for the general reader. He sought not to glorify war, but to portray it in all its aspects. His writing was said to possess a Homeric quality – "Australia's Iliad and Odyssey" – surely a pleasing comment for a man who enjoyed the classics. Certainly his volumes ranked among the best war histories and justly won a high reputation overseas

Bean's writings gained additional significance because they helped fashion national sentiment in Australia. World War I aroused emotions far stronger than did federation and stood out as a national event of great importance. Bean was conscious of this and through his writings and support for the Australian War Memorial, helped create both the Anzac legend and the "Digger" who became a new folk-hero. Both were built around the qualities of bravery, resilience, initiative, and capacity to withstand hardship that he first perceived at Gallipoli. Such qualities, he thought, reflected the fact that most soldiers came from the bush, where the struggle with nature prepared them for the field of battle. "The bush dweller," he observed, "learns something of half the arts of a soldier by the time he is ten years old." Recent research has cast doubts on some of his

conclusions. It has been estimated that only 17 per cent of the troops in 1915 were bush dwellers, while "mateship" was evident among soldiers of other nations. Bean's writings are no longer accepted to the extent they once were. Even so they exerted a profound influence and continue to occupy an important place in Australian historiography. indeed, not the least of his achievements was to add new dimensions to a historical literature previously often regarded as staid and lacking in issues of real moment.

BRIAN H. FLETCHER

See also Australia; World War I

Biography

Charles Edwin Woodrow Bean. Born Bathurst, New South Wales, 18 November 1879, son of an emigrant English classics teacher. Educated at All Saints' College, Bathurst; then in England at Brentwood Grammar School; Clifton College; MA, Hertford College, Oxford. Assistant master, Brentwood School, 1903, and Sydney Grammar School, 1904; called to Bar, Inner Temple, 1903; admitted to Bar, Supreme Court, New South Wales, 1904; associate to Sir William Owen, 1905–07; junior reporter, Sydney *Morning Herald*, 1908: London correspondent, 1910–13, leader-writer, 1914, official correspondent with the Australian Forces, 1914–18; led historical mission to Gallipoli, 1919; acting director, Australian War Museum, 1919; official Australian Government historian of World War I, 1919–42; various chairmanships and presidencies of civic and professional organizations. Married Ethel Young, 1921. Died Sydney, 30 August 1968.

Principal Writings

On the Wool Track, 1910
The Dreadnought of the Darling, 1911
Flagships Three, 1912
The Anzac Book, 1916
Letters from France, 1917
In Your Hands, Australians, 1918
Editor, *The Official History of Australia in the War of 1914–18*, 12 vols., 1921–42; abridged as *Anzac to Amiens*, 1946
The Story of Anzac, 2 vols., 1921–24
"Sidelights of the War on Australian Character," *Journal of the Royal Australian Historical Society* 13 (1927), 211–21
"The Writing of the Australian Official History of the Great War: Sources, Methods and Some Conclusions," *Journal of the Royal Australian Historical Society* 24 (1938), 85–112
"The Technique of a Contemporary War Historian," *Historical Studies, Australia and New Zealand* 2 (November 1942), 65–79
War Aims of a Plain Australian, 1945
Gallipoli Mission, 1952
Two Men I Knew: William Bridges and Brudenell White, Founders of the AIF, 1957
Gallipoli Correspondent: The Frontline Diary of C.E.W. Bean, edited by Kevin Fewster, 1968

Further Reading

Andrews, Edward M., "Bean and Bullecourt: Weaknesses and Strengths of the Official History of Australia in the First World War," *Revue Internationale d'Histoire Militaire* 72 (1990), 25–47
Andrews, Edward M., *The Anzac Illusion: Anglo-Australian Relations during World War I*, Cambridge: Cambridge University Press, 1993
Bazley, A.W., "C.E.W. Bean," *Historical Studies* 14 (1969), 147–54
Inglis, Kenneth, *C.E.W. Bean, Australian Historian*, St. Lucia: University of Queensland Press, 1970

Inglis, Kenneth, "C.E.W. Bean," in Bede Nairn *et al.*, eds., *Australian Dictionary of Biography*, Melbourne, London, and New York: Melbourne University Press, 1979

McCarthy, Dudley, *Gallipoli to the Somme: The Story of C.E.W. Bean*, Sydney: Ferguson, and London: Secker and Warburg, 1983

Thomson, Alistair, "'Steadfast until Death'? C.E.W. Bean and the Representation of Australian Military Manhood," *Australian Historical Studies* 23 (1989), 462–78

White, Richard, *Inventing Australia: Images and Identities, 1688–1980*, Sydney and Boston: Allen and Unwin, 1981

Winter, Denis, *Making the Legend: The War Writings of C.E.W. Bean*, St. Lucia: University of Queensland Press, 1992

Beard, Charles A. 1874–1948
US economic historian

Beard, Mary Ritter 1876–1958
US women's historian

Charles Beard's progressive view of history was formed at DePauw University, at Oxford University (including his activities on behalf of Ruskin Hall and its aim to educate the working class), and, finally, by a group of reform-minded professors at Columbia University. Already in 1901, Beard published his *The Industrial Revolution*, where he maintained that the great economic changes would bring about a beneficent adjustment in the thought and institutions of Western culture. In this stipulation of an inherently progressive tendency of history, Beard's activism would find its strength and his empiricism and pragmatism its limit. The perceived obligation to support this tendency shaped Beard's works in history and political science, social reform, and urban administration (the latter in the New York Bureau of Municipal Research and as adviser to Tokyo's mayor). All obstacles to the historically mandated adjustment to industrialization Beard explained by what today is called the "hermeneutic of suspicion": reactionary forces obstructed the needed radical democratization of society. He did so when he linked economic realities and interests to the shaping of the American Constitution in *An Economic Interpretation of the Constitution of the United States* (1913). The work, based on an early prosopographical study, made Beard both famous and controversial with the thesis that the direct economic interests of those who won at the Philadelphia Convention (primarily the public creditors), rather than thoughtful deliberations guided by age-old wisdom, inspired the provisions of the Constitution. The losers were those with reality interests (debtors, especially mortgage holders) and, although not noted, those not represented at the convention (women, poor, slaves). The dualistic scheme represented a stark economic determinism, which Beard later disowned. He continued this line of inquiry in the *Economic Origins of Jeffersonian Democracy* (1915) and in a series of lectures published only in 1922, *The Economic Basis of Politics*. World War I convinced Beard that America should remain uninvolved abroad and should dedicate itself to the construction of a truly modern society. By the mid-1920s, however, Beard had shifted his interest to the writing of survey history. Together with James Harvey Robinson he had published the highly successful *The Development of Modern Europe* (1907), which had been intended to realize the program of a "New History" – one that de-emphasized the history of states, battles, and treaties, in favor of economic and cultural (especially scientific and technological) developments. The masses were praised as an important historical agent, but the work only replaced the "old" backward-looking elite with a "good" democratic elite that led the masses, suspected to be inert.

In 1927, Charles Beard and his wife, Mary Ritter Beard, published the first two volumes of *The Rise of American Civilization*. Splendidly written, it would be a shaping force for a generation of young intellectuals as well as a favorite of the general public. It stayed within Beard's economic interpretation of history, and viewed the Civil War, not as a struggle over slavery, but as the "Second American Revolution" in which the industrial and commercial North and East won lasting hegemony over the rural South. The work made the Beards financially independent and brought fame to Charles Beard in particular. The volumes were also a sort of *summa* of the American Progressive school of history with the stipulated certainty of an ever-increasing rationality expected to result in ever greater justice, civic virtue, and happiness. In the 1930s that certainty became a temporary casualty of Charles Beard's turn to radical historiographical relativism under the influence of the New Physics and German historicism – best manifested in his presidential address to the American Historical Association in 1934 ("Written History as an Act of Faith"). Progress became merely Beard's subjective choice over chaos or determinism, because it made social activism feasible. Ironically, Beard also wrote works that advocated the reform of American society in those years, guided by the insights of the certainties of the social sciences. After 1936, fearing another American intervention in Europe, Beard's interest shifted back to foreign policy. In history he found substantial reasons for warning against any direction of American energy abroad lest it obstruct the building of the "Good Society" at home (*A Foreign Policy for America*, 1940). Increasingly isolated after America's entry into the war, he wrote the remaining volumes of *The Rise of American Civilization* with Mary Beard in order to recall to Americans the true mission of their country. His anxiety about the decline of the American Republic and his deep resentment of Franklin D. Roosevelt's substitution of external intervention for full social reform shaped his *President Roosevelt and the Coming of the War, 1941* (1948). Although its influence faded rapidly in the post-1945 powerful and prosperous USA, Charles Beard's historical work remains an outstanding example of American Progressive history.

Although overshadowed by the reputation of her husband, Mary Ritter Beard was a formidable historian in her own right. She was an influential co-author of *The Rise of American Civilization*, and her special interest in various reform movements was manifest in it. Aside from works on suffrage and labor issues, she was a pioneer in what came to be known as women's history with her *Woman as Force in History* (1946), which tried to demonstrate the power of women in all ages and areas of life so as to end the view of women as a subjected gender without influence on history.

ERNST BREISACH

See also Bailyn; Cott; Croce; Curti; France: French Revolution; Gipson; Hofstadter; Jensen; LaFeber; Lerner; Morison; Parrington; Political; Robinson; Schlesinger; Spruill; Stampp; United States: Colonial; United States: 19th Century; United States: 20th Century; United States: Historical Writing, 20th Century, Williams, W.; Women's History: North America; Woodward

Biography

Charles Austin Beard. Born Knightstown, Indiana, 27 November 1874. Studied at DePauw University, PhB 1898; then Oxford University where, with Walter Vrooman, he founded Ruskin Hall [now College], 1899; returned to US, and studied at Cornell University, 1899–1901; and Columbia University, MA, 1903, PhD 1904. Taught (rising to professor of politics), Columbia University, 1904–17: resigned on political grounds; helped found New School for Social Research; training school director, New York Bureau of Municipal Research, 1917–22. Independent lecturer/writer, 1917–48. Married Mary Ritter, historian, 1900 (1 daughter, 1 son). Died New Haven, 1 September 1948.

Principal Writings

The Industrial Revolution, 1901
With James Harvey Robinson, *The Development of Modern Europe*, 2 vols., 1907–08; enlarged 1929–30
An Economic Interpretation of the Constitution of the United States, 1913
With Mary Ritter Beard, *American Citizenship*, 1914
Economic Origins of Jeffersonian Democracy, 1915
The Economic Basis of Politics, 1922; enlarged 1945
With Mary Ritter Beard, *The Rise of American Civilization*, 4 vols., 1927–42
The Devil Theory of War: An Inquiry into the Nature of History and the Possibility of Keeping Out of War, 1936
A Foreign Policy for America, 1940
With Mary Ritter Beard, *A Basic History of the United States*, 1944
President Roosevelt and the Coming of the War, 1941: A Study in Appearance and Realities, 1948

Further Reading

Beale, Howard K., ed., *Charles A. Beard: An Appraisal*, Lexington: University of Kentucky Press, 1954
Borning, Bernard C., *The Political and Social Thought of Charles A. Beard*, Seattle: University of Washington Press, 1962
Breisach, Ernst, *American Progressive History: An Experiment in Modernization*, Chicago: University of Chicago Press, 1993
Hofstadter, Richard, *The Progressive Historians: Turner, Beard, Parrington*, New York: Knopf, 1968; London: Cape, 1969
Nore, Ellen, *Charles A. Beard: An Intellectual Biography*, Carbondale: Southern Illinois University Press, 1983
Strout, Cushing, *The Pragmatic Revolt in American History: Carl Becker and Charles Beard*, New Haven: Yale University Press, 1958

Biography

Mary Ritter Beard. Born Indianapolis, 5 August 1876, daughter of a lawyer. Received BA, DePauw University, 1897; graduate study, Columbia University. Involved in feminist politics and also wrote books mostly on feminist issues. Married Charles Austin Beard, 1900 (died 1948; 1 daughter, 1 son). Died Scottsdale, Arizona, 14 August 1958.

Principal Writings

With Charles A. Beard, *American Citizenship*, 1914
A Short History of the American Labor Movement, 1920
With Charles A. Beard, *The Rise of American Civilization*, 4 vols., 1927–42
On Understanding Women, 1931
Editor, *America Through Women's Eyes*, 1933
With Charles A. Beard, *A Basic History of the United States*, 1944
Woman as Force in History: A Study in Traditions and Realities, 1946
The Force of Women in Japanese History, 1953
The Making of Charles A. Beard: An Interpretation, 1955

Further Reading

Cott, Nancy F., ed., *A Woman Making History: Mary Ritter Beard through Her Letters*, New Haven: Yale University Press, 1991
Lane, Ann J., ed., *Mary Ritter Beard: A Sourcebook*, New York: Schocken, 1977
Turoff, Barbara K., *Mary Beard as Force in History*, Dayton, OH: Wright State University, 1979

Becker, Carl L. 1873–1945
US historian

Carl L. Becker's initial historical views were shaped by Frederick Jackson Turner at the University of Wisconsin, James Harvey Robinson at Columbia University, and a natural skepticism. His studies caused a break with the certainties of small-town, Protestant America that launched him on a search for a new certainty conducted in intellectual history. For some years, that certainty was provided by the tenets of the prevailing Scientific history and the Progressive movement although Becker's skepticism surfaced as early as 1910 in the article "Detachment and the Writing of History." In it Becker criticized the over-reliance on "facts" and the neglect of "imagination" in the epistemology and composition of historical accounts. While traces of positivist certainties, including a progressive telos in history, remained present in his educational texts and some works for the broader public, even after his views had shifted away from the progressive position (especially in *Progress and Power*, 1935), they soon were expunged from his scholarly publications.

After Becker's disenchantment by World War I and its aftermath, epistemological doubts engulfed his entire historical thought, producing a view of the cosmos and history as being without any inherent meaning. During the 1920s – a period in which he wrote little – Becker struggled with the implications of his philosophical shift and began to unlink gradually the historian's account of the past from any permanent features and from certainties about the representations of the past. In his *Eve of the Revolution* (1918) and *The Declaration of Independence* (1922) Becker detached the thoughts and actions of people from the notion of timeless ideas and ideals, relocating the latter within the limits of specific time and space contexts – originating there and being relative to them. A paper given in 1926 offered a glimpse at the maturation of Becker's relativism that manifested itself fully in Becker's 1931 presidential address to the American Historical Association: "Everyman His Own Historian" (later reprinted in a collection with the same title, 1935). Although he granted that histories with a short range could be pragmatically tested, those with a long-range nexus between the past, present, and the expectations for the future took on an imaginary quality. As "facts" lost their experiential certainty and became constructs, historical accounts came to resemble more or less mythical adaptations of whatever happened in the past. Historians no longer were the builders of factually accurate accounts of the past, but more the guardians of a society's myths, including Becker's once-held progressive views on history.

Accordingly, Becker's best-known work *The Heavenly City of the Eighteenth-Century Philosophers* (1932) treated Western culture's decisive turn from Christianity's concept of history to that of the Enlightenment as a mere shift of modes of thought. Neither view had any claim to truth but only to being a more or less useful myth. But despite its radically relativistic message, Becker's in this case particularly elegant writing made the book a success in a still strongly positivist scholarly environment. After 1936, Becker's historical work showed a new intellectual and personal struggle. The threat from totalitarian regimes made the defense of liberal democracies an issue for Becker who, although skeptical, cherished the Enlightenment's message of tolerance and rationality. However, his pronounced relativistic view of the cosmos and history provided him no good basis for a defense. The post-1935 books – based on lecture series on American history he had delivered – carried the visible traces of his struggle. In the end, he resolved that skepticism should spare some of the basic elements of the American tradition, on which could then be constructed a new American history and a democracy with a better collective spirit and organization. His historical work represents less a witness to American Progressive history and more a prefiguration of those later American views on history that abandoned the concept of progress and the certainties connected with it.

ERNST BREISACH

See also Croce; Curti; Gipson; Jensen; Parrington; Social; United States: American Revolution

Biography

Carl Lotus Becker. Born Lincoln Township, Black Hawk County, Iowa, 7 September 1873. Studied at Cornell College, Mount Vernon, Iowa; then at University of Wisconsin with Charles Homer Haskins, BA 1896, PhD 1907; and with James Harvey Robinson, Columbia University, 1898–99. Taught at Pennsylvania State College, 1899–1901; Dartmouth College, 1901–02; then, rising to professor, University of Kansas, 1902–16; University of Minnesota, 1916–17; and Cornell University, 1917–41 (emeritus). Married Maude Hepworth Ranney, 1901 (1 son). Died Ithaca, New York, 10 April 1945.

Principal Writings

The History of Political Parties in the Province of New York, 1760–1776, 1909
"Detachment and Writing in History," *Atlantic Monthly* 106 (1910), 524–36
Eve of the Revolution: A Chronicle of the Breach with England, 1918
The Declaration of Independence: A Study in the History of Political Ideas, 1922
The Heavenly City of the Eighteenth-Century Philosophers, 1932
Everyman His Own Historian: Essays on History and Politics, 1935
Progress and Power, 1935
New Liberties for Old, 1941
How New Will the Better World Be? A Discussion of Post-War Reconstruction, 1944; in UK as *Making a Better World*, 1945
Freedom and Responsibility in the American Way of Life, 1945

Detachment and the Writing of History: Essays and Letters of Carl L. Becker, edited by Phil L. Snyder, 1958
"What Is the Good of History?" Selected Letters of Carl L. Becker, 1900–45, edited by Michael Kammen, 1973

Further Reading

Breisach, Ernst, *American Progressive History: An Experiment in Modernization*, Chicago: University of Chicago Press, 1993
Brown, Robert Eldon, *Carl Becker on History and the American Revolution*, East Lansing, MI: Spartan, 1970
Smith, Charlotte Watkins, *Carl Becker: On History and the Climate of Opinion*, Ithaca, NY: Cornell University Press, 1956
Strout, Cushing, *The Pragmatic Revolt in American History: Carl Becker and Charles Beard*, New Haven: Yale University Press, 1958
Wilkins, Burleigh Taylor, *Carl Becker: A Biographical Study in American Intellectual History*, Cambridge, MA: MIT Press, 1961

Bede *c.672/3–735*
Anglo-Saxon chronicler

Although most often thought of as a historian, Bede's principal literary output was in the form of biblical commentaries and teaching texts. It was through the latter that he began to be involved in the writing of history, an aspect of his work that became particularly important in the later years of his life. Entered at the age of seven as a novice into the monastery of Wearmouth, recently founded by the Northumbrian nobleman Biscop Baducing (Benedict Biscop), Bede remained a monk of the house until his death. His earliest writings date from around the year 703, very soon after he was ordained a priest. By this time he was probably teaching in the monastery, and he began writing texts to instruct his pupils. Possibly his first work was the brief treatise that he called the *Liber de temporibus* ("On Time"), which very briefly categorized the divisions of time into hours, days, years, annual cycles and ultimately the Six Ages of the Universe. To illustrate the latter he compiled a very brief chronicle, which, although unoriginal in its contents, represents his earliest historical writing.

He returned to the same subject in 725, when he wrote a considerably expanded and augmented version of the earlier treatise, under the title of *De temporibus ratione* ("On the Computation of Time"). For this he composed a new and much longer chronicle, which in later manuscript tradition could circulate as a separate work in its own right, under the title of "The Greater Chronicle" (to distinguish it from the "Lesser Chronicle" accompanying the *Liber de temporibus*). This is a work of considerable sophistication, for which Bede drew upon a wide variety of sources, including the most recent version of the *Liber pontificalis*, a collection of papal biographies that was being kept up to date pontificate by pontificate. His handling of his sources was deft and critical; he selected with care and rewrote what he borrowed if he felt the original was poorly expressed. The work also indicates how much Bede knew both of a past that he saw extending back into the biblical world with which he was concerned in his commentaries on Samuel (c.716) and on the Books of Kings (c.725), and of the contemporary events throughout much of western Europe and the Mediterranean in his own day.

Although it is important to be aware of the generic differences between history and hagiography, Bede's lives of saints contain much information of historical value, and have been much appreciated for that. He applied the same critical guidelines in accumulating information and assessing its value in composing them as he did in his works of history. Particularly important are his two versions of the *Life of St. Cuthbert*. The first of these was written in verse some time in the years 705 to 716, at the request of the community of the island monastery of Lindisfarne, where Cuthbert had been both prior and briefly bishop (685–87). He wrote a more substantial prose *Life of Cuthbert* around 721 to supplement his earlier work, which itself was intended to replace a previous anonymous *Life* that the monks of Lindisfarne found unsatisfactory. In his writings on Cuthbert Bede developed the concept of the *opus geminatum* or "twinned work," in which the treatment of the same subject in both prose and verse was held to form the perfect unified view of it.

From his work for the monks of Lindisfarne it was a natural step to turn to the history of his own monastery. It is possible that Bede may have been involved in the composition of an anonymous *Life* of its second abbot, Ceolfrid (d. 716), which is important for being the earliest known work to date events by years of the Incarnation (our modern AD dating). Around 730 he completed his *Historia abbatum* (History of the Abbots of Wearmouth and Jarrow). Following a brief account of Benedict Biscop's earlier life this took the history of the two components of the twin monastery, which he founded in 674 and 680/1 respectively, up to the abdication and death of his successor Ceolfrid in 716. It is thus a unique source for 7th and early 8th century Northumbrian monasticism, made all the more remarkable by being a strictly historical account that avoided any reference to the miraculous.

That Bede did not himself regard historical narrative and tales of miracles as antithetical can be seen from his greatest undertaking, the *Historia ecclesiastica gentis Anglorum* or "Ecclesiastical History of the English People," that he completed in 731. This substantial work in five books, to which he probably made minor revisions and additions in 732/3, recounted the history of the establishment of the Angles and the Saxons in Britain, their conversion to Christianity, and many features of the political and ecclesiastical developments that then took place up to Bede's own time. Two slightly different versions exist, one of which is represented in manuscripts written within a few years at most of Bede's death in 735. Brief continuations in chronicle form of 8th-century events have been added to a few of the manuscripts. Bede's original text is by far and away the most important source for not just Anglo-Saxon, but also British and Pictish history in the 7th and early 8th centuries, and its value is enormously enhanced by Bede's careful selection of his sources and the critical judgments he applied to them, a process that he describes in the preface to the work. In his choice of title he aligned himself with a tradition of Christian historiography that went back to Eusebius of Caesarea (*c*.265–339); following whom he included original documents in his narrative. The skill with which Bede organized his materials and arranged his narrative, together with the critical acumen that he displays, makes him by far the greatest of the writers of history in the early medieval West.

ROGER COLLINS

See also Britain: Anglo-Saxon; Britain: 1066–1485; Knowles; Levison; Medieval Historical Writing; Orderic; Saxo; Stenton

Biography
Born Northumbria, *c*.672/3. Entered monastery of Wearmouth, then moved to Jarrow, 669/70. Died Jarrow, Northumbria, 735; canonized 1899.

Principal Writings
Life of St. Cuthbert, verse, *c*.705–716; prose, *c*.721
De temporibus ratione (On the Computation of Time), 725
Historia abbatum (History of the Abbots of Wearmouth and Jarrow), 730
Historia ecclesiastica gentis Anglorum (Ecclesiastical History of the English People), 731

Further Reading
Blair, P. Hunter, *The World of Bede*, London: Secker and Warburg, 1970; New York: St. Martin's Press, 1971
McClure, Judith, and Roger Collins, eds., *The Ecclesiastical History of the English People: The Great Chronicler Bede's Letter to Egbert*, Oxford and New York: Oxford University Press, 1994
Wallace-Hadrill, J.M., *Bede's Ecclesiastical History of the English People: A Historical Commentary*, Oxford: Oxford University Press, 1988

Begriffsgeschichte (History of Concepts)

Although the word *Begriffsgeschichte* (history of concepts) was evidently coined by Hegel, the term today designates an approach to intellectual history devised in western Germany in the 1960s, associated particularly with the scholarly vision of Reinhart Koselleck and the methods and goals of two ambitious reference works: the *Geschichtliche Grundbegriffe: historisches Lexikon zur politisch-sozialen Sprache in Deutschland* (Historical Concepts: A Historical Dictionary of Political and Social Language in Germany, 1972–), and the *Handbuch politisch-sozialer Grundbegriffe in Frankreich, 1680–1820* (Handbook of Political and Social Concepts in France, 1680–1820, 15 vols. to date, 1985–). Though less innovative in conception, a third postwar German reference work may also be considered under this heading: the *Historisches Wörterbuch der Philosophie* (Historical Dictionary of Philosophy, 8 vols. to date, 1971–). These works – and particularly the first two – are designed to overcome perceived shortcomings in traditional ways of studying the history of ideas.

With strong roots in 18th-century philosophical idealism, jurisprudence, and philology, modern German historiography has always displayed a pronounced interest in interpreting the mental life of the past, including language and symbolic meaning. Between the late 19th century and the 1950s, German scholars typically studied ideas in the terms of what was called *Geistesgeschichte* (history of the spirit, or mind) and *Ideengeschichte* (history of ideas) – traditions associated with Wilhelm Dilthey (1833–1911) and Friedrich Meinecke (1862–1954). In the spirit of 19th-century German *Historismus* (historism, or historicism) these approaches strove to explain ideas by situating them in their distinctive contexts of politics and elite culture – frameworks of the *Zeitgeist* (spirit of the times) and state power. Yet with the 20th-century growth of interest in creating a broader, transpolitical, social and economic basis for historical studies – one that attended to social structures, socioeconomic change, and the experiences of ordinary people as opposed to elites – the approaches of Meinecke and Dilthey began to look increasingly narrow. *Begriffsgeschichte* was conceived as a way to relate the life of the mind more closely to the overall contexts of society, social change, and social communication in which ideas were produced and disseminated.

The approach is best conveyed in the research strategy and programmatic goals of the *Geschichtliche Grundbegriffe* (GG), announced in 1967 by Koselleck together with the medievalist Otto Brunner and the social historian Werner Conze. In the format of an encyclopedic dictionary, these men initiated a collaborative project to map semantic shifts in the German language relating specifically to social and political discourse in Central Europe between 1750 and 1850. In lengthy articles written by specialists or teams of specialists, they chose to focus on key categories of social communication – concepts covering broad semantic fields such as "citizen," "democracy," "society," "revolution," "state," and "nation" – in the age of the Enlightenment and revolutionary upheaval, when German Europe embarked upon the process of social "modernization" (secularization, democratic and industrial transformation). Unearthing the story of shifting meanings in public discourse, they hypothesized, would reveal major permutations in social consciousness. This would clarify not only the diverse ways that German speakers responded, emotionally and intellectually, to rapid change in what Koselleck termed the *Sattelzeit* (or "saddle period" between premodern and modern times), but would reveal how new or altered terms, contested meanings, and syntax helped to either constrain or spur social, political, and economic change. For evidence of socio-linguistic change, the editors of GG asked their contributors to examine a wide sampling of sources, such as speeches, newspapers, popular pamphlets, literary works, and personal letters as well as 18th- and early 19th-century dictionaries, administrative documents, and the published works of philosophers and social theorists; presumably, such materials would sustain reconstruction of popular as well as elite usage. The result, produced over a period of more than 20 years, is a compendium of lengthy articles – some of them scholarly monographs in themselves which run to over 100 pages. Grandiose in conception, many historians would now agree that Koselleck and his team have produced a model of scholarly thoroughness, a richly detailed and documented record of social consciousness at the advent of European democratization and industrialization.

The *Historisches Wörterbuch der Philosophie* (HWP), also initiated in western Germany in 1967, is more sweeping in scope, but less methodologically innovative than the GG. Launched and edited by Joachim Ritter and Karlfried Gründer, its purpose was to define the technical terms and enduring problems of philosophy relating to all periods of world history, especially as they are understood in the German language. Its emphasis is on the conceptual history of systematic philosophy – that is, an aspect of high culture – and the vastness of its scope rules out the kind of close attention to socio-linguistic change in specific historical settings that characterizes the GG. In this regard, the HWP remains more closely tied to the traditions of *Geistesgeschichte*.

This is not true, however, of the *Handbuch politisch-sozialer Grundbegriffe in Frankreich* (HGF) which – by blending the assumptions of sociology of knowledge, selective use of quantitative analysis, and new theories of popular culture together with a revised version of the non-quantitative methods of Koselleck – attempts to go beyond the GG in its study of the social basis of linguistic and conceptual change. Focusing on political and social discourse in France in the era of the Old Regime and French Revolution (1680–1820), the HGF began to appear in 1985 under the editorship of Rolf Reichard (a former student of Koselleck) and Eberhard Schmitt. By employing quantitative reasoning, discourse analysis, and other techniques – e.g., the interpretation of such non-conventional forms of evidence as prints, popular imagery, games, songs, festivals, and political primers or catechisms – they and their collaborators (both French and German) seek to delve even more deeply beneath elite usage to construct the language and *mentalités* (collective mentalities) of other, less literate social groups.

HARRY RITTER

See also Conze; Koselleck

Further Reading

Carr, David, Review of Reinhart Koselleck, *Futures Past*, *History and Theory* 26 (1987), 197–204

Koselleck, Reinhart, "Einleitung" (Introduction) in Otto Brunner, Werner Conze, Reinhart Koselleck, eds., *Geschichtliche Grundbegriffe: historisches Lexikon zur politisch-sozialen Sprache in Deutschland*, vol. 1, Stuttgart: Klett, 1972

Koselleck, Reinhart, *Historische Semantik und Begriffsgeschichte* (The Semantics of History and Begriffsgeschichte), Stuttgart: Klett-Cotta, 1979

Koselleck, Reinhart, "Begriffsgeschichte and Social History" in Koselleck, *Futures Past: On the Semantics of Historical Time*, Cambridge, MA: MIT Press, 1985

Koselleck, Reinhart, "Sozialgeschichte und Begriffsgeschichte," in Wolfgang Schieder and Volker Sellin, eds., *Sozialgeschichte in Deutschland*, vol. 1, Göttingen: Vandenhoeck & Ruprecht, 1986

Meier, H.G., "Begriffsgeschichte," *Historisches Wörterbuch der Philosophie*, vol. 1, Basel: Schwabe, 1971

Popkin, Jeremy D., "Recent West German Work on the French Revolution," *Journal of Modern History* 59 (1987), 737–50

Rayner, Jeremy, "On Begriffsgeschichte," *Political Theory* 16 (1988), 496–501

Rayner, Jeremy, "On Begriffsgeschichte Again," *Political Theory* 18 (1990), 305–07

Reichardt, Rolf et al., eds., *Handbuch politisch-sozialer Grundbegriffe in Frankreich, 1680–1820* (Handbook of Political and Social Concepts in France, 1680–1820), Munich: Oldenbourg, 1985[–]

Richter, Melvin, "Conceptual History (*Begriffsgeschichte*) and Political Theory," *Political Theory* 14 (1986), 604–37

Richter, Melvin, "*Begriffsgeschichte* and the History of Ideas," *Journal of the History of Ideas* 48 (1987), 247–63

Richter, Melvin, "Understanding Begriffsgeschichte: A Rejoinder," *Political Theory* 17 (1989), 296–301

Richter, Melvin, *The History of Political and Social Concepts: A Critical Introduction*, New York: Oxford University Press, 1995

Sheehan, James J., "*Begriffsgeschichte*: Theory and Practice," *Journal of Modern History* 50 (1978), 312–19

Tribe, Keith, translator's introduction, in Reinhart Koselleck, *Futures Past: On the Semantics of Historical Time*, Cambridge, MA: MIT Press, 1985

Tribe, Keith, "The *Geschichtliche Grundbegriffe* Project: From History of Ideas to Conceptual History" [review article], *Comparative Studies in Society and History* 31 (1989), 180–84

Veit-Brause, Irmline, "A Note on Begriffsgeschichte," *History and Theory* 20 (1981), 61–68

Beloch, Karl Julius 1854–1929

Italian (German-born) historian of ancient Italy

Beloch was the founder of the modern study of ancient history in Italy. He was also the founder of the study of ancient demography and played a leading role in the history of European demography.

His fundamental interests and contributions were revealed by his earliest book, *Campanien* (Campania, 1879); this superseded earlier studies that merely listed sources and monuments. Beloch combined archaeology and history in a brilliant bringing to life of a neglected part of ancient Italian history which was a melting-pot of Oscan, Greek, Etruscan, and Roman influences. Beloch himself recognized that it contained many errors, but it was a pioneering work on which all later studies are based.

His horizons broadened with *Der italische Bund* (The Italian Federation, 1880), again a path-breaking work on the organization of Italy in all its complexity. Beloch combined constitutional history with statistics, notably on the territories of the Italian states and the development of Rome's control through colonies and self-governing municipalities, but questions were raised over his assessment of sources. Most importantly, the book began his feud with Theodor Mommsen, who declared that rarely had a work been written with such neglect of specialist research or a scientific "mystery tour" undertaken with such light baggage. The chance of a chair in Germany was virtually out of the question.

Die Bevölkerung der griechisch-römischen Welt (Population of the Greco-Roman World, 1886) was, in Beloch's own words, the first attempt to describe population movement on an extensive scale and over a long period by the systematic and critical examination of all evidence. It had previously been claimed that nothing could be known about such matters. Beloch stated that he had been collecting the evidence since he was 14 years old. His method was to determine the area of a state, then assemble all given figures for the population, to subject them to analysis and to put them in the context of paradigms such as economic history. Population was the result of historical and economic factors, and where these were known, the population could be calculated. Beloch admitted that there was a margin of error of 25 per cent either way with the free population, and 50 per cent either way with the slave population, but his figures were probable minimums, and were to serve as a working basis for historians. This book was the stimulus to a projected history of population in Europe, and Beloch spent every summer for decades in archives all over Europe collecting data.

Beloch's most important contribution otherwise to ancient history was his multivolume *Griechische Geschichte* (Greek History, 1893–1904), which rendered obsolete the previous work of Ernst Curtius, Georg Busolt, and Adolf Holm. By Beloch's own account, he should never have undertaken it, because it absorbed all his energies. He visited Greece six times, the last visit being in 1909. He "smashed to pieces the conventional picture," subjecting the early period to ruthless criticism and rejecting everything not vouched for by monuments, literary sources, or logic. The history of the 4th century was completely rewritten, and economic and cultural history were given their full due. In all of this there was not a superfluous word. This was his life's work and it gave him the recognition in his fifties that he had previously lacked.

The work was full of his individual insights, and remains the unchallenged classic of the 20th century. He opposed the over-valuation of great individuals but was deeply interested in them. Themistocles was the greatest Athenian politician. He attacked the myth of Leonidas: his death cleared the way for Pausanias, who won the great victory over the Persians at Plataia. Pericles was guilty of the greatest crime in Greek history in causing the Peloponnesian War. Beloch saw himself as a modern Theramenes, caught between the proletariat and the Junkers.

In matters of causation, Beloch emphasized "force of circumstances," and saw humans as driven by needs. The Greeks had to defeat the Persians, because of their moral and intellectual superiority.

The main focus of his interest – despite his commitment to freedom as the greatest human good – was on the attempts to unify Greece, where he praised Dionysius, Isocrates, and Philip of Macedon. This meant that Alexander was regarded as inferior to his father as a general and statesman. For Beloch, Greek history was the most important page in the history of mankind, because the Greeks began the eternal struggles – for truth, freedom and justice.

After the tragedy of World War I and his restriction to the teaching of Greek history, Beloch finally produced a *Römische Geschichte* (Roman History, 1926), only down to 264 BCE. It was not a narrative history but a series of specialist studies, notably on the sources. He applied a most severe criticism to the lists of magistrates, dismissing early plebeian consuls and most of the early dictators. He revised his account of Italy given in the study of 1880. In his reconstruction of Roman history, Beloch was most famous for his view that the dictator formed a link between the monarchy and the Republic in the first half of the 5th century.

Beloch was for the most part a materialist, who saw the laws of history in society and economics, and was famous as a "mathematical" historian, reducing everything to statistics and tables. His source criticism was often attacked as subjective and inconsistent. His writing was marred by endless feuds, against rivals past and present, and an appalling anti-Semitism. He denounced philologists who understood nothing of history and its methods. He remained a patriotic German to the end of his life, yet he spent almost all of it abroad, fighting for recognition; in his middle age he lost everything and had to begin all over again. No one has probably ever known more about Italian geography, which Beloch ceaselessly surveyed. He had no successor in his combination of so many specialist disciplines.

RONALD T. RIDLEY

See also Greece: Ancient; Sanctis

Biography

Born Petschendorf (now in Poland), 21 January 1854. Privately educated by mother after father's death; because of his bronchitis, educated in Italy (naturalized 1923); attended University of Parma, 1872; University of Heidelberg, 1873, PhD 1875. Professor, University of Rome, 1877–1912, 1913–14: dismissed due to war (interned Siena, then Florence); reinstated, 1924; professor, University of Leipzig, 1912–13. Founded *Studi di Storia antica*, 1891, and *Biblioteca de Geografia Storica*, 1900. Married Bella Bailey, 1879 (died 1918; 2 daughters). Died Rome, 6 February 1929.

Principal Writings

Campanien (Campania), 1879

Der italische Bund unter Roms Hegemonie (The Italian Federation under Rome's Leadership), 1880

Die attische Politik seit Perikles (Athenian Politics after Perikles), 1884

Die Bevölkerung der griechisch-römischen Welt (Population of the Greco-Roman World), 1886

"La popolazione d'Italia nei secoli XVI, XVII e XVIII (The Population of Italy in the 16th to 18th Centuries)," *Bulletin de l'Institut international de Statistique* 3 (1888), 1–42; reprinted in Carlo Cipolla, ed., *Storia dell'economia italiana*, 1959

Griechische Geschichte (Greek History), 3 vols., 1893–1904

Contributor, *Die Geschichtswissenschaft der Gegenwart in Selbstdarstellungen* (Current Historiography in Self-Portraits), edited by S. Steinberg, 1926

Römische Geschichte bis zum Beginn der punischen Kriege (Roman History to the Outbreak of the Punic Wars), 1926

Bevölkerungsgeschichte Italiens (History of Population in Italy), 3 vols., 1937–61

Further Reading

Christ, Karl, *Von Gibbon zu Rostovtzeff: Leben und Werk führender Althistoriker der Neuzeit* (From Gibbon to Rostovtzeff: The Life and Work of the Leading Ancient Historians of Modern Times), Darmstadt: Wissenschaftliche Buchgesellschaft, 1972

Momigliano, Arnaldo, "Beloch, Karl Julius," in *Dizionario biografico degli italiani*, vol. 8, 1966

Polverini, Leandro, "Bibliografia degli scritti di Giulio Beloch" (Bibliography of the Writings of Julius Beloch), *Annali della Scuola Normale di Pisa* (1979), 1429–62; (1981), 825–27

Polverini, Leandro, ed., *Aspetti della storiografia di Giulio Beloch* (Aspects of the Historiography of Julius Beloch), Naples: Edizioni Scientifiche Italiane, 1990

Berlin, Isaiah 1909–1997

British historical philosopher

Isaiah Berlin is a historian of ideas known for his wide learning, his luminous historical imagination, and his passionate commitment to the view that there are no final and absolute truths in history. Born in Latvia and educated in England, Berlin was at home in three different intellectual traditions – the Anglo-American, the Russian, and the Jewish. As a young man he was a member of the "Oxford circle" of philosophers whose discussions about language, knowledge, and meaning helped shape the mode of linguistic analysis which dominated philosophy in the English-speaking world in the 1940s and 1950s. More recently he had considerable influence as a moral and political philosopher. His seminal essay "Two Concepts of Liberty" (1958) deepened and enriched modern liberal political philosophy, as did his continuing defense of "value pluralism" – the idea that since moral goods are both multiple – and incompatible, there can never be a single set of values or a single ideal society to which all should aspire. Berlin was also active as a critic of music and literature and as a commentator on Jewish affairs. But his most significant contributions to the intellectual life of the late 20th century may well be his essays in the history of ideas and the philosophy of history.

As a philosopher of history Berlin was a steadfast critic of deterministic theories which claim that the historical process is governed by laws dictating the course of events. Among such theories he focused his criticism especially on those that treat historical knowledge as a species of scientific knowledge, with aims and methods similar to those of the natural sciences. Historical knowledge, he argued, concerns human motives and human agency, an understanding of which requires a kind of insight and intuition far removed from the testable hypotheses of natural science. Retrospectively the historical process may seem explicable in terms of causal chains and impersonal social forces, but a genuine understanding of the past requires the imagination to enter into the mental world of historical figures and to discern the range of possibilities open to them.

Berlin's approach to the history of ideas is of a piece with his philosophical writing. He was not an author of historical monographs but an essayist, a master of the essay form, whose discussion of a thinker often took him beyond formal arguments in search of a central vision of the world and of man's place in it. Thus in writing about the French theocrat Joseph de Maistre, his focus was not on Maistre's arguments for the existence of God or the necessity of authority, but on points Maistre chose not to argue – his dark vision of human nature and his insistence on the force of blind tradition and irrational instinct. Likewise, in Berlin's stimulating and richly textured essays on the Russian radical Alexander Herzen, his emphasis was not on Herzen's Hegelianism or his socialism but on his "sense of the movement of nature and of its unpredictable possibilities."

Berlin's essays on the history of ideas centered around two poles: Russian history and literature, and the history of a "Counter-Enlightenment" tradition that Berlin himself did much to define. In addition to the essays on Herzen (who was clearly one of Berlin's heroes), the Russian writings include *The Hedgehog and the Fox* (1953), a searching exploration of tensions in Tolstoi's views of history and human nature, as well as the brilliant essays on the emergence of the Russian intelligentsia in *A Marvellous Decade* (1954). Berlin's Counter-Enlightenment is rooted in a relativist and skeptical tradition stretching back to antiquity. But its central figures are Vico, Herder, and J.G. Hamann, whom Berlin saw as united not only in their rejection of Enlightenment rationalism, but also in their belief that all truth is particular, that every culture is unique, and that "to understand a religion, or a work of art, or a national character, one must 'enter into' the unique conditions of its life."

There are several qualities that make Berlin's historical writing absolutely distinctive. One is his prose style which, with its breathless run-on sentences, its interminable paragraphs, its unforgettable metaphors, its dazzling mixture of exuberance and nuance, leaves the reader both exhausted and exhilarated.

Another quality is Berlin's ability to evoke succinctly but vividly both the personalities of thinkers and the intellectual contexts within which they lived and worked. The history of ideas for Berlin is not the study of disembodied concepts and categories. It is the study of the thought and feeling of particular individuals living at specific times and places. Thus Berlin's writing includes pithy evocations of Marx's Paris, Vico's Naples, and the rarefied intellectual atmosphere within the Moscow circles of the 1840s. The personalities of his thinkers are also vividly sketched – especially in the case of Russians like Belinskii and Chaadaev who were not original minds but who were remarkable for their ability to pursue the ideas and arguments of others to their most extreme consequences.

The most impressive of all Berlin's qualities as a historian, however, is his extraordinary capacity for empathy – his ability to enter into the minds of thinkers whose views are sometimes antithetical to his own. This quality, which Berlin admired in the novelist Turgenev and the philosopher Herder, was clearly a key to his own success in bringing the history of ideas to life.

JONATHAN BEECHER

See also Anderson, P.; Kołakowski; Nationalism; Russia: Modern

Biography
Born Riga, Latvia, 6 June 1909; emigrated to England, 1920. Educated at St. Paul's School, London; BA, Corpus Christi College, Oxford, 1932, MA 1935. War service: Ministry of Information, New York, 1941–42; Washington embassy, 1942–46. Taught philosophy at Oxford University, from 1932: attached to New College, 1932, 1938–50; All Souls College, 1932–38, 1950–66, and from 1975; Chichele professor of social and political theory, 1957–67; president, Wolfson College, 1966–75. President, British Academy, 1974–78. Knighted 1957. Married Aline Elizabeth Yvonne de Gunzbourg, 1956. Died 6 November 1997.

Principal Writings
Karl Marx: His Life and Environment, 1939
The Hedgehog and the Fox: An Essay on Tolstoy's View of History, 1953
A Marvellous Decade [lectures], 1954
Two Concepts of Liberty, 1958 [lecture]; reprinted in Four Essays on Liberty, 1969
Four Essays on Liberty, 1969
Vico and Herder: Two Studies in the History of Ideas, 1976
Concepts and Categories: Philosophical Essays, edited by Henry Hardy, 1978
Russian Thinkers, edited by Henry Hardy and Aileen Kelly, 1978
Against the Current: Essays in the History of Ideas, edited by Henry Hardy, 1979 [includes bibliography]
Personal Impressions, edited by Henry Hardy, 1981
The Crooked Timber of Humanity: Chapters in the History of Ideas, edited by Henry Hardy, 1990

Further Reading
Annan, Noel, Introduction to Isaiah Berlin, Personal Impressions, London: Hogarth Press, 1980; New York: Viking, 1981
Galipeau, Claude J., Isaiah Berlin's Liberalism, Oxford and New York: Oxford University Press, 1940
Gray, John, Isaiah Berlin, London: HarperCollins, 1995; Princeton: Princeton University Press, 1996
Hausheer, Roger, Introduction to Isaiah Berlin, Against the Current, London: Hogarth Press, 1979; New York: Viking, 1980

Jahanbegloo, Ramin, Conversations with Isaiah Berlin, New York: Scribner, 1991; London: Halban, 1992
Lieberson, Jonathan, and Sidney Morganbesser, "The Questions of Isaiah Berlin" and "The Choices of Isaiah Berlin," New York Review of Books (March 6 and 20, 1980)
Macpherson, C.B., "Berlin's Division of Liberty," in his Democratic Theory: Essays in Retrieval, Oxford: Oxford University Press, 1973
Magee, Bryan, Men of Ideas: Some Creators of Contemporary Philosophy, London: British Broadcasting Corporation, 1978; New York: Viking, 1979
Margalit, Edna, and Avishai Margalit, eds., Isaiah Berlin: A Celebration, London: Hogarth Press, and Chicago: University of Chicago Press, 1991
Momigliano, Arnaldo, "On the Pioneer Trail," New York Review of Books (11 November 1976), 33–38
Ryan, Alan, ed., The Idea of Freedom: Essays in Honor of Isaiah Berlin, Oxford and New York: Oxford University Press, 1979
Walzer, Michael, "Are There Limits to Liberalism," New York Review of Books (19 October 1995), 28–31
Williams, Bernard, Introduction to Isaiah Berlin, Concepts and Categories, London: Hogarth Press, 1978

Bernal, Martin 1937–
British ancient historian

As one of the most controversial historians of the ancient Mediterranean world, Martin Bernal has set out to challenge what he has described as the racist, "Aryan Model," of 19th-century historiography and to emphasize the Egyptian and Near Eastern (Afro-Asiatic) sources of Greek culture that he believes have been minimized by traditional classical studies. A sinologist who spent his early career analyzing Chinese socialism, in the 1970s and 1980s Bernal turned to the study of the ancient world. Although these scholarly pursuits and their tools seem quite disparate, Bernal's consistent focus in each field has been on "origins" and "foreign influences." In his first publication, Chinese Socialism to 1907 (1976), Bernal analyzed the European introduction of socialism to China with its various subsequent adaptations. In Bernal's work on the ancient Mediterranean he has argued for a conglomerate of interacting cultures that was dominated, particularly in the 2nd millennium BCE by Egypt, which eventually influenced many of the more important elements of Greek culture including art, religion, and philosophy.

Bernal's most important publications have been his on-going multivolume work entitled, Black Athena: The Afroasiatic Roots of Classical Civilization (1987–91). The first volume, subtitled "The Fabrication of Ancient Greece," primarily presented a survey of 19th- and 20th-century scholarship, an assault on the "Aryan Model," and a call for a return to what Bernal termed the "Ancient Model" which had been suppressed by European scholarship. This dominant model was located by Bernal in Greek literature in the form of affirmations of Egyptian and Phoenician influences. Black Athena is copiously documented, although Bernal has been criticized for his heavy reliance on secondary source material.

His theory was further elaborated in volume 2 of Black Athena subtitled, "The Archaeological and Documentary Evidence," in which he gathered the supporting material for his "Revised Ancient Model," including what he saw as a Semitic

(Hyksos) colonization of Mycenae – a huge Middle-Kingdom Egyptian hegemony that covered the Aegean as well as areas of the Caucasus Mountains – and his claim of "massive" Egyptian influence on the Minoan civilization in Crete. The physical evidence Bernal used in establishing these claims emerges, generally, from the late Bronze Age (c.600–c.1000, BCE) and includes, in addition to textual evidence, more than 800 objects mostly from the Near East but also from Egypt. This material is the foundation of his paradigm, that Greek culture had its most essential origins in the cultures of both Egypt and the Near East. Bernal plans to add yet another volume that will cover the etymological and linguistic evidence for his theory.

Bernal's work has been informed and critiqued by two schools of thought. The first of these schools, represented initially by Michael C. Astour and Cyrus Herzl Gordon, as well as – more recently – E. Cline, W.V. Davies and Lily Schofield, has postulated that evolving Greek culture participated in a variety of levels of reciprocal interaction with the ancient Near East and Egypt. Such relationships, dating from as early as 1600 BCE during the Minoan period, are supported by linguistic and archaeological data as well as a later written tradition found in Herodotus, Plato, and others that speak of Afro-Asiatic influences on Greek culture. That this school has only recently received a greater acceptance among classicists is evidence for Bernal of the racism that he asserted has continued to stymie the study of the ancient Mediterranean. Agreement between Bernal and these scholars is found on many points. However, it is significant that many of Bernal's most ardent critics have also emerged from this school. They assert that in Bernal's thesis of Egyptian hegemony in the Aegean he has made too much of a body of evidence that certainly suggests a reciprocal and even somewhat cosmopolitan situation, but only moderate interaction between Egypt, the Near East and the Aegean Greeks.

The Afrocentrist movement is the second school of thought to influence Bernal's historiography. This group is represented by its earlier proponents, D. Walker, H. Easton, Henry Highland Garnet and Cheikh Anta Diop as well as more recent scholars such as George G.M. James, Jacob H. Carruthers, and M. Delaney, all of whom have emphasized a racially and culturally black or Ethiopian Egypt. Bernal refers those who have held to this position as the "Black Champions of Ancient Egypt." However, many scholars disagree with Bernal's dating of Egyptian-Aegean evidence as well with his theory about the racial make-up of Egypt, and with the insights that modern discussions on race might bring to the study of the ancient world. Most interesting, however, has been the criticism that has emerged from the Afrocentrists regarding Bernal, who is often perceived by them as an outsider, falling short of full-blown Afrocentrism since he has acknowledged too few black (Ethiopian) pharaohs and because he has placed a greater emphasis on Mesopotamian civilizations than on the Nile River culture when describing the development of world civilizations.

In his writings Bernal has often identified his own work as a "revolution," referring to Thomas Kuhn's theory of the paradigm shifts necessary to reconceptualize a theoretical problem. He has described his efforts as part of a shift away from the old, outdated paradigm represented by the "Aryan Model" towards a new, more complete explanation of the evidence. Such a claim has been attacked by detractors on all sides.

However, Bernal must certainly be acknowledged as one who has forced a new consideration of the Afro-Asian-Aegean evidence that was indeed deemed insignificant by those who viewed the origins of Greek culture as a predominantly Eurocentric phenomenon.

KENNETH R. CALVERT

See also Africa: North; Diop; Egypt: Ancient; Kuhn

Biography
Martin Gardiner Bernal. Born London, 10 March 1937, son of a scientist and a writer. Served with the Royal Air Force, becoming a senior aircraftsman. Attended school in Cambridge; studied at King's College, Cambridge, BA, MA, PhD, then fellow, 1965–73; postdoctoral studies, University of California, Berkeley, 1962–65; and Harvard University, 1964. Professor of government, Cornell University, from 1972. Married 1) Judith Pace Dunn, 1960 (marriage dissolved 1975); 2) Leslie Miller, sociologist, 1979 (1 daughter, 3 sons).

Principal Writings
Chinese Socialism to 1907, 1976
Black Athena: The Afroasiatic Roots of Classical Civilization, 2 vols. to date, 1987–91
Cadmean Letter: The Transmission of the Alphabet to the Aegean and Further West Before 1400 BC, 1990
"Black Athena: Hostilities to Egypt in the Eighteenth Century," in Sandra Harding, ed., *The "Racial" Economy of Science*, 1993
"The Image of Ancient Greece as a Tool for Colonialism and European Hegemony," in G.C. Bond and Angela Gilliam, eds., *Social Construction of the Past: Representation as Power*, 1994

Further Reading
Carruthers, Jacob H., "Outside Academia: Bernal's Critique of Black Champions of Ancient Egypt," *Journal of Black Studies* 22 (1992), 459–76
"The Challenge of *Black Athena*," *Arethusa* (1989) [special issue]
Delaney, M., *The Origins of Races and Color*, Baltimore: Black Classics Press, 1991
Lefkowitz, Mary R., and Guy MacLean Rogers, eds., *Black Athena Revisited*, Chapel Hill: University of North Carolina Press, 1996
Lefkowitz, Mary R., *Not Out of Africa: How Afrocentrism Became an Excuse to Teach Myth as History*, New York: Basic Books, 1996
Palter, R., "*Black Athena*, Afro-Centrism, and the History of Science," *History of Science* 31 (1993), 227–87

Bīrūnī, Abū Rayhān al-, 973–c.1050
Arab historian of India

There is some disagreement about the birthplace, even the spelling of al-Bīrūnī's name. His full name has been rendered as Abu'l-Rayhān al-Bīrūnī as well as Abu-Rihan Muhammad. Many simply refer to him as al-Bīrūnī, "The Master." His place of birth is also disputed, as several cultures claim him as their own, although present day Iran is most probably correct.

Positioned between Hellenistic and Oriental cultures, al-Bīrūnī's Arabian location played a significant role in his ability to evaluate and to refine a diverse body of scientific and humanistic literature. Although limited by unreliable translations, he examined his sources with an unusually objective commitment to truth, and without allegiance to any long-standing intellectual tradition. He approached his craft with a refreshing degree of innovative thinking. He was not timid about asking questions that challenged accepted ways of thinking. Finally, he brought new methods to bear upon scholarly investigation, providing one of the earliest examples of scientific experimentation. Based upon these qualities, it is not surprising that many scholars suggest that al-Bīrūnī is the foremost scientist of the Islamic world.

Though he enjoyed official protection toward the close of the first millennium CE his intellectual inquiry commonly took place in challenging and stressful circumstances. He was trained in mathematics and the sciences in the court of a Sāmānid king, Mansur II ibn Nuh, in southwestern Asia near the Aral Sea. It was at this time that he produced his first major work, "Chronology of Ancient Nations." Herein he examined different chronological systems used among various cultures and presented a great deal of historical, astronomical, and linguistic information. Later he was "assigned" to study Indian philosophy and science, accompanying the Ghaznavid sultan, Mahmūd of Ghazna in his Islamic conquest of India.

Success in science can often be measured by one's willingness to step outside of accepted norms by taking calculated but very necessary risks. This involves breaking with tradition and establishing a new course in pursuit of a new solution to an old problem. Several examples may be found in history, such as with Galileo. Al-Bīrūnī stands out among the scientists of history as one who readily challenged, questioned, and spoke out against accepted norms, careless scholarship, and the tendency to yield to scientific principles based upon the reputation of the original scientist. Al-Bīrūnī took advantage of several opportunities to offer a critical review of Greek and Indian science as he studied Aristotelian and Hindu philosophy. Approximately 500 years prior to Copernicus' published work on a heliocentric solar system, al-Bīrūnī sought the endorsement of this model. Yet, he could not convince his contemporaries who adhered to the Aristotelian school of geocentrism. Finally, he abandoned his efforts. He criticized Indian scientists such as Balabhadra, who he said preferred tradition to his own observations. In general, he believed that Indian learning was based on superstition among the masses and that there were few individuals who thought to check and verify knowledge.

Modern science, rich in experimental methodology, is rooted in ancient philosophy which knew nothing of experimentation. Logic, observation, and reasoning were the tools used then to open the intellectual doorway to knowledge and understanding. As noted, al-Bīrūnī's approach to "pursuing truth" was unusual because of his unwillingness to accept traditional views and his insistence on verification through experiments, ushering in the new paradigm of modern science. Many examples of his experimental methodology could be cited. One of the more interesting examples, however, involved emeralds and adders. The former were reputed to cause blindness in the latter. He tested this hypothesis, repeated his experiment, and found the notion to be absolutely false.

The intellectual stature and productivity of this Islamic scientist and historian alone distinguish him as one of the outstanding thinkers recorded on the pages of history. Yet, the cultural position occupied by this man, his critical eye, and his tendency toward experimental verification of scientific theories set him apart as a true genius.

WILLIAM T. JOHNSON

See also Science

Biography

Born probably in Khwārazm (now Kloving, Iran), 973, of Persian parents. In his youth studied history, chronology, mathematics, astronomy, philosophy, and medicine. Because of political unrest, traveled to India, where he taught Greek philosophy; then settled in Ghazna, Afghanistan, 1017. Died c.1050.

Principal Writings

Al-Athār al-baqiya; in English as *The Chronology of Ancient Nations*, 1879

Tafhim li-awa'il sin'at al-tanjim; in English as *The Book of Instruction in the Elements of the Art of Astrology*, 1934

Kitab tahqīq mā lil-Hind, c.1030; in English as *Alberuni's India: An Account of the Religions, Philosophy, Literature, Geography, Chronology, Astronomy, Customs, Laws, and Astrology of India*, 1910

Kitāb tahdid nihayat al-amakin litashih masafat al-masakin; in English as *The Determination of the Coordinates of Positions for the Correction of Distances Between Cities*, 1967

Further Reading

Boilot, D.J., "L'Oeuvre d'al Beruni: essai bibliographique" (The Works of al-Biruni: A Bibliographical Essay), *Mélanges de l'Institut dominicain d'études orientales* 2 (1955), 161–225; and "Corrigenda d'addenda," 3 (1956), 391–96

Nasr, Seyyed Hossein, *Al-Bīrūnī: An Annotated Bibliography*, Tehran: High Council of Culture and Art, 1973

Said, Hakim Mohammed, *Al-Bīrūnī: His Times, Life and Works*, Karachi: Hamdard, 1981

Blainey, Geoffrey 1930–
Australian historian

Geoffrey Blainey's influence on the writing of Australian history has been fourfold. He first came to prominence in the 1950s as a pioneer in the neglected field of Australian business history. Using the skills developed in those studies, he produced during the 1960s and 1970s a number of surveys of Australian history in which explanation was organized around the exploration of the impact of a single factor (distance, mining, pre-settlement Aboriginal society). While continuing in these veins, Blainey next turned to the rhythms of global history in the industrial period. Because of his authority as a historian, he was increasingly in demand as a commentator on Australian public affairs, attracting criticism that at times threatened to obscure the merits of his contributions to the writing of Australian history. He remains nevertheless a productive and distinguished figure in Australian historiography, eluding easy categorization.

Blainey was trained in R.M. Crawford's school of Melbourne historians during the post-1945 years when its reputation was at its height and debate between Marxists, social democrats, and Catholics extremely vigorous. Unlike many of his contemporaries, Blainey eschewed overt ideology; unlike nearly all the academically gifted he did not attempt postgraduate study in Britain. Instead for nearly a decade he worked as a freelance historian, accepting commissions from mining companies, banks, his university, and a suburban municipality. In these works he developed skills in interpreting technological change in admirably lucid narratives that appealed both to specialist and non-specialist audiences. He also refined his characteristic technique of turning a received orthodoxy on its head and considering under-explored alternatives. The obvious, he found, was often overlooked. Blainey communicated this process of sifting with attractive gusto. His arguments were presented modestly and tentatively, although once having arrived at a conclusion he sometimes seemed reluctant to shift further.

Appointment to the staff of the University of Melbourne in 1962 afforded him opportunity for more ambitious works. *The Rush That Never Ended* (1963), still the standard history of mining in Australia, won immediate acclaim, its wide and diverse sweep integrated into a persuasive narrative. Implicit in its argument lay a repudiation of the theories of class conflict favored by many Australian academic historians. Blainey, who wrote with empathy about working miners, portrayed them as exemplars of "redshirt capitalism," with the potential to share in the wealth generated by managers and investors who ventured their capital. *The Tyranny of Distance* (1966) could be seen as a series of interlinked essays on the effect on Australian society of big distances, both within the continent and in relation to the parent societies of Britain and Europe. In the opening chapter Blainey challenged the traditional account of modern Australia's origins by arguing that Britain's occupation of New South Wales in 1788 was motivated more by its potential for producing flax and timber for naval purposes than by any need for a convict colony. Extensive debate followed. More than thirty years later most would accept that strategic and commercial motives buttressed the penal purposes of Australian colonization. Without convincing his peers of his entire hypothesis, Blainey could be credited with identifying an issue highly relevant to contemporary Australia's sense of national identity.

Of his more ambitious works, *The Causes of War* (1973) sought to locate the origins of international conflict in economic factors; its arguments owed little to Marxist critiques of capitalism, but suggested that fluctuations in commercial confidence influenced the readiness of nations to risk armed hostilities. This interest in collective morale also informed *The Great Seesaw* (1988), a survey of world history since 1750, which attempted to trace swings between optimism and pessimism in western civilization. Some critics found this book too determinist, others questioned Blainey's account of recent movements such as environmentalism; few engaged in detailed analysis of his arguments. By this time Blainey had become embroiled in public controversy; this was somewhat unexpected, since until the early 1980s his abilities had received bipartisan recognition. One of the earliest appointees to the Order of Australia, he was a deft and respected chairman of the Australia Council (1977–81) and chairman of the Australia-China Council (1979–84). In a speech in 1984 he questioned the Hawke Labour government's policies of multiculturalism and increased Asian immigration as proceeding too quickly to avoid racial disharmony. Accused of fomenting racism and rebutted by major authorities on immigration policy, Blainey

stood his ground, basing his views on his historian's perception of the reactions of "the average Australian." His apologia, *All for Australia* (1984), provoked a rejoinder from a group of historians, *Surrender Australia?* (1985), which attacked not only his stance on immigration but also his writing of history. This embittered controversy left Blainey something of an academic isolate, although well regarded in conservative circles. He resigned his university post in 1988 and resumed his freelance status. He remained a frequent commentator on public affairs, and in 1998 was nominated by the federal government as a delegate to the constitutional convention on a potential Australian republic (he was skeptical).

In 1994 Blainey published *A Shorter History of Australia*, a blueprint for a larger work of interpretation. Its main theme sketched the emergence of a sense of national identity as a people of largely European origins came to terms with the Australian environment. In this process the collective experience of the Australian people, the ingenious application of technological skills, and the energizing power of business could be seen as more significant than government policies seeking to force the pace of change. If this outlook struck some as conservative, it was undeniable that Blainey's ideas on the interplay of technological and social change in Australia had influenced many subsequent historians, among them Graeme Davison and K.T. Livingston. His experiences in the public arena suggest that, as with Manning Clark, Australians tend to place heavy responsibilities on the historian as social commentator.

GEOFFREY BOLTON

See also Australia; Maritime

Biography

Geoffrey Norman Blainey. Born Melbourne, 11 March 1930, son of a clergyman. Educated Ballarat High School; Wesley College, Melbourne; Queen's College, University of Melbourne. Freelance historian, 1952–61; taught (rising to professor) University of Melbourne, 1962–88. Order of Australia, 1975. Married Ann Warriner Heriot, historian, 1957 (1 daughter).

Principal Writings

The Peaks of Lyell, 1954

Gold and Paper: A History of the National Bank: A History of the National Bank of Australasia Ltd., 1958; revised edition, with Geoffrey Hutton, 1983

Mines in the Spinifex: The Story of Mount Isa Mines, 1960; revised 1970

The Rush That Never Ended: A History of Australian Mining, 1963; revised 1993

The Tyranny of Distance: How Distance Shaped Australia's History, 1966; revised 1982

The Causes of War, 1973; 3rd edition 1988

Triumph of the Nomads: A History of Ancient Australia, 1975; revised 1982

A Land Half Won, 1980

The Blainey View, 1982

All for Australia, 1984

With R.M. Crawford and Manning Clark, *Making History*, 1985

The Great Seesaw: A New View of the Western World, 1750–2000, 1988

A Game of Our Own: The Origins of Australian Football, 1990

Blainey, Eye on Australia: Speeches and Essays of Geoffrey Blainey, 1991

A Shorter History of Australia, 1994

Further Reading

Laster, Kathy, "The Historian as Prophet: Geoffrey Blainey and the Asianization of Australia," *Meanjin* (June 1984), 305–11

Markus, Andrew, and Merle Calvin Ricklefs, eds., *Surrender Australia? Essays in the Study and Uses of History: Geoffrey Blainey and Asian Immigration*, Sydney and Boston: Allen and Unwin, 1985

Pascoe, Rob, *The Manufacture of Australian History*, Melbourne, Oxford, and New York: Oxford University Press, 1979

Bloch, Marc 1886–1944

French social and economic historian

One of the most innovative French historians in the first half of the 20th century, Bloch stands as a prominent representative of the generation that rejected positivist orientations, and laid the foundation for an entire renewal of the historical discipline. Together with Lucien Febvre, Bloch is the father of the Annales school, thus named after the journal that the two founded in 1929 – the *Annales d'histoire économique et sociale* – which, under a similar title, is still issued. Bloch acknowledged his debt to Henri Pirenne, and was a lifetime friend and collaborator of Febvre. At the University of Strasbourg, in particular, Bloch benefited from disciplinary exchanges with his colleagues, historians and social scientists such as Maurice Halbwachs, Gabriel Le Bras, Charles Blondel, André Piganiol, Charles-Edmond Perrin, and Georges Lefebvre. Bloch's research focused on medieval France and Europe, his interests ranging from social and economic to political and cultural history, with special regard to rural societies.

Rather indifferent to philosophical matters, Bloch did not outline a coherent methodological theory; still, each of his studies broke new ground, and set the agenda for further developments. Meditations on the nature of his profession, and on explanation and causation in history can be found in the notes that he drafted while in the army, during both world wars, and then in the Resistance. In *Apologie pour l'histoire* (1949; *The Historian's Craft*, 1953), Bloch formulated his "regressive method," as he labeled the need to understand the past through the present no less than the present through the past.

Bloch's first major book, and possibly the most influential in the long run, ploughed the fertile field of what has come to be known as *mentalités*. In 1983, a new edition of *Les Rois thaumaturges* (1924; *The Royal Touch*, 1973) appeared with a preface by Jacques Le Goff, who cited Bloch as a pioneer in the history of collective representations and anthropological political history. In this book, Bloch highlighted the rituals performed by French and English kings (from about the 11th century, until respectively 1825 and 1714) in order to heal those who suffered from scrofula. Having evaluated a considerable amount of evidence according to criteria inspired by the "psychology of the testimony," Bloch concluded that the kings' miracles were nothing but "gigantic false news," in analogy with the contemporary war phenomena he had described in his 1921 article "Réflexions d'un historien sur les fausses nouvelles de la guerre" (A Historian's Observations on the False News of War). As he argued, from studying the dispersion of irrational popular beliefs in the Middle Ages – ever after

the favorite domain of the history of *mentalités* – historians could gain insight into deeper mental structures.

The Royal Touch comprised many significant elements of Bloch's historical investigation: the comparative perspective; the interdisciplinary approach; the preference for anonymous masses and social groups rather than for individuals. In this book, Bloch was also a forerunner in the use of iconographic sources, and in the social history of medicine and the body. Moreover, he inaugurated the combination of Marxist structural analysis with the Durkheimian concept of "collective consciousness," thereafter a distinctive trait of French historiography.

Later in his career, Bloch devoted his attention to French rural history, of which his second book is a major synthesis. *Les Caractères originaux de l'histoire rurale française* (1931; *French Rural History*, 1966) was primarily a work in historical geography. Bloch relied on the teaching of Vidal de La Blache, on his personal observation of the French countryside, and on cartography – especially on those land-registry maps that illustrated what he called the "anatomy of the soil." By establishing interrelations between field patterns, agricultural techniques, and customary practices of community life, Bloch divided France into three different regions. He was particularly concerned with the process of enclosures, with the emergence of the much debated agrarian individualism. *French Rural History* also introduced topics which he discussed fully in *La Société feodale* (1939–40; *Feudal Society*, 1961). Now a classic in medieval history, it analyzed interdependence ties within the frame of medieval social structure, pointing at both legal status and an economic definition of class, with an emphasis on the antithesis between freedom and serfdom. *Feudal Society* eventually attempted to capture similarities and differences between European and Japanese feudal institutions and class relations. Bloch thus pushed forward what he had labelled as the "historical comparison," as opposed to the "universal comparison" advocated by linguists, and wider in scope. In his 1928 essay "Pour une histoire comparée des sociétés européennes" ("A Contribution Toward a Comparative History of European Societies"), Bloch had maintained that, by comparison, historians should expect to test their explanations and hypotheses rather than search for universals. This pragmatic disposition was later favored by William Sewell and Sylvia Thrupp, while challenged by Alette and Boyd Hill for its lack of rigor.

Bloch's individual contribution cannot be judged separately from the evolution of the French "new history," which reached its height in the 1960s and 1970s. The interdisciplinary approach, the notion of *mentalités*, and even Braudel's "long duration" and "total history" owe a lot to Bloch's pioneering explorations in the new terrain of historical analysis. Meanwhile, his posthumous works presented Bloch to a larger public, both as a scholar and as a man personally involved in the tragic events of his time. Besides the very popular *Historian's Craft*, his other memoirs were also published – *L'Etrange Défaite* (1946; *Strange Defeat*, 1949) and *Souvenirs de guerre, 1914–1915* (1969; *Memoirs of War*, 1980). A collection of his articles and essays, *Mélanges historiques* (1963), also became available in accessible English translations (*Land and Work in Medieval Europe*, 1967, and *Slavery and Serfdom in the Middle Ages*, 1975).

FRANCESCA TRIVELLATO

See also Agrarian; Anderson, P.; Annales School; Anthropology; Barkan; Boorstin; Braudel; Burke; Chevalier; Duby; Environmental; Europe: Modern; Febvre; Feudalism; France: 1000–1450; Fustel; Ganshof; Haller; Hilton; Labrousse; Lefebvre; Literature; Lopez; Mabillon; McNeill; Mentalities; Pirenne; Postan; Power; Rashid; Reformation; Renouvin; Rörig; Seignobos; Simiand; Social; Spain: Modern; Vovelle; Weber, E.; White, L.

Biography

Marc Léopold Benjamin Bloch. Born Lyon, 6 July 1886, son of Gustave Bloch, Roman historian. Trained at Ecole Nationale Supérieure, Paris; University of Leipzig; and University of Berlin. Served in French army during World War I. Lecturer, later professor of medieval history, University of Strasbourg, 1919–36; professor of economic history, the Sorbonne, 1936–40. Founded (with Lucien Febvre), *Annales d'histoire économique et sociale*, 1929. Married Simone Vidal in 1919 (6 children). Army volunteer, 1939–40; leader, Franc-Tireur group, French resistance, Lyon, 1942–44. Captured, tortured, and executed by Gestapo near Lyon, 16 June 1944.

Principal Writings

L'Ile de France: les pays autour de Paris, 1913; in English as *The Ile-de-France: The Country around Paris*, 1971

"Réflexions d'un historien sur les fausses nouvelles de la guerre" (A Historian's Observations on the False News of War), *Revue de Synthèse Historique* (1921)

Les Rois thaumaturges: étude sur le caractère surnaturel attribué à la puissance royale, particulièrement en France et en Angleterre, 1924; in English as *The Royal Touch: Sacred Monarchy and Scrofula in England and France*, 1973

"Pour une histoire comparée des sociétés européennes," *Revue de Synthèse Historique* (1928); in English as "A Contribution Toward a Comparative History of European Societies," in his *Land and Work in Medieval Europe*, 1967

Les Caractères originaux de l'histoire rurale française, 1931; in English as *French Rural History: An Essay on Its Basic Characteristics*, 1966

La Société féodale, 2 vols., 1939–40; in English as *Feudal Society*, 2 vols., 1961

L'Etrange Défaite: témoignage écrit en 1940, 1946; in English as *Strange Defeat: A Statement of Evidence Written in 1940*, 1949

Apologie pour l'histoire, ou, métier d'historien, 1949; in English as *The Historian's Craft*, 1953

Mélanges historiques, 2 vols., 1963; selections in English as *Land and Work in Medieval Europe: Selected Papers*, 1967, and as *Slavery and Serfdom in the Middle Ages: Selected Papers*, 1975

Souvenirs de guerre, 1914–1915, 1969; in English as *Memoirs of War, 1914–15*, 1980

Marc Bloch, Lucien Febvre et les Annales d'Histoire Economique et Sociale: Correspondance (Marc Bloch, Lucien Febvre and the *Annales*: Correspondence), edited by Bertrand Müller, 1994

Further Reading

Atsma, Hartmut, and André Burguière, eds., *Marc Bloch aujourd'hui: histoire comparée et sciences sociales* (Marc Bloch Today: Comparative History and the Social Sciences), Paris: Editions de l'Ecole des Hautes Études en Sciences Sociales, 1990

Bedarida, François, and Denis Peschanski, eds., *Marc Bloch à Etienne Bloch: lettres de la "drole de guerre"* (Marc Bloch to Etienne Bloch: Letters on the Phony War), Paris: Institut d'Histoire du Temps Présent, 1991

Boutruche, Robert, "Marc Bloch vu par ses élèves" (Marc Bloch Through the Eyes of His Students), in University of Strasbourg Faculty of Letters, *Mémorial des années 1939–1945*, Paris: Belles Lettres, 1947

Burguière, André, "La Notion de 'mentalités' chez Marc Bloch et Lucien Febvre: Deux conceptions, deux filiations" (The Idea of "Mentalities" in Marc Bloch and Lucien Febvre: Two Concepts, Two Legacies), *Revue de Synthèse* 104 (1983), 333–48

Dollinger, Philippe, "Notre maître Marc Bloch: l'historien et sa méthode" (Our Master Marc Bloch: The Historian and His Method), *Revue d'histoire économique et sociale* 27 (1948–49), 109–26

Fink, Carole, *Marc Bloch: A Life in History*, Cambridge and New York: Cambridge University Press, 1989

Hill, Alette Olin, Boyd H. Hill, Jr., *et al.*, "American Historical Review Forum: Marc Bloch and Comparative History," *American Historical Review* 85 (1980), 828–57

Lenkova, Grozdanka, "La conception historique de Marc Bloch" (The Historical Conception of Marc Bloch), *Bulgarian Historical Review* 18 (1990), 74–78

Lyon, Bryce, and Mary Lyon, eds., *The Birth of Annales History: The Letters of Lucien Febvre and Marc Bloch to Henri Pirenne, 1921–1935*, Brussels: Académie Royale de Belgique, 1991

Mastrogregori, Massimo, *Il genio dello storico: le consideragioni sulla storia di Marc Bloch e Lucien Febvre e la tradizione metodologica francese* (The Genius of the Historian: Considerations on the History of Marc Bloch and Lucien Febvre and the French Methodological Tradition), Naples: Edizione Scientifichi Italiane, 1987

Pluet-Despatin, Jacqueline, ed., *Ecrire la société: lettres à Henri Berr, 1924–1943* (Writing Society: Letters to Henri Berr), Paris: IMEC, 1992

Revel, Jacques, and Lynn Hunt, eds., *Histories: French Constructions of the Past*, New York: New Press, 1995

Rhodes, Robert Colbert, "Emile Durkheim and the Historical Thought of Marc Bloch," *Theory and Society* 5 (1978), 45–73

Sewell, William H., Jr., "Marc Bloch and the Logic of Comparative History," *History and Theory* 6 (1967), 208–18

Walker, Lawrence, "A Note on Historical Linguistics and Marc Bloch's Comparative Method," *History and Theory* 19 (1980), 154–64

Blum, Jerome 1913–1993
US historian of modern Europe

Jerome Blum was one of America's leading historians of rural Europe. In a career that spanned fifty years, he produced a series of major studies of the relationship between lords and peasants: first in Austria, then in Russia, and finally, in Europe at large.

Blum wrote his dissertation at Johns Hopkins University under the direction of Frederic Lane, an outstanding economic historian whose studies of Venetian shipbuilding and commerce were admired by no less a figure than Fernand Braudel. Blum derived from his mentor a conviction of the primacy of economic and material factors in history. If Lane began with ships, Blum began with trains: his first major article was a study of the impact of the advent of the railways (and improved roads) in Austria. His dissertation showed how improvements in communications generated larger markets, and convinced a significant number of landowners to opt for profit-oriented agricultural production. Here was the solution to a paradox: why the Austrian nobility, ostensibly the beneficiaries of the hereditary subjection of the peasantry, provided the impetus for peasant emancipation during the 1840s. Paid labor, they discovered, was more efficient and profitable than the servile variety (the *robot*).

Accepting a position at Princeton University, where he would spend his entire career, Blum began to expand the chronological and geographical range of his work. An important article of 1957 examined the rise of serfdom in Eastern Europe from the 15th century onward. And in 1961 Blum published his magisterial *Lord and Peasant in Russia*, a book that encompassed a thousand years of Russian history, with particular emphasis on the Russian variant of serfdom. Why was the subjection of the Russian peasants so radical and so prolonged? Blum traced the roots of Russia's peculiar institution to the mutually advantageous bargain the tsars made with their nobles at the expense of the peasants in the formative period of absolutism. But just as the autocracy, by withdrawing from the lord-peasant relationship, collaborated in the rise of serfdom, so in the 19th century the tsars played a crucial role in its abolition. In the last portion of this impressive book Blum examined the movements and pressures that led to the emancipation decree of 1861, and suggested why the outcome of emancipation was ultimately so unsatisfactory for Russia's peasants.

In his next major work, *The End of the Old Order in Rural Europe* (1978), Blum continued and extended his analysis of the demise of servile obligations. Here the chronological range is restricted to a single century (roughly, from 1770 to 1870), but the geographical range is vastly expanded to include more than a dozen European lands. The author handled the enormous diversity of his materials with exemplary clarity, so that the emancipation of peasantries in both the western and eastern zones of the continent appeared as a unified, pan-European process. He began with an exquisitely detailed description of rural society on the eve of emancipation, then moved to the factors and pressures that gradually eroded the old order, and finally analyzed the precipitants and consequences of the reforms that eliminated the hereditary subjection of Europe's peasants in the interests of liberty, equality, and efficiency. The result is an extraordinarily comprehensive and erudite analysis of the transition from the society of orders, based on privilege and inequality, to the society of classes, in which legal (though not economic) equality is the general rule.

All of Blum's books were studies in the vicissitudes of human freedom and the prerequisites of modernity. In his last book, *In the Beginning* (1994), he returned to his starting point: the 1840s as the seedbed of the modern era. Again the perspective was panoramic and comparative, with case studies ranging from Britain to Russia. The first and most important chapter analyzed "the revolution in communications," from the huge corporations spawned by the railroads to the extraordinary impact of the humble postage stamp. Without underestimating the extent of human misery and political folly in that crucial decade, the book nevertheless contrived to place the accent on enhanced prospects for freedom and prosperity. This great historian of Europe's nobles and peasants ended his distinguished career with a celebration of the advent of bourgeois society.

BRUCE THOMPSON

See also Agrarian; Austro-Hungarian; Russia: Early Modern

Biography

Born Baltimore, 27 April 1913. Educated at Johns Hopkins University, BA 1933, PhD 1947. Served in US Army Field Artillery as captain, 1942–46. Taught (rising to professor) at Princeton University, 1947–81 (emeritus). Died 7 May 1993.

Principal Writings

"Transportation and Industry in Austria, 1815–1848," *Journal of Modern History* 15 (1943), 24–38

Noble Landowners and Agriculture in Austria, 1815–1848: A Study of the Origins of the Peasant Emancipation of 1848, 1948

"The Rise of Serfdom in Eastern Europe," *American Historical Review* 62 (1957), 807–36

The European Peasantry from the Fifteenth to the Nineteenth Century, 1960

Lord and Peasant in Russia from the Ninth to the Nineteenth Century, 1961

The European World since 1815: Triumph and Transition, 1966

"The European Village as Community: Origins and Functions," *Agricultural History* 45 (1971), 157–78

"The Internal Structure and Polity of the European Village Community from the Fifteenth to the Nineteenth Century," *Journal of Modern History* 43 (1971), 541–76

The End of the Old Order in Rural Europe, 1978

"Agricultural History and Nineteenth-Century European Ideologies," *Agricultural History* 56 (1982), 621–31

Editor, *Our Forgotten Past: Seven Centuries of Life on the Land,* 1982

In the Beginning: The Advent of the Modern Age, 1994

Further Reading

Behrens, C.B.A., "The End of Servility," *New York Review of Books* (14 June 1979), 35–38

Gerschenkron, Alexander, "Lord and Peasant in Russia," in his *Continuity in History and Other Essays,* Cambridge, MA: Harvard University Press, 1969

Gillispie, Charles, "Jerome Blum," *Proceedings of the American Philosophical Society,* 138 (1994), 407–12

Boahen, A. Adu 1932–

Ghanaian historian

One of West Africa's pre-eminent historians, A. Adu Boahen forced a change in the way Africa's recent history has been written since the 1960s. Following several influential articles and his address to the watershed International Congress of African Historians, held in Dar es Salaam in 1965, Boahen has virtually overseen a shift in Africanist historiography. Whereas the literature had previously been written from a Eurocentric perspective that emphasized the positive aspects of colonial contact in African history – or at least was invariably preoccupied with, in Boahen's words, "the origins, structure, operation and impact of colonialism" – the "Dar es Salaam school," as those influenced by Boahen came to call themselves, began to place colonialism within the larger context of a broader African history and started to examine the colonial experience from an African point of view.

To this end, Boahen's most important contributions to date have stemmed from his work on volume 7 of the UNESCO General History of Africa: *Africa under Colonial Domination, 1880–1935,* which he edited and which was originally published in 1985. The work intended to present the state of the art of African history at its publication; under Boahen's watchful eye it did so somewhat radically, synthesizing available knowledge and broad trends in research while covering the breadth of the continent and examining relationships among its regions. Most importantly, 21 of the work's 35 contributing authors were Africans, reflecting Boahen's belief that for the historical knowledge of Africa to reach its fullest potential, African history would have to be written in large part by Africans.

Boahen published *African Perspectives on Colonialism* in 1987, a version of his well-received James S. Schouler lectures delivered at Johns Hopkins University in 1985, which drew heavily on the materials he had edited in the UNESCO General History and which made them even more accessible for undergraduate and lay audiences. By this date the premise that Africanist literature relied too heavily on a Eurocentric perspective when assessing colonialism was hardly fresh (Boahen himself had published an article arguing against Eurocentrism but at the same time favoring an even-handed assessment of colonialism and its aftermath almost twenty years earlier), but it was one that bore repeating, especially in 1985, the 25th anniversary of the overthrow of colonialism in much of Africa. Arguing that precolonial Africa "was certainly not in a Hobbesian state of nature" but rather stood on the cusp of an African Renaissance on the eve of its most sudden and rapid takeover, Boahen nevertheless tallied the "positive" social and economic changes that came alongside the violence, randomness, and wanton destruction that characterized Africa's colonization.

Unlike some historians who claimed to be neutral or apolitical, Boahen explicitly addressed his historical interpretations to Africa's policymakers. Boahen clearly hoped that an honest appraisal of Africa's past experiences, be they proud or pathetic, could improve those policymakers' chances of making well-informed and beneficial decisions for Africa's independent nations. His conclusions to the two works cited above contained "ledgers" that weighed the good that came of Africa's colonial experience against the bad. As a few critics have noted, this exercise by itself may spark a few debates but could ultimately be pointless. Boahen, however, intended for this exercise, as he may have intended for the bulk of his work, to establish a firm foundation upon which present and future decisions could be made for the people of Africa, not to stamp the imprimatur of "good" or "bad" on a period of history and a historical relationship.

Boahen practiced what he preached in 1992, when he ran for Ghana's presidency as the representative of the New Patriotic party. Although he was defeated in what his and other opposition parties maintained was a rigged election, Boahen has continued to press for democratization in Ghana and throughout West Africa. Adu Boahen effectively welded his academic concerns to political ones, but his lasting contribution to African historiography is likely to be his insistence on the addition of an African perspective to African history.

J. TODD MOYE

See also Oliver

Biography

Albert Adu Boahen. Born Osien, Ghana (formerly Gold Coast), 24 May 1932. Received BA, University of Ghana, 1956; PhD, University of London, 1959. Teaches at the University of Ghana.

Principal Writings

Britain, the Sahara, and the Western Sudan, 1788–1861, 1961
Topics in West African History, 1966
Ghana: Evolution and Change in the Nineteenth and Twentieth Centuries, 1975
Editor, *Africa under Colonial Domination, 1880–1935*, 1985 [UNESCO General History of Africa, vol. 7]
African Perspectives on Colonialism, 1987

Further Reading

Copans, Jean, *La Longue Marche de la modernité africaine: savoirs, intellectuels, démocratie* (The Long March of African Modernity: Knowledge, Intellectuals, Democracy), Paris: Karthala, 1990
International Congress of African Historians, *Perspectives nouvelles sur l'histoire africaine* (Historical Perspectives on the History of Africa), Paris: Présence Africaine, 1971
Jewsiewicki, Bogumil, and David Newbury, eds., *African Historiographies: What History for Which Africa?* Beverly Hills, CA: Sage, 1986
Neale, Caroline, *Writing "Independent" History: African Historiography, 1960–1980*, Westport, CT: Greenwood Press, 1985

Bock, Gisela 1942–
German social and feminist historian

Gisela Bock is one of the few internationally well known German women historians. Her reputation is founded on her original and incisive contributions to feminist theory but also on her impressively broad empirical research ranging from women industrial workers in the USA, the role of political thinkers of Renaissance Italy, and Nazi eugenic policies, to social welfare in early modern and modern Europe. Her influence was no doubt helped by her command of numerous foreign languages, and by her personal and professional contacts in the USA, Italy, France, and Britain helped by lengthy research and teaching affiliations abroad.

Bock's article "Women's History and Gender History" (1989), inaugurating the journal *Gender and History*, was as much an exposition of the "state of the art" as a clarion call for future research. It stressed the significance of women's history yet urged more gender history. She argued that women's history was more than "restoring women to history" and demonstrating that their experiences of the past, even of time itself, could be vastly different from men's. Further, Bock noted that the course of women's history is no less complex than that of men's, and that this necessarily affected all history, entailing, for example, the overturn of "hierarchies between the historically important and unimportant." Moreover, Bock was concerned to link women's history to history in general by conceptualizing women "as a sociocultural group, i.e. as a sex." This use of gender as a historical category would, she argued, affect our view of men, too, as they become visible as sexual beings. For her, the importance of gender history was that it challenged the "sex blindness" of traditional historiography and other preconceived ideas, such as that gender differences are static and universal because derived from "biological" differences between men and women, when in fact they are historically specific and dependent on social, political, and cultural factors. In fact, Bock went as far as urging historians to do away with the word "biology" altogether because it has distorted an understanding of the gendered past. Furthermore, gender history also entailed "thinking in relations," not only those between the sexes but within the sexes, that is, between men and women but also among women and among men so that we are aware of cooperation but also of conflict. This does not mean that gender relations should be studied to the exclusion of all other sociocultural relations, such as class, race, age, sexuality, but that gender relations affect all other social relations.

In *Beyond Equality and Difference* (1992) which she co-edited with the Cambridge philosopher Susan James, Bock reconsidered the significance of the dichotomous concepts of gender "equality" and "difference" which have long been central in feminist history. By careful contextualization, these terms were revealed not as timeless but dependent on specific social situations, specific personalities at specific times. But historical interpretations also depend on different national and academic perspectives. Debates among women's historians point to interesting "national types" of feminism, for example, the Anglo-Saxon tendency to concentrate almost exclusively on equality, while French and Italian feminists have tended to celebrate female difference. The volume offered reasons for such diversity but at the same time dispelled crude beliefs in national stereotypes.

The duality of the two concepts were rooted in the divergent aims of the women's liberation movements, in history as well as at the present: the right to be equal or to be different. Bock and James argued that both objectives were inherently problematic, the first because of its tendency to seek an assimilation by women to men without first changing the flawed male-defined culture, the second as it could easily become misogynist in that references to women's differences are often invoked to justify sexual inequality. In fact, as the editors argued, the two concepts need not be mutually exclusive; for example, some feminists regard gender difference as a starting point and equality as a goal while others strive for equality as a way of guaranteeing the right to female difference.

As one of the pioneers of women's history Bock helped to integrate the subject of female labor into research on family structure and the economy. In 1976, as an academic assistant at the Free University of Berlin, she was one of the leading founder members of the "Berlin summer university" hoping to stimulate feminist research among women inside and outside academia, and more generally, to empower all women in society. True to its motto, "the personal is also political and academically significant" the meeting gave center stage to topics affecting all women's lives and yet previously ignored by academics. Bock and Barbara Duden spoke on the historical development of housework, subsequently published in the conference volume as "Arbeit aus Liebe/Liebe als Arbeit" (Labor of Love/Love as Labor). Housework, they argued, has remained invisible in western society because women themselves belittle their own domestic skill and activity; because as a "labor of love" housework is unpaid, taken for granted, and therefore never accounted for in either family or national economy; thus historians had always ignored it, thinking of it as an essential and therefore unchanging and ahistorical part of female nature. Bock and Duden were among the first to reject this notion, calling housework instead a social construct.

They pointed out that housework as we know it today and as the target of the post-1945 women's movement, had evolved only in the 19th century when the bourgeois model of the family had been imposed on the working classes. The authors also established the crucial link between women's unwaged and waged work and their low pay and inferior status in society. Their call for wages for housework to end women's subjugation and the undervalued and invisible domestic labor boosted the campaigns by the West German women's movement of the 1970s and 1980s. Among social and feminist historians the article remains seminal.

But it was Bock's path-breaking *Zwangssterilisation im Nationalsozialismus* (Compulsory Sterilization in National Socialism, 1986) which secured her position as one of the most prominent women's historians in Germany and as the expert on Nazi population policy. Her meticulous research in official papers and contemporary publications revealed the view from above, but the careful sifting of nearly a thousand criminal cases of various sterilization courts made visible for the first time the experience of women victims. Bock argued compellingly that in the Third Reich sexism and racism were inseparable: Nazi women's policy was not only misogynist but also deeply racist, and Nazi racism was also profoundly sexist. Thus the study not only shed new light on Nazi population policy but radically revised previous views of women's policy and racial hygiene under Hitler. Bock undermined the hitherto dominant view that the program of sterilizations was merely a precursor of the extermination policy of 1939. Instead she presented sterilization as an essential part of the Nazi population policy. This led her also to reject the belief that a "cult of motherhood" was the most distinctive feature of Nazi women's policy. While previously Nazi pronatalism was either portrayed in positive terms (for making motherhood respectable again after Weimar Germany's libertarianism) or as profoundly antifeminist (because it reduced women to breeders), Bock contested both views. She argued that it was not so much pronatalism but a profound and repressive antinatalism – an attempt to prevent the birth of racially "inferior" children – that was at the heart of Nazi population policy. Far from targeting only certain "dysgenic" women, Bock claimed Nazi antinatalism potentially victimized all women by threatening them with compulsory abortion or sterilization when they did not conform to eugenic standards of fitness. This was most forcefully realized by the roughly 400,000 compulsory sterilizations on eugenic grounds carried out between 1934 and 1945. Although men and women were affected in equal numbers, Bock insisted that the effects of sterilization were more serious for women than men: childlessness has different meanings for the two sexes and sterilized women often became victims of sexual abuse; many more female than male sterilization candidates attempted and committed suicides; many more women than men died as a result of the operation. Bock called these deaths "not an unfortunate 'side effect' of reproductive policies . . . rather they were planned and deliberate mass murder."

In later publications she further refined the gendered nature of Nazi racism/population policy. Bock argued, for example, that the Nazi state privileged fathers over mothers and celebrated fatherhood rather than motherhood. Bock also insisted that genocide was gendered because after 1939 state antinatalism was aimed almost exclusively at women through compulsory abortions and sterilization of Polish and Russian women in forced labor and concentration camps. Women were also the majority of those killed in the gas chambers of the death camps while men entered forced labor. In fact, Himmler justified this need to kill women in order to stop children growing up as avengers.

Bock's verdict that "National Socialist racism was no more gender neutral than National Socialist sexism was race neutral" influenced subsequent research about the Third Reich and the Weimar republic. But her assertion that the experience of the minority of compulsorily sterilized women could and should be projected onto the general situation of all women in Nazi Germany proved controversial. Bock was also criticized for what many considered to be her overemphasis of antinatalism at the expense of pronatalism. New research has proven conclusively that far from being mere propaganda, pronatalism had often taken on a tangible reality: for example, positively when mothers and their children received financial benefits and negatively when access to abortion was significantly reduced for Aryan and eugenically "fit" women and when in 1943 the death penalty was introduced for certain categories of abortions.

Bock's critical exchange with the American historian Claudia Koonz sparked off a passionate debate within the present German women's movement and feminist research on women's agency in the Third Reich. This has been dubbed a "Historikerinnenstreit," a women historians' dispute echoing the "Historikerstreit" in Germany and North America in the late 1980s, the historians' dispute over how the recent German past should be interpreted.

CORNELIE USBORNE

See also Hausen

Biography
Born Karlsruhe, Germany, 28 February 1942, daughter of a chemist. Taught at Free University of Berlin, 1971–83; European University Institute, Florence, 1985–89; and University of Bielefeld from 1989.

Principal Writings
Thomas Campanella: politisches Interesse und philosophische Spekulation (Thomas Campanella: Political Interest and Philosophical Speculation), 1974
Die andere Arbeiterbewegung in den USA von 1905–1922 (The Other Workers' Movement in the USA from 1905 to 1922), 1976
With Barbara Duden, "Arbeit aus Liebe/Liebe als Arbeit: zur Entstehung der Hausarbeit im Kapitalismus" (Labor of Love/Love as Labor: On the Origins of Housework under Capitalism), in Gruppe Berliner Dozentinnen, eds., *Frauen und Wissenschaft: Beiträge zur Berliner Sommeruniversität für Frauen, Juli 1976*, 1977
Zwangssterilisation im Nationalsozialismus: Studien zur Rassenpolitik und Frauenpolitik (Compulsory Sterilization in National Socialism: Studies in Racial and Women's Policy), 1986
"Women's History and Gender History: Aspects of an International Debate," *Gender and History* 1 (1989), 7–30
Editor with Pat Thane, *Maternity and Gender Policies: Women and the Rise of the European Welfare States, 1880s–1950s*, 1991
Editor, with Susan James, *Beyond Equality and Difference: Citizenship, Feminist Politics, and Female Subjectivity*, 1992

Bodin, Jean 1529/30–1596
French jurist and legal historian

Born in Angers of a middle-class family, Bodin entered the Carmelite order in 1545, destined for a career in the church. He moved to the Carmelite house in Paris in 1547, where he obtained a thorough humanistic education. His search for religious truth led to a heresy charge in 1547, when he recanted. Leaving the Carmelites, he became a student of law, and in the 1550s a teaching assistant at the University of Toulouse, where he was attracted to academic jurisprudence. Unable to gain a professorship, he tried to promote a new humanist college for the city's youth, which also failed. In his speech to the Senate (*Oratio*, 1559), he drew the foundations for a liberal arts college that would rival the Collège de France in Paris.

Bodin returned to Paris in 1561 as a barrister to the Parlement, but spent most of his time working on an encyclopedic program of research and writing in historical jurisprudence. His first work, the *Methodus* (1566), broke new ground as the first guide to the study of universal history. This was followed by his response to Malestroit (1568), in which he attributed the price revolution of the 16th century to the influx of bullion from the Americas, and presented the first quantitative theory of money in what would become the modern field of political economy. Virtually overnight he entered the service of Francis, Duke of Alençon, and became one of the major public figures of his era.

Charles IX appointed Bodin to several administrative and political missions in 1570, and he entered the court of the new king, Henry III, in 1574. His major political work, the *République* (1576), brought him instant acclaim as well as a lucrative marriage. In this systematic exposition of French and universal public law he developed an absolutist theory of royal sovereignty within a framework of traditional restraints on state government. He was chosen deputy for the Third Estate to the States General in the same year, which brought him brief notoriety. Henry III proposed new taxes for the enforcement of religious uniformity. Bodin, defending the over-taxed Estate and opposed to more civil war, became a leader of the opposition that defeated the tax. Losing royal favor, he left Paris for Laon, the seat of his wife's family. He became king's attorney there in 1587, a position which he held until his death in 1596.

The last years of Bodin's life were challenging ones that brought much despair. In the Civil War that followed the assassination of Henry III in 1589, Laon came under Catholic control. Bodin collaborated with the Catholic League in order to preserve his office and property, even though it despised his principles of non-resistance and toleration. He was often questioned for his religious views, and when he was captured by Catholic League rioters in 1590 his house was searched and library burned. Many of his hidden manuscript books, however, were unpublished at his death. These included five books on Roman public law which he ordered to be burned, and the *Colloquium heptaplomeres* (Colloquium of the Seven, 1584). The latter was so controversial that it was not published until 1857. It did, however, circulate freely in manuscript among intellectuals. The work consists of conversations on true religion between Catholics, Jews, Lutherans, Muslims,

Zwinglians, and philosophical skeptics. Bodin's position was that all historical religions were deviations from an original natural religion that could be known only through speculative reason. Bodin was accused of being a Jew, Catholic, Calvinist, and atheist, and there is little doubt why the work was not published.

His two most influential works were the *Methodus* and the *République*. The *Methodus* was the most philosophical book on history in the 16th century. Bodin defined history as public history – constitutions and states. He began with writing the history of communities and their laws from Moses to the Greeks, Romans, pagans, Apostles, Arabs, later Europeans, Turks, Africans, and the Indians of the Americas. In the *République*, he saw the state as a lawful government of many families who held in common a *puissant* (mighty) sovereignty. Its purpose was to cultivate man's welfare. An institution that was evolving by natural processes, it was subject to divine and natural law, but not human law. The latter belonged to the king, who possessed sovereignty that conferred his control of the law. Such sovereigns had to decide which old human laws should be kept, and what new ones should be enacted. Question the authority of kings, and states would disassemble, followed by peasant uprisings, banditry, and revolution.

Thoughts such as this brought Bodin to the position of a *politique* (one of the politicals). A proponent of religious peace, toleration, and a reformed moderate government, he became the theoretician of the *politiques*. But the death of his patron the Duke of Alençon in 1584, and his public criticisms of various governments for the price revolution, monopolies, and overspending they allowed (*Malestretti*, 1568), made him dispensable. He also became obsessed with witches, stating (from witches' testimony) that a witch-cult was emerging across Europe. Since this was caused by women's "bestial" sexuality, unless it was stamped out, male witches might use peasant discontent to lead revolts against the king (*Démonomanie*, 1580). Beliefs such as these tarnished his image as a *politique*, but not as a scholar.

Bodin saw himself as a jurist in the humanist tradition, striving to trace law to its origins. But the original Roman law, the thorny medieval law, and the medieval philosophy of grammarians ("jugglers of syllables") and philologists, had destroyed the vision of the past and negated the promise of the future. What was needed was a secular legal science based on a comparative synthesis of the total juridical experience of all advanced states. Using Ramist methodology, Bodin would find the best laws of all states, correlate them with their backgrounds and environments, and put together those that were relevant as universal public law. This synthetic approach inspired all his work on both law and history, and marked him as the founding author of the *jus gentium* – the fundamental law of people.

In the end, Bodin's political and legal ideas were keyed to his religious perceptions. He saw a future of progress, a constant expansion of peoples, economies, and states leading to a world commonwealth. In this future the security of the people must be the supreme law. Prudence and moral virtues must rule passions. But once there is a breakdown in government, when people do not accept law, lack fear of God, and accept evil and blasphemy, then God dispenses divine justice. The Civil Wars were God's scourge on the people, and the scourge would last until people's hearts changed to receive true universal religion and law, and the accompanying moral and civic virtues. Not until then could Bodin the historian, jurist, politician, and sage rest in peace.

LOUIS A. KNAFLA

See also France: to 1000; Historiology; Legal; State

Biography

Born Angers, 1529/30. Trained as a Carmelite novice in Angers, then Paris; may have taken orders, but certainly released from them by 1548. Studied law in Toulouse. Independent lecturer before settling in Paris where he practiced law at the Parlement from 1561; king's attorney (prosecutor), Laon, from 1587. Occasional emissary of Charles IX, served the Duke of Alençon, and was deputy at the States General of Blois, 1576. Married in Laon, 1584. Died Laon, June 1596.

Principal Writings

Oratio de instituenda in republica juventute ad senatum populumque tolosatem (Oration to the Senate and People of Toulouse on the Education of the Youth of the Commonwealth) 1559
Methodus ad facilem historiarum cognittonem, 1566; in English as *Method for the Easy Comprehension of History*, 1945
Responsio ad paradoxa Malestretti (Response to the Malestroit Paradox), 1568
Les Six Livres de la République, 1576; in English as *The Six Bookes of the Commonweale*, 1606, reprinted and annotated, 1962; *Six Books of the Commonwealth*, 1955; and as *On Sovereignty: Four Chapters from the Six Books of the Commonwealth*, 1992
Iuris universi distributio (The Classification of Universal Law), 1578; reprinted 1985
De la Démonomanie des sorciers, 1580; in English as *On the Demon-Mania of Witches*, 1995
Colloquium heptaplomeres (Colloquium of the Seven), written 1584; first published 1857
Selected Writings on Philosophy, Religion and Politics, edited by Paul Lawrence Rose, 1980

Further Reading

Denzer, Horst, ed., *Jean Bodin: Proceedings of the International Conference on Bodin in Munich*, Munich: Beck, 1973
Franklin, Julian H., *Jean Bodin and the Sixteenth-Century Revolution in the Methodology of Law and History*, New York: Columbia University Press, 1963
Gottschalk, Eduard Guhrauer, *Das Heptaplomeres des Jean Bodin: zur Geschichte der Kultur und Literatur im Jahrhundert der Reformation*, Berlin: Eichler, 1841; reprinted Geneva: Slatkine, 1971
Goyard-Fabre, Simone, *Jean Bodin et le droit de la République*, Paris: Presses Universitaires de France, 1989
Kelley, Donald R., *Foundations of Modern Historical Scholarship: Language, Law, and History in the French Renaissance*, New York: Columbia University Press, 1970
Moreau-Reibel, Jean, *Jean Bodin et le droit publique comparé dans ses rapports avec la philosophie de l'histoire*, Paris: Vrin, 1933
Rose, Paul Lawrence, *Bodin and the Great God of Nature: The Moral and Religious Universe of a Judaiser*, Geneva: Droz, 1980

The Body

Viewed as a stable, naturalistic object best studied by the sciences, the human body's role in history had been – prior to the late 1970s – restricted to that of a biological structure of history. The history of the body, except for periodic appearances in demographic or medical history, had remained as a result largely unwritten, taken for granted as an ahistorical organism which – as everyone was thought to understand through their own personal bodily experience – requires sustenance, reproduces, is disabled by disease, and dies.

One of the first important body histories was thus not a history of the body itself, but rather of its representations in metaphor and iconography. *The King's Two Bodies* by Ernst Kantorowicz (1957) used bodily metaphor to illuminate the political theology of European kingship in the Middle Ages, which represented the monarch as a politically hermaphroditic individual, possessing simultaneously the mortal body of the king and the immortal body of kingship, the individual body of the ruler, and the collective body politic of the ruled.

This theme of the body politic would be picked up again and elaborated in the late 1960s not by a historian but rather by the anthropologist Mary Douglas, in her highly influential work *Purity and Danger* (1966) and later in *Natural Symbols* (1970). According to Douglas, metaphors of a body politic exist because the human body is in fact the most readily available image of a social system. At the same time, the social body tends to constrain concepts of the human body as a result of the continual exchange of meanings between the two kinds of bodily experience: a demand for conformity in the social body, for example, may manifest a greater demand for self-control of the physical body (which is then itself placed firmly outside the increasingly important social discourse).

A similar thesis had been introduced back in 1939 by sociologist Norbert Elias in *The History of Manners*, as part of his influential 2-volume work *The Civilizing Process*. The proliferation of etiquette treatises in Europe beginning with the early modern period, he argued, had resulted from (and contributed to) the growing inhibition of bodily impulses and increasingly internalized embarrassment of them, which themselves coincided with changes in the structure of the upper and middle ranks of European society.

Thus the body which these ranks of society were rejecting in these social processes was essentially that of the lower classes. Describing this body in *Gargantua and Pantagruel*, literary critic Mikhail Bakhtin formulated in *Rabelais and His World* (1965, translated 1968) his important concept of the "popular" or "grotesque" body: a body which was not a closed, completed unit but rather constantly outgrowing itself and transgressing its own limits in the acts of eating, drinking, copulation, giving birth, and death, and which in the early modern period was rejected by the upper ranks of society in favor of a body fenced off from other bodies and whose orifices and protrusions were either controlled or eliminated.

The translation into English of Bakhtin and Elias in the late 1970s coincided closely with that of the works of Michel Foucault who, by suggesting that the human body is a social construct, moved body studies into the realm of historical investigation. Throughout *The Birth of the Clinic* (1963, translated 1973), *Discipline and Punish* (1975, translated 1977), and *The History of Sexuality* (1976–84), Foucault asserted that in the modern period power discourses did not merely lend meaning to the body but in fact constituted it entirely.

While problematic, starting in the early 1980s Foucault's writings inspired many historians of gender to re-examine cultural constructions of the "naturalistic" body upon which social inequalities and prejudices had been traditionally justified. In rapid succession Rudolph M. Bell (*Holy Anorexia*, 1985) and Caroline Walker Bynum (*Holy Feast and Holy Fast*, 1987) examined medieval women's renunciation of food and found therein not necessarily a rejection of female corporeality but rather a maximization of its potentialities and an expression of autonomy; and Peter Brown (*The Body and Society*, 1988) and Margaret R. Miles (*Carnal Knowing*, 1989) interpreted early Christian and medieval asceticism not as a mere dualistic rejection of the body or as ritualized misogyny but a means of the body's rehabilitation into a positive component of a Christian's self-identity.

Other historians investigated the historical construction of the female body by the dominant discourse in other contexts: Londa Schiebinger (*The Mind Has No Sex?*, 1989) and Thomas Laqueur (*Making Sex*, 1990) have outlined a shift in the sciences and philosophy during the late 18th and early 19th centuries from a biological model of the sexes as two versions of the same body to a model of essentially two different, incommensurable bodies, which was then used – particularly according to Schiebinger – to justify the lack of women's participation in society's public sphere on one hand, and – according to Dorinda Outram in *The Body and the French Revolution* (1989) – their political disenfranchisement on the other.

Historians of Judaism (such as Howard Eilberg-Schwartz, *People of the Body*, 1992, and Sander Gilman, *The Jew's Body*, 1991), homosexuality (Siobhan Somerville, "Scientific Racism and the Emergence of the Homosexual Body," 1994), and of African Americans (John Saillant, "The Black Body Erotic and the Republican Body Politic, 1790–1820," 1994–95) have used similar techniques to examine the cultural constructions of the body among members of those groups, and conversely by the dominant discourse which arose from and were then used to justify social inequality, including the conflicting ways in which the body was constructed and hence medicated, as by the English and Indians in the work of David Arnold (*Colonizing the Body*, 1993).

Social historians and historians of medicine have likewise begun, *vis-à-vis* the influences of Kantorowicz, Douglas, Elias, Bakhtin, and Foucault, to reconsider the historical role of the body's metaphors, representations, and constructions. Natalie Zemon Davis has, for example, examined conflicting social metaphors of the body between Catholics and Protestants in post-Reformation France ("The Sacred and the Body Social in Sixteenth-Century Lyon," 1980), while the experience of health and sickness *within* the body has been the subject of research by Barbara Duden (*The Woman Beneath the Skin*, 1987, translated 1991). Katherine Park on the other hand has investigated the cultural history of anatomy ("The Criminal and Saintly Body: Autopsy and Dissection in Renaissance Italy," 1994 and "The Life of the Corpse: Division and Dissection in Late Medieval Europe," 1993) and, as in the work of social historian Peter Linebaugh ("The Tyburn Riot Against the Surgeons," 1975), even the historical role of the dead body as a cultural object.

Despite the multicultural focus of collections like the forty historical, anthropological, philosophical, and photographic articles collected by Michel Feher in *Fragments for a History of the Human Body* (1989, note Barbara Duden's unparalleled bibliography of body studies, "A Repertory of Body History," in vol. 3), the major concentration of historical writing on the body has stayed in the field of European history where it first began, and awaits expansion to other historical specializations.

MICHELLE A. LAUGHRAN

See also Brown; Davis, N.; Foucault; Kantorowicz

Further Reading

Armstrong, David, *Political Anatomy of the Body: Medical Knowledge in Britain in the Twentieth Century*, Cambridge and New York: Cambridge University Press, 1983

Arnold, David, *Colonizing the Body: State Medicine and Epidemic Disease in Nineteenth-Century India*, Berkeley: University of California Press, 1993

Bakhtin, Mikhail, *Tovrchestvo Fransua Rable: narodnaia kul'tura srednevekov'ia i Renessansa*, written 1940, suppressed until 1965; in English as *Rabelais and His World*, Cambridge, MA: MIT Press, 1968

Bell, Rudolph M., *Holy Anorexia*, Chicago: University of Chicago Press, 1985

Bremmer, Jan, and Herman Roodenburg, eds., *A Cultural History of Gesture from Antiquity to the Present Day*. Cambridge: Polity Press, 1991; Ithaca, NY: Cornell University Press, 1992

Brown, Peter, *The Body and Society: Men, Women, and Sexual Renunciation in Early Christianity*, New York: Columbia University Press, and London: Faber, 1988

Bynum, Caroline Walker, *Holy Feast and Holy Fast: The Religious Significance of Food to Medieval Women*, Berkeley: University of California Press, 1987

Bynum, Caroline Walker, *The Resurrection of the Body in Western Christianity, 200–1336*, New York: Columbia University Press, 1995

Camporesi, Piero, *La carne impassible*, Milan: Seggiature, 1983; in English as *The Incorruptible Flesh: Bodily Mutation and Mortification in Religion and Folklore*, Cambridge: Cambridge University Press, 1988

Ceard, Jean, Marie Madeleine Fontaine, and Jean-Claude Margolin, eds., *Le Corps à la Renaissance* (The Renaissance Body), Paris: Aux Amateur de Livres, 1990

Culianu, Ioan P., "A Corpus for the Body," *Journal of Modern History* 63 (1991), 61–80

Davis, Natalie Zemon, "The Sacred and the Body Social in Sixteenth-Century Lyon," *Past and Present* 90 (1980), 40–70

Douglas, Mary, *Purity and Danger: An Analysis of Concepts of Pollution and Taboo*, New York: Praeger, and London: Routledge, 1966

Douglas, Mary, *Natural Symbols: Explanations in Cosmology*, London: Cresset Press, and New York: Pantheon, 1970

Duden, Barbara, *Geschichte unter der Haut: ein Eisenacher Arzt und seine Patientinnen um 1730*, Stuttgart: Klett Cotta, 1987; in English as *The Woman Beneath the Skin: A Doctor's Patients in Eighteenth-Century Germany*, Cambridge, MA: Harvard University Press, 1991

Eilberg-Schwartz, Howard, *People of the Body: Jews and Judaism from an Embodied Perspective*, Albany: State University of New York Press, 1992

Elias, Norbert, *Über den Prozess der Zivilisation: Soziogenetische und Psychogenetische Untersuchungen*, 2 vols., Basel: Falken, 1939; in English as *The Civilizing Process*, 2 vols., New York: Urizen (vol. 1) and Pantheon (vol. 2), and Oxford: Blackwell, 1978–82

Farr, James R., "The Pure and Disciplined Body: Hierarchy, Morality, and Symbolism in France during the Counter-Reformation," *Journal of Interdisciplinary History* 21 (1991), 391–414

Featherstone, Mike, Mike Hepworth, and Bryan S. Turner, eds., *The Body: Social Process and Cultural Theory*, Newburg Park, CA and London: Sage, 1991

Feher, Michel, with Ramona Naddaff and Nadia Tazi, eds., *Fragments for a History of the Human Body*, 3 vols., New York: Zone, 1989

Foucault, Michel, *Naissance de la clinique: une archéologie du regard médical*, Paris: Presses Universitaires de France, 1963; in English as *The Birth of the Clinic: An Archaeology of Medical Perception*, New York: Pantheon, and London: Tavistock, , 1973

Foucault, Michel, *Surveiller et punir: naissance de la prison*, Paris: Gallimard, 1975; in English as *Discipline and Punish: The Birth of the Prison*, New York: Pantheon, and London: Allen Lane, 1977

Foucault, Michel, *Histoire de la sexualité*, 3 vols., Paris: Gallimard, 1976–84; in English as *The History of Sexuality*, 3 vols., New York: Pantheon, 1978–86, London: Allen Lane, 1979–88

Gallagher, Catherine, and Thomas Laqueur, eds., *The Making of the Modern Body: Sexuality and Society in the Nineteenth Century*. Berkeley: University of California Press, 1987

Gilman, Sander, *The Jew's Body*, New York: Routledge, 1991

Hunt, Lynn, ed., *Eroticism and the Body Politic*, Baltimore: Johns Hopkins University Press, 1991

Jones, Colin, and Roy Porter, editors, *Reassessing Foucault: Power, Medicine and the Body*, London and New York: Routledge, 1994

Kantorowicz, Ernst, *The King's Two Bodies: A Study in Mediaeval Political Theology*, Princeton: Princeton University Press, 1957

Laqueur, Thomas, "Bodies, Death, and Pauper Funerals," *Representations* 1 (1983), 109–31

Laqueur, Thomas, "Bodies, Details, and the Humanitarian Narrative," in Lynn Hunt, ed., *The New Cultural History*, Berkeley: University of California Press, 1989

Laqueur, Thomas, *Making Sex: Body and Gender from the Greeks to Freud*, Cambridge, MA: Harvard University Press, 1990

Linebaugh, Peter, "The Tyburn Riot Against the Surgeons," in Douglas Hay *et al.*, eds., *Albion's Fatal Tree: Crime and Society in Eighteenth-Century England*, New York: Pantheon, and London: Allen Lane, 1975

Martin, Emily, *The Woman in the Body: A Cultural Analysis of Reproduction*, Boston: Beacon Press, 1988

Miles, Margaret R., *Carnal Knowing: Female Nakedness and Religious Meaning in the Christian West*, Boston: Beacon Press, 1989; Tunbridge Wells: Burns and Oates, 1992

O'Neill, John, *Five Bodies: The Human Shape of Modern Society*, Ithaca, NY: Cornell University Press, 1985

Outram, Dorinda, *The Body and the French Revolution: Sex, Class, and Political Culture*, New Haven: Yale University Press, 1989

Park, Katherine, "The Life of the Corpse: Division and Dissection in Late Medieval Europe," *Journal of the History of Medicine* 50 (1993), 111–32

Park, Katherine, "The Criminal and Saintly Body: Autopsy and Dissection in Renaissance Italy," *Renaissance Quarterly* 47 (1994), 1–33

Porter, Roy, "Bodies of Thought: Thoughts about the Body in Eighteenth Century England," in Joan H. Pittock and Andrew Wear, eds., *Interpretation and Cultural History*, London: Macmillan, and New York: St. Martin's Press, 1991

Porter, Roy, "History of the Body," in Peter Burke, ed., *New Perspectives on Historical Writing*, Cambridge: Polity Press, 1991; University Park: Pennsylvania State University Press, 1992

Rousselle, Aline, *De la maitrise du corps à la privation sensorielle: IIe-IVe siècles de l'ere chrétienne*, Paris: Presses Universitaires de France, 1983; in English as *Porneia: On Desire and the Body in Antiquity*, Oxford: Blackwell, 1988

Saillant, John, "The Black Body Erotic and the Republican Body Politic, 1790–1820," *Journal of the History of Sexuality* 5 (1994–95), 403–28

Schiebinger, Londa, *The Mind Has No Sex?: Women in the Origins of Modern Science*, Cambridge, MA: Harvard University Press, 1989

Schiebinger, Londa, *Nature's Body: Gender in the Making of Modern Science*, Boston: Beacon Press, and London: Pandora Press, 1993

Shilling, Chris, *The Body and Social Theory*, Newbury Park, CA: Sage, 1993

Somerville, Siobhan, "Scientific Racism and the Emergence of the Homosexual Body," *Journal of the History of Sexuality* 5 (1994–95), 243–66

Steinberg, Leo, *The Sexuality of Christ in Renaissance Art and Modern Oblivion*, New York: Pantheon, 1983; London: Faber, 1984

Suleiman, Susan R., ed., *The Female Body in Western Culture: Contemporary Perspectives*, Cambridge, MA: Harvard University Press, 1986

Turner, Bryan S. *The Body and Society: Explorations in Social Theory*, Oxford and New York: Blackwell, 1984

Usbourne, Cornelie, *The Politics of the Body in Weimar Germany: Women's Reproductive Rights and Duties*, London: Macmillan, and Ann Arbor: University of Michigan Press, 1992

Bolland, Jean 1596–1665

Flemish hagiographer

The corpus of early literature on the lives of the saints was disdained by the humanists both for its naive disregard for historical accuracy and for its stylistic crudity. Protestants rejected it along with the entire cult of the saints. A Dutch Jesuit, Héribert Rosweyde, trained in philology and interested in church history, proposed in 1606 a plan for publication of critically edited versions of some 1300 lives of saints supplemented by volumes of commentary explaining difficulties and evaluating the provenance and reliability of each account. After Rosweyde's death in 1629, Jean Bolland accepted direction of the work, immediately expanding the project to include not only saints of northwest Europe but those of the entire world, not only the saints of the official Roman Martyrology but also those venerated by local Christian communities. He judged that it would be sensible to publish some critical apparatus along with rather than as supplement to the vitae and to give order to the whole by publishing the vitae in the order in which saints were commemorated in the Christian liturgical calendar. Where no vita was available, he would compile an entry from original sources. Beginning with January, he selected those saints whose vitae could be included, edited the texts, attached discussions of the particulars of the way in which the saint was venerated in liturgy and popular piety, and prefaced each account with some discussion of provenance, authorship, reliability, locations of manuscript(s), variant readings, and annotations.

In 1635, finding that he had collected enough documents to quadruple the extensive corpus left by Rosweyde, he recruited to assist him a former pupil, Godefroid Henschens, who expanded Bolland's method by comparing variant biographies of individual saints and providing *explication de texte* utilizing the material and methods of several scholarly disciplines. Bolland involved him in revising the January material, published in two folio volumes in 1643, before they moved to completing the February material, published in three volumes in 1658. Each volume contained, in addition to the vitae, prodigious amounts of material on church history, chronology, geography, law, government, literature, and the arts. Though the format devised by Henschens was now normative, the General of the Jesuits had already recognized the pivotal role of Bolland by using the term "Bollandist" to describe the project, whose practitioners to this day are known as "Bollandists."

Invited to Rome by Pope Alexander VII in 1659 to mine the resources of the Vatican Library, Bolland was too ill to travel and sent Henschens and a new recruit, Daniel Papebroch, planning their Itinerary in detail and traveling with them as far as Cologne. Visiting not only Rome but libraries in Germany, Italy, and France, they returned with more than 1400 new vitae as well as other documents and materials for their enterprise. At the time of his death in 1665 the March volumes were within three years of publication and the Bollandist library was the foremost repository of hagiographic materials in the world.

JOSEPH M. McCARTHY

See also Catholicism; Levison; Mabillon; Muratori

Biography

Born Julémont, near Liège, 11 August 1596. Entered the Jesuit novitiate at Malines, 1612; ordained, 1625; prefect of studies, Malines, 1625–30; appointed successor editor, *Fasti Sanctorum* (The Feasts of the Saints), 1630. Died Antwerp, 12 September 1665.

Principal Writings

Acta Sanctorum (Acts of the Saints) [with Godefroid Henschens *et al.*], 67 vols., 1643–1940

Further Reading

Carnandet, Jean-Baptiste, and J. Fèvre, *Les Bollandistes et l'hagiographie ancienne et moderne* (The Bollandists and Hagiography, Ancient and Modern), Lyon: Gauthier, 1866

Coens, Maurice, *Recueil d'études bollandiennes* (A Collection of Bollandist Studies), Brussels: Société des Bollandistes, 1962

Dehaisnes, Chrétien César Auguste, *Les Origines des "Acta Sanctorum" et les protecteurs des Bollandistes dans le nord de la France* (The Origins of the "Acta Sanctorum" and the Patrons of the Bollandists in Northern France), Douai: Dechristé, 1869

Delehaye, Hippolyte, *Les Légendes hagiographiques* (Hagiographic Legends), Brussels: Bureaux de la Société du Bollandists, 1906; in English as *The Legends of the Saints*, London and New York: Longman, 1907; reprinted 1962

Delehaye, Hippolyte, *A travers trois siècles: l'oeuvre des bollandistes, 1615–1915*, 1920; in English as *The Work of the Bollandists Through Three Centuries, 1615–1915*, Princeton: Princeton University Press, 1922

Delehaye, Hippolyte, *Cinq leçons sur la méthode hagiographique* (Five Lessons in Hagiographic Method), Brussels: Société des Bollandistes, 1934

Gaiffier, Baudouin de, "Hagiographie et critique: quelques aspects de l'oeuvre des Bollandistes au XVIIe siècle" (Hagiography and Criticism: Some Aspects of the Work of the Bollandists in the 17th Century) in his *Etudes critiques d'hagiographie et d'iconologie*, Brussels: Société des Bollandistes, 1967

Gautier, Léon, *Les Acta Sanctorum: étude sur le recueil des Bollandistes* (The *Acta Sanctorum*: A Study of the Bollandist Collection), Paris: Palme, 1863

Grafton, Anthony, *Defenders of the Text: The Traditions of Scholarship in the Age of Science, 1450–1800*, Cambridge, MA: Harvard University Press, 1991

Knowles, David, "The Bollandists," in his *Great Historical Enterprises*, London and New York: Nelson, 1963

Lechat, Robert, "Les *Acta Sanctorum* des Bollandistes" (The *Acta Sanctorum* of the Bollandists), *Catholic Historical Review* 6 (1920), 334–42

Palmieri, Aurelio, "The Bollandists," *Catholic Historical Review* new series 3 (1923), 341–57

Papebroch, Daniel, "Tractatus praeliminarius de vita, operibus et virtutibus Johannis Bollandi" (Preliminary Treatise on the Life, Works, and Virtues of John Bolland), *Acta Sanctorum martii*, Antwerp: J. van Meurs, 1668

Peeters, Paul, *L'Oeuvre des Bollandistes* (The Work of the Bollandists), Brussels: Palis des Académies, 1942; revised 1961

Pitra, Jean Baptiste, *Etude sur la collection des Actes des saintes par les RR. PP. Jésuites Bollandistes* (A Study of the Acts of the Saints by the Bollandist Jesuits), Paris: Lecoffre, 1850

Smedt, Charles De, "Les Fondateurs de Bollandisme" (The Founders of Bollandism); in *Mélanges Godefroid Kurth*, Paris: Champion, 1908

Sullivan, Donald, "Jean Bolland and the Early Bollandists," in Helen Damico and Joseph B. Zavedil, eds., *Medieval Scholarship: Biographical Studies in the Formation of a Discipline*, New York: Garland, 1995, 3–14

Bolton, Herbert E. 1870–1953

US historian of Spanish America

Determined to correct the notion that American colonization proceeded from east to west, Herbert E. Bolton's prolific writings argued consistently that Spanish explorers and missionaries arrived before the English or French and that New World settlement also moved south to north. His challenge to the Anglo-American interpretation of colonial history earned Bolton the title "Father of Spanish Borderlands history," and throughout his long career as professor of US history and director of the Hubert Howe Bancroft Library, he elaborated on the theme.

A Wisconsin native educated at the University of Pennsylvania, Bolton joined the Department of History at the University of Texas, Austin, in 1901 and almost immediately discovered the nearly forgotten, largely unused Spanish archives. He began to visit Mexico in order to survey and catalog materials concerning the Spanish presence in roughly the southernmost third of the US from Atlantic to Pacific. His *Guide to Materials for the History of the United States in the Principal Archives of Mexico* (1913) established Bolton as scholar of colonial Spanish North America, a field he almost single-handedly developed, and his list of publications grew longer every year.

Bolton's *Texas in the Middle Eighteenth Century* (1915) and *Spanish Exploration in the Southwest, 1542–1706* (1916) were but preludes, however, to his great synthesis, *The Spanish Borderlands* (1921), which directly challenged traditional colonial American history. *Arrendondo's Historical Proof of Spain's Title to Georgia* (1925) and *The Debatable Land* (1925) reinforced his thesis that the 1607 settlement of Jamestown by the English was not the opening shot in America's story. On the contrary, in 1513, Ponce de León was perhaps the first European to lay eyes on Florida, and by the time John Smith met Pocahontas, Spain had planted permanent colonies in the Southwest, while missionaries reported thousands of conversions among Indians. Bolton also challenged Frederick Jackson Turner's 1893 thesis that virtually ignored non-Anglo Europeans and argued that frontier existence bred rugged individualism and democracy. Neither, Bolton discovered, seemed to have occurred among Spanish pioneers or institutions.

Wooed from Texas to the University of California, Berkeley, Bolton taught and directed the expansive Bancroft Library, adding works on Spanish North America, and continued to shape study of the Spanish Borderlands. He researched individuals and began a lifelong fascination with Father Eusebio Francisco Kino, the Jesuit who extended Mexico's mission frontier into the lower Colorado and Gila River regions of Arizona and worked among Pima Indians. *Historical Memoir of Pimeria Alta* (1919) was Bolton's first foray into translating this priest's works. He published a short sketch of Kino, *The Padre on Horseback* (1932), followed by a full biography, *Rim of Christendom* (1936). *Pageant in the Wilderness* (1950) detailed attempts by Fathers Silvestre Velez de Escalante and Francisco Atanasio Dominguez to chart a route from Mexico City to the California coast. As he often did when researching explorations, Bolton retraced the route using original maps and making corrections when required.

Bolton wrote extensively on explorers, as in *Coronado* (1949) and the 5-volume edition of *Anza's California Expeditions* (1930). Spanish institutions, in particular missions and presidios, were also subjects of numerous articles. Bolton's specialized monographs led scholars into new and intriguing aspects of Borderlands study, but also tended to leave central themes undeveloped and methodology disjointed – problems that continue to plague this field.

Bolton produced two texts in which the first third is devoted to events prior to the English debut in America. They also reveal European involvement in North America by the Dutch, Swedes, Russians, and Portuguese. Thus, Bolton's demand that colonial studies embrace more than just the original 13 colonies enlarged the scope of US history and encouraged historians to look beyond political boundaries to a greater hemispheric history.

In addition, Borderlands study expanded the field of US Western history, which Turner's focus on the closing frontier tended to retard. Since the 1960s, scholars have gone beyond Bolton's concern with biography and institutions and embraced archaeological and anthropological methods, environment and historical geography, the study of disease, social and cultural history, as well as Native American history and ethnohistory. The field attempts to acknowledge and explain the Spanish legacy that remained alive in California, New Mexico, Arizona, and Texas, long after Spanish departure in 1821, and challenges the "Black Legend" that depicted Spanish involvement in the New World as uniquely cruel to indigenous populations.

At the same time, because Spanish control ended in 1821, Borderlands history is often classified as colonial history, even though some scholars argue that 1848 – when Mexico ceded the Southwest to the US – better represents the end of Spanish involvement, while still others make a convincing case for continuation of Borderlands study into the 20th century. It has also fragmented in the years since Bolton's death, identified to some extent with Latin American, not US, history. Historians of Southeast Borderlands tend to be isolated from those of Southwest Borderlands, the first falling generally into Southern and second into Western history. Only a few Bolton disciples – John Francis Bannon, *The Spanish Borderlands Frontier, 1513–1821* (1970) and David J. Weber, *The Spanish Frontier in North America* (1992) – have tried to unite the two regions and identify common themes and questions.

Bolton's importance, however, is undisputed. His writings, particularly *The Spanish Borderlands*, still challenge traditional views of colonial and frontier history. They raise significant questions, such as the role of frontier on Spanish institutions and Spanish-Indian versus Anglo-Indian relations. The search for common historical elements between North and South America remains an open subject, and the call for a greater hemispheric history has yet to be answered. Bolton taught enthusiastically until 1953 when he died at the age of 82, and left hundreds of graduate students, who have expanded Borderlands history and seek to make it relevant to 20th-century history.

KATHLEEN EGAN CHAMBERLAIN

See also Borah; Hanke

Biography

Herbert Eugene Bolton. Born Tomah, Monroe County, Wisconsin, 20 July 1870. Attended Tomah High School and Milwaukee Normal School; then briefly a school principal, Fairchild, Wisconsin; studied with Frederick Jackson Turner, receiving BA, University of Wisconsin, 1895; PhD in medieval history, University of Pennsylvania, 1899. Taught at Milwaukee Normal School, 1899–1901; University of Texas, 1901–09; Stanford University, 1909–10; and University of California at Berkeley, 1911–44. Married Gertrude Janes, 1895 (7 children). Died 30 January 1953.

Principal Writings

Guide to Materials for the History of the United States in the Principal Archives of Mexico, 1913
Texas in the Middle Eighteenth Century: Studies in Spanish Colonial History and Administration, 1915
Editor, *Spanish Exploration in the Southwest, 1542–1706*, 1916
"The Mission as a Frontier Institution in the Spanish-American Colonies," *American Historical Review* 23 (1917), 42–61
Editor and translator, *Historical Memoir of Pimería Alta: A Contemporary Account of the Beginnings of California, Sonora, and Arizona, 1683–1711*, 2 vols., 1919
With Thomas Maitland Marshall, *The Colonization of North America, 1492–1783*, 1920
The Spanish Borderlands: A Chronicle of Old Florida and the Southwest, 1921
"The Location of LaSalle's Colony on the Gulf of Mexico," *Southwest Historical Quarterly* 27 (1924), 171–89
Editor, *Arrendondo's Historical Proof of Spain's Title to Georgia: A Contribution to the History of One of the Spanish Borderlands*, 1925
With Mary Ross, *The Debatable Land: A Sketch of Anglo-Spanish Contest for the Georgia Country*, 1925
Editor and translator, *Fray Juan Crespi: Missionary Explorer on the Pacific Coast, 1769–1774*, 1927
Editor and translator, *Anza's California Expeditions*, 5 vols., 1930
Outpost of Empire: The Story of the Founding of San Francisco, 1931
The Padre on Horseback: A Sketch of Eusebio Francisco Kino, SJ, Apostle to the Pimas, 1932
"The Black Robes of New Spain," *Catholic Historical Review* 21 (1935), 257–82
Rim of Christendom: A Biography of Eusebio Francisco Kino, Pacific Coast Pioneer, 1936
Wider Horizons of American History, 1939
Coronado on the Turquoise Trail: Knight of Pueblos and Plains, 1949
Editor and translator, *Pageant in the Wilderness: The Story of the Escalante Expedition to the Interior Basin, 1776*, 1950

Further Reading

Bannon, John Francis, ed., *Bolton and the Spanish Borderlands*, Norman: University of Oklahoma Press, 1964 [includes bibliography]
Bannon, John Francis, *The Spanish Borderlands Frontier, 1513–1821*, New York: Holt Rinehart, 1970
Bannon, John Francis, *Herbert Eugene Bolton: The Historian and the Man*, Tucson: University of Arizona Press, 1978
Hanke, Lewis, ed., *Do the Americas Have a Common History? A Critique of the Bolton Theory*, New York: Knopf, 1964
Hurtado, Albert L., "Herbert E. Bolton, Racism, and American History," *Pacific Historical Review* 62 (1993), 127–42
Jacobs, Wilbur R., John W. Caughey, and Joe B. Frantz, eds., *Turner, Bolton, and Webb: Three Historians of the American Frontier*, Seattle: University of Washington Press, 1965
Magnaghi, Russell M., "Herbert E. Bolton and Sources for American Indian Studies," *Western Historical Quarterly* 6 (1975), 33–46
Ogden, Adele, and Engel Sluiter, eds., *Greater America: Essays in Honor of Herbert Eugene Bolton*, Berkeley: University of California Press, 1945 [includes bibliography]
Poyo, Gerald E., and Gilberto M. Hinojosa, "Spanish Texas and Borderlands Historiography in Transition: Implications for United States History," *Journal of American History* 75 (1988), 393–416
Scardaville, Michael C., "Approaches to the Study of the Southeastern Borderlands," in R. Reid Badger and Lawrence A. Clayton, eds., *Alabama and the Borderlands from Prehistory to Statehood*, University: University of Alabama Press, 1985
Weber, David J., "Turner, the Boltonians, and the Borderlands," *American Historical Review* 91 (1986), 66–81
Weber, David J., *Myth and the History of the Hispanic Southwest: Essays*, Albuquerque: University of New Mexico Press, 1988
Weber, David J., *The Spanish Frontier in North America*, New Haven: Yale University Press, 1992
Worster, Donald, "Herbert Eugene Bolton: The Making of a Western Historian," in Richard W. Etulain, ed., *Writing Western History: Essays on Major Western Historians*, Albuquerque: University of New Mexico Press, 1991, 193–213

Boorstin, Daniel J. 1914–

US intellectual historian

Daniel Boorstin is one of the most widely published American historians, and his contributions to the study of history can be found in the libraries of prestigious academic institutions and in the pages of popular magazines. His capacity to communicate what are often sophisticated and complex concepts in an accessible manner has won him a wide audience and even wider professional acclaim.

In many ways, Boorstin's work is comparable to those efforts associated with the concept of total history. This perspective, perhaps first associated with the French historians Fernand Braudel and Marc Bloch and the journal *Annales*, is, at least in part, an attempt to demonstrate the interrelationships between the diverse array of factors that have profoundly affected human society. In so doing, total history often violated the boundaries of what some traditionalists regard as history in favor of a more interdisciplinary (and often more sophisticated) view increasingly popular among modern scholars.

Several significant differences distinguish Boorstin from many of the other academicians seeking to bring together such seemingly disparate elements of human history. Not the least of these is an extraordinary and diverse professional and scholarly background that provides Boorstin wide-ranging expertise.

After receiving his doctorate from Yale, Boorstin trained as a lawyer, taught in several elite institutions around the world, was director of the National Museum of History and Technology and senior historian at the Smithsonian Institution in Washington, DC, and, finally, served as the twelfth Librarian of Congress, a position he held until retiring in 1987.

Boorstin's scholarly contributions are equally wide-ranging, and he has been the recipient of the Pulitzer, the Bancroft and the Parkman prizes. Among his most respected works is the trilogy *The Americans* (1958–73). In many ways these volumes are comparable in scope to Braudel's work on the Mediterranean in that each examined a specific society over an extended period, tracing what Boorstin termed "countless, little-noticed revolutions." Indeed a prevalent concern for Boorstin was the impact of such subtle "revolutions" as the concept of time and the improvement of building materials. Coincidentally, he addressed the more "usual" topics – exploration, technology, politics, and religious and intellectual thought – weaving them together into a fascinating description of mankind's development.

Boorstin distinguishes between "revolutions" and "turning points," a distinction which he argues is too often misunderstood. In his 1991 article "History's Hidden Turning Points," Boorstin contended that true revolutions are not necessarily those episodes commonly described as such. Further, he suggested that the most important revolutions may even be initially unnoticed by society, their impact gradually unfolding over time. As evidence, Boorstin noted the scant media attention given the Food and Drug Administration's approval of the first birth control pill in 1960.

The most significant revolutions, he argued, may well exist outside the narrow confines of traditional social, political, and economic definitions and are often those seemingly simple technological innovations regularly given short shrift by the scholarly community. To Boorstin, however, they are the building materials of progress, literally the concrete foundations of human development as described in *The Creators* (1992). On cursory glance, *The Creators* appears to be an assessment of the achievements of such cultural icons as Plato, Benjamin Franklin, Herman Melville, and Claude Monet. In reality, like his earlier book *The Discoverers* (1983), it is a much more ambitious and sophisticated study of mankind's ongoing quest to understand both the internal and the external world. It is a similarly ambitious quest that drives Boorstin's scholarship, the hope that in understanding the past, one can comprehend the present and perhaps better prepare for the future.

Boorstin is in a particularly favorable position to accomplish such a goal. An extraordinarily talented and engaging author, he willingly embraces what "elitist" scholars eschew – the belief that a fundamental purpose of intellectual and academic pursuit is to educate and enlighten the masses. In so doing, he provides a profoundly valuable service to an audience all too often forgotten by his professional colleagues.

ROBERT E. BARNETT

See also Hartz; Media; Morison; Popular; Potter; United States: 19th Century

Biography

Daniel Joseph Boorstin. Born Atlanta, Georgia, 1 October 1914, son of a lawyer. Grew up in Tulsa, Oklahoma; received BA, Harvard University, 1934; BA, Oxford University, 1936, BCL 1937; JSD, Yale University, 1940. Taught at Harvard University, 1938–42; Harvard Law School, 1939–42; Swarthmore College, 1942–44; and University of Chicago (rising to professor), from 1944. Director, National Museum of History and Technology, Smithsonian Institution, 1969–73; senior historian, 1972–75. Librarian of Congress, 1975–87. Called to the Bar: Inner Temple, London, 1937; Massachusetts, 1942. Married Ruth Carolyn Frankel, 1941 (3 sons). Received Pulitzer prize, 1974.

Principal Writings

The Mysterious Science of the Law: An Essay on Blackstone's Commentaries, 1941
The Lost World of Thomas Jefferson, 1948
The Americans, 3 vols., 1958–73
America and the Image of Europe: Reflections on American Thought, 1960
The Image; or, What Happened to the American Dream, 1962
Editor, *American Civilization*, 1972
The Discoverers, 1983
"History's Hidden Turning Points," *US News and World Report* 110 (22 April 1991), 52–65
The Creators, 1992
Cleopatra's Nose: Essays on the Unexpected, edited by Ruth F. Boorstin, 1994

Borah, Woodrow 1912–
US social and economic historian of Latin America

Woodrow Wilson Borah belongs to that generation of post-World War II Latin American historians that revolutionized the study of Latin American history by concentrating on the study of the influence of institutions on the social and economic life of colonial Latin America. Along with Sherburne F. Cook and Lesley Bird Simpson, the Berkeley school of demographic and economic history emphasized the utilization of economic and social sources overlooked by previous historians of Latin America. Prior to this development, studies on colonial Latin America concentrated on institutions and personalities.

During the early 20th century, US writing on colonial Spanish America, based on the work of 19th-century US historians, presented Spanish colonization in the New World positively. These historians sought to banish the "Black Legend" of Spain's unique cruelty that plagued the interpretation of Spain's colonization since the 16th century with the publication of Las Casas' writings. These revisionist historians were also responsible for establishing the infrastructure for the study of Latin America in the US. As initiators, they concentrated on both those relatively accessible documents issued by colonial institutions, and on writing biographies. Many of these studies concentrated on elites and presented a caricature of the masses, especially the Indian peoples.

Borah had a tremendous impact on this scholarly environment by shifting the focus of the analysis to social and economic topics. Earlier members of the Berkeley school came from fields outside the discipline of history to provide insights that would transform the study of colonial Latin America. The historian/geographer Carl O. Sauer, who some consider the founder of the school, studied the native population of Mexico prior to and after the Spanish conquest. Another early member of the school was Sherburne F. Cook, an environmental physiologist, who studied numerous topics concerning the influence of the environment on the pre- and post-conquest native population. It was these contributions from other fields that created the unique focus of the Berkeley school on demographics and economic history.

Borah arrived in Berkeley in 1936 and worked with Herbert E. Bolton, historian of the Spanish Borderlands, and Sauer on his dissertation concerning the silk industry in colonial Mexico. He based this study, later published as *Silk Raising in Colonial Mexico* (1943), on 14 months of research in Mexico, searching the nation's regional archives for tithe records as a means to discover the amount of silk produced. At this time very few historians of Latin America conducted research in regional archives. Borah's use of tithe records, to which he was introduced through his work in medieval history, contributed greatly to the reorientation of Latin American colonial history.

From 1942 to 1947, World War II interrupted Borah's scholarly career when he went to work for the Office of Strategic Services. In 1948, he returned to Berkeley as a professor in the Speech Department. He continued his research on colonial Mexico and published *New Spain's Century of Depression* (1951), which established him as a leading scholar of colonial Mexico. Previously historians accepted the interpretation that during the colonial period New Spain's economy had a period of continuous economic growth. Borah challenged this interpretation by contending that the decline of the Indian population contributed to a period of economic decline that began in the late 16th century and lasted until the 18th century. New Spain's agricultural and mining production especially suffered through labor shortages. The Spaniards created numerous labor control mechanisms, such as debt peonage, to assure themselves of a steady flow of labor to their various economic enterprises. Also, the rise of the hacienda could be traced to this period as these large agricultural production units provided the necessary foodstuffs for the cities and mining centers. This tentative hypothesis, based on archival research and Cook and Simpson's work on the Indian population of the 16th century, has consequently been developed and accepted as a valid interpretation by other historians.

Subsequently, Borah began his major work with Cook on population studies in the 1950s and 1960s. Researching the Mixteca Alta, he initially approached Cook for his statistical knowledge, thus beginning a collaboration that revolutionized the study of colonial Latin America. Their conclusion on the preconquest Indian population living in central Mexico, which they estimated at 25.2 million, caused heated debate in the field. They published their findings in numerous monographs, most notably in *The Aboriginal Population of Central Mexico on the Eve of the Spanish Conquest* (1963). Utilizing abundant archival sources, such as the second Spanish Register of Tributes, they applied statistical analysis to the tribute-paying population to arrive at the figure of the preconquest population. Their conclusions reignited the controversy surrounding the "Black Legend" concerning Spain's colonization of the Americas.

Their monumental 3-volume work, *Essays in Population History* (1971–79), applied their methodology to other areas of Latin America. For Hispaniola, they arrived at a figure of four to eight million for the Indian population at the time of initial European contact. This figure also caused controversy because many historians considered Friar Bartolomé de Las Casas' figure of four million as hyperbole to support his arguments against Spanish treatment of the Indians in the Indies. Borah and Cook blamed the drastic decline of the Indian population of Hispaniola on excessive labor obligations, the disruption of indigenous social and economic organization, and European diseases.

Borah continued his individual research on various Mexican colonial topics. He returned to an earlier study, originally a collaboration with Lesley Bird Simpson that began in 1931, of the General Indian Court. This work, published as *Justice by Insurance* (1983), analyzed this institution as a response to the conflicting demands of the conquered and the conquerors in the New Spain context. Borah not only analyzed the institutional structure, but also the social and economic structure in which it operated until the end of colonial rule in the early 19th century.

Borah's demographic, social and economic research and scholarship influenced the agenda of a generation of Latin American historians that studied in the 1960s and 1970s. Subsequent scholars confirmed many of his findings on the colonial history of Latin America in general and Mexico in particular. His paradigms, with their emphasis on social and economic issues, shaped the future direction of Latin American historical scholarship and research not only in the United States, but also in Latin America and Europe.

CARLOS PÉREZ

See also Latin America: Colonial; Spain: Imperial

Biography

Woodrow Wilson Borah. Born Utica, Mississippi, 22 December 1912. Received BA, University of California, Los Angeles, 1935, MA 1936; PhD in history and geography, University of California, Berkeley, 1940. Taught at Princeton University, 1941–42; then served as an analyst for the Office of Strategic Services and the US Department of State, 1942–47. Taught (rising to professor), at University of California, Berkeley, 1948–80 (emeritus). Married Therese Levy, 1945 (1 son, 1 daughter).

Principal Writings

Silk Raising in Colonial Mexico, 1943
New Spain's Century of Depression, 1951
Early Colonial Trade and Navigation between Mexico and Peru, 1954
Price Trends of Some Basic Commodities in Central Mexico, 1551–1570, 1958
The Indian Population of Central Mexico, 1531–1610, 1960
The Population of Central Mexico in 1548: An Analysis of the suma de visitas de pueblos, 1960
With Sherburne F. Cook, *The Aboriginal Population of Central Mexico on the Eve of the Spanish Conquest*, 1963
With Sherburne F. Cook, *The Population of the Mixteca Alta, 1520–1960*, 1968
"Latin America, 1610–1660," *New Cambridge Modern History*, vol. 4, 1970
With Sherburne F. Cook, *Essays in Population History: Mexico and the Caribbean*, 3 vols., 1971–79
Justice by Insurance: The General Indian Court of Colonial Mexico and the Legal Aides of the Half-Real, 1983
Price Trends of Royal Tribute Commodities in Nueva Galicia, 1557–1598, 1992

Further Reading
Keen, Benjamin, "Main Currents in United States Writings on Colonial Spanish America, 1884–1984," *Hispanic American Historical Review* 65 (1985), 657–82
Wilkie, James W., and Rebecca Horn, "An Interview with Woodrow Borah," *Hispanic American Historical Review* 65 (1985), 401–41

Bourdieu, Pierre 1930–

French theorist

Pierre Bourdieu is a multidisciplinary investigator of social structures and practices. He is positioned at the pragmatic intersection where a variety of rich but partial theoretical traditions of the last century become useful to practical understanding. Difficult to encapsulate, his work grows out of sensible appreciations of the historical sociologies of Marx, Durkheim, and Weber; hermeneutics, phenomenology, and existentialism; structuralism and poststructuralism. For Bourdieu these are not mutually annihilating theoretical positions, but toolboxes that offer contextually productive or unproductive resources to the study of how humans think and live. A distiller of theoretical insights, Bourdieu is not insensitive to theoretical wrangling and disciplinary turf wars, he is impatient with them.

Bourdieu is especially fascinated with "homologies," the reproduction in one social sphere or context of practices and relationships native to another. In his early work on the sociology of education, investigating the cultural politics of communication and misunderstanding, he pointed out that structural relations of social class are reproduced homologously in the classroom by (among other things) lectures that communicate only to students already bearing cultural capital accumulated via their families' position in class hierarchies. The lecture form reflects a politics of knowledge; the lecturer speaks at people presumed already to be like her, reproduces herself in those few who are pre-equipped to respond at the "proper" level, and reconsigns the rest (bad students) to silence. Here, as elsewhere, Bourdieu engages in an anthropology of the familiar, attempting to show the effect of common sense in hiding the power dynamics wrapped up in "normal" practices. As a precondition to such investigations, he counsels against "defense mechanisms of bad faith" designed to dismiss, minimize, or relativize his findings (especially as they appear to be "only" about France or Algeria) for our own practices. Bourdieu insists above all on rigorous methodological self-reflection, denying that intellectual practices have any automatic autonomy from the grimy practical dynamics of social positions in conflict (indeed, the claim to such autonomy is one of the weapons of intellectual politics). *Homo Academicus* (1984, translated in 1988) capped this ongoing research focus with a startling excavation of the politics of intellectual culture in the academy.

The term "cultural capital" points to Bourdieu's effort to identify the practical logics that make "class" effective as a structure and practice rather than an *a priori* category. In his concrete, specific studies (often collaborative) on "high" and "middlebrow" art, education, academic culture, games and sports, language, and on the sociology of cross-cultural communication, among others, Bourdieu has shown that "cultural" fields are sites of competition and domination in which practical oppositions of class distinction are played out. Within these fields, social actors position and identify themselves according to symbolic "tastes and preferences" that contain their practical assessment of the types and weights of capital (economic, political, cultural, intellectual, physical) that they are able to deploy or "cash in" for social advantage (*Distinction: A Social Critique of the Judgement of Taste*, 1979, translated 1984, is the most elaborate demonstration and a good place to start). Consequently, there is a relatively autonomous, relatively dependent homology between the economic violence of workplace exploitation, the political violence of the State, and the "symbolic violence" of dominant cultural forms and patterns of consumption.

Bourdieu breaks down the Manichaean oppositions of reductive class analysis to show that classes are internally divided into "class fractions" by the dispersion of capitals (calling intellectuals, for example, the "dominated fraction of the dominating class"). Gender, cultural formation (or generation), social position, social origin, and ethnic origin are some of the factors that sort and distribute capitals into class fractions. Once positioned, each class fraction has an interest in fortifying and normalizing its position with respect to other competing positions, *distinguishing* itself from "others" by using them (and being used by them) to describe what it is *not* (in this context he calls attention to the use of paired adjectives of the "good/evil" variety, e.g.,"rigorous/sloppy – pedantic/creative"). Such distinguishing practices cannot be well understood in isolation, but only in relation to particular social-historical spaces of possible positions.

This practical logic of distinction (or *Classification*) with respect to competing positions produces what Bourdieu calls the "habitus," a situated commonsense conception of the world that structures knowledge and action, and reciprocally reinforces the structural positioning that produced it. In this sense, all social actors participate actively in their positioning, "choosing" what they are already by making virtue of necessity. This dynamic significantly complicates questions of "domination," "consent," "resistance," and "submission," and reveals the absurdity of abstract, mutually-defining dichotomies (what he calls "mirror traps') such as "free will or determinism," "meaning or structure," "interpretation or science."

Bourdieu's investigative practice will look familiar in some of its particulars to many historians who are either working with parts of the vast conceptual field that Bourdieu has distilled, or who have "independently" come to homologous conclusions. As yet, his direct influence on historians and historiography has been limited, but the well-stocked toolbox he offers to historians of the social politics of culture has already begun to look attractive to some practitioners of the "new cultural history," especially as the productive phase of the interpretive anarchy of postmodernism wanes.

CARL DYKE

See also Chartier; Consumerism

Biography
Born Denguin, 1 August 1930. Received agrégation in philosophy, Ecole Normale Supérieure, 1954. Taught philosophy, Lycée de Moulins, 1954–55; then sociology, University of Algiers, 1958–60; University of Paris, 1960–61; professor, University of Lille, 1961–64; Ecole des Hautes Etudes, from 1964, and Collège de France, from 1981. Married Marie-Claire Brizard, 1962 (3 sons).

Principal Writings

Un Art moyen: essai sur les usages sociaux de la photographie,
1965; in English as *Photography: A Middle-Brow Art*, 1990

Editor, with Jean-Claude Passeron and Monique de Saint Martin,
Rapport pédagogique et communication, 1965; in English as
*Academic Discourse: Linguistic Misunderstanding and Professorial
Power*, 1994

With Alain Darbel, *L'Amour de l'art, les musées et leur public*,
1966; in English as *The Love of Art: European Art Museums and
Their Public*, 1991

With Jean-Claude Passeron and Jean-Claude Chamboredon, *Le Métier
de sociologue*, 1968; in English as *The Craft of Sociology*, 1991

With Jean-Claude Passeron, *La Reproduction: éléments pour une
théorie du système d'enseignement*, 1970; in English as
Reproduction in Education, Society and Culture, 1977

*Esquisse d'une théorie de la pratique: précédé de trois études
d'ethnologie kabyle*, 1972; in English as *Outline of a Theory of
Practice*, 1977

Algérie 60: structures économiques et structures temporelles, 1977;
in English as *Algeria 1960: The Disenchantment of the World,
The Sense of Honour, The Kabyle House or the World Reversed:
Essays*, 1979

La Distinction: critique sociale du jugement, 1979; in English as
Distinction: A Social Critique of the Judgment of Taste, 1984

Questions de sociologie, 1980; in English as *Sociology in Question*,
1993

Le Sens pratique, 1980; in English as *The Logic of Practice*, 1990

Ce que parler veut dire: l'économie des échanges linguistiques, 1982;
in English as *Language and Symbolic Power*, 1991

Homo Academicus, 1984; in English as *Homo Academicus*, 1988

Choses dites, 1987; in English as *In Other Words: Essays Towards
a Reflexive Sociology*, 1990

L'Ontologie politique de Martin Heidegger, 1988; in English as *The
Political Ontology of Martin Heidegger*, 1991

Les Règles de l'art: genèse et structure du champ littéraire, 1992; in
English as *The Rules of Art: Genesis and Structure of the
Literary Field*, 1996

With Loïc Waquant, *Réponses: pour une anthropologie réflexive*
(Responses: On an Introspective Anthropology), 1992

The Field of Cultural Production: Essays on Art and Literature,
edited by Randal Johnson, 1993

With Hans Haacke, *Libre échange*, 1994; in English as *Free
Exchange*, 1995

Raisons pratiques: sur la théorie de l'action, 1994

Further Reading

Adamson, Walter L., *Avant-Garde Florence: From Modernism to
Fascism*, Cambridge, MA: Harvard University Press, 1993

Brubaker, Rogers, "Rethinking Classical Sociology: The Sociological
Vision of Pierre Bourdieu," *Theory and Society* 14 (1985), 745–75

Calhoun, Craig, Edward LiPuma, and Moishe Postone, eds.,
Bourdieu: Critical Perspectives, Chicago: University of Chicago
Press, and Cambridge: Polity Press, 1993

Harker, Richard, Cheleen Mahar, and Chris Wilkes, eds., *An
Introduction to the Work of Pierre Bourdieu: The Practice of
Theory*, Basingstoke: Macmillan, and New York: St. Martin's
Press, 1990

Hunt, Lynn, ed., *The New Cultural History*, Berkeley: University of
California Press, 1989 (see the essays by Aletta Biersack and
Roger Chartier)

Ringer, Fritz, *Fields of Knowledge: French Academic Culture in
Comparative Perspective, 1890–1920*, Cambridge and New York:
Cambridge University Press, 1992

Robbins, Derek, *The Work of Pierre Bourdieu: Recognizing Society*,
Boulder, CO: Westview Press, and Milton Keynes: Open
University Press, 1991

Urbizagástegui Alvarado, Rubén, *Pierre Bourdieu: A Bibliography*,
Riverside, CA: Waira, 1993

Boxer, C.R. 1904–
British historian of Portugal

Periodically the works and reputation of a single historian come
to dominate a given field for one or two generations. The writings of Charles Boxer have played such a role for the English-
language interpretation of the history of the Portuguese empire
and its colonial dependencies, and have played a pivotal role
in Portuguese-language historiography as well. Boxer is one
of those remarkable scholars who has been instrumental in
defining the character and scope of his field; his works have
become touchstones to the essential investigations of Portuguese
history. Boxer has the capacity to speak equally persuasively
and authoritatively to audiences in Europe, the United States
and Latin America, and his work has had a substantial impact
on the fields of Portuguese, Brazilian, and Asian history.

An author of prodigious output (a bibliography compiled
in 1984 when Boxer was 80 years old lists more than 300
published works), Boxer published his first articles in the 1920s
and continued writing actively into the 1980s. His writing epitomizes the best aspects of the documentary-scientific approach
to historical analysis and is characterized by a comprehensive
use of documentation integrated into an effective narrative and
analytical framework. Boxer has been a pioneer, along with
several Portuguese and Brazilian scholars, in establishing the
documentary and institutional framework of the colonial
Portuguese experience.

An important component of his work has been the publication of key documents illustrating this history, but his contribution extends far beyond a mere antiquarian interest, and his
reputation and influence rest primarily upon several substantial
studies. The most important of his publications include: *The
Christian Century in Japan* (1951), *Salvador de Sá and the
Struggle for Brazil and Angola, 1602–1686* (1952), *The Dutch
in Brazil, 1624–1654* (1957), *The Golden Age of Brazil,
1695–1750* (1962), *The Dutch Seaborne Empire* (1965) and
The Portuguese Seaborne Empire (1969). He has also published
biographies of prominent 17th-century Brazilian figures, a book
investigating race relations in the Portuguese world, an exploration of gender issues in Iberian society, and an examination
of the Iberian ecclesiastical tradition. As this list suggests, the
scope of his research is both topically and geographically broad.
These works have established the basic outline of the Portuguese
experience throughout the world and form the backbone of its
interpretation in English.

While Boxer's importance stems in part from his role as a
pioneer and definer of the field, his influence also results from
his ability to elucidate the significance of an event by placing
it within its broader social, political and economic context.
Although published in the 1950s, his *Salvador de Sá* addressed
social and economic issues that are now being confronted by
historians of Africa. His works on Brazil reflect an awareness
of the importance of local institutions, such as the town council
and local lay religious associations, in the development of the
social matrix of colonial society. His study of race relations in
Brazil set the agenda for a generation of scholars of this essential topic, while he was one of the first scholars seriously to
address the issue of gender relations in *Mary and Misogyny:
Women in Iberian Expansion Overseas* (1975).

Boxer has also exerted an important influence on Portuguese studies through his professional activities. He has inspired two generations of scholars, both in England and the United States, and has maintained an active profile in professional organizations and meetings. Significantly, his influence has not been limited to the English-speaking world, but he has maintained a close contact with the most prominent scholars of Portugal and Brazil as well. Indicative of the esteem in which he is held is the list of awards and honors bestowed upon him. These include honorary degrees from universities in Brazil, England, The Netherlands, Hong Kong, and Portugal and, among other honors, the Premio D. Pedro II awarded him by the Brazilian government in 1986.

The breadth and depth of Boxer's writing mark him as one of the most outstanding historians in any field in the mid-20th century. Within the field of Portuguese history his work has played an essential role in establishing a foundation upon which a systematic and vibrant picture of the Portuguese and Brazilian experience can be constructed.

LINCOLN A. DRAPER

See also Brazil; World

Biography

Charles Ralph Boxer. Born Isle of Wight, England, 8 March 1904. Educated at Wellington and Sandhurst. Served in the British Army, 1923–47, much of this time in Japan: prisoner of war, 1941–45, later member of the British delegation of the Far East Commission; resigned from the Army, 1947. Camões Chair of Portuguese, University of London, 1947–67; first professor of Far Eastern history, School of Oriental and African Studies, 1951–53. After retirement, held professorships at Indiana University; and Yale University, 1969–72. Married the writer Emily Hahn, 1945 (died 1997; 2 daughters).

Principal Writings

The Christian Century in Japan, 1951
Salvador de Sá and the Struggle for Brazil and Angola, 1602–1686, 1952
The Dutch in Brazil, 1624–1654, 1957
The Golden Age of Brazil, 1695–1750: Growing Pains of a Colonial Society, 1962
The Dutch Seaborne Empire, 1600–1800, 1965
The Portuguese Seaborne Empire, 1415–1825, 1969
Mary and Misogyny: Women in Iberian Expansion Overseas, 1975

Further Reading

Rodrigues, José Honório, "C.R. Boxer," *Revista do Instituto Histórico e Geográfico Brasileiro* 147 (1986), 1108–13
Wehling, Arno, "Recepçao de C.R. Boxer no Instituto de Filosofia e Ciencias Sociais da Universidade Federal do Rio de Janeiro" (Reception of C.R. Boxer at the Institute of Philosophy and Social Science at the Federal University of Rio de Janeiro), *Revista do Instituto Histórico e Geográfico Brasileiro*, 147 (1986), 1113–18
West, George S., *A List of the Writings of Charles Ralph Boxer Published Between 1926 and 1984*, London: Tamesis, 1984

Bracher, Karl Dietrich 1922–
German historian and political scientist

A leading interpreter of Weimar and Nazi Germany and the ideologies that have shaped Europe's modern history, Karl Dietrich Bracher has contributed significantly to our understanding of the course of 20th-century history. Having grown up during the 1920s and 1930s, Bracher built his career and established his reputation during the early Cold War. This was a time when many young West Germans not only had to come to grips with their nation's recent history, but also with the Soviet challenge – a real presence in postwar Germany. However, Bracher and his generation also had the opportunity to acquaint themselves with American democracy, which, because of its optimistic view of history, made a deep impression on the young historian. Initially drawing lessons for his own country from the ongoing battle between democracy and dictatorship, Bracher later also discussed this struggle in European terms.

After World War II, Bracher studied ancient and modern history, philosophy, and classical philology in Tübingen, completing his doctorate in 1948. The classics, Bracher wrote later, had served his family as a spiritual antidote to the atmosphere of the Nazi era and after the war they continued to be one of his points of orientation. After participation in the Salzburg Seminar for American Studies, one year at Harvard, and six as a teacher at the Free University at Berlin, Bracher in 1955 completed his postdoctoral thesis, *Die Auflösung der Weimarer Republik* (The Disintegration of the Weimar Republic). In 1958 he was appointed to a professorship at the Free University; in 1959 he accepted a professorship in Bonn which became his permanent academic home.

If there is one theme that permeates all of Bracher's work, it is the fragility of democracy. And while a cool-headed analyst, Bracher has been the opposite of a detached observer. His work is characterized by persistent arguing on behalf of a proper appreciation of liberal democracy's fundamental elements of pluralism, human rights, and constitutionality – along with the advocacy of his country's allegiance to the West. Bracher's advocacy is fueled by the concern that the threat of totalitarianism – from the right or left – is always lurking around the corner, that too many people are too easily wooed by utopian schemes promising quick radical change. In his eyes, democracy's beneficiaries too easily take their basic freedoms for granted or underestimate their true value, or they are impatient with democracy's inescapable rule of compromise.

What distinguishes Bracher's work on Germany between 1919 and 1945 and made it innovative at the time of publication is its integration of structural and functional analysis with a narrative deeply rooted in historical fact. His three major works on the era – *Die Auflösung der Weimarer Republik*, *Die nationalsozialistische Machtergreifung* (The National-Socialist Seizure of Power, 1960), and *Die deutsche Diktatur* (1969; *The German Dictatorship*, 1970) – not only relate in meticulous detail the course of events leading to the German catastrophe, they also offer a clear and precise analysis of how and why the Weimar system stopped working and the Nazi alternative proved so effective for so long. The innovative nature of Bracher's approach caused it to be controversial as well. Historians (especially in the Federal Republic – less so in the

United States) did not see *Die Auflösung der Weimarer Republik* or its sequels as true works of history but rather as political science; yet political scientists often charged the opposite. But the achievement of two of Bracher's major objectives has proven lasting: the demystification of the rise of national socialism (making it the work of real people making real choices, instead of blaming impersonal notions such as a singular German "fate," capitalist or communist "conspiracies," or foreign influences) and the establishment of the case of Weimar as a model for the decline of democracy in a more general sense.

During the 1970s and 1980s, Bracher became one of the more vocal critics of what he saw as the defeatist and impatient mood of the time in which he recognized many of the destructive elements that during the 1920s and 1930s had brought down Weimar. As he wrote in the introduction to the English translation of *Zeit der Ideologien* (1982; *The Age of Ideologies*, 1984): "When the realization of high-pitched political expectations was found to come up against certain limits, there was a revival of the confrontation of power and spirit, politics and ideal – a confrontation especially painful in Germany and one that was generally believed to have been overcome." He was especially wary of movements questioning, or operating partially outside and against, the constitutional system in his country, such as the "Green" and "Peace" movements. The danger remains, he said, that the sequence: crisis of confidence – radical, utopian alternative – erosion of democratic processes or worse, will repeat itself.

Bracher also protested against the devaluation of the notion of "totalitarianism" and the discrediting of its users as "anti-communists." Unlike many others, he believed there remained much to be learned from applying the term to the communist world, particularly in regard to communism's fundamental differences with the West. The end of the Cold War confirmed his views but, Bracher warned in *Wendezeiten der Geschichte* (1992; *Turning Points in Modern Times*, 1995) this is no reason for triumphalism. Although the chances for building resilient democratic systems in Europe were much better than at the beginning of the short, ideological 20th century (1917–89), there were no guarantees. Democracy is the state form "of self-limitation and insight into the imperfection of man, just as dictatorship is the rule of man's ideological arrogance." There is no alternative to the hard work of maintaining a civil society, nor can this work ever be considered done. To understand why, there will scarcely be a better place to go than the works of Bracher.

RUUD VAN DIJK

See also Broszat; Germany: 1800–1945; Germany: since 1945; Miller, S.; Nietzsche

Biography
Born Stuttgart, 13 March 1922. Received PhD, University of Tübingen, 1948; postgraduate study, Harvard University, 1949–50. Taught (rising to professor), Free University, Berlin, 1950–58; and University of Bonn from 1959. Married Dorothee Schleicher, 1951 (1 son, 1 daughter).

Principal Writings
Verfall und Fortschritt im Denken der frühen römischen Kaiserzeit: Studien zum Zeitgefühl und Geschichtsbewusstsein des Jahrhunderts nach Augustus (Decline and Progress in Early Imperial Roman Thought: Studies in the Sense of Time and Historical Consciousness in the Century Following Augustus), written 1948; published 1987

Die Auflösung der Weimarer Republik: eine Studie zum Problem des Machtverfalls in der Demokratie (The Disintegration of the Weimar Republic: A Study on the Problem of the Decline of Power in a Democracy), 1955

Die nationalsozialistische Machtergreifung: Studien zur Errichtung des totalitären Herrschaftssystems in Deutschland 1933–34 (The National-Socialist Seizure of Power: The Construction of the Totalitarian Ruling System in Germany, 1933–34), 1960

Deutschland zwischen Demokratie und Diktatur: Beiträge zur neueren Politik und Geschichte (Germany between Democracy and Dictatorship: Contributions to the New Politics and History), 1964

Die deutsche Diktatur: Entstehung, Struktur, Folgen des Nationalsozialismus, 1969; in English as *The German Dictatorship: The Origins, Structure, and Consequences of National Socialism*, 1970

Das deutsche Dilemma: Leidenswege der politischen Emanzipation, 1971; in English as *The German Dilemma: The Throes of Political Emancipation*, 1974, and as *The German Dilemma: The Relationship of State and Democracy*, 1975

Die Krise Europas, 1917–1975 (The Crisis of Europe, 1917–1975), 1976; revised as *Europa in der Krise: Innengeschichte und Weltpolitik seit 1917* (Europe in Crisis: Internal History and World Politics since 1917), 1979

Zeitgeschichtliche Kontroversen: Um Faschismus, Totalitarismus, Demokratie (Controversies of Contemporary History: Over Fascism, Totalitarianism, Democracy), 1976

Geschichte und Gewalt: Zur Politik im 20. Jahrhundert (History and Force: On Politics in the 20th Century), 1981

Zeit der Ideologien: Eine Geschichte politischen Denkens im 20. Jahrhundert, 1982; in English as *The Age of Ideologies: A History of Political Thought in the Twentieth Century*, 1984

Die totalitäre Erfahrung (The Totalitarian Experience), 1987

Wendezeiten der Geschichte: Historisch-politische Essays, 1987–1992, 1992; in English as *Turning Points in Modern Times: Essays on German and European History*, 1995

Further Reading
Funke, Manfred *et al.*, eds., *Demokratie und Diktatur: Geist und Gestalt politischer Herrschaft in Deutschland und Europa, Festschrift für Karl Dietrich Bracher* (Democracy and Dictatorship: The Spirit and Form of Political Power in Germany and Europe), Düsseldorf: Droste, 1987 [includes bibliography]

Braham, Randolph L. 1922–
US (Romanian-born) political scientist

Born in Romania, but an emigrant to the US just after World War II, Braham is generally regarded as the foremost historian of the Nazi Holocaust in Hungary. Braham's research interests in political science center around comparative government and government policy in Eastern Europe, the Soviet Union, and Israel, and he is the author of a number of textbooks such as *Soviet Politics and Government: A Reader* (1965). He has also published monographs on the educational systems of Israel and Romania, and edited a book on *Social Justice* (1981).

Braham's central and most important work concerns the Holocaust in Hungary, a topic on which he has published nearly twenty books and dozens of articles. He has also written widely on Romanian Jews during the Holocaust, on the Eichmann trial, on anti-Semitism in Eastern Europe, and on related topics. Braham's best known and most important work is *The Politics of Genocide*, a 2-volume work published in 1981 and revised in 1994. *The Politics of Genocide* is arguably among the half-dozen finest works ever to appear on the Nazi Holocaust, and is a model of everything that a work of scrupulous scholarship should be. It presents in a magisterial way a detailed almost day-by-day account of the Nazi extermination of Hungarian Jewry, the last national group of Jews to be deported and murdered by the Nazis. Between May and July 1944, the Nazi SS (which had effectively seized control of Hungary in March 1944) deported approximately 350,000 Jews, chiefly from rural Hungary and Transylvania, to Auschwitz, where nearly all were murdered. Killings organized by the pro-Nazi Arrow Cross continued without mercy after the deportations were halted until Hungary was liberated by the Soviet Union in early 1945. About 120,000 Jews in Budapest survived the war, some because of the efforts of Raoul Wallenberg and other foreign diplomats. Because the Hungarian phase of the Holocaust occurred shortly before liberation, and because there were many survivors, more is known about it than about other aspects of the Nazi genocide. Nevertheless, much remains highly controversial and heavily debated, especially the alleged efforts of SS leaders Heinrich Himmler and Adolf Eichmann to "trade" hundreds of thousands of Jews for Allied trucks and supplies, and the role of Hungarian Jewish leaders like Rudolf Kastner in these alleged proposals. On the controversial issues relating to the Holocaust in Hungary, Braham has been extremely dubious of the suggestions by some historians, for example Yehuda Bauer, that a deal for Jewish lives with the Nazis was realistically possible, and has viewed Eichmann's alleged proposals for such a deal as a smokescreen to mislead Hungarian Jewry's Budapest leadership. *The Politics of Genocide* is also notable for the extraordinarily wide range of primary sources that Braham mastered, and is a monument of deep primary scholarship although it deals with events that occurred less than forty years before it was published.

Braham has also published numerous other books on the Holocaust, especially in Hungary, and has edited more than a dozen books of collected essays and documents in this field. Most recently he has edited *The Tragedy of Romanian Jewry* (1994), dealing with one of the least explored and most obscure phases of the Holocaust.

W.D. RUBINSTEIN

See also Holocaust

Biography

Randolph Lewis Braham. Born Bucharest, Romania, 20 December 1922; emigrated to US, 1948; naturalized 1953. Received BA, City College of New York, 1948, MS 1949; PhD, New School for Social Research, 1952. Research associate, YIVO-Institute for Jewish Studies, 1954–59; taught political science (rising to professor), City College (now City University) of New York, 1959–92; director, Institute for Holocaust Studies, City University of New York, from 1980. Married Elizabeth Sommer, 1954 (2 sons).

Principal Writings

The Hungarian Jewish Catastrophe: A Selected and Annotated Bibliography, 1962; revised 1984

The Destruction of Hungarian Jewry: A Documentary Account, 2 vols., 1963
Soviet Politics and Government: A Reader, 1965
Hungarian Jewish Studies, 2 vols., 1966–69
The Eichmann Case: A Source Book, 1969
The Politics of Genocide: The Holocaust in Hungary, 2 vols., 1981; revised 1994
Editor, *Social Justice*, 1981
Genocide and Retribution: The Holocaust in Hungarian-Ruled Northern Transylvania, 1983
The Holocaust in Hungary: Forty Years Later, 1985
Editor, *The Psychological Perspectives of the Holocaust and of Its Aftermath*, 1988
Editor, *The Tragedy of Romanian Jewry*, 1994

Braudel, Fernand 1902–1985
French socio-cultural historian

Fernand Braudel was a historian of encyclopedic knowledge and universal vision. According to one of his disciples, Georges Duby, Braudel's "monumental" contribution surpassed that of the twin founders of *annaliste* history – Marc Bloch and Lucien Febvre. Few 20th-century historians have exerted a more powerful influence over the discipline, an influence which was backed by the institutional authority of the 6th section of the Ecole Pratique des Hautes Etudes, an interdisciplinary research center which Braudel headed after 1956, and the Maison des Sciences de l'Homme, his home from 1962 until his death.

Braudel was 47 when he published the work that was to establish his international reputation, *La Méditerranée et le monde méditerranéen à l'époque de Philippe II* (1949; *The Mediterranean World in the Age of Philip II*, 1972–73). The most extraordinary fact about this extraordinary, exuberant work was that it was written, for the most part, during the author's five-year imprisonment during World War II. Some critics have explained the relegation of politics to the third and arguably least important section of the work by invoking the trauma, for France and Braudel, of the "strange defeat" of 1940. A more convincing explanation for the now-famous tripartite division of *La Méditerranée* was its long period of gestation in the 1920s and 1930s during which time Braudel was a highschool (*lycée*) teacher in Algiers, a researcher in the Spanish archives, then a university lecturer in Brazil. His friendship with Lucien Febvre, whom he met fortuitously on board the ship carrying them both back to Europe from Latin America in 1937, strengthened the interdisciplinary nature of Braudel's work, which was already founded upon the firm conviction that history was the *primus inter pares* of the social sciences. The decision to divide his work into three parts, with *la longue durée* representing the geographic and climatic forces acting upon the human species, *la moyenne durée* covering socio-economic factors, and *la courte durée*, the more fleeting influence of politics and diplomacy, elicited praise from many, criticism from a few, and imitation from hardly anyone. More than any of his works, perhaps, *The Mediterranean* places the author in a very French tradition which begins with the relativist Montesquieu and runs through sociologists and synthesizers like Emile Durkheim and Henry Berr.

In 1967, Braudel published volume one of his *Civilisation matérielle et capitalisme, XVe–XVIIIe siècle* (*Capitalism and*

Material Life, 1400–1800, 1973) to be followed a decade later by volume 2 which, to preserve the tripartite formula, was divided into two parts. Volume 3 is entitled, typically, "The Perspective of the World." Concentrating on the economic aspect of Western hegemony, and revealing Braudel's knowledge of the work of German scholars such as Werner Sombart, this volume charts the course of commerce between continents before focusing on the impact of the Industrial Revolution. *Civilisation and Capitalism* is both an act of homage to the transforming power of capitalism and a critique of the Marxist distinction between commercial and "modern" industrial capitalism. By adopting the universal and the *longue durée* approach, Braudel degutted the revolutionary content of the Marxist analysis of history and capitalism. Critics have suggested the methodology was adopted for precisely this reason.

Braudel's last, unfinished work, *L'Identité de la France* (1986; *The Identity of France,* 1988–90), is both his most personal and human but, in many respects, his least satisfying book. It is as if the weight of his profound love for and knowledge of France was too heavy for the overworked triadic, universalist, structuralist methodology. However, both completed volumes reveal the essential Braudel, with Romans and Barbarians clashing on the Vistula, Christians and Muslims battling it out in the Middle East, sweeps and cycles of history, neomarxist "infrastructures" and "superstructures." The time-scale is based on millennia and centuries, not decades and years. The fundamental concern (unlike that of Marx) is with geography and culture, the *bourg* and *patois: histoire totale* held in the wide embrace of time and place. France, somewhat romantically and nostalgically one feels, given the author's "peasant" roots, is seen as the invention of her geography, the product of her diverse cultural past, her peasant *mentalité* surviving the disruptive, and dehumanizing, impact of modern capitalism. Having finished the thousand pages, Maurice Barrès's dictum comes to mind: "Nous sommes la continuité du passé" (We are the heirs of the past). This last work reveals no weakening of the resolve to borrow freely from the social, and indeed the natural, sciences. We move from population studies to "palynology," paleontology to "retrospective hematology." Little wonder that Braudel found a warmer welcome – like *Annaliste* history in general – in America and Australia than in Britain, with its traditional Oxbridge concern for empirical, individualist historiography. It has been suggested that Rockefeller funds in the 1950s brought Braudel into the orbit of a "cultural Cold War," and that the Annales scholar was recruited – often unknowingly – for the battle of Western "civilization" against Eastern Marxist "barbarism."

And yet, for all the *structures* and *conjonctures,* for all the prioritization of Latin civilization, the existentialist striving of ordinary human beings can be traced throughout Braudel's oeuvre. A few years after his death, his wife and most loyal disciple, Paule Braudel, revealed the poetic vision that informed the work of her husband. In his early years he had expressed the wish to be a poet, and when asked about *The Mediterranean* he had explained that his ultimate objective was not, in essence, dissimilar from that of Matisse – to discover some form and meaning in the colors of life.

GWYNNE LEWIS

See also Anderson, P.; Annales School; Anthropology; Barkan; Basadre; Bloch; Blum; Boorstin; Burke; Cahen; Chaudhuri; Chevalier; China: Late Imperial; Cipolla; Consumerism; Conze; Environmental; Europe: Modern; France: 1000–1450; Góngora; González; Halperín-Donghi; Historiology; Hobsbawm; Kula; Labrousse; Le Roy Ladurie; Parker; Polanyi; Poliakov; Renouvin; Southeast Asia; Semple; Simiand; Social; Spain: Modern; Spain: Imperial; Stone; Vovelle; Wallerstein; World

Biography

Born Luméville-en-Ornois, Meuse, 24 August 1902. Educated at Lycée Voltaire, Paris; then studied at the Sorbonne, agrégation 1923, and PhD, 1947. Taught at University of Algiers, 1923–32; Lycée Condorcet and Lycée Henri IV, Paris, 1932–35; and University of São Paulo, 1935–38. Returned to France to be an instructor, 4th section, Ecole Pratique des Hautes Etudes, 1937–38, but was captured while serving during World War II and spent remainder of war in a German prisoner of war camp. Returned to the Sorbonne where he served as co-director and later director, *Annales,* 1946–85; professor, Collège de France, 1949–72; president, 6th section, Ecole Pratique des Hautes Etudes, 1956–72. Married Paule Pradel, 1933 (2 daughters). Died Saint-Gervais, Haute-Savoie, 28 November 1985.

Principal Writings

La Méditerranée et le monde méditerranéen à l'époque de Philippe II, 2 vols., 1949, revised 1966; in English as *The Mediterranean and the Mediterranean World in the Age of Philip II,* 2 vols., 1972–73

Civilisation matérielle et capitalisme, XVe–XVIIIe siècle, Paris: Colin, 1967, reprinted as vol. 1 of *Civilisation matérielle, économie et capitalisme, XVe–XVIII siècle,* 1979; in English as *Capitalism and Material Life, 1400–1800,* 1973

Ecrits sur l'histoire, 1969; in English as *On History,* 1980

"Personal Testimony," *Journal of Modern History* 44 (1972), 448–67

Afterthoughts on Material Civilization and Capitalism, 1977

Civilisation matérielle, économie et capitalisme, XVe–XVIIIe siècle, 3 vols., 1979; in English as *Civilization and Capitalism, 15th–18th Century,* 3 vols., 1981–84 [includes revised translation of *Capitalism and Material Life*]

L'Identité de la France, 2 vols. in 3, 1986; in English as *The Identity of France,* 2 vols., 1988–90

Grammaire des civilisations, 1987; in English as *A History of Civilizations,* 1994

Le modèle italien, 1989; in English as *Out of Italy, 1450–1650,* 1991

Further Reading

Bailyn, Bernard, "Braudel's Geohistory: A Reconsideration," *Journal of Economic History* 11 (1951), 277–82

Bessmertny, Youri, "Les *Annales* vues de Moscou" (The *Annales* as Seen from Moscow), *Annales: ESC* 47 (1992), 245–59

Braudel, Paule, "Braudel," in John Cannon, ed., *The Historian at Work,* London and Boston: Allen and Unwin, 1980

Braudel, Paule, "Les Origines intellectuelles de Fernand Braudel: un témoignage" (The Intellectual Origins of Fernand Braudel: A Testimony), *Annales: ESC* 47 (1992), 239–44

Gemelli, Giuliano, *Fernand Braudel e l'Europa universale* (Fernand Braudel and Universal Europe), Venice: Marsilio, 1990

Hexter, J.H., "Fernand Braudel and the *monde Braudelien*," *Journal of Modern History* 44 (1972), 480–539

Hunt, Lynn, "French History in the Last Twenty Years: The Rise and Fall of the Annales Paradigm," *Journal of Contemporary History* 21 (1986), 209–24

Kinser, Samuel, "Annaliste Paradigm? The Geohistorical Structuralism of Fernand Braudel," *American Historical Review* 86 (1981), 63–105

Péguy, C.-P., "L'Univers géographique de Fernand Braudel" (The Geographical Universe of Fernand Braudel), *Espaces-Temps* 34-35 (1986)

Trevor-Roper, Hugh, "Fernand Braudel, the Annales, and the Mediterranean," *Journal of Modern History* 44 (1972), 468-79

Wallerstein, Immanuel *et al.*, "The Impact of the *Annales* School on the Social Sciences," *Review* 2 (1978) [special issue]

Wesseling, H.L. *et al.*, "Fernand Braudel," *Itinerario* 5 (1981), 15-52

Brazil

Brazil's multicultural and multi-ethnic background has fascinated historians, economists, and other social scientists. After independence from Portugal, Brazil deviated from the typical patterns of social, political, and economic development that spread through the Spanish-speaking Latin American countries. Under a military government, the "Brazilian Miracle" of 1968-73 propelled the nation into the ranks of the world's largest economies. Scholars have sought to discern the unique pattern of development of the only Portuguese-speaking Latin American country.

This search has led to a study of Brazil's colonial past. In 1500, the fortuitous circumstance of a storm first brought the Portuguese to Brazil's shores. Initially, the Portuguese concentrated on their African and Asian possessions in the evolving Portuguese empire. Sebastião da Rocha Pita's *História da América portuguêsa* (The History of Portuguese America, 1730), the first general history of Brazil that covered the period from the discovery to 1724, incorporated some of the earliest accounts of Portuguese colonization of Brazil. The English, Portugal's steadfast ally, followed with Robert Southey's 3-volume classic *History of Brazil* (1810-19), the first history of Brazil written in English.

Twentieth-century scholars have also taken an interest in Brazil's early colonial history. Alexander Marchant's *From Barter to Slavery* (1942) examined the early contacts between the Indians and Portuguese, as well as the donatary captaincy system established by the Portuguese as a means to administer the new territories. Few scholars have continued the investigation of the important topic of early Portuguese and Indian encounters during the early years of colonization. The development of Portugal's Indian policy during the 17th century is explored in Mathias C. Kiemen's *The Indian Policy of Portugal in the Amazon Region, 1614-1693* (1954; revised 1973). This study probed the relationship between the church and state in the colonization and Europeanization of the Indians of the Amazon region. John Hemming's *Red Gold* (1978) extended the scope of this investigation to include the conquest of the Brazilian Indians to 1760, the year that the Portuguese crown expelled from Brazil the Jesuits, the religious order responsible for Indian welfare. His subsequent work, *Amazon Frontier* (1987), traced the history of the Amazon Indians' relationship with the Portuguese and their Brazilian descendants until 1910.

Sugar replaced Brazil's initial lucrative export – brazilwood – by the mid-16th century, as exploration and colonization continued. Various historians have explored the importance of sugar as the motor of the Brazilian colonial economy. This monoculture production required vast quantities of labor. Since Portuguese raiding on Indian villages did not fulfill the labor demand of the large landowners, importing African slaves became the solution for the problem of acquiring a reliable labor source. The three elements of a monoculture, slave labor, and large landholdings contributed to the rise of Brazil's plantation society and culture. The Brazilian-anthropologist-turned-historian Gilberto Freyre, with works such as *Casa-grande e senzala* (1933; *The Masters and the Slaves*, 1946), *Sobrados e mucambos* (1936; *The Mansions and the Shanties*, 1963), *Ordem e progresso* (1959; *Order and Progress*, 1970), and *Brazil: An Interpretation* (1945; revised as *New World in the Tropics*, 1959) provided an idyllic and relatively benign view of plantation society and culture in the formation of the Brazilian character. These works, the first two originally published in Brazil in the 1930s, influenced the work of numerous scholars, such as Frank Tannenbaum's *Slave and Citizen* (1946). This comparative work, although not exclusively about Brazilian slavery, utilized many Brazilian examples for Tannenbaum's thesis that Latin American slavery was milder than that of the southern United States. This difference emerged because Iberian laws regarding slavery still considered the slave a human being regardless of his position in the social order, while English law considered slaves to be property.

In the 1960s, many of Freyre's and Tannenbaum's conclusions came under closer scrutiny as a new focus emerged based on a closer analysis of archival sources. These historians called into question the notion that slavery in Brazil was milder than its United States counterpart. One important legacy of Freyre's work was that it directed attention away from the study of institutions and politics to an interest in social, economic, and cultural issues regarding slavery. Not much work has been done on the history of early colonial slavery in Brazil. Representative of these few studies is Stuart B. Schwartz's *Sugar Plantations in the Formation of Brazilian Society* (1985), which focused on northeast Brazil, the center of sugar production. It was a social history centered on the emergence of the plantation society that developed around sugar production. Besides its analysis of the system of slavery, it also presented a picture of the slaves themselves as they experienced that system. Kátia M. Queirós Mattoso's *Etre esclave au Brésil* (1979; *To Be a Slave in Brazil*, 1986) carried the investigation of the everyday life of the slave up to the abolition of the institution in 1888. Recently social history has also concentrated on the importance of the family, although few studies of the family during the colonial period exist. Alida C. Metcalf contributed to our understanding of the colonial family on the Brazilian frontier in her *Family and Frontier in Colonial Brazil* (1992). One particular aspect of the transfer of wealth from one generation to the next, the dowry, was examined by Muriel Nazzari in *Disappearance of the Dowry* (1991), which sought to explain why this institution disappeared by the end of the 19th century.

Portugal's control of the lucrative export, sugar, attracted other European powers to Brazil's shores. The Dutch were one of Portugal's most persistent European rivals for control of its overseas colonies and trade during the 17th century. Charles R. Boxer, the pre-eminent historian of this rivalry, investigated the period of the Dutch occupation of Brazil in *The Dutch in Brazil, 1624-1654* (1957) and in *Salvador de Sá and the Struggle for Brazil and Angola, 1602-1686* (1952). Besides studying this important period, Boxer also explored Brazil's role within Portugal's empire in *The Portuguese Seaborne Empire* (1969).

Before Portugal's union with Spain (1580–1640), Brazil's colonial administration developed slowly as a result of the concentration of its colonial population along the coast and the existence of an export, sugar, easily taxed in Lisbon. A.J.R. Russell-Wood treated one important early institution, the Santa Casa da Misericórdia of Bahia, a lay brotherhood that provided social services to Bahia's needy, in *Fidalgos and Philanthropists* (1968). Stuart B. Schwartz conducted a prosopographical study of the members of another early colonial institution, the High Court of Bahia, in *Sovereignty and Society in Colonial Brazil* (1973), demonstrating the dual relationship of the judges to the colonial bureaucracy and local society.

The discovery of gold in the 1690s transformed Brazil as the Portuguese crown shifted its attention to this relatively neglected colony with the growth of numerous mining centers. Boxer's *The Golden Age of Brazil, 1695–1750* (1962), a socioeconomic study of the various mining regions during the gold boom, is still the classic work on this period. During the 18th century, the influence of the Enlightenment, especially through the policies of the Marquis of Pombal, minister of state from 1750 to 1777, contributed to an administrative and economic reorganization of Portugal's American colony. In 1763, with the creation of a viceroyalty in Rio de Janeiro, the Portuguese crown recognized the shift of economic and political power from the northeast, in Pernambuco and Bahia, to southern Brazil, in Minas Gerais and Rio de Janeiro, as a result of the mining boom. Dauril Alden's *Royal Government in Colonial Brazil* (1968) is a study not only of the administration of the Marquis of Lavradio, viceroy from 1769 to 1779, but also of the development of Portuguese imperial policy from the discovery of Brazil to the early 19th century.

The first stirrings of Brazilian nationalism and the pursuit of independence occurred during the second half of the 18th and the early 19th centuries. In contemporary historiography one of the most important precursor movements of Brazilian independence was the *Inconfidência Mineira*. The eminent Brazilian historian João Capistrano de Abreu did not include this episode in his early masterful and influential work, *Capítulos de história colonial 1500–1800* (Chapters in Colonial History 1500–1800), originally published in 1907. Recent studies, such as Kenneth Maxwell's *Conflicts and Conspiracies* (1973), have given this plot a central role in the conflicts between colonial and metropolitan interest groups that engulfed Portugal's American colony as a result of Pombal's colonial policy.

Few historians have examined the pivotal transitional period from colony to kingdom to nation. In 1808, with the arrival of the Portuguese crown and court, fleeing Napoleon's army, Brazil's position within the empire changed dramatically as Rio de Janeiro became the capital of the Portuguese empire. Brazil's elevation within the empire contributed to the creation of a new sense of identity *vis-à-vis* Portugal and subsequent independence in 1822. Roderick Cavaliero's *The Independence of Brazil* (1993) covered the important transitional phases from 1808 to 1831. Significant in this transition was the formation of a national identity, ably treated in Roderick Barman's *Brazil* (1988), which examined the role the national elite played in creating the nation-state. Dom Pedro I, who established Brazil's constitutional monarchy, was responsible for the relatively smooth transition of Brazil from colony to nation by avoiding the disintegration that the Spanish American empire experienced. Neill Macaulay's 1986 biography offered a comprehensive analysis of the man and his reign. Originally written between 1962 and 1975, *The Brazilian Empire* (1985), a collection of essays in translation by Emília Viotti da Costa, examined and dispelled prior conclusions about the empire, especially those surrounding José Bonifácio de Andrada e Silva, the emperor's adviser and minister, credited with inspiring the idea of independence in Dom Pedro. In 1831, Dom Pedro I's abdication in favor of his son, Dom Pedro II, completed the transition to full Brazilian independence from Portugal.

The period of the regency, from 1831 to 1840, was especially critical as a result of numerous republican and separatist revolts. João José Reis' *Rebelião escrava no Brasil* (1986; *Slave Rebellions in Brazil*, 1993) investigated one – the most important urban slave rebellion – and also contributed to an understanding of slave life during this critical period. Mary C. Karasch also surveyed slave life during this period in *Slave Life in Rio de Janeiro, 1808–1850* (1987). Freyre and Tannenbaum are two figures that historians of slavery have had to contend with as a result of their earlier influential writing on the topic. Robert Toplin's *The Abolition of Slavery in Brazil* (1970) challenged Tannenbaum's thesis that Brazil abolished slavery in a gradual and peaceful manner. He argued that there was a radicalization of the abolitionists that threatened social and political upheaval. Other studies adding to our understanding of slavery, the slave trade, and its abolition under the empire are Leslie Bethell's *The Abolition of the Brazilian Slave Trade* (1970) as well as Robert Edgar Conrad's *The Destruction of Brazilian Slavery, 1850–1888* (1973) and *World of Sorrow* (1986). These works all attacked the idea of the benign nature of slavery and demonstrated its cruelty and inhumanity. Exploring the individual lives of 19th-century Afro-Brazilians remains much more difficult. Eduardo da Silva reconstructed the life and times of Candido da Fonseca Galvão, an Afro-Brazilian, in *Prince of the People* (1993), an important contribution that added a rich dimension to the understanding of the life of an Afro-Brazilian during the 19th century.

In 1840, Dom Pedro II ascended the throne and continued nation-state development along a more centralized path by reversing the federalist experiment attempted during the regency. When examining nation-state development during the Second Empire, scholars have focused on institutional studies. The National Guard, an institution created during the regency in 1831, played a pivotal role in guaranteeing order and as a counterweight to the regular army. Fernando Uricoechea's *The Patrimonial Foundations of the Brazilian Bureaucratic State* (1980) provided an analysis of this important institution utilizing the Weberian concept of patrimonial bureaucracy. Richard Graham's study, *Patronage and Politics in Nineteenth-Century Brazil* (1990), continued along the same line by examining patronage as an important mechanism in the functioning of the Second Empire. Eul-Soo Pang scrutinized the role of the economic and political elites in *In Pursuit of Honor* (1988) through an examination of the empire's titled nobility.

Another important pillar of the empire was the patriarchal family. Since the 1960s there has been a new emphasis on the study of the family influenced by Freyre's seminal work noting the significance of the patriarchal family in Brazilian history, an interpretation accepted by scholars until recently. Although still in its infancy, the new Brazilian family history has begun to question some of the assumptions of the patriarchal model, especially the nature of its predominance in society. Darrell Levi's *The Prados of São Paulo* (1987), an important study in the new Brazilian family history, examined the influence of one São Paulo elite family on the political, economic, and cultural life of the nation from 1840 to 1930. Another important study of the family during the late 19th century and the first half of the 20th century is Dain Borges' *The Family in Bahia, Brazil, 1870–1945* (1992), which explored the influence of the modern state on the evolution of the family.

To a limited extent, economic development during the second half of the 19th century has also interested historians searching for the roots of Brazil's economic development. Continuing the colonial export model of tropical products, coffee and sugar continued to play an important role for capital accumulation for subsequent investment in industrialization. When discussing economic development during the 19th century, many authors have followed a dependency approach for an explanation of the nation's experience. This approach highlighted the dominant role that Britain played in continuing a neocolonial model of economic development. Peter L. Eisenberg's *The Sugar Industry in Pernambuco* (1974) provided such an approach by examining how British demand in the 1840s stimulated sugar production, until the export crisis when European beet sugar replaced Brazilian sugar. As with most studies of the plantation economy, this one also took slavery into consideration, as the author examined the transition from slavery to free labor.

Coffee, another major export, also structured Brazilian economic development during the 19th century and entered into crisis through overproduction in the early 20th century. Stanley Stein's classic work *Vassouras* (1957) broke new ground as a result of his use of archival sources from the notarial offices and municipal councils. In the past, many historians had depended on the use of foreign observers and on similar primary and secondary sources. This ground-breaking study examined the effects of the world economy on the local level by concentrating on one municipality, Vassouras. It also called into question the predominant theme of earlier studies on the plantation about the benign nature of the master-slave relation.

Warren Dean, following Stein's lead, investigated a different coffee producing region in *Rio Claro* (1976). During the 1960s, there was a new emphasis in social history on writing history from below by concentrating on previously neglected social actors. Dean's work centered not only on the slaves but also on the immigrants who arrived during the mid-19th century. Verena Stolcke's *Coffee Planters, Workers, and Wives* (1988), a work of historical anthropology, also fixed on previously neglected social groups by studying the development of labor on the coffee plantations of western São Paulo. Also, since the 1960s and 1970s, there has been a focus on gender issues in historical studies as demonstrated by Stolcke's study. Another important contribution in the study of gender was June E. Hahner's *Emancipating the Female Sex* (1990), which explored the development of the women's movement in a social, economic, and political context. Hahner also offered another contribution to the literature on neglected social groups in her

study *Poverty and Politics* (1986). Instead of examining previously neglected rural social groups, she concentrated on the urban masses, especially those of Rio de Janeiro, in order to analyze how the urban poor transformed itself from an unorganized mob to an organized mass in order to pursue its interests. The work also scrutinized the elite's response to these efforts. Another contribution to the new social history focusing on gender and class issues was Sandra Lauderdale Graham's *House and Street* (1988) which exposed the lives of the female work force employed in domestic service. Another aspect of 19th-century social history that has captured historians' attention is that of the social construction of crime and the criminal. An important contribution to this field was Thomas H. Holloway's *Policing Rio de Janeiro* (1993), which surveyed the modernization of law enforcement as well as the influence of the elite on policing in order to maintain public order and protect private property. Elite and urban studies have also enhanced our understanding of the 19th century as can be seen in Jeffrey D. Needell's *A Tropical Belle Epoque* (1987), which analyzed the cultural dependency of Brazil's elite as it patterned itself on European models.

Historians have studied the boom/bust cycle of the Brazilian economy as an explanation for the country's underdevelopment. The Amazon rubber boom is the typical example that has fascinated many diverse individuals, scholars and laymen alike, since the boom brought fabulous prosperity for Brazil. Barbara Weinstein's *The Amazon Rubber Boom, 1850–1920* (1983), utilizing a dependency approach, studied the impact of the rubber boom on the lower Amazon and the city of Belém from the empire to the early 20th century. Environmental history, which examines the relationship of people and their environment, is a relatively new discipline. A study of the rubber boom provided many insights into the impact that people have had on their environment and vice versa. Warren Dean's environmental history, *Brazil and the Struggle for Rubber* (1987), explored the oft-cited story that it was the British removal of rubber seeds from Brazil that led to the bust of the rubber boom. Dean argued that it was biological factors that contributed to Brazil's inability to establish the rubber plantations needed for rational production and export in order to sustain the boom. In a monumental contribution to Latin American environmental history this author analyzed the destruction of Brazil's Atlantic forest from the colonial period to the present in *With Broadax and Firebrand* (1995), contributing to our overall understanding of the subject and providing many fertile avenues for further research.

During the empire there were also early efforts at incipient industrialization. Anyda Marchant's *Viscount Mauá and the Empire of Brazil* (1965) examined the role of one of the promoters of this industrialization, Irineu Evangelista de Sousa, Viscount Mauá. Stein explored the development of one industry, textile manufacturing, in his pioneering study *The Brazilian Cotton Manufacture* (1957) from the end of the 18th century to 1950. He probed the relationship of the industrialist-entrepreneur with the state, and the events that shaped that relationship. An important regional study on the relationship between coffee production and industrialization was Warren Dean's *The Industrialization of São Paulo, 1880–1945* (1969). It was the wealth generated by coffee production that contributed to industrialization and economic development.

The role of Britain in stimulating demand for Brazilian goods during the empire has been an area of particular importance since British investment stimulated export production. Alan K. Manchester's classic work *British Preëminence in Brazil* (1933) revealed how Britain utilized its Portuguese base in the colonial period to expand into Brazil. During the greater part of the 19th century, Britain maintained its supremacy until challenged by Germany at the end of that century and, finally, was replaced by the United States during the 20th century. Richard Graham in his pioneering work, *Britain and the Onset of Modernization in Brazil, 1850–1914* (1968), argued that the British were responsible for the spread of coffee culture in Brazil. The British played an ambiguous role in Brazil since their investments in the economy created the conditions for modernization but also led to the nation's underdevelopment. Scholars have paid scant attention to the role of British and other foreign merchants in Brazil's economic development during the 19th century. Eugene Ridings' important study *Business Interest Groups in Nineteenth-Century Brazil* (1994) filled in this lacuna in the literature. British investment in mining was treated by Marshall Eakin in *British Enterprise in Brazil* (1989), which challenged one of the dominant dependency theses that foreign concerns wielded inordinate political power in Brazil.

Historians have also gravitated to the study and explanation of the factors that led to the fall of the empire in 1889. Earlier studies suggested that the abolition of slavery without compensation had contributed to the downfall of the emperor in that he lost the support of an important group, the landowners. The military, which became an important institution in Brazilian politics after the War of the Triple Alliance (1865–70), played a decisive role in the overthrow of the emperor. The transition from empire to republic was traced through the life of one man, Marshal Mânoel Deodoro da Fonseca, the military officer responsible for the coup d'état against the emperor, in Charles Willis Simmons' *Marshal Deodoro and the Fall of Dom Pedro II* (1966). Studies on the military as an institution emerged in the 1960s as a result of the various military regimes that were in control in various Latin American countries, including Brazil. June Hahner explored the earlier political role played by the military in *Civilian-Military Relations in Brazil, 1889–1898* (1969), which looked at not only the role of the military in the coup d'état but also subsequent developments in the first decade of the First Republic (1889–1930) when civilian rule supplanted military rule.

One of the most curious episodes of this decade was the millenarian movement in Canudos led by Antônio the Counselor from 1893 to 1897 in the backlands of the state of Bahia. Historians of social banditry and millenarian movements, influenced by the works of E.J. Hobsbawm, conceived of the phenomena as a result of capitalist penetration and the breakdown of traditional society. Euclides da Cunha, a Brazilian journalist who followed the military expedition against Canudos, originally wrote about his experiences in *Os sertões* (1902; *Rebellion in the Backlands*, 1944). This work, a classic in Latin American literature, was also a statement about Brazilian nationalism as the author contended that the true Brazilian, the authentic Brazil, was in the backlands and not in the Europeanized urban centers of the coast. Robert M.

Levine's *Vale of Tears* (1992) gathered together much of the revisionist history on Canudos since da Cunha's classic work. Subsequently, the Peruvian novelist Mario Vargas Llosa fictionalized this episode in *The War of the End of the World* (1981, translated 1984). Another millenarian movement that has captured the attention of historians is the Contestado Rebellion of the early 20th century. Todd A. Diacon, in *Millenarian Vision, Capitalist Reality* (1991), explained this millenarian movement through examining the breakdown of the patron-client relationship resulting from the penetration of international capital into the Contestado region.

As a result of the political crisis of 1893, the coffee elite won the presidential elections of 1894, replacing the military and their middle sector allies in government. The coffee oligarchy, from the states of São Paulo, Minas Gerais, and Rio de Janeiro, would control the government for its own benefit for 36 years. Since 1945, historiography has increasingly focused on the First Republic and its political, social, and economic development. Previous historiography had considered the Brazilian state during the First Republic as a model of liberal economic development. Current research has demonstrated that the Brazilian state during this period was an interventionist one. Steven Topik's *The Political Economy of the Brazilian State, 1889–1930* (1987) argued that 1930 did not usher in a new period of state intervention in the economy, but continued a pattern of state intervention. Previous historiography had emphasized the heavy dominance of the coffee oligarchy over Brazil's economic development during the First Republic. The extent of that dominance has been questioned by Winston Fritsch in *External Constraints on Economic Policy in Brazil, 1889–1930* (1988), which analyzed the outside constraints on decisions concerning economic policy, such as working against the coffee planters' interests to placate the London and New York bankers in order to secure foreign capital.

Scholars have also analyzed this period's political history. The figure of the *coronel*, a local political boss, dominated political life in rural Brazil. Victor Nunes Leal's *Coronelismo* (1948; translated 1977) was a classic study by a Brazilian political scientist on the roots of local political control by the *coronéis*. Another important locus of regional political power in rural Brazil is the extended elite family or kinship group. Linda Lewin's *Politics and Parentela in Paraíba* (1987) examined this subject by studying the emergence of the cotton export sector in the state of Paraíba and the shifting *parentela* realignments on the level of state politics during the First Republic.

Other historians have also studied regionalism as a method of understanding Brazilian politics during the First Republic. During the First Republic, political power, centralized during the empire, shifted to the states. Therefore, one important aspect of this period was the heightened regionalism of this federal republic. An initial ground-breaking study was Joseph Love's *Rio Grande do Sul and Brazilian Regionalism, 1882–1930* (1978), initially a doctoral dissertation at Columbia University, an institution that has been at the forefront of Brazilian studies since the 1960s. The author's main thesis is that it is impossible to understand either national or regional politics in isolation. It is necessary to take into consideration the relationship between the two in order to have a deeper understanding of politics during the First Republic. Subsequently other studies emerged on important Brazilian regions as a result of a collaborative research effort between Love, Robert M. Levine, and John D. Wirth. Levine studied Pernambuco, one of the most important states in northeast Brazil, the previous dynamic sugar producing region, in *Pernambuco and the Brazilian Federation, 1889–1937* (1978), which suffered political and economic decline during the First Republic. Eul-Soo Pang has considered the other important northeastern state, Bahia, in *Bahia in the First Brazilian Republic* (1979), which explored the *coronéis* and the political system they developed in the state. Wirth wrote on Minas Gerais, a politically powerful state during this period, in *Minas Gerais and the Brazilian Federation, 1889–1937* (1977). Love examined São Paulo, the most politically and economically powerful state of the First Republic, in *São Paulo in the Brazilian Federation, 1889–1937* (1980). The author analyzed the relationship between the Paulista elite and its dependence on coffee as the Achilles heel that finally led to its downfall. These studies by Love, Levine, and Wirth, following a similar methodology, not only explored regionalism but also pondered questions about the states' political elites and the process of capitalist modernization.

The 1929 world economic crisis destroyed the stability of the First Republic since the nation was vulnerable to the economic fluctuations of the world market because of its heavy dependence on exports and foreign loans. In 1930, Getúlio Vargas came to power with the support of the urban bourgeois groups who were against the coffee oligarchy. The urban bourgeois groups blamed the coffee oligarchy for the depression. Besides the increased class antagonism, regional conflict increased contributing to a breakdown of the coffee oligarchy's alliance. The first important political symptom of the crisis of the First Republic was the *tenente's* (junior officers) revolt of 1922, which denounced the coffee oligarchy. In 1924, another military revolt broke out in São Paulo that eventually spread to other states. In Rio Grande do Sul, Captain Luis Carlos Prestes revolted and joined the Paulista, forming the Prestes column, which penetrated the interior of the country in an attempt to launch a peasant revolt. Neill Macaulay studied this episode in *The Prestes Column* (1974), which was the first English-language account of this important movement. Another important symptom presaging the ultimate crisis of the First Republic was the establishment of the Brazilian Communist party in 1922. The struggle between the communists and the anarchists for control of the working-class movement was examined in John W.F. Dulles, *Anarchists and Communists in Brazil, 1900–1935* (1973). Dulles continued his study of the Brazilian Communist party's role during the Vargas years in *Brazilian Communism, 1935–1945* (1983). The Brazilian Communist party has also attracted the attention of other historians such as Ronald Chilcote's *The Brazilian Communist Party* (1974), which covered the period from 1922 to 1972.

Vargas himself has received some attention from historians as demonstrated by John W.F. Dulles' *Vargas of Brazil* (1967), subtitled a political biography, which examined Vargas' role in Brazilian politics from 1930 until his suicide in 1954 in a chronological manner without any political, social, or economic analysis of the period. On the other hand, Robert M. Levine inspected Vargas' machinations to establish the centralized rule that would be embodied by the Estado Nôvo in *The Vargas Regime* (1970). Thomas E. Skidmore's *Politics in Brazil, 1930–1964* (1967), in his attempt to explain the 1964 coup, took into consideration Vargas and examined the 20-year period of democratic politics that followed the Estado Nôvo. In terms of regional politics during the period covered by Skidmore, Carlos E. Cortés analyzed the influence of Rio Grande do Sul on national politics in *Gaúcho Politics in Brazil* (1974).

Brazilian historiography considers 1930 a turning point as the state under Vargas instituted a policy of industrialization as a solution to the economic crisis. John Wirth analyzed the overall economic development of Brazil during the Vargas years (1930–1954) in *The Politics of Brazilian Development* (1970), emphasizing the three main issues of his economic policy during his two presidential administrations, foreign trade, steel, and petroleum. Particular industries have also been studied by historians. With the opening of the Volta Redonda steelworks, Vargas, as well as many other Brazilians, considered this step as symbolizing Brazil's economic emancipation. The steel industry, actively promoted by Vargas, was studied by Werner Baer in *The Development of the Brazilian Steel Industry* (1969), which investigated the development of the steel industry from the colonial period to the 1960s. Nathaniel Leff's *The Brazilian Capital Goods Industry, 1929–1964* (1968) examined theories of economic development in light of Brazil's capital goods industry and its relation to overall economic growth. Baer's *Industrialization and Economic Development in Brazil* (1965) provided an overall economic analysis of the period from 1945 to 1964 and the effects of industrialization on various sectors of the economy.

Labor history in the past twenty years has also contributed to our understanding of Brazilian history by investigating various aspects of the development of the Brazilian working class. Labor historians' research on the 20th-century working class allows us to understand how political, social, and economic factors contributed to this development. In an analysis of working-class politics from the 1930s to 1950s, John French's *The Brazilian Workers' ABC* (1992) explained the reasons that workers, in order to advance their interests, opted for supporting populist politicians, who often betrayed them. Another study concerning the São Paulo working class was Joel Wolfe's *Working Women, Working Men* (1993), which, by examining the role of textile workers and metalworkers, allowed the author to explore the issue of gender in the working-class movement. This study also explored the rise of factory commissions, first created by the female textile workers, as well as workers' support for Vargas.

After the coup of 1964, Brazil underwent a period of tremendous economic growth under the military governments that instituted a policy emphasizing foreign investment, industrialization, economic growth, and internal repression. Thomas E. Skidmore examined the effects of the 1964 coup in *The Politics of Military Rule, 1964–85* (1988), a sequel to his earlier study on Brazilian politics. He also explored the process of political liberalization that led to redemocratization in 1985. The role of business elites in recent Brazilian history is examined in Leigh Payne's *Brazilian Industrialists and Democratic Change* (1994), which surveyed the regime preferences of Brazil's capitalist class. Payne investigated the contention that one of the cornerstones of the military governments was Brazil's capitalist class by conducting a series of interviews with 155 São Paulo industrialists. She concludes that they did not have a firm commitment to authoritarian rule and have accepted the broader Brazilian democracy of the 1980s.

Much of the post-1964 historical literature has focused on Brazil's economic growth and subsequent economic crisis in the 1980s and 1990s. An excellent analysis of the overall economic development from the colonial period to the early 1990s was Werner Baer's *The Brazilian Economy* (4th edition, 1995). More specific studies have examined particular industries and their contribution to economic growth. Import-substitution and government intervention played an important role in Brazil's economic growth. In *Engines of Growth* (1994), Helen Shapiro analyzed the role of state intervention in attracting foreign investment for the development of a durable goods industry, concluding that the state's import-substitution policy was successful. Brazil's import-substitution policy was also studied by Jorge Chami Batista in *Debt and Adjustment Policies in Brazil* (1992), which examined the Segundo Plano Nacional de Desenvolvimento (Second National Development Plan) of the 1970s, an attempt to establish basic and capital goods industries through state investment. Keith Rosenn explores the costs of foreign investment in *Foreign Investment in Brazil* (1991) by analyzing the legal system regulating that investment. Brazil's economic growth also had its victims, namely the country's masses. In a study of Brazil's working class during this period, Salvador Sandoval, in *Social Change and Labor Unrest in Brazil since 1945* (1993), emphasized political factors over economic ones in the growth of labor militancy.

Historians of Brazil have been especially productive for the last thirty years and have examined many aspects of this complex and fascinating nation. Its cultural, political, social, and economic transformations, as well as the underlying continuities, have given rise to many questions and debates in the field. Many unexplored areas of its colonial, imperial, and national past still require research. Numerous questions are still open for exploration as Brazil enters a new phase of its history in the late 20th century with the attempt to establish a stable democracy.

CARLOS PÉREZ

See also Boxer; Cardoso; Degler; Freyre; Holanda; Latin America: National; Prado Júnior; Rodrigues; Slavery: Modern; Stein; Varnhagen; Women's History: Latin America

Further Reading

Abreu, João Capistrano de, *Capítulos de história colonial 1500–1800* (Chapters in Colonial History), Rio de Janeiro: Orosco, 1907; 7th edition, 1988
Alden, Dauril, *Royal Government in Colonial Brazil: With Special Reference to the Administration of the Marquis of Lavadio, Viceroy, 1769–1779*, Berkeley: University of California Press, 1968
Baer, Werner, *Industrialization and Economic Development in Brazil*, Homewood, IL: Irwin, 1965
Baer, Werner, *The Development of the Brazilian Steel Industry*, Nashville: Vanderbilt University Press, 1969
Baer, Werner, *The Brazilian Economy: Its Growth and Development*, Columbus, OH: Grid, 1979; 4th edition, *The Brazilian Economy: Growth and Development*, Westport, CT: Praeger, 1995
Barman, Roderick J., *Brazil: The Forging of a Nation, 1798–1852*, Stanford, CA: Stanford University Press, 1988
Batista, Jorge Chami, *Debt and Adjustment Policies in Brazil*, Boulder, CO: Westview Press, 1992

Bethell, Leslie, *The Abolition of the Brazilian slave trade: Britain, Brazil, and the Slave Trade, 1807–1869*, Cambridge: Cambridge University Press, 1970
Bethell, Leslie, ed., *Colonial Brazil*, Cambridge and New York: Cambridge University Press, 1987
Borges, Dain, *The Family in Bahia, Brazil, 1870–1945*, Stanford, CA: Stanford University Press, 1992
Boxer, C.R., *Salvador de Sá and the Struggle for Brazil and Angola, 1602–1686*, London: University of London Press, 1952
Boxer, C.R., *The Dutch in Brazil, 1624–1654*, Oxford: Clarendon Press, 1957
Boxer, C.R., *The Golden Age of Brazil, 1695–1750: Growing Pains of a Colonial Society*, Berkeley: University of California Press, 1962; reprinted 1995
Boxer, C.R., *The Portuguese Seaborne Empire, 1415–1825*, London: Hutchinson, and New York: Knopf, 1969
Burns, E. Bradford, *The Unwritten Alliance: Rio-Branco and Brazilian-American Relations*, New York: Columbia University Press, 1966
Burns, E. Bradford, ed., *Perspectives on Brazilian History*, New York: Columbia University Press, 1967
Burns, E. Bradford, *Nationalism in Brazil: A Historical Survey*, New York: Praeger, 1968
Burns, E. Bradford, *A History of Brazil*, New York: Columbia University Press, 1970; 3rd edition, 1993
Cavaliero, Roderick, *The Independence of Brazil*, London: British Academic Press, and New York: St. Martin's Press, 1993
Chandler, Billy Jaynes, *The Bandit King: Lampião of Brazil*, College Station: Texas A&M Press, 1978
Chilcote, Ronald H., *The Brazilian Communist Party: Conflict and Integration, 1922–72*, New York: Oxford University Press, 1974
Conrad, Robert Edgar, *The Destruction of Brazilian Slavery, 1850–1888*, Berkeley: University of California Press, 1973
Conrad, Robert Edgar, *Children of God's Fire: The Politics of Rio Grande do sul, 1930–64*, Princeton: Princeton University Press, 1983
Conrad, Robert Edgar, *World of Sorrow: The African Slave Trade to Brazil*, Baton Rouge: Louisiana State University Press, 1986
Cortés, Carlos E., *Gaúcho Politics in Brazil*, Albuquerque: University of New Mexico Press, 1974
Costa, Emília Viotti da, *The Brazilian Empire: Myths and Histories*, Chicago: University of Chicago Press, 1985
Cunha, Euclides da, *Os sertões*, Rio de Janeiro: Laemmert, 1902, reprinted 1946; in English as *Rebellion in the Backlands*, Chicago: University of Chicago Press, 1944
Dean, Warren, *The Industrialization of São Paulo, 1880–1945*, Austin: University of Texas Press, 1969
Dean, Warren, *Rio Claro: A Brazilian Plantation System, 1820–1920*, Stanford, CA: Stanford University Press, 1976
Dean, Warren, *Brazil and the Struggle for Rubber: A Study in Environmental History*, Cambridge and New York: Cambridge University Press, 1987
Dean, Warren, *With Broadax and Firebrand: The Destruction of the Brazilian Atlantic Forest*, Berkeley: University of California Press, 1995
Degler, Carl N., *Neither Black nor White: Slavery and Race Relations in Brazil and the United States*, New York: Macmillan, 1971
Denslow, David, *Sugar Production in Northeast Brazil and Cuba, 1858–1900*, New York: Garland, 1987
Diacon, Todd A., *Millenarian Vision, Capitalist Reality: Brazil's Contestado Rebellion, 1912–1916*, Durham, NC: Duke University Press, 1991
Diffie, Bailey Wallys, *A History of Colonial Brazil, 1500–1792*, Malabar, FL: Krieger, 1987
Dulles, John W.F., *Vargas of Brazil: A Political Biography*, Austin: University of Texas Press, 1967
Dulles, John W.F., *Anarchists and Communists in Brazil, 1900–1935*, Austin: University of Texas Press, 1973

Dulles, John W.F., *Brazilian Communism, 1935–1945: Repression during World Upheaval*, Austin: University of Texas Press, 1983

Duncan, Julian, *Public and Private Operation of Railways in Brazil*, New York: Columbia University Press, and London: King, 1932

Eakin, Marshall Craig, *British Enterprise in Brazil: The St. John d'el Rey Mining Company and the Morro Velho Gold Mine, 1830–1960*, Durham, NC: Duke University Press, 1989

Eisenberg, Peter L., *The Sugar Industry in Pernambuco: Modernization without Change, 1840–1910*, Berkeley: University of California Press, 1974

Evans, Peter B., *Dependent Development: The Alliance of Multinational, State and Local Capital in Brazil*, Princeton: Princeton University Press, 1979

French, John, *The Brazilian Workers' ABC: Class Conflict and Alliances in Modern São Paulo*, Chapel Hill: University of North Carolina Press, 1992

Freyre, Gilberto, *Casa-grande e senzala: formação da família brasileira sob o regime de economia patriarcal*, Rio de Janeiro: Maia & Schmidt, 1933; in English as *The Masters and the Slaves: A Study in the Development of Brazilian Civilization*, New York: Knopf, 1946, London: Secker and Warburg, 1947

Freyre, Gilberto, *Sobrados e mucambos: decadência do patriarcado rural e desenvolvimento do urbano*, São Paulo: Nacional, 1936; in English as *The Mansions and the Shanties: The Making of Modern Brazil*, New York: Knopf, 1963

Freyre, Gilberto, *Brazil: An Interpretation*, New York: Knopf, 1945; revised as *New World in the Tropics: The Culture of Modern Brazil*, 1959

Freyre, Gilberto, *Ordem e progresso*, 2 vols., Rio de Janeiro: Olympio, 1959; in English as *Order and Progress: Brazil from Monarchy to Republic*, New York: Knopf, 1970, London: Secker and Warburg, 1972

Fritsch, Winston, *External Constraints on Economic Policy in Brazil, 1889–1930*, Pittsburgh: University of Pittsburgh Press, 1988

Furtado, Celso, *Formação econômica do Brasil*, Rio de Janeiro: Cultura, 1959, 17th edition 1980; in English as *The Economic Growth of Brazil: A Survey from Colonial to Modern Times*, Berkeley: University of California Press, 1963

Graham, Richard, *Britain and the Onset of Modernization in Brazil, 1850–1914*, Cambridge: Cambridge University Press, 1968

Graham, Richard, "Brazil: The National Period," in Roberto Esquenazi-Mayo and Michael C. Meyer, eds., *Latin American Scholarship since World War II*, Lincoln: University of Nebraska Press, 1971

Graham, Richard, *Patronage and Politics in Nineteenth-Century Brazil*, Stanford, CA: Stanford University Press, 1990

Graham, Sandra Lauderdale, *House and Street: The Domestic World of Servants and Masters in Nineteenth-Century Rio de Janeiro*, Cambridge: Cambridge University Press, 1988; Austin: University of Texas Press, 1992

Hahner, June Edith, *Civilian-Military Relations in Brazil, 1889–1898*, Columbia: University of South Carolina Press, 1969

Hahner, June Edith, *Poverty and Politics: The Urban Poor in Brazil, 1870–1920*, Albuquerque: University of New Mexico Press, 1986

Hahner, June Edith, *Emancipating the Female Sex: The Struggle for Women's Rights in Brazil, 1850–1940*, Durham, NC: Duke University Press, 1990

Hemming, John, *Red Gold: The Conquest of the Brazilian Indians*, Cambridge, MA: Harvard University Press, and London: Macmillan, 1978

Hemming, John, *Amazon Frontier: The Defeat of the Brazilian Indians*, Cambridge, MA: Harvard University Press, and London: Macmillan, 1987

Holloway, Thomas H., *The Brazilian Coffee Valorization of 1906: Regional Politics and Economic Dependence*, Madison: University of Wisconsin Press, 1975

Holloway, Thomas H., *Immigrants on the Land: Coffee and Society in São Paulo, 1886–1934*, Chapel Hill: University of North Carolina Press, 1980

Holloway, Thomas H., *Policing Rio de Janeiro: Repression and Resistance in a Nineteenth-Century City*, Stanford, CA: Stanford University Press, 1993

Karasch, Mary C., *Slave Life in Rio de Janeiro, 1808–1850*, Princeton: Princeton University Press, 1987

Kiemen, Mathias Charles, *The Indian Policy of Portugal in the Amazon Region, 1614–1693*, Washington, DC: Catholic University of America Press, 1954; revised New York: Octagon, 1973

Lang, James, *Portuguese Brazil: The King's Plantation*, New York: Academic Press, 1979

Leal, Victor Nunes, *Coronelismo: enxada e voto: o município e o regime representativo no Brasil*, Rio de Janeiro, 1948; in English as *Coronelismo: The Municipality and Representative Government in Brazil*, Cambridge and New York: Cambridge University Press, 1977

Leff, Nathaniel H., *The Brazilian Capital Goods Industry, 1929–1964*, Cambridge, MA: Harvard University Press, 1968

Leff, Nathaniel H., *Underdevelopment and Development in Brazil*, Boston and London: Allen and Unwin, 1982

Levi, Darrell E., *The Prados of São Paulo: An Elite Family and Social Change, 1840–1930*, Athens: University of Georgia Press, 1987

Levine, Robert M., *The Vargas Regime: The Critical Years, 1934–1938*, New York: Columbia University Press, 1970

Levine, Robert M., *Pernambuco and the Brazilian Federation, 1889–1937*, Stanford, CA: Stanford University Press, 1978

Levine, Robert M., *Vale of Tears: Revisiting the Canudos Massacre in Northeastern Brazil, 1893–1897*, Berkeley: University of California Press, 1992

Lewin, Linda, *Politics and Parentela in Paraíba: A Case Study of Family-Based Oligarchy in Brazil*, Princeton: Princeton University Press, 1987

Lockhart, James, and Stuart B. Schwartz, *Early Latin America: A History of Colonial Spanish America and Brazil*, Cambridge and New York: Cambridge University Press, 1983

Love, Joseph L., *Rio Grande do Sul and Brazilian Regionalism, 1882–1930*, Stanford, CA: Stanford University Press, 1978

Love, Joseph L., *São Paulo in the Brazilian Federation, 1889–1937*, Stanford, CA: Stanford University Press, 1980

Luz, Nicia Villela, "Brazil" in Roberto Cortés Conde and Stanley J. Stein, eds., *Latin America: A Guide to Economic History, 1830–1930*, Berkeley: University of California Press, 1977

Macaulay, Neill, *The Prestes Column: Revolution in Brazil*, New York: New Viewpoints, 1974

Macaulay, Neill, *Dom Pedro: The Struggle for Liberty in Brazil and Portugal, 1798–1834*, Durham, NC: Duke University Press, 1986

McDowall, Duncan, *The Light: Brazilian Traction, Light and Power Company Limited, 1899–1945*, Toronto: University of Toronto Press, 1988

Manchester, Alan Krebs, *British Preëminence in Brazil, Its Rise and Decline: A Study in European Expansion*, Chapel Hill: University of North Carolina Press, 1933

Marchant, Alexander, *From Barter to Slavery: The Economic Relations of Portuguese and Indians in the Settlement of Brazil, 1500–1580*, Baltimore: Johns Hopkins Press, 1942

Marchant, Alexander, "The Unity of Brazilian History" in Howard F. Cline, ed., *Latin American History: Essays on Its Study and Teaching, 1898–1965*, vol. 2, Austin: University of Texas Press, 1967

Marchant, Anyda, *Viscount Mauá and the Empire of Brazil: A Biography of Irineu Evangelista de Sousa, 1813–1889*, Berkeley: University of California Press, 1965

Mattoso, Kátia M. de Queirós, *Etre esclave au Brésil: XVIe–XIXe*, Paris: Hachette, 1979; in English as *To Be a Slave in Brazil, 1550–1888*, New Brunswick, NJ: Rutgers University Press, 1986

Mauro, Frédéric, "Recent Works on the Political Economy of Brazil in the Portuguese Empire," *Latin American Research Review* 19 (1984), 87–105

Maxwell, Kenneth, *Conflicts and Conspiracies: Brazil and Portugal, 1750–1808*, Cambridge: Cambridge University Press, and New York: New York University Press, 1973

Metcalf, Alida C., *Family and Frontier in Colonial Brazil: Santana de Parnaíba, 1580–1822*, Berkeley: University of California Press, 1992

Morse, Richard M., "Some Themes of Brazilian History" in Howard F. Cline, ed., *Latin American History: Essays on Its Study and Teaching, 1898–1965*, vol. 2, Austin: University of Texas Press, 1967

Nazzari, Muriel, *Disappearence of the Dowry: Women, Families, and Social Change in São Paulo, Brazil, 1600–1900*, Stanford, CA: Stanford University Press, 1991

Needell, Jeffrey D., *A Tropical Belle Epoque: The Elite Culture of Turn-of-the-Century Rio de Janeiro*, Cambridge and New York: Cambridge University Press, 1987

Pang, Eul-Soo, *Bahia in the First Brazilian Republic: Coronelismo and Oligarchies, 1889–1934*, Gainesville: University Presses of Florida, 1979

Pang, Eul-Soo, *In Pursuit of Honor: Noblemen of the Southern Cross in Nineteenth Century Brazil*, Tuscaloosa: University of Alabama Press, 1988

Payne, Leigh A., *Brazilian Industrialists and Democratic Change*, Baltimore: John Hopkins University Press, 1994

Pereira, Luiz Carlos Bresser, *Desenvolvimento e crise no Brasil entre 1930 e 1967*, Rio de Janeiro: Zahar, 1968; revised in English as *Development and Crisis in Brazil, 1930–1983*, Boulder, CO: Westview Press, 1984

Prado Júnior, Caio, *A revolução brasileira* (The Brazilian Revolution), São Paulo: Editôra Brasiliense, 1966

Reis, João José, *Rebelião escrava no Brasil: a história do levante dos malês, 1835*, São Paulo: Brasiliense, 1986; in English as *Slave Rebellions in Brazil: The Muslim Uprising of 1835 in Bahia*, Baltimore: Johns Hopkins University Press, 1993

Ridings, Eugene, *Business Interest Groups in Nineteenth-Century Brazil*, New York and Cambridge: Cambridge University Press, 1994

Rocha Pita, Sebastião da, *História da América portuguêsa* (The History of Portuguese America), 1730

Rosenn, Keith S., *Foreign Investment in Brazil*, Boulder, CO: Westview Press, 1991

Russell-Wood, A.J.R., *Fidalgos and Philanthropists: The Santa Casa de Misericórdia of Bahia, 1550–1755*, Berkeley: University of California Press, 1968

Russell-Wood, A.J.R., *The Black Man in Slavery and Freedom in Colonial Brazil*, New York: St. Martin's Press, and London: Macmillan, 1982

Russell-Wood, A.J.R., "United States Contribution to the Historiography of Colonial Brazil," *Hispanic American Historical Review* 65 (1985), 683–723

Sandoval, Salvador A.M., *Social Change and Labor Unrest in Brazil since 1945*, Boulder, CO: Westview Press, 1993

Schwartz, Stuart B., "Brazil: The Colonial Period," in Roberto Esquenazi-Mayo and Michael C. Meyer, eds., *Latin American Scholarship since World War II*, Lincoln: University of Nebraska Press, 1971

Schwartz, Stuart B., *Sovereignty and Society in Colonial Brazil: The High Court of Bahia and its Judges, 1609–1751*, Berkeley: University of California Press, 1973

Schwartz, Stuart B., *Sugar Plantations in the Formation of Brazilian Society: Bahia, 1550–1835*, Cambridge and New York: Cambridge University Press, 1985

Schwartz, Stuart B., *Slaves, Peasants, and Rebels: Reconsidering Brazilian Slavery*, Urbana: University of Illinois Press, 1992

Seckinger, Ron, *The Brazilian Monarchy and the South American Republics, 1822–1831*, Baton Rouge: Louisiana State University Press, 1984

Shapiro, Helen, *Engines of Growth: The State and Transnational Auto Companies*, Cambridge and New York: Cambridge University Press, 1994

Silva, Eduardo da, *Prince of the People: The Life and Times of a Brazilian Free Man of Colour*, London and New York: Verso, 1993

Simmons, Charles Willis, *Marshal Deodoro and the Fall of Dom Pedro II*, Durham, NC: Duke University Press, 1966

Skidmore, Thomas E., *Politics in Brazil, 1930–1964: An Experiment in Democracy*, New York: Oxford University Press, 1967

Skidmore, Thomas E., "The Historiography of Brazil, 1889–1964" *Hispanic American Historical Review*, part 1: 55 (1975), 716–48; part 2: 56 (1976), 81–109

Skidmore, Thomas E., *The Politics of Military Rule, 1964–85*, New York: Oxford University Press, 1988

Southey, Robert, *History of Brazil*, 3 vols., London: Longman, 1810–19

Stein, Stanley J., *The Brazilian Cotton Manufacture: Textile Enterprise in an Underdeveloped Area, 1850–1950*, Cambridge, MA: Harvard University Press, 1957

Stein, Stanley J., *Vassouras: A Brazilian Coffee County, 1850–1900: The Roles of Planter and Slave in a Plantation Society*, Cambridge, MA: Harvard University Press, 1957

Stein, Stanley J., *The Historiography of Brazil, 1808–1889*, Durham, NC: Duke University, 1960

Stolcke, Verena, *Coffee Planters, Workers, and Wives: Class Conflict and Gender Relations on São Paulo Plantations, 1850–1980*, New York: St. Martin's Press, and London: Macmillan, 1988

Sweigart, Joseph, *Coffee Factorage and the Emergence of a Brazilian Capital Market, 1850–88*, New York: Garland, 1987

Tannenbaum, Frank, *Slave and Citizen: The Negro in the Americas*, New York: Knopf, 1946

Topik, Steven, *The Political Economy of the Brazilian State, 1889–1930*, Austin: University of Texas Press, 1987

Topik, Steven, "History of Brazil," in Paula H. Covington and David Block, eds., *Latin America and the Caribbean: A Critical Guide to Research Sources*, New York: Greenwood Press, 1992

Toplin, Robert Brent, *The Abolition of Slavery in Brazil*, Cambridge: Cambridge University Press, 1970; New York: Atheneum, 1972

Trebat, Thomas J., *Brazil's State-Owned Enterprises: A Case Study of the State as Entrepreneur*, Cambridge and New York: Cambridge University Press, 1983

Uricoechea, Fernando, *The Patrimonial Foundations of the Brazilian Bureacratic State*, Berkeley: University of California Press, 1980

Vargas Llosa, Mario, *La guerra del fin del mundo*, Barcelona: Seix Barral, 1981; in English as *The War of the End of the World*, New York: Farrar Straus, 1984, London: Faber, 1985

Vianna Moog, Clodomir, *Bandeirantes e pioneiros: paralelo hetre duas culturas*, Rio de Janeiro: Globo, 1954; in English as *Bandeirantes and Pioneers*, New York: Braziller, 1964

Weinstein, Barbara, *The Amazon Rubber Boom, 1850–1920*, Stanford, CA: Stanford University Press, 1983

Wirth, John D., *The Politics of Brazilian Development, 1930–1954*, Stanford, CA: Stanford University Press, 1970

Wirth, John D., *Minas Gerais and the Brazilian Federation, 1889–1937*, Stanford, CA: Stanford University Press, 1977

Wolfe, Joel, *Working Women, Working Men: São Paulo and the Rise of Brazil's Industrial Working Class, 1900–1955*, Durham, NC: Duke University Press, 1993

Breasted, James Henry 1865–1935
US Orientalist

James Henry Breasted was America's first Egyptologist and the greatest Orientalist of his generation in his country. His works were pioneering and remain fundamental. Only 78 years after Champollion had cracked the code of the hieroglyphs, the young graduate spent some six years in European libraries and in an epigraphical survey of Egypt and Nubia to collect and translate all the sources for Egyptian history. The first scientific dictionary of Egyptian was still in progress, so he compiled his own as he went. The five resulting volumes, *Ancient Records of Egypt* (1906–07) were published by the time Breasted was forty and would have been creditable as a life's work. The translations have stood the test of time, and there has been no replacement for English-language students.

Having collected the sources, he then wrote the history. *A History of Egypt* appeared first in 1905, and was the first such history in a modern sense. Breasted was able to use some work of predecessors, such as his teacher Erman, and Meyer, Maspero, and Wiedemann, but his major forerunner in English was Petrie, whose history was simply a catalogue of kings and monuments. Breasted's was history in the widest sense, with political, military, and architectural events as a framework, and a full description of the social, religious, and cultural development of Egypt. The main documentation was his own *Ancient Records*. His ability to breathe life into such scattered and fragmentary sources amazed contemporary scholars, and the famous elegance of his style was already apparent. *A History of Egypt* was translated into German by Ranke, French by Moret, into Russian and Arabic, and there was also a Braille edition. A second edition appeared in 1909, and it was endlessly reprinted.

In *A History of Egypt* Breasted stated that the study of Egyptian religion had barely begun, and that it would be decades before a survey would be possible. Seven years later he wrote it. The *Development of Religion and Thought in Ancient Egypt* (1912) began as the Morse lectures. More than half the book is devoted to the most difficult texts of all, the Pyramid Texts, which Sethe had begun to publish in 1908. The more than 700 "spells" are a vast mixture of funerary rituals, magical charms, ancient rites, hymns, prayers, and myths. Breasted's genius was in disentangling the many strata going back to prehistoric times, in order to give a coherent account of Egyptian religion in the third millennium. He demonstrated the conflict between the Solar and Osirian cults for control of the dead king, but more importantly the growth of moral concepts, "perhaps the most fundamental step in the evolution of civilisation." Here he discussed the many examples of "Wisdom literature" which he had excluded from his *Records*. It was Breasted who gave the name "Coffin Texts" to the Middle Kingdom funerary texts from the period when the Osirian cult triumphed, and he traced the changing rituals from the Pyramid Texts through to the "Book of the Dead." Breasted's fundamental interest in moral development is shown in his regret that the Solar cult was overtaken; the cult stressed morality during life and not merely after death, and that morality was circumvented by resort to magic to overcome the perils of the afterlife, including the final judgment. The book ends with the figure who held such fascination for Breasted, Akhenaton, the first monotheist, the first individual in history.

These themes were restudied in the later more popular *The Dawn of Conscience* (1933), which was devoted to the analysis of the contribution of Egyptian to Hebrew thought. In this Breasted firmly rejected the interpretations of human history by pessimists such as Spengler.

During his early career as a university teacher, Breasted had had to eke out his meager salary by endless public lectures. In 1916 he published one of the best-selling history books of the century (selling up to 120,000 copies a year), *Ancient Times*, a history of the ancient world from the stone ages to the barbarian invasions. It was remarkable for the hundreds of illustrations, all fully explained, and dozens of maps. Not merely political history, it paid attention to economics, thought, art, literature, and everyday life. Its influence was enormous; it did more than any other single work to propagate a general knowledge of the debt of modern civilization to the Ancient Near East; with its stress on sources it was a fine training manual for students; it was read with pleasure by multitudes and translated into Arabic and Swedish and a shorter version into Japanese and Malay; and it was instrumental in bringing forth vast sums of money for Near Eastern archaeology. Imbued with Breasted's humanist ideals, it was cited by both sides in the Scopes' trial on teaching evolution in schools in 1925.

Although Breasted's life after this was largely devoted to administration, honorable place is held by his translation of one of the most difficult of all texts, the Edwin Smith Surgical Papyrus, dating from the 17th century BCE, but perhaps going back to the third millennium, and called by Breasted "the earliest known scientific document." The vast edition with translation and commentary took him ten years; he was assisted by Arno Luckhardt. Once again there was no extant glossary for such technical terms in ancient Egyptian.

The realization that so little remained from so many centuries of Egyptian history convinced Breasted that every effort had to be made to find more material. He convinced John Rockefeller Jr. to provide vast sums of money and the result was the Oriental Institute, established in 1919. By the time of Breasted's death it was working in Egypt, Iraq, Syria, Palestine, Anatolia, and Iran. As its director Breasted was the greatest organizer of archaeological research the world had yet seen, and the results of its work have revolutionized our understanding of the history of the Near East.

Breasted devoted his life to the reconstruction of the earliest history of mankind, and to mapping the development of human nature. If he had a weakness it was his predilection for the Egyptians, but he expanded his interests to take in the entire preclassical world.

RONALD T. RIDLEY

See also Egypt: Ancient; Near East

Biography

Born Rockford, Illinois, 27 August 1865. Educated at North Central College, BA 1888; Chicago College of Pharmacy; Chicago Theological Seminary, 1888–90; Yale University, MA 1892; University of Berlin, PhD 1894. At University of Chicago: assistant in Egyptology, 1894–96; assistant director, Haskell Oriental Museum, 1895–1901, director, 1901–31; taught Egyptology and Semitic languages (rising to professor of Egyptology and Oriental history), 1896–1933 (emeritus); director, Oriental Institute, 1919–35. Married Frances Hart, 1894 (2 sons, 1 daughter). Died New York, 2 December 1935.

Principal Writings

A History of Egypt, from the Earliest Times to the Persian Conquest, 1905; revised 1909

Ancient Records of Egypt, 5 vols., 1906–07

The Development of Religion and Thought in Ancient Egypt, 1912

Ancient Times: A History of the Early World, 1916
The Edwin Smith Surgical Papyrus, 2 vols., 1930
The Dawn of Conscience, 1933

Further Reading

Bierbrier, M., ed., *Who Was Who in Egyptology*, London: Egypt Exploration Society, 1995

Breasted, Charles, *Pioneer to the Past: The Story of James Henry Breasted, Archaeologist*, New York: Scribner, 1943; London: Jenkins, 1948

Wilson, John A., *Signs and Wonders upon Pharaoh: A History of American Egyptology*, Chicago: University of Chicago Press, 1964

Brenner, Robert 1943–

US economic historian

When Robert Brenner published his article "Agrarian Class Structure and Economic Development in Pre-Industrial Europe" in *Past and Present* in 1976, he sparked one of the liveliest debates in the long and distinguished history of that journal. The article fired salvos at two major targets: neo-Smithians who proposed urban commerce as the primary solvent of agrarian feudalism, and neo-Malthusians who argued for the primacy of demographic trends in early modern economic history. The pull of markets and the pressures of population must be understood, Brenner argued, within a larger context conditioned by class and property relations. His article offered a fresh perspective on the old problem of "the transition from feudalism to capitalism." But where Marxists had traditionally directed their attention toward the revolutionary role of the bourgeoisie, Brenner focused his analysis on the conflict between landlords and peasants. In England, he suggested, the aristocracy was the principal agent of the breakthrough to modernity.

How and why did the breakthrough occur first in England? Feudalism, for Brenner, was a system of surplus-extraction based on coercion, the lords' ability to subject peasants to arbitrary levies and prohibitions. According to the neo-Malthusian model, this system broke down in Western Europe during the 14th and 15th centuries in the aftermath of plague and demographic collapse: peasants used their own scarcity to improve their bargaining position and to win their freedom. But the outcome varied in different regions, according to Brenner, depending upon the relative strength of the contending classes and their allies. In England, the lords were too weak to re-impose serfdom and the crown was too weak to impose absolutism. But the lords were strong enough to prevent their customary tenants from achieving full property rights to plots of land. Rising rents enabled them to evict the majority of their tenants and to subject the rest to competition for leases. This competition, in turn, encouraged innovation, efficiency, and production for the market rather than subsistence agriculture. Here was the crucial breakthrough: no longer a zero-sum game of surplus-extraction, but a symbiotic relationship between profit-oriented landlords and improving tenants.

Agrarian capitalism in England, then, was the unintended result of the landlords' search for higher revenues from their increasingly large estates. Elsewhere in Europe, tax-paying peasants were able to achieve partial property rights while the state compensated the nobility with offices and privileges (France), or the peasants were dispossessed completely as the lords were strong enough to impose serfdom (Eastern Europe). In either case political absolutism was accompanied by continuing agricultural crisis. One of the strengths of Brenner's account was its insistence on comparative analysis, and each successive article deepened and extended the argument to encompass eventually all of the regions of Europe.

In England the failure of the peasants to establish property rights deprived the monarchy of a potential financial base in the peasantry (the French pattern). Instead, the crown depended on the support of the landed classes represented in Parliament, and on revenues derived from taxes on overseas traders. Brenner's second major contribution was a long-awaited study of these overseas traders and the role they played in the politics of the English revolution and civil war. *Merchants and Revolution*, published in 1993, was based on Brenner's doctoral dissertation completed in 1970. It was dedicated to his dissertation supervisor, Lawrence Stone, and it applied to London's overseas traders the same method Stone had used so brilliantly in his classic studies of the aristocracy: prosopography, the biography of a group. Having examined lords and peasants in a series of path-breaking articles on the roots of agrarian capitalism, Brenner now turned his attention to merchant capitalism. There was, in Stuart England, a revolutionary bourgeoisie after all: that sector of London's merchant community, intricately bound by ties of kinship and partnership, which owed its fortunes to the American trade. These "new merchants," accustomed to risk, were allied with one of the major factions in Parliament, and they enjoyed close relations with the London populace as well. For Brenner this hitherto overlooked coalition was at once the sparkplug and the pacemaker of the English revolution.

Brenner has intervened decisively in two classic historiographical debates: on the transition from feudalism to capitalism, and on the bourgeois revolution. In the first case he employed the combination of a wide-ranging comparative method and close attention to specific historical patterns of development; in the second, detailed archival investigation of intricate biographical networks. In both cases, he has offered densely textured examples of class analysis. With Eric Hobsbawm, Victor Kiernan, and Perry Anderson (who gave us the most searching appreciation of *Merchants and Revolution*), Brenner is among the most original and accomplished historians still at work in the Marxist tradition.

BRUCE THOMPSON

See also Le Roy Ladurie; Marxist Interpretation; Poland: to the 18th Century

Biography

Robert Paul Brenner. Born New York City, 28 November 1943. Received BA, Reed College, 1964; MA, Princeton University, 1966; PhD 1970. Taught at University of California, Los Angeles, from 1968.

Principal Writings

"The Social Basis of English Commercial Expansion, 1550–1650," *Journal of Economic History* 32 (March 1972), 361–84

"The Civil War Politics of London's Merchant Community," *Past and Present* 58 (February 1973), 53–107

"Agrarian Class Structure and Economic Development in Pre-Industrial Europe," *Past and Present* 70 (February 1976), 30–74

"The Origins of Capitalist Development: A Critique of Neo-Smithian Marxism," *New Left Review* 104 (July–August 1977), 25–92

"Dobb on the Transition from Feudalism to Capitalism," *Cambridge Journal of Economics* 2 (1978), 121–40

"The Agrarian Roots of European Capitalism," *Past and Present* 97 (November 1982), 16–113

"Bourgeois Revolution and Transition to Capitalism," in A.L. Beier, David Cannadine, and James M. Rosenheim, eds., *The First Modern Society: Essays in English History in Honour of Lawrence Stone*, 1989

"Economic Backwardness in Eastern Europe in Light of Developments in the West," in Daniel Chirot, ed., *The Origins of Backwardness in Eastern Europe: Economics and Politics from the Middle Ages until the Early Twentieth Century*, 1989

Merchants and Revolution: Commercial Change, Political Conflict, and London's Overseas Traders, 1550–1653, 1993

"Uneven Development and the Long Downturn: The Advanced Capitalist Economies from Boom to Stagnation, 1950–1998," *New Left Review* (1998), 1–265

Further Reading

Anderson, Perry, "Maurice Thomson's War," *London Review of Books* 15 (4 November 1993), 13–17

Aston, Trevor, and C.H.E. Philpin, eds., *The Brenner Debate: Agrarian Class Structure and Economic Development in Pre-Industrial Europe*, Cambridge: Cambridge University Press, 1985

Briggs, Asa 1921–

British historian

In the years after the death of A.J.P. Taylor, Asa Briggs was the most widely known British historian, achieving a degree of recognition and popular appeal attained by very few. This reflected his skills as a communicator, his empathy for historical periods, places, and individuals, and his ability to encapsulate the complexities of historical change in simple and straightforward language. It was also a product of the range of his interests and his prodigious output as writer, broadcaster, and administrator. By the mid-1990s Briggs had published nearly 40 books (on subjects as diverse as the wine of Haut Brion, the department store Lewis's, Britain 1780–1867, the BBC, and the occupation of the Channel Islands during World War II), as well as a multitude of articles, essays, and introductions, and innumerable reviews. Indeed, the sheer eclecticism of his output and the range of his organizational responsibilities militated against him producing the one magisterial work of historical interpretation that could have confirmed his maturity and individuality as a great historian.

The nearest Briggs came to such a work is undoubtedly the monumental 6-volume history of the British Broadcasting Corporation, somewhat misleadingly entitled *The History of Broadcasting in Britain*, whose publication spanned the 35 years from 1961 to 1996. Although dominated by the figure and ideals of Lord Reith, for whose values Briggs clearly had much sympathy, this is more an official history of the creation and functioning of the ideal of public service broadcasting than an interpretive study. Lauded for its minutely detailed accounts of the evolution of a complex institution, it has also been criticized for being diffuse and lacking in cogent summary: too much historical raw material, and not enough historical art. Significantly, while historians have enthusiastically mined the *History* for materials for their own analyses, the work has had marginal influence in cognate disciplines such as media and communications studies.

Eschewing abstractions for concrete historical events and experiences is, however, very much Briggs' historical method, and it lies at the heart of his significance in the development of social history. In the years after 1945 when the British historical establishment was dominated by conservative political history, and nonpolitical historians largely wrote within a confirmed Marxist perspective, Briggs' aphorism that social history was not history with the politics left out, but history with the economics put in, enabled him to carve a distinctive kind of history from below, which fused social, economic, and political concerns in a broad, almost "total" history, overtly left of center in sympathy, but outside the restrictions of Marxist theory. This approach lay behind his study, *The Age of Improvement, 1783–1867* (1959), which became one of the most durable history textbooks of the following decades, as well as his later *A Social History of England* (1983).

Briggs' nontheoretical empiricism encouraged not merely the flowering of social history, but in particular the emergence of many of its constituent elements as distinct sub-disciplines. The volume of essays he edited, *Chartist Studies* (1959), and the first, in particular, of the three volumes co-edited with John Saville, *Essays in Labour History* (1960–77), consolidated the common ground between Marxist and non-Marxist social and labor historians through which the study of British labor history flourished. *Chartist Studies* also demonstrated Briggs' firm commitment to the importance of the locality, and to the use of the specific to illuminate the general, which helped to elevate local history above parochial antiquarianism.

His *History of Birmingham*, Vol. 2: *Borough and City, 1865–1938* (1952), and especially his sharply perceptive *Victorian Cities* (1963), played an important part in the turn to urban history by the group of historians led by H.J. Dyos (although Dyos regretfully abandoned *Victorian Cities* as a model for urban history on the basis that it was "a work of such singular virtuosity that it almost certainly could not be followed up by anyone else"). Nevertheless, the theme developed in this book, of a class-divided Manchester ceding cultural and political leadership in the 1850s and 1860s to a more collaborationist Birmingham, proved an enduring framework not merely for British urban history, but also for the history of the 19th century more generally.

Victorian Cities was also the second in Briggs' trilogy of books on Victorian Britain, which commenced with *Victorian People* (1954), and concluded with *Victorian Things* (1988), which provided the foundation of Briggs' most enduring achievement. The latter, in its presentation of an idiosyncratic and apparently unordered selection of interesting facts and anecdotes, perhaps indicated too clearly the limitations of Briggs' historical method, and helps to explain not only the degree to which in the 1980s he appeared increasingly marginalized within the interdisciplinary study of Victorian culture and society, as it came increasingly under the sway of postmodern cultural theory, and the reasons why a new generation of scholars, committed to many of his most cherished ideals (comparativeness, interdisciplinarity), came to regard his brand of empiricism with hostility. Nevertheless, *Victorian People* and *Victorian Cities* did more than any other texts to rescue the Victorian period from the condescending hostility of critics such as Lytton Strachey, and to promote the interdisciplinary study of the period fostered by the journal *Victorian Studies*.

Briggs was a member of the original editorial board of *Victorian Studies*; he was also (to identify but a fraction of his immense organizational efforts) a founder of the Society for the Study of Labour History, president of the Social History Society and of the Local History Society, chair of the Standing Conference on Local History, of the Victorian Society, and of the William Morris Society, and chancellor of the Open University. This activity serves both as a measure of Briggs' importance, and an explanation of its limits, for ultimately, although Briggs' significance as a historian is undoubted, there being few areas in the historiography of 19th- and 20th-century Britain in the 1990s that do not bear some marks of his influence, this significance derives more from his organizational and institutional energies than from any enduring interpretive innovations.

MARTIN HEWITT

See also Britain: since 1750; Cole; Consumerism; Urban

Biography
Born Keighley, Yorkshire, 7 May 1921. Educated at Keighley Grammar School; Sidney Sussex College, Cambridge, BA 1941, BSc in economics, University of London, 1941. Served in the Intelligence Corps, 1942–45. Fellow, Worcester College, Oxford, 1945–55; reader in recent social and economic history, Oxford University, 1950–55; professor of modern history, University of Leeds, 1955–61; and University of Sussex, 1961–76: dean, school of social studies, 1961–65, pro-vice-chancellor, 1961–67, and vice-chancellor, 1967–76; provost, Worcester College, Oxford, 1976–91; chancellor, Open University, from 1978. Married Susan Anne Banwell, 1955 (2 sons, 2 daughters). Created life peer, Baron Briggs of Lewes, 1976.

Principal Writings
History of Birmingham, vol. 2: *Borough and City, 1865–1938*, 1952
Victorian People: Some Reassessments of People, Institutions, Ideas, and Events, 1851-1867, 1954
The Age of Improvement, 1783–1867, 1959
Editor, *Chartist Studies*, 1959
Editor with John Saville, *Essays in Labour History*, 3 vols., 1960–77
The History of Broadcasting in Britain, 6 vols., 1961–96
Victorian Cities, 1963
A Social History of England, 1983; revised 1994
Victorian Things, 1988
Editor with Daniel Snowman, *Fins de siècle: How Centuries End, 1400–2000*, 1996

Further Reading
Cannadine, David, "The Macaulay of the Welfare State," *London Review of Books* (6 June 1985)
Fraser, Derek, ed., *Cities, Class and Communication: Essays in Honour of Asa Briggs*, London: Harvester, 1990

Britain: Anglo-Saxon

Several of the major English medieval chroniclers, such as William of Malmesbury and Roger of Wendover, gave some attention to Anglo-Saxon history, mainly derived from Bede and the *Anglo-Saxon Chronicle*, but it was not until the rise of antiquarian studies in the 16th century that interest in Roman Britain began to develop. This was particularly marked by such works as the *Britannia* of William Camden (1551–1623), published in 1586, and the 1611 *Historie of Great Britaine* by John Speed (1552?–1629). The same period also saw a new scholarly interest in the early history of the Anglo-Saxons. Archbishop Matthew Parker (1504–75) formed a particularly important collection of manuscripts, and sponsored an edition of Asser. While Richard Verstegen's *Restitution of Decayed Intelligence in Antiquities Concerning the Most Noble and Renowned English Nation* of 1605 represented the first attempt at writing an interpretive history of the early Anglo-Saxons.

Oxford (especially Queen's College) and to a slightly lesser degree Cambridge were the main centers of Anglo-Saxon literary, linguistic, and historical studies throughout the 17th and early 18th centuries, particularly associated with such scholars as George Hickes (1642–1715), Henry Wharton (1664–94) and Thomas Hearne (1678–1735). Some rather spurious historical arguments concerning the Anglo-Saxons and their supposed liberties were also bandied about during the political and constitutional conflicts of these years. More significantly a number of important editions were produced, such as Sir James Ware's 1664 *editio princeps* of Bede's *Historia abbatum*, Edmund Gibson's *Chronicon Saxonicum* (1692) and John Smith's remarkable 1722 edition of Bede's *Historia ecclesiastica*. In some cases these have preserved texts that were subsequently lost in the Cotton Library fire of 1731. With the rise of the Enlightenment, which regarded such postclassical periods as barbaric, fashion dramatically changed, and it was not until the mid-19th century that interest in the Anglo-Saxon period revived. Even then it remained largely subordinate to study of the Norman and Angevin periods, and Old English texts were seriously under-represented in the editions of the Rolls series.

The late 19th and early 20th centuries saw Anglo-Saxon studies put on a new basis with the appearance of critical editions of many major sources, influenced by recent German textual scholarship. Charles Plummer quietly revolutionized the study of the period through the production of the first modern editions of Bede (1896) and of the Anglo-Saxon Chronicle (1892), both of which remain authoritative. A multivolume edition of the *Chronicle*, under the general editorship of David Dumville, is starting to publish each manuscript of the text individually, and Sir Roger Mynors and Bertram Colgrave edited and translated Bede in 1969, with the assistance of the very early St. Petersburg manuscript of the *Historia ecclesiastica* not known to Plummer. A full critical edition that they planned never appeared, but Colgrave did edit most of the informative Latin saint's lives of the early Anglo-Saxon period, including the important *Vita Wilfridi*.

The numerous law codes of the Anglo-Saxon kingdoms were magisterially edited by Felix Liebermann between 1903 and 1916, and a new edition of Asser was published by W.H. Stevenson in 1904. The documentary records of the period had already been collected and edited, not entirely critically, by J.M. Kemble in his *Codex Diplomaticus Aevi Saxonici* (1839–48) and partially again in Walter de Grey Birch's *Cartularium Saxonicum* (1885–93). These are now gradually being replaced by new editions, sponsored by the British Academy, which devote individual volumes to each of the main archives of Anglo-Saxon charters. A distinctive late form of Old English governmental text attained publication in Florence Harmer's *Anglo-Saxon Writs* (1952). More literary texts in Old English, including many of considerable importance for historical study, have been published in the long-running Early English Text Society series. Paralleling this establishment of a firm textual basis for the historical study of the period, has been the rapid opening up of its archaeological record in the decades following the discovery of the important Sutton Hoo burial site in 1939. The subject has established its absolute autonomy, successfully distancing itself from the tradition of literary studies out of which it grew. The archaeology of Roman Britain was already much more firmly grounded, due to the greater prestige of classics, with which it was always associated, and the significant lack of literary texts upon which any alternative approach to the period could be based.

The interpretation of Anglo-Saxon history developed alongside the emergence of new critical editions. A pioneering figure, often unjustly neglected, was Hector Munro Chadwick, whose *Studies on Anglo-Saxon Institutions* (1905) broke new ground in eschewing a narrative approach in favor of an analytical discussion of social, administrative, and political structures. The narrative framework, in the light of all the developments in textual studies, was provided magisterially by Sir Frank Stenton in his 1943 contribution to the Oxford History of England, entitled *Anglo-Saxon England*. Through this and a substantial body of articles, collected after his death, Stenton, who had a remarkable understanding of the relationship between history and topography, imposed his views on a succeeding generation of scholars. His emphasis, if anywhere, lay in the later part of the period, and he had the fewest new things to say about the 6th to early 8th centuries, in which Latin rather than Old English was the dominant language of record. This feature was reflected in the work of such of his disciples as Dorothy Whitelock, who tended, unlike Stenton, to be more literary scholars than historians. This ambiguity continues to be reflected in such specialist journals as *Anglo-Saxon England*, which began its run in 1972.

The study of the "Age of Bede" was revolutionized by the Oxford Ford lectures of the German exile Wilhelm Levison published as *England and the Continent in the Eighth Century* (1946). The approach to the period that integrated British and Continental developments was followed up most strongly by J.M. Wallace-Hadrill, in his own Ford lectures, published as *Early Germanic Kingship in England and on the Continent* (1971), and in his posthumously published commentary on Bede's *Historia Ecclesiastica* (1988). This tradition is continued in the work of his former pupils, such as Patrick Wormald (on law), Judith McClure (on Bede's exegesis) and Alf Smyth (on the Viking period). It has been given renewed importance through the recent work on Archbishop Theodore of Canterbury (668–90), led by Michael Lapidge and largely resulting from his and Bernhard Bischoff's 1994 edition of the remains of Theodore's exegetical writings. Continental influences are also now more keenly appreciated in the study of the period

of monastic reform in the 10th century. The literature and the documentary record of that period have been subject to groundbreaking study by Eric John, C.R. Hart, David Dumville, and again Michael Lapidge. Simon Keynes' *The Diplomas of King Æthelred "the Unready"* (1980) has helped revolutionize understanding of the workings of the old English state in its final period, as have a series of fundamental articles by James Campbell.

Both Scotland and Wales were affected by the strong currents of antiquarianism that ran through the 16th and 17th centuries. But late medieval Scottish chroniclers, such as Fordun and Bower, who tried to provide the all-embracing national histories to be found in the works of their English and European counterparts, lacked real evidence for the earlier centuries and thus were led to include much nonsense in their narratives. This tended to be repeated with little critical challenge in the national histories that were written up to and during the Enlightenment. The almost complete lack of literary and documentary records from pre-12th century Scotland is at the heart of a modern debate as to whether such materials once existed and have virtually all been lost or whether they were never produced in significant quantities, thus making of this an almost preliterate society. While the latter case was strongly argued by Kathleen Hughes in a posthumously published paper, recent work by Elizabeth Okasha and others indicates the presence of a higher level of literacy in the pre-9th century Pictish kingdoms than was once assumed. This would suggest that what materials were not destroyed in the period of Viking activity in Scotland and the Isles were lost following the anglicization of the Scottish court and the upper levels of society from the late 11th century onwards, which rendered the earlier Celtic records incomprehensible and obsolete.

What has survived began to be collected and studied in a genuinely scholarly way in the late 19th century. William Skene gathered the brief narrative texts, including ones from Irish and English sources, in his *Chronicles of the Picts, Chronicles of the Scots and Other Early Memorials of Scottish History* (1867). The only genuinely early and indigenous items from this collection have received more recent study in John Bannerman's 1974 edition and translation of the *Senchus Fer nAlban* (in his *Studies in the History of Dalriada*) and Marjorie O. Anderson's publication of the regnal lists and related texts in her *Kings and Kingship in Early Scotland* (1973). She and her husband Alan O. Anderson had previously produced what remains the standard edition of Adamnán's *Life of Columba* (1961; revised 1991), the main source for the foundation and earliest history of the monastery of Iona.

The dearth of written evidence has led to the placing of greater emphasis on the interpretation of the material culture of Pictish and early Scottish society, as particularly represented in the symbol stones. A pioneering survey of the artistic and archaeological remains was offered in Joseph Anderson's 2-volume *Scotland in Early Christian Times* (1881), and the entire corpus of the carved and inscribed stones was recorded in J. Romilly Allen and Joseph Anderson's *Early Christian Monuments of Scotland* (1903). While Romilly Allen's classification of the stones remains fundamental, their purpose and meaning continues to provide lively debate in the interpretations offered by historians, archaeologists, and anthropologists such as Isobel Henderson, Anthony Jackson, and Ross Samson.

More general studies of Pictish and early Scottish history, initiated by W.F. Skene's classic 3-volume *Celtic Scotland: A History of Ancient Alban* (1876), have grown in recent years, as the subject has become increasingly popular, not least as a reflection of growing awareness of and aspirations towards cultural and political autonomy in Scotland. H.M. Chadwick's last work, *Early Scotland* (1949), was a brief attempt to bring Skene up to date, but the crucial event in modern Pictish studies was the conference at Dundee in 1952 that produced *The Problem of the Picts*, edited by F.T. Wainwright, which opened up new areas of linguistic, archaeological, and historical study. The first really modern general survey to follow this was that of Isobel Henderson in *The Picts* (1967).

Wales was more fortunate in the survival of early texts, although their interpretation was rarely easy. The 19th-century movement to encourage publication of national records had its Welsh manifestation in the two volumes of *Ancient Laws and Institutes of Wales* (1841), which actually included much material of post-Conquest date. Only relatively recently have the genuinely early, 10th- and 11th-century legal texts been extracted and translated by Dafydd Jenkins in his *The Law of Hywel Dda* (1986). The body of probably – if controversially – early charters pertaining to the bishopric of Llandaff was another candidate for Victorian editing, with the cartulary known as the *Liber Landavensis* being published in 1840 under the auspices of the newly founded Welsh Manuscript Society. As this edition did not use the earliest manuscript of the work, it was superseded in 1893 by that of J. Gwenogvryn Evans, *The Text of the Book of Llan Dâv Reproduced from the Gwysaney Manuscript*. The first serious attempt to interpret this material was made by Wendy Davies in *The Llandaff Charters* (1979). Gwenogvryn Evans also began a series of private publications of facsimiles and transcriptions of some of the early Welsh poetry, including the work that has become known as the *Gododdin*, which contains brief elegies on a series of warriors who fought for the British kingdom of Gododdin (centered on Edinburgh) around the year 600. So difficult was this text to understand that Evans, in his *The Book of Aneirin* (1922), interpreted it as referring to a battle fought by the Earl of Chester in Anglesey in 1098. Only the researches of Sir Ifor Williams have brought real light to this and the whole corpus of early verse in Welsh, making possible new editions by himself and more recently by A.O.H. Jarman.

Other more directly historical texts have also been made available, although the earliest of them, the *Annales Cambriae* is still only to be found in an unsatisfactory edition in the Rolls series. The late 13th-century *Brut y Tywysogion*, which contains entries extending back to the 7th century, has been edited in its two manuscript versions by Thomas Jones, as has the comparable *Brenhinedd y Saesson*. Early medieval genealogical texts, comparable to those from Ireland, were edited by P.C. Bartrum in 1966. Although Sir John Rhys' *Celtic Britain* of 1882 led the way, the production of a substantial account of early Welsh history and society, on the basis of these sources, was first achieved by Sir John Lloyd in the first volume of his ground-breaking *History of Wales from the Earliest Times to the Edwardian Conquest* (1911), and the subject has been brought up to date in the more analytical *Wales in the Early Middle Ages* (1982) by Wendy Davies.

ROGER COLLINS

See also Anglo-Saxon Chronicle; Bede; Camden; Hughes, K.; Levison; Roger; William of Malmesbury

Further Reading

Allen, John Romilly, and Joseph Anderson, *The Early Christian Monuments of Scotland: A Classified Illustrated, Descriptive List of the Monuments with an Analysis of Their Symbolism and Ornamentation*, Edinburgh: Neill, 1903; reprinted 1993

Anderson, Alan O., and Marjorie O. Anderson, eds., *Adamnán's Life of Columba*, London and New York: Nelson, 1961; revised edition, Oxford and New York: Oxford University Press, 1991

Anderson, Joseph, *Scotland in Early Christian Times*, 2 vols., Edinburgh: D. Douglas, 1881

Anderson, Marjorie O., *Kings and Kingship in Early Scotland*, Edinburgh: Scottish Academic Press, 1973, Totowa, NJ: Rowman and Littlefield, 1974; revised edition, London: Chatto and Windus, 1980

Bannerman, John, ed., *Studies in the History of Dalriada*, Edinburgh: Scottish Academic Press, 1974

Bartrum, Peter Clement, ed., *Early Welsh Genealogical Tracts*, Cardiff: Wales University Press, 1966

Birch, Walter de Grey, ed., *Cartularium Saxonicum: A Collection of Charters Relating to Anglo-Saxon History*, 3 vols., London: Whiting, 1885–93; reprinted 1964

Bischoff, Bernhard, and Michael Lapidge, eds., *Biblical Commentaries from the Canterbury School of Theodore and Hadrian*, Cambridge and New York: Cambridge University Press, 1994

Camden, William, *Britannia*, London: Newbery, 1586; in English 1610

Campbell, James, *Essays in Anglo-Saxon History*, London: Hambledon Press, 1986

Chadwick, Hector Munro, *Studies on Anglo-Saxon Institutions*, Cambridge: Cambridge University Press, 1905; reprinted New York: Russell and Russell, 1963

Chadwick, Hector Munro, *Early Scotland: The Picts, the Scots, and the Welsh of Southern Scotland*, Cambridge: Cambridge University Press, 1949

Colgrave, Bertram, ed., *Vita Wilfridi* (The Life of Bishop Wilfrid) by Eddius Stephanus, Cambridge: Cambridge University Press, 1927

Colgrave, Bertram, and Roger Mynors, eds., *Bede's Ecclesiastical History of the English People*, Oxford: Oxford University Press, 1969; revised 1991

Davies, Wendy, *The Llandaff Charters*, Aberystwyth: National Library of Wales, 1979

Davies, Wendy, *Wales in the Early Middle Ages*, Leicester: Leicester University Press, and Atlantic Highlands, NJ: Humanities Press, 1982

Douglas, David C., *English Scholars*, London: Cape, 1939; revised 1951

Dumville, David, ed., *Britons and Anglo-Saxons in the Early Middle Ages*, Aldershot, Hampshire: Variorum, 1993

Evans, J. Gwenogvryn, *The Text of the Book of Llan Dâv Reproduced from the Gwysaney Manuscript*, 1893; reprinted Aberystwyth: National Library of Wales, 1979

Evans, J. Gwenogvryn, *The Book of Aneirin: The Text of Y Gododdin*, 2 vols., Pwllheli, 1908–22

Gibson, Edmund, ed., *Chronicon Saxonicum*, Oxford, 1692

Harmer, Florence, *Anglo-Saxon Writs*, Manchester: Manchester University Press, 1952; reprinted Stamford: Watkins, 1989

Hart, Cyril James Roy, *The Early Charters of Eastern England*, Leicester: Leicester University Press, 1966

Henderson, Isobel, *The Picts*, New York: Praeger, and London: Thames and Hudson, 1967

Hughes, Kathleen, *Celtic Britain in the Early Middle Ages*, Woodbridge, Suffolk: Boydell, and Totowa, NJ: Rowman and Littlefield, 1980

Jackson, Anthony, *The Symbol Stones of Scotland: A Social Anthropological Resolution of the Problem of the Picts*, Kirkwall: Orkney Press, 1984

Jarman, Alfred Owen Hughes, ed., *Y Gododdin: Britain's Oldest Heroic Poem*, Llandysul: Gomer, 1988

Jenkins, Dafydd, ed., *The Law of Hywel Dda: Law Texts of Medieval Wales*, Dyfed: Gomer, 1986; revised 1990

John, Eric, *Reassessing Anglo-Saxon England*, Manchester: Manchester University Press, 1997

Jones, Thomas, ed., *Brut y Tywysogion; or, The Chronicle of the Princes: Red Book of Hergest Version*, Cardiff: University of Wales Press, 1955

Jones, Thomas, ed., *Brenhinedd y Saesson; or, The King of the Saxons*, Cardiff: University of Wales Press, 1971

Kemble, John Mitchell, ed., *Codex Diplomaticus Aevi Saxonici*, 6 vols., Cardiff, 1839–48

Kendrick, T.D., *British Antiquity*, London: Methuen, 1950; New York: Barnes and Noble, 1970

Keynes, Simon, *The Diplomas of King Æthelred "the Unready" (978–1016): A Study in Their Use as Historical Evidence*, Cambridge and New York: Cambridge University Press, 1980

Knowles, David, *Great Historical Enterprises* [and] *Problems in Monastic History*, London and New York: Nelson, 1963

Lapidge, Michael, ed., *Archbishop Theodore: Commemoration Studies on His Life and Influence*, Cambridge and New York: Cambridge University Press, 1995

Levison, Wilhelm, *England and the Continent in the Eighth Century*, Oxford: Oxford University Press, 1946

Liber Landavens, Llyfrteilo; or, The Ancient Register of the Cathedral Church of Llandaff, Llandovery: W. Rees, 1840

Liebermann, Felix, *Die Gesetze der Angelsachsen* (The Law of the Anglo-Saxons), 3 vols., Halle: Niemayer, 1903–16

Lloyd, John, *History of Wales from the Earliest Times to the Edwardian Conquest*, Cambridge and New York: Longman, 1911

McClure, Judith, "Bede's Old Testament Kings," in Patrick Wormald, Donald Bullough, and Roger Collins, eds., *Ideal and Reality in Frankish and Anglo-Saxon Society*, Oxford: Blackwell, 1983

Okasha, Elizabeth, *Corpus of Early Christian Inscribed Stones of South-east Britain*, Leicester: Leicester University Press, 1993

Owen, Aneurin, *Ancient Laws and Institutes of Wales, Comprising Laws Supposed to be Enacted by Howel the Good, Modified by Subsequent Regulations under the Native Princes Prior to the Conquest by Edward the First, and Anomalous Laws* [Code of Hywel Dea], 2 vols., London: Eyre and Spottiswoode, 1841

Plummer, Charles, ed., *Anglo-Saxon Chronicle: Two of the Saxon Chronicles Parallel with Supplementary Extracts from Others*, 2 vols., Oxford: Oxford University Press, 1892–99

Plummer, Charles, ed., *Bede*, 2 vols., Oxford: Oxford University Press, 1896

Rhys, John, *Celtic Britain*, London: Society for Promoting Christian Knowledge, and New York: E.J.B. Young, 1882; revised 1884

Samson, Ross, ed., *Social Approaches to Viking Studies*, Glasgow: Cruithne Press, 1991

Skene, William Forbes, ed., *Chronicles of the Picts, Chronicles of the Scots and Other Early Memorials of Scottish History*, Edinburgh: HM General Register House, 1867

Skene, William Forbes, *Celtic Scotland: A History of Ancient Alban*, 3 vols., Edinburgh: Edmonston and Douglas, 1876–80; reprinted Freeport, NY: Books for Libraries Press, 1971

Smith, John, ed., *Historia ecclesiastica gentis Anglorum* (Ecclesiastical History of the English People) by Bede, Cambridge, 1722

Smyth, Alfred P., *Scandinavian Kings in the British Isles, 850–880*, Oxford and New York: Oxford University Press, 1977

Speed, John, *Historie of Great Britaine, under the Conquests of the Romans, Saxons, Danes, and Normans . . . from Iulius Caesar, to Our Most Gracious Sovereigne, King James*, London: Hall and Beale, 1611

Stenton, F.M., *Anglo-Saxon England*, Oxford: Oxford University Press, 1943

Verstegen, Richard, *Restitution of Decayed Intelligence in Antiquities Concerning the Most Noble and Renowned English Nation*, Antwerp: Bruney, 1605

Wainwright, Frederick Threlfall, ed., *The Problem of the Picts*, Edinburgh: Nelson, 1955; New York: Philosophical Library, 1956

Wallace-Hadrill, J.M., *Early Germanic Kingship in England and on the Continent*, Oxford: Oxford University Press, 1971

Wallace-Hadrill, J.M., *Bede's Ecclesiastical History of the English People: A Historical Commentary*, Oxford: Oxford University Press, 1988

Ware, James, ed., *Historia abbatum* by Bede, Dublin: Crook, 1664

Williams, Ifor, *The Beginnings of Welsh Poetry*, Cardiff: University of Wales Press, 1972

Williams, John, ed., *Annales Cambriae*, London: Longman, 1860; reprinted 1965

Wormald, Patrick, "*Lex Scripta* and *Verbum Regis*: Legislation and Germanic Kingship from Euric to Cnut," in Peter H. Sawyer and Ian N. Wood, eds., *Early Medieval Kingship*, Leeds: School of History, 1977

Britain: 1066–1485

British medieval history has been shaped by and has shaped the way the nation perceives itself. Both the sources and earlier histories were in general the work of the literate on behalf of the powerful. Bede's *Ecclesiastical History of the English People*, written in 731 was a model for later writers. Historical writings continued through such narratives as the *Anglo-Saxon Chronicle* into the period after the Norman Conquest. The compilation of chronicles flourished in monastic and urban scriptoria until the 15th century. Like newspapers of the past, they contained elements of myth, history, and current affairs. A distinction may be made between annalists, who merely recorded events, and chroniclers, who placed them in a narrative framework. William of Malmesbury, the most sophisticated historian of the 12th century, named his sources and subjected them to careful evaluation. Matthew Paris, one of the renowned St. Albans chroniclers, was a prolific author who wrote in the 13th century on recent and contemporary political events. His work was scholarly but biased by his own views. The *Polychronicon* or Universal Chronicle of Ranulph Higden, a 14th-century monk of Chester, was encyclopedic in its learning and advanced a complete theory of history as a succession of world empires. Their works were widely copied by contemporaries. Two 12th-century Welshmen made significant contributions to history. Giraldus Cambrensis (Gerald of Wales) wrote on the topography, history, and politics of Ireland, Wales, and England; and from Geoffrey of Monmouth's *Historia regum Britanniae* (History of the Kings of Britain, 1135–39) the English derived their knowledge of the ancient British legend of King Arthur, which became part of their national mythology. Later Shakespeare drew on Holinshed's *Chronicles of England, Scotland and Ireland* (1577) for his history plays, propaganda on behalf of the Tudors.

During the 16th century, Renaissance scholarship, the dispersal of monastic libraries, and the need to justify the Reformation, were all factors that led to more exact historical enquiry. Various strands of medieval knowledge evolved into more modern forms. Matthew Parker, Archbishop of Canterbury under Elizabeth I, published editions of various medieval chronicles. He was ideally placed to make his collection of former monastic manuscripts, which he bequeathed to Corpus Christi College, Cambridge. William Camden, the most famous historian of his age published *Britannia* in 1586. Following the ideas of his predecessor John Leland he described the geography, history, genealogy, and antiquities of the British isles county by county. This scheme provided the framework for subsequent antiquarian writings, which transmitted much information from the Middle Ages to future scholars. On account of his learning Camden was made Clarenceux King of Arms, one of the chief heralds, in 1597. The fascination with chivalry and noble pedigrees, passed down orally by the heralds, and from 1484 in the records of the College of Arms, broadened to become the study of genealogy. William Dugdale, another herald, was the greatest antiquarian scholar of the 17th century. Central government records, notably Domesday Book, had always been consulted to settle private property disputes. In the earlier 17th century, documents such as Magna Carta were used by lord chief justice Edward Coke and others to further constitutional conflicts with the Stuart monarchs. During the Civil War oppression under the "Norman Yoke" featured in the antimonarchist propaganda of the levellers and other radical groups.

The Restoration era saw further antiquarian activity, which culminated in Parliament's publication of *The Rolls of Parliament* in 1767 and *Domesday Book* in 1783. In 1838 Parliament founded the Public Record Office as the repository of the nation's history. This encouraged further waves of publication of historical documents by national and local record societies. In Britain the Enlightenment made its strongest impact on Scottish intellectual life. There the philosopher David Hume produced his *History of England* from 1754 which asserted the superiority of the Scots and the Tories. The "Glorious Revolution" of 1688 and the subsequent introduction of the Hanoverian dynasty caused anxiety among the Whig faction. A justification for the deposition of a reigning monarch was needed. Thus originated Thomas Babington Macaulay's *History of England* (1849–61) and what Herbert Butterfield later termed "the Whig interpretation of history." This was associated with the idea of progress, and in the 19th century with political and constitutional history. Parliamentary reform and the export of British institutions to the Empire led William Stubbs and F.W. Maitland to explore the medieval roots of government. Their work dominated research interests until the mid-20th century. Both were influenced by German scholarship and links between scholars of both countries remained close until World War I. Stubbs at Oxford, Maitland at Cambridge and T.F. Tout and James Tait of the Manchester school of medieval history were among the first university historians. They introduced a scientific approach to the evidence of the past. Nationalistic pride was expressed through interest in the origins of the English language. Examples of English literature from the time of Chaucer were published in the volumes of the Early English Text Society. Reaction against the machine age led to a fascination with the Middle Ages. The novels of Walter Scott and Benjamin Disraeli popularized a romantic nostalgia for medieval chivalry. Auguste Pugin and the Pre-Raphaelites, especially William Morris created a revival of interest in medieval architecture and interior design. Many everyday objects and buildings, notably the new Houses of Parliament, were designed in the fashionable "Victorian Gothic" style. The Catholic Revival stimulated interest in the medieval church. This was not without its ideological battles, exemplified in the controversies between the Roman Catholic historian Cardinal Gasquet and his Protestant opponent G.C. Coulton. Economic and social history developed in response to the impact of industrialization and the widening of the franchise. Charles Gross in America and George Unwin in Britain were pioneers in the medieval aspect of this field. Socialist writers such as Beatrice and Sidney Webb and their protégé Unwin inaccurately saw the origins of the trades unions in the medieval guilds.

Focus on the institutions of political, ecclesiastical, and economic life continued into the 20th century, aided by the publication and exploration of a widening range of source materials and enormous developments in archive and museum curatorship. Scientific discipline gave precedence to the empirical collection and analysis of data, and theoretical approaches favored on the continent were generally treated with suspicion. Continuities remained strongest in political and constitutional history, which were long overshadowed by Stubbs and other Victorian pioneers. V.H. Galbraith was the first historian to deride their moral judgmentalism. However, their work on Parliament has been refined by the extensive researches of H.G. Richardson and G.O. Sayles, and on royal administration by W.L. Warren and S.B. Chrimes among others. Features of the royal household which G.R. Elton identified with the "Tudor revolution in government" were found to be already present in the 15th century. New biographies of the medieval monarchs and leading nobles resulted from detailed research. Authors concentrated less on the actions of the central individuals than Victorian biographers and more on the political context. Political history was enriched by K.B. McFarlane's use of a broader range of sources, and his students constituted a school engaged in research on the aristocracy and the gentry. The concept of the affinity, or following, proved a useful tool, as in D.B. Crouch's *The Beaumont Twins* (1986) and Simon Walker's *The Lancastrian Affinity* (1990). Jean Le Patourel, John Gillingham, and Malcolm Vale contributed to a broader understanding of English political society through research on its links with continental Europe, especially France and the Low Countries.

While the bulk of 20th-century research remained empirically based, it evolved from the study of governmental institutions largely through interaction with the social sciences and the influence of immigrant and foreign scholars. Michael Postan and Eileen Power of the London School of Economics stimulated the application of economic laws to medieval history. Postan's ideas were controversial: after Power's early death he wrote little that was general, but his work was continued by his students Edward Miller and John Hatcher. A useful overview of debates in economic history was provided by J.L. Bolton's *The Medieval English Economy* (1980). In the late 19th and early 20th centuries Gross, Maitland, and Tait focused urban history on early medieval boroughs and their documents. Later historians turned their attention to the more problematic evidence for the period after the Black Death. The inconclusive 1970s debate about late medieval urban decay generated useful research on individual towns, for example Charles Phythian-Adams' *Desolation of a City: Coventry and* the *Urban Crisis of the Late Middle Ages* (1979). Archaeology and local history have contributed to the development of urban history, as seen in the work of Colin Platt and Derek Keene. Complex statistical and interdisciplinary models are now being tested by Derek Keene and the London Centre for Metropolitan History.

Feminist theory has introduced new insights into the history of medieval women. Increased urban employment opportunities for women immediately after the Black Death are discussed by various authors in two edited collections: Lindsey Charles and Lorna Duffin's *Women and Work in Preindustrial England* (1985) and P.J.P. Goldberg's *Woman is a Worthy Wight* (1992). Judith Bennett in *Women in the Medieval English Countryside* (1987) and elsewhere illuminated the lives of peasant women. George Homans, an American sociologist, applied his knowledge to medieval peasant communities in *English Villagers of the 13th Century* (1941) and H.C. Darby initiated the study of historical geography. Rodney Hilton and the Birmingham school used Marxist theory to explore the oppression of peasants in feudal society, while their rivals J. Ambrose Raftis and the Toronto school used manorial documents instead to emphasize the autonomous activities undertaken by peasant communities, independent of lordly control.

Perspectives derived from anthropology have been influential in social history, particularly among North American scholars. For example, social roles occupied at particular phases of the life-cycle have been discussed by Barbara Hanawalt in *The Ties That Bound* (1986) and in Caroline M. Barron and Anne Sutton's *Medieval London Widows, 1300–1500* (1994). Both Barbara Hanawalt at the Center for Medieval and Renaissance Studies at the University of Minnesota and Caroline Barron at London University encouraged students and colleagues to undertake research in a wide range of new areas. Richard Smith and Marjorie McIntosh, both associated with the Cambridge Group for the History of Population and Social Structure must be credited with introducing techniques and ideas pioneered for the early modern period into medieval history.

In church history the institutional bias of David Knowles and others has been redressed by work on lay piety. Pioneering work was done by Christopher Brooke for the earlier and Dorothy Owen for the later Middle Ages. Clive Burgess encouraged research on parish life in an important series of articles, and various local studies on the contribution of religious guilds and fraternities are now being published.

As history has benefited from the discerning use of theory, so medieval literature studies have benefited from the new historicism. Historical and literary studies have grown closer together in the last decades of the 20th century, as may be seen in the *Records of Early English Drama*, edited by Canadian and North American scholars. Works on Lollardy by Anne Hudson and Margaret Aston also stressed the rise of literacy in late medieval society. More recent research on popular religion and manuscript and print culture, along with Eamon Duffy's *The Stripping of the Altars* (1992), have overturned the previously held belief that the late medieval church was in decline and reformation inevitable.

In general the historiography is biased toward England, but research in Welsh, Scottish, and Irish universities, especially that of Rees Davies, has done much to correct the balance. In writings on European developments and cultural developments,

Britain's role tends to be marginal. Over the course of the 20th century the foundations laid by earlier generations of historians have enabled more recent scholars to develop a more complex understanding of medieval Britain. The focus of research has shifted from the early to the later Middle Ages, and periodization has been eroded. Greater continuities are now perceived between pre- and post-Conquest society and developments associated with early modern society have been traced back into the Middle Ages.

VIRGINIA R. BAINBRIDGE

See also Anglo-Saxon Chronicle; Bede; Camden; Cheney; Elton; Hilton; Holinshed; Knowles; Maitland; Postan; Power; Stubbs; William of Malmesbury; Webb

Further Reading

Aston, Margaret E., *Lollards and Reformers: Images and Literacy in Late Medieval England*, London: Hambledon, 1984

Bainbridge, Virginia R., *Gilds in the Medieval Countryside: Social and Religious Change in Cambridgeshire, c.1350–1558*, Woodbridge, Suffolk: Boydell, 1996

Barlow, Frank, *The English Church, 1066–1154: A History of the Later Anglo-Saxon Chronicles*, London and New York: Longman, 1979

Barron, Caroline M., and Anne F. Sutton, eds., *Medieval London Widows, 1300–1500*, London and Rio Grande, OH: Hambledon, 1994

Bean, John Malcolm William, *The Decline of English Feudalism, 1215–1540*, Manchester: Manchester University Press, and New York: Barnes and Noble, 1968

Bede, *Historia ecclesiastica gentis Anglorum* (Ecclesiastical History of the English People), 731

Bennett, Judith M., *Women in the Medieval English Countryside: Gender and Household in Brigstock before the Plague*, Oxford and New York: Oxford University Press, 1987

Bolton, James L., *The Medieval English Economy, 1150–1500*, London: Dent, and Totowa, NJ: Rowman and Littlefield, 1980

Brand, Paul, *The Origins of the English Legal Profession*, Oxford and Cambridge, MA: Blackwell, 1992

Britnell, Richard H., and A.J. Pollard, eds., *The McFarlane Legacy: Studies in Late Medieval Politics and Society*, Stroud: Sutton, and New York: St. Martin's Press, 1995

Brooke, C.N.L., *Medieval Church and Society: Collected Essays*, London: Sidgwick and Jackson, 1971; New York: New York University Press, 1972

Brown, Jennifer M., ed., *Scottish Society in the 15th Century*, London: Arnold, and New York: St. Martin's Press, 1977

Burgess, Clive, "'By Quick and by Dead': Wills and Pious Provision in Late Medieval Bristol," *English Historical Review* 102 (1987), 837–58

Burrow, John Wyon, *A Liberal Descent: Victorian Historians and the English Past*, Cambridge and New York: Cambridge University Press, 1981

Camden, William, *Britannia*, London: Newbery, 1586; in English 1610

Cantor, Norman F., *Inventing the Middle Ages: The Lives, Works, and Ideas of the Great Medievalists of the Twentieth Century*, New York: Morrow, 1991; Cambridge: Lutterworth Press, 1992

Charles, Lindsey, and Lorna Duffin, eds., *Women and Work in Preindustrial England*, London: Croom Helm, 1985

Chrimes, Stanley Bertram, *An Introduction to the Administrative History of Medieval England*, Oxford: Blackwell, and New York: Macmillan, 1952

Clanchy, M.T., *From Memory to Written Record: England, 1066–1307*, Cambridge, MA: Harvard University Press, and London: Arnold, 1979; revised 1993

Clanchy, M.T., *England and Its Rulers, 1066–1272*, Oxford: Blackwell, and Totowa, NJ: Barnes and Noble, 1983

Corfield, Penelope J., and Derek Keene, *Work in Towns, 850–1850*, Leicester: Leicester University Press, 1990

Crouch, David, *The Beaumont Twins: The Roots and Branches of Power in the Twelfth Century*, Cambridge and New York: Cambridge University Press, 1986

Darby, Henry Clifford, ed., *A New Historical Geography of England*, Cambridge: Cambridge University Press, 1973

Davies, Robert Rees, *Conquest, Coexistence, and Change: Wales, 1063–1415*, Oxford and New York: Oxford University Press, 1987; reprinted as *The Age of Conquest: Wales 1063–1415*, 1991

Davies, Robert Rees, ed., *The British Isles, 1100–1500: Comparisons, Contrasts, Connections*, Edinburgh: Donald, and Atlantic Highlands, NJ: Humanities Press, 1988

Duffy, Eamon, *The Stripping of the Altars: Traditional Religion in England, c.1400–c.1580*, New Haven and London: Yale University Press, 1992

Dyer, Christopher, *Standards of Living in the Later Middle Ages: Social Change in England, c.1200–1520*, Cambridge and New York: Cambridge University Press, 1989

Ewan, Elizabeth, *Townlife in Fourteenth-Century Scotland*, Edinburgh: Edinburgh University Press, 1990

Frame, Robin, *The Political Development of the British Isles, 1100–1400*, Oxford and New York: Oxford University Press, 1990

Fussner, F. Smith, *The Historical Revolution: English Historical Writing and Thought, 1580–1640*, London: Routledge, and New York: Columbia University Press, 1962

Galbraith, Vivian Hunter, *Kings and Chroniclers: Essays in English Medieval History*, London: Hambledon, 1982

Geoffrey of Monmouth, *Historia regum Britanniae* (History of the Kings of Britain), 1135–39

Gibson, Gail McMurray, *The Theater of Devotion: East Anglian Drama and Society in the Late Middle Ages*, Chicago: University of Chicago Press, 1989

Gillingham, John, *The Angevin Empire*, London: Arnold, and New York: Holmes and Meier, 1984

Goldberg, P.J.P., ed., *Woman is a Worthy Wight: Women in English Society, c.1200–1500*, Gloucester: Sutton, 1992

Gransden, Antonia, *Historical Writing in England*, 2 vols., London: Routledge, and Ithaca, NY: Cornell University Press, 1974–82

Gross, Charles, *The Guild Merchant: A Contribution to British Municipal History*, 2 vols., Oxford: Oxford University Press, 1890

Hanawalt, Barbara A., *The Ties That Bound: Peasant Families in Medieval England*, Oxford and New York: Oxford University Press, 1986

Harper-Bill, Christopher, *The Pre-Reformation Church in England, 1400–1530*, London and New York: Longman, 1989; revised 1996

Higden, Ranulph, *Polychronicon* (Universal Chronicle), 1327–52

Hilton, Rodney, *The English Peasantry in the Later Middle Ages*, Oxford and New York: Oxford University Press, 1975

Holinshed, Raphael *et al.*, *The Chronicles of England, Scotland and Ireland*, 1577

Hollister, Charles Warren, *The Military Organisation of Norman England*, Oxford: Oxford University Press, 1965

Holt, J.C., *Magna Carta*, Cambridge: Cambridge University Press, 1965

Homans, George C., *English Villagers of the Thirteenth Century*, Cambridge, MA: Harvard University Press, 1941

Howell, Margaret, *Eleanor of Provence: Queenship in Thirteenth-Century England*, Oxford: Blackwell, 1998

Hudson, Anne, *The Lollards and Their Books*, London: Hambledon, 1985

Hume, David, *History of England*, 6 vols., 1754–62

Keen, Maurice, *England in the Later Middle Ages: A Political History*, London: Methuen, 1973; London and New York: Routledge, 1988

Keene, Derek, *Survey of Medieval Winchester*, 2 vols., Oxford and New York: Oxford University Press, 1985

Knowles, David, *The Monastic Order in England: A History of Its Development from the Times of St. Dunstan to the Fourth Lateran Council, 943–1216*, Cambridge: Cambridge University Press, 1940; 2nd edition [with dates 940–1216] 1963

Knowles, David, *The Religious Orders in England*, 3 vols., Cambridge: Cambridge University Press, 1948–59

Le Patourel, H.E. Jean, *The Norman Empire*, Oxford: Oxford University Press, 1976

Leyser, Henrietta, *Medieval Women: A Social History of Women in England, 450–1500*, London: Weidenfeld and Nicolson, and New York: St. Martin's Press, 1995

Macaulay, Thomas Babington, *The History of England from the Accession of James II*, 5 vols., London: Longman, 1849–61

McFarlane, K.B., *The Nobility of Later Medieval England*, Oxford and New York: Oxford University Press, 1974

McIntosh, Marjorie Keniston, *Autonomy and Community: The Royal Manor of Havering-atte-Bowe, 1200–1500*, Cambridge and New York: Cambridge University Press, 1986

McKisack, May, *Medieval History in the Tudor Age*, Oxford: Oxford University Press, 1971

Maitland, F.W., *Township and Borough*, Cambridge: Cambridge University Press, 1898

Maitland, F.W., *The Constitutional History of England*, Cambridge: Cambridge University Press, 1908

Meale, Carol M., ed., *Women and Literature in Britain 1150–1500*, Cambridge: Cambridge University Press, 1993

Mertes, Kate, *The English Noble Household, 1250–1600: Good Governance and Political Rule*, Oxford and New York: Blackwell, 1988

Miller, Edward, and John Hatcher, *Medieval England: Rural Society and Economic Change, 1086–1348*, London and New York: Longman, 1978

Otway-Ruthven, Annette J., *A History of Medieval Ireland*, London: Benn, and New York: Barnes and Noble, 1968; reprinted 1980

Owen, Dorothy, *Church and Society in Medieval Lincolnshire*, Lincoln: Lincolnshire Local History Society, 1971

Phythian-Adams, Charles, *Desolation of a City: Coventry and the Urban Crisis of the Late Middle Ages*, Cambridge and New York: Cambridge University Press, 1979

Platt, Colin, *Medieval England: A Social History and Archaeology from the Conquest to 1600AD*, London: Routledge, and New York: Scribner, 1978

Pocock, J.G.A., *The Ancient Constitution and the Feudal Law: A Study of English Historical Thought in the Seventeenth Century*, Cambridge: Cambridge University Press, 1957; revised 1987

Pollock, Frederick, and Frederic William Maitland, *The History of English Law before the Time of Edward I*, 2 vols., Cambridge: Cambridge University Press, and Boston: Little Brown, 1895; revised 1898

Postan, M.M., *The Medieval Economy and Society: An Economic History of Britain in the Middle Ages*, London: Weidenfeld and Nicolson, 1972; Berkeley: University of California Press, 1972 [with subtitle *An Economic History of Britain, 1100–1500*]

Power, Eileen, *The Wool Trade in English Medieval History*, London and New York: Oxford University Press, 1941

Prestwich, Michael, *The Three Edwards: War and State in England, 1272–1377*, London: Weidenfeld and Nicolson, and New York: St. Martin's Press, 1980

Raftis, James Ambrose, *Tenure and Mobility: Studies in the Social History of the Medieval English Village*, Toronto: Pontifical Institute of Medieval Studies, 1964

Records of Early English Drama, Toronto: University of Toronto Press, 1982–

Reynolds, Susan, *An Introduction to the History of English Medieval Towns*, Oxford: Oxford University Press, 1977

Sawyer, Peter H., ed., *Domesday Book: A Reassessment*, London: Arnold, 1985

Sayles, George Osborne, *The King's Parliament of England*, New York: Norton, 1974

Smith, Richard M., ed., *Land, Kinship and Lifecycle*, Cambridge and New York: Cambridge University Press, 1984

Stubbs, William, *The Constitutional History of England in Its Origin and Development*, 3 vols., Oxford: Oxford University Press, 1874-78

Swanson, Heather, *Medieval Artisans: An Urban Class in Late Medieval England*, Oxford and New York: Blackwell, 1989

Swanson, Robert Norman, *Church and Society in Late Medieval England*, Oxford and New York: Blackwell, 1989

Tait, James, *The Medieval English Borough*, Manchester: Manchester University Press, 1936

Tout, Thomas Frederick, *Chapters in the Administrative History of Medieval England*, 6 vols., Manchester: Manchester University Press, 1920-33

Unwin, George, *The Guilds and Companies of London*, London: Methuen, 1908; reprinted 1963

Vale, Malcolm, *War and Chivalry: Warfare and Aristocratic Culture in England, France and Burgundy at the End of the Middle Ages*, London: Duckworth, and Athens: University of Georgia Press, 1981

Wagner, Anthony Richard, *English Genealogy*, London: Oxford University Press, 1960; revised 1972

Walker, Simon, *The Lancastrian Affinity*, Oxford and New York: Oxford University Press, 1990

Warren, Wilfred Lewis, *The Governance of Norman and Angevin England, 1086-1272*, London: Arnold, and Stanford, CA: Stanford University Press, 1987

Wright, S.J., ed., *Parish, Church and People: Local Studies in Lay Religion, 1350-1750*, London: Hutchinson, 1988

Britain: 1485-1750

In both style and content, British political historiography has changed beyond all recognition in the last fifty years. Increasingly sophisticated research has unhorsed the grand narratives of the 19th-century liberal tradition. It is now far more specialized, with the canon endlessly subdividing; its principal preoccupations, however – the emergence of the state, the Protestant Reformation and the causes of civil wars and revolutions – remain largely the same. By contrast, the past fifty years have seen economic, social and cultural historians fill huge gaps in what we know about the everyday lives of ordinary people.

D.C. Coleman, W.G. Hoskins, and the Cambridge Group for the History of Population and Social Structure have established the key economic and social determinants of early modern English life. With the help of hundreds of local historians, they have pieced together a story of population expansion from the late 15th century, price inflation and agrarian underdevelopment. Consequent economic hardship down to the mid-17th century helped polarize rich and poor as never before. The English smallholder gradually disappeared, the landless, wage-dependent population expanded, their impoverishment giving a violent push to the growing pull of the towns.

Although widely accepted, the consequences of these findings for the history of early modern English society have proved highly contentious. Fierce debate once surrounded the fortunes of landowners. Economics was made to explain the troubled nature of English politics in the period. R.H. Tawney,

Christopher Hill and Lawrence Stone claimed that the gentry (or bourgeoisie), stuffed with the wealth of the church redistributed during the Reformation, fought for political parity with an old, economically backward ruling class, choosing the House of Commons as the institution through which to assert the liberties of the (landed) subject to constitutional self-determination. Hence civil war and revolution. The empirical heart has been ripped out of this argument by numerous critics and "the storm over the gentry" has long since blown out. But its effects linger, especially the doubts cast on the reliability of economic determinism in historical explanation.

Appetite for controversy, however, remains healthy. The civil wars and revolution of the mid-17th century continue to excite some of the most vigorous, sometimes rancorous debates. "Revisionists" have disputed the traditional idea that conflict was somehow inevitable. There was no "high-road to civil war." On the one hand, A.F. Pollard's Tudor despots have been exposed as paper tigers, K.B. McFarlane and Penry Williams demonstrating that the so-called "new monarchy" ruled cooperatively with its mightiest subjects, who ran the increasingly ramshackle machinery of English local government and taxation on its behalf, often to their own ends. By the close of Elizabeth I's reign, royal imprudence and inflation had brought the English crown to the brink of bankruptcy. On the other hand, Sir Geoffrey Elton, Conrad Russell, and Kevin Sharpe have denied the supposed initiative, autonomy, and self-confidence of the Tudor and early Stuart House of Commons, which took its lead in legislative and fiscal matters from the upper House and from the royal court. Indeed, they have argued that the existence of a widely held consensus about the supremacy of royal authority made conflict over political principle impossible.

Furthermore, since the 1960s local historians have successfully questioned the primacy of burning issues of constitutional significance in people's lives. Alan Everitt, Anthony Fletcher, and Peter Clark on 16th- and 17th-century Kent, Sussex, and Essex respectively, have all argued that early modern Englishmen felt their strongest allegiance to their county. Its social structures gave local politics a reassuring unity and continuity, typified by the process of parliamentary "selection" described by Mark Kishlansky. Here was consensuality at work – elections rarely descended into contests, as candidates were effectively appointed by the prearranged mutual consent of political elites in the shires and towns. Far better to preserve and maintain the dignity of the *cursus honorum* than to subject the fragile local social order to periodic trials by ballot. This "localist" attachment to the preservation of introverted regional elites determined the common response to the coming of war in 1642 – the widespread self-preservationist neutralism identified by Brian Manning and John Morrill.

Ann Hughes, Clive Holmes and William Hunt have demonstrated more recently, however, that the so-called "county communities" were in fact riven by long-standing social, political, and religious conflicts far stronger than the notional bonds of local loyalties. Such conflicts patterned the politics of the provincial shires and towns with generational competition over social standing, honor, and respectability among kin, neighbors, tenants, and dependants. They were often little more serious than disputes over precedence, but were remarkably easily galvanized into trials of blood and strength when crossed with the constitutional struggles which increasingly occupied early

Stuart politics. Johann Sommerville has stressed the tension between ideas about the nature of political authority, based on the one hand, on divine right, and on the other, on the "social contract" between rulers and ruled. The power of the supposed political consensus to maintain order was seriously compromised by contemporary disagreements about the relationship between royal prerogative and the rule of law. Perhaps most significant is the extent and sophistication of contemporary awareness of and engagement with such issues – these seem to have been so advanced that historians have begun to talk of a genuinely popular political culture. Derek Hirst, Tom Cogswell, and Richard Cust have each highlighted this level of widespread popular debate with regard to English politics in the 1620s. Against the backdrop of the European religious wars of the age, conflict over fundamental principles of property rights and personal freedom infected a political process riven and distorted by the pace at which Charles I manfully battled with its anachronisms. The teleology of Whig historians may have discredited the search for ideological causes of the English Civil War. That does not mean that there were none.

Work on the deeper structures of society and culture in early modern England has done much to reinforce this view. Margaret Spufford and David Underdown have made much from an imaginative analysis of those contrasting rural communities which characterized early modern society. They have sought connections between the cultural characteristics, religion and political allegiances of rural English men and women and the very landscape in which they lived, the nature of the economy that the locality supported, and attendant structures of manorial and ecclesiastical authority. In socially atomized and market-oriented pasture regions there seems to have been greater religious and political freedom than in tightly controlled, subsistence-based arable regions. This thesis has attracted its critics – there are plenty of exceptions disproving the rule – but work of this nature has helped lift the barrier which once divided social and political history, as well as demonstrating the political awareness of ordinary people, and their powerful influence over political debate and events.

Equally fruitful debates have arisen over the conflicts within communities under the pressure of social, economic, and cultural change in the period. English peasant risings, food riots, and protest against agricultural "improvement" have been studied in the pioneering work of Buchanan Sharp, Keith Lindley, and John Walter. In their influential study of Terling in Essex, Keith Wrightson and David Levine detected a more peaceful yet barely less traumatic polarization of village society. The swelling ranks of the poor came to depend on the increasingly pious paternalism of their social superiors. Cultural estrangement was both the cause and consequence of a campaign for "the reformation of manners" conducted by the godly magistrate, concerned to tame the moral turpitude of the masses. For many historians, this kind of sociocultural conflict has been overemphasized. Martin Ingram's study of church court presentments has indicated that cultural conflict was far less prevalent than has been claimed, probably no greater than it had ever been, and muted by the contiguity between "elite" and "plebeian" patterns of belief and behavior. The cultural change associated with the Protestant Reformation brought not just conflict but also encouraged the public rationalization of private charity, exemplified by the Elizabethan poor laws.

Religious change was probably the most significant feature of the early modern period. In the past 25 years conventional thinking on the progress and success of the Reformation has been jettisoned, be it Sir Geoffrey Elton's statutory coercion "from above," or A.G. Dickens' contrasting rapid popular conversion "from below." As Eamon Duffy has established, the late medieval church was by no means moribund, corrupt, and "ripe for reformation," but rather a vibrant and popular institution. John Bossy and Christopher Haigh have described the survival of popular Catholicism as a result of this vitality, as well as the political and factional vicissitudes at court upon which the spiritual reform of the country depended. The generally moderating influence of the state was offset by the "privatization" of the English church by the laity, described by Claire Cross. Having appropriated huge amounts of church land, a landed and urban elite wielded an important influence over the emergence of a radical Protestantism often at odds with the moderate *via media* of the established church.

The immense cultural impact of the Reformation is captured in a seminal work by Sir Keith Thomas, itself a triumph for the reconstitution of popular mentalities amongst those hitherto considered historiographically dumb. For him, the Reformation killed a form of Christianity whose animistic qualities, such as the powerful magic of intercessory prayer and the protection of saintly patrons, was not easily replaced at a popular level by a Protestantism that fuelled moral torment rather than spiritual satisfaction. In the work of Patrick Collinson, however, Protestantism is itself described as a popular form of culture, bibliocentric and introverted, but which nevertheless served to unite countless godly communities, rich and poor, and ultimately the Protestant nation.

In some respects 17th-century politics have been rewritten as a category of religious history. In the analyses of Peter Lake and Nicholas Tyacke, by 1600 orthodox Calvinist Protestantism had established a firm hold, yet never exercised a complete monopoly over spiritual life, finally losing its grip altogether in the 1620s, when it came under attack from archbishop William Laud and his episcopal hierarchy. Conflict, when it came in the 1640s, was not the "Puritan revolution" conjured by 19th-century historians such as Samuel Gardiner; it was a reaction against a perceived "counter revolution" which, for many, threatened to push England back into the clutches of papal Rome – in John Morrill's phrase, not so much the first modern revolution, as the last war of religion. The fear of Catholicism, described by Robin Clifton, Caroline Hibbard and Peter Lake as a vital unifying element in English Protestantism, was unleashed with a violence that was to unsettle society for half a century. Where once the politics of the Restoration era epitomized unprincipled cynicism, historians such as Tim Harris, Mark Knights and Jonathan Scott have done much to restore a sense of ideological tension in the period. Apart from disputing with one another the evolution of party politics, a feature of the historiography of the period which once seemed utterly unshakable, they have revealed in all its deadly shades the outline of an ideological "cold war" characterized by heated crises over religious dissent and popish plotting which kept Englishmen at each others' throats at least until the intervention of William of Orange in 1688. Thereafter, England was far less prey to the destructive forces of religious heterogeneity, as dissent was effectively co-opted to the business of preserving order throughout Britain. Now demons were sought elsewhere – namely France.

The descent into "the second hundred years' war" in the 18th century provides the backdrop to the final chapter of another key theme of recent historiography – the emergence of state authority. The renovation of the English state from the end of the 15th century has been the subject of intense debate, dominated by Geoffrey Elton's thesis of a "Tudor revolution in government," centered on the reforms of Thomas Cromwell, and the correctives to it provided by his own students. Elton's belief that the 1530s witnessed the sudden and dramatic replacement of the royal household by an efficient bureaucracy as the seat of government has been almost entirely refuted by John Guy, who disputed the timing of the "revolution," urging the importance of the earlier reforms of Cardinal Wolsey; and David Starkey, who has demonstrated that the politics of personality, encapsulated in the factional politics of the king's bedchamber, often had a far more important influence than the rational dictates of policy. On the other hand, Christine Carpenter and Simon Payling's studies of 15th-century political society in Warwickshire and Nottinghamshire respectively show that it was from the preservation of good order at the local level that wider political stability derived, the evolution of personal "good lordship" underpinning the emergence of the early modern state. By examining related cultural patterns, such as codes of honor and the rise of a Renaissance ethic of public service to the prince, Mervyn James added great depth and subtlety to the history of state formation. Ideas (even ideals) underlay the blunt reality of the Tudors' "monopoly of violence."

Another key feature in the development of state authority was the partial victory of the English lowlands over the highlands of the British Isles in the 16th century, their colonization in the 17th and eventual subjection in the 18th. Henry VIII's assumption of an Irish crown has been described by Brendan Bradshaw as a liberal "constitutional revolution," aimed at tying together the English king and his Irish subjects with bonds of mutual respect and responsibility. But in the absence of adequate resources to implement open policies of repression, the maintenance of the early modern "English Empire" depended almost entirely upon the incorporation of ambitious and opportunistic Celtic and colonial elites into a system of consular administration, examined by Ciaran Brady and Steven Ellis for Ireland and J. Gwynfor Jones for Wales.

After centuries of uneasy relations across their borders, the union of England with her northern neighbor came altogether more peacefully, yet created disastrous tensions in the medium term. Conrad Russell has mooted a "British problem" fatally undermining Stuart regal governance. The simultaneous government of three very different kingdoms, crossed with the pathological urge for uniformity across all three exhibited by Charles I and his closest advisers led to the triple catastrophe of rebellion and revolution all across the British Isles between 1637 and 1655. It was not until the defeat of the Jacobite rebellion between 1689 and 1691, and the establishment of the "Protestant ascendancy" in Ireland, recently reassessed by S.J. Connolly, as well as the parliamentary union with Scotland in 1707, reappraised by Patrick Riley, that the way was cleared for the emergence of a British "superstate." The chief characteristic of this new entity was the burgeoning executive limb

of government at Westminster and Whitehall, as well as the regional centers of naval and fiscal administration. Lewis Namier and Sir John Plumb have suggested that this vast new structure promoted a stability hitherto elusive in English politics. Government established an interest (and a payroll) among those parties, Whig and Tory, whose emergence and increasing organization also did a great deal to subsume the tensions in English politics, so devastating in earlier periods, into a civil parliamentary political process.

This achievement was made easier by the existence of a mighty "enemy without." The new state was designed to assure England's effective involvement as a well-armed protagonist in the "second hundred years' war" with France. Britain's first steps on the world stage were paid for by the instruments of a financial revolution, described by Henry Roseveare, and in particular a national bank and a system of deficit finance underwritten by Parliament. Since commitments to creditors could be met only from regular tax income, it simply became impossible to govern without Parliaments. The political consequences of the events of 1689, recognized by John Miller and W.A. Speck as neither glorious nor revolutionary, were far more important than any principled motives behind them. Political pragmatism provided considerable motive force to that "constitutional progressivism" which 19th-century historians liked to think of as the English nation's true genius.

SEAN KELSEY

See also Cambridge Group; Dickens; Elton; Hill; Russell; Plumb; Protestantism; Reformation; Stone; Tawney; Thomas, K.; Wrigley

Further Reading

Amussen, Susan Dwyer, *An Ordered Society: Gender and Class in Early Modern England*, Oxford and New York: Blackwell, 1988

Aylmer, Gerald Edward, *The King's Servants: The Civil Service of Charles I, 1625–42*, New York: Columbia University Press, and London: Routledge, 1961; revised 1974

Aylmer, Gerald Edward, *The State's Servants: The Civil Service of the English Republic, 1649–60*, London and Boston: Routledge, 1973

Bossy, John, *The English Catholic Community, 1570–1850*, London: Darton Longman and Todd, 1975

Bradshaw, Brendan, *Irish Constitutional Revolution of the Sixteenth Century*, Cambridge and New York: Cambridge University Press, 1979

Brady, Ciaran, *The Chief Governors: The Rise and Fall of Reform Government in Tudor Ireland, 1536–1588*, Cambridge and New York: Cambridge University Press, 1994

Carpenter, Christine, *Locality and Polity: A Study of Warwickshire Landed Society, 1401–1499*, Cambridge and New York: Cambridge University Press, 1992

Clark, Peter, and Paul Slack, eds., *Crisis and Order in English Towns, 1500–1700: Essays in Urban History*, Toronto: University of Toronto Press, and London: Routledge, 1972

Clark, Peter, and Paul Slack, eds., *English Towns in Transition, 1500–1700*, London and New York: Oxford University Press, 1976

Clifton, Robin, "Fear of Popery," in Conrad Russell, ed., *The Origins of the English Civil War*, London: Macmillan, and New York: Barnes and Noble, 1973; reprinted with corrections 1975

Cogswell, Thomas, *The Blessed Revolution: English Politics and the Coming of War, 1621–4*, Cambridge and New York: Cambridge University Press, 1989

Coleman, D.C., *The Economy of England, 1450–1750*, London and New York: Oxford University Press, 1977

Colley, Linda, *In Defiance of Oligarchy: The Tory Party, 1714–1760*, Cambridge and New York: Cambridge University Press, 1982

Collinson, Patrick, *The Religion of Protestants: The Church in English Society, 1559–1625*, Oxford: Oxford University Press, 1982

Connolly, Sean, *Religion, Law and Power: The Making of Protestant Ireland, 1660–1760*, Oxford and New York: Oxford University Press, 1992

Cowan, Ian Borthwick, *The Scottish Reformation: Church and Society in Sixteenth-Century Scotland*, London: Weidenfeld and Nicolson, and New York: St. Martin's Press, 1982

Cross, Claire, *Church and People, 1450–1660: The Triumph of the Laity in the English Church*, London: Fontana, and Atlantic Highlands, NJ: Humanities Press, 1976

Cust, Richard, *The Forced Loan and English Politics, 1626–28*, Oxford and New York: Oxford University Press, 1987

Dickens, A.G., *The English Reformation*, London: Batsford, and New York: Schocken, 1964; 2nd edition Batsford, 1989, University Park: Pennsylvania State University Press, 1991

Duffy, Eamon, *The Stripping of the Altars: Traditional Religion in England c.1400–c.1580*, New Haven: Yale University Press, 1992

Ellis, Steven G., *Tudor Frontiers and Noble Power: The Making of the British State*, Oxford and New York: Oxford University Press, 1995

Elton, G.R., *The Tudor Revolution in Government: Administrative Changes in the Reign of Henry VIII*, Cambridge: Cambridge University Press, 1953

Elton, G.R., *Policy and Police: The Enforcement of the Reformation in the Age of Thomas Cromwell*, Cambridge: Cambridge University Press, 1972

Erickson, Amy Louise, *Women and Property in Early Modern England*, London and New York: Routledge, 1993

Everitt, Alan Milner, *The Community of Kent and the Great Rebellion, 1640–60*, Leicester: University of Leicester Press, 1966

Fletcher, Anthony J., *Reform in the Provinces: The Government of Tudor and Stuart England*, New Haven and London: Yale University Press, 1986

Foster, Roy, *Modern Ireland, 1600–1972*, London: Allen Lane, and New York: Penguin, 1988

Guy, John Alexander, *Tudor England*, Oxford and New York: Oxford University Press, 1988

Haigh, Christopher, *English Reformations: Religion, Politics and Society under the Tudors*, Oxford and New York: Oxford University Press, 1993

Harris, Tim, with Paul Seaward and Mark Goldie, eds., *The Politics of Religion in Restoration England*, Oxford and Cambridge, MA: Blackwell, 1990

Harris, Tim, *Politics under the Later Stuarts: Party Conflict in a Divided Society, 1660–1715*, London and New York: Longman, 1993

Hibbard, Caroline, *Charles I and the Popish Plot*, Chapel Hill: University of North Carolina Press, 1983

Hill, Christopher, *The Century of Revolution, 1603–1714*, Edinburgh: Nelson, and New York: Norton, 1961; revised 1972

Hirst, Derek, *The Representative of the People? Voters and Voting in Early Stuart England*, Cambridge and New York: Cambridge University Press, 1975

Holmes, Clive, "The County Community in Stuart Historiography," *Journal of British Studies* 19 (1980), 54–73

Hoskins, William George, *The Making of the English Landscape*, London: Hodder and Stoughton, 1955; revised 1992

Hughes, Ann, *Politics, Society and Civil War in Warwickshire, 1620–1660*, Cambridge and New York: Cambridge University Press, 1987

Hughes, Ann, *The Causes of the English Civil War*, London: Macmillan, and New York: St. Martin's Press, 1991

Hunt, William, *The Puritan Moment: The Coming of Revolution in an English County*, Cambridge, MA: Harvard University Press, 1983

Ingram, Martin, *Church Courts, Sex and Marriage in England, 1570–1640*, Cambridge and New York: Cambridge University Press, 1987

James, Mervyn Evans, *Family, Lineage and Civil Society: A Study of Society, Politics and Mentality in the Durham Region, 1500–1640*, Oxford: Oxford University Press, 1974

Jones, J. Gwynfor, *Early Modern Wales, c.1525–1640*, London: Macmillan, and New York: St. Martin's Press, 1994

Kishlansky, Mark, *Parliamentary Selection: Social and Political Choice in Early Modern England*, Cambridge and New York: Cambridge University Press, 1986

Knights, Mark, *Politics and Opinion in Crisis, 1678–81*, Cambridge and New York: Cambridge University Press, 1994

Lake, Peter, *Moderate Puritans and the Elizabethan Church*, Cambridge and New York: Cambridge University Press, 1982

Lindley, Keith, *Fenland Riots and the English Revolution*, London: Heinemann, 1982

McFarlane, K.B., "Bastard Feudalism," *Bulletin of the Institute of Historical Research* 20 (1943–44), 161–80

Miller, John, *The Glorious Revolution*, London and New York: Longman, 1983

Mitchison, Rosalind, *Lordship to Patronage: Scotland, 1603–1745*, London: Arnold, 1983

Morrill, John Stephen, *The Revolt of the Provinces: Conservatives and Radicals in the English Civil War, 1630–1650*, London: Allen and Unwin, and New York: Barnes and Noble, 1976

Namier, Lewis, *The Structure of Politics at the Accession of George III*, London: Macmillan, 1929; New York: St. Martin's Press, 1957

Neale, John E., *The Elizabethan House of Commons*, New Haven: Yale University Press, and London: Cape, 1950

Neale, John E., *Elizabeth I and Her Parliaments, 1559–1601*, 2 vols., London: Cape, 1953–57; New York: St. Martin's Press, 1958

Notestein, Wallace, *The Winning of the Initiative by the House of Commons*, Oxford: Oxford University Press, 1924

Payling, Simon, *Political Society in Lancastrian England: The Greater Gentry of Nottinghamshire*, Oxford and New York: Oxford University Press, 1991

Plumb, J.H., *The Growth of Political Stability in England, 1675–1725*, London: Macmillan, 1967; as *The Origin of Political Stability: England, 1675–1725*, Boston: Houghton Mifflin, 1967

Pollard, Albert Frederick, *The History of England from the Accession of Edward VI to the Death of Elizabeth, 1547–1603*, London and New York: Longman, 1923

Riley, Patrick William Joseph, *The Union of England and Scotland: A Study in Anglo-Scottish Politics on the Eighteenth Century*, Manchester: Manchester University Press, and Totowa, NJ: Rowman and Littlefield, 1978

Roseveare, Henry, *The Financial Revolution, 1660–1760*, London and New York: Longman, 1991

Russell, Conrad, *The Crisis of Parliaments: English History, 1509–1660*, Oxford and New York: Oxford University Press, 1971

Russell, Conrad, *Parliaments and English Politics, 1621–1629*, Oxford and New York: Oxford University Press, 1979

Schwoerer, Lois G., ed., *The Revolution of 1688–1689: Changing Perspectives*, Cambridge and New York: Cambridge University Press, 1992

Scott, Jonathan, *Algernon Sidney and the Restoration Crisis, 1677–1683*, Cambridge and New York: Cambridge University Press, 1991

Sharp, Buchanan, *In Contempt of All Authority: Rural Artisans and Riot in the West of England, 1586–1660*, Berkeley: University of California Press, 1980

Sharpe, James A., *Crime in Early Modern England, 1550–1750*, London and New York: Longman, 1984

Sharpe, Kevin, ed., *Faction and Parliament: Essays on Early Stuart History*, Oxford and New York: Oxford University Press, 1978

Sommerville, J.P., *Politics and Ideology in England, 1603–1640*, London and New York: Longman, 1986

Speck, W.A., *Reluctant Revolutionaries: Englishmen and the Revolution of 1688*, Oxford and New York: Oxford University Press, 1988

Spufford, Margaret, *Contrasting Communities: English Villagers in the Sixteenth and Seventeenth Centuries*, Cambridge and New York: Cambridge University Press, 1974

Starkey, David, *The Reign of Henry VIII: Personalities and Politics*, London: G. Philip, 1985

Stone, Lawrence, *The Crisis of the Aristocracy, 1558–1641*, Oxford and New York: Oxford University Press, 1965

Tawney, R.H., "The Rise of the Gentry, 1558–1640," *Economic History Review* 11 (1941), 1–38

Thirsk, Joan, ed., *The Agrarian History of England and Wales*, vol. 4: *1500–1640*, Cambridge and New York: Cambridge University Press, 1967

Thomas, Keith, *Religion and the Decline of Magic: Studies in Popular Beliefs in Sixteenth- and Seventeenth-Century England*, London: Weidenfeld and Nicolson, and New York: Scribner, 1971

Trevor-Roper, Hugh, "The Gentry 1540–1640," *Economic History Review* (1953), Supplement 1

Tyacke, Nicholas, *Anti-Calvinists: The Rise of English Arminianism, 1590–1640*, Oxford and New York: Oxford University Press, 1987

Underdown, David, *Revel, Riot and Rebellion: Politics and Culture in England, 1603–1660*, Oxford and New York: Oxford University Press, 1985

Walter, John, "Grain Riots and Popular Attitudes to the Law: Maldon and the Crisis of 1629," in John Brewer and John Styles, eds., *An Ungovernable People: The English and Their Laws in the Seventeenth and Eighteenth Centuries*, London: Hutchinson, and New Brunswick, NJ: Rutgers University Press, 1980

Williams, Penry, *The Tudor Regime*, Oxford and New York: Oxford University Press, 1979

Worden, Blair, *The Rump Parliament, 1648–1653*, Cambridge: Cambridge University Press, 1974

Wormald, Jenny, *Court, Kirk and Community: Scotland, 1470–1625*, London: Arnold, and Toronto: University of Toronto Press, 1981

Wrightson, Keith and David Levine, *Poverty and Piety in an English Village: Terling, 1525–1700*, New York: Academic Press, 1979; revised Oxford and New York: Oxford University Press, 1995

Wrightson, Keith, and David Levine, *The Making of an Industrial Society: Whickham, 1560–1765*, Oxford and New York: Oxford University Press, 1991

Wrigley, E.A., and Roger S. Schofield, *The Population History of England, 1541–1871: A Reconstruction*, London: Arnold, and Cambridge, MA: Harvard University Press, 1981

Zagorin, Perez, *The Court and the Country: The Beginning of the English Revolution*, London: Routledge, and New York: Atheneum, 1969

Britain: since 1750

With the world's first industrial revolution, an empire, and a sophisticated democracy as subject matter, modern British history has acquired an importance far beyond Britain's shores as a paradigm of modernity. The narrative of British development has been characterized by the absence of revolutionary ruptures and by slow change.

Studies of the second half of the 18th century have been dominated by political history and the debate over whether George III was a constitutional monarch or a tyrant. The most influential work here is undoubtedly Lewis Namier's *The Structure of Politics at the Accession of George III* (1929) with its defense of the king and its portrait of politics as a network of interest groups devoid of ideology. Namier's ideas were later debated in Richard Pares' *King George III and the Politicians* (1953) and in Herbert Butterfield's *George III and the Historians* (1957). The later 18th century has been the focus of historical attention not only because of the Industrial Revolution but because it witnessed the first stirrings of political movements in favor of democracy and equal rights. The history of the English crowd was opened up by George Rudé in *Wilkes and Liberty* (1962) and then by John Brewer in *Party Ideology and Popular Politics at the Accession of George III* (1976). Brewer argued that the 1760s witnessed the expansion of popular political culture and identified the period between 1754 and 1789 as the time when oligarchical politics broke down to be replaced by a party system.

E.P. Thompson characterized 18th-century society as one divided between patricians and plebeians in his *Customs in Common* (1991), a model based on social conflict. By contrast, Paul Langford's *Public Life and the Propertied Englishman* (1991) emphasized the rise of the bourgeoisie, interpreting the 18th century in terms of consensus. Another consensual (and much debated) interpretation was provided by J.C.D. Clark in *English Society, 1688–1832* (1985) who argued that Britain throughout the "long 18th century" was a "confessional state" (dominated by the monarchy, the aristocracy, and the Church of England). A very different model was presented in John Brewer's *The Sinews of Power* (1989) which demonstrated the way in which Britain during the 18th century became a "fiscal-military state" in which repeated warfare revolutionized the relationship between government and people. Linda Colley's *Britons* (1992) also showed how warfare alongside Protestantism helped construct a distinctive national identity in the later 18th century.

Victorian historians viewed their own century through the lens of the Whig theory of history. The liberal constitution of the mid-Victorian years was interpreted as the product of the gradual unfolding of "progress" that had characterized British development since Magna Carta. Victorian values came into disrepute in the early 20th century, a shift often associated with Lytton Strachey's *Eminent Victorians* (1918), a classic debunking of four heroes of the previous century. However, it was G.M. Young's *Portrait of an Age* (1936) that set the agenda for modern historiography, portraying the 19th century, in reaction to Strachey, as a time of progress and modernization which found stability through the rigors of Evangelicalism. Young distinguished between early Victorian Britain (a time of social tension), the calm and confidence of mid-Victorian Britain, and the growing sense of crisis evident in the late Victorian period.

Between 1945 and 1980, studies of the 19th century burgeoned, reflecting both the professionalization of history in new universities and the expansion of social and economic history. Historians tried to explain how modern Britain with its distinctive class structure had come to be. All concurred that the 19th century was a dynamic period that had remodeled both social relations and the landscape. This was well caught by Asa Briggs' influential textbook, *The Age of Improvement* (1959) and by George Kitson Clark in *The Making of Victorian England* (1962). E.P. Thompson in *The Making of the English Working Class* (1963) and the new labor historians revealed how class conflict was central to the emergence of modern society. New attention was devoted to protest movements and working-class associations. Some of this literature was pre-occupied with the question of how Britain managed to avoid revolution, a problem introduced into the literature at the beginning of the 20th century by Elie Halévy who argued that Methodism pacified the working class. Following the lead of E.J. Hobsbawm's *Labouring Men* (1964), many historians focused on the role of the labor aristocracy (the skilled workers) in abandoning revolutionary class politics. The most well known work in this vein was John Foster's *Class Struggle and the Industrial Revolution* (1974).

Nineteenth-century social history was a particularly fertile area after 1945. In one of the most ambitious overviews, Harold Perkin's *Origins of Modern English Society* (1969) asserted that public administration had been dominated by the "aristocratic ideal" up to the 1830s when it had been replaced: first, by the "entrepreneurial," and later, in the 1870s, by the "professional" ideal. The modern welfare state inspired an interest in its antecedents with studies devoted to developments in health, factory legislation, and poor relief. Samuel Finer's 1952 biography of Sir Edwin Chadwick exemplified this new administrative history, but the key work was Oliver MacDonagh's "The Nineteenth-Century Revolution in Government", detailing the process by which abuses were dealt with and the way in which the modern centralized state began to emerge.

Political historians after the war concentrated on the coming of democracy and a two party political system. The senior political historian of early Victorian Britain was undoubtedly Norman Gash who established the importance of Sir Robert Peel as the architect of Victorian stability. Maurice Cowling's *1867: Disraeli, Gladstone and Revolution* (1967) was an anti-Whiggish account of the creation of mass democracy. Robert Blake became the most important historian of Conservatism with his 1966 biography of Disraeli and *The Conservative Party from Peel to Thatcher* (1970; revised 1985) while *Origins of the Labour Party* (1954) were treated by Henry Pelling. John Vincent's *The Formation of the British Liberal Party* (1966) was a path-breaking study, making possible the social history of Victorian politics. Similarly, H.J. Hanham's *Elections and Party Management* (1959) detailed the way in which the Victorian electoral system operated.

Since 1980, trends in research have included a greater interest in the bourgeoisie. Leonore Davidoff and Catherine Hall's *Family Fortunes* (1987) showed how gender was integral to the formation of the middle class, reflecting the new women's history. There has, however, been a shift away from an interest in class identities, evident in many of the contributions to the 1990 *Cambridge Social History of Britain, 1750–1950* edited by F.M.L. Thompson. Thompson's own *The Rise of Respectable Society* (1988) caught this mood by demonstrating the consensual nature of Victorian society where previous historians had tended to emphasize conflict. During the 1980s, there were divisions over the success, or failure, of the Victorian economy. W.D. Rubinstein studied the wealth structure of modern Britain and concluded that the Industrial Revolution was relatively unimportant, the return on financial capital being greater than that on industry. In a widely read work, *English Culture and the Decline of the Industrial Spirit* (1981), Martin Wiener argued that capitalist values had not triumphed in the world's first industrial nation, and that the new entrepreneurs increasingly copied the values of the old elite after mid-century, creating a culture that was hostile to capitalism and providing an explanation for subsequent economic failure. Since the 1980s, political history has been characterized by a concentration on the vitality of liberalism evident in J.P. Parry's *The Rise and Fall of Liberal Government in Victorian Britain* (1993), Peter Mandler's *Aristocratic Government in the Age of Reform* (1990), and Eugenio Biagini's *Liberty, Retrenchment and Reform* (1992).

Foreign policy is best approached through Kenneth Bourne's *The Foreign Policy of Victorian England* (1970) and Muriel E. Chamberlain, *"Pax Britannica"? British Foreign Policy* (1988).

Following Helen Lynd's *England in the Eighteen-Eighties* (1945), historians have concentrated on the crisis in liberal thought that emerged in the later 19th century, a reaction to poverty at home and perceived economic failure, propelling politicians to conceive of the state in new ways and launching the "New Liberalism." The modern approach to the state produced by the rediscovery of poverty in the 1880s inspired much debate. Pat Thane's *Foundations of the Welfare State* (1982) traced the growth of the state. The reaction of the Conservative party to poverty was discussed in E.H.H. Green's *The Crisis of Conservatism* (1995) which dealt with the Tariff Reform campaign. Ellen Ross' *Love and Toil* (1993) recounted the experience of poverty, while the best study of the responses to poverty is Gareth Stedman Jones' *Outcast London* (1971). In contrast, both *The Invention of Tradition* (1983), edited by E.J. Hobsbawm and Terence Ranger, and *Englishness* (1986), edited by Robert Colls and Philip Dodd, identified 1880–1920 as the heyday of invented tradition and a renewed discovery of "Englishness" as a counterweight to the crisis in the state.

Inevitably, the 20th century is a relatively new field of study. It has been framed to some extent by narratives of decline, whether in economic, political, or social and moral terms, or the end of empire. At the same time, there has also been a stress on success as shown by rising living standards, the creation of new industries, and victory in two world wars (see Peter Clarke's *Hope and Glory*, 1996). "Decline" was, however, evident in one of the most important early works, George Dangerfield's *The Strange Death of Liberal England* (1935). Part of the same debunking spirit that produced Strachey's *Eminent Victorians*, it dramatically told the story of how the Liberal party was torn apart in the years 1910–14 by three forces that it could not control: labor militancy, the struggle for female suffrage, and the Irish Home Rule movement. By contrast, more recent historians such as Peter Clarke and Duncan Tanner have demonstrated the underlying strength of pre-1914 Liberalism.

Much modern historiography has been taken up with the role of war in transforming the state and social relations. Arthur Marwick's *The Deluge* (1965) argued that World War I launched modern society with its new roles for women and the working class. The discussion of interwar Britain has been dominated by the experience of economic depression. Historical accounts such as Robert Skidelsky's *Politicians and the Slump* (1967) were colored by Keynesian assumptions making the key question "Why was Keynes not listened to?" Charles Loch Mowat and others tended to follow Churchill in assuming that the politicians of the period were "second class brains," which explained not only economic failure but also appeasement. The image of the 1930s as the "Devil's Decade" was challenged by John Stevenson and Chris Cook's *The Slump* in 1977 (updated in 1994 as *Britain in the Depression*). While not denying the appalling poverty and misery of the period, they pointed to the rise of new industries and improved living standards, suggesting that the roots of consumer society could be found before the war.

World War II is now usually seen as a "People's War" that created the basis for the postwar welfare state, the substance of Paul Addison's *The Road to 1945* (1975). James Cronin's *The Politics of State Expansion* (1991), an important study of taxation and state development, saw the war as a key moment in state development when the Treasury for the first time lost control of the economy and fiscal policy was transformed. Twentieth-century foreign policy is explored in David Reynolds' *Britannia Overruled* (1991), C.J. Bartlett's *British Foreign Policy in the Twentieth Century* (1989), and, most importantly, Paul Kennedy's *The Realities Behind Diplomacy* (1981).

Post-1945 political history has been limited by the operation of the Public Record Office's "thirty year rule," restricting access to government documents. The steady release of records is making possible studies of the early postwar administrations, of which the best example is Kenneth O. Morgan's *Labour in Power* (1984). Less positive about the postwar settlement, Corelli Barnett's *The Audit of War* (1986) argued that the British economy failed because of investment in the welfare state rather than in new technology. Postwar politics were dominated by corporatism up to 1979, a theme explored in Keith Middlemas' *Power, Competition and the State* (1986–91). The emerging social history of the postwar period has been characterized by the themes of affluence, consumerism, and consensus and has been well summarized by the contributors to Paul Johnson's *Twentieth-Century Britain* (1994), a useful collection covering social and economic history. While most historians of modern Britain have taken it as axiomatic that modernization has been an essential theme of British history, there has been a growing trend toward exploring the politics of tradition and nostalgia in Britain, of which Patrick Wright's *On Living in an Old Country* (1985) and Raphael Samuel's *Theatres of Memory* (1994) are good examples.

ROHAN MCWILLIAM

See also Briggs; Butterfield; Davidoff; Economic; Hobsbawm; Industrial Revolution; Ireland; Jones, G.; Namier; Protestantism; Rudé; Thompson, E.; Thompson, F.

Further Reading

Addison, Paul, *The Road to 1945: British Politics and the Second World War*, London: Cape, 1975

Bailey, Peter, *Leisure and Class in Victorian England: Rational Recreation and the Contest for Control, 1830–1885*, Toronto and Buffalo: University of Toronto Press, 1978; revised London and New York: Methuen, 1987

Barnett, Corelli, *The Audit of War: The Illusion and Reality of Britain as a Great Nation*, London: Macmillan, 1986

Bartlett, Christopher J., *British Foreign Policy in the Twentieth Century*, Basingstoke: Macmillan, 1989

Biagini, Eugenio F., *Liberty, Retrenchment and Reform: Popular Liberalism in the Age of Gladstone, 1860–1880*, Cambridge and New York: Cambridge University Press, 1992

Blake, Robert, *Disraeli*, London: Eyre and Spottiswoode, 1966; New York: St. Martin's Press, 1967

Blake, Robert, *The Conservative Party from Peel to Thatcher*, London: Eyre and Spottiswoode, 1970, New York: St. Martin's Press, 1971; revised 1985

Bourne, Kenneth, *The Foreign Policy of Victorian England, 1830–1902*, Oxford: Clarendon Press, 1970

Brewer, John, *Party Ideology and Popular Politics at the Accession of George III*, Oxford and New York: Oxford University Press, 1976

Brewer, John, *The Sinews of Power: War, Money, and the British State, 1688–1783*, London: Unwin Hyman, and New York: Knopf, 1989

Briggs, Asa, *The Age of Improvement, 1783–1867*, London and New York: Longman, 1959

Briggs, Asa, *Victorian Cities*, London: Odhams Press, 1963; New York: Harper, 1965

Butterfield, Herbert, *George III and the Historians*, London: Collins, 1957; revised New York: Macmillan, 1959

Cannon, John, *Parliamentary Reform, 1640–1832*, Cambridge: Cambridge University Press, 1972

Chadwick, Owen, *The Victorian Church*, 2 vols., London: A. & C. Black, and New York: Oxford University Press, 1966–70

Chamberlain, Muriel E., *"Pax Britannica"? British Foreign Policy, 1789–1914*, London and New York: Longman, 1988

Clark, J.C.D., *English Society, 1688–1832: Ideology, Social Structure, and Political Practice During the Ancien Regime*, Cambridge and New York: Cambridge University Press, 1985

Clarke, Peter F., *Lancashire and the New Liberalism*, Cambridge: Cambridge University Press, 1971

Clarke, Peter F., *Hope and Glory: Britain, 1900–1990*, London: Allen Lane, 1996

Colley, Linda, *Britons: Forging the Nation, 1707–1837*, New Haven and London: Yale University Press, 1992

Colls, Robert, and Philip Dodd, eds., *Englishness: Politics and Culture, 1880–1920*, London: Croom Helm, 1986

Cowling, Maurice, *1867: Disraeli, Gladstone and Revolution: The Passing of the Second Reform Bill*, Cambridge: Cambridge University Press, 1967

Cronin, James, *The Politics of State Expansion: War, State and Society in Twentieth-Century Britain*, London and New York: Routledge, 1991

Dangerfield, George, *The Strange Death of Liberal England*, New York: Smith and Haas, 1935; London: Constable, 1936

Davidoff, Leonore, and Catherine Hall, *Family Fortunes: Men and Women of the English Middle Class, 1780–1850*, London: Hutchinson, and Chicago: University of Chicago Press, 1987

Dickinson, H.T., ed., *Britain and the French Revolution, 1789–1815*, Basingstoke: Macmillan, and New York: St. Martin's Press, 1989

Dyos, H.J., and Michael Wolff, eds., *The Victorian City: Images and Realities*, 2 vols., London: Routledge, 1973

Finer, Samuel Edward, *The Life and Times of Sir Edwin Chadwick*, London: Methuen, 1952; New York: Barnes and Noble, 1970

Floud, Roderick, and Donald McCloskey eds., *The Economic History of Britain since 1700*, 2nd edition, 3 vols., Cambridge: Cambridge University Press, 1994

Foster, John, *Class Struggle and the Industrial Revolution: Early Industrial Capitalism in Three English Towns*, London: Weidenfeld and Nicolson, and New York: St. Martin's Press, 1974

Gash, Norman, *Politics in the Age of Peel: A Study in the Technique of Parliamentary Representation, 1830–1850*, London and New York: Longman, 1953

Green, E.H.H., *The Crisis of Conservatism: The Politics, Economics, and Ideology of the British Conservative Party, 1880–1914*, London and New York: Routledge, 1995

Halévy, Elie, *Histoire du peuple anglais au XIXe siècle*, 4 vols., Paris: Hachette, 1912–32; in English as *A History of the English People in the Nineteenth Century*, 5 vols., London: Unwin-Benn, 1924–34

Hammond, J.L., and Barbara Hammond, *The Village Labourer, 1760–1832: A Study in the Government of England before the Reform Bill*, London and New York: Longman, 1912

Hanham, H.J., *Elections and Party Management: Politics in the Time of Disraeli and Gladstone*, London: Longman, 1959; Hamden, CT: Archon, 1978

Harris, José, *Private Lives, Public Spirit: A Social History of Britain, 1870–1914*, Oxford and New York: Oxford University Press, 1994

Harrison, J.F.C., *Robert Owen and the Owenites in Britain and America: The Quest for the New Moral World*, London: Routledge, 1969

Hilton, Boyd, *The Age of Atonement: The Influence of Evangelicalism on Social and Economic Thought, 1795–1865*, Oxford and New York: Oxford University Press, 1988

Hobsbawm, Eric J., *Labouring Men: Studies in the History of Labour*, London: Weidenfeld and Nicolson, 1964; New York: Basic Books, 1965

Hobsbawm, Eric J., *Industry and Empire: An Economic History of Britain since 1750*, London: Weidenfeld and Nicolson, and New York: Pantheon, 1968

Hobsbawm, Eric J., and Terence O. Ranger, eds., *The Invention of Tradition*, Cambridge and New York: Cambridge University Press, 1983

Johnson, Paul, ed., *Twentieth-Century Britain: Economic, Social, and Cultural Change*, London and New York: Longman, 1994

Jones, Gareth Stedman, *Outcast London: A Study in the Relationship Between Classes in Victorian Society*, Oxford: Clarendon Press, 1971; New York: Pantheon, 1984

Jones, Gareth Stedman, *Languages of Class: Studies in English Working-Class History, 1832–1982*, Cambridge and New York: Cambridge University Press, 1983

Kennedy, Paul M., *The Realities behind Diplomacy: Background Influences on British External Policy, 1865–1980*, London and Boston: Allen and Unwin, 1981

Kitson Clark, George, *The Making of Victorian England*, London: Methuen, and Cambridge, MA: Harvard University Press, 1962

Langford, Paul, *Public Life and the Propertied Englishman, 1689–1798*, Oxford and New York: Oxford University Press, 1991

Lynd, Helen Merrell, *England in the Eighteen-Eighties: Toward a Social Basis for Freedom*, London and New York: Oxford University Press, 1945

MacDonagh, Oliver, "The Nineteenth-Century Revolution in Government: A Reappraisal," *Historical Journal* 1 (1958), 52–67

McKibbin, Ross, *Ideologies of Class: Social Relations in Britain, 1880–1950*, Oxford and New York: Oxford University Press, 1990

Mandler, Peter, *Aristocratic Government in the Age of Reform: Whigs and Liberals, 1830–1852*, Oxford and New York: Oxford University Press, 1990

Marwick, Arthur, *The Deluge: British Society and the First World War*, London: Bodley Head, and Boston: Little Brown, 1965

Middlemas, Keith, *Power, Competition and the State*, 3 vols., Basingstoke: Macmillan, and Stanford, CA: Stanford University Press, 1986–91

Morgan, Kenneth O., *Labour in Power, 1945–51*, Oxford: Clarendon Press, 1984

Morgan, Kenneth O., *The People's Peace: British History, 1945–89*, Oxford and New York: Oxford University Press, 1990

Mowat, Charles Loch, *Britain Between the Wars, 1918–1940*, London: Methuen, and Chicago: University of Chicago Press, 1955

Namier, Lewis, *The Structure of Politics at the Accession of George III*, London: Macmillan, 1929; New York: St. Martin's Press, 1957

Pares, Richard, *King George III and the Politicians*, Oxford: Clarendon Press, 1953

Parry, Jonathan Philip, *The Rise and Fall of Liberal Government in Victorian Britain*, New Haven and London: Yale University Press, 1993

Pelling, Henry, *Origins of the Labour Party, 1880–1900*, London: Macmillan, and New York: St. Martin's Press, 1954

Perkin, Harold, *Origins of Modern English Society, 1780–1880*, London: Routledge, 1969

Prothero, I.J., *Artisans and Politics in Early Nineteenth-Century London: John Gast and His Times*, Baton Rouge: Louisiana State University Press, 1979

Reynolds, David, *Britannia Overruled: British Politics and World Power in the Twentieth Century*, London and New York: Longman, 1991

Ross, Ellen, *Love and Toil: Motherhood in Outcast London, 1870–1918*, Oxford and New York: Oxford University Press, 1993

Rubinstein, William D., *Capitalism, Culture, and Decline in Britain, 1750–1990*, London and New York: Routledge, 1993

Rudé, George, *Wilkes and Liberty: A Social Study of 1763 to 1774*, Oxford: Clarendon Press, 1962

Samuel, Raphael, *Theatres of Memory*, London and New York: Verso, 1994

Skidelsky, Robert, *Politicians and the Slump: The Labour Government of 1929–1931*, London: Macmillan, 1967

Stevenson, John, and Chris Cook, *The Slump: Society and Politics during the Depression*, London: Cape, 1977; revised as *Britain in the Depression: Society and Politics, 1929–39*, London and New York: Longman, 1994

Strachey, Lytton, *Eminent Victorians: Cardinal Manning, Florence Nightingale, Dr. Arnold, General Gordon*, London: Chatto and Windus, and New York: Putnam, 1918

Tanner, Duncan, *Political Change and the Labour Party 1900–1918*, Cambridge and New York: Cambridge University Press, 1990

Taylor, A.J.P., *English History, 1914–45*, Oxford and New York: Oxford University Press, 1965

Thane, Pat, *Foundations of the Welfare State*, London: Longman, 1982; revised 1996

Thompson, Dorothy, *The Chartists*, London: Temple Smith, and New York: Pantheon, 1984

Thompson, E.P., *The Making of the English Working Class*, London: Gollancz, 1963; New York: Pantheon, 1964

Thompson, E.P., *Customs in Common*, London: Merlin Press, and New York: New Press, 1991

Thompson, F.M.L., *English Landed Society in the Nineteenth Century*, London: Routledge, 1963

Thompson, F.M.L., *The Rise of Respectable Society: A Social History of Victorian Britain, 1830–1900*, London: Fontana, and Cambridge, MA: Harvard University Press, 1988

Thompson, F.M.L., ed., *The Cambridge Social History of Britain, 1750–1950*, 3 vols., Cambridge and New York: Cambridge University Press, 1990

Vincent, J.R., *The Formation of the British Liberal Party*, London: Constable, and New York: Scribner, 1966; revised 1976

Webb, Sidney, and Beatrice Webb, *The History of Trade Unionism*, London and New York: Longman, 1894; revised 1920

Wiener, Martin, *English Culture and the Decline of the Industrial Spirit, 1850–1980*, Cambridge and New York: Cambridge University Press, 1981

Wright, Patrick, *On Living in an Old Country: The National Past in Contemporary Britain*, London: Verso, 1985

Young, George Malcolm, *Portrait of an Age: Victorian England*, London: Oxford University Press, 1936; reprinted Oxford and New York: Oxford University Press, 1957

British Empire

The British empire was acquired and lost between the late 16th and mid-20th centuries, and was the largest and most extensive in history. Literature devoted to Britain's imperial enterprise is considerable and covers virtually every aspect of the empire's existence, reflecting the size and diversity of the empire itself. Two recent works covered the whole imperial narrative: Lloyd's *The British Empire, 1558–1983* (1984) took the story up to the Falkland Islands war, perhaps the last of Britain's imperial conflicts; while James' *The Rise and Fall of the British Empire* (1994) attempted to show how the empire influenced the British and their worldview.

In general, the historiography is divided into three parts. The first covers the acquisition and loss of the American colonies (1600–1783), which, including the Caribbean, were the main focus of British interests. North America became the preferred area for British emigrants, although the entire region was developed economically, the dominant trades being tobacco in America and sugar in the West Indies, both of which relied on slaves. McFarlane's *The British in the Americas, 1480–1815* (1994) linked the history and development of both regions and argued that this is necessary to understand fully Britain's involvement in the "New World." The economic contribution of these colonies to Britain's burgeoning North Atlantic trading system has been the focus of much debate among historians: for a good introduction on the importance of slavery and sugar see Sheridan's *Sugar and Slavery* (1974). The principal work on the slave trade is Curtin's *The Atlantic Slave Trade* (1969). More controversially, Williams in his *Capitalism and Slavery* (1944, reprinted 1964), connected the slave trade with the development of Britain's industrial revolution. This view has been widely challenged, especially in Ward's "The Profitability of Sugar Planting in the British West Indies, 1650–1834" (1978). Other scholars have gone further by examining the effects of the colonial economies as a whole on Britain's industrial and economic development: Rule's *The Vital Century* (1992) provides a good overview of the debate.

The constitutional relationship between Britain and its American colonies was dealt with by Greene in his *Peripheries and Center* (1986). He argued that for the most part Britain ruled the American colonies on sufferance and that when the British tried to impose their will the colonists revolted. The literature on the American revolution is vast, but two good starting points are Countryman's *The American Revolution* (1985) and Bonwick's *The American Revolution* (1991). For a good overview which argued that the war in America was essentially a "people's war" and thus the first of the modern wars see Conway's *The War of American Independence, 1775–1783* (1995).

The British were also involved in India through the auspices of the East India Company. During the 18th century the Company transformed itself from a trading concern into a major imperial power backed by the British government. This evolution has been dealt with in Lawson's comprehensive account *The East India Company: A History* (1993).

The loss of the American colonies ended the "first" British empire, and it was often said that the second began when Britain concentrated on the east following the end of the French wars in 1815. Bayly's *Imperial Meridian* (1989) disputed this and showed that the empire grew immensely between 1780 and 1830, particularly in India and by the conquest of Dutch, French, and Spanish territories in South Africa (Cape Colony), the Indian Ocean, and the West Indies during the Napoleonic Wars. According to Bayly, there was no significant break therefore between the end and beginning of the first and second empires.

During the 19th century the British empire expanded to a size hitherto unprecedented. The whole of India (including modern Pakistan and Burma) was acquired, as were vast areas of Africa and southeast Asia. The process of imperial expansion was completed after the defeat of the German and Turkish empires in 1918, when Britain gained more African territory and, importantly, much of the Middle East. Unlike the first period, there are several good surveys: Hyam's *Britain's Imperial Century, 1815–1914* (1976) covered the main phase of expansion, while Porter's *The Lion's Share* (1975) ended following decolonization. More recently, Judd's *Empire* (1996) took a thematic approach to explain expansion and examines the influence of the empire on British identity.

The literature for this period is vast and there are many explanations and themes. To contemporaries, particularly missionary societies, Britain moved abroad to bestow true religion, justice, and firm but compassionate rule for the "natives." This idea of "benevolent imperialism" motivated many adventurers, such as David Livingstone. For work on the missionaries and their outlook in the tropical empire see Stanley *The Bible and the Flag* (1990). Rather than settling in the tropics, British emigrants preferred to colonize Canada, Australia, and New Zealand. Seeley's *Expansion of England* (1883) regarded these white colonies as essentially "England" abroad, the colonists bringing with them English notions of freedom and the rule of law. Later historians developed this idea by claiming that these colonies followed a natural progression within British imperialism. Once they were deemed mature, they were given constitutions and self-government, coming together with Britain in a commonwealth of free nations: the volumes of the *Cambridge History of the British Empire*, written mostly in the 1920s and 1930s, were the high-water mark of this trend. In Oxford, this was taken a step further by scholars such as Coupland in *The Empire in These Days* (1935) and Hancock in his 2-volume *Survey of British Commonwealth Affairs* (1937–42). They argued that the nonwhite colonies could, through British guidance, also achieve self-government, and join a multiracial commonwealth tied together by shared allegiances and interests. Mansergh's *The Commonwealth Experience* (1969; revised 1982) took the story further, to the era of decolonization and the establishment of the Commonwealth. Mansergh concluded that the national interests of the new independent states had proved too strong for the sort of relationship envisaged by earlier British historians and politicians. Instead the Commonwealth emerged as an organization designed to further social, economic, and cultural ties. In this way the Commonwealth has endured and this is an achievement in itself and should be seen as such.

A theme which has produced abundant and controversial literature is one devoted to economic explanations of British expansion. Initially, Hobson's *Imperialism* (1902) argued that Britain operated an aggressive imperialist policy because of the demands of capitalists for new territory for capital investment. This idea proved popular with later Marxist analysts, who believed governments acted at the behest of pugnacious businessmen. Later, Gallagher and Robinson disagreed, first in their "The Imperialism of Free Trade" (1953), and then in their more substantial *Africa and the Victorians* (1961), arguing that Britain preferred to dominate local economies indirectly and used annexation as a last resort. British expansion was not driven by the needs of capitalists but by governments determined to secure British interests, both economic and strategic. British intervention owed more to the collapse of local societies under pressure from British and western economic penetration. More recently, however, Cain and Hopkins took Hobson's views a step further in their 2-volume *British Imperialism* (1993). They argued that since the 18th century British economic expansion has been driven by a collection of southern English elite groups, including the City of London, whom they termed "gentlemanly capitalists." This group influenced government policy in order to secure their own needs and interests over 200 years. This view has been rigorously challenged by, for example, Porter in his article, "'Gentlemanly Capitalism' and Empire" (1990), which contended that the various regions of the empire were not bound solely by the interests of "gentlemanly capitalists," a term which takes no account of the divergent concerns within Britain's economic elites. Porter suggested that other areas of Britain and the empire played their part in economic and territorial expansion as well.

The impact of the empire on British society has added a major topic to imperial historiography. Politicians used the empire to gain popular support, while the people were influenced by calls for imperial defence and by the way empire pervaded popular culture, for instance in schooling and the music halls. Works written and edited by Mackenzie, especially his *Imperialism and Popular Culture* (1986), have spearheaded this approach, and have added an important dimension to British, as well as to imperial history.

Decolonization, essentially the period between 1945 and 1965, is the third part of Britain's imperial story, and has generated its own historiography. For a good overview see Darwin's *The End of the British Empire* (1991). Darwin argued that there are numerous causes which explain why Britain shed its empire in the space of twenty years. Various factors need to be considered: Britain's domestic difficulties; changes in world power and economics that adversely affected Britain; and the rise of colonial nationalism. Nevertheless, vestiges of the empire remain, in Bermuda and Gibraltar, for example; while Hong Kong reverted to China only in 1997. However, Britain still retains strong links with its former colonies as the existence and apparent vitality of the Commonwealth testifies.

KEITH SURRIDGE

See also Curtin; Greene; India; Seeley; Subaltern; Williams, E.

Further Reading

Bayly, C.A., *Indian Society and the Making of the British Empire*, Cambridge and New York: Cambridge University Press, 1988

Bayly, C.A., *Imperial Meridian: The British Empire and the World, 1780–1830*, London and New York: Longman, 1989

Bond, Brian, ed., *Victorian Military Campaigns*, London: Hutchinson, and New York: Praeger, 1967

Bonwick, Colin, *The American Revolution*, London: Macmillan, and Charlottesville: University Press of Virginia, 1991

Brown, Judith M., *Modern India: The Origins of an Asian Democracy*, Delhi, Oxford, and New York: Oxford University Press, 1985; 2nd edition 1994

Cain, Peter J., *Economic Foundations of British Overseas Expansion, 1815–1914*, London: Macmillan, 1980

Cain, Peter J., and Anthony G. Hopkins, *British Imperialism: Innovation and Expansion, 1688–1914* and *Crisis and Deconstruction, 1914–1990*, 2 vols., London and New York: Longman, 1993

Cambridge History of the British Empire, 8 vols., Cambridge: Cambridge University Press, 1929–63

Chaudhuri, K.N., *The Trading World of Asia and the English East India Company, 1660–1760*, Cambridge: Cambridge University Press, 1978

Conway, Stephen, *The War of American Independence, 1775–1783*, London and New York: Arnold, 1995

Countryman, Edward, *The American Revolution*, New York: Hill and Wang, and London: Tauris, 1985

Coupland, Reginald, *The Empire in these Days: An Interpretation*, London: Macmillan, 1935

Curtin, Philip D., *The Atlantic Slave Trade: A Census*, Madison: University of Wisconsin Press, 1969

Darwin, John, *Britain and Decolonisation: The Retreat from Empire in the Post-War World*, London: Macmillan, and New York: St. Martin's Press, 1988

Darwin, John, *The End of the British Empire: The Historical Debate*, Oxford and Cambridge, MA: Blackwell, 1991

Davenport, Thomas, *South Africa: A Modern History*, London: Macmillan, and Toronto: University of Toronto Press, 1977; revised 1987, 1991

Fieldhouse, D.K., *Economics and Empire, 1830–1914*, London: Weidenfeld and Nicolson, and Ithaca, NY: Cornell University Press, 1973

Gallagher, John, and Ronald Robinson, "The Imperialism of Free Trade," *Economic History Review* 6 (1953), 1–15

Greene, Jack P., *Peripheries and Center: Constitutional Development in the Extended Polities of the British Empire and the United States, 1607–1788*, Athens: University of Georgia Press, 1986

Hancock, W.K., *Survey of British Commonwealth Affairs*, 2 vols., London and New York: Oxford University Press, 1937–42; reprinted 1964

Havinden, Michael, and David Meredith, *Colonialism and Development: Britain and Its Tropical Colonies, 1850–1960*, London and New York: Routledge, 1993

Hobson, J.A., *Imperialism: A Study*, London: Nisbet, 1902, revised 1938; 3rd edition, London: Unwin Hyman, 1988

Hyam, Ronald, *Britain's Imperial Century, 1815–1914: A Study of Empire and Expansion*, New York: Barnes and Noble, and London: Batsford, 1976

James, Lawrence, *The Rise and Fall of the British Empire*, London: Little Brown, and New York: St. Martins Press, 1994

Judd, Denis, *Empire: The British Imperial Experience from 1765 to the Present*, London: HarperCollins, 1996

Lawson, Philip, *The East India Company: A History*, London and New York: Longman, 1993

Lloyd, Trevor Owen, *The British Empire, 1558–1983*, Oxford and New York: Oxford University Press, 1984

Louis, William Roger, general editor, *The Oxford History of the British Empire*, Oxford: Oxford University Press, 1998–

McFarlane, Anthony, *The British in the Americas, 1480–1815*, London and New York: Longman, 1994

MacKenzie, John M., ed., *Imperialism and Popular Culture*, Manchester: Manchester University Press, 1986

McNaught, Kenneth, *The Pelican History of Canada*, London and Baltimore: Penguin, 1969; revised 1988

Madden, Frederick, and D.K. Fieldhouse, eds., *Oxford and the Idea of Commonwealth*, London: Croom Helm, 1982

Mansergh, Nicholas, *The Commonwealth Experience*, London: Weidenfeld and Nicolson, and New York: Praeger, 1969; revised in 2 vols., London: Macmillan, and Toronto: University of Toronto Press, 1982

Marshall, P.J., *Problems of Empire: Britain and India, 1757–1813*, London: Allen and Unwin, and New York: Barnes and Noble, 1968

Marshall, P.J., *Bengal, the British Bridgehead: Eastern India, 1740–1828*, Cambridge and New York: Cambridge University Press, 1988

Marshall, P.J., ed., *The Cambridge Illustrated History of the British Empire*, Cambridge and New York: Cambridge University Press, 1996

Molony, John, *The Penguin History of Australia*, New York: Viking, and London: Penguin, 1988

Morris, James, *The Pax Britannica Trilogy*, 3 vols., London: Faber, and New York: Harcourt Brace, 1968–78

Parry, J.H., Philip Sherlock, and Anthony Maingot, *A Short History of the West Indies* London: Macmillan, and New York: St. Martin's Press, 1956; 4th revised edition, 1987

Porter, Andrew, and A. Stockwell, eds., *British Imperial Policy and Decolonization, 1938–64*, 2 vols., London: Macmillan, 1987–89

Porter, Andrew, "'Gentlemanly Capitalism' and Empire: The British Experience since 1750?" *Journal of Imperial and Commonwealth History* 18 (1990), 265–95

Porter, Andrew, ed., *The Atlas of British Overseas Expansion*, London: Routledge, and New York: Simon and Schuster, 1991

Porter, Bernard, *The Lion's Share: A Short History of British Imperialism, 1850–1970*, London and New York: Longman, 1975; 3rd edition [with dates 1850–1995], 1996

Rice, Geoffrey, ed., *The Oxford History of New Zealand*, Oxford and New York: Oxford University Press, 1992

Robinson, Ronald, and John Gallagher with Alice Denny, *Africa and the Victorians: The Official Mind of Imperialism*, London: Macmillan, and New York: St. Martin's Press, 1961; revised 1981

Rule, John, *The Vital Century: England's Developing Economy, 1714–1815*, London and New York: Longman, 1992

Seeley, J.R., *The Expansion of England: Two Courses of Lectures*, London: Macmillan, 1883; New York: Macmillan, 1904

Sheridan, Richard B., *Sugar and Slavery: An Economic History of the British West Indies 1623–1775*, Baltimore: Johns Hopkins University Press, 1974

Simmons, Richard C., *The American Colonies: From Settlement to Independence*, London: Longman, and New York: McKay, 1976

Stanley, Brian, *The Bible and the Flag: Protestant Missions and British Imperialism in the Nineteenth and Twentieth Centuries*, Leicester: Apollos, 1990

Ward, J.R., "The Profitability of Sugar Planting in the British West Indies, 1650–1834," *Economic History Review* 31 (1978), 197–213

Warwick, Peter, ed., *The South African War: The Anglo-Boer War, 1899–1902*, Harlow: Longman, 1980

Williams, Eric, *Capitalism and Slavery*, Chapel Hill: University of North Carolina Press, 1944; London: Deutsch, 1964

Broszat, Martin 1926–1989
German historian

As with most West German historians of his generation, Martin Broszat was heavily influenced by his personal experience of the Third Reich and the war. Almost all of his work as a historian can be understood as an attempt to come to grips with the Nazi past in a double sense: first, in a scientific sense, that is by trying to develop satisfactory historical explanations for this troublesome and traumatic period in German history, and, second, to combat the mystifications and the repression of the Nazi period and especially of the Holocaust. His historical scholarship was also meant as "historical pedagogy" (*kritische Aufklärungsarbeit*) for the postwar German public at large.

Being one of the founders of German contemporary history (*Zeitgeschichte*) after World War II he gained most of his fame as the director of the Institut für Zeitgeschichte in Munich between 1972 and 1989. As its administrator and as an author he was widely known inside and outside of Germany. In his work four main themes can be discerned. First, he explained the content and role of national socialist ideology. Second, he examined the institutional structure of the "Hitler state" and the explanation of the Holocaust. Third, he revealed the ways ordinary Germans had experienced Nazi rule and the ways in which they had resisted its "total" claims. And finally, he exposed the problematical ways German historians have handled the Nazi past and the desirability of a "historicization" (*Historisierung*) of the Third Reich.

In his first book, *Der Nationalsozialismus* (1960; *German National Socialism*, 1966), Broszat analyzed the worldview of national socialism. In contrast to the totalitarian interpretations of national socialism, as developed by Ernst Nolte and Karl Dieter Bracher, Broszat emphasized the unsystematic character of this ideology. He singled out anti-Semitism, antibolshevism, and the notion of *Lebensraum*, as its core ideas, and argued that they functioned as legitimations for the real core of Nazi ideology: the longing for a "rebirth" of "the German nation," hatred, and a pathological need to "act." The last was directed against all groups inside and outside the German borders classified by the Nazis as "foreign to the German race" (*Volksfremde*) and "enemies of the German Volk" (*Volksfeinde*). National socialist ideology appealed primarily to the anxiety-ridden middle classes who felt threatened by the economic crisis and hyperinflation.

At the same time Broszat emphasized that the Nazi takeover and national socialist politics could not be interpreted as the realization of a political program, as had been done by the Nazis themselves and was still done by historians such as Andreas Hillgruber, Klaus Hildebrand, and Eberhard Jäckel. According to Broszat, Nazi politics should be interpreted not so much as the result of the conscious intentions and ideas of Hitler, but primarily as the outcome of the institutional structure and dynamics of the Nazi state. Against so-called "intentionalist" interpretations, which stressed the importance of Hitler's anti-Semitic intentions, Broszat developed – together with Hans Mommsen – the so-called "structuralist" or "functionalist" interpretation of the Third Reich. In this interpretation Hitler's power and policies are primarily explained as a function of the political structure of Nazi Germany. In this way he countered the widely held "demonological" interpretations that reduced the Third Reich to the "demon" Hitler and a bunch of "Nazi criminals."

In his book *Der Staat Hitlers* (1969; *The Hitler State*, 1981), Broszat developed his structuralist interpretation of Nazi politics. The foundation of this interpretation was the so-called double structure of the Nazi state. By this Broszat referred to the fact that after the Nazi movement had taken over political power in Germany, it had created an organizational political structure parallel to the existing institutions of the state and in direct competition with them. Formally the leaders of these new organizations, such as the "Gauleiter," got their instructions from Hitler and were responsible only to him. In fact they developed a high measure of initiative and autonomy – partly because of the vagueness of Hitler's orders. A chaotic division of formal responsibilities was the result – and a permanent struggle for power among the competing organizations and their leaders. In this political "struggle for survival" the radicals usually proved to be "the fittest" with a process of "cumulative radicalization" in politics the result.

The fact that this radicalization of Nazi policy acquired such a murderous character was explained by Broszat not primarily by Nazi ideology, but by a process of "negative selection." As the Nazis were dependent on the cooperation of the traditional German power elites in the economy, the military, and the civil service, their ideological rhetoric concerning "a revolution of society" could be transformed into political action only in those domains, where no conflicts with these vested interests were to be expected. Therefore the political energy of the Nazis was increasingly channeled towards their "negative" goals: the battle against the *Volksfeinde* and *Volksfremde* inside and outside of Germany. Inside Germany this amounted to the segregation, isolation, and, finally, elimination of racially defined minorities that were of no importance to the elites, such as the mentally and hereditary ill, the homosexuals, the Gypsies, and the Jews. Outside Germany it meant – a racially defined – war of aggression.

In the context of the rapid German advances on the Eastern front in 1941–42, when the majority of the European Jews came within reach of Nazi Germany, the vague ideological slogans concerning the "solution of the Jewish problem" thus changed into a policy and a practice of hitherto unimaginable mass murder. So according to Broszat the extreme radical and murderous character of Nazi policies was primarily a result of the structure and dynamics of the "Hitler state" and only secondarily a result of a centrally orchestrated, intentional policy. In contrast with Nazi propaganda, Hitler in fact had been a "weak dictator" and Nazi Germany a polycracy instead of a monocracy.

In line with his earlier attacks on the totalitarian and intentionalist interpretations of national socialism was Broszat's last major project, a history of Nazi Germany from the perspective of "everyday life" (*Alltagsgeschichte*). In the multivolume *Bayern in der NS-Zeit* (Bavaria in the National-Socialist Period, 1977–83) he and his collaborators tried to show on a local and regional level that many ordinary Germans and ordinary institutions (such as the army, churches, and the civil service) withstood the Nazi claim to total power and continued to function – more or less – according to their traditional values. For this relative "immunity" to Nazi domination he introduced the (biological) notion of *Resistenz*. In this way Broszat and his followers have tried to restore the continuity in German history that had been lost in most demonological and totalitarian interpretations. Restoring the continuity in German history over the Nazi period was necessary in Broszat's view to break through the "insulation" of this period from the rest of German history and its treatment as an empire of pure evil. What was needed was a bracketing of ahistorical, moral categories and the application of scientific, historical method to the period: in short, the "historicization" of the Third Reich. Therefore the historians had to roll the history of Nazi Germany forward and not backward and look at it through the eyes of (German) contemporaries while bracketing the knowledge of its disastrous outcome. This also meant necessarily a relativization of "Auschwitz," because its central importance *after* 1945 did not correspond to its marginal importance *before* 1945 – at least for the majority of the ordinary Germans. Black and white contrasts, such as the contrast between the (bad or evil) collaboration with the Nazis and the (good or heroic) resistance against them were to be supplanted by a more "realistic" coloring of the behavior of ordinary Germans in the various shades of grey. Only by such a "historicization" of the Third Reich could its history lose its moralistic, pedagogical overtones and become really "historical." In the *Historikerstreit* of 1986–87 this argument was, totally contrary to Broszat's intentions, taken over by Ernst Nolte and Andreas Hillgruber to whitewash modern German history. Therefore his ideas in this respect – including the notion of *Resistenz* – have been heavily criticized and debated.

On balance Broszat's "structuralist" interpretation has been very important in both the academic and public debate about the character of Nazi Germany, although few historians today defend it in its original form. Many critics, such as Christopher Browning and Ian Kershaw, have rejected Broszat's radical downplaying of the role of intentionality, ideology, and the individual Hitler. His proposal to "historicize" the period has also been criticized for its apologetic potential, by Saul Friedländer and Dan Diner. Nevertheless, no serious historian of the Third Reich can afford to ignore Broszat's interpretation and arguments.

CHRIS LORENZ

See also Germany: 1800–1945; Germany: since 1945; Mommsen, H.; Schieder; Srbik

Biography
Martin Broszat. Born Leipzig, 14 August 1926. Studied at University of Leipzig, 1944–49; University of Cologne, 1949–52, PhD 1952. Taught at University of Cologne, 1954–55; Institute of Contemporary History, University of Munich, 1955–69: head, 1972–89; and University of Konstanz, 1969–80 (emeritus). Married Alice Welter, 1953 (1 son, 2 daughters). Died Munich, 14 October 1989.

Principal Writings
Der Nationalsozialismus: Weltanschauung, Programm und Wirklichkeit, 1960; in English as *German National Socialism, 1919–1945*, 1966

With Ladislaus Hory, *Der kroatische Ustascha-Staat, 1941–1945* (Croatian Ustaša State, 1941–1945), 1964

Der Staat Hitlers: Grundlegung und Entwicklung seiner inneren Verfassung, 1969; in English as *The Hitler State: The Foundation and Development of the Internal Structure of the Third Reich*, 1981

Editor with others, *Bayern in der NS-Zeit* (Bavaria in the National-Socialist Period), 4 vols., 1977–83

Die Machtergreifung: der Aufstieg der NSDAP und die Zerstörung der Weimarer Republik, 1984; in English as *Hitler and the Collapse of Weimar Germany*, 1987

Nach Hitler: der schwierige Umgang mit unserer Geschichte (After Hitler: The Difficult Handling of Our History), 1987

Further Reading
Henke, Klaus-Dietmar, and Claudio Natoli, eds., *Mit dem Pathos der Nüchternheit: Martin Broszat, das Institut für Zeitgeschichte und die Erforschung des Nationalsozialismus* (With the Pathos of Soberness: Martin Broszat, the Institute of Contemporary History, and the Research of National Socialism), Frankfurt and New York: Campus, 1991

Pätzold, Kurt, "Martin Broszat und die Geschichtswissenschaft in der DDR" (Martin Broszat and East German Historiography), *Zeitschrift für Geschichtswissenschaft* 39 (1991), 663–76

Broué, Pierre 1926–

French historian of 20th-century Europe

Atypical among French leftist historians in his early rejection of Stalinism, Broué was one of the first western scholars to perform extensive research in the government archives that opened with the collapse of the Soviet Union. This allowed him the satisfaction of documenting many points on which he had previously only speculated.

Broué's numerous historical works have influenced more than a generation of students and scholars. His *La Révolution et la guerre d'Espagne* (1961; *The Revolution and Civil War in Spain*, 1972) rejected the conventional interpretations of both the left and right while putting forth new insights into the 1936–39 period. The motivation for this work was initially personal; he had discussed the Spanish events with participants his own age, who, according to Broué, shared impressions and interpretations absent from published studies.

Among his other major works are *Le Parti bolchévique* (The Bolshevik Party, 1963), *Révolution en Allemagne* (Revolution in Germany, 1971), *Les Procès de Moscou* (The Moscow Trials, 1964) and *Léon Sedov* (1993). Broué's *Trotsky* (1988) has become something of a bestseller among historical works available in the French-speaking world. This work is at odds with the classic Isaac Deutscher trilogy which, Broué asserts, offers a cursory analysis of the most important documents and contains much speculation without factual support. In addition, Broué has served as director of the Leon Trotsky Institute as well as editor of the journal *Cahiers Léon Trotsky* (Archives Leon Trotsky).

What marks Broué's work as unique is his commitment to a critical Trotskyist interpretation of history. He regards Trotsky's *History of the Russian Revolution* as a text that provides a methodology which can bring the historian closer to the "truth." Using this and other of Trotsky's writings as guides, Broué has developed a school of historical thought quite different from other intellectual tendencies. For example, until the collapse of the USSR, within the French historical profession most scholars were influenced either by the pro-Stalin Communist party or the anticommunist right. Broué, however, was critical of both tendencies, arguing that both wrote "in shades of day and night."

Despite his admiration for Trotsky, Broué's work has been widely criticized by members of the far left who consider much of his work to be too moderate and critical of Trotsky. His response is that he refuses to allow his personal feelings to obscure his historical judgment. Thus, in *Trotsky*, he points to the contradictions and defects of his subject while basing his own evaluations upon documentation that often shatters cherished myths.

WILLIAM A. PELZ

Biography

Born France, 8 May 1926. Received diplome d'études supérieure, University of Grenoble, 1952; doctorate, University of Paris, Nanterre, 1972. Taught at lycées in Nyons, Switzerland; Beaune, Paris; and Monereau-faut-Yonne, France, 1948–65; and at Institut d'Etudes Politiques, St. Martin d'Hères (rising to professor), from 1965. Married Andrée Jacquenet, teacher (2 sons, 3 daughters).

Principal Writings

With Emile Témime, *La Révolution et la guerre d'Espagne*, 1961; in English as *The Revolution and the Civil War in Spain*, 1972

Le Parti bolchévique: histoire du P.C. de' U.R.S.S. (The Bolshevik Party), 1963

Les Procès de Moscou (The Moscow Trials), 1964

Révolution en Allemagne, 1917–1923 (Revolution in Germany), 1971

L'Assassinat de Trotsky: 1940 (The Assassination of Trotsky), 1980

Trotsky, 1988

Léon Sedov: fils de Trotsky, victime de Staline (Leon Sedov: Son of Trotsky, Victim of Stalin), 1993

Further Reading

Pelz, William A., "From the French Resistance to Marxist History: An Interview with Professor Pierre Broué," *Left History*, 3/1 (Spring/Summer 1995), 123–29

Brown, Peter 1935–

British historian of late antiquity

The period from 250 to 750 CE was one in which much of Europe was fought over between the representatives of the Germanic and Classical civilizations. That battle has been recommenced in our own century between those wishing to extend the boundaries of the "early Middle Ages" and those who desire to advance the sway of Ancient History. It is probably fair to say that at the turn of the century, the former had command of the situation. Ancient History at Oxford then (and still today) was divided from "Modern History" at the accession of Diocletian in 284 CE. The period after that, with particular regard to the establishment of Christian dominance in the empire, was seen as medieval or Byzantine. This position has elsewhere suffered steady erosion. Classicists realized that they could re-label "decline" as "transformation," and there was a move to reclaim the Latin and Greek literature of the later age which had long been neglected because of its seeming "degeneracy" from classical standards.

While there had been considerable interest in the period of *Spätantike* in Germany from the start of this century, that enthusiasm did not spread widely in the English-speaking world until the 1960s. For British historiography, perhaps the two great landmarks of that movement were the appearance of A.H.M. Jones' monumental multivolume *Later Roman Empire, 284–602* (1964) and the densely argued intellectual biography *Augustine of Hippo* (1967) by Peter Brown. Though he has now long worked in America, Brown sprang from the Oxford tradition and his early work shows both great rigor and zest toward Brown's source material as well as an unusually intense feeling of rapport with it. *Augustine of Hippo* demonstrates these qualities to a high degree. Above all, it imparts a feeling of an almost magisterial knowledge of the very substantial corpus of Augustine's work and a remarkable ability to identify with changes in Augustine's attitude through the course of his lifetime. It was immediately regarded as a classic work, and it perhaps remains Brown's most substantial.

Brown's influence, however, was also advanced by a number of important articles, perhaps the most influential of which was his "The Rise and Function of the Holy Man in Late

Antiquity" (1971). This study demonstrated the way in which Brown had developed away from textual analysis into investigating new ways of understanding the ancient world. Religious "holy men" were seen as figures of power in local society, as village patrons and intercessors between ordinary people and other forms of authority. This radical approach was mirrored by Brown's subsequent analysis of relics, the fullest exposition of which appears in *The Cult of the Saints* (1981). Tombs and the remains of the bodies of saints were understood to "operate" much as the persons and cult of holy men had done. The tombs of the "Very Special Dead" were seen as centers of power, and places at which communication was effected between the suppliant and the authority of the sublime. Brown was himself a major factor in the rise of interest in his period of specialism. The very term "late antiquity" is often associated directly with Brown's work and, especially in America, a whole series of works on saints, relics, "the Holy," and their "active operation" in late Roman and medieval society was initiated largely by the inspiration of his example through the 1970s and 1980s.

Brown's particular genius is an ability to draw the reader sympathetically into a vanished world. The sights, colors, and smells of late antiquity are summoned up for us: cities bustle, crowds shout and jostle, priests chant, and mosaics glisten. He also possesses a remarkable flair for summing up the rhythms of time and change: slow and imperceptible as life drowses on around the Mediterranean, or in sudden sweeps down from the north or out of the desert. It is perhaps true that Brown at times appears so self-enchanted that his argument can seem to shimmer out of focus before the attention of those who lack his perception. But if more recent works, such as *The Body and Society* (1988), have failed to shock us anew with quite such vivid visions of the past, his achievement to date has inspired a whole generation of students to ponder the fascinating enigma that is late Roman society.

DOMINIC JANES

See also Body; Cameron; Momigliano; Roman

Biography

Peter Robert Lamont Brown. Born 26 July 1935. Educated at Aravon School, Bray, County Wicklow, Ireland; Shrewsbury School; New College, Oxford, MA. Fellow, All Souls College, Oxford, 1956–75; lecturer in medieval history, Merton College, Oxford, 1970–75; special reader in Byzantine history, 1970–73; reader, 1973–75; professor, Royal Holloway College, University of London, 1975–78; University of California, Berkeley, 1978–86; and Princeton University, from 1986. Married 1) Friedl Esther Löw-Beer, 1959 (2 daughters); 2) Patricia Ann Fortini, 1980; 3) Elizabeth Gilliam, 1989.

Principal Writings

Augustine of Hippo: A Biography, 1967
"The Rise and Function of the Holy Man in Late Antiquity," *Journal of Roman Studies* 61 (1971), 80–101
Religion and Society in the Age of Saint Augustine, 1972
The Social Context to the Religious Crisis of the Third Century AD, 1975
The Making of Late Antiquity, 1978
The Cult of the Saints: Its Rise and Function in Latin Christianity, 1981

Society and the Holy in Late Antiquity, 1982
The Body and Society: Men, Women, and Sexual Renunciation in Early Christianity, 1988
Power and Persuasion in Late Antiquity: Towards a Christian Empire, 1992
Authority and the Sacred: Aspects of the Christianisation of the Roman World, 1995

Browne, Edward G. 1862–1926
British historian of Iran and of Persian literature

E.G. Browne was the son of a wealthy shipbuilder, steered automatically via Eton to Cambridge University, where he reluctantly qualified as a physician at his father's insistence, but his background gave no hint of his future calling. As a teenager during the Russo-Turkish war of 1877–78, he found his sympathies aroused for the Turks, and spent the summer of 1882 in Istanbul; he subsequently enrolled in the Cambridge Indian Languages Tripos to learn Arabic and Persian, and as a fellow of Pembroke College in 1887 spent a year in Iran. His early interest in international politics, a propensity to support the underdog, and a fascination for religious phenomenology and Persian poetry, henceforth characterized his activities and writings. As a historian, his principal topics were Babism (a chiliastic religious and revolutionary social movement in Iran, an offshoot of Iranian Shi'ism and the ancestor of Baha'ism); the Iranian Constitutional Revolution; and the literary history of Iran in Islamic times.

Even before his year in Iran, Browne had read Gobineau's account of the Babi revolt and its suppression (1848–52), and was impressed by the heroism of its martyrs. He devoted much of his journey to a clandestine search for Babis and their manuscripts, and in 1890 visited both the leader of the minority sect, the Azalis, on Cyprus, and leaders of the majority sect, the Baha'is, at Acre. He published an edited translation of an account of Babi and Baha'i history (*A Traveller's Narrative*, 1891) and several further translations and editions up until 1918 (*Materials for the Study of the Babi Religion*); his obituary of 'Abd al-Bahâ' in 1921 approvingly noted the Baha'i leader's promotion of racial unity in the segregated United States. However, Browne's conviction that the Azalis were closer to the "original" form of the religion and his treatment of their accounts as more authentic has drawn criticism from Baha'i scholars.

From 1905 until 1911 Browne was caught up in Iran's Constitutional movement, characteristically on the side of the revolutionaries and against the repressive Qajar monarchy and its Russian supporters. As vice-chairman of the Persia Committee, a pressure group composed of writers, journalists and MPs of both parties, he opposed the Anglo-Russian Convention of 1907 (which had established Russian and British zones of influence in Iran), and lobbied in vain through lectures and pamphlets for the withdrawal of Russian troops from Iran and the resignation of foreign minister Edward Grey. The main scholarly results of his involvement are his 1910 book, *The Persian Revolution of 1905–1909*, and *The Press and Poetry of Modern Persia* (1914). The latter in particular, with its extensive quotations of patriotic and political verse of the time, is a celebration of the democratic ideals Browne saw embodied in Iran's vigorous free press, and a broadside aimed at those in Britain who (in the pages of the *Times*, among other vehicles) dismissed Iranians as decadent and unfit to govern themselves. Both works remain unique sources for the intellectual life of Iran of the period, since Browne personally knew several of the Iranian nationalists then exiled in France and England.

Browne's monumental *Literary History of Persia* (1902–24), spanning the period from the 10th to the early 20th century, has never been surpassed in either scope or depth by Western scholarship, and has only one rival among modern works in Persian. Based on original sources, most of them as yet in manuscript and many available to Browne alone, it included excerpts of major works in Persian and in translation, and digressed broadly into the political and social history of Iran. Volume 1 has been faulted for essentially duplicating the existing histories of ancient Persia and the Arab conquest, but Browne's innovative prolegomena constituted a useful corrective to the Arabocentric historiography of the early Islamic period. Volume 4 perpetuated several prejudices which Browne derived from (or at least shared with) contemporary Iranian scholars, notably the tradition that "post-classical" Persian literature of the past three centuries (in particular that of the 18th) was of generally poor quality, all artifice and no art. This view is now being revised.

Among Browne's many other contributions to Orientalist scholarship were his editions and translations of Arabic and Persian manuscripts, including Mostawfi's universal history (the *Ta'rikh-i-Guzida*) and Ebn Esfandyâr's history of Tabaristan, and his completion of E.J.W. Gibb's *A History of Ottoman Poetry* on his colleague's untimely death in 1901. He also attracted candidates in the consular and colonial services to an academic training, producing such later historians of the Middle East as Sir Reader Bullard and Laurence Lockhart; and the school of modern Middle Eastern languages so formed became the nucleus of the later Middle East Centre at Cambridge.

Browne was a maverick. Although his activism on behalf of the Iranian Constitutionalists (as also on behalf of the Boers and for Irish Home Rule) fell mainly on deaf ears and cost him some deserved recognition, and his enthusiasm for the followers of the Bab seems to have led him along a side stream, he contributed to a timely change of orientation in British scholarship of the East. Hitherto, Islamic studies in Britain had meant classical Arabic; Persian was an ancillary, the borrowed classical language of administration and intellectual contact in India, and Iran a geopolitical appendage of the Raj. Browne's predecessor as a historian of Iran, Sir John Malcolm (1769–1863), exemplified this attitude as an amateur, an envoy from the Indian empire who entered Iran by the "back door" of the Persian Gulf and chose to chronicle Persia's past. Browne, a professional academic entering literally and figuratively by the "front door" of contemporary Iran, opened the way to the full range of Islamic and modern Iranist scholarship.

JOHN R. PERRY

See also Iran

Biography

Edward Granville Browne. Born Uley, near Dursley, England, 7 February 1862. Educated at Glenalmond and Eton; then studied medicine and Oriental languages, Pembroke College, Cambridge, 1879–84; and St. Bartholomew's Hospital. Never practiced medicine; travelled in Persia, 1887–88; lecturer, later professor of Persian, Cambridge University, 1888–1926, and fellow, Pembroke College. Married Alice Caroline Blackburne Daniell, 1906 (died 1925; 2 sons). Died 5 January 1926.

Principal Writings

Editor and translator, *A Traveller's Narrative*, by Abdul Baha, 1891
A Year Among the Persians, 1893
Editor, *A History of Ottoman Poetry* by E.J.W. Gibb, vols. 2–6, 1901–09
A Literary History of Persia, 4 vols., 1902–24
The Persian Revolution of 1905–1909, 1910
Editor, *The Ta'rikh-i-Guzida; or, Select History of Hamdu'llah/Mustawfi-i-Qazwini*, 1910
The Press and Poetry of Modern Persia, 1914
Materials for the Study of the Babi Religion, 1918
Arabian Medicine, 1921
Selections from the Writings of E.G. Browne on the Babi and Baha'i Religions, edited by Moojan Momen, 1987

Further Reading

Arberry, A.J., *Oriental Essays: Portraits of Seven Scholars*, London: Allen and Unwin, and New York: Macmillan, 1960
Arnold, T.W., and R.A. Nicholson, eds., *A Volume of Oriental Studies Presented to E.G. Browne on His 60th Birthday*, Cambridge: Cambridge University Press, 1922
Balyuzi, H.M., *Edward Granville Browne and the Baha'i Faith*, London: Ronald, 1970
McLean, D., "English Radicals, Russia and the Fate of Persia, 1907–1913," *English Historical Review* 93 (1978), 338–52
Nicholson, R.A., *A Descriptive Catalogue of the Oriental mss. Belonging to the Late E. G. Browne*, Cambridge: Cambridge University Press, 1932 (by Browne, completed by Nicholson)

Brunner, Otto 1898–1982

Austrian historian

Otto Brunner was an avid pan-German who served in World War I and taught at the University of Vienna. In 1943 he joined the Nazi party, which resulted in his losing his post in 1945 during Allied denazification. Allegations of right-wing sentiments have clouded judgments about the value of Brunner's work ever since. After only a short retirement, in 1954 Brunner became a full professor at the University of Hamburg. He strongly believed in and practiced a historical theory which incorporated many disciplines, and he objected to all single-minded schools as too limited in scope. His own work is marked with a distinctive blend of social and political theory.

Brunner has never been widely translated into English, largely due to the complexity of his prose. What is widely regarded as his most important work, *Land und Herrschaft* (1939; *Land and Lordship*, 1992) has only recently become available in an English edition. This work explored the origins of the social and legal position of the south German nobility and was immensely controversial at its publication. Brunner protested that medieval history had too often been conceptualized as a precursor of the 19th-century nation-state. He found no such model in his research, in which he examined early medieval, Austrian, and Bavarian sources. Brunner found that no "state," as such, existed, and that the public and private spheres could not be so well defined in the past as they are in the modern era. Brunner did, however, allow that a long tradition of legal and constitutional forms, based on the rights of the nobility to own and defend land, did exist. *Land and Lordship* went to great lengths to explain the importance of the relationship between the nobility and the land. Brunner has been criticized in modern studies, which place more emphasis on the nobility, for over-stating this relationship, but this in no way diminishes the impact of this highly original work.

Originally published in 1939 the book has undergone some significant alterations. Earlier versions were tainted with Nazi sympathies. Brunner has often been criticized for his references to the German *Volk*, for expounding a philosophy of German unity, and even for his usage of Südostdeutschlands (southeast Germany) in the book's original subtitle in place of Österriech (Austria). Brunner, a well known pan-German, was also accused of harboring sympathies for the Anschluss – the forced merger of Austria with Germany in 1938. Although this may be the case, Kaminsky and Melton pointed out in the preface to the English edition, Brunner's choice of language reflected his approach to history, as much as, if not more than, his political affiliations. Furthermore, Brunner's work is not tainted with Nazi ideology, that is, racism and anti-Semitism. In any case Brunner removed much of the controversial language in the 4th edition, published in 1959.

STEPHEN K. CHENAULT

See also Begriffsgeschichte; Conze; Koselleck; Universal

Biography

Born Mödling, Lower Austria, 21 April 1898. Served on the Italian front in World War I. Studied history and geography, University of Vienna, PhD 1922; historian and archivist, Institut für Österreichische Geschichtsforschung, 1921–22. Archivist, Haus-, Hof-, und Staatsarchiv, Vienna, 1923–31; professor of Austrian history, University of Vienna, 1931–45: director, Institut für Österrechische Geschictsforschung, 1940–45; dismissed at end of World War II; professor of economic history, University of Hamburg, from 1954. Died 12 June 1982.

Principal Writings

Die Finanzen der Stadt Wien von den Anfängen bis ins 16. Jahrhundert (Municipal Finance in Vienna from Its Founding to the 17th Century), 1929

Land und Herrschaft: Grundfragen der territorialen Verfassungsgeschichte Österreichs im Mittelalter, 1939, 4th edition 1959; in English as *Land and Lordship: Structures of Governance in Medieval Austria*, 1992

Adeliges Landleben und europäischer Geist: Leben und Werk Wolf Helmhards von Hohbert, 1612–1688 (Noble Rural Life and European Culture), 1949

Die Rechtsquellen der Städte Krems und Stein (Legal Sources of the Towns Krems and Stein), 1953

Abendländisches Geschichtsdenken (Western Historical Thought), 1954

Neue Wege der Sozialgeschichte: Vorträge und Aufsatze, 1956; revised as *Neue Wege der Verfassungs und Sozialgeschichte* (New Paths of Constitutional and Social History), 1968

Editor with Werner Conze and Reinhart Koselleck, *Geschichtliche Grundbegriffe: historisches Lexikon zur politisch-sozialen Sprache in Deutschland* (Historical Concepts: A Historical Dictionary of Political-Social Language in Germany), 1972–

Sozialgeschichte Europas im Mittelalter (European Medieval Social History), 1978

Further Reading

Bergengrün, Alexander, and Ludwig Deike, eds., *Alteuropa und die moderne Gesellschaft: Festschrift für Otto Brunner* (Old Europe and Modern Society), Göttingen: Vandenhoeck & Ruprecht, 1963

Zöllner, Erich, "Otto Brunner," *Mitteilungen des Instituts für Österreichische Geschichtsforschung* 90 (1982), 519–22

Zum Gedenken an Otto Brunner (1898–1982) (In Memory of Otto Brunner), Hamburg: Pressestelle der Universität, 1983

Buckle, Henry Thomas 1821–1862

British positivist historian

An independent scholar of considerable means, Henry Thomas Buckle identified with the French positivist philosophy advanced by Auguste Comte. Buckle emerged as an apologist for a structured and predicable view of history; he viewed history as a system and a science. Critical of the antiquarians, biographers, and chroniclers of his day, Buckle anticipated that he would emerge as the first of a new generation of British historians who would clarify historical values, introduce a new methodology, and eliminate the prevailing views of history.

Buckle received no formal higher education; after traveling throughout Europe during the late 1830s and early 1840s, he established a residence in London in 1842. He read all of the available sources and developed a plan in 1853 for a multivolume *History of Civilization in England*; the first volume was published in 1857 and was discussed widely. This volume was an expostulation of Buckle's methodology and his critique of "contemporary" history; a second volume focused on Spain and Scotland was published in 1861, the year before Buckle's untimely early death from "fever" in Damascus. Thus, Buckle never did formally address England in his study. In 1872 Helen Taylor edited additional notes and writings in *Miscellaneous and Posthumous Works*.

Historiographers have continued to be attracted by Buckle's independence of thought and the boldness of his argumentation; nonetheless, most argued that Buckle's use of statistical data was flawed and that any claim of his objectivity lacks justification. Some contend that Buckle was not an historian at all; rather, that he was by method and mentality a 19th-century sociologist. However, Buckle's positivism has continued to attract discussion, especially in Eastern Europe where positivism and history as a science were part of the orthodoxy of the communist world. Theorists there continued to grapple with his theories into the 1990s.

WILLIAM T. WALKER

See also Historiology; Lecky; Positivism; Solov'ev; Villari

Biography

Born Lee, Kent, 24 November 1821, to a wealthy merchant family. Lived and traveled as a gentleman scholar. Died Damascus, 29 May 1862.

Principal Writings

History of Civilization in England, 2 vols., 1857–61

Miscellaneous and Posthumous Works, edited by Helen Taylor, 3 vols., 1872; re-edited by J.M. Robertson, 1904

Further Reading

Diamond, Solomon, "Buckle, Wundt, and Psychology's Use of History," *Isis* 75 (1984), 143–52

Hanham, H.J., ed., "Introduction," to *Buckle on Scotland and the Scotch Intellect*, Chicago: University of Chicago Press, 1970

Huth, Alfred Henry, *The Life and Writings of Henry Thomas Buckle*, London: Low Marston Searle and Rivington, and New York: Scribner and Welford, 1880

Robertson, John Mackinnon, *Buckle and His Critics: A Study in Sociology*, London: Sonnenschein, 1895

St. Aubyn, Giles, *A Victorian Eminence: The Life and Works of Henry Thomas Buckle*, London: Barrie, 1958

Shavit, Yaacob, "Ha-simus sel maskilim yehudim be-mizrah eyropah be-misnato sel Henri Tomas Baql" (The Works of Henry Thomas Buckle and Their Application by the Maskilim of Eastern Europe), *Zion* 49 (1984), 401–12

Zub, Alexandru, "The Buclean Impact on Romanian Culture," *Annuarul Institutului de Istorie si Arheologie "A.D. Xenopol"* [Romania] supplement 4 (1983), 189–99

Bugis and Makasar (Sulawesi) Chronicles

The Bugis and Makasar peoples of South Sulawesi in Indonesia share a tradition of history-writing in a "state chronicle" form. The writing of chronicles was probably inspired by European models (one chancellor of Makassar had a library of European books) although an early version of the Malay Annals (Sejarah Melayu) may have been known in Makassar. A chronicle is in essence a history of the ruling of a kingdom. A succession of rulers is set out and historical events are located within their reigns. The chronicles are written in a terse, matter-of-fact style and supernatural events are generally found only at the beginning. The Bugis author of the Chronicle of Boné distances himself from these supernatural events by use of the words *gareq* (so the story goes) and *riasengngi* (it is said).

Bugis and Makasar chronicles are concerned largely with events in the 16th and 17th centuries but contain the names of rulers as early as the 14th. There is clear evidence of a rigorous selection process, and most chronicles are short: that of Boné, an important west coast kingdom, consists of 17 manuscript pages. The indigenous word for chronicle, (Bugis) *attoriolong* and (Makasar) *pattorioloang*, "that which concerns people of the past," is the general term for any narrative prose text of a historical nature. Chronicles contain no dates (the use of dates in contemporary diaries suggests that this was a stylistic convention) but their chronology, which is by days, months, years and reign-lengths, is remarkably accurate when examined against evidence from contemporary Dutch sources. By Javanese and Malay standards, Bugis and Makasar chronicles exhibit a singular historical consciousness and objectivity. Their authors are unknown but had access to court archives and were unafraid to state the truth plainly: one ruler is described as lacking intelligence and possessing a bad temper. Nevertheless, the chronicles make claims through history and ancestry for the legitimacy of rulers and a hereditary ruling class.

Important though they are, chronicles make up a only a small proportion of Bugis and Makasar historical writings. The kingdoms of Goa, Talloq, Boné, and Wajoq, as well as the minor kingdom of Tanétté, have chronicles, but the kingdoms of Luwuq, Soppéng, and Sidénréng have none. Diaries, treaties, legal records, correspondence, king lists, genealogies, and short accounts of single subjects in the form of notes or a narrative make up the greater part of the corpus of Bugis historical texts. These sources were used by chroniclers, and some can be identified in surviving codices. The information they contain extends back to about 1300, the approximate date of the development of writing in South Sulawesi.

Bugis and Makasar chronicles are written in the Bugis-Makasar script, a near-syllabary modelled on a South Sumatran script derived, ultimately, from India. Writing was originally on long strips of palm leaf but was replaced after 1600 by imported European paper, bound into books. Makasar historical sources are fewer than Bugis and traditionally date from the invention of the Old Makasar script by a harbor master of Makassar in the first half of the 16th century. The Old Makasar script was replaced by the Bugis-Makasar script in the 18th century.

One of the first uses of writing in Bugis-speaking areas was the recording of genealogies for the purpose of marriage alliances. Important genealogies are headed by a *tomanurung* (a heavenly-descended being) or a *totompoq* (one who arose from the underworld) or both. These supernatural beings, of either sex, account for the origin of status, which in theory was always ascriptive and which legitimized political authority. Genealogies record the transmission, through women, who were in principle not allowed to marry beneath themselves, of status, and thus the right to rule. The kingdom of Goa alone developed a patrilineal transmission of office. The wide distribution of genealogies among the upper classes and their veracity (as witnessed by the ability to cross-reference individuals in the genealogies of different kingdoms) enable the construction of a historical chronology for the period before 1600, a period for which there are few European sources. Also important are the court diaries, which belong mostly to the 16th century and provide precise dates for the events they record. Poems in the *toloq* meter are often woven around historical individuals and events.

Short texts in narrative or note form dealing with a single subject are common in Bugis codices but do not represent such a distinct genre as the chronicles, and their historicity has to be established on an individual basis. Many narrative texts are evidently of oral origin and some are plainly legends. Nevertheless, they are more numerous than chronicles and may in time yield much useful information on South Sulawesi's past.

Traditional historical forms survived until the 20th century but have since been replaced in all but the most remote regions by modern historical forms originating in Europe.

I.A. CALDWELL

See also Ali Haji

Further Reading

Blok, R., *History of the Island of Celebes*, 4 vols., Calcutta: Calcutta Gazette Press, 1817

Caldwell, I.A., "Power, State and Society among the pre-Islamic Bugis," *Bijdragen tot de Taal-, Land- en Volkenkunde* 151 (1995), 394–421

Cense, A.A., "Old Buginese and Makassarese Diaries," *Bijdragen tot de Taal-, Land- en Volkenkunde* 122 (1966), 416–28

Macknight, C.C., "The Rise of Agriculture in South Sulawesi before 1600," *Review of Indonesian and Malaysian Affairs* 17 (1983), 92–116

Noorduyn, J., "Some Aspects of Makassar-Buginese Historiography," in D.G.E. Hall, ed., *Historians of South East Asia*, London: Oxford University Press, 1961

Noorduyn, J., "Origins of South Celebes Historical Writing" in M.A. Soedjatmoko *et al.*, eds., *An Introduction to Indonesian Historiography*, Ithaca, NY: Cornell University Press, 1965

Pelras, C., "Introduction à la littérature Bugis" (Introduction to Bugis Literature), *Archipel* 20 (1975), 239–67

Reid, Anthony, "The Rise of Makassar," *Review of Indonesian and Malaysian Affairs* 17 (1983), 117–60

Zainal Abidin, Andi, "Notes on the Lontara as Historical Source," *Indonesia* 12 (1971), 159–72

Bultmann, Rudolf 1884–1976

German theologian and New Testament scholar

The German Lutheran theologian Rudolf Bultmann was one of the most influential biblical scholars of the 20th century. As Professor of New Testament studies at the University of Marburg from 1921 to 1951, Bultmann was the major figure in the development of "form criticism" which held that the synoptic gospels (Matthew, Mark, and Luke) of the New Testament were collections of religious traditions and ideas already existing in the primitive church when they were written by their evangelist authors. Bultmann claimed that these narratives were determined by the concerns of the early church and thus primarily reflect the church's working out of its doctrinal and cultural position at that time. The evangelists edited the stories of Jesus and those statements attributed to him in the gospels as forms of *kerygma* (preaching) placed within a historical narrative used to reinforce the doctrinal positions of the early church. The problem now is that the mythology and historical circumstances upon which the gospels depend serves in the modern age to render our knowledge of Jesus problematic, as neither those mythological nor historical conditions still apply.

Bultmann's *Die Geschichte der synoptischen Tradition* (1921; *The History of the Synoptic Tradition*, 1963), along with the work of Martin Dibelius and Karl Ludwig Schmidt, was to prove very controversial, as critics held that form criticism eroded confidence in the historicity of the New Testament. The Form Critics applied themselves to classifying groups of things in the gospels such as miracle stories and pronouncements attributed to Jesus in order to determine their historical reliability, and believed that the *form* of these passages indicated their probable dates. Early in his career Bultmann was allied with the so-called "dialectical theologians" such as Karl Barth, who rejected the late 19th-century liberalization of German Protestant theology. For Bultmann the greatest area of concern was the liberal focus on the historicality of the person of Jesus. Bultmann argued that the central hurdle in Christian belief rested between the life of Jesus, the historical information about him in the gospel narratives, and his being the Christ of Christian faith. The issue of faith had to move beyond the historical to focus on the problem of being.

At the heart of his theology Bultmann attempted to pass over the historicity of Jesus in order to focus on the ways in which Christ was significant for individuals today. Jesus' history is merely our knowledge of his existence. The larger issues concerning the nature of Christ, Christ as the means of Christian understanding, the proclamation of the gospel, and the work of the holy spirit, are the true subject of theology. Thus historical knowledge of Jesus receded before concerns that stressed the believer's experience of God through the risen Lord. With this as his focus Bultmann moved theology beyond the distinction between "fact" and myth, to focus on finding the authentic meaning of Christ's divine nature.

Bultmann was greatly influenced by his Marburg contemporary Martin Heidegger and in particular Heidegger's *Sein und Zeit* (1927; *Being and Time*, 1962). Bultmann came to see the human condition as determined by a search for self-understanding and meaning. He found the answer in the individual Christian's encounter with the resurrected Lord. Thus Bultmann's theology trafficked in existential issues and language when he claimed that the gospel writers presupposed the concern with being so typical of religious existentialism. Bultmann's union of existentialism and his analysis of the problems inherent in New Testament mythology form the substance of his "Neues Testament und Mythologie" (1948; "New Testament and Mythology," 1953). He argued for the *Entmythologisierung* or "demythologizing program" that would render the mythological statements of the New Testament meaningful in the modern context through translating them into the language of being, that is, human existence, which could be understood only in existential terms. The notion of being was the common ground between the gospels and the modern age.

Bultmann's prominence was due mostly to the controversial nature of Form Criticism and his project for "demythologizing" the gospels. In both areas he suggested abandoning the search for the historical grounding of Christian faith. His critics justifiably claimed that his focus on the existential was won at a cost of denying the ontological aspects of any notion of God. At the same time Bultmann contributed greatly to modern scholarship on the origins of the Christian church, church historiography, the development of the science of hermeneutics, as well as his own unification of philosophical and theological concerns. All of this work proved to be a major attempt to reiterate the significance of Jesus Christ in modern theology. His enormous influence from the late 1940s through the 1960s was due in no small part to his courageous opposition to Nazism as a member of the Confessing Church in Germany and as a leading German academic. Nevertheless, since his death Bultmann's theology has proven vulnerable to criticism for its connection to Heidegger as well as for its reductionism. His exegesis of biblical texts has also proven to be highly problematic and is now questioned widely.

SEÁN FARRELL MORAN

See also Christianity

Biography

Rudolf Karl Bultmann. Born Wiefelstede, 20 August 1884, son of a parson. Studied at the universities of Tübingen, Berlin, and Marburg, degree in theology, 1910. Taught New Testament studies, University of Marburg, 1912–16; University of Breslau (now Wrocław, Poland), 1916–20; University of Giessen, 1920–21; and University of Marburg, 1921–51 (emeritus). Married Helene Feldmann, 1917 (3 daughters). Died Marburg, 30 July 1976.

Principal Writings

Die Geschichte der synoptischen Tradition, 1921; in English as *The History of the Synoptic Tradition*, 1963; revised 1968

Jesus, 1926; in English as *Jesus and the Word*, 1934

Glauben und Verstehen, 4 vols., 1933–65; vol. 2 in English as *Essays Philosophical and Theological*, 1955, vol. 1 in English as *Faith and Understanding*, 1969

Das Evangelium des Johannes, 1941; in English as *The Gospel of John: A Commentary*, 1971

"Neues Testament und Mythologie," in Hans Werner Bartsch, ed., *Kerygma und Mythos*, 1948; in English as "New Testament and Mythology" in Hans Werner Bartsch, ed., *Kerygma and Myth: A Theological Debate*, vol. 1, 1953

Theologie des Neuen Testaments, 3 vols. 1948–53; in English as *Theology of the New Testament*, 2 vols., 1951–55

Das Urchristentum im Rahmen der antiken Religionen, 1949; in English as *Primitive Christianity in Its Contemporary Setting*, 1956

With Karl Jaspers, *Die Frage der Entmythologisierung*, 1954; in English as *Myth and Christianity: An Inquiry into the Possibility of Religion Without Myth*, 1958

History and Eschatology, 1957

Existence and Faith: Shorter Writings, 1960

Further Reading

Fergusson, David, *Bultmann*, London: Geoffrey Chapman, 1991; Collegeville, MN: Liturgical Press, 1992

Henderson, Ian, *Rudolf Bultmann*, London: Carey Kingsgate, 1965; Richmond: John Knox Press, 1966

Johnson, R.A., ed., *Rudolf Bultmann: Interpreting Faith for the Modern Era*, London and San Francisco: Collins, 1987

Jones, S. Gareth J., *Bultmann: Towards a Critical Theology*, Cambridge: Polity Press, and Cambridge, MA: Blackwell, 1991

Macquarrie, John, *An Existentialist Theology: A Comparison of Heidegger and Bultmann*, London: SCM Press, and New York: Macmillan, 1955

Macquarrie, John, *The Scope of Demythologizing: Bultmann and His Critics*, London: SCM Press, 1960; New York: Harper, 1961

Painter, John, *Theology as Hermeneutics: Rudolf Bultmann's Interpretation of the History of Jesus*, Sheffield: Almond, 1987

Schmithals, Walter, *An Introduction to the Theology of Rudolf Bultmann*, London: SCM Press, and Minneapolis: Augsburg Press, 1968

Young, Norman James, *History and Existentialist Theology: The Role of History in the Thought of Rudolf Bultmann*, Philadelphia: Westminster Press, and London: Epworth, 1969

Burckhardt, Jacob 1818–1897

Swiss cultural historian

Jacob Burckhardt's major achievements lay in his refinement of the Renaissance as a concept in historical periodization, and in the methodological innovations of his research in cultural history.

The son of a clergyman who wrote history, Burckhardt received a thorough classical education in his native Basel. In 1839 he went to the University of Berlin for four years, studying with Leopold von Ranke, the most famous historian of the day, and with Franz Kugler, the great art historian. After returning to Switzerland, Burckhardt combined lecturing at the University of Basel with newspaper work. For a few years he edited a conservative newspaper, but increasingly resented the time that journalism took away from his historical research.

The success that he enjoyed in publishing his research enabled him to secure a chair of history at the Zurich Polytechnic where he taught from 1855 to 1858. Burckhardt then returned to the University of Basel and remained there for the rest of his life.

Burckhardt's research dealt with the cultural history of Italy, where the lifelong bachelor made frequent aesthetic pilgrimages and research trips. Cultural history as a field of scholarly research had long since developed its own characteristic features, emphasizing in particular the daily life of people in society. In many ways, cultural history as it was then practiced resembled the social history of today. Burckhardt inherited this tradition of cultural history, but revolutionized the field by expanding it to include the prominent classes and by singling out the great individuals who best reflected the spirit of the age, the *Zeitgeist*, as the prime specimens for historical research.

Two turning points in Italian culture, with profound implications for the general history of Europe, preoccupied Burckhardt in his principal works. In *Die Zeit Constantins des Grossen* (1853; *The Age of Constantine the Great*, 1949), Burckhardt imaginatively portrayed the downfall of classical antiquity at the hands of triumphant Christianity. He had tried to fit this book into the standard pattern of cultural history, but the personality of Constantine had emerged nonetheless as a vivid example of how exceptional individuals alter the historical process. With his first step Burckhardt had created a new approach to the history of ideas by combining a detailed analysis of elites in the context of cultural history's traditional emphasis on social themes.

He used the same general scholarly approach in his masterpiece, *Die Cultur der Renaissance in Italien* (1860; *The Civilization of the Renaissance in Italy*, 1904). In this book he sought to explain why the Middle Ages had ended in Italy sooner than elsewhere and why the Renaissance had begun there. The first historian to recognize the sharp break between these two periods, Burckhardt entertained a complex and substantially negative view of the Renaissance. Its immense cultural energy and originality thrilled him and inspired his unstinting praise. Nonetheless, the strongly conservative Burckhardt saw in the Renaissance the beginnings of the amoral modern state, which he feared, and of the soulless culture of modern times, which he detested.

He traced the good and the bad in the Renaissance to the concept of individualism with which, for better and worse, the Middle Ages had virtually nothing to do. Burckhardt sought to show how this concept had arisen in the particular social and political context of late medieval Italy, and what its intellectual antecedents had been in antiquity. In a series of brilliantly original and socially framed vignettes from high Italian culture, Burckhardt built his case for understanding the Renaissance as the historical moment when the human ego, unimpeded by medieval restraints, began its initially magnificent but increasingly dreadful odyssey in the modern world.

The moral dilemma of the Renaissance issued from the humanist movement. The humanists, whose scholarly researches into antiquity and celebration of the individual human personality inspired much of Renaissance art, did not intend to undermine Christianity, but they undermined it just the same. Humanism evolved into an ambiguous but essentially pagan supplement to Christianity with an implicit and sometimes explicit tendency to substitute itself for scripturally based values. This moral ambiguity transformed Italy into "a school for scandal."

With the spread of humanism beyond the Alps, the rest of Europe eventually found itself in the same moral crisis that had befallen the Italians. Hence, Burckhardt's famous description of the Italians as "the first born among the sons of Europe" contains a decidedly dubious element. Vague and noncommittal about his own religious views, Burckhardt neither desired to return to the Middle Ages nor thought it possible to do so. No modern man "could pass but one hour in the Middle Ages," and he repeatedly expressed his thanks for the artistic achievements of the Renaissance. The problem of how to maintain morality without the sanction of religious value remained, however, and Burckhardt grew increasingly pessimistic about the West's chances of ever solving it.

Praised by many of its admirers as one of the most original works of history ever written, The Civilization of the Renaissance in Italy also gave occasion for many famous attacks. Its candidly elitist assumptions and values make it a controversial book still. Even Burckhardt's critics, however, have been forced to answer the questions he raised in his seminal book, and it remains the most influential work of Renaissance scholarship and of cultural history ever published.

Burckhardt, only 42 when The Civilization of the Renaissance in Italy appeared, never completed another scholarly work. He did write two handbooks: one on travel, Der Cicerone (1855; The Cicerone, 1908), and another on art appreciation that dealt with architecture only, Die Geschichte der Renaissance in Italien (The History of the Renaissance in Italy, 1867). He devoted most of the rest of his career to teaching. His lectures inspired much admiration in Basel, notably on the part of his younger colleague, Friedrich Nietzsche, for their astringent irony and immense learning. Burckhardt conducted no graduate seminars and taught few doctoral students, but one of his pupils, Heinrich Wölfflin, succeeded him and perpetuated his influence in the field of art history. Although Burckhardt only taught small classes at a university with a relatively undistinguished reputation, he became famous as one of the leading historians in Europe because of the recognition that The Civilization of the Renaissance in Italy brought him.

Several more books, edited by Burckhardt's friends, appeared after his death. Three of these posthumous publications contributed significantly to his reputation as a historian of genius. In the four volumes of Griechische Kulturgeschichte (1898–1902; The History of Greek Culture, 1963), derived from his lectures, he returned to one of his favorite themes: the threat posed by the state to the individual. This problem had become much worse in modern times, as he observed in Weltgeschichtliche Betrachtungen (1905; Reflections on History, 1943) and Historische Fragmente aus dem Nachlass (1929; Judgments on History and Historians, 1958), both based on his historiography lectures, but permeated with prophetic ruminations about the cataclysmic future of Europe. With Europe's moral center gone, Burckhardt could see nothing but disaster ahead.

RICHARD DRAKE

See also Burke; Cantimori; Chabod; Cultural; Gilbert; Ginzburg; Góngora; Greece: Ancient; Haskins; Huizinga; Intellectual; Italy: Renaissance; Kristeller; Literature; Martines; Morison; Niebuhr; Nietzsche; Philosophy of History; Ranke; Reformation; Renaissance Historical Writing; Roman; Schieder; Schnabel; Schorske; Ullman; Weber, M.; White, H.

Biography

Jacob Christopher or Jakob Christoph Burckhardt. Born Basel, 25 May 1818, to a patrician clerical family. Received a classical education; then briefly studied theology, University of Basel before rejecting this course of study; studied history with Leopold von Ranke and Johann G. Droysen, University of Berlin, PhD 1843, Habilitation 1844. Traveled widely. Taught briefly at Basel, then at Polytechnic Institute, Zurich, 1855–58; professor, University of Basel, 1859–93. Died Basel, 8 August 1897.

Principal Writings

Die Zeit Constantins des Grossen, 1853; in English as The Age of Constantine the Great, 1949
Der Cicerone: eine Anleitung zum Genuss der Kunstwerke italiens, 1855; in English as The Cicerone: An Art Guide to Painting in Italy for the Use of Travellers and Students, 1908
Die Cultur der Renaissance in Italien, 1860; in English as The Civilization of the Renaissance in Italy, 2 vols., 1904
Die Geschichte der Renaissance in Italien (The History of the Renaissance in Italy), 1867
Griechische Kulturgeschichte, 4 vols., 1898–1902; in English as The History of Greek Culture, 1963
Weltgeschichtliche Betrachtungen, 1905; in English as Reflections on History, 1943
Historische Fragmente aus dem Nachlass, 1929; in English as Judgments on History and Historians, 1958
The Greeks and Greek Civilization, edited by Oswyn Murray, 1998

Further Reading

Central Renaissance Conference, Jacob Burckhardt and the Renaissance: A Hundred Years After, Lawrence: University of Kansas Press, 1960
Dru, Alexander, ed., The Letters of Jacob Burckhardt, London: Routledge, and New York: Pantheon, 1955
Ferguson, Wallace K., The Renaissance in Historical Thought: Five Centuries of Interpretation, Boston: Houghton Mifflin, 1948
Gilbert, Felix, History: Politics or Culture? Reflections on Ranke and Burckhardt, Princeton: Princeton University Press, 1990
Janssen, E.M., Jacob Burckhardt und die Renaissance, Assen, Netherlands: van Gorcum, 1970
Kaegi, Werner, Jacob Burckhardt: eine Biographie, 7 vols., Basel: Schwabe, 1947–82

Burke, Peter 1937–

British social and cultural historian of early modern Europe Peter Burke began his career as a historian of the Renaissance, but one who broke with the traditional view of the Renaissance, à la Jacob Burckhardt, as a uniquely Italian phenomenon focused on "individualism" and "modernity." Burke, siding with numerous medievalists, notably Erwin Panofsky and Johan Huizinga, argued that "renaissances" (as revivals of classical culture) were not temporally bound – they occurred for example under the Carolingians and during the high Middle Ages. Nor, argued Burke, following Arnold Toynbee, were "renaissances" geographically bound – having occurred not only in Italy but also in Byzantium, in Islam, and even in the

Far East. In discussions of the Italian Renaissance, Burke also advocated the power of continuity over the argument for radical change. In the best-known works of the Italian Renaissance, Machiavelli's *Prince* and Castiglione's *Courtier*, Burke noted powerful medieval trends. Just because Petrarch and other "Renaissance men" argued that the Renaissance signaled a radical break with the past, argued Burke, that was no reason necessarily to believe them. In revising the traditional periodization, Burke was in league with E.H. Gombrich, who argued that the Italian Renaissance should be viewed more as a "movement" than a "period."

Burke's historiographic sympathies lie with the French Annales school, founded by Lucien Febvre and Marc Bloch, with such notable heirs as Fernand Braudel, Pierre Chaunu, Pierre Goubert, and Emmanuel Le Roy Ladurie. Burke has edited the works of *annalistes* in two collections. In the first, *Economy and Society in Early Modern Europe* (1972), a collection of essays that appeared in the journal *Annales* from 1955 to 1966, Burke's choice of essays demonstrated the variety of approaches for studying the *longue durée*. In the second, *A New Kind of History* (1973), Burke brought the writings of Lucien Febvre to English readers. Burke's *The French Historical Revolution* (1990) is a history and critique of the Annales school from 1929 to 1989. According to Burke, the *annaliste* movement unfolded in three phases – rebellion, transformation, and rebellion again – each represented by a different generation. Febvre and Bloch fought against the dominance of traditional political narrative and sought to replace it with "problem-oriented, analytical history" that would take into account the whole range of human activities. Braudel transformed this rebellion into a school, whose students (the third generation of *annalistes*) rebelled against their "fathers" in the aftermath of the 1968 student uprisings. Although Burke saw the Annales movement as "effectively over," he nonetheless advocated the writing of what Braudel termed "total history." According to Burke, this was "not an account of the past including every detail, but one which emphasizes the connections between different fields of human endeavor."

Burke himself also ventured into historiography. According to Burke, the tireless advocate for social history, historians have traditionally viewed sociologists as "people who state the obvious in barbarous and abstract jargon," while sociologists have viewed historians as "myopic fact-collectors without system or method." In *History and Social Theory* (1992), Burke attempted to find common ground, and argued that while theory (the domain of sociologists) can never be "applied" to the past (the domain of historians), nonetheless sociologists and historians have much to learn from each other. While Burke cited many contemporary theorists and historians in this work, he admitted that Marx and Durkheim, Weber and Malinowski "still have much to teach us." In another historiographic work, *Varieties of Cultural History* (1997), Burke attempted to bridge a different gap, that between traditional, positivist historians, who practice an "empiricism confident that 'the documents' will reveal 'the facts,'" and cultural historians, who are often prone to the pitfalls of "contructivism," the notion that reality is culturally constructed. In this work, Burke tackled not only earlier historians such as Bloch and Huizinga, but also modern cultural theorists, including Sigmund Freud, Mikhail Bakhtin, and Michel Foucault.

Burke is perhaps best known by his masterwork *Popular Culture in Early Modern Europe* (1978). The ambitious design of this book was nothing less than the description and interpretation of popular culture, the culture of the "subordinate classes," from 1500 to 1800 in the whole of Europe. In less capable hands, the study of such a vast temporal and geographic span might devolve into a mass of incomprehensible facts or facile generalizations, but Burke wove together a broad base of examples, using methodologies ranging from anthropology and ethnography to art history, to create a synthetic interpretation of the regionalized worlds of pre-industrial European society. But social history for Burke has not been limited to the study of history from below. In *Venice and Amsterdam* (1974), he used comparative prosopography to look at the lives of 17th-century elites. This focus on particular social groups in specific regions is reminiscent of the work of E.P. Thompson on the English working class, of Lawrence Stone on the English peerage, and of Le Roy Ladurie on the French peasants of Languedoc.

In the 1990s, Burke turned his attention to the importance of language as a cultural phenomenon. Here he drew on (among others) the controversial work of the American linguist Benjamin Whorf, who claimed that the very grammatical structure of language was responsible for shaping culture. Language has played such a critical role in history, Burke argued, that it is "too important to leave to the linguists." Burke's writing in this area has been influenced by other British historians, e.g., Raphael Samuel, Gareth Stedman Jones, Jonathan Steinberg, and most notably Roy Porter, the social historian of medicine, with whom Burke edited three collections of essays on the social history of language.

PHILLIP C. ADAMO

See also Agrarian; Annales School; Anthropology; East Central Europe; Febvre; Foucault; France: 1450–1789; Gurevich; Italy: Renaissance; Labrousse; Lefebvre; Le Roy Ladurie; Local; Mentalities; Mousnier; Poland: to the 18th Century; Poland: since the 18th Century; Sarpi; Social; Sociology; Vovelle; Xenophon

Biography

Ulick Peter Burke. Born London, 16 August 1937, son of a bookseller. Educated at St. Ignatius' College, Stamford Hill, London; St. John's College, Oxford, 1957–69; St. Antony's College, Oxford, BA 1960, MA 1964. Taught at University of Sussex, 1962–79; and Emmanuel College, Cambridge, from 1979. Served in the British Army, Singapore District Signal Regiment, 1956–57. Married 1) Susan Patricia Dell, 1972 (marriage dissolved 1983); 2) Maria Lúcia García Pallares, historian of 18th- and 19th-century Brazil, 1988.

Principal Writings

The Renaissance Sense of the Past, 1969
Culture and Society in Renaissance Italy, 1420–1540, 1972; revised as *Tradition and Innovation in Renaissance Italy: A Sociological Approach*, 1974, and as *The Italian Renaissance: Culture and Society in Italy*, 1987
Editor, *Economy and Society in Early Modern Europe: Essays from the Annales*, 1972
Editor, *A New Kind of History: From the Writings of Febvre*, 1973
Venice and Amsterdam: A Study of Seventeenth-Century Elites, 1974
Popular Culture in Early Modern Europe, 1978

Sociology and History, 1980

Montaigne, 1981

Editor with Antoni Mączak and Henryk Samsonowicz, *East-Central Europe in Transition: From the Fourteenth to the Seventeenth Century*, 1985

Vico, 1985

The Historical Anthropology of Early Modern Italy: Essays on Perception and Communication, 1987

The Renaissance, 1987

Editor with Roy Porter, *The Social History of Language*, 1987

The French Historical Revolution: The Annales School, 1929–89, 1990

Editor with Roy Porter, *Language, Self and Society: A Social History of Language*, 1991

Editor, *New Perspectives on Historical Writing*, 1991

Editor, *Critical Essays on Michel Foucault*, 1992

The Fabrication of Louis XIV, 1992

History and Social Theory, 1992

The Art of Conversation, 1993

The Fortunes of the Courtier: The European Reception of Castiglione's Cortegiano, 1995

Editor with Roy Porter, *Languages and Jargons: Contributions to a Social History of Language*, 1995

Varieties of Cultural History, 1997

Burns, Robert Ignatius 1921–

US medievalist

Burns began his career studying the role of Jesuits in the American northwest in the 19th century, particularly with regard to their role as intermediaries in the struggles between Amerindians and white settlers and government. At the same time, he began to study a more distant frontier, that separating Christians and Muslims in medieval Valencia. His first extended work on Spain, *The Crusader Kingdom of Valencia* (1967) demonstrated how the Church provided a template for the local organization of the conquered territories.

In *Islam under the Crusaders* (1973), Burns examined the sharp acculturative pressures to which the Muslims of Valencia were subjected in the decades after the Christian conquest. There he noted the persistence of traditional social forms. For Burns, the greatest factor affecting the acculturation of Mudéjars was their need to participate in commerce. (Looking at 15th-century Valencia twenty years later, Mark Meyerson would conclude that participation in the Christian legal system was the most powerful acculturating factor.) In examining the roots of James I's "tolerance" Burns concluded that he had no personal ethnic or cultural policies, but simply represented those of his own society. Burns depicted a colonized Muslim majority with a certain level of autonomy which, in Burns's view, was an impediment to their assimilation. He described a situation in which two exclusivist social systems had to coexist, creating a situation in which tolerance was scarcely distinguishable from intolerance inasmuch as the tolerance that preserved the alien group also condemned it to isolation. Burns was especially eloquent on the nature of James I's understanding of law. He was one of the prime movers behind the revival of Roman law, but he also had an understanding – advanced for the time – of the Muslims' concept of *sunna*, which he understood as the comprehensive law of the community, *any* community (thus the king referred to the sunna of the Jews and described Islamic sunna in a charter as "the privileges and customs which the Saracens were accustomed to have"). Sunna – customary law – was equated with xara (*sharia* or religious law) and both were equated to Furs – fueros – the comprehensive Romanizing code of the Christians.

Burns' views of Valencian feudalism were influenced by an increasingly discredited notion that Iberian feudalism was somehow "incomplete" when compared to the customs of northern European countries. He regarded Catalonia as feudal in structure, but with "an unfeudal soul" inhabiting the body. The vassal/lord relationship was a formal, not a dynamic one. Burns tried to develop an interpretation of feudalism that fit the peculiar circumstances of a frontier kingdom, where the lords did not form a feudal hierarchy, where their status was not so different of that from non-nobles, and where there was a "democratic air" about the landholding system. Recent research on Valencian feudalism in the 14th and 15th centuries tends to confirm Burns' analysis; Valencian feudalism was contractual: "fiefs" were bought and sold much like commodities and the association of family and tenancy so characteristic of the feudal heartland of Europe was never in evidence in the kingdom of Valencia.

Burns' best pages are devoted to how Christian misperception of Muslim institutions came to influence or change them. Thus the *amīn*, the central figure in the *aljama* or local Islamic community, became a bailiff. The Christians viewed the *aljama* as a kind of town council, imposed new roles on it and institutionalized them. Thus under this kind of pressure, a tribal council was transformed, by the 14th century, into a body of elected representatives, a dramatic example of directed cultural change.

Burns asserted that his goal was to read every document available for 13th-century Valencia – the documents which, now at the end of career, he has been publishing in his *Diplomatarium*. This meticulous study of a single universe of documents permitted what he styled "documental archeology": data that appears peripherally in a large number of documents takes on substantive meaning through repetition. An example would be persons known only from their mention as abutters in a number of field perambulations.

In the introductory volume of his *Diplomatarium*, Burns presents an extended discussion on the nature of the paper-based administrative revolution of the 13th century – an intelligent contribution to the history of communication technology somewhat reminiscent of Harold Innis in *The Bias of Communication* (1951). The revolution was initiated with the Catalan conquest of the Muslim paper industry at Játiva, whereupon the Christians had not only the stores of paper at their disposal, but the pool of technicians who could impart information about its production. For Burns, James I's territorial expansion brought with it an increasingly complex administration that encouraged bureaucrats to keep cheap paper copies of the parchment charters they dispatched in the form of the register, a kind of information retrieval system that made possible administrative oversight of an entire kingdom with an unprecedented degree of efficiency. (Innis would have turned the equation around: paper itself stimulated administrative complexity and made possible the efficient management of newly-acquired territory.) Thus the "control of Játiva's paper was the factor that dictated the scope and redefined the purpose of [James]' registers." Registers, in turn, strengthened the legal system by making possible a system of customary law based on precedents that could be studied at a central repository. Thus, government was the motive force pushing the diffusion of literate habits and modes: legal texts were the basis of a distinctive Catalan urban prose which only subsequently became a literary language.

THOMAS F. GLICK

See also Spain: Islamic; Spain: to 1450

Biography
Born San Francisco, 16 August 1921. Entered the Jesuit order, 1940; ordained 1954. Received BA, Gonzaga University, 1943, MA 1945; MA, Fordham University, 1949; PhD, Johns Hopkins University, 1958; Doc ès Sc. Hist., University of Fribourg, Switzerland, 1961. Taught at University of San Francisco, 1947–76; and University of California, Los Angeles, from 1976.

Principal Writings
The Jesuits and the Indian Wars of the Northwest, 1966
The Crusader Kingdom of Valencia: Reconstruction on a Thirteenth-Century Frontier, 1967
Islam under the Crusaders: Colonial Survival in the Thirteenth-Century Kingdom of Valencia, 1973
Medieval Colonialism: Postcrusade Exploitation of Islamic Valencia, 1975
Moors and Crusaders in Mediterranean Spain: Collected Studies, 1978
Muslims, Christians, and Jews in the Crusader Kingdom of Valencia: Societies in Symbiosis, 1984
Society and Documentation in Crusader Valencia, 1985
Editor, Diplomatarium Regni Valentiae, 2 vols. to date, 1985–
Jews in the Notarial Culture: Latinate Wills in Mediterranean Spain, 1200–1350, 1996

Further Reading
McCrank, Lawrence L., "R.I. Burns as Ethnologist and Historian of the Old World and the New," in Larry Simon, ed., Iberia and the Mediterranean World of the Middle Ages: Essays in Honor of Robert I. Burns, S.J., vol. 2, Leiden: Brill, 1996

Bury, J.B. 1861–1927
British classicist and historian of Byzantium

John Bagnell Bury probably best deserves to be remembered as a founding father of modern British Byzantine studies, although he was by training a classicist. This interest, which appeared early in his scholarly life, may have stemmed from his unusually wide-ranging linguistic abilities. In 1880 he studied Sanskrit, Hebrew, and Syriac for six months at the University of Göttingen, while still working for his first degree in classics at Trinity College, Dublin. Also, while still an undergraduate, he collaborated in editing Euripides' Hippolytus. Further editions of classical authors, notably Pindar, followed, but in the 1880s he began to turn his attention to later periods. He learned Russian in 1887, at a time when much of the best in Byzantine studies was being written in that language, as he himself would later point out in the introduction to his edition of Gibbon. Thereafter he always remained alert to the literature on his subject in a variety of Slavonic languages.

His first contributions were his articles of 1888 on Theophylact Simocatta and of 1889 on Michael Psellos. His work on these two Byzantine historians paralleled the preparation of his first large-scale publication, the earlier version of 2-volume History of the Later Roman Empire (1889). This covered a broad chronological span, from the late 4th to the early 9th centuries. Although he then turned his attention back to classical studies, working on histories of both ancient Greece and the early Roman empire up to the death of Marcus Aurelius, he was elected professor of modern history at Trinity College, Dublin in 1893. He moved from this chair to that of Greek in 1898, and published his influential A History of Greece in 1900.

In the later 1890s Bury had also been working on one of his most important projects, an edition in seven volumes of Edward Gibbon's History of the Decline and Fall of the Roman Empire, which appeared in stages between 1896 and 1900. This remains the best edition of this classic work, not only for the quality of its text, but also for the important notes and introduction that Bury contributed, which assessed both Gibbon's own contributions and the development of studies of the subject since Gibbon's day. It is equally clear from the introduction how highly Bury prized Gibbon's qualities of skepticism and sound judgment, which he consciously sought to emulate in his own writings.

In 1902 Bury became Regius professor of modern history at Cambridge, and perhaps in consequence of his move from Ireland, promptly turned his attention to the study of his homeland's patron saint. His Life of St. Patrick appeared in 1905 and was ground-breaking in its application of critical scrutiny to the confused mass of materials of various periods and even more variable worth relating to its subject. Several of Bury's judgments on sources and many of his individual arguments would now be rejected, but he opened up the modern scholarly study of this elusive figure, initiating an intense, often vitriolic, debate on Patrick's origins, identity, chronology and achievements that has extended over most of the 20th century.

Bury returned to Byzantine studies, with articles appearing in 1906 and 1907 on the life and writings of emperor Constantine Porphyrogenitos. These served as prolegomena to a major, though now superseded, book on the subject of The Imperial Administrative System in the Ninth Century, which was published in 1911. In the same period he continued to lecture and publish on the ancient Greek historians. Bury's health began to decline from 1910 onwards, but he continued to write at a prodigious rate, producing a History of the Eastern Roman Empire in 1912 and a small book, A History of Freedom of Thought, in 1913.

Following the ending of World War I, he turned his attention to a hitherto neglected period of Greek history, with the publication in 1923 of The Hellenistic Age. The same year also saw the appearance of an entirely new version of his History of the Later Roman Empire. Like that of 1889, this was in two volumes, but it covered only the period from 395 to 565, with the second volume being entirely devoted to the reign of Justinian. As Bury himself said of it, "the reader will find here a fuller account of the events of the reign than in any other single work," a claim that is still true as far as works in English are concerned. Of all his Byzantine and Late Roman studies this remains the most significant in terms of the wide range of sources upon which it drew and the careful narrative it offers. The postwar years also saw Bury undertaking the general editorship of and contributing articles to the multivolume *Cambridge Ancient History*, which long remained a standard work of reference on Greek and Roman history up to the 4th century CE, and which is only now being replaced by a new edition.

In his work on both classical and Byzantine history Bury's primary concern was the measured evaluation of evidence, which he saw as central to his aim of establishing historical studies on a new "scientific" basis. He was reacting against an earlier Victorian tendency to see the subject primarily as a branch of literature, and he hoped to demonstrate rigorously objective principles in the assessment of evidence, that would lift historical analysis into what he regarded as a higher level of undertaking. *The Idea of Progress* (1920) similarly demonstrated his belief in the wider transformation of society through the application of rational principles. He cultivated a deliberately detached style, applying the dictum that he had used of Gibbon, that "enthusiasm is inconsistent with intellectual balance." While the historiographical objectivity that he sought might now seem unattainable, it reflected contemporary views on scientific method and the nature of scientific truth, as well as on linear social development, that now appear equally dated. However, Bury's concern with the rigorous assessment of evidence and the preservation of a tradition of skeptical enquiry deriving from Gibbon give continuing value to his work. Much, though not all of it may now seem outdated in terms of the limitations of some of the methodologies employed and the interpretations offered, but Bury remains important for the influence of his work on succeeding generations of historians, and for the way that he opened up so many individual texts and topics of Greek, Roman, Byzantine, and Irish history to modern critical study.

ROGER COLLINS

See also Byzantium; Greece: Ancient; Literature; Psellos; Roman; Runciman; Trevelyan; Universal

Biography
John Bagnell Bury. Born County Monaghan, Ireland, 16 October 1861, son of a cleric. Attended Foyle College, Londonderry; Trinity College, Dublin, BA in classics and mental and moral philosophy, 1882. Fellow, Trinity College, Dublin, 1885–1903: professor of modern history, 1893–1902; Regius professor of modern history, Cambridge University, 1902–27. Married Jane Bury, his second cousin, 1885 (1 son). Died Rome, 1 June 1927.

Principal Writings
Editor, *The History of the Decline and Fall of the Roman Empire*, by Edward Gibbon, 7 vols., 1896–1900
"The Chronology of Theophylaktos Simokatta," *English Historical Review* 3 (1888), 310–15
"Roman Emperors from Basil II to Isaac Komnenos (AD 976–1057)," *English Historical Review* 4 (1889), 41–64 and 251–85; reprinted in *Selected Essays*, 1930
A History of the Later Roman Empire from Arcadius to Irene, 395 AD to 800 AD, 2 vols., 1889
A History of Greece to the Death of Alexander the Great, 1900, revised in 2 vols., 1902; abridged as *History of Greece for Beginners*, 1903, and as *A Student's History of Greece*, 1907

The Life of Saint Patrick and His Place in History, 1905
"The Ceremonial Book of Constantine Porphygennetos," *English Historical Review* 22 (1907), 209–27 and 417–39
The Ancient Greek Historians, 1909
The Imperial Administrative System in the Ninth Century, 1911
A History of the Eastern Roman Empire from the Fall of Irene to the Accession of Basil I, AD 802–867, 1912
A History of Freedom of Thought, 1913
The Idea of Progress: An Inquiry into Its Origin and Growth, 1920
With others, *The Hellenistic Age: Aspects of Hellenistic Civilization*, 1923
History of the Later Roman Empire from the Death of Theodosius I to the Death of Justinian, AD 395 to AD 565, 2 vols., 1923
General editor, *Cambridge Ancient History*, 12 vols., 1923–
The Invasion of Europe by the Barbarians, 1928
Selected Essays, edited by Harold Temperley, 1930

Further Reading
Baynes, Norman H., *A Bibliography of the Works of J.B. Bury*, Cambridge: Cambridge University Press, 1929
Dowling, Linda, "Roman Decadence and Victorian Historiography," *Victorian Studies* 28 (1985), 579–607

Business History

Business history, a relatively new field of scholarly inquiry, came into existence as a response to the rise of big business, first in the United States and then elsewhere. The first organizations to promote it were the Business History Society, founded along with the *Business History Review* at Harvard University in 1926, and the Business Archives Council, established in Great Britain in 1934. Since then, the field has spread around the world, although institutionally it remains strongest in the United States, where its major anchors are large-scale industry and business schools.

Business history's institutional basis in the United States has helped shape the themes and issues it addresses. Two additional factors shaping the field are its relationship with cognate fields and a strong and growing critical tradition.

The field's initial subjects were individual companies and the unique great men who founded them, and company histories and biographies of key businessmen continue to account for much of business history's output. The correspondence of interest between business historians and their subjects was especially obvious in the early literature: historians required archival materials and financial support; firms and prominent businessmen used their wealth, provision of access, and sometimes employment opportunities to help shape the stories historians told, often to a broad public. This is not to imply that business historians were or are particularly vulnerable to influence from large firms and wealthy individuals. In fact, this is generally not true. But the coincidence of interest between business historians and their subjects has frequently resulted in a literature that focuses primarily on the large manufacturing firm, on "correct" decisions made within it, and on the successful entrepreneur.

Business history's other crucial institutional anchor in the United States, the business school, has also had a major impact. Robert Locke has shown that business training took on a modern, more "scientific" basis beginning in the 1940s. In the

United States, and in particular at Harvard Business School, history formed a vital part of such training even before this paradigm shift. Along with military studies and law, business education frequently employed the case study, often prepared by the professional business historian. This admirable attempt to create a usable past also affected the field's content: criteria such as immediate applicability, the individual firm (without reference to the context within which it operates), and "good" vs. "bad" managerial decisions often set the agenda.

Perhaps more than any other historical field, one university, Harvard, and one individual, Alfred Dupont Chandler, Jr., have set the tone for business history since the early 1960s. Chandler's *Strategy and Structure* (1962) took the study of the firm to a new level by comparing case studies of companies in different industries in order to establish the common determinants and attributes of business decision-making and administration. His argument that a firm's structure emerged from the strategy it followed and from general characteristics of its industrial sector (including markets and technology) was later expanded and refined in two additional books. *The Visible Hand* (1977) dealt with a much larger number of American firms than did his earlier work; *Scale and Scope* (1990) compared developments in the United States with those in Great Britain and Germany. Chandler's influence has extended worldwide, inspiring similar histories of business strategy and structure in Germany, Japan, France, Britain, and elsewhere.

Smaller groups of established business historians have focused on a variety of topics that range beyond decision-making within the firm. One area of particular interest, especially recently, has been multinational corporations (e.g., Jones, 1996). Some have also turned their attention to the framework within which business operates, in particular to issues related to regulation (e.g., Vietor, 1994), or to the relationship between internal firm decision-making and macroeconomic factors affecting those decisions (e.g., Porter, 1990). Finally, a few business historians have considered the role of values and culture in firm structure and performance (e.g., Hirschmeier and Yui, 1975).

The closest historical subdiscipline to business history has always been economic history, which has provided theoretical foundations and economic context for the study of the firm. Still, the insistence of key business historians – not least Chandler – on empirical studies of and on internal decision-making within particular firms has kept some distance between business and economic history.

Chandler has been largely responsible for close relations with a much newer historical subfield, history of technology. His emphasis on technology's role as a crucial constraint on decision-making within firms lent itself well to the emerging new discipline, and a number of historians of technology have successfully integrated their field with business history (e.g., Hounshell and Smith, 1988; Hirsh, 1989).

Business history has also increasingly influenced and been influenced by other fields, both historical and otherwise. Diplomatic historians such as Michael Hogan (1987) have emphasized the centrality of businessmen and big business to the conduct of US foreign policy, and businessmen and their companies now routinely populate the pages of other mainstream historians, too. Business historians nowadays continue to be influenced by other historians, but are as likely to draw upon the work of social theoreticians, anthropologists, sociologists, ethicists, or theoretical practitioners of business studies.

The third major determinant of the evolution of business historiography has been two categories of critical tradition, one mildly revisionist and one strongly critical.

Most revisionist business historians question neither the utility nor most of the findings of mainstream business history. Instead, they want the field to extend its grasp, in particular to managers below the very top levels, to businesses outside of the manufacturing sector, and to small and medium-sized firms.

Histories of business that are more strongly critical, both of their subject and of the usual treatment of it, have a long tradition, stretching back to Ida Tarbell's work on Standard Oil (1904). But harsh criticism of business among its historians has become much more commonplace since the 1960s, in part owing to developments in Western political culture, and in part owing to the expansion of the field, which has made dissent more viable. One of the major issues at stake has been instances of undemocratic influence of business on party politics and labor relations. The general emphasis of big business on profits above all other concerns – including, for instance, local communities, worker welfare, and the environment – has also been a target of some business histories (e.g., Noble, 1977).

Critiques of traditional business history and changing relationships with cognate fields have altered the field substantially. Rather than focus simply on successful decision-making within the firm, recent business historiography is apt to look closer at the broader context within which business operates, and at poor and mediocre performance, failure as well as success.

RAYMOND G. STOKES

See also Chandler; Economic

Further Reading

Blackford, Mansel, and K. Austin Kerr, *Business Enterprise in American History*, Boston: Houghton Mifflin, 1986; revised 1994

Chandler, Alfred D., Jr., *Strategy and Structure: Chapters in the History of the American Industrial Enterprise*, Cambridge, MA: MIT Press, 1962

Chandler, Alfred D., Jr., *The Visible Hand: The Managerial Revolution in American Business*, Cambridge, MA: Harvard University Press, 1977

Chandler, Alfred D., Jr., and Herman Daems, eds., *Managerial Hierarchies: Comparative Perspectives on the Rise of the Modern Industrial Enterprise*, Cambridge, MA: Harvard University Press, 1980

Chandler, Alfred D., Jr., *Scale and Scope: The Dynamics of Industrial Capitalism*, Cambridge, MA: Harvard University Press, 1990

Hannah, Leslie, *The Rise of the Corporate Economy*, London: Methuen, and Baltimore: Johns Hopkins University Press, 1976

Hirsh, Richard, *Technology and Transformation in the American Electric Utility Industry*, Cambridge and New York: Cambridge University Press, 1989

Hirschmeier, Johannes, and Tsunehiko Yui, *The Development of Japanese Business, 1600–1973*, Cambridge, MA; Harvard University Press, and London: Allen and Unwin, 1975

Hogan, Michael J., *The Marshall Plan: America, Britain, and the Reconstruction of Western Europe, 1947–1952*, Cambridge and New York: Cambridge University Press, 1987

Hounshell, David A., and John Kenly Smith, Jr., *Science and Corporate Strategy: Du Pont R & D, 1902–1980*, New York: Cambridge University Press, 1988

Jones, Geoffrey, *The Evolution of International Business*, London: Routledge, 1996

Lazonick, William, *Business Organization and the Myth of the Market Economy*, Cambridge: Cambridge University Press, 1991

Locke, Robert R., *Management and Higher Education since 1940: The Influence of America and Japan on West Germany, Great Britain, and France*, Cambridge: Cambridge University Press, 1989

Noble, David F., *America by Design: Science, Technology, and the Rise of Corporate Capitalism*, New York: Knopf, 1977; Oxford: Oxford University Press, 1979

Porter, Michael E., *The Competitive Advantage of Nations*, London: Macmillan, and New York: Free Press, 1990

Tarbell, Ida M., *The History of the Standard Oil Company*, New York: McClure Phillips, 1904

Vietor, Richard, *Contrived Competition: Regulation and Deregulation in America*, Cambridge, MA: Belknap Press, 1994

Wilson, John F., *British Business History, 1720–1994*, Manchester: Manchester University Press, 1995

Butterfield, Herbert 1900–1979

British political historian and philosopher of history

Following his mentor Harold Temperley, Herbert Butterfield began his long career at Cambridge studying diplomatic history. With the publication of *The Historical Novel* (1924) and *The Whig Interpretation of History* (1931), he quickly made his mark in the realm of historiography. Throughout his career Butterfield devoted his attention to questions concerning the philosophy and technique of history, as well as to the promotion of historical thinking among the British public.

Butterfield's strictly historical writing was limited to *The Peace Tactics of Napoleon, 1806–1808* (1929), a brief biography for the Great Lives series, *Napoleon* (1939), then *The Statecraft of Machiavelli* (1940) and *George III, Lord North and the People, 1779–80* (1949). The latter was a detailed narrative analysis of a crisis in the English monarchy. Subsequently Butterfield wrote *George III and the Historians* (1957) as a historiographical critique of Sir Lewis Namier and other historians who contended that George III had undermined Parliament and blocked its proper constitutional primacy. Butterfield argued for a more traditional interpretation, that George III was acting to recoup royal power he believed had been lost by his predecessors. The debate demonstrated Butterfield's concern to bring out the complexity and unpredictability of history. For him, the historical process was a search for dissimilarity between present and past – the attempt to understand the past solely according to its own terms.

Butterfield's historiographical publications are many and varied, including critiques of the problem of hindsight in historical writing; reflections on his Christian philosophy of history; efforts to bring history to the public; and suggestions for new directions for history writing. The essence of his historiographical thinking is contained in his best known work, *The Whig Interpretation of History* (1931). In it he attacked "the tendency in many historians to write on the side of the Protestants and the Whigs, to praise revolutions provided they have been successful, to emphasize certain principles of progress in the past and to produce a story which is the ratification if not the glorification of the present." He decried the dispensing of moral judgments through history writing, especially implicit ones based on an artificial search for similarities between the past and present. The Whig approach obscured the true diversity of history and betrayed a lack of historical understanding. For Butterfield, the modern world was not "the victory of the children of light over the children of darkness in any generation" but rather the product of a continual "clash of wills" creating unpredictable and inconsistent outcomes.

In *Christianity and History* (1949) and in *History and Human Relations* (1951), Butterfield applied his concern for proper historical understanding to the relationship between his Christian faith and his view of history. He asserted that history was altogether unable to provide "an interpretation of life on the earth." Historians ought to concentrate on "technical history," the scientific, research-based attempt to arrive at an "historical explanation." Butterfield neither attempted to find the hand of God in history, nor believed it could be done; but he did argue that history "uncover[ed] man's universal sin." Therefore, "the historian cannot give a judgment on particular human beings that can be admitted as a final moral judgment ... save in the sense that he can say: 'All men are sinners.'" According to Butterfield, the only basis for any more explicit Christian view of history was an individual's personal experience of God, not technical history.

Butterfield was also dedicated to presenting the fruits of academic history to the British public. Almost all of his published historiographical reflections originated as special university lectures or as radio broadcasts on the BBC. For instance, *Christianity and History* began as a series of broadcast lectures given in the spring of 1949, and was then published in the BBC journal *The Listener*; this served as the basis for a lecture series delivered to the divinity faculty at Cambridge, which was then published in final book form. In 1958 Butterfield founded and chaired the British Committee on the Theory of International Politics, attempting to apply his historical expertise to current issues. With Martin Wight, he edited *Diplomatic Investigations: Essays in the Theory of International Politics* (1966), a published expression of the British Committee's mandate to examine "the nature of the international state-system, the assumptions and ideas of diplomacy, the principles of foreign policy, the ethics of international relations and war."

Ironically, when he published *The Origins of Modern Science, 1300–1800* (1949), Butterfield was accused of succumbing to the Whiggish desire to seek out the roots of modern science, distorting its true and invariably complex historical context. Nonetheless, he successfully identified the need to broaden historical research beyond the narrow limits of political history and demonstrated that past scientific advancements were often more significant to modern civilization than concurrent political events.

KYLE JANTZEN

See also Acton; Britain: 1066–1485; Britain: since 1750; Ecclesiastical; Gatterer; Germany: 1450–1800; Macaulay; Schlözer; Science; Trevelyan; Whig

Biography

Born Oxenhope, Yorkshire, 7 October 1900. Educated at Trade and Grammar School, Keighley; Peterhouse, Cambridge, MA, 1922. Visiting fellow, Princeton University, 1924–25; fellow, Peterhouse,

Cambridge, 1928–79: master, 1955–68; professor of modern history, Cambridge University, 1944–63: vice-chancellor, 1959–61, Regius professor, 1963–68 (emeritus, 1968–79). Editor, *Cambridge Historical Journal*, 1938–52. Knighted 1968. Married Edith Joyce [Pamela] Crawshaw, 1929 (3 sons). Died Sawston, Cambridge, 20 July 1979.

Principal Writings

The Historical Novel, 1924
The Peace Tactics of Napoleon, 1806–1808, 1929
The Whig Interpretation of History, 1931
Napoleon, 1939
The Statecraft of Machiavelli, 1940
The Englishman and His History, 1944
Lord Acton, 1948
Christianity and History, 1949
George III, Lord North and the People, 1779–80, 1949
The Origins of Modern Science, 1300–1800, 1949
History and Human Relations, 1951
Reconstruction of an Historical Episode: The History of the Enquiry into the Origins of the Seven Years' War, 1951
Liberty in the Modern World, 1952
Christianity, Diplomacy and War, 1953
Man on His Past: The Study of the History of Historical Scholarship, 1955
George III and the Historians, 1957; revised 1959
Editor with Martin Wight, *Diplomatic Investigations: Essays in the Theory of International Politics*, 1966

Further Reading

Chadwick, Owen, "Acton and Butterfield," *Journal of Ecclesiastical History* 38 (1987), 386–405
Coll, Alberto R., *The Wisdom of Statecraft: Sir Herbert Butterfield and the Philosophy of International Politics*, Durham, NC: Duke University Press, 1985
Elliott, J.H., and H.G. Koenigsberger, eds., *The Diversity of History: Essays in Honour of Sir Herbert Butterfield*, Ithaca, NY: Cornell University Press, and London: Routledge, 1970
Elton, G.R., "Herbert Butterfield and the Study of History," *Historical Journal* 27 (1984), 729–43
Thompson, Kenneth W., ed., *Herbert Butterfield: The Ethics of History and Politics*, Washington, DC: University Press of America, 1980

Byzantium

Byzantium (Greek *Byzantion*), a small Greek city-state by the straits of Bosporos founded *c.*657 BCE by Byzas of Megara, and recolonized in the 5th century by the Spartans, like ancient Babylon and Rome, lent its name to an empire (330–1453 CE). The citizens of the city were called Byzantines, but in the 16th century the Frenchman Jerome Wolf applied the term to include all the people of the empire ruled from Byzantium, now renamed Constantinople. Its inhabitants however called it *Basileion ton Romaion*, Kingdom of the Romans, and themselves *Rhomaioi* (Romans). Since 212 CE, when all the free people of the Roman empire were enfranchised and became Roman citizens, the "Byzantines" viewed themselves as Romans and their state as a continuation of the Roman empire.

But Western European (Latin, Germanic, Frankish), Russian, Khazarian Hebrew, and other non-Greek sources speak of the "Byzantines" as Greeks, and of their state as *Graecia*, or "land of the Greeks." Near Eastern people, Armenians, Georgians, and Semites of several nations called the "Byzantines" *Yoyn, Yavani* or *Yunani* (Ionians) and their empire as *Yunastan, Yavan, Yawan* (Ionia).

The chronology of the empire is conventionally divided into three periods. The early period – from Byzantium's inauguration as the new capital of the Roman empire in 330 CE to 610 – were years of transition. In the middle centuries, from the beginning of the 7th century to the sack of Constantinople by the Fourth Crusade in 1204, the empire went through several reforms, revivals, and readjustments, reaching its golden age between the 9th and the 11th centuries. The period between 1204 and 1453 was one of decline and fall, even though it witnessed some brilliance in learning, the arts, theology and the sciences.

During the proto-Byzantine period, Christianity became the dominant religion and contributed to the formation of the empire's new ethos. During the first three centuries, the empire retained much of the past inheritance and remained a multi-ethnic, multireligious, and multilingual empire. Beginning with the 7th century, when several less Hellenized provinces were lost to the Arabs and to Slavic tribes in the Balkans, ethnologically, linguistically, and religiously the empire became more homogeneous. The dominant Greek and Hellenized population's unity was strengthened through a common language and a common religion. Ethnic and religious minorities in the empire were called by their ethnic and sectarian names (Armenian, Slav, Jew, Paulician, Monophysite, and the like). But after the sack of Constantinople in 1204, even though Constantinople was recovered by the Greeks and Greek kingdoms and principalities were reunited in 1261, the empire declined.

Through eleven centuries, the Byzantine empire remained in a constant state of alarm to defend itself against old and new formidable enemies – Persians and Arabs, Huns, Goths, Slavs, Bulgarians, Russians, Petchenegs, Magyars, Franks, and Venetians, Turks, and other lesser known tribes. The Byzantine empire included most of the territories that had been under Roman rule before Constantine the Great's reign. But over eleven centuries, the empire expanded and condensed, and was at its largest under Justinian in the 6th century. From the 7th to the 12th centuries the empire included the Balkan peninsula, from the Danube river in the north to the island of Crete in the south, parts of the Italian peninsula, and Asia Minor in the east.

With the invasion of Turkish nomadic tribes in the east and the Normans in the west, the empire began shrinking again. After its dismemberment by the Fourth Crusade the empire fragmented into principalities and kingdoms never to be united again. The restoration of the empire in 1261 was ephemeral and did not prevent its final collapse.

The scholarship of the last 75 years has demonstrated that the Byzantine empire was great in several respects: political, military, economic, intellectual. It produced great statesmen, diplomats, generals, law givers, renowned scholars, and reformers. Its highly developed system of law and an admirable administrative machinery enabled it not only to maintain order and stability, but also helped it to endure for more than a millennium, although it was subject to changes and reforms, renewals and continuities. The noted historian F.M. Powicke summarized the modern view as: "Far from being a moribund society ... it was the greatest, most active and most enduring political organism that the world has yet seen, giving for centuries that opportunity for living which we associate with the spacious but transitory peace of Augustus or Hadrian." Among the scholars of the Byzantine empire, historians occupied a prominent position.

The historiography of the Byzantine empire starts in the 4th century with Eusebius of Caesarea. His *Ecclesiastical History* (311–25) exerted an enormous influence and contributed greatly to the kind of relationship that existed between church and state in the Byzantine millennium. Socrates Scholasticus' *Ekklesiastike Historia* (*The Ecclesiastical History*) surpassed Eusebius in objectivity and documented historical research, and remains an invaluable source for both church and secular history of the period from 305 to 439 CE.

Zosimus' *Nea Historia* (c.450–502; *New History*, 1982) treated the history of the 4th century down to 410 from a non-Christian point of view. He was perhaps the last pagan historian. More important for the historiography of the early Byzantine period is Procopius, whose history of his own time in eight books described Justinian's wars against the Persians, Vandals, and Ostrogoths. His preference for secular over religious causation brings him closer to Thucydides than Herodotus.

The historiography of the period between the 7th and the 15th centuries includes historical works whose authors used the terms *historia* and *chronographia* as synonyms. There were some important historians and some who are more properly designated as *chronographoi* or chroniclers. Agathias' works imitated those of Procopius, but he concentrated on general Narses' campaigns in Italy. His account remains valuable for the attention he paid to events of social and intellectual significance. Theophylact Simocatta's *Oikoumenike Historia* (7th century; *The History of Theophylact Simocatta*, 1986) is the main source for the reign of Maurice. Theophanes the Confessor's *Chronographia* (9th century; *The Chronicle of Theophanes*, 1997) is the most important source for the 7th and 8th centuries. He incorporated in his work much information from other sources no longer extant. The *Chronographies* of George Hamartolos, Joseph Genesios, Leo Diakonos, John Skylitses, George Kedrenos, John Zonaras, and Michael Glykas have not been translated, but all include valuable information on cultural, religious, prosopographical, and artistic history of the 9th to the 12th centuries. Michael Psellos' *Chronographia* (11th century; *Fourteen Byzantine Rulers: The Chronographia*, 1966) is a history of the emperors from the accession of Basil II (976) to the reign of Michael VII (1071–78). Equally important is Anna Komnene's *The Alexiad* (1138–48; translated 1969), the history of her father's reign (1081–1118) modeled after the classical Greek style of historiography. John Kinnamos' *Chronikai* (12th century; *Deeds of John and Manuel Comnenus*, 1976) took over where Anna Komnene left off and treated the reigns of both John II and Manuel II (1118–80). He consciously imitated the methods of classical Greek historians including Procopius. His style was more forceful than that of his predecessors.

The historiography of the last centuries of the Byzantine empire (1204–1453) consciously imitated the ancient historians. The Fourth Crusade and the fragmentation of the Empire into Greek kingdoms and Latin municipalities provoked much interest and promoted a nostalgia for the glories of the past. Niketas Choniates' *Chronike Diegesis* (12th century; *O City of Byzantium*, 1984) is the most important source for the period, and for the capture of Constantinople in the Fourth Crusade in particular. Important authors not yet translated into English include George Akropolites, whose 13th-century chronicle covers one of the most critical periods of the empire's history (1203–61); George Pachymeres' account, the most detailed source for the second half of the 13th century; Nikephoros Gregoras' analytical history for 1320–59; and one of the most important historians on economic and administrative aspects of the period, Ioannes Kantakouzenos' chronicle, a source of information for 1320–56. Two historians of the last century of Byzantium must also be noted. Doukas's *Historia* (15th century; *Decline and Fall of Byzantium to the Ottoman Turks*, 1975) is a valuable source for Greek and Turkish affairs, especially between 1204 and 1391, and the siege of Constantinople down to 1462. George Sphrantzes' 15th-century *Chronikon* is a combination of two *Chronika*. The part known as *Chronikon minus* is authentic and has been translated as *The Fall of the Byzantine Empire* (1980) and it is an important eyewitness source for the events between 1413 and 1477.

Interest in the study of the Byzantine empire in Western Europe began in the 16th century with Wolf's edition of the series *Corpus Byzantinae Historiae* (1645–70). Next, Charles Du Cange (1610–88) produced not only a series of major volumes on history, genealogies, families, topographies, and numismatics, but also an indispensable thesaurus of the Greek language in the Byzantine era. Palaeography, diplomacy, and topography continued to interest several successors of Du Cange. Byzantine studies declined as a result of the dismissive analysis of the empire by writers such as Montesquieu, Voltaire, Gibbon, and Charles Le Beau. Georges Finlay, and Barthold G. Niebuhr, the founder of the Bonn edition of *Corpus Scriptorum Historiae Byzantinae*, revived interest in the study of Byzantium in the 19th century.

Therefore, Byzantine studies as a respected academic discipline was established only at the end of the 19th century when Karl Krumbacher became professor of Byzantine studies in Munich and published the monumental and still useful *Geschichte der byzantinischen Literatur* (History of Byzantine Literature, 1891). The Munich School of Byzantinology inaugurated the leading journal *Byzantinische Zeitschrift*, and it has produced several influential specialists, including Franz Dölger and Hans Georg Beck.

In addition to Munich, there are today major schools of Byzantine studies in Paris, Palermo, Brussels, London, Birmingham, Athens, Belgrade, Moscow, Thessaloniki, and Washington, DC. The first Byzantine studies chair in Paris was occupied by Charles Diehl, a pioneer in the study of the women of Byzantium. Under the leadership of Paul Lemerle, the School of Byzantine studies in Paris has trained several leading Byzantinists. Also in Paris, the Assumptionist Fathers research center made major contributions in the study of chronology, topography, sigillography, codicology, and related fields. In Russia, whose religion and religious culture owe much to Byzantium, a school under the leadership of Vasilii Grigor'evich Vasilievskii, an outstanding editor of sources and the founder of *Vizantijskij Vremennik*, trained several scholars including A.A. Vasiliev, whose *Istoriia Vizantii* (1923; *History of the*

Byzantine Empire, 1928–29) remains a valuable text to the present day.

Interest in Byzantine studies among the Greeks, for whom the story of Byzantium is part of the history of their nation, developed soon after the end of the first phase of the Greek War of Independence in 1832. The monumental 6-volume work of Konstantinos Paparregopoulos, *Historia tou hellenikou ethnous* (History of the Greek People, 1860–77) – some 3,685 pages – was continued by Spyridon Lampros who prepared the way for the establishment of two centers for Byzantine studies in Greece: Athens and Thessaloniki. Konstantinos Amantos and Dionysios Zakythinos of the University of Athens trained several Byzantinists including John Karayannopoulos, the founder of the Center for Byzantine Studies in Thessaloniki. Italy's centers include Palermo under Bruno Lavagnini, Ravenna under G. Bonini, and the Vatican City through its Institute for Oriental Studies; each made major contributions with the publication of original works, critical editions, or monographs and periodical literature. In the United States, it was Vasiliev who introduced the study of Byzantium as an autonomous discipline. He was followed by his first student, Peter Charanis, who trained several Byzantinists. Dumbarton Oaks Center for Byzantine Studies, the center par excellence for research in the history and civilization of the Byzantine empire, has published several outstanding books, original sources, and the annual Dumbarton Oaks Papers.

Byzantine historiography of the last 50 years has contributed much to a revision and a better understanding of all facets of Byzantium's development. The demographic issue and the question of continuity versus discontinuity between the Byzantine empire and the ancient Greek world were extensively researched in the second half of our century. Charanis' *Studies on the Demography of the Byzantine Empire* (1972) has been the authority on the subject and today – according to Kazhdan and Cutler – the prevailing opinion is that:

> Notwithstanding the various tribes and peoples that settled on the territory of the [Byzantine] Empire . . . the prevailing population was as Greek or Hellenized as it had been in the Balkans and Asia Minor during the 4th through 6th centuries (AD). Certainly, there were ethnic minorities there . . . (Italians, Bulgarians, Armenians and so on), but the main ethnic substratum consisted, throughout Byzantine history, of Greek and Hellenized constituents. The language [Greek] remained unchanged.

Even though the name "Byzantine" has been accepted today, scholars from as early as the 17th century have described the Byzantine empire as the Greek empire. More recent historians have treated the history of the Byzantine empire as a portion of the history of the Greek nation. In *Geschichte des byzantinischen Staates* (1940; *History of the Byzantine State*, 1956; revised 1969) George Ostrogorsky noted that "Byzantine history properly speaking is the history of the medieval Greek Empire." The Hellenistic character of the empire's civilization and the continuity between the ancient and the Byzantine Greek worlds has been convincingly resolved in favor of continuity, in *The "Past" in Medieval and Modern Greek Culture* (1978), edited by Speros Vryonis.

Contemporary Byzantine historiography has demonstrated that the Byzantine empire's economic, intellectual, administrative, and spiritual powers, although differing from century to century, kept it vigorous and alive, and helped it to exert permanent influences on many nations and peoples of Eastern and Western Europe, and the Near East. Byzantium's social structure, its attitude toward war and peace, its kind of government, diplomacy, defenses, administration, and administrative machinery, its religion and church, its education and art, its domestic and external problems, its economy and daily life, its strengths and weaknesses, and above all its influence and contribution to its people and to others have become subjects of intensive study.

Much has been done by Nicolas Svoronos in the area of law and legislation as it applied to taxation and the economic reforms of the middle Byzantine centuries, and by John Karayannopoulos in terms of economy, diplomacy, and finances. Palaeography and manuscript catalogs have been continued while much attention has been given to vernacular literature by Herbert Hunger. Learning and education have had a long history in Byzantine studies and in the last fifty years major contributions have been made.

But life and civilization in the Byzantine world was never static and Byzantine scholars, though never unanimous in several areas of research, have emphasized certain important traits of the empire's institutions, ideologies, and practices. Throughout its history, the empire was ruled by an emperor, or Basileus, a system of monarchy checked by several institutions, providing more flexibility and preventing the evolution of the monarchy into an absolute power. The divine right of the emperor was curtailed by the divine right of the people, who insisted that the government was a form of *ennomos basileia*, a kingship subject and obedient to the law. In the eyes of the people, the emperor who violated and abused the law was subject to deposition and even death. Authority that rested with the people implied that no body, civil or ecclesiastical, could act in violation of established creed, law, or custom. Moral, legal, and religious barriers prevented the emperor from becoming an absolute monarch.

In the spirit of equality under the law, the relations between church and state, civil and ecclesiastical, were determined by the principle of *harmonia* (harmony) with a specific definition of roles. Spiritual authority oversaw the spiritual needs of the empire's people, while civil authority was responsible for the secular aspects. This principle does not mean that some emperors did not attempt or practice Caesaropapism. Some patriarchs aspired to introduce Papocaesarism, placing ecclesiastical authority over imperial authority. The rule that governed both was the principle of dyarchy (*dyarchia*).

The administrative relationship between the central and provincial governments was closer to the Greek than the Roman model. When Constantine the Great transferred the capital to a Greek city, he followed Greek models in several of the government's reforms. He made civil and military authorities separate. His administrative structure allowed more autonomy to each branch of the government. In contrast to the Roman imperial system of centralized authority, the Byzantine empire's organization was founded on the Greek experience which allowed cities to function as political entities, retaining their civic pride, their individuality, even though politically parts of the empire. Furthermore, provincial governors had purely civil responsibilities leaving military functions to military commanders.

While in the first and last centuries of the empire's existence there were disparities and a wealthy class in contrast to a very poor class, in the middle Byzantine centuries there was a strong middle class of artisans and farmers. Social mobility allowed a poor peasant to move to the capital for work and ultimately emerge as emperor or patriarch. A free agricultural peasantry, as well as artisans and technicians organized in guilds, were supervised by governmental appointees. Western European feudalism was introduced in the East by the Crusades, but free small landholders survived to the very end of the empire's existence, argued Angeliki Laiou in *Peasant Society in the Late Byzantine Empire* (1977).

In terms of culture and civilization, Byzantine historiography of the last fifty years, such as the work of Phaideon Koukoules, has concentrated on daily life, popular religiosity, lives of saints as sources for the study of daily life, social institutions, and the social ethos of Byzantine society. The study of Byzantine civilization and its influence on the Slavic and Western European world has preoccupied several leading Byzantinists including Dmitri Obolensky and John Meyendorff. The nature of civilization has been revealed in its art and architecture, literature, religious thought and theology, hymnology and epic poetry. All these subjects have received much attention, which has resulted in outstanding contributions. Other aspects of Byzantine history such as topography, institutions, and the cities, have been extensively treated.

Attacked from east and west, north and south, the empire fought many wars and ultimately it succumbed. Relations with both allies and enemies have been the areas of much scholarly research with first-rate monographs and original studies such as that of Speros Vryonis.

Byzantine theological thought, church hymnography, ecclesiastical liturgies and music have been greatly influential and of interest to the Christian world down to the present time. Scholars such as Hans Georg Beck and John Meyendorff have devoted their lives to the study of the church and theology of the Byzantine world. Unlike archaeology and architecture – both relatively young fields of scholarly research – art has become the subject of many important studies. Although it has been viewed as one of Byzantium's original contributions, Ernst Kitzinger argued that art, too, manifested a "perennial Hellenism." It did not originate in the Iranian world, as some earlier historians maintained, but in the Hellenic and hellenized Greek world. In the light of this, the iconoclastic controversy of the 8th century has been seen not only as a religious issue, but also as a conflict between the Hellenic and the Semitic worldviews. If concern for human welfare and the vulnerable members of society is a measure of a civilized people, Demetrios Constantelos argued, Byzantium must have been a more civilized state than its critics would have us believe.

Our knowledge of Byzantine history and civilization has been greatly enriched and enlarged by many critical editions of sources by devoted philologists, historians, theologians, and others. The student of the Byzantine empire should constantly consult the bibliographies in professional journals such as *Byzantinische Zeitschrift*, *Byzantion*, *Revue des Etudes Byzantines*, *Byzantina*, *Epeteris Etairias Byzantinon Spoudon*, *Vizantijskij Vremennik*, and *The Oxford Dictionary of Byzantium*.

DEMETRIOS J. CONSTANTELOS

See also Brown; Bury; Cameron; Cassiodorus; Eastern Orthodoxy; Halecki; Kazhdan; Komnene; Lopez; Middle East; Obolensky; Ostrogorsky; Procopius; Psellos; Roman; Runciman; Russia: Medieval; Russia: Early Modern; Vasiliev

Further Reading

Agathias, *De imperio et rebus gestis Iustiniani*, written 565; in English as *The Histories*, New York: de Gruyter, 1975

Ahrweiler, Hélène, *Byzance et la mer* (Byzantium and the Sea), Paris: Presses Universitaires de France, 1966

Ahrweiler, Hélène, *L'Idéologie politique de l'Empire byzantin* (The Political Ideology of the Byzantine Empire), Paris: Presses Universitaires de France, 1975

Akropolites [Acropolites], George, *Chronike Syngraphe*, written 13th century; in English as *A Translation and Historical Commentary of George Akropolites' History*, 1978

Angold, Michael, *The Byzantine Empire, 1025–1204: A Political History*, London and New York: Longman, 1984

Barker, John W., *Manuel II Palaeologus (1391–1425): A Study in Late Byzantine Statesmanship*, New Brunswick, NJ: Rutgers University Press, 1969

Barnes, Timothy David, *The New Empire of Diocletian and Constantine*, Cambridge, MA: Harvard University Press, 1982

Baynes, Norman H., *Byzantine Studies and Other Essays*, London: Athlone Press, 1955

Beck, Hans Georg, *Kirche und theologische Literatur im byzantinischen Reich* (Church and Theological Literature in the Byzantine Empire), Munich: Beck, 1959

Beck, Hans Georg, *Geschichte der byzantinischen Volksliteratur* (The History of Popular Byzantine Literature), Munich: Beck, 1971

Beck, Hans Georg, *Das byzantinische Jahrtausend* (The Byzantine Millennium), Munich: Beck, 1978

Beckwith, John, *Early Christian and Byzantine Art*, Harmondsworth: Penguin, 1970; revised 1979

Brand, Charles M., *Byzantium Confronts the West, 1180–1204*, Cambridge, MA: Harvard University Press, 1968

Brehier, Louis, *Le Monde byzantin* (The Byzantine World), 3 vols., Paris: Michel, 1947–50

Browning, Robert, *The Byzantine Empire*, New York: Scribner, and London: Weidenfeld and Nicolson, 1980; revised 1992

Browning, Robert, *Medieval and Modern Greek*, Cambridge, MA: Harvard University Press, and Cambridge: Cambridge University Press, 1983

Bryer, Anthony, and David Winfield, *The Byzantine Monuments and Topography of the Pontos*, 2 vols., Washington DC: Dumbarton Oaks, 1985

Cameron, Alan, *Literature and Society in the Early Byzantine World*, London: Variorum, 1985

Chalandon, Ferdinand, *Les Comnène: études sur l'empire byzantin au XIe et XIIe siècles* (The Comnenes: Studies on the Byzantine Empire, 11th and 12th Centuries), 2 vols., Paris: Picard, 1900–12; reprinted New York: B. Franklin, 1960

Charanis, Peter, *Studies on the Demography of the Byzantine Empire*, London: Variorum, 1972

Choniates, Niketas, *Chronike Diegesis*, written before 1204; in English as *O City of Byzantium: Annals of Niketas Choniates*, Detroit: Wayne State University Press, 1984

Christophilopoulou, Aikaterinee, *Byzantine Historia*, Athens, 1984; in English as *Byzantine History*, Amsterdam: Hakkert, 1986

Conomos, Dimitri E., *The Late Byzantine and Slavonic Communion Cycle: Liturgy and Music*, Washington, DC: Dumbarton Oaks, 1985

Constantelos, Demetrios J., *Byzantine Philanthropy and Social Welfare*, New Brunswick, NJ: Rutgers University Press, 1968; revised 1991

Constantelos, Demetrios J., *Poverty, Society and Philanthropy in the Late Medieval Greek World*, New Rochelle, NY: Caratzos, 1992

Dagron, Gilbert, *Naissance d'une capitale: Constantinople et ses institutions de 330 à 451* (Birth of a Capital: Constantinople and Its Institutions, 330–451), Paris: Presses Universitaires de France, 1974

Doukas [Ducas], *Historia byzantina*, written 15th century; in English as *Decline and Fall of Byzantium to the Ottoman Turks*, Detroit: Wayne State University Press, 1975

Dvornik, Francis, *Byzantine Missions among the Slavs: Saints Constantine-Cyril and Methodius*, New Brunswick, NJ: Rutgers University Press, 1970

Geanakoplos, Deno John, *Byzantium: Church, Society and Civilization*, Chicago: University of Chicago Press, 1984

Gero, Stephen, *Byzantine Iconoclasm during the Reign of Leo III*, Louvain: Secrétariat du Corpussco, 1973

Gero, Stephen, *Byzantine Iconoclasm during the Reign of Constantine V*, Louvain: Secrétariat du Corpussco, 1977

Gregoras, Nikephoros, *Historia Rhomaike* (Byzantine History), 37 vols., written c.1351–58

Hendy, Michael F., *Coinage and Money in the Byzantine Empire, 1081–1261*, Washington, DC: Dumbarton Oaks, 1969

Hendy, Michael F., *Studies in the Byzantine Monetary Economy c.300–1450*, Cambridge and New York: Cambridge University Press, 1985

Holum, Kenneth, *Theodosian Empresses: Women and Imperial Dominion in Late Antiquity*, Berkeley: University of California Press, 1982

Hunger, Herbert, *Reich der neuen Mitte: Der christliche Geist der byzantinischen Kultur* (The Empire of the New Center: The Christian Spirit of Byzantine Culture), Graz: Styria, 1965

Hunger, Herbert, *Die hochsprachliche profane Literatur der Byzantiner* (The Literate Secular Literature of the Byzantines), 2 vols., Munich: Beck, 1978

Hussey, Joan M., *Church and Learning in the Byzantine Empire, 867–1185*, London: Oxford University Press, 1937

Hussey, Joan M., *The Orthodox Church in the Byzantine Empire*, Oxford: Oxford University Press, 1986

Jeffreys, Elizabeth M., and Michael J. Jeffreys, *Popular Literature in Late Byzantium*, London: Variorum, 1983

Kaegi, Walter Emil, Jr., *Byzantine Military Unrest, 471–843: An Interpretation*, Amsterdam: Hakkert, 1981

Kaegi, Walter Emil, Jr., *Army, Society and Religion in Byzantium*, London: Variorum, 1982

Kantakouzenos, Ioannes [John Cantacuzenus], *Historia*, written c.1362–69

Karayannopoulos, John [Karagiannopoulos, I.E.], *Das Finanzwesen des frühbyzantinischen Staates* (The Financial Structure of the Early Byzantine State), Munich: Oldenbourg, 1958

Karayannopoulos, John [Karagiannopoulos, I.E.], *Istoria Byzantinou Kratous* (History of the Byzantine State) 3 vols., Thessaloniki: Vanias, 1978–81

Kazhdan, A.P., and Anthony Cutler, "Continuity and Discontinuity in Byzantine History," *Byzantion* 52 (1982), 429–78

Kazhdan, A.P., and Giles Constable, *People and Power in Byzantium: An Introduction to Modern Byzantine Studies*, Washington, DC: Dumbarton Oaks, 1982

Kazhdan, A.P., and Ann Wharton Epstein, *Change in Byzantine Culture in the Eleventh and Twelfth Centuries*, Berkeley: University of California Press, 1985

Kazhdan, A.P., ed., *The Oxford Dictionary of Byzantium*, 3 vols., New York and Oxford: Oxford University Press, 1991

Kinnamos, John, *Epitome* (Résumé), written 1180–83; in English as *Deeds of John and Manuel Comnenus*, New York: Columbia University Press, 1976

Kitzinger, Ernst, *Byzantine Art in the Making: Main Lines of Stylistic Development in Mediterranean Art, 3rd–7th centuries*, Cambridge, MA: Harvard University Press, and London: Faber, 1977

Komnene [Comnena], Anna, *The Alexiad*, written 1138–48; in English as *The Alexiad of Anna Comnena*, Harmondsworth and Baltimore: Penguin, 1969

Koukoules, Phaideon, *Byzantinon bios kai politismos* (Life and Civilization of the Byzantines), 6 vols., Athens, 1948–57

Kriaras, Emmanoucl, *Vyzantina Hippotika Mythistoreemata* (Byzantine Chivalric Fiction), Athens: Aetus, 1955

Krumbacher, Karl, *Geschichte der byzantinischen Litteratur von Justinian bis zum Ende des Oströmischen Reiches (527–1453)* (History of Byzantine Literature from Justinian to the End of the Eastern Roman Empire), Munich: Beck, 1891

Kulakovskij, Julian A., *Istoriia Vizantii* (Byzantine History), 3 vols., Kiev, 1912–15; reprinted 1973

Laiou, Angeliki E., *Constantinople and the Latins: The Foreign Policy of Andronicus II, 1282–1328*, Cambridge, MA: Harvard University Press, 1972

Laiou, Angeliki E., *Peasant Society in the Late Byzantine Empire: A Social and Democratic Study*, Princeton: Princeton University Press, 1977

Lemerle, Paul, *Le premier humanisme byzantin: notes et remarques sur l'enseignement et la culture à Byzance des origines au Xe siècles*, Paris: Presses Universitaires de France, 1970; in English as *Byzantine Humanism, the First Phase: Notes and Remarks on Education and Culture in Byzantium from its Origins to the Tenth Century*, Canberra: Australian Association for Byzantine Studies, 1986

Lemerle, Paul, *The Agrarian History of Byzantium from the Origins to the Twelfth Century: The Sources and Problems*, Galway: Galway University Press, 1979

Maguire, Henry, *Art and Eloquence in Byzantium*, Princeton: Princeton University Press, 1981

Mango, Cyril, *The Art of the Byzantine Empire, 312–1453: Sources and Documents*, Englewood Cliffs, NJ: Prentice Hall, 1972; reprinted Toronto: University of Toronto Press, 1986

Mango, Cyril, *Byzantium: The Empire of New Rome*, London: Weidenfeld and Nicolson, and New York: Scribner, 1980

Mathews, Thomas F., *The Early Churches of Constantinople: Architecture and Liturgy*, University Park: Pennsylvania State University Press, 1971

Meyendorff, John, *Byzantine Theology: Historical Trends and Doctrinal Themes*, New York: Fordham University Press, and London: Mowbrays, 1974

Meyendorff, John, *Byzantium and the Rise of Russia: A Study of Byzantino-Russian Relations in the Fourteenth Century*, Cambridge and New York: Cambridge University Press, 1981

Miller, Timothy S., *The Birth of the Hospital in the Byzantine Empire*, Baltimore: Johns Hopkins University Press, 1985

Mitsakis, Kariophiles, *Byzantine Hymnographia*, Thessalonika: Patriochikon Hidryma Paterikon Meleton, 1971

Moravcsik, Gyula, *Byzantinoturcica* (Turkish Byzantium), 2 vols., Berlin: Akademie, 1958

Nicol, Donald M., *The Last Centuries of Byzantium, 1261–1453*, London: Hart Davies, and New York: St. Martin's Press, 1972

Norwich, John Julius, *Byzantium*, 3 vols., London: Viking, 1988–95; New York: Knopf, 1989–96

Obolensky, Dimitri, *The Byzantine Commonwealth: Eastern Europe, 500–1453*, London: Weidenfeld and Nicolson, and New York: Praeger, 1971

Oikonomides, Nicolas, *Hommes d'affaires grecs et latins à Constantinople (XIIIe–XVe siècles)* (Relations Between Greeks and Latins of Constantinople, 13th–15th Centuries), Montreal: Institut d'études medievales Albert-le-Grand, 1979

Oikonomides, Nicolas, ed., *Studies in Byzantine Sigillography*, Washington, DC: Dumbarton Oaks, 1987

Orlandos, Anastasios, *Monasteriake architektonike* (Monastic Architecture), Athens: Hestia, 1958

Ostrogorsky, George, *Geschichte des byzantinischen Staates*, Munich: Beck, 1940; in English as *History of the Byzantine State*, Oxford: Blackwell, 1956; New Brunswick, NJ: Rutgers University Press, 1957; revised 1968

Pachymeres, George, *Syngraphikai historiai* or *Hromaike Historia* (Roman [Eastern] History), 13 vols., written 13th and 14th centuries

Papadakis, Aristeides, *Crisis in Byzantium: The Filioque Controversy in the Patriarchate of Gregory II of Cyprus (1283–1289)*, New York: Fordham University Press, 1983

Paparregopoulos, Konstantinos, *Historia tou hellenikou ethnous* (History of the Greek People), 6 vols., Athens: Passaree, 1860–77; abridged in French as *Histoire de la civilisation hellénique*, Paris: Hachette, 1878

Patlagean, Evelyne, *Structure sociale, famille, chrétienté à Byzance: IVe–XIe siècle* (Social Structure, the Family, Byzantine Christendom: 4th–11th Centuries), London: Variorum, 1981

Podskalsky, Gerhard, *Theologie und Philosophie in Byzanz* (Theology and Philosophy in Byzantium), Munich: Beck, 1977

Powicke, F.M., *Modern Historians and the Study of History*, London: Odhams Press, 1956

Psellos, Michael, *Chronographia*, c.1059–78; in English as *The Chronographia of Michael Psellus*, New Haven: Yale University Press, 1953, revised as *Fourteen Byzantine Rulers*, 1966

Runciman, Steven, *The Fall of Constantinople, 1453*, Cambridge: Cambridge University Press, 1965

Runciman, Steven, *The Great Church in Captivity: A Study of the Patriarchate of Constantinople from the Eve of the Turkish Conquest to the Greek War of Independence*, Cambridge: Cambridge University Press, 1968

Scholasticus, Socrates [Scholastikos, Sokrates], *Ekklesiastike Historia*, written c.439; in English as *The Ecclesiastical History*, Grand Rapids, MI: Eerdmans, 1952

Ševčenko, Ihor, *Ideology, Letters and Culture in the Byzantine World*, London: Variorum, 1982

Ševčenko, Ihor, *Society and Intellectual Life in Late Byzantium*, London: Variorum, 1981

Simocatta, Theophylact, *Oikoumenike Historia*, written early 7th century; in English as *The History of Theophylact Simocatta*, Oxford and New York: Oxford University Press, 1986

Sphrantzes, George, *Chronikon*, written 1450s; in English as *The Fall of the Byzantine Empire: A Chronicle*, Amherst: University of Massachusetts Press, 1980

Stratos, Andreas N., *To Byzantion ston hebdomon abiona*, 5 vols., Athens: Hestas, 1965–; in English as *Byzantium in the Seventh Century*, 5 vols., Amsterdam: Hakkert, 1968–80

Svoronos, Nicolas, *Etudes sur l'organisation intérieure, la societé et l'économie de l'Empire Byzantin* (Studies on the Inner Organization, the Society, and the Economy of the Byzantine Empire), London: Variorum, 1973

Theophanes the Confessor, *Chronographia*, written 810–14; in English as *The Chronicle of Theophanes Confessor: Byzantine and Near Eastern History, AD284–813*, Oxford and New York: Oxford University Press, 1997

Treadgold, Warren T., *The Byzantine Revival, 780–842*, Stanford, CA: Stanford University Press, 1988

Vasiliev, A.A., *Istoriia Vizantii*, 3 vols., St. Petersburg: Academia, 1923; in English as *History of the Byzantine Empire*, 2 vols., Madison: University of Wisconsin Press, 1928–29; revised as *History of the Byzantine Empire, 324–1453*, Madison: University of Wisconsin Press, 1952

Vikan, Gary, and John Nesbit, *Security in Byzantium: Locking, Sealing and Weighing*, Washington, DC: Dumbarton Oaks, 1980

Vryonis, Speros, Jr., *Byzantium: Its Internal History and Relations with the Muslim World*, London: Variorum, 1971

Vryonis, Speros, Jr., *The Decline of Medieval Hellenism in Asia Minor and the Process of Islamization from the Eleventh Through the Fifteenth Century*, Berkeley: University of California Press, 1971

Vryonis, Speros, Jr., ed., *The "Past" in Medieval and Modern Greek Culture*, Malibu, CA: Undena, 1978

Wilson, Nigel Guy, *Scholars of Byzantium*, London: Duckworth, and Baltimore: Johns Hopkins University Press, 1983

Wolf, Jerome [Heironymous], series editor, *Corpus byzantinae historiae*, 17 vols., Paris, 1645–70

Zakythinos, Dionysius A., *Le Despotat grec de Morée* (The Greek Despotat of the Morea [Peloponnese]), 2 vols., Paris: Belle Lettres, 1932–53; revised 1975

Zakythinos, Dionysius A., *Vyzantine Istoria* (Byzantine History), Athens: Myrtide, 1972

Zosimos [Zosimus], *Nea Historia* or *Historia Nova*, written c.450–502; in English as *New History*, Canberra: Australian National University Press, 1982

C

Caesar, Julius 100–44 BCE

Roman historian

According to Greco-Roman criteria Caesar was not a historian. His extant works – C. Iuli Caesaris, Commentarii rerum gestarum (Gaius Julius Caesar's Notes on His Achievements) – belong to a tradition of historical *hypomnemata*, or *aides-mémoire*, compiled as sources for historians who would develop these raw notes into a creative work of art. The dictator Sulla was one of Caesar's most prolific predecessors in the genre.

Much has been made of Caesar's supposedly cynical adoption of certain stylistic features to add plausibility to essentially personal propaganda, but the unadorned Attic style of oratory was the norm for *Commentarii*; the conventional use of the third person by the author when referring to himself seems to have begun with Xenophon's *Anabasis*; analysis and comment have no place in this genre: the facts must be allowed to speak for themselves. However, a plain, fast-moving style with straightforward, orthodox syntax and vocabulary no doubt suited both Caesar's temperament and his purposes. In this kind of writing, he advises, one should avoid unusual words "like rocks at sea." The form itself encourages the inference that here is the unvarnished truth from a no-nonsense military man.

De bello Gallico (*The Gallic War*) covers Caesar's systematic conquest of Gaul between 58 and 52 BCE, beginning with the subjugation of the Helvetii and ending with the siege of Alesia and defeat of Vercingetorix, in book 7. This hard-won victory, an irrefutable demonstration of Caesar's tactical ability and the capacity of a well-trained Roman army, made a suitably impressive climax to the whole work. An eighth book, dealing with mopping-up operations, was added by his lieutenant, Aulus Hirtius. Caesar was renowned for his speed in writing as well as in forced marches and he needed to get his narrative into the public domain quickly.

Each book was probably written at the end of the annual campaign season and at first had a limited circulation. The work then seems to have been edited as a whole and published more widely in 51. At this point Caesar may have added the valuable geographical digressions on the Suebi (5.12–14), Britain (6.11–18) and the Hyrcanian Forest (6.11–28), perhaps supplementing his firsthand knowledge from a written source, now unknown.

An author may of course play down events that do not fit the image he wishes to convey but books 5 and 6 present a catalogue of disasters and dangers for the Romans. Despite the detachment demanded by the *Commentarius* form, Caesar does not conceal the urgency of these crises nor, for example, his grief at the death of Curio – the only passage of direct speech in *De bello civile* (*The Civil War*). There is only one place where Caesar's account of the facts has been convincingly challenged. At *Bello Gallico* 1.12, he apparently fails to mention the leading role of his most trusted lieutenant, Labienus, in the defeat of the Tigurini, although he is usually scrupulous in acknowledging the merits of his subordinates. The *Commentaries* bore ample witness to Caesar's achievements, amplifying his official despatches to the Senate, keeping him in the public eye, and frustrating his political opponents during his long absences from Rome.

In *The Civil War* Caesar is more obviously writing in self-justification. As a public enemy he was fighting to preserve his career, as well as his life, against the Senate's general, Pompey. The three books cover the years 49–48 but the record is not complete, especially for the latter stages of the war, ending with Pompey's murder and the chaos in Alexandria. Caesar attempts a calm assessment of the process of war on both sides and, as in *The Gallic War*, gives due credit to the enemy, even to the deserter Labienus. Here his account can be checked against contemporary sources. The letters of Cicero, for whom Caesar was "the right man on the wrong side," are particularly revealing. Short continuations of *The Civil War* in Egypt, Africa, and Spain were added by officers of Caesar's, the *Bellum Hispaniense* (*The Spanish War*) being of interest for its un-literary quality.

Caesar's was the art that conceals art. His lucid, spare but intense style was admired from the start by Cicero among others, who warned that no-one but a fool would attempt to "improve" upon it. Hirtius's preface to *The Gallic War* book 8 remarks similarly that Caesar had not offered historians material but had effectively precluded them from ever writing on the subject. Caesar's reputation as an orator was second only to Cicero's and he must have foreseen that his work would stand on its own merits.

The Gallic War contains a unique record of the Celtic and Teutonic peoples, notably book 6.1–18 on the customs of the Gauls, including the Druids, and the Germans; it became popular again in the Renaissance with the rise of nationalism in Europe. From the 16th to 19th centuries the *Commentaries* were consulted as handbooks of military tactics and organization; Napoleon declared them essential reading for any aspiring general. Caesar was that rare combination – brilliant general and literary genius.

MARILYNNE BROMLEY

See also Egypt: Ancient; France: to 1000; Machiavelli; Roman

Biography

Gaius Julius Caesar. Born Rome, 100 BCE, descended from a patrician family. In army in Asia, 81–c.70; quaestor, 69; in province of Further Spain, 68–64/3 and 61–60; elected high priest (Pontifex Maximus), 63; praetor, 62; consul, 59 (and 4 more times); conquered Gaul, and was made governor, 58–50; invaded Britain, 55 and 54; defeated Pompey and republicans in civil war, 49–45; dictator, 49 (and 3 more times). Married 1) Cornelia, daughter of Lucius Cornelius Cinna, 84 (died 68; 1 daughter); 2) Pompeia, granddaughter of Sulla, c.68 (divorced c.61); 3) Calpurnia, 59. Assassinated Rome, 15 March 44 BCE.

Principal Writings

De bello Gallico, 52 BCE; in English as *The Gallic War* (Loeb edition), translated by H.J. Edwards, 1917

De bello civile, 48 BCE; in English as *The Civil Wars* (Loeb edition), translated by A.G. Peskett, 1914

Further Reading

Adcock, Frank E., *Caesar as Man of Letters*, Cambridge: Cambridge University Press, 1956

Bradford, Ernle Dusgate Selby, *Julius Caesar: The Pursuit of Power*, London: Hamish Hamilton, 1984

Carter, J.M., Introduction to his translation of *The Civil War, Books 1 and 2*, Warminster: Aris and Phillips, 1991

Chevallier, Raymond, ed., *Présence de César*, Paris: Belles Lettres, 1985

Ellis, Peter Berresford, *Caesar's Invasion of Britain*, New York: New York University Press, 1980; London: Orbis, 1994

Gelzer, Matthias, *Caesar: der Politiker und Staatsmann*, Stuttgart: Deutsche Verlags-Anstalt, 1921; in English as *Caesar, Politician and Statesman*, Oxford: Blackwell, and Cambridge, MA: Harvard University Press, 1968

Mutschler, Fritz-Heiner, *Erzählstil und Propaganda in Caesars Kommentarien* (Narrative Style and Propaganda in Caesar's Commentaries), Heidelberg: Winter, 1975

Pascucci, G., "Interpretazione linguistica e stilistica del Cesare autentico" (Linguistic and Stylistic Analysis of the Genuine Caesar), in Hildegard Temporini, ed., *Aufstieg und Niedergang der römischen Welt*, vol.1, Berlin: de Gruyter, 1973

Rambaud, Michel, *L'Art de la déformation historique dans les "Commentaires" de César* (The Art of Historical Distortion in the "Commentaries" of Caesar), Paris: Belles Lettres, 1952

Ruebel, James S., ed., *Caesar and the Crisis of the Roman Aristocracy: A Civil War Reader*, Norman: University of Oklahoma Press, 1994

Yavetz, Zvi, *Caesar in der Öffentlichen Meinung*, Dusseldorf: Droste, 1979; in English as *Julius Caesar and His Public Image*, London: Thames and Hudson, and Ithaca, NY: Cornell University Press, 1983

Cahen, Claude 1909–1991

French historian of the Middle East

Generally acknowledged as one of the foremost historians of the Middle East in the 20th century, Claude Cahen determined very early to devote himself to historical research. To his classical formation as a historian, he added the learning of Arabic, Turkish and Persian, which he used as a tool to open new historical prospects. He chose economic and social history, then a neglected field, particularly on the Islamic world.

From his earliest articles Cahen showed his masterly ability to explore medieval chronicles and derive from them unprecedented data on comparative historical understanding, mainly on feudalism. His thorough study of primary sources included precious information from rarely exploited sources collected on missions, notably at Istanbul in 1936–37. Having established his historical method, he wrote his monumental thesis *La Syrie du Nord à l'époque des croisades et la Principauté franque d'Antioche* (Northern Syria in the Era of the Crusades and Frankish Antioch), published in Paris (1940) together with his complementary thesis *Le régime féodal de l'Italie normande* (Feudalism in Norman Italy). During his five years of imprisonment in a German stalag (1940–45), he pursued his reflections on history, notably through informal lectures he gave to his companions. He joined the French Communist party in 1939 when it was still illegal, but he never belonged to a school or movement, found the Marxist theory of the Asiatic mode of production inadequate, and kept apart from the Annales group. He preferred to publish in the *Revue Historique* and Orientalist periodicals, although he refused to be categorized as an Orientalist. He saw in the traditional Orientalist method two possible drifts. The first one, ideological, put forward a comparative analysis of religious and philological doctrines and based its social analysis on the imperatives of Islam. The second one, philological or linguistic, allowed grammarians or theoreticians of language to impose their understanding of texts on historians. He vigorously defended his idea that European medieval civilization included the whole Mediterranean world and the Middle East. This area was, until the 15th century, not radically different from Europe. Its study needed to be brought within the mainstream of methods elaborated to study European medieval history. One of his main concerns was that the historian has no right to ignore any social group. He opened a considerable field in socioeconomic history of the Orient by approaching politics through taxation and coinage. From very early in his career, he was a discoverer of new sources in various languages (Latin, Greek, Arabic, Persian, Turkish, Syriac, Armenian, among others). He would immediately disclose his findings in articles. He always kept himself informed about primary and secondary sources and transmitted his knowledge to colleagues, disciples, and students.

Cahen exposed his general ideas on his historical method in his article "Pour la science de l'histoire" (On Historical Science, 1946) in which he defended a subtle historical materialism independent of Marxist theories. Although he remained a Marxist, his method was mainly based upon empirical research, extensive erudition, and broad historical understanding. Throughout his career, he remained a *universitaire* and, unlike Braudel, never joined the Ecole Pratique des Hautes Etudes. One of his main concerns was to transmit his knowledge and experience, and he continued to write annotated bibliographies and textbooks for advanced students. His collaboration was sought by foreign publishers who translated and published some of his books before the French original text came out. Such was the case with *L'Islam, des origines au début de l'empire ottoman* (Islam from Its Origins to the Beginning of the Ottoman Empire, 1970), first published in German (1968), Italian (1969), then in Spanish and Arabic (1972) and Turkish (1990). His *Pre-Ottoman Turkey* (1968), largely predated its French edition, *La Turquie pré-ottomane* (1988).

One of Cahen's main concerns remained Turkish domination and expansionism over a vast area that, in its western part, was to become the Ottoman empire. He was also the first to retrace the strong Persian influence, expressed in Arabic as well as Persian, in cultural and administrative fields, inherited from Sassanian tradition and further through emigration. Since he was always very cautious and critical when using Islamic historiography, his method and achievements have not been seriously challenged by the new English historical school (essentially Patricia Crone and her disciples) which, from the mid-1970s reinterpreted early Islamic history. Many of Cahen's disciples and students still derive much profit from his works, advice and methodology, and transmit it to younger students.

Cahen's self-identification was by no means based on his Jewish ancestry. His personal identity was built mainly upon his scholarship and political commitments. But he was above all a tolerant free thinker. Extremely modest, he never sought for honors. Through his reputation he was elected to the Académie des inscriptions et belles-lettres (1973), and was president of the Société Asiatique (1974). He was also, with W.F. Leemans, the founder of the *Journal of the Economic and Social History of the Orient* (JESHO), first issued in 1957, and its director until 1986. He was the dean of the editorial committee of *Studia Iranica* and a member of the directorial committee of *The Encyclopaedia of Islam*. In his last years, he became increasingly deaf and blind. Although he endeavored to pursue his task, his pioneering work on Arabic papyri was taken over by Yousouf Ragheb. Other scholars or disciples, such as Thierry Bianquis, Jacqueline Chabbi, and Jean-Claude Garcin, remain inspired by Cahen's methods, which were also applied by his close disciple Françoise Micheaud to study the history of non-religious learning in medieval Islam. They continue to publish studies dedicated to his thought and memory.

JEAN CALMARD

See also Ibn al-Athīr; Lewis; Middle East

Biography

Born Paris, 26 February 1909. Studied in Paris at Lycée Louis-le-Grand; Ecole Normale Supérieure, 1928–32, degree in history and geography, 1932; studied Arabic, Turkish, and Persian, Ecole des langues orientales, 1931. Taught at lycées in Amiens and Rouen; then at the Ecole des langues orientales, 1937–40. Prisoner of war, 1940–45. Taught (rising to professor), University of Strasbourg, 1945–59; Ecole des langues orientales, 1945–55; and the Sorbonne, 1959–79. Married Pauline Olivier [Annette Blain], 1948 (5 sons, 1 daughter). Died 18 November 1991.

Principal Writings

La Syrie du Nord à l'époque des croisades et la Principauté franque d'Antioche (Northern Syria in the Era of the Crusades and Frankish Antioch), 1940
Le Régime féodal de l'Italie normande (Feudalism in Norman Italy), 1940
"Pour la science de l'histoire" (On Historical Science), *La Pensée* 8 (1946)
Pre-Ottoman Turkey: A General Survey of the Material and Spiritual Culture and History, c.1071–1330, 1968; in French as *La Turquie pré-ottomane*, 1988
L'Islam des origines au début de l'empire ottoman (Islam from Its Origins at the Beginning of the Ottoman Empire), 1970

Turcobyzantina et Oriens christianus (Turkish Byzantium and Eastern Christianity), 1974
Makhzûmiyyât: Etudes sur l'histoire économique et financière de l'Egypte médiévale (Makhzûmiyyât: Studies in the Economic and Financial History of Medieval Egypt), 1977
Les Peuples musulmans dans l'histoire médiévale (Moslem Peoples in Medieval History), 1977 [collected articles]
Introduction à l'histoire du monde musulman médiéval, VIIe–XVe siècles (Introduction to the History of the Medieval Muslim World, 7th–15th Centuries), 1982
Orient et Occident au temps des croisades (Orient and Occident at the Time of the Crusades), 1983

Further Reading

Cheikh-Moussa, A., D. Gazagnadou, and F. Michaeu, eds., "L'Oeuvre de Claude Cahen: lectures critiques," *Arabica* 43/1 (1996)
Curiel, Raoul, and Rika Gyselen, eds., *Itinéraires d'Orient: Hommage à Claude Cahen*, Bures-sur-Yvette: Groupe pour l'étude de la civilisation du Moyen-Orient, 1994

Cam, Helen 1885–1968
British medievalist

Helen Maud Cam was one of Britain's pre-eminent historians of the Middle Ages. Her work clearly reveals the nature of the transition from the approach of the revered Victorian authorities to the new techniques and concerns of 20th-century medievalists. Educated at home by her parents, she was "eating and drinking Greek" at an early age, and her solid grounding in classical languages served the future scholar well. After graduating from London University she began the work for her MA in Anglo-Saxon and Frankish studies during a fellowship year in the United States, presenting her thesis at London University in 1909.

Even from this early period two of the elements which were to define Cam's approach to history were already apparent. Her interests and research methods were catholic; she was never to be of the insular, "ivory towered" school of British medievalists. It is significant that she began and was to conclude her academic career in the United States. After a career spent first at London University and then at Girton College, Cambridge, her last years of teaching before her retirement in 1954 took her to another Cambridge; Cam was awarded a chair at Harvard and from there she exerted a powerful influence on a generation of American medievalists.

Her approach to her discipline, while always punctilious and often narrowly focused, could also be wide-ranging, drawing unhesitatingly on the latest findings of North American scholarship, in conjunction with the most eminent British Victorians, and her more popular writing was alluring enough to draw non-specialists, whether British or North American, into the wonders of the very distant past.

The second defining element is evident in the published title of her MA thesis, *Local Government in Francia and England, 768–1034*. The intricacies of local government, especially in later medieval England, were to be a source of continuing fascination for Cam, and it is largely through her work in this area, particularly on the hundred rolls, that her reputation was established.

The world of English medieval scholarship which Cam entered with the publication of her thesis in 1912 was one in which the dominant authorities were William Stubbs (1825–1901) and F.W. Maitland (1850–1906), men whose historical preoccupations had been primarily constitutional, legal, and administrative. Nurtured on their works, Cam never rejected their insights. Rather, her scholarship attempted to augment and, where she felt it necessary, gently correct the panoramic historical picture they had provided.

While Stubbs, particularly in his great *Constitutional History* (1874–78), and Maitland in his *History of English Law* (1895), had approached the structures of medieval English government from the top down, concentrating chiefly upon king, Parliament and the offices of state, Cam was to find her scholarly focus in the records of local government and local law enforcement. It is entirely appropriate that the introduction to the first group of her collected essays, *Liberties and Communities in Medieval England* (1944), a volume that drew together articles written between 1923 and 1942, should bear the title "In Defence of the Study of Local History."

The essays which appeared in the second collected volume, *Law-Finders and Law-Makers in Medieval England* (1963), dedicated to "The Historians of Harvard, My Friends and Fellow-workers 1948–1954," are somewhat more theoretical, the product of a mature, confident historian, undaunted by the challenges of such thorny topics as "The Rule of Law in English History" and "The Theory and Practice of Representation in Medieval England," and yet even here Cam never strays far from the shire, the hundred and the vill, her points of entry to the medieval world.

The *Law-Finders and Law-Makers* collection also includes Cam's eloquent tributes to the two historians she most revered: "Stubbs Seventy Years After" and "Maitland – the Historians' Historian." These essays clearly reveal the qualities that Cam prized most in those who write history. While she wrote of her regret concerning Stubbs' "acceptance of the unconscious assumptions of his age and his subjection to the influence of contemporary circumstances," she concludes her careful examination of his faults of omission and commission with a celebration of his "vital and magnificent achievement."

Cam admitted that she was one of those "who love Maitland this side idolatry" and she lamented the neglect of his work. She acknowledged, however, that "law was his guiding light and the legal approach to history is too impersonal for the average reader, who demands incident and characterization from his historical writers." Cam had learned her lessons well; for her, as for Maitland, "the history of law was not a specialized sub-section of the history of England; it was an integral part of it." As G.M. Trevelyan said of Maitland, Cam also used aspects of the legal practice of medieval England "as a tool to open the mind of medieval man." Both great medievalists used the law as a mechanism to reveal what Maitland called "the common thoughts of our forefathers about common things."

Unlike much of Maitland's work, Cam's writing could, when circumstances required it, capture "the average reader"; 1950 saw the first edition of her popular *England before Elizabeth*, a panoramic work which combined scholarship with lively writing, and one of her last publications was a Historical Association pamphlet, *Historical Novels* (1961), a survey which boldly accorded categories for "quality" to all the fictional

works discussed. In her assessment of historical fiction Cam was no less demanding and discerning than she was of the work of scholarly historians; the best of it "can arouse the critical faculty and stimulate investigation for the verification or disproof of unfamiliar facts, leading to firsthand acquaintance with original sources." Cam appears to have approached her own work with the same goals in mind, answering, throughout her long career, Stubbs' call to the historian "to rest content with nothing less than attainable truth."

KATHLEEN E. GARAY

See also Britain: Anglo-Saxon; Maitland; Stubbs

Biography

Helen Maud Cam. Born Abingdon, 22 August 1885. Educated at home; studied at Royal Holloway College, University of London, BA 1908, MA 1909. Fellow in history, Bryn Mawr College, 1908–09; assistant mistress in history, Cheltenham Ladies' College, 1909–12; assistant lecturer in history, Royal Holloway College, 1912–17, staff lecturer, 1919–21; at University of Cambridge: research fellow, Girton College, 1921–26, lecturer, 1926–48, and university lecturer, 1930–48; Zemurray Radcliffe professor in history, Harvard University, 1948–54. Died Orpington, Kent, 9 February 1968.

Principal Writings

Local Government in Francia and England, 768–1034, 1912
Studies in the Hundred Rolls: Some Aspects of Thirteenth-Century Administration, 1921
The Hundred and the Hundred Rolls, 1930
Liberties and Communities in Medieval England: Collected Studies in Local Administration and Topography, 1944
England before Elizabeth, 1950; revised 1960
Historical Novels, 1961
Law-Finders and Law-Makers in Medieval England: Collected Studies in Legal and Constitutional History, 1963

Cambridge Group

The Cambridge Group for the History of Population and Social Structure has revolutionized the study of English demographic history. Formed in 1964 with the support of a grant from the Gulbenkian Foundation, the Cambridge Group has been funded by the SSRC (Social Science Research Council) since 1968, and was granted the status of research unit of the SSRC in 1974. The three most renowned members of the group, Anthony Wrigley, Roger Schofield, and Peter Laslett, have all been involved since 1964, and have produced a huge number of books and articles on an array of subjects, including the history of social and family structure, numerous aspects of historical demography, and research techniques such as family reconstitution and aggregative analysis.

The first work to appear from the Cambridge Group was *An Introduction to English Historical Demography*, published in 1966. The work contained a number of articles dealing with some of the methodological issues surrounding demographic history and could be regarded as a handbook for historical demographers. The late 1960s also saw the release of Wrigley's ground-breaking work on the Devon village of Colyton, which went a long way toward establishing the group's reputation – a reputation that was further enhanced by the publication of Wrigley's *Population and History* in 1969. J.D. Chambers, emeritus professor of economic and social history at Nottingham and himself a historical demographer of some note, praised *Population and History* as "the most interesting contribution to demographic discussion since Malthus."

The Cambridge Group has produced numerous influential works, however it was Wrigley and Schofield's *The Population History of England* (1981) that really assured the group an international reputation. In a contemporary review by Leslie Bradley the work was lauded as "required reading for the really serious historical demographer . . . the definitive work in this field for many years to come." The highly innovative study was based on two sophisticated techniques devised by the Cambridge Group: "back projection" and "family reconstitution," which involved working back from population totals devised from 19th-century census records, and tracing parish records of baptisms, marriages, and burials. Wrigley and Schofield analyzed a dataset of 3.7 million monthly totals from a sample of 404 parishes and generated estimates for the population of England as far back as the 16th century, together with birthrates, marriage rates, and mortality rates. Their ground-breaking approach was described as "the most detailed and the most sophisticated attempt to provide an adequate set of demographic series."

However, the work has not been without its critics. In an article in *Population Studies* in 1985, Ronald Lee queried the accuracy of the back projection algorithm, and suggested some amendments to the formula which he put forward in his own theory of "inverse projection" and which have led to revisions by Wrigley and Schofield. Furthermore, in *Essays in English Population History* (1994), Peter Razzell questioned the reliability of the late 18th- and early 19th-century parish records on which many of their calculations were based, and challenged Wrigley and Schofield's claim that there was an insignificant fall in mortality in the 18th century. There have also been several articles discussing other methodological conundrums raised by the group's work, such as the reliability of age data and the difficulties of tracing migrants; and Laslett's claim that premodern England was a "one-class society" in *The World We Have Lost* (1965) remains highly contentious. However, the wealth of literature generated by the group's work should, perhaps, be seen as a testament to its continuing importance.

The Population History of England, like much of the group's work, relied heavily on the use of modern information technology; indeed it is inconceivable to imagine that the book would have been possible without computers. As Wrigley and Schofield themselves pointed out, "The formidable size of the dataset and the complexity of the operations that were required . . . would have represented an insuperable obstacle . . . at any time before the availability of electronic computers." This has ensured that the group has established and maintained close links with the historical computing community.

Links with other groups of academics and researchers are kept up through journals such as *Local Population Studies*, which carries updates of work in progress at Cambridge in every issue. The journal grew out of a news-sheet to which the group contributed and which was distributed to the large number of the group's voluntary helpers. *Local Population Studies* received funding and frequent contributions from the group and, until

very recently, Roger Schofield sat on the editorial board. In 1986 the group launched a new journal, *Continuity and Change*, which concentrates on three main areas of interest for the group: the history of household, family kinship, and social relations; legal institutions; and social structure.

The constant innovation and sheer mass of research produced by the Cambridge Group over the years has ensured that its contribution to English demographic history has been unique. Indeed it continues to be so, for in addition to the work produced at Cambridge, students and ex-members of the group continue to develop and disseminate the skills developed at Cambridge at institutions all over the world. The significance of the group's work, and the contribution of one member of the group in particular, was celebrated recently by the knighthood of Anthony Wrigley and his appointment as chairman of the British Academy.

RICHARD BAXELL

See also Demography; Wrigley

Further Reading

Anderson, Michael, ed., *British Population History: From the Black Death to the Present Day*, Cambridge and New York: Cambridge University Press, 1996

Bonfield, Lloyd, Richard M. Smith, and Keith Wrightson, eds., *The World We Have Gained: Histories of Population and Social Structure*, Oxford and New York: Blackwell, 1986

Chambers, J.D., "Some Aspects of E.A. Wrigley's *Population and History*," *Local Population Studies* 3 (Autumn 1969), 18–28

Eversley, D.E.C., Peter Laslett, and E.A. Wrigley, eds., *An Introduction to English Historical Demography*, London: Weidenfeld and Nicolson, and New York: Basic Books, 1966

Laslett, Peter, *The World We Have Lost*, London: Methuen, 1965, New York: Scribner, 1966; revised 1984

Laslett, Peter, and Richard Wall, eds., *Household and Family in Past Time: Comparative Studies in the Size and Structure of the Domestic Group over the Last Three Centuries in England, France, Serbia, Japan, and Colonial North America*, Cambridge and New York: Cambridge University Press, 1972

Laslett, Peter, *Family Life and Illicit Love in Earlier Generations: Essays in Historical Sociology*, Cambridge and New York: Cambridge University Press, 1977

Laslett, Peter, Karla Oosterveen, and Richard M. Smith, eds., *Bastardy and Its Comparative History: Studies in the History of Illegitimacy and Marital Nonconformism in Britain, France, Germany, Sweden, North America, Jamaica and Japan*, London: Arnold, and Cambridge, MA: Harvard University Press, 1980

Lee, Ronald, "Inverse Projection and Back Projection: A Critical Appraisal, and Comparative Results for England, 1539–1871," *Population Studies* 39 (1985), 233–48

Razzell, Peter, *Essays in English Population History*, London: Caliban, 1994

Schofield, Roger S., "Historical Demography: Some Possibilities and Some Limitations," *Transactions of the Royal Historical Society* 21 (1971), 119–32

Schofield, Roger S., "The Standardisation of Names and the Automatic Linking of Vital Records," *Annales de démographie historique* (1972), 359–64

Wrigley, E.A., "Marriage and Fertility in Pre-Industrial England," *The Listener* 75 (10 February 1966), 199–201

Wrigley, E.A., "Mortality in Pre-Industrial England: The Example of Colyton, Devon over Three Centuries," *Daedalus* (Spring 1968), 546–80; reprinted in D.V. Glass and Roger Revelle, eds., *Population and Social Change*, London: Arnold, and New York: Crane Russak, 1972

Wrigley, E.A., *Population and History*, London: Weidenfeld and Nicolson, and New York: McGraw Hill, 1969

Wrigley, E.A., ed., *Nineteenth Century Society: Essays in the Use of Quantitative Methods for the Study of Social Data*, Cambridge: Cambridge University Press, 1972

Wrigley, E.A., ed., *Identifying People in the Past*, London: Arnold, 1973

Wrigley, E.A., and Roger S. Schofield, *The Population History of England, 1541–1871: A Reconstruction*, London: Arnold, and Cambridge, MA: Harvard University Press, 1981

Wrigley, E.A., and Roger S. Schofield, *English Population History from Family Reconstitution, 1580–1837*, Cambridge and New York: Cambridge University Press, 1997

Camden, William 1551–1623
English historian

William Camden was the most significant British historian of his time. His work followed the tradition of antiquarian scholarship, which originated in the Middle Ages and was absorbed into Tudor historiography. However, it also displayed the Renaissance emphasis on careful evaluation of sources and the use of classical models. He advanced rational explanations for the course of events and discussed them in a broader context. Like his contemporary Francis Bacon, who placed history within a universal scheme of knowledge, he stands at the beginning of the scientific revolution.

After his education at St. Paul's School and Oxford University, Camden returned to London and taught at Westminster School. He became known for his historical scholarship and was a friend of the leading intellectuals of his day, notably Robert Cotton the manuscript collector. He corresponded with continental scholars, including the Italian humanist Blondus, the French historian de Thou and the Dutch geographer Ortelius. The latter encouraged him to write *Britannia*, published in 1586. This was a gazetteer of the British Isles, describing the topography, history, genealogy, and ancient monuments of each county, grouped according to their ancient tribal occupants. This work drew on John Leland's writings of a generation earlier, but was more sophisticated. Its scholarly apparatus included the careful footnoting of sources, among which were manuscripts, coins, architectural remains and monuments, and local tradition. *Britannia* was published in Latin for an international audience and went through six editions in Camden's lifetime. It was first printed in English in 1610.

Camden's celebrity led to his appointment as chief herald, Clarenceux King of Arms in 1597. This position enabled him to collect additional material to update successive editions. Subsequently he was approached by Lord Burleigh, Queen Elizabeth's chief secretary, to write a history of her reign. The Tudors were always aware of the importance of the right publicity. With the *Annales Rerum Anglicarum et Hibernicarum Regnante Elizabetha* (The Annals of Events in England and Scotland during the Reign of Elizabeth), Camden turned his attention to contemporary history. As models he used Polybius and Tacitus, political historians of the Roman republic. Through Lord Burleigh he had privileged access to important contemporary documents, but had to tread a cautious path in what he wrote. He did not footnote his sources but quoted where he felt it necessary. Only work covering the years up to 1588 was published in 1615 and the rest not until after Camden's death in 1625. Its appearance in Latin limited its circulation, as Camden considered its subject inappropriate for English-only readers. Camden's writings were those of a patriot and he was always deferential to the queen. However his view of her actions as pragmatic and politically moderate has been borne out by subsequent research and his work remains an important source for Elizabeth's reign. He left manuscript notes on the main events of James I's reign, which provide a brief history of this time.

A year before he died Camden endowed the first chair of history at Oxford University. His enduring legacy was the provision of a conceptual framework for the transmission of historical knowledge and its influence on local and antiquarian scholarship up to the 19th century. *The Victoria History of the Counties of England* is in some respects an heir to this tradition. Soon after his death he was considered worthy of biography and the publication of his letters. In 1840 the Camden Society, which exists for the publication of historical records, was named after him.

VIRGINIA R. BAINBRIDGE

See also Archaeology; Britain: Anglo-Saxon; Britain: 1066–1485; Trevor-Roper

Biography
Born London, 2 May 1551, son of a painter. Educated at Oxford University. Schoolmaster, Westminster School, c.1577–1597; appointed Clarenceux King of Arms, 1597. Died Chislehurst, 9 November 1623.

Principal Writings
Britannia (in Latin), 1586; English edition 1610
Annales Rerum Anglicarum et Hibernicarum Regnante Elizabetha (The Annals of Events in England and Scotland during the Reign of Elizabeth), part 1 1615, part 2 1625, English edition 1630

Further Reading
Kendrick, T.D., *British Antiquity*, London: Methuen, 1950; New York: Barnes and Noble, 1970
Levy, Fred Jacob, *Tudor Historical Thought*, San Marino, CA: Huntingdon Library, 1967
McKisack, May, *Medieval History in the Tudor Age*, Oxford: Oxford University Press, 1971
Piggott, Stuart, *William Camden and the Britannia* [lecture], London: Cumberlege, 1953
Trevor-Roper, Hugh, *Queen Elizabeth's First Historian: William Camden and the Beginnings of English "Civil History"*, London: Cape, 1971

Cameron, Averil 1940–
British historian of Byzantium

The study of Byzantine history has never been a particular strength of the British. This may partly be a reflection of the linguistic challenges posed by the sources for this thousand-year empire. Ancient texts in Greek, Latin, Arabic, Coptic, and Syriac are joined by extensive modern commentaries not only in the west European languages but also in those of the Slavic east. Nevertheless, certain elements of east Mediterranean history have remained actively studied, primarily the Crusades, but also, in recent decades, the period of late antiquity. Chronological divisions between major historical periods are bound on occasion to be somewhat arbitrary and that between antiquity and Byzantium is especially unclear, for the simple reason that the one society evolved smoothly into the other. So, while Averil Cameron's work frequently employs the word "Byzantine," nevertheless her over-riding interest in the 6th century places her likewise within the age of late antiquity as understood by A.H.M. Jones and Peter Brown. These two writers, perhaps more than any others, have caused a resurgence of studies on this period. Cameron can be seen as following in their wake, not only in general terms, but also in her style. Jones studied institutions through employing a remarkable if rather dry reading of original sources, while Brown used these in a different way to build up a highly charismatic vision of the social functioning of late antique society. The particular success of Cameron's work is that she manages to combine elements of both these approaches.

Cameron cut her teeth on textual studies of early Byzantine authors, as in *Agathias* (1970) and *Corripus* (1976). In these studies and editions she reaffirmed the importance of writers hitherto neglected because they did not conform to classical standards. The panegyric of Corripus in praise of Justin, for example, is now recognized as a valuable source for the presentation of imperial power and ceremony. More recently, Cameron has addressed perhaps the greatest writer of her period in *Procopius and the Sixth Century* (1985). She has been keen to develop her interests in images as well as in texts and to bring into the discipline modern literary theories of source criticism, a pioneering move demonstrated to most spectacular effect in *Christianity and the Rhetoric of Empire* (1991). It is perhaps significant that the work for this study of "reading" Christian texts was carried out at and published by the University of California. British scholarship remains far less open to such detailed use of theory in textual analysis. A further area in which she has embraced wider trends in scholarship and so brought a new focus to the study of Byzantium has been women's studies. Her examination of the cult of the Virgin Mary is of particular note, as is her editorship of *Images of Women in Antiquity* (1983), which followed the modern trend toward comparative study by contrasting in its chapters the practices of a wide range of ancient civilizations.

Cameron is very much of her time in her concern for the distinctiveness of different cultures and of their interaction. She upholds the idea of late antiquity as a period of vibrant cultural activity during which economic stagnation was but a periodic and regional ill. She is keen to stress the mutual influence of Greeks and non-classical cultures in this period. Two volumes of collected essays have been published, *Continuity and Change in Sixth-Century Byzantium* (1981) and *Changing Cultures in Early Byzantium* (1996). These volumes collect together work carried out over many years, before her current appointment as Warden at Keble College, Oxford, when she was professor of late antique and Byzantine studies at King's College, London. But although she has long worked at the frontier of research, she will further increase her influence among students and future scholars through her much-needed modern text-

books covering the whole late antique period, *The Later Roman Empire, AD 284–430* (1993) and *The Mediterranean World in Late Antiquity, AD 395–600* (1993). These put together the work of Jones and Brown to give a concise description of interdependent institutional and cultural change. Her period is now perhaps being studied by more students than ever before, a situation which, through specialized studies as well as the new student texts, she has done much to promote.

DOMINIC JANES

See also Eastern Orthodoxy; Procopius; Roman

Biography
Averil Millicent Sutton Cameron. Born 8 February 1940. Attended Westwood Hall Girls' High School, Leek, Staffordshire; Somerville College, Oxford, BA, MA 1962; University of Glasgow; PhD, University College, London. Taught (rising to professor), King's College, London, 1965–94: director, Centre for Hellenic Studies, 1988–94; Warden, Keble College, Oxford, from 1994. Married Alan Douglas Edward Cameron, 1962 (marriage dissolved, 1980; 1 son, 1 daughter).

Principal Writings
Agathias, 1970
Corripus, 1976
Continuity and Change in Sixth-Century Byzantium, 1981
Editor with Amelie Kuhrt, *Images of Women in Antiquity*, 1983
Procopius and the Sixth Century, 1985
Christianity and the Rhetoric of Empire: The Development of Christian Discourse, 1991
The Later Roman Empire, AD 284–430, 1993
The Mediterranean World in Late Antiquity, AD 395–600, 1993
Changing Cultures in Early Byzantium, 1996

Canada

For most of its evolution, the historical writing of French and English Canada followed separate paths, and thus will be treated in turn here. The two historiographies, though, did move closer together after the changes of the 1960s and 1970s ushered in a new brand of social history.

French Canada/Quebec
The beginnings of French Canadian historiography can be dated to the publication of François-Xavier Garneau's *Histoire du Canada* (1845–48). Here, Garneau established the theme of "survivance" which would dominate the province's historical writing up to the present. Writing within the context of the 1837 rebellions and Lord Durham's claim that French Canada had no history, Garneau produced a 3-volume narrative describing the history of his people as a centuries-long struggle for survival. For Garneau, this struggle did not end with the conquest in 1759–60, when the British forces defeated the French in North America – a tragic yet formative event – but was taken up by French Canadian politicians in the parliamentary realm.

In the century after *Histoire du Canada*, as the influence of the Catholic church rose in Quebec, French Canadian historiography was dominated by clerical writers. While rejecting

Garneau's more liberal and political interpretation, priest historians such as Jean-Baptiste-Antoine Ferland and Henri-Raymond Casgrain adapted the former's nationalist ideals to their own clerical and conservative interpretation. The Catholic church now stood as the bastion of French Canadian survival, while language, the traditional family and a rural way of life provided additional safeguards. The clerical dominance of Quebec historiography lasted into this century, a dominance best represented by Lionel Groulx. Through works such as *La Naissance d'une race* (Birth of a Race, 1919) and *Histoire du Canada français depuis la découverte* (History of French Canada since its Discovery, 1950–52), a 4-volume summary of his life's work, Groulx emerged as the first historian to rival Garneau in importance. Groulx gave new life to the theme of "survivance," adapting it to what he saw as the threats of urbanization and industrialization through a combination of Garneau's nationalism, traditional Catholic ideology and notions of racial pride and destiny.

Only after World War II did secular, professional historians unseat the domination of clerical history. Historians took part in the rapid secularization of Quebec which reached full momentum during the "Quiet Revolution" of the 1960s. History departments were established at universities in Montreal and Laval by 1947, and the *Revue d'histoire de l'Amérique française* was launched. The national question remained a dominating one for the new historians, but the latter looked more to material forces in addressing it, and, in doing so, lively historiographical debate erupted. The main issue was the economic inferiority of French Canada, an issue of particular contemporary relevance given the control over Quebec's economy by largely external, anglophone interests.

At the University of Montreal, a neo-nationalist school emerged that placed a secular spin upon the central event of traditional historiography. Guy Frégault, Maurice Séguin, and Michel Brunet argued that the conquest had disrupted the "normal" social and economic development of French Canada by "decapitating" its homegrown bourgeoisie. Denied access to trade, capital, and real political power, French Canadian society fell back upon agriculture and the Catholic church for survival. Historians at Laval University disputed the neo-nationalist claim that New France had produced a bona fide bourgeois class. Jean Hamelin and Fernand Ouellet asserted that it was not the conquest but a lack of skilled labor, commercial agriculture, and capital, along with a mentality hostile to capitalist development, that thwarted French Canadian development. Whereas the neo-nationalists and previous historians had located the source of Quebec's problems outside the province, Hamelin and Ouellet pointed to factors internal to French Canadian society to explain its failure to develop.

Ouellet's work was a watershed in French Canadian historiography – because of the methodology it introduced, rather than the particular arguments it made. Ouellet's assertions concerning the mentality of French Canadian inhabitants and the resulting agricultural crisis have been hotly and effectively contested, most particularly by Gilles Paquet and Jean-Pierre Wallot. However, Ouellet's *Histoire économique et sociale du Québec* (1966) ushered in a new age of "scientific," social history. Influenced by the Annales school, Ouellet used quantitative methods to present an exhaustive study of the underlying social and economic structures of Lower Canada, while incorporating shorter term conjunctures such as grain price fluctuations. After Ouellet, historians focused upon the social structure of French Canada, turning away from the traditional image of a harmonious, united people to study the formation of a class society. Louise Dechêne's *Habitants et marchands de Montréal au XVIIe siècle* (1974; *Habitants and Merchants in Seventeenth-Century Montreal*, 1992) is perhaps the clearest example of work based upon the best of contemporary historical methods.

Over the past twenty years, French Canadian historiography has moved more in line with historical trends elsewhere – notably in the dominance of social history and the attention paid to class and gender. While Ouellet's work provided the foundation for the examination of Quebec as a class society, women's history has become the fastest growing field in the past decade. A synthesis of existing work was presented in Le Collectif Clio's *L'Histoire des femmes au Québec depuis quatres siècles* (1982; *Quebec Women*, 1987), with a 1992 edition incorporating subsequent studies. Overall, recent historical writing in French has downplayed the traditional focus on Quebec as different or exceptional, arguing instead that the province had gone through the same process of modernization (industrialization and accompanying class conflict, urbanization, the rise of the state) as other societies. Paul-André Linteau, Jean-Claude Robert, and René Durocher's *Histoire du Québec contemporain* (1979–86; *Quebec: A History*, 1983; *Quebec since 1930*, 1991) presented the picture of Quebec as a modern, pluralistic society; the text also reveals the abiding influence of the Annales school, with its focus on the *longue durée* and the structures of Quebec society.

English Canada

The "national question" – this time the emergence of Canada itself as a self-governing state – also was an abiding issue for Canadian historians writing in English. However, English Canada was less cohesive and compact than French Canada and its historiography revealed more regional variation.

The earliest historical writing in English was largely promotional and localist. Works such as Thomas Chandler Haliburton's *An Historical and Statistical Account of Nova-Scotia* (1829) tried to promote the growth of a region or colony, while also stressing British imperial connections. In the wake of the Durham Report (1839), a distinct Reform historiography emerged which added the theme of constitutional evolution (responsible government, unity among the British North American colonies) to the 19th-century concern for material progress. Historians like John Mercier McMullen further argued that Canada West/Ontario best represented and embodied the values of Reform history. The tradition of viewing Ontario's development as "national" history, and that of other provinces as "regional," gained momentum with Confederation. After Confederation, a "national school" emerged which adapted the major themes of Reform historiography to the vision of a geographically expanding yet unified Canada, centered in Ontario.

Through the 19th century, historical writing in English was the product of amateur historians; William Kingsford's 10-volume *The History of Canada* (1887–98) was a testimony to the energy of these amateur enthusiasts. By the end of the century, English Canadian history had moved toward a professionalization of the discipline, closely following trends in the United States and Europe. History departments were set up at Toronto and Queen's universities, and the *Review of Historical Publications Relating to Canada* started publication (the *Canadian Historical Review* replaced it in 1920). Under George Wrong, Toronto's History department became the center of a renewed nationalist historiography. Inspired in part by the political focus of British Whig history, and later fueled by pride for Canada's contribution in World War I, this school focused on constitutional history, and most particularly on responsible government, Confederation and the evolution from colonial to national status. W.P.M. Kennedy's *The Constitution of Canada* (1922) and Chester Martin's *Empire and Commonwealth* (1929) were exemplars of this constitutional history, while Arthur Lower's *Colony to Nation* (1946) revealed the lasting influence of the "colony-to-nation" school.

The interwar years saw a movement away from political and constitutional history to a focus upon environmental and economical forces. Toronto political economist Harold Innis was the most original and influential scholar in this movement. Through a number of exhaustive studies – most notably *The Fur Trade in Canada* (1930) – Innis argued that the social, political, and economic development of Canada depended upon geographical features and the exploitation of a series of staple resources (fur, fish, timber, wheat). The staples thesis also posited that resource exploitation in the hinterland was dependent upon markets in metropolitan centers such as Britain, and it was the expansion of the metropolis into the hinterland that characterized Canadian history. Innis' work inspired other historians in their search for made-in-Canada interpretations of Canadian history. In *The Commercial Empire of the St. Lawrence* (1937), Donald Creighton advanced a thesis that would dominate historical writing into the 1960s. The Laurentian thesis argued that a coherent market economy had been built upon a unified geographic system, the St. Lawrence basin. In search of staples for export, this commercial empire expanded outward along natural trade routes, laying the foundations for a transcontinental Canadian economy and nation.

After World War II, there was a return to political and national history among English Canadian historians. Spurning the "impersonal" focus of geographic and economic history, but concerned to maintain a "national" perspective, historians turned to political biography. Creighton masterfully reconciled the Laurentian thesis and biographical history in the 2-volume *John A. Macdonald* (1952–55). Here, Macdonald personified the drive to build a unified nation outward from the St. Lawrence basin; his two greatest achievements – Confederation and the Canadian Pacific Railway – brought the old dream of commercial empire to the Pacific shore. Other political figures such as George Brown, Arthur Meighen, and J.S. Woodsworth also attracted biographers; meanwhile, work on the multi-volume *Dictionary of Canadian Biography* got under way in 1960.

Ironically, amid a heightened popular nationalism brought on by Canada centennial celebrations, English Canadian historians began to question the nationalist focus that had guided their work for so long. Growing weary of the search for a national identity which always seemed out of grasp, Ramsay Cook and J.M.S. Careless exhorted their colleagues to examine the "limited identities" of region, class, and ethnicity. Indeed, despite the hegemony of a centrist "national" historiography, regional writing had a strong and abiding tradition. Manitoban W.L. Morton was critical of the Laurentian school's dominance, and in his own work contributed to the history and regional consciousness of the west. Margaret Ormsby provided a sweeping and literary narrative of Canada's westernmost province, while to the east, W.S. MacNutt produced *New Brunswick, a History* (1963). Regional history received a boost with the founding of journals (*Acadiensis, BC Studies, Prairie Forum*) and, within the last few years, the publication of updated histories. Even Ontario, which for so long was treated as the exemplar of national history, is now properly considered a region, as evidenced in the Ontario Historical Studies series.

Over the past two decades, a focus on social history has come to dominate English Canadian writing. Journals such as *Social History/Histoire Sociale* and *Labor/Le travail* emerged, while the *Canadian Historical Review* increasingly provided room for social historians. Influenced by currents from Britain and the United States, Canadian writers turned to analytical categories such as class and gender to recreate the life of "ordinary" Canadians, rather than political leaders. Until the 1970s, studies of class and the working class in English Canada had focused on the formation of trade unions and labor's role in left-wing politics. Spurning this institutional focus, and inspired by the work of E.P. Thompson, a younger generation of Marxist historians took a more comprehensive approach, studying the lived experiences of all working-class people, organized or not. Bryan Palmer and Gregory Kealey led the way, arguing that class consciousness and cultural formation were crucial to class formation and were forged in resistance to capitalism.

English Canadian historians have been slow to heed the role of gender in Canada's past. Catherine Cleverdon's *The Woman Suffrage Movement in Canada* (1950) stands out as an early and isolated look at Canadian women. Yet over the past decade, women's history has been one of the most fruitful fields in English Canadian writing. Much of this work was synthesized in the multi-authored survey text, *Canadian Women: A History* (1988), edited by Alison Prentice *et al.* As with the studies it drew upon, *Canadian Women* sought to recover the experiences of women in Canada's past and to show their contributions. It also argued that a distinct "women's culture" had formed as women struggled against the inequities of a patriarchal society. Most recently, some historians have moved away from this exclusive focus on women in history, toward a broader gender history. Joy Parr's *The Gender of Bread-winners* (1990) is an example of this approach, which studies the ways in which gender (masculine and feminine) has been constructed historically, most particularly in conjunction with class.

Finally, the turn to social history has heightened interest in Canada's native peoples, largely neglected until recently. Harold Innis demonstrated that native Indians played an important role in developing Canada's first staple resource industry, furs. Through the 1970s and 1980s, Arthur Ray, Robin Fisher, and Sylvia Van Kirk portrayed native peoples as active participants in the fur trade, further arguing that the trade was largely beneficial to both natives and Europeans. More recently, the efforts of Prairie natives to adjust to the agricultural society of European newcomers has been studied by Sarah Carter in *Lost Harvests* (1990). Meanwhile, ethnohistorians have looked at native societies themselves, making innovative use of oral and material sources to supplement the written record. Here, the work of Bruce Trigger is most notable.

CHAD REIMER

See also Britain: British Empire; Creighton; Crime; Eccles; Ethnicity; Ethnohistory; Frégault; Groulx; Innis; Legal; Lower; McLuhan; Morton; Ormsby; Parkman; Popular; Séguin; Trigger; Women's History: North America; World War I

Further Reading

Barman, Jean, *The West Beyond the West: A History of British Columbia*, Toronto: University of Toronto Press, 1991

Berger, Carl, *The Writing of Canadian History: Aspects of English-Canadian Historical Writing, 1900–1970*, Toronto: Oxford University Press, 1976; 2nd edition Toronto: University of Toronto Press, 1986

Berger, Carl, ed. *Contemporary Approaches to Canadian History*, Toronto: Copp Clark Pitman, 1987

Bernard, Jean-Paul, "L'Historiographie canadienne récente (1964–94) et l'histoire des peuples du Canada" (Recent Canadian Historiography and the History of the Peoples of Canada), *Canadian Historical Review* 76 (1995), 321–53

Brunet, Michel, *Canadians et Canadiens: études sur l'histoire et la pensée des deux Canadas* (English and French Canadians: Studies on the History and Ideas of the Two Canadas), Montreal: Fides, 1954

Buckner, Phillip, and John G. Reid, eds., *The Atlantic Region to Confederation: A History*, Toronto: University of Toronto Press, 1994

Carter, Sarah, *Lost Harvests: Prairie Indian Reserve Farmers and Government Policy*, Montreal: McGill-Queen's University Press, 1990

Cleverdon, Catherine, *The Woman Suffrage Movement in Canada*, Toronto: University of Toronto Press, 1950

Le Collectif Clio, *L'Histoire des femmes au Québec depuis quatres siècles*, Montreal: Les Quinze, 1982, revised 1992; in English as *Quebec Women: A History*, Toronto: Women's Press, 1987

Creighton, Donald Grant, *The Commercial Empire of the St. Lawrence, 1760–1850*, Toronto: Ryerson Press, and New Haven: Yale University Press, 1937

Creighton, Donald Grant, *John A. Macdonald*, 2 vols., Toronto: Macmillan, 1952–55

Dechêne, Louise, *Habitants et marchands de Montréal au XVIIe siècle*, Paris: Plon, 1974; in English as *Habitants and Merchants in Seventeenth-Century Montreal*, Montreal: McGill-Queen's University Press, 1992

Fisher, Robin, *Contact and Conflict: Indian-European Relations in British Columbia, 1774–1890*, Vancouver: University of British Columbia Press, 1977

Forbes, Ernest R., and Delphin Andrew Muise, *The Atlantic Provinces in Confederation*, Toronto: University of Toronto Press, 1993

Frégault, Guy, *La Guerre de la conquête*, Montreal: Fides, 1955; in English as *Canada: The War of the Conquest*, Toronto: Oxford University Press, 1969

Friesen, Gerald, *The Canadian Prairies: A History*, Lincoln: University of Nebraska Press, 1986; Toronto: University of Toronto Press, 1987

Gagnon, Serge, *Le Québec et ses historiens*, Quebec: Presses de l'Université Laval, 1978; in English as *Quebec and Its Historians, 1840–1920*, Montreal: Harvest House, 1982, and *Quebec and Its Historians: The Twentieth Century*, Harvest House, 1985

Garneau, François-Xavier, *Histoire du Canada, depuis sa découverte jusqu'a nos jours*, 3 vols., Quebec, 1845–48; in English as *History of Canada: From the Time of Its Discovery till the Union Year*, 3 vols., Montreal: Lovell, 1860

Groulx, Lionel, *La Naissance d'une race* (Birth of a Race), Montreal: Bibliothèque d'Action Française, 1919

Groulx, Lionel, *Histoire du Canada français depuis la découverte* (History of French Canada since Its Discovery), 2 vols., Montreal: L'Action National, 1950–52

Haliburton, Thomas Chandler, *An Historical and Statistical Account of Nova-Scotia*, 2 vols., Halifax: Howe, 1829

Hamelin, Jean, *Economie et société en Nouvelle-France* (Economy and Society in New France), Québec: Presses de l'Université Laval, 1968

Innis, Harold, *The Fur Trade in Canada: An Introduction to Canadian Economic History*, London: Oxford University Press, and New Haven: Yale University Press, 1930; revised 1956

Kealey, Gregory S., *Toronto Workers Respond to Industrial Capitalism, 1867–1892*, Toronto: University of Toronto Press, 1980

Kennedy, W.P.M., *The Constitution of Canada: An Introduction to Its Development and Law*, Oxford and New York: Oxford University Press, 1922

Kingsford, William, *The History of Canada*, 10 vols., Toronto: Resford and Hutchison, 1887–98; reprinted New York: AMS Press, 1968

Linteau, Paul-André, René Durocher, and Jean-Claude Robert, *Histoire du Québec contemporain*, 2 vols., Montreal: Boréal, 1979–86; in English as *Quebec: A History, 1867–1929* and *Quebec since 1930*, Toronto: Lorimer, 1983–91

Lower, A.R.M., *Colony to Nation*, Toronto and New York: Longman, 1946

McMullen, John Mercier, *The History of Canada, from Its First Discovery to the Present Time*, Brockville: McMullen, 1855; revised 1868, 1892

McNaught, Kenneth, *The Pelican History of Canada*, London and Baltimore: Penguin, 1969; revised 1988

MacNutt, William Stewart, *New Brunswick: A History, 1784–1867*, Toronto: Macmillan, 1963

Martin, Chester, *Empire and Commonwealth: Studies in Governance and Self-Government in Canada*, Oxford: Clarendon Press, 1929

Morton, W.L., *The Progressive Party in Canada*, Toronto: University of Toronto Press, 1950

Morton, W.L., *Manitoba: A History*, Toronto: University of Toronto Press, 1957; revised 1967

Ormsby, Margaret, *British Columbia: A History*, Toronto: Macmillan, 1958

Ouellet, Fernand, *Histoire économique et sociale du Québec, 1760–1840*, Montreal: Fides, 1966; in English as *Economic and Social History of Quebec, 1760–1850*, Toronto: Gage, 1980

Ouellet, Fernand, *Le Bas-Canada, 1791–1840: changements structuraux et crise*, Ottawa: Editions de l'Université d'Ottawa, 1976; in English as *Lower Canada, 1791–1840: Social Change and Nationalism*, Toronto: McClelland and Stewart, 1980

Ouellet, Fernand, *The Socialization of Quebec Historiography since 1960*, Toronto: Robarts Centre for Canadian Studies, 1988

Palmer, Bryan D., *A Culture in Conflict: Skilled Workers and Industrial Capitalism in Hamilton, Ontario, 1860–1914*, Montreal: McGill-Queen's University Press, 1979

Paquet, Gilles, and Jean-Pierre Wallot, *Lower Canada at the Turn of the Nineteenth Century: Restructuring and Modernization*, Ottawa: Canadian Historical Association, 1988

Parr, Joy, *The Gender of Breadwinners: Women, Men and Change in Two Industrial Towns, 1880–1950*, Toronto: University of Toronto Press, 1990

Prentice, Alison et al., *Canadian Women: A History*, Toronto: Harcourt Brace, 1988

Ray, Arthur, *Indians in the Fur Trade: Their Role as Trappers, Hunters, and Middlemen in the Lands Southwest of Hudson Bay, 1660–1870*, Toronto: University of Toronto Press, 1974

Séguin, Maurice, *La "Nation canadienne" et l'agriculture (1760–1850): essai d'histoire économique* (The "Canadian Nation" and Agriculture, 1760–1850: Essays in Economic History), Trois Rivières: Boréal, 1970

Shore, Marlene, "'Remember the Future': The *Canadian Historical Review* and the Discipline of History, 1920–95," *Canadian Historical Review* 76 (1995), 410–63

Taylor, M. Brook, *Promoters, Patriots and Partisans: Historiography in Nineteenth-Century English Canada*, Toronto: University of Toronto Press, 1989

Trigger, Bruce G., *The Children of Aataentsic: A History of the Huron People to 1660*, 2 vols., Montreal: McGill–Queen's University Press, 1976

Trigger, Bruce G., *Natives and Newcomers: Canada's "Heroic Age" Reconsidered*, Montreal: McGill–Queen's University Press, 1985; Manchester: Manchester University Press, 1986

Van Kirk, Sylvia, *"Many Tender Ties": Women in Fur-Trade Society in Western Canada, 1670–1870*, Winnipeg: Watson and Dwyer, 1980; Norman: University of Oklahoma Press, 1983

Cantimori, Delio 1904–1966
Italian historian of the 16th century

Delio Cantimori was a prolific writer; his bibliography of 581 items published between 1926 and 1969 includes substantial monographs, numerous articles, collections of the latter – friendship with the publisher Giulio Einaudi ensured even reviews were included – editions of texts, translations from German and from English into Italian, and entries for compilations. His interests remained consistent over his adult life, and reflected to an exceptional degree his upbringing and personality. Typically *romagnolo*, he was fiercely politically-minded, sharply polemical, often controversial with oscillating opinions.

His pithy "Italy and the Papacy" in the Reformation volume of *The New Cambridge Modern History* (1958) is available to readers in English only. It signposts his major contribution as a historian: new light on 16th-century Italian heretics. A slim volume published in 1929 had set the tone in examining Bernardino Ochino as a Renaissance man and Church reformer; in this revision of his university thesis, Cantimori made modifications to answer questions raised when he read Lucien Febvre's *Martin Luther* of the previous year. Cantimori indicated that Ochino's religious beliefs were grounded in the humanistic philosophy of Ficino and Pico, hence were Italian and not akin to those of Protestant reformers beyond the Alps. He maintained that religion was the core element of any culture, of which no two people's was the same. For him Italian culture was identifiable and superior – itself a concept of the Italian Renaissance. Hence religion was a moral force reflecting racial characteristics. As Cantimori extended his researches to other Italian reformers, the originality of his contribution was less in his views as to why Italian reformers made little impact on the Italian peninsula (although he did embrace this), than in what happened to these reformers in exile, above all in the peak period of their emigration between 1540 and 1560. He judged them as long remaining Italian in culture in Geneva, London, or wherever, with aspirations other than those of their continental and English *confrères*.

These views (essentially the wider application of those on Ochino) were ably expounded in *Eretici italiani del cinquecento* (Italian Heretics of the 16th Century, 1939), which complemented documents on the subject that Cantimori had garnered and published two years earlier. Where Cesare Cantù's chronologically extensive vista of almost a century before had focused on the idiosyncrasies of individual Italian heretics, Cantimori's approach was to underline those factors that had produced them, and secondly and primarily he sought to chart how the heretics responded to persecution on the Italian peninsula, and to life abroad in exile. He deemed that the failure of the movement for reform on the Italian peninsula was not due to suppression by the Inquisition, or the absence of state intervention, but rather to "a lack of energy": individuals with authority cared insufficiently. Cantimori failed to indicate in this regard that those with authority actually had a vested interest in preserving the *status quo*, since the Church provided them with rich pickings. Overall Cantimori's approach, while original and stimulating, is not definitive. In his last years he returned to the subject, projecting in 1960 a vast study of the relationship between humanism and religious life on the Italian peninsula from Savonarola to Sarpi. Work in progress was published posthumously as *Umanesimo e religione nel rinascimento* (Humanism and Religion in the Renaissance, 1975).

Cantimori was highly critical of terms such as Renaissance, Counter-Reformation, Baroque. The first of these became a preoccupation with him, which became clear in a series of articles covering a very wide spectrum on what it meant to De Sanctis, Weber, Armando Sapori, Huizinga, and Jacob Burckhardt. For none of them did the term Renaissance encapsulate what Cantimori considered a key element: the close relationship between Renaissance humanism and the thought of 16th-century Italian Church reformers. Cantimori's general view as to the value of history was that it formed the basis of political education. In practice, as applied to his own career, it could be taken as learning to have an eye for the main chance. From 1926 he was a card-carrying fascist, while during World War II he became a member of the Italian Communist party, which he left in 1956. A charitable view is that he was an idealist who was several times disillusioned. His political writings underline this interpretation. It was not coincidental that during World War II Cantimori took consolation in examining the aspirations of the foremost Italian Jacobins; his *Utopisti e riformatori italiani* (Italian Utopian and Reformist Thinkers, 1943) devoted a chapter to each. Later he edited a selection of their writings under the title *Giacobini italiani* (The Italian Jacobins, 1956–64), thereby paralleling his work on Italian heretics.

CECIL H. CLOUGH

See also Ginzburg; Pieroni Bortolotti

Biography
Born Russi, near Ravenna, 30 August 1904; his father was a republican in the Mazzini tradition. Studied at Scuola Normale Superiore, 1924–27; and University of Pisa, 1924–27. Schoolmaster and independent researcher, 1929–34; assistant director, Institute of Germanic Studies, Rome, 1934–43; assistant in modern history, University of Rome, 1937–40; professor of modern history, University of Pisa, 1948–51; and University of Florence, 1951–66. Died Florence, 13 September 1966.

Principal Writings

Bernardino Ochino, uomo del rinascimento e reformatori
(Bernadino Ochino, Renaissance Man and Reformer), 1929

Per la storia degli eretici italiani del secolo XVI in Europa: testi
(Contributions towards the History of Italian Heretics in the 16th
Century: Texts), 1937

Eretici italiani del cinquecento: richerche storiche (Italian Heretics of
the 16th Century: Historical Researches), 1939

Utopisti e riformatori italiani, 1794–1847: Richerche storiche
(Italian Utopian and Reformist Thinkers, 1794–1847: Historical
Researches), 1943

Editor with Renzo de Felice [vol. 2 only], *Giacobini italiani: Testi*
(The Italian Jacobins: Texts), 2 vols., 1956–64

"Italy and the Papacy," in *The New Cambridge Modern History*,
vol.2: *The Reformation, 1520–1559*, 1958

Studi di storia (Historical Studies), 1959

Editor and translator, *Meditazioni sulla storia universale* (Reflections
on History) by Jacob Burckhardt, 1959

Prospettive di storia ereticale italiana (Perspectives on the History of
16th-Century Italian Heresy), 1960

Umanesimo e religione nel rinascimento (Humanism and Religion in
the Renaissance), 1975

Politica e storia contemporanea: scritti (1927–1942) (Writings on
Politics and Contemporary History, 1927–1943), edited by Luisa
Mangoni, 1991

Further Reading

Berengo, Marino, "La ricerca storica di Delio Cantimori" (The
Historical Research of Delio Cantimori), *Rivista Storica Italiana*
79 (1967), 902–43

Ciliberto, M., *Intellettuali e fascismo: saggio su Delio Cantimori*
(Intellectuals and Fascism: A Study of Delio Cantimori), Bari: De
Donato, 1977

Cochrane, Eric, and John Tedeschi, "Delio Cantimori: Historian
(1904–1966)," *Journal of Modern History* 39 (1967), 438–45

Miccoli, Giovanni, *Delio Cantimori: la ricerca di una nuova critica
storiografica* (Delio Cantimori: Research Towards a New Critical
Historiography), Turin: Einaudi, 1970; a revision of *Nuova rivista
storica* 51 (1967); 52 (1968); of the bibliography in *Rivista
storica italiana* 79 (1967); and of the course and seminar listings
in *Belfagor* 22 (1967)

Tenenti, A., "Delio Cantimori, storico del Cinquecento" (Delio
Cantimori, Historian of the 16th Century), *Studi storici* 14
(1968), 20–28

Cardoso, Fernando Henrique 1931–
Brazilian social scientist and politician

Fernando Henrique Cardoso contributed greatly to the development of dependency theory during the 1960s and the 1970s. Dependency theory emerged as a critique of neoclassical economic explanations of modernization and development. His major contribution to the theory was contained in his collaborative work with Enzo Faletto, *Dependencia y desarrollo en América Latina* (1969; *Dependency and Development in Latin America*, 1979). Cardoso and Faletto worked on their ideas while researching and studying at the Latin American Institute for Social and Economic Planning (ILPES) in Santiago, Chile. They never used the term "dependency theory," but instead spoke about "situations of dependency."

Initially, Cardoso worked on the question of Brazilian slavery along with other Brazilian social scientists in a project funded by UNESCO. His research, originally conducted for his doctoral dissertation, was published as *Capitalismo e escravidão* (Capitalism and Slavery, 1962), a study of Brazilian slavery in Rio Grande do Sul. Using a structural analysis, he argued against the prevalent view presented by Gilberto Freyre about the relatively benign relationship between slave and master. His analysis stressed that although slavery linked southern Brazil to the export sector, it prevented modern forms of capitalist development.

Subsequently, Cardoso shifted his research interests to a study of the Brazilian entrepreneur and economic development, which was published as *Empresário industrial e desenvolvimento econômico* (Industrial Entrepreneurs and Economic Underdevelopment, 1964). He conducted a series of interviews in 1961 and 1962 with various industrialists around the country. Extrapolating from these interviews, he analyzed the current trend of Brazilian development, and argued that a crisis was imminent. Since 1930 three sectors had emerged – the traditional exporting agricultural-commercial elite, the new industrial bourgeoisie, and the urban masses – whose divergent economic and political interests were difficult to balance, creating a governmental crisis that only a military coup could resolve. Presciently, Cardoso had been working on this study in the years prior to Brazil's 1964 coup.

Fleeing Brazil as a result of the coup, Cardoso went to Santiago and worked at ILPES, a branch of the United Nations Economic Commission for Latin America (ECLA). At the institute, Cardoso met and worked with Enzo Faletto, a Chilean social scientist, on the ideas that evolved into a general theory of dependency. Influenced not only by Marxism but also functionalism and structuralism, their ideas elaborated on the ECLA model of development formulated by Raúl Prebisch. ECLA's model stressed the necessity of increasing industrial production and the formation of a Latin American Common Market as a means of countering the deteriorating terms of trade for Latin America's primary exports. Instead of concentrating exclusively on external economic factors and social groups, Cardoso and Faletto shifted their focus to internal economic factors and social groups. They argued for the importance of analyzing the relationship of the interests of the national dominant classes with those of the international dominant classes. Not only was this relationship pivotal, but also the relationship of the national dominant classes with the internal dominated groups and classes needed examination.

In 1965, he presented his initial ideas on dependency that were the basis for *Dependency and Development*. The study provided a historical analysis of Latin America's dependent situation, which began with its political independence from Spain and Portugal. In the 19th century, England, as a trading partner, became the dominant economic power and demanded a steady supply of raw materials for its own burgeoning industrial economy. Latin America's local elites consisted of a dynamic sector, the merchants and plantation owners producing for the world market, as well as the hacienda owners who produced for internal consumption. These groups formed alliances in order to control the lower classes that provided the necessary labor. Alliances also allowed access to land for export production. These fragile alliances sometimes broke out into struggles between the two groups, characterized by the struggle between the regions against the center. Although the alliance did allow the consolidation of the national state by subordinating the regional *caudillos* (military strongmen), it also contributed to economic stagnation.

For Cardoso and Faletto, local national elites produced one type of economic development in Latin America. The demands of the world market for particular export products conditioned the decisions of national elites, but local political, social, and economic power remained in their hands. Metropolitan countries, especially England, channeled external investment into the infrastructure for exports and provided credit. The local military, political, and economic elites were allowed to rule by the metropolitan powers. With economic growth, there came the creation of a middle class to staff the burgeoning bureaucratic structure. It was necessary for the ruling elites, especially those of the dynamic export sector, to maintain social control in order to appropriate land and labor for economic growth.

Cardoso and Faletto also analyzed another type of economic development, that of the enclave economy. This type of development differed from the previous model because export production was directly controlled by foreign capital. This dependency situation occurred in productive activities, such as mining and some forms of agricultural production, that required heavy capital investment that local elites were not able to generate. This type of development had no linkages with the national economy but was outwardly oriented. Capital came from outside, very little labor was required, and profits were not reinvested into the national economy but sent to the metropolis where decisions on the enterprise were made.

After this sketch of 19th-century Latin American economic growth, there was a transitional phase at the beginning of the 20th century. With the expansion of the export economy, there was not only a growth of the urban middle class, but also of the working class. With the growth of the middle class and working class, each Latin American country experienced a unique political crisis prior to the 1929 depression, depending on the relative strength of its contending political groups. Previously, economic historians had focused on the depression, the disruption of trade during World War II, and the push for the development of an internal market, as the period when these crises had occurred. Cardoso and Faletto saw the roots of the crisis as coming earlier, based on the need of the ruling oligarchy to incorporate the middle class and working class into the political structure. The world crisis of 1929 would affect each country differently depending on its internal political realignments and the success of incorporating the middle sectors and the working class. Whether the economy was controlled by local capital or was an enclave economy, as well as the type of enclave, also determined the type of internal developments in the national market after World War II.

After the war, Latin American countries instituted a policy of industrialization based on a balance of the nationalist and populist forces within each country. Since no strong industrial bourgeoisie existed, this weakened group found it necessary to make alliances with other groups in order to push the state into industrialization, since it was necessary to transfer agricultural export profits into the development of industry. These alliances were either with the national agricultural export group, the urban middle class and working class, or with the state. In the late 1950s and 1960s, with the declining terms of trade for agricultural exports, this period of import-substitution and populism, the dominant ideology, came under strain as the urban masses increased their demands for economic redistribution and political participation. In many Latin American countries, this crisis led to the emergence of military governments in order to solve both the political and the economic crisis and to reassure foreign investors. Foreign capital increasingly came to control economic growth, determining which industries would expand within the country, creating a situation of dependency.

Cardoso and Faletto provided a critique of many of the abstract models that conceived of economic development as unilinear and universal. Those models, whether Marxist or neoclassical, spoke about stages that each country had to go through in order to become "modern." Cardoso and Faletto merged history into their analysis as a means to counteract the tendency of academic theorists, such as Walt W. Rostow, to reify the developmental process. Cardoso believed in the study of concrete situations of dependency as a means of combining theory with empirical analysis.

In the milieu of the late 1960s and 1970s Cardoso's ideas were favorably received as an explanation for Latin America's underdevelopment. One of the reasons is that there were other Latin American scholars working on similar problems during this period. Outside of Latin America, these ideas were also well received by the scholarly community, particularly in the United States. Many consider Cardoso's collaborative work with Faletto as the classic work on dependency that is essential for an understanding of Latin American history.

Cardoso's analysis also challenged André Gunder Frank's writings on dependency. Frank argued that dependency invariably led to underdevelopment in the peripheral countries. Cardoso countered with his idea of dependent capitalist development, which postulated that development could take place in a situation of dependency. This situation benefited those national groups associated with international capital, while it harmed the nation's traditional economic elites – agrarian producers for the domestic market and national entrepreneurs and merchants not associated with international capital. This situation could lead to a political crisis, as contradictions between those groups associated with international capital and those associated with national capital emerged. This dependency situation contributed to the rise of bureaucratic-authoritarian regimes.

Subsequently, Cardoso examined the rise of the bureaucratic-authoritarian regime in Latin America, utilizing the 1964 Brazilian military coup as a model. These regimes could be either military or civilian, but each had a similar goal: to promote capitalist development. In order to achieve this goal, these regimes needed to neutralize the popular and middle classes demands for economic redistribution and social justice. Also, they promoted the expansion of the state bureaucracy and public enterprises as a means to achieve capitalist development. Many of these state enterprises were (and are) associated with multinational corporations, and found a political, social, and economic climate amenable to their economic interests. This unique convergence of public and private economic interests contributed to the rise of an entrepreneurial capacity within the bureaucratic strata. Whether a bureaucratic-authoritarian regime was military or civilian depended on the extent of the political crisis engendered by the popular and middle classes in their search for social justice and economic redistribution. When the ruling classes could not control the upsurge of popular protest, the military intervened. Initially, these military regimes were extremely repressive, and repression continues to be a defining feature. This repression is considered necessary as a means for engendering capital accumulation.

After years of exile, Cardoso returned to Brazil in 1968 to participate in the political life of the nation. In 1986, he was elected to the Senate and, in 1988, he participated in organizing a political party, the Partido da Social Democracia Brazileira (Brazilian Social-Democratic Party). He has also participated in various Brazilian governments as foreign minister and finance minister. In 1994, while running for president, he rejected many of his own ideas concerning dependency during his campaign. Subsequently, he won the election and was inaugurated in 1995.

CARLOS PÉREZ

See also Freyre; Latin America: Nationalism

Biography
Born Brazil, 18 June 1931. Studied and taught at the University of São Paulo, 1949–64; exiled to Chile after the 1964 Brazilian coup; worked at the Latin American Institute for Social and Economic Planning, 1964–67; returned to University of São Paulo in 1968, but "retired" by the right-wing government, December 1968. Founder, Brazilian Center for Analysis and Planning. Elected to the Brazilian Senate, 1986. Organizer, Partido da Social Democracia Brasiliera (Brazilian Social-Democratic Party), 1988. Foreign minister, 1992; finance minister, 1993; president of Brazil from 1995.

Principal Writings
Capitalismo e escarvidão no Brasil meridional: o negro na escravocrata do Rio Grande do Sul (Capitalism and Slavery in Southern Brazil: The Negro in the Slave Society of Rio Grande do Sul), 1962

Empresário industrial e desenvolvimento econômico no Brasil (Industrial Entrepreneurs and Economic Underdevelopment in Brazil), 1964

With Enzo Faletto, *Dependencia y desarrollo en América Latina: ensayo de interpretación sociológica*, 1969; in English as *Dependency and Development in Latin America*, 1979

Política e desenvolvimento em sociedades dependentes: ideologias do empresariado industrial argentino e brasileiro (Politics and Underdevelopment in Dependent Societies), 1971

Dependency Revisited, 1973

"On the Characterization of Authoritarian Regimes in Latin America," in David Collier, ed., *The New Authoritarianism in Latin America*, 1979

Further Reading
Bath, C. Richard, and Dilmus D. James, "Dependency Analysis of Latin America: Some Criticisms, Some Suggestions," *Latin American Research Review* 11:3 (1976), 3–54

Bodenheimer, Susanne J., *The Ideology of Developmentalism: The American Paradigm-Surrogate for Latin American Studies*, Beverly Hills, CA: Sage, 1971

Cavarozzi, Marcelo, "El 'desarrollismo' y las relaciones entre democracia y capitalismo dependiente en *Dependencia y desarrollo en América Latina*," *Latin American Research Review* 17 (1982), 152–65

Chase-Dunn, Christopher, "A World-System Perspective on *Dependency and Development in Latin America*," *Latin American Research Review* 17 (1982), 166–71

Chilcote, Ronald H., *Theories of Development and Underdevelopment*, Boulder, CO: Westview Press, 1984

Halperín-Donghi, Tulio, "'Dependency Theory' and Latin American Historiography," *Latin American Research Review* 17 (1982), 115–30

Kahl, Joseph A., *Modernization, Exploitation, and Dependency in Latin America: Germani, González Casanova, and Cardoso*, New Brunswick, NJ: Transaction, 1976

Kahl, Joseph A., *Three Latin American Sociologists: Gino Germani, Pablo Gonzales Casanova, Fernando Henrique Cardoso* [sic], New Brunswick, NJ: Transaction, 1988

Love, Joseph L., "The Origins of Dependency Analysis," *Journal of Latin American Studies* 22 (February 1990), 143–68

Packenham, Robert A., "Plus ça change . . .: The English Edition of Cardoso and Faletto's *Dependencia y desarrollo en América Latina*," *Latin American Research Review* 17 (1982), 131–51

Roxborough, Ian, "Unity and Diversity in Latin American History," *Journal of Latin American Studies* 16 (May 1984), 1–26

Carlyle, Thomas 1795–1881
British historian

From a humble background in lowland Scotland, Thomas Carlyle rose to be the social commentator who above all others set the intellectual tone of early Victorian England. In the 1820s and 1830s, his contributions to the great 19th-century reviews introduced a generation to the writers of the German Enlightenment, to Kant, Schiller, Fichte, and Goethe. Then, in the early years of Victoria's reign, his social critiques established the parameters of the dominant debate of the 1840s, which in *Chartism* (1839) he styled "the Condition-of-England" question.

Carlyle's historical writing cannot be understood in isolation from his wider social criticism, for indeed it was essentially part of it. The essential core of his philosophy was summed up in his first major work, *Sartor Resartus* (1836), acknowledged today as the most significant of all his works. In this book Carlyle developed his famous "philosophy of clothes," an ingenious allegory for his transcendental beliefs. Here clothes – the outward appearance – are presented as both revealing and obscuring the body – the inner reality – just as the outward forms of the contemporary world might be said to shroud its inner – or transcendental – reality.

For Carlyle this inner reality was truth, or, in historical terms, the hidden workings of divine providence. This placed paradoxical pressures on his conception of the historian's task, and produced a historiography at odds with the prevailing historicism of Ranke. Ultimately Carlyle was uninterested in the painstaking recovery and careful presentation of historical facts. He did not believe that the past could be encapsulated in either abstraction or narrative. As he wrote in his 1830 essay "On History": "Narrative is *linear*, Action is *solid*." Instead, through allowing the past to speak to the present in the form of contemporary records, and through the operation of imagination on such primary sources, he sought to recreate the past. His aim was to enable the reader to be present, to see the events he described, and above all to know the central figures whose biographies he considered the very stuff of history.

Detail was subordinated to insight, accuracy to veracity. To this end he deployed not only an unparalleled genius for making the past concrete, but also a writing style so fractured, so exuberant, and with such wilful disregard for normal rhetorical structures, that it has challenged readers ever since. As one of his contemporary critics suggested, he was "rather a poet writing on history, than a historian." Hence perhaps the most powerful of all Carlyle's historical writings occur in *Past and Present* (1843), in the fictive form of a history of Abbot Samson of the Abbey of St. Edmundsbury (a transparent rendition of Bury St. Edmunds, on whose recently published records Carlyle's account was based).

Carlyle's reputation as a historian, however, was made by his 3-volume *The French Revolution* (1837), which he wrote in the three years following his move from Scotland to London in 1834 – even rewriting the first volume from scratch when the manuscript was burnt by mistake while on loan to John Stuart Mill. Carlyle's history was a series of dramatic set pieces written in the present tense, designed to encapsulate the Revolution, and to reinterpret it not as the blind, mob-driven, cataclysm of contemporary wisdom, but as a just apocalypse, a retribution on the empty sham of the French *ancien régime*. His portraits of the leading protagonists, especially Mirabeau, Danton, and Robespierre, and his powerful description of the storming of the Bastille endure as defining representations of the Revolution, notwithstanding the slender documentary basis of his writing, and its supercession long since as a reliable historical account.

If *The French Revolution* retains significance only as great literature, this is not true of the second of Carlyle's major historical works, *Oliver Cromwell's Letters and Speeches* (1845). Carlyle, true to the Scottish Calvinist tradition in which he had been reared, had long had a fascination for the mid-17th century, and for a while planned a full-scale history of the Puritan revolution, paralleling his study of the French revolution. Progressively this was narrowed down to a collection of Cromwell's letters and speeches, with Carlyle's own annotations and elucidations. Despite some memorable historical descriptions, *Cromwell* lacked the literary power of *The French Revolution*. But it also overthrew the prevailing picture of Cromwell as a fanatical political adventurer, hypocrite, and traitor, establishing in its stead a religious idealist, struggling with the dilemmas of his career. It also represented the most complete affirmation of Carlyle's desire to let the past speak for itself: by the standards of his time he was an assiduous editor, and as a documentary collection the volume has retained at least some of its historical authority.

If Carlyle's apparently ready acceptance of Cromwell's drift to authoritarianism made uneasy reading for many of Carlyle's disciples, it was an unease deepened by the last of his great historical works, the 6-volume study of the 18th-century Prussian king, *Frederick the Great* (1858–65). Carlyle's interest had been aroused by a battlefield visit while staying in Germany in 1852, and it is thus fitting that the battle accounts are the highpoint of this study which, for all its great length, managed to skip over the last 23 years of Frederick's reign in half a volume. Nevertheless, not only was the book long-used as a teaching text by the German General Staff, but it continues to be cited as an authority by modern historians.

The completion of *Frederick* marks virtually the end of Carlyle's writings. His advancing age, and the death of his wife, Jane Carlyle, in 1866 dampened the fires of his genius. In any case, the increasingly antidemocratic tone of his writings, clearly visible in his lectures of 1840, *On Heroes, Hero-worship, and the Heroic in History* forthrightly expressed in his *Latter-Day Pamphlets* (1850), and visibly untempered in his study of Frederick II, had lost him the ear of the educated public. Nevertheless, despite attempts in the mid-20th century to arraign him as an influence on fascist ideologies, there was little in Carlyle's thought that travelled well abroad. Even within Britain, although he retained fervent disciples, including J.A. Froude, he had founded no school and wrought no lasting influence on historical writing.

MARTIN HEWITT

See also Froude; Lecky; Literature; Macaulay; Masculinity; Nevins; Popular; Reformation; Schama; Trevelyan; Wilamovitz-Möllendorff; Williams, R.

Biography

Born Ecclefechan, Scotland, 4 December 1795, son of a dissenting stonemason. Educated in Scottish schools and University of Edinburgh. Private tutor and schoolmaster, then freelance writer; lived in London from 1834. Married Jane Baillie Welsh, 1826 (died 1866). Died London, 5 February 1881.

Principal Writings

Sartor Resartus, 1836
The French Revolution, 3 vols., 1837
Chartism, 1839
On Heroes, Hero-worship, and the Heroic in History, 1841
Past and Present, 1843
Oliver Cromwell's Letters and Speeches, 2 vols., 1845
Latter-Day Pamphlets, 1850
Frederick the Great, 6 vols., 1858–65

Further Reading

Campbell, Ian, *Thomas Carlyle*, London: Hamish Hamilton, 1974
Cobban, Alfred, "Carlyle's 'French' Revolution," *History* 48 (1963), 306–16
Dale, Peter Allan, *The Victorian Critic and the Idea of History: Carlyle, Arnold, Pater*, Cambridge, MA: Harvard University Press, 1977
Froude, J.A., *Thomas Carlyle: A History of His Life in London, 1834–81*, London: Longman, 1884; New York: Harper, 1885
Gooch, G.P., *History and Historians in the Nineteenth Century*, London and New York: Longman, 1913; revised 1952
Kenyon, John, *The History Men: The Historical in England since the Renaissance*, London: Weidenfeld and Nicolson, 1983; Pittsburgh: University of Pittsburgh Press, 1984
Le Quesne, A. Lawrence, *Carlyle*, Oxford and New York: Oxford University Press, 1982
Sanders, Charles R., ed., *The Collected Letters of Thomas and Jane Welsh Carlyle*, 24 vols., Durham, NC: Duke University Press, and Edinburgh: Edinburgh University Press, 1970–95
Seigel, Jules Paul, *Thomas Carlyle: The Critical Heritage*, London: Routledge, and New York: Barnes and Noble, 1971
Tarr, Rodger L., *Thomas Carlyle: A Descriptive Bibliography*, Oxford and New York: Oxford University Press, and Pittsburgh: University of Pittsburgh Press, 1989
Williams, Raymond, *Culture and Society, 1780–1950*, London: Chatto and Windus, and New York: Columbia University Press, 1958

Carr, E.H. 1892–1982

British historian of modern Europe

Edward Hallett Carr's dedication to democratic and humanist ideals, combined with a pragmatic dialectical method, was applied to a tremendous range of subjects in works that remain as relevant today as when they were first written. It is not easy to characterize a scholar whose works include the epic 14-volume *A History of Soviet Russia* (1950–78), as well as literary investigations and art criticism (such as *Dostoevsky* [1931] and *The Romantic Exiles* [1933]). However Carr will be remembered first and foremost as an international historian and philosopher of history. He should also be remembered as one of the first modern international political economists.

An abiding fascination with the dual themes of ideational-material dialectic and historic transformation permeated his texts. Like R.G. Collingwood before him, Carr was principally concerned with the consequences of the expansion of reason in social affairs, as seen in his important *What Is History?* (1961). The transformation of society (domestic or international), it was noted, had been achieved either by war or revolution. Both were unsatisfactory but nevertheless necessary until humankind recognized that as modes of change they were far too costly and inexact. Revolution, in the French case – of which Carr was fond – had provided the impetus behind freedom and democracy, but had gone astray due to a failure to provide mechanisms through which these powerful ideas could be realized. Consequently, innovation had to be tempered by an appreciation of the realistic limits of potential action thereby generating the evolution of viable institutions. Carr firmly believed that in an interdependent, industrialized setting, hard bargaining, rather than revolution and war, was a superior method of achieving evolutionary change "toward goals which can be defined only as we advance towards them, and the validity of which can only be verified in a process of attaining them."

Present at the Versailles Peace Conference and serving twenty years in the British Foreign Office (for a time as an adviser on League of Nations affairs), Carr famously criticized interwar international politics in *The Twenty Years' Crisis 1919–1939* (1939). He was certain that those who framed the 1919 settlement did not understand that 19th-century laissez-faire economic practices, combined with the nationalism inspired by the principal of national self-determination, were unsuited to the political realities of postwar Europe. British, French and especially American politicians were roundly criticized by Carr for imposing a "sterile" politico-economic status quo on a new era. This powerful and much acclaimed thesis – the rejection of "utopianism" – became a clarion-call for a "realist" reassessment of international politics that was subsequently to grip the emerging discipline of international relations. Few have acknowledged, however, the dialectic in *Crisis* that sought an interplay, if not synthesis, between utopianism and realism. Of realism, Carr said that it lacks "a finite goal, an emotional appeal, a right of moral judgment and a ground for action." He argued for a constant renegotiation between the competing forces of utopia and reality to guide both theorists and practitioners.

In one of his less-cited works, *Conditions of Peace* (1942), Carr elaborated the theme of systemic change and in so doing he concentrated much more on the economic content of the ideas and policies he sought to discourage. The crux of his argument was that the democratic powers had to seize the initiative and renegotiate economics and politics into constructive forces for positive change – a challenge Carr viewed as the core moral crisis facing the democracies. In the darkest days of World War II he advocated a thoroughgoing commitment to European reconstruction, with Germany at the heart of arrangements, that would eventually devolve to a "European Planning Authority" supported by a "Bank of Europe" responsible for financing trade, investment, liquidation of claims, and currency control. The key to the creation of a new order was wedded to the resolution of unemployment and the spread of mass democracy.

Just as history had shown that war and other social disorders flourished in economic malaise, so too the demand for equality "has been at the root of every recent revolution and of most recent wars." "The driving force behind any future international order," Carr later wrote, "must be a belief ... in the value of individual human beings irrespective of national affinities or allegiance" (*Nationalism and After*, 1945). Just as the military was subordinated to popular control, so too, argued Carr, must "the holders of economic power ... be responsible to, and take their orders from, the community in exactly the same way." Liberty, in this scheme, would apply in terms of "maximum social and economic opportunity." This was indeed a radical strategy. Carr wanted an international political economy based on a redistribution of wealth and the transfer of economic power to popular control. A system where profit was balanced against equality, liberty against obligation, "increased consumption [for] social stability, [and] equitable distribution [for] maximum production." Such views, largely ignored by realists, were severely criticized, in the House of Lords for example, as "an active danger," when Carr expressed them during his assistant editorship of the *Times* during and just after the war.

The frictions in the interaction between territorial power and international economics that Carr perceived, and for which he subsequently recommended a combination of state and international remedies, have been transformed and intensified, but not alleviated in the late 20th century. Worse still, the marginalization of great masses of increasingly powerless people that Carr argued was the basis of discontent contributing to World War II is again prevalent.

ADAM COBB

See also Central Europe; Davies, R.; Diplomatic; Frontiers; Russia: Modern; Russia: Russian Revolution; Taylor

Biography

Edward Hallett Carr. Born London, 28 June 1892. Educated at Merchant Taylors' School, London; Trinity College, Cambridge, BA 1915, MA 1916. Served in Foreign Office, 1916–36: at the Paris peace conference, 1919; and at Riga, Geneva, and London. Wilson professor of international politics, University College Wales, Aberystwyth, 1936–47; director of foreign publicity, Ministry of Information, 1939–40; assistant editor, the *Times*, 1941–46; tutor in politics, Balliol College, Oxford, 1953–55; fellow, Trinity College, Cambridge, 1955–82. Married 1) Anne Ward Howe, 1925 (1 son); lived with Joyce Marion Stock Forde, 1946–64; 2) Betty Behrens, historian, 1966. Died Cambridge, 3 November 1982.

Principal Writings

Dostoevsky, 1931

The Romantic Exiles: A Nineteenth-Century Portrait Gallery, 1933

Karl Marx: A Study in Fanaticism, 1934

International Relations since the Peace Treaties, 1937; revised as *International Relations Between the Two World Wars, 1919–1939*, 1947

Michael Bakunin, 1937

The Twenty Years' Crisis, 1919–1939: An Introduction to the Study of International Relations, 1939

The Future of Nations: Independence or Interdependence?, 1941

Conditions of Peace, 1942

Nationalism and After, 1945

The Soviet Impact on the Western World, 1946

"The Moral Foundations for World Order," in E.L. Woodward, ed., *Foundations for World Order*, 1948

A History of Soviet Russia, 14 vols., 1950–78 (vols. 9–10, *Foundations of a Planned Economy*, with R.W. Davies)

Studies in Revolution, 1950

German-Soviet Relations Between the Two World Wars, 1919–1939, 1951

The New Society, 1951

What Is History?, 1961

1917: Before and After, 1969; in US as *The October Revolution: Before and After*, 1969

ABC of Communism, 1969

From Napoleon to Stalin, and Other Essays, 1980

The Twilight of the Comintern, 1930–1935, 1982

The Comintern and the Spanish Civil War, edited by Tamara Deutscher, 1984

Further Reading

Cobb, Adam C., "Economic Security: E.H. Carr and R.W. Cox – The Most Unlikely Bedfellows," *Cambridge Review of International Studies* 9 (1995)

Fox, William R.T., "E.H. Carr and Political Realism: Vision and Revision," *Review of International Studies* 11 (1985), 1–16

Howe, Paul, "The Utopian Realism of E.H. Carr," *Review of International Studies* 20 (1994), 277–97

Jenkins, Keith, *On "What Is History?" From Carr and Elton to Rorty and White*, London and New York: Routledge, 1995

Carr, Raymond 1919–

British historian of Spain

Although he has written on subjects as diverse as contemporary Latin America, Swedish history, and fox hunting, it is as a pioneer of the history of contemporary Spain that Raymond Carr is best known. When his epic *Spain 1808–1939* was published in 1966 the study of contemporary Spanish history was still relatively unknown. This was true not only of British universities, where it was unfashionable, but also of academic institutions in Francoist Spain where political reasons made it "unsuitable." There were exceptions, notably Gerald Brenan and Jaime Vicens Vives, for whom Carr professed great admiration and whom he often cited as important influences. It would be mistaken, however, to attribute his success simply to good timing. *Spain 1808–1939* was innovative in both content and approach, and not only did it establish itself immediately as the standard historical text on late modern Spain but, significantly, it has managed to retain this status to the present day.

In this book Carr rejected the then current view that Spain's turbulent and problematic recent history had a uniquely "Spanish" cause in favor of a more sophisticated and analytical approach. Spain, he argued, was not "different" and the roots of her problems could be uncovered and identified in the same way as those of any other country. Though incorporating some social and economic history, it was primarily an example of orthodox political history in which political decisions and their consequences took precedence over structural factors: he once wrote that "accident and personal choice are the stuff of history." His conclusion was that much of recent Spanish history revolved around the search for a legitimate political system that was not reliant on force. A search, he would later argue in *Modern Spain 1875–1980* (1980), that finally ended with the transition to democracy of the 1970s. More specifically, Carr believed that many of Spain's problems resulted from the tensions caused by the imposition of advanced liberal institutions on a socially and economically backward society that was essentially conservative. Nowadays, of course, this analysis sounds fairly standard, but thirty years ago it was genuinely innovative.

In many respects the depth and range that were features of Carr's writing made him the ideal historian to produce such an extensive and pioneering historical text. Yet the comprehensive nature of what was his first book, along with the freely admitted fact that he felt little attraction toward the more detailed and in-depth type of research required for the writing of theses or scholarly monographs, may have limited his subsequent options. Certainly, while his later books would encompass sociocultural as well as political matters and continue to be analytical and argumentative, they could sometimes give the impression of covering similar ground from familiar perspectives. This may partly explain why, in spite of his undoubted influence and the great respect in which he is held, he has seldom been considered definitive on any particular issue; Carr, it is said, has posed far more questions than he has provided answers. In 1980 the shorter *Modern Spain 1875–1980* was published, providing an accessible synthesis of his earlier work.

Carr typically employed an eclectic method that was quite prepared to utilize any historical perspective, be it conservative, liberal, or Marxist. In *The Spanish Tragedy* (1977), for example, both religion and class conflict were presented as the fundamental causes of the Spanish Civil War. Similarly, despite his preference for the political, he showed little aversion to employing structural explanations where he felt them appropriate. This, allied with a willingness to look at any situation from all sides and consider all points of view, resulted in his work attracting criticism as well as praise. On the one hand, he was paid tribute for what some see as his range, objectivity, and understanding. Such was the opinion of the reviewer who commended the *Spanish Tragedy* for displaying "judgment that was, paradoxically, sound but fair to all concerned." His critics, on the other hand, described him as haphazard and inconclusive.

Although the changes taking place in Spanish society during the 1960s and 1970s would probably have stimulated and facilitated academic interest in contemporary Spain irrespective of Carr, his personal role was nonetheless significant. Besides writing about Spain, he was an eager participant in many debates (including a particularly acrimonious public disagreement over Spanish anarchism) while, at Oxford University, he supervised and encouraged many future hispanists from both Britain and Spain, Paul Preston among them. Carr himself always rejected the idea of an "Oxford school" of Spanish historians, but the influence of his approach and method can be detected in the work of several scholars of contemporary Spain.

STUART BLYTH

See also Spain: Modern

Biography

Albert Raymond Maillard Carr. Born Bath, England, 11 April 1919. Educated at Brockenhurst School; Christ Church, Oxford, BA 1941. Lecturer, University College, London, 1945–56; at Oxford University, 1946–87: fellow, All Souls College, 1946–53, fellow, New College, 1953–64, director, Latin American Centre, 1964–68, fellow, St. Antony's College, from 1964 and warden, 1968–87. Knighted 1987. Married Sarah Strickland, 1950 (3 sons, 1 daughter).

Principal Writings

Spain, 1808–1939, 1966; revised as *Spain, 1808–1975*, 1982
The Spanish Tragedy: The Civil War in Perspective, 1977; reprinted as *The Civil War in Spain, 1936–1939*, 1986
With Juan Pablo Fusi Aizpúrua, *Spain: Dictatorship to Democracy*, 1979
Modern Spain, 1875–1980, 1980
Puerto Rico: A Colonial Experiment, 1984
"Introduction: The Spanish Transition in Perspective," in Robert Clark and Michael Haltzel, eds., *Spain in the 1980s: The Democratic Transition and a New International Role*, Cambridge, MA: Ballinger, 1987

Further Reading

Lannon, Frances, and Paul Preston, eds., *Elites and Power in Twentieth-Century Spain: Essays in Honour of Sir Raymond Carr*, Oxford and New York: Oxford University Press, 1990

Cassiodorus *c.487–c.585*
Roman historian

Cassiodorus was one of the leading figures in the history of Italy in the 6th century, and he is also one of those most responsible for our knowledge of it. He held high posts in the civil service under Theoderic and the other Ostrogothic kings who held power in post-Roman Italy, and spent some time in Constantinople while Italy was being conquered by the armies of the Byzantine emperor Justinian. Later he returned to Italy and established a monastery on his family estate at Vivarium, in Bruttium, at which the monks were to lead a more scholarly life than St. Benedict had recently envisaged in his Rule. Both the secular and monastic parts of his life saw him engage in historical activities.

The best known work of Cassiodorus is his *Variae*, a collection of the letters he wrote on behalf of various Gothic sovereigns between 507 and 537. The digressions characteristic of the more formal of these letters contain much historical material, some of it reflecting a mood of traditionalism and a desire to represent the administration of the Goths as restoring the glories of the past. The letters also purport to convey

information concerning the history of the Goths, in particular the Amal family of which Theoderic was a member. Indeed, Cassiodorus mentions a Gothic history he wrote at the command of Theoderic in which he "made the origin of the Goths to be Roman." This work has not survived, but when, in 551, the monk Jordanes wrote his own work on the Goths, he drew on the lost work of Cassiodorus. Estimates of the indebtedness of Jordanes to Cassiodorus vary widely. Jordanes was in Constantinople when he wrote his work, and as Cassiodorus was then in that city it has been suggested that he stood behind the labors of Jordanes. The hypothesis is alluring, but lacks proof.

A historical work of Cassiodorus that has come down to us is his *Chronica*, that he represented as having been composed at the behest of the consul for 519, Theoderic's son-in-law Eutharic. It was written in accordance with the traditional method of the Christian world chronicle, beginning with Adam and proceeding to the present. For most of this work Cassiodorus used material that had been gathered by the pioneer of the genre, Eusebius, and his continuators Jerome and Prosper of Aquitaine, but from 455 his material is original. The work was in the traditional format of a chronicle, providing information on a year-by-year basis. Again, Cassiodorus developed a pro-Gothic interpretation of history; for example, he describes the Goths as having sacked Rome in 410 "in a clement fashion," and it is with no sense of discontinuity that he presents the consulship of the Goth Eutharic as having followed those which had been held by Romans for more than a millennium.

The collapse of the Gothic kingdom before the armies of Justinian rendered irrelevant the works of history that Cassiodorus had hitherto written and the political agenda they served, and increasingly his thoughts turned to religion. But his interest in history persisted. At the monastery of Vivarium he wrote his *Institutiones*, a work designed to provide an introduction to books his monks would find useful. Among the works he evaluates are those of a number of historians, among them Josephus, whom he describes as "almost a second Livy," an unexpected allusion to a historian outside the Judaeo-Christian tradition. He also mentions the ecclesiastical historians Eusebius, Socrates, Sozomen and Theodoret, and the Latin authors Orosius, Marcellinus, Prosper, and Jerome.

Cassiodorus' last involvement with the writing of history was part of another project of his monastic period, that of having a number of Greek works with a bearing on theology translated into Latin. Among them were the *Jewish Antiquities* of Josephus and the works of three ecclesiastical historians of the 5th century, Socrates, Sozomen, and Theodoret. By this time the emperor Justinian, of whose empire Italy was now a part, was campaigning against a theological tendency observable in the works of one of the 5th century authors, and it may well be that Cassiodorus saw himself as showing resistance to the policies of the emperor by way of this historical undertaking.

Cassiodorus' life was a long one, marked by great changes in society and in his own way of life. His lasting enthusiasm for history is evident; perhaps not quite so obvious are the ways in which he persistently sought to use history for the furtherance of political ends.

JOHN MOORHEAD

See also Byzantium; Momigliano; Roman; Tacitus; Velleius

Biography
Flavius Magnus Aurelius Cassiodorus. Born Scylacium (now Squillace), southern Italy, c.487. Served Ostrogoth king Theoderic in various capacities, 514–24, then secretary or chief minister to other kings; lived in Constantinople, c.550. Founded a monastery at Vivarium, Calabria, to which he retired. Died c.585.

Principal Works
Chronica, c.519
Variae, 12 books, 537; as *The Letters*, translated by Thomas Hodgkin, 1886; as *The Variae*, translated by S.J.B. Barnish, 1992
Institutiones divinarum et humanarum litterarum, as *An Introduction to Divine and Human Readings*, translated by Leslie Webber Jones, 1946
Texts in *Patrologiae cursus completus*, series Latina, edited by J.-P. Migne, vols. 69–70

Further Reading
Barnwell, P.S., *Emperors, Prefects, and Kings: The Roman West, 395–565*, London: Duckworth, and Chapel Hill: University of North Carolina Press, 1992
Heather, Pete J., "Cassiodorus and the Rise of the Amals: Genealogy and the Goths under Hun Domination" *Journal of Roman Studies* 79 (1989), 103–28
Krautschick, Stefan, *Cassiodor und die Politik seiner Zeit* (Cassiodorus on the Politics of His Time), Bonn: Habelt, 1983
Leanza, Sandro, ed., *Atti della Settimana di studi su Flavio Magno Aurelio Cassiodoro*, Soveria Mannelli: Rubbetino, 1986
Momigliano, Arnaldo, "Cassiodorus and Italian Culture of His Time," *Proceedings of the British Academy* 41 (1955), 207–46
Momigliano, Arnaldo, "Cassiodoro," in *Dizionario biografico degli Italiani*, vol.21 (1978)
Moorhead, John, *Theoderic in Italy*, Oxford and New York: Oxford University Press, 1992
O'Donnell, James J., *Cassiodorus*, Berkeley: University of California Press, 1979
Stone, Harold, "The Polemics of Toleration: The Scholars and Publishers of Cassiodorus' *Variae*," *Journal of the History of Ideas* 46 (1985), 147–66

Cassirer, Ernst 1874–1945
German historian of philosophy

A Kantian, Cassirer is best known for his ability to take abstract ideas, place them in concrete circumstances, and bring them to life for the reader. His view of the world was that all experience is a dynamic field. He argued that the world can be discussed and organized, and that morals and ethics are amenable to scientific description and cataloging. This concern is most evident in what he considered to be the focus of his major work.

In this he argued that people are by nature experience-rich creatures. They use symbols to make sense out of their world and the world about them. If one is to understand how people create reality and make order out of chaos in all fields of human endeavor from the natural sciences to politics to art, Cassirer says, we must analyze and interpret symbolic interactions. Reality is not always what science says it is, but what individuals construct it to be. This artificial reality portrays a type of objectivity, but it is an interior objectivity not related to the world of commonsense perception.

Some have suggested that Cassirer's typological organization of human existence and cognition is so broad as to be practically meaningless, while others see this openness to diversity and creativity as the core of his importance, allowing him to be ready to interpret and dissect new phenomena, as his constructs are not as tied, as those of other theorists, to current ideas. Cassirer's theories can be used, they argue, to create a base for cultural, economic, and political ideas not yet clearly articulated or not yet even formed.

Cassirer claimed that his flexibility allowed him to let those who are creating reality to create that reality, and allowed him to chart their course along general but recognizable paths: individuals are symbol- and myth-creating. *A priori* predictability is not what Cassirer wished to accomplish. He wanted to develop a system where human existence can be observed as it unfolds. This allows one to analyze the movement of ideas as they form, and creates an analytic framework with implications not only for constructive but reconstructive work.

Cassirer was one of the few philosophers who was able to speak to the growing storm of oppression that was then sweeping over Europe and threatening to engulf the world. His approach to history and philosophy provided positive, broad-based, yet specific recommendations for coping with the problems of modern societies.

What is Cassirer's importance to the craft of history? He looked at the whole historical process and saw history as an ever-changing human parade, which could be seen adequately only in motion. This "motion" brings both historians and their times alive for the reader. Cassirer's procedure allows historians to capture ideas and action, and, by merging them together, creates a more dynamic, lived synthesis than would be possible with each category perceived as distinct.

PAUL BARTON-KRIESE

See also German: 1450–1800; Italy: Renaissance; Nietzsche; Panofsky; Renaissance Historical Writing; Schramm

Biography
Born Breslau, 28 July 1874. Attended Breslau Gymnasium, then studied at universities of Berlin, Heidelberg, Munich, and Marburg, receiving his PhD from Marburg, 1899. Taught philosophy at University of Berlin, 1905–19; professor of philosophy, University of Hamburg, 1919–33: forced to resign because of Nazi race laws; taught at Oxford University, 1933–35; professor of philosophy, University of Gothenburg, Sweden, 1935–41; moved to US and taught at Yale University, 1941–44; and Columbia University, 1944–45. Married Toni Bondy, 1902 (2 sons, 1 daughter). Died New York City, 13 April 1945.

Principal Writings
Substanzbegriff und Funktionsbegriff, 1910; in English as *Substance and Function*, 1923
Zur Einstein'schen Relativitätstheorie, 1921; in English as *Einstein's Theory of Relativity*, 1923
Philosophie der symbolischen Formen, 3 vols., 1923–29; in English as *The Philosophy of Symbolic Forms*, 3 vols., 1953–57
Sprache und Mythos: ein Beitrag zum Problem der Götternamen, 1925; in English as *Language and Myth*, 1946
Individuum und Kosmos in der Philosophie der Renaissance, 1927; in English as *The Individual and the Cosmos in Renaissance Philosophy*, 1963
Die Philosophie der Aufklärung, 1932; in English as *The Philosophy of the Enlightenment*, 1951

An Essay on Man: An Introduction to a Philosophy of Human Culture, 1944
The Myth of the State, 1946
Symbol, Myth, and Culture: Essays and Lectures of Ernst Cassirer, 1935–1945, edited by Donald Phillip Verene, 1979

Further Reading

Ferretti, Sylvia, *Cassirer, Panofsky, and Warburg: Symbol, Art, and History*, New Haven: Yale University Press, 1989
Schilpp, Paul Arthur, *Ernst Cassirer*, Stuttgart: Kohlhammer, 1949
Schilpp, Paul Arthur, ed., *The Philosophy of Ernst Cassirer*, Evanston, IL: Library of Living Philosophers, 1949

Cassius Dio *c.*150–235 CE

Roman historian

Cassius Dio (also known as Dio Cassius) was of a Nicaean family prominent in the Roman government. He wrote in Greek not Latin. *Rhomaike* (*Roman History*), his only surviving work, shows that he identified with the Roman empire and its institutions, epitomizing the bicultural nature of the Roman empire.

Of the original 80 books of *Roman History*, those surviving cover the period 68 BCE to 40 CE (Books 36–60); it is therefore an important source for the reign of Augustus (31 BCE–14 CE). In this portion of the work, Cassius Dio presented contradictory pictures of Augustus. The remaining portions, covering from the founding of Rome to 229 CE, survive in summary form in the works of the Byzantine historians Constantine VII Porphyrogenitus, John VIII Xiphilinus, and John Zonaras.

Cassius Dio was involved in politics at the highest levels during a career in Rome which gave him access to the emperors. The surviving summaries of his work during the reigns of emperors Marcus Aurelius (121–80), Commodus (180–92), Septimius Severus (192–211), Caracalla (211–17), Macrinus (217–18), and Elagabalus (218–22) give us his personal reactions to these men. Cassius Dio's personal observations of Roman personalities, politics, and life make his work important today. Based on his literary style, analysis of events, and accuracy, Cassius Dio ranks as a second-rate historian among ancient writers. However, for the modern historian the value of his work rests in its corroboration of the work of other ancient authors, and in its detail.

Cassius Dio described from personal experience the philosopher-emperor, Marcus Aurelius' habit of walking the streets of Rome clad in a dark cloak and with no torchbearer to light his way. He contrasted this modest emperor with his son, Commodus, who dressed in a white silk tunic embroidered in gold to receive the greetings of his courtiers, Cassius Dio among them. Commodus then donned a jeweled crown and two purple garments with gold spangles for the multitudes. Later, he would cool himself with chilled wine after hunting wild animals in the public amphitheaters. Details such as these are his unique if not epic contributions to history.

A main fault of his writing is his retrospective projection. Cassius Dio projected the imperial situation of his own day onto the era of Augustus. He manufactured an exchange between the Augustan figures Agrippa and Maecenas that was

in essence a discourse on the monarchical institutions of his own day. This bias did not allow him to draw an accurate picture of the gradual transition from the principate of Augustus to the emperors of the 3rd century CE.

During the reign of Caracalla Cassius Dio retired from public life to write the *Roman History*. His influences were two ill-matched Greek authors, Thucycides the historian and Demothenes the orator. Accordingly, his work is sparely written in the Attic style, and his language is correct, reflecting the social status of his family, and free from affectation.

Knowing that the problems of the empire were too many to group accurately, Cassius Dio none the less established a broad chronological structure for Roman history that was accurate and systematic. He is a trustworthy source and his was the first major history written since Livy; he may have used Suetonius, Seneca, Tacitus, and Augustus' biographer, Cremutius Cordus, as his sources. Although Byzantine scribes copied Cassius Dio's writings, there seems to have been little interest in his work after his death. The author of the *Roman History* knew that the absolutism prevailing in his day kept important information from him. Also, his lack of knowledge of Roman republican institutions is evident in that portion of his work.

NANCY PIPPEN ECKERMAN

Biography

Born Nicaea, Bithynia (now Iznik, Turkey), *c.*150, son of a Roman senator, Marcus Cassius Apronianus. Studied in Italy. Entered Senate before 192; praetor, 194; consul 204 and (with Severus Alexander), 229; appointed governor of various provinces including Africa, Dalmatia, and Pannonia Superior; served several emperors; retired due to ailing health after 229. Died Nicaea, 235.

Principal Works

Rhomaike (Roman History), 207–22; as *Dio's Roman History* (Loeb edition), translated by Earnest Cary, 9 vols., 1914–27

Further Reading

Barnes, Timothy David, "The Composition of Cassius Dio's *Roman History*," *Phoenix* 38 (1984), 240–55
Gowing, Alain M., *The Triumviral Narratives of Appian and Cassius Dio*, Ann Arbor: University of Michigan Press, 1992
Grant, Michael, ed., *Readings in the Classical Historians*, New York: Scribner, and London: Maxwell Macmillan, 1992
Millar, Fergus, *A Study of Cassius Dio*, Oxford: Clarendon Press, 1964

Castro, Américo 1885–1972

Spanish (Brazilian-born) medievalist and literary historian

Américo Castro was a student of Ramón Menéndez Pidal and the early part of his career was devoted to standard philological and literary subjects. Around 1940, in the wake of liberal Spain's defeat in the Spanish Civil War (1936–39), he began to consider the historical roots of what he identified as Spain's insecurity as an internalization of its apparent cultural, political, and social failings with respect to the rest of Europe. The result was a monumental reconsideration of the country's medieval history and a view of the crystallization of "Spanish" culture in the Middle Ages under the influence of interaction with its Muslim enemies and Jewish minorities.

Castro's critique of traditional Spanish historiography is directed at two kinds of generalizations current in the literature. Many Spanish historians have held that the national culture has fixed parameters which have remained constant from the time of the Iberians until the present. This fallacy Castro labels "pan-Hispanism." The second generalization is that of "Spanish decadence," ostensibly associated with the lack of fit between the inbred values of pan-Hispanism and the progressive values associated with modern Europe. Castro's answer is that the culture we call Spanish is not an eternal entity but one which came into being in the centuries following the Muslim invasion of 711, and that culture was one whose idiosyncrasies can be explained by the interaction of Christians with Muslims and Jews. Inasmuch as the Christian "caste" depended upon Muslims and Jews for economic and agricultural skills and for scientific and technological expertise, the inferiority feelings of modern Spaniards with respect to the rest of Europe are simple reflections of age-old insecurities held by Spanish Christians regarding the worth of manual labor and intellectual activities.

Both Castro's theory of history and his methodology depend upon factors that he understands to have a historifiable (historiable) dimension. Castro continually redefined historiable, a necessity as the term has no objectifiable reality. But in one of his more succinct definitions he defines it as the processes by which systems of values are created. This is the concept at its most intelligible level, and Castro's analysis of the process of value creation in medieval Castile is the most significant aspect of his work. The central role that accords to collective self-awareness of nationhood is the major reflection of Wilhelm Dilthey's influence on Castro, and themes of history such as self-knowledge (Selbstbesinnung) and experiential awareness (Erlebnis) recur throughout his work. Yet he also admits the action of unconscious processes, such as unconscious imitation by Christians of Muslim or Jewish customs, practices, or habits of thought.

Castro's affirmation of the normativity of the Islamic society and culture of Al-Andalus met with entrenched resistance from Spanish historians long accustomed to essentialist criteria. That is why he was so insistent on rejecting culturally contradictory terms like "Hispano-Arabs" (in cultural terms, one could not be a Spaniard and an Arab at the same time) and why he could not accept the legitimacy of the term Reconquest, because it wrongly implied that the persons who regained Spain were culturally and socially the same as those who had lost it in 711.

In order to explicate his theory Castro, who had no acquaintance at all with modern social science, coined words to convey concepts that are perfectly well understood in contemporary cultural anthropology. Thus instead of culture (in the anthropological sense) he uses the term morada vital, which he himself rendered in English as "the dwelling place of life." The notion of experience – the conscious level of the largely unconscious processes contributing to the formation of culture – he rendered as vividura ("functional context") or vivencia ("conscious experience"). These terms have tended to obfuscate the simple concepts they were meant to describe. Moreover, believing that

he required some theoretical base, he attached himself to the idealism of Dilthey which further obscured the nature of the culture contact that he was attempting to describe. Finally, just like his mentor Menéndez Pidal, he was a neo-Lamarckian (although without perhaps knowing it), a perspective that reveals itself both in the rhetoric of the "ascent" of a particular society, but also in the notion of a kind of internal drive that is powering the ascent.

These nuances of his work conspire to make it difficult to perceive the solid ground on which his concepts are based. First, his notion of how medieval Spanish culture crystallized in the crucible of acculturative pressures emanating from Islamic and, to a lesser degree, Jewish culture is amply corroborated by hundreds of studies of cultural contact and acculturation. Second, his insistence on the conscious element of cultural crystallization, which seemingly runs counter to the general anthropological emphasis on unconscious processes, conforms well with some contemporary views of cultural change. Like Anthony Giddens, for example, Castro is insistent on the recursive, constant, and slow-paced nature of cultural change, which is dependent on the accretion of lived experience. Thus Castro states that the "dwelling place [culture] is built in the process of transcending daily routine."

Castro initiated a rage for searching Spanish history and literature for evidence of Jewish and Muslim cultural survivals. His own contribution included the Christian appropriation of Islamic holy war (jihad), the pilgrimage to Santiago de Compostela as a substitute for that to Mecca, and his masterful reading of the Archpriest of Hita's Libro de Buen Amor for its Muslim references. More controversial is his identification of "Jewish" traits among Spanish converso intellectual and religious elites of the 16th century (Fernando de Rojas and Fray Luis de León, for example). He even sought to establish the roots of the Inquisition in the exclusivism of medieval Judaism.

THOMAS F. GLICK

See also Basadre; Domínguez-Ortiz; Maravall; Menéndez Pidal; Sánchez-Albornoz; Spain: Islamic; Spain: to 1450; Spain: Modern

Biography

Born Rio de Janiero, 1885. Educated in Spain. Professor, University of Madrid, 1913–36: founded the university's Research Center for Humanist Studies. Spanish ambassador to Germany, 1931–32, but left Spain for the US after Franco's rise to power in 1936. Adviser to the Guggenheim Foundation, then taught at University of Wisconsin, 1937–39; University of Texas, 1939–40; and Princeton University, from 1940. Married Carmen Madinaveitia, 1911 (1 daughter, 1 son). Died Spain, 26 July 1972.

Principal Writings

España en su historia: cristianos, moros y judíos, 1948; in English as The Structure of Spanish History, 1954; revised as The Spaniards: An Introduction to Their History, 1971
La realidad histórica de España (The Realities of Spanish History), 1954, revised 1962
An Idea of History: Selected Essays of Américo Castro, 1977

Further Reading

Araya, Guillermo, Evolución del pensamiento histórico de Américo Castro (The Development of Américo Castro's Historical Thinking), Madrid: Taurus, 1969

Araya, Guillermo, *El pensamiento de Américo Castro: estructura intercastiza de la historia de España* (The Thinking of Américo Castro: The Rigid Structure of the History of Spain), Madrid: Alianza, 1983

Cuenca Toribio, José Manuel, "Américo Castro: historiador" (Américo Castro, Historian), *Cuadernos Hispanoamericanos* 426 (1985), 51–56

Cuenca Toribio, José Manuel, "Exilio e historiografía: un binomio simbolico" (Exile and Historiography: A Symbolic Binomial), *Cuadernos hispanoamericanos* 473–74 (1989), 93–99

Glick, Thomas F., "Darwin y la filología española" (Darwin and Spanish Philology), *Boletín de la Institución Libre de Enseñanza*, 2nd epoch, 12 (1991)

Gómez-Martínez, José Luis, *Américo Castro y el origen de los españoles: historia de una polémica* (Américo Castro and the Origins of the Spanish: History of a Controversy), Madrid: Gredos, 1975

Hillgarth, J.N., "Spanish Historiography and Iberian Reality," *History and Theory* 24 (1985), 23–43

Hornik, Marcel, ed., *Collected Studies in Honor of Américo Castro's Eightieth Year*, Oxford: Lincombe Lodge Research Library, 1965 [includes bibliography]

Laín Entralgo, Pedro, ed., *Estudios sobre la obra de Américo Castro* (Studies on the Works of Américo Castro), Madrid: Taurus, 1971

Surtz, Ronald E., Jaime Ferran, and Daniel P. Testa, *Américo Castro, the Impact of His Thought: Essays to Mark the Centenary of his Birth*, Madison, WI: Hispanic Seminary of Medieval Studies, 1988

Catholicism/Catholic Church

The investigation and description of the temporal development of Christianity embrace not only narrowly institutional history but also the history of Christian theology, of Christian life and worship, and of the relationship of Christianity to culture and society. Historians of Christianity have traditionally distinguished three eras in its development. In the first, beginning with the *Acts of the Apostles* and extending through late antiquity, historians such as Eusebius, Augustine, and Orosius sought to locate the events of the Christian experience in a history of salvation, the story of God's interventions in history to bring redemption to fallen humanity. In the second, roughly contemporaneous with the western Middle Ages, this tradition continued to provide the framework for chronicles, but the dominant thrust of church history was the description of local jurisdictions and personages in the form of annals, *gesta*, and hagiography. The third period began with the Protestant Reformation and engendered the historiography of the Roman Catholic church as distinct from Christian historiography in general. The first great contribution to this historiographic tradition was a general history of the Christian church, *Historia ecclesiae Christi* (7 vols.; 1559–74), by Mathias Flacius Illyricus and other Lutheran theologians. This immense compendium of data, organized by centuries, attacked the popes and the institutions of the Roman church as fundamentally anti-Christian. It evoked a powerful and scholarly refutation, *Annales ecclesiastici* (1588–1607), by Caesar Baronius, which aimed to demonstrate the substantial identity of the Roman Catholic church of the 17th century with the Christian church of the 1st century. With these works, the fundamental critical and apologetic standpoints were staked out, the "Roman Catholic" tradition was either distinguished from or identified with the totality of the Christian experience of the first fifteen centuries of the common era.

Not all of the controversy was between Protestants and Catholics. A great deal of it was internal. Pietro Pallavicini's *Storia del Concilio di Trento* (History of the Council of Trent, 1656–57) and the collections of conciliar documents that culminated in Mansi's *Nova et amplissima collectio* (The New and Most Complete Collection of the Sacred Councils, 1759–98) were a reaction to the critique of the Council of Trent by the Venetian friar Paolo Sarpi, whose disgust at the excesses of papal conduct and power had led him to portray the Council as a political struggle and to underestimate its religious and spiritual dimensions. Polemic purposes engendered Claude Fleury's *Histoire ecclésiastique* (Ecclesiastical History, 1698–1720), which argued the Gallican position, and Bonaventure Racine's *Abrégé de l'histoire ecclésiastique* (Epitome of Ecclesiastical History, 1762–67), which advanced the cause of Jansenism. Controversy was also a powerful stimulus to the development of historical methodology. The Bollandist development of a scientific hagiography, a work that still continues, was stimulated in part by the Protestant rejection of the cult of the saints. The work of the Benedictines of St. Maur in collecting and editing manuscripts led to Mabillon's development of a science of diplomatics, as well as other advances in textual criticism.

The advent of Romanticism and nationalism stimulated change and growth no less in Roman Catholic church history than in other historiographical demesnes, fostering a fresh appreciation of the positive elements of medieval civilization and creating a new spirit of critical scholarship as well as a new interest in historical sources. The publication of abbé Jacques-Paul Migne's monumental series *Patrologia Latina* (Latin Patrology, 1844–80) and *Patrologia Graeca* (Greek Patrology, 1857–66), as well as the opening of the Vatican archives to scholars in 1883, were fruits of this interest. Johann Adam Möhler strove in *Symbolik* (1832; *Symbolism*, 1997) to clarify the differences between Catholicism and other forms of Christianity and put the study of Catholic church history on a thoroughly scientific foundation. Unfortunately, he also led Catholic historiography back from the moderating influences of the Enlightenment to bitter and triumphalist polemic. His lectures, posthumously published as *Kirchengeschichte* (Church History, 1867–68), and his founding of a school of ecclesiastical history at Tübingen, encouraged a generation and more of historians, the most important of whom was Karl Josef Hefele, whose *Conciliengeschichte* (1855–74; *A History of the Christian Councils*, 1872–96), continued by others, is still a vital resource for understanding the councils of the church. His contemporary, Johann Ignaz von Döllinger, founded at Munich another powerful school of ecclesiastical history, whose influence was felt in the historical works of Charles de Montalembert, most notably *Les Moines d'Occident depuis saint Benôit jusqu'à saint Bernard* (1860–77; *The Monks of the West from Saint Benedict to Saint Bernard*, 1861–79) and *Pie IX et la France en 1849 et en 1859* (1860; *Pius IX and France in 1849 and 1859*, 1861), and in the essays of his pupil, Lord Acton, the founding editor of *The Cambridge Modern History*.

Döllinger's career also called attention to the dangers awaiting church historians. A priest as well as a professor, Döllinger was also his university's representative to the Bavarian Landtag, and leader of the Catholic Right in the Frankfurt National Assembly of 1848–49. From a position favoring papal claims, his studies in the history of the early church led him strongly to oppose Pius IX's increasingly monarchical tendencies and to reject the proclamation of papal infallibility in 1870. Excommunicated, he spent the last two decades of his life supporting the Old Catholic church formed by opponents of the infallibility dogma, a work in which he was joined by the historian of canon law, Johann von Schulte. In the next generation, Louis Duchesne fell victim to the papacy's efforts to root out an ill-defined heresy referred to as Modernism. Although Duchesne's ecclesiastical career did not suffer, his brilliant *Histoire ancienne de l'église* (1905–22; *Early History of the Christian Church*, 1909–24), which was seen as downplaying the divine origins of the church and overemphasizing the sociopolitical origins of its institutions, was placed on the Index of Forbidden Books, where it remained until the Index was abolished after the Second Vatican Council. More recently, Hans Küng, a theologian at the University of Tübingen, had his license to teach theology revoked by Vatican authorities for his questioning of the historical basis of church doctrines in such works as *Rechtfertigung* (1957; *Justification*,1964), *Die Kirche* (1967; *The Church*, 1971), and *Unfehlbar: eine Anfrage* (1970; *Infallible?*, 1971).

The climate within the Roman Catholic bureaucracy between the two Vatican councils thus favored safe and ultramontane viewpoints. The great works of church history written in this period, such as Ludwig Pastor's *Geschichte der Päpste* (1886–1933; *The History of the Popes*, 1891–1953), and Augustin Fliche and Victor Martin's *Histoire de l'église catholique* (History of the Catholic Church, 1934–63), are therefore exemplary in scholarship without venturing onto dangerous ground. Indeed, in an age of growing ecumenism, some of the most penetrating studies of the Catholic church in general and the papacy in particular were the work of nonCatholics, as in the case of Kenneth Scott Latourette's treatment of Catholicism in *A History of the Expansion of Christianity* (1937–45) and Erich Caspar's *Geschichte des Papsttums* (1935). As the 20th century drew to a close, Roman Catholic historiography was grappling with the implications of the views of the church enunciated in the Second Vatican Council and with the new emphases contributed to the writing of history by quantitative methods, social history, cultural studies, and systems thinking. Increasingly, the linkages of Catholicism with other religions and thought systems were being explored, along with the impact of economic and social change upon the church polity. Vigorous investigation and debate focused on every era of Christian experience and every part of the world. One major historiographical problem stood out as a challenge to Catholic historians: the exploration and clarification of the behavior of Pope Pius XII and the Vatican bureaucracy with regard to the Nazi persecution of the Jews, of which the publication of archival documents in *Actes et documents du Saint Siège relatifs à la seconde guerre mondiale* (Acts and Documents of the Holy See Regarding World War II, 1965–81) was only the first step.

JOSEPH M. MCCARTHY

See also Acton; Bolland, Cantimori; Chadwick; Eusebius; Mansi; Momigliano; Sarpi

Further Reading

Actes et documents du Saint Siège relatifs à la second guerre mondiale (Acts and Documents of the Holy See Regarding World War II), 11 vols., Vatican City: Libreria Editrice Vaticana, 1965–81

Acton, Lord, *Essays on Church and State*, edited by Douglas Woodruff, London: Hollis and Carter, 1952; New York: Crowell, 1968

Antón, Angel, *El misterio de la Iglesia: evolución histórica de las ideas eclesiológicas* (The Mystery of the Church: Historical Evolution of Ecclesiological Ideas), 2 vols., Madrid: Autores Cristianos, 1986–87

Augustine, St., *De civitate dei*, written 413–26; in English as *The City of God*

Baronius, Caesar, *Annales ecclesiastici* (Ecclesiastical Annals), 12 vols., Rome, 1588–1607

Bauman, Michael, and Martin Klauberer, eds., *Historians of the Christian Tradition: Their Methodologies and Impact on Western Thought*, Nashville: Broadman and Holman, 1995

Bellenger, D.A., ed., *Opening the Scrolls: Essays in Catholic History in Honour of Godfrey Anstruther*, Bath: Downside Abbey, 1987

Bischof, Franz Xaver, *Theologie und Geschichte: Ignaz von Döllinger (1799–1890), in der zweiten Hälfte seines Lebens* (Theology and History: Ignaz von Döllinger in the Second Half of His Life), Stuttgart: Kohlhammer, 1997

Blet, Pierre, *Pie XII et la Seconde Guerre mondiale d'après les archives du Vatican* (Pius XII and the Second World War According to the Vatican Archives), Paris: Perrin, 1997

Blockx, Karel, *A Bibliographical Introduction to Church History*, Leuven: Acco, 1982

Bradley, James E., and Richard A. Muller, *Church History: An Introduction to Research, Reference Works, and Method*, Grand Rapids, MI: Eerdmans, 1995

Caspar, Erich, *Geschichte des Papsttums* (History of the Papacy), 2 vols., Tübingen: Mohr, 1935

Chadwick, Owen, *Catholicism and History: The Opening of the Vatican Archives*, Cambridge and New York: Cambridge University Press, 1978

Döllinger, Johann Ignaz von, *Der Papst und das Concil* (The Pope and the Council), Frankfurt: Minerva, 1968

Döllinger, Johann Ignaz von, *Hippolytus und Kallistus; oder, Die Römische Kirche in der ersten Hälfte des 3. Jahrhunderts* (Hippolytus and Calixtus; or, The Roman Church in the First Half of the Third Century), Aalen: Scientia, 1977

Duchesne, Louis, *Histoire ancienne de l'église*, 4 vols., Paris: Fontemoing, 1905–22; in English as *Early History of the Christian Church, from Its Foundation to the End of the Fifth Century*, 3 vols., London: Murray, 1909–24, New York: Longman, 1912–24; reprinted 1957

Eusebius of Caesarea, *Historia ecclesiastica*, written 311–25; in English as *The Ecclesiastical History* and *The History of the Church from Christ to Constantine*

Fleury, Claude, *Histoire ecclésiastique* (Ecclesiastical History), 13 vols., Paris: Mariette, 1698–1720

Fliche, Augustin, and Victor Martin, eds., *Histoire de l'Eglise* (History of the Church), 21 vols. and supplements, Paris: Bloud & Gay, 1934–63

Gooch, G.P., *History and Historians in the Nineteenth Century*, London and New York: Longman, 1913; revised 1952

Guilday, Peter, *Church Historians*, New York: Kenedy, 1926

Hefele, Karl Josef von, *Conciliengeschichte*, 7 vols., Freiburg: Herder, 1855–74; in English as *A History of the Christian Councils: From the Original Documents*, 5 vols., Edinburgh: Clark, 1872–96; reprinted New York: AMS Press, 1972

Illyricus, Mathias Flacius, *Historia ecclesiae Christi* (History of the Christian Church), 7 vols., Basel: Oporini, 1559–74

Jedin, Hubert, "General Introduction to Church History," in Hubert Jedin and John Dolan, eds., *History of the Church*, 10 vols., London: Burns and Oates, and New York: Seabury Press, 1965–81, vol. 1, 1–56

Jedin, Hubert, "Ecclesiastical Historiography," *New Catholic Encyclopedia*, 18 vols., New York: McGraw Hill, 1967–89, vol. 7, 5–13

Kaufmann, Franz Xavier, and Arnold Zingerle, eds., *Vatikanum II und Modernisierung: historische, theologische und soziologische Perspektiven* (Vatican II and Modernization: Historical, Theological, and Sociological Perspectives), Paderborn: Schoningh, 1996

Kirsch, J.P., "Ecclesiastical History," *The Catholic Encyclopedia*, 15 vols., New York: Appleton, 1907–12, vol. 7, 365–80

Küng, Hans, *Rechtfertigung: die Lehre Karl Barths und eine katholische Besinnung*, Einsiedeln: Johannes, 1957; in English as *Justification: The Doctrine of Karl Barth and a Catholic Reflection*, New York: Nelson, 1964, London: Burns and Oates, 1965

Küng, Hans, *Die Kirche*, Freiburg: Herder, 1967; in English as *The Church*, London: Burns and Oates, and New York: Sheed and Ward, 1971

Küng, Hans, *Unfehlbar: eine Anfrage*, Zurich: Bensinger, 1970; in English as *Infallible? An Inquiry*, Garden City, NY: Doubleday, and London: Collins, 1971; expanded as *Infallible? An Unresolved Inquiry*, New York: Continuum, 1994

Latourette, Kenneth Scott, *A History of the Expansion of Christianity*, 7 vols., New York: Harper, 1937–45; reprinted 1970

Lautenschläger, Gabriele, *Joseph Lortz, 1887-1975: Weg, Umwelt und Werk eines katholischen Kirchenhistorikers* (Joseph Lortz: Method, Milieu, and Work of a Catholic Church Historian), Würzburg: Echter, 1987

Mabillon, Jean, *De re diplomatica* (The Science of Diplomatic), Paris: Billaine, 1681

Mansi, Giovanni Domenico, *Sacrorum conciliorum nova et amplissima collectio* (The New and Most Complete Collection of the Sacred Councils), 31 vols., 1759–98 [reprinted and continued by L. Petit and J.B. Martin, 53 vols., Paris: 1901–27]

Migne, J.-P., ed., *Patrologiae cursus completus*, series Graeca (or *Patrologia Graeca*; Greek Patrology), 161 vols., Paris, 1857–66

Migne, J.-P., ed., *Patrologiae cursus completus*, series Latina (or *Patrologia Latina*; Latin Patrology), 221 vols., Paris, 1844–80

Möhler, Johann Adam, *Symbolik*, Mainz, 1832; in English as *Symbolism*, New York: Crossroad, 1997

Möhler, Johann Adam, *Kirchengeschichte* (Church History), 3 vols., Regensburg: Manz, 1867–68

Momigliano, Arnaldo, *The Classical Foundations of Modern Historiography*, Berkeley: University of California Press, 1990

Monseigneur Duchesne et son temps (Monsignor Duchesne and His Times), Rome: Ecole Française de Rome, 1975

Montalembert, Charles de, *Les Moines d'Occident depuis saint Benôit jusqu'à saint Bernard*, 7 vols., 1860–77; in English as *The Monks of the West from Saint Benedict to Saint Bernard*, 7 vols., Edinburgh, Blackwood, 1861–79; in 2 vols., New York: Kenedy, 1905; reprinted in 6 vols., New York: AMS Press, 1966

Montalembert, Charles de, *Pie IX et la France en 1849 et en 1859*, 2nd edition, Paris: Douniol, 1860; in English as *Pius IX and France in 1849 and 1859*, Boston: Donahoe, 1861

Morghen, Raffaello, *Tradizione religiosa nella civiltà dell'Occidente cristiano: saggi di storia e di storiografia* (Religious Tradition in Western Christian Civilization: Essays in History and Historiography), Rome: Istituto Storico Italiano per il Medio Evo, 1979

Nigg, Walter, *Die Kirchengeschichtsschreibung* (Ecclesiastical Historiography), Munich: Beck, 1934

Orosius, Paulus, *Historiae adversum paganos*, written from 417; in English as *The Seven Books of History against the Pagans*, Washington, DC: Catholic University Press, 1964

Overath, Joseph, *Kirchengeschichte: Orientierungshilfen, Standpunkte, Impulse für heute* (Church History: Orientation, Viewpoints, Impetus for the Present), Frankfurt: Lang, 1987

Pallavicini, Pietro, *Storia del Concilio di Trento* (History of the Council of Trento), 2 vols., Rome, 1656–57

Pastor, Ludwig, *Geschichte der Päpste*, 16 vols., Freiburg: Herder, 1886–1933; in English as *The History of the Popes: From the Close of the Middle Ages*, 40 vols., London: Hodges, 1891–1953, St. Louis: Herder, 1936–61; reprinted Nendeln, Liechtenstein: Kraus, 1968–69

Racine, Bonaventure, *Abrégé de l'histoire ecclésiastique* (Epitome of Ecclesiastical History), 13 vols., Paris, 1762–67

Sarpi, Paolo, *Istoria del Concilio Tridentino*, 1619; in English as *History of the Council of Trent*, 1620

Schatz, Klaus, *Allgemeine Konzilien: Brennpunkte der Kirchengeschichte* (General Councils: Flashpoints of Church History), Paderborn: Schoningh, 1996

Schulte, Johann von, *Die Geschichte der Quellen und Literatur des kanonisches Rechts* (History of the Sources and Literature of Canon Law), 3 vols., Stuttgart: Enke, 1875–80

Seeliger, Hans R., *Kirchengeschichte, Geschichtstheologie, Geschichtswissenschaft* (Church History, History of Theology, Historical Science), Düsseldorf: Patmos, 1981

Vollmar, E.R., "Catholic Historical Scholarship in the US," *New Catholic Encyclopedia*, 18 vols., New York: McGraw Hill, 1967–89, vol. 7, 3–5

Wagner, Harold, *Johann Adam Mühler (1796-1838), Kirchenvater der Moderne* (Johann Adam Mühler, Modern Father of the Church), Paderborn: Bonifatius, 1996

Central America

Coming to terms with the historical literature on Central America presents a significant challenge. While the region possesses a certain conceptual and analytical unity, it is also composed of five distinct political, social, and economic entities whose collective experiences are not readily condensed into consistent generalizations. Nevertheless, the experiences of Guatemala, Nicaragua, Honduras, El Salvador, and Costa Rica, while unique, are related to each other and cannot be adequately comprehended without understanding the historical experience of the region as a whole. The historical writing on Central America consists of a mixture of works that attempt to synthesize the history of the region and a much more numerous collection of works that focus on the history of individual countries. Regardless of the scope of the writing, the best work on Central America consistently points to the diverse ethnic character of these countries and attempts to elucidate the manner in which the various cultural groups have affected the course of the historical experience.

The historical literature of Central America covers four major periods: pre-Columbian, colonial, national, and 20th-century. The literature on the pre-Columbian period, generally written by anthropologists or archaeologists, constitutes a field unto itself. Studies on the Maya, in particular, are numerous and examine the full range of pre-Columbian experience. Probably the basic resource for this period is the multivolume and frequently updated *Handbook of Middle American Indians* (1964–76) edited by Robert Wauchope. A good source for the non-Mayan regions is Doris Stone's *Pre-Columbian Man Finds Central America* (1972). Surveys on the Maya include: Norman Hammond's *Ancient Maya Civilization* (1982) and J.S. Henderson's *The World of the Ancient Maya* (1981). Also provocative is the discussion of the collapse of the lowland Maya civilization in *The Classic Maya Collapse* (1973) edited by Patrick Culbert.

While descriptions of Central America by Spaniards during the colonial period are not as numerous as those written about Mexico or Peru, the region figures prominently in some of the more notable colonial writings. Gonzalo Fernández de Oviedo y Valdés provided a vivid (if partisan) account of the conquest of the Isthmus in his classic *Historia general y natural de las Indias* (General and Natural History of the Indies, 1519). Bartolomé de Las Casas told his side of the story in *Brevísima relación de la destrucción de las Indias* (1552; *The Tears of the Indians*, 1656). Details from Central America also figured in Toribio de Motolinia's *Memoriales e historia de los indios de la Nueva España* (Memorials and History of the Indians in New Spain, c.1560). A notable synthesis of the history of the region is *Historia general de las Indias occidentales, y particular de la gobernacion de Chiapa y Guatemala* (A General History of the West Indies, in Particular the Governing of Chiapa and Guatemala, 1619) written by Antonio de Remesal.

Although the historiography of Central America has tended to follow trends pioneered for other regions, several path-breaking works on the region's colonial period have been written. H.H. Bancroft's *History of Central America* (1886–87) is a classic that remains useful despite its overt articulation of the late 19th-century progressive view of history. More recent studies reflecting the development of sophisticated social and economic models of interpretation are Murdo MacLeod's *Spanish Central America* (1973) and William L. Sherman's *Forced Native Labor in Sixteenth-Century Central America* (1979). Nancy Farriss' study of the Maya during the colonial period, *Maya Society under Colonial Rule* (1984) integrated anthropology and history in an incisive study of the impact of colonial rule on the indigenous people of the region. Another work that successfully assessed the relationship between Spaniard and Indian in the colonial world is Inga Clendinnen's *Ambivalent Conquests* (1987). Clendinnen examined the ideological stance underlying the Spanish conquest of the Yucatan (from both a military and religious point of view) and then used the same documentation to examine the character of the Indian response. This book is one of the best attempts to elucidate the psycho-social character of the conquest, and should be required reading for students of any region of colonial Latin America.

Tracking the history of Central America during the 19th century becomes much more complex, as the countries of the region began to follow their own individual courses and to acquire unique identities. Moreover the history of the 19th century has not received as much attention as either the colonial period or the 20th century. It has also been skewed by studies emphasizing the importance of the liberal governments while neglecting the impact of the conservative regimes. Typical of this latter type of liberal history is the *Reseña histórica de Centro América* (Historical Overview of Central America, 1878–87) by Lorenzo Montúfar. This work influenced Bancroft's treatment of the 19th-century republics and so has had a significant impact in both Spanish and English. In English probably the best work dealing with the history of the entire region is Ralph Lee Woodward Jr.'s *Central America* (2nd edition 1985). Woodward emphasized the characteristics that unify the region while detailing the numerous local forces that have prevented an effective regional entity from emerging. He also provided an excellent introduction to the literature of

the region and an extensive topical bibliography completed the work. *Central America* is probably the single best starting point in English for an introduction to the history of this complex area.

While the 19th century witnessed the formation of the five separate republics, it also produced the first encounters with the imperialistic aspirations of the United States. By mid-century the tension between the growth of national sovereignties and a dependence on the economic, political, and technological power of North America had become one of the fixed themes of the region's experience. The experience of the foreign adventurers known as "filibusters," especially that of William Walker, became a preoccupation of the literature. Still of value on this theme is W.O. Scroggs, *Filibusters and Financiers* (1916). On a related theme, the attempts to build a transportation route across the isthmus figure prominently and confront the issue of dependence and sovereignty. A good overview of these efforts is Thomas Schoonover's "Imperialism in Middle America: United States, Britain, Germany, and France Compete for Transit Rights and Trade, 1820s–1920s," (1983). On the building of the canal in Panama, David McCullough's *A Path Between the Seas* (1977) is probably the best overview, while Michael Conniff's *Black Labor on a White Canal* (1985) explored the labor patterns and racial attitudes that conditioned the construction process.

The issue of foreign domination and foreign intervention has continued to provide a focus for studies of the events of the 20th century. Closely related to these themes are works that examine the revolutionary movements that have figured so prominently since World War II. One of the most controversial episodes (from a North American point of view) is the "revolutionary" movement started by Jacobo Arbenz in Guatemala and his subsequent overthrow and assassination. The two classic works on this event are Richard Immerman's *The CIA in Guatemala* (1982) and Stephen Schlesinger and Stephen Kinser's *Bitter Fruit* (1982). On the Sandinista revolution in Nicaragua, the best two works are J.A. Booth's *The End and the Beginning* (1982) and David Nolan's *The Ideology of the Sandinistas and the Nicaraguan Revolution* (1984). For the crisis in El Salvador consult *El Salvador in Transition* (1982) by Enrique Baloyra and *Revolution in El Salvador* (1982) by Tommie Sue Montgomery. Also useful in interpreting the roots of the conflict is *Matanza* (1971), Thomas P. Anderson's account of the popular uprising in the early 1930s and its brutal repression.

The interpretation of the history of Central America remains a very fluid and ill-defined field. It is probably safe to say that the predominance of local identities and the persistence of sharp class and ethnic divisions militates against efforts to produce a satisfactory regional synthesis. The process by which local and topical studies are incorporated into a broader synthesis – a difficult enterprise at best – is made even more difficult by the lack of a clear regional identity to give impetus to such a project. Unless and until Central America coalesces into some sort of viable unity it is likely that its history will continue to be written from a local point of view, making it a fruitful area for insightful topical studies, but a daunting challenge to the generalist seeking to establish broad interpretations.

LINCOLN A. DRAPER

See also America: Pre-Columbian; Bancroft; Las Casas

Further Reading

Anderson, Thomas P., *Matanza: El Salvador's Communist Revolt of 1932*, Lincoln: University of Nebraska Press, 1971

Baloyra, Enrique, *El Salvador in Transition*, Chapel Hill: University of North Carolina Press, 1982

Bancroft, H.H., *History of Central America*, 3 vols., San Francisco: Bancroft, 1886–87

Booth, John A., *The End and the Beginning: The Nicaraguan Revolution*, Boulder, CO: Westview Press, 1982; revised 1985

Clendinnen, Inga, *Ambivalent Conquests: Maya and Spaniard in Yucatan, 1517–1570*, Cambridge and New York: Cambridge University Press, 1987

Conniff, Michael, *Black Labor on a White Canal: Panama, 1904–1985*, Pittsburgh: University of Pittsburgh Press, 1985

Culbert, Patrick, ed., *The Classic Maya Collapse*, Albuquerque: University of New Mexico Press, 1973

Farriss, Nancy M., *Maya Society under Colonial Rule: The Collective Enterprise of Survival*, Princeton: Princeton University Press, 1984

Fernández de Oviedo y Valdés, Gonzalo, *Historia general y natural de las Indias* (General and Natural History of the Indies), 1519; reprinted in 5 vols., Madrid: Atlas, 1959

Hammond, Norman, *Ancient Maya Civilization*, New Brunswick, NJ: Rutgers University Press, 1982

Henderson, John S., *The World of the Ancient Maya*, Ithaca, NY: Cornell University Press, 1981

Immerman, Richard H., *The CIA in Guatemala: The Foreign Policy of Intervention*, Austin: University of Texas Press, 1982

Las Casas, Bartolomé de, *Brevísima relación de la destrucción de las Indias*, 1552; in English as *The Tears of the Indians*, 1656, and *The Devastation of the Indies: A Brief Account*, New York: Seabury Press 1974

McCullough, David, *A Path Between the Seas: The Creation of the Panama Canal, 1870–1914*, New York: Simon and Schuster, 1977

MacLeod, Murdo J., *Spanish Central America: A Socioeconomic History, 1520–1720*, Berkeley: University of California Press, 1973

Montgomery, Tommie Sue, *Revolution in El Salvador: Origins and Evolution*, Boulder, CO: Westview Press, 1982

Montúfar, Lorenzo, *Reseña histórica de Centro América* (Historical Overview of Central America), 7 vols., Guatemala City: El Progreso, 1878–87

Motolinía, Toribio, *Memoriales e historia de los indios de la Nueva España* (Testimonials and History of the Indians of New Spain), reprinted Madrid: Atlas, 1970

Nolan, David, *The Ideology of the Sandinistas and the Nicaraguan Revolution*, Coral Gables, FL: University of Miami Press, 1984

Remesal, Antonio de, *Historia general de las Indias occidentales, y particular de la gobernacion de Chiapa y Guatemala* (General History of the West Indies, in Particular the Governing of Chiapa and Guatemala), 1619; reprinted in 2 vols., Madrid: Atlas, 1964–66

Schlesinger, Stephen, and Stephen Kinser, *Bitter Fruit: The Untold Story of the American Coup in Guatemala*, Garden City: Doubleday, 1982

Schoonover, Thomas, "Imperialism in Middle America: United States, Britain, Germany, and France Compete for Transit Rights and Trade, 1820s–1920s," in Rodri Jeffreys-Jones, ed., *Eagle Against Empire: American Opposition to European Imperialism, 1914–1982*, Aix-en-Provence: EEAS, 1983

Scroggs, William O., *Filibusters and Financiers: The Story of William Walker and His Associates*, New York: Macmillan, 1916

Sherman, William L. *Forced Native Labor in Sixteenth-Century Central America*, Lincoln: University of Nebraska Press, 1979

Stone, Doris, *Pre-Columbian Man Finds Central America*, Cambridge, MA: Peabody Museum Press, 1972

Wauchope, Robert *et al.*, eds., *Handbook of Middle American Indians*, 16 vols., Austin: University of Texas Press, 1964–76, with later supplements

Woodward, Ralph Lee, Jr., *Central America: A Nation Divided*, New York: Oxford University Press, 1976, 2nd edition 1985

Central Asia: since 1850

Comprising the modern-day countries of Kazakhstan, Kyrgyzstan, Uzbekistan, Turkmenistan, and Tajikistan, Central Asia is a region that has never been a single political unit. From the middle of the 19th century most of the territory was located within the tsarist Russian empire; subsequently, in the 20th century, it was incorporated into the Soviet Union. As a result, the Russian factor has played a significant role in shaping Central Asian history. Studies of the 19th century have focused on the motivations and effects of Russian conquest and administration on the region's political development. Soviet historians, applying Lenin's ideas of imperialism as a stage of capitalism, have emphasized economic concerns as the driving force behind Russian conquest. The work of N.A. Khalfin is typical of this interpretation. In *Russia's Policy in Central Asia* (1960; translated 1964) Khalfin argued that, as Russia entered the phase of capitalist development, Russian capitalists influenced government officials to pursue an expansionist policy in Central Asia in order to secure raw cotton supplies for Russian textile industrialists and to acquire a protected market for Russian light industry. Western scholars, while acknowledging that economic considerations did exist, have tended to emphasize the quest for frontier security and strategic competition with Britain as the dominant element in tsarist expansion. In *Russia's Protectorates in Central Asia* (1968) Seymour Becker rejected Khalfin's interpretation in favor of an explanation that stressed Russian desire to preserve law and order on the frontier. Becker stressed the role of local military commanders in advancing into Turkestan without authorization from their superiors in St. Petersburg. A similar view was held by Richard A. Pierce in *Russian Central Asia, 1867–1917* (1960). More recently, David MacKenzie elaborated on the role of military leaders in his article "The Conquest and Administration of Turkestan, 1860–85" (1988) by showing the strategic importance that Russian leaders placed on the region and their desire to gain imperial prestige by filling the power vacuum on the border.

The impact of colonial rule was the subject of Edward Dennis Sokol's study *The Revolt of 1916 in Russian Central Asia* (1954), in which he suggested that tsarist administrative policy had been a complete failure. Sokol concluded that Russia "effected no significant influence intellectually or culturally upon Asia," and that the material conditions for most of the local population under Russian rule had become worse. A less pessimistic assessment was offered by Becker in "Russia's Central Asian Empire, 1885–1917," (1988) where he pointed to urban growth and the integration of Central Asia into the Russian economy as beneficial for the region in the long run, even though Russian rule disrupted the traditional local economy.

Social and cultural developments have also received attention since the mid-1960s in studies that have bridged the tsarist and Soviet eras. Edward Allworth dealt with intellectual trends among Central Asian writers in "The Changing Intellectual and Literary Community," a chapter in his collection *Central Asia: A Century of Russian Rule* (1967). Identity formation has been the center of attention in the work of Hélène Carrère d'Encausse. Her book *Islam and the Russian Empire* (1981; translated 1988) examined the Muslim reaction to Russian rule, and emphasized the nationalist and reformist elements in Turkestan and Bukhara and by placing the Islamic reformist movement in Bukhara into a broader context of Muslim intellectual responses to the arrival of European conquest generally. Elizabeth E. Bacon offered an anthropological approach to Central Asian history in her work, *Central Asians under Russian Rule* (1966). Writing in the 1960s, Bacon noted that religious practices and old patterns of social organization continued to persist among Central Asian peoples even despite official Soviet efforts to transform them. Nevertheless, she did observe a new sense of growing national identity.

Studies of Central Asia in the Soviet era (1917–91) have primarily looked at Soviet nationalities policies and the topic of nationalism in Central Asia. Historians writing in the late 1950s and 1960s were largely informed by notions of modernization and development. Alexander G. Park's *Bolshevism in Turkestan, 1917–1927* (1957) treated the aims, methods, and achievements of Soviet policy. Park saw Soviet policy as a reversal of tsarist policy, which had treated Central Asia as a mere supplier of raw materials and food. He presented Soviet nationality policies as essentially economic, because they had as their main goal the equal distribution of industry throughout the Soviet Union, and he concluded that the failure of these policies arose from trying to develop all nations according to identical models. Geoffrey Wheeler credited Soviet policies with successfully modernizing the traditional way of life in *The Modern History of Soviet Central Asia* (1964). In particular, Wheeler argued that nomadism had disappeared, tribal loyalties were no longer dominant, education had become entirely secular, and Islamic law was no longer operative. Thus, in his view modernization had brought higher standards of living to the Central Asian peoples. A similar positive assessment for the Soviet modernization of Tajikistan can be found in Teresa Rakowska-Harmstone's *Russia and Nationalism in Central Asia* (1970).

The changes in the Soviet Union under Gorbachev and the subsequent collapse of the USSR in 1991 have opened up new research questions. Most strikingly, the emergence of newly independent Central Asian countries has called for a changing focus away from Central Asia as a whole and towards studies of the particular countries. Anticipating the end of Soviet rule in Central Asia, Michael Rywkin's *Moscow's Muslim Challenge* (1982) examined historical, cultural, demographic, and economic aspects of Soviet rule and looked to an imminent end to Moscow's control. An example of the new studies can be found in James Critchlow's *Nationalism in Uzbekistan* (1991), and Donald S. Carlisle's "Soviet Uzbekistan: State and Nation in Historical Perspective" (1994).

JONATHAN A. GRANT

Further Reading

Allworth, Edward, ed., *Central Asia: A Century of Russian Rule*, New York: Columbia University Press, 1967; revised as *Central Asia: 120 Years of Russian Rule*, Durham, NC: Duke University Press, 1989

Bacon, Elizabeth A., *Central Asians under Russian Rule: A Study in Culture Change*, Ithaca, NY: Cornell University Press, 1966

Becker, Seymour, *Russia's Protectorates in Central Asia: Bukhara and Khiva, 1865–1924*, Cambridge, MA: Harvard University Press, 1968

Becker, Seymour, "Russia's Central Asian Empire, 1885–1917," in Michael Rywkin, ed., *Russian Colonial Expansion to 1917*, London: Mansell, 1988

Carlisle, Donald S., "Soviet Uzbekistan: State and Nation in Historical Perspective," in Beatrice F. Manz, ed., *Central Asia in Historical Perspective*, Boulder, CO: Westview Press, 1994

Critchlow, James, *Nationalism in Uzbekistan: A Soviet Republic's Road to Sovereignty*, Boulder, CO: Westview Press, 1991

Encausse, Hélène Carrère d', *Réforme et révolution chez les musulmans de l'empire russe*, Paris: Presses de la Fondation Nationale des Sciences Politiques, 1981; in English as *Islam and the Russian Empire: Reform and Revolution in Central Asia*, Berkeley: University of California Press, and London: Tauris, 1988

Khalfin, Naftula Aronovich, *Politika Rossii v Srednei Azii, 1857–1868*, Moscow: Izd-vo vostochnoi lit-ry, 1960; abridged in English as *Russia's Policy in Central Asia*, London: Central Asian Research Centre, 1964

MacKenzie, David, "The Conquest and Administration of Turkestan, 1860–85," in Michael Rywkin, ed., *Russian Colonial Expansion to 1917*, London: Mansell, 1988

Park, Alexander G., *Bolshevism in Turkestan, 1917–1927*, New York: Columbia University Press, 1957

Pierce, Richard A., *Russian Central Asia, 1867–1917: A Study in Colonial Rule*, Berkeley: University of California Press, and Cambridge: Cambridge University Press, 1960

Rakowska-Harmstone, Teresa, *Russia and Nationalism in Central Asia: The Case of Tadzhikistan*, Baltimore: Johns Hopkins Press, 1970

Rywkin, Michael, *Moscow's Muslim Challenge: Soviet Central Asia* Armonk, NY: Sharpe, and London: Hurst, 1982; revised Sharpe, 1990

Sokol, Edward Dennis, *The Revolt of 1916 in Russian Central Asia*, Baltimore: Johns Hopkins Press, 1954

Wheeler, Geoffrey, *The Modern History of Soviet Central Asia*, New York: Praeger, and London: Weidenfeld and Nicolson, 1964

Central Europe

One of the most controversial geopolitical terms of modern history, Central Europe has often been defined in historical writing as a concept or political theme, rather than an indisputable fact of geography. Consequently, the historiography of what is sometimes termed the "imaginary region" tends to consist of polemical essays and period studies, while there have been no attempts to write a comparative history of the states in the heart of Europe.

Opinion is divided on whether Central Europe can be regarded as a separate entity, "the third historical region of the continent," or whether it should be seen as the mere borderland of Western or Eastern European civilization. In a ground-breaking work of Hungarian historiography, Jenő Szűcs argued that in the Middle Ages Central Europe belonged to the Eastern periphery of Western Europe, becoming the Western outpost of Eastern Europe in certain periods of modern history. Accordingly, in recent works the middle zone of Europe has frequently been likened to a ferry drifting between East and West.

The historical debate on the definition of Central Europe dates back to World War I. In 1915 Friedrich Naumann's

Mitteleuropa (published a year later in English as *Central Europe*) introduced the political concept of German domination in the middle zone of the continent and the strategy of expansion along the Berlin-Baghdad axis. As J.W. Headlam-Morley observed, the idea of *Mitteleuropa* at the end of the war attracted "far more attention in enemy and allied countries, and has been more freely discussed, than any official or ministerial pronouncements." Naumann's work was followed in Germany and Austria by numerous books and articles on "the region where Germans live either in solid mass or isolated national groups in the midst of other peoples." This German interpretation of Central Europe was immediately challenged both in the territory of the Habsburg monarchy and in Western Europe. In 1917, even such well-known advocates of German-Christian civilization as the Hungarian Gyula Szekfª found it impossible to use the term Central Europe without distancing themselves from Naumann's views. Opponents of German cultural and political influence in the heart of Europe, such as the Czech T.G. Masaryk (1850–1937) and historians of the British New Europe group, launched a campaign in London against a pan-German *Mitteleuropa*. Headlam-Morley, R.W. Seton-Watson, Lewis Namier, and a few other historians and Central European experts in British government service, sought to counterbalance German propaganda by championing the creation of a "zone of small nations." Their Central European scheme pointedly excluded Germany. Accordingly, after the war Seton-Watson, the first Masaryk chair of Central European history at London University, limited the geographical scope of his studies to the countries "East and South of Germany." Other British historians, such as E.H. Carr, followed the approach of the Foreign Office, simultaneously adopting a wider interpretation of Central Europe, which included Germany, the Balkans, and the Danubian lands as well as using a narrower definition which was limited to the former component parts of the Habsburg empire.

In the interwar years the idea of a Central European federation and the projects aiming for Customs Union became dominant themes in the historiography of the region. Western European historians of differing political persuasions and national sympathies, ranging from the pro-Czech R.W. Seton-Watson to the Hungarophile C.A. Macartney, argued for a Danubian, or Central European union between Germany and Russia. In 1940 in the United States, the scholarly *Journal of Central European Affairs* was founded to promote a united "New Central Europe."

After World War II scholarly interest in Central European ideas diminished. Although some native historians in Western exile continued to defend the distinctive cultural heritage of Central European states, in postwar historiography the political term Eastern Europe came to be used.

The late 1980s witnessed a resurgence in the Central European idea both in political and historical writing. It proved difficult, however, to draw the historical boundaries between Eastern and Central Europe without erecting a political wedge between them. Eric Hobsbawm went as far as to claim that the notion of Central Europe is inherently racist, reinvented to divide the countries of "Eastern Europe." This position was contested by Hungarian historians, who generally agreed that the descendant states of the former Austro-Hungarian monarchy constitute Central Europe.

Many efforts have been made to replace the inflammatory political term Central Europe with either a more exact or a more general geographical description of the region. American works tend to favor the term East Central Europe while some historians native to the region prefer the use of Central Eastern Europe. Several scholarly works refer to the area as Danubian Europe, or *Zwischeneuropa*, namely the lands between Germany and Russia. In any case, these more recent terms of historical geography have proved as controversial as the one they are intended to replace.

GÁBOR BÁTONYI

See also Carr, E.; Namier; Seton-Watson, H.; Seton-Watson, R; Szekfű

Further Reading

Borsody, Stephen, *The Tragedy of Central Europe: Nazi and Soviet Conquest and Aftermath*, New Haven: Yale Concilium on International and Area Studies, 1980

Campbell, Gregory F., *Confrontation in Central Europe: Weimar Germany and Czechoslovakia*, Chicago: University of Chicago Press, 1975

Dvornik, Francis, *The Making of Central and Eastern Europe*, London: Polish Research Centre, 1949; Gulf Breeze, FL: Academic International Press, 1974

Graubard, Stephen R., *Eastern Europe . . . Central Europe . . . Europe*, San Francisco: Westview Press, 1991

Gross, Feliks, *Crossroads of Two Continents: A Democratic Federation of East-Central Europe*, New York: Columbia University Press, 1945

Halecki, Oscar, *Borderlands of Western Civilization: A History of East Central Europe*, New York: Ronald Press, 1952

Hanák, Péter, "Central Europe: An Alternative to Disintegration," *New Hungarian Quarterly*, 33/127 (1992), 3–10

Havránek, Jan, "Central Europe, East-Central Europe and the Historians, 1940–1948," in Éva Somogyi, ed., *Verbürgerlichung in Mitteleuropa*, Budapest: MTA Történettudományi Intézet, 1991

Headlam-Morley, J.W., *Studies in Diplomatic History*, London: Methuen, and New York: King, 1930

Headlam-Morley, J.W., *A Memoir of the Paris Peace Conference, 1919*, edited by Agnes Headlam-Morley, London: Methuen, 1992

Meyer, Henry Cord, *Mitteleuropa in German Thought and Action, 1815–1945*, The Hague: Nijhoff, 1955

Naumann, Friedrich, *Mitteleuropa*, Berlin: Reimer, 1915; in English as *Central Europe*, London: King, 1916, New York: Knopf, 1917

Palmer, Alan W., *The Lands Between: A History of East-Central Europe since the Congress of Vienna*, London: Weidenfeld and Nicolson, and New York: Macmillan, 1970

Schöpflin, George, and Nancy Wood, eds., *In Search of Central Europe*, Cambridge: Polity Press, 1989

Seton-Watson, Hugh, "Is There an East-Central Europe" in Sylva Sinanian, István Deák, and Peter C. Ludz, eds., *Eastern Europe in the 1970s*, New York: Praeger, 1972

Seton-Watson, Hugh, *The "Sick Heart" of Modern Europe: The Problem of the Danubian Lands*, Seattle: University of Washington Press, 1975

Szűcs, Jenő, *Vázlat Európa három történeti régiójáról* (Outline of Three Historical Regions of Europe), Budapest: Magvetô, 1983

Chabod, Federico 1901–1960

Italian historian

Federico Chabod belonged to the generation of Italian scholars that came of age during the difficult interwar years. Their work, while perhaps not enjoying the international recognition of their Annales school contemporaries, nonetheless had a significant influence on modern Italian historiography. Chabod's reputation as a historian was not founded on methodological innovations, indeed in many ways he was a traditionalist whose Rankean historicism was informed by Benedetto Croce's ethical-political philosophy of history. Instead, his influence lies in expanding Italian historiography from its traditional insularity by inserting it into a broader, European context. Italian historiography prior to this period had often been characterized by provincialism and regionalism, a tendency that was particularly pronounced in the interwar years when fascist political ideology encouraged a patriotic focus on Italian historical topics. Chabod's fascination with issues of the cultural and political identity of nations would appear repeatedly throughout his career.

Chabod's first studies were on Machiavelli: he published several essays in the mid-1920s that were later revised and translated for the 1958 collection *Machiavelli and the Renaissance*. In these, by situating Machiavelli firmly within his 16th-century context, Chabod tried to liberate him from the politically presentist interpretations that flourished under fascism. While he is perhaps best known outside Italy for these early publications, Chabod's most important work came after he turned his attention to the two topics that would occupy the rest of his scholarly career, the Milanese state under Charles V, and Italy's post-unification foreign relations.

Chabod's study of Milan spanned a 25-year period in which he published several essays and books that culminated in his unfinished opus, *L'epoca di Carlo V* (The Epoch of Charles V) in the Treccani *Storia di Milano*, published posthumously in 1961. At the core of these books were issues that informed all of his work: the nature of Italy's position within a broader European context, the interplay between external and internal forces and events, and their impact on the course of Italian history. By focusing on the often conflictual relationship between the center and peripheral states, Chabod was able to show how the profound social, economic, and political transformation Milan experienced in the 16th century was intimately tied to Charles V's imperial program and the unfolding of events within the empire as a whole.

As part of his studies on Milan, Chabod also confronted the question of the modernity of Renaissance states, something that historians, since Burckhardt's evocation of the state as a work of art, have debated at great length. In contrast to the generally accepted chronology among contemporary historians which traced the birth of modernity to Italy's heroic golden days of the 12th and 13th centuries, Chabod dated it to the 15th and 16th centuries. As evidence of the nascent modernity of this era, he pointed to the beginnings of a modern bureaucratic structure and ethos in Charles V's empire. In Milan, a new hierarchy of administrators and functionaries whose loyalty was to the state apparatus, rather than the person of the ruler, came increasingly into conflict with the traditional, semi-feudal hierarchy of imperial officials whose relationship to the sovereign was based on personal ties of loyalty and devotion. These bureaucrats, as Chabod identified them, believed their positions derived not from the good favor of the sovereign, but rather from a sort of *rason d'office*, that is, from their increasingly important role in administering the burgeoning requirements of a vast, complex state. Chabod's musings on the modernity of the Renaissance state were most provocatively posited in a brief 1956 essay, "Y a-t-il un état de la Renaissance?" (Was There a Renaissance State?). This work significantly influenced the subsequent course of the debate on the Renaissance state among historians, who it must be said, have since presented a number of serious challenges to Chabod's fundamental assumptions and conclusions on the modernity of these administrative structures and officials, and the states that they served.

The other principal area of Chabod's research was post-unification Italy. In the mid-1930s he became involved in a team project to write a history of Italy's foreign relations from 1870 to 1914. Though interrupted by the war and his subsequent political involvements, in 1951 Chabod published what some consider his greatest work, *Storia della politica estera italiana dal 1870 al 1896* (*Italian Foreign Policy*, 1996). While nominally a history of Italian diplomacy, this book dealt with much more than just the negotiations, diplomats and treaties that were the focus of most traditional diplomatic histories. Chabod's objective was to write a new type of diplomatic history in which internal and external affairs were studied not in isolation, but as part of the larger historical whole. Thus, in his treatment of Italian foreign policy he focused on internal political, cultural, and socioeconomic conditions, and demonstrated how they informed the policies and course of Italian foreign relations. *Italian Foreign Policy* was much more than just a history of Italian diplomacy, it represented a comprehensive history of Italian society in the post-Risorgimento years. As in his work on Milan, at the core of Chabod's treatment was the belief that seemingly regional or national issues could not be understood in isolation, but only within their complete internal and external context. If in the intervening years certain of his historical conclusions have been challenged, the influence of Chabod's expansive approach to Italian history on subsequent generations of historians, particularly in Italy, cannot be denied.

ERIC R. DURSTELER

See also De Felice; Machiavelli; Italy: Renaissance; Procacci; Renaissance Historical Writing; Romeo; Sarpi

Biography

Born Val d'Aosta, Piedmont, 23 February 1901. Studied at the University of Turin with Gaetano Salvemini, 1924–25, then with Friedrich Meinecke in Berlin. Taught at University of Perugia, 1935–38; and University of Milan, 1938–46; professor, University of Rome, 1946–60. Director, Croce Institute, Naples. Editor, *Rivista storica italiana*. Married Jeanne Rohr, 1930. Died Rome, 14 July 1960.

Principal Writings

L'Italie contemporaine: conférences faites a l'Institut d'études politiques de l'Université de Paris, 1950; in English as *A History of Italian Fascism*, 1963

Storia della politica estera italiana dal 1870 al 1896, 1951; in English as *Italian Foreign Policy: The Statecraft of the Founders*, 1996

Machiavelli and the Renaissance, 1958

"Y a-t-il un état de la Renaissance?" (Was There a Renaissance State?) in *Actes de Colloque sur la Renaissance*, 1958, 57–78

L'epoca di Carlo V (The Epoch of Charles V), 1961
L'idea di nazione (The Idea of Nation), edited by Armando Saitta
 and Ernesto Sestan, 1961
Storia dell' idea d'Europa (History of the Idea of Europe), 1961
Storia di Milano (History of Milan), 1961
Opere (Works), 3 vols. in 5, 1964–85

Further Reading

Bertelli, Sergio, ed., *Per Federico Chabod (1901-1960): atti del
 seminario internazionale* (For Federico Chabod), 2 vols., Perugia:
 Università di Perugia, 1981
Sasso, Gennaro, *Il guardiano della storiografia: profilo di Federico
 Chabod e altri saggi* (The Guardian of History: Profile of
 Federico Chabod and Other Essays), Naples: Guida, 1985
Vigezzi, Brunello, ed., *Federico Chabod e la "nuova storiografia"
 italiana dal primo al secondo dopoguerra, 1919–1950* (Federico
 Chabod and the New Italian Historiography from the End of the
 First to the End of the Second World War), Milan: Jaca, 1984

Chadwick, Owen 1916–

British religious historian

Owen Chadwick has made a profound contribution to British
church history in the last few decades. He has produced books
on many subjects from early asceticism to the fate of the
churches in the Cold War.

Chadwick's style is attractive and the best of his writing has
considerable literary merit. He writes from within the Christian
tradition, but although he is a priest in the Church of England
he does not write clerical history. In his *Victorian Miniature*
(1960) Chadwick described the often strained relationship
between a liberal squire and an evangelical vicar in a Norfolk
village. Chadwick's sympathies were clearly with the socially
concerned landowner rather than the ardent Calvinist cleric.
It is a basic sympathy discernible in all his work.

Indeed, Chadwick wrote a number of short works that illuminate his general approach to historical study. His 1954 book
on the founding of Cuddesdon, an Anglican college for training
priests, is a good example. It is much more than a conventional account of one institution, and its real interest lies in
the fact that it was a plea for a tolerant, humane and scholarly approach to religious life. An informed tolerance and
moderation are the distinctive features of Chadwick's approach
to his subjects. This enables him to discuss complex issues with
clarity, but at times it lapses into blandness and a tendency to
underestimate the importance of conflict in human affairs.

Chadwick explored the possibility of using biography to
approach wider historical developments. His biographies offer
clear illustrations both of the strength and of the limitation of
his method. In 1983 Chadwick published a life of Hensley
Henson (a controversial Bishop of Durham in the interwar
years), and in 1990 a life of archbishop Michael Ramsey
appeared. Both volumes offered sympathetic and engaging
accounts of their subjects in the course of which Chadwick
described the changing role of Christianity in England, as it
moved from the center to somewhere near the margin of public
life. The writing was characteristically assured and urbane.
However, perhaps the urbanity of the author disguised the
significance of the conflicts in which his subjects had engaged.

Chadwick's portrait of Henson made him appear mellower
than he was and understated his capacity for self-destructive-
ness. Similarly, while Chadwick offered a powerful description
of Ramsey's attempt to fuse the life of the prayer with public
witness, important questions about Ramsey's leadership were
not analyzed.

Chadwick's first published work was on the early church. In
his writing on John Cassian and the Christian ascetics he discussed the process by which Christianity changed from being a
sectarian movement which stressed separation from the world
to being the dominant ideology of the Western world. The
growth of Christendom was crucial, and much of Chadwick's
later work was a description of how this idea came under
increasing pressure. His book on the general history of the
Reformation described the breakdown of the medieval order of
Europe, and the intellectual disturbance that accompanied it.
However, Chadwick focused chiefly on the fate of Christianity
in the post-Enlightenment world.

Two of his most important works were concerned with the
19th century. *The Secularization of the European Mind in
the Nineteenth Century* (1975) was the only book in which
Chadwick devoted extensive attention to non-Christian
thinkers. He sought to evaluate the criticisms of traditional religion offered by Marx and Engels, and to analyze the response
of the churches to Darwinism, sociology, and agnostic humanism. Chadwick remained optimistic about the intellectual credibility of Christianity in the light of these challenges.

The work for which Chadwick is probably best known is the
two volumes of *The Victorian Church* (1966–70). This was a
wide-ranging account of Christian experience in a time of social
and intellectual upheaval. Chadwick demonstrated how the
British churches sought to respond to industrialization and
urbanization, while at the same time charting the rise of the Free
Churches and the resurgence of Roman Catholicism. Chadwick's
psychological insight and gift for biography were demonstrated
as a number of sketches of key figures were offered to illustrate
general themes. He paid a great deal of attention to the Christian
response to Darwin, arguing that there was no incompatibility
between religion and science. Similarly, Chadwick gave a sympathetic account of those scholars and theologians who came to
terms with biblical criticism, and saw it as an ally in the pursuit
of truth. His basic approach is summed up in the final words of
the first volume: "the inmost soul of Christianity knew that all
truth is of God." *The Victorian Church* relates the story of the
institutional churches, and the ideas of articulate and educated
believers. The experience of religion of the mass of people is
not touched upon and as a resource for social history its value
is limited. Nonetheless, given its aims it remains a magisterial
introduction to the subject.

Chadwick has written comparatively little about the 20th
century. This is regrettable as many of the secularizing forces
he analyzed earlier reached a certain culmination in the 20th
century. His account of the experience of the churches in the
Cold War is relatively short and is modest in its claims for
the significance of religion in ending communist domination
of Eastern Europe. It is informative, but the tone is curiously
flat in comparison with his earlier work. Chadwick's *Britain
and the Vatican during the Second World War* (1986) shows
considerable skill in handling diplomatic history, but it does
not explore or develop the themes that dominated his earlier

writing. If Chadwick had extended the analysis of the intellectual assaults on Christianity into the 20th century he might have been less optimistic in his conclusions.

It is hard to judge how influential Chadwick has been in the development of English historiography, as many general works of history underestimate the importance of religion. However, his works on religious matters will continue to be read for their religious insight, intelligence, and generosity of mind.

MARK RICHARD DORSETT

See also Acton; Britain: Anglo-Saxon; Britain: since 1750; Butterfield; Catholicism; Muratori; Trevelyan

Biography

William Owen Chadwick. Born 26 July 1916. Educated Tonbridge School; St. John's College, Cambridge. Took holy orders; fellow, Trinity Hall, Cambridge, 1947–56; master, Selwyn College, Cambridge, 1956–83; Dixie professor of ecclesiastical history, Cambridge University, 1958–68, Regius professor of modern history, 1968–83, and vice-chancellor, 1969–71; chancellor, University of East Anglia, 1985–94. Married Ruth Hallward, 1949 (2 sons, 2 daughters).

Principal Writings

John Cassian: A Study in Primitive Monasticism, 1950; 2nd edition 1968
The Founding of Cuddesdon, 1954
The Mind of the Oxford Movement, 1960
Victorian Miniature, 1960
General editor, The Pelican History of the Church, 6 vols., 1961–70
The Reformation, 1964
The Victorian Church, 2 vols., 1966–70
The Secularization of the European Mind in the Nineteenth Century, 1975
Catholicism and History: The Opening of the Vatican Archives, 1978
The Popes and European Revolution, 1981
Hensley Henson: A Study in the Friction Between Church and State, 1983
Britain and the Vatican during the Second World War, 1986
Michael Ramsey: A Life, 1990
The Christian Church in the Cold War, 1992
Acton and History, 1998

Further Reading

Beales, Derek, and Geoffrey Best, eds., History, Society, and the Churches: Essays in Honour of Owen Chadwick, Cambridge and New York: Cambridge University Press, 1985
Gilley, Sheridan, "The Historian and the Church," International History Review 8 (1986), 613–19

Chandler, Alfred D., Jr. 1918–

US business historian

Alfred Chandler is probably the world's leading contemporary business historian. Chandler broke with the tradition of American business history, which concentrated upon studies of individual business leaders and firms, often treating them either hagiographically or with hostility, as either pillars or enemies of society, focusing instead upon problems of organization, structure, integration, and management. Heavily influenced by the work of the sociologists Max Weber and Talcott Parsons, Chandler focused upon large corporations primarily as bureaucratic and organizational structures, an approach consonant with the emphasis upon the emergence of big institutions and the professionalization of various facets of American life that characterized much historical writing on the United States in the 1960s and 1970s. While New Left historians have argued that his emphasis on large corporations as productive and efficient organizations promoting economic rationalization served to justify the role of big business in society and the economy, Chandler always followed the value-free social science tradition in which he was trained. Chandler's history is essentially impersonal, focusing on economic and institutional forces and trends rather than individuals. This is the case even in his biographical studies of his great-grandfather Henry Varnum Poor and of Pierre du Pont, and in his editorship of several volumes of presidential papers of both Theodore Roosevelt and Dwight D. Eisenhower. In all these cases he focused, not on the personalities of the men studied, but on administrative and organizational aspects of their careers.

Chandler's most notable works are Strategy and Structure (1962); The Visible Hand (1977); and Scale and Scope (1990). All concentrated on the development of the American business corporation from the mid-19th to the mid-20th centuries; the last put this development in the context of a comparative study, focusing on the United States, Britain, and Germany. Strategy and Structure elaborated themes previously discussed by Chandler in several articles of the 1950s, most notably "The Beginnings of 'Big Business' in American Industry" (1959). Concentrating upon Du Pont, General Motors, Standard Oil, and Sears, Roebuck, he recounted the organizational innovations adopted by American big business organizations in the later 19th and early 20th centuries, especially the evolution of vertically-integrated companies structured in separate divisions, to take advantage of new forces in the economy. These forces included railroads, large urban markets for both industrial and consumer goods, electrification and the internal combustion machine, and specialized research and development. In response to the economic difficulties of the 1880s and 1890s, mass production was combined with mass marketing to produce major economies of scale. Like all of Chandler's work, this study was extensively researched in numerous business archives and contemporary publications.

Both this book and its successor, The Visible Hand, which took these themes further, won the Newcomen prize in business history. In the second work Chandler drew attention to the emergence of hierarchical administration, a new managerial class, revised procedures in large corporations, and the dichotomy between closely integrated, centralized, one-product corporations and more decentralized multiproduct, multi-market firms, which gained in flexibility and so were able to explore new fields. He also suggested that rather than relying on the workings of the market and Adam Smith's "invisible hand," American corporations chose to operate as a more "visible hand" and to integrate suppliers of raw materials, manufacturing, and marketing into one vertically-integrated and well-administered enterprise, thus attaining major efficiencies of scale and scope, which enabled them to drive out less well-integrated competitors. The first firm to adopt such a strategy tended to enjoy important competitive advantages over any emulators. Chandler also argued that, due to its large and homogeneous domestic market, the United States experienced these developments sooner than other industrialized economies.

Chandler's most recent major work, *Scale and Scope*, built on his previous one, comparing the American experience of the late 19th and early 20th centuries with those of Germany and Britain. He blamed sluggish British economic growth on the failure to invest in manufacturing, marketing, and management, and on the reluctance of businessmen to cede personal ownership and control of their firms by establishing extensive management hierarchies. In Germany, by contrast, manufacturers, encouraged by the government's support for cartels and their close relations with their bankers, followed the American pattern, thus breaking into British domestic markets. Some critics allege that Chandler takes an overly optimistic view of the benefits of hierarchical management, contending that large, hierarchical bureaucratic structures have often proved inefficient in practice. Even so, he has clearly set the terms of a major ongoing debate in business history.

Indeed, overall Chandler's work tends to dominate the field of contemporary business history. His writings, including not only several major books but numerous influential essays and articles and several edited collections, his tireless industry, his throng of well-trained graduate students, now themselves holding influential academic posts, and his eminent position at the Harvard Business School, the leading center of business history in the United States and the home of the *Business History Review*, ensure that his impact on business history will continue into the next century.

PRISCILLA M. ROBERTS

See also Business; Fogel; Hughes, T.; United States: 19th Century; United States: Historical Writing, 20th Century

Biography

Alfred Dupont Chandler, Jr. Born Guyencourt, Delaware, 15 September 1918. Educated at Phillips Exeter Academy; received BA, Harvard University, 1940, MA 1947, PhD 1952; attended University of North Carolina, 1945–46. Served in US Navy during World War II. Held a research post at Massachusetts Institute of Technology, 1950–63; taught at Johns Hopkins University, 1963–71; Straus professor of business history, Graduate School in Business Administration, Harvard University, from 1971. Married Fay Martin, 1944 (3 sons, 1 daughter).

Principal Writings

Henry Varnum Poor: Business Editor, Analyst, and Reformer, 1956
"The Beginnings of 'Big Business' in American Industry," *Business History Review* 33 (1959), 1–31; reprinted in *The Essential Alfred Chandler*, 1988
Strategy and Structure: Chapters in the History of the American Industrial Enterprise, 1962
With Stephen Salsbury and Adeline Cook Strange, *Pierre S. Du Pont and the Making of the Modern Corporation*, 1971
The Visible Hand: The Managerial Revolution in American Business, 1977
With Richard S. Tedlow, *The Coming of Managerial Capitalism: A Casebook on the History of American Economic Institutions*, 1985
The Essential Alfred Chandler: Essays Toward a Historical Theory of Big Business, edited by Thomas K. McCraw, 1988
Scale and Scope: The Dynamics of Industrial Capitalism, 1990

Further Reading

Chandler, Alfred D., Jr., Roy Church, Albert Fishlow, Neil Fligstein, Thomas P. Hughes, Jürgen Kocka, Hidemasa Morikawa, and Frederic M. Scherer, "*Scale and Scope*: A Review Colloquium," *Business History Review* 64 (1990), 690–788
Du Boff, Richard B., and Edward S. Herman, "Alfred Chandler's New Business History: A Review," *Politics and Society* 10 (1980), 87–110
Galambos, Louis, "The Emerging Organizational Synthesis in Modern American History," *Business History Review* 44 (1970), 279–90
Galambos, Louis, "Technology, Political Economy, and Professionalization: Central Themes of the Organizational Synthesis," *Business History Review* 57 (1983), 471–93
John, Richard R., "Elaborations, Revisions, Dissents: Alfred D. Chandler's *The Visible Hand* after Twenty Years," *Business History Review* 71 (1997), 151–200
Lamoreaux, Naomi R., "Chandler's Own Economies of Scope," *Reviews in American History* 19 (1991), 391–95
Lévy-Leboyer, Maurice, "The Quintessential Alfred Chandler," *Business History Review* 62 (1988), 516–21
McCraw, Thomas K., "The Challenge of Alfred D. Chandler, Jr.: Retrospect and Prospect," *Reviews in American History* 15 (1987), 160–78
McCraw, Thomas K., Introduction to McCraw, ed., *The Essential Alfred Chandler: Essays Toward a Historical Theory of Big Business*, Boston: Harvard Business School Press, 1988
Parker, William N., "The Scale and Scope of Alfred D. Chandler, Jr." *Journal of Economic History* 51 (1991), 958–63
Teece, David J., "The Dynamics of Industrial Capitalism: Perspectives on Alfred Chandler's *Scale and Scope*," *Journal of Economic Literature* 31 (1993), 199–225

Chartier, Roger 1945–

French cultural historian

Roger Chartier first garnered wide recognition in the 1970s and he remains a leading light in the "fourth generation" of French Annales school historians. His public engagement with the work of a number of American historians has brought their endeavors to the attention of French scholars and made him one of the French historians most well-known to English-speaking audiences. His publications, new and old, play an important role in current debates about the past, on subjects ranging from popular culture, urbanity and marginality to the history of the book and cultural or "representational" history.

Chartier began his career by exploring educational forms, co-producing *L'Education en France aux XVIème et XVIIème siècles* (Education in France in the 16th and 17th Centuries, 1976). This early work announces its Annaliste genealogy; the authors depended on charts and statistics to make their argument. The thesis, that French education served to reproduce dominant groups, is indebted to the claims of sociologist Pierre Bourdieu. Chartier also co-edited *L'Histoire de l'édition française* (History of French Publishing) (1982–86), one of the defining works of the history of the book. Along with other Annalistes such as Henri-Jean Martin, Daniel Roche, and Frédéric Barbier, Chartier established this approach to intellectual history. They considered the printed word as a historical factor, attempting to reconstruct literary culture in its totality.

Chartier's work has expanded the focus of the field from books to all forms of printed material, such as pamphlets and broadsides. While he continues to be interested in the dissemination of printed material, he has more recently drawn analytic attention to how practices of reading took place. In this effort he has examined both the material form of read objects and the changing contexts in which reading occurs. His attention to the way format determines how reading transpires has proven compelling and original, although his privileging of the demands imposed by material design has been criticized as potentially ahistorical. This work is one element of Chartier's critical re-evaluation of both serial or quantitative analyses and the "history of mentalities" approaches intimately associated with the Annales school. To this end he has written cogent expositions of the writings of Michel Foucault, Norbert Elias, Bourdieu, and Jürgen Habermas, all of whom have influenced his critical outlook.

Chartier has pursued an extended examination of systems of representation, exploring how people were ordered or classed in the early modern period. In his contribution to *Les Marginaux et les exclus dans l'histoire* (The Marginal and the Excluded in History, 1979) he describes a widespread 15th-century French conviction that marginal populations structured themselves on a monarchical model, thus were popularly thought to follow a local "king of thieves." Using sources from the arrest of a group of "guex" in Paris in 1448 and the trial of the "Coquillards" in 1445 Dijon, he explored how this understanding operated and resonated with other 14th- and 15th-century conceptions of group organization. In his insistence that this royal model does not reflect how marginal peoples lived, he brought to the foreground a continuing theoretical underpinning of his writings.

Chartier is always careful to distinguish between representations produced by the dominant elites, whether ecclesiastical, economic, or political, and the "daily reality which always overflows" such classifications. A similar awareness informs his hesitation in treating all past phenomena as texts. In a much-noted review of Robert Darnton's *The Great Cat Massacre* (1984) and in his own books and essays, Chartier mobilizes an analysis of symbols to approach the lived existence of the lower orders. In contrast, his treatment of first-person narratives, written by members of the literate strata, insists on the importance of "intentionality and originality" of formulation. Chartier manifests an attachment to a radical disjuncture between writing and speech cultures. While the former is all that the historian can access, an interrogation of representations is primarily useful for approximating the palpable experience of the latter.

In *Les Origines culturelles de la Révolution française* (1990; *The Cultural Origins of the French Revolution*, 1991) Chartier provides a compelling re-evaluation of intellectual and political interpretations of how the Revolution took hold and proceeded, as well as offering the first synthesis of the outpouring of monographs on the revolutionary period which appeared in the 1980s. In answer to the self-posed question "Did books cause the Revolution?" Chartier proposed a deftly layered response. He challenged assumptions about the role of certain authors and titles in setting up the possibility of Revolution. He insisted that the Revolution invented the Enlightenment, retrospectively uniting diverse texts into a coherent intellectual paternity. It was the explosion of written material that preceded 1789, Chartier submitted, that helped produce the conditions in which French people were able to understand and accept the destruction of the monarchy and the society of orders. More than the novelty of ideas published or the increased diffusion of such texts, he saw a general change in the reception of printed materials as critical. New genres and new methods of distribution contributed to the emergence of "a solitary and privileged relation of reader to book." This new way of reading reshaped the cultural appreciation of the existing regime. Chartier made compelling use of Habermas' formulations of the public sphere to explain the importance of dechristianization and desacralization in late 18th-century France. As some critics have complained, Chartier's discussion does not attempt or is unable to explain why the Revolution actually began.

The ambition and chronological breadth of Chartier's efforts are suggested by the subtitle of a recent book, *Forms and Meanings: Texts, Performances, and Audiences from Codex to Computer* (1995). Among the questions addressed in this set of studies (which are united by their exploration of how "the form that transmits a text to its readers or hearers constrains the production of meaning") is Chartier's expansion of his critique of the category "popular culture." He dismantled the bipolar interpretations of "popular culture" as either a space of freedom, separate from dominant understandings and practices, or as a passive appropriator of dominant conceptions. He insists that the historian, by interrogating discourses ("almost always written texts") yet remaining aware of the "irreducibility of experience to discourse" can trace a more accurate description of non-elite lives and practices. Chartier is cognizant of domination but attentive to the dominated's inventiveness and originality, committed to archival research yet attuned to theoretical sophistication regardless of discipline; his research and writings mediate with verve and insight the tensions that, after the linguistic turn, stymie so many historians.

TODD DAVID SHEPARD

See also Anthropology; Bourdieu; Cultural; Darnton; Davis, N.; France: 1485–1789; Habermas; Mentalities

Biography
Born Lyon, 9 December 1945. Received agrégation in history at the Ecole Normale Supérieure de Saint-Cloud, 1969. Taught at University of Paris I, 1970–76; and Ecole des Hautes Etudes en Sciences Sociales, from 1976. Married Anne-Marie Trepier, teacher, 1967 (1 son, 1 daughter).

Principal Writings
With Dominque Julia and Marie-Madeleine Compère, *L'Education en France aux XVIème et XVIIème siècles* (Education in France in the 16th and 17th Centuries), 1976

Les Marginaux et les exclus dans l'histoire (The Marginal and the Excluded in History), 1979

General editor with Henri-Jean Martin, *L'Histoire de l'édition française* (History of French Publishing), 4 vols., 1982–86

"Texts, Symbols, and Frenchness," *Journal of Modern History* 57 (1985), 682–95

The Cultural Uses of Print in Early Modern France, 1987

Editor, *Les Usages de l'imprimerie (XVe–XIXe siecle)*, 1987; in English as *The Culture of Print: Power and the Uses of Print in Early Modern Europe*, 1989

Lectures et lecteurs dans la France d'Ancien Regime (Reading and Readers in *Ancien Régime* France), 1987

*Frenchness in the History of the Book: From the History of
    Publishing to the History of Reading*, 1988
Cultural History: Between Practices and Representations, 1988
Les Origines culturelles de la Révolution française, 1990; in English
    as *The Cultural Origins of the French Revolution*, 1991
*L'Ordre des livres: lecteurs, auteurs, bibliothèques en Europe entre
    XIVè et XVIIIe siècle*, 1992; in English as *The Order of Books:
    Readers, Authors and Libraries in Europe Between the Fourteenth
    and Eighteenth Centuries*, 1994
*Forms and Meanings: Texts, Performances, and Audiences from
    Codex to Computer*, 1995

Further Reading

Carrard, Philippe, *Poetics of the New History: French Historical
    Discourse from Braudel to Chartier*, Baltimore: Johns Hopkins
    University Press, 1992
Darnton, Robert, "The Symbolic Element in History," *Journal of
    Modern History* 58 (1986), 218–34
Fernandez, James, "Historians Tell Tales: Of Cartesian Cats and
    Gallic Cockfights," *Journal of Modern History* 60 (1988), 113–27
Kaplan, Steven L., *Farewell Revolution: Disputed Legacies: France,
    1789/1989*, Ithaca, NY: Cornell University Press, 1995
LaCapra, Dominick, "Chartier, Darnton, and the Great Symbol
    Massacre," *Journal of Modern History* 60 (1988), 95–112

Chaudhuri, K.N. 1934–

Indian historian

The new intellectual course established by K.N. Chaudhuri with
regard to Asian economic development adopts the intellectual
position that influences which guided economic growth were
the same in Asia as in Europe, America, or any other region.
This is contrary to the traditionally held view that the Asian
economy operated largely in a vacuum under the influence of
unique and primitive factors. This view is, to some degree, based
on the influence of Fernand Braudel and what he called *la
longue durée*, an interwoven complex of common elements that
determined the fundamental economic structure over time.
Based upon Chaudhuri's research, the common elements of
supply and demand economics forged a strong commercial,
capitalistic economy in Asia where markets operated in the
same fashion as those in other countries. Chaudhuri states that
trade ultimately depended on the "ability of local economic
elements to create a surplus, over and above the subsistence
demand and to maintain this level of production over a sufficiently long period of time." Thus, trade in Asia was a rational
rather than a backward operation. Some of Chaudhuri's
groundbreaking assertions are more controversial, however. He
claims, for instance, that the introduction of armed trade by
the Portuguese contributed to the failure of regional powers
in Asia fully to exploit oceanic trade. Other scholars such as
G.V. Scammell of Pembroke College, Cambridge argue that this
view is illogical.

While scholars have studied the economic aspects of Asian
history for years, it should be noted that the quantitative
methodology incorporated by Chaudhuri establishes a new
window through which we may view history. This sets him
apart as a pioneer, with a stronger voice and a bolder pen than
many of his predecessors. This aspect of Chaudhuri's work
opens fruitful research possibilities. Chaudhuri digitized the

accountant's figures from the English East India Company after
1709 and subsequently derived hundreds of tables from which
to determine important trends. Combining this raw data with
other Company information, he has been able to single out
many of the Company's commodities such as pepper, tea, and
various textiles and to find how the decision making process
evolved, how patterns of production developed, and what
factors most influenced competition. Chaudhuri's theoretical
approach is based on systems analysis in an effort to add clarity
and rigor to his views. Yet he is wary of models as over-
simplifications of reality.

In spite of many admirable qualities, Chaudhuri's approach
to historiography is not without its critics. Some have
concluded that the results of all the number-crunching are
unsurprising. For example, Chaudhuri says, "If the present
study of Indian Ocean trade points in the direction of any
systematic conclusion at all, it is that the process of economic
change was shaped by the social and political systems of
different civilizations and their attitudes towards one another."
Some claim that the historian's subjective analysis may be just
as valid as the statistical analysis. Nor is it surprising that
many historical questions remained unsolved, and that new
ones have been raised.

WILLIAM T. JOHNSON

See also British Empire; Indian Ocean; Middle East; World

Biography

Kirti Narayan Chaudhuri. Born 8 September 1934, son of the
prominent writer/broadcaster Nirad C. Chaudhuri. Educated
privately in India; received BA, University of London, 1959, PhD
1961. Taught (rising to professor), School of Oriental and African
Studies, University of London, 1961–91; Vasco da Gama professor
of the history of European expansion, European University Institute,
Florence, from 1991. Married, 1961 (1 son).

Principal Writings

*The English East India Company: The Study of an Early Joint-stock
    Company, 1600–1649*, 1965
*The Trading World of Asia and the English East India Company,
    1660–1760*, 1978
*Trade and Civilisation in the Indian Ocean: An Economic History
    from the Rise of Islam to 1750*, 1985
*Asia before Europe: The Economy and Civilisation in the Indian
    Ocean from the Rise of Islam to 1750*, 1990

Chen Yinke [Chen Yinque], 1890–1969

Chinese historian

By the general consensus of the Chinese intellectual world Chen
Yinke was undoubtedly one of the most original and creative
historians in 20th-century China. His originality and creativity
emerged in his sustained effort to develop paradigms, concepts,
and methods adequate to the double task of analyzing Chinese
historical sources and formulating problems unique to Chinese
history. Unlike most Chinese historians of his generation,
whose imaginations had been captivated by the Western
idea of "scientific history" or theories of social evolution

governed by inexorable laws, he belonged to a small scholarly coterie of cultural conservatives who refused to accept theories and practices in Western historiography as universally valid, and insisted that Chinese history must be understood on its own terms. As a cultural conservative he held fast to his basic Confucian values even in extreme adversity such as the onslaught of the Cultural Revolution during the last three years of his life. His faith in his own tradition was strengthened rather than weakened by his early exposure to the classical culture of the West. He reinterpreted basic Confucian values in terms of Platonic ideas that transcend time and are therefore not subject to change. However, as a historian Chen's unusually keen mind made him sensitive to the most minute and subtle changes in history.

From early childhood he was given the best education of his day, both old and new. It began with private tutoring in Chinese classics and history and continued with modern schooling in Tokyo. Between 1909 and 1925 he studied at a number of European and American universities. He had a natural penchant for classical languages including Greek, Latin, Sanskrit, and Pali, but also learned many other languages directly relevant to the study of the history between China and its inner and central Asian neighbors such as Mongolian, Manchu, Tibetan, Turkish, and Persian. The thorough training in Oriental languages he received from Charles Rockwell Lanman at Harvard and Henrich Luders at Berlin (1921–25) proved to be particularly fruitful. By the late 1910s he had already made up his mind to pursue history as his vocation. He intended to make good use of the many languages at his disposal and from the 1920s to the early 1930s his research work was focused on comparative studies of Buddhist sutras in the Chinese, Sanskrit, and Tibetan texts and of historical sources of alien dynasties in the Chinese, Mongolian, Tibetan, Manchu, and Persian languages. However, his avowed purpose was a comprehensive reconstruction of Chinese history between 220 and 960 CE when Chinese civilization underwent a fundamental transformation due to both the invasion of Buddhism and the conquests of various "barbarian" groups.

Free from traditional Sino-centric biases, Chen's historical reconstruction consisted in objective analyses of how forces of non-Chinese origins reshaped Chinese culture, society, polity, and economy. In his overall assessment, while these forces did work to hasten the disintegration of the first Chinese empire they also contributed in the long run to the rise of a second one of a more cosmopolitan character. In two brief but brilliant volumes of historical synthesis, one on T'ang political history and another on the origins of Sui and T'ang institutions, he succeeded in establishing a paradigm for the study of T'ang history that has won him worldwide recognition as the foremost authority on medieval China. Historians of the T'ang period everywhere can argue either with him or against him but never without him.

From the mid-1930s the emphasis of Chen's research gradually shifted from China's contact with the outside world to its internal growth and development. Taking advantage of his encyclopedic command of Chinese sources of all types he began to combine poetry and fiction with historical documents to illustrate the subtle changes in T'ang society and culture. This is an entirely new approach to Chinese history, never attempted before so systematically and with such a high degree of sophis-

tication. It began in a trickle in short essays but ended in a flood with the publication in 1950 of a book called, in his usual modest manner, "a draft annotated interpretation of poems of Yuan Zhen (779–831) and Bai Ju-yi (772–846)." Chen also turned increasingly hermeneutical in methodology while still retaining the same high standard of philological precision.

The last stage of his life and work from 1949 to 1969 can best be described as a heroic tragedy. He became blind in 1945, but nevertheless he continued to teach and write with the help of research assistants in postwar Peking. He flew out of the besieged city in December 1948 but could not go any further when the communists in October 1949 occupied Canton, where he was on the faculty of a Christian college. In 1953 he had the remarkable courage to decline the offer of the Academy of Science to serve as director of the Institute of Medieval History in Peking, giving the explicit reason that he could not possibly accept Marxism-Leninism as the only theoretical framework for the study of history. He even quoted the famous motto of Patrick Henry: "Give me liberty or give me death" to show his determination to fight for intellectual freedom and independence. Needless to say, he paid heavily for this in the years to come. However, his last and also by far his largest research project must be considered a miracle in the entire history of Chinese historiography. It is a detailed study of the life of a well-known courtesan-artist Liu Rushi (1618–64) during the Ming-Ching transition, built on the basis of hundreds of 17th-century historical and literary sources of all types. From memory he gave instructions to his assistant as to where relevant records could be found and then had them read to him for further research. It took him a whole decade (1954–64) to complete the writing, and more than a decade after his death for it to see light of day in 1980 in three volumes. But what is most remarkable is that the book is as much about Chen, the 20th-century historian, as about the 17th-century courtesan-artist. According to his interpretation Liu never yielded to the Manchu rule because the Manchu conquerors showed every intention of distorting and destroying the basic values of Chinese culture. By her quiet but unwavering defiance Liu embodied the Confucian principle of moral integrity and thereby contrasted sharply to those scholars who were only too eager to serve the new dynasty. From his other writings, and particularly his poetry of this period, we know for certain that Liu's was exactly the same lofty principle that Chen had all along set for himself to follow under the new historical circumstances.

YING-SHIH YU

Biography

Born Changsha, 1890. Classical Chinese education, then studied philology at universities in Berlin, 1909–11, Switzerland, 1911–12, and Paris, 1913–14; at Harvard University, 1919–21; and in Berlin, 1921–25. Taught and researched, Tsing Hua College, 1925–49; and Linnan University, Guangzhou, 1949–52. Because of war unable to take up professorship of sinology, Oxford University, 1938; arrived 1946, but forced to resign due to incipient blindness, 1956. Head, National Research Institute of History and Philology, Academia Sinica; director, Palace Museum; editorial board member, Qing Archives. Died Guangzhou, 1969.

Principal Writings

Suitang zhidu yuanyuan luelungao (Draft Essays on the Origins of Sui and Tang Institutions), 1943

Tangdai zhengzhishi shulunkao (Draft Outline of Tang Political History), 1943

Yan Bai shijian zhenggao, 1955

Liu Rushi biezhuang, 3 vols., 1980

Further Reading

Boorman, Howard L., and Richard C. Howard, eds., *Biographical Dictionary of Republican China*, 4 vols., New York: Columbia University Press, 1967–1971, vol.1, 259–261

Demieville, Paul, "Tch'en Yin-ko (1890–1969): Necrologie," *T'oung Pao* 57 (1971), 136–43

Jian Tianshu, *Chen Yinque Xiansheng biannian shiji* (Chen Yinke: A Chronological Account of His Life), Shanghai: Guji Press, 1981

Lu Chiandong, *Ch'en Yin-k'o ti tsui hou 20 nien* (The Last 20 Years of Ch'en Yin-ke), Peking: Sanlien Press, 1995

Yü Ying-shih, *Ch'en Yin-k'o wan nien shih wen shih cheng* (An Annotated Interpretation of Chen Yinke's Writings and Poems, 1949–1969), Taipei: China Times Press, 1984; revised 1986

Cheney, C.R. 1906–1987

British medievalist

C.R. Cheney was one of the 20th century's most eminent and respected medievalists. His reputation rests primarily on his technical assurance as a great editor of texts and on his outstanding contributions to the history of the medieval Church.

"Records," he wrote, "like the little children of long ago, only speak when they are spoken to, and they will not talk to strangers." As an expert in the science of diplomatic (the critical study of historical documents), he immersed himself in the forms and formulas of medieval ecclesiastical records, their legal significance, and, not least, the procedures of the administrative agencies for which they were written. As he put it, "diplomatic commits the critic of texts to a study of the office which produced the texts." He also urged the necessity of reconstructing as far as possible the totality of the products of particular administrations: "we cannot draw a picture of the administrative office in just proportions unless we make the effort to collect the fragments and reconstitute scattered *fonds*."

In his editions of texts, replete with extensive commentaries, he set new standards of documentary scholarship, and ensured almost single-handedly that England leapt to the forefront in medieval diplomatic. The second volume of *Councils and Synods* (1964) – a definitive edition of documents concerning the law and legislation of the English Church (1205–1313) – was begun in collaboration with Sir Maurice Powicke; but the finished product, issued in two parts and some 1,500 pages long, was in essence Cheney's work, despite the formal attribution of joint editorship to Powicke. A triumph of scholarly detective work and precision, it is one of the great achievements of English historical scholarship. With his wife, Mary Cheney, "the best of collaborators," he collected and edited Pope Innocent III's correspondence relating to England and Wales in *Letters of Pope Innocent III* (1967) – the fruits of extensive researches not only in the Vatican archives but among the surviving muniments of every potential recipient. In 1973 he founded the British Academy's *English Episcopal Acta*

series, set up to locate and publish the extant official written acts of English prelates from 1066 to the 13th century. He was himself largely responsible for two volumes on Canterbury, and saw the enterprise firmly established as a seminal resource for the history of English church government.

But Cheney was far from regarding the editing of texts as an end in itself. In a series of masterly monographs, he wrote extensively on ecclesiastical records and record-making – *English Bishops' Chanceries* (1950) and *Notaries Public* (1972) are of special importance – and took a particular interest in the history of the English Church and Anglo-papal relations in the period 1154–1216. Such themes as the growth and operation of papal government, the interlocking administration of church and state, the power and patronage of the crown over the clergy, and the conflict between ecclesiastical and secular law, were dealt with in *From Becket to Langton* (his revised 1955 Ford lectures) and in his classic biography *Hubert Walter* (1967) – in which he dealt sympathetically with the career of a worldly-wise archbishop of Canterbury who was also royal justiciar and chancellor. His most influential book, however, is generally recognized to be *Pope Innocent III and England* (1976), a magisterial and deeply learned study in which he deployed to the full his unrivalled knowledge of the available sources. He also produced numerous carefully crafted articles, most of which were collected and published in three volumes: *Medieval Texts and Studies* (1973), *The English Church and Its Laws* (1982), and *The Papacy and England* (1982).

Cheney was not much inclined to philosophizing about the historian's craft. He took its relevance and importance for granted, and his enduring influence lies preeminently in his expertise and dedication as a practitioner. He was a pioneer in demonstrating that ecclesiastical records, even those of the most technical sort, could also provide evidence for historians in other fields. Acutely sensitive to the complexity and contradictions of medieval society, he conveyed a vivid sense of the gulf that often existed between governmental claims and actual performance, and of how people coped with their often conflicting loyalties and duties. His judgments were scrupulously fair and renowned for their human insight. As he wrote of Hubert Walter: "Those who would be leaders in the Church needed a training which was sad preparation for the contemplative life or the strict application of Christian principles. They must temporize. They must be politicians. Perhaps the medieval Church made impossible demands of her prelates, requiring of them all the Christian virtues and all the mundane arts besides. The fact remains that Hubert Walter, for all his faults, was . . . perhaps as good a head as the English Church could expect to have."

Cheney's school of research students was not large, but he trained them to uphold the most rigorous standards; and his generosity in the help he gave to other scholars was legendary. He recognized the importance of collaborative ventures long before they became common in the humanities, and he operated firmly in the mainstream of the international academic community. He, more than most, appreciated that "every historian's path is full of pitfalls." But no English medievalist has been better equipped to identify and avoid them; and few scholars have written so authoritatively about the workings of both papal government and national ecclesiastical politics. "Yet," as Christopher Brooke concluded in his British Academy obituary, he will perhaps be remembered in future generations – when the monographs . . . of our day have been buried and forgotten – as an immortal editor; as one who taught us by learning, ingenuity, deep skill, and perception of how scribes worked and how manuscripts were made, and who constructed his editions by application of . . . a common sense utterly uncommon and a sense of craftsmanship, which set him among the immortals.

K.J. STRINGER

Biography

Christopher Robert Cheney. Born Banbury, Oxfordshire, 20 December 1906, son of a printer. Educated at Banbury County School; Wadham College, Oxford, BA 1928. Taught at University College, London, 1931–33; University of Manchester, 1933–37; Oxford University, 1937–45: fellow, Magdalen College, 1938–45; University of Manchester, 1945–55; Cambridge University, 1955–72: fellow, Corpus Christi College, 1955–87. Married Mary Gwendolen Hall, 1940 (2 sons, 1 daughter). Died Cambridge, 19 June 1987.

Principal Writings

Episcopal Visitation of Monasteries in the Thirteenth Century, 1931; revised 1983

English Synodalia of the Thirteenth Century, 1941

Editor, *Handbook of Dates for Students of English History*, 1945

English Bishops' Chanceries, 1100–1250, 1950

Editor and translator with W.H. Semple, *Selected Letters of Pope Innocent III Concerning England (1198–1216)*, 1953

From Becket to Langton: English Church Government, 1170–1213, 1956

Editor with F.M. Powicke, *Councils and Synods, with Other Documents Relating to the English Church*, part 2: AD 1205–1313, 1 vol. in 2 parts, 1964

Hubert Walter, 1967

Editor with Mary G. Cheney, *The Letters of Pope Innocent III (1198–1216) Concerning England and Wales*, 1967

Notaries Public in England in the Thirteenth and Fourteenth Centuries, 1972

Medieval Texts and Studies, 1973

Pope Innocent III and England, 1976

Editor with Mary G. Cheney, *Studies in the Collections of Twelfth-Century Decretals*, 1979

The English Church and Its Laws, 12th–14th Centuries, 1982

The Papacy and England, 12th–14th Centuries: Historical and Legal Studies, 1982

Editor with Bridgett E.A. Jones, *English Episcopal Acta 2: Canterbury, 1162–1190*, 1986

Editor with E. John, *English Episcopal Acta 3: Canterbury, 1193–1205*, 1986

Further Reading

Brooke, C.N.L., D.E. Luscombe, G.H. Martin and Dorothy Owen, eds., *Church and Government in the Middle Ages: Essays Presented to C.R. Cheney on His 70th Birthday*, Cambridge: Cambridge University Press, 1976

Brooke, C.N.L., "Christopher Robert Cheney, 1906–1987," *Proceedings of the British Academy* 73 (1987), 425–46

Chevalier, François 1914–

French historian of Mexico

François Chevalier offers an example of a historian who became famous with his first monograph: *La Formation des grands domaines au Mexique* (1952; *Land and Society in Colonial Mexico*, 1963). The formation of the "hacienda" or "great estate" in the 17th century is the topic of this narrative. The focus is principally on the geographical area of the north of Mexico. This truly monumental work represented the first exhaustive research from the archives in Mexico and in Seville in Spain on 17th-century Mexico. Until Chevalier wrote *Land and Society in Colonial Mexico* little was known about this period. Unlike the preceding century in Spanish America, which inspired a great number of works, the 17th century was a forgotten time because it had little to offer in terms of great events. It was a century sandwiched in between the conquest of Mexico and its independence from Spain.

However, it was no accident that this scholar chose to write about the 17th century. His intellectual mentors Lucien Febvre, Marc Bloch, and Fernand Braudel suggested that history should not necessarily focus on great events and figures, but rather on long-term trends and on groups. Thus the Annales school's concept of *la longue durée* shaped Chevalier's work. He was a great advocate of economic and demographic research which he argued were the foundations of history. He started his graduate career with his adviser and mentor, Marc Bloch, whose *Les Caractères originaux de l'histoire rurale française* (1931; *French Rural History*, 1966) combined history, geography, and culture. Chevalier, too, was to blend geography in the broad sense with archival research. He was a great traveler and spent seven years in Mexico learning, as he stated in a interview, not only from the archives, but from living in Mexico itself. His study of the environment led him to focus on long-term trends, especially the formation of great land estates, which was particularly relevant for the history of Mexico in view of its agrarian revolution in 1910. Chevalier wrote his doctoral thesis in the late 1940s and early 1950s after the Mexican government of Cardenas had redistributed 44 million acres of land in the late 1930s. Chevalier sought not only to understand the endurance of large plantations, but also their eventual elimination. For Chevalier, in order to understand the eventual demise of the haciendas one needs to explore the *mentalité*, or mind-set of their owners. This enabled him to propose that for many Mexicans land was a means to achieve status. He also suggested that the contraction of a silver-based economy led Mexican elites to devise other strategies for survival. As Eric Young pointed out in an article on the historiography of colonial Mexico, Chevalier maintained that a process of feudalization took place when silver production stagnated. Attempting to locate when and how colonial Mexico became feudal, Chevalier became part of the ongoing Marxist debate about whether Latin America was "feudal" or already capitalistic in its colonial era. This intellectual debate had important political ramifications, since characterizing the Mexican colonial era as "feudal" signified that the Mexican Revolution of 1910 should be perceived as a "Bourgeois Revolution."

As Young noted, in *The Aztecs under Spanish Rule* (1964) Charles Gibson refuted Chevalier's thesis of the feudalization of the Mexican countryside. Young suggested that Gibson, by demonstrating that haciendas in the Central Valley of Mexico were highly commercial and its workforce mobile, showed that haciendas in Mexico were not necessarily "feudal."

Chevalier's work was strongly influenced and enriched by his close collaboration with Mexican historians such as Silvio

Zavala and Daniel Cosio Villegas. Chevalier advanced the importance of indigenous culture, an insight he gained from his travels through Mexico. His discussion of pre-Hispanic land patterns and his sense of the complexity of the Aztec state are truly remarkable. Chevalier pioneered the importance of culture in understanding Latin America thirty years before cultural history became the vogue. His work also led other historians to understand the importance of placing cultural history in a economic and demographic context. A passion for Latin America in general and Mexico in particular permeates his work.

Chevalier has published more than fifty articles on a variety of topics. He wrote not only about Mexico, but Peru, Venezuela, and even Colombia. This breadth of knowledge is evident in his last major work, *L'Amérique Latine de l'Indépendance à nos jours* (Latin America from Its Independence to Present Day, 1977), where his effort to contribute work useful to historians is particularly manifest. The first chapter of this work comprises an extensive bibliography not only on Latin America, but for all the major nations within the region; it has proven invaluable in helping other researchers. Chevalier's insistence on the role of history in understanding the present is clear throughout this latest work.

BRETT TROYAN

See also Gibson; Latin America: Colonial; Mexico

Biography
François George Chevalier. Born Montluçon, 27 May 1914, son of a university professor. Attended school at Grenoble; licentiate in history and geography, Ecole Nationale des Chartes, diploma as an archivist-paleographer; docteur ès lettres, Casa Velázquez, Madrid. Second Lieutenant during World War II. Academic career: Institut Français de Mexico 1946–49, director, 1949–62; Faculté des Lettres, University of Bordeaux, 1962–66; director, Casa Velázquez, 1967–79; the Sorbonne, 1969–83 (emeritus). Married Josèphe Charvet, 1949 (3 sons).

Principal Writings
La Formation des grands domaines au Mexique: terre et société aux XVI–XVII siècles, 1952; in English as *Land and Society in Colonial Mexico: The Great Hacienda*, 1963
L'Amérique Latine de l'Indépendance à nos jours, 1977

Further Reading
Palafox, Ricardo Avila, Carlos Martínez Assad, and Jean Meyer, eds., *Las formas y las políticas del dominio agrario: homenaje a François Chevalier*, Guadalajara: Editorial Universidad de Guadalajara, 1992
Van Young, Eric, "Mexican Rural History since Chevalier: The Historiography of the Colonial Hacienda," *Latin American Research Review* 18 (1983), 5–62

Childhood

Until relatively recently, children and childhood have been missing dimensions within historical writing. Autobiographical and biographical works contained reference to childhood experience, while institutional studies – in the field of education

especially – explored the evolution and application of policies and practices designed with children in mind. The potential of the history of children and childhoods as a subject for investigation by historians lay virtually untapped until the publication in 1960 of Philippe Ariès' *L'Enfant et la vie familiale sous l'Ancien Régime* (*Centuries of Childhood*, 1962) prompted a significant change of emphasis.

Drawing essentially upon European evidence, Ariès argued in this seminal work that childhood was a social construction. He maintained that no concept of childhood existed in the Middle Ages or earlier; that children had been perceived to be miniature adults, not individuals with different needs. However, by a process commencing during the 17th century and completed by the mid-18th, the notion of childhood as a distinct state gradually came to be accepted. Neither Ariès' assertions nor his use of evidence were to remain long unchallenged, but his key role in stimulating the exploration of childhood in history is indisputable.

Since the early 1960s, historians interested in redressing this missing dimension have tended to follow one of two main lines of enquiry. Initially, a great deal of the research and publication revolved around the central issue of the history of childhood as a social construction. Among the leading supporters of Ariès' basic thesis were John Demos whose *A Little Commonwealth* (1970) concluded that the Puritan founders of Massachusetts society in the 1630s did not view children as a group with special needs; and Edward Shorter whose survey history, *The Making of the Modern Family* (1976) upheld Ariès' contention that modern child-centered parenting practices were superior to those of earlier centuries. Lloyd deMause emerged as the most extreme exponent of the viewpoint that the further one went back into history, the more brutally children were treated. The argument contained in his essay on "The Evolution of Childhood" in *The History of Childhood* (1974) has subsequently been dismissed by specialist researchers, and the early influence of psychohistory on the development of the history of children has waned accordingly.

More widespread and more productive of detailed information has been the other significant line of investigation into the history of children, an approach that can incorporate questions about the concept of childhood but which, by its very nature, deals much more extensively with children's experiences in the past. A useful survey of such publications is contained in the first chapter of Linda Pollock's *Forgotten Children* (1983). Among the most outstanding of more recent monographs are Shulamith Shahar's *Yaldut bi-Yeme-ha-benayim* (1990; *Childhood in the Middle Ages*, 1990); Barbara Hanawalt's *Growing Up in Medieval London* (1993); Eric Hopkins' *Childhood Transformed* (1994); and Anna Davin's *Growing Up Poor* (1996).

By far the most comprehensive guide to the richness of this developing field, is the volume edited by American scholars Joseph Hawes and Ray Hiner's *Children in Historical and Comparative Perspective* (1991). The bibliographical essays surveying the nature of research in fifteen different countries confirm Hawes and Hiner's impression that studying the history of children is a multidisciplinary undertaking. The earlier emphasis on policy, reflected in such works as Ivy Pinchbeck and Margaret Hewitt's 2-volume *Children in English Society* (1969–73) and Robert Bremner's 3-volume documentary collection, *Children and Youth in America* (1970–74) has since been augmented by research that is enhanced by the insights of other disciplines. The term "childhood history" does not, therefore, denote a developing sub-discipline of social, family, or women's history: it is simply a convenient means of referring to child-centered histories of children and childhood at different times and in different cultures.

Relatively few scholars working in the field have been concerned to debate methodology, although Australian researcher Jan Kociumbas sought to promote discussion with her 1984 article in *Labour History*, "Childhood History as Ideology." Hawes and Hiner proposed a useful framework for investigation in the introduction to their *Growing Up in America* (1985), suggesting that historians of children should explore adult attitudes towards children and childhood; the conditions shaping the development of children; the subjective experience of being a child in the past; children's influence on adults and each other; and the social, cultural, and psychological functions of children. Most historians have been primarily concerned to uncover the experiences of children in the past. The very nature of the subject matter means that, for the most part, the findings draw most heavily upon adult perceptions of children and childhood, since child-centered source material produced by children themselves is a relatively rare form of evidence prior to the development of compulsory elementary education, and most oral testimony is of childhood experience filtered through adult recollection.

The youth movements of the 1960s, the expansion of social history, an associated awareness that the experiences of both women and children were largely missing from historical narratives, and a gradual realization that the size of the youth presence in populations at any given time was such that it should not be ignored: all of these factors coincided with the publication of Ariès' work and contributed to a rapid expansion of scholarly interest in the experiences of children in the past. Both the diversity of childhoods and the variety of ways in which the history of children continues to be explored ensure that "childhood history" will remain as lively a field of historical enquiry as the subjects who are central to its existence.

JEANINE GRAHAM

See also Ariès; Pinchbeck

Further Reading

Ariès, Philippe, *L'Enfant et la vie familiale sous l'Ancien Regime*, Paris: Plon, 1960; in English as *Centuries of Childhood: A Social History of Family Life*, London: Cape, and New York: Knopf, 1962

Bremner, Robert, *Children and Youth in America*, 3 vols., Cambridge, MA: Harvard University Press, 1970–74

Cunningham, Hugh, *The Children of the Poor: Representations of Childhood since the Seventeenth Century*, Cambridge, MA and Oxford: Blackwell, 1991

Davin, Anna, *Growing Up Poor: Home, School and Street in London, 1870–1914*, London: Rivers Oram, 1996

deMause, Lloyd, ed., *The History of Childhood*, New York: Psychohistory Press, 1974

Demos, John, *A Little Commonwealth: Family Life in Plymouth Colony*, New York: Oxford University Press, 1970

Gil'adi, Avner, *Children of Islam: Concepts of Childhood in Medieval Muslim Society*, Basingstoke: Macmillan, and New York: St. Martin's Press, 1992

Hanawalt, Barbara A., *Growing Up in Medieval London: The Experience of Childhood in History*, Oxford and New York: Oxford University Press, 1993

Hawes, Joseph M., and N. Ray Hiner, eds., *American Childhood: A Research Guide and Historical Handbook*, Westport, CT: Greenwood Press, 1985

Hawes, Joseph M., and N. Ray Hiner, eds., *Growing Up in America: Children in Historical Perspective*, Urbana: University of Illinois Press, 1985

Hawes, Joseph M., and N. Ray Hiner, eds., *Children in Historical and Comparative Perspective: An International Handbook and Research Guide*, Westport, CT: Greenwood Press, 1991

Hawes, Joseph M., *The Children's Rights Movement: A History of Advocacy and Protection*, Boston: Twayne, 1991

Hetherington, Penelope, ed., *Childhood and Society in Western Australia*, Nedlands: University of Western Australia Press, 1988

Hopkins, Eric, *Childhood Transformed: Working-Class Children in Nineteenth-Century England*, Manchester: Manchester University Press, 1994

Kociumbas, Jan, "Childhood History as Ideology," *Labour History* [Australia] 47 (November 1984), 1–17

Magnússon, Sigurður Gylfi, "From Children's Point of View: Childhood in Nineteenth-Century Iceland," *Journal of Social History* 29 (1995), 295–323

Pinchbeck, Ivy, and Margaret Hewitt, *Children in English Society*, 2 vols., London: Routledge, 1969–73

Pollock, Linda, *Forgotten Children: Parent–Child Relations from 1500 to 1900*, Cambridge and New York: Cambridge University Press, 1983

Shahar, Shulamith, *Yaldut bi-Yeme-ha-benayim*, Tel Aviv: Devir, 1990; in English as *Childhood in the Middle Ages*, London and New York: Routledge, 1990

Shorter, Edward, *The Making of the Modern Family*, New York: Basic Books, 1975; London: Collins, 1976

Sutherland, Neil, *Children in English-Canadian Society: Framing the Twentieth-Century Consensus*, Toronto: University of Toronto Press, 1976

Sutherland, Neil, Jean Barman, and Veronica Strong-Boag, eds., *Canadian Childhood History Project: A Bibliography of Canadian Childhood*, Vancouver: Department of Social and Educational Studies, University of British Columbia, 1987

Sutherland, Neil, "When You Listen to the Winds of Childhood, How Much Can You Believe?," *Curriculum Inquiry* 22 (1992), 235–56

Walvin, James, *A Child's World: A Social History of English Childhood, 1800–1914*, Harmondsworth: Penguin, 1982

Werner, Emmy E., *Pioneer Children on the Journey West*, Boulder, CO: Westview Press, 1995

Wilson, Adrian, "The Infancy of the History of Childhood: An Appraisal of Philippe Ariès," *History and Theory* 19 (1980), 132–53

Zelizer, Vivianna, *Pricing the Priceless Child: The Changing Social Value of Children*, New York: Basic Books, 1985

China: Ancient (*c.*1500–221 BCE)

Antiquity or the past (*gu*) has long been a subject of Chinese interest, though it is more difficult to assert that this was a concern with "history" per se. Perhaps owing to the enduring cultural significance of the cult of the dead (popularly, and inappropriately, known as "ancestor worship"), the past has been the chief organizing principle and most common narrative device of Chinese life stories. Kong-zi (551–479 BCE), the legendary classical figure familiar to us in the West as Confucius, offered one of the most fitting statements of antiquity's significance when he said, "I receive, I do not invent. I trust and love the past." His putative avowal of devotion to *gu* contributed much toward a presumption enshrined in the Han dynasty (206 BCE–221 CE) that Kong-zi had written, edited, and/or assembled all the literary and historical works of the *sandai* ("Three Ages": Xia [legendary], Shang [1576–1046 BCE], and Zhou [1045–771 BCE]) comprising the Chinese canon. This figurative predication was a critical part of a normative narration of antiquity wherein the *sandai* forged a definitive cultural pattern according to which all subsequent time was measured.

The era before the *sandai* was China's age of heroes; it was an extended interval of slow time or, rather, time out of time, where the great culture heroes *Sanhuang* (Three Emperors) and *Wudi* (Five Sovereigns) mapped the heavens and ordered the earth. For their myriad descendants they left: divination (Fu Xi), fire (Sui Ren), the digging stick (Shen Nong), pacific civilization (Huang Di), meritocracy (Yao), diking and irrigation (Yu). The last of the sovereigns, Shun, appointed Yu to succeed him, in recognition of his control of the deluge that threatened to destroy the *zhongyuan* (North China Plain), the putative core of sinitic civilization. And it was Yu who founded the Xia dynasty and the first of the three eras. This first age, until very recently, was considered purely legendary, a time of pre- and post-diluvian heroes whose achievements and failures were loftily described in the *Shiji* (*The Grand Scribe's Records*, c.90 BCE), China's first comprehensive history, but of which there was scant artifactual evidence and, most importantly, no written records. From the Xia, we move to the historical time of the Shang and Zhou and, later, the first institutional experiments with centralized rule, the Qin (221–208 BCE) and the Han (206 BCE –221 CE). In this manner, the normative account insists on a common racial and ethnic descent of all Chinese from a core cultural complex (*huaxia*) in the North China Plain (*zhongyuan*).

Yet, ancient time has a history and the story of how it has been episodically construed has been told often in this century, as China's grand transformation from celestial empire to modern nation-state inspired many to explore with critical self-consciousness the imperial past both as artifact and idea. It was a newly emergent scholarly criticism of antiquity by modern historians Zhang Binglin, Hu Shi, and Gu Jiegang, combined with the ground-breaking paleographic work of Wang Guowei, Luo Zhenyu, Guo Moruo, and Dong Zuobin that created the conditions for a re-imagining of Chinese history in both its sweep and breadth. In a period of intense cultural questioning in the 1920s and 1930s, these revisionist efforts occurred along distinct, parallel trajectories: the former text-criticism cohort subjecting received works to scientific analysis; the latter paleography group parsing out the language of China's earliest written records on bone, shell, and bronze. Remarkable as their work was in establishing the historicity of the Shang through decipherment of the oracle bone inscriptions (*jiaguwen*), fleshing out the ceremonial political organization of the Zhou through translation of their inscribed bronzes (*jinwen*), and disclosing the mythic character of the canonical texts, the antiquity they reconstructed confounded a persistent national mythology of common descent.

Gu Jiegang's conclusive account of the received record of antiquity, in digest, may be found in a line from Saloustios not unfamiliar to the Western student of myth: "These things never happened, but are always." This is the lesson of antiquity's records according to Gu, whose efforts in *Gushi bian* (Critiques of Ancient History, 1926–41) to sort out the archival bulk of China's past led to the conclusion that much of ancient history, rather than a record of actual events, was a pious fabrication of latter-day archivists and literary figures who gave the past a history through embellishment and invention. Yet, unlike the march away from myth in the name of "objectivity" so evident in the history written in the West, history in China has remained bound in certain distinct ways to the mythical. This commingling of myth and history is explicit in the preservation of a chronology of antiquity first advanced in the Han and in the enduring commonplace that Chinese are all "children of the Yellow Emperor (Huangdi, first of the Five Sovereigns)."

It is in the context of the creative tension between a normative transmission that effaces the diversity of traditions of China's past and archaeological and exegetical work devoted to recuperating that diversity that 20th-century historiography of ancient China is best understood. Left as heritage, this unresolved tension has been taken up as a task by contemporary scholars of early China, whose techniques and approaches differ little from Chinese scholars of 60 years ago, except that paleography and the study of textual traditions have converged to yield a novel understanding of Chinese antiquity which has come at the expense of long-cherished conceptions of the past.

As a contemporary field of study, the history of early China is arguably the most vigorous of all branches of sinology and its scholarly health is the result of new readings and/or interpretations of received texts, as well as an astonishing number of archaeological discoveries, many of which have effected more significant revision in the inherited portrait of ancient China, others of which have affirmed the new readings of ancient texts, and still others that have compelled redaction of received texts. The field is marked by a broad front of diverse scholarly activity – excavation, transcription, dating, translation, and reconstruction – its vitality exemplified in the recent publication of special monographs, such as Michael Loewe's *Early Chinese Texts* (1993) and Edward L. Shaughnessy's *New Sources of Early Chinese History* (1997).

Expanding work of this sort on the research tools requisite for the understanding of ancient texts is the consequence of a steady flow of archaeological finds. A great number of these excavations occurred in the 1970s and yielded thousands of inscribed oracle bone fragments (virtually all from the late Shang period), hundreds of bronze vessels (many of them inscribed and most from the Zhou era), thousands of wood and bamboo covenant texts (most dating from just before the Warring States era, c.490 BCE), and copious manuscript finds (from the later Warring States, c.300 BCE, Qin, 217 BCE, and early Han, 168 BCE) some previously known, others unattested. However, it is only in the last few years that their contents have been disclosed through the publication in Chinese scholarly journals of photographs, rubbings, and transcriptions. The increasing availability of the manuscripts, in particular those recovered from Tomb 3 at Mawangdui near Changsha, Hunan in south central China, has made possible a staggering number of translations, many of them intended for the general reader.

Ballantine Books has teamed up with several eminent scholars of early China, some of whom have been negotiating with the Chinese government to publish excavated texts more rapidly, to produce English translations for the non-specialist of the *Yijing* (Classic of Changes), *De Dao Jing* (or *Laozi*), *Sunzi bingfa* (Master Sun's Methods of Combat), *Sun Bin bingfa* (Sun Bin's Methods of Combat), *Huang-Lao boshu* (Silk Manuscripts of the Yellow Emperor-Old Man), and the *Lunyu* (Selected Sayings or Analects [of Confucius]). The Mawangdui silk manuscript "*Laozi A*," more popularly known as the *Dao De Jing* (Tao Te Ching), exemplifies the contemporary convergence of paleography and text-based study while illustrating the peril of maintaining an uncritical attitude toward the received canon. The *Laozi* A also discloses the critical dialectical relationship between a living, transmitted text and its buried exemplar, for it was discovered that the received version of the text was in reverse order, the second part (*Dao*, the way) preceding the first (*De*, mana). A silk manuscript *Yijing* (the earliest yet discovered) and commentaries, also removed from Tomb 3, differed as well from the received text of the classic with respect to the sequence and graphic identity of some of the hexagrams. A discovery in 1973 at Dingxian, Hebei (Northern China) of a *Lunyu* manuscript in 20 chapters just like the received canonical 20, along with other manuscripts different from their transmitted counterparts, points to a pre-imperial China composed of diverse textual communities whose lives were underwritten by work on locally transmitted and edited texts and where information circulated widely. While these excavations from tomb libraries all over China have received much attention (most notably in the work of Donald Harper, Roger Ames, and Robert Henricks), scholars working on earlier paleographic texts and recovered objects are re-mapping the territory of late neolithic China (c.2100–1800 BCE) with dramatic consequences for the theory of its independent origin.

The orthodox conception of unitary cultural development from a northern core strains under the weight of mounting evidence that the peoples of ancient China were actors within a wide-ranging cultural ecology. On this latter point, a firestorm of controversy has been sparked by Victor Mair's report in *Archaeology* on the well-preserved Caucasian mummies uncovered in the Tarim Basin region in northwest China and dating from approximately 1200 BCE. The discovery provides confirmation of work underway in reconstructing the great arcs of human contact reaching from Central Asia and southern Siberia to northern China, the culturally pluralistic dimensions of which are breathtakingly explicit in the international scholarship produced on the subject in Mair's forthcoming edited anthology, *The Bronze Age and Iron Age Peoples of Eastern Central Asia*.

Recent work in archaeology, metals, pottery, and culture contact has provided evidence of an early Chinese civilization (the Qijia) in the northwest contemporaneous and interacting with cultures of Central Asia. Much of this can be found in a recent study by Louisa Fitzgerald-Huber of cross-cultural contact in the late neolithic (c.2000 BCE). Reasoning on the basis of an impressive collection of evidence, she successfully revised our understanding of a unified Chinese culture in favor of a broad multi-stranded cultural arc reaching from Bactria to Siberia, to northwestern China, and to north central China.

Regardless of how ancient Chinese civilization assumed its historic forms, once in place it generated a mass of documentation impressive in its volume, range, and complexity. The welter of documentation of their past, both real and imagined, and the task of parsing out this past and attempting to determine whether it was endowed with "historicity" has been the subject of decades of historical inquiry by Chinese, Japanese, and Western scholars. The earliest extant textual sources, while they are not histories in the modern sense of the term, provide us a window on the formation of early historic civilization. The oracle bone inscriptions (*jiaguwen*, literally "inscriptions on shell and bone") are the first written records of the Chinese, although some scholars, such as David Pankenier, are convinced that "Chinese writing predates the earliest oracle bone inscriptions by a very considerable time."

To date, more than 200,000 fragments of such inscribed texts, all of which were produced from 1200 to 1046 BCE, have been found, of which approximately 50,000 have been published as rubbings. From this growing corpus a great deal has been learned of the functioning of the Bronze Age theocracy known as the Shang which maintained a measure of control over the region of the North China Plain. These unique inscriptions and their decipherment by Shima Kunio, Takashima Ken-ichi, and David Keightley, have revealed much about the Shang quotidian: the lengths of the day and week, their concept of space, their sacrificial economy, their itinerancy, but above all, the profound significance of their ancestors, specifically the dead kings of the early Shang. The importance of the dead is unmistakable in the surviving inscriptional record, for divinations about them constitute roughly 80 per cent of the excavated total. However, the oracle bone inscriptions also speak of Shang territory (*wotian*, literally, "our fields"), offensive and defensive engagements with adversaries, progresses and hunts, and frequent mention of the names other tribal groups gave themselves.

The Shang were not alone, being one of a number of tribes within a contiguous complex of groups, and, thus, spoke for themselves. Indeed, the reconstruction of numerous sites of parallel cultural development has been one of the obvious consequences of the feverish archaeological activity of the past 20 years. The work, first of Virginia Kane, and more recently of Robert Bagley, has cast a needed clarifying light on regional bronze metallurgy during the 2nd to 1st millennium BCE, disclosing the existence of a considerable number of groups contiguous with the Shang who were capable of producing ritual vessels. Knowing that bronze was sacred and used exclusively for rites that gave order to clan life, the evidence of regional bronze-making cultures suggests that there were other worlds, other cosmologies, and perhaps other, as yet undiscovered, inscribed texts. Nevertheless, it is from the surviving records of the Shang theocracy that some scholars – having identified cultural traits such as sericulture, divination, bronze metallurgy, and ancestor worship all prefigurative of later developments – have drawn historical lines of descent to the present.

The Zhou left, as well, a generous archival record consisting of some divinatory bone inscriptions (unearthed in 1976 at Qishan, Shaanxi near the ancient Zhou homeland in northwest China), and an increasing number of inscribed bronze vessels, many of which have been catalogued by Chinese (Zhou Fagao, Guo Moruo) and Japanese scholars (Shirakawa Shizuka), and a few of which have been analyzed and translated by Edward L. Shaughnessy in *Sources of Western Zhou*

History (1991). Ritual bronzes, like oracle bone inscriptions, though offering little in the way of evidence of a Chinese "historical sense," do provide records of ancient liturgy and religious performance, as Jessica Rawson has pointed out in her monumental survey of the early Zhou bronzes in the Arthur M. Sackler Collections. They are assuredly not primary documents. The vessels were cast to celebrate and record formal occasions of the conferring of a fief or title on members of cadet lineages bound by either blood or mutual self-interest with the ruling Ji clan of the Zhou. A record of investiture to a loyal scribe was publicly announced at the royal palace of the Ji clan, transcribed onto bamboo, then transported by the scribe to his natal fief whereupon a bronze vessel was cast bearing the original charge along with a dedication by the scribe to his ancestors. Ritual bronzes – food and drink vessels, cooking and serving utensils, bells – so inscribed and placed in the lineage temple are thus several layers removed from the event and, as Shaughnessy and Lothar von Falkenhausen have demonstrated, were not literal transcripts but the negotiated products of royal decrees to subordinates. Bronzes, then, are less primary sources than exemplars of a curious Zhou "inter-textuality" wherein contiguous tribal groups were bound in a pacific confederacy through the exchange of inscribed gifts and offerings to lineage forebears.

A change in the composition of this cultic confederacy may be recognized in an extraordinary cache of bronze vessels, all valued possessions of several generations of a single clan of scribes named Wei, unearthed in 1976 in Shaanxi from a pit where they had been placed for safekeeping when the Zhou was overcome by its former dependants in 771 BCE. The cache of 103 bronze vessels, 74 of which bore inscriptions containing a narrative genealogy of the clan and accounts of events crucial to the Zhou conquest of the region, the Zhuangbai hoard 1, has proven invaluable in clarifying the chronology of events attested in received accounts from the *Shang shu* (Revered Documents, Book of History, *c.*600–200 BCE) in addition to permitting scholars to organize vessel styles into a sequenced stratigraphy. More valuable than this, however, is the subtle evidence contained in bronzes cast by the last lineage head, named Xing, of symbolic abduction wherein reverence for ancestors is replaced by an assertive sense of the greatness of the present generation.

In the Springs and Autumns (*Chunqiu*, 770–479 BCE) and Warring States periods (*Zhan'guo shidai*, 479–221 BCE) that followed, the violent consequences of this symbolic abduction were worked out. In this interval preceding the formation of centralized imperial rule, the peoples of China underwent an extraordinary transformation with the appearance of multiple urban centers, water control, cavalry, the crossbow, burgeoning handicraft industries and trade, legal codes, and most notably, an avalanche of texts. A common emphasis in studies of this era neglects the violence explicit in its title for an attention to the texts as emblematic of a "golden age" of Chinese philosophy. This was the era of the so-called *baijia* (100 schools), the peripatetic persuaders such as the *ru* (weaklings or "Confucians"), *fa* (methods or "Legalists"), *nong* (tillers), *dao* (way or "Daoists"), whose teachings formed a natural philosophical, ritual, administrative, medical, and legal reservoir from which was drawn the intellectual heritage of all subsequent Chinese civilization.

An inspired reconstruction of this history from received texts and recent excavations is Mark Edward Lewis' *Sanctioned Violence in Early China* (1990) which described this period of textual productivity against the backdrop of the aggressive resolution of the myriad tribal kingdoms of the post-Zhou era into a single dynastic state. Lewis' work effects a complete re-conceptualization of the formative history of the imperium by placing violence in the forefront and treating Warring States texts as epiphenomena. War raged over the landscape of Iron Age China, occurring between, and within, kingdoms from 770 to 221 BCE, as the aristocratic clans constituting the familial backbone of the early Chinese state eliminated each other. The records of the period show that, amidst this havoc, a new warrior elite was created, one sustained by slaughter the resulting spoils of which were not respectfully offered as gifts to the dead. Instead, war was justified as necessary to the maintenance of a social order imitative of that given by the great culture heroes who had fashioned order from chaos, and effective campaigns could be prosecuted only through strategy, that is the expertise brought from the study of texts.

What distinguished this Warring States mutation was the loosening of the bonds of violence to the cult of the dead and releasing it upon the cosmos. Violence was naturalized and now necessary to the forging of a state under the absolute rule of a commander. The martial commander, holding power over life and death, emerged as the metaphorical authority in Warring States society and this model, in an age of growing literacy and wandering persuaders, was cast back upon antiquity, resulting in the invention of the Three Emperors and the Five Sovereigns as authoritarians who acted at the behest of heaven in creating humanity by tearing it violently from nature. Yet, the revised portrait of contending states governed by a rapacious warrior elite offered by Lewis stands in contrast to evidence from other late Warring States texts like the *Zhou li* (Rites of Zhou), which indicate movement away from martial fiefs toward a bureaucratic state. Thus the increasingly common envisioning of the state as the inspired product of the necessary, violent excess of a sage-king or similar exemplar reflects not the ascendance of the warrior, but instead the competing strains of a declining feudal ethic and its bureaucratic successor.

Thus, in stressing a Warring States version of absolute kingship justified by appeal to heaven and the examples of the culture heroes, Lewis invoked Gu Jiegang's argument for a layered invention of antiquity according to which the earlier a figure is seen in China's mythic strata, the later it is invented. Also, he placed the intellectual history of the period in a new light by portraying the *baijia* as a contentious collection of advocacies aimed at enhancing, limiting, or eliminating the absolute authority of kingship.

This view of the traditions of Warring States thought is convincingly reinforced by the most exciting text-based scholarship on Chinese antiquity, that of E. Bruce Brooks and A. Taeko Brooks. They labored in relative isolation for more than two decades, but their efforts to establish a reliable chronology for selected texts of the 5th to 3rd centuries BCE gained a scholarly forum in 1993 with the creation of the Warring States Working Group. The group treats texts as living traditions and, relying on a typology of texts in which the genuine/spurious dichotomy is enriched by the addition of an accretional model of text information, has been able to propose full or partial stratifications or dating for many of the heterogeneous works brought forward in the Warring States avalanche. Texts of this era are considered as an evolving "record of an advocacy position over decades and sometimes even centuries." Reliable dates are considered assignable to textual strata alone, never to an entire work unless that work can be demonstrated to be integral, and thus the matter of authenticity remains ongoing. Moreover, strata may be compared with parallel texts of the same time in China, or even with texts from another culture, to consider the diverse provenance and history of transmission of the work. The results have been impressive: the first example of a text fully analyzed by this method – *The Original Analects: The Sayings of Confucius and His Successors* (1998) – was recently published. In the coming years it is hoped to give equally thorough treatment to other major texts, among them *Mengzi* (Book of Master Meng or Mencius), *Sunzi bingfa* (Master Sun's Art of War), the *Dao De Jing* and the *Chunqiu* (Springs and Autumns Chronicle), and to produce summary accounts of the *Shijing* (Classic of Poetry) and of the general development of Warring States thought and society. As with archaeological excavations and a new historicist paleography, the Brooks' endeavor provides an impressive corrective to the narrative of China's unitary cultural evolution.

Taken as a whole, the contemporary study of Chinese antiquity would encourage the adventurer to explore the increasingly accessible reaches of ancient China and to distrust received images of uniformity and continuity in favor of the matter-of-fact usages of a cultural complexity heretofore only marginally represented. China is a place of many pasts, and with the especially intense engagement of scholars of many disciplines with antiquity, we are acquiring more and more insight into the diverse sources of ancient Chinese life. China's past was never as inert as the monolithic metaphor, "the world's longest continuous culture," would suggest and that is perhaps the most obvious consequence of the recent upsurge in the study of antiquity by scholars in China, Japan, Europe, and the United States. Thus, as the close of our millennium approaches and the events of Chinese antiquity recede further from view, we know and understand more than ever before about ancient Chinese whose lives were left in numerous evidentiary shards of bronze, bone, tortoise shell, wood, bamboo, and silk.

LIONEL JENSEN

See also Eberhard; Gu; Kong-zi; Sima Qian

Further Reading

Akatsuka Kiyoshi, *Chūgoku kodai no shūkyō to bunka: In ōchō no saishi* (China's Ancient Religion and Culture: The Sacrifices of the Yin Dynasty), Tokyo: Kadokawa Shoten, 1977
Allan, Sarah, *The Shape of the Turtle: Myth, Art, and Cosmos in Ancient China*, Albany: State University of New York Press, 1991
Ames, Roger T., trans., *Sun-tzu: The Art of Warfare*, New York: Ballantine, 1993
Ames, Roger T., and Henry Rosemont, Jr., trans., *The Confucian Analects: A Philosophical Translation*, New York: Ballantine, 1998
Bagley, Robert W., *Shang Ritual Bronzes in the Arthur M. Sackler Collections*, Cambridge, MA: Harvard University Press, 1987
Birrell, Anne, *Chinese Mythology: An Introduction*, Baltimore: Johns Hopkins University Press, 1993
Boltz, William, *The Origin and Early Development of the Chinese Writing System*, New Haven: American Oriental Society, 1994
Brooks, E. Bruce, and A. Taeko Brooks, *The Original Analects: The Sayings of Confucius and His Successors*, New York: Columbia University Press, 1998
Chang Kwang-chih, *Art, Myth, and Ritual: The Path to Political Authority in Ancient China*, Cambridge, MA: Harvard University Press, 1983
Eberhard, Wolfram, *Lokalkulturen im alten China*, vol. 2: *Die Lokalkulturen des Südens und Ostens*, Leiden: Brill, 1942; in English as *The Local Cultures of South and East China*, Leiden: Brill, 1968
Falkenhausen, Lothar von, *Suspended Music: Chime-bells in the Culture of Bronze Age China*, Berkeley: University of California Press, 1993
Fitzgerald-Huber, Louisa, "Qijia and Erlitou: The Question of Contacts with Distant Cultures," *Early China* 20 (1995), 17–67
Granet, Marcel, *Danses et légendes de la Chine ancienne* (Dances and Legends of Ancient China) 2 vols., Paris: Alcan, 1926
Gu Jiegang [Ku Chieh-kang], *Gushi bian* (Critiques of Ancient History) 7 vols., 1926–41; reprinted 1982
Harper, Donald, *Early Chinese Medical Literature: The Mawangdui Medical Transcripts*, New York: Columbia University Press, 1997
Henricks, Robert G., trans., *Lao-tzu Te-tao Ching: A New Translation Based on the Recently Discovered Ma-wang-tui Texts*, New York: Ballantine, 1989; London: Rider, 1991
Hsü Cho-yün and Katheryn Linduff, *Western Chou Civilization*, New Haven and London: Yale University Press, 1988
Hulsewé, Anthony F.P., *Remnants of Ch'in Law: An Annotated Translation of the Ch'in Legal and Administrative Rules of the Third Century BC, Discovered in Yün-meng Prefecture, Hu-pei Province, in 1975*, Leiden: Brill, 1985
Jensen, Lionel M., *Manufacturing Confucianism: Chinese Traditions and Universal Civilization*, Durham, NC: Duke University Press, 1997
Kane, Virginia C., "The Independent Bronze Industries in the South of China Contemporary with the Shang and Zhou Dynasties," *Archives of Asian Art* 28 (1974–75), 77–107
Karlgren, Bernhard, "Legends and Cults in Ancient China," *Bulletin of the Museum of Far Eastern Antiquities* 18 (1946), 199–365
Keightley, David N., *Sources of Shang History: The Oracle Bone Inscriptions of Bronze Age China*, Berkeley: University of California Press, 1978
Lau, Dim Cheuk, ed., *The ICS Ancient Chinese Texts Concordance Series*, Hong Kong: Commercial Press, 1992–
Lau, Dim Cheuk, and Roger T. Ames, trans., *Sun Pin: The Art of Warfare*, New York: Ballantine, 1996
Lewis, Mark Edward, *Sanctioned Violence in Early China*, Albany: State University of New York Press, 1990
Li Xueqin, *Eastern Zhou and Qin Civilizations*, New Haven and London: Yale University Press, 1985
Loewe, Michael, ed., *Early Chinese Texts: A Bibliographical Guide*, Berkeley, CA: Institute of East Asian Studies, 1993
Mair, Victor H., "The Mummies of the Tarim Basin," *Archaeology* 48 (1995), 28–35
Mair, Victor H., ed., *The Bronze Age and Iron Age Peoples of Eastern Central Asia*, 2 vols., Philadelphia: University of Pennsylvania Museum of Archaeology and Anthropology, forthcoming
Matsumaru Michiō and Takashima Ken-ichi, eds., *Kōkotsumoji jishaku sōran* (Comprehensive Guide to Interpretations of Oracle Bone Graphs), Tokyo: Tokyo University Press, 1994
Pankenier, David, "The Cosmo-political Background of Heaven's Mandate," *Early China* 20 (1995), 121–76
Peerenboom, Randall P., *Law and Morality in Ancient China: The Silk Manuscripts of Huang-Lao*, Albany: State University of New York Press, 1993

Porter, Deborah Lynne, *From Deluge to Discourse: Myth, History, and the Generation of Chinese Fiction*, Albany: State University of New York Press, 1996

Rawson, Jessica, *Western Zhou Ritual Bronzes from the Arthur M. Sackler Collections*, Washington, DC: Arthur M. Sackler Gallery of Art, and Cambridge, MA: Arthur M. Sackler Museum, 1990

Schwartz, Benjamin I., *The World of Thought in Ancient China*, Cambridge, MA: Harvard University Press, 1985

Shaughnessy, Edward L., *Sources of Western Zhou History: Inscribed Bronze Vessels*, Berkeley: University of California Press, 1991

Shaughnessy, Edward L., trans., *I Ching: The Classic of Changes*, New York: Ballantine, 1997

Shaughnessy, Edward L., ed., *New Sources of Early Chinese History: An Introduction to the Reading of Inscriptions and Manuscripts*, Berkeley, CA: Institute of East Asian Studies, 1997

Shima Kunio, *Inkyo bokuji sorui* (Collected Inventory of the Oracle Texts from the Wastes of Yin), Tokyo: Taian, 1964; revised 1971

Sima Qian, *The Grand Scribe's Records*, edited by William H. Nienhauser, Jr., Bloomington: Indiana University Press, 1994–

Vandermeersch, Léon, *Wangdao, ou, la voie royale: Recherches sur l'esprit des institutions de la Chine archaïque* (Wangdao; or, The Royal Way: Researches on the Spirit of the Institutions of Ancient China), 2 vols., Paris: Ecole Française d'Extrême-Orient, 1977–80

Wen Fong, ed., *The Great Bronze Age of China: An Exhibition from the People's Republic of China*, New York: Metropolitan Museum of Art, and London: Thames and Hudson, 1980

Wu Hung, *Monumentality in Early Chinese Art and Architecture*, Stanford, CA: Stanford University Press, 1995

Yates, Robin D.S., trans., *Five Lost Classics: Tao, Huang-Lao, and Yin-yang in Han China*, New York: Ballantine, 1997

China: Early and Middle Imperial

(221 BCE–959 CE)

The unification of China under the power of the Qin state in 221 BCE initiated 21 centuries of centralized imperial government over eight major dynasties. Central government under the control of a single dynasty remained a powerful, though often distant, ideal even during periods of division. Under the unifying force of the first emperor, Qin armies defeated each rival, and initiated reforms that went far toward abolishing the decentralized structure of the Zhou and extended the influence of the state. Especially important was the division of the empire into 36 commanderies, which in turn were subdivided into counties, with all levels ultimately accountable to the central government – a system that persisted in its broad form throughout much of the imperial period.

Qin also initiated a more central control through the standardization of scripts, weights, measures, and currency, and began the process of building thousands of miles of imperial highways and waterways to connect China's various regions – even beginning work on northern fortifications that would, more than a millennium later, be represented by the Great Wall. The vast process of standardization and centralization would play a major role – both practically and symbolically – in later periods, as the unification became the model of central government that would persist throughout Chinese history. The most significant survey of this period is Denis Twitchett and Michael Loewe's *The Cambridge History of China*, vol. 1: *The Ch'in and Han Empires, 221 BC–AD 220* (1986), of which Derk

Bodde's first chapter forms a major overview of the Qin unification. Other important works on this still relatively understudied period include A.F.P. Hulsewé's *Remnants of Ch'in Law* (1985), Yang Kuan's *Qin Shihuang* (The First Emperor of Qin, 1956), and Derk Bodde's still useful translation of three biographies of major Qin figures, *Statesman, Patriot, and General in Ancient China* (1940).

China's first imperial dynasty endured for less than two decades, and had only two emperors. The Han dynasty succeeded Qin, when Liu Bang, a commoner, assumed the title of emperor in 202 BCE. Building upon the strengths of Qin unification, but carefully backing away from its excesses, Han saw 400 years of rule, interrupted in the first decade of the common era by a 15-year challenge from Wang Mang's Xin dynasty (9–23 CE). Although the period has traditionally been characterized for its effective central rule and stability, in fact the periods marked by dynastic strength and stable administration were relatively few. For much of the Former Han uneasy relations with northern groups, particularly the Xiongnu, were predominant, and several reigns in the Later Han were characterized by palace intrigue and corruption at court.

The Han bureaucracy solidified many aspects of state power during its first century while dealing with the delicate balance created by having rewarded followers of Liu Bang with hundreds of estates shortly after the dynasty's founding. Pressures from relatives of empresses and other "unofficial" members of the court, who at times wielded enormous influence, also formed a long-term challenge to Han's rulers. In addition to the *Cambridge History*, notable surveys on the Han include Wang Zhongshu's *Han Civilization* (1982), Michele Pirazzoli-t'Serstevens' *La Chine des Han* (1982; *The Han Dynasty*, 1982), Hans Bielenstein's *The Bureaucracy of Han Times* (1980), and Michael Loewe's *Crisis and Conflict in Han China* (1974). Among the important monographs on this period's growing scholarship are A.F.P. Hulsewé's *Remnants of Han Law* (1955) and *China in Central Asia* (1979), Hsü Cho-yün's *Han Agriculture* (1980), Yü Ying-shih's *Trade and Expansion in Han China* (1967), and Michael Loewe's *Everyday Life in Early Imperial China* (1968).

The Han, weakened by internal pressures in the 2nd century CE, gave way to 350 years of division, in which China was split, first into the three kingdoms of Wei, Wu, and Shu during the 3rd century, and again into a succession of northern and southern dynasties over the next three centuries. Although the period has not been studied with the same thoroughness of earlier and later periods of central rule, several works provide useful documentation, including Achilles Fang's translation of relevant sections of the exemplary Sima Guang's *Zizhi tongjian* and Rafe de Crespigny's *Northern Frontier* (1984), which treated issues of northern policy that would set the theme for the next four centuries.

During the period of disunion, Buddhism gained followers in the fragmented kingdoms as state Confucianism went into decline. Buddhism spread throughout China, laying a foundation for its central place in the unified states of Sui and T'ang. Important works on Chinese Buddhism during this period include Kenneth Chen's *Buddhism in China* (1964), and Erik Zürcher's *The Buddhist Conquest of China* (1959). The period of disunion was also a time for a flourishing of Daoist writings, art, and eclectic thought, as well as the continued power of an aristocracy that gained power in the Han. Recent scholarship includes Patricia Ebrey's *The Aristocratic Families of Early Imperial China* (1978), Albert Dien's *State and Society in Early Medieval China* (1990), and David Johnson's *The Medieval Chinese Oligarchy* (1977).

The centuries of re-established unity under the Sui (581–617) and T'ang (618–906) dynasties saw the return to a single polity of vastly changed northern and southern territories, after three centuries of division. The Sui founder, Yang Jian, from a part-nomad northern family, had the difficult task of reuniting north and south through a centralized legal code, new roads, and waterways – tasks that call to mind Qin's short-lived centralization seven centuries earlier. Sui Yangdi, the second and last emperor of the dynasty, who undertook the largest centralizing efforts early in his reign, combined this work with large-scale military efforts, including an attempt to gain control of the Korean peninsula, only to be defeated there and beset by internal rebellion in China. It is as though Qin and Sui, overwhelmed by the internal and external demands of reinventing central rule, were unable to reign for more than two generations. The major general work on this period is Twitchett and Fairbank's *Cambridge History of China*, vol. 3: *Sui and T'ang China, 589–906*, part 1 (1979). Arthur Wright's *The Sui Dynasty* (1978) is a fine overview of the dynastic founding, and represents an impressive sensitivity to the historiographical peculiarities of his sources, especially the *Zizhi tongjian* and the *T'ang Shu*.

The T'ang, not unlike the Han before it, gained control of China during the confusion of the last years of the short-lived Sui. The T'ang founders inherited Sui's centralizing achievements, and quickly moved to solidify the state and display its military strength to the always problematic north. In both geographic expanse and cultural achievements T'ang has traditionally been regarded among Chinese readers as the height of imperial China, and a lasting model for later periods. From its capital in Chang'an, which became one of the richest and most cosmopolitan cities the world would see for many centuries, T'ang slowly solidified a modified bureaucratic structure that would persist throughout the imperial period and began, under the leadership of the second emperor, Gaozong (reigned 649–683), to expand its military influence in all directions, including into Vietnam, Korea, and much of Central Asia.

Solidification of T'ang rule continued unabated, even throughout what traditional historians considered the despotic reign of empress Wu (reigned 684–705), who came to power, first as a regent and then in her own right, in the late 7th century. The T'ang saw its height, as well as the seeds of its demise, during the reign of the emperor Xuanzong (reigned 713–755). The early decades of the reign saw perhaps the greatest cultural displays China had ever known, as well as a capable and efficient government machinery. The later years of his reign saw the solid framework of the first century of T'ang rule undone by an emperor and bureaucracy meandering aimlessly through more than a decade of a leadership vacuum that resulted in command of frontier armies being turned over to alien generals and palace intrigue on a monumental scale. Although traditional historians point out the familiar villains – eunuchs, maternal relatives, and (in this case) a lovely concubine – it is clear that a combination of misrule and larger social and economic changes contributed to the mid-T'ang crisis,

which came to a head when a Turkish general rebelled, leading his troops toward Luoyang and then Chang'an, while Xuanzong and his court fled southward into Sichuan in one of the most famous exoduses in Chinese history.

The An Lushan rebellion from 755 to 763 was extremely destructive and, even though T'ang's power was restored, the next 150 years reflected a severely weakened state, with increasing difficulties with northern groups and ineffective central institutions. In addition to the *Cambridge History*, prominent works on T'ang government and history include a good introduction to period in Howard Wechsler's *Mirror to the Son of Heaven* (1974), David McMullen's *State and Scholars in T'ang China* (1988), Charles Hartman's *Han Yü and the Search for T'ang Unity* (1986) and John Perry and Bardwell Smith's edited collection *Essays on T'ang Society* (1976). Major works on cultural issues include Edward Schafer's *The Golden Peaches of Samarkand* (1963), *The Vermilion Bird* (1967), and *Pacing the Void* (1977), as well as Stephen Teiser's *The Ghost Festival in Medieval China* (1988).

The fall of the T'ang led to another period of division, the Five Dynasties, in which China was again divided between north and south. What are traditionally termed the Ten Kingdoms rose in succession in the south, largely unhindered by the more powerful northern states. None was strong enough to consolidate the south, or approach unification of the empire. In the north, five dynasties rose and fell, each lasting only a matter of years, as military influence passed from one set of rulers to another. Among the relatively few works devoted to the period are Wang Gung-wu's *The Structure of Power in North China during the Five Dynasties* (1963), Shu Fen's *Liao shi gao* (Investigations into the Liao Period, 1984), and thorough studies by the Japanese scholar Shimada Masao, such as *Ryō no shakai to bunka* (Liao Society and Culture, 1956) and *Ryōchō shi no kenkyū* (Studies in Liao History, 1979).

The first twelve centuries of imperial rule in China thus saw a pattern of unity and division that echoes the beginning of the Ming (1368–1644) novel *Three Kingdoms* – "The empire, long divided, must unite; long united, must divide." Although the profound political, social, and economic factors behind this pattern are specific to each period, the traditional rendering remains persuasive in its broad brushstrokes.

ROBERT A. LaFLEUR

See also Chen; Sima Guang

Further Reading

Bielenstein, Hans, *The Bureaucracy of Han Times*, Cambridge and New York: Cambridge University Press, 1980

Bodde, Derk, *Statesman, Patriot, and General in Ancient China: Three Shih-chi Biographies of the Ch'in Dynasty (255–206 BC)*, New Haven: American Oriental Society, 1940; reprinted New York: Kraus, 1967

Chen, Kenneth S., *Buddhism in China: A Historical Survey*, Princeton: Princeton University Press, 1964

Cheng Qianfan, *T'angdai jinshi xingjuan yu wenxue* (T'ang Dynasty Literature and Jinshi Candidate Literary Portfolios), Shanghai, 1980

Crespigny, Rafe de, *Northern Frontier: The Policies and Strategy of the Later Han Empire*, Canberra: Australian National University Press, 1984

Dien, Albert E., ed, *State and Society in Early Medieval China*, Stanford, CA: Stanford University Press, 1990

Ebrey, Patricia Buckley, *The Aristocratic Families of Early Imperial China: A Case Study of the Po-ling Ts'ui Family*, Cambridge and New York: Cambridge University Press, 1978

Fu Xuanzong, *T'angdai keju yu wenxue* (The T'ang Dynasty Examination System and Literature), Sian, 1986

Gao Buying, *T'ang Song wen juyao* (Essentials of T'ang and Song Literature), 3 vols., Hong Kong, 1976

Hartman, Charles, *Han Yü and the Search for T'ang Unity*, Princeton: Princeton University Press, 1986

Hsü Cho-yün, *Han Agriculture: The Formation of Early Chinese Agrarian Economy*, 206 BC–AD 220, Seattle: University of Washington Press, 1980

Hulsewé, Anthony F.P., *Remnants of Han Law*, Leiden: Brill, 1955

Hulsewé, Anthony F.P., *China in Central Asia: The Early Stage, 125 BC to AD 23: An Annotated Translation of Chapters 61–96 of the History of the Former Han Dynasty*, Leiden: Brill, 1979

Hulsewé, Anthony F.P., *Remnants of Ch'in Law: An Annotated Translation of the Ch'in Legal and Administrative Rules of the 3rd Century BC*, Leiden: Brill, 1985

Johnson, David G., *The Medieval Chinese Oligarchy*, Boulder, CO: Westview Press, 1977

Loewe, Michael, *Everyday Life in Early Imperial China during the Han Period*, 202 BC–AD 220, New York: Putnam, 1968; London: Carousel, 1973

Loewe, Michael, *Crisis and Conflict in Han China, 104 BC–AD 9*, London: Allen and Unwin, 1974

Luo Genze, *Wan T'ang Wudai wenxue piping shi* (A History of Literary Criticism in the T'ang and Five Dynasties), Shanghai, 1945

Luo Genze, *Sui T'ang wenxue piping shi* (A History of Literary Criticism in the Sui and T'ang), Taipei, 1981

McMullen, David, *State and Scholars in T'ang China*, Cambridge and New York: Cambridge University Press, 1988

Perry, John Curtis, and Bardwell L. Smith, eds., *Essays on T'ang Society: The Interplay of Social, Political, and Economic Forces*, Leiden: Brill, 1976

Pirazzoli-t'Serstevens, Michele, *La Chine des Han: histoire et civilisation*, Paris: Presses Universitaires de France, 1982; in US as *The Han Dynasty*, New York: Rizzoli, 1982; in UK as *The Han Civilization of China*, Oxford: Phaidon, 1982

Qian Mu, *Guoshi dagang* (Outline of Chinese History), Shanghai, 1948

Schafer, Edward H., *The Golden Peaches of Samarkand: A Study of T'ang Exotics*, Berkeley: University of California Press, 1963

Schafer, Edward H., *The Vermilion Bird: T'ang Images of the South*, Berkeley: University of California Press, 1967

Schafer, Edward H., *Pacing the Void: T'ang Approaches to the Stars*, Berkeley: University of California Press, 1977

Shimada Masao, *Ryō no shakai to bunka* (Liao Society and Culture), Tokyo, 1956

Shimada Masao, *Ryōchō shi no kenkyū* (Studies in Liao History), Tokyo, 1979

Shu Fen, *Liao shi gao* (Investigations into the Liao Period), Wuhan, 1984

Sima Guang, *The Chronicle of the Three Kingdoms*, translated by Achilles Fang, 2 vols., Cambridge, MA: Harvard University Press, 1952–65

Teiser, Stephen F., *The Ghost Festival in Medieval China*, Princeton: Princeton University Press, 1988

Twitchett, Denis, and John K. Fairbank, eds., *The Cambridge History of China*, vol. 3: *Sui and T'ang China, 589–906*, part 1, Cambridge and New York: Cambridge University Press, 1979

Twitchett, Dennis, and Michael Loewe, eds., *The Cambridge History of China*, vol. 1: *The Ch'in and Han Empires, 221 BC–AD 220*, Cambridge and New York: Cambridge University Press, 1986

Utsunomiya Kiyoyoshi, *Chūgoku kodai chūseishi kenkyū* (Studies of Ancient and Medieval Chinese Philosophy), Tokyo, 1977

Wang Gung-wu, *The Structure of Power in North China during the Five Dynasties*, London: Oxford University Press, and Stanford, CA: Stanford University Press, 1963

Wang Zhongshu, *Han Civilization*, New Haven and London: Yale University Press, 1982

Wechsler, Howard, *Mirror to the Son of Heaven: Wei Cheng at the Court of T'ang T'ai-Tsung*, New Haven and London: Yale University Press, 1974

Wright, Arthur, *The Sui Dynasty: The Unification of China, AD 581–617*, New York: Knopf, 1978

Xiao Gongquan, *Zhongguo zhengzhi sixiang shi*, 6 vols., Taipei, 1954; in English as *The History of Chinese Political Thought*, one vol. to date, Princeton: Princeton University Press, 1979

Yang Kuan, *Qin Shihuang* (The First Emperor of Qin), Shanghai: Renmin chubanshe, 1956

Yü Ying-shih, *Trade and Expansion in Han China: A Study in the Structure of Sino-Barbarian Economic Relations*, Berkeley: University of California Press, 1967

Zürcher, Erik J., *The Buddhist Conquest of China: The Spread and Adaptation of Buddhism in Early Medieval China*, 2 vols., Leiden: Brill, 1959

China: Late Imperial (960–1911)

The Song dynasty represents a shift in historical – and hence, historiographical – emphasis towards what many scholars have termed a "great divide," or "neo-traditional society." With roots in the T'ang, as early as the 8th century, and continuing on throughout the Song, China saw a profound, but slow-moving, shift in social, economic, technological, and material life. These deep changes, which echo Fernand Braudel's second level of historical change, have been the emphasis of a number of major works in the past quarter century, including Mark Elvin's *The Pattern of the Chinese Past* (1973), Robert Hymes's study of elite families in two localities, *Statesmen and Gentlemen* (1986), Richard Davis's *Court and Family in Sung China* (1986), and Patricia Ebrey's introduction and translation, *Family and Property in Sung China: Yüan Tsai's Precepts for Social Life* (1984). Works on economy and commerce have included Paul Smith's *Taxing Heaven's Storehouse* (1991), Richard von Glahn's *The Country of Streams and Grottoes* (1987) which analyzed the role of migration on China's frontier, and Shiba Yoshinobu's *Sōdai Shōgyō-shi Kenykū* (1968; *Commerce and Society in Sung China*, 1970), which provided an introduction to the massive changes in society and economy during the Song.

The Song has been characterized in 20th-century historiography not only for its major long-term changes, but also (following more traditional historians) for its enormous political intrigue, intellectual achievements, and uneasy relations with northern groups, who would play a major role in each of China's subsequent dynasties. The Northern Song (960–1127), which denotes the time before the capital was forced southward by the increasingly prominent Jin state, was a time of great intellectual growth, and represented the solidification of the examination system, which would become the primary means of entering bureaucratic service during the late imperial period. Major scholarship on these themes has included John Chaffee's *The Thorny Gates of Learning in Sung China* (1985), Thomas Lee's *Government Education and Examinations in Sung China* (1985), and Winston Lo's *An Introduction to the Civil Service of Sung China* (1987), as well as Miyazaki Ichisada's *Kakyo Gōkyō* (1946; *China's Examination Hell*, 1976), which provides a basic introduction to the examinations from Song through Qing.

Works on the important intellectual changes of this time include James T.C. Liu's survey of these issues, *China Turning Inward* (1988) and Peter Bol's meticulously researched *"This Culture of Ours"* (1992). On Song Neo-Confucianism, prominent works include Thomas Metzger's *Escape from Predicament* (1977), Wing-tsit Chan's *Chu Hsi: Life and Thought* (1987) and *Chu Hsi: New Studies* (1989), as well as Daniel Gardner's *Chu Hsi and the Ta-hsueh* (1986). Other major Song intellectual figures have been treated in fine biographies, such as Anne Birdwhistell's *Transition to Neo-Confucianism* (1989), Jonathan Chaves' *Mei Yao-ch'en and the Development of Early Sung Poetry* (1976), and Hoyt Tillman's *Utilitarian Confucianism* (1982), as well as Ronald Egan's *The Literary Works of Ou-yang Hsiu* (1984) and *Word, Image, and Deed in the Life of Su Shi* (1994).

Finally, studies of popular culture and social history have achieved a new prominence in recent historiography with works such as Valerie Hansen's *Changing Gods in Medieval China, 1127–1276* (1990), Stephen Teiser's *The Ghost Festival in Medieval China* (1988), Patricia Ebrey's *The Inner Quarters: Marriage and the Lives of Chinese Women in the Sung Period* (1993), Priscilla Chung's *Palace Women in the Northern Sung* (1981), and Brian McKnight's *Law and Order in Sung China* (1992).

The move of the Song capital to Hangzhou, under pressure from Ruzhen invaders who set up their Jin capital in Kaifeng in 1126, signaled the end of decades of precarious peace with the north and marked a long period – Southern Song (1127–1279) and the Yuan Dynasty (1279–1368) of the Mongols – during which much, if not all, of China's traditional territory was ruled by "outsiders." Scholarship on the Liao, Jin, Xia, and Mongol empires has been relatively sparse when compared to periods such as the T'ang, Song, or Ming, but a flurry of important scholarship in the past few decades has begun to remedy the situation. The major works on Inner Asia during this period are *The Cambridge History of Early Inner Asia* (1990) edited by Denis Sinor, and *The Cambridge History of China*, vol. 6: *Alien Regimes and Border States, 907–1368* (1994) edited by Herbert Franke and Denis Twitchett. Other important works on these empires are Morris Rossabi's *China among Equals* (1983), *China under Jurchen Rule* (1995) edited by Hoyt Tillman and Stephen West, Ruth Dunnell's *The Great State of White and High: Buddhism and State Formation in Eleventh-Century Xia* (1996), Chan Hok-lam's *The Historiography of the Chin Dynasty* (1970) and *Legitimation in Imperial China* (1984), as well as Tao Jing-shen's, *The Jurchen in Twelfth Century China* (1976) and *Two Sons of Heaven* (1988).

Few "outsiders" have had as powerful an impact on China as the Mongols in the 13th and 14th centuries. Although not directly related to the history of China, the development of the Mongolian empire under the leadership of Chinggis Khan and the conquests of much of Europe and Asia are a significant part of world history. A recent survey is David Morgan's *The Mongols* (1986). Francis Cleaves' translation of *The Secret History of the Mongols* (1982) is relevant to the formation of the empire. The Mongols annihilated the Jin in 1234, and completed their conquest of Southern Song in 1279. In the four decades between these dates, the Mongols controlled north China and solidified their rule of "all under heaven," as the Chinese called their territory.

Mongol rule in China during the Yuan dynasty has been the subject of a great deal of scholarship in both China and the West. Important works on Yuan government include Morris Rossabi's *Khubilai Khan* (1988), Herbert Franke's *China under Mongol Rule* (1994) and *From Tribal Chieftain to Universal Emperor and God* (1978), John Langlois' edited work: *China under Mongol Rule* (1981), Ch'i-ch'ing Hsiao's *The Military Establishment of the Yüan Dynasty* (1978), John Dardess' *Conquerors and Confucians* (1973), and Elizabeth Endicott-West's *Mongolian Rule in China* (1989). More specialized studies on social and cultural issues have also developed apace, the most prominent of which include Paul Ch'en's *Chinese Legal Tradition under the Mongols* (1979), James Cahill's *Hills Beyond a River* (1976), Sherman Lee and Wai-Kam Ho's *Chinese Art under the Mongols* (1968), and Stephen West's *Vaudeville and Narrative* (1977).

Mongol rule lasted less than a century, although its after-effects would remain prominent over the next two dynasties. During the nearly three centuries of the Ming, China saw a resurgence that destroyed the Mongol state under the organizing work of the dynastic founder, Zhu Yuanzhang, who ruled as the Hongwu emperor for the first thirty years of the period. As the second emperor (after Gaozu in the Han) to rise from peasant origins, the Hongwu emperor has captured the imagination of Chinese readers over the past five centuries, and the Ming was, for traditional historians, a high point of Chinese culture sandwiched between two "alien" dynasties. The major survey on the Ming is *The Cambridge History of China*, vol. 7: *The Ming Dynasty, 1368–1644* (1988) edited by Frederick W. Mote and Denis Twitchett. On the founding of the Ming, Edward Dreyer's excellent *Early Ming China* (1982), John Dardess' *Confucianism and Autocracy* (1983), and Edward Farmer's *Early Ming Government* (1976) are prominent, as is an entire body of work by the Chinese scholar Wu Han, whose *Zhu Yuanzhang juan* (Biography of Zhu Yuanzhang, 1949) was an imaginative reconstruction of the founding years.

Major studies of Ming institutions are Charles Hucker's *The Censorial System of Ming China* (1966), and Ray Huang's *Taxation and Governmental Finance in Sixteenth Century Ming China* (1974). As Huang points out, by the mid-Ming, serious financial problems had beset the dynasty after decades of poor fiscal management. Eunuch management of palace expenditures, according to both traditional and more recent historiography, became a major factor in the weakening of the state. Factional politics, echoing bureaucratic divisions in the Song, also prevailed in the mid- to late Ming. Important works on Ming government and society include Hilary Beattie's *Land and Lineage in China* (1979), Albert Chan's *The Glory and Fall of the Ming Dynasty* (1982), Chang Chun-shu's *Crisis and Transformation in Seventeenth Century China* (1992), Jerry Dennerline's *The Chia-ting Loyalists* (1981), and James Parsons' *The Peasant Rebellions of the Late Ming Dynasty* (1970).

The Ming also saw a profound growth in social, cultural, and intellectual realms, including advances in printing and the growth of the vernacular novel. The last thirty years has seen a great deal of research on these issues, including prominent translations and studies of Ming literature. Major works include Andrew Plaks' *Four Masterworks of the Ming Novel* (1987), David Roy's *The Plum in the Golden Vase* (1993), Anthony Yu's *The Journey to the West* (1977–83), Jonathan Spence's *The Memory Palace of Matteo Ricci* (1984), and James Cahill's *Parting at the Shore* (1978) and *The Distant Mountains* (1982).

The transition from Ming to Qing was a decades-long process that included the debilitation of the Ming from within and the building of the Manchu state, which would be ruled in the 17th and 18th centuries by two of China's longest-reigning emperors, Kangxi and Qianlong. On the century from roughly 1550 to 1650, which formed the heart of the transition, see Jonathan Spence and John Wills' *From Ming to Ch'ing* (1979), Ray Huang's *1587: A Year of No Significance* (1981), and Lynn Struve's *Southern Ming, 1644–1662* (1984), which portrayed the struggles of Ming loyalists after the establishment of Qing. The most prominent work on the development of the Manchu state and early Qing governance is Fredric Wakeman's *The Great Enterprise* (1985). Important works on 17th- and 18th-century rule from a variety of perspectives include Jonathan Spence's *Emperor of China* (1974), Philip Kuhn's magnificent *Soulstealers* (1990), R. Kent Guy's *The Emperor's Four Treasuries* (1987), Harold Kahn's *Monarchy in the Emperor's Eyes* (1971), and Madeleine Zelin's *The Magistrate's Tael* (1984).

Major studies of Qing institutions include the extremely useful analysis of Beatrice Bartlett's *Monarchs and Ministers* (1991), Pierre-Etienne Will's *Bureaucratie et famine en Chine au dix-huitième siècle* (1980; *Bureaucracy and Famine in Eighteenth-Century China*, 1990), John Watt's *The District Magistrate in Late Imperial China* (1972), and Fredric Wakeman's *Conflict and Control in Late Imperial China* (1975). Studies of legal mechanisms include *Law in Imperial China, Exemplified by 190 Ch'ing Dynasty Cases* (1967) edited by Derk Bodde and Clarence Morris, and Ch'ü T'ung-tsu's *Law and Society in Traditional China* (1961). Because of the intimate relationship between the Manchu rulers and the rest of Inner Asia, the northern frontier played a major role in Qing history. The most detailed work concerning these issues is *The Cambridge History of China*, vol. 10: *Late Ch'ing, 1800–1911* (1978) edited by Joseph Fletcher and John Fairbank.

Studies of Qing intellectual achievements include Benjamin Elman's significant books *From Philosophy to Philology* (1984) and *Classicism, Politics, and Kinship* (1990), which analyzed the growth of schools of thought and major works of the period.

The history of China from the mid-19th century onward provided a very different set of themes than can be found during the early, middle, and late imperial periods. Nonetheless, the early 19th century, before the height of the Western impact, has been the subject of a number of major studies, including Jonathan Spence's *The Search for Modern China* (1990), which provided an account of Chinese history since the late Ming. Other useful works on the early to mid-19th century include the first two volumes of Jean Chesneaux, Marianne Bastid, and Marie-Claire Begère's *Histoire de la Chine* (1969–72; selections as *China from the Opium Wars to the 1911 Revolution*, 1976), and Frederic Wakeman's *The Fall of Imperial China* (1975).

The history of late imperial China is inextricably intertwined with powers beyond the traditional borders of the Middle Kingdom – from Mongolia and Manchuria to Western Europe. The manner in which Chinese rulers and literati responded to these influences forms a major theme in the last four dynasties of imperial history, but so too does the rich, interconnected institutional and cultural flowering of the late imperial period show intimate connections to China's early history.

ROBERT A. LAFLEUR

See also Ma; Mongol; Naitō; Needham; Spence

Further Reading

Araki Toshikazu, *Sōdai kakyo seido kenkyō* (A Study of the Song Dynasty Examination System), Kyoto: Toyoshi kenkyukai, 1969

Bartlett, Beatrice S., *Monarchs and Ministers: The Grand Council in mid-Ch'ing China (1723–1820)*, Berkeley: University of California Press, 1991

Beattie, Hilary J., *Land and Lineage in China: A Study of T'ung-ch'eng County, Anhwei, in the Ming and Ch'ing Dynasties*, Cambridge and New York: Cambridge University Press, 1979

Birdwhistell, Anne D., *Transition to Neo-Confucianism: Shao Yung on Knowledge and Symbols of Reality*, Stanford, CA: Stanford University Press, 1989

Bodde, Derk, and Clarence Morris, eds., *Law in Imperial China, Exemplified by 190 Ch'ing Dynasty Cases*, Cambridge, MA: Harvard University Press, and Oxford: Oxford University Press, 1967

Bol, Peter K., *"This Culture of Ours": Intellectual Transitions in T'ang and Sung China*, Stanford, CA: Stanford University Press, 1992

Cahill, James, *Hills Beyond a River: Chinese Painting of the Yüan Dynasty*, New York: Weatherhill, 1976

Cahill, James, *Parting at the Shore: Chinese Painting of the Early and Middle Ming Dynasties, 1368–1580*, New York: Weatherhill, 1978

Cahill, James, *The Distant Mountains: Chinese Painting of the Late Ming Dynasty, 1570–1644*, New York: Weatherhill, 1982

Chaffee, John W., *The Thorny Gates of Learning in Sung China: A Social History of Examinations*, Cambridge: Cambridge University Press, 1985; Albany: State University of New York Press, 1995

Chan Hok-lam, *The Historiography of the Chin Dynasty: Three Studies*, Wiesbaden: Steiner, 1970

Chan Hok-lam, *Legitimation in Imperial China: Discussion under the Jurchen-Chin Dynasty (1115–1234)*, Seattle: University of Washington Press, 1984

Chan, Albert, *The Glory and Fall of the Ming Dynasty*, Norman: University of Oklahoma Press, 1982

Chan, Wing-tsit, *Chu Hsi: Life and Thought*, New York: St. Martin's Press, 1987

Chan, Wing-tsit, *Chu Hsi: New Studies*, Honolulu: University of Hawaii Press, 1989

Chang, Chun-shu, *Crisis and Transformation in Seventeenth Century China: Society, Culture, and Modernity in Li Yu's World*, Ann Arbor: University of Michigan Press, 1992

Chaves, Jonathan, *Mei Yao-ch'en and the Development of Early Sung Poetry*, New York: Columbia University Press, 1976

Ch'en, Paul, *Chinese Legal Tradition under the Mongols: The Code of 1291 as Reconstructed*, Princeton: Princeton University Press, 1979

Chesneaux, Jean, Marianne Bastid, and Marie-Claire Bergère, eds., *Histoire de la Chine*, vols. 1–2, Paris: Hatier, 1969–72; selections in English as *China from the Opium Wars to the 1911 Revolution*, New York: Pantheon, 1976, Hassocks, Sussex: Harvester Press, 1977

Ch'ü T'ung-tsu, *Law and Society in Traditional China*, The Hague: Mouton, 1961

Chung, Priscilla, *Palace Women in the Northern Sung, 960–1126*, Leiden: Brill, 1981

Cleaves, Francis Woodman, ed. and trans., *The Secret History of the Mongols*, vol. 1, Cambridge, MA: Harvard University Press, 1982

Dardess, John, *Conquerors and Confucians: Aspects of Political Change in Late Yüan China*, New York: Columbia University Press, 1973

Dardess, John, *Confucianism and Autocracy: Professional Elites and the Founding of the Ming Dynasty*, Berkeley: University of California Press, 1983

Davis, Richard L., *Court and Family in Sung China, 960–1279: Bureaucratic Success and Kinship Fortunes for the Shih of Ming-chou*, Durham, NC: Duke University Press, 1986

Dennerline, Jerry, *The Chia-ting Loyalists: Confucian Leadership and Social Change in Seventeenth Century China*, New Haven and London: Yale University Press, 1981

Dreyer, Edward L., *Early Ming China: A Political History, 1355–1435*, Stanford, CA: Stanford University Press, 1982

Dunnell, Ruth, *The Great State of White and High: Buddhism and State Formation in Eleventh-Century Xia*, Honolulu: University of Hawaii Press, 1996

Ebrey, Patricia Buckley, trans., *Family and Property in Sung China: Yüan Tsai's Precepts for Social Life*, Princeton: Princeton University Press, 1984

Ebrey, Patricia Buckley, *The Inner Quarters: Marriage and the Lives of Chinese Women in the Sung Period*, Berkeley: University of California Press, 1993

Egan, Ronald C., *The Literary Works of Ou-yang Hsiu*, Cambridge and New York: Cambridge University Press, 1984

Egan, Ronald C., *Word, Image, and Deed in the Life of Su Shi*, Cambridge, MA: Harvard University Press, 1994

Elman, Benjamin A., *From Philosophy to Philology: Intellectual and Social Aspects of Change in Late Imperial China*, Cambridge, MA: Harvard University Press, 1984

Elman, Benjamin A., *Classicism, Politics, and Kinship: The Ch'ang-chou School of New Text Confucianism in Late Imperial China*, Berkeley: University of California Press, 1990

Elvin, Mark, *The Pattern of the Chinese Past*, Stanford, CA: Stanford University Press, and London: Eyre Methuen, 1973

Endicott-West, Elizabeth, *Mongolian Rule in China: Local Administration in the Yuan Dynasty*, Cambridge, MA: Harvard University Press, 1989

Farmer, Edward L., *Early Ming Government: The Evolution of Dual Capitals*, Cambridge, MA: Harvard University Press, 1976

Fletcher, Joseph F., and John K. Fairbank, eds., *The Cambridge History of China*, vol. 10: *Late Ch'ing, 1800–1911*, Cambridge and New York: Cambridge University Press, 1978

Franke, Herbert, *From Tribal Chieftain to Universal Emperor and God: The Legitimation of the Yüan Dynasty*, Munich: Bayerische Akademie der Wissenschaften, 1978

Franke, Herbert, and Denis Twitchett, eds., *The Cambridge History of China*, vol.6: *Alien Regimes and Border States, 907–1368*, Cambridge and New York: Cambridge University Press, 1994

Franke, Herbert, *China under Mongol Rule*, Aldershot: Variorum, 1994

Gardner, Daniel K., *Chu Hsi and the Ta-hsueh: Neo-Confucian Reflection on the Confucian Canon*, Cambridge, MA: Harvard University Press, 1986

Glahn, Richard von, *The Country of Streams and Grottoes: Expansion, Settlement, and the Civilizing of the Sichuan Frontier in Song Times*, Cambridge, MA: Harvard University Press, 1987

Guy, R. Kent, *The Emperor's Four Treasuries: Scholars and the State in the Late Ch'ien-lung Era*, Cambridge, MA: Harvard University Press, 1987

Hansen, Valerie, *Changing Gods in Medieval China, 1127–1276*, Princeton: Princeton University Press, 1990

Hsiao, Ch'i-ch'ing, *The Military Establishment of the Yüan Dynasty*, Cambridge, MA: Harvard University Press, 1978

Huang, Ray, *Taxation and Governmental Finance in Sixteenth Century Ming China*, Cambridge and New York: Cambridge University Press, 1974

Huang, Ray, *1587: A Year of No Significance: The Ming Dynasty in Decline*, New Haven and London: Yale University Press, 1981

Hucker, Charles O., *The Censorial System of Ming China*, Stanford, CA: Stanford University Press, 1966

Hymes, Robert P., *Statesmen and Gentlemen: The Elite of Fu-chou, Chiang-hsi, in Northern and Southern Sung*, Cambridge and New York: Cambridge University Press, 1986

Johnson, David, Andrew J. Nathan, and Evelyn S. Rawski, eds., *Popular Culture in Late Imperial China*, Berkeley: University of California Press, 1985

Kahn, Harold L., *Monarchy in the Emperor's Eyes: Image and Reality in the Ch'ien-lung Reign*, Cambridge, MA: Harvard University Press, 1971

Kuhn, Philip A., *Soulstealers: The Chinese Sorcery Scare of 1768*, Cambridge, MA: Harvard University Press, 1990

Kusumoto Masatsugu, *Sō Min jidai jugaku shisō no kenkyū* (Studies of Song and Ming Confucian Thought), Chiba: Hiroike Gakuen Shuppanbu Shōwa 37, 1962

Langlois, John, ed., *China under Mongol Rule*, Princeton: Princeton University Press, 1981

Lee, Sherman, and Wai-Kam Ho, *Chinese Art under the Mongols: The Yüan Dynasty (1279–1368)*, Cleveland: Cleveland Art Museum, 1968

Lee, Thomas H.C., *Government Education and Examinations in Sung China*, New York: St. Martin's Press, 1985

Liu, James T.C., *China Turning Inward: Intellectual-Political Changes in the Early Twelfth Century China*, Cambridge, MA: Harvard University Press, 1988

Lo, Winston, *An Introduction to the Civil Service of Sung China, with Emphasis on Its Personnel Administration*, Honolulu: University of Hawaii Press, 1987

McKnight, Brian E., *Law and Order in Sung China*, Cambridge and New York: Cambridge University Press, 1992

Metzger, Thomas A., *Escape from Predicament: Neo-Confucianism and China's Evolving Political Culture*, New York: Columbia University Press, 1977

Miyazaki Ichisada, *Kakyo Gōkyō*, 1946; in English as *China's Examination Hell: The Civil Service Examinations of Imperial China*, New Haven and London: Yale University Press, 1976

Morgan, David, *The Mongols*, Oxford and New York: Blackwell, 1986

Mote, Frederick W., and Denis Twitchett, eds., *The Cambridge History of China*, vol. 7: *The Ming Dynasty, 1368–1644*, Cambridge and New York: Cambridge University Press, 1988

Okada Takehiko, *Sō Min tetsugaku josetsu* (Introduction to Song and Ming Philosophy), Tokyo: Bungensha Shōwa 52, 1977

Parsons, James Bunyan, *The Peasant Rebellions of the Late Ming Dynasty*, Tucson: University of Arizona Press, 1970

Plaks, Andrew H., *Four Masterworks of the Ming Novel*, Princeton: Princeton University Press, 1987

Qian Mu, *Guoshi dagang* (Outline of Chinese History), Shanghai, 1948

Rao Zongyi, *Zhongguo shixue shang zhi zhengtong lun* (Legitimation Theory in Chinese Historiography), Hong Kong, 1977

Ren Jiyu, *Zhongguo zhexue shi* (The History of Chinese Philosophy), 4 vols., Beijing, 1979

Rossabi, Morris, *China among Equals: The Middle Kingdom and Its Neighbors, 10th–14th Centuries*, Berkeley: University of California Press, 1983

Rossabi, Morris, *Khubilai Khan: His Life and Times*, Berkeley: University of California Press, 1988

Roy, David T., trans., *The Plum in the Golden Vase*, Princeton: Princeton University Press, 1993

Shiba Yoshinobu, *Sōdai Shōgyō-shi Kenkyū*, Tokyo: Kazama Shobō, 1968; in English as *Commerce and Society in Sung China*, Ann Arbor, Center for Chinese Studies, University of Michigan, 1970

Sinor, Denis, ed., *The Cambridge History of Early Inner Asia*, Cambridge and New York: Cambridge University Press, 1990

Smith, Paul, *Taxing Heaven's Storehouse: Horses, Bureaucrats, and the Destruction of the Sichuan Tea Industry, 1074–1224*, Cambridge, MA: Harvard University Press, 1991

Spence, Jonathan D., *Emperor of China: Self Portrait of K'ang-hsi*, New York: Knopf, 1974; in UK as *K'ang-hsi: Emperor of China*, London: Cape, 1974

Spence, Jonathan D., and John E. Wills Jr., eds., *From Ming to Ch'ing: Conquest, Region, and Continuity in Seventeenth-Century China*, New Haven and London: Yale University Press, 1979

Spence, Jonathan D., *The Memory Palace of Matteo Ricci*, New York: Penguin, 1984; London: Faber, 1985

Spence, Jonathan D., *The Search for Modern China*, London: Hutchinson, and New York: Norton, 1990

Struve, Lynn A., *Southern Ming, 1644–1662*, New Haven and London: Yale University Press, 1984

Tao Jing-shen, *The Jurchen in Twelfth Century China: A Study of Sinicization*, Seattle: University of Washington Press, 1976

Tao Jing-shen, *Two Sons of Heaven: Studies in Sung-Liao Relations*, Tucson: University of Arizona Press, 1988

Teiser, Stephen, *The Ghost Festival in Medieval China*, Princeton: Princeton University Press, 1988

Tillman, Hoyt Cleveland, *Utilitarian Confucianism: Ch'en Liang's Challenge to Chu Hsi*, Cambridge, MA: Harvard University Press, 1982

Tillman, Hoyt Cleveland, and Stephen West, eds., *China under Jurchen Rule*, Albany: State University of New York Press, 1995

Umehara Kaoru, *Sōdai kanryō seido kenkyū* (Studies of the Song Bureaucratic System), Kyoto: Dōhōsha Shōwa 60, 1985

Utsunomiya Kiyoyoshi, *Chūgoku kodai chūseishi kenkyū* (Studies of Ancient and Medieval China), Tokyo, 1977

Wakeman, Frederic, Jr., and Carolyn Grant, eds., *Conflict and Control in Late Imperial China*, Berkeley: University of California Press, 1975

Wakeman, Frederic, Jr., *The Fall of Imperial China*, New York: Free Press, 1975; London: Collier Macmillan, 1977

Wakeman, Frederic, Jr., *The Great Enterprise: The Manchu Reconstruction of Imperial Order in Seventeenth-Century China*, 2 vols., Berkeley: University of California Press, 1985

Watt, John Robertson, *The District Magistrate in Late Imperial China*, New York: Columbia University Press, 1972

West, Stephen, *Vaudeville and Narrative: Aspects of Chin Theater*, Wiesbaden: Steiner, 1977

Will, Pierre-Etienne, *Bureaucratie et famine en Chine au dix-huitième siècle*, Paris: Mouton, 1980; in English as *Bureaucracy and Famine in Eighteenth-Century China*, Stanford, CA: Stanford University Press, 1990

Wu Han, *Zhu Yuanzhang juan* (Biography of Zhu Yuanzhang), Shanghai, 1949; revised edition 1965

Yu, Anthony C., trans., *The Journey to the West*, 4 vols., Chicago: University of Chicago Press, 1977–83

Zelin, Madeleine, *The Magistrate's Tael: Rationalizing Fiscal Reform in Eighteenth Century Ch'ing China*, Berkeley: University of California Press, 1984

China: Modern (since 1911)

When does modern China start? In much of the 19th-century historiography of China, the arrival of Europeans at the court of the Qianlong emperor in 1793 was seen as a landmark which permanently shattered the Middle Kingdom's sense of cultural superiority and ushered China into an era of modernity. With hindsight, 1793 may well have been a year of no significance, but the meanings ascribed in Europe to the mission, from its aftermath to World War II, became central to historical narratives which portrayed that encounter as a "clash of civilizations." The question of the koutou, the Qing's court dismissal of the British gifts, and the Qianlong emperor's letter to George III were all thought by historians to be the emblems of profound cultural differences imagined between an "immobile" and "stagnant" China in its "confrontation" with a "dynamic" Europe. In this vein, early historical narratives such as W.E. Soothill's *China and the West* (1925) remained confined to a political account of China's encounter with the West and its gradual "opening up" after a series of "humiliations," in particular the so-called "Opium War" (1839–42), the second treaty settlement (1857–60), and the expedition against the Boxers (1900). A similar explanatory framework also characterized the Harvard school under J.K. Fairbank, who was one of the first professionally to train students as historians of modern China. In pioneering works such as *China's Response to the West* (1954), Fairbank and others interpreted the history of modern China as a "response" to the "challenge" of the West: based on the assumption that the basic social structure and cultural beliefs of China had remained unchanged for two thousand years, the abandonment of "tradition" for the benefits of "modernization" became the main focus of historical analysis. This approach, which has been described as the "Western impact – Chinese response" paradigm, emphasized the role of Western traders, missionaries, and other "cultural intermediaries" as the principal agents of change who brought enlightenment to China, while new knowledge was in turn disseminated from top to bottom through society via their Chinese disciples. Treaty ports and other Western enclaves – seen as the main locations where modernization took place – were also favorite objects of historical investigation. Historical movements that originated inside China, such as peasant uprisings and popular rebellions, were generally interpreted as "traditional" or "xenophobic" forces unleashed by the intrusion of the West. The "failure" of the Chinese empire to "modernize," on the other hand, was seen to be largely the consequence of a static and arrogant culture, embodied in particular by the tribute system, symbol of fundamental differences between "traditional China" and the "modern West."

In China, the study of history developed vigorously between the two world wars, notably under the impulse of nationalism. If noted scholars such as Liang Qichao, Gu Jiegang and Luo Zhenyu had criticized traditional historiographical methods and transformed the study of history into a more empirically based social science, they also prudently avoided entering into the more recent history of their country. In the hands of nationalist scholars, however, the events which had unfolded since the Opium War were thought to be the very key to understanding China's inferior position in the contemporary world. The history of the nation, in their view, had been a long series of humiliating encounters that demanded redress. National history – seldom written with a real interest in verification – was seen as a means to instil a sense of outrage in all national subjects, and "imperialist powers" became the constitutive outsiders against whom the nation should unite. The agreements made by the Qing empire were described as "unequal treaties," and the "intrusions" and "encroachments" of the West became privileged objects of investigation.

The political agenda of nationalist historians in China was to a great extent replicated by historians in Europe and the

United States during the 1960s, a period marked by a shift of interest away from the study of political figures, institutions, and diplomacy – the terrain of traditional history – towards social and economic models of historical change: revolutions, peasants, and the working class became new objects of historical inquiry, as in Ramon Myers' *The Chinese Peasant Economy* (1970). Often heavily influenced by Marxist scholarship, social and economic historians portrayed the Opium War as the first chapter of a painful history of imperialist onslaught which had impeded the "normal" development of Chinese economy and society and had reduced that country to a "semi-feudal" and "semi-colonized" appendage of the Western capitalist system. Although such developments were less marked in countries such as Britain, the Netherlands, and Germany, where sinological circles retained a strong preference for the study of more ancient historical periods, they also dominated the modern historiography of China in France, in particular in the readers on modern China edited under Jean Chesneaux. Similar to the "reception studies" that continued to flourish in the United States, these historiographical developments not only perpetuated Eurocentric notions of "modernization," but also failed to take into account historical transformations which took place in parts of China independently of any foreign presence. People and events in that country, moreover, were represented as passive entities which merely "responded" to outside influences. The history of modern China, in that view, was very much the history of the West in China.

In an important book entitled *Discovering History in China* (1984), Paul Cohen argued in favor of the more China-centered view that has steadily gained ground in the historical understanding of China's recent past since the early 1970s. In contrast to the more Eurocentric approaches which had represented the only significant historical changes in China as a consequence of or a response to the "Western impact," a number of historians took a more interior view, specifically concerned with Chinese problems in a Chinese context. Instead of interpreting the late Qing reformer Liang Qichao as an alienated intellectual who responded to a "foreign challenge," as Joseph R. Levenson had done in his influential work *Liang Ch'i-ch'ao and the Mind of Modern China* (1953), more critical historians stressed that the reform movement which contributed so much to the invention of new social identities in modern China operated to a large extent out of complex interactions and fusions of different indigenous schools of thought, dominated by New Text Confucianism and statecraft scholarship (*jingshi*) and influenced even by classical noncanonical philosophies (*zhuzixue*) and Mahayana Buddhism. An increased awareness of the internal dynamics and indigenous context of social movements also characterized other important historical studies on the 1911 and 1949 revolutions, as a shift towards a more China-centered perspective gradually started to take shape. Even the rise of the Communist party, one of the conventional issues addressed by social historians, was thoroughly rewritten, as new scholarship, more focused in time and space, undermined the general characterizations that marred much of the traditional historiography. Far from seeing the thought of Mao Zedong in terms of a "sinification of Marxism," as used to be the case in most historical analyses of "Maoism," Werner Meissner, for instance, went as far as to demystify the debate

around "dialectical materialism" in the 1930s, seeing it as no more than a secret code in which "philosophical terms" stood as political symbols to convey the correct military strategy for adoption in the struggle against the Guomindang from high to low cadres in the Chinese Communist party. A shift away from Eurocentrism also characterized the work of a number of economic historians, who highlighted the very active role Chinese businessmen and entrepreneurs, often in symbiosis with foreign merchants, played in a 19th-century commercial revolution which may well still be unfolding in China today. Where some historians of the 1950s perceived "inveterate unity," moreover, new approaches highlighted important changes over time, significant regional differences and great variety in cultural levels. This strategy of spatial differentiation, often inspired by the work of G. William Skinner, revealed significant differences, not only between the littoral and the hinterland, but also between regions and provinces. From social disorder in 19th-century Guangdong to the rise of warlordism in Hunan, an increasing number of province-centered studies illuminated the great diversity of modern China. A better awareness of and interest in social stratification also led to a shift away from the more usual focus on elites (governors, warlords, political leaders, and prominent intellectuals) and toward an exploration of the lower reaches of society (popular religions, rural society).

The conventional knowledge about what constitutes "modern China," in other words, has gradually changed over the last couple of decades. The Opium War, traditionally seen as the starting point of modern history in China, is no longer viewed by all historians as a significant time marker between "tradition" and "modernity," and a number of scholars have pointed at the continuities between the late imperial period and the 20th century. If the "tradition" of many aspects of life in the People's Republic of China is justifiably highlighted, the potential "modernity" of the late empire is in turn underlined by historians who have found staggering cultural, economic, and social changes in an era previously seen as stagnant and unchanging: a commercial revolution, unprecedented urbanization, greater social mobility, and the spread of print culture are but some of the factors that are thought to have profoundly marked the two centuries preceding the arrival of foreign ships in Canton, thus actively shaping an experience of modernity which is both similar to and distinct from that of Europe. It has been suggested that the beginnings of modernity in China might well have to be sought as far back as the 16th century.

Social theory heavily influenced the historiography of China in the 1960s and 1970s, but since the 1980s younger generations have preferred to turn to cultural anthropology and literary theory. This recent shift towards the history of culture is marked by an interest in theories of knowledge and the semiotics of discourse, as social practices are thought to depend on the representations people use to make sense of their world. Recent trends in cultural history do not necessarily subscribe to the existence of any "natural" categories such as "women," for instance, since gender is interpreted as a system of cultural representation that actively shapes the meanings social groups assign to sex differences. These new developments have infused the study of modern China with a new vigor, although not all cultural historians are equally balanced in their use of new theoretical tools. All too often, for instance, the deployment of undigested high theory has been used as a substitute for critical thought, while indulgence in cultural relativism has led to a disregard for evidence based on primary sources. Postmodernist approaches, moreover, have often replicated the more antiquated categories which characterized the "Western impact – Chinese response" paradigm. Little effort is made to understand China in its own terms, and China is once again reduced to playing the role of a passive victim of "colonialism" and "cultural imperialism." On the other hand, a more eclectic use of theoretical resources has allowed other historians to build upon the foundations established by the more China-centered approach of the last two decades. Cultural historians have been most successful in the exploration of early modern China. Craig Clunas, for instance, has highlighted the importance of material culture in the quest for social status in the late Ming. The existence of parallels between early modern Europe and China, which had once been suggested by Chinese historians such as Liang Qichao and Hu Shi, are increasingly seen to be historically significant by some of these cultural historians. Frank Dikötter has analyzed dominant discourses of self, gender, and "race" in the modern period on the basis of new empirical evidence to show that they cannot so much be interpreted as a mere derivation from the West, but rather as a distinct version of modernity largely reconfigured from indigenous sources. Other studies in the field of culture and society have also pointed to the enduring capacity of social groups to appropriate and indigenize foreign thought in contemporary China, including Christianity and Marxism. From a backwater in the early decades of this century, "modern China" has thus emerged as a site of contestation between very different historical interpretations, and these tensions continue to stimulate debate and enrich our understanding of this vital part of the contemporary world.

FRANK DIKÖTTER

See also Fairbank; Liang; Spence

Further Reading

Barrett, Timothy H., *Singular Listlessness: A Short History of Chinese Books and British Scholars*, London: Wellsweep, 1989

Beasley, William G., and Edwin G. Pulleyblank eds., *Historians of China and Japan*, London: Oxford University Press, 1961

Bergère, Marie-Claire, *L'Age d'or de la bourgeoisie chinoise, 1911–1937*, Paris: Flammarion, 1980; in English as *The Golden Age of the Chinese Bourgeoisie, 1911–1937*, Cambridge: Cambridge University Press, 1989

Chang Hao, *Chinese Intellectuals in Crisis: Search for Order and Meaning, 1890–1911*, Berkeley: University of California Press, 1987

Ch'en, Jerome, *China and the West: Society and Culture, 1815–1937*, London: Hutchinson, and Bloomington: Indiana University Press, 1979

Chen Yung-fa, *Making Revolution: The Communist Movement in Eastern and Central China, 1937–1945*, Berkeley: University of California Press, 1986

Clunas, Craig, *Superfluous Things: Material Culture and Social Status in Early Modern China*, Cambridge: Polity Press, and Urbana: University of Illinois Press, 1991

Cohen, Paul A., *Discovering History in China: American Historical Writing on the Recent Chinese Past*, New York: Columbia University Press, 1984

Dikötter, Frank, *The Discourse of Race in Modern China*, London: Hurst, and Stanford, CA: Stanford University Press, 1992

Dikötter, Frank, *Sex, Culture and Modernity in China: Medical Sciences and the Construction of Sexual Identities in the Early Republican Period*, London: Hurst, and Honolulu: University of Hawaii Press, 1995

Fairbank, John K., and Ssu-yü Teng, eds., *China's Response to the West: A Documentary Survey, 1839–1923*, Cambridge, MA: Harvard University Press, 1954

Fairbank, John K., ed., *The Chinese World Order: Traditional China's Foreign Relations*, Cambridge, MA: Harvard University Press, 1968

Feuerwerker, Albert, *Rebellion in Nineteenth-Century China*, Ann Arbor: University of Michigan Press, 1986

Hao Yen-p'ing, *The Commercial Revolution in Nineteenth-Century China: The Rise of Sino-Western Capitalism*, Berkeley: University of California Press, 1986

Ladany, Laszlo, *The Communist Party of China and Marxism, 1921–1985: A Self-Portrait*, London: Hurst, and Stanford, CA: Stanford University Press, 1988

Levenson, Joseph R., *Liang Ch'i-ch'ao and the Mind of Modern China*, Cambridge, MA: Harvard University Press, 1953; revised 1959

Liang Qichao [Liang Ch'i-ch'ao], *Intellectual Trends in the Ch'ing Period*, Cambridge, MA: Harvard University Press, 1959 (Chinese original, 1920)

Meissner, Werner, *Philosophie und Politik in China: die Kontroverse über den dialektischen Materialismus in den dreissiger Jahren*, Munich: Fink, 1986; in English as *Philosophy and Politics in China: The Controversy over Dialectical Materialism in the 1930s*, London: Hurst, and Stanford, CA: Stanford University Press, 1990

Myers, Ramon H., *The Chinese Peasant Economy: Agricultural Development in Hopei and Shantung, 1890–1949*, Cambridge, MA: Harvard University Press, 1970

Rawski, Thomas G., *Economic Growth in Prewar China*, Berkeley: University of California Press, 1989

Rowe, William T., *Hankow: Commerce and Society in a Chinese City, 1796–1889*, Stanford, CA: Stanford University Press, 1984

Schwartz, Benjamin I., *In Search of Wealth and Power: Yen Fu and the West*, Cambridge, MA: Harvard University Press, 1964

Skinner, G. William, editor, *The City in Late Imperial China*, Stanford, CA: Stanford University Press, 1977

Soothill, W.E., *China and the West: A Sketch of Their Intercourse*, London: Oxford University Press, 1925

Spence, Jonathan D., *The Search for Modern China*, London: Hutchinson, and New York: Norton, 1990

China: Historical Writing, Ancient

(c.1100–221 BCE)

The period under discussion extends from the last years of the Shang dynasty (c.1600–1100 BCE) to the end of the Zhou (c.1100–221 BCE). The long Zhou dynasty again divided into the Western Zhou (c.1100–771) and the Eastern Zhou (770–221). Eastern Zhou further divided into the Chunqiu (Spring and Autumn, 770–404) and Zhanguo (Warring States, 403–221) periods. In historical development, the Western Zhou was generally characterized as feudal China; the Eastern Zhou was the era of the decline and disintegration of China's feudal order, and by 403 the feudal states under the Zhou all virtually became independent and were at war with one another. In 221, the state of Qin defeated all other states and established a unified centralized bureaucratic empire to replace the old Zhou feudal order. That was the end of ancient China and the beginning of Imperial China.

Historical consciousness and thought has been a major component in all Chinese philosophical discourse since the

Golden Age of Philosophers from the 6th to 3rd centuries BCE. But the earliest roots of Chinese historical thought and consciousness go back even further, to the 11th century when China's earliest classics, such as *The Book of Change*, *The Book of History*, and *The Book of Songs*, began to take their definitive forms. These canons suggested that history was the discernible pattern of past human conduct and could serve as a guide for human action. Such historical thought was based on a profound understanding of natural law: that the universe was constantly changing and that human beings also evolve each day, in order to survive. This was the prevailing belief of the time. It was also these books that produced a dialectic interpretation of all change in the universe. For example, a life that just begins also begins the process of its ending, and the final ending is the birth of a new life. History, to the Chinese of the 11th century BCE, recorded the process of the change of human life and activities. One must learn from history to improve one's life in the world of change. This was the concept of history in the world of the most ancient Chinese canons.

Historical thought became more diverse and broad in China's Golden Age of Philosophers. In this period of tremendous socio-economic, political, and cultural changes, the great thinkers considered the effect of history on men's view of life. Confucius (Kong-zi, 551–479) saw the moral function of history and its goodness for mankind. Mencius (Meng Ke, 371–289) also recognized the moral importance of history but held that the pattern of history was cyclical rather than progressive. The Daoists, for their part, doubted that history had any meaning or any use, given that it was simply the record of the decline of human freedom and individualism. In contrast, Mo Di (fl.479–438), the founder of Mohism, held that history reflected the progress of human civilization in social order and political stability. Mo Di believed that human society progressed in the complex structure of a developing "social contract" between the "great man" and the masses. The Legalists, such as Han Fei (280–233), proposed that human history was always in linear progress, and hence voiced the view that past history had no use for mankind in any way. The great philosophers of this period also considered whether history had a purpose, or the existence of a prime mover behind human destiny. Both Confucianists and Mohists argued for the profound purpose of history, but the Daoists, the Legalists, and Xun Qing (fl.298–238) questioned the validity and sensibility of such a view. Human history, they believed, was a natural process, and there could not be a grand divine design behind human affairs.

Historical writings in ancient China included six broad categories: compilation of historical documents; annals or chronicles; regional history; biographies; monographs on special subjects; and historical criticism. The *Shangshu* (or *Shujing*, The Book of History) was the earliest historical writing in China. Compiled first in the 11th century, it was a collection of imperial decrees, speeches, declarations, political theories, historical records, and royal instructions. The book went through several enlargements and the final version included materials from the 4th century. Originally one hundred chapters, its current version has only 29, including materials composed from the 11th century to the 4th century. It is the most important source for the history, institutions, and culture of the Western Zhou period (1100–771 BCE). A sequel, titled

Zhoushu (later *Yi Zhoushu*, History of the Zhou) in 71 chapters, was compiled in the 4th century. It covers the period from the 11th century to the first decades of the 6th century, but all except two of the documents in the book were composed in the Zhanguo period (403–221 BCE).

Among the chronicles of ancient China, five major works have been considered the representative writings. The earliest was the *Chunqiu* (The Spring and Autumn Annals). It is a chronicle of ancient China from 722 to 481, and its authorship was traditionally ascribed to Confucius. Although an annal of only 16,572 words, it contains certain views on the pattern of history and on the moral function of history – that is, how history should be used to praise the good and to blame the bad (the principle of *bao-bian*). History is considered a book of judgment on political and social actions. Writing history was perceived not as an objective pursuit but as a subjective intellectual undertaking. On the historiographic side, the *Chunqiu* laid down the basic structure of chronicles in the history of Chinese historical writing. In interpreting the history of the period, the author saw it as a process of the breakdown of the feudal order that ruled the Western Zhou. Specifically, it was marked by the decline of the king's power and the disintegration of the old class system under the feudal structure. The *Zuoshi chunqiu* (Zuo's Spring and Autumn Annals) was the best-written chronicle in ancient China. Covering the years 805 to 454 – with main entries from 722 to 468 – in more than 196,845 words, it is better written than the *Chunqiu*. Traditionally it was considered a commentary on the *Chunqiu* and has been titled *Zuozhuan* (Zho's Commentary on the Chunqiu); its author was identified as Tso Qiuming, a contemporary of Confucius, but modern studies have convincingly shown that it was actually composed in the late 4th century. Unlike the *Chunqiu*, which covered mainly political and military events and was often written in extreme brevity (sometimes just one word in an entry), the *Zuoshi chunqiu* included political, economic, social, military, diplomatic, and intellectual events, and each entry was written as a complete essay in a lively and elegant prose narrative. On more than fifty occasions, the author also expressed his views on the event in question in a commentary introduced by a special format which began with "The Author Comments." The author of the *Zuoshi chunqiu* had similar views on the concept and function of history as the author of *Chunqiu*, but unlike him saw the period that he wrote about as an age of progressive changes – the breakdown of the old feudal which was to create a new political, economic, and social order that would eventually bring about peace and prosperity.

In the 3rd century two elaborate versions of commentary on the *Chunqiu* were composed. One was by Gongyang Gao and called *Gongyang Zhuan* (The Gongyang Commentary) and one by Guliang Chi and called *Guliang Zhuan* (The Guliang Commentary). They were detailed annotations of the historical events only briefly sketched or outlined in the *Chunqiu*, but each also attempted to interpret the events and personalities by a strict moralistic viewpoint, in line with the *Chunqiu*'s "principle of praise and blame." Both also added cosmological and religious implications to the historical facts. The two books passed among devoted students through oral transmission for generations until the mid-2nd century when they were transmitted to written text.

The first chronicle covering the long span of ancient Chinese history from the period of the legendary Five Emperors (traditionally in the 3rd millennium BCE) to 299 BCE was composed in the 3rd century. It was the *Zhushu jinian* (Bamboo Annals). This was a heterogeneous annalistic account of events spanning some 2500 years of ancient China. Unfortunately the complete text of the book has not survived; only fragments are still available for examination.

Among the earlier writings on the history of regional states in ancient China, two stood out as the most important: the *Guoyu* (Discourses of the States) and the *Zhanguo ce* (Stratagems of the Warring States). The *Guoyu* covered the events of eight feudal states from 967 to 453: Zhou, Lu, Qi, Jin, and Zheng in north China; Chu, Wu, and Yue in south China. The accounts were narrated through quoting the original text of discourse between and among key figures in the particular event under discussion. The author of the *Guoyu* thus made three unique contributions to Chinese historiography: regional history as a category of historical writing; historical objectivism in the sense of "let the facts speak for themselves"; and writing history as storytelling. The *Zhanguo ce* was similar to the *Guoyu* in structure and organization but with a much narrower scope: it included only political, military, and diplomatic matters. Covering the twelve independent states in China from the mid-5th century to the end of the 3rd century, it was the history of China during the Warring States through the life, words, and political career of the ambitious sophists who tried to sell their political ideas to different rulers to change their own personal circumstances and to turn the tide of political change. The various proposals of these men form the contents of the book. In a larger intellectual perspective, the book shows how the individuals changed the course of history during a period of chaos and war. Different versions of the *Zhanguo ce* were present before 221. Liu Xiang (80–9 BCE) of the Han dynasty edited all the different versions into one that is the current text of the book. In December 1973, another version of the book was discovered in a tomb in Hunan province in south China and more than 60 per cent of its material is not found in the current text. Without title itself, it has now been entitled *Zhanguo zongheng jia shu* (The Book of the Sophists of the Warring States Period).

In the category of biographies, two types of writing were developed. One was in the form of genealogical records, which included lists of emperors, kings, chief nobles, and high officials; and one was chronological biography, a biography arranged year by year. The representative work of the former was *Shiben* (Genealogical Records) and of the latter the *Mu Tianzi Zhuan* (Chronological Biography of King Mu). The *Shiben* covers the period from the legendary Yellow Emperor (traditionally 2698) to 481. King Mu of the Zhou dynasty reigned in the 9th century and the book gave a detailed account of his daily activities. Neither book, unfortunately, has survived; only fragments are still extant.

The monographs in ancient China all dealt with a specialized subject, such as economy, geography, and regional culture. The two representative works of this category are *Shanhai jing* (The Mountain and Sea Classic) and *Yugong* (Tribute of King Yu). The *Shanhai jing* is a treatise on cultural and physical geography in historical context. For example, it discusses the lore and history of more than 130 plants, 260 animals, and 226 areas of mineral deposits such as gold, silver, copper, iron, and tin. It also deals with ethnic groups and religious belief in ancient China. It may be considered the first work on the history of science and religion in China. Although its first version was composed in the 4th century, the current text is the result of several revisions and includes many later additions, probably compiled in the early 2nd century. The *Yugong* is a book of cultural, historical, economic, and administrative geography. It was originally written as one separate work in the 4th century, but was incorporated as a chapter into *The Book of History* in the 3rd century.

There was no complete book of historical criticism produced in ancient China. But separate essays of criticism on historical events and personages were present in various historical works and philosophical writings. The comments introduced by "Junzi yue" in the *Zuoshi chunqiu* discussed earlier were good examples. Others can be found in the works of Mencius, Xun Qing, and Han Fei. The *Lüshi chunqiu* (Lü's Spring and Autumn Annals) by Lü Buwei (*fl.*285–235) and others in 239 also contains extensive essays. These essays generally show the authors's views on certain historical events and their ideas on the nature, pattern, and moving forces of history.

Ancient China produced a considerable amount of writing in history and historical thought. A good variety of historiographic styles and approaches developed, which began a sophisticated historiographical tradition that has since become an essential part of Chinese intellectual life and political culture.

CHUN-SHU CHANG

See also Kong-zi

Further Reading

Beasley, William G., and Edwin G. Pulleyblank, eds., *Historians of China and Japan*, London: Oxford University Press, 1961

Chang Chun-shu, *The Making of China: Main Themes in Premodern Chinese History*, Englewood Cliffs, NJ: Prentice Hall, 1975

Chunqiu [Ch'un ch'iu] (Spring and Autumn Annals); in English as *The Ch'un Ts'ew* in *The Chinese Classics*, vol. 5, Hong Kong: Hong Kong University Press, 1960

Du Weiyung, *Zhongguo shixue shi* (History of Chinese Historical Writing), vol. 1, Taibei: Sanmin, 1993

Gardner, Charles S., *Chinese Traditional Historiography*, Cambridge, MA: Harvard University Press, 1938; revised 1961

Gongyang Gao [Kung yang Kao], *Gongyang zhuan* (The Gongyang Commentary)

Guliang Chi [Ku Liang Ch'ih], *Guliang zhuan* (The Guliang Commentary)

Guoyu (Discourses of the State)

Ho, Ping-ti, *The Cradle of the East: An Inquiry into the Indigenous Origins of Techniques and Ideas of Neolithic and Early Historic China, 5000–1000 BC*, Chicago: University of Chicago Press, 1975

Jin Yufu [Chin Yü fu], *Zhongguo shixue shi* (History of Chinese Historical Writing), revised editions, Beijing: Zhonghua shuju, 1962

Keightley, David N., *Sources of Shang History: The Oracle Bone Inscriptions of Bronze Age China*, Berkeley: University of California Press, 1978

Li Zongtong [Li Tsung-t'ung], *Zhongguo shixue shi* (History of Chinese Historical Writing) Taibei: Zhonghua wenhua, 1955

Lu Buwei [Lü Pu-wei], *Lüshi chunqiu* (Lü's Spring and Autumn Annals)

Mu tianzi zhuan (Chronological Biography of King Mu); in French as *Le Mu tianzi zhuan: traduction annotée, études critiques* (The Mu tianzi zhuan: Annotated Translation and Critical Study), Paris: Presses Universitaires de France, 1978

Naitō Torajirō, *Shina shigakushi* (History of Chinese Historical Writing), Tokyo: Kōbundō, 1949

Qu Wanli [Ch'ü Wan-li], *Shuyung lunxue ji* (Collected Essays), Taibei: Kaimin shudian, 1969

Shanhai jing (The Mountain and Sea Classic); in French as *Chan-hai-king, antique géographie chinoise*, Paris, 1891

Shangshu or *Shujing* [*Shih Ching*] (The Book of History); in English as *The Shoo King* in *The Chinese Classics*, vol. 3, Hong Kong: Hong Kong University Press, 1960

Shiben bazhong (Genealogical Records), Shanghai: Shangwu yingshuguan, 1957

Yi Zhou Shu (History of the Zhou)

Yugong (Tribute of King Yu)

Zhang Menglun [Chang Meng-lun], *Zhongguo shixue shi* (History of Chinese Historical Writing) vol. 1, Gansu: Gansu Renmin chubanshe, 1983

Zhang Xincheng [Chang Hsin-che'ng], *Gujin weishu tongkao* (A Comprehensive Study of Forged Books), Shanghai: Shangwu yingshuguan, 1959

Zhanguo ce (Intrigues of the Warring States); translated as *Chan-kuo T'se*, London: Oxford University Press, 1970; Ann Arbor: University of Michigan Center for Chinese Studies, 1996

Zhanguo zongheng jia shu (The Book of the Sophists of the Warring States Period), Beijing: Wenwu chubanshe, 1976

Zuozhuan [*Tso chuan*] (Zuo's Commentary on the Spring and Autumn Annals); in English as *Tso Chuen*, in *The Chinese Classics* vol. 5, Hong Kong: Hong Kong University Press, 1960

Zhushu jinian (Bamboo Annals); in English as *Annals of the Bamboo Annals*, Lawrence, KS: Coronado Press, 1972

China: Historical Writing, Early and Middle Imperial (221 BCE–959 CE)

In 221 BCE the Qin dynasty (221–207 BCE) unified China and established a centralized bureaucratic empire to replace the Zhou feudal system. This was the beginning of Imperial China, which lasted to 1911 CE, when Republican China was founded. The long history of Imperial China was divided into three periods: Early Imperial, 221 BCE–220 CE; Middle Imperial, 221–959; Late Imperial, 960–1911. This essay covers the Early and Middle periods, including the major dynasties of Qin, Han (202 BCE–8 CE, 25–220), Jin (265–420), Sui (589–618), and T'ang (618–907). The period between 220 and 589 was also referred to as the Six Dynasties.

Both historical thought and historiography made significant advance in early imperial China. Sima Qian (*c.*145–*c.*87 BCE), the father of Chinese historiography, advanced the most comprehensive system of historical thought. Through his imaginative and original thinking, he set forth his views of history in his immortal *Shiji* (Historical Records) in 130 books (that is, chapters). History as the past, according to Sima Qian, is the creative process of interaction among human beings in accordance with the will of a supreme divine force; in a larger sense, civilization was created in this process. History, as a literary text, is the record of past events, national and local, large and small, and the story of all those persons who stand out with special achievements and unique skills. History is written, on this view, to advise, educate, and admonish the present world and the living. Therefore, the duty of a historian is not only to record, but also to evaluate and judge human affairs as well as to discern the will of the supreme divine mover and the pattern of history. To achieve this goal, Sima Qian designed a special format for writing history that has five parts: Imperial Annals (*benji* or *ji*); biographies (*liezhuan* or *zhuan*); tables (*biao*); hereditary houses (*shijia*); and monographs (*shu*). He also emphasized that writing history is more than recording the facts; it is a lively, creative undertaking. The historian not only writes history, but *creates* history with great power of imagination and the liberty to interpret and to add interesting details. Sima Qian thus defined the nature and purpose of history, expounded the dimension and function of historical knowledge, explored the scope of historiography, and emphasized the primacy of the unity of history and literature – the creative and imaginative edge in writing history.

Sima Qian's *Historical Records* is a comprehensive history of China from the Yellow Emperor (traditionally 2698 BCE) down to his own time, the reign of Emperor Wu (reigned 141–87 BCE) of the Han dynasty. Each component of his style and format of writing history may have its origin traced back to ancient China, such as the earlier annals, regional histories, biographies, monographs, and storytelling history-writing, but combining them together into one coherent structure of discourse in historical representation was his ingenious creation. He also made historical criticism a regular part of his work – at the end of almost every chapter he makes his commentary on the subject of the chapter in a special paragraph introduced by *Taishi gong yue* (The Grand Historian remarks), a device whose origin goes back to the *Junzi yue* in the *Zuoshi chunqiu* of the 4th century.

Sima Qian defined the historian's craft in an age of grand philosophical synthesis, the Han dynasty. His craft then became the standard way of compiling and writing history (*zhengshi*). He was followed by the great Han historian Ban Gu (32–92 CE) in writing his *Hanshu* (History of the Former Han Dynasty). In 100 books (120 books by later count), the *Hanshu* covered the history of the Han dynasty from 206 BCE to 23 CE. It was written in the same structure as the *Historical Records*, but with expansion in the scope of some categories such as monographs and the incorporation of the "hereditary houses" into the biographies. Since it covers only one dynasty, it later became the model for writing the official history of one dynasty, termed "dynastic history," in Imperial China. As the writing of dynastic history became an established institution in Imperial China after the Han dynasty, there was at least one official history written for every major dynasty in Chinese history. Altogether there have been 26 such histories in 4,052 chapters covering the history of China from the Yellow Emperor to the end of the last dynasty, the Qing (1644–1911). Ban Gu followed Sima Qian's historiographical style but held different views on history and historiographical approaches. History, in Ban's view, has a purpose and moves according to a grand design by a divine prime mover. All natural phenomena of the cosmic order manifest the divine will of Heaven and should serve as the guidance for human affairs. Writing history includes recording all notable human events and natural happenings so that the present can benefit from the past and the future from the present. Therefore historiographic endeavor is not a subjective intellectual undertaking, but an objective task of recording the past and decoding the present. Objective recording of the facts, however, is also a process of selection, as one cannot record all that is taking place in the natural world and human society. But selection necessarily follows certain criteria, and such criteria must be based on a value system. To Ban Gu, that value system in his standard of selection was exclusively from the established Han Confucianism formulated and propagated by Dong Zhongshu (179–104 BCE) since emperor Wu's time (141–87 BCE). Ban Gu, thus, may be said to be the first influential Confucian historian. Both the structure and contents of the *Hanshu* reflect this intellectual propensity.

The Han period also saw a flourishing in the writing of history in other historiographic styles. For the dynastic transition from the Qin to the Han, Lu Chia's (c.250–175 BCE) *Chu-Han Chunqiu* (The History of the Chu-Han Period, 206–202 BCE) stood out as the most detailed and interpretive work on the struggle between Liu Bang (247–195) and Xiang Yu (232–202). In chronicles, Xun Yue's (148–209 CE) *Hanji* (The Annals of the [Former] Han Dynasty) was one of the most important works in Han historiography. Covering the years 206 BCE to 23 CE in over 200,000 words, it followed the tradition of the earlier classic *Zuoshi chunqiu* and was based on the *Hanshu*. But it stood out with its use of new sources to supplement and correct the *Hanshu* and with its profound commentary on all major historical issues which constitutes 10 per cent of the book. In regional histories, the *Wu-Yue chunqiu* (The History of Wu and Yue) by Zhao Ye (died 83 CE) and the *Yue jue shu* (Yue History) by Yuan Kang (*fl.* 1st century BCE) are the best works. Both focused on the history of the Wu and Yue states in the 5th century and re-created the critical events and personalities based on both historical records and local legends and folklore. History was thus written as a subjective process of imaginative re-creation.

Two new genres in Chinese historiography began in the Han dynasty. One was history of statecraft and the other was women's history. Liu Xiang (79–8 BCE) was the originator of both. His *Shuoyuan* (Discourses on Statecraft and Ethics), in twenty books, is a history of the major ideas on government, military, and interstate relations that were advanced during Chunqiu and Zhanguo periods (722–222). Liu examined all those ideas in their historical and political contexts. Liu Xiang's *Lienü zhuan* (A Biography of Famous Women) contained perceptive portraits of 105 women from high antiquity to the Zhanguo period (403–222). He classified his subjects in seven categories by moral criteria ranging from model mothers to mischievous beauties whose immoral conduct led to the disgrace and downfall of their men. Liu considered biography a source of inspiration and moral lesson and as an agent for cultivating the compassionate and righteous mind of political leaders. The *Lienü zhuan* is an important source of social history; it reveals the social status, educational level, and political power of women in ancient China, when women played a much more important role in Chinese society than their later counterparts. In fact, the Han society also manifested much of this difference. It had the first woman historian, Ban Zhao (c.48–c.120) in Chinese history. She was Ban Gu's sister and wrote the sections of "Tables" and "Treatise on Astronomy" of the *Hanshu*. She was respected as one of the most learned scholars of her time.

In the Early Imperial period, more than 300 historical works were written, representing a large variety of historiographical forms and styles, but the most important advancement in Chinese historical writing in this period was made by Sima Qian, who actually engendered a revolution in Chinese historiography by creating a new form of history writing. This new form was later referred to as the *jizhuan* (annal-biography) style and was followed in the writing of all dynastic histories. The new historiographical form was also one of universal history, since it sets out to cover the whole world known to the Chinese. For example, both the *Historical Records* and *Hanshu* include the history and current conditions in Korea, Central Asia, and other regions outside China. The Han historians further consolidated the practical purpose of history and in many ways considered history as moral and political treatises. Han Confucianism connected Heaven and Earth and Sima Qian's definition of history was based on that theory. Thus history had a definite purpose of discerning and understanding the Divine Will of Heaven, and historians would have to formulate histories in order to preserve the continuity of past, present, and future.

In the Han period, the state gave a clear focus to history and began the practice of compiling its history by an official institution in the court. That was the writing of the Eastern Han history in the Eastern Lodge of the Southern Palace (Dongguan), which eventually produced an official dynastic history, called *Dongguan Hanji* (History of the [Eastern] Han Written in the Eastern Lodge), in some 143 books by the collective labor of more than twenty historians extending from 62 to 225. This marked the beginning of compiling the official history of a dynasty by a government apparatus. It was to become a permanent institution in Imperial and early Republican China. Seventeen of the 24 Dynastic Histories after the Han dynasty were compiled by such official apparatus, the last of which functioned from 1914 to 1927.

In the Middle Imperial period (221–959), the historians and thinkers were enormously influenced by Sima Qian's and Ban Gu's craft in writing and thinking about history. But they also placed new emphasis on certain issues in their thought about history and in their search for its meaning. Xun Xu (died 289) and Li Chung (*fl.* early 4th century) undertook to define the territory of history. They divided all known human writings (both published and unpublished) into four categories: classics, history, philosophy, and literature. History included thirteen categories of writings: standard histories (*Shiji* and *Hanshu* types); annals and chronicles; history of ruling houses and rulers; records of contending independent states; court diaries and veritable records; ancient affairs and traditions; treatises on functions of offices; rites, ceremonials, and etiquettes; punishments and laws; biographies and stories; geography and maps; genealogical records; and bibliographies and catalogues. As this fourfold classification of writings henceforth became the standard system in China, this definition of the territory of history was also followed by later historians and scholars.

In the search for the nature, meaning, and pattern of history, some historians and thinkers of this period considered social change to be the focus for examining the motive forces in the historical process; that is, to understand history was to discern the forces of change at work in human society. To others, however, the lives of individuals, contained in biographies, became of central concern; for this group, the center of history was man himself. In general, the relationship between fate and free will, and the role of the "great man" versus the commoner in making history provided another focus for the historiographical and intellectual pursuits of a variety of historians and philosophers. Liu Yiqing (403–444), Han Yu (768–824), and Liu Zongyuan (773–819) were the leading voices raising these questions. Still others made the idea of progress versus the force of tradition the central concern of their historical thought. The great Liu Zhiji (661–721) of the T'ang dynasty, author of the great classic on historical criticism *Shitong* (Study of Historiography), was one such writer in this last category. Some historians believed that the key to understanding the historical process was through the structure and evolution of the governmental organization and administration and its related social and economic matters. Du You (735–812) was the representative voice and best known advocate of this view. His monumental *Tongdian* (Comprehensive Institutes), in 200 books, set a format and style of institutional history. The work is divided into nine sections: the economic system, civil service examinations, the official system, rites, music, the military system, the legal system, political geography, and border affairs; and in each the period covered extends from the earliest historical times (traditionally 3rd millennium BCE) down to 755 CE.

Chinese historiography in the Middle Imperial period produced more than 1,100 titles in the thirteen categories of historical writings listed above. Its most important advances were made in three areas. First, the writing of biographies. More than 350 biographies were composed in this period and they manifested highly innovative approaches in form, style, and tone over an infinite variation of subjects, from the living to the dead, from the mortal to the immortal, from the noble to the lowly, from Chinese to non-Chinese, and from priests to laymen. Second, the writing of dynastic histories. Sixty-six dynastic histories were written during the period; they all followed the *jizhuan* style and covered fourteen dynasties of the period. Thirteen of these works were later recognized as the official Dynastic Histories, with a total of 1,271 books. Third, the government's systematic effort to compile an official history of the current dynasty. Following the Eastern Han court's establishment of an official apparatus to compile an official dynastic history, a Bureau of History was formally set up as a regular component of the governmental structure and headed by the chief minister of the state by the Northern Qi dynasty (555–577) in the 6th century. It henceforth remained a permanent institution throughout the history of Imperial China. The authority of composing dynastic history by the Bureau was further enhanced by the decree in 593 of emperor Wen (reigned 581–604) of the Sui dynasty that banned any private effort to write dynastic history. Under the T'ang, the Bureau was enlarged and empowered with higher status in the court. It now took the exclusive responsibility of selecting, processing, and editing official records, and composing histories for both the current and earlier dynasties. As a result, it produced the official histories in 371 books of six previous dynasties: Jin (265–420), the Liang (502–557), the Chen (557–589), the Northern Qi (550–557), the Northern Zhou (557–581), and the Sui (581–618). The Bureau also composed eight editions (versions) of the official history, National History

(*Guoshi*), of the T'ang dynasty from 618 to 762, the last of which consisted of 130 books. The dynastic histories so composed by the Bureau all took after the historiographical tradition of Sima Qian and Ban Gu and followed the common assumptions about the function and pattern of historical writing as the mirror of the past for the benefit of the present. In addition, history also came to be considered a unique means to legitimizing new dynasties. Thus history became inseparable from the destiny of a dynasty.

The Middle Imperial period also marked a new trend in Chinese historiography – the rising interest in the history and cultures of foreign countries. More than forty important works about the "world" (*shijie*) and "foreign countries" (*waiguo*) were written from 221 to 907. They represented the new effort of Chinese historians and scholars to search for a new understanding and representation of the world outside China. The Chinese world from the 4th century on was under political and military challenge from North and Central Asia and religious impact from Central and South Asia. In response, China grew to be a cosmopolitan empire in the T'ang dynasty. The new historiographical world of foreign peoples and countries came to manifest how the Chinese intellectual world was stimulated and transformed during that long period of foreign challenge.

The writing of local history was another major focus of historiographical venture in the Middle Imperial period. More than 120 works were written about a large range of topics in local history, including monographs on large and small administrative regions, imperial capitals, major urban centers, and mountains and waters. Representative works are the *Huayang guozhi* (A History of the Region South of Mt. Hua) by Chang Qu (fl. 265–316), the history of Sichuan, southern Shanxi, and northeastern Yunan from high antiquity to 347 CE; the *Shuijing zhu* (A Commentary on the Classic of Waters) by Li Daoyuan (467–527), a detailed study of the history, lore, and current conditions of 1,252 waterways in the Chinese empire; the *Luoyang qialan ji* (A Record of the Buddhist Monasteries of Lo-Yang) by Yang Xuanzhi (fl. 528–555), a history of Loyang through the account of the famous Buddhist monasteries in the city from 493 to 547; and the *Yuanhe junxian tuzhi* (A Gazetteer with Maps of the T'ang Empire in Prefectures and Districts Written in the Yuanhe Period [813]) by Li Jifu (758–814), a detailed history and account of current conditions of all the prefectures, districts, and counties of the T'ang empire. These local histories were composed for different historiographical purposes. First, they examined local knowledge and worldviews of the regions to show how they differed from the national customs and ethos. Second, they revealed how local changes were linked to the fate of the empire. Third, they manifested their authors' special interpretation and evaluation of history. For example, Yang Xuanzhi saw Buddhism as one of the major causes for the decline and fall of the Northern Wei dynasty (386–534), and he used his account of the Buddhist monasteries in its capital Loyang to make his point. In the early 6th century, the city had 1,367 Buddhist monasteries with more than 100,000 monks and nuns in a population of 500,000. As a result, the court drained its resources by building grand Buddhist temples and weakened its authority by granting too much power and wealth to Buddhist priests. On the other hand, Li Jifu, the chief minister and director of the Bureau of History in 813, used the *Yuanhe junxian tuzhi* to show the grandeur and wealth of the great T'ang empire, thus showing the role of the local regions in the empire-building of the T'ang dynasty.

Liu Zhiji's *Shitong*, written from 702 to 710, was a revolutionary work of historical criticism and historiographical method. It has three parts: one is a critique of all major historical works before the T'ang dynasty, including the *Chunqiu* (The Spring and Autumn Annals) attributed to Confucius (Kong-zi) and the *Shiji* by Sima Qian; one deals with historical method, including comprehensive treatments of historiographical style, problems of documentation, language skills, research techniques (such as internal and external criticism), and the theory of history; and the last one is a history of Chinese historical writing before the T'ang, with special focus on the origins of Chinese historiography, major types of writings, and different historiographical ideas. In writing history, the historian, in Liu's view, should maintain strict objectivity and make no moral nor any nonfactual judgment; he should faithfully abide by the spirit of doubting the well-established theories and construct his argument by wider evidence and fairer deliberations. In his research and representation, the historian should always remind himself of the importance of comprehensive study of all possible sources and of the interdependence of cultural, social, economic, and intellectual factors in a historical event. In the final analysis, he was to write a comprehensive history from a detached and critical standpoint.

In the Early and Middle Imperial periods, Chinese historical thought and historiography reached unprecedented development from Sima Qian to Liu Zhiji. Almost all major intellectual issues and methodological approaches in interpreting, writing, and evaluating human history were explored and forcefully engaged. Major breakthroughs were made in every direction of historical studies, and more than 1,400 works of varying styles and forms were produced to examine the total human past. Historical consciousness came to be a critical component of the Chinese mind, and it continued to be so throughout Imperial China to present day.

CHUN-SHU CHANG

See also Ban; Liu; Sima Qian

Further Reading

Ban Gu [Pan Ku], *Hanshu*; partially translated as *The History of the Former Han Dynasty*, 3 vols., Baltimore: Waverly Press, and London: Kegan Paul, 1938–55, and as *Courtier and Commoner in Ancient China*, New York: Columbia University Press, 1974

Beasley, William G., and Edwin G. Pulleyblank, eds., *Historians of China and Japan*, London: Oxford University Press, 1961

Chang Chun-shu, "The Periodization of Chinese History: A Survey of Major Schemes and Hypotheses," *Bulletin of the Institute of History and Philology, Academia Sinica* 45 (1973), 157–79

Chang Chun-shu, "Qin-Han China in Review," *Studies in Chinese History* 4 (1994), 47–59

Chang Qu [Ch'ang Ch'ü], *Huayang guozhi* (A History of the Region South of Mount Hua)

Dongguan Hanji (History of the [Eastern] Han Written in the Eastern Lodge)

Du You [Tu Yu], *Tongdian* (Comprehensive Institutes)

Gardner, Charles S., *Chinese Traditional Historiography*, Cambridge, MA: Harvard University Press, 1938; revised 1961

Holcombe, Charles, *In the Shadow of the Han*, Honolulu: University of Hawaii Press, 1994

Jin Yufu [Chin Yü-fu], *Zhongguo shixue shi* (History of Chinese Historical Writing), revised editions, Beijing: Zhonghua shuju, 1962

Jiu Tangshu, (Old History of the T'ang Dynasty) compiled by Liu Xu [Liu Hsu] *et al.*

Li Daoyuan [Li Tao-yuan], *Shuijing zhu* (A Commentary on the Classic of Waters)

Li Jifu [Li Chi-fu], *Yuanhe junxian tuzhi* (A Gazetteer with Maps of the T'ang Empire in Prefectures and Districts Written in the Yuanhe Period)

Li Zongtong [Li Tsung-t'ung], *Zhongguo shixue shi* (History of Chinese Historical Writing), Taibei: Zhonghua wenhua, 1953

Liu Xiang [Liu Hsiang], *Lienü zhuan* (A Biography of Famous Women)

Liu Xiang [Liu Hsiang], *Shuoyuan* (Discourses on Statecraft and Ethics)

Liu Zhiji [Liu Chih-chi], *Shitong* (Study of Historiography)

Lu Jia [Lu Chia], *Chu-Han Chunqiu* (The History of the Chu-Han Period)

McMullen, David, *State and Scholars in T'ang China*, Cambridge and New York: Cambridge University Press, 1988

Naitō Torajirō, *Shina shigakushi* (History of Chinese Historical Writing), Tokyo: Kōbundō, 1949

Sima Qian [Ssu-ma Ch'ien], *Shiji* [Shih-chi]; as *Records of the Grand Historian*, translated by Burton Watson, 2 vols., New York: Columbia University Press, 1961, revised 1993; and as *Historical Records*, translated by Raymond Dawson, Oxford and New York: Oxford University Press, 1994; as *The Grand Scribe's Records*, edited by William H. Nienhauser, Jr., Bloomington: Indiana University Press, 1994–

Suishu (History of the Sui Dynasty), compiled by Wei Zheng [Wei Cheng] *et al.*

Swann, Nancy Lee, *Pan Chao, the Foremost Woman Scholar of China, First Century AD: Background, Ancestry, Life, and Writings of the Most Celebrated Woman of Chinese Letters*, London and New York: Century, 1932

Twitchett, Denis, *The Writing of Official History under the T'ang*, Cambridge and New York: Cambridge University Press, 1992

van der Sprenkel, O.B., *Pan Piao, Pan Ku, and the Han History*, Occasional Paper 3, Canberra: Australian University Centre of Oriental Studies, 1964

Xin Tangshu (New History of the T'ang Dynasty), compiled by Ouyang Xiu [Ou-yang Hsiu], Song Qi [Sung Ch'i], *et al.*

Xun Yue [Hsun Yueh], *Hanji* [The Annals of the [Former] Han Dynasty)

Yang Xuanzhi [Yang Hsuan-chih], *Luoyang qialan ji*; in English as *A Record of Buddhist Monasteries in Lo-Yang*, Princeton: Princeton University Press, 1984

Yuan Kang [Yuan K'ang], *Yue jue shu* (Yue History)

Zhang Menglun [Chang Meng-lun], *Zhongguo shixue shi* (History of Chinese Historical Writing), vol. 1, Lanzhou: Gansu Renmin chubanshe, 1983

Zhao Ye, *Wu-Yue chunqiu* (The History of Wu and Yue)

China: Historical Writing, Late Imperial (960–1911)

Late Imperial China extended from 960 to 1911, through four successive major dynasties: the Song (960–1279), the Yuan (1279–1368), the Ming (1368–1644), and the Qing (1644–1911). The characteristic historical development of the long period was the persistent non-Chinese challenge on the one hand and tremendous economic and cultural progress on the other. Two of the four dynasties were not even Chinese, the Yuan being a Mongol regime and the Qing a Manchu regime. The Song also lost north China to the Jurcheds in 1126 and controlled only south China from 1127 to 1279 when it was conquered by the Mongols. But in political, economic, cultural, intellectual, and scientific developments, China was so advanced that it actually had entered the early modern age in Song times and the modern age in late Ming times in the 17th century. Chinese historical thought and historiography of this long period of 700 years reflected both of these trends by having adapted the old traditions to meet the new challenge and create a new world of modernity.

The Song dynasty was an age of economic prosperity and military crisis. The Chinese empire was constantly being pressed by non-Chinese peoples, the Tanguts, the Khitans, the Jurchens, and the Mongols, and Song China's primary concern was how to deal with one military crisis after another. The need for reform and revitalization provided a continuing theme among Song statesmen, who were in traditional China also among the leading thinkers and historians.

In such a national context, historical thought during Song times returned to the earliest and most fundamental Chinese conception of history: namely, the practical use of history. Leading Song historians and thinkers such as Wang Qinruo (962–1025), Yang Yi (947–1020), Song Qi (998–1061), Ouyang Xiu (1007–72), Sima Guang (1019–86), Zheng Qiao (1104–62), Lu You (1125–1210), Zhu Xi (1130–1200), Lu Zuqian (1137–81), and Tang Zhongyu (1138–88), all held that history is the most essential guide to statecraft, and that both institutions and the intelligent individual should consult history in planning successful action. History, as they all proceeded to elaborate in their various forms of discourse, shows the merits and demerits of past institutions, the scope and operation of social forces, the role of ideas in various social and political processes, the diversity of the human conscience, models of behavior, the myriad facets of human affairs and natural environment, and the place of social change in general, and of progress in particular. History was thus conceived of not just as a mirror of the past, but as a guidebook for the active citizen and statesman. Moreover, these scholars also argued that writing history and compiling historical records were both necessary and noble responsibilities for the intellectual, whose primary pursuit in life was to serve the state and the people, and to lead the common people in the right direction. As for the type of history that could best serve the purpose of history so defined, two schools stood out as the most influential. One focused on examining history by a special period (such as the history of only one dynasty) or through a special subject (such as the history of political system), and one insisted on looking upon history as a continuous stream, necessitating the writing of general history comprehensive in subject coverage and *longue durée* in time span. Among the representative works of the former were the *Xin Tangshu* (A New History of the T'ang Dynasty, 618–907), in 225 chapters, by Ouyang Xiu and Song Qi; the *Wuda shi* (The History of the Five Dynasties, 907 [875]–960), in 152 chapters, by Xue Juzheng (912–981) and others; the *Xin Wudai shi* (A New History of the Five Dynasties), in 74 chapters, by Ouyang Xiu; the *Nantang shu*

(A History of the Southern T'ang Dynasty, 937–975), in 18 chapters, by Lu You; the *Lida zhidu xiangshuo* (A Comprehensive History of the Administrative Systems Throughout the Ages), in 13 chapters, by Lü Zuqian; and the *Tang huiyao* (Comprehensive Institutes of the T'ang Dynasty), in 100 chapters, by Wang Pu (922–981). Zheng Qiao's *Tongzhi* (General Treatise) was the best-known work of the school of comprehensive general history. Written from 1149 to 1161, it was modeled after Sima Qian's *Shiji* in six major sections in 200 chapters: imperial annals, biographies, hereditary houses, chronological tables, records of independent kingdoms, and monographs. The period covered extends from earliest historical times down to the end of the T'ang dynasty in 907. Zheng Qiao also held that in making history useful the historian must write it with a strict adherence to objectivity and let the facts speak for themselves. He took issue with those who believed that history had a divine purpose and that writing history was making a moral judgment. Sima Guang's celebrated *Zizhi tongjian* (Comprehensive Mirror for Aid in Government) also belongs to this school. Written from 1066 to 1084 and based on 341 sources, this book chronicled the history of China of 1,362 years from 403 BCE to 959 CE in 294 chapters. Year by year, it treated the major political and military events in detail and with strict principle of objectivity. To Sima Guang, history was a political treatise and as such its usefulness rested with the fullness and objectiveness of its representation.

Since history was given such an immense function in directing human affairs, some Song scholars, such as Zhu Xi and Lu You, began to see the power of history as the power to influence and teach. They argued accordingly that history should be written with a sense of enormous responsibility and with strong moral and political beliefs. It should be seen as a divine design to uphold the eternal justice in all human affairs. In doing so, they were going back to the ideas of both Sima Qian (145–86 BCE) and even Confucius (Kong-zi, 551–479 BCE). In the end, however, they also held that the writing of history was a matter of creative choice and was thus a subjective, not objective, intellectual undertaking. In history, a thinker finds his intellectual autonomy and power, beyond and above any mundane human concerns and political restrictions.

Sung historiography also stood out in several other directions. First, the issue of political legitimacy and nationalism forged the major themes in many Song historical writings. The *Zizhi tongjian gangmu* (The String and Mesh of the Comprehensive Mirror for Aid in Government) by Zhu Xi and his disciples was the best-known such work. Condensing and restructuring Sima Guang's *Zizhi tongjian* into 59 chapters according to Confucian political ethics and nationalism, it came to serve as a textbook to put forth the Confucian cardinal standards of historical judgment and prescribed principles of historical writing. For example, regimes that came to power by illegal means such as usurpation were denounced as illegitimate or eliminated from the pages of the *Zizhi tongjian gangmu*. As Zhu Xi was to become the most influential thinker after the Song dynasty, this book gradually became the most influential historical work in late Imperial China. Second, new genres were created in Song historiography. The most important of the new genres was the *jishi benmo* style, by which history is examined by a series of major topics arranged in a time sequence with discourses on each topic proceeding in chronological order. This combination of topical and annal-istic approaches created a new type of history, a revolution in Chinese historiography. Yuan Shu (1131–1205) devised this new historiographical style in his *Tongjian jishi benmo* (Comprehensive Mirror in Narration of Events from Beginning to End), written in 1173, which covers the history of China from 403 BCE to 959 CE in 305 topics; and it has since rivaled the *jizhuan* (annal-biography) style as the most commonly followed form in history writing. Every dynasty and signifi-cant period in late Imperial China had a standard history written in the *jishi benmo* style. Altogether, more than 110 works of this style were written from the Song to the end of the Qing dynasty in 1911.

The Song period also saw the rise of intense interest in writing contemporary history by individual historians. Since the 6th century, the writing of contemporary history was gener-ally undertaken by the Bureau of History or under Imperial auspices; individual historians ventured only to compile histo-ries of past dynasties. The new emphasis on the practical func-tion of history for statecraft and the need to re-examine the failures in dealing with the external non-Chinese challenge and of domestic policies engendered a blossoming of the writing of contemporary history. Two representative works of this new historiographical trend were the *Sanchao beimeng huibian* (A Documentary Study of the Song-Jin Relations during the Three Reigns of Hui, Qin, and Gao Emperors, 1117–1161) by Xu Mengxin (1124–1205) and the *Jianyan yilai chaoye zaji* (Studies on the National Affairs from the Court to the Regions since the Jianyan Reign, 1127) by Li Xinchuan (1164–1234). The former, completed in 1194 in 250 chapters, chronicled the Song relations with the Jurchen Jin dynasty (1115–1234) from 1117 to 1162 with reference to over 200 public and private sources. It is a monumental work of diplomatic history with each key issue documented by original sources. Hsu used the original sources to show the erroneous policy and harmful measures that the Song government took in dealing with the Jurchen challenge. Li Xinchuan's *Jianyan yilai chaoye zaji*, completed in 1216 in 40 chapters, is a comprehensive treat-ment of the history and institutions of Song China from 1127 to 1216 in thirteen topics ranging from economic conditions to contemporary affairs. Some of these contemporary histories presented the most immediate assessment and evaluation of recent and contemporary issues in the Song empire, and with the benefit of the advanced printing press in widespread use they had reached a large segment of Song intellectuals and offi-cials. That made historians potent political critics and policy advisers at a time of political upheaval and national crisis. For this and many other reasons discussed above, the Song was a special era of Chinese historiography; it produced more than 1,300 historical works, a number that was unmatched in Chinese history except for the last dynasty, the Qing, which had a total of 5,478 historical works for its 267 years from 1644 to 1911.

The Yuan dynasty produced fewer historical works and still fewer major historians. Under the direction of T'o T'o (1313–1355) the Bureau of History completed three major Dynastic Histories in the later part of the dynasty. The *Songshi* (History of the Song Dynasty, 960–1279) was written from 1343 to 1345 in 496 chapters; the *Liaoshi* (History of the Liao [Khitan] Dynasty, 916–1125) was completed in 1344 in 116

chapters; and the *Jinshi* (History of the Jin Dynasty, 1115–1234), written in 1344 in 135 chapters. These histories, of 747 chapters altogether, had been written in a short period, from 1343 to 1345, and followed the established dynastic history style and principle of compilation. But some new elements were also created. For example, a special section of Neo-Confucianism (*Daoxue zhuan*) was added in the *Songshi*, which reflected the rising influence of the new Confucian doctrines in the Song dynasty. All three histories also reflected the influence of nationalism and race issues in their contents and structure.

The *Wenxian tongkao* (Comprehensive History of Civilization), in 348 chapters, by Ma Duanlin (c.1250–1325) stood out as the best-known major historical writing of the Yuan period. Completed in 1307, this is a comprehensive history of Chinese civilization from high antiquity down to 1224 in 24 broad categories ranging from the tax system and monetary system to the military and foreign relations. Ma, an official under the Song and retired under the Mongol Yuan dynasty, wrote the book with a systematic interpretive frame-work and made penetrating commentaries on every important issue and event. He believed that misgovernment and corrup-tion led to the decline and fall of the Song empire. Ma Dualin's views on history and historiography were similar to those of Zheng Qiao: both placed emphasis on the importance of writing comprehensive general history and on the primacy of objectivity in presenting the fact in historical research.

Ming historians continued the established historiographical tradition on the one hand, and created new directions and emphases in history writing on the other. Following tradition, the historians of the Bureau of History under the direction of Song Lian (1310–1381) compiled the official history of the defunct preceding dynasty, *Yuanshi* (History of the Yuan Dynasty), in 1370. In 210 chapters, it covers the history of the Mongols from the rise of Genghis Khan (c.1162–1227) in 1206 to the death of the last Yuan ruler in China, emperor Shun (Shundi, reigned 1333–1368), in 1370. In the new direction of historical studies, Ming historians came to advance a new theory of history writing. They asserted that the influence of history was equal to that of the great Confucian classics in directing human affairs and that the classics were in fact orig-inally all historical works (*Liujing jieshi*). Thus history writing from the very beginning of Chinese intellectual tradition had wielded an extraordinary degree of influence. The great philoso-pher Wang Shouren (Yangming, 1472–1529) first advanced the thesis that the cardinal Confucian classics were but the contemporary historical records of China's ancient past to the Zhou dynasty (c.1100–222 BCE) in a conversation in 1514 with his disciple Xu Ai (1487–1517) recorded in the *Chuanxi lu* (Instructions for Practical Living). Later, Wang Shizhen (1526–90) explored this view in full in his *Yanzhou shanren sibu gao* (Treatises on Classics, History, Philosophy, and Literature, 1576), and it was further elaborated by his con-temporary, Li Zhi (1527–1602) in his *Fenshu* (Collected Works, 1590). The Ming historians also picked up on one stream of Song thought by moving the individual more decisively to the center of their historical thought. History was made by man and should take biography, the story of man, as its central task. More interestingly, history could be the moving story of an individual's struggle to survive and to achieve. History thus was the story of the human spirit, from its most pitiful weakness to its most incredible strength, and the story of each person's struggle for survival in the face of national, social, or personal crisis.

In Ming historical writing, two unique developments stand out: the unusual blossoming of compilations of Ming history and contemporary events by private effort and the unprecedented output of biographical and autobiographical materials. Of the former, more than 350 titles were written, and of the latter at least 200 biographies and 250 autobiographies. Three representative works of the former are given here: the *Huang Ming shi gai* (A Comprehensive History of the Ming Dynasty), in 120 chapters, was completed by Zhu Guozhen (1557–1632?) in 1632; the *Yenshan tang bieji* (Collection of Treatises on Ming History), in 100 chapters, by Wang Shizhen in 1590; and the *Mingshi qie* (An Unauthorized History of the Ming Period), in 105 chapters, by Yin Shouheng (1552?–1634?) in 1634. All three were composed in the style and form of official dynastic history and covered the history of the Ming dynasty from its founding to their own time – to 1627 in Zhu Guozhen, to 1589 in Wang Shizhen, and to the early 1600s in Yin Shouheng. They not only composed the history of their dynasty and their specific times, but also offered new interpretation and criticism of critical political issues and major institutional changes. The interest and devotion in history writing among Chinese intellectuals and the place of historians' role in society and state affairs all reached a new watershed in the Ming period.

Among the biographies and autobiographies of the Ming period, the *Cangshu* (Hidden Books) and *Xu Cangshu* (A Sequel to Hidden Books) by Li Zhi stood out as revolutionary in historical thought. The *Cangshu*, in 68 chapters, was written in 1599, and *Xue cangshu*, in 27 chapters, in 1602. The former comprises critical biographies of 800 historical figures from the 5th century BCE to the end of the Yuan dynasty in 1368; the latter, biographies of 400 personages of the Ming dynasty from its founding in the 14th century to Li Zhi's own time in 1572. Through these 1,200 biographies, which were based on dynastic histories and other traditional sources, Li Zhi criticized the then divine Confucius and the Confucian concepts and judgment of history and recast the lives of his subjects by new criteria of evaluation; he also rejected the traditional status of women. He held that all historical judgment was a reflection of contemporary values and values changed with time. Thus he turned the villains in traditional Confucian historiography into heroes. Both his historical thought and his historiography were truly radical, so much so that he was eventually put in jail for his revolutionary views. Late Ming China in the late 16th and early 17th centuries was a time of national and political crisis, social breakdown, economic uprooting, and intellectual and literary revolution, all of which gave birth to the age of modernity in Chinese history. Li Zhi was one of the cataclysmic thinkers of this new age and his biographical writing a harbinger of the new historiography. In essence, Li Zhi's historical thought was that history was the most important among all literary genres and that it should make the life story of man its central subject, rather than that of the state or society, as in traditional historiography.

The long Qing dynasty of 268 years was divided into two periods, with the Opium War (1839–42) as the dividing line. China was left to itself before the war and became part of the world system after it. The development of Chinese historiography also reflected this change although it was at a slower pace than in the political realm. Hence this essay will cover only the Qing period before the Opium War.

The early Qing period, 1630–1700, was an age of dynastic transition, with the fall of the Chinese Ming and the rise of the Manchu Qing dynasty. It was marked with bloody wars and destruction and continuing human struggle for power and survival. These and other common factors associated with a dynastic change in Chinese history provided tempting themes for historians to write about: they set out to ask why the Ming declined and fell, why the Manchu rose to power, why the peasant rebels failed to establish a new dynasty after they first brought down the Ming regime in the spring of 1644, what was the rightful place that each individual should take between the two dynasties, and who were the villains, and who the heroes? In the end, by the close of the transition period more than 1,100 private historical works about these issues were written by numerous historians of different standing during this tumultuous era, the largest number of historical works ever composed in a period of seven decades in the history of China.

The subject matter of this enormous amount of historical writing falls into five categories: the history of the Ming dynasty, the Ming-Qing dynastic transition, biographies of both heroes and villains, history of ideas, and historical thought and method. Representative works of the first category are the *Guoque* (A Critical History of the [Ming] Dynasty) by Tan Qian (1593–1658) and the *Zuiwei lu* (A History of the Ming Dynasty) by Zha Jizuo (1610–76). Tan's work was completed in 1653 in 104 chapters plus four introductory chapters. It covers the history of the Ming from 1328 to 1645 in the annalistic pattern, arranged in year-month-day fashion. It stands out with its discriminating evaluation of issues, objective narration, and biting commentaries on critical events. Zha's work, completed around 1670 in 102 chapters, followed the form of the official histories (the annal-biography style). Its coverage of the Ming dynasty from its founding to 1663 when the Manchu regime finally defeated all Ming forces in south China makes it one of the most comprehensive of Ming histories compiled privately during this time; it also examines Ming history from a standpoint free of any political influence from the Manchu Qing regime. Among the numerous works on the Ming-Qing dynastic transition, those of Ji Liuqi (1622–after 1687) and Zhang Dai (1597–1684) stand out as among the most important historical writings in this period. Ji wrote the *Mingji beilue* (Records of the Late Ming in the North) in 24 chapters and *Mingji nanlue* (Records of the Late Ming in the South) in 16 chapters, both completed in 1671 in the annalistic-topical form. The former covers the years from 1595 to mid-1644 in 674 topics and the latter the years from mid-1644 to 1665 in 446 topics. In the two books, Ji not only detailed the last seven decades of the Ming regime and the process of the Ming-Qing transition, but also offered systematic interpretation of the causes that led to the Ming demise, such as lack of good ministers and generals, factional strife, eunuch tyranny and corruption, natural disasters, domestic rebellion, and external Manchu attack. Zhang Dai wrote *Shigui shu houji* (A History Book Stored in the Stone Case) around 1670 in 63 chapters. Covering 1627–63, it comprises three chapters of imperial annals, three chapters of hereditary houses (imperial princes), and 57 chapters of biographies. It was written in the form of the official histories but without the tables and monographs. Through the biographies and annals the causes and the processes of the Ming-Qing dynastic transition revealed themselves. Zhang held that the Ming fell not due to misrule of its last emperor Chongzhen (reigned 1627–44), but from the corruption of eunuchs under the notorious Wei Zhongxian (1568–1627) that affected the demise beyond return under Chongzhen's predecessor, emperor Tianqi (reigned 1621–27).

Among the many biographies of heroes and villains, different approaches were taken, such as national versus regional, individual versus collective, and moralistic versus realistic. Zha Jizuo's *Guoshou lu* (Record of Heroes Who Died for the Ming Regime), written around 1650, narrated in detail the heroic efforts of 209 persons who died for the Ming regimes from 1644 to 1650. The moving portraits articulated the strengths, weaknesses, and indomitable spirit of humans in the face of insurmountable odds.

In two areas the historiography of the Ming-Qing transition period produced significant breakthroughs. In intellectual history, the creation of the *xue-an* (school of thought) form by Huang Zongxi (1610–95) was the most innovative in Chinese historiography in this time. In 1676, Huang wrote a comprehensive history of Ming thought in 62 chapters, the *Mingru xue-an* (A Complete Treatise on Ming Thought by Schools). In the book, he grouped more than 200 thinkers of the Ming period into 19 distinctive schools, and for each school, careful accounts of its intellectual lineage and critical evaluations of the life and teachings of each thinker are given with extensive selections of representative writings. Huang created a new form in historical writing and was followed by later scholars in writing intellectual history.

In historical thought and method two historians, Gu Yanwu (1613–82) and Wang Fuzhi (1619–92), stood out as the most accomplished of the Ming-Qing transition period. Gu's representative work was the *Rizhi lu* (Record of Daily Learning) in 32 chapters and Wang's *Dutong jianlun* (On Reading the *Comprehensive Mirror for Aid in Government*) in 30 chapters and *Songlun* (On the History of the Song Dynasty) in 15 chapters. Both Gu and Wang believed in the progressive view of history and a historian's attention should be more on the modern and contemporary events than on the ancient. As social customs, political institutions, and intellectual system all changed with time, the historian should examine the process of these changes as reference for the present, since the human mind is a product of history. Gu held that in writing history, the historian should place, Gu held, historical judgment in the structure of the text. In research, the historian should use the inductive method to draw his views and conclusions; in gathering sources, he should ascertain the authenticity by both internal and external evidence and note the difference between the primary and the secondary; in making a judgment, he should collect the greatest amount of sources possible and then be led only by the facts without any subjective proclivities; for the investigation of a historical event, a historian should look into its origin, development, and consequences and then secure a full understanding of a historical experience. Wang Fuzhi further maintained that since historians study the thought and actions of the past, they need to re-live the past in order to know the deliberations of past agents as if they were their own at the present time. In making historical criticism – criticism of historical events and personages – one should place oneself in the time, place, and special situation of the subject matter and try to see how would one respond to the same peculiar environment. One should not make sweeping generalizations; any criticism should be specific and concrete. Following his words, Wang wrote the monumental *Dutong jianlun* and *Songlun*, the first two complete books of historical criticism in Chinese historiography, which provided a new and at times a revisionist look into the major historical events and personages of Chinese history from 403 BCE to 1279 CE. When Gu and Wang expounded the nature of historical understanding and the rules of historical method, they aspired to establish a new way to achieve correct historical knowledge, for they believed that the Ming dynasty fell because its intellectuals failed to make full and correct use of history as guidance for their service to the state. As Gu and Wang saw it, these late Ming scholars paid little attention to history and only indulged in talks about speculative ideas and mistaken philosophical principles without historical foundation; hence they, as pillars of the state, failed to draw up concrete and effective plans to save the empire from collapse. To Gu and Wang, a sound and effective human mind is the product of concrete empirical inquiries producing a balanced and concrete knowledge of the past in order to understand the present and plan for the future. This intellectual conviction of Gu and Wang characterizes the world views of almost all the historians who toiled on the writing of history during the tumultuous era of Ming-Qing dynastic transition. They wrote history with a strong sense of political mission.

The years from 1700 to 1840 saw three major developments in Chinese historiography. First came the completion of the official history of the Ming dynasty, *Mingshi* (History of the Ming Dynasty) in 336 chapters, in February 1736. The *Mingshi* was the work of the official Bureau of History, but it was the final achievement of the labor of many great scholars and historians from 1679 to 1736 who composed the monumental work in official and unofficial capacities, among them Yu Tong (1618–1704), Mao Qiling (1623–1716), Zhu Yizun (1629–1709), and Wan Sitong (1638–1702). Its first version was written by Wan Sitong in 500 chapters in 1702; then it was edited and changed to 416 chapters; then it was revised by Wang Hongxu (1645–1723) to 310 chapters in 1714–23; and finally it was revised to its final version of 316 chapters from 1723 to 1736 under the chief editor Zhang Tingyu (1672–1755). It was printed by the Palace Printing Office in the Wuying Hall in the autumn of 1739. The *Mingshi* has been praised for its good organization, strict objectivity, and lucid writing; it has been considered the best of the official Dynastic Histories since the T'ang dynasty (618–907). It was also the last such dynastic history compiled during the Imperial period which ended in 1911 (the last two dynastic histories after the *Mingshi* were written during the Republican period).

The 18th century was an era of intense intellectual repression in China. Large-scale literary inquisitions were carried out in the empire to persecute any real or perceived criticism of Manchu rule or the state-endorsed ideology. Scholars were afraid to discuss subjects that concerned recent history, historical personages of uncertain moral evaluation, or political issues. As a result, they chose safe subjects: intellectually detached studies of ancient texts and hermeneutical topics, and the intellectual characterization *kaoju xue* or *kaozheng xue* (literally, textual criticism or evidential research). This was the age of *Kaoju Xue*. The historians of this period also turned their creative energies to annotations, collations, criticism, emendations, editing, and recovery of ancient and earlier historical texts, and avoided writing innovative and grand new works. Their works all contributed to solid scholarship, but produced no path-breaking creations. There were some 60 leading historians of this intellectual trend, but the following four stood out: Wang Mingsheng (1722–97), the author of *Shiqi shi shangque* (A Critical Study of the Seventeen Dynastic Histories) in 100 chapters in 1788; Zhao Yi (1727–61), the author of *Nian-er shi zhaji* (Notes on the 22 Dynastic Histories) in 43 chapters in 1795; Qian Daxin (1728–1804), the author of *Nian-er shi kaoyi* (On the Discrepancies in the 22 Dynastic Histories) in 100 chapters in 1797; and Cui Dongbi (1740–1810), the author of *Kaoxin lu* (Inquiries into the Authenticity of Some Major Issues in Ancient History) in 36 chapters. The main contributions of these scholars may be summed up as follows in the context of the dynastic histories they examined: 1) textual criticism and annotations; 2) explanation and elucidation of institutional and official structures, and social systems; 3) criticism of individual historical works; 4) commentary on major historical events and personages; 5) inquiry into the authenticity of certain critical historical assumptions; and 6) new views on forged texts and skepticism of long-held understanding of sacred texts and legends in ancient China. While all four made enormous critical contributions in their defined domain, Cui Dongbi was considered the most challenging and bold in his attack on some of the long-standing sacred mythical traditions in ancient Chinese history, such as his criticism of the sacred aspects of the life of Confucius and the authenticity of the texts attributed to him in Chinese history.

Some scholars, however, chose not to follow the prevailing trend of research in historical studies and made significant contributions, although their works were in general not printed until the 19th century when intellectual repression faded away as the Manchu rule in China began to decline. Quan Zuwang (1705–55) was one of the most distinguished of these scholars. Working from an unfinished manuscript by Huang Zongxi, he completed a monumental history of thought of the Song and Yuan periods (960–1368), the *Song Yuan xue-an* (A Complete Treatise on Song and Yuan Thought by Schools) in 1755. Quan labored on the work for the last 11 years of his life, 1744–55, but the book was not completed at the time of his death. The project began with Huang Zongxi and followed the style of Huang's *Mingru xue-an*, but he died with only 25 schools of thought completed and 17 partly finished. Quan resumed the work with some changes in historiographical style such as treating all schools equally; he completed the 17 unfinished schools and wrote 45 new ones. Still by 1755 when he died, not all of Quan's original plan of 91 schools was completed. The unfinished work was later revised and supplemented to 100 chapters to cover all 91 schools for the 410 years as Quan planned and was first printed in 1838. Together with the *Mingru xue-an* it now stands as one of the two best works on intellectual history in Imperial China.

In the 19th century, a series of works on the intellectual history of the Qing period were written, such as the *Guochao xue-an xiaoshi* (A Short History of Thought of the Current [Qing] Dynasty) by Tang Jian (1778–1861) in 1845 and the *Guochao Hanxue shicheng ji* (Biographies of the Great Masters of Han Learning [Evidential Research] of the Current [Qing] Dynasty) in 1812 and *Guochao Songxue yuanyuan ji* (Biographies of the Great Masters of Song Learning [Neo-Confucian] of the Current [Qing] Dynasty) by Jiang Fan (1761–1833), and the *Hanxue shangdui* (Discussions on the Importance of Han Learning) in 1824 and 1838 by Fang Dongshu (1772–1851). But none of these approached the magnitude and quality of Huang's and Quan's works.

Zhang Xuecheng (1738–1801) has been considered the most accomplished historian of the 18th century for his broad discussion of the nature and uses of historical knowledge, of historical method, and of the theory of history. A grand treatise on all these is presented in his book *Wenshi tongyi* (General Meaning of Literature and History), a collection of 122 essays written from 1772 to 1800 and first printed in 1832. In these essays, Zhang expounded the nature of history as the record of the past experience of human life, and he asserted that the moving force behind history is the continuing interaction between the human world and the natural world, that the basic concepts of history are change and particularity, and that the function of history is education. Following these fundamental assumptions, he proceeded to make elaborate discussions on certain basic issues in Chinese historical thought and theory. First, he affirmed that the cardinal Confucian classics were but the records of the human experience in ancient times, and thus as Ming historians so forcefully argued, were but history texts and should be viewed as such. Second, since change was a basic concept of history, human experience made linear progress, but each of the stages in this process was particular and in this sense the past could not be useful for the present. However, the principles of construction and change behind past experiences and institutions must be learned as stimuli to human imagination and to guide present life. That is, although we might admire the classical age, we should not try to restore the old systems and institutions; instead we should try to understand the principles behind them for these principles are valid for all the time. The study of contemporary affairs should thus be more beneficial as they are more relevant than ancient history. Zhang therefore criticized the current climate of evidential research for its emphasis on the study of ancient texts and its lack of interest in contemporary studies. Zhang also believed that history was made as a result of the interaction of the human world with the natural world, and hence he questioned the role of heroes in making history. Individuals could respond only to the environment in which they acted; they could not change the prevailing tide to create new worlds. Finally, Zhang maintained that only after these basic assumptions about history and historical knowledge were clarified, could one learn from history to make history the explanation and guidance for the life of the present day.

In actual historiography, Zhang Xuecheng emphasized the total, comprehensive history of the *longue durée*. A good historical work should be: 1) structured in a sound and systematic interpretive framework; 2) lucidly written in an absorbing narrative; 3) based on abundant research data; and 4) strict in factual objectivity. He then went on to propose a new form of history writing. It should have three parts: first, a detailed chronological treatment of the period in question as an overview of the major events and personalities; then, a series of topics treating in monographic form the institutions, political systems, biographies, thought, literature, and special issues and problems of the period; and third, maps, tables, charts, illustrations and other quantitative materials to supplement and complement the first two parts. Zhang also promoted the writing of local history, with a clear understanding of the link between the empire and the regions, between local knowledge and national worldview, and between the core and the periphery. He proposed a new form of local history to include four main parts: 1) a chronology of major events; 2) biographies; 3) monographs on special topics such as local geography, economy, taxation system, social customs, political institutions, religious activities and ceremonies, and thought and literature; and 4) maps, tables, charts, and other quantitative materials. In composing local history, the historian should also follow four principles: broadness in view, fairness in judgment, completeness in sources, and factual objectivity in representation. Zhang compiled at least six local histories by his own craft, among which the most monumental was the *Hubei tongzhi* (A History of Hubei Province) in 152 chapters in 1794. Zhang Xuecheng's grand treatise on the historical thought and historiography summed up some of the fundamental issues and enduring concerns in the Chinese historiographical tradition. When it was printed in 1832, China was about to begin a new phase in history. It fittingly closes this long inquiry of 900 years of Late Imperial Chinese historical thought and historiography. Zhang's work sought a new historiography based on tradition, and led to modern Chinese historical studies in the late 19th and 20th centuries.

CHUN-SHU CHANG

See also Gu; Liang; Ma; Mongol; Naitō; Needham; Sima Guang; Sima Qian; Wang; Zhang

Further Reading

Beasley, William G., and Edwin G. Pulleyblank, eds., *Historians of China and Japan*, London: Oxford University Press, 1961

Chang Chun-shu, and Shelley Hsueh-lun Chang, *Crisis and Transformation in Seventeenth-Century China: Society, Culture, and Modernity*, Ann Arbor: University of Michigan Press, 1992

Chang Chun-shu, and Shelley Hsueh-lun Chang, *Redefining History*, Ann Arbor: University of Michigan Press, 1997

Chang, Shelley Hsueh-lun, *History and Legend: Ideas and Images in Ming Historical Novels*, Ann Arbor: University of Michigan Press, 1990

Cui Dongbi, *Kaoxin lu* (Inquiries into the Authenticity of Some Major Issues in Ancient History)

Du Lianzhe [Tu Lien-che], *Mingren zizhuan wenchao* (An Anthology of Autobiographies of Ming Times), Taibei: Yiwen Yinshuguan, 1977

Fang Dongshu [Fang Tung-shu], *Hanxue shangdui* (Discussion on the Importance of Han Learning), 1824, 1838

Gardner, Charles S., *Chinese Traditional Historiography*, Cambridge, MA: Harvard University Press, 1938; revised 1961

Gu Jiegang [Ku Chieh-kang], *Dangdai Zhongguo shixue* (Contemporary Chinese Historiography), Nanjing: Shengli chuban gongsi, 1947

Gu Yanwu [Ku Yen-wu], *Rizhi lu* (Record of Daily Learning)

Huang Zongxi [Huang Tsung-hsi], *Mingru xue-an* (A Complete Treatise on Ming Thought by Schools)

Ji Liuqi [Chi Liu-ch'i], *Mingji beilue* (Records of the Late Ming in the North)

Ji Liuqi [Chi Liu-ch'i], *Mingji nanlue* (Records of the Late Ming in the South)

Jiang Fan [Chiang Fan], *Guochao Hanxue shicheng ji* (Biographies of the Great Masters of Han Learning [Evidential Research] of the Current [Qing] Dynasty), 1812

Jiang Fan [Chiang Fan], *Guochao Songxue yuanyuan ji* (Biographies of the Great Masters of Song Learning [Neo-Confucian] of the Current [Qing] Dynasty)

Jin Yufu [Chin Yü-fu], *Zhongguo shixue shi* (History of Chinese Historical Writing), revised editions, Beijing: Zhonghua shuja, 1962

Li Xinchuan [Li Hsin-ch'uan], *Jianyan yilai chaoye zaji* (Studies on the National Affairs from the Court to the Regions since the Jianyan Reign)

Li Zhi [Li Chih], *Cangshu* (Hidden Books), 1599

Li Zhi [Li Chih], *Fenshu* (Collected Works), 1590

Li Zhi [Li Chih], *Xu Cangshu* (A Sequel to Hidden Books), 1602

Li Zongtong [Li Tsung-t'ung], *Shixue gaiyao* (An Introduction to Chinese Historiography), Taibei: Zhengzhong shuji, 1968

Liang Qichao [Liang Ch'i-ch'ao], *Zhongguo jin sanbainian xueshu shi* (A History of Chinese Thought and Scholarship over the Past 300 Years), Shanghai: Zhonghua shuji, 1936

Lu You [Lu Yu], *Nantang shu* (A History of the Southern T'ang Dynasty)

Lü Zuqian [Lü Tsu-ch'ien], *Lida zhidu xiangshuo* (A Comprehensive History of the Administrative Systems Throughout the Ages)

Ma Duanlin [Ma Tuan-lin], *Wenxian tongkao* (Comprehensive History of Civilization)

Mingshi (History of the Ming Dynasty)

Naitō Torajirō, *Shina shigakushi* (History of Chinese Historical Writing), Tokyo: Kobundo, 1949

Ouyang Xiu [Ou-yang Hsiu] and Song Qi [Sung Ch'i], compilers, *Xin Tangshu* (A New History of the T'ang Dynasty)

Ouyang Xiu [Ou-yang Hsiu], *Xin Wudai shi* (A New History of the Five Dynasties)

Qian Daxin [Ch'ien Ta-hsin], *Nian-er shi kaoyi* (On the Discrepancies in the 22 Dynastic Histories), 1797

Qian Mu [Ch'ien Mu], *Zhongguo jin sanbainian xueshu shi* (History of Chinese Thought and Scholarship over the Past 300 Years), Shanghai: Shangwu yinshuguan, 1937

Quan Zuwang [Ch'üan Tsu Wang], *Song Yuan xue-an* (A Complete Treatise on Song and Yuan Thought by Schools), 1755

Sima Guang [Ssu-ma Kuang], *Zizhi tongjian* (Comprehensive Mirror for Aid in Government)

Tan Qian [Tan Ch'ien], *Guoque* (A Critical History of the [Ming] Dynasty), 1653

Tang Jian [T'ang Ch'ien], *Guochao xue-an xiaoshi* (A Short History of Thought of the Current [Qing] Dynasty), 1845

Wang Fuzhi [Wang Fu-chih], *Dutong jianlun* [*Du Tongjian lun*] (On Reading the *Comprehensive Mirror for Aid in Government*)

Wang Fuzhi [Wang Fu-chih], *Songlun* (On the History of the Song Dynasty)

Wang Mingsheng [Wang Ming-sheng], *Shiqi shi shangque* (A Critical Study of the Seventeen Dynastic Histories), 1788

Wang Pu [Wang P'u], *Tang huiyao* (Comprehensive Institutes of the T'ang Dynasty)

Wang Shizhen [Wang Shih-chen], *Yanzhou shanren sibu gao* (Treatises on Classics, History, Philosophy, and Literature)

Wang Shizhen [Wang Shih-chen], *Yenshan tang bieji* (Collection of Treatises on Ming History), 1590

Wang Shouren [Wang Shou-jen], *Chuanxi lu* (Instructions for Practical Living)

Xu Mengxin [Hsu Meng-hsin], *Sanchao beimeng huibian* (A Documentary Study of the Song-Jin Relations during the Three Reigns of Hui, Qin, and Gao Emperors)

Xue Juzheng [Hsueh Chü-cheng], *Wuda shi* (The History of the Five Dynasties)

Yang Lien-sheng, *Excursions in Sinology*, Cambridge, MA: Harvard University Press, 1969

Yin Shouheng, *Mingshi qie* (An Unauthorized History of the Ming Period), 1634

Yuan Shu, *Tongjian jishi benmo* (Comprehensive Mirror in Narration of Events from Beginning to End)

Zha Jizuo [Cha Chi-tso], *Guoshou lu* (Record of Heroes Who Died for the Ming Regime), 1650

Zha Jizuo [Cha Chi-tso], *Zuiwei lu* (A History of the Ming Dynasty), 1670

Zhang Dai [Chang Tai], *Shigui shu houji* (A History Book Stored in the Stone Case)

Zhang Menglun [Chang Meng-lun], *Zhongguo shixue shi* (History of Chinese Historical Writing), vol. 2, Lanzhou: Gansu Renmin chubanshe, 1986

Zhang Xuecheng [Chang Hsueh-ch'eng], *Hubei tongzhi* (A History of Hubei Province), 1794

Zhang Xuecheng [Chang Hsueh-ch'eng], *Wenshi tongyi* (General Principles of Literature and History), written 1772–1800; printed 1832

Zhao Yi [Chao Chi], *Nian-er shi zhaji* (Notes on the 22 Dynastic Histories), 1795

Zheng Hesheng [Cheng Ho-sheng], *Zhongguo shibu mulu xue* (A Bibliographical Study of Chinese Historiography), Shanghai: Shangwu yinshuguan, 1929

Zheng Qiao [Cheng Ch'iao], *Tongzhi* (General Treatise)

Zhu Guozhen [Chu Kuo-chen], *Huang Ming shi gai* (A Comprehensive History of the Ming Dynasty), 1632

Zhu Xi [Chu Hsi], *Zizhi tongjian gangmu* (The String and Mesh of the *Comprehensive Mirror for Aid in Government*)

Christianity

The influence of Christianity, and, more specifically, the Christian worldview, on historical writing in the Western world has been immense. Christian historical perspectives have affected our ideas of history as process, as linear, as universal, encompassing all peoples in all places and all times, as having a definite beginning and quite possibly an end, as meaningful, purposive, and positive. Beginning with two traditional sources, the Hebrew scriptures and Greco-Roman historiography, Christian authors, from the writers of the Gospels through Augustine in the 4th century CE, fashioned a new method of historical writing emphasizing time as the space in which God did his redemptive work.

Hebrew historiography, embodied most directly in the Torah and other writings, stressed divine purpose in history. The God of the Hebrews acted directly in human affairs. The writing of history, such as in the books of Genesis, Exodus, Judges and Kings, was thus an effort to elaborate on and explain the working out of the covenant with God. Human decisions, affairs, and conflicts were given meaning through their relationship to the liberation of the people of Israel from Egypt, their trials in the wilderness, and the establishment of the Israelites in the Promised Land. Subsequent history, such as that of King David or the Babylonian exile, was interpreted in the light of this historical dynamic.

Greco-Roman histories, in contrast, focused on origin myths, founding stories, and personalities, especially of divine rulers, and tended towards description and cataloging. From the 8th century BCE through the 2nd century CE, Homer, Herodotus, Strabo, and Plutarch helped define this tradition. By the time of the emperor Augustus at beginning of the Common Era, history was seen as the place where the divine purposes of the empire – order, prosperity, and peace – were carried out. It was also a time when the eventual unity of all peoples could be foreseen, and a universal history written.

Both of these traditions were firmly incorporated into Christian historical writing. Signs of divine intervention, miraculous events, and the efficacy of the church as an instrument of salvation all had parallels in the Hebrew and Greco-Roman ideas of history, either in the events of the Exodus or the creation of the empire. The earliest Christian histories exist in the Gospels and The Acts of the Apostles. The events of the life of Jesus and his earliest followers are recounted here in such a way as to give their theological significance priority over their historical actuality. Nevertheless, each also acts as a history of Jesus and the early Church. These accounts reveal a central aspect of the Christian historical worldview: the events of the past gather their significance to the extent they reveal the salvific purposes of God and the establishment of his kingdom here on Earth.

Early Christian histories from the 3rd through 5th centuries, such as Eusebius of Caesarea's *Historia ecclesiastica* (*Church History*, 311–25), St. Augustine's *De civitate dei* (*The City of God*, 413–26) and *Confessiones* (*Confessions*, 397), developed a chronological approach that supported this basic premise. They saw history as divided into various world ages, each building on the other until their culmination in the age of Christ. To this, Augustine added a transcendent theme of great influence: history as the struggle between good (the City of God) and evil (the City of Earth). This dynamic view of history as a process in which those dedicated to God would eventually triumph over those dedicated to themselves became a dominant motif of Western historical writing. For these men, and for the medieval writers to follow, history possessed three dominant ages (with many sub-periods interspersed, depending on the writer) through which this process unfolded. Jesus represented the beginning of the current age, the age of the Holy Spirit, the last and most advanced age in the history of humanity, which would end with the *eschaton*, the last days.

The age of the Renaissance and Reformation undermined many of the old assumptions and added new dimensions to the Christian telling of history. Humanist scholars, intent on uncovering the core of ancient texts through textual criticism, removed the source naivety of many medieval authors. Protestant scholars, through their attacks on the institutional church, separated the church from the historical working-out of God's redemption of humanity. The explorations of the New World challenged the concepts of universal history and unitary world ages. The result was the gradual secularization of the Christian historical worldview. Sacred history was no longer accepted automatically as coterminous with human history.

The Enlightenment of the 17th and 18th centuries pushed this secularization even further. Writers reinterpreted the progress of humanity towards emancipation not as the work of divine salvation but as the development of reason, shifting from a theocentric to an anthropocentric worldview. The three world ages now became the familiar ancient, medieval, and modern, removing the birth of Jesus from its central place in history and relegating explicit Christian frameworks to an earlier, less rational age. Christian historiography continued to focus on church history, accentuating the division between the sacred and the profane.

Nevertheless, much of the Christian framework was maintained, even if the content was changed, well into the 19th and 20th centuries. This can be seen dramatically in the work of the idealist philosopher G.W.F. Hegel's *Phänomenologie des Geistes* (1807; *The Phenomenology of Mind*, 1910) which emphasized history as the self-realization of pure consciousness. Hegel placed the Christian God, philosophically rendered as pure spirit or mind, fully within human history, rather than as a force outside of history that occasionally intervened. Writers in this tradition in the 20th century, such as Pierre Teilhard de Chardin, author of *Comment je crois* (1969; *Christianity and Evolution*, 1971) saw history as the progressive unfolding of human consciousness while retaining the Christian God as the endpoint of history.

The terrors of the 20th century undermined this generally progressive, secularized Christian worldview. The writings of theologians, such as Rudolf Bultmann's *Die Geschichte der synoptischen Tradition* (1921; *The History of the Synoptic Tradition*, 1963) and *Das Urchristentum im Rahmen der antiken Religionen* (1949; *Primitive Christianity in Its Contemporary Setting*, 1956), Paul Tillich's *A History of Christian Thought* (1956), and Reinhold Niebuhr's *Beyond Tragedy* (1937) tried to reassert the Christian view of evil as central to an understanding of history. An ironic approach to historical writing, one that eliminates divine influence on temporal affairs, has dominated modern Christian interpretations of history to the point that one can question whether an explicitly Christian perspective on history continues to exist. On the one hand, the division between the traditional Christian historian, who sees divine purpose within human events, and the modern, secular, scientific historian seems to be great. On the other hand, many Christian authors have adopted a secular, humanistic approach to history that leaves the action of God, divine purpose, and redemption out of their historical narratives.

DOUGLAS CREMER

See also Bultmann, Eusebius; Hegel; Niebuhr; Religion

Further Reading

Augustine, St., *Confessiones*, 397; in English as *Confessions*
Augustine, St., *De civitate dei*, written 413–426; in English as *The City of God*
Breen, Quirinus, *The Impact of the Church upon Its Culture: Reappraisals of the History of Christianity*, Chicago: University of Chicago Press, 1968
Breisach, Ernst, *Historiography: Ancient, Medieval, and Modern*, Chicago: University of Chicago Press, 1983; revised 1994
Bultmann, Rudolf, *Die Geschichte der synoptischen Tradition*, Göttingen: Vandenhoeck & Ruprecht, 1921; in English as *The History of the Synoptic Tradition*, New York: Harper, and Oxford: Blackwell, 1963, revised 1968
Bultmann, Rudolf, *Das Urchristentum im Rahmen der antiken Religionen*, Zurich: Artemis, 1949; in English as *Primitive Christianity in Its Contemporary Setting*, London and New York: Thames and Hudson, 1956
Eusebius of Caesarea, *Historia ecclesiastica*, written 311–25; in English as *The Ecclesiastical History* and *The History of the Church from Christ to Constantine*

Hegel, G.W.F., *Die Phänomenologie des Geistes*, Bamberg: Goebhardt, 1807; in English as *The Phenomenology of Mind*, 2 vols., London: Sonnenschein, and New York: Macmillan, 1910, 2nd edition London: Allen and Unwin, and New York: Macmillan, 1931; as *Phenomenology of Spirit*, Oxford: Clarendon Press, 1977
Johnson, Paul, *A History of Christianity*, New York: Atheneum, and London: Weidenfeld and Nicolson, 1976
Kee, Howard Clark, *Christianity: A Social and Cultural History*, New York: Macmillan, 1991
Küng, Hans, *Christianity: Essence, History, Future*, New York: Continuum, and London: SCM Press, 1995
McIntire, C.T., ed., *God, History, and Historians: An Anthology of Modern Christian Views of History*, New York and Oxford: Oxford University Press, 1977
Niebuhr, Reinhold, *Beyond Tragedy: Essays on the Christian Interpretation of History*, New York: Scribner, 1937; London: Nisbet, 1938
Richardson, Alan, *History Sacred and Profane*, Philadelphia: Westminster Press, and London: SCM Press, 1964
Teilhard de Chardin, Pierre, *Comment je crois*, Paris: Seuil, 1969; in English as *Christianity and Evolution*, New York: Harcourt Brace, and London: Collins, 1971
Tillich, Paul, *A History of Christian Thought*, Providence, RI: privately printed, 1956; New York: Harper, and London: SCM, 1968

Cipolla, Carlo M. 1922–

Italian economic historian of the Renaissance

Carlo Cipolla has been described as "the master of the short historical monograph" and has been praised for his "pithy and often penetrating analysis." The author of many microhistories on Renaissance Italian economics, particularly in Tuscany from the 14th through 17th centuries, Cipolla is known for his studies of particular problems. Among his most controversial writings are those that focus on the so-called "economic depression of the Renaissance," in which he entered a lively debate with Robert Lopez and Harry Miskimin in the journal *Economic History Review* in the 1960s. Cipolla had, in the same journal in 1949, discussed a recession in the 14th century followed by an upward trend in the 15th century, produced not by technology or bullion movements, but by increased investment. Lopez and Miskimin instead characterized the European economic trends of the Renaissance as a depression, based in part on their conclusion that growth in the 15th century was not equal to that in the 13th. Cipolla criticized their data as well as their conclusions, labeling both historians "stagnationists."

Several of Cipolla's works have focused entirely on money, its forms, and its movements; others on specific towns in Tuscany. However, Cipolla's work has not been confined to such micro-studies; he was also the editor of *The Fontana Economic History of Europe* (1972–76) and the author of both introductory and synthetic works on European economic history, as well as studies of science and technology, European expansion, and literacy. His studies, replete with graphs, charts, maps, and pictures, make monetary and economic history understandable even to the innumerate. Admitting that divisions of historical periods and disciplines are always somewhat arbitrary, even absurd, Cipolla developed his own disciplines with relish. He sought to bridge the gap between history and economics. This gap produces serious difficulties: economics is concerned with the present and the future as well as the past, history only with past; history does not seek laws, economics necessitates them. These divergences are perhaps most visible in the way in which scholars formulate questions. Historians tend to limit themselves to what questions *can* be asked of particular sources, which sometimes leads the economist to think that historians are ignorant of the role and importance of economic factors in history. On the other hand, economists tend to formulate models based on problems of economics – without attention to the sources and the information they can provide. Cipolla's own answers to this inevitable confrontation are the microhistories he has written, e.g., plague in a small Tuscan town; the monetary policy of Florence in the 14th and 15th centuries; and the development of clocks.

Cipolla, however, delves deeper than a single issue. At one point, he compared the writing of history to staging a theatrical show: the work necessary behind the scenes is far less organized than the finished product, which is intended to present a coherent and logical progression of events. Cipolla is interested in showing the process as well as the product. This, in combination with his desire to produce interdisciplinary studies, demonstrates his belief that economic history does not operate in a vacuum but must also involve social and cultural considerations, making his work compatible with that of the practitioners of the history of *mentalités*. In any given economic history, Cipolla studies transportation, coinage, products, values, labor, interest rates, and monetary policy. He has accused European economic historians, including Pirenne and Braudel, of being weak on economic theory, and seeks to integrate economic as well as historical theory into his own work to redress the problems that ignorance of one may cause.

KATHLEEN COMERFORD

See also Demography; Industrial Revolution; Italy: Renaissance; Italy: since the Renaissance; Renaissance Historical Writing; World

Biography

Carlo Maria Cipolla. Born Pavia, 15 August 1922. Graduate in political science, University of Pavia; studied in Paris and London, late 1940s. Taught economic history at universities of Genoa, Venice, Pavia, and California, Berkeley; professor of economic history, Scuola Normale Superiore de Pisa, from 1982 to retirement.

Principal Writings

Le avventure della lira (The Adventures of the Lira), 1958
The Economic History of World Population, 1962
With Robert S. Lopez, and Harry A. Miskimin, "Economic Depression of the Renaissance?", *Economic History Review* 2nd series, 16 (1964), 519–29
Guns and Sails in the Early Phase of European Expansion, 1400–1700, 1965; in US as *Guns, Sails, and Empires: Technological Innovation and the Early Phases of European Expansion, 1400–1700*, 1965
Clocks and Culture, 1300–1700, 1967
Literacy and Development in the West, 1969
The Economic Decline of Empires, 1970
European Culture and Overseas Expansion, 1970 [combines *Guns and Sails*, 1965, and *Clocks and Culture*, 1967]
Editor, *The Fontana Economic History of Europe*, 6 vols., 1972–76

Storia economica dell'Europa pre-industriale, 1974; in English as *Before the Industrial Revolution: European Society and Economy, 1000–1700*, 1976
Storia economica dell'Europa pre-industriale, 1975; in English as *Before the Industrial Revolution: European Society and Economy, 1000–1700*, 1976
Cristofano e la peste: un caso di storia del sistema sanitario in Toscana nell'eta di Galileo, 1976; in English as *Cristofano and the Plague: A Study in the History of Public Health in the Age of Galileo*, 1973
Public Health and the Medical Profession in the Renaissance, 1976
The Basic Laws of Human Stupidity, 1976
Chi ruppe i rastelli a Monte Lupo?, 1977; in Britain as *Faith, Reason, and the Plague: A Tuscan Story of the Seventeenth Century*, 1979; in US as *Faith, Reason, and the Plague in Seventeenth-Century Tuscany*, 1979
With Derek Birdsall, *The Technology of Man: A Visual History*, 1979
Contro un nemico invisibile: epidemie e strutture sanitarie nell'Italia del Rinascimento (Against an Invisible Enemy: Epidemics and Public Health Organizations in Renaissance Italy), 1985
La moneta a Firenze nel Cinquecento, 1987; in English as *Money in Sixteenth-Century Florence*, 1989
Tra due culture: introduzione alla storia economica, 1988; in English as *Between Two Cultures: An Introduction to Economic History*, 1991
Le tre rivoluzioni e altri saggi di storia economica e sociale (The Three Revolutions and Other Essays in Social and Economic History), 1989
Miasmi ed umori: ecologia e condizioni sanitarie in Toscana nel Seicento, 1989; in English as *Miasmas and Disease: Public Health and the Environment in the Pre-Industrial Age*, 1992

Further Reading

Bullock, Alan, *Is History Becoming a Social Science? The Case of Contemporary History*, London and New York: Cambridge University Press, 1977
Fischer, Wolfram, R. Marvin McInnis, and Jurgen Schneider, eds., *The Emergence of a World Economy, 1500–1914: Papers of the IX International Congress of Economic History*, Wiesbaden: Steiner, 1986
Lopez, Robert S., and Harry A. Miskimin, "The Economic Depression of the Renaissance," *Economic History Review*, 2nd series 14 (1961–62), 400–26
Solow, R.E., "Economics: Is Something Missing?", in William N. Parker, ed., *Economic History and the Modern Economist*, Oxford: Blackwell, 1986

Clapham, J.H. 1873–1946

British economic historian

Along with R.H. Tawney and George Cunningham, J.H. Clapham effectively established the discipline of economic history in Britain during the interwar years. His first economic history book appeared in 1921, a study of *The Economic Development of France and Germany, 1815–1914*. As the first substantial treatment in English of the two countries' economic histories, it was an important study in its own right, but it also illustrated the value of comparative history. However, it was remarked by one critic that the juxtaposition of Germany and France was in fact not a very fruitful one, although it was one often made by subsequent writers. As a follow up, Clapham planned and initiated the huge collaborative volumes published as the *Cambridge Economic History of Europe*.

As long ago as 1897 the economist Alfred Marshall had told Lord Acton that the lack of a proper history of Britain's industrial economy was "a disgrace." He added that John Clapham, who had studied economic history and worked as a researcher for Marshall himself, was by far the best equipped man to undertake such a work. His hopes were realized when Clapham's major book, *An Economic History of Modern Britain*, appeared in three volumes between 1926 and 1938. It was the first comprehensive treatment of Britain's economic history, a theme not previously treated as a whole, except superficially. Written on a scale more usually associated with general national history, it is magisterial in scope, extending even to discussion of such relative minutiae as the development of the children's toy industry, yet successfully integrating economic developments into the broader political and social contexts. Its qualities, not least the fine turn of phrase and ability to convey the excitement of technological innovation, were widely acknowledged, although it has not been accepted uncritically. Its handling of social concepts such as class is uncertain, even vague, and for the most part discussion of social matters is very traditional, confined mainly to the type of issues that interested economists – population growth, urban development, public health, education and the like. This was in marked contrast to the strongly sociological history coming from contemporaries such as Tawney. In part, no doubt, this was because, unlike Tawney and some of his fellow radical historians, Clapham's interest in the past was not inspired primarily by moral or philosophical questions. "The variety of human life," he professed in his inaugural Cambridge lecture, published in 1929, "is attraction in itself . . . [The historian] cares for the beginnings of things as such." Despite the fact that he had come strongly under the influence of Alfred Marshall, Clapham was skeptical about the utility of economic theory for the historian, doubting that the past could be reduced to the neat order and logic posited by so much economic theory. Although his well known paper of 1922, "On Empty Economic Boxes," was dismissed as naive by A.C. Pigou, Clapham remained undeterred, and his major work employed very little theory – at least not overtly. This should not be pushed too far, however, since his interpretation of Britain's economic history did reflect the static partial equilibrium economics he had learned with Marshall. Thus the *Economic History of Modern Britain* is stronger on issues on economic organization than on development, and the reader is given relatively little idea of how and why the state of the national economy changed over time. Indeed, there is a certain Whiggishness inherent in Clapham's interpretation of the Industrial Revolution as a success story and in his implicit acceptance of capitalism. This brought him into conflict with the those who, writing from a leftish perspective, popularized an alternative and negative view. In particular, he disagreed with the Hammonds' denigration of the Industrial Revolution, and used statistical measures to support his contention that industrialization produced rising real wages. This disagreement sparked off a long-running debate about the impact of the Industrial Revolution on working-class living standards and if subsequent contributions often assumed ideological overtones, it is important to remember that Clapham's original difference with the Hammonds was not rooted in ideology: it came about because he was convinced that their pessimism had no valid statistical foundation, a conviction that later contributors generally conceded.

To a large extent it was precisely Clapham's concern with measurement that gave his major book its unique place in the development of economic history in Britain. In the range of issues he explored, the type of economic questions he asked, and by applying to everything the simple question "how much?," Clapham not only revolutionized the handling of modern economic history but also set the agenda for succeeding generations of researchers. That the agenda has now moved on and the statistical issues are now approached in a far more sophisticated manner cannot detract from the importance of his contribution. Indeed, his intuitive grasp of the importance of human motivation in establishing causality prevented him from descending into the sort of statistical determinism that was later to characterize the worst sort of econometric history.

It has been suggested by W.H.B. Court that Clapham's historical strengths were most in evidence, his weaknesses least so, in his final major work, a commissioned history of the Bank of England, two volumes of which were published in 1944 shortly before his death. They were certainly wider in scope than the title might imply, but Clapham's canvas was narrower, allowing him to focus not on a whole nation but on a single institution which he understood well, and also on a clearly defined social group whose work and motivations he knew. The social history in this book is thus more convincing than that in *The Economic History of Modern Britain*. Not everyone would agree with Court's assertion that Clapham was "the greatest of English economic historians," but few would contest the significance of his contribution to the development of his discipline.

KENNETH D. BROWN

See also Economic; Hammond; Industrial Revolution; Power

Biography

John Harold Clapham. Born Broughton, Salford, Lancashire, 13 September 1873. Educated at Leys School, Cambridge; King's College, Cambridge, BA 1895. At Cambridge University: fellow, King's College, 1898–1904, and 1908–46; lecturer, rising to professor of economic history, 1898–1902 and 1908–46; professor of economics, University of Leeds, 1902–08. Seconded to the Board of Trade, 1916–18. Married Mary Margaret Green, 1905 (1 son, 3 daughters). Knighted 1943. Died 29 March 1946.

Principal Writings

The Economic Development of France and Germany, 1815–1914, 1921
An Economic History of Modern Britain, 3 vols., 1926–38
The Study of Economic History, 1929
Editor with Eileen Power, *The Cambridge Economic History of Europe*, vol. 1, 1941
The Bank of England: A History, 2 vols., 1944
A Concise Economic History of Britain from the Earliest Times to 1750, 1949

Further Reading

Clark, G.N., "Sir John Harold Clapham," *Proceedings of the British Academy* 32 (1947), 334–52
Court, William Henry Bassano, *Scarcity and Choice in History*, London: Arnold, and New York: A.M. Kelley, 1970

Floud, Roderick, "Words, Not Numbers: John Harold Clapham," *History Today* 39 (April 1989), 42–47

Gunn, J., ed., *John Harold Clapham, 1873–1946: Fellow, Tutor, and Vice-Provost: A Memoir*, Cambridge: Cambridge University Press, 1949

Harte, N.B., ed., *The Study of Economic History: Collected Inaugural Lectures, 1893–1970*, London: Cass, 1971

Clark, Alice 1874–1934

British economic and women's historian

Alice Clark wrote only one book, *Working Life of Women in the Seventeenth Century* (1919). But that one book is probably the most influential work of the 20th century on English women of the early modern period. From a liberal Quaker background, Clark knew many prominent reformers as family friends. After leaving school she took a housewifery course and then entered the family shoe firm (at the bottom), where she was to spend most of her adult life (as a director from 1904). In 1912 she moved to London to serve on the Executive Committee of the Union of Suffrage Societies. In 1913, aged 38, she was awarded Mrs. Bernard Shaw's research studentship and began to study history at the London School of Economics. She followed Eileen Power as research student there, and, like her, was supervised by Lilian Knowles (professor from 1919). R.H. Tawney was also a significant influence. In the first third of this century more women were active in the field of economic history than at any time since, but Clark's personal relation to other women historians is unknown. It seems likely that her own background played the most significant role in determining her choice of subject matter. From two years of research in the British Library she produced *Working Life*. Ten years after moving to London she returned to work in the family factory in Street, Somerset, until her death.

Working Life traces the shift over a long 17th century from "domestic industry" (what we might call a subsistence economy) in which wives and husbands contributed jointly and equally to household subsistence, through "family industry," a regime in which some members of the family worked for wages but that work was still carried out mainly within the household, to "capitalistic industry," in which virtually all production was commercial and took place outside the home in factories. Clark's tripartite development is still largely accepted today, although the terminology has changed. The significance of the development and its chronology, however, are highly disputed.

Working Life remains the leading exposition of the pessimistic view that capitalist industry seriously eroded women's status, which had been higher, perhaps even equal to that of men, in the pre-capitalist and pre-industrial past. She found in medieval and early modern "domestic industry" a model of women's self-sufficiency, productive labor, and self-respect to be applied to her own day. Many medievalists of Clark's day and later shared her pessimism. Historians who studied the 18th and 19th centuries (notably Ivy Pinchbeck, who published *Women Workers and the Industrial Revolution, 1750–1850* a decade after *Working Life*) took a more optimistic view of the effects of capitalism and industrialization on women's work, emphasizing freedom of choice in employment. Today, the question of women's status in the past is usually less clear-cut than it was for Clark or Pinchbeck. Ideas either of a medieval golden age or of industrial progress are rejected. The most outspoken advocate of historical continuity in women's status from the 14th century to the present day is the medievalist Judith Bennett.

The debate on women's status has largely been carried on among feminist historians. Clark herself had no influence on the men who wrote so-called "standard" histories of the early modern economy or family, which make virtually no mention of women's work. Now, nearly eighty years after *Working Life*, feminist historians are only beginning to have some impact on history textbooks insofar as "people" have at least to be acknowledged as of two genders, with potentially significant differences of experience. To some extent, Clark's influence in the field of women's history is the result of *Working Life* having been reprinted in 1968 and again in 1982, coinciding with two waves of feminist history. It still offers the most comprehensive introduction to women's everyday lives in the early modern period.

AMY LOUISE ERICKSON

See also Pinchbeck; Power; Scott, Joan

Biography

Born Street, Somerset, 1874, to a Quaker shoe-manufacturing family. Took a housewifery course, then entered family business at a low level in 1897, working her way up to life director, 1904. Suffered severe bouts of illness, mainly tuberculosis, 1893 and 1909. Traveled in Europe and Middle East, 1909–12. Executive committee member, National Union of Women Suffrage Societies, London, 1912–13. Research student, London School of Economics, 1913–17. Returned to family firm, part-time, 1917–22, full-time, 1922–34. Died 1934.

Principal Writings

Working Life of Women in the Seventeenth Century, 1919

Further Reading

Berg, Maxine, "The First Women Economic Historians," *Economic History Review* 45 (1992), 308–29

Erickson, Amy Louise, Introduction to Alice Clark, *Working Life of Women in the Seventeenth Century*, London: Routledge, 1992

Gillett, Margaret Clark, "Alice Clark of C. & J. Clark Ltd, Street, Somerset," Oxford: privately printed, n.d. [before 1935]

Clark, Manning 1915–1991

Australian historian

One of Australia's foremost historians of the 20th century, Manning Clark became an Australian nationalist who renounced British Australia. Clark was born in Sydney and educated in Melbourne, and these two cities formed the basis of his ideas. From his early years, Clark was interested in philosophy, poetry, painting, and music. Later he came strongly to oppose change, social improvement, and optimism. In his *A Short History of Australia* (1963) and the 6-volume *A History of Australia* (1962–87), Clark certainly implicitly argued for a reform agenda and saw classes and individuals as shaping Australian history. Only later in life did he become more "metaphysical" and "pessimistic" in approach. As Stephen Holt explains in *Manning Clark and Australian History* (1982), Clark was a "believer in individual as opposed to social regeneration and devoted to metaphysics as opposed to politics, pessimistic about human nature and skeptical as to the uplifting possibilities of political action and moral idealism."

As Australia's most widely read historian, one of Clark's roles was to reveal a unique Australian "national identity." In doing so, he posed a fundamental question, "Did [Australians] have anything of [their] own to replace what had been swept so abruptly into history's overflowing rubbish bin of discarded human dreams?" Australian history began to be taught as an undergraduate subject in Australian universities only in the 1940s. Today it attracts hundreds of first-year undergraduates in Australian universities. Australian history, according to Clark, has a different approach from other national histories as the origins of the white Australian identity arose in the bush rather than in the cities. This may be disputed, as the "rural" basis of national history also applies to countries such as the United States and Argentina. In Australia, though, the rural community played an exceptionally important role in the exploration of the country, and Clark's *A Discovery of Australia* (1976) was centered on this theme. Following the ideas of Russell Ward, Clark stressed that Australia's history took root in the Australian outback and from the Australian outback emerged its national character. In order to form a national character, he wrote, Australia had to create a culture of its own. Furthermore, emphasized Stephen Holt, "Australia had to break away from Europe and develop a national and virile culture of its own." Clark's hope for an Australian identity was further boosted in 1979 when he delivered the annual James Duhig Memorial Lecture at the University of Queensland in Brisbane (later published as *The Quest for an Australian Identity*, 1980). In these lectures, Clark stressed that the colonial Europeans believed Australia was inferior to Western Europe in every respect. Clark's message therefore suggested that every effort had to be made to establish an Australian identity.

Clark's most influential work was his 6-volume *A History of Australia*. In the *History*, Clark argued that white Australian institutions and culture were transposed from Europe: particularly important were Catholicism, Protestantism, and the Enlightenment. Furthermore, adds Carl Bridge in *Manning Clark: Essays on His Place in History* (1994), "The *History* told of the clash – of Catholicism, Protestantism, and the Enlightenment – of the rape of the land, the annihilation of the Aborigines, and of the 'fatal flaws' that brought down a gallery of desperate men (and occasionally women) in the Australian emptiness." More importantly, however, Clark used his *History* to tell his fellow Australians who they were, what they stood for, and what might become of them. Clark's first sentence in the book was: "Civilization did not begin in Australia until the last quarter of the 18th century." The Australian Aborigines who were the indigenous people of Australia, claimed Clark, created "cultures" but not "civilization."

The ideas of history could be conveyed well only through indirect narrators. This was evident in the *History*, where Clark described the Aborigines from the European point of view. As a result, the Aborigines were often referred to as "cannibals" or "savages," although the Aborigines were by no means seen that way by all white Australians. Clark also stressed that history was best told with many examples, written from the thoughts of historians. Therefore, he used the *History* to convey his personal opinion: that the coming of Western civilization to Australia was tragic.

Throughout the *History* Clark was influenced by debates and events affecting his own generation. His analysis changed through time, especially during the 25-year period it took to publish the *History*. Like those of many historians, his works received criticism, particularly for oversimplifying the exposition of Australian history. Whatever the criticisms, Clark's works have earned him a prominent place both in the history of Australia, and in the writing of its history.

YEONG-HAN CHEONG

See also Australia; Blainey

Biography

Charles Manning Hope Clark. Born Burwood, New South Wales, 13 March 1915, son of an Anglican cleric, and descended from early settlers on his mother's side. Attended Melbourne Grammar School, University of Melbourne, and Balliol College, Oxford. Taught at Blundell's School, then returned to Australia and taught at Geelong Grammar School; taught political science, University of Melbourne, 1944–46; professor of history, University College, Canberra (later Australian National University), 1949–75 (emeritus). Married Dymphna Lodewyckx, 1939 (5 sons, 1 daughter). Died Canberra, 23 May 1991.

Principal Writings

Editor with L.J. Pryor, *Selected Documents in Australian History*, 2 vols., 1950–55
Sources of Australian History, 1957
Meeting Soviet Man, 1960
A History of Australia, 6 vols., 1962–87
A Short History of Australia, 1963
Disquiet and Other Stories, 1969
The Beginning of an Australian Intelligentsia, 1973
A Discovery of Australia, 1976
In Search of Henry Lawson, 1978
David Campbell, 1915–1979: Words Spoken at His Funeral, 1979
Occasional Writings and Speeches, 1980
The Quest for an Australian Identity, 1980
Australia Felix: Chap Wurrung and Major Mitchell, 1987
Writing a History of Australia, 1989
The Quest for Grace, 1990
The Puzzles of Childhood [autobiography], 1990
A Discovery of Australia: The 1976 ABC Boyer Lectures and Their 1988 Postscript, 1991
A Historian's Apprenticeship, 1992
Manning Clark's History of Australia, abridged by Michael Cathcart, 1993

Further Reading

Bridge, Carl, ed., *Manning Clark: Essays on His Place in History*, Carlton: Melbourne University Press, 1994
Crawford, Raymond Maxwell, *An Australian Perspective*, Parkville: Melbourne University Press, 1960
Crawford, Raymond Maxwell, *A Bit of a Rebel: The Life and Work of George Arnold Wood*, Sydney: Sydney University Press, 1975
Crawford, Raymond Maxwell, *Making History: R.M. Crawford, Manning Clark, Geoffrey Blainey*, Fitzroy: McPhee Gribble, and New York: Penguin, 1985

Gammage, Bill, "Charles Manning Hope Clark, 1915–1991," *Australian Historical Association Bulletin* 66–67 (1991)

Holt, Stephen, *Manning Clark and Australian History, 1915–1963*, St Lucia: University of Queensland Press, 1982

Macintyre, Stuart, *A History for a Nation: Ernest Scott and the Making of Australian History*, Carlton: Melbourne University Press, 1994

Pascoe, Rob, *The Manufacture of Australian History*, Melbourne, Oxford, and New York: Oxford University Press, 1979

Ryan, Peter, "Manning Clark," *Quadrant* 299 (1993)

Scott, Ernest, *History and Historical Problems*, London: Oxford University Press, 1925

Throssell, Ric, *For Valour*, Sydney: Currency Press, 1976

Cobb, Richard 1917–1996

British historian of revolutionary France

Richard Cobb, one of the great British historians of France, is best known for his absorbing, richly evocative studies of the impact of the French Revolution on the lives of ordinary people. A master of both French and English prose, Cobb possessed a novelist's eye for the significant detail, a genius for the vivid description of people and places, and an unparalleled command of the archival sources for the revolutionary period. In all his work his main concern was to look at the great events of the 1790s through the eyes of the *petit peuple* and to tell the story of the Revolution in ways that illuminated the experience, the hopes, and the fears of men (and occasionally women) with ordinary vices and unheroic ambitions.

Early in life Cobb left behind the sheltered world of Tunbridge Wells and acquired a second "identity" as a Frenchman. A lover of the French language and of French writers (such as Raymond Queneau), with an ear for popular speech, he wrote in 1967 that for more than thirty years he had "walked French popular history, drunk it, seen it, heard it, participated in it." France was his home for many of these years, and he was over fifty when his first book in English was published. He was already well known, however, through the publication of two dozen articles in French provincial journals and of a monumental French doctoral thesis.

Les Armées Révolutionnaires (1961–63; *The People's Armies*, 1987) was a study of the citizen armies created in 1793 to combat rural counter-revolution, to enforce revolutionary price-controls, and to assist in the requisition of food and supplies. Born at a time of administrative anarchy and popular revolution, these groups of armed citizens were conceived as a vanguard necessary to bring the Terror to the countryside and combat the greed and inertia of provincial elites. They came to be both feared and hated; and when the crisis of 1793 had passed the revolutionary government disbanded them, accusing their leaders of complicity in the alleged Hébertist conspiracy. From Cobb's perspective their breakup marked the end of the "anarchic Terror" and the beginning of a period of "administered" and "policed" Terror under the direct control of the revolutionary dictatorship.

On its appearance *The People's Armies* was recognized as a major contribution to the study of "history from below" during the French Revolution. The book was seen as complementing the work of Albert Soboul on the Parisian *sans-culottes* and of George Rudé on revolutionary crowds. But whereas Soboul and Rudé had stressed the political aims and organization of the "popular movement," and the economic and social determinants of its "ideology," Cobb focused on the varying attitudes, temperaments and prejudices of his revolutionaries, the mixing of high and low motives, of zealotry and ambition. Whereas Soboul and Rudé had sought to generalize about group behavior, Cobb's concern was with individuals. His book can be seen as a vast set of artfully arranged vignettes, conveying a sense of the irreducible complexity of people and events. As Cobb himself put it: "The Terror in the village was as complex as life itself . . . . We must rest content with conclusions which are almost entirely negative and always imprecise, avoiding the temptation to impose a false sense of unity and simplicity on a subject which had neither."

The idiosyncratic features of Cobb's approach to "history from below" became more pronounced in his later works. In *The Police and the People* (1970), *Reactions to the French Revolution* (1972), and *Paris and Its Provinces* (1975) he focused on ordinary people at odds with authority. He distanced himself explicitly from "the altogether too respectable Crowd" of Professor Rudé and from the precise Marxist choreography of Soboul's "historical ballet of the Year II." His subjects were outsiders – misfits, criminals, outcasts, and individualists – who sought to escape the constraints of both conventional society and ideological orthodoxy. Cobb also became fascinated by the history of private life and of private perspectives on public events. In discussing "private calendars" and "fringe occupations" and in an enthralling essay on seduction and pregnancy in revolutionary Lyon, he showed how tangential, and even how irrelevant "great" events could seem when viewed from the perspective of people struggling to survive.

Underlying all of Cobb's historical writing was an attitude that might be termed extreme historical nominalism. Distrusting broad patterns, rigid categories, and reductive explanatory schemes, Cobb argued that individuals and unique events are the stuff of history. The best the historian could do was to use individual "case histories" in order to illustrate attitudes and assumptions prevalent at a given time and place. Good historical writing was necessarily impressionistic. Abstraction and generalization tended to falsify and trivialize our sense of the past. The problems posed by this conception of history are obvious. When the Revolution is viewed "from below" and in terms of the experience of individuals, the events, movements, and institutions confidently described in textbooks and monographs lose their clear outlines and the Revolution itself dissolves into a confusion of personal calendars, private passions, local conflicts, local loyalties, family vendettas, violence, and alcohol.

But Cobb's "nominalism," is also the key to some of his most distinctive contributions to our understanding of French history. These include his capacity for empathy with outsiders, his insistence on the endless variety of French provincial life, on the persistence of regional ties, and on the danger of generalizations on a national scale. A passionate believer in the value of local and regional history, Cobb was convinced that politics, even revolutionary politics, centered around local issues and local interests. In his writing this perspective was given added resonance by his sensitivity to French topography – his "sense of place." For one of the most striking features of his work was his ability to evoke, often in startlingly vivid terms, the look, the sounds, and the feel of the Paris banlieue, the backstreets of Lyon, and the wet, flat countryside of northern France.

JONATHAN BEECHER

See also France: French Revolution; History from Below; Hufton; Rudé; Schama; Soboul; Social

Biography

Richard Charles Cobb. Born 20 May 1917. Educated at Shrewsbury School; Merton College, Oxford, BA in modern history, 1939. Studying French history in France at outbreak of war; served in the British forces, eventually as liaison to Czech Army. Resumed research in France after war; returned to England, 1955; taught at University College, Aberystwyth, 1955–61; University of Leeds, 1961–62; and Oxford University, 1962–87: fellow/tutor, Balliol College, 1962–73, university professor, 1973–84, and professorial fellow, then research fellow, Worcester College, 1973–87. Married 1) in 1951 (marriage dissolved: 1 son); 2) Margaret Tennant, 1963 (3 sons, 1 daughter). Died 15 January 1996.

Principal Writings

Les Armées Révolutionnaires, 1961–63; in English as The People's Armies: The Armées Révolutionnaires, Instrument of the Terror in the Departments, April 1793 to Floréal Year II, 1987
Terreur et subsistances, 1793–1795 (Terror and Subsistence), 1965
A Second Identity: Essays on France and French History [autobiography], 1969
The Police and the People: French Popular Protest, 1789–1820, 1970
Reactions to the French Revolution, 1972
Paris and Its Provinces, 1792–1802, 1975
A Sense of Place, 1975
Raymond Queneau, 1976
Tour de France [collected essays], 1976
Death in Paris: The Records of the Basse-Géole de la Seine, October 1795–September 1801, Vendémiaire Year IV–Fructidor Year IX, 1978
Promenades: A Historian's Appreciation of Modern French Literature, 1980
The Streets of Paris, 1980
French and Germans, Germans and French: A Personal Interpretation of France under Two Occupations, 1914–1918/1940–1944, 1983
Still Life: Sketches from a Tunbridge Wells Childhood [autobiography], 1983
A Classical Education [autobiography], 1985
People and Places, 1985
Something to Hold Onto: Autobiographical Sketches, 1988
Editor with Colin Jones, Voices of the French Revolution, 1988
The End of the Line [autobiography], 1997

Further Reading

Darnton, Robert, "French History: The Case of the Wandering Eye," New York Review of Books (5 April 1973), 25–30
Gilmour, David, "Diary," London Review of Books (21 May 1987), 250
Lewis, Gwynne, and Colin Lucas, eds., Beyond the Terror: Essays in French Regional and Social History, 1794–1815, Cambridge and New York: Cambridge University Press, 1983
Paxton, Robert O., "Living with the Enemy," New York Review of Books (16 June 1983), 9–10
Weitz, Margaret Collins, "Histoire populaire: An Interview with Richard Cobb," Contemporary French Civilization 7 (1982), 82–87
Woloch, Isser, Review of Les Armées Révolutionnaires, Journal of Modern History 37 (1965), 245–47

Cobban, Alfred 1901–1968

British historian of France

Alfred Cobban was a historian of unusual intellectual range. Reader then Professor of French history at University College, London from 1937 to his retirement 30 years later, he published no less extensively in the fields of political theory and international affairs. He will, though, be remembered principally for his part in the remarkable transformation that historical scholarship on the French Revolution has undergone in the second half of the 20th century.

Cobban was the first historian to challenge the interpretation of the Revolution as a quintessentially bourgeois revolution. Although elaborated by French historians working within a home-grown Republican-Marxist tradition, by the 1930s this view had come to dominate academic thinking and research world-wide. Cobban delivered his initial onslaught on the orthodoxy in 1954, in his inaugural lecture "The Myth of the French Revolution." Ten years later he made his "revisionist" case at greater length and to a far wider audience in The Social Interpretation of the French Revolution (1964).

His starting point was that what had come to be seen as a common-sense version of events was, like all history, the work of particular historians working within a specific historiographic tradition. Cobban's deconstruction of this tradition focused on the influence of Marxist-Leninism within it. Unlike many of his British followers, Cobban's did not deny a place for theory in historical study; what he objected to was the deterministic character of the theory in question and its mechanistic application by "orthodox" historians. In interpreting the Revolution in terms of the "substitution of a capitalist bourgeois order for feudalism," they were forcing the events of a few years at the end of the 18th century into a pre-determined Marxist schema of the whole of human history.

This brief ideological critique rested on a relentless empirical one. Cobban himself had done little or no archival research on Revolutionary France; instead he used data gathered by orthodox historians to show that the findings of recent research could no longer be accommodated within their theoretical model. Feudalism as a system had withered away long before the Revolution abolished its last vestiges in the form of seigniorial rights. Far from advancing emergent capitalism, the Revolution was largely responsible for France's economic retardation relative to "evolutionary" Britain. Most crucially, there was simply no self-conscious, capitalist bourgeois class to mastermind its own revolution. Empirical research revealed in its place a loose collection of disparate social groupings. The one which provided the personnel of the Revolution consisted not of industrialists and businessmen but of officeholders and lawyers. Nor did these revolutionaries act as unofficial spokesmen for the forces of capitalism: their principal commitment was to the new state machine and their own survival in office. Insofar as they served any wider sectional interest, it was that of landowning society, to which they themselves belonged.

Cobban acknowledged he had no coherent vision of the Revolution to offer. He did, however, have some positive views to put forward. His best known formulations came from simply inverting the tenets of the orthodoxy (the Revolution was *against* not for capitalism; its agents the *declining* not rising bourgeoisie), and were surely intended for their polemical effect – "publicity stunts" was how one critic described them. Other suggestions, though, have proved more fruitful: for example, the importance in revolutionary conflicts of social divisions other than class (rich versus poor, town versus country).

Already before his death in 1968 the reception given to his *Social Interpretation* had revealed that the orthodoxy's hold on English-language scholarship was in fact tenuous. In France, however, it would take another decade of fierce academic in-fighting before revisionists under Furet's leadership gained the upper hand. By then Cobban's call for a new approach to the Revolution had been answered: "1789" was the work of a mixed noble-bourgeois elite of notables who survived the Terror to become the masters of 19th-century France. This positive revisionist interpretation never dominated the academic scene as the old paradigm had done; less because of neo-Marxist resistance than as a result of the emergence of another revisionist or "post-revisionist" approach, which abandoned social categories – some would say, human agency – altogether for the study of political culture both of the Revolution and the *ancien régime* from which it sprang.

Cobban's reputation has itself undergone some revision over the years. Marxists no longer simply dismiss him as a Cold War warrior and grant that he pinpointed certain reductionist tendencies within the classic interpretation. Conversely, latter-day revisionists now place greater stress on the negative character of his work and point to assumptions it is said to have shared with the old paradigm. (It is often said that he was merely replacing a Marxist with a "non-Marxist economic interpretation.") This reading not only tends to cut him off from subsequent developments in the scholarship but has even resulted in a move to place others – specifically, G.V. Taylor and Richard Cobb – above him in the revisionist pantheon.

The full story of the overthrow of the Marxist paradigm would require a considerable cast. (It would also need to be set in the wider context of the changing international and French political scene from the antifascist popular front of the 1930s and 1940s through the outbreak of the Cold War and the Hungarian rising to the events of April and May 1968 and beyond.) However, while the full extent of Cobban's influence on French revisionists remains problematic, among early Anglo-Saxon revisionists he was surely pre-eminent. It was after all his *Social Interpretation* that succeeded in making the bourgeois revolution thesis the object of intensive – and overdue – international debate. Undoubtedly his part in the renewal of scholarship thereafter was not so significant. It did not, though, take a huge imaginative leap on the part of second-generation revisionists to go from his and Taylor's denial of class conflict to the assertion of noble-bourgeois collaboration as a key revolutionary impulse. Doubtless through his part in the rediscovery of the Tocquevillian perspective of the Revolution as continuity – as well as change – he performed a more enduring service to the historiography.

Although his textbook *A History of Modern France* (1957–61) continues to sell well, Cobban's writings on the Revolution are now read mainly by those interested in past historiographical battles. That is not to say that today's specialists have nothing to learn from them. His work remains exemplary for its evident respect for the scholarly contribution of the Marxist historians whose views he was attacking; and his call for a genuinely social interpretation of the Revolution freed from dogmatic Marxism remains as relevant today as when it was made.

JOHN DUNNE

See also Carlyle; France: 1450–1789; France: French Revolution; France: since the Revolution; Furet; Hufton; Soboul

Biography
Born London, 1901. Educated at Latymer Upper School, London; Gonville and Caius College, Cambridge, 1919–25: research fellow, 1923–25. Taught at University College, Newcastle upon Tyne, 1926–37; and University College, London (rising to professor), 1937–68. Married Kathleen Muriel Hartshorn, 1929 (2 daughters). Died London, 1 April 1968.

Principal Writings
Edmund Burke and the Revolt Against the Eighteenth Century: A Study of the Political and Social Thinking of Burke, Wordsworth, Coleridge, and Southey, 1929
Dictatorship: Its History and Theory, 1939
Editor, *The Debate on the French Revolution, 1789–1800*, 1950
A History of Modern France, 2 vols., 1957–61; revised in 3 vols., 1962–65
The Social Interpretation of the French Revolution, 1964
Aspects of the French Revolution, 1968

Further Reading
Behrens, C.B.A., "Professor Cobban and His Critics," *Historical Journal* 9 (1966), 236–40
Bosher, J.F., ed., *French Government and Society 1500–1850: Essays in Memory of Alfred Cobban*, London: Athlone Press, and New York: Humanities Press, 1973
Cavanaugh, Gerald C., "The Present State of French Revolutionary Historiography: Alfred Cobban and Beyond," *French Historical Studies* 7 (1972), 587–606
Comninel, George C., *Rethinking the French Revolution: Marxism and the Revisionist Challenge*, London: Verso, 1987
Doyle, William, *Origins of the French Revolution*, Oxford and New York: Oxford University Press, 1980
Greenlaw, Ralph W., ed., *The Social Origins of the French Revolution: The Debate on the Role of the Middle Classes*, Lexington, MA: Heath, 1975
Hobsbawm, Eric J., *Echoes of the Marseillaise: Two Centuries Look Back on the French Revolution*, London: Verso, and New Brunswick, NJ: Rutgers University Press, 1990
McLennan, Gregor, *Marxism and the Methodologies of History*, London: New Left Books, and New York: Schocken, 1981
Soboul, Albert, *Understanding the French Revolution*, London: Merlin Press, and New York: Interaction, 1988

Cole, G.D.H. 1889–1959
British labor historian

G.D.H. Cole was a lifelong political activist, deeply involved with various aspects of the contemporary labor movement and a leading mentor of the Labour Party. Although his political interests led him almost inevitably to the study of history, his intellectual horizons stretched much further and his historical writings constituted only part of a vast corpus of work that he produced on political and economic subjects. His mission, he asserted in his inaugural professorial lecture, was to penetrate other men's minds and other times in order to unravel the values on which societies had rested in the past. This task, he added, was undertaken "not primarily as historian or recorder or for the purpose of analysis and comparison – important as these are – but for the practical purpose of suggesting to anyone I can influence, and above all to the society in which I belong, what is the right pattern of social thought to guide social action in the circumstances of here and now." Cole's first major book appeared in 1913 but it was not really until the 1920s and his appointment to a readership in economics at the University of Oxford that labor history as such began to claim an increasing share of his attention. Thereafter, as E.P. Thompson told Cole's wife, "he showed us all the way."

For all its rather pedestrian style, Cole's *A Short History of the British Working-Class Movement* (1925) was significant as the first serious attempt by a British writer to describe the historical experiences and activities of ordinary people. As such, it represented a major advance on the Webbs' narrower and rather inadequately revised *The History of Trade Unionism*. It was followed by a number of books and articles on similar themes. One of the most successful, *The Common People, 1746–1938* (1938), was produced collaboratively with his brother-in-law, Raymond Postgate, who added some color to Cole's lucid but generally somber prose, thereby doing much to ensure the book's long popularity. Although its approach and interpretations – particularly its pessimistic view of the impact of industrialization upon working-class living standards – were all later challenged on ideological and methodological grounds, particularly in a number of other general surveys from the late 1970s few other works rested on such a grasp of primary material or ranged over such a long period of time. If Cole's *History of the Labour Party since 1914* (1948) has now been replaced by more considered studies, his *British Working Class Politics* (1941), a detailed survey of radical and labor efforts to secure parliamentary representation, still remains a useful reference work.

The familiarity with contemporary sources that characterized much of Cole's historical writing reflected his belief that it was the best way to bring the past to life for his readers. He was an avid gatherer of early radical literature, producing edited versions of much of it. The important collection that appeared under the title *British Working Class Movements: Selected Documents, 1789–1875* (1951) again pioneered a type of publication which other labor historians subsequently emulated, though not always with such success.

To the modern reader some of Cole's work now seems rather dated and old-fashioned. For one thing, it tends to be dominated by the history of institutional development: what Cole meant by labor history was essentially the history of movements. Despite its geographical and chronological scope, even the monumental 5-volume *History of Socialist Thought*, which appeared between 1953 and 1960 and was hailed by a leading French scholar as irreplaceable, has been criticized for being more a study of parties and trade unions than of ideas. For another, Cole was no theorist. Although he found Marx's historical method useful, his own innate empiricism ensured that he eschewed the facile determinism that reduced history

to dogma. Sometimes, too, his historical writing displayed a certain Whiggishness, not least in the belief, advanced during his Oxford inaugural lecture, that it was legitimate for the historian to make moral judgments. "I have to make, throughout, judgments of value. I have to proclaim certain ends as good, and to denounce others as evil." Individuals were similarly judged according to how far they had fostered the values which Cole himself prized, such as truth, rationality, toleration, comradeship, democracy, liberty, and social security. He was a firm believer in the role of the individual in shaping the past. He knew a great deal about the lives of early labor leaders and in *Chartist Portraits* (1941) he used biography very effectively to draw attention to the variegated nature of the Chartist movement. More than anything else, perhaps, this book pointed the way for the reassessment of Chartism undertaken by following generations of scholars. An earlier study of Robert Owen (1925) is curiously unsatisfactory, probably because Cole did not actually care very much for his subject, despite sharing many of his underlying convictions. His most successful individual biography was his first, a study of William Cobbett (1924), an individual whose radicalism, trenchant views, and love of the English countryside were much to Cole's own taste.

Cole's death in 1959 may have prevented him from witnessing the great upsurge of interest in working-class history which followed the foundation of the Society for the Study of Labour History in 1960, but it was more than fitting that in the same year *Essays in Labour History*, edited by Asa Briggs and John Saville, should appear. Originally intended as a *Festschrift* to Cole, it proved an appropriate memorial volume to his pioneering role in developing the historical study of the working classes: as an Oxford colleague told Mrs. Cole, her husband "practically invented Labour history as a subject."

KENNETH D. BROWN

See also Economic; Social; Tawney

Biography

George Douglas Howard Cole. Born 25 September 1889. Educated at St. Paul's School; Balliol College, Oxford. At Oxford University: fellow, Magdalen College, 1912–19, University College, 1925–44, All Souls College, 1944–57, and Nuffield College, 1957–59; university reader in economics, 1925–44; and professor of social and political theory, 1944–57. Also active in Labour Party, and president, Fabian Society, 1952–59; contributor, *New Statesman*. Married the writer Margaret Isabel Postgate, 1918 (1 son, 2 daughters), with whom he wrote many books, both political treatises and mystery novels. Died 14 January 1959.

Principal Writings

The Life of William Cobbett, 1924
Robert Owen, 1925; as *The Life of Robert Owen*, 1930
A Short History of the British Working-Class Movement, 3 vols., 1925–27
With Raymond Postgate, *The Common People, 1746–1938*, 1938, revised [with dates 1746–1946], 1946; in US as *The British Common People, 1746–1938*, 1939, revised as *The British People*, 1947
Persons and Periods, 1938
British Working Class Politics, 1832–1914, 1941
Chartist Portraits, 1941
A History of the Labour Party from 1914, 1948

Editor, with A.W. Filson, *British Working Class Movements: Selected Documents, 1789–1875*, 1951
Attempts at General Union: A Study in British Trade Union History, 1818–1834, 1953
A History of Socialist Thought, 5 vols., 1953–60

Further Reading
Briggs, Asa, and John Saville, eds., *Essays in Labour History*, vol. 1: *In Memory of G.D.H. Cole, 25 September 1889–14 January 1959*, London: Macmillan, and New York: St. Martin's Press, 1960
Carpenter, L.P., *G.D.H. Cole: An Intellectual Biography*, Cambridge: Cambridge University Press, 1973
Cole, Margaret, *Growing Up into Revolution*, London and New York: Longman, 1949
Cole, Margaret, *The Life of G.D.H. Cole*, London: Macmillan, and New York: St. Martin's Press, 1971
Wright, Anthony, *G.D.H. Cole and Socialist Democracy*, Oxford: Clarendon Press, 1979

Collingwood, R.G. 1889–1943
British philosopher and historian

R.G. Collingwood was one of the most important and original philosophers of history of the 20th century. His work is often associated with that of Benedetto Croce, who did influence Collingwood early on; nevertheless, Collingwood's linking of history and philosophy has proven to be a unique and major achievement in modern historiography.

The son of a friend, secretary, and biographer of John Ruskin, Collingwood went to study at Rugby School and University College, Oxford, before becoming a fellow at Pembroke College in 1912 where he remained for the rest of his career as a professor of metaphysics. Collingwood's education was very broad; he was a brilliant classics scholar as an undergraduate and proved to be an important archaeological theorist on Roman Britain and ancient Rome in addition to his work in philosophy.

In *An Autobiography* (1939), Collingwood claimed that his thinking about history remained consistent, but it is obvious that his ideas changed considerably over time. Early in his career his work was characterized by his rejection of the realism influential at Oxford in the 1920s. His earliest writings, such as *Religion and Philosophy* (1916), reflected the Hegelian idealism that had dominated Oxonian philosophy during the previous generation. His first important work, *Speculum Mentis* (1924), clearly showed Crocean influences as Collingwood examined what he held to be five forms of human experience – art, religion, science, history, philosophy – ranked in ascending order according to degrees of truth he felt were possible in each. Collingwood saw history as superior to science, which he held to be excessively speculative and abstract, and found history's superiority in its treatment of experience as a concrete, albeit temporal, process. But history was inferior to philosophy because the latter offers knowledge of the self in a way history cannot, and philosophical experience can come only after the other forms of experience have been already been attained. The mind is the locus of this self-awareness, it is infinite and is capable of using philosophy to know what is true in the lesser forms of experience, including history, and can escape their limitations.

The primacy of philosophy, as well as idealism, in Collingwood's scheme lessened with time. In *An Essay on Philosophical Method* (1933), Collingwood had already come to see that history, along with science, was not inferior to philosophy in terms of truth, but was limited to seeking categorical propositions about individuals and events – philosophy on the other hand had all of being as its concern. The critical element here was that metaphysical knowledge was possible only through knowledge of history, thus historical experience had moved to an absolutely essential position in any philosophical knowledge of being.

This merger of philosophy and history was to become a dominant theme of Collingwood's later work, and by 1940 in *An Essay on Metaphysics*, he had come to see philosophy as intellectual history. In part this was a result of work he had first presented in his pamphlet *The Philosophy of History* (1930), and in a series of lectures in 1936 which revealed that Collingwood had begun seeing history as a series of historical acts alien to the historian. The historian surrenders the past, through a process of verification that Collingwood insisted was essentially "Baconian," to questioning that can result in a variety of plausible reconstructions as long as any single reconstruction of the past will yield consequences consistent with the evidence, or if other reconstructions do not yield consequences that directly contradict it. By the time Collingwood's lectures were published posthumously in his now most famous work, *The Idea of History* (1946), the historian was seen as not only uncovering the acts of the past but also unearthing the thought expressed in those acts. Thought informs and explains the act so it is essential for historians to study the thought processes at work in any historical act because as Collingwood put it "All history is the history of thought" – all history is definable as, and is only comprehensible as, the actions of autonomous individuals with beliefs, perceptions, ideas, and thoughts.

Collingwood's philosophy of history represented an important rejection of neopositivism and its attempt to assimilate history within the natural sciences and have it conform to more "scientific" standards of inquiry and analysis. Collingwood believed in history's claim to a unique kind of knowledge, a morphological position shared by Michael Oakeshott and even analytical philosophers of history such as William Gallie and William Dray. Historical understanding can come only through "re-enactment" of the thought of individuals in the past on the basis of evidence, thus it is essentially narrative in form.

Collingwood also made substantial contributions in archaeology, where his reputation as a practicing historian largely lies, and he developed an important reputation as a speculative thinker, as well as a philosopher of art and religion. He added original contributions to metaphysics, especially his "theory of presuppositions," which many critics think foreshadows Thomas Kuhn's "paradigms" in scientific revolutions. Collingwood's masterful prose style played a role in his enormous influence and legacy, while at the same time his work produced no obvious "school" following his lead.

SEÁN FARRELL MORAN

See also Carr, E.; Croce; Cultural; Historiology; Intellectual; Literature; Memory; Metahistory

Biography
Robin George Collingwood. Born Cartmel Fell, Lancashire, 22 February 1889. Educated at Rugby School; University College, Oxford, BA 1912. Served with the Admiralty 1915–19. Fellow,

tutor, and librarian, Pembroke College, Oxford, 1912–35; university lecturer in philosophy and Roman history, 1912–35, and professor of metaphysical philosophy, 1935–41, Oxford University. Married 1) Ethel Winifred Graham, 1918 (marriage dissolved 1942; 1 son, 1 daughter); 2) Kathleen Frances Edwardes, 1942 (1 daughter). Died Coniston, Lancashire, 9 January 1943.

Principal Writings

Religion and Philosophy, 1916
Roman Britain, 1923; revised 1932
Speculum Mentis; or, the Map of Knowledge, 1924
Outlines of a Philosophy of Art, 1925
The Archaeology of Roman Britain, 1930
The Philosophy of History, 1930
An Essay on Philosophical Method, 1933
With J.N.L. Myres, *Roman Britain and the English Settlements*, 1936
The Principles of Art, 1938
An Autobiography, 1939
An Essay on Metaphysics, 1940
The New Leviathan; or, Man, Society, Civilization and Barbarism, 1942
The Idea of Nature, edited by T.M. Knox, 1945
The Idea of History, edited by T.M. Knox, 1946; revised edition, with *Lectures 1926–1928*, edited by Jan van der Dussen, 1993
Essays in the Philosophy of Art, edited by Allen B. Donagan, 1964
Essays in the Philosophy of History, edited by William Debbins, 1965
Faith and Reason: Essays in the Philosophy of Religion, edited by L. Rubinoff, 1968

Further Reading

Donagan, Alan, *The Later Philosophy of R.G. Collingwood*, Oxford: Oxford University Press, 1962
Johnston, William M., *The Formative Years of R.G. Collingwood*, The Hague: Nijhoff, 1967
Kransz, Michael, *Critical Essays on the Philosophy of R.G Collingwood*, Oxford: Oxford University Press, 1972
Rubinoff, L., *Collingwood and the Reform of Metaphysics: A Study in the Philosophy of the Mind*, Toronto: University of Toronto Press, 1970
Taylor, Donald S., "A Bibliography of the Publications and Manuscripts of R.G. Collingwood, with Selective Annotations," *History and Theory* 24 (1985), 1–89

Commager, Henry Steele 1902–1998

US constitutional historian

Henry Steele Commager was a leading 20th-century historian of the United States, whose major concern was to interpret the country's history in a manner accessible to the general reader. His career spanned the rise of the US to world power after World War II, and his preoccupations were to a considerable degree the product of contemporary developments, whose influence the evolution of his thinking and career reflected. His ultimate aim was to ensure, in the words of one of his biographers, "that his readers might become more informed and responsible participants in the great experiment launched in the eighteenth century to make a free, democratic, and bountiful society a reality on the North American continent." Despite misgivings at various times over McCarthyism and US involvement in Vietnam, overall his faith in the United States never wavered, and he took an essentially optimistic view of his country.

Commager was one of the most visible and authoritative historians of his time, whose works were used by generations of undergraduates, highschool students, and laymen. For fifty years college students used successive revisions of *The Growth of the American Republic* (1930), a survey textbook produced in collaboration with the Harvard historian Samuel Eliot Morison. For high schools he produced *Our Nation* (1941), and for the general reader *America: The Story of a Free People* (1942), which he wrote in collaboration with Allan Nevins. In general, these works provided a liberal rather than radical interpretation of American history. Commager's clear, limpid style gave his message additional force.

Commager was both a convinced Jeffersonian and a liberal supporter of the New Deal, who believed that the United States still represented the ideals of its founders. He resolved any contradictions among his assorted loyalties to the decentralizing Jefferson and the centralizing Franklin D. Roosevelt by arguing that the US had changed since 1800; that the individual states could not deal with the social and economic challenges facing them in the 20th century; and that therefore the federal government had been forced to step into the breach to meet society's overwhelming needs. A student of the progressive historian Vernon Parrington, who originally accepted revisionist historians' condemnation of American involvement in World War I, by the mid-1940s Commager had become a strong supporter of a greater international role for his country. His commitment to liberal values remained firm, nonetheless, during both the Cold War and the Vietnam War.

During the late 1940s and 1950s Commager strongly condemned McCarthyism and the ensuing demands for conformity, arguing that such attempts to restrain thought would inevitably stifle clear thinking and put an end to American creativity and, ultimately, society. He articulated these themes in his essay published in the joint collection *Civil Liberties under Attack* (1951) and in those gathered in *Freedom, Loyalty, Dissent* (1954), in which he commented: "The great danger that threatens us is neither heterodox thought nor orthodox thought, but the absence of thought." Commager presciently argued that McCarthyite attacks on American diplomats would render them afraid to offer unpopular advice, with deleterious consequences for US international policies; moreover, the fate of Western civilization rested on the United States, which therefore should be obliged to preserve free inquiry and tolerate dissent. During the Vietnam War era, he demanded that the government exhibit greater accountability and provide the public with more information, arguing that its failure to do so was destroying its credibility. He also told foreigners that the ensuing protest and social ferment in the US was an indication of the health of American society rather than the reverse.

Commager's single most influential work was *The American Mind* (1950), his attempt to sketch the "American character" as such avatars as Alexis de Tocqueville and Lord Bryce had done before him. He argued that since the 1890s, a decade he considered a watershed in American history, and despite the great changes in scientific thinking in particular that had occurred in the interim, his countrymen had been optimistic, materialistic, friendly, partial to experimentation and to quantification, and possessed of a sense of conscious superiority to the rest of the world. He expressed fears that a centralized political economy would lead to the loss of American cultural diversity, but ultimately was optimistic that Americans would rise to the challenge of the future. In *The Search for a Usable Past* (1967), *Jefferson, Nationalism, and the Enlightenment* (1975), and *The Empire of Reason* (1977), Commager continued to affirm his fundamental faith in the underlying ideals of the United States, whatever challenges these might appear to face, and however many flaws one might perceive in the country. He felt his single most important task as a historian was to awaken Americans to their heritage and their obligation to live up to the traditions that had formed their history. He never abandoned his efforts to this end and, despite occasional misgivings in his later years, ultimately he remained confident that his compatriots would respond to this call.

PRISCILLA M. ROBERTS

See also Adams; Link; Morison; Nevins

Biography

Born Pittsburgh, 25 October 1902. Received PhB, University of Chicago, 1923, MA 1924, PhD 1928. Taught at New York University (rising to professor), 1926–38; Columbia University, 1938–56; and Amherst College, 1956–72 (emeritus). Served with Office of War Information during World War II. Married 1) Evan Carroll, 1928 (1 son, 2 daughters); 2) Mary Powlesland, 1979. Died Amherst, Massachusetts, 2 March 1998.

Principal Writings

With Samuel Eliot Morison, *The Growth of the American Republic*, 1930; 5th edition 1962
Documents of American History, 1934
Theodore Parker, 1936
Our Nation, 1941
With Allan Nevins, *America: The Story of a Free People*, 1942
The American Mind: An Interpretation of American Thought and Character since the 1880s, 1950
With Allan Nevins, *The Heritage of America: The Blue and the Gray*, 1950
Living Ideas in America, 1951
"The Pragmatic Necessity for Freedom," in Clair Wilcox, ed., *Civil Liberties under Attack*, 1951
Freedom, Loyalty, Dissent, 1954
The Spirit of America, 1958
The Search for a Usable Past, and Other Essays in Historiography, 1967
Jefferson, Nationalism, and the Enlightenment, 1975
The Empire of Reason: How Europe Imagined and America Realized the Enlightenment, 1977
Commager on Tocqueville, 1993

Further Reading

Cobb, Lawrence Wells, "Henry Steele Commager," in Clyde N. Wilson, ed., *Twentieth-Century American Historians*, Detroit: Gale, 1983 [*Dictionary of Literary Biography*, vol. 17]
Dawidoff, Robert, "Commager's *The American Mind*: A Reconsideration," *Reviews in American History* 12/3 (September 1984), 449–62
Fowler, Robert Booth, *Believing Skeptics: American Political Intellectuals, 1945–1965*, Westport, CT: Greenwood Press, 1978
Hyman, Harold M., and Leonard W. Levy, eds., *Freedom and Reform: Essays in Honor of Henry Steele Commager*, New York: Harper, 1967

Kraus, Michael, and Davis D. Joyce, *The Writing of American History*, revised edition, Norman: University of Oklahoma Press, 1985
Lemisch, Jesse, *On Active Service in Peace and War: Politics and Ideology in the American Historical Profession*, Toronto: New Hogtown Press, 1975
Skotheim, Robert Allen, *American Intellectual Histories and Historians*, Princeton: Princeton University Press, 1966

Commons, John R. 1862–1945
US labor historian

John R. Commons was fundamentally an economist, and his principal contribution historiographically was the first major synthesis of material on the development and role of organized labor in the US. As Sean Wilentz has noted, every labor historian owes a debt to Commons for the foundations he and his collaborators laid in the progressive era. Although his work reflected the institutional bias of the times, as well as the emphasis on economic factors that went with his primary occupation, his research provided the basis for the further study of labor history.

As an economist and social activist, Commons integrated many of the new statistical techniques of late 19th-century German history with the searching moral and experimental consciousness of a midwestern progressive. He is considered one of the founding theorists of "institutional economics" (along with Thorstein Veblen and Simon Patten), ascribing to functional groups a key negotiating role in the economic process. Thus one of his important contributions to economic history was a comprehensive analysis of the place of organized labor in the evolution of the American industrial economy (volumes 3 through 10 of *The Documentary History of American Industrial Society* [1910] and the *History of Labour in the United States* [1918–35]).

Commons life informed his approach to history. Born in Ohio to abolitionist parents, he attended Oberlin College. To help pay for his college education he worked in a print shop, where he was educated about unions and where he read Henry George's *Progress and Poverty* (1884). George's single tax approach to social reform played a key role in Commons' thinking, and he acknowledged this influence in *The Distribution of Wealth* (1893). From Oberlin he went to graduate school at Johns Hopkins University, where the twin influences of the German historical method and the economic theory of marginal utility became core elements of his thinking, and where Richard T. Ely, a founder of the American Economic Association, became a mentor. While at Johns Hopkins he also met E.A. Ross, who would become a prominent sociologist and later a colleague at the faculty at the University of Wisconsin.

Commons' history-writing developed as a part of his involvement in a number of social reform organizations, as well as a part of the progressive era efforts of Robert La Follette and others in Wisconsin. In 1893, for instance, he co-founded the American Proportional Representation League (advocating collective bargaining), served as vice-president of the National League for Promoting the Public Ownership of Monopolies, and promoted, along with Ely, the Institute of Christian

Sociology. That same year his first book, *The Distribution of Wealth* – an outgrowth of notes forming a course taught at Indiana University – appeared, and he also prepared a second book, *Social Reform and the Church* (1894). In the latter he argued that equality of opportunity was the logical ethical outcome of Christian teachings.

From Indiana University Commons moved to the University of Wisconsin where he played an important role in the development of the "Wisconsin Idea." He served on state committees for La Follette in 1905 and 1907. He worked with the Milwaukee socialists to organize the Bureau of Economy and Efficiency (1910–11). And on the national level he consulted with the National Civic Union in 1901 and 1906, and served as a member of Woodrow Wilson's Industrial Relations Commission from 1913 to 1915.

His two major works on labor, *The Documentary History of American Industrial Society* and the *History of Labour in the United States*, emerged from this period in Wisconsin. In them he argued that labor organizations arose as a response to growing markets (demand) and coincidental downward pressure on wages from price competition. That emphasis on the economic environment reflected his marginal value schooling, although in *Institutional Economics* (1934) he later argued he had stepped away from marginalist theory. As an institutional economist, he studied the role of organized groups reacting to economic change.

Commons' other works, most notably *Institutional Economics* and *Legal Foundations of Capitalism* (1924), interpreted the history of ideas in political economy, as well as continuing his analysis of the institutional (especially legal) bases for development. By 1934 he described his project as follows: "The problem now is not to create a different kind of economics – 'institutional economics' – divorced from previous schools, but how to give to collective action, in all its varieties, its due place throughout economic theory."

Commons' institutional approach to labor history, as practiced at the University of Wisconsin by his student Selig Perlman and by Perlman's student Philip Taft, remained dominant until challenged by the "new labor history" in the 1960s. Writers of the new labor history such as Anthony F.C. Wallace and David Montgomery argued that Commons missed broader patterns, cultural and social developments behind working-class experience in the United States, and that even in discussing the institutional history of unions he underestimated the role played by ideas and the importance of the struggle over power on the shopfloor. While some of Montgomery's work builds broadly on Commons' institutional studies, the main thrust of the new labor history builds "from the bottom up," with an emphasis on culture that comes from the work of E.P. Thompson.

With the 1930s and the coming of the New Deal, Commons' influence was ambiguous. He continued to champion collective action, but remained strongly committed to government action at the state rather than the federal, level and he advocated structural reform rather than deficit spending. Thus while his proposals for government recognition of organized labor may be seen to have influenced significant New Deal legislation, Commons became marginal to the larger Keynesian revolution in economic thinking and social policy.

DONALD R. PALM

See also Foner, P.; Gutman; Labor

Biography
John Rogers Commons. Born Hollansburg, Ohio, 13 October 1862. Received BA, Oberlin College, 1888; studied with economist Richard T. Ely at Johns Hopkins University, 1888–90. Taught economics at Wesleyan University, 1890–91; Oberlin College, 1891–92; Indiana University, 1892–95; and Syracuse University, 1895–99; political researcher, 1899–1904; taught political economy, University of Wisconsin, 1904–32. Married Ella Brown Downey, 1890 (died 1928; 5 children, of whom 2 survived infancy). Died Raleigh, North Carolina, 11 May 1945.

Principal Writings
The Distribution of Wealth, 1893
Social Reform and the Church, 1894
Races and Immigrants in America, 1907
With others, *The Documentary History of American Industrial Society*, 11 vols., 1910
With John B. Andrews, *Principles of Labor Legislation*, 1916
With others, *History of Labour in the United States*, 4 vols., 1918–35
Trade Unionism and Labor Problems, 1921
The Legal Foundations of Capitalism, 1924
Institutional Economics: Its Place in Political Economy, 1934
Myself, 1934
The Economics of Collective Action, edited by Kenneth H. Parsons, 1950

Further Reading
Brody, David, "The Old Labor History and the New: In Search of an American Working Class," *Labor History* 20 (1979), 111–26
Brody, David, "Reconciling the Old Labor History and the New," *Pacific Historical Review* 62 (1993), 1–18
Dubofsky, Melvin, *The State and Labor in Modern America*, Chapel Hill: University of North Carolina Press, 1994
Fink, Leon, "John R. Commons, Herbert Gutman, and the Burden of Labor History," in Fink, ed., *In Search of the Working Class: Essays in American Labor History and Political Culture*, Urbana: University of Illinois Press, 1994
Harter, Lafayette G., Jr., *John R. Commons: His Assault on Laissez-Faire*, Corvallis: Oregon State University Press, 1962
Isserman, Maurice, "'God Bless Our American Institutions': The Labor History of John R. Commons," *Labor History* 17 (1976), 309–28
Kimeldorf, Howard, "Bringing Unions Back In (Or Why We Need a New Old Labor History)," *Labor History* 32 (1991), 91–103
Montgomery, David, *Workers' Control in America: Studies in the History of Work, Technology, and Labor Struggles*, Cambridge and New York: Cambridge University Press, 1979
Wallace, Anthony F.C., *Rockdale: The Growth of an American Village in the Early Industrial Revolution*, New York: Knopf, 1978

Comparative History

The objective of the comparative method is to test for social or cultural differentiation in the historical development of common institutions, ideas, and social, political, and economic structures. That means that the unit of analysis (e.g., a state, a social class, an institution, or an idea) must be carefully defined and controlled. Moreover, if the "levels of socio-economic integration" of the societies being compared are sharply different (e.g., rural/urban, traditional/modern), the differential in level must be factored into the comparison. The contextual variables tested for must also be carefully defined. Normally, the comparative method implies cross-cultural comparison, but similar objectives can be pursued by comparing, for example, the reception of a number of different ideas in one society. Such a study would identify the social, institutional, and cognitive variables of reception, but not the cultural ones.

Modern comparative history arose from what in the 19th century was called the Comparative Method, which Burrow argues "consists in the recognition of similarities between the practices and beliefs of contemporary primitive or barbaric peoples and those recorded in the past history of civilization." The method was in fact developed earlier, in particular in schemes of social evolution devised by Scottish political economists such as Adam Smith, Adam Ferguson, and John Millar, who, in formulating a scheme of human civilization, classified societies according to their structures, whether higher or lower, possibly on an analogy with comparative anatomy.

In the mid-19th century, Sir Henry Maine (1822–88) was also influential from the perspective of comparative law and historical jurisprudence. In *Ancient Law* (1861), *Village Communities in the East and West* (1871), and other works, Maine developed a view of comparative history based on the assumption of common origins of European culture, first in Greece, and later (under the influence of comparative philology) in India. Thus his comparativism implied both diffusionism as a central mechanism of cultural growth, and change and evolutionism, in the same sense used by political economists.

In spite of the breadth of 19th-century comparativism, particularly among early anthropologists, contemporary comparative history is most likely inspired by Marx, who formulated a general theory of social action and then applied it to different societies. Marxian "historical materialism" also promoted an evolutionary scheme based on characteristic forms of property: tribal or communal, state (as in ancient or Oriental despotism), feudal, and capitalist. Such a scheme led to a particular periodization of Western history as well as a method for comparing the social structure of different societies both synchronically and historically.

After Marx, Max Weber wrote a number of influential, broad-gauged comparative works comparing systems of religious values, bureaucracies, and agriculture. His approach was typological, grouping different civilizational forms together under ideal types: modern bureaucracies of the West, ancient bureaucracies of the old empires, patrimonialism (e.g., feudalism), hierocracy (where priests rule), and Caesaro-papism (where civil authorities adopted priestly roles). These models could be compared with others, used as blueprints for evaluating subtypes, or applied simultaneously to explicate different aspects of a single case. Weber described an ideal type as "a purely ideal limiting concept with which a real situation of action is compared and surveyed." Thus any account of the "essence" of Christianity must necessarily be only relatively valid for any time or place, but may be of great value when used as a device for "comparison and . . . measurement of reality."

Among more recent theorists Arnold J. Toynbee, in his massive *A Study of History* (1934–61) made civilizations – initially 21 of them – the base unit of analysis. These were seen as environmentally sensitive entities, called into being by responses to specific environmental stimuli. Toynbee was criticized for using (although perhaps unconsciously) the history of Rome as an ideal type against which other civilizations were measured, and for privileging Christianity. Nevertheless the encyclopedic range and sophistication of his discussion remains insightful for the dynamics of specific civilizations and interactions among them. In world systems theory, only world-empires (in the historical past) and, more recently, world-economies are valid units of analysis. Moreover, the latter are viewed as comprised of only three functionally-described types: core-states (first-world economic and political powers), peripheral areas, and semi-peripheral areas, which play a variety of mediation roles between core and periphery. Marshall Hodgson formulated five types of "motif" on the basis of which inter-regional comparisons could be made: 1) common events (the Black Death); 2) parallel developments (the evolution of scriptural religions); 3) supraregional effects (expansion of civilizations, changing local balances of power); 4) activity motifs (the practice of science or monasticism); 5) the interregional role of specific regions. Hodgson also considered the units of historical comparison (Oikoumene, civilization, region, cultural area, civilized tradition).

Comparative intellectual history, to cite a more bounded and less open-ended instance of comparative method, generally works by holding an idea or set of ideas constant and examining them in different social and cultural contexts. Thus, to cite some examples from the comparative history of scientific ideas, Darwinism, relativity, Freudian psychology, Lavoisier's new chemistry, and the set of ideas and attitudes comprising the scientific revolution have all been studied as cognitive systems whose content, emphases, and ideological associations were reconfigured as they crossed national and cultural boundaries. Such studies, as a whole, have worked against the notion promoted by many scientists that science is "international" and has a truth component that is not subject to cultural inflections.

While comparative analysis need not necessarily lead to the extreme cultural relativism of Oswald Spengler, who upheld the equal validity of all belief systems, it does call into question any notion of normativity – that historians can decide what kind of actions and experiences can be held as normative – or rather demonstrates that normativity can be adduced to confirm an observer's value judgments.

THOMAS F. GLICK

See also Hodgson; Religion: Comparative; Toynbee; Wallerstein

Further Reading

Bensaude-Vincent, Bernadette, and Ferdinando Abbri, eds. *Lavoisier in European Context: Negotiating a New Language for Chemistry*, Canton, MA: Science History Publications, 1995

Burrow, John Wyon, *Evolution and Society: A Study in Victorian Social Theory*, Cambridge and New York: Cambridge University Press, 1966

Glick, Thomas F., ed., *The Comparative Reception of Darwinism*, Austin: University of Texas Press, 1974; reprinted Chicago: University of Chicago Press, 1988

Glick, Thomas F., ed., *The Comparative Reception of Relativity*, Dordrecht and Boston: Reidel, 1988

Hodgson, Marshall G.S., *Rethinking World History: Essays on Europe, Islam and World History*, edited by Edmund Burke III, Cambridge and New York: Cambridge University Press, 1993

Kalberg, Stephen, *Max Weber's Comparative Historical Sociology*, Chicago: University of Chicago Press, and Cambridge: Polity Press, 1994

Montague, M.F. Ashley, ed., *Toynbee and History: Critical Essays and Reviews*, Boston: Porter Sargent, 1956

Porter, Roy, and Mikuláš Teich, *The Scientific Revolution in National Context*, Cambridge and New York: Cambridge University Press, 1992

Roth, Günther, "Max Weber's Comparative Approach and Historical Typology," in Ivan Vallier, ed., *Comparative Methods in Sociology: Essays on Trends and Applications*, Berkeley: University of California Press, 1971

Toynbee, Arnold J., *A Study of History*, 12 vols., Oxford and New York: Oxford University Press, 1934–61

Wallerstein, Immanuel, *The Modern World-System*, 3 vols., New York and London: Academic Press, 1974–89

Computers and Computing, History of

The history of computing, as a professional activity, began in the 1960s, shortly after the development of the modern computer and the realization of the computer both as a catalyst of social transformation and as a commercial product. Nearly all of the early writing in the field was by computer professionals. Those involved in the study of the history of computing now include professional historians (in many fields), journalists, and, still, some computer professionals. The historical writing includes strands from the history of technology, the history of science, information technologies, business history, popular accounts and memoirs, or personal accounts.

Just as the modern computer includes two converging elements – machine logic and machine calculation – so the history of computing includes two elements or threads. Logic and calculation converged in the stored-program electronic digital computers of the late 1940s and early 1950s. However, as historian Michael Mahoney noted in "History of Computing" (1988), the threads in the history of computing "come together" but "they do not unite." One approach, focused on the logic, is generally grounded in intellectual history or history of science and traces the development of logic and cognitive science. Examples of this approach are the works of Howard Gardner, Pamela McCorduck, and J. David Bolter which focus on intellectuals, theorists, and concepts within mathematics, logic, information theory, cognitive science and artificial intelligence. With the trend-setting work of Jean Sammet (1969), this thread began to include work on the history of software and programming languages.

However the main thread of the history of computing is machine calculation and this generally falls within history of technology, business history, or economic history. This thread weaves together the story of engineers, scientists, businesses and, to a lesser extent, the use of the machines. Most early work in this thread focused on internal aspects of computational development by emphasizing specific people, machines, and, sometimes companies involved in the commercial development of the computer.

While the field of the history of computing began in earnest in the 1960s, there were some works as early as the 19th century on the early mechanical calculators, considered predecessors to the modern computer. In most cases, work before the mid-1970s was written by technical professionals personally involved in development, such as Herman Goldstine, Jean Sammet, Maurice Wilkes, and others. Computer professionals provided authoritative, vivid, and technical accounts which were "insider" history, full of "facts" and "firsts." According to Mahoney, many of these accounts tended to "take as givens (often technical givens) what a more critical, outside viewer might see as choices." In the 1980s, the work of computer professionals developed a more historical, multidimensional approach and advanced the field by broadening the subject areas covered in historical writings (e.g., programming languages, personal workstations, and the computer industry).

By the 1960s, history of computing also included journalistic and popular accounts, which continue to form part of the field today and which often focus on "social impacts" of computer technology. These works tend to be vivid and to capture the personal spirit of the actors, but are often skewed toward the unusual or the spectacular and rely on self-evaluation of their subjects. The work of Stan Augarten and of Tracy Kidder are notable examples of journalistic accounts that do add to historical work in the field. The history of the Internet is one area in which popular and journalistic accounts are pointing to new subjects for traditional historical works.

In the 1970s historians such as Arthur Norberg, I. Bernard Cohen, Uta Merzbach and Thomas Smith, brought the development of computing to the attention of mainstream historians. Around the end of the decade a group of scholars trained in history as well as science and technology completed dissertations in the field of computing. The work of William Aspray, Paul Ceruzzi, and Nancy Stern, among others, brought a multidimensional approach that often included economics, politics, organizational structure, culture, and technical detail. A group of historians of computing developed in Europe including Brian Randell and Martin Campbell-Kelly in England, Jan van den Ende in the Netherlands, and Donald MacKenzie in Scotland.

Several important general trends in the approach to the history of computing have occurred over time. Early works often used the approach of biography (of men or machines), with technical details, "Whiggishness," and concepts of progress and revolution driving the narrative. The early "internalist" approach, with a focus on the design of the technology itself, was countered with a "contextualist" approach, with the consideration of social and cultural contexts, in the 1980s by an influx of historians, especially those of technology and science. The growth of areas of research and approaches was assisted by the American Federation of Information Processing (AFIPS)-Smithsonian Institution oral history project (1967–73), the establishment of the Charles Babbage Institute for the History of Information Processing (1978), the establishment of a journal by the AFIPS, *Annals of the History of Computing* (1979), and the establishment of Association for Computing Machinery (ACM) and AFIPS conferences on the history of computing.

Areas that remain under-researched include labor history (shop-floor practices) and the organization of work, the systems in which computers have become embedded, and computer users (including businesses) and applications, among others. New trends in the history of technology have begun to affect the kinds of questions posed and the methods of study, and have expanded work into some of these neglected areas. The origins and formation of the group of new computer professionals is being studied by Atsushi Akera. The work of Donald MacKenzie and Boelie Elzen uses a "social construction of technology" approach. In *The Closed World* (1995), Paul Edwards studied the computer using the concepts of metaphor, discourse, and contingency. Edwards and David Mindell are researching the role of the government in the development of systems. JoAnne Yates approached the development of early calculating machines as part of the business machine industry and the rise of a professional managerial class. The rapid growth of the Internet has stimulated research into the users of computers by Juan Rogers and popular views of computers by Paul Ceruzzi; it has also encouraged the approach used in studies of communication/information technologies.

A problem for current historical work in the field of computing is the incredible diffusion and diversity of computers in today's society. According to Mahoney: "historians stand before the daunting complexity of a subject that has grown exponentially in size and variety." As computers developed, they became "embedded in the worlds of science, technology, industry and business which structured computing even as they changed in response to it." Thus, computing history is an amalgamation of history of technology, science, business, industry, communications, information, and popular culture.

LINDA EIKMEIER ENDERSBY

Further Reading

Akera, Atsushi, "Exploring the Architecture of an Early Machine: The Historical Significance of the ENIAC Machine Architecture," *Annals of the History of Computing* 18 (1996)

Aspray, William, "Literature and Institutions in the History of Computing," *Isis* 75 (1984), 162–70

Aspray, William, ed., *Computing before Computers*, Ames: Iowa State University Press, 1990

Aspray, William, "The History of Computing within the History of Information Technology," *History and Technology* 11 (1994), 7–20

Augarten, Stan, *Bit by Bit: An Illustrated History of Computers*, New York: Ticknor and Fields, 1984

Beniger, James, *Control Revolution: Technological and Economic Origins of the Information Society*, Cambridge, MA: Harvard University Press, 1986

Berkeley, Edmund C., *Giant Brains or Machines That Think*, New York: Wiley, 1949

Bolter, J. David, *Turing's Man*, Chapel Hill: University of North Carolina Press, and Harmondsworth: Penguin, 1984

Campbell-Kelly, Martin, *ICL: A Business and Technical History*, Oxford and New York: Oxford University Press, 1989

Ceruzzi, Paul E., *Reckoners: The Prehistory of the Digital Computer, From Relays to the Stored Program Concept, 1935–1945*, Westport, CT: Greenwood Press, 1983

Cohen, I. Bernard, "Babbage and Aiken," *Annals of the History of Computing* 10 (1988), 171–93

Cohen, I. Bernard, "Howard Aiken and the Computer," in Stephen G. Nash, ed., *A History of Scientific Computing*, Reading, MA: Addison Wesley, 1990

Cohen, I. Bernard, "Howard H. Aiken, Harvard University, and IBM: Cooperation and Conflict," in Clark A. Elliot and Margaret W. Rossiter, eds., *Science at Harvard University*, Bethlehem, PA: Lehigh University Press, 1992

Cortada, James W., ed., *A Bibliographic Guide to the History of Computing, Computers, and the Information Processing Industry*, Westport, CT: Greenwood Press, 1990

Cortada, James W., *Before the Computer: IBM, NCR, Burroughs, and Remington Rand and the Industry They Created, 1865–1956*, Princeton: Princeton University Press, 1993

Edwards, Paul N., *The Closed World: Computers and the Politics of Discourse in Cold War America*, Cambridge, MA: MIT Press, 1995

Elzen, Boelie, and Donald MacKenzie, "From Megaflops to Total Solutions: The Changing Dynamics of Competitiveness in Supercomputing," in William Aspray, ed., *Technological Competitiveness*, New York: Institute of Electrical and Electronics Engineers, 1993

Elzen, Boelie, "The Social Limitations of Speed: The Development and Use of Supercomputers," *Annals of the History of Computing* 16 (1994), 46–61

Ende, Jan van den, "Tidal Calculations in the Netherlands, 1920–1960," *Annals of the History of Computing* 14 (1992), 23–33

Ende, Jan van den, "The Number Factory: Punched Card Machines at the Dutch Central Bureau of Statistics," *Annals of the History of Computing* 16 (1994), 15–24

Ende, Jan van den, "The Turn of the Tide: Computerization in Dutch Society, 1900–1965," *Annals of the History of Computing* 17 (1995), 82–95

Feigenbaum, Edward, and Julian Feldman, eds., *Computers and Thought*, New York: McGraw Hill, 1963

Flamm, Kenneth, *Creating the Computer: Government, Industry, and High Technology*, Washington, DC: Brookings Institution, 1987

Flamm, Kenneth, *Targeting the Computer: Goverment Support and International Competition*, Washington, DC: Brookings Institution, 1987

Gardner, Howard, *The Mind's New Science: A History of the Cognitive Revolution*, New York: Basic Books, 1985

Goldstine, Herman, *The Computer from Pascal to von Neumann*, Princeton: Princeton University Press, 1972

Hendry, John, *Innovating for Failure: Government Policy and the Early British Computer Industry*, Cambridge, MA: MIT Press, 1989

Hyman, Anthony, *Charles Babbage: Pioneer of the Computer*, Princeton: Princeton University Press, 1982

Hyman, Anthony, "Whiggism in the History of Science and the Study of the Life and Work of Charles Babbage," *Annals of the History of Computing* 12 (1990), 62–67

Kidder, Tracy, *The Soul of a New Machine*, Boston: Little Brown, 1981

Lee, J.A.N., ed., *International Biographical Dictionary of Computer Pioneers*, Chicago and London: Fitzroy Dearborn, 1995

McCorduck, Pamela, *Machines Who Think: A Personal Investigation into the History and Prospects of Artificial Intelligence*, San Francisco: Freeman, 1979

MacKenzie, David, *Inventing Accuracy: An Historical Sociology of Nuclear Missile Guidance*, Cambridge, MA: MIT Press, 1990

MacKenzie, David, and Boelie Elzen, "From Megaflops to Total Solutions," in William Aspray, ed., *Technological Competitiveness: Contemporary and Historical Perspectives on the Electrical, Electronics, and Computer Industries*, New York: Institute of Electrical and Electronics Engineers Press, 1993

Mahoney, Michael S., "The History of Computing in the History of Technology," *Annals of the History of Computing* 10 (1988), 113–25

Merzbach, Uta, *Georg Scheutz and the First Printing Calculator*, Washington, DC: Smithsonian Institution Press, 1977

Metropolis, Nicholas, Jack Howlett, and Gian-Carlo Rota, eds., *A History of Computing in the Twentieth Century*, New York: Academic Press, 1980

Mindell, David, "Anti-Aircraft Fire Control and the Development of Integrated Systems at Sperry, 1925–1940," *IEEE Control Systems* 15 (April 1995), 108–13

Mindell, David, "Automation's Finest Hour: Bell Labs and Automatic Control in World War II," *IEEE Control Systems* 15 (December 1995), 72–80

Nash, Stephen G., ed., *A History of Scientific Computing*, Reading, MA: Addison Wesley, 1990

Norberg, Arthur L., "Another Impact of the Computer: The History of Computing," *IEEE Transactions on Education* 27 (1984), 197–203

Pugh, Emerson W., *Memories That Shaped an Industry: Decisions Leading to IBM System/360*, Cambridge, MA: MIT Press, 1984

Pugh, Emerson W., *Building IBM: Shaping an Industry and Its Technology*, Cambridge, MA: MIT Press, 1995

Randell, Brian, ed., *Origins of Digital Computers: Selected Papers*, Berlin and New York: Springer, 1973

Redmond, Kent C., and Thomas M. Smith, *Project Whirlwind: The History of a Pioneer Computer*, Bedford, MA: Digital Press, 1980

Rogers, Juan, "Implementation of a National Information Infrastructure: Science and the Building of Society," PhD dissertation, Virginia Polytechnic and State University, 1996

Sammet, Jean E., *Programming Languages: History and Fundamentals*, Englewood Cliffs, NJ: Prentice Hall, 1969

Smith, Thomas M., "Project Whirlwind: An Unorthodox Development Project," *Technology and Culture* 17 (1976), 447–64

Stern, Nancy, *From ENIAC to UNIVAC: An Appraisal of the Eckert-Mauchly Computers*, Bedford, MA: Digital Press, 1981

Turck, J.A.V., *Origin of Modern Calculating Machines: A Chronicle of the Evolution of the Principles That Form the Generic Make-up of the Modern Calculating Machine*, Chicago: Western Society of Engineers, 1921

Wexelblat, Richard L., ed., *History of Programming Languages*, New York: Academic Press, 1981

Wilkes, Maurice V., *Memoirs of a Computer Pioneer*, Cambridge, MA: MIT Press, 1985

Williams, Michael R., *A History of Computing Technology*, Englewood Cliffs, NJ: Prentice Hall, 1985

Yates, JoAnne, *Control Through Communication: The Rise of System in American Management*, Baltimore: Johns Hopkins University Press, 1989

Computing and History

The use of computers for the storage, retrieval, and analysis of historical data dates back to the early ground-breaking projects of the 1960s, which required large mainframe computers that required highly complex programming and cumbersome means of input. The generally quantitative and statistical focus, employing methodologies borrowed from the social sciences, meant that many non-computing historians of the time were rather skeptical of the value of this new "school" of historical computing. Remarks such as "the historian of tomorrow will be a programmer or he will be nothing" (made by Emmanuel Le Roy Ladurie) did not help to enamor the new field to more "traditional" historians. Thus an antipathy developed among many historians who questioned the value of the new technology to "high" or narrative history, though there was less criticism of computers' applicability to areas such as record-linkage and demography.

In fact it was demography that produced one of the most significant and celebrated works to have come out of historical computing, Wrigley and Schofield's *The Population History of England*, published in 1981. Using a technique called "family reconstitution" Wrigley and Schofield built up a comprehensive picture of the population of England over three centuries, a task that without computers would have been inconceivable. Their work presented a serious challenge to traditional demography and to views on the nature of the family in English history. Likewise, in the United States early historical computing was also responsible for the questioning of long established historical paradigms. R.W. Fogel's *Railroads and American Economic Growth* (1964) and Fogel and Engerman's *Time on the Cross* (1974) attacked the established wisdom of views on the effects of the railways on industrialization in the US and the economics of slavery respectively. Both works were highly controversial and created a lasting impact.

From this mainly quantitative approach of the early days, historical computing has expanded into most areas of historical analysis, from social and economic history to art history, and from historical geography to textual analysis. While quantitative analysis remains a major strand (witness the burgeoning literature on issues such as living standards in the Industrial Revolution in Britain), the manipulation of text has now become a central component of historical computing; after all, a large proportion of historical sources come in the form of text. As R.J. Morris established, "since the 1970s there has been an important though subtle move from data set to data base." Within the UK the use of databases has established something of a hegemony in historical computing, contributing to areas such as prosopography and business history. Most database projects have used standard commercial relational database management systems such as Paradox and Access, but there have been significant criticisms of the suitability of commercial relational database software to the vagaries of historical sources. A notable attempt to overcome this problem has been made at the University of Göttingen in Germany as part of the historical workstation project. The database system *clio* (named after the history muse) makes a bold attempt to deal with the problems familiar to those historians working with medieval or early modern sources, such as obscure and archaic dating formats and "fuzzy" or incomplete data.

These improvements in data retrieval and analysis have been shadowed by advances in data storage. The setting up of archives holding machine readable data has been another important development in historical computing. Early computer projects, constrained by the hardware, often resorted to complicated coding schemes to alleviate storage demands. This limitation is no longer as significant, allowing the possibility of much more comprehensible and accessible datasets to be stored in archives such as the Economic and Social Research Council (ESRC) data archive, which was set up at the University of Essex in 1967 and now contains more than 7000 datasets. PhD students with ESRC scholarships are now required to offer their datasets for deposit to the data archive, which should guarantee a considerable amount of machine readable versions of primary source material for both research and teaching.

Although computing has expanded into many areas of historical research, there is still some way to go. The schism between the worlds of the computing and non-computing historians still exists and historical computing is still a minority occupation. However, within universities the use of computers is becoming more widespread, and few history departments have been immune to the impacts of the new technology. The popular use of word processing and, more recently, electronic mail (e-mail), has encouraged academics who might not otherwise use a computer to experiment with OPAC library catalogues and, increasingly, the Internet.

This progress is probably due to the rapid advances in computer technology over the last thirty years. Following the advent of the IBM PC in 1981, hardware, while decreasing in size, has become much faster and able to store ever greater amounts of data, while simultaneously decreasing in price. Likewise, software has become more "user friendly" due to the increasing reliance on industry standard operating systems, particularly Microsoft's Windows, itself based on the graphical operating system of the Apple Macintosh. As W.A. Speck pointed out, most software applications now require little more than "knowing which buttons to press." Furthermore, the linking together of computers into small Local Area Networks (LANs) has enabled the sharing of resources and the possibility now exists of almost limitless information when LANs are themselves combined into Wide Area Networks (WANs) such as the British academic network JANET, and the Internet. In short, research projects that even the most skilled programmer would have balked at are now possible without leaving the office. As Morris recently declared, "for readers and researchers, the physical constraints of library walls are becoming increasingly meaningless."

RICHARD BAXELL

See also Fogel; Wrigley

Further Reading

Denley, Peter, Stefan Fogelvik, and Charles Harvey, eds., *History and Computing* 2, Manchester: Manchester University Press, and New York: St. Martin's Press, 1989

Denley, Peter, "Models, Sources and Users: Historical Database Design in the 1990s," *History and Computing* 6 (1994), 33–43

Denley, Peter, "Computing Techniques for Historical Research," in L.J. Butler and Anthony Gorst, eds., *Modern British History: A Guide to Study and Research*, London: Tauris, 1998, 95–118

Fogel, Robert William, *Railroads and American Economic Growth: Essays in Econometric History*, Baltimore: Johns Hopkins Press, 1964

Fogel, Robert William, and Stanley L. Engerman, *Time on the Cross: The Economics of American Negro Slavery*, 2 vols., Boston: Little Brown, and London: Wildwood, 1974

Greenstein, Daniel, "A Source-orientated Approach to History and Computing: The Relational Database," *Historical Social Research* 14 (1989), 9–16

Greenstein, Daniel, *A Historian's Guide to Computing*, Oxford and New York: Oxford University Press, 1994

Harvey, Charles, and Jon Press, *Databases in Historical Research: Theory, Methods, and Applications*, London: Macmillan, 1995; New York: St. Martin's Press, 1996

Kenny, Anthony, *The Computation of Style: An Introduction to Statistics for Students of Literature and Humanities*, Oxford and New York: Pergamon Press, 1982

Lewis, Myrddin John, and Roger Lloyd-Jones, *Using Computers in History: A Practical Guide*, London and New York: Routledge, 1996

Mawdsley, Evan, N. Morgan, L. Richmond, and Richard Trainor, *History and Computing* 3, Manchester and New York: Manchester University Press, 1990

Mawdsley, Evan, and Thomas Munck, *Computing for Historians: An Introductory Guide*, Manchester and New York: Manchester University Press, 1993

Morris, Robert J., "Computers and the Subversion of British History," *Journal of British Studies* 34 (October 1995), 503–28

Prescott, Andrew, "History and Computing," in Christine Mullings *et al.*, eds., *New Technologies for the Humanities*, London: Bowker Saur, 1996

Schürer, Kevin, "Historical Research in the Age of the Computer: An Assessment of the Present Situation," *Historical Social Research* 36 (1985), 43–54

Shorter, Edward, *The Historian and the Computer: A Practical Guide*, Englewood Cliffs, NJ: Prentice Hall, 1971

Southall, Humphrey, and Ed Oliver, "Drawing Maps with a Computer . . . or Without?," *History and Computing* 2 (1990), 146–54

Speck, William A., "History and Computing: Some Reflections on the Achievements of the Past Decade," *History and Computing* 6 (1994), 28–32

Winchester, I., "What Every Historian Needs to Know about Record Linkage in the Microcomputer Era," *Historical Methods* 25 (1992), 149–65

Wrigley, E.A., and Roger S. Schofield, *The Population History of England, 1541–1871: A Reconstruction*, London: Arnold, and Cambridge, MA: Harvard University Press 1981

Comte, Auguste 1798–1857

French sociologist and theorist

Proclaimed the father of sociology, Auguste Comte is both much more and much less than that title indicates. He is the originator of the term positivism (along with other terms such as biology and altruism), although contemporary understanding of the term positivism would be almost unrecognizable to him. Positivism has come to mean an empirical, statistical, rigid application of pure scientific method to all aspects of human experience and knowledge. There is an implication of sterility and formalism in the term, an implication of trying to fit the square peg of human emotional action into the round hole of atomistic, scientific explanation. This, however, was not the positivism that Comte intended and originated. His philosophical system never ignored the emotional and moral side of human nature. The perversion came about as a result of Comte's advocacy of applying scientific methodology to the creation of a political system.

Comte began his life during the ferment of post-revolutionary France. The societal upheavals left a strong desire on Comte's part to create political order from the disorder that he observed around him; and this despite his own very rebellious nature. After being thrown out of the Ecole Polytechnic in Paris, and briefly flirting with the idea of emigrating to America, he became the personal secretary of Henri de Saint-Simon and there began work on the foundation of his philosophy. Saint-Simon's ideas, particularly the idea of applying scientific knowledge to the workings of society, were very influential on Comte, something that he was to continue to deny the rest of his life.

His first major work, an essay entitled "Plan des travaux scientifiques nécessaires pour réorganiser la société" (Plan of the Scientific Operations Necessary for Reorganising Society), was first published in 1822. In this long essay, Comte proposed that politics become a science, and consequently follow science's requirements for empirical observations, rather than the dogma of politics. If this were accomplished, then social theory would approach the certitude of science.

This new science would consist of two principles. The first principle was that of progression of the intellect, and political and social evolution, through three stages of history – the theological, the metaphysical, and the positive stage. The second principle was the classification of the sciences, determining the order in which the sciences were established. The term positivism was used, as opposed to negativism, in order to distinguish between a positive and negative attitude to science as the ultimate source of knowledge. The two principles reflected the same core ideas: that science and scientific methods are superior in actually determining the best political structure for a stable, coherent society. If science was applied to all of man's ideas, they would become homogeneous, and with homogeneous ideas, a stable, prosperous society can be created.

Comte completed a number of other essays and major writings in his career. The two major works delineating his positivist philosophy were the 6-volume *Cours de philosophie positive* (1830–42; *The Positive Philosophy of Auguste Comte*, 1853), and the 4-volume *Système de politique positive* (1851–54; *A System of Positive Polity*, 1875–77).

The *Cours* reviewed the principles of the natural sciences and sociology, thereby attempting to establish positivism's scientific credentials. Comte's *Systeme* was an attempt to reconcile the rational, scientific aspects of positivism found in the *Cours* with the emotional aspects of human existence. Comte insisted that there was a genuine consistency between the two works, to the point of including in the appendix of *Système* six of his early essays.

These two books described Comte's philosophy of positivism. This philosophy required a general understanding of the sciences and the scientific method. This understanding, when applied to all of human knowledge, would create a new science of society. It then followed that this new science would become the basis for reordering society and creating a social consensus. Social consensus would be reached through the scientific observation of facts, and the development of theories that would explain human action. Comte felt that if society were explained in this way, all would see the obvious truth and would reach agreement on the validity of the societal structures created from this positivist approach. Comte saw as his end goal the creation of political structures based upon this social consensus.

Positivism, as outlined by Comte, consisted of two main elements: "humanity" and the "general milieu." Specifically, the "milieu" was comprised of three "modes"; the mathematical or astronomical, the physical, and the chemical. "Humanity" was comprised of two "modes"; the individual and society, studied by biology and sociology respectively. The study of "humanity" was subordinate to the study of the "milieu." This was justified on logical and scientific grounds. The simpler sciences needed to be studied first, as the originators of the positivist method. In addition, the science of the three modes should be understood before advancing to the more complex science of the individual and society.

Positivism was important to political structures in that it forced the view of the whole, the social point of view, by requiring the observation of the progressive links of the simple to the complex. Positivism would teach individuals to understand their actions in the present as having value, and thus enforce a more practical approach to their daily lives. Individuals working to improve their individual lives would, as a result, improve their collective well-being.

Comte's primary contribution was not his theory of positivism, or his fundamental work in sociology, but rather the extension of the scientific method to an entirely new realm, the realm of society and the individual. This approach is hardly considered revolutionary today but was a real intellectual advance by Comte. While his writings offer little empirical support for his theories – a severe contradiction to his positivist philosophy – Comte's insistence on applying scientific methodology to the individual and society was his greatest contribution to intellectual history. Without the path broken by Comte, much contemporary political, historical, and sociological work could not have been written.

TIMOTHY P. COON

See also Adams; Annales School; Buckle; Dubnov; Ecclesiastical; Historiology; Media; Philosophy of History; Religion; Sociology

Biography

Isidore Auguste Marie François Xavier Comte. Born Montpellier, 19 January 1798, son of a tax collector. Studied at Ecole Polytechnique, 1812–14, then expelled; remained in Paris teaching mathematics. Secretary to Henri Saint-Simon, 1818–24; spent remainder of life teaching, writing, and lecturing. Died Paris, 5 September 1857.

Principal Writings

Cours de philosophie positive, 6 vols., 1830–42; in English as *The Positive Philosophy of Auguste Comte*, 1853
Discours sur l'ensemble du positivisme, 1849; in English as *A General View of Positivism*, 1865
Système de politique positive, ou, traité de sociologie instituant la religion universelle de l'humanité, 4 vols., 1851–1854; in English as *A System of Positive Polity; or, Treatise on Sociology Instituting the Religion of Humanity*, 4 vols., 1875–77
Catéchisme positiviste, ou, sommaire exposition de la religion universelle de l'humanité, 1852; in English as *The Catechism of Positive Religion*, 1858

Further Reading

Andreski, Stanislav, ed., *The Essential Comte*, London: Croom Helm, and New York: Barnes and Noble, 1974
Caird, Edward, *The Social Philosophy and Religion of Comte*, Glasgow: Maclehose, 1885, New York: Macmillan, 1893; reprinted 1968
Hawkins, Richmond, *Auguste Comte and the United States (1816–1853)*, Cambridge, MA: Harvard University Press, 1936
Lenzer, Gertrude, ed., *Auguste Comte and Positivism: The Essential Writings*, New York: Harper, 1975
Lévy-Bruhl, Lucien, *La Philosophie d'Auguste Comte*, Paris: Alcan, 1900; in English as *The Philosophy of Auguste Comte*, New York: Putnam, and London: Sonnenschein, 1903
Mill, John Stuart, "Auguste Comte and Positivism," *Westminster Review* (1865); reprinted in his *Auguste Comte and Positivism*, London: Trübner, 1865, Philadelphia: Lippincott, 1866; reprinted Ann Arbor: University of Michigan Press, 1961
Pickering, Mary, "New Evidence of the Link Between Comte and German Philosophy," *Journal of the History of Ideas* 50 (1989), 443–63
Pickering, Mary, *Auguste Comte: An Intellectual Biography*, London: Cambridge University Press, 1993
Pickering, Mary, "Auguste Comte and the Saint-Simonians," *French Historical Studies* 18 (1993), 211–36

Confucius *see* Kong-zi

Consumerism and Consumption

Consumption is a multifaceted topic. Initially studied by economic and social historians, in the last four decades anthropology, sociology, cultural studies, and human geography have all influenced the historical study of consumption. In the pre- and postwar years the French Annales school of history profoundly shaped the study of consumption with remarkable contributions such as Fernand Braudel's *Civilisation matérielle, économie et capitalisme* (1979; *Civilization and Capitalism*, 1981–84) and Emmanuel Le Roy Ladurie's *Montaillou* (1975; translated 1978). In such heroic reconstructions of economic and social structures of *la longue durée*, food, drink, and clothing figured as part of the texture of everyday life that linked material forces to collective mentalities.

From the 1960s structuralism and poststructuralism nuanced the emphasis on the role of economics in the shaping of cultural practices and stressed the symbolic role of goods in social patterns. Since then Annales-oriented studies have investigated not only nutrition, water supplies, and the distribution of grains, but also the semiotics of food in documents such as the Bible or Diderot's *Encyclopédie*. Historical anthropology has also produced a variety of works on foodstuffs and material culture in the contexts of industrialization and trade. In *Sweetness and Power* (1985) Sidney W. Mintz investigated the social aspects of the role of sugar and showed how production and consumption were mutually determining. As sugar was put to new uses and took on new meanings, it was transformed from "curiosity and luxury into commonplace and necessity." Such studies reflected the broadening of the focus of historical inquiry to include consumption and market culture as well as the revision of the rigid Marxist position that emphasized structure over superstructure.

Such trends led to the proliferation of works on consumption since the 1980s by two groups of historians. Practitioners of the New Social History applied quantitative analysis to estate inventories in order to determine the practices of different social classes, while cultural historians employed the method developed in anthropology and literary criticism to view material objects as a system of signs that provided windows for bygone societies. For the latter group the study of material culture came to include the subject of shopping, defined as the purchasing of nonessential items, and was linked not only with leisure but with the formation of class identity. One of the earliest theorists of consumption, Thorstein Veblen, had argued in *The Theory of the Leisure Class* (1899) that the bourgeois activity of consumption was motivated by the desire to emulate social superiors, namely the aristocrats. Scholars have revised Veblen's thesis by arguing that distinctly middle-class values emerged in the 17th and the 18th centuries, at least in Europe, and that through the 19th century the tension between egalitarianism and capitalism, asceticism, and materialism all informed production and consumption. Veblen's main achievement was in locating consumption as a part of modern society's power relations.

Another crucial strand in the study of consumption originated with the Marxian Frankfurt school, led by Theodor Adorno and Max Horkheimer. Disciplined in the tradition of German philosophy and sociology, the Frankfurt school conceptualized commodification and the culture industry. In *Dialektik der Aufklärung* (1944; *Dialectic of Enlightenment*, 1972) Adorno and Horkheimer viewed modernization, culminating in the historical legacy of the 20th century, as a process in which advanced capitalism and rationalization would produce a kind of a cultural equivalent to political fascism. Disindividuation and a totalizing domination by mass and commodity culture would ensue. While the Frankfurt school had most influence in political theory and cultural criticism, the notion of commodification and a focus on the material objects of mass culture also resonated in historical studies. Walter Benjamin, who was of the same cohort as the Frankfurt school, was especially influential in the study of urban consumption. His unfinished Arcade project on 19th-century Parisian urban culture made use of the concept of the *flâneur* (a leisurely stroller), a figure who emerged in early 19th-century Paris and who has been interpreted both as symbolizing urban modernity and as the male counterpart to the female shopper.

Related to the *flâneur* is the idea of the spectator. Guy Debord's *La Société du spectacle* (1967; *The Society of the Spectacle*, 1970) criticized the passive consumption of visual entertainments. The idea of the spectacle has since been applied in works as varied as those on court rituals, festivals, cafe culture and the advent of the department store, and mass entertainment. The sociologist Pierre Bourdieu's argument in *La Distinction: critique sociale du jugement* (1979; *Distinction: A Social Critique of the Judgement of Taste*, 1984), that no aesthetic judgment is innocent but is formed through social factors, including the desire to emulate, has also influenced historical studies on taste and style. Debates continue as to the role of the spectator – whether active or passive – and the relevance of historical specificity.

Another main source of debate is the periodization of consumer culture. Scholars have located consumer revolutions in 17th- or 18th-century England and America and in 19th-century France. In *The Birth of a Consumer Society* (1982) Neil McKendrick, John Brewer and J.H. Plumb described a rapid increase in consumption in all sectors of society and linked middle-class fascination with goods with the spirit of scientific inquiry, improvement, and secularization as well as with social emulation and class competition. Simon Schama in *The Embarrassment of Riches* (1987) described the 17th century as a society in the throes of commercialization, while Chandra Mukerji in *From Graven Images* (1983) questioned the idea of a consumer revolution itself by arguing that commercial capitalism, having developed in 15th- and 16th-century Europe, actually preceded industrial capitalism.

The issue of gender has been crucial in the study of consumption. The historical process in which shopping became an activity of the interior and a pleasurable one has been interpreted by feminist theories as both empowering and alienating. Questions arise as to whether commercial capitalism led to the individuation of women and provided a realm of cultivation and sociability or whether the arena of consumption consists of a mere substitute public sphere and a false projection of the utopian dimension of human aspirations. Others argued that for many women consumption requires confronting complex and contradictory systems of values and impulses and that in this way shopping is only one aspect of a larger everyday world in which such challenges occur constantly, particularly as merchandising, design, display, and advertising have become ubiquitous. Recent studies have emphasized the need to investigate the relationship of commercial culture with formal politics and modern communication systems and also the need to analyze multiple versions of identity for both men and women. The rural area and the suburb have reappeared as sites of material culture. This was in part spurred by human geography, which demonstrated that a series of spatial reorganizations occurs in the development of industrial societies and that spaces and places constitute a system of representation pivotal to identity formation.

H. Hazel Hahn

See also Bourdieu; Braudel; Britain: since 1750; Davidoff; Design; de Vries; Dress; Habermas; Labrousse; Lasch; Leisure; Merton; Plumb; Potter; Quantitative; Wilson; Women's History: Africa

Further Reading

Adshead, Samuel Adrian M., *Material Culture in Europe and China, 1400–1800: The Rise of Consumerism*, New York: St. Martin's Press, and Basingstoke: Macmillan, 1997

Agnew, Jean-Christophe, *Worlds Apart: The Market and the Theatre in Anglo-American Thought, 1550–1750*, Cambridge and New York: Cambridge University Press, 1986

Appadurai, Arjun, ed., *The Social Life of Things: Commodities in Cultural Perspective*, Cambridge and New York: Cambridge University Press, 1986

Baudrillard, Jean, *La Société de consommation: ses mythes, ses structures* (The Society of Consumption: Its Myths, Its Structures), Paris: Denoël, 1970

Bermingham, Ann, and John Brewer, ed., *The Consumption of Culture, 1600–1800: Image, Object, Text*, London and New York: Routledge, 1995

Bourdieu, Pierre, *La Distinction: critique sociale du jugement*, Paris: Minuit, 1979; in English as *Distinction: A Social Critique of the Judgment of Taste*, Cambridge, MA: Harvard University Press, and London: Routledge, 1984

Braudel, Fernand, *Civilisation matérielle, économie et capitalisme, XVe–XVIII siècle*, 3 vols., Paris: Colin, 1979; in English as *Civilization and Capitalism, 15th–18th Century*, London: Collins, 1981–84, New York: Harper, 1982–84

Brewer, John, and Roy Porter, eds., *Consumption and the World of Goods*, London and New York: Routledge, 1993

Briggs, Asa, *Victorian Things*, London: Batsford, 1988; Chicago: University of Chicago Press, 1989

Brown, Gillian, *Domestic Individualism: Imagining the Self in Nineteenth-Century America*, Berkeley: University of California Press, 1990

Bryson, Phillip J., *The Consumer under Socialist Planning: The East German Case*, New York: Praeger, 1984

Campbell, Colin, *The Romantic Ethic and the Spirit of Modern Consumerism*, Oxford and New York: Blackwell, 1987

Carter, Erica, *How German Is She? Postwar West German Reconstruction and the Consuming Woman*, Ann Arbor: University of Michigan Press, 1997

Certeau, Michel de, *Arts de faire* [vol. 1 of *L'Invention du quotidien*], Paris: Union Générale d'Editions, 1980; in English as *The Practice of Everyday Life*, Berkeley: University of California Press, 1984

Cohen, Lizabeth, *Making a New Deal: Industrial Workers in Chicago, 1919–1939*, Cambridge and New York: Cambridge University Press, 1990

Cross, Gary S., *Time and Money: The Making of Consumer Culture*, London and New York: Routledge, 1993

Debord, Guy, *La Société du spectacle*, Paris: Buchet/Chastel, 1967; in English as *The Society of the Spectacle*, Detroit: Black and Red, 1970

De Grazia, Victoria, and Ellen Furlough, eds., *The Sex of Things: Gender and Consumption in Historical Perspective*, Berkeley: University of California Press, 1996

Forster, Robert, and Orest A. Ranum, eds., *Food and Drink in History: Selections from the Annales*, Baltimore: Johns Hopkins University Press, 1979

Fox, Richard Wightman, and T.J. Jackson Lears, eds., *The Culture of Consumption: Critical Essays in American History, 1880–1980*, New York: Pantheon, 1983

Gibb, James G., *The Archaeology of Wealth: Consumer Behavior in English America*, New York: Plenum, 1996

Goldthwaite, Richard, *Wealth and the Demand for Art in Italy, 1300–1600*, Baltimore: Johns Hopkins University Press, 1993

Gregory, Derek, *Geographical Imaginations*, Oxford: Blackwell, 1994

Horkheimer, Max, and Theodor W. Adorno, *Dialektik der Aufklärung: Philosophische Fragmente*, Amsterdam: Querido, 1947 [revised edition of *Philosophische Fragmente*, 1944]; in English as *Dialectic of Enlightenment*, New York: Seabury Press, 1972, London: Allen Lane, 1973

Jordan, William C., *Women and Credit in Pre-Industrial and Developing Societies*, Philadelphia: University of Pennsylvania Press, 1993

Kaplan, Steven L., *The Bakers of Paris and the Bread Question, 1700–1775*, Durham, NC: Duke University Press, 1996

Lears, T.J. Jackson, *Fables of Abundance: A Cultural History of Advertising in America*, New York: Basic Books, 1994

Lebergott, Stanley, *Pursuing Happiness: American Consumers in the Twentieth Century*, Princeton: Princeton University Press, 1993

Le Roy Ladurie, Emmanuel, *Montaillou: village occitan de 1294 à 1324*, Paris: Gallimard, 1975; in English as *Montaillou: The Promised Land of Error*, New York: Braziller, 1978, and as *Montaillou: Cathars and Catholics in a French Village, 1294–1324*, London: Scolar Press, 1978

MacCannell, Dean, *The Tourist: A New Theory of the Leisure Class*, New York: Schocken, and London: Macmillan, 1976; revised 1989

McClain, James L., John M. Merriman, and Ugawa Kaoru, eds., *Edo and Paris: Urban Life and the State in the Early Modern Era*, Ithaca, NY: Cornell University Press, 1994

McCracken, Grant David, *Culture and Consumption: New Approaches to the Symbolic Character of Consumer Goods and Activities*, Bloomington: Indiana University ress, 1988

McKendrick, Neil, John Brewer, and J.H. Plumb, *The Birth of a Consumer Society: The Commercialization of Eighteenth-Century England*, Bloomington: Indiana University Press, and London: Europa, 1982

Migiel, Marilyn, and Juliana Schiesari, eds., *Refiguring Woman: Perspectives on Gender and the Italian Renaissance*, Ithaca, NY: Cornell University Press, 1991

Miller, Daniel, ed., *Acknowledging Consumption*, London and New York: Routledge, 1995

Miller, Michael B., *The Bon Marché: Bourgeois Culture and the Department Store, 1869–1920*, Princeton: Princeton University Press, and London: Allen and Unwin, 1981

Mintz, Sidney W., *Sweetness and Power: The Place of Sugar in Modern History*, New York: Viking, and London: Sifton, 1985

Mort, Frank, *Cultures of Consumption: Masculinities and Social Space in Late Twentieth-Century Britain*, London and New York: Routledge, 1996

Mukerji, Chandra, *From Graven Images: Patterns of Modern Materialism*, New York: Columbia University Press, 1983

Orlove, Benjamin, ed., *The Allure of the Foreign: Imported Goods in Postcolonial Latin America*, Ann Arbor: University of Michigan Press, 1997

Prételle, Edmond, and Jean-Pierre Terrail, *Capitalism, Consumption, and Needs*, Oxford and New York: Blackwell, 1985 (French original)

Quimby, Ian M.G., ed., *Material Culture and the Study of Material Life*, New York: Norton, 1978

Reddy, William, *The Rise of Market Culture: The Textile Trade and French Society, 1750–1900*, Cambridge and New York: Cambridge University Press, 1984

Roche, Daniel, *La Culture des apparences: une histoire du vêtement (XVIIe–XVIIIe siècle)*, Paris: Fayard, 1989; in English as *The Culture of Clothing: Dress and Fashion in the Ancien Régime*, Cambridge and New York: Cambridge University Press, 1994

Schama, Simon, *The Embarrassment of Riches: An Interpretation of Dutch Culture in the Golden Age*, New York: Knopf, 1987; London: Collins, 1988

Scitovsky, Tibor, *The Joyless Economy: An Inquiry into Human Satisfaction and Consumer Dissatisfaction*, Oxford and New York: Oxford University Press, 1976; revised 1992

Tiersten, Lisa, "Redefining Consumer Culture: Recent Literature on Consumption and the Bourgeoisie in Western Europe," *Radical History Review* 57 (1993), 116–59

Veblen, Thorstein, *The Theory of the Leisure Class: An Economic Study in the Evolution of Institutions*, New York: Macmillan, 1899; London: Allen and Unwin, 1924

Walvin, James, *Fruits of Empire: Exotic Produce and British Taste, 1660–1800*, New York: New York University Press, and Basingstoke: Macmillan, 1997

Williams, Rosalind, *Dream Worlds: Mass Consumption in Late Nineteenth Century France*, Berkeley: University of California Press, 1982

Wilson, Elizabeth, *Adorned in Dreams: Fashion and Modernity*, London: Virago Press, 1985; Berkeley: University of California Press, 1987

Conze, Werner 1910–1986

German historian

Werner Conze was one of Germany's most prolific historians after World War II. He crucially influenced the emergence of German social historiography, the history of the working class, and *Begriffsgeschichte*, and played a major role in the organization of historical studies. Conze was enormously productive and left a wide-ranging oeuvre matched by few of his contemporaries. His works on German-Polish history in World War I (*Polnische Nation und deutsche Politik im Ersten Weltkrieg* [The Polish Nation and German Politics in World War I], 1958), on German-Russian relations, and on German history between 1890 and 1933 are generally considered his most important contributions. Nation-building and the history of the nation-state formed one of the major themes of his work. His initiatives in the field of contemporary history, for example, as one of the founders of the journal *Vierteljahreshefte für Zeitgeschichte* (1953), and his commitment to social history had a lasting impact on several generations of German historians. He was a pupil of Hans Rothfels whose far-reaching influence can be traced in many of Conze's works. A pioneer in the teaching of contemporary history, which he championed as early as 1948, Conze developed a special interest in the Weimar Republic, particularly in chancellor Brüning's cabinet.

Conze understood social history not merely as a part of general history but as its synthesis. In his view history could no longer be written as the narrative of individual lives or of states but only in respect to the masses. Thus he called for closer cooperation between history and sociology, political science, and economics; a synthesis of their methods and terminologies could overcome the over-specialization of the historian. In his path-breaking article "Vom 'Pöbel' zum 'Proletariat'" (From "Mob" to "Proletariat," 1954) he formulated his ideas of social change as exemplified by *Vormärz* society. In 1957 Conze founded the Arbeitskreis für moderne Sozialgeschichte (Workshop for Modern Social History) and presided over it until his death. It has published the series *Industrielle Welt* since 1962 as well as 43 edited volumes. This workshop, probably Conze's most influential organizational achievement, was based on the interdisciplinary research of about twenty historians, sociologists, economists, lawyers, and social anthropologists. It was this interdisciplinary social history that was his objective.

Contrary to expectation Conze did not really formulate any theory of social history. When founding the workshop, he believed in pragmatic, empirical research. He was, therefore, often criticized by a younger theory-oriented generation of social historians (for example, Jürgen Kocka and Hans-Ulrich Wehler), who emphasized social and economic factors and their impact on politics and culture. From the 1960s the program of a "Historische Sozialwissenschaft" emerged against Conze's structural model. He was further criticized for not having distinguished precisely enough between social and structural history, and for having suggested that early modern history was primarily the history of events. Conze also had to defend himself constantly against the accusation that he intended to subordinate social history to economic history. Although in 1979 he joined the editorial board of the journal *Vierteljahrschrift für Sozial- und Wirtschaftsgeschichte*, he did not himself found a special journal devoted entirely to social history. Instead he aimed to synthesize all aspects of history and tried to find a compromise between social and political history.

Conze thought that the distinction between the social sciences (*Sozialwissenschaften*) and political sciences (*Staatswissenschaften*), which predated that between social and political history, was the result of the separation of state and society in the modern world. Consequently in his 1962 study of the *Vormärz* he explored the conflict between state and society in early 19th-century Germany, which he placed into the context of modern nation-building. As long as this separation was a historical reality Conze accepted the distinction between social and political history, but for the period after 1945 he could no longer accept it. For him the reunification of history and sociology was a central aim possibly to be achieved by social history. Thus social and economic history concentrated on society while social and constitutional history concentrated on questions concerning the state. In both cases social history had a bridge-building function. His commitment to these ideas certainly made Conze unique among postwar German historians. He could thus resume his own prewar research as he had distanced himself from the problematic *völkisch* ideology of Gunther Ipsen, although he had been fascinated by Ipsen's sociological methodology for studying population and agrarian society.

In addition to his German background Conze was also influenced by American community studies. He may be regarded as one of the first German historians to have no reservations about the American sociological school, which he accepted as early as in the 1950s. Moreover, Conze acknowledged the significance of French sociological studies of elections for German research on the history of political parties. Conze systematically tried to formulate an integral social history in contrast to the hitherto predominant sectoral one. He called it *Strukturgeschichte* in order to have a more definite term; here he built on Fernand Braudel's ideas of a *histoire des structures* which can best be traced in his *Die Strukturgeschichte des technisch-industriellen Zeitalters als Aufgabe für Forschung und Unterricht* (The Structural History of the Technological-Industrial Age as a Challenge for Research and Teaching, 1957). This emphasized structures and processes in history and attempted to replace traditional hermeneutics with empirical analysis. In Germany at this time Conze had only few colleagues who would have accepted his ideas.

On the basis of his workshop Conze, with Otto Brunner and Reinhart Koselleck, founded and helped edit the highly influential and voluminous compendium *Geschichtliche Grundbegriffe* (1972–). His contributions included the articles: Adel, Arbeit, Bauer, Fanatismus, Freiheit, Klasse, Mittelstand, Militarismus, Proletariat, Rasse, Säkularisation, and Schutz. Conze's interest in *Begriffsgeschichte* grew out of his concern for social-historical questions, and his belief that the revolutionary period of around 1800 had had an impact on the development of political language. Thus he thought that studying the history of political terms could help us to understand historical processes. He believed that the historical turning point of around 1800 produced by the Industrial, the American, and the French revolutions, was even more significant than those of 1500 or 1917. This became one of the fundamental ideas of the *Geschichtliche Grundbegriffe*.

Another process identified by Conze was the workers' movement torn between state and society. His political standpoint and personal circumstances meant that Conze was not close to the workers' interests. Nonetheless the Institut für Sozial- und Wirtschaftsgeschichte which he founded at the University of Heidelberg brought the study of the workers' movement to the center of his attention. He intended to integrate it into a social history of Germany. With Dieter Groh he wrote a book that investigated the workers' movement in the context of the national movement. Both aspects, the social and the national, were considered to be equally important in forming the basis of social democracy. This was an attempt to bridge the national and the social movements. In the early 1970s Conze's interests shifted towards the history of the workers themselves, and later he advocated the study of family history.

BENEDIKT STUCHTEY

See also Begriffsgeschichte; Brunner; Germany: since 1945; Kocka; Koselleck; Wehler

Biography

Born Neuhaus, Elbe, 31 December 1910. Professor of modern history, University of Posen, 1944–45; University of Münster, 1952–57; and University of Heidelberg, 1957–79. Founded Arbeitskreis für moderne Sozialgeschichte, 1957. Married Gisela Pohlmann, 1936. Died Heidelberg, 28 April 1986.

Principal Writings

Hirschenhof: Die Geschichte einer deutschen Sprachinsel in Livland (Hirschenhof: History of a Linguistic Enclave in Livonia), 1934

Agrarverfassung und Bevölkerung in Litauen und Weissrussland (Agrarian Constitution and Population in Lithuania and Belorussia), 1940

Leibniz als Historiker (Leibniz as Historian), 1951

Editor, *Deutschland und Europa: historische Studien zur Völker- und Staatenordnung des Abendlandes* (Germany and Europe: Historical Studies of Peoples and States in the West), 1951 [Festschrift]

"Vom 'Pöbel' zum 'Proletariat': Sozialgeschichtliche Voraussetzungen für den Sozialismus in Deutschland" (From "Mob" to "Proletariat": Social-Historical Preconditions for the Emergence of Socialism in Germany), in *Vierteljahrsschrift für Sozial- und Wirtschaftsgeschichte* 41 (1954), 333–64

Die Strukturgeschichte des technisch-industriellen Zeitalters als Aufgabe für Forschung und Unterricht (The Structural History of the Technological-Industrial Age as a Challenge for Research and Teaching), 1957

Polnische Nation und deutsche Politik im Ersten Weltkrieg (The Polish Nation and German Politics in World War I), 1958

Editor, *Staat und Gesellschaft im deutschen Vormärz, 1815–1848* (State and Society in the German Vormärz), 1962

Die deutsche Nation: Ergebnis der Geschichte, 1963; in English as *The Shaping of the German Nation: A Historical Analysis*, 1979

Die Zeit Wilhelms II. und die Weimarer Republik: Deutsche Geschichte 1890 bis 1933 (The Age of William II and of the Weimar Republic: German History, 1890–1933), 1964

Möglichkeiten und Grenzen der liberalen Arbeiterbewegung in Deutschland: das Beispiel Schulze-Delitzschs (Opportunities and Limitations of the Liberal Labor Movement in Germany: The Example of Schulze-Delitzschs), 1965

With Dieter Groh, *Die Arbeiterbewegung in der nationalen Bewegung: die deutsche Sozialdemokratie vor, während, und nach der Reichsgründung* (The Labor Movement as Part of the National Movement: German Social Democracy before, during, and after the Foundation of the Reich), 1966

Editor with Otto Brunner and Reinhart Koselleck, *Geschichtliche Grundbegriffe: historisches Lexikon zur politisch-sozialen Sprache in Deutschland* (Historical Concepts: A Historical Dictionary of Political-Social Language in Germany), 1972–

Editor with Ulrich Engelhardt, *Arbeiter im Industrialisierungsprozess: Herkunft, Lage und Verhalten* (Workers in the Process of Industrialization: Origin, Condition, and Behavior), 1979

Der Strukturwandel der Familie im industriellen Modernisierungsprozess (Changes in Family Structure in the Industrial Process of Modernization), 1979

Further Reading

Kocka, Jürgen, *Sozialgeschichte: Begriff, Entwicklung, Probleme* (Social History: Concept, Development, Problems), Göttingen: Vandenhoeck & Ruprecht, 1977

Kocka, Jürgen, "Werner Conze und die Sozialgeschichte in der Bundesrepublik Deutschland" (Werner Conze and Social History in West Germany), *Geschichte in Wissenschaft und Unterricht* 37 (1986), 595–602

Koselleck, Reinhart, "Werner Conze: Tradition und Innovation," *Historische Zeitschrift* 45 (1987) 529–43

Ritter, Gerhard, "Die neuere Sozialgeschichte in der Bundesrepublik Deutschland" (Recent Social History in West Germany), in Jürgen Kocka, ed., *Sozialgeschichte im internationalen Überblick: Ergebnisse und Tendenzen der Forschung*, Darmstadt: Wissenschaftliche Buchgesellschaft, 1989, 19–88

Schieder, Wolfgang, "Sozialgeschichte zwischen Soziologie und Geschichte: Das wissenschaftliche Lebenswerk Werner Conzes" (Social History between Sociology and History: The Scholarly Life Work of Werner Conze), *Geschichte und Gesellschaft* 13 (1987), 244–66

Schulze, Winfried, *Deutsche Geschichtswissenschaft nach 1945* (German Historical Science since 1945), Munich: Oldenbourg, 1989

Coquery-Vidrovitch, Catherine 1935–
French historian of Africa

Catherine Coquery-Vidrovitch is among the greatest names in French African studies. She has been a tireless supporter of Africa and Africans, and has assisted in opening up several new areas of African studies research. In addition, she has helped in breaking down the French attitude of paternalism in relation to Africa, inherited from the colonial era.

Coquery-Vidrovitch is best known for her mode of production interpretations. Her analyses link the mode of production to the economic structure, gender roles, and spatial organization of African societies. Some have called her perspective Marxist, a label that somewhat bewilders Coquery-Vidrovitch, yet has continued to remain with her throughout her career. Her studies have sparked numerous other "materialist" studies of African societies.

Coquery-Vidrovitch's work on the African mode of production was built on Jean Suret-Canale's work, which suggested that the model of the Asiatic mode of production be applied to Africa. But, says Coquery-Vidrovitch, just as Marx and Engels sketched out an alternative mode of production with the "Asiatic mode of production" in order to take the peculiarities of Asian societies into account, so must the same be done for Africa. Simply acknowledging the African mode of production as different from that of Europe is not enough. African peculiarities such as the lineage system, decentralized government, mass migration, long-distance trade, and the absence of huge despotic governments all make the African mode of production distinct from the Asian model. While perhaps more applicable than the European model, the Asian model is also inadequate. The importance of long-distance trade throughout African history and its regions suggests that exchange, in relation to production, would also be a fruitful path of investigation in Africa.

In *The Workers of African Trade* (1985), edited with Paul Lovejoy, Coquery-Vidrovitch put a new twist on research done on long-distance African trade by examining the work inputs and lives of the workers involved, rather than simply the trade networks themselves, as had been the traditional means of investigation. This means of analysis was one of the ways in which Coquery-Vidrovitch wove together production and exchange, providing a more complete economic picture of African history. In this sense, she has also added to the growing field of African social history.

Another of Coquery-Vidrovitch's contributions to African historiography is her work dealing with women and their marginalization during colonialism. She has helped focus attention on Africa's women and the ways in which European value and production systems transformed and marginalized many of the roles of women in Africa. Rather than follow some of the traditional social science explorations of gender dealing primarily with kinship systems and gender roles, Coquery-Vidrovitch has injected the themes of economic productivity and labor into the analysis. The growing focus on African women will ensure that her work and precedents will be relevant for a long time to come.

Urbanism has also become a recent research focus of Coquery-Vidrovitch. She has been instrumental in defining and examining the process of African urbanization and its effects on Africans and their economic system. Her overview paper in *African Studies Review* (1994), stands as a definitive summation of the study of African urbanization. In it Coquery-Vidrovitch points to a number of directions in which research should move. One theme is to examine urbanism as a phenomenon in itself, and not as a colonial legacy or as a product of capitalism, and another is the inspection of urban households as a source of resource-generation. Lastly, the conclusion contains sensible advice for all Africanists, namely, a traditional African mode of thinking should not be opposed to a Western modern mode of thinking. Since African thought is not static, the modes of thought should not be dichotomized but should instead be seen as two components of the same process.

TOYIN FALOLA and JOEL E. TISHKEN

See also Africa: Central; Women's History: Africa

Biography
Catherine Marion Coquery-Vidrovitch. Born Paris, 25 November 1935, daughter of an engineer and an acoustician. Studied at the Lycée Victor-Dury, Lycée Fénelon, and the Ecole Normale Supérieure de jeunes filles, agrégation in history and geography, and doctorate. Taught history at a lycée, Chartres, then at the lycées Carnot and Buffon, Paris, 1959–61; Ecoles Pratiques des Hautes Etudes, 1962–71; and University of Paris VII (rising to professor), from 1971. Married Michel Coquery, university lecturer, 1958 (3 daughters, 1 son).

Principal Writings
La Découverte de l'Afrique: l'Afrique noire atlantique des origines au XVIII siècle (The Discovery of Black Atlantic Africa from Its Origins to the 18th Century), 1955

Brazza et la prise de possession du Congo: la mission de l'ouest africain, 1883–1885 (Brazza and the Capture of the Ownership of the Congo: The West African Mission, 1883–1885), 1969

With Samir Amin, *Histoire économique du Congo, 1880–1968: du Congo Français à l'union douanière et économique d'Afrique Centrale* (The Economic History of the Congo, 1880–1968: From the French Congo to the Economic and Customs Union of Central Africa), 1969

Le Congo au temps des grandes compagnies concessionaires, 1898–1930 (The Congo in the Period of the Great Concessionary Companies, 1898–1930), 1972

With Henri Moniot, *L'Afrique noire de 1800 à nos jours* (Black Africa from 1800 to the Present), 1974

"Recherches sur un 'mode de production' africain" (Research on the African Mode of Production) in David Seddon, ed., *Relations of Production: Marxist Approaches to Economic Anthropology*, 1978

Afrique noire: permanences et ruptures, 1985; in English as *Africa: Endurance and Change South of the Sahara*, 1988

Editor with Paul E. Lovejoy, *The Workers of African Trade*, 1985

With Alain Forest, *Décolonisation et nouvelles dépendances:
modèles et contremodèles idéologiques et culturels dans les pays
du Tiers-Monde* (Decolonization and New Dependencies:
Ideological and Cultural Models and Countermodels in the Third
World), 1986
L'Histoire des femmes en Afrique (African Women's History), 1987
Histoire des villes d'Afrique noire: des origines à la colonisation
(Black African Urban History from Its Origins to Colonization),
1993
*Les Africaines: histoire des femmes d'Afrique noire du XIXème
siècle au XXème* (Black African Women's History from the 19th
to the 20th Centuries), 1994
With Michel Coquery, "The Process of Urbanization in Africa, from
the Origins to the Beginning of Independence: An Overview
Paper," *African Studies Review* 34 (1994), 1–98

Corbin, Alain 1936–

French social historian

Alain Corbin may be the least predictable of France's contemporary historians. In a profession where the demands of
specialization have encouraged most people to stake out a small
piece of intellectual territory and to cling to it tenaciously,
Corbin continually seeks out new subjects of interrogation. He
has been among the pioneers in the historical profession who
have incorporated methods of cultural anthropology into their
historical research and analysis. The thread that ties all of his
work together is a belief that the ways people imagine, express,
and understand their world helps to structure its very existence. In all of his studies, Corbin focuses on debates over
meaning, because he sees them as the cultural expression of
intense social and political conflict. Whether his subject is
health reformers troubling over the dangers of excrement or
peasants engaging in a seemingly inexplicable orgy of violence,
Corbin teases out the questions of power at stake in words
and in acts.

Corbin began his academic career – as was more or less
expected of French historians of his generation – with an enormous regional thesis, in his case, on the southwestern region
of the Limousin, published as *Archaïsme et modernité en
Limousin au XIX siècle, 1845–1880* (Tradition and Modernity
in the Limousin in the 19th Century, 1975). Along with
Maurice Agulhon's research on the Var, Corbin's study was
one of the first in France to draw attention to the importance
of particular local factors in the development of left-wing politics. Both masons and peasants in the Limousin, he shows,
developed their political expectations out of the egalitarian
forms of sociability that structured their everyday life. Corbin
argues that both Socialist Democrats in 1848–49 and Radicals
and Socialists in the last third of the century were able to win
the support of these rural peasants and workers because they
were able to present themselves effectively as the champions
of equality and democracy.

After studying the Limousin, Corbin turned his attention to
structural, behavioral, discursive, and political factors that
helped to define the practice and control of prostitution in
France from the mid-19th century to the present. *Les Filles de
noce* (1978; *Women for Hire*, 1990) charts the regulation of
the sex trade from strict confinement in the 1850s, to limited
regulation under the Second Empire and the Third Republic,

to the loosening of police surveillance in the 20th century.
Inspired by Michel Foucault's theories of power, Corbin
analyzes the stakes that various concerned parties – including
public health officials, police officers, feminists, and prostitutes
themselves – had in controlling prostitution. Underlying his
study is the argument that most government attempts at regulation or prohibition ultimately served to distance prostitutes
from the economic control of their own labor.

While these first two works were well received by the scholarly community, it was Corbin's third book that earned him
the reputation of being among the most path-breaking and
controversial of contemporary historians. In *Le Miasme et la
jonquille* (1982; *The Foul and the Fragrant*, 1986), Corbin
examines shifting beliefs about odor and scent in the 18th and
19th centuries. His analysis of discourses of smell reveals that
assumptions about odor had important consequences on the
physical sciences, urban reform, and cultural sensibilities. In
the end, Corbin takes what seems to be a trivial topic and
persuasively argues that collective imagination has been a
powerful force in determining forms of public control as well
as of private reflection on the self and others.

All of Corbin's later work elaborates on the importance of
collective imagination in conditioning social structures and
relations. *Le Territoire du vide* (1988; *The Lure of the Sea*,
1994) traces the evolution of the seashore environment as a
desirable site in French, British, and German cultural perceptions. Corbin argues that prior to the Enlightenment, the sea
was viewed as an untamable source of anxiety, but in the mid-
18th century, European ruling classes, and later, Romantic
artists latched on to the seashore as a representative environment free of the scars of urbanization and technological
change. Similarly, Corbin's most recent book, *Les Cloches de
la terre* (The Bells of the Earth, 1994) examines the passions
and controversies surrounding village belltowers in 19th-
century France. Clergy, notables, and peasants all put great
cultural weight on controlling the bells which lent resonance
to the countryside. Although today these bells evoke little more
than nostalgia for a picturesque past, Corbin argues that in
the 19th century they were at the center of the collective imagination of village life, at times ringing out municipal solidarity,
at others, sounding the deep religious and social schisms that
divided even the smallest hamlet.

Between these two projects, Corbin wrote a small but powerful book about the ritualized group torture and murder of a
minor nobleman in the Dordogne on an unfortunate August day
in 1870 entitled *Le Village des cannibales* (1990; *The Village of
Cannibals*, 1992). In retelling the horrific event, Corbin shows
why the torturers – otherwise "normal" peasant men – came to
see in an inconsequential nobleman the combined threat of
republicans, nobility, priests, and Prussians. Corbin gives great
weight in his analysis to the importance of rumors, and his
methodology will undoubtedly serve as a source of inspiration
for cultural historians in the years to come.

Finally, for anyone interested in tracing Corbin's intellectual
trajectory, many of his past essays and articles were republished in 1991 under the title *Le Temps, le désir, et l'horreur*
(Time, Desire, and Horror). In this collection, as in his body
of work as a whole, the breadth and novelty of Corbin's work
is striking. Overall, Corbin's influence on the profession has
been his insistence that the historian's craft is based on

"detecting and not dictating" human sensibilities and passions. As to what subjects Corbin might detect in the future, that is undoubtedly the least predictable question of all.

MONA L. SIEGEL

See also Europe: Modern; Foucault; France: since the Revolution

Biography
Alain Michel Marie Antoine Corbin. Born Courtomer, Orne, 12 January 1936, son of a doctor. Studied at the Ecole du Sacré-Coeur, Domfront; the Sorbonne; University of Caen, agrégation in history and doctorate. Taught at the lycée Gay-Lussac, Limoges, 1959–68; University of Limoges (rising to professor of contemporary history), 1968–86; director, humanities faculty, University of Tours, 1977–80; professor of contemporary history, University of Paris I, from 1987. Married Annie Lagore, teacher, 1963 (2 sons).

Principal Writings
Archaïsme et modernité en Limousin au XIX siècle, 1845–1880 (Tradition and Modernity in the Limousin in the 19th Century), Paris: Rivière, 1975
Les Filles de noce: misère sexuelle et prostitution: 19e et 20e siècles, 1978; in English as Women for Hire: Prostitution and Sexuality in France after 1850, 1990
Editor, La Prostitution à Paris au XIXe siècle, 1981
Le Miasme et la jonquille: l'odorat et l'imaginaire social, XVIIIe–XIXe siècles, 1982; in English as The Foul and the Fragrant: Odor and the French Social Imagination, 1986
Editor with Michelle Perot, De la Révolution à la Grande guerre, vol. 4 of Histoire de la vie privée, 1987; in English as From the Fires of Revolution to the Great War, vol. 4 of A History of Private Life, 1990
Le Territoire du vide: l'Occident et le désir du rivage, 1750–1840, 1988; in English as The Lure of the Sea: The Discovery of the Seaside in the Western World, 1750–1840, 1994
Le Village des cannibales, 1990; in English as The Village of Cannibals: Rage and Murder in France, 1870, 1992
Le Temps, le désir, et l'horreur: essais sur le dix-neuvieme siècle, Paris: Aubier, 1991; in English as Time, Desire, and Horror: Towards a History of the Senses, 1995
Les Cloches de la terre: paysage sonore et culture sensible dans les campagnes aux XIX siècle (The Bells of the Earth: Sonorous Landscape and Sensitive Cultivation in the Countryside of the 19th Century), 1994

Further Reading
Bouyssy, M., "Alain Corbin; ou, le terrier d'Alice de l'histoire" (Alain Corbin; or, The Rabbit-hole of History), Esprit 213 (1995), 74–85

Cosío Villegas, Daniel 1898–1976
Mexican historian

Born in Mexico City, Cosío Villegas studied widely before he became an economist, taking a year of engineering, seven years of law, and two years of philosophy in Mexico. Abroad he took courses in economics at Harvard University, in agricultural economy at the University of Wisconsin, in poultry farming at Cornell University, and in agriculture at the London School of Economics. This broad academic background made Cosío Villegas an unusually well prepared intellectual for his time, well suited for the administrative jobs which he assumed

early on in his career during the 1920s. After the Mexican Revolution of 1910–17, when the old regime's bureaucrats were partially replaced by revolutionary cadres, Cosío Villegas brought innovative ideas to his undertakings at the National Autonomous University of Mexico, the Foreign Ministry, the Ministry of Education, the Ministry of Treasury, and the Bank of Mexico.

Cosío Villegas also distinguished himself as an independent intellectual and journalist, as a teacher of philosophy, sociology, history, and economics. As an economist interested not only in teaching his discipline but also in discussing and popularizing it, in 1933 Cosío Villegas founded and directed Mexico's first school of economics. In the same year he founded the enduring editorial house, Fondo de Cultura Económica, which has become a major publisher and distributor of a wide variety of books throughout Latin America. in 1934 Cosío Villegas founded and directed the academic journal, El Trimestre Económico, modeled after Economic Quarterly. Following the defeat of the Spanish Republic in 1939 and the forced exile of Spanish intellectuals, Cosío Villegas was instrumental in bringing many of them to Mexico and in harnessing their talents to Mexico's educational needs. From an original place of Spanish refuge, the House of Spain, in which they used to gather and lecture, evolved into a prestigious undergraduate and graduate college, El Colegio de México. As the Colegio's secretary, Cosío Villegas took the initiative to create its internal disciplinary divisions and endow each with its own journal: the Center for Historical Studies with Historia Mexicana; the Center for International Studies with Foro Internacional.

As one of his many contributions to Mexico's historiography, in the late 1940s Cosío Villegas launched the thesis that there was a historical continuity between the ancien régime of Porfirio Díaz, overthrown by the revolutionaries in 1910, and the postrevolutionary regime. Cosío Villegas based his provocative argument on the observation that following the progressive period of Lázaro Cárdenas' presidency (1934–40), the agrarian and the nationalizing endeavors came to an end. What came in their stead were policies aiming at economic growth exactly as had been the case during the Porfirian period. Once again material progress took precedence over justice because the revolution had failed to accomplish a radical break with the previous regime.

Cosío Villegas' fears that Mexico was regressing into a neo-Porfiriato were published first as an essay in 1947 under the title "La Crisis de México" (Mexico's Crisis). The same concern motivated him to inquire further into the vagaries of the Porfirian era (1877–1911). The investigation led Cosío Villegas to publish Porfirio Díaz en la revuelta de la Noria (Porfirio Díaz during the Noria Riot, 1953). This book was to be a by-product of the multivolume Historia moderna de México (Modern History of Mexico) published under his editorship. These volumes, ten in all, came out between 1955 and 1974 and were based on the previously unpublished documents from the Porfirio Díaz archives. Written by eleven historians, the volumes covered the period following the republican restoration after the French-imposed monarchy had been defeated and after liberalism had triumphed over the conservative reaction which had supported it. The volumes included social, political, and economic history and the history of Mexico's foreign relations.

According to Cosío Villegas, the political stability that Mexico reached by 1867 was the watershed between the old and the contemporary era and also the starting point of the first volume of Mexico's modern history. The 10th volume followed Mexico's historical trajectory to 1910 when the 44 year-old regime ran its course and the autocratic government which had embodied it was overthrown.

While editing the history of the Porfirian period, Cosío Villegas was a keen observer of his own times. His observations and reflections turned into several books. In *El sistema político mexicano* (Mexico's Political System, 1972), Cosío Villegas examined the two central pieces of Mexico's political system: the official state party of the institutionalized revolution (El Partido de la revolución institucionalizada, PRI) and the presidential figure. Cosío Villegas pointed out that Mexico's presidents governed not subject to laws and institutions but to their temperaments and moods. This book was followed in 1974 by *El estilo personal de gobernar* (The Personal Style of Rule) and in 1975 by *La sucesión presidencial* (The Presidential Succession). In all three books Cosío Villegas subjected Mexico's political regime to scathing criticism, suggesting that the president was endowed with exaggerated power which needed to be curtailed. Similarly, the state party, which the president had at his disposal, left no room for the development of a democratic competitive party system.

Cosío Villegas' memoirs were published posthumously in 1976. they provide a window on a good part of Mexico's 20th century and depict the human frailties and magnanimity of Cosío Villegas' friends, collaborators, and bosses, and of Mexico's public figures with whom he had come into a personal contact.

DANIELA SPENSER

See also Latin America: National; Mexico

Biography
Born Mexico City, 23 July 1898. Studied at National Preparatory School; National School of Jurisprudence, law degree, 1925; University of Wisconsin; Harvard University; London School of Economics; Ecole Libre des Sciences Politiques, Paris; and Cornell University, MA. Taught at National Preparatory School; National School of Jurisprudence; and Schools of Law and of Philosophy and Letters, Autonomous National University. General secretary, Autonomous National University; director/founder, National School of Economics, 1933. Founder/editor, *El trimestre económico*, 1934–48; founder/director, Fondo de Cultura Económica publishing house, 1935–49; co-founder, Colegio de México, 1940: president, 1958–63; founder/editor, *Historia Mexicana*, 1951–61; and *Foro Internacional*. Economic adviser to finance minister; special ambassador to UN Economic and Social Council, 1957–68. Died Mexico City, 10 March 1976.

Principal Writings
Porfirio Díaz en la revuelta de la Noria (Porfirio Díaz during the Noria Riot), 1953
Editor, *Historia moderna de México* (Modern History of Mexico), 10 vols., 1955–74
Estados Unidos contra Porfirio Díaz, 1956; in English as *The United States versus Porfirio Díaz*, 1963
El sistema político mexicano: las posibilidades de cambio (Mexico's Political System), 1972

Historia mínima de México, 1973; in English as *A Compact History of Mexico*, 1974
El estilo personal de gobernar (The Personal Style of Rule), 1974
La sucesión presidencial (The Presidential Succession), 1975
Memorias, 1976

Further Reading
Florescano, Enrique, and Ricardo Pérez Montfort, eds., *Historiadores de México en el siglo XX* (Mexican Historians of the 20th Century), Mexico City: FCE & CONACULTA, 1995
Krauze, Enrique, *Daniel Cosío Villegas: una biografía intelectual*, 2nd edition, Mexico City: Mortiz, 1991

Cott, Nancy F. 1945–
US women's and social historian

One of the pioneers of women's history, Nancy F. Cott emerged from the flowering of social history that took place in the 1960s. Cott shaped the field of women's history from its inception. She turned her attention to those previously neglected by the historical canon, using the tools of social history to reconstruct the experiences of ordinary women in the past. Second wave feminism as well as social history inspired her interest in women's history. She first defined and explored one of the central dilemmas of women's history in the 19th century: the simultaneous social constraints and social activism of middle-class women. Later, she explored one of women's history's most perplexing eras – the period after suffrage – providing one of the most ambitious studies of 20th-century women's organizations and activism. Recently she has turned to the life and letters of an earlier women's history pioneer, Mary Beard.

The Bonds of Womanhood (1977) outlined the uses women made of their sphere and the opportunities that their affiliation with reform provided. This was one of the first explorations of women's culture and the strength that women drew from relationships with one another. As Cott found, such instances of "sisterhood" led to the assumption of a more public voice in the 19th century. For example, women's religious and missionary societies became effective fundraisers and provided organizational acumen for its members. These reformers could then springboard to abolition, and a few moved onward to women's rights.

In "Passionlessness: An Interpretation of Victorian Sexual Ideology, 1790–1850" (1978–79), Cott explored the construction of women's sphere more deeply. Women were not the pliant victims of male ideals of feminine behavior, she argued. In fact, women themselves helped to create key elements of 19th-century ideal womanhood – virtue and sexual passionlessness. Women writers exalted the superior moral qualities of the female sex and turned these into the basis for greater autonomy on the domestic front. Women's morality and freedom from the baser male lusts, such writers claimed, gave them a source of authority. The ideology of passionlessness, in part created by women, gave women the right of refusal in the marriage bed. Given the decline in the 19th-century birthrate and the male cooperation necessary to achieve it, Cott's argument supported the thesis that enhanced power for women in the middle-class home developed in the 19th century.

In *The Grounding of Modern Feminism* (1987), Cott showed the connections between pre- and post-suffrage women's activism in the proliferation of voluntarism in the 1920s. She also brought out the diversity of women's groups, their different goals and definitions of feminism, which the umbrella goal of the vote had glossed over. After suffrage, without the unifying force of that goal, conflict rather than consensus would characterize women's politics. In *Grounding*, Cott pointed out the theoretical differences within feminism and how they spread to tactical differences in the 1920s. The equality versus difference debate did not begin in the 1920s, but the issue caused splintering among women activists such as the divisions between reformers such as Florence Kelley and Equal Rights Amendment advocate Alice Paul over both strategies and goals. Moreover, the greater variety of public options opened to women in the 1920s because of consumerism, employment, and educational change helped to fray an already unraveling feminist consensus.

Cott cautioned historians and feminists against interpreting the periods of 1912–1919 and 1967–74 as norms for women's activism and consciousness. She noted the inevitability of fragmentation among women, discarding declensionist arguments about the 1920s and the late 1970s. Women differ according to class, ethnic, racial, family, political, and sexual identity. Few women, she wrote, can afford to lose sight of their complex identities and adopt the singular identity "woman." The lack of the ballot in a culture that defined individualism by political participation gave diverse women a common goal at a unique moment in history, giving rise to what Cott identified as "not unity but strategic coalition." Cott argued for a feminism that encompasses sexual difference and differences among women leading to coalition building, as opposed to monolithic and unattainable unity. She also situated feminism historically. In both seven-year periods of 20th-century feminist activism, it existed in the social and political context of reform. Internalist analyses of the "failure of feminism" that ignore the wax and wane of political radicalism and reform have little utility for contemporary feminists, Cott suggested.

In the 1990s Cott turned her attention to a foremother in the field of women's history, Mary Beard. She edited a collection of Beard's letters and analyzed her historical contributions on her own and as co-author with her husband Charles Beard, restoring Beard's place as influence and collaborator. Cott highlighted the role Mary Beard played in broadening the topics encompassed in their collaborative work, by insisting that the "cultural side" was as much history as were war and politics. She also revealed Charles' influence on Mary's thought, including her most famous work, *Women as a Force in History*. Issues of feminism, diversity, identity, and women's history itself link Cott's many contributions to historical thought.

JESSICA WEISS

See also Kerber; United States: 19th Century; Women's History: North America

Biography

Nancy Falik Cott. Born Philadelphia, 8 November 1945. Received BA, Cornell University, 1967; PhD, Brandeis University, 1974. Taught at Wheaton College, 1971; Clark University, 1972; Wellesley College, 1973–74; and Yale University, from 1975. Married Lee Cott, 1969 (1 child).

Principal Writings

Roots of Bitterness: Documents of the Social History of American Women, 1972

The Bonds of Womanhood: "Woman's Sphere" in New England, 1780–1835, 1977

"Passionlessness: An Interpretation of Victorian Sexual Ideology, 1790–1850," *Signs* 4 (1978–79), 219–36

Editor, *A Heritage of Her Own: Toward a New Social History of American Women*, 1979

"Feminist Theory and Feminist Movements: The Past Before Us," in Juliet Mitchell and Ann Oakley, eds., *What Is Feminism?*, 1986

The Grounding of Modern Feminism, 1987

"Two Beards: Coauthorship and the Concept of Civilization," *American Quarterly* 42 (1990), 274–301

Editor, *A Woman Making History: Mary Ritter Beard Through Her Letters*, 1991

Editor, *History of Women in the United States: Historical Articles on Women's Lives and Activities*, 20 vols., 1992–

Counter-Reformation

In 1946 the German historian of the Counter-Reformation, Hubert Jedin, wrote, "Historical terms are like coins: normally one lets them through one's fingers without looking carefully at their minting," while in 1968 the English historian of the Counter-Reformation, H.O. Evennett, asked if there had "not been a certain tendency for post-medieval ecclesiastical history to become imprisoned within its own categories?" Both of these authors had pointed to a particular interest of historians in the history of the terms and categories used to analyze late medieval and early modern ecclesiastical histories. There appears to be a connection between the subject and the categories used to study and discuss that subject.

The standard story of the history of the term "Counter-Reformation" (or in German, *Gegenreformation*) has been repeatedly written. According to Albert Elkan, the term was first found (in the plural) in the works of the German jurist Johann Stephen Pütter in the late 18th century. Pütter used the term to refer to the forceful taking over of jurisdictions by authorities claiming rights designated to Roman Catholics in the period following the Peace of Augsburg in 1555. These legal claims were particularly pressed in the Holy Roman empire, including the kingdom of Bohemia, and Pütter's use of the term reflected the particular juridical context of the Holy Roman empire in the period between 1555 and his own time, a juridical context where rights were associated with particular historically-legitimated jurisdictions.

Although Pütter began writing of the "Counter-Reformations" in the 1770s, it appears that the term found general usage only in the 1830s. Even then, it continued to be used in the plural and as a specific political or legal designator, not as the general label for a movement or an epoch. According to Elkan, Jedin, and Evennett, it was the famous German historian Leopold von Ranke who, influenced by ideas labeled "Romantic," began to use the term to refer to an entire period, an "epoch" of European history that shared certain characteristics in a variety of fields. He used it in reference to the period 1555–1648. Ranke was intrigued by the idea that forces which seem to have been defeated could resurface and be accepted. In his *History of the Popes*, in addition to the concept of Counter-Reformation(s), Ranke used terms such as "reconstruction," "restoration," "reformation," and "regeneration."

The term began to achieve widespread acceptance (in the singular) by the 1860s and 1870s, only to engender a reaction on the part of the German historian Wilhelm Maurenbrecher, who argued what came to be known as the "Spanish Thesis." This pointed out the importance of Iberian predecessors to the "Counter-Reformation(s)," placing the latter into a larger history of "Catholic Reform" or "Catholic Reformation" and underlining the internal vitality of Latin Christian institutions independent of the influence of Luther or other Protestant reformers. This split showed a general characteristic of the debate over the term "Counter-Reformation(s)": Protestant-leaning historians tended to accept its legitimacy; Catholic-leaning historians tended to be more circumspect in its application, preferring not to legitimate the Protestant movements by labeling Roman Catholic actions as simply responses.

By the late 19th century, many historians writing in various western European national historical traditions had accepted the German term "Counter-Reformation" to refer to ecclesiastical developments in the late 16th and early 17th centuries, although few historians used it in the general sense that German historians did. (Western European historians would tend to – and still tend to – refer instead to the period of the "Wars of Religion" or to a particular ruler's reign, i.e. "Elizabethan England.")

In the 1940s, Jedin proposed to bridge the historiographical gap which had developed between advocates of the term "Counter-Reformation" and advocates of the term "Catholic Reformation." His important book, *Katholische Reformation oder Gegenreformation?* (Catholic Reformation or Counter-Reformation?, 1946) clearly outlined what he took to be the major differences between the two terms. Jedin proposed to use Pütter and Ranke's term *Gegenreformation* to help analyze precisely those developments, institutions, and ideas which had been the result of people's actions in response to the Protestants. These included various types of controversial theology, religious orders such as the Capuchins or the Jesuits, sermonizers and painters who were responding to various Protestant points, and other administrative initiatives and innovations. To Jedin, both the "spontaneous" developments within Roman Catholicism and the "dialectical" ones which were the result of Protestantism were necessary to understand the period.

More recently, historians, building on the works of von Pastor and others, have emphasized the role of Italians in the Counter-Reformation, looking at social movements and ecclesiastical politics in Italy. Work has also been undertaken on the implementation of this "Counter-Reformation" (now in the singular) across Europe in places such as France, Poland, and the Central European Habsburg lands, as well as abroad in the missionized territories of the Americas, Africa, and Asia. The Counter-Reformation, which began as a specific legal term developed in the context of the late-18th century Holy Roman empire, has become a historical coin of exchange of almost worldwide acceptance.

JOSEPH F. PATROUCH

See also Dickens; Reformation

Further Reading

Dickens, A.G., *The Counter Reformation*, New York: Harcourt Brace, and London: Thames and Hudson, 1969

Elkan, Albert, "Entstehung und Entwicklung des Begriffs Gegenreformation" (Genesis and Development of the Term Counter-Reformation), *Historische Zeitschrift* 112 (1914), 473–93

Evennett, Henry O., "The Counter-Reformation," in Joel Hurstfield ed., *The Reformation Crisis*, London: Arnold, 1965; New York: Barnes and Noble, 1966

Evennett, Henry O., *The Spirit of the Counter-Reformation*, Cambridge: Cambridge University Press, 1968

Jedin, Hubert, *Katholische Reformation oder Gegenreformation? Ein Versuch zur Klärung der Begriffe nebst einer Jubiläumsbetrachtung über das Trester Konzil* (Catholic Reformation or Counter-Reformation? An Attempt to Clarify the Concepts), Lucerne: Stocker, 1946

Jedin, Hubert, "Catholic Reform and Counter Reformation," in Erwin Iserloh, Joseph Glazik, and Hubert Jedin, eds., *Reformation and Counter Reformation*, London: Burns and Oates, and New York: Seabury Press, 1980 [German original 1967]

Jones, Martin D.W., *The Counter Reformation: Religion and Society in Early Modern Europe*, Cambridge and New York: Cambridge University Press, 1995

McGinniss, Frederick J., "The Counter Reformation in Italy," in William S. Maltby, ed., *Reformation Europe: A Guide to Research* 2, St. Louis: Center for Reformation Research, 1992

Pütter, Johann Stephen, *Historische Entwicklung der heutigen Staatsverfassung des deutschen Reichs*, 3 vols., Göttingen: Bandenhoeck, 1786–87; in English as *A Historical Development of the Present Political Constitution of the Germanic Empire*, 3 vols., London: Payne, 1790

Ranke, Leopold von, *Die römischen Päpste in den letzten vier Jahrhunderten*, 3 vols., Leipzig: Duncker & Humblot, 1834–36; in English as *The Ecclesiastical and Political History of the Popes of Rome during the Sixteenth and Seventeenth Centuries*, 3 vols., London: Murray, 1840, Philadelphia: Lea and Blanchard, 1841; and as *The History of the Popes*, 3 vols., London: Bell, 1907

Schmidt, Kurt Dietrich, *Die Katholische Reform und die Gegenreformation* (Catholic Reform and the Counter-Reformation), Göttingen: Vandenhoeck & Ruprecht, 1975

Zeeden, Ernst Walter, "Zeitalter der europäischen Glaubenskämpfe, Gegenreformation, Katholische Reform" (The Period of the European Religious Struggles, Counter-Reformation, Catholic Reform), *Saeculum* 7 (1956), 321–68

Creighton, Donald Grant 1902–1979

Canadian historian

Like his friend and colleague Harold Adams Innis, Donald Grant Creighton was deeply interested in the relationship between human society and the environment it inhabited. In a long and prolific life as a working historian, Creighton made two major contributions to Canadian history: his Laurentian thesis, formulated alongside Innis' staples thesis, to explain the development of the nation; and his skill as a storyteller, which carried Canadian historical writing to new heights.

Creighton's earliest work, placing the Lower Canadian Rebellion of 1838 in the context of a struggle between the economic conservatism of French-Canadian society and the aggressive commercialism of Anglo-American business elites, led him to look more carefully at the motivation of those elites. At the heart of their activity he found the St. Lawrence River system, the water highway that led directly into the North

American hinterland. He became fascinated by the river's role in the development of Canada and laid out his thesis in his first major work, *The Commercial Empire of the St. Lawrence* (1937). Creighton believed that Canada's destiny was shaped by the great river system that penetrated it; the St. Lawrence fired the imagination of explorers, merchants, and capitalists, who saw it as a way to link the natural wealth of North America directly to European markets. Ultimately, however, the river dashed the very hopes it spawned. Broken at all too frequent intervals by impassable sections, it was eclipsed by American railways.

And yet the dream of the St. Lawrence did not die. After taking his Laurentian thesis back in time and superimposing it on the earliest days of the French presence in Canada (*Dominion of the North*, 1944), Creighton returned to the merchant elites of the 19th century and interpreted Confederation as an expression of their frustration over failed hopes for a commercial empire. Because rapids and waterfalls stood in the way of that empire, they turned instead to a political empire – the Confederation of British North America – as a poor second choice. This thesis underlay Creighton's *The Road to Confederation: The Emergence of Canada* (1964), but came out especially strongly in his two-volume biography of Canada's first prime minister, John A. Macdonald, entitled *The Young Politician* (1952) and *The Old Chieftain* (1955). In Creighton's eyes, Macdonald was the heir to generations of Canadians who had been moved by the St. Lawrence. For the hard-drinking and jovial lawyer-turned-politician of the biography, Confederation was a way to breathe life into the political version of the empire of the St. Lawrence.

Creighton's fondness for Macdonald and his Conservative successors is clear, but nowhere more so than in his writings on 20th-century Canadian history. In those books, primarily *Canada's First Century* (1970) and *The Forked Road: Canada, 1939–57* (1976), prime minister Robert Borden was Canada's last great national leader, and World War I was the pinnacle of Canadian nationhood. Everything afterwards had been a slow process of integrating Canada into the United States. In this long decline, Creighton knew full well who the villains were: the Liberal prime minister Mackenzie King and the progenitors of the liberal interpretation of Canadian history. They had considered the country's colonial heritage as a stain, all traces of which had to be eradicated as soon as possible, so that Canada could proudly don the emperor's new clothes of independence from Britain. For Creighton this was heresy. The colonial heritage was not an embarrassment, but rather the prop of modern Canada; Britain had carefully fostered Canadian nationhood, while at the same time protecting the fledgling country from the great republic to the south. With this in mind, Creighton attacked the liberal interpretation with all of the righteous indignation with which his Methodist upbringing had endowed him.

Although more recent historians have decried Creighton's anglo-centrism, none can deny his consummate skill as a writer. Particularly in his biographies (and in this regard *The Commercial Empire of the St. Lawrence* might be called the biography of a river), he displayed an unusual gift for combining history and literature. Creighton wanted to get as far away as possible from the 19th-century tradition of dense, impenetrable biographies which he derided as "fat funereal volumes"

and in this he succeeded admirably. As J.M.S. Careless put it, he was a master at capturing the juncture of character and circumstance. It is this skill that makes the best of Creighton's work, whatever one thinks of the politics that lay behind it, a delight to read.

JONATHAN F. VANCE

See also Canada; Lower; Morton; Ormsby

Biography

Born Toronto, 15 July 1902. Received BA, University of Toronto, 1925; BA, Oxford University, 1927, MA 1930. Taught at University of Toronto (rising to professor) from 1927. Married Luella Bruce, 1926 (1 son, 1 daughter). Died Brooklin, Ontario, 1979.

Principal Writings

The Commercial Empire of the St. Lawrence, 1760–1850, 1937
Dominion of the North: A History of Canada, 1944
John A. Macdonald, 2 vols., 1952–55
Harold Adams Innis: Portrait of a Scholar, 1957
The Road to Confederation: The Emergence of Canada, 1863–1867, 1964
Canada's First Century, 1867–1967, 1970
The Forked Road: Canada, 1939–57, 1976
The Passionate Observer: Selected Writings, 1980

Further Reading

Berger, Carl, *The Writing of Canadian History: Aspects of English-Canadian Historical Writing, 1900–1970*, Toronto: Oxford University Press, 1976; 2nd edition Toronto: University of Toronto Press, 1986
Cook, Ramsay, *The Craft of History*, Toronto: Canadian Broadcasting Corporation, 1973
Levitt, Joseph, *A Vision Beyond Reach: A Century of Images of Canadian Destiny*, Ottawa: Deneau, 1982
Moir, John S., ed., *Character and Circumstance: Essays in Honour of Donald Grant Creighton*, Toronto: Macmillan, 1970

Crime and Deviance

The history of crime is a subject fraught with difficulties. It can be studied on a global scale, and it must be perceived in a historical sense, as well as in a topical, geographical, or demographic one. With a continent that has such a long recorded history as Europe, it can be divided into medieval, early modern, and modern: from the rise of local communities and towns, to the rise and disintegration of monarchical governments and the emergence of secular nation-states. Topically, crime includes the classical "sins" in the Hebraic-Judaic-Christian tradition of murder and theft which are called "crime," as well as the accretion of regulations of behavior called "offenses" which were introduced over time by communities and the state. "Deviance" refers to behavior that does not conform to the norms of communities or the state, and deviant acts can be classified as crimes or offenses depending on the circumstances in which the act was committed. Historically, the creation of nation-states and legal systems, law enforcement bodies, political parties, and governmental bureaucracies contributed to a reshaping of elites, a redefinition of public order, and the creation of new forms of social control that are still with us today.

Most modern historians of crime and deviance work from records and literary evidence, which contain as many problems in their usage as they provide illumination of their subject. Many nation-states, for example, generate their own national statistics on crime, and have a vested interest in the propagation of these statistics to the exclusion of other sources of information. This can be seen, for example, in the career of Adolphe Quetelet (1796–1874), the earliest criminal statistician, who was also one of the earliest social scientists. It can also be seen in the rise and use of modern statistics in all countries. Historians, while often providing a useful corrective to impressionistic evidence that comes from novelists, newspaper reporters, and other observers, still lack an effective model for the recreation of the criminal past. Some models, however, like those of Benoît Garnot, Eric H. Monkkonen, and Lawrence Friedman have been useful.

The study of recorded crime has been aided by the recovery and accessibility of court and other legal records, a process that has increased dramatically since the late 19th century. The records of the central state now pose a formidable resource. The organization of these records, however, together with the problems of accessibility and finding aids and indexes, still remain major deterrents to all but the most committed researchers. Too often writers have adhered to the records of the central courts and the central state, ignoring the rich archives of local courts and authorities, which range from the police to municipal courts and magistrates. These local records are often not retained, but where they are extant, significant studies such as John Beattie's *Crime and the Courts in England* (1986) are possible. The records of most police forces are generally closed to researchers. In more modern times, where they do survive, they can underlie such insightful studies as David Arnold's *Police Power and Colonial Rule* (1986), Richard Hill's *Policing the Colonial Frontier* (1986), John Weaver's *Crimes, Constables, and Courts* (1995), and *Policing in Australia* (1987), edited by Mark Finnane.

There have been a number of major shifts in the study of crime in recent years. One of these is the examination of crime in the household and in the workplace. This new focus on white- and blue-collar crime in the workplace, domestic violence in the family, and regulatory offenses in the community is best seen in Florike Egmond's *Underworlds* (1993) and Bernard Schnapper's *Voies nouvelles en histoire du droit* (New Paths in the History of Law, 1991). We lack, however, effective methodologies to study these crimes and offenses at the level of the community, as well as across the national divides, in terms of structure (the long durée), conjuncture (mid-term development), and "event" (the particular moment). The best methodologies come from Europe; these are not always easily applicable to other cultures and countries but they do make comparative studies possible, as in Clive Emsley's and Louis Knafla's *Crime History and Histories of Crime* (1996).

A further problem is the ever-changing definition of what constitutes crime or criminous activity. For example, in modern times we have lost much of our knowledge of petty theft because authorities – on whom the burden of prosecution now rests – have become increasingly reluctant to prosecute low-valued monetary crimes because of the increasing cost of the public prosecutorial system. But we have also seen a tremendous rise in sexual crimes, as society's sensitivity has changed from tolerating unsolicited male acts upon women to no longer accepting them, as both Judith Allen's *Sex and Secrets* (1990) and Judith R. Walkowitz's *City of Dreadful Delight* (1992) have demonstrated. With regard to individual crimes of violence, for example, we have lost the crime of infanticide since at least the mid-19th century, and in some countries have gained the crime of abortion, as Lionel Rose has shown in *Massacre of the Innocents* (1986). Moreover, child abuse and wife-beating, activities that were once permitted and at times extolled, are now among the most prominent crimes in Western society. Indeed, these ever-changing definitions of what constitutes crime have also affected "serious" and "violent" crime.

The role of the central state in the history of crime and criminal justice has been a prominent one since the 16th century. Its historiography in modern times was spurred by the work of Charles, Richard, and Louise Tilly in the 1960s and 1970s, which was funded by numerous programs of the Ford Foundation and the Social Science Research Council, featured in sessions of the Social Science History Association, and followed up by scholars and institutes in France and the Netherlands, in particular in the work of Pieter Spierenburg. The totality of this work posed the proposition that Europe was in cultural, religious, and social disarray from the 16th to the 18th centuries, and that its older authoritarian structures were in various stages of disintegration. The rise of the nation-state was seen as a response to war and threats to order. The creation of national taxation, armies, police, foreign colonies, and industrialization enabled an alliance to be forged between landed and commercial elites to form strong central states. An important result was that communities lost control of public space and the distribution of goods and services, and that workers lost control of the means of production. Thus Howard Zehr's *Crime and the Development of Modern Society* (1976) and Andrew Scull and Stanley Cohen's edited collection *Social Control and the State* (1983) equated the rise of the nation-state with the rise of social control.

However, more recent research, in Robert P. Weller and Scott Evan Guggenheim's edited collection *Power and Protest in the Countryside* (1982) and Stuart Woolf's *The Poor in Western Europe in the Eighteenth and Nineteenth Centuries* (1986), has shown that crime as an expression of rural or civic unrest is not so easily identified. This research has also demonstrated that patterns of policing have reflected variant and often conflicting interests, and that forms of punishment – the ultimate weapon of the central state for enforcing its hegemony upon society – reflected social, economic, and psychological concerns that developed independently of the interests of the state. While the police may determine who gets arrested and who is prosecuted, the interests of the central state may often be at variance with those of local communities or their social structures, as can be seen in Douglas Hay and Francis Snyder's edited collection *Policing and Prosecution in Britain* (1980), Alf Lüdtke's *"Gemeinwohl" Polizei und "Festungspraxis"* (1982; *Police and State in Prussia*, 1989), and Greg Marquis' *A History of the Canadian Association of Chiefs of Police* (1993).

State control may indeed be a heavily nuanced subject. On the one hand, it may be exercised by the elite, but it often requires tacit approval by large sections of society. On the other hand, most violence is actually at the expense of the working classes, both in terms of physical injury and property damage. Since these people are in the least favorable position to recoup their losses, we must also see that, according to Stanley Cohen's *Visions of Social Control* (1985) and *Labour, Law and Crime* (1987) edited by Francis Snyder and Douglas Hay, they fear the "dangerous" elements among themselves as much, if not more, than the elites above them who have at their hands the means for defending life and property – arms, money, and government. Too often the history of crime is written with little regard to class or race.

Thus it is interesting to note that there is little contemporary work that looks historically at crimes of the well-to-do, such as the "white collar" crime that is being studied in today's society. These crimes were given great scope with the development of the nation-state and its bureaucracies, contracts, commerce, and promotion of industrialization, and through the technological revolution. Moreover, as George Robb noted in *White-Collar Crime in Modern England* (1992), the sources of these crimes are seldom found in the records of the state. They are discovered more often in the records of private and public companies, and in the interstices of legitimate and fraudulent business practices. David Johnson suggested in *Illegal Tender* (1995) that the investigation of such crimes is often driven as much by political agendas and bureaucratic conflict as it is by scientific technology.

More work is needed on the roles played by non-statal organizations in the informal criminal justice system that affects definitions of crime and criminal prosecutions. For example, John A. Davis' *Conflict and Control* (1988) and Steven C. Hughes' *Crime, Disorder and the Risorgimento* (1994) suggested that the Mafia in Italy can be seen not only as organized groups of criminals committing crimes, but also as 1) mediators in disputes who maintain the older, traditional forms of honor and socioeconomic status, and 2) as a collective force to keep the peace on the streets and in the workplace. Brigands in Italy and Spain can be seen in the same roles, as can the Robin Hood tradition in England, gunslingers in the United States, and bandits in Mexico and South America. At times these people are simply groups who are so labelled by the state for the purpose of extinguishing them. Their activities are little different from the use of violence by authorities of the state to maintain the exercise of fear over a segment of the population, thereby legitimizing violent crime. Examples would include the Ku Klux Klan in the United States, Hitler's youth gangs in Germany, and the apartheid state in South Africa. Citizens, too, have often accepted state officials using violence on their behalf. *Policing Western Europe* (1991) edited by Clive Emsley and Barbara Weinberger, David R. Johnson's *Policing the Urban Underworld* (1979), and Wilbur Miller's *Cops and Bobbies* (1977) all included examples of this phenomena, which could also include the gendarmes in France and the police in the United States.

Once crime has been defined and its parameters explored, long-term trends in the history of criminality can be established. An early debate centered on Ted Robert Gurr's "Historical Trends in Violent Crime" (1981), Lawrence Stone's "Interpersonal Violence in English Society" (1983), and J.A. Sharpe's critique of Stone in *Past and Present* (1985). Recorded serious crime per person rose from the 15th century to the early 17th, then went into a long decline until the late 18th or early 19th century. There was then no clear pattern until the mid- or late 19th century, when it began a gradual increase that is now approaching the early 17th-century peak. Terence Morris' *Crime and Criminal Justice since 1945* (1989) suggested that the real increase, however, has been since World War II. Given the rich archival studies that have been undertaken since the early 1980s, the time has come for another debate.

There are, however, several problems with this paradigm. First, homicide may not be the best index of criminality for the long durée, and, as J.S. Cockburn demonstrated in "Patterns of Violence in English Society" (1991), the real trend may be somewhat different. Moreover, it has been shown, in *Crime and the Law* (1980) edited by V.A.C. Gatrell, Bruce Lenman, and Geoffrey Parker, that the great decrease in capital crimes between 1600 and 1800 was accompanied by an equally significant increase in petty crimes. There are also other indicators that may be even more important than homicides. Domestic violence, for example, was not a crime at all before the late 19th century. In some countries – such as Britain and the United States – the police were told not to become involved in family disputes down to the early 1990s.

Another element of criminality involves class. The old paradigm of crime as an activity of the poor or unemployed against the "propertied," and the resulting theory of the criminal law as a tool of the state to maintain class control and the supremacy of the elite, has not been challenged sufficiently. The "Warwick School," with its influence on the profession still significant, can be seen in E.P. Thompson's *Whigs and Hunters* (1975), *Albion's Fatal Tree* (1975) edited by Douglas Hay, and Dag Lindström and Eva Österberg's *Crime and Social Control in Medieval and Early Modern Swedish Towns* (1988). Crime as an innate element of the human condition involves a large proportion of the "unpropertied" committing crimes against themselves or the land (as in such property crimes as the theft of wood), just as the elite does to one another (such as the ancient duel or the modern stock fraud).

What is needed, perhaps, are some new theories of criminality to explain record evidence for the role of class, occupation, and gender in recorded criminality. Recent studies such as Nancy Stepan's *"The Hour of Eugenics"* (1991) have begun to emerge on both occupational and gender crime, and there is considerable room for the development of the larger view in both Europe and the Americas. Malcolm Feeley's "The Decline of Women in the Criminal Process" (1994) contributed to the current debate on the question of female versus male criminality in the long durée. While this is an extremely controversial topic, considerable research has appeared in Elaine Abelson's *When Ladies Go A-Thieving* (1989), Judith Allen's *Sex and Secrets*, and Lucia Zedner's *Women, Crime and Custody in Victorian England* (1991), and in other work, as more young scholars become engaged in this topic.

Criminality has been linked increasingly to poverty, as well as to place: to pockets of society, groups of people, districts of cities, and the rural countryside. In other words, criminality is being found to be situationally determined. As Emsley demonstrated in *Crime and Society in England* (1987), work on collective action, protest, and "social crime" in national contexts in the past two decades has necessitated the creation of alternative definitions. The cunning woman in England, the *muchachos* and *caballeristas* in Spain, the *strollica* in Italy, the *znakhar* in Russia, the *caudillo* in Mexico, and the role of *charivari* and *samosud* as cultural artefacts reflect the complex structure of social relations and order on the rural landscape. Moreover, the emphasis on the impact of industrialization and urbanization has perhaps been overdone. A peasant, or working-class, *mentalité* incorporates their recourse to, and participation in, the law as well as serving the grist of much of its operation.

There has also been considerable work on the "marginal" groups at the fringe of traditional criminality, ranging from women and children to non-conformists, the insane, and the mentally "disordered" in Roger Lane's *Violent Death in the City* (1979), David Rothman's *Conscience and Convenience* (1980), Michael MacDonald and Terence Murphy's *Sleepless Souls* (1990), Lucia Zedner's *Women, Crime and Custody*, and Andrew Scull's *The Most Solitary of Afflictions* (1993). Decades of active research on witchcraft have provided ideas and methods for the study of more modern forms of marginalization in Richard Evans' *The German Underworld* (1988), Michael Kunze's *Highroad to the Stake* (1987), and Brian Levack's *The Witch-Hunt in Early Modern Europe* (1987). Moreover, the life of indigenous peoples living under their colonizers or conquerors has complicated the problem of crime in modern society.

Other groups have been equally determined to maintain their rights and their cultures. Examining criminality in a broader perspective, pioneering books for American society include Lawrence Friedman and Robert Percival's *The Roots of Justice* (1981) and the award-winning *The Transformation of Criminal Justice* (1989) of Allen Steinberg. This has encouraged more comparative studies at a sociolegal and geographic level on crime as a phenomenon of borderlands, for example, *Law for the Elephant, Law for the Beaver* (1992) edited by John McLaren, Hamar Foster, and Chet Orloff. Richard Brown's *No Duty to Retreat* (1991), John Phillip Reid's "The Layers of Western Legal History" (1992), and Louis Knafla's "Violence on the Western Canadian Frontier" (1995), have contributed to the further study of crime and violence at the apex of the western North American frontier.

Considerations such as these lie at the heart of the historiography of crime and criminal justice in Europe and the Americas as well as in Asia and the Pacific. In *Crime History* Emsley and Knafla argued that what is needed is not only specialized research into localities and nation-states, but also thought and ideas that will eventually form the bridges that link the experiences of peoples and societies laterally. There have been a number of recent attempts to establish such links, including the work of anthropologists and criminologists as well as historians and lawyers; for example, David Anderson and David Killingray's *Policing the Empire* (1991), Paula Byrne's *Criminal Law and the Colonial Subject* (1993), and Louis Knafla and Susan Binnie's *Law, Society, and the State* (1995). These links and experiences can be analyzed from late medieval times into the early 19th century, and from the emergence of the state out of the communal worlds of a rural environment to the worlds of the Enlightenment, Revolution, and the modern bureaucratic nation-state.

Finally, the subject of punishment has been dominated by those philosophical works that have examined its history. The writings of Antonio Gramsci and Michel Foucault are prominent

in this regard. They have provided broad, interpretive sweeps, but are not research oriented. Current studies, however, reveal a shift to the history of punishment based on archival work. Fascinating histories of executions are found in Pieter Spierenburg's *The Spectacle of Suffering* (1984), V.A.C. Gatrell's *The Hanging Tree* (1994), and Richard Evans' *Rituals of Retribution* (1996). The history of prisons, however, is developing into one of the most highly sophisticated areas. Prominent examples of different forms of incarceration from several countries include Alan Frost's *Botany Bay Mirages* (1994), David Garland's *Punishment and Modern Society* (1990), Michael Stephen Hindus' *Prison and Plantation* (1980), Estelle Freedman's *Their Sisters' Keepers* (1981), Lawrence Friedman and Robert Percival's *The Roots of Justice*, Michael Ignatieff's *A Just Measure of Pain* (1978), David Philips and Susanne Davies' *A Nation of Rogues?* (1994), Alexander Pisciotta's *Benevolent Repression* (1994), John Pratt's *Punishment in a Perfect Society* (1992), Nicole Rafter's *Partial Justice* (1985), Philippe Robert and René Lévy's "Histoire et question pénale" (1985), Pieter Spierenburg's *The Prison Experience* (1991), Richard van Dülmen's *Theater des Schreckens* (1985; *Theatre of Horror*, 1990), and André Zysberg's *Les Galériens* (Galley Slaves, 1987). These works reveal not only how far the field has advanced in this decade, but also what a rich historical tradition has been established for future writers.

LOUIS A. KNAFLA

See also Brazil; Davis, N.; Furnivall; Italy: since the Renaissance; Legal; Ortiz; Radzinowicz; Rudé; Thompson, E.

Further Reading

Abelson, Elaine S., *When Ladies Go A-Thieving: Middle Class Shoplifters in the Victorian Department Store*, Oxford and New York: Oxford University Press, 1989
Allen, Judith, *Sex and Secrets: Crimes Involving Australian Women since 1880*, Melbourne, Oxford, and New York: Oxford University Press, 1990
Anderson, David M., and David Killingray, eds., *Policing the Empire: Government, Authority, and Control*, Manchester: Manchester University Press, 1991
Arnold, David, *Police Power and Colonial Rule: Madras, 1859–1947*, Delhi, Oxford, and New York: Oxford University Press, 1986
Beattie, John Maurice, *Crime and the Courts in England, 1660–1800*, Princeton: Princeton University Press, and Oxford: Oxford University Press, 1986
Brown, Richard Maxwell, *No Duty to Retreat: Violence and Values in American History and Society*, New York: Oxford University Press, 1991
Brown, Richard Maxwell, "Law and Order on the American Frontier: The Western Civil War of Incorporation," in John McLaren, Hamar Foster, and Chet Orloff, eds., *Law for the Elephant, Law for the Beaver: Essays in the Legal History of the North American West*, Regina, Saskatchewan: Canadian Plains Research Center, University of Regina, and Pasadena, CA: Ninth Judicial Circuit Historical Society, 1992
Byrne, Paula J., *Criminal Law and the Colonial Subject: New South Wales, 1810–1830*, Cambridge and New York: Cambridge University Press, 1993
Cockburn, J.S., "Patterns of Violence in English Society: Homicide in Kent, 1560–1985," *Past and Present* 130 (1991), 70–106
Cohen, Stanley, *Visions of Social Control: Crime, Punishment and Classification*, Cambridge: Polity Press, and New York: Blackwell, 1985

Davis, John A., *Conflict and Control: Law and Order in Nineteenth Century Italy*, Basingstoke: Macmillan, and Atlantic Highlands, NJ: Humanities Press, 1988

Dülmen, Richard van, *Theater des Schreckens: Gerichtspraxis und Strafrituale in der frühen Neuzeit*, Munich: Beck, 1985; in English as *Theatre of Horror: Crime and Punishment in Early Modern Germany*, Cambridge: Polity Press, and Cambridge, MA: Blackwell, 1990

Egmond, Florike, *Underworlds: Organized Crime in the Netherlands, 1650–1800*, Cambridge: Polity Press, 1993

Emsley, Clive, *Crime and Society in England, 1750–1900*, London and New York: Longmans, 1987

Emsley, Clive, and Barbara Weinberger, eds., *Policing Western Europe: Politics, Professionalization and Public Order, 1850–1940*, New York: Greenwood Press, 1991

Emsley, Clive, and Louis A. Knafla, *Crime History and Histories of Crime: Studies in the Historiography of Crime and Criminal Justice in Modern History*, Westport, CT: Greenwood Press, 1996

Evans, Richard J., ed., *The German Underworld: Deviants and Outcasts in German History*, London and New York: Routledge, 1988

Evans, Richard J., *Rituals of Retribution: Capital Punishment in Germany, 1600–1987*, Oxford and New York: Oxford University Press, 1996

Feeley, Malcolm, "The Decline of Women in the Criminal Process: A Comparative Study," *Criminal Justice History* 15 (1994), 235–74

Finnane, Mark, ed., *Policing in Australia: Historical Perspectives*, Kensington: New South Wales University Press, 1987

Foucault, Michel, *Surveiller et punir: naissance de la prison*, Paris: Gallimard, 1975; in English as *Discipline and Punish: The Birth of the Prison*, New York: Pantheon, and London: Allen Lane, 1977

Freedman, Estelle B., *Their Sisters' Keepers: Women's Prison Reform in America, 1830–1930*, Ann Arbor: University of Michigan Press, 1981

Friedman, Lawrence M., and Robert V. Percival, *The Roots of Justice: Crime and Punishment in Alameda County, California, 1870–1910*, Chapel Hill: University of North Carolina Press, 1981

Friedman, Lawrence M., *Crime and Punishment in American History*, New York: Basic Books, 1993

Frost, Alan, *Botany Bay Mirages: Illusions of Australia's Convict Beginnings*, Carlton: Melbourne University Press, 1994

Garland, David, *Punishment and Modern Society: A Study in Social Theory*, Chicago: University of Chicago Press, and Oxford: Oxford University Press, 1990

Garnot, Benoît, *Histoire et criminalité de l'antiquité au XXe siècle: nouvelles approches* (History and Criminality from Antiquity to the 20th Century: New Approaches), Dijon: Editions Universitaires de Dijon, 1992

Gatrell, V.A.C., Bruce Lenman, and Geoffrey Parker, eds., *Crime and the Law: The Social History of Crime in Western Europe since 1500*, London: Europa, 1980

Gatrell, V.A.C., *The Hanging Tree: Execution and the English People, 1770–1868*, Oxford and New York: Oxford University Press, 1994

Gramsci, Antonio, *Quaderni del carcere*, 6 vols., written 1926–37, published Turin: Einaudi, 1948–51, critical edition, 4 vols., 1975; in English as *Selections from the Prison Notebooks*, London: Lawrence and Wishart, 1971, New York: International Publishers, 1972

Gurr, Ted Robert, "Historical Trends in Violent Crime: A Critical Review of the Evidence," *Crime and Justice* 3 (1981), 295–353

Hay, Douglas *et al.*, eds., *Albion's Fatal Tree: Crime and Society in Eighteenth-Century England*, New York: Pantheon, and London: Allen Lane, 1975

Hay, Douglas, and Francis G. Snyder, eds., *Policing and Prosecution in Britain, 1750–1850*, Oxford and New York: Oxford University Press, 1980

Hill, R.S., *Policing the Colonial Frontier: The Theory and Practice of Coercive Social and Racial Control in New Zealand, 1767–1867*, Wellington: Ward, 1986

Hindus, Michael Stephen, *Prison and Plantation: Crime, Justice, and Authority in Massachusetts and South Carolina, 1767–1878*, Chapel Hill: University of North Carolina Press, 1980

Hughes, Steven C., *Crime, Disorder and the Risorgimento: The Politics of Policing in Bologna*, Cambridge and New York: Cambridge University Press, 1994

Ignatieff, Michael, *A Just Measure of Pain: The Penitentiary in the Industrial Revolution*, London: Macmillan, and New York: Pantheon, 1978

Johnson, David R., *Policing the Urban Underworld: The Impact of Crime on the Development of American Policing, 1800–1887*, Philadelphia: Temple University Press, 1979

Johnson, David R., *Illegal Tender: Counterfeiting and the Secret Service in Nineteenth-Century America*, Washington, DC: Smithsonian Institution Press, 1995

Knafla, Louis A., and Susan Binnie, *Law, Society, and the State: Essays in Modern Legal History*, Toronto and Buffalo: University of Toronto Press, 1995

Knafla, Louis A., "Violence on the Western Canadian Frontier: A Historical Perspective," in Jeffrey Ian Ross, ed., *Violence in Canada: Sociopolitical Perspectives*, Don Mills, Ontario and New York: Oxford University Press, 1995

Kunze, Michael, *Highroad to the Stake: A Tale of Witchcraft*, Chicago: University of Chicago Press, 1987

Lane, Roger, *Violent Death in the City: Suicide, Accident and Murder in Nineteenth-Century Philadelphia*, Cambridge, MA: Harvard University Press, 1979

Levack, Brian P., *The Witch-Hunt in Early Modern Europe*, London and New York: Longmans, 1987

Lindström, Dag, and Eva Österberg, *Crime and Social Control in Medieval and Early Modern Swedish Towns*, Stockholm: Almqvist & Wiksell, 1988

Lüdtke, Alf, *"Gemeinwohl," Polizei und "Festungspraxis": staatliche Gewaltsamkeit und innere Verwaltung in Preussen, 1815–1850*, Göttingen: Vanderhoeck & Ruprecht, 1982; in English as *Police and State in Prussia, 1815–1850*, Cambridge and New York: Cambridge University Press, 1989

MacDonald, Michael, and Terence R. Murphy, *Sleepless Souls: Suicide in Early Modern England*, Oxford and New York: Oxford University Press, 1990

McLaren, John, Hamar Foster, and Chet Orloff, eds., *Law for the Elephant, Law for the Beaver: Essays in the Legal History of the North American West*, Regina, Saskatchewan: Canadian Plains Research Center, University of Regina, and Pasadena, CA: Ninth Judicial Circuit Historical Society, 1992

Marquis, Greg, *A History of the Canadian Association of Chiefs of Police*, Toronto and Buffalo: University of Toronto Press, 1993

Miller, Wilbur R., *Cops and Bobbies: Police Authority in New York and London, 1830–1870*, Chicago: University of Chicago Press, 1977

Monkkonen, Eric H., ed., *Crime and Justice in American History: The Colonies and the Early Republic*, 2 vols., Westport, CT: Meckler, 1991

Morris, Terence, *Crime and Criminal Justice since 1945*, Oxford and New York: Blackwell, 1989

Philips, David, and Susanne Davies, *A Nation of Rogues? Crime, Law, and Punishment in Colonial Australia*, Carlton: Melbourne University Press, 1994

Phillips, Jim, Tina Loo, and Susan Lewthwaite, eds., *Crime and Criminal Justice: Essays in the History of Canadian Law*, Toronto and Buffalo: University of Toronto Press, 1994

Pisciotta, Alexander W., *Benevolent Repression: Social Control and the American Reformatory-Prison Movement*, New York: New York University Press, 1994

Pratt, John, *Punishment in a Perfect Society: The New Zealand Penal System, 1840–1939*, Wellington: Victoria University Press, 1992

Quetelet, Adolphe, *Recherches sur la population, les naissances, les décès, les prisons, les dépôts de mendicité, etc. das le royaume des Pays-Bas* (Research on the Population, Births, Deaths, Prisons, Medical Provision, etc., of the Low Countries), Brussels: Tarlier, 1827

Rafter, Nicole Hahn, *Partial Justice: Women in State Prisons, 1800–1935*, Boston: Northeastern University Press, 1985; London: Transaction, 1990

Reid, John Phillip, "The Layers of Western Legal History," in John McLaren, Hamar Foster, and Chet Orloff, eds., *Law for the Elephant, Law for the Beaver: Essays in the Legal History of the North American West*, Regina, Saskatchewan: Canadian Plains Research Center, University of Regina, and Pasadena, CA: Ninth Judicial Circuit Historical Society, 1992

Robb, George, *White-Collar Crime in Modern England: Financial Fraud and Business Morality, 1845–1929*, Cambridge and New York: Cambridge University Press, 1992

Robert, Philippe, and René Levy, "Histoire et question pénale," *Revue d'histoire moderne et contemporaine* 32 (1985), 481–526

Rose, Lionel, *Massacre of the Innocents: Infanticide in Great Britain, 1800–1939*, London and New York: Routledge, 1986

Rothman, David, *Conscience and Convenience: The Asylum and Its Alternatives in Progressive America*, Boston: Little Brown, 1980

Rousseau, Xavier, "Criminality and Criminal Justice History in Europe, 1250–1850: A Select Bibliography," *Criminal Justice History* 14 (1993), 159–81

Schnapper, Bernard, *Voies nouvelles en histoire du droit: la justice, la famille, la répression pénale, XVIe–XXe siècles* (New Paths in the History of Law: Justice, Family, and Penal Repression, 16th–20th Centuries), Paris: Presses universitaires de France, 1991

Scull, Andrew, and Stanley Cohen, eds., *Social Control and the State: Historical and Comparative Essays*, Oxford: Blackwell, and New York: St. Martin's Press, 1983

Scull, Andrew, *The Most Solitary of Afflictions: Madness and Society in Britain, 1700–1900*, New Haven and London: Yale University Press, 1993

Sharpe, James A., *Crime in Early Modern England, 1550–1750*, London and New York: Longman, 1984

Sharpe, James A., and Lawrence Stone, "Debate: The History of Violence in England," *Past and Present* 108 (1985), 206–24

Slatta, Richard, *Cowboys of the Americas*, New Haven and London: Yale University Press, 1990

Snyder, Francis G., and Douglas Hay, eds., *Labour, Law and Crime: An Historical Perspective*, London and New York: Tavistock, 1987

Spierenburg, Pieter, ed., *The Emergence of Carceral Institutions: Prisons, Galleys and Lunatic Asylums, 1550–1900*, Rotterdam: Erasmus University Press, 1984

Spierenburg, Pieter, *The Spectacle of Suffering: Executions and the Evolution of Repression: From a Preindustrial Metropolis to the European Experience*, Cambridge and New York: Cambridge University Press, 1984

Spierenburg, Pieter, ed., *The Prison Experience: Disciplinary Institutions and Their Inmates in Early Modern Europe*, New Brunswick, NJ: Rutgers University Press, 1991

Steinberg, Allen, *The Transformation of Criminal Justice: Philadelphia, 1800–1880*, Chapel Hill: University of North Carolina Press, 1989

Stepan, Nancy Leys, *"The Hour of Eugenics": Race, Gender, and Nation in Latin America*, Ithaca, NY: Cornell University Press, 1991

Stone, Lawrence, "Interpersonal Violence in English Society, 1300–1980," *Past and Present* 101 (1983), 22–33

Thompson, E.P., *Whigs and Hunters: The Origin of the Black Act*, London: Allen Lane, and New York: Pantheon, 1975

Tilly, Charles, "Reflections on the History of European State-Making," in Charles Tilly, ed., *The Formation of National States in Western Europe*, Princeton: Princeton University Press, 1975

Tilly, Charles, Louise A. Tilly, and Richard Tilly, *The Rebellious Century, 1830–1930*, Cambridge, MA: Harvard University Press, 1975

Vigier, Philippe, ed., *Maintien de l'ordre et polices en France et en Europe au XIXe siècle* (The Maintenance or Order and Policing in France and Europe from the 19th Century), Paris: Créaphis, 1987

Walkowitz, Judith R., *City of Dreadful Delight: Narratives of Sexual Danger in Late-Victorian London*, Chicago: University of Chicago Press, and London: Virago, 1992

Weaver, John C., *Crimes, Constables, and Courts: Order and Transgression in a Canadian City, 1816–1970*, Montreal: McGill–Queen's University Press, 1995

Weller, Robert P., and Scott Evan Guggenheim, eds., *Power and Protest in the Countryside: Studies of Rural Protest in Asia, Europe, and Latin America*, Durham, NC: Duke University Press, 1982

Woolf, Stuart, ed., *The Poor in Western Europe in the Eighteenth and Nineteenth Centuries*, London and New York: Methuen, 1986

Zedner, Lucia, *Women, Crime and Custody in Victorian England*, Oxford and New York: Oxford University Press, 1991

Zehr, Howard, *Crime and the Development of Modern Society: Patterns of Criminality in Nineteenth-Century Germany and France*, London: Croom Helm, and Totowa, NJ: Rowman and Littlefield, 1976

Zysberg, André, *Les Galériens: vies et destin de 60,000 forçats sur les galères de France, 1680–1748* (Galley Slaves: Lives and Destiny of 60,000 Convicts in the Galleys of France, 1680–1748), Paris: Seuil, 1987

Croce, Benedetto 1866–1952
Italian philosopher and historian

Perhaps Italy's foremost spokesperson on matters of philosophy, history, art, and literary studies in the first half of the 20th century, the figure of Benedetto Croce became synonymous with intellectual endeavor in humanist disciplines and unrelenting opposition to the Italian fascist regime. His notorious phrase "all true history is contemporary history" reflects his brand of historicism that sees historical consciousness as the supreme form of knowledge and the role of the historian as actively investing history with meaning by moral, ethical, and political responses to her/his present circumstances and philosophical speculation on historical development. This "absolute historicism," as he called it, rests upon Croce's view of human development as an ever-creative process that reacts against incessant flux and change. The principles of coherence in history were to be found in the cognitive procedures of the historian who worked in the knowable present and who thereby unified the universal and the particular. Croce's theories collapsed philosophy into the category of history and proposed new responsibilities for historians as intellectuals that gave them a pre-eminent role in cultural life.

Croce belonged to a generation of Italian intellectuals (such as the philosopher Giovanni Gentile, the historian Gaetano Salvemini, the economist Luigi Einaudi, the radical priest Romolo Murri, the writer Giovanni Papini, the poet-artist Ardengo Soffici) that came to prominence in the Giolittian period of Italian politics (1901–14) and heralded a crusade of "Neo-liberalism" against what they saw as the prevalent materialism of their epoch with its resultant debasement of life wrought by the processes of industrialization, modernization, and the attendant doctrines of positivism, socialism, and democracy. Like many others of his time, Croce was schooled with a classical humanist education that seemed ill-fitted to the opportunities offered to the technocrats and industrial workers in a rapidly changing Italian society that left unemployed and educated middle classes ready to vent their anger and frustration in print. Scorning the university culture of his day, especially academic philosophy, Croce embarked upon a program of self-instruction and participation in debate which resulted in his corpus of 4659 individual writings that comprised books, articles, reviews, and letters on the subjects of philosophy, literature, and history, often scattered throughout various newspapers and journals, but especially in *La Critica*, the journal which he founded himself in 1903.

Croce's philosophical treatises culminated in what he called the "philosophy of the spirit" which he developed over a series of works from the beginning of the century to the 1920s. The theory is based on rationalist principles of classical Romantic philosophy in attempting to create a homogenous and all-encompassing "system" that could accommodate every human endeavor to understand both the physical universe and the social world. The main principle of the "spirit" (that is, human consciousness) is its circularity within the structure of a system formed by constraints of aesthetics, logic, economics, ethics, and historical time.

Croce eventually abandoned the schematism of these earlier works in response to more profound attempts to explore methodological considerations of history and historiography. His *La storia come pensiero e come azione* (1938; *History as the Story of Liberty*, 1941) signaled his apotheosis of history as the supreme meditative subject for all philosophical inquiry. In this work, and later expounded more fully in *Filosofia, poesia, storia* (1951; *Philosophy, Poetry, History*, 1966), can be found Croce's doctrine of "absolute historicism," where the "spirit" is considered to be completely spontaneous and free of predetermined structure, but becomes manifest in the flow of historical action and thought. His insistence on the spirituality and essential creativity of the human agent in history led him to argue that written history must in turn be committed and personal in its exposition of human development, and that the historian must eschew pretensions of being detached or scientific. The humanistic philosophical foundations of Croce's view of the primarily ethical nature of the historian's task often isolated him from more systemizing theoreticians such as the schools of German historicism or the Marxists, the latter of whom, especially Antonio Gramsci, dismissed Croce's work as an example of outdated conservatism and elitist oratory.

The practical results of Croce's historical theorizing and exhortation of ethical-political historiography can be seen in the histories he wrote in the interwar period and in his obvious protest against the fascist regime and the contemporary currents of political and historical thought. His *Storia del regno di Napoli* (1925; *History of the Kingdom of Naples*, 1970) argued against positivistic historical accounts that colored explanations of the poverty of southern Italy with quasi-naturalistic theories of land use, climate, and racial characteristics. Croce instead highlighted the existence of a Neapolitan civic tradition that flowed into unified Italy and exhorted the Neapolitan intellectual and political elite to recognize and capitalize upon the positive aspects of their past (hence his history as "preparing action"). The *Storia del storiografia italiana nel secolo decimonono* (The History of Italian Historiography in the 19th Century, 1921) was written to counter fascism's denigration of the preceding liberal period. Croce tried to show that despite its faults Italian political liberalism had its achievements and respectability, and that the cultural phenomena which led to fascism (romantic decadence, nationalism, imperialism, political radicalism, and violence) were not exclusive to Italy but common to all of Europe. The invitation to take up the liberal agenda once again was further expressed in the *Storia d'Europa nel secolo decimonono* (1932; *History of Europe in the Nineteenth Century*, 1934), in which the narrative pivots on the decline of the vitality of liberalism in the decades after 1871 and focuses on demonstrating how an intellectual vacuum was filled by the positivistic cults of science and naturalistic determinism which in turn led to the Neoromantic over-reaction evident in Croce's own time. In all of these works there is an attempt to balance a contemporary concern with genuine historical inquiry. *The History of the Kingdom of Naples* is the most successful and most interesting, while the moralizing *History of Europe* appears today as unnecessarily abstract and somewhat vacuous.

Croce's centrality to the intellectual life of Italy from the beginning of the century to the end of World War II has often been characterized as a benevolent dictatorship. His philosophical aloofness from the practical world of politics, his contempt of academic culture, and his uncompromising criticism of others made him many enemies, including a great number contemporary intellectuals and the Catholic church who placed his complete works on the Index in 1932. Croce's propensity to abstraction on the subjects of history and historiography should be understood in the context of his career as an all-round intellectual whose interests in history stemmed from his primary concern with philosophy. For him history was the "matter" of philosophy and philosophy the "method" of history, and he called the concept of "philosophy of history" a "contradictio in adiecto." In 1947 he founded the Istituto Italiano per gli Studi Storici (Italian Institute for Historical Studies) at his home in Naples. His disciples include Raffaello Franchini, Carlo Antoni, Alfredo Parente, and Gennaro Sasso. R.G. Collingwood translated much of Croce's historical theory for the English-speaking world, and Crocean historicism was welcomed by the American historians Carl Becker and Charles Beard who incorporated it into the debates surrounding "New History." International admiration for Croce's work during and after his lifetime, his incessant activity in diverse aspects of Italian cultural life, and his staunch defense of individual rights and liberalism against an oppressive fascist regime have ensured his fame and influence as a historian and a champion of the importance of historical understanding.

NICHOLAS EVERETT

See also Chabod; Collingwood; De Sanctis; Garin; Ginzburg; Gombrich; Gramsci; Halperín-Donghi; Historiology; Italy: Renaissance; Italy: since the Renaissance; Literature; Oral; Renaissance Historical Writing; Romeo; Salvemini; Spriano; White, H.

Biography
Born Pescasseroli, 25 February 1866, to a wealthy family. Lived with his cousin, Silvio Spaventa, statesman/philosopher of the "Historical Right" after his parents' death in an earthquake, 1883.

Educated in Catholic schools, Naples. Founder/editor *La Critica* 1903–43. Married Adele Rossi, 1914 (4 daughters). Died Naples, 20 November 1952.

Principal Writings

Croce's voluminous corpus is difficult to disentangle; many of his works are collections of pieces published previously in *La Critica* and elsewhere. Later editions were often revised and considerably altered by Croce himself. The indispensable bibliographical guides are:

Fausto, Nicolini, ed., *L'"editio ne varietur" delle opere di Benedetto Croce*, Naples: Biblioteca dell'Archivio Storico del Banco di Napoli, 1960

Borsari, Silvano, ed., *L'opera di Benedetto Croce: Bibliografia*, Naples: Istituto Italiano per gli Studi Storici, 1964

Selected works with regard to Croce's philosophy and practice of history:

La rivoluzione napoletana del 1799 (The Neapolitan Revolution of 1799), 1897

Materialismo storico ed economia marxista, 1900; in English as *Historical Materialism and the Economics of Karl Marx*, 1914

Filosofia della pratica, economia ed etica, 1909; in English as *Philosophy of the Practical, Economic and Ethic*, 1913

La Spagna nella vita italiana durante la Rinascenza (Spain in Italian Life during the Renaissance), 1917

Teoria e storia della storiografia, 1917; in English as *Theory and History of Historiography*, 1921, and as *History: Its Theory and Practice*, 1921

Storie e leggende napoletane (Neapolitan Stories and Legends), 1919

Storia della storiografia italiana nel secolo decimonono (The History of Italian Historiography in the 19th Century), 2 vols., 1921

Etica e politica, 1922; selections in English as *The Conduct of Life*, 1924, *An Autobiography*, 1927, and *Politics and Morals*, 1946

Elementi di politica (Elements of Politics), 1925

Storia del regno di Napoli, 1925; in English as *History of the Kingdom of Naples*, 1970

Uomini e cose della vecchia Italia (Men and Facts of Old Italy), 2 vols., 1927

Storia d'Italia dal 1871 al 1915, 1928; in English as *A History of Italy, 1871–1915*, 1929

Storia dell'età barocca in Italia (History of the Baroque Age in Italy), 1929

Storia d'Europa nel secolo decimonono, 1932; in English as *History of Europe in the Nineteenth Century*, 1934

Vite di avventure, di fede e di passione (Lives of Adventure, Faith, and Passion), 1936

La storia come pensiero e come azione, 1938; in English as *History as the Story of Liberty*, 1941

Il carattere della filosofia moderna (The Nature of Modern Philosophy), 1941

Per la nuova vita dell'Italia (For the New Life of Italy), 1944

Discorsi di varia filosofia, 2 vols., 1945; selections in English as *My Philosophy, and Other Essays on the Moral and Political Problems of Our Time*, 1949

Pagine politiche (Political Pages), 1945

Pensiero politico e politica attuale (Political Theory and Contemporary Politics), 1946

Due anni di vita politica italiana (Two Years of Italian Political Life), 1948

Quando l'Italia era tagliata in due (estratto di un diario), 1948; in English as *Croce, the King and the Allies: Extracts from a Diary, July 1943–June 1944*, 1950

Filosofia e storiografia (Philosophy and Historiography), 1949

Filosofia, poesia, storia: pagine tratte da tutte le opere, 1951; in English as *Philosophy, Poetry, History: An Anthology of Essays*, 1966

Scritti e discorsi politici (1943–1947) (Political Writings and Speeches), 1963

Further Reading

Badaloni, Nicola, and Carlo Muscetta, *Labriola, Croce, Gentile*, Rome: Laterza, 1977

Bausola, Adriano, *Filosofia e storia nel pensiero crociano* (Philosophy and History in Croce's Thought), Milan: Vita e Pensiero, 1965

Bazzoli, Maurizio, *Fonti del pensiero politico di Benedetto Croce* (Sources of Benedetto Croce's Political Thought), Milan: Marzorati, 1971

Benedetti, Ulisse, *Benedetto Croce e il fascismo* (Benedetto Croce and Fascism), Rome: Volpe, 1967

Biscione, Michele, *Interpreti di Croce* (Interpreters of Croce), Naples: Giannini, 1968

Boulay, Charles, *Benedetto Croce jusqu' en 1911: trente ans de vie intellectuelle* (Benedetto Croce up to 1911: Thirty Years of Intellectual Life), Geneva: Droz, 1981

Caponigri, A. Robert, *History and Liberty: The Historical Writings of Benedetto Croce*, London: Routledge, 1955

Carini, Carlo, *Benedetto Croce e il partito politico* (Benedetto Croce and the Political Party), Florence: Olschki, 1975

Caserta, Ernesto G., "Croce and Marxism," *Journal of the History of Ideas* 44 (1983), 141–49

Ceccarini, Ennio, ed., *Benedetto Croce: la storia, la libertà* (Benedetto Croce: History, Freedom), Rome: Edizione della Voce, 1967

Coli, Daniela, *Croce, Laterza e la cultura europea* (Croce, Laterza, and European Culture), Bologna: Mulino, 1983

De Gennaro, Angelo A., *The Philosophy of Benedetto Croce: An Introduction*, New York: Citadel Press, 1961

Gramsci, Antonio, *Il materialismo storico e la filosofia di Benedetto Croce* (Historical Materialism and the Philosophy of Benedetto Croce), Turin: Einaudi, 1948

Jacobitti, Edmund E., "Hegemony before Gramsci: The Case of Benedetto Croce," *Journal of Modern History* 52 (March 1980), 66–84

Jacobitti, Edmund E., *Revolutionary Humanism and Historicism in Modern Italy*, New Haven: Yale University Press, 1981

Leone de Castris, Arcangelo, *Croce, Lukács, Della Volpe: Estetica ed egemonia nella cultura del Novecento* (Croce, Lukács, Della Volpe: Aesthetics and Hegemony in the Culture of the 19th Century), Bari: De Donato, 1978

Leone de Castris, Arcangelo, *Egemonia e fascismo: il problema degli intellettuali negli anni Trenta* (Hegemony and Fascism: The Problems of Intellectuals in the 1930s), Bologna: Mulino, 1981

Mack Smith, Denis, "Benedetto Croce: History and Politics," *Journal of Contemporary History* 8 (1973), 41–61

Murray, Gilbert, Maulio Brosio, and Guido Calagero, eds., *Benedetto Croce: A Commemoration*, London: Istituto Italiano di Cultura, 1953

Palmer, Lucie M., and Henry S. Harris, eds., *Thought, Action and Intuition: A Symposium on the Philosophy of Benedetto Croce*, Hildesheim and New York: Olms, 1975

Pois, Robert A., "Two Poles within Historicism: Croce and Meinecke," *Journal of the History of Ideas* 31 (1970), 253–72

Roberts, David D., *Benedetto Croce and the Uses of Historicism*, Berkeley: University of California Press, 1987

Sasso, Gennaro, *Benedetto Croce: la ricerca della dialettica* (Benedetto Croce: The Research of Dialectics), Naples: Morano, 1975

Setta, Sandro, *Croce, il liberalismo e l'Italia post-fascista* (Croce, Liberalism, and Post-Fascist Italy), Rome: Bonacci, 1979

Sprigge, Cecil, *Benedetto Croce: Man and Thinker*, New Haven: Yale University Press, and Cambridge: Bowes and Bowes, 1952

Valiani, Leo, *Fra Croce e Omodeo: storia e storiografia nella lotta per la libertà* (Between Croce and Omodeo: History and Historiography in the Struggle for Freedom), Florence: Le Monnier, 1984

White, Hayden V., "The Abiding Relevance of Croce's Idea of History," *Journal of Modern History* 35 (1963), 109–24

White, Hayden V., *Metahistory: The Historical Imagination in Nineteenth-Century Europe*, Baltimore: John Hopkins University Press, 1973, 375–425

Crosby, Alfred W., Jr. 1931–

US environmental historian

The publication of Alfred W. Crosby's *The Columbian Exchange* (1972) marked a major turning point in the study of European expansion, indigenous-newcomer relations, and environmental history. Rarely has a single book had such a profound and sweeping impact on so many different parts of the historical profession. Although written primarily about North and Central America, *The Columbian Exchange* raised methodological and conceptual questions of relevance throughout the world. As such, this seminal study attracted international attention and marked the emergence of a major new historian.

The Columbian Exchange is a simple story, based on unique insight and told in a manner that is at once convincing and accessible. Historians had, before Crosby, been studying the question of the impact of epidemic disease on North American indigenous populations and were engaged in a lengthy and complex debate about the number and distribution of pre-European contact peoples. There had, as well, been a small number of commentaries about other ecological transitions attending the arrival of the Europeans, such as the introduction of the horse and other livestock by early explorers and settlers. Crosby brought these disparate strands together and added additional questions and observations. He examined, in an admittedly preliminary fashion, the impact of European diseases on indigenous peoples and the possibility that syphilis was transported from North America to Europe. His studies of the impact of introduced animals, birds, and plants, and his equally insightful comments about the consequences of taking North American plants to Europe, opened up a vital field of historical inquiry. Crosby's ideas were of particular importance in the field of indigenous history, where the concept of the "Columbian exchange" helped explain many of the difficult transitions faced by indigenous peoples in the first years of European encounter.

Crosby's work emerged at a time of growing environmental awareness and, of equal importance, when world historians were expanding their analysis of the connections between peoples and continents. Through *The Columbian Exchange*, Crosby challenged scholars to take this analysis to its most fundamental level, and to investigate the biological transitions and transformations that attended human movements. Crosby broadened his investigations, working on a more comprehensive study, *Ecological Imperialism*, which he published in 1986. This study was more sweeping in scope, but built directly on the lines of analysis brought forward in his first work in the field. Most significantly, and reflecting the benefits of extensive international research, Crosby's new book provided numerous non-North American examples of the relevance of global connections in environmental history. He continued his investigations in the field of environmental history, publishing *Germs, Seeds, and Animals* in 1994 as well as a study of the 1918 influenza epidemic. Through these works, and the continuing interest expressed in his studies of ecological imperialism, Crosby established himself as one of the world's leading environmental historians.

Crosby's next work took him in a substantially different direction. In 1997, he published *The Measure of Reality*, in which he examined the transitions in mathematical thought and expression and connected these developments to the expansion of Europe. Crosby argued that quantification permitted radically different analyses of reality and that developments in visualization allowed for profoundly important representations of those understandings. These developments in quantification provided Europeans with a unique combination of the abstract and practical, the conceptual and the representational, which aided in their efforts to understand and then explore the broader world. As with his earlier studies in ecological history, Crosby sought to explain a broad phenomenon – the scientific and commercial evolution of Europe – through comprehensive and multigenerational assessments.

Crosby has contributed a series of valuable studies to the growing fields of environmental, scientific, and world history. His work is sweeping in nature, seeking to find understanding in broad patterns and comparative aspects rather than in detailed studies of a specific case. As such, it carries with it all the strengths and weaknesses of bold generalizations and global analysis. Particularly through *The Columbian Exchange*, *Ecological Imperialism*, and *The Measure of Reality*, Crosby has attempted to explain several of the key themes in world history. While his work never claimed to provide all of the answers, Crosby did, in a manner that is both unique and vital, ask important new questions, prodding other scholars to follow his lead into promising fields of historical inquiry. It is a true measure of his impact on the historical profession that many have done just that, with scholars from many countries seeking to ascertain the applicability of Crosby's ideas and methods in their area of study.

KEN COATES

See also Environmental; Imperial; Medicine; Native American; United States: Colonial; World

Biography

Alfred Worcester Crosby, Jr. Born Boston, 15 January 1931, son of a commercial artist. Received BA, Harvard University, 1952, MA 1956; PhD, Boston University, 1961. Served in US Army, 1952–55. Taught at Albion College, 1960–61; Ohio State University, 1961–65; San Fernando Valley State College, 1965–66; and Washington State University, 1966–77; professor, University of Texas, Austin, from 1977. Married 1) (1 son); 2) Barbara Stevens, 1964 (1 daughter); 3) Frances Karttunen, 1983 (2 stepchildren).

Principal Writings

America, Russia, Hemp, and Napoleon: American Trade with Russia and the Baltic, 1783–1812, 1965

The Columbian Exchange: Biological and Cultural Consequences of 1492, 1972

Epidemic and Peace, 1918, 1976; in UK as *America's Forgotten Pandemic: The Influenza of 1918*, 1989

Ecological Imperialism: The Biological Expansion of Europe, 900–1900, 1986

The Columbian Voyages, the Columbian Exchange, and Their Historians, 1987

Germs, Seeds, and Animals: Studies in Ecological History, 1994
The Measure of Reality: Quantification and Western Society,
     1250–1600, 1997

Crusades

The historiography of crusading is the history of crusading itself. Since Pope Urban II called the first crusade at Clermont in November 1095, each generation has redefined the purpose and identity of crusading.

From the beginnings of the movement each crusade attracted much analysis. Commentators sought to show God's working in the events of the campaign while extolling the heroic deeds of leading warriors and giving bloody blow-by-blow accounts of battles as in the epic tradition. Although most of the commentators wrote in Latin, the language of scholarship, the crusades also inspired verse and prose works in the vernacular and by the end of the 12th century a full-blown epic "Crusade cycle" had been composed in French verse. Some accounts were written to excuse the failure of a campaign; others set out to assess the last crusade campaign for the benefit of the next one or to assist with planning and encourage recruitment. By the late 13th century analysis was being developed further, with the writing of theoretical crusade plans.

For Christians, the crusade was both a pilgrimage and a holy war, the duty of pious kings. For the Muslims likewise the war was a holy one against the enemies of God and was the duty of the pious sultan. Powerful sultans such as Saladin and Baybars were depicted by their biographers as indefatigable in their efforts to root out the Christians from Palestine. Saladin's biographer Bahā al-Dīn also depicted him intending to invade Europe and destroy the Christians utterly.

In Europe the crusade always had its critics, but in the 16th century the concept received its most significant challenge yet from Martin Luther. In his "Explanation of the 95 theses" (1518) he stated that Ottoman attacks on Christendom were God's punishment for Christians' sins and that the Church authorities should not resist them by arms, only by prayer. Later in "On war against the Turk" (1529) he stated that it was the responsibility of the prince rather than the Church to defend the people in battle.

Early Protestant historians followed him in blaming the failure of crusades on the spiritual errors of the Roman Catholic crusaders and their clergy. However, Thomas Fuller in *The Historie of the Holy Warre* (1639) also identified strategic and organizational flaws in the campaigns, underlining the weakness of the Christian kingdom of Jerusalem as a fundamental problem.

For these writers, Islam in the form of the Ottoman Turks was still a real threat to Christendom; part of their purpose in writing was to discover how Christendom could repel that threat. By the 18th century the danger had receded and historians wrote from a position of secure detachment. To the rational historians of the Enlightenment, crusading was a regrettable expression of irrational superstition and violence, although they applauded individual heroism against what they considered to be the barbarism of Islam. For Edward Gibbon in his *Decline and Fall of the Roman Empire* (1776–88) the

crusades had "checked rather than forwarded the maturity of Europe," but he believed that they had at least undermined the feudal aristocracy and aided the rise of the peasants and middle classes.

The 19th-century Romantic movement revived popular and academic interest in the crusades; the crusaders' valor was admired, although their intolerance was disliked. Nationalism also stimulated crusading studies, particularly in France where the crusades offered the reassurance of a glorious national past after the upheaval of the Revolution and the Napoleonic wars. Renewed German interest in the late 19th century also owed something to nationalist interests, reflecting an expansionist policy in the Middle East. In this era French and German scholars led the field in meticulous examination of the sources, laying the foundations of modern crusading scholarship.

Between the world wars crusading studies developed on both sides of the Atlantic. In 1935 Carl Erdmann laid down in *Die Entstehung des Kreuzzugsgedankens* (The Origin of the Idea of the Crusade, 1977) a theory of how the ideology behind crusading developed, which has been seriously challenged only recently by the work of John Gilchrist.

The period since 1945 has seen a great expansion of crusading studies and new debates. Steven Runciman's *A History of the Crusades* (1951–54) repeated the traditional Protestant, rationalist condemnation of the crusades as "a long act of intolerance in the name of God." However a new generation of crusade historians led by Jonathan Riley-Smith contends that the crusades were "a genuinely popular devotional activity" whose monetary costs were greater than the expected gains. These views have been challenged by Hans Mayer who argued in his *Geschichte der Kreuzzüge* (1965; *The Crusades*, 1972) that hope of gain was in fact a major motivation for crusaders. Modern debate also centers on the definition and scope of crusading, tracing the continuation of crusading tradition down to the fall of Malta to Napoleon in 1798; and expanding its scope to include campaigns in Spain, the Balkans, and northeastern Europe.

The field of research has also expanded to include the social and national origins of crusaders, the preaching and organization of crusades, and attitudes towards crusading, all drawing on a wide variety of source material ranging from government archives to fictional literature. Another rapidly expanding area of research is the study of the military religious orders set up to defend pilgrims traveling to the holy places and the crusader states. Led by the research of Joshua Prawer and Jean Richard, the history of the crusader states has become a separate area of study in its own right.

The crusades attract much interest in the Islamic world, although western scholars complain that Islamic scholars have appeared reluctant to adopt a critical approach to the sources. Israeli scholars, seeing a parallel between the crusader states and the modern state of Israel, have been at the forefront of crusading studies. With holy wars still raging in many parts of the world it is clear that the history of the crusades has considerable contemporary relevance.

HELEN J. NICHOLSON

See also Burns; Byzantium; Cahen; Eastern Orthodoxy; France: 1000–1450; Ibn al-Athīr; Jewish; Komnene; Middle East; Orderic; Otto; Runciman; Russia: Medieval; Sybel; William of Tyre

Further Reading

Boase, T.S.R., "Recent developments in Crusading Historiography," *History* 22 (1937), 110–25

Brundage, J., "Recent Crusade Historiography: Some Observations and Suggestions," *Catholic Historical Review* 49 (1964), 493–507

Erdmann, Carl, *Die Enstehung des Kreuzzugsgedankens*, Stuttgart: Kohlhammer, 1935; in English as *The Origin of the Idea of the Crusade*, Princeton: Princeton University Press, 1977

Gabrieli, Francesco, *Storici Arabi delle crociate*, Turin: Einaudi, 1963; in English as *Arab Historians of the Crusades*, London: Routledge, and Berkeley: University of California Press, 1969

Gilchrist, John, "The Erdmann Thesis and the Canon Law, 1083–1141," in Peter W. Edbury, ed., *Crusade and Settlement*, Cardiff: University College Cardiff Press, and Atlantic Highlands, NJ: Humanities Press, 1985

Gilchrist, John, "The Papacy and the War against the Saracens, 795–1216," *International History Review* 10 (1988), 174–97

Heath, Michael J., *Crusading Commonplaces: La Noue, Lucinge, and Rhetoric Against the Turks*, Geneva: Droz, 1986

Holt, Peter Malcolm, *The Age of the Crusades: The Near East from the Eleventh Century to 1517*, London and New York: Longman, 1986

Housley, Norman, *The Later Crusades, 1274–1580: From Lyons to Alcazar*, Oxford: Oxford University Press, 1992

Kedar, Benjamin Z., *Crusade and Mission: European Approaches toward the Muslims*, Princeton: Princeton University Press, 1984

La Monte, J.L., "Some Problems in Crusading Historiography," *Speculum* 15 (1940), 57–75

Maalouf, Amin, *Les Croisades vues par les Arabes*, Paris: J'ai Lu, 1983; in English as *The Crusades through Arab Eyes*, London: Al Saqi, 1984; New York: Schocken, 1985

Mayer, Hans E., *Geschichte der Kreuzzüge*, Stuttgart: Kohlhammer, 1965; in English as *The Crusades*, London: Oxford University Press, 1972

Prawer, Joshua, *Toldot mamlekhet ha'tsalbanim be-Erets Yisrael*, 2 vols., Jerusalem: Mosad Bialik, 1963; in French as *Histoire du royaume de Jérusalem* (History of the Kingdom of Jerusalem), Paris: Editions du Centre National de la Recherche Scientifique, 1969–70

Prawer, Joshua, *The Latin Kingdom of Jerusalem*, London: Weidenfeld and Nicolson, 1972; as *The Crusaders' Kingdom: European Colonialism in the Middle Ages*, New York: Praeger, 1972

Prawer, Joshua, *Crusader Institutions*, Oxford and New York: Oxford University Press, 1980

Richard, Jean, *Le Comté de Tripoli sous la dynastie toulousaine, 1102–1187* (The County of Tripoli under the Toulouse Dynasty), Paris: Geuthner, 1945; reprinted New York: AMS Press, 1980

Richard, Jean, *Le Royaume latin de Jérusalem*, Paris: Presses Universitaires de France, 1953; in English as *The Latin Kingdom of Jerusalem*, Amsterdam: North Holland, 1979

Riley-Smith, Jonathan, *What Were the Crusades?*, London: Macmillan, and Totowa, NJ: Rowman and Littlefield, 1977

Riley-Smith, Jonathan, *The First Crusade and the Idea of Crusading*, London: Athlone Press, and Philadelphia: University of Pennsylvania Press, 1986

Riley-Smith, Jonathan, *The Crusades: A Short History*, London: Athlone Press, and New Haven: Yale University Press, 1987

Riley-Smith, Jonathan, ed., *The Oxford Illustrated History of the Crusades*, Oxford and New York: Oxford University Press, 1995

Runciman, Steven, *A History of the Crusades*, 3 vols., Cambridge and New York: Cambridge University Press, 1951–54

Setton, Kenneth M., *A History of the Crusades*, 6 vols., Madison: University of Wisconsin Press, 1955–89

Siberry, Elizabeth, *Criticism of Crusading, 1095–1274*, Oxford and New York: Oxford University Press, 1985

Siberry, Elizabeth, "The Crusades: Tales of the Opera," *Medieval History* 3 (1993), 21–25

Tyerman, Christopher, *England and the Crusades, 1095–1588*, Chicago: University of Chicago Press, 1988

Tyerman, Christopher, "Were There Any Crusades in the Twelfth Century?" *English Historical Review* 110 (1995), 553–77

Cuba

After 1959, with the advent of the Cuban Revolution, interest in Cuban history soared as governments and scholars sought to explain the emergence of a socialist regime ninety miles from the shores of the United States, the 20th century's foremost imperial power. The relationship of this Caribbean island to the imperial centers of Madrid and Washington has influenced its ideological, political, social, and economic development from 1492 to the present. Historical scholarship on Cuba has focused on the explanatory power of this relationship for an understanding of the internal dynamics of its history.

An early historical work demonstrating the relationship of the Cuban Revolution to renewed interest in Cuban studies was Charles E. Chapman's *A History of the Cuban Republic*. Originally proposed by the US ambassador to Cuba, Enoch H. Crowder, in the 1920s and published in 1927, it reappeared in 1971 as a response to the dearth of material on Cuba prior to the Revolution. Since the 1960s, historians examining and analyzing various aspects of Cuban history have contributed numerous studies to fill in this lacuna.

Cuba under Spanish colonial rule attracted the attention of historians at the beginning of the 20th century, since it would provide the framework for understanding and justifying the US imperial role in the Caribbean after 1898. Irene A. Wright's *The Early History of Cuba, 1492–1586* (1916) was an original contribution to the study of the Spanish discovery, conquest, and colonization of Cuba. Based on solid archival research, it remains a classic work for an understanding of the island's formative colonial period. More recently other works have appraised the role of Cuba and the Caribbean within Spain's empire. Kenneth R. Andrews' *The Spanish Caribbean* (1978), although not exclusively about Cuba, incorporated a broad analysis focusing on the importance of the Caribbean in Spain's early imperial policy. As a result of the crown's subsequent colonial policy, the Caribbean suffered economic decline and an increase in contraband and pirate activity. John Robert McNeill researched the 18th century, a period of tumultuous political, social, and economic change for Cuba, in *Atlantic Empires of France and Spain* (1985), which used a comparative approach that delved into the role of colonial seaports in mediating the relations between the metropolis and the colonial periphery. The author probed the process of colonial development through the interplay of 18th-century imperial policy with colonial reality.

Historians have also undertaken institutional studies of the colonial military, the linchpin of imperial policy. During the 18th-century, the military emerged as a dominant institution in Cuba as a result of British imperial policy in the Caribbean. The British occupation of Havana from 1762 to 1763 completely transformed Cuba and contributed to a program of fiscal and military reforms under the Spanish king Charles III. Allan J. Kuethe evaluated how Bourbon imperial policy affected not only the military but also Cuban society after the British occupation in *Cuba, 1753–1815: Crown, Military, and Society* (1986). He demonstrated that the Bourbon monarchs maintained the loyalty of the Cuban elites through commercial concessions even as the monarchy collapsed in Spain and mainland Spanish America challenged its rule. Historians have not only investigated the broader question of imperial policy but have also concentrated on the social history of colonial Cuba during the crucial period of the late 18th and early 19th centuries. Larry R. Jensen considered the role of the press during the period of imperial crisis in *Children of Colonial Despotism* (1988) which exploited a neglected primary source, the periodical press. The author scrutinized the role of the Cuban "sugarocracy" during the political vicissitudes of constitutionalism as reflected in the press. One of the critical questions that Jensen explored was the reason Cuba remained faithful to Spain in the midst of imperial disintegration.

Economic history has received a predominant place in the study of Cuba because of the importance of sugar and tobacco in the island's export economy. Although sugar has received considerable attention, tobacco was the leading export in Cuba's economy during the first three centuries of colonial rule. Fernando Ortiz's *Contrapunteo cubano* (1940; *Cuban Counterpoint*, 1947) examined the pivotal role that these two tropical products had on the early development of the island's society. In the late 18th and early 19th centuries, sugar displaced tobacco as the primary export. The classic work on the development of the Cuban sugar industry from its colonial beginnings is Ramiro Guerra y Sanchez's *Azúcar y población en las Antillas* (1927; *Sugar and Society in the Caribbean*, 1964). For Guerra, the key to understanding Cuban social, political, and economic development was the plantation. After the Cuban Revolution, Marxist analysis penetrated the study of the sugar economy. A detailed analysis of the multifaceted nature of the sugar economy published in Cuba after the Revolution was Manuel Moreno Fraginals' *El ingenio* (1964; *The Sugarmill*, 1976). The author probed the technical side of sugar production by studying archival and other sources made available after the Revolution.

Slavery, the predominant labor system on the sugar plantations, has been the subject of numerous inquiries by social historians. Various factors, such as the northern migration of blacks from the southern US after World War II and the decolonization process in Africa, contributed to the flourishing interest in research on slavery undertaken in the 1960s and 1970s. The influential comparative studies by Frank Tannenbaum and Stanley Elkins regarding the differences between the evolution of slavery in Latin America and the United States provided the model for the early investigations of Cuban slavery. Herbert S. Klein's *Slavery in the Americas* (1967) showed how the institutional differences in Cuba's and Virginia's slave systems contributed to the divergence in subsequent developments regarding the incorporation of blacks in their respective societies after the abolition of slavery. Gwendolyn Midlo Hall's *Social Control in Slave Plantation Societies* (1971) also employed a comparative approach in analyzing the fundamental problem of social control in two distinct slave systems, the French and Spanish. Racism emerged in both societies as an important component for the ideological justification of the slave system and contributed to maintaining social control.

Franklin W. Knight's *Slave Society in Cuba during the Nineteenth Century* (1970) provided a comprehensive view of the socioeconomic context for Cuban slave society by emphasizing the contradictions emerging from the inherent nature of a system based on unskilled labor at a time when planters introduced a technology requiring skilled technicians. Employing a demographic analysis, Kenneth F. Kiple utilized census data in *Blacks in Colonial Cuba* (1976) in order to clarify figures contained in the earlier works by Klein and Knight regarding Cuban slavery. Another work, applying a quantitative methodology based on the work of a research team of 24 students from Cuba and the US who gathered slave prices from notarial records and official sales tax lists, was the impressive study by Laird W. Bergad, Fe Iglesias García, and María del Carmen Barcia: *The Cuban Slave Market* (1995). This study, as well as a recent one by Rebecca J. Scott, challenged Manuel Moreno Fraginal's assertion that after 1850 – and the introduction of technology on the sugar plantations – slavery was not profitable. After mid-century, the demand for slaves continued, as revealed by rising slave prices, until the eve of abolition.

During the 19th century, a major issue that engaged Madrid and the Cuban creole planter class was the British pressure for the abolition of slavery. The Anglo-Spanish treaty of 1817, the first significant effort to end the trade, influenced subsequent diplomacy between the British and the Spanish. Historians, engaging in extensive archival research in Spain and England, have explored the diplomacy behind the suppression and abolition of the slave trade. An early effort in understanding this diplomacy was Arthur F. Corwin's *Spain and the Abolition of Slavery in Cuba* (1967), which traced Spanish policy from 1817 to the abolition of slavery in 1886. David Murray concentrated on British efforts to end the trade in *Odious Commerce* (1980).

Besides the external British efforts, there were internal attempts to bring an end to the system, the most notable being the 1844 Escalera conspiracy. Inside Cuba, historians have critically examined this conspiracy for an understanding of colonial history and the social contradictions existing in a slave society. Some have questioned the existence of the conspiracy, while others have perceived it as an aborted social revolution. The conspiracy has received far less attention outside of Cuba; Robert L. Paquette is one of the few historians in the English-speaking world who has critically inspected it, in *Sugar Is Made with Blood* (1988). Rebecca J. Scott in *Slave Emancipation in Cuba* (1985) also studied the slaves' struggle for freedom. In addition, her work focused on the plantation owners' adaptations to the new reality emerging with abolition, by creating control mechanisms that would allow them access to labor. Another aspect of 19th-century Cuban slave society that has received attention is the life of the free colored. To understand the relationship between racism and economic exploitation, Verena Stolcke investigated the institution of marriage in *Marriage, Class and Colour in Nineteenth-Century Cuba* (1974). Aline Helg in a ground-breaking study explored the fate of Afro-Cubans after independence in *Our Rightful Share* (1995). It refuted earlier studies by Tannenbaum, Klein, and other US historians that upheld the myth of the relatively benign nature of Latin American slavery and presumed racial equality. Helg's study, based on extensive research, exploded this myth as did the earlier works by Knight and Hall. One important contribution from this study was the exploration of the 1912 racist massacre of Afro-Cubans that suppressed the Partido Independiente de Color. In academic studies it is most difficult to give a human face to the slave's suffering. Esteban Montejo's *Biografía de un cimarrón* (1966; *The Autobiography of a Runaway Slave*, 1968), as oral history and social document, provided a mirror into the world of a Cuban slave during the 19th century with all of its horrors and hopes.

Social and economic historians have also focused on 19th-century Cuba's rural society. The growth of the sugar industry totally transformed rural life, as capital penetrated into the countryside. The demand for land displaced many peasants. Laird W. Bergad researched this transformation in *Cuban Rural Society in the Nineteenth Century* (1990). As a result of the displacement experienced by the peasantry, social banditry emerged as a powerful rural protest movement against the effects of an encroaching capitalism. Influenced by the works of Eric J. Hobsbawm, historians have explored social banditry for an understanding of Cuban social and rural history. During the mid-19th century the impending collapse of the slave labor system, capital penetration, and the aftermath of the Ten Years' War (1868–78) for Cuban independence led to social and economic breakdown in the countryside. Many peasants affected by these transformations turned to social banditry. Louis A. Pérez, Jr., in *Lords of the Mountain* (1989), investigated the convergence of social banditry with Cuba's political struggles for independence that engulfed the latter half of the 19th and early 20th centuries. Rosalie Schwartz disagreed with Hobsbawm and Pérez regarding the nature of social banditry. Whereas Hobsbawm and Pérez viewed the social bandit as emerging from a displaced peasantry, Schwartz concluded in *Lawless Liberators* (1989) that the social bandit operating in the Havana region had clearly political aims.

The role of the United States in Cuban history during the 19th century is pivotal for an understanding of subsequent events in the 20th century. After the Cuban Revolution, historians concentrated on the political, social, and economic relationship between the US and Cuba in order to understand how a socialist country could emerge ninety miles from the most advanced capitalist country. Lester D. Langley's *The Cuban Policy of the United States* (1968) summarized US policy towards the island from the late 18th century to the 20th century. He focused primarily on the 19th century since more documentation was available to him. One of the earliest post-revolutionary studies was Philip S. Foner's *A History of Cuba and its Relations with the United States* (1962–65) which traced Cuban historical development from 1492 to the Second War for Independence (1895–98). Foner sought to interpret the inevitability of the Cuban Revolution in light of the political and economic dominance of the US over Cuban affairs. During this period southern interests in the US looked longingly toward Cuba in order to extend slavery and continue the plantation economy vital to the survival of the southern elites. Sectors of the Cuban *criollo* planter elite also sought annexation to the US as a solution to a declining slave system that was under assault by the British and internal abolitionist forces. Robert E. May's *The Southern Dream of a Caribbean Empire* (1973) analyzed this episode in the wider context of the southern US strategy of expanding into the Caribbean, primarily Cuba, Nicaragua, and Mexico, to insure the survival

of slavery and the plantation system. Josef Opatrny examined the US and Cuban motives behind the annexationist movement in *U.S. Expansionism and Cuban Annexationism in the 1850s* (1990). The author argued that the movement contributed to a sense of Cuban identity as well as an understanding of armed struggle as one of the avenues for resolving the political crisis with Spain.

After the Ten Years' War, or the first War for Independence, the US continued to intervene in Cuban affairs as it sought to insure that Cuba would remain thoroughly within the US political and economic orbit after the inevitable independence from Spain. The interim period between the first and second war for Cuban independence in 1895 has also received the attention of historians. Earlier historiography on the Spanish-American War emphasized the vital US role in securing Cuban independence from Spain. Louis A. Pérez, Jr.'s *Cuba Between Empires* (1983) provided an analysis of the interwar period and subsequent US intervention in the second war for Cuban independence. The author contended that the Cuban patriots were on the verge of winning their struggle for independence against Spain when the US intervened. The Cuban elites sought intervention in order to avoid a social revolution. In an earlier study, Philip S. Foner investigated US intervention during the Spanish-Cuban-American war (1895–98), the name preferred by Cuban historians for the Spanish-American War and introduced to the English-speaking public by Samuel Flagg Bemis in 1959. This study, *The Spanish-Cuban-American War and the Birth of American Imperialism* (1972), continued Foner's analysis of 19th-century US-Cuban affairs. Foner's was a controversial revisionist appraisal because he argued for the primacy of the Cuban patriots in securing their own independence, thereby diminishing the US role. The major controversial thesis of Foner's study is that US intervention in Cuba in 1898 marked the beginning of US imperialism as a result of monopoly capitalism and the search for markets. Foner's was a Marxist analysis that underscored the economic roots of US policy towards Cuba. Both authors ended their historical analysis with the establishment of the Cuban republic in 1902. John L. Offner offered a diplomatic history of the period in *An Unwanted War* (1992) that disagreed with Foner's and Pérez's slighting of the US role in winning Cuban independence. He also challenged those historians who argued that the war was inevitable, contending that neither party involved in the conflict wanted the war.

Antonio Maceo and José Martí, two patriots that contributed significantly to Cuban independence, have fascinated historians. Both Foner and Pérez treated these two individuals in their analysis of Cuban independence, but biographies on Maceo and Martí abound. Foner analyzed the controversial figure of Maceo in his interpretive study *Antonio Maceo: The "Bronze Titan" of Cuba's Struggle for Independence* (1977). Magdalen M. Pando, in a more recent study, wrote a panegyric narrative in *Cuba's Freedom Fighter* (1980) that exalted Maceo's figure and his accomplishments during the second war of independence. After the Cuban Revolution, the controversial figure of Martí, the father of Cuban independence, received the most attention from biographers, since both sides claimed him as a precursor to their respective movements. Some considered him a typical 19th-century Latin American liberal, while others cast him as a precursor to Cuba's Marxist revolutionary tradition. Representative biographies are those by Richard B. Gray and John M. Kirk. Gray's 1962 study not only surveyed Martí's life and thought but also traced the development of Martí as a patriotic symbol. He further charted how various political factions gained popular support by using Martí as a justification for their political actions. Kirk's 1983 biography, based on Martí's extensive writings, evaluated the influences, both liberal and socialist, on the development of his political, moral, social, and economic ideas in order to clarify the debate regarding his figure. Gerald E. Poyo explored the 19th-century expatriate milieu that Cubans forged for themselves in the US in *"With All, and for the Good of All"* (1989). This expatriate community contributed to Martí's intellectual, political, and nationalist development.

The US occupation of Cuba in 1898, treated by the works cited earlier by Foner and Pérez, has also captured the attention of historians. Although the Platt Amendment prevented annexation, Cuba entered into a dependent relation with the US. David F. Healy's political history, *The United States in Cuba* (1963), examined how the occupation contributed to the rise of an informal empire in Cuba. James H. Hitchman's *Leonard Wood and Cuban Independence* (1971), an institutional and biographical history, provided a detailed study of the US occupation sympathetic to the memory of Governor-General Leonard Wood and his achievements on the island. On the other hand, Foner's work, a predominantly economic analysis, questioned Wood's role during the occupation and the subsequent creation of the Cuban Republic in 1902. Pérez's study also demonstrated how the US made Cuba into a semicolony by promoting its dependence.

In its analysis of the controversial Platt Amendment of 1902, Hitchman's work concluded that the amendment guaranteed Cuban stability and allowed the nation to build its institutions and foster economic prosperity. Other historians disagreed with this conclusion, arguing that the amendment, which survived until 1934, marred the birth of the Cuban republic since it transformed the new nation into a US dependency. Pérez probed political life during this period in *Cuba under the Platt Amendment* (1986). He analyzed the relationship between the Cuban political elites and Washington, arguing that many times, due to the weakness of the government, they clashed around fundamental issues of patronage that was beneficial to the politicians but detrimental to US economic interests. Allan Reed Millett scrutinized one particular episode from this period, the second US intervention from 1906 to 1909, in *The Politics of Intervention* (1968). His political history emphasized the role of US army officers in influencing the Provisional Government's policies during the occupation. Pérez continued his research on US political hegemony over Cuban affairs during the early 20th century in his monograph *Intervention, Revolution, and Politics in Cuba* (1978). Attempting to avoid direct military intervention, the dominant economic influence of the US guaranteed increased political and diplomatic intervention into Cuban affairs.

Seeking an explanation for the 1959 Cuban Revolution, some historians considered the 1933 Cuban Revolution an opening act for Fidel Castro's success. It provided the framework for the subsequent revolutionary transformation of Cuba in the 1960s, as it contained the seeds of a new nationalism as well as a radical social and economic program. Luis E.

Aguilar in *Cuba 1933* (1972) traced the continuity between the ideals and aspirations of 1933 and their subsequent realization in 1959. Samuel Farber's *Revolution and Reaction in Cuba* (1976), one of the few studies of the period between 1940 and 1952, also considered the continuities between 1933 and 1959. He maintained that after the defeat of the 1933 Revolution Bonapartism and populism dominated Cuban politics, considering Fulgencio Batista's government as Bonapartist, the 1940s civilian governments as populist, and Castro's movement as Bonapartist.

Scholars have investigated the US role in determining the course and subsequent defeat of the 1933 Revolution. In the 1960s and 1970s, dependency theory influenced the historical analysis of Latin America. Jules Robert Benjamin's *The United States and Cuba* (1977) provided a dependency analysis of Cuba which primarily concentrated on the years 1925–34. Besides examining the Cuban Revolution of 1933 and its threat to US hegemony over the island, he also evaluated the rise of the US Good Neighbor policy. Some historians have considered the Good Neighbor policy as indicative of a change in US policy towards Latin America, in general, and Cuba, in particular, since the US did not engage in direct military intervention in the region. Irwin F. Gellman contradicted this position in his diplomatic history *Roosevelt and Batista* (1973) by stressing the continuity of intervention in Cuban affairs through diplomatic, political, and especially through economic means.

Historians have not neglected the study of institutional history, fixing on one of the most important Cuban institutions, the military. Rafael Fermoselle's *The Evolution of the Cuban Military* (1987) tracked the historical development of the military from the colonial period to the present revolutionary regime. Louis A. Pérez, Jr., on the other hand, focussed on the role of the military in the 20th century in *Army Politics in Cuba* (1976). With the occupation of Cuba in 1898, the US disbanded the Cuban independence army and created a new army out of the Rural Guard, a corrupt police force. Emphasizing the continuity of the military as an institution, Pérez analyzed the role of the military since Gerardo Machado's regime of the 1920s. In both Batista's and Castro's governments, diametrically opposed ideologically, the military played a predominant role in government. José M. Hernández also explored the US role in the rise of militarism in *Cuba and the United States* (1993) and concluded that the military influence in politics cannot be directly related to US policies but instead resembled the historical pattern of Latin America in general.

Since the Revolution's triumph scholars have advanced numerous explanations on its origins. An early example of this genre is Ramón Eduardo Ruiz's *Cuba: The Making of a Revolution* (1968), which argued that the Cuban Revolution culminated a struggle that had its roots in the 19th century. Its success resulted from Cuba's revolutionary tradition, its nationalism directed against the US, and from a strong figure, Fidel Castro, who had antecedents in the nation's past. Also, for Ruiz, Castro gained the support of the Cuban people by claiming that his movement embodied the ideals of José Martí. Diplomatic historians have also provided explanations for the Revolution by focusing on the role of nationalism. In an early study, Robert F. Smith examined the mixture of political and economic factors in determining foreign policy in *The United*

States and Cuba (1960). He investigated how the conflict between Cuban nationalism and US economic interests since 1898 contributed to the Revolution. Jules Robert Benjamin's *The United States and the Origins of the Cuban Revolution* (1990) provided an innovative diplomatic history that explained the success of the Revolution by examining how nationalism contributed to the struggle against US political and economic domination. Its unique analysis arose from its examination of US hegemony as the author skilfully disentangled the roots of the institutions and culture that gave rise to that hegemony. Benjamin argued that US institutions and culture blinded the US to the contradictions its policies were producing within Cuban society as it sought stability while attempting change.

The Cuban Revolution has generated a plethora of historical studies not only concentrating on its origins, but also on the revolutionary struggle itself. Scholars have focused on various of the social groups that participated in the struggle against Batista. Since events surrounding the struggle are fairly recent, many historians have made use of the various memoirs of participants as well as interviews with them. Jaime Suchlicki's *University Students and Revolution in Cuba* (1969) employed interviews with Cuban exiles to trace the development of student participation in the nation's political struggles. He analyzed how the students from the University of Havana contributed to Batista's overthrow by engaging in acts of urban guerrilla warfare. A different treatment of the years preceding the revolutionary victory of 1959 is *The Cuban Insurrection* (1974) by Ramón L. Bonachea and Marta San Martín. These two authors examined the rarely studied urban guerrilla struggle as well as those revolutionary movements not directly associated with the rural guerrilla struggle. Two newspapermen, John Dorschner and Roberto Fabricio, employed US State Department documents, secondary sources, and newspapers, and conducted numerous interviews to present a historical narrative on the final months of 1958 leading up to Castro's victory in *The Winds of December* (1980). The authors also investigated a question that has perplexed scholars and laymen alike: did Castro's Marxist-Leninist ideology emerge before or after the victory of the Revolution?

Intellectual historians have also explored the roots of Cuban socialism as well as the evolution of Castro's ideas and their influence on the Revolution. Sheldon B. Liss explored the radical tradition in Cuban thought in *Roots of Revolution* (1987). He maintained that the Cuban Revolution inherited the radical program contained in the various strands of the ideology espoused by numerous Cuban thinkers. Other scholars have examined Castro's reasons for radicalizing the primarily middle-class 1959 Revolution. The anticommunist Cuban exiles who left the island proclaimed that Castro "betrayed the Revolution" when he declared his Marxist-Leninist leanings. Lionel Martin contended that Castro had contact with radical ideas prior to the Revolution in *The Early Fidel* (1978). During his student days at the University of Havana, Castro's involvement in student politics exposed him to radical ideas and actions. Liss investigated the profundity of Castro's mature ideas on numerous topics in *Fidel!* (1994). He studied the European and Latin American intellectual background that contributed to the development of Castro's ideas. Loree Wilkerson's *Fidel Castro's Political Programs from*

Reformism to "Marxism-Leninism" (1965) researched the influence of Castro's ideology on the transition from a reform political program to one of increased radicalization in the early years of the Revolution.

The transformation of the Cuban Revolution in the early 1960s attracted the attention of historians, as well as laymen, to the socialist experiment in Cuba. This fascination produced an abundance of works charting the radical course of the Revolution from the 1960s to the 1990s. The works were written from the full spectrum of political viewpoints and highlighted the polemical nature of the Revolution's transformation. Theodore Draper presented the "official" US position in two works, *Castro's Revolution* (1962) and *Castroism* (1965). Draper argued, as did many others, that Castro had betrayed the original ideals of the Revolution. In keeping with the "revolution betrayed" thesis, Andrés Suárez disagreed with the historical explanation that the transition occurred as a result of popular pressures from below in *Cuba: Castroism and Communism* (1967). Motivated by foreign policy considerations regarding the benefits of Soviet nuclear power, the author suggested that Castro alone was responsible for the turn of events in Cuba. K.S. Karol also charted the transformation by concentrating on the Stalinization and militarization of the initial attempt by the Revolution to create a different model of national development in *Les guérilleros au pouvoir* (1970; *Guerrillas in Power*, 1970). Karol, initially sympathetic to the Revolution, assessed the negative role of the Soviet Union in transforming Cuban society and politics by extinguishing the liberated spirit of the early revolutionary years. Jorge I. Domínguez furnished a comprehensive analysis of the Cuban Revolution in *Cuba: Order and Revolution* (1978) which exposed the disorderly nature of Cuban politics, society, and economy before 1959 and the order imposed on the nation by the revolutionary government. After imposing order, the revolutionary legislation enacted in the first two years transformed all aspects of Cuban politics, society, and economy.

Economic historians and others have focused on the performance of the Cuban socialist economy as well as its dependence on the Soviet Union. Many issues associated with the performance of the Cuban economy are also polemical in nature. Some contended that the Revolution's emphasis on education, health, income distribution, and other social services demonstrated the overall success of the Revolution's goals. Others pointed to Cuban dependence on a monoculture economy, its lack of sustained economic growth, and its relationship to the USSR as evidence of the Revolution's failure. An early work investigating the Revolution during its tenth anniversary from a sympathetic Marxist perspective was Leo Huberman and Paul M. Sweezy's *Socialism in Cuba* (1969). The authors examined the political and economic problems of the Revolution in light of the policies instituted by the revolutionary government. James O'Connor's *The Origins of Socialism in Cuba* (1970) looked at the early exultant years of the Cuban socialist experiment to the mid-1960s. Providing a brief economic background of the prerevolutionary period, the author's primary investigation concentrated on those early years of revolutionary political and economic planning. On the other hand, Carmelo Mesa-Lago critically studied the success and failure of the Cuban economy in its first twenty years in *The Economy of Socialist Cuba* (1981), which provided a sober analysis of the social and economic components of the Revolution. Another work that statistically probed the economic reality was *The Cuban Economy* (1989) by Andrew Zimbalist and Claes Brundenius.

Sociologists and political scientists have produced works on the Revolution's impact on the ordinary lives of the Cubans who remained on the island. These studies will provide historians with a wealth of data for future historical studies on the development of the Cuban Revolution under Castro. In 1962 Maurice Zeitlin conducted a series of interviews with members of the Cuban working class, industrial workers who benefited from the triumph of the Revolution. In *Revolutionary Politics and the Cuban Working Class* (1967), which provided information on the years from the 1930s to the 1950s, the author investigated the attitudes of these workers towards the transformations they were experiencing.

Influenced by the rise of feminism in the 1960s and 1970s, historians have not neglected gender studies. Seeking to understand the transformations of women's lives under the Revolution, scholars have studied the earlier Cuban feminist movement looking for continuities with subsequent developments. The years from 1898 to 1940 saw the emergence of a Cuban feminist movement that challenged the prevailing view on the legal status of women. K. Lynn Stoner offered an analysis of this movement in *From the House to the Streets* (1991) which traced the struggle of middle- and upper-class women for the expansion of women's rights. Lois M. Smith and Alfred Padula studied the impact of the Revolution on women in *Sex and Revolution* (1996), which explored the role of women in prerevolutionary Cuba and how, after the Revolution, state power transformed women's lives in the political, social, and economic spheres.

Marifeli Pérez-Stable's social history *The Cuban Revolution* (1993) investigated the prerevolutionary Cuban society previously neglected by historians in their treatment of Cuba. The author also depicted how workers responded to the call for unselfish contributions to the Revolution for the collective well-being of the nation. Pérez-Stable concluded that the radical phase of the Revolution ended in 1970 as it became institutionalized after that year. Oral history has also made inroads into Cuban historical studies by providing insight into the ordinary lives of Cubans undergoing the radical reorganization of their society. The works by Oscar Lewis, Ruth Lewis, and Susan Rigdon are representative of this historical genre.

The Revolutionary government benefited the Cuban masses by extending education and health services to those previously deprived of them. Richard R. Fagen provided a comprehensive investigation of the formal and informal educational institutions that changed the lives of the average Cuban in *The Transformation of Political Culture in Cuba* (1969). He studied the government's campaign against illiteracy, the Committees for Defense of the Revolution, and the Schools of Revolutionary Instruction and their contribution to the formation of a new political culture and a new conception of citizenship. The Revolutionary government also fulfilled another promise of the Revolution by expanding health services to the masses. Ross Danielson's social history, *Cuban Medicine* (1979), dissected the social, political, and economic factors that influenced the development of Cuban medicine from the colonial period to the present socialist government. An analysis of Cuban medicine

under the Revolutionary government was Julie Margot Feinsilver's *Healing the Masses* (1993), which illustrated the Cuban achievements in medicine when contrasted with the rest of Latin America and the developing world. The author concluded that Cuba is a world-class power in medicine and an example for other nations to follow.

The ubiquitous US role in Cuban affairs continues to influence historical developments in the late 20th century. The Cold War conditioned the US response to the Cuban Revolution. The US perceived Cuba as a Soviet surrogate threatening hemispheric stability by exporting revolution to Latin America. Lynn Darrell Bender explored the development of the mutual hostility between the US and Cuba after the Revolution in *The Politics of Hostility* (1975). The hostile relationship between the two countries determined the direction of US foreign policy towards Cuba during the period of Soviet influence. Continuing the theme of US/Cuban hostility, Michael J. Mazarr's *Semper Fidel* (1988) postulated that this hostility had its roots in the mutually contradictory aims of US dominance over Cuban affairs coupled with rising Cuban nationalism. Dependency theory also influenced the study of US/Cuban relationships after the Revolution, as is clear in Morris Morley's *Imperial State and Revolution* (1987). Morley contended that the US, as a capitalist imperialist state, has historically promoted policies for capital accumulation in the interest of the multinational corporate community. When the Revolution challenged this economic model, the US reacted by attempting to isolate Cuba from the capitalist world in order to undermine this example for the rest of Latin America. Although US foreign policy towards Cuba has dominated the field of diplomatic history, Jorge I. Domínguez significantly reinforced our understanding of Cuban foreign policy in *To Make a World Safe for Revolution* (1989). The author deviated from those historians who perceived Cuban policy purely as an extension of Soviet policy. Granting autonomy to Cuba's foreign policy, he argued that the nation has acted pragmatically with governments or revolutionary movements to insure the survival of the Revolution.

Except for José Martí, no Cuban figure has elicited more ink from the pens of historians, political scientists, journalists, and pundits than Fidel Castro. Many have considered it necessary to understand Castro in order to understand the Revolution. A few representative works are those by Lee Lockwood, Enrique Meneses, Herbert L. Matthews, and Tad Szulc. Lockwood, a journalist, conducted a series of perceptive interviews with Castro during the summer of 1965 for his book *Castro's Cuba, Cuba's Fidel* (1967). As a primary source document this collection of interviews is invaluable for comprehending Castro's ideas on numerous topics concerning the Revolution. Along similar journalistic lines was Meneses' 1966 biography, which offered a portrait of Castro in the Sierra Maestra in 1958, and Matthews' 1969 one, which provided a personal portrait of Castro. The only analytical biography written in English is Szulc's *Fidel: A Critical Portrait* (1986), which was based on interviews with government officials and friends, on newspapers and on secondary sources. It gave the most thorough account of Castro's relationship to the Revolution before and after taking power. Robert E. Quirk, an author who has not had access to Castro, based his 1993 psychological study on an analysis of Castro's speeches, archival research in the National

Library of Cuba, and numerous secondary sources including declassified US government documents. By immersing Castro's figure in the events surrounding late 20th-century Cuba, Quirk produced a historical summary of the last few decades of revolutionary transformations on the island as well as the influence of international politics on the development of the Revolution.

The Revolution stimulated historical writing on Cuba in order to discover what intellectual, political, social, and economic factors contributed to its ultimate success in the face of US opposition. Although the polemical nature of earlier studies clouded the objective analysis of these factors, the last two decades have produced a wealth of critical works. After the fall of the Soviet Union, the shifting fortunes of the Revolution have captured the attention of historians and other social scientists. In the coming decades historians will continue to explore the nation's past in order to understand its present and prepare for its future.

CARLOS PÉREZ

See also LaFeber; Latin America: National; Moreno Fraginals; Ortiz; Pérez; Thomas, H.; Women's History: Latin America

Further Reading

Aguilar, Luis E., *Cuba 1933: Prologue to Revolution*, Ithaca, NY: Cornell University Press, 1972

Andrews, Kenneth R., *The Spanish Caribbean: Trade and Plunder, 1530–1630*, New Haven: Yale University Press, 1978

Bemis, Samuel Flagg, *A Short History of American Foreign Policy and Diplomacy*, New York: Holt, 1959

Bender, Lynn Darrell, *The Politics of Hostility: Castro's Revolution and U.S. Policy*, Hato Rey, Puerto Rico: Inter-American University Press, 1975

Benjamin, Jules Robert, *The United States and Cuba: Hegemony and Dependent Development, 1880–1934*, Pittsburgh: University of Pittsburgh Press, 1977

Benjamin, Jules Robert, *The United States and the Origins of the Cuban Revolution*, Princeton: Princeton University Press, 1990

Bergad, Laird W., *Cuban Rural Society in the Nineteenth Century: The Social and Economic History of Monoculture in Matanzas*, Princeton: Princeton University Press, 1990

Bergad, Laird W., Fe Iglesias García, and María del Carmen Barcia, *The Cuban Slave Market, 1790–1880*, Cambridge and New York: Cambridge University Press, 1995

Bonachea, Ramón L., and Marta San Martín, *The Cuban Insurrection, 1952–1959*, New Brunswick, NJ: Transaction, 1974

Bourne, Peter G., *Fidel: A Biography of Fidel Castro*, New York: Dodd Mead, and London: Macmillan, 1986

Bradford, Richard H., *The "Virginius" Affair*, Boulder: Colorado Associated Press, 1980

Chapman, Charles Edward, *A History of the Cuban Republic: A Study in Hispanic American Politics*, New York: Macmillan, 1927; reprinted Westport, CT: Greenwood Press, 1971

Corbitt, Duvon C., "Cuban Revisionist Interpretations of Cuba's Struggle for Independence," *Hispanic American Historical Review* 43 (1963), 395–404

Corbitt, Duvon C., *A Study of the Chinese in Cuba, 1847–1947*, Wilmore, KY: Asbury Press, 1971

Corwin, Arthur F., *Spain and the Abolition of Slavery in Cuba, 1817–1886*, Austin: University of Texas Press, 1967

Dalton, Thomas C., *"Everything within the Revolution": Cuban Strategies for Development Since 1960*, Boulder, CO: Westview Press, 1993

Danielson, Ross, *Cuban Medicine*, New Brunswick, NJ: Transaction, 1979

Domínguez, Jorge I., *Cuba: Order and Revolution*, Cambridge, MA: Harvard University Press, 1978

Domínguez, Jorge I., *To Make a World Safe for Revolution: Cuba's Foreign Policy*, Cambridge, MA: Harvard University Press, 1989

Dorschner, John, and Roberto Fabricio, *The Winds of December*, New York: Coward McCann, and London: Macmillan, 1980

Draper, Theodore, *Castro's Revolution: Myths and Realities*, New York: Praeger, and London: Thames and Hudson, 1962

Draper, Theodore, *Castroism: Theory and Practice*, New York: Praeger, 1965

Dubois, Jules, *Fidel Castro: Rebel-Liberator or Dictator?*, Indianapolis: Bobbs Merrill, 1959

Fagen, Richard R., *The Transformation of Political Culture in Cuba*, Stanford, CA: Stanford University Press, 1969

Farber, Samuel, *Revolution and Reaction in Cuba, 1933–1960: A Political Sociology from Machado to Castro*, Middletown, CT: Wesleyan University Press, 1976

Feinsilver, Julie Margot, *Healing the Masses: Cuban Health Politics at Home and Abroad*, Berkeley: University of California Press, 1993

Fermoselle, Rafael, *The Evolution of the Cuban Military, 1492–1986*, Miami: Universal, 1987

Foner, Philip S., *A History of Cuba and Its Relations with the United States*, 2 vols., New York: International Publishers, 1962–65

Foner, Philip S., *The Spanish-Cuban-American War and the Birth of American Imperialism, 1895–1902*, 2 vols., New York: Monthly Review Press, 1972

Foner, Philip S., *Antonio Maceo: The "Bronze Titan" of Cuba's Struggle for Independence*, New York: Monthly Review Press, 1977

Gellman, Irwin F., *Roosevelt and Batista: Good Neighbor Diplomacy in Cuba, 1933–1945*, Albuquerque: University of New Mexico Press, 1973

Goizueta-Mimó, Félix, *Bitter Cuban Sugar: Monoculture and Economic Dependence from 1825–1899*, New York: Garland, 1987

Gray, Richard B., *José Martí, Cuban Patriot*, Gainesville: University of Florida Press, 1962

Guerra y Sanchez, Ramiro, *Azúcar y población en las Antillas*, Havana: Cultural, 1927; in English as *Sugar and Society in the Caribbean: An Economic History of Cuban Agriculture*, New Haven: Yale University Press, 1964

Hall, Gwendolyn Midlo, *Social Control in Slave Plantation Societies: A Comparison of St. Domingue and Cuba*, Baltimore: John Hopkins Press, 1971

Halperin, Maurice, *The Rise and Decline of Fidel Castro: An Essay in Contemporary History*, Berkeley: University of California Press, 1972

Healy, David F., *The United States in Cuba, 1898–1902: Generals, Politicians, and the Search for Policy*, Madison: University of Wisconsin Press, 1963

Helg, Aline, *Our Rightful Share: The Afro-Cuban Struggle for Equality, 1886–1912*, Chapel Hill: University of North Carolina Press, 1995

Hernández, José M., *Cuba and the United States: Intervention and Militarism, 1868–1933*, Austin: University of Texas Press, 1993

Higgins, Trumbull, *The Perfect Failure: Kennedy, Eisenhower, and the CIA at the Bay of Pigs*, New York: Norton, 1987

Hitchman, James H., *Leonard Wood and Cuban Independence, 1898–1902*, The Hague: Nijhoff, 1971

Huberman, Leo, and Paul M. Sweezy, *Socialism in Cuba*, New York: Monthly Review Press, 1969

Jensen, Larry R., *Children of Colonial Despotism: Press, Politics, and Culture in Cuba, 1790–1840*, Tampa: University Presses of Florida, 1988

Karol, K.S., *Les guérilleros au pouvoir: l'itinéraire politique de la révolution cubaine*, Paris: Laffont, 1970; in English as *Guerrillas in Power: The Course of Cuban Revolution*, New York: Hill and Wang, 1970; London: Cape, 1971

Kiple, Kenneth F., *Blacks in Colonial Cuba, 1774–1899*, Gainesville: University of Florida Press, 1976

Kirk, John M., *José Martí: Mentor of the Cuban Nation*, Tampa: University Presses of Florida, 1983

Klein, Herbert S., *Slavery in the Americas: A Comparative Study of Virginia and Cuba*, Chicago: University of Chicago Press, and London: Oxford University Press, 1967

Knight, Franklin W., *Slave Society in Cuba during the Nineteenth Century*, Madison: University of Wisconsin Press, 1970

Kuethe, Allan J., *Cuba, 1753–1815: Crown, Military, and Society*, Knoxville: University of Tennessee Press, 1986

Langley, Lester D., *The Cuban Policy of the United States: A Brief History*, New York: Wiley, 1968

Lewis, Oscar, Ruth M. Lewis, and Susan M. Rigdon, *Four Men: Living the Revolution, an Oral History of Contemporary Cuba*, Urbana: University of Illinois Press, 1977

Lewis, Oscar, Ruth M. Lewis, and Susan M. Rigdon, *Four Women: Living the Revolution, an Oral History of Contemporary Cuba*, Urbana: University of Illinois Press, 1977

Lewis, Oscar, Ruth M. Lewis, and Susan M. Rigdon, *Neighbors: Living the Revolution, an Oral History of Contemporary Cuba*, Urbana: University of Illinois Press, 1978

Liss, Sheldon B., *Roots of Revolution: Radical Thought in Cuba*, Lincoln: University of Nebraska Press, 1987

Liss, Sheldon B., *Fidel! Castro's Political and Social Thought*, Boulder, CO: Westview Press, 1994

Lockwood, Lee, *Castro's Cuba, Cuba's Fidel: An American Journalist's Inside Look at Today's Cuba in Text and Pictures*, New York: Macmillan, 1967

McNeill, John Robert, *Atlantic Empires of France and Spain: Louisbourg and Havana, 1700–1763*, Chapel Hill: University of North Carolina Press, 1985

Martin, Lionel, *The Early Fidel: Roots of Castro's Communism*, Secaucus, NJ: Lyle Stuart, 1978

Matthews, Herbert L., *Fidel Castro*, New York: Simon and Schuster, 1969; as *Castro: A Political Biography*, London: Allen Lane, 1969

May, Robert E., *The Southern Dream of a Caribbean Empire, 1854–61*, Baton Rouge: Louisiana State University Press, 1973

Mazarr, Michael J., *Semper Fidel: America and Cuba, 1776–1988*, Baltimore: Nautical and Aviation Publishing, 1988

Meneses, Enrique, *Fidel Castro*, Madrid: Aguado, 1966; in English, New York: Taplinger, and London: Faber, 1968

Mesa-Lago, Carmelo, *The Economy of Socialist Cuba: A Two-Decade Appraisal*, Albuquerque: University of New Mexico Press, 1981

Millett, Allan Reed, *The Politics of Intervention: The Military Occupation of Cuba, 1906–1909*, Columbus: Ohio State University Press, 1968

Montejo, Esteban, *Biografía de un cimarrón*, Havana: Instituto de Etnología, 1966; in English as *The Autobiography of a Runaway Slave*, edited by Miguel Barnet, London: Bodley Head, 1968

Moreno Fraginals, Manuel, *El ingenio: el complejo económico social cubano del azúcar, 1760–1860*, Havana: Comisión Nacional Cubana de la UNESCO, 1964, revised in 3 vols., Havana: Editorial de Ciencias Sociales, 1978; vol. 1 in English as *The Sugarmill: The Socioeconomic Complex of Sugar in Cuba, 1760–1860*, New York: Monthly Review Press, 1976, London: Macmillan, 1993

Morley, Morris, *Imperial State and Revolution: The United States and Cuba, 1952–1986*, Cambridge and New York: Cambridge University Press, 1987

Murray, David, *Odious Commerce: Britain, Spain and the Abolition of the Cuban Slave Trade*, Cambridge and New York: Cambridge University Press, 1980

O'Connor, James, *The Origins of Socialism in Cuba*, Ithaca, NY: Cornell University Press, 1970

Offner, John L., *An Unwanted War: The Diplomacy of the United States and Spain over Cuba, 1895–1898*, Chapel Hill: University of North Carolina Press, 1992

Opatrny, Josef, *U.S. Expansionism and Cuban Annexationism in the 1850s*, Prague: Charles University, 1990; Lewiston, NY, and Lampeter, Wales: Mellen, 1993

Ortiz, Fernando, *Contrapunteo cubano del tabaco y el azúcar*, Havana: Montero, 1940; in English as *Cuban Counterpoint: Tobacco and Sugar*, New York: Knopf, 1947; reprinted 1995

Pando, Magdalen M., *Cuba's Freedom Fighter: Antonio Maceo, 1845–1896*, Gainesville, FL: Felicity Press, 1980

Paquette, Robert L., *Sugar Is Made with Blood: The Conspiracy of La Escalera and the Conflict Between Empires over Slavery in Cuba*, Middletown, CT: Wesleyan University Press, 1988

Pérez, Louis A., Jr., *Army Politics in Cuba, 1898–1958*, Pittsburgh: University of Pittsburgh Press, 1976

Pérez, Louis A., Jr., *Intervention, Revolution, and Politics in Cuba, 1913–1921*, Pittsburgh: University of Pittsburgh Press, 1978

Pérez, Louis A., Jr., "In the Service of the Revolution: Two Decades of Cuban Historiography, 1959–1979," *Hispanic American Historical Review* 40 (1980), 79–89

Pérez, Louis A., Jr., *Historiography in the Revolution: A Bibliography of Cuban Scholarship, 1959–1979*, New York: Garland, 1982

Pérez, Louis A., Jr., *Cuba Between Empires, 1878–1902*, Pittsburgh: University of Pittsburgh Press, 1983

Pérez, Louis A., Jr., *Cuba under the Platt Amendment, 1902–1934*, Pittsburgh: University of Pittsburgh Press, 1986

Pérez, Louis A., Jr., *Cuba: Between Reform and Revolution*, Oxford and New York: Oxford University Press, 1988

Pérez, Louis A., Jr., *Lords of the Mountain: Social Banditry and Peasant Protest in Cuba, 1878–1918*, Pittsburgh: University of Pittsburgh Press, 1989

Pérez, Louis A., Jr., *Cuba and the United States: Ties of Singular Intimacy*, Athens: University of Georgia Press, 1990

Pérez, Louis A., Jr., *Essays on Cuban History: Historiography and Research*, Gainesville: University Press of Florida, 1995

Pérez, Louis A., Jr., *José Martí in the United States: The Florida Experience*, Tempe: Arizona State University Center for Latin American Studies, 1995

Pérez-Stable, Marifeli, *The Cuban Revolution: Origins, Course and Legacy*, Oxford and New York: Oxford University Press, 1993

Poyo, Gerald E., *"With All, and for the Good of All": The Emergence of Popular Nationalism in the Cuban Communities of the United States, 1848–1898*, Durham, NC: Duke University Press, 1989

Quirk, Robert E., *Fidel Castro*, New York: Norton, 1993

Riera Hernández, Mario, *Cuba Libre, 1895–1958*, Miami: Colonial Press, 1968

Ripoll, Carlos, *José Martí, the United States, and the Marxist Interpretation of Cuban History*, New Brunswick, NJ: Transaction, 1984

Ruiz, Ramón Eduardo, *Cuba: The Making of a Revolution*, Amherst: University of Massachusetts Press, 1968

Schwartz, Rosalie, *Lawless Liberators: Political Banditry and Cuban Independence*, Durham NC: Duke University Press, 1989

Scott, Rebecca Jarvis, *Slave Emancipation in Cuba: The Transition to Free Labor, 1860–1899*, Princeton: Princeton University Press, 1985

Smith, Lois M., and Alfred Padula, *Sex and Revolution: Women in Socialist Cuba*, New York: Oxford University Press, 1996

Smith, Robert F., *The United States and Cuba: Business and Diplomacy, 1917–1960*, New York: Bookman, 1960

Smith, Robert F., "Twentieth-Century Cuban Historiography," *Hispanic American Historical Review* 44 (1964), 44–73

Stolcke, Verena, *Marriage, Class and Colour in Nineteenth-Century Cuba: A Study of Racial Attitudes and Sexual Values in a Slave Society*, London and New York: Cambridge University Press, 1974

Stoner, K. Lynn, *From the House to the Streets: The Cuban Women's Movement for Legal Reform, 1898–1940*, Durham NC: Duke University Press, 1991

Stubbs, Jean, *Tobacco on the Periphery: A Case Study in Cuban Labour History, 1860–1958*, London and New York: Cambridge University Press, 1985

Suárez, Andrés, *Cuba: Castroism and Communism, 1959–66*, Cambridge, MA: MIT Press, 1967

Suchlicki, Jaime, *University Students and Revolution in Cuba, 1920–1968*, Coral Gables: University of Miami Press, 1969

Suchlicki, Jaime, *Cuba: From Columbus to Castro*, New York: Scribner, 1974; revised London and Washington, DC: Brassey's, 1990

Szulc, Tad, *Fidel: A Critical Portrait*, New York: Morrow, 1986; London: Hutchinson, 1987

Thomas, Hugh, *Cuba: The Pursuit of Freedom*, New York: Harper, and London: Eyre and Spottiswoode, 1971; abridged as *The Cuban Revolution*, Harper, 1977

Turton, Peter, *José Martí, Architect of Cuba's Freedom*, London: Zed, 1986

Welch, Richard E., Jr., *Response to Revolution: The United States and the Cuban Revolution, 1959–1961*, Chapel Hill: University of North Carolina Press, 1985

Wilkerson, Loree, *Fidel Castro's Political Programs from Reformism to "Marxism-Leninism,"* Gainesville: University of Florida Press, 1965

Wright, Irene A., *The Early History of Cuba, 1492–1586*, New York: Macmillan, 1916

Zeitlin, Maurice, *Revolutionary Politics and the Cuban Working Class*, Princeton: Princeton University Press, 1967

Zimbalist, Andrew S., and Claes Brundenius, *The Cuban Economy: Measurement and Analysis of Socialist Performance*, Baltimore: John Hopkins University Press, 1989

Cultural History

Cultural history was formerly associated with the examination of art and intellectual activity among cultivated elites, but its scope has been broadened so that it has become the study of – as Raymond Williams puts it – "a whole way of life," its language, and its systems of representation. At the end of the 20th century cultural history has moved into the forefront of professional history: its practitioners may be relatively few but its visibility is high. In part, this trend in historiography reflects similar transformations in the human sciences as a whole: everywhere we are confronted with the concentration on symbolic and linguistic systems that has done much to erode the authority of older, inherited positivisms. In part, this can also be explained by the breathtaking acceleration of the culture industries, representing a quantum expansion in the symbolic worlds we all inhabit. This reordering of lived experience is reflected in the sorts of questions that historians are prompted to ask of the past, seeing new things in the past that had been previously invisible.

But the revitalization of cultural history at this moment may also derive from profound questions about history itself. Essentially, history is about the relations between the past and the present. Yet reflection on the connections between past and present is hardly the preserve of professional historians. It is a process that underwrites our public cultures. And it is a process that is deeply inlaid into private, subjective lives: in this context it is called memory. The imaginative properties of both private remembering and of professional or historio-graphical remembering are more apparent now than a generation or two ago. The very practices of history are founded on given cultural codes. These too are now becoming visible in new ways. Those who have turned to cultural history are concerned with the manner in which, at the turn of the millennium, history itself – the relations between past and present – can be most fruitfully imagined.

In the traditions of modern European thought, from the time of the Enlightenment, history was conventionally cultural history. It was concerned with the issue of civilization. The job of the historian was to chart the rise and fall of civilizations. And to an important degree civilization was judged in terms of high culture. The sharpest expression of such a historiography, emanating from the putative father of cultural history, can be found in the histories of Jacob Burckhardt. And, broadly, the philosophical imprimatur for such historiography came from Hegel.

The intellectual roots of contemporary cultural historiography are complex and diverse; indeed, a distinguishing feature of much of the most engaging cultural history of our own times is its willed conceptual eclecticism. In such a context generalization is dangerous. But it can be suggested that in the 20th century cultural history has been re-formed in the long, uneven break with Hegelianism. A number of dominating lines of transformation can be identified. Each, in a different manner, moves away from the totalizing ambition of classical Hegelianism.

First is the route from Nietzsche. From this purview the modern world is perceived not as the realization of reason but of unreason. "Monumental histories," legitimating the idea of evolutionary or teleological development bringing about progress, were condemned by Nietzsche in favor of a method that was both less inscribed in the protocols of rationalist explanation and that also attempted to discover the rational core of apparently irrational behavior. There is a direct connection between Nietzsche at the end of the 19th century and Foucault at the end of the 20th. There is an entire raft of Foucauldian cultural histories in our own times that aim to turn inside-out the connotations associated with the rational founding principles of western civilization, showing how unseen relations of power have been inscribed deep inside the much-vaunted freedoms of the West. In these explorations, the workings of culture have a privileged role. This Nietzschean perspective, revived most notably by Foucault, has been especially influential in contemporary studies of the formation of sexualities – where professional history has been confronted by the dynamics of sexual politics.

Second is the tradition that was concerned with collective mentalities. This is a tradition that, in its earliest moments, can be identified with Durkheim and with Marcel Mauss, and that in the 1920s and 1930s was a formative presence in the historiography of the Annales school. The emphasis on the unconscious forms of a culture – as opposed to its conscious content – was in turn to feed into that most beguiling of 20th-century intellectual revolutions, structuralism. In the work of structural anthropology, and most dramatically in the person of Levi-Strauss, a structural sociology converged with structural linguistics, or semiotics. The impact of this model of structural anthropology was profound, touching every corner of the humanities. This was a theoretical approach that directly addressed the question of cognition itself (taken up in the wonderfully challenging cultural history of Carlo Ginzburg). And, potentially at least, it was a mode of thinking that was peculiarly fruitful for historians, for the whole drift of structuralism was to suggest that culture itself derived, not from the innate human capacities of peculiarly gifted individuals, but from social and historical convention. It is difficult to think of any historian who regards him or herself as a direct inheritor of structural anthropology in the Levi-Strauss model, for there was much in this method that was inimical to the practice of history; but equally it is difficult to think of any of the great cultural historians of our own times whose very conception of culture has not been touched by this inheritance.

Third, there is the route out from Hegel represented by Dilthey, and by the notion of the close immersion in a text or culture signalled by the term *Verstehen* (understanding). This was to open up many fields of qualitative sociology (participant observation, for example) as well, again, of anthropology (not to mention Collingwood's philosophy of history). The methods of "thick description," advocated principally by Clifford Geertz, for example, can be found to have a direct correlate in the cultural historiography of Robert Darnton.

Fourth, mention must be made of Freud and traditions of psychoanalysis. The connections between historiography and psychoanalysis in the 20th century have always been representative of a minority interest. But in the field of cultural history they have been innovative. The more cultural historians have investigated issues associated with the imagination, the unconscious and those fantasies that drive the inner life, the more central the psychoanalytical traditions have become.

This is a necessarily schematic mapping. The interconnections between these different modes of thought are of most significance. But the effect of these (and other) perspectives has been to allow the reinvention of cultural history in our own times. Owing to the impact of, first, structuralism, and then poststructuralism, this has been identified, most frequently, as evidence of the "linguistic turn" in historiography – a not altogether appropriate term to describe the very different conceptual impulses at work. Even so, two very broad tendencies can be discerned underlying the shift described. The first is a move away from the positivist inheritance of historiography, a positivism that has been in place since the institutionalization of history as an academic discipline at the end of the 19th century. The second – more complex in nature – is the move away from faith in the Hegelian notion of totality: cultural history today is as likely to be concerned with the margins as with the center; with the micro rather than with the macro; and with symbolic or "morphological" connections rather than with strict questions of causality.

This represents a palpable break. It affects, as I suggest in a moment, not only matters of content – what is appropriate for historiographical inquiry – but also, critically, the means of historiographical representation (or how the story is told). But it allows too the cultural dimension of historiography, both in terms of object of study and in terms of method of inquiry, to be more explicitly conceptualized. If one looks at the generation of British historians, for example, who were either writing or who came of age in the 1930s, one can see that time and again they insisted that whatever the scientific properties of history, it needed also to be "poetic." This difficult

formulation suggested, in metaphorical idiom, that essentially aesthetic notions – the imaginative capacities of the author, recognition of the power of the inner life on the shaping of ideas, the rhetorical power of language – all needed to be recognized as formal components of historical as much as of literary studies. Thus there are continuities as well as breaks.

In the anglophone world, an important recognition of these shifts appeared in a lecture delivered by E.H. Gombrich, which was subsequently published as *In Search of Cultural History* (1969). Here Gombrich was explicit about the need to break from the metaphysics of Hegel, while salvaging as many of his methods, at a lower level of abstraction, as remained viable. He recognized too the "chastening" insight that "no culture can be mapped out in its entirety," advocating instead the value of establishing the "interconnectedness" of historical relations.

Since the late 1960s, various manifestos for, or readers on, "the new cultural history" have proliferated, emanating from the English-speaking world, from Western Europe, and from Latin America (Brazil in particular, which is not without its connections to Levi-Strauss and his intellectual milieu). More to the point, some impressively rich empirical historiography has appeared. Much of this is modest and low-key, appearing in small journals, and then forgotten in the vast tides of print that envelop all readers in this period; a handful of practitioners can boast a global reputation – one thinks of Carlo Ginzburg, Robert Darnton, or Natalie Zemon Davis.

The full range of this work cannot be summarized. A final point will have to suffice. The protracted break from the positivist legacy has undermined an unadorned faith in truth and in its empirical foundations. The contingencies of historical knowledge, shifting from generation to generation and from place to place, appear now of far greater consequence than in the first half of the century. Indeed, it has been the cultural historians who have been most ready to look to literary models in order to think through the complexities of historical truth. And it has been the cultural historians who have been most daring in recasting received notions of history by inventing new narrative forms.

Dominic La Capra has argued that the modernist revolution, which a hundred years ago swept through the imaginative arts, has come to historiography only belatedly. Narratives driven by multiple perspectives; the conscious employment of variant rhetorical strategies, carrying different voices and different tones; the suspicion of an incontrovertible, monologic conclusiveness: all these increasingly appear in the new cultural histories. They do not negate the principal methodologies (or the ethics) of the jobbing historian. Natalie Zemon Davis talks of consciously making her rhetoric work for her; and of a history that generates not so much proofs as "historical possibilities." This does launch, to pick up an earlier point, a new poetics of historical study, in which historical truth lies as much in form as in content. This is a historiography that is itself a new cultural form. But as we see in its most exciting manifestations, it also promises a means of representation adequate to capture those "memories" of the past which are alive in our own culture today.

BILL SCHWARZ

See also Anthropology; Art; Body; Bourdieu; Braudel; Burckhardt; Burke; Chartier; Chevalier; China: Modern; Consumerism; Corbin;

Darnton; Davis, D.; Davis, N.; Europe: Modern; Freyre; Garin; Gay; Ginzburg; Hanke; Herder; Huizinga; Hunt; Intellectual; Köprülü; Lamprecht; Mentalities; Mexico; Miliukov; Mosse; Mumford; Ozouf; Schorske; Soboul; Theatre; Thomas, K.; Thompson, E.; Vico; Vovelle; Williams, R.; Zeldin

Further Reading

Bederman, Gail, *Manliness and Civilization: A Cultural History of Gender and Race in the United States, 1880–1917*, Chicago: University of Chicago Press, 1995

Burckhardt, Jacob, *Die Cultur der Renaissance in Italien*, 2 vols., Basel: Schweighauss, 1860; in English as *The Civilization of the Renaissance in Italy*, 2 vols., New York: Macmillan, and London: Swan Sonnenschein, 1904

Chartier, Roger, *Cultural History: Between Practices and Representations*, Ithaca, NY: Cornell University Press, and Cambridge: Polity Press, 1988

Confino, Alon, "Collective Memory and Cultural History: Problems of Method," *American Historical Review* 102 (1997), 1386–1403

Darnton, Robert, *The Great Cat Massacre and Other Episodes in French Cultural History*, New York: Basic Books, and London: Allen Lane, 1984

Davis, Natalie Zemon, *Society and Culture in Early Modern France: Eight Essays*, Stanford, CA: Stanford University Press, and London: Duckworth, 1975

Fox, Richard Wightman, and T.J. Jackson Lears, eds., *The Power of Culture: Critical Essays in American History*, Chicago: University of Chicago Press, 1993

Geertz, Clifford, *The Interpretation of Cultures: Selected Essays*, New York: Basic Books, 1973; London: Hutchinson, 1975

Gilroy, Paul, *The Black Atlantic: Modernity and Double Consciousness*, Cambridge, MA: Harvard University Press, and London: Verso, 1993

Ginzburg, Carlo, *Il formaggio e i vermi: il cosmo di un mugnaio del '500*, Turin: Einaudi, 1976; in English as *The Cheese and the Worms: The Cosmos of a Sixteenth-Century Miller*, London: Routledge, and Baltimore: Johns Hopkins University Press, 1980

Gombrich, E.H., *In Search of Cultural History*, Oxford: Oxford University Press, 1969

Hunt, Lynn, ed., *The New Cultural History*, Berkeley: University of California Press, 1989

Schorske, Carl E., *Fin-de-Siècle Vienna: Politics and Culture*, New York: Knopf, 1979; London: Weidenfeld and Nicolson, 1980

Schwarz, Bill, *The Expansion of England: Race, Ethnicity and Cultural History*, London and New York: Routledge, 1996

Susman, Warren, *Culture as History: The Transformation of American Society in the Twentieth Century*, New York: Pantheon, 1984

Williams, Raymond, *Culture and Society, 1780–1950*, London: Chatto and Windus, and New York: Columbia University Press, 1958

Winter, Jay, *Sites of Memory, Sites of Mourning: The Great War in European Cultural History*, Cambridge and New York: Cambridge University Press, 1995

Curti, Merle 1897–1996

US social and intellectual historian

Perhaps the most influential American historian between the Progressive generation of the early 20th century and the Consensus school of the 1950s, Merle Curti wrote pioneering works in American intellectual and social history, peace research, and the history of education. Curti's remarkably long and prolific career, stretching over sixty years, is significant not only – perhaps not even primarily – for its impact on current historical debate. Indeed, there is no "Curti school" or "Curti thesis" that currently engages historians in active debate. Curti's career uniquely illuminates the development of the American historical profession since the Progressive era, even though his actual writings are cited less frequently by historians.

Perhaps due to his upbringing in the Populist-Progressive ferment of small-town midwestern America, Curti's sympathies from the start were broadly democratic and critical of laissez-faire industrial capitalism. Curti's oeuvre is heavily influenced by the Progressive historians, especially Charles Beard, Carl Becker, and Frederick Jackson Turner (Curti was a Turner student at Harvard College). While not a Marxist in any strict or orthodox way, he undoubtedly absorbed Marx through the Progressive historians and later through John Dewey, his colleague at Columbia University Teacher's College in the 1930s. In contrast to the sometimes coarse economic determinism of the Progressives, Curti leavened his historical analysis with insights gained from Dewey's instrumentalist approach. So while Curti's awareness of economic interests was always keen, he avoided clumsy class struggle analyses by situating conflict within its broader social, cultural, and institutional setting.

Curti's earliest work examined the origins and development of the American peace movement. His doctoral dissertation was published in 1929 as *The American Peace Crusade, 1815–1860*; he expanded this study with *Peace or War: The American Struggle, 1636–1936* (1936). While highly sympathetic to his subject – he was a pacifist until the rise of Hitler's Germany convinced him otherwise – he did not let this compatibility blind him to critical social analysis. While the "history of this [peace] crusade ... is a stirring one," he wrote, the middle-class constituency of the movement prevented it from taking any radical stance against "social injustice, class conflict, and the profit motive."

Curti's next major project came as a result of an invitation from the American Historical Association's Commission on Social Studies in the Schools. *The Social Ideas of American Educators* (1935) had a profound impact on the history of education, bringing it into the mainstream of historical writing. Rather than narrowly focusing on particular institutions or educational policymaking, Curti placed the history of American education clearly within the context of American capitalism and the class interests inherent in an industrializing society. Mainly a series of intellectual-biographical sketches of such figures as Horace Mann and Booker T. Washington, *Social Ideas* was similar to Curti's peace research in that he expressed sympathy with progressive reformers while recognizing the limitations class interests placed on their reforms. While Curti's assessments of individual educators are perhaps obsolete, his emphasis on examining the social purposes of education continues to be a main feature of American historiography.

Curti is known primarily as an intellectual historian, a reputation based chiefly on his masterful synthesis, *The Growth of American Thought* (1943, 4th edition 1982). Today readers of *American Thought* often underestimate the work, due in part to its encyclopedic scope and resulting lack of detailed analysis, and (by today's standards) its loose theoretical underpinnings. While these criticisms are legitimate enough, Curti's achievement still commands respect; a 1952 poll of American historians voted *American Thought* the "most favored" historical work published between 1936 and 1950, a testament to its significance.

No doubt *American Thought* gained this status because before Curti invented it, there was no such field as American Intellectual History. While precursors such as Edward Eggleston, Bliss Perry, and Vernon L. Parrington had published works in what today is classified as intellectual history, they treated almost exclusively literary and religious figures. Curti broadened the scope of inquiry by including thinkers from across the intellectual spectrum (including scientists), serious writers as well as popularizers. Dime novels and Darwinism, Dewey as well as the advertiser Bruce Barton all met Curti's criteria for inclusion.

The Growth of American Thought is rarely used in classrooms today, and historians are more likely to use it as a handy encyclopedia or handbook than to read it as a compelling interpretation of American thought. Such use, however, does not diminish its importance. Curti's approach, placing ideas within their economic and social contexts, is his legacy to the writing of intellectual history. The alternative approach, exemplified by Arthur O. Lovejoy in European history and Perry Miller in early American history, treats ideas autonomously, as the play of minds isolated from the social contexts in which the thinkers lived. While the Lovejoy-Miller history of ideas approach has its adherents (John P. Diggins, for example), the "ecological" approach pioneered by Curti is today the dominant strain in American historiography.

Besides its position as a founding text of intellectual historiography, *American Thought* brought the entire Progressive historiographical project to a crucial point. Critics of Progressive historiography had long objected to its relativism and presentism. *American Thought* clearly evinced these traits. Furthermore, while Curti displayed a mastery of material, he failed to provide a consistent theory of the role ideas played in society. For example, when progressive-democratic reforms succeeded in having an impact on society, Curti attributed their success to their rationality; when they failed, however, he tended to emphasize the stifling effect of economic and social interests. On the other hand, the presentism inherent in Progressive historiography never seemed to bother Curti. In an approving review of Becker's *Everyman His Own Historian* (1935), he urged historians to "select and emphasize those memories of the past that will impel men to seek and build a more desirable future." The problems of relativism and lack of explanatory theory, however, were not so easily ignored.

Fortuitously, Curti reached this impasse at the same time as the American historical profession did. To a number of American historians, the social sciences seemed to provide the theoretical model that could solve what Peter Novick called the "objectivity problem." To this end, the Social Science Research Council funded an investigation into employing social science methodology in historical writing, the committee of which Curti chaired. The resulting report, *Theory and Practice in Historical Study* (SSRC Bulletin no. 54, 1946) did not, of course, solve the "objectivity problem"; nor did Curti and his committee colleagues uncritically embrace positivistic social science as a model for historical writing. But the report, with its employment of social scientific terminology (e.g., "frames of reference"), nevertheless drew historical practice closer to the social sciences.

The next major project Curti tackled was in some respects a natural outgrowth of his earlier work: first, because democracy had always been a central concern; second, because it examined his mentor Turner's frontier thesis; and third, by its attempt to address the problems of objectivity and relativism raised in *Theory and Practice*. Written with his wife, Margaret W. Curti, and three other associates at the University of Wisconsin, *The Making of an American Community* (1959) is important for its enormously innovative methodology and sources. In this test case for the applicability of the frontier thesis to 19th-century Templealeau County, Wisconsin, Curti and his colleagues were among the first scholars to use census records, record linkage, and statistical analysis as the basis for writing social history. Never before had these sources and methods been used to test a historical hypothesis (generally confirming Turner's view that the frontier had a democratizing influence on social structure), and *The Making of an American Community* became a milestone work, presaging the rise of the New Social History of the 1960s and 1970s, and blazing the trail for a generation of community studies by historians such as Philip Greven and Stephen Thernstrom.

Merle Curti's influence on American historiography can no longer be traced through current citation indexes because, more than most historians, his impact transcends his bibliography. His renown continues in other ways: the Organization of American Historians' prize for best book in intellectual and social history bears his name; and he is remembered as an inspiring teacher who mentored more than a generation of graduate students, including Richard Hofstadter, Warren Sussman, and John Higham. For the better part of the 20th century, Curti's career has both shaped and reflected the writing and practice of history in the United States.

CHRISTOPHER BERKELEY

See also United States: Historical Writing, 20th Century

Biography

Merle Eugene Curti. Born Papillon, Nebraska, 15 September 1897. Received BA, Harvard University, 1920, MA 1921, PhD 1927; additional postgraduate study at the Sorbonne, 1924–25. Instructor, Beloit College, 1921–22; professor, Smith College, 1925–37; and Columbia University Teachers College, 1937–42; Frederick Jackson Turner professor of history, University of Wisconsin, Madison, 1943–68 (emeritus). Married Margaret Wooster, 1925 (died 1961; 2 daughters). Died Madison, 9 March 1996.

Principal Writings

The American Peace Crusade, 1815–1860, 1929
The Social Ideas of American Educators, 1935; revised 1959
Peace or War: The American Struggle, 1636–1936, 1936
The Growth of American Thought, 1943; 4th edition 1982
The Roots of American Loyalty, 1946
Editor, *Theory and Practice in Historical Study: A Report of the Committee on Historiography*, New York: Social Science Research, 1946 [Bulletin 54]
With Vernon Carstensen, *The University of Wisconsin: A History, 1848–1925*, 2 vols., 1949
Probing Our Past, 1955
With Robert Daniel, Shaw Livermore, Jr., Joseph Van Hise, and Margaret W. Curti, *The Making of an American Community: A Case Study of Democracy in a Frontier County*, Stanford, CA: Stanford University Press, 1959
Human Nature in American Thought: A History, 1980

Further Reading

Dawidoff, Robert, "*The Growth of American Thought*: A Reconsideration," *Reviews in American History* 14 (1986), 474–86

Ekirch, Arthur A., Jr., *American Intellectual History: The Development of a Discipline*, Washington, DC: American Historical Association, 1963

Henretta, James A., "*The Making of an American Community*: A Thirty-Year Retrospective," *Reviews in American History* 16 (1988), 506–12

Higham, John, *History: Professional Scholarship in America*, New York: Harper, 1965; revised edition, Baltimore: Johns Hopkins University Press, 1989

Higham, John, and Paul K. Conkin, eds., *New Directions in American Intellectual History*, Baltimore: Johns Hopkins University Press, 1979

Skotheim, Robert Allen, *American Intellectual Histories and Historians*, Princeton: Princeton University Press, 1966

Curtin, Philip D. 1922–

US historian of Africa

Philip D. Curtin has led the growth of African history in the United States, defined a comparative style of world history, and contributed significantly to the development of intellectual history, historical demography, economic history, and medical and environmental history in Africa and other non-European regions. He is best known among European and American historians for his seminal quantitative assessment of the volume and directions of the Atlantic slave trade (*The Atlantic Slave Trade: A Census*, 1969). Curtin served as president of the (US) African Studies Association (1970–71) and of the American Historical Association (1983) and represented the American historical profession nationally and internationally. Two of his books won prizes in quite distinct subfields of history: the Robert Livingstone Schuyler prize of the American Historical Association for *The Image of Africa* (1964) and the Welch medal of the American Association for the History of Medicine for *Death by Migration* (1989).

Curtin made his principal contributions to African history in the United States through his development of programs in African and comparative tropical (later: world) history at the University of Wisconsin, Madison, between the early 1960s and 1975, where – with his equally eminent colleague, Jan Vansina, and later also Steven Feierman – he trained a generation of students who became prominent in a range of subfields of African history that reflected the breadth of his own accomplishments. With Vansina and Feierman, and joined by Leonard Thompson, Curtin authored a standard African history text. He also coauthored the widely read semi-popular introduction to the study of Africa, *Africa and Africans* (1971). Curtin joined the Johns Hopkins University Department of History in 1975 and from that base he developed his long-standing professional and scholarly interests in world history through leadership of the fledgling World History Association.

Like most other members of the founding generation of African historians in the 1950s, Curtin entered "non-western" history from a background in the history of Europe. His doctoral research at Harvard led to a first book contrasting imperial and local interests in 19th-century Jamaica, and to an enduring interest in the history of Latin America. He then turned to intellectual history, exploring the increasingly racist European outlook in *Image of Africa* (1964). His emphasis on the growth of European racist thought carried through to *Africa and Africans*, where he introduced beginners to the continent by identifying the racist myths in modern western culture that surround Africa. At a time when Africa's past still seemed beyond the reach of established specializations in the historical discipline, Curtin explored the potential of Africans' intellectual history in two edited volumes, *Africa Remembered* (1967), and *Africa and the West* (1972).

Further definitive contributions to contemporary understanding of Africa's past came from Curtin's demonstration that formal economic history techniques could be applied to Africa, at a time when Africans' "economic rationality" was being questioned and when few dared hope for evidence from Africa amenable to economic analysis. His *Census* of the Atlantic slave trade offered the first systematic research into the volume and direction of the "odious commerce," revealing an unsuspected quantity and variety of evidence from all sides of the Atlantic basin and narrowing the existing wide range of estimates to a statistically determined figure in the vicinity of 10 to 12 million Africans landed alive in the New World. Hundreds of subsequent studies have modified the detailed timing and geographical distribution of the trade, and, although a few have attempted to raise the aggregate total for the trade as high as 15 million, the scholarly consensus still takes Curtin's approach as a starting point. It was ironic, in view of Curtin's intellectual history of European racism, that other professional circles, equally dedicated to exposing the harmful effects of racial stereotyping, interpreted the aggregate totals and quantitative style in the *Census* as diminishing the moral heinousness of the trade, by comparison to much higher, though undocumented, earlier estimates of its scale.

The patterns of Atlantic trade that Curtin defined in the *Census* framed his principal economic history monograph, *Economic Change in Precolonial Africa* (1975). In relation to the Atlantic trade, Curtin applied rational choice theory to African economic behavior in the grasslands and Saharan margins on the westernmost edge of the continent. He established a program in African economic history at the University of Wisconsin, which published the journal *African Economic History*. Curtin's emphasis on African economic inventiveness, even as slavers, encountered sustained criticism from other scholars who emphasized moral issues and the sufferings of the slaves, as well as from political economists who were simultaneously stressing Africa's "underdevelopment" – the thesis that Africa's contact with the world economy had impoverished the continent through forced "unequal exchange."

Curtin's interest in historical demography also contributed to the development of population history in Africa, which some of his students carried to sophisticated levels. His own work in this field remained global in scale and culminated in the appearance of *Death by Migration* (1989). In tracing the lethal effects of tropical pathogens on Europeans – often military men – who ventured into the tropics in the era before modern chemical medicine, this book combined population history with medical history and the history of disease to develop a subtheme that had emerged from Curtin's early work on European imperial history and had matured into calculations of slave mortality at sea that Curtin had appended to the *Census*.

The secondary emphasis on the influence of droughts and epidemics on the Senegambian desert margins in Curtin's *Economic Change* added the history of climate to Africa's past. Environmental change, expanded to incorporate human contributions to disasters often misperceived as "natural," has subsequently become a prominent aspect of studies of the experiences of Africans from early times to the present.

Curtin consistently, and distinctively, placed the history of Africa in its broader world-historical context. This broad vision positioned his teaching of African history, structured his textbook writing, and led his economic, population, and medical monographic research repeatedly out into the Atlantic and beyond. Curtin's approach to world history resonated more with William McNeill's many writings than with the highly structured political economy of André Gunder Frank or with the historical sociology of Immanuel Wallerstein that prevailed during the 1970s and 1980s. Curtin compared historical instances of similar phenomena, as he examined trading diaspora in *Cross-Cultural Trade in World History* (1984) or plantations, sugar, and slavery in *The Rise and Fall of the Plantation Complex* (1990). In these and several dozen essays and other shorter works, Curtin's career-long vision of methodologically sophisticated, rigorously documented, broad, and balanced history brought Africa's past onto the world stage, and has contributed significantly to the most profound and positive developments in the discipline during the second half of the 20th century.

JOSEPH C. MILLER

See also Africa: North; Africa: West; Britain: British Empire; Imperial; Indigenous; Latin America: National; Maritime; Migration; Quantitative; Slavery: Modern; Vansina; World

Biography

Philip De Armond Curtin. Born Philadelphia, 22 May 1922. Received BA, Swarthmore College, 1948; MA, Harvard University, 1949, PhD 1953. Taught at Swarthmore College, 1953–56; University of Wisconsin, Madison, 1956–75; and Johns Hopkins University from 1975. Married Anne Gilbert, 1957 (3 sons).

Principal Writings

Two Jamaicas: The Role of Ideas in a Tropical Colony, 1830–1865, 1955
The Image of Africa: British Ideas and Action, 1780–1850, 1964
Editor, *Africa Remembered: Narratives by West Africans from the Era of the Slave Trade,* 1967
The Atlantic Slave Trade: A Census, 1969
With Paul Bohannan, *Africa and Africans,* 1971
Editor, *Africa and the West: Intellectual Responses to European Culture,* 1972
Economic Change in Precolonial Africa: Senegambia in the Era of the Slave Trade, 2 vols., 1975
With Steven Feierman, Leonard Thompson, and Jan Vansina, *African History,* 1978
Cross-Cultural Trade in World History, 1984
Death by Migration: Europe's Encounter with the Tropical World in the Nineteenth Century, 1989
The Rise and Fall of the Plantation Complex: Essays in Atlantic History, 1990

Further Reading

Lovejoy, Paul E., ed., *Africans in Bondage: Studies in Slavery and the Slave Trade: Essays in Honor of Philip D. Curtin on the Occasion of the Twenty-Fifth Anniversary of African Studies at the University of Wisconsin,* Madison: University of Wisconsin Press, 1986

D

Darnton, Robert 1939–

US historian of France

Robert Darnton has been called a *maître du livre* and the description is not inaccurate. Over the past thirty years he has taken the study of the written word to new heights, proving along the way that Marshall McLuhan was correct when he stated that the medium is the message; in the case of Darnton, the medium first consisted of thousands of letters requesting books – the archives of the Société typographique de Neuchâtel, which Darnton realized created an ethnographic archive for the study of the social composition of 18th-century France. Through his work with these records, Darnton has expanded the frontiers of historical study and has enabled researchers to observe new facets of past literate cultures. Darnton has advanced this approach in his various books, such as *The Literary Underground of the Old Regime* (1982), but he has not restricted his interests in cultural history to the records of the Société typographique.

As a graduate student in the 1960s Darnton was introduced to the vast collections of pre-revolutionary French pamphlets held by the New York Public Library, and recognized their value not only as a record of what had occurred, but also as an integral part of those actions and events. Later, to his delight, he discovered the archival collections of the Société, then a virtually untouched collection of documents including requests for specific texts, many of them outlawed within France. Drawing on the sociological tools at his disposal, Darnton used these records to discover what literate France wanted to read. In doing so his work has gone beyond that of mere deconstructionists, that is, he went beyond the literary devices used in constructing the literary work, and proceeded to demonstrate in a very real and tangible way how the desire to read these books and pamphlets reflected the social and political mores of the period.

The archives of the Société contain thousands of letters from French bookdealers and booksellers from the 18th century, which Darnton immediately recognized for their potential value as a barometer of social unrest, individual longings, and, more generally, as a microcosm of literate French society. Over the following years he mined this precious lode in order to illuminate the underground world of literary France, the areas that interested the people, the topics that were popular.

Using this methodological approach to the holdings of other archives and the texts of printed works, Darnton has shown the accuracy of his perceptions of pre-revolutionary France and has made known to historians and public alike the value of understanding what the populace of a given time or place wants to read. To add to this understanding, he has also made use of anthropological tools; for example, in an essay from his collection *The Great Cat Massacre* (1984), "Peasants Tell Tales: The Meaning of Mother Goose," Darnton examined the lives of ordinary *citoyens* of the *ancien régime* through one of their more common surviving sources, the fairy tale. Employing theories and methods developed by cultural anthropologists and folklorists, such as Claude Lévi-Strauss, Antii Aarne and Stith Thompson, he provided the reader with insight into the background thoughts, emotions, and history embodied in such tales. In doing so, Darnton endeavored to portray the context of the written word, illustrating some of the complexities of 18th-century French culture.

As an analyst and observer of pre-revolutionary French culture Darnton has been without peer. As a literary observer of the printed word and what it represents, he has helped place it in its proper context. As a student of culture, he has shown the value of employing anthropological tools in historical studies. And as a historian, he has greatly benefited the profession, introducing the student and the specialist to fertile areas for study and to new methodologies.

DANIEL M. GERMAN

See also Anthropology; Chartier; Cultural; France: 1450–1789; France: French Revolution; Mentalities

Biography

Born New York City, 10 May 1939. Received BA, Harvard University, 1960; BPhil, Oxford University, 1962, PhD 1964. Junior fellow, Harvard University, 1965–68; taught at Princeton University (rising to professor), from 1972. Married 1963 (3 children).

Principal Writings

Mesmerism and the End of the Enlightenment in France, 1968
The Widening Circle: Essays on the Circulation of Literature in Eighteenth-Century Europe, 1976
The Business of Enlightenment: A Publishing History of the Encyclopédie, 1775–1800, 1979
The Literary Underground of the Old Regime, 1982
The Great Cat Massacre and Other Episodes in French Cultural History, 1984
The Kiss of Lamourette: Reflections in Cultural History, 1990
The Corpus of Clandestine Literature in France, 1769–1789, 1995
The Forbidden Best-Sellers of Pre-Revolutionary France, 1995

Further Reading

Fernandez, James, "Historians Tell Tales: Of Cartesian Cats and Gallic Cockfights," *Journal of Modern History* 60 (1988), 113–27

LaCapra, Dominick, "Chartier, Darnton, and the Great Symbol Massacre," *Journal of Modern History* 60 (1988), 95–112

Mah, Harold, "Suppressing the Text: The Metaphysics of Ethnographic History in Darnton's Great Cat Massacre," *History Workshop* 31 (1991), 1–20

Daube, David 1909–

British (German-born) legal historian

David Daube is perhaps the 20th century's foremost historian of ancient law. His work spans a 60-year period (from 1932 to the early 1990s) and is based on a remarkably thorough, indeed dazzling, grasp of the whole of classical literature, Roman law, biblical and Near Eastern law, the Talmud, and the New Testament. It is notable for its originality and penetrating insight, as well as for its extraordinary breadth, and for the felicity, lucidity, and wit of the writing.

Daube pioneered the modern study of biblical law as a subject of historical inquiry distinct from the study of biblical religion; he introduced techniques of biblical "form criticism" and emphasis on the original context and social situation of particular ideas and utterances into the study of Roman law; and he deployed a formidable knowledge of Rabbinic Judaism to produce profound insights both into the setting of particular pronouncements reported in the Talmud and into the background and significance of sayings and teachings recorded in the New Testament.

Daube was the product of an orthodox Jewish upbringing and a German classical education; he was guided into legal history by the great Roman lawyer, Otto Lenel, at the University of Freiburg, and studied for a doctorate at two universities (Göttingen and Cambridge) notorious for exact critical scholarship. His earliest publications, before he left Germany in 1933, concerned biblical and Talmudic law. He continued writing on biblical law in England and his early articles on the subject culminated in his first book, *Studies in Biblical Law*, completed in 1943, but published only in 1947.

The book marked an important new direction in biblical legal scholarship and in comparative legal history. It sounded themes typical of much of Daube's work on biblical law: for instance, the insistence that ancient Hebrew law is a field of legal study that should be approached as such and dissociated from the religious character given to it by the priestly authors of the Bible; the recognition that the actual operation of biblical law and the development of legal thought in biblical times can be sometimes better recovered by looking at legal concepts and categories implicit in biblical narratives and at nuances to be found in the language of those narratives; and the perception that certain ideas derived from the law of the time provided patterns that came to have a profound influence on biblical theology. A notable example of the latter is the powerful effect of ancient legal practices regarding the redemption of poor kinsfolk who have been sold into slavery on the formulation of concepts of Redemption in both the Old and New Testaments – a theme to which Daube returned in detail in *The Exodus Pattern in the Bible* (1963).

Daube's earliest article on Roman law, "On The Third Chapter of the *Lex Aquilia*," was published in 1936; it presented a brilliant and original interpretation of the history of the basic Roman statute on damage to property (including slaves). It was the first of a long line of articles that brought Daube international recognition as one of the most prominent living Roman lawyers. Much of his work on Roman law has been concerned with what analysis of linguistic forms can reveal about a particular text and with the misunderstandings that arise when scholars fail to pay attention to how ideas and institutions develop (but old linguistic forms persist) in the face of changing circumstances. The concern with linguistic analysis is particularly evident in his two books on Roman law: *Forms of Roman Legislation* (1956) and *Roman Law: Linguistic, Social, and Philosophical Aspects* (1969).

Daube's first studies of the New Testament also go back to the 1930s and initially took the form of papers prepared for C.H. Dodd's New Testament seminar at Cambridge. These early New Testament studies culminated in another book: the lectures *The New Testament and Rabbinic Judaism* delivered at the School of Oriental and African Studies of the University of London in 1952 and published in 1956. Daube's work on the New Testament emphasized its Jewish background, but a Jewish background more varied and open than 1st-century Judaism is traditionally supposed to be. It is the work of a scholar steeped in Rabbinic modes of exegesis (as few students of the New Testament are) and has yielded wide-ranging and brilliant insights into the power and persistence of Jewish elements in early Christianity.

In various other works, Daube has been concerned with the moral dilemmas faced by politically oppressed groups, with the position of marginalized "have nots" and women, and with problems of tyranny, obedience, and revolt. These themes are pursued, for instance, in the lectures later incorporated into his books *Collaboration with Tyranny in Rabbinic Law* (1965), *Civil Disobedience in Antiquity* (1972), and *Appeasement or Resistance, and Other Essays on New Testament Judaism* (1987).

Daube's work typically begins by focusing on a problematic detail, often a curious mode of expression, that others have overlooked in a text or tradition. Using that to illuminate other details, it builds up – in an almost magical way – to a startling, yet compelling, new view of the subject. For all its emphasis on context, however, his work has been primarily concerned with deciphering the meaning of texts rather than with the systematic reconstruction of their social setting. Daube's is a style of scholarship that, indeed, eschews systematic exposition and seeks to read riddles and solve problems rather than survey the answers arrived at by others. Hints of the Daubean style are evident in the work of a few immediate pupils (such as Calum Carmichael and Alan Watson); but, for the most part, his work is the product of a unique and peculiarly erudite genius whose working methods have not been readily assimilable by others.

EDWARD M. WISE

See also Watson

Biography

Born Freiburg, 8 February 1909. Educated at Berthold Gymnasium, Freiburg; studied law, University of Freiburg; doctor of law,

University of Göttingen, 1932; PhD, Cambridge University, 1936. Fellow, Caius College, Cambridge, 1938–46; lecturer in law, Cambridge University, 1946–51; professor of jurisprudence, University of Aberdeen, 1951–55; Regius professor of civil law, and fellow, All Souls College, Oxford University, 1955–70 (emeritus); professor, School of Law, University of California, Berkeley, 1970–77 (emeritus); director, Robbins Hebraic and Roman Law Collection, 1970–89. Married 1) Herta Babette Aufseesser, 1936 (marriage dissolved 1964; 3 sons); 2) Helen Margolis Smelser, 1986.

Principal Writings

Studies in Biblical Law, 1947
Editor with William David Davies, *The Background of the New Testament and Its Eschatology*, 1955
Forms of Roman Legislation, 1956
The New Testament and Rabbinic Judaism, 1956
Editor, *Studies in the Roman Law of Sale: Dedicated to the Memory of Francis de Zulueta*, 1959
The Exodus Pattern in the Bible, 1963
The Sudden in the Scriptures, 1964
Collaboration with Tyranny in Rabbinic Law, 1965
Roman Law: Linguistic, Social, and Philosophical Aspects, 1969
Civil Disobedience in Antiquity, 1972
Ancient Jewish Law: Three Inaugural Lectures, 1981
Appeasement or Resistance, and Other Essays on New Testament Judaism, 1987
Collected Studies in Roman Law, edited by David Cohen and Dieter Simon, 2 vols., 1991
Collected Works, vol. 1, *Talmudic Law*, edited by Calum M. Carmichael, 1992

Further Reading

Bammel, Ernst, Charles Kinsley Barrett, and W.D. Davies, eds., *Donum Gentilicium: New Testament Studies in Honour of David Daube*, Oxford: Oxford University Press, 1978
Carmichael, Calum M., ed., *Essays on Law and Religion: The Berkeley and Oxford Symposia in Honour of David Daube*, Berkeley, CA: Robbins Collection, 1993
Jackson, Bernard S., ed., *Studies in Jewish Legal History in Honour of David Daube*, London: Jewish Chronicle Publications, 1974
Watson, Alan, ed., *Daube Noster: Essays in Legal History for David Daube*, Edinburgh: Scottish Academic Press, 1974

Davidoff, Leonore 1932–

US/British feminist historian

Leonore Davidoff is best known for *Family Fortunes* (1987), her ground-breaking reassessment of the making of the English provincial middle class, written in conjunction with a fellow feminist historian, Catherine Hall. By using a gendered analytical framework, they created a nuanced portrait of a particular class in England that was the product of a long-term study of class and gender in 19th-century British society based on their training in the British sociological tradition. Davidoff the sociologist moved into history early in her career because "Edwardian, even Victorian, culture cast a long shadow over the lives of older women, as well as molding the institutions of post-war England."

Davidoff's first book was *The Best Circles* (1973). A study of high society, etiquette, and the social season, it heralded Davidoff's main interests; domestic life, housekeeping, domestic service, domestic and family relationships, and women's employment were to be emphasized in different ways throughout her most important works. In *The Best Circles* she introduced intriguing views of the ways in which upper- and middle-class women maintained the fabric of "Society" through ever-changing social rituals, particularly the etiquette of card leaving and "calling" that regulated social intercourse and ensured that those with higher status maintained control over social relationships. One of the most compelling aspects of the book is Davidoff's attempt to "look at Society in detail as a linking factor *between* the family and political and economic institutions." Far from being "private" and ephemeral, these practices prevented the aristocracy from remaining a rigid social category. Individuals and families whose wealth was based upon the professions, commerce, and industry were carefully vetted, and often admitted to the highest social ranks. In turn, this influenced the shift to broader-based politics and culture; and economically, the etiquette rituals stimulated major shifts in patterns of consumption. While these connections were sometimes more implicit than explicit, they provided a fleeting foretaste of the monumental effort made in *Family Fortunes* to deconstruct the public/private divide by demonstrating their close interdependence in the growth of the middle class in Britain. But at a simpler level, this slim volume furnished splendid thumbnail sketches of the extraordinary practices of the privileged in the 19th century: of masked balls and private music parties; of ladies-in-waiting squabbling over seating order at dinner; of the stiff formality of daily family worship made absurd by the perceptions of a child. Davidoff's eye for the telling detail that keeps the reader entranced – the mark of historians who turn their craft into art – was already keenly developed in 1973.

During the process of researching and writing *Family Fortunes*, Davidoff also edited in collaboration with Belinda Westover a very useful collection of articles examining aspects of women's work in the 20th century through the use of oral history. *Our Work, Our Lives, Our Words* (1986) yielded sometimes poignant reminders of both the continuities and changes in the home and work experiences of women from one generation to another. In *Our Work* we again see Davidoff's concern to break down dichotomies and boundaries: oral history she sees as a particularly important methodology for making links between work and family (the "public" and "private") and also for drawing connections between individual life experiences and the wider historical context.

Family Fortunes was widely reviewed in both history and sociology journals, being recognized immediately as an important work of synthesis between class and gender analysis. Davidoff and Hall supplied extraordinarily rich and suggestive detail about the lives of banking, trading, farming, and professional families in industrial and suburban Birmingham and rural Essex and Suffolk. We see into their churches, chapels, voluntary and charitable organizations; industrial, commercial, and farming enterprises; parlors, sickrooms, schoolrooms, and gardens; and we read of family and kinship relations at all levels of business, intimacy, and duty. Some considered the book insufficiently theoretical, but the insights were subtly embedded in the substantive material. The book accomplished brilliantly the difficult task of writing gender history rather than women's history: old masculinist models of what is significant for economic history were jettisoned; yet both men and women remained firmly within the frame of reference. The authors contended that the family was the institution central to the development of the middle class in their period. Strong domestic values motivated both women and men, and were legitimated by the strength of evangelical belief, both Anglican and Dissenting. These British capitalists pursued Mammon guided by a vision of earthly domestic bliss leading to eternal salvation. At the same time, these religious values buttressed and elaborated an already existing sexual division of labor so that on one level, the middle-class world came to be divided into increasingly segregated "public" and "private" spheres, to which men and women were respectively assigned. But the mutability of these rhetorical spheres was also demonstrated. One reviewer put it perfectly: "'The public world of men' ... is a concept which disappears before our eyes," as Davidoff and Hall demonstrated the ways in which the allegedly autonomous entrepreneur depended upon women and family, and the manifold ways in which women contributed to family enterprise in both direct and hidden ways. The central importance of domesticity to middle-class masculinity was also beautifully illustrated. There is much that is controversial in the book: the authors' emphasis upon the similarities between Anglican evangelicals and Nonconformists rather than on the bitter political differences between the Established Church and Dissent; putting gender at the center of economic history; and, indeed, the use of "separate spheres" as a significant guiding concept, to name just a few areas. As a landmark history, the book has quite rightly resulted in argument.

During the years between the publication of *The Best Circles* and *Family Fortunes* Davidoff's work appeared as a steady stream of scholarly articles, the most important of which have been republished in the collection *Worlds Between* (1995). Read together, these essays make a powerful argument that domesticity as a concept and the home as a place received important new emphases in the 19th century, across all classes and in both rural and urban areas. Davidoff argued that this affected diverse areas of social and political life: religious practices (particularly within the evangelical movement); individual experiences of masculinity and femininity; desires, sexuality and reproduction; work and production; and claims for political and social inclusion and leadership that were made by various groups among the middle and working classes. If any doubt had been possible about her position on the "public/private" debate after publication of *Family Fortunes*, this is removed by reading the collection as a whole, and the last chapter in particular where she discusses this key problem in detail. For Davidoff, "public" and "private" should not be considered as conceptual absolutes, but rather as a minefield of "huge rhetorical potential," unstable, mutable, and shifting in meanings and implications. On the material and experiential level, this dualism has affected our institutions, organizations, economies, language, family patterns, and psyches. But Davidoff does not see public and private as fixed, separate entities. Always in her work she is looking for the ways in which they overlap, influence each other, interpenetrate: she points out the areas of this dualism's operation, together with its contradictions and the hidden interrelationships that belie the rhetoric. In short, her work taken as a whole explores in fascinating detail the significance of the "public" and "private" as a system of meaning organizing modern English society,

while also deconstructing these notions. Far from being trapped within a redundant conceptual framework, Davidoff's accumulated work has provided us with rich and nuanced understandings of diverse aspects of women's and men's lives understood in the wider context of the evolving class structure and cultural framework of modern England.

MARGARET L. ARNOT

See also Britain: since 1750; Family

Biography
Born New York City, 31 January 1932. Received BA, Oberlin College, 1953; MS, London School of Economics, 1956; PhD, University of Essex, 1983. Research assistant, Department of Social Sciences, University of Birmingham, 1956–57; taught at University of London Extramural Department, 1955–60; senior member, Lucy Cavendish College, Cambridge, 1964–68; supervisor in sociology for economics tripos, Cambridge University, 1965–68; researcher and lecturer (rising to professor), University of Essex, from 1969. Married David Lockwood, 1956 (3 sons).

Principal Writings
The Best Circles: Society, Etiquette and the Season, 1973
Editor with Belinda Westover, *Our Work, Our Lives, Our Words*, 1986
With Catherine Hall, *Family Fortunes: Men and Women of the English Middle Class, 1780–1850*, 1987
Worlds Between: Historical Perspectives on Gender and Class, 1995

Further Reading
Newton, Judith, "*Family Fortunes*: 'New History' and 'New Historicism'," *Radical History Review* 43 (1989), 5–22
Vickery, Amanda, "Golden Age to Separate Spheres? A Review of the Categories and Chronology of English Women's History," *Historical Journal* 36 (1993), 383–414

Davidson, Basil 1914–
British historian of Africa

Basil Davidson has grown to become one of the most recognized names in African studies. Davidson worked as a journalist from 1938 to 1962 for a number of publications including the *Economist* and the London *Times*. During World War II he served in the British Army in the Balkans. The war exposed him to the excesses of nationalism and allowed him to see several African cities when he travelled to the Balkan war theater via Africa. He returned to his career of journalism following the war, with the additional intention of writing history. His plans to study Eastern European history faded as the Cold War made access difficult, so he turned to African history in 1951.

Davidson was active in defining the field and was among the first to write academic histories of the continent. His early works, such as *Old Africa Rediscovered* (1959), and *Black Mother* (1961, revised 1980), remain seminal works in African history. It has been said that the works of Davidson helped to usher in "the golden age" of African historiography.

The liberation of Africans still under colonial domination was an intense interest of Davidson's, and explains his staunch support for African nationalism. He travelled in the war theaters of Angola and knew well the nationalist leaders of Portuguese Africa, Agostino Neto and Amilcar Cabral. Davidson wrote about the nationalist movements in Portuguese Africa to inform the apathetic European and American public about the real social conditions in these nations. His anticolonial thinking led to the publication of *The Liberation of Guine* (1969), *In the Eye of the Storm* (1972), *The People's Cause* (1981) and *The Black Man's Burden* (1992). Davidson argued that the most important cultural event of 20th-century Africa was the culmination of nationalism and all its implications. Davidson's activities earned him the label of a radical, a tag he has given little effort to shedding: that European imperialism was cancerous, retrogressive, and brutal have remained central to Davidson's thinking.

As part of the nationalist school, Davidson has spent a good deal of time highlighting the glories of the African precolonial past. While interpreted today as biased and selective, nationalist historiography served a very real need in post-independence Africa. After decades of subjugation, obfuscation, and outright denial of the accomplishments of the African past by the European powers, nationalist historiography reclaimed the glory of the African past, giving back to Africans part of their sense of identity. A challenge for Davidson was to define "glorious" so it suited Africans, not Europeans. Despite this, Davidson succeeded in selecting themes and events that appealed to Western audiences and yet at the same time asserted the greatness of the African past.

One of the main features of Davidson's writings is his commitment to cross-disciplinary investigation of the past. For him, the discipline of history does not have a monopoly on ways to study the past. In the early years of African historiography, when secondary writings on many subjects were scant, a synthetic researcher was a practical one. Later, Davidson's synthetic research style became central to his writings as he investigated the interrelatedness of African societies to one another and the rest of the world. Among his studies that employ a cross-disciplinary research methodology are: *The African Past* (1964), *The Africans* (1969), *Africa in Modern History* (1978), *Modern Africa* (1983), *Africa* (TV series, 1984), *The Story of Africa* (1984), and *The Search for Africa* (1994).

Davidson has campaigned against ignorance of Africa in the West and to destroy many of the myths surrounding Africa in today's world; this has often led him to write on topics concerning the entire continent. This has widened his appeal to a large reading public, and his works have been translated into 17 languages.

This wide appeal has also attracted criticism, yet his works are superbly written, well documented, and have provided an abundance of further research avenues. Two generations of scholars have been influenced by his works. Many Africans, Europeans, and North Americans owe a great deal of the way they see African history to Basil Davidson.

TOYIN FALOLA and JOEL E. TISHKEN

See also Africa: Central; Nationalism; Ogot

Biography

Basil Risbridger Davidson. Born 9 November 1914. Served in the British Army, 1940–45, in the Balkans, North Africa, and Italy. Early career mainly as journalist: editorial staff member, the *Economist*, 1938–39; diplomatic correspondent, the *Star*, 1939; Paris correspondent, the *Times*, 1945–47, and chief foreign leaderwriter, 1947–49; special correspondent, the *New Statesman*, 1950–54; and the *Daily Herald*, 1954–57; leader-writer, *Daily Mirror*, 1959–62. Visiting professor in Ghana, 1964, at University of California, Berkeley, 1971, and at Edinburgh, Manchester, Birmingham, and Turin universities. Married Marion Ruth Young, 1943 (3 sons).

Principal Writings

The African Awakening, 1955
Old Africa Rediscovered, 1959; also as *The Lost Cities of Africa,* 1959
Black Mother: Africa – the Years of Trial, 1961; in US as *Black Mother: The Years of the African Slave Trade,* 1961; revised as *Black Mother: Africa and the Atlantic Slave Trade,* 1980
The African Past: Chronicles from Antiquity to Modern Times, 1964
Africa: History of a Continent, 1966
Africa in History: Themes and Outlines, 1967
East and Central Africa to the Late Nineteenth Century, 1967; revised as *A History of East and Central Africa to the Late Nineteenth Century,* 1969
The Africans: An Entry to Cultural History, 1969; also as *The African Genius: An Introduction to African Cultural and Social History,* 1970
The Liberation of Guine: Aspects of an African Revolution, 1969
In the Eye of the Storm: Angola's People, 1972
Can Africa Survive? Arguments Against Growth Without Development, 1974
Africa in Modern History: The Search for a New Society, 1978
The People's Cause: A History of Guerrillas in Africa, 1981
Modern Africa, 1983
Africa: A Voyage of Discovery (TV series), 1984
The Story of Africa, 1984
African Civilization Revisited: From Antiquity to Modern Times, 1991
The Black Man's Burden: Africa and the Curse of the Nation-State, 1992
The Search for Africa: A History in the Making, 1994; in US as *The Search for Africa: History, Politics, and Culture,* 1994

Further Reading

Egerton, F. Clement C., *Angola Without Prejudice*, Lisbon: Agency-General for the Overseas Territories, 1955
Eriksen, Tore Linne, *Modern African History: Some Historical Observations*, Research Report no. 55, Uppsala, Sweden: Scandinavian Institute of African Studies, 1979
Fyfe, Christopher, ed., *African Studies since 1945: A Tribute to Basil Davidson*, London: Longman, 1976

Davies, Norman 1939–
British historian of Poland

Among the foremost historians of Poland writing in the English language, Norman Davies is the author of the most satisfactory history of that country since Oskar Halecki's 1942 *History of Poland*. Unlike Halecki, who specialized in late medieval and Renaissance history, Davies' field is modern Poland. Nevertheless, Davies has, in many ways, become the intellectual successor to Halecki in that both men are able to comprehend the entire scope of the Polish past, and, of equal importance, place Polish history in its European context.

Furthermore, both moved from an early specialization on Poland to writing more broadly on European history, in effect using the complexity of Poland's history to help explain Europe's past, and refocusing European history on all of Europe, not simply the westernmost portion. This is most noticeable in Davies' *Europe: A History* (1996).

Davies' first book, a study of the Polish-Soviet War of 1919–20, was the first significant scholarship on that important conflict in English. A.J.P. Taylor described it as "a very remarkable book . . . a permanent contribution to historical knowledge and international understanding." *God's Playground* (1981), Davies' best-known book to date, is a synthetic, 2-volume work that provides a coherent and up-to-date narrative account of the Polish past, incorporating the work of both Polish and non-Polish scholars. His third book, *Heart of Europe* (1984), is, perhaps, his most interesting work stylistically. It covers Polish history in a series of essays, beginning with the Solidarity era and working backward to the Middle Ages. Meant primarily for a non-Polish audience, *Heart of Europe* is at its best in explaining the impact of history on the Polish consciousness, and the interplay of past and present that made history supremely relevant to Poles struggling under foreign oppression. More recently, Davies has focused on topics such as the Polish community in Britain, and the impact of World War II on East Central Europe. Davies' works often receive praise from reviewers for their scholarship as well as for the author's command of prose.

Historiographically, Davies tends to forego large, all-encompassing theories in favor of description and analysis. His works are strongest in the area of politics and government policy, subjects he seems to prefer over economics. Neither of his histories of Poland spend a great deal of time on the economics of peasant agriculture or industrialization, and emigration from the Polish lands receives virtually no coverage at all. Despite his descriptive approach, however, Davies is quite capable of drawing broad conclusions from the evidence, and drawing parallels across time, something that is essential in the study of Polish history and in understanding the Polish view of history.

As one of the foremost interpreters of East European history in the English-speaking world, Davies is at his most forceful in decrying the myths that many hold about Eastern Europe and its people. In a 1994 lecture he noted that despite all the attention paid to the 50th anniversary of the Allied invasion of France, World War II was primarily fought in Eastern Europe. Much of the history of that war has been written, he noted, without any accurate information about the Soviet Union – one of the war's major players. This has led to numerous distortions and a selective remembrance of the history of World War II that overemphasizes the role of the Western Allies.

Davies' ability to point out the fallacies and myths about controversial subjects – such as Polish-Jewish relations – has occasionally resulted in his being attacked in the popular press. Despite this, however, the depth and comprehensiveness of his books and articles insures that Davies will remain the most widely read historian of Poland working in a non-Polish language.

JOHN RADZILOWSKI

See also East Central Europe; Europe: Modern; Poland: to the 18th Century; Poland: since the 18th Century

Biography

Born Bolton, Lancashire, 1939. Studied history, Magdalen College, Oxford; University of Grenoble; and University of Sussex; doctorate, Jagiellonian University, Kraków. Research fellow, St. Antony's College, Oxford, 1969–71; lecturer, then reader in Polish history, School of Slavonic and East European Studies, University of London, from 1971.

Principal Writings

White Eagle, Red Star: The Polish–Soviet War, 1919–20, 1972
"Great Britain and the Polish Jews, 1918–20," *Journal of Contemporary History* 8/2 (1973), 119–42
Editor, *Poland, Past and Present: A Select Bibliography of Works on Polish History in English*, 1977
God's Playground: A History of Poland, 2 vols., 1981
Heart of Europe: A Short History of Poland, 1984
Sobieski's Legacy: Polish History, 1683–1983: A Lecture, 1985
Cataclysm: The Second World War and Eastern Europe, 1939–1945, 1988
"The Growth of the Polish Community in Great Britain, 1939–50," in Keith Sword with Davies and Jan Ciechanowski, *The Formation of the Polish Community in Great Britain, 1939–50*, 1989
Editor with Antony Polonsky, *Jews in Eastern Poland and the USSR, 1939–46*, 1991
Europe: A History, 1996

Davies, R.W. 1925–
British historian of Russia

R.W. Davies is the leading British economic historian of 20th-century Russia. From 1958 he was the collaborator of E.H. Carr in his history of Soviet Russia in the 1920s, which Davies has continued into an exploration of the 1930s and collectivization, with 1936 as the projected completion point for his investigations. After war service Davies studied Russian and then turned to economics and economic history to work under the leading émigré scholar Alexander Baykov at the University of Birmingham. Apart from a brief interlude, Davies then made his career at the University of Birmingham, where he succeeded Baykov to head a newly formed Centre for Russian and East European Studies (CREES), one of a number of such centers established by the British government in the early 1960s to assist in understanding the development of the Soviet bloc. Davies remained in charge until 1979, establishing its reputation as the leading center in Western Europe. He attracted world-class scholars such as Moshe Lewin and encouraged a formidable postgraduate research program. This was financed in part by winning OECD support for a pioneering study of Soviet science policy (which developed into an innovative study of technology levels) and later by gaining British Social Science Research Council support for an investigation of Soviet economic history. This allowed the publication of CREES working papers covering major aspects of Russian social and economic history. Despite this entrepreneurialism Davies remained an accessible, enthusiastic scholar, and it was characteristic that he relinquished control in 1979 to better concentrate on his historical work and supervision.

Here Davies insisted on empirical accuracy to break through the myths and the accusations of history informed by Cold

War perspectives, something made possible by the extensive acquisition of printed primary sources in the Alexander Baykov library at the university. In the 1980s this led Davies and his team into important technical debates about Soviet economic growth, especially in the New Economic Policy period. This field had witnessed much controversy over the prospects for growth, and even sharper political debates as new work suggested that the costs of Stalinism, though horrific, had been exaggerated in some accounts. In addition to his own accounts, Davies has also made available key documents on which the new economic history of Russia is being built, and reworked earlier classic estimates of growth rates. His concern has gone beyond narrow economic history to try to unravel the interaction of economics and politics, and in this sense, despite the use of modern economic and statistical concepts, his concerns remain more those of traditional historiography.

Davies, however, eschewed direct involvement in the wider debate on the nature of the USSR. When the Soviet Union invaded Hungary in 1956 he broke with the British Communist party, though he was not a part of the influential debates among ex-Communist party historians in Britain. Despite subsequent sharp criticism of the USSR and friendship with historians who fell foul of the regime, he rejected both Trotsky's arguments and more radical left-wing critiques and saw the system as having an element of "socialism." For Davies, Stalinism was a distorted "adaptation of Marxism" that could be overcome by reform. This led him to a positive view of *perestroika*, arguing at the time that "in 1987 and 1988 we have seen nothing less than the rebirth of Soviet Marxism. The Marxist analysis of the Soviet experience is now one of the focal points of the whole debate." He even allowed himself to speculate on the "alluring" prospect of "a golden Soviet future." When this prospect did not materialize he returned to his more detailed investigations of Soviet economic history which will remain an essential part of the foundations on which a more adequate analysis of the nature of the Soviet system will be built.

MICHAEL HAYNES

See also Carr, E; Russia: Modern

Biography

Robert William Davies. Born London, 23 April 1925. Educated at Westcliff High School; then served in radio communications including in Egypt for the Royal Air Force during World War II. Received BA in Russian studies, School of Slavonic and East European Studies, University of London, 1950; PhD in commerce, University of Birmingham, 1954. Taught at University of Glasgow, 1954–56; and University of Birmingham (rising to professor), from 1956: director, Centre for Russian and East European Studies, 1963–79. Married 1953 (1 son, 1 daughter).

Principal Writings

The Development of the Soviet Budgetary System, 1958
With others, *Science Policy in the U.S.S.R.*, 1969
With E.H. Carr, *Foundations of a Planned Economy, 1926–1929*, 2 vols., 1969–78
Editor with Ronald Amann and Julian Cooper, *The Technological Level of Soviet Industry*, 1977
Editor, *The Soviet Union*, 1978
The Socialist Offensive: The Collectivisation of Agriculture, 1929–1930, 1980

The Soviet Collective Farm, 1929–1930, 1980
"'Drop the Glass Industry': Collaborating with E.H. Carr," *New Left Review* 145 (May/June, 1984), 56–70
Editor with S.G. Wheatcroft, *Materials for a Balance of the Soviet National Economy, 1928–1930*, 1985
The Soviet Economy in Turmoil, 1929–1930, 1989
Soviet History in the Gorbachev Revolution, 1989
Editor, *From Tsarism to the New Economic Policy: Continuity and Change in the Economy*, 1990
"Gorbachev's Socialism in Historical Perspective," *New Left Review* 179 (January/February, 1990), 5–28
With J.M. Cooper and M.J. Ilic, *Soviet Official Statistics of Industrial Production: Capital Stock and Capital Investment, 1928–1941*, 1991
Editor with Mark Harrison and S.G. Wheatcroft, *The Economic Transformation of the Soviet Union, 1913–1945*, 1994
Crisis and Progress in the Soviet Economy, 1931–1933, 1995

Further Reading

Cooper, Julian, Maureen Perrie, and E.A. Rees, eds., *Soviet History, 1917–1953: Essays in Honour of R.W. Davies*, Basingstoke: Macmillan, 1995

Davis, David Brion 1927–
US cultural historian

David Brion Davis is one of the world's leading historians of the cultural and ideological aspects of slavery and antislavery. His first book, *Homicide in American Fiction, 1798–1860* (1957) stemmed from an initial interest in the movement to abolish capital punishment. Davis gradually shifted his scholarly focus to an investigation of the origins of antislavery. The result was *The Problem of Slavery in Western Culture* (1966; revised 1988). In a panoramic overview, Davis demonstrated historical continuities in the tensions and rationalizations of slavery from ancient through early modern times. He then traced the breakdown of the traditional system and the accompanying rise of antislavery thought during the first three quarters of the 18th century. Never before had the arguments for and against slavery been reviewed so comprehensively or with such emphasis on the ambiguities and ironies within the traditional religious and philosophical discourse. Moving through a broadly chronological sequence of individual writers, Davis' methodological premise was that, in the final analysis, descriptions of general intellectual trends are only abstractions. Antislavery opinion required the specific decisions and commitments of individual men to engender the age of abolition. The *Problem of Slavery* was received with almost universal and unreserved acclaim, and was awarded a Pulitzer prize in 1967. Davis' stress on the overriding importance of individual intellectual agents as the catalysts of the age of abolition elicited one sobering critique. Classical historian Moses Finley noted that the ending of slavery in America required the translation of intellectual fervor and commitment into political and military power. Nothing was more difficult and necessary in analyzing the history of slavery than to explain how new moral perceptions became effective in action. Finley implied that Davis' approach had limited the relevance of his history of antislavery to the contemporary world.

Davis' next major study, *The Problem of Slavery in the Age of Revolution, 1770–1823* (1975) was in part a response to

Finley's challenge. Here Davis explicitly set himself the task of explaining the breakthrough and success of abolition in Britain during the age of the American and French revolutions. Drawing upon a combination of Freudian and Marxian models, he accounted for this first major triumph of antislavery in class terms. British antislavery ideology, argued Davis, was especially attractive to the dominant political and economic classes of Great Britain during the early stages of its Industrial Revolution. By mobilizing British culture against the horrors of the slave trade, antislavery ideology could be read unconsciously in a way that displaced attention, among all classes, from industrial chains being forged closer to home. Davis' hypothesis of hegemonic displacement attracted more criticism than any argument in the first volume.

From this perspective, the second volume was historiographically far more stimulating and controversial than the first. Some historians objected to Davis' attempt to use Freudian dynamics to demonstrate the link between antislavery and class interest. Others challenged Davis' almost exclusive focus upon the attitudes of the dominant political and economic class in accounting for the political appeal or victories of British antislavery. After two decades of extended debate Davis himself reworked his analysis of the problem of capitalism and antislavery to take account of the critiques (see the revised *The Problem of Slavery in Western Culture*, 1988).

Davis' third major study of antislavery, *Slavery and Human Progress* (1984), was a return to the first volume's history of ideas. Davis again surveyed developments over two millennia, but with more emphasis on collective intellectual trends than on individual thinkers. In geographical scope the third volume went well beyond the Classical/Christian tradition of the first. *Slavery and Human Progress* cut against a previously dominant historiographical perspective. Davis envisioned the relationship between slavery and progress as extending far back into the pre-abolitionist era. Before the 18th century "progress" was linked to the expansion, not to the eradication of slavery. With the rise of antislavery occurred an inversion of the traditional connection. Yet Davis also showed that even during the age of abolition the idea of progress was often used to rationalize inaction and to defend slavery against antislavery. As with Davis' first study of antislavery, *Slavery and Human Progress*, with its subtle analysis of paradoxes and rationalizations, was appreciated for its encyclopedic sweep and magisterial grasp of multiple meanings.

Davis' impact to date is therefore a dual one. He has been the source of first resort for any analysis of antislavery thought and of its major cultural representatives, and he enormously expanded the range of theoretical perspectives that had previously been brought to bear on the history of antislavery. The scholarly debate that he stirred up is still reverberating.

SEYMOUR DRESCHER

See also African American; Genovese; Slavery: Ancient; Slavery: Modern; United States: Colonial; United States: American Revolution

Biography

Born Denver, 16 February 1927. Received BA, Dartmouth College, 1950; MA, Harvard University, 1955, PhD 1956. Taught at Dartmouth College, 1953–54; Cornell University (rising to professor), 1955–69; Yale University from 1972. Married 1) Frances Warner, 1948 (marriage dissolved 1971; 1 son, 2 daughters); 2) Toni Hahn, 1971 (2 daughters).

Principal Writings

Homicide in American Fiction, 1798–1860: A Study in Social Values, 1957
The Problem of Slavery in Western Culture, 1966, revised 1988
Editor, *Ante-Bellum Reform*, 1967
The Slave Power Conspiracy and the Paranoid Style, 1969
The Problem of Slavery in the Age of Revolution, 1770–1823, 1975
Slavery and Human Progress, 1984
From Homicide to Slavery: Studies in American Culture, 1986
Revolutions: Reflections on American Equality and Foreign Liberations, 1990

Further Reading

Bender, Thomas, ed., *The Anti-Slavery Debate: Capitalism and Abolitionism as a Problem in Historical Interpretation*, Berkeley: University of California Press, 1992
Drescher, Seymour, "The Antislavery Debate" [review essay], *History and Theory* 32 (1993), 311–29
Oostindie, Gert, ed., *Fifty Years Later: Antislavery, Capitalism, and Modernity in the Dutch Orbit*, Leiden: KITLV, 1995; Pittsburgh: University of Pittsburgh Press, 1996

Davis, Natalie Zemon 1928–
US historian of early modern Europe

A brilliantly scholarly historian, grasping the interest of her reader with the artistry of her superbly written books: these words of praise encapsulate critics' reception of Natalie Zemon Davis' books. With the addition of comments on her dazzling erudition, her innovative and imaginative way of exercising social history, we have the portrait of a ground-breaking historian.

The key word of her approach to 16th- to 18th-century France is dialogue. In her historical practice, dialogue with the past is not a simple metaphor, but a deliberate effort of listening to the voices of men and women beyond the centuries. Her attempt to capture the lives of the common people, of those who are usually absent from the historian's conventional archival sources, orients her methodological choices. Her frames of reference are the French school of "mentalities" which tries to reconstruct ordinary lives in the context of their larger social schemes of behavior, and her British predecessor and counterpart E.P. Thompson with his attention to the function of ritual. Davis' point of observation is also the intersection of society and culture.

What interests her is how collective and individual identities are constructed and transformed through cultural choices. More precisely, she wants to see how individuals shape themselves in relation to larger structures, be it the family or communities like the church. She never sees people as determined by the conditions and constraints framing their lives or limiting their actions. She presents them as actors maneuvering to cope with their conditions, and even succeeding in changing things, as she likes to show with reference to women.

Such a perspective characterizes her conception of popular culture as the outcome of a constant exchange with learned and high culture. While others oppose static dichotomies – learned/popular, literate/illiterate, male/female – Davis observes and analyzes intersections and a dynamic process of interactions. Her method tries to answer to a double challenge. The first is to bring into relief voices heard only through the interstices of traditional sources; the second, to give an accurate account of the multidimensional character of sociocultural realities. Her originality in the latter respect also comes from her skillfulness in establishing a dialogue with and between scholarly theories. She integrates literary history and theory in the study of typical cases. To retrieve the evidence of a popular culture, she reads social and cultural events as anthropologists and folklorists do.

In three of her books, she engages in multilayered analysis of case studies. Her first volume, *Society and Culture in Early Modern France* (1975), assembled eight essays on diverse aspects of 16th-century France. They are perfect demonstrations of the way social and cultural contexts act upon groups and individuals who, in their turn, contribute to shape them. This applies to religious dissent among male artisans or urban women or to ritual and festive traditions, particularly those involving "carnavalesque" demeanor of turning the world upside-down. Reversals and riots accomplish more than a blowing off of steam. They have close connections with the society's hierarchies and dominant values, and thus represent not the pathological but the normal.

The Return of Martin Guerre (1983) presents the ideal test case for Davis to illustrate the interplay between the shaping of individual identities and broader social and cultural considerations. This fascinating tale of an impostor who, for three years, took Martin Guerre's place in his village, family, and wife's bed, is a perfect context for Davis' multilayered analysis. The story presents aspects of peasants' life with their aspirations, constraints, property customs, and the way they manage their land. It puts into relief the value they invest in marriage and family links. The events are known through an account by Jean de Coras, doctor of laws, responsible for the case before the Parlement of Toulouse where the false Martin Guerre, Arnaud du Tihl, was tried and sentenced to death in 1560. This account gives the historian access to the way a lawyer and man of letters shaped peasants' experience.

Davis' third book does not totally contradict her confidence in ordinary people's capacity for maneuvering within the constraints of their fate, in spite of the situations of violence and crime presented. *Fiction in the Archives* (1987) examines letters of remission. They are requests for pardon addressed to the king of France by perpetrators of homicides, from 1523 until 1568. Their interest lies in the almost direct contact they provide with ordinary people's experiences. Legal experts who shaped the narratives did not overshadow their voices nor radically change the stories told to avoid execution. Pardon letters constitute one of the best sources about the lower orders of society. Davis begins by situating the legal and political context of the pardon letters, stressing their role in enhancing the king's power. She then devotes a chapter to stories of men killing men. They invoke as attenuating circumstances an excess of hot anger, often during ritual and festive times. By contrast, women's crimes are said to occur after years of sufferings.

However, Davis does not focus exclusively on their documentary interest. She considers them for their fictional value, the art with which men and women crafted their tales in comparison with contemporary literary short stories. Her technique of cross-fertilizing the reading of her sources through the interplay of different disciplines is particularly successful. Beyond sociological, political, and legal analysis, she opens new territories for the historian with her recourse to the domains of folklore studies, literary theory, and psychology.

MADELEINE JEAY

See also Agrarian; Anthropology; Body; Cultural; Feminism; France: 1450–1789; Kantorowicz; Mentalities; Pieroni Bortolotti; Women's History: Europe

Biography
Born Detroit, 8 November 1928. Attended Kingswood School, Detroit; Smith College, BA 1949; Radcliffe College, MA 1950; University of Michigan, PhD 1959. Taught history at Brown University, 1959–63; economics, then history, at University of Toronto, 1956–71; professor, University of California, Berkeley, 1971–77; and, Princeton University, 1977–96. Married Chandler Davis, mathematician, 1948 (3 children).

Principal Writings
"Some Tasks and Themes in the Study of Popular Religion," in Charles Trinkaus and Heiko Oberman, eds., *The Pursuit of Holiness in Late Medieval and Renaissance Religion: Papers from the University of Michigan Conference*, Leiden: Brill, 1974
Society and Culture in Early Modern France: Eight Essays, 1975
The Return of Martin Guerre, 1983
Fiction in the Archives: Pardon Tales and their Tellers in Sixteenth-Century France, 1987
"Iroquois Women, European Women," in Margo Hendricks and Patricia Parker, eds., *Women, Race and Writing in the Early Modern Period*, 1994
Women on the Margins: Three Seventeenth-Century Lives, 1995

Further Reading
Chartier, Roger, *Cultural History: Between Practices and Representations*, Cambridge: Polity Press, and Ithaca, NY: Cornell University Press, 1988
Diefendorf, Barbara B., and Carla Hesse, eds., *Culture and Identity in Early Modern Europe (1500–1800): Essays in Honor of Natalie Zemon Davis*, Ann Arbor: University of Michigan Press, 1993

Debo, Angie 1890–1988
US historian of Native Americans

In the preface to her textbook on American Indians, *A History of the Indians of the United States* (1970), Angie Debo tells the story of searching for an Indian church in Oklahoma. "Anybody can tell you where it is," an Oklahoma Creek assured her. Yet finding herself lost amid the rolling hills and brush, she stopped at a schoolhouse to ask the way. The white teachers claimed never to have heard of the place. The Indian students, on the other hand, immediately pointed out the spot, which stood a mere quarter mile away, shrouded by foliage. Debo explained, however, "there was a denser thicket in the minds of those teachers of Indian children obscuring their intellectual and spiritual view." It was this barrier that Debo sought to remove, and her most significant contributions to American history lie in her ability to explore the Native American view-point without preconception or prejudice and to present the history of first Americans to a broad US audience.

Debo battled two forms of prejudice as she began her career after earning her doctorate in 1933 from the University of Oklahoma. She taught briefly at West Texas State Teachers College, but discovered that, despite her qualifications, when most universities advertised for a professorship, women need not have applied. Thus, Debo spent most of her lengthy career as a freelance historian. Moreover, her initial attempts to write an honest history of American Indians were met not with open arms, but with hostility. Her second, and to many her most significant work, *And Still the Waters Run*, written in 1936, clearly pointed out the greed and exploitation that motivated whites who seized Indian lands, particularly those of the "five Civilized Tribes" removed to Oklahoma after 1830. She reserved the most biting criticism not for the military or frontiersman, but the wave of land sharks, corrupt lawyers, and politicians who followed the tribes to Indian Territory to plunder their farmlands, forests, mineral and oil resources. What resulted, Debo clearly wrote, was an orgy of exploitation almost beyond belief. Because many of those responsible still lived in Oklahoma in 1936, publication of *And Still the Waters Run* did not occur until 1940, and then only by an out-of-state publisher. The result was severe censure in some cases and charges of libel in others.

Nevertheless, exploitation of Native Americans was a theme Debo explored often. Her first work, for example, *The Rise and Fall of the Choctaw Republic* (1934) examined the impact of the US Civil War on the Choctaw people and revealed for the first time that Indians of Indian Territory also participated in that conflict, often with devastating results once the war ended. Neither did Debo entirely let the uninformed off the hook. Her works often reminded students of US history that much damage to native culture was also done by the well-meaning missionary or the reformer with ready solutions to problems he barely understood. Through her diligent return to this theme, Debo laid much of the groundwork for the ethnohistorical study of Native Americans that began to grow in the 1980s. As such, Debo was a true pioneer of Native American historical research.

In addition, Debo published a number of regional studies that veered sharply away from her exposé of white-native relations. These offer an in-depth look at frontier Oklahoma and early 20th-century communities, sometimes with a Wild West flair. One of the first, *Tulsa: From Creek Town to Oil Capital* (1943) was a history of the growth of a wild, booming frontier community. Thus, Debo made significant contributions to the historiography of US Western history and to the regional study of Indian Territory, or Oklahoma.

Debo's final publication, *Geronimo: The Man, His Time, His Place* (1976), was a return to the subject for which she will be best remembered, and in 1983, she wrote the preface to the 7th printing of *A History of the Indians of the United States*, a text based on a seven-week course in Indian history designed and taught by Debo for teachers of Indian children. In this final preface, Debo announced the correction of a previous error, an error made originally by negotiators of an 1804 treaty, which she unknowingly perpetuated. "I am glad," she wrote, "to correct my own account." Similarly, as a result

of Debo's lengthy and prolific career and her absolute determination to present the history of Oklahoma Indians honestly, it can be said that she caused many historians and other Americans to correct their own mistaken accounts of their nation's first inhabitants.

KATHLEEN EGAN CHAMBERLAIN

See also Native American

Biography

Born Beattie, Kansas, 30 January 1890. Moved with family to farm in Oklahoma, 1899. Educated at Marshall High School, Oklahoma, 1913; University of Oklahoma, BA 1918, PhD 1933; University of Chicago, MA 1924. Taught at West Texas State Teachers College, 1934–43; for most of her career was independent historian. Died Enid, Oklahoma, February 1988.

Principal Writings

The Rise and Fall of the Choctaw Republic, 1934
And Still the Waters Run: The Betrayal of the Five Civilized Tribes, 1940
The Road to Disappearance, 1941
Tulsa: From Creek Town to Oil Capital, 1943
Oklahoma, Foot-Loose and Fancy-Free, 1949
The Five Civilized Tribes of Oklahoma: Report on Social and Economic Conditions, 1951
A History of the Indians of the United States, 1970
Geronimo: The Man, His Time, His Place, 1976

Further Reading

Fey, Harold E., and D'Arcy McNickle, *Indians and Other Americans: Two Ways of Life Meet*, New York: Harper, 1959
Schrems, Suzanne H., and Cynthia J. Wolff, "Politics and Libel: Angie Debo and the Publication of *And Still the Waters Run*," *Western Historical Quarterly*, 22 (1991), 184–203

De Felice, Renzo 1929–1996
Italian political historian

Renzo De Felice was among the most controversial historians of Italian fascism. His notoriety, however, did not diminish his reputation as one of the most respected students of the subject and as the author of certainly the greatest biography of Benito Mussolini, a multivolume project for the Einaudi publishing house that, after thirty years, was on the verge of completion at the time of his death. De Felice's first volume, *Mussolini il rivoluzionario, 1883–1920* (Mussolini the Revolutionary, 1883–1920), was issued in 1965, and was followed by six more. The last, uncompleted, volume was to be a study of the dictator's last years as head of Germany's doomed puppet state, the Italian Social Republic. Along with the biography, De Felice wrote other important works on Italian history, from early studies on Italian Jacobinism and on the Jews under the fascist regime to *Il fascismo* (Fascism, 1970). He also edited letters and memoirs of many important 20th-century figures such as Gabrielle D'Annunzio, Alceste De Ambris, and Dino Grandi. In addition, as founder and editor of the important journal, *Storia Contemporanea*, De Felice enjoyed considerable influence in Italian academic life.

Besides presenting scholars with the most ambitious biography of the Duce, with its famously impressive footnotes, De Felice enriched the debate on fascism. He insisted that notions of generic fascism, although not without validity, are dangerous at some point and that important distinctions should be drawn between Italian fascism and its German cousin, National Socialism. While De Felice recognized other variations throughout Europe, he believed that a search for real fascism beyond there was a futile task.

De Felice's interpretation of fascism, particularly in its "movement" phase, as a middle-class revolution with roots in the Enlightenment, also provoked debate. He elaborated on this thesis until he reached the conclusion that the fascist revolt of society's middle ranks was not based on fear, but rather was an assertive bid for power by an emergent class. De Felice therefore accorded authentic revolutionary motives to Mussolini and gave fascism a certain status as a valid political idea unto itself, in the Enlightenment tradition, and not one to be explained away in what he criticized as "simple" Marxist terms. Finally, De Felice claimed that Mussolini's regime reached a height of genuine "consensus" popularity in 1936 with the conquest of Ethiopia.

De Felice's interpretations of Mussolini and fascism launched a major intellectual debate in Italy. While some drew what they believed to be De Felice's own conclusions, or apologies, from his texts, he was reluctant to label and embrace avowed interpretations. His clearest attempts to put his own synthesis in print came only in the mid-1970s with an entry on "Fascism" for the *Enciclopedia del novecento*, a final chapter of *Le interpretazioni del fascismo* (1969; *Interpretations of Fascism*, 1977), and an interview with the American scholar, Michael Ledeen, *Intervista sul fascismo* (1975; *Fascism: An Informal Introduction*, 1976).

While the first volume of De Felice's biography of Mussolini was noteworthy, the harshest criticisms erupted after the publication of *Intervista sul fascismo*. In 1975 Italy's fascist experience still weighed heavily on its historiography and many, particularly Marxist scholars, condemned De Felice's and other studies that failed to exhibit explicitly antifascist viewpoints. In his attempts to credit fascism as an authentically revolutionary movement with intellectual anchors in respectable philosophical traditions, important figures from the academic left such as Giuliano Procacci, Nicola Tranfaglia, and Paolo Alatri worried that De Felice had elevated apologias for fascism into serious historical discourse. De Felice answered these criticisms with accusations that Italy's historical "establishment" was too doctrinaire and rushed too easily to left-wing conclusions. Unfortunately his death leaves this question unresolved.

ROY PALMER DOMENICO

See also Italy: since the Renaissance; Salvemini; Spriano

Biography

Born Rieti, 1929. Studied under Delio Cantimori and Federico Chabod, University of Naples, where he was also a youthful activist in the Italian Communist party. Professor of history, Faculty of Political Sciences, University of Rome. Married Livia De Ruggiero, daughter of the historian Guido De Ruggiero. Died Rome, May 1996.

Principal Writings

Storia degli ebrei italiani sotto il fascismo (History of Italian Jews under Fascism), 1961
Mussolini, 7 vols., 1965–92
Le interpretazioni del fascismo, 1969; in English as *Interpretations of Fascism*, 1977
Il fascismo: le interpretazioni dei contemporanei e degli storici (Fascism: Interpretations of Contemporaries and Historians), 1970
Intervista sul fascismo, edited by Michael Ledeen, 1975; in English as *Fascism: An Informal Introduction to Its Theory and Practice*, 1976
Ebrei in un paese arabo: gli ebrei nella Libia contemporanea tra colonialismo, nazionalismo arabo e sionismo (1835–1970), 1978; in English as *Jews in an Arab Land: Libya, 1835–1970*, 1985

Further Reading

Ledeen, Michael, "Renzo De Felice and the Controversy over Italian Fascism," *Journal of Contemporary History* 11 (1976), 269–83
Painter, Borden W., Jr., "Renzo De Felice and the Historiography of Italian Fascism," *American Historical Review* 95 (1990), 391–405

Degler, Carl N. 1921–
US historian

Carl N. Degler, one of the leading post-1945 historians of the United States, has pursued a career which encapsulates many of the developments in American history during that period. Never a dogmatist or ideologue, in his work he represents many of the most fruitful developments of postwar liberal history, particularly the increasing emphasis given to social history and to the study of groups, once largely ignored, including ethnic minorities and women. Degler was ready to cross disciplinary boundaries and to use the insights of comparative history; he was also willing to challenge conventional pieties. His major works include a 1-volume synthesis of United States history and substantial studies of race, the South, American women, and most recently of the role of Darwinism in American social thought.

Degler's first major work, *Out of Our Past* (1959), provided a readable and accessible overview of the history of the United States. It concentrated, not upon facts, dates, and narrative, but rather on the evocation of the American past through the evidence both of the social sciences and of diaries, letters, literary sources, and the accounts of foreign observers. Degler dealt extensively with the changing lives and experiences of average Americans, especially those of the working class and trade unionists, and with women, the family, immigrants, and blacks, and the social effects of urbanization and industrialization. He also suggested that the scale and scope of the changes wrought in the United States by Franklin D. Roosevelt's New Deal amounted to a "third American revolution," the successor of the original revolution of the 1770s and 1780s, and the epochal Civil War. His work was an implicit answer to those historians who attempted to minimize the importance of the social and economic reforms of the 1930s.

Degler's interest in social history, coinciding as it did with the upheavals of the 1960s, led him to a comparative examination of slavery and race relations in the United States and Brazil, *Neither Black nor White* (1971). Degler attempted to explain why it was that Brazil had by the late 19th century dismantled its segregationist legislation, whereas the United States did not do so until the 1960s. He concluded that, although racism undoubtedly existed in Brazil, the ambiguous halfway status of the mulatto moderated many of its worst effects; moreover, the hierarchical nature of Brazilian society and the lack of full democracy to some degree protected blacks. In the United States, by contrast, and particularly after universal manhood suffrage became prevalent, all Americans with some African blood were defined as black and subjected to humiliating segregatory legislation, since in a mobile and competitive society blacks posed an economic and social threat to working-class whites. Degler followed this work with *The Other South* (1974), a study of 19th-century southern intellectual opponents of slavery and racism. Inevitably written with the contemporary southern situation in mind, this volume concluded that, while a discernible white southern dissenting, antiracist and antislavery tradition existed, by the late 19th century its proponents had largely been driven out of the South, not to be replaced until the 1950s. To the debate of the 1950s and early 1960s as to whether post-World War II Americans were conformist, Degler contributed *Affluence and Anxiety* (1968), in which he argued that, even in the 19th century, Alexis de Tocqueville and other foreign observers had commented upon the prevalence of such traits in the United States.

After tackling the topical theme of race, Degler turned to the equally timely issue of women's rights, producing *At Odds* (1980), an early synthesis of the history of American women and the family, a volume largely based upon his own extensive research in this area. He argued forcefully that the demands of American women for equality and personal fulfillment were often in opposition to and hampered by the calls made upon them by their family roles, especially the bearing and raising of children, which would have to change drastically if American women were ever to achieve full equality.

In some ways, the arguments that Degler put forward in his most recent and controversial work, *In Search of Human Nature* (1991), in particular his endorsement of current theories that men and women are biologically and psychologically unalike, which implies that they naturally tend to fill different social roles, seem to contradict his previous book's support for greater equality, and to reflect the growing social conservatism of the Reagan-Bush years. In this new study, subtitled *The Decline and Revival of Darwinism in American Social Thought*, Degler once more broke new ground, as he tried to marry the insights of the new discipline of sociobiology to those of history. After detailing the original rise of Social Darwinism in the United States, and its challenge in the early 20th century by theories that culture and nurture, not nature, were responsible for most differences between human beings, Degler detailed the rise of sociobiology, the attempt to apply behavioral rules derived from the study of other animals to the human species. While praising his attempt to introduce historians and the lay reader to the concepts of sociobiology, critics charged that he was unfamiliar with all the relevant literature and had too readily accepted the theories of those who argued that most human behavior was biologically determined, while ignoring the scholarship of those who qualified or dissented from this view.

Despite such caveats, in his lengthy career Degler produced some of the most stimulating, well-researched, and accessible liberal scholarship on themes of absorbing contemporary interest, and is "a man known for his tolerance and good sense." His work won him substantial public and professional recognition, including a Beveridge prize (1971), a Pulitzer prize (1972), and a Bancroft prize (1972), a chair at Stanford University, and service as president of both the Organization of American Historians and the American Historical Association, the two major United States professional historical organizations.

PRISCILLA M. ROBERTS

See also Brazil; Latin America: National; Slavery: Modern; United States: 20th Century; Women's History: North America

Biography

Carl Neumann Degler. Born Orange, New Jersey, 6 February 1921. Educated at Upsala College, New Jersey, BA 1942; Columbia University, MA 1947, PhD 1952. Taught at Hunter College, 1947–48; New York University, 1947–49; Adelphi College, 1950–51; City College of New York, 1952; Vassar College (rising to professor), 1952–68; Stanford University, 1968–90 (emeritus). Married Catherine Grady, 1948 (1 son, 1 daughter).

Principal Writings

Out of Our Past: The Forces That Shaped Modern America, 1959; 3rd edition 1984

Affluence and Anxiety: 1945–Present, 1968; 2nd edition as *Affluence and Anxiety: America since 1945*, 1975

Neither Black nor White: Slavery and Race Relations in Brazil and the United States, 1971

The Other South: Southern Dissenters in the Nineteenth Century, 1974

Place over Time: The Continuity of Southern Distinctiveness, 1977

At Odds: Women and the Family in America from the Revolution to the Present, 1980

In Search of Human Nature: The Decline and Revival of Darwinism in American Social Thought, 1991

Further Reading

Boylan, Anne M., "The Family of Woman," *Reviews in American History* 8/4 (December 1980), 431–36

Fass, Paula S., "Of Genes and Men," *Reviews in American History* 20/2 (June 1992), 235–41

Kraus, Michael, and Davis D. Joyce, *The Writing of American History*, revised edition, Norman: University of Oklahoma Press, 1985

Sternsher, Bernard, *Consensus, Conflict, and American Historians*, Bloomington: Indiana University Press, 1975

Delbrück, Hans 1848–1929
German military and political historian

Hans Delbrück paved the way for the investigation and study of the art of warfare, especially as it related to political history. Following completion of his university studies in Heidelberg, Greifswald, and Bonn, Delbrück volunteered for combat in the Franco-Prussian War of 1870–71 (battle of Gravelotte, siege of Metz). These wartime experiences provided the basis for his later research.

After the completion of his dissertation on Lambert von Hersfeld (1873), Delbrück obtained the position of tutor for the younger son of the crown prince of Prussia, Waldemar. This position, which Delbrück held for five years until the death of Waldemar (1879), allowed him to research and prepare himself for a university teaching career. During this period, he edited the papers of the Prussian field marshal Gneisenau and wrote his biography (1882). This work marked Delbrück's entry into the field of military history.

With Delbrück's Habilitation (the publication necessary to gain promotion at the university) began the first major disputes of his career, since the Philosophical Faculty at the University of Berlin refused to accept his area of interest as a historical topic. In the end, it took until 1895 for him to get a professorship, and then only because the Prussian cultural minister Althof pulled strings. Delbrück remained as professor of history until his retirement in 1921.

Delbrück was no stranger to controversy. His first publications dealing with military-historical problems were subjected to harsh criticism. His *Die Perserkriege und der Burgunderkrieg* (The Persian Wars and the Burgundy War, 1887) and *Die Strategie des Perikles: erläutert durch die Strategie Friedrich des Grossen* (The Strategy of Pericles Explained Through the Strategy of Frederick the Great, 1890) were greeted with disbelief and amazement in military circles because of their comparison of historical military events greatly separated in time and place. If this was a failing of his works, Delbrück did manage to shed new light on older historical problems. By means of rational calculation, he was able to argue that the armies of antiquity were not as large as had previously been believed.

In addition, Delbrück introduced the use of a new general criticism, rather than the older critical evaluation of sources, to the study of history. Because this method substantially revised the existing picture of ancient military history and, therefore, ancient history in general, he was shunned by his fellow historians and academic colleagues. Although the advantages of Delbrück's general criticism have been viewed by many as "incalculable," its weaknesses are also clear. General criticism readily exposes contradictions, inconsistencies, and improbabilities in the sources that it analyzes, but cannot offer firm conclusions, only theories and hypotheses.

Delbrück's great "mistake" in *Die Strategie des Perikles* was that he attacked the philosophy of the "war of attrition" and thus implied that the German national hero Frederick the Great was unheroic. This turned the military establishment against him. Only after the storm of controversy about Delbrück's methods and conclusions had passed was a balanced criticism of his work possible.

The isolation of his work resulted not only from his methodology, especially his general criticism, but also from his historical philosophy which stood in opposition to the spirit of the Wilhelmine age. He brought rationally argued, scientific analysis to an area of history which had previously been based on emotions. Delbrück's point of view was in agreement with the new technological age and did not fit with the emotional warrior spirit prevalent among the soldiers and scholars of his day.

Delbrück's major work, *Geschichte der Kriegskunst im Rahmen der politischen Geschichte* (1900–20; *History of the Art of War within the Framework of Political History*, 1975–85), encapsulated all of his theories. Although the fourth volume continued Delbrück's battle with his critics, it was actually the other volumes that were at the center of his contribution. *History of the Art of War* was, without a doubt, one of the most original contributions by a German historian in the 19th or 20th century, as no comparable study had been undertaken prior to it. With this work Delbrück reached the peak of his creativity.

It is interesting to note that these four volumes, which established Delbrück's reputation as a historian, came near the end of his career. Despite its failings in the area of social history, *History of the Art of War* was masterful in its use of sources and in the historical questions it posed. However, this did not prevent other major historians of the age from greeting it with skepticism (Leopold von Ranke) or disregard (Theodor Mommsen). In volume 4, Delbrück differentiated between the war of attrition and the war of destruction and argued successfully that Frederick the Great embodied the first, and Napoleon the second of these concepts. Delbrück's renewed criticism of Frederick the Great made him a national pariah, and his critics were quick to attack all the small mistakes in logic and research that he had made. Despite this controversy, Delbrück's broad knowledge, clear writing, and original thinking established him as one of the premier historians of his age.

In addition to *History of the Art of War* Delbrück later completed a 5-volume *Weltgeschichte* (World History, 1923–28) based on his university lectures from 1896 onwards. Delbrück's *Weltgeschichte* was the last world history written entirely by a German historian, albeit with the help and advice of colleagues for specific chapters. The scope of his *Weltgeschichte* was enormous. Delbrück covered general world history from its beginnings until Bismarck's resignation as German chancellor, concentrating on difficult historical questions that attested to his mental sharpness even at the age of 70.

In both *History of the Art of War* and *Weltgeschichte*, Delbrück was the first historian to undertake a study of the art of war in its relation to political history. This originality in his thinking set him apart from his contemporaries and made him a target for those who supported more traditional views of military history. Through his work, Delbrück revolutionized the process for evaluating and writing military history and almost singlehandedly established it as a modern academic discipline at the university level in Germany.

Delbrück's distance from the power politics of the military establishment may well have been the key to his eventual success. By observing military matters from the outside, he was not influenced by internal pressures and was, thus, able to offer an unbiased interpretation of events as he saw them, not as the military wanted them to be portrayed.

Although many aspects of Delbrück's work continue to be controversial, most historians today admit that without him our understanding of military-political history would be much less extensive. The strong reactions that Delbrück elicited from his contemporaries sparked historical debates that still remain important today, some 70 years after his death.

GREGORY WEEKS

See also Germany: 1450–1800; Military; Napoleonic Wars

Biography

Hans Gottlieb Leopold Delbrück. Born Bergen auf Rügen, 11 November 1848. Studied history at Heidelberg, Greifswald, and Bonn. Fought in Franco-Prussian War. Tutor of German crown princes, 1874–79; professor, University of Berlin, from 1885.

Free-Conservative deputy, in Prussian "Land" Parliament, 1882–85; Reichstag member, 1884–90. Editor with Heinrich von Treitschke, *Preussische Jahrbücher*, 1883–90, solely, 1890–1919. Married Lina Thiersch, 1884 (3 sons, 4 daughters). Died Berlin, 14 July 1929.

Principal Writings

Das Leben des Feldmarschalls Grafen Neithart v. Gneisenau (The Life of Gneisenau), 2 vols., 1882

Historische und Politische Aufsätze (Historical and Political Essays), 1887; republished as *Erinnerungen, Aufsätze und Reden* (Memoirs, Essays, and Speeches), 1902

Die Perserkriege und der Burgunderkrieg: Zwei kombinierte kriegsgeschichtliche Studien (The Persian Wars and the Burgundy War: Two Combined Military-Historical Studies), 1887

Die Strategie des Perikles: erläutert durch die Strategie Friedrich des Grossen (The Strategy of Pericles Explained Through the Strategy of Frederick the Great), 1890

Friedrich, Napoleon, Moltke: Ältere und neuere Strategie (Frederick, Napoleon, Moltke: Older and Newer Strategy), 1892

Die Polenfrage (The Poland Question), 1894

Geschichte der Kriegskunst im Rahmen der politischen Geschichte, 4 vols., 1900–20; in English as *History of the Art of War within the Framework of Political History*, 4 vols., 1975–85

Numbers in History: How the Greeks Defeated the Persians, the Romans Conquered the World, the Teutons Overthrew the Roman Empire, and William the Norman Took Possession of England, 1913

Bismarcks Erbe (Bismarck's Inheritance), 1915

Ludendorffs Selbstporträt (Ludendorff's Self-Portrait), 1922

Government and the Will of the People: Academic Lectures, 1923

Weltgeschichte, 5 vols., 1923–28

Vor und nach dem Weltkrieg: politische und historische Aufsätze, 1902–1925 (Before and after the World War: Political and Historical Essays), 1926

Der Friede von Versailles (The Peace of Versailles), 1930

Further Reading

Bucholz, Arden, *Hans Delbrück and the German Military Establishment: War Images in Conflict*, Iowa City: University of Iowa Press, 1985

Christ, Karl, "Hans Delbrück," in his *Von Gibbon zu Rostovtzeff: Leben und Werk führender Althistoriker der Neuzeit* (From Gibbon to Rostovtzeff: The Life and Work of the Leading Ancient Historians of Modern Times), Darmstadt: Wissenschaftliche Buchgesellschaft, 1972

Craig, Gordon A., "Delbrück: The Military Historian," in Edward M. Earle, ed., *Makers of Modern Strategy: Military Thought from Machiavelli to Hitler*, Princeton: Princeton University Press, 1941

Daniels, Emil, Karl Lehmann, and Gustav Roloff, eds., *Delbrück-Festschrift* (Delbrück *Festschrift*), Berlin: Stilke, 1908

Daniels, Emil, and Paul Rühlmann, eds., *Am Webstuhl der Zeit: Eine Erinnerungsgabe, Hans Delbrück dem Achtzigjährigen von Freunden und Schülern dargebracht* (A *Festschrift* for Hans Delbrück), Berlin: Hobbing, 1928

Deutsche Staatsbibliothek, *Der Nachlass Hans Delbrücks* (The Papers of Hans Delbrück), Berlin: Deutsche Staatsbibliothek, 1980

Gut, G., *Studien zur Entwicklung Hans Delbrücks als politischer Historiker* (Studies on the Development of Hans Delbrück as a Political Historian), dissertation, Free University of Berlin, 1951

Harnack, A. von, "Hans Delbrück als Historiker und Politiker (Hans Delbrück as Historian and Politician), *Neue Rundschau* 63 (1952), 408–26

Meinecke, Friedrich, "Nachruf" (Obituary), *Historische Zeitschrift* 140 (1929), 702–04

Rassow, Peter, "Hans Delbrück als Historiker und Politiker" (Hans Delbrück as Historian and Politician), *Die Sammlung* 4 (1949), 134–44

Schleier, Hans, "Hans Delbrück," in Gustav Seeber, ed., *Gestalten der Bismarckzeit*, Berlin: Akademie, 1978

Schwabe, Klaus, *Wissenschaft und Kriegsmoral: Die deutschen Hochschullehrer und die politischen Grundfragen des Ersten Weltkrieges* (Science and War Morality: The German University Teachers and the Basic Political Questions of the First World War), Göttingen: Musterschmidt, 1969

Thimme, Annelise, *Hans Delbrück als Kritiker der Wilhelminischen Epoche* (Hans Delbrück as a Critic of the Wilhelmine Epoch), Düsseldorf: Droste, 1955

Ziekursch, Johannes, "Hans Delbrück," *Deutsches Biographisches Jahrbuch* 11 (1929), 89–95

Delisle, Léopold 1826–1910

French historian, archivist/librarian, and paleographer

Delisle was a key agent of the transition in history from antiquarianism to a modern academic discipline. As a founder of the modern Bibliothèque Nationale and organizer of its manuscript collections he shaped technical and methodological approaches in France and beyond. His main work in the 1850s and early 1860s centered on the Bibliothèque's Latin manuscripts. He was largely responsible for more than doubling the number (static for over a century) of catalogued manuscripts, and then launched himself upon the French manuscripts. This brought him the directorship of the manuscript department in 1871, and further promotion thereafter.

These cataloging activities were of such historiographical importance as to make him a central figure in his profession very early. No medievalist was in a better position to monitor and mine the Bibliothèque's hitherto confused collections. His humble position at the Bibliothèque, where promotion was largely by seniority, long contrasted with a growing academic reputation. His debut *Etudes sur la condition de la classe agricole en Normandie au Moyen Age* (Studies in the Condition of the Agrarian Class in Medieval Normandy, 1851) was an early contribution to the emerging genre of rural economy. It won the Prix Gobert and secured him remarkably exalted provincial job-offers. Membership of the Institut de France at the age of 31 was consequent upon publication of *Classe agricole* (The Agrarian Class, 1851), *Notice sur Orderic Vital* (Notice on Orderic Vitalis, 1855), and *Catalogue des actes de Philippe Auguste* (Catalog of the Acts of Philip Augustus, 1856).

The last of these works showcased his skills as a diplomatist. Its importance lay in establishing a basic classification of the procedures of the French royal chancery in the forty years either side of 1200. Delisle went on to repeat the feat for the reigns of Philip VI and Charles V. His *Mémoire sur les actes d'Innocent III* (Essay on the Acts of Innocent III, 1857) was the point of departure for comparable descriptions of the papal chancery which would culminate in the Ecole Française de Rome's publication of 13th- and 14th-century papal registers. His *Recueil des actes de Henri II roi d'Angleterre* (Acts of Henry II, King of England) began the work of dating the acts of that king, a lifelong interest.

Delisle was a prolific editor of primary sources, and his history was notable for a relentless insistence on documentary basis. In combination with his extraordinary output, this made him a miniaturist, but also in larger matters a difficult polemicist to confront. The access he could command to archives extended well beyond public collections: his *Histoire du château et des sires de Saint Sauveur le Vicomte* (History of the Castle and Lords of Saint-Sauveur-le-Vicomte, 1867) is an example of work drawing heavily on private sources, some of which have not again seen the light of day. His *Mémoire sur les opérations des templiers* (Essay on the Operations of the Templars, 1889) showed how the order developed as a financial network.

At the head of the Bibliothèque Delisle was adept at manipulating a propagandist rivalry with the British Museum to secure funds for reorganization – although it was upon practice at London that the key reforms in the management of collections were modeled. In aggressive campaigns against the market in stolen manuscripts he combined scholarship with political and strategic sense – notably in respect of the Ashburnham collection. He became a predator of the auction rooms as expenditure on acquisitions rose by over 50 per cent. He also earned a reputation as an assiduous wooer of gifts and bequests – and on occasion integrated his academic work with strategies of acquisition. Delisle's outstanding achievement was an extension of his career among the manuscript collections. It was under his direction that the vast enterprise of cataloging the Bibliothèque's 1.5 million printed volumes was undertaken, although it was to be 1897 before the first volume appeared. It was this career that led Pottier to ascribe to Delisle "a genius for bibliography."

For him there was no distinction between his bibliographical work, historiography, diplomatic studies, and art history. All were rooted in skills that earned him the reputation of the greatest paleographer of the late 19th century. In *Le Cabinet des manuscrits de la Bibliothèque Imperiale* (Cabinet of Manuscripts of the Bibliothèque Imperiale, from 1868), he laid out a history of the book – writing, calligraphy, binding – and the book market at Paris in the medieval centuries. By the 1880s he was becoming interested in new technologies of reproducing manuscripts, perhaps as a consequence of his failure to acquire for the Bibliothèque the Vatican's first register of Philip Augustus, which he produced in facsimile in 1883. He went on to pioneer heliographic reproduction. He became skilled at pressuring publishers into producing costly editions of illustrated manuscripts, increasingly in tandem with exhibitions.

Delisle's interest in medieval art and design was of long standing, and naturally focused on illuminators. Beginning with his *Psautier de la reine Ingeburg femme de Philippe Auguste* (Psalter of Queen Ingeburg, Wife of Philip Augustus, 1867), he sought to give ascription on stylistic bases a viable documentary underpinning. It was Delisle who attributed the *Très Riches Heures du Duc de Berry* to the Limbourg brothers. He also identified or elaborated upon a string of other illuminators of the 14th century in Paris and the Netherlands. The effect of a large number of major and minor treatises was to generate a new vitality in the study of French art in the 13th and 14th centuries, which climaxed in the 1904 exhibition of *Primitifs français* at the Pavillon de Marsan and Bibliothèque Nationale.

From the Bibliothèque Delisle established a degree of influence over the French historiographical professions not seen again until the heyday of Annales. The sheer scale of his bibliography obstructs a full appreciation of his career: at his death some 2,102 items were attributed to him, a figure that excludes the pseudonymous or unsigned notes he contributed routinely to newspapers and local learned journals. This testament to a ferocious application defies specialization, though a certain emphasis on his native Normandy and on the 12th–14th centuries may be detected. Delisle's work was not of the kind that develops an explicit polemical or philosophical stance, but his career makes him the incarnation of the positivist moment in historiography.

GARETH PROSSER

See also France: 1000–1450; Orderic

Biography

Léopold Victor Delisle. Born 24 October 1826. Privately educated, Valognes, Manche; studied at the Ecole des Chartes, 1846–50; member, Institut de France 1857; member, Conseil de Perfectionnement, Ecole des Chartes, 1858: président, 1878. Offered but declined post of archivist, Archives Départementales of Seine-Inférieure, Rouen, 1851; entered Bibliothèque Nationale 1852: *employé première classe* 1857; *bibliothècaire* 1866; in the absence of his predecessor (retired) took responsibility for preserving the manuscript collections through the siege and revolution of 1870–71, at some personal risk: the Commune voted his removal but fell before the decision could be implemented; the Versailles government formalized his position as *conservateur en chef* of the manuscript department; *administrateur-général* at the Bibliothèque Nationale, 1874; forcibly retired by vote in the National Assembly, 1905. Married Laure Burnouf, daughter of the linguist and Orientalist Eugène Burnouf, 1857 (died 1905). Died Chantilly, 22 July 1910.

Principal Writings

Monograph

Etudes sur la condition de la classe agricole en Normandie au Moyen Age (Studies in the Condition of the Agrarian Class in Medieval Normandy), 1851

Critical Editions

Notice sur Orderic Vital (Notice on Orderic Vitalis), 1855

Catalogue des actes de Philippe Auguste (Catalog of the Acts of Philip Augustus), 1856

Mémoire sur les actes d'Innocent III (Essay on the Acts of Innocent III), 1857

Inventaire des manuscrits des fonds latin de la Bibliothèque Impériale ou Nationale (Inventory of the Manuscripts of the Latin Collections of the Imperial or National Library), 1863–71

Recueil des historiens des Gaules et de la France (Sources on the History of Gaul and of France), vols. 22–24, 1865–1904

Rouleaux des morts du XIe au XVe siècles, 1866

Psautier de la reine Ingeburg femme de Philippe Auguste (Psalter of Queen Ingeburg, Wife of Philip Augustus), 1867

Histoire du château et des sires de Saint-Sauveur-le-Vicomte (History of the Castle and Lords of Saint-Sauveur-le-Vicomte), 1867

Le Cabinet des manuscrits de la Bibliothèque Impériale (Cabinet of Manuscipts of the Bibliothèque Impériale), 1868–81; reprinted as *Cabinet des manuscrits de la Bibliothèque Nationale*, 1974

Notes sur quelques manuscrits de la bibliothèque de Tours (Notes on Some Manuscripts in the Tours Library), 1868

Actes normands de la Chambre des comptes sous Philippe de Valois (1328–1350) (Norman Acts of the Treasury of Philip of Valois), 1871

Chronique de Robert de Torigni, abbé du Mont-Saint-Michel (Chronicle of Robert de Torigni, Abbot of Mont-Saint-Michel), 2 vols., 1872–73

Mandements et actes divers de Charles V (1364–1380) (Various Mandates and Acts of Charles V) 1874

Inventaire général et methodique des manuscrits français de la Bibliothèque Nationale (Methodical General Inventory of French Manuscripts in the Bibliothèque Nationale), 2 vols., 1876–78

Notice sur un livre à peintures executé en 1250 dans l'abbaye de Saint-Denis (Notice on a Book of Paintings Done in the Abbey of Saint Denis in 1250), 1877

Bible de Théodulphe (Théodulphe's Bible), 1879

Livre d'Heures d'Ailly (Ailly's Book of Hours), 1879

Trois manuscrits de la bibliothèque de Leyde (Three Manuscripts from the Leyde Library), 1879

Mélanges de Paléographie et de bibliographie (A Collection of Paleography and Bibliography), 1880

Le Premier registre de Philippe-Auguste (The First Register of Philip Augustus), facsimile edition, 1883

"Les livres d'Heures du duc de Berry" (The Duke of Berry's Book of Hours), *Gazette des Beaux-Arts*, 1884

Les Collections de Bastard d'Estang à la Bibliothèque Nationale (The Collections of Bastard d'Estang at the Bibliothèque Nationale), 1885

Album paléographique ou recueil des documents importants relatifs à l'histoire et à la littérature nationales (Paleographic Album or Collection of Important Documents Relating to National History and Literature), facsimile collection, 1887

Les manuscrits des fonds Libri et Barrois (The Manuscripts of the Libri and Barrois Collections), 1888

Mémoire sur les opérations des templiers (Essay on the Operations of the Templars), 1889

Catalogue général des livres imprimés de la Bibliothèque Nationale (Catalogue of Books Published by the Bibliothèque Nationale), 1897–

Recherches sur la librairie de Charles V (Research on Charles V's Library), 3 vols., 1907

Recueil des actes de Henri II, roi d'Angleterre et duc de Normandie, concernant les provinces françaises et les affaires de France (The Acts of Henry II, King of England and Duke of Normandy, Concerning the French Provinces and the Affairs of France), edited by Elie Berger, 3 vols., 1909–27

Further Reading

Lacombe, Paul, *Bibliographie des travaux de M. Léopold Delisle* (A Bibliography of the Work of Léopold Delisle), Paris: Imprimerie National, 1902; and *Supplément, 1900–1910*, Paris: Leclerc, 1911

Delumeau, Jean 1923–

French social historian of early modern religion

Jean Delumeau is a French *annaliste*, primarily concerned with the Reformation and Catholic or Counter-Reformation in France and the world. Focusing on the spiritual deficiencies of the Middle Ages, including theological confusion and the lack of a respectable and educated priesthood, Delumeau considered how the actions of Luther and his contemporaries made necessary changes in the way theology was taught and religion was practiced, within the Catholic church and outside it. Delumeau's view of early modern Catholicism was essentially negative: reform and renewal could not have occurred without the catalyst of the Protestant Reformation. However, this Reformation was preventable: had there been an ecumenical council on the scale of Trent before 1517, a more organized response on the part of Rome, and an acceptance of the role of councils in doctrinal policy, there would have been no Reformation at all. Instead, by the time the Council of Trent was called, prevention was impossible. The significance of that council was to give "those who remained faithful to Rome what all western Christians aspired to at the threshold of the modern age: a catechism and pastors."

The common ground among reformers of all religious persuasions – the need for better understanding of the faith – is at the center of Delumeau's thesis. In the 16th and 17th centuries, Christian society "on both sides of the confessional abyss" was preoccupied with sin and the fear of God. Delumeau used retrospective sociology to examine a culture that could produce such fear and such a punitive interpretation of religion; thus, his source base was particularly influential. He examined pastoral visitations, private parish records, registers of ecclesiastical and lay courts, synodal statutes, devotional literature, and geographical distributions of sodalities, confessions, pilgrimages, and confraternities, and extrapolated what he called the characteristics of devotion. He studied how popular attitudes toward superstitions changed as Christianity adapted and camouflaged folk rituals and beliefs rather than suppressing or superseding them. As the "two Christian Reformations" became more established and accepted on the popular levels, fear of the devil diminished, a claim that William Monter later quantified. Delumeau attributed the decline to the scientific revolution and the emergence of a new pastoral elite and a new mentality that left everyone more reassured, because the people felt "better protected by the Bible (especially in Protestantism), the sacraments (especially in Catholicism), and the catechism (in both)." The Catholic church institutionalized the separation between priest and parishioner by policing the morals and behavior of the clergy and by building seminaries. The new priests were to convert the masses in more ways than one: missionaries were sent to rural areas to preach to the public, using processions, book burnings, and hymns in the vernacular set to popular tunes. Once the average person was shocked into belief, the parish priest taught him or her how to assimilate the belief into everyday life.

Delumeau argued that medieval Europe was never properly converted to Christianity, but rather practiced a superstitious folk religion that looked Christian. He pointed to the lack of contact the average believer had with the formal doctrines of his or her religion, the testimony of contemporaries regarding the merits of certain clerics, and the continuance of superstitions and magical practices among uneducated believers. He traced a heightened awareness of and preoccupation with the deadly sins, as well as the clergy's desire to introduce a guilt mentality, to engender anguish in the population, to convert them or to strengthen their beliefs. This was at the root of the Reformation crisis and demonstrated that Enlightenment Europe was not "de-Christianized" because Europe had never been Christianized. Critics have suggested that Delumeau reached this conclusion because of his ignorance of medieval history; an excellent rehearsal of these arguments is found in John van Engen's "The Christian Middle Ages as an Historiographical Problem" (1986). A.N. Galpern and Louis Chatellier based their challenges to Delumeau not on medieval history, but on the French context. Chatellier demonstrated the existence of a Catholic society by 1750, when Delumeau saw it as only beginning. Galpern argued that Delumeau judged the religiosity of the Reformation era by later standards and postulated too large a gulf between elite and peasant. J.K. Powis noted that Delumeau failed to consider outside forces, for example the crises of the 14th century, the Muslim threat, and the Protestant Reformation, all of which all led to great fear and a feeling of human responsibility, thus resulting in greater clerical control. According to Powis and Keith Luria, Delumeau exaggerated the evidence, using the clergy as a barometer of what people thought and believed, rather than what they were *taught* to believe. André Vauchez criticized Delumeau for ignoring the individual and positive aspects of piety and not acknowledging the rather obvious possibility that *mentalités* might differ, thus leading to different levels or types of Christianization.

Delumeau's controversial theses do have supporters; for example, Thomas Tentler and Steven Ozment both argued that during the late Middle Ages the Catholic church exerted great social control by priest-confessors who were given the power of absolution in the sacrament of penance. This created anxiety in Christians and focused on confession, producing a flawed and unsatisfying piety and a feeling of betrayal in the believer. A.D. Wright showed that Delumeau responded to earlier detractors by a more critical approach, and lauded Delumeau's talent for comparisons between Catholic and Protestant developments.

Delumeau characterized the Catholic Reform movement as a long-term process, from Luther to Voltaire, extending beyond the traditional boundary of the Peace of Westphalia (1648). In writing a broad history of Christianity, Delumeau considered three main themes: sin, guilt, and reassurance. He interpreted medieval church history as an "evolution toward a culture of guilt," which significantly expanded the powers of the clergy by imposing compulsory confession on each Christian. This idea of social control revisited, somewhat more positively, Henry C. Lea's *A History of Auricular Confession and Indulgences in the Latin Church* (1896), which suggested a confrontation between priest and penitent, in which confession was rather like torture.

Delumeau's impact on the historical understanding of the late Middle Ages and Reformation era is profound and lasting: a broadened source base, an integration of world history into the study of a European phenomenon, and a focus on questions of personal responses to changes in the practice of faith. Even his detractors recognize his importance: he created and maintained a series of historical debates concerning the type and depth of religious belief in premodern Europe.

KATHLEEN COMERFORD

Biography

Born Nantes, 18 June 1923. Studied at Institut Fénelon, Grasse; Lycée Masséna, Nice; Lycée Thiers, Marseilles; Lycée Henri IV, Paris; agrégation in history, Ecole Normale Supérieure, 1947, PhD 1955. Served in French Army, 1944–46. Taught at lycées in Bourges, 1947–48, Rome, 1948–50, and Rennes, 1950–54; attached to Centre Nationale du Recherche Scientifique (CNRS), 1954–56; taught at University of Rennes, 1957–70; director of studies, Ecole Pratique des Hautes Etudes, from 1963; professor of history, University of Paris I, from 1970; and Collège de France, from 1974. Married Jeanny Le Goff, physician, 1947 (2 sons; 1 daughter).

Principal Writings

Vie économique et sociale de Rome dans la seconde moitié du XVIe siècle (Economic and Social Life of Rome in the Second Half of the 16th Century), 2 vols., 1957–59

L'Alun de Rome, XVe–XIXe siècle (Alum in Rome, 15th–19th Centuries), 1962

Naissance et affirmation de la réforme (Birth and Establishment of the Reform), 1965

With others, *Le Mouvement du port de Saint-Malo, 1681–1720, bilan statistique* (The Activity of the Port of Saint-Malo, 1681–1720: A Balance Sheet), 1966

La Civilisation de la Renaissance (The Civilization of the Renaissance), 1967

Editor, *Histoire de la Bretagne* (History of Brittany), 1969

Le Catholicisme entre Luther et Voltaire, 1971; in English as *Catholicism Between Luther and Voltaire: A New View of the Counter-Reformation*, 1977

Editor, *Documents de l'histoire de la Bretagne* (Documents on the History of Brittany), 1971

Rome au XVIe siècle (Rome in the 16th Century), 1975

La Mort des pays de Cocagne: comportements collectifs de la Renaissance à l'âge classique (The Death of the Land of Plenty: Collective Behavior of the Renaissance and the Classical Age), 1976

Le Christianisme va-t-il mourir? (Is Christianity Dying?), 1977

La Peur en Occident, XIVe–XVIIIe siècles: une cité assiégée (Fear in the West, 14th–18th Centuries: A City Surrounded), 1978

Le Diocèse de Rennes (The Diocese of Rennes), 1979

Histoire vécue du peuple chrétien (History as Lived by the Christian People), 2 vols., 1979

Un Chemin d'histoire: chrétienté et christianisation (One Path of History: Christianity and Christianization), 1981

Le Cas Luther (The Case of Luther), 1983

Le Péché et la peur: la culpabilisation en Occident, XIIIe–XVIIIe siècles, 1983; in English as *Sin and Fear: The Emergence of a Western Guilt Culture, 13th–18th Centuries*, 1990

Ce que je crois (What I Believe), 1985

Les Malheurs des temps: histoire des fléaux et des calamités en France (The Misfortunes of Time: History of Plagues and Disasters in France), 1987

L'Aveu et le pardon: les difficultés de la confession XIII–XVIIe siècle (Admission and Pardon: The Difficulties of Confession), 1990

Editor with Daniel Roche, *Histoire des pères et de la paternité* (History of Fathers and Paternity), 1990

Une Histoire du paradis, 2 vols. to date, 1992–; partially translated as *A History of Paradise: The Garden of Eden in Myth and Tradition*, 1995

La Religion de ma mère: les femmes et la transmission de la foi (My Mother's Religion: Women and the Transmission of Faith), 1992

Arezzo, espace et sociétés, 715–1230: recherches sur Arezzo et son contado du VIIIe au début du XIIIe siècle (Arezzo, Space and Society 715–1230: Research on Arezzo and Its Contado from the 8th through the Beginning of the 13th Century), 1996

L'Historien et la foi (The Historian and Faith), 1996

Homo Religiosus (Religious Man), 1997

Further Reading

Powis, J.K., "Repression and Autonomy: Christians and Christianity in the Historical Works of Jean Delumeau," *Journal of Modern History* 64 (1992), 366–74

van Engen, John, "The Christian Middle Ages as an Historiographical Problem," *American Historical Review* 91 (1986), 519–52

Demography

Interest in the demographic trends of the past developed out of the growing field of economic history. Economic historians wanted to improve their understanding of the population implications of industrial and agricultural revolution within the

British context. Rising population was seen as part of the explanation for the momentous and self-perpetuating epoch of the Industrial Revolution in the 18th century, notwithstanding the suggestions by contemporary commentators that the population was falling.

The earliest attention focused on mortality because of the supposed connections with an improving food supply and standard of living. In particular, McKeown argued that mortality fell in the 18th century due to increased resistance to disease through improved nutrition. This thesis has subsequently been discredited, most forcefully by Livi-Bacci.

It was in continental Europe that most attention was given to developing methods of historical demography. Here the focus was on ascertaining the "natural fertility" of communities. Louis Henry was significant in drawing up rules of family reconstitution as a method of linking together information on individuals and families from registers of baptism, marriage, and burial. This provided information on age at marriage, remarriage, birth intervals, average life expectancy, and infant and child mortality. A social historian, Pierre Goubert, looked at early modern subsistence crises and suggested that the price of wheat could be seen as a barometer of demographic change. Historians of the Annales school were also interested in reproduction as an insight into *mentalité*. Some countries already had very high quality statistical sources, for example, in Sweden listings of inhabitants, called *husförhörslängder*, which gave information on literacy levels and migrations, were collected from the late 17th century and state organized from 1740.

In Britain, Tony Wrigley adopted the family reconstitution method for his study of the parish of Colyton in Devon. After the formation of the Cambridge Group for the History of Population and Social Structure in 1964, the efforts of large numbers of local historians who carried out reconstitutions for parishes with good quality records dating back into the 16th century were coordinated. Some pitfalls remain with the family reconstitution method. It is still most effective for small communities and the results are inhibited by the extent of migration. Marriage irregularities were certainly more prevalent in the early modern period, and nonconformity in a community can distort the results. The Cambridge Group have augmented the reconstitution picture by simultaneously developing a large dataset of high quality Anglican registers for aggregate analysis.

Over the past thirty years, historical demography has become more sophisticated in a number of ways. The use of computers has become vastly more effective, and carrying out reconstitutions by computer has immensely speeded up what was previously an extremely time-consuming task of nominal linkage by hand. Demographic historians have also developed far more understanding of the drawbacks of sources which were not originally designed for demographic purposes, such as parish registers and the census. Their methods now range from the construction of model life tables, to the subjection of aggregative data to methods of back projection that take account of migration to produce estimates of population size.

From the extensive research which has been carried out, Wrigley and Schofield have argued that three quarters of population growth in the English case was due to the rapid rise in fertility, although this took place within the context of falling mortality. Couples needed a threshold of income to be able to marry and Wrigley and Schofield linked the age of marriage data they produced to real wage indexes. However, it was notably female marriage ages that showed most variation, falling by an estimated 3.1 years in the long 18th century. Wrigley and Schofield have been criticized for excessive economic determinism and failure to make satisfactory links with the economic and social context, for example, the long lags of up to forty years in their explanation between wage changes and demographic adjustment are now thought unconvincing.

Nevertheless, the work of historical demographers has produced an entirely new insight into population changes over time in England which has changed the historical understanding of many other aspects of society. The late 16th and early 17th centuries emerge as a period of population growth that was birthrate led, but by contrast the late 17th century saw population stagnation. Illegitimacy and prenuptial pregnancies were found to follow similar trends to marital fertility. There also appeared to be significant changes in celibacy although non-marriage is difficult to measure. It may have changed from some 20 per cent in late 17th-century England to just 3–4 per cent in the early 19th century. These discoveries have been influential in developing an increased historical awareness of the shape of past households. Michael Anderson's work, for example, has been influential in exploring demographic influences on the lifecycle. Hajnal argued that Western Europe was characterized by both a high age of marriage and celibacy.

However, attempts to define a uniform Western European demographic pattern in terms of birth and death rates have now been abandoned. As more information has become available it has become apparent that individual countries had very different population regimes. Indeed, the well-studied English pattern contrasts with other countries where mortality generally seems to hold more sway than fertility. Scandinavian countries in general seem to have had a falling death rate along with a stable or slowly falling birth rate. It is also the case that similar scenarios sometimes had contrasting outcomes. Late 18th-century Ireland and France both had predominantly Catholic populations and peasant economies, but whereas population pressure in Ireland led to cataclysmic famine in 1845–46, France was the first country where people controlled their reproduction.

Large-scale demographic history investigations have ranged from the Princeton project on the European demographic transition post-1850 (from a high to a low regime of both fertility and mortality) to analysis of the changing historical patterns of the French Canadian population. There is still a need to develop ways of looking at population change in less well recorded countries. Eastern European countries did not have censuses until the end of the 19th century and very little is known about Southern Europe. Recently more attention has been paid to historical demography in Asia and Africa.

PAMELA SHARPE

See also Annales School; Ariès; Barkan; Beloch; Borah; Brenner; Cambridge Group; Computing; Curtin; Family; Fügedi; Habakkuk; Henry; Latin America: Colonial; Le Roy Ladurie; Malin; Marriage; Migration; Quantitative; Sexuality; Tilly, L.; Wrigley

Further Reading

Anderson, Michael, *Population Change in North-Western Europe, 1750–1850*, London: Macmillan, 1988

Anderson, Michael, "The Social Implications of Demographic Change," in F.M.L. Thompson, ed., *The Cambridge Social History of Britain, 1750–1950*, vol. 2, Cambridge and New York: Cambridge University Press, 1990

Coale, Ansley J., and Susan Cotts Watkins, ed., *The Decline of Fertility in Europe*, Princeton: Princeton University Press, 1986

Cook, Sherburne F., and Woodrow Borah, *Essays in Population History: Mexico and the Caribbean*, 3 vols., Berkeley: University of California Press, 1971–79

de Vries, Jan, *European Urbanization, 1500–1800*, Cambridge, MA: Harvard University Press, and London: Methuen, 1984

Duben, Alan, and Cem Behar, *Istanbul Households: Marriage, Family and Fertility, 1880–1940*, Cambridge and New York: Cambridge University Press, 1991

Dyson, Tim, ed., *India's Historical Demography: Studies in Famine, Disease and Society*, London: Curzon Press, 1989

Gillis, John R., Louise A. Tilly, and David Levine, *The European Experience of Declining Fertility, 1850–1970*, Oxford and Cambridge, MA: Blackwell, 1992

Hajnal, John, "European Marriage Patterns in Perspective," in D.V. Glass and D.E.C. Eversley, eds., *Population in History: Essays in Historical Demography*, London: Arnold, and Chicago: Aldine, 1965

Hanley, S., "The Influences of Economic and Social Variables on Marriage and Fertility in Eighteenth and Nineteenth Century Japanese Villages," in Ronald D. Lee, ed., *Population Patterns in the Past*, New York: Academic Press, 1977

Heywood, C., "The Growth of Population," in Pamela M. Pilbeam, ed., *Themes in Modern European History, 1780–1830*, London and New York: Routledge, 1995

Higman, B.W., *Slave Populations of the British Caribbean, 1807–34*, Baltimore: Johns Hopkins University Press, 1984

Ho, Ping-ti, *Studies on the Population of China, 1368–1953*, Cambridge, MA: Harvard University Press, 1959

Houston, Robert Allan, *The Population History of Britain and Ireland, 1500–1750*, London: Macmillan, 1992

Knodel, John, *Demographic Behaviour in the Past: A Study of Fourteen German Village Populations in the Eighteenth and Nineteenth Centuries*, Cambridge and New York: Cambridge University Press, 1988

Landers, John, *Death and the Metropolis: Studies in the Demographic History of London, 1670–1830*, Cambridge and New York: Cambridge University Press, 1993

Livi-Bacci, Massimo, *Popolazione e alimentazione: saggio sulla storia demografia europea*, Bologna: Mulino, 1987; in English as *Population and Nutrition: An Essay on European Demographic History*, Cambridge and New York: Cambridge University Press, 1991

McKeown, Thomas, *The Modern Rise of Population*, London: Arnold, and New York: Academic Press, 1976

Malthus, Thomas, *An Essay on the Principle of Population*, London: Johnson, 1798

Reher, David, *Town and Country in Pre-Industrial Spain: Cuenca, 1540–1870*, Cambridge and New York: Cambridge University Press, 1990

Reher, David, and Roger S. Schofield, *Old and New Methods in Historical Demography*, Oxford: Oxford University Press, 1993

Rotberg, Robert I., and Theodore K. Rabb, eds., *Hunger and History: The Impact of Changing Food Production and Consumption Patterns on Society*, Cambridge and New York: Cambridge University Press, 1983

Schofield, Roger S., David Reher, and Alain Bideau, eds., *The Decline of Mortality in Europe*, Oxford and New York: Oxford University Press, 1991

Smith, R., "Fertility, Economy and Household Formation in England over Three Centuries," *Population and Development Review* 7 (1981), 595–622

Viazzo, Pier Paolo, *Upland Communities: Environment, Population and Social Structure in the Alps since the Sixteenth Century*, Cambridge and New York: Cambridge University Press, 1989

Vinovskis, Maris A., ed., *Studies in American Historical Demography*, New York: Academic Press, 1979

Woods, Robert I., *The Population of Britain in the Nineteenth Century*, London: Macmillan, 1992

Wrigley, E.A., *Population and History*, London: Weidenfeld and Nicolson, and New York: McGraw Hill, 1969

Wrigley, E.A., and Roger S. Schofield, *The Population History of England, 1541–1871: A Reconstruction*, London: Arnold, and Cambridge, MA: Harvard University Press, 1981

Wrigley, E.A., "The Growth of Population in Eighteenth-Century England: A Conundrum Resolved," *Past and Present* 98 (1983), 121–50

Dening, Greg 1931–

Australian ethnohistorian of the Pacific

A central member of the "Melbourne group" of ethnohistorians, Greg Dening is significant in that he began the rescue of the peoples of the Pacific from anthropology, and that he helped rescue the discipline of history, especially in Australia, from the empiricists.

Dening inherited his love of the sea from his father, a ship radio operator based in Fremantle after World War I. Dening finds an inner peace in contemplating the ocean: "waves are my worry-beads." Coastlines and beaches are a constant theme in his writing. Dening attended Jesuit schools in Perth and Melbourne and entered the Order himself at age 16; he left the priesthood in 1968 after a disagreement with church authorities. His time as a priest taught him the importance of "performance": the rhythms and the silences of a well-sung Mass Dening sees as transferable to the theatricality of history-writing and lecturing. It is this common interest in "performance" that he sees as linking the history he studied at Melbourne and the anthropology he undertook at Harvard. His view of history enraged many of the traditionalists in Australia: one spoke of "the viper in our midst" after Dening's inaugural professorial lecture at Melbourne in 1971; another retorted after Dening's famous "History as a Social System" address that "Dening is too subtle for me." Dening persevered and during his 20 years at Melbourne gathered a school around him across several local universities, including LaTrobe, Monash, and Victoria.

The Pacific has been Dening's main research area. Having originally trained as a Jesuit himself, he understood the difficulties faced by the missionaries heading off to the South Seas. They and the beachcombers like Edward Robarts fascinated him because they "crossed the beach" from one culture into another. Dening wanted to understand why some people "go native," that is, adopt the customs and practices of exotic cultures. The discipline of history, in which he had been trained, should also "go native," in his view, leaving the comforts of its familiar surrounds and attempting to understand the cultures of the Other. Hence his interest in the contact history of the Pacific, which Dening began to see as a "two-sided history," a tragic and devastating tale worthy of a wider audience. His first project was the Marquesas, the isolated island group in the southeast Pacific.

Dening's first publication, the edited journal of Robarts, failed to win a large readership, but this did not deter him from his task of bringing the Marquesan story to the English-language reading publics on either side of the Pacific. *Islands and Beaches* (1980) is the main product of this project, a book which wove the Marquesan story into a larger historiographical framework of how history ought to be pursued in the post-modern era. The "natives" and the "strangers" not only met in tragic circumstances, but constructed "performances" for each other. Little did the foreign sailors realize, for example, that the Marquesan girls who swam onto their ships and performed exciting dances were not naive harlots but had in fact carefully practiced their routines on makeshift dancefloors designed to resemble ship-decks.

Dening then applied this approach to a commissioned account of his alma mater, Xavier College, a fashionable Jesuit school in Melbourne. The elaborate rituals of elite schools make them ideal candidates for ethnohistory, of course, and this work stands out from the more conventional institutional histories. Personally the project enabled Dening to interrogate his own scholarly and religious origins more carefully, and also to challenge the sentimentality that dominates Irish-Australian historiography.

His third major project was a novel account of the *Bounty*. Dening's argument is that Bligh was not as tyrannical as the typical captains of his period, and that the famous mutiny should be understood as a highly political "performance." While this thesis may not have won over all readers, it is clear that Dening's interest in ritual is very helpful in understanding the routines of shipboard life.

His fourth main project, an ethnographic account of the killing of astronomer William Gooch at Oahu in 1792, is partly autobiographical. Dening describes Gooch's socialization at Cambridge University as if he were talking anthropologically of a "native."

The importance of Dening and the Melbourne Group is the linking together of an anthropology focused on ritual processes with a history concerned to reposition Pacific peoples as agents rather than mere victims. The ethnohistorians want to describe what "actually" happened rather than what "really" occurred.

ROBERT PASCOE

See also Pacific

Biography

Gregory Moore Dening. Born Newcastle, New South Wales, 29 March 1931. Studied history, University of Melbourne, BA 1957; theology, Canisius College, New South Wales, 1957–63; and anthropology, Harvard University, MA and PhD, 1972. Taught history and anthropology, University of Hawaii, 1968; lectured in sociology and history, LaTrobe University, 1969–71; professor of history, University of Melbourne, 1971–91 (emeritus). Married Donna Merwick, American historian, 1971 (1 son deceased).

Principal Writings

"History as a Social System," *Historical Studies* 15 (1973), 673–85
Editor, *The Marquesan Journal of Edward Robarts*, 1974
Xavier: A Centenary Portrait, 1978
Islands and Beaches: Discourse on a Silent Land, Marquesas, 1774–1880, 1980
The Death of William Gooch: A History's Anthropology, 1988

Mr. Bligh's Bad Language: Passion, Power, and Theatre on the Bounty, 1992
Performances, 1996

Further Reading

Cathcart, Michael *et al.*, *Mission to the South Seas: The Voyage of the Duff, 1796–1799*, Melbourne: Melbourne University History Monograph no.11, 1990
Merwick, Donna, ed., *Dangerous Liaisons: Essays in Honour of Greg Dening*, Melbourne: Melbourne University History Monograph no.19, 1994

De Sanctis, Francesco 1817–1883
Italian literary historian and critic

The most famous literary historian of 19th-century Italy, Francesco De Sanctis has remained a seminal force in the study of Italian literature. He epitomized the politically engaged Romantic intellectual, and his many books and essays reflected the liberal aspirations of the era. It is impossible to separate his political involvements from his monumental scholarly achievements.

De Sanctis grew up in Morra Irpina, near Naples, in a society only just beginning to emerge from feudalism. Although belonging to the relatively privileged class of small landowners and professionals, De Sanctis came to think of this reactionary society as the negative pole of history from which Italy should distance itself as rapidly as possible. From his youth onwards, De Sanctis sided wholeheartedly with the cause of modernization, which he understood as the struggle for progressive liberal ideas about education, politics, and economics.

A gifted student, De Sanctis began to teach and to publish while still in his teens. As a result of his involvement in radical politics and in the failed 1848 revolution in Naples, De Sanctis lost his teaching position, spent 30 months in prison, and then suffered banishment. The exiled scholar, further radicalized by his traumatic experiences, eventually reached Piedmont, a gathering place for political refugees from all over Italy.

In Piedmont from 1853 to 1856, De Sanctis taught Italian in a girls' school and continued with his scholarly writing on Italian literature. Still progressive in general outlook, De Sanctis for pragmatic reasons began to moderate his political views and became a supporter of the Piedmontese monarchy.

He moved to Zurich in 1856 and began teaching Italian literature at the polytechnic there. As his time in Turin had transformed his southern Italian outlook into a national one, so the four years that he spent in Zurich made him more cosmopolitan in a European sense. De Sanctis returned to Italy in 1860 after Garibaldi's invasion of Sicily dramatically accelerated the process of unification. For the next few years he busied himself with politics, a period that culminated in his election to Parliament and a brief period as minister of public instruction.

Frustrated and disillusioned by the growing conservatism of Italian governments, De Sanctis withdrew from politics. He had married in 1863, but not happily. His financial situation, which had always been precarious, grew worse. In this troubled political and personal frame of mind, he returned to scholarly research and writing as his principal activity. During an intense six-year period, 1866–72, De Sanctis published the books that secured his fame as one of the great literary critics and historians of modern Italian history.

The first of these books, *Saggi critici* (Critical Essays, 1866), contained the newspaper articles that he had written during his exile. The *Saggio critico sul Petrarca* (Critical Essay on Petrarch, 1869), also based on work that he had done in exile, displayed his mature thought about literary criticism: a rich eclectic mixture of Enlightenment, Romantic, Vichian, and Hegelian ideas coupled with an insistence that no single systematically applied theory could do full justice to the infinite variety of literature, which at its highest level issued not from erudition at all, but from a spontaneous act of the imagination.

In his masterpiece, *Storia della letteratura italiana* (1870–71; *The History of Italian Literature*, 1930), De Sanctis applied the critical ideas of the Petrarch book to Italian literature as a whole. He took a fundamentally Hegelian view of the country's great literary achievements, which in a dialectical way both reflected and promoted the cultural, civic, and moral progress of the Italian people. The dialectic moved slowly and uncertainly, to be sure. Retrograde periods often followed the most perfect literary manifestations of the sublime. Yet at every stage of the country's literary history, great figures, on the world-historical order of Hegelian theorizing, had appeared. His critical method became centered on the analysis of the origins, the evolution, and the climax of each stage.

Machiavelli stood out as the most heroic figure in all of Italian literature, for the Florentine chancellor alone at the time of freedom's collapse in Italy clearly had understood the reasons for the country's weakness and had proposed a resolute plan of reform along the lines of civic humanism. De Sanctis downplayed the notorious moral issues that, in his judgment, had obscured Machiavelli's real worth as a coolly astute analyst of Italy's eternal problems. Italy still needed Machiavelli's program of civic humanism, as all of the country's greatest citizens and writers from that day to this had come, often by very different ways, to realize.

In 1871, the University of Naples offered De Sanctis a chair in comparative literature, and he taught there for the next four years. He continued to maintain a heavy schedule of scholarly publishing, particularly on the theme of realism in literature, understood not in the sense then in vogue as result of Zola's novels, but as "the ideal set in the real," and its importance in the modernization of Italian culture as a whole.

Also during the years at the University of Naples, De Sanctis resumed political activity, but soon became disillusioned anew by the country's failure to undertake serious reforms. In 1878, De Sanctis did agree to serve for a second time as minister of public instruction. A serious eye ailment forced him out of office in 1880. He then began to dictate the memoirs that were left uncompleted at the time of his death in Naples in 1883.

Although famous and admired throughout Italy in his lifetime, De Sanctis wrote against the positivist grain of the age. Other scholars often attacked him for deficient research, and negative critical judgments marred the initial reception of his books, including *The History of Italian Literature*. Full critical rehabilitation and elevation to canonical status came toward the end of the century. As a result of Benedetto Croce's admiring reappraisal, De Sanctis became a totemic figure for the idealists who dominated Italian culture after 1900. More support came from the paladin of Italian Marxism, Antonio Gramsci, who in the posthumously published *Quaderni del carcere* (1948–51; *Selections from the Prison Notebooks*, 1971) hailed De Sanctis as an exemplar for politically and morally engaged writers. From abroad, where knowledge of him had been slight, De Sanctis attracted increasing attention in the postwar period. His life and work continue to be the subject of a vast scholarly literature.

RICHARD DRAKE

See also Cantimori; Guicciardini; Villari

Biography

Born Morra Irpina, Avellino, 28 March 1817, to a gentry family. Taught in Naples, 1839–48; Turin, 1854–55; Zurich, 1856–60; and Naples, 1871–76. Imprisoned as a supporter of Mazzini, Naples, 1850–53; exiled 1853–61. Served as minister of public instruction, 1862, 1879–80. Married Maria Testa, 1863. Died Naples, 29 December 1883.

Principal Writings

Saggi critici (Critical Essays), 1866; selections in English as *De Sanctis on Dante*, 1957
Saggio critico sul Petrarca (Critical Essay on Petrarch), 1869
Storia della letteratura italiana, 1870–71; in English as *The History of Italian Literature*, 2 vols., 1930

Further Reading

Breglio, Louis Anthony, *Life and Criticism of Francesco De Sanctis*, New York: Vanni, 1941
Croce, Benedetto, *Gli scritti di Francesco De Sanctis e la loro fortuna: Saggio bibliografica* (The Writings of Francesco De Sanctis and Their Critical Fortunes: A Bibliographical Essay), Bari: Laterza, 1917
Croce, Elena, and Alda Croce, *Francesco De Sanctis*, Turin: UTET, 1964
Prete, Antonio, *Il realismo di De Sanctis* (The Realism of De Sanctis), Bologna: Cappelli, 1970
Russo, Luigi, *Francesco De Sanctis e la cultura napoletana, 1860–1885* (Francesco De Sanctis and Neapolitan Culture, 1860–1885), Venice: Nuova Italia, 1928
Villari, Pasquale, *Studies: Historical and Critical*, London: Unwin, and New York: Scribner, 1907
Wellek, René, *A History of Modern Criticism*, vol. 4: *The Later Nineteenth Century*, New Haven: Yale University Press, 1965; London: Cape, 1966

Design History

Design history is an academic discipline that applies a cross-disciplinary approach to the study of design. This stands apart from "history of design" which is more appropriately seen as an aspect of the discipline of design history. Design history is object-led, yet it is more than an examination of the object within a chronology. Rather, it is concerned with understanding and finding explanations of the past and present by evaluating, selecting, and ordering data with reference to the object or product. The role played by design is summarized in *Design in Context* (1987) where Penny Sparke writes that the "product is the mediator between manufacture and the consumer, and its design is the container of the message that is mediated." Nonetheless, design remains a complex concept, for not only has it been assigned different meanings at different periods of history, but it is both the heuristic process (conception and/or sketch or model) and the result of that process (the end-product).

A continuum within descriptive literature is that design has been recognized as the intellectual or rational part of a work of art and is therefore capable of influencing society. Whether one examines the writings of the Renaissance art theorist Giorgio Vasari or the 19th-century social historian John Ruskin, one finds the assumption that "good" design is capable of having a positive effect or, perhaps more meaningfully, "bad" design a negative influence on society. Thus the Design Reform movement of the mid-19th century held that design was fraught with moral implications and could serve as a powerful vehicle for social reform. More recently advertisers would have us believe that adding the label "design" to an object (e.g., designer jeans, designer drugs) signifies social status or style.

Recognizing that every element of a product has been "designed" and is, by definition, a construction with numerous voices, encourages contextualization. This leads to an examination of the underpinnings of the society, the ideologies, and the practices that promote specific choices and encourage final acceptance or rejection of a product. Design historians are often engaged in discourse analysis as they attempt to come to terms with reading the ideas and theories embodied within the objects. With the physical object at the center of a series of relationships, the design historian is therefore interested in any of a myriad of processes: the initial conception, the selection of materials, manufacturing, marketing, taste, and consumption. Even after initial consumption the object continues to gain semiotic weight as it communicates new meanings and values.

As an area of study, design history developed in the 1960s within Britain's art colleges and polytechnics in answer to the growing demand for an art history that addressed the specific needs of craft and industrial design students as well as those in fashion and graphics. These new courses, confusingly titled History of Design and/or Design History, were meant to focus on design issues rather than following a traditional art history format that prioritized the fine arts. If art history was the birthing chamber for the new discipline it was a very public arena, for art history was also undergoing profound changes. Traditional methods of interpreting art were being questioned and the revisionist views adopted as the New Art History made inroads into even the most conservative of campuses (Attfield). The academic roots that anchor the discipline of design history, while less established, are also in place in the United States, Canada, and Australia; however, in many European countries, the related associations and publications have traditionally reflected an industrial design bias.

Design History's mixed heritage is evident in the choice of models scholars have applied to it. The most cited of the early texts is art and architectural historian Nikolaus Pevsner's *Pioneers of the Modern Movement* (1936) which introduced the student to designers and their ideas. While ground-breaking as a chronology of designers, it said little about the objects and it is generally agreed that it was Sigfried Giedion who first wrote about design from a societal rather than an individual

perspective. In *Mechanization Takes Command* (1948) Giedion attempted to investigate the relationship between design and societal change. Despite the possibilities of this new approach most authors were content to identify the designers and study what they thought and did. An interesting result of this traditional form of scholarship was the creation of a market for goods by prominent designers.

A watershed in design history came in 1972 with the Open University's course History of Architecture and Design, 1890–1930. For many this was the first opportunity to consider the role design played in everyday life, as topics such as the electric home, raised by Adrian Forty, were addressed. The growing interest in design is reflected in the formation of the Design History Society (1977), the publication of *Design Issues* (Chicago, 1984), the *Journal of Design History* (London, 1988), and in 1989 the opening of the Design Museum in London. However as design history continued to draw freely from other fields (anthropology, social history, art history, sociology, women's studies, archaeology) its identity was questioned. "[I]n the sense of a single, organized discipline with defined aims and objects, [design history] does not exist," Clive Dilnot argued in "The State of Design History" (1984).

Nevertheless, the majority rejoiced in the discipline's cross-disciplinary and proposed democratic nature. The use of methods from philosophy, political economy, linguistics, psychoanalysis, and cultural studies were recognized as an important intellectual stimulus to the discipline and found voice in cross-disciplinary journals such as *Block* (Middlesex, 1979). John A. Walker's *Design History and the History of Design* provides an excellent overview of the discipline as well as outlining the shift away from production towards the themes of "consumption, reception and taste" as the focus of scholastic endeavor.

It is perhaps symptomatic of postmodern and postcolonial thought that throughout the 1990s design historians have continued to broaden the boundaries that they have only so recently set for themselves. This has been done through the continual questioning of the dominant value systems – most recently the roles of gender and ethnicity (identity) in the production and consumption of the designed object.

JENNIFER E. SALAHUB

See also Art; Cultural

Further Reading

Attfield, Judy, "Form/female Follows Function/male: Feminist Critiques of Design," in John A. Walker, *Design History and the History of Design*, London: Pluto Press, 1989

Banham, Reyner, *Theory and Design in the First Machine Age*, London: Architectural Press, and New York: Praeger, 1960

Barthes, Roland, *Mythologies*, Paris: Seuil, 1957; selections in English as *Mythologies*, London: Cape, 1972, New York: Hill and Wang, 1973

Bayley, Stephen, *Taste: An Exhibition about Values in Design*, London: Victoria and Albert Museum, 1983

Conway, Hazel, ed., *Design History: A Students' Handbook*, London and Boston: Allen and Unwin, 1987

Dilnot, Clive, "The State of Design History," parts 1 and 2, *Design Issues: History, Theory, Criticism* 1/1 (1984), 3–23 and 1/2 (1984), 3–20

Forty, Adrian, *Objects of Desire: Design and Society, 1750–1980*, London: Thames and Hudson, and New York: Pantheon, 1986

Giedion, Sigfried, *Mechanization Takes Command: A Contribution to Anonymous History*, New York: Oxford University Press, 1948

Hebdige, Dick, "Object as Image: The Italian Scooter Cycle," *Block* 5 (1981), 44–64

Margolin, Victor, ed., *Design Discourse: History, Theory, Criticism*, Chicago: University of Chicago Press, 1989

Pevsner, Nikolaus, *Pioneers of the Modern Movement from William Morris to Walter Gropius*, London: Faber, 1936; as *Pioneers of Modern Design*, New York: Museum of Modern Art, 1949

Sparke, Penny, *Design in Context*, London: Bloomsbury, 1987

Sparke, Penny, *As Long as It's Pink: The Sexual Politics of Taste*, London: Pandora, 1995

Walker, John A., *Design History and the History of Design*, London: Pluto Press, 1989

Woodham, Jonathan M., "Redesigning a Chapter in the History of British Design: The Design Council Archive at the University of Brighton," *Journal of Design History* 8 (1995), 225–29

Deutscher, Isaac 1907–1967
Polish-born historian of Russia

Isaac Deutscher was a historian, biographer, and prolific essayist and commentator on developments in the communist world until his unexpected death from a heart attack. Deutscher's outstanding contribution is his 3-volume life of Trotsky based on a detailed reading of Trotsky's works and privileged access to the Trotsky archive at Harvard. This work remains a fundamental reference point for the study of 20th-century Russia and the equal of any historical biography in any language. Unfortunately, the quality and timelessness of much of the rest of Deutscher's work is more questionable. An understanding of this is best found in an analysis of Deutscher's ambiguous political relationship to Trotsky himself.

Deutscher was born near Kraków in Poland. Revolting against a strict Jewish upbringing, he turned to poetry and literary criticism before joining the then banned Polish Communist party (PCP) in 1926. Vigorous political activity led him to a deeper study of history and the social sciences. Disappointed by a visit to Russia in 1931 and further alienated by the "third period" policies of the Third International which treated social democracy as as big an enemy as fascism, Deutscher was expelled from the PCP as part of a small anti-Stalinist opposition in 1932. Thereafter he was a "freelance" figure on the left, sympathetic to Trotsky, but now hounded both by the authorities and the Stalinist Communist party. He fled to England in April 1939 and learned the language so quickly and thoroughly that he was soon able to establish himself as a journalist and eventually to write history of high literary quality, inspired in part by his reading of Gibbon and Macaulay. He married his wife Tamara Lebenhaft in 1947 and she acted as his researcher and editor, continuing after his death.

Trotsky had argued that Stalin's rule represented the "betrayal of the revolution." At first, Trotsky had seen this as a product of a political degeneration, but during the 1930s he increasingly stressed the deeper social roots of Stalin's system while denying that it had yet overturned the economic base of socialism in the form of nationalized property. This analysis produced powerful but contradictory insights. Trotsky papered over the contradictions by suggesting that the regime was unstable and would not survive World War II. Socialists had therefore to organize for an anticapitalist revolution in the West and a revolution in the East that would restore a genuine socialism. The strengthening of the position of the Soviet Union as a result of World War II put a huge questionmark over this analysis. Orthodox Trotskyism turned Trotsky's ideas into dogma, defending the letter of his last writings. Less orthodox Trotskyists revised the argument, suggesting either that Russia had become a form of state capitalism or a new class society, neither capitalist nor socialist.

Deutscher could accept neither of these positions and effectively solved the problem by retreating from the sharpness of Trotsky's late 1930s critique of the Soviet Union. This was reinforced by his doubts about the capacity of the working class for independent action, and the value of organized political engagement at a time when the choice seemed to be to line up either with Moscow or with Washington. He famously described his general intellectual position as being an "honorable" withdrawal to the "watchtower" from which the world could be observed "with detachment and alertness ... au-dessous de la melée." He also saw himself as a Jewish heretic in the tradition of Spinoza, Heine, Marx, Trotsky, and Freud, being both an intellectual and a physical exile from much of the Jewish tradition as well as that of the then orthodox left. This attitude was reflected in his increasing lack of sympathy with Trotsky's positions in the last volume of his biography. In Deutscher's wider writing it was reflected in his hopes that the ruling bureaucracies within the communist bloc would generate an internal momentum for reform to complete what he called in 1967 "the unfinished revolution." This optimism was continually disappointed and it undermined much of his commentary where he showed himself credulous to gossip and insufficiently self-critical.

The resulting contradictions were exposed during his lifetime in essays by Leopold Labedz from the right, and, even more ruthlessly from the left, by Tony Cliff. At the time however these made little impression on Deutscher's admirers who continued immediately after his death to praise and republish his essays. The critiques, however, seem to have better stood the test of time. Deutscher hoped that his 1949 biography of Stalin, the trilogy on Trotsky, and an unfinished biography of Lenin, of which only fragments have been published, would constitute "a single essay in a Marxist analysis of the revolution of our age." But aside from the Trotsky trilogy Deutscher's legacy has contributed little to our understanding of Soviet history or wider discussions in western Marxism, and this despite the influence of "history from below" on the analysis of the Stalin years.

MICHAEL HAYNES

See also Broué

Biography
Born near Kraków, Poland, 3 April 1907, son of a printer. Educated in Kraków. Journalist in Poland, 1924–39; member, Communist party of Poland, 1926–32; expelled from party for leading an anti-Stalinist opposition, 1932; Polish correspondent in London, 1939; editorial staff member, the *Economist*, 1942–49, and the *Observer* (pen-name Peregrine), 1942–47; roving European correspondent, 1946–47; independent author. Served in Polish Army, 1929–30, 1940–41. Married Tamara Lebenhaft, 1947 (1 son). Died Rome, 19 August 1967.

Principal Writings

Stalin: A Political Biography, 1949
Soviet Trade Unions: Their Place in Soviet Labour Policy, 1950
Russia after Stalin, 1953
The Prophet Armed: Trotsky, 1879–1921, 1954
Heretics and Renegades, and Other Essays, 1955
The Prophet Unarmed: Trotsky, 1921–1929, 1959
The Great Contest: Russia and the West, 1960
The Prophet Outcast: Trotsky, 1929–1940, 1963
Ironies of History: Essays on Contemporary Communism, 1966
The Unfinished Revolution: Russia, 1917–1967, 1967
The Non-Jewish Jew, edited by Tamara Deutscher, 1968
Lenin's Childhood, 1970
Russia, China and the West: A Contemporary Chronicle, 1953–1966, edited by Fred Halliday, 1970
Marxism in Our Time, edited by Tamara Deutscher, 1971
The Great Purges, edited by Tamara Deutscher, 1984
Marxism, Wars and Revolutions: Essays from Four Decades, edited by Tamara Deutscher, 1984

Further Reading

Beilharz, Peter, "Isaac Deutscher: History and Necessity," *History of Political Thought* 7 (1982), 375–92
Cliff, Tony, "The End of the Road: Deutscher's Capitulation to Stalinism," in his *Neither Washington nor Moscow: Essays on Revolutionary Socialism*, London: Bookmarks, 1982
Horowitz, David, ed., *Isaac Deutscher: The Man and his Work*, London: Macdonald, 1971
Labedz, Leopold, "Isaac Deutscher: Historian, Prophet, Biographer," *Survey* 30/1–2 (March 1988), 33–93
Rosenberg, J., "Isaac Deutscher and the Lost History of International Relations," *New Left Review* 215 (January/February 1996), 3–15

de Vries, Jan 1943–

US (Netherlands-born) economic historian of early modern Europe

Despite being interested in economic factors, many historians have found scholarship in economic history difficult to apply to their own work. As the divide between the disciplines of history and economics has widened, Jan de Vries has stood out as a scholar able to speak to both sides. Fully conversant with economic theory, he has still demonstrated a sensitivity to historical complexity, a capacity for archival research, and, perhaps most impressively, a felicitous and witty writing style few can match. Trained and employed as a historian, he holds a joint appointment as a professor of economics and history at Berkeley and has been chosen president of the Economic History Association, a group largely composed of economists.

De Vries' scholarly contributions fall into two major categories, although both types of scholarship aim towards the same end. First, his work on the Netherlands in the early modern period has argued that the Dutch economy was both highly advanced and yet static. Second, his wide-ranging, synthetic interpretations of early modern European economic history have portrayed the period as the crucial foundation for the Industrial Revolution.

His concern in both kinds of writing has been to rethink the transition that western Europe made from a pre-industrial to an industrial way of life. Through the 1960s, most economic history focused on the Industrial Revolution of the 19th century as a decisive break, one characterized by new technology, the rise of great cities, and a distinctive capitalist ethos. De Vries has been part of what he himself terms the "revolt of the early modernists" who, beginning in the 1970s, have demonstrated the importance of the changes that occurred before the 19th century. At the same time, de Vries has argued against the view that economic development happened at a constant rate. Instead, parts of the European economy reached high but stationary levels of economic sophistication. Many regions declined while only a few made the later transition into industrialization. Widespread migration, the growth of the state, and immense pressure on the family were all, de Vries has suggested, costs accompanying early industrialization.

In his studies of the Netherlands, de Vries has argued that the Dutch created a highly capitalist economy in the early modern period without moving toward industrialization. The Netherlands had already reached a very high level of agricultural productivity in the 16th century. Similarly, using their intricate system of canals, the Dutch had succeeded in moving goods and people extremely efficiently for an economy without railroads. At the same time, de Vries has argued, an intricate web of institutional controls and cultural habits prevented the modernity of early modern Netherlands from jumping into continuous, sustained growth and an industrial revolution. Guilds, town and provincial councils, and merchant companies maintained great power, taxes remained very high, and investors preferred safe investments rather than commerce or industry. Yet, until the mid-19th century with full-scale industrialization in Britain, de Vries estimates, the Netherlands probably was the wealthiest country in Europe. The Dutch achieved a relatively high level of economic development, but once they reached that level they elected not to make the necessary institutional and cultural changes that were probably necessary to expand still further.

De Vries' work is part of a larger debate by European and American scholars on the Dutch economy. He has played a major role in international efforts to reconstruct the long term growth rates for the Netherlands. The exact lines of growth play a major role in the debate over de Vries' argument. Earlier historians suggested that the Dutch economy boomed in the 17th century and then declined. De Vries argues that the Netherlands had a large amount of growth already early in the 16th century and that the economy declined only in relative, not absolute terms in the 18th century.

At the same time, however, de Vries has also sought to go beyond arguing that industrialization grew out of a high rate of earlier growth. As he has maintained in his interpretations of the European economy as a whole, the critical changes in the early modern period that lay the foundation for later industrialization did not necessarily create growth in the short run for the overall economy. Rather, he argues, change in form and function laid the foundation for the industrialization that would follow.

Older economic history scholarship has argued that in pre-industrial Europe the fundamental problem was that supply did not meet demand. Societies were poor and could not produce the goods that the populace wanted. Much of this older scholarship has suggested that new technology, urbanization, and a freeing of market forces broke this pre-industrial pattern. De

Vries has argued that the decisive forces were not technology first of all but new commercial links between regions, not large-scale urbanization but rural industry, and not the market *per se* but actions of the state and changes in consumption.

The new commercial links, the importance of rural industry, and the role of the state can all be seen, de Vries argues, in the unique pattern of urbanization that arose during the early modern period. The innovation of the early modern period was the creation of an "urban system": a few large cities concentrated in northwestern Europe – England, northern France, and the Netherlands – which directed the flows of capital and raw materials between rural industrial or proto-industrial areas. Between 1600 and 1750, de Vries has shown, 80 per cent of all urban growth in Europe occurred in just 38 out of approximately 200 cities and of these 38, thirty were political capitals, ports, or both. The capitals were the cities growing most consistently. The state concentrated capital and commerce in a relatively few cities, and then, in turn, merchants in these cities reorganized the rural industrial regions of Europe in order to achieve a higher level of productivity.

This urban system, in turn, led to the other innovation of the early industrial revolution, one which almost all previous scholars before de Vries missed: the growth of a large number of small towns, whose economy had been based on rural industry, into larger industrial towns. Industrialization began, in other words, "from below." Only later, with the full impact of the railroad and the inventions of the second Industrial Revolution was industrialization, according to de Vries, accompanied by the relative growth of large cities.

De Vries also attacks the earlier focus on the relation of supply and demand by employing the more pragmatic concept of effective demand. The problem in pre-industrial Europe was how consumers could translate their preferences into concrete actions in a market. De Vries suggests that during the early modern era many ordinary western Europeans abandoned some of their fatalism and began working harder in order to obtain more and better goods. The result was a gradual, but important rise in demand that helped stimulate a growth in commercial and industrial capitalism. The expansion of rural industry and commercial agriculture was, in de Vries' telling, an "industrious revolution" which was perhaps as important as the later Industrial Revolution. One of the intriguing aspects of de Vries' concept of "industriousness" is that it puts women at the center of the story. Often, it was their work and their decisions about saving and consumption which determined how households would allocate their labor, production, and savings.

CARL STRIKWERDA

See also Demography; Low Countries; Religion; Urban

Biography
Born Duivendrecht, the Netherlands, 14 November 1943. Studied at Columbia University, AB 1965; Yale University, PhD 1970. Taught at Michigan State University, 1970–73; professor of economics and history, University of California, Berkeley, from 1973. Married Jeannie Grace Green, 1968 (1 son, 1 daughter).

Principal Writings
"On the Modernity of the Dutch Republic," *Journal of Economic History* 33 (1973), 191–202

The Dutch Rural Economy in the Golden Age, 1500–1700, 1974
Economy of Europe in an Age of Crisis, 1600–1750, 1976
Barges and Capitalism: Passenger Transportation in the Dutch Economy, 1632–1839, Utrecht: HES, 1981
"Poverty and Capitalism," *Theory and Society* 12 (1983), 245–55
"The Decline and Rise of the Dutch Economy, 1675–1900," in Gary Saxonhouse and Gavin Wright, eds., *Technique, Spirit and Form in the Making of the Modern Economies, Research in Economic History*, supplement 3, 1984
European Urbanization, 1500–1800, 1984
"The Population and Economy of the Preindustrial Netherlands," *Journal of Interdisciplinary History* 15 (1985), 661–82
"Welvaren Holland" (Holland of Prosperity), *Bijdragen en medelingen betreffende de geschiedenis der Nederlanden* 102 (1987), 229–39
Editor with Ad van der Woude and Akira Hayami, *Urbanization in History: A Process of Dynamic Interactions*, 1990
Editor with David Freedberg, *Art in History, History in Art: Studies in Seventeenth Century Dutch Culture*, 1991
"Between Purchasing Power and the World of Goods: Understanding the Household Economy in Early Modern Europe," in John Brewer and Roy Porter, eds., *Consumption and the World of Goods*, 1993
"The Industrial Revolution and the Industrious Revolution," *Journal of Economic History* 54 (1994), 249–70
With Ad van der Woude, *Nederland, 1500–1815: De eerste ronde van moderne economische groei*, 1995; in English as *The First Modern Economy: Success, Failure, and Perseverance of the Dutch Economy, 1500–1815*, 1996

Further Reading
Strikwerda, Carl, "The City in History Revisited: New Overviews of European Urbanization," *Journal of Urban History* 13 (1987), 426–50

Díaz del Castillo, Bernal c.1492–1584
Spanish historian

Bernal Díaz del Castillo is unusual in that he came to history late in his life. Earlier he had been a conquistador who took park in three expeditions to Mexico between 1517 and 1519. His most famous campaign was the conquest of the Aztec empire by Hernando Cortés in 1519. In 1568, at the age of 76, he wrote a memoir of his exploits called the *Historia verdadera de la conquista de la Nueva España* (published c.1575; *The Conquest of New Spain*, 1963).

He wrote his work as a rebuttal to the published work of Cortés' confessor, Francisco López del Gómara, which gave a history of Cortés' conquests of Mexico. Díaz del Castillo felt that López de Gómara had distorted the facts of Cortés's conquest over the Aztecs, and wrote his memoirs to set the record straight. This work has great historical importance since Díaz del Castillo was an eyewitness to the capture and destruction of the Aztec capital of Tenochtitlán.

Díaz del Castillo had no formal historical training, and constructed a simple narrative of events. Since he did not consider himself a historian, he did not worry about being objective in his work. With this latitude in style and content, Díaz del Castillo was able to write in a very personal manner that overlooked little. One of the strengths of his work is that he showed a great deal of curiosity. Díaz del Castillo chronicled events and described objects that a "professional" historian might have overlooked as insignificant. This attention to the minute and the commonplace makes this work important, since few other accounts of the society he described remain.

The work is important on many levels. It is the only eyewitness account of the contact between the Spanish and the Aztecs. It is also an insight into the thinking and the mindset of the Spanish who set out to conquer the New World. By his own admission, Díaz del Castillo was no scholar, but a conqueror of New Spain. How the Catholic Spaniards viewed their place in the world and how they viewed the indigenous people they came into contact with are dealt with in detail in this work.

The True History gives an insight into the nature and manner of warfare in the early 16th century in the New World. The various battles between the Spanish and the Aztecs are described in some detail. More importantly, from a historical standpoint, one of the greatest contributions of Díaz del Castillo's work is that it offers one of the few descriptions of the Aztec people and their city of Tenochtitlán. Díaz del Castillo provided a vivid narrative of the layout of the city, describing in detail the royal residence of the Aztec emperor Montezuma and the various religious buildings around Montezuma's court.

Díaz del Castillo also supplies a vivid description of some aspects of daily life in Aztec society, describing food, clothing, and rituals. Particularly interesting are his accounts of human sacrifice as practiced by the Aztecs. Perhaps the most poignant aspect of the book is the description of the final destruction of the Aztec capital by the armies of Cortés.

As important as *The True History* is in understanding the Spanish conquest, the work is not without its weaknesses. One of the most obvious is that it was written fifty years after the fact, and mainly from memory. Nonetheless, Díaz del Castillo's work is still one of the most important chronicles of the period of Spanish history. *The True History* is the de facto standard reference for histories on the Spanish conquest.

DREW PHILIP HALEVY

See also European Expansion; Latin America: Colonial

Biography

Born Medina del Campo, Spain, *c*.1492. Went to the Indies, eventually serving as a conquistador with several expeditions, most notably that of Cortés in 1519. Returned to Spain twice to claim compensation, 1540 and 1550. Eventually settled in Guatemala, where he married Teresa Becerra, daughter of a fellow conquistador, retired to his *encomendero*, and wrote his memoirs. Died Santiago de los Caballeros, Guatemala, 3 February 1584.

Principal Writings

Historia verdadera de la conquista de la Nueva España, written 1568, published *c*.1575; in English as *The Discovery and Conquest of Mexico, 1517–1521*, 1928, and as *The Conquest of New Spain*, 1963

Further Reading

Adorno, Rolena, "The Discursive Encounters of Spain and America: The Authority of Eyewitness Testimony in the Writing of History," *William and Mary Quarterly* 49 (1992), 210–28

Cerwin, Herbert, *Bernal Díaz: Historian of the Conquest*, Norman: University of Oklahoma Press, 1963

Hagen, Victor Wolfgang Von, *Recia guerra: Díaz del Castillo escribe su Historia de la Conquista* (Stout War: Díaz del Castillo Writes the History of the Conquest), Mexico City: Mortiz, 1969

Dickens, A.G. 1910–
British historian of the Reformation

The distinguished career of A.G. Dickens as historian may be conveniently divided into three phases – Oxford, Hull, and London. His studies at Magdalen College, Oxford were followed by a period as fellow and tutor of Keble College, interrupted by five years' war service. From 1949 to 1962 he was professor of history at the University of Hull. Since 1962 he has been based in London, first as professor of history at King's College, and second, as director of the Institute of Historical Research from 1967 to 1977. Since then he has enjoyed a very active and productive retirement. These career movements were intimately related to Dickens' research priorities and to his sense of historical vocation.

A Yorkshireman by birth, he turned to research into Tudor Yorkshire as early as 1932, with (by his own account) two major objectives – "to study on all the social levels one particular crisis in our history: the English Reformation and its sequels" and "to build up local and biographical studies into regional histories which in turn would some day help to augment and reshape our national history." His preference was "to examine the nation's grass roots rather than its political and institutional pinnacles." In this way he defined himself as a social historian long before the term became fashionable. Reflecting later on this early period he recorded the pleasure of his discovery that "the middle and lower orders of society had mental and even cultural lives, which included personal responses to religion."

A number of individual publications during the 1930s and in the period immediately after World War II culminated in 1959 in the book *Lollards and Protestants in the Diocese of York, 1509–1558*, published a decade after his return from Oxford to Yorkshire to take up the chair of history at Hull, a move which had both symbolized and cemented his leadership in the field of northern regional history. Widely regarded as one of Dickens' most enduring contributions to historical writing, this work was in essence a general history of early Protestantism in Yorkshire and Nottinghamshire, and one of its principal effects was to encourage many younger scholars to pursue parallel local and regional research.

A biographical study, *Thomas Cromwell and the English Reformation* (1959), was followed shortly by *The English Reformation* (1964) which quickly established Dickens' reputation as the most authoritative interpreter of the English movement. Rejecting the traditional notion that the English Reformation could be summed up as "an act of state," he was concerned to delineate the development of genuine Protestant conviction in English society both before and after Henry VIII's conflict with the papacy, and criticized the tendency of earlier historians to allow ordinary men and women "to fall and disappear through the gaps between the kings, the prelates, the monasteries and the prayer books." With characteristic balance, however, he acknowledged that "governments and leaders remain important" and that "the story will not cohere in their absence."

From the mid 1960s Dickens increasingly turned his attention beyond England to the Reformation on the European continent, and a number of works swiftly flowed from his pen – a biography of Luther and textbooks on the Protestant and Catholic Reformations. Unlike his studies of England, these were not based on personal archival research, but they demonstrated his considerable ability to absorb a vast body of research and to reinterpret it for an English-speaking audience in lively and readable style. The most important of these works was the 1974 volume *The German Nation and Martin Luther* which placed Luther's movement firmly in the context of German society, especially the dynamic urban environment which had become the cutting edge of Reformation research.

This European interest was entirely congruent with the new direction that Dickens' career took after his appointment in 1967 to the directorship of the Institute of Historical Research, the largest institution for postgraduate historical studies in Britain and a key focal point in the international scholarly network. Building on personal contacts established in Germany after the war, and strengthened by his appointment as foreign secretary of the British Academy, Dickens played a major role for the next decade in promoting joint international conferences and other fruitful scholarly contacts for academics and students. It was his firm conviction that no position of leadership in the historical arena was more important or influential than the directorship of the Institute that led him to decline a number of opportunities to return to the more rarefied world of Oxford.

From the mid-1970s, Dickens had been planning to undertake the daunting task of writing a comprehensive historiographical study of the Reformation. A fortuitous meeting with an Australian scholar engaged in a similar enterprise led to eight years of collaborative research and culminated in the publication in 1985 (with John Tonkin) of *The Reformation in Historical Thought*, now a standard reference work on the subject.

While this achievement might have seemed an appropriate conclusion to a life of prolific publication, much more was to come. The massive output of scholarly research and writing in more than two decades since the 1964 publication of *The English Reformation*, and some trenchant criticisms of Dickens' interpretation by younger scholars, led him in his mid-seventies to accept the challenge of producing a new edition. Two important articles in 1987 answered his critics on key points, while the second edition of *The English Reformation* in 1989 was far more than a reissue of a classic. New and rewritten chapters brought it genuinely up-to-date. Dickens patiently corrected his critics' misconceptions while qualifying his own views where necessary in the light of new research. The essential perspective of the earlier work was emphatically restated for a new generation, with the caveat that "for every historian who embarks upon so great a theme, humility must become at once the alpha and omega."

In his early eighties Dickens took up one further task which had been on his agenda for two decades – a substantial study of Erasmus, which was written jointly with Whitney Jones and published in 1994. By then he could look back on an extraordinarily prolific career in which he had made a vast and complex subject his own and presented it with flair and lucidity to an international and multilingual audience.

JOHN TONKIN

See also Britain: 1485–1750; Counter-Reformation; Protestantism; Reformation

Biography

Arthur Geoffrey Dickens. Born Yorkshire, 6 July 1910. Educated at Hymers College, Hull; Magdalen College, Oxford, BA 1932, MA 1936. Served in the British Army, 1940–45. Fellow/tutor, Keble College, Oxford, 1933–49, and university lecturer, 1941–49; taught at Hull University, 1949–62; and King's College London, 1962–67; director, Institute of Historical Research, University of London, 1967–77. Married Molly Bygott, 1936 (died 1978; 2 sons).

Principal Writings

Lollards and Protestants in the Diocese of York, 1509–1558, 1959
Thomas Cromwell and the English Reformation, 1959
The English Reformation, 1964; 2nd edition 1989
Reformation and Society in Sixteenth-Century Europe, 1966
Martin Luther and the Reformation, 1967
Editor with Dorothy Carr, *The Reformation in England: To the Accession of Elizabeth I*, 1967
The Counter Reformation, 1968
The Age of Humanism and Reformation: Europe in the Fourteenth, Fifteenth and Sixteenth Centuries, 1972
The German Nation and Martin Luther, 1974
Editor, *The Courts of Europe: Politics, Patronage and Royalty, 1400–1800*, 1977
Contemporary Historians of the German Reformation, 1979
Reformation Studies [collected articles], 1982
With John Tonkin, *The Reformation in Historical Thought*, 1985
"The Early Expansion of Protestantism in England, 1520–1558," *Archiv für Reformationsgeschichte* 28 (1987), 187–221
"The Shape of Anticlericalism and the English Reformation," in E.I. Kouri and Tom Scott, eds., *Politics and Society in Reformation Europe*, 1987
With Whitney Jones, *Erasmus the Reformer*, 1994
Late Monasticism and the Reformation [collected articles], 1994

Further Reading

Brooks, Peter Newman, ed., *Reformation Principle and Practice: Essays in Honour of Arthur Geoffrey Dickens*, London: Scolar, 1980
Dickens, A.G., and John Tonkin, *The Reformation in Historical Thought*, Cambridge, MA: Harvard University Press, and Oxford: Blackwell, 1985: chapter 3
O'Day, Rosemary, *The Debate on the English Reformation*, London: Methuen, 1986

Dilthey, Wilhelm 1833–1911

German philosopher and historian

In the history of Western thought the possibility of knowledge in general and of historical knowledge in particular has been continuously called into question by various schools of skepticism. While Kant in his *Critique of Pure Reason* endeavored to put our knowledge of the physical world on the "secure path of science," Wilhelm Dilthey's lifelong ambition was to escape skepticism by providing the same epistemological foundation for our knowledge of the human-historical world. This latter project presupposed a clear distinction between the natural sciences (*Naturwissenschaften*) and the human sciences (*Geisteswissenschaften*). In his *Einleitung in die Geisteswissenschaften* (1883; *Introduction to the Human Sciences*, 1989), Dilthey took the position that the distinction was justified on the basis of their different subject matter. The first deals with the general, the universal, and the law-like; the second with the particular, the individual, and the unique. Later he revised this view and suggested that at the basis of the distinction lay two different modes of experiencing reality: "outer sensory experience" (*Erfahrung*) versus an "inner lived experience" (*Erlebnis*). In other words, the foundation of the human sciences turned out to be psychology, the same discipline that his neo-Kantian rivals, such as Wilhelm Windelband and Heinrich Rickert regarded as one of the natural sciences.

It was Dilthey's contention that nature as a datum is "closed" to us, not accessible via immediate and concrete experiential awareness, whereas the mental world of society, culture, and history is known to us from "inside" as lived experience. Extending the fundamental Kantian question, "How is experience in general possible?" Dilthey asked how *meaningful* experience was possible. In answering this he argued that the primary datum of lived experience was not a mass of disconnected facts, or "sensations," or "impressions," as the positivists would have it, but units of meaning, that is, facets of life already organized, interpreted, and, therefore, meaningful. The principles by which we organize our social and historical experience are the "categories of life" such as *value* through which we experience the present, *purpose* through which we anticipate the future, and *meaning* through which we recall the past.

Dilthey shared the premise of the German historical school (for example, Droysen and Ranke) that there was no such thing as a universal subject, only historical individuals. He rejected Hegelian speculative philosophy which assigned the meaning of history to a transcendental subject coming to absolute self-consciousness. "Behind life we cannot go," he insisted. History is neither the forward march of reason nor the unfolding of a divine plan. The first condition of the possibility of a science of history is that we ourselves are historical beings. We, humans, study the history we ourselves make.

The Geisteswissenschaften have a common subject matter: humanity. For Dilthey, history assumes the central role among the human sciences because in his view all human manifestations are part of a historical process and should be interpreted, or explained in historical terms. This, combined with his further tenets that different ages and individuals can be understood only by an imaginative assimilation to their specific point of view, and that the historian's point of view is always the product of his own age, amount to historicism, a position with which Dilthey is most commonly associated today.

It is important to note that the path he cut for himself in the intellectual wilderness of 19th-century speculative philosophy and positivism eventually led him far away from the "clearing" of Kantian critical philosophy. For Dilthey's project of a critique of historical reason, although meant to be a completion of Kant's work, entailed not merely the notion that a special variety of reason is employed in historical thinking but also that reason itself is historical. Contrary to the conclusion of the *Critique of Pure Reason*, the very conditions of knowledge, historical or otherwise, are subject to historical change.

In spite of this demonstration of intellectual independence Dilthey thought of himself as belonging to a Kantian generation. He also benefited from the ideas of Husserl whose analysis of "structure" and "significance" made a profound impression on him. His own discussion of temporality left a clear mark on Heidegger's *Being and Time*, and his writings on psychology clearly affected Jaspers' thinking. Others influenced by Dilthey include Max Weber, Ernst Troeltsch, Karl Löwith, Georg Lukács, Hans-Georg Gadamer, and Jürgen Habermas.

Dilthey left many unfinished writings behind him and was unable to work his ideas into a definitive system. This may have been to do with his suspicion of rationally constructed edifices of theory. A more likely explanation, however, is the unresolved tension between his sympathy for historicism and his equally strong concern for valid criteria of knowledge. If all consciousness is historically conditioned then the only permanent feature connected with both the natural and the human sciences is the philosopher's frustration in trying to provide an epistemological foundation for them.

JANOS SALAMON

See also Begriffsgeschichte; Castro; Cultural; Historiology; Hourani; Intellectual; Protestantism; Religion

Biography
Wilhelm Christian Ludwig Dilthey. Born Biebrich, Hesse, 19 November 1833. Attended school at Wiesbaden; studied theology at the University of Heidelberg, and philosophy and history at the University of Berlin, PhD 1864. Appointed as extraordinarius in philosophy at University of Basel, 1866; professor of philosophy, University of Kiel, 1868–71; University of Breslau, 1871–82; and as successor to Lotze, University of Berlin, 1882–1905. Died Seis bei Basen, 1 October 1911.

Principal Writings
Einleitung in die Geisteswissenschaften, 1883; in English as *Introduction to the Human Sciences*, 1989
Der Aufbau der geschichtlichen Welt in den Geisteswissenschaften, 1910; in English in *Hermeneutics and the Study of History*, 1996 [*Selected Works*, vol. 4]

Further Reading
Betti, Emilio, *Die Hermeneutik als allgemeine Methode der Geisteswissenschaften* (Hermeneutics as a General Method of the Humanities), Tübingen: Mohr, 1972
Ermarth, Michael, *Wilhelm Dilthey, The Critique of Historical Reason*, Chicago: University of Chicago Press, 1978
Habermas, Jürgen, *Erkenntnis und Interesse*, Frankfurt: Suhrkamp, 1968; in English as *Knowledge and Human Interests*, Boston: Beacon Press, 1971, London: Heinemann, 1972
Heussi, Karl, *Die Krisis des Historismus* (The Crisis of Historicism), Tübingen: Mohr, 1932
Johach, Helmut, *Handelnder Mensch und objektiver Geist: Zur Theorie der Geistes- und Sozialwissenschaften bei Wilhelm Dilthey* (Man of Action and Objective Spirit: On Dilthey's Theory of Spiritual and Social Studies), Meisenheim: Hain, 1974
Plantinga, Theodore, "Commitment and Historical Understanding: A Critique of Dilthey," *Fides et Historia* 14 (1982), 29–36
Rickman, H.P., *Meaning in History: Wilhelm Dilthey's Thoughts on History and Society*, London: Allen and Unwin, 1961

Dio Cassius *see* Cassius Dio

Diodorus Siculus *c.104–c.20 BCE*
Greek historian

Diodorus Siculus undertook probably the most ambitious project in historiography known from the ancient world: to compile the history of the world, from the origins of human culture to his own day. After incurring censure from 19th-century commentators, his reputation for discrimination in use of sources and for soundness of historical judgment has begun to be rehabilitated.

Diodorus has often been criticized for not doing what he never intended to do. His choice of the unique title *Bibliotheke Historike* (Historical Library) indicates his purpose and acknowledges the work's limitations. His *koinai praxeis* (general events) or *koinai historiai* (general histories) were to provide a sourcebook for "those who are more able" as historians; he expressly distanced himself from the "expert in one war" such as Thucydides with whom he has been unfavorably compared as an analyst of events.

The experiment in universal history had been tried before, for example by Ephorus, one of Diodorus' most reliable sources, but by Diodorus' standards no predecessor was truly universal. He insisted that the mythological period before the Trojan War and the legends of non-Greek peoples should be included for completeness, despite the difficulties involved. Of the forty books of the *Bibliotheke Historike*, books 1–5 – containing legends and customs of early Egypt, the Near and Middle East, India, and Africa; myths and legends of the Greek gods and early heroes; the Western islands and their peoples – are complete, as are books 11–20, containing Mediterranean history from 480 to 302. Books 6–10 (from the Trojan War to 480) and books 21–40 (from 301–60/59) are fragmentary, although a complete copy is said to have been extant in Constantinople until as late as 1453, when the city was sacked by the Turks.

In his general introduction, Diodorus outlines a rationale and overall plan for his work, partly to forestall "pirates" who might publish his material prematurely without acknowledgement, or mutilate it as part of their own compilations. For books 1–6 his approach was ethnographical and topographical; for the historical period he uses a double-referenced chronological system, attempting to combine parallel treatment of events across the nation-states, within an annalistic framework of Greek Olympiads and Archon years, synchronized as closely as possible with Roman consular years. This excessively complex arrangement militated against the production of either an accessible account or accurate causal analysis. As a basic structure he used the Chronology of Apollodorus of Athens, supplemented by that of Castor of Rhodes for the mythological period and the years after 120/119, where Apollodorus ends.

Diodorus' usual working method seems to have been, like Livy's, to follow what he considered to be the most reliable source until that source ran out, but occasionally to supplement it from as many as four further sources, sometimes resulting in a confusion which Diodorus does not deem it necessary or possible to unravel. For the years after 411 he was using sources now no longer extant, except in fragments. Since the discovery in 1906 of a papyrus fragment of the "Oxyrhynchus Historian" (*Hellenica Oxyrhynchia*), estimates of Diodorus' sources and his use of them have been revised in his favor. The close correspondence between Diodorus and the Oxyrhynchus Historian, Ephorus' own source, has reassured scholars that Diodorus recognized and was faithful to the best available. He echoed Polybius in stressing the necessity of firsthand information and claimed to have visited a substantial part of Europe and Asia, although there is no evidence that he went further than Egypt, Sicily, and Rome where, apparently having learned Latin in Sicily, he was able to consult the abundant records.

More than any other Hellenistic historian, Diodorus reflects the Stoic tenet that history should be profitable as a source of moral examples, rather than merely pleasurable. This antithesis can be traced back at least to Plato, was discussed by Thucydides, evident in Xenophon, and appeared to be resolved by Polybius who declared that the serious student will naturally take pleasure in what is morally beneficial. Diodorus was also concerned that the role of divine providence should be recognized in events, seeing divine intervention or retribution where others would not. However, he explicitly rejected his contemporaries' other besetting passion – overblown rhetoric – in all its forms.

Diodorus has rightly been valued as a mine of information on long-lost historians, but he is much more. For several periods he is our only or most important source: early Egypt, Sicily (a tribute to his birthplace), and the years 480–430 and 362–302. As an annalist, he often filled gaps left by more specialist historians and provided important supplementary information on, for example, Greek mythology and early Rome. He is indispensable to any student of the life of Alexander, preserving a version that has features in common with Quintus Curtius and Justinus – the so-called Vulgate or Peripatetic Tradition – but is substantially at variance with Arrian and Plutarch.

This "immense labor" produced, as Diodorus intended, "a great fountain for those who are fond of study." Whatever his shortcomings as compiler and analyst, Diodorus showed an extraordinary breadth in both his concept of history and his vision of the universal nature of humanity. Diodorus may have been influenced here by the Stoic doctrine of the brotherhood of humankind, but he was far ahead of his time in offering such clear and full evidence of it.

MARILYNNE BROMLEY

See also Egypt: Ancient; Machiavelli

Biography
Born Agyrium, Sicily, *c.*104 BCE. Traveled in Egypt, *c.*60–56; settled in Rome, *c.*56. Died *c.*20 BCE.

Principal Writings
Bibliotheke Historike (Historical Library), completed *c.*30
Works (Loeb edition), translated by C.H. Oldfather *et al.*, 12 vols., 1933–67

Further Reading
Barber, Godfrey Louis, *The Historian Ephorus*, Cambridge: Cambridge University Press, and Chicago: Ares, 1935

Burton, Anne, *Diodorus Siculus*, Leiden: Brill, 1972

Drews, Robert, "Diodorus and His Sources," *American Journal of Philology* 83 (1962), 383–92

Hammond, Nicholas Geoffrey Lempriere, *Three Historians of Alexander the Great: The So-Called Vulgate Authors: Diodorus, Justin and Curtius*, Cambridge and New York: Cambridge University Press, 1983

Pavan, M., "La teoresi storica di Diodoro Siculo" (The Historical Theory of Diodorus Siculus), *Rendiconti dell'Accademia dei Lincei* 16 (1961)

Sacks, Kenneth, *Diodorus Siculus and the First Century*, Princeton: Princeton University Press, 1990

Spoerri, Walter, *Späthellenistische Berichte über Welt, Kultur und Götter* (Late Hellenistic Accounts of Society, Culture, and Religion), Basel: Reinhardt, 1959

Verdin, H., G. Schepens, and E. de Keyser, eds., *Purposes of History: Studies in Greek Historiography from the 4th to the 2nd centuries* BC, Louvain: Catholic University, 1990

Vuillemin, Jules, *Nécessité ou contingence: l'aporie de Diodore et les systèmes philosophiques*, Paris: Minuit, 1984; in English as *Necessity or Contingency? The Master Argument and Its Philosophical Solutions*, Cambridge: Cambridge University Press, 1995

Dionysius of Halicarnassus

*c.*60–after 7 BCE
Greek historian

Little is known of Dionysius' life other than he came to Italy around 30 BCE from Halicarnassus (now Bodrum) in Caria, Asia Minor. His arrival in Rome coincided with the end of the civil war between Augustus and Antony. He taught rhetoric to the sons of wealthy Roman families. Scholars regard his critical works on rhetoric and his literary criticism as his best efforts, rather than his historical work.

Dionysius' 20-book history of Rome from prehistoric times to the beginning of the First Punic War in 265 BCE, *The Roman Antiquities*, is a valuable source of the history of early Rome. Only 10 of the 20 books are extant. Most of the other books have survived in fragments and in Plutarch's biography of Camillus. Classicist Richard Jebb characterized Dionysius' *Roman Antiquities* as an introduction to Polybius' history of Rome.

Roman Antiquities exhibits Dionysius' skills in literary criticism and rhetoric. However, the premise of the work is problematic. His object in writing the history was to acquaint the Greeks with the origins of Rome. He felt that by doing so he could reconcile the Greeks, who believed that a race of barbarians had conquered them, to the Roman domination of the Mediterranean. Dionysius claimed Roman victory was due to the piety and righteousness of the Romans; Roman success proved that they had the approval of the gods. He linked the Romans culturally and ethnically with the Greeks, making the Etruscans an amalgam of Greek peoples coming together in Italy. Earlier this century some historians gave credence to this theory of the origins of the Etruscans.

Roman Antiquities was never a popular history. Several reasons for the history's lack of a readership are apparent. Dionysius was the champion of the Attic style of writing rather than the popular, flowery Asiatic style. Livy related most of the stories Dionysius tells without the moralizing and rhetoric.

Moreover, Dionysius' misunderstanding of the origins of Roman politics, religion, and social classes may have been obvious to his contemporaries.

Modern classicists and historians can appreciate Dionysius' quotation of source documents. Instead of footnotes, he addresses the reader directly saying that he has consulted many sources. While scholars have dismissed Dionysius' *Roman Antiquities* as rhetoric or fiction, his robust, cynical attitude remains fresh, as does his struggle to remain objective while fighting the inherent tendency of the historian to personalize a historical text. His methods of addressing this problem differ from those of the contemporary scholar and the reader will see that he did not always win this struggle.

NANCY PIPPEN ECKERMAN

See also Beloch

Biography
Born Halicarnassus, *c.*60 BCE. Settled in Rome to write and teach rhetoric, *c.*29. Died after 7 BCE.

Principal Writings
The Roman Antiquities (Loeb edition), translated by Earnest Cary, 7 vols., 1937–50
The Critical Essays (Loeb edition), translated by Stephan Usher, 2 vols., 1974–85

Further Reading
Bonner, Stanley Frederick, *The Literary Treatises of Dionysius of Halicarnassus: A Study of the Development of Critical Method*, Cambridge: Cambridge University Press, 1939

Bowersock, Glen Warren, *Augustus and the Greek World*, Oxford: Oxford University Press, 1965; Westport, CT: Greenwood Press, 1981

Breisach, Ernst, *Historiography: Ancient, Medieval, and Modern*, Chicago: University of Chicago Press, 1983; revised 1994

Fox, Matthew, "History and Rhetoric in Dionysius of Halicarnassus," *Journal of Roman Studies* 83 (1993), 31–48

Gabba, Emilio, *Dionigi e la storia di Roma arcaica*, Paris: Actes IXe Congrès, 1974; in English as *Dionysius and the History of Archaic Rome*, Berkeley: University of California Press, 1991

Klotz, Alfred, *Livius und seine Vorgäneger* (Livy and His Predecessors), Amsterdam: Hakker, 1964

Schwartz, Eduard, *Griechische Geschichtsschreiber* (Greek Historians), Leipzig: Tübner, 1940–41

Diop, Cheikh Anta 1923–1985
Senegalese historian of Africa

A Senegalese scholar whose work became a central pillar of the Afrocentric movement, Cheikh Anta Diop was a committed Pan-Africanist who argued that the origins of ancient Egypt were African and that Black Africa possessed a fundamental cultural unity. He pushed his commitment beyond the realm of scholarship and was a key figure in the Senegalese political opposition from the early 1960s until his death in 1985. Labelling Diop as a scholar is not an easy task. Although his books deal with history and argue that the histories of Africa and the West need to be understood in light of the African origins of civilization, many historians have found it difficult to accept his work. Diop himself wrote of a key text, *L'Afrique noire précoloniale* (1960; *Precolonial Black Africa*, 1987), that it was "not, strictly speaking, a history book, but an auxiliary tool indispensable to the historian." Further complications arise when considering Diop's polymathic training and publications: history, archaeology, Egyptology, linguistics, and physics were all fields that he studied and in which he published. His reputation first developed among French-speaking Africans and Africanists during the 1950s and 1960s; in the 1970s African American scholars in the United States began translating his books into English, thus facilitating the growth of his reputation as one of the seminal thinkers in Afrocentricism.

Diop formulated his ideas while studying at the Sorbonne in the late 1940s and early 1950s. Postwar Paris was an exciting place for African intellectuals as the Négritude literary movement associated with the poets Léopold Senghor and Aimé Césaire was in full swing and the journal *Présence africaine* was establishing itself as a premier forum for the discussion of African political, artistic, and historical issues. Diop was very active in anticolonial activities organized by African students, and produced articles for *Présence africaine.* In 1954, he turned to the journal to publish his doctoral thesis on the Egyptian origin of African civilization after it was rejected by his committee. *Nations nègres et culture* (Negro Nations and Culture) appeared in 1955 and created an immediate sensation among French-speaking African intellectuals. The book critiques previous scholarship and assumptions concerning ancient Egypt and asserts that all available sources prove without a doubt that the ancient Egyptians were a Black African people. By denying this, European scholarship had stripped Black Africa of its cultural heritage. Diop cited similarities in concepts of totem, circumcision practices, monarchy organization, cosmological beliefs, caste systems, and matriarchal social structure as evidence for Africa's Egyptian ancestry. He then turned to comparative linguistics to argue for a genetic relationship between the language of ancient Egypt and the Senegalese language, Wolof.

Diop was a noteworthy participant in two international congresses organized by *Présence africaine* and in 1960 obtained his doctorate from the Sorbonne after a memorable thesis defense. He returned to Senegal to assume a research post at the Institut Fondamental d'Afrique Noire (IFAN) where he established a radiocarbon laboratory to pursue his interests in archaeology and physics. In the meantime, he published his most controversial book, *L'Unité culturelle de l'Afrique noire* (1959; *The Cultural Unity of Black Africa*, 1962). Here Diop draws from 19th-century European debates about the origins of civilization to argue that there existed northern and southern cradles of civilization. The northern cradle was located in Eurasia; it was marked by patriarchy, nomadism, and pastoralism. The southern cradle was found in Africa and was in essence matriarchal, sedentary, and agricultural. The two came into contact in the Mediterranean and this cross-fertilization led to the rise of the ancient Greece.

Historians have criticized the sweeping nature of this kind of argumentation, asserting that it inaccurately represents rather more complex historical realities. Several French scholars writing in the early 1960s considered Diop's work politically useful in that it promoted African unity, but at the same time derided its lack of scholarly objectivity. Diop responded that his scholarship was objective and that his books were misunderstood because European and African historians had different concerns when it came to writing African history. The Senegalese scholar believed that African historians must be concerned with finding synthesis in African history and that they should be writing "History" from a macro-perspective. This was in contrast to the detailed microhistorical studies of Western historians "whose goal seems to be to dissolve collective African historical consciousness in the pettiness of details."

In the 1970s, Diop's reputation grew as English translations of his books were integrated into African American scholarly traditions long concerned with exploring the links between ancient Egyptian and African civilization. His wide learning and unwavering belief that "Egypt is to the rest of Black Africa what Greece and Rome are to the West" had a profound impact among the group of African American intellectuals who developed Afrocentrism in the 1980s. Diop and his most important disciple, the Congolese historian Théophile Obenga, were key contributors to the multivolume UNESCO *General History of Africa*. At a 1974 UNESCO-sponsored conference in Cairo on the peopling of ancient Egypt, Diop and Obenga created a stir by forcefully arguing that the first inhabitants of the Nile were Black Africans; several French Egyptologists were persuaded that the evidence from comparative linguistics was not fortuitous and should be pursued further. Diop published an elaboration in 1977, *Parenté génétique de l'égyptien pharaonique et des langues négro-africaines* (Genetic Relationship of Pharaonic Egyptian and Negro-African Languages). Diop's contribution to the UNESCO collection, "Origin of the Ancient Egyptians" in *Ancient Civilizations of Africa* (vol.2 of the *General History*), was not acceptable to all the members of the editorial committee and thus a note was appended to the text indicating this disagreement.

Diop died in February 1985 just as his international reputation was reaching its peak. In Senegal, IFAN and the National University were renamed in his honor. His books continue to appear in new editions and serve as essential texts for students of Afrocentrism and African intellectual history.

CHRISTOPHER GRAY

See also Africa: North; Bernal

Biography

Born Diourbal, Senegal, 1923. Studied at the Sorbonne, received doctorate 1960. Returned to Senegal to take up a research post at the Institut Fondamental d'Afrique Noir. Founded Bloc des Masses Senegalaises and Front National Senegalais; both parties later outlawed by the government. Died Dakar, 7 February 1985.

Principal Writings

Nations nègres et cultures, 1955, revised as 2 vols., 1979; selections translated in *The African Origin of Civilization: Myth or Reality*, 1974

L'Unité culturelle de l'Afrique noire: domaines du patriarcat et du matriarcat dans l'antiquité classique, 1959; in English as *The Cultural Unity of Black Africa: The Domains of Patriarchy and of Matriarchy in Classical Antiquity*, 1962

L'Afrique noire précoloniale, 1960; in English as *Precolonial Black Africa: A Comparative Study of the Political and Social Systems of Europe and Black Africa, from Antiquity to the Formation of Modern States*, 1987

*Les Fondements culturels techniques et industriels d'un futur état
fédéral d'Afrique noire*, 1960; revised as *Les fondements
économiques et culturels d'un état fédéral d'Afrique noire*, 1974;
in English as *Black Africa: The Economic and Cultural Basis for
a Federated State*, 1978
Antériorité des civilisations nègres: mythe ou vérité historique?,
1967; in English as *The African Origin of Civilization: Myth or
Reality*, 1974
*Parenté génétique de l'égyptien pharaonique et des langues négro-
africaines: processus de sémitisation* (Genetic Relationship of
Pharaonic Egyptian and Negro-African Languages), 1977
Civilisation ou barbarie: anthropologie sans complaisance, 1981; in
English as *Civilization or Barbarism: An Authentic Anthropology*,
1991
"Origin of the Ancient Egyptians," in G. Mokhtar, ed., *Ancient
Civilizations of Africa*, 1981 [UNESCO General History of
Africa, vol. 2]
Egypte ancienne et Afrique noire (Ancient Egypt and Black Africa),
1989
*Alerte sous les tropiques: articles, 1946–1960: culture et
développement en Afrique noire* (Alarm in the Tropics: Articles,
1946–1960: Culture and Development in Black Africa), 1990

Further Reading

Asante, Molefi Kete, *Kemet, Afrocentricity, and Knowledge*, Trenton,
NJ: Africa World Press, 1990
Bernal, Martin, *Black Athena: The Afroasiatic Roots of Classical
Civilization*, vol. 1: *The Fabrication of Ancient Greece,
1785–1985*, London: Free Association Press, and New Brunswick,
NJ: Rutgers University Press, 1987
Ela, Jean-Marc, *Cheikh Anta Diop, ou, l'honneur de penser* (Diop;
or, The Honor of Thinking), Paris: L'Harattan, 1989
Gray, Chris, *Conceptions of History in the Works of Cheikh Anta
Diop and Théophile Obenga*, London: Karnak House, 1989
"Hommage à Cheikh Anta Diop," *Présence africaine* 1–2 (1989)
[special issue]
Obenga, Théophile, *L'Afrique dans l'antiquité: Egypte pharaonique,
Afrique noire* (Africa in Antiquity: The Egypt of the Pharaohs
and Black Africa), Paris: Présence africaine, 1973
Saakana, Amon Saba, *Ancient Egypt and Black Africa: A Student's
Handbook for the Study of Ancient Egypt in Philosophy,
Linguistics and Gender Relations*, London: Karnak House, 1992
Samb, Djibril, *Cheikh Anta Diop*, Dakar: Nouvelles Editions
Africaines du Sénégal, 1992
Van Sertima, Ivan, and Larry Williams, eds., *Cheikh Anta Diop*,
New Brunswick, NJ: Transaction, 1986

Diplomatic History/International Relations

Diplomatic history or international history is essentially the study of the history of international relations. It is concerned with the analysis of all forms of political interaction between states, including treaties, wars, and trade. Strictly speaking, diplomatic history is different from international history, as it is possible to write a diplomatic history of a single country's foreign policy, while the latter by definition deals with the complex interplay of relations between two or more countries. The discipline of international relations is different again in that it is concerned primarily either with the study of contemporary diplomacy or the formulation of theoretical models that seek to explain the workings of the international system.

The study of diplomatic history as a distinct type of history had its origins in the 19th century with the work of Leopold von Ranke and his disciples. From Ranke came two of the most traditional aspects of the discipline: first, that the research should be based on official archival material, and second, that it should provide a detached, objective, and non-judgmental account of events. At first, however, the work on diplomacy was largely an offshoot of political history, and it was not until the start of the 20th century that the discipline took on more distinctive features. It was at this point that it began to focus on more recent events, a tendency that began with a series of books on early 19th-century diplomacy. Probably the most important of these volumes was Charles Webster's *The Congress of Vienna* (1919), but this period also saw a series of influential monographs on 19th-century European diplomatic history by historians such as H.W.V. Temperley, A.F. Pribram, R.H. Lord, and B.E. Schmitt. These books, building on Ranke's legacy, set the tone for much of the work that followed. However, there were in addition books that dealt with even more recent events such as the Franco-Prussian War and the origins of World War I.

The writing of such volumes was inspired by the publication by states of official diplomatic correspondence. The increasing willingness of governments to publish documents, such as the French publication from 1910 of documents on the origins of the Franco-Prussian War, was a particularly important development for the discipline. This more than anything else allowed diplomatic history to generate one of its most notable characteristics, which is that in contrast to other branches of history, it has always shown an interest in the recent past. This trend was most evident in the years following World War I, when various participants in the conflict published volume upon volume of their diplomatic correspondence from the period before August 1914. Germany led the way in this field, closely followed by Britain, when the diplomatic historians G.P. Gooch and H.W.V. Temperley were asked to edit the series. The publication of the German and British documents helped to spark a debate about the origins of World War I, and encouraged the publication of a number of works on the subject, such as S.B. Fay's *Origins of the First World War* (1928), B.E. Schmitt's *The Coming of the War* (1930), and Luigi Albertini's *Le origini della guerre del 1914* (1942–43; *The Origins of the War of 1914*, 1952–57). The tendency in the debate, fitting the objective tone of diplomatic history, was that no one power was guilty for causing the war; it was rather the result of universal miscalculation.

The works that appeared in the next three decades largely followed the limited methodology outlined above. It soon became clear that the problem with this approach was that it led to vastly detailed histories which often lacked an analytical edge and which did little to explain how foreign policy was constructed in the first place. This was, however, not true of all the writers in the field, for some were capable of producing memorable work that tackled broader concepts such as the ideas of a balance of power. Most notable in this respect were the works of A.J.P Taylor, and in particular his *The Struggle for Mastery in Europe* (1954). Also important were books by historians such as W.N. Medlicott, Pierre Renouvin, and W.L. Langer. It was, however, clear that diplomatic history was in danger of becoming a cul de sac in which orthodox views held too great a sway; this became even more evident when historians started to consider the origins of World War II.

Even before the end of World War II, the study of the origins of that conflict had been started by E.H. Carr's *The Twenty Years' Crisis* (1939), and after the war the trickle became a flood. This trend was encouraged once again by the almost immediate publication of government documents, but also significant was the appearance of the first part of Winston Churchill's war memoirs, *The Gathering Storm* (1948), which set in stone an orthodox view on war origins that damned the British and French appeasement of an insatiable Nazi Germany. It did not take long for this orthodoxy to be challenged. In 1961 A.J.P. Taylor produced his *The Origins of the Second World War*, which postulated that the war over Poland in 1939 was the result of diplomatic blundering rather than part of Hitler's blueprint for world domination. Taylor's work caused intense debate, and it opened the gates for others to follow. In particular the 1960s and 1970s saw historians such as D.C. Watt, David Dilks, and George Peden begin to analyze the motives behind British appeasement of Germany and to demonstrate that military, economic, and financial factors had been as important for Britain as diplomatic concerns. In addition, such studies displayed an increasing interest in the way both public and private perceptions were formed, which led in turn to new offshoots from purely diplomatic history such as the study of intelligence and propaganda. It became clear that the discipline was becoming more sophisticated.

Another important reason for the shift in diplomatic history from the 1960s onwards was the influence of the changes that were going on in history as a whole, as the discipline moved away from political history towards social, economic, cultural, and intellectual history. In particular the new history of the Annales school raised a challenge as it was overtly hostile to diplomatic history, regarding it as a nothing more than a history of elites. This criticism rang home, for diplomatic history was still overwhelmingly concerned with high politics and was based primarily on the documents of foreign ministries and their ambassadors. In order to overcome the limitations of diplomatic history some of its practitioners started to devote attention to the economic, social, cultural, and military factors that influenced foreign policymaking. The most significant of such scholars was the West German historian Fritz Fischer who, in his book *Griff nach der Weltmacht* (1961; *Germany's Aims in the First World War*, 1967), reopened the debate about the origins of that conflict by demonstrating how Germany's economic and colonial ambitions had contributed to the outbreak of war. Fischer's thesis provoked a bitter debate, but away from the specifics of his subject matter his approach showed that to study foreign policy in isolation from domestic factors was a grave error. In addition, a similar influence was exerted by the rise of international relations as a discipline within political science. The application of a social science methodology to relations between states showed that it was possible to move away from complete empiricism towards more theoretical explanations. Historians such as F.H. Hinsley and Christopher Thorne took up the challenge from international relations and showed how broader frameworks of analysis could be applied to diplomatic history.

In addition to influences from inside the discipline of history, external factors also had a role in changing the agenda of diplomatic history. One key fact was that, unlike World War I, World War II had been a truly global conflict involving war in the Pacific as well as Europe. This meant that for virtually the first time a non-European subject, the origins of the Pacific War, became of concern for diplomatic historians, and this in turn helped to open up interest in the history of diplomatic relations between the East Asian states and the West. In particular, an interest in Japan was to be seen in works by such historians as Chihiro Hosoya, Ian Nish, and Akira Iriye. World War II was also significant because by weakening the European states and their colonial empires it shifted the spotlight of world events away from Europe towards the newly independent states of Southeast Asia and the Middle East. The complex history of decolonization in these areas and the subsequent diplomatic maneuverings of the Cold War rivals, the Soviet Union and the United States, opened up new uncharted arenas for diplomatic historians.

Contemporary events could also be influential in affecting the diplomatic history agenda. The most obvious postwar example was the effect of the Vietnam War on the way in which historians approached the history of America's foreign relations. Opposition to the war led a number of historians to move away from straightforward accounts of diplomatic history to an attempt to understand the motivations and ideology that lay behind American foreign policy. The result was a number of books on subjects such as American imperialism at the end of the 19th century, the role of the United States in East Asia in the 20th century, and the origins of the Cold War, which utilized some of the tools of economic, social, and cultural history. Once again the result was to cause a major debate within the discipline which continues to reverberate with undiminished vigor to the present day, particularly in the pages of *Diplomatic History*, the journal of the Society of Historians of American Foreign Relations.

Diplomatic history is thus in a position, after a time of external criticism and self-doubt, to produce once again interesting and challenging work. The field has benefited enormously from the influx of ideas of social history and international relations and from the ending of its former Eurocentricity.

SAHO MATSUMOTO

See also Ambrose; Annales regni; Butterfield; Chabod; Droysen; Elliott; Europe: Modern; Fischer; Gilbert; Intelligence; Jelavich; Kedourie; Kennedy; Kolko; LaFeber; Mattingly; Mayer; Motley; Renouvin; Rodrigues; Taylor; Vagts; Williams, W.

Further Reading

Albertini, Luigi, *Le origini della guerre del 1914*, 3 vols., Milan: Bocca, 1942–43; in English as *The Origins of the War of 1914*, 3 vols., London: Oxford University Press, 1952–57

Carr, E.H., *The Twenty Years' Crisis, 1919–1939: An Introduction to the Study of International Relations*, London: Macmillan, 1939; New York: St. Martin's Press, 1962

Churchill, Winston, *The Second World War*, vol. 1: *The Gathering Storm*, London: Cassell, and Boston: Houghton Mifflin, 1948

Dilks, David, "'We Must Hope for the Best and Prepare for the Worst': The Prime Minister, the Cabinet and Hitler's Germany, 1937–1939," *Proceedings of the British Academy* 73 (1987), 309–52

Fay, Sidney Bradshaw, *Origins of the First World War*, 2 vols., New York: Macmillan, 1928

Fischer, Fritz, *Griff nach der Weltmacht: die Kriegszielpolitik des kaiserlichen Deutschland, 1914–18*, Düsseldorf: Droste, 1961; in English as *Germany's Aims in the First World War*, London: Chatto and Windus, and New York: Norton, 1967

Gooch, G.P., *Before the War: Studies in Diplomacy*, 2 vols., London: Longman, 1936

Hinsley, Francis Harry, *Power and the Pursuit of Peace: Theory and Practice in the History of Relations Between States*, Cambridge: Cambridge University Press, 1963

Hogan, Michael J., ed., *America in the World: The Historiography of American Foreign Relations since 1941*, Cambridge and New York: Cambridge University Press, 1995

Hosoya, Chihiro, "Miscalculations in Deterrent Policy: Japanese–US Relations, 1938–1941," *Journal of Peace Research* 2 (1968), 97–115

Hunt, Michael H., *Ideology and US Foreign Policy*, New Haven: Yale University Press, 1987

Iriye, Akira, *Power and Culture: The Japanese-American War, 1941–1945*, Cambridge, MA: Harvard University Press, 1983

Joll, James, *Europe since 1870: An International History*, London: Weidenfeld and Nicolson, and New York: Harper, 1973

Langer, William Leonard, *European Alliances and Alignments, 1871–1890*, New York: Knopf, 1931; revised 1950

Lord, R.H., *The Second Partition of Poland: A Study in Diplomatic History*, Cambridge, MA: Harvard University Press, 1915

Mayer, Arno J., *Political Origins of the New Diplomacy, 1917–1918*, New Haven: Yale University Press, 1959

Medlicott, W.N, *Bismarck, Gladstone and the Concert of Europe*, London: Athlone Press, 1956

Nish, Ian Hill, *Alliance in Decline: A Study in Anglo-Japanese Relations, 1908–23*, London: Athlone Press, 1972

Peden, G., *British Rearmament and the Treasury, 1932–1939*, Edinburgh: Scottish Academic Press, 1979

Pribram, A.F., *Austrian Foreign Policy, 1908–1918*, London: Allen and Unwin, 1923

Renouvin, Pierre, *La Crise européenne et la grande guerre, 1904–1918* (The European Crisis and the Great War), Paris: Allan, 1934

Robertson, Esmonde M., ed., *The Origins of the Second World War: Historical Interpretations*, London: Macmillan, 1971

Schmitt, Bernadotte E., *The Coming of the War, 1914*, New York: Scribner, 1930

Taylor, A.J.P., *The Struggle for Mastery in Europe, 1848–1918*, London and New York: Oxford University Press, 1954

Taylor, A.J.P., *The Origins of the Second World War*, London: Hamish Hamilton, and New York: Atheneum, 1961

Temperley, H.W.V., *The Foreign Policy of Canning, 1822–1827: England, the Neo-Holy Alliance, and the New World*, London: Bell, 1925

Thorne, Christopher, *Border Crossings: Studies in International History*, Oxford and New York: Blackwell, 1988

Watt, Donald Cameron, *How War Came: The Immediate Origins of the Second World War, 1938–1939*, London: Heinemann, and New York: Pantheon, 1989

Webster, C.K., *The Congress of Vienna, 1814–15*, London and New York: Oxford University Press, 1919

Documentary Film

Since its inception film has acted both as an instrument of information and as a source of entertainment. The documentary film, a term not popularized until the 1920s, began with the origins of film technology. The documentary film, however, has changed over time, shifting along with the technological as well as political, social, and culture landscape.

As filmmaking emerged in the 1890s, the documentarists distinguished their work from other filmmakers by their focus on real people and real events. In the 20th century's first decade, the "nickelodeon" era, in which single reel films lasted from one to ten minutes, the film of fact gave way to entertainment. The documentary's rebirth resulted from distinct American and Soviet impulses. The first great American documentarist, Robert Flaherty, began as an explorer and prospector in northern Canada, but soon filming dominated his trips. In 1922 he released, *Nanook of the North*. While private benefactors financed *Nanook*, Flaherty's second film, *Moana* (1926), about Polynesian culture, received American commercial film studio support. In the same period, Dziga Vertov and other Soviet documentarists glorified their new order. Three traditions predominated in the 1920s: the American romantic tradition; the Soviet propaganda style; and continental realism.

In reviewing Flaherty's *Moana*, John Grierson, a documentarist employed by the British government's film unit, popularized the term documentary to describe an "actuality-based" work. Grierson, who had just embarked on a decades-long career as a director and producer of government-sponsored documentaries in Britain, sought to promote filmmaking outside of the commercial film industry, believing that films should educate the public. Debate raged, however, about whether documentaries captured "truth." Documentarists like Vertov believed a film remained authentic even if the artist conveyed a generalized poetic feeling from facts. Grierson later altered his definition to account for the creative interpretation (as opposed to treatment) of actuality. Filmmakers and critics agreed that documentaries mixed social and artistic sensibilities and thus transcended mere fact or mere entertainment.

American filmmakers, unlike their European counterparts, did not receive state support, until the Depression and the New Deal altered the American status quo. During the 1930s the US government subsidized projects that captured the American experience. Pare Lorentz created two famous documentaries, *The Plow That Broke the Plains* (1936), and *The River* (1937), for a New Deal agency. Lorentz's films fit into a larger documentary impulse sweeping the nation's artistic communities.

During the anxious years of depression, the documentary gained importance as a means of national propaganda. In Nazi Germany Leni Riefenstahl's *Triumph of the Will* (1935) and *Olympia* (1938) stood as powerful artistic statements celebrating the fascist state. War temporarily institutionalized the documentary as propaganda. In Britain, for example, just a short step carried Grierson from making movies that explained the British economy, *Housing Problems* (1935), to ones that showcased the Royal Air Force, *The Lion Has Wings* (1939). American commercial film director Frank Capra produced the Why We Fight series under the eye of the American government.

During the 1930s a parallel documentary tradition, the newsreel, surged. At times, more than 20 million people a month viewed Time-Life Inc.'s March of Time series, which began in 1935. The newsreel tradition dated from film's earliest days, but they had their strongest appeal during the war. Technological factors shaped the newsreel style. Because of the limitations in recording live events (especially battles), newsreel producers opted for a reportial style and they re-enacted key events. Until 1945, and the introduction of 16mm safety film, filmmakers could not shoot uninterrupted for more than ten minutes.

In the 1950s the newsreel continued on a new medium, television. In postwar America, corporations sponsored documentarists. Standard Oil of New Jersey invested $175,000 in Flaherty's *Louisiana Story* (1948), which dramatized the arrival of oil exploration in the Louisiana bayou. Film sponsorship by big business, big charities, government, and television brought commercial styles into the field. While in some cases television's sponsorship moderated the tone and restricted the selection of topics, television also widened the audience for coverage of compelling issues, such as McCarthyism and the civil rights movement.

Television's immediacy gave viewers a sense of being there amidst the action. The cultural shift augmented technological innovations, such as small lightweight hand-held cameras with portable tape recorders that made it easier to capture action and sound and lessened the need for large crews, further altering documentary technique. As part of a widespread search for "truth" during the 1960s, documentarists attempted to capture life without preconceived notions. An early example of the cinéma-vérité style, Richard Leacock's *Primary* (1960), chronicled the 1960 Democratic presidential primary. In seeking to dramatize current events, the cinéma-vérité documentarists acted as the story's catalyst, provoking reactions to create their story. More versatile cameras and easier editing also eased the return of the feature-length documentary.

The confrontational style proceeded into the 1970s, a decade marked by the emergence of women filmmakers. Barbara Kopple's *Harlan County, USA* (1976), captured the gritty essence of a coal miners' strike. The Vietnam War provided material for scores of films, reinforcing the documentarist's role as social critic. This was even more striking with the postwar confrontation of the Holocaust, from Alain Resnais' elegant *Nuit et brouillard* (*Night and Fog*, 1955), to Claude Lanzmann's epic *Shoah* (1985), and Marcel Ophuls' investigation into French complicity with its Nazi invaders in *Le Chagrin et la pitié* (*The Sorrow and the Pity*, 1971).

The documentary continues to evolve. Commercial docudramas, an unsteady mixture of fiction and fact, and public relations films have corrupted the documentary's expository legacy. In attempting to explain weighty topics, historical documentaries, such as Ken Burns' Civil War and baseball films on American public television, rely on extant footage, archival sources, and expert commentary. No longer just a chronicle of current events, documentaries also function as an oracle of history. The encroachment upon the historian's turf has ignited the old debate about whether filmmakers document or distort the truth.

CHRISTOPHER MACGREGOR SCRIBNER

See also Film; Media

Further Reading

Barnouw, Erik, *Documentary: A History of Non-Fiction Film*, London and New York: Oxford University Press, 1974; revised 1983

Barsam, Richard, *Nonfiction Film: A Critical History*, New York: Dutton, 1973, London: Allen and Unwin, 1974; revised 1992

Campbell, Craig, *Reel America and World War I: A Comprehensive Filmography of Motion Pictures in the United States, 1914–1920*, Jefferson, NC: McFarland, 1985

Jacobs, Lewis, ed., *The Documentary Tradition*, New York: Hopkinson and Blake, 1971; revised 1979

Pronay, Nicholas, and David W. Spring, eds., *Propaganda, Politics, and Film, 1918–45*, London: Macmillan, 1982

Smith, Paul, ed., *The Historian and Film*, Cambridge and New York: Cambridge University Press, 1976

Swann, Paul, *The British Documentary Film Movement, 1926–1946*, Cambridge and New York: Cambridge University Press, 1989

Domínguez Ortiz, Antonio 1909–

Spanish historian

Born in Seville in 1909, with university degrees in history from Seville and Madrid, Antonio Domínguez Ortiz is one of the foremost specialists of early modern Spanish history and one of the truly great Spanish historians of this century. He belongs to a generation of historians which blossomed during the regime of Francisco Franco, receptive to much of the innovative historical scholarship being undertaken outside the Spain in the French and Anglo-Saxon worlds, yet still distinctly Spanish in their choice of topics and the way they analyzed them. Far removed from the penchant for macro-explanations of the development of Spanish history – so characteristic of the great historians and thinkers of the first half of this century (Claudio Sánchez Albornoz, Américo Castro, José Ortega y Gasset, among others) – Domínguez Ortiz's work, like that of others in his generation, has been centered on the more modest but equally important goal of enlarging our understanding of Spanish history a little bit at a time. In a sense this work is less ambitious than the preceding generation's, but far more fruitful because it has helped lay out the path which many social, economic, and political historians have followed up until the present.

Throughout his long and extraordinarily prolific career, Domínguez Ortiz has concentrated on the history of Spain between the reign of the Catholic kings and the end of the *ancien régime*, from the late 15th century to the late 18th. He has made significant contributions to our understanding of many aspects of the Spanish past ranging from population development to intellectual history. It is in his studies of Spanish society, however, that the work of Domínguez Ortiz has been most fruitful. He is a social historian in the best possible sense, open to advances in the social sciences and keenly interested in how society works, how different social groups are structured, and how they interact. His work is basically non-quantitative and is firmly grounded in his own archival work and in a vast knowledge of both contemporary and historical accounts of past events, processes, and characters. His approach to history is also decidedly non-ideological. His shadow has been a long one among younger generations of historians, not only because of the way he has written history, but also because many of the subjects and interpretations he emphasized have subsequently gained favor among younger historians. It is impossible to research early modern Spanish history today without being keenly aware of his legacy. Domínguez Ortiz's work continues to constitute the point of departure for most serious research on a wide range of social groups and institutions of *ancien régime* society in Spain.

His classic studies of 17th- and 18th-century Spanish society – *La sociedad española en el siglo XVIII* (18th-Century Spanish Society, 1955) and *La sociedad española en el siglo XVII* (17th-Century Spanish Society, 1963–70) are arguably his two most influential works. In them Domínguez Ortiz pointed to a society that was a nexus of interest groups, each with specific interests of its own which were played out in given structural contexts which constrained their actions. Money and economic position were central to the way each group developed in society, but so were prestige, honor, lineage, and the prevailing levels of social and religious tolerance. This way of approaching society was strongly influenced by many of the advances made by the social sciences during the central decades of this century, although Domínguez Ortiz seldom emphasized this point. The way he dealt with the nobility and the clergy was characteristic of this approach. With the nobility, his work was one of the first to treat it as a specific social group. It was a group whose position within the society of the *ancien régime* was based on status (honor, prestige, social consideration, privilege) rather than merely on wealth; although within the nobility itself, more often than not wealth, especially rents, was the key to its own internal hierarchy. When studying the clergy, the basic approach remained the same. Both clergy and nobility were estates, because their social position was based on tradition and legal privilege, yet both revealed very sharp internal differences defined mainly by wealth. Priests and nobles wielded considerable social, political, and economic influence within the sphere of Spanish society, although this influence was conditioned by their position within each estate.

The work of Domínguez Ortiz on minority groups has also had a far-reaching influence on Spanish historiography. Of particular importance was his pioneering study of converts from Judaism (*conversos*) during the early modern period (*La clase social de los conversos en Castilla en la Edad Moderna* (The Social Class of the *conversos* in Early Modern Castile, 1955). He was one of the very first to treat them not as crypto-Jews but rather as a heterogeneous social group, urban-based, often elite but with no established position in an estate society bent on protecting its own vested interests and on excluding any sign of religious or social divergence. In his work on the *moriscos* (Muslim converts to Christianity), which began in 1949 and which culminated in his *Historia de los moriscos* (History of the *moriscos*, 1978, written with Bernard Vincent), Domínguez Ortiz explored the social makeup of the *morisco* minority, the difficulties of their assimilation into Spanish society and the reasons for and consequences of their expulsion, first from Granada, and then from Spain in 1609. Typically he was concerned more with the way they fit into society than he was with the political or religious debates involving their expulsion. Domínguez Ortiz's research has led him to study other minority groups in society (slaves, foundlings, Gypsies), periods of civil unrest (especially during the 17th century), urban history (especially of his native Seville), popular religion, Bourbon reformism, the fiscal policy of Philip IV, different aspects of the Enlightenment in Spain, the population history both of his native Andalusia and of Spain as a whole, the role of doctors in society, and a host of other subjects all of which related to his pervasive interest

in the makeup and the way premodern Spanish society functioned.

Although he is one of the most eminent Spanish historians, it is ironic that Domínguez Ortiz never became a university faculty member. How a historian of his stature could spend his entire teaching career in secondary education is one of those mysteries of Spain that is near impossible to fathom. Yet the true stature of an historian is not given by his institution but by his work, and the work of Domínguez Ortiz stands high indeed. His studies of 17th- and 18th-century Spanish society, clearly written yet laced with vast but unpretentious erudition (so uncommon among more contemporary historians), are an unending source of pleasure and understanding of the way Spanish society worked. It is unfortunate that more of his work is not available in English.

DAVID REHER

See also Spain: Imperial

Biography
Born Seville, 1909. Received degrees in history from universities of Seville and Madrid. Taught geography and history in Seville, Granada, and Madrid. Retired 1979.

Principal Writings
Orto y ocaso de Sevilla (Rise and Decline of Seville), 1946; 2nd edition, 1974

La clase social de los conversos en Castilla en la Edad Moderna (The Social Class of the *conversos* [Converts] in Early Modern Castile), 1955

La sociedad española en el siglo XVIII (18th-Century Spanish Society), 1955; revised as *Sociedad y Estado en el siglo XVIII español* (Society and State in 18th-Century Spain), 1976

Política y hacienda de Felipe IV (Politics and Finances of Philip IV), 1960

La sociedad española en el siglo XVII (Spanish Society in the 17th Century), 2 vols., 1963–70; reprinted 1992

Crisis y decadencia en la España de los Austrias (Crisis and Decadence in Habsburg Spain), 1969

The Golden Age of Spain, 1516–1659, 1971

Los judeoconversos en España y América (The Jewish *conversos* in Spain and America), 1971

Alteraciones andaluzas (Andalusian Upheavals), 1973

El Antiguo Régimen: los Reyes Católicos y los Austrias (The *Ancien Régime*: The Catholic Kings and the Habsburgs), 1973

Las clases privilegiadas en el Antiguo Régimen (The Privileged Classes during the *Ancien Régime*), 1973

Hechos y figuras del siglo XVIII español (Events and Personalities of 18th-Century Spain), 1973

Desde Carlos V a la Paz de los Pirineos, 1517–1660 (From Charles V to the Peace of the Pyrenees, 1517–1660), 1974

With Francisco Aguilar Piñal, *El barroco y la ilustración* (The Age of the Baroque and the Enlightenment), 1976

With Bernard Vincent, *Historia de los moriscos: vida y tragedia de una minoría* (History of the *moriscos*: Life and Tragedy of a Minority), 1978

Política fiscal y cambio social en la España del siglo XVIII (Fiscal Policy and Social Change in 18th-Century Spain), 1984

Historia de Sevilla: la Sevilla del siglo XVII (History of Seville in the 17th Century), 1984

Instituciones y sociedad en la España de los Austrias (Institutions and Society in Habsburg Spain), 1985

Estudios de historia económica y social de España (Studies in the Social and Economic History of Spain), 1987

Carlos III y la España de la Ilustración (Charles III and the Spain
of the Enlightenment), 1988
Editor, *Historia de España* (History of Spain), 12 vols., 1988–91
Los judeoconversos en la España moderna (The Jewish *conversos* in
Early Modern Spain), 1992

Further Reading
"La història social a España a partir de l'obra de D. Antonio
Domínguez Ortiz" (The Social History of Spain from the Works
of Domínguez Ortiz), *Manuscrits: Revista d'Història Moderna* 14
(January 1996), 15–118

Dopsch, Alfons 1868–1953
Austrian social and economic historian

Alfons Dopsch was an eminent social and economic historian
noted for his spirited revision of Western European medieval
history and his love of lively academic debate. He based his
work not on economic or sociological theory but on comparative archaeology supplemented by literary sources. Evidence
obtained from archaeological excavations particularly appealed
to him because it allowed historians to survey longer periods
of time than was possible using literary sources. Many earlier
medievalists, using only written sources, had developed a legal
and constitution methodology that treated each historical
period as distinct from its predecessor. Their work admitted
little or no historical continuity, but Dopsch maintained that,
viewed from the perspective of economics and society, continuity not separation accurately characterized cultural change.

In 1904 Dopsch first attracted attention as a promising
scholar with the publication of Austrian land registers, *Die
Landesfürstlichen Urbare* (Austrian Domainal Feudal Land
Registers), that he had edited. His first monograph, *Die ältere
Sozial- und Wirtschaftsordnung der Alpenslawen* (The Early
Economic and Social Order of the Alpine Slavs, 1909), established his revisionist bent by proving that historians had understated the number of Slavs living in the Alpine region. For his
second major work, *Die Wirtschaftsentwicklung der Karolingerzeit* (The Economic Development of the Carolingian Age,
1912–13), he broadened his inquiries to include the entire area
of the Roman empire affected by the German invasions. In this
work and later in *Naturalwirtschaft und Geldwirtschaft in der
Weltgeschichte* (Natural Economy and Money Economy in
World History, 1930) he attacked Karl Bücher's closed
economy (*geschlossene Hauswirtschaft*) theory. Bücher, a practitioner of the legal and constitutional methodology, assumed
that economic systems owed little or nothing to their predecessors, and argued that the decline of towns, and with them
trade and money, had forced early medieval Europeans to base
their economy on self-sufficient agricultural estates. Dopsch
countered that the Germans had trickled into the Roman
empire and destroyed neither town life, trade, nor the use of
money during the 6th and 7th centuries. Furthermore, rather
than a peasantry attached to large manorial estates, numerous
free peasant holdings persisted during these years.

From this evidence and the conclusions he derived from it
came Dopsch's crowning blow to the historical status quo. In
the pages of his most important work, *Wirtschaftliche und*

*soziale Grundlagen der europäischen Kulturentwicklung aus
der Zeit von Cäsar bis auf Karl den Grossen* (1918–20;
abridged as *The Economic and Social Foundation of European
Civilization*, 1937), he proclaimed that the fall of the Roman
empire in Western Europe was not the catastrophic destruction
(*Katastrophentheorie*) of advanced Roman civilization by
German barbarians. On the contrary, the Middle Ages had
evolved in an orderly fashion because the Germans preserved
and absorbed Roman culture. Armed with this thesis, he rehabilitated the much maligned Merovingians by arguing that the
Carolingian Renaissance only completed what the Franks had
begun during the 5th and 6th centuries. In his last major study,
Herrschaft und Bauer in der deutschen Kaiserzeit (Lord and
Peasant during the Medieval German Empire, 1939), Dopsch
extended his uninterrupted economic evolution thesis to the
early modern era.

During the nearly seventy years that have passed since
Dopsch published his last major work, medievalists have significantly altered many of his conclusions, partly because new
archaeological research has cast doubt on some of the evidence
he employed, and partly because his thesis exaggerated and
oversimplified the origins and development of the Middle Ages.
While the contemporary literary sources magnified the catastrophic impact of the Germans on the Roman empire, Dopsch
understated the regional differences involved in the process.
For example, the Rhinelands suffered an economic decline
worse than most other parts of the Roman empire. Ruralization
was also more widespread than Dopsch maintained. Towns
declined to villages in most cases except for those few located
on the main trade routes. Finally, Dopsch's strong advocacy of
continuity forced him to underemphasize the important
German contributions to medieval culture. Nevertheless,
Dopsch had a significant effect on medieval studies by forcing
historians to give more consideration to economic and social
factors and to the issue of continuity.

ROBERT F. FORREST

See also Power; Sánchez-Albornoz; Srbik

Biography
Born Lobositz, Bohemia, 14 June 1868. Studied at Institut für
Österreichische Geschichtsforschung. Professor, University of Vienna,
1898–1936. Married Marie Ficker, 1900 (1 son, 1 daughter). Died
Vienna, 1 September 1953.

Principal Writings
Die ältere Sozial- und Wirtschaftsordnung der Alpenslawen (The
Early Economic and Social Order of the Alpine Slavs), 1909
*Die Wirtschaftsentwicklung der Karolingerzeit, vornehmlich in
Deutschland* (The Economic Development of the Carolingian Age,
Particularly in Germany), 2 vols., 1912–13
*Wirtschaftliche und soziale Grundlagen der europäischen
Kulturentwicklung aus der Zeit von Cäsar bis auf Karl den
Grossen* (Economic and Social Foundations of European
Civilization from Caesar to Charlemagne), 2 vols., 1918–20;
abridged in English as *The Economic and Social Foundation of
European Civilization*, 1937
Naturalwirtschaft und Geldwirtschaft in der Weltgeschichte (Natural
Economy and Money Economy in World History), 1930
Herrschaft und Bauer in der deutschen Kaiserzeit (Lord and Peasant
during the Medieval German Empire), 1939

Dress

The history of dress has its origins in the cataloging of the appearance, apparel, and customs of people of different nationalities and localities. The encyclopedic works which these antiquarian practices first produced continue to comprise a significant portion of the literature of the field. Influenced perhaps by conventional perceptions of dress itself as the purview of the "feminine" segment of society, the study of dress has until recently been perceived by the academy as comparable to the study of the so-called lesser genres – portraiture, still-life, landscape – within the academy of the fine arts. Despite the fact that during the early part of the 20th century the study of dress increasingly incorporated its social and economic contexts, only rarely did scholars in the field focus on the dress of the working or middle classes, or consider in any depth the implications of dress in the politics of gender and race. The history of dress continued to be primarily concerned with the decorous, upper-class, *haute couture* inhabitants of the drawing room and high society, until the scholarship of the last twenty to thirty years embraced the revisionist influences of outside disciplines such as gender studies, material culture studies, and social history, bringing to the study of dress not only new methodologies, but also the element of cross-disciplinary collaboration.

The informal beginnings of the history of dress can be traced as far back as the engraved costume books of the 16th and 17th centuries. These books were printed in Western Europe by such artists as Jost Amman and Cesare Vecellio in a period of extensive transcontinental exploration and anthropological curiosity about the habits and appearances of people in foreign lands. Olian has described the books, which illustrated and commented upon the dress worn in various segments of society throughout the known world, as "geographies and histories of clothing and manners." They established what was to be a primary framework for the discussion of dress well into the 20th century: that of nationalism.

Other early works, including a history of "Male and Female Costume" attributed to George Bryan (Beau) Brummell (1822), took up the study of the dress of historical cultures as the basis of a critique of that of their own time and nationality. Brummel proposed thereby to influence current trends in taste and style and to document the changes that resulted: "to make regular half-yearly additions to the work, in each of which an accurate drawing and a critical description of the actual progress of the public taste in costume will be given." His work elaborated on the post-Renaissance construction of the Englishman – notorious for adopting the fashions of a patchwork of European nations – as lacking a sense of national identity and presenting a ludicrous amalgam of foreign eccentricities. Nineteenth-century works spawned by British and American movements for dress reform would likewise appeal to the simpler, more organic dress of the past in contrast to the limitations of the fashionable dress of the day for both men and women.

In the wake of the publication of Diderot's influential *Encyclopédie* (1751–65) – which devoted considerable attention in its volumes to the production of textiles and apparel – and promoted, perhaps, by the passion for taxonomy that thrived in late 18th- and 19th-century Europe, a number of encyclopedic works dealing with dress were generated during the latter half of the 19th century. Once again, the strong association of modes of dress with national identity played its part. These works either studied monographically the history of a single country's dress (see, for example, both Fairholt and Quicherat) or divided broader surveys according to national and local trends. Particularly notable in this latter category is Planché's *A Cyclopedia of Costume* (1876–79), the format and ambitions of which were carried on in such standard reference works of the 20th century as Millia Davenport's *The Book of Costume* (1948) and François Boucher's *Histoire du costume en Occident* (1965; 20,000 *Years of Fashion*, 1967). The Eurocentric agenda of the earlier works was perpetuated by Davenport and Boucher, who noted Asiatic and Middle Eastern customs and costume only by way of background for the scrutiny of those of the West; references to African, South American, and Eastern European dress were few. Euro- and Anglo-centrism continue to dominate the field to this day. In museums throughout the Western world, Asiatic costumes tend to be collected and retained under the auspices of departments of Asiatic arts, and African costumes under those of African and Oceanic artifacts, rather than by departments of textiles and costumes. The study of ethnographic costume has more often fallen under the rubric of ethnography than that of the history of dress.

Juxtaposed with the taxonomical and antiquarian works that launched the discipline as such, works of scholars concerned with the social history of dress also emerged at the turn of the 20th century. Among the most influential of these scholars, Max von Boehn, whose multivolume set *Die Mode* (1907–19; *Modes and Manners*, 1909–27) was written in the first decade of the 20th century and reprinted and translated numerous times during the following fifty years, addressed the course of fashion as one element of the social, artistic, and nationalistic agendas of each chronological period in the modern history of Western Europe. The American economist Thorstein Veblen, in his best-known work, *The Theory of the Leisure Class* (1899), indicted fashionable dress as a sign of conspicuous consumption and thereby complicit in perpetuating a culture driven by the inequitable distribution and display of wealth. Indeed, Veblen's construction of the woman in this "pecuniary culture" as the enforcedly indolent site of her husband's "vicarious leisure" echoed the battle cry of many a 19th-century advocate for dress reform and woman's enfranchisement, who argued that the physical constraints of fashionable dress (corsetted waists, weighty skirts, and tightly-fitted bodices) both enforced and emblematized women's societally-prescribed uselessness. Veblen's social and economic critiques engendered the support of Quentin Bell in his 1947 work *On Human Finery*, in which he described Veblen's work as "undoubtedly the most valuable contribution yet made to the philosophy of clothes . . . [though] strangely neglected by our historians of fashion; his works contain a challenge which, in this country [England] at all events, has been ignored." Bell declared it the "purpose and the justification" of his own book to "represent" Veblen's work.

The historians of dress who dominated the discipline at the time Bell wrote his defense of Veblen included several affiliated with the Victoria and Albert Museum in London, an institution devoted to the collection and preservation of the decorative, as well as the fine, arts. In this milieu, James Laver, keeper of the

Department of Prints and Drawings and of Paintings at the museum from 1938 through 1959, wrote of the aesthetics of, and changing tastes in, fashionable dress, as well as of its documentation and representation in paintings and prints. Laver's social and aesthetic history of dress was revisionist for its time. He and his colleagues, however – as Bell pointed out – continued to concern themselves with the interrelationships between visual imagery provided by court portraits and documentation of the dress of the well-to-do, apparently regardless of such questions as Veblen had raised about the role played by dress in asserting and perpetuating class, gender, and economic distinctions.

Laver's colleague at the Victoria and Albert Museum, John L. Nevinson, annotated various reprint editions of historical texts concerning the manners, morals, and practicalities of dress from the Renaissance forward. By the 1960s, Nevinson became the first scholar to study and write on the origins, early history, and social influence of fashion plates, an area of research taken up during the 1970s by Madeleine Ginsburg, another member of the Victoria and Albert Museum curatorial staff. Nevinson distinguished between fashion plate images and those provided by painted or engraved portraits, proposing that fashion plates were viewed by those who produced and consumed them as portraits of costume in which the particular human figure was conceived as of secondary importance. Nevinson's work implicitly cautioned against the difficulties inherent in seeking documentary evidence of dress from images that privileged the human figure, face, or identity, defining a methodological break with earlier historians in the field.

With the rise of museology in the late 19th century, archaeological, artifact-centered scholarship in the history of dress came into its own. Indeed, much of the scholarly work in the field today continues to be associated with museum collections and exhibitions, and is carried out by historians linked in some way with the museum milieu. The scholarship of the latter half of the 20th century is generally distinguished from that of earlier periods, which commonly sought its "evidence" in the images of dress supplied by contemporary visual arts, by a new insistence upon the integration of the material evidence of surviving garments themselves with the corollary contexts of literary and visual documents. This increased emphasis on material culture within the field parallels an increased legitimation of material culture studies in other areas of historical scholarship during the last twenty to thirty years. The works of Norah Waugh, which diagrammed and analyzed the cut and construction of a range of Western European men's and women's clothing in the context of excerpts from contemporary documents, comprised the first "practicum" in this material approach to the history of dress. Studies from the 1950s by English costume historians C. Willett Cunnington and Phillis Cunnington had contributed to this realignment of priorities, elevating the pragmatics of dress – cut, construction, fabrication – to the stature of socially and economically significant elements in their own right and of prime importance to the understanding of the outward appearance on which von Boehn had focused in his influential works. The legacy of the Cunningtons was carried on by such scholars as Anne Buck, who both collaborated with Phillis Cunnington and continued to negotiate the pragmatics of English and European dress in works of her own on the 18th and 19th centuries. It was not, however, until the publication of Waugh's works and the subsequent works of Janet Arnold that the archaeological aspects of the discipline and the pursuit of the tangible artifact received first priority.

Scholars associated with the History of Dress department at the Courtauld Institute of Art have, for the past twenty to thirty years, fortified the relationship between the work of the museum and the work of historians of dress. Aileen Ribeiro, the program's current director and a specialist in 17th- and 18th-century European dress, has been instrumental in reformulating that relationship. As has been said, from the 19th through the mid-20th centuries, historians of dress derived much of the information for their work from the visual arts, conceiving of painted and engraved images as reliable, contemporary documents of changing fashions. Ribeiro and other members of the Courtauld school have posited instead that, while individual works of art may indeed supply evidence of certain broadly-based vogues of dress, these representations are subject to the filters of sitter / artist intention and convention which must be taken into account in appealing to such representations for chronologically "accurate" testimony on the specifics of contemporary dress. Indeed, representations of dress in portraits, just as in history paintings, may be intended in some cases to be viewed purely iconographically, playing on intentional anachronisms or elaborations of historical ideals (as Ribeiro pointed out, for instance, in her 1975 dissertation on the interrelationships between depictions of women in fancy dress in 18th-century English portraits and the fancy dress worn at masquerades during the same period).

Ribeiro and her colleagues have generated a new discourse between historians of art and historians of dress. Historians of art have come to rely on their cross-disciplinary counterparts in resolving questions of dating, provenance, and attribution that can be clarified by knowledgeable analysis of the works in the context of the current state of research on dress. The pages of recent fine art exhibition catalogues attest to this shift of priority, often including scholarly essays on the social history of dress and its particular ramifications for the works of art on view.

The conventional exclusion of middle- and working-class topics from the canon of the discipline (although the early costume books referred to at the beginning of this article were generally consistent in representing the burgher and even peasant archetypes of the localities they explored) can be attributed in part to the dearth of extant material and documentary evidence of the clothes worn by these classes. Yet scholarly initiatives in gender and class studies have prompted new research in these areas by historians of dress and their collaborators in the last twenty years. It may therefore be that the conventionally "decorous" nature of the discipline until recently tended to exercise certain restrictions upon the subjects it comfortably treated.

While certain sectors of the American community of historians of dress maintain earlier antiquarian agendas, advances in broadening the discipline's parameters to encompass the previously disenfranchised topics of working-class dress and the politics of dress, to name just two, as well as revisionist methodologies, have been particularly strong in the United States. Claudia Kidwell, associated with the National Museum of American History of the Smithsonian Institution, has emphasized these areas in her exhibitions and publications of the last twenty years. Valerie Steele, an American historian associated with the Museum Studies program of the Fashion Institute of Technology (FIT) in New York, has collaborated with Kidwell and, in her own work, has revisited conventionally studied subjects such as the lives and output of *couturières* and the social history of dress in the Jazz Age (treated by Laver in 1964) from feminist and psychoanalytic points of view. Richard Martin, previously Steele's colleague at FIT and now at the Metropolitan Museum of Art, a historian of art by training, has similarly transgressed canonic bounds of decorum within museum walls, turning on its head the conventional notion of dress as a lesser genre, subordinate to the fine arts, with such exhibitions as *Fashion and Surrealism* (1987), which reconsidered the collaborations of 20th-century *couture* designers and fine artists as a means of understanding the designers themselves as fine artists. He has irreverently undercut the traditional decorum of the discipline with exhibitions on *Jocks and Nerds* (1989), revolving around menswear, and on *Infra-apparel* (1993), a history of underwear.

As an academic discipline, the history of dress owes its recent evolution largely to the outside influences of parallel disciplines. Disciplines such as gender studies, the study of material culture, and social history have contributed to the strength and breadth of the study of dress through its reformation as an interdisciplinary enterprise.

SUSAN SHIFRIN

Further Reading

Arnold, Janet, *Patterns of Fashion: Englishwomen's Dresses and Their Construction*, 2 vols., London: Wace, 1964–66; New York: Drama Book, 1972

Arnold, Janet, *Patterns of Fashion: The Cut and Construction of Clothes for Men and Women, c.1560–1620*, London: Macmillan, and New York: Drama Book, 1985

Arnold, Janet, *A Handbook of Costume*, London: Macmillan, 1973; New York: Drama Book, 1985

Baines, Barbara Burman, *Fashion Revivals from the Elizabethan Age to the Present Day*, London: Batsford, 1981

Barthes, Roland, *Le Système de la mode*, Paris: Seuil, 1967; in English as *The Fashion System*, New York: Hill and Wang, 1983; London: Cape, 1985

Bell, Quentin, *On Human Finery*, London: Hogarth Press, 1947, New York: Wyn, 1949; revised 1976

Boehn, Max von, *Die Mode: Menschen und Moden im achtzehnten Jahrhundert*, 4 vols., Munich: Bruckmann, 1907–19; in English as *Modes and Manners*, 4 vols., London: Harrap, and New York: Putnam, 1909–27

Boucher, François, *Histoire du costume en Occident, de l'Antiquité à nos jours*, Paris: Flammarion, 1965; in English as *20,000 Years of Fashion: The History of Costume and Personal Adornment*, New York: Abrams, 1967, and as *A History of Costume in the West*, London: Thames and Hudson, 1987

Breward, Christopher, *The Culture of Fashion: A New History of Fashionable Dress*, Manchester: Manchester University Press, 1995

Brummel, Beau [George Bryan], *Male and Female Costume: Grecian and Roman Costume, British Costume from the Roman Invasion until 1822, and the Principles of Costume Applied to Improved Dress of the Present Day*, edited by Eleanor Parker, written c.1820, first published New York: Doubleday, 1932; reprinted 1978

Buck, Anne, *Dress in Eighteenth-Century England*, New York: Holmes and Meier, and London: Batsford, 1979

Callahan, Colleen, "Dressed For Work: Women's Clothing on the Job, 1900–1990," *Labor's Heritage* 4 (1992), 28–49

Challamel, Augustin, *Histoire de la mode en France: la toilette des femmes depuis l'époque gallo-romaine jusqu'à nos jours*, Paris: Bibliothèque du Magasin aux Demoiselles, 1875; in English as *The History of Fashion in France; or, The Dress of Women from the Gallo-Roman Period to the Present Time*, London: Low Marston, and New York: Scribner, 1882

Cunnington, Cecil Willett, and Phillis Cunnington, *Handbook of English Costume in the Seventeenth Century*, London: Faber, and Philadelphia: Dufour, 1957

Cunnington, Cecil Willett, and Phillis Cunnington, *The History of Underclothes*, London: Joseph, 1951; reprinted London: Faber, 1981, New York: Dover, 1992

Davenport, Millia, *The Book of Costume*, New York: Crown, 1948

De Marly, Diana, *Working Dress: A History of Occupational Clothing*, New York: Holmes and Meier, and London: Batsford, 1986

Diderot, Denis *et al.*, *Encyclopédie, ou, Dictionnaire raisonné des sciences, des arts et des métiers* (The Encyclopedia; or, Dictionary of the Sciences, the Arts, and the Professions), 17 vols., Paris, 1751–65

Ewing, Elizabeth, *Everyday Dress, 1650–1900*, London: Batsford, 1984; New York: Chelsea House, 1989

Fairholt, Frederick William, *Costume in England: A History of Dress from the Earliest Period till the Close of the Eighteenth Century*, London: Chapman and Hall, 1846

Garber, Marjorie, *Vested Interests: Cross-Dressing and Cultural Anxiety*, New York: Routledge, 1992; London: Penguin, 1993

Hollander, Anne, *Seeing Through Clothes*, New York: Viking, 1978

Kidwell, Claudia Brush, and Margaret C. Christman, *Suiting Everyone: The Democratization of Clothing in America*, Washington, DC: Smithsonian Institution Press, 1974

Kidwell, Claudia Brush, and Valerie Steele, eds., *Men and Women: Dressing the Part*, Washington, DC: Smithsonian Institution Press, 1989

Kunzle, David, *Fashion and Fetishism: A Social History of the Corset, Tight-Lacing and Other Forms of Body-Sculpture in the West*, Totowa, NJ: Rowman and Littlefield, 1982

Laver, James, *Taste and Fashion, from the French Revolution to the Present Day*, London: Harrap, 1937; New York: Dodd Mead, 1938; revised 1945

Laver, James, *Women's Dress in the Jazz Age*, London: Hamish Hamilton, 1964

Laver, James, *The Age of Illusion: Manners and Morals, 1750–1848*, London: Weidenfeld and Nicolson, 1966; New York: McKay, 1972

Laver, James, *The Age of Optimism: Manners and Morals, 1848–1914*, London: Weidenfeld and Nicolson, 1966

Laver, James, *A Concise History of Costume*, London: Thames and Hudson, and New York: Abrams, 1969; revised as *Costume and Fashion: A Concise History*, London: Thames and Hudson, and New York: Oxford University Press, 1983

Laver, James, *Modesty in Dress: An Inquiry into the Fundamentals of Fashion*, London: Heinemann, and Boston: Houghton Mifflin, 1969

Lurie, Alison, *The Language of Clothes*, New York: Random House, and London: Heinemann, 1981

Maeder, Edward, ed., *An Elegant Art: Fashion and Fantasy in the Eighteenth Century*, Los Angeles: Los Angeles County Museum of Art, and New York: Abrams, 1983

Martin, Richard, *Fashion and Surrealism*, New York: Rizzoli, and London: Thames and Hudson, 1987

Martin, Richard, and Harold Koda, *Jocks and Nerds: Men's Style in the Twentieth Century*, New York: Rizzoli, 1989

Martin, Richard, and Harold Koda, *Infra-apparel*, New York: Metropolitan Museum of Art, 1993

Martin, Richard, and Harold Koda, *Orientalism: Visions of the East in Western Dress*, New York: Metropolitan Museum of Art, 1994

Nevinson, J.L., "Origin and Early History of the Fashion Plate," *United States National Museum Bulletin* 250 (1967)

Olian, Jo Anne, "Sixteenth-Century Costume Books," *Dress: The Journal of the Costume Society of America* 3 (1977), 20–48

Planché, James Robinson, *A Cyclopaedia of Costume, or, Dictionary of Dress Including Notices of Contemporaneous Fashion on the Continent*, London: Chatto and Windus, 1876–79; New York: Bouton, 1877

Quicherat, Jules, *Histoire du costume en France depuis les temps les plus reculés jusqu'à la fin du XVIIIe siècle* (The History of Costume in France from the Most Distant Times to the End of the 18th Century), Paris: Hachette, 1875

Ribeiro, Aileen, *The Dress Worn at Masquerades in England, 1730 to 1790, and Its Relation to Fancy Dress in Portraiture*, New York: Garland, 1984

Ribeiro, Aileen, *Dress and Morality*, London: Batsford, and New York: Holmes and Meier, 1986

Ribeiro, Aileen, *Fashion in the French Revolution*, London: Batsford, and New York: Holmes and Meier, 1988

Ribeiro, Aileen, *The Art of Dress: Fashion in England and France, 1750 to 1820*, New Haven: Yale University Press, 1995

Roberts, Helene E., "The Exquisite Slave: The Role of Clothes in the Making of the Victorian Woman," *Signs: Journal of Women in Culture and Society* 2 (1977), 554–69

Squire, Geoffrey, *Dress, Art, and Society, 1560–1970*, New York: Viking, and London: Studio Vista, 1974

Steele, Valerie, *Fashion and Eroticism: Ideals of Feminine Beauty from the Victorian Era to the Jazz Age*, New York and Oxford: Oxford University Press, 1985

Steele, Valerie, *Paris Fashion: A Cultural History*, Oxford and New York: Oxford University Press, 1988

Steele, Valerie, *Women of Fashion: Twentieth-Century Designers*, New York: Rizzoli, 1991

Strutt, Joseph, *A Complete View of the Dress and Habits of the People of England, from the Establishment of the Saxons in Britain to the Present Time*, 2 vols., London: Bohn, 1842

Veblen, Thorstein, *The Theory of the Leisure Class: An Economic Study in the Evolution of Institutions*, New York: Macmillan, 1899; London: Allen and Unwin, 1924

Waugh, Norah, *Corsets and Crinolines*, New York: Theatre Arts, and London: Batsford, 1954; reprinted 1991

Waugh, Norah, *The Cut of Men's Clothes, 1600–1900*, New York: Theatre Arts, and London: Faber, 1964

Waugh, Norah, *The Cut of Women's Clothes, 1600–1930*, New York: Theatre Arts, and London: Faber, 1968

Droysen, J.G. 1808–1884
German historian

J.G. Droysen's scholarly career was marked by major publications in two seemingly disparate fields. In the 1830s, as a philologist become historian, he published a life of Alexander the Great and a 2-volume history of Hellenism that combined intellectual and political history in a strongly positive and original interpretation of Hellenism. A decade later, after the disappointment of his hopes during the 1848 revolution, he began to write Prusso-German history as a means of showing the necessity of German unification under and by Prussia. These two periods are linked by his political efforts in the 1840s and the historical theory behind them. His work as a student at the University of Berlin, where he supported himself as tutor to Felix Mendelssohn and as a translator of classical Greek, is very helpful in understanding his later work.

His chief teachers were August Boeckh (1785–1886) and Friedrich August Wolf (1759–1824), both of whom pioneered the study of texts and, thereby, of major ideas in historical context. Droysen learned better from them the historical methods needed for his later work than he would have from such history faculty as the young Leopold von Ranke – whom Droysen always detested for his conservatism – or the less celebrated Friedrich Wilken or Friedrich von Raumer. Droysen's philosophical training was as important as his philological. He found G.W.F. Hegel's ideas deeply exciting. Over three years, he followed Hegel's entire lecture series (Droysen's notes were detailed and meticulous enough to be used by Kuno Fischer in editing the definitive edition of Hegel's works). His poetic inclination, not exhausted in writing occasional lyrics for Mendelssohn's *Lieder*, was also strong.

Droysen's first publications were his translations. His still revered rendering of Aeschylus appeared in 1832 and his Aristophanes translation in 1836. The appendix to the Aeschylus translation offered his first overview of the place of ancient Greece in world history. This view informed his very successful *Geschichte Alexanders des Grossen* (Life of Alexander the Great, 1833) and the sequel *Geschichte des Hellenismus* (History of Hellenism, 1836–43). The content of his argument was original, though its shape remained Hegelian; the ancient Greeks had discovered freedom, but not in a stable form. In consequence, Hellenic freedom undercut itself, but first produced universal ideas spread east by Alexander the Great's armies after 331 BCE This made Hellas (not Judaea) ancestral to the Christianity Droysen revered, and meant, crucially, that Hellenism was historically progressive, and furthermore meant that Christianity received the agenda for creating stable, enduring human freedom.

Droysen elaborated these ideas in his insightful but tendentious modern historical writings while at Kiel, in Schleswig-Holstein, after he became professor there in 1840. The move was good for him. The agitation over the national status of the duchies Schleswig-Holstein launched him into national politics, and Droysen wrote and spoke for their Germanization. At the same time, his solo teaching of the service course in modern European history forced him to reconfigure the modern past. The results of this reconfiguration appear in his published *Vorlesungen über die Freiheitskriege* (Lectures on the Wars of Freedom, 1836–43). Briefly stated, modern history was a progressive evolution, destined by God, away from absolutist "powers" (*Mächte*) to free "states" (*Staaten*). The Reformation and the peculiar political interests of Hohenzollern Prussia assured that Prussia would one day create a unified German "state," steeped in Protestant truth, that would lead a peaceful, liberated Europe.

During the Revolution of 1848, as an influential and outspoken deputy from Kiel to the National Assembly in Frankfurt, Droysen was able to work for the realization of this program. As a leader in the right center *Casinopartei* and member of the Constitution Committee, Droysen saw history being made. Rudolf Hübner collected Droysen's diary and incidental writings in *Aktenstücke und Aufzeichnungen* (1924), while Droysen's minutes of constitutional committee meetings appeared in 1849. The series of political defeats between March 1849 (when Frederick William IV of Prussia declined to be German monarch) and November 1850 (when the Convention of Olmütz between Austria and Prussia ended the last effort at Prussian national leadership) forced Droysen and other nationalist liberals to rethink both strategy and tactics. Predictably, his re-evaluation of politics profoundly changed his historiography.

Changes appeared in three ideas, present before 1848 in his thinking, but now greatly emphasized. First, Droysen saw that human inclinations decided events and used history to provide heroes and villains for imitation and avoidance. This common-place didacticism is marked in his *Das Leben von Feldmarschall Graf York von Wartenburg* (Life of Fieldmarshal York von Wartenburg, 1851–52) in which he celebrated as he detailed the life of Wartenburg, who shifted Prussia to the anti-French alliance at a key moment after Napoleon's defeat in Russia in 1812. Second, Droysen, always aware of self-interest in politics, now acknowledged that this play might lead to merely relatively happy outcomes. He hoped to teach political players never to the lose the good in the hopeless pursuit of the best. Finally, his reliance on Prussia as the only possible unifier of Germany became complete. All three elements combine in his monumental, never completed, and surely little read, 14-volume *Geschichte der preussischen Politik* (History of Prussian Politics, 1855–86). This became his life's work, and in it he tried to show that Prussia's rulers, in chasing their particularist Prussian state interest, had consistently acted in the German self-interest as well. Meticulously researched in the Prussian archives he loved, the contents are narrowly diplomatic and military.

Droysen's imagination did not fail him, however. He remained a gifted prose writer and a popular lecturer at Jena, where he went after Kiel, and later at the University of Berlin, where he returned as full professor. There he taught and wrote when unification did come in 1866 and 1870–71, and there he felt deep ambivalence about Germany's new-found status. There, too, he annually delivered lectures on the philosophy of history in the last three decades of his career. These are published as his *Historik* (the outline of which is published in English as *Outlines of the Principles of History*) and in them he developed and explicated his notion that historians properly merge scholarship and partisanship by seeking "to understand through research" (*forschend zu verstehen*). This is a suitable motto for his career.

ROBERT FAIRBAIRN SOUTHARD

See also Dilthey; Germany: 1800–1945; Gilbert; Greece: Ancient; Hintze; Historiology; Meyer; Mommsen, T.; Savigny; Sybel; Wilamovitz-Möllendorff

Biography

Johann Gustav Bernhard Droysen. Born Treptow, Pomerania, 6 July 1808, son of an army chaplain. Studied classics at the Stettin Gymnasium, and University of Berlin. Taught school in Berlin, 1829–35; gave formal lectures on classical philology, University of Berlin, 1835–40; professor of history, University of Kiel, Schleswig-Holstein, 1840–51; University of Jena, Thuringia, 1851–59; and University of Berlin, 1859–84. Married 1) Marie Mendel, 1835 (died 1847); 2) Emma Michaelis, 1849 (2 sons, 1 daughter). Died Berlin, 19 June 1884.

Principal Writings

Geschichte Alexanders des Grossen (Life of Alexander the Great), 1833
Geschichte des Hellenismus (History of Hellenism), 2 vols., 1836–43
Vorlesungen über die Freiheitskriege (Lectures on the Wars of Freedom), 2 vols., 1836–43

Verfassungsausschuss (Minutes of Constitutional Meetings), 1849
Das Leben von Feldmarschall Graf York von Wartenburg (Life of Fieldmarshal York von Wartenburg), 2 vols., 1851–52
Geschichte der preussischen Politik (History of Prussian Politics), 14 vols., 1855–86
Grundriss der Historik, 1868, revised 1882; abridged in English as *Outline of the Principles of History*, 1893
Aktenstücke und Aufzeichnungen zur Geschichte der Frankfurter Nationalversammlung (Diary and Incidental Writings on the History of the Frankfurt Assembly, 1849), edited by Rudolf Hübner, 1924

Further Reading

Birtsch, Günther, *Die Nation als sittliche Idee: Der Nationalstaatsbegriff in Geschichtsschreibung und politischer Gedankenwelt Johann Gustav Droysens* (The Nation as Moral Idea: The National State Concept in the Historical Writing and Thinking of Johann Gustav Droysen), Cologne: Bohlau, 1964
Bravo, Benedetto, *Philologie, Historie, Philosophie de l'Histoire: étude sur J. G. Droysen, Historien de l'Antiquité* (Philosophy, History, Philosophy of History: Studies on Droysen, Historian of Antiquity), Wrocław: Zakład Narodowy, 1968
Gilbert, Felix, *Johann Gustav Droysen und die preussisch-deutsche Frage* (Johann Gustav Droysen and the Prussian German Question) Berlin: Oldenbourg, 1931
Rüsen, Jörn, *Begriffene Geschichte: Genesis und Begründung der Geschichtstheorie J. G. Droysens* (History Comprehended: Genesis and Foundation of the Historical Theory of J.G. Droysen), Paderborn: Schöning, 1969
Southard, Robert Fairbairn, *Droysen and the Formation of the Prussian School*, Lexington: University of Kentucky Press, 1995

Dubnov, Simon 1860–1941
Russian-born Jewish historian and thinker

One of the pioneers of Jewish history, Simon Dubnov (or Dubnow) wrote a number of monumental works on the Jewish past and in so doing developed and articulated a secular Jewish nationalism. As historian, ideologist, literary critic, and journalist, Dubnov put forward the idea that the Jewish people were more than just coreligionists, but in fact constituted a people whose common bond was a shared culture. His work influenced nearly every historian of the Jewish people who came after him, even though the vital intellectual world of East European Jewry, in which Dubnov was such an important figure, was destroyed by German Nazism and Soviet Communism.

Born into a line of distinguished religious scholars, Dubnov received his early education in Talmudic studies, but at the age of 14 began attending a state school, and soon came to reject his religious upbringing. He received little training beyond the secondary level, but read widely and deeply in many areas. Like many of his contemporary Russian counterparts, Dubnov was captivated by positivism, and the works of Comte, J.S. Mill, and their allies, which reached Russia in the late 19th century by way of Germany, proved to be a major influence. He was a strong adherent of the Jewish Enlightenment (*Haskalah*). Even though his views on religion moderated greatly as he grew older, Dubnov was a confirmed secularist who never gave up his belief in the promise of 1789 and the attainability of liberty and equality under the law. Like many contemporary historians, Dubnov was influenced too by the prevailing Darwinian views of human development as applied to nations. Nevertheless, Dubnov saw human evolution as overcoming the need for and the effectiveness of brute force as a factor in human affairs. Instead, the survival of nations and peoples would be increasingly based on advances in culture and learning. Even the horrors of the Kishnev pogroms, World War I, and the Russian Revolution (in which Dubnov lost faith after it failed to produce true democracy in Russia) did not shake his fundamental belief in human evolution.

Although Dubnov wrote numerous short articles for Russian-Jewish newspapers and journals, along with textbooks and shorter works, he is perhaps best known for two large multivolume works – *Istoriia evreiskogo naroda na vostoka* (1903; *History of the Jews in Russia and Poland*, 1916–20) and *Die Weltgeschichte des jüdischen Volkes* (1925–30; *History of the Jews*, 1967–73) – and a collection of essays, *Pis'ma o starom i novom evreistve, 1897–1907* (1907; *Nationalism and History: Essays on Old and New Judaism*, 1958). In these works, Dubnov developed his theory of secular Jewish nationalism – which he called autonomism. Although he was not the first to conceive of diaspora nationalism, he emerged as its most articulate and scholarly proponent. After the destruction of the Jewish state in 70 CE and the subsequent diaspora, the Jewish people, Dubnov believed, had remained a nation, despite being scattered. The Jews were "a people whose home is the entire world." This provided a basis, Dubnov felt, for Jews to claim minority rights in the nations where they lived, without compromising loyalty to the state or assimilating. Thus, to be a Jew was more than a matter of religion, and this led Dubnov to reject assimilation. At the same time, he keenly felt the need to reform Jewish religious practices and modernize the Jewish people – particularly the conservative communities of Eastern Europe – in order for them to take their rightful place among the nations. There is also some evidence that Dubnov felt this approach to nationalism could work for other stateless peoples as well.

For Dubnov, the development of nations followed a clear, three-part course: first, tribal; second, political-territorial; and finally, cultural-historical. The Jewish people, Dubnov believed, had reached the third state. "We have seen many examples . . . of nations that have disappeared from the scene after they had lost their land and become dispersed . . . We find only one instance, however, of a people that has survived for thousands of years despite dispersion and loss of homeland . . . the people of Israel." This was due, he felt, to the Jews having attained the highest level of nationhood – that of the "spiritual nation." The ideal of the spiritual nation was one Dubnov saw as "the anchor for all progressive Jews." As a result, Dubnov strongly opposed Zionism and the move to create a territorial Jewish homeland which, in his worldview, would be a step backwards for the Jewish people.

Although Dubnov's work tended to focus on large historical processes and the actions of the rulers rather than the ruled, and his direct influence on Jewish historiography was lessened by the impact of the Holocaust and the establishment of the state of Israel, his works continue to be a primary reference point for Jewish history, and his philosophy of Jewish existence is still very relevant to modern Jewish life.

JOHN RADZILOWSKI

See also Jewish

Biography

Simon Markovich Dubnov (Semon Dubnow). Born Mstislavl, Russia (now Belarus), 18 September 1860. Self-taught; lived (sometimes illegally) in St. Petersburg, Mstislavl, Vilna, and Odessa, 1880–1906. Lecturer on Jewish history, Institute for Jewish Studies, St. Petersburg, 1908. Founder, Jewish Historical-Ethnographical Society; editor, *Jewrelskala Starina*, 1908–18. Organized Folkspartei, 1906. Moved to Berlin after promised chair of Jewish history in Kowno, Lithuania (promise not fulfilled), 1922; lived in Berlin, 1922–33, then in Riga, Latvia. Participated in conference on protection of Jewish rights, 1927. Married Ida Freidlin, 1883 (2 daughters, 1 son). Murdered by a Nazi soldier in the Riga ghetto, 8 December 1941.

Principal Writings

Chto takoe evreiskaia istoriia, 1896–97; in English as *Jewish History: An Essay in the Philosophy of History*, 1903
Istoriia evreiskogo naroda na vostoka, 1903; in English as *History of the Jews in Russia and Poland*, 3 vols., 1916–20
Pis'ma o starom i novom evreistve, 1897–1907, 1907; *Nationalism and History: Essays on Old and New Judaism*, 1958
An Outline of Jewish History, 3 vols., 1925
Die Weltgeschichte des jüdischen Volkes, 10 vols., 1925–30; in English as *History of the Jews*, 5 vols., 1967–73
Kniga zhizni [autobiography], 3 vols., 1930–40
A Short History of the Jewish People, 1936

Further Reading

Dubnov-Erlich, Sophie, *The Life and Work of S.M. Dubnov: Diaspora Nationalism and Jewish History*, Bloomington: Indiana University Press, 1991
Goodman, Saul, "Simon Dubnov: A Revaluation," *Commentary* 30 (1960), 511–15
Niger-Charney, Samuel, "Simon Dubnow as Literary Critic," *YIVO Annual of Jewish Social Science* 1 (1946), 305–17
Pinson, Koppel S. "The National Theories of Simon Dubnow," *Jewish Social Studies* 10 (1948), 335–58
Steinberg, Aaron, ed., *Simon Dubnow, L'homme et son oeuvre: publié à l'occasion du centenaire de sa naissance (1860–1960)* (Simon Dubnow, The Man and His Work: A Memorial Volume on the Occasion of the Centenary of His Birth (1860–1960), Paris: World Jewish Congress, 1963

Du Bois, W.E.B. 1868–1963
US scholar and activist

Author of more than twenty books and more than a hundred scholarly articles, editor of the *Crisis*, and tireless civil rights advocate, William Edward Burghardt Du Bois is one of the dominant figures in 20th-century African American history. Along with Carter G. Woodson, Du Bois was one of the first scholars to explore the black experience in the United States in a serious and systematic way.

Du Bois was a graduate of Fisk University and the first black to be awarded a PhD from Harvard (1895); his doctoral dissertation on the suppression of the Atlantic slave trade moved almost immediately into print and started him on a promising academic career. He commenced with a brief stint as an instructor at the University of Pennsylvania, where he researched his landmark sociological study, *The Philadelphia Negro* (1899). In 1897 he moved to Atlanta University, where he presided over the annual conferences of historians and sociologists that resulted in several path-breaking studies of contemporary black life. Collectively known as the Atlanta University Publications on the Study of Negro Problems, these volumes remain indispensable tools for students of black history.

Never wholly comfortable within academia, Du Bois brought black history to a wider audience through a constant stream of articles in popular journals such as the *Atlantic Monthly*, *Nation*, *New Republic*, *Horizon*, *Chicago Defender*, *Pittsburgh Courier*, *Amsterdam News*, and *Negro Digest*. His concern with the black masses led to political engagement as well. Between 1905 and 1910, he emerged as a leader and key public voice of the Niagara movement, a group of African American intellectuals and journalists dedicated to the full integration of blacks into the nation's social and economic life. This goal, and the Niagara movement's outspoken opposition to all forms of racial discrimination, contrasted sharply with the emphasis of Du Bois' main rival, Booker T. Washington, upon vocational training and acquiescence to segregation and disfranchisement. Du Bois' most important work in this period of his long career was *Souls of Black Folk* (1903), probably the most well-known and enduring of his many publications. It was in this collection of essays that he first articulated many of the ideas and concepts to which he later returned and elaborated upon, including the metaphor of black life existing behind a "veil," invisible to the dominant white society but vibrant, culturally dynamic, and invaluable to America nonetheless.

Du Bois' increasing commitment to the black freedom struggle pulled him out of university life. A founder of the National Association for the Advancement of Colored People (NAACP), Du Bois moved in 1910 to New York City, to edit that organization's influential monthly organ, *The Crisis*. For the next 24 years his primary role was, in the words of one biographer, a "propagandist of protest." Often embroiled in controversy, Du Bois led the NAACP to national prominence in this era. He also grew interested in anticolonial struggles, taking part in the first three Pan-African Congresses, and working tirelessly to bring African issues to the attention of his readers. A 1934 dispute with the NAACP's directors over tactics in the fight against segregation led to his resignation and return to Atlanta University.

This temporary retreat allowed Du Bois to research and publish his most important historical work, *Black Reconstruction* (1935). A detailed, eloquent dissent from the racist orthodoxy of the time, *Black Reconstruction* firmly rejected the notion that the post-Civil War treatment of the defeated South had been a "tragic mistake," a doomed experiment in racial equality undone by corrupt northern business interests and the freedpeople's inability to grasp the responsibilities of citizenship. The book anticipated the revisionist scholarship of the 1960s and 1970s by placing the activity of black slaves at the center of the Civil War drama and by stressing the achievements and limitations of the Reconstruction experiment. Rather than focus upon national politics or congressional initiative, the book highlighted the ways in which emancipation and Reconstruction unfolded at the grass roots level, exploring the changing relationship between poor whites and blacks at a time when few historians considered ordinary people worthy of serious study. Its lyrical style – treading a fine line between poetry and prose for several hundred pages – and its passion further distinguished it from contemporary historical writing. A final chapter, entitled "The Propaganda of History" excoriated professional historians for distorting of this era of southern history in order to justify the segregation and disfranchisement that followed on its heels. Understandably, this combative stance won Du Bois few allies. For the most part, the book was ignored by the major historical journals of the day, a reflection of the marginal status of black scholars and African American history at the time. "Rediscovered" in the 1960s, *Black Reconstruction* is now acknowledged as one of the masterpieces of American historical literature.

Returning to the NAACP in 1944 as director of special research, Du Bois continued to write about black history. In the postwar era, he increasingly turned his attention to Africa and the new nations emerging on that continent. Following the publication of *The World and Africa* (1947), another pioneering work in which he reacted against the widely-held notion that the "dark continent" had always been underdeveloped, Du Bois, now 79 years old, devoted his still formidable talents to the domestic campaign against the Cold War. Politically, he moved close to the Communist left, running in 1950 as a candidate for the US Senate on the American Labor Party ticket. Harassed mercilessly by federal authorities in the 1950s, Du Bois left the United States in 1961 to reside in Ghana at the invitation of president Kwame Nkrumah. At the time of his death in August 1963, he was working on his last great project, the *Encyclopedia Africana*, a projected multivolume survey of African anthropology, politics, and history sponsored by Nkrumah's government. The project was never completed.

RICK HALPERN

See also African American; African Diaspora; Foner, P.; James; Lewis, D.; Stampp; United States: 19th Century; United States: Historical Writing, 20th Century

Biography

William Edward Burghardt Du Bois. Born Great Barrington, Massachusetts, 23 February 1868. Studied at Fisk University, BA 1888; Harvard University, BA 1890, MA 1891, PhD 1895; University of Berlin, 1892–94. Taught at Wilberforce University, 1894–95; instructor in sociology, University of Pennsylvania, 1896–97; professor of economics and economic history, Atlanta University, 1897–1910, where he coordinated the annual Atlanta University Studies Conferences and edited its publications. Cofounder and general secretary, Niagara movement, 1905–10; member, board of directors of the National Association for the Advancement of Colored People (NAACP): director of publicity and research, and editor of *The Crisis*, 1910–34. Professor of sociology, Atlanta University, 1934–44. Director of special research, NAACP, 1944–49. Active in Council on African Affairs, 1949–54. Left US and settled in Ghana, 1961. Married 1) Nina Gomer, 1896 (died 1950; 1 son, 1 daughter); 2) Shirley Lola Graham, 1951. Died Accra, Ghana, 27 August 1963.

Principal Writings

The Suppression of the African Slave Trade to the United States of America, 1638–1870, 1896
The Philadelphia Negro: A Social Study, 1899

Souls of Black Folk: Essays and Sketches, 1903
John Brown, 1909
Darkwater: Voices from within the Veil, 1920
The Gift of Black Folk: Negroes in the Making of America, 1924
*Black Reconstruction: An Essay Toward a History of the Part
    Which Black Folk Played in the Attempt to Reconstruct
    Democracy in America, 1860–1880*, 1935; as *Black
    Reconstruction in America*, 1964
*Black Folk, Then and Now: An Essay in the History and Sociology
    of the Negro Race*, 1939
*Dusk of Dawn: An Essay Toward an Autobiography of a Race
    Concept*, 1940
*The World and Africa: An Inquiry into the Part Which Africa Has
    Played in World History*, 1947
*The Autobiography of W.E.B. Du Bois: A Soliloquy on Viewing My
    Life from the Last Decade of Its First Century*, 1968

Further Reading

Andrews, William L., ed., *Critical Essays on W.E.B. Du Bois*,
    Boston: Hall, 1985
Aptheker, Herbert, ed., *Annotated Bibliography of the Published
    Writings of W.E.B. Du Bois*, Millwood, NY: Kraus, 1973
Horne, Gerald, *Black and Red: W.E.B. Du Bois and the Afro-
    American Response to the Cold War, 1944–1963*, Albany: State
    University of New York Press, 1986
Lester, Julius, ed., *The Seventh Son: The Thought and Writings of
    W.E.B. Du Bois*, 2 vols., New York: Random House, 1971
Lewis, David Levering, *W.E.B. Du Bois: Biography of a Race,
    1868–1919*, New York: Holt, 1993
Marable, Manning, *W.E.B. Du Bois: Black Radical Democrat*,
    Boston: Twayne, 1986
Moore, Jack B., *W.E.B. Du Bois*, Boston: Twayne, 1981
Rampersad, Arnold, *The Art and Imagination of W.E.B. Du Bois*,
    Cambridge, MA: Harvard University Press, 1976
Rudwick, Elliott M., *W.E.B. Du Bois: A Study in Minority Group
    Leadership*, Philadelphia: University of Pennsylvania Press, 1960

Duby, Georges 1919–1996

French social and economic historian

Widely regarded as one of the most outstanding postwar medieval historians, Georges Duby has offered theories on 11th- and 12th-century French society, the rise of knighthood, changes in family structure, and the development of the medieval economy that have become accepted dogma to such an extent that the younger generation of historians are sometimes apt to accept them uncritically as fact. Duby was originally inspired by the writings of Marc Bloch, although the two never met. Consequently his work reflects the influence of the so-called Annales school of history which developed from Bloch's and Lefebvre's journal of that name: an interdisciplinary approach which may borrow from anthropology, sociology and economics, art and culture as well as the history of ideas in the cause of historical analysis, and which concentrates on problems and themes rather than historical narrative. His focus was always on French society in the 11th and 12th centuries, which he regarded as a period of fundamental change; but his range was wide, as was demonstrated by collaborative histories such as *Histoire de la vie privée* (1985–87; *A History of Private Life*, 1987–91).

He sprang to fame with the publication in 1953 of his first major work, *La Société aux XIe et XIIe siècles dans la région maçonnaise* (Society in the 11th and 12th Centuries in the Mâcon Region); which was, in the Annales tradition, a detailed analysis of a small area applied to large historical problems. His research built on and consolidated much of Bloch's work on feudalism, although in the process he also amended Bloch's conclusions. Most importantly, he showed that the knightly class was recognized as being part of the nobility by the mid-11th century. He traced the practice of granting land to vassals in return for military service, a fundamental factor in the development of feudalism. He also studied the origins of the aristocracy of the 12th-century Mâconnais and concluded that, although Bloch had seen them as a "new" nobility, they were actually descended from the great families of Carolingian times. However, marriage and inheritance were now tightly controlled in order to retain the patrimony intact and so preserve the family's wealth and nobility.

This study has been so influential in modern research into medieval society that it is astonishing that no English edition has yet been published. Much of Duby's subsequent work stemmed from his initial discoveries in the Mâconnais, notably the essays published in English as *The Chivalrous Society* (1977) on the nature and development of knighthood, and his research into the changing status of noble marriage and noblewomen. Some of his conclusions on the development of knighthood were later superseded by his own research and the research of his pupil Jean Flori, which revealed that the position of knighthood in the Mâconnais was exceptional; elsewhere knights did not begin to claim nobility until the late 11th century or much later. In *Fiefs and Vassals* (1994) Susan Reynolds questioned Duby's use and interpretation of evidence for the development of the fief.

Duby developed his exploration of the growth of the feudal aristocracy in his *L'Économie rurale et la vie des campagnes dans l'Occident médiéval* (1962; *Rural Economy and Country Life in the Medieval West*, 1968) and *Guerriers et paysans* (1973; *The Early Growth of the European Economy*, 1974). He concluded that the feudal lords' need for money was the crucial factor in stimulating economic growth, rather than the growth of trade, as had been argued by Henri Pirenne. Initially lords accumulated capital as booty from feudal wars; then, as private warfare became less profitable, they turned to encouraging peasant production, creaming off their profits in tolls and dues. Duby's work opened up research into the medieval economy and commercial growth, although much remains to be explained.

Duby did not limit himself to traditional historical areas, also examining mental attitudes, culture, and ideologies. In *Le Dimanche de Bouvines* (1973; *The Legend of Bouvines*, 1990), he discussed not only the course of a decisive battle but also the changing mental representations of that battle. This radical approach to history is only now becoming widely accepted by medieval historians. In 1978 Duby published *Les Trois Ordres, ou, l'imaginaire du féodalisme* (*The Three Orders*, 1980), hailed by Jacques Le Goff as "one of the major historical works of our time." This is a treatment of the medieval concept, previously studied by Le Goff and others, that society was divided into three orders: those who pray, those who fight, and those who work. Duby asked why this concept was expressed at certain times and not others, and who articulated it. This work has become a classic, yet in a 1986 article Elizabeth

Brown noted serious shortcomings: the study was so limited geographically and chronologically as to be misleading to the unwary reader, and it would be more useful to tackle the fundamental problem of why medieval people were so concerned to devise these ideological concepts.

Duby was most severely criticized for his work on medieval marriage and the changing status of women, particularly his apparent assumption that all women were always regarded as passive figures inferior to men. As Kimberly LoPrete pointed out, this approach is unbalanced and misleading and appears to ignore evidence from and about women. She concluded: "Duby has yet to confront what may well be deforming ideological structures at the core of his own readings of historical texts." It would be ironic if this progressive historian who did so much to reshape our understanding of the Middle Ages was himself limited by his own fundamental preconceptions.

HELEN J. NICHOLSON

See also Annales School; Braudel; Europe: Modern; France: to 1000; France: 1000–1485; Hilton; Marriage; Mentalities; Poland: to the 18th Century; Sexuality; Urban; Vovelle; Women's History: Europe

Biography

Georges Michel Claude Duby. Born Paris, 7 October 1919. Educated at Lycée de Mâcon, then received his agrégation and doctorate. Taught at University of Lyon, 1944–50; University of Besançon, 1950–51; University of Aix-Marseille, 1951–70; and Collège de France, 1970–96. Elected to the Académie Française, 1987. Married Andrée Combier, 1942 (1 son, 2 daughters). Died Aix-en-Provence, 2 December 1996.

Principal Writings

La Société aux XIe et XIIe siècles dans la région mâconnaise (Society in the 11th and 12th Centuries in the Mâcon Region), 1953

L'Economie rurale et la vie des campagnes dans l'Occident médiéval: France, Angleterre, Empire, IX–XV siècles, 1962; in English as Rural Economy and Country Life in the Medieval West, 1968

Le Dimanche de Bouvines: 27 juillet 1214, 1973; in English as The Legend of Bouvines: War, Religion, and Culture in the Middle Ages, 1990

Guerriers et paysans, VIIe–XIIe siècle: premier essor de l'économie européene, 1973; in English as The Early Growth of the European Economy: Warriors and Peasants from the Seventh to the Twelfth Century, 1974

The Chivalrous Society, 1977

Editor with Jacques Le Goff, Famille et parenté dans l'Occident médiéval (Family and Kinship in the Medieval West), 1977

Medieval Marriage: Two Models from Twelfth-Century France, 1978

Les Trois Ordres, ou, l'imaginaire du féodalisme, 1978; in English as The Three Orders: Feudal Society Imagined, 1980

Editor, Histoire de la France urbaine (A History of Urban France), 5 vols, 1980–83

Le Chevalier, la femme et le prêtre: le mariage dans la France féodale, 1981; in English as The Knight, the Lady, and the Priest: The Making of Modern Marriage in Medieval France, 1983

Editor with Philippe Ariès, Histoire de la vie privée, 5 vols., 1985–87; in English as A History of Private Life, 5 vols., 1987–91

Mâle Moyen Age: de l'amour et autres essais, 1988; in English as Love and Marriage in the Middle Ages, 1994

Editor with Michelle Perrot, Storia delle donne in Occidente, 5 vols., 1990–92; in English as A History of Women in the West, 5 vols., 1992–94

L'Histoire continue, 1991; in English as History Continues, 1994

Further Reading

Brown, Elizabeth A.R., "Georges Duby and the Three Orders," Viator 17 (1986), 51–64

Ditcham, B.G.H., "The Feudal Millennium? Social Change in Rural France circa 1000 in Recent French Historiography," Medieval History 3 (1993), 86–99

Flori, J., L'Essor de la chevalerie: XIe–XIIe siècles (The Development of Chivalry, 11th–12th Centuries), Geneva: Droz, 1986

Le Goff, Jacques, "Les Trois Fonctions au Moyen Age" (The Functions of the Three Orders in the Middle Ages), Annales 34 (1979), 1187–1215

LoPrete, Kimberly, "Review of Georges Duby: Love and Marriage in the Middle Ages," Speculum 70 (1995), 607–09

Moore, R.I., "Duby's Eleventh Century," History 69 (1984), 36–49

Oexle, Otto Gerhard, "Die 'Wirklichkeit' und das 'Wissen': ein Blick auf das Sozialgeschichtliche Oeuvre von Georges Duby" (Reality and Knowledge: A Look at the Sociohistorical Work of Georges Duby), Historische Zeitschrift 232 (1981), 61–91

Reynolds, Susan, Fiefs and Vassals: The Medieval Evidence Reinterpreted, Oxford and New York: Oxford University Press, 1994

Duhem, Pierre 1861–1916
French historian of science

The historical writings of Pierre Duhem are notable for their pioneering attempt to situate the history of science in its wider historical context and for their recognition of the real interest of the Middle Ages for the historicizing of science. Duhem was also an early proponent of the view that Christianity had a positive role in the development of modern science. All of this, however, came late in a career spanning some three decades, and like the philosophical writings they are hardly to be separated from, they were the outgrowth of his main and continuing interests in theoretical physics. Like many scientists before and since, Duhem felt it appropriate to use history in defence of his scientific positions. But this is not to say that his works are purely propaganda or devoid of non-scientific interest; his wide interests in philosophy and theology became more pronounced as his career progressed, particularly in the voluminous works on medieval science for which he is now best known. His work is best regarded as falling into three distinct phases, notwithstanding the inevitable overlaps between them.

His early work consisted largely of brilliant essays in a sort of philosophical history. The phrase "historical and critical" often appeared in their subtitles, and their style bore a strong resemblance to that of Duhem's Austrian contemporary, Ernst Mach. The topics of these essays cover Duhem's main interests in the theory of heat, physical chemistry, the theory of light, and electricity. The philosophy underpinning this species of critical history is somewhat reminiscent of positivism but is indebted to many other sources – its relation to positivism has been thoroughly explored by Maiocchi. These essays provided the epistemological framework that controls a highly normative, though subtle and sensitive, treatment of the historical material. At this stage there was no trace of the interest in medieval science that was to be basis of his later fame.

The next phase can be dated to the middle of November 1903, when, perhaps as a result of a postcard from Paul

Tannery, Duhem discovered what he took to be genuine medieval physics in the work of Jordanus de Nemore. This discovery led to what seems like an orgy of indiscriminate fact-hunting under extraordinarily difficult conditions, conducted with little apparent regard for overall consistency. When he made this discovery Duhem had been working on a 2-volume study of statics. In it he first denied that there had been any worthwhile science in the Middle Ages and then went on to give the evidence to the contrary. From the same period is the even more famous *Etudes sur Léonard de Vinci* (Studies on Leonardo da Vinci, 1906–13), in reality explorations of putative medieval antecedents of Galileo's mechanics. Here in the chaos of new facts and fluctuating judgments, we meet Duhem's historiographic prejudices – his loyalty to the Catholic church, and his loyalty to France – rather than his considered judgments. To this period also belongs his *Sozein ta phainomena: Essai sur la notion de théorie physique de Platon à Galilée* (1908; *To Save the Phenomena*, 1969), the brilliant short essay on the history of astronomy that superficially reads like a direct normative application of Duhem's philosophical principles to a reassessment of the Galileo case, and foreshadows the incomplete multivolume *Le Système du monde* (1913–59; abridged as *Medieval Cosmology*, 1985) of the final phase of Duhem's career.

It is in this latter work that Duhem finally found his bearings, though this fact has not been visible to historians because it was incomplete at the time of his death in 1916, and because half of what was finished remained unpublished for some 40 years. In it Duhem offered a coherent model of what science as intellectual history could be: integrated into the philosophical, theological, and political background so that their mutual relations could be seen. There is no longer any trace of the positivist model of science as an autonomous discipline, independent of philosophy and theology, that dominated his earlier writings. Instead we have the historical question as to what the relations of science to philosophy and theology actually are. This is not the type of social history that became fashionable in the 1970s and 1980s, but broad-band intellectual history of the type developed by Alexandre Koyré and his pupils in the postwar period, though from a different standpoint. In this work Duhem also developed his view that the intellectual climate of the Christian Middle Ages was not purely Aristotelian – far from it, the resistance of the ecclesiastical authorities to dogmatic Aristotelianism paved the way for modern science.

This and other claims still reflected his prejudices, but on examination his works are much less favorable to the Aristotelianizing scholasticism favored by the Catholic authorities than many commentators believed, or than some of Duhem's earlier remarks would have led the reader to expect. The true nature of his final commitments is still open for debate, and remains controversial. The user of his work needs to be aware of these commitments, for, whatever else he abandoned of his earlier historiographical attitudes, he continued to adhere to the critical history he had learned in his youth, rejecting the pretence of the objective description of neutral historical fact in favor of critical engagement with the material.

R.N.D. MARTIN

See also Mach; Sarton; Science

Biography

Pierre Maurice Marie Duhem. Born Paris, 10 June 1861, son of a commercial traveler. Educated Collège Stanislas and Ecole Normale Supérieure, 1882–87, doctorate 1887. Taught at universities of Lille 1887–93; Rennes 1893–94; and Bordeaux 1894–1916. Died Cabréspine, Aude, 14 September 1916.

Principal Writings

Le Mixte et la combinaison chimique (Mixture and Chemical Combination), 1902
Les Théories électriques de J. Clerk Maxwell (The Electrical Theories of J. Clerk Maxwell), 1902
L'Evolution de la mécanique, 1903; in English as *The Evolution of Mechanics*, 1980
Les Origines de la statique, 2 vols., 1905–06; in English as *The Origins of Statics*, 1991
Etudes sur Léonard de Vinci (Studies on Leonardo da Vinci), 3 vols., 1906–13
La Théorie physique, son objet et sa structure, 1906; in English as *The Aim and Structure of Physical Theory*, 1954
Sozein ta phainomena: Essai sur la notion de théorie physique de Platon à Galilée, 1908; in English as *To Save the Phenomena: An Essay on the Idea of Physical Theory from Plato to Galileo*, 1969
Le Système du monde: histoire des doctrines cosmologiques de Platon à Copernic, 10 vols., 1913–59; abridged in English as *Medieval Cosmology: Theories of Infinity, Place, Time, Void, and the Plurality of Worlds*, 1985
La Science allemande, 1915; in English as *German Science: Some Reflections on German Science and German Virtues*, 1991
La Chimie est-elle une science française? (Is Chemistry a French Science?), 1916
Notice sur les travaux scientifiques de Duhem (Report on Duhem's Academic Works), *Mémoires de la Société des Sciences Physiques et Naturelles de Bordeaux*, 7/1 (1917), 71–169
Prémices philosophiques (Philosophical First Fruits), edited by Stanley L. Jaki, 1987
Essays in the History and Philosophy of Science, edited by Roger Ariew and Peter Barker, 1996

Further Reading

Ariew, Roger, and Peter Barker, eds, *Pierre Duhem: Historian and Philosopher of Science*, Synthèse 83 (1990), 177–453
Duhem, Hélène, 1936, *Un Savant français . . .: Pierre Duhem* (A French Scientist), Paris: Plon, 1936
Jaki, Stanley L., *Uneasy Genius: The Life and Work of Pierre Duhem*, The Hague: Nijhoff, 1984 [includes bibliography]
Jaki, Stanley L., *Reluctant Heroine: The Life and Work of Hélène Duhem*, Edinburgh: Scottish Academic Press, 1992
Jordan, E., "Duhem, Pierre," *Mémoires* [Société des Sciences Physiques et Naturelles de Bordeaux] 7 (1917), 3–40
Maiocchi, Roberto, *Chimica e filosofia, scienza, epistemologia, storia e religione nell'opera di Pierre Duhem* (Chemistry and Philosophy, Epistemology, History and Religion in the Work of Pierre Duhem), Florence: Nuova Italia, 1985 [includes bibliography]
Martin, R.N.D. *Pierre Duhem: Philosophy and History in the Work of a Believing Physicist*, La Salle, IL: Open Court, 1991
Miller, D.M., "Duhem, Pierre Maurice Marie," *Dictionary of Scientific Biography*, vol. 4, New York: Scribner, 1971
Paul, Harry W., *The Edge of Contingency: French Catholic Reaction to Scientific Change from Darwin to Duhem*, Gainesville: University Presses of Florida, 1979

Dunning, William A. 1857–1922

US historian of the American South

Retrieving the issue of post-Civil War Reconstruction from the prerogative of amateur and politically motivated historians, William A. Dunning initiated a field of inquiry which provoked waves of acceptance and reaction well into the 1960s. In particular, Dunning's *Reconstruction: Political and Economic* (1907) set forth a historical interpretation that dominated the professional discussion throughout the first half of the 20th century. The "Dunning school," embodied in a generation of graduate students and intellectual heirs, expanded this powerful interpretation and offered a vision of Reconstruction from the state level. These works, however, began to gather significant threads of opposition by the 1930s, and faced an increasingly hostile reception thereafter. By the mid-1960s, the revolution against the Dunning thesis was complete, as Kenneth M. Stampp's synthetic account, *The Era of Reconstruction, 1865–1877* (1965), reflected new consensus in the field. Though discredited, Dunning's work yet retains a monumental place in the history of Reconstruction, as the first and prevailing interpretation for several generations of historiography.

Dunning's early writings coalesced around the issue of the Constitution in the post-Civil War period, which he portrayed as increasingly powerful on the national level. Asked to write the volume on Reconstruction for the *American Nation* series, Dunning sought to offer a newly holistic account of the period: westward expansion, economic growth and change, racial policy, foreign affairs, constitutional issues, and partisan politics embodied within a single narrative. A lack of primary research by Dunning, however, led to an over-reliance on secondary sources and on the writings of his students. Positing that the course of Reconstruction had been overthrown in the aftermath of Lincoln's assassination and the acerbic 1866 elections, Dunning regarded the rise of Radical Reconstruction (1867–73) as the ominous forerunner of tumult in the South. With northern carpetbaggers and southern scalawags aligned against southern institutions, according to this thesis, the policies of the national government and black-controlled state legislatures in the South effectively crippled the prevailing political and social order. Only in the intervention of the Panic of 1873 and white resurgence in the South was the resumption of "home rule" finally possible, as "Redeemers" successfully restored order to the region. By 1877, according to Dunning, the dark period in US history had ended, and the South had reclaimed its own sovereignty and respect.

The interpretive framework thus advanced by Dunning was bolstered by numerous state studies completed by his graduate students at Columbia University. The works of James Garner, Walter Fleming, J.G. de Roulhac Hamilton, C. Mildred Thompson, and Charles Ramsdell were at the core of the "Dunning school" of historiography, and offered considerable sympathy for white southerners. Still, Dunning and his "school" proved valuable correctives for one another: while Dunning sought a national and political approach, his students' tendencies toward regional and social history furnished depth to the interpretation. As a professor, Dunning demanded his students perform at the highest standards of critical inquiry,

but responded with a genial friendship in return. Evidence of their significant relationship is revealed not only in their shared vision of Reconstruction, but also in three separate historical volumes to Professor Dunning, which his students warmly dedicated to "the Old Chief."

Active in professional organizations for both history and political science, Dunning achieved a prominence that reflected the enduring respect of his contemporaries. President first of the American Historical Association (1913) and later of the American Political Science Association (1922), he opposed the increasing disjunction between the fields. He likewise saw the fragmentation brought on by historical monographs as an unfortunate seed of division. Nonetheless, Dunning's books in political science were heralded by an audience different from that of his histories, though with much the same positive reception. His three-volume *History of Political Theories* (1902–20), the particular intellectual and personal preoccupation of Dunning's career, gathered significant acclaim among political scientists and stands as perhaps his most important work of scholarship, if largely ignored by historians.

Associated with Columbia University for nearly fifty years – from college matriculation in 1877 until his death in 1922 – Dunning led one of the most respected history departments of his era. He was devoted to the scientific inquiry of the past, and students noted that his books were written slowly, but with few later changes. His primary concern was to be seen as neither prejudiced nor reckless in his conclusions. It is ironic, then, that this scholar who had hoped especially to eliminate the prejudice in interpretation that had characterized Reconstruction history would be seen by later generations as the author of a particularly racist historiographic tradition. The Dunning interpretation of Reconstruction, powerful in its time, no longer remains viable. It is, however, the powerful legacy of an influential professor and his intellectual heirs, who together comprised a "school" of United States historiography.

DAVID T. BURRELL

See also African American; Foner, E.; Litwack; Phillips; Stampp; United States: 19th Century

Biography

William Archibald Dunning. Born Plainfield, New Jersey, 12 May 1857. Newspaper reporter, New York City, 1875–77. Attended Dartmouth College briefly before being expelled for a prank; received BA, Columbia University, 1881, MA 1884, PhD 1885. Taught (rising to professor), Columbia University, 1886–1922. Married Charlotte E. Loomis, 1888 (died 1917). Died 25 August 1922.

Principal Writings

Essays on the Civil War and Reconstruction and Related Topics, 1898; reprinted 1965
History of Political Theories, 3 vols., 1902–20
Reconstruction: Political and Economic, 1866–1877, 1907; reprinted 1968
The British Empire and the United States: A Review of Their Relations during the Century of Peace Following the Treaty of Ghent, 1914; reprinted 1969
Truth in History, and Other Essays, 1937; reprinted 1965

Further Reading

Current, Richard N., ed., *Reconstruction in Retrospect: Views from the Turn of the Century*, Baton Rouge: Louisiana State University Press, 1969

Hamilton, J.G. de Roulhac, Introduction to William A. Dunning, *Truth in History, and Other Essays*, New York: Columbia University Press, 1937; reprinted Port Washington, NY: Kennikat Press, 1965

Harper, Alan D., "William A. Dunning: The Historian as Nemesis," *Civil War History* 10 (1964), 54–66

Hosmer, John Harelson, "William A. Dunning: 'The Greatest Historian,'" *Mid-America* 68 (1986), 57–78

Muller, Philip R., "Look Back Without Anger: A Reappraisal of William A. Dunning," *Journal of American History* 61 (1974), 325–38

Pressly, Thomas J., "Racial Attitudes, Scholarship, and Reconstruction: A Review Essay," *Journal of Southern History* 32 (1966), 88–93

Stephenson, Wendell Holmes, *Southern History in the Making: Pioneer Historians of the South*, Baton Rouge: Louisiana State University Press, 1964

Dutt, R.C. 1848–1909

Indian historian and politician

R.C. Dutt's career spanned scholarship, literature, the Indian Civil Service, and later politics, and he wrote at a time when much of the Indian elite did not envisage an end to British rule in India. Dutt's early writings never set out to subvert the British position and it was his moderate stance that made him acceptable to many British commentators. In his later works Dutt was developing as a political thinker and he began to challenge the "divine right of conquerors," helping to establish the foundations of India's nationalist movement in the 20th century.

Dutt's first book, *Three Years in Europe* (1872), revealed his great powers of observation and evinced his strong belief in the plight of the poor in all nations. This continued with *The Peasantry of Bengal* (1874) in which he described the growing discontent of an agrarian population who were suffering under Zamindar overlordship.

Although most of Dutt's works were published in English, he did contribute to the growth in Bengali literature pioneered by Bankim Chunder Chatterjee. Influenced by Chatterjee, Dutt wrote six historical novels between 1870 and 1893, three of which were later translated into English. In 1885 Dutt translated the *Rig Veda* into Bengali much to the despair of the Hindu religious elite who were in consternation at the thought of a non-Brahmin handling the ancient Hindu scriptures.

Dutt's first solely historic work was a broad description of the development of Hindu civilization, and, although containing no new analysis, *History of Civilization in Ancient India* (1889–90) grew from his conviction that most historians were producing few works for the general reader.

With the publication of *England and India: A Record of Progress during 100 Years* (1897) Dutt's writings became more politically charged: he called for an extension of the popular share in legislation and administration in India and was very critical of the effects that mass-produced British goods had on India's domestic industries. This book stands out as the first academic work by an Indian that sought to analyze critically the economic consequences of British rule and to challenge the orthodox view that imperial economic policy was increasing Indian prosperity.

Famines in India (1900) contained five "open letters" to Lord Curzon, the British viceroy of India, suggesting changes in government policy that would alleviate the persistent threat of famine. Dutt argued for a relaxation of the heavy tax burden placed on some of India's poorest producers; however, colonial officials dismissed much of Dutt's evidence as inaccurate. Perhaps seeking to vindicate his own views Dutt continued his analysis in *The Economic History of British India* (1902), covering 1757 to 1837, and *India in the Victorian Age* (1904). These works were regarded by many Indian nationalists as documentary proof of the exploitation inherent in British rule.

Although Dutt remained a constitutional nationalist, his later works were an important contribution to a growing critique of British rule in India. The "drain of wealth theory," pioneered by writers such as Dadabhai Naoroji, came to be a foundational precept of the India's nationalist movement in the early 20th century.

BILLY FRANK

Biography

Romesh Chunder Dutt. Born Calcutta, 13 August 1848. Educated at Hare's School; Presidency College, Calcutta; University College, London; passed Indian Civil Service examination, England, 1868; studied law, Middle Temple, 1871: called to the Bar. Returned to India, and entered Indian Civil Service, 1871; assistant magistrate, later magistrate, rural Bengal, 1871–81; collector, 1881–94; commissioner, 1894–97; resigned and settled in England, 1897; lecturer, University College, London, 1898–1904; returned to India, 1904; revenue minister, Baroda, 1904–09. Married 1864 (5 daughters, 1 son). Died Baroda, 30 November 1909.

Principal Writings

Three Years in Europe, 1872; revised and expanded, 1896
The Peasantry of Bengal, Being a View of Their Condition under the Hindu, the Mahomedam and the English Rule, 1874
History of Civilization in Ancient India, 2 vols., 1889–90
England and India: A Record of Progress during 100 Years, 1785–1885, 1897
Famines in India, 1900
The Economic History of British India: A Record of Agriculture and Land Settlements, Trade and Manufacturing Industries, Finance and Administration, from the Rise of the British Power in 1757 to the Accession of Queen Victoria in 1837, 1902
India in the Victorian Age: An Economic History of the People, 1904

Dyos, H.J. 1921–1978

British urban historian

H.J. Dyos was the founder of the modern study of urban history. His only monograph was *Victorian Suburb* (1961), which was the first evocative portrait of what he christened "suburbania," and which drew upon his own childhood knowledge of London south of the Thames. The great metropolis always remained at the center of his interests, but his inexhaustible energies were poured into collaborative and editorial enterprises to draw together the many existing disciplines which had separately contributed to an understanding of the history of towns and cities. Dyos himself encouraged urban historians to learn established disciplines, even while he made them tributary to his own. His training at the London School of Economics after his wartime service was as an economic historian; he was appointed to a lectureship in the subject at University College, Leicester in 1952, and went on make the new University of Leicester, with its strengths in local history and Victorian studies, a highly congenial base for the rest of his career. Dyos had begun by elucidating the impact of railway building on housing in Victorian London, not least in the mass displacement of the city's poor, and he retained a special love of transport history. He encouraged the development of quantitative and statistical methods of study, as in computerizing census data, though he rejected the abstract inhumanity of some its practitioners, and his work was always informed by an economist's sense of the financial systems underlying the 19th-century building and housing industries in London especially, and of how these dictated the exploitation of urban land and space, and shaped the formation of both slum and suburb.

Dyos, however, also had a humanist's concern for both social reform (especially in the matter of housing) and for the present and future of the city, as lying at the heart of the present and future of humanity, and he achieved an international and a theoretical view of his subject as the study of the city as a whole. He was, however, the least dogmatic of men, and his views were always based in the Anglo-Saxon manner on close empirical study, not least on the city's study of itself. While he ascribed a decisive role in the emergence of a global urbanism in the 19th century to the development of industrial technology, he was equally alive to the interaction of such processes with inherited tradition, religious and secular, and took a vital interest in how the modern urban experience had both created new kinds of consciousness and re-created old ones. Dyos convened the first meeting of the Urban History Group as part of the conference of the Economic History Society in 1963; his typed and cyclostyled Urban History Newsletter, much of which he wrote himself, was followed by the Urban History Yearbook (in 1974). The discipline could he said to have been fairly launched with a conference in Leicester in September 1966, whose proceedings were edited by Dyos as The Study of Urban History (1968). Dyos also founded the series Studies in Urban History,

Themes in Urban History, and Explorations in Urban Analysis. The subject attained an early maturity in the beautifully produced 2-volume work The Victorian City (edited with Michael Wolff, 1973). He had a strongly developed aesthetic sense and a love of 19th-century architecture, and succeeded Sir Nikolaus Pevsner as Chairman of the Victorian Society in 1976. Dyos was a great hunter of new talent among the young, and his sudden and premature death at the very height of his powers deprived the world he had created of a genial and kindly patron and promoter, and it orphaned a generation of young scholars. He gave the study of urban history in Britain its multiform and multidisciplinary character, while, by his very generosity of spirit and lack of egotism and of selfishness, he centered all its activities upon himself. No single scholar in the field of urban studies has since arisen to succeed him.

SHERIDAN GILLEY

See also Briggs; Britain: since 1750; Urban

Biography

Harold James Dyos. Born London, 1921. Served in Royal Artillery, World War II. Received BA, London School of Economics, University of London, 1949, PhD 1952. Taught (rising to professor), University College, Leicester, later University of Leicester, 1952–78. Married Olive Dyos (1 daughter). Died Leicester, 22 August 1978.

Principal Writings

Victorian Suburb: A Study of the Growth of Camberwell, 1961
Editor, *The Study of Urban History*, 1968
With Derek H. Aldcroft, *British Transport: An Economic Survey from the Seventeenth Century to the Twentieth*, 1969
Editor with Michael Wolff, *The Victorian City: Images and Realities*, 2 vols., 1973
Exploring the Urban Past: Essays in Urban History, edited by David Cannadine and David Reeder, 1982

Further Reading

Mandelbaum, Seymour J., "Harold James Dyos and British Urban History," *Economic History Review* 38 (1985), 437–47
Reeder, David, "Introduction: H. J. Dyos and the Urban Process" and David Cannadine, "Urban History in the United Kingdom: The 'Dyos Phenomenon' and After," in David Cannadine and David Reeder, eds., *Exploring the Urban Past: Essays in Urban History by H.J. Dyos*, Cambridge and New York: Cambridge University Press, 1982

E

East Central Europe

The terms "East Central Europe" or "Eastern Europe," used to describe the lands between Germany and Russia (or the former USSR) are curious, considering that the region is close to the geographic center of the European continent. The latter term is the more recent of the two, having appeared at the beginning of the Cold War to describe a series of formerly independent states under Soviet domination. (The term was further applied to Yugoslavia, but not to Greece.) The former term came into use after World War I, particularly among Polish historians. It has come reflect a historiographic emphasis on the links this region shares with Western Christendom. By contrast, the term Eastern Europe seemed to symbolize the separation of these lands from Europe proper. Piotr Wandycz has defined east central Europe as Poland, Hungary, and Bohemia/Czechoslovakia, so that this cultural/geographic region has at sometimes been very large and other times quite small.

Most historical surveys of "Europe" or "Western Civilization" ignore east central Europe, or, at best, treat it as peripheral to the main streams of European history. This stems, in part, from the turbulent history of the region during the past two centuries and the resulting political importance attached to competing historical interpretations of past events. During the 19th century, at a time when the discipline of history was becoming increasingly scientific and professional, many of these nations had lost their independence and despite periodic national uprisings, such as in Poland in 1830 and 1863, and in Hungary in 1848, they remained largely submerged until after World War I. The prime interpreters of the histories of these nations were often Germans or Russians, who had a vested interest in demonstrating that once-powerful nations like Poland-Lithuania were historical failures, and who invoked prevailing Darwinian theories of national development to drive home their arguments. Native historians, by contrast, were influenced by their respective nationalisms, and often sought to present heroic or even messianic views of the past. Debates over historical events – even those in the distant past – were highly charged with contemporary meaning.

Each nation in East Central Europe has developed its own distinctive historiography, sometimes quite old, as in the case of Poland and Hungary, and sometimes quite new, as in case of Slovakia and Bulgaria. Nevertheless, a few common themes run through all of their historiographies. Westernizers have looked to Western Europe for historical models, either to emphasize historical links with the West (in the case of Poland, Hungary, and Bohemia), or to explain why the nation has failed to develop properly (as in the case of Romania). Traditionalists, by contrast, have sought roots of national development in the distant tribal past or in the strength of idealized peasant folkways. The differences between these two groups (who are similar to the better-known Slavophiles and Westernizers in Russian historiography) have been the least pronounced in nations with the strongest links to the West, such as Poland and Hungary.

Historians in East Central Europe have, moreover, been far more involved in the making of history than elsewhere, and this sense of political immediacy adds an edge to the historiography of the region. Historians in this region have had a front-row seat, unfortunately, for many of the 20th century's most terrible wars and atrocities. The region has long been a highway for powerful foreign armies. In Poland, for example, historians struggled painfully in the aftermath of the partitions and various national uprisings, to explain why their nation was subject to such disasters and tragedies. The role of historians as keepers of their nations' collective memories has imposed special burdens on the regions' scholars. Historians (and other academics) came to the fore in great numbers after the collapse of communism in 1989. Viewed as honest brokers after the end of party hegemony, historians headed governments in Poland and Hungary, while a playwright led Czechoslovakia (and later the Czech Republic) and a musician was president of Lithuania.

Since 1989, historians from both inside and outside East Central Europe have again emphasized the region as an integral part of Europe. (Whether historians of Western Europe take notice is another matter.) The old, Cold War notion of Eastern Europe as a distinct region encompassing everything from the southern Baltic littoral (including eastern Germany but not Lithuania) to the Balkans (exclusive of Greece) has fallen out of favor, in part because it had little historical basis and was predicated on a political situation that proved quite transitory. The recent work of Wandycz, Norman Davies, and others harkens back to the earlier writings of Oskar Halecki and Francis Dvornik, who conceived of east central Europe as a political and cultural transitional zone between Germany and Russia. Indeed, Wandycz's East Central Europe, although it has varied drastically in size over the centuries, now seems a far more durable concept than the Cold War concept of "Eastern Europe."

JOHN RADZILOWSKI

See also Balkans; Burke; Central Europe; Davies, N.; Fischer; Halecki; Poland: to the 18th Century; Rothschild; Sugar

Further Reading

Banac, Ivo, "Historiography of the Countries of Eastern Europe: Yugoslavia," *American Historical Review* 97 (1992), 1084–1104

Berend, Tibor Iván, and György Ránki, *Khozép-Kelet-Európa gazdasági fejlodése a 19–20 században*, Budapest: Konyvkiado, 1976; in English as *Economic Development in East-Central Europe in the Nineteenth and Twentieth Centuries*, New York: Columbia University Press, 1974

Burke, Peter, Antoni Mączak, and Henryk Samsonowicz, eds., *East-Central Europe in Transition: From the Fourteenth to the Seventeenth Century*, Cambridge and New York: Cambridge University Press, 1985

Burks, Richard Voyles, "East European History: An Ethnic Approach," American Historical Association Pamphlet 425, 1973

Crampton, R.J., *Eastern Europe in the Twentieth Century*, London: Routledge, 1994

Davies, Norman, *Heart of Europe: A Short History of Poland*, New York and Oxford: Oxford University Press, 1984

Davies, Norman, *Europe: A History*, Oxford and New York: Oxford University Press, 1996

Deák, István, "Historiography of the Countries of Eastern Europe: Hungary," *American Historical Review* 97 (1992), 1041–65

Dvornik, Francis, *The Making of Central and Eastern Europe*, London: Polish Research Centre, 1949; Gulf Breeze, FL: Academic International Press, 1974

Dvornik, Francis, *The Slavs: Their Early History and Civilization*, Boston: American Academy of Arts and Sciences, 1956

Garton Ash, Timothy, *The Magic Lantern: The Revolution of '89 Witnessed in Warsaw, Budapest, Berlin, and Prague*, New York: Random House, 1990

Halecki, Oskar, *The Limits and Divisions of European History*, London and New York: Sheed and Ward, 1950

Halecki, Oskar, *Borderlands of Western Civilization: A History of East Central Europe*, New York: Ronald Press, 1952

Halecki, Oskar, "Jadwiga of Anjou and the Rise of East Central Europe," *Polish Review* 19 (1974), 157–69

Hitchins, Keith, "Historiography of the Countries of Eastern Europe: Romania," *American Historical Review* 97 (1992), 1064–83

Kann, Robert A., and Zdeněk David, *The Peoples of the Eastern Habsburg Lands, 1526–1918*, Seattle: University of Washington Press, 1984

Király, Bela K., ed. *The Crucial Decade: East Central European Society and National Defense, 1859–1870*, New York: Brooklyn College Press, 1984

Koralka, Jirí, "Historiography of the Countries of Eastern Europe: Czechoslovakia," *American Historical Review* 97 (1992), 1026–40

Magocsi, Paul Robert, *Historical Atlas of East Central Europe*, Seattle: University of Washington Press, 1993

Rothschild, Joseph, *East Central Europe Between the Two World Wars*, Seattle: University of Washington Press, 1974

Rothschild, Joseph, *Return to Diversity: A Political History of East Central Europe since World War II*, Oxford and New York: Oxford University Press, 1989; revised 1993

Sedlar, Jean W., *East Central Europe in the Middle Ages, 1000–1500*, Seattle: University of Washington Press, 1994

Seton-Watson, Hugh, *Eastern Europe Between the Wars, 1918–1941*. Cambridge: Cambridge University Press, 1945; 3rd edition, 1962

Sukiennicki, Wiktor, *East Central Europe during World War I: From Foreign Domination to National Independence*, 2 vols. Boulder, CO: East European Monographs, 1984

Sussex, Roland, and J. C. Eade, eds., *Culture and Nationalism in Nineteenth-Century Eastern Europe*, Columbus, OH: Slavica, 1983

Todorova, Maria, "Historiography of the Countries of Eastern Europe: Bulgaria," *American Historical Review* 97 (1992), 1105–17

Turnock, David, *Eastern Europe: An Historical Geography, 1815–1945*, London and New York: Routledge, 1989

Walters, E. Garrison, *The Other Europe: Eastern Europe to 1989*, Syracuse, NY: Syracuse University Press, 1987

Wandycz, Piotr S., *Lands of Partitioned Poland, 1795–1918*, Seattle: University of Washington Press, 1975

Wandycz, Piotr S., "Historiography of the Countries of Eastern Europe: Poland," *American Historical Review* 97 (1992), 1011–25

Wandycz, Piotr S., *Price of Freedom: A History of East Central Europe from the Middle Ages to the Present*, London and New York: Routledge, 1992

Eastern Orthodoxy

The Eastern Orthodox church numbers around 250 million members throughout the world, but especially in Eastern Europe, the former Soviet Union, and along the coasts of the Mediterranean. It constitutes a family of local, self-governing churches, each of which follows identical doctrine, discipline, and spiritual practices. The Orthodox church is an Eastern church in the sense that it is the product of Middle Eastern, Hellenic, and Slavic history and culture. The term "Eastern" extends beyond geographical or cultural conditions, signifying rather the identity of the Orthodox church with the tradition and centers of the early church. The term "Orthodox" is a qualification that describes much more than the form of this church, implying rather its integrity in terms of both doctrine and liturgy. Constantine, the first Roman emperor to put an end to the age of persecution and martyrdom, espoused the Christian faith in the early part of the 4th century and rendered Christianity a state religion. He founded a new capital for the empire, Constantinople, which was to rival and replace the "Old Rome" in splendor and significance. This empire played a dominant role in the history of the Eastern Orthodox church for more than a thousand years.

Historiography flourished during this early period, in the form of both formal history and informal chronicle, although the Byzantines themselves never clearly distinguished between the two. Two main types of history may be discerned: the genre of church history, as it was created by Eusebius in the 4th century (with his *Ecclesiastical History*), and the more secular story, as it was told by Procopius and Agathias in the 6th century (with their writings on wars). Eusebius of Caesarea (c.260–339) experienced and described the persecution of Christians by Diocletian. His history covered events from the foundation of the church to 324. He greatly admired Constantine, whose biography he composed. Eusebius was the first to adapt to Christian thought the ancient Hellenistic theory of the monarch as the image of God. His objective was to show the heroic progress of Christianity. For him, history acquired a dimension of providence (*pronoia*) and teleology. Time was perceived as linear, not circular; it looked towards Christ's *parousia* or Second Coming. Geographically, historians were normally concerned with the territory within the Byzantine empire.

Later church historians such as John of Ephesus and Evagrius introduced more secular material. Evagrius Scholasticus (536–600) wrote an ecclesiastical history in six books, a sequel to the apologetic histories of Gelasius of Caesaria, Philostorgius,

Socrates, Sozomen, and Theodoret, covering the years from 431 to 593. The first full-length chronicle appeared in the 6th century and was written by John Malalas. Written in simple Greek, it comprises an uncritical compilation of biblical, mythical, and historical material. This work was extremely popular and was used by all subsequent chroniclers. It too adopted the linear concept of time, varying in its approach from the strictly chronological to the more biographical.

A series of councils convened by the emperor – seven of them between 325 and 787 – enabled the bishops to examine false teachings and to express fundamental truths of the church. These decisions – enforced as law in the Eastern Roman empire – confirmed the principle of honor and order of prestige among the influential cities: Rome and Constantinople (the capitals of the Western and Eastern parts of the empire respectively), followed by Alexandria, Antioch, and Jerusalem. With the conversion of the Slavs in the 10th century, Moscow would later seek to be added to this hierarchical list.

The iconoclastic controversies of the 7th and 8th centuries caused a break in historiography until the early 9th century. In his *Bibliotheca* (*The Library of Photius I*), patriarch Photius outlined many historical works lost during this period. At this time, the estrangement between East and West became more marked, aggravated by rivalry over missionary jurisdiction and controversy over theological issues. About this time, George Synkellos devised chronological tables, and Theophanes the Confessor began a detailed chronicle. The purpose was increasingly for the religious edification and education of readers. In fact, historiography of the 10th century was again narrowly apologetic and partisan (see, for example, the chronicle of Symeon Magistros). The 10th-century history of Leo the Deacon is more objective in its approach, based on eyewitness accounts, and more inclusive in its scope. The growing tension between East and West in both civil and church matters inevitably led to divergence, ultimately ending in division (1054). In spite of formal and informal attempts at reunion – two significant councils were held in Lyon (1274) and in Florence (1438–39) – the rift was never healed, especially after the indelible mark left by the crusaders in the Middle East (1098–99) and in Asia Minor (1204).

The Eastern Orthodox church was not only both in tension and in dialogue with the Western church over the centuries, but from the 7th century it also found itself in conflict with Islam. This tension became the focus of attention in the historical literature that followed.

The leading intellectual of the 11th century was Michael Psellos, who revealed fresh possibilities in Byzantine historiography. This learned and literary tradition of historiography was furthered in the writings of Nikephoros Bryennios (with his history), John Kinnamos (with his *Epitome*), and the rhetorical Niketas Choniates.

The only woman historian that Byzantium produced comes from this period. Anna Komnene (1083–1153) was the daughter of Emperor Alexios I and the wife of Nikephoros Bryennios. In her forced retirement, she devoted herself to scholarship and to the composition of her celebrated *Alexiad*, a panegyric of her father's reign. It is a gem of Byzantine literature, written in an erudite Greek by an astonishingly cultured woman. Very personal and scarcely impartial, this work nonetheless remains our major source of information regarding the empire's revival and its confrontation with the crusaders and the Seljuk Turks.

Historical works of this period in the Slavic tradition include the *Povest' vremennykh let* (*The Russian Primary Chronicle*, 1953), attributed to the 11th-century Kievan monk Nestor, and an account from the 12th-century ruler Vladimir Monomakh. The various saints' lives also assume great historiographical significance.

During the 12th century there were three major, and largely rhetorical, chroniclers: John Zonaras, Constantine Manasses, and Michael Glykas. The first of these was a court official in Constantinople, later tonsured a monk. His world chronicle spans from Creation to the year 1118; it is characterized by a certain sophistication. Zonaras provided unique details, as well as a valuable check on the *Alexiad*. The works of the next century were less fanciful, but it was during the 14th century that the Eastern Orthodox church saw a flowering in historiography. Kallistos Xanthopoulos returned to the Eusebian genre of history, with his ecclesiastical history based on earlier church historians and some hagiographical texts. Nikephoros Gregoras (d.1361), one of the greatest polymaths of his time, was an opponent of the Hesychast revival and as a result fell out with his friend, John Kantakouzenos. He was condemned by the church in 1351, but his *Historia Rhomaike* (Byzantine History) is a major source for the period between 1320 and 1359. Emperor John VI Kantakouzenos (d.1383) had many ideas for the revival of his empire. Distrusted, however, by his people, he was forced to retire and wrote several theological treatises, as well as a history composed in the form of memoirs, an apologia for his career between 1320 and 1357. Secular historiography survived until the end of the Eastern empire in 1453: the leading historians were John Kananos and George Sphrantzes, the latter even witnessing the fall of the imperial city. The fall of Constantinople (1453) marked the beginning of a period of decline in Eastern Orthodoxy: it was a time of geographical and intellectual confinement.

Under Islam, the church was not entirely extinguished – especially since the Koran recognized Jesus as "a great prophet," and his followers as another "people of the Book" – but its dynamism was based more on lay piety and monastic spirituality. The classic texts on prayer and the spiritual life were compiled during this period by St. Nikodemus the Hagiorite (1749–1809) in his *Philokalia* (*The Philokalia*, 1979–). Orthodox Christians were in effect segregated from mainstream social and political life. Their religious attitude became narrow, their lifestyle defensive, and their doctrine apologetic in tone. Their theological discourse was deeply marked by conservatism and westernization. In terms of church life and administration, the situation was still more disheartening, presenting a picture of degradation and decadence. Patriarchs were removed and reinstated at whim with bewildering rapidity. The church became corrupt under Turkish oppression, and it was also humiliated and persecuted. This was the age of the "new martyrs." Eyewitness accounts of these martyrdoms are given in Papadopoulos and Lizardos' translation, *New Martyrs of the Turkish Yoke* (1985).

Paradoxically, the patriarch's position and prestige were strengthened as he was invested with civil and church power. This permitted some degree of organization, as well as an extended jurisdiction over the faithful adherents of Eastern Orthodoxy. The ethnarchic system introduced by the Ottomans thus brought most of the autocephalous Orthodox churches under the authority and direction of Constantinople. Yet the outward conditions remained deplorable, allowing for neither stability in church life nor missionary growth.

Independence from the Turkish yoke in the 19th century, accompanied by the general growth of national consciousness in Europe at the time, resulted in the creation of the modern national churches. The first of these, the Church of Greece, was recognized by the Ecumenical Patriarchate of Constantinople in 1850. Serbia claimed control in 1879, Romania in 1885, Bulgaria in 1860. This in turn led to a parallel interest in local historiography. Scholarship during this period in the area of church history was influenced by Western methodology. Major works appeared by K. Kontogiannis, and by Philaretos Vapheides of the Halki Theological School in Constantinople. A.D. Kyriakos produced a church history in three volumes.

Historiographical literature during this dark period generally lacked the vigor and versatility of the early and Byzantine eras. The approach was often restrictive in terms of confessional understanding, of ecclesiastical jurisdiction, and of national background. The schools and seminaries – predominantly, although not only in Greek-speaking regions – encouraged education and growth, but the historiography of Eastern Orthodoxy largely declined in quality, even after the establishment of printing presses. (Representatives of this period are Laonikos Halkokondylis in the 15th century, Patriarch Dositheos of Jerusalem in the 16th, Meletios of Athens who wrote an ecclesiastical history in three volumes in the 17th, the encyclopaedist Evgenios Voulgaris in the 18th, and Patriarch Konstantios I in the 19th century.) As in the early centuries of Christianity, history was largely written out in blood, not in ink during these years.

The Slavic churches also witnessed a revival at this time, particularly in Russia. P. Alexieff (d.1801) composed a multivolume history of the Greco-Russian church, and metropolitans Plato and Evgeny further produced significant works. Archbishop Philaret of Moscow (1782–1867) published a history of the Russian church, as did both Makarios and Golubinsky. Just as the Byzantine empire was falling to the Moslems, the seeds of the Russian empire were taking root in Moscow, marking the beginning of a remarkable spiritual and liturgical renewal. Russia freed itself from dependence on Constantinople (effectively from as early as 1448) and of subjection to Mongol invaders. There developed an almost messianic mentality.

In the early 18th century, Peter the Great endeavored to bring the traditional ways of the Russian church into greater conformity with Western European ways. Yet, while Orthodox Russia alone escaped the fate of the rest of Eastern Orthodoxy during the four hundred years of Ottoman rule, in the 20th century it was fiercely persecuted. For the Russian church, the 20th century has proven to be, until only recently, a time of gradual and methodical strangulation of church policy and polity. Of all the Eastern Orthodox churches that gained new independence when the Turks yielded their sovereignty to Christian rulers, only the Church of Greece found itself free of communist repression.

During the 20th century numerous historical publications both in the form of collected volumes and monographs have been produced. Academicians in Greece presented more "scholarly" work: Vasileios Stephanides (1878–1958) and Gerasimos Ioannou Konidaris (1905–87). The more "political" approach was espoused in Russia and Paris by Antonii Kartashev (1875–1960). A more "institutional" profile is offered by Vasil Istavridis of the Halki Theological School.

In recent years, Georges Florovsky combined a keen sense of history, a profound depth of theology, and a sincerely irenic attitude. Florovsky proved greatly influential on other contemporary Church historians, such as John Meyendorff and Vlasios Pheidas.

JOHN CHRYSSAVGIS

See also Byzantium; Cameron; Crusades; Eusebius; Greece: Modern; Komnene; Ottoman; Psellos

Further Reading

Bidez, Joseph, and Léon Parmentier, eds., *The Ecclesiastical History of Evagrius with the Scholia*, London: Methuen, 1898; reprinted Amsterdam: Hakkert, 1964, New York: AMS Press, 1979

Bryennios, Nicephorus, *Historia* (History), written early 12th century

Cameron, Averil, *Agathias*, Oxford: Oxford University Press, 1970

Cameron, Averil, *Procopius and the Sixth Century*, London: Duckworth, and Berkeley: University of California Press, 1985

Chalkokondyles, Laonikos, *Historiarum*, written 15th century; reprinted as *Laonikou Chalkokondylou Apodeixis Historian Deka* (History: The Ten Books), in *Patrologiae cursus completus*, series Graeca [*Patrologia Graeca*], edited by J.-P. Migne, vol.159, Paris, 1866

Choniates, Niketas, *Chronike Diegesis*, written before 1204; in English as *O City of Byzantium: Annals of Niketas Choniates*, Detroit: Wayne State University Press, 1984

Corpus scriptorum historiae Byzantinae, 50 vols., Bonn, 1828–97

Croke, Brian, and Alanna Emmett, eds., *History and Historians in Late Antiquity*, Oxford and New York: Pergamon Press, 1983

Drake, Harold Allen, *In Praise of Constantine: A Historical Study and New Translation of Eusebius' Tricennial Orations*, Berkeley: University of California Press, 1976

Ellis, Jane, *The Russian Orthodox Church: A Contemporary History*, London: Croom Helm, and Bloomington: Indiana University Press, 1986

Eusebius of Caesarea, *Historia ecclesiastica*, written 311–25; in English as *The Ecclesiastical History* and *The History of the Church from Christ to Constantine*

Evagrius Scholasticus, *Historia ecclesiastica*, written 6th century; in English as *Ecclesiastical History*, London: Methuen, 1898; New York: AMS Press, 1979

Filaret [Philaret] of Moscow, *Istoriia russkoi tserkvi* (History of the Russian Church), Moscow, 1848–53; in German as *Geschichte der Kirche Russlands*, 2 vols., Frankfurt: Baer, 1872

Florovsky, Georges, *Puti russkogo bogosloviia*, Paris: YMCA Press, 1937; in English as *Ways of Russian Theology*, Belmont, MA: Nordland, 1972

Geanakoplos, Deno John, *Medieval Western Civilization and the Byzantine and Islamic Worlds: Interaction of Three Cultures*, Lexington, MA: Heath, 1979

Georgios Synkellos [Georgius Syncellus], *Ekloge Chronographias* (Selections from the Chronographers), edited by Alden Mosshammer as *Ecloga Chronographica*, Leipzig: Teubner, 1984

Glykas, Michael, *Biblos chronike* (World Chronicle), written 12th century

Golubinskii, Evgenii, *Istoriia russkoi tserkvi* (History of the Russian Church), 2 vols. in 4, 1880–81; reprinted The Hague: Mouton, 1969

Gregoras, Nikephoros, *Historia Rhomaike* (Byzantine History), 37 vols., written c.1351–58

Heisenberg, August, *Quellen und Studien zur spätbyzantinischen Geschichte* (Sources and Studies in Later Byzantine History), London: Variorum, 1973

Henry, René, ed., *Photius: Bibliothèque*, 9 vols., Paris: Belles Lettres, 1959–91

Hunger, Herbert, *Die hochsprachliche profane Literatur der Byzantiner* (The Literate Secular Literature of the Byzantines), 2 vols., Munich: Beck, 1978

Hussey, Joan M., *The Orthodox Church in the Byzantine Empire*, Oxford: Oxford University Press, 1986

John of Ephesus, *Commentarii de beatis orientalibus*, written 6th century; in English as *Lives of the Eastern Saints*, edited by E.W. Brooks, Paris: Firmin-Didot, 1923–25

Kaegi, Walter Emil, *Byzantium and the Decline of Rome*, Princeton: Princeton University Press, 1968

Kananos, John [Cananus, Joannes], *De Constantinopolis obsidione* (On the Siege of Constantinople), written 1422; reprinted as *Johannis Canani de Constantinopolis obsidione*, edited by E. Pinto, Naples: Scientifica, 1968

Kantakouzenos, Ioannes [John Cantacuzenus], *Historia*, written c.1362–69

Karayarmopoulos, John [Karagiannopoulos, I.E.], and Günter Weiss, *Quellenkunde zur Geschichte von Byzanz (324–1453)* (Sources of Byzantine History, 324–1453), 2 vols., Wiesbaden: Harrassowitz, 1982

Kartashev, Anton Vladimirovich, *Ocherki po istorii russkoi tserkvi* (Essays on the Russian Church), 2 vols., Paris: YMCA, 1959

Kinnamos, John, *Epitome* (Résumé), written 1180–83; in English as *Deeds of John and Manuel Comnenus*, New York: Columbia University Press, 1976

Komnene [Comnena], Anna, *The Alexiad*, written 1138–48; in English as *The Alexiad of Anna Comnena*, Harmondsworth and Baltimore: Penguin, 1969

Konidares, Gerasimos Ioannou, *Ekklesiastike historia* (General Ecclesiastical History), 2 vols., Athens, 1954–70

Kyriakos, A. Diomedes, *Geschichte der orientalischen Kirchen von 1453–1898* (History of the Eastern Church from 1453 to 1898), Leipzig: Deichart, 1902

Leo the Deacon [Diakonos Leon], *Historia* (History), written before 992

Magoulias, Harry J., ed. and trans., *Doukas: Decline and Fall of Byzantium to the Ottoman Turks: An Annotated Translation of "Historia Turco-Byzantina,"* Detroit: Wayne State University Press, 1975

Malalas, John, *Chronographia*, written 6th century; in English as *The Chronicle of John Malalas: A Translation*, Melbourne: University of Melbourne Press, 1986

Maloney, George, *A History of Orthodox Theology since 1453*, Belmont, MA: Nordland, 1976

Manasses, Constantine, *Synopsis historike*, written 12th century; in English as *The Chronicle of Constantine Manasses from the Creation of the World to the Reign of Constantine the Great*, Washington, DC: Dumbarton Oaks, 1995

Mansi, Giovanni Domenico, *Sacrorum conciliorum nova et amplissima collectio* (The New and Most Complete Collection of the Sacred Councils), 31 vols., 1759–98 [reprinted and continued by L. Petit and J.B. Martin, 53 vols., Paris: 1901–27]

Meletios of Athens, *Ekklisiastike historia* (Ecclesiastical History), 2 vols., Vienna, 1783

Meyendorff, John, *L'Eglise orthodoxe: hier et aujourd'hui*, Paris: Seuil, 1960, revised 1995; in English as *The Orthodox Church: Its Past and Role in the World Today*, London: Darton Longman and Todd, and New York: Pantheon, 1962

Nestor, *Povest' vremennykh let*, completed 1013–15; in English as *The Russian Primary Chronicle: Laurentian Text*, Cambridge, MA: Mediaeval Academy of America, 1953

Nicol, Donald M., *The Last Centuries of Byzantium, 1261–1453*, London: Hart Davis, and New York: St. Martin's Press, 1972

Nikodemus the Hagiorite, Saint, *Philokalia*, compiled 18th century; in English as *The Philokalia: The Complete Text*, London: Faber, 1979–

Papadopoulos, L., and G. Lizardos, trans., *New Martyrs of the Turkish Yoke*, Seattle: St. Nectarios Press, 1985

Pheidas, Vlasios, *Ekklesiastike historia tes Rossias, 988–1988* (Ecclesiastical History of Russia, 988–1988), Athens: Apostolike Diakonia tes Ekklesias tes Hellados, 1988

Philippides, Marias, *Emperors, Patriarchs, and Sultans of Constantinople, 1373–1513: An Anonymous Greek Chronicle of the Sixteenth Century*, Brookline, MA: Hellenic College, 1990

Photius, Patriarch, *Bibliotheca*, written 9th century; in English as *The Library of Photius I: Saint Patriarch of Constantinople*, London: SPCK, 1920, and as *The Bibliotheca: A Selection*, London: Duckworth, 1994

Pospielovsky, Dimitry, *The Russian Church under the Soviet Regime, 1917–1982*, 2 vols., Crestwood, NY: St. Vladimir's Seminary Press, 1984

Psellos, Michael, *Chronographia*, c.1059–78; in English as *The Chronographia of Michael Psellus*, New Haven: Yale University Press, 1953, revised as *Fourteen Byzantine Rulers*, 1966

Roberson, Ronald G., *The Eastern Christian Churches: A Brief Survey*, 5th revised edition, Rome: Pontifical Oriental Institute, 1995

Runciman, Steven, *The Great Church in Captivity: A Study of the Patriarchate of Constantinople from the Eve of the Turkish Conquest to the Greek War of Independence*, Cambridge: Cambridge University Press, 1968

Schmitt, John, ed., *The Chronicle of Morea: A History in Political Verse, Relating the Establishment of Feudalism in Greece by the Franks in the Thirteenth Century*, Groningen: Bouma, 1967; New York: AMS Press, 1979

Schwartz, Edward, ed., *Acta conciliorum oecumenicorum*, 12 vols., Berlin: de Gruyter, 1914–84

Sphrantzes, George, *Chronikon*, written 1450s; in English as *The Fall of the Byzantine Empire: A Chronicle*, Amherst: University of Massachusetts Press, 1980

Stavrides, Vasileios [Istavridis, Vasil], *Historia tou Oikoumenikou Patriarcheiou* (History of the Ecumenical Patriarchate), Athens, 1967

Stephanides, Vasileios [Basilius], *Ekklisiastike historia* (Ecclesiastical History), Athens: Aster, 1948

Theophanes the Confessor, *Chronographia*, written 810–14; in English as *The Chronicle of Theophanes Confessor: Byzantine and Near Eastern History, AD 284–813*, Oxford and New York: Oxford University Press, 1997

Vapheides, Philaretos, *Ekklesiastike historia: apo tou Kyriou emon Iesou Christou mechri ton kath emas chronon* (Ecclesiastical History: From Our Lord Jesus Christ to Our Times), Constantinople: Voutyra, 1884

Vlasto, A.P., *The Entry of the Slavs into Christendom: An Introduction to the Medieval History of the Slavs*, Cambridge: Cambridge University Press, 1970

Ware, Timothy, *The Orthodox Church*, Harmondsworth and Baltimore: Penguin, 1963; revised 1994

Ware, Timothy, *Eustratios Argenti: A Study of the Greek Church under Turkish Rule*, Oxford: Oxford University Press, 1964

Wilson, Nigel Guy, *Scholars of Byzantium*, London: Duckworth, and Baltimore: Johns Hopkins University Press, 1983

Xanthopoulos, Nikephoros Kallistos [Callistus], *Ecclesiasticae historiae* (Ecclesiastical History), written 14th century; reprinted in *Patrologiae cursus*, series Graeca [*Patrologia Graeca*], edited by J.-P. Migne, vols. 145–47

Zonaras, Joannes, *Chronikon*, 18 books, written 12th century; in English as *Zonaras' Account of the Neo-Flavian Emperors: A Commentary*, Ann Arbor, MI: University Microfilms International, 1977

Eaton, Richard Maxwell 1940–

US social historian of South Asia and Islam

Richard Maxwell Eaton has devoted his career to understanding and explaining the process by which over a quarter of the population of South Asia converted to Islam, comprising over a third of all Muslims in the world today. His control over the relevant primary texts, particularly his extensive use of Persian language sources, has enabled him to explain the process of conversion to Islam during the 13th–18th centuries in particularly nuanced ways. For several regions of Pakistan, India, and Bangladesh, he has analyzed the interrelationships among the policies of Muslim rulers, the diverse roles of Muslim religious institutions and individuals, and the socio-economic transformations concomitant with conversion to Islam.

Eaton's work sheds much light on the contested issue of what being "Muslim" means in South Asia. Muslim identity has been highly politicized in the troubled development of nationalism in India, Pakistan, and Bangladesh. The idea that Muslims comprised a distinct nation led the British to "partition" India and Pakistan in 1947, leaving between 10 and 15 million dead or homeless. Subsequently, within Pakistan itself, regional identities have frequently outweighed Islamic nationalism, leading to bloody civil wars. The most decisive of these conflicts culminated in 1971, when eastern Bengal split off as Bangladesh. For its part, India continues to be wracked by communal conflict over the place of Muslim identity in a predominantly Hindu country. By studying conversion to Islam in regions in each of these countries, Eaton has done much to help us understand the roots of these conflicts.

The issue of Muslim identity has also divided scholars. Aziz Ahmad, S.M. Ikram, Ayesha Jalal, I.H. Qureshi, Francis Robinson, and Farzana Shaikh, among others, emphasize – in different ways – Muslim national identity. Through case studies across South Asia, Eaton demonstrates the complexity of conversion to Islam, showing it to be the result not of state policy by Muslim rulers but rather of the assimilation of local traditions with Islamic rituals, cosmologies, and literatures, creating a distinctly regional synthesis. Paralleling his approach, scholars such as Imtiaz Ahmad, Christopher Bayly, Paul Brass, Ashgar Ali Engineer, Peter Hardy, Mashirul Hasan, and Mattison Mines stress the regional component in South Asian Muslim communities.

Eaton's early work concentrated on the place of Muslim holy men in society and politics in the Deccan region (south-central India). His doctorate became the basis of his first monograph: *Sufis of Bijapur, 1300–1700* (1978). His "Sufi Folk Literature and the Expansion of Indian Islam" (1974) analyzed songs about women's domestic work as a medium for the transmission of Islamic values. His *Firuzabad* with George Mitchell (1990), specifically explored the architectural expressions of Islamic religious and political institutions. His forthcoming *Social History of the Deccan* (in The New Cambridge History of India series) will survey scholarship on the premodern history of this region.

In the 1970s, Eaton undertook an intensive study of the vital province of Punjab in the upper Indus plain. His pathbreaking work on this region demonstrated how non-Muslim pastoral nomadic peoples, particularly Jats, settled down in the rich but arid lands of west Punjab. Their harnessing of irrigation technology from West Asia and their connections with the prestigious Sufi lineages combined to transform them into Muslim sedentary peasants. Among Eaton's most influential articles on this region are "Court of Man, Court of God" (1982) and "The Political and Religious Authority of the Shrine of Baba Farid in Pakpattan, Punjab" (1982). Each of these articles demonstrates a different aspect of the complex interaction between Sufi shrines and both the local population and the Mughal imperial and British colonial states.

Most recently, Eaton has examined conversion to Islam in eastern Bengal, today the largest community of Muslims in the world. A combination of Mughal and Turkish political expansion, sedentization (through technological paradigm shifts, particularly from swidden to wet rice agriculture), and charismatic Sufis inspired mass conversion to Islam among the lightly Hinduized population. The mosques and *madrasas* (Islamic religious schools), which the Muslim settlers constructed on the frontier as it gradually moved eastward across Bengal, formed focal points for the newly converted and settled peasantry. Eaton's *The Rise of Islam and the Bengal Frontier, 1204–1760* (1993) received due recognition through both the 1994 Albert Hourani book award from the Middle East Studies Association and also the 1995 Ananda Kentish Coomaraswamy book prize from the Association of Asian Studies; no other book has ever been so honored. For this book, Eaton drew heavily on Mughal sources, with the addition of local Bengali records and chronicles, coins, architecture, stone inscriptions, and folk traditions to demonstrate the complexity of the process of blending Islamic ideas and institutions into Bengali regional culture.

Eaton has over the years also turned his attention to other regions of South Asia. He has examined the south Indian state of Kerala – in "Multiple Lenses" (1993) – and Afghanistan – in his master's thesis "The First Afghan War" (1967). His "Conversion to Christianity among the Nagas, 1876–1971" (1984) takes up the issue of tribal conversion to Christianity in the British colonial context in the northeast corner of India; this article forms the theoretical and methodological basis for his subsequent work on conversion to Islam in India. Further, Eaton has located South Asian Islam in the larger contexts of West Asia and the world through his *Islamic History as Global History* (1990), commissioned by the American Historical Society.

MICHAEL H. FISHER

Biography
Born Grand Rapids, Michigan, 8 December 1940. Received BA, College of Wooster, 1962; MA, University of Virginia, 1967; PhD, University of Wisconsin, Madison, 1969. Taught at Walton High School, Virginia, 1964–65; and University of Arizona, from 1972.

Principal Writings
"The First Afghan War," MA thesis, University of Virginia, 1967
"Sufi Folk Literature and the Expansion of Indian Islam," *History of Religions* 14 (1974), 117–27
Sufis of Bijapur, 1300–1700: Social Roles of Sufis in Medieval India, 1978
"Court of Man, Court of God: Local Perceptions of the Shrine of Baba Farid, Pakpattan, Punjab," in Richard C. Martin, ed., *Islam in Local Contexts*, 1982

"The Political and Religious Authority of the Shrine of Baba Farid in Pakpattan, Punjab," in Barbara Metcalf, ed., *Moral Conduct and Authority: The Place of "Adab" in South Asian Islam*, 1982

"Conversion to Christianity among the Nagas, 1876-1971," *Indian Economic and Social History Review* 21 (1984), 1-44

With George Mitchell, *Firuzabad: Palace City of the Deccan*, 1990

Islamic History as Global History, 1990

"Multiple Lenses: Differing Perspectives of 15th-century Calicut," in Laurie Sears, ed., *Autonomous Histories, Particular Truths: Essays in Honor of Professor John Smail*, 1993

The Rise of Islam and the Bengal Frontier, 1204-1760, 1993

Eberhard, Wolfram 1909–1989

German sociologist and social historian

A scholar of the history, society, and culture of Western, Central, and Eastern Asia, Wolfram Eberhard wrote works that examined the fields of history, sociology, frontier studies, folklore, religion, popular literature, and the history of astronomy.

Eberhard's training in both classical sinology as well as modern sociological and ethnological research methodologies enabled him to pursue research in history and social institutions over the entire span of Chinese history, as well as conducting field work on social institutions in China, Korea, Turkey, and Central Asia. He could study problems in ancient texts, and equally well engage in contemporary field research, devise and carry out surveys, and work with statistical data.

Eberhard was one of the pioneers in going beyond the limits of the conventional "Confucian" perspective of Chinese history and pursuing serious scholarship on the origins of Chinese society, the characteristics of regional cultures underneath the "great China culture," and the relations between the Chinese and the various non-Chinese peoples on the frontiers of the constantly changing areas of Chinese settlement and control. Following on the momentum of the Chinese folklore studies movement of the 1920s, he contributed pioneering research to folklore collecting and analysis, and delved into numerous aspects of the life and culture of the Chinese lower classes whom the Confucian tradition had largely overlooked. In many aspects of Chinese studies, he opened up avenues of scholarship that are now regarded as common areas for research. His broad scholarship inspired a generation of students who have pursued insightful research along the many paths he first explored. Unfortunately, some younger scholars have been too quick to criticize his errors while forgetting his groundbreaking scholarship, on which their own research rests.

In the latter half of the 1930s Eberhard began to publish theoretical work on the origins and development of Chinese society, its diverse ethnic composition, and its complex social structure. He argued that Chinese society was the result of the fusion of various tribal groups into local cultures, which ultimately fused into a larger Chinese society, with the earlier local cultures creating regional distinctions. Some of the original tribes were fully absorbed into the resulting Chinese society while others survived as minority groups under pressure to assimilate into the larger and more technologically advanced Chinese culture. This research is discussed in his two-volume *Lokalkulturen im alten China* (1942-43; vol. 2 as *The Local Cultures of South and East China*, 1968) and other works.

His *Social Mobility in Traditional China* (1962) argued that there was greater social mobility in premodern China than in other pre-industrial societies, which strongly contributed to the striking continuity of Chinese culture.

His research on the peoples on the Chinese frontiers and the Chinese interactions with them appeared in several major works such as *Conquerors and Rulers* (1952; revised 1964) and *China's Minorities* (1982).

Many of Eberhard's articles were reprinted along with some newly published essays in the six volumes of his collected papers. His publications reveal his enduring interests in Chinese and Turkish folklore and folklife, and in the geographically, ethnically, and socially marginal people of China.

From 1937 to 1948, Eberhard taught history at Ankara University and contributed significantly to the development of sinological scholarship in Turkey. During this period he published on a wide variety of subjects, including Chinese folklore, popular literature, history, minorities and local cultures in China, the relations between the Chinese and the peoples of Central Asia, and Turkish history, society, and popular culture. The first edition of his *A History of China* (1947) was published in Turkish and later translated into German, English, and French.

Eberhard's voluminous publications on Chinese and Turkish folklore and folklife spanned his entire career. The results of his folklore collecting and research appeared in several compilations as well as in many other collections of Chinese folktales, songs, theater plays, novels, and parables. Some of these collections are comprised of a voluminous amount of data with only preliminary analysis, since he believed that it was his responsibility to make his data available for research by other scholars even though his analysis was incomplete. The publication of his *Typen chinesischer Volksmärchen* (Types of Chinese Folktales, 1936) provided the topological framework for bringing Chinese folktales into the systematic study of world folktales. He also published numerous studies analyzing the content, structure, and transmission of Chinese folktales and folk customs. Many of these analyses may be seen in his second and fourth volumes of collected papers: *Studies in Chinese Folklore and Related Essays* (1970), and *Moral and Social Values of the Chinese* (1971). Eberhard's sociological viewpoint also influenced his research on folktale transmission. Not only was he concerned with the tale-teller, the audience, and the social context, but he also showed that the respective genders, ages, and family relationships of tale-tellers and audiences have a marked influence on the content of a tale. His research on this aspect of tale-telling is the theme of his *Studies in Taiwanese Folktales* (1970).

In collaboration with P.N. Boratav, Eberhard published *Typen türkischer Volksmärchen* (Types of Turkish Folktales, 1953), thereby providing a topological framework for the study and comparison of Turkish folktales within a worldwide context. This was preceded and followed by several related publications, including his *Minstrel Tales from Southeastern Turkey* (1955).

Eberhard's interest in the culture of ordinary people included extensive research on Chinese popular religion. His *Guilt and Sin in Traditional China* (1967) analyzed the widely distributed moralistic tracts (shan-shu) as a source for Chinese moral and social values outside the orthodox Confucian tradition. In another pioneering example of research methodology, his long article "Temple-building Activities in Medieval and Modern China: An Experimental Study" (1964) demonstrated the way statistical data gathered from local histories can be used to study certain historical aspects of religion in China. His publications on Chinese popular religion influenced many of the younger scholars who founded the Society for the Study of Chinese Religions and its journal (1976).

Eberhard also turned his attention to the constantly recurring problem of the interpretation of symbols in folk literature, art, and religion. His *Lexikon chinesischer Symbole* (1983; *Dictionary of Chinese Symbols*, 1986) examined symbols for their historical, literary, religious, and metaphorical implications, and also showed that many symbols have sexual implications not previously recognized. His earlier interest in symbols can also be seen in the series of studies on Chinese dreams published from 1966 to 1978, including *Chinesische Träume und ihre Deutung* (Chinese Dreams and Their Interpretation, 1971).

Eberhard cofounded the Asian Folklore and Social Life monographs series (Taipei) which hosted the publication of many scholars' works on relevant topics in Eastern, Central, and Western Asia, and also reprinted several series of valuable and long out-of-print Chinese monographs and collections relating to Chinese folklore.

ALVIN P. COHEN

See also China: Ancient

Biography

Born Potsdam, 17 March 1909, son of an astrophysicist. Attended the Victoria Gymnasium, Potsdam; studied classical Chinese and social anthropology at Berlin University, PhD 1933; and modern Chinese at the seminar for Oriental languages in Berlin, diploma 1929. Worked in the Berlin Anthropological Museum: first trip to China in 1934, to collect ethnographic materials for the museum; taught German and Latin at universities in Peking. Director, Grassi Museum Asiatic section, Leipzig, 1936–37. Received a Moses Mendelssohn fellowship in 1937 to travel and lecture in the US. Also traveled through Japan to China and Hong Kong; since he opposed the Nazis, he could not return to Germany; while in Hong Kong, he received the offer of a professorship at Ankara University, where his family joined him and he lived as a stateless resident and taught, 1937–48; taught sociology, University of California, Berkeley, 1948–76 (emeritus); then independent researcher. Married 1) Alide Roemer, 1934 (2 sons); 2) Irene Ohnesorg, 1985. Died 15 August 1989.

Principal Writings

Typen chinesischer Volksmärchen (Types of Chinese Folktales), 1936
Chinese Fairy-tales and Folk-tales, 1937; revised as *Folktales of China*, 1965
Kultur und Siedlung der Randvölker Chinas (Culture and Settlement of the Marginal People of China), 1942
Lokalkulturen im alten China, 2 vols., 1942–43; vol. 2 revised in English as *The Local Cultures of South and East China*, 1968
Çin Tarihi, 1947; in German as *Chinas Geschichte*, 1948; in English as *A History of China*, 1950, revised 1969; 4th edition, 1977
Das Toba-Reich Nordchinas, eine soziologische Untersuchung (The Toba Empire of North China: A Sociological Investigation), 1949
Chinese Festivals, 1952; revised 1972
Conquerors and Rulers: Social Forces in Medieval China, 1952; revised 1964

With Pertev Naili Boratav, *Typen türkischer Volksmärchen* (Types of Turkish Folktales), 1953
Minstrel Tales from Southeastern Turkey, 1955
Social Mobility in Traditional China, 1962
"Temple-building Activities in Medieval and Modern China: An Experimental Study," *Monumenta Serica* 23 (1964): 264–318; reprinted in his *Moral and Social Values of the Chinese: Collected Essays*, 1971
Erzählungsgut aus Südost-China (Narratives from Southeast China), 1966
Guilt and Sin in Traditional China, 1967
Settlement and Social Change in Asia, 1967
Sternkunde und Weltbild im alten China (Astronomy and Conceptions of the World in Ancient China), 1970
Studies in Chinese Folklore and Related Essays, 1970
Studies in Taiwanese Folktales, 1970
Chinesische Träume und ihre Deutung (Chinese Dreams and Their Interpretation), 1971
Moral and Social Values of the Chinese, 1971
China und seine westlichen Nachbarn: Beiträge zur mittelalterlichen und neueren Geschichte Zentralasiens (China and Her Western Neighbors: Contributions to the History of Central Asia in the Middle Ages and Modern Times), 1978
China's Minorities: Yesterday and Today, 1982
Life and Thought of Ordinary Chinese, 1982
Lexikon chinesischer Symbole: Geheime Sinnbilder in Kunst und Literatur, Leben und Denken der Chinesen, 1983; in English as *A Dictionary of Chinese Symbols: Hidden Symbols in Chinese Life and Thought*, 1986

Further Reading

Allan, Sarah, and Alvin P. Cohen, eds., *Legend, Lore, and Religion in China: Essays in Honor of Wolfram Eberhard on His Seventieth Birthday*, San Francisco: Chinese Materials Center, 1979

Eccles, W.J. 1917–

Canadian (British-born) historian of French Canada

The most influential modern English-language historian of New France, W.J. Eccles was intimately associated with most major historical enterprises of the second half of the 20th century in Canada and the United States: the Centenary series, the *Dictionary of Canadian Biography*, the Histories of the American Frontier, the New American Nation series, the *Historical Atlas of Canada*, and the *Encyclopedia of the North American Colonies*. His iconoclastic treatment of French experience in North America stressed the uniqueness of Canadian history and of the society it shaped.

Until the 1960s, the history of New France in the English-speaking world was synonymous with the works of Francis Parkman, who perceived the struggle for empire in North America as one that pitted the forces of Protestant progress against those of Catholic reaction. Although the French colony had some heroic figures, its inhabitants were firmly under the sway of the Roman Catholic church which condemned them to obedience to autocracy, ignorance, and superstition. The British conquest of 1760 was a "happy calamity," freeing them from despotic oppression. As a student, Eccles accepted the Parkman's views but, while researching his thesis on governor Frontenac, sources in the French archives suggested a very different interpretation. On the one hand, Eccles was impressed with the efficacy of military government in meeting challenges and, on the other, he admired a state that put the well-being of citizens above the market. This vision has led Matteo Sanfilippo to label Eccles a "red tory."

Eccles first made his mark in this thesis debunking governor Frontenac, one of Parkman's heroes, by portraying him as an impecunious noble bent on enrichment and self-aggrandizement, an inept administrator whose greatest talent was to be able to mislead both his minister and historians. He followed up this by a scathing attack on Parkman and the Anglo-Protestant disdain for New France shared by many of his colleagues in a paper published in the *William and Mary Quarterly* in 1961. His reputation as a revisionist made, Eccles turned to writing syntheses that progressively widened the scope of his enquiry. New France was not just another New World society but a unique blend of Europe and America fashioned by its location as an outpost of empire that produced a warrior ethos. This view was most clearly defined in his important 1971 essay – "The Social, Economic, and Political Influence of the Military Establishment in New France." Here he posited that the military was a major staple of the Canadian economy draining "a goodly quantity of the available supply of brains, initiative and ability." His work on the military was pursued mainly in a score of individual biographies and the introductory essay, "French Forces in North America during the Seven Years' War," that he wrote for vol. 3 of the *Dictionary of Canadian Biography*.

Interest in the military naturally evolved into a study of the place of the fur trade in French imperialism and the role of native peoples. In 1979 he challenged the accepted interpretation of H.A. Innis and contributed in reopening debates on the nature of the fur trade (1987). This interest brought Eccles to examine more closely relations between the native peoples and French imperialism. As a result of his unsuccessful defence of an Ontario tribe's land claims, he produced "Sovereignty Association, 1534–1783" in 1984, which argued that the French never controlled the lands occupied by native peoples (1987). This influential article served as historical background evidence for the multitude of similar cases argued before the courts in recent years.

Because Eccles' major syntheses – *The Canadian Frontier* (1969) and *France in America* (1972) – were widely adopted as required readings in early Canadian history survey courses in universities across the country, English Canada's vision of New France was shaped by his interpretation of a paternalistic society ruled by a military aristocracy that did not exploit the peasantry. He succeeded in overcoming the Anglo-Protestant historiographical tradition that denied legitimacy to New France and also in establishing the French experience as a vital component of Canada's uniqueness. His impact in French Québec was not as great, however. This was not because his works were unknown (although only an abridged version of his *Frontenac* was translated into French) or not respected. But francophone historians rejected his emphasis on the importance of the military and aristocracy, concentrating instead on the main subjects of social history that had a greater resonance in their own society – merchants, artisans, and the peasantry. Thus, despite his sympathy for Quebec's distinct society, Eccles did not completely succeed in bridging the gap that separates the country's two solitudes.

JOHN A. DICKINSON

See also Parkman

Biography

William John Eccles. Born in Thirsk, Yorkshire, 17 July 1917; moved to Canada, 1928. Served in the Royal Canadian Air Force during World War II. Attended McGill University, Montreal, BA 1948, MA 1951, PhD 1955; and the Sorbonne, 1951–52. Taught at University of Manitoba, 1953–57; University of Alberta, 1957–63; and University of Toronto (rising to professor), 1963–83 (emeritus). Married Margaret Jean Jaffray, 1948 (2 sons, 1 daughter).

Principal Writings

Frontenac: The Courtier Governor, 1959
"The History of New France According to Francis Parkman," *William and Mary Quarterly* 18 (1961), 163–75
Canada under Louis XIV, 1664–1701, 1964
The Canadian Frontier, 1534–1760, 1969
"The Social, Economic, and Political Significance of the Military Establishment in New France," *Canadian Historical Review* 52 (1971), 1–22; also in his *Essays on New France*
France in America, 1972; revised 1990
Essays on New France, 1987

Further Reading

Codignola, Luca *et al.*, "A Forum on W.J. Eccles," *British Journal of Canadian Studies* 11 (1996), 66–89

Ecclesiastical History

The writing of ecclesiastical history within the Christian tradition is closely linked to the evolution of ideas about the relationship between the sacred and the secular. The understanding of this relationship was originally derived from the Jewish historical consciousness with its paradoxical blending of the prophetic and apocalyptic traditions: the traditions in which, on the one hand, God was seen to reveal himself to mankind through the events of history and to be responsible for those events, and on the other hand, where it was believed that God would irrevocably alter the course of history and in effect bring time itself to an end.

The Christian adaptation of apocalyptic categories emphasizes the resurrected Christ and his dual role as redeemer and judge at the end of time. This idea produces an ecclesiology in which the sacred and the secular are understood to exist in conflictual tension and in which the supreme redemptive act (Christ's sacrifice on the cross) came into history from outside of time. The implication of this is that the process of human history (ordinary time) in and of itself does not lead to salvation and does not possess any necessary correlation to divine objectives. The task of the church in this view is to maintain the efficacy of Christ's message in the face of a world and society overtly hostile to sacred ends. With its overtones of social conflict this interpretation has been most influential during periods in which Christianity and the church lay outside the established power structure and emphasized the transformative character of the Christian message.

In contrast the prophetic tradition, with its concept of history as an immanent process, while socially radical in origin, has been very influential with thinkers for whom the ends of church and society are seen to be harmonious and complementary. In this view the church perfects a society that is infused with divinely ordained structures. Its role is that of the leaven in the lump rather than the agent of fundamental transformation. Redemption is understood to be an incremental process over which the church presides; but it is not seen to be antithetical to the surrounding social environment. Both of these traditions have coexisted within Christian ecclesiastical writing and not infrequently have been blended together by the same author. The tension between these two modes of interpretation established the fundamental issues of Christian ecclesiastical history and have provided a structure within which the significance of its development can be understood.

In the first generations after the death of Christ, Christian thought had not yet developed a clearly defined sense of history, nor had the church acquired an articulated institutional profile. The image that emerged, however, suggested that the church was seen to fit into the apocalyptic model of history. The authors of the New Testament believed they were living in the end of time and they looked to the church to prepare the people of God for the imminence of the second coming. Functioning within a context in which their beliefs and values conflicted overtly with those of the dominant pagan society, they saw in their rituals and institutions a divine mechanism distinct from and leading to the ultimate judgment and redemption of the world.

This apocalyptic understanding of the church dominated Christian thinking up to the time of Constantine. His conversion to Christianity transformed the church from a persecuted institution into the guardian of the dominant ideology of the Roman empire. This transformation necessitated a rearticulation of the relationship of the church to the rest of society. Eusebius of Caesarea (c. 260–339) provided this new interpretation with his *Ecclesiastical History* (written 311–325). For Eusebius history was a process guided by divine providence that culminated in the creation of a Christian empire by Constantine. He explicitly identified the emperor as an agent of God's grace, thus integrating secular polity, church, and society into a complementary whole. In constructing his theory of a Christian empire, Eusebius reached back to the Jewish tradition – stemming from the prophets – that recognized the empires of the world to be active agents of God's will. In so doing he recapitulated for the Christian tradition the idea that the secular world functioned as a means to the divine ends intended by God, and he integrated the significance of time into the historical process itself.

St. Augustine of Hippo pushed the idea of historical process even further and effectively integrated the apocalyptic and prophetic traditions. In *The City of God* he described history as a conflict between two principles manifested in opposing social orders: the City of Man and the City of God. These two orders existed side by side and intermingled with each other, but they were distinguished by the ends that ruled their course. The City of Man was guided by the selfish ambitions of unredeemed humanity while the City of God developed in accordance with divine ends. The City of Man was capable of accomplishing some notable tasks – Augustine saw political institutions as a barrier against the most unbridled forms of human passion – but the frailty of human nature inevitably dragged the secular institutions of the world into rapacious conflicts. The course of history, then, when considered apart from divine grace, was marked by the cyclical rise and fall of monuments to the mistaken quest for power and domination.

Tempering this pessimistic view of human affairs was Augustine's vision of the role of grace and love – the fundamental principles of the City of God. Moving against the destructive forces of fallen mankind, the unifying force of love, given to the world through the sacrifice and grace of Christ, made possible the progressive creation of the City of God. The church formed the visible sacramental manifestation of this order, but was itself subject to the degrading activity of the secular city. Ultimately the City of God was built over time by individuals who chose allegiance to the sacred rather than the secular principle thereby enabling the divine purpose of God to become manifest within human society. Complementing this concept of progressive development Augustine also looked to the events of the second coming to complete the process of history and to reveal the City of God in its full triumph.

Augustine's system successfully blended the apocalyptic and immanent traditions of Christian thought. His skeptical view of secular institutions, however, did not harmonize well with the very different social conditions of the Middle Ages, and the dynamic component of his system was discarded in favor of a more static vision of society and the church. Medieval authors were influenced by both modes of thought, but deemphasized the sense of urgency associated with the apocalyptic tradition. Medieval thought transmuted the end of time into a distant future that had little impact on the course of human events. At the same time, the human condition was believed to be permeated with the divine and to be a microcosm of the hierarchical structure of the universe. The sacred and the profane intermingled on every level. The genre of the lives of the saints pointed repeatedly to the presence of the eternal within human experience, while the development of an elaborate liturgical ritual underlined the sacramental character of daily life and the dependence of the political realm on the religious. In general the outlook of the medieval world was ahistorical. The dominant pattern of time was cyclical (bounded by the distant linearity of the "end times") and the significance of worldly events could be understood only within the context of Christian doctrine.

As the political structures of Europe became more complex and more differentiated from ecclesiastical culture, an image of society began to develop that made possible for the first time positive interpretations of secular social processes. In his *De monarchia*, Dante turned the traditional medieval relationship between church and state around and identified the Holy Roman empire as a holy city designated by God to fulfill the natural ends of mankind. Machiavelli went one step further and divorced the ends of the state from any dependence on divine intervention. For him, the church became one tool among many that could be used for the acquisition of power. While his point of view was rejected by the majority of his contemporaries, and the extremity of his secularism was not to be duplicated until the 19th century, Machiavelli nevertheless was the first writer to extract the church from its religious claims and to interpret it in strictly secular terms.

The Reformation dealt additional blows to medieval ecclesiastical triumphalism by destroying the church's claim to universal authority. While the alliance between church and state may have persisted as a social reality, the reformers' rupture with tradition necessitated a new ecclesiology to justify the break with the past and to rationalize the new political-religious relationships. Protestant reformers tended to reach back to the apocalyptic tradition to justify their defiance of the institutional church, but frequently recast their social ideas within the framework of the immanent tradition – in an effort to identify the new institutional structures with the will of God – as soon as their reforms became the new status quo. They sought to articulate continuity within change by linking their actions with the ideal apostolic church (Augustine's City of God) that they believed themselves to be making manifest.

The cumulative impact of the critiques of the Renaissance and the religious challenges of the Reformation was to shatter the integrity of the religious model of historical interpretation. Over the course of the 17th and 18th centuries the fundamental premises of intellectual discourse shifted away from the traditional reliance on doctrine and authority, and increasingly looked to reason and nature as the touchstones of understanding. Ecclesiastical history started to be distinguished from human history, and as time went on came to be written in reaction to principles articulated for the secular sphere. Throughout this period, histories of the church continued to be written that adhered to the old model, but interpretations reflective of the new emphasis on man as a creature of nature were also composed. Characterized by an emphasis on the universal character of the human experience, and by the universality of the principle of progress, the new historical model traced the development of reason within human culture over time and identified its triumph within the countries of Western Europe in the 18th century. To explain reason's failure prior to this point in time, the advocates of this point of view stated that the progressive forces of society had been obscured and retarded by the forces of superstition and ignorance – typically represented by organized religion.

This period marks the apogee of the immanent tradition of historical interpretation. While the church was frequently treated with skepticism, the structure of history itself continued to be identified with the workings of divine purpose. God was identified as the architect of nature while history was understood to be the mechanism by which mankind was educated in God's plan. Ultimately this educational process would lead to the unification of the spiritual, rational, and historical worlds. This belief in progress transformed the traditional Christian spiritual teleology into a secular process; one in which historical categories played a central role in forging the patterns of thought of the time.

Under the influence of German idealism, traditional historical topics ceased to be regarded as fixed and essential categories (determined by God), but came to be seen as relative elements whose meaning was derived from their historical context. Biblical stories lost much of their typological significance and were reinterpreted within the context of their own time. Christianity itself was discussed within the context of other faiths, and while it continued to be regarded as the epitome of religious expression, historians began to think of it as one example of a broader cultural process that transcended the limits of the Western experience.

This increasing awareness of the relativity of historical periods and of the need to understand the past on its own terms led in the 19th century to the development of historical science. Founded in Germany and predicated on the need to base historical assessments on critically verified documentation, this tradition soon came to dominate historical writing. Within this orientation the church was seen to be one element of society whose significance needed to be determined on the basis of its written record and not on *a priori* doctrinal judgments. But while the church was looked at in secular terms, the founder of the movement, Leopold von Ranke, saw a transcendent divine principle to be the motive force of the historical process. In general this tradition was marked by an overt confidence in the progressive improvement of the human condition and even writers such as Auguste Comte and Karl Marx, who overtly rejected the idea of the divine as a historical reality, based their systems on a belief in progressive development.

An inherent tension existed, however, between the organization of historical ideas around the idea of progress and the scientific methodology requiring that historical judgments be based on unbiased empirical evidence. The logic of the latter pointed to the necessity of eliminating all transcendent principles – not just traditional Christian ones. By rejecting the validity of transcendent principles, however, historians had to define an organizing concept of enquiry that could adequately impose an order and significance on increasingly relative historical constructs. The problem was that the various solutions (idealism, positivism, historical materialism) were themselves extra-historical ideals that could be challenged by the same criteria that had undermined the centrality of traditional Christian concepts. The ability of scientific history to formulate a definitive interpretation of the past was eventually seen to be illusory. As a result, by the 1930s historians were actively seeking new modes of interpretation that could reintegrate ideas and historical criticism. This period saw the flourishing of Marxist and fascist efforts to incorporate ideology into their interpretations, but it also witnessed a revival of overtly Christian interpretations of history.

Responding to the failure of the progressive model occasioned by the disillusionment of World War I and II, writers such as Pierre Teilhard de Chardin, Reinhold Niebuhr, Paul Tillich, and Karl Barth looked back to elements of the Christian tradition to fashion a view of history that could incorporate the experience of evil, demonstrated by the events of the 20th century, and a faith in the efficacy of Christian redemption. Rejecting the optimism of the 19th century, these writers came to the conclusion that the sacred and the profane could never be totally reconciled within history. They saw history as an arena of conflict and not of progress, and they shifted the emphasis back to the apocalyptic tradition by separating events within time from the process of redemption. Typically, the ecclesiology of the post-World War II period emphasized that the church needed to act in opposition to the secular forces of society, and revived the Augustinian distinction between the apostolic and the institutional church.

The most recent developments in ecclesiastical history have followed current historiographical trends. Religious questions – both spiritual and institutional – are being approached from the point of view of social, cultural, and economic history, and historians are incorporating methodologies from other disciplines into their interpretations. In general, the confessional and institutional focus of the past has given way to an acceptance of the multidimensional character of the church's role in society and most recent studies of religion and the church seek to explain religious experience as an outgrowth of other social processes. Typically the study of religion today is thought of as a topical specialty, and the use of Christian principles as the fundamental premise of historical thought is no longer possible in studies addressed to the general population. The effort to incorporate the essentially ahistorical posture of faith into the secular historical worldview still continues as a social tendency, but up to now has had little impact on formal historical studies.

LINCOLN A. DRAPER

See also Butterfield; Comte; Counter-Reformation; Eusebius; Gibbon; Machiavelli; Niebuhr; Ranke; Reformation

Further Reading

Acosta, Jose de, *Historia natural y moral de las Indias*, written 1590, 2 vols., London: Hakluyt Society, 1880; in English as *The Natural and Moral History of the Indies*, edited by Edward Grimeston, New York: Franklin, 1964

Augustine, St., *De civitate dei*, written 413–426; in English as *The City of God*

Barth, Karl, *Die kirchliche Dogmatik*, vol.3, part 1: *Die Lehre von der Schöpfung*, Zollikon: Evangelischer, 1945; in English as *Church Dogmatics 3: The Doctrine of Creation*, Edinburgh: Clark, and New York: Scribner, 1958

Breisach, Ernst, *Historiography: Ancient, Medieval, and Modern*, Chicago: University of Chicago Press, 1983; revised 1994

Butterfield, Herbert, *Christianity and History*, London: Bell, 1949; New York: Scribner, 1950

Dante Alighieri, *De monarchia*, written 1310–13, first printed 1559; in English as *On World-Gorvernment*, 1957

Dawson, Christopher, *The Dynamics of World History*, edited by John J. Mulloy, New York: Sheed and Ward, 1956

Dix, Gregory, *The Shape of the Liturgy*, London: Dacre, 1943; reprinted San Francisco: Harper, 1982

Eusebius of Caesarea, *Historia ecclesiastica*, written 311–25; in English as *The Ecclesiastical History* and *The History of the Church from Christ to Constantine*

Gale, Richard M., ed., *The Philosophy of Time: A Collection of Essays*, Garden City, NY: Anchor, 1967; London: Macmillan, 1968

Gibbon, Edward, *The History of the Decline and Fall of the Roman Empire*, 6 vols., London: Strahan and Cadell, 1776–88

Goodfield, June, and Stephen Toulmin, *The Discovery of Time*, New York: Harper, and London: Hutchinson, 1965

Gutierrez, Gustavo, *Teología de la liberación: perspectives*, Lima: CEP, 1971; in English as *A Theology of Liberation: History, Politics, and Salvation*, Maryknoll, NY: Orbis, 1973, London: SCM Press, 1974

Iggers, Georg G., *The German Conception of History: The National Tradition of Historical Thought from Herder to the Present*, Middletown, CT: Wesleyan University Press, 1968; revised 1983

Lotz, David W., "Philip Schaff and the Idea of Church History", in *A Century of Church History: The Legacy of Philip Schaff*, edited by Henry W. Bowden, Carbondale: Southern Illinois University Press, 1988

Machiavelli, Niccolò, *Il principe*, written 1513–16, printed 1532; in English as *The Prince*

McIntire, C.T., ed., *God, History, and Historians: An Anthology of Modern Christian Views of History*, Oxford and New York: Oxford University Press, 1977

Markus, R.A., *Saeculum: History and Society in the Theology of St. Augustine*, Cambridge: Cambridge University Press, 1970

Niebuhr, Reinhold, *Faith and History: A Comparison of Christian and Modern Views of History*, New York: Scribner, and London: Nisbet, 1949

Ranke, Leopold von, *Die römischen Päpste in den letzten vier Jahrhunderten*, 3 vols., Leipzig: Duncker & Humblot, 1834–36; in English as *The Ecclesiastical and Political History of the Popes of Rome during the Sixteenth and Seventeenth Centuries*, 3 vols., London: Murray, 1840, Philadelphia: Lea and Blanchard, 1841; and as *The History of the Popes*, 3 vols., London: Bell, 1907

Richardson, Alan, *History Sacred and Profane*, Philadelphia: Westminster Press and London: SCM Press, 1964

Smalley, Beryl, *Historians in the Middle Ages*, London: Thames and Hudson, and New York: Scribner, 1974

Tillich, Paul, *The Interpretation of History*, New York: Scribner, 1936

Ecology

Ecology is a word the meaning of which varies considerably, depending on whether the object of analysis is ecology as nature, ecology as a science, ecology as a movement, or ecology as an ideology. The concept originated in the late 1870s in the work of the German zoologist Ernst Haeckel. Like "economy" before it, it was derived from the Greek word *oikos*, or household management. In the early 20th century the science of ecology developed into what was then a minor tradition in the biological sciences, dealing with the interactions of living organisms and their physical environments. But beginning in the 1960s, as a result of a growing sense of ecological crisis, the influence of ecology within the biological sciences increased; meanwhile the term increasingly came to be used as a substitute for the concept of nature in all of its numerous connotations, as a label for the rapidly expanding environmental movement, and to refer to a new form of political ideology, sometimes called "ecologism."

Historical research into environmental questions today can scarcely be imagined apart from the influence exerted by this ideology that emerged with the modern ecological movement. In *Green Political Thought* (1990) Andrew Dobson distinguished between environmentalism, or non-radical environmental politics, and ecologism (best represented by thinkers like British Green Party spokesperson Jonathon Porritt). In this interpretation, ecologism is characterized by its insistence that 1) there is a growing ecological crisis; 2) ecological conditions demand radical changes in social organization; 3) there are definite ecological limits to economic growth; 4) technology cannot provide a quick fix for ecological problems; 5) the exploitation of the planet is tied to the exploitation of people; 6) the environment has intrinsic value apart from human beings; and 7) nature provides a model for the organization of society. Deep ecologists such as Arne Naess, Bill Devall, and George Sessions go even further, arguing for a biocentric ethics in which human beings are accorded no more importance than any other organism. Other variants of radical ecology include ecofeminism (as in the work of Carolyn Merchant), ecoanarchism (represented by Murray Bookchin and Robyn Eckersley) and ecosocialism (as in the writings of David Pepper and James O'Connor).

For historians the rise of ecologism (on top of what is widely perceived to be a global ecological crisis) has raised a number of problems. Foremost among these is the extent to which nature as we know it is a human product. For William Cronon in *Uncommon Ground* (1995), the problem was a dual one: "On the one hand we need somehow to persuade scientists and environmentalists who assume 'nature' to be natural, wholly external to human culture, that there is something profoundly important and useful in recognizing its cultural connectedness. On the other hand, we need no less to persuade humanists and postmodernists that although ideas of nature may be the projected ideas of men and women, the world onto which we project those ideas is by no means entirely of our own making."

Historians have thus tried to explore not only the changing nature of ecology, but the changing understanding of what ecology is. At times this has led to conflicts with the naturalistic and scientific bases of ecologism. Although ecology as an ideology has generally sought to root its prescriptions in scientific conceptions of nature, ecological science has recently shifted from an early 20th-century ecology that emphasized order, harmony, stability, diversity, and succession (exemplified by the work of Frederic Clements) to a view of nature's ecology as one of disorder or chaos. Political ecologists thus frequently rely on a conception of ecological science that is no longer as widely adhered to within the scientific community – although today's ecological science like yesterday's, Donald Worster cautioned in *The Wealth of Nature* (1993), cannot be "assumed to be all-knowing, all-wise, or eternally true," making it a mistake simply to jettison the concept of natural order.

The issue of what constitutes ecology has thus not been free of the relativistic concerns of our "postmodernist" times, and historians have played an increasingly important role in tracing out these changing conceptions. What is often discovered is that, as Raymond Williams wrote in *Problems in Materialism and Culture* (1980), "the idea of nature is the idea of man; and this not only generally, or in ultimate ways, but the idea of man in society, indeed the ideas of kinds of societies." In this view, the central issue has always been whether nature includes humanity and needs to be linked organically with human society, or whether nature can be treated as an "other" to be conquered. For thinkers like Williams and Cronon, those who insist that nature or ecology exists only outside society adopt a view which, though frequently sympathetic toward nature, merely reinforces the prevailing outlook that nature is the "other." "It will be ironic," Williams wrote, "if one of the last forms of the separation of abstracted Man and abstracted Nature is an intellectual separation between economics and ecology. It will be a sign that we are beginning to think in some necessary ways when we can conceive these becoming, as they ought to become, a single discipline."

Some ecological scientists with a historical bent have also warned against an abstracted Ecology from which models for society are to be derived. Thus Yrjö Haila and Richard Levins contended in *Humanity and Nature* (1992) "that a view of 'nature' as a straightforward material entity giving rules to be followed in constructing society lacks any clear meaning." Nature is in fact highly complex and variable. Nor does knowledge of ecosystems provide a direct model for human society. For example, while it is often thought that ecosystems with greater diversity are more stable, ecological science has recently proven otherwise: the more interconnections within a system the more unstable the system is. This however says nothing about how we should organize society or why. Nevertheless, Haila and

Levins argued that historians should study the development of ecohistorical periods and ecoformations with the goal of establishing a relatively sustainable social relation to nature that meets the needs of all humanity. This is all the more important since we live today in a "new stage of global history" that is characterized by ecological crisis. There is therefore a rich agenda for historians and social scientists seeking to reassess the changing human relation to nature.

JOHN BELLAMY FOSTER

See also Africa: Eastern; Africa: West; America: Pre-Columbian; Archaeology; Australia; Cronon; Crosby; Curti; Environmental; Imperialism; Le Roy Ladurie; McNeill; Malin; Marks; Merchant; Ogot; Sauer; Semple; Worster

Further Reading

Bookchin, Murray, *The Ecology of Freedom: The Emergence and Dissolution of Hierarchy*, Palo Alto: Cheshire, 1982
Bramwell, Anna, *Ecology in the Twentieth Century: A History*, New Haven and London: Yale University Press, 1989
Clements, Frederic, *Plant Succession: An Analysis of the Development of Vegetation*, Washington, DC: Carnegie Institution, 1916
Cronon, William, ed., *Uncommon Ground: Toward Reinventing Nature*, New York: W Norton, 1995
Devall, Bill, and George Sessions, *Deep Ecology*, Salt Lake City, UT: Gibbs Smith, 1985
Dobson, Andrew, *Green Political Thought: An Introduction*, London and Boston: Routledge, 1990
Eckersley, Robyn, *Environmentalism and Political Theory: Toward an Ecocentric Approach*, Albany: State University of New York Press, and London: University College London Press, 1992
Foster, John Bellamy, *The Vulnerable Planet: A Short Economic History of the Environment*, New York: Monthly Review Press, 1994
Haila, Yrjö, and Richard Levins, *Humanity and Nature: Ecology, Science and Society*, London: Pluto Press, 1992
Harvey, David, "The Nature of the Environment: Dialectics of Social and Environmental Change," in Ralph Miliband and Leo Panitch, eds., *The Socialist Register 1993*, London: Merlin, 1993
Merchant, Carolyn, *Radical Ecology: The Search for a Livable World*, London and New York: Routledge, 1992
Merchant, Carolyn, *Earthcare: Women and the Environment*, London and New York: Routledge, 1996
Naess, Arne, *Ecology, Community and Lifestyle: Outline of an Ecosophy*, Cambridge and New York: Cambridge University Press, 1989
O'Connor, James, "Capitalism, Nature, Socialism: A Theoretical Introduction," *Capitalism, Nature, Socialism* 1 (1988), 11–38
Pepper, David, *The Roots of Modern Environmentalism*, London: Croom Helm, 1984
Porritt, Jonathon, *Seeing Green: The Politics of Ecology Explained*, Oxford and New York: Blackwell, 1986
Williams, Raymond, *Keywords: A Vocabulary of Culture and Society*, London: Croom Helm, and New York: Oxford University Press, 1976; revised 1983
Williams, Raymond, *Problems in Materialism and Culture: Selected Essays*, London: Verso, 1980; New York: Schocken, 1981
Williams, Raymond, *Resources of Hope: Culture, Democracy, Socialism*, London: Verso, 1989
Worster, Donald, *Nature's Economy*, Cambridge and New York: Cambridge University Press, 1977; 2nd edition 1994
Worster, Donald, ed., *The Ends of the Earth: Perspectives on Modern Environmental History*, Cambridge and New York: Cambridge University Press, 1988
Worster, Donald, *The Wealth of Nature: Environmental History and the Ecological Imagination*, New York: Oxford University Press, 1993

Economic History

Economic history emerged as an academic discipline in Britain in the late 19th century. It was however connected to a much longer tradition of social and economic commentary and analysis that had characterized English and Scottish political economy for the previous two centuries. Interest in economic history increased among academics in the late 19th century because of a rejection by some historians of "drum and trumpet" history (the history of elites, diplomacy, and wars) in favor of a history of the mass of the population and of agriculture, industry, and commerce. But a more important and immediate cause of the emergence of economic history was an alienation on the part of some economists from the marginalist revolution of the 1880s and 1890s (the increasing dependence in economics upon formal profit-maximizing and market clearing models as guides to understanding economic behavior). The abstract, deductive, individualistic, and present-centered nature of this formalism in economics encouraged some economists to study the history of the economic past using less formal methods. The *laissez-faire* policy views of orthodox political economy from the 1880s also encouraged an economic history (seen particularly in the work of the Webbs) that examined the excesses and inequalities of industrializing society in order to highlight the need for more government intervention and regulation. William Cunningham, who wrote the first proper economic history text in 1882, objected to the idea of economic man and was against making assumptions about maximizing utilities. He favored the study of societies in their own time and with their own special social and cultural attitudes and motivations. These views came out in his controversies with Alfred Marshall, the leading exponent of the marginalist revolution in economics. Although Marshall himself saw economics as "the study of mankind in the ordinary business of life," the method that he helped to establish encouraged economists to specialize in abstract theorizing about the working of the economy at macro level. Economic history thus came to thrive in anti-Marshallian centers such as the London School of Economics and the University of Birmingham. Other late 19th-century figures contributing to the separation of economic history from economics included Arnold Toynbee, who was the first to popularize the phrase "industrial revolution," writing about this at length in his London lectures of 1883, and William Ashley, who was the first British economic historian deliberately to adopt a periodization not derived from political history. In other countries the origins and nature of the subject have been rather different. For example, in France it emerged largely from the 1920s as part of the Annales approach – emphasizing the need for history to turn away from a narrative of political events to study the geographical, ecological, and demographic aspects of material life over long time perspectives. In the United States economic history remained closely linked with neoclassical economics and with economic theory.

Economic history expanded in the 1920s in England with the foundation of the Economic History Society and the *Economic History Review*. Much research appeared that used previously neglected historical documents, such as the censuses of production, overseas trade figures, local municipal records, parliamentary papers, and business archives. Theoretical analysis was not a major feature in the early decades of the subject, though the best empirical work of this period always included interesting arguments about cause and effect.

Economic history had made a break from economics but had not set up an alternative or distinctive methodology in the sense of a distinctive set of theoretical underpinnings. According to D.C. Coleman in his *History and the Economic Past* (1987), two distinct strains were apparent in British economic history by the early 20th century. First was the "rationalist" or "neutralist" tradition exemplified by the works of John Clapham, Herbert Heaton, A.P. Wadsworth, and Julia de Lacey Mann. This was characterized by a more or less exclusively economic focus, lack of social or political context, an emphasis upon statistical measures, and a general lack of interest in long-term cause or effect. The second strain was the "political" tradition represented in the work of R.H. Tawney, Barbara and John Hammond, G.D.H. Cole, and others. These writers were influenced by some variety of socialist thought (either Christian socialism, Fabianism, or Marxism). They sought connections with other developing fields of the social sciences and attempted to answer major questions of causality, reasons for the decline of feudalism, for example, and the rise of capitalism. They also wrote for a popular audience, relied much less upon quantitative indicators, and were motivated by moral and social issues: "Too much time," Tawney wrote, "is spent today piling up statistics and facts . . . [we] . . . need to get to the moral questions and relationships which lie at the heart of economic ones."

From 1931 Tawney held the first chair in Economic History at the London School of Economics. But these writers, in general, were, and are, regarded somewhat condescendingly by the historical establishment – seen as romantic and lacking objectivity. At this time economic history was a broadly based branch of historical enquiry which took in social and political as well as strictly economic history and had a broad definition of "the economic sphere." It also had a broad chronological perspective, which saw the development of a strong medieval component in these years: first in the classic study of Paul Vinogradoff and then in the social and economic analyses of M.M. Postan, Eileen Power, and E.M. Carus Wilson. Economic history developed institutional roots in several British universities often, as at Birmingham, in conjunction with business and commercial studies. But the subject was also at home and immensely popular in university extramural classes and in the Workers' Educational Association. The subject appealed to people across the political spectrum, for different reasons, from members of the Historians Group of the Communist Party to liberal academics from economics and business studies backgrounds, such as T.S. Ashton who succeeded Tawney to the London chair but whose work included the best-selling *The Industrial Revolution* (1948), which was written in an accessible and popular style for a general readership. What most economic historians had in common at this time was a nontechnical approach to their subject and the production of widely read popular works.

By 1950 economic history had largely fallen into the hands of the "rationalist" approach and in the late 1940s and 1950s there was a move to incorporate theoretical insights from branches of economics, especially development and trade cycle theory. This resulted in some classic studies of trade cycles (following a pattern set by N.D. Kondratieff and Joseph Schumpeter as early as the 1920s and 1930s) and the composition of GNP in different phases of economic growth. There was a growing tendency at this time to view the experiences of western, and specifically British industrialization, as a model that could throw light on the solutions to Third World development problems: this is seen most clearly in the work of W.W. Rostow. Many formative accounts of particular industries or sectors of the economy also appeared in the 1950s and 1960s (for example Mathias on brewing and Coleman on paper) and "business history" grew in popularity. Large, often highly successful and long-lived firms commissioned academics to write their histories. Classic works appeared such as Wilson on Unilever and Coleman on Courtaulds, but there was a general bias in business history in favor of heroic and unrepresentative accounts. During the 1960s increasing numbers of separate departments of economic history were established in British universities. This accompanied the general expansion of the university sector and of the social sciences and economics in particular. These separate departments did not generally confine themselves to a narrowly defined area of economic life in the past, but integrated a great deal of the increasingly popular social history of the period, especially where that social history had a materialist basis: the history of popular protest, labor, social conditions, and class – a history from below rather than from elite perspectives. These were inspired by Marxist and socialist approaches and seen particularly in the work of Christopher Hill, E.P. Thompson, E.J. Hobsbawm, and Rodney Hilton.

From the early 1960s the so-called "New economic history" or cliometrics became popular. This arose first in the United States where economic history had always retained closer connections with economics, usually staying within rather than separating from economics departments in universities. The "new economic history" involved applying economic theory and economic "models" to historical evidence: "A cliometrician is an economist applying economic theory . . . to historical facts . . . in the interest of history," McCloskey noted. The most vigorous exponents of cliometrics claimed that it would eventually provide definitive answers to many of the most fundamental questions asked by economic historians. The implication was that this approach would put economic history back on an objective or scientific path of discovering truths.

The new economic history was more theoretically driven than the "old" economic history of both Tawney and Clapham. It appeared to be a clean break from the past, but it shared similarities with a longer tradition of economic history that had begun to neglect social and political context and to favor quantitative approaches. The statistical and quantitative character of cliometrics was boosted by increasing use of computer technology, not only producing graphs and statistical breakdowns, but also enabling model-building, back-projection, and counterfactual developments. Model-building was dominated by the construction of models of historical sectors or economies based on the assumptions of neoclassical economics and/or upon national income accounting. Back-projection or the estimation of what figures might have been for periods where evidence does not exist, on the basis of later periods where statistics do exist, created some thought-provoking results. For example Wrigley and Schofield, with the assistance of the demographer R.D. Lee, used back-projection to estimate 18th-century population growth figures from the 1851 Census in their definitive work of 1981. But the most controversial

technique arising from the "new economic history" was "counterfactual history": the calculation of the advantages of a historical innovation by comparing economic growth in the presence of the innovation with economic growth as it might have been without it (the latter estimated by building up an alternative model of the economy in the absence of the innovation – in other words, a counterfactual model). A great deal of railway history was considered in this way, as was the economics of slavery. The path-breaking work was R.W. Fogel's *Railroads and American Economic Growth* (1964). In this Fogel constructed a model of what the US economy might have looked like in 1890 if railways had never existed. He showed that the role of railways in American economic growth had been overstated. He also worked with Stanley Engerman on *Time on the Cross* (1974), a controversial *tour de force* on the economics of slavery and abolition.

Cliometrics never entirely came to dominate economic history in Britain as it did for a period in the United States. It came close but, by the 1980s, the problems of the approach were increasingly exposed. Most important were the dubious assumptions made about human behavior and motivation in the past on the basis of neoclassical economics. The core of econometric analysis is the neoclassical scenario of a competitive regime of production and exchange where the price system allocates resources in a semi-automatic way (market clearing). The further back in time one went the less applicable the basic assumptions of modern economic theory were likely to be, as Polanyi demonstrated in *The Great Transformation* (1944). In addition, the complete separation of cliometrics from other types of history often resulted in a serious lack of context. And lack of interest in broader social, political, and cultural issues together with attempts to quantify the unquantifiable, weakened the reputation of the approach. Because the method also generally adopted a highly abstract, technical, and quantitative mode of communication, it was difficult for the nonspecialist to understand or criticize. This resulted in what often appeared to be an exclusive group of specialists writing for each other with little regard for the rest of the historical establishment.

Although the heyday of cliometrics has passed, the identification of this method with economic history has been and remains strong, while economic history generally has remained more oriented toward quantitative methods and to strictly defined "economic" issues than it was in its earliest years. This has resulted in an alienation of many historians from the subject. Interest in economic change has also waned in recent decades because of a declining interest in materialist approaches to history and a strong anti-Marxist tendency in the social sciences that rejects any approach suggestive of economic or structuralist determinism. At the same time, there has been enormous growth in the popularity of social and cultural history. This has resulted in a contraction of economic history as fewer recruits to academic history enter the discipline. There has been only limited development of new theoretical tools in economic history to assist in the understanding of past economies, although institutional approaches for a time looked set to signal change. The tools of anthropology (with their stress on "cultural otherness") have, for example, been little engaged to study production and exchange in the past, and interdisciplinary approaches have remained much more limited in Britain than in France or the United States. Generally speaking there has been an unfortunate separation between the study of economies in the past and their social and cultural aspects.

Some see this as a time of crisis for economic history. Institutionally, this is certainly the case in Britain as economic retrenchment in the education system has meant the closure of many small independent economic history departments. The way forward would seem to be to resurrect the integrated approach to the economic, social, and cultural life in the past that characterized the best writing of economic history in its earliest years. This was, after all, the original reason for the emergence of the subject.

PAT HUDSON

See also Beard; Cardoso; Cipolla; Cole; Hammond; Hill; Hilton; Hobsbawm; Industrial Revolution; Otsuka; Polanyi; Postan; Power; Tawney; Thompson, E.; Vinogradoff

Further Reading

Ashley, William James, *An Introduction to English Economic History and Theory*, 2 vols., New York: Putnam, and London: Rivington, 1888–93

Ashton, T.S., *Iron and Steel in the Industrial Revolution*, Manchester: Manchester University Press, and New York: Longman, 1924

Ashton, T.S., *The Industrial Revolution, 1760–1830*, London: Oxford University Press, 1948

Carus-Wilson, E. M., "An Industrial Revolution in the Thirteenth Century," *Economic History Review* 11 (1941), 39–60

Clapham, John Harold, *An Economic History of Modern Britain*, 3 vols., Cambridge: Cambridge University Press, 1926–38

Clapham, John Harold, *The Bank of England: A History*, 2 vols., Cambridge: Cambridge University Press, 1944

Cole, G. D. H., and Raymond Postgate, *The Common People, 1746–1938*, London: Methuen, 1938, revised [with dates 1746–1946], 1946; in US as *The British Common People, 1746–1938*, New York: Knopf, 1939, revised as *The British People*, 1947

Coleman, D.C., *The British Paper Industry, 1495–1860: A Study in Industrial Growth*, Oxford: Oxford University Press, 1958; Westport, CT: Greenwood Press, 1975

Coleman, D.C., *Courtaulds: An Economic and Social History*, 3 vols., Oxford: Oxford University Press, 1969–80

Coleman, D.C., *History and the Economic Past: An Account of the Rise and Decline of Economic History in Britain*, Oxford and New York: Oxford University Press, 1987

Court, William Henry Bassano, *The Rise of the Midland Industries, 1600–1838*, London: Oxford University Press, 1938

Cunningham, William, *The Growth of English Industry and Commerce*, 2 vols., Cambridge: Cambridge University Press, 1882; 4th edition 1905–07

Dobb, Maurice, *Studies in the Development of Capitalism*, London: Routledge, 1946; New York: International Publishers, 1947

Floud, Roderick, and Donald McCloskey, eds., *The Economic History of Britain since 1700*, 2nd edition, 3 vols., Cambridge: Cambridge University Press, 1994

Fogel, Robert William, *Railroads and American Economic Growth: Essays in Econometric History*, Baltimore: Johns Hopkins Press, 1964

Fogel, Robert William, and Stanley L. Engerman, *Time on the Cross: The Economics of American Negro Slavery*, 2 vols., Boston: Little Brown, and London: Wildwood, 1974

Hammond, J.L., and Barbara Hammond, *The Village Labourer, 1760–1832: A Study in the Government of England before the Reform Bill*, London and New York: Longman, 1911

Hammond, J.L., and Barbara Hammond, *The Town Labourer, 1760–1832: The New Civilisation*, London and New York: Longman, 1917

Harte, N.B., ed., *The Study of Economic History: Collected Inaugural Lectures, 1893–1970*, London: Cass, 1971

Heaton, Herbert, *The Yorkshire Woollen and Worsted Industries*, Oxford: Oxford University Press, 1920

Hill, Christopher, *Puritanism and Revolution: Studies in Interpretation of the English Revolution of the 17th Century*, London: Secker and Warburg, 1958; New York: Schocken, 1964

Hilton, Rodney, *Bond Men Made Free: Medieval Peasant Movements and the English Rising of 1381*, London: Temple Smith, and New York: Viking, 1973

Hobsbawm, Eric J., *On History*, London: Weidenfeld and Nicolson, and New York: New Press, 1997

Kadish, Alon, *Historians, Economists and Economic History*, London and New York: Routledge, 1989

McCloskey, Donald, *Econometric History*, Basingstoke: Macmillan, 1987

Marshall, Alfred, *Principles of Economics: An Introductory Volume*, 9th edition, London: Macmillan, 1963

Mathias, Peter, *The Brewing Industry in England, 1700–1830*, Cambridge: Cambridge University Press, 1959

Pinchbeck, Ivy, *Women Workers and the Industrial Revolution, 1750–1850*, London: Routledge, 1930; reprinted 1969

Polanyi, Karl, *The Great Transformation*, New York: Farrar and Rinehart, 1944; as *Origins of Our Time: The Great Transformation*, London: Gollancz, 1945

Pollard, Sidney, *The Genesis of Modern Management: A Study of the Industrial Revolution in Great Britain*, Cambridge, MA: Harvard University Press, and London: Edward Arnold, 1965

Postan, M.M., *The Medieval Economy and Society: An Economic History of Britain in the Middle Ages*, London: Weidenfeld and Nicolson, 1972; Berkeley: University of California Press, 1972 [with subtitle *An Economic History of Britain, 1100–1500*]

Power, Eileen, *Medieval People*, London: Methuen, and Boston: Houghton Mifflin, 1924

Rogers, James Edward Thorold, *Six Centuries of Work and Wages: The History of English Labor*, New York: Putnam, and London: Sonnenschein, 1884

Rostow, W.W., *The Stages of Economic Growth: A Non-Communist Manifesto*, Cambridge: Cambridge University Press, 1960, New York: Cambridge University Press, 1965; 3rd edition 1990

Schumpeter, Joseph Alois, *Theorie der wirtschaftlichen Entwicklung*, Leipzig: Duncker & Humblot, 1912; in English as *The Theory of Economic Development: An Inquiry into Profits, Capital, Credit, Interest, and the Business Cycle*, Cambridge, MA: Harvard University Press, 1936

Tawney, R.H., *The Agrarian Problem in the Sixteenth Century*, London: Longman, 1912

Tawney, R.H., *Religion and the Rise of Capitalism*, New York: Harcourt Brace, 1926; London: Murray, 1933

Thompson, E.P., *The Making of the English Working Class*, London: Gollancz, 1963; New York: Pantheon, 1964

Toynbee, Arnold, *Lectures on the Industrial Revolution in England*, London: Rivington, 1884; as *Lectures on the Industrial Revolution of the Eighteenth Century in England*, New York: Humboldt, 1884

Unwin, George, *Industrial Organisation in the Sixteenth and Seventeenth Centuries*, Oxford: Oxford University Press, 1904; reprinted Clifton, NJ: A.M. Kelley, 1973

Unwin, George, *Studies in Economic History*, London: Macmillan, 1927; reprinted New York: A.M. Kelley, 1966

Vinogradoff, Paul, *The Growth of the Manor*, London: Swan Sonnenschein, and New York: Macmillan, 1905; revised London: Allen and Unwin, and New York: Macmillan, 1911

Wadsworth, Alfred P., and Julia de Lacey Mann, *The Cotton Trade and Industrial Lancashire, 1600–1750*, Manchester: Manchester University Press, 1931

Webb, Sidney, and Beatrice Webb, *English Local Government from the Revolution to the Municipal Corporations Act*, 9 vols., London and New York: Longman, 1906–29

Wilson, Charles H., *The History of Unilever: A Study in Economic Growth and Social Change*, 3 vols., London: Cassell, 1954–68

Wrigley, E.A., and Roger S. Schofield, *The Population History of England, 1541–1871: A Reconstruction*, London: Arnold, and Cambridge, MA: Harvard University Press, 1981

Egypt: Ancient

Modern research into ancient Egypt did not begin until Napoleon's expedition of 1798, which took with it 175 scientists and scholars, surveying instruments, and a large library. However, Western perspectives of the Egyptian past started with the Greeks, and some have endured into the 20th century. Hecataeus of Miletus, in the later 6th and early 5th centuries BCE, visited Egypt and described it in his *Periegesis* (Descriptive Geography). The work has not survived, and surmises about Hecataeus' research have been far-fetched. However, the historian Herodotus of Halicarnassus, who visited Egypt about the middle of the 5th century BCE cited Hecataeus, and both in the ancient and modern world he has been charged with plagiarism from his predecessor. However, Herodotus did independent research in Egypt and consulted Egyptian informants including a temple scribe; his description of the country and his effort to write a history of the pharaonic period is the best account that has survived from ancient Greece. Yet he shows the difficulty of the task. He began Egyptian history with Menes, who united Upper and Lower Egypt, and it is generally agreed that this reflects Egyptian tradition correctly, but his list of Egyptian kings is muddled and overlaid by folktale. He knew nothing of the predynastic period which has been revealed by modern archaeologists. Moreover, although he claimed to have sailed as far south as the first cataract, his knowledge of Upper Egypt was sketchy. His veracity was attacked by later writers, and lately some modern scholars, particularly Detlev Fehling in Germany and Stephanie West in Britain have revived the charges, but we can be sure that he did not purposely mislead and that he based his account on what he saw and what he was told. He was convinced of Egypt's importance as the source of Greek civilization, even insisting that the Greek gods came from Egypt.

After the death of Alexander the Great in 323 BCE, a Macedonian dynasty was founded in Egypt by one of Alexander's generals, Ptolemy, who brought in Greek settlers and made his capital at Alexandria which developed into a great center of Greek culture. Under Ptolemy I, Hecataeus of Abdera produced a history of Egypt that popularized the idea that Egypt was the source of civilization. After Hecataeus, however, a sounder account was produced by a priest of Sebennytos, Manetho, the prophet of the temple at Heliopolis, who dedicated his history of Egypt to Ptolemy II. Neither Hecataeus' history nor Manetho's, which corrected it, has survived, but Manetho was accepted as an authority by later Jewish and Christian writers who used him to establish biblical chronology. He divided Egyptian history into 31 dynasties, grouped into three main periods, the Old, Middle, and New Kingdoms, which correspond to Egyptian history as modern Egyptologists have reconstructed it. It is clear that he consulted temple archives; and the king-list at Turin, which while intact contained the names of the Egyptian kings up to the 19th dynasty, gives us some idea of the documents which Manetho could have consulted.

Diodorus Siculus, who was a contemporary of Julius Caesar and the emperor Augustus and wrote a world history in 40 books, devoted his first book to Egypt, and his main source is generally agreed to have been Hecataeus of Abdera. That is the most likely theory, although it cannot be proved, for Diodorus cited Hecataeus once only – for his description of the monument of Osymandias, which was probably the Ramesseum at Thebes. But Rome's interest in Egypt was more as a source of grain than as a source of civilization, and knowledge of Egypt's ancient history remained shadowy, although there was widespread interest in Egyptian mystery religions, such as the cult of Isis and Serapis. Plutarch wrote an essay on Isis and Osiris relating the myth of the battle between Osiris and his brother Typhon, the Egyptian Seth, for which our oldest source is the Pyramid Texts.

The temples of Egypt fell on hard times in the 3rd century CE even before the victory of Christianity in the 4th century, and once the temples were abandoned, knowledge of hieroglyphic writing died out. Even the demotic script developed for the Egyptian language under the Ethiopian dynasty c.700 BCE was abandoned, and its place was taken by Coptic which was devised for Christian writings. In late antiquity, Horapollo wrote a *Hieroglyphica* which purported to explain hieroglyphs as picture writing, and his authority bedeviled the first modern efforts to decipher hieroglyphic writing, for he interpreted hieroglyphs as sacred symbols rather than as a script. Egypt's ancient monuments decayed and with the Arab invasion of the 7th century, Egypt itself became unknown to Europeans.

Credit for the rediscovery of ancient Egypt can go to the savants who accompanied Napoleon on his Egyptian campaign, and to the unknown French soldier who discovered the Rosetta Stone a short distance northwest of Rosetta on the Nile. This inscription was a trilingual decree passed by a synod of Egyptian priests in 196 BCE in honor of Ptolemy V Epiphanes and transcribed in hieroglyphic, demotic, and Greek. Using this, Jean-François Champollion deciphered hieroglyphic script in 1821. Champollion was appointed to a newly-created chair of Egyptian antiquity at the Collège de France in 1831, and is justly considered the father of modern Egyptology, although his decipherment was widely rejected in England and Germany after his death. However, it was vindicated by the discovery in 1866 of the Canopus Decree – trilingual like the Rosetta Stone – by Karl Richard Lepsius who took up where Champollion left off. Lepsius' monumental 12-volume *Denkmäler aus Aegypten und Aethiopien* (1849–56; *Discoveries in Egypt, Ethiopia, and the Peninsula of Sinai*, 1852) marked a new achievement in Egyptology, for it made the evidence of Egyptian remains available to European scholars. The other two great names in Egyptology of the 19th and early 20th centuries were Auguste Mariette (1821–81) and W.M. Flinders Petrie (1853–1942). Mariette's most famous find was the tombs of the sacred Apis bulls at Saqqara. But his greatest service was to put an end to the disorganized plundering of Egyptian antiquities as the chief supervisor of all excavations in Egypt and director of antiquities, an office to which he was appointed by the khedive of Egypt. It was Mariette who founded the Bulaq Museum which has become the great Cairo museum. Petrie, Edwards professor of Egyptology at University College, London from 1892, put archaeology on a scientific footing by developing sequence dating based on potsherds, a method he first applied in Palestine in 1890. Widely doubted at the time, sequence dating has now become standard procedure.

In addition, Egyptologists also have a powerful mechanism for dating in the Egyptian civil calendar of 365 days, to which the Egyptians remained faithful until the Christian period. Because it is shorter than the astronomical year, it corresponds with it exactly only once every 1,460 years. But the 3rd-century Roman grammarian Censorinus had preserved the information that in 139 CE the new year of the civil calendar corresponded with the heliacal rising of the star Sirius, which the Egyptians called Sothus, and thus we can compute "Sothic cycles" at 1314, 2770, and 4228 BCE. We also have an epigraphical record that in the 7th year of the Middle Kingdom pharaoh Senusert III, the heliacal rising of Sirius took place on day 16 of the 8th month of the calendar, which gives us 1872 BCE, the earliest fixed date in history. Egyptian dates in turn have been used to establish a chronology for the prehistory of the eastern Mediterranean. Thus there is now a degree of consensus for the date when the dynastic period began with the union of Upper and Lower Egypt by the pharaoh Menes, which Champollion dated to 5867 BCE and Lepsius at 3892. James Breasted dated it to 3400, Sir Alan Gardiner 3289 or 3189; John A. Wilson 3100; and Pierre Montet about the beginning of the 3rd millennium.

Before Menes, there stretches the predynastic period, where archaeologists have identified various cultures: Egypt appears to have been a melting pot of immigrants not only from the Libyan desert and the Sudan, but also from Asia and the Mediterranean. The emergence of the dynastic period represented an abrupt and sudden flowering for which scholars offer divergent explanations. One is Arnold Toynbee's "Challenge and Response" hypothesis: newcomers driven into the Nile valley by the progressive desiccation of northern Africa had to clear the Nile river jungle and control the annual flood in order to survive, and their culture and society were their solution to the problem. Another is V. Gordon Childe's urban revolution hypothesis, which proposed that primitive agriculturalists began to group together in villages where some undertook specialized occupations resulting in increased productivity, which in turn produced a surplus of wealth that served as the economic basis for a ruling class. This revolution may have taken place in the Delta where the archaeological evidence for it is now buried deep in the mud. Yet many Egyptologists still believe that it was a new intrusion of migrants from southern Mesopotamia that sparked the sudden change; there is clear evidence of early borrowings from Mesopotamia in Egypt, but none so far from Egypt have been found in Mesopotamia. But present opinion, summarized by Hoffman's Egypt before the Pharaohs (1991), has swung back to the theory of a Nilotic origin and Africanists have labelled the "Dynastic Race" theory "Aryanist."

Dynasty III marks the start of the Old Kingdom, the era of the great pyramids, the first of which were the stepped pyramid of Djoser at Saqqara. Later Dynasty III pharaohs followed Djoser's example but with the founder of the next dynasty Snofru, true pyramids emerged: at Medum he reconstructed a

stepped pyramid built by the last king of Dynasty III, Huni, and at the village of Dashur he built two pyramids, including the curious "Bent Pyramid." But the best-known pyramids of Dynasty IV (2650–2500 BCE) were built at Gizeh where the pharaoh Khufu built the "Great Pyramid," Egypt's most famous monument, which has given rise to many theories and odd notions: Petrie's first work in Egypt was undertaken to prove the theories of Piozzi Smith about Khufu's pyramid, and his first achievement as an Egyptologist was to disprove them.

Imperial splendor reached its height under Amenhotep III and his queen Tiye. The temples Amenhotep erected changed the appearance of Thebes. However historians have noted that Amenhotep named his state barge "Radiance of Aten," thus recognizing the solar deity Aten whose cult was to convulse Egypt under his son, and perhaps even before Amenhotep III's death, for a number of Egyptologists argue that Amenhotep made his son co-regent at the end of his life: Cyril Aldred for instance postulated a co-regency of at least twelve years. The evidence, however, leaves room for skepticism.

Most of what we know about the failed religious revolution of Amenhotep IV, who took the name Akhenaten, comes from the excavations at Amarna, the modern name of the new capital Akhetaten (Seat of the Aten) which Akhenaten built halfway between Memphis and Thebes. Akhenaten's religious revolution has provoked great interest, in part because of supposed connections with Hebrew monotheism which were popularized by Sigmund Freud in his Der Mann Moses und die monotheistische Religion (1939; Moses and Monotheism, 1939), but he was a religious zealot who neglected affairs of state and his reign was disastrous.

Akhenaten's successor Smenkhare reigned no more than three years, and he was succeeded by the boy Tutankamun (1352–44), probably his brother, who died violently, for his mummy shows a head wound caused probably by an arrow. The discovery in 1922 of his tomb, untouched by grave robbers, by Howard Carter and Lord Carnarvon, has been the most sensational achievement of Egyptology and has given Tutankamun a celebrity that history would otherwise have denied him. Under him, Akhetaten was abandoned and priesthood of Amon resumed its dominance.

Egypt's long history, its generally reliable chronology, its connections with the Bible, and its ancient reputation as the birthplace of civilization have given ancient Egypt a fascination and importance outweighing all other antique cultures. The Swedish prehistorian, Oscar Montelius, in his Der Orient und Europa (1899) propounded the first coherent view of European prehistory by positing a migration of culture and technology from the Orient into the West, and later his system was pushed to extremes by Elliott Smith, who in his book The Ancient Egyptians (1911) set forth a hyperdiffusionist doctrine that was further developed by his disciple W. J. Perry. Their hypothesis, which remained popular until World War II, argued that small groups of people set out from Egypt, mainly by sea, to colonize and civilize the world, bringing with them the techniques of mummification and megalithic building. The central axiom of the diffusionist school was that no invention was ever made twice, and thus if similar technology is found in two prehistoric cultures, however far apart, there must be a connection. Thus if pyramids appeared in Central America, the source of the idea had to be Egyptian.

But at the same time as Elliott Smith and Perry were over-stating their doctrines, V. Gordon Childe was elaborating a moderate diffusionist model which held the field until the development of Carbon-14 dating. His model, set forth in various editions of his *Dawn of European Civilization* (1925), put forward the hypothesis that civilization moved westwards from the twin sources of Egypt and Mesopotamia, via Crete and Anatolia to Greece and Italy and thence to northern Europe. The value of this model for dating is obvious, for Egyptian history had a reliable chronology which could be used for comparative dating. Thus the stages of the Minoan civilization discovered by Sir Arthur Evans on Crete in 1900 could be dated from Egyptian imports found there.

All these diffusionist models have now been rendered dubious by Carbon-14 dating, modified by tree-ring calibration. The megalithic monuments of northern Europe must now be dated earlier than once suspected, and the earliest stone temples on Malta predate the pyramids. However, Egyptian chronology based on its calendar and king-lists has been vindicated, and Carbon-14 has not seriously challenged the accepted chronology of the prehistoric Aegean area. Yet there has been reluctance to abandon the ancient idea that Egypt was the source of civilization, which was reflected in the recent multi-volume work of Martin Bernal, *Black Athena* (1987–), which, among other claims, argued that modern scholars have conspired to deny Egypt the credit it deserves. Among the African American proponents of "Black History," it is generally accepted that ancient Egypt was a great African civilization, which was, in fact, considered a respectable hypothesis before Napoleon's expedition initiated the modern study of Egyptology.

J.A.S. EVANS

See also Archaeology; Bernal; Diodorus; Herodotus; Near East

Further Reading

Albright, William Foxwell, *From the Stone Age to Christianity: Monotheism and the Historical Process*, Baltimore: Johns Hopkins Press, 1940

Aldred, Cyril, *Akhenaten, King of Egypt*, London and New York: Thames and Hudson, 1988

Armayor, O. Kimball, *Herodotus' Autopsy of the Fayoum: Lake Moeris and the Labyrinth of Egypt*, Amsterdam: Gieben, 1985

Bernal, Martin, *Black Athena: The Afroasiatic Roots of Classical Civilization*, 2 vols. to date, London: Free Association Press, and New Brunswick, NJ: Rutgers University Press, 1987–91

Breasted, James Henry, *A History of Egypt from the Earliest Times to the Persian Conquest*, New York: Scribner, 1905, revised 1909; London: Murray, 1938

Childe, Vere Gordon, *Dawn of European Civilization*, London: Kegan Paul Trench Trübner, and New York: Knopf, 1925; revised 1939, 1947, 1950, 1957

Childe, Vere Gordon, *What Happened in History*, Harmondsworth: Penguin, 1942; New York: Penguin, 1946

Daniel, Glyn, and Colin Renfrew, *The Idea of Prehistory*, 2nd edition, Edinburgh: Edinburgh University Press, 1988 [1st edition, by Daniel only, 1962]

Emery, Walter B., *Archaic Egypt*, Harmondsworth and Baltimore: Penguin, 1961

Fakhry, Ahmed, *The Pyramids*, Chicago: University of Chicago Press, 1961

Fehling, Detlev, *Die Quellenangaben bei Herodot: Studien zur Erzählkunst Herodots*, Berlin: de Gruyter, 1971; in English as *Herodotus and His "Sources": Citation, Invention and Narrative Art*, Leeds: Cairns, 1990

Freud, Sigmund, *Der Mann Moses und die monotheistische Religion*, Amsterdam: Lange, 1939; in English as *Moses and Monotheism*, New York: Knopf, and London: Hogarth Press, 1939

Gardiner, Alan Henderson, *Egypt of the Pharaohs*, Oxford and New York: Oxford University Press, 1961

Hoffman, Michael, *Egypt before the Pharaohs*, Austin: University of Texas Press, 1991

James, Thomas Garnet Henry, *Pharaoh's People: Scenes from Life in Imperial Egypt*, London: Bodley Head, and Chicago: University of Chicago Press, 1984

Lefkowitz, Mary R., *Not Out of Africa: How Afrocentrism Became an Excuse to Teach Myth as History*, New York: Basic Books, 1996

Lefkowitz, Mary R., and Guy MacLean Rogers, eds., *Black Athena Revisited*, Chapel Hill: University of North Carolina Press, 1996

Lepsius, Karl Richard, *Denkmäler aus Aegypten und Aethiopien*, 12 vols., Berlin: Nickolaische, 1849–56; abridged in English as *Discoveries in Egypt, Ethiopia, and the Peninsula of Sinai*, London: Bentley, 1852

Lipke, Paul, *The Royal Ship of Cheops: A Retrospective Account of the Discovery, Restoration, and Reconstruction*, Oxford: BAR, 1984

Mokhtar, Gamel, ed., *Ancient Civilizations of Africa*, London: Heinemann, and Berkeley: University of California Press, 1981

Montelius, Oscar, *Der Orient und Europa: Einfluss der orientalischen Cultur auf Europa bis zur Mitte des letzten Jahrtausends v. Chr* (The Orient and Europe: The Influence of Oriental Culture on Europe until the Middle of the Last Millennium BCE), Stockholm, 1899

Montet, Pierre, *L'Egypte éternelle*; in English as *Eternal Egypt*, London: Weidenfeld and Nicolson, and New York: New American Library, 1964

Murdock, George Peter, *Africa: Its Peoples and Their Culture History*, New York: McGraw Hill, 1959

Perry, W.J., *The Growth of Civilization*, New York: Dutton, and London: Methuen, 1924

Petrie, William Matthew Flinders, *A History of Egypt*, 6 vols., London: Methuen, 1898–1905; reprinted 1989

Redford, Donald B., *History and Chronology of the Eighteenth Dynasty of Egypt*, Toronto: University of Toronto Press, 1967

Redford, Donald B., *Akhenaten: The Heretic King*, Princeton: Princeton University Press, 1984

Renfrew, Colin, *Before Civilization: The Radiocarbon Revolution and Prehistoric Europe*, London: Cape, and New York: Knopf, 1973

Seters, John Van, *The Hyksos: A New Investigation*, New Haven: Yale University Press, 1966

Smith, Elliott, *The Ancient Egyptians and Their Influence on Civilization*, London and New York: Harper, 1911, revised 1923; reprinted 1970

Trigger, Bruce G., *A History of Archaeological Thought*, Cambridge and New York: Cambridge University Press, 1989

West, Stephanie, "Herodotus' Epigraphical Interests," *Classical Quarterly* 79 (1985), 278–305

Wilson, John A., *The Burden of Egypt: An Interpretation of Ancient Egyptian Culture*, Chicago: University of Chicago Press, 1951; reprinted as *The Culture of Ancient Egypt*, 1956

Egypt: since the 7th Century CE

The history of Egypt since the Arab conquest in 639–44 down to the arrival of Napoleon in 1798 has been a poor relation of ancient, Roman, and modern Egypt. Despite the fact that Egypt in the Middle Ages became the greatest power in the Near East, and despite the wealth of its archival materials, the period remains understudied and little known outside academic circles for want of any great international, that is Western, interest in the Islamic period and its civilization. Meanwhile the subject itself has not proved easy to define. From the 7th to the 18th century, Egypt was either a province of wider empires such as the Arab from the 7th to the 10th centuries and the Ottoman from the 16th century onwards. Or, as the seat of such empires centered on Cairo, it was ruled by dynasties such as the Arab Fatimids, 969–1171; the Kurdish Ayyubids, 1171–1250; and the Turkish Mamluks, 1250–1517, who were variously perceived by themselves, by their subjects, and subsequently by historians as foreign to the country and its people. This is especially true of the Albanian Muhammad 'Ali, the so-called founder of modern Egypt, 1805–49, whose dynastic ambition to carve out a new empire in the region was restricted to Egypt itself only by British intervention and British rule, 1881–1922. Even then, after the final creation of an Egyptian nation-state, Nasser aspired between 1953 and 1970 to lead a much wider Arab nation in the Middle East.

The 7-volume French *Histoire de la nation égyptienne* (History of the Egyptian Nation, 1931–40), edited by Gabriel Hanotaux, thus divided the Islamic period into volumes on the Middle Ages, the Ottoman period, and the 19th and 20th centuries. Of the comparable, though earlier, English *History of Egypt*, only Stanley Lane-Poole's *A History of Egypt in the Middle Ages*, (1901; revised 1914) is still in general use, followed by P.M. Holt's *Egypt and the Fertile Crescent, 1517–1922* (1966). David Ayalon, Robert Irwin, and Hassanein Rabie each dealt with the Mamluk and J. Stanford Shaw with the Ottoman period; otherwise the reader must go to more general histories of the Middle East such as that by Endress. Janet Abu-Lughod, Stanley Lane-Poole, Carl F. Petry, André Raymond, and Susan Jane Staffa have each described the history of Cairo; otherwise, studies of social and cultural history remain scattered. In the early Islamic period, the question is complicated by the substitution of perishable paper for the papyrus documentation of Roman Egypt, by the conversion of the bulk of the population from Christianity to Islam, and by the change of language, written and vernacular, from Coptic and Greek to Arabic. The outcome at the beginning of the 19th century was memorably described by E.W. Lane's *The Manners and Customs of the Modern Egyptians* (1836); but the changes have been imperfectly understood, despite the work of S.D. Goitein on the medieval Jewish Geniza documents, and that of Michael Winter on the Ottoman period. Nevertheless, from the time of Ibn 'Abd al-Hakam and al-Kindi in the 9th and 10th centuries, there was in literate Muslim Egyptians a strong streak of patriotism, which culminated in the 15th century in the voluminous works of al-Maqrizi, most notably his *Khitat* or "Places": a topographical account of the country which is the framework for an encyclopedic description of its history, manners, and customs. Such patriotism reappeared in the historical work of al-Jabarti at the beginning of the 19th century, and inspired the first generation of westernized intellectuals in the middle of the century. The major authors of the medieval period then found their way into print, with Maqrizi as the model for the *Khitat* of the engineer 'Ali Mubarak (1886–89), which provided a modern description of the country.

In this way the state, created by Muhammad 'Ali and placed by him at the center of the modern history of the Middle East and Africa, became the focus of historical writing by Egyptians and western Europeans, beginning with the British and the French, and well surveyed by P.J. Vatikiotis' *The Modern History of Egypt* (1969). Egypt variously figured in histories of the Middle East such as Malcolm Yapp's; in histories of imperialism in Africa, especially Robinson and Gallagher's *Africa and the Victorians* (1961); and in particular in histories of the Nile such as Collins' *The Waters of the Nile* (1990). Studies of Egypt's economic history have grown out of reports on economic policy such as Charles Issawi's, while increasing attention is being paid to social history as in the work of Ehud Toledano. Egypt's political history as a nation-state developed from a French model of revolutionary nation-building against a British preference, in the years of British rule, for a model of Oriental passivity (well shown in the 9th, 10th and 11th editions of the *Encyclopaedia Britannica*). In the very large literature of the modern subject, the most vigorous Egyptian exponent has been Afaf Lutfi al-Sayyid Marsot, while the most celebrated French work is Berque's *L'Egypte: impérialisme et révolution* (1967; *Egypt: Imperialism and Revolution*, 1972). On the underlying theme of conflict between tradition and modernity, the standard work by P.J. Vatikiotis, *The Modern History of Egypt*, concluded pessimistically on the subject of the continued gulf between state and people, seeing little hope for the plural democracy favored by the majority of contemporary historians. This disapproval of the way in which the government of independent Egypt has remained authoritarian is a major feature of the literature, of political as well as historical importance.

MICHAEL BRETT

See also Goitein; Ottoman

Further Reading

Abu-Lughod, Janet L., *Cairo: 1001 Years of the City Victorious*, Princeton: Princeton University Press, 1971

Ayalon, David, *Gunpowder and Firearms in the Mamluk Kingdom: A Challenge to Medieval Society*, London: Valentine Mitchell, 1956; Totowa, NJ: Frank Cass, 1978

Ayalon, David, *Studies on the Mamluks of Egypt (1250–1517)*, London: Variorum, 1977

Berque, Jacques, *L'Egypte: impérialisme et révolution*, Paris: Gallimard, 1967; in English as *Egypt: Imperialism and Revolution*, London: Faber, and New York: Praeger, 1972

Collins, Robert O., *The Waters of the Nile*, Oxford and New York: Oxford University Press, 1990

Efendi, Huseyn, *Ottoman Egypt in the Age of the French Revolution*, translated by J. Stanford Shaw, Cambridge, MA: Harvard University Press, 1964

Endress, Gerhard, *Einführung in die islamische Geschichte*, 2 vols., Munich: Beck, 1982; in English as *An Introduction to Islam*, Edinburgh: Edinburgh University Press, and New York: Columbia University Press, 1988

Goitein, S.D., *A Mediterranean Society: The Jewish Communities of the Arab World as Portrayed in the Documents of the Cairo Geniza*, 6 vols., Berkeley: University of California Press, 1967–93

Hanotaux, Gabriel, ed., *Histoire de la nation égyptienne* (History of the Egyptian Nation), 7 vols., Paris: Société de l'Histoire Nationale, 1931–40

Holt, Peter Malcolm, *Egypt and the Fertile Crescent, 1517–1922: A Political History*, London: Longman, and Ithaca, NY: Cornell University Press, 1966

Irwin, Robert, *The Middle East in the Middle Ages: The Early Mamluk Sultanate, 1250–1382*, London: Croom Helm, and Carbondale: Southern Illinois University Press, 1986

Issawi, Charles, *Egypt: An Economic and Social Analysis*, London and New York: Oxford University Press, 1947; revised 1954

Issawi, Charles, *An Economic History of the Middle East and North Africa*, New York: Columbia University Press, 1982

Lane, Edward William, *The Manners and Customs of the Modern Egyptians*, London, 1836; reprinted London: Dent, and New York: Dutton, 1966

Lane-Poole, Stanley, *A History of Egypt in the Middle Ages*, London: Methuen, and New York: Scribner, 1901; revised Methuen, 1914

Lane-Poole, Stanley, *The Story of Cairo*, London: Dent, 1902

Marsot, Afaf Lutfi al-Sayyid, *Egypt and Cromer: A study in Anglo-Egyptian Relations*, London: Murray, and New York: Praeger, 1968

Marsot, Afaf Lutfi al-Sayyid, *Egypt's Liberal Experiment, 1922–1936*, Berkeley: University of California Press, 1977

Marsot, Afaf Lutfi al-Sayyid, *Egypt in the Reign of Muhammad Ali*, Cambridge and New York: Cambridge University Press, 1984

Marsot, Afaf Lutfi al-Sayyid, *A Short History of Modern Egypt*, Cambridge and New York: Cambridge University Press, 1985

Mubarak, 'Ali, *Al-Khitat al-tawfiqiyya al-jadida* (The New Book of Fortunate Places), 20 vols., Cairo, 1886–89

Petry, Carl F., *The Civilian Elite of Cairo in the Later Middle Ages*. Princeton: Princeton University Press, 1981

Rabie, Hassanein, *The Financial System of Egypt, AH 564–741/AD 1169–1341*, London and New York: Oxford University Press, 1972

Raymond, André, *Le Caire* (Cairo), Paris: Fayard, 1993

Robinson, Ronald, and John Gallagher with Alice Denny, *Africa and the Victorians: The Official Mind of Imperialism*, London: Macmillan, and New York: St. Martin's Press, 1961; revised 1981

Shaw, J. Stanford, *The Financial and Administrative Organization and Development of Ottoman Egypt, 1517–1798*, Princeton: Princeton University Press, 1962

Staffa, Susan Jane, *Conquest and Fusion: The Social Evolution of Cairo, AD 642–1850*, Leiden: Brill, 1977

Toledano, Ehud R., *State and Society in mid-Nineteenth-Century Egypt*, Cambridge and New York: Cambridge University Press, 1990

Vatikiotis, Panayiotis J., *The Modern History of Egypt*, London: Weidenfeld and Nicolson, and New York: Praeger, 1969; 4th edition, 1991

Winter, Michael, *Egyptian Society under Ottoman Rule, 1517–1798*, London and New York: Routledge, 1992

Yapp, Malcolm E., *The Making of the Modern Near East, 1792–1923*, London and New York: Longman, 1987

Yapp, Malcolm E., *The Near East since the First World War: A History to 1995*, 2nd edition, London and New York: Longman, 1991; revised 1996

Einhard *c.*770–840

Frankish chronicler

Einhard was a Frank who was the main biographer of the emperor Charlemagne. As the biographer of such a famous king, he sheds light on a significant era of medieval history. Einhard was educated in a monastery in Hesse (near Frankfurt, Germany). He mastered Latin and absorbed many of the writings of the ancient Romans, and this background would have a profound influence on his subsequent historical writings.

During the late 8th century, Charlemagne gathered scholars from all over Europe to come to his palace school at Aachen. In 791, Einhard was sent to the palace school by his abbot. While there, he came to the attention of Charlemagne and became the emperor's adviser and friend. Einhard stayed at court and was in a position to observe imperial policies and the emperor himself until Charlemagne's death in 814. Einhard remained in favor with Charlemagne's son and successor, Louis I (the Pious), but he soon retired to his estates. It was during his retirement that the aging courtier wrote his surviving works.

We have four surviving works by Einhard. One is a collection of his letters, two are religious tracts, and the most famous is his *Life of Charlemagne*. It is this last work, written probably between 829 and 836, that has earned Einhard the reputation as an influential writer of history.

Einhard's biography of Charlemagne is a short work divided into five parts: 1) Charlemagne's predecessors, the early Carolingians; 2) Charlemagne's wars; 3) the emperor's private life; 4) his last years and death; and 5) Charlemagne's last will and testament. Einhard explicitly wrote of his motivation for writing this historical biography. He said that he wanted to preserve the memory of the deeds of the great man both because of their importance, and because of the kindness that Charlemagne had showed him throughout his life. Furthermore, Einhard said that there was no one else who could relate the history with the accuracy of an eyewitness to the events. To supplement his personal experience, Einhard drew from his knowledge of the written documents of the period as he produced his history.

Einhard's *Life of Charlemagne* was the first medieval biography of a secular figure. That distinction, combined with his firsthand knowledge of the events discussed, makes it a valuable source. However, the source has remained a controversial one for historians. Since Einhard was breaking new territory in writing a secular biography, he drew from precedents that were familiar. In structure and content, Einhard creates his *Life* based on Suetonius' *Lives of the Caesars* (*c.*121–22 CE), in particular the "Life of Augustus." Many of the descriptions of Charlemagne's life are taken directly from Suetonius, so historians are unsure whether we can actually learn about Charlemagne from the man who knew him so well. Either Einhard was attempting to recreate the Frankish emperor in the mould of the Roman one, or he selected those passages from Suetonius that accurately described his patron.

Einhard himself serves as an excellent model of the court of Charlemagne, in which Germanic and Roman cultural elements were combined with new creative force. Einhard used elegant Latin and copied Roman historical models as he wrote the biographical eulogy for the Frankish emperor. While modern historians might wish that the biography were free from the ambiguities and errors created by Einhard's use of Suetonius, nevertheless, medievalists cannot ignore this important biography written by an eyewitness to the significant events of Charlemagne's reign.

JOYCE E. SALISBURY

See also France: to 1000; Ganshof; Suetonius

Biography

Einhardus, also known as Eginhard. Born Maingau, East Franconia, *c.*770. Studied at monastery of Fulda. Joined Charlemagne's entourage, 796: on ambassadorial missions, 806, 813; secretary to Louis the Pious; tutor of Lothair, Louis's eldest son, 817. Abbot of Fontenelle; retired first to Fontenelle, 828, then to Seligenstadt, which he founded. Married Irma, later an abbess (died 836). Died Seligenstadt, 14 March 840.

Principal Writings
Vita Caroli Magni, c.830; in *Two Lives of Charlemagne*, translated by Lewis Thorpe, 1969

Further Reading
Ganshof, F.L., "Notes critiques sur Eginhard, biographe de Charlemagne," *Revue Belge de Philologie et d'Histoire* 3 (1924), 725–58

Elkins, Stanley 1925–
US historian of slavery

Stanley Elkins is best known for his attempt to apply social psychology, specifically the literature that emerged from studying the Holocaust, to the historical problem of slavery in the US.

In *Slavery* (1959) he created controversy by analyzing the basic slave personality as the "Sambo" archetype, and slaves as exhibiting virtually no resistance to their condition as slaves. Using role psychology and personality theory models, he ascribed this behavior to a complete breakdown of slaves' personalities brought on by the physical and mental tortures of the Middle Passage and perpetuated through the all-embracing, repressive institutional practices of American slavery, and the associated development of slaves' personalities based upon a limited available repertoire of models, standards, and attitudes. "Sambo," according to Elkins, was docile but irresponsible, loyal but lazy, humble but deceitful. Thus the old stereotype of racial inferiority, which described very similar traits, was replaced with a new argument for psychological and cultural damage inflicted by the institutions of slavery, which has become known as the "Elkins thesis."

Essentially, Elkins hoped to portray the moral and practical consequences of unrestrained capitalism, but in the process he unleashed a new debate about the nature of the American slave personality and culture. By forcing the concentration camp analogy, he left many survivors from each side of the analogy – African Americans and Jews – uncomfortable with the comparison.

The reaction to Elkins' book, along with that to Daniel Patrick Moynihan's report on the black family and the general political atmosphere of the civil rights movement, provided impetus for a whole generation of new research in slavery. Such phrases as, "the slave personality," "the slave community," and "slave culture," are all to varying degrees responses to Elkins. Eugene Genovese's neo-Marxist *Roll, Jordan, Roll* (1974), John Blassingame's *The Slave Community* (1972), Herbert Gutman's *The Black Family in Slavery and Freedom* (1976), and Lawrence Levine's anthropological *Black Culture and Black Consciousness* (1977), all responded to the Sambo type by describing the complexity and originality of the slave culture under the mature 19th-century world of American slavery. Other writers, notably Peter Wood (*Black Majority*, 1974), have extended the research in slave culture back into the colonial era, describing important ways in which black culture shaped the development of American culture and institutions.

Elkins' original purposes in writing the book were lost in the debate over the Sambo type. He argued that the problem of slavery offered a crucial case study for understanding the useful role played by institutions in limiting the material ambitions of capitalism and in offering a location for the purposeful activity of intellectuals. He followed Richard Hofstadter's lead in criticizing American society on both counts. Discussing capitalism, he used comparative slavery studies (especially Frank Tannenbaum's *Slave and Citizen*, 1947) to argue that the competing Spanish institutions of church and state – the Catholic church, aristocratic tradition, and heritage of Roman law – had created a less absolute, and thus more moral, slavery than had the unfettered individualistic capitalism of colonial America. He then argued that individualism and crumbling institutions had left American intellectuals without an adequate environment within which to propose and develop the kinds of careful critiques of slavery or the concrete programs for emancipation that had allowed the European nations to end slavery without resorting to civil war and to the vague programs for integrating the freedmen that marked the post-emancipation era. Other historians, notably Genovese, and Peter Kolchin in his *Unfree Labor: American Slavery and Russian Serfdom* (1987), have argued that the evolution of slave cultures provides a stronger basis for such comparison of the institutions of slavery.

Elkins also contributed to the debates over the nature of the early American republic, with an essay (co-authored with Eric McKitrick in 1968), in which the Founding Fathers are portrayed as "young men of the revolution." That work has been extended to a much more comprehensive analysis of the political ideas and practice of the first decade of US history in *The Age of Federalism* (1993).

Although most of his conclusions regarding slavery have been rejected, Elkins' ambitious thesis has been enormously fruitful in the debate and research that it provoked.

DONALD R. PALM

See also African American; Cuba; Fogel; Levine; Slavery: Modern

Biography
Stanley Maurice Elkins. Born Boston, 27 April 1925. Received BA, Harvard University 1949; MA, Columbia University, 1951, PhD 1959. Taught at Fieldston School, 1951–54; University of Chicago, 1955–60; and Smith College, from 1960. Married 1947 (4 children).

Principal Writings
Slavery: A Problem in American Institutional and Intellectual Life, 1959; 3rd edition 1976
With Eric McKitrick, "The Founding Fathers: Young Men of the Revolution," in Jack P. Greene, *The Reinterpretation of the American Revolution, 1763–1787*, 1968
With Eric McKitrick, *The Age of Federalism: The Early American Republic, 1788–1800*, 1993

Further Reading
Blassingame, John, *The Slave Community: Plantation Life in the Antebellum South*, New York: Oxford University Press, 1972; revised 1979

Lane, Ann J., ed., *The Debate over Slavery: Stanley Elkins and His Critics*, Urbana: University of Illinois Press, 1971

Parish, Peter J., *Slavery: History and Historians*, New York: Harper, 1989

Elliott, J.H. 1930–

British historian of early modern Europe

John H. Elliott's life work has been to examine the little-studied Hispanic world of the 16th and 17th centuries. In the process he has helped to chart the boundaries between the medieval and modern worlds. He has traced the dramatic rise to power of Spain and its failed attempt to dominate Europe and its larger world. Implicitly he believes that Spain, as the first European power with a world empire, traveled part of the way down the road to modernity before the rest of Europe, and its starts and stops and ultimate failure to arrive until recently, serve to illuminate the successes of those that did. The slow path to modernity holds haunting, unresolved paradoxes, dilemmas, and contradictions left over from times past that Elliott has examined in the quicksilver light of Spanish history.

Lacking the monographic base for Spain that was the stock in trade of historians writing about other European countries, Elliott was forced to be selective, especially given the seemingly never-ending paper trail left by the Spanish bureaucracy. He chose to concentrate on what he perceived to be a crucial turning point in Spanish history, the ministry of the Count-Duke of Olivares (1621–43), when a program of reform was adopted to counteract the perceived decline of Spain. Looking for, but not initially finding state policy papers that recorded the decision-making process by which Spain tried to recover its former glory led Elliott out to the periphery where he produced a case study of how the center lost and then kept Catalonia. The result was his *The Revolt of the Catalans* (1963) where he described Spain's success and failure in ruling much of the world, the symbiotic relationship between Crown or central government and the provincial elites, and the latter's rule of the others. The Spanish state's working relationships with regional elites, and its inability to break through this upper strata and establish deeper ties of loyalty and allegiance with lower-level groups based on mutual benefits, are keys to understanding Spain's initial success and ultimate failure. The efficiencies and economies of action that accrue when such a breakthrough takes place never benefited Spain, unlike those countries where such a link was established.

Not having an adequate larger context within which to locate his regional study of Catalonia forced Elliott to write a general history, *Imperial Spain, 1469–1716* (1963). This general survey still stands as the finest interpretive overview of the period and well illustrates the seductive powers of Elliott's elegant, hypnotic prose that draws the reader into a contemplation of the macro-forces of history, which in this book are the rewards and perils of imperialism. The personal, interior dialogue with the reader with Socratic point and counterpoint is an enduring feature of Elliott's writing and accounts for its dramatic tension and engaging effect. After setting the Spanish stage with his general survey, Elliott felt compelled to map out a European-wide synthesis, and this resulted in his *Europe Divided, 1559–1598* (1968). Here he argued for a basic European social unity, but one comprising diversity of cultures and faiths whose tensions stimulated a divergence between the Mediterranean South and the Atlantic North.

The expanse of Elliott's vision and synthesis led to an invitation to deliver the Wiles lectures at the Queen's University of Belfast for 1969 where he reversed the usual order for study of the discovery of the New World and considered its impact on 16th- and early 17th-century Europe. These lectures appeared as *The Old World and the New, 1492–1650* (1970), initiated the Cambridge Early Modern History monograph series, and helped establish the period as a separate field of European history. Elliott was a general editor of the series and sought to publish those works bridging the period from the 15th to the 18th centuries showing continuity and change that underscored the transition from the medieval to the modern. His appointment to the Institute for Advanced Study at Princeton University in 1973 allowed him to return to what he considered a watershed in Spanish history, the crucial period of the Olivares ministry, and to his plan for a comprehensive political biography of the Count-Duke. Collecting, collating, and determining the main texts of the Count-Duke's papers led to their 2-volume publication with extensive commentary as *Memoriales y cartas del Conde Duque de Olivares* (Reports and Letters of the Count-Duke of Olivares, 1978–80). These were to become the main documentary basis for the political biography. Elliott also became increasingly aware of the cultural legacy of the Count-Duke in his building and furnishing of the Buen Retiro palace in Madrid for Philip IV (1621–65). The outcome of Elliott's foray into cultural history was *A Palace for a King* (with Jonathan Brown, 1980) where we see political and social history combined with the history of art in Elliott's characteristically panoramic view. Olivares' mobilization of intellectuals, artisans, and writers in the service of the state has a particularly modern resonance.

Invited to give the Trevelyan lectures at Cambridge University for 1983, Elliott chose to contrast the remarkably similar contemporary careers of Europe's two main rival statesmen, Cardinal Richelieu and the Count-Duke of Olivares, each plotting and maneuvering to outdo the other in the creation of a viable European state. In *Richelieu and Olivares* (1984), Elliott argued that posterity had disproportionately rewarded the victor and ignored the loser, thus distorting the reality of 17th-century Europe. Elliott's exacting examination showed that the race was very close and that contemporaries were never convinced of the inevitability of Spain's decline and France's ascent.

Finally his monumental *The Count-Duke of Olivares* appeared in 1986. For the first half of 17th-century Spanish history it serves as the point of departure for those wanting to understand what went before and what came afterwards. As a result, other historians have undertaken a sustained re-examination of the so-called decline of Spain. The cumulative effect of Elliott's biography along with this re-examination has been to push the debate back from the 17th to the 16th century, and, like all of Elliott's work, it forced a broader reformulation of the issue not just as a question in economic history but as single fabric woven with political and diplomatic threads, statecraft, finance, economics, cultural attitudes, and structural components.

With the Olivares biography behind him, Elliott brought together in *Spain and Its World, 1500–1700* (1989) some of his most important essays from various journals and books. Elliott's introduction and commentary on each piece provide important clues to his thinking and the direction of his work.

Elliott's recent public lectures – *National and Comparative History* (1991), *Illusion and Disillusionment: Spain and the Indies* (1992), and *Britain and Spain in America: Colonists and Colonized* (1995) – suggest a movement away from Spain to the subject of Spain and Britain in America as a point of comparison and contrast in the larger drama of the making of the modern world.

MAURICE P. BRUNGARDT

See also Latin America: Colonial; Maravall; Parker; Spain: Imperial

Biography

John Huxtable Elliott. Born Reading, England, 23 June 1930. Educated at Eton College, 1943–48; Trinity College, Cambridge, BA 1952, PhD 1955. Fellow of Trinity College, Cambridge, 1954–67: honorary fellow since 1991; taught at Cambridge University, 1957–67; professor of history, King's College, London, 1968–73; Institute for Advanced Study, Princeton, 1973–90; Regius professor of modern history, and fellow of Oriel College, Oxford University, since 1990. Knighted 1994. Married Oonah Sophia Butler, 1958.

Principal Writings

Imperial Spain, 1469–1716, 1963
The Revolt of the Catalans: A Study in the Decline of Spain, 1598–1640, 1963
Europe Divided, 1559–1598, 1968
The Old World and the New, 1492–1650, 1970
Editor with José F. de la Peña, *Memoriales y cartas del Conde Duque de Olivares*, (Reports and Letters of the Count-Duke of Olivares) 2 vols., 1978–80
With Jonathan Brown, *A Palace for a King: The Buen Retiro and the Court of Philip IV*, 1980
Richelieu and Olivares, 1984
"Spain and America in the Sixteenth and Seventeenth Centuries" and "The Spanish Conquest and Settlement of America," in Leslie Bethell, ed., *The Cambridge History of Latin America*, vol. 1, 1984
The Count-Duke of Olivares: The Statesman in an Age of Decline, 1986
Spain and Its World, 1500–1700: Selected Essays, 1989
Editor, *The Hispanic World: Civilization and Empire; Europe and the Americas; Past and Present*, 1991
National and Comparative History, 1991
Illusion and Disillusionment: Spain and the Indies, 1992
Britain and Spain in America: Colonists and Colonized, 1995

Further Reading

Kagan, Richard L., and Geoffrey Parker, eds., *Spain, Europe, and the Atlantic World: Essays in Honour of John H. Elliott*, Cambridge and New York: Cambridge University Press, 1995
Thompson, I.A.A., and Bartolomé Yun Casalilla, eds., *The Castilian Crisis of the Seventeenth Century: New Perspectives on the Economic and Social History of Seventeenth-Century Spain*, Cambridge and New York: Cambridge University Press, 1994

Elton, G.R. 1921–1994

British (German-born) political historian

A German-born Jew who fled Prague in 1939 in order to escape Hitler, G.R. Elton was the greatest Tudor historian of the century. He was particularly associated with the notion of a Tudor revolution in government – the title of his first book – published in 1953 – but was important more generally as an interpreter of the century and as a supervisor at Cambridge of postgraduates, many of whom disseminated his views of the period. Elton tended to adopt a bureaucratic perspective. He saw society as precarious and public order as something that had to be striven for and then protected. His main hero was Thomas Cromwell, Henry VIII's principal administrator in the 1530s, whom Elton viewed as the crucial figure in the definition of English legislative sovereignty, the maintenance of order during the Henrician Reformation, and the development of a modern state structure. These themes were advanced in *Policy and Police*, originally the Ford lectures for 1972, and in *Reform and Renewal: Thomas Cromwell and the Common Weal*, the Wiles lectures for 1972.

Elton's influence rested in part on his willingness not only to advance his particular interpretation of the 1530s in monographs and a large number of essays and articles, but also on his engagement with a wider audience through a series of textbooks. His *England under the Tudors* (1955) was for three decades the most widely read book on the period at sixth form and undergraduate level and was a model of erudition and clarity. It was supplemented, though not supplanted, by *Reform and Reformation* (1977).

Unlike most British historians who were, and are, resolutely either British or "European," Elton was expert in both British and continental European history. He edited volume 2 of the *New Cambridge Modern History* (1990), which dealt with the early 16th century, and had earlier published *Reformation Europe* (1963), an important volume in the very successful Fontana History of Europe series.

Elton's influence did not simply rest on his publications. He was also a figure of consequence in academic politics and patronage. The series of offices and honors he accumulated, developed, and utilized was by any standard impressive. Elton was powerful in Cambridge, where he was a professor from 1967 and Regius professor of modern history from 1983 to 1988. As a leading figure in the faculty and as a postgraduate supervisor, Elton played a major role in molding many of the academics of the next generation at a time when the expansion of the profession created many opportunities. The five *Festschriften* Elton received are a powerful testimony to his influence. He was, however, less successful in his opposition to borrowing of ideas from the social sciences and to new departures in teaching, themes that he outlined in his *The Practice of History* (1967).

On the national scale Elton rose to be an energetic president of the Royal Historical Society, 1972–76, and to be publication secretary of the British Academy, 1981–90, and his importance was acknowledged with a knighthood in 1986. He was an active patron of scholarly initiatives, including the monograph series Studies in History, but it cannot be said that he was a supporter of innovation in teaching or research.

Partly because of this, Elton's long-term legacy is likely to be limited. His interpretation of his own period was novel in analysis but not method, and had little to offer those working on other subjects. His last book, *The English* (1992), was provocative rather than definitive.

Yet he was very impressive not least because of his energy and personality. While Regius professor, Elton took part in a student balloon debate in which participants impersonated famous individuals and explained why they should not be thrown from a rapidly falling balloon in order to save their fellow travellers. Elton gave a solid performance as Thomas Cromwell. One of the students pretended to be Elton. It is difficult to imagine any other Regius professor taking part in such an occasion – or any other being thought interesting enough to be impersonated by a student.

JEREMY BLACK

See also Britain: 1066–1485; Britain: 1485–1750; Plumb; Political; Quantitative; State; Tawney; Thomas, K.; Trevelyan

Biography

Geoffrey Rudolph Elton, originally Gottfried Rudolph Ehrenberg. Born Tübingen, 17 August 1921. Attended school in Prague, then emigrated to England, 1939 (naturalized 1947); attended Rydal School, Colwyn Bay, then taught there while taking an External BA, University of London, 1943; Derby student, University College, London, 1946–48, PhD 1949. Served in the British Army in Italy, 1944–46. Taught at Glasgow University, 1948–49; Cambridge University (rising to Regius professor), 1949–88: fellow of Clare College from 1954. Knighted 1986. Married Sheila Lambert, 1952. Died 4 December 1994.

Principal Writings

The Tudor Revolution in Government: Administrative Changes in the Reign of Henry VIII, 1953
England under the Tudors, 1955
The Tudor Constitution: Documents and Commentary, 1960
Reformation Europe, 1517–1559, 1963
The Practice of History, 1967
Political History: Principles and Practice, 1970
Policy and Police: The Enforcement of the Reformation in the Age of Thomas Cromwell, 1972
Reform and Renewal: Thomas Cromwell and the Common Weal, 1973
Studies in Tudor and Stuart Politics and Government: Papers and Reviews, 4 vols., 1974–92
Reform and Reformation: England, 1509–1558, 1977
F.W. Maitland, 1985
Editor, *The New Cambridge Modern History,* 2nd edition, vol. 2: *The Reformation,* 1990
The English, 1992

Further Reading

Cross, Claire, David Loades, and J.J. Scarisbrick, eds., *Law and Government under the Tudors: Essays Presented to Sir Geoffrey Elton, Regius Professor of Modern History in the University of Cambridge, on the Occasion of his Retirement,* Cambridge and New York: Cambridge University Press, 1988
Guth, DeLloyd J., and John W. McKenna, eds., *Tudor Rule and Revolution: Essays for G.R. Elton from His American Friends,* Cambridge and New York: Cambridge University Press, 1982
Scott, Tom, and E.I. Kouri, eds., *Politics and Society in Reformation Europe: Essays for Sir Geoffrey Elton on his Sixty-Fifth Birthday,* London: Macmillan, 1986

Slavin, Arthur J., "G.R. Elton: On Reformation and Revolution," *History Teacher* 23 (1990), 405–31

Engels, Friedrich 1820–1895
German theoretician and historian

While Friedrich Engels is commonly known as the co-founder, with Karl Marx, of modern socialist theory, less frequently acknowledged is his contribution to the development of a radical approach to historical studies. His first major work, *Die Lage der arbeitenden Klasse in England* (1845; *The Condition of the Working Class in England,* 1887), emphasized the importance of class and gender and thus broke with the traditional "great man" approach to history that characterized the bulk of historical writing from Livy into the 20th century. Engels renounced any attempt to substitute individual personality for historical forces.

While he acknowledged that "men make history themselves," Engels also pointed out that

> they do so however in a given environment, which conditions them, and on the basis of actual, already existing relations, among which the economic relations – however much they may be influenced by other, political and ideological, relations – are still ultimately the decisive ones.

Throughout *The Condition of the Working Class in England* and his other his historical writings, Engels regarded the common people not just as the objects of history, but as the agents of historical change. His contributions to understanding the importance of class are many but among the most significant are: 1) discerning the importance of the popular masses in history; 2) understanding how common people express themselves within the culture and language of their times; 3) demonstrating how historical consciousness is necessary for radical change; 4) stressing class struggle as the motor which moves forward historical development.

Throughout his *Der deutsche Bauernkrieg* (1870; *The Peasant War in Germany,* 1926), Engels looked behind the openly stated religious causes of peasant rebellion to argue that the fundamental causes were rooted in class relations. According to Engels his book endeavored to reveal how religious and political theories were used by participants to understand their own actions while seeking "to prove that the political and religious theories were not the causes, but the results of that stage in the development of agriculture, industry, land and waterways, commerce and finance, which then existed in Germany."

When most were content to leave women out of history or, at best, portray them as minor players on a broad stage, Engels demonstrated how historical development was instrumental in the transformation of women's role in society. Among his contentions concerning gender are: 1) the importance of gender in understanding human development and history; 2) detailing the economic basis of women's oppression; 3) outlining women's role in society while arguing gender is a historically and socially determined concept, and thus not biologically preordained.

In contrast to intellectuals who accepted women's position within society as the natural result of "the female nature," Engels looked for the historical factors that led to male dominated structures. Engels contended that the rise of private property, controlled by men, led women to a position of subordination. He maintained

> as wealth increased, it, on the one hand, gave the man a more important status in the family than the woman, and, on the other hand, created a stimulus to utilize this strengthened position in order to overthrow the traditional order of inheritance in favor of the children. But this was impossible as long as descent according to mother right prevailed. This had, therefore, to be overthrown, and it was overthrown ... The overthrow of mother right was the *world-historic defeat of the female sex.* The man seized the reins in the house too, the woman was degraded, enthralled, became the slave of the man's lust, a mere instrument for breeding children.

Historians have found many factual errors in Engels historical writings, which is not surprising since he mainly relied on secondary sources easily available to him. This does not, however, diminish his importance as a major contributor to what is known as the "Marxist" school of history which emphasizes the primacy of economic and social forces over the individual or the political. Yet even among non-Marxist historians, much of Engels' work has proved instrumental in shaping a vision of the past – particularly in the field of social history. Thus, one might say that Engels' importance is due more to the questions he asked than to the specifics he cited.

WILLIAM A. PELZ

See also Chadwick; Coquery-Vidrovitch; Feminism; Feudalism; Germany: 1800–1945; Kołakowski; Labor; Marx; Marxist Interpretation; Nationalism; Niebuhr; Philosophy of History; Science; State; Urban

Biography

Born Barmen near Wuppertal, Germany, 28 November 1820, son of a manufacturer. Had a commercial apprenticeship before settling in Manchester to manage family's English holdings, 1842–69; moved to London, 1869; private scholar and polemicist. Died London, 5 August 1895.

Principal Writings

With Karl Marx, "Die deutsche Ideologie," written 1845–46; published in *Historisch-kritische Gesamtausgabe: Werke, Schriften, Briefe,* vol. 5, edited by David Rjazanov and V.V. Adoratskij, 1932; in English as *The German Ideology,* 1964

With Karl Marx, *Die heilige Familie, oder Kritik der kritischen Kritik,* 1845; in English as *The Holy Family; or, Critique of Critical Critique,* 1956

Die Lage der arbeitenden Klasse in England, 1845; in English as *The Condition of the Working Class in England in 1844,* 1887

Der deutsche Bauernkrieg, 1870; in English as *The Peasant War in Germany,* 1926

Der Ursprung der Familie, des Privateigenthums und des Staats, 1884; in English as *The Origin of the Family, Private Property, and the State,* 1891

With Karl Marx, *Collected Works,* 1975–

Further Reading

Bartel, Horst, and Walter Schmidt, "Friedrich Engels zu einigen Grundproblemen der Geschichte des deutschen Volkes im 19. Jahrhundert" (Friedrich Engels on the Fundamental Problems of the History of the German People in the 19th Century), *Jahrbuch der Geschichte* 6 (1972)

Wolf, Eric R., "The Peasant War in Germany: Friedrich Engels as Social Historian," *Science and Society* 51 (1987), 82–92

Zhukov, E.M., *Engel's i problemy istorii* (Engels and the Problems of History), 1970

Enlightenment Historical Writing

Many of the *philosophes,* the leading French intellectuals of the 18th century, disparaged much of the past: the Middle Ages for being barbaric, the age of the Reformation for being fanatical, and the reign of Louis XIV for its supposed obsession with *gloire,* and found that history could not provide the logical principles and ethical suppositions that were required to support the immutable laws they propounded.

Despite the Enlightenment's strong interest in the future, there was also an interest and sense of continuity with the past. Giambattista Vico (1668–1744), professor of rhetoric at Naples, emphasized the historical evolution of human societies in his *La scienza nuova* (1725; *The New Science,* 1948) and advanced a cyclical theory of history. In the German states historiographical traditions of imperial reform, imperial history, and Latin humanism were very much alive. The Sicilian cleric Rosario Gregorio (1753–1809) used scholarly methods to challenge false views of the medieval past of the island. In Sweden, Olof von Dalin (1708–63) wrote a scholarly history of his country which was commissioned by the Estates and refuted the Gothicist myths of Sweden's early history. Sven Lagerbring (1707–87) introduced the criticism of source material into Swedish history.

Voltaire (1694–1778) and Bolingbroke (1678–1751) propounded the notion of history as *belles-lettres,* of "philosophy teaching by example." They did so to great commercial effect, reflecting the growth of a reading market interested in history. Authors wrote for a large and immediate readership, producing a clearly commercial product, in contrast to the classical model of history for the benefit of friends and a posthumous public. In 1731 Voltaire brought dramatic near-contemporary history to a huge readership, with his history of Charles XII receiving ten printings in its first two years. His works on Louis XIV and the war of 1741 were similarly successful.

There was also a strong interest in the idea of an impartial enquiry into the past, and an emphasis on history as scholarship. Historical research was well developed in England where scholars studied both the Anglo-Saxon period and the more recent past, with the 17th century a particular focus of discussion and research.

Many of the greatest historians were British. The Scottish cleric William Robertson (1721–93) acquired a European reputation with his works, which were praised by Catherine II, D'Holbach, and Voltaire, and resulted in his election to academies in Madrid, Padua, and St. Petersburg. Robertson was a thorough researcher, noting in the preface to his *History of the Reign of Charles V* (1769), "I have carefully pointed out the sources from which I have derived information." The Scottish philosopher David Hume (1711–76) was best known in his lifetime as the author of a *History of England* (1754–62). The great critic of the French Revolution, Edmund Burke (1729–97), wrote an unpublished essay on English history (1757–60) which ascribed the development of human society to Providence's role in providing suitable conditions.

The greatest historical work of the century was Edward Gibbon's *The History of the Decline and Fall of the Roman Empire* (1776–88). This was a work of ambition, range, and scholarship that had a very favorable critical and commercial reception. A master of irony, Gibbon offered an exemplary tale that explained the history of Europe until it reached its contemporary condition of multiple statehood and Italian decadence. He wrote in a clear, narrative form, and included interesting people and events, dramatic occurrences, and often theatrical details for the domestic reader. History as an exemplary tale was generally accepted because politics and morality were not differentiated, either on the individual or on the communal scale. As with other works of history of the period, Gibbon offered essentially a political account, and the notion of rulership, governance and political life as moral activities were such that history was seen in that light by Gibbon, other historians, and their readers. Morality served to provide both an instructive story and an enlightening approach to the complexity of the past.

JEREMY BLACK

See also Gibbon; Hume; Vico; Voltaire

Further Reading

Black, John Bennett, *The Art of History: A Study of Four Great Historians of the Eighteenth Century*, London: Methuen, and New York: Crofts, 1926

Bowersock, Glen Warren, John Clive, and Stephen R. Graubard, eds., *Edward Gibbon and the Decline and Fall of the Roman Empire*, Cambridge, MA: Harvard University Press, 1977

Brumfitt, J.H., *Voltaire: Historian*, Oxford: Oxford University Press, 1958

Carrithers, David, "Montesquieu's Philosophy of History," *Journal of the History of Ideas* 47 (1986), 61–80

Forbes, Duncan, *Hume's Philosophical Politics*, Cambridge and New York: Cambridge University Press, 1975

Gibbon, Edward, *The History of the Decline and Fall of the Roman Empire*, 6 vols., London: Strahan and Cadell, 1776–88

Hume, David, *History of England*, 6 vols., 1754–62

Okie, Laird, *Augustan Historical Writing: Histories of England in the English Enlightenment*, Lanham, MD: University Press of America, 1991

Phillipson, Nicholas, *Hume*, London: Weidenfeld and Nicolson, and New York: St. Martin's Press, 1989

Reill, Peter Hanns, *The German Enlightenment and the Rise of Historicism*, Berkeley: University of California Press, 1975

Robertson, William, *History of the Reign of Charles V: With a View of the Progress of Society in Europe, from the Subversion of the Roman Empire, to the Beginning of the Sixteenth Century*, 3 vols., London: Strahan, 1769

Trevor-Roper, Hugh, "The Historical Philosophy of the Enlightenment," *Studies on Voltaire and the Eighteenth Century* 27 (1963), 1667–87

Vico, Giambattista, *La scienza nuova*, 1725, revised 1730; in English as *The New Science*, Ithaca, NY: Cornell University Press, 1948

Wexler, Victor G., *David Hume and the History of England*, Philadelphia: American Philosophical Society, 1979

Ennen, Edith 1907–

German constitutional, economic, and social historian

Central to Edith Ennen's historical work is the productive way she has combined constitutional history with economic and social history in her investigation of the Middle Ages. In Ennen's studies of regional and urban history her sphere of interest frequently has extended as far as the 19th century.

Ennen completed her PhD in 1933, under the supervision of Franz Steinbach: its subject was *Die Organisation der Selbstverwaltung in den Saarstädten* (The Organization of Self-Government in the Cities of the Saar), during the early modern period. This meant that she was closely connected with the Institut für Geschichtliche Landeskunde des Rheinlandes (Rhineland Institute for Regional History) at Bonn University during the early part of her academic career: this institute has recently been attacked for infiltrating German regional history with nationalist ideology. However, Ennen did not express *völkisch* or racist opinions like her colleague Franz Petri and did not join the NSDAP (the National Socialist Party), partly due to her strong Catholic beliefs. During the National Socialist period she stayed in the background, qualified as an archivist, and published small studies on specific questions relating to medieval and regional history. In 1974 she took up the position of town archivist in Bonn.

Ennen's first major work, *Frühgeschichte der europäischen Stadt* (The Early History of the European City, 1953), represented an important step away from the earlier ideological climate of the Rhineland Institute. It is true that Ennen did start out with the question, much-debated in the 1930s and 1940s, of how far urbanization was a dangerous thing for a nation. However, in her detailed historical investigation of the origins of particular cities she clearly distanced itself from the view that the city was an unnatural phenomenon, emphasizing its superiority to the rural way of life. Ennen's particular innovation in urban historical research was to introduce typological comparisons of various central European cities; she also used the geographic method, which had previously been employed mainly for research into dialects and popular traditions. This enabled her to progress beyond the doyens of urban history in the 1930s – Henri Pirenne, Fritz Rörig, and Hans Planitz – who had concentrated predominantly on investigating one particular urban type, as represented by the oldest German cities: the northwest European trading and industrial cities. Ennen was able to trace the origins of the earliest cities in northwest Europe using a group of clearly defined criteria: the construction of walls around the medieval merchant settlements, the spread of the term *burgensis*, the emergence of free districts, and weekly markets. Ennen observed that particular regions – especially the area between the Schelde, the Maas, and the Rhine, along with the Rhône-Saone region – were at the forefront of urban development, explaining this through their strategic location on the border of the Romance and Germanic cultures. Here, Mediterranean urban culture (which had survived from classical times despite mass migration) met the settlements of Germanic merchant culture with its cooperative style of organization, and this combination produced the characteristically medieval style of urban development. Ennen had produced preliminary studies for the *Frühgeschichte* in the 1930s and 1940s. She was able to add a new perspective to the process of urbanization in the Germanic region and in Europe as a whole by setting it in the larger context of the development of advanced urban cultures, beginning in the Near East in the 7th millennium BCE. This innovative work brought her international recognition and established her reputation as an eminent urban historian.

In 1961 Ennen was given a temporary professorship in Bonn. In 1964 she became a regular professor in Saarbrücken and in 1968 in Bonn. In 1962 she published *Geschichte der Stadt Bonn* (A History of the City of Bonn), in which she combined a series of smaller studies to form a rounded picture. She has retained close connections with the city of Bonn and with her home town of Merzig in the Saarland throughout her life. From 1968 until her retirement Ennen was director of the Rhineland Institute for Regional History and co-editor of the *Rheinische Vierteljahresblätter* (Rhineland Quarterly), which dated from 1932. She was also closely involved in the Rhineland urban atlas.

In 1972 Ennen published *Die europäische Stadt des Mittelalters* (*The Medieval Town*, 1979), inspired by research during her work on the *Frühgeschichte* and by later discussions with colleagues. This work also brought her international acclaim. In it Ennen extended the geographical framework of her examination (previously limited to the cities of the Schelde, the Maas, the Rhineland, and northern Italy), in order to present a fuller, more complex picture of the urban landscape of Europe. This is still a key reference work for European urban history; it was translated and reprinted a number of times.

Ennen devoted herself to her academic work with exceptional self-discipline and never married (her motto was *aut liberi, aut libri* – either children or books); she continued her academic work after her retirement in 1974. In 1979, together with archaeologist Walter Janssen, she published *Deutsche Agrargeschichte* (German Agricultural History), extending from the neolithic age to the end of the 18th century; this work is notable for its interdisciplinarity, drawing on both archaeological and documentary sources.

In the 1980s Ennen moved into a new field of enquiry. Her book *Frauen im Mittelalter* (Women in the Middle Ages, 1984) is a richly documented work; it did not, however, align itself with the emerging field of research into women's historical studies. This reference work has also been translated into a number of languages and reprinted several times.

Ennen is convinced of the layperson's right to look to history for answers to the moral questions of their time, and she started out from the basic assumption that historians have something to say to their own age. Thus in her own works she discussed the negative developments associated with urbanization and traced the city-dweller's ambivalent feeling towards the city back to classical times. In Ennen's view an understanding of history is vital to enable us to take responsibility for our shared urban heritage.

Ennen played an important part in developing the disciplines of urban and regional history in Germany after 1945, and it is in this area that her influence is most clearly apparent. Her students have become regional historians and archivists, although few of them (Klaus Fehn of Bonn, Walter Janssen of Würzburg, and Franz Irsigler of Trier) have taken up university teaching posts. She has also had a lasting influence on the work of historical societies and archives. A series of commemorative publications reflects the widespread appreciation of her work in both research and teaching.

RITA GUDERMANN

Biography

Born Merzig, Saar, Germany, 29 October 1907, daughter of a doctor. Studied at University of Freiburg; University of Berlin; and with Franz Steinbach, receiving PhD, University of Bonn, 1933. Taught briefly in the Bonn Gymnasium, then archivist in Berlin, 1934–47; and Bonn, 1947–64; professor, University of Saarbrücken, 1964–67; and University of Bonn, 1968–74 (emerita).

Principal Writings

Die Organisation der Selbstverwaltung in den Saarstädten vom ausgehenden Mittelalter bis zur Französischen Revolution (The Organization of Self-Government in the Cities of the Saar), 1933
Frühgeschichte der europäischen Stadt (The Early History of the European City), 1953
Geschichte der Stadt Bonn (A History of the City of Bonn), 1962
With D. Höroldt, *Kleine Geschichte der Stadt Bonn* (A Short History of the City of Bonn), 1967
Die europäische Stadt des Mittelalters, 1972; in English as *The Medieval Town*, 1979
With Walter Janssen, *Deutsche Agrargeschichte: vom Neolithikum bis zur Schwelle des Industriezeitalters* (German Agricultural History: From the Neolithic to the Industrial Age), 1979
Frauen im Mittelalter (Women in the Middle Ages), 1984

Further Reading

Besch, Werner *et al.*, eds., *Die Stadt in der europäischen Geschichte: Festschrift für Edith Ennen* (The City in European History: Festschrift for Edith Ennen), Bonn: Röhrscheid, 1972
Frau Professor Dr Edith Ennen zum 60. Geburtstag in dankbarer Verehrung dargebracht von ihren Schülern (To Edith Ennen on Her 60th Birthday, in Grateful Admiration from Her Students), Saarbrücken: University of Saarbrücken, 1967
Oberkrome, Willi, *Volksgeschichte: methodische Innovation und völkische Ideologisierung in der deutschen Geschichtswissenschaft, 1918–1945* (National History: Methodological Innovation and Nationalist Ideology in German History, 1918–1945), Göttingen: Vandenhoeck & Ruprecht, 1993

Environmental History

Although environmental history has emerged as a distinct historical field only since the late 1960s, it has a long ancestry. The idea that human society (and hence history) is profoundly affected by physical environment can be traced back at least as far as ancient Greece; ideas of climatic and geographical determinism were also widespread in 18th- and early 19th-century Europe. Modern environmental history has, however, been shaped by the development of historical geography and agrarian history, by attempts to establish a more scientific base for history, and, since the 1960s, by growing concern about environmental degradation. Modern environmental history can also be understood as part of a wider reaction against an older history of nations, states and "great men and women."

Donald Worster argued in 1988 that environmental history operates at three different, but often interrelated, levels – the historical study of nature, the study of humans' socio-economic interaction with the environment, and the environment as understood through changing ideas about nature. The first of these, sometimes described as "ecological history" in order to emphasize its grounding in the natural sciences, is concerned with the study of nature in both its organic and inorganic forms, and the ways in which specific environments or environmental factors functioned in the past and affected human activities. Thus, historians have investigated evidence for climatic change and its impact on vegetation, farming, and human health. Other scholars (notably Alfred W. Crosby) have examined the consequences of epidemic diseases and transoceanic plant and animal exchanges, especially in the wake of the first European voyages of discovery, or (as in the case of James C. Malin's study of the North American grasslands) they have looked at the changing character and human uses of specific types of landscape over an extended time-period. While some of these studies focused on the complex ecologies of small areas, environmental history frequently operates on a grand scale, spanning continents and even encompassing the entire globe. This strand of environmental history has likewise emphasized the importance of "natural disasters," such as volcanic eruptions and epidemics (like the Black Death of the 14th century), over which human beings had seemingly little control. Nature thus provides the essential dynamic for historical change.

The second level Worster identified is more anthropocentric, seeing the environment as a realm of human activity and interaction. It focuses on how the forms of nature, such as soils, forests, seasons, diseases, and water resources shaped human modes of production and patterns of social organization, or how human beings changed the landscape according to their own needs and practices. Here environmental history is allied to agrarian history: the stress is generally in terms of an emerging symbiosis, worked out over many generations, between people and the places they inhabit. The work of the Annales school in France provides several examples of this approach, although the emphasis varies – Marc Bloch's study of French rural history offers a less determinist approach than Fernand Braudel's study *La Méditerranée et le monde méditerranéen à l'époque de Philippe II* (1949; *The Mediterranean and the Mediterranean World in the Age of Philip II*, 1972) with its powerful plea for the geographical underpinning of human history, while Emmanuel Le Roy Ladurie's discussion of the role of climate in history forcefully contests the claims of more crudely deterministic writers on the subject.

Worster's third category identified the historical study of the environment with human beliefs and perceptions, and aligned environmental history with the history of ideas rather than with the natural sciences. This approach emphasizes how environments are understood or represented at different points in time or from different cultural perspectives. This form of environmental history is exemplified by the work of Clarence J. Glacken, who traced ideas about the natural world in European thought from the ancient Greeks to the late 18th century. Controversy has, however, raged mainly around what Lynn White in 1967 called the "historic roots of our present ecologic crisis." He argued that the Judeo-Christian tradition had shown an exceptional hostility towards nature, believing firmly in the divinely ordained subordination of nature to humankind. Other writers have rejected this claim as far too sweeping and have sought to place responsibility for changing attitudes elsewhere, for instance (in the case of Carolyn Merchant) in the Scientific Revolution of the 17th century. White's suggestion that other cultures were more empathetic toward nature has helped to give rise to an often stark dichotomy between Western exploitation and aggression, and the protective and sustainable environmental practices of non-Western cultures. Historical studies of the non-Western world have sometimes supported this view, but others have pointed to a discrepancy between cultural precepts and environmental practices.

The best environmental history (like William Cronon's masterly *Changes in the Land*, 1983) has succeeded in combining at least two of these strands, using the perceptual to inform the material, or has shown the contrast between different sets of cultural values and conflicting or alternative uses of the environment. But as environmental history has developed a number of areas of controversy have emerged, often arising from the use of very different kinds of sources or methodological approaches. By concentrating almost exclusively on biological or climatic factors, some historians have produced a strongly deterministic history, which identified the role of conscious human agency as secondary to the forces lying largely beyond human control. Other historians have contested this line of argument, either because the evidence is inconclusive or because monocausal explanations are deemed inadequate for complex historical phenomena.

A second point of contention relates to the extent to which a present-day sense of global environmental crisis can be read back into the past. Overturning old ideas of a developing and largely creative symbiosis with nature, some recent writers, such as Clive Ponting, have seen virtually the whole of human history as a tale of environmental degradation. Others have taken a far less pessimistic position, arguing instead that environmental history provides many examples of successful and sustainable relationships between people and their environment, and that environmental catastrophe is a very recent concept which should not be allowed to distort our understanding of the past.

DAVID ARNOLD

See also Annales School; Brazil; Chevalier; Corbin; Crosby; Curtin; Ecology; Freyre; Historical Geography; Le Roy Ladurie; Malin; Merchant; Semple; World; Worster

Further Reading

Bloch, Marc, *Les Caractères originaux de l'histoire rurale française*, Oslo: Aschehoug, and Cambridge, MA: Harvard University Press, 1931; in English as *French Rural History: An Essay on Its Basic Characteristics*, Berkeley: University of California Press, and London: Routledge, 1966

Braudel, Fernand, *La Méditerranée et le monde méditerranéen à l'époque de Philippe II*, 2 vols., Paris: Colin, 1949, revised 1966; in English as *The Mediterranean and the Mediterranean World in the Age of Philip II*, 2 vols., London: Collins, and New York: Harper, 1972–73

Bruun, Ole, and Arne Kalland, eds., *Asian Perceptions of Nature: A Critical Approach*, Copenhagen: Nordic Institute of Asian Studies, 1992; Richmond, Surrey: Curzon, 1995

Cronon, William, *Changes in the Land: Indians, Colonists, and the Ecology of New England*, New York: Hill and Wang, 1983

Crosby, Alfred W., Jr., *The Columbian Exchange: Biological and Cultural Consequences of 1492*, Westport, CT: Greenwood Press, 1972

Crosby, Alfred W., Jr., *Ecological Imperialism: The Biological Expansion of Europe, 900–1900*, Cambridge and New York: Cambridge University Press, 1986

Glacken, Clarence J., *Traces on the Rhodian Shore: Nature and Culture in Western Thought from Ancient Times to the End of the Eighteenth Century*, Berkeley: University of California Press, 1967

Le Roy Ladurie, Emmanuel, *Histoire du climat depuis l'an mil*, Paris: Flammarion, 1967; in English as *Times of Feast, Times of Famine: A History of Climate since the Year 1000*, Garden City, NY: Doubleday, 1971, London: W.H. Allen, 1972

Le Roy Ladurie, Emmanuel, *Le Territoire de l'historien*, 2 vols., Paris: Gallimard, 1973–78; selections in English as *The Territory of the Historian*, Brighton: Harvester Press, and Chicago: University of Chicago Press, 1979, and as *The Mind and Method of the Historian*, 1981

McNeill, William H., *Plagues and Peoples*, Garden City, NY: Doubleday, 1976; Oxford: Blackwell, 1977

Malin, James C., *The Grassland of North America: Prolegomena to Its History*, Lawrence, KS: Malin, 1947

Merchant, Carolyn, *The Death of Nature: Women, Ecology, and the Scientific Revolution*, San Francisco: Harper, 1980

Nash, Roderick, *Wilderness and the American Mind*, New Haven: Yale University Press, 1967

Pepper, David, *The Roots of Modern Environmentalism*, London: Croom Helm, 1984

Ponting, Clive, *A Green History of the World: The Environment and the Collapse of Great Civilizations*, London: Sinclair Stevenson, 1991; New York: St. Martin's Press, 1992

Post, John D., *The Last Great Subsistence Crisis in the Western World*, Baltimore: Johns Hopkins University Press, 1977

Rotberg, Robert I., and Theodore K. Rabb, eds., *Climate and History: Studies in Interdisciplinary History*, Princeton: Princeton University Press, 1981

White, Lynn, Jr., "The Historical Roots of Our Ecologic Crisis," *Science* 155 (1967), 1203–07

Worster, Donald, *Nature's Economy*, Cambridge and New York: Cambridge University Press, 1977; 2nd edition 1994

Worster, Donald, "Doing Environmental History," in Donald Worster, ed., *The Ends of the Earth: Perspectives on Modern Environmental History*, Cambridge and New York: Cambridge University Press, 1988

Erikson, Erik H. 1902–1994

US (German-born) psychohistorian

The use of Freudian psychology in historical writing dates from shortly after the turn of the 20th century. Psychoanalysts and historians alike recognized the strong lines of continuity in research, analysis, and narrative creation that the two fields share. Yet as late as the 1950s a theoretical foundation for and concrete examples of psychohistory were lacking. Erik H. Erikson's life cycle theory, provided the theoretical anchors, and his psychobiographical works the examples needed for the field of psychohistory. His work reached a wide public audience and influenced several generations of historians. The common currency of terms such as "identity" and "identity crisis" is testimony of his profound influence on our self-understanding. Revived historical focus on the importance of identity and of childhood and adolescent experiences continues to evoke

Erikson's vision and testifies to his continued influence on conceptualizations of the past.

Erikson's psychoanalytic clinical work, begun under Anna Freud in Vienna after 1927, permitted him insight into the dynamics of growing up and growing old which he brought to his historical work. In *Childhood and Society* (1950) he expanded Freud's psychosexual stages of development from three (oral, anal, phallic) to eight. Each of these stages represents a set of emotional and developmental challenges strongly influenced by history and culture that continue into old age. The successful resolution of the crisis in which each stage culminates constitutes personality development and permits an individual to grow and contribute. Erikson categorized each of his eight stages on a spectrum which needed exploration and balance for an individual to avoid dysfunction: 1) infancy: trust versus mistrust; 2) early childhood: autonomy versus shame and doubt; 3) preschool: initiative versus guilt; 4) school age: industry versus inferiority; 5) puberty: identity versus identity confusion; 6) young adulthood: intimacy versus isolation; 7) middle adulthood: generativity versus stagnation; and 8) late adulthood: integrity versus despair. Stage five, puberty, is the source of our common understanding of the term "identity crisis." In *Young Man Luther* (1958), Erikson defined these crises as products of a lifelong psychosocial process: "At a given age, a human being, by dint of his physical, intellectual and emotional growth, becomes ready and eager to face a new life task, that is, a set of choices and tests which are in some traditional way prescribed and prepared for him by his society's structure. A new life task presents a *crisis* whose outcome can be a successful graduation, or alternatively an impairment of the life cycle . . . each crisis lays one more cornerstone for the adult personality." In his major psychobiographies, *Young Man Luther* and *Gandhi's Truth* (1969), Erikson used this paradigm to explicate the origins of Luther's and Gandhi's behavior and beliefs.

An additional Eriksonian contribution to historical thought was the clinical observation that historians have affective relationships with their material. Known as *countertransference* in psychoanalytic terminology, the awareness of one's own emotional state and the acceptance of the necessity of coming to terms with the implications of that relationship upon scholarly work create a context in which historical work is simultaneously more accurate, enriching, and human. Erikson's "A Personal Word" to Gandhi (and his readers) in *Gandhi's Truth* is an emulated model of self-disclosure, reflection, and insight.

Emigrating to the United States on Hitler's assumption of power in 1933, Erikson obtained a university professorship without formal academic training on the strength of his psychoanalytic theories. In a 1942 article of historical interest, "Hitler's Imagery and German Youth," Erikson applied his nascent ideas as a contribution to wartime psychology. He achieved some notoriety in 1950 when he resigned from, and was subsequently reinstated by court order to, the Berkeley campus of the University of California on account of the institution of system-wide loyalty oaths which Erikson refused to sign. The popularity of his biographies (*Gandhi's Truth* won the Pulitzer prize) spread his ideas widely. A reviewer later commented that "Erikson is probably the closest thing to an intellectual hero in American culture today."

The complexities of his own family background gave Erikson a particular sensitivity to social margins. The biological son of a

Danish father and a Danish-Jewish mother, but raised as the son of a German-Jewish pediatrician (Homburger), Erikson struggled with and researched religious belief intensely. Collaborating with anthropologists Scudder Mekeel (researching Sioux Native American children) and Alfred Kroeber (working with the Yurok Native Americans of northern California), Erikson became sensitized to anthropological perspectives of the individual, the family, and society. From these experiences he drew the conclusion that although cultural forms of institutions may vary, they nonetheless bear remarkable similarities by virtue of their function as social mitigators of personality development. "It would seem almost self-evident," Erikson wrote in *Life History and the Historical Moment* (1975) "how the concepts of 'identity' and 'identity crisis' emerged from my personal, clinical, and anthropological observations." Erikson's historical analyses remain influential in no small part because of his awareness of the psychosocial origins of his work.

DAVID D. LEE

See also Freud; Gay; Mentalities; Nietzsche

Biography

Erik Homburger Erikson. Born Frankfurt, Germany, 15 June 1902; emigrated to US, 1933; naturalized 1939. Graduate, Vienna Psychoanalytic Clinic, 1933; studied with Anna Freud and at Harvard Psychological Clinic. Practicing psychoanalyst, 1933–94. Teacher and researcher: Harvard University School of Medicine, 1934–35; Yale University School of Medicine, 1936–39; University of California, Berkeley, 1939–50; Austen Riggs Center, Stockbridge, Massachusetts, 1951–60; Harvard University, 1960–70 (emeritus). Married Joan Mowat Serson, 1930 (3 children). Died Harwich, Massachusetts, 12 May 1994.

Principal Writings

"Hitler's Imagery and German Youth," *Psychiatry* 5 (1942), 475–95
Childhood and Society, 1950; revised 1963
Young Man Luther: A Study in Psychoanalysis and History, 1958
Identity and the Life Cycle, 1959
Insight and Responsibility: Lectures on the Ethical Implications of Psychoanalytic Insight, 1964
Identity: Youth and Crisis, 1968
Gandhi's Truth: On the Origins of Militant Nonviolence, 1969
Life History and the Historical Moment, 1975
The Life Cycle Completed: A Review, 1982
With Joan M. Erikson and Helen Q. Kivnick, *Vital Involvement in Old Age*, 1986

Further Reading

Albin, Mel, ed., *New Directions in Psychohistory: The Adelphi Papers in Honor of Erik H. Erikson*, Lexington, MA: Lexington Books, 1980
Capps, Donald, Walter H. Capps, and M. Gerald Bradford, eds., *Encounter with Erikson: Historical Interpretation and Religious Biography*, Missoula, MT: Scholars Press, 1977
Coles, Robert, *Erik H. Erikson: The Growth of His Work*, Boston: Little Brown, 1970
Evans, Richard I., *Dialogue with Erik Erikson*, New York: Harper, 1967
Roazen, Paul, *Erik H. Erikson: The Power and Limits of a Vision*, New York: Free Press, 1976
Wallulis, Jerald, *The Hermeneutics of Life History: Personal Achievement and History in Gadamer, Habermas, and Erikson*, Evanston IL: Northwestern University Press, 1990

Wright, J. Eugene, Jr., *Erikson, Identity, and Religion*, New York: Seabury Press, 1982
Zock, Hetty, *A Psychology of Ultimate Concern: Erik H. Erikson's Contribution to the Psychology of Religion*, Amsterdam: Rodopi, 1990

Ethnicity and "Race"

Ethnicity is a fundamental feature of human history: there may be as many as 1800 ethnic groups in Africa alone. Ethnic and "race" groups are characterized both by "environmental" differences – such as language, religion, territory, and popular memory – and by differences in their biology, such as their physical appearance, genetic pool, and epidemiological characteristics. Almost by definition historians have favored the "environmental" interpretation of ethnicity over the "genetic" alternative. The classic nature/nurture debate in the area of "race" and ethnicity greatly revolves around the kinds of evidence the protagonists are willing to use, and since historians mostly employ social and individual data they are far more inclined to emphasize human agency and free will. This is at the expense of the more social-scientific considerations emphasized by sociobiologists such as Pierre van den Berghe.

Although it is clear that "race" exists as an important linguistic category in the discourse of most people, professional historians, especially in the United States, have tended not to write about "race" as a category of people in the postwar period. (The term "race," however, continues to be used less ashamedly in postwar Britain and Europe.) Although racism existed in classical antiquity, there was no systematic treatment of "race" until the Enlightenment. "Race" first appeared as an intellectual category in the work of Johann Friedrich Blumenbach in the 1780s, was a powerful explanatory tool in the 19th century, and then was downplayed when the terrible events of the Holocaust became widely known. Racism is now understood to be a cultural construct, an extreme form of the differentiation to which people resort when trying to explain social life.

Another set of categories which provide the framework for historical debate include "nations," "peoples," and "tribes," each carrying heavy political baggage. The technical term "Creole" has been popularized by Benedict Anderson to denote the ruling immigrant group, such as the Anglo Americans. (This is the opposite of its vernacular meaning.) There is also a sub-category of ethnic groups known as the "caste," a form of *enforced* ethnicity. In certain societies (notoriously India) people are obliged to remain within fixed, and quite official, ethnic groupings. Partha Chatterjee's *The Nation and Its Fragments* (1993) is the most recent work to explore this subject. Pierre van den Berghe has attempted to extend the concept of "caste" to (pre-Mandela) South Africa and to the United States. Since ethnicity has much to do with naming (and being *named* by others), the work of Virginia Dominguez is significant and theoretically useful. This Cuban anthropologist first came to notice with her study of "Creole Louisiana" in *White by Definition* (1986), while the language of ethnic differentiation in contemporary Israel is the theme of her *People as Subject, People as Object* (1989).

Historical arguments thus come down to a series of interesting debates. The importance of these historical debates obviously varies from one country to the next, but the views of historians in the shaping of public opinion are arguably more influential on this topic than on many others. After all, appeals to "history" are fundamental to many of the debates around "race" and ethnicity. The most pressing of these are those with direct policy implications for the United States, and many of the historiographical contours of ethnic history have been shaped by US discussions. Such is the strength of national boundaries, however, that insights from one area of study are not always historiographically obvious in another, even in studies of the same groups of people viewed at different stages of their migration process. The outstanding example of this myopic tendency is that of the European groups who made up the immigrant minorities in the United States: only late in their history, from the 1980s, were they understood to have a pre-migration experience, a life before Ellis Island.

For most of the 20th century, the world's most powerful (and pluralist) nation saw itself as a large "melting pot." Israel Zangwill's influential American play, *The Melting-Pot* (1909) coincided with the major inquiry by the Immigration Commission on the history and future prospects of immigration into the United States. Then followed World War I and the passing of the Quota Laws, severely restricting immigration into the US. At this moment of intense "Americanization" appeared the first two recognizably professional historical accounts of the "new immigrants": Robert Foerster's fine study of the Italians, and the epic story of the Polish peasantry offered by William Thomas and Florian Znaniecki. Both works swam against the tide of American public policy, however, and it was not until the work of Marcus Lee Hansen and Oscar Handlin in the 1940s that immigration history again resurfaced as an important theme. Handlin, Brooklyn-bred himself and one of the first Jews to make it at Harvard, wrote a lyrical masterwork, *The Uprooted*, (1951), which took Thomas and Znaniecki's work to a higher level. Hansen devised the "Law" that perpetuates his name: that while the children of the immigrants would do all they could to deny their ancestry, the third generation would be just as anxious to rediscover their ethnic roots. Hansen's Law explains the huge growth in interest among hyphenate Americans in their past, especially during the 1960s. The anchor to this work was a remarkable paper given at Stockholm in 1960 by Frank Thistlethwaite, who placed "the Atlantic crossing" at the center of modern history.

The "ethnic revival" historiography is best reflected in the work of John Bodnar, Raymond Breton, Dino Cinel, Donna Gabaccia, Jon Gjerde, Tamara Hareven, Robert Harney, Michael La Sorte, Stephan Thernstrom, and Rudolph Vecoli. Despite important differences within this group, these historians were linked by an interest in "history from the bottom up," by the use of the "chain migration" tool crafted by Australian demographers influenced by Charles Price, by a tendency to see their subjects as "migrants" (again an Australian term) rather than "emigrants" or "immigrants," by a focus on the "placemaking" process through which groups constructed their own settlements, and, most assuredly, by a rejection both of the earlier simple push-pull models beloved by economic historians and of the filiopietistic historiography common among amateur ethnic historians. So Breton spoke of "institutional

completeness" to describe the reconstruction of ethnic folkways in a new setting, and Harney adopted the Italian word *ambiente* to connote the application of this principle in the case of Little Italies. Bodnar pointed to the stubborn survival of ethnic and class identities in the New World, and argued that these immigrants were "the transplanted" rather than "the uprooted." Cinel showed that there was an unconscious replication of traditional Italian settlement patterns on the other side of the world when the *contadini* settled in San Francisco. Tamara Hareven's study of French Canadians in the New England mill town Amoskeag examined the relationship between immigrant kinship patterns and the strictures of industrial discipline. La Sorte undertook a group biography of "greenhorn" Italo Americans based on six autobiographies and a diary. Kerby Miller used a Gramscian notion of cultural hegemony to demonstrate the persistence among Irish Americans of "holy Ireland," a sentimental version of their ethnic roots.

The major collective product of this "ethnic revival" school was the *Harvard Encyclopedia of American Ethnic Groups* (1980), drawn together by Thernstrom. It contains 106 group entries, ranging from "Afro-Americans" and "Italians" to "Yankees," and 29 thematic essays, such as "American identity and Americanization." Ethnic history in the US has registered significant methodological progress. Much of the earlier work was based on qualitative material, such as the letters of immigrants that feature in Charlotte Erickson's *Invisible Immigrants* (1972). Quantitative evidence became more common: an early example was E.P. Hutchinson's *Immigrants and Their Children* (1956), which made use of the US national censuses of 1910, 1920, and 1950. Thernstrom's *The Other Bostonians* (1973) took the quantitative method to a new level, with long-run time-series data drawn from several sources. This quantitative approach was criticized for its apolitical tendency, and a more balanced style followed. The "ethnic revival" school was influential outside North America, as evidenced in Robert Pascoe's 1987 study of Italians in Australia.

The pressure for "ethnic revival" history coincided with the entry of minority students into the mass university system of North America. Many universities and colleges introduced a major in Ethnic Studies (or some variant). Numerous museums and specialist libraries began actively to collect materials, especially in Toronto (Multicultural History Society of Ontario), New York (Center for Migration Studies), Philadelphia (Balch Institute), Minneapolis (Immigration History Center), and Rome (Centro Studi Emigrazione). By the 1990s there were at least 58 scholarly journals in North America specializing in the field, and a section of H-Net on the Internet devoted to Ethnic History, and several specialist websites based around the history of particular groups.

During the 1980s and 1990s, historians of the blacks and the new immigrant groups, particularly the Hispanics, adopted many of the techniques and methods of the older ethnic historians in order to write their own histories. This later work is generally more political, and more directly confronts racism.

Racism is coming to be seen as linked to slavery, that "peculiar institution," central to American history, but of ancient origins. Indeed, one way to understand the difference between an ethnic group and a "race" is to say that a race is denied a heritage by those who define a subordinate group in their midst as a "race." Nowhere is this truer than in the case of slaves. As Orlando Patterson showed, the "social death" in slavery is the condition of "natal alienation," the genealogical isolation of those who became slaves. This was a more fundamental fact than color or religious difference, and also explained the genocidal effect of removing indigenous people from their families (as was common in Australia) or from land associated with ancestors (as evident in North America). Patterson defined slavery as "the permanent, violent domination of natally alienated and generally dishonored persons." It logically follows that slaves could have no ethnicity, by definition, and Patterson's analysis of the dozens of slaveholding societies revealed that slaves were therefore never defined as "outcast" or belonging to a subordinate "caste." Slavery has been far more common that most imagine: at the time of Domesday Book in England (1086), for instance, 21 per cent of the Cornish were slaves, and even indigenous peoples owned slaves. But endoservitude was relatively uncommon, because people are far less likely to enslave others of their own ethnicity: this after all goes back to Patterson's definition of slavery, natal alienation. The biological differences that gave credibility to racism were by-products of slavery, for slaves have usually been distinguished by bodily aspects; even when their skin color was not black, slaves were branded, tattooed, had their hair shorn, or their ears cropped.

The levels of racism among white-immigrant groups from Europe with regard to indigenous African and Hispanic peoples in the North American case (and Asian people in the Australian case) may be linked to their own experiences of racism. When that racism comes to be regarded as normative, it can be "passed along," and atrocious behavior excused as "normal." But contests over land-use are the more fundamental difficulty, and local studies such as that by William Cronon in New England illustrate the enormous environmental changes that result from the imposition of new land-use practices brought about by settlers.

Ethnic history moved during the 1980s into a set of larger questions. What is the relationship between ethnic minorities and the state? What is the historical experience of these minorities in older societies (such as Europe) compared with the six "Anglo fragment societies" (United States, Australia, South Africa, Rhodesia, New Zealand, Canada)? Is the Iberian experience fundamentally different? How valid is the concept of "internal colonization" (Hechter) in explaining the making of societies such as the United Kingdom? Where does "national identity" come from? Is ethnic heritage merely a social construct, "an invention of tradition," or is there more to it than that? Does the policy of cultural diversity assist in the process of decolonization? Or is it merely a new form of exploitation carried out by the Creole elite on an unsuspecting pluralist population?

Instead of understanding debates about distant ethnicity as merely filiopietistic and the province of amateur historians making a special case for their ancestors, professional historians have become more interested in the question conceptualized by Anthony D. Smith as *The Ethnic Origins of Nations* (1986). The senior American historian Bernard Bailyn's later work on the ethnicity of early America can be seen in this same light, linking immigrant aspiration to national development. Bodnar's *Remaking America* (1992) offered an interesting account of different ways in which the American past has been commemorated by social and ethnic groups. Bodnar described the problem as one of "collective memory." A comparable analysis of ethnic festivals based on work such as Orsi's study of Italian Harlem would be invaluable.

According to Benedict Anderson, the precondition for the modern nation was the development of print technology, which assembled the readership of books and newspapers as members of an "imagined community." The model of nation-state which proved successful was the American one, copied throughout Latin America and (later) Asia and Africa. The American "people," as they were called in the Declaration of Independence, had become a "nation" 13 years later in the US Constitution. These Creole wars of independence, argues Anderson, were caused as much by a fear of indigenous and slave rebellions as by a desire to oust the colonial power. Magnus Mörner agreed with Anderson that the emergence of the state in Latin America was precocious. Ethnic groups were fundamental to the emergence of the nation-state in Latin America, either in the wishful albeit futile legislation of the Spanish metropole that restricted areas of Mexico to non-indigenous people, the same policy as the Jesuits in the border country of Venezuela, or in the dramatic impact of Italian and Spanish immigrants throughout Argentina.

Whether there was an exact moment of nationalism's appearance is debated among historians: Benedict Anderson contended that it dated to the American Revolution, while Anthony D. Smith saw it as much more incremental. His *National Identity* (1991) took the ideas of his earlier work forward into the modern period. Smith defined the modern nation as "a named human population sharing an historic territory, common myths and historical memories, a mass, public culture, a common economy and common legal rights and duties for all members." This definition suggests a variety of combinations with other kinds of identity – class, religious, or ethnic, for the nation is above all multidimensional. In this respect the nation is more complex than the state, which refers to those public institutions that are separate from civil society. The nation's specifically *ethnic* aspects (and origins) soon recede from view. There is thus an intrinsic conflict between nationalism and minority ethnicity. Martin Thom, in *Republics, Nations and Tribes* (1995), posited an interesting variant of this thesis, that there was a step in the formation of the nation-state associated with the European city-state, which deserves analysis in its own right.

An important counterpoint to the nationalist paradigm in history-writing is the situation of minorities whose claim to a history extends across national boundaries. Prominent examples are the Chinese dispersed through Southeast Asia and the Jews across several continents. As Abeyashere explains, the Dutch ruled Batavia (Jakarta) by parcelling each indigenous and immigrant group into its own *kampung* (neighborhood), a pattern of ethnic classification also favored in other parts of Asia. The history of the Jews has often been trivialized down to the level of "middlemen minorities" (to use the phrase of Pierre van den Berghe), a category also used to describe the Lebanese in West Africa, Indians in East Africa, and the Chinese in Southeast Asia. These groups must be understood as having a reality larger than their specialized economic function, even though it is that "shopkeeper" position which makes them a visible and vulnerable minority. *Nanyang* (overseas) Chinese are the subject of Victor Purcell's and of Charles Coppell's works. Broadly, there is a growing literature on ethnic minorities in Asia, such as the minorities in the People's Republic of China. There has been a resurgence among the ethnic minorities of China, officially 55 in number, during the 1980s and 1990s, largely as a reaction to the excesses of the Han majority during the Cultural Revolution. The process is described by Colin Mackerras. Stevan Harrell theorizes the Han treatment of the minorities as a "civilizing project," and compares it to earlier programs of integration carried out by the Confucians and the Christians.

This discussion may be usefully concluded by a consideration of Eastern Europe, for it is the latest battleground in which these endless debates around ethnicity and "race" are being fought out. Here all the themes come together to produce a series of terrible confrontations. For outsiders, the people of Eastern Europe might appear to be relatively homogenous in appearance ("race"), but they are incompatibly divided by territorial association, language, religion, and the self-perpetuating grudges born of a torrid history. The practice of *naming* others as belonging outside one's own group has encouraged the genocidal practice of "ethnic cleansing" common to this region. The apparently innocent name of "Macedonia" has generated violent reactions on the Greek border, a conflict that has spread to Macedonian émigré communities in Canada and Australia. As Lorig Danforth explains, appeals to history remain central to these debates. Curiously, however, the word "ethnicity" here takes on the pejorative overtones usually associated with "race," and the most innocent readings of an "ethnic history" in this region become overburdened by political considerations. On particular occasions during the 20th century, the region has reverberated with the forced removal of specific populations from one country to another, producing "natal alienation" for thousands of people. Populations have also been forbidden to speak particular languages. Victims of such policy are not literally slaves, but are certainly conscripts for the ongoing ethnic wars. The failed nations of the region, especially the entity known as Yugoslavia, can be explained historically as societies that were impossibly compromised by their ethnic makeup. A nation such as modern Greece requires powerful "dream-work", that is, it has to be imagined into existence, according to Stathis Gourgouris. The American model of nation-building has proved to be inapplicable to many parts of the world, including Eastern Europe, where perhaps the intervening stage of the city-state has kept the full development of nationalism in check. After all, cities like Skopje, Thessaloniki, Zagreb, and Sarajevo exercise a powerful but localized hegemony and do not readily coalesce into nations.

ROBERT PASCOE

See also Agrarian; Anthropology; Balkans; Bock; Cultural; Indigenous; Labor; Nationalism; Slavery: Modern; Social; South Africa; Sugar; United States: 19th Century; United States: 20th Century

Further Reading

Abeyashere, Susan, *Jakarta: A History*, Singapore: Oxford University Press, 1987

Anderson, Benedict, *Imagined Communities: Reflections on the Origin and Spread of Nationalism*, London and New York: Verso, 1983; revised 1991

Bailyn, Bernard, *The Peopling of British North America: An Introduction*, New York: Knopf, and London: Tauris, 1986

Blumenbach, Johann Friedrich, *The Anthropological Treatises* (includes "On the Natural Variety of Mankind"), edited by Thomas Bendyshe, London: Longman, 1865 (German original 1775, 1795)

Bodnar, John, *Immigration and Industrialization: Ethnicity in an American Mill Town, 1870–1940*, Pittsburgh: University of Pittsburgh Press, 1977

Bodnar, John, *Remaking America: Public Memory, Commemoration, and Patriotism in the Twentieth Century*, Princeton: Princeton University Press, 1992

Breton, Raymond, and Pierre Savard, eds., *The Quebec and Acadian Diaspora in North America*, Toronto: Multicultural History Society of Ontario, 1982

Chatterjee, Partha, *The Nation and Its Fragments: Colonial and Postcolonial Histories*, Princeton: Princeton University Press, 1993

Cinel, Dino, *From Italy to San Francisco: The Immigrant Experience*, Stanford, CA: Stanford University Press, 1982

Coppell, Charles, *Indonesian Chinese in Crisis*, Kuala Lumpur: Oxford University Press, 1983

Cronon, William, *Changes in the Land: Indians, Colonists, and the Ecology of New England*, New York: Hill and Wang, 1983

Danforth, Loring M., *The Macedonian Conflict: Ethnic Nationalism in a Transnational World*, Princeton: Princeton University Press, 1995

Davis, Arthur Paul, *From the Dark Tower: Afro-American Writers, 1900–1960*, Washington, DC: Howard University Press, 1974

Domínguez, Virginia R., *White by Definition: Social Classification in Creole Louisiana*, New Brunswick, NJ: Rutgers University Press, 1986

Domínguez, Virginia R., *People as Subject, People as Object: Selfhood and Peoplehood in Contemporary Israel*, Madison: University of Wisconsin Press, 1989

Erickson, Charlotte, ed., *Invisible Immigrants: The Adaptation of English and Scottish Immigrants in Nineteenth-Century America*, London: London School of Economics/Weidenfeld and Nicolson, and Coral Gables: University of Miami Press, 1972

Foerster, Robert Franz, *The Italian Emigration of Our Times*, Cambridge, MA: Harvard University Press, 1919

Gabaccia, Donna R., *From Sicily to Elizabeth Street: Housing and Social Change among Italian Immigrants, 1880–1930*, Albany: State University of New York Press, 1984

Gjerde, Jon, *From Peasants to Farmers: The Migration from Balestrand, Norway, to the Upper Middle West*, Cambridge and New York: Cambridge University Press, 1985

Gourgouris, Stathis, *Dream Nation: Enlightenment, Colonization, and the Institution of Modern Greece*, Stanford, CA: Stanford University Press, 1996

Handlin, Oscar, *The Uprooted: The Epic Story of the Great Migrations That Made the American People*, Boston: Little Brown, 1951, revised 1973; as *The Uprooted: From the Old World to the New* London: Watts, 1953

Hansen, Marcus Lee, *The Atlantic Migration, 1607–1860: A History of the Continuing Settlement of the United States*, Cambridge, MA: Harvard University Press, 1940

Hareven, Tamara, *Family Time and Industrial Time: The Relationship Between the Family and Work in a New England Industrial Community*, Cambridge and New York: Cambridge University Press, 1982

Harney, Robert F., and J. Vincenza Scarpaci, eds., *Little Italies in North America*, Toronto: Multicultural History Society of Ontario, 1981

Harrell, Stevan, ed., *Cultural Encounters on China's Ethnic Frontiers*, Seattle: University of Washington Press, 1994

Hartz, Louis, ed., *The Founding of New Societies: Studies in the History of the United States, Latin America, South Africa, Canada, and Australia*, New York: Harcourt Brace, 1964

Hechter, Michael, *Internal Colonialism: The Celtic Fringe in British National Development, 1536–1966*, London: Routledge, and Berkeley: University of California Press, 1975

Holloway, Thomas H., *Immigrants on the Land: Coffee and Society in São Paulo, 1886–1934*, Chapel Hill: University of North Carolina Press, 1980

Hutchinson, Edward Prince, *Immigrants and Their Children, 1850–1950*, New York: John Wiley, and London: Chapman and Hall, 1956

La Sorte, Michael, *La Merica: Images of Italian Greenhorn Experience*, Philadelphia: Temple University Press, 1985

MacDonald, John S., and Leatrice MacDonald, "Chain Migration, Ethnic Neighborhoods and Social Networks," *Millbank Memorial Fund Quarterly* 42 (1962), 82–97

Mackerras, Colin, *China's Minority Cultures: Identities and Integration since 1912*, Melbourne: Longman, and New York: St. Martin's Press, 1995

Martellone, Anna Maria, *Una Little Italy nell'Atene d'America: la comunità italiana di Boston dal 1800 al 1920* (A Little Italy in the Athens of America: The Italian Community of Boston, 1800–1920), Naples: Guida, 1973

Miller, Kerby A., *Emigrants and Exiles: Ireland and the Irish Exodus to North America*, New York and Oxford: Oxford University Press, 1985

Mörner, Magnus, *Region and State in Latin America's Past*, Baltimore: Johns Hopkins University Press, 1993

Orsi, Robert Anthony, *The Madonna of 115th Street: Faith and Community in Italian Harlem, 1880–1950*, New Haven and London: Yale University Press, 1985

Pascoe, Rob, *Buongiorno Australia: Our Italian Heritage*, Melbourne: Greenhouse, 1987

Patterson, Orlando, *Slavery and Social Death: A Comparative Study*, Cambridge, MA: Harvard University Press, 1982

Piore, Michael J., *Birds of Passage: Migrant Labor and Industrial Society*, Cambridge, MA: Cambridge University Press, 1979

Purcell, Victor, *The Chinese in Southeast Asia*, Oxford and New York: Oxford University Press, 1951

Scobie, James R., *Revolution on the Pampas: A Social History of Argentine Wheat, 1860–1910*, Austin: University of Texas Press, 1964

Smith, Anthony D., *The Ethnic Origins of Nations*, Oxford: Blackwell, 1986

Smith, Anthony D., *National Identity*, London: Penguin, and Reno: University of Nevada Press, 1991

Smith, Judith E., *Family Connections: A History of Italian and Jewish Immigrant Lives in Providence, Rhode Island, 1900–1940*, Albany: State University of New York Press, 1985

Solberg, Carl E., *Immigration and Nationalism: Argentina and Chile, 1890–1914*, Austin: University of Texas Press, 1970

Solomon, Barbara Miller, *Ancestors and Immigrants: A Changing New England Tradition*, Cambridge, MA: Harvard University Press, 1956; reprinted Chicago: University of Chicago Press, 1972

Thernstrom, Stephan, *The Other Bostonians: Poverty and Progress in the American Metropolis, 1880–1970*, Cambridge, MA: Harvard University Press, 1973

Thernstrom, Stephan, ed., *Harvard Encyclopedia of American Ethnic Groups*, Cambridge, MA: Harvard University Press, 1980

Thistlethwaite, Frank, "Migration from Europe Overseas in the Nineteenth and Twentieth Centuries" and "Postscript," in Rudolph J. Vecoli and Suzanne M. Sinke, eds., *A Century of European Migrations, 1830–1930*, Urbana: University of Illinois Press, 1991

Thom, Martin, *Republics, Nations and Tribes*, London and New York: Verso, 1995

Thomas, William I., and Florian Znaniecki, *The Polish Peasant in Europe and America*, 5 vols., Boston: Badger, 1918–20, London: Constable, 1958; edited and abridged by Eli Zaretsky, Urbana: University of Illinois Press, 1984

van den Berghe, Pierre, *The Ethnic Phenomenon*, New York and London: Elsevier, 1981

Vecoli, Rudolph J., and Suzanne M. Sinke, eds., *A Century of European Migrations, 1830–1930*, Urbana: University of Illinois Press, 1991

Ethnohistory

Ethnohistory is an interdisciplinary approach, applied primarily to the history of non-European societies that produce little or no written documentation; it combines the methods of ethnology (a division of the overall discipline of anthropology) with those of history. Although fusions of these methodologies can be traced in the works of earlier scholars, the first major study to bear the unmistakable imprint of ethnohistorical technique was Bailey's *The Conflict of European and Eastern Algonkian Cultures, 1504–1700* (1937). Published in eastern Canada with a small print run, Bailey's book attracted little attention in the United States, where a separate process of scholarly evolution was foreshadowed by the appearance of anthropological works – such as Ralph Linton's *Acculturation in Seven American Indian Tribes* (1940) – that addressed the nature of culture change in North American aboriginal societies. The creation of the Indian Claims Commission by the US Congress in 1946 gave a further stimulus, and the increasing recognition by ethnologists of the importance of historical evidence and analysis was reflected in the foundation of the journal *Ethnohistory* in 1954. Also by that time a few major studies such as Wallace's *King of the Delawares* (1949) had drawn attention to the need for sustained scholarly analysis of the native experience. The publication of Trelease's *Indian Affairs in Colonial New York* (1960) is widely regarded as an important landmark, being the first substantial work of ethnohistory published in the United States by a historian rather than an anthropologist. Meanwhile, studies such as Gibson's *Tlaxcala in the Sixteenth Century* (1952) and *The Aztecs under Spanish Rule* (1964) exemplified the application of ethnohistorical techniques outside North America.

The intellectual origins of ethnohistory can be attributed in part to the shortcomings of the both history and anthropology. Few professional historians, prior to the middle decades of the 20th century, showed any serious interest in aboriginal peoples. This reflected a widespread assumption that native societies were simple and static, and therefore unworthy of the attention of a discipline that specialized in evaluating the complexities of change through time. Furthermore, peoples who were not literate in any European sense produced no original documentation that was comprehensible to historians schooled in archival research. The solution was to ignore such societies, except insofar as they might be peripherally relevant to other historical fields. This observation could not be applied to anthropologists, as the ethnology of native North American peoples had been one of the principal elements of the emergent discipline of anthropology in the late 19th century. Yet the "synchronic" approach of ethnologists – the portrayal, chiefly based on field research, of a society as it existed at a particular time – tended to produce studies that neglected the existence of change through time, or treated it simplistically. Ethnohistorical method prompted both ethnologists and historians to be open to a wider variety of techniques. Those trained in ethnology came to make greater use of documentary evidence and to attend more closely to the dynamics of sociocultural change. Historians were brought to recognize the value of oral evidence, as well as evidence based on material culture and environmental adaptations, while also becoming sensitized to the demands made by cross-cultural study on the practitioners of a discipline that had European intellectual roots, but professed to encompass the entire human past in its potential scope.

From the late 1960s onwards, the ethnohistorical approach was used with increasing sophistication. Many important studies appeared in North America, including Wallace's *The Death and Rebirth of the Seneca* (1970), and the full-blooded assault on the complacencies of North American colonial history launched by Jennings in *The Invasion of America* (1975). Trigger's *The Children of Aataentsic* (1976) showed the ability of an ethnohistorian to write a detailed narrative account of a native society, both before and after non-native contact, and at the same time to reshape important interpretive themes affecting both aboriginal and colonial history. Brown's *Strangers in Blood* (1980) was one of several works that dealt with gender issues as well as intercultural exchanges in fur trade society, while Axtell's *The Invasion Within* (1985) was one of a number of substantial studies in which he explored religious and other interactions between native inhabitants and North American colonists. The field as a whole was invigorated by debates between advocates of a "cultural-relativist" approach to native history, and those who argued that aboriginal-colonial interactions could best be explained on a basis of shared rationality.

During the 1980s and the 1990s the flow of ethnohistorical studies became a flood. As well as such specifically dedicated journals as *Ethnohistory*, other anthropological and historical periodicals – notably *William and Mary Quarterly* – regularly published articles grounded in ethnohistory. The approach, legitimately regarded as North American in its origins, was used extensively in other geographical contexts. Among the themes now prominent was the study of the autonomy – limited though it might be in some circumstances – exercised by aboriginal peoples in their dealings with colonists and colonial powers. Examples included Comaroff's *Body of Power, Spirit of Resistance* (1985), Clendinnen's *Ambivalent Conquests* (1987), Merrell's *The Indians' New World* (1989) and White's *The Middle Ground* (1991). At the same time, significant questions were raised about the future of ethnohistory. Had increasing interdisciplinary sharing of research methods made a specifically interdisciplinary approach such as ethnohistory obsolete? Alternatively, should ethnohistory be recognized as a discipline in itself? Or, from a different critical direction, did the continuing practice of ethnohistory preponderantly by non-aboriginal scholars represent an undue appropriation of aboriginal history and culture? These questions will undoubtedly continue to be debated, but in the late 1990s continuing productivity suggests that ethnohistory remains a useful methodological framework for historians and others.

JOHN G. REID

See also Anthropology; Axtell; Bolton; Dening; Gibson; Indigenous; Native American; Trigger

Further Reading

Axtell, James, "The Ethnohistory of Early America: A Review Essay," *William and Mary Quarterly*, 3rd series, 35 (1978), 110–44
Axtell, James, *The Invasion Within: The Contest of Cultures in Colonial North America*, New York: Oxford University Press, 1985

Bailey, Alfred Goldsworthy, *The Conflict of European and Eastern Algonkian Cultures, 1504–1700: A Study in Canadian Civilization*. Saint John: New Brunswick Museum, 1937
Bailey, Alfred Goldsworthy, "Retrospective Thoughts of an Ethnohistorian," Canadian Historical Association, *Historical Papers/Communications historiques* (1977)
Brown, Jennifer S.H., *Strangers in Blood: Fur Trade Company Families in Indian Country*, Vancouver: University of British Columbia Press, 1980
Clendinnen, Inga, *Ambivalent Conquests: Maya and Spaniard in Yucatan, 1517–1570*, Cambridge and New York: Cambridge University Press, 1987
Comaroff, Jean, *Body of Power, Spirit of Resistance: The Culture and History of a South African People*, Chicago: University of Chicago Press, 1985
Gibson, Charles, *Tlaxcala in the Sixteenth Century*, New Haven: Yale University Press, 1952
Gibson, Charles, *The Aztecs under Spanish Rule: A History of the Indians of the Valley of Mexico, 1519–1810*, Stanford, CA: Stanford University Press, 1964
Jennings, Francis, *The Invasion of America: Indians, Colonialism, and the Cant of Conquest*, Chapel Hill: University of North Carolina Press, 1975
Linton, Ralph, ed., *Acculturation in Seven American Indian Tribes*, New York: Appleton Century, 1940
Merrell, James H., *The Indians' New World: Catawbas and Their Neighbors from European Contact Through the Eve of Removal*, Chapel Hill: University of North Carolina Press, 1989
Trelease, Allen W., *Indian Affairs in Colonial New York: The Seventeenth Century*, Ithaca, NY: Cornell University Press, 1960
Trigger, Bruce G., *The Children of Aataentsic: A History of the Huron People to 1660*, 2 vols., Montreal: McGill–Queen's University Press, 1976
Trigger, Bruce G., "Ethnohistory: Problems and Prospects," *Ethnohistory*, 29 (1982)
Trigger, Bruce G., "Alfred G. Bailey, Ethnohistorian," *Acadiensis* 18 (1989), 3–21
Trigger, Bruce G., "Early Native North American Responses to European Contact: Romantic versus Rationalistic Interpretations," *Journal of American History*, 77 (1990–91)
Wallace, Anthony F.C., *King of the Delawares: Teedyuscung, 1700–1763*, Philadelphia: University of Pennsylvania Press, 1949
Wallace, Anthony F.C., *The Death and Rebirth of the Seneca*, New York: Knopf, 1970
White, Richard, *The Middle Ground: Indians, Empires, and Republics in the Great Lakes Region, 1650–1815*, Cambridge and New York: Cambridge University Press, 1991

Europe: Modern

The uneven development caused by cultural, economic, social, political, and geographical diversity within Europe has problematized a definition of the beginning of "modern" Europe. Throughout the 19th century, the Romantic historians František Palacký, Joachim Lelewel, Nikolai Karamzin, and Thomas Babington Macaulay eulogized their respective countries and established strictly national chronologies. In this vein, the French historian Jules Michelet portrayed the French Revolution as the practical realization of the Enlightenment *philosophes*. Since Lord Acton's *Cambridge Modern History* (edited by A.L. Ward *et al.*, 1902–12) most historians have enshrined the revolution as a cornerstone in the advance of liberty and a caesura in European history.

Marxist historians accepted the revolution's universality, although they followed Georges Lefebvre's *Quatre-vingt-neuf*

(1939; *The Coming of the French Revolution*, 1947) in looking beyond the ideological to the material roots and documenting economic motivations of a highly literate capitalist class straining under feudal restrictions. In the 1980s, the new cultural history moved beyond politicization to focus instead on the revolution's cultural meaning. Lynn Hunt's influential *Politics, Culture, and Class* (1984) typified this approach in its rejection of socioeconomic determinism and its use of Clifford Geertz's social and cultural anthropology, Carlo Ginzburg's microhistory, and Sven-Olof Linquist's "dig where you stand" approach.

Only the Industrial Revolution has been accorded equal responsibility for the transformation and modernization of Europe. Clive Trebilcock described its technical innovations – led by the steam engine, factory system, and a specialized, capital intensive economy – in *The Industrialization of the Continental Powers* (1981), but the effects of economic changes transcended the workplace.

Historians, especially from Ranke's historicist school, praised industrialization as the handmaiden of democracy and free trade. Using historicism's empiricist methodology, Treitschke's *Deutsche Geschichte im neunzehnten Jahrhundert* (1879–94; *History of Germany in the Nineteenth Century*, 1915–19) typified the supreme faith in the industrialized nation-state, European civilization, and progress. His basic assumptions echo today in M.S. Anderson's *The Ascendancy of Europe* (1972), and in arguments for historical objectivity.

In the early 20th century, however, works such as J.L. and Barbara Hammond's *The Village Labourer* (1911) showed a darker side to industrialization as old social networks based on hand production and village life gave way to the impersonal, economic calculation of the factory and city life. Marxist historiography, although restricted before the 1950s to such notable works as Maurice Dobb's *Studies in the Development of Capitalism* (1946), Jan Romein's *De lage landen bijde zee* (The Lowlands by the Sea, 1934), and Emilio Sereni's *Il capitalismo nelle campagne* (Capitalism in the Countryside, 1947), explored economic and social development and reversed the liberal ethos and valuation of industrialization, while nonetheless retaining a narrative of unilinear European progress.

Since 1950 the new social and economic histories encouraged innovative research into the 19th century, bringing Marxism into the mainstream. *English Social History* (1942) by G.M. Trevelyan had already redefined social history as "history of the people with the politics left out." Demographic historians studied the phenomenon of urbanization in A.F. Weber's *The Growth of Cities in the Nineteenth Century* (1899) and Thomas McKeown's *The Modern Rise of Population* (1976). Lucien Febvre and Marc Bloch established the quantitative structuralism of the Annales school, while Fernand Braudel pioneered "total history" and influenced a generation of labor historians. The Communist Party History Group in Britain produced Eric Hobsbawm and E.P. Thompson, whose *The Making of the English Working Class* (1963) set a controversial standard for histories of the working class and working-class consciousness. The working class was synonymous with the socialist and trade union movement as in Vernon Lidtke's examination of the working-class milieu, *The Outlawed Party* (1966). Newer historiography nuanced this simplification with Weberian models in the Bielefeld school of Hans-Ulrich Wehler or Jürgen Kocka, or

with modernization theory in Katznelson and Zolberg's edited volume, *Working-Class Formation* (1986). Klaus Tenfelde's *Alltagsgeschichte* and "history from below" brought further new perspectives by looking beyond institutions. Ultimately, deconstructivist techniques found application here, too. Gareth Stedman Jones *Languages of Class* (1983) and Barry Hindess' *Politics and Class Analysis* (1987) challenged structuralist class analysis as misrepresentative of workers' reality.

Outside social history, historians examined the ideological forces unleashed in the 19th century. Hans Kohn's *Nationalism* (1955) and J.J. Sheehan's *German Liberalism in the Nineteenth Century* (1978) explored the transformation of ideologies in a social context. Theodore S. Hamerow described the political implications of social change in the formation of the modern German state in *The Social Foundations of German Unification* (1969–74).

By the 1970s, studies of 19th-century Europe included the dynamic middle classes. Charles S. Maier's *Recasting Bourgeois Europe* (1975) analyzed their attempted return to normalcy after World War I in a Europe plagued with systemic economic and political crises. Peter Gay's *The Bourgeois Experience* (1984–95) and David Blackbourn and R.J. Evans' *The German Bourgeoisie* (1991) showed how the middle classes participated increasingly in politics and culture, as the nation-state became the center of political and economic life. Bonnie Smith's *Ladies of the Leisure Class* (1981) helped move women away from the margins into mainstream research as part of a general trend towards interest in the marginal and exceptional.

Diplomatic and political history produced fertile research on the origins of the two world wars, although standard works such as William L. Langer's *European Alliances and Alignments* (1931) and Paul Kennedy's *The Rise of Anglo-German Antagonism* (1980) generally concentrated on diplomatic alliances and statesmen. Instead of sharp breaks, historians concentrated now on continuity. The question of how responsible big business was for Hitler's rise to power was the starting point for a dispute about David Abraham's *The Collapse of the Weimar Republic* (1981). Abraham had contended that decisions by business had helped destabilize the Weimar republic, while his initial adversary, Henry Turner, asserted that it did not. The debate, however, quickly spiraled into a controversy about questionable research methodology, which Peter Novick scrutinized in *That Noble Dream* (1988). The Fischer thesis launched the first wave of the German *Historikerstreit* by proposing a continuity of German politics from Bismarck to Hitler in *Germany's Aims in the First World War* (1961, translated 1967). Arno Mayer examined the domestic origins of war in *The Persistence of the Old Regime* (1981) and, in contrast to the assertion that Europe was bourgeoisified during the 19th century, both he, and Martin Wiener in his *English Culture and the Decline of the Industrial Spirit* (1981), argued the failure of capitalist values as the bourgeoisie feudalized itself in imitation of the old aristocratic elite. William Sewell's *Work and Revolution in France* (1988) looked for the persistence of attitudes from the Old Regime in 19th-century France.

Recently scholars have focused on war's social impact. The changed nature of war itself could be explored in L.F. Haber's *The Poisonous Cloud* (1986) and John Keegan's *The Face of Battle* (1976). Gail Braybon's *Women Workers in the First World War* (1981) and J.M. Winter and R.M. Wall's *The*

Upheaval of War (1988) showed the dramatic changes for women and the family. Indeed, Modris Eksteins' *Rites of Spring* (1989) saw the very birth of the modern age in World War I.

Histories of postwar Europe still tend to be overshadowed by the relative "newness" of the recent past. Also, the diversification of history, inspired by Michel Foucault and the literary theory of Jacques Derrida, has brought a wave of postmodernist and deconstructivist histories on virtually every topic. Alain Corbin's *Le Miasme et la jonquille* (1982; *The Foul and the Fragrant*, 1986), a history of odor, or Philippe Ariès and Georges Duby's *Histoire de la vie privée* (1985–87; *A History of Private Life*, 1987–91) show how broadly defined the history of modern Europe has become.

ROBERT GOODRICH

See also Acton; Ariès; Bloch; Braudel; Broué; Conze; Corbin; Duby; Febvre; Fischer; Gay; Geertz; Ginzburg; Hammond; Hobsbawm; Hunt; Jones, G.; Karamzin; Keegan; Kocka; Lefebvre; Lelewel; Macaulay; Michelet; Palacký; Ranke; Thompson, E.; Treitschke; Trevelyan; Wehler

Further Reading

Abraham, David, *The Collapse of the Weimar Republic: Political Economy and Crisis*, Princeton: Princeton University Press, 1981

Anderson, Matthew Smith, *The Ascendancy of Europe: Aspects of European History, 1815–1914*, London: Longman, and Totowa, NJ: Rowman and Littlefield, 1972

Ariès, Philippe, and Georges Duby, eds., *Histoire de la vie privée*, 5 vols., Paris: Seuil, 1985–87; in English as *A History of Private Life*, 5 vols., Cambridge, MA: Harvard University Press, 1987–91

Blackbourn, David, and Richard J. Evans, *The German Bourgeoisie: Essays on the Social History of the German Middle Classes from the Late Eighteenth to the Early Twentieth Century*, London and New York: Routledge, 1991

Braybon, Gail, *Women Workers in the First World War: The British Experience*, London: Croom Helm, and Totowa, NJ: Barnes and Noble, 1981

Breunig, Charles, *The Age of Revolution and Reaction, 1789–1850*, New York: Norton, 1970; London: Weidenfeld and Nicolson, 1971

Corbin Alain, *Le Miasme et la jonquille: l'odorat et l'imaginaire social, XVIIIe–XIXe siècles*, Paris: Aubier Montaigne, 1982; in English as *The Foul and the Fragrant: Odor and the French Social Imagination*, Cambridge, MA: Harvard University Press, and Leamington Spa: Berg, 1986

Davies, Norman, *Europe: A History*, Oxford and New York: Oxford University Press, 1996

Dobb, Maurice, *Studies in the Development of Capitalism*, London: Routledge, 1946; New York: International Publishers, 1947

Eksteins, Modris, *Rites of Spring: The Great War and the Birth of the Modern Age*, Boston: Houghton Mifflin, and London: Bantam, 1989

Evans, Eric J., *The Forging of the Modern State: Early Industrial Britain, 1783–1870*, London and New York: Longman, 1983

Fischer, Fritz, *Griff nach der Weltmacht: die Kriegszielpolitik des kaiserlichen Deutschland, 1914–18*, Düsseldorf: Droste, 1961; in English as *Germany's Aims in the First World War*, London: Chatto and Windus, and New York: Norton, 1967

Fitzpatrick, Sheila, *The Russian Revolution, 1917–1932*, Oxford and New York: Oxford University Press, 1982

Fussell, Paul, *The Great War and Modern Memory*, Oxford and New York: Oxford University Press, 1975

Gay, Peter, *The Bourgeois Experience: Victoria to Freud*, Oxford and New York: Oxford University Press, 1984–

Haber, Ludwig Fritz, *The Poisonous Cloud: Chemical Warfare in the First World War*, Oxford and New York: Oxford University Press, 1986

Hamerow, Theodore S., *The Social Foundations of German Unification, 1858–71*, 2 vols., Princeton: Princeton University Press, 1969–74

Hammond, J.L. and Barbara Hammond, *The Village Labourer, 1760–1832: A Study in the Government of England before the Reform Bill*, London and New York: Longman, 1911

Hardach, Gerd, *The First World War, 1914–1918*, Berkeley: University of California Press, and London: Allen Lane, 1977 (German original)

Hindess, Barry, *Politics and Class Analysis*, Oxford and New York: Blackwell, 1987

Hobsbawm, Eric J., *Industry and Empire: An Economic History of Britain since 1750*, London: Weidenfeld and Nicolson, and New York: Pantheon, 1968

Hunt, Lynn, *Politics, Culture, and Class in the French Revolution*, Berkeley: University of California Press, 1984; London: Methuen, 1986

Jones, Gareth Stedman, *Languages of Class: Studies in English Working-Class History, 1832–1982*, Cambridge and New York: Cambridge University Press, 1983

Katznelson, Ira, and Aristide R. Zolberg, eds., *Working-Class Formation: Nineteenth-Century Patterns in Western Europe and the United States*, Princeton: Princeton University Press, 1986

Keegan, John, *The Face of Battle*, London: Cape, and New York: Viking, 1976

Kennedy, Paul M., *The Rise of Anglo-German Antagonism, 1860–1914*, London and Boston: Allen and Unwin, 1980

Kocka, Jürgen, *Klassengesellschaft im Krieg: Deutsche Sozialgeschichte, 1914–1918* (Class Society during War), Göttingen: Vandenhoeck & Ruprecht, 1973; in English as *Facing Total War: German Society, 1914–1918*, Cambridge, MA: Harvard University Press, and Leamington Spa: Berg, 1984

Kohn, Hans, *Nationalism: Its Meaning and History*, Princeton: Van Nostrand, 1955; revised 1965

Langer, William Leonard, *European Alliances and Alignments, 1871–1890*, New York: Knopf, 1931; revised 1950

Lefebvre, Georges, *Quatre-vingt-neuf*, Paris: Maison du livre français, 1939; in English as *The Coming of the French Revolution*, Princeton: Princeton University Press, 1947

Lidtke, Vernon L., *The Outlawed Party: Social Democracy in Germany, 1878–1890*, Princeton: Princeton University Press, 1966

Lüdtke, Alf, *Alltagsgeschichte: zur Rekonstruktion historischer Erfahrungen und Lebensweisen*, Frankfurt: Campus, 1989; in English as *The History of Everyday Life: Reconstructing Historical Experiences and Ways of Life*, Princeton: Princeton University Press, 1995

McKeown, Thomas, *The Modern Rise of Population*, London: Arnold, and New York: Academic Press, 1976

Maier, Charles S., *Recasting Bourgeois Europe: Stabilization in France, Germany, and Italy in the Decade after World War I*, Princeton: Princeton University Press, 1975

Mayer, Arno J., *The Persistence of the Old Regime: Europe to the Great War*, New York: Pantheon, and London: Croom Helm, 1981

Novick, Peter, *That Noble Dream: The "Objectivity Question" and the American Historical Profession*, Cambridge and New York: Cambridge University Press, 1988

Pipes, Richard, *The Russian Revolution*, New York: Knopf, and London: Collins, 1990; concise version, 1995

Pollard, Sidney, *Peaceful Conquest: The Industrialization of Europe, 1760–1970*, Oxford and New York: Oxford University Press, 1981

Roche, Daniel, *Le Peuple de Paris: essai sur la culture populaire au XVIIIe siècle*, Paris: Aubie Montaigne, 1981; in English as *The People of Paris: An Essay in Popular Culture*, Berkeley: University of California Press, and Leamington Spa: Berg, 1987

Romein, Jan, *De lage landen bijde zee* (The Lowlands by the Sea), Utrecht: de Haan, 1934

Schapiro, Jacob S., *Liberalism: Its Meaning and History*, Princeton: Van Nostrand, 1958

Sereni, Emilio, *Il capitalismo nelle campagne (1860–1900)* (Capitalism in the Countryside, 1860–1900), Turin: Einaudi, 1947

Sewell, William H., Jr., *Work and Revolution in France: The Language of Labor from the Old Regime to 1848*, Cambridge and New York: Cambridge University Press, 1988

Sheehan, James J., *German Liberalism in the Nineteenth Century*, Chicago: University of Chicago Press, 1978

Smith, Bonnie G., *Ladies of the Leisure Class: The Bourgeoises of Northern France in the Nineteenth Century*, Princeton: Princeton University Press, 1981

Tenfelde, Klaus, *Sozialgeschichte der Bergarbeiterschaft an der Ruhr im 19. Jahrhundert* (Social History of the Ruhr Miners in the 19th Century), Bonn: Neue Gesellschaft, 1977

Thompson, E.P., *The Making of the English Working Class*, London: Gollancz, 1963; New York: Pantheon, 1964

Trebilcock, Clive, *The Industrialization of the Continental Powers, 1780–1914*, London and New York: Longman, 1981

Treitschke, Heinrich von, *Deutsche Geschichte im neunzehnten Jahrhundert*, 5 vols., Leipzig: Hirzel, 1879–94; in English as *Treitschke's History of Germany in the Nineteenth Century*, 7 vols., London: Jarrold, and New York: McBride, 1915–19

Trevelyan, G.M., *English Social History: A Survey of Six Centuries, Chaucer to Queen Victoria*, London and New York: Longman, 1942

Turner, Henry Ashby, Jr., *German Big Business and the Rise of Hitler*, New York and Oxford: Oxford University Press, 1985

Ward, A.L. *et al.*, eds., *The Cambridge Modern History*, Cambridge: Cambridge University Press, and New York: Macmillan, 1902–12

Weber, Adna Ferrin, *The Growth of Cities in the Nineteenth Century: A Study in Statistics*, New York: Columbia University Press, 1899

Wehler, Hans-Ulrich, *Das deutsche Kaiserreich, 1871–1918*, Göttingen: Vandenhoeck & Ruprecht, 1973; in English as *The German Empire, 1871–1918*, Leamington Spa: Berg, 1985

Wiener, Martin, *English Culture and the Decline of the Industrial Spirit, 1850–1980*, Cambridge and New York: Cambridge University Press, 1981

Winter, Jay, and Richard Wall, eds., *The Upheaval of War: Family, Work and Welfare in Europe, 1914–1918*, Cambridge and New York: Cambridge University Press, 1988

European Expansion

The historiography of European expansion, a period defined by the emergence of Portugal in the early 15th century and ending with the birth of the Enlightenment during the early 18th century, has undergone significant changes in both tone and breadth. The compelling accounts of first contact from conquistadors and missionaries reveal a great deal about the mindset of Europe on the eve of global domination. Fortune hunters and clerics wrote with agendas that sometimes conflicted with each other, but whether riches or converts were the goal, the belief that Europe was inherently superior to the cultures they encountered was a shared value. Modern historians resurrected these eyewitness accounts and wrote self-congratulatory works extolling the indomitable spirit of Europeans involved in expansion. Authors regarded European expansion as the culmination of a special brand of European genius demonstrable throughout the ages. Not until recently have historians expanded upon ethnocentric interpretations and addressed alternative explanations for Europe's rapid advance to global hegemony. Current historiography is diverse: historians have recently published scholarship on pre-Columbian civilization, European advances in sailing and military technology, and the psychology of a Europe motivated and transformed by discovery.

The first "historian" of the Spanish conquest of Mexico was a barely literate colleague of Hernando Cortés by the name of Bernal Díaz. Writing for wealth and recognition near the end of his life, Díaz published *Historia verdadera de la conquista de la Nueva España* (published *c.* 1575; *The Conquest of New Spain*, 1963) as an attempt to publicize the remarkable accomplishments of conquistadors other than Cortés and to defend the reputation of the 1519 expedition from clerics and royal bureaucrats intent on controlling the conquistadors. One reason Díaz published his work was to counter the negative publicity generated by Bartolomé de Las Casas' *Brevísima relación de la destrucción de las Indias*, (1552; *The Tears of the Indians*, 1656; and *The Devastation of the Indies: A Brief Account*, 1974). A Dominican priest, Las Casas was one of many missionaries who objected to the economic exploitation of the natives, but not necessarily to their systematic conversion. Las Casas pleaded his case to a sympathetic Spanish crown interested in excuses to consolidate the conquistadors' unprecedented acquisitions without granting them freedom of action in the New World.

Cortés was a true adventurer beholden to no authority. His fabled action of burning his ships on the Mexican shores was symbolic of his intent to achieve wealth and titles without interference from royal agents. Cortés did not want royal enemies, however, so he made sure to update his superiors of his adventures through a series of letters to Charles V. Written between 1519 and 1526 Cortés' famous five letters are masterpieces of self-promotion and, like Díaz's memoir, a fascinating story of a European's first impressions after contact. The Aztec perspective was disregarded for centuries until historians and anthropologists reinterpreted Aztec symbols recorded by Spanish observers. The Aztecs invested Cortés' landings with cosmic significance and adopted the comforting prophecy that the whirlwind conquest of their ancient civilization by a few hundred marauders was beyond their control. A modern interpretation of the Aztec position is found in Miguel León-Portilla's *Visión de los vencidos* (1959; *Broken Spears*, 1962).

The story of European expansion, according to most historians, began with Portugal's conquest of the Moorish island of Ceuta in 1415. Upstart Portugal, benefiting from a unified crown, the able leadership of Henry the Navigator, and the timely assault of the Mongols upon Christendom's arch-rival, Islam, was able to utilize borrowed technology for their fleet and establish themselves first as Islam's competitor and then, rather quickly, as the dominant seafaring power. J.H. Parry was one of the most influential historians of European expansion and the architect of the argument that European expansion was the natural outcome of a persistent crusading impulse and the legacy of the Renaissance. The most precise presentation of Parry's thesis is found in his brief but authoritative work, *The Establishment of the European Hegemony* (revised 1961). Parry granted that imperialism was undoubtedly motivated by economic gain, but he also maintained that imperialism was tempered by the missionary tradition. Europe, in Parry's view, accepted responsibility with its empire. Implicit in Parry's argument is that Europeans enlightened the conquered peoples and were in turn themselves enlightened by the discovery of the New World. The curiosity that defined the Renaissance was compounded by the remarkable events at the turn of the 16th century.

Parry's scholarship is impressive and essential to any study of European expansion, but it is also a traditional interpretation. G.V. Scammell examined the same time period and arrived at markedly different conclusions. Scammell's *The First Imperial Age* (1989) incorporates economic history, social history, and the European attitude toward the indigenous peoples to conclude that Europe closed its mind in the face of discovery. Europe's expansion, in Scammell's view, was not the glorious culmination of underlying constructive forces evident since medieval times, but rather the successful employment of technology and political organization in the service of greed. Scammell demonstrated that empire was a financial burden that bankrupted Spain and Portugal while the Dutch and English got rich by avoiding empire, at least during the first imperial age. Scammell further maintained that instead of a rich source of opportunity for lower-class men to make their fortune, expansion served the rich and weakened the mother countries by excluding a significant portion of the male population from contributing to needed domestic growth. Empire also provided another excuse for Europe's competing families to wage war with one another. In his most provocative conclusion Scammell stated that "European culture evolved with little benefit from acquaintance with the wider world." Discovery increased cynicism, prejudice, and contempt. Trade centered on exotic novelties and remained subordinate to the existing economic order. Scammell's critique of the traditional school embodied by Parry asserted that the only indomitable spirit that triumphed in Europe as a result of expansion was complacent arrogance.

1992 was the 500th anniversary of Columbus' "discovery" of the New World, and a formidable crop of historical scholarship coincided with the observance. Some of this scholarship was innovative and filled existing gaps in the historiography, while many of the publications descended into mindless revisionism. Not only historians contribute to the current historiography of European expansion; literary critics interested in the language and symbols of both the conquerors and the conquered have widened the scope of research, while anthropologists struggled to reconstruct the history of cultures with no written record. Stephen Greenblatt addressed the power of words and interpreted the narratives of explorers and conquistadors regarding their impressions of the New World. In *Marvelous Possessions* (1991) Greenblatt emphasized the meaning of "wonder" in seeking answers to the question of what went through the minds of the Europeans who first set foot in the New World. The European vanguard that confronted the New World used language to demystify, rationalize, and by implication, subject the discoveries to the European paradigm. Patricia Seed expanded upon this thesis in her article "Taking Possession and Reading Texts (1992)." Tzvetan Todorov's *La conquête de l'Amérique* (1982; *The Conquest of America*, 1984) examined the various issues surrounding communication between the conquistadors and the natives. The central issue revolved around Cortés and Montezuma's reaction to each other. Cortés saw the Aztec emperor as the savage equivalent of a European monarch interested in negotiation while Montezuma regarded Cortés as a demigod. The clash of two worlds is a complex and elusive subject, involving numerous

disciplines that continues to occupy much of the contemporary historical writing on European expansion.

While the conquest of Mexico may be the most popular topic for historians of expansion, some scholars follow Parry's example and continue to study the big picture. Geoffrey Parker's *The Military Revolution* (1988) detailed Europe's advances in military technology and its success in projecting military power abroad. Parker discussed both land warfare and naval technology and concluded, in an argument some critics dismissed as "technological determinism," that these innovations initiated the necessary political and military centralization required for Europe's successful expansion. William H. McNeill wrote in *The Pursuit of Power* (1982) that Europe's penchant for adopting new technology was an integral part of its success abroad, but McNeill also suggests that Europe's easy victories originated from Europe's *will* to use technology invented in other cultures for expansionist goals those cultures never themselves pursued.

J.H. Parry ended *The Establishment of European Hegemony* with the 18th century because by then there were permanent European settlements comprised of merchants, missionaries, and colonists on every continent except Australia and Antarctica. These settlements were in some way or another dependent upon the mother countries. Recently, ethnographers, archaeologists, literary critics, and scholars studying the drastic changes in North America's ecology after European contact have joined forces with historians and contributed to the historiography of European expansion. European expansion between 1415 and 1715 encompasses a diverse historiography as old as expansion itself. Memoirs and autobiographies from the 16th century gave way to traditional historians applauding European values in the 19th and 20th centuries. The last twenty years witnessed the inclusion of every conceivable discipline in the debates surrounding European expansion. There is every indication that the field of European expansion will continue to be provocative and diverse considering the number of unexplored avenues remaining.

BRIAN CRIM

See also Díaz; Las Casas; Parker; Spain: Imperial

Further Reading

Abu-Lughod, Janet L., *Before European Hegemony: The World System, AD 1250–1350*, New York: Oxford University Press, 1989

Adorno, Rolena, "The Discursive Encounter of Spain and America: The Authority of Eyewitness Testimony in the Writing of History," *William and Mary Quarterly* 49 (1992), 210–28

Berler, Beatrice, *The Conquest of Mexico: A Modern Rendering of William H. Prescott's History*, San Antonio, TX: Corona, 1988

Cerwin, Herbert, *Bernal Díaz: Historian of the Conquest*, Norman: University of Oklahoma Press, 1963

Colston, Stephen A., "'No Longer Will There be a Mexico': Omens, Prophecies, and the Conquest of the Aztec Empire," *American Indian Quarterly* 9 (1985), 239–58

Díaz del Castillo, Bernal, *Historia verdadera de la conquista de la Nueva España*, written 1568, published c.1575; in English as *The Discovery and Conquest of Mexico, 1517–1521*, New York: Harper, and London: Routledge, 1928, and as *The Conquest of New Spain*, London: Penguin, 1963

Greenblatt, Stephen, *Marvelous Possessions: The Wonder of the New World*, Chicago: University of Chicago Press, and Oxford: Oxford University Press, 1991

Greenblatt, Stephen, ed., *New World Encounters*, Berkeley: University of California Press, 1993

Las Casas, Bartolomé de, *Brevisima relación de la destrucción de las Indias*, 1552; in English as *The Tears of the Indians*, 1656, and *The Devastation of the Indies: A Brief Account*, New York: Seabury Press 1974

León-Portilla, Miguel, ed., *Visión de los vencidos: relaciones indígenas de la conquista*, México City: UNAM, 1959; in English as *The Broken Spears: The Aztec Account of the Conquest of Mexico*, Boston: Beacon Press, 1962

McAlister, Lyle N., *Spain and Portugal in the New World, 1492–1700*, Minneapolis: University of Minnesota Press, 1984

McNeill, William H., *The Pursuit of Power: Technology, Armed Force, and Society since AD 1000*, Chicago: University of Chicago Press, 1982; Oxford: Blackwell, 1983

Parker, Geoffrey, *The Military Revolution: Military Innovation and the Rise of the West, 1500–1800*, Cambridge and New York: Cambridge University Press, 1988

Parry, J.H., *Europe and a Wider World*, London: Hutchinson, 1949, revised 1961; as *The Establishment of the European Hegemony, 1415–1715: Trade and Exploration in the Age of the Renaissance*, New York: Harper, 1961

Parry, J.H., *The Age of Reconnaissance*, Cleveland: World, and London: Weidenfeld and Nicolson, 1963

Scammell, G.V., *The World Encompassed: The First European Maritime Empires, c.800–1650*, Berkeley: University of California Press, and London: Methuen, 1981

Scammell, G.V., *The First Imperial Age: European Overseas Expansion, c.1400–1715*, London and Boston: Unwin Hyman, 1989

Seed, Patricia, "Taking Possession and Reading Texts: Establishing the Authority of Overseas Empires," *William and Mary Quarterly* 49 (1992), 184–209

Thomas, Hugh, *The Conquest of Mexico*, London: Hutchinson, 1993; as *Conquest: Montezuma, Cortés, and the Fall of Old Mexico*, New York: Simon and Schuster, 1993

Todorov, Tsvetan, *La Conquête de l'Amérique: la question de l'autre*, Paris: Seuil, 1982; in English as *The Conquest of America: The Question of the Other*, New York: Harper, 1984

Eusebius of Caesarea c.265–339 CE

Early Christian historian

Eusebius lived in Caesarea on the shores of Palestine during the years that Christians experienced their final persecutions under Roman rule and achieved their final acceptance under the emperor Constantine. As a young man, Eusebius studied Christian thought, and later served the church as a presbyter of Caesarea. Eusebius' intimate involvement with the Christian church during this crucial time meant that he was also intimately involved with the politics of empire. He observed martyrdoms and their impact; he gained the respect of Constantine and enjoyed the emperor's confidence throughout his life; and he became involved in the theological controversies of the day (specifically the Christian struggle against Arianism) that had strong political consequences. Eusebius' impact as a historian is due in large part to his central participation in the formation of a Christian empire, a historical event of profound consequence.

Eusebius was a prolific writer. He is credited with writing 46 works, of which only 15 have survived intact. His writings reflect his overwhelming religious interest, and include works that engaged the religious controversies of the day. He also wrote many biblical works, such as commentaries on scripture and works on biblical place-names and geography. However, the works that are most influential today are his historical works: The *Martyrs of Palestine*, the *Life of Constantine*, the *Chronological Tables*, and best-known, *The History of the Church*.

The History of the Church is an influential work both for its content and for its method. In content, Eusebius presumes to write the history of the progress of the Christian church from the time of Christ through its victory in the time of Constantine. Within the ten books of this history, Eusebius offers testimony to the major events of Christian history. This work remains a crucial source for historians of this period.

Eusebius approached his historical study from a method similar to that of his biblical analysis. He proceeded from the point of view that his present was a fulfillment of that which had gone before, in the same way that the coming of Christ was a fulfillment of the Old Testament prophecies. History, for Eusebius, was a linear progression of cause and effect, so when he included accounts of persecutions, martyrdoms, and disagreements, it was from the optimistic view that these events were leading to the ultimate victory of the church during the time of Constantine. This approach foreshadowed and influenced many historical accounts.

Eusebius' history was not simply a personal recollection, and this increased its importance. He included quotations or summaries of more than a hundred texts to prove the validity of his history. Many of these texts would have been lost if it had not been for their reproduction by Eusebius.

Eusebius furthermore did not simply quote his sources uncritically. He compared differing accounts of the same event. For example, he compared the version of an event recorded in the scriptural account in Acts with that recounted by the Roman historian Josephus, to reconcile any discrepancies (*History of the Church*, book 1, 11). While his analysis would not hold up to modern critical methodology, it nevertheless established principles of analysis of historical sources.

Eusebius was an historian of a critically important time in the formation of Western culture. He offers information unavailable elsewhere, and he offered a model of historical study, both in his expression of a linear, causal history and in his use of historical methods, that was influential for at least a millennium.

JOYCE E. SALISBURY

See also Bauer; Bede; Byzantium; Cassiodorus; Catholicism; Christianity; Eastern Orthodoxy; Ecclesiastical; Josephus; Medieval Chronicles

Biography

Eusebius or Eusebios. Born Palestine c.265 CE. Disciple of Pamphilos; imprisoned with him in anti-Christian persecutions of Diocletian, 303–11; elected bishop of Caesarea, c.313, adviser to emperor Constantine, 323; participated in first Council of Nicaea, 325, and Council of Tyre, 335. Died 339.

Principal Writings

Texts in *Patrologiae cursus completus*, series Graeca (*Patrologia Graeca*), edited by J.-P. Migne, vols. 19–24; and in *Die griechischen christlichen Schriftsteller* (Berlin Academy series): Ecclesiastical History edited by Eduard Schwartz, 1908; Life of Constantine edited by Friedhelm Winkelmann, revised 1992

The Ecclesiastical History (Loeb edition), translated by Kirsopp Lake and J.E.L. Oulton, 2 vols., 1926–32

The History of the Church from Christ to Constantine, translated by G.A. Williamson, 1965

Further Reading

Barnes, Timothy David, *Constantine and Eusebius*, Cambridge, MA: Harvard University Press, 1981

Baynes, Norman H., "Eusebios and the Christian Empire," in *Mélanges Bidez* [Essays in honor of Joseph Bidez], vol. 1, Brussels, 1934, 13–18

Croke, Brian, and Alanna Emmett, eds., *History and Historians in Late Antiquity*, Oxford and New York: Pergamon Press, 1983

Grant, Robert M., *Eusebius as Church Historian*, Oxford: Clarendon Press, 1980

Lawlor, H.J., *Eusebiana: Essays on the Ecclesiastical History of Eusebius, Bishop of Caesarea*, Oxford: Clarendon Press, 1912

Markus, R.A., *From Augustine to Gregory the Great: History and Christianity in Late Antiquity*, London: Variorum, 1983

Mosshammer, Alden, *The Chronicle of Eusebius and Greek Chronographic Tradition*, Lewisburg, PA: Bucknell University Press, 1979

Sirinelli, Jean-François, *Les Vues historiques d'Eusèbe de Césarée durant la période prénicéenne* (The Historical Views of Eusebius during the pre-Nicene Period), Dakar: Université de Dakar, 1961

Wallace-Hadrill, David S., *Eusebius of Caesarea*, London: Mowbray, 1960; Westminster, MD: Canterbury Press, 1961

F

Fairbank, John K. 1907–1991

US historian of China

Most historians of modern China recognize John K. Fairbank as a pivotal figure in our understanding of developments in the "Middle Kingdom" over the past two centuries. Fairbank's importance rests on his abundant scholarship, his cultivation of a talented cadre of graduate students at Harvard, and his shaping of Asian and Chinese studies programs in universities, particularly in North America. Although many may take issue with Fairbank's historical interpretations, political preferences, or administrative absorption, few will dispute that he was largely responsible for taking Chinese studies from the narrow confines of philology and diplomacy in the early 20th century and placing it within the ordinary curriculum of late 20th-century university departments, especially history.

Fairbank graduated from Harvard in 1929 with a degree in history, but his embryonic interest in China was not nurtured until he arrived at Oxford on a Rhodes scholarship and had the opportunity to study under Hosea Ballou Morse. Morse, a former official in the Chinese Imperial Maritime Customs Service, encouraged Fairbank to go to China, counseling the young graduate student that any serious study of China needed to be grounded in language competence. Living in Beijing (then Peiping) from 1932 to 1936, he worked under T.F. Tsiang (Jiang Tingfu), head of the History department at Tsing Hua (Qinghua) University, where he also lectured and conducted research for his doctorate. Fairbank received a DPhil from Oxford in 1936 and returned to teach at Harvard, beginning an academic relationship with his alma mater that continued until his death.

From the outset, China's prevalent adversities influenced Fairbank's scholarship. In an article that appeared in the September 1937 *Amerasia*, he attempted to draw a parallel between Western imperialism in the 19th century and the recent Japanese invasion. The civil war between the Nationalists and Communists (1945–49) prompted his classic *The United States and China* (1949), which sought to explain the Chinese political situation to an America entering the Cold War. With the Communist victory in 1949 came an effort to account for yet another tumultuous political upheaval with *A Documentary History of Chinese Communism* (1952). By the early 1950s, a heated debate raged in the United States over why the Communists succeeded in China. Many China specialists who had been associated with American policy formulation toward China were accused of being either too sympathetic to the Communists, or too critical of the Nationalists, or both. As Fairbank had worked for the American government in China during and after World War II and was not affectionate toward the Nationalists, he became a target. The extent to which the political climate stifled his scholarship and commentary is difficult to measure, but until Richard Nixon's trip to China in 1972, when China analysts again came into vogue, Fairbank produced a prodigious amount of academic and popular literature. One student recalls Fairbank introducing with fulsome praise Owen Lattimore to a Harvard audience in the late 1950s, suggesting that the Harvard professor stood his ground.

To Fairbank it was obvious that one needed to understand the broad contours of China's past, and that of the 19th century in particular, if one hoped to fathom the eruptions of the 20th century. Since very little work had been done to develop such an understanding, he plunged into the task of producing rudimentary knowledge about the preceding century so that scholars could at least ask sophisticated questions. The estimable *Trade and Diplomacy on the China Coast* (1953) became a model for young China specialists because of its thorough research and nuanced portrait of Confucian China confronting the West. Fairbank and collaborators facilitated further research with such works as *Ch'ing (Qing) Administration* (1960), which provided insights into the Manchu bureaucracy in operation; *Ch'ing (Qing) Documents* (1952, revised 1965), a guide to the literary language of the bureaucracy; *China's Response to the West* (1954), a translation of documents accompanied by a useful bibliography; and *Japanese Studies of Modern China* (1955), an annotated list of Japanese research, created on the assumption that the Japanese had long studied China and could thus render valuable insights. *A History of East Asian Civilization* (1958), a 2-volume text that has undergone several transformations, continues to provide a solid reference for undergraduates. Perhaps the culmination of Fairbank's efforts to make China research more accessible is found in *The Cambridge History of China* (1977–), which he edited with Denis Twitchett. It is a multivolume project consisting of state-of-the-field articles, many written by Fairbank's students.

In addition to his scholarly production, Fairbank trained scholars who staff the leading universities of North America. A few, such as Benjamin Schwartz and Philip Kuhn, teach at Harvard; other leading centers of Asian studies read like the roster of a Fairbank seminar: Albert Feuerwerker at Michigan; the late Lloyd Eastman at Illinois; the late Joseph Levenson at Berkeley; Japanologists Robert Scalapino of Berkeley, Peter

Duus of Stanford, and Marius Jansen of Princeton also came under Fairbank's tutelage. Outside of the academy, newspaper writers Theodore White and Fox Butterfield were his students. And Robert Irick has been toiling in Taiwan since the 1960s to reprint much of China's written legacy for the research universities of the world. This represents just a small sampling of a much larger body of sinologists whom Fairbank trained and influenced over the decades.

Fairbank's students invariably have fond memories of their mentor. They often disagreed with his historical emphases or political positions, but this did not lessen their respect for the man. For example, Lloyd Eastman wanted to work on 20th-century China while at Harvard; Fairbank insisted on a 19th-century topic for his dissertation: Eastman dutifully produced a solid study of the Sino-French War of the 1880s, and he then proceeded to become the leading authority on the Nationalist period (1927–49), while remaining close friends with his teacher. In an early May 1995 discussion on the Internet of Fairbank's influence, former student Marilyn Young related that "Fairbank and I disagreed – sometimes virulently – on the subject of imperialism, on the best ways to oppose the Vietnam War, etc. But he was open, flexible, and above all intellectually skeptical and always ironic." Upon his death, students and colleagues wrote brief reflections about the man and his impact on them, published as *Fairbank Remembered*, which provides insight into the many facets of the scholar and the gentleman.

Fairbank nonetheless had critics – in the United States on the new left and on the right, and in China from both the Nationalists and the Communists. Some of the complaints were chiefly political. Thus many in the Committee of Concerned Asian Scholars, a new left organization formed during the Vietnam War, viewed Fairbank as a cold warrior. In mainland China, historians since the Communist revolution have usually characterized Fairbank as an apologist for imperialism. In Taiwan he fared little better, being labelled a minion of Moscow. Anticommunists in the United States, such as Karl Wittfogel, considered Fairbank much too sympathetic to the Chinese Communists. Yet as the Chinese revolution moderated with the ascendancy of Deng Xiaoping in the late 1970s and the Cold War concluded in the late 1980s, the political vitriol receded as well.

More absorbing are the assessments of Fairbank's scholarship. In *China Misperceived* sinologist Steven Mosher argues that the Fairbank school places too much emphasis on the continuities between China's despotic past and the totalitarian present. Actually, "far more striking than any connections between China past and present . . . was the organizational, ideological, and policy isomorphism between" the People's Republic of China and the Soviet Union. That same criticism came from Marxist social scientists, who maintained that Communist China represents a sharp break with that despotic past. One Taiwan historian assailed Fairbank's contention that a Chinese society imbued with Confucian values could not modernize. This position, most fully developed in Mary Wright's *The Last Stand of Chinese Conservatism*, held sway during the 1960s and 1970s but has since been questioned given the rise of the "Four Dragons." Fairbank also reproached himself for faulty analysis. In the posthumously published *China: A New History* (1992), Fairbank acknowledged that

his assessment of the Communist revolution as "the best thing" that had occurred in China in centuries was "sentimental sinophilia."

Conceivably the most consequential legacy of Fairbank will be the institutions he created or utilized to spread Chinese and Asian studies. The East Asian Center at Harvard became a prototype for other universities, whether or not they were staffed by Fairbank's students. His election to the presidencies of the Association of Asian Studies and the American Historical Association reflect the high esteem in which he was held by peers. But former student Thomas Metzger best sums up Fairbank's importance: "he not only turned modern Chinese history into one of the world's most interesting historiographical fields but also did more than anyone else to develop an interdisciplinary approach to this field."

THOMAS D. REINS

See also China: Modern

Biography

John King Fairbank. Born Huron, South Dakota, 24 May 1907. Received BA in history, Harvard University, 1929; Rhodes scholarship, then DPhil, Oxford University, 1936 with study at Tsing Hua (Qinghua) University, Beijing, 1932–36. Taught at Harvard University 1936–77: director, East Asian Research Center, 1959–73; and chairman, Council on East Asian Studies, 1972–77 (emeritus from 1977). Special assistant to American ambassador, China, 1942–43; Office of Strategic Services and Office of War Information, 1942–45; director, US Information Service, China, 1945–47. Married Wilma Cannon, 1932 (2 daughters). Died 14 December 1991.

Principal Writings

Monographs
The United States and China, 1949; 4th edition 1979
Trade and Diplomacy on the China Coast: The Opening of the Treaty Ports, 1842–1854, 1953
China Perceived: Images and Policies in Chinese-American Relations, 1974
Chinabound: A Fifty Year Memoir, 1982
The Great Chinese Revolution, 1800–1985, 1986
China Watch [collected essays], 1987
China: A New History, 1992

Edited Works
With Conrad Brandt and Benjamin Schwartz, *A Documentary History of Chinese Communism*, 1952
Ch'ing Documents: An Introductory Syllabus, 2 vols., 1952; revised 1959, 1965
With Ssu-yu Teng, *China's Response to the West: A Documentary Survey, 1839–1923*, by Liang Qichao, 1954
With Masataka Banno, *Japanese Studies of Modern China: A Bibliographical Guide to Historical and Social Science Research on the 19th and . . . 20th Centuries*, 1955
Chinese Thought and Institutions, 1957
With Edwin O. Reischauer and Albert Craig, *A History of East Asian Civilization*, 2 vols., 1958–60
With Ssu-yu Teng, *Ch'ing Administration: Three Studies*, 1960
The Chinese World Order: Traditional China's Foreign Relations, 1968
With Frank A. Kierman, Jr., *Chinese Ways in Warfare*, 1974
Series editor with Denis Twitchett, *The Cambridge History of China*, 1977–
With Suzanne Wilson Barnett, *Christianity in China: Early Protestant Missionary Writings*, 1985

Further Reading

Cohen, Paul A., and Merle Goldman, eds., *Fairbank Remembered*, Cambridge, MA: Harvard University Press, 1992

Evans, Paul M., *John Fairbank and the American Understanding of Modern China*, Oxford and New York: Blackwell, 1988

Gordon, Leonard H.D., and Sydney Chang, "John K. Fairbank and His Critics in the Republic of China," *Journal of Asian Studies*, 30 (1970), 137–49

Mosher, Steven W., *China Misperceived: American Illusions and Chinese Reality*, New York: Basic Books, 1990

Wright, Mary C., *The Last Stand of Chinese Conservatism: The T'ung-Chih Restoration, 1862–1874*, Stanford, CA: Stanford University Press, 1957

The Family

The history of the family originated in the study of individual family lines, but in the past thirty years it has incorporated the insights of demography, anthropology, sociology, feminism, and economic history to transform the way the family is treated historically. It has been used to reshape the way historians understand the past, and been employed by politicians to try to mold current policies.

Genealogy first dominated family history, with a stress on the continuity of discrete elite family lines. From biblical tracings of family trees to African oral traditions, genealogy accented lineage, with an emphasis on powerful families. Peasant families, on the other hand, were assumed to be historically unrecoverable, leaving few written records.

In the middle of the 19th century the French social scientist Frédéric LePlay created a model to describe the historical family. He delineated three family types: the patriarchal, the stem, and the unstable. The patriarchal family centered on a male head of household, who continued to command blood kin even after they had left his household. The stem he characterized as large, with several generations under one roof. The unstable family had no powerful center, and was variable in form. LePlay argued that the stem, not the patriarchal family, had been the most prevalent form in pre-industrial Europe; he saw it as the most stable of all patterns. In contrast he feared the rise of the unstable family which he characterized as typical of the new industrial areas. LePlay's theories came to predominate in thinking about the historical family.

In the postwar period, several new disciplines emerged with theories that reinvigorated the study of the family. Population studies, or demography, assisted historians in discovering what the family structures of the past had been in practice, rather than in theory. Family structure encompassed many issues, including completed family size, composition of the household, and age of marriage. Most historians had followed LePlay in assuming that the pre-industrial era was dominated by the stem family. However, the work of Peter Laslett of the Cambridge Group for Population History and Social Structure on the records of early modern England contradicted LePlay's model. In *The World We Have Lost* (1965) Laslett argued that the typical early modern family was a nuclear one, although servants might also be included as family members. The Cambridge Group used family reconstitution (originally developed by French historical demographer Louis Henry) painstakingly to link different types of records about a small community. Family reconstitution has since been employed wherever sufficient records might exist to explore other cultures. More recently studies from other European locales have challenged Laslett's findings by revealing that family form varied widely within similar geographical areas and cultures. Indeed, Martine Segalen's study of *ancien régime* France illustrated that family form could vary over a small geographical area.

Furthermore, Michael Anderson's work suggested that the extended family was likely to exist in industrialized cultures, such as 19th-century England, where life expectancy was lengthening and age of marriage was lowering. Demographers also traced the changing size of the family, noting that the large pre-industrial family was closer in size to the modern family than might have been expected, due to late marriage and a high infant mortality rate. Completed family size only really began to drop in the industrial period. Whether this was due to more effective birth control or parental decisions which saw the small family as more economically viable is still being debated.

Kinship bonds were another way of examining the history of the family. How did families deal with their kin? How did they interact within their communities? What were their patterns of inheritance? This anthropological approach (especially in the work of Jack Goody) was particularly helpful in exploring how families functioned in medieval Europe and Asia. Nonliterate cultures, whose histories had been assumed lost, suddenly re-emerged as peasant culture was elucidated from archaeological and manorial records. In *L'Enfant et la vie familiale* (1960; *Centuries of Childhood*, 1962), Philippe Ariès investigated the crucial relationship between parent and child that was central to most family life. Although his contentions that only recently has childhood come to be seen as a separate category and that most parents in the early modern world sought to distance themselves from their children have been effectively countered by Linda Pollock and others, his study of the *mentalité* of family life inspired much work on the social relations within families.

This inspired deeper scrutiny of the modern family. How did the family change and survive in the industrial period? Feminist historians Louise Tilly and Joan Scott traced the shift of work from the home in the pre-industrial period to the public sphere in the 19th century. A by-product of this was the transformation of the family from a place of work to one where sentiment ruled. In *The Family, Sex and Marriage in England* (1977), Lawrence Stone located the rise of this sentimental family in the aristocratic families of early modern England, while Edward Shorter investigated the middle-class household. Christopher Lasch added a psychological element in his exploration of the middle-class home as a "haven in a heartless world." All agreed that the modern family was distinguished by its separation from the workplace. However, historians of the working-class family have demonstrated that work did not disappear from home and that for them, the family was not quite the oasis depicted in Lasch's writings. Ellen Ross' work on family strategies in late 19th-century London illustrated ways the working-class families integrated occasional work into family life.

Class formation was another crucial role of the family. In the 1980s, three 19th-century studies, Mary Ryan's of upstate

New York, Bonnie Smith's of France, and Leonore Davidoff and Catherine Hall's of England, located the establishment of a family's class status solidly in the family, particularly through the gender roles of the men and women within. They proposed that class formation resided in the social relations a family constructed, particularly the informal ties constructed by women of the family.

Current political debates often suggested paths for study. Black family life was examined by Herbert Gutman in order to counter current assumptions that the experience of slavery meant that African Americans were incapable of sustaining family affinities. He demonstrated that the family had been alive, well, and adaptive within African American culture from its earliest inception. However, the recent work of Ann Patton Malone challenges Gutman's analysis through a family reconstitution of several slave families in Louisiana. She emphasized the flexibility needed to endure the constant threats to family life in the antebellum South.

The growth of family history as an academic discipline was spurred by postwar fears about the instability of family forms. Most historians have demonstrated that the current expansion of family forms has historical antecedents. The field is now moving into an exploration of relationships within the family between siblings, domesticity, and how families evolve over time. The life-course approach has been especially helpful in understanding how families deal with different stages in their existence, from early marriage to retirement. All these approaches will continue to be applied more rigorously to a range of subjects.

KELLY BOYD

See also Ariès; Cambridge Group; Davidoff; Demography; Gutman; Henry; Lasch; Scott, Joan; Stone; Tilly, L.

Further Reading

Anderson, Michael, *Family Structure in Nineteenth-Century Lancashire*, London: Cambridge University Press, 1971

Anderson, Michael, *Approaches to the History of the Western Family, 1500–1914*, London: Macmillan, 1980; New York: Cambridge University Press, 1995

Ariès, Philippe, *L'Enfant et la vie familiale sous l'Ancien Regime*, Paris: Plon, 1960; in English as *Centuries of Childhood: A Social History of Family Life*, London: Cape, and New York: Knopf, 1962

Boyer, Richard E., *Lives of the Bigamists: Marriage, Family, and Community in Colonial Mexico*, Albuquerque: University of New Mexico Press, 1995

Burguière, André, ed., *Histoire de la famille*, Paris: Colin, 1986; in English as *A History of the Family*, 2 vols., Cambridge, MA: Harvard University Press, and Cambridge: Polity Press, 1996

Davidoff, Leonore, and Catherine Hall, *Family Fortunes: Men and Women of the English Middle Class, 1780–1850*, London: Hutchinson, and Chicago: University of Chicago Press, 1987

Demos, John, *Past, Present and Personal: The Family and the Life Course in American History*, Oxford and New York: Oxford University Press, 1986

Engel, Barbara Alpern, *Between the Fields and the City: Women, Work and Family in Russia, 1861–1914*, Cambridge and New York: Cambridge University Press, 1994

Flandrin, Jean-Louis, *Familles: parenté, maison, sexualité dans l'ancienne société*, Paris: Hachette, 1976; in English as *Families in*

Former Times: Kinship, Household and Sexuality, Cambridge and New York: Cambridge University Press, 1979

Gillis, John R., *A World of Their Own Making: Myth, Ritual, and the Quest for Family Values*, New York: Basic Books, 1996; and as *A World of Their Own Making: A History of Myth and Ritual in Family Life*, Oxford: Oxford University Press, 1997

Goody, Jack, Joan Thirsk, and E.P. Thompson, eds., *Family and Inheritance: Rural Society in Western Europe, 1200–1800*, Cambridge and New York: Cambridge University Press, 1976

Goody, Jack, *The Oriental, the Ancient and the Primitive: Systems of Marriage and the Family in the Pre-Industrial Societies of Eurasia*, Cambridge and New York: Cambridge University Press, 1990

Grubb, James S., *Provincial Families of the Renaissance: Private and Public Life in the Veneto*, Baltimore: Johns Hopkins University Press, 1996

Gutman, Herbert G., *The Black Family in Slavery and Freedom, 1750–1925*, New York: Pantheon, and Oxford, Blackwell, 1976

Hareven, Tamara, ed., *Transitions: The Family and the Life Course in Historical Perspective*, New York and London: Academic Press, 1978

Journal of Family History: Studies in Family, Kinship and Demography, 1976–

Kertzer, David I., and Richard P. Saller, eds., *The Family in Italy from Antiquity to the Present*, New Haven and London: Yale University Press, 1991

Lasch, Christopher, *Haven in a Heartless World: The Family Besieged*, New York: Basic Books, 1977; London: Norton, 1995

Laslett, Peter, *The World We Have Lost*, London: Methuen, 1965; New York: Scribner, 1966; revised 1984

Laslett, Peter, and Richard Wall, eds., *Household and Family in Past Time: Comparative Studies in the Size and Structure of the Domestic Group over the Last Three Centuries in England, France, Serbia, Japan and Colonial North America*, Cambridge and New York: Cambridge University Press, 1972

Le Play, Frédéric, *L'Organisation de la famille selon le vrai modèle signalé par l'histoire de toutes les races et de tous les temps*, Paris: Téqui, 1871; in English as *Frédéric Le Play on Family, Work, and Social Change*, Chicago: University of Chicago Press, 1982

Levine, David, *Family Formation in an Age of Nascent Capitalism*, New York and London: Academic Press, 1977

Malone, Ann Patton, *Sweet Chariot: Slave Family and Household Structure in Nineteenth-Century Louisiana*, Chapel Hill and London: University of North Carolina Press, 1992

Medick, Hans, "The Proto-industrial Family Economy: The Structural Function of Household and Family during the Transition from Peasant to Industrial Capitalism," *Social History* 1 (1976), 291–316

Metcalf, Alida C., *Family and Frontier in Colonial Brazil: Santana de Parnaíba, 1580–1822*, Berkeley: University of California Press, 1992

Mitterauer, Michael, and Reinhard Sieder, *Vom Patriarchat zur Partnerschaft zum Strukturwandel die Familie*, Munich: Beck, 1982; in English as *The European Family: Patriarchy to Partnership from the Middle Ages to the Present*, Chicago: University of Chicago Press, and Oxford: Blackwell, 1982

Moxnes, Halvor, *Constructing Early Christian Families: Family as Social Reality and Metaphor*, London and New York: Routledge, 1997

O'Day, Rosemary, *The Family and Family Relationships, 1500–1900: England, France, and the United States of America*, London: Macmillan, and New York: St. Martin's Press, 1994

Pollock, Linda, *Forgotten Children: Parent–Child Relations from 1500 to 1900*, Cambridge and New York: Cambridge University Press, 1983

Ross, Ellen, *Love and Toil: Motherhood in Outcast London, 1870–1918*, Oxford and New York: Oxford University Press, 1993

Rudolph, Richard L., *The European Peasant Family and Society: Historical Studies*, Liverpool: Liverpool University Press, 1995

Ryan, Mary P., *Cradle of the Middle Class: The Family in Oneida County, New York, 1790–1865*, Cambridge and New York: Cambridge University Press, 1981

Segalen, Martine, *Sociologie de la famille*, Paris: Colin, 1981; in English as *Historical Anthropology of the Family*, Cambridge and New York: Cambridge University Press, 1986

Shorter, Edward, *The Making of the Modern Family*, New York: Basic Books, 1975; London: Collins, 1976

Smith, Bonnie G., *Ladies of the Leisure Class: The Bourgeoises of Northern France in the Nineteenth Century*, Princeton: Princeton University Press, 1981

Stevenson, Brenda E., *Life in Black and White: Family and Community in the Slave South*, Oxford and New York: Oxford University Press, 1996

Stone, Lawrence, *The Family, Sex and Marriage in England, 1500–1800*, London: Weidenfeld and Nicolson, and New York: Harper, 1977

Tilly, Louise A., and Joan Wallach Scott, *Women, Work, and Family*, New York: Holt Rinehart, 1978; London: Methuen, 1987

Turner, Barry, and Tony Rennell, *When Daddy Came Home: How Family Life Changed Forever in 1945*, London: Hutchinson, 1995

Wall, Richard, ed., *Family Forms in Historic Europe*, Cambridge and New York: Cambridge University Press, 1982

Wrigley, E.A. *et al.*, *English Population History from Family Reconstitution, 1580–1837*, Cambridge and New York: Cambridge University Press, 1997

Febvre, Lucien 1878–1956

French historian

As a founder of the Annales school, Lucien Febvre was one of French historiography's most influential figures. Febvre's contribution began early as a contributor to Henri Berr's *Revue de synthèse* (founded 1900). Along with Marc Bloch he began publication of *Annales d'histoire économique et sociale*, which became the *Annales d'histoire sociales*, later the *Mélanges d'histoire sociale*, and finally the *Annales: économies, sociétés, civilisations* (or *Annales: ESC*) in 1929. Finally, he was instrumental in the creation of Section 6 (Social and Economic Sciences) in the Ecole Pratique des Hautes Etudes of the University of Paris, the most important center for historical study in France. Underlying this was Febvre's belief in the necessity of synthesizing all knowledge in a historical framework.

The essence of Febvre's approach was to abolish the barriers between the human sciences and the social sciences. Through the *Annales* he argued that in practice there should be no distinction between history and geography, history and economy, history and sociology, history and politics, history and psychology, history and religion, and so on. The individual works of Febvre are essentially steps in the direction of putting this proposal into action.

A major characteristic of Febvre's work was his attitude toward knowledge. He was open to a wide variety of sources and types of analysis at a time when most historians were wedded either to archives or to literary sources. His openness helped to cast him as a rebel in the academic world. He was severe to the narrow-minded criticisms typical of highly specialized academics. In a 1933 letter written to "a dear friend," Febvre commented on the plan for an encyclopedia noting: "an Encyclopedia is a work in perpetual evolution, hence, year by year, it will be completed, reformed, redone. Finally, a third argument – and then our separation is very clear. You tell me "Where is Geography in all that?.' My dear friend, it is everywhere and nowhere. The same as the History of Art. The same as Law. The same as Moral. The same as . . ., well, I will not continue. Why? Because I am not writing an Encyclopedia of the Sciences." Febvre could not accept barriers between disciplines; he believed in the unity of knowledge. He applied the same criticism to history based solely on specifics, which he termed, following Berr, *histoire historisante*.

This does not mean Febvre wished to eliminate facts from historical analysis. But he believed that history as a discipline embraced more than the political and diplomatic topics thought traditionally to be the heart of history. He also gave much thought to the study of personalities. Thus the intimate relations between history and psychology – both a psychology of individuals who might be considered the makers of history, and a psychology of the masses – were crucial to his work. Although devoted to the study of the work of some individuals and of the corresponding social repercussions, Febvre did not concentrate on class. Febvre recognized that the social environment is an organic reality which attracts the individual, thus is a determinant in the creative process. Hence, the individual and the social are not in conflict, but complement each other. These views are clearly illustrated in his important review of the works of Arnold Toynbee and Oswald Spengler, written in 1953. Febvre said about the latter "Let us not judge him; to judge is not proper for a historian; let us try to understand him, what does it mean, in his case, to relate his book and his success with the needs of a Germany then already building up what would become Hitler's national socialism." This defined, in his own words, the idea of what it means to be a historian. And he revealed himself to be caustic in his criticism. Of Toynbee he wrote: "What *A Study of History* brings us which deserves to be lauded is not new. And what it brings new is not noteworthy."

Febvre's works reflected the evolution of his teaching and in a sense can be interpreted as intellectual history. This is very clear in his most important work, *Le Problème de l'incroyance au XVIe siècle* (1942; *The Problem of Unbelief in the Sixteenth Century*, 1982). In this influential book, Febvre produced not a mere relation of facts, but a study of Rabelais' mental processes. This desire to integrate a range of approaches was central to his historiographical contribution.

UBIRATAN D'AMBROSIO

See also Agrarian; Annales School; Anthropology; Barkan; Bloch; Braudel; Burke; Cantimori; Chevalier; Europe: Modern; France: 1000–1450; France: 1450–1789; Frontiers; Ganshof; Labrousse; Mentalities; Michelet; Needham; Pirenne; Power; Reformation; Renouvin; Seignobos; Semple; Vovelle; Weber

Biography

Lucien Paul Victor Febvre. Born Nancy, Lorraine, 22 July 1878. Educated at Ecole Normale Supérieure; received doctorate, the Sorbonne, 1912. Taught at University of Dijon, 1912–14; served in French Army, 1914–18; lecturer, University of Strasbourg, 1919–33; founded (with Marc Bloch), *Annales d'histoire économique et sociale*, 1929; professor, Collège de France, 1933–50; founder/president, 6th section, Ecole Pratique des Hautes Etudes, from 1948. Married Suzanne Dognon, 1921 (3 children). Died Saint-Amour, Jura, 27 September 1956.

Principal Writings

Philippe II et la Franche-Comté: étude d'histoire politique, religieuse et sociale (Philip II and la Franche-Comté: A Study of Political, Religious, and Social History), 1911

La Terre et l'évolution humaine: introduction géographique à l'histoire, 1922; in English as *A Geographical Introduction to History*, 1925

Un destin: Martin Luther, 1928; in English as *Martin Luther: A Destiny*, 1929

Le Problème de l'incroyance au XVIe siècle: la religion de Rabelais, 1942; in English *The Problem of Unbelief in the Sixteenth Century: The Religion of Rabelais*, 1982

Autour de l'Heptaméron, amour sacré, amour profane: les classiques de la liberté: Michelet (On the Heptameron, Sacred Love, Profane Love: The Classics of Liberty), 1944; as *Michelet et la Renaissance* (Michelet and the Renaissance), 1992

Combats pour l'Histoire (Battles for History), 1953

Au coeur religieux du XVIe siècle (The Heart of 16th-Century Religion), 1957

With Henri-Jean Martin, *L'Apparition du livre*, 1958; in English as *The Coming of the Book: The Impact of Printing, 1450–1800*, 1976

Pour une histoire à part entière (For a Fully-Fledged History), 1962; selections in English as *Life in Renaissance France*, 1977

A New Kind of History: From the Writings of Febvre, edited by Peter Burke, 1973

Further Reading

Burguière, André, "La Notion de 'mentalités' chez Marc Bloch et Lucien Febvre: Deux conceptions, deux filiations" (The Idea of "Mentalities" in Marc Bloch and Lucien Febvre: Two Concepts, Two Legacies), *Revue de Synthèse* 104 (1983), 333–48

Lyon, Bryce, and Mary Lyon, eds., *The Birth of Annales History: The Letters of Lucien Febvre and Marc Bloch to Henri Pirenne, 1921–1935*, Brussels: Académie Royale de Belgique, 1991

Mastrogregori, Massimo, *Il genio dello storico: le considerazioni sulla storia di Marc Bloch e Lucien Febvre e la tradizione metodologica francese* (The Genius of the Historian: Considerations on the History of Marc Bloch and Lucien Febvre and the French Methodological Tradition), Naples: Edizioni Scientifiche Italiene, 1987

Raminelli, Ronald, "Lucien Febvre no caminho das mentalidades" (Lucien Febvre on the Road to Mentalities), *Revista de Historia* 122 (1990), 97–115

Rhodes, Colbert, "Emile Durkheim and the Socio-Historical Thought of Lucien Febvre," *International Journal of Contemporary Sociology* 25 (1988), 65–82

Wessel, Marleen, "Lucien Febvre und Europa: An den Grenzen der Geschichte" (Lucien Febvre and Europe: At the Boundaries of History), *Comparativ* 3 (1993), 28–39

Wootton, David, "Lucien Febvre and the Problem of Unbelief in the Early Modern Period," *Journal of Modern History* 60 (1988), 695–730

Feierman, Steven 1940–
US historian of Africa

Steven Feierman received his training in the late 1960s and early 1970s and can be considered to be among the second generation of historians of Africa in the United States. He has made a number of important historiographical contributions by creating changes in ways of analyzing oral tradition, health, and resistance to colonialism.

Feierman began his academic career as a historian of oral traditions. His dissertation, which was later published as *The Shambaa Kingdom* (1974), used Shambaa oral tradition in its investigation into the precolonial past of Shambaa. Feierman employed two research strategies simultaneously for this study. First, he collected and organized Shambaa oral traditions, much like the first generation of Africanist historians had done. The oral traditions provided the basis for the study's history and chronology. Second, Feierman also conducted a study of Shambaa culture and society, much like traditional anthropological fieldwork. This data was then used to supplement the oral traditions, providing a more well rounded investigation into Shambaa history. Feierman did not see this undertaking as a dichotomized methodology involving two separate projects. Rather he saw them as one, and researched them accordingly. While previous oral historians had certainly not neglected culture, it was Feierman who discussed a methodology for its study.

Feierman is best known for the numerous contributions he has made to research on African health and healing. The historiography of African health until the late 1970s described health systems as existing at the level of the ethnic group. Therapeutic systems were held to be similar throughout an ethnic group; variations did not exist among practitioners of the same ethnic group. The new interpretation, instead, held that healing systems varied from practitioner to practitioner. This is not to say that healing systems were mutually incomprehensible. Coherent systems can spread across an ethnic group, a nation, or even several nations. But the theory that healing systems are contained within ethnic boundaries is no longer held to fit African reality. Feierman was an instrumental figure in propagating a nonethnic mode of analysis for African health research.

Health and healing have numerous linkages to social structure and culture as well, claimed Feierman. One cannot understand health in Africa unless one understands African social structure and culture as well. How disease, the body, and life and death are defined are all culturally determined. Health practitioners work within their own cultural milieu and interpret health and wellness accordingly. Society and culture also influence the patient as one's social network affects the choices and interpretations one makes concerning health. In most communities several kinds of healers work side by side, including biomedical physicians, Islamic or Christian religious healers, spirit possession cult leaders, indigenous religious leaders, and many others. Which of them one attends, or attends first, is determined by the social network of the patient. Kin, friends, and community leaders can all influence the sort of health care an individual seeks.

Health and healing are also intimately related to the environment. A study of African health cannot be divorced from space. The social, political, and economic choices that a community makes have repercussions in the natural world. Decisions on whether to invest in sanitation, education, health care, or agriculture all have important effects on a community's health. Colonialism becomes an important factor when considering health because it removed a portion of these choices from the Africans themselves. As Feierman illustrated in "Struggles for Control" (1985), the colonial system made a number of developmental choices which had severe repercussions upon African health. Decisions to dam rivers, cut forests, and alter African agricultural patterns all changed the disease climate of Africa by increasing the size of ecosystems favored by particular pathogens and/or their carriers.

Feierman recently made a research request to Africanists to rejoin healing and religion in their studies. In research relating to resistance to colonialism, healing was split from religion. Yet, says Feierman in "Healing as Social Criticism" (1995), they were intimately linked in precolonial Africa. Religious leaders of territorial religions or affliction religions were thought of as healers of the land. Their patrons were entire communities who depended on them for rain, the dispelling of plagues or insects, or the eradication of witchcraft. But there is little doubt that they were considered healers by Africans themselves. These religious leaders were often involved in resistance to colonialism, which has been well researched for many regions. Yet this research does not recognize these leaders as healers. Healing as merely a transaction between a healer and an individual patient is just a portion of the story regarding African healing systems.

Feierman has made a number of important contributions to African studies. He has been a major voice in promoting the study of an Africa free of Western-imposed intellectual categories (such as those of religion and health) which do not apply to African reality. The legitimization of oral traditions also received support from Feierman. But Feierman is perhaps best known for his contributions to the study of African health, with which his name is almost synonymous.

TOYIN FALOLA and JOEL E. TISHKEN

See also Curtin; Vansina

Biography

Steven Mark Feierman. Born New York City, 12 December 1940. Received BA, Columbia University 1961; MA, Northwestern University 1962, PhD 1970; diploma in social anthropology, Oxford University, 1965, PhD 1972. Taught at University of Wisconsin, Madison, from 1969; then moved to University of Florida. Married Elizabeth Karlin, 1964 (1 son, 1 daughter).

Principal Writings

The Shambaa Kingdom: A History, 1974
"The Social History of Disease and Medicine in Africa," *Social Science and Medicine* 13B:4 (1979), 239–43
"History of Pluralistic Medical Systems: Change in African Therapeutic Systems," *Social Science and Medicine* 13B:4 (1979), 277–84
"Therapy as a System in Action in Northeastern Tanzania," *Social Science and Medicine* 15B:3 (1981), 353–60
The Social Origins of Health and Healing in Africa, 1984
"Struggles for Control: The Social Roots of Health and Healing in Modern Africa," *African Studies Review* 28 (1985), 73–147
Peasant Intellectuals: Anthropology and History in Tanzania, 1990
Editor with John M. Janzen, *The Social Basis of Health and Healing in Africa*, 1992
"African Histories and the Dissolution of World History," in Robert Bates and others, eds., *Africa and the Disciplines*, 1993
"Healing as Social Criticism in the Time of Colonial Conquest," *African Studies* 54:1 (1995), 73–88

Feminism

The resurgence of European and Anglo-American feminism in the 1960s and 1970s engendered women's history as a discipline and prodded historians to reconceptualize the practice of history. The large number of women who rode the crest of second-wave feminism, and who joined the historical profession in the 1970s, transformed the historical field entirely, urging historians to ask different questions, seek alternative sources, and apply new methods to old historical problems. Feminist historians tried to merge grassroots activism with scholarly rigor, hoping that by uncovering women's narratives they would enrich our understanding of the past and help dismantle the patriarchy of the present. Since the 1970s, feminist historians have successfully taken up the challenge presented by Natalie Zemon Davis in "'Women's History' in Transition: The European Case" (1976) to use "the study of the sexes" to "help promote a rethinking of some of the central issues faced by historians – power, social structure, property, symbols, and periodization."

At least four streams of feminist historical writing have evolved over the last five centuries. One stream, represented by the arguably protofeminist 15th-century writer Christine de Pizan, or the 19th-century feminist Grimké sisters, highlighted the accomplishments of notable women in history, to legitimate their own demands for equality in the social, political, or legal spheres. Another group of feminist writers incorporated the Marxist analyses of Friedrich Engels and August Bebel, or the existentialist-feminist approach of Simone de Beauvoir, to trace the origins of patriarchy. These feminists, who were most active in the 1970s, viewed all historical inequality as a reflection of men's desire to oppress women, an approach that Gerda Lerner (1969) dubbed the "oppression model." In the 1970s and 1980s, another strand of feminist historiography sought to uncover women's contributions to major historical events such as the American Revolution, the French Revolution, and World War I, events that had been traditionally written about as if men had been the sole participants. Titles such as *Becoming Visible* (1976) and *Hidden from History* (1973) reflected this desire to place women back into the grand narrative of history. And most recently, in the 1980s and 1990s, feminist scholarship, with the help of anthropology, literary criticism, psychoanalysis, and poststructuralism, has transformed historical scholarship by challenging such time-honored tools of the profession as historical periodization.

The contemporary practice of feminist history grew out of the subjects and methods of social history. Using what were once thought to be non-traditional sources, – e.g., parish and inquisitional records, folktales – social historians uncovered the history of those who could not write, those who fell outside of the traditional centers of power. By combining these sources with social historians' demographic studies, for example, feminist historians began interpreting social historians' statistics to show continuities and discontinuities in women's marriage, reproductive, and working patterns.

The changing role of women during the Industrial Revolution is a case in point. For example, it had been long assumed by Marxists that the political and social status of women improved with their entry into the industrial economy. Paradoxically, many historians claimed that the rise of the Industrial Revolution contributed to the evolution of "separate spheres" for men and women by taking "productive" labor out of the household and leaving middle-class women economically dependent upon their husbands and confined to the domestic sphere. In *Women, Work, and Family* (1978) Louise Tilly and Joan Scott incorporated social history to show that "wage work in itself represented a change but not an improvement in women's social position and did not dramatically alter the relationship of women . . . to their families."

One of the most radical effects of feminism on historical scholarship is its challenge to traditional historical periodization. In her path-breaking essay, "Did Women Have a Renaissance?" (1974), Joan Kelly-Gadol argued that the period long known to historians as the Renaissance was decidedly not a Renaissance for women, and in fact the changing social relations brought about by emerging states and early capitalism produced a restriction in the number of roles available to women. This application of feminist thought begat a whole series of studies determined to break down these traditional periodizations by looking at history through the lens of gender. Joan Landes' *Women and the Public Sphere in the Age of the French Revolution* (1988) undercut the idea of an Enlightenment by demonstrating how ideologies of Republican motherhood perpetuated by writers such as Rousseau, shunted public, educated women into the private sphere. Some feminist historians, such as Juliet Mitchell, went so far as to call for a new periodization based on a woman's life cycle, using marriage, childbirth, and sexuality as historical markers.

Feminism has also affected the practice of non-Western history. Many feminist historians have employed feminist critiques to study non-Western cultures. In *Feminism and Nationalism in the Third World* (1986) Kumari Jayawardena traced the history of feminist movements in Asia and the Middle East, and posited that feminism in many Third World countries was an indigenous ideology, not one imposed by the Western world. Margaret Strobel and Nupur Chaudhuri each demonstrated that Western feminism often relied on an ideology of imperialism.

Most contemporary feminist historians have now moved away from the mono-causal "oppressed group model" – whereby all women across time and place were oppressed by patriarchy – to explain women's political, social, and economic inequality. Historians have criticized this model for being ahistorical and essentialist. They have also veered from studying women in isolation, calling instead for studies that are relational. These studies demonstrate how the effects of structural changes differ among men and women, and among women of different classes and races. One way to achieve this goal, Joan Scott argued in "Gender: A Useful Category of Historical Analysis" (1986; reprinted in *Gender and the Politics of History*, 1988) is to use gender – "the social organization of the relationship between the sexes" – as a category of historical analysis. Employing gender as an analytical tool, and combining it with poststructuralist theories, she has claimed, will produce more fruitful historical analyses for contemporary scholars.

Contemporary feminist historiography is going through tumultuous but exciting times. Some feminist historians feel that the influence of postmodern theories have gutted the political agenda of early feminist histories and have rendered women without historical agency. Others claim that these new methods of historical inquiry provide a greater texture to the histories of women and men. For example, in what is known in feminist academic circles as the "equality/difference debate," some historians now claim that feminism cannot be defined solely in terms of women's attempts to attain equal rights, but that feminism sometimes implies "equality in difference," i.e., that women are different from but complementary to men. Though the meaning of second-wave feminism is still being debated today among feminist historians, there is no doubt that the questions raised by feminist historiography have touched all fields of historical inquiry, including family history, diplomatic and military history, and the history of science.

SANDIE HOLGUÍN

See also Davis, N.; Lerner; Women's History

Further Reading

Bridenthal, Renate, and Claudia Koonz, eds., *Becoming Visible*, Boston: Houghton Mifflin, 1977; revised with Susan Mosher Stuard, 1987

Chaudhuri, Nupur, "Memsahibs and Motherhood in Nineteenth-Century Colonial India," *Victorian Studies* 31 (1988), 417–37

Davis, Natalie Zemon, "'Women's History' in Transition: The European Case," *Feminist Studies* 3 (1976), 83–103

Hartman, Mary S., and Lois W. Banner, eds., *Clio's Consciousness Raised: New Perspectives on the History of Women*, New York: Harper, 1974

Jayawardena, Kumari, *Feminism and Nationalism in the Third World*, New Delhi: Kali for Women, London: Zed, and Totowa, NJ: Biblio, 1986

Kelly, Joan, *Women, History, and Theory: The Essays of Joan Kelly*, Chicago: University of Chicago Press, 1984 [includes "Did Women Have a Renaissance?" (1974)]

Kessler-Harris, Alice, *Women Have Always Worked: A Historical Overview*, Old Westbury, NY: Feminist Press, 1981

Landes, Joan B., *Women and the Public Sphere in the Age of the French Revolution*, Ithaca, NY: Cornell University Press, 1988

Lerner, Gerda, "New Approaches to the Study of Women in American History," *Journal of Social History* 3 (1969), 53–62

Mitchell, Juliet, *Woman's Estate*, Harmondsworth: Penguin, 1971; New York: Pantheon, 1972

Offen, Karen, "Defining Feminism: A Comparative Historical Approach," *Signs* 14 (1988), 119–57

Rowbotham, Sheila, *Women, Resistance and Revolution*, London: Allen Lane, and New York: Pantheon, 1972

Rowbotham, Sheila, *Hidden from History: 300 Years of Women's Oppression and the Fight Against It*, London: Pluto, 1973; New York: Pantheon, 1975

Scott, Joan Wallach, *Gender and the Politics of History*, New York: Columbia University Press, 1988

Scott, Joan Wallach, ed., *Feminism and History*, Oxford and New York: Oxford University Press, 1996

Strobel, Margaret, *European Women in British Africa and Asia*, New York: Holt Rinehart, 1978

Tilly, Louise A., and Joan Wallach Scott, *Women, Work, and Family*, New York: Holt Rinehart, 1978; London: Methuen, 1987

Vicinus, Martha, ed., *Suffer and Be Still: Women in the Victorian Age*, Bloomington: Indiana University Press, 1972; London: Methuen, 1980

Feudalism

Feudalism is a model or construct devised to encompass a specified constellation of political and institutional elements present in medieval European societies. The word originates with the Latin *feudum*, fief, and was coined by English and European legal scholars of the 16th through the 18th centuries to define a set of land-tenure relationships thought characteristic of the European nobility of the Middle Ages.

For "feudalism" we should understand a limited number of related heuristic models: first, an institutional one, commonly known as "feudo-vassalic"; second, a more encompassing social one, such as Marc Bloch's concept of "feudal society"; and third, a Marxist notion based on a "feudal" mode of production and considered as a universal stage in human history.

The feudo-vassalic model was most completely schematized by Ganshof, for whom the linkage of fief and vassalage was basic to an institutional conception of feudalism. But Ganshof omitted what, for Strayer and others, is the defining element of the system: public power privately exercised. Bloch's model was less formalistic (fiefs and vassalage were not inevitably linked), and more inclusive, since for Bloch the relationship of peasants to lords was parallel to that of vassals to men of higher rank.

Marx described feudal society as an extension of early Germanic tribal society in which the nobility exercised a kind of communal ownership of land, worked by a dependent peasantry. There are a number of problems with the Marxist approach. First, there is considerable confusion over the owner of the means of production. In fact, this was shared by the nobility and the peasantry, which makes little sense in Marxist social theory. Second, Engels (in a letter to Marx of 15 December 1882) defined a "second serfdom" which began in the 15th century and extended to the end of the Old Regime in France. Bloch accepted the reality of post-medieval feudalism, especially in the form of rural seignories.

The transition from "ancient society" to feudalism has attracted recent attention. For Wickham, the transition occurred whenever and wherever more rents are paid to lords than are taxes paid into a public treasury. Inasmuch as the Roman fiscal system had collapsed by the 6th century, such a rule would push the transition to an earlier date than the watershed year of 1000 CE favored by other historians. Bois suggested a multiple criteria for the transition: How long did rural slavery last? When did the smallholder become subject to a lord? When did the water-powered gristmill cease being one of the motors of peasant economic expansion and become an instrument of seignorial oppression? These indicators point to a 10th- or 11th-century transition in central and southern France and in Catalonia in particular. Reynolds, in an extreme revisionist stance, concluded that feudo-vassalic relations were a kind of legalist overlay on a very different underlying social reality, and not, in any case, the product of early medieval governmental disintegration, but rather of bureaucratic, legalistic royal administrations of the 12th century and later.

Another group of theorists led by Pierre Toubert has centered the transition on the phenomenon of *incastellamento* – the re-organization of the countryside into "castral units" wherein the peasantry is dominated by feudal castellans. This movement began in the mid-10th century in northern Italy, Provence, and Catalonia, somewhat later in central and northern France and southern Italy. Note that *incastellamento* promotes instrumentalist criteria rather than the formal or legalistic insistence on the presence of specific forms of fiefs or vassalage.

In spite of consistent complaints about the limited value of any such construct, feudalism has been a tremendously successful model because it has generated an impressive amount of research, (see, for example, the 1272 citations in *Historical Abstracts*, 1960–96), which is a good yardstick by which to measure the value of a hypothesis to any specific generation of historians. It has been a universalizing hypothesis that has forced virtually every medieval historian to come to grips with it and weigh their own evidence against it, even though it is not a unified model but rather a multifocal one. In historical analysis generally, and comparative history even more so, the most fruitful models are those with many elements. Feudalism is such a model: it is loaded with formal elements (e.g., fief, vassalage, homage, etc.) whose substantive content displays regional and chronological variation.

There is then the further issue of what elements of feudalism ought to be considered as normative. Traditionally, the institutions of areas identified as the "hearth" of an innovation are taken as normative – in this case, the feudal institutions of northern France, western Germany, the Low Countries, and England. But this is a purely conventional distinction and, in comparative perspective, normativity tends to dissolve as an issue.

Feudalism has been a highly successful model in terms of generating significant research. But Brown suggests that just as happens in natural science, a reigning paradigm should be overthrown when enough anomalies build up to discredit it. The epistemology of social science is quite different however. Here, paradigms change over time and among different disciplinary groups, depending on a variety of mainly exogenous factors, including general social values or shifts in the research programs of different groups of scholars. Anomalies, instead of destroying paradigms, may simply force them to broaden. This explains why a single term like feudalism can have so many different meanings, each defined by a different disciplinary tradition.

The construct has been criticized as oversimplified; yet (based on Ganshof only) the feudo-vassalic model has a minimum of fifty variables. Indeed the richness and complexity of the model account for its longevity and success. There is the further problem of the inevitable confusion of feudalism as a conventional, popular term ("feudal" as a synonym of "medieval" in common parlance) with a variety of technical meanings. Medieval scholars themselves frequently mix technical and conventional usages.

THOMAS F. GLICK

See also Bloch; Ganshof

Further Reading

Bloch, Marc, "Feudalism," in Edwin R.A. Seligmann, ed., *Encyclopedia of the Social Sciences*, 15 vols., New York: Macmillan, 1930–35

Bloch, Marc, *La Société féodale*, 2 vols., Paris: Michel, 1939–40; in English as *Feudal Society*, 2 vols., Chicago: University of Chicago Press, and London: Routledge, 1961

Bois, Guy, *La Mutation de l'an mil: Lournand, ville mâconnaise de l'antiquité au féodalisme*, Paris: Fayard, 1989; in English as *The Transformation of the Year One Thousand: The Village of Lournand from Antiquity to Feudalism*, Manchester: Manchester University Press, 1992

Brown, Elizabeth A.R., "The Tyranny of a Construct: Feudalism and Historians of Medieval Europe, 1063–88," *American Historical Review* 79 (1974), 128

Ganshof, F.L., *Qu'est-ce que la féodalité?*, Brussels: Lebègue, 1944; in English as *Feudalism*, London: Longman, 1952, New York: Harper, 1961

Marx, Karl, *Formen, die der kapitalistischen Produktion vorhergehen* [part of *Grundrisse der Kritik der politischen Ökonomie*], Berlin: Dietz, 1952; abridged translation as *Pre-Capitalist Economic Formations*, London: Lawrence and Wishart, 1964, New York: International, 1965

Reynolds, Susan, *Fiefs and Vassals: The Medieval Evidence Reinterpreted*, Oxford and New York: Oxford University Press, 1994

Strayer, Joseph R., "Feudalism," in Strayer, ed., *Dictionary of the Middle Ages*, 13 vols., New York: Scribner, 1985, 5:82–89

Toubert, Pierre, ed., *Structures féodales et féodalisme dans l'Occident méditerranéen: Xe–XIIIe siècles* (Feudal Structures and Feudalism in the Western Mediterranean from the 10th to the 13th Centuries), Rome: Ecole Française de Rome, 1980

Wickham, Chris, "The Other Transition: From the Ancient World to Feudalism," *Past and Present* 103 (1984), 3–36

Film

Film, which marked its centenary in 1995, has become an important field of historical inquiry in the last 25 years, enriched by the domains of literature, psychoanalysis, and philosophy. While the field tended to follow categories of genres, national industries, individual filmmakers, silent/sound films, and theory/history, recent comparative and interdisciplinary studies have also broken down such categories. Although historical films and the relationship between film and history have only occasionally received systematic attention, there has been a flourishing of excellent works that analyze film industries and film contents in the context of larger economic, political, social, and cultural trends.

From its inception film was received both as a form of mass culture and of modern art. It is the last invention of mass communication to be conceived as both, and this tension between mass culture and elite art has informed film scholarship. This was true of one of the earliest attempts at a general history of cinema, Paul Rotha's *The Film till Now* (1930), which insisted on the aesthetic qualities of film. Siegfried Kracauer in *From Caligari to Hitler* (1947) identified certain Weimar films as carrying political ideology. Although he reduced the complexity and ambiguity of film contents to ideology, he was a pioneer in using close reading and in the very taking up of film as a subject matter for cultural analysis. Kracauer argued that the radical potential of film was distorted by capitalism, which led to the production of sleek entertainments with artistic value. He suggested that the early cinema appealed to the urban crowd because of its fragmented form. The earliest cinema indeed emphasized not coherent and emotional narrative but display and showmanship, forming what Tom Gunning termed the "cinema of attractions." The idea that cinema formed one element of modern entertainment is underlined in *Cinema and the Invention of Modern Life* (1995), edited by Leo Charney and Vanessa Schwartz, who argued that modern life was cinematic before the event. Kracauer's notion that fragmented form was popular has been modified by findings, for instance, that early Soviet audiences preferred Hollywood films to Soviet masterpieces such as Eisenstein's *Battleship Potemkin* (1925).

From the 1970s scholarly debate concerning both film theory and film history flourished. Christian Metz's psychoanalytic theory of the filmic apparatus and the spectator transformed film theory and was in turn modified by feminist critics challenging the idea that cinema appealed to male pleasure. Patrice Petro in *Joyless Streets* (1989) aimed to unravel the historical argument underpinning the psychoanalytic theory. At the same time, film history moved away from accounts of technological developments and canonical films, to the study of cinema as an economic and social institution as well as a cultural phenomenon. Klaus Kreimeier's *Die UFA- Story* (1992; *The UFA Story*, 1996), for instance, thoroughly examined one film industry. The impetus of theory and history also propelled studies on spectatorship as a matrix of perceptual response and subjectivity. Miriam Hansen in *Babel and Babylon* (1991) pointed out that commercial and cultural exigencies influenced the shifting conceptions of the spectator as mass or elite, and that the formation of a unique public sphere of a mixed audience was both celebrated and denigrated.

Scholars have investigated the relationship between aesthetic, ideological, and economic dimensions of film. The ideological facet of film is most clearly delineated in uses as propaganda and in instances of censorship. While some cinemas born in wartime tended to be realistic (Italian neorealism or Korean cinema), from early on escapism has been a tremendously popular strand in cinema. The happy endings of Hollywood tended to resolve conflicts over cultural values, just as Nazi films more explicitly affirmed a communal worldview and sought to help the spectators sift through disorienting reality. Roland Barthes in *Mythologies* (1957; translated 1972) pointed out that belief systems such as capitalism, democracy, Christianity, and the nuclear family are constructions of modern myth, which naturalizes history and creates "common sense" out of complex issues. Such a concept of myth has been used in the study of cinema. In *Fascism in Film* (1986) Marcia Landy noted that fascist myths – about youth, family, sexuality, heroism, or sacrifice – are not just about transcending or escaping reality but are about the tension between the real and the imaginary, about the transgression of the boundaries between the two. It is the "fusion of social and psychological conflicts with the elements of myth that constitutes [the fascist] ideological discourse." Heide Fehrenbach also argued in *Cinema in Democratizing Germany* (1995) that Heimat films of the 1950s underscored a communal ideal that comforted the survivors of the war but was in turn rejected as outmoded by the younger generation. She emphasized the highly politicized role of the cinema in the reconstruction of German political legitimacy and national identity. Such studies highlight the importance of popular films as historical subject. Richard Stites pointed out that popular films carry the "treasury of symbols and codes."

In the 1990s historians have debated the role of historical film and what Hayden White termed "historiophoty" (image-based representation of historical discourse). They acknowledged the superiority of film for capturing elements such as landscape, atmosphere, and emotional content. Robert Rosenstone in *Revisioning History* (1995) pointed out that the visual media have become the principal carrier of historical messages, and that the historical film should be seen as a mode of envisioning the past with its own rules of representation. He emphasized that the aim of new historical films is to understand the historical legacy rather than to entertain, and that filmmakers have often focused on certain subjects before historians. Latin American films of the 1960s depicting colonialism, and African equivalents a decade later, were produced by political and cultural movements and preceded historiographies treating the same themes. *New Latin American Cinema* (1997), edited by Michael T. Martin, suggested that while Hollywood cinema has been internationally predominant, some national cinemas have other independent outlets. Indian cinema – Bollywood – is the second-largest in the world, and Indian films are widely exported to the Middle East and Africa. Aimed at a mostly illiterate audience, these romances underscore the power of the universal language of film.

Historians have also made a major contribution to the archaeology of cinema. For example, Kevin Brownlow's *The Parade's Gone By* (1968) was an accessible study of silent cinema based on extended interviews with the early pioneers of film. Brownlow himself played a major role in the restoration of silent films, most notably Abel Gance's *Napoleon* (1927), which he, in effect, rediscovered. Archaeologists of cinema have also reached further back in time. Laurent Mannoni's *Luce e movimento* (1995; *Light and Movement*, 1995) investigated the rich field of pre-cinematographic moving images. Film history is now a thriving and sophisticated discipline drawing on academic and non-academic specialists.

H. HAZEL HAHN

See also Documentary; Media; White, H.

Further Reading

Abel, Richard, ed., *French Film Theory and Criticism: A History/Anthology, 1907–1939*, 2 vols., Princeton: Princeton University Press, 1988

Balio, Tino, ed., *The American Film Industry*, Madison: University of Wisconsin Press, 1976

Barthes, Roland, *Mythologies*, Paris: Seuil, 1957; selections in English as *Mythologies*, London: Cape, 1972, New York: Hill and Wang, 1973

Brownlow, Kevin, *The Parade's Gone By*, London: Secker and Warburg, and Berkeley: University of California Press, 1968

Bruno, Giuliana, *Streetwalking on a Ruined Map: Cultural Theory and the City Films of Elvira Notari*, Princeton: Princeton University Press, 1993

Carnes, Mark C., ed., *Past Imperfect: History According to the Movies*, New York: Holt, 1995, revised 1996; London: Cassell, 1996

Charney, Leo, and Vanessa Schwartz, eds., *Cinema and the Invention of Modern Life*, Berkeley: University of California Press, 1995

Fehrenbach, Heide, *Cinema in Democratizing Germany: Reconstructing National Identity after Hitler*, Chapel Hill: University of North Carolina Press, 1995

Ferro, Marc, *Cinéma et histoire*, Paris: Denoël, 1977; in English as *Cinema and History*, Detroit: Wayne State University Press, 1988

Gunning, Tom, *D.W. Griffith and the Origins of American Narrative Film: The Early Years of Biograph*, Urbana: University of Illinois Press, 1991

Hansen, Miriam, *Babel and Babylon: Spectatorship in American Silent Film*, Cambridge, MA: Harvard University Press, 1991

Hay, James, *Popular Film Culture in Fascist Italy: The Passing of the Rex*, Bloomington: Indiana University Press, 1987

Kracauer, Siegfried, *From Caligari to Hitler: A Psychological History of the German Film*, Princeton: Princeton University Press, and London: Dobson, 1947

Kreimeier, Klaus, *Die UFA-Story: Geschichte eines Filmkonzerns*, Munich: Hauser, 1992; in English as *The UFA Story: A History of Germany's Greatest Film Company, 1918–1945*, New York: Hill and Wang, 1996

Landy, Marcia, *Fascism in Film: The Italian Commercial Cinema, 1931–1943*, Princeton: Princeton University Press, 1986

Mannoni, Laurent, *Luce e movimento: incunaboli dell'immagine animata*, Gemona: Giornate del Cinema Muto, 1995; in English as *Light and Movement: Incunabula of the Motion Picture, 1420–1896*, 1995

Martin, Michael T., ed., *New Latin American Cinema*, 2 vols. to date, Detroit: Wayne State University Press, 1997

Metz, Christian, *Le Significant Imaginaire: psychanalyse et cinéma*, Paris: Union Générale d'Editions, 1977; in English as *Psychoanalysis and Cinema: The Imaginary Signifier*, London: Macmillan, 1982

Murray, Bruce A., and Chris J. Wickham, eds., *Framing the Past: The Historiography of German Cinema and Television*, Carbondale: Southern Illinois University Press, 1992

Orr, John, *Cinema and Modernity*, Cambridge: Polity Press, and Cambridge, MA: Blackwell, 1993

Petro, Patrice, *Joyless Streets: Women and Melodramatic Representations in Weimar Germany*, Princeton: Princeton University Press, 1989

Richards, Jeffrey, *Visions of Yesterday*, London: Routledge, 1973

Rosenstone, Robert, *Revisioning History: Film and the Construction of a New Past*, Princeton: Princeton University Press, 1995

Rotha, Paul, *The Film till Now: A Survey of the Cinema*, London: Cape, 1930; revised edition London: Vision, 1949, 1960, New York: Funk and Wagnalls, 1949

Sorlin, Pierre, *European Cinemas, European Societies, 1939–1990*, London and New York: Routledge, 1991

Stites, Richard, "Soviet Movies for the Masses and for Historians," *Historical Journal of Film, Radio and Television* 11 (1991), 243–52

von Geldorn, James, ed., *Mass Culture in Soviet Russia: Tales, Poems, Songs, Movies, Plays and Folklore, 1917–1953*, Bloomington: Indiana University Press, 1995

Youngblood, Denise J., *Soviet Cinema in the Silent Era, 1918–1935*, Ann Arbor, MI: UMI Research Press, 1985

Finley, M.I. 1912–1986

British (US-born) ancient historian

Moses Finley was one of the most important ancient historians to emerge in the English-speaking world during the last fifty years. Although from the United States, Finley had the most remarkable and dominating effect on the Cambridge University faculty of classics, which then, as now, was one of the most important of its kind in Britain. His role was to bring a new prominence to social and economic issues within ancient history and to the use of models in the solving of historical problems and disputes. The reason for this may lie in his training in law and history rather than in traditional classics. Britain must thank McCarthyism for Finley's move from Rutgers to Cambridge in the early 1950s.

His first major work was *Studies in Law and Credit in Ancient Athens, 500–200 BC* (1952), but he gained world recognition with his *The World of Odysseus* (1954). Using anthropological ideas on kinship, he pioneered in identifying the power of families and households in the pre-archaic Greek world (as differentiated from the archaic period of the *Iliad*). Finley was keen to stress the primitive nature of classical antiquity. He thought that many classicists looked on their period of specialism with rose-tinted spectacles and he emphasized that, in many ways within the social and economic sphere, antique Europe was a strange and backward place.

Finley was an outstanding thinker and writer, who was at pains to extract the maximum from his sources while accounting for, and bemoaning, their inadequacies. After all, reliable figures are hard to find from the ancient world and so it is best, perhaps, to concentrate on the ways that things happened, to concentrate on a qualitative as well as on a quantitative analysis. Over time, Finley's interests developed in two main directions: the study of the social and economic order of ancient society, and historiography. Particular themes were a recurring interest of his, especially slavery, perhaps best represented by *Ancient Slavery and Modern Ideology* (1980), and ancient political processes, as in *Politics in the Ancient World* (1983). He also pioneered a strong vision of the ancient city-state as a parasitic organism within its hinterland, as spelt out in *The Ancient Economy* (1973).

Finley's interest in theory stemmed from his strong desire for explanatory models with which to make sense of the ancient world. He was passionately interested in the question of the historian's imaginative and constructive role, as can be seen from *The Use and Abuse of History* (1975) and *Ancient History: Evidence and Models* (1985). However, his enemies may have overestimated his radicalism, as he never departed from the traditional basics of textual analysis. He employed models from outside his discipline as aids rather than as goals. He was always careful not to place too much reliance on sociology, anthropology, or archaeology, in the belief that these subjects can inform the historian, but cannot be his or her salvation.

Finley did not find universal approval, despite the undoubted quantity and quality of his output over a long career. He was not afraid to attack others whose approaches he did not look on with respect. There is no question, however, that he strongly influenced the Cambridge Classics Faculty for a generation, and was very widely read in both the English- and non-English-speaking worlds. He gave an enormous boost to the study of the social and economic history of the ancient city-state. Finley can be seen as part of the postwar movement toward social analysis in history, which, in turn, has led to the modern concern with cultural studies. His particular contribution was to take his place at the forefront of these general historiographical trends in the sphere of ancient history.

DOMINIC JANES

See also Davis, D.; Greece: Ancient; Polanyi; Rostovtzeff; Slavery: Ancient

Biography

Moses I. Finley. Born Moses Finkelstein, New York, 20 May 1912, son of a mechanical engineer. Attended Syracuse Central High School; received BA in psychology, Syracuse University, 1927; MA in public law, Columbia University, 1929, PhD in history 1950. Worked briefly as a legal clerk, 1929; researcher/editorial assistant, *Encyclopedia of the Social Sciences*, 1930–33; taught at City College of New York, 1934–42; also held research fellowship, Columbia University, 1934–35; editor/translator, Institute for Social Research, (then affiliated with Columbia University), 1937–39. Held executive posts with wartime relief agencies, 1942–47. Taught at Rutgers University, 1948–52; but emigrated to England after attacks by McCarthy, 1954 (naturalized 1962); taught (rising to professor), Cambridge University, 1964–79 (emeritus): fellow, Jesus College, 1957–86; master, Darwin College, 1976–82. Knighted 1979. Married Mary Moscowitz Thiers, teacher, 1932 (died 22 June 1986). Died Cambridge, 23 June 1986.

Principal Writings

Studies in Law and Credit in Ancient Athens, 500–200 BC, 1952
The World of Odysseus, 1954
The Greek Historians: The Essence of Herodotus, Thucydides, Xenophon, Polybius, 1959
Aspects of Antiquity: Discoveries and Controversies, 1968
The Ancient Economy, 1973
The Use and Abuse of History, 1975
Ancient Slavery and Modern Ideology, 1980
Economy and Society in Ancient Greece, edited by Brent D. Shaw and Richard P. Saller, 1981 [includes bibliography]
Politics in the Ancient World, 1983
Ancient History: Evidence and Models, 1985

Fischer, Fritz 1908–
German historian

Arguably the most important German historian of the 20th century, Fritz Fischer effected a radical reappraisal not only of the politics of imperial Germany prior to and during World War I, but also of the other world powers. He also postulated a continuity of imperialist aggression on the part of Germany from the Kaiser's time to the Third Reich. His first post-World War II book, *Griff nacht der Weltmacht* (1961; *Germany's Aims in the First World War*, 1967), created an unprecedented and acrimonious debate among, first, German colleagues, and then internationally within the entire discipline of modern European diplomatic and political history. Fischer had been conventionally trained in the established Hegelian-Rankean paradigm, conservative in his basic historical-philosophical assumptions, and with a strong Protestant formation. This is reflected in his biographies of Ludwig Nicolovius (Prussian educationalist during the era of Baron vom Stein) and Moritz August von Bethmann Hollweg (1795–1877, minister for education and religious affairs in Prussia, 1858–62) published prior to World War II).

However, the various postwar explanations for the Nazi period, such as that by Friedrich Meinecke, which exculpated the Prussian military tradition, and the antiliberal political culture fostered by the educated elite in Germany, especially after the foundation of the Reich by Bismarck, appeared to Fischer as threadbare.

Fischer was the first notable German intellectual effectively to agree with earlier Western interpretations of the course of German history, namely that the failure of the development of a vigorous liberal parliamentary political culture from the time of the Reformation allowed the Prussian militarist tradition to triumph in Germany. This tradition had not only been celebrated by German intellectual leaders as superior to that of the West, it also developed a sense of world mission to impose itself on the rest of the world. At the first German historians' congress after the war, in Munich 1949, Fischer adumbrated his later theses in a powerful address on Protestantism and politics in 19th-century Germany. In this he berated the Lutheran heritage which recognized the ruler of the state as occupying a divinely sanctioned office that had to be obeyed. This tradition sustained a dangerously different political consciousness in the German middle and upper classes and stifled the modernizing political process that evolved into parliamentary democracy in the West. Here the political culture had been shaped by Calvinist (as opposed to Lutheran) ideas and values that placed the ruler under the law rather than above it. Fischer at that time made an open appeal to his colleagues to appropriate this Western tradition. Conservatives such as Gerhard Ritter were bitterly opposed to this interpretation of the course of German history and to the remedy prescribed.

Fischer insisted in his Hamburg seminars that the Third Reich had not been the result of a tragic breakdown in German politics caused by the unjust imposition in 1919 of the Treaty of Versailles. Rather it was the consequence of military, political, and commercial ambitions of the entire German power-elite whose aims in 1933–45 were all traceable back to aims developed prior to 1914 and which had merely been frustrated by the unexpected loss of World War I and the subsequent era of the Weimar republic. Thus Fischer maintained the thesis of *continuity* of German war aims from 1914 to 1945. *Germany's Aims in the First World War* sought to establish the origins and implementation of these aims 1914–18. In doing so he departed from conventional diplomatic history to investigate the various pressure groups within the Reich which had military, territorial, and commercial ambitions in Central and Eastern Europe, the Balkans, and Asia Minor, as well as Africa. All these appeared in memoranda in various ministries and not all were compatible. Nevertheless, a consensus of these aims (the "September Program") was tabled by the Reich chancellor, Bethmann Hollweg, on the eve of the Battle of the Marne, in mid-September 1914, when the Schlieffen plan for the Western Front seemed on the brink of success.

The "September Program" proposed first the annexation of Belgium and the eastern industrialized parts of France, and second the conquest of East Central Europe at the expense of Russia, which would be driven back beyond the Urals. This redrawing of the map of Europe was to be for "imaginable time." Despite the many setbacks, Fischer showed that the German power-elite maintained the essence of this series of objectives right up until October–November 1918.

Fischer reaffirmed his analysis with a massive investigation of German politics from the time of the appointment of Hollweg as chancellor in 1911 to the outbreak of war in 1914, in *Krieg der Illusionen* (1969; *War of Illusions*, 1975). This work portrays the politics behind the diplomacy and reveals the Kaiser Reich as a state desperate to preserve the authoritarian-bureaucratic Bismarckian constitution against the rising tide of social democracy on the one hand, while on the other seeking to establish itself as a great colonial and naval power, not only alongside but at the expense of the others, especially Britain, France, and Russia.

With these assessments Fischer provoked others to reinvestigate the origins of Reich domestic and foreign policy and the links between them. He also challenged the profession to abandon previous exculpating historiography which down-played the aggressiveness of German policy, and forced an across-the-board revision of traditional interpretations of Prussian-German

history in the 19th and 20th centuries. Although Fischer has been criticized for not balancing his research by equivalent assessments of the other Great Powers, his findings have stood the test of time and succeeded in showing that both the Kaiser Reich and the Third Reich were dominated by capitalist elites who shared the same anti-Western, racist, and imperialist consciousness.

JOHN A. MOSES

See also Diplomatic; East Central Europe; Europe: Modern; Germany: 1800–1945; Hartung; Joll; Kennedy; Ritter; Wehler; World War I

Biography

Born in Ludwigstadt, Upper Franconia in Bavaria, 5 March 1908, son of a railway inspector. Attended grammar schools in Ansbach and Eichstätt, 1917–26, and the universities of Erlangen and Berlin, studying Protestant theology, history, philosophy, and pedagogics, with the church historians Erich Seeberg and Hans Lietzmann and the educationalist and philosopher Eduard Spranger; later studied constitutional history under the influence of Fritz Hartung, and national history under A.O. Meyer, Hermann Oncken, and Wilhelm Schüssler. Research was interrupted by war service and a period as prisoner of war, which postponed until 1947 his taking up his appointment in 1942 to the chair of medieval and modern history at University of Hamburg: taught until 1978. Married Margarete Lauth-Volkmann, 1942 (1 son, 1 daughter).

Principal Writings

Moritz August von Bethmann-Hollweg und der Protestantismus (Bethmann-Hollweg and Protestantism), 1938

Ludwig Nikolovius: Rokoko, Reform, Restauration (Ludwig Nikolovius: Rococo, Reform, Restoration), 1939

Griff nach der Weltmacht: die Kriegszielpolitik des kaiserlichen Deutschland, 1914–18, 1961; in English as *Germany's Aims in the First World War*, 1967

Krieg der Illusionen: Die deutsche Politik von 1911 bis 1914, 1969; in English as *War of Illusions: German Policies from 1911 to 1914*, 1975

Bündnis der Eliten: Zur Kontinuität der Machtstrukturen in Deutschland, 1871–1945, 1979; in English as *From Kaiserreich to Third Reich: Elements of Continuity in German History, 1871–1975*, 1986

Hitler war kein Betriebsunfall: Aufsätze (Hitler Was No Industrial Accident: Essays), 1992

Further Reading

Fletcher, Roger, Introduction to Fritz Fischer, *From Kaiserreich to Third Reich*, London and Boston: Allen and Unwin, 1986

Geiss, Imanuel, *Studien über Geschichte und Geschichtswissenschaft* (Studies in History and Historical Sciences), Frankfurt: Suhrkamp, 1972

Geiss, Imanuel, and Bernd Jürgen Wendt, eds., *Deutschland in der Weltpolitik des 19. und 20. Jahrhunderts: Fritz Fischer zum 65. Geburtstag* (Germany in the World Politics of the 19th and 20th Centuries: Fritz Fischer on His 65th Birthday), Düsseldorf: Bertelsmann Universitätsverlag, 1973 [includes bibliography]

Moses, John A., *The Politics of Illusion: The Fischer Controversy in German Historiography*, London: Prior, and New York: Barnes and Noble, 1975

Fleck, Ludwig 1896–1961

Polish-Israeli historian of science

The work of Ludwig Fleck has been represented as a road not taken in the history of science. Or is it? Fleck's notion of the "scientific community" and his attention to the rituals of that community in many ways anticipated later work on the sociology of scientific practice. Fleck's argument in part derived from Durkheim, but provided a basis for much of Thomas Kuhn's formulation of the "structures" of scientific practice. Indeed, Kuhn wrote that Fleck's work, together with that of Francis X. Sutton, "made me realize that [scientific ideas] might require to be set in the sociology of the scientific community," suggesting the huge impact of Fleck's discussion of the creative role of the *Denkkollektiv* in forming a historic "thought style" (*denkstil*) of a community. Fleck's concerns for the cultural conditioning of scientific practice and thought have often been traced to a 1928 stay in Vienna as a medical intern. But his work did not focus on the language of scientists, so much as it rejected the transparency attributed to scientific knowledge. Fleck's later consideration of the experiment as an artifact of scientific practice used sociological models as a way to analyze the role of "experience" in medical and scientific knowledge and laboratories. At a remove of 60 years, his work echoes some of the central concerns of postmodern critiques of scientific knowledge.

Fleck's *Entstehung und Entwicklung einer wissenschaftlichen Tatsache* (1935; *Genesis and Development of a Scientific Fact*, 1979) provided a sociologically rooted model of the formation and legitimation of scientific knowledge by focusing on laboratory practice, scientific literature, and the social practices of the scientific community. The work won little attention after its first publication, both due to the circumstances of its publication in Switzerland and to Fleck's position as a Jewish microbiologist in Poland before and during World War II. The value of Fleck's work was recognized only after Kuhn's work called attention to the notion of a "paradigm" and to the social constraints on scientific practice. Fleck was less interested in the means by which one model of thought or model of experience displaced another, than in the construction of the notion of experience within the experimental process. This is suggested in his careful reading of the Wasserman reaction as a test for specific antigens as being based on a new conception of syphilis as an infectious disease.

Fleck's discussion of epistemological structures that constrained the perception of scientific experience, and the professional rituals that validated observations as a scientific "fact" used sociological models to understand current changes in scientific practice. His emphasis on professional communication and patterns of thought as collective practices was strongly indebted to Durkheim's discussion of collective ritual: for Fleck, individual knowledge is constantly negotiated with the collective. Fleck emphasized the genesis of science both in patterns of scientific practice and local "thought-styles" and professional customs that constrained laboratory experiments; science was defined by the mindset and rituals that animated a collective enterprise. In describing the validation of knowledge in specialized literature as a collective practice, Fleck sketched a historical sociology for experimental knowledge. Scientific knowledge gained validation first in specialized literature before being popularized as "textbook" knowledge.

Inspired by a rejection of Kantian categories to describe scientific practices, Fleck coined a series of terms that would express the social and imaginative constraints on how science works. Fleck paid considerable attention to the linguistic practices that define truth, but rejected the tacit assumption that scientific language remained outside social conventions. He examined how medical and scientific understandings of disease were conditioned by the mental structures by which disease was understood (*Denkbegriffe*) and how social forces conditioned not only scientific experiments, but their reception within the collective world of scientists. "Scientific knowledge" was not a constant or an objective process: the replication of scientific knowledge within a field was itself conditioned by mental structures, and followed a path that set the terms on which scientists continued in their own work. The course of an experiment was due to the particular notion of scientific experience to which few had access, but which determined new ways of reacting to the data of experimental models; it was the moment when the scientist altered his own behavior against the models which he shared with the collectivity.

The attention Fleck paid to the terms of scientific discovery questioned the linearity of progress, but at the same time it emphasized the different levels of dialectic between scientist and scientific community. While Fleck's work prefigured some of Kuhn's concerns and points of investigation, his interest in the construction of knowledge and social reproduction of science is not mirrored in Kuhn's work. Kuhn was familiar with Fleck's arguments, but seems to have brought his own meaning to them; Fleck's terms were appropriated within Kuhn's notion of the "paradigm." The rediscovery of Fleck's concern with the rituals and collective rules of science had a greater influence on post-Kuhnian thought, however, and was early championed by Steven Shapin, and historians whose work is increasingly inflected with sociological concerns. Fleck's arguments parallel recent interest in both scientific writing and the relativity and indeterminacy of laboratory practice, but call into question the cognitive styles of practitioners, rather than the relativity of meaning.

Fleck was primarily concerned with historical change. It is tempting to see the delays of recognizing either Fleck's typhus vaccine or the *Genesis* as representative of the social constraints he discussed. Yet to do so confuses Fleck's interest in the sociological constraints of the acceptance of knowledge as a fact with the influence of social prejudice or racism on scientific knowledge. Fleck's interest in the structures by which facts and vaccines are recognized concerns the construction of scientific knowledge in "normal" conditions, and the day to day constraints of specialized literature. Awareness of social constraints no doubt however increased the irony of his work in Lwów's ghetto and laboratories in Auschwitz and Buchenwald. Fleck headed an institute of microbiology in Poland after the war. He emigrated to Israel in 1956 and worked at the Institute for Biological Research in Ness-Ziona until his death.

DANIEL BROWNSTEIN

Biography

Born Lwów, Poland (formerly Austrian-occupied Galicia, now Lvov, Ukraine), 11 July 1896, son of an artist. Studied medicine, Jan Kazimerz University. Worked primarily as a microbiologist;

researcher with Rudolf Weigl, and later his assistant at University of Lwów; founded a private laboratory, 1923, and served as a consultant, Lwów General Hospital, 1923–39; doctor in the Jewish ghetto, and worked as a microbiologist when held in Auschwitz and Buchenwald. Allowed to emigrate to Israel with family, 1956. Worked for Institute for Biological Research, Ness Ziona, Israel, 1956–61. Married Ernestina Waldman, 1923 (1 son). Died Ness Ziona, 1961.

Principal Writings

Entstehung und Entwicklung einer wissenschaftlichen Tatsache: Einführung in die Lehre vom Denkstil und Denkkollektiv, 1935; in English as *Genesis and Development of a Scientific Fact*, 1979

Further Reading

Baldamus, Wilhelm, "Ludwig Fleck and the Development of the Sociology of Science," in Peter R. Gleichman, Johan Goudsblom, and Hermann Korte, eds., *Human Figurations: Essays for/Aufsätze für Norbert Elias*, Amsterdam: Amsterdams Sociologisch Tijdschift, 1977

Cohen, Robert S., and Thomas Schnelle, eds., *Cognition and Fact: Material on Ludwig Fleck*, Dordrecht: Reidel, 1986

Kuhn, Thomas S., Foreword, to Fleck, *Genesis and Development of a Scientific Fact*, edited by Thaddeus J. Trenn and Robert K. Merton, Chicago: University of Chicago Press, 1979

Löwy, Ilana, *The Polish School of Philosophy of Medicine: From Tytus Chalubinski (1820–1889) to Ludwig Fleck (1896–1961)*, Dordrecht: Kluwer, 1990

Fogel, Robert William 1926–

US economic historian

Although Robert Fogel's main intent has been the creation and elaboration of cliometrics (the use of statistics and measurement to advance historical knowledge), he has become best known because of the controversial theses he and his co-authors have advanced on two central historiographical issues: the role of transport in the development of the US economy, and the economic analysis of slavery.

His first major book, *Railroads and American Economic Growth* (1964), argued that trains were not the central force in industrializing the United States that others, such as Alfred D. Chandler, had suggested. Fogel argued that the nation's infrastructure of canals was the crucial economic link. That work has since been largely refuted, as historians believe that it rested on questionable assumptions and that it failed to credit the secondary economic effects of the railroads, both in creating markets and in offering new engineering solutions.

Fogel's second major work, *Time on the Cross* (1974), co-authored with Stanley Engerman, presented a revision of the history of slavery in the US. In an analysis that many historians viewed as dangerously close to that of Ulrich Phillips, Fogel and Engerman used statistical records to describe the slave system as one governed by economic rationality. Where Phillips had described the slave system as mild but inefficient, and Kenneth Stampp saw a system that was harsh but profitable, Fogel and Engerman described slavery as both relatively mild and profitable. This was especially telling, in their analysis, when slave conditions were compared with those of northern workers of the same era. Slaves, they argued, were on average more efficient and industrious. They worked shorter hours, fewer days, and were less frequently whipped than had been estimated. And all this was made possible because of a complex set of incentives for performance – incentives, they argued, that outweighed punishment as a motivation for slaves. In this analysis, Fogel and Engerman were expanding and refocusing pioneering econometric work done in comparative slavery by Alfred H. Conrad and John R. Meyer.

Fogel and Engerman were quite different from Phillips, who believed in black racial inferiority, in that they allowed for the role of the development of an African American culture within slavery. In that way they also reflected the literature that responded to Stanley Elkins' work, but that allowance for slave culture did not offset the general feeling among historians that *Time on the Cross* underplayed the harshness of the daily experience of slavery and made the slaveholders seem relatively benign. The criticism of the book took two forms. Most commonly, it questioned the assumptions behind the analysis, in much the same way that Fogel's earlier work on the railways had been critiqued. For example, in Paul David's collection *Reckoning with Slavery* (1976), Herbert Gutman and Richard Sutch critiqued the book as having applied the econometric model too rigidly, used too little data, and having relied too often on unique or unusual data. More fundamentally, critics questioned the possibility of doing good history of an essentially immoral institution by looking only at the economic record.

Subsequently Fogel has continued to work on refining and expanding the usefulness of cliometric approaches. He has directed an expanded effort to collect and analyze data relating to the slave problem, which culminated in the publication of an additional book on the subject, *Without Consent or Contract* (1989), along with several volumes of supporting data. That book does not depart significantly from the conclusions of *Time on the Cross*, but it has created less controversy. The study more consistently relies upon the significant body of literature establishing the complex nature of the slave culture. This may well have helped with the book's reception, as may the additional care that was taken with the analysis. In addition, the book appeared in a less charged political atmosphere.

DONALD R. PALM

See also African American; Computing; Economic; Gutman; Quantitative; Slavery: Modern; Stampp; United States: 19th Century

Biography

Born New York City, 1 July 1926. Received BA, Cornell University, 1948; MA, Columbia University, 1960; PhD, Johns Hopkins University, 1963. Taught at Johns Hopkins University, 1958–59; University of Rochester, 1960–64 and 1968–75; University of Chicago, 1964–75 and from 1981; and Harvard University, 1975–81. Awarded Nobel prize for economics, 1993. Married Enid Cassandra Morgan, 1949 (2 sons).

Principal Writings

The Union Pacific Railroad: A Case in Premature Enterprise, 1960
Railroads and American Economic Growth: Essays in Econometric History, 1964

With Stanley Engerman, *Time on the Cross: The Economics of American Negro Slavery*, 2 vols., 1974
Without Consent or Contract: The Rise and Fall of American Slavery, 2 vols., 1989
Economic Growth, Population Theory, and Physiology: The Bearings of Long-Term Processes on the Making of Economic Policy, 1994

Further Reading

Conrad, Alfred H., and John R. Meyer, "The Economics of Slavery in the Ante-Bellum South," *Journal of Political Economy* 66 (1958), 95–130
David, Paul, Herbert G. Gutman, Richard Sutch, Peter Temin, and Gavin Wright, *Reckoning with Slavery: A Critical Study in the Quantitative History of American Negro Slavery*, New York: Oxford University Press, 1976
Goldin, Claudia, and Hugh Rockoff, eds., *Strategic Factors in Nineteenth Century American Economic History: A Volume to Honor Robert W. Fogel*, Chicago: University of Chicago Press, 1992
Parish, Peter J., *Slavery: History and Historians*, New York: Harper, 1989

Foner, Eric 1943–

US historian

Eric Foner's interpretation of the history of the decades surrounding America's Civil War provided a completely new way of comprehending that turbulent time. The Civil War and Reconstruction have understandably generated more debate, in terms of quantity and intensity, than any other period in American history. The literature concerning Reconstruction has itself undergone at least two major revisions and countless minor ones; Foner's *Reconstruction: America's Unfinished Revolution, 1863–1877* (1988) synthesized the latest major wave of revisionist literature, that of the 1960s and 1970s, but it also offered a new framework for the interpretation of the period, and the Union, as a whole.

Foner first put forward his framework, which stressed the centrality of "free labor" ideology in *Free Soil, Free Labor, Free Men* (1970), a study of the ideological underpinnings of the pre-Civil War Republican party. His interpretations addressed one of the major historical questions of the period – why the Civil War started in the first place – but shifted the focus of the debate as it then existed. According to Foner, Republican ideology of the period centered on a passionate belief in the worth, even the necessity, of free and independent labor. This line of thought held that the Republicans' political antislavery campaign was not antiracist (an assessment with which even the most sympathetic historian of Republicans of the period would find it difficult to disagree) so much as it was "an affirmation of the superiority of the social system of the North – a dynamic, expanding capitalist society" whose success depended upon "the dignity and opportunities which it offered the average laboring man" – opportunities that were denied to black slaves and white workers in the South, and which therefore threatened liberty throughout the Union and helped create the atmosphere necessary for civil war.

This form of analysis proved equally fruitful for the period of Reconstruction, which Foner expanded to include the years

of the Civil War in which rebellious southern slaves forced northerners to alter their definition of "free labor" and their expectations for African Americans in the new political order. Foner placed the struggle over the control of labor in an emerging capitalist order at the center of *Reconstruction*. In Foner's fresh analysis labor control and the changing definition of free labor itself became a common theme which he used to integrate and explain the history of the years from roughly 1850 to 1880. This was no small feat; Foner was arguably the first to fashion a coherent narrative out of issues and themes as disparate as the transition from slavery to a "free" labor force on the part of southern blacks, the power struggle between the presidency and the Congress, the evolving definition of "Reconstruction" itself, the violence perpetrated against new political actors in the South, and the nation's rapidly changing economy (particularly in the Northeast and the West). He was able to do so by expanding his analysis in a way that few if any before him had done: Foner's *Reconstruction* was a reconstruction of the Union, not just of the South – although that region was certainly ground zero of the conflict. By defining Reconstruction as a struggle over labor rather than a struggle over issues of race – the traditional lens of analysis for the period, particularly among members of the Dunning, or "New South," school of Reconstruction and the line of thought that Foner's generation of historians revised – Foner shifted the terms of historiographical debate, but he also put his work at the forefront of race theory as it was developing in the 1980s. Foner treated race not as a characteristic that dictated attitudes and actions for historical actors, but as a social construction whose shape was altered from time to time by dominant political debates.

Significantly Foner's was the first major synthesis on Reconstruction to emerge from the generation of American historians who came of age during the civil rights revolution of the 1950s and 1960s, which itself is often referred to as the Second Reconstruction. Their experience during that period clearly manifested itself in their work, in which they sought to write history "from the bottom up" – in this case giving historical voice to the African Americans who made the difficult transition from slavery to freedom. Foner's work clearly placed him at the forefront of this revolution in historical writing.

J. TODD MOYE

See also African American; Litwack; Political; United States: American Revolution; United States: 19th Century

Biography

Born New York City, 7 February 1943. Received BA, Columbia University, 1963, PhD 1969; BA Oxford University 1965. Taught at City College, City University of New York, 1972–82; and Columbia University, 1969–73 and from 1982. Married 1) 1965; 2) Lynn Garafola, 1980.

Principal Writings

Free Soil, Free Labor, Free Men: The Ideology of the Republican Party before the Civil War, 1970
Nat Turner, 1971
Tom Paine and Revolutionary America, 1976
Politics and Ideology in the Age of the Civil War, 1980

Nothing but Freedom: Emancipation and Its Legacy, 1983
Reconstruction: America's Unfinished Revolution, 1863–1877, 1988; abridged as *A Short History of Reconstruction*, 1990
Editor, *The New American History*, 1990
Freedom's Lawmakers: A Directory of Black Officeholders during Reconstruction, 1993

Foner, Philip S. 1910–1994

US labor historian

A prolific writer and editor who was denied university employment on political grounds for most of his career, Philip S. Foner was one of the first professionally trained historians to dedicate himself to labor history and African American history. Foner received his doctorate from Columbia University, where he studied under Allan Nevins, and began to teach at City College in 1932. His first book, *Business and Slavery: The New York Merchants and the Irrepressible Conflict* (1941), was a study of relations between the cotton-producing South and New York bankers, manufacturers, and merchants in the 1850s. Northern business interests, Foner held, were eager to conciliate the slave South and advocated aggressive action by the Lincoln administration only when secession erupted in the spring of 1861. *Business and Slavery* showed Foner's interest in political history and epochal events, but it contained remarkably little reference to workers, slaves, and free blacks, the groups that later would interest him most.

Along with Herbert Aptheker, Foner became one of the best-known American historians to join the Communist party. In 1941, Foner's academic career was cut short when, along with dozens of other faculty members in New York's city colleges, he was denounced by a state legislative committee. The teachers were suspended, even though no specific abuses of position could be identified. Foner's perjured denial of Party membership did not help his case, and a Board of Higher Education committee voted 2–1 to dismiss him. Three of Foner's brothers – including his twin Jack, like him a historian at City College – also lost their jobs as a result of the anticommunist purge.

After his dismissal, Foner entered publishing as a principal and chief editor of Citadel Press. During World War II the Communist party, which threw itself behind the war effort, tried to construct a Popular Front tradition of patriotic radicalism out of the American past. Foner edited booklets of writings by Thomas Paine, Thomas Jefferson, Abraham Lincoln, George Washington, and Franklin Delano Roosevelt, and wrote two topical works, *Morale Education in the American Army* (1944) and *The Jews in American History, 1654–1865* (1945).

In the postwar period, the publication of the first volume of his *History of the Labor Movement in the United States* (1947) and a massive monograph, *The Fur and Leather Workers Union* (1950), put Foner in the forefront of labor history. The *History* was Foner's magnum opus, an unfolding project with sporadic installments that appeared, on average, once every five years. When he died ten volumes were in print, with two more in preparation. Foner intended his work as a grand Marxist synthesis of labor history. He conceived of it as a deliberate alternative to the earlier work of John R. Commons and others, whose *History of Labour in the United States* (4 vols., 1918–35) argued that American workers possessed only "job consciousness," not class consciousness, and that Samuel Gompers' combination of craft unionism and nonpartisan politics was most sensible for American labor.

As labor history exploded in the 1960s and 1970s, Foner won recognition for his pioneering efforts, but he also came in for criticism by practitioners of the "new labor history" inspired by the example of E.P. Thompson. The new historians acknowledged the impressive detail in the multivolume *History*, but many considered Foner's methods just as limited as those of Commons. Both, they pointed out, mainly wrote about formal institutions such as trade unions, political organizations, and labor law. Each was oblivious to everyday working-class experience, including family, neighborhood, religion, recreation, and education. Foner's dramas of heroes and villains, martyrs and misleaders, inevitable conflict and steady progress, his critics argued, was mechanical, predictable, and unable to explain why left-wing politics rarely had much appeal for American workers. Foner, however, doggedly stuck to his approach of amassing empirical detail and making firm political judgments. He returned fire at the new historians in the preface to *History*'s sixth volume: "Not a few of the 'new' labor historians have left the working class without any outlets through which they can voice their discontent and change their conditions."

Foner was the author or editor of more than 110 books, chiefly in labor and radical history, African American studies, and anti-imperialism. He edited documentary collections on black workers, Asian Americans, factory girls, and labor songs. He oversaw editions of writings by Paul Robeson, W.E.B. Du Bois, Frederick Douglass, Jack London, Joe Hill, Helen Keller, and Mother Jones. His works of black history – including *Frederick Douglass* (1964), *Organized Labor and the Black Worker* (1974), *Blacks in the American Revolution* (1976), *American Socialism and Black Americans* (1977), and *Essays in Afro-American History* (1978) – are packed with facts, but some critics faulted him for an almost total neglect of black women (unlike his labor histories, which did routinely include the study of women, if not of gender).

History for Foner had a direct – too direct, some said – political relevance. He frequently timed his books for commemorative dates. In 1967, Foner issued a compilation of favorable articles about the Soviet revolution culled from American newspapers and intellectuals in 1917. In 1977 and 1986, he published books on the centenaries the massive strike wave of 1877 and the inaugural May Day in 1886. In 1976 he published several books about the American revolution. Union militants and political activists often found these works informative, but critics charged that Foner was overly selective and celebratory, guided by tidy preconceptions and political needs rather than open-ended inquiry.

Foner regained an academic post in 1967 when he began teaching at Lincoln University, where he remained until his retirement in 1979. In 1981, forty years after the anticommunist purge, the City University of New York Board of Trustees passed a resolution apologizing to Foner and his colleagues, admitting to the violation of their academic freedom, and promising that it would not happen again. From retirement, Foner continued to publish prodigiously, and in 1994 the New York Labor History Association honored him with its award for lifetime achievement in labor history.

CHRISTOPHER PHELPS

See also Cuba; Labor; Marx

Biography

Philip Sheldon Foner. Born New York City, 14 December 1910. Received BA, City College, New York, 1932; MA, Columbia University, 1933, PhD 1940. Taught at City College, New York, 1933–41, but was denounced with others as a communist and dismissed. Entered publishing as chief editor, Citadel Press, 1945–67. Re-entered academe as professor of history, Lincoln University, Pennsylvania, 1967–79. Married 1941 (2 children). Died New York City, 13 December 1994.

Principal Writings

Business and Slavery: The New York Merchants and the Irrepressible Conflict, 1941

Morale Education in the American Army: War for Independence, War of 1812, Civil War, 1944

The Jews in American History, 1654–1865, 1945

History of the Labor Movement in the United States, 10 vols. 1947–92

The Fur and Leather Workers Union, 1950

A History of Cuba and Its Relations with the United States, 2 vols., 1962–65

Frederick Douglass, 1964

Editor, *The Bolshevik Revolution: Its Impact on American Radicals, Liberals, and Labor*, 1967

The Spanish-Cuban-American War and the Birth of American Imperialism, 1895–1902, 2 vols., 1972

Organized Labor and the Black Worker, 1974

History of Black Americans, 3 vols., 1975–83

Blacks in the American Revolution, 1976

American Socialism and Black Americans: From the Age of Jackson to World War II, 1977

Antonio Maceo: The "Bronze Titan" of Cuba's Struggle for Independence, 1977

The Great Labor Uprising of 1877, 1977

Essays in Afro-American History, 1978

Women in the American Labor Movement, 2 vols., 1979–80

British Labor and the American Civil War, 1981

May Day, 1986

With David Roediger, *Our Own Time: A History of American Labor and the Working Day*, 1989

Further Reading

Dubofsky, Melvin, "Give Us That Old Time Labor History: Philip S. Foner and the American Worker," *Labor History* 26 (1985), 118–37

Miller, Sally M., "Philip Foner and 'Integrating' Women into Labor History and African-American History," *Labor History* 33 (1992), 456–69

Montgomery, David, "To Study the People: The American Working Class," *Labor History* 21 (1980), 485–512

Schrecker, Ellen W., *No Ivory Tower: McCarthyism and the Universities*, New York: Oxford University Press 1986

Von Gelder, Lawrence, obituary of Foner, *New York Times* (15 December 1994), B20

Foucault, Michel 1926–1984

French social theorist

Michel Foucault is famous for the concept of "discourse" and for his dazzling explorations of madness, medicine, punishment, and sexuality. These may appear unconnected: the dry theoretical elaborations seem to stand apart from the detailed case studies which constitute his major impact on historiography. Yet theory and history were deeply entwined in his work.

Foucault's theory of discourses rejected the conventional history of great thinkers and their ideas, portrayed as precursors of modern intellectual or scientific achievements. It sought instead to locate ideas in a wider context of fundamental forms of thought. A discourse, defined as a collection of ideas and practices with a common object and mode of discussion, emerges from an intellectual framework or *épistème*, which unconsciously shapes the form of knowledge and theory in each historical period. The "archaeology" of a discourse therefore involves placing it alongside all its contemporaries, however irrational or eccentric they seem, within the context of a common *épistème*. Both "magic" and "science" may coexist within the same framework, and to emphasize one at the expense of the other would be a serious misinterpretation. Shifts from one *épistème* to another constitute radical transformations in conceptualizing knowledge and in examining, describing, and controlling the world: these changes may not involve any continuities, and therefore cannot be viewed as stages in an inevitable process of cumulative "scientific" progress. In Foucault's outline of Western history, Renaissance discourses were characterized by a legendary or magical form of knowledge: the world revealed its meanings in superficial resemblances between things and words, connected in chains of, to the modern mind, arbitrary significance. The following "classical" age was more empirical and logical, believing that reality could be accurately represented through directly demonstrable terms. Every object or species, properly categorized, had its place in the orderly, logical structure of a world that could be subjugated by reason. In the modern age, as all things, particularly humans themselves, became objects of study in isolated disciplines, there are no possibilities of such an integrated view, and no guarantees of rational certainty in knowledge. We are only too conscious of our historical limitations and incompatible perspectives. At the end of *Les Mots et les choses* (1966; *The Order of Things*, 1970), Foucault famously proclaimed the death of the supremely rational "Man" as classically conceived.

Underlying this schema was a deep skepticism about the possibilities of rational progress. Foucault's most famous equation, that of discourse with *power*, suggests that, in their everyday influences as well as through "expert" applications, discourses shape individuals' identities and ensure their conformity. In his first major study, *Folie et déraison* (1961; *Madness and Civilization*, 1965), he described the "great confinement" of the "classical" age, in which everyone deviating from the dominant culture of reason was imprisoned indiscriminately in places such as Louis XIV's new General Hospitals – the mad, sexual deviants, unemployed vagrants, and criminals together. At the end of the 18th century each of these groups became the object of specialized, if connected, discourses, with their own professional practices and institutions. Usually portrayed as founders of modern civilized policies, 19th-century reformers in essence changed nothing: the mad, like many defined as "other," were still repressed and voiceless. As Macey argued, for Foucault a history of madness had to be the archaeology of silence. His account of penal changes in *Surveiller et punir* (1975; *Discipline* and *Punish*, 1977) was equally striking and critical: the old bodily punishments, the theater of blood which dominated most legal systems before 1800, were swept aside in many countries in the 19th century (though he notes England and Russia were exceptions to this apparent reform movement). The "civilized" alternative, the prison, like the lunatic asylum, enclosed convicts, and, through pressure on the mind, imposed the "stifling anguish of responsibility" for their own reform. Through switching the focus from body to mind, using procedures of all-round surveillance, the prison introduced a new discipline, both on its inmates and the society outside the walls. The penitentiary generated the "punitive city," as the influence of criminological discourse spread throughout the social fabric. In these narratives Foucault created a legacy of persuasive perceptions: power is all-pervasive, indivisible from the ideas of the "sciences" which study human dilemmas, and has throughout history taken the body and mind as mechanisms of social discipline. The excluded, those controlled by the discourses of power, are nevertheless portrayed as far from passive, since even in silence they have at times refused to accept their labels without a struggle.

With the study of punishment and his last works on sexuality, Foucault had moved from archaeology of discourses to their "genealogy." By tracing lines of power, he wanted (after Nietzsche) to write "effective history," a more explicit, openly committed and "curative" account: unlike the "traditional" historian, he did not claim objectivity. The themes of domination and resistance naturally became the focus of the work on sexuality where Foucault explored processes of silence and repression in sexual discourses (which, as a gay man, he felt very keenly). Writing history became a search for the roots of resistance today.

At the end of his life, Foucault seemed to have become more committed, if no less academic, in his work. Much of his theoretical obfuscation derived from his desire to skirt the pitfalls of identifying with warring intellectual camps in France such as Marxism and structuralism. "Do not ask who I am and do not ask me to be the same," he said in *L'Archéologie du savoir* (1969; *The Archaeology of Knowledge*, 1972). He has proved equally contentious for historians. His avoidance of conventional scholarship has allowed empirical rejection of his bold characterizations of historical transformations. Infuriating in his poetic style, studiedly vague about his explanations of historical change, Foucault nevertheless remains essential reading. As Peter Burke has said, "those who reject his answers are unable to avoid his questions."

PETER RUSHTON

See also Althusser; Ariès; Body; Burke; Chartier; Corbin; Crime; Cultural; Europe: Modern; Gender; Greece: Ancient; Homosexuality; Intellectual; Medicine; Mentalities; Musicology; Orientalism; Postmodernism; Science; Scott, Joan; Sexuality; Social; United States: 20th Century; Walkowitz

Biography

Michel Paul Foucault. Born Poitiers, 15 October 1926, son of a doctor. Studied philosophy, Ecole Normale Supérieure, then researched in psychology; received his licence, 1948, 1950, and diploma, 1952. Taught philosophy and French literature, universities of Lille, Uppsala, Warsaw, Hamburg, Clermont-Ferrand, São Paulo,

and Tunis, 1960–68; professor, University of Paris-Vincennes, 1968–70; professor of the history of systems of thought, Collège de France, 1970–84. Died Paris, 25 June 1984.

Principal Writings

Folie et déraison: histoire de la folie à l'âge classique, 1961, abridged as *Histoire de la folie*, 1961; in English as *Madness and Civilization: A History of Insanity in the Age of Reason*, 1965

Naissance de la clinique: une archéologie du regard médical, 1963; in English as *The Birth of the Clinic: An Archaeology of Medical Perception*, 1973

Les Mots et les choses: une archéologie des sciences humaines, 1966; in English as *The Order of Things: An Archaeology of the Human Sciences*, 1970

L'Archéologie du savoir, 1969; in English as *The Archaeology of Knowledge*, 1972

Surveiller et punir: naissance de la prison, 1975; in English as *Discipline and Punish: The Birth of the Prison*, 1977

Histoire de la sexualité, 3 vols., 1976–84; in English as *The History of Sexuality*, 3 vols, 1978–86

Editor, *Herculine Barbin dite Alexina B.*, 1978; in English as *Herculine Barbin, Being the Recently Discovered Memoirs of a Nineteenth-Century French Hermaphrodite*, 1980

Power/Knowledge: Selected Interviews and Other Writings, 1972–1977, edited by Colin Gordon, 1980

The Foucault Reader, edited by Paul Rabinow, 1984

Dits et écrits, 1954–1988, 4 vols., 1994

Further Reading

Burke, Peter, *History and Social Theory*, Cambridge: Polity Press, 1992; Ithaca, NY: Cornell University Press, 1993

Dean, Mitchell, *Critical and Effective Histories: Foucault's Methods and Historical Sociology*, London and New York: Routledge, 1994

Goldstein, Jan, ed., *Foucault and the Writing of History*, Oxford and Cambridge, MA: Blackwell, 1994

Gutting, Gary, *Michel Foucault's Archaeology of Reason*, Cambridge and New York: Cambridge University Press, 1989

Kelly, Michael, ed., *Critique and Power: Recasting the Foucault/Habermas Debate*, Cambridge, MA: MIT Press, 1994

Macey, David, *The Lives of Michel Foucault*, London: Hutchinson, and New York: Pantheon, 1993

McNay, Lois, *Foucault: A Critical Introduction*, Cambridge: Polity Press, and New York: Continuum, 1994

O'Farrell, Clare, *Foucault: Historian or Philosopher?*, London: Macmillan, and New York: St. Martins Press, 1989

Poster, Mark, *Foucault, Marxism, and History: Mode of Production versus Mode of Information*, Cambridge: Polity Press, and New York: Blackwell, 1994

Sheridan, Alan, *Michel Foucault: The Will to Truth*, London and New York: Tavistock, 1980

Foxe, John 1516–1587

English historian

Although the author of diverse works, from dramatic verse (*Christus triumphans*, 1556) to sermons and religious translations, John Foxe is known as the author of *Acts and Monuments*, or, more commonly, the "Book of Martyrs." First published in England in 1563, *Acts and Monuments* underwent three revised editions during Foxe's lifetime (1570, 1576 and 1583), and, next to the Bible, was the most widely read text of 16th-century England. A copy of the 1570 *Acts and*

Monuments was ordered by the 1571 Convocation to be placed in every cathedral, and many parishes followed suit, increasing the availability of Foxe's work to the general population. The numerous woodcut illustrations provided the illiterate with vivid memorials to the martyrs, and upheld the ideal of an imperial Christianity embodied in the portrayal of Elizabeth I as a second Constantine.

The provenance of Foxe's work lies with the Latin edition published in 1554 in Strasburg where Foxe and his family lived in exile during the reign of Mary Tudor. Upon the succession of Elizabeth in 1558, Foxe returned to England and undertook the research and publication of subsequent editions of *Acts and Monuments* as his life's work, incorporating in the text the stories of hundreds of martyrs burned during Mary's reign, as well as expanding the scope of the Strasburg edition, which was complete to only 1500.

The *Acts and Monuments* is representative of 16th-century historical writing in its attempt to establish the legitimacy of the Protestant church by creating a history of persecution linking the early Christian martyrs with the Marian martyrs, whose stories comprise the greater part of the text. For evidence, Foxe used standard published documents for those martyrs who gave their lives in the distant past. For the more recent martyrs of the 16th century, Foxe relied on eyewitness testimonials and accounts supplied by the martyrs themselves, or by family members and other witnesses who were present at the persecutions. Evidence was under constant review as it came available in order to correct errors or to fill in gaps in the text. In this regard, Foxe's work stands as a monument to the lives of those traditionally silent in the historical record: artisans, apprentices, women, and those from the lower orders of society. His work informed the Protestant authors John Bunyan and John Milton and was dramatized in *Thomas Lord Cromwell*, a chronicle play of the late 16th century. *Acts and Monuments* provided evidence for subsequent accounts of the Marian persecutions, such as David Hume's 18th-century *History of England*. Foxe's collection of documents and transcripts has been preserved among the Harleian and Landsdowne manuscripts at the British Library.

Until the mid-19th century, criticism of Foxe originated within Catholic polemic and focused on Foxe himself rather than on the validity of his work. There has been no doubt that the burnings under Mary occurred, but whether Foxe's martyrs should be considered such, rather than heretics, has raised considerable ire among Catholic apologists. The first attack came in 1566 by Nicholas Harpsfield (*Sex Dialogi*), and was followed in 1603–04 by the Jesuit Robert Parsons in his *A Treatise of Three Conversions of England*. Both critics condemned the character of Foxe, his book as blasphemy, and his martyrs as criminals. However, *Acts and Monuments* attained a pre-eminence of position among the English Protestant faithful and provided a basis for the history of the Church of England, until a series of attacks from the Anglican historian S.R. Maitland, published in the *British Magazine* during the period 1835–49. At this time, two new editions of *Acts and Monuments* appeared: the abridged two-volume family edition edited by Michael Hobart Seymour (*Book of Martyrs*, 1838), and the 8-volume scholarly edition edited by Stephen Reed Cattley (1831–41). It was Cattley's edition on which Maitland vented his scorn. Maitland questioned the veracity of the incidents related in the *Acts and Monuments*, and unearthed numerous factual mistakes and errors in translation by referring to many of the extant source documents. Maitland, and his successors in the campaign, J.S. Brewer and James Gardiner, accused Foxe of tampering with documents and editing evidence to suit his purpose and that of the Puritan cause. During the next hundred years his reputation fell deeper into disrepute except for a few defenders who excused Foxe his errors by emphasizing the mass of information collected by him. With the publication of *John Foxe and His Book* (1940), J.F. Mozley defended Foxe from his assailants through a detailed analysis of several questionable cases. Although Mozley was able to vindicate evidential judgments made by Foxe, he cautioned against a too heavy reliance on *Acts and Monuments* as factually accurate; it must be viewed as a product of, and not only a source for, the period from which it emerged, and as such it contains biases informed by religious beliefs, just as do papist publications of the same time.

Although the accuracy of the *Acts and Monuments* is questionable, its usefulness as a historical document has not diminished. Foxe as historian has metamorphosed into Foxe as myth-maker, as contemporary analysis of his work moves beyond the evidence toward the interpretation placed on the evidence. The charge that Foxe included persons who could not be considered true martyrs to the Protestant (Anglican) cause has been used by his detractors to challenge his interpretation of evidence. Rather than limiting his martyrology to those who adhered to an orthodox Protestant theology, Foxe's martyrs possessed all manner of sectarian opinions, and this illustrates Foxe's belief that a church which tortured and burned unbelievers could not be the true church, and that all who perished at her hands, regardless of theological stripe, proved the point.

MARGARET SHKIMBA

See also Reformation

Biography

Born Boston, Lincolnshire, 21 December 1516. Studied at Brasenose College, Oxford, 1532, BA 1537, MA 1543; fellow, Magdalen College, Oxford, 1539–45, resigned. Briefly a tutor, then settled in London; tutor to the orphaned children of the executed earl of Surrey. Became a deacon, 1550, but as a Protestant, eventually left England after Mary I came to the throne; settled in Frankfurt, 1554; then Basel; returned to England, 1559; ordained 1559/60. Married Agnes Randall, 1546/47 (3 sons, 2 daughters). Died 1587.

Principal Writings

Acts and Monuments, 1563, revised 1570, 1576, 1583; subsequently known as *Book of Martyrs*

Further Reading

Collinson, Patrick, "Truth and Legend: The Veracity of John Foxe's Book of Martyrs," in A.C. Duke and C.A. Tamse, eds., *Clio's Mirror: Historiography in Britain and the Netherlands*, Zutphen: De Walburg Pers, 1985

Facey, Jane, "John Foxe and the Defence of the English Church," in Peter Lake and Maria Dowling, eds., *Protestantism and the National Church in Sixteenth Century England*, London: Croom Helm, 1987

Haller, William, *The Elect Nation: The Meaning and Relevance of Foxe's "Book of Martyrs,"* New York: Harper, 1963; as *Foxe's "Book of Martyrs" and the Elect Nation*, London: Cape, 1963

Knott, John R., *Discourses of Martyrdom in English Literature, 1563–1694*, Cambridge and New York: Cambridge University Press, 1993

Maitland, Samuel Raffey, *Twelve Letters on Fox's "Acts and Monuments," Originally Published in the British Magazine in the Years 1837 and 1838*, London: Rivington, 1841

Mozley, James Frederic, *John Foxe and His Book*, London: SPCK, and New York: Macmillan, 1940; reprinted New York: Octagon, 1970

Olsen, V. Norskov, *John Foxe and the Elizabethan Church*, Berkeley: University of California Press, 1973

Wooden, Warren W., *John Foxe*, Boston: Twayne, 1983

France: to 1000

For several centuries a major problem in French historiography has been the precise chronological setting of the origins of France. This took the form of questioning whether the French were primarily the descendants of the Gallic tribes conquered by Caesar or whether their national identity derived from the Franks who, under Clovis, conquered most of Roman Gaul in the late 5th century CE. The answers given from the late 15th century onwards often related directly to more immediate problems of where the eastern frontiers of France should run and what was the nature of the relationship between the French and their German neighbors. All of this frequently led to fierce if quite unhistorical debates on such matters as whether Charlemagne (747–814) should be classed as a Frenchman or a German. Likewise, as was equally true in Britain, arguments over the nature and working of social and political institutions in the early medieval period could also have a direct bearing on contemporary politics. Thus, in the 17th and 18th centuries, debates on the character of the annual Merovingian and Carolingian assemblies were used as a vehicle for expressing both radical and conservative political ideas during a period of monarchical absolutism.

Such arguments dominated approaches to the early history of France from the 16th century onwards. The birth of the French tradition of antiquarian scholarship was marked by the publication in 1495 of the *Compendium de origine et gestis Francorum* (On the Origin and Deeds of the Franks) of Robert Gaguin (1433–1501), which was also notable for its skeptical attitude toward the medieval legends of Charlemagne and the supposedly Trojan origins of the Franks. In the 16th century French historians and jurists developed even more polemical arguments concerning their early history. In this they were in part spurred on by religious divisions among themselves, but were reacting to claims being made in the works of their Italian and German counterparts. Notable among them were François Hotman (1524–90), who in his book *Francogallia*, published in 1573, presented the Franks as the saviours of the Celtic population of Gaul from the Romans, and his Catholic counterpart Jean Bodin (1530–96), who tried to make the French out to be descendants of the Greeks. History was also used to justify royal policies, as in the paralleling of Charlemagne's conquest of Italy in 793–94 with Charles VIII's intervention in Italy in 1495.

While few of these historical interpretations really advanced the understanding of the realities of Roman Gaul and the ensuing Frankish kingdoms of the Merovingian (c.480–751) and Carolingian (751–987) dynasties, it did give further impetus to the collecting of manuscripts and the editing of texts relating to the history of these periods by French, German, and Swiss scholars. Gregory of Tours (538/39–594/95), whose *Historiae* (Histories, known as *History of the Franks*) constitutes the main narrative source for the 6th-century Merovingian kingdoms was first edited in 1512, and the discovery of increasing numbers of manuscripts led to the publication of several new versions, before the appearance of the impressive edition of the Maurist Thierry Ruinart in 1699. Other texts were slower to be discovered. Thus the *editio princeps* of the 7th-century *Chronicle of Fredegar* dates only from 1568, and the writings of the major ecclesiastical authors of the Carolingian period were all first edited in the 17th century. The later part of that century is marked by a proliferation of new editions of a much higher standard than their predecessors, including those of legal and administrative texts, such as the Carolingian capitularies. These were given an impressive new edition in 1677 by Etienne Baluze. Baluze was librarian to Jean Baptiste Colbert, minister of Louis XIV, who was one of the most avid and successful collectors of medieval manuscripts at this time. The same period saw the formation of valuable multivolume collections, notably the *Gallia Christiana* of 1715, which published documents relating to all of the French episcopal dioceses. Likewise, advances were made in the scholarly evaluation of such texts, not least through the establishment by the Maurist Jean Mabillon (1632–1707) of criteria for the authenticating and dating of manuscripts, including charters, in his *De re diplomatica* (The Science of Diplomatic) of 1681.

Although arguments based on supposed Frankish precedents were used by some contemporary political writers, the period of the Enlightenment saw a severe decline in interest in the post-Roman history of France. Voltaire (1694–1778), for example, castigated Charlemagne for allowing the church to gain so much power, for the savagery of his laws, and for being little better than a brigand. A revival in the scholarly study of early medieval France was largely generated by the rise of Romantic nationalism in Germany in the period following the end of the Napoleonic wars. In 1819 the Freiherr von Stein (1757–1831), who had previously played a central role at the Prussian court, set up a society called the Gesellschaft für Deutschlands ältere Geschichtskunde, dedicated to the collecting and editing of texts relating to early German history. Various different series were planned, to cover chronicles, law codes, charters, letter collections, and "antiquities," all under the general title of *Monumenta Germaniae Historica*. The first volume of the first of these series was published in 1821, and contained editions of a large number of chronicles and annals, mostly concerned with the 8th to 10th centuries. Under the general editorship from 1823 until 1873 of Georg Heinrich Pertz (1795–1876) and then of Georg Waitz (1813–86), the wider program of publication was successfully launched, albeit with various modifications. This resulted in the production of the first, and in many cases still the only, modern critical editions of such central works for the history of this period as the *Historiae* of Gregory of Tours, the so-called *Chronicle of Fredegar* (late 7th-century with mid-8th-century continuations), and the anonymous *Liber Historiae Francorum* of *c*.726/7, all of which were edited by Bruno Krusch (1857–1940), who was also responsible for a further five volumes of hagiographical texts of Merovingian and Carolingian date. For the latter period the activities of the various scholars associated with the *Monumenta* proved particularly important, especially in the years leading up to World War I. Critical editions of the letter collection of Alcuin (*c*.737–804), and of the charters and capitulary legislation of Charlemagne were followed by many more volumes of legal and administrative texts. Some gaps still remain: no edition yet exists of the charters of Charlemagne's son Louis the Pious (778–840).

In France, despite the earlier efforts of Augustin Thierry (1795–1856), in his *Lettres sur l'histoire de France* of 1827, the real revival of scholarly and popular interest in the early medieval centuries did not come until the later 19th century. This was influenced not least by the appearance in 1888 and 1892 of the Merovingian and Carolingian volumes of the *Histoire des institutions politiques de l'ancienne France* (History of the Political Institutions of Medieval France) of Numa Denis Fustel de Coulanges (1830–89). At the same time, his younger contemporaries were attempting to match German textual scholarship, initiating new series of editions and studies, such as Gabriel Monod's *Etudes critiques sur les sources de l'histoire mérovingienne* (Critical Studies on the Sources for Merovingian History, 1872–85), and the much more substantial and chronologically wide ranging *Collection de textes pour servir à l'étude et à l'enseignement de l'histoire* (Collection of Texts to Help in the Study and Teaching of History, 1886–) produced by the Société historique. While Monod published a valuable diplomatic edition of the earliest manuscript of Fredegar (1885), texts of Gregory of Tours' *Historiae* in two parts were among the first products of the *Collection de textes*. This series numbered Ferdinand Lot (1866–1952) among its earliest editors. A pupil of Arthur Giry, the modern founder of charter studies in France, and of Gabriel Monod, he went on to make significant contributions to both Roman and Frankish studies. A program for the publication of the charter collections of the West Frankish monarchs from Charles the Bald (823–77), who was seen as the first unequivocally French Carolingian king, was also initiated in rivalry with the Monumenta's *Diplomata Karolinorum* series. Louis Halphen (1880–1950), who studied under Lot and later collaborated with him in a volume concerned with the first decade of the reign of Charles the Bald, edited the first of these volumes, devoted to the reigns of Lothar and Louis V (*c*.967–87), in 1908. He subsequently produced a critical edition of Einhard's *Vita Karoli* in 1923 and a major study, *Charlemagne et l'empire carolingien* (1947; *Charlemagne and the Carolingians*, 1977), as well as much work on later periods. This editorial program, under the auspices the Academie des Inscriptions, then floundered, but revived with a series of volumes in the 1940s and early 1950s, and was then continued under the direction of another generation of scholars, such as Georges Tessier and Robert-Henri Bautier, who edited the *acta* of the non-Carolingian Odo (d. 898) in 1967.

At the same time, however, the interpretive study of the early medieval period on the part of French historians was in many ways adversely affected by the rise of the Annales school. By concentrating on structural analysis and the *longue durée*, scholars such as Georges Duby (1919–96) threw valuable light on the social and economic development of many regions of France (and Italy) over extended periods. However, the fashion for such regional theses, whose chronological dimensions are conditioned by the availability of local records, led in almost all cases to their starting no earlier than the 9th century and more usually in the 10th. This has resulted in a quite surprising collapse of interest among French historians in earlier periods and in more purely political aspects of the Carolingian centuries. This neglect over several decades is only now starting to be reversed in the work of such scholars as Michel Rouche, Régine Le Jan and Stefane Lebecq.

In the meantime many of the most important contributions to the study of the Merovingian period have come from the German Historical Institute in Paris, whose former director, Karl Ferdinand Werner, produced the first synoptic overview of early French history, as well as much detailed smaller-scale work on the period. The Institute has also been involved through the collaboration of Hartmut Atsma with Jean Vezin in the production of photographic facsimiles of all the extant early Frankish charters, in several volumes of the series *Chartae Latinae Antiquiores*. In Germany, too, Merovingian and Carolingian Frankish scholarship has been far more active than in France itself in recent decades. Leading roles have been played in this both before and after World War II by Heinz Löwe, and more recently by Eugen Ewig, a former student of Wilhelm Levison, whose own disciples, such as Rudolf Schieffer, Hans Hubert Anton, Ulrich Nonn, Jörg Jarnut, and others, have continued the tradition. Friederich Prinz has been the leading figure in the study of Merovingian and early Carolingian monasticism. As well as in more purely political and institutional studies, Germany has also long led the way in the investigation of Carolingian art. E.H. Zimmermann's important *Vorkarolingische Miniaturen* (Pre-Carolingian Miniatures) of 1916 was a milestone in this, and the numerous and substantial publications of Percy Ernst Schramm and Florentine Mütherich have uncovered much of the court-based and regional schools of manuscript painting of the period. German scholars have also dominated and directed the study of Frankish palaeography, with a formidable tradition being established in Munich under Ludwig Traube, Paul Lehmann, and Bernhard Bischoff.

A significant tradition of Frankish studies has developed in Belgium. The way was led by Henri Pirenne (1862–1935), who had studied in both France and Germany, with his famous thesis that the achievements of the Carolingian period depended upon the prior destruction of the economic unity of the Mediterranean by the Arabs. François Louis Ganshof, who had been a pupil of Ferdinand Lot in Paris, was the first to offer a major analysis of the nature and purpose of the Carolingian capitularies and produced a series of vital studies of Frankish institutions, particularly of the age of Charlemagne. His argument that the final years of that monarch's reign represented a period of decline continues to provoke discussion. More recently Alain Dierkens has studied the ecclesiastical history of the Carolingian northeast and has questioned long unchallenged views of the importance of the Irish contributions to Frankish monasticism.

In Britain and the United States the tradition of scholarly interest in early medieval France goes back at least to the 1930s. The Oxford historian J.M. Wallace-Hadrill was the foremost

British historian of, first, the Merovingian and then, as his interests changed, of the Carolingian period. He re-edited part of the *Chronicle of Fredegar* (1960) and wrote a substantial study, *The Frankish Church* (1983), as well as numerous articles and reviews. His influence on Carolingian studies is in part carried on in the work of Donald Bullough, who has established a reputation as the foremost authority on the work of Alcuin, as well as in numerous related areas. In Cambridge, Walter Ullmann, although more concerned with later periods, published his Birkbeck lectures on the Carolingian Renaissance in 1969. His former students Janet Nelson and Rosamond McKitterick have been among the most influential of current British historians of the Carolingian period, opening up areas of study, such as literacy and the reign of Charles the Bald, that had been neglected or ignored in continental scholarship.

In America the European roots of much of the current interest in early French history can be seen in the work of such scholars as Luitpold Wallach. The latter's long, and somewhat acrimonious, debate with Ann Freeman over the authorship of the *Libri Carolini* opened up an important subject, leading to Freeman's new edition of the work. Richard E. Sullivan has led the way in looking at the missionary activities of the Frankish church, and has exerted considerable influence on subsequent generations of American historians. Others have continued to turn directly to European traditions of interpretation. Patrick Geary, who is particularly close to the Austrian school of Frankish historiography, dominated by Heinrich Fichtenau and Herwig Wolfram, has given renewed impetus to the subject in the US, not least through innovative investigations of such overlooked areas as the theft of relics, the treatment of death, and the role of memory. In Canada Walter Goffart has trenchantly challenged and revised much received wisdom on a whole range of subjects, from the processes of accommodating the barbarians in the late Roman period, through the historiography of Gregory of Tours, Fredegar, and Paul the Deacon, to the Le Mans forgeries. Likewise, Alexander C. Murray has provided important new ideas on problems of Merovingian institutional and social history, and the Francophone Canadian scholar Alain Stoclet has contributed not least an important study of abbot Fulrad of Saint-Denis.

ROGER COLLINS

See also Bodin; Duby; Einhard; Fustel; Gregory of Tours; Krusch; Mabillon; Pirenne; Schramm; Ullmann; Voltaire; Waitz

Further Reading

Anton, Hans Hubert, *Fürstenspiegel und Herrscherethos in der Karolingerzeit* (Mirrors for Princes and the Ethics of Leadership in the Carolingian Age), Bonn: Röhrscheid, 1968

Baluze, Etienne, ed., *Capitularia regum francorum* (The Capitularies of the Frankish Kings), 2 vols., Paris: Muguet, 1677

Bautier, Robert-Henri, and Georges Tessier, eds., *Recueil des actes d'Eudes, roi de France (888–898)* (Collection of the Documents of Odo, King of France, 888–898), Paris: Klincksieck, 1967

Bischoff, Bernhard, *Die Südostdeutschen Schreibschulen und Bibliotheken in der Karolingerzeit* (Scribal Schools and Libraries of Southeastern Germany in the Carolingian period), 2 vols., Leipzig: Harrassowitz, 1940–80

Bruckner, Albert, and Robert Marichal, eds., *Chartae Latinae Antiquiores: Facsimile Edition of the Latin Charters Prior to the Ninth Century*, Zurich: Graf, 1954–

Brühl, Carlrichard, *Deutschland-Frankreich: die Geburt zweier Völker* (Germany/France: The Birth of Two Peoples), Cologne: Böhlau, 1990

Bullough, Donald, *The Age of Charlemagne*, London: Elek, 1965; New York: Putnam, 1966

Collins, Roger, *Fredegar*, Aldershot: Variorum, and Brookfield, VT: Ashgate, 1996

Dierkens, Alain, *Abbayes et chapitres entre Sambre et Meuse (VIIe–XIe siècles)* (Abbeys and Cathedral Chapters Between the Sambre and the Meuse) Sigmaringen: Thorbecke, 1985

Duby, Georges, *Guerriers et paysans, VIIe–XIIe siècle: premier essor de l'économie européene*, Paris: Gallimard, 1973; in English as *The Early Growth of the European Economy: Warriors and Peasants from the Seventh to the Twelfth Century*, London: Weidenfeld and Nicolson, and Ithaca, NY: Cornell Unversity Press, 1974

Einhard, *La Vie de Charlemagne* (Vita Karoli/The Life of Charlemagne), edited by Louis Halphen, Paris: Champion, 1923; revised 1947

Ewig, Eugen, *Trier im Merowingerreich: Civitas, Stadt, Bistum* (Trier in the Merovingian Period), Trier: Paulinus, 1954

Fichtenau, Heinrich, *Das karolingische Imperium: soziale und geistige Problematik eines Grossreiches*, Zurich: Fretz & Wasmuth, 1949; in English as *The Carolingian Empire: The Age of Charlemagne*, Oxford: Blackwell, 1957, New York: Harper, 1964

Fredegar, *Fredegarii chronicon*; in English as *The Fourth Book of the Chronicle of Fredgar with its Continuations*, edited by John Michael Wallace-Hadrill, London and New York: Nelson, 1960

Freeman, Ann, "Thedulf of Orléans and the *Libri Carolini*," *Speculum* 32 (1957), 663–705

Fustel de Coulanges, Numa, *Histoire des institutions politiques de l'ancienne France* (History of the Political Institutions of Medieval France), 6 vols., Paris: Hachette, 1875–92

Gaguin, Robert, *Compendium de origine et gestis Francorum* (On the Origins and Deeds of the Franks), Paris: Gerlerii, 1497

Gallia Christiana (Christian Gaul), 16 vols., Paris: Clognard, 1715–1874

Ganshof, F.L., *The Carolingians and the Frankish Monarchy*, London: Longman, and Ithaca, NY: Cornell University Press, 1971

Geary, Patrick, *Living with the Dead in the Middle Ages*, Ithaca, NY: Cornell University Press, 1994

Goffart, Walter, *Rome's Fall and After*, London: Hambledon Press, 1989

Halphen, Louis, *Charlemagne et l'empire carolingien*, Paris: Michel, 1947; in English as *Charlemagne and the Carolingians*, Amsterdam: North-Holland, 1977

Hotman, François, *Francogallia*, 1573; reprinted with parallel English text, Cambridge: Cambridge University Press, 1972

Jarnut, Jörg, Ulrich Nonn, and Michael Richter, eds., *Karl Martell in seiner Zeit* (Charles Martel in His Day), Sigmaringen: Thorbecke, 1994

Lebecq, Stéfane, *Marchands et navigateurs frisons du haut Moyen Age* (Early Medieval Frisian Merchants and Seamen), 2 vols., Lille: Presses Universitaires, 1983

Lehmann, Paul, *Erforschung des Mittelalters* (Medieval Researches), 5 vols., Stuttgart: Hiersemann, 1959–62

Le Jan, Régine, *Famille et pouvoir dans le monde franc (VIIe–Xe siècles): essai d'anthropologie sociale* (Family and Power in the Frankish World), Paris: Publications de la Sorbonne, 1995

Levison, Wilhem, *England and the Continent in the Eighth Century*, Oxford: Oxford University Press, 1946

Lot, Ferdinand, ed., *Diplomata Karolinorum: recueil de reproductions en facsimile des actes originaux des souverains carolingiens conservés dans les archives et bibliothèques de France* (Diplomata Karolinorum: Collection of Facsimile Reproductions of the Original Acts of the Carolingian Sovereigns Held in the Archives and Libraries of France), 2 vols., Paris: Didier, 1936–40

Löwe, Heinz, *Handbuch der deutschen Geschichte* (Handbook of German History), Munich: Deutscher Taschenbuch, 1979

Mabillon, Jean, *De re diplomatica* (The Science of Diplomatic), Paris: Billaine, 1681

McKitterick, Rosamond, *The Carolingians and the Written Word*, Cambridge and New York: Cambridge University Press, 1989

Monod, Gabriel, *Études critiques sur les sources de l'histoire mérovingienne* (Critical Studies on the Sources for Merovingian History), 2 vols., Paris: Francke, 1872–85

Morrissey, Robert John, *L'Empereur à la barbe fleurie: Charlemagne dans la mythologie et l'histoire de France* (Charlemagne in French History and Mythology), Paris: Gallimard, 1997

Murray, Alexander C., *Germanic Kinship Structure: Studies in Law and Society in Antiquity and the Early Middle Ages*, Toronto: Pontifical Institute, 1983

Mütherich, Florentine, and Percy Ernst Schramm, *Denkmäle der deutschen Könige und Kaiser* (Monuments of German Kings and Emperors), Munich: Prestel, 1962

Nelson, Janet L., *Charles the Bald*, London: Longman, 1992

Pirenne, Henri, *Mahomet et Charlemagne*, Paris: Alcan, 1937; in English as *Mohammed and Charlemagne*, London: Allen and Unwin, New York: Norton, 1939

Rouche, Michel, *Clovis*, Paris: Fayard, 1996

Schieffer, Rudolf, *Die Entstehung des päpstlichen Investiturverbots für den deutschen König* (The Origin of the Papal Investiture Ban for German Kings), Stuttgart: Hiersemann, 1981

Société historique, *Collection de textes pour servir à l'étude et à l'enseignement de l'histoire* (Collection of Texts to Help in the Study and Teaching of History), 1886–

Stoclet, Alain, *Autour de Fulrad de Saint-Denis (v.710–784)* (On Fulrad of Saint-Denis), Geneva: Droz, 1993

Sullivan, Richard E., *Christian Missionary Activity in the Early Middle Ages*, Aldershot: Variorum, 1994

Thierry, Augustin, *Lettres sur l'histoire de France* (Letters on the History of France), Paris: Pontheiu, 1827

Traube, Ludwig, *Nomina Sacra: Versuch einer Geschichte der christlichen Kürzung* (*Nomina Sacra*: An Attempted History of the Christian Latin Abbreviations), Munich: Beck, 1907; reprinted 1967

Ullmann, Walter, *The Carolingian Renaissance and the Idea of Kingship*, London: Methuen, 1969

Wallace-Hadrill, J.M., *The Frankish Church*, Oxford and New York: Oxford University Press, 1983

Wallach, Luitpold, *Alcuin and Charlemagne: Studies in Carolingian History and Literature*, Ithaca, NY: Cornell Unversity Press, 1959

Werner, Karl Ferdinand, *Histoire de France*, vol.1: *Les origines (avant l'an mil)* (The History of France, vol. 1: The Origins, before the year 1000), Paris: Fayard, 1988

Wolfram, Herwig, *Die Geburt Mitteleuropas: Geschichte Österreichs vor seiner Entstehung, 378–907* (The Birth of Central Europe), Vienna: Siedler, 1987

Zimmermann, Ernst Heinrich, ed., *Vorkarolingische Miniaturen* (Pre-Carolingian Miniatures), Berlin: Im Slebstverlage des Deutschen Vereins für Kunstwissenschaft, 1916

France: 1000–1450

During the Middle Ages France was better defined by language and culture than by political or geographical boundaries. Between 1000 and 1450 the territories and formal authority of its kings expanded greatly, but the history of the medieval kingdom strictly defined would exclude substantial parts of modern France, notably the duchies of Brittany and Burgundy, Artois, Alsace-Lorraine, the Franche-Comté and Haute Savoie, and smaller lordships in the south including Béarn and Nice.

There was always, however, a larger area in which the French language and French culture predominated, and all through the Middle Ages the influence and indirect power of the kings of France extended far beyond the bounds of their own domain. The wide currency of the works of Jean Froissart (c.1337–after 1404), historian of the Hundred Years' War and the world of chivalry, is a witness to that cultural hegemony. The process by which the French kings exploited and consolidated their influence, and the resources which they used to that end, is a large part of the history of the age.

The kingdom of France emerged from the wreckage of the Carolingian empire when the descendants of Hugh Capet (c.941–96, proclaimed king in 987) imposed and maintained a tenuous authority over their feudatories from a strategic seat in the Ile de France. When their vassal William duke of Normandy (1027–1087) conquered England he became a rival of equal rank, and the marriage of his granddaughter Matilda to the count of Anjou, and of their son Henry II (1133–89) to Eleanor, heiress of Aquitaine made the king of England the lord of western France. A cycle of conflict and precarious settlement followed which issued in the Hundred Years' War (1337–1453) and ultimately left the English with only Calais. The French prevailed by their tenacity, skilful diplomacy – which was greatly aided by their influence in the papal court during the popes' residence at Avignon (1309–78) – and careful husbanding of their resources. The practice from the late 13th century of assigning great fiefs such as Burgundy and Berri as appanages for the younger princes of the royal house, although it sometimes fomented rivalries, allowed them to assimilate very disparate territories. First and last, however, they enjoyed pre-eminence in the culture of the day. From the reign of Louis IX (1215–70), who died on crusade, they were the Most Christian Kings, the arbiters of chivalry, and even their rivals and their enemies shared their idiom and their values.

France made an early contribution to the study of medieval history through the work of the Maurists, members of the reformed Benedictine congregation of St-Maur, founded at St-Germain-des-Prés in 1618, which became a notable house of scholarship. Jean Mabillon's *De re diplomatica* (The Science of Diplomatic, 1681) is the first modern critical work on historical texts, and the *Recueil des historiens des Gaules et de la France* (Collection of the Historians of the Gauls and of France, 1737–86) stood as a model for later collections. The Maurists were dispersed at the Revolution, but the harm done then to many archival collections and libraries was offset by the foundation in 1789 of the Archives Nationales, and in 1839 by the establishment of a school of archival science the journal of which, the *Bibliothèque de l'Ecole des Chartes*, is a major repository of diplomatic and paleographical studies. The Société de l'Histoire de France (1834–) concurrently undertook the critical publication of historical texts.

An early name among the distinguished graduates of the Ecole des Chartes is that of Léopold Delisle, who also contributed to the development of the school. Delisle was a master of manuscript studies, whose works, including his *Catalogue des actes de Philippe Auguste* (Catalogue of the Acts of Philip Augustus, 1856) and *Recueil des Actes de Henri II* (Collection of the Acts of Henry II; with Elie Berger, 1909–27), besides his liturgical and other codicological studies, are outstanding examples of diplomatic science.

The modern world inherited from the Middle Ages a tradition of history as a story of notable events, like the *Grandes Chroniques de France* (Grand Chronicle of France), of the lives of those associated with them, like Jean Chartier's *Chronique de Charles VII* (Chronicle of Charles VII, 1858), and of particular places and parts, like the *Histoire du Comté de Bourgogne* (A History of the County of Burgundy, 1740) by F.I. Dunod de Charnage. That tradition is not yet spent, but it has been augmented over the last two centuries, a period that has achieved remarkable feats in social organization, by an urgent interest in the conventions and structure of society at large.

In France such issues are the subject of frequent and intense debate. The 19th century searched for scientific truth in history, and found it either in determinism, especially Marxist determinism, or in a rigorous pursuit of the transcendent individual whose significant actions, the true substance of history, can be appreciated only when they are cleansed of irrelevance and subjective misapprehension. The classic statement of such objective historical science is the *Introduction aux études historiques* (1898; *Introduction to the Study of History*, 1898) of C.V. Langlois and Charles Seignobos, but the *histoire événémentielle* for which it strives is inevitably tempered by other considerations. In the 19th century, when representative government was a general preoccupation, historians concerned themselves with constitutional history in England, as in the work of William Stubbs, and with the forms of government and its institutions in France, notably in the *Histoire des institutions politiques de l'ancienne France* (History of the Political Institutions of Medieval France, 1875–92) of Numa Fustel de Coulanges. That durable work was complemented as late as 1959–62 by a comprehensive and scholarly, though conceptually a notably old-fashioned survey, *Histoire des institutions françaises du Moyen Age* (History of French Institutions in the Middle Ages, 1951) by Ferdinand Lot and Robert Fawtier, in three volumes covering seignorial, royal, and ecclesiastical institutions respectively.

The emergence and early fortunes of the Capetian kings obviously marks a critical period in French medieval history, and one that has received constant attention from historians. Achille Luchaire published *Histoire des institutions monarchiques de la France sous les premiers Capétiens (987–1180)* (History of Royal Institutions of France under the First Capetians) in 1883, and followed it with other studies including *Les Communes françaises à l'époque des Capétiens directs* (The French Communes under the Capetian Kings, 1890). Those and many similar studies were summarized in synthetic works such as the *Histoire de France* of Ernst Lavisse, published in 9 volumes between 1900 and 1911, and the *Histoire générale* begun by Gustave Glotz, of which nine volumes on the Middle Ages appeared between 1925 and 1945. The *Histoire de l'Eglise* (History of the Church) edited by Augustin Fliche and Victor Martin (1934–) is still incomplete, and does not cover the years of the Avignon papacy, but there is a general account of that period in Guillaume Mollat, *Les Papes d'Avignon* (1912; *The Popes at Avignon, 1305–78*, 1963), and a specialized structural study by Bernard Guillemain, *La Cour pontificale d'Avignon* (The Papal Court of Avignon, 1962).

A new and lively style of inquiry arose after World War I from the work of two historians at the University of Strasbourg. Lucien Febvre was a medievalist who turned to early modern history, and coined the term *outillage mentale*, which has gained general acceptance as *mentalité*, for the object of his quest: the active mind of the past. His younger colleague Marc Bloch was a committed medievalist of wide sympathies, a luminous and powerfully influential scholar, with certainly the most charismatic appeal of his generation of historians. In 1929 they founded the periodical *Annales d'histoire économique et sociale*, presenting an agenda for themselves and their contributors that had an enduring effect on historical studies. Bloch began his career in economic history, publishing *L'Ile de France* (1913; *The Ile-de-France*, 1971), and returned to the theme with an impressively wide-ranging study, *Les Caractères originaux de l'histoire rurale française* (1931; *French Rural History*, 1966). His deeper qualities emerged, however, in *Les Rois thaumaturges* (1924; *The Royal Touch*, 1973), a delicately learned study of the complex of myth, superstition, and politics embodied in the doctrine of the royal touch as a cure for scrofula, "the king's evil," and in his masterpiece, *La Société féodale* (1939–40; *Feudal Society*, 1961). Block combined intellectual gifts and humane sympathy to an uncommon degree; he was a Jew and a patriot as well as an outstanding scholar. He rejoined the army in 1939, the Resistance in 1942, and was captured and shot by the Nazis.

La Société féodale is over-ambitious in its scope, and inevitably flawed. Medieval society was never a system, and Bloch knew well that he was distorting it by discussing it. The book nevertheless displayed his talents on every page in its engaging acuity, subtlety, and learning. The influence of Bloch's writings was often as strong as his direct influence as a teacher, and his declaration of scholarly faith, *Apologie pour l'histoire* (1949; *The Historian's Craft*, 1953), struck a chord with writers and readers of history both in France and abroad.

Annales, retitled *Annales: économies, sociétés, civilisations* (or *Annales: ESC*) in 1946, also became influential abroad, but under the direction of Fernand Braudel – whom Febvre had encouraged to expand his study of Philip II's policies to the whole area of the Mediterranean – its pages were increasingly occupied by studies of the early modern period. In recent decades the general influence of the periodical has diminished, chiefly because its field has broadened, but its ideology has been defined and vigorously defended in a manual entitled *Faire de l'Histoire* (1974; partially translated as *Constructing the Past*, 1985) by Jacques Le Goff and Pierre Nora.

Annales had long since made its mark on medievalists, who after 1945 carried Bloch's principles into a wide range of studies. They gave particular attention to the economic and demographic crisis of the 14th century and to the effects of the Hundred Years' War. Robert Boutruche's *La Crise d'une société* (A Society in Crisis, 1947) is a detailed review of a rich, highly specialized, and particularly vulnerable region. What might be described as the culture of war is cogently discussed by Philippe Contamine in *Guerre, état, et société* (War, the State, and Society, 1972), a study enlarged by Contamine's *Des Pouvoirs en France* (Authority in France, 1992). The social upheavals of late medieval society are examined by Michel Mollat and Philippe Wolff in *Ongles bleus, Jacques et Ciompi* (Journeymen, Rustics, and Chumps, 1970). The proceedings of a conference held by the Troisième Congrès National des Sociétés savantes on *La France anglaise au Moyen Age* (English France in the Middle Ages, 1988), explored the interaction of the French and the English in the territories variously held by the English in the course of some four centuries: a richly ambivalent theme.

In the meantime the development of economic history had enlarged the study of medieval towns much beyond earlier concerns with the communal movement and the workings of municipal government. In an extensive field, Elizabeth Chapin's *Les Villes des foires de Champagne* (Towns and Fairs in Champagne, 1937) examined a commercial focus of international importance; Jean Schneider's *La Ville de Metz aux XIII et XIV siècles* (The City of Metz in the 13th and 14th Centuries, 1950) was a study of the whole community; and Philippe Wolff's *Commerce et marchands de Toulouse* (The Trade and Merchants of Toulouse, 1954) discussed both the local and long-distance trade of the city.

Among those who although not pupils of Bloch found themselves inspired by his writings, Georges Duby moved from an intensive, and widely influential study of a region – *La Société aux XIe et XIIe siècles dans la région mâconnaise* (Society in the 11th and 12th Centuries in the Mâcon Region, 1953) – and a survey of economic development in western Europe at large – *L'Economie rurale et la vie des campagnes dans l'Occident médiéval* (1962; *Rural Economy and Country Life in the Medieval West*, 1968) – to deeper explorations of the constituents and articulation of the medieval hierarchy. *Les Trois Ordres* (1978; *The Three Orders*, 1980) and *Le Chevalier, la femme, et le prêtre* (1981; *The Knight, the Lady and the Priest*, 1983) moved smoothly between documentary material and theory, and in its discussion of kinship, the concept and nature of knighthood, and relations between the sexes it touched on many themes of wider significance. At the other end of the social scale, Emmanuel Le Roy Ladurie's *Montaillou* (1975; translated 1978) used the documents of an inquisitorial process against heresy to reconstruct a village community in the Languedoc. The vivid detail of reported conversations, and the startling nature of both the familiar and the unfamiliar in the daily lives of the inhabitants have made the book probably the most widely-read historical study of recent times.

Recent studies of French history by British and American scholars have illuminated both traditional and current themes. The Capetian monarchy is examined by J.W. Baldwin in *The Government of Philip Augustus* (1986), and over a longer period by Elizabeth Hallam, in *Capetian France* (1980). Two of the great duchies embroiled in the Hundred Years' War were studied in M.G.A. Vale's *English Gascony, 1399–1453* (1970) and M.C.E. Jones' *Ducal Brittany, 1364–99* (1970). The last phase of the war is documented in C.T. Allmand's *Lancastrian Normandy* (1983). The first period of the French recovery from the early impact of the war was covered by a great work of traditional scholarship, *L'Histoire de Charles V* (1901–31) by Roland Delachenal, and by P.S. Lewis' *Later Medieval France* (1968), which surveyed the reintegrated kingdom. There is now in progress a learned and lively study of the whole war in *The Hundred Years War* by Jonathan Sumption, of which the first volume, *Trial by Battle*, covering the years from 1328 to 1347, appeared in 1990.

The demographic studies that *Annales* nurtured and in which French scholars formulated much of the current methodology were issued in 1988 in a 3-volume *Histoire de la population française* (A History of the Population of France), edited by Jacques Dupaquier and others. The first volume, *Des origines à la Renaissance* (From the Earliest Times to the Renaissance), covered the whole period of the Middle Ages.

GEOFFREY H. MARTIN

See also Bloch; Delisle; Duby; Febvre; Froissart; Fustel; Le Goff; Le Roy Ladurie; Mabillon; Seignobos; Stubbs

Further Reading

Allmand, Christopher Thomas, *Lancastrian Normandy: The History of a Medieval Occupation*, Oxford and New York: Oxford University Press, 1983

Baldwin, John Wesley, *The Government of Philip Augustus: The Foundations of French Power in the Middle Ages*, Berkeley: University of California Press, 1986

Bautier, Robert-Henri, ed., *La France de Philippe Auguste: le temps des mutations* (The France of Philip Augustus: An Age of Change), Paris: Editions du Centre National de la Recherche Scientifique, 1982

Bloch, Marc, *L'Ile de France: les pays autour de Paris*, Paris: Cerf, 1913; in English as *The Ile-de-France: The Country around Paris*, Ithaca, NY: Cornell University Press, and London: Routledge, 1971

Bloch, Marc, *Les Rois thaumaturges: étude sur le caractère surnaturel attribué à la puissance royale, particulièrement en France et en Angleterre*, Paris: Colin, 1924; in English as *The Royal Touch: Sacred Monarchy and Scrofula in England and France*, London: Routledge, 1973

Bloch, Marc, *Les Caractères originaux de l'histoire rurale française*, Oslo: Ascheoug, and Cambridge, MA: Harvard University Press, 1931; in English as *French Rural History: An Essay on Its Basic Characteristics*, Berkeley: University of California Press, 1966

Bloch, Marc, *La Société féodale*, 2 vols., Paris: Michel, 1939–40; in English as *Feudal Society*, 2 vols., Chicago: University of Chicago Press, and London: Routledge, 1961

Bloch, Marc, *Apologie pour l'histoire, ou, métier d'historien*, Paris: Colin, 1949; in English as *The Historian's Craft*, New York: Knopf, 1953, Manchester: Manchester University Press, 1954

Boutruche, Robert, *La Crise d'une société: seigneurs et paysans en Bordelais pendant la Guerre de Cent ans* (A Society in Crisis: Lords and Peasants in the Bordelais during the Hundred Years' War), Paris: Belles Lettres, 1947

Bur, Michel, *Suger, abbé de St-Denis et régent de France* (Suger, Abbot of St. Denis and Regent of France), Paris: Perrin, 1991

Cazelles, Raymond, *La Société politique et la crise de la royauté sous Philippe de Valois* (The Political Community and the Crisis of Monarchy under Philippe de Valois), Paris: Librairie d'Argences, 1958

Chapin, Elizabeth, *Les Villes des foires de Champagne, des origines au début du XIV siècle* (Towns and Fairs in Champagne from Their Beginnings to the 14th Century), Paris: Champion, 1937

Chartier, Jean, *Chronique de Charles VII: roi de France* (Chronicle of Charles VII: King of France), Paris: Jannet, 1858

Contamine, Philippe, *Guerre, état et société à la fin du Moyen Age: études sur les armées des rois de France, 1337–1494* (War, the State, and Society at the End of the Middle Ages: Studies of the Royal Armies of France), Paris: Mouton, 1972

Contamine, Philippe, *Des Pouvoirs en France, 1300–1500* (Authority in France, 1300–1500), Paris: Presses de l'Ecole Normale Supérieure, 1992

Delachenal, Roland, *L'Histoire de Charles V* (The History of Charles V), 5 vols., Paris: Picard, 1909–31

Delisle, Léopold, ed., *Catalogue des actes de Philippe Auguste* (Catalogue of the Acts of Philip Augustus), Paris: Durand, 1856

Delisle, Léopold, and Elie Berger, eds., *Recueil des actes de Henri II, roi d'Angleterre et duc de Normandie, concernant les provinces françaises et les affaires de France* (The Acts of Henry II, King of England and Duke of Normandy, Concerning the French Provinces and the Affairs of France), 3 vols., Paris: Imprimerie Nationale, 1909–27

Duby, Georges, *La Société aux XIe et XIIe siècles dans la région mâconnaise* (Society in the 11th and 12th Centuries in the Mâcon Region), Paris: Colin, 1953

Duby, Georges, *L'Economie rurale et la vie des campagnes dans l'Occident médiéval: France, Angleterre, Empire, IX–XV siècles*, Paris: Aubier, 1962; in English as *Rural Economy and Country Life in the Medieval West*, Columbia: University of South Carolina Press, and London: Arnold, 1968

Duby, Georges, *The Chivalrous Society*, London: Arnold, and Berkeley: University of California Press, 1977

Duby, Georges, *Les Trois Ordres, ou, l'imaginaire du féodalisme*, Paris: Gallimard, 1978; in English as *The Three Orders: Feudal Society Imagined*, Chicago: University of Chicago Press, 1980

Duby, Georges, *Le Chevalier, la femme et le prêtre: le mariage dans la France féodale*, Paris: Hachette, 1981; in English as *The Knight, the Lady, and the Priest: The Making of Modern Marriage in Medieval France*, New York: Pantheon, 1983, London: Allen Lane, 1984

Dulud, Michel, *Du Guesclin* (Bertrand du Guesclin, c.1320–1380), Paris: Editions de Paris, 1958

Dunod de Charnage, François Ignace, *Histoire du Comté de Bourgogne* (A History of the County of Burgundy), Besançon, 1740

Dupaquier, Jacques, *Histoire de la population française* (A History of the Population of France), 4 vols., Paris: Presses Universitaires de France, 1988

Favier, Jean, *Philippe le Bel* (Philip the Fair, 1268–1314), Paris: Fayard, 1978

Fawtier, Robert, *Les Capétiens et la France: leur rôle dans sa construction*, Paris: Presses Universitaires du France, 1942; in English as *The Capetian Kings of France: Monarchy and Nation, 987–1328*, London: Macmillan, and New York: St. Martin's Press, 1960

Fawtier, Robert, *Les Sources de l'histoire de France des origines à la fin du XV siècle* (Sources for the History of France from its Origins to the End of the 15th Century), Paris: Picard, 1971

Fliche, Augustin, and Victor Martin, eds., *Histoire de l'Eglise* (History of the Church), 21 vols. and supplements, Paris: Bloud & Gay, 1934–63

Fustel de Coulanges, Numa, *Histoire des institutions politiques de l'ancienne France* (History of the Political Institutions of Medieval France), 6 vols., Paris: Hachette, 1875–92

Gies, Frances, *Joan of Arc: The Legend and the Reality*, New York: Harper, 1981

Glotz, Gustave, *Histoire générale: histoire ancienne* (General History: Ancient History), 9 vols., Paris: Presses Universitaires de France, 1925–45

Guillemain, Bernard, *La Cour pontificale d'Avignon, 1309–76: étude d'une société* (The Papal Court of Avignon, 1309–76: A Study of a Society), Paris: Boccard, 1962

Hallam, Elizabeth M., *Capetian France, 987–1328*, London and New York: Longman, 1980

Higounet, Charles, *Bordeaux pendant le haut Moyen Age* (Bordeaux in the High Middle Ages), Bordeaux: Fédération Historique de Sud-Ouest, 1963

Holmes, George, ed., *The Oxford Illustrated History of Medieval Europe*, Oxford: Oxford University Press, 1988

Jones, Michael C.E., *Ducal Brittany, 1364–99: Relations with England and France during the Reign of Duke John IV*, London: Oxford University Press, 1970

Langlois, Charles Victor, and Charles Seignobos, *Introduction aux études historiques*, Paris: Hachette, 1898; in English as *Introduction to the Study of History*, London: Duckworth, 1898; New York: Holt, 1913

Lavisse, Ernest, general editor, *Histoire de France depuis les origines jusqu'à la révolution* (A History of France from Its Origins to the Revolution), 9 vols., Paris: Hachette, 1900–11

Le Goff, Jacques, and Pierre Nora, *Faire de l'Histoire*, 3 vols., Paris: Gallimard, 1974; translated in part as *Constructing the Past: Essays in Historical Methodology*, Cambridge and New York: Cambridge University Press, 1985

Le Roy Ladurie, Emmanuel, *Montaillou, village occitan de 1294 à 1324*, Paris: Gallimard, 1975; in English as *Montaillou: The Promised Land of Error*, New York: Braziller, 1978, and as *Montaillou: Cathars and Catholics in a French Village, 1294–1324*, London: Scolar Press, 1978

Lewis, Peter Shervey, *Later Medieval France: The Polity*, London: Macmillan, and New York: St. Martin's Press, 1968

Lot, Ferdinand, and Robert Fawtier, *Histoire des institutions françaises du Moyen Age* (History of French Institutions in the Middle Ages), 3 vols., Paris: Presses Universitaires de France, 1951

Luchaire, Achille, *Histoire des institutions monarchiques de la France sous les premiers Capétiens (987–1180)* (A History of the Royal Institutions of France under the First Capetians), 2 vols., Paris: Imprimerie Nationale, 1883

Luchaire, Achille, *Les Communes françaises à l'époque des Capétiens directs* (The French Communes under the Capetian Kings), Paris: Hachette, 1890

Mabillon, Jean, *De re diplomatica* (The Science of Diplomatic), Paris: Billaine, 1681

Mollat, Guillaume, *Les Papes d'Avignon, 1305–1378*, Paris: Lecoffre, 1912; 9th edition, 1963; in English as *The Popes at Avignon, 1305–78*, London and New York: Nelson, 1963

Mollat, Michel, and Philippe Wolff, *Ongles bleus, Jacques et Ciompi: les révolutions populaires en Europe aux XIV et XV siècles* (Journeymen, Rustics, and Chumps: Popular Revolt in Europe in the 14th and 15th Centuries), Paris: Calmann Lévy, 1970

Panofsky, Erwin, ed., *Abbot Suger on the Abbey Church of St-Denis and Its Art Treasures*, Princeton: Princeton University Press, 1946

Renouard, Yves, *Bordeaux sous les rois d'Angleterre* (Bordeaux under the Kings of England), Bordeaux: Fédération Historique du Sud-Ouest, 1965

Richard, Jean, *Les Ducs de Bourgogne et la formation du duché du XI au XIV siècle* (The Dukes of Burgundy and the Formation of the Duchy from the 11th to the 14th Centuries), Paris: Belles Lettres, 1954

Richard, Jean, *St. Louis: roi d'une France féodale, soutien de terre sainte*, Paris: Fayard, 1983; in English as *Saint Louis: Crusader King of France*, Cambridge and New York: Cambridge University Press, 1992

Schneider, Jean, *La Ville de Metz aux XIII et XIV siècles* (The City of Metz in the 13th and 14th Centuries), Nancy: Georges Thomas, 1950

Sumption, Jonathan, *The Hundred Years War*, vol. 1: *Trial by Battle*, London: Faber, 1990; Philadelphia: University of Pennsylvania Press, 1991

Troisième Congrès National des Sociétés savantes, *La France anglaise au Moyen Age* (English France in the Middle Ages), Paris: CTHS, 1988

Vale, Malcolm, *English Gascony, 1399–1453: A Study of War, Government, and Politics during the Late Stages of the Hundred Years' War*, London: Oxford University Press, 1970

Vale, Malcolm, *Charles VII*, Berkeley: University of California Press, 1974

Vaughan, Richard, *Valois Burgundy*, Hamden, CT: Archon, and London: Allen Lane, 1975

Warner, Marina, *Joan of Arc: The Image of Female Heroism*, London: Weidenfeld and Nicolson, and New York: Knopf, 1981

Wolff, Philippe, *Commerce et marchands de Toulouse, vers 1350–1450* (The Trade and Merchants of Toulouse, c.1350–1450), Paris: Plon, 1954

Wood, Charles T., *The French Appanages and the Capetian Monarchy*, Cambridge, MA: Harvard University Press, 1966

France: 1450–1789

When Voltaire observed that Louis XIV's regime had "succeeded in transforming a hitherto turbulent people into a peace-loving nation who were dangerous only to their foes after having been their own enemies for more than a hundred years," he touched on the problem that has most captivated recent historians of early modern France: the emergence and social impact of a political regime known later as "absolutism." To be sure, historians sharply differed in their definitions and explanations of absolutism; some – mostly British – historians, such as Roger Mettam and Nicholas Henshall, rejected the notion altogether as hopelessly inadequate for the reality it was supposed to describe; and others, notably those of the Annales school, nearly disregarded absolutism altogether in the search for long-term socioeconomic structures (the *longue durée*). Still, a regime that fielded 400,000 troops at one time, restored law and order among its subjects, redefined their legal status (within limits), and projected French culture to the ends of Europe understandably provided the majority of historians of early modern France with their central bearings in a wide and complex field.

Following World War II, research on the Old Regime continued to reflect the institutional emphasis imparted to it by prewar French historians such as Ernest Lavisse and Georges Pagès, but it was soon apparent that infusions of social history were widening and deepening older approaches. Such was apparent in the inescapable work of Roland Mousnier, whose countless publications – such as his early *La Vénalité des offices sous Henri IV et Louis XIII* (The Venality of Offices under Henry IV and Louis XIII, 1945) and magisterial synthesis *Les Institutions de la France sous la monarchie absolue, 1598–1789* (1974–80; *The Institutions of France under the Absolute Monarchy, 1598–1789*, 1979–84) – reflected older ideas of a rationalizing monarchy ruling from above, but also posed questions regarding the social basis of political support and opposition. Although Mousnier's notion of a transition from a society of orders to a society of classes was largely discredited, his examination of popular revolts and his debate with the Soviet historian Boris Porchnev over their social constituency helped illuminate the setbacks that the monarchy experienced in its development and the compromises it was obliged to make. This was a point reinforced by a number of other studies on the machinery of government, some by British historians, such as Richard Bonney's *Political Change in France under Richelieu and Mazarin, 1624–1661* (1978) and David Potter's *A History of France, 1460–1560* (1995), and some by Americans, such as Orest Ranum's *Richelieu and the Councillors of Louis XIII* (1963), Sharon Kettering's *Patrons, Brokers, and Clients in Seventeenth-Century France* (1986), and William Beik's *Absolutism and Society in Seventeenth-Century France* (1985). Further fleshing out these matters were such grand syntheses of political and social history as Pierre Goubert's *L'Ancien Régime* (1969–73; vol. 1 as *The Ancien Régime*, 1973) and Emmanuel Le Roy Ladurie's *L'Ancien Régime de Louis XIII à Louis XV* (1991; *The Ancien Régime*, 1996), and such smaller scale overviews as Denis Richet's *La France moderne* (Modern France, 1973), which is arguably the best short introduction to the Old Regime ever published, and David Parker's *The Making of French Absolutism* (1983). If all these works had a common theme, it was that the early modern state bore little resemblance to the model of bureaucratic rationality described by Max Weber, and that the French government and French society coexisted in a state of constant tension throughout the Old Regime.

But what were the origins of absolutism? Post-World War II historians surely acknowledged the role of military demands

on a monarchy facing challenges from English kings in the Hundred Years' War and from Habsburg powers that threatened France on the east and south. Yet as military/diplomatic history lost the prestige it had enjoyed before 1945, historians of the last half-century came to focus more intently on the domestic politics of state consolidation. In a series of important publications culminating in *Representative Government in Early Modern France* (1980), J. Russell Major elaborated a process of state-building involving a distinct Renaissance phase, when the monarchy governed primarily through consultation with pre-existing institutions, followed by a distinct absolutist phase, when it imposed control from above. This model underwent much criticism, both from historians like R.J. Knecht, who in his *Renaissance Warrior and Patron* (1994) argued that the French state operated along absolutist lines already in the early 16th century, and from historians like Beik, who noted more reliance on negotiation under Louis XIV than Major allowed. Yet Major's notions were in their broadest outline corroborated by an influential group of ceremonialist historians including Ralph Giesey, Sarah Hanley, and Richard Jackson. Working under the influence of the medievalist Ernst Kantorowicz's *The King's Two Bodies* (1957), this group found a gradual dissolving of traditional oppositions between representations of the king's mortal person and representations of the state within the royal funeral, the *lit de justice* of the *parlements* (royal sovereign courts), and the royal coronation by the early 17th century, thereby confirming the idea of a distinct absolutist stage – indicated by the joining of the king's two bodies – dating from the accession of Henri IV. In the 1980s and 1990s, as feminist historiography began to exert influence on the field, Hanley broadened her approach in a series of articles that rooted state-building in a "family-state compact," a joint enterprise of parents and jurists to regulate family succession through a highly gendered political authority. Other important works dealing with the ideological background to absolutism included Donald Kelley's *Foundations of Modern Historical Scholarship* (1970) and Nannerl Keohane's *Philosophy and the State in France* (1980).

As Marxist "materialism" and sociology lost influence to anthropology and linguistics, historians of recent decades rediscovered religion as a force to reckon with in the construction of the Old Regime. Partly on the inspiration of Emile Durkheim, who had stressed the role of religion in generating forms of collective self-representation, and of the *Annaliste* Lucien Febvre, who had characterized the French Reformation as an effort to develop new forms of spirituality, historians in the 1970s began to look at the religious conflicts of the 16th century as truly "about" religion and its cultural implications, not as mere ideological projections of conflicts with more "material" origins. Robert Kingdon's fine studies of Genevan Calvinism helped prepare the way for revision, but it was Natalie Zemon Davis who, in the essays eventually published in *Society and Culture in Early Modern France* (1975), broke new ground most decisively. Davis argued that behind late 16th-century local violence lay not economic stress but conflict between two competing religious communities with different ways of symbolically defining and purifying themselves in the sight of God. Once religion was "rescued" from reductionism, the task remained to re-integrate it within the fabric of political and social history. J.H.M. Salmon's masterful synthesis, *Society in Crisis* (1975), was one such effort at non-reductionist integration, as were the more narrowly focused studies of Philip Benedict, *Rouen during the Wars of Religion* (1981), Barbara Diefendorf, *Beneath the Cross* (1991), and Michael Wolfe, *The Conversion of Henri IV* (1993). To be sure, differences remained between those like Robert Descimon who, in his *Qui étaient les Seize?* (Who Were the Sixteen?, 1983), placed greater emphasis on politics than on popular theology as a driving force, and those like Denis Crouzet who, in his *Les Guerriers de Dieu* (The Warriors of God, 1990), did just the reverse. Yet the majority of historians appeared to agree by the 1990s that religious and non-religious forces could best be understood with reference to each other and that the construction of Bourbon absolutism represented the victory not of a "secular" *politique* faction over Catholic and Protestant fanaticism, as had been argued since Voltaire's time, but rather of a particular Gallican form of Catholicism, as inherently religious as any of its rivals. That the *raison d'état* promoted in the 17th century by Cardinal Richelieu was rooted in religious principles had already been argued by William Church in his *Richelieu and Reason of State* (1972). But the fullest elaboration of this approach – which showed that political history, too, had a *longue durée* – appeared in Dale K. Van Kley's *The Religious Origins of the French Revolution* (1996). In this ambitious work, the author recast the political history of the entire Old Regime as a struggle between two parties – one motivated by a Catholic form of spirituality associated with the Jesuits and the other by Protestant/Jansenist spirituality – and tracked the ultimately unsuccessful efforts of the monarchy to rise above them through the propagation of "sacral absolutism."

Because the 17th century witnessed the high tide of absolutism, historians working on this period most closely associated French history with the history of the monarchy, even if, as already pointed out, they recognized that the monarchy's authority was frequently challenged and rested on compromise. One fortunate result of this association was the appearance of many fine biographies of the first three Bourbon kings, who were on a whole much better served by scholars than were their immediate Valois predecessors or Bourbon successors; among such works were David Buisseret's *Henry IV* (1984), Elizabeth Marvick's *Louis XIII* (1986), A. Lloyd Moote's *Louis XIII, the Just* (1989), John B. Wolf's *Louis XIV* (1968), François Bluche's *Louis XIV* (1986; translated 1990), and Andrew Lossky's *Louis XIV and the French Monarchy* (1994). Strangely enough, these biographies and the institutional studies noted above were not accompanied by much new serious study of the royal court, which in the 17th century experienced a major expansion and exerted such a great social and political influence. It was possibly for this reason that historians rediscovered and, for a time, celebrated the pre-World War II work of Norbert Elias, notably *Über den Prozess der Zivilisation* (1939; *The Civilizing Process*, 1978–82), which appeared in new French and English editions. More recently Elias' work has been criticized, notably in Daniel Gordon's *Citizens Without Sovereignty* (1994).

As the major disruption of absolutist rule in the 17th century, the Fronde inspired a number of studies written from different perspectives. Ernest Kossman's *La Fronde* (1954), A. Lloyd Moote's *The Revolt of the Judges* (1972), and Orest Ranum's *The Fronde* (1993) examined the main political narrative.

Hubert Carrier's *La Presse et la Fronde* (The Press and the Fronde, 1989–91) and Christian Jouhaud's *Mazarinades* (1985) dealt with the propaganda war. Richard M. Golden's *The Godly Rebellion* (1981) revealed a little-known Jansenist sequel to the Fronde that pointed to the troubles the crown would have from that quarter in the next century.

Although the biographies by Wolfe, Bluche, and Lossky covered the length of Louis XIV's reign, no comprehensive general treatment of the period appeared in the post-World War II period that could rival Ernest Lavisse's work published early in the century, even if Pierre Goubert's *Louis XIV et vingt millions de français* (1966; *Louis XIV and Twenty Million Frenchmen*, 1970) did offer a brief, but now obsolete survey. It was in the more specialized studies that cutting-edge research appeared, many of these studies devoted to the cultural and ideological aspects of the reign; among them were Henri-Jean Martin's *Livre, pouvoirs et société* (Books, Power, and Society, 1969) (which also covered the early 17th century), Lionel Rothkrug's *Opposition to Louis XIV* (1965), Robert Isherwood's *Music in the Service of the King* (1973), Orest Ranum's *Artisans of Glory* (1980), and Peter Burke's *The Fabrication of Louis XIV* (1992). Another primary focus of research was the late reign, which Goubert and Rothkrug described in terms of crisis and decline, but which a younger generation of historians showed to be far more resilient than previously thought; Joseph Klaits' *Printed Propaganda under Louis XIV* (1976) illuminated the efforts of foreign minister Colbert de Torcy's stable of monarchist propagandists to respond to critics in their own language of history and law during the War of the Spanish Succession, while Thomas Schaeper's *The French Council of Commerce* (1983) demonstrated the vitality of mercantilist principles among French merchants and the innovative bureaucratic measures taken by the monarchy to enlist the merchants' counsel.

If the historiography of the 17th century was oriented toward the triumph of absolutism, the historiography of the next century was dominated by the search for the origins of 1789. Here the main historiographical development was the collapse of the dominant Marxist social theory of the French Revolution, which had featured a "rising" bourgeoisie chafing against "feudal" limits imposed by the aristocracy, a theory that was largely consistent with older institutionalist notions of a reforming monarchy blocked by "special interests." Robert R. Palmer in his multivolume synoptic *The Age of the Democratic Revolution* (1959–64) began to move toward a more political and less social version of the Marxist theory, but it was Alfred Cobban in his *The Social Interpretation of the French Revolution* (1964), followed by François Furet in his *Penser la Révolution française* (1978; *Interpreting the French Revolution*, 1981) and William Doyle in his *Origins of the French Revolution* (1980), who attacked the whole social argument and put political contestation back at the top of the historiographical agenda.

Although some historians, notably Michel Antoine in his *Le Conseil du roi sous le règne de Louis XV* (The Royal Council during the Reign of Louis XV, 1970) and *Louis XV* (1989), maintained the idea of a competent, well-intentioned monarchy brought down by dark, subversive forces concentrated in the aristocratic *parlements*, fresh examinations of *parlement* opposition, such as J.H. Shennan's *The Parlement of Paris* (1968) and Jean Egret's *Louis XV et l'opposition parlementaire* (Louis

XV and *Parlement* Opposition, 1970), argued that these institutions, far from representing only the narrow interests of the aristocracy, reflected the broad consensus of the nation genuinely disturbed by the inefficiency and "despotic" tendencies it perceived in the state. Although royal tax increases generated much of the opposition faced by the crown, a growing number of studies – B. Robert Kreiser's *Miracles, Convulsions, and Ecclesiastical Politics in Early Eighteenth-Century Paris* (1978), Dale K. Van Kley's *The Damiens Affair and the Unraveling of the Ancien Régime* (1984), Jeffrey Merrick's *The Desacrilization of the French Monarchy* (1990), David Bell's *Lawyers and Citizens* (1994), and Peter Campbell's *Power and Politics in Old Regime France* (1996) – held that even more than taxes, it was the monarchy's largely unconsidered persecution of a dissident Catholic sect, the Jansenists, undertaken in the wake of its persecution and expulsion of Protestants under Louis XIV, that energized the Jansenist-led *parlements* and other judicial bodies in their subversion of royal authority through attacks on its "despotism." Enhancing this perspective, Sarah Maza's *Private Lives and Public Affairs* (1993) revealed how well-publicized trials regarding domestic abuse at the end of the Old Regime made the threat of "despotism" seem all the more real for having roots in the politics of the family.

But why could the supposedly absolute monarchy not have simply crushed opposition to its policies, including harassment by the *parlements*, institutions that could be legally compelled to register royal edicts? This was in part, argued some historians, because of the development of "public opinion," which *parlementaires* and their allies used to maintain growing pressure on the monarchy. Building upon the notion of a newly emergent "public sphere" developed by Jürgen Habermas in his *Strukturwandel der Öffentlichkeit* (1962; *The Structural Transformation of the Public Sphere*, 1989), Keith Baker argued in *Inventing the French Revolution* (1990) that politics broke out of the absolutist mold in the later 18th century when the "public" gained an authority formerly vested in the monarchy and "public opinion," informed by Enlightenment *philosophes* among others, became the arbiter of political truth. This essentially rhetorical approach inspired many other studies of the public and its opinion, among them Dena Goodman's study of Enlightenment salons, *The Republic of Letters* (1994). Another approach was taken by Robert Darnton who, in a series of books culminating in *The Forbidden Best-Sellers of Pre-Revolutionary France* (1995), investigated the history of publishing, in particular the rise of defamatory political pornography. In combination with the works of the High Enlightenment, Darnton argued, this Grub Street literature weakened the authority of the crown and thereby prepared the way for 1789. Darnton's widely read work remained controversial and was attacked in particular by Roger Chartier in *Les Origines culturelles de la Révolution française* (1990; *The Cultural Origins of the French Revolution*, 1991), wherein Chartier argued that delegitimization derived less from Grub Street pornography than from subtle changes in authority structures readers brought to the reading of defamatory literature rather than derived from them.

Given that the standoff between the monarchy and its critics ended with the financial crisis of the late 1780s, it was not surprising historians paid considerable attention to the long-

and short-term reasons for the monarchy's fiscal collapse. The development of the Old Regime's fiscal structure was studied by, among others, Martin Wolfe in *The Fiscal System of Renaissance France* (1972), Richard Bonney in *The King's Debts* (1981), James B. Collins in *Fiscal Limits of Absolutism* (1988), and Daniel Dessert in *Argent, pouvoir et société au Grand Siècle* (Money, Power, and Society in 17th-Century France, 1984). State fiscality in the 18th century was studied, with varying amounts of attention paid to political implications, in Herbert Lüthy's *La banque protestante en France* (Protestant Banking in France, 1959–61), J.F. Bosher's *French Finances, 1770–1795* (1970), Steven L. Kaplan's *Bread, Politics, and Political Economy in the Reign of Louis XV* (1976), Robert D. Harris's *Necker* (1979), James C. Riley's *The Seven Years War and the Old Regime in France* (1986), and Thomas E. Kaiser's "Money, Despotism, and Public Opinion" (1991). In a number of penetrating articles – the most broadly conceived being "Old Regime Origins of Democratic Liberty" (1994) – David Bien argued that it was paradoxically the monarchy's need to borrow money on the much superior credit of privileged bodies like the clergy that prevented it from eliminating the tax exemptions that contributed to the fiscal crisis of 1789. Bien's re-examination of Old Regime corporate institutions was continued in the work of some of his students, most notably by Gail Bossenga in her study of urban politics and finance, *The Politics of Privilege* (1991).

By the 1990s it could be no longer said, as it had been earlier, that the collapse of the old social interpretation of 1789 left historians in a "somewhat painful void." On the contrary, historians now enjoyed a multiplicity of political, financial, religious, cultural, and feminist interpretive frameworks with which to explain the collapse – and rise – of the Old Regime. Yet none of these alone could provide a satisfactory general theory. It seemed that for at least the reasonably near future there would be no royal road to the problem of absolutism.

THOMAS E. KAISER

See also Burke; Chartier; Darnton; Davis, N.; Febvre; Furet; Goubert; Habermas; Kantorowicz; Lavisse; Le Roy Ladurie; Voltaire

Further Reading

Antoine, Michel, *Le Conseil du roi sous le règne de Louis XV* (The Royal Council during the Reign of Louis XV), Geneva: Droz, 1970

Antoine, Michel, *Louis XV*, Paris: Fayard, 1989

Baker, Keith, *Inventing the French Revolution: Essays on French Political Culture in the Eighteenth Century*, Cambridge and New York: Cambridge University Press, 1990

Beik, William, *Absolutism and Society in Seventeenth-Century France: State Power and Provincial Aristocracy in Languedoc*, Cambridge and New York: Cambridge University Press, 1985

Bell, David Avrom, *Lawyers and Citizens: The Making of a Political Elite in Old Regime France*, New York and Oxford: Oxford University Press, 1994

Benedict, Philip, *Rouen during the Wars of Religion: Popular Disorder, Public Order, and the Confessional Struggle*, Cambridge and New York: Cambridge University Press, 1981

Bien, David D., "Old Regime Origins of Democratic Liberty" in Dale K. Van Kley, ed., *The French Idea of Freedom: The Old Regime and the Declaration of Rights of 1789*, Stanford, CA: Stanford University Press, 1994

Bluche, François, *Louis XIV*, Paris: Fayard, 1986; *Louis XIV*, Oxford: Blackwell, and New York: Watts, 1990

Bonney, Richard, *Political Change in France under Richelieu and Mazarin, 1624–1661*, Oxford and New York: Oxford University Press, 1978

Bonney, Richard, *The King's Debts: Finance and Politics in France, 1589–1661*, Oxford: Clarendon Press, and New York: Oxford University Press, 1981

Bosher, J.F., *French Finances, 1770–1795: From Business to Bureaucracy*, Cambridge: Cambridge University Press, 1970

Bossenga, Gail, *The Politics of Privilege: Old Regime and Revolution in Lille*, Cambridge and New York: Cambridge University Press, 1991

Buisseret, David, *Henry IV*, London and Boston: G. Allen and Unwin, 1984

Burke, Peter, *The Fabrication of Louis XIV*, New Haven and London: Yale University Press, 1992

Campbell, Peter, *Power and Politics in Old Regime France, 1720–1745*, London and New York: Routledge, 1996

Carrier, Hubert, *La Presse et la Fronde (1648–1653): Les mazarinades* (The Press and the Fronde [1648–1653]: The Mazarinades), 2 vols., Geneva: Droz, 1989–91

Chartier, Roger, *Les Origines culturelles de la Révolution française*, Paris: Seuil, 1990; in English as *The Cultural Origins of the French Revolution*, Durham NC: Duke University Press, 1991

Church, William F., *Richelieu and Reason of State*, Princeton: Princeton University Press, 1972

Cobban, Alfred, *The Social Interpretation of the French Revolution*, Cambridge: Cambridge University Press, 1964

Collins, James B., *Fiscal Limits of Absolutism: Direct Taxation in Early Seventeenth-Century France*, Berkeley: University of California Press, 1988

Crouzet, Denis, *Les Guerriers de Dieu: la violence au temps des troubles de religion (vers 1525–vers 1610)* (The Warriors of God), 2 vols., Seyssel: Champ Vallon, 1990

Darnton, Robert, *The Forbidden Best-Sellers of Pre-Revolutionary France*, New York: Norton, 1995

Davis, Natalie Zemon, *Society and Culture in Early Modern France: Eight Essays*, Stanford, CA: Stanford University Press, and London: Duckworth, 1975

Descimon, Robert, *Qui étaient les Seize? Mythes et réalités de la ligue parisienne, 1585–1594* (Who Were the Sixteen?: Myths and Realities of the Paris League, 1585–1594), Paris: Klincksieck, 1983

Dessert, Daniel, *Argent, pouvoir et société au Grand Siècle* (Money, Power, and Society in 17th-Century France), Paris: Fayard, 1984

Diefendorf, Barbara B., *Beneath the Cross: Catholics and Huguenots in Sixteenth-Century Paris*, New York and Oxford: Oxford University Press, 1991

Doyle, William, *Origins of the French Revolution*, Oxford and New York: Oxford University Press, 1980

Egret, Jean, *Louis XV et l'opposition parlementaire, 1715–1774* (Louis XV and Parlement Opposition, 1715–1774), Paris: Colin, 1970

Elias, Norbert, *Über den Prozess der Zivilisation: Soziogenetische und Psychogenetische Untersuchungen*, 2 vols., Basel: Falken, 1939; in English as *The Civilizing Process*, 2 vols., New York: Urizen (vol. 1) and Pantheon (vol. 2), and Oxford: Blackwell, 1978–82

Furet, François, *Penser la Révolution française*, Paris: Gallimard, 1978, revised 1983; in English as *Interpreting the French Revolution*, Cambridge and New York: Cambridge University Press, 1981

Giesey, Ralph E., *The Royal Funeral Ceremony in Renaissance France*, Geneva: Droz, 1960

Golden, Richard M., *The Godly Rebellion: Parisian Curés and the Religious Fronde, 1652–1662*, Chapel Hill: University of North Carolina Press, 1981

Goodman, Dena, *The Republic of Letters: A Cultural History of the French Enlightenment*, Ithaca, NY: Cornell University Press, 1994

Gordon, Daniel, *Citizens Without Sovereignty: Equality and Sociability in French Thought, 1670–1789*, Princeton: Princeton University Press, 1994

Goubert, Pierre, *Louis XIV et vingt millions de français*, Paris: Fayard, 1966; in English as *Louis XIV and Twenty Million Frenchmen*, London: Allen Lane, and New York: Pantheon, 1970

Goubert, Pierre, *L'Ancien Régime*, 2 vols., Paris: Colin, 1969–73; vol. 1 translated as *The Ancien Régime: French Society, 1600–1750*, New York: Harper, and London: Weidenfeld and Nicolson, 1973

Habermas, Jürgen, *Strukturwandel der Öffentlichkeit: Untersuchungen zu einer Kategorie der bürgerlichen Gesellschaft*, Neuwied: Luchterhand, 1962; in English as *The Structural Transformation of the Public Sphere: An Inquiry into a Category of Bourgeois Society*, Cambridge, MA: MIT Press, and London: Polity Press, 1989

Hanley, Sarah, *The "Lit de justice" of the Kings of France: Constitutional Ideology in Legend, Ritual, and Discourse*, Princeton: Princeton University Press, 1983

Hanley, Sarah, "Engendering the State: Family Formation and State Building in Early Modern France," *French Historical Studies* 16 (1989), 4–27

Hanley, Sarah, "Social Sites of Political Practice in France: Lawsuits, Civil Rights, and the Separation of Powers in Domestic and State Government, 1500–1800," *American Historical Review* 102 (1997), 27–52

Harris, Robert D., *Necker: Reform Statesman of the Ancien Régime*, Berkeley: University of California Press, 1979

Henshall, Nicholas, *The Myth of Absolutism: Change and Continuity in Early Modern European Monarchy*, New York and London: Longman, 1992

Isherwood, Robert M., *Music in the Service of the King: France in the Seventeenth Century*, Ithaca, NY: Cornell University Press, 1973

Jackson, Richard A., *Vive le Roi! A History of the French Coronation from Charles V to Charles X*, Chapel Hill: University of North Carolina Press, 1984

Jouhaud, Christian, *Mazarinades: La Fronde des mots* (The Mazarinades: The Fronde of Words), Paris: Aubier, 1985

Kaiser, Thomas E., "The Abbé de Saint-Pierre, Public Opinion and the Reconstitution of the French Monarchy," *Journal of Modern History* 55 (1983), 618–43

Kaiser, Thomas E., "Money, Despotism, and Public Opinion in Early Eighteenth-Century France: John Law and the Debate on Royal Credit," *Journal of Modern History* 63 (1991), 1–28

Kantorowicz, Ernst, *The King's Two Bodies: A Study in Mediaeval Political Theology*, Princeton: Princeton University Press, 1957

Kaplan, Steven L., *Bread, Politics, and Political Economy in the Reign of Louis XV*, 2 vols., The Hague: Nijhoff, 1976

Kelley, Donald R., *Foundations of Modern Historical Scholarship: Language, Law, and History in the French Renaissance*, New York: Columbia University Press, 1970

Keohane, Nannerl O., *Philosophy and the State in France: The Renaissance to the Enlightenment*, Princeton: Princeton University Press, 1980

Kettering, Sharon, *Patrons, Brokers, and Clients in Seventeenth-Century France*, New York and Oxford: Oxford University Press, 1986

Kingdon, Robert McCune, *Geneva and the Coming of the Wars of Religion in France, 1555–1563*, Geneva: Droz, 1956

Klaits, Joseph, *Printed Propaganda under Louis XIV: Absolute Monarchy and Public Opinion*, Princeton: Princeton University Press, 1976

Knecht, R.J., *Renaissance Warrior and Patron: The Reign of Francis I*, Cambridge and New York: Cambridge University Press, 1994

Kossmann, E.H., *La Fronde* (The Fronde), Leiden: Universitaires Pers Leiden, 1954

Kreiser, B. Robert, *Miracles, Convulsions, and Ecclesiastical Politics in Early Eighteenth-Century Paris*, Princeton: Princeton University Press, 1978

Lavisse, Ernest, *Louis XIV*, 2 vols., Paris: Hachette, 1911

Le Roy Ladurie, Emmanuel, *L'Ancien Régime de Louis XIII à Louis XV, 1610–1774*, 2 vols., Paris: Hachette, 1991; in English as *The Ancien Régime: A History of France, 1610–1774*, Oxford and Cambridge, MA: Blackwell, 1996

Lossky, Andrew, *Louis XIV and the French Monarchy*, New Brunswick, NJ: Rutgers University Press, 1994

Lüthy, Herbert, *La banque protestante en France de la révocation de l'édit de Nantes à la Révolution* (Protestant Banking in France from the Revocation of the Edict of Nantes to the French Revolution), 2 vols., Paris: SEVPEN, 1959–61

Major, James Russell, *Representative Government in Early Modern France*, New Haven and London: Yale University Press, 1980

Martin, Henri-Jean, *Livre, pouvoirs et société à Paris au XVIIe siècle (1598–1701)* (Books, Power, and Society in Paris during the 17th Century) 2 vols., Geneva: Droz, 1969

Marvick, Elizabeth Wirth, *Louis XIII: The Making of a King*, New Haven and London: Yale University Press, 1986

Maza, Sarah, *Private Lives and Public Affairs: The Causes Célèbres of Prerevolutionary France*, Berkeley: University of California Press, 1993

Merrick, Jeffrey W., *The Desacralization of the French Monarchy in the Eighteenth Century*, Baton Rouge: Louisiana State University Press, 1990

Mettam, Roger, *Power and Faction in Louis XIV's France*, Oxford and New York: Blackwell, 1988

Moote, Alanson Lloyd, *The Revolt of the Judges: The Parlement of Paris and the Fronde, 1643–1652*, Princeton: Princeton University Press, 1972

Moote, Alanson Lloyd, *Louis XIII, the Just*, Berkeley: University of California University Press, 1989

Mousnier, Roland, *La Vénalité des offices sous Henri IV et Louis XIII* (The Venality of Offices under Henry IV and Louis XIII), Rouen: Maugard, 1945; revised 1971

Mousnier, Roland, *Les Institutions de la France sous la monarchie absolue, 1598–1789*, 2 vols., Paris: Presses Universitaires de France, 1974–80; in English as *The Institutions of France under the Absolute Monarchy, 1598–1789*, 2 vols., Chicago: University of Chicago Press, 1979–84

Pagès, Georges, *La monarchie de l'ancien régime en France* (The Monarchy of the Old Regime in France), Paris: Colin, 1928

Palmer, R.R., *The Age of the Democratic Revolution: A Political History of Europe and America, 1760–1800*, 2 vols., Princeton: Princeton University Press, 1959–64

Parker, David, *The Making of French Absolutism*, New York: St. Martin's Press, and London: Arnold, 1983

Porchnev, Boris, *Narodnye vosstanii vo frantsii pered frondoi, 1623–48*, Moscow: Akademiia Nauk, 1948; in French as *Les Soulèvements populaires en France de 1623 à 1648* (Popular Revolts in France from 1623 to 1648), Paris: SEVPEN, 1963

Potter, David, *A History of France, 1460–1560: The Emergence of a Nation State*, Basingstoke: Macmillan, and New York: St. Martin's Press, 1995

Ranum, Orest A., *Richelieu and the Councillors of Louis XIII: A Study of the Secretaries of State and Superintendents of Finance in the Ministry of Richelieu, 1635–42*, Oxford: Clarendon Press, 1963

Ranum, Orest A., *Artisans of Glory: Writers and Historical Thought in Seventeenth-Century France*, Chapel Hill: University of North Carolina Press, 1980

Ranum, Orest A., *The Fronde: A French Revolution, 1648–1652*, New York: Norton, 1993

Richet, Denis, *La France moderne: l'esprit des institutions* (Modern France: The Spirit of Institutions), Paris: Flammarion, 1973

Riley, James C., *The Seven Years War and the Old Regime in France: The Economic and Financial Toll*, Princeton: Princeton University Press, 1986

Rothkrug, Lionel, *Opposition to Louis XIV: The Political and Social Origins of the French Enlightenment*, Princeton: Princeton University Press, 1965

Salmon, John Hersey Macmillan, *Society in Crisis: France in the Sixteenth Century*, London: Benn, 1975

Schaeper, Thomas J., *The French Council of Commerce, 1700–1715: A Study of Mercantilism after Colbert*, Columbus: Ohio State University Press, 1983

Shennan, J.H., *The Parlement of Paris*, Ithaca, NY: Cornell University Press, and London: Eyre and Spottiswoode, 1968

Van Kley, Dale K., *The Damiens Affair and the Unraveling of the Ancien Régime, 1750–1770*, Princeton: Princeton University Press, 1984

Van Kley, Dale K., *The Religious Origins of the French Revolution: From Calvin to the Civil Constitution, 1560–1791*, New Haven and London: Yale University Press, 1996

Wolf, John Baptist, *Louis XIV*, New York: Norton, and London: Gollancz, 1968

Wolfe, Martin, *The Fiscal System of Renaissance France*, New Haven: Yale University Press, 1972

Wolfe, Michael, *The Conversion of Henry IV: Politics, Power, and Religious Belief in Early Modern France*, Cambridge, MA: Harvard University Press, 1993

France: French Revolution

Whether or not Mao Tse-tung, when asked about the significance of the French Revolution, actually replied that it was too early to judge, "1789" has unquestionably dominated the world's political and ideological agenda for the last two centuries. Edmund Burke knew that it would. In 1796 he wrote: "out of the tomb of the murdered monarchy in France has arisen a vast, tremendous, unformed spectre, in a far more terrific guise than any which ever yet have overpowered the imagination." A few years ago, the communist historian Albert Soboul closed his *Précis d'histoire de la Révolution française* (1962; *The French Revolution, 1787–1799*, 1974) with these words: "Still admired and still feared, the Revolution lives on in our minds."

The universal appeal of 1789 has proved to be both a blessing and a curse. During the first half of the 19th century, the Fall of the Bastille or the Jacobin Terror was frequently invoked to legitimize – or denounce – radical, revolutionary, even conservative movements. In France, long before Karl Marx injected new, historic meaning into the word "bourgeois', François Guizot was celebrating the Revolution as "the triumph of the bourgeoisie." Further to the right of the political spectrum, Joseph de Maistre and Louis de Bonald had constructed their Catholic royalist denunciation of the "godless revolution" by the 1820s, founding a tradition which passed through the pen of Charles Maurras to today's Action Française movement. The revolutions of 1848 and 1871 would help to destroy the links between constitutional monarchy, Bonapartism, and revolution: henceforth, republicanism and the French Revolution would walk through history, hand in hand. The association between republicanism, revolution, and respectability was strengthened in 1891 by the appointment of Alphonse Aulard as the first incumbent of the chair of French Revolutionary Studies in the Sorbonne.

On the left, the link between socialism and the Revolution – first forged by Philippe Buonarroti with his account of Babeuf's 1828 conspiracy of the equals – was given "scientific" respectability by the advent of Marxism. Although Marx himself was ambivalent about the *political* significance of 1789 (bourgeois Frenchmen dressed up in Roman togas!), most historians on the left looked to the Revolution for the origins of socialism and democracy; the "classic historiography" of the Revolution, which stretched from Buonarrotti, through Jean Jaurès and Albert Mathiez, to the great socialist and communist historians of the 20th century, Georges Lefebvre and Albert "Marius" Soboul, had been conceived. But it was not only in France that the Revolution dictated the political and historical agenda. From the beginning of the 19th century the spirit of 1789 had been invoked by revolutionary leaders as far apart as Mexico and Greece. The Declaration of the Rights of Man had become universal property: its influence can easily be detected in the Charter of the United Nations after World War II.

If 1848 and 1871 in France had fused the Revolution with Republicanism, the Russian Revolution of 1917 seemed to confirm the validity of Marx's class-based theory of historical change, the "bourgeois" revolution of 1789 being followed by the "proletarian" revolution of 1917. According to the revisionist historian, François Furet, Marxist-Leninists would now appropriate the Jacobin Terror as a model for the world communist revolution – a temporary dictatorship would be translated into a law of history. Robespierre would become "the failed Lenin."

However, from the fall of the Bastille to the fall of the Berlin Wall two centuries later, the universalism of the Revolution was continually being undermined by its identification with French nationalism. It was only with the triumph of the Soviet Union in World War II (followed by the Chinese Revolution of 1949 which would refocus attention on the revolutionary potential of the peasantry in history) and the patriotic role of communists in the French Resistance that the Marxist and Marxist-Leninist analysis of the French Revolution would really dominate French Revolutionary studies. The work of scholars worldwide – Tagahashi in Japan, Ado in the Soviet Union, Markov in East Germany, Soboul in France, Hobsbawm and Rudé in Britain – promoted the idea of the French Revolution as the undertaker of feudal regimes and of the artisan and shopkeeper as the prerevolutionary vanguard of the proletarian revolution. In America, liberal historians like R.R. Palmer preferred to see the Revolution as part – albeit the most significant – of an 18th century movement towards modern democracy which linked events in America with those in Europe. With its emphasis on the language and rhetoric of modern democracy, as well as on the force of ideas in history, Palmer's work should be seen as an important part of that American tradition which emphasizes intellectual and political history, a tradition which stretches from Charles Beard to Keith Baker and which informs recent revisionist accounts of the Revolution.

As the 20th century reaches its end, the attraction of 1789 shows little sign of diminishing, and not only among radical historians. Simon Schama's *Citizens* (1989) praises the cultural and political achievements of the *ancien régime* and the early Revolution while vilifying the violent "mob." François Furet, Keith Baker, and Colin Lucas recently produced a 4-volume work that enshrines the revisionist theme – that modern democratic institutions and ideas were gradually emerging during the 18th century, only to be temporarily drowned in blood during the Revolution. This unseemly rush to bury the "social/socialist" French Revolution – a move not unrelated to political events in Russia and Eastern Europe during the 1980s – has been checked only by the global celebration of the bicentenary of the Revolution as well as by the rise to prominence of women's history and cultural history. According to Harriet Applewhite and Darline Levy "Gender, together with race, class, ideology, and power politics, shaped revolutionary outcomes in the age of the democratic revolution," a conclusion that links the "New History" with the tradition of R.R. Palmer.

The French Revolution retains its power to attract and fascinate then, and probably will continue to do so as long as exploitation, social, racial, political, and economic, persists in our world. The words of the famous Declaration of the Rights of Man, ambiguous as they are, will not be forgotten in the 21st century.

GWYNNE LEWIS

See also Guizot; Hobsbawm; Lefebvre; Rudé; Schama; Soboul

Further Reading

Applewhite, Harriet, and Darline Levy, *Women and Politics in the Age of the Democratic Revolution*, Ann Arbor: University of Michigan Press, 1993

Baker, Keith, *Inventing the French Revolution: Essays on French Political Culture in the Eighteenth Century*, Cambridge and New York: Cambridge University Press, 1990

Blanning, Tim, *The Origins of the French Revolutionary Wars*, London and New York: Longman, 1986

Buonarroti, Philippe, *Conspiration pour l'égalité dite de Babeuf: suivi du procès auquel elle donna lieu, et des pièces justicatives, etc., etc.*, 2 vols., Brussels: Librairie Romantique, 1828; in English as *Buonarroti's History of Babeuf's Conspiracy for Equality*, London: Hetherington, 1836; reprinted New York: A.M. Kelley, 1965

Burke, Edmund, "Letters on a Regicide Peace," in his *Works*, 8 vols., 1792–1827, vol.5

Cobb, Richard, *The Police and the People: French Popular Protest, 1789–1820*, Oxford: Oxford University Press, 1970

Cobban, Alfred, *The Social Interpretation of the French Revolution*, Cambridge: Cambridge University Press, 1964

Darnton, Robert, *The Business of Enlightenment: A Publishing History of the Encyclopédie, 1775–1800*, Cambridge, MA: Harvard University Press, 1979

Doyle, William, *The Oxford History of the French Revolution*, Oxford and New York: Oxford University Press, 1989

Fehér, Ferenc, ed., *The French Revolution and the Birth of Modernity*, Berkeley: University of California Press, 1990

Forrest, Alan, *The French Revolution and the Poor*, Oxford: Blackwell, and New York: St. Martin's Press, 1981

Furet, François, Keith Baker, and Colin Lucas, eds., *The French Revolution and the Creation of Modern Political Culture*, 4 vols., Oxford and New York: Pergamon Press, 1987–94

Furet, François, and Mona Ozouf, eds., *Dictionnaire critique de la Révolution française*, Paris: Flammarion, 1988; in English as *A Critical Dictionary of the French Revolution*, Cambridge, MA: Harvard University Press, 1989

Furet, François, *Le Passé d'une illusion: essai sur l'idée communiste au XXe siècle*, (An Illusion of the Past: An Essay on the Idea of Communism) Paris: Laffont, 1995

Gough, Hugh, *The Newspaper Press in the French Revolution*, London: Routledge, and Chicago: Dorsey, 1988

Hampson, Norman, *The Enlightenment*, Harmondsworth: Penguin, 1968; New York: Penguin, 1976

Hunt, Lynn, *Politics, Culture, and Class in the French Revolution*, Berkeley: University of California Press, 1984; London: Methuen, 1986

Jones, Colin, *The Longman Companion to the French Revolution*, London: Longman, 1988

Jones, Peter M., *The Peasantry in the French Revolution*, Cambridge and New York: Cambridge University Press, 1988

Kennedy, Emmet, *A Cultural History of the French Revolution*, New Haven: Yale University Press, 1989

Lefebvre, Georges, *La Révolution française*, Paris: Alcan, 1930; in English as *The French Revolution*, 2 vols., London: Routledge and Paul, and New York: Columbia University Press, 1962–64

Lewis, Gwynne, *The French Revolution: Rethinking the Debate*, London and New York: Routledge, 1993

Melzer, Sarah, and Leslie Rabine, eds., *Rebel Daughters: Women and the French Revolution*, Oxford: Oxford University Press, 1992

Rose, R.B., *Gracchus Babeuf: The First Revolutionary Communist*, London: Arnold, and Stanford, CA: Stanford University Press, 1978

Rudé, George, *The Crowd in the French Revolution*, Oxford: Clarendon Press, 1959; New York: Oxford University Press, 1967

Schama, Simon, *Citizens: A Chronicle of the French Revolution*, New York: Knopf, and London: Viking, 1989

Slavin, Morris, *The Left and the French Revolution*, Atlantic Highlands, NJ: Humanities Press, 1995

Soboul, Albert, *Les Sans-culottes parisiens en l'an II: mouvement populaire et gouvernement révolutionnaire, 2 Juin 1793–9 Thermidor An II*, Paris: Clavreuil, 1958; abridged and revised as *Mouvement populaire et gouvernement révolutionnaire en l'an II (1793–1794)*, Paris: Flammarion, 1973; in English as *The Parisian Sans-Culottes and the French Revolution, 1793–4*, Oxford: Clarendon Press, 1964, and as *The Sans-Culottes: The Popular Movement and Revolutionary Government, 1793–1794*, New York: Doubleday, 1972

Soboul, Albert, *Précis d'histoire de la Révolution française*, Paris: Editions Sociales, 1962, expanded as *La Révolution française*, 1982; in English as *The French Revolution, 1787–1799*, London: NLB, 1974, New York: Random House, 1975

Sutherland, Donald, *France, 1789–1815: Revolution and Counter-revolution*, London: Fontana, and New York: Oxford University Press, 1985

Tilly, Charles, *The Vendée*, London: Arnold, 1964; Cambridge, MA: Harvard University Press, 1968

France: since the Revolution

It is often suggested that the French Revolution of 1789 laid the foundations of modern democratic politics, and the way in which it did so has dominated debate for the past 200 years. Parliamentary representation and direct democracy, which existed side by side during the revolutionary period, created two diverging traditions in French political life based on separate understandings of the concept of popular sovereignty. This was further complicated by the emergence of an authoritarian tendency within the revolutionary tradition which culminated under Napoleon I. Opposition to the revolutionary process led to the beginnings of another strand in French political life: reactionary politics.

Historians have identified several contentious issues in their studies of modern France: continuity versus discontinuity, tradition versus modernity, change versus stagnation. Whatever the debate, the French Revolution remains a crucial point of reference. Therefore, the temptation has been to present the period since 1789 as a succession of revolutionary and reactionary periods interspersed with occasional periods of authoritarianism.

Alongside continuing debates about the nature of the French Revolution, historians have discussed the nature and role of the Napoleonic era in relation to the Revolution and the Restoration. Often this has taken the form of biography, as in Georges Lefebvre's or Vincent Cronin's portraits of Napoleon. Pieter Geyl's *Napoleon: voor en tegen in de Franse geschiedschrijving* (1946; *Napoleon: For and Against*, 1949) gathered together much of the early writing on the emperor and demonstrated the extreme stances he evoked. Most discussion revolved around a few key questions. Was the First Empire an inevitable consequence of the conquests of the Revolution, which allowed the generals of the revolutionary armies to acquire enormous power? Was the First Empire a necessity due to the inability of successive revolutionary governments to create a stable political system within which the nation could recognize itself? Bonaparte exploited his revolutionary pedigree (was he not the victor at Toulon, the savior of the Republic in Vendemiaire Year III?) to argue that his role was to end the Revolution as well as to consolidate its achievements. Of course Louis XVI had spoken very much in the same vein when he signed the 1791 Constitution, but the Revolution, far from ending, had taken on a much more radical turn. As Louis Bergeron's *L'Episode napoléonien, 1799–1815* (1972; *France under Napoleon*, 1981) demonstrated, the Emperor's reorganization of France's administrative, legal, and financial systems benefited in the short term from distorted war demands as well as control of vast areas of continental Europe. In the longer term, the collapse of French Atlantic interests meant a major geographical shift in the industrial base of the country from the Atlantic coast to the north and northeastern borders; it also meant a transfer of wealth, which left the western part of the country much weakened economically. Napoleon's political legacy reinforced centralization and authoritarianism, creating continuity with the *ancien régime*, albeit in a new legal context with guaranteed rights afforded to individuals by the Revolution. Frank A. Kafker and James M. Laux's edited collection, *Napoleon and His Times* (1989), provides an overview of recent debates.

The Restoration (1814–30) and the July Monarchy (1830–48) have presented historians with a similar set of problems. Guillaume de Bertier de Sauvigny's survey, *La Restauration* (1955; *The Bourbon Restoration*, 1967) suggested that the Bourbons did much to stabilize France. But did the return of the Bourbons bring back the centralized authority of the Old Regime and eliminate the experiment of the Revolution and the Empire? In his detailed analysis of the two regimes, *Le Libéralisme en France de 1814 à 1848* (Liberalism in France, 1814–1848, 1967), Louis Girard argued that there was in fact no way back to the old days of the *ancien régime* and that the period 1815–48 represented the first – albeit clumsy – attempt at a parliamentary regime, inspired by the British example. The bicameral organization of legislative power in the Charter of 1814 (revised in 1830) did allow for some form of parliamentary debate, but the influence of the monarchs remained, and the very limited franchise did little to widen political participation during these years. In this respect, the rise to power of Louis Philippe, despite his own revolutionary heritage (his father, Philippe d'Orléans, had voted for the execution of his cousin Louis XVI in 1793, and he himself had served in the revolutionary armies at Jemappes in 1793), brought little significant change. However, historians such as David Pinkney in *Decisive Years in France* (1986) have credited the July Monarchy with success in the economic field, identifying the 1840s as the years in which France started on the road toward industrialization. But the boom was short-lived and collapsed with the mid-century economic crisis that culminated in the revolutions of 1848. In his seminal article "Comment naissent les Révolutions?" (How are Revolutions Born?, 1948), Ernest Labrousse identified the political, economic, and social causes that coincided in time to bring about the events of 1848.

The impact that the February and June days of 1848 had on France is a question that has been hotly debated. George Duveau's *1848* (1965; translated 1967) offered a survey of the events, while Frederick De Luna's *The French Republic under Cavaignac* (1969) also provided a good account. The most durable achievement of 1848 was the reintroduction of universal male suffrage. Although curtailed between 1849 and 1851, it was to be challenged again only between 1940 and 1944. Equally significant in 1848 was the formulation of a new constitution that, while adhering faithfully to the principle of the separation of powers, vested popular sovereignty in a single chamber and in a president elected by universal male suffrage. Without any system of checks and balances between executive and legislature, the scene was set for a dangerous rivalry that would hinge on the personality of the elected president. These issues are treated in Peter Amann's *Revolution and Mass Democracy* (1975) as well as Maurice Agulhon's *1848* (1973; *The Republican Experiment*, 1983). Thus the possible return of another authoritarian regime was set in motion. The long-term legacy of 1848 is not so significant, although the Second Republic did try to address the issue of social equality, without any success. Indeed, both Maurice Agulhon's *La République au village* (1970; *The Republic in the Village*, 1982) and John Merriman's *The Agony of the Republic* (1978) argued that conservative agrarian and industrial forces in France used the social reforms put forward by the Second Republic to ensure the failure of the regime and to frighten an inexperienced electorate into believing that revolution meant an end to property. Ted Margadant's *French Peasants in Revolt* (1979) extended the argument to reveal rural resistance to Louis Napoleon's 1851 coup. For some conservative thinkers the new challenge faced by the French elites after 1848 was how best to devise measures that would allow these elites to control universal suffrage. Tocqueville's answer was to accept universal suffrage, but to offset its impact through a process of de-centralization that would reinforce the power of the local landed proprietors against the influence of the mob in Paris. Roger Price's *The French Second Republic* (1972) provides a useful survey of the period. Mention should also be made of Theodore Zeldin's *France, 1848–1945* (1973), a magisterial survey of the social history of the century that followed the 1848 revolution.

Control of democratic politics could take a different form. Indeed the 1848 Constitution provided the opportunity for another bout of authoritarian rule. Louis Napoleon campaigned on the themes of peace and prosperity to secure his election in 1849, before resorting to a coup supported by the army in 1851 in order to retain the presidency and with it increased powers, as expressed in the establishment of the Second Empire a year later. Louis Napoleon's career has been much studied. Stuart L. Campbell's *The Second Empire Revisited* (1978) assessed the historical debates from the Third Republic to the end of World War II, while James McMillan's *Napoleon III* (1991) has drawn together more recent appraisals.

Historians such as Guy Palmade in *Capitalisme et capitalistes français au XIXe siècle* (1961; *French Capitalism in the Nineteenth Century*, 1972) and Maurice Lévy-Leboyer and François Bourguignon in *L'Economie française au XIXe siècle* (1985; *The French Economy in the Nineteenth Century*, 1990) have argued that the Second Empire represented a period of success for the French economy, thanks to political stability and social acquiescence. Peter McPhee's *A Social History of France* (1992) placed this degree of social acquiescence in the context of political repression at the beginning of the regime. The degree to which the Empire was actually responsible for fostering economic development is not a straightforward matter. Napoleon III benefited from an upturn in economic conditions worldwide, with an increased level of demand for European heavy goods paralleled by a stabilization of currencies due to the discovery of gold mineral reserves in the New World. It is true that the Empire fostered such developments by setting up a modern banking system, including joint stock companies designed to entice investments on a large scale. Contrary to commonly held belief, the French state did not intervene directly in the running of the economy, except most obviously in the signing of the trade treaty with Britain in 1860, and similar measures (including monetary agreements) with other European states. In most cases of industrial policy, the state acted as a guarantor to small investors, as was the case with the reorganization of the railway network from 1851 onwards. Increases in the production of heavy goods industry should not hide difficulties in other sectors, such as textiles, or, indeed, agriculture, where no major restructuring took place. Hugh D. Clout's *Agriculture in France on the Eve of the Railway Age* (1979) argued that the agricultural sector exhibited no change in patterns of land ownership or land use, and that the levels of investment remained low and consequently the use of new technology was quite rare. This was confirmed in Roger Price's *The Modernization of Rural France* (1983). The image of a prosperous Second Empire may well be one that is exaggerated. The reality was probably less clearcut, with cyclical crises, in 1855 for example. Further difficulties emerged in the late 1860s.

The apparent popular support given to the regime between 1851 and 1859 should not overshadow the resistance to the takeover well documented for the provinces in the works of Peter McPhee, Roger Price, and Maurice Agulhon. Nor should one ignore the growing opposition to the regime that culminated with the elections of 1869 and the emergence of the radical program of government articulated by Gambetta and others, known as the "Programme de Belleville." The political practices of official candidates and physical pressures at polling stations point to an authoritarian and corrupt regime, which does not fit well in the tradition of democratic politics, either at parliamentary level or at the level of rank and file organization. The so-called liberalization of the regime from the 1860s must be related to the difficulties in foreign policy, following the semi-fiasco of the Italian initiative (1859) and the total collapse of the Mexican adventure (1867). Indeed foreign policy loomed large in the image building of a powerful France in Europe and the world. Napoleon III's involvement in the Crimea, Italy, Mexico, and the Far East aimed at a revision of the 1815 settlement. Successful to a degree, the Second Empire played a role in unleashing nationalisms throughout Europe with no need to measure the consequences of such a policy. In particular, its inability to comprehend the significance of the battle of Sadowa (1866) opened the road to defeat during the Franco–Prussian War in 1870. With surrender came the collapse of the regime. Clearly the years 1815–70 did not produce political stability. The succession of various regimes interrupted by revolutions (1830 and 1848) tend to present an image of discontinuity with little genuine economic change. Could defeat produce a different picture?

The Third Republic that slowly emerged from defeat and revolution has often been ridiculed for its inability to foster political stability. General studies of the Third Republic include the appropriate volumes of general histories such as Alfred Cobban's *A History of Modern France* (1965), but more often studies have focused on shorter spans of time or events: for example, the Commune, the Belle Epoque, the Dreyfus affair, World War I, or the Popular Front. This reflects the dissatisfaction of historians with the period. The Third Republic has been attacked for its lack of vision in bringing about reforms, as indicated by the numerous debates concerning income tax, which came into effect only in 1917. It has been harshly criticized for the way in which it expired in 1940. Yet in many ways the 1875 laws that served as a constitutional text for the Third Republic ushered in a period of remarkable stability, continuity, and a degree of modernity.

The Commune, part of the larger fiasco of the Franco–Prussian War, has fascinated historians concerned with revolutionary upheavals. Stewart Edwards' *The Paris Commune, 1871* (1971) placed the events in context and discussed the intensity of its repression. Alistair Horne's *The Fall of Paris* (1965) offered a blow-by-blow account of the larger event. The Dreyfus affair has loomed large in the historiography of the late 19th century. Jean-Denis Bredin's *L'Affaire* (1983; *The Affair*, 1986) examined the case and the trials in great detail, while Eric Cahm's *L'Affaire Dreyfus* (1994; *The Dreyfus Affair*, 1996) set the event in its social context. Michael Burns' *Rural Society and French Politics* (1984) revealed the lack of impact of the Dreyfus affair on rural communities. Burns' book also dealt with the phenomenon of Boulangism and how the Third Republic responded to the perceived internal threat of the authoritarian general.

The Dreyfus affair had rocked the stability of the Republic by calling into question authority, tradition, and past glories. In this context, Charles Maurras (1868–1942) tried to create a coherent alternative to individual liberties, based on the values of royalism, while others, such as Count Gobineau (1816–82),articulated a racist and nationalistic discourse designed to remove the influence of the Declaration of the Rights of Man. Both condemned the idea of a general will and stood firmly against the concept of society being the result of a free association among equals. Historians have argued that the Third Republic countered such attacks by articulating a program of nation building. The education policies of the 1880s were particularly significant in this respect: compulsory free primary schools delivered a structured curriculum designed to present a unified perception of the country, around the principles of 1789. Teaching was delivered in French,which played a role in the unifying process towards the creation of a modern nation. Donald N. Baker and Patrick J. Harrigan's edited collection *The Making of Frenchmen* (1980) contains a variety of perspectives on the system. However, Eugen Weber's *Peasants into Frenchmen* (1976) argued that it was not until World War I that backward peasants became Frenchmen. Not surprisingly, this thesis has been challenged. Both Peter McPhee's *A Social History of France* (1992) and Vivien Gruder's "Can We Hear the Voices of Peasants?" (1993) have reviewed the evidence and concluded that French was used as a common language for trade and exchange at local levels as early as the 18th century. With the establishment of primary schools, peasants had been recast as Frenchmen long before World War I. Further pioneering studies have investigated the discourse chosen by the Republic to create consensus in the nation. In particular, Maurice Agulhon's *Marianne au combat* (1979; *Marianne into Battle*, 1981) analyzed the transformation of the national symbol. Jean-Marie Mayeur and Madeleine Rebérioux's *Les Débuts de la Troisième République, 1871–1898* (1973; *The Third Republic from Its Origins to the Great War*, 1984) provides a good survey of this crucial period for the Third Republic.

The Republic was also preoccupied with its own legitimacy and survival, which would play a fateful role as World War I approached. Its international vision was considerably hampered by the defeat of 1870 and the isolation that followed. Jules Ferry (1832–93) and his successors as premier tackled the situation by advocating colonial development which led to rivalry with Great Britain, exemplified by the Fashoda incident in the Sudan of 1899. Henri Brunschwig's *Mythes et réalités de l'impérialisme colonial français, 1871–1914* (1960; *French Colonialism, 1871–1914*, 1964) argued that France's imperial adventures were to some extent not economically motivated, but served to divert public attention from the debacle of the Franco–Prussian War. The progressive build-up of an alliance system in the early 1900s led to agreements with Russia and Britain, but none of these had any military dimension. All the same these contributed to the increase of international tensions in the years preceding 1914. The responsibility of France in the debate about the origins of World War I has been hotly debated, with some historians arguing that France's desire to regain Alsace-Lorraine was paramount in fostering an aggressive policy on the part of the Republic. John F.V. Keiger's *France and the Origins of the First World War* (1983) suggested that diplomats had little room for maneuver in trying to avoid the war. Jean-Jacques Becker's two works, *1914* (1977) and *Les Français dans la Grand Guerre* (1980; *The Great War and the French People*, 1986) explored the ways in which the French people were drawn into the war and their later response to the devastation it created. What is certain is that the consequences of the war on France were catastrophic. Economically and demographically, the losses were immense and victory was hollow. This view led to the presentation of the war as a watershed in French history. The development of cultural history has added to the war's portrayal as the dividing line between the "traditional" prewar and the "modern" postwar periods. Jay Winter's *Sites of Memory, Sites of Mourning* (1995) contradicts this thesis. Winter sees an important intersection between the "old" and the "new," and refuses to accept a teleological approach that would neatly divide "precursors" and "exponents" of modernism.

The interwar period led to a renewal of the old confrontation between revolutionary and counter-revolutionary forces in a new international context that opposed democracy to fascism and bolshevism. Like other European states, France was struggling to maintain some sort of balance in the aftermath of World War I and the global economic instability of the period. Philippe Bernard's *La Fin d'un monde* (1975) and Henri Dubief's *Le Déclin de la Troisième République* (1976; combined in *The Decline of the Third Republic*, 1985), traced the developments of the period. The experiment of the "Front Populaire" reaffirmed the revolutionary heritage of 1789 and took some inspiration from the social program of 1793. Julian Jackson's *The Popular Front in France* (1988) is a good introduction to the movement. The Popular Front returned to the 1848 idea of a limitation of the working week, further introducing two weeks paid holiday. Thus was born one of the key reference points for the French left in the 20th century. French communism's roots were explored in Robert Wohl's *French Communism in the Making* (1966). The right has been examined as well, in Eugen Weber's *Action Française* (1962), William Irvine's *French Conservatism in Crisis* (1979), and Malcolm Anderson's *Conservative Politics in France* (1974).

However, the revolutionary continuity between 1789, 1848, and 1936 was interrupted by World War II and the Vichy regime of Marshal Petain. The Vichy regime had its own internal logic and agenda. It perceived Nazi occupation as a unique opportunity to defeat French revolutionary traditions. Maurras' "divine surprise" was meant to erase 150 years of history in order to renew it with monarchical tradition and clerical influence. This ignored external realities and exemplified the inward looking attitudes that were dominant in some circles of French society.

The level of collaboration of the Vichy state with the Nazi war machine started to be discussed openly only in the 1960s. Robert Paxton's *Vichy France* (1972) opened the floodgates. His joint effort with Michael Marrus, *Vichy France and the Jews* (1981), pushed the investigation further; they demonstrated that the Vichy government had pre-empted German demands, particularly in regard to anti-Jewish legislation. The debate remains open, fluctuating from outright condemnation to a more nuanced view.

The issue is further complicated by the powerful myth created by de Gaulle on his return to France in 1944. In order to legitimize his own position, he argued that the Vichy state was not the French state that had existed before 1939 and was reborn in 1944. He presented himself as the savior of his people, stressed the importance of the Resistance, and proceeded to ignore what had actually happened in France during five years of occupation. The silence imposed by a portrait of glorious regeneration explains the recent renewal of interest in the war years, now that de Gaulle's influence is fading. It has also led to a deconstruction of the myth created by de Gaulle regarding the Vichy regime and the Resistance movements. Of the studies of the Resistance, H.R. Kedward's *Resistance in Vichy* (1978) is particularly important.

The world that emerged after 1945 owed little to the world before 1939. In France, World War II represents another watershed. Nevertheless, debates concerning the nature of the political system, the ideals of social equality, and the solutions given to economic problems ensured that ties with various traditions emerged again. Politically, the Fourth Republic retained some of the characteristics of the Third Republic. In this respect, Jean Lacouture has shown that de Gaulle failed to impose his vision of a powerful head of state, standing above party politics in the Napoleonic tradition. The regime was renewed with the traditional separation of powers, a lower and upper house, and a president of the Republic with no power. For the first time, women were given the vote. A good account of this is in Andrew Shennan's *Rethinking France* (1989). The Fourth Republic also ushered in radical economic and social change. Agriculture and industry were transformed while the population started to expand again. Some historians have likened these developments to an industrial revolution. The process of recovery benefited from the Marshall Plan. It was also conceived as a process of cooperation with other European states, first West Germany with the Coal and Steel agreement, and as such presaged the signing of the Treaty of Rome in 1957. Recovery was implemented through high levels of state intervention, including the nationalization of key industries – coal, railways, electricity – and economic planning. As M.C. Cleary has suggested, agriculture was transformed beyond recognition into an efficient and profitable sector of the economy, combining high levels of productivity in the northern plains with specialized types of production in other areas. This was helped by the process of *remembrement* (regrouping of land) designed to eliminate inefficient peasant smallholdings. Some of them still remain but agriculture today employs less than 10 per cent of the active population of the country. Despite all these changes, the Fourth Republic was short-lived and troubled as shown in Philip Williams' *Crisis and Compromise* (1964) and Jean-Pierre Rioux's *La France de la IVe République* (1980; *The Fourth Republic*, 1987).

The economic successes and the social achievements (a health service and welfare system) of the Fourth Republic have often been often contrasted with its political failures. It was unable to produce majorities in parliament due to the multiplicity of political parties, and this led to numerous parliamentary crises and to a succession of governments unable to take or enforce decisions. Perhaps more crucially, the regime also failed to work out the colonial issues that had followed European decline on the world stage after 1945. Although Pierre Mendès France did resolve the Indochina conflict at Geneva in 1954, the Fourth Republic then became embroiled in nationalist uprisings in North Africa. In particular, it sent troops to Algeria, where it took eight years to reach peace and disengagement. As John Talbott described in *The War Without a Name* (1980), by 1958 the Republic had collapsed under the threat of a military coup in Algiers. This gave de Gaulle his second chance at power. Brought to defend "Algerie Française," he finally concluded peace with the representatives of the FNL (Forces Nationales de Liberation) in Evian in 1962, granting independence to Algeria. As Robert Aldrich and John Connell's *France's Overseas Frontier* (1992) demonstrated, this opened up a period of neocolonialism, best represented by the appearance of French troops in Chad and other former French colonies in black Africa.

After 1958, the Fifth Republic renewed the links between democratic politics and authoritarianism in French political life. It created a presidential regime whose attractions were the Gaullist myths of "legitimacy" and "grandeur." This dealt with the consequences of the 1940 defeat and the dark years of occupation and collaboration. De Gaulle presided over a period of remarkable economic development in the very favorable world economic context of the 1960s, fostered by the establishment of the EEC. The eleven years of Gaullist rule were otherwise dominated by nationalistic outbursts, which ranged from support for an independent Quebec to more ambitious moves to proclaim France's independence in world affairs. France cooperated with Soviet Russia, recognized China, and supported the emerging Third World. All three policies were designed to challenge the authority of the United States. This was combined with obstinate positions in most European negotiations within the EEC, in the name of the French national interest. De Gaulle's European policy was based on Franco–German cooperation, which dominated the early years of the EEC. Its economic results were reinforced by political will, closer cultural ties, and unique military cooperation, which have been surveyed in the many editions of Jacques Chapsal's *La Vie politique sous la Cinquième République* (Political Life under the Fifth Republic, 1990). Under de Gaulle, France quit NATO and developed its own nuclear deterrent. Economic success and political posturing did not prevent de Gaulle from facing an increasingly active opposition. The presidential elections of 1965 had brought together the various formations of the left and center left (old left-wing parties and small radical clubs) in an effort to establish a possible alternative to the rule of the Right. The effort fell short, but the 1965 elections marked the start of François Mitterand's challenge. Gains at the legislative elections of 1967 brought the coalition of the Left in sight of gaining a majority in parliament, but May 1968 delayed any further achievements. It renewed the tradition of rank and file politics on the streets, only to guarantee a huge right-wing majority at the hastily organized elections of June 1968. In the end the reconstituted Socialist party under Mitterand's leadership had to wait another thirteen years to win both the presidential and the legislative elections in 1981. A good introduction to the events of the 1960s is Bernard E. Brown's *Protest in Paris* (1974), while Adrien Dansette's *Mai 1968* (1971) and Hervé Hamon and Patrick Rotman's *Génération* (1987–88) focus more directly on the period of crisis.

Alternation in power within a somewhat presidential constitution was finally achieved 200 years after the French Revolution had heralded the practice of modern democratic politics. The practice of rotation in power between left and right, reinforced by the sharing of power between a right-wing president and a left-wing prime minister or vice-versa, has been portrayed by François Furet in *La République du centre* (1988) as symbolizing an end to civil strife in France. According to him, France is now a mature democracy that has left behind the divisions of the past. This is echoed in the collection of essays edited by George Ross, Stanley Hoffmann, and Sylvia Malzacher, *The Mitterand Experiment* (1987). Yet direct democracy appealed to students and workers in 1968 and direct action retains its attraction for various social groups who may feel frustrated in an economic downturn. Consensus politics may still hide deep-seated differences, witnessed by the rise of Jean-Marie Le Pen's National Front, which is treated

in Nonna Mayer and Pascal Perrineau's collection, *Le Front National à découvert* (Uncovering the National Front, 1989). Only the next century will prove whether the complex and sometimes contradictory ideas of the French Revolution have finally been digested by the French people.

MARTINE BONDOIS MORRIS

See also Cobban; Geyl; Lefebvre; Marrus; Napoleonic Wars; Ozouf; Weber, E.; World War I; Zeldin

Further Reading

Agulhon, Maurice, *La République au village: les populations du Var de la Révolution à la Seconde République*, Paris: Plon, 1970; in English as *The Republic in the Village: The People of the Var from the French Revolution to the Second Republic*, Cambridge and New York: Cambridge University Press, 1982

Agulhon, Maurice, *1848, ou, l'apprentissage de la République, 1848–1852*, Paris: Seuil, 1973; in English as *The Republican Experiment, 1848–1852*, Cambridge and New York: Cambridge University Press, 1983

Agulhon, Maurice, *Marianne au combat: l'imagerie et la symbolique républicaines de 1789 à 1880*, Paris: Flammarion, 1979; in English as *Marianne into Battle: Republican Imagery and Symbolism in France, 1789–1880*, Cambridge and New York: Cambridge University Press, 1981

Agulhon, Maurice, *La République*, 2 vols., Paris: Hachette, 1990; in English as *The French Republic, 1879–1992*, Oxford: Blackwell, 1993

Aldrich, Robert, and John Connell, *France's Overseas Frontier: Départements et Territoires d'Outre-Mer*, Cambridge and New York: Cambridge University Press, 1992

Aminzade, Ronald, *Ballots and Barricades: Class Formation and Republican Politics in France, 1830–1871*, Princeton: Princeton University Press, 1993

Amman, Peter H., *Revolution and Mass Democracy: The Paris Club Movement in 1848*, Princeton: Princeton University Press, 1975

Anderson, Malcolm, *Conservative Politics in France*, London: Allen and Unwin, 1974

Anderson, Robert David, *Education in France, 1848–1870*, Oxford: Oxford University Press, 1975

Anderson, Robert David, *France, 1870–1914: Politics and Society*, London and Boston: Routledge, 1977

Baker, Donald N., and Patrick J. Harrigan, eds., *The Making of Frenchmen: Current Directions in the History of Education in France, 1679–1979*, Waterloo, Ontario: Historical Reflections Press, 1980

Becker, Jean Jacques, and Stéphane Audoin-Rouzeau, eds., *1914: comment les Français sont entrés dans la guerre: contribution à l'étude de l'opinion publique printemps-été 1914* (1914, or Why the French Entered the War: Contributions to the Study of Public Opinion in the Spring and Summer of 1914), Paris: Presses de la Fondation Nationale des Sciences Politiques, 1977

Becker, Jean Jacques, *Les Français dans la Grande Guerre*, Paris: Laffont, 1980; in English as *The Great War and the French People*, Leamington Spa: Berg, and New York: St. Martin's Press, 1986

Berenson, Edward, *Populist Religion and Left-Wing Politics in France, 1830–1852*, Princeton: Princeton University Press, 1984

Bergeron, Louis, *L'Episode napoléonien, 1799–1815*, 2 vols., Paris: Seuil, 1972; in English as *France under Napoleon*, Princeton: Princeton University Press, 1981

Bernard, Philippe, *La Fin d'un monde*, Paris: Seuil, 1975; in English as *The Decline of the Third Republic, 1914–38*, New York and Cambridge: Cambridge University Press, 1980

Bertier de Sauvigny, Guillaume de, *La Restauration*, Paris: Flammarion, 1955; in English as *The Bourbon Restoration*, Philadelphia: University of Pennsylvania Press, 1967

Best, Geoffrey, ed., *The Permanent Revolution: The French Revolution and Its Legacy, 1789–1989*, London: Fontana, 1988; Chicago: University of Chicago Press, 1989

Bezucha, Robert J., *The Lyon Uprising of 1834: Social and Political Conflict in the Early July Monarchy*, Cambridge, MA: Harvard University Press, 1974

Bredin, Jean-Denis, *L'Affaire*, Paris: Julliard, 1983; in English as *The Affair: The Case of Alfred Dreyfus*, New York: Braziller, 1986, London: Sidgwick and Jackson, 1987

Brogan, Denis William, *The Development of Modern France, 1870–1939*, London: Hamish Hamilton, 1940; in US as *France under the Republic: The Development of Modern France, 1870–1939*, New York: Harper, 1940, revised 1967

Brogan, Denis William, *The French Nation from Napoleon to Petain*, London: Hamish Hamilton, and New York: Harper, 1957

Brown, Bernard E., *Protest in Paris: Anatomy of a Revolt*, Morristown, NJ: General Learning Press, 1974

Brunschwig, Henri, *Mythes et réalités de l'impérialisme colonial français, 1871-1914*, Paris: Colin, 1960; in English as *French Colonialism, 1871-1914: Myths and Realities*, New York: Praeger, 1964, revised London: Pall Mall Press, 1966

Burns, Michael, *Rural Society and French Politics: Boulangism and the Dreyfus Affair, 1886–1900*, Princeton: Princeton University Press, 1984

Bury, John Patrick Tuer, *Gambetta and the National Defence: A Republican Dictatorship in France*, London and New York: Longman, 1936

Bury, John Patrick Tuer, *France, 1814–1940*, Philadelphia: University of Pennsylvania Press, and London: Methuen, 1949; revised 1969

Bury, John Patrick Tuer, *Napoléon III and the Second Empire*, London: English University Press, 1964; New York: Harper, 1968

Bury, John Patrick Tuer, and Robert Tombs, *Thiers, 1797–1877: A Political Life*, London and Boston: Allen and Unwin, 1986

Cahm, Eric, *L'Affaire Dreyfus: histoire, politique et société*, Paris: Livre de Poche, 1994; in English as *The Dreyfus Affair in French Society and Politics*, London and New York: Longman, 1996

Campbell, Peter, *French Electoral Systems and Elections, 1789-1957*, New York: Praeger, and London: Faber, 1958

Campbell, Stuart L., *The Second Empire Revisited: A Study in French Historiography*, New Brunswick, NJ: Rutgers University Press, 1978

Caron, François, *Histoire économique de la France, XIXe-XXe siècles*, Paris: Colin, 1981; in English as *An Economic History of Modern France*, New York: Columbia University Press, 1979

Chapsal, Jacques, *La Vie politique sous la Cinquième République* (Political Life under the Fifth Republic), 2 vols., 5th ed., Paris: Presses Universitaires de France, 1990

Charle, Christophe, *Histoire sociale de la France au XIXe siècle*, Paris: Seuil, 1991; in English as *A Social History of France in the Nineteenth Century*, Oxford: Berg, 1994

Charlton, Donald Geoffrey, *Secular Religions in France, 1815–1870*, London and New York: Oxford University Press, 1963

Chevalier, Louis, *Classes laborieuses et classes dangereuses à Paris pendant la première moitié du XIXe siècle*, Paris: Plon, 1958; in English as *Laboring Classes and Dangerous Classes in Paris during the First Half of the Nineteenth Century*, Princeton: Princeton University Press, and London: Routledge, 1973

Cleary, M.C., *Peasants, Politicians and Producers: The Organisation of Agriculture in France since 1918*, Cambridge and New York: Cambridge University Press, 1989

Clout, Hugh D., *Agriculture in France on the Eve of the Railway Age*, London: Croom Helm, and Totowa, NJ: Barnes and Noble, 1979

Cobban, Alfred, *A History of Modern France*, 2 vols., Harmondsworth: Penguin, 1957–61; revised edition, 3 vols., London: Cape, 1962–65, New York: Braziller, 1965

Collingham, H.A.C., *The July Monarchy: A Political History of France, 1830–1848*, London and New York: Longman, 1988

Corbin, Alain, *Les Filles de noce: misère sexuelle et prostitution: 19e et 20e siècles*, Paris: Aubier Montaigne, 1978; in English as

Women for Hire: Prostitution and Sexuality in France after 1850, Cambridge, MA: Harvard University Press, 1990

Corbin, Alain, *Le Village des cannibales*, Paris: Aubier, 1990; in English as *The Village of the Cannibals: Rage and Murder in France, 1870*, Cambridge, MA: Harvard University Press, and Cambridge: Polity Press, 1992

Crafts, N.F.R, "Economic Growth in France and Britain, 1830-1910: A Review of the Evidence," *Journal of Economic History* 44 (1984), 49–67

Cronin, Vincent, *Napoleon*, London: Collins, 1971; in US as *Napoleon Bonaparte: An Intimate Biography*, New York: Morrow, 1972

Crossley, Ceri, *French Historians and Romanticism: Thierry, Guizot, the Saint-Simonians, Quinet, Michelet*, London and New York: Routledge, 1993

Dansette, Adrien, *Histoire religieuse de la France contemporaine*, 2 vols., Paris: Flammarion, 1948–51; revised 1965; in English as *A Religious History of Modern France*, 2 vols., Edinburgh: Nelson, and Freiburg and New York: Herder, 1961

Dansette, Adrien, *Mai 1968*, Paris: Plon, 1971

Dedman, Martin, *The Origins and the Development of the European Union, 1945–1995: A History of European Integration*, London and New York: Routledge, 1996

De Luna, Frederick A., *The French Republic under Cavaignac, 1848*, Princeton: Princeton University Press, 1969

Devlin, Judith, *The Superstitious Mind: French Peasants and the Supernatural in the Nineteenth Century*, New Haven: Yale University Press, 1987

Dubief, Henri, *Le Déclin de la Troisième République*, Paris: Seuil, 1976; in English as *The Decline of the Third Republic, 1914–1938*, New York and Cambridge: Cambridge University Press, 1985

Duveau, Georges, *1848*, Paris: Gallimard, 1965; in English as *1848: The Making of a Revolution*, London: Routledge, and New York: Pantheon, 1967

Edwards, Stewart, *The Paris Commune, 1871*, London: Eyre and Spottiswoode, 1971; Chicago: Quadrangle, 1973

Fehér, Ferenc, ed., *The French Revolution and the Birth of Modernity*, Berkeley: University of California Press, 1990

Furet, François, and Denis Richet, *La Révolution*, 2 vols., Paris: Hachette, 1965–66, as *La Révolution française*, Paris: Fayard, 1973; in English as *French Revolution*, London: Weidenfeld and Nicolson, and New York: Macmillan, 1970, and as *Revolutionary France, 1770–1880*, Oxford: Blackwell, 1992

Furet, François, and Jacques Ozouf, *Lire et écrire: l'alphabétisation des Français de Calvin à Jules Ferry*, 2 vols., Paris: Minuit, 1977; in English as *Reading and Writing: Literacy in France from Calvin to Jules Ferry*, Cambridge and New York: Cambridge University Press, 1982

Furet, François, and Mona Ozouf, eds., *Dictionnaire critique de la Révolution française*, Paris: Flammarion, 1988; in English as *A Critical Dictionary of the French Revolution*, Cambridge, MA: Harvard University Press, 1989

Furet, François, *La République du centre: la fin de l'exception française*, Paris: Calmann Lévy, 1988

Geyl, Pieter, *Napoleon: voor en tegen in de Franse geschiedschrijving*, Utrecht: Oosthoek, 1946; in English as *Napoleon: For and Against*, London: Cape, and New Haven: Yale University Press, 1949

Gibson, Ralph, *A Social History of French Catholicism, 1789–1914*, London and New York: Routledge, 1989

Gildea, Robert, *The Past in French History*, New Haven: Yale University Press, 1994

Girard, Louis, *Le Libéralisme en France de 1814 à 1848: doctrine et mouvement* (Liberalism in France, 1814–1848: Doctrine and Movement), 3 vols., Paris: Centre de Documentation Universitaire, 1967

Goldberg, Harvey, *The Life of Jean Jaurès*, Madison: University of Wisconsin Press, 1962

Gruder, Vivien, "Can We Hear the Voices of Peasants?," *History of European Ideas* 17 (1993), 167–90

Hamon, Hervé, and Patrick Rotman, *Génération*, 2 vols., Paris: Seuil, 1987–88

Hanagan, Michael, *Nascent Proletarians: Class Formation in Post-Revolutionary France*, Oxford: Blackwell, 1989

Harris, Ruth, *Murders and Madness: Medicine, Law, and Society in the Fin de Siècle*, Oxford and New York: Oxford University Press, 1989

Hayward, Jack Ernest Shalom, *After the French Revolution: Six Critics of Democracy and Nationalism*, New York: New York University Press, and Hemel Hempstead: Harvester Wheatsheaf, 1991

Hemmings, Frederick William John, *Culture and Society in France, 1848–1898: Dissidents and Philistines*, London: Batsford, 1971; New York: Scribner, 1972

Higgs, David C., *Nobles in Nineteenth-Century France: The Practice of Inegalitarianism*, Baltimore: Johns Hopkins University Press, 1987

Horne, Alistair, *The Fall of Paris: The Siege and the Commune, 1870–71*, London: Macmillan, 1965; New York: St. Martin's Press, 1966

Hutton, Patrick H., *The Cult of the Revolutionary Tradition: The Blanquists in French Politics, 1864–1893*, Berkeley: University of California Press, 1981

Irvine, William D., *French Conservatism in Crisis: The Republican Federation of France in the 1930s*, Baton Rouge: Louisiana State University Press, 1979

Jackson, Julian, *The Popular Front in France: Defending Democracy, 1934–38*, Cambridge and New York: Cambridge University Press, 1988

Jardin, André, and André-Jean Tudesq, *La France des notables*, 2 vols., Paris: Seuil, 1973; in English as *Restoration and Reaction, 1815–1848*, Cambridge and New York: Cambridge University Press, 1983

Jardin, André, *Alexis de Tocqueville, 1805–59*, Paris: Hachette, 1984; in English as *Tocqueville: A Biography*, New York: Farrar Straus, and London: Halban, 1988

Kafker, Frank A., and James M. Laux, eds., *Napoleon and His Times: Selected Interpretations*, Malabar, FL: Krieger, 1989

Katznelson, Ira, and Aristide R. Zolberg, eds., *Working-Class Formation: Nineteenth-Century Patterns in Western Europe and the United States*, Princeton: Princeton University Press, 1986

Kedward, H.R., *Resistance in Vichy France: A Study of Ideas and Motivation in the Southern Zone, 1940–42*, Oxford and New York: Oxford University Press, 1978

Keiger, John F.V., *France and the Origins of the First World War*, London: Macmillan, and New York: St. Martin's Press, 1983

Kennan, George F., *The Fateful Alliance: France, Russia and the Coming of the First World War*, Manchester: Manchester University Press, and New York: Pantheon, 1984

Labrousse, Ernest, "Comment naissent les Révolutions?" (How are Revolutions Born?) in *Actes du Congrès historique du centenaire de la révolution de 1848*, Paris: Presses Universitaires de France, 1948

Labrousse, Ernest, ed., *Aspects de la crise et de la dépression de l'économie française au milieu du dix-neuvieme siècle, 1846–1851* (Aspects of the French Economic Crisis and Depression in the mid-19th Century), La Roche-sur-Yon: Imprimerie Centrale de l'Ouest, 1956

Lacouture, Jean, *De Gaulle*, 3 vols., Paris: Seuil, 1984–86; abridged in English as *De Gaulle*, 2 vols., London: Collins Harvill, and New York: Norton, 1990–92

Larkin, Maurice, *Church and State after the Dreyfus Affair: The Separation Issue in France*, New York: Barnes and Noble, and London: Macmillan, 1974

Lefebvre, Georges, *Napoléon*, Paris: Alcan, 1935, revised 1965; in English as *Napoleon*, 2 vols., New York: Columbia University Press, and London: Routledge, 1969

Lehning, James R., *Peasant and French: Cultural Contact in Rural France during the Nineteenth Century*, Cambridge and New York: Cambridge University Press, 1995

Lévy-Leboyer, Maurice, and François Bourguigon, *L'Economie française au XIXe siècle: analyse macro-économique*, Paris: Economica, 1985; in English as *The French Economy in the Nineteenth Century: An Essay in Econometric Analysis*, Cambridge: Cambridge University Press, 1990

Logue, William, *From Philosophy to Sociology: The Evolution of French Liberalism*, DeKalb: Northern Illinois University Press, 1983

Lyons, Martyn, *Napoleon Bonaparte and the Legacy of the French Revolution*, London: Macmillan, and New York: St. Martin's Press, 1994

McManners, John, *Church and State in France, 1870–1914*, New York: Harper, and London: SPCK, 1972

McMillan, James F., *Napoleon III*, London and New York: Longman, 1991

McPhee, Peter, *A Social History of France, 1780–1880*, London and New York: Routledge, 1992

Magraw, Roger, *France, 1815–1914: The Bourgeois Century*, London: Collins, 1983; New York: Oxford University Press, 1986

Magraw, Roger, *A History of the French Working Class*, 2 vols., Oxford: Blackwell, 1992

Margadant, Ted W., *French Peasants in Revolt: The Insurrection of 1851*, Princeton: Princeton University Press, 1979

Marrus, Michael R., and Robert O. Paxton, *Vichy France and the Jews*, New York: Basic Books, 1981

Mayer, Nonna, and Pascal Perrineau, eds., *Le Front National à découvert* (Uncovering the National Front), Presses de la Fondation Nationale des Sciences Politiques, 1989

Mayeur, Jean-Marie, and Madeleine Rebérioux, *Les Débuts de la Troisième République, 1871–1898*, Paris: Seuil, 1973; in English as *The Third Republic from Its Origins to the Great War*, Cambridge and New York: Cambridge University Press, 1984

Merriman, John M., *The Agony of the Republic: The Repression of the Left in Revolutionary France, 1848–1851*, New Haven: Yale University Press, 1978

Mitchell, Allan, *The German Influence in France after 1870: The Formation of the French Republic*, Chapel Hill: University of North Carolina Press, 1979

Nère, Jacques, *The Foreign Policy of France from 1914 to 1945*, London and Boston: Routledge, 1975

Nicolet, Claude, *L'Idée Républicaine en France, 1789–1924: essai d'histoire critique*, Paris: Gallimard, 1982

Noiriel, Gérard, *Les Ouvriers dans la société française, XIXe–XXe siècle*, Paris: Seuil, 1986; in English as *Workers in French Society in the Nineteenth and Twentieth Centuries*, New York: Berg, 1990

Nora, Pierre, ed., *Les Lieux de mémoire*, 3 vols., Paris: Gallimard, 1984–92; abridged in English as *Realms of Memory: Rethinking the French Past*, 2 vols., New York: Columbia University Press, 1996–97

Nord, Philip, *The Republican Moment: Struggles for Democracy in Nineteenth-Century France*, Cambridge, MA: Harvard University Press, 1995

O'Brien, Patrick, and Caglar Keyder, *Economic Growth in Britain and France, 1780–1914: Two Paths to the Twentieth Century*, London and Boston: Allen and Unwin, 1978

Palmade, Guy, *Capitalisme et capitalistes français au XIXe siècle*, Paris: Colin, 1961; in English as *French Capitalism in the Nineteenth Century*, New York: Barnes and Noble, and Newton Abbot, Devon: David and Charles, 1972

Paxton, Robert O., *Vichy France: Old Guard and New Order, 1940–44*, New York: Knopf, and London: Barrie and Jenkins, 1972

Perrot, Michelle, *Les Ouvriers en grève: France, 1871–1890*, The Hague: Mouton, 1974; abridged in English as *Workers on Strike: France, 1871–1890*, New Haven: Yale University Press, 1987

Pilbeam, Pamela M., *The Middle Classes in Europe, 1789–1914: France, Germany, Italy, and Russia*, Basingstoke: Macmillan, and Chicago: Lyceum, 1990

Pilbeam, Pamela M., *Republicanism in Nineteenth-Century France, 1814–1871*, New York: St. Martin's Press, 1995

Pinkney, David H., *Decisive Years in France, 1840–1847*, Princeton: Princeton University Press, 1986

Plessis, Alain, *De la fête impériale au mur des fédérés, 1852–1870*, Paris: Seuil, 1973; in English as *The Rise and Fall of the Second Empire, 1852–1872*, Cambridge and New York: Cambridge University Press, 1985

Poidevin, Raymond, and Jacques Bariéty, *Les Relations franco–allemandes, 1815–1975* (Franco–German Relations, 1815–1975), Paris: Colin, 1977

Price, Roger, *The French Second Republic: A Social History*, Ithaca, NY: Cornell University Press, and London: Batsford, 1972

Price, Roger, ed., *Revolution and Reaction: 1848 and the Second French Republic*, London: Croom Helm, and New York: Barnes and Noble, 1975

Price, Roger, *The Modernization of Rural France: Communications Networks and Agricultural Market Structures in Nineteenth-Century France*, London: Hutchinson, and New York: St. Martin's Press, 1983

Price, Roger, *A Social History of Nineteenth Century France*, London: Hutchinson, and New York: Holmes and Meier, 1987

Rémond, René, *Le Droite en France de 1815 à nos jours: continuité et diversité d'une tradition politique*, Paris: Aubier, 1954; in English as *The Right Wing in France from 1815 to de Gaulle*, Philadelphia: University of Pennsylvania Press, 1969

Rendall, Jane, *The Origins of Modern Feminism: Women in Britain, France, and the United States, 1780–1860*, New York: Schocken, 1984; London: Macmillan, 1985

Reynolds, Siân, ed., *Women, State and Revolution: Essays in Power and Gender in Europe since 1789*, Brighton: Wheatsheaf, 1986; Amherst, University of Massachusetts Press, 1987

Rioux, Jean-Pierre, *La France de la IVe République*, Paris: Seuil, 1980; in English as *The Fourth Republic, 1944–1958*, Cambridge and New York: Cambridge University Press, 1987

Rosanvallon, Pierre, *Le Moment Guizot*, Paris: Gallimard, 1985

Rosanvallon, Pierre, *Le Sacre du citoyen: histoire du suffrage universel en France*, Paris: Gallimard, 1992

Ross, George, Stanley Hoffmann, and Sylvia Malzacher, eds., *The Mitterand Experiment: Continuity and Change in Modern France*, New York: Oxford University Press, and Cambridge: Polity Press, 1987

Sauvy, Alfred, *Histoire économique de la France entre les deux guerres* (French Economic History between the Wars), 4 vols., Paris: Fayard, 1965–75

Sewell, William H., Jr., *Work and Revolution in France: The Language of Labor from the Old Regime to 1848*, Cambridge and New York: Cambridge University Press, 1988

Shennan, Andrew, *Rethinking France: Plans for Renewal, 1940–1946*, Oxford and New York: Oxford University Press, 1989

Shorter, Edward, and Charles Tilly, *Strikes in France, 1830–1968*, Cambridge and New York: Cambridge University Press, 1974

Sirinelli, Jean François, and Pascal Ory, *Les Intellectuels en France: de l'affaire Dreyfus à nos jours*, Paris: Colin, 1986

Stone, Judith F., *The Search for Social Peace: Reform Legislation in France, 1890–1914*, Albany: State University of New York Press, 1985

Sutton, Michael, *Nationalism, Positivism and Catholicism: The Politics of Charles Maurras and French Catholics, 1890–1914*, Cambridge and New York: Cambridge University Press, 1982

Talbott, John E., *The War Without a Name: France in Algeria, 1954–62*, New York: Knopf, 1980; London: Faber, 1981

Tombs, Robert, *France, 1814–1914*, London and New York: Longman, 1996

Trebilcock, Clive, *The Industrialization of the Continental Powers, 1780–1914*, London and New York: Longman, 1981

Weber, Eugen, *Action Française: Royalism and Reaction in Twentieth-Century France*, Stanford, CA: Stanford University Press, 1962

Weber, Eugen, *Peasants into Frenchmen: The Modernization of Rural France, 1870–1914*, Stanford, CA: Stanford University Press, and London: Chatto and Windus, 1976

Welch, Cheryl, *Liberty and Utility: The French Idéologues and the Transformation of Liberalism*, New York: Columbia University Press, 1984

Williams, Philip M., *Crisis and Compromise: Politics in the Fourth Republic*, 3rd edition, London: Longman, and Hamden, CT: Archon, 1964 [originally published as *Politics in Post-war France*, 1955]

Winter, Jay, *Sites of Memory, Sites of Mourning: The Great War in European Cultural History*, Cambridge and New York: Cambridge University Press, 1995

Wohl, Robert, *French Communism in the Making, 1914–1924*, Stanford, CA: Stanford University Press, 1966

Wright, Gordon, *France in Modern Times*, 5th edition, New York: Norton, 1995

Zeldin, Theodore, *France, 1848–1945*, 2 vols., Oxford and New York: Oxford University Press, 1973–77, revised in 5 vols., 1979–81; as *A History of French Passions*, 2 vols., 1993

Franklin, John Hope 1915–

US historian of American South

There are those who would characterize John Hope Franklin as a black historian, but he would deny this. Throughout his life he maintained that he is a historian of the South. In both subject matter and within the profession he has been an integrationist. "He has," in the words of historians August Meier and Elliott Rudwick, "constantly striven to make black history not a Jim Crow specialty, but an integral part of the fabric of American history-writing." In the same vein, he sought to bring blacks into the mainstream of the history profession. Neither process, however, has been without isolation, alienation, and racism. Franklin has condemned these negatives and noted that one response to these conditions would be for black scholars to isolate themselves from a world that isolates them. But as Franklin noted in *Race and History* (1989), he believes "that the proper choice for the American Negro scholar is to use his knowledge and ingenuity, his resources and talents, to combat the forces that isolate him and his people and, like the true patriot that he is, to contribute to the solution of the problems that all Americans face in common."

Franklin's seminal work, *From Slavery to Freedom*, was first published in 1947 and revised and reprinted into the 1990s. It was this exhaustive scholarly assessment of the Negro experience that gained Franklin international recognition and earned him praise from both black and white historians. Franklin was part of a new wave in black historiography that shifted emphasis from prominent black individuals to the experience of the black masses. Franklin took this new approach further and was successful in his "conscious effort to write the history of the Negro in America with due regard for the forces at work which have affected his development. This has involved a continuous recognition of the main stream of American history and the relationship of the Negro to it. . . . It would have been impossible to trace the history of the Negro in America without remaining sensitive to the main currents in the emergence of American civilization."

Brought up in the segregated South, Franklin noted that his developing years were fundamentally grounded in race and poverty. But they were also molded by supportive, learned, and instructive parents, neither of whom would "voluntarily accept segregation." According to Franklin, his post-secondary educational experiences at Fisk University – a black university with a biracial faculty – and Harvard were relatively free of racism. The same could not be said, however, of the historical associations of which he became a member. Until the 1960s, Franklin faced discrimination and racism within such organizations as the Mississippi Valley Historical Association, the American Historical Association, and the Southern Historical Association. Supporters and advocates such as C. Vann Woodward and Kenneth Stampp notwithstanding, it was not until the 1960s that most of the barriers, and indignities, were eradicated.

According to Meier and Rudwick, their extensive interviews of black and white historians of the South and of black history reveal a greater influence of "value considerations and social purpose than most other historical specialties." Certainly Franklin found this to be the case. While he sought to place the experience of the Negro in the continuum of mainstream American history, he maintains that "I could not have avoided being a social activist even if I had wanted to." Thus, concurrent with his scholarship was his advocacy of black civil rights. In 1961 he took the opportunity to challenge and disprove the negative assessments of Reconstruction, and in 1976 he condemned American society for its failure to deliver on the postwar promise of an end to racism against blacks. In his presidential address to the American Historical Association in 1980, he noted the racist remarks that remain in a well-known college textbook, and lamented the author's lack of "commitment to sobriety and accuracy." And yet, at the same time and throughout his career, Franklin adamantly asserted the need for history that was free of polemics. Black pride and personal commitment to black civil rights should not turn black history into a soapbox at the expense of accuracy. "It is important to make certain that zeal for revision does not become a substitute for truth and accuracy and does not result in the production of works that are closer to political tracts than to histories."

Franklin assessed his own commitment to the field of history in his 1988 lecture A Life of Learning. There were three goals he had set out to attain. First, in pursuing different components of southern history, he sought to "write a monograph, a general work, a biography, a period piece, and edit some primary source and some work or works, perhaps by other authors, to promote an understanding of the field." By the time of this lecture, he had completed them all. Second, he decided "to explore new areas or fields, whenever possible, in order to maintain a lively, fresh approach to the teaching and writing of history." And finally, he pledged his time and energy to professional associations and journals, both in the United States and abroad. Franklin was once called the "dean of today's Negro historians"; this 1968 tribute might be dated, but Franklin's teaching, scholarship, and professional service contributions to the field of history – as a southerner, a black man, and, most importantly as a historian – cannot be denied.

ELIZABETH B. ELLIOT-MEISEL

See also African American; Litwack; United States: 19th Century

Biography

Born Rentiesville, Oklahoma, 2 January 1915. Received BA, Fisk University, 1935; MA, Harvard University, 1936, PhD 1941. Taught at Fisk University 1936–37; St. Augustine's College, 1939–43; North Carolina College, 1943–47; Howard University, 1947–56; Brooklyn College, 1956–64; University of Chicago, 1964–82; and Duke University, 1982–85 (emeritus). Married Aurelia E. Whittington, 1940 (1 son).

Principal Writings

The Free Negro in North Carolina, 1790–1860, 1943
"The Enslavement of Free Negroes in North Carolina," Journal of Negro History 29 (1944), 401–28
From Slavery to Freedom: A History of American Negroes, 1947; 7th edition, with Alfred A. Moss, Jr., as From Slavery to Freedom: A History of African Americans, 1994
The Militant South, 1800–1861, 1956
Reconstruction: After the Civil War, 1961
The Emancipation Proclamation, 1963
Racial Equality in America, 1976
A Southern Odyssey: Travellers in the Antebellum North, 1976
"A Mirror for Americans: A Century of Reconstruction History," American Historical Review (1980), 1–14
George Washington Williams: A Biography, 1985
A Life of Learning, 1988
Race and History: Selected Essays, 1938–1988, 1989
The Color Line: Legacy for the Twenty-First Century, 1993

Further Reading

Anderson, Eric, and Alfred A. Moss, Jr., eds., The Facts of Reconstruction: Essays in Honor of John Hope Franklin, Baton Rouge: Louisiana State University Press, 1991
Hine, Darlene Clark, ed., The State of Afro-American History: Past, Present, Future, Baton Rouge: Louisiana State University Press, 1986
Holton, F., "John Hope Franklin, Scholar," University of Chicago Magazine 73 (September 1980), 14–18
Meier, August, and Elliott M. Rudwick, Black History and the Historical Profession, 1915–1980, Urbana: University of Illinois Press, 1986

Frégault, Guy 1918–1977
French Canadian historian

After World War II, two new schools of French Canadian historiography emerged. The first, centered on l'Université de Laval, conceived of the history of New France in the tradition of the Annalistes. The second, based at l'Université de Montréal, worked in the positivist tradition and practiced the histoire événementielle so deplored by the Annalistes. Among the young historians at Montreal was Guy Frégault.

A student of Lionel Groulx and the Jesuit historian Jean Delanglez, who converted him to positivism at Loyola University in Chicago, Frégault was slow to adopt the neo-nationalist approach that Maurice Séguin had pioneered. By the late 1940s, Séguin and other neo-nationalists at Montréal had embarked upon a revision of the traditional view that French Canada had always been a pastoral society, maintaining instead that the Canadiens were commercial and entrepreneurial by nature. According to the neo-nationalist interpretation, they were driven onto the land only by the devastating consequences of the conquest of French Canada by the British in 1759.

Although he would later become one of the strongest proponents of this view, Frégault's early work remained firmly within the Groulx framework. His 1948 biography of François Bigot, French Canada's last *intendant*, was a solid if standard tale of corruption and debasement in the French society of Louis XIV. The *intendant* was portrayed as one of a small coterie of government suppliers and contractors determined to take advantage of the Seven Years' War for its own profit. This view was later criticized for being too hard on a man who was the product of a corrupt and inefficient system rather than its creator. Frégault himself may have come to rue his characterization of the *intendant*; according to Yves Zoltvany, Frégault might have written a very different biography had he done so as a full-fledged neo-nationalist historian.

In 1954, Frégault publicly signalled his conversion to the neo-nationalist school. In *Canadian Society in the French Regime*, he argued that historians had interpreted French Canada by reading history backwards; they had described the nature of the society after the conquest, and then superimposed those same characteristics onto the period before 1763. By doing this, they arrived at the mistaken conclusion that French Canadians had always been children of the soil. Not so, maintained Frégault, and he described a society that was driven by trade and commerce in which businessmen played the dominant social role. That society, however, could not survive without the support of the metropolis. When New France was cut off from France, its demise was ensured.

This is precisely the process that Frégault detailed the following year in *La guerre de la conquête* (1955; *Canada: The War of the Conquest*, 1969). This study of the fall of New France in 1759 stressed the profound dislocation caused by the British takeover. Because of inadequate support of the colony and French bureaucratic ineptness (not to mention the venality of Bigot and his cronies), French Canada was no match for the English invaders and succumbed in short order. But the Conquest was not simply a military defeat. It was also a defeat in political, social, and even cultural terms. The society of the Canadiens was disrupted, its political structure destroyed, and the people left isolated within a progressively more anglicized region. "The framework of the Canadian community, destroyed in the crisis," wrote Frégault, "was never properly rebuilt."

But Frégault brought more than just neo-nationalist revisionism to the study of French Canada. By focusing on a succession of oligarchies which jostled for power and influence within the colony, he forced historians to rethink the traditional notion that political squabbles were a consequence of a carefully crafted system of checks and balances intended to ensure that neither the governor nor the *intendant* became too powerful. He did not deny that the French crown fully intended the two key administrators to fight among themselves in a sort of divide-and-rule strategy, but emphasized that nascent lobby groups exerted considerable influence in shaping government policy in the colony.

Even in such arguments that were apparently strictly historical in nature, Frégault's deep commitment to modern French Canadian nationalism was evident. By asserting that power and influence resided in the colony as well as in the metropolis, he characterized New France as an embryonic French-Canadian nation. For this reason, according to Frégault, 1759

was a defining moment in the identity of French Canadians, a fact that made the tragedy of the conquest even more profound.

JONATHAN F. VANCE

See also Canada; Séguin

Biography

Born Montreal, 16 June 1918. Educated at University of Montreal, BA 1938, L et L, 1940; Loyola University, Chicago, PhD 1949. Taught at University of Montreal, 1942–59; director, Institute of History, University of Ottawa, 1959–77. Died 1977.

Principal Writings

La Civilisation de la Nouvelle-France (1713–1744) (The Civilization of New France), 1944
François Bigot: administrateur français (François Bigot: French Administrator), 1948
Le Grand Marquis, Pierre de Rigaud de Vaudreuil et la Louisiane (The Grand Marquis, Pierre de Rigaud de Vaudreuil and Louisiana), 1952
Canadian Society in the French Regime, 1954
La Guerre de la conquête, 1955; in English as *Canada: The War of the Conquest*, 1969
Pierre LeMoyne d'Iberville, 1968
Chronique des années perdues (Chronicle of the Lost Years), 1976

Further Reading

Lamarre, Jean, *Le Devenir de la nation québécoise selon Maurice Séguin, Guy Frégault et Michel Brunet, 1944–1969* (The Future of the Quebec Nation According to Maurice Séguin, Guy Frégault, and Michel Brunet, 1944–1969), Sillery, Quebec: Septentrion, 1993
Ouellet, Fernand, *The Socialization of Quebec Historiography since 1960*, Toronto: Robarts Centre for Canadian Studies, 1988
Savard, Pierre, ed., *Guy Frégault, 1918–1977*, Montreal: Bellarmin, 1981
Zoltvany, Yves F., *The Government of New France: Royal, Clerical, or Class Rule?* Scarborough, Ontario: Prentice Hall, 1971

Freud, Sigmund 1856–1939
Austrian psychoanalyst

It is often, and rightly, observed that the influence of Sigmund Freud on 20th-century culture is matched only by that of Karl Marx. The comprehensive theoretical systems these thinkers constructed can be said to complement each other: psychoanalysis gives an account of the inner, subjective workings of the individual while Marxism deals with the individual's external, objective reality. If this distinction is an oversimplification, it is not because Marx showed a sustained theoretical interest in the subjective realm, but because Freud, especially in his later writings, developed a social metaphysics.

Although suspicious of metaphysical speculation – perhaps because he dreaded nothing more than the conflation of his work with untestable flights of imagination – Freud was convinced that the insights gained through the analysis of the individual psyche are applicable to the human condition in general, and that they can help us better understand the history, the meaning, and the value of civilization. It was with this aim in mind that he wrote *Das Unbehagen in der Kultur* (1930;

Civilization and Its Discontents, 1930). One of the main premises of this book is the old idea that society is humanity writ large. This idea, most famously used in Plato's *Republic*, was further developed by Freud's claim that the individual's psyche and mankind's psyche evolved from the same starting point – a primitive stage of direct instinct-gratification – to the same destination – a civilized stage of controlled or sublimated instincts. In Freud's view, such evolution did not necessarily spell progress. For the happiness derived from the satisfaction of a wild instinctual impulse was incomparably more intense than that derived from satisfying an already tamed instinct. "It is easy for a barbarian to be healthy; for a civilized man the task is hard," he wrote.

The central thesis of Freud's social metaphysics is that the origin of civilization is instinctual renunciation. The "progress" of civilization, the world of cultural achievement, is won only by denying to the sexual and aggressive instincts the direct gratification which they seek. The essential unhappiness of civilized man, his malaise or discontent (*Unbehagen*) is a manifestation of his unconscious sense of guilt. The origin of this guilt is the Oedipus-complex, that is, the conflict between the need for the authority's – the father's – love, and the urge towards instinctual satisfaction, whose inhibition by this authority produces the inclination to aggression. The suppression of the aggressive impulse which is now added to the original suppression of the sexual instinct, provides energy for neurotic substitutes. The net result is individual psychosis. But Freud regarded society itself as psychotic, and psychotic on its own, not merely as the sum of its sick members. The source of this is the eternal struggle that takes place on the collective level between civilization's internal erotic impulsion (Eros), which causes human beings to unite, and the instinct of destruction that derives its energy from the instincts sacrificed for the sake of this unity.

When aggressive impulses are repressed for the sake of civilization, they become internalized, or displaced inwards. Their management is taken over by the "super-ego," an agency set up for this purpose both on the individual and the collective level. The collective, or "cultural" super-ego is the voice of conscience and will be as harsh or violent in its dealing with the collective ego as is the sense of guilt derived from that eternal conflict between the forces of unity (Eros) and destruction (Death). The cultural super-ego produces a set of demands in the form of ethics, moral precepts, and religious commandments.

The greatest threat to the existence of civilization is the constitutional inclination of its members to be aggressive to one another. The cultural super-ego attempts to solve this problem by issuing the command to love one's neighbor as oneself, and to love one's enemies – a command, Freud notes, painfully impossible to fulfill. "What a potent obstacle to civilization aggressiveness must be," he adds, "if the defense against it can cause as much unhappiness as aggressiveness itself!" It is typical of the super-ego to take insufficient account of the strength of the id, the storehouse of instincts, and of the objective limitations presented by the external environment. Therefore, therapy both on the individual and the collective level must often include an opposition to the super-ego in order to reduce the patient's consuming sense of guilt, the ultimate source of his unhappiness.

It should be stressed here that by therapeutic opposition to the super-ego Freud certainly did not mean the destruction of it. He may have been sympathetic to civilized man's malaise resulting from the brutal domestication of his instincts but he was not a Romantic anarchist. He saw culture not just as deprivation but also as a means of individual fulfillment. Although he thought it quite impossible to adjust the claims of the sexual instinct to the demands of civilization, he accepted the inevitability of the conflict between the individual and society, and sought ways of maximizing individualism within a social context.

In the Freudian system the balance between the id (inner needs) and super-ego (outer actualities) is maintained by the ego. But critics have often objected that the system itself fails to do justice to outer actualities, that is, it fails to take historical and social difference into account. For instance, one of these critics, Erik Erikson suggested that while the patients of early psychoanalysis suffered most from inhibitions which prevented them from being what they perceived themselves to be, the patients of today suffer most from a dizzying sense of being unable to perceive just who or what they are. In other words, the horizon of psychoanalysis is too narrow to allow for the vista of a cultural shift from overt symptoms, especially conversion hysteria, to modern "character neurosis."

It would be rash to conclude that Freud was unaware of the different forms emotional conflicts can take under varying historical conditions. He called attention, for example, to the different manifestations of the intent of self-injury throughout the ages. In modern times, it has to hide itself behind something accidental; formerly it was a customary sign of mourning; and in other periods it could express trends towards piety and renunciation of the world. He thought that modern neurosis carries on the function of the monastery: both serve as refuge for those who are unwilling or unable to face the world. Nevertheless, it is clear that ultimately Freud's interest lay more in discovering timeless truths than in investigating unique historical developments.

Unlike Marx, who thought of history as a story with a happy ending, Freud took a more pessimistic, or perhaps more realistic view of the same subject. He saw no wholesale solution to the problem of human unhappiness, and occasionally wondered if civilization was worth the entrance fee, the suppression of raw instincts.

JANOS SALAMON

See also Althusser; Art; Burke; Cultural; Davis, D.; Egypt: Ancient; Erikson; Gay; Gender; Ginzburg; Hofstadter; Homosexuality; Hunt; Lasch; Mach; Marxist Interpretation; Memory; Nietzsche; Schorske; Sexuality; United States: Historical Writing, 20th Century

Biography

Born Freiberg, Moravia, 6 May 1856, son of a textile manufacturer. Attended Sperl Gymnasium, Vienna; University of Vienna, 1873–82; entered the General Hospital in Vienna as a clinical assistant to the psychiatrist Theodor Meynert, 1882; studied with J.M. Charcot, Paris; then appointed lecturer in neuropathology, University of Vienna, 1885; began private practice in Vienna, 1886. Married Martha Bernays, 1886 (3 sons; 3 daughters, including the psychoanalyst Anna Freud). Left Vienna, 1938; settled in London. Died London, 23 September 1939.

Principal Writings

Eine Kindheitserinnerung des Leonardo da Vinci, 1910; in English as *Leonardo da Vinci: A Psychosexual Study of Infantile Reminiscence*, 1916

Totem und Tabu: Über einige Übereinstimmungen im Seelenleben der Wilden und der Neurotiker, 1913; in English as *Totem and Taboo: Resemblances Between the Psychic Drives of Savages and Neurotics*, 1917

Das Unbehagen in der Kultur, 1930; in English as *Civilization and Its Discontents*, 1930

Der Mann Moses und die monotheistische Religion, 1939; as *Moses and Monotheism*, 1939

Gesammelte Werke, 17 vols., 1940–52

The Standard Edition of the Complete Psychological Works of Sigmund Freud, 24 vols., 1953–74

Further Reading

Bonaparte, Marie, Anna Freud, and Ernst Kris, eds., *Aus den Anfängen der Psychoanalyse*, London: Imago, 1950; in English as *The Origins of Psycho-analysis*, London: Imago, and New York: Basic Books, 1954

Dorer, Maria, *Historische Grundlagen der Psychoanalyse* (Historical Foundations of Psychoanalysis), Leipzig: Meiner, 1962

Gay, Peter, *Freud for Historians*, New York: Oxford University Press, 1985

Gay, Peter, *Freud: A Life for Our Time*, New York: Norton, 1988

Hutton, Patrick H., "Sigmund Freud and Maurice Halbwachs: The Problem of Memory in Historical Psychology," *History Teacher* 27 (1994), 145–58

Jones, Ernest, *Sigmund Freud: Life and Work*, 3 vols., London: Hogarth Press, 1953–57; as *The Life and Work of Sigmund Freud*, New York: Basic Books, 1953–57

Madison, Peter, *Freud's Concept of Repression and Defense*, Minneapolis: University of Minnesota Press, 1961

Smith, Joseph H., ed., *Telling Facts: History and Narration in Psychoanalysis*, Baltimore: Johns Hopkins University Press, 1992

Steiner, George, "The Historicity of Dreams (Two Questions to Freud)," *Salmagundi* 61 (Fall 1983), 6–21

Freyre, Gilberto 1900–1987

Brazilian historical sociologist and essayist

Gilberto Freyre's trilogy on the cultural history of Brazil – *Casa-grande e senzala* (1933; *The Masters and the Slaves*, 1946), *Sobrados e mucambos* (1936; *The Mansions and the Shanties*, 1963) and *Ordem e progresso* (1959; *Order and Progress*, 1970) – pioneered in the history of the family and childhood and also sparked debates on comparative slavery and comparative race relations.

Freyre's complex history of Brazil can best be described as a nostalgic fable of the rise and decline of the sugar plantations of the Northeast. *The Masters and the Slaves* told how the specially "miscible" Portuguese founded a multiracial tropical colony. For three centuries, the self-sufficient plantation shaped Brazilian civilization. In the cane fields, plantation slavery divided Brazilians into masters and slaves, and left a legacy of authoritarianism. But in the bedrooms and kitchens of the Big House, plantation paternalism harmonized Brazilians, and left a legacy of racial fraternity. Indians, Portuguese, and Africans fused both sexually and culturally into Brazilians; the resulting civilization was culturally hybrid, "Oriental," and, in its own way, Christian.

The Mansions and the Shanties described the decline of this plantation patriarchy. The arrival of the exiled Portuguese king in 1808 brought taxation, centralization, urbanization, and finally, a "re-Europeanization" of customs. In the early 19th century, plantation families moved from the Big House to the city mansion. Gradually, new institutions such as the school, the family doctor, and "the street" infiltrated the mansion, emancipating the woman and the child from patriarchal tutelage. By the mid-19th century, upwardly mobile mulatto men of talent had entered the mansions to marry the daughters of patriarchal planters and form a new, "semipatriarchal" establishment. *Order and Progress* argued that the abolition of slavery in 1888 and the symbolically parricidal overthrow of the emperor in 1889 completed the disintegration of patriarchy. Traces of patriarchal racial harmony ameliorated the "social question" of industrial modernity.

Freyre's essays transformed Brazilian debates on national identity. Following the abolition of slavery, Brazilian historians and writers had avoided speaking of its impact on society. Instead, they had diagnosed their people as the sad victims of race mixture and a tropical climate. In *The Masters and the Slaves*, Freyre claims that Brazilians are the happy mestizo heirs of the slave plantation's fusion of cultures and races. His uninhibited exploration of intimate details of domestic life gave Brazilian readers a shock of self-recognition and won over the general public. His profuse documentation of colonial folkways, using eclectic sources, offered social scientists a plausible cultural, rather than racial, explanation of the nation. Since *The Masters and the Slaves*, all Brazilian historiography has contended with Freyre's argument that slavery and the patriarchal family were central formative institutions. From the 1950s onward, Marxian sociologists and historians, centered at the Universidade de São Paulo, have agreed that slavery shaped society, but have sharply corrected Freyre's claims that paternalism characterized Brazilian plantation slavery. They have preferred to analyze the nation not as a cultural tradition but as the outcome of class conflicts. Social historians have also supplemented Freyre's monolithic image of the family, for example, by showing that many colonial Brazilians lived in female-headed households.

Studies in the United States influenced Freyre, and his ideas in turn shaped United States and Caribbean historiography. Freyre studied at Baylor University, where he witnessed southern segregation and lynchings, and at Columbia University, where he absorbed cosmopolitan avant-garde trends. His social-science influences included Franz Boas (antiracist cultural anthropology, the community study method), W.G. Sumner (folkways), F.H. Giddings, and the Progressive historians. His Columbia master's thesis, "The Social Life in Brazil in the Middle of the Nineteenth Century" (1922), broke new ground with its virtuoso combination of social and political history. In time, American historians such as Frank Tannenbaum and Eugene Genovese responded to Freyre's comparisons of Brazilian slavery and race relations with the United States.

Freyre's work after 1945 shifted toward developing "Luso-tropicology," the comparative study of adaptations of Portuguese culture in tropical colonies of Asia, Africa, and the Americas. Lusotropicology isolated him from the mainstream, for it offended most scholars as a conservative apology for Portuguese colonialism. And neither his textbook, *Sociologia* (1945), nor his essay, *Como e porque sou e não sou sociólogo* (How and Why I Am and Am Not a Sociologist, 1968), persuaded readers as a guide to his eclectic method. Specifically, neither clarified the muddle of causal variables and paired symbolic types (e.g., "the masters" and "the slaves") in his historical analysis.

Because of the polemical reaction against his work, some of Freyre's innovative experiments and solid contributions remain unacknowledged and unexploited. He conceived the idea of "a history of childhood" in the 1920s, before French social historians did likewise. He pioneered environmental history in *Nordeste* (1937), a history of the sugar plantation complex. He experimented with oral history in *Order and Progress*. He tried presenting historical arguments in two "seminovels," *Dona Sinhá e o filho padre* (1964; *Mother and Son*, 1967) and *O outro amor do Dr. Paulo* (The Other Love of Dr. Paulo, 1977). He published useful monographs (notably on the English in 19th-century Brazil and on Brazilian domestic architecture) along with a stream of minor essays (on sugar, ghosts, ironworking, tombstones, engineers, Jesuits, tropical medicine, nutrition and cuisine, among other topics) that mixed insights and folkloric trivia. Urban anthropologists such as Roberto Da Matta began a rereading of Freyre in the 1980s; it has not yet reached Brazilian historians.

DAIN BORGES

See also Brazil; Cardoso; Holanda; Latin America: National; Slavery: Modern; Stein

Biography
Gilberto de Mello Freyre. Born Recife, Brazil, 15 March 1900. Studied at Baylor University, Waco, Texas, BA 1920; Columbia University, 1920–22, MA. Secretary to governor of Pernambuco, 1926–30; political exile 1930; visiting professor, Stanford University, 1931; sponsor of "Afro-Brazilian Congress" symposia, 1934 and 1937; professor of sociology, University of Distrito Federal, 1935–38. Federal deputy and member of Constituent Assembly, 1946–50; Brazilian member of Social and Cultural Commission, General Assembly of United Nations, 1949. Founder, 1948, and later director of Joaquim Nabuco Institute, Recite. Active in anticommunist journalism and politics after 1950, notably in platforms of the Aliança Renovadora Nacional (ARENA) party, 1960s. Married Magdalena Guedes Pereira, 1941 (1 son, 1 daughter). Died Recife, 18 July 1987.

Principal Writings
"The Social Life in Brazil in the Middle of the Nineteenth Century," *Hispanic American Historical Review* 2 (1922), 597–630

Casa-grande e senzala: formação da família brasileira sob o regime de economia patriarcal, 1933; in English as *The Masters and the Slaves: A Study in the Development of Brazilian Civilization*, 1946

Sobrados e mucambos: decadência do patriarcado rural e desenvolvimento do urbano, 1936; in English as *The Mansions and the Shanties: The Making of Modern Brazil*, 1963

Nordeste: aspectos da influência da canna sobre a vide e a paizagem do nordeste do Brasil (The Northeast), 1937

Brazil: An Interpretation, 1945; revised as *New World in the Tropics: The Culture of Modern Brazil*, 1959

Sociologia, 2 vols., 1945

Ordem e progresso, 2 vols., 1959; in English as *Order and Progress: Brazil from Monarchy to Republic*, 1970

Dona Sinhá e o filho padre (Mother and Son), 1964 [novel]; in English as *Mother and Son: A Brazilian Tale*, 1967

Como e porque sou e não sou sociólogo (How and Why I Am and Am Not a Sociologist), 1968

Tempo morto e outros tempos: trechos de um diário de adolescência e primeira mocidade, 1915–1930 (Fallow Time and Other Times: Passages from a Diary), 1975

O outro amor do Dr. Paulo (The Other Love of Dr. Paulo), 1977 [fiction]

Further Reading
Araújo, Ricardo Benzaquen de, *Guerra e paz: Casa-Grande & senzala e a obra de Gilberto Freyre nos anos 30* (War and Peace: *The Masters and the Slaves* and the Work of Gilberto Freyre in the 1930s), Rio de Janeiro: Editora 34, 1994

Dinneen, Mark, "Gilberto Freyre" in Verity Smith, ed., *Encyclopedia of Latin American Literature*, London and Chicago: Fitzroy Dearborn, 1997

Ferrer, Ada, "Gilberto Freyre: A Problem in the Historiography of Brazilian Slavery," *Inter-American Review of Bibliography* 38 (1988), 196–211

Matta, Roberto Da, "A originalidade de Gilberto Freyre" (The Originality of Gilberto Freyre), *BIB: Boletim Informativo e Bibliográfico de Ciências Sociais* 24 (1987), 3–10

Morse, Richard M., "Balancing Myth and Evidence: Freyre and Sergio Buarque," *Luso-Brazilian Review* 36 (1995), 47–57

Needell, Jeffrey D., "Identity, Race, Gender, and Modernity in the Origins of Gilberto Freyre's Oeuvre," *American Historical Review* 100 (1995), 51–77

Skidmore, Thomas E., "Gilberto Freyre and the Historiography of the Early Brazilian Republic: Some Notes on Methodology," *Comparative Studies in Society and History* 6 (1964), 490–505

Froissart, Jean [Jehan] *c.*1337–after 1404
French chronicler

Jean Froissart is one of the best known chroniclers of European chivalry and of the events of the Hundred Years' War. Many of the leading figures were personally known to him and he may be likened to a journalist in his access to firsthand information, his interviewing of eyewitnesses, and the vivid style with which he narrated events.

Like his near-contemporary, Jean Le Bel, he came from a bourgeois family in the Duchy of Hainault. He served at the court, probably first as a page and later as a secular priest in minor orders. His literacy skills were useful and he did not find it necessary to be ordained until offered a benefice in 1373. His writings recorded the myths and rituals of a warlike and often brutal society. Ancient codes of conduct found their most sophisticated expression in the interrelated court circles of France, Burgundy, and England of Froissart's time. The language spoken by the aristocracy of these regions was French and Froissart catered for this market, where the reading aloud of romances and histories was a popular pastime. Earlier in his career he was better known as a poet, but his fame rests on the *Chroniques* (Chronicles) eventually covering the period 1325–1400 in four books. Book 2 contains the so-called *Chronique des Flandres* (Chronicle of Flanders).

The *Chronicles* survive in three versions, modified to suit successive patrons, all connected with the ducal house of Hainault. In about 1360 Froissart travelled to England and became a clerk to Philippa of Hainault, queen of Edward III. He presented her with an early chronicle about the martial prowess of her husband. In her service and later, Froissart travelled widely. After Philippa's death, Froissart entered the service of Robert duke of Namur, her brother-in-law, who encouraged him to write the first version of the *Chronicles*. Namur was an ally of Edward III and the *Chronicles* were sympathetic to the English position in the war against France.

About ten years later Froissart produced a new version with a neutral slant. By then he was chaplain to Guy duke of Blois and he included a eulogy to this patron. The first version of the *Chronicles* covered the years up to 1369, and relied heavily on Jean Le Bel's Chronicle which ended in 1361. The second version went up to 1385 and followed Le Bel less closely. By this time, Froissart had assembled additional information from heralds and knights who had witnessed events. Towards the end of his life Froissart wrote a third version, which brought the *Chronicles* up to 1400. His negative attitude toward England may have reflected disappointment with his reception at the English court on his visit in 1395. Although Richard II rewarded him generously for gifts of his writings, all his friends were dead. Nevertheless, the *Chronicles* are an important source for the Peasants' Revolt of 1381 and other events of Richard's reign. The first version was the most popular, surviving in about fifty manuscripts, the second in two and the third in only one copy.

There is the question of Froissart's reliability as an historical source. Certainly the early part of his *Chronicles* is derived from Jean Le Bel and Froissart changed his interpretation of events to suit his patrons. Nevertheless his writings reflect the range of confidences to which a man of his position was privy. Froissart was a cosmopolitan individual and a skilled historical writer, who exercised critical judgment over the information he included. Although he romanticized the lives of the elite, whom he served, he was honest about the contradiction between chivalric ideals and the messy realities of war. His subject matter and the exquisite contemporary illustrations of his works represent a lasting memorial to a vanished social and political world.

VIRGINIA R. BAINBRIDGE

See also France: 1000–1450; Reformation

Biography

Born Valenciennes, Nord, c.1337. Entered princely service in early life, moving often: served Queen Philippa of Hainaut, wife of Edward III, London, and other English and Scottish lords, 1361–69. Took orders in 1370s: curate of Les Estinnes, near Mons, 1373; canon of Chimay, 1384; visited England, 1394–95. Died Chimay, after 1404.

Principal Writings

Chroniques (Chronicles): version 1, 1369; version 2, 1385; version 3, c.1400; as *The Chronicles*, translated by Geoffrey Brereton, 1968

Further Reading

Dembowski, Peter F., *Jean Froissart and His Meliador: Context, Craft and Sense*, Lexington, KY: French Forum, 1983
Keen, Maurice, "Chivalry, Heralds and History," in R.H.C. Davis and J.M. Wallace-Hadrill, eds., *The Writing of History in the Middle Ages: Essays Presented to Richard William Southern*, Oxford and New York: Oxford University Press, 1981
Palmer, J.J.N., ed., *Froissart: Historian*, Woodbridge, Suffolk: Boydell, and Totowa, NJ: Rowman and Littlefield, 1981
Shears, Frederick Sidney, *Froissart: Chronicler and Poet*, London: Routledge, 1930
Vale, Juliet, *Edward III and Chivalry: Chivalric Society and Its Context*, Woodbridge, Suffolk: Boydell, 1982
Vale, Malcolm, *War and Chivalry: Warfare and Aristocratic Culture in England, France and Burgundy at the End of the Middle Ages*, London: Duckworth, and Athens: University of Georgia Press, 1981

Frontiers

The study of frontiers traditionally belongs to the interdisciplinary subject of historical geography, but it has been enriched by specialist works on international law, political geography, and the theory of international relations.

Since the 17th century, historical geographers have been concerned with the study of conquests: changes in the territorial possessions of states, empires, and royal houses. In 1881, in *The Historical Geography of Europe*, the Oxford scholar E.A. Freeman described the task of historical geographers as to "mark the boundaries" and "trace out the extent of territory which the different states and nations of Europe and the neighbouring lands have held at different times in the world history." At the same time, political thinkers such as Alberico Gentili, Hugo Grotius, and Emmerich de Vattel linked the question of frontiers directly to the study of war. They were particularly preoccupied with the legal problem of the right to conquer and annex foreign lands. Consequently, by the beginning of the 20th century frontiers were seen by both scholars and politicians, in Lord Curzon's often quoted words, as "the razor's edge on which hang suspended the modern issues of war and peace, of life or death to nations." The former viceroy of India claimed that in modern history "wars of religion, of alliances, of rebellion, of aggrandizement, of dynastic intrigue or ambition" were "replaced by frontier wars." Yet, Curzon, who had personal experience of drawing the boundaries of a number of states, insisted that scientifically delimited frontiers were "capable of being converted into the instruments and evidences of peace."

From the 19th century the examination of frontiers was closely related to the emerging modern nationalism; John Stuart Mill described "the geographical limits of states" as catalysts of the "feeling of nationality." As Lucien Febvre put it in a polemic essay, after the French Revolution national boundaries were "backed up by a second, moral frontier."

The strong link between national character and the expanding territory of the state was clearly illustrated by the American historian Frederick Jackson Turner. In *The Significance of the Frontier in American History* (1893), Turner argued that the historical development of America gradually moved away from its European origins as a result of the western march across the continent between the 17th and 19th centuries. The Turner hypothesis was based on the assumption that a vast area of free land made the western frontier of the US no more than a notional and temporary line, one that facilitated further expansion rather than delimited it.

In Europe a similarly determinist "frontier concept" was advocated by Friedrich Ratzel. The German geographer argued that the evolution of national boundaries originated in human desire to economize and make the best use of increasingly overpopulated land. Ratzel's "space conception" was based on the assumption that according to the general law of growth "the borders of the larger areas embrace the smaller ones." This doctrine was taken up by in the 1920s by Karl Haushofer and the German school of *Geopolitik*. In line with Ratzel, they characterized borders as temporary dividing lines, which followed the shifts in international politics.

This thesis was repudiated by the French Annales school. Lucien Febvre illustrated the concern of modern nations "to mark out their limits across deserts, unproductive marshlands or barren rocky territory," and urged that historians should discuss the evolution of frontiers in relation to the territorial sovereignty of the state.

The research of frontiers gained momentum after World War I, partly as a result of competing claims of national historiographies in Central and Eastern Europe. The territorial disputes centered around the question of national self-determination, but they were complicated by the strategic, economic, historical, and geographical approaches to frontier-making. In the vanquished states, most of all in Hungary, frontier revision became by far the most popular topic of international relations. In "The Distress of the East European Small States" (1946, translated 1991) István Bibó contended that preoccupation with boundary problems was the prime cause of the hopeless tangle of ethnic conflicts in Eastern Europe.

By the time of World War II, according to E.H. Carr "the tradition which made the drawing of frontiers the primary and most spectacular part of peacemaking has outlived its validity." Hence, in postwar historical writing the question of frontiers was often linked to the examination of theoretical problems, such as the origin of nationalism. In *Nations and States* (1977), Hugh Seton-Watson argued that the nationalism of "old nations," which inhabited their sovereign state within well-defined territorial limits, widely differed from those of "new nations," which acquired national consciousness before their state-formation. Thus, Seton-Watson described territorial nationalism in terms of the nations' drive for sovereignty.

Decolonization from 1947 onwards caused a proliferation of new states, which had frontiers that corresponded to no significant geographical, economic, or cultural unit. The resulting large number of new border disputes inspired a great volume of legal, political, and military studies. Consequently, in modern historiography there has been a persistent tendency to discuss frontiers as they facilitate local wars, or national, political, and economic conflicts.

GÁBOR BÁTONYI

See also Historical Geography; Turner

Further Reading

Bibó, István, "The Distress of East European Small States" in *Democracy, Revolution, Self-Determination: Selected Writings*, New York: Columbia University Press, 1991 [Hungarian original, 1946]
Butlin, Robin A., *Historical Geography: Through the Gates of Space and Time*, London: Arnold, 1993
Carr, E.H., *Conditions of Peace*, London and New York: Macmillan, 1942
Curzon, George Nathaniel, *Frontiers*, Oxford: Clarendon Press, 1907; reprinted 1976
De Martini, Raymond J., *The Right of Nations to Expand by Conquest*, Washington, DC: Catholic University Presses of America, 1947
Fawcett, Charles Bungay, *Frontiers: A Study in Political Geography*, Oxford: Oxford University Press, 1918
Febvre, Lucien, *La Terre et l'évolution humaine: introduction géographique à l'histoire*, Paris: Renaissance du livre, 1922; in English as *A Geographical Introduction to History*, London: Trench Trübner, and New York: Knopf, 1925; reprinted 1974
Febvre, Lucien, "*Frontière*: The Word and the Concept," in Peter Burke, ed., *A New Kind of History: From the Writings of Febvre*, London: Routledge, and New York: Harper, 1973
Freeman, Edward Augustus, *The Historical Geography of Europe*, London: Longman, 1881
Macartney, C.A., *National States and National Minorities*, London: Oxford University Press, 1934; reprinted New York: Russell and Russell, 1968
Powell, Philip W. *et al.*, *Essays on Frontiers in World History*, Austin: University of Texas Press, 1981
Prescott, John Robert Victor, *Political Frontiers and Boundaries*, London and Boston: Unwin Hyman, 1987; revised and expanded 1990
Ratzel, Friedrich, *Politische Geographie: oder die Geographie der Staaten, des Verkehres und des Krieges* (Political Geography: On the Geography of State, Commerce, and War), Berlin: Oldenbourg, 1897
Seton-Watson, Hugh, *Nations and States: An Enquiry into the Origins of Nations and the Politics of Nationalism*, London: Methuen, and Denver: Westview Press, 1977
Taylor, A.J.P., *How Wars End*, London: Hamish Hamilton, 1985
Thompson, L.M., and Howard Lamar, eds., *The Frontier in History: North America and Southern Africa Compared*, New Haven: Yale University Press, 1981
Turner, Frederick Jackson, *The Significance of the Frontier in American History*, Madison: State Historical Society of Wisconsin, 1894 [as lecture 1893]

Froude, J.A. 1818–1894

British historian and man of letters

One of the most prolific of Victorian historians, J.A. Froude was also a belletrist, a man of political affairs, an editor, and, ultimately, a professor of history.

Froude was among the first historians of his generation to conduct extensive research in archives and repositories. He did his own research, refusing to employ assistants or secretaries to translate and copy documents. He kept his use of secondary sources to a minimum. Ostensibly, his objective as a historian was to attempt to see all sides of an issue before reaching a conclusion. Likewise, as the editor of the influential journal *Fraser's Magazine* from 1860 to 1874, he often published timely articles on public affairs that ran counter to his own opinions. Froude's work as a historian and essayist, however, was by no means an example of the positivist approach to history. He doubted that a thorough search of the sources would eventually yield the truth about the past. His principal interest lay in using historical sources to fashion a dramatic story about the past. Froude achieved this objective; he was a brilliant prose stylist who attracted a wide readership.

Froude's judgments on history and current affairs were shaped by deeply held cultural biases and personal convictions. As a result, his historical and literary publications antagonized his opponents and often failed to please his friends. Over time, he attracted the enmity of Oxonians, Roman Catholics, economists, liberals, socialists, Irish nationalists and colonists throughout the empire, other historians, and literary critics. He occasionally responded in print to his adversaries, and the continual attempts to demolish his work and question his probity caused him immense concern.

The attacks on his work began when he published *Nemesis of Faith* (1849) which criticized the tractarian influences at Oriel College, Oxford. The book was publicly burned at Exeter and Froude subsequently resigned his clerical office. Soon after he met Thomas Carlyle, who became his friend and literary mentor. Carlyle exercised a powerful influence on Froude, particularly in the writing of biography, which became one of his fortes. Froude's great work, the *History of England from the Fall of Wolsey to the Death of Elizabeth* (1856–70), emphasized the roles of Henry VIII and Burghley and exalted the maritime power of England. No history published to that date had been based on so much previously unseen primary source material. The *History of England* was an immediate success. Nevertheless, Froude's conclusion that the Protestant Reformation was beneficial because it triumphed over authority, superstition, and barbarism was sharply called into question by Catholic scholars who claimed that his personal biases undermined the validity of his interpretations.

Froude then launched his next important project, *The English in Ireland in the Eighteenth Century* (1872–74). Froude was an ardent Conservative, and the purpose of the work was to point out the errors of the Liberal government's policies in Ireland, including the disestablishment of the Protestant Church of Ireland and land reform. A storm of criticism ensued from Irish nationalists and unionists, alike. Nationalist public speakers and journalists maintained that Froude blamed the victims of English imperialism for their misfortunes: he believed the Irish were a savage population and were born to be ruled. Fifty years later, nationalist historians were still combating Froude's analysis of Irish sources and refuting his interpretations of key events in Irish history. Unionist historian W.E.H. Lecky, one of Froude's friends, criticized his offensive and intemperate language, intolerance, and errors in interpretation, among other shortcomings.

Meanwhile, Froude's work was under heavy attack from A.E. Freeman, the Regius professor of history at Oxford. Freeman charged that Froude was a careless scholar who was too often inaccurate in his use of sources. Froude was caught out on numerous mistakes, which he claimed were minor, but the attacks dealt a permanent blow to his reputation as a scholar.

The greatest controversy over Froude's work followed the publication of his multivolume biography of Thomas Carlyle and the other materials which had been entrusted by Carlyle to him as literary executor. Froude tried to follow Carlyle's rather confusing directions that the biography should serve as Carlyle's posthumous act of penance for his own harshness as a biographer. Froude also believed that Carlyle would have applauded a biography that broke through the hagiographic conventions that defined the genre. The result was an extremely critical examination of Carlyle's life which broke those bounds by disclosing personal aspects of Carlyle's life. The biography caused great offense to Carlyle's family and friends. Moreover, Froude's technique in editing Carlyle's papers for publication also came under fire; he was accused of manipulating the meaning of some documents and of suppressing others. Carlyle

had been Froude's friend for thirty years; the criticism of the biography was especially hurtful.

In 1892, at age 74, Froude succeeded Freeman as Regius professor at Oxford; the irony of accepting the appointment was too much for Froude to resist. He labored with his usual intensity on his lectures, which were well attended and subsequently published. The arduous responsibilities of the position, however, may have hastened his death.

Froude was invariably mentioned in contemporary memoirs and in assessments of Victorian writers, but he has not attracted much sustained or critical attention in the 20th century.

LAWRENCE W. McBRIDE

See also Carlyle; Lecky; Trevelyan

Biography

James Anthony Froude. Born Dartington, Devon, 23 April 1818, to a landed clerical family. Attended Westminster School, 1830–33; then privately educated, 1833–35; studied at Oriel College, Oxford, BA 1842, MA 1843; fellow, Exeter College, Oxford, 1840–49; took deacon's orders, 1844, but resigned 1872. Editor, *Fraser's Magazine*, 1860–74. Named Regius professor of modern history, Oxford University 1892. Married 1) Charlotte Maria Grenfell, 1849 (died 1860; 1 daughter); 2) Henrietta Elizabeth Warre, 1861 (died 1874; 1 son, 1 daughter). Died Salcombe, Devon, 20 October 1894.

Principal Writings

The Nemesis of Faith, 1849
History of England from the Fall of Wolsey to the Death of Elizabeth, 12 vols., 1856–70
The English in Ireland in the Eighteenth Century, 3 vols., 1872–74
Editor, *Reminiscences*, by Thomas Carlyle, 2 vols., 1881
Thomas Carlyle: A History of the First Forty Years of His Life, 1795–1835, 2 vols., 1882
Luther: A Short Biography, 1883
Thomas Carlyle: A History of His Life in London, 1834–81, 2 vols., 1884
My Relations with Carlyle, 1886
Oceana; or, England and Her Colonies, 1886
The English in the West Indies; or, The Bow of Ulysses, 1888
The Two Chiefs of Dunboy; or, An Irish Romance of the Last Century, 1889
Lord Beaconsfield, 1890
The Spanish Story of the Armada, and Other Essays, 1892
Lectures on the Council of Trent, 1893
Life and Letters of Erasmus, 1893
English Seamen in the Sixteenth Century, 1895

Further Reading

Burke, Thomas N., *English Misrule in Ireland: A Course of Lectures, Delivered . . . in Reply to J.A. Froude*, New York: Lynch Cole and Mechen, 1873
Dunn, Waldo Hilary, *Froude and Carlyle: A Study of the Froude-Carlyle Controversy*, New York and London: Longman, 1930; reprinted Port Washington, NY: Kennikat Press, 1969
Dunn, Waldo Hilary, *James Anthony Froude: A Biography*, 2 vols., Oxford: Oxford University Press, 1961–63
Fussner, F. Smith, *Tudor History and the Historians*, New York: Basic Books, 1970
Gilbert, Elliot L., "Rescuing Reality: Carlyle, Froude, and Biographical Truth-Telling," *Victorian Studies* 34 (1991), 295–314
Goetzman, Robert, *James Anthony Froude: A Bibliography of Studies*, New York: Garland, 1977

Harrison, Frederic, "The Historical Method of J.A. Froude," *Nineteenth Century* 44 (1898), 373–85; reprinted in his *Tennyson, Ruskin, Mill, and Other Literary Estimates*, London: Macmillan, 1899

Lecky, W.E.H., "Mr. Froude's *English in Ireland*," *Macmillan's Magazine* 27 (January 1873), 246–64; and 30 (June 1874), 166–84

Mitchel, John, *1641: Reply to the Falsification of History by James A. Froude, Entitled "The English in Ireland,"* Glasgow: Cameron and Ferguson, 1873

Paul, Herbert, *The Life of Froude*, London: Pitman, and New York: Scribner, 1905

Skelton, John, *The Table Talk of Shirley: Reminiscences of and Letters from Froude, Thackeray, Disraeli, Browning, Rossetti, Kingsley, Baynes, Hurley, Tyndall and others*, Edinburgh: Blackwood, 1895

Fruin, Robert 1823–1899

Dutch historian

Robert Fruin was the most influential Dutch historian of the 19th century, playing a central role in the transformation of history into a professional discipline in his country. In his exhaustive *History and Historians in the Nineteenth Century*, G.P. Gooch called him "a miniature Ranke." Fruin was awarded the first chair of Dutch history created in the Netherlands and held it for 34 years. His work consisted largely of detailed studies in institutional and political history, in which he often seems guilty of a naive positivism. His repeated calls for historians to be impartial seem to confirm the impression that he believed "the facts speak for themselves," but Fruin's conception of history needs to be placed within the context of his time.

While teaching at Leiden's City Gymnasium from 1849 to 1859, Fruin wrote his best-known work, *Tien jaren uit de Tachtigjarige Oorlog* (Ten Years of the Eighty Years' War, 1857–58). This was one of the first studies of the Dutch revolt to make critical use of archival sources. In it, Fruin described the crucial period from 1588 to 1598, when the infant republic made the transition from unstable confederacy to political and economic Great Power. His combination of political analysis with an examination of economic and religious history was innovative at the time. The book won wide praise and led to his appointment as professor at the University of Leiden.

In his inaugural lecture at Leiden, *De onpartijdigheid van den geschiedschrijver* (The Impartiality of the Historian, 1860), Fruin called for historians to avoid writing history from ideological or religious perspectives. This appeal was aimed at winning recognition for history as an independent profession, one which created knowledge useful for purposes beyond justifying religious beliefs or providing ammunition for political battles. Indeed, Fruin hoped that greater research into Dutch history from a variety of angles would help unify his nation, by reducing conflict between Calvinists and Catholics as well as reconciling those who favored and those who opposed the constitutional monarchy of the Netherlands under the House of Orange.

Fruin provided an example of what he meant by impartial historiography in his *Het voorspel van den Tachtigjarigen Oorlog* (The Prologue of the Eighty Years' War, 1859–60), arguing that the revolt was not a religiously-inspired Calvinist fight against Catholic oppression, but was instead a nationalist rebellion against foreign rule, one that included both Calvinist and Catholic elements. *Het voorspel* was a response to J.L. Motley's *Rise of the Dutch Republic* (1856) which had identified the tyranny of the Spanish with the Catholic church.

These studies brought Fruin face to face with the question of how to judge the struggle between the stadholders of the House of Orange and the town oligarchies represented in the States-General, a conflict which had dominated the politics of the republic. Fruin tended to favor the stadholders in his work, an admiration which grew out of his wish for national unity. He believed the survival of the Netherlands in his own time depended on its centralized structure, and so he praised the stadholders' attempts to push the republic in a more centralized direction and deplored the particularism of the oligarchies.

Most of Fruin's work consisted of short essays, minutely detailed investigations of a circumscribed topic, sometimes only a single document (most published in *Verspreide geschriften* [Collected Essays], 1900–05). Critics have censured him for an extreme empiricism that prevented him from ever writing a synthesis, but Dutch historians still measure themselves against the research standards he set. Fruin is probably the only 19th-century Dutch historian whose work is still studied today.

MARYBETH CARLSON

See also Low Countries; Motley

Biography

Robert Jacobus Fruin. Born Rotterdam, 1823. Taught at City Gymnasium, Leiden, 1849–59; professor, Rijksuniversiteit, Leiden, 1860–94. Died Leiden, 1899.

Principal Writings

Tien jaren uit de Tachtigjarige Oorlog, 1588–1598 (Ten Years of the Eighty Years' War), 1857–58

Het voorspel van den Tachtigjarigen Oorlog (The Prologue of the Eighty Years' War), 1859–60

De onpartijdigheid van den geschiedschrijver (The Impartiality of the Historian), 1860

De drie tijdvakken der Nederlandsche geschiedenis (Three Periods of Dutch history), 1865

Het beleg en ontzet der stad Leiden in 1574, 1874; in English as *The Siege and Relief of Leyden in 1574*, 1927

Over de plaats die de geschiedenis in de kring der wetenschappen inneemt (On the Place of History among the Sciences), 1878

Afscheidsrede (Valedictory Address), 1894

Verspreide geschriften (Miscellaneous Essays), 11 vols., 1900–05

Geschiedenis der staatsinstellingen in Nederland tot den val der republiek (Constitutional and Institutional History of the Northern Netherlands), 1901

Further Reading

Blaas, P.B.M., "The Touchiness of a Small Nation with a Great Past: The Approach of Fruin and Blok to the Writing of the History of the Netherlands," in A.C. Duke and C.A. Tamse, eds., *Clio's Mirror: Historiography in Britain and the Netherlands*, Zutphen: De Walburg Pers, 1985

Blok, Petrus Johannes, "Robert Fruin," in his *Verspreide studiën op het gebied der geschiedenis* (Miscellaneous Studies in the Field of History), Groningen: Wolters, 1903

Byvanck, Willem Geertrud Cornelis, "Robert Fruin," in his *Literarische en historische studiën* (Literary and Historical Studies), Zutphen: Thieme, 1918

Colenbrander, Herman Theodor, "Robert Fruin" in his *Historie en leven* (History and Lives), Amsterdam: Van Kampen en Zoon, 1915–20, vol. 3, 179–85

Kernkamp, Gerhard Wilhelm, "Robert Fruin," in his *Van Menschen en Tijden* (Of Men and Times), Haarlem: Willink & Zoon, 1931, vol. 1, 97–176

Smit, Jacobus Wihlemus, *Fruin en de partijen tijdens de republiek* (Fruin and the Parties during the Republic), Groningen: Wolters, 1958

Tollebeek, Jo, *De toga van Fruin: denken over geschiedenis in Nederland sinds 1860* (Fruin's Toga: Thinking about History in the Netherlands since 1860), Amsterdam: Wereldbibliotheek, 1990

Wesseling, H.L., "Robert Fruin: de geschiedenis van een reputatie" (Robert Fruin: The History of a Reputation), in his *Onder historici: opstellen over geschiedenis en geschiedschrijving* (Among Historians: Essays about History and Historical Writing), Amsterdam: Bakker, 1995

Fügedi, Erik 1916–1993
Hungarian medievalist

Any attempt to evaluate the historical contribution and influence of Erik Fügedi must inevitably take account of the geographical and political as well as the intellectual environment from which he emerged. To say that all historians are the products of their time and place is to repeat a truism, but the statement is remarkably appropriate in Fügedi's case. Born in 1916 in Vienna, when it was still the western capital of the Austro-Hungarian empire, Fügedi was educated in Budapest, the formerly glittering eastern capital city, but which, following World War I, became merely the center of a dismembered and defeated country.

Fügedi has been said to belong to a generation "which inherited both the values and problems of historical Hungary" and which attempted to "rescue its intellectual achievements while overcoming its national and social prejudices." Early in his career, as a student of the eminent Hungarian medieval historians Imre Szentpétery, Imre Hajnal, and Elemér Mályusz, Fügedi developed two fundamental views of history which were to shape his work. The young scholar achieved the realization that careful and detailed studies of earlier societies were more valuable than the rhetorical generalizations that had characterized much of 19th-century scholarship. He concluded also that the historical problems of the Danube Basin region could be more incisively addressed if researchers troubled to investigate the language and culture of neighboring nations.

Among Fügedi's earliest works, appearing during the late 1930s, are review articles of both Slovak and Hungarian historical studies, all published in *Századok*, the journal of the Hungarian Historical Association, but written in both Hungarian and Slovak. Following World War II, Fügedi returned to his position at the National Archives to find himself placed in charge of the salvage and conservation of endangered private libraries and archives. His friend and admirer János Bak has speculated that "it may have been from the experiences of those years, when Dr. Fügedi visited castles and manor houses, some still inhabited, others looted and in desperate shape, that he received a major impetus to study the history and structure of the nobility of old Hungary, since he had the chance to meet its last representatives."

The nobility however was to form only one aspect of Fügedi's multifaceted research and publication activity during his most productive period, from the early 1960s to the late 1970s. Despite obstacles, which included a ten-year political "banishment" to a canning factory, Fügedi had already begun to publish articles on Hungarian urban history during the late 1950s, and his work from this period onwards shows an increasing appreciation for topographical and demographic evidence. In 1965 he joined the newly established Historical Demography Research Group and headed the team for ten years until his retirement in 1980. This small but important institution "was first among the centers of Hungary where methods of new history – quantification, complex analysis, application of demographic and sociological perspectives – were pursued and propagated."

Informed by these new techniques, Fügedi continued his investigations of urban history, an area little explored by previous Hungarian historians, who had tended to limit their focus to matters of high politics and to the activities of the aristocracy. The fact that many of the early urban settlers in Hungary were of foreign, primarily German origin, with a smaller proportion of Italians, may explain both their neglect by earlier historians and their attraction for the more ethnically inclusive Fügedi. In seminal essays, published between 1956 and 1981 in French and German as well as Hungarian, Fügedi documented the historical development of individual towns and the emergence of the urban class in late medieval Hungary.

His work on the towns provides clear evidence that Fügedi was not merely an archaeological or demographic historian – he was also concerned with the pursuit of ideas and identities. Looking back in the mid-1980s, Fügedi noted that his first scholarly visit to Paris introduced him to that area of research which he considered to be his "home ground": sociological and psychological approaches to the history of society, especially of its elites. He examined the role of immigrants in medieval Hungarian society in a 1974 article and analyzed aspects of the medieval Hungarian intelligentsia in studies published in 1980 and 1981 (all reprinted in *Kings, Bishops, Nobles and Burghers in Medieval Hungary*, 1986). His last years were spent in the preparation of a major study of the Hungarian medieval aristocracy.

Fügedi's contacts with the French Annales school seem also to have fostered the combination of ecclesiastical, social, and urban history which emerged in such essays as "La Formation des villes et les ordres mendiants en Hongrie" (The Development of Towns and the Mendicant Orders in Hungary, 1970). Perhaps the best monographic example of the interlaced, multidisciplinary nature of Fügedi's work available in English is his 1986 study *Castle and Society in Medieval Hungary (1000–1437)*. In this work Fügedi used topographical evidence, demographic data, and a wealth of intensive documentary analysis to support what almost amounts to a brief social and political history of medieval Hungary.

While he possessed all the skills of the specialist, Fügedi never limited his vision or restricted his analyses to merely antiquarian matters. Although more recent archaeological data and comparative studies have updated and in some cases revised the details of his findings, his expertise in using a variety of analytical techniques combined with the sheer scope of his investigations have ensured that Fügedi's work will remain central to the study of the Hungarian Middle Ages.

KATHLEEN E. GARAY

Biography

Born Vienna, 22 September 1916. Educated in Budapest at Péter Pázmány University. Worked briefly at the national archives, before active service during World War II. In charge of rescue and conservation of private collections, libraries, and archives, 1945–49; briefly head, Archival Research Center, 1950, then, after political persecution, clerk in a cannery for ten years; research fellow, Historical Association, 1961; joined demography research group and eventually became head, 1965–80; professor, Eötvös Loránd University, from 1980. Died 1993.

Principal Writings

A 15. századi magyar aristokrácia mobilitása (The Social Mobility of the 15th-Century Hungarian Aristocracy), 1970

"La Formation des villes et les ordres mendiants en Hongrie" (The Development of Towns and the Mendicant Orders in Hungary), *Annales: ESC* 25 (1970), 966–87

Uram, királyom . . .: A XV. századi Magyarország hatalmasai (My Lord, My King . . .: The Powerful Men of 15th-Century Hungary), 1974

Vár es társadalom a 13–14. századi Magyarországon (Castle and Community in 13th–14th-Century Hungary), 1977

With Kálmán Benda, *A magyar korona regénye* (The Story of the Hungarian Crown), 1979

Kolduló barátok, polgarok, nemesek: tanulmányok a magyar középkorról (Mendicant Friars, Burgesses, Nobility: Studies in the Hungarian Middle Ages), 1981

"Medieval Castles in Existence at the Start of the Ottoman Advance" in J. M. Bak and Béla Kiraly, eds., *From Hunyadi to Rákóczi: War and Society in Medieval and Early Modern Hungary*, 1982

"Some Characteristics of the Medieval Hungarian Noble Family," *Journal of Family History* 7 (1982), 27–39

Castle and Society in Medieval Hungary, 1000–1437, 1986

Ispánok, bárok, kiskirályok: a középkori magyar arisztokrácia fejlodése (Stewards, Barons, Minor Monarchs: The Evolution of the Medieval Hungarian Aristocracy), 1986

Kings, Bishops, Nobles and Burghers in Medieval Hungary edited by J.M. Bak, 1986 [includes bibliography]

Könyörülj, bánom, könyörülj (Mercy, my Lord, Mercy), 1986

Az Elefánthyak: a középkori magyar nemés es klánja (The Elefánthy: The Medieval Hungarian Nobleman and His Kindred), 1992

Furet, François 1927–1997

French historian

Like most French intellectuals who came to maturity after World War II, Furet as a young man felt the attraction of communism, and what he later called "Stalino-Marxist historicism." He was one of those whose adherence to such views was relatively brief, and whose subsequent development was strongly influenced by the need to exorcise youthful error. This meant that he has devoted much of his life to reflection on the French Revolution of 1789, and on the revolutionary tradition in France, becoming the leader of what is called the Revisionist school. There was an institutional, as well as an intellectual aspect to the conflict between the revisionists and the adherents of the orthodox view of the Revolution. The latter were to be found in the university faculties, and were led by the successive holders of the chair of the history of the Revolution at the Sorbonne (University of Paris), notably Albert Soboul. Furet's career, however, progressed outside the faculties, and in research institutions – the Centre National de la Recherche Scientifique, the Ecole des Hautes Etudes en Sciences Sociales, and finally the Institut Raymond Aron. An additional feature of his career has been its transatlantic nature. From early on he was a frequent visitor to American universities, and in later years he was able to combine his Parisian responsibilities with a post at the University of Chicago.

Furet began with some quantitative work on the 18th-century bourgeoisie, but after joining the Ecole des Hautes Etudes in 1961, he largely abandoned archival research for a broader interpretive sweep. Since then most of his work has taken two forms, narrative histories intended for the general public, and an immense output of interpretive essays, mainly on historiography. Another feature of his career has been the frequency with which he has edited joint works and cooperated with other authors. Thus he has come to be seen as the leader of a school of like-minded revisionist historians.

His first major work was a general narrative history, *La Révolution* (1965–66; *French Revolution*, 1970) in cooperation with Denis Richet. Consisting of two lavishly illustrated volumes, it was intended for the general reader. Nevertheless it was a serious academic contribution, and diverged enough from the standard French line to be seen as controversial. To some extent this resulted from the utilization of perspectives that had been developed by British and American scholars, notably Alfred Cobban. The overall view expressed in this work was that in its first years the Revolution had a positive character, but that after 1792 it had "skidded" off course into the fanaticism and extremism of the Terror. The outbreak of war was essential to this, not seen as an extraneous event, but as the outcome of the Revolution itself, a view long held by non-French historians. As his views developed, Furet came to emphasize more strongly the way in which there was a natural progression from 1789 to the Terror of 1792–94, thus abandoning his "skidding" theory for a virtual return to the view of the Revolution as a "bloc," but seen in a negative light, as it had been by opponents of the Revolution from Burke onwards. The other major characteristic of Furet's revisionism, a feature of his work throughout, was his concentration on the political aspects, and his neglect of the search for economic and social causes.

Over the next fifteen years, apart from joint editorship with Jacques Ozouf of *Lire et écrire* (1977; *Reading and Writing*, 1982), a study of the development of literacy in France, Furet's work consisted largely of essays and articles on the historiography of the Revolution. The most important of these were collected in *Penser la Révolution Française* (1978; *Interpreting the French Revolution*, 1981), including an article first published in *Annales* in 1970, on "the revolutionary catechism." This was an attack on the views of Soboul and Mazauric, on the traditional "Marxist" line. In fact Furet argued that there was not a great deal of Marx in this; he edited a translation of every passage that could be excavated from Marx's works on the subject to show that Marx himself had not said much on the French Revolution specifically. Rather, Furet argued, the traditional views expressed the revolutionaries' own estimates of their role, and thus was Jacobin rather than Marxist.

It was natural that the controversy between Furet's revisionist school and the traditionalists, now led by Vovelle, Soboul's successor in the Sorbonne chair, should be prominent in the explosion of publications that accompanied the bicentenary of the Revolution in 1989. Furet's main contributions were to bring together the different authors of a multivolume *Dictionnaire critique de la Révolution française* (1988; *A Critical Dictionary of the French Revolution*, 1989), to introduce an anthology of speeches, *Orateurs de la Révolution française* (Orators of the French Revolution, 1989), and to take part in the production of the bilingual work *The French Revolution and the Creation of Modern Political Culture* (1987–94). In all of these activities, he continued to work in characteristic fashion in large-scale collaborative projects. In 1992 Furet returned to narrative history with a volume on the period 1770–1879 in a 5-volume general history of France. In this his narrative centered on the working out of the implications of the 1789 Revolution, until they produced the Third Republic. He saw the survival and relative success of this regime as marking the first termination of the cycle of conflict and instability opened in 1789. However the collapse of 1940 and the subsequent years of political and constitutional instability meant, he said, that the definitive termination of the Revolution came only with the bicentenary itself. He expressed this view in his chapter in *La République du Centre* (1988), saying that French exceptionalism, which had begun in 1789, had at last ended. The controversy over the commemoration of the Revolution in the following year suggested that this verdict might have been premature.

Although Furet continued to write on the significance of the Revolution, his most recent work took him into apparently different territory. *Le Passé d'une illusion* (The Past of an Illusion, 1995) deals with the history of the rise and fall of communism in the 20th century. Nevertheless the symbiosis between 1789 and 1917 means that even here he is not far from his continuing preoccupation. For while Mathiez, one of the apostolic succession of those who had expounded the "revolutionary catechism," had defended Bolshevism in 1917–20 by comparing it to Jacobinism, the discrediting of communism in the eyes of French intellectuals over the last twenty years has powerfully strengthened the impact of Furet's revisionist views on Jacobinism, and the Revolution of 1789.

DAVID ROBIN WATSON

See also Annales School; Cobban; France: 1450–1789; France: French Revolution; France: since the Revolution; Ozouf; Poliakov; Political; Social

Biography

Born Paris, 27 March 1927. Studied at Lycée Janson-de-Sailly; agrégation from Faculté des Lettres, Paris. Worked at Centre National de la Recherche Scientifique, 1956–66, before moving to the Ecole des Hautes Etudes en Sciences Sociales, where he was president, 1977–85; director, Institut Raymond Aron, 1985–97; also held a joint appointment with the University of Chicago from 1985. Married 1) Jacqueline Nora (marriage dissolved; 1 son); 2) Deborah Kun, 1986 (1 daughter). Died 12 July 1997.

Principal Writings

With Denis Richet, *La Révolution*, 2 vols., 1965–66, as *La Révolution française*, 1973; in English as *French Revolution*, 1970, and as *Revolutionary France, 1770–1880*, 1992

Editor with Jacques Ozouf, *Lire et écrire: l'alphabétisation des Français de Calvin à Jules Ferry*, 2 vols., 1977; in English as *Reading and Writing: Literacy in France from Calvin to Jules Ferry*, 1982

Penser la Révolution française, 1978, revised 1983; in English as *Interpreting the French Revolution*, 1981

L'Atelier de l'histoire, 1982; in English as *In the Workshop of History*, 1984

La Gauche et la Révolution française au milieu du XIXe siècle: Edgar Quinet et la question du jacobinisme, 1865–1870 (The Left and the French Revolution in the Middle of the 19th Century: Edgar Quinet and the Question of Jacobinism, 1865–1870), 1986

Marx et la Révolution française, 1986; in English as *Marx and the French Revolution*, 1988

Editor with Mona Ozouf, *Dictionnaire critique de la Révolution française*, 1988; in English as *A Critical Dictionary of the French Revolution*, 1989

La République du centre: la fin de l'exception française (The Republic of the Center: The End of French Exceptionalism), 1988

Orateurs de la Révolution française (Orators of the French Revolution), 1989

Editor with Mona Ozouf, *Terminer la Révolution: Mounier et Barnave dans la Révolution française* (Ending the Revolution: Mounier and Barnave in the French Revolution), 1990

Editor with Mona Ozouf, *La Gironde et les Girondins* (The Gironde and the Girondins), 1991

Editor with Mona Ozouf, *The French Revolution and the Creation of Modern Political Culture*, vol.3: *The Transformation of the Political Culture, 1789–1848*, 1991

Editor with Mona Ozouf, *Le Siècle de l'avènement républicain* (The Century of Republican Accession), 1993

Le Passé d'une illusion: essai sur l'idée communiste au XXe siècle (The Past of an Illusion: An Essay on the Idea of Communism), 1995

Further Reading

Langlois, Claude, David D. Bien, Donald Sutherland, and François Furet, "François Furet's Interpretation of the French Revolution," *French Historical Studies*, 16 (1990), 766–80

Furnivall, J.S. 1878–1960

British colonial administrator and scholar of Burma

J.S. Furnivall was noted principally for his writings on colonial policy and practice. As an Indian civil servant, he wrote numerous classified and official reports on various topics of Burmese society. Furnivall had a deep understanding of Burmese culture and was regarded as a knowledgeable and sympathetic commentator on contemporary Burma.

Dubbed the "Grand Old Man of Burmese Scholarship" by the *Guardian*, in April 1960, Furnivall was a prolific writer of broad surveys and introductory texts on the tropical East Indies. He wrote numerous articles and book reviews for more than than two dozen major journals such as the *Journal of the Burma Research Society* and *Public Affairs*, but much of what he wrote is now seen as highly Eurocentric.

In 1908 after seeing a copy of the *Journal of the Siam Society*, Furnivall collaborated with Charles Dinoiselle, former Professor of Pali in Rangoon College, and U May Oung, a barrister, in founding the Burma Research Society in 1910, "for the investigation and encouragement of Arts, Sciences and Literature in relation to Burma and neighbouring countries." The society produced its own journal and attempted to steer clear of politics, but because of the difficulties the society had with the government, it came to be classified as a political organization.

Furnivall placed a very high priority on education and his concern about the shortage of books for Burmese students in the English language led him to found the Burma Book Club and *World of Books* magazine in 1924. The Book Club was a meeting ground for young intellectuals, such as U Thant who supported this venture. To provide opportunities for adult education, Furnivall became a founding member of the Burma Education Extension Association in 1928. He wrote on the relationship of education and economics, noting that the problem of education was one of demand rather than supply, and, furthermore that there was a need to educate the Burmese and prepare them for self-rule (*Educational Progress in Southeast Asia*, 1943). Not all of his views were heeded; for example, during World War II he wrote that the Allies should cooperate with the Burmese to establish a government that was acceptable and capable of governing Burma.

The publication of *An Introduction to the Political Economy of Burma* (1931) aroused much public interest. Written as a set of lectures for university students, the book analyzed the precolonial economy of Burma and the devastating impact the capitalistic West had on the Burmese way of life. Much of Furnivall's information was derived from personal experience and observation, as well as from statistical information. He appealed to the British government of Burma to rebuild the country's economy. He described Burma as a "plural society"; one that consisted "of several groups living side by side but separately, not united for the common welfare or for any common end but divided from one another by the common desire for individual profit."

Netherlands India (1939) is a survey of economic progress and sociopolitical development of Indonesia under Dutch colonial rule. While the indigenous people were active participants in the economic process, the Regents and the native heads were excluded from foreign trade. In turn this led to a loss in their prestige, and an increase in idleness and crime. The Dutch thought they had introduced new land schemes but by encouraging the growth of wealth, they created greater divisions in Javanese society. The educational opportunities for the Javanese were restricted and some "could merely pick up in the vernacular crumbs of European learning such as would qualify them for menial or subordinate clerical positions." Though less acquainted with Indonesia, Furnivall hoped that the Dutch experience would offer the British government of Burma valuable insights on how Burma should be governed. Comparing British and Dutch rule, Furnivall observed that "in Burma the British have from the first relied on western principles of rule, on the principles of law and economic freedom; in Netherlands India the Dutch have tried to conserve and adapt to modernize the tropical principles of custom and authority." Herein, for Furnivall, lay the examples of direct and indirect rule, even though in practice there was no sharp division between the two.

Furnivall's most influential work was *Colonial Policy and Practice* (1948). The book was written at the request of the British government of Burma in their search for solutions to the socioeconomic and political problems that arose after World War II. He analyzed the origins and structures of the colonial governments in Burma and the Dutch East Indies. In Burma, colonial rule destroyed the social structure which was based "on personal authority, custom and religion." Villages lost their autonomy and monastic schools their effectiveness. Furthermore, colonial rule in Burma aided in the rise of a polarized society, which led to racial division in labor and the growth of crime, the latter especially evident in Lower Burma.

Two of Furnivall's later publications were *The Governance of Modern Burma* (1958) and *Experiment in Independence: The Philippines* (1974). In the former, Furnivall analyzed the forms and structures of government in Burma and argued that the main concern of local government should be to encourage the Burmese "to want what they need." The latter publication, published posthumously and edited by Frank N. Trager, is a brief account of the impact of Spanish and American rule, and of the economic and political structures after March 1934 when the Tydings-McDuffie Act was passed. Furnivall's main goal was to publish a comprehensive study of colonial policy and practice in Southeast Asia, a project that did not materialize. But he did complete his intensive study *The Social and Economic History of Burma, 1862–1947*, commissioned by the government of the Union of Burma, but never published by them. Much of the research was based on Furnivall's previous writings on the history of Burma and the consequences of colonial rule in Burma.

After the independence of Burma Furnivall served as an adviser on national planning with the U Nu administration. He was more than a colonial administrator and a scholar; he was an activist concerned about social justice, education, progress, and welfare.

ERNEST A. LeVos

Biography

John Sydenham Furnivall. Born 14 February 1878. Attended Royal Medical Benevolent College, Epsom, 1892–97; Trinity Hall, Cambridge, BA 1900; passed Indian Civil Service examination, 1902. Administrator in Burma, 1903–23: founded Burma Research Society, 1910, and Burma Book Club, 1924; visited and studied in the Netherlands and Java, 1933–35; lecturer, University of Rangoon; and Cambridge University, 1936–41; lived in Burma 1948–60; adviser on planning to the Government of the Union of Burma. Married Margaret Ma Nyun Toungoo (2 daughters). Received Order of Thado Thiri Thudhamna, 1949. Died Cambridge, 7 July 1960.

Principal Writings

An Introduction to the Political Economy of Burma, 1931
The Fashioning of Leviathan: The Beginnings of British Rule in Burma, 1939
Netherlands India: A Study of Plural Economy, 1939
Progress and Welfare in South-East Asia: A Comparison of Colonial Policy and Practice, 1941
Educational Progress in Southeast Asia, 1943
Colonial Policy and Practice: A Comparative Study of Burma and Netherlands India, 1948
The Governance of Modern Burma, 1958
Experiment in Independence: The Philippines, edited by Frank N. Trager, 1974

Further Reading

Cowan, C.D., and Oliver William Wolters, eds., *Southeast Asian History and Historiography: Essays Presented to D.G.E. Hall*, Ithaca, NY: Cornell University Press, 1976

Hall, D.G.E., ed., *Historians of South East Asia*, London: Oxford University Press, 1961

Trager, Frank N., ed., *Furnivall of Burma: An Annotated Bibliography of the Works of John S. Furnivall*, New Haven: Yale University Press, 1963

Fustel de Coulanges, Numa 1830–1889

French historian

Numa Fustel de Coulanges' first great work, *La Cité antique* (1864; *The Ancient City*, 1877), was founded on his thorough knowledge of classical languages and careful reading in ancient texts. It contended that religion was the sole factor in the evolution of ancient Greece and Rome, that the bonding of family and state was the work of religion, that because of ancestor worship the family, drawn together by the need to engage in the ancestral cults, became the basic unit of ancient societies, expanding to the *gens*, the Greek phratry, the Roman tribe, to the patrician city state, and that decline in religious belief and authority in the moral crisis provoked by Roman wealth and expansion doomed the republic and resulted in the triumph of Christianity and the death of the ancient city state. This controversial thesis was welcome enough in the Second Empire to lead Victor Duruy to select Fustel to tutor the empress Eugénie in history. A few years later, under the Third Republic, it marked Fustel as dangerously antisecular but he never retreated from his conclusions.

Fustel felt the humiliation of France in the War of 1870 all the more keenly because of his residence in Strasbourg and, while producing a historical refutation of German claims to Alsace, he was led to re-examine the entire question of Germanic influence on French history. The result was the publication in 1875 of what he intended to be the first volume of *Histoire des institutions politiques de l'ancienne France* (History of the Political Institutions of Ancient France). This dealt with the period of the Germanic invasions and was to be followed by three more volumes dealing respectively with feudalism, the later Middle Ages, and the *ancien régime*. The thesis of this first volume was that the Germanic invasions were gradual and peaceful rather than sudden and violent, that they produced no new economic or political institutions, so that Merovingian Gaul merely continued the practices of the late Roman empire. In Fustel's view, the feudal transformation and the growth of aristocracy arose from private methods of property organization and protection. The Franks did not bring about this change, only contributed to it via the teutonic judicial system and the *comitatus*. This thesis drew so much criticism from both French and German historians that Fustel set to work to prove his contentions in detail, in a work that took the remainder of his life, was published in full in six volumes only after his death, and then extended only as far as the Carolingian years. He managed to produce enough scholarly work not directly related to his great investigation to fill three volumes of miscellaneous studies.

Fustel prided himself on the rigorousness of his method. He told his students that no presuppositions, not even a working hypothesis can be allowed to influence the developing investigation. He took no account of evidence except for contemporary documents (literary and philosophical as well as official) which he examined and interrogated minutely. Above all, he insisted that the historian guard against reading present ideas or concerns backward into the past. He claimed to have founded his method entirely on Descartes, but was surely influenced by the positivism of his own day and was perhaps naively confident of his ability to arrive at the truth, even to the point of claiming to be able to enumerate exactly how many "truths" he had uncovered. His insistence on using only documents not only blocked him from taking adequate account of the insights of his fellow historians but was also deeply flawed by his complete ignorance of some methods of documentary analysis. Trained initially in ancient history, he never studied diplomatics, which is central to the understanding and interpretation of medieval charters and chancery documents, so that he based some of his analyses on forgeries that were recognized as such by other researchers. When taxed with this, he dismissed the criticism on the ground that a good forger was perforce using the methods and concepts of the time in which the document was supposed to have originated, so that a good forgery was as useful to him as an authentic document. Critics also noticed that the origins of his great study in his emotional reaction to the War of 1870 put paid to his claims not to read the past through a hypothesis based on the concerns of the present, a circumstance that explains why the ultra-nationalist Charles Maurras claimed Fustel as a patron saint of anti-Germanism. Nonetheless, he maintained an exalted notion of his own importance, even to cautioning a class of students, "Do not applaud me. It is not I that speak to you but History that speaks through my mouth!"

JOSEPH M. MCCARTHY

See also Agrarian; France: to 1000; France 1000–1450

Biography

Numa Denis Fustel de Coulanges. Born Paris, 18 March 1830; orphaned at a young age. Studied at the Lycée Charlemagne; graduated from the Ecole Normale Supérieure, 1853, then spent two years at the Ecole Française d'Athènes; received his agrégation, 1857. Professor at the lycée in Amiens; doctorat-ès-lettres, Paris, 1858; professor of history at Strasbourg, 1860–70; and Ecole Normale Supérieure, 1870–75; professor of ancient history, 1875–78, and medieval history, 1878–80, 1883–89, the Sorbonne; director, Ecole Normale Supérieure, 1880–83. Married Blanche Hermine Julienne Demarquat, 1856. Died Massy, Essonne, 12 September 1889.

Principal Writings

La Cité antique, 1864; in English as *The Ancient City: A Study on the Religion, Laws and Institutions of Greece and Rome*, 1877

Histoire des institutions politiques de l'ancienne France (History of the Political Institutions of Medieval France), 6 vols., 1875–92

Recherches sur quelques problèmes d'histoire (Research on Some Historical Problems), 1885; includes "Le problème des origines foncières," translated as *The Origin of Property in Land*, 1891

Nouvelles recherches sur quelques problèmes d'histoire (New Research on Some Historical Problems), edited by Camille Juliann, 1891

Questions historiques (Historical Questions), edited by Camille Juliann, 1893

Further Reading

Arbois de Jubainville, H. d', *Deux manières d'écrire l'histoire: critique de Bossuet, d'Augustin Thierry, et de Fustel de Coulanges* (Two Ways of Writing History: A Critique of Bossuet, Thierry and Fustel de Coulanges), Paris: Bouillon, 1896

Aulard, Alphonse, "Fustel de Coulanges, patriote, politique, philosophe" (Fustel de Coulanges: Patriot, Politician, Philosopher), *La révolution française* (1916), 385–99

Bloch, Marc, "Fustel de Coulanges, historien des origines françaises" (Fustel de Coulanges, Historian of French Origins), *Revue internationale de l'enseignement* (1930), 168–78

Bourgeois, Emile, "Fustel de Coulanges," *Revue internationale de l'enseignement* (1890), 121–51

Galateo Adamo, Andrea, *Le mura e gli uomini: società e politica in N.D. Fustel de Coulanges* (Walls and Men: Society and Politics in N.D. Fustel de Coulanges), Naples: Edizioni Scientifiche Italiane, 1987

Gaxotte, Pierre, "Fustel de Coulanges, historien sous le boisseau" (Fustel de Coulanges: Historian under a Bushel), *Le Purgatoire* (1982), 83–90

Gérin-Ricard, Lazare de, *L'Histoire des institutions politiques de Fustel de Coulanges* (Fustel de Coulanges' History of Political Institutions), Paris: Malfère, 1936

Guiraud, Paul, *Fustel de Coulanges*, Paris: Hachette, 1896

Hartog, François, *Le XIXe siècle et l'histoire: le cas Fustel de Coulanges* (The 19th Century and History: The Case of Fustel de Coulanges), Paris: Presses Universitaires de France, 1988

Herrick, Jane, *The Historical Thought of Fustel de Coulanges*, Washington, DC: Catholic University of America Press, 1954

Maurras, Charles M.P., *Devant l'Allemagne éternelle: Gaulois, Germains, Latins: chronique d'une résistance* (Against Everlasting Germany: Gauls, Germans, Latins: A Chronicle of Resistance), Paris: Etoile, 1937

Monod, Gabriel, "Fustel de Coulanges," *Revue historique* (1889), 277–85

Tourneur-Aumont, Jean-Mederic, *Fustel de Coulanges, 1830–1889*, Paris: Boivin, 1931

G

Gall, Lothar 1936–

German historian of modern Germany

Lothar Gall ranks first among living historians of 19th-century Germany. Gall has written the standard German-language biography of Germany's first chancellor, Otto von Bismarck, *Bismarck: Der weisse Revolutionär* (1980; *Bismarck: The White Revolutionary*, 1986). He has also published extensively on 19th-century liberalism and on the development of the *Bürgertum* and *Mittelstand*, the German middle class. Gall has edited what many consider the standard German-language text on the history of German liberalism, *Liberalismus* (Liberalism, 1976).

The publication of *Bismarck* heralded the rebirth of political biography as a legitimate genre in German historiography, now firmly re-established with such works as Theodor Schieder's 1986 biography of Frederick the Great, and John C.G. Röhl's two-volume biography of Wilhelm II. According to Gall, Bismarck was a conservative because he wanted desperately to maintain the quasi-absolutist Prussian monarchy. Yet, Bismarck was revolutionary in his methods. Unable to resolve this tension between goal and method, Bismarck – described by Gall as the "sorcerer's apprentice" – created a regime he himself was unable to control and which would be unable to exist without him: "Nothing, absolutely nothing remains" of Bismarck's achievements. Most biographers no longer consider historical greatness an interesting or even a legitimate standard against which to measure their subjects. Nonetheless, Gall has done so profitably. According to Gall, the historical individual's ability to recognize as mere tools what contemporaries can only identify as goals is what lends the figure greatness. Thus, Bismarck, despite the failure of his life's work, was great.

Just as Gall's interest in the great historical individual signifies a rejection of much of German historiography of the 1970s, his research on the *Bürgertum* has shown an interest in a better understanding of the role the middle class played in Germany's failure to establish the western-style democracy that Ralf Dahrendorf idealized in *Society and Democracy in Germany* (1967), an ideal which German historians have made their own. In *Bürgertum in Deutschland* (The Middle Class in Germany, 1989), Gall narrated the history of the Bassermann family. Gall described them as the quintessential *Bürger* of the 19th century, *mittelständisch*. The Bassermanns' 18th-century ancestors were not urban patricians, nor did they rise into the middle class through the civil service. They were self-made men, measuring their self-worth by their own achievement. Although it is difficult to consider the Bassermanns representative of the *Bürgertum* in general, Gall convincingly describes what happened to the *Mittelstand* after 1848. Contributing to the re-evaluation of late 19th-century German society and politics begun by David Blackbourn and Geoff Eley in *The Peculiarities of German History* (1984), Gall stressed the Bassermanns' involvement in those bodies that Blackbourn and Eley correctly identified as the middle class's political home: the extra-parliamentary bodies, especially the many voluntary associations, Germany's *Vereine*. Gall's important contribution to the work begun by Blackbourn and Eley, however, is his differentiation between the different strata of the *Bürgertum*. Blackbourn and Eley explained how the uppermost levels and lowest levels of the middle class politically expressed themselves. The *Bürger* in the uppermost levels of the middle class found ways to influence the regime by their increasing economic importance; those in the lowest levels quickly sank into the petty bourgeoisie, the trusted supporters of the Wilhelmine regime. Gall described the fate of the original *Mittelstand* which occupied the middle of the middle-class social strata, those Germans who led Germany's early industrialization and who brought forth the industrialists of the late 19th and early 20th centuries. Economically increasingly marginalized but able to avoid falling to the levels of the petty bourgeoisie, members of this *Mittelstand* became members of an interest group like any other in German society, renouncing all ties to the ideals of 1848, or they joined the middle levels of the civil service, became academics or professionals, or they rejected both their heritage and the hollow shell of Wilhelminism and became artists.

With his research, Gall has contributed significantly to a new and more differentiated understanding of the 19th century, discarding old epochal descriptors as the age of nationalism, of revolution, of industrialization. Gall perhaps best summarized his historiographical position in his contribution to the Oldenbourg History Outlines series: *Europa auf dem Weg in die Moderne, 1850–1890* (Europe on Its Way to Modernity, 1984). According to Gall, the 19th century was an age of transitions, of developments overlapping in time; no one type of development dominated the epoch. Perhaps most important to Gall is the interconnection between national and European developments.

Gall has remained outside the fray of methodological controversies in German historiography such as the *Historikerstreit*.

While this is easier for a historian of the 19th century than for a contemporary historian, he has not avoided exposure in the public sphere. As contributor to the exhibition *Fragen an die deutsche Geschichte* (Questions in German History, 1974) in Berlin's parliament building, Gall edited the accompanying catalog. This exhibition serves as a model of neutral, sober – occasionally too sober – presentation of history. In the exhibition, Gall's assessment of the totality of German history became clear: the continuity in German history lies in its discontinuity, its frequent, far-reaching political, cultural, and socioeconomic change.

Gall's greatest contribution to the study of 19th-century Germany history is his emphasis on its transitional character. His works mark the beginning of a transition from the methodologically and thematically narrow research foci of the 1960s and 1970s to a more comprehensive definition of the age.

MARTIN R. MENKE

See also Germany: 1800–1945

Biography

Born Lötzen, East Prussia, 3 December 1936. Received doctorate, 1960; Habilitation, 1967. Taught at University of Giessen, 1968–72; Free University of Berlin, 1972–75; and University of Frankfurt, from 1975.

Principal Writings

Benjamin Constant: Seine politische Ideenwelt und der deutsche Vormärz (Benjamin Constant: His Political Ideas and Germany before the Revolution of 1848), 1963

Der Liberalismus als regierende Partei: Das Grossherzogtum Baden zwischen Restauration und Reichsgründung (Liberalism as a Governing Party: The Grand Duchy of Baden Between Restoration and the Establishment of the Reich of 1871), 1968

Editor, *Das Bismarck-Problem in der Geschichtsschreibung nach 1945* (The Question of Bismarck in German Historiography after 1945), 1971

With others, *Fragen an die deutsche Geschichte* (Questions in German History), 1974 [exhibition catalog]

"Liberalismus und 'bürgerliche Gesellschaft': Zu Charakter und Entwicklung der liberalen Bewegung in Deutschland" (Liberalism and Bourgeois Society), *Historische Zeitschrift* 220 (1975), 324–56

"Bismarck und der Bonapartismus" (Bismarck and Bonapartism), *Historische Zeitschrift* 223 (1976), 618–37

Editor, *Liberalismus* (Liberalism), 1976

Bismarck: Der weisse Revolutionär, 1980; in English as *Bismarck: The White Revolutionary*, 2 vols., 1986

Editor, *Die grossen Reden* (The Great Speeches [of Otto von Bismarck]), 1981

"Die Bundesrepublik in der Kontinuität der deutschen Geschichte" (West Germany in the Continuity of German History), *Historische Zeitschrift* 239 (1984), 603–13

Europa auf dem Weg in die Moderne, 1850–1890 (Europe on Its Way to Modernity), 1984

Editor, *Die grossen Deutschen unserer Epoche* (The Great Germans of Our Age), 1985

"Theodor Schieder, 1908–1984," *Historische Zeitschrift* 241 (1985), 1–25

Bürgertum in Deutschland (The Middle Class in Germany), 1989

"Von der ständischen zur bürgerlichen Gesellschaft" (From Feudal to Bourgeois Society), in Peter Blickle, ed., *Enzyklopädie deutscher Geschichte*, vol.25, 1993

"Die Gegenwart der Vergangenheit: Zum Lebenswerk von Thomas Nipperdey" (The Present of the Past: On the Life's Work of Thomas Nipperdey), *Historische Zeitschrift* 256 (1993), 297–308

Editor with others, *Die Deutsche Bank, 1870–1995*; in English as *The Deutsche Bank, 1870–1995*, 1995

Bürgertum, Liberale Bewegung und Nation: Ausgewählte Aufsätze (Middle Class, Liberal Movement, and Nation: Selected Essays), edited by Dieter Hein, Andreas Schulze, and Eckhart Triechel, 1996

Further Reading

Schulze, Winfried, *Deutsche Geschichtswissenschaft nach 1945* (German Historical Science since 1945), Munich: Oldenbourg, 1989

Gallagher, John 1919–1980

British imperial historian

John Gallagher was not a prolific historian, and was unusual in that most of his important work was published in collaboration, especially with Ronald Robinson. Much of his significance lies in his influence over a generation of imperial historians, most especially of British India (the Cambridge school), whose work transformed the historiography of this subject in the 1960s and 1970s. Nevertheless, in collaboration with Robinson, Gallagher was responsible for three works, an article, a chapter in the *New Cambridge Modern History* (1962), and a book, *Africa and the Victorians* (1961), which turned the study of 19th-century imperial expansion on its head.

Prior to the publication of "The Imperialism of Free Trade" (1953), the historiography of 19th-century European imperialism had been dominated by attempts to explain the apparently dramatic late century reversal of indifference to empire which seemed to lie behind the "Scramble for Africa" and for the Pacific, and by debate over the "Hobson-Lenin thesis" that expansion resulted from crisis in the European economy. Robinson and Gallagher challenged this sense of discontinuity, arguing that the mid-19th century had not been an era of anti-imperialism, but that – at least in the case of the British – the whole century shared certain attitudes to empire: that the expansion of trade and British interests were desirable, but should be achieved at the minimum possible cost and the least possible political commitment. The motto, they suggested, could have been "trade without control if possible; trade with control if necessary." The determinants which made the shift from "informal control" to formal annexation necessary were identified not – or at least not usually – in Europe, but in Africa and Asia themselves.

These ideas were developed in *Africa and the Victorians* (1961). Here Robinson and Gallagher, assisted by Alice Denny, argued that the fulcrum of the Scramble for Africa was the British "occupation" of Egypt in 1882. This intervention, they suggested, set in motion a chain of diplomatic events that led ultimately to the Berlin conference of 1886. The reason presented for this intervention was not a seachange in British policy, but rather the crumbling of the Khedival regime in Egypt, through which Britain and France had previously exercised informal control.

At the same time, the book also introduced two other themes. Almost as an afterthought, Robinson and Gallagher formulated the concept of the "official mind" of imperialism, suggesting that ultimately the motives for imperial expansion could not be derived from broad analysis of the needs of the economy, any more than from the rhetoric of politicians, but only through painstaking analysis of the thoughts, assumptions, and viewpoints of unheralded civil servants of the Foreign and Colonial offices, whose collective consciousness amounted to an "official mind" in which the key decisions were taken. For this official mind, it was emphasized, each element of empire was rarely treated in isolation, or from an economic perspective alone, but was usually treated strategically, with reference to its place in the complete imperial system. The imperative to bolster British control in Egypt rested on the Suez Canal, and the significance of the canal was as a vital imperial artery linking the British Isles to India. Thus the African empire was little more than a "giant footnote" to the history of the Indian empire.

Of greatest significance, however, was the central place that these works, and especially the chapter on "The Partition of Africa" which Gallagher co-wrote with Robinson for the *New Cambridge Modern History* vol. 11 (1962), gave to the notion of "collaboration," and hence to the operation of historical forces at the imperial frontier. This notion in particular, but also these three works in general, formed the foundations of the "ex-centric" or peripheral approaches to European imperialism taken up by D.K. Fieldhouse and others.

Unlike Robinson, who continued to elaborate the notion of collaboration, Gallagher avoided becoming embroiled in the sustained historical controversy which these early publications produced. Enduring after 1963 what he considered a Babylonian exile in Oxford, before returning to Cambridge in 1971, his personal publications were few. Much of the considerable work he did on India during this period was never written-up; all that appeared were snatches, such as his essay "Nationalisms and the Crisis of Empire, 1919–22," eventually published in 1981. Nevertheless, through the work of his pupils, Gallagher helped to rewrite the history of modern India, shifting the focus from high diplomacy to what has since been described as "the brutal scramble for resources by politicians at the more humble level where the pickings lay," and pointing out both the frugality of much imperial control, and the crucial role of neglect in the maintenance of empire.

By the later 1970s, Gallagher's work was increasingly circumscribed by illness. As a result his Ford Lectures of 1973–74 were revised and published only after his death. Although retaining many of the stylistic quirks appropriate to oral delivery, the resulting volume, *The Decline, Revival and Fall of the British Empire* (1982), developed his ideas of empire as a coherent entity to be studied holistically as a continual historical process. It rejected common assumptions that envisaged imperialism as undergoing a unidirectional trajectory of decay, leading eventually and inevitably to independence, with nationalism as much an element in the process of imperial control as it was a response to it, and argued instead that empire had to be seen as an uneven and cyclical process, in which imperial fortunes could wax as well as wane. Here Gallagher also developed his influential analysis of the three levels in the imperial environment: international, national, and colonial, arguing that it was the shifting balance of forces at each of these levels, rather than changes – however dramatic – in any one, that ultimately determined the course of imperial histories.

Like most historiographical revolutions, Gallagher's work did not gain universal acceptance. The early work with Robinson prompted a long-running historical controversy that ultimately spawned studies in its own right. His later work has been seen as a pale reflection of what he might have achieved. Nevertheless, there can be no doubt that Gallagher's works transformed the study of European empire.

MARTIN HEWITT

See also British Empire; Egypt: since the 7th Century; Imperial

Biography
John Andrew Gallagher. Born 1 April 1919. Educated at Birkenhead Institute; Trinity College, Cambridge, MA 1937. Served in Royal Tank Regiment, 1939–45. Fellow, Trinity College, Cambridge, 1948–63: dean, 1960–63, senior research fellow, 1971–72; university lecturer, Cambridge University, 1953–63; Beit professor of the history of the British commonwealth, Oxford University, 1963–70; fellow, Balliol College, Oxford, 1963–70; Vere Harmsworth professor of imperial and naval history, Cambridge University, 1971–80. Died 5 March 1980.

Principal Writings
With Ronald Robinson, "The Imperialism of Free Trade," *Economic History Review* 6 (1953), 1–15; reprinted in *The Decline, Revival and Fall of the British Empire*, 1982

With Ronald Robinson and Alice Denny, *Africa and the Victorians: The Official Mind of Imperialism*, 1961; revised 1981

With Ronald Robinson, "The Partition of Africa," *The New Cambridge Modern History* vol. 11, Cambridge: Cambridge University Press, 1962; reprinted in *The Decline, Revival and Fall of the British Empire*, 1982

The Decline, Revival and Fall of the British Empire: The Ford Lectures and Other Essays, edited by Anil Seal, 1982

Further Reading
Atmore, A.E., "The Extra-European Foundations of British Imperialism: Towards a Reassessment," in C.C. Eldridge, ed., *British Imperialism in the Nineteenth Century*, Basingstoke: Macmillan, and New York: St. Martin's Press, 1984

Fieldhouse, D.K., "'Imperialism': An Historiographical Revision," *Economic History Review* 14 (1961), 187–209

Fieldhouse, D.K., *Economics and Empire, 1830–1914*, London: Weidenfeld and Nicolson, and Ithaca, NY: Cornell University Press, 1973

Louis, William Roger, ed., *Imperialism: The Robinson and Gallagher Controversy*, New York: New Viewpoints, 1976

Platt, Desmond Christopher Martin, *Finance, Trade and Politics in British Foreign Policy, 1815–1914*, Oxford: Oxford University Press, 1968

Platt, Desmond Christopher Martin, "The Imperialism of Free Trade: Some Reservations," *Economic History Review* 21 (1968), 296–306

Robinson, Ronald, and Anil Seal, "Professor John Gallagher, 1919–80," *Journal of Imperial and Commonwealth History* 9 (1981), 119–24

Stokes, Eric, "Late Nineteenth Century Colonial Expansion and the Attack on the Theory of Economic Imperialism: A Case of Mistaken Identity?," *Historical Journal* 12 (1969), 285–301

Ganshof, F.L. 1895–1980

Belgian medievalist

One of the most eminent medieval historians of the mid-20th century, F.L. Ganshof was the direct successor of Henri Pirenne at the head of the famous "Ghent school" of medievalists established by Pirenne at the University of Ghent, Belgium. Emerging from the troubled times of World War I and the bitter struggle within Belgium between Dutch and French speakers, Ganshof helped preserve the fame of Ghent after it became completely Dutch-speaking after 1930. His work was shaped by his legal studies – he practiced law for a short time in the 1920s – and in working out many of the implications of Pirenne's theoretical arguments, particularly with regard to the centrality of the Carolingian era in European history. Possessed of formidable expertise in source criticism as well as enormous energy and zest in the hunt for documents, Ganshof was passionate about writing history based on a meticulous and close reading of the sources. He distrusted historical theory and ended the earlier contacts of Ghent with the then-fledgling Annales school of Marc Bloch and Lucien Febvre.

No area better showed the dominant traits of Ganshof's approach to history than his publications on the Frankish period, c.500–900. This period was congenial and fascinating to him both because his teacher Pirenne, in *Mahomet et Charlemagne* (1937; *Mohammed and Charlemagne*, 1939), had marked it as the transition point between the late Roman and medieval periods and because, as he told his students, it was the last era of human history whose sources could be mastered by a single scholar. Eschewing Pirenne's theoretical and economic methodology, however, Ganshof produced dozens of articles all marked by a thoroughgoing institutional and legal approach to his subject based upon important documents surviving from the period. Among these documents were the Polyptics, Einhard's biography of Charlemagne, the capitularies, and others. These articles appeared in a variety of journals, conference proceedings, and *Festschriften*, and only some were collected by Bryce and Mary Lyon, appearing in English as *Frankish Institutions under Charlemagne* (1968) and *The Carolingians and the Frankish Monarchy* (1971). Several of these pieces remain the starting point for further research in a number of areas. An important summary of many of Ganshof's conclusions about the organization of the early medieval countryside can be found in his article for the first *Cambridge Economic History* (1941).

By far Ganshof's most enduring and popular work was a short textbook, *Qu'est-ce que la féodalité?* (1944; *Feudalism*, 1952). Especially in North America, it became a perennial bestseller in survey classes on the European Middle Ages and is the only work by Ganshof still in print. The book's virtues for teaching were many: it defined the crucial legal and institutional aspects of feudalism in a concise and lavishly documented form. By drawing on documents originating from the region between the Loire and Rhine rivers, Ganshof was able to lay bare, he believed, the basic legal and institutional structure of medieval society of the 9th through 11th centuries, which in turn served as the foundation for the growth of the great national kingdoms of the High Middle Ages. Here again we find Ganshof's conviction, inherited from Pirenne, of the central importance of the Carolingian age, and the corresponding importance of the

Frankish heartland as the microcosm of Europe. His views have proven very congenial to American historians of the Middle Ages, several of whom, such as Carl Stephenson and Joseph Strayer, published significant works on the same subject.

The third area of Ganshof's historical interests had to do with the history of Belgium and the Low Countries in general. He was the author of a number of important works on the region, including a history of the first counts of Flanders, a history of Belgium in the Carolingian period, and a general history of urban institutions in the region between the Loire and Rhine in the Middle Ages. Together with numerous articles and extended critical essays, Ganshof made a major contribution to the historical writing about his own country.

Lastly, there was Ganshof the internationalist. Partly by upbringing and early experience as an attaché at the Paris Peace Conference of 1919, Ganshof was at home in the cosmopolitan world of a postwar Europe bent on some form of unification. His work on the Frankish period in general and Charlemagne in particular threw light on the "pre-national" period of European history when, as he believed, the essential traits of European culture were formed. He also helped rehabilitate the image of Charlemagne, who had been claimed as an imperial ancestor by the Nazis, but who emerged in Ganshof's work as the "Father of Europe." This was precisely the title of a major exhibition on Charlemagne and his age held at Aachen in 1965 under the auspices of the European Community. Ganshof's influence extended to the United States in the form of a visiting appointment at the University of California at Berkeley for the 1963–64 academic year.

In many ways Ganshof was the last of the great historical positivists, whose first question was always "What does the source say?" Before the end of his life, this approach to history had been discarded as old-fashioned by many, particularly those inspired by the methodological approaches of the Annales school. Even at the University of Ghent, the focus has evolved away from source criticism and institutional history in favor of social and economic history. Ganshof's ideas about feudalism have also been challenged as being too far removed from reality, as well as anachronistic. Thus, despite international renown nearly equal to that of Henri Pirenne during his lifetime, the influence of Ganshof's work has receded much faster than his master's. Nonetheless Ganshof will remain an important figure for the understanding of Carolingian history for some time to come.

JAMES M. MURRAY

See also Annales regni; Feudalism; France: to 1000

Biography

François-Louis Ganshof. Born Bruges, Belgium 14 March 1895, son of a lawyer. Attended Athenée Royal; attaché, Belgian delegation, Paris Peace Conference, 1919; studied law and history, University of Ghent, where he was supervised by Henri Pirenne, DLit 1921, LLD 1922; postgraduate study with Ferdinand Lot at University of Paris. Law practice, Brussels, 1922–23. Taught (rising to professor), University of Ghent, 1923–61. Married Nelly Kirkpatrick, 1920 (2 sons, 2 daughters). Died Brussels, 1980.

Principal Writings

Etude sur les ministériales en Flandre et en Lotharingie (A Study of "Ministeriales" in Flanders and Lotharingia), 1926

"Medieval Agrarian Society at Its Prime," in *The Cambridge Economic History of Europe*, 1941

Qu'est-ce que la féodalité?, 1944; in English as *Feudalism*, 1952

Le Moyen Age, 1953; in English as *The Middle Ages: a History of International Relations*, 1971

La Belgique carolingienne (Carolingian Belgium), 1958

Karl der Grosse in seiner Aachener Pfalz während der Jahre 802 und 803 ... Das karolingische Erbe im Osten, 1959; abridged in English as *Frankish Institutions under Charlemagne*, 1968

The Carolingians and the Frankish Monarchy, 1971

Further Reading

Milis, Ludo, "Nécrologie: Francois-Louis Ganshof," *Revue Belge de Philologie et d'Histoire* 59 (1981), 518–28

Simons, Walter, "The *Annales* and Medieval Studies in the Low Countries," in Miri Rubin, ed., *The Work of Jacques Le Goff and the Challenges of Medieval History*, Woodbridge, Suffolk: Boydell and Brewer, 1996

Garcilaso de la Vega 1539–1616

Peruvian chronicler

Garcilaso de la Vega, known as "El Inca," was born in Cuzco, Peru, the son of Captain Sebastián Garcilaso de la Vega, a prominent Spaniard, and Isabel, the granddaughter of the Incan ruler Tupac Yupanqui. This mixed heritage would prove to be the guiding influence in Garcilaso's life and historical importance. Garcilaso's father divorced his mother and disowned them both, but upon his father's death, Garcilaso traveled to Spain to attempt to claim part of the family inheritance. He would never return to Peru, making the Old World his new home. During his years in Spain, Garcilaso served in the army of the Spanish monarch Philip II, and rose to the rank of captain. Following his military career he took minor religious orders. He also turned to the writing profession as a source of income. It would be Garcilaso's Peruvian-Spanish heritage that would become the major influence of his writings.

La Florida del Inca (1605; *The Florida of the Inca*, 1951), was his first historical work. Although not as widely known as his later work, this look at the Hernando de Soto expedition was based upon the recollections of a soldier in the de Soto entourage, Gonzalo Silvestre. Garcilaso's work on the pre-Hispanic period of Peruvian history, *Comentarios reales de los Incas* (*Royal Commentaries of the Incas*, 1966), became widely read and greatly respected following its publication in 1609. In addition to Garcilaso's personal recollection of stories that his mother had told him while he was growing up, the work also utilized the written account by a Jesuit priest, Blas Valera, that had come into the possession of Garcilaso when he lived in Spain. Furthermore, he had requested Incan documents from friends still living in Peru and these became another source of information for his writings. Accordingly, part of the book resembles a memoir, but the rest of it was based on Spanish chroniclers who worked in Peru.

Garcilaso's importance to the historical profession lies in the fact that he had a true sense of the times and of the Incan people. As such, he was able to provide the native side of Peruvian history, especially for the period prior to the arrival of the Spaniards. Garcilaso combined his knowledge of Peruvian history with an elegant writing style, a style that has led some to call him one of the greatest prose writers of colonial Spain.

Although authoritative from the perspective of Incan events, Garcilaso's works also contained the bias that was found in the Spanish accounts (such as Pedro Sarmiento de Gambóa's *Historia de los incas* [*History of the Incas*]) that he denounced. In addition to the criticism noted above, Garcilaso's writings were also criticized for a lack of historical analysis. It is worth noting, however, that Garcilaso had not been trained as a historian. Moreover, he should not be considered a historian in the modern-day sense, but rather a chronicler who added literary style to his stories. His major historical contribution can be found in his compilation of the facts about the Incan customs, legends, and beliefs, and the passing down of that knowledge to later generations.

Garcilaso lived and wrote during the era of several noted Spanish historical writers who collectively developed a Latin American historiography. Among them were Alonso de Ercilla y Zúñiga (*La Araucana* [The Araucanan]), Bernardo de Balbuena (*La grandeza mexicana* [Mexican Grandeur]), Francisco Cervantes de Salazar (*Mexico en 1554* [Mexico in 1554]), and Pedro de Cieza de León (*La crónica del Perú* [Chronicle of Peru]). For his major contribution, Garcilaso was the first chronicler/historian to offer a nativist account of Peruvian history. In this regard, the mestizo's work was accepted with such admiration for the authenticity of its presentation of the Incan story to European society that *Royal Commentaries* was translated into French around 1633 and into English in 1688.

Garcilaso also worked on a history of Spanish Peru, *Historia general del Perú* (*General History of Peru*, 1688), which was published the year following his death in Córdoba in 1616.

H. MICHEAL TARVER

See also Latin America: Colonial

Biography

Garcilaso [Gómez Suárez de Figueroa]. Born Cuzco, Peru (then capital of the Inca empire), 12 April 1539, son of Spanish captain and Inca princess. Spent childhood with mother's family; taken to live with father and given new family name, Gómez Suárez de Figueroa, which he used until adulthood; tutored privately in Latin and Spanish. After father's death, left Peru for Spain, and settled with uncle at Montilla, near Córdoba, 1560; served in military until 1574, then retired to farm and breed horses; left Montilla for Córdoba where he took orders and served as chief steward, Immaculate Conception Hospital, from 1590. Died Córdoba, Spain, 23 April 1616.

Principal Writings

La Florida del Inca o historia del Adelantado Hernando de Soto, 1605; in English as *The Florida of the Inca*, 1951

Comentarios reales de los Incas, 1609 (*Primera parte* [First Part]); in English as *First Part of the Royal Commentaries of the Yncas*, 2 vols., 1869–71

Historia general del Perú, 1617 (*Segunda parte* [Second Part] of *Comentarios reales*); in English as *General History of Peru*, 1688

Works: A Critical Text with Bibliography, edited by Hayward Keniston, 1925

Royal Commentaries of the Incas and General History of Peru, translated by Harold V. Livermore, 2 vols., 1966

Further Reading

Adorno, Rolena, "El Inca Garcilaso de la Vega" in Verity Smith, ed., *Encyclopedia of Latin American Literature*, London and Chicago: Fitzroy Dearborn, 1997

Aranda, Antonio Garrido, ed., *El Inca Garcilaso entre Europa y America*, Córdoba: Caja Provincial de Ahorros de Córdoba, 1994

Instituto Cambio y Desarrollo, *Ynca Garcilaso de la Vega: primer mestizo de America: estudios*, Lima: Instituto de Investigaciones Cambio y Desarrollo, 1993

Miró Quesada, Aurelio, *El Inca Garcilaso*, Lima: Scheuch, 1945

Sanchez, Luis Alberto, *Garcilaso Inca de la Vega, primer criollo*, Santiago: Ercilla, 1939

Slick, Sam L., "Garcilaso de la Vega," in James Olson, ed., *Historical Dictionary of the Spanish Empire, 1402–1975*, Westport, CT: Greenwood Press, 1992

Thomas, Jack Ray, *Biographical Dictionary of Latin American Historians and Historiography*, Westport, CT: Greenwood Press, 1984

Varner, John Grier, *El Inca: The Life and Times of Garcilaso de la Vega*, Austin: University of Texas Press, 1968

Volpi, Giorgio, "Storiografia della non-storia e modernita storiografica nell'inca Garcilaso de la Vega" (Historiography of Nonhistory and Modern Historiography in Garcilaso del la Vega), *Storia della Storiografia* 5 (1984), 19–45

Gardiner, Samuel Rawson 1829–1902

British historian

Few works of Victorian scholarship have had a more profound effect on succeeding historiography than Samuel Rawson Gardiner's narrative of English history from 1603 to 1658. For nearly a century Gardiner's work has provided a framework for debate regarding the causes and consequences of the English revolution of the 1640s. Yet his achievement is as complex as it is influential. A descendant of Oliver Cromwell, Gardiner was born in 1829 to a gentry family which belonged to the Catholic Apostolic church or Irvingites, a millennialist, anti-revolutionary sect with universal claims. Gardiner's religious affiliation did not prevent him from receiving a First Class BA from Christ Church, Oxford, but he was apparently forced by the dean and chapter to resign his studentship shortly thereafter. Having married Isabella Irving, daughter of the church's eponymous preacher, Gardiner began his authorial career by translating a work on Christian family life by a German convert to Irvingism who had researched 17th-century England. Gardiner subsequently began to investigate the early Stuart era himself, working in the British Museum library, Public Record Office, and national archives throughout Europe. Soon Gardiner's research notes produced a ripple of controversy in *Notes and Queries* and his narrative began to appear, two volumes at a time. The installments of 1863 and 1869, examining the reign of James I from 1603 to 1623, sold few copies and received unenthusiastic reviews.

Only in the 1870s, after Gardiner had left the Catholic Apostolic church and ventured nearer to the familiar historical territory of civil war, did contemporaries begin to perceive the value of his minutely detailed narrative. By 1884 installments covering the years 1603 to 1642 had been revised and reissued in a 10-volume *History of England*. Meanwhile, contributions to the Hegelian *Academy* and other periodicals as well as a history of the Thirty Years' War established Gardiner as an authority on 17th-century history. Later years brought a civil list pension, research fellowships at Oxford, the editorship of the *English Historical Review* and, after Isabella's death, a historian second wife, Bertha Meriton Cordery. Recognized for his dogged exactitude, Gardiner felt both confident and wary enough to decline the Regius professorship at Oxford in 1894, but in 1896 he accepted the invitation to give the Ford lectures which became *Cromwell's Place in History*. He was not as successful at excising contemporaneity as legend would suggest, engaging near the end of his career in exchanges with Father Gerard over Gunpowder Plot and with the irascible J.H. Round over Charles I and the earl Glamorgan. When Gardiner died in 1902 his narrative, by then acknowledged to be monumental, had not reached 1658, but he had added to his *History of England* a pair of multivolume narratives, the *History of the Great Civil War* and *History of the Commonwealth and Protectorate*. His burial at Sevenoaks with the Anglican rite and the installation of a memorial plaque in his honor in Christ Church Cathedral signaled how much he and the English establishment had changed in half a century.

Because neither his friendships nor marriages spanned both his zealous and professional years, panegyric guesswork became a necessity for Gardiner's eulogists, who touted him as a prototype of Victorian virtue: an industrious, humble family man and humanitarian who had found the 17th century polemical, and left it historical. Yet examination of Gardiner's oeuvre exposes the difference between his historical and historiographical personae. Using sources ranging from the Thomason Tracts at the British Museum to Spanish government documents at Simancas, Gardiner precisely reconstructed the motives of 17th-century parties and personages, allowing their actions to unfold more explicably. His highly descriptive work avoided the Whiggish censoriousness of his predecessors T.B. Macaulay and John Forster and outdid David Hume's *History of England* in its understanding of religious motivations and in its breadth and depth of research. Specifically, Gardiner revised Sir Anthony Weldon's snide appraisal of James I, insisted that Strafford was not the apostate of Whig legend, and discovered a powerful peace party in the English Civil War. He presented Cromwell as a visionary tolerationist whose Mosaic dispensation dissipated in the imperialistic adventures of the Protectorate. Gardiner's "Puritan Revolution" disclaimed the hauteur which Hume and Macaulay had lavished upon Puritans and suggested instead that the Puritan spirit had been absorbed into the character of English institutions. His lectures and textbooks reveal that a dialectical and conventionally nationalistic approach underlay his narrative. His empiricism, indeed, was merely a separable part of his historical philosophy, a means to the end of narrating a truly national epic, one in which Whig and Tory, Anglican and dissenter made indispensable contributions to a tolerationist synthesis.

Gardiner's impact on early Stuart studies has been great, partly because his work, produced in an age of Flaubertian reductionism, is resistant to its own methods. His judgments betray a minimum of assumptions and display literally first-hand knowledge of a broad range of primary materials, many of which he preserved in standard editions for various record societies. Readers may easily extrude Gardiner's narrative descriptions from his analytical excurses, allowing for an early version of interactive history. But his work, with its emphasis upon an immanent tolerationism, was more Hegelian than has previously been allowed. Part of Gardiner's posthumous appeal, moreover, lies in a comprehensiveness that has rendered his work compatible with a number of collateral interpretations. It has made several returns to historiographical fashion, even recovering from R.G. Usher's withering attack in 1915 on its inconsistencies and reputedly false taxonomies. For 20th-century socioeconomic historians such as R.H. Tawney, Lawrence Stone, and Christopher Hill, Gardiner provided an irreplaceable account of the political superstructure of a revolution. Neo-Whigs like J.H. Hexter, who regard the early 17th century as the seedbed of English liberties, as well as revisionists of the 1970s and 1980s, who emphasized the contingencies which occasioned the Civil War, have held up Gardiner's work as the standard which their unreconstructed opponents cannot meet. Although Gardiner's analytical categories, "the nation" and war and peace parties, for example, have been rejected or refined, his narrative has never been entirely superseded. Even recent discussions of Nicholas Tyacke's "Arminian revolution" and Conrad Russell's "British problem" are precedented to a limited extent in Gardiner's treatment, respectively, of Laudianism and the politics of the three kingdoms. Latter-day narratives, which sharpen Gardiner's episodic focus, seek to transcend his accomplishments through imitation of his methods. These include works by Thomas Cogswell, Richard Cust, and John Reeve on the 1620s, Kevin Sharpe on the 1630s, Anthony Fletcher, Valerie Pearl, Mark Kishlansky, Robert Ashton, and David Underdown on the 1640s, and Blair Worden on the Rump Parliament. During an age of epistemological destabilization and new historicism, Gardiner's work remains not merely a symbol but a reservoir of empiricist vigor.

MYRON C. NOONKESTER

See also Britain: 1485–1750; Hill; Naval

Biography

Born Ropley, Hampshire, 4 March 1829, a descendant of Oliver Cromwell. Educated at Winchester School, 1841–47; Christ Church, Oxford, BA 1851. Deacon in Irvingite or Catholic Apostolic church, 1851–66. Taught at Bedford College, London, 1863–81; King's College, London (rising to professor), 1872–84; research fellow, Oxford University, at All Souls College, 1884–92, and Merton College 1892–1902. Editor, *English Historical Review*, 1891–1901. Married 1) Isabella Irving, daughter of Edward Irving (founder of Irvingite church), 1856 (died 1878); 2) Bertha Meriton Cordery, historian of French Revolution, 1882 (6 sons, 2 daughters). Died Sevenoaks, Kent, 23 February 1902.

Principal Writings

The Thirty Years' War, 1618–1648, 1874
The First Two Stuarts and the Puritan Revolution, 1603–1660, 1876
History of England from the Accession of James I to the Outbreak of the Civil War, 10 vols., 1883–84 [collected edition of 5 works published 1863–82]
History of the Great Civil War, 1642–1649, 1888–91; 2nd edition, 1893
History of the Commonwealth and Protectorate, 1649–1660, 3 vols., 1894–1901
Cromwell's Place in History, 1897
What Gunpowder Plot Was, 1897
Oliver Cromwell, 1899

Further Reading

Adamson, J.S.A., "Eminent Victorians: S.R. Gardiner and the Liberal as Hero," *Historical Journal* 33 (1990), 641–57
Fahey, David M., "Gardiner and Usher in Historical Perspective," *Journal of Historical Studies* 1 (1968) 137–50
Finlayson, Michael G., *Historians, Puritanism and the English Revolution: The Religious Factor in English Politics before and after the Interregnum*, Toronto: University of Toronto Press, 1983
Firth, C.H., "Two Oxford Historians," *Quarterly Review* 195 (1902), 547–66
Jann, Rosemary, "Changing Styles in Victorian Military History," *Clio* 11 (1982), 155–64
Kenyon, John, *The History Men: The Historical Profession in England since the Renaissance*, London: Weidenfeld and Nicolson, 1983; Pittsburgh: University of Pittsburgh Press, 1984
Lang, Timothy, *The Victorians and the Stuart Heritage: Interpretations of a Discordant Past*, Cambridge and New York: Cambridge University, 1995
Shaw, William Arthur, ed., *Bibliography of the Historical Works of Dr S.R. Gardiner*, London: Royal Historical Society, 1903; reprinted New York: Burt Franklin, 1969
Tyacke, Nicholas, "An Unnoticed Work of Samuel Rawson Gardiner," *Bulletin of the Institute of Historical Research* 47 (1974), 244–45
Usher, Roland G., *Critical Study of the Historical Method of Samuel Rawson Gardiner*, St. Louis: Washington University, 1915

Garin, Eugenio 1909–
Italian intellectual historian

Eugenio Garin has been, quietly, a formidable scholarly historian and public intellectual of the left in Italy since World War II. In both capacities his work has been shaped by the same imperatives that motivated many others among the generations that passed consciously through the fascist period: to explain how the Italy of Garibaldi and Mazzini became the Italy of Mussolini, and to prevent this happening again. Garin works in the intellectual and cultural history of Italy since the 12th century, and he has sought to identify therein impulses and blockages to human liberation. He was a historian of cultural politics well before the "new cultural history," but although he is sensitive to popular culture, his field of investigation has always been "high" philosophy and ideas. This has allowed him to float above some of the debates that would normally attend a scholar of his political orientation, as have his massive scope, erudition, and subtlety. Consequently, his influence has been broad but unremarked.

Garin's basic orientation toward the politics of culture is linked to Antonio Gramsci (although his influence would be hard to gauge as Garin's intellectual formation preceded his exposure to Gramsci's writings). Of course the concern with culture is in no way a Gramscian invention, being a monolith of Italian intellectual life. Gramsci, however, understood culture to be endowed with a particularly revolutionary power. With Gramsci, Garin elaborated the key idea of the "conception of the world" (or worldview), a comprehensive (and often internally conflicted) cognitive framework that orders and conditions human material practices relatively autonomously, and that is both the product and instrument of culture in revolution. Thus, he examines people's ideas and cultures as effective forces (or weapons) within historical fields (and conflicts) that are also conditioned and constrained by material forces and structures.

Also linked to Gramsci is Garin's methodology, elaborated most explicitly in *La filosofia come sapere storico* (Philosophy as Historical Knowledge, 1959), which involves the minute primary examination of historical detail, and the attempt to locate individuals and ideas within their well-defined and concrete "historical situation." Garin elaborated this view of the practice of history as properly conducted in the realm of the individual, of "multiplicity and distinction," in direct opposition to Croce, Gentile, and others in the Italian idealist tradition. (Garin recently edited and wrote an important introduction to Gentile's *Opere filosofiche* [Philosophical Works], 1991.) Garin took Gentile to task for his adherence to abstract unities that can be found in no particular historical case. For Garin this view, which posits a supra-historical unity of Philosophy, and on its basis claims to be able to reconstruct any historical philosophy from fragments, collapses history into reductive metaphysics and makes historical investigation pointless from the outset. Garin suggested instead "the search for nexuses, linkages, relationships, concrete unities that connect different aspects of culture and civilization." For Garin, the unities in history must be discovered by historical examination of diverse elements in tension.

This suspicion of *a priori* historical continuity and periodization (easily seen as an early form of the current rejection of "metanarratives") led Garin to some of the main questions in *Scienza e vita civile nel Rinascimento italiano* (1965; *Science and Civic Life in the Italian Renaissance*, 1969). In particular, he aligned himself against those who attempt to impose continuity on the Renaissance by sorting its components into clear-cut oppositions, and tracing reductive linearities through the "scholastic classifications" that remain. Like so many intellectuals of the 20th century, Garin's fundamental presupposition is a field of "differences" from which only provisional unities can be constructed. In this vein, and in Gramscian terminology, Garin proposed that rather than in continuity with the Middle Ages, the significance of the Renaissance may be seen in decisive *rotture*, breaks or ruptures that occurred precisely in the articulation of "conceptions of the world": "In an extremely complex, and disconcerting, weave, new ideas and new hypotheses were fermenting. One way of understanding reality was disappearing, while entirely original positions were affirming themselves." The provisional substance of this new conception of the world was a deeply conflicted yet hopeful commitment to the ability of humans to overcome *fortuna* through their own *virtù*, breaking from the cyclical fatalism of medieval thought.

Venturing into the history of science, Garin found the concrete historical break again in Galileo. Here, the shift of consciousness was not to a liberating humanism, but away from the now sterile formulation of Aristotelianism and to an entirely new worldview suggested by Copernicus. Thus, the picture that might be assembled from the mosaic of particular instances of rupture that Garin laid out in *Science and Civil Life* and other studies spanning the medieval, Renaissance, and Enlightenment periods, is of the rebellion of the humanists against the medieval scholastic tradition, in favor of a liberating use of the classics to promote the advance of man and of reason. This would be followed by the formalization of this approach, and then by the renewed liberation of Galileo's break from the Aristotelian view of science altogether, followed by

another formalization, and so on. Attention to the liberating effects of emergent conceptual breaks (virtually simultaneous, it should be noted, with both Kuhn's famous theory of paradigm shifts and Althusser's assertion of an "epistemological break" in Marx's thought) is Garin's most powerful conceptual tool.

Garin has very fruitfully applied this approach to specific studies of changing modes and forms of culture and cultural politics well into the current century. In engaging with discussions on school reform (e.g., in *L'educazione in Europa 1400–1600* [Education in Europe, 1400–1600], 1957), he used his method to clarify historically just what did constitute the *studia humanitatis* as a multiple and contested historical formation. Garin noted the emergence of the early universities as places where the techniques of reading, of scholasticism, are taken to their maximum. In this tradition, conflicts are resolved through the refinement of reading techniques; reference to the world itself becomes distant; and authority is located in the author, not in nature or experience. In fact, the object of knowledge is not man, or nature, but the text. Where medieval learning used the classics as tools to understand and defend the faith, the humanists used the classics instead as a model of moral practice and an instrument of human formation. Nor should the struggle be seen as purely an academic one: it was a concrete revolt for the control of culture. Garin argued that the cultural conditions of this formalism and the revolt against it remain in tension in contemporary educational practices, and will remain so for as long for as the impulse to liberty in the academy remains unsupported by liberty in the particular social world that dictates the academy's terms of existence.

CARL DYKE

See also Italy: Renaissance

Biography

Born Rieti, 9 May 1909. Professor of history of philosophy, University of Florence. Married Maria Soro.

Principal Writings

Der italienische Humanismus, 1947; in Italian as *L'umanesimo italiano: filosofia e vita civile nel Rinascimento*, 1952; in English as *Italian Humanism: Philosophy and Civic Life in the Renaissance*, 1965

Medioevo e rinascimento: studi e ricerche (Middle Ages and Renaissance: Studies and Research), 1954

Cronache di filosofia italiana, 1900–1943 (Chronicles of Italian Philosophy, 1900–1943), 1955

L'educazione in Europa 1400–1600: problemi e programmi (Education in Europe, 1400–1600: Problems and Programs), 1957

La filosofia come sapere storico (Philosophy as Historical Knowledge), 1959

La cultura filosofica del Rinascimento italiano: ricerche e documenti (The Philosophical Culture of the Italian Renaissance: Research and Documents), 1961

La cultura italiana tra '800 e '900: studi e ricerche (Italian Culture Between the 19th and 20th Centuries), 1963

Scienza e vita civile nel Rinascimento italiano, 1965; in English as *Science and Civic Life in the Italian Renaissance*, 1969

Storia della filosofia italiana (The History of Italian Philosophy), 3 vols., 1966

La cultura del Rinascimento: profilo storico (The Culture of the Renaissance: Historical Profiles), 1967

Portraits from the Quattrocento, 1972
Intellettuali italiani del XX secolo (Italian Intellectuals of the Twentieth Century), 1974
Rinascite e rivoluzioni: movimenti culturali dal XIV al XVIII secolo (Renaissances and Revolutions: Cultural Movements from the 14th to the 18th Centuries), 1975
Lo zodiaco della vita: la polemica sull'astrologia dal Trecento al Cinquecento, 1976; in English as *Astrology in the Renaissance: The Zodiac of Life*, 1983
Il tumulto dei Ciompi: un momento di storia fiorentina ed europea (The Ciompi Revolt: A Moment in Florentine and European History), 1981

Further Reading
Bibliografia degli scritti di Eugenio Garin, 1929–1979, Rome: Laterza, 1979 [bibliography]

Gatterer, Johann Christoph 1729–1799
German historian

Often mentioned in connection with Schlözer, Spittler, Michaelis, Achenwall, and Heyne, Gatterer belonged to the school of historians that made the University of Göttingen a famous German center of learning in the 18th century. Gatterer promoted the ancillary sciences, helping them to become established in the general theological and philological as well as the historical syllabus. Thus he helped to transmit historico-critical knowledge in subjects such as statistics, numismatics, heraldry, geography, chronology, and diplomatics, and he played a major role in mediating between the different disciplines. The many manuals he edited expanded the methodological arsenal available to the historian. He could not claim to be the first advocate of the study of these subjects, but he was definitely one of its staunchest supporters. Gatterer was convinced that all things in life were connected with each other. Therefore a mere political and diplomatic history was, in his view, inadequate. In order to write a truly universal history, it would be necessary to include cultural, social, and economic aspects, as well as the history of morals, languages, and religions.

As a result Gatterer has often been characterized as having no interest in politics. By standing back from a Reichs-centered, legal view of history with mainly political concerns, Gatterer opened the way for an intensive debate with works of West European historiography by Voltaire and Montesquieu, Hume and Robertson. Although Gatterer's historico-philosophical ideas were rooted in a German tradition, it was the French and British art of writing history which he regarded as exemplary. Gatterer believed that the ancillary sciences deeply influenced the truth of historical cognition; only they could guarantee that history was approached and written in a proper scientific way. Moreover, they not only aided but also constituted an important part of history. On this point he differed from, for example, Voltaire.

Gatterer also became known as an advocate of history as a professional discipline. Here he could build on a Göttingen tradition which he developed by systematizing history and making it independent of other subjects. Especially with regard to his discourses on theoretical and methodological questions, Gatterer's work influenced the following generations. His rediscovery of

world history was of considerable influence on historical thinking until the time of Ranke, leaving traces, for example, in the universal-historical ideas that Ranke expressed in his *Die grossen Mächte*.

Gatterer's theoretical concerns and his emphasis on professionalizing history went together with his call for an institutionalization of the historical sciences. Consequently he established a special seminar, "Historisches Institut," in Göttingen in 1764, founded the "Historische Encyclopädia" (a general introduction to the study of history), and published the journals *Allgemeine Historische Bibliothek* from 1767 to 1771 and *Historisches Journal* from 1772 to 1781 (each 16 vols.). In this respect Gatterer was highly influential in forming modern views of the professional study of history.

His epistemology formed a bridge between the 18th and the 19th centuries and enriched the discussion about the scientific nature of history with its emphasis on the relativity of historical understanding. According to Gatterer history was an individualizing undertaking, and therefore it needed the historian's intuitive understanding of the past. He expressed his epistemological ideas in a large number of articles, among which the most important are "Von der Evidenz in der Geschichtskunde" (Evidence in History, 1767) and "Abhandlung vom Standort und Gesichtspunkt des Geschichtsschreibers" (Treatise Concerning the Position and Perspective of the Historian, 1768).

In his article "Vom historischen Plan" (1765) Gatterer explained what he thought the historian's tasks were. He believed that the history of the Reich would always have to be seen from a European perspective, and he also tried to combine a chronological with a synchronous method. Gatterer therefore demanded that the historian should recognize, in Friedrich Meinecke's words, both horizontal and vertical moments in the course of history. Universal history made sense only when it was written in such a way that the history of nations revealed the basic formulas of hegemony or dependency. Here the parallel histories of nations confirmed the rules of synchronism and succession. Basically any system of universal history could be written in a philosophical, systematic manner showing that all aspects of life were related to each other.

Accordingly only the histories of nations reflected the philosophy that all things were interrelated, a system that, having once reached the necessary universal level of perception, could be extended to what Gatterer famously termed "*Nexus rerum universalis.*" Thus in contrast to the mere addition of national histories which had hitherto passed for a universal history, Gatterer launched a philosophical idea that served as a frame for a world history. This idea was that the history of humanity could be understood according to one scientific principle, namely the historical. And this principle itself was based on a systematic, philosophical structure of history.

As Gatterer put it in his *Abriss der Universalhistorie* (1765), the historian should aim not only for historical representation, but also for understanding. This meant that his task was to choose his material and to interpret it. The epistemological dilemma between the claim to possess objective historical knowledge and necessarily subjective historical understanding could not, however, be resolved. Under this premise the historian had to distinguish between important and unimportant facts, the account of which he structured according to both a chronological and a synthetic procedure. In his eight universal histories

Gatterer tried to find a compromise between the different methods of organization. Finally he combined the chronological approach with a synchronic pattern. Gatterer belonged to a generation of Enlightenment historians who deeply influenced historical thinking and hermeneutic ideas, and tried to give history a theoretical basis.

BENEDIKT STUCHTEY

See also Schlözer

Biography
Born Lichtenau (bei Ansbach), 13 July 1729. Studied at the University of Altdorf; then taught at a local Gymnasium, before taking a post at the University of Göttingen, 1759. Died Göttingen, 5 April 1799.

Principal Writings
Handbuch der Universalhistorie (Handbook of Universal History), 2 vols., 1761–65
Abriss der Universalhistorie (Outline of Universal History), 1765
"Vom historischen Plan und der darauf sich gründenden Zusammenfügung der Erzählung" (Concerning the Historical Plan and the Narrative Based upon It), *Allgemeine Historische Bibliothek* 1 (1765), 15–89
"Von der Evidenz in der Geschichtskunde" (Evidence in History), in D.F.E. Boysen, ed., *Die Allgemeine Welthistorie* 1 (1767), 3–38
"Abhandlung vom Standort und Gesichtspunkt des Geschichtsschreibers" (Treatise Concerning the Position and Perspective of the Historian), *Allgemeine Historische Bibliothek* 5 (1768), 3–29
Einleitung in die synchronistische Universalhistorie (Introduction to synchronistic universal history), 2 vols., 1771
Ideal einer allgemeinen Weltstatistik (Ideal of General World Statistics), 1773
Abriss der Geographie (Outline of Geography), 1775
Abriss der Chronologie (Outline of Chronology), 1777
Abriss der Diplomatik (Outline of Diplomacy), 1778

Further Reading
Butterfield, Herbert, *Man on His Past: The Study of the History of Historical Scholarship*, Cambridge: Cambridge University Press, 1955; Boston: Beacon Press, 1960
Hammerstein, Notkar, *Jus und Historie: Ein Beitrag zur Geschichte des historischen Denkens an deutschen Universitäten im späten 17. und im 18. Jahrhundert* (Law and history: a contribution to the history of historical thinking at German universities in late 17th and early 18th Centuries), Göttingen: Vandenhoeck & Ruprecht, 1972
Iggers, Georg G., "The University of Göttingen, 1760–1800, and the Transformation of Historical Scholarship," *Storia della Storiografia* 2 (1982), 11–37
Reill, Peter Hanns, "History and Hermeneutics in the *Aufklärung*: The Thought of Johann Christoph Gatterer," *Journal of Modern History* 45 (1973), 24–51
Reill, Peter Hanns, *The German Enlightenment and the Rise of Historicism*, Berkeley: University of California Press, 1975
Reill, Peter Hanns, "Johann Christoph Gatterer," in Hans-Ulrich Wehler, ed., *Deutsche Historiker*, vol.6, Göttingen: Vandenhoeck & Ruprecht, 1980, 7–22

Gay, Peter 1923–
US (German-born) intellectual historian of Europe

Peter Gay is one of the world's leading modern intellectual historians. His most important works have been on the Enlightenment and the history of ideas, Weimar Germany, and most recently on Sigmund Freud and the role of human emotions in the making of history.

Gay's first book, his Columbia University dissertation, *The Dilemma of Democratic Socialism*, was published in 1952 and proved to be the start of a voluminous writing career that now has lasted more than four decades. During the ten years following the publication of his dissertation, Gay focused almost exclusively on the history of ideas in the Enlightenment. His second book, *Voltaire's Politics* (1959), like his first, was on the development of political ideas. In this case, Gay was interested specifically in Voltaire's role not only as a philosopher but also as a politician in the Enlightenment and how politics influenced his thinking and writing. This proved to be a new and untried approach to the study of Voltaire's life and helped establish Gay's academic reputation as well as secure him a place as an intellectual historian of high rank.

Gay continued the Enlightenment emphasis in his work with the first volume of his ambitious *The Enlightenment: An Interpretation* (1966), which was subtitled *The Rise of Modern Paganism*. For this, he received both the National Book award and the Mecher Book award; he then wrote a second, less successful *Enlightenment* volume with the subtitle *The Science of Freedom* (1969).

At the same time that *The Rise of Modern Paganism* was being praised by reviewers, Gay published his first major book on European intellectual history, *Weimar Culture* (1968), a social and cultural history of the Weimar years in Germany. *Weimar Culture* was the first study of the failures and successes of the Weimar republic using cultural rather than political history. Gay's new perspective on this period proved groundbreaking and dramatically changed the way cultural history was viewed in historical circles.

In 1978, Gay published his second major book on modern European intellectual history, *Freud, Jews and Other Germans*. Sigmund Freud proved to be a fruitful field for Gay who published a number of works on the man and his work during the following years. As a result of his Freud research, Gay most recently has been instrumental in applying psychoanalysis to the study of history, and has argued that Freud's psychoanalysis is one of the most revolutionary methods ever developed for gaining an understanding of human emotions and the human psyche as well as for learning about culture and its influence on the human personality. Gay's use of psychoanalytic historical methods has enabled him to explain in great detail historical-cultural trends and human actions.

The psychoanalytic approach to history was not first used by Gay but by the child development and education expert Erik Erikson in his work *Young Man Luther* (1958). However, it was Gay who popularized this approach, made it accessible to the masses, and advocated its use throughout his career.

The thought-provoking analyses and novel approaches in Gay's works have made his writings a must-read for anyone interested in intellectual or social history. His contributions, especially on the Enlightenment and Freud, have helped us to better understand the intellectual development and traditions of our own modern industrialized society. For this reason, his work has been and continues to be enormously influential.

GREGORY WEEKS

See also Europe: Modern; Nietzsche

Biography

Peter Jack Gay [né Frölich]. Born Berlin, 20 June 1923. Left Germany with family, 1939; arrived US, 1941; naturalized, 1946. Received BA, University of Denver, 1946; MA, Columbia University 1947, PhD in political science, 1951. Taught political science (rising to professor), Columbia University, 1948–55, taught history, 1956–69; professor, Yale University, from 1969 (emeritus). Married Ruth Slotkin, writer, 1959 (3 stepdaughters).

Principal Writings

The Dilemma of Democratic Socialism: Eduard Bernstein's Challenge to Marx, 1952
Voltaire's Politics: The Poet as Realist, 1959
The Party of Humanity: Essays in the French Enlightenment, 1964
The Enlightenment: An Interpretation, 2 vols., 1966–69
A Loss of Mastery: Puritan Historians in Colonial America, 1966
Weimar Culture: The Outsider as Insider, 1968
The Bridge of Criticism: Dialogues on the Enlightenment, 1970
With R.K. Webb, *Modern Europe*, 1973
Style in History, 1974
Art and Act: On Causes in History – Manet, Gropius, Mondrian, 1976
Freud, Jews and Other Germans: Masters and Victims in Modernist Culture, 1978
The Bourgeois Experience: Victoria to Freud, 1984–
Freud for Historians, 1985
A Godless Jew: Freud, Atheism and the Making of Psychoanalysis, 1987
Freud: A Life for Our Time, 1988
"The German-Jewish Legacy – and I: Some Personal Reflections," *American Jewish Archives* 40 (1988), 203–10
Editor, *A Freud Reader*, 1989
Reading Freud: Explorations and Entertainments, 1990
Sigmund Freud and Art: His Personal Collection of Antiquities, 1993
The Enlightenment and the Rise of Modern Paganism, 1995
My German Question: Growing Up in Nazi Berlin, 1998

Further Reading

Toews, John E., "Historicizing Psychoanalysis: Freud in His Time and for Our Time," *Journal of Modern History* 63 (1991), 504–45

Geertz, Clifford 1926–

US cultural anthropologist

Historians have always needed to determine precisely how their "evidence" – fragments of writings, structures, artifacts, tracings on the earth – related to the understandings of the men and women who had made them. Anthropologists, by demonstrating how differently different societies conduct and order themselves, have provided useful warnings against the notion that we need simply apply "common sense" to understand the doings of other peoples in other times and other places, but too often the models of analysis they offered can seem at once too abstract and too rigid. Here the work of the American anthropologist Clifford Geertz has been of major importance. Within his home discipline Geertz played a major role in the revolution that established "Symbolic Anthropology," the systematic study of meaning and the vehicles of meaning, at its center (for his engaging and illuminating retrospections on his career, see *After the Fact*, (1995). Geertz has been at least equally influential in the disciplines adjacent to his own: politics, literary criticism, and, most especially, history.

In his first collection of essays, *The Interpretation of Cultures* (1973), addressed to a broad academic audience, Geertz presented a newly refined theory of "culture." He declared his position in the introductory essay, "Thick Description: Towards an Interpretive Theory of Culture": "Believing, with Max Weber, that man is an animal suspended in webs of significance he himself has spun, I take culture to be those webs, and the analysis of it to be therefore not an experimental science in search of law but an interpretive one in search of meaning." Social conduct was not to be understood by the accumulation of instances and the establishment of regularities, but by way of "thick description," the "setting down [of] the meanings particular social actions have for the actors whose actions they are." The identification of those meanings is difficult, because they are complex, layered, and typically coded: "Doing ethnography is like trying to read (in the sense of 'construct a reading of') a manuscript: – foreign, faded, full of ellipses, incoherencies, suspicious emendations, and tendentious commentaries, but written not in conventionalized graphs of sound but in transient examples of shaped behavior." But because culture is shared and public, the meanings will be reiterated in a number of observable forms, and the observer will therefore be able to test and refine initial guesses by further observations, over different areas of social life.

Action as metaphorical text; culture as "acted document." The attraction for historians is obvious. If intentions are contained and revealed in social actions, historians need not be restricted to (potentially misleading) first-person claims about intentions. With records of observed action made amenable to systematic, principled interpretation, historians are empowered to decipher the motives and meanings of people excluded from direct participation in the written record. (The contemporaneous but independent work of the great British social historian E.P. Thompson, different in its intellectual origins, was very similar in its implications for historical practice.)

Geertz's theory, while responsive to historians' traditional concern for concrete detail, also authorized different levels of generalization: the analyst's task was "to uncover the conceptual structures that inform our subjects' acts . . . and to construct a system of analysis in whose terms what is generic to those structures . . . will stand out against the other determinants of human behavior." It will then be possible to state "what the knowledge thus attained demonstrates about the society in which it is found, and beyond that, about social life as such." In that same volume Geertz provided a series of exemplary demonstrations, most famously in "Deep Play: Notes on the Balinese Cockfight." Here, after "thickly describing" the complex of human actions surrounding the fight, and mining them for their psychological, aesthetic, moral, and political import, he was able to demonstrate to his readers that "this apparent amusement and seeming sport" was, in the minds of the players, a tense and dangerous political battle: a "status bloodbath." The cockfight analysis became an important model for social historians intent on exploring the cultural meanings of popular pastimes as well as other more solemn forms of social action. A decade later came a second essay collection which included the influential "'From the Native's Point of View': On the Nature of Anthropological Understanding," a restatement of his approach in more accessible terms. Later Geertz was to make his own contribution to political history with *Negara* (1980), in which he demonstrated that state rituals we might be tempted to dismiss as "mere" theater were the dynamic as well as the expression of a complex politics.

Another contribution is more difficult to demonstrate. It relates to how we write. At a time when social theorists typically mimed an addled "scientism," Geertz wrote with wit, grace, and economy. Furthermore, he admitted his presence on the page, engaging the reader in conversation. He had made his interest in writing strategies and styles explicit in his *Works and Lives* (1988). That book, and his own example, have led others in the human sciences to acknowledge and respond to the peculiar challenges and possibilities of academic writing.

In recent years Geertz has been recognized as one of the few North American intellectuals ready and able to challenge the anti-humanist implications of postmodernism in its several guises (an early essay is entitled "Thinking as a Moral Act"). His declared goal is to expand the role of reason in human affairs, to generate "usable truths," and to enlist "the power of the scientific imagination to bring us into touch with the lives of strangers," so that we will acknowledge them as moral realities too.

INGA CLENDINNEN

See also Anthropology; Cultural; Europe: Modern; Goitein; Indigenous; Religion; Science; Southeast Asia; Stone

Biography
Clifford James Geertz. Born San Francisco, 23 August 1926. Served in the US Navy, 1943–45. Studied at Antioch College, BA 1950; Harvard University, PhD 1956. Taught briefly at Harvard before a research fellowship at Massachusetts Institute of Technology, 1956–58, which included a year in Indonesia; research fellow, Stanford University, 1958–59. Taught anthropology, University of California, Berkeley, 1959–60; and University of Chicago (rising to professor), 1960–70; moved to Institute for Advanced Study, Princeton, 1970; Linder professor of social science, Princeton University, from 1982. Married Hildred Storey, 1948 (2 children).

Principal Writings
The Religion of Java, 1960
Agricultural Involution: The Process of Ecological Change in Indonesia, 1963
The Interpretation of Cultures: Selected Essays, 1973
Negara: The Theatre State in Nineteenth-Century Bali, 1980
Works and Lives: The Anthropologist as Author, 1988
After the Fact: Two Countries, Four Decades, One Anthropologist, 1995

Gender

Gender has evolved as a category of historical analysis in the course of the increasingly sophisticated research into women's history inspired by second-wave feminism. Initially, when women's history was struggling for recognition within the discipline, "gender" was used as a synonym for "women" so as to render research into women more acceptable by camouflaging the objects of enquiry.

The subsequent understanding of gender as a social category imposed on a sexed body remained descriptive and associated with matters concerning women. Nevertheless, this distinction between sex and its social organization – gender – represents a major insight of feminist scholarship, transposing women as objects of study from the realm of biology to that of history. While restoring history to women, this usage retains the body as an ahistorical entity.

The concept's theoretical potential became apparent when it began to be employed, from the 1970s onward, to conceptualize the general issues that had emerged from the largely descriptive case studies proliferating in the historiography of women. Conceiving of women as a social group – a gender – allows historians to account for continuities and discontinuities in women's history, for persistent inequalities as well as radically different social experiences. Gender differentiation has been shown to be a universal, all-pervasive characteristic of society. Along with class and race, gender forms one of the main axes along which inequalities of power are organized. This understanding of gender does not aim to explain why men and women are positioned differently in society, rather it is a tool for alerting historians to the wide variety of forms that the relationship between men and women may take in different periods and cultures.

During most of the 1970s and 1980s, historical analysis of gender fell into three main approaches. First, there was the attempt to explain the origins of patriarchy, for example, in Shulamith Firestone's work on men's domination of women. While offering an analysis internal to the gender system itself, this approach presupposes the primacy of that system in all social organization, failing to show how gender inequality is related to other forms of inequality. Furthermore, it is based on physical difference, thus positing the body as an ahistorical entity.

Second, ways of integrating feminist critiques into a Marxian tradition were sought by economists such as Heidi Hartmann, by sociologists, and by historians such as Joan Kelly. Here, gender was treated as a by-product of economic structures with no independent analytic status of its own.

Third, following Juliet Mitchell's *Psychoanalysis and Feminism* (1974), recourse was taken to different schools of psychoanalysis to explain the production and reproduction of the subject's gendered identity. The feminist rereading of Freud through Jacques Lacan – for example in Sally Alexander's work – has been particularly influential in explaining the constitution of female subjectivity in and through language. These approaches not only involved a shift of focus from social systems to the individual and his or her immediate social environment, such as the family or the household, they have also tended to see gender – understood as a system of binary opposition – as a human universal.

More recently, gender has come to be defined as a relational category, denoting both inter- and intra-relations of men and women. From conceiving of women as a gender group, it follows that men form one, too. Thus, gender has paved the way for the study of men and masculinity, but also, and more fundamentally, it has helped to reconceptualize history as a series of events shaped by groups of gendered beings over time. This view has laid the theoretical base for a rewriting of history in the light of the ubiquity of gender.

Influenced by French poststructuralism, in 1986 Joan Scott proposed a definition of gender as a volatile system of classification which results from a continuous struggle for the power to determine meanings. Following Michel Foucault, she conceived of knowledge as the socially produced understanding of human relationships, including those between women and men. According to this view, the uses and meanings of knowledge are contested as well as constitutive of power relations. Thus gender denotes both the knowledge of sexual difference and the social organization of that difference. By producing knowledge of the changes in that system of classification over time, historiography itself becomes embroiled in the contest for power.

Thus a concept of gender as a discursively produced construct has emerged. Following Jacques Derrida, methods of textual analysis, mostly borrowed from literary criticism, are employed to unravel – deconstruct – a multiplicity of meanings of masculinity and femininity, meanings that derive from each term's oppositional definition rather than from the signification of actual men and women. For feminist historians such as Denise Riley, this entails a dilemma in that the group that has spurred the political project of feminist historiography dissolves as a fixed point of reference. This understanding of gender has been criticized for obliterating both the experience of domination suffered by women and their historical agency. Experience and agency have become questionable as concepts of a historical analysis that is concerned with representation rather than with the pursuit of a discernible and retrievable historical reality. Because of its focus on the text, this kind of analysis also runs the risk of excluding consideration of those social groups not likely to leave written records.

In the deliberate move away from the last vestiges of essentialism in favor of all-encompassing historicization, the understanding of gender as a social construct has led historians to discard the concept of sex as the biologically given and hence unchangeable physical essence or core. By highlighting the multifaceted, not of necessity exclusively linguistic, process of social construction, gender is focused as an arena of struggle in which the meanings of femininity and masculinity are contested and renegotiated.

The concept of gender represents a major theoretical advance in historical analysis and is likely to continue to prove its potential of radically transforming the writing of history.

JUTTA SCHWARZKOPF

See also Bock; Feminism; Masculinity; Scott, Joan; Women's History

Further Reading

Alexander, Sally, "Women, Class and Sexual Differences in the 1830s and 1840s: Some Reflections on the Writing of a Feminist History," *History Workshop* 17 (1984), 125–49
Butler, Judith, *Gender Trouble: Feminism and the Subversion of Identity*, London and New York: Routledge, 1990
Butler, Judith, and Joan Wallach Scott, eds., *Feminists Theorize the Political*, New York and London: Routledge, 1992
Canning, Kathleen, "Feminist History after the Linguistic Turn: Historicizing Discourse and Experience," *Signs* 19 (1994), 368–404
Firestone, Shulamith, *The Dialectic of Sex: The Case for a Feminist Revolution*, New York: Morrow, 1970; London: Cape, 1971
Gender and History, Oxford: Blackwell, 1988–
Hall, Catherine, "Politics, Poststructuralism and Feminist History," *Gender and History* 3 (1991), 204–10
Hartmann, Heidi, "The Unhappy Marriage of Marxism and Feminism: Towards a More Progressive Union," *Capital and Class* 8 (1979), 1–33
Kelly, Joan, "The Doubled Vision of Feminist Theory," in her *Women, History, and Theory: The Essays of Joan Kelly*, Chicago: University of Chicago Press, 1984
Mitchell, Juliet, *Psychoanalysis and Feminism*, New York: Pantheon, and London: Allen Lane, 1974
Mitchell, Juliet, and Jacqueline Rose, eds., *Feminine Sexuality: Jacques Lacan and the école freudienne*, London: Macmillan, and New York: Norton, 1982
Poovey, Mary, "Feminism and Deconstruction," *Feminist Studies* 14 (1988), 51–65
Riley, Denise, *"Am I That Name?" Feminism and the Category of "Women" in History*, Minneapolis: University of Minnesota Press, and London: Macmillan, 1988
Rubin, Gayle, "The Traffic in Women: Notes on the Political Economy of Sex," Rayna R. Reiter, ed., *Toward an Anthropology of Women*, New York: Monthly Review Press, 1975
Scott, Joan Wallach, "Gender: A Useful Category of Historical Analysis," *American Historical Review* 91 (1986), 1053–75
Scott, Joan Wallach, *Gender and the Politics of History*, New York: Columbia University Press, 1988
Walkowitz, Judith R., Myra Jehlen, and Bell Chevigny, "Patrolling the Borders: Feminist Historiography and the New Historicism," *Radical History Review*, 43 (1989), 23–43

Genovese, Eugene D. 1930–

US historian of American slavery

During the 1960s and 1970s Eugene D. Genovese emerged as America's most influential, and certainly its most controversial, historian of black slavery and the antebellum South. A Marxist scholar, he emphasized the importance of class formation and class exploitation in the Old South. This, according to Genovese, set the region apart dramatically from the antebellum North. While sensitive to the power of white racism, Genovese nonetheless believed that the South's social and economic relationships, most significantly between masters and slaves, provided the clearest analytical framework with which to understand its antebellum history.

In his early writings Genovese examined the "world" of the master class. In *The Political Economy of Slavery* (1965), *In Red and Black* (1968), and *The World the Slaveholders Made* (1969) he defined the Old South as precapitalist, prebourgeois, premodern. Drawing on comparative slavery studies, Genovese interpreted the civilization of the Old South as "seigneurial" – a distinctive society in which slaveholders, specifically large planters, maintained hegemony by owning the factors of production. The planter elite, Genovese explained, set the Old South's social, economic, and intellectual tone. Nonslaveholders, who aspired to own slaves themselves, never challenged their rule.

In his landmark book, *Roll, Jordan, Roll* (1974), Genovese drew on insights from the work of pioneer historian Ulrich B.

Phillips, and integrated blacks as a class into a complex "world" that the slaves in fact helped to shape. The Old South, Genovese argued, was a closed society, an organic whole, "a historically unique kind of paternalist society." "Cruel, unjust, exploitative, oppressive," he wrote, "slavery bound two peoples together in bitter antagonism while creating an organic relationship so complex and ambivalent that neither could express the simplest human feelings without reference to the other." Slaveholders understood plantation paternalism as "the involuntary labor of the slaves as a legitimate return to their masters for protection and direction." The slaves, however, viewed it differently. "Paternalism's insistence," Genovese said, "upon mutual obligations – duties, responsibilities, and ultimately even rights – implicitly recognized the slaves' humanity." In *Roll, Jordan, Roll* Genovese underscored the slaves' religion and their cultural expression as modes of resistance and survival. Afro-Christianity, he explained, "gave the slaves the one thing they absolutely had to have if they were to resist being transformed into the Sambos they had been programmed to become. It fired them with a sense of their own worth before God and man." According to Genovese, then, the slaves both accommodated and resisted their enslavement. In terms of slavery's impact on the black family life, for example, he found "as much evidence of resistance and of a struggle for a decent family life as of demoralization." Writing in 1995, historian David Brion Davis considered *Roll, Jordan, Roll* "still the most vivid, imaginative, and comprehensive picture we have of slave life in the South."

Following *Roll, Jordan, Roll*, Genovese refined and added texture to his arguments. Drawing upon his early interest in comparative slavery, in *From Rebellion to Revolution* (1979) he explained the shift in slave uprisings in the Americas "from attempts to secure freedom from slavery to attempts to overthrow slavery as a social system." In the 1980s Genovese continued to underscore the tensions between slavery and bourgeois property. In *Fruits of Merchant Capital* (1983) he and Elizabeth Fox-Genovese argued that slavery was "a hybrid system" that "raised a regionally powerful ruling class of a new type, at once based on slave relations of production and yet deeply embedded in the world market and hostage to its internationally developed bourgeois social relations of production. In this essential respect, the Old South emerged as a bastard child of merchant capital and developed as a noncapitalist society increasingly antagonistic to, but inseparable from, the bourgeois world that sired it."

Genovese's latest research focuses on the cultural and intellectual lives of the master class, 1790–1861, a topic he introduced in *The Slaveholders' Dilemma* (1992) and continued to explore in *The Southern Tradition* (1994) and *The Southern Front* (1995). Focusing closely on the intellectual origins of southern conservatism, Genovese sees important historic parallels between southern conservatives and the Marxist left. Both cautioned against the dangers of unrestrained capitalism. According to Genovese, southern conservatism "contains much of intrinsic value that will have to be incorporated in the world view of any political movement, inside or outside the principal political parties, that expects to arrest our plunge into moral decadence and national decline." As historian and social critic, Genovese deplores white racism but champions what he considers to be the positive contributions of both antebellum and modern southern conservative thinkers. He admires, for example, their belief in human depravity, their reverence for family and community, and their repudiation of extreme individualism. Much as he did three decades ago, Genovese continues to interpret the South and southerners as distinct and different from the North and northerners. Insightful, complex, and often inflammatory, Genovese's writings on slavery and the South remain among the most important in US historical literature. Few scholars have pondered these topics with such sophistication and depth.

JOHN DAVID SMITH

See also African American; Elkins; Freyre; Gramsci; Gutman; Hobsbawm; James; Lasch; Marx; Political; Slavery: Modern; Stampp; Thompson, E.; United States: 19th Century; Women's History: African American; Zinn

Biography
Born Brooklyn, New York, 19 May 1930. Received BA, Brooklyn College, 1953; MA, Columbia University 1955, PhD 1959. Taught history and economics, Polytechnic Institute of Brooklyn, 1958–63; taught history, Rutgers University 1963–67; Sir George Williams University, 1967–69; and University of Rochester, 1969–86; joint appointments at University of Georgia, Georgia Institute of Technology, and Georgia State University, from 1986. Married Elizabeth Fox, historian, 1969.

Principal Writings
The Political Economy of Slavery: Studies in the Economy and Society of the Slave South, 1965
In Red and Black: Marxian Explorations in Southern and Afro-American History, 1968
The World the Slaveholders Made: Two Essays in Interpretation, 1969
Roll, Jordan, Roll: The World the Slaves Made, 1974
From Rebellion to Revolution: Afro-American Slave Revolts in the Making of the Modern World, 1979
With Elizabeth Fox-Genovese, *Fruits of Merchant Capital: Slavery and Bourgeois Property in the Rise and Expansion of Capitalism*, 1983
The Slaveholders' Dilemma: Freedom and Progress in Southern Conservative Thought, 1820–1860, 1992
The Southern Tradition: The Achievement and Limitations of an American Conservatism, 1994
The Southern Front: History and Politics in the Cultural War, 1995

Further Reading
Boles, John B., and Evelyn Thomas Nolen, eds., *Interpreting Southern History: Historiographical Essays in Honor of Sanford W. Higginbotham*, Baton Rouge: Louisiana State University Press, 1987
Davis, David Brion, "Southern Comfort," *New York Review of Books* (5 October 1995), 43–46
Meier, August, and Elliott M. Rudwick, *Black History and the Historical Profession, 1915–1980*, Urbana: University of Illinois Press, 1986
Parish, Peter J., *Slavery: History and Historians*, New York: Harper, 1989
Roper, John Herbert, "Marxing through Georgia: Eugene Genovese and Radical Historiography for the Region, *Georgia Historical Quarterly* 80 (1996), 77–92
Shalhope, Robert E., "Eugene Genovese, the Missouri Elite, and Civil War Historiography," *Bulletin of the Missouri Historical Society* 26 (July 1970), 271–82
Steirer, William F., Jr., "Eugene D. Genovese: Marxist-Romantic Historian of the South," *Southern Review* 10 (1974), 840–50

Germani, Gino 1911–1979

Argentine (Italian-born) sociologist

Gino Germani was a sociologist of Italian origin who worked mainly in Argentina and the United States. He is known for his work on development, based on the central role played in his thinking by the ideas of modernization, mobilization, and marginality. Although he adopted a structural-functionalist approach in some of his work, Germani did not adhere to one theoretical orthodoxy in particular. In the world of Argentine sociology, he studied and disseminated the thinking of Weber, Simmel, and Mannheim.

Germani is known as the founder of "scientific" sociology in Argentina, and as one of the prime movers of its establishment in Latin America. In his work *La sociología en América Latina* (Sociology in Latin America, 1964) he analyzed the evolution of the subject in the region and set out a scientific program for its development based on the professionalization of its personnel, the promotion of empirical research, the updating of its study programs, and the deepening of the dialogue between Latin American sociologists. His plan was to distance sociological thought from the speculative and philosophical mode that prevailed in academic circles and to orient the discipline towards an empirical approach, while not overlooking theoretical work. He promoted systematic research into the structural configuration of Argentina.

In 1955 Germani published *Estructura social de la Argentina* (The Social Structure of Argentina), his first and one of his most important works. It has been recognized as the first systematic study of the totality of the country's social structure and its development during the period 1850–1950. Germani set about this task from the perspective of social morphology, thus recognizing the influence of the French school of Durkheim. Based on census data, he studied the volume and spatial distribution of the country's principal groups and subgroups and their reciprocal relations. What makes his conceptualization of social structure important is his consideration of the entire network of interactions between groups – all dimensions and not just the socio-economic are relevant to its comprehension.

Germani's work in building an institutional structure for academic sociology reached its peak from 1957. With the creation of a course in sociology at the University of Buenos Aires, Germani succeeded in systematizing the education of the first graduates in sociology, in a program that included research into Argentine social structure and academic studies abroad.

The phenomenon of modernization was one of the central themes in Germani's work, a theme that was emerging in the preoccupations of European intellectuals in the postwar period, but which he applied in an original way to Latin American societies.

The transition of traditional societies with little industrialization to modernized, secularized, and developed societies must be understood not only in economic terms. Germani saw the process of modernization as a problem of political systems and in this sense he saw it as the integration of the masses into political life by means of representative democracy. These ideas are expressed in *Política y sociedad en una época en transición* (Politics and Society in an Era of Transition, 1962), in which he indicates that modernization takes place in three basic elements of the social structure: "the type of social action, the attitude to the change, and the degree of specialization of the institutions."

The process of modernization in Latin American countries has different characteristics from that in Europe: the asynchrony of social change, the role played by the sense of identification with the nation in the political integration of the masses, and the imbalance between a modernized society and a political system with restricted participation. In his analysis of societies in transition, Germani assigned a significant role to internal and external migration in relation to structural transformations. The notion of social and political mobility allowed Germani to understand the role played by the working classes in the formation of innovatory alliances with elites that were not necessarily based on revolutionary socialist processes. Mobilization signifies a break with the traditional political passivity and makes a number of actions available.

In his later studies Germani worked with these ideas to find an explanation for the phenomenon of popularism in Argentina. His reflections on the relations between the masses and the political system had formed in the 1950s, when he experienced the establishment of a government that had broad popular support and an authoritarian tendency. The formation of a new urban proletariat, a result of the expulsion of peasants and inhabitants from the interior to large urban centers, was associated with the social and economic consequences of the crisis of 1930. This new sector coexisted with the "old laborers" and their traditional forms of relationship with the state, a coexistence that reconstituted the bases for forming political alliances within the context of social mobilization.

In this way Germani defined a comprehensive framework for understanding the relations between the conservative masses and modernizing elites, and for identifying political and psychosocial aspects of the working classes with respect to their behavior within a system of representative democracy. Furthermore, this framework also made possible an approach to an analysis of political authoritarianism in societies in the process of modernization.

Even though Germani at that time maintained – typically for his generation – an optimistic vision of the possibilities offered by modernization as a means of access to social and economic development in the societies of Latin America, he nevertheless warned of the risks of social disintegration that might result from the processes of change. In the Third World, society in transition is complex and contradictory, giving rise to the typical phenomenon of marginality. Germani made clear his doubts about the political consequences of the processes of change in Latin American societies which, when subjected to powerful structural changes, can become exposed to political authoritarianism.

This totality of considerations regarding the modernization of society, social migrations, and political phenomena was taken up again in the final years of Germani's career, during his time in the United States. He re-elaborated his conclusions about totalitarianism and populism from a comparative perspective, analyzing fascism in Italy, the Franco system in Spain, and Peronism in Argentina.

MARIA ELINA ESTEBANEZ

See also Latin America: National

Biography

Born Rome, 4 February 1911. Attended University of Rome, 1930–34. Expelled from Italy by the fascist regime; arrived Argentina, 1934. Graduated in philosophy, University of Buenos Aires, 1943; then research under direction of historian Ricardo Levene, Institute of Sociological Research, to 1946. In internal exile, 1946–55; during which time taught at Colegio Libre de Estudios Superiores, Buenos Aires and Rosario. Returned to University of Buenos Aires, 1956–66; director, Institute of Sociological Research; founder, Argentina's first academic course in sociology. Emigrated to US for political reasons, 1966; professor, Harvard University, 1966–76. Returned to Italy and continued his work there, at the University of Naples, 1976–79. Married Celia Carpi, 1954 (1 son; 1 daughter). Died 1979.

Principal Writings

Estructura social de la Argentina (The Social Structure of Argentina), 1955

La sociología científica (Scientific Sociology), 1955

Política y sociedad en una época en transición (Politics and Society in an Era of Transition), 1962

La sociología en América Latina (Sociology in Latin America), 1964

Sociología de la modernización: estudios teóricos, metodológicos, y aplicados a América Latina, 1969; in English as *The Sociology of Modernization: Studies on Its Historical and Theoretical Aspects with Special Regards to the Latin American Case,* 1981

Editor, *Modernization, Urbanization, and the Urban Crisis,* 1973

Autoritarismo, fascismo e classi sociali, 1975; in English as *Authoritarianism, Fascism, and National Socialism,* 1978

Marginality, 1980

The Sociology of Modernization: Studies on Its Historical and Theoretical Aspects with Special Regard to the Latin American Case, 1981

Further Reading

Graciarena, Jorge, Introduction to Gino Germani, *Estructura social de la Argentina,* Buenos Aires: Solar, 1987

Jorrat, Jorge and Ruth Sautu, *Después de Germani: exploraciones sobre Estructura social de la Argentina,* Buenos Aires: Paidos, 1992

Kahl, Joseph, *Modernization, Exploitation, and Dependency in Latin America: Germani, Gonzalez Casanova, and Cardoso,* New Brunswick, NJ: Transaction, 1976

Neiberg, Federico, "La invención del peronismo y la constitución de la sociología en Argentina," doctoral thesis, Federal University of Rio de Janeiro, Museo Social, 1993

Germany: to 1450

The origins of the antiquarian study of German history may be traced to the arrival in Rome around 1455 of the unique manuscript of the *Germania* of the Roman historian Cornelius Tacitus, composed around 98 CE. The manuscript itself, written in the Loire valley in the mid-9th century, had been preserved in the library of the monastery of Hersfeld in Hesse, but all knowledge of the work had otherwise been lost until 1425, when the existence of this codex was first revealed. Finally brought to Italy thirty years later, it was avidly studied by Italian and then by German humanists. Twenty-nine extant manuscript copies were made in the 15th and early 16th centuries, and the first printed version appeared in Venice in 1470. This was soon followed by the first German edition,

published in Nuremburg in 1473. Tacitus's work was used as a source by Aeneas Sylvius Piccolomini – soon to be pope Pius II – in his *De ritu, situ, moribus et conditione Germaniae descriptio* of 1457. As papal representative to the Diet held at Frankfurt in 1454, Piccolomini had already attempted to arouse the national selfconsciousness of the German princes, largely with the aim of uniting against the threat he saw posed by the Ottomans, following their capture of Constantinople the previous year. In his published address, *De Constantinople clade et bello contra Turcos,* he praised the Germans as victors over the Romans, alluding to the defeat of Augustus's legions in 9 BCE.

Such historical references and the unlooked-for wealth of information relating to the German past revealed in Tacitus's long-lost work inspired interest in the antiquity and the distinctiveness of German civilization. Such aspirations once aroused soon led, as elsewhere in Europe at this time, to the fabrication of new sources. In 1498 Annius of Viterbo published what he claimed was the 5-volume work of the Babylonian priest Berosus. In this nonsensical narrative appeared a certain Tuysco, who was claimed as the eponymous ancestor of the Germans (*gli Tedeschi* in Italian), and a direct descendant of Noah. He in turn had a series of descendants with the names of some of the principal Germanic peoples mentioned by Tacitus. Although quickly denounced in Italy, these claims were taken up by German humanists such as Franciscus Irenicus, alias Franz Friedlieb, who could thereby argue that Germany enjoyed an antiquity greater than that of Greece, Rome, or any other part of Europe.

The interest in Roman literary sources for the early history of the Germans soon led to a cult of supposed national leaders from that heroic past. The first and most durable of these was Arminius, explicitly described by Tacitus in his *Annales* as the "liberator of Germany," who had led the confederacy that had overwhelmed Varus's army in 9 BCE. Ulrich von Hutten was the first to single him out, initially in his *Brutus Germanicus* of 1515, dedicated to the archbishop of Mainz, and then in a series of other letters and polemical addresses, culminating in his posthumous *Arminius* of 1529. The main theme of these works was the presentation of Arminius as the liberator of Germany from Roman tyranny, at a time when such arguments had a powerful contemporary resonance. This emphasis on conflict with Rome was not lost on the early Protestant reformers, such as Luther's friend Georg Spalatin, who in his *Von dem theuren Deudschen Fürsten Arminio* (From the German Prince Arminius) of 1535 created the anachronistic Germanization of his subject's name as "Herman," by which he was generally thereafter known.

While it seemed easy to make a correlation, though by no means historically correct, between the German lands and populations described by Tacitus with those of later medieval and modern Germany, other periods presented problems. The conquest of Gaul by the Franks, who had come from east of the Rhine but had rapidly ceased to be identifiable as linguistically Germanic, raised the question of the historical relationship between the French and the Germans. This was no neutral issue in the light of a tradition of almost continuous political conflict over culturally ambiguous regions such as Alsace and Lorraine, extending from the 9th century to the present. This first took on a scholarly dimension in the light of the new interest in the German past. In 1501 in his *Germania* Jakob Wimpfeling argued that the Germans had been established on the western bank of the Rhine since time immemorial – a view flatly contradicted the following year by Thomas Murner of Strasbourg, who argued in his *Germania Nova* that the disputed lands were quintessentially French and always had been.

As in the case of Arminius/Herman, the arguments came to crystalize around the interpretations put upon the achievements of a number of heroic conquerors, in particular the Merovingian Frankish king Clovis and the first Carolingian emperor Charlemagne. In brief, were they French or German? In the case of Clovis his exclusively French area of operation made him hard to claim as a father figure for the medieval German state, but a better case could be made for Charlemagne, much of whose time was spent campaigning in Saxony and Bavaria. In the controversy between Wimpfeling and Murner, the former claimed him as a German, while the latter saw him as French. These cultural and chronological uncertainties remain to the present. Thus, for example, Friedrich Prinz in writing the first volume of a series called Neue Deutsche Geschichte under the title of *Grundlagen und Anfänge: Deutschland bis 1056* (Antecedents and Origins: Germany to 1056, 1985) started his account with the accession of Clovis in 481, whereas Josef Fleckenstein, in composing the equivalent volume of a similar series, under the title of *Grundlagen und Beginn der deutschen Geschichte* (1974; *Early Medieval Germany*, 1974) began with Charlemagne.

Modern historical scholarship on the German Middle Ages could be said to owe its origins to the foundation in Hannover in 1819 of a small but select society, which would grow into the source of the best and most prolific series of editions and studies relating to this period, not only in Germany but in the world. This is the body that came to be known from the general title of its publications as the *Monumenta Germaniae Historica*. Following the Enlightenment, which had been as dismissive of German antiquity and medieval civilization as it had of the Anglo-Saxons and other nonclassical peoples and periods, Romantic nationalists of the early 19th century took up these discarded subjects with new zeal. In particular, Heinrich Friedreich Karl, Freiherr von und zum Stein, once a reforming minister at the Prussian court and adviser to Tsar Alexander I, turned to the revitalizing of historical studies after the failure of his attempts to secure German political unification at the Congress of Vienna. For this purpose he founded the society called the Gesellschaft für Deutschlands ältere Geschichtskunde, which was to devote itself to the publication of historical records relating to early German history. Similar scholarly interests were being pursued at this time in old German philology and the collection of folktales on the part of the brothers Grimm, and in the study of medieval as well as Roman law by Friedrich Karl von Savigny – all of whom, like Goethe, were friends of Stein or were influenced by him.

Although the initial pace of publication was slow, with only two volumes of the *Scriptores* series appearing before 1839, materials were collected that could serve editors working decades later. Thus the manuscript collations made in libraries in Austria and Italy in 1821–22 by Georg Heinrich Pertz, who became the society's first official editor in 1823, were still being used by his successors at the end of the century. The net was cast very widely, with the first volume being devoted to Carolingian texts. From 1839 the rate of production speeded up, particularly when Pertz was succeeded by his former assistant Georg Waitz, under whose direction several new series were introduced and some of the works included in the *Scriptores* were reprinted in smaller and cheaper volumes.

The program of editions in most of these series was chronologically structured, with both the Merovingian and Carolingian periods being included within the remit. Indeed, the *Auctores Antiquissimi* series, initiated in 1877, encompassed a range of late Roman texts of greater or lesser relevance to Germanic antiquity that extended the chronological parameters of the project even further. In general this led to the publication of a series of magisterial editions; notable among them were the seven hefty volumes of Merovingian historiography and saints' lives edited between 1888 and 1937 by Bruno Krusch, the numerous contributions of the great classicist Theodor Mommsen to the *Auctores Antiquissimi*, and the volumes of the collections of Carolingian letters and poetry for which Ernst Dümmler and Ludwig Traube, the founding father of modern paleographical study, were primarily responsible.

While all of this was to the great gain of the early periods, later centuries have in general had to wait their turn until more recent times. While a number of valuable series of annals of central medieval date were included in the stately folio volumes of the *Scriptores* series, which effectively ground to a halt in the late 1880s, most other middle and late medieval records began to be edited only in the course of the 20th century and many still await treatment. Thus, currently, the editing of the charters of the German kings and emperors has reached only as far as the reign of Henry VI, and the series of volumes of the royal and imperial constitutions has now just arrived at 1356. Although there have been numerous publications elsewhere in Germany of a variety of regional, legal, economic, and political records, there has been something of a neglect of the later Middle Ages in German scholarship, awaiting the appearance of the authoritative editions of royal and imperial documents. This is in marked contrast to the flurry of scholarly activity that has long surrounded the succeeding Reformation period.

While the main concern of the *Monumenta Germaniae Historica* has always been with the editing of texts, this gave rise to various valuable off-shoots in the form of scholarly journals and subsidiary series of studies and handbooks. The most significant current periodical relating to medieval studies, both for the publishing of articles and for the quantity and status of its reviews is the *Deutsches Archiv für Erforschung des Mittelalters*, which first appeared under the slightly different title of *Deutsches Archiv für Geschichte des Mittelalters* in 1937. Its ancestry is, however, much older. In founding his society in 1819, the Freiherr von Stein had also planned for it to have a journal in which the manuscript researches of the editors might appear. The first volume of this *Archiv der Gesellschaft für ältere deutsche Geschichtskunde* appeared in 1820, six years before the corresponding first volume of the *Scriptores*, but it proved erratic. Only 12 volumes were ever published, in the years to 1874. Under Waitz it was replaced in 1876 by the *Neues Archiv*, which managed annual publication up to 1935, except during and immediately after World War I. In this journal editors such as Krusch published lengthy articles on the manuscript underpinning of their editions, which have to be taken account of alongside the published texts themselves.

From 1938 the *Monumenta* began publishing its *Schriften*, a series of studies, that have included such major contributions to historical literature as Karl Bosl's *Die Reichsministerialität der Salier und Staufer* (The Imperial "Ministeriales" under the Salian and Hohenstaufen Emperors, 1950–51), Percy Ernst Schramm's 3-volume *Herrschaftszeichen und Staatssymbolik* (Signs and Symbols of Rulership, 1954–56), and Josef Fleckenstein's *Die Hofkapelle der deutschen Könige* (The Palace Chapel of the German Kings, 1959–66), and the *Einfluss und Verbreitung der pseudoisidorischen Fälschungen* (The Influence and Spread of the Pseudo-Isidoran Forgeries, 1972–74) of Horst Fuhrmann. To this ongoing series has been added the smaller format *Studien und Texte* and the new *Hilfsmittel* handbooks, which include Hubert Mordek's magisterial 1995 survey of the manuscripts containing Carolingian capitularies.

While the *Monumenta* has played a central, even dominant, role in German medieval scholarship during the last two centuries, it has been a far from exclusive one. Numerous surveys and studies of particular periods and reigns have been written from the late 19th century onwards, often with a particular regional emphasis, by professors at the numerous German universities. Notable among the earliest of these was Karl Hampe, who wrote a book in 1894 on the Hohenstaufen king Conradin and then produced a very influential survey of the whole Salian and Hohenstaufen period in his *Deutsche Kaisergeschichte in der Zeit der Salier und Staufer* (1909; *Germany under Salian and Hohenstaufen Emperors*, 1973). The preceding dynasty received similar treatment in Robert Holtzmann's *Geschichte der sächsischen Kaiserzeit* (History of the Saxon Empire, 1941). By the time this appeared the direction and character of historical scholarship in Germany was largely, though not entirely, dictated by the Nazi regime. Even historians who were not sympathetic to the political ideology could display the influence of the general ethos that gave rise to Nazism in their works. This is true of Ernst Kantorowicz in his famous 1931 study of Frederick II. Others actively pandered to the historical fantasies prompted by Himmler, who believed himself to be a reincarnation of the first Ottonian ruler, Henry the Fowler, not least in their discussions of potentially sensitive subjects such as Charlemagne's harsh treatment of the Saxons. A number of historians, including the then president of the *Monumenta*, Theodor Mayer, who had written on the reign of Frederick Barbarossa, went into early retirement in 1945.

After the war and the overthrow of Nazism, a reaction set in, especially in the treatment of subjects and periods that seemed to glorify conquest and national self-aggrandizement. An important example of such works was the very critical treatment of the reign of Charlemagne in *Das Karolingische Imperium* (1949; *The Carolingian Empire*, 1957) by the Austrian historian Heinrich Fichtenau. A return to more celebratory mode, particularly of his cultural achievements, became possible with the 1965 Aachen conference on Charlemagne, which produced the 5-volume *Karl der Grosse* (1966–68), edited by Helmut Beumann and others. Later periods also received new critical scrutiny, not least in surveys such as Horst Fuhrmann's *Deutsche Geschichte im hohen Mittelalter* (1978; *Germany in the High Middle Ages*, 1986) and Alfred

Haverkamp's *Aufbruch und Gestaltung, Deutschland 1056–1273* (1984; *Medieval Germany*, 1988).

In the English-speaking world pioneering work in making available the fruits of German scholarship was done by Geoffrey Barraclough who studied in Munich under the distinguished paleographer Paul Lehmann in the early 1930s. He published translations of essays by leading German historians in the second volume of his *Mediaeval Germany* (1938), and produced a highly influential survey of the whole of German history (taken as starting in 919) in his *The Origins of Modern Germany* (1946). This was all the more important in the light of the unfortunate history of the third volume of *The Cambridge Medieval History* (1922), *Germany and the Western Empire*. Subsequently, translations of medieval German texts began to appear, not least in the Columbia Records of Civilization series, and Boyd Hill produced a very useful selection of royal documents in English in his *Medieval Monarchy in Action* (1972). Several of the recent major German works have been translated, including the surveys by Hampe, Fuhrmann, and Haverkamp, and Karl Jordan's 1979 study of Henry the Lion, the formidable Bavarian rival of Frederick Barbarossa. Original work on post-Carolingian German history in Britain owes most to Karl Leyser, who left four volumes of significant articles, mainly though not exclusively devoted to the Ottonian period. His pupil Timothy Reuter has been responsible for editing Leyser's posthumous publications, translating some of the fundamental works of modern German scholarship, and producing his own ground-breaking *Germany in the Early Middle Ages* (1991). For later periods, still neglected in comparison, the way has been opened by F.R.H. Du Boulay's *Germany in the Later Middle Ages* (1983).

ROGER COLLINS

See also Barraclough; Krusch; Leyser; Savigny; Tacitus

Further Reading

Barraclough, Geoffrey, ed. and trans., *Mediaeval Germany, 911–1250: Essays by German Historians*, 2 vols., Oxford: Blackwell, 1938; New York: Barnes and Noble, 1967

Barraclough, Geoffrey, *The Origins of Modern Germany*, Oxford: Blackwell, 1946, revised 1947; New York: Capricorn, 1963

Beumann, Helmut *et al.*, eds., *Karl der Grosse: Lebenswerk und Nachleben* (Charlemagne's Life and Legacy), 5 vols., Düsseldorf: Schwann, 1966–68

Bosl, Karl, *Die Reichsministerialität der Salier und Staufer: ein Beitrag zur Geschichte des hochmittelalterlichen deutschen Volkes, Staates und Reiches* (The Imperial "Ministeriales" under the Salian and Hohenstaufen Emperors) 2 vols., Stuttgart: Hiersemann, 1950–51

Brühl, Carlrichard, *Deutschland-Frankreich: die Geburt zweier Völker* (Germany/France: The Birth of Two Peoples), Cologne: Böhlau, 1990

Du Boulay, F.R.H., *Germany in the Later Middle Ages*, London: Athlone Press, and New York: St. Martin's Press, 1983

Fichtenau, Heinrich, *Das karolingische Imperium: soziale und geistige Problematik eines Grossreiches*, Zurich: Fretz & Wasmuth, 1949; in English as *The Carolingian Empire: The Age of Charlemagne*, Oxford: Blackwell, 1957, New York: Harper, 1964

Fleckenstein, Josef, *Die Hofkapelle der deutschen Könige* (The Palace Chapel of the German Kings), 2 vols., Stuttgart: Hiersemann, 1959–66

Fleckenstein, Josef, *Grundlagen und Beginn der deutschen Geschichte*, Göttingen: Vandenhoeck & Ruprecht, 1974; in English as *Early Medieval Germany*, Amsterdam and New York: Elsevier, 1974

Fuhrmann, Horst, *Einfluss und Verbreitung der pseudoisidorischen Fälschungen: von ihrem Auftauchen bis in die neuere Zeit* (The Influence and Spread of Pseudo-Isidoran Forgeries), 3 vols., Stuttgart: Hiessemann, 1972–74

Fuhrmann, Horst, *Deutsche Geschichte im hohen Mittelalter*, Göttingen: Vandenhoeck & Ruprecht, 1978; in English as *Germany in the High Middle Ages, c.1050–1200*, Cambridge and New York: Cambridge University Press, 1986

Gwatkin, H.M., and J.P. Whitney, eds., *The Cambridge Medieval History*, vol.3: *Germany and the Western Empire*, Cambridge: Cambridge University Press, and New York: Macmillan, 1922

Hampe, Karl, *Geschichte Konradins von Hohenstaufen* (The History of Conrad of Hohenstaufen), Innsbruck: Wagner, 1894

Hampe, Karl, *Deutsche Kaisergeschichte in der Zeit der Salier und Staufer*, Leipzig: Queller Meyer, 1909; in English as *Germany under Salian and Hohenstaufen Emperors*, Oxford: Blackwell, and Totowa, NJ: Rowman and Littlefield, 1973

Haverkamp, Alfred, *Aufbruch und Gestaltung, Deutschland 1056–1273*, Munich: Beek, 1984; in English as *Medieval Germany, 1056–1273*, Oxford and New York: Oxford University Press, 1988, revised 1992

Hill, Boyd, Jr., *Medieval Monarchy in Action: The German Empire from Henry I to Henry IV*, London: Allen and Unwin, and New York: Barnes and Noble, 1972

Holtzmann, Robert, *Geschichte der sächsischen Kaiserzeit, 900–1024* (History of the Saxon Empire), Munich: Callwey, 1941

Jordan, Karl, *Heinrich der Löwe: eine Biographie*, Munich: Beek, 1979; in English as *Henry the Lion: A Biography*, Oxford and New York: Oxford University Press, 1986

Kantorowicz, Ernst, *Kaiser Friedrich der Zweite*, Berlin: Bondi, 1927, revised 1931; vol. I in English as *Frederick the Second, 1194–1250*, London: Constable, and New York: R.R. Smith, 1931

Linehan, Peter, "The Making of the *Cambridge Medieval History*," *Speculum* 57 (1982), 463–94

Mordek, Hubert, *Bibliotheca capitularium regum Francorum manuscripta: Überlieferung und Traditionszusammenhang der fränkischen Herrscherlasse* (The Manuscripts of the Frankish Royal Capitularies), Munich: Monumenta Germaniae Historica, 1995

Prinz, Friedrich, *Grundlagen und Anfänge: Deutschland bis 1056* (Antecedents and Origins: Germany to 1056), Munich: Beek, 1985

Reuter, Timothy, *Germany in the Early Middle Ages 800–1056*, London and New York: Longman, 1991

Schramm, Percy Ernst, *Herrschaftszeichen und Staatssymbolik: Beiträge zu ihrer Geschichte vom dritten bis zum sechzehnten Jahrhundert* (Rulers' Insignia and State Symbology: Contributions to Their History from the 3rd to the 16th Centuries), 3 vols., Stuttgart: Hiersemann, 1954–56

Werner, Karl Ferdinand, *Das NS-Geschichtsbild und die deutsche Geschichtswissenschaft* (The Nazi View of History and German Historical Scholarship), Stuttgart: Kohlhammer, 1967

Germany: 1450–1800

Every national history is unique, but some histories are more unique than others, a distinction with which German historians are perfectly happy. From before the emergence of modern historiography, the idea that, in comparison with the nation-states of Britain and France, Germany has followed a special historical path, or *Sonderweg*, has been a commonplace. For the early German historian Leopold von Ranke this special path was all the more important, in that he placed central emphasis on the historical importance of the development of the state. All the positive developments of German history from the Protestant Reformation to the rise of Prussia were to be seen in the light of state-building. Conversely, the consistent opponent of these developments, the Habsburg dynasty, was seen as committed to an impossible or pernicious program of universal monarchy that led it to oppose German aspirations to statehood until defeated by Prussia. In Vienna, the capital of the other German nation, an antipathy towards German nationalism led Austrian official historiography to emphasize a different but not necessarily contradictory picture. Led by Alfred von Arneth, they portrayed the Habsburgs as state-builders in competition with Prussia.

It was the Holocaust that most forcibly demanded the revival of the *Sonderweg*. Against an earlier generation of German historians who insisted that Hitler had been an anomaly in German culture, Hans-Ulrich Wehler (in his *Deutsche Gesellschaftsgeschichte* (German History, 1987) argued that the roots of both the terrible crimes of the Nazis and Hitler and the lesser ones of the *Kaiserreich* (1871–1918) were rooted deep in the German past. Yet Wehler's criticisms were not new, or even confined to anti-Nazis. Heinrich von Srbik, in his *Deutsche Einheit* (German Unity, 1935–42) also saw the *Kaiserreich* as a crippled state defined by the sheer power politics of Prussian hegemony rather than any valid program of nation-building. Srbik's call for the expansion of the boundaries of a new "Great Germany" to embrace all linguistic/racial Germans has, not surprisingly, been generally repudiated, not least by Srbik. However, other historians have gingerly picked at the idea, arguing that the old "Holy Roman Empire of the German Nation" should not be understood in the terms of 19th-century nationalism. The old Reich was polylingual, multicultural, proto-federalist, even capable of tolerating multiple state churches. Some German historians have even suggested *sotto voce* that it has served as implicit model for the European Community. (For many of these arguments expressed boldly, if eccentrically, see Friedrich Heer's *Das Heilige Römische Reich*, 1967; *Holy Roman Empire*, 1968). One intriguing confirmation of this notion is its place in the dissertation that French career Eurocrat, Charles Boutant finished and published in his retirement, *L'Europe au grand tournant des années 1680* (Europe at the Great Turning Point of the 1680s, 1985). At the very least, there has been a trend in German political and constitutional historiography away from concentration on individual states such as Prussia and toward histories of either the whole multi-state complex, or at least the middle states, regional governments, and free cities whose history makes sense only within the framework of the Holy Roman empire.

But how is a German political/constitutional history as now conceived to be written? The best way to answer this question is to look at an outstanding general survey from the previous generation, Hajo Holborn's *A History of Modern Germany* (1959–69), and compare it to two recent ones, Volker Press' *Kriege und Krisen* (War and Crisis, 1991), and John Gagliardo's *Germany under the Old Regime* (1991). Each of these writers revealed a significant historical continuity. All three divided

German history sometime in the 17th century between a Reformation and true early modern era, but where Holborn took 1648 as a starting point of the second period, the later authors found 1600 a more appropriate dividing line. The crucial difference between the two periods was not any breach in constitutional or confessional history, but a century long economic downturn/collapse of political legitimacy, known as the "General Crisis of the Seventeenth Century" (see the essays collected in Geoffrey Parker and Lesley M. Smith's *The General Crisis of the Seventeenth Century*, 1978). Even after 1648, German history can still be understood within the framework of the old Reich.

A literature on the internal constitutional/administrative, and legal history of the old Reich has existed in Germany, naturally enough, since the legal profession would require it even if historians did not, but it also has an established tradition in English. Henry F. Schwarz's *The Imperial Privy Council in the Seventeenth Century* (1943) was perhaps the earliest such study. An excellent overall review can also be found in John Gagliardo's *Reich and Nation* (1980). In German, the growing corpus of Karl Otmar von Aretin's work on institutional history, most notably the recent *Das alte Reich* (The Old Reich, 1993) is a good source. Of the old Reich's overarching institutions – the "Circles of the Empire," or provincial governments – little is available in English, but what there is, such as James Allen Vann's *The Swabian Kreis* (1975), is good. A companion study, Reinhard von Neipperg's *Kaiser und schwäbischer Kreis* (Emperor and Swabian Circle, 1991), is well worth tackling. To these works might be added the whole corpus of Mack Walker, and above all, F.L. Carsten, whose *Princes and Parliaments in Germany from the Fifteenth to the Eighteenth Century* (1959), represents an intriguing attack on the early modern *Sonderweg*.

Another very traditional type of history is the biography of the great figure. As guides to a period, biographies of rulers and great statesmen have their advantages, and English is blessed with some very good biographies of figures such as Frederick the Great and Maria Theresa. G.P. Gooch's *Frederick the Great* (1947), C.A. Macartney's *Maria Theresa and the House of Austria* (1969), Charles Ingrao's *In Quest and Crisis* (1979), John Spielman's *Leopold I of Austria* (1977), and Derek Beales' *Joseph II* (1987) stand out. Astonishingly, there is no scholarly study of Charles VI (reigned 1712–40) in any language, but Verlag Styria's series of commissioned biographies of the Holy Roman emperors has to some extent filled the gap with Bernd Rill's *Karl VI* (Charles VI, 1992). These biographies are brilliantly complemented by Andrew Wheatcroft's cultural study of the Habsburgs public relations tradition in *The Habsburgs* (1995).

R.J.W. Evans' *Rudolf II and His World* (1973) arguably belongs in the section above, but its explicit commitment to the intellectual history of a public figure and his court make it a much more ambitious and important work than might be expected of a biography. Although the work itself is characterized by an unfortunate enthusiasm for the excesses of Frances Yates, it clearly signalled a departure in the intellectual history of the period. While this has been thoroughly described in many traditional intellectual histories, even excellent works such as Ernst Cassirer's *Die Philosophie der Aufklärung* (1932; in English as *The Philosophy of the Enlightenment*, 1951) have

tended to tell us more about their authors than their subjects. This is a problem shared by all "internalist" history, and is no reason not to read the classics, but it has inevitably led to a skewed understanding of the contemporary intellectual climate. As Evans demonstrated, particularly in his later *The Making of the Habsburg Monarchy, 1500–1700* (1979), one could hardly come to a proper understanding of contemporary thought by ignoring such (for the period) vital issues as alchemy and secret writing. Recent works such as John Stoye's *Marsigli's Europe, 1680–1730* (1994) – unfortunately not reliable on the details of Marsigli's later life – and Pamela Smith's *The Business of Alchemy* (1994), confirmed the continuing fertility of this historicized approach to intellectual endeavor. Another potentially fruitful departure is David Sorkin's revelation of the considerable religious dimension of the Enlightenment, sketched in his *Moses Mendelssohn and the Religious Enlightenment* (1996), and to be developed further in the future.

No review of traditional German historiography could omit military affairs, for which, in the early modern period at least, the first resort should still be to the Prussian and Austro-Hungarian staff histories. For all their limitations, these works in most cases still represent the only products of really thorough archival research of the kind that is second nature in diplomatic history. Nonetheless, they should be read with due attention to the effective and entertainingly polemical critiques contained in the fourth volume of Hans Delbrück's *Geschichte der Kriegskunst* (1900–20; *History of the Art of War*, 1975–85). However, Delbrück himself is not always reliable. For an English-language synthetic narrative, we have *The Thirty Years' War* (1984) edited by Geoffrey Parker, and the voluminous oeuvre of Christopher Duffy, but readers with a less intensive interest may wish to skip directly to literature by Michael Roberts and Geoffrey Parker developing the currently lively debate over the "Military Revolution." Roberts and Parker each see European military practice as having been profoundly transformed by a series of organizational (Roberts), or technological (Parker) changes in the period 1500–1700. Several authors, most notably Brian Downing in his recent *The Military Revolution and Political Change* (1991), have argued that the Revolution led to militarization, which had a decisive effect in stunting the growth of western-style bourgeois democracy. Perhaps more worthy of note is the emphasis that Roberts placed on the "Protestant Lions," Maurice of Nassau, Cromwell, Gustavus Adolphus, and Frederick the Great. Such emphasis was dangerously reminiscent of the Rankeans' assumption of the racial/confessional superiority of Protestant north Germans over Latin Catholicism. Thus, while the "Military Revolution" has been under sustained attack by John Lynn, and others, Cornelis Schulten's succinct source criticism, "Une nouvelle approche de Maurice de Nassau" (A New Approach to Maurice of Nassau) in Pierre Chaunu's *Le Soldat, la stratégie, la mort* (The Soldier, Strategy, and Death, 1989) is by far the most damaging blow struck against it.

The rich field of urban history is the most characteristic traditional form of early modern German social history. Mack Walker's *German Home Towns* (1971) makes a good introduction to this field, but there are numerous local studies that repay attention. A good overview is C.R. Friedrichs' *The Early Modern City* (1995). Such works seem to provide an appropriate scale for the treatment of the vexed question of social organization, especially the debate over whether early modern society should be seen as divided by class in the Marxist, or "estate" in some more rigorously historicist sense.

Other social divisions within the small German city feature various "peoples without history" at the margins of burgher society: Jews, women, and, although the literature has scarcely developed, gays, and children. Among treatments of the relationship between Jew and Gentile in early modern Germany, Ronnie Po-Chia Hsia's *The Myth of Ritual Murder* (1988) stands out. For women's history, Merry Wiesner's *Working Women in Renaissance Germany* (1986) quickly emerged as a standard, but Heide Wunder's *"Er ist die Sonn', sie ist der Mond"* ("He is the Sun, She is the Moon," 1992) also attracted considerable attention. Isabel Hull's, *Sexuality, State, and Civil Society in Germany, 1700–1815* (1996) provides a more recent interpretation, informed by developments in gender and gay history. It is probably from historians of these liminal figures, or perhaps the proponents of "the history of everyday life," or *Alltagsgeschichte*, that the next generation of German historians will derive their attacks on, and defenses of, the *Sonderweg*.

ERIK A. LUND

See also Cassirer; Delbrück; East Central Europe; Macartney; Parker; Ranke; Srbik; Wehler

Further Reading

Anderson, Matthew Smith, *Historians and Eighteenth Century Europe, 1715–1789*, Oxford and New York: Oxford University Press, 1979

Anderson, Matthew Smith, *The War of the Austrian Succession, 1740–1748*, London and New York: Longman, 1995

Aretin, Karl Otmar von, *Das alte Reich, 1648–1806*, vol. 1: *Föderalistische oder hierarchische Ordnung (1648–1684)* (The Old Reich, 1648–1806, vol. 1: Federal or Hierarchical Order, 1648–1684), Stuttgart: Klett Cotta, 1993

Arneth, Alfred, *Prinz Eugen von Savoyen*, 3 vols., Vienna: Anstalt, 1858

Arneth, Alfred, *Geschichte Maria Theresia's* (History of Maria Theresa), 10 vols., Vienna: Braumüller, 1863–79

Asprey, Robert B., *Frederick the Great: The Magnificent Enigma*, New York: Ticknor and Fields, 1986; Tunbridge Wells: Costello, 1988

Barker, Thomas Mack, *Double Eagle and Crescent: Vienna's Second Turkish Siege and Its Historical Setting*, Albany: State University of New York Press, 1967

Barker, Thomas Mack, "Military Entrepreneurship and Absolutism: Habsburg Models," *Journal of European Studies* 4 (1974), 19–42

Bayerische Akademie der Wissenschaften, ed., *Neue deutsche Biographie* (New German Biography), 18 vols to date, Berlin: Duncker & Humblot, 1953–

Beales, Derek, *Joseph II*, Cambridge and New York: Cambridge University Press, 1987

Beese, Christian, *Markgraf Hermann von Baden (1628–1691): General, Diplomat, und Minister Kaiser Leopolds I*, Stuttgart: Kohlhammer, 1991

Benecke, Gerhard, "The Westphalian Circle, the County of Lippe, and Imperial Currency Control," in James Allen Vann and Steven W. Rowan, eds., *The Old Reich: Essays on German Public Institutions*, Brussels: Editions de la Librairie Encyclopédique, 1974

Benecke, Gerhard, *Maximilian I (1459–1519): An Analytical Biography*, London and Boston: Routledge, 1982

Berdahl, Robert M., *The Politics of the Prussian Nobility, 1770–1848*, Princeton: Princeton University Press, 1988

Bérenger, Jean, *Finances et absolutisme autrichien dans la seconde moitié du XVIIème siècle* (Austrian Finances and Absolutism in the Second Half the 17th Century), 2 vols., Paris: Champion, 1975

Boutant, Charles, *L'Europe au grand tournant des années 1680: la succession palatine* (Europe at the Great Turning Point of the 1680s: The Palatine Succession), Paris: Société d'Edition d'Enseignement Supérieur, 1985

Braubach, Max, *Prinz Eugen von Savoyen*, 5 vols., Munich: Oldenbourg, 1963–65

Broman, Thomas, "Rethinking Professionalization: Theory, Practice, and Professional Ideology in Eighteenth-Century German Medicine," *Journal of Modern History* 67 (1995), 835–72

Broucek, Peter, *Der Geburtstag der Monarchie: die Schlacht bei Kolin, 1757* (The Birthday of the Monarchy: The Battle of Kolin, 1757), Vienna: ÖBV, 1982

Büsch, Otto, *Militärsystem und Sozialleben im alten Preussen, 1713–1807: Die Anfänge der sozialen Militarisierung der preussisch-deutschen Gesellschaft* (Military System and Social Life in Old Prussia, 1713–1807: The Origins of the Social Militarization of Prusso-German Society), Berlin: de Gruyter, 1962

Bush, M.L., *The European Nobility*, 2 vols., Manchester: Manchester University Press, 1988

Butterfield, Herbert, *Reconstruction of an Historical Episode: The History of the Enquiry into the Origins of the Seven Years' War*, Glasgow: Jackson, 1951

Carsten, Francis, *Princes and Parliaments in Germany from the Fifteenth to the Eighteenth Century*, Oxford: Oxford University Press, 1959

Caspar, Max, *Johannes Kepler*, Stuttgart: Kohlhammer, 1948; in English as *Kepler*, New York: Abelard Schuman, 1959

Cassirer, Ernst, *Die Philosophie der Aufklärung*, Tübingen: Mohr, 1932; in English as *The Philosophy of the Enlightenment*, Princeton: Princeton University Press, 1951

Chance, James Frederick, *The Alliance of Hanover: A Study of British Foreign Policy in the Last Years of George I*, London: Murray, 1923

Chaunu, Pierre, ed., *Le Soldat, la stratégie, la mort: mélanges André Corvisier* (The Soldier, Strategy, and Death: Contributions In Honor of André Corvisier), Paris: Economica, 1989

Coxe, William, and Franz Hartig, *History of the House of Austria*, 5 vols., London: Hansard, 1807; revised 1820; expanded 1853

Damen, Richard, ed., *Fischer Lexikon: Geschichte* (The Fischer Guide: History), Frankfurt: Fischer, 1990

Delbrück, Hans, *Geschichte der Kriegskunst im Rahmen der politischen Geschichte*, 4 vols., Berlin: Stilke, 1900–20, reprinted Berlin: de Gruyter, 1962–66; in English as *History of the Art of War within the Framework of Political History*, 4 vols., Westport, CT: Greenwood Press, 1975–85

Dickson, Peter George Muir, *Finance and Government under Maria Theresia, 1740–1780*, Oxford and New York: Oxford University Press, 1987

Downing, Brian, *The Military Revolution and Political Change: Origins of Democracy and Autocracy in Early Modern Europe*, Princeton: Princeton University Press, 1991

Duden, Barbara, *Geschichte unter der Haut: ein Eisenacher Arzt und seine Patientinnen um 1730*, Stuttgart: Klett Cotta, 1987; in English as *The Woman Beneath the Skin: A Doctor's Patients in Eighteenth-Century Germany*, Cambridge, MA: Harvard University Press, 1991

Duffy, Christopher, *The Army of Maria Theresa: The Armed Forces of Imperial Austria*, Newton Abbot: David and Charles, and New York: Hippocrene, 1977

Duffy, Christopher, *Siege Warfare*, London: Routledge, 1979

Duffy, Christopher, *The Fortress in the Age of Vauban and Frederick the Great*, London: Routledge, 1985

Duffy, Christopher, *Frederick the Great: A Military Life*, London: Routledge, 1985

Evans, Robert John Weston, *Rudolf II and His World: A Study in Intellectual History, 1576–1612*, Oxford: Oxford University Press, 1973

Evans, Robert John Weston, *The Making of the Habsburg Monarchy, 1500–1700: An Interpretation*, Oxford and New York: Oxford University Press, 1979

Feldzüge des Prinzen Eugen (The Campaigns of Prince Eugene), 21 vols., Vienna, 1876–91

Frevert, Ute, *Frauengeschichte: zwischen bürgerlicher Verbesserung und neuer Weiblichkeit*, Frankfurt: Suhrkamp, 1986; in English as *Women in German History from Bourgeois Emancipation to Sexual Liberation*, Oxford and New York: Berg, 1989

Frey, Linda, and Marsha Frey, *A Question of Empire: Leopold I and the War of the Spanish Succession, 1701–05*, New York: Columbia University Press, 1983

Frey, Linda, and Marsha Frey, *Frederick I: The Man and His Times*, New York: Columbia University Press, 1984

Friedrichs, Christopher R., *Urban Society in an Age of War: Nördlingen, 1580–1720*, Princeton: Princeton University Press, 1979

Friedrichs, Christopher R., *The Early Modern City, 1450–1750*, London and New York: Longman, 1995

Gagliardo, John, *Reich and Nation: The Holy Roman Empire as Idea and Reality, 1763–1806*, Bloomington: Indiana University Press, 1980

Gagliardo, John, *Germany under the Old Regime, 1600–1790*, London and New York: Longman, 1991

Gooch, G.P., *Frederick the Great*, London and New York: Longman, 1947

Gross, Hanns, *Empire and Sovereignty: A History of Public Law Literature in the Holy Roman Empire, 1599–1804*, Chicago: University of Chicago Press, 1973

Heer, Friedrich, *Das Heilige Römische Reich*, Vienna: Scherz, 1967; in English as *Holy Roman Empire*, New York: Praeger, and London: Weidenfeld and Nicolson, 1968

Holborn, Hajo, *A History of Modern Germany*, 3 vols., New York: Knopf, and London: Eyre and Spottiswoode, 1959–69

Hsia, R. Po-Chia, *Society and Religion in Münster, 1535–1618*, New Haven: Yale University Press, 1984

Hsia, R. Po-Chia, *The Myth of Ritual Murder: Jews and Magic in Reformation Germany*, New Haven and London: Yale University Press, 1988

Hsia, R. Po-Chia, *Social Discipline in the Reformation: Central Europe, 1550–1750*, London and New York: Routledge, 1989

Hughes, Michael, *Law and Politics in Eighteenth Century Germany: The Imperial Aulic Council in the Reign of Charles V*, Woodbridge, Suffolk: Boydell, 1988

Hull, Isabel, "Feminist and Gender History Through the Literary Looking Glass: German Historiography in Postmodern Times," *Central European History* 22 (1989), 279–300

Hull, Isabel, *Sexuality, State, and Civil Society in Germany, 1700–1815*, Ithaca, NY: Cornell University Press, 1996

Ingrao, Charles W., *In Quest and Crisis: Emperor Joseph I and the Habsburg Monarchy*, West Lafayette, IN: Purdue University Press, 1979

Ingrao, Charles W., *The Habsburg Monarchy, 1618–1815*, Cambridge and New York: Cambridge University Press, 1994

Ingrao, Charles W., ed., *State and Society in Early Modern Austria*, West Lafayette, IN: Purdue University Press, 1994

Jähns, Max, *Geschichte der Kriegswissenschaften vornehmlich in Deutschland* (The History of Military Science as Practiced in Germany), 3 vols., Munich: Oldenbourg, 1889–91; reprinted New York: Johnson, 1965

Kann, Robert A., *A History of the Habsburg Empire, 1526–1918*, Berkeley: University of California Press, 1974

Killy, Walther, ed., *Deutsche biographische Enzyklopädie* (German Biographical Dictionary), 5 vols. to date, Munich: Saur, 1995–

Königliche Akademie der Wissenschaften, ed., *Allgemeine deutsche Biographie* (General German Biography), 56 vols., Leipzig: Duncker & Humblot, 1875–1912

Kopitzsch, Franklin, "Die deutsche Aufklärung: Leistungen, Grenzen, Wirkungen" (The German Enlightenment: Achievement, Limits, and Effects), *Archiv für Sozialgeschichte* 23 (1983), 1–22

Die Kriege Friedrichs des Grossen (The Wars of Frederick the Great), 3 series, 19 vols., Berlin: Mittler, 1890–1914

Kuhn, Thomas S., *The Copernican Revolution: Planetary Astronomy in the Development of Western Thought*, Cambridge, MA: Harvard University Press, 1957

Kunisch, Johannes, *Der kleine Krieg: Studien zum Heerwesen des Absolutismus* (The Little War: Studies in the Absolutist Practice of War), Wiesbaden: Steiner, 1973

Langsam, Walter C., *Francis the Good: The Education of an Emperor, 1768–1792*, New York: Macmillan, 1949

Lynn, John, "The Pattern of Army Growth, 1445–1945," in John Lynn, ed., *Tools of War: Instruments, Ideas and Institutions of Warfare, 1445–1871*, Urbana: University of Illinois Press, 1990

Lynn, John, "Food, Funds, and Fortresses: Resource Mobilization and Positional Warfare in the Campaigns of Louis XIV," in John Lynn, ed., *Feeding Mars: Logistics in Western Warfare from the Middle Ages to the Present*, Boulder, CO: Westview Press, 1993

Macartney, C.A., *Maria Theresa and the House of Austria*, London: English Universities Press, 1969

McKay, Derek, *Prince Eugene of Savoy*, London: Thames and Hudson, 1977

Magenschab, Hans, *Josef II: Revolutionär von Gottes Gnaden* (Joseph II: Revolutionary by God's Grace), Graz: Styria, 1979

Magocsi, Paul Robert, *Historical Atlas of East Central Europe*, Seattle: University of Washington Press, 1993

Melton, James Van Horn, "The Nobility in the Bohemian and Austrian Lands, 1620–1780," in Hamish M. Scott, ed., *The European Nobilities in the Seventeenth and Eighteenth Centuries*, 2 vols., London: Longman, 1995

Midelfort, H.C. Erik, *Witch Hunting in Southwestern Germany, 1562–1684: The Social and Intellectual Foundations*, Stanford, CA: Stanford University Press, 1972

Neipperg, Reinhard von, *Kaiser und schwäbischer Kreis (1714–1733): Ein Beitrag zur Reichsverfassung, Kreisgeschichte und kaiserlichen Reichspolitik am Anfang des 18. Jahrhunderts* (Emperor and Swabian Circle: A Contribution to the Study of Imperial Administration, Local History, and Imperial National Policy at the Beginning of the 18th Century), Stuttgart: Kohlhammer, 1991

Oberhammer, Evelin, ed., *Der ganzen Welt ein Lob und Spiegel: Das Fürstenhaus Liechtenstein in der frühen Neuzeit* (A Compliment and Mirror to the Whole World: The Princely House of Liechtenstein in the Early Modern Period), Vienna: Verlag für Geschichte und Politik, 1990

Österreichischer Erbfolgekrieg, 1740–1748 (The War of the Austrian Succession, 1740–1748), 9 vols. in 10 parts, Vienna: Siedel, 1896–1905

Parker, Geoffrey, and Lesley M. Smith, eds., *The General Crisis of the Seventeenth Century*, London and Boston: Routledge, 1978; 2nd edition 1997

Parker, Geoffrey, ed., *The Thirty Years' War*, London and Boston: Routledge, 1984; revised 1997

Peham, Helga, *Leopold II: Herrscher mit weiser Hand* (Leopold II: Master with a Wise Hand), Graz: Styria, 1987

Pelzer, Erich, *Der elsässischer Adel im Spätfeudalismus: Tradition und Wandel einer regionalen Elite zwischen dem Westfälischen Frieden und der Revolution (1648–1790)* (The Alsatian Nobility in Late Feudalism: Tradition and Change in a Regional Elite Between the Peace Period of Westphalia and the Revolution, 1648–1790), Munich: Oldenbourg, 1990

Press, Volker, "Österreichische Grossmachtbildung und Reichsverfassung" (Austria's Rise as a Great Power and the Reich Constitution), *Mitteilungen des Institutes für österreichische Geschichtsforschung*, 98/1–2 (1990), 131–54

Press, Volker, *Kriege und Krisen: Deutschland, 1600–1715* (War and Crisis: Germany, 1600–1715), Munich: Beck, 1991

Redlich, Oswald, *Das Werden einer Grossmacht: Österreich von 1700 bis 1740* (The Development of a Great Power: Austria from 1700 to 1740), Vienna: Rohrer, 1938

Redlich, Oswald, *Weltmacht des Barock: Österreich in der Zeit Leopolds I* (World Power of the Baroque: Austria in the Time of Leopold I), Vienna: Rohrer, 1961

Rill, Bernd, *Karl VI.: Habsburg als barocke Grossmacht* (Charles VI: Habsburg as World Power of the Baroque), Graz: Styria, 1992

Roberts, Michael, "The Military Revolution, 1560–1660," in Clifford J. Rogers, ed., *The Military Revolution Debate: Readings on the Military Transformation of Early Modern Europe*, Boulder, CO: Westview Press, 1995

Roider, Karl A., *Austria's Eastern Question, 1700–1790*, Princeton: Princeton University Press, 1982

Schreiber, Georg, *Franz I. Stephan: An der Seite einer grossen Frau* (Francis Stephen I: At the Side of a Great Woman), Graz: Styria, 1986

Schroeder, Paul W., *The Transformation of European Politics, 1763–1848*, Oxford: Clarendon Press, 1994

Schlumbohm, Jürgen, *Lebensläufe, Familien, Höfe: Die Bauern und Heuerleute des osnabrückischen Kirchspiels Belm in proto-industrieller Zeit, 1650–1860* (Life, Family, Home: The Farmers and Day Laborers of the Osnabruck Parish of Belm in the Proto-Industrial Era, 1650–1860), Göttingen: Vandenhoeck & Ruprecht, 1994

Schwarz, Henry F., *The Imperial Privy Council in the Seventeenth Century*, Cambridge, MA: Harvard University Press, and London: Oxford University Press, 1943; reprinted 1972

Scott, Tom, *Freiburg and the Breisgau: Town-Country Relations in the Age of Reformation and Peasants' War*, Oxford and New York: Oxford University Press, 1986

Showalter, Dennis, *German Military History, 1648–1982: A Critical Bibliography*, New York: Garland, 1984

Sicken, Bernhard, *Der fränkische Reichskreis: Seine Ämter und Einrichtungen im 18. Jahrhundert* (The Franconian Circle of the Empire: Its Officers and Direction in the 18th Century), Würzburg: Schöningh, 1970

Smith, Pamela, *The Business of Alchemy: Science and Culture in the Holy Roman Empire*, Princeton: Princeton University Press, 1994

Sorkin, David J., *Moses Mendelssohn and the Religious Enlightenment*, London: Halben, and Berkeley, CA: University of California Press, 1996

Spielman, John Philip, *Leopold I of Austria*, London: Thames and Hudson, and New Brunswick, NJ: Rutgers University Press, 1977

Spielman, John Philip, *The City and the Crown: Vienna and the Imperial Court, 1600–1740*, West Lafayette, IN: Purdue University Press, 1993

Srbik, Heinrich von, *Deutsche Einheit: Idee und Wirklichkeit vom heiligen Reich bis Königgratz* (German Unity: Ideal and Reality from the Holy Empire to Koniggratz), 4 vols., Munich: Bruckmann, 1935–42

Srbik, Heinrich von, *Wien und Versailles, 1692–1697: Zur Geschichte von Strassburg, Elsass, und Lothringen* (Vienna and Versailles, 1692–97: On the History of Strasbourg, Alsace, and Lorraine), Munich: Bruckmann, 1944

Stoye, John, *The Siege of Vienna*, London: Collins, 1964; New York: Holt Rinehart, 1965

Stoye, John, *Marsigli's Europe, 1680–1730: The Life and Times of Luigi Ferdinando Marsigli, Soldier and Virtuoso*, New Haven and London: Yale University Press, 1994

Sutton, John L., *The King's Honor and the King's Cardinal: The War of the Polish Succession*, Lexington: University Press of Kentucky, 1980

Szabo, Franz A.J., *Kaunitz and Enlightened Absolutism 1753–1780*, Cambridge and New York: Cambridge University Press, 1994

Vann, James Allen, *The Swabian Kreis: Institutional Growth in the Holy Roman Empire, 1648–1715*, Brussels: Editions de la Librairie Encyclopédique, 1975

Vierhaus, Rudolf, *Ranke und die soziale Welt* (Ranke and the Social World), Münster: Aschendorffsche Verlagsbuchhandlung, 1957

Waddington, Richard, *La Guerre de sept ans: histoire diplomatique et militaire* (The Seven Years' War: Diplomatic and Military History), 5 vols., Paris: Firmin Didot, 1899–1907

Walker, Mack, *German Home Towns: Community, State, and General Estate, 1648–1871*, Ithaca, NY: Cornell University Press, 1971

Walker, Mack, *The Salzburg Transaction: Expulsion and Redemption in Eighteenth Century Germany*, Ithaca, NY: Cornell University Press, 1992

Wandruszka, Adam, *Das Haus Habsburg: die Geschichte einer europäischen Dynastie*, Stuttgart: Vorweck, 1956; in English as *The House of Habsburg: Six Hundred Years of a European Dynasty*, London: Sidgwick and Jackson, and New York: Doubleday, 1964

Wehler, Hans-Ulrich, *Deutsche Gesellschaftsgeschichte* (German Society in History), 3 vols. to date, Munich: Beck, 1987–

Wheatcroft, Andrew, *The Habsburgs: Embodying Empire*, New York: Viking, 1995

Wiesner, Merry E., *Working Women in Renaissance Germany*, New Brunswick, NJ: Rutgers University Press, 1986

Wunder, Heide, *"Er ist die Sonn', sie ist der Mond": Frauen in der frühen Neuzeit*, ("He is the Sun, She is the Moon": Women in the Early Modern Period), Munich: Beck, 1992

Wurzbach, Constantin, *Biographisches Lexikon des Kaiserthums Österreich* (Biographical Dictionary of the Austrian Empire), 60 vols., Vienna: Hof, 1856–91; reprinted New York: Johnson, 1966

Zedinger, Renate, *Hochzeit im Brennpunkt der Mächte: Franz Stephan von Lothringen und Erzherzogin Maria Theresia* (Marriage at the Flashpoint of the Powers: Francis Stephen of Lorraine and Archduchess Maria Theresa), Vienna: Böhlau, 1994

Zedler, Johann Heinrich, and Carl Günther Ludovici, eds., *Grosses vollständiges Universal-Lexikon* (Grand Comprehensive Encyclopedia), 64 vols., Halle: Zedler, 1732–50; reprinted Graz: Akademisches, 1961–64

Zophy, Jonathan W., *The Holy Roman Empire: A Dictionary Handbook*, Westport, CT: Greenwood Press, 1980

Germany: 1800–1945

The turbulent history of modern Germany has posed a variety of challenges for historians. Because of the impact of World War II on the interpretation of German history, the subject is best approached by dividing it into the pre- and post-World War II eras.

Up to World War II, the history of 19th-century Germany was largely influenced by the Rankean concept of history and its emphasis on the importance of the state. The classic work in this regard is Heinrich von Treitschke's *Deutsche Geschichte im neunzehnten Jahrhundert* (1879–94; *History of Germany in the Nineteenth Century*, 1915) which, although addressing some cultural and religious developments, is above all concerned with tracing Prussia's rise to greatness and its contributions to German unity. As in Droysen's 1868 *Geschichte der preussischen Politik* (A History of Prussian Politics), Treitschke's superbly written account emphasized people in power as important, referring to them as "historical heroes."

Because the unification of Germany was interpreted as Germany's great historical event of the 19th century, historians emphasized the political actors and processes that were involved in this event, with a particular consideration of Bismarck. The first major account of this era was Heinrich von Sybel's colossal 7-volume *Die Begründung des Deutschen Reiches durch Wilhelm I* (1889–95; *The Founding of the German Empire by William I*, 1890–98), which portrayed Prussia as the glorious founder of the new empire and a new age. The story of the foundation of the empire was told from a viewpoint sympathetic with the "blood and iron" approach to German unity, as testified in Erich Brandenburg's *Die Reichsgründung* (The Founding of the Empire, 1916), or Dawson's *The German Empire* (1919). The literature on Bismarck himself was correspondingly flattering. Hans Rothfels portrayed him as a protector against the nationalism of the masses and their wayward ideas of social democracy. Even British historians such as Grant Robertson expressed reserved admiration for Bismarck.

At the same time, however, there was a moderate opposing school of thought. Meinecke in *Nach der Revolution* (After the Revolution, 1919) was critical of Prussian militarism and the social tensions of the second empire, a sentiment echoed in Lamprecht's *Zur jüngsten deutschen Vergangenheit* (On the Most Recent German Past, 1902–04). Similarly, Ziekursch claimed that the empire had been founded against the liberal spirit of the time. Arthur Rosenberg's *Die Entstehung der deutschen Republik 1871–1918* (1928; *The Birth of the German Republic*, 1931) showed, through a Marxist approach, the emergence of antisocialist industrialists and Junkers which hindered the development of democracy in Germany. Eckart Kehr's provocative *Schlachtflottenbau und Parteipolitik 1894–1901* (1930; *Battleship Building and Party Politics in Germany 1894–1901*, 1973) considered the internal dimension of foreign policy, specifically the pressure that economic groups brought to bear. His work, largely ignored at the time, emphasized not the traditional "Primat der Aussenpolitik" but the "Primat der Innenpolitik."

Although most historiography dealt with Bismarck's era, some attention was paid to other aspects of 19th-century Germany. The extent to which Stein and the early Prussian reforms were influenced by the French Revolution were debated between Max Lehmann in his 3-volume biography *Freiherr von Stein* (1902–05), and Ernst von Meier in *Französische Einflüsse auf die Staats- und Rechtsentwicklung Preussens im 19. Jahrhundert* (French Influences on the Development of Prussia's State and Law in the 19th Century, 1907). In the economic sphere, the importance of the 1834 Customs Union in German unification received consideration in Henderson's *The Zollverein* (1939). Valentin's comprehensive history of 1848 gave a liberal-democratic interpretation of this revolution, with clear sympathy for the democratic aspirations of the reformers. His treatment was a more positive portrayal than Sybel and Treitschke, who believed in Bismarck's *Realpolitik* as the only way to achieve the national goals of the reformers. A leftist interpretation of the 1848 events emerged at this time as well. *Germany: Revolution and Counter-Revolution* (1933), with contributions by Marx and Engels, interpreted the revolution as a revolt of the working classes. Leftist interpretations were also to be found in Franz Mehring's *Zur deutschen Geschichte* (On German History, 1931).

Works on social aspects of 19th-century Germany were scant. Schnabel's masterpiece *Deutsche Geschichte im neunzehnten Jahrhundert* (A History of Germany in the Nineteenth Century, 1929) addressed the developments of the arts, religion, and science of 19th-century Germany, but within the framework of national and liberal movements.

With the advent of World War II, historiography of 19th-century Germany began a considerable transformation. Erich Eyck, one of a number of German historians who had emigrated during the war – others included Veit Valentin, Gustav Mayer, Arthur Rosenberg, Hajo Holborn, Hans Rothfels, and Golo Mann – wrote his 3-volume biography of Bismarck between 1941 and 1944. In it, he portrayed Bismarck as crushing the noble aspirations of the national-liberal movement of the 1860s. In contrast to the former praise of Bismarck's *Realpolitik*, Eyck expressed regret that German unity was achieved through violence, and that Bismarck had not shown more respect for the constitution. This critical appraisal of the *Kaiserreich* did not last into the immediate postwar era, however.

In the decade after the war, historians were concerned above all with the notion of *Sonderweg*. The questions centered around whether Germany had a flawed historical development, compared to her West European counterparts, which created the conditions necessary for Hitler's rise, or if he was simply a *Betriebsunfall*, an accident on an otherwise respectable historical path. Meinecke's *Die deutsche Katastrophe* (1946; *The German Catastrophe*, 1950) downplayed continuity in German history, as did Ritter's *Staatskunst und Kriegshandwerk* (1954–68; *The Sword and the Scepter*, 1969–73), where he portrayed the Prussian military tradition as one relatively free from militarism and imperialism, the roots of both of which being in any case readily found in modern western European industrial societies in general. The theme of Hitler's detachment from German historical development runs through early works on German resistance to Hitler, such as Rothfels' *Die deutsche Opposition gegen Hitler* (1951; *The German Opposition to Hitler*, 1961) or Ritter's 1954 biography on the conservative resistance fighter Carl Goerdeler. Similarly in *Europa und die deutsche Frage* (1948; *The German Problem*, 1965), Ritter saw the roots of militarism in western society overall, and as a product of the French Revolution which broke down civilian/military barriers. Other works that appeared outside of Germany did, however, suggest that Nazism had roots in German history. A.J.P. Taylor's *The Course of German History* (1945) pointed in this direction with his emphasis on obedience and duty as a German trait, as did Gordon Craig's *Politics of the Prussian Army* (1955) with his emphasis on the importance of the military and its influence on diplomacy throughout German history.

With Fritz Fischer's *Griff nach der Weltmacht* (1961; *Germany's Aims in the First World War*, 1967), the *Sonderweg* debate took on new life. Fischer's interpretation that World War I was the result of German aggressive designs, was pathbreaking. It suggested a continuation between the expansionist plans of the Second and Third Reichs, and seriously questioned the accepted stance of the "accident" interpretation of Hitler. Fischer's thesis on internal politics dictating Germany's foreign policy also caused a stir. Armed with the new paradigms of social history, a plethora of works on continuity in German history began appearing in the 1960s, with an emphasis on internal affairs of Bismarck's empire. Economic history played a key role in several interpretations. Hans Rosenberg in *Grosse Depression und Bismarckzeit* (Great Depression and the Era of Bismarck, 1967) provided a new interpretation of the second empire by focusing on the role that economic crises played in the decline of German liberalism, the search for colonies, and the climate of ideas such as anti-Semitism. Rosenberg's interpretation of Bismarck's empire as one where the main characters acted within a structural framework beyond their control, a clear sign of Weberian historical sociology, began a new era of dealing with the German past. Hans-Ulrich Wehler also focused on economic developments in *Bismarck und der Imperialismus* (Bismarck and Imperialism, 1969), arguing that foreign expansion was a function of a shrinking economy that threatened traditional elites. Witt in *Die Finanzpolitik des Deutschen Reiches, 1903–1913* (The Finance Policies of the German Empire, 1903–1913; 1970) also explored political and economic developments, and concluded that civilian officials were aware of the military plans before the war. Other works centered on specific interest groups. Puhle determined that the Agrarian League was the most important anti-Semitic movement of the empire. The main thrust of these works revolved around the failure of German liberalism, attributing it to, among other reasons, the domination of Junkers, the "feudalization" of the bourgeoisie, and Bismarck's lack of respect for parliament.

The new criticisms of Bismarck's empire reached a zenith in Wehler's *Das deutsche Kaiserreich* (1973; *The German Empire*, 1985), where Wehler set out to prove the origins of Nazism in the Wilhelmine era, by emphasizing the structural similarities between late 19th-century Germany and the Nazi regime. He portrayed the Second Reich as a dictatorship rather than a constitutional monarchy. Wehler's tract is a classic of the Bielefeld school of history, of which Jürgen Kocka is also a key figure, that developed in West Germany in the late 1960s and 1970s.

The accepted interpretation of the *Sonderweg* in German history was brought into question at the beginning of the 1980s by Blackbourn and Eley's *Mythen deutscher Geschichtsschreibung* (1980; *The Peculiarities of German History*, 1984). The two British historians proposed to put Hitler in context, by describing him as neither an accident of history nor an inevitability, but rather as a contingency. Their argument challenged the idea that one needs a successful bourgeois revolution for successful capitalist development, and questioned whether Britain should be the standard by which German history is judged. Lothar Gall's *Bismarck: Der weisse Revolutionär* (1980; *Bismarck: The White Revolutionary*, 1986) has also offered some redress of the negative interpretation of Bismarck as well.

The post-1945 era also witnessed an attempt to understand the immediate conditions behind the rise of Nazism. Karl Dietrich Bracher in his 1955 study on the Weimar republic emphasized the structural conditions that allowed the rise of Nazism, as well as pointing out chancellor Bruning's contributions to Hitler's ascent. In the 1970s, Knut Borchardt argued that the Weimar republic was doomed to failure because it lacked the necessary room to maneuver in order to counter the mounting economic problems. His conclusions were debated by Harold James in *The German Slump* (1986), who argued that the republic was not inherently doomed, and that there were a variety of viable economic options available. The role of big business in Hitler's rise has also come under recent scrutiny. David Abraham has argued in *The Collapse of the Weimar Republic* (1981) that industrialists were largely at fault for the rise of National Socialism, a conclusion challenged by Henry Turner in *German Big Business and the Rise of Hitler* (1985).

There is, of course, no shortage of literature on the Nazi era itself. Debates in this field have focused primarily around the intent of Hitler and the Nazi regime, specifically with regards to the Holocaust. On the one hand are "functionalist" historians such as Hans Mommsen and Martin Broszat, who play down the purposive elements of Hitler's leadership. Instead, they place Nazism within the context of German history and stress the role that traditional elites played in the establishment and running of the Third Reich. An analysis of the structures of the Nazi regime, with their overlapping jurisdictions, has led Mommsen to his controversial conclusion that Hitler was a "weak dictator." Broszat in *Der Staat Hitlers* (1969; *The Hitler State*, 1969) documented the internal chaos from a structuralist point of view, emphasizing the tensions between party and state. In short, they subscribe to Karl Schleunes' approach in *The Twisted Road to Auschwitz* (1970). Karl Dietrich Bracher and Klaus Hildebrand, on the other hand, belong to the "intentionalist" camp. They believe that Hitler's intentions were clear from the outset, and that he unwaveringly pursued the mass murder of Jews from his takeover of power.

Social history of Nazi Germany has also become more prolific in recent years. Michael Kater's *The Nazi Party* (1983), for example, has provided an analysis of the socioeconomic backgrounds of the party's members, while Claudia Koonz in *Mothers in the Fatherland* (1986) has addressed women's organizations. Tim Mason's *Arbeiterklasse und Volksgemeinschaft* (The Working Class and the National Community, 1975) investigated the limitations of Nazi policy in dealing with labor at home, and suggested that Hitler was forced to launch the war earlier than planned due to potential labor unrest. The debate about society in the Third Reich has pitted Ian Kershaw, who claims that no social revolution took place in Nazi Germany because Hitler did not overly concern himself with internal matters, against David Schoenbaum, who agrees with Ralf Dahrendorf that a social revolution did indeed take place.

The debate about the Third Reich was given additional energy during the *Historikerstreit* (historians' debate) that erupted in the Federal Republic in 1986. This debate pitted leading historians such as Ernst Nolte, Joachim Fest, and Andreas Hillgruber, against a field led primarily by Jürgen Habermas. Nolte argued that it was time to historicize the Third Reich. In so doing, he claimed, one would find that Hitler was acting defensively to protect Western civilization from the Bolshevik threat, and that the Holocaust was not unique, but one of a series of genocides throughout the world. Habermas argued that this approach would lead to a trivializing of the Holocaust.

The extent to which the *Historikerstreit*, and also the German unification in 1990, will have an impact on the writing of modern German history remains to be seen.

GARY S. BRUCE

See also Bock; Bracher; Broszat; Conze; Droysen; Fischer; Gall; Habermas; Hillgruber; Holocaust; Kehr; Kocka; Koonz; Lamprecht; Mason; Meinecke; Mommsen, H.; Ritter; Rosenberg, A.;

Rosenberg, H.; Schnabel; Sybel; Taylor; Treitschke; Wehler; World
War I; World War II

Further Reading

Abraham, David, *The Collapse of the Weimar Republic: Political
Economy and Crisis*, Princeton: Princeton University Press, 1981

Barkin, K.D., "From Uniformity to Pluralism: German Historical
Writing since World War I," *German Life and Letters* 34
(1980–81), 234–47

Berghahn, Volker, "West German Historiography Between
Continuity and Change," *German Life and Letters* 34 (1980–81),
248–59

Blackbourn, David and Geoff Eley, *Mythen deutscher
Geschichtsschreibung: die gescheiterte bürgerliche Revolution von
1848*, Frankfurt: Ullstein, 1980; revised in English as *The
Peculiarities of German History: Bourgeois Society and Politics in
Nineteenth-Century German History*, Oxford: Oxford University
Press, 1984

Blanke, Horst Walter, *Historiographiegeschichte als Historik* (The
History of Historiography), Stuttgart: Frommann-Holzboog, 1991

Borchardt, Knut, *Wachstum, Krisen, Handlungsspielräume der
Wirtschaftspolitik: Studien zur Wirtschaftsgeschichte des 19. und
20. Jahrhunderts*, Göttingen: Vandenhoeck & Ruprecht, 1982; in
English as *Perspectives on Modern German Economic History
and Policy*, Cambridge: Cambridge University Press, 1991

Bracher, Karl Dietrich, *Die Auflösung der Weimarer Republik: eine
Studie zum Problem des Machtverfalls in der Demokratie* (The
Disintegration of the Weimar Republic: A Study on the Problem
of the Decline of Power in a Democracy), Stuttgart: Ring, 1955

Bracher, Karl Dietrich, *Die deutsche Diktatur: Entstehung, Struktur,
Folgen des Nationalsozialismus*, Cologne: Kiepenheuer & Witsch,
1969; in English as *The German Dictatorship: The Origins,
Structure, and Consequences of National Socialism*, New York:
Praeger, 1970; London: Weidenfeld and Nicolson, 1971

Brandenburg, Erich, *Die Reichsgründung* (The Founding of the
Empire), 2 vols., Leipzig: Quelle & Heger, 1916

Broszat, Martin, *Der Staat Hitlers: Grundlegung und Entwicklung
seiner inneren Verfassung*, Munich: Deutscher Taschenbuch, 1969;
in English as *The Hitler State: The Foundation and Development
of the Internal Structure of the Third Reich*, London and New
York: Longman, 1981

Craig, Gordon A., *Politics of the Prussian Army, 1640–1945*,
Oxford: Clarendon Press, 1955

Dahrendorf, Ralf, *Gesellschaft und Demokratie in Deutschland*,
Munich: Piper, 1965; in English as *Society and Democracy in
Germany*, Garden City, NY: Doubleday, and London: Weidenfeld
and Nicolson, 1967

Dawson, W.H., *The German Empire, 1867–1914, and the Unity
Movement*, New York: Macmillan, and London: Allen and
Unwin, 1919

Droysen, J.G., *Geschichte der preussischen Politik* (History of
Prussian Politics), 14 vols., 1855–86

Eley, Geoff, "Viewpoint: Nazism, Politics and Public Memory:
Thoughts on the West German *Historikerstreit*," *Past and Present*
121 (1988), 171–208

Engels, Friedrich, *Germany: Revolution and Counter-Revolution*,
London: Lawrence, 1933

Evans, Richard J., "Rethinking the German Past," *West European
Politics* 4 (1981), 131–48

Evans, Richard J., "From Hitler to Bismarck: The 'Reich' and
Kaiserreich in Recent Historiography," *Historical Journal* 26
(1983), 485–97 and 999–1020

Evans, Richard J., *Rethinking German History: Nineteenth-Century
Germany and the Origins of the Third Reich*, London and
Boston: Allen and Unwin, 1987

Eyck, Erich, *Bismarck*, 3 vols., Zurich: Rentsch, 1941–44; abridged
in English as *Bismarck and the German Empire*, London: Allen
and Unwin, 1950

Faulenbach, Bernd, *Geschichtswissenschaft in Deutschland:
traditionelle Positionen und gegenwärtige Aufgaben*, Munich:
Beck, 1974

Fischer, Alexander, and Gunther Heydemann, eds.,
Geschichtswissenschaft in der DDR, 2 vols., Berlin: Duncker &
Humblot, 1988–90

Fischer, Fritz, *Griff nach der Weltmacht: die Kriegszielpolitik des
kaiserlichen Deutschland, 1914–18*, Düsseldorf: Droste, 1961; in
English as *Germany's Aims in the First World War*, London:
Chatto and Windus, and New York: Norton, 1967

Ford, Franklin L., "Strands of History, Mostly German," *Journal of
Modern History* 52 (1980), 477–86

Gall, Lothar, *Bismarck: Der weisse Revolutionär*, Frankfurt:
Propylean, 1980; in English as *Bismarck: The White
Revolutionary*, 2 vols., London: Allen and Unwin, 1986

Grab, Walter, "German Historians and the Trivialization of Nazi
Criminality," *Australian Journal of Politics and History* 33
(1987), 273–78

Henderson, William Otto, *The Zollverein*, Cambridge: Cambridge
University Press, 1939; Chicago: Quadrangle, 1959

Hildebrand, Klaus, *Deutsche Aussenpolitik, 1933–1945: Kalkül oder
Dogma?*, Stuttgart: Kohlhammer, 1971, revised 1980; in English
as *The Foreign Policy of the Third Reich*, Berkeley: University of
California Press, and London: Batsford, 1973

Hildebrand, Klaus, *Das Dritte Reich*, Munich: Oldenbourg, 1979; in
English as *The Third Reich*, London and Boston: Allen and
Unwin, 1984

Iggers, Georg G., *The German Conception of History: The
National Tradition of Historical Thought from Herder to the
Present*, Middletown, CT: Wesleyan University Press, 1968;
revised 1983

Iggers, Georg G., *New Directions in European Historiography*,
Middletown, CT: Wesleyan University Press, 1975; revised 1984

Iggers, Georg G., "The Tragic Course of German Historiography:
The Political Function of Historical Scholarship in Germany in
the Nineteenth and Twentieth Centuries," *German Life and
Letters* 34 (1980–81), 222–47

James, Harold, *The German Slump: Politics and Economics,
1924–1936*, Oxford: Clarendon Press, 1986

Kater, Michael, *The Nazi Party: A Social Profile of Members and
Leaders, 1919–45*, Cambridge, MA: Harvard University Press,
and Oxford: Blackwell, 1983

Kater, Michael, "Nazism and the Third Reich in Recent
Historiography," *Canadian Journal of History* 20 (1985), 85–101

Kehr, Eckart, *Schlachtflottenbau und Parteipolitik, 1894-1901*,
Berlin: Ebering, 1930; in English as *Battleship Building and Party
Politics in Germany, 1894-1901: A Cross-Section of the Political,
Social, and Ideological Preconditions of German Imperialism*,
Chicago: University of Chicago Press, 1973

Kershaw, Ian, *The Nazi Dictatorship: Problems and Perspectives of
Interpretation*, London: Arnold, 1985; 3rd edition 1993

Kocka, Jürgen, "Der 'Deutsche Sonderweg' in der Diskussion" (The
Special German Path in Discussion), *German Studies Review* 5
(1982), 365–79

Kohn, Hans, *German History: Some New German Views*, London:
Allen and Unwin, 1954

Koonz, Claudia, *Mothers in the Fatherland: Women, the Family, and
Nazi Politics*, New York: St. Martin's Press, 1986; London: Cape,
1987

Lamprecht, Karl, *Zur jüngsten deutschen Vergangenheit* (On the
Most Recent German Past), 2 vols., Berlin: Gaertners, 1902–04
[*Deutsche Geschichte*]

Lehmann, Max, *Freiherr von Stein*, 3 vols., Leipzig: Hirzel, 1902–05

Maier, Charles S., Stanley Hoffmann, and Andrew Gould, *The Rise
of the Nazi Regime: Historical Reassessments*, Boulder, CO:
Westview Press, 1985

Maier, Charles S., *The Unmasterable Past: History, Holocaust, and
German National Identity*, Cambridge, MA: Harvard University
Press, 1988

Mason, Tim, *Arbeiterklasse und Volksgemeinschaft: Dokumente und Materialien zur deutschen Arbeiterpolitik, 1936–1939* (The Working Class and the National Community: Documents and Material on German Worker Politics), Opladen: Westdeutscher, 1975

Mattheisen, Donald, "History as Current Events: Recent Works on the German Revolution of 1848," *American Historical Review* 88 (1983), 1219–37

Mehring, Franz, *Zur deutschen Geschichte* (On German History), Berlin: Soziologische Verlagsanstalt, 1931

Meier, Ernst von, *Französische Einflüsse auf die Staats- und Rechtsentwicklung Preussens im 19. Jahrhundert* (French Influences on the Development of Prussia's State and Law), 2 vols., Leipzig: Duncker & Humblot, 1907–08

Meinecke, Friedrich, *Nach der Revolution: geschichtliche Betrachtungen über unsere Lage* (After the Revolution: Historical Observations on Our Situation), Munich: Oldenbourg, 1919

Meinecke, Friedrich, *Die deutsche Katastrophe: Betrachtungen und Erinnerungen*, Wiesbaden: Brockhaus, 1946; in English as *The German Catastrophe: Reflections and Recollections*, Cambridge, MA: Harvard University Press, 1950

Moeller, Robert, "The Kaiserreich Recast? Continuity and Change in Modern German Historiography," *Journal of Social History* 17 (Summer 1984), 655–80

Mommsen, Hans, *From Weimar to Auschwitz: Essays in German History*, Princeton: Princeton University Press, and Cambridge: Polity Press, 1991

Moses, John A., "Restructuring the Paradigm: West German Historians Between Historicism and Social History," *Australian Journal of Politics and History* 29 (1983), 368–78

Puhle, Hans-Jurgen, *Agrarische Interessenpolitik und preussischer Konservatismus im wilhelminischen Reich, 1893–1914* (Agrarian Interest Groups and Prussian Conservatism in the Wilhelmine Empire), Hanover: Literatur und Zeitgeschehen, 1967

Ritter, Gerhard, *Europa und die deutsche Frage: Betrachtungen über die geschichtliche Eigenart des deutschen Staatsdenkens*, Munich: Munchner Verlag, 1948, revised as *Das deutsche Problem*, 1962; in English as *The German Problem: Basic Questions of German Political Life, Past and Present*, Columbus: Ohio State University Press, 1965

Ritter, Gerhard, *Carl Goerdeler und die deutsche Widerstandsbewegung*, Stuttgart: Deutsche Verlags-Anstalt, 1954; in English as *The German Resistance: Carl Goerdeler's Struggle against Tyranny*, London: Allen and Unwin, and New York: Praeger, 1958

Ritter, Gerhard, *Staatskunst und Kriegshandwerk: das Problem des "Militarismus" in Deutschland*, 4 vols., Munich: Oldenbourg, 1954–68; in English as *The Sword and the Scepter: The Problem of Militarism in Germany*, Coral Gables: University of Miami Press, 1969–73, London: Allen Lane, 1972–73

Robertson, Grant, *Bismarck*, London: Constable, 1918; New York: Holt, 1919

Rosenberg, Arthur, *Die Entstehung der deutschen Republik, 1871–1918*, Berlin: Rowohlt, 1928; in English as *The Birth of the German Republic, 1871–1918*, London: Oxford University Press, 1931; New York: Russell and Russell, 1962

Rosenberg, Hans, *Grosse Depression und Bismarckzeit: Wirtschaftsablauf, Gesellschaft und Politik in Mitteleuropa* (Great Depression and the Bismarck Era), Berlin: de Gruyter, 1967

Rothfels, Hans, *Bismarck und der Staat: Ausgewählte Dokumente* (Bismarck and the State), Stuttgart: Kohlhammer, 1925

Rothfels, Hans, *Die deutsche Opposition gegen Hitler: eine Würdigung*, Krefeld: Scherpe, 1951; in English as *The German Opposition to Hitler: An Appraisal*, London: Regency, 1961

Schleunes, Karl, *The Twisted Road to Auschwitz: Nazi Policy toward German Jews, 1933–39*, Urbana: University of Illinois Press, 1970

Schnabel, Franz, *Deutsche Geschichte im neunzehnten Jahrhundert* (A History of Germany in the 19th Century), 4 vols., Freiburg: Herder, 1929–37

Schoenbaum, David, *Hitler's Social Revolution: Class and Status in Nazi Germany*, London: Weidenfeld and Nicolson, and Garden City, NY: Doubleday, 1966

Schroeder, Paul W., "Once More, the German Question," *International History Review* 9 (1987), 95–107

Schulze, Winfried, *Deutsche Geschichtswissenschaft nach 1945* (German Historical Science since 1945), Munich: Oldenbourg, 1989

Sheehan, James, "What Is German History: Reflections on the Role of the Nation in German History?" *Journal of Modern History* 53 (1981), 1–23

Sybel, Heinrich von, *Die Begründung des deutschen Reiches durch Wilhelm I*, Munich: Oldenbourg, 7 vols., 1889–94; in English as *The Founding of the German Empire by William I*, New York: Crowell, 1890–97

Taylor, A.J.P., *The Course of German History: A Survey of the Development of Germany*, London: Hamish Hamilton, 1945; New York: Coward McCann, 1946

Treitschke, Heinrich von, *Deutsche Geschichte im neunzehnten Jahrhundert*, 5 vols., Leipzig: Hirzel, 1879–94; in English as *Treitschke's History of Germany in the Nineteenth Century*, 7 vols., London, Jarrold, and New York: McBride, 1915–19

Turner, Henry Ashby, Jr., *German Big Business and the Rise of Hitler*, New York: Oxford University Press, 1985

Valentin, Veit, *Geschichte der deutschen Revolution von 1848–9*, Berlin: Ullstein, 1930–31; abridged in English as *1848: Chapters of German History*, London: Allen and Unwin, 1940; Hamden, CT: Archon, 1965

Wehler, Hans-Ulrich, *Bismarck und der Imperialismus* (Bismarck and Imperialism), Cologne: Kiepenheuer & Witsch, 1969

Wehler, Hans-Ulrich, ed., *Deutsche Historiker*, Göttingen: Vandenhoeck & Ruprecht, 1971–

Wehler, Hans-Ulrich, *Das deutsche Kaiserreich, 1871–1918*, Göttingen: Vandenhoeck & Ruprecht, 1973; in English as *The German Empire, 1871–1918*, Leamington Spa: Berg, 1985

Williamson, D.G., "The Bismarck Debate," *History Today* 34 (September 1984), 47–49

Witt, Peter-Christian, *Die Finanzpolitik des Deutschen Reiches, 1903–1913* (The Finance Policies of the German Empire, 1903–1913), Lübeck: Matthiesen, 1970

Ziekursch, Johannes, *Politische Geschichte des neuen deutschen Kaiserreichs* (A Political History of the New German Empire), 3 vols., Frankfurt: Frankfurter Societats, 1925–30

Germany: since 1945

The historiography of postwar Germany, the political histories of Germany after the defeat of the Third Reich in 1945, and the subsequent division of Germany are closely related. Communist East Germany – the German Democratic Republic or GDR – adopted a Marxist historiography that was largely subservient to the interests of the communist regime and interpreted postwar German history in a distinctly partial way. East German history had not received much attention from western historians prior to 1990, primarily due to a lack of primary sources; thus, the analysis of the GDR was left to political scientists, economists, and sociologists. The *DDR-Handbuch* (GDR Handbook; 1975, 1979, 1985), published by the West German Federal Ministry of Intra-German Relations, has been a highly useful compilation of knowledge on various aspects of East Germany, and has reflected in its subsequent editions the state of research on the GDR in West Germany. With the unification of Germany in 1990 and the opening of East

German archives, those findings, and the history of the GDR, can be re-evaluated.

The early historiography of the Federal Republic of Germany was dominated by publicists, political scientists, and sociologists who worked in the field of contemporary history and set the tone for an interpretation of postwar history that emphasized the caesura of 1945 and the end of the German *Sonderweg* with Germany's integration in the West and the conditions of democratization in West Germany. Fritz René Allemann's title *Bonn ist nicht Weimar* (Bonn Is Not Weimar, 1956) not only captured the main difference between the failed democracy of the Weimar republic and that of the Federal Republic after 1949, but also reflected the self-image of the Federal Republic.

The dependency of Germany on the framework created by Allied decisions during and after World War II has been a major point of reference, especially with regard to the division of Germany and the founding of two German states. Hans-Peter Schwarz's book *Vom Reich zur Bundesrepublik* (From Reich to Federal Republic, 1966) systematically analyzed the limited latitude of German politics during the occupation period of 1945 to 1949. The Federal Republic of Germany was a product of necessity rather than choice. This has particularly affected foreign policy; Wolfram Hanrieder's studies have emphasized the impact of the international system on West German foreign policy, while Waldemar Besson's *Die Aussenpolitik der Bundesrepublik* (The Foreign Policy of the Federal Republic, 1970) focused on the formulation of national interests in West Germany's foreign policy.

The caesura of 1945 has been interpreted as the hour zero – a new start. This was true in many respects, although on the whole a peculiar mixture of new beginning and restoration persisted. Ralf Dahrendorf, in his 1965 study *Gesellschaft und Demokratie in Deutschland* (*Society and Democracy in Germany*, 1967), had pointed to continuities of social stratification, elites, and attitudes after 1945, and historians such as Conze and Lepsius, and Broszat, Henke and Woller, have further elaborated on these continuities.

The question of German unification has always been a major part of postwar German history. The political debates of the 1950s instigated studies by both Steininger and Foschepoth which questioned chancellor Adenauer's commitment to German unification, but their theses arguing Adenauer's indifference towards unification or of "missed opportunities" have been refuted by Hans-Peter Schwarz's voluminous biography of the first chancellor. The fierce debates of the new *Ostpolitik* of the Brandt government after 1969 have left little trace in postwar German historiography. Moreover, with the benefit of hindsight, the effects of West German *Ostpolitik* appeared in a different light following Germany's unification in 1990. Timothy Garton Ash's *In Europe's Name* (1993) thoroughly analyzed the effects *Ostpolitik* had on unification. The unification also called into question the prevailing perspective of separate histories of East and West Germany that had characterized the historiography of postwar Germany, particularly the multi-volume survey *Geschichte der Bundesrepublik Deutschland* (A History of the Federal Republic of Germany, 1981–87), edited by Bracher and others. The interdependence of West and East German history, which has been the focus of studies by Klessmann and by Birke, might prove more fruitful for a comprehensive understanding of postwar Germany in the future. In the historians' debate (*Historikerstreit*) in the mid-1980s, divergent interpretations of the history of the Third Reich have already highlighted different views on postwar German identity and historiography. In essence, the debate addressed the question of whether German identity and history are still under the shadow of the Third Reich or whether the Germans should become a "normal" nation, thus historicizing the Third Reich. The unification of Germany in 1990, which has ended Germany's postwar history, may have served as a catalyst to open up the historiographical perspective on postwar Germany and on modern German history in general. The consequences and ramifications of those historiographical shifts remain yet to be seen.

MATTHIAS ZIMMER

See also Bracher; Broszat; Conze; Kocka; Weber, H.

Further Reading

Allemann, Fritz René, *Bonn ist nicht Weimar* (Bonn is Not Weimar), Cologne: Kiepenheuer & Witsch, 1956

Baring, Arnulf, *Machtwechsel: Die Ära Brandt-Scheel* (Transition of Power: the Brandt-Scheel era), Stuttgart: Deutsche Verlags-Anstalt, 1982

Bark, Dennis L., and David R. Gress, *A History of West Germany*, 2 vols., Oxford and New York: Blackwell, 1993

Besson, Waldemar, *Die Aussenpolitik der Bundesrepublik: Erfahrungen und Massstäbe* (The Foreign Policy of the Federal Republic: Experience and Standards), Munich: Piper, 1970

Birke, Adolf M., *Nation ohne Haus: Deutschland, 1945–1961* (Nation without a house: Germany 1945–1961), Berlin: Siedler, 1989

Bracher, Karl Dietrich, Theodor Eschenburg, Joachim C. Fest, and Eberhard Jäckel, eds., *Geschichte der Bundesrepublik Deutschland* (A History of the Federal Republic of Germany), 5 vols., Stuttgart: Deutsche Verlags-Anstalt, and Mannheim: Brockhaus, 1981–87

Broszat, Martin, Klaus-Dietmar Henke, and Hans Woller, eds., *Von Stalingrad zur Währungsreform: Zur Sozialgeschichte des Umbruchs in Deutschland* (From Stalingrad to the Currency Reform: The Social History of Radical Change in Germany), Munich: Oldenbourg, 1988

Bundesministerium für Innerdeutsche Beziehungen [West German Federal Ministry of Intra-German Relations], *DDR-Handbuch* (GDR Handbook), Cologne: Wissenschaft & Politik, 1975, 1979, 1985

Conze, Werner, and M. Rainer Lepsius, eds., *Zur Sozialgeschichte der Bundesrepublik Deutschland: Beiträge zum Kontinuitätsproblem* (On the Social History of the Federal Republic of Germany: Articles on the Problem of Continuity), Stuttgart: Klett-Cotta, 1983

Dahrendorf, Ralf, *Gesellschaft und Demokratie in Deutschland*, Munich: Piper, 1965; in English as *Society and Democracy in Germany*, Garden City, NY: Doubleday, and London: Weidenfeld and Nicolson, 1967

Evans, Richard J., *In Hitler's Shadow: West German Historians and the Attempt to Escape from the Nazi Past*, New York: Pantheon, and London: Tauris, 1989

Foschepoth, Josef, ed., *Adenauer und die deutsche Frage* (Adenauer and the German Question), Göttingen: Vandenhoeck & Ruprecht, 1988

Fulbrook, Mary, *Anatomy of a Dictatorship: Inside the GDR, 1949–1989*, Oxford and New York: Oxford University Press, 1995

Garton Ash, Timothy, *In Europe's Name: Germany and the Divided Continent*, London: Cape, and New York: Random House, 1993

Hacke, Christian, *Weltmacht wider Willen: Die Aussenpolitik der Bundesrepublik Deutschland* (The Reluctant World Power: The Foreign Policy of the Federal Republic of Germany), Stuttgart: Klett-Cotta 1988; revised and expanded edition Frankfurt: Ullstein 1993, 1997

Haftendorn, Helga, *Sicherheit und Entspannung: Zur Aussenpolitik der Bundesrepublik Deutschland, 1955–1982*, Baden-Baden: Nomos, 1983; in English as *Security and Detente: Conflicting Priorities in German Foreign Policy*, New York: Praeger, 1985

Hanrieder, Wolfram F., *West German Foreign Policy, 1949–1963: International Pressure and Domestic Response*, Stanford, CA: Stanford University Press 1967

Hanrieder, Wolfram F., *Germany, America, Europe: Forty Years of German Foreign Policy*, New Haven and London: Yale University Press, 1989

Klessmann, Christoph, *Die doppelte Staatsgründung: Deutsche Geschichte, 1945–1955* (The Dual State Founding: German History, 1945–1955), Göttingen: Vandenhoeck & Ruprecht, 1982

Klessmann, Christoph, *Zwei Staaten, eine Nation: Deutsche Geschichte, 1955–1970* (Two States, One Nation: German History, 1955–1970), Göttingen: Vandenhoeck & Ruprecht, 1988

Knowlton, James, and Truett Cates, trans., *Forever in the Shadow of Hitler? Original Documents of the Historikerstreit, the Controversy Concerning the Singularity of the Holocaust*, Atlantic Highlands, NJ: Humanities Press 1993

Kocka, Jürgen, *Vereinigungskrise: Zur Geschichte der Gegenwart* (The Crises of Unification: The Present as History), Göttingen: Vandenhoeck & Ruprecht, 1995

Köhler, Henning, *Adenauer: Eine politische Biographie* (Adenauer: A Political Biography), Berlin: Propyläen, 1994

McAdams, A. James, *Germany Divided: From the Wall to Reunification*, Princeton: Princeton University Press, 1993

Maier, Charles S., *The Unmasterable Past: History, Holocaust, and German National Identity*, Cambridge, MA: Harvard University Press, 1988

Morsey, Rudolf, *Die Bundesrepublik Deutschland: Entstehung und Entwicklung bis 1969* (The Federal Republic of Germany: Origin and Development to 1969), Munich: Oldenbourg, 1987

Schwarz, Hans-Peter, *Vom Reich zur Bundesrepublik: Deutschland im Widerstreit der aussenpolitischen Konzeptionen in den Jahren der Besatzungsherrschaft, 1945–1949* (From Reich to Federal Republic: Germany and the Clashing Foreign Policy Conceptions during the Years of Occupation, 1945–1949), 2 vols., Berlin: Luchterhand, 1966; revised 1980

Schwarz, Hans-Peter, *Adenauer*, 2 vols., Stuttgart: Deutsche Verlags-Anstalt 1986–91; vol. 1 in English as *Konrad Adenauer: From the German Empire to the Federal Republic, 1876–1952*, Providence, RI and Oxford: Berghahn, 1995

Steininger, Rolf, *Eine vertane Chance: Die Stalin-Note vom 10. März 1952 und die Wiedervereinigung: Eine Studie auf der Grundlage unveröffentlichter britischer und amerikanischer Akten*, 2 vols., Berlin: Dietz, 1985; in English as *The German Question: The Stalin Note of 1952 and the Problem of Reunification*, New York: Columbia University Press, 1990

Weber, Hermann, *Die DDR, 1945–1986* (The German Democratic Republic, 1945–1986), Munich: Oldenbourg, 1988; revised [with dates 1945–1990] 1993

Geyl, Pieter 1887–1966
Dutch historian

Probably the best-known Dutch historian outside his own land, Pieter Geyl challenged standard views of the separate development of Dutch and Belgian cultures and won international fame based on his work as a historical critic. In his time, Dutch intellectual, political, and social life was divided into liberal, Calvinist, and Catholic categories (pillarization), a division that had given much Dutch historical writing a dogmatic character. Geyl's work, while ignoring the social and economic dimensions which were then providing new insights into an understanding of the Dutch past, did help break down these ideological categories.

Originally attracted to a career as a poet or novelist, Geyl discovered an interest in history while a student at the University of Leiden. It was also at this time that the Flemish revival first caught his attention. This movement had arisen in Belgium, where French speakers controlled the government and intellectual life, and Geyl's sympathies with it would eventually lead him to rethink the assumptions about history upon which the separate Dutch and Belgian states were based.

After completing the research for his doctoral thesis in Venice, and receiving his doctorate in 1913, Geyl taught in a Gymnasium for a short time, and then became the London correspondent for the *Nieuwe Rotterdamsche Courant*, the most prominent daily newspaper in the Netherlands, a post that eventually led to his appointment to the chair in Dutch studies at the University of London, which had just been created with the support of the Dutch government. Much of Geyl's scholarly writing in these years, particularly the books, *Willem IV en Engeland tot 1748* (William IV and England until 1748, 1924) and *Oranje en Stuart, 1641–72* (1939; *Orange and Stuart*, 1969), focused on Anglo-Dutch relations. In these, Geyl argued that the Dutch republic's stadholders had depended on English support, fortified by marriage alliances between the princes of Orange and the English royal families, to advance their power within the republic. Such an argument questioned the then-dominant monarchist tradition of Dutch historiography, which tended to criticize the urban patriciates of the republic's States' party for placing their particularist concerns above national interests.

While in London, Geyl also put forward the argument that would be the basis of much of his life's work: that the Dutch and Flemish peoples were divided between two states as the result of an accident of history and geography. At that time, the standard view held that the separation of the northern and southern Netherlands during the revolt of the Low Countries against Spain in the late 16th and early 17th centuries was the climax of a split that had been evolving over centuries. This interpretation had won wide acceptance after Henri Pirenne made a forceful argument for it in his *Histoire de Belgique* (1899–1932), and it legitimized the separate Dutch and Belgian national states. But Geyl publicly rejected this view in his lectures at the University of London, and in 1925 published an alternative model in his *De Groot-Nederlandsche gedachte* (The Greater-Netherlands Idea, 1925). He expanded his argument in what he viewed as his major work, *De geschiedenis van de Nederlandsche Stam* (1930–59; revised as *The Netherlands in the Seventeenth Century*, 1961–64). In these he maintained that the Low Countries were divided into two states at the end of the revolt against the Spanish only because the Spanish were unable to regain control of the north, since their army could not move freely north of the barrier formed by the Rhine and Meuse rivers. While Geyl's incorporation of geographic factors into historical explanation was influential, later historians have seen flaws in his linking of language and national self-consciousness in the early modern period.

Geyl assumed the chair of history at the University of Utrecht in 1936, overcoming opposition to his appointment by those who found his Flemish sympathies too radical and his view of the royal house too critical. He gradually became estranged from extremists in the Flemish movement who sympathized with the Nazis, leading to his arrest after the German invasion in 1940 and deportation to Buchenwald along with approximately 100 other Dutch leaders. Held hostage there for 13 months, he was then transferred back to the Netherlands where his internment continued until 1944. After his release, he worked for the Resistance while writing *Napoleon, voor en tegen in de Franse geschiedschrijving* (1946; *Napoleon: For and Against*, 1949), which analyzed changes in French historians' work on Napoleon over 150 years, showing how their views were influenced by events of their own times.

Geyl's studies of historiography continued after the war's end, as he resumed his position at the University of Utrecht. A central theme in his postwar work was his passionate attack on systems of universal historical laws. He became one of the foremost critics of Arnold Toynbee, defending the study of the nation-state and of individuals against Toynbee's universalism. He also disapproved of the system-building of Jan Romein, the University of Amsterdam's influential Marxist historian.

Geyl's contributions to Dutch historical scholarship and to historical criticism are linked by his belief that a history guided by ideological principles is a history that neglects the actual diversity of the past. He has sometimes been characterized as the "last of the great 19th-century historians," due to his distrust of theoretical approaches to history, his exclusive attention to political history, and his love of narrative. But his fresh approach to the traditional questions of Dutch history was anything but 19th-century.

MARYBETH CARLSON

See also France: since the Revolution; Low Countries; Toynbee

Biography

Pieter Catharinus Arie Geyl. Born Dordrecht, 15 December 1887. Studied Dutch language and literature, Leiden University, 1906–11, PhD 1913. London correspondent, *Nieuwe Rotterdamsche Courant*, 1913–19. Professor of Dutch history, University College, London, 1919–36; and State University of Utrecht, 1936–58 (held hostage and dismissed from university, 1940–44). Married 1) Maria Cornelia van Slooten, 1911 (died 1933; 2 children); 2) Garberlina Kremer, 1934. Died Utrecht, 31 December 1966.

Principal Writings

Christofforo Suriano: resident van de Serenissime Republiek van Venetië in Den Haag, 1616–1623 (Christofforo Suriano: Envoy of the Serene Republic of Venice in The Hague, 1616–1623), 1913

Willem IV en Engeland tot 1748 (William IV and England until 1748), 1924

De Groot-Nederlandsche gedachte (The Greater-Netherlands Idea), 1925

De geschiedenis van de Nederlandsche Stam, 3 vols., 1930–59; abridged in English as *The Revolt of the Netherlands, 1555–1609*, 1932, and *The Netherlands Divided, 1609–1648*, 1936; revised and expanded as *The Netherlands in the Seventeenth Century*, 2 vols., 1961–64

Oranje en Stuart, 1641–72, 1939; in English as *Orange and Stuart, 1641–1672*, 1969

Napoleon: voor en tegen in de Franse geschiedschrijving, 1946; in English as *Napoleon: For and Against*, 1949

De Patriottenbeweging, 1780–1787 (The Patriot Movement), 1947

The Pattern of the Past: Can We Determine It?, 1949

Debates with Historians, 1955

Studies en strijdschriften (Studies and Debates), 1958

Encounters in History, 1961

Pennestrijd over staat en historie: opstellen over de vaderlandse geschiedenis aangevuld met Geyl's levensverhaal (tot 1945) (Controversy about State and History: Essays on the History of the Fatherland, supplemented with Geyl's Life Story), 1971

Further Reading

Boogman, J.C. "Pieter Geyl (1887–1966)," *Bijdragen voor de Geschiedenis der Nederlanden* 21 (1966–67), 269–77

Dunk, H.W. von der, "Pieter Geyl: History as a Form of Self-Expression" in A.C. Duke and C.A. Tamse, eds., *Clio's Mirror: Historiography in Britain and the Netherlands*, Zutphen: De Walburg Pers, 1985

Mehta, Ved, *Fly and the Fly-Bottle: Encounters with British Intellectuals*, London: Weidenfeld and Nicolson, 1962

Rogier, L.J., "Herdenking van P. Geyl" (Remembrance of P. Geyl), *Mededelingen van de Koninklijke Nederlandse Akademie van Wetenschappen, Afdeling Letterkunde*, nieuwe reeks 30, number 12, Amsterdam: Noord-Hollandsche, 1967

Rowan, Herbert H., "The Historical Work of Pieter Geyl," *Journal of Modern History* 37 (1965), 35–49

Tollebeek, Jo, *De toga van Fruin: denken over geschiedenis in Nederland sinds 1860* (Fruin's Toga: Thinking about History in the Netherlands since 1860), Amsterdam: Wereldbibliotheek, 1990

Giannone, Pietro 1676–1748

Italian historian of the Cartesian school

Pietro Giannone's *L'Istoria civile del regno di Napoli* (1723; *The Civil History of the Kingdom of Naples*, 1729–31) charted for Edward Gibbon "the progress and abuse of sacerdotal power." From 1698 until early in 1723 Giannone practiced in Naples as an advocate, pleading with emphasis on legal doctrine rather than case precedence. Since the mid-16th century the kingdom of Naples had become increasingly subservient to the clerical authority of the church of Rome, exerted particularly on the Italian peninsula with the intent of exterminating Protestantism there in any form. From his legal practice Giannone found that though in theory civil justice was a matter of state, in actuality it was often subject to ecclesiastical restraints. To substantiate the cases of his advocacy Giannone consulted legal archives in Naples and elsewhere in the kingdom, and read its regional histories, such as those of Summonte and Parrino, as well as extending his interest to Machiavelli's writings and Guicciardini's *History of Italy*. After more than a decade's legal experience Giannone began his own history; a study of his sources has appeared recently. The printing of his work in Naples extended over almost two years, and it appeared in four substantial volumes. This *Civil History* is the work on which Giannone's standing as a historian rests.

He defined the work in his introduction as the demonstration that in the Roman Catholic world civil and ecclesiastical history were inseparably intertwined; accordingly the focus was on the Roman Catholic church as a political force in western Christendom. The forty books of text furnished the examples, ranging chronologically from Augustus to the early 18th century, and based on the region that became the kingdom of Naples. The approach was original, since unlike previous histories it was not a narration of civil and of ecclesiastical events; instead, legal evidence was marshalled to illustrate laws, institutions, and customs. The whole sought to reveal how from its earliest years the church of Rome had organized itself as an undying institution to further its own interests. The church's economic policy, be it tenths, donations, acquisitions of land, or property, with which Giannone had much experience from his legal practice, was covered in depth. An institution, therefore, was delineated for the first time as an influential factor in history. Moreover Giannone was the first scholar to signal the potential of legal materials as a historical source.

There were negative features of his history, not least because it paid scant attention to the fact that institutions are not static, and also because Giannone totally disregarded the part played by individuals. His work can be summed up as the first application of Cartesian method to history. Cartesianism depended on fixed values, which functioned consistently under exactly defined laws. Giannone provided what in effect were his own concepts of law, state, and sovereignty, as though immutable over some 17 centuries. Despite the cyclic concept favored in antiquity and reborn during the Italian Renaissance, history is not essentially the repetition of a set pattern. Giannone's methodology inevitably resulted in serious manipulation of evidence and in distortions. His state was consistently portrayed as progressive, a civilized entity for the good of all its subjects, while the church was presented as regressive and fraudulent – the very antithesis of all inherent in its Christian message. Not surprisingly to some contemporaries of Roman Catholic and of Protestant credence alike the work was deemed more propaganda than true history, which had serious consequences for its author.

Giannone was excommunicated immediately after publication, and the following year the work was placed on the Index. Giannone had fled to Vienna, where over the next four years he wrote justifying his stance. This new work was eventually printed in 1895 as Triregno (Three Kingdoms), not his title but one that reflects its tripartite division: the heavenly harmony of body and soul, earthly life, the nature of the pope's earthly kingdom. The first two were philosophy, the last little other than a synthesis of his Civil History, reasserted in another context. In his last years in prison Giannone wrote two further works of a historical character: Discourses on the Decades of Livy, echoing Machiavelli's title, and on the church under Gregory the Great, perhaps conceived as a counterblast to those who had criticized his neglect of individuals in his previous works. Both testified to a growing caution on the author's part, since he professed his belief in the tenets of the Roman Catholic faith, but otherwise they essentially encapsulated his Civil History and Triregno.

Once the Civil History was on the Index it was little read on the Italian peninsula; even the attack on it by Eusebio Filopatro, published in two volumes in 1728, of necessity feigned a Cologne printing (actually Naples). During Giannone's lifetime a few manuscript copies of his other writings were circulated, principally in Naples, publication on the peninsula being considered an unacceptable risk: testimony in its own way of Giannone's thesis. In Protestant countries, however, Giannone's

Civil History was welcomed as being an attack from within the Italian peninsula on the Roman church. An English translation was printed in London between 1729 and 1731, a French one emanated from Switzerland with the author's additions and corrections in 1742. There were also a number of Swiss and Dutch reprints of his history, as well as the publication of some of his other writings, in the course of the 18th century. It was the author's revised text, first printed in 1753, that has been recently reprinted, regrettably without critical apparatus.

CECIL H. CLOUGH

Biography
Born Ischitella, 7 May 1676. Moved to Naples to read law, 1692, taking his doctorate in civil and canon laws, University of Naples, 1698. Practiced law, first with Gaetano Argento, 1689–1702, then on his own, 1702–1723. Following excommunication for anticlericalism, forced to flee to court of Charles VI in Vienna, 1723, then to Venice, 1734, Modena, and Geneva; tricked into attending mass within Savoy and captured, April 1736; held in prison, Turin, 1737–48. Died Turin, 7 March 1748.

Principal Writings
L'Istoria civile del regno di Napoli, 4 vols., 1723; in English as The Civil History of the Kingdom of Naples, 2 vols., 1729–31; revised 1753
Vita scritta da lui medesimo [autobiography], written 1735, published 1890
Il Triregno: ossia del regno del cielo, della terra, e del papa (Three Kingdoms: that is the Kingdom of Heaven, that on Earth, and that of the Pope), 3 vols., published 1895

Further Reading
Ajello, Raffaele, "Pietro Giannone fra libertini e illuministi" (Pietro Gianonne between the "Libertines" and the "Illuminists"), in Rivista storica italiana 87 (1975), 104–31; reprinted in his Arcana juris: diritto e politica nel Settecento italiano, Naples: Jovene, 1976
Ajello, Raffaele, ed., Pietro Giannone e il suo tempo: (Pietro Giannone and His Times), 2 vols., Naples: Jovene, 1980 [conference papers]
Bertelli, Sergio, Giannoniana: autografi, manoscritti e documenti della fortuna di Pietro Giannone (Giannoniana: Autographs, Transcripts, and Documents Illustrative of Pietro Giannone's Reputation), Naples: Ricciardi, 1968
Bonnat, G., "Pietro Giannone à Genève et la publication de ses oeuvres en Suisse au XVIIIe et au XIXe siècles" (Pietro Giannone in Geneva and the Publication of His Works in Switzerland in the 18th and 19th Centuries), Annali della scuola speciale per archivisti e bibliotecari dell' Università di Roma 3 (1963), 119–38
Fiorentino, F., "Le fonti dell Istoria civile di Pietro Giannone" (The Sources of Pietro Giannone's Civil History), Belfagor 19 (1964), 141–53, 397–410, 517–33
Niccolini, Fausto, Gli scritti e la fortuna di Pietro Giannone: ricerche bibliografiche (Pietro Giannone's Writings and Reputation: Bibliographical Researches), Bari: Laterza, 1914

Gibbon, Edward 1737–1794
British historian of Rome and universal historian

Ever since the completion of his magnum opus, The History of the Decline and Fall of the Roman Empire (1776–88), Edward Gibbon has been regarded as the greatest of all

Enlightenment historians, an assessment which has been strengthened rather than undermined by modern revisionism. Without depreciating his remarkable personal gifts, this elevated status owes a good deal to context. Gibbon was at least a generation younger than men such as Voltaire, Montesquieu, and Hume, who are rightly seen as the "founding fathers" of a new Enlightenment historicity. For "founding fathers" one may as well read "absolute beginners," since the new outlook transferred the basis of history's message and significance away from the authoritative record of the recent past – a model common to all "Histories" between Thucydides and Clarendon – to the "philosophic" sifting of the meaning of the past in its entirety: a truly daunting expansion of scope, but one that established modern history as we know it. While the previous generation had stumbled down uncharted paths towards history writing as a second or third career, which was commonly reached (or not) in early middle age, Gibbon could record that, "I *know*, by experience, that from my early youth I aspired to the character of an historian." He thus grew up an omnivorous reader of history in all its forms – ancient and modern, philosophic and antiquarian – and also the detached spectator of the inevitable *gaucheries* of his predecessors, when confronted by their new and essentially impossible task. He is thus truly the historian's historian, having always been preoccupied with strictly historiographical concerns. However, a question has always hung over him as a result: was there not some cost attached to this narrowing of focus, away from the wider intellectual brilliancy of his predecessors? might not his *History* lack philosophic depth as a result?

The second critical component in Gibbon's intellectual formation was his reading of the *Mémoires* of the French Academy of Inscriptions when at Lausanne in his teens, in particular the works of the "great," the "celebrated" Nicholas Freret, whom he revered. It was Freret, Gibbon decided, who had supplied him with a working model of history that blended the broad conceptual approach of the new "philosophic" history with the scrupulous accuracy and hitherto narrower focus of the "antiquarian" or "erudite" tradition – another post-Renaissance development, but one which had never enjoyed the same esteem as either the humanist writing of "History" or the new "philosophy." Nonetheless, the marriage of organizing concepts with accurately established data – a recipe for excellence in historical writing that has not yet been improved – is one that we may fairly associate with Gibbon's name: Freret and the Academicians only illustrated how this might work at the level of the learned article for a small audience of *cognoscenti*; Gibbon carried it up to the level of a great world history, which made an indelible impact on educated opinion throughout Western Europe. It is a mark of the difficulty of this transition that, having made significant programmatic statements about *how* to write history in the *Essai sur l'étude de la littérature* (published rather by accident in 1761), it was another 12 years before he was successfully embarked on a project that could put these ideas into practice. Still, the upshot was a work that made a major contribution to the definition of modern "history" at a formative moment, siting it precisely midway between an individuated data base and "philosophical" concepts. Of course that process of definition was taking place in many forms and at many levels; but Gibbon's combined literary, commercial, scholarly, and intellectual triumph was unique in its day,

and it may well be that the subsequent profile of "conjectural history" or "sociology" would have been significantly higher without it.

Apart from attempts to place Gibbon within Western historical tradition and much patient exploration of his work in its innumerable local contexts (historical and historiographical), criticism of the *History* falls into two principal strands: analytic and genetic. Because it is a universal history, and so lacks a specific thesis which might then be argued out, critics have been tempted to follow the work through its several stages, seeking to unlock its secrets this way. The fact of its publication in unequal installments, the clear caesuras at the end of the third and fourth volumes (out of six), and the drastic change of focus at the beginning of the fifth, all indicate that the design and structure of the work were based on piecemeal accumulation rather than classical symmetry; indeed the last two volumes may in a real sense be regarded as virtually a new project. But though this narrative of a narrative is an extremely important commentary on Gibbon's makeup and methods, historians have not been convinced that any significant change in his substantive views took place during the long years of composition (1773–88). We are thus driven back on a more analytical approach.

Although the *History* has no overall thesis – the classical view that Rome fell because of its moral decadence applies only to its first half – it supplies an account of human nature at work in world history which, though it emerges only via the detail of the narrative, is in fact one of remarkable consistency. Gibbon appears as a traditional moralist – simple, flexible, and still plausible to the unillusioned readers of today; he believes that man's condition is "imperfect," but is neither a pessimist nor a fatalist. Although he allows for material progress and, by passing out of barbarism into civilization, for significant changes in mankind's mental outlook, he remains the historian of a constant human nature and emphatically not of progress. The change from barbarism to civilization is a unique one, not a continuous process of upward evolution, and its principal point is not an access of material comfort – though Gibbon does not sneer at that – but radically altered time horizons for human achievement and mental outlook. Civilized man (of whom the Romans were supreme exemplars) produces buildings, artifacts and writings so durable as to approximate to unchanging and immortal truth, human and natural; and he views his life, if not quite in the context of eternity, still with an awareness of the remote past and of "posterity," that is, like a philosophic historian. The moralizing element in this is not especially distinctive; it lacks the schematic nicety of a philosophically derived account (such as Hume's); and it could also be argued that some analogue might be found for it in contemporary Christian doctrine: but this is to miss the point. The point was to supply a complete, secular account of human nature which was historically derived; an induction from 2,000 years of historical record, which would as a result be different in kind from either philosophical or theological accounts. Here was Gibbon's contribution to the greatest of all Enlightenment "projects" – the construction of a secular science of man.

There are then two interdependent ways we may judge Gibbon: as a pioneer in historical method who helped shape modern "history" at a formative moment, and as an author who described a universal human condition in historical terms. The former is more visible and constitutes an obvious claim on our attention; the latter was at least as important to Gibbon himself and, though it was rapidly rendered passé after 1790 by schemes of historical progress and evolution, it is surely a significant underlying element when explaining his astonishingly sustained popularity throughout a 20th century which has witnessed a continued paring away of the encumbrances of progressive thinking.

PETER GHOSH

See also Bury; Byzantium; Crusades; Deutscher; Enlightenment; Guizot; Karamzin; Momigliano; Montesquieu; Pirenne; Popular; Roman; Scriptores; Syme; Weber, M.; Whewell; William of Tyre

Biography

Born Putney, 8 May 1737. Entered Magdalen College, Oxford, 1752; expelled after converting to Catholicism, 1753 (reconverted to Protestantism, 1754). Sent by his father to Lausanne, 1753; returned to England, 1758; captain in the Hampshire militia, 1760–62; toured Italy, 1763–65; began writing his *History*, 1773; member of Parliament, 1774–80, 1781–83: commissioner of trade, 1779–82; retired to Lausanne to live more cheaply, 1783; returned to England for a visit, 1793, but became ill. Died London, 16 January 1794.

Principal Writings

Essai sur l'étude de la littérature, 1761; in English as *An Essay on the Study of Literature*, 1764
Critical Observations on the Sixth Book of the Aeneid, 1770
The History of the Decline and Fall of the Roman Empire, 6 vols., 1776–88
A Vindication of Some Passages in the Fifteenth and Sixteenth Chapters of "The History of the Decline and Fall of the Roman Empire," 1779
Miscellaneous Works of Edward Gibbon with Memoirs of His Life and Writings, edited by John, Lord Sheffield, 3 vols., 1796, revised 1814, 1837

Further Reading

Baridon, Michel, *Edward Gibbon et le mythe de Rome: histoire et idéologie au siècle des lumières*, Paris: Champion, 1977
Bowersock, Glen Warren, John Clive, and Stephen R. Graubard, eds., *Edward Gibbon and the Decline and Fall of the Roman Empire*, Cambridge, MA: Harvard University Press, 1977
Burrow, John Wyon, *Gibbon*, Oxford and New York: Oxford University Press, 1985
Carnochan, W.B., *Gibbon's Solitude: The Inward World of the Historian*, Stanford, CA: Stanford University Press, 1987
Cartledge, Paul, "The 'Tacitism' of Edward Gibbon," *Mediterranean Historical Review* 4 (1989), 251–70
Ghosh, Peter, "Gibbon Observed," *Journal of Roman Studies* 81 (1991), 132–56
Ghosh, Peter, "Gibbon's First Thoughts: Rome, Christianity and the *Essai sur l'étude de la littérature*, 1758–61," *Journal of Roman Studies* 85 (1995), 148–64
Giarrizzo, Giuseppe, *Edward Gibbon e la cultura europea del Settecento*, Naples: Istituto Italiano, 1954
McKitterick, Rosamond, ed., *Edward Gibbon and Empire*, Cambridge: Cambridge University Press, 1996
Momigliano, Arnaldo, *Studies in Historiography*, London: Weidenfeld and Nicolson, and New York: Harper, 1966
Pocock, J.G.A., "Edward Gibbon in History," Sterling M. McMurrin, ed., *The Tanner Lectures on Human Values* vol. 11, Salt Lake City: Utah University Press, 1990
Porter, Roy, *Edward Gibbon: Making History*, London: Weidenfeld and Nicolson, 1988
Trevor-Roper, Hugh, "Gibbon and the Publication of *The Decline and Fall*," *Journal of Law and Economics* 19 (1976), 489–506
Trevor-Roper, Hugh, "The Historical Philosophy of the Enlightenment," *Studies on Voltaire and the 18th Century* 27 (1963), 1667–87
Womersley, David, *The Transformation of The Decline and Fall of the Roman Empire*, Cambridge and New York: Cambridge University Press, 1988
Womersley, David, ed., *Edward Gibbon: Bicentenary Essays*, Oxford: Voltaire Foundation, 1997
Wootton, David, "Narrative, Irony and Faith in Gibbon's *Decline and Fall*," *History and Theory* [theme issue] 33 (1994), 77–105

Gibson, Charles 1920–1985

US historian of colonial Latin America

Charles Gibson was one of the most notable and influential historians of colonial Latin America. His importance to the field rests primarily on two works: *Tlaxcala in the Sixteenth Century* (1952) and *The Aztecs under Spanish Rule* (1964). Working at a time when the study of Latin America was still in a formative stage, his investigations and methodology were instrumental in laying the groundwork for incorporating the experience of the indigenous peoples of America into the historical narrative. Prior to the publication of *Tlaxcala*, no one had examined native society or articulated the significance of its structures to the development of postconquest society. After *Tlaxcala*, and even more notably after the publication of *The Aztecs*, it was impossible to ignore this question. In categorical terms, Gibson brought the discipline of ethnohistory to the study of Latin America and highlighted the fertility of cross-disciplinary investigations. Both *Tlaxcala* and *The Aztecs* stand as formidable pieces of research and remain essential reading for an understanding of colonial Mexico.

To appreciate fully the importance of Gibson's insights into postconquest society it is necessary to recall that he was writing at a time when the heroic quality of the Spanish experience in America – characterized by the writings of Hubert H. Bancroft, Edward G. Bourne, Eugene Bolton, and Robert Ricard – dominated the field. As Gibson was publishing his work on Tlaxcala their romantic interpretation was undergoing considerable revision. Clarence Haring (*Spanish Empire in America*) and Lesley Byrd Simpson (*The Encomienda in New Spain*) brought institutional studies to a new level of sophistication, while the population studies Simpson undertook with Sherburne F. Cook mapped out the essential contours of the demographic transformations wrought by the conquest.

Gibson's work fitted into this revisionary climate, but possessed the unique quality of shifting the focus from the Spanish actors to the hitherto silent indigenous actors. While simple in concept, this shift of focus represented a fundamental reorientation of interpretation and necessitated the investigation of a new set of documents. Unlike the majority of his contemporaries, Gibson concentrated his research in the local archives of Mexico (*Tlaxcala* examines in detail the records of the Indian municipal council of Tlaxcala) leaving the archives in Spain relatively untouched. This research strategy tended to emphasize the importance of activity occurring on the local level while de-emphasizing the significance of actions taken on the imperial level in Spain.

By working through the details of local administration Gibson transformed the image of the impact of the Indian within colonial society. His crucial discovery was that far from being passive victims of a process of social transformation, the Indians played an active role in giving shape to the postconquest world. They tended to be selective in their adaptations to Spanish culture; in fact by the selective quality of their acquiescence and resistance they limited the actions the Spaniards were able to take. Moreover, Gibson's analysis pointed out for the first time that the structures of Indian society remained intact after the conquest and formed the organizational skeleton of colonial administration. Spanish authority below the level of the Indian town relied on a sensitive cultural, religious, economic, and political process of negotiation with a native elite for its effectiveness.

Gibson's conclusions transformed the traditional understanding of the impact of the conquest and led to a new type of study. The proliferation of regional studies, arguably the dominant genre of investigation for the past twenty years, owes its inspiration to Gibson's model (especially *Tlaxcala*), while his characterization of the indigenous role in society has been duplicated in other regions over and over again and today forms the basis for a consensus among most colonial scholars.

The significance of Gibson's work transcends his methodological innovations. The experience of reading either *Tlaxcala* or *The Aztecs* immerses the reader in a meticulously crafted pattern of detail. His work is not for the faint of heart or the impatient reader. Gibson understood his role to be a channel for the transmission of the facts revealed by the documents, and he was reticent about drawing overt conclusions from the information he presented. This lack of an explicit conceptual framework can make his writing difficult to grasp as a whole, but the lasting value of his investigations derives from his implicit understanding of the complete picture and of the way in which each detail related to the totality. While he did not inform the reader in so many words about the significance of his observations, his presentation of evidence was structured by such an understanding and holds together on that account.

As monumental as these two studies may be, they are not definitive or complete in every respect. *Tlaxcala* covered only the 16th century, and while *The Aztecs* purports to survey the entire colonial period, Gibson's coverage is decidedly weaker on the later period than for the 16th century. This weakness in his work has prompted subsequent scholars to investigate this period more thoroughly than he was able to, and in many cases they have revised his conclusions. His studies, particularly *The Aztecs*, possess a heavy corporate emphasis. As such the role played by unique individuals tends to be obscured, and the importance of psychological variables over the course of events remains totally unacknowledged. Most profoundly – and this is perhaps the most pressing problem for colonial historians to solve – his work failed to present an adequate picture of the nature of the interaction between Spaniard and Indian. Since it was this dynamic process that gave colonial society its unique character, the difficulty of sketching the contours of this interaction is a major gap in our understanding. But while Gibson did not solve this problem – or even address himself to it – without his primary insight about

the importance of indigenous structures to the development of the colonial world the question could not even be asked.

Gibson's reputation and significance rest on the scholarship that produced *Tlaxcala* and *The Aztecs*. But in the later phase of his career he continued to play a prominent role in the profession, and produced a number of bibliographical articles in which he identified the important scholars who helped to build the field of Latin American history.

LINCOLN A. DRAPER

See also Chevalier; Ethnohistory; Latin America: Colonial; Mexico; Spain: Imperial

Biography
Born Buffalo, New York, 12 August 1920. Received BA, Yale University, 1941, PhD 1950; MA, University of Texas, 1947. Taught at University of Iowa, 1949–65; and University of Michigan, Ann Arbor, 1965–85. Married (1 daughter, 3 sons). Died Plattsburgh, New York, 22 August 1985.

Principal Writings
Tlaxcala in the Sixteenth Century, 1952
The Aztecs under Spanish Rule: A History of the Indians of the Valley of Mexico, 1519–1810, 1964
Spain in America, 1966
The Spanish Tradition in America, 1968
The Black Legend: Anti-Spanish Attitudes in the Old World and the New, 1971

Further Reading
Chevalier, François, "Charles Gibson (1920–1985)," *Hispanic American Historical Review* 66 (1986), 349–51
Garner, Richard L., and William B. Taylor, eds., *Iberian Colonies, New World Societies: Essays in Memory of Charles Gibson*, privately printed after appearing in parts in *Bibliotheca Americana*, 1985
Keen, Benjamin, "Main Currents in United States Writings on Colonial Spanish America, 1884–1984," *Hispanic American Historical Review* 65 (1985), 657–82
Lockhart, James, *Charles Gibson and the Ethnohistory of Postconquest Central Mexico*, La Trobe University Institute of Latin American Studies, Occasional Paper no. 9 (1987)

Giesebrecht, Wilhelm von 1814–1889
German medieval historian

Wilhelm von Giesebrecht was a renowned medieval scholar and an important advocate of Ranke's critical method. He was born into a Prussian intellectual family with a tradition of becoming pastors, teachers, or writers. Giesebrecht followed suit. After a brief flirtation with drama, he became a professor of history.

Giesebrecht was the second of Ranke's students to gain worldwide fame. In Ranke's seminar, Giesebrecht learned the importance of the critical method, the methodology that professionalized historical study. It emphasized careful preparation and training, strict impartiality, and a critical examination of primary sources. The use of secondary sources, which was common among early 19th-century historians, was to be limited to the extent that they could be verified by primary source material. Giesebrecht eagerly adopted Ranke's teachings, and using these methods, he meticulously reconstructed the lost annals of the time of Henry III. When a copy of the annals was discovered a generation later, the accuracy of Giesebrecht's work was widely acclaimed. The publication of the lost annals earned him a stipend for study; for three years, from 1843 to 1845, he travelled through Austria and Italy visiting archives and libraries. The immediate result of his travels was a dissertation on medieval Italian letters, *De litterarum studiis apud Italos primis medii aevi saeculis* (1845). Even more importantly, his travels allowed him to amass an extensive collection of primary medieval source material. From this collection, Giesebrecht would write his monumental masterpieces.

In 1855, he published the first volume of his *Geschichte der Deutschen Kaiserzeit* (History of the German Imperial Era). This work began a 6-volume study of German history in the High Middle Ages. The six volumes described in brilliant prose three centuries of medieval history from the Carolingian empire to the reign of Barbarossa. Giesebrecht invented the term *Kaiserzeit* to denote the period when the German emperors controlled the destiny of Europe and when "the German man counted for most in the world and the German name was famous." Giesebrecht was not a racial advocate, but he was a fervent nationalist who wanted Germany to be unified. By his own admission he hoped that his work would in some small way aid the process of unification. He wrote that, "the science of German history is a torch which lights our path and throws its beam forward as well as backward." The work was a tremendous success. The breadth of his knowledge, the artistry of his narrative prose, and his nationalistic message captured the minds of the public – both German and non-German. The accuracy of the text and the detailed notes on the source materials and the so-called authorities of the field won him accolades for his scholarship. Although some of his colleagues denigrated his prose style, the consensus was that the volumes were masterpieces. Böhmer praised him as the soundest of all medieval scholars. Contemporary criticism was limited: the Prussian school resented his position that the achievements of medieval Germany were due to the efforts of the central and south Germans, and Sybel rejected Giesebrecht's main premise that the empire was both national and beneficial. Sybel argued that the empire led Germany into needless wars that wasted its wealth and blood and retarded its development. Despite Giesebrecht's obvious romantic glorification of the empire, numerous historians defended his thesis. Ficker accused Sybel of applying contemporary concepts to the period and of ignoring the context of the time. Today historians recognize several limitations in the work. By our standards, the volumes are not completely objective. Giesebrecht wrote a brilliant narrative history, but it did have a manifest purpose (to further unification). Despite its impressive scholarship, the work ignored constitutional, economic, and intellectual issues, though to be fair, this absence reflects its time and not Giesebrecht's negligence.

The popularity of the volumes won Giesebrecht first a chair in Königsberg and then the professorship of history in Munich in 1862. As a professor, he altered German historiography. He was a brilliant, witty lecturer, but his greatest impact was on the curriculum. He persuaded the Bavarian schools to adopt history as a subject in its own right and he organized and

taught a seminar modeled after Ranke's teachings. He served on the Historical Commission and acted as its president for many years. Today, Giesebrecht is honored both for his role in continuing Ranke's professionalization of history and the merit of his six medieval volumes. Although his medieval studies are flawed by current standards, they remain impressive historical works and a testament to Giesebrecht's scholarship and brilliance.

FRED HOOVER

Biography

Friedrich Wilhelm Benjamin von Giesebrecht. Born Berlin, 5 March 1814. Studied with Ranke. Taught at universities of Königsberg, 1857–62; and Munich, 1862–89. Married Dorothea Schwendy Reissner, 1846 (1 stepson, 1 son). Died Munich, 18 December 1889.

Principal Writings

De litterarum studiis apud Italos primis medii aevi saeculis, 1845
Geschichte der Deutschen Kaiserzeit (History of the German Imperial Era), 6 vols., 1855–95; many editions

Further Reading

Gooch, G.P., *History and Historians in the Nineteenth Century*, London and New York: Longman, 1913; revised 1952
Heimpel, Hermann, "Friedrich Wilhelm Benjamin van Giesebrecht," *Neue Deutsche Biographie*, 1964, vol. 6, 379–82
Riezler, Sigmund, *Gedächtnisrede auf Wilhelm von Giesebrecht*, Munich: Akademie, 1891
Sybel, Heinrich von, "Giesebrecht und Döllinger," in his *Vorträge und Abhandlungen*, Munich: Oldenbourg, 1897

Gilbert, Felix 1905–1991

US (German-born) Renaissance historian

Felix Gilbert, one of the great masters of Italian Renaissance studies, was an outstanding member of the generation of German émigré historians that contributed so decisively to American scholarship in the postwar era. Although his Florentine and Venetian studies were the principal foci of his research, he also wrote authoritative works on the origins of American foreign policy, on 19th- and 20th-century German historiography, and on 20th-century political, diplomatic, and military history. His generosity was as legendary as his erudition, and his gift for friendship made him a cherished mentor to several generations of historians on both sides of the Atlantic.

Born in 1905 in Baden-Baden into a liberal and cultivated family prominent in business and the professions, he was related on his mother's side to the Mendelssohn and Oppenheim clans of musicians and bankers. He knew from an early age both the privileged sense of security of the prewar bourgeoisie and the anxieties of war, political violence, and hyperinflation. In *A European Past: Memoirs, 1905–1945* (1988), a product of his ninth decade, he gave a lively and engaging account of the experiences that shaped his vocation as a historian. Many of his books and articles would deal with the genesis of intellectual innovation and vocational commitment in periods of political crisis. One collection of his historical essays is aptly titled *History: Choice and Commitment* (1977).

In the late 1920s Gilbert was a participant in Friedrich Meinecke's prestigious seminar at the University of Berlin. At Meinecke's suggestion he wrote his dissertation on the historian J.G. Droysen before embarking on his Italian Renaissance studies. He was in Italy when Hitler came to power, and would not return to Germany until the end of World War II. After some years in London, he found refuge at Princeton's Institute for Advanced Study, where he began to publish his work on Machiavelli. As an assistant to Edward Mead Earle he contributed, with his friend Gordon Craig, to the classic volume *Makers of Modern Strategy* (1941); forty years later they would contribute to the second edition of the book edited by Peter Paret. During the war Gilbert worked as a research analyst for the Office of Strategic Services (OSS), while forming lasting friendships with the next generation of American historians, including Carl Schorske, Leonard Krieger, Franklin Ford, and H. Stuart Hughes. Many of these historians contributed to *The Diplomats, 1919–1939*, a pioneering collection of essays edited by Craig and Gilbert. After the war Gilbert taught for many years at Bryn Mawr, where he incubated the studies that would blossom into his Bancroft prize-winning *To the Farewell Address: Ideas of Early American Foreign Policy* (1962) and his classic *Machiavelli and Guicciardini: Politics and History in Sixteenth-Century Florence* (1965).

When Gilbert arrived in the United States, intellectual history as a branch of historical study was in its infancy. Indeed the field had not yet been baptized: according to Gilbert, Perry Miller was the first scholar to use the term "intellectual history" in its modern sense, in his classic study of Puritanism as a system of thought and a view of the world, *The New England Mind* (1939). A.O. Lovejoy, whose *The Great Chain of Being* (1936) offered a competing paradigm for the field, preferred the term "history of ideas." A potential problem with Lovejoy's method was the tendency of the ideas under study to float free from their historical contexts. Miller's method, on the other hand, could even in the work of less subtle historians produce a totalizing history of the Zeitgeist. "This solution of the problem is questionable," Gilbert wrote in "Intellectual History: Its Aims and Methods" (1971), "because every society consists of various social strata and each has its own intellectual outlook; if we go beyond reconstructing the outlook of the ruling group the picture becomes diffuse."

In Gilbert's own work ideas are never disembodied; they always emerge from a precisely delineated milieu. His Machiavelli studies, for example, marry the close textual analysis he had practiced in Meinecke's seminar with the interest in the social and institutional bases of politics that he shared with such members of his own generation as Eckart Kehr. His classic essay on Bernardo Rucellai (1949), locates the origins of political science in a particular discussion circle with a specific ideological agenda. It showed how humanist idealism was modulated into political realism in tandem with the transformation of Florentine factions into political parties. And *To the Farewell Address*, which studied the dialectic of idealism and realism in the context of American foreign policy, offered a brilliant demonstration of the Hamiltonian origins of Washington's valedictory. It placed Hamilton's thought squarely in the school of power politics and *raison d'état*, and thus revealed Washington's address, that quintessentially American document, as an example of a European genre: the Political Testament.

In 1962, Gilbert accepted a post at the Institute for Advanced Study, where he remained until his death in 1991 at the age of 85. Through his participation in Princeton's Davis seminars he kept abreast of new developments in the field of social history. He wrote often on historiographical issues, introducing Meinecke, Otto Hintze, and Aby Warburg to American readers in masterly essays. He wrote too about the history of his own family, the Mendelssohn clan of musicians, bankers, and professors. His interest in the role of banking in history in turn produced *The Pope, His Banker, and Venice* (1980), a brilliant study of economic diplomacy during the papacy of Julius II. And his last book, *History: Politics or Culture?* (1990), offered a reassessment of Ranke and Burckhardt, and made a delightful coda to his long and distinguished career. Although he was far too modest and skeptical to say so, no one was better qualified than he to carry on and to transmit the legacy of the great 19th-century historians.

BRUCE THOMPSON

See also Italy: Renaissance; Muratori

Biography

Born Baden-Baden, Germany, 21 May 1905, son of an English doctor settled in Germany. Studied at the universities of Heidelberg, Munich, and Berlin; received PhD, University of Berlin, 1931, where he studied with Friedrich Meinecke. Left Germany in the late 1920s, eventually settling in the US after living in Britain, 1933–36; naturalized US citizen. Taught at Scripps College, 1936–37; Institute for Advanced Study, Princeton, 1939–43, 1962–91; and Bryn Mawr College, 1946–62. Research analyst, Office of Strategic Services and US State Department, 1943–46. Married Mary Raymond, 1956. Died 14 February 1991.

Principal Writings

Johann Gustav Droysen und die preussisch-deutsche Frage (Johann Gustav Droysen and the Prussian German Question), 1931

Editor with Edward M. Earle and Gordon Craig, *Makers of Modern Strategy: Military Thought from Machiavelli to Hitler*, 1941

"Bernardo Rucellai and the Orti Oricellari: A Study on the Origin of Modern Political Thought," *Journal of the Warburg and Courtauld Institutes* 12 (1949), 101–31; reprinted in *History: Choice and Commitment*, 1977

Editor with Gordon Craig, *The Diplomats, 1919–1939*, 1953

To the Farewell Address: Ideas of Early American Foreign Policy, 1962

With John Higham and Leonard Krieger, *History: The Development of Historical Studies in the United States*, 1965

Machiavelli and Guicciardini: Politics and History in Sixteenth-Century Florence, 1965

The End of the European Era, 1890 to the Present, 1970, 4th edition, 1991

With Stephen Grabard, *Historical Studies Today*, 1972

History: Choice and Commitment, 1977

The Pope, His Banker, and Venice, 1980

A European Past: Memoirs, 1905–1945, 1988

History: Politics or Culture? Reflections on Ranke and Burckhardt, 1990

Further Reading

Craig, Gordon A., "Insight and Energy: Reflections on the Work of Felix Gilbert," in Hartmut Lehmann, ed., *Felix Gilbert as Scholar and Teacher*, Washington, DC: German Historical Institute, Occasional Paper no.6, 1992

Ford, Franklin L., Introduction, to Felix Gilbert, *History: Choice and Commitment*, Cambridge, MA: Harvard University Press, 1977

Lehmann, Hartmut, and James J. Sheehan, eds. *An Interrupted Past: German-Speaking Refugee Historians in the United States after 1933*, Cambridge: Cambridge University Press, 1991

Schorske, Carl E., "Survivor of a Lost World," *New York Review of Books* (10 November 1988)

Gilson, Etienne 1884–1978

French historian of medieval philosophy

Beginning with his doctoral thesis, Etienne Gilson studied the impact of medieval philosophy on Descartes. Concluding that the metaphysical systems of the 17th century were strongest where they preserved the heritage of medieval metaphysics and that the Cartesian system made sense only against the background of Thomistic metaphysics, Gilson turned to the closer study of Aquinas, then to Augustine, Bonaventure, Bernard of Clairvaux, and others. His research convinced him that it was idle to attempt to describe a philosophy common to them, since their philosophies were forged in opposition to one another. In his view, the essence of philosophy lay in the act of philosophizing rather than in its product. This being the case, the historian of medieval philosophy needed to study the thinking of individuals rather than aiming to elaborate a synthesis of the thought of ten centuries. This insight was reinforced when Gilson studied Augustine in order to understand what ideas of his had imprinted themselves on medieval philosophy. In trying to understand Augustine's thought from Augustine's own viewpoint rather than that of later commentators, Gilson was impressed more by the organic uniqueness of that thought than by any likeness to or appropriation by later thinkers. The medieval philosophy based on Aristotle, although it used Augustinian terminology, did not evolve from Augustine. Gilson aimed, then, to study the evolution of philosophy from the Church Fathers to the end of the 14th century by placing the different authentic philosophies elaborated by individuals into the context of the intellectual culture of the Middle Ages. For him, medieval philosophy commenced with the contact of Christianity and Greek philosophy and always pivoted on the reconciliation of faith and reason.

The key to Gilson's historical method was outlined in the bibliographical notes of his *Saint Thomas d'Aquin* (1925; *Moral Values and the Moral Life*, 1961): read, reread, and reflect on Thomas' writings; resort to *explication de texte* and learn the author's technical terminology, characteristic style, and vocabulary; observe how Thomas used the analytic order; establish the reasoning in the synthetic order from principle to consequences and remove examples; and remember that nothing is faithful to a philosopher's thought except his own text in the original language. While these principles were for general use, it is noteworthy that Gilson enunciated them in writing of St. Thomas Aquinas, for the study of Aquinas was for him the central study of medieval philosophy. The emergence of a full-blown Aristotelian thought was characteristic of the Christian age, and Gilson contended – contrary to other historians - that it did not evolve gradually in Thomas' thought but was substantially discernable in *De veritate* (1256–59)

and had changed only accidentally by the *Summa theologiae* (1266–73).

The core point of Gilson's activity was the assertion of the existence and validity of a distinctively Christian philosophy that was authentically philosophical and which represented the autonomous activity of human reason within the context of divine revelation, the human intellect providing demonstrations of theological truths arrived at through authentic philosophical method. The integrity of the study of medieval thought can only be maintained by refusing to isolate the activity of philosophy from that of theology. While the distinction between them is conceptually valid and necessary, it is unhistorical to remove from its theological setting a philosophy in which the very selection of problems and themes was dictated by theological ends. Gilson held that such a philosophy, truly perennial, could vigorously address modern problems. Along with Jacques Maritain, he took neo-Thomism from being a narrow preserve of clerics and brought it forcefully into academic and socio-political dialogue.

JOSEPH M. MCCARTHY

See also Reformation

Biography

Etienne Henry Gilson. Born Paris, 13 June 1884, son of businessman. Educated at the Petit Séminaire de Notre-Dame-des-Champs and Lycée Henri IV, 1895–1903; received agrégation in philosophy, the Sorbonne, 1907, PhD 1913. Taught in provincial lycées, 1907–13; taught philosophy and education, University of Lille, 1913–19. Served in the French Army in World War I: captured at Verdun. Taught philosophy, University of Strasbourg, 1919–21; and the history of medieval philosophy, the Sorbonne, 1921–32; and Collège de France, 1932–51. Founded *Etudes de philosophie médiévale*, 1922, and *Archives d'histoire doctrinale et littéraire du Moyen Age*, 1926. Elected to the Académie Française, 1946. Married Thérèse Ravisé, 1908 (2 daughters, 1 son). Died Cravant, France, 19 September 1978.

Principal Writings

Index scholastico-cartésien, 1913

La Liberté chez Descartes et la théologie (Liberty and Theology in Descartes), 1913

Le Thomisme: introduction au système de S. Thomas d'Aquin, 1919, several revisions; in English as *The Philosophy of St. Thomas Aquinas*, 1924, and as *The Christian Philosophy of St. Thomas Aquinas*, 1956

La Philosophie au Moyen Age des origines patristiques à la fin du XIVe siècle (Philosophy in the Middle Ages from Its Patristic Origins to the End of the 14th Century), 2 vols., 1922; revised 1944, 1962

La Philosophie de Saint Bonaventure, 1924, revised 1943; in English as *The Philosophy of Saint Bonaventure*, 1938

Saint Thomas d'Aquin, 1925; in English as *Moral Values and the Moral Life: The Ethical Theory of St. Thomas Aquinas*, 1961

Introduction à l'étude de S. Augustin, 1929; in English as *The Christian Philosophy of Saint Augustine*, 1960

Etudes sur le rôle de la pensée médiévale dans la formation du système cartésien (Studies on the Role of Medieval Thinking in the Forming of the Cartesian System), 1930

La Théologie mystique de Saint Bernard, 1934; in English as *The Mystical Theology of St. Bernard*, 1990

Reason and Revelation in the Middle Ages, 1938

God and Philosophy, 1941

L'Etre et l'essence, 1948; in English as *Being and Some Philosophers*, 1949

Jean Duns Scot: introduction à ses positions fondamentales (Duns
  Scotus: Introduction to His Fundamental Beliefs), 1952
History of Christian Philosophy in the Middle Ages, 1955
Elements of Christian Philosophy, 1960
Le Philosophe et la théologie, 1960; in English as *The Philosopher
  and Theology*, 1962
With Thomas Langan, *Modern Philosophy: Descartes to Kant*, 1963
With Thomas Langan and Armand Maurer, *Recent Philosophy:
  Hegel to the Present*, 1966

Further Reading

Facco, Maria Luisa, *Etienne Gilson: storia e metafisica* (Etienne
  Gilson: History and Metaphysics), Japadre: L'Aquila, 1992
Gouhier, Henri, *Etienne Gilson: trois essais* (Gilson: Three Essays),
  Paris: Vrin, 1993
Livi, Antonio, *Etienne Gilson: filosofía cristiana e idea del límite
  crítico* (Gilson: Christian Philosophy and the Idea of a Critical
  Boundary), Pamplona: Ediciones Universidad de Navarra, 1970
McGrath, Margaret, *Etienne Gilson: A Bibliography*, Toronto:
  Pontifical Institute of Medieval Studies, 1982
Madiran, Jean, *Gilson: chroniques philosophiques* (Gilson:
  Philosophical Chronicles), Paris: Editions Difralivre, 1992
Maritain, Jacques *et al.*, *Etienne Gilson: philosophe de la chrétienté*
  (Gilson: Philosopher of Christendom), Paris: Cerf, 1949
Quinn, John Michael, *The Thomism of Etienne Gilson: A Critical
  Study*, Villanova, PA: Villanova University Press, 1971
Schmitz, Kenneth L., *What Has Clio to do with Athena: Etienne
  Gilson, Historian and Philosopher*, Toronto: Pontifical Institute of
  Medieval Studies, 1987
Shook, Laurence K., *Etienne Gilson*, Toronto: Pontifical Institute of
  Medieval Studies, 1984
Toso, Mario, *Fede, ragione e civiltà: saggio sul pensiero di Etienne
  Gilson* (Faith, Reason, and Civilization: Essay on the Thought of
  Etienne Gilson), Rome: LAS, 1986

Ginzburg, Carlo 1939–

Italian cultural historian of early modern Italy

Son of the distinguished writer Natalia Ginzburg, Carlo
Ginzburg was born in Turin but spent his early years confined
with his family to a village in Abruzzi because of his father's
antifascist activities. His father, Leone Ginzburg, was a teacher
of Russian literature and one of the founders of the publishing
firm Einaudi. Leone was also one of the handful of Italian
academics who resigned from teaching in 1932 rather than
swear allegiance to fascism, and was a leader of the left-wing
group *Giustizia e Libertà*. When the regime collapsed in 1943
he returned to Rome, was arrested by the Germans in
November, and died in the notorious Regina Coeli prison early
in 1944. A flavor of the Ginzburg family history is given by
Natalia in her *All Our Yesterdays* (1952). Carlo Ginzburg grew
up with Natalia and a stepfather, Gabriele Baldini, living in
Turin, Rome, and London. Baldini, who died in 1969, was a
professor of English literature, and so Carlo was raised in an
intensely intellectual household dominated by books and ideas.

Carlo Ginzburg's first inclination was to become a novelist,
and his theoretical reading in the mid-1950s was a diet of
Lukács, Gramsci, Croce, Leo Spitzer, the philologist Erich
Auerbach, and Gianfranco Contini. Two projects drew him
along, and these have remained his historical passion: the question of the "meanings" we can attach to artworks, particularly in the Western realist tradition, and the sources of cultural

dissent, especially in the early modern period. (No evidence
exists of Ginzburg attempting to write fiction, although he did
try his hand at painting.) At the prestigious Scuola Normale
Superiore in Pisa, he was taught by Delio Cantimori (1904–66),
the Italian translator of Marx's *Capital*, vol.1, a historian of
heresies, and a writer on Jacob Burckhardt and other cultural
historians. Ginzburg's first article, in 1961, when he was 22,
concerned a witchcraft trial in 1519, and was published in the
Scuola's journal. With Cantimori's support, Ginzburg took up
what was in the early 1960s an obscure subject, the fertility
rituals of Italian peasants. The choice of such a marginal group
in part reflects Ginzburg's own intensely private self: his own
intellectual and secular background marked him off from mainstream academic life.

Yet ironically Ginzburg succeeded where many of his contemporaries failed: in communicating with a broader reading
public in both the Italian and the English-speaking world. The
first secret of his success lay in his method: in describing the
peasant rituals he did not emplot his work like a conventional
Italian historian, with a lengthy contextual introduction, but
told a story. Ginzburg took the reader through the inquisition
trials on a journey of discovery, contrasting the official worldview of the inquisitors with the half-formed populist views of
those being interrogated. He revealed a forgotten premodern
world where peasants waged mock outdoor battles under cover
of night, jousting with sticks of fennel and sorghum – ostensibly to increase the fertility of their fields. As readers we are
taken to this startling image of these warriors (*benandanti*) by
the gradual inquisitional process. In doing so, Ginzburg reconstructed for the lay reader the pleasure which the historian
derives from the detective work that constitutes archival
research. Professional critics attacked *I benandanti* (1966; *The
Night Battles*, 1983) for its refusal to contextualize the fertility
rituals: how common were they? what was their philosophical
rationale? and so on. Ginzburg reacted by writing a far more
formal historical account of another group of heretics, the
Nicodemites, and then later regretted this concession, for *Il
nicodemismo* (1970) did not attract a large readership. The
lesson learned, he improved on his formula, and international
success came first with his third book, the celebrated *Il formaggio e i vermi* (1976; *The Cheese and the Worms*, 1980) an
account of the heretical miller from Pordenone, Menocchio.

The second secret to Ginzburg's formula is also a novelistic
strategy, that is, to give us a character with whom we can
follow the story. Instead of his proper name, Domenico
Scandella, the miller's nickname *Menocchio* is used throughout.
Having been permitted this intimacy, the reader gets to see the
world through Menocchio's eyes, so far as the documents will
allow. Even the title of the book comes from Menocchio's
mouth, for it turns out that this heretic believes the cosmos
was made like cheese is churned, and living things appeared,
including God, just as worms can spawn in cheese. We read
the same books as Menocchio; we can imagine his worldview
as being entirely consistent and congruent with what he can
know. In short, a profoundly heretical view is normalized, and
our intellectual conceit is stripped away. The book quickly
went into an English edition, the earliest book was also translated, and three of Ginzburg's subsequent books found ready
translation into English. He took up visiting appointments in
various US universities.

Although Ginzburg came to the notice of English-speaking social historians early in his career, he has not developed a school around him. This is partly a matter of his personality, and partly that his subject matter is perhaps not broad enough. But his "detective" method does have much broader applicability. The key to Ginzburg's notion of history as "detective" work is to be found in his well-known essay on clues (reprinted in *Miti, emblemi, spie* (1986; *Clues, Myths, and the Historical Method*, 1989). In that essay he uses the story of art historian Giovanni Morelli to demonstrate the cross-disciplinary significance of minute clues. Morelli tested the authenticity of masterworks in the Western oils tradition by careful scrutiny of minor details such as the shape of ears and fingers: since artists usually depict these according to their formulaic routine, these details are the fingerprints by which we can recognize the hand of each master. So too, Ginzburg reminds us, did Sherlock Holmes solve his crimes and Sigmund Freud conduct his analyses. The historian must do likewise. Equally, if we trace the history of the divination of these clues back in time, we find that all cultures depend upon them. The hunters found their quarry through tracks; the first human alphabets derived from the observance of natural signs, such as bird tracks on a river's sandy bank. By this neat example, Ginzburg wants literate official culture to recognize its debt to Menocchio's premodern peasant world.

ROBERT PASCOE

See also Anderson, P.; Anthropology; Cultural; Europe: Modern; Indigenous; Mentalities; Oral

Biography

Born Turin, 1939, son of novelist Natalia Ginzburg and publisher/political activist Leone Ginzburg. Studied at Scuola Normale Superiore, Pisa; held fellowships at Harvard University Center for Italian Renaissance Studies in Florence, and Warburg Institute, London, 1964. Lecturer in modern history, University of Rome; then professor of modern history (*professore incaricato*), University of Bologna, from 1970. Married 2) Luisa Ciammitti, museum curator (2 daughters).

Principal Writings

I benandanti: richerche sulla stregoneria e culti agrari tra Cinquecento e Seicento, 1966; in English as *The Night Battles: Witchcraft and Agrarian Cults in the Sixteenth and Seventeenth Centuries*, 1983

Il nicodemismo: simulazione e dissimulazione religioso nell'Europa del '500 (Nicodemism: Religious Simulation and Dissimulation in 16th-Century Europe), 1970

Il formaggio e i vermi: il cosmo di un mugnaio del '500, 1976; in English as *The Cheese and the Worms: The Cosmos of a Sixteenth-Century Miller*, 1980

Indagini su Piero: il Battesimo, il Ciclo di Arezzo, la Flagellazione di Urbino, 1981; in English as *The Enigma of Piero: Piero della Francesca*, 1985

Miti, emblemi, spie: morfologia e storia [collected essays], Turin: Einaudi, 1986; in English as *Clues, Myths, and the Historical Method*, 1989

Storia notturna: una decifrazione del sabba, 1989; in English as *Ecstasies: Deciphering the Witches' Sabbath*, 1990

Il giudice e lo storico: considerazioni in margine al processo Sofri (The Judge and the Historian), 1991

Further Reading

Luria, Keith, "The Paradoxical Carlo Ginzburg," and (with Romulo Gandolfo) "Carlo Ginzburg: An Interview," *Radical History Review* 35 (1986), 80–111

Martin, John, "Journeys to the World of the Dead: The Work of Carlo Ginzburg," *Journal of Social History* 25 (1992), 613–26

Schutte, Anne Jacobson, "Carlo Ginzburg," *Journal of Modern History* 48 (1979), 296–315

Giovio, Paolo *c.*1486–1552

Italian humanist historian

Paolo Giovio's reputation as a historian rests on his classically inspired *Historiae sui temporis* (The History of His Own Times, 1550–52), a work harshly criticized on publication and undervalued today. It had been his most consuming interest over almost forty years, and its preface explained that it covered events of the world – hence it was a universal history as formulated by Polybius and underlined by Leonardo Bruni. Its range was from 1494 to 1547, the year in which Henry VIII and Francis I died, but following its classical models dates and sources were rarely indicated. As published it comprised 45 books, though books 5–10 and 19–24 were mere outlines, in imitation of the lost books of Livy's *Ab Urbe Condita* (From the Founding of the City) – the fictitious parallel being that Giovio's books likewise had been lost in a sack of Rome, though actually they were never written. Giovio was interested in the broadening Christendom, taking in Muscovy in the east, which he hoped would counter Turkish expansion, and the New World in the west. This emphasis of his overshadowed any disintegration within Western Christendom itself inflicted by Luther and Protestantism. For Giovio, as likewise for Guicciardini, the invasion of the Italian peninsula by the French in 1494 was the watershed, bringing long-term ruin for the peninsula in its wake (it should be noted that Giovio had read Guicciardini's *Storia d'Italia* [1561; *The History of Italy*, 1753–56] in manuscript). Columbus and the discovery of the New World in 1492 received brief treatment, being before his watershed, and featured in the context of explaining that the gold and silver from the New World furnished Spain with the means for warfare, thereby enabling her domination of the Italian peninsula. The first book of his history mentioned as existing (the text of books 13 and 14 as published) late in 1515 was concerned with affairs in Central Europe and also with the Turkish-Persian conflict of 1514, to which a brief account of events in Western Christendom for the year was an appendix. For Italians like Giovio at this time the close-at-hand threat of the Turks was of greater direct political importance than the New World.

The work, published at the expense of the first grand duke of Florence, was printed in Florence by Lorenzo Torrentino, printer to the duke. The first volume appeared in August 1550, the second in September 1552, only three months before Giovio's death in Florence. His death was hastened by pressures of seeing the work through the press. Although helped – particularly by Benedetto Varchi – Giovio feverishly composed missing portions, revised, and proof-corrected. Almost simultaneously Torrentino printed an Italian version (1552–53), translated from the original Latin by Lodovico Domenichi. The work was virtually uncensored (of those changes that Charles V sought only the most minor were actually incorporated) and there was no revision by others. However, Giovio throughout working on the *History* depended on patronage, and he admitted that truth should not be stated too bluntly. The author's consistent aim was to titillate, while gratifying the illustrious, particularly the emperor. Unsurprisingly this resulted in the work on publication being castigated as prejudiced, even unprincipled, as well as flawed by factual errors: Varchi, ungenerously, given his assistance, listed a hundred for the most part relating to Florence, which essentially were inconsequential. Giovio's emphasis on deeds worthy of imitation on the part of the illustrious, together with his highlighting of wickedness – features typical of 15th-century humanistic history – inevitably meant that those ill-favored sneered at the supposedly virtuous as having bought the historian's favor. Hence venality was added to the work's supposed untrustworthiness. In his *Elogia* (1546; that portion relating to scholars published as *An Italian Portrait Gallery*, 1935), Giovio had commented that the historian of contemporary events was writing "of the sport of Fortune, with envy always watching," a fitting epithet for his *History*'s reception. Existing manuscript versions, with the author's correspondence, broadly indicate the *History*'s development over the years. Leo X on the evidence of the portion relating to 1514 believed the *History* likely to be the outstanding one of the century. In the event that accolade went to Guicciardini's *History of Italy*, which was not a universal history and much less classical in style. Furthermore, where Guicciardini based his work on archival and written sources, which could be checked, Giovio had drawn heavily on eyewitness accounts, often from personal interviews, and this oral tradition, itself classical, could not be verified, and could descend to gossip. The work's classical emphasis was largely out of favor by the time of its publication. Even so, Giovio's vivid writing and what were savored as slights ensured that in the two decades following publication his *History* was widely read on the Continent, even if it tended to be cited only to denigrate it, as has been the case subsequently. By 1567 there had appeared at least ten printings of the very lengthy Latin text, and by 1572 ten of Domenichi's Italian; by 1570 there were three printings of a French translation, a Spanish one was printed in 1562 and a German one eight years later; neither the *History* entire nor selections have ever been translated into English.

Within the scope of history as defined in his day, Giovio wrote several other works, information from which was reworked in his *History*: for instance, his *Comentario de le cose de' Turchi* (A Commentary on Turkish Affairs, 1532) formed the basis of his *History*'s account of Albanian struggles against the Turks. In 1548 he published a description of the British Isles derived from classical authorities and Polydore Vergil's *Anglica Historia* (The History of the English, 1534). His biographies of twelve Visconti and Sforza princes of Milan was well received, as were those of several generals. His lives of Leo X and Adrian VI were more eulogistic, written with an eye to potential papal patronage. None of these works was documented, and he referred to his forthcoming *History* for the sources. In the villa that he built at Como he incorporated a *musaeum*, as he termed it, comprising almost four hundred portraits in oils of illustrious men, and some women. These portraits were universal in geographical range and included individuals of the classical and medieval worlds, though the focus was on Giovio's contemporaries. Many of these latter were painted from life, or from an authentic likeness. Woodengravings taken from his portraits enhanced the published text of his Eulogies and of some of his biographies. These engravings, like the portraits in his gallery, reflected contemporary (and classical) assumptions that physiognomy was a guide to character, and hence helped explain actions and history. Giovio's *History* and his biographies furnished thumbnail descriptions of the physical characteristics of an individual, picked out as influencing events. The oil portraits were copied for other portrait galleries and these, as well as published engravings taken from the originals or copies, have served as illustrations of the persons concerned to the present day (frequently with the original source not indicated) – one of Giovio's achievements as a historian not to be underestimated.

CECIL H. CLOUGH

See also Renaissance

Biography

Also known as Paulus Jovius. Born Como, Duchy of Milan, probably in 1486, son of a notary. Educated in Como, Milan, and Padua, where he studied medicine. Moved to Rome, 1512, where he practiced medicine while carrying out a parallel career in philosophy and literature; made bishop of Nocera, 1527. Died Florence, 10 December 1552.

Principal Writings

Historiae sui temporis (The History of His Own Times), written from 1514; published, 1550–52
Comentario de le cose de' Turchi (A Commentary on Turkish Affairs), 1532
Elogia veris clarorum virorum imaginibus apposita (Eulogies of Illustrious Men with a Likeness from Life Alongside Each), 1546; section published in English as *An Italian Portrait Gallery*, 1935
Descriptio Britanniae (The Description of Britain), 1548
Illustrium virorum vitae (The Lives of Illustrious Men), 1551

Further Reading

Clough, Cecil H., "A Manuscript of Paolo Giovio's *Historiae sui temporis, Liber VII*: More Light on the Career of Ludovico degli Arrighi," *Periodico della Società Storica Comense* 53 (1989), 53–83
Clough, Cecil H., "The New World and the Italian Renaissance," in Cecil H. Clough and P.E.H. Hair, eds., *The European Outthrust and Encounter, the First Phase, c.1400–c.1700: Essays in Tribute to David Beers Quinn, on His Eightieth Birthday*, Liverpool: Liverpool University Press, 1994
Fasola, B., "Per un nuovo catalogo della collezione giovana" (Towards a New Catalogue of Giovio's Portrait Gallery), in *Atti de Convegno Paolo Giovio: Il rinascimento e la memoria*, Como: Presso la Società a Villa Gallia, 1985
Müntz, P., "Le Musée de portraits de Paul Jove" (Paolo Giovio's Portrait Collection), *Mémoires de l'Institut National de France: académie des Inscriptions et Belles-Lettres* 36 (1901), 249–343
Zimmermann, T.C. Price, *Paolo Giovio: The Historian and the Crisis of Sixteenth-Century Italy*, Princeton: Princeton University Press, 1995

Gipson, Lawrence Henry 1880–1971
US historian of the British empire

With his mentor, Charles McLean Andrews, Lawrence Henry Gipson provided the central texts of the Imperial school. They interpreted early American history in the context of British imperial development, emphasizing institutional and economic data.

The goals of the members of the Imperial school contrast with those of their contemporaries, the "Progressive" historians (e.g., Carl Becker, Charles Beard, and Arthur Schlesinger, Sr.). Where the Progressives described the economic conflicts (between colonies and empire and between the colonists themselves) that surrounded the origins and meaning of the American revolution, the Imperial school based its analysis upon the economic and administrative problems faced by British colonial rulers. For Gipson, British imperial administrators were on the whole honest, fair-minded men, concerned with running an empire, not with establishing tyranny.

The multiple volumes of *The British Empire before the American Revolution* (1939–70) represent a lifetime of trans-Atlantic research into the details of administration. It rivals George Bancroft's earlier *History of the United States from the Discovery of the American Continent* (1834–74) in ambition, and answers Bancroft's emphasis on the American search for liberty with a comprehensive analysis of the freedoms provided Americans under British protection. Gipson's *The Coming of the Revolution, 1763–1775* (1954) distills that argument, with a particular focus on the development of American nationalism within the perceived imperial constraints.

Gipson used economic data to place political history in social context, and he discussed US history in the broader scope of British imperial relations, as a part of the Atlantic community and in the world context. Seeing the colonies in that context, he interpreted the revolution of 1776 as one of resentment in the face of change. For instance, the colonists were resisting a series of taxes brought on because of the Seven Years' War (a war in which the role of the colonists had been problematic); they resented new laws concerning trade, although their own ill-considered trade practices brought on those laws; and they bridled at the restrictions on their westward expansion, when coherent, economical, and peaceful imperial organization dictated such limits. Thus the revolution was less one of principle than one of reaction to external pressures and economic change.

Both groups, the Progressives and the Imperial school, held that the key slogans of the revolution – liberty, equality, democracy – were politically convenient but had little to do with the actual reasons for the revolt. In looking for the latent causes of the rebellion, the Imperial school, like the Progressives, opened new sources of information on both sides of the Atlantic. They provided a wealth of new documentation for the day-to-day operations and concerns of the empire, and they provided the first comprehensive description of the economic fortunes and pressures that went with building the empire.

The first responses to the Imperial school argument asserted that the political principles did, in fact, count. For instance, Edmund S. Morgan and Helen M. Morgan provided a first book in this "consensus" effort (*The Stamp Act Crisis*, 1953, revised 1963), and Jack P. Greene's book, *The Quest for Power* (1963) provided an analysis of the political networks from which those ideas emerged.

The impact of the Imperial school is difficult to separate from that of the Progressives. Both provided new economic and institutional data, as well as a strong dose of skepticism about the ideals and intentions of the revolutionary generation.

As such, both groups have influenced the growth of the "neo-Progressives" (ranging from the revisionists, such as William Appleman Williams, to the new social historians, such as James Henretta).

As a member of the editorial boards of the *American Historical Review* and the *William and Mary Quarterly*, Gipson was influential in encouraging the 1950s explosion of research and writing about early America. He also sat on the board of directors for the Institute of Early American History and Culture during that important growth period. His extensive collections of documents and notes have been preserved as the central resources of the Lawrence Henry Gipson Institute for Eighteenth-Century Studies at Lehigh University.

DONALD R. PALM

Biography

Born Greeley, Colorado, 7 December 1880, son of a newspaper editor. Attended College of Idaho; received BA in journalism, University of Idaho, 1903; studied with Charles M. Andrews, Yale University, BA 1903, PhD 1918; Rhodes scholar, Oxford University, 1904–07. Taught at College of Idaho, 1907–10; Farnham fellow, Yale University, 1910–11; taught at Wabash College, 1911–24; and Lehigh University (rising to professor), 1924–52 (emeritus). Married Jeannette Reed, 1909. Died Pennsylvania, 26 September 1971.

Principal Writings

Jared Ingersoll: A Study of American Loyalism in Relation to British Colonial Government, 1920; reprinted as *American Loyalist: Jared Ingersoll*, 1971
The British Empire before the American Revolution, 15 vols., 1939–70; revised 1958–70
The American Revolution as an Aftermath of the Great War for the Empire, 1754–1763, and Other Essays in American Colonial History, 1950
The Coming of the Revolution, 1763–1775, 1954

Further Reading

Morris, Richard B. "The Spacious Empire of Lawrence Henry Gipson," in Alden T. Vaughan and George Athan Billias, eds., *Perspectives on Early American History: Essays in Honor of Richard B. Morris*, New York: Harper, 1973
Shaw, Diane Windham, editor, *Guide to the Papers of Lawrence Henry Gipson*, Bethlehem, PA: Gipson Institute for Eighteenth-Century Studies, Lehigh University, 1984

Global History *see* World History

Godechot, Jacques Léon 1907–1989
French historian of the Revolutionary and Napoleonic era

A prolific scholar, Jacques Godechot devoted his long career to studying the French Revolutionary and Napoleonic eras. He was attracted to the period while still a young student and published his first scholarly article when he was only 19. With the encouragement of his dissertation director, the eminent historian Albert Mathiez, Godechot prepared a substantial thesis on the civilian commissioners attached to the armies during the Directory. His research led him to consult, not only the archives of France but also those of Belgium, the Netherlands, Switzerland, Germany, and Italy. As a result, Godechot gained an unusually wide understanding of the Revolution and its international impact.

Godechot expanded his outlook further when, after World War II, he published a history of the Atlantic Ocean. He had grown interested in the topic while teaching courses on maritime history at the French naval academy during the late 1930s. In his book Godechot first provided a detailed geographical description of the body of water, then crafted a clear narrative account of the colonial and naval conflicts that marked it from the voyages of Columbus through the two world wars.

This work helped convince him that the various revolutions that had taken place in the late 1700s were interrelated events, linked by economic, social, and political forces. In Godechot's eyes, not France alone but all of western and central Europe underwent similar experiences. Drawing on recent publications on historical demography, he developed the idea that rapid population growth during the 18th century contributed to the revolutionary ferment.

In 1954 his scholarship caught the attention of the American historian R.R. Palmer, professor at Princeton. He invited Godechot to conduct research there as well as to collaborate on a paper dealing with the "problem of the Atlantic from the 18th to the 20th century" that would be presented at the International Congress of Historical Sciences in 1955. Together they reached the conclusion that a revolutionary, democratic movement had encompassed both sides of the Atlantic basin, agitating colonial America and most of western Europe. They also insisted that greater unity existed in the trans-Atlantic community in the 1700s than in the 1900s. Each historian later developed this "Atlantic Revolution" thesis in individual ways.

Their work stirred considerable controversy for ideological and historiographical reasons. Leftist historians charged them with buttressing the Atlantic alliance organized under the auspices of the United States, an accusation that Godechot vigorously denied. Orthodox historians, especially those in France, criticized them for minimizing the importance and uniqueness of the French experience by subordinating it to an international upheaval. While accepting the supreme role of France's revolution, Godechot envisioned a "Western Revolution" occurring in several phases, with the American Revolution marking the initial episode and the French having crucial significance.

Developing this thesis preoccupied Godechot for several more years. He expanded upon his ideas in a volume that covered the period 1770–99: *Les Révolutions* (1963; *France and the Atlantic Revolution*, 1965). But Godechot also realized how fiercely opposition to the Revolution had raged inside and outside France. In a synthetic work, *La Contre-Révolution* (1961; *The Counter-Revolution*, 1971), he closely examined reactionary theorists such as Burke and Maistre who fought it ideologically, as well as popular uprisings that attempted to defeat it by force of arms. These two studies, aimed at a general audience, fully demonstrated Godechot's ability to range widely across Europe, incorporating sources written in some half-dozen languages.

He also produced solid works on a variety of specialized topics. These included the capture of the Bastille on 14 July 1789; Europe and America during the Napoleonic era; major

historians of the Revolution; daily life under the Directory; the Revolution in the Toulouse region; and a detailed chronology for the period 1787–99. Remarkably, Godechot found time to write hundreds of articles and book reviews for scholarly journals. In addition, during the quarter-century that he taught at the University of Toulouse, he directed scores of dissertations on local history and the press. In this way Godechot trained a new generation of scholars of the Revolution.

Godechot's importance as a historian lies in his willingness to view the French Revolution in an international context. He considered it part of a "Western Revolution" that shook the Atlantic world in the late 18th century and whose impact extended well into the 19th. Open to new approaches and undogmatic in his interpretations, Godechot proved a highly versatile scholar. His capacity to compress his numerous archival discoveries into readable texts accessible to trained specialists and ordinary readers alike, widely disseminated knowledge of the revolutionary period.

JAMES FRIGUGLIETTI

Biography

Born Lunéville, 3 January 1907. Educated at University of Nancy, licence-ès-lettres 1927; the Sorbonne, University of Paris, doctorate 1938. Served in French army, 1929–30. Taught at Lycée Kléber, Strasbourg, 1933–35; and Ecole Navale, 1935–40; dismissed from teaching post by Vichy regime and lived clandestinely during German occupation; rejoined army, 1944–45. Professor, University of Toulouse, 1945–80 (emeritus). Married Arlette Lambert, 1932 (3 sons, 1 daughter). Died 24 August 1989.

Principal Writings

Les Commissaires aux armées sous le Directoire: contribution à l'étude des rapports entre les pouvoirs civils et militaires (The Commissioners with the Armies under the Directory: A Contribution to the Study of Civil-Military Relations) 2 vols., 1937

Histoire de l'Atlantique (History of the Atlantic Ocean), 1947

Les Institutions de la France sous la Révolution et l'Empire (The Institutions of France under the Revolution and the Empire), 1951

La Grande Nation: l'expansion révolutionnaire de la France dans le monde de 1789 à 1799 (The Great Nation: French Revolutionary Expansion, 1779–1799), 1956

La Contre-Révolution, doctrine et action, 1789–1804, 1961; in English as *The Counter-Revolution: Doctrine and Action, 1789–1804*, 1971

Les Révolutions, 1770–1799, 1963; in English as *France and the Atlantic Revolution of the Eighteenth Century, 1770–1799*, 1965

La Prise de la Bastille, 14 juillet 1789, 1965; in English as *The Taking of the Bastille, July 14th, 1789*, 1970

Un Jury pour la Révolution (A Jury for the Revolution), 1974

La Vie quotidienne en France sous le Directoire (Daily Life in France under the Directory), 1977

Regards sur l'époque révolutionnaire (Aspects of the Revolutionary Era), 1980

Le Comte d'Antraigues: un espion dans l'Europe des émigrés (The Count of Antraigues: A Spy in a Europe of Emigrés), 1986

La Révolution française dans le Midi toulousain (The French Revolution in the Toulouse Region), 1986

Further Reading

Forster, Robert, R.R. Palmer, James Friguglietti, and Emmet Kennedy, "American Historians Remember Jacques Godechot," *French Historical Studies* 16 (1990), 879–92

Goitein, S.D. 1900–1980

German-born historian of Jewry in the medieval Arabic world

S.D. Goitein studied Islamic history in Germany with Carl H. Becker and was influenced in his approach to civilizations by Michael I. Rostovtzeff. His knowledge of Arabic was forged in editing the *Ansāb al-Ashrāf* of al-Balādhurī and his work on Judeo-Arabic texts in the 1930s. He was also well-read in British social anthropology, which guided him in the formulation of a questionnaire he used to write a book (in Hebrew) on the Jews of Yemen, based on techniques of oral history.

Goitein's career was closely linked to the Cairo Geniza, a room attached to a synagogue where papers of all kinds were deposited so that the name of God might not inadvertently be destroyed. Of the quarter million pieces – mainly literary – surviving, around 7000 were judged by Goitein as "documents of historical value." These he mined for many years (starting in 1950), finding "a true mirror of life, often cracked and blotchy, but very wide in scope and reflecting each and every aspect of the society that originated it." This research led to his magisterial work, *A Mediterranean Society* (1967–93), whose six volumes are devoted, respectively, to Economic Foundations, The Community, The Family, Daily Life, The Individual, and an index volume. Goitein retrospectively characterized the project as "interpretive historical sociography," which he came to associate with the objectives of cultural anthropology as explicated by Clifford Geertz in *The Interpretation of Cultures* (1973). The Geniza fragments lent themselves to a "thick description" of Jewish life in the medieval Arabic world, even though Goitein realized that "cultural analysis is intrinsically incomplete."

Goitein forged a view of Jewish life and culture in the medieval Arabic world based on the nature of the bourgeois revolution in the medieval Muslim world and the idiosyncratic adaptation that Jews made to it. Because Islamic civilization was, paradoxically, largely secular in nature, non-Muslims could also feel part of its cultural traditions. By accepting the norms of the Muslim middle class, the Jewish populations of those countries transformed themselves from the agricultural class of late antiquity to the commercially-oriented urban Jewish culture of the Islamic Middle Ages. The civilization of the High Middle Ages (roughly 850 to 1250) Goitein characterized as an "intermediate" civilization – intermediate chronologically between Hellenistic late antiquity and the Renaissance; intermediate in character, between the secular culture of the Roman world and the clerical world of medieval Europe; and in geography between Europe and the Far East. The civilization of this period was marked by the cultural and economic leadership of the middle class and by the "all pervading influence of Greek science in both matter and spirit."

The bourgeois revolution involved, among other facets, the movement of capital, merchants, and craftsmen through what Goitein described as a Muslim customs union or free trade zone extending from Spain to India. He viewed the India trade as "the backbone of medieval international economy" and for years worked on a project, still unpublished, whose working title was the "India Book," based on Geniza materials documenting Jewish participation in that commercial network.

The garrison towns of the early Arab empire were transformed into consumer centers, linked by improved infrastructure – including roads, caravan routes, and commercial shipping. Because law in the Islamic world was conceived as personal and not territorial, freedom of communication and travel were virtually total, and medieval documents convey little sense of "national" boundaries. Arabic was the vehicle of both high culture and commerce. Judeo-Arabic, a literary vernacular based on local speech, was a more flexible vehicle of expression than was standard literary Arabic, because unlike Arabs, Jews were not bound by the conventions of Koranic usage. By the end of the 11th century Arabic was used in all Jewish commercial and religious court transactions.

In the 10th through the 12th centuries the merchant class was the vital core of Muslim civilization. This class supported the great body of scholars who codified Islamic law and, among the autonomous Jewish subculture of the Islamic world, the same relation between commerce, law, language, and travel for learning was found. Among Jews and Christians, as well as Muslims, individuals moved easily between leadership roles in the separate spheres of commerce, law, and religion. Finally, as Goitein himself stressed, his work, while centered on Jewish actors, is about medieval Islamic society and culture, because that was the everyday context of Jewish life in the Arabic-speaking world.

THOMAS F. GLICK

See also Egypt: since the 7th Century; Middle East; Poliakov; Spain: Islamic; Spain: to 1450

Biography

Shlomo Dov Goitein. Born Burgkunstadt, Germany, 3 April 1900, son of a rabbi. Received PhD, University of Frankfurt, 1923. Emigrated to Israel, 1923, and the US, 1957. Taught school, Haifa, 1923–27; rose to professor, Hebrew University, Israel, 1928–57: director, School of Oriental Studies, 1949–56; professor of Arabic, University of Pennsylvania, 1957–71; affiliate, Institute for Advanced Study, Princeton, 1971–80. Married Theresa Gottlieb, 1929 (2 daughters, 1 son). Died 1980.

Principal Writings

Editor, *Ansāb al-Ashrāf* by al-Balādhurī, 1936–38
From the Land of Sheba, 1947
Jews and Arabs: Their Contacts through the Ages, 1955; revised 1974
Studies in Islamic History and Institutions, 1966
A Mediterranean Society: The Jewish Communities of the Arab World as Portrayed in the Documents of the Cairo Geniza, 6 vols., 1967–93
Letters of Medieval Jewish Traders, 1973
Editor, *Religion in a Religious Age*, 1974

Further Reading

Attal, Robert, *A Bibliography of the Writings of Prof. Shelomo Dov Goitein*, Jerusalem: Hebrew University, 1975
Diem, Werner, *A Dictionary of the Arabic Material of S. D. Goitein's A Mediterranean Society*, Wiesbaden: Harrassowitz, 1994

Goldman, Eric 1915–1989

US historian

Eric Goldman was a leading early historian of the American liberal reformist tradition, whose works *Rendezvous with Destiny* (1952) and *The Crucial Decade* (1956) won wide popularity with both college students and general readers. Goldman's early works included studies of the historian John Bach McMaster (1943) and of the reformer Charles J. Bonaparte (1943), together with a textbook, *The World's History* (1947). His true métier, however, was the exposition of near-contemporary history, a predilection almost certainly encouraged by several years spent working as a journalist for *Time* magazine before he finally, in 1943, opted for an academic career at Princeton University.

Goldman's first major work, *Rendezvous with Destiny*, was a narrative history of reform in the United States, from the Grant administration to 1948. Lively, well-written, and highly readable, it provided an overview of eight decades of reformers, complete with arresting vignettes of numerous individuals, and stressed the continuities among successive American reform movements. Writing at the height of the Cold War, he also argued that the fundamental liberal tradition of the United States was moderate, centrist, and incrementalist, and decidedly non-socialist and non-totalitarian. While broadly sympathetic to the cause of American reform, Goldman was far from uncritical toward his subjects, faulting progressives of World War I for their lukewarm reception of the League of Nations, American reformers of the 1920s for their emphasis on freedom of lifestyles rather than economic reform, and those of the 1930s for their overly tolerant attitude toward Soviet Russia. His views of past American reformers encapsulated the conventional, liberal, centrist orthodoxy of the early 1950s, from its support for anticommunism and international activism abroad and New Deal-style big government at home, to its condemnation of McCarthyism. *The Crucial Decade*, a narrative account of the ten – later fifteen – years after World War II ended, had the strengths and weaknesses of its predecessor. Easy in style, it assumed that New Deal-Fair Deal social welfare assumptions and material prosperity had become permanent features of the American landscape, and that international affairs should be given higher priority than domestic. Although his work was essentially celebratory, in 1960 Goldman echoed the Democratic presidential candidate John F. Kennedy's criticism that the Eisenhower years had left the United States deficient in a sense of national purpose, with no higher goals than those of materialism, but expressed his optimism that his countrymen would rise to the new challenges likely to face them in the 1960s.

Goldman's emphasis on immediate contemporary history reflected his own interest in politics and his conception "of the role of the university professor as including participation in certain types of public affairs." He frequently lectured overseas on behalf of the State Department, wrote numerous articles for popular journals, including *Harper's*, *Holiday*, the *New Republic*, the *Saturday Review*, the New York *Times*, and the New York *Herald Tribune*, and often appeared on television programs. He was also active in Democratic politics. The apogee of Goldman's public career was reached in late 1963,

when President Lyndon B. Johnson, eager to enhance his ties to and image with American intellectuals, invited him to join the White House staff as a special consultant, his duties primarily to further these goals. Goldman's bestselling account of his three years in the Johnson administration, *The Tragedy of Lyndon Johnson* (1969), gave a poignant picture of the president, whom the author admired and described as a "[s]trange, complex man in strange, complex circumstances – too astute not to know how seriously things had gone wrong, too limited by background and by self to grasp what had really happened." It could also serve as a manual describing the pitfalls that may await the academic who ventures into the political arena, and the disillusionment likely to overcome the intellectual when forced to choose between his principles and his personal loyalties. An admirer of Johnson, Goldman came to disagree with him over the Vietnam War and the president's attitude toward intellectuals, and in September 1966 chose to leave his service.

However professionally illuminating Goldman's White House years may have been, it seems that they also brought an end to the most productive phase of his career. Although he continued to write reviews and articles for popular journals, his volume on Johnson was the last major work he published. As the liberal American tradition that Goldman had both represented and chronicled fell into increasing disarray, he appeared unable to tackle any further lengthy projects. His personal files at Princeton University for the 1970s and 1980s house a depressing litany of complaints as to his salary, teaching, office space, housing, colleagues, leave, and other matters. Goldman simultaneously continued to win numerous awards as best teacher, his scintillating lecturing style and personal political experience attracting huge classes of enthusiastic undergraduates. Yet, overall, the career of this politically engaged academic and scholar of American reform serves as a cautionary tale of the dangers that await the historian tempted to become a protagonist on the stage he chronicles.

PRISCILLA M. ROBERTS

Biography

Eric Frederick Goldman. Born Washington, DC, 17 June 1915. Grew up in Baltimore; received BA, Johns Hopkins University, 1935, PhD 1938. Taught at Johns Hopkins University, 1938–41; staff member, *Time* magazine, 1940–43; taught at Princeton University from 1943. Special adviser to president Lyndon Johnson, 1963–66. Married Joanna Ruth Jackson, 1952. Died 19 February 1989.

Principal Writings

Charles J. Bonaparte, Patrician Reformer: His Earlier Career, 1943
John Bach McMaster, American Historian, 1943
Rendezvous with Destiny: A History of Modern American Reform, 1952
The Crucial Decade: America, 1945–1955, 1956, revised and expanded as *The Crucial Decade – And After: America, 1945–1960*, 1960
The Tragedy of Lyndon Johnson, 1969

Further Reading

Fowler, Robert Booth, *Believing Skeptics: American Political Intellectuals, 1945–1965*, Westport, CT: Greenwood Press, 1978
Kraus, Michael, and Davis D. Joyce, *The Writing of American History*, revised edition, Norman: University of Oklahoma Press, 1985

Lemisch, Jesse, *On Active Service in War and Peace: Politics and Ideology in the American Historical Profession*, Toronto: New Hogtown Press, 1975

Morton, Marian J., *The Terrors of Ideological Politics: Liberal Historians in a Conservative Mood*, Cleveland: Press of Case Western Reserve University, 1972

Skotheim, Robert Allen, *American Intellectual Histories and Historians*, Princeton: Princeton University Press, 1966

Sternsher, Bernard, *Consensus, Conflict, and American Historians*, Bloomington: Indiana University Press, 1975

Gombrich, E.H. 1909–

British (Austrian-born) art historian

All art historians seek to explain art in a clear and understandable manner, but few have achieved this to the same extent as Ernst Gombrich. His *Story of Art*, written in 1950, is a very readable introduction to the history of art and remains popular today. On a more scholarly level, he has been no less successful and, surprisingly, no less readable. He served as director of the Warburg Institute in London for many years, but nevertheless produced a impressively steady stream of publications throughout his long career.

In a number of essays, including the well-known "Meditations on a Hobby Horse" (1951), and in *Art and Illusion* (1960) Gombrich presents a unique view on how art is created. He opposes the traditional view that art reproduces what the artist sees. Rather, he maintains, art is created from what the artist knows, what is basic to that object on a psychological level (or, at least initially, on the level of physical need). Art is *made* and then the result is compared or *matched* against what the artist sees when he/she looks at the world. Art is learned through this process of making and matching (schemata and corrections) and progresses in this way. Conceptual art, such as the art of ancient Egypt or the Middle Ages, is art that chooses to focus on schemata; naturalistic/illusionistic art, such as that of ancient Greece and the Renaissance, uses schemata as its starting point – but the development of schemata remains the basis of art in all cases.

This theory of artistic creation explains the existence of various styles both within the history of art in general and in the oeuvre of a particular artist specifically. Each period and each artist within that period learned – and relied upon – certain schemata for creating art which, in turn, provided the means by which viewers of art can identify and categorize styles.

Gombrich supports his theories with data from psychological experiments, and he has been specifically influenced by the work of psychologist/philosophers Ernst Kris and Karl Popper. Beyond this clear connection with psychology, however, Gombrich's work is difficult to classify. Within art historical circles he was influenced by his teacher, Julius von Schlosser, who, in turn, was a student of Benedetto Croce. Crocean theory maintained that there was no history of art, that every piece of art was an individual, totally autonomous creation. Gombrich did not follow this philosophy, but it may in part account for his focus on the problem of artistic creation in itself. He is somewhat allied with the philosophy of iconology as championed by Erwin Panofsky and he wrote a number of essays utilizing it, but Gombrich also warned against its

excesses in the introduction of *Symbolic Images* (1972). He is often typecast as one who is interested exclusively in the "illusionistic" tradition, but he successfully applied his theories to the decorative arts in *The Sense of Order* (1979).

Gombrich's most obvious contributions are his ability to focus on the link between art and psychology in a scientifically credible manner, and his discussions concerning the history of styles. His approach is not a methodology *per se*, but it forces a reconsideration of the artistic process in terms of what we know about human beings, and thus has significant applications within a number of different methodologies.

JULIET GRAVER ISTRABADI

See also Art; Burke; Cultural; Panofsky

Biography

Ernst Hans Josef Gombrich. Born Vienna, 30 March 1909, son of a lawyer and a pianist. Educated at Theresianum, Vienna; Vienna University, PhD. Worked for BBC Monitoring Service, 1939–45. Taught at Warburg Institute, University of London, 1936–59; and University College, London, 1956–76; director, Warburg Institute, 1959–76. Married Ilse Heller, 1936 (1 son). Knighted 1972.

Principal Writings

The Story of Art, 1950; 16th edition 1995

Art and Illusion: A Study in the Psychology of Pictorial Representation, 1960

Meditations on a Hobby Horse, and Other Essays on the Theory of Art, 1963

Norm and Form, 1966

In Search of Cultural History, 1969

Aby Warburg: An Intellectual Biography, 1970

Symbolic Images, 1972

The Heritage of Apelles, 1976

Ideals and Idols: Essays on Values in History and in Art, 1979

The Sense of Order: A Study in the Psychology of Decorative Art, 1979

The Image and the Eye: Further Studies in the Psychology of Pictorial Representation, 1982

New Light on Old Masters, 1986

Reflections on the History of Art: Views and Reviews, edited by Richard Woodfield, 1987

With Didier Eribon, *Ce que l'image nous dit*, 1991; in English as *Looking for Answers*, 1993

Topics of our Time: Twentieth-Century Issues in Learning and in Art, 1991

Further Reading

Pavar, Claude N., "Restoring Cultural History: Beyond Gombrich," *Clio* 20 (1991), 157–67

Pinto, Eveline, "Ernst Gombrich: la recherche d'une histoire culturelle et la découverte de la logique des situations," *Revue de Synthèse* 106 (1985), 61–80

Góngora, Mario 1915–1985

Chilean social, legal, and intellectual historian

Born in Santiago in 1915, Mario Góngora represented the synthesis of 20th-century conservative thought in Chile. Respected for his vast knowledge, his erudition, and the consistency of his interpretations, Góngora rejected the previous generation's devotion to liberal principles and progress and used the concept of "juridical convictions" to argue that modern Chilean society had its roots in Spanish colonial institutions and their ethos. Although he originally supported the Pinochet military regime's *Declaración de Principios del Gobierno* (Declaration of the Principles of Government, 1974), which called for a restoration of a strong central government buttressed by popular support, Góngora later criticized Pinochet for betraying his earlier platform and destroying Chilean national identity by handing the state over to neoliberals in *Ensayo histórico sobre la noción de estado en Chile en los siglos XIX y XX* (Historical Essay on the Idea of the State in Chile in the 19th and 20th Centuries, 1981). Echoing the views of many others, Simon Collier has called Góngora "the outstanding Chilean historian of his generation."

Beginning his career as a law student, Góngora co-founded the Conservative Youth in 1935 and edited its official journal *Lircay* until he broke with the party three years later. In 1938, Góngora visited France for the first time, initiating a lifelong intellectual and spiritual connection with European history, its historians, and their ideas. Upon his return to Chile, he joined the Communist party, edited its journal *Principios* (Principles), studied pedagogy at the National University and retired from from active politics in 1944. Góngora recalled these years, 1931–45, as "the decisive period of my intellectual biography," during which he formed strong attachments to the French Catholic renaissance of Charles Péguy and Jacques Maritain, and began to look for the roots of Chile's instability in its past. Attracted to the global, systemic interpretations of Jacob Burckhardt, Jules Michelet, Johan Huizinga, Friedrich Meinecke, Leopold von Ranke, and especially Oswald Spengler, Góngora also drew upon the work of earlier Chilean historians Benjamín Vicuña Mackenna, Alberto Edwards, and Francisco Antonio Encina to situate the role of the state in Chilean society.

Góngora made a decisive research trip to Madrid and Seville in 1947–48, where he worked in the Archive of the Indies and began his investigations into the colonial history of Chile and Spanish America. While there he met Professor Alfonso García Gallo at Madrid's Central University and later recalled that both these experiences determined the future direction of his work, convincing him of the centrality of historico-legal and institutional processes for the development of a national identity. Góngora took several more research trips to Europe, believing that European and Latin American history could not be separated. He attended Fernand Braudel's classes at the Ecole Pratique des Hautes Etudes whenever he could, and accepted visiting professorships at Cologne, Oxford, and Yale. Although Braudel's quantitative methodology and socioeconomic orientation of the Annales school differed from his own approach to the study of history, Góngora wholeheartedly agreed with their idea of the "long duration," and believed that patterns of Chilean historical experience have persisted from colonial times to the present, including language, the Catholic religion, the idea of a strong central executive power, folklore, the arts, and the absence of any authentic industrial capitalist ethos. Toward this end he wrote several books on the institutional and social history of Chile's colonial period, always with one eye on the present. In each of these works, Góngora examined an element in Chile's colonial society or economy to reveal how those early processes determined the direction of national development and affected its national identity. This approach offered a dramatic contrast to previous interpretations by Diego Barros Arana, Miguel Luís and Domingo Amunátegui, and José Victorino Lastarria, Chile's major 19th-century historians who used their histories to champion liberal ideals of order and material progress.

In the late 1960s and early 1970s, as Chile's political spectrum became increasingly divided among Salvador Allende's Marxist socialists, the traditionalist Christian Democrats and an interventionist military, Góngora's historical studies assumed an obvious contemporary relevance. He turned his attention to Chilean intellectual history – a condemnation of the liberal-positivist experiments of the 19th century and their historian-apologists had always underpinned his work – and produced *Estudios de historia de las ideas y historia social* (Studies in the History of Ideas and Social History, 1980). The arguments set forth in *Estudio* foreshadowed those developed more explicitly a year later in his last major publication, *Ensayo histórico sobre la noción de estado en Chile en los siglos XIX y XX*. In this critique of the Pinochet regime, Góngora drew upon a wide range of conservative thinkers, including Novalis, Möser, Burke, de Maistre, Schmitt, and Edwards, to argue that the state historically had defined Chilean identity. By incorporating neoliberalism's emphasis on free markets and individuals in competition, Góngora believed that Pinochet had turned away from Chile's traditions and therefore broken his pact with the historical nation. Instead, Góngora argued in his *Ensayo*, Chile should return to that state-directed form of industrial development which had been its tradition since the colonial days of warfare against the Araucanian Indians. If the roots of Chile's problems could be found in its history, Góngora also believed the past contained directions to success in the future.

Góngora was the major Chilean historian of the last half of the 20th century. Rejecting the liberal-positivist orientation of the 19th-century Chilean historians, he synthesized the thought of earlier conservative writers Edwards, Encina, Jaime Eyzaguirre, and Osvaldo Lira to define a Chilean national identity that had its roots in the Hispanic colonial past. In the Latin American tradition of the engaged intellectual, Góngora used his historical studies to comment on the present condition of his country and to identify firm cultural foundations for future economic development and the role of government in society. His wide-ranging knowledge, strict attention to the accuracy of his sources, and devotion to the philosophy of history influenced a generation of Chilean students at the University of Chile, where he taught for thirty years, and at the Catholic University, where he ended his career.

KAREN RACINE

See also Latin America: Colonial; Latin America: National

Biography

Mario Góngora del Campo. Born Santiago, Chile, 22 June 1915. Studied at the Liceo San Agustín; University of Chile. Taught mainly at the University of Chile from 1944, before finally moving to the Catholic University of Chile. Died 1985.

Principal Writings

El estado en el derecho indiano: época de fundación, 1492–1570 (The State in the Law of the Indies), 1951

With Jean Borde, *Evolución de la propiedad rural en el Valle del Puangue* (Evolution of Rural Property in the Valley of Puangue), 2 vols., 1956

Origen de los 'inquilinos' de Chile central (Origin of the Sharecroppers of Central Chile), 1960

Los grupos de conquistadores en Tierra Firme 1509–1530: fisonomía histórico-social de un tipo de conquesta (Conquistador Groups on the Spanish Main, 1509–1530: Historical and Social Physiognomy of a Style of Conquest), 1962

Encomenderos y estancieros: estudios acerca de la constitución social aristocrática de Chile después de la conquista, 1580–1660 (Encomenderos and Landowners: Studies in the Aristocratic Social Composition of Chile since the Conquest), 1970

Studies in the Colonial History of Spanish America, 1975

Estudios de historia de las ideas y de historia social (Studies in the History of Ideas and Social History), 1980

Ensayo histórico sobre la noción de estado en Chile en los siglos XIX y XX (Historical Essay on the Idea of the State in Chile in the 19th and 20th Centuries), 1981

Further Reading

Carmagnani, Marcelo, "Mario Góngora, 1915–1985," *Hispanic American Historical Review* 66 (1986), 770–72

Collier, Simon, "Interview with Mario Góngora," *Hispanic American Historical Review* 63 (1983), 663–75

Cristi, Renato, and Carlos Ruíz, "Conservative Thought in Twentieth Century Chile," *Canadian Journal of Latin American and Caribbean Studies* (1990), 27–60

González Celis, Fernando, "Ensayo histórico sobre la noción de estado en Chile, del historiador Mario Góngora: los primeros pasos de la geografía política en la ciencia occidental de Chile" (Historical Essay on the Notion of the State in Chile, by Historian Mario Góngora: The First Steps of Political Geography in the Western Science of Chile), *Revista chilena de historia y geografía* 158 (1990), 149–59

Ibáñez de Santa María, Adolfo, "Estatismo y tradicionalismo en Mario Góngora" (Statism and traditionalism in Mario Góngora), *Historia* 22 (1987), 5–23

Krebs, Ricardo, "El historiador Mario Góngora" (The historian Mario Góngora), *Historia* 20 (1985), 5–9

Ruíz-Tagle, Carlos, "Góngora, el antifrívolo" (Góngora: The antifrivolous), *Atenea* 452 (1985), 201–04

Tau Anzoátegui, Víctor, "Las convicciones jurídicas: un aporte metológico de Mario Góngora" (Juridical Convictions: A Methodological Contribution of Mario Góngora), *Historia* 22 (1987), 325–33

González Casanova, Pablo 1922–

Mexican historian

Born in 1922, Pablo González Casanova was one of the first students of El Colegio de México, a college-level institution founded by the Spanish Republican refugees in Mexico. There he obtained a master's degree in historical sciences in 1947; in 1949 he obtained his doctoral degree in sociology from the University of Paris under the guidance of Fernand Braudel.

For many years González Casanova directed the Faculty of Political and Social Sciences of Mexico's National Autonomous University (UNAM), and between 1966 and 1970 headed its Institute for Social Science Research. González Casanova was UNAM's chancellor from 1970 until 1972. In that capacity he broadened the scope of high-school education by promoting the foundation of high school level preparatory schools of science and humanities, and university education by sponsoring the establishment in Mexico of the English-style open university system.

González Casanova's intellectual work began under the influence of his Spanish mentors such as José Gaos and José Miranda, among others, and his first published works were histories of ideas. In 1955 he published his first book on the sociology of knowledge. However, few works have had such a profound and enduring impact on Mexico's and Latin America's intellectuals, politicians, and the reading public in general as *La democracia en México* (1965; *Democracy in Mexico*, 1970). A rigorous examination of Mexico's economic, social, and political structures, the book was written with the intention of making a clear exposition of Mexico's reality hidden behind official rhetoric and propaganda of the unrealized postulates of the Mexican Revolution. As González Casanova put it: "It is not enough to establish democratization formally in the underdeveloped countries in order to accelerate development, nor to imitate all of the specific forms of classic democracy in order to have democracy: democracy exists to the extent that the people share the income, culture, and power; anything else is democratic folklore or rhetoric."

In his subsequent works, González Casanova returned to theoretical sociology, refining concepts in confrontation with the Mexican and Latin American reality. *La sociología de la explotación* (Sociology of Exploitation, 1969) belongs to the genre in which the author takes a critical Marxist approach to the question of exploitation, the theory of surplus value during the economic phase of monopoly competition, and neocolonialism, among others.

In the 1980s, González Casanova coordinated a number of collective studies in order to bring into focus Latin American reality and highlight its common and divergent characteristics. This was an especially turbulent period in Latin America's turbulent history, with violent confrontations between authoritarian regimes and popular and middle-class insurgencies on the one hand, and open interventions or low intensity counterinsurgency policies carried out by local military forces under the auspices of the United States government on the other. Under González Casanova's creative coordination several collections were published on self-determination, the Latin American labor movement, the history of the military in Latin American politics, and the theory and practice of the state in Latin America throughout its history.

In his subsequent theoretical work, González Casanova returned to his reflections on exploitation. He examined the nature of power relations and advocated a popular national and a concerted international struggle against imperialism and in favour of socialism. During the 1980s, González Casanova centered his work on examining contemporary Mexican politics from different angles, contributing to the debate on the future of the nation and democracy. These concerns led him to organize the publication of works on elections in Mexico.

González Casanova's concern with the role of social and political actors in history led him to supervise a multivolume study of the Mexican labor movement spanning the colonial period to the 1980s, under the title *La clase obrera en la historia de México* (The Working Class in Mexico's History, 1980–89). He himself contributed a volume in which he analyzed the politics of the first constitutional government headed by Venustiano Carranza between 1917 and 1920. González Casanova examined the government's politics, oscillating between its intention to impose an authority similar to the one the revolutionaries sought to abolish, and the need to govern in an environment in which it was imperative for the state's stability to reckon with the labor movement.

In his most recent work, González Casanova returned to one of his earlier interests, and coordinated a 4-volume collection of essays in which the authors surveyed the role of the university in present-day society. In another collection of essays, following the presidential elections in 1988, González Casanova edited a collective effort aimed at re-examining, at a critical juncture in Mexico's history, the experience of struggling for a genuine democracy. The essays contained in *Primer informe sobre la democracia: México, 1988* (The First Report on Democracy: Mexico, 1988) and *Segundo informe sobre la democracia* (The Second Report on Democracy, 1990) sought to explain from within the political, social, and economic texture of Mexico's society and the prospect for Mexico's transition toward democracy.

DANIELA SPENSER

See also Latin America: National

Biography
Born Toluca, Mexico, 11 February 1922, to an academic family. Educated at National Preparatory School, 1939–40; studied law, El Colegio de México, 1940–42, and history, 1943–46, MA 1947; studied sociology, University of Paris, 1947–50, PhD 1949. Taught sociology and history (rising to professor), Autonomous University of Mexico, from 1952: director, Institute for Social Science Research, 1970–72.

Principal Writings
La ideología norteamericana sobre inversiones extranjeras (The North American Ideology of Foreign Investment), 1955
La democracia en México, 1965; in English as *Democracy in Mexico*, 1970
La sociología de la explotación (Sociology of Exploitation), 1969
Editor, *América Latina historia de medio siglo* (Latin America: The History of Half a Century), 2 vols., 1977–81
En el primer gobierno constitucional (1917–1920) (In the First Constitutional Government, 1917–1920), 1980
Editor, *La clase obrera en la historia de México* (The Working Class in Mexico's history), 17 vols., 1980–89
La nueva metafísica y el socialismo (New Metaphysics and Socialism), 1982
No intervención, autodeterminación y democracia en América Latina (Non-Intervention, Self-Determination, and Democracy in Latin America), 1983
Historia del movimiento obrero en América Latina (History of the Latin American Labor Movement), 4 vols., 1984–85
Las elecciones en México: evolución y perspectivas (Elections in Mexico: Evolution and Perspectives), 1985
Editor with Héctor Aguilar Cambin, *México ante la crisis* (Mexico before the Crisis), 2 vols., 1985–86
Historia y sociedad (History and Society), 1987
Editor with Jorge Cadena Roa, *Primer informe sobre la democracia: México, 1988* (The First Report on Democracy: Mexico, 1988), 1988
México, el 6 de julio de 1988: Segundo informe sobre la democracia (The Second Report on Democracy: Mexico 6 July 1988), 1990
Latin America Today, 1994

Further Reading
Florescano, Enrique, and Ricardo Pérez Montfort, eds., *Historiadores de México en el siglo XX* (Mexican Historians of the 20th Century), Mexico City: FCE & CONACULTA, 1995
Knight, Thomas J., "A Mexican View of Utopianism: Pablo González Casanova," *Revista Interamericana* 9 (1979–80), 529–42

Gopal, Sarvepalli 1923–
Indian historian

Sarvepalli Gopal is noted for his ability to open the lives of those he has studied. His personal involvement in the contemporary history of India has made him uniquely qualified to publish in this area. He has also demonstrated sound judgment and objectivity in his writings despite a personal attachment to some of the objects of his study.

If we accept as one aspect of history biographies of great individuals, then Gopal has made a significant contribution to his field. Biography is more than a sequence of events, however. It is adding the human element to those events in such a way as to offer unique historical insights via the lives of others. An obvious instance of Gopal's success at this task is his work on the life of Jawaharlal Nehru. Projecting the many-faceted personality of Nehru is a daunting task. Gopal's work breaks new ground in the already large volume of extant material on Nehru through a sensitive examination of the international and domestic issues in which Nehru was involved and by illuminating the lives of many of Nehru's friends and professional associates.

One tendency that may develop from this emphasis on the individual is that subjectivity begins to undermine the historian's perspective. Gopal has done well to resist such a tendency in his biographical treatment of his own father, Sarvepalli Radhakrishnan, a philosopher and a president of India. In fact, some have found it difficult to find the personal side of this subject in Gopal's work. Once again Gopal is able to offer something new to the autobiographical and other material published on Radhakrishnan, at least in the arena of personal and political concerns. Religious matters appear more difficult to grapple with, and Gopal suggests that the modern trend to neglect religious tendencies is perilous.

Gopal's emphasis on the human element of history may derive from the fact that he is writing about the contemporary history of a nation, much of which he has witnessed, contributed to, or been personally affected by. Some explanation for the novelty he brought to his work on Nehru was his fortunate, first access to Nehru's personal papers; this gave a great sense of authority to his writings. A unique perceptiveness has been attributed to Gopal, to the point that many are amazed with his insights. This level of scholarship is difficult to attain without a very focused approach. For example, Gopal has not been drawn into an analysis of India's history, and hardly mentions the caste system in India in his trilogy on Nehru. The purpose of his work is biography and Gopal stays true to his purpose. While those less familiar with the historical period may dwell solely upon Nehru's idealistic and rhetorical aspects, Gopal instead reveals the practical qualities of Nehru's imagination in a fresh way.

Gopal is unable to ignore other members of India's leadership during this formative period, and is not timid about their troubled personal relationships. Rajendra Prasad is ranked as prominent in medievalisms and Rajagopalachari is characterized as intellectually arrogant and vindictive. It may be said that some of India's political leaders, although seeming allies, often proved to be as much trouble to one another as their opponents. Gopal's bold judgment makes his subjects more tangible. His works dispel many of the biases published in the 1960s, especially in regard to the interaction between India's leadership and foreign powers such as China.

It should come as no surprise that some historians are more critical of Gopal's biographies, claiming for example that aspects of his work on Nehru merely reinforce Nehru's own view of himself. In this light, the reader leaves the rather mild and predictable outcome with a sense that the work is inconclusive. A number of paradoxical views also leave one puzzled. For example, Nehru is blamed by some for a preference for large-scale projects that only increased the disparity between the poor and the wealthy. Gopal fudged the issue by claiming that Nehru was interested in small-scale economic improvements, designed to raise the standard of living in rural areas; yet, the Second Plan emphasized the building of heavy industry. In spite of these criticisms, Gopal's historical work is seen as occupying a special place in the historiography of southern Asia.

WILLIAM T. JOHNSON

See also India

Biography
Born Madras, 23 April 1923, son of Sir Sarvepalli Radhkrishnan (1888–1975), philosopher and president of India. Attended Mill Hill School; BL, MA, Madras University; MA, PhD, Oxford University. Taught at Andhra University, Waltair, 1948–52; assistant director, National Archives of India, 1952–54; director, historical division, Ministry of External Affairs, New Delhi, 1954–66; commonwealth fellow, Trinity College, Cambridge, 1963–64; reader in South Asian history, Oxford University 1966–71; professor of contemporary history, Jawaharlal Nehru University, New Delhi, 1972–83 (emeritus).

Principal Writings
The Permanent Settlement in Bengal and Its Results, 1949
The Viceroyalty of Lord Ripon, 1880–1884, 1953
British Policy in India, 1858–1905, 1965
Jawaharlal Nehru: A Biography, 3 vols., 1975–84
Radhakrishnan: A Biography, 1989
Editor, *Anatomy of a Confrontation: The Babri Masjid–Ramjanmbhumi Issue*, 1991

Further Reading
Bhattacharya, Sabyasachi, and Romila Thapar, eds., *Situating Indian History: For Sarvepalli Gopal*, Delhi: Oxford University Press, 1986

Gordon, Linda 1940–
US women's historian

Linda Gordon has played a formative role in the development of both women's history and the history of sexuality, forcing whole new topics of investigation onto the historical agenda as a result of her pioneering research on previously untapped source materials. Her acclaimed work on the politics of birth control was followed by ground-breaking studies of family violence and of single motherhood; she has examined the ways in which each of these issues has been culturally and politically constructed in America from the end of the 19th century to the present day. She has charted meticulously the interaction of the public with the private, the political with the personal.

In *Women's Body, Women's Right*, (1976), Gordon argued that birth control was not so much a question of technology as "an issue of politics." She identified three separate stages in the American birth control movement; each had its own terms of reference that were closely linked to wider political agendas. In the second half of the 19th century feminists had used the term "voluntary motherhood" to argue for choice, freedom, and reproductive autonomy for women. Between 1910 and 1920, socialist feminists campaigned for "birth control" to revolutionize society and empower working-class women and men. The "planned parenthood" movement of the 1940s associated well-managed families with national strength. Gordon's own research project was concurrent with and, indeed, part of a fourth stage – the feminist campaigns of the 1970s which took the legalization of abortion as their focus.

Gordon's work has combined a rigorous historical approach with a strong commitment to feminist politics. As a historian she has declared her interests readily; as a feminist, she has clearly been inspired by the belief that history has an important contribution to make to the contemporary women's movement. Thus she concluded her study of birth control with a call for reproductive self-determination and liberation for women. Similarly, she has been unafraid to draw moral conclusions in her articles on incest and family violence, arguing that "the presence or absence of a strong feminist movement makes the difference between better and worse solutions to the social problem of child sexual abuse."

Gordon has stressed repeatedly the importance of considering resistance and individual agency in women's history, aiming to position women and children as subjects rather than objects, as individual actors rather than passive victims of social control or male patriarchy. The issue of agency was signposted as crucial in the title of her book on family violence, *Heroes of Their Own Lives* (1988), taken from Charles Dickens' *David Copperfield*: "Whether I shall turn out to be the hero of my own life, or whether that station will be held by anybody else, these pages must show." Gordon aimed to demonstrate that women and children actively fought or prosecuted their abusers, initiated contact with protection societies, and resisted the interpretations placed on their cases by social workers. She rejected poststructuralist approaches to the history of gender (such as that of Joan Scott) arguing that they obscure personal agency, silence women, and ignore physical experience. Scott has, in turn, criticized Gordon's interpretation of agency as autonomy, and her failure to consider how agency can be constructed through discourse.

Gordon's work on family violence was based on a relatively new set of source materials – the case records of social work agencies. She explored the way in which such mediated and constructed accounts, written by social workers, could provide insights on the lives of clients, often members of poor immigrant families. Gordon also used her study of agencies working in Boston to chart changes in the construction of family violence and in the attitudes of social workers from the 1870s to the 1970s; she demonstrated that notions of gender played a crucial role. Late 19th-century child-savers, influenced by the temperance, social purity, and feminist movements, attributed both wife-beating and incest to "male depravity" associated with "the lower classes." In the period 1910–30 agencies focused on child neglect which they associated with environmental degradation and the problem of single motherhood; girls who had been sexually abused were labelled as delinquent and placed in industrial schools. Gordon linked this shift to the decline of feminism and the professionalization of social work. During the 1940s and 1950s the blame shifted to women – wives were seen as responsible for their husbands' violence and even, through negligence, for incestuous abuse.

Such a massive endeavor as *Heroes of Their Own Lives* has not escaped criticism. Gordon's explanation of family violence in terms of "power struggles" between family members has been described as unconvincing; neither does she fully articulate the links between feminism and the 19th-century child-saving movement. Her strengths lie in her thorough archive work and her ability to write wonderfully poignant and readable history that is equally pertinent to specialists and non-specialists alike.

LOUISE AINSLEY JACKSON

See also United States: Historical Writing, 20th Century; Women's History: North America

Biography

Irene Linda Gordon. Born Chicago, 19 January 1940, daughter of a social worker and a child welfare activist. Received BA, Swarthmore College, 1961; MA, Yale University, 1963, PhD 1970. Taught (rising to professor), University of Massachusetts, Boston, 1968–84; University of Wisconsin, Madison, from 1984. Married (1 daughter).

Principal Writings

Woman's Body, Woman's Right: A Social History of Birth Control in America, 1976
Heroes of Their Own Lives: The Politics and History of Family Violence: Boston, 1880–1960, 1988; revised 1990
Editor, *Women, the State, and Welfare*, 1990
Pitied but Not Entitled: Single Mothers and the History of Welfare, 1890–1935, 1994

Further Reading

Herman, Judith Lewis, "Review of Linda Gordon: *Heroes of Their Own Lives*," *Gender and History*, 1 (1989), 109–11
Scott, Joan Wallach, "Book Review: *Heroes of Their Own Lives* by Linda Gordon" (followed by Gordon's response and review of Scott's *Gender and the Politics of History*), *Signs*, 15 (1990), 848–60

Graetz, Heinrich 1817–1891
Jewish historian and Bible scholar

Heinrich Graetz was one of the leading practitioners of *Wissenschaft des Judentums* (The Academic Study of Judaism), the 19th-century German Jewish intellectual enterprise which

applied the tools of critical analysis to the Jewish past. Founded by a group of young Jewish intellectuals who were trained at German universities in the early 19th century, the proponents of *Wissenschaft* attempted to remove the study of the Jewish past from the exclusive purview of rabbinical scholars. Isaac Jost's 10-volume *Geschichte der Israeliten* (History of the Israelites, 1820–47) is considered by most to be the first important product of the *Wissenschaft* movement and, more importantly, the beginning of modern Jewish historiography.

Graetz's work was profoundly influenced by Hegelian philosophy and the historic ideas of Leopold von Ranke. Graetz drew upon the conceptual apparatus of Hegel regarding the unfolding of the "World spirit" to examine the progressive unfolding of the idea of Judaism. The debt to Ranke was even more pronounced. Like Ranke, Graetz based his studies on a critical evaluation of the available source material and looked for the "deeper connections" that lay behind the numerous details. In addition, both Ranke and Graetz focused on the personalities of leading individuals to illuminate the characteristics of a given age. Yet, in spite of their similar approaches to the study of history, Ranke and Graetz parted ways over one issue: whereas Ranke rejected all national theories of history, Graetz was the enthusiastic historian of the Jewish people.

The life work of Graetz was a multivolume historical study of the Jewish people entitled *Geschichte der Juden von den ältesten Zeiten bis auf die Gegenwart* (1853–75; *History of the Jews*, 1891–98). Most of his other writings were either preliminary studies or supplements to his *magnum opus*. The *History of the Jews* offers a passionate description of the trials and tribulations of the Jewish people, and it presents an unabashedly nationalist and multifaceted definition of Judaism. Graetz's *History of the Jews* publicly declared that the essence of Judaism was comprised of both a religious and political component, the twin axes around which Jewish history revolved.

The nationalist orientation of Graetz's history paralleled the prevailing nationalist spirit of contemporary German historiography. Unlike Christian theologians who had denied the Jews a national history after the destruction of the Second Temple in 70 CE and Isaac Jost who rejected lines of continuity between the age of the Prophets and the Rabbis, Graetz insisted that all periods of Jewish history were connected and that each period displayed the national character of Judaism. Historiographically, the *History of the Jews* was based on previously ignored literary sources and it succeeded in illuminating many obscure episodes in Jewish history. The glaring weaknesses of Graetz's 11-volume study of Jewish history is that it neither evaluated the Jews of Poland, Russia, or Turkey, nor did it evaluate the social and economic aspects of Jewish history. The work was criticized by Jewish scholars as containing "stories but not history" and it was publicly attacked by the German historian Heinrich von Treitschke as further evidence of the unwillingness of German Jews to become Germans once and for all. In spite of its flaws and critics, the *History of the Jews* was a pioneering effort in modern Jewish historiography that still retains its influence on Jewish historians.

KEITH H. PICKUS

See also Baron, S.; Jewish

Biography

Heinrich Hirsch Graetz. Born Xions, Posen [now Poznań, Poland], 31 October 1817. Spent his early years in Posen, Zerkow, and Wolstein [Wolsztyn], before going to Oldenbourg to study with Samson Raphael Hirsch; received PhD, University of Jena. Schoolteacher, Breslau, 1845–48; and Lundenburg, 1850–52; lecturer, Jewish Theological Seminary, Breslau, from 1853; honorary professor, University of Breslau, 1869. Died Munich, 7 September 1891.

Principal Writings

Die Konstruktion der jüdischen Geschichte (written 1846), 1936; in English as *The Structure of Jewish History, and Other Essays*, 1975

Geschichte der Juden von den ältesten Zeiten bis auf die Gegenwart, 11 vols., 1853–75; in English as *History of the Jews*, 6 vols., 1891–98

Editor, *Monatsschrift für Geschichte und Wissenschaft des Judentums* (Monthly on the History and Philosophy of Judaism), 1892–94

Further Reading

Baron, Salo Wittmayer, *History and Jewish Historians: Essays and Addresses*, Philadelphia: Jewish Publication Society of America, 1964

Bloch, Philipp, *Heinrich Graetz*, Posen: Alkalay, 1898; revised 1904

Cohen, Arthur A., *The Natural and the Supernatural Jew: An Historical and Theological Introduction*, New York: Pantheon, 1962; London: Vallentine Mitchell, 1972

Deutsch, Gotthard, *Heinrich Graetz: A Centenary*, 1917

Meisl, Josef, *Heinrich Graetz . . . zu seinem 100. Geburtstag* (Heinrich Graetz on His 100th Birthday), 1917

Gramsci, Antonio 1891–1937

Italian cultural historian

As a founder of the Italian Communist party (PCI) and prominent antifascist, Antonio Gramsci was better known during his lifetime as a revolutionary political activist and journalist than as a historian. However, his imprisonment in November 1926 by Mussolini gave Gramsci time to make a systematic study of history, politics, and philosophy. Writing in a fascist prison severely compromised his work, as he had to contend with both censorship and a scarcity of sources, but, despite the obstacles, by the time of his death in 1937, he had filled 34 notebooks with reflections on various aspects of history and philosophy. Clearly shaped by classical Marxism, these writings commonly called the *Quaderni del carcere* (1948–51; *Prison Notebooks*, 1971) also show the influence of Italian idealist philosopher, Benedetto Croce, as well as Machiavelli's *The Prince*.

Because Gramsci often consciously obscured his writings to outmaneuver the watchful eye of censors, his work is more open to interpretation than that of most intellectuals. The most widely noted insight of Gramsci's work is the development of the concept of "hegemony" – the way the predominance of certain ideas produces acceptance of the existing order. In contrast to dogmatic Marxists who saw civil society as an almost automatic reflection of economic relations, he emphasized the myriad of beliefs, social relations, and institutions that produce acceptance of the status quo. Gramsci argued that

force alone is seldom sufficient to maintain a ruling class. State coercion in alliance with hegemony, however, can protect the privileges of the powerful few. For example, he examined the 19th-century unification of Italy as a case of a "passive revolution" because most peasants – while not enthusiastic about the process – gave their passive consent.

Central to his theory of hegemony was the study of the historical role of intellectuals. For Gramsci, intellectuals could be divided into two clearly different groups. Those he termed traditional intellectuals normally served the current ruling class and had a worldview that can be traced to earlier periods of historical development. Roman Catholic intellectuals who defended the power of the church against various anticlerical or secular demands would be examples of this traditional category. On the other hand, there also existed organic intellectuals whose skills and beliefs critical of the established order helped create a new counter-hegemonic world view for a new progressive class. A prime example of this would be the working class in capitalist society. This is vital because in normal times without this development "subaltern classes, by definition, are not united and cannot unite."

The history of why and how the oppressed classes have functioned is one of the tasks of the organic intellectual. Particularly since the 1960s these ideas have influenced a generation of historians such as the American Eugene Genovese, to look to the complex web of belief, tradition, and institutional power to explain the actions of the common people. Critics, such as Perry Anderson, have argued in response that Gramsci overemphasized the importance of consent while downplaying the power of the state as a repressive historical force. Be that as it may, Gramsci's attempt to add a less deterministic and more cultural element to traditional Marxism has inspired a wealth of rich historical work.

The writings of Gramsci have especially been a touchstone for historians, such as Harvey Kaye, who seek to understand the interplay of ideas and action – of the rulers and the ruled. Gramsci's intellectual framework provides an alternative embraced by many historians as they seek to avoid the twin pitfalls of dogmatic Marxism and conservative "end of history" proponents. Neither wedded to an economic determinist theory nor joined to a fanciful theory of "great men," Gramsci prompted historians to re-examine the importance of culture and ideas within a Marxist framework. Even those historians who reject many basic Marxist tenets are nonetheless compelled to acknowledge the usefulness of Gramsci's contribution.

WILLIAM A. PELZ

See also African American; Anderson, P.; Crime; Croce; De Sanctis; Garin; Ginzburg; Halperín-Donghi; Joll; Leisure; Marxist Interpretation; Oral; Pieroni Bortolotti; Rudé; Scott, James; Scribner; Spriano; State; Subaltern; Takaki; United States: 19th Century

Biography

Born Ales, Sardinia, 23 January 1891. Studied linguistics and philosophy, University of Turin, 1911–14. Journalist: founder/editor, *La Città Futura*, and *L'Ordine Nuova*, 1919; political organizer: Italian representative to the Comintern, 1922–23; general secretary, Italian Communist party, 1924–26; elected parliamentary deputy, 1924. Imprisoned by fascist regime, 1926–37. Married Giulia Schuct in Soviet Union (1 son). Died Rome, 27 April 1937.

Principal Writings

Quaderni del carcere, 6 vols., written 1926–37, published 1948–51; selections in English as *Selections from the Prison Notebooks*, 1971

Lettere del Carcere, 1947; selections in English as *Letters from Prison*, 1973 and 2 vols., 1994

Opere di Antonio Gramsci (Collected Works), 12 vols., 1947–72

History, Philosophy and Culture in the Young Gramsci, 1975

Selections from Political Writings, 2 vols., 1977–78

Selections from Cultural Writings, 1984

A Gramsci Reader: Selected Writings, 1916–1935, edited by David Forgacs, 1988

Further Reading

Anderson, Perry, "The Antinomies of Antonio Gramsci." *New Left Review*, no.100 (November 1976–January 1977), 5–80

Genovese, Eugene D., "On Antonio Gramsci," *Studies on the Left* 7(2) (March-April, 1967), 83–107

Joll, James, *Antonio Gramsci*, New York: Viking, 1977; London: Penguin, 1978

Kaye, Harvey J., *The Powers of the Past*, Minneapolis: University of Minnesota Press, and London: Harvester Wheatsheaf, 1991

Sassoon, Anne Showstack, *Gramsci's Politics*, New York: St. Martin's Press, and London: Croom Helm, 1980

Greece: Ancient

The history of ancient Greece is traditionally divided into three periods, whose titles are drawn from art history: the Archaic period, from the 8th century BCE to the Persian invasions of Greece in 490–479 BCE; the Classical period, from 479 to the death of Alexander the Great in 323 BCE; and the Hellenistic period, from 323 to the annexation of the Ptolemaic Egypt by the Romans in 30 BCE. Archaeological work continues to throw light on the period before the 8th century, but the absence of significant written evidence makes it impossible to consider a history of the period.

The historiography of Greece started in the 5th century BCE with Herodotus, whose *Histories* described relations between the Greeks and their Eastern neighbors down to the period of the Persian invasions. Thucydides, while ostensibly writing a history of the Peloponnesian War (431–404), provided a narrative of earlier 5th-century history that linked his work with that of Herodotus. Thucydides' account broke off at 411, and a number of writers continued the narrative: one of these accounts, Xenophon's *Hellenica*, survives, taking the narrative down to 362. By this time a tradition was established of writing what were essentially narratives of the recent past and of contemporary events; this tradition continued in the Greek world throughout antiquity. Didorus Siculus, writing in the 1st century BCE, and basing his work on earlier writers, produced a history of the world in 40 books from the myths of the Egyptians and others down to c.60, of which the first half, going down to 301, and focusing on the Greek world, including Sicily, survives largely intact, but the rest only in fragments. Not much remains from the Hellenistic period, but substantial parts of the work of Polybius do survive, covering the period 264–146. His *Universal History* was a conscious attempt to link the histories of the various parts of the Mediterranean, and thus covered Rome and Carthage as well as the Greek world.

Between antiquity and the late 18th century there was little significant historiographical work on ancient Greece, beyond the editing and translation of the ancient writers. In the 18th century interest in the surviving monuments of Greece increased, but this antiquarianism was not accompanied by an interest in re-examining the history of the period, until the American War of Independence stimulated a renewed interest in Greek history.

The first modern narrative political histories of Greece were William Mitford's *The History of Greece* (1784–1810), and John Gillies' *The History of Ancient Greece* (1786). Neither author was a professional historian, and both works were intended to highlight the dangers of democracy. The history of Athens in the 5th century BCE was put forward as a warning for democrats who sympathized with the American cause. In the fourth volume of his work Mitford drew an explicit contrast between the constitution of Britain on the one hand, and classical Athens and revolutionary France on the other. In opposition to the antidemocratic ideology of Mitford, George Grote published his very influential *History of Greece* in 1846–56. Grote divided Greek history into two parts, "legendary Greece," and "Grecian History," covering the period down to about 280, which he saw as marking the end of Greek freedom. Grote's defence of Athenian democracy was regarded as overzealous, but the work was enormously influential, dominating approaches to Greek history not only in Britain but also in Germany until the end of the century. The most important history by a German scholar was probably that of K.J. Beloch (1893), and he further influenced Gaetano de Sanctis in Italy, whose history of Athens was published in 1898. The influence of these 19th-century historians was immense. The basic narrative of history established by Grote has not been significantly challenged, and much of his interpretation is still accepted. J.B. Bury published a history of Greece in 1900 which, edited by Russell Meiggs in 1975, remains a standard school textbook in Britain at the end of the 20th century.

Interest in the history of Greece inevitably meant above all interest in classical Athens, and as well as political histories there were attempts to use epigraphic and numismatic evidence, for example in August Böckh's *Die Staatshaushaltung der Athener* (1817; *The Public Economy of Athens*, 1828), and later in the century Jacob Burckhardt's *Griechische Kulturgeschichte* (1898–1902; *The History of Greek Culture*, 1963). The 19th century also saw histories of the Hellenistic period, the first being Gillies' *The History of the World from the Reign of Alexander to That of Augustus* (1807), whose narrative of a divided Greek world eventually overcome by Rome has been seen as reflecting the condition of Europe facing Napoleon. J.G. Droysen's *Geschichte des Hellenismus* (History of Hellenism, 1836–43), covering the same period, had a rather different agenda, arguing that the fusion of Greek and Oriental cultures in the Near East after the conquests of Alexander provided the conditions for the birth of Christianity.

The main developments in the study of ancient Greece in the first half of the 20th century resulted from the work of archaeologists, who radically changed perceptions of the earliest periods of Greek history and prehistory, and from developments in comparative philology and anthropology. These latter led to increased interest in social life, and perhaps above all in Greek religion, with the publication in 1903 of the first edition of Jane Ellen Harrison's *Prolegomena to the Study of Greek Religion*. Archaeology added greatly to knowledge about Greek colonization in the Archaic period, and this brought an increased interest in areas such as trade and commerce, scarcely mentioned in the literary sources on which history had been largely based. Epigraphy and papyrology also contributed to the understanding of the Hellenistic period, with substantial contributions to the history of the Hellenistic world; in England by W.W. Tarn, and in particular in France by Maurice Holleaux and Claire Préaux.

The study of Greek and Roman history has always been closely linked with the study of classical literature, and one of the consequences of this has been that, especially in the German- and English-speaking worlds, a resistance to what are seen as ideologically driven approaches to history. Rather there has been a Rankean concern with establishing the facts. In part this is due to the nature of the subject, since there are large areas of Greek history where even the most basic outline of events is hard to establish. As a result Greek history has seldom been characterized by major debates about interpretation. Marxism has had some influence on Greek historiography, for example Rostovtzeff's *The Social and Economic History of the Hellenistic World* (1941) and G.E.M. de Ste Croix, *The Class Struggle in the Ancient Greek World* (1981), but the theses of these works have not won widespread acceptance.

An important and influential attempt to bring more method into Greek history was the work of Moses Finley. His *The Ancient Economy* (1973) put forward a Weberian analysis of economic activity in the ancient world that had previously been argued for by Hasebroek in *Staat und Handel im alten Griechenland* (1928; *Trade and Politics in Ancient Greece*, 1933), but had not been much noticed. Finley's picture of trade as more or less marginal to the social and political life of the ancient Mediterranean has won considerable acceptance as far as it applies to the Greek world, even if it is less attractive to Roman historians. Finley's other contribution was a general emphasis on method, most explicitly in his final book, *Ancient History: Evidence and Models* (1985). He criticized the failure of ancient historians to make use of models, and was particularly hostile to regional studies based on detailed analysis of archaeological, epigraphic, papyrological, and literary evidence, which, because of their lack of any theoretical approach, he dismissed as antiquarianism.

Although classical archaeology has been dominated by art historical scholarship, some archaeologists have produced work of wider historical importance. In particular A.M. Snodgrass, following the approach of V. Gordon Childe, has used archaeology to cast light on social developments not only in Archaic Greece but also during the Classical period. An area of study that has developed, particularly in the 1980s and afterwards, has been the emergence of the Greek city-states from the so-called Dark Age in the 8th century BCE. Here evidence from Greek literature, archaeology, and comparative anthropology have been used fruitfully by Snodgrass and other scholars influenced by him.

Very important work on Greek social history has been done by French structuralist scholars, above all J.-P. Vernant, but also Vidal-Naquet and Marcel Detienne. The interest in areas such as myth and its relationship with the culture and society of ancient Greece has had wider implications. Institutions of Greek cities that have previously been seen as the subject of traditional political history or even of military history, for example the hoplite phalanx, can be shown to relate to the basic structures of Greek thought that are the subject of myth and are articulated in art as well as literature. Above all this approach has produced important work on religion, and has indicated how thoroughly religion pervaded all areas of Greek life.

One of the effects of this kind of structuralist approach has been to raise new questions about that nature of politics in the ancient world. Finley emphasized the differences between ancient and modern ideas of politics and democracy, and more recent examinations of the workings of the Athenian democracy, such as those of M.H. Hansen, have emphasized the need to analyze Greek political systems on their own terms, rather than introducing anachronistic ideological assumptions. This has also led to a recognition that social and cultural activities cannot be divorced from politics. Following the work of Michel Foucault, the second volume of whose history of sexuality is concerned with ancient Greece, there has been considerable work on homosexuality and on issues of gender. One of the most important writers in this area has been Winkler.

The nature of the evidence has meant that Athens has been the best-studied Greek city-state, but important work has been done on Sparta, above all by Paul Cartledge, who has moved from a basically Marxist position to one that draws on post-structuralist ideas.

There is a steady stream of general works on the major areas, of which a few are listed below. Sometimes they conceal a polemical agenda beneath an apparently straightforward title, but they are the best route to recent research.

HUGH BOWDEN

See also Beloch; Burckhardt; Diodorus; Droysen; Finley; Foucault; Rostovtzeff; Sanctis; Thucydides; Universal; Vernant; Xenophon

Further Reading

Böckh, August, *Die Staatshaushaltung der Athener*, 2 vols., Berlin: Realschulbuchhandlung, 1817; in English as *The Public Economy of Athens*, 2 vols., London: Murray, 1828

Burckhardt, Jacob, *Griechische Kulturgeschichte*, 4 vols., Berlin; Spemann, 1898–1902; in English as *The History of Greek Culture*, New York: Ungar, 1963

Bury, J.B., *A History of Greece to the Death of Alexander the Great*, London: Macmillan, 1900, revised in 2 vols., 1902; 4th edition, 1975

Cartledge, Paul, *Agesilaos and the Crisis of Sparta*, London: Duckworth, and Baltimore: Johns Hopkins University Press, 1987

Cartledge, Paul, *The Greeks: A Portrait of Self and Others*, Oxford and New York: Oxford University Press, 1993

Davies, John Kenyon, *Democracy and Classical Greece*, Hassocks, Sussex: Harvester, and Atlantic Highlands, NJ: Humanities Press, 1978; revised 1993

de Ste. Croix, G.E.M., *The Class Struggle in the Ancient Greek World: From the Archaic Age to the Arab Conquests*, London: Duckworth, and Ithaca, NY: Cornell University Press, 1981

Detienne, Marcel, *Les Maîtres de vérité dans la Grèce archaïque*, Paris: Maspero, 1967; in English as *The Masters of Truth in Archaic Greece*, New York: Zone, 1996

Droysen, J.G., *Geschichte des Hellenismus* (History of Hellenism), 2 vols., Hamburg: Perthes, 1836–43

Finley, Moses I., *The Ancient Economy*, London: Chatto and Windus, and Berkeley: University of California Press, 1973

Finley, Moses I., *Ancient History: Evidence and Models*, London: Chatto and Windus, 1985; New York: Viking, 1986

Foucault, Michel, *Histoire de la sexualité*, vol. 2: *Les Usages des plaisirs*, Paris: Gallimard, 1980; in English as *The History of Sexuality*, vol. 2: *The Use of Pleasure*, New York: Pantheon, and London: Allen Lane, 1985

Gillies, John, *The History of Ancient Greece, Its Colonies and Conquests: From the Earliest Accounts till the Division of the Macedonian Empire in the East*, 2 vols., London: Strahan Cadell, 1786

Gillies, John, *The History of the World from the Reign of Alexander to That of Augustus*, London: Strahan Cadell and Davies, 1807; Philadelphia: Farrand Mallory, 1809

Gordon, Richard Lindsay, ed., *Myth, Religion, and Society: Structuralist Essays*, Cambridge and New York: Cambridge University Press, 1981

Green, Peter, *Alexander to Actium: The Historical Evolution of the Hellenistic Age*, London: Thames and Hudson, and Berkeley: University of California Press, 1990

Grote, George, *History of Greece*, 12 vols., London: Murray, 1846–56; New York Harper, 1853–72

Hansen, Mogens H., *Die athenische Volksversammlung im Zeitalter des Demosthenes*, Constance: Universitäts Verlag, 1984; in English as *The Athenian Assembly in the Age of Demosthenes: Structure, Principals, and Ideology*, Oxford and New York: Blackwell, 1987

Harrison, Jane Ellen, *Prolegomena to the Study of Greek Religion*, Cambridge: Cambridge University Press, 1903

Hasebroek, Johannes, *Staat und Handel im alten Griechenland: Untersuchungen zur antiken Wirtschaftsgeschichte*, Tübingen: Mohr, 1928; in English as *Trade and Politics in Ancient Greece*, London: Bell, 1933; New York: Biblo and Tannen, 1967

Holleaux, Maurice, *Rome, la Grèce et les monarchies hellénistiques au III siècle (273–205) avant J.C.* (Rome, Greece and the Hellenistic Monarchies 273-205 BCE, Paris: Boccard, 1921; reprinted 1969

Mitford, William, *The History of Greece*, 5 vols., London: Murray and Robson, 1784–1810

Momigliano, Arnaldo, *Studies in Historiography*, London: Weidenfeld and Nicolson, and New York: Harper, 1966

Murray, Oswyn, *Early Greece*, Brighton: Harvester, and Atlantic Highlands, NJ: Humanities Press, 1980; 2nd edition, 1993

Préaux, Claire, *Le Monde hellénistique: la Grèce et l'Orient de la mort d'Alexandre à la conquête romaine de la Grèce, 323–146, avant J.C.* (The Hellenistic World: Greece and the Orient from the Death of Alexander to the Roman Conquest of Greece, 323-146 BCE), 2 vols., Paris: Presses Universitaires, 1978–92

Rostovtzeff, M.I., *The Social and Economic History of the Hellenistic World*, Oxford: Oxford University Press, 1941; revised 1953

Snodgrass, Anthony M., *Archaic Greece: The Age of Experiment*, London: Dent, and Berkeley: University of California Press, 1980

Snodgrass, Anthony M., *An Archaeology of Greece: The Present Shape and Future Scope of the Discipline*, Berkeley: University of California Press, 1987

Tarn, William Woodthorpe, and Guy Thompson Griffith, *Hellenistic Civilisation*, London: Arnold, 1927; revised 1952

Vernant, Jean-Pierre, *Mythe et société en Grèce ancienne*, Paris: Maspero, 1974; in English as *Myth and Society in Ancient Greece*, Hassocks, Sussex: Harvester, and Atlantic Highlands, NJ: Humanities Press, 1980

Vidal-Naquet, Pierre, *Le Chausseur noir: formes de pensée et formes de société dans le monde grec*, Paris: Maspero, 1981; in English as *The Black Hunter: Forms of Thought and Forms of Society in the Greek World*, Baltimore: Johns Hopkins University Press, 1986

Walbank, Frank W., *The Hellenistic World*, Brighton: Harvester, and Atlantic Highlands, NJ: Humanities Press, 1981; revised 1992

Winkler, John J., *The Constraints of Desire: The Anthropology of Sex and Gender in Ancient Greece*, New York: Routledge, 1990

Greece: Modern

The year 1821 is indisputably regarded as the beginning of modern Greek history. The revolutionary struggle that started in this year, and led to the establishment of an independent Greek state eleven years later, placed Greece back on the European map after more than three centuries of Ottoman rule. In the ensuing years, Greek history has reflected the attempts of the state to find an effective formula of government, to accommodate its territorial ambitions, to unite its population, and to modernize, both politically and economically. Distinct events have changed its course: apart from the Revolution, the eventful reign of king Otto, the defeat of 1897 by the Ottoman empire, the Balkan Wars (1912–13), the two World Wars, the defeat of 1922, the Civil War (1946–49), and the military dictatorship (1967–74). Historiography on modern Greece has mainly concentrated on these watersheds, assessing their importance for the course of modern Greek history.

The struggle for independence has attracted considerable attention, both as a movement for national self-determination and from the viewpoint of its international repercussions. In *The Struggle for Greek Independence* (1973), a volume edited by Richard Clogg, the intellectual preparation carried out by Greek Enlightenment thinkers was underlined, but at the same time emphasis was placed upon foreign support for the struggle in the form of *Philhellenism*. The same author has edited *The Movement for Greek Independence, 1770–1821* (1976), an invaluable collection of translated primary material that provides an analysis of the intellectual and social forces that paved the way for the revolution. Another interesting approach to the Greek struggle for independence was offered by Douglas Dakin in *The Greek Struggle for Independence, 1821–1833* (1973), which attempted to incorporate the revolution into a wider European context of intellectual and political change. The author noted the impact of European thought upon Greek intellectuals, but also traced the gradual resuscitation of a Greek identity as the Ottoman grip became less and less effective. Finally, the translation of General Makriyannis' *Memoirs* (1966) provided a fresh, disarmingly honest, and vividly narrated contemporary account of the struggle from the viewpoint of an illiterate, yet conscientious and idealistic 19th-century military man.

The period between independence and World War I is presented by the historiography as a struggle for internal modernization and territorial expansion. The ambitious, yet failed attempts of the first governor of modern Greece to modernize the state were analyzed in C.M. Woodhouse's *Capodistrias* (1973). At the same time, the emergence of the vision of a Greater Greece – often known as the "Great Idea" – has been perceived as the point of reference for Greek foreign policy from the 1860s until 1922. Douglas Dakin's *The Greek Struggle in Macedonia, 1897–1913* (1966, reprinted 1993) recorded the systematic policies of the Greek state to expand northwards and eastwards. The book revealed that such was the political momentum of the Great Idea that, despite the humiliating defeat of 1897, Greece multiplied its efforts to incorporate Macedonia, culminating in the highly successful campaigns of the two Balkan Wars (1912–13). On the other hand, Michael Llewellyn Smith's *Ionian Vision* (1973) analyzed the last chapter of the Great Idea, reaching its peak with the Treaty of Sèvres (1920) and collapsing irreversibly with the defeat of 1922 and with the

1923 Treaty of Lausanne. The year 1923 is generally presented as the cataclysmic end to an illusion of greatness, which established Greece's geographical position and redirected the efforts of the Greek state into the goal of domestic consolidation and modernization.

The implications of World War II for Greece are mainly analyzed from the viewpoint of the Nazi occupation (1941–44) and the ensuing Civil War (1946–49). The implementation of the Nazi "New Order" in Greece was meticulously examined in Mark Mazower's *Inside Hitler's Greece* (1995). The liberation in 1944 found Greece divided, both ideologically and socially, and Heinz Richter's *British Intervention in Greece* (1985) traced the origins of this divide that, by 1946, had escalated into the bloody civil war. Richter also concentrated on the significance of British foreign policy toward Greece during the crucial period 1945–46. L.S. Wittner's *American Intervention in Greece, 1943–1949* (1982) approached the same issues from the viewpoint of the American interests in the region, and supplied an account of the international implications of the struggle until its conclusion in 1949. Another interesting and more recent contribution to the study of the Greek Civil War is the volume edited by Lars Baerentzen, John O. Iatrides, and Ole L. Smith: *Studies in the History of the Greek Civil War* (1987). Again, apart from the domestic aspects of the conflict, emphasis was placed on the international dimensions of the Civil War, as a prelude and symptom of the growing confrontation between western and eastern blocs.

The military dictatorship of 1967–74 and the subsequent complications over Cyprus constitute the final clear watershed in modern Greek history. In the long endeavor of Greek society for stability and modernization the April 1967 coup and the junta are regarded as traumatic setbacks. In their *I "Figli del sole"* (1965; *Fascism Today*, 1969) Angelo Del Boca and Mario Giovana emphasized the "fascist" element of the regime and viewed the junta as one part of a reactionary revival not only within Greece, but also in the whole of Europe after 1945. Richard Clogg and George Yannopoulos edited the volume *Greece under Military Rule* (1972), in which they examined the ideology of the regime and assessed its impact upon the political and social structures of postwar Greece. However, implicit in the analysis is the realization that the collapse of the regime in 1974 initiated a new chapter in Greek history, with the promise of a more unwavering progress toward democracy and socioeconomic modernization. In this vein, Clogg's *Parties and Elections in Greece* (1987), and the collection of contributions in *Greece in the 1980s* (1983), edited by the same author, highlighted the emergence of a new, more stable political framework in Greece and accounted for the dramatic changes in the make-up of Greek society and economy – changes that have brought the country closer to a definite European orientation.

General historical accounts of modern Greece broach all the above major issues and at the same time offer a comprehensive overview of the continuities and discontinuities in the course of modern Greek history. Among a number of such works, Clogg's *A Short History of Modern Greece* (1979) has provided a concise, yet poignant analysis of the main trends and developments. Similar coverage is found in C.M. Woodhouse's *The Story of Modern Greece* (1968). Finally, *Modern Greece* (1968), by John Campbell and Philip Sherrard, placed equal emphasis

on the analysis of both developments and institutions, thus highlighting factors such as the diachronical social significance of the Orthodox church and the long-term qualities of the Greek state, economy, and culture.

ARISTOTLE A. KALLIS

See also Eastern Orthodoxy; Ottoman

Further Reading

Baerentzen, Lars, John O. Iatrides, Ole L. Smith, eds., *Studies in the History of the Greek Civil War*, Copenhagen: Museum Tusculanum Press, 1987

Campbell, John, and Philip Sherrard, *Modern Greece*, London: Benn, and New York: Praeger, 1968

Clogg, Richard, and George Yannopoulos, eds., *Greece under Military Rule*, London: Secker and Warburg, and New York: Basic Books, 1972

Clogg, Richard, *The Struggle for Greek Independence*, London: Macmillan, and Hamden, CT: Archon, 1973

Clogg, Richard, ed. and trans., *The Movement for Greek Independence, 1770–1821: A Collection of Documents*, London: Macmillan, 1976

Clogg, Richard, *A Short History of Modern Greece*, Cambridge: Cambridge University Press, 1979; New York: Cambridge University Press, 1986

Clogg, Richard, ed., *Greece in the 1980s*, London: Macmillan, and New York: St. Martin's Press, 1983

Clogg, Richard, *Parties and Elections in Greece: The Search for Legitimacy*, London: Hurst, and Durham, NC: Duke University Press, 1987

Dakin, Douglas, *The Greek Struggle in Macedonia, 1897–1913*, Thessaloniki: Institute for Balkan Studies, 1966; reprinted 1993

Dakin, Douglas, *The Greek Struggle for Independence, 1821–1833*, Berkeley: University of California Press, and London: Batsford, 1973

Del Boca, Angelo, and Mario Giovana, *I "Figli del sole,"* Milan: Feltrinelli, 1965; in English as *Fascism Today*, New York: Pantheon, 1969, London: Heinemann, 1970

Finlay, George, *History of the Greek Revolution*, 2 vols., Edinburgh: Blackwood, 1861

Gordon, Thomas, *History of the Greek Revolution*, 2 vols., London: Cadell, 1832

Llewellyn Smith, Michael, *Ionian Vision: Greece in Asia Minor, 1919–1922*, London: Allen Lane, and New York: St. Martin's Press, 1973

Makrygiannes, Ioannes, *Apomnemoneumata*, Athens: Vagionake, 1947; in English as *The Memoirs of General Makriyannis, 1797–1864*, London: Oxford University Press, 1966

Mazower, Mark, *Inside Hitler's Greece*, New Haven: Yale University Press, 1995

Richter, Heinz A., *British Intervention in Greece: From Varkiza to Civil War, February 1945 to August 1946*, London: Merlin, 1985

Wittner, Lawrence S., *American Intervention in Greece, 1943–1949*, New York: Columbia University Press, 1982

Woodhouse, Christopher M., *The Story of Modern Greece*, London: Faber, 1968

Woodhouse, Christopher M., *Capodistrias: The Founder of Greek Independence*, London and New York: Oxford University Press, 1973

Woodhouse, Christopher M., *Modern Greece: A Short History*, London: Faber, 1977; revised 1991

Green, Alice Stopford 1847–1929

Irish political historian

Alice Stopford had an eclectic, largely autodidactic, liberal education which affected her work as a historian. Her father was an archdeacon in the Church of Ireland in Kells, County Meath, and she had the run of his library, teaching herself German, Greek, and metaphysics by the age of 16. In 1873, she attended lectures in physics in Dublin's College of Science. After the death of her father, Alice settled in Chester with her mother and sister. She began to visit the lively households of family and friends in London where she came into contact with the denizens of London's bohemian world, as well as intellectuals and political figures, including her future husband, the historian John Richard Green, who had recently completed his *A Short History of the English People* (1874). After they married, in 1877, they collaborated on *A Short Geography of the British Islands*, which appeared in 1879. She then worked as her husband's research assistant and secretary until his death in 1883. J.R. Green had been an important influence on her thinking as a historian; his death was a devastating loss.

After her husband's death, Green determined to make a career for herself. She began by preparing a revised edition of his *Short History*. Shortly afterwards, in 1888, she published a brief life of Henry II aimed at school-age students. Over the next few years, she conducted research on a pioneering historical work: the 2-volume *Town Life in the Fifteenth Century* (1894). Concentrating on a neglected period that had attracted the attention only of political historians, the book's emphasis on aspects of European social history made it an important early work in the field. It assured Mrs. Green, as she was often referred to in print, that her thoughts on historical topics would be respected by other members of the profession.

Green made the best of her position and reputation as a woman of letters and a scholar. According to her biographer, R.B. McDowell, she loved the company of other intellectuals and was robust in conversation on any topic. Her London home remained a favorite meeting place for scholars, politicians, and social and political activists until, in 1918, she returned to Ireland, where she continued to welcome a wide range of guests in her home in Dublin. She was active in many causes of the day. She gave away one-third of her income each year; visited captured Boer soldiers on St. Helena; and in 1901 founded the Africa Society, serving as its vice-president and helping to edit its journal. Green interpreted British imperial problems in Africa in the light of her Irish nationalist perspective, which had begun to develop under her late husband's influence.

By 1900 she had become absorbed by the Irish nationalist struggle for independence and the Gaelic revival, a movement which aimed to preserve the Irish language and culture. Her writing during the next twenty years combined her scholarly research interests with political propaganda, a genre which attracted dozens of nationalist and unionist historians and intellectuals during this vibrant period. The Irish scholar Eoin MacNeill provided her with information about and translations of Irish sources for the medieval period in the Historical Manuscripts Commission, the Calendars of the State Papers, and the Public Record Office, enabling her to work as a historian again.

In her first work in Irish history, *The Making of Ireland and Its Undoing, 1200–1600* (1908), Green described Ireland's flourishing commercial networks, manufacturers, and learning which she maintained were destroyed by Tudor imperialism in Ireland. *The Old Irish World* (1912) and several subsequent articles and essays responded to some critics' charges that she had not made a convincing case that Ireland had been as flourishing as she maintained. She returned to her favorite theme in 1925 in her last book, *The History of the Irish State to 1014*. Her most important book during this period, however, was *Irish Nationality* (1911). Dedicated to "The Memory of the Irish Dead," she surveyed Irish history from the arrival of the ancient Gaels through the 19th century. She declared that ancient Ireland was characterized by the shaping of a true democracy: the masses participated in a diversified national life and shared a common ethos. Subsequent Irish history, she continued, was the record of the people consciously acting within the spirit of that nation to safeguard its traditions from the cultural conquest of foreigners. She believed that, over time, the people of Ireland had become divided racially and culturally; nevertheless, she stated that all of the Irish people maintained their claim to a government of their own, one that would bind together the whole nation and create prosperity. As such, she was one of a number of nationalist writers in this period who praised the spirit of a nation that was largely Gaelic and Catholic but, at the same time, attempted to convince Irish unionists and Protestants that their place in an Irish state under a home rule government would be both secure and valued. Her writing, however, proved more useful to nationalist propagandists than convincing to unionists. During the Irish war for independence, 1916–21, she wrote two political pamphlets, *Ourselves Alone in Ulster* and *Loyalty and Disloyalty: What It Means in Ireland*, in which she attacked unionists for their determined, and ultimately successful, effort to partition the country.

After independence, she supported the pro-Treaty side during the Irish Civil War, 1922–23. She served in the Irish Senate, where she spoke in favor of reconciliation. The last few years of her life were spent writing her *History of the Early Irish State* and some textbooks for Irish schools.

LAWRENCE W. MCBRIDE

Biography

Alice Sophia Amelia Stopford Green. Born Kells, County Meath, Ireland, 1847. Educated by governesses, but largely self-taught. Married historian J.R. Green 1877 (died 1883). Active in London and Dublin intellectual circles; helped to found the Africa Society, 1901, and the School of Irish Studies, 1903; active in the Irish nationalist and Gaelic revival movements. Member, Irish Senate, 1922–29. Died Dublin, 28 May 1929.

Principal Writings

With J.R. Green, *A Short Geography of the British Islands*, 1879
Henry II, 1888
Town Life in the Fifteenth Century, 2 vols., 1894
"Women's Place in the World of Letters," *Nineteenth Century* (June 1897)
The Making of Ireland and Its Undoing, 1200–1600, 1908
Irish Nationality, 1911
The Old Irish World, 1912
The Irish National Tradition, 1917

Loyalty and Disloyalty: What it Means in Ireland, 1918
Ourselves Alone in Ulster, 1918
The Government of Ireland, 1921
The Irish and the Armada, 1921
The History of the Irish State to 1014, 1925
Studies from Irish History, vols. 1–2, 1927

Further Reading

McDowell, Robert Brendan, *Alice Stopford Green: A Passionate Historian*, Dublin: Figgis, 1967

Greene, Jack P. 1931–

US historian of colonial and revolutionary America

A prolific essayist, master of synthesis, editor of 18th-century pamphlets and Landon Carter's seminal diary; editor and co-editor of a substantial number of collections of conference papers on colonial and revolutionary themes, of works on historiography and of reference as well as documentary collections for student use; one-time editor of the *William and Mary Quarterly* and long-time professor of History at Johns Hopkins University, Jack P. Greene is also the author of four major interpretive studies in political, constitutional, social and intellectual history.

Never reluctant to acknowledge the influence of an earlier generation of scholars, or to challenge the latest orthodoxy, Greene has excelled in discerning historiographical trends and imposing order on the ever burgeoning and increasingly fragmented field of social history while pushing forward the historian's agenda. Though his interest in political ideas, structures of power, personal and political identities, and patterns of behavior could be construed as elitist and his interpretation of the Virginia gentry has been challenged, Greene was among the first scholars to embrace the concept of an Atlantic world and to recognize its myriad influences in shaping American developments. Not only do his writings incorporate grand theory, they are also duly sensitive to cross-cultural developments.

Greene's talent for delineating structures of power and identifying political processes was evident in his first major published work, *The Quest for Power* (1963), in which he examined the specific powers acquired by representative legislatures. Although the theme was hardly new, his systematic and quantitative approach served to clarify the constitutional position that the colonists sought to defend from the very real threat posed by Parliament and the even greater challenge presented by the king and his ministers. Thus, the Declaration of Independence was "a fairly accurate statement of grievances as the signers saw them."

Standing much 20th-century scholarship on its head, Greene argued in *Peripheries and Center* (1986) that the transition from colonial status to nationhood was marked not by discontinuity but rather by continuity. While the problem of where ultimate authority lay had led to the dissolution of the early British empire, separation from Britain did not settle the question nor was it resolved by the creation of the federal Constitution. In this volume Greene moved towards the view propounded by Black, Reid, and Gray on the legitimacy of the colonial cause arguing that where authority and ideology at the center were weak and local power and traditions were strong, "local institutions and customs may be at least as important in determining existing legal and constitutional arrangements as those at the center." Underpinning the movement for independence, the emergence of American national government, and an American nationality were the overlapping processes of Americanization and Anglicization.

The issue of Americanization and Anglicization was more fully explored in Greene's masterly synthesis *Pursuits of Happiness* (1988) which drew together much of the new social history of the previous twenty years. Arguing that there was a common pattern of development among the regions of Britain's early Atlantic empire – the Chesapeake, the Middle Colonies, the Lower South, New England, the Atlantic islands of Bermuda and (to a much lesser extent) the Bahamas, and the West Indian islands – where, after an initial period of social simplification, creolized variants of institutions, structures, and values found in England were articulated and elaborated in the settler societies. Furthermore after 1660, the differences between regions were diminished by a powerful process of social and cultural convergence whereby the regions of British colonial America became both more creole and more metropolitan. New England excepted, these regions had possessed "little common purpose and no unified social vision."

In his examination of the changing contemporary definitions of America from Columbus to the American Revolution and the creation of the republic, *The Intellectual Construction of America* (1993), Greene explored European responses to America and the meanings given to its discovery. Although initially America was a place which Europeans interpreted in terms of their own past and whose inhabitants they classified according to Christian and classical categories, in British America especially, the Revolution lifted Americans' "own sense of self," sharpening the concept of America as an exceptional country where land and resources were boundless. The idea of American exceptionalism was firmly rooted in this period; it was not the creation of 19th-century American historians, although their ideas would be subsequently supplemented and distorted by postwar consensus writers. Greene rejected the notion advanced by some critics that Americanization and Anglicizisation invalidated the exceptionalist argument. That the colonies were more like Europe at the point when they separated from it, the recognition of deep social divisions in American society, and the knowledge that much of the success associated with early America was facilitated by the killing and removal of Native Americans and the exploitation of African slaves were not incompatible with contemporary perceptions of America as a special place, a rankless rather than a classless society "in which all free people occupied the same social status in relationship to the law and enjoyed an equality of opportunity to strive for and earn respect."

The causes and consequences of the American Revolution are central to an understanding of Greene's work. His position on the causes of the Revolution, essentially a conservative one and unchanged over the decades, is clear enough: it was a conflict undertaken to secure for British Americans the same individual rights and autonomy that Englishmen enjoyed at home, becoming a quest for independence only when compromise proved impossible on both sides. In the 1970s he wrote a series of essays devoted to defining the character of the

Revolution and elaborating its rhetoric. The emergence of a "new republican paradigm" and the demand for a more inclusive history together with the recognition that victory brought new and unforeseen problems shifted the focus of historians from causes to consequences. Greene edited *The American Revolution: Its Character and Limits* (1987), which addressed problems raised but not resolved by the winning of independence. This was followed by *Understanding the American Revolution: Issues and Actors* (1995), which posed the question of why from the perspective of its leaders the Revolution remained incomplete. By looking at the quarter century after the war, it was possible to define the specific limits of the revolutionary impulse. Consistent with the emergent culture he identified in *Pursuits of Happiness* Greene maintained that the primary concerns of most independent Americans "were private rather than public." Civic virtue was not the foundation of the new republic. The private orientation of American society set limits on the political potentialities of the American Revolution. The pursuit of individual happiness was "the primary shaping social value. "

GWENDA MORGAN

See also Bailyn; British Empire; Gipson; United States: Colonial; United States: American Revolution

Biography

Jack Phillip Greene. Born Lafayette, Indiana, 12 August 1931. Received BA, University of North Carolina, 1951; MA, Indiana University, 1952; graduate study, University of Nebraska, 1952–55, University of Bristol, 1953–54; PhD, Duke University, 1956. Served in the US Army Reserve, Military Intelligence, 1956–63. Taught at Michigan State University, 1956–59; Case Western Reserve University, 1959–65; University of Michigan, 1965–66; and Johns Hopkins University from 1966. Married 1) Sue Neuenswander, 1953 (marriage dissolved 1990; 1 son, 1 daughter); 2) Amy Turner Bushnell, 1990.

Principal Writings

The Quest for Power: The Lower Houses of Assembly in the Southern Royal Colonies, 1689–1776, 1963
Editor, *The Diary of Colonel Landon Carter of Sabine Hall, 1752–1778*, 2 vols., 1965
Editor, *Settlements to Society, 1584–1763*, 1966
Editor, *Colonies to Nation, 1763–1789*, 1967
Editor, *The Reinterpretation of the American Revolution, 1763–1789*, 1968
Editor with Robert Forster, *Preconditions of Revolution in Early Modern Europe*, 1970
Editor with David W. Cohen, *Neither Slave nor Free: The Freedmen of African Descent in the Slave Societies of the New World*, 1972
"The Social Origins of the American Revolution: An Evaluation and an Interpretation," *Political Science Quarterly* 88 (1973), 1–22
All Men Are Created Equal: Some Reflections on the Character of the American Revolution, 1976
"Society, Ideology and Politics: An Analysis of the Political Culture of Mid-Eighteenth-Century Virginia" in Richard M. Jellison, ed., *Society, Freedom and Conscience: The American Revolution in Virginia, Massachusetts, and New York*, 1976
Editor with J.R. Pole, *Colonial British America: Essays in the New History of the Early Modern Era*, 1984
Editor, *Encyclopedia of American Political History*, 3 vols., 1984
Peripheries and Center: Constitutional Development in the Extended Polities of the British Empire and the United States, 1607–1788, 1986

Political Life in Eighteenth-Century Virginia, 1986
Editor, *The American Revolution: Its Character and Limits*, 1987
Pursuits of Happiness: The Social Development of Early Modern British Colonies and the Formation of American Culture, 1988
Editor with J. R. Pole, *The Blackwell Encyclopedia of the American Revolution*, 1991
Imperatives, Behaviors and Identities: Essays in Early American Cultural History, 1992
The Intellectual Construction of America: Exceptionalism and Identity from 1492 to 1800, 1993
Negotiated Authorities: Essays in Colonial Political and Constitutional History, 1994
Understanding the American Revolution: Issues and Actors, 1995
Interpreting Early America: Historiographical Essays, 1996

Gregory of Tours 538/9–594/5
Frankish historian

Among the historians who described the events of the immediately post-Roman period in western Europe, it was bishop Gregory of Tours who wrote the biggest book. His *Historiae* (Histories), conventionally but misleadingly known as the *History of the Franks*, is for the most part concerned with the history of Gaul, both secular and religious. Gregory begins with the creation of Adam, but his account becomes steadily more detailed as he approaches his own time, and the final six of his ten books offer a detailed account of the period 575–591.

Much of Gregory's narrative is taken up with the history of the Franks, who came to power over most of Gaul in the late 5th and early 6th centuries, and his presentation of their deeds demands of the reader a strong stomach. It moved from the time of Clovis (481–511), a "great and outstanding fighter" whose career is represented as a succession of wars and murders relieved by baptism, to that of Gregory's contemporaries, whom he warned to desist from their incessant fighting lest they be defeated by foreign enemies. Like many subsequent authors, Gregory was made uneasy by the vigor and bellicose tendencies of the early Merovingian dynasty.

He seems to have begun writing soon after becoming bishop of Tours in 573. It is therefore not surprising that his work emphasizes the importance of the episcopacy in the society of the 6th century, although some passages suggest that not everyone saw eye to eye with the bishops as to the desirability of this situation. A man with a firm conviction of his own orthodoxy, Gregory speaks as a member of the establishment, in the voice of a Catholic bishop from a good family. Hence his enthusiasm for the conversion to Catholicism of king Clovis, an event which he saw as being similar to the conversion of the emperor Constantine, and his detestation for the kingdoms ruled over by heretical Arians, the history of whom he was not above distorting.

Gregory's convictions ensured that he had a lively sense of the supernatural, which can create problems for modern readers. Unlike many medieval authors who were content to tell stories of miracles of which other people were the beneficiaries, Gregory described them as happening to himself, as when the presence of relics of saints saved him and other people on a boat from drowning. His surviving minor works tell of the lives and posthumous miracles worked by a number of saints, in particular St. Martin of Tours, the patron of the see over which Gregory presided, and suggest an optimistic view of the world that may be implied in the *Histories* but which is not always to the fore.

There is no doubt that Gregory makes demands on his readers. Sometimes he gives the appearance of finding his subject matter out of control; the sheer press of facts and the lack of clear focus or overt organizing principle can be disconcerting. This apparent confusion has implausibly been held to reflect the confusion of his times, or to be connected with his Latin style, which is less tightly-ordered than that of classical historians. But Gregory's apparent incoherence owes much to his method of organizing his material chronologically, often on a year-by-year basis, which necessarily makes the development of themes hard to trace, and to his penchant for interrupting the flow of the narrative with colorful stories, frequently of a kind that demonstrate the power of the episcopal class of which he was a member. These stories are among the most interesting parts of the *Histories*, and they often include dialogue, the presentation of which Gregory clearly enjoyed. While they are enlivening, they lend parts of the work an anecdotal character.

It is largely because of Gregory that the history of post-Roman Gaul is known in such detail. We may probe his work in vain to discover general theories, but had Gregory spelt one out it would hardly have been of a kind to appeal to modern susceptibilities. The wealth of information he provides, however irritating and biased its presentation may be, ensures that, among the former provinces of the Roman empire in the West, the basic outline of events is better known for Gaul than for any other region.

JOHN MOORHEAD

See also France: to 1000

Biography
Georgius Florentius Gregorius. Born Arvernus (now Clermont-Ferrand), 30 November 538/9, from important Gallo-Roman clerical families on both sides. Entered church as boy; studied under archdeacon Avitus at Clermont, then deacon to bishop Nicetius; appointed bishop of Tours, 573. Died Tours, 17 November 594/5.

Principal Writings
Historiae (Histories); in English as *History of the Franks*, 1927
Works, in *Monumenta Germaniae Historica: Scriptores rerum Merovingicarum*, 1951

Further Reading
Auerbach, Erich, *Mimesis: dargestellte Wirklichkeit in der abendländischen Literatur*, Bern: Francke, 1946; in English as *Mimesis: The Representation of Reality in Western Literature*, Princeton: Princeton University Press, 1953
Auerbach, Erich, *Literatursprache und Publikum in der lateinischen Spätantike und im Mittelalter*, Bern: Francke, 1958; in English as *Literary Language and Its Public in Late Latin Antiquity and the Middle Ages*, New York: Pantheon, and London: Routledge, 1965
Bonnet, Max, *Le Latin de Grégoire de Tours* (The Latin of Gregory of Tours), Paris: Hachette, 1890
Goffart, Walter, *The Narrators of Barbarian History* (AD550–800): *Jordanes, Gregory of Tours, Bede, and Paul the Deacon*, Princeton: Princeton University Press, 1988
Hellmann, Siegmund, "Studien zur mittelalterlichen Geschichts-schreibung, 1: Gregor von Tours" (Studies in Medieval Historical Writing: Gregory of Tours), *Historische Zeitschrift* 107 (1911), 1–43
Monod, Gabriel, *Etudes critiques sur les sources de l'histoire mérovingienne* (Critical Studies on the Sources for Merovingian History), 2 vols., Paris: Francke, 1872–85
Nie, Giselle de, *Views from a Many-Windowed Tower: Studies of Imagination in the Works of Gregory of Tours*, Amsterdam: Rodopi, 1987
Oldoni, M., "Gregorio di Tours e i *Libri Historiarum*, letture e fonti, metodi e ragioni" (Gregory of Tours and the *Books of Histories*: Readings and Sources, Methods and Motives), *Studi Medievali* 13 (1972), 563–700
Pietri, Luce, *La Ville du Tours de IVe au VIe siècle: naissance d'une cité chétienne* (The City of Tours from the 4th to the 6th Centuries: Birth of a Christian City), Rome: Ecole Française de Rome, 1983
Thürlemann, Felix, *Der historische Diskurs bei Gregor von Tours: Topoi und Wirklichkeit* (The Historical Discourse in Gregory of Tours: Topoi and Reality), Bern: Lang, 1974
Wallace-Hadrill, J.M., *The Frankish Church*, Oxford and New York: Oxford University Press, 1983
Weidemann, Margarete, *Kulturgeschichte der Merowingerzeit nach den Werken Gregors von Tours* (The Cultural History of the Merovingian Period in the Works of Gregory of Tours), 2 vols., Mainz: Verlag des Romisch-Germanischen Zentralmuseums, 1982
Wood, Ian N., *The Merovingian Kingdoms, 450–751*, London: Longman, 1994

Grimshaw, Patricia 1938–
Australian (New Zealand-born) feminist historian

One of Australia's leading feminist and family historians, Patricia Grimshaw has also contributed to the historiography of New Zealand and the United States. Since her early publications in the 1970s, she has maintained a commitment to the retrieval function of feminist history and to the importance of exploring women's agency.

Her 1972 publication, *Women's Suffrage in New Zealand*, stands as the path-breaking work in New Zealand feminist historiography, although as Grimshaw herself has noted, the study was largely written in the 1960s before either the development of "women's history" or the emergence of second wave feminism in New Zealand. Nevertheless, as a work that sought to retrieve a group which previously had been "hidden from history," it heralded one of the dominant themes in Australian and New Zealand women's history during the 1970s and beyond, the need to recover a hitherto ignored past.

Grimshaw's more recent contribution to American historiography through her work on American missionary wives in 19th-century Hawaii, *Paths of Duty* (1989), demonstrates her continuing dual commitment to resurrecting previously ignored groups of women and interpreting their lives within a framework that emphasizes women's agency while simultaneously acknowledging the social structures which constrained them.

It is through her combination of interests in both the history of families and the history of women that Grimshaw has established herself as one of Australia's best known historians. In 1979 she argued for the need to combine the work of historians of the family with those who examined women's public role: "it is imperative that studies which offer a broad overview of historical change in women's history attempt to synthesize the two approaches." Her emphasis on the role of women within the context of familial relations led her to reject the interpretations offered by the first major feminist histories in Australia, published in the 1970s, which presented Australian women as profoundly and perhaps uniquely oppressed. Instead, Grimshaw argued that there was "a fair degree of sexual equality" within the colonial family.

Although she would subsequently modify her stance on the degree of equality that existed within Australian colonial families, Grimshaw's rejection of what she regards as the "woman as victim" analysis of some feminists remained constant. Her concomitant emphasis on women's capacity to negotiate and actively construct their own lives has been central to many of her publications in the 1980s and 1990s; these include studies of Australian families in the 19th and 20th centuries, the feminist and temperance advocate Bessie Lee Harrison, and the reactions of late 19th-century Australian socialists, both male and female, to "the woman question." Grimshaw's investigation of the experiences of women of European heritage in Australia and New Zealand offers a rare instance of a comparative approach within the feminist historiography of these countries.

While primarily interested in the history of Anglo-Celtic families, Grimshaw has also contributed to Aboriginal history. In particular, her 1981 chapter, "Aboriginal Women: A study of Culture Contact" is significant as one of the earliest studies by a white feminist academic in Australia that recognized the fundamentally different historical experiences of Aboriginal and non-Aboriginal women.

Grimshaw's major role, however, remains as a historian of white women and their families, particularly in the 19th century. She further explores these themes as a co-author of *Creating a Nation* (1994), the first general history of Australia to foreground women's experiences. In addition to her role as an author, Grimshaw has facilitated the development of her two major fields of inquiry, family and feminist history, through her role as a co-editor. *Families in Colonial Australia* (1985) remains the major collection on the former subject, while Grimshaw's co-editorship of *Australian Women: Feminist Perspectives* (1981) and *Studies in Gender* (1992) represent important contributions to the latter area.

JOANNE SCOTT

See also Australia; Women's History: Australia

Biography

Patricia Ann Grimshaw. Born Patricia Ann Sinclair, Auckland, 16 December 1938. Studied at University of Auckland, BA 1960, MA 1963; University of Melbourne, PhD 1986. Taught (rising to professor) University of Melbourne, from 1977. Married Roger Hamilton Grimshaw, 1961 (2 daughters, 2 sons).

Principal Writings

Women's Suffrage in New Zealand, 1972
"Women and the Family in Australian History: a Reply to *The Real Matilda*," *Historical Studies* 18 (1979), 412–21
Editor with Norma Grieve, *Australian Women: Feminist Perspectives*, 1981
Editor with Lynne Strahan, *The Half-Open Door: Sixteen Modern Australian Women Look at Professional Life and Achievement*, 1982
Editor with Chris McConville and Ellen McEwen, *Families in Colonial Australia*, 1985

"Bessie Harrison Lee and the Fight for Voluntary Motherhood" in Marilyn Lake and Farley Kelly, eds., *Double Time: Women in Victoria – 150 Years*, 1985, 139–47
"'Man's Own Country': Women in Colonial Australian History" in Norma Grieve and Ailsa Burns, eds., *Australian Women: New Feminist Perspectives*, 1986, 182–209
With John Lack, "Households," in Bill Gammage and Peter Spearritt, eds., *Australians 1938*, 1987, 197–221
"Tasman Sisters: Lives of 'the Second Sex'" in Keith Sinclair, ed., *Tasman Relations: New Zealand and Australia, 1788–1988*, 1987, 224–45
"Only the Chains Have Changed," in Verity Burgmann and Jenny Lee, eds., *Staining the Wattle: A People's History of Australia since 1788*, 1988, 66–86
Paths of Duty: American Missionary Wives in Nineteenth-Century Hawaii, 1989
Editor with Ruth Fincher and Marion Campbell, *Studies in Gender: Essays in Honour of Norma Grieve*, 1992
"The 'Equals and Comrades of Men?': *Tocsin* and 'the Woman Question,'" in Susan Magarey, Sue Rowley, and Susan Sheridan, eds., *Debutante Nation: Feminism Contests the 1890s*, 1993, 100–13
With Marilyn Lake, Ann McGrath and Marian Quartly, *Creating a Nation*, 1994
With Andrew May, "'Inducements to the Strong to Be Cruel to the Weak': Authoritative White Colonial Male Voices and the Construction of Gender in Koori Society," in Norma Grieve and Ailsa Burns, eds., *Australian Women: Contemporary Feminist Thought*, 1994, 92–106
Editor with Marian Quartly and Susan Janson, *Freedom Bound 1: Documents on Women in Colonial Australia*, 1995

Further Reading

Janson, Susan, "Writing Australian Women's History," *Melbourne Historical Journal* 13 (1981), 40–44

Groulx, Lionel 1878–1967
French Canadian historian

Lionel Groulx was arguably the most important French-Canadian historian of the 20th century. During a career that spanned over six decades he was both a significant public personality committed to the use of history as a tool that might instill a sense of nationalism among French-speaking Quebecers and a leading figure in the professionalization of historical writing in Quebec.

Groulx was initially attracted to the study of the past in the midst of the significant changes that Quebec was experiencing in the late 19th and early 20th centuries. While Quebec had been conquered by the British in the late 18th century, French-speakers had managed to avoid assimilation, from Groulx's perspective, by having remained relatively isolated in rural areas where their language and their Catholic heritage had kept them apart from the conquerors who were largely English-speaking and Protestant. By the start of the 20th century, however, French-speakers were increasingly moving to cities, with the result that well-educated young men such as Groulx were concerned that their people might soon be assimilated. These men formed various nationalistic organizations designed to encourage French Canadians to remain true to their roots, and Groulx, a newly ordained priest, calculated that he could best contribute by teaching young Quebecers about their past.

Groulx never entirely abandoned this selfconscious use of history as a nationalistic tool. He wrote and spoke extensively to a general audience in order provide Quebecers with the means to confront the problems of the day. Along the way he invariably referred to the past in order to remind French-speakers of their roots, often depicting them as having hailed from a small band of religious-minded people who had long ago made the journey from France. In the process, he tended to be critical of those who had emigrated to Quebec since the end of French rule, and he was particularly harsh in his depiction of the Jews who had come to Quebec in significant numbers in the early 20th century.

Because of Groulx's anti-Semitism, he has been shunned over the past three decades by historians, largely lay persons with a more professional training, who have tended to depict him as a primitive historian from some distant past. In Groulx's own mind, however, there was a distinction between the "popular" and the professional historian. The first had an obligation to inform the masses about "their past in order to recognize the fragility of their nation. While [he] should never distort the past, he needs to focus upon those facts which might encourage a sense of patriotism . . ." On the other hand, there was the more professional historian who needed "to be completely free to develop an objective view of the past based upon the use of appropriate historical methods."

Groulx's more professional side was evident, for instance, in the way in which his depiction of the Quebec past evolved over the course of the century. At the start of his career, he held a view of Quebec history that focused on the struggle of his people for survival in the face of the English conquerors, and he gave a special role to Catholicism for having provided a bulwark against assimilation. He went so far in some of his early writing as to suggest that French-speakers had been blessed with a providential mission in North America. This perspective distinguished Groulx from earlier historians who had played down either the cataclysmic nature of the conquest or the central role of Catholicism. Over the course of his career, this perspective evolved as Groulx, in spite of his lack of professional training, proved to be a conscientious researcher who remained relatively well informed about changing trends in the discipline. Accordingly, his later works, and in particular his *Histoire du Canada français* (A History of French Canada, 1950–52), his grand overview of the history of French Canada from its beginnings up to the end of World War II, dispensed with the notion that much of the French-Canadian experience had been dictated by a higher power. Instead he now recognized that material factors had played a major role in shaping the fate of his people, in the process pushing the role of religion to the side.

By the 1950s, however, Quebec society was urbanizing at an unprecedented rate and its French-speaking majority was beginning to play a more central role in the economy. Groulx's own increasingly materialistic view of the past reflected these changes in the larger society, but he could not keep up with the younger, postwar historians who viewed French Canadian history from an entirely materialistic perspective. Ironically, however, these historians had profited from Groulx's role in establishing the infrastructure for a more professional view of the past. Over the course of the 1940s Groulx had been the driving force behind the establishment of the first formally

constituted history department in a French-language university, and had established both the professional association of and the professional journal for Quebec historians.

In the final analysis, Groulx's legacy was an ambiguous one. On the one hand, he held certain views that were ill-suited to a secular, urban, and ethnically diverse society. On the other hand, he was a modern historian whose views, within certain limits, were subject to change and who believed in the value of both archival research and the free exchange of views among historians who belonged to a common profession.

RONALD RUDIN

See also Canada; Frégault; Séguin

Biography
Lionel-Adolphe Groulx. Born Vaudreuil, 13 February 1878, son of a farmer. Studied classics and theology at Sainte-Thérèse, Valleyfield, and Montreal seminaries; doctoral study in philosophy and theology, Rome, 1906–08. Ordained 1903; taught literature, Valleyfield, 1903–06, 1908–15; professor of history, University of Montreal, 1915–48. Contributor/editor, *Action Française*, 1920–28; contributor, *Action Nationale*, 1920–28; founder/editor, *Revue d'Histoire de l'Amérique Française*, 1946–67. Died Vaudreuil, 23 May 1967.

Principal Writings
Histoire du Canada français depuis la découverte (A History of French Canada since Its Discovery), 2 vols., 1950–52
Notre grande aventure: l'empire français en Amérique du nord, 1535–1760 (Our Grand Adventure: The French Empire in North America, 1535–1760), 1958
Le Canada français missionnaire: une autre grande aventure (French Canadian Missionaries: Another Great Adventure), 1962

Further Reading
Berger, Carl, *The Writing of Canadian History: Aspects of English-Canadian Historical Writing, 1900–1970*, Toronto: Oxford University Press, 1976; 2nd edition Toronto: University of Toronto Press, 1986
Delisle, Esther, *Le Traître et le juif: Lionel Groulx, le devoir et le délire du nationalisme d'extrême droite dans la province du Québec, 1929–1939*, Outrement, Quebec: L'Etinelle, 1992; in English as *The Traitor and the Jew: Anti-Semitism and Extreme Right-Wing Nationalism in Quebec from 1929 to 1939*, Toronto: Davies, 1993
Frégault, Guy, *Lionel Groulx: tel qu'en lui-mème* (Lionel Groulx: As He Was), Ottawa: Leméac, 1978
Gaboury, Jean-Pierre, *Le Nationalisme de Lionel Groulx: aspects idéologiques* (Ideological Aspects of the Nationalism of Lionel Groulx), Ottawa: Editions de l'Université d'Ottawa, 1970
Gagnon, Serge, *Le Québec et ses historiens*, Quebec: Presses de l'Université Laval, 1978; in English as *Quebec and Its Historians, 1840–1920*, Montreal: Harvest House, 1982, and *Quebec and Its Historians: The Twentieth Century*, Harvest House, 1985
Lamarre, Jean, *Le Devenir de la nation québécoise selon Maurice Séguin, Guy Frégault et Michel Brunet, 1944–1969* (The Future of the Quebec Nation According to Maurice Séguin, Guy Frégault, and Michel Brunet, 1944–1969), Sillery, Quebec: Septentrion, 1993
Rudin, Ronald, "Revisionism and the Search for a Normal Society: A Critique of Recent Quebec Historical Writing," *Canadian Historical Review* 73 (1992), 30–61
Trofimenkoff, Susan Mann, ed., *Abbé Groulx: Variations on a Nationalist Theme* Toronto: Copp Clark, 1973
Trofimenkoff, Susan Mann, *Action française: French Canadian Nationalism in the Twenties*, Toronto: University of Toronto Press, 1975

Gsell, Stéphane 1864-1932

Swiss historian of North Africa

Born to a Swiss Protestant family from St. Gall which had recently moved to Paris, Stéphane Gsell was educated at the Ecole Normale Supérieure and then spent four years at the Ecole Française de Rome, where he worked on a thesis on the emperor Domitian. Published in 1894, it provided the dominant view on many aspects of Domitian's life and reign for several decades. As a biography of the emperor it has only just been replaced by Brian W. Jones' 1992 work. In Rome Gsell also developed archaeological interests, conducting highly praised excavations of an Etruscan cemetery at Vulci. The influence of the ecclesiastical historian Louis Duchesne led him to become increasingly committed to the study of late antiquity and particularly the history and archaeology of North Africa, most of which was then under French rule.

In 1890 Gsell was appointed to a teaching post at the Ecole des Lettres in Algiers, and in the following year became involved in the excavations at Tipasa. Here in 1892 he discovered the site of the large 4th-century basilica, containing an important mosaic inscription, and he also uncovered the martyrium of the town's patron saint, Salsa. After the Tipasa excavations he accompanied Henri Graillot on an expedition in 1893-94 to record postclassical antiquities in the area north of the Aurès mountains. Their report was published in the *Mélanges de l'Ecole Française de Rome* and provided a substantial amount of information on the Donatist presence in this region. This was one of Gsell's major contributions to illuminating the history of this long-lived schismatic group. Gsell's very unfavorable 1895 review of the ground-breaking study by the young German scholar Walter Thümmel, which tried to identify Donatism with indigenous cultural opposition to Rome and therefore to the Catholic church in North Africa, may well have been another, even if it did not succeed in putting a permanent end to such interpretations.

From 1895 to 1904 Gsell, now appointed professor in the Ecole in Algiers, contributed an annual account of current excavations in North Africa to the Rome *Mélanges*, under the title of "Chronique archéologique africaine." In 1901, having become inspector of antiquities in Algeria, he published his important 2-volume *Monuments antiques d'Algérie* (Ancient Monuments of Algeria), which recorded all the then known ancient buildings in the region, organized by category, and included a large corpus of early Christian monuments. This was followed from 1902 by the gradual compiling of his *Atlas archéologique de l'Algérie* (Archaeological Atlas of Algeria), which he completed in 1911. This consisted of fifty maps, with a scale of 1/200,000, accompanied by more than 500 pages of commentary, and it continues to serve as a vital research tool in the study of Roman and Byzantine sites in Algeria, especially at present since the country is now almost inaccessible.

From his time in Rome onwards Gsell collected and published new inscriptions. He devised a plan for a large-scale edition with commentary of *Les Inscriptions latines d'Algérie* (Latin Inscriptions of Algeria), of which the initial volume appeared in 1922. This was devoted to the area of the Roman province of Africa Proconsularis, and it substantially augmented the collection of inscriptions to be found in the equivalent volume of the

Corpus Inscriptionum Latinorum (Corpus of Latin Inscriptions) of 1881. Unfortunately, this project remained incomplete at the time of Gsell's death. He continued to take an active part in excavations, notably of the church at Henchir Akhrib in Numidia, and at Thibilis. In general, Gsell's involvement in the excavation, study, and publication of numerous early Christian sites in Algeria probably represents his scholarly activity with the greatest long-term significance. Married in 1909, he lost his wife in childbirth the following year. This contributed to his decision to leave Algeria, and in 1912 he returned to Paris, where he had been appointed to a professorship of North African history in the Collège de France. He did, however, retain his office of inspector of monuments and museums, and returned to Algeria for extended visits each year thereafter.

In Paris Gsell devoted himself to preparing a monumental *Histoire ancienne de l'Afrique du Nord* (Ancient History of North Africa, 1913-28). By the time of his death he had published eight volumes of this work, but it had only extended as far as the end of the Mauritanian kingdom of Juba II in 39 CE. Being exceedingly well grounded in the epigraphic and literary sources, his work has retained much of its authority as a detailed narrative of events. More recent archaeological work, however, such as the Anglo-American excavations in Carthage, and modern methodological advances in historical scholarship have diminished its value as an interpretation of pre-Roman North Africa. On a smaller scale, in 1927 he contributed the opening section of a *Histoire d'Algérie* (History of Algeria), which he wrote together with Georges Marçais and Georges Yver. This was actually a revision of a small book, *L'Algérie dans l'antiquité* (Algeria in Antiquity), that he had first published in 1900.

Throughout his scholarly career Gsell published articles and reviews. Some of these proved exceedingly influential, notably "La Tripolitaine et le Sahara au IIIe siècle de notre ère" (Tripolitania and the Sahara in the Third Century CE, 1926). In this particular case, his view that the camel was introduced into North Africa only during the Roman period, with significant consequences for the development of nomad raiding, has been shown to be mistaken. Even so, Gsell's standing as one of the founding fathers of the study of the Christian archaeology of North Africa remains unassailable, and it is for his *Monuments antiques* and his *Atlas archéologique*, perhaps much more than for his unfinished *Histoire*, that he will be remembered.

ROGER COLLINS

Biography

Stéphane Charles Emile Gsell. Born Paris, 7 February 1864, to a Swiss family recently settled in France. Educated at the Lycée Louis-le-Grand; Ecole Normale Supérieure, 1883-86; Ecole Française, Rome, 1886-90. Taught (rising to professor) at Ecole des Lettres, Algiers, 1890-1904; involved in archaeological work from 1891: inspector of antiquities for Algeria, 1901-32; professor of North African history, Collège de France, 1912-32. Married, 1909 (wife died 1910). Died 1 January 1932.

Principal Writings

Essai sur le règne de l'empereur Domitien, 1894
L'Algérie dans l'antiquité (Algeria in Antiquity), 1900; revised 1903
Monuments antiques d'Algérie (Ancient Monuments of Algeria), 2 vols., 1901

Atlas archéologique de l'Algérie (Archaeological Atlas of Algeria), 1911
Histoire ancienne de l'Afrique du Nord (Ancient History of North Africa), 8 vols., 1913–28
Les Inscriptions latines d'Algérie (Latin Inscriptions of Algeria), 1922
"La Tripolitaine et le Sahara au IIIe siècle de notre ère" (Tripolitania and the Sahara in the Third Century CE), *Mémoires de l'Académie des Inscriptions et Belles-Lettres* (1926)
With Georges Marçais and Georges Yver, *Histoire d'Algérie* (History of Algeria), 1927

Further Reading
Albertini, Eugène, "Stéphane Gsell," *Revue Africaine* 73 (1932), 20–53
Frend, William H.C., *The Archaeology of Early Christianity: A History*, London: Geoffrey Chapman, and Minneapolis: Fortress Press, 1996

Gu Jiegang [Ku Chieh-kang] 1893–1980
Chinese historian

Gu Jiegang's most significant contribution as a historian was his theory on the layered construction of ancient Chinese history, which first gained major influence in 1923. This theory has already been analyzed and summarized by many scholars. Its main ideas can be presented as follows: 1) the accounts of the early "history" of China reached further back into antiquity the more recently they were produced; 2) the central figures of these early legends tend to appear more idealized in records composed in more recent periods; 3) even if we cannot discover all the true facts of early Chinese antiquity, at least we can find the earliest forms these legends took in "historical" records; 4) the study of the evolution of the legends about Chinese antiquity is an important field in itself.

In the development of his own intellectual paradigm, Gu Jiegang had several sources of inspiration. The first was the new intellectual atmosphere propagated by the May Fourth movement of 1919. After the movement, Chinese intellectuals had a greater tendency to doubt all aspects of the Chinese tradition. Leading intellectuals such as Hu Shi (1891–1962) called for a critical re-examination of the intellectual and scholarly heritage of China.

Second, Gu Jiegang found inspiration in his enjoyment of folk theater. He found that when several operas described the same story, the operas written in later periods tended to have more elaborate plots. This fact led him to wonder whether historical accounts about ancient sage emperors evolved in the same way.

Third, Gu Jiegang adapted and developed the research of Confucian classicists of the "New Text" tradition. Some New Text classicists of the late Qing (1644–1911) period argued that Confucian classics of the "Ancient Text" tradition were actually forgeries composed in the 1st century CE. While Gu Jiegang generally accepted New Text classicists' conclusions concerning the Ancient Text classics, he did not share their reverence for the New Text classics. In fact, Gu Jiegang also used Ancient Text classicists' criticism on the New Text classics to show that these texts were not reliable sources of ancient history either. To Gu Jiegang, Confucian classics were no longer to be viewed as sacred texts to be studied with faith, but as historical sources to be analyzed and questioned.

Gu Jiegang's theory of layered construction launched him to the leadership in the field of ancient history in China. Indeed, the large amount of work on ancient texts and on ancient history inspired by his theory has been known as the *Gushi bian* (Critiques of Ancient History) movement, named after the title of a 7-volume collection of essays by various scholars published under his supervision from 1926 to 1941.

Some of Gu Jiegang's particular conclusions about ancient texts and ancient history have since been overturned. However, his general idea of layered construction of ancient Chinese history is still an inspiration to historians of early China. Moreover, Gu Jiegang's influence on Chinese historical studies reached beyond the spread of his own theory. He showed a genuine interest in helping fellow historians in the development of their careers, even when they disagreed with his ideas about history. He even included essays refuting his own ideas in the volumes of *Gushi bian*. In this way, Gu Jiegang encouraged intellectual tolerance and open debate by his own example.

XIAO-BIN JI

See also China: Ancient; China: Modern

Biography
Born Suzhou, 1893, from a scholar-gentry family. Tutored in Chinese classics before studying philosophy, University of Beijing, 1913–20. Taught at University of Beijing, 1920–26; editor, Commercial Press, 1922–24; professor of history, universities in Zhongshan, 1927–29; Nanjing, 1929–31; Beijing, 1931–37; Yunnan, 1938–39; Qilo, 1939–41; National Central, 1941–43; Fudan, 1943–46; and Shanghai, 1949–54; appointed head of History Department, Academia Sinica (now Academy of Social Sciences), 1954: executive member, 1977–80. Died Beijing, 1980.

Principal Writings
With others *Gushi bian* (Critiques of Ancient History), 7 vols., 1926–41; reprinted 1982; preface in English as *The Autobiography of a Chinese Historian*, 1931
Dangdai Zhongguo shixue (Contemporary Chinese Historiography), 1947

Further Reading
Gray, J., "Historical Writing in Twentieth-Century China: Notes on Its Background and Development," in William G. Beasley and Edwin G. Pulleyblank, eds., *Historians of China and Japan*, Oxford: Oxford University Press, 1961
Gu Chao, *Gu Jiegang nianpu* (Chronological Biography of Gu Jiegang), Beijing: Zhongguo shehui kexue, 1993
Hummel, Arthur W., "What Chinese Historians Are Doing in Their Own History," *American Historical Review*, 34 (1929), 715–24
Richter, Ursula, "Gu Jiegang: His Last Thirty Years," *China Quarterly* 90 (1982), 286–95
Richter, Ursula, *Zweifel am Altertum: Gu Jiegang und die Diskussion über Chinas Alte Geschichte als Konsequenz der "Neuen Kulturbewegung,"* c.1915–1923 (Doubts on Antiquity: Gu Jiegang and the Discussion on China's Ancient History as a Consequence of the New Culture Movement, 1915–23), Stuttgart: Steiner, 1992
Schneider, Laurence A., *Ku Chieh-kang and China's New History: Nationalism and the Quest for Alternative Traditions*, Berkeley: University of California Press, 1971

Wang Fansen, *Gu shi bian yundong de xingqi, yige sixiangshi de fenxi* (The Rise of the "Critiques of Ancient History" Movement: An Analysis in Intellectual History), Taibei: Yunchen, 1987

Wang Xuhua, *Gu Jiegang xuanji* (Selected Works of Gu Jiegang), Tianjin: Tianjin renmin, 1988

Yoshihiko Ogura, *Kōnichi senka no Chūgoku chishikijin: Ko Ketsu-gō to Nihon* (A Chinese Intellectual during the War of Resistance against the Japanese: Gu Jiegang and Japan), Tokyo, 1987

Yü Ying-shih, "Gu Jiegang, Hong Ye yu Zhongguo xiandai shixue" (Gu Jiegang, William Hung and Modern Historiography of China), in Yü Ying-shih, *Shixue yu chuantong* (History and Tradition), Taibei: Shibao wenhua, 1982

Guha, Ranajit 1922–

Indian historian

Ranajit Guha has made original and important contributions to the study of the history of India under European colonialism and to anticolonial historiography. His first monograph, *A Rule of Property of Bengal* (1963), traced the influence of French physiocratic ideas on British land-management policy in 18th-century colonial Bengal. Its methodological innovation consisted of finding a place for the autonomy of intellectual history in the study of colonial economic policy, usually treated, before Guha's book and Eric Stoke's *The English Utilitarians and India* (1959), simply as a matter of colonial administrative response to historical exigencies. Guha's second monograph, *Elementary Aspects of Peasant Insurgency in Colonial India* (1983), was published after he started editing the *Subaltern Studies* series. Both *Elementary Aspects* and *Subaltern Studies*, which initially brought together a band of nine younger historians from India, Australia, and the UK and for whom Guha was an intellectual mentor, pursued an agenda of history-writing that was novel and somewhat different from the "history from below" approach that English historians had developed. The distinguishing marks were the emphases that Guha and his colleagues placed on various kinds of relationships of domination and subordination in studying the history of "subaltern" or socially subordinated groups – the word "subaltern" was Gramscian in origin – in colonial South Asia and elsewhere. Indeed, colonialism itself was treated in this history as akin to domination.

In *Elementary Aspects* and in articles published in the 1980s and the 1990s, Guha broached a series of new questions with regard to the ways peasant rebellions in South Asia had been understood and depicted in elitist colonial and nationalist archives, and proposed certain innovative strategies for reading these archives so that the peasant or the subaltern could be seen as the subject(s) of their own histories. It would not be an exaggeration to say that Guha introduced into Indian historiography the Benjaminian practice of reading the archives "against the grain." By drawing on the insights of literary criticism, Sanskrit grammar and of structural anthropology and linguistics, Guha produced some original suggestions as to how the presence of relationships of power – and hence of peasant-agency as well – could be tracked in documents left by ruling groups and classes. At the same time, the book drew attention to subaltern modes of mobilization and communication for the purpose of resistance to oppression. Guha's point was to underline the (relative) autonomy of subaltern lives *vis-à-vis* the cultures of both nationalist and colonial elites. *Elementary Aspects* contains the first serious discussion, for example, of the role and structures of rumors in peasant insurgencies of colonial India. Guha also argued, both here and in a series of articles in *Subaltern Studies* and elsewhere, his thesis that there were two domains of politics in Indian modernity, the elite-domain based on European/bourgeois grammar of constitutionalism and organized public life, and a relatively autonomous domain of subaltern politics, both coming together in the workings of Indian democracy but operating on distinctly different understandings of power and rule. In a celebrated article, "Chandra's Death," where he examined a fragmentary early 19th-century court document bearing on the death of a low-caste Bengali woman forced to undergo abortion, Guha extended and modified this argument to take account of the inequalities of gender.

Another interest of Guha's has been the question of history itself. His Sakharam Ganesh Deuskar lectures, delivered at the invitation of the Centre for Studies in Social Sciences, Calcutta in 1987, and published as *An Indian Historiography of India* (1988), raised the question of the relationship between history-writing and colonial domination. He disputed the received view that, for Indians, the modern sense of history was something of a "gift" from the West. He situated the possibility for "an Indian historiography of India" within two struggles: nationalist struggles against colonialist rendering of India's pasts, and an internal struggle, among Indians, over the very nature of the past itself, between the "puranic" (*puranas*: mythical stories about Indian divinities) conception of time and the modern linear one that underlines secular history. Guha's work connects the issues of time, memory and history to some of the central questions of subaltern historiography itself. Are the memories of the subordinate classes – often expressed in puranic and other mythic times – to be subordinated to historiographies that can only serve the state? This is the central question at the heart of his essay "The Small Voice of History"; it is also at the very core of the critique he mounts of the so-called Cambridge school in his article entitled, "Dominance Without Hegemony and Its Historiography" (1989). Here, again, Guha returns to a fundamentally Gramscian problematic of *Subaltern Studies*: the nature of power of the state in India. It is his contention that precisely because the codes and understanding of power in India cannot be completely assimilated to the modern conception of power within which the state emerges, Indian history could not be written as though it were some kind of a spiritual biography of the colonial or modern Indian state. Instead, Guha attempts to approach the question of power in India by effecting a series of displacements in the fundamental terms of the usual vocabulary with which historians and political scientists speak of the Indian state.

His more recent writings, as yet unpublished, demonstrate a deepening interest in philosophies of language (both Indian and Western) and in representations of memory and time. A short note on "History as Cultural Criticism" appeals to Indian systems of logic to understand how the idea of "translation" was itself assimilated in many North Indian languages to a term that actually means "speaking after" (*anuvada*). His essay "Not at Home in Empire" studies some writings of Rudyard Kipling and George Orwell in order to understand modern colonialists' anxiety about being imperial, and a recent essay, "The Migrant's Time," turns to Heidegger in an effort to investigate questions of nostalgia, memory, and history among South Asians outside the subcontinent.

In summary, it may be said that Guha's work has been seminal in creating a variety of history which acts as a means for serious critical-theoretical reflection on the problem of modern colonialism and its intellectual and cultural legacies in the non-Western world.

DIPESH CHAKRABARTY

See also India; Subaltern

Biography
Born Siddhakati village, Bakarganj district, East Bengal, 23 May 1922, of a minor landowning family and son of a judge. Received BA, Presidency College, Calcutta; MA, University of Calcutta, 1946. Communist party activist, 1942–56. Went to Paris, 1947, and traveled widely in Europe, Asia, and North Africa, 1947–53; returned to academic career, 1953, teaching at colleges in Calcutta area; taught history, Jadavur University, 1958–59, and in England at University of Manchester, 1959–62; and University of Sussex, 1964–79; senior research fellow, Research School of Pacific Studies, Australian National University, 1980–87 (emeritus). Founder/editor, *Subaltern Studies: Writings on South Asian History and Society*, 1982–89. Married twice.

Principal Writings
The English Utilitarians and India, 1959
A Rule of Property of Bengal: An Essay on the Idea of Permanent Settlement, 1963
"On Some Aspects of the Historiography of Colonial India," *Subaltern Studies* 1 (1982)
Elementary Aspects of Peasant Insurgency in Colonial India, 1983
"The Prose of Counter Insurgency," *Subaltern Studies* 2 (1983)
"The Career of an Anti-God in Heaven and on Earth," in Ashok Mitra, ed., *The Truth Unites: Essays in Tribute to Samar Sen*, 1985
"Chandra's Death," *Subaltern Studies* 5 (1987), 135–65
An Indian Historiography of India: A Nineteenth-Century Agenda and Its Implications, 1988
Editor with Gayatri Chakravorty Spivak, *Selected Subaltern Studies*, 1988
"Dominance Without Hegemony and Its Historiography," *Subaltern Studies* 6 (1989), 210–309
"The Authority of Vernacular Pasts," *Meanjin* 51 (1992), 299–307
"Discipline and Mobilize," in Partha Chatterjee and Gyanendra Pandey, eds., *Subaltern Studies* 7 (1992), 69–120
"The Small Voice of History," in Shahid Amin and Dipesh Chakrabarty, eds., *Subaltern Studies* 9 (1996)

Further Reading
Amin, Shahid, and Gautam Bhadra, "Ranajit Guha: A Biographical Sketch," and Gautam Bhadra, "A Bibliography of Ranajit Guha's Writings," in David Arnold and David Hardiman, eds., *Essays in Honour of Ranajit Guha*, Delhi and New York: Oxford University Press, 1994 [*Subaltern Studies* 8]
Gupta, Dipankar, "On Altering the Ego in Peasant History: Paradoxes of the Ethnic Option," *Peasant Studies* 13 (1985), 5–24
Sathyamurthy, T.V., "Indian Peasant Historiography: A Critical Perspective on Ranajit Guha's Work," *Journal of Peasant Studies* 18 (1990), 92–144

Guicciardini, Francesco 1483–1540
Florentine humanist historian

Francesco Guicciardini's heavily detailed history of the Italian wars prior to 1535 so impressed Francesco De Sanctis (1817–83) that, despite his aversion to its author's code of conduct, he evaluated it as the most impressive intellectual work written by any Italian. Guicciardini's reputation as a historian has tended to fluctuate with intellectual trends. During the classical revival Lord Bolingbroke was to prefer "in every respect" Guicciardini's history to that of Thucydides; 75 years later Leopold von Ranke, whose paramount concern was the rigorous treatment of data, virtually destroyed the standing of Guicciardini's history in deeming it both derivative of secondary authorities and unreliable.

Unusually for a 16th-century work, virtually all of Guicciardini's autograph notes, drafts, and related papers for his history are extant and in one location, so its genesis can be reliably ascertained. It was drafted with much care over the last four years of the author's life, with some portions being reworked as many as seven times; it remained but a little unfinished at his death. Reportedly on his deathbed he asked that his history be destroyed. Doubtless he knew that his harsh anticlerical sentiments would prove unacceptable, as already the Council of Trent was strengthening sacerdotal authority. Probably his request for the work's destruction was not meant seriously, and was little more than a conscious classical echo, perhaps of Virgil regarding his *Aeneid*. Indeed Guicciardini had been determined that posterity should know him for his history: the Florentine artist Giuliano Bugiardini, when painting his portrait (now in Yale University Art Gallery), was instructed to depict the sitter glancing up from the page on which he had just written his history's opening words. From about 1543 the work was privately censored by the historian's nephew, Agnolo; this allowed it to be published in Florence, where its first 16 books were printed in 1561. The unfinished last four books, likewise edited by Agnolo, were first printed in Venice in 1564. From its initial publication the work bore the title *Storia d'Italia* (1561; *The History of Italy*, 1753–56), which, although not the writer's – he provided none – aptly epitomized the work's theme: how, over the forty years from 1494, the Italian peninsula's wealth and cultural preeminence in terms of Western Christendom was dissipated by the unified states of France and Spain, which through military might came in succession to control the politics of the peninsula.

Though written in Italian, *The History of Italy* had features associated with the humanistic histories of previous generations. Guicciardini had transcribed from Cicero's *De oratore* a passage with rules for the writing of history, which were placed facing his own text to serve as a guide. In his work the rhetoric of antiquity was retained with avowedly invented, paired orations, numbering some thirty in all. These, ostensibly declaimed by the two opposing generals on the eve of the battle, or by two statesmen with contrasting views at a time of crisis, were set-pieces to furnish the pros and cons of the situation. Second, only very occasionally did Guicciardini's text provide a date. Third, and to a degree that Polybius would have approved, Guicciardini's work focused on motives and on causes. Moreover his narrative was consciously annalistic in style, reminiscent of Livy and of Tacitus. The objective of such a presentation was to enable the reader to appreciate how events unfolded, and thus to reveal that what had been thought likely to happen by those involved in making decisions was but rarely the eventuality: by this means the historian avoided hindsight. The character of a person of influence (the only persons considered by Guicciardini) was given *ad seriatim*, so as to show how it changed over time in consequence of circumstances.

A humanist's view of history combined rhetoric and ethics in seeking to provide a code of conduct for present and future action. It was here that Guicciardini most radically parted from tradition. He concluded that individuals were consistently motivated by self-interest (as he himself certainly was). The consequence, when formulated as *raison d'état*, was the complete failure of the Italian powers to cope with foreign invasions, and so to avert the peninsula's ruin. For Guicciardini events never repeated themselves in their entirety, as the minute details he provided in his history were intended to demonstrate, and hence he had no models to offer. This view was reinforced for him because "Fortune" and God played their parts in human affairs, but were beyond human calculation. Accordingly for him there was an inevitability that rendered human action ineffective. Despite Ranke's adverse strictures, *The History of Italy* went far beyond the genre of humanist history in its provision of accurate details, based on firsthand information, as Guicciardini's notes, which Ranke never knew, make abundantly evident; a thorough study of his sources, however, is still lacking.

The History of Italy, written in Guicciardini's maturity, was his third attempt. Two previous histories concerned with Florence had been begun only to be abandoned in the interest of promoting his career; both were untitled and very far from complete. The so-called *Storie fiorentine dal 1378 al 1509* (1859; *History of Florence*, 1970) was begun in 1508 and left aside the following year. It was intended to be a continuous narrative from the Ciompi revolt of 1378 to at least 1509, with events from 1494 treated in depth. From late in 1527 until 1531 Guicciardini worked sporadically on what is called his *Florentine Affairs* (or *Florentine History*) (first published in 1945). Seemingly more traditional than his previous work, it commenced with the foundation of Florence. Though both these works are fragmentary, they have a value in revealing stages in Guicciardini's development as a historian. Strikingly, it is evident that Guicciardini made strenuous efforts to verify facts and extensively consulted primary and secondary materials in that quest. In all three of his histories there is, in varying degrees, the same stress on egotistical motives and on cause and effect. Guicciardini was not without personal bias, which on occasion came foremost. *The History of Italy* testifies to his hatred of the Borgia family, and that loathing ensured his acceptance as true contemporary calumnies directed at pope Alexander VI and his family. The work also exhibits unjustifiable self-praise and an undue stress on his own role in important events. Even so it remains the most perceptive history written in the late Italian Renaissance.

CECIL H. CLOUGH

See also Giannone; Gilbert; Giovio; Italy: Renaissance; Renaissance Historical Writing; Sarpi

Biography

Born Florence, 6 March 1483; son of Piero Guicciardini, of a distinguished patrician Florentine family. Enrolled to study law, University of Florence, 1498; transferred to University of Ferrara, 1501; and to University of Padua, doctorate in civil law 1505. Returned to Florence, where he established a lucrative legal practice and taught law at the university. Elected Florentine ambassador to king Ferdinand of Aragon, 1511. Following the Medici's return to power in Florence in 1512, gained that family's favor, obtaining prestigious and financially rewarding posts in papal service, commencing with that of governor of Modena, 1516; one of the chief advisers to Alessandro de' Medici, 1534–37; after Alessandro's assassination dismissed by Cosimo, his successor; retired from public life to write his history, 1537. Married into the powerful Salviati family, 1508. Died Florence, 22 May 1540.

Principal Writings

Storie fiorentine dal 1378 al 1509, written from 1508, but never completed; published in *Opere inedite* edited by Giuseppe Canestrini, 10 vols., 1857–67; authoritative critical edition as *Storie fiorentine dal 1378 al 1509*, edited by Roberto Palmarocchi, 1931; in English as *The History of Florence*, 1970

Storia d'Italia, written from 1534; published 1561; extended by *Dell'historia d'Italia . . . gli ultimi quattro libri non più stampati*, 1564; authoritative critical edition as *Storia d'Italia*, edited by Alessandro Gherardi, 4 vols., 1919; in English as *The History of Italy*, 1753–56

Le cose fiorentine ora per la prima volta pubblicate (Concerning Florence, for the First Time Published), edited by Roberto Ridolfi, 1945

Further Reading

Bondanella, Peter, *Francesco Guicciardini*, Boston: Twayne, 1976

Gilbert, Felix, *Machiavelli and Guicciardini: Politics and History in Sixteenth-Century Florence*, Princeton: Princeton University Press, 1965

Hale, John R., Introduction to Guicciardini, *History of Italy and History of Florence*, New York: Washington Square Press, 1964

Palmarocchi, Roberto, *Studi guicciardini*, Florence: Macri, 1947

Phillips, Mark, *Francesco Guicciardini: The Historian's Craft*, Toronto: University of Toronto Press, 1977

Ridolfi, Roberto, *Genesi della Storia d'Italia guicciardiniana* (The Genesis of Guicciardini's *History of Italy*), Florence: Olschki, 1939; reprinted in his *Opuscoli di storia letteraria e di erudizione: Savonarola, Machiavelli, Guicciardini, Gianotti* (Studies in Literary History and Scholarship: Savonarola, Machiavelli, Guicciardini, Gianotti), 1942

Rubinstein, Nicolai, "The *Storie fiorentine* and the *Memorie di famiglia* by Francesco Guicciardini," *Rinascimento* 4 (1953), 171–225

Guichard, Pierre 1939–

French medievalist, archaeologist, and Arabist

Pierre Guichard's scholarly career divides into two distinct phases. In the first (1969–78) he was occupied with defining the tribal nature of settlement in Al-Andalus (Islamic Spain) of the 8th and 9th centuries, mixing anthropological methods with analysis of historical texts and, in particular, place-name evidence. In the second phase (1978–91) he turned to extensive archaeology which yielded a full-fledged model of rural settlement.

In a 1969 study of the settlement of the Valencian region, Guichard concluded that the area (known as Sharq al-Andalus in Arabic sources) was much less Arabized than had once been thought and that the region was heavily settled by Berbers, whose geographical distribution he sketched out. This adumbration was fully worked out in *Al-Andalus: estructura antropológica de una sociedad islámica en Occidente* (Al-Andalus: The Anthropological Structure of an Islamic Society in the West, 1976) whose objective was to demonstrate the segmentary nature of early Andalusi society. Inasmuch as a tribal polity replaced – and for centuries coexisted with – the non-tribal Hispano-Roman population that was already in place, the processes of conversion and acculturation involved the assimilation of the indigenous population to tribal norms. Rather than the ethnic fusion that Lévi-Provençal and other Arabists presumed to have taken place rather quickly, Guichard argued for the persistence of substantial cleavages in accord with segmentary norms of social organization. In the second half of the book he turned to the special problem of Berber settlement, analyzing tribal place-names, the typical settlement pattern of clans dispersed in hamlets, and evidence of segmentary political structures. Here there is a detailed excursus on the high incidence place-names in Beni- (e.g., Benicasim, "sons of Qāsim") in Sharq al-Andalus, which reflect the association between a given territory and an agnatic group. Only with the political and social stability of the Umayyad caliphate did tribalism weaken as a significant social force.

In 1978, Guichard presented a paper on the problem of the existence of feudal-type structures at the now-famous Rome meeting on *incastellamento* organized by Pierre Toubert. He argued that although the high incidence of castles in Sharq al-Andalus might look like a feudalized countryside and that the Christian conquerors of the region clearly took it as such, those castles were non-feudal in nature and played different social and political roles. His views on the non-feudal nature of Andalusi society proved influential in a concurrent re-examination of the nature of medieval Iberian feudalism and the overthrow of the 19th-century liberal doctrine that feudalism there had been "incomplete" with regard to the rest of Europe. As a new generation of scholars under the influence of Toubert, particularly in Catalonia and Valencia, questioned the received view of feudalism, their views were shaped by Guichard's carefully constructed analysis of non-feudal castral districts which thereby provided a kind of negative template against which to evaluate feudalism in the Christian kingdoms.

In partnership with the archaeologist André Bazzana, he then began to study the castles of Sharq al-Andalus using the methods of extensive archaeology. From this work there emerged a novel interpretation of the organization of the countryside of al-Andalus. Guichard found that the segmentary settlements that he had described in his 1976 book formed a distinctive pattern that reappeared consistently throughout the study area. A number of villages (Spanish *alquerías*; Arabic *qurā*, s. qarya), from six to ten typically, were arrayed in the environs of a castle (*hisn*), situated on a hillside or hilltop, forming a discrete castral district. These castles did not control their districts, however, but simply served as places of refuge in times of insecurity and were not permanently garrisoned. The *qā'id* in charge of a *hisn* was in no way a feudal castellan, but rather a government official with administrative and military duties. *Qurā* were clan-based settlements (hence the frequency of place names beginning with Beni-) and were held in common. Alongside them, and particularly in the environs of towns, there were private

parcels called *rahal/s*, usually owned by government officials or wealthy individuals. Guichard's hypothesis set off a disciplinary war pitting medieval archaeologists against Arabists. The latter were unwilling to endorse the demographic or cultural weight that Guichard accorded to Berbers, attacked the segmentary interpretation of Beni- place-names, insisted on the social control function of *husūn*, and asserted that *rahal/s* were cattle pens. However, a younger generation of scholars, not attached to any party in this polemic, has produced substantial new data that tends to confirm Guichard's hypothesis.

In a number of papers, and particularly in his 2-volume thesis *Le musulmans de Valence et la Reconquête* (1990–91) Guichard takes up the 13-century transition from Muslim to Christian rule and its effect on the distinctive landscape that he had described. In the Christian kingdom of Valencia, castles were enlarged to house a feudal castellan and permanent garrison, while village fields, previously unbounded, were surveyed and parceled out to individual settlers (whether Muslim or Christian), thus depriving a clan-based society of an important support of social cohesion.

Guichard's work has been controversial in Spain because his approach crosses the boundaries between medieval history and Arabism, two professional cultures that had hardly interacted before. Moreover his methodology, which stresses the "association of text and terrain" proved difficult for textually-oriented scholars of whatever discipline to grasp. The eclecticism that characterizes his approach has had a strong formative influence on a younger generation of medieval historians, Arabists, and archaeologists who have built on his work to revise substantively our understanding of rural society, social, ethnic, and cultural change in Islamic Spain, as well as of the contrasting meaning of rural social organization in Al-Andalus and the feudal crown of Aragón.

THOMAS F. GLICK

See also Spain: Islamic; Spain: to 1450

Biography
Born La Côte St. André, 5 November 1939. Received agrégation in history, 1966, and doctorate, 1987. Taught at universities of Toulouse and Lyon.

Principal Writings
"La peuplement de la région de Valence aux deux premiers siècles de la domination musulmane" (The Peopling of the Region of Valencia in the First Two Centuries of Muslim Domination)," *Mélanges de la Casa de Velázquez* 5 (1969), 103–56

Al-Andalus: estructura antropológica de una sociedad islámica en Occidente (Al-Andalus: The Anthropological Structure of an Islamic Society in the West), 1976

Structures sociales "orientales" et "occidentales" dans l'Espagne musulmane ("Oriental" and "Occidental" Social Structures in Muslim Spain), 1977

With André Bazzana and Patrice Cressier, *Les Châteaux ruraux d'al-Andalus: histoire et archéologie des husun du sud-est de l'Espagne* (Rural Castles in Islamic Spain: History and Archaeology of Fortresses of Southeastern Spain), 1988

L'Espagne et la Sicile musulmanes aux XIe et XIIe siècles (Spanish and Sicilian Muslims in the 11th and 12th Centuries), 1990

"Faut-il en finir avec les berbères de Valence?" (Shouldn't We be Finished with the Berbers of Valence?), *Al-Qantara* 11 (1990), 161–73

Les musulmans de Valence et la Reconquête: XIe–XIIIe siècles (The Muslims of Valencia and the *Reconquista*: 11th–12th Centuries), 2 vols., 1990–91

La España musulmana: Al-Andalus omeya (siglos VIII–XI) (Muslim Spain: Umayyad Al-Andalus from the 8th to 11th Centuries), 1995

Further Reading

Barceló, Carmen, "¿Galgos o podencos? Sobre la supuesta berberización del país valenciano en los siglos VIII y IX" (On the Supposed Berberization of the Valencian Region in the 8th and 9th Centuries), *Al-Qantara* 11 (1990), 429–60

Glick, Thomas F., *From Muslim Fortress to Christian Castle: Social and Cultural Change in Medieval Spain*, Manchester: Manchester University Press, 1995

Torró, Josep, "Producció, reproducció i colonització: una comentaris a pròposit de l'obra de Pierre Guichard" (Production, Reproduction and Colonization: Some Comments on the Work of Pierre Guichard), *Revista d'Història Medieval* (Valencia) 4 (1993), 229–41

Guizot, François 1787–1874

French historian and statesman

François Guizot is more readily identified for his political career than for his history-related accomplishments. Under the July Monarchy (1830–48) he served as minister of the interior, minister of public instruction, ambassador to Britain, minister of foreign affairs, and prime minister. He is nevertheless an important figure in 19th-century French historiography. His contributions were manifested in his teaching, his writing, and his intense efforts to enhance the historical profession in his country.

Guizot was born into a Protestant family at Nîmes in 1787, and experienced the French Revolution in a deeply personal way: his father was guillotined in 1794. Guizot's mother moved her children to Geneva, where, in a highly moral and intellectual atmosphere, young Guizot studied law and philosophy. He turned to history only after his return to Paris at the age of 18 and his collaboration with Pauline de Meulan (whom he married in 1812) on a critical French edition of the work of Edward Gibbon.

Guizot's teaching and writing were intimately linked. His professorial career was launched at the Sorbonne, where he was appointed to a chair in modern history in 1812. His teaching was interrupted by the fall of the Empire and his subsequent engagement in political affairs, including a series of administrative positions in the early Restoration government. Later, however, Guizot's influential lectures earned him recognition, along with his colleagues Victor Cousin and Abel François Villemain, as part of the "triumvirate of the Sorbonne." The lectures he offered from 1828 to 1830, in particular, demonstrated Guizot's innovative attempts to construct a history of civilization, and were published as the *Cours d'histoire moderne* (1828–30; *The History of Civilization* and *The History of France*). Divided into two parts, one focusing on Europe, the other on France, the *Cours* remains perhaps Guizot's most respected work. Here he sought to identify general ideas running through the thread of civilization, especially when they contained a moral message. He was less concerned with individuals than with the larger influences that culminated in the emergence of strong, stable states. His historical writing was informed throughout by a strong sense of divine Providence.

It also relied on a decidedly progressive perspective. Guizot wrote that "[t]he idea of progress, of development, appears to me to be the fundamental idea contained in the word *civilisation*" (quoted in Crossley, p.83). He acknowledged the existence of crisis moments throughout history, but in his view these crises served to advance the generally moral, rational, and ordered cause of civilization. In his eyes the confusion and instability that followed the fall of the Roman empire were succeeded by feudalism, which, with its attendant struggles between church and state had been followed by the emergence of absolutism. His own lifetime, Guizot believed, had witnessed the final dismantling of absolutism – as evidenced by the French Revolution, for example – and advancement to another, better phase.

At this point it is necessary to consider how Guizot's historical studies influenced his political ideologies, how he employed his historical knowledge for practical purposes. Guizot extolled the rise in stature of the bourgeois elements of the Third Estate as among the Revolution's most positive results. To consolidate the Revolution's gains, this conservative thinker maintained that the bourgeois population must form the basis of a representative government similar to the English constitutional monarchy model. It was not quite democracy, but it was emblematic of the liberal thinking of his time.

Along these lines, Guizot was preoccupied for much of his life with the question of why England's 17th-century Revolution had yielded a system of government so unified, so stable, so orderly, while his own country had not yet achieved a similar result. His interest in this issue is reflected in his *Histoire de la révolution d'Angleterre* (1854–56; *A Popular History of England*, 1876), which, while never completed, was nonetheless an influential and well-respected work, and in an important 1850 essay, "Pourquoi la Révolution d'Angleterre a-t-elle réussi?" (Why Did the English "Glorious Revolution" Succeed?)

Guizot is also credited with having advanced the cause of French historical scholarship in an unprecedented manner. In particular, he implemented the systematic collection and edition of archival materials and promoted the stature and professionalization of the discipline. In these efforts he was vastly assisted by the resources available to him by virtue of his political position. In 1833, while minister of public instruction, he established the Société de l'Histoire de France, a professional organization to which many of France's most eminent historians have belonged. Also in 1833, Guizot secured the king's support for the creation of a government-sponsored committee charged with publishing French historical source material. The massive, multivolume *Collection des documents inédits relatifs à l'histoire de France* (Collection of Previously Unpublished Documents Relating to French History) began to appear in 1836. In addition, one must consider the indirect effects of the influence Guizot exerted on other great historical minds of his era, many of whom, such as Jules Michelet, were among his pupils and protégés.

Finally, Guizot is recognized for his tripartite vision of the historian's task. First, he envisaged the historian as an anatomist, one who must dissect the body – the facts and events – of history. Second, he perceived the historian as a physiologist who must understand and explain the functions and interrelationships between the various structures of the body. But these efforts alone were not sufficient. In the end, the historian was also responsible for conveying a sense of external reality, a living physiognomy, restoring the past to a vibrant and vital condition. Over the generations, however, many have criticized Guizot for having failed to attain his own standards.

ERIKA DREIFUS

See also France: French Revolution; Manzoni; Mathiez; Michelet; Motley; Political; Reformation; Thierry

Biography

François Pierre Guillaume Guizot. Born Nîmes, 4 October 1787, to a bourgeois Protestant family; his father was executed during the reign of terror, 1794. Fled with family to Geneva, 1794, where he was educated; returned to Paris to study law, 1805.
Lecturer/professor, the Sorbonne, 1812–15, 1820–25, 1828–30.
Political career: minister of the interior, 1830; minister of public instruction, 1832–36; and minister of foreign affairs, 1840–48.
Married 1) Pauline de Meulan, writer, 1812 (died 1827; 1 son died in infancy; 1 son died 1837); 2) Elisa Dillon, 1828 (died 1833; 2 sons; 1 son died in infancy). Died Val-Richer, 12 September 1874.

Principal Writings

Histoire des origines du gouvernement représentatif en Europe, 1821–22; in English as *History of the Origin of Representative Government in Europe*, 1852
Essai sur l'histoire de la France, 1823
Cours d'histoire moderne, 2 vols., 1828–30, comprising *Histoire générale de la civilisation en Europe, depuis la chute de l'empire romain jusqu'à la Révolution française* and *Histoire de la civilisation en France, depuis la chute de l'empire romain jusqu'en 1789*; in English as *The History of Civilization from the Fall of the Roman Empire to the French Revolution*, 3 vols., 1846, and *The History of France from the Earliest Times to 1848*, completed by Madame Guizot de Witt, 8 vols., 1856 (as *France*, 8 vols., 1898)
Histoire de la révolution d'Angleterre, 6 vols., 1854–56; in English as *A Popular History of England*, 5 vols., 1876
Mémoires pour servir à l'histoire de mon temps, 9 vols., 1858–68; in English as *Memoirs to Illustrate the History of My Time*, 8 vols., 1858–67

Further Reading

Barnes, Harry Elmer, *A History of Historical Writing*, Norman: University of Oklahoma Press, 1937
Crossley, Ceri, *French Historians and Romanticism: Thierry, Guizot, the Saint-Simonians, Quinet, Michelet*, London and New York: Routledge, 1993
Gooch, G.P., *History and Historians in the Nineteenth Century*, London and New York: Longman, 1913; revised 1952
Johnson, Douglas W., *Guizot: Aspects of French History, 1787–1874*, London: Routledge, 1963
O'Connor, Mary Consolata, *The Historical Thought of François Guizot*, Washington, DC: Catholic University of America Press, 1955
Rosanvallon, Pierre, *Le Moment Guizot*, Paris: Gallimard, 1985
Thompson, James Westfall, *A History of Historical Writing*, vol. 2: *The Eighteenth and Nineteenth Centuries*, New York: Macmillan, 1942

Gunki monogatari
Japanese war chronicle tales

Gunki monogatari constitute a genre of medieval Japanese historical literature, recounting, often in highly fictionalized or tendentious form, major military conflicts and the political events surrounding them. Most deal with the civil disturbances that occurred between 1156 and 1221, weakening the imperial government and giving rise to shogunal or military rule.

In contrast to the courtly literature, including the historical tales (*rekishi monogatari*) of the Heian period (794–1185), the war chronicles employ simple grammar, numerous Chinese terms, and frequent allusions to Chinese history. While the courtly literature sensitively depicts human emotions such as longing, love, and melancholy, the *gunki monogatari* describe heroic deeds in vigorous detail, and celebrate such martial values as bravery and loyalty. Often anonymously composed, the tales were in most cases chanted by itinerant, blind performers called *biwa hōshi* (lute-monks).

The first major work in this genre is the *Hōgen monogatari*, which recounted events in 1156, the first year of the Hōgen era (1156–58). During this year a succession dispute at the imperial court in Kyoto led for the first time to military intervention, and the seizure of power by the samurai leader Taira Kiyomori (1118–81). The *Hōgen monogatari*, however, focuses upon the role of Minamoto Tametomo (1139–77), a warrior who fought against Kiyomori, suffering banishment in consequence. The key theme of this work is how tragedy results from the violation of proper family relationships as prescribed by Confucian teachings. The *Heiji monogatari* is an account of events during the Heiji era (1159–60), when the samurai leader Minamoto Yoshitomo, who had been allied with Kiyomori during the earlier disturbance, attempted to seize power with the aid of the court noble Fujiwara Nobuyori. This effort was crushed by Kiyomori, whose family thereafter exercised complete control over the court until 1185. Both of these works seem to have been chanted, in various versions, from the 13th century; the latter survives in 33 different texts.

The *Heike monogatari* (*The Tale of the Heike*) was commonly acknowledged as the greatest of these works, a masterpiece comparable in its literary influence to the classic 11th-century novel *Genji monogatari* (The Tale of Genji). It briefly recounted the events of 1156–60, but focused upon the struggle between the ruling Taira and insurgent forces led by Yoshitomo's sons, Minamoto Yoritomo and Yoshitsune, culminating in Yoritomo's triumph in 1185. The first of the tale's three sections centered around Kiyomori, his arrogant ambition and callousness. The second and third focused upon two of Yoritomo's generals, his cousin Yoshinaka and half-brother Yoshitsune. The Buddhist theme of impermanence, and the ultimate futility of human effort, pervades the work and provides its aesthetic.

Often described as an epic, the orally-recited *Heike monogatari* combined summary historical narrative with close-up scenes of specific battles. The supernatural frequently played a role. The language of the *Heike*, and the other *gunki monogatari*, rarely attains the rich sweep of Homeric literature, although there are occasional passages of considerable power and beauty. The opening lines are among the best-known in all Japanese literature: "The proud do not endure, they are like a dream on a spring night; the mighty fall at last, they are as dust before the wind."

There are 88 extant versions of the *Heike*, and all are no doubt of composite authorship. The most authoritative text, however, may have been compiled by the courtier Fujiwara Yukinaga in the early 13th century, although another tradition credits this achievement to a *biwa hōshi* named Kakuichi in 1371. The *Genpei suiseiki* (Chronicle of the Rise and Fall of the Genji and Heike) is considered a variant of the *Heike monogatari*, but is far longer and designed for reading rather than recitation.

The *Shōkyūki* (or *Jōkyūki*) is an account of the Shōkyū War (1221). This conflict resulted from an effort by an abdicated emperor, Go-Toba, to overthrow the Kamakura shogunate and restore direct imperial rule. The attempt failed and in fact led to the complete eclipse of imperial power. Another abortive bid for the restoration of direct imperial rule is described in the 14th-century work *Taiheiki* (Chronicle of Great Pacification). This highly fictionalized text portrayed the events surrounding the overthrow of the Kamakura shogunate, and the establishment of the Muromachi shogunate by Ashikaga Takauji in 1336. Its internal inconsistencies and differences in style suggest composite authorship, although a 14th-century source credits its composition to a monk named Kojima (d. 1374).

The fanciful *Soga monogatari* (Tale of the Soga, 14th century) and *Gikeiki* (Tale of Yoshitsune, 15th century) are set in the late 12th century, and deal with the period in which the first military regime or shogunate was established. The *Ōninki* (Chronicle of Onin) described the civil war of 1467–77, and the *Taikōki* (Chronicle of the Taikō) the career of the great warlord Toyotomi Hideyoshi (1536–98).

The war chronicles are prefigured by the 10th-century *Shōmonki* (or *Masakado-ki*, Chronicle of Masakado), 11th-century *Mutsu waki*, and section 25 of the 12th-century *Konjaku monogatari* (Tales of Present and Past). While often unreliable as histories (a Japanese scholar in 1891 wrote that "The *Taiheiki* is worthless as a historical source"), these works are invaluable sources of information on the values, customs, beliefs, and fighting styles of the medieval military class.

GARY P. LEUPP

See also Japan; Japanese Chronicles

Further Reading

Cogan, Thomas J., trans., *The Tale of the Soga Brothers*, Tokyo: University of Tokyo Press, 1987

Hiroshi Kitagawa, and Bruce T. Tsuchida, trans., *The Tale of Heike*, 2 vols., Tokyo: University of Tokyo Press, 1975

McCullough, Helen Craig, trans., *The Taiheiki: A Chronicle Medieval Japan*, New York: Columbia University Press, 1959

McCullough, Helen Craig, trans., *Yoshitsune: A Fifteenth-Century Japanese Tale*, Stanford: Stanford University Press, 1966

McCullough, Helen Craig, trans., *The Tale of the Heike*, Stanford, CA: Stanford University Press, 1988

McCulloch, William H., trans., "Shōkyūki: An Account of the Shōkyū War of 1221," *Monumenta Nipponica* 19 (1964)

Reischauer, Edwin O., and Joseph K. Yanagita, "The Heiji Monogatari" in *Translations of Early Japanese Literature*, Cambridge, MA: Harvard University Press, 1951

Wilson, William R., trans., *Hōgen monogatari: Tale of the Disorder in Hōgen*, Tokyo: Sophia University, 1971

Gurevich, Aron 1924–

Russian medieval social historian

Aron Gurevich is one of the best-known modern Russian medieval historians, second only to Mikhail Bakhtin in international repute. He is famous not only for his studies of Norse sagas and European cultural history, but for his theoretical writings on "the science of history." A self-taught *Annaliste*, he spent the majority of his career cut off from personal interaction with the French practitioners of the history of *mentalités*, due to the political and intellectual climate of the Soviet Union. Despite this comparative academic isolation, Gurevich displays a great familiarity with the work of the *Annalistes* and enjoys a following in the West. Among his goals has been the opening of the West to Russian historians, by making documents and historical studies from the West available to Russia; he has also helped to make Russian historical work more available to the West.

Gurevich studied agrarian history in Moscow University, under the "non-Party Marxist" Evgenii Kosminskii. As a student there, he espoused the "Westernizer" view of Russian history, in which the evils of Russian society and history were attributed to the influence of the Byzantine empire. Western society, from which Russia was isolated, was seen as progressive and desirable. This view is to be contrasted with the Slavophile viewpoint, which saw the Westernization of Peter the Great as the source of weakness in Russian society. Part of this debate has focused on the understanding of legal institutions. Westernizers (such as Gurevich) have always seen Western law as superior. He developed an interest in Western legal systems based on his negative personal experience as well as the historical experience of Russian/Soviet society.

The problems facing Russian scholars of the West – mostly issues of access to documents and secondary reading – were exacerbated by his personal choice of not joining the Communist party. After great difficulties in finding a job, Gurevich was eventually employed in relatively remote Kalinin at the Pedagogical Institute; he regularly travelled the 100 miles to Moscow to conduct research in libraries there. In 1988 he made his first trip to the West. While studying the Anglo-Saxon peasantry, he realized his focus had been on the peasants as objects of exploitation or sources of income, but not as people. This realization led him to turn to the related disciplines of historical and social anthropology. The concern with a more "total" history informs all of his work. As he noted in his preface to a collection of essays, *Historical Anthropology of the Middle Ages* (1992), the historian "needs to find a method of reading texts (texts in their widest, semiological, meaning) that will help to disclose the secrets of other epochs by revealing the *mentalité* which lays its imprint upon the whole life of their society."

Gurevich has been concerned with defining as well as practicing social history, in an effort to discover "the human content of social history." Having explicitly repudiated the techniques of Marxist historians, partially on the basis of Marx's own disclaimers regarding the tendencies of his followers to apply the "base/superstructure" model to all situations, Gurevich instead insists on studying small groups to gain a more accurate perspective on human behavior and to avoid reductionism. This necessitates an understanding of the *mentalités* and cultures of small groups. A firm believer in and practitioner of micro-analysis, Gurevich described his own work in 1990 as focusing on "all possible aspects of social life," noting "intimate connections between presumably unconnected aspects, including wealth and religion, or property relations and magic." Neglecting aspects of social behavior leads, he stated, to false or incomplete conclusions – because these aspects were found in the same individuals or groups and considered to be connected on a natural and real level, they must not be separated by the historian. "In this sense, contemporary social history cannot but be historical anthropology, or anthropologically oriented history," he stated.

The sources Gurevich uses to study this "total history" include sagas, *exempla*, and *summae confessorum*. He is concerned with texts, contexts, and what other social historians such as Craig Harline and R. Po-Chia Hsia, have termed "points of contact" between higher and lower levels of society. In *Problemy srednevekovoi narodnoi kul'tury* (1981; *Medieval Popular Culture*, 1988), his study of "'low-level' medieval culture" which has been translated into German and English, Gurevich concluded that the only way to determine the true character of medieval religiosity was to study the sources in detail, not only for what the texts themselves said, but also by paying attention to the audience of those texts. He cautioned against using a few texts to create a complete picture of medieval culture, since texts can only be representative of a slice of that culture.

KATHLEEN COMERFORD

See also Poland: to the 18th Century

Biography

Aron Iakovlevich Gurevich. Born 1924. Studied under Neusykhin and Kosminskii, University of Moscow, mid-1940s, received PhD 1950. Held professorships, Pedagogical Institute, Kalinin; Institute of Philosophy; and Institute of General History, Russian Academy of Sciences, Moscow.

Principal Writings

Pokhody vikingov (The Viking Expeditions), 1966
Svobodnoe krestianstvo feodal'noi Norvegii (The Free Peasantry of Feudal Norway), 1967
Problemy genezisa feodalizma v zapadnoi Evrope (Problems of the Genesis of Feudalism in Western Europe), 1970
Istoriia i saga (History and Saga), 1972
Kategorii srednevekovoi kul'tury, 1972; in English as *Categories of Medieval Culture*, 1985
Norvezhskoe obshchestvo v rannee srednevekov'e: problemy sotsial'nogo stroia i kul'tury (Norwegian Society in the Early Middle Ages: Problems of Social Structure and Culture), 1977
Edda i saga (Edda and Saga), 1979
Problemy srednevekovoi narodnoi kul'tury, 1981; in English as *Medieval Popular Culture: Problems of Belief and Perception*, 1988
Kul'tura i obshchestvo srednevekovoi Evropy glazami sovremennikov: exempla XIII veka (The Culture and Society of Thirteenth-Century Europe through the Eyes of Contemporaries), 1989
Odissei: chelovek v istorii, issledovaniia po sotsial'noi istorii i istorii kul'tury (Odysseus, Man in History), 1989
Chelovek i kul'tura: individual'nost' v istorii kul'tury, 1990
Srednevekovyi mir: kul'tura bezmolvstvuiushchego bol'shinstva (The World of the Middle Ages: The Culture of the Silent Majority), 1990

Historical Anthropology of the Middle Ages, 1992
Istoricheskii sintez i shkola "Annalov," 1993
"The Double Responsibility of the Historian," *Diogenes*, 168 (1994), 65–84
"The Literacy of Waldensianism from Valdes to 1400," in Peter Biller and Anne Hudson, eds., *Heresy and Literacy, 1000–1530*, 1994
The Origins of European Individualism, 1995 [Russian original]

Further Reading

Burke, Peter, "Bakhtin for Historians," *Social History* 13 (1988), 85–90
Burke, Peter, "Popular Culture Reconsidered," *Storia della Storiografia* 17 (1990), 41–50
Howlett, Jana, "Preface" to Aaron Gurevich, *Historical Anthropology of the Middle Ages*, Chicago: University of Chicago Press, 1992

Gutman, Herbert G. 1928–1985

US social historian

A creative, deeply empirical, historical thinker, Herbert G. Gutman symbolized the ascent of social history in the United States in the 1970s. His 1973 article, "Work, Culture, and Society in Industrializing America, 1815–1919," placed the face of a coal miner on the cover of the *American Historical Review*. Ranging across time and space, the essay insisted that ordinary Americans mattered as much as the oft-written about politicians and businessmen. Gutman focused on obscured humanity – immigrants, workers, mill girls, rural blacks – situating such people in historical periods that framed their experience and that they themselves influenced. He probed obvious sources and events as well as digging in uncharted ground, always reaching for new meaning and understanding of the recurrent tensions associated with work and life in a changing America.

Gutman, whose origins lay at the intersection of New York City's Jewish and left milieux, wrote his first histories in the consensus-dominated 1950s. He studied workers and the Depression of the 1870s and over the course of the 1960s published a series of articles that explored the workers' search for power in Gilded Age America. It was, at the time, a marginal topic, pursued in marginal institutions, but in the words of his friend and collaborator Ira Berlin it made Gutman "a spokesman for a history that as yet had no name." Gradually, by the close of the 1960s, after establishing a friendship with E.P. Thompson and sharpening the focus of his writing by polemicizing against the institutional narrowness of the John R. Commons-led Wisconsin school of economistic labor studies, Gutman became recognized as perhaps the leading figure in the emerging field designated the "new" working-class history. Appointments to the University of Rochester and later the Graduate Center of the City University of New York followed, and it was there that Gutman supervised a score of talented, highly politicized working-class historians.

No book would ever appear summarizing Gutman's massive researches into the history of 19th-century labor. While he worked fastidiously in archives and printed sources, Gutman wrote with difficulty; like the history he studied, his prose and the organization of his thought had a tortured and rambling quality and he could never quite bring himself to see it finished. Manuscripts piled up and were sent across the country in typescript; many never found their way into print, including a massive volume on workers in Paterson, New Jersey. The "Work, Culture, and Society" essay, after years of *samizdat*-like circulation, was finally published. Meant to be an opening statement of reinterpretation, it proved, ironically, to be more of a closing chapter in a set of studies of class formation that were never to be completed. Two collections of essays, one published posthumously, stand as the published mark of this phase of Gutman's historical practice.

Gutman began reconsidering what he had invested twenty years thinking through. Never adept at theoretical nuances, he had gravitated to modernization theory in the 1960s and adopted some of the language of this analytic edifice. He soon came to reconsider the flattening homogeneity of terms such as premodern and traditional. It was perhaps not accidental that his self-questioning paralleled a shift in his concerns away from the factory, mine, and mill workers of the late 19th century and toward the slave South and the plantation.

Early in the 1970s Gutman shared a podium with Stanley Engerman, Robert Fogel, and Eugene Genovese as the four Rochester scholars discussed new directions in black history. The symposium masked quite acute personal differences, and within a few years tensions hardened into an acrimonious falling out. Fogel and Engerman's *Time on the Cross* (1974), a much publicized concoction of high-tech "cliometrics" and ideological posturing, proclaimed, to the interest of *Time* magazine, that slavery had not been so bad after all. Gutman was outraged. When the *Journal of Negro History* asked him for a review (he had not reviewed a book for a scholarly journal since 1968), he immersed himself in the task, subjecting Fogel and Engerman to a rigorous cross-examination. Gutman's invective reached its boiling point over the undemocratic use and abuse of history, over how Fogel and Engerman had constructed a pseudohistory out of pseudostatistics, hiding behind their mastery of a mere technique, which they then used to distort the past. You did not need regression analysis to know that slavery was an absolute evil, Gutman's scorched prose proclaimed, nor could any manipulation of numbers arithmetically do away with the resistance and struggle for life sustained by enslaved African Americans.

The passion of political commitment eased Gutman back into the flow of writing. His "review" of *Time on the Cross* came relatively quickly and easily. It stands as something of a historiographic landmark, unique in its relentless critical engagement with a text. When published it took up the entire 175 page issue of the journal, and it appeared as a book (*Slavery and the Numbers Game*, 1975) almost immediately.

Gutman's polemical attentions had also long been drawn to issues of race, slavery, and slave resistance and adaptation through his opposition to Daniel Patrick Moynihan's 1965 report on the historical origins of racial inequalities. Moynihan argued that the "pathologies" of black America were rooted in the slave system's destruction of the black family: African Americans were stripped of the fundamental resource required to sustain meaningful relationships and social advancement. In *The Black Family in Slavery and Freedom* (1976) Gutman argued that far from being destroyed by slavery, the black family was cherished, preserved, and valued by blacks who, over many generations, defended themselves and their kin from slavery's arsenal of degradation. Aimed at Moynihan, Gutman also raised his polemical sights at Genovese, whose *Roll, Jordan, Roll* (1974) structured the history of slaves too much into the ideological and cultural universe of the masters for Gutman's taste. By the late 1970s Gutman and Genovese were routinely exchanging counter-denunciations.

Immersion in the polemics over slave culture energized Gutman, but it also trapped him in a rut of personalized antagonism. He found it difficult to even hear the word "hegemony" without wincing in almost physical pain at the thought of this Genovese-import into the theoretical language of social history. He spent the remainder of his life wrestling with demons and trying to restart his research and conceptualization of class formation. But he was now an international figure, bombarded with requests to attend conferences, visit foreign lands, and explore the meaning of history with scholars who claimed they needed his guidance. His energies remained almost contagious, but there was too much that he was doing, and too little time: he worked with others in teaching middle-level trade unionists the history of United States workers; he struggled to find the proper voice, medium, and analytic tone to disseminate a truly popular and synthetic history of American labor; with Steve Brier he organized the American Social History Project, which would eventually produce a stunning oeuvre of work encompassing films, CD-Roms, and the much-acclaimed 2-volume *Who Built America* (1989–92); and with Ira Berlin he explored the demographic making of the US working class.

All of these projects were left for others to complete. Over the course of his 25 years of researching and writing history Gutman had a profound impact. He did more than add workers to the history of the nation: he changed how historians think. His legacy, yet to be fulfilled, is to change the present face of the nation, a political project that, he believed, begins with understanding the past.

BRYAN D. PALMER

See also African American; Elkins; Family; Fogel; Labor; Marriage; Slavery: Modern; Social; Stampp; Thompson, E.; United States: 19th Century; United States: Historical Writing, 20th Century; Women's History: African American

Biography

Herbert George Gutman. Born New York City, 18 March 1928. Received BA, Queens College, New York, 1949; MA, Columbia University 1950; PhD, University of Wisconsin, 1959. Taught at Fairleigh Dickinson University, 1956–63; State University of New York, Buffalo, 1963–66; University of Rochester, 1966–72; City College of New York, 1972–76; and Graduate Center, City University of New York, 1976–85. Married Judith Mara, 1950 (2 children). Died Nyack, New York, 21 July 1985.

Principal Writings

"The Workers' Search for Power: Labor in the Gilded Age," in H. Wayne Morgan, ed., *The Gilded Age: A Reappraisal*, 1963; reprinted in *Power and Culture*, 1987

"Industrial Invasion of the Village Green," *Trans-Action* 4 (May/June 1966), 19–24

"The Knights of Labor and Patrician Anti-Semitism: 1891," *Labor History* 13 (1972), 63–67

With Stanley L. Engerman, Robert W. Fogel, and Eugene D. Genovese, "New Directions in Black History: A Symposium," *Forum* 1 (1972), 22–41

"Le Phénomène invisible: la composition de la famille et du foyer noir après la Guerre de Sécession" (Invisible Phenomenon: Family Composition and the Black Household after the Civil War), *Annales: ESC* 27 (1972), 1197–1218

"Work, Culture, and Society in Industrializing America, 1815–1919," *American Historical Review* (1973), 531–88; reprinted in *Work, Culture, and Society in Industrializing America*, 1976

Slavery and the Numbers Game: A Critique of Time on the Cross, 1975

The Black Family in Slavery and Freedom, 1750–1925, 1976

With Paul David, Richard Sutch, Peter Temin, and Gavin Wright, *Reckoning with Slavery: A Critical Study in the Quantitative History of American Negro Slavery*, 1976

Work, Culture, and Society in Industrializing America: Essays in American Working-Class and Social History, 1976

"La Politique ouvrière de la grande entreprise américaine de 'l'âge du clinquant': le cas de la Standard Oil Company" (The Politics of Labor and Large Industry in Gilded Age America: The Case of Standard Oil), *Le Mouvement Social* 102 (1978), 68–99

Power and Culture: Essays on the American Working Class, edited by Ira Berlin, 1987

Further Reading

Abelove, Henry *et al.*, eds., *Visions of History*, by MARHO: The Radical Historians Organisation, Manchester: Manchester University Press, and New York: Pantheon, 1983

Berlin, Ira, "Introduction: Herbert G. Gutman and the American Working Class," in Herbert G. Gutman, *Power and Culture*, New York: Pantheon, 1987

Dubofsky, Melvyn, "Workers, Jews, and the American Past," *Tikkun*, 3 (1988)

Fink, Leon, "John R. Commons, Herbert Gutman, and the Burden of Labor History," in Fink, ed., *In Search of the Working Class: Essays in American Labor History and Political Culture*, Urbana: University of Illinois Press, 1994

Kealey, Gregory S., "Herbert Gutman, 1928–1985, and the Writings of Class History," *Monthly Review* 31 (May 1986), 22–30

Kealey, Gregory S., "Gutman and Montgomery: Politics and Direction of Labor and Working-Class History in the United States," *International Labor and Working-Class History* 37 (1990), 58–68

Levine, Susan, "Class and Gender: Herbert Gutman and the Women of 'Shoe City'," *Labor History* 29 (1988), 344–55

Meier, August, and Elliott M. Rudwick, *Black History and the Historical Profession, 1915–1980*, Urbana: University of Illinois Press, 1986

Montgomery, David, "Gutman's Nineteenth-Century America," *Labor History* 19 (1978), 416–29

Montgomery, David, "Gutman's Agenda for Future Historical Research," *Labor History* 29 (1988), 299–312

Rodgers, Daniel T., "Tradition, Modernity, and the American Industrial Worker: Reflections and Critique," *Journal of Interdisciplinary History* 7 (1977), 655–81

Roediger, David R., "The Greatness of Herbert Gutman," in his *Towards the Abolition of Whiteness: Essays on Race, Politics, and Working-Class History*, New York: Verso, 1994

Thompson, E.P., "The Mind of a Historian," *Dissent* 35 (Fall 1988), 493–96

Wiener, Jonathan M., "Radical Historians and the Crisis in American History," in his *Professors, Politics and Pop*, London and New York: Verso, 1991

H

Habakkuk, H.J. 1915–

British social and economic historian

John Habakkuk is probably the only historian to be associated with two influential theses, both known as "the Habakkuk thesis." Although in diverse fields each has generated much debate and resulted in many publications of case studies and theoretical works proving or disproving Habakkuk's case.

Habakkuk entered economic history in the 1930s when it was still a new discipline and seen as non-traditional and radical in an academic sense. He was particularly influenced by M.M. Postan as his mentor. His work has been distinguished by the application of economic theory to history, and a spell in the Economics Faculty at Cambridge led him to search for deeper forces beneath the apparent accidents of economic history, particularly regarding the limitations of land scarcity. He was also motivated to look for the economic origins of human behavior as a result of the 1930s Depression and was subsequently involved in the development of high level economic theories and applications while doing war work in the Foreign Office and Board of Trade from 1940 to 1946.

Habakkuk is something of a polymath – his first research topic was the impact of the Dutch theologians on 17th-century thought – and his earliest work was an article on empire and overseas expansion. He became interested in free trade, and in particular the flow of British capital to India for railway building. However, he became well-known by developing his "landownership thesis." He was impressed by the incredible continuity of power of the oldest landed families apparent before World War II. In his article in *Economic History Review*, published in 1940, he argued that, in the period 1680–1740 a very active land market became progressively concentrated into fewer hands to such an extent that the economic gap between large landowners and the gentry widened. The thesis was based on the only family papers then available in the earliest extant record offices for Northamptonshire and Bedfordshire. When more papers became available, his thesis was subject to criticism, for example, by Clay, Beckett, and Bonfield. It is also the case, however, that once the heat had gone out of the "rise of the gentry" debate, landownership largely went out of fashion as attention in social and economic history turned to "history from below." However, Habakkuk's *Marriage, Debt and the Estates System* (1994), the publication of his Ford lectures of 1984–85, consolidated his long interest in landownership, and demonstrated his grasp of complex legal issues.

Landownership had given Habakkuk an insight into the importance of marriage patterns, and in the 1950s he turned his attention to demography. He was present at the genesis of demographic history, entering the field when mortality factors still carried most weight in explanations of demographic change and before the field became overly statistical. Within this context, Habakkuk was among the first to point to the influence of fertility and marriage factors.

Spells of teaching in the United States, and the development of new lecture courses, led Habakkuk to consider technology and develop another "Habakkuk thesis," this time regarding the "American system of manufactures." Published as *American and British Technology in the Nineteenth Century* (1962), his argument was that the late 19th-century North American economy was rich in land relative to labor. As a result labor costs were high, so it was rational to substitute capital for labor. Criticism has been levelled at the thesis by Rosenberg and Landes, for instance, particularly at the supposed wage differential between skilled and unskilled labor. More recently, it has been argued that the thesis is flawed by concentrating on male wages, whereas the labor force was predominantly women and children.

After becoming principal of Jesus College, Oxford in 1967, Habakkuk became more involved in university administration, becoming vice-chancellor of Oxford University from 1973–77, and during the early 1980s chairing several public committees. He has encouraged generations of research students with diverse research interests, from quantitative demographic and economic historians such as Roderick Floud to social historians such as Gareth Stedman-Jones.

PAMELA SHARPE

See also Thompson, F.

Biography

Hrothgar John Habakkuk. Born Barry, South Wales, 13 May 1915. Educated at Barry County School; St. John's College, Cambridge, BA 1936. Taught at Cambridge University, first at Pembroke College, and then as university lecturer, 1938–50. Temporary civil servant, Foreign Office, 1940–42, and Board of Trade, 1942–46. At Oxford University: professor of economic history, 1950–67, vice-chancellor, 1973–77, pro-vice-chancellor, 1977–83; fellow, All Souls College, 1950–67, and from 1988; principal, Jesus College, 1967–84. President, University College, Swansea, 1975–84. Knighted 1976. Married Mary Richards, 1948 (1 son, 3 daughters).

Principal Writings

"English Landownership, 1680–1740," *Economic History Review*
    10 (1940), 2–17
American and British Technology in the Nineteenth Century, 1962
General editor with M.M. Postan, *The Cambridge Economic
    History of Europe*, 2nd edition, 1966–89
*Marriage, Debt and the Estates System: English Landownership,
    1650–1950*, 1994

Further Reading

Landes, David S., "Factor Costs and Demand: Determinants of
    Economic Growth: A Critique of Professor Habakkuk's Thesis,"
    Business History 7 (1965), 15–33
Thompson, F.M.L,. ed., *Landowners, Capitalists and Entrepreneurs:
    Essays for Sir John Habakkuk*, Oxford and New York: Oxford
    University Press, 1994

Habermas, Jürgen 1929–

German philosopher

Jürgen Habermas is a contemporary philosopher who has exerted considerable influence on the theory and writing of history. Since the 1960s he has maintained the tradition of critical theory that flourished in the work of Max Weber and, later, the Frankfurt School (of which he was a member).

Habermas' reputation is based on the thesis set forth in his 1961 Marburg Habilitation and subsequent book, *Strukturwandel der Öffentlichkeit* (*The Structural Transformation of the Public Sphere*, 1989). Not only is this his most historical work but it has proved to be the work that has most influenced historians. Habermas located the emergence of a bourgeois public sphere in late 17th- and 18th-century Europe. Evident in coffee houses, salons, lending libraries, and the embryonic press, this "public" constituted a category of society separate from the family and the state. It became possible to speak of "public opinion" for the first time. This essentially elitist world expanded and developed alongside the rise of the market economy. Characterized by the presumption of a rough equality among its members, it stood in opposition to 18th-century absolutism. The bourgeois public sphere was based on rationality and claimed to uphold universal and liberal principles. Habermas argued that the public sphere declined in the 19th and 20th centuries through the rise of commercialization and modern culture industries as well as the extension of state bureaucracy. What was left was a "pseudo-public or sham-private world of cultural consumption." Thus the press, for example, was no longer the organ of information that it had once been, but merely a purveyor of entertainment. Habermas' larger political purpose was therefore to question the whole nature of democracy.

Habermas was well known among historians in France and Germany, but the impact of his work on an English-speaking audience was delayed until the translation of *Strukturwandel* in 1989. His influence can be seen particularly in recent debates on the origins of the French Revolution. Historians such as Roger Chartier and Keith Baker have engaged with Habermas in a discussion of how the public sphere and public opinion established the framework within which the Revolution became possible. Hence the importance attached to clubs and newspapers in the creation of civil society outside the state. Joan B. Landes has argued that one of the chief characteristics of the French public sphere in the age of the Revolution was that it was gendered. Despite its claims to uphold universal values, its ethos was masculine (derived from the classical republican tradition) and excluded women. The 1989 conference on Habermas and the public sphere (whose proceedings were edited by Craig Calhoun) included contributions from several historians including Keith Baker and Geoff Eley. Habermas himself offered further thoughts on the subject. Much of the recent historical work on the separate spheres of public and private is in his debt.

In later work, Habermas argued that the dilemmas of modern society can be traced to the effects of modern technology. He argued, for example, that a barrier had developed between the public sphere and the scientists who create new technologies. Furthermore, he rejected the liberal political tradition of the modern state, doubting that constitutional change could have much effect on politics. In a somewhat autocratic sense he favored new controls to create a genuine democracy, perceiving modern mass man as a victim of technology bereft of any identity.

In keeping with the tradition of social criticism he inherited from 19th-century German thinkers such as Karl Marx and Werner Sombart, Habermas still believes that capitalism will pass through a series of inevitable stages. Sombart believed that the disintegration of culture could be linked to the last stages of capitalism. Habermas has projected this stage of late capitalism into an indefinite future. He argued in *Legitimationsprobleme im Spätkapitalismus* (1973; *Legitimation Crisis*, 1976) that it has been modern technology that has produced crises of the kind that lead to an inevitable collapse. Once the stage of late capitalism is reached, there will be a legitimation crisis of the first order.

Responding to criticism from the evolutionary sociologist Niklas Luhmann at the 1974 German Sociology Congress, Habermas argued that one could reconstruct social evolution as part of a historical process. He postulated a three-stage evolution from a period before civilization to an archaic civilization, then to a highly developed civilization. This evolutionary theory was not presented as a theory of history. Its function was to open an avenue for practical discussion. Habermas saw historical writing as dependent on a narrative form rooted in basic concepts. For him, historical writing describes social action, interprets motives, understands values and worldviews. In the past, the world seemed divided into many distinct histories and few historians found a common pattern to it. In contrast, Habermas pointed out in *Theorie und Praxis* (1963; *Theory and Practice*, 1973) that the transition to a modern world society revealed a universal structure of human consciousness. Therefore, history does have meanings and these meanings require explanation. However, in the absence of scientific rigor, meaning becomes symbolic. It acquires the status of fact, even when it is not.

Under the influence of Talcott Parsons' theories of social action, Habermas published a 2-volume work, *Theorie des kommunikativen Handelns* (1982; *Theory of Communicative Action*, 1984), which treated diverse themes of communicative rationalism. In it, he went beyond the theory of social action and worked with theories of systems and the paradoxes of the modern world.

In a more concrete form, Habermas was able to link ideas, the existentialist ones of Heidegger for example, to political rather than economic events. By 1984 he had realized that Heidegger's idea of the history of existence was tied to the collectivist politics of the 1930s rather than to individual suffering. It was the political influence of that philosophy that he rejected. It was also his more sociological understanding of the world that led him to defend the idea that even a well-developed idea of universal history can never replace the general theories of the social and human sciences.

HELEN LIEBEL-WECKOWICZ

See also Chartier; Dilthey; France: 1450–1789; Germany: 1800–1945; Media

Biography

Born Düsseldorf, 18 June 1929. Studied at University of Göttingen; PhD, University of Bonn, 1954; Habilitation, University of Marburg, 1961. Taught philosophy, University of Heidelberg, 1962–64; professor of philosophy and sociology, University of Frankfurt, 1964–71 and from 1982; director, Max-Planck-Institut zur Erforschung der Lebensbedingungen der wissenschaftlich-technischen Welt, 1971–82. Married Ute Wesselhoeft, 1955 (1 son, 2 daughters).

Principal Writings

Strukturwandel der Öffentlichkeit: Untersuchungen zu einer Kategorie der bürgerlichen Gesellschaft, 1962; in English as The Structural Transformation of the Public Sphere: An Inquiry into a Category of Bourgeois Society, 1989
Erkenntnis und Interesse, 1968; in English as Knowledge and Human Interests, 1971
Theorie und Praxis: sozial-philosophische Studien, 1963, revised and expanded, 1971; abridged in English as Theory and Practice, 1973
Zur Logik der Sozialwissenschaften (On the Logic of the Social Sciences), 1967; revised 1970
Technik und Wissenschaft als "Ideologie," 1968; selected essays in English as Toward a Rational Society: Student Protest, Science and Politics, 1970
Legitimationsprobleme im Spätkapitalismus, 1973; in English as Legitimation Crisis, 1976
"The Public Sphere: An Encyclopedia Article", New German Critique 3 (1974), 44–55
Zur Rekonstruktion des historischen Materialismus, 1976; selected essays translated in Communication and the Evolution of Society, 1979
Theorie des kommunikativen Handelns, 2 vols., 1982; in English as The Theory of Communicative Action, 2 vols., 1984

Further Reading

Calhoun, Craig, ed., Habermas and the Public Sphere, Cambridge, MA: MIT Press, 1993
Castiglione, Dario, and Lesley Sharpe, eds., Shifting the Boundaries: Transformation of the Languages of Public and Private in the Eighteenth Century, Exeter: University of Exeter Press, 1995
Johnson, Christopher H., "Lifeworld, System and Communicative Action: The Habermasian Alternative in Social History," in Lenard R. Berlanstein, ed., Rethinking Labor History: Essays on Discourse and Class Analysis, Urbana: University of Illinois Press, 1993
Kelly, Michael, ed., Critique and Power: Recasting the Foucault/Habermas Debate, Cambridge, MA: MIT Press, 1994
Landes, Joan B., Women and the Public Sphere in the Age of the French Revolution, Ithaca, NY: Cornell University Press, 1988

McCarthy, Thomas A., The Critical Theory of Jürgen Habermas, London: Hutchinson, and Cambridge, MA: MIT Press, 1978
Nathans, Benjamin, "Habermas's 'Public Sphere' in the Era of the French Revolution," French Historical Studies 16 (1990), 620–44
White, Stephen K., ed., The Cambridge Companion to Habermas, Cambridge: Cambridge University Press, 1995

Halecki, Oskar 1891–1973

US (Austrian-born) historian of Poland and Europe

Oskar Halecki was among the best known and most respected East European émigré scholars in the West following World War II. His early work focused on the history of Poland-Lithuania, and he was one of the pioneers of Byzantine studies in interwar Poland. Following the war, however, he expanded his scholarly interests to include the entire European state system and the role played by East Central Europe in European history. Throughout his career he emphasized the essential spiritual and cultural unity of the Latin West, including the region that he called "the borderlands of Western civilization" – Poland-Lithuania, Hungary, Bohemia, and the Balkans. In the West, he was the most learned and forceful of the many east European scholars who have argued that East Central Europe is more than simply an appendage of Western Europe.

Born in the multinational Habsburg empire and educated at the foremost institution of Polish learning, the Jagiellonian University in Kraków, Halecki came of age at the time when Poland regained its independence after 123 years of foreign domination. The ongoing debates about what form the new nation should take found Poles divided into two camps: those who held to the "Piast" vision of a smaller but more ethnically homogeneous Poland, and those who wanted a Poland modeled along the lines of the old multinational Polish-Lithuanian commonwealth wherein "Polishness" depended more on political citizenship than on language, religion, or ethnic bloodlines. These debates had an important impact on Halecki, who was an adherent of the latter position.

Like most historians of his day, Halecki's history was one of grand historical processes, and, like his contemporaries, he gave politics, wars, and the actions of rulers their due. Yet, for Halecki, the key to understanding the past lay in culture and religion above all else. This led him to the conclusion that despite its deep divisions, the history of Christian Europe, and especially the Latin West, could be understood as a unified whole, across a millennium, provided due attention was paid to Byzantium and East Central Europe. Although he placed great importance on the role that Christian Europe had played in human advancement, he had little regard for notions of European superiority. His experiences as a Pole led him to reject all forms of imperialism, and to subscribe to the notion – following Lord Acton and the Polish anthropologist Bronisław Malinowski – that freedom and civilization were inseparable, and that in the European history of whatever century "freedom in its various aspects is simply the problem, the basis of all others." This belief, along with his Catholicism and his emphasis on culture and spirit, led him to reject all forms of materialism – whether Marxist or capitalist. For Halecki, unlike Machiavelli, the ideal ruler based his or her actions on Christian principles.

Halecki is best known in the West as a historian of Poland. For him, the Polish past had a strong spiritual and cultural unity. In his later years, however, most of his published works focused on Europe as a whole, a subject to which he brought a phenomenal command of primary sources. One of Halecki's most interesting contributions was a reclassification of European history to account for the role played by all European nations, a problem he had been pursuing through several published works, but which appeared in its final form only in a posthumous book, *Jadwiga of Anjou* (1991). Halecki saw two geographical/cultural fault lines dividing Europe: the first ran from the North Sea through the Rhine Valley to the Ligurian Sea; the second ran from the Baltic Sea, through the Vistula Basin, to the Black Sea, encompassing much of Poland and Ukraine. Along these basic divisions, the story of Europe played itself out. In his two transitional zones – Swiss/Burgundian and Polish/Ukrainian – conflicts between cultures and worldviews were enacted.

Although Halecki's vision of European history fell out of fashion even before his death, his impact on present historiography is clear. His *History of Poland*, reprinted many times, was for decades the best source on Poland in the English-speaking world, even though it has been criticized as being too nationalistic and too favorable toward the Poles. Yet, Halecki's work, particularly his belief in the importance of culture and religion in macrohistory, may be best remembered as being a forerunner of the resurgence of "World History" in the early 1990s.

JOHN RADZILOWSKI

See also Davies, N.; East Central Europe; Poland: since the 18th Century

Biography

Born Vienna, 26 May 1891, son of a Polish officer in the Austrian army. Attended Jagiellonian University, Kraków, 1909–13, lecturer, 1916–18. Held chair of the history of Eastern Europe, Warsaw University, 1918–39, but spent 1918–28 chiefly as Polish representative to a range of international political organizations. In Switzerland at the outbreak of World War II. Moved to Paris to organize a Polish university in exile; but fled to the United States, July 1940 (naturalized 1947). Professor of East European history, Fordham University, 1944–61. Awarded Order of St. Gregory the Great by Pope Paul VI, 1966. Married Helen de Sulima Szarlowska (died 1964). Died White Plains, New York, 17 September 1973.

Principal Works

Un Empereur de Byzance à Rome: vingt ans de travail pour l'union des églises et pour la défense de l'Empire d'Orient, 1355–1375 (One Emperor from Byzantium to Rome: Twenty Years of Work for the Union of the Churches and the Defence of the Eastern Empire), 1930

La Pologne de 963 à 1914: essai de synthèse historique, 1933; in English as *A History of Poland: An Essay in Historical Synthesis*, 1942, 9th edition 1976

Nowe uwagi krytyczne o wyprawie warenskiej, 1939; in English as *The Crusade of Varna: A Discussion of Controversial Problems*, 1943

Editor, *The English Atlas: Moses Pitt (1654–96)*, New York: Tebinka, 1943

Polish–Russian Relations: Past and Present, Notre Dame: Notre Dame University Press, 1943

The Two World Wars: A Comparison, 1946 [lectures]

The Limits and Divisions of European History, 1950

Eugenio Pacelli, Pope of Peace, 1951; also as *Pius XII*, 1953

Borderlands of Western Civilization: A History of East Central Europe, 1952

Editor, *Poland*, 1957

From Florence to Brest (1439–1596), 1958

"The Renaissance Origins of Pan-Slavism," *Polish Review* 3, 1–2 (Winter-Spring 1958), 7–19

"The Problem of Federalism in the History of East Central Europe," *Polish Review* 5, 3 (Summer 1960), 5–19

The Millennium of Europe, 1963

Jadwiga of Anjou and the Rise of East Central Europe, 1991

Further Reading

Lewalski, Kenneth F., "Oscar Halecki," in Hans A. Schmitt, ed., *Historians of Modern Europe*, Baton Rouge: Louisiana State University Press, 1971

Halévy, Elie 1870–1937
French historian of Britain

Elie Halévy was one of the few French historians who made the study of the British the centerpoint of his work, and as such was one of the best known of French historians in British historical circles during his lifetime. To subsequent generations of students his works on liberalism and utilitarianism, on religion and especially Methodism, and on the history of socialist thought were primary texts. They provided a first systematic analysis of subjects and figures who became key historical issues in the rise of social history from the 1950s. Halévy was also a distinctive French historian. Though of the same generation as the early Annales school, he was not part of this movement, and indeed appears to have had little contact with it. He was a historian of ideas, a historian of the 19th and 20th centuries, and his major interests were in England, and in the origins and impact of World War I on European politics. His background, while certainly formed in the social sciences praised by the Annales school, was much more fundamentally connected to philosophy and politics.

Halévy was born into a talented and wealthy secular Jewish family which identified with the Third Republic. His grandfather Léon was a poet and one of the disciples of Saint-Simon. His father worked in the theater as a librettist and wrote belles lettres. His younger brother Daniel was a well-known author and publicist. The Halévy brothers attended the elite academic institutions in France – the Lycée Condorcet then the Ecole Normale Supérieure, where Elie studied philosophy. When the Dreyfus affair split France forcing a confrontation with the arbitrary justice of the military elite and its anti-Semitism, Halévy defended Dreyfus on republican and liberal principles. These principles became the program for the philosophic journal he took a major part in founding in 1893, the *Revue de Métaphysique et de Morale*, and the guide to all his later historical works. Halévy took up a teaching post at the Ecole Libre des Sciences Politiques, the institution founded to train civil servants, administrators, and diplomats, and stayed there all his professional life. He later turned down posts at the rival Sorbonne, and preferred the modern atmosphere of a policy-oriented environment similar to the London School of

Economics, with its emphasis on the social sciences, modern history, international relations, administration, public law, and modern languages.

Halévy started his study of the philosophic radicals, the early English utilitarians, while a student at the Ecole Normale, and in the period 1895–1905 decided that history rather than philosophy or sociology was to be his vocation. The first two volumes of *La Formation du radicalisme philosophique* (*The Growth of Philosophic Radicalism*, 1928) were published in 1901, the third in 1904. Halévy defended the utilitarians, arguing for the proactive impact of their doctrines which fitted the needs of a class of merchants and manufacturers, but also noted the collectivist implications of a number of their positions and projects.

Halévy found at the heart of English liberalism not just the secular individualistic ideas of the utilitarians, however, but the religious beliefs of evangelical Protestantism. Ideas together with beliefs underlay basic English institutions and helped to explain political action. Halévy described the revival of the Puritan religious impulse in national consciousness at the turn of the 19th century, asking why was it that England, which experienced so much social and economic chaos in the process of industrialization, did not experience political revolution. This became the famous "Halévy thesis," debated more narrowly as a comment on the social impact of Methodism. This was argued at greater length in the first volume of his *Histoire du peuple anglais* in 1912, *L'Angleterre en 1815*. This volume of his social and intellectual history of the English was followed by subsequent volumes taking his narrative up to World War I, and an uncompleted volume on the Victorians. The series was published in English as *History of the English People* (1924–34).

During this time of writing his volumes on the English, Halévy also wrote the works on the history of socialism for which he became most famous in France. He wrote an early volume on the English radical Thomas Hodgskin, followed by his *Histoire du socialisme europeén* (History of European Socialism, 1948), and by his essay and edition of *La Doctrine de Saint-Simon* (The Doctrine of Saint-Simon), a short biography of Sismondi, and later essays published in his *L'Ere des tyrannies* (1938; *The Era of Tyrannies*, 1965). The war marked a turning point in his hopes for socialism. Where he earlier wrote about its democratic potential, his later work focused on authoritarianism and statism.

Like many of his contemporary historians, Halévy was politicized by World War I. Already 44 at its outbreak, he was turned away from the nationalism of many of his contemporaries, seeking a postwar role in enhancing a broad European culture and liberal, democratic institutions. He spent more time in England, and interacted closely with Graham Wallas, H.A.L. Fisher, Ernest Barker, G.P. Gooch, the Hammonds, and the Webbs. He lectured and wrote on the impact of the war, publishing the Rhodes Memorial lectures he gave in Oxford as *The World Crisis of 1914–1918* (1930). He organized a conference in 1936 on themes of socialism and revolution, war, nationalism, and totalitarianism, published after his death in *The Era of Tyrannies*. Here the libertarian themes he had once sought in the socialist tradition were overtaken by pessimistic themes of the growth of state power and the kinship of socialism with both communism and fascism.

MAXINE BERG

See also Britain: since 1750

Biography
Born Etretat, Normandy, 6 September 1870, son of a playwright. Educated at Lycée Condorcet; agrégation in philosophy, Ecole Normale Superieure, 1892, doctorate 1900. Professor, Ecole Libre des Sciences Politiques, Paris, from 1898; founder/director, *Revue de Métaphysique et de Morale*, 1893. Married Florence Noufflard, 1901. Died Sucy-en-Brie, 21 August 1937.

Principal Writings
La Formation du radicalisme philosophique, 3 vols., 1901–04; in English as *The Growth of Philosophic Radicalism*, 1928
Thomas Hodgskin (1787–1869), 1903; in English as *Thomas Hodgskin*, 1956
Histoire du peuple anglais au XIXe siècle, 1912–32; in English as *A History of the English People in the Nineteenth Century*, 1924–34
Editor with Celestin Bougle, *La Doctrine de Saint-Simon: exposition, première année, 1829*, 1924
The World Crisis of 1914–1918: An Interpretation, 1930
Sismondi, 1933
L'Ere des tyrannies: études sur le socialisme et la guerre, 1938; in English as *The Era of Tyrannies*, 1965
Histoire du socialisme européen (History of European Socialism), 1948

Further Reading
Chase, Myrna, *Elie Halévy: An Intellectual Biography*, New York: Columbia University Press, 1980
Halévy, Elie, *Correspondance (1891–1937)*, Paris: Fallois, 1996
Hughes, H. Stuart, *Consciousness and Society: The Reorientation of European Social Thought, 1890–1930*, New York: Knopf, 1958, London: MacGibbon and Kee, 1959; revised New York: Vintage, 1977
Walsh, John, "Elie Halévy and the Birth of Methodism," *Transactions of the Royal Historical Society* 5th series, 25 (1975), 2–20

Haller, Johannes 1865–1947
German medievalist

Principally a historian of the papacy, the German *Reich*, and the relations between them in the medieval period, Johannes Haller was arguably the most significant, and certainly the most widely read, representative of politically and methodologically conservative historism in his generation. His consistency through decades of political and intellectual turmoil in Germany from the outbreak of World War I to the end of World War II testifies to the resilience of statist historiography in the face of challenges from the left and from the racialist right.

Haller's interest in the papacy was inspired by commingled loathing and admiration. He was a Protestant and a German nationalist for whom the *Kulturkampf* never ended. Even in the Third Reich, he hinted darkly at continuing ultramontane conspiracies in Germany. Profoundly convinced that the interests of the Vatican and Germany were mutually incompatible, Haller squeezed his sources for every last drop of evidence of the mutual antagonism of pope and emperor. And where he could no longer find it, this inveterate Rankean, feared by other scholars for the withering rebukes he would deliver were he to catch them in the unprofessional use of sources, invented the evidence freely. However, he read papal power politics as a model of its kind, suggesting lessons from which German statesmen of his own age might still learn. Even though his awe of papal *Realpolitik* arose out of jealousy, Haller did not allow his imagination to run away with him so as to over-shadow his scholarship. A similar admixture of contempt and love ran through his various encounters with French history, and especially his *Tausend Jahre deutsch-französische Bezie-hungen* (1930; *France and Germany*, 1932).

The same cannot be said of Haller's interventions in debates on German war aims and domestic policies in 1914–18. In this case, he used the past to legitimize aggressive annexation policies in the present. Such abuse of academic authority is perfectly illustrated by his sending students Christmas cards depicting "Luther in a U-boat."

In the aftermath of defeat and of the November Revolution of 1918, Haller overcame a crisis of political confidence to write his best-known work, *Die Epochen der deutschen Geschichte* (1923; *The Epochs of German History*, 1930). In it he developed what amounted to a theoretical statement of classic historism. In periods of German ascendancy, he argued, *Führer* first integrated the *Volk* into the nation-state and then allowed the proper function of the nation-state – the pursuit of power politics – to develop. It was an approach to German history that relegated the *Volk* to putty, which a leader of genius could mould at will.

This view of historical process had ambiguous political consequences. On the one hand, it helps explain both Haller's unstinting hostility toward parliamentary democracy and the Weimar republic and his public acclaim for Hitler during the 1930s. On the other, it brought him into sometimes brutal exchanges with proponents of a racial determinism that saw in the *Volk* the motor of history. In close collaboration with his former student and successor to the chair of medieval history at Tübingen, Heinrich Dannenbauer, Haller poured scorn over reworked Tacitean myths of the superiority of Germanic tribesmen to degenerate Romans, derided claims that the first Germans had Nordic origins, and dismissed the notion that Germans were Aryan. Marc Bloch, in his review articles on German historiography published in the *Annales* and the *Revue Historique*, noted that Haller's and Dannenbauer's work represented an adherence to scholarly standards under difficult circumstances, and testified to their "civic courage."

Haller did not contribute propaganda in World War II as he had done in World War I. By the end of his life, his faith in Nazism and his faith in German nationalism had collapsed. Nor could he find any meaning in history to replace either. His last work verged on nihilism. The hand of God was visible indeed in history. But it was cruel, incomprehensible, or both.

PETER A. LAMBERT

Biography

Born Keinis, Ostland, 15 October 1865, son of a cleric. Studied at University of Heidelberg, 1891; received Habilitation, University of Basel, 1897; Prussian Historical Institute, Rome, 1901–02. Taught at University of Marburg, 1902–13; professor, University of Tübingen, 1913–32 (emeritus). Married Elisabeth Fueter, 1904 (2 sons, 2 daughters). Died Tübingen, 24 December 1947.

Principal Writings

Die Epochen der deutschen Geschichte, 1923; in English as *The Epochs of German History*, 1930
Aus dem Leben des Fürsten Philipp zu Eulenburg-Hertefeld, 1924; in English as *Philip Eulenburg: The Kaiser's Friend*, 2 vols., 1930
Tausend Jahre deutsch-französische Beziehungen, 1930; in English as *France and Germany: The History of One Thousand Years*, 1932
Das Papsttum: Idee und Wirklichkeit (The Papacy: Ideology and Reality), 3 vols. in 5, 1934–45

Halperín-Donghi, Tulio 1926–

Argentine intellectual, political, social, and economic historian

Tulio Halperín-Donghi has contributed much to our knowledge of Latin America in general and Argentina in particular. He has been a prolific writer since the 1950s, and his work embodies Benedetto Croce's observation that a historian writes history with present interests in mind. His approach has energized the field of Latin American history, as he both analyzes economic, social, political, and intellectual factors and investigates their relationship to each other in order to provide a comprehensive view of the past. His writings have ranged through numerous historical fields to illuminate the seemingly confusing Latin American past by providing a framework within which to understand it.

Halperín-Donghi initially began his studies in chemistry but soon abandoned that field for the study of history. During the late 1940s and early 1950s he enrolled in the University of Buenos Aires. A brilliant student, he began his career as a historian by publishing his initial essays while attending university. During the 1950s and 1960s he had a close relationship with those scholars who had been denied positions at the university under the Peronist regime. These scholars continued their work by contributing to the journals *Imago Mundi* and *Sur* as well as to the cultural supplement of the newspaper *La Nación*. José Luis Romero, a principal figure behind *Imago Mundi* and a historian of ideas, and Claudio Sánchez Albornoz, a historian of medieval Spain, convinced Halperín-Donghi to study European history. In Europe he studied at the University of Turin, where he was influenced by the ideas of Croce and Antonio Gramsci. He also attended the Ecole des Hautes Etudes in Paris, where he came into contact with Fernand Braudel and the Annales school of French historians.

After his excursion into European history, Halperín-Donghi returned to the study of the history of Argentina and Latin America. Focusing on 19th-century Argentina, he wrote what many scholars consider to be his most original work: *Revolución y guerra* (1972; *Politics, Economics and Society in Argentina in the Revolutionary Period*, 1975), an investigation of the many forces that led to Argentine independence. Although he thought of the work as a political history, it also wove together strands of regional, intellectual, political, social, and economic history. Organized chronologically, the book began with the colonial economic antecedents to independence, tracing the growth of Buenos Aires and its maritime provinces. This growth affected the interior provinces and contributed to the disarray and regional conflicts after independence. During the period of the war for independence, Buenos Aires became the site of struggles between the military and political leadership for dominance and influence over the emerging republican order. This new group of career revolutionaries challenged the power of the traditional social groups, the colonial merchants and bureaucrats. Halperín-Donghi's analysis did not lose sight of the alliances between the new elites and the old. This interregnum between the dissolution of the old order and the emergence of the new had unintended consequences, because it unleashed unforseen social forces that contributed to the chaos and fragmentation that arose after 1820. The rise of Juan Manuel de Rosas, Argentina's quintessential *caudillo* (political boss), was the logical consequence of the attempt by the revolutionary elites to transform the political, social, and economic structures, because he imposed order on the chaos they had wrought. Scholars have valued Halperín-Donghi's grasp of the period's broad trends, which he elucidated by studying the protagonists' confrontation with economic, social, and regional forces. Furthermore, Halperín-Donghi linked the invention of the new political order with the creation of new social and economic links among elites during the dissolution of the colonial order. He considered the emergence of this new elite to be the central factor in the transformation from a colonial to a republican order.

Another important contribution emphasized by scholars is Halperín-Donghi's analysis of the rise of Argentina's *terrateniente* (landlord) class. Previous historiography had focused on the colonial roots of this landed class as well as the dominance of livestock breeding in the countryside. This traditional historiography, identifying the *terratenientes* with cattle breeders, postulated that their growing economic power gave them an unimpeded social pathway into the avenues of political power. It also conceptualized the urban and rural elites as distinctive entities with conflicting interests. Halperín-Donghi challenged this view with his perceptive examination of Argentina's late colonial urban and rural elites, which he perceived as having intertwined interests and personal ties. Contradicting the accepted gospel that the landlord class had colonial roots, he proposed that the wealth of colonial Buenos Aires was based on commerce and silver, not on rural production. This had resulted from the city's position as the seat of the new Viceroyalty of the Rio de la Plata, which included present-day Bolivia and its silver wealth from Potosí.

In Latin American historiography, the question of whether haciendas, *estancias*, or other large landed properties functioned under feudal systems of production or as capitalist enterprises has been paramount for an understanding of the region's social and economic structures and their transformation over time. Halperín-Donghi argued that by 1820 *estancias* appeared that functioned as capitalist enterprises, since they employed free-wage labor and did not depend on merchant or usurious capital, two important defining characteristics. In terms of labor, he has demonstrated that prior to 1820 there was a predominance of free-wage labor in the *estancia* and that the process accelerated after that date. However, during this same period, the *estancia* was reliant on merchant or usurious capital. After 1820, the *estancia* became independent not as a result of massive capital accumulation but because of the modest capital requirements for livestock production. This process coincided with the emergence of the Rosas regime, which favored it and, therefore, contributed to its consolidation.

Halperín-Donghi entered the debate on the relative autonomy of the state, and the relationship between the landlord class, the political elite, and the state is another theme that he explored in order to understand the complexity of the connection between class and political power. For him, the state had already developed and consolidated before the landlord class emerged as a dominant economic actor. One of the consequences of the revolution in the Rio de la Plata was the divorce between the landowners and the administrators of power. This divorce between economic and political power was more complete in Buenos Aires than in the provinces. The political elites, therefore, were not totally subordinated to the dictates of the landlord class. The introduction of universal male suffrage during the 1820s, which politicized the urban masses, threatened the political power of the governing elites. They maintained their hold on political power by finding a counterpoise in the less politicized character of the rural masses. The direct influence of the landlord class was also limited, because the electoral laws organized the entire countryside into one electoral district.

In earlier writings on the development of the landowning class, Halperín-Donghi suggested that this class was not only the beneficiary of the expansion of the export sector but also the agent guiding this development in a conscious manner. In later writings he reversed his position, stating that this class was the creation of the process of export expansion resulting from the profound restructuring of rural society entailed in the process. The state took on a new-found importance as the agent of the transformations by relegating the landowning class to the position of captive allies under the Rosas regime.

Another contribution of Halperín-Donghi has been in the field of 19th- and 20th-century Argentine intellectual history and the history of ideas. While at university he studied two seminal thinkers from the Generation of 1837, Domingo Faustino Sarmiento and Esteban Echeverría. His first book, *El pensamiento de Echeverría* (The Philosophical Ideas of Echeverría, 1951), explored the ideas of this romantic writer, who wrote *Dogma socialista* (1839) and opposed the Rosas regime. Halperín-Donghi assigned the intellectuals an important role in forging the Argentine nation during the 19th century.

Halperín-Donghi's exile from Argentina after the 1966 military coup widened his understanding of Argentine history by placing it in the larger Latin American context. He devoted numerous studies to contemporary Argentine history by concentrating on the figure of Juan Domingo Perón and Peronism. In an initial study, *Argentina en el callejón* (Argentina in a Cul-de-Sac, 1964), he explained the rise of Perón by an analysis of the 1930 crisis of the liberal economic model of export-led growth. In a subsequent study, *La larga agonía de la Argentina peronista* (The Long Agony of Peronist Argentina, 1994), he redated the beginning of the crisis of the Argentine state to the period 1852–1930. In another revision of his early views, he saw the "Peronist Revolution" as primarily an economic revolution and only secondarily as a political or cultural one.

Halperín-Donghi also analyzed wider Latin American trends in three important studies, *Storia dell'America Latina* (1968; *The Contemporary History of Latin America*, 1993), *Hispanoamérica después de la independencia* (1972; *The Aftermath of Revolution in Latin America*, 1973), and *Reforma y disolución de los imperios ibéricos, 1750–1850* (Reform and the

Breakdown of the Iberian Empires, 1750–1850, 1985), as well as in other significant works. Since its initial publication, the first work, in its Spanish translation, has influenced numerous Spanish-speaking university students as a basic text for a holistic study of Latin America. The author, influenced by Fernand Braudel, sought a middle course between anecdotal narrative and unchanging structures. He concentrated on examining the historical processes of social and economic change as the colonial compact with Spain and Portugal broke down and a neocolonial order emerged with the industrial powers during the 19th century.

After his exile, Halperín-Donghi initially taught at Oxford and Harvard before settling at the University of California in 1971. His years of exile have contributed tremendously to his understanding of Argentina within the larger Latin American context, and he continues to write and influence the field of Latin American history by his perspicacious observations on the past, present, and future of the region.

CARLOS PÉREZ

See also Argentina

Biography
Born Buenos Aires, 27 October 1926. Studied in the Faculty of Philosophy and Letters and Faculty of Law, University of Buenos Aires, PhD 1955; then at University of Turin and Ecole des Hautes Etudes, Paris. Taught at University of Rosario, 1955–61; and University of Buenos Aires, 1959–66; after coup in 1966 left Argentina and taught at Harvard University, 1967–70; Oxford University, 1970–71; and University of California, Berkeley, 1971–94 (emeritus).

Principal Writings
El pensamiento de Echeverría (The Philosophical Ideas of Esteban Echeverría), 1951
Un conflicto nacional: moriscos y cristianos viejos en Valencia, Cuadernos de Historia de España (A National Conflict: New Christians and Old Christians in Valencia, Chronicles of Spanish History), 1957
Tradición política española e ideología revolucionaria de Mayo (The Spanish Political Tradition and the Revolutionary Ideology of May, 1810), 1961
Argentina en el callejón (Argentina in a Cul-de-Sac), 1964
Storia dell'America Latina, 1968; in Spanish as Historia contemporánea de América Latina, 1969; in English as The Contemporary History of Latin America, 1993
El revisionismo histórico Argentino (A Revisionist History of Argentina), 1971
Argentina: de la revolución de la independencia a la confederación rosista (Argentina: From the Revolutionary Period to Rosas' Confederation), 1972
Hispanoamérica después de la independencia: consecuencias sociales y económicas de la emancipación, 1972; in English as The Aftermath of Revolution in Latin America, 1973
Revolución y guerra: formación de una élite dirigente en la Argentina criolla, 1972; in English as Politics, Economics, and Society in Argentina in the Revolutionary Period, 1975
Proyecto y construcción de una nación: Argentina, 1846–1880 (The Project of Constructing a Nation: Argentina, 1846–1880), 1980
Guerra y finanzas en los orígenes del estado argentino, 1791–1850 (War and Finance in the Origins of the Argentine State, 1791–1850), 1982
José Hernández y sus mundos (José Hernández and His World), 1985

Reforma y disolución de los imperios ibéricos, 1750–1850 (Reform and the Breakdown of the Iberian Empires, 1750–1850), 1985
El espejo de la historia: problemas argentinos y perspectivas hispanoamericanas (The Mirror of History: Argentine Problems and Latin American Perspectives), 1987
La larga agonía de la Argentina peronista (The Long Agony of Peronist Argentina), 1994
Ensayos de historiografía (Historiographical Essays), 1996

Further Reading
Chiaramonte, José Carlos, and Oscar Terán, "Tulio Halperín-Donghi: de voluntades y realidades" (Tulio Halperín-Donghi: Of Intentionality and Reality), Todo es Historia 301 (1992), 58–71
Hora, Roy, and Javier Trímboli, "Tulio Halperín-Donghi: como no hay alternativas de fondo, el debate ideológico se hace poco interesante. Hoy no hay disenso sobre el pasado porque no lo hay sobre el presente" (Tulio Halperín-Donghi: Since there are no radical alternatives, the ideological debate is of little interest. Today there are no debates over the past because there are none over the present), in Roy Hora and Javier Trímboli, eds., Pensar la Argentina: los historiadores hablan de historia y política, Buenos Aires: Cielo por Asalto, 1994, 36–54
Hora, Roy, and Javier Trímboli, eds., Discutir Halperín: siete ensayos sobre la contribución de Tulio Halperín-Donghi a la historia argentina (Discussing Halperín: Seven Essays on Tulio Halperín-Donghi's Contribution to Argentine History), Buenos Aires: Cielo por Asalto, 1997

Hammond, J.L. 1872–1949 and Barbara Hammond 1873–1961
British economic and social historians

The Hammonds were, separately and together, authors of a series of controversial books between 1911 and the 1930s that reshaped historical understanding of early 19th-century British social history. Their trilogy of studies of the working class – The Village Labourer (1911), The Town Labourer (1917), and The Skilled Labourer (1919), together adding up to around 450,000 words of sustained historical argument – were particularly influential and controversial.

John Hammond's first historical study, an account of the political career of Charles James Fox, settled the customary debt of a young reformer to the great Whig leader. The Village Labourer, co-authored with his wife Barbara, was a much more innovative and contentious work. It was an unambiguous political intervention in Edwardian debates about the future of traditional landed society. The picture it gave of the rule of landed gentlemen before 1832 exploded nostalgia for the good old days when the county families were undisputed masters of the English countryside. Their power and wealth were shown to be built on exploitation, fraud, and violence. The small farmer, the cottager, the squatter were deprived of their traditional common rights by the chicanery of parliamentary enclosure while the rural labourer saw his wages beaten down to a bare subsistence level. This brutal regime culminated in the desperate Swing Riots of 1830 and the Great Reform Act of 1832, the latter the first in a series of political reforms that were to bring gradually to its close the disastrous reign of the landed interest.

The Town Labourer and The Skilled Labourer provided equally grim accounts of the impact of economic and social change on the urban worker. The Industrial Revolution meant longer and harder hours of work and an impoverished and unhealthy life in the squalor of new factory towns: "For the revolution that had raised the standard of comfort for the rich had depressed the standard of life for the poor." This social polarization was justified by the doctrines of political economy and by evangelical Christianity. It was also maintained by state power which denied any means – the parliamentary vote, trade unionism – by which working people could act together to improve their situation. Terrified by the French Revolution, the rulers of early 19th-century England saw only one purpose for government: the maintenance of order. This meant, according to the Hammonds, that law and justice became "the sentinels of a new and more terrible inequality between man and man."

Each of these three studies ended, at around 1832, on a bleak and hopeless note. *The Village Labourer* closed with the failure of the 1830 Swing Riots: "So perished the last hope of reform and reparation for the poor." *The Skilled Labourer* finished with the threat of civil war. And *The Town Labourer* concluded that "the soul of man was passing into a colder exile" in which social fellowship was dead. And yet civil war was averted, social and political reforms were introduced, working-class living standards did ultimately improve. It was left to later books to explain this. *The Rise of Modern Industry* (1925), in particular, argued that the chaos of early industrialization was reformed by two main agencies. First, the influence of "the educated class," working through the civil service, the factory inspectorate, and the professions, began to control some of the harmful effects of laissez-faire. And second, less emphasized by the Hammonds, the trade union movement.

The central thrust of the Hammonds' account of early 19th-century England provoked considerable debate throughout the 1920s and 1930s. Some of their key arguments were disputed. In particular, none of their books provided much in the way of precise empirical evidence for their contention about declining living standards. Their periodization of this decline was vague and there was little attempt to distinguish the precise experience of different sections of the working class or different regions of the country. J.H. Clapham's criticisms of the absence of precise quantitative data on wages and prices was especially influential. In several articles in the late 1920s Barbara and John Hammond responded to their critics. They made some concessions, but they also effectively defended their positions on solid empirical grounds and vindicated their credentials as historians. Responsive to the expansion of research in their field, they incorporated new material in revised editions of each of the *Labourer* volumes during the 1920s.

[By the 1930s the Hammonds had pretty much retired from the field of early 19th-century social history. *The Bleak Age* (1934) was a condensation of their 1930 book *The Age of the Chartists*. John Hammond, increasingly frail (he suffered a major heart attack in 1937), concentrated on a massive study published in 1938: *Gladstone and the Irish Nation*. At the same time their mode of writing history fell from favor. However, the growth of a new social history in the 1960s vindicated the continuing relevance of the work of the Hammonds. E.P. Thompson's *The Making of the English Working Class* in particular, though critical of specific aspects of the their interpretation of the period, is a successor of the *Labourer* trilogy.

JOHN SEED

See also Clapham; Economic; Europe: Modern; Halévy; Hobsbawm; Social; Tawney

Biography

John Lawrence Le Breton Hammond. Born Drighlington, Yorkshire, 18 July 1872, son of Rev. Vavasour Hammond, Vicar of Drighlington, near Bradford. Educated at Bradford Grammar School; St. John's College, Oxford, BA 1895. Political journalist: editor of the pro-Boer *Speaker* 1899–1907; occasional leader writer for the *Tribune* and the *Daily News*. Secretary to the Civil Service Commission, 1907–13. Served, despite his age, in the Royal Field Artillery, 1914–15, subsequently working in the Ministry of Reconstruction. Special correspondent and editorial writer, *Manchester Guardian*, 1919–39. Married Barbara Bradby, historian, 1901. Died near Hemel Hempstead, 7 April 1949.
Lucy Barbara Bradby Hammond. Born July 1873, daughter of a clergyman and public school headmaster. Attended St. Leonard's School, St. Andrews; Lady Margaret Hall, Oxford; later fellow. Married John Lawrence Hammond, historian, 1901 (died 1949). Died 14 November 1961.

Principal Writings

Barbara Hammond
William Lovett, 1800–1877, 1922
"Urban Death-Rates in the Early Nineteenth Century," *Economic History: A Supplement of the Economic Journal* 1 (1926–28), 419–28

J.L. Hammond
"Colonial and Foreign Policy" in Francis W. Hirst, Gilbert Murray, and J.L. Hammond, *Liberalism and Empire: Three Essays*, 1900
Charles James Fox: A Political Study, 1903
"New Light on the Industrial Revolution," *Contemporary Review* 131 (1927), 741–46
"The Industrial Revolution and Discontent," *Economic History Review* 2 (1929–30), 215–28
C.P. Scott of the Manchester Guardian, 1934
Gladstone and the Irish Nation, 1938
With M.R.D. Foot, *Gladstone and Liberalism*, 1952

Joint Publications
The Village Labourer, 1760–1832: A Study in the Government of England before the Reform Bill, 1911
The Town Labourer, 1760–1832: The New Civilization, 1917
The Skilled Labourer, 1760–1832, 1919
Lord Shaftesbury, 1923
The Rise of Modern Industry, 1925; revised 1937
The Age of the Chartists, 1832–54: A Study of Discontent, 1930
James Stansfeld: A Victorian Champion of Sex Equality, 1932
The Bleak Age, 1934

Further Reading

Ashton, T.S., entry on the Hammonds in David L. Sills, ed., *International Encyclopedia of the Social Sciences*, 19 vols., New York: Macmillan, 1968, vol. 6, 316–17
Clarke, Peter F., *Liberals and Social Democrats*, Cambridge and New York: Cambridge University Press, 1978
Hartwell, R.M., "The Rise of Modern Industry: A Review," in his *The Industrial Revolution and Economic Growth*, London: Methuen 1971
Johnson, Richard *et al.*, eds., *Making Histories: Studies in History-Writing and Politics*, London: Hutchinson, and Minneapolis: University of Minnesota Press, 1982
Kaye, Harvey J., *The British Marxist Historians: An Introductory Analysis*, Cambridge: Polity Press, 1984; New York: St. Martin's Press, 1995

Lovell, John, general introduction to J.L. and Barbara Hammond, *The Town Labourer*, London and New York: Longman, 1978

Mingay, G.E., general introduction to J.L. and Barbara Hammond, *The Village Labourer*, London and New York: Longman, 1978

Rule, John, general introduction to J.L. and Barbara Hammond, *The Skilled Labourer*, London and New York: Longman, 1979

Tawney, R.H., "J.L. Hammond, 1872–1949," *Proceedings of the British Academy* 46 (1960), 167–94

Thomis, Malcolm, *The Town Labourer and the Industrial Revolution*, London: Batsford, and New York: Barnes and Noble, 1974

Thompson, E.P., *The Making of the English Working Class*, London: Gollancz, 1963; New York: Pantheon, 1964

Winkler, Henry R., "J.L. Hammond" in Hans A. Schmitt, ed., *Historians of Modern Europe*, Baton Rouge: Louisiana State University Press, 1971

Handlin, Oscar 1915–

US social historian

It is difficult to categorize Oscar Handlin. He is one of the most prolific authors of 20th century US social and ethnic history, and his topics have been as varied as his approaches, which often included the use of related disciplines such as psychology or sociology.

Handlin was fond of beginning his research with a good question, and that question frequently revolved around the twin themes of immigration and acculturation. These themes have dominated some of his best known works, including *The Uprooted*, first published in 1951, and *Children of the Uprooted* (1966). Like many of his social histories, these continued the work of Handlin's mentor, Arthur Schlesinger, Sr., and contributed significantly to the growing fields of urban and ethnic history. In *The Uprooted*, for example, Handlin became one of the first to explore the psychological alienation of immigrants in American society, and at the same time the estrangement between immigrants and their American-born offspring, a subject continued in *Children of the Uprooted*. These books asked if the American dream of opportunity and a better life was worth the high price paid by the first generation of immigrants, and concluded that to millions it probably was.

Moreover, these seminal works examined the "new" immigrants from eastern and southern Europe who arrived late in the 19th century and whose language and cultural differences erected barriers to immediate acculturation. He returned to the question of new immigrants and America's so-called melting pot in *The Newcomers: Negroes and Puerto Ricans in a Changing Metropolis* (1959), where he explored the additional dimension of race. In this work, as in others before it, Handlin endorsed the importance of education in the acculturation process, but denied that these groups are prone to violence or criminal behavior as many xenophobic Americans have claimed.

Handlin's interests have straddled many subjects, and after his retirement in 1978 he supervised the dissertations of some 72 PhD candidates, whose scholarly research ranged from the colonial period to the 20th century, from Revolutionary War ideology to post-Civil War industrialization. His courses reportedly dealt with everything from immigrants and urbanization, to religion, politics, and literature. Similarly, his own research interests ranged from slavery to 20th-century civil rights movements, from immigration to American affluence, and from youth culture to the role of liberty in American history. Handlin liked to concern himself primarily with ordinary lives, making him a pioneer in the field of history from the bottom up. His use of social sciences, literature, geography, economics, and psychology opened vistas for his own historical inquiry and that of his students. His clear, engrossing writing style and ability to turn out nearly a book per year made him popular with the reading public as well.

Although Handlin welcomed an interdisciplinary approach to history, he admonished historians who rely too heavily on theory or mold findings to fit into it. Theory, he claimed, is useful only when historians understand it well enough to apply it – and they frequently do not – and only when it serves to enhance bona fide research. Moreover, Handlin opposed fads in history, from the consensus approach of the 1950s to the proliferation of fragmented areas of study in the 1970s and beyond. The array of new methodologies such as quantification, he has said, have the potential of undermining basic skills and procedures of the historical profession and should, therefore, be used with caution.

Handlin was also a critic of the large 1960s university expansions and the unrest, which he attributed to this rapid increase in the student body. He was especially disparaging of what he called the "go-go" mentality in universities and the tendency to bypass professional training and ethics in favor of career advancement. In his series of essays titled *Truth in History* (1979), Handlin especially criticized his profession's current tendency to try to serve up "nostrums to dissolve current and future problems." Historians must, he said, rededicate themselves to the discipline of history, not to trying to solve the dilemmas of the modern world.

Handlin also feared a loss of autonomy and critical freedom among historians as scholars become more and more financially dependent on government and private foundations to support themselves and their research. On the other hand, he could not entirely deny the narrower opportunities for historians in the latter decades of the 20th century, and perhaps longed for a return to the elitism of earlier days, an elitism no longer feasible – or acceptable.

Even so, Handlin's own place in history is secure. It rests solidly on his contributions to urban and social history. Many historians would argue that there are very good reasons to explore a multitude of paths, and that temporary fragmentation is a fair price to pay for finally being able to include large segments of American society heretofore omitted from traditional history books. Similarly, there are historians who would defend new methodologies, claiming they enhance, rather than undermine the old methods. Handlin might agree, but within limits. His lengthy, distinguished career represents an unending quest to find truth in history and the absolute belief that history must be done the right way.

KATHLEEN EGAN CHAMBERLAIN

See also Bailyn; Ethnicity; Migration; Scott, A.; Slavery: Modern; United States: Historical Writing, 20th Century; Urban; Williams, W.

Biography

Born Brooklyn, New York, 29 September 1915, son of Jewish immigrants. Attended Brooklyn College, BA 1934; Harvard

University, MA 1935, PhD 1940. Taught at Brooklyn College, 1936–38; and Harvard University (rising to professor), 1939–78 (emeritus); director, Harvard University Library, 1979–85. Married 1) Mary Flug, historian, 1937 (died 1976; 1 son, 2 daughters); 2) Lilian Bombach, 1977.

Principal Writings

Boston's Immigrants, 1790–1865: A Study in Acculturation, 1941; revised and enlarged 1959

With Mary Flug Handlin, *Commonwealth: A Study of the Role of Government in the American Economy: Massachusetts, 1774–1861*, 1947; revised 1969

Editor, *This Was America: True Accounts of People and Places, Manners and Customs, as Recorded by European Travelers to the Western Shore in the Eighteenth, Nineteenth, and Twentieth Centuries*, Cambridge: Harvard University Press, 1949

The Uprooted: The Epic Story of the Great Migrations That Made the American People, 1951, revised 1973; in UK as *The Uprooted: From the Old World to the New*, 1953

Chance or Destiny: Turning Points in American History, 1955

Race and Nationality in American Life, 1957

Al Smith and His America, 1958

Editor, *Immigration as a Factor in American History*, 1959

The Newcomers: Negroes and Puerto Ricans in a Changing Metropolis, 1959

Fire-Bell in the Night: The Crisis in Civil Rights, 1964

Children of the Uprooted, 1966

With Mary Flug Handlin, *Facing Life: Youth and the Family in American History*, 1971

With Mary Flug Handlin, *The Wealth of the American People: A History of American Affluence*, 1975

Truth in History, 1979

Abraham Lincoln and the Union, 1980

The Distortion of America, 1981

With Lilian Handlin, *A Restless People: Americans in Rebellion, 1770–1787*, 1982

Further Reading

Bringhurst, Newell G., *Brigham Young and the Expanding American Frontier*, Boston: Little Brown, 1986

Bushman, Richard L. *et al.*, eds., *Uprooted Americans: Essays to Honor Oscar Handlin*, Boston: Little Brown, 1979

Stave, Bruce, ed., *The Making of Urban History: Historiography Through Oral History*, Beverly Hills: Sage, 1977

Hanke, Lewis 1905–1993

US social and cultural historian of Latin America

Viewed as the dean of North American Latin Americanists, Lewis Hanke emerged as one of the most influential revisionist Latin American historians of the 20th century. Hanke's contributions to the furtherance of Latin American studies as both a discipline and as an integral part of American and world history encompass an unprecedented number of academic monographs and articles as well as active involvement in archival work, editorship, and teaching. Trained in Latin American history at Harvard University under the prominent Latin Americanist Clarence H. Haring during the 1930s, Hanke became interested in the life and work of the Spanish theologian, Bartolomé de Las Casas.

His first two studies on Las Casas, *Las teorías politicas de Bartolomé de Las Casas* (The Political Theories of Bartolomé de Las Casas) and *The First Social Experiments in America*

were published in 1935. Although these works laid the basis for his later studies of Las Casas, they did not receive the acclaim accorded to his magisterial work, *The Spanish Struggle for Justice in the Conquest of America* (1949). Hanke's most influential work was premised on a debate between two famous 15th-century Spanish theologians, Bartolomé de Las Casas and Juan Gines de Sepulveda, held before the Spanish monarch Charles V. Hanke's presentation of Las Casas's vision of Indian humanity versus Sepulveda's belief in the application of Aristotle's doctrine of natural slavery to Native Americans helped redefine the traditional interpretation of the Spanish conquest in the 15th and 16th centuries, and most importantly the Spanish role. This role was commonly referred to as the "Black Legend", and historians prior to Hanke characterized the Spanish conquest of the New World as particularly cruel and unjust. In Hanke's mind, Las Casas' ideas on Christian charity and the universal nature of mankind discredited the validity of this legend. By extension, Las Casas becomes a symbol for Spanish humanity in the midst of a brutal conquest as he attempts to redefine the relationship between the interlopers and the native populations.

Hanke's reinterpretation of the Spanish role in the conquest has been labeled by its opponents as the "White Legend," an unsophisticated attempt to replace a legend of Spanish cruelty with another legend of Spanish beneficence. Hanke has also been criticized for overemphasizing the importance of religion as well as social and cultural factors in his work on Las Casas. Despite the controversy surrounding his reinterpretation of the Spanish conquest, Hanke's reassessment provided and still provides useful insights into the social, cultural, and religious rationale underlying these events. Hanke's interest in Las Casas was a lifelong obsession. Hanke admired the vision and courage of Las Casas in confronting Spanish authority. Throughout his career he continued to publish articles as well as conduct symposia on various aspects of Las Casas' career.

Hanke's research interests ranged far and wide, but always returned to Las Casas. He conducted ground-breaking studies on the urban history of Potosi, a colonial mining center in present-day Bolivia. Ironically, Hanke's studies of Potosi emanated from a research trip to Sucre, Bolivia to examine Las Casas manuscripts in a monastery. He also compiled a multivolume collection of Spanish viceregal reports on the Indies. These documents provide exacting detail on institutional as well as social and cultural aspects of colonial Spanish society. By compiling these documents, Hanke also filled a critical void in the literature on Spanish America which neglected the role of viceroys and their administrations. Hanke's fundamental belief in the importance of primary documents also lent more depth and complexity to the study of Spanish America.

Hanke was an advocate of social and cultural history, and his work on Las Casas demonstrates his commitment to expanding the bounds of historical interpretation. Hanke's pioneering work in Latin American studies did not preclude an interest in teaching. He is responsible for training a generation of prominent Latin Americanists. True to form, Hanke's interest in Las Casas, the embodiment of his concerns regarding justice, social and cultural history, and revisionist history, never waned. In an obituary written by another prominent Latin Americanist, Benjamin Keen, Keen pointed out that Hanke at age 84 – shortly before his death – was attempting to prepare a volume to be called *The Fundamental Ideas and Convictions of Bartolomé de Las Casas*. This total commitment to academic production in the form of editorship and authorship combined with archival work and teaching distinguishes Hanke as a truly gifted and significant historian of the 20th century.

STEPHEN GILROY HALL

See also Latin America: Colonial; O'Gorman; Spain: Imperial

Biography

Lewis Ulysses Hanke. Born Oregon City, Oregon, 2 January 1905. Received BS, Northwestern University 1924, MA 1925; PhD Harvard University 1936. Taught at American University, Beirut, 1927–30; Harvard University 1934–39; director, Hispanic Foundation, Library of Congress, 1939–51; taught at University of Texas, 1951–56: director, Institute of Latin American Studies, 1951–58; taught at Columbia University, 1961–67; University of California, Irvine, 1967–69; and University of Massachusetts, Amherst, 1969–93. Married Kate Gilbert, poet. Died Amherst, Massachusetts, 26 March 1993.

Principal Writings

The First Social Experiments in America: A Study in the Development of Spanish Indian Policy in the Sixteenth Century, 1935

Las teorías politicas de Bartolomé de Las Casas (The Political Theories of Bartolomé de Las Casas), 1935

The Spanish Struggle for Justice in the Conquest of America, 1949

Las Casas, historiador, estudio preliminar a la Historia de las Indias, 1951; in English as *Bartolomé de Las Casas, Historian: An Essay in Spanish Historiography,* 1952

Editor, *Hispanic American Historical Review,* 1954–60

Aristotle and the American Indians: A Study in Race Prejudice in the Modern World, 1959

Editor, *Do the Americas Have a Common History? A Critique of the Bolton Theory,* 1964

History of Latin American Civilization: Sources and Interpretations, 2 vols., 1967

All Mankind is One: A Study of the Disputation between Bartolomé de Las Casas and Juan Gines de Sepulveda in 1550 on the Intellectual and Religious Capacity of the American Indians, 1974

"American Historians and the World Today: Responsibilities and Opportunities," *American Historical Review* 80 (February 1975), 1–20

Selected Writings of Lewis Hanke on the History of Latin America, 1977

"The Early Development of Latin American Studies in the United States," in David J. Robinson, ed., *Studying Latin America: Essays in Honor of Preston E. James,* 1980

Further Reading

Bushnell, David, and Lyle N. McAlister, "An Interview with Lewis Hanke," *Hispanic American Historical Review* 68 (1988), 653–74

Gibson, Charles, "Latin America and the Americas," in Michael G. Kammen, ed., *The Past Before Us: Contemporary Historical Writing in the United States* Ithaca, NY: Cornell University Press, 1980.

Keen, Benjamin. "Obituary: Lewis Hanke (1905–1993)," *Hispanic American Historical Review* 73 (November 1993), 663–65

Rodríguez, Celso, "The Writings of Lewis Hanke," *Revista Inter-Americana de Bibliographia* 36 (1986), 427–51

Hargreaves, John D. 1924–

British historian of African legal history

John D. Hargreaves was one of a small group of scholars who, as Britain and other European powers began to lose their overseas empires in the aftermath of World War II, began to shed new light on those empires, the motives behind their establishment, and their impact on both the imperialist Europeans and the dominated subjects. Like other researchers at the time, with the historiography of most of Africa during the colonial period still in its infancy, he had to base his work very much on primary, archival material in order to create a foundation upon which others could subsequently build. Hargreaves' area of special interest, and the base for his major contributions to historical knowledge, awareness, and understanding, was West Africa. Unlike most other British historians at the time, he paid particular attention to French involvement in the region. In this he was a leader in the trend that gave rise to greater interest in Francophone sub-Saharan Africa among British and United States historians than among their French colleagues who, with only a few exceptions, have concentrated more on North Africa, especially Algeria. Hargreaves' work subsequently become wider in scope.

By his own account, Hargreaves' historical writing was strongly influenced by his undergraduate studies and subsequent postgraduate work on Anglo-French relations in the early 20th century under Lewis B. Namier at Manchester University. There he received what he was later to characterize as an excellent education in European history; his war service in Malaya roused his interest in extending this to other societies. This interest began to flourish during his years as a lecturer at Fourah Bay College in Sierra Leone and fuelled his concern to put the African point of view rather more than was the general rule. In this vein his first published book was a brief biography of Sir Samuel Lewis, the Sierra Leonean barrister and the first African to receive a British knighthood.

Hargreaves' impact began to be felt more forcibly with his *Prelude to the Partition of West Africa* (1963), one of the first studies to explore the impact on the region of the relationship between the French and British, based on thorough use of archival material. This set a standard for careful, solidly based empirical research which was to become one of his hallmarks. The logical continuation of this prelude was *West Africa Partitioned* (1974–85). Able to make more use of secondary material, Hargreaves maintained his high standards of care, filling gaps with further primary research.

In the meantime his interest in the French empire was reflected in a succinct survey, *West Africa: The Former French States* (1967). Once again his lucid analysis was coupled to an unwillingness to become trapped in arguments about the nature of imposed colonial boundaries, permitting useful comparisons with the neighboring British colonies, resulting in what was then unquestionably the best work on those colonies in the English language.

An area of African history to which Hargreaves also turned his attention was reflected in another major work, *Decolonization in Africa* (1988). Again combining thorough reading of the secondary literature with the limited archival sources then available, Hargreaves set a high standard for those who followed him in this field. Like any historian of colonial Africa, or indeed the British empire, Hargreaves became aware of the significant role played by Scots. Unlike most other historians, however, he turned this into an interesting study, *Aberdeenshire to Africa* (1981). Focusing on a range of individuals, some obscure, some more well known, he provided a useful picture of the individuals, their impact on the regions in which they worked, and, perhaps more significantly, the impact of their work on them.

In all his work Hargreaves avoided becoming involved in the creation or defence of complex theoretical frameworks, and was careful not to go beyond his sources in analysis or conjecture. Although some criticized him for excessive caution, he served and serves as a model for those historians who still feel that part of our craft and art is to simply tell a story as clearly and accurately as possible. In a wider sense he also stands as a model for academics' becoming involved in practical postimperial issues, notably the problems facing Africans, particularly students, in Britain and larger issues of racism, in both of which he has shown an active concern. Academically and personally, Hargreaves has earned the respect of all those in the African history field and of those outside it familiar with his work.

SIMON KATZENELLENBOGEN

See also Imperial

Biography

John Desmond Hargreaves. Born Colne, Lancashire, 25 January 1924. Educated at Skipton Grammar School; Bootham School; BA, Manchester University, 1943, MA 1948. Served in British Army in Germany and Malaga, 1943–46. Assistant principal, War Office, 1948; taught at Manchester University, 1948–52; Fourah Bay College, Sierra Leone, 1952–54; and Aberdeen University (rising to professor), 1954–85. Married Sheila Elizabeth Wilks, 1950 (2 daughters, 1 son).

Principal Writings

A Life of Sir Samuel Lewis, 1958
Prelude to the Partition of West Africa, 1963
West Africa: The Former French States, 1967
West Africa Partitioned, 2 vols., 1974–85
The End of Colonial Rule in West Africa: Essays in Contemporary History, 1979
Aberdeenshire to Africa: Northeast Scots and British Overseas Expansion, 1981
Decolonization in Africa, 1988; 2nd edition 1996

Hartung, Fritz 1883–1967
German constitutional historian

During a long career Fritz Hartung made important contributions to the development of constitutional history, emphasizing the importance of the politics of power in a field that had traditionally been dominated by lawyers and legal interpretations. Following in the footsteps of Otto Hintze, Hartung published several specialized monographs on the political history of Ansbach-Bayreuth, the Franconian Circle, Saxony, and Prussia. As an editor he was responsible for the publication of important periodicals and collections of primary sources. As a professor in Berlin, he instructed generations of future archivists

and university professors (among them Gerhard Oestreich and Fritz Fischer) in political history and the arcane details of German constitutional law.

In addition to his extensive scholarly output Hartung published numerous articles on current affairs in which he expressed his conservative viewpoint. An admirer of Frederick the Great and Bismarck, Hartung, a national conservative, rejected the republican principles of the Weimar era. During the Nazi era, he maintained, as did so many other German professors, an "unpolitical" stance while continuing his teaching and research. After the war, Hartung declined an offer to join the newly established Free University, and the opportunity to help create a new university in the Western zone, but retained his position with the University of Berlin (Humboldt) until his retirement in 1949.

Hartung's first study analyzed the politics of Karl August von Hardenberg during his tenure in Ansbach-Bayreuth, a principality in southern Germany which belonged to the Prussian crown from 1791 to 1806. Whereas contemporaries and other scholars were dismayed by the strong-arm tactics employed by Hardenberg in his effort to impose Prussian rule, Hartung presented the work of the Prussian administrator as an attempt to modernize the region. The experiences in Ansbach-Bayreuth, Hartung argued, provided Hardenberg with a blueprint for his policies during the Prussian Reform era. In his study on Charles V and the German estates Hartung again emphasized the power of *Realpolitik* over the subtleties of legal interpretation. Several studies on domestic politics in regions of the Holy Roman empire during the 16th century followed before Hartung published his most popular study, his often reprinted *Deutsche Verfassungsgeschichte vom 15. Jahrhundert bis zur Gegenwart* (German Constitutional History from the 15th Century to the Present, 1914). This work remains his most important contribution to a historicized representation of constitutional law. Building on the work of Otto Hintze, he traced the development of institutions and legal codes from the time of the German estates through absolutism and the parliamentary phase to the age of modern dictatorship, emphasizing the importance of political developments and placing the constitutional questions in a broader perspective.

In the earlier editions of his general works on political history, including his *Deutsche Geschichte von 1871 bis 1914* (German History from 1871 to 1914, 1920), Hartung emphasized the role of Bismarck and the centrality of Prussia in the founding of the Wilhelmine empire. After World War I, Hartung, who vigorously opposed the idea of Germany's war guilt, but was not uncritical of the role of monarchy or the Prussian institutes, presented the Wilhelmine empire as the foundation of a modern Germany. However, after World War II he concluded that 1914 had marked the end of an old era to which Germany could not return.

FRANK SCHUURMANS

Biography

Born Saargemünd, 12 January 1883. Professor of history, Humboldt University, Berlin, 1923–49. Died West Berlin, 24 November 1967.

Principal Writings

Hardenberg und die preussische Verwaltung in Ansbach-Bayreuth von 1792 bis 1806 (Hardenberg and Prussian Administration in Ansbach-Bayreuth from 1792 to 1806), 1906

Karl V und die deutschen Reichsstände von 1546 bis 1555 (Charles
V and the German States of the Empire from 1546 to 1555),
1910
*Deutsche Verfassungsgeschichte vom 15. Jahrhundert bis zur
Gegenwart* (German Constitutional History from the 15th
Century to the Present), 1914
Deutsche Geschichte von 1871 bis 1914 (German History from
1871 to 1914), 1920; revised 1924, 1952
"Der aufgeklärte Absolutismus" (Enlightened Absolutism),
Historische Zeitschrift 180 (1955); in English as *Enlightened
Despotism*, 1957

Further Reading

Dietrich, Richard, ed., *Forschungen zu Staat und Verfassung:
Festgabe für Fritz Hartung* (Research on State and Constitution:
Festschrift), Berlin: Duncker & Humblot, 1958
Oestreich, Gerhard, "Fritz Hartung als Verfassungshistoriker" (Fritz
Hartung as a Constitutional Historian), in *Der Staat* [Berlin], 7
(1968), 447–69
Sochow, Werner, "Bibliographie Fritz Hartung," *Jahrbuch für die
Geschichte Mittel- und Ostdeutschlands* [Berlin] (1954), 211–40

Hartz, Louis 1919–1986

US historian

Louis Hartz's most influential work by far was his seminal
volume *The Liberal Tradition in America* (1955), which was
awarded at the time of publication with the American Political
Science Association's Woodrow Wilson prize, and was one of
the three or four most prominent works of the "consensus"
historians of the 1950s. Hartz, a professor of government at
Harvard University, argued that almost all citizens of the
United States, whatever their precise political labels, shared
allegiance to a common liberal tradition and thus adhered to
a broader consensus as to political, social, and economic aims
and forms. Even before the American Revolution the American
colonies, in his opinion, were distinguished from West
European societies by the absence of genuine feudal institutions, and their adherence to a modified Lockean liberal
ideology. The fact that Americans never had to rebel against
or reject a feudal *ancien régime* was responsible for their later
failure to develop either a strong socialist or a true conservative movement. Even those Americans who called themselves
conservatives in fact believed in a centrist consensus based
upon classic liberal tenets, political equality, and democratic
institutions. The one exception to this rule was the pre-Civil
War American South, which did attempt to furnish an intellectual rationale for a hierarchical, nonegalitarian society based
both on slavery and on a well-defined class system, an experiment that ended in failure in 1865, when the South lost the
Civil War.

Hartz's work addressed one issue which had preoccupied
many American historians: the question why, despite its rapid
industrialization in the late 19th century, the United States
never developed a strong socialist movement to match those
of the West European countries. Appearing as it did at the
height of the Cold War, this study also helped to explain to
Americans' satisfaction why their country opposed both
fascism and communism so strongly, thus answering to certain
prevailing intellectual anxieties. Some readers and reviewers of

the book struck a distinctly self-congratulatory note when
agreeing with its thesis, which they felt affirmed their country's
political superiority. Hartz himself, however, argued that the
centrist consensus to which virtually all Americans adhered put
them at a grave disadvantage when dealing with other countries that did not share this unique heritage of being born into
equality. In particular, the lack of a genuine revolutionary
heritage made it almost impossible for Americans to understand why other peoples turned to revolution to win equality
and defeat oppression, a major source of difficulties for post-
World War II United States policymakers in dealing with a
world where revolutionary change was endemic. Moreover,
Hartz argued, Americans, who shared a common heritage of
escape from a Europe which they found unsympathetic, were
unable simply to accept a world in which other countries
were markedly different from their own; instead, "[a]n absolute
national morality is inspired either to withdraw from 'alien'
things or to transform them" in its own image. Hartz was one
of several historians and social scientists of the 1950s, among
them Daniel Bell, Daniel Boorstin, Richard Hofstadter, and
David Potter, who stressed the broad consensus of political
aims and ideology which the majority of Americans had shared.
Although the New Left attacked this school during the 1960s
and 1970s, on the grounds that it ignored large numbers of
Americans who were excluded from the ruling consensus, many
of its basic theses still retain their plausibility and validity.

Hartz's work in the United States reflected his broader
concern with the comparative examination and explanation of
the national heritages of various countries as the product of
their differing histories. He was particularly interested in the
interrelationships of old and new cultures, and of colonial
countries and their colonies. These preoccupations were
apparent in his first work, *Economic Policy and Democratic
Thought: Pennsylvania, 1776–1860* (1948), and in a collection
of essays which he edited, *The Founding of New Societies*
(1964), in which he and other colleagues compared Latin
America, Canada, South Africa, and Australia with the
European cultures which settled them. He suggested that, when
Europeans colonized other areas, they took with them ideas
current in their own countries, which then tended to become
ossified and immobile in their new abodes. In his final two
decades severe illness ended Hartz's teaching and writing
career, but he still retained his interest in research in other
cultures, and, until he died, he attempted to work on a great
historical synthesis that would explain the differences between
the East and the West. He will, however, be best remembered
for *The Liberal Tradition in America*, a work which is still
read and remains influential.

PRISCILLA M. ROBERTS

See also Political; Potter; United States: 19th Century

Biography

Born Youngstown, Ohio, 8 April 1919, son of Russian immigrants.
Grew up in Omaha, Nebraska; attended Omaha Technical High
School; received BA, Harvard University, 1940, PhD 1946. Taught
at Harvard University (rising to professor of government), 1945–74;
Chairman, Commission on American Civilization, 1955–58.
Married (marriage dissolved; 1 son). Died Istanbul, 20 January
1986.

Principal Writings

Economic Policy and Democratic Thought: Pennsylvania, 1776–1860, 1948

The Liberal Tradition in America: An Interpretation of American Political Thought since the Revolution, 1955

Editor, *The Founding of New Societies: Studies in the History of the United States, Latin America, South Africa, Canada, and Australia*, 1964

The Necessity of Choice: Nineteenth-century Political Thought, edited by Paul Roazen, 1990

Further Reading

Barber, Benjamin R., "Louis Hartz," *Political Theory* 14 (1986), 355–58

Diggins, John Patrick, "Knowledge and Sorrow: Louis Hartz's Quarrel with American History," *Political Theory* 16 (1988), 355–76

Fowler, Robert Booth, *Believing Skeptics: American Political Intellectuals, 1945–1965*, Westport, CT: Greenwood Press, 1978

Hartshorne, Thomas L., *The Distorted Image: Changing Conceptions of the American Character since Turner*, Cleveland: Press of Case Western Reserve University, 1968

Higham, John, "The Cult of the American Consensus: Homogenizing American History," *Commentary* 27 (1959), 93–101

Higham, John, "Beyond Consensus: The Historian as a Moral Critic," *American Historical Review* 67 (1962), 609–25

Higham, John, with Leonard Krieger and Felix Gilbert, *History: The Development of Historical Studies in the United States*, Englewood Cliffs, NJ: Prentice Hall, 1965

Hofstadter, Richard, *The Progressive Historians: Turner, Beard, Parrington*, New York: Knopf, 1968; London: Cape, 1969

Kraus, Michael, and Davis D. Joyce, *The Writing of American History*, revised edition, Norman: University of Oklahoma Press, 1985

Lemisch, Jesse, *On Active Service in War and Peace: Politics and Ideology in the American Historical Profession*, Toronto: New Hogtown Press, 1975

Meyers, Marvin, Leonard Krieger, Harry V. Jaffa, and Louis Hartz, "Symposium," *Comparative Studies in Society and History* 5 (April 1963), 261–84

Morton, Marian J., *The Terrors of Ideological Politics: Liberal Historians in a Conservative Mood*, Cleveland: Press of Case Western Reserve University, 1972

Riemer, Neal, *American Political Theory*, vol. 1, Princeton: Princeton University Press, 1967

Riley, Patrick, "Louis Hartz, The Final Years: The Unknown Work," *Political Theory* 16 (1988), 377–99

Sternsher, Bernard, *Consensus, Conflict, and American Historians*, Bloomington: Indiana University Press, 1975

Tyrrell, Ian, *The Absent Marx: Class Analysis and Liberal History in Twentieth-Century America*, Westport, CT: Greenwood Press, 1986

Wise, Gene, *American Historical Explanations: A Strategy for Grounded Inquiry*, Homewood, IL: Dorsey Press, 1973; revised Minneapolis: University of Minnesota Press, 1980

Haskins, Charles Homer 1870–1937

US medievalist

Charles Homer Haskins is best remembered for his groundbreaking work in medieval European history. However, this polymath also played a crucial role in the evolution of American higher education, as the dean of the Harvard Graduate School, and in the development of American foreign policy, as an adviser to president Woodrow Wilson. His work was notably influential in the progressive historiography and politics that often dominated the American scene in the 20th century.

By age six, Haskins had mastered Latin and Greek. By age 13 he had entered Allegheny College where his father was a faculty member. Considered too young by Harvard, Haskins transferred to Johns Hopkins University at age 15 where he took a degree in law and, being too young for the bar, returned as a graduate student of American history. During these advanced studies, Haskins met his lifetime associates Frederick Jackson Turner and Woodrow Wilson. Significant for all three was the influence of Herbert Baxter Adams who attempted to institute a Rankean historiography and German seminar format that would divorce the study of American history from romantic and religious idealism. It was Adams' goal to focus the search for American institutional roots in their "Teutonic" origins rather than in some brilliant spontaneous generation. While Turner remained focused on American origins, Haskins turned to medieval studies. However, a deep interest in American institutions always informed his work. Indeed, Haskins, Turner, and Wilson were all dedicated to peculiar mixtures of Rankean historiography and American idealism.

Among Haskins' scholarly achievements was his successful assault on the European domination of medieval studies. Through intensive archival research in France, Italy, Spain, and Germany, Haskins shifted the field away from the imbedded nationalistic interests of European scholarship toward the theory that the Normans, more than the "Teutons" or any other of the diverse medieval influences, were most central to the development of European, particularly English, culture. In his work, *The Normans in European History* (1915), Haskins observed that this group had created strong, unifying connections between France, England, and Sicily as well as with Ireland and Scotland. The Norman contribution laid the foundations of what would emerge as distinctly European institutions. This pan-European history challenged many of the assumptions that dominated early 20th-century European historiography. While some questioned his achievements, Haskins' work also found much high praise.

Among those impressed were Tory-leaning Britons who had long argued for the Norman, rather than the Anglo-Saxon, roots of the English aristocracy. The Tory historian Sir Frederick Powicke praised Haskins as an oddity among American scholars whom he viewed as prone to religious and political bias. He stated that, "[Haskins] did more than anyone in recent years to give a much-needed sense of the value of discipline and direction to the study of History in America." In his *Norman Institutions* (1918), the second work of this project, Haskins provided the overall data supporting the pan-European theory. This work was also found useful by scholars who focused their attention on the sources of English institutions. At one and the same time, Haskins' work had broadened medieval historiography, brought new respect for American scholarship, and provided new impetus for partisan historiography.

His other great work, *The Renaissance of the Twelfth Century* (1927), had an even greater impact. Here he directly attacked Jacob Burckhardt and the prevailing scholarly opinion that the Middle Ages was a "dark" and "superstitious" period, broken only by the 15th-century Renaissance. The "Haskins theory" stated that earlier renaissances, or a series of cultural advances, ultimately led to the Italian Renaissance. Informing these developments was a synthesis of Arabic, Greek, and European learning, an interaction that took place, according to Haskins, in Spain as well as in the Norman kingdom of Sicily where some of the earliest universities were established. Haskins explored this topic further in *The Rise of Universities* (1923) and *Studies in the History of Mediaeval Science* (1924). He postulated that through these gates came scientific and philosophic, mainly Aristotelian, works that had been lost to the West. It was here that the foundations of European science and medicine were established, not to mention European unity. Though at first ignored, Haskins' theory came to be hailed for its great innovation.

Essential in the development of this scholarship was the influence of Frederick Jackson Turner. The two were colleagues in American history at the University of Wisconsin before Haskins pursued his medieval interests. In 1902 Haskins began a long career at Harvard University and in 1910 convinced Turner to leave Wisconsin for the Ivy League school. Turner is well-known for his frontier thesis wherein he rejected Adams' Teutonic theory and postulated the origins of American institutions in the ordering of the frontier. Though this period had ended, the "frontier conditioned" society would continue to seek to order new frontiers most prominently represented, for Turner, in the progressive state and its universities. Haskins predictably found in the Norman transformation of England a strong parallel to Turner's American frontier. Like Turner, he postulated a frontier situation in medieval England which was brought to order through innovative Norman institutions that were eventually served by the emerging universities. Haskins' student, Joseph Strayer, further linked such themes in his study on the medieval origins of the modern state.

None of this scholarship was without practical application. During his 35 years at Harvard University Haskins helped to further this school's rising scholarly reputation. In the early 1900s institutional theory was a focus of political and historical research at Harvard, and the efforts of Haskins and Turner were well-suited to this emphasis. As the dean of the Graduate School Haskins was able to establish interdisciplinary studies at Harvard and to participate in wide-ranging discussions regarding the nature and direction of American collegiate education. During World War I Haskins was influential in setting the pattern of higher education, particularly through the introduction of "Western Civilization" courses that brought to students a progressive understanding of the Western heritage and America's dominant position in that history. This was seen by many as essential to the academic support of Western, particularly American, democratic ideals against the rise of tyranny. In this work Haskins often included not only a Rankean "scientific" methodology but also an American romanticism that conveyed the notion that the United States represented the height of Western development.

The political manifestations of Haskins' scholarship were found primarily in their attachment to Woodrow Wilson's progressive "democratic liberalism." Wilson believed in the ability of the state to order society. Hence, the historiography of his classmates included the historical "lessons" that Wilson needed to support his political program. For Haskins, service

to Wilson came first as a member of the American team assigned to assess possible hindrances in peace negotiations after World War I and then as interpreter and adviser to the President at the 1918–19 Paris Peace Conference. As head of the Western Division, which structured the peace agreement for the crucial frontiers of Germany, Belgium, and Denmark, Haskins applied his understanding of European history and society. As a pro-French interpreter for Wilson to Clemenceau, Haskins had an unusual position of influence in the peace process, particularly in the implementation of the Wilsonian policy that the historical analysis of American (and Norman) institutions could somehow be applied to the modern European "frontiers" that had been so crucial in the disputes leading to the war.

After the peace conference Haskins wrote the first, often uncritical, works regarding the negotiations, its personalities, and the problems that led to the failure of peace in Europe. Also during these years Haskins produced a number of works supporting his various theses. Before succumbing to Parkinson's Disease in 1937, Haskins had produced a large quantity of material while also serving as the head or founder of a number of scholarly societies. In his 67 years Haskins had been a key figure in transforming not only medieval studies, but also American higher education and politics.

KENNETH R. CALVERT

See also White, L.

Biography

Born Meadville, Pennsylvania, 21 December 1870. Studied Latin and Greek from early age; entered Allegheny College, 1883; transferred to Johns Hopkins University, BA 1887, PhD (supervised by Herbert Baxter Adams), 1890; studied in Berlin and at the Ecole des Chartes, Paris. Taught (rising to professor) Johns Hopkins University, 1889–92; University of Wisconsin, 1892–1902; and Harvard University, 1902–37: dean, Harvard Graduate School, 1908–24. Married Clare Allen, lecturer in Romance languages at Radcliffe College, 1912 (2 sons, 1 daughter). Died Cambridge, Massachusetts, 14 May 1937.

Principal Writings

With Dean Putnam Lockwood, *The Sicilian Translators of the Twelfth Century and the First Latin Version of Ptolemy's Almagest*, 1910
The Ancient Trade Guilds and Companies of Salisbury, 1912
The Normans in European History, 1915
Norman Institutions, 1918
The Rise of Universities, 1923
Studies in the History of Mediaeval Science, 1924
The Renaissance of the Twelfth Century, 1927
Studies in Medieval Culture, 1929

Further Reading

Benson, Robert L., Giles Constable, and Carol D. Lanham, eds., *Renaissance and Renewal in the Twelfth Century*, Cambridge, MA: Harvard University Press, and Oxford: Oxford University Press, 1982
Cantor, Norman F., *Inventing the Middle Ages: The Lives, Works, and Ideas of the Great Medievalists of the Twentieth Century*, New York: Morrow, 1991; Cambridge: Lutterworth Press, 1992
Powicke, F.M., "Charles Homer Haskins," *English Historical Review* 52 (1937), 649–56

Taylor, Charles Holt, and J.L. La Monte, eds., *Anniversary Essays in Mediaeval History, by Students of Charles Homer Haskins, Presented on His Completion of Forty Years of Teaching*, Boston: Houghton Mifflin, 1929

Vaughn, Sally N. "Charles Homer Haskins," in Clyde N. Wilson, ed., *American Historians, 1866–1912*, Detroit: Gale, 1986 [*Dictionary of Literary Biography*, vol. 47]

Hausen, Karin 1938–

German women's and gender historian

Perhaps best known for her collaboration with both national and international scholars, Karin Hausen has challenged the German social sciences throughout her career to re-evaluate the positioning of women historically. In addition to other notable feminist historians of the so-called second wave, she has helped to legitimize the focus on women as a viable subject of historical investigation. In her role as mentor, colleague, and contributing academic, lending shape and contour to some of the major debates concerning women's roles in the family, the workplace, and society in general, Hausen has argued that the writing of history is never a neutral act. A product of the terrain within which it is written, history according to Hausen is rarely static, ever evolving, and always constrained by social and political determinants. By invoking the category of gender as an essential part of the process of both identity formation and the practice of historical writing, Hausen's contribution to the annals of history may in fact have little to do with explaining the past as it was. Rather, her attention to the discourses and practices of social inequalities, articulated through the lens of gender, have represented the attempt to think critically about the past as it unfolds through the subjective experiences of the here and now.

Emerging onto the scene in the wake of the turbulent student revolts of the late 1960s, second-wave German feminism called for equality and representation in all aspects of society. One such arena was the conservative German university, left virtually unaffected by post-1945 attempts at institutional reform. Itself a site of continual debate well into the 1970s, the university in general and certain academic disciplines specifically were subjected to intense public scrutiny, and German feminists took this opportunity to stress the issue of women's self-determination on campus and in the lecture halls. The gradual proliferation of Women's Studies centers in Germany, now almost commonplace but not wholly uncontested, is a testament to the ongoing struggle that Hausen has engaged in since the mid-1970s in her role as historian and now director of the Center for Interdisciplinary Women's and Gender Studies at the Technical University of Berlin.

Hausen was awarded her doctorate for her 1969 dissertation on German colonial rule in Cameroon. Although she published a portion of her doctoral dissertation in article form, she moved away from this topic to a more thorough investigation of women's role in the 19th and 20th-century German family. In early articles, Hausen's research mirrored the prevalent "insert woman here" methodology of the day, which attempted to expose women's historical contributions to a past that had heretofore been written from the perspective of, and by, men alone. No longer would women be forced to "search for their history" (*Frauen suchen ihre Geschichte* [Women Search for Their History], 1982); instead women's experiences would be central not peripheral to the historical narrative. Although this approach helped fill the cavernous empirical void, one question remained underanalyzed: how and in what ways is women's inferiority central to their ongoing struggle for autonomy and acceptance in modern German society?

By the early to mid-1980s, Hausen's many collaborative works began to break down this now outdated paradigm. No longer content with simply documenting the ways in which women were marginalized by society, Hausen, along with other prominent German women's historians such as Annette Kuhn, Gisela Bock, Karen Hagemann, and Heide Wunder, began to investigate "the completeness," for lack of a better word, of the social construction of power relations, in this case the perceived totality of woman's inferiority over and against man's almost eternal superiority. Simply stated, are women victims or actors in the unfolding drama of the past? Or, as Hausen argues, does women's status vary from site to site, from historical context to historical context, from the family, to the workplace and home again? This shift away from mere documentation toward a more theoretical engagement with gender as both femininity and masculinity has forced German feminist historians to think critically about what society has invested in what it means to be a man or a woman, and how these values are changed and contested through history as it evolves on the page.

Undeniably part of a growing trend to institutionalize and thereby legitimize Gender Studies as part of the university curriculum, Hausen's role as director of the Center for Interdisciplinary Women's and Gender Studies has undoubtedly opened doors for such analyses. Now common to many universities in the former West Germany and in the new German states, such centers serve an important function in fostering greater communication among scholars from a variety of disciplinary backgrounds. By increasing awareness on university campuses on both sides of the Atlantic, Karin Hausen has helped redefine the parameters of women's/gender history through her sustained and informed questioning, altering the form and function of historical writing in the process.

JENNIFER V. EVANS

Biography

Born 1938. Received PhD, Free University, Berlin, 1969. Director, Center for Interdisciplinary Women's and Gender Studies, Technical University, Berlin.

Principal Writings

Deutsche Kolonialherrschaft in Afrika: Wirtschaftsinteressen und Kolonialverwaltung in Kamerun vor 1914 (German Colonial Rule in Africa: Business Interests and Colonial Government in Cameroon before 1914), 1970

"Die Polarisierung der 'Geschlechtscharaktere': Eine Spiegelung der Dissoziation von Erwerbs- und Familienleben" (The Polarization of Gendered Characteristics: An Examination of the Disassociation of Work and Family Life), in Werner Conze, ed., *Sozialgeschichte der Familie in der Neuzeit Europas*, 1976

"The Family and Role Division," in Richard J. Evans and W.R. Lee, eds., *The German Family: Essays on the Social History of the Family in Nineteenth- and Twentieth-Century Germany*, 1981

Editor, *Frauen suchen ihre Geschichte: Historische Studien zum 19. und 20. Jahrhundert* (Women Search for Their History: Historical Studies of the 19th and 20th Centuries), 1982

Editor with Helga Nowotny, *Wie Männlich ist die Wissenschaft?* (How Masculine are the Social Sciences?) 1986

Editor with Heide Wunder, *Frauengeschichte – Geschlechtergeschichte* (Women's History – Gender History), 1992

Editor with Gertraude Krell, *Frauenerwerbsarbeit: Forschungen zu Geschichte und Gegenwart* (Women's Work: Research on the Past and Present), 1993

Editor, *Geschlechterhierarchie und Arbeitsteilung: zur Geschichte ungleicher Erwerbschancen von Männern und Frauen* (Gender Hierarchies and the Division of Labor: Towards a History of the Unequal Workforce Opportunities Between Men and Women), 1993

"Die 'Frauenfrage' war schon immer eine 'Männerfrage': Überlegungen zum historischen Ort von Familie in der Moderne" (The 'Woman Question' Was Always Already a 'Man's Question': Thoughts on the Historical Location of Family in Modernity), 1994

Hayashi School

The Hayashi school was a quasi-official school of Japanese historians during the period of the Tokugawa shogunate (1603–1868). Founded by Hayashi Razan (1583–1657), the school applied orthodox neo-Confucian historiographical principles to the study of the Japanese past. Its major works include *Honchō tsugan* (Comprehensive Mirror of the Japanese Court, 1670), *Ōdai ichiran* (Outline of Generations of Rulers, 1650), and *Tokugawa jikki* (True Record of the Tokugawa, 1809–49).

In 1608 the eclectic neo-Confucian scholar Fujiwara Seika recommended Razan as personal tutor to the shogun Tokugawa Hidetada. Razan thereafter acquired considerable influence in the government, and in the drafting of laws, and was a key figure in Japan's diplomacy with Korea and in the formulation of anti-Christian policies. But his key project was the compilation of *Honchō tsugan*, beginning in 1644.

Razan's work was continued by his son Gahō and grandson Hōkō. In 1691, during the reign of the ardent Confucian shogun Tokugawa Tsunayoshi, Hōkō was asked to relocate his school to the Yushima district of Edo (modern Tokyo). The school was renamed Shōhei-kō (School of Prosperous Peace), and Hōkō was appointed *Daigaku no kami* (Head of the University). This title became hereditary, and nine other members of the Hayashi family were to receive it up to the end of the Tokugawa period (1868), when the was school taken over by the new Meiji regime. During the Kansei reforms (1787–93), when all schools of Confucian thought other than Zhu Xi neo-Confucianism were banned, the school was reorganized, and an official shogunal academy (*gakumonsho*) established alongside it. The school was briefly taken over by the Meiji government in 1868, and discontinued in 1870.

The *Honchō tsugan* is largely modelled after Sima Guang's *Zi-zhi tong-jian* (Comprehensive Mirror for Aid in Government); it is written in Chinese and follows the Chinese chronological (*hennen*) style. It does not, however, follow the traditional Chinese practice of including the author's own interpretation of events, and thus fails to offer a distinctive historical viewpoint. Even so it, and other Hayashi school works, convey a basic rationalism, a view that *li* (principle) is at work in human affairs. It reflects a basic humanism, emphasizing the activities of human beings with few references to the supernatural, and treats the study of history as a fundamentally didactic project. In *Honchō tsugan*, the Chinese ethnocentrism found in neo-Confucian works is adjusted to Japanese ruling-class needs; while never failing to value China, the Hayashi school writers came to estimate Japan as the greatest of nations, and to emphasize the gulf between Japan and the "barbarian" nations.

The *Tokugawa jikki*, compiled mostly by Hayashi Jussai (1768–1841) and completed in 1849, recounts the reigns of the first 10 Tokugawa shoguns (from 1603 to 1786); a sequel, *Zoku Tokugawa jikki* (True Record of the Tokugawa, Continued), was never completed.

The generations of Hayashi family leaders, who oversaw official historical writing throughout the Tokugawa shogunate, include: Razan (1583–1657); Gahō (1618–1680); Hōkō (1644–1732); Ryūkō (1681–1758); Hōkoku (1721–1773); Hōtan (1761–1787); Kinpō (1767–1793); Jusai (1768–1841) [adopted heir]; Teiu (1791–1844); Sōkan (1828–1853); Fukusai (1800–1859); and Gakusai (1833–1906).

GARY P. LEUPP

See also Arai; Japan; Mito; Sima Guang

Further Reading

Blacker, Carmen, "Japanese Historical Writing in the Tokugawa Period," in William G. Beasley and Edwin G. Pulleyblank, eds., *Historians of China and Japan*, London: Oxford University Press, 1961

Nakai, Kate Wildman, "Tokugawa Confucian Historiography: The Hayashi, the Early Mito School, and Arai Hakuseki," in Peter Nosco, ed., *Confucianism and Tokugawa Culture*, Princeton: Princeton University Press, 1984

"Neo-Confucian Orthodoxy," in Ryusaku Tsunoda, William Theodore de Bary, and Donald Keene, eds., *Sources of Japanese Tradition*, New York: Columbia University Press, 1958

Heckscher, Eli F. 1879–1952

Swedish economic historian

Author of a masterpiece on mercantilism, published for the first time in the early 1930s and recently reprinted in English, Eli Filip Heckscher, the founding father of economic history in Sweden, still remains well-known internationally today, both within the discipline and as a great contemporary economist. The latter fame originates mainly from his decisive contribution to the Heckscher-Ohlin theorem in international trade theory, which he first formulated through a paper issued in 1919 and only translated three decades later, but which finally resulted, in the late 1970s, in the awarding of a Nobel prize in Economics to one of his former students, Bertil G. Ohlin (1899–1979).

These better-known works represent no more than a small part of Heckscher's academic production, most of which is available only in Swedish. His stature as an economic historian is at its greatest in epistemological and methodological terms. In his own country Heckscher's standing is based on all his numerous writings, which are generally seen to be part of economic history, and not economic theory. Economic history was the field in which his truly pioneering work was done, and to which he devoted most of his intellectual and organizational efforts. Only within this tradition can we see the continuity and coherence of his output. These qualities are not to be found in his political and journalistic work or his writings as a social or monetary polemicist. From 1911 to the end of World War I, Heckscher co-edited a conservative newspaper called *Svensk Tidskrift*, only to become, after the war, a staunch liberal and an active contributor to *Dagens Nyheter*, a quite opposite periodical. On the other hand, in 1917, he founded the Political Economy Club, a scientific elite organization, partly in order to provide Knut Wicksell (1851–1926) with a forum after his retirement from the chair of economics at the University of Lund. Although Wicksell remained at its center until his death, Heckscher was also one of its most active members. He produced some first-class theoretical papers in those years, including the one mentioned above. But he did this only intermittently and he withdraw altogether from the Club after the 1929 economic crash, mainly to concentrate on his studies in economic history.

These had begun more than a quarter of century before, with his licentiate thesis of 1903, presented in the following year at the University of Uppsala, but published only in 1908. That work, on *Produktplakatet* (the Swedish Navigation Act of 1724), already contained the essentials of Heckscher's two main historiographical themes: the development of Sweden's economy from the 16th and the 17th centuries on; and the nature and functioning of the "mercantile system," not only in his own country but in Europe as a whole. Those were to be the themes, respectively, of his monumental (but unfinished) study on Sweden's economic history since the reign of Gustav Vasa, the first two volumes of which were published in 1935–36, while the last two appeared in 1950; and of the better known and more rounded two volumes on mercantilism, issued in Swedish in 1931 and almost immediately translated to several other languages.

Merkantilisment is Heckscher's crowning achievement in general economic history. It is fundamentally a history of economic policies, which views mercantilism successively as a unifying system (the discussion of which comprises the whole first volume), as a system of power, a system of protection, a monetary system, and a conception of society that, according to Heckscher, was a transitional one which extended from its medieval origins to modern liberalism. Heckscher's starting points in this book were the earlier works by Adam Smith, whose *Wealth of Nations* (1776) he much admired, and by Gustav von Schmoller (1838–1917), whom he strongly criticized. But his main theoretical inspiration came directly from Alfred Marshall's *Principles of Economics* (1890).

As for the economic history of his country, non-Swedish readers must be satisfied with a glimpse into Heckscher's intentions and results through a work of synthesis that he issued in the early 1940s, and whose revised version was later translated and published posthumously in the United States as *An Economic History of Sweden* (1954). Most of his other historical and theoretical writings seem to have been rooted in, or related to, one of these two main themes.

Such assertions can be made, for instance, with regard to his doctoral dissertation of 1907, on the significance of railroads for Sweden's economic development, an economic and statistical account which had originated from an assignment provided by the Swedish State Railways on the 50th anniversary of its foundation. They also apply to his 1918 book on the Continental System, translated into English in 1922, which clearly had to do with Heckscher's work on mercantilism; as well as to his long chapter on monetary history from 1914 to 1925. Despite their intrinsic value, these two studies did not get the recognition that they deserved, in contrast to Heckscher's course notes on the Industrial Revolution, which were first published in 1931, and which, for more than forty years, remained a standard text in Swedish universities.

There still remains a last group of writings that were destined to have an independent and more definitive value. This strand was inaugurated in 1904 by the very first paper that he published, which contained an initial version of his well-known "plea for theory" within economic history research. Several times improved and rewritten, it stated the tasks, the scope, and the methods of economic history. In retrospect this can be seen as one of his greatest contributions to the study and teaching of the discipline. Fortunately, in this case, a better elaborated version was published in English in 1929. All these served to make Heckscher one of the founding fathers of modern economic history.

TAMÁS SZMRECSÁNYI

See also Sweden

Biography

Eli Filip Heckscher. Born Stockholm, 24 November 1879, to a Jewish family; his father, a lawyer by training, was Danish consul general stationed in Sweden. Attended University of Uppsala, where he studied history with Harald Hjärne and economics with David Davidson; licentiate, 1904; doctorate, 1907. Appointed lecturer in economics at the University of Stockholm, 1907, to work under the supervision of Gustav Cassel; chair of economics and statistics, Stockholm Business School, 1909–29, then research professor in economic history, 1929–49. Married (1 son). Died Stockholm, 23 December 1952.

Principal Writings

"Ekonomisk historia: några antydningar," *Historisk Tidskrift* 24 (1904), 167–98; reprinted in his *Ekonomi och historia*, 1922; in English as "A Plea for Theory in Economic History," *Economic History* 1 (1929) supplement, 525–34

Till beysning av järnvägarnas betydelse för Sveriges ekonomiska utveckling (Clarifying the Significance of Railways for Sweden's Economic Development), 1907

Produktplakatet och dess förutsättningar: bidrag till merkantilsystemets historia i Sverige (The Navigation Act and Its Determinations: A Contribution to the History of the Mercantile System in Sweden), 1908

Kontinentalsystemet, 1918; in English as *The Continental System: An Economic Interpretation*, 1922

"Utrikeshandelns verkan på inkomstfördelningen," *Ekonomisk Tidskrift* 21 (1919), 1–32; in English as "The Effect of Foreign Trade on the Distribution of Income," American Economic Association, *Readings in the Theory of International Trade*, 1949

Editor with Kurt Bergendal, *Bidrag till Sveriges ekonomiska och sociala historia under och efter världskriget* (Contribution to the Economic and Social History of Sweden during and after the World War), 1926

"Penningväsende och penningpolitik från krigsutbrottet till den internationella guldmyntfotens återställelse, 1914–25," in his *Bidrag till Sveriges ekonomiska och sociala historia under och efter världskriget*, 1926; in English as "Monetary History from 1914 to 1925 in Its Relations with Foreign Trade and Shipping," in Kurt Bergendal, Wilhelm Keilhau, Einard Cohn, and Thorsteinn Thorsteinsson, eds., *Sweden, Norway, Denmark, and Iceland in the World War*, 1930

Merkantilisment: ett led i den ekonomiska politikens historia, 2 vols., 1931; in English as *Mercantilism*, 2 vols., 1935, revised 1955

Sveriges ekonomiska historia från Gustav Vasa (Swedish Economic History since the Reign of Gustav Vasa), 4 vols., 1935–50

Ekonomisk-historiska studer (Economic-Historical Studies), 1936

Industrialismen: den ekonomiska utvecklingen sedan 1750 (Industrialism: The Economic Development since 1750), 1938

"Quantitative Measurement in Economic History," *Quarterly Journal of Economics* 53 (1939), 167–93

Svenskt arbete och liv från medeltiden till nutiden, 1941; in English as *An Economic History of Sweden*, 1954

With Bertil Ohlin, *Heckscher-Ohlin Trade Theory*, 1991

Further Reading

Coleman, D.C., "Eli Heckscher and the Idea of Mercantilism," *Scandinavian Economic History Review* 5 (1957), 3–25

Gerschenkron, Alexander, Preface, in Heckscher, *An Economic History of Sweden*, Cambridge, MA: Harvard University Press, 1954

Henriksson, Rolf G.H., "Eli F. Heckscher: The Economic Historian as Economist," in Bo Sandelin, ed., *The History of Swedish Economic Thought*, London: Routledge, 1991

Magnusson, Lars, "Eli Heckscher and Mercantilism: An Introduction," in Heckscher, *Mercantilism*, London: Routledge, 1994

Montgomery, Arthur, "Eli F. Heckscher," in J.T. Lambie, ed., *Architects and Craftsmen in History: Festschrift für Abbot Payson Usher*, Tübingen: Mohr, 1956

Hegel, G.W.F. 1770–1831

German philosopher

G.W.F. Hegel's philosophy of history dominated the first half of the 19th century and his theories still remain influential today. Few other historians have attracted either the praise or the denunciation that has followed his historical legacy. Since his death, historians have debated the meaning and the relevance of his metaphysical system.

Hegel studied at a theological seminary and the works of Rousseau and Kant made a profound impression upon him. After becoming a professor of philosophy, he created a metaphysical system that transcended philosophy and exerted a powerful influence on social, political, and historical theory. Hegel showed little interest in most facets of the historical practice, but the ramifications of his "speculative" philosophy fundamentally altered the study of history. Hegel's main works revealed his metaphysical system and outlined a new developmental pattern of world history. He synthesized important elements of the Reformation view of history, in which man struggled through the arena of life furthering God's will, with the Enlightenment's secular views on rationality and reason triumphant. Employing his famous dialectic model – that thesis and antithesis interact to create a new synthesis which represents what is most essential to each of the originals – he

merged these two separate worldviews into a new coherent model. Beneath the surface confusion of events and actions, and despite the discordant goals of humanity, history was the embodiment of God's will. History was the progressive development of reason through distinct stages of humanity's existence. Reason and rationality were both the goal of the essence of the ultimate "Spirit." In this system, humanity followed reason and strove for freedom. However, Hegel's "Idea of Freedom" was based on the submission of "Right and Law" as established by the "State." Political systems based on reason and the law and populated with dutiful enlightened citizens were thus the ultimate manifestation of God's will.

Hegel's philosophy bridged the chasm separating Christian scholars and secular philosophers. He provided enough God to satisfy liberal Christians and an emphasis on reason that appeased the rationalists. In the process, he established new paradigms that swept through academia. His macrohistorical approach widened the sphere of historical studies. It illustrated the benefits of expanding the studies that had hitherto been limited to political history and biographical works. New possibilities in social history were avidly accepted by the next generation of historians, including Karl Marx. Efforts were made to link separate histories into an all-encompassing world history. Hegel's division of history into four great epochs (the Oriental, the Greek, the Roman, and the German) convinced many historians that different eras and cultures were fundamentally dissimilar and had to be evaluated within their own contexts and in recognition of the specific "needs of that age." Hegel's insistence that motives often differed from those professed, led to a more critical appraisal of source materials. Actions, motives, and repercussions were increasingly scrutinized for consistency, and causal relationships became more and more important. The dialectic model had less immediate impact, but in later generations it has become a staple tenet in many historical interpretations.

Although few credible historians would refute Hegel's impact, many have leveled scathing criticisms on his philosophy of history. Certain contemporary historians claimed Hegel's God was not a true personal God and that he was in effect preaching atheism. Hegel's view of the state led critics to label him an apologist for imperial Germany. The complexity of his works allowed different historians to accuse him of advocating either revolutionary rebellion or reactionary state repression. His Germanic model of western Europe was warped by critics into a racial philosophy of intolerance. The error in this interpretation was profoundly revealed when the Nazis castigated his works – mainly because his emphasis on rationalism and critical evaluation contradicted the Nazi efforts to create a new German mythos. Modern criticism focuses mainly on his methodology. Hegel's speculative style is inconsistent with today's analytical methods. His macrohistorical approach has largely been rejected and replaced with theories of limited range that can be tested against specific historical incidents. He has been accused of employing an *a priori* system that defies the objective reality. The claim that Hegel is not scientifically objective is perhaps the most damaging and the most credible. However, he must be evaluated as a historian from his era. He does not meet today's academic standards, but he did set the stage for Marx and Ranke who in turn created much of the methodology still employed today.

FRED HOOVER

See also Althusser; Art; Begriffsgeschichte; Berlin; Christianity; Collingwood; Cultural; De Sanctis; Dilthey; Droysen; Fischer; Gardiner; Graetz; Historiology; Hourani; Jewish; Kołakowski; Lecky; Maruyama; Marxist Interpretation; Meinecke; Metahistory; Nietzsche; Pevsner; Philosophy of History; Polanyi; Popper; Ranke; Reformation; Religion; Sanctis; Solov'ev; Spengler; Sybel; Ullmann; Universal; Villari; Weber, M.; Wellhausen

Biography

Georg Wilhelm Friedrich Hegel. Born Stuttgart, 27 August 1770, son of a revenue officer. Studied theology, University of Tübingen, 1788–93. Tutor, Bern and Frankfurt am Main, 1793–1801. Private lecturer, then professor, University of Jena, 1801–06; editor in Bamberg, 1807; headmaster in Nuremberg, 1808–16; full professor, University of Heidelberg, 1816–18; and University of Berlin, 1818–31. Married Marie von Tucher, 1811 (2 sons); plus one further son. Died Berlin, 14 November 1831, of cholera.

Principal Writings

Die Phänomenologie des Geistes, 1807; in English as *The Phenomenology of Mind*, 1910, and *Phenomenology of Spirit*, 1977

Wissenschaft der Logik, 3 vols., 1812–16; in English as *Hegel's Science of Logic*, 1929

Grundlinien der Philosophie des Rechts oder Naturrecht und Staatswissenschaft im Grundrisse, 1820–21; in English as *The Philosophy of Right and Law*, 1952

Vorlesungen über die Philosophie der Geschichte, 1837; in English as *Lectures on the Philosophy of World History*, 1975

Werke, 20 vols., 1986

Further Reading

O'Brien, George Dennis, *Hegel on Reason and History: A Contemporary Interpretation*, Chicago: University of Chicago Press, 1975

Smith, Page, *The Historian and History*, New York: Knopf, 1964

Ritter, Joachim, *Hegel und die französische Revolution*, Cologne: Westdeutscher, 1957; in English as *Hegel and the French Revolution: Essays on the Philosophy of the Right*, Cambridge, MA: MIT Press, 1982

Wilkins, Burleigh Taylor, *Hegel's Philosophy of History*, Ithaca, NY: Cornell University Press, 1974

Heilbron, J.L. 1934–

US historian of physics

J.L. Heilbron has had an illustrious academic career starting as a doctoral student of Thomas Kuhn and culminating as dean of the University of California at Berkeley and editor of the journal *Historical Studies in the Physical and Biological Sciences*. He has written on topics covering almost half a millennium: from John Dee, an English mathematician-cum-magician, in the 16th century, to the history of particle accelerators in the late 20th. This great span in time has been bought at the expense of a strict limitation in the subject matter. To use a metaphor that Heilbron repeatedly uses himself: he is looking for a small signal against a vast background of noise, the signal being the history of physics and the noise being all other history. Of course, the metaphor is taken from physics itself. Heilbron has (co-)published monographs on John Dee, on the Royal Society at the time of Newton's presidency, on quantification in the 18th century, especially within the field

of electricity, on Henry G. Moseley (an early 20th-century English physicist whose promising career was cut short in the battle of Gallipoli), on Max Planck (a German physicist of great renown in the development of quantum physics in the early 20th century), and finally on the Lawrence Berkeley Laboratory of the mid-20th century.

Heilbron's book on Moseley (which grew out of his doctoral dissertation) examined the intellectual development of a physicist from within the British elite educational system (Eton, Oxford) to his influential but brief work with Ernest Rutherford, one of the towering figures in the history of atomic and nuclear physics. Heilbron employed Moseley's correspondence extensively, pointing to a style that is vigorous in thought and economical in expression. Indeed, Heilbron's own style can also be described in this way.

The book on Moseley contains a biography and Moseley's correspondence. Heilbron has continued to work on making the writings of physicists more readily available; the book on John Dee contains an English translation of Dee from the Latin; and Heilbron has edited searching tools for literature (especially correspondence) on the history of 20th-century physics. This activity is of course also aptly described by the metaphor of finding a signal within a vast background of noise.

The metaphor implies that there is much that is irrelevant for Heilbron's stories. Contextualization is always defined by what is necessary to explain the physics in question – no more and no less. In his history of electricity in the 17th and 18th centuries, his history of the Royal Society, his co-authored statistics of funding for physics around 1900, and his history of the 20th-century particle accelerators, Heilbron took funding to be the relevant context. Funding enables physics to advance. The social or institutional context never has an influence upon scientific theory beyond that of enabling. For that reason, Heilbron's narratives have separated the cognitive from the social and institutional context. Heilbron has not doubted that the signal (cognitive progress) can be recognized by virtue of its similarity with what we now consider true, correct, and rational. The following quotation from *Electricity in the 17th and 18th Centuries* (1979) illustrates both Heilbron's vigorous style and his perfect hindsight: "No doubt this salve, made among other things of skull moss, mummy, and the fat and blood of a dead man, would be most beneficial when used as directed, *viz.*, smeared upon a stick or napkin previously dipped in the wound and kept far away from the patient."

In his study of electricity, Heilbron emphasized that experimental work and theory construction can be separated from metaphysical commitments such as a paradigm. This is not only against the teachings of his PhD supervisor, it also situates Heilbron explicitly on one side of the fault line in the historiography of science of the late 20th century: scientific theory is not sociologically constructed but a result of experimental evidence, the interpretation of which is unproblematic in the sense that it is not significantly influenced by the historical context of the observer.

Weighing Imponderables (1993) has since located the history of electricity of the 18th century within a more general history of quantification, which is truly a history of enlightenment. Much of the book deals with the technicalities of devising quantifying techniques in the sciences of heat and geodesy. Quantification in science was enabled in part by the burgeoning (if rudimentary) numeracy in the population at large due to the growth of commerce. General history has thus enabled the progress of straight thinking, the best representative of which is (quantitative) physics.

Two of Heilbron's books – *John Dee* (1978) and *The Dilemmas of an Upright Man* (1986) – could be said to engage directly in historiographical debates in which he energetically defended his conception of historical signal and historical noise. *John Dee* engaged with Frances Yates' argument that the "irrational" hermetic tradition provided an important resource for the scientific revolution. Heilbron separated the positive and negative influences of the hermetists: their (experimental) study of topics depreciated or ignored in the schools and their promise of ultimate knowledge versus their secretiveness, their acceptance of reports of prodigies, and their anti-rationalism. Heilbron found that the translation of Dee provided in the book confirmed that such a neat separation of the beneficial and the maleficent in the history of rationality is justified. *The Dilemmas* described Max Planck's opposition to Ernst Mach and Niels Bohr's insistence that physics cannot reach reality beneath the appearances. Heilbron never became explicit about the purpose of this book, but the narrative connects Planck's opposition to Mach and Bohr with his opposition to the Nazis, and he made the dilemma of the "upright man" (Planck, the dean of German physics) resemble the dilemma of a philosophical realist (Heilbron, the dean of Berkeley) faced with the sociology of knowledge in the 1980s. The same theme was treated in an article written contemporaneously with the Planck book on Bohr's brand of quantum mechanics. Heilbron argued implicitly against Paul Forman, a fellow and contemporary Kuhn PhD student. In an article well known to historians of physics, Forman had argued that cultural influences in the 1920s were at least partly responsible for the indeterminism that became a part of the new quantum physics. Heilbron contended that quantum mechanics succeeded because of quantitative agreement with experiment and despite Bohr's "unsystematic" philosophy, just as he argued with Dee. Wider culture or society thus played no role in the history of science other than providing funds.

Heilbron's co-written history of the Lawrence Berkeley Laboratory (and the pilot study that covered both the Lawrence Berkeley and the Lawrence Livermore up to about 1970) did not disguise the relevance of a social, political, and economic context. It is very clear that the support of the military was what enabled the development of this blueprint for particle accelerators, which have dominated physics during the second half of the 20th century. Again, Heilbron sought a signal in the vast amount of historical sources available, and the signal is physics. While the narrative points to, say, high politics, or the changes in work practice of male and female workers, or the medical uses of accelerators, these topics are covered only in so far as they have an impact on the history of physics. As a result, we have an engaging story of modern big science from the perspective of the "main" scientific discipline involved.

ARNE HESSENBRUCH

Biography

John Lewis Heilbron. Born San Francisco, 17 March 1934. Received BA, University of California, Berkeley, 1955, MA 1958, PhD 1964. Assistant director, Sources in the History of Quantum Physics, Berkeley and Copenhagen, 1961–64; taught at University of Pennsylvania, 1964–67; University of California, Berkeley, from 1967. Married in 1959.

Principal Writings

H.G.J. Moseley: The Life and Letters of an English Physicist, 1887–1915, 1974

Introduction, *John Dee on Astronomy*, translated by Wayne Shumaker, 1978

Electricity in the 17th and 18th Centuries: A Study of Early Modern Physics, 1979

Historical Studies in the Theory of Atomic Structure, 1981

With Robert W. Seidel and Bruce R. Wheaton, *Lawrence and His Laboratory: Nuclear Science at Berkeley, 1931–1961*, 1981

Elements of Early Modern Physics, 1982

The Dilemmas of an Upright Man: Max Planck as Spokesman for German Science, 1986

With Robert W. Seidel, *Lawrence and His Laboratory : A History of the Lawrence Berkeley Laboratory*, 1989

Editor with Tore Frängsmyr and Robin A. Rider, *The Quantifying Spirit in the 18th Century*, 1990

Weighing Imponderables and Other Quantitative Science around 1800, 1993

Henry, Louis 1911–1991
French demographic historian

Louis Henry contributed to the development of almost every aspect of the methodology of demographic science. He is best known for developing the concept of natural fertility (marital fertility where couples do not alter their reproductive behavior according to the number of children already born), and analyzing the reasons for population growth. However, he was as much interested in explaining Third World population trends as European population history. He is also associated with the evolution of an understanding of infant mortality and of the analytical use of censuses and projection methods. Most of his career was spent at the University of Paris.

Henry came to historical demography relatively late in life when he became a research associate, in the newly established Institut National d'Etudes Démographiques (INED) at the age of 34, following World War II. From the late 1940s his articles started to dominate the pages of the journal *Population*. In a precomputer age, these developed the theoretical basis of historical demography by the scientific measurement of facts and social phenomenon, and the development of mathematical models. In 1953 he published *Fécondité des mariages* (*Fertility of Marriage*, 1980).

In the same year, he began work, with Etienne Gautier, on the parish register of Crulai in Normandy and became the pioneer of the technique of family reconstitution. The results were published in 1958 as a prototype village monograph, *La Population de Crulai* (The Population of Crulai). The development of reconstitution techniques were a tool in Henry's search for natural fertility. This study showed how much birth intervals narrowed when the preceding child died before its first birthday. He argued the death of the earlier child permitted a new conception, rather than that the new conception increased the risk to the living child. At the same time the study established scientific rules for the calculation of mortality rates in communities.

A prior project had used parish registers and genealogy to study the bourgeois of Geneva and was published in 1956 as *Anciennes familles genevoises* (Old Genevan Families). Here Henry found that while wet nursing increased the fertility of the elite in the early 17th century, a reaction developed in the second half of the century. After 1650 reduced opportunities caused young men to leave Geneva and to have smaller families than their predecessors. This study demonstrated for the first time that in the 17th and 18th centuries levels of fertility were low relative to natural fertility and quite variable between groups affected by late marriage and birth spacing. By this means, Henry incorporated not only social and economic but also biological factors into his analysis.

These ideas became more widely known through his articles on fertility and family that appeared in *Population* between 1957 and 1961. A collection of these writings, *On the Measurement of Human Fertility* (1972), made him well known in English-speaking countries. In this book he aimed to establish a system of analyzing given data on family histories and the timing of events, for example marriages and births, using mathematical models, to consider how physiological functions related to matters of reproduction, and to question at what point a population starts to use contraception. This work was particularly influential for those such as E.A. Wrigley, who were to become major figures in the development of demographic history.

In the late 1950s, Henry started work on a project focusing on the study of the French population since Louis XIV, with a particular emphasis on dukes and peers. He also published a manual of demographic history. Scrupulous in his practice, and somewhat intransigent in manner, Henry set up a series of rules for demography that have had an enormous influence in ensuring standardization of method in the subsequent study of demographic history.

PAMELA SHARPE
with translation assistance from Kathryn Limb

See also Annales School; Demography; Family; Wrigley

Biography

Born St. Girous, France, 19 February 1911. Studied at the Ecole Polytechnique, 1931–39. Captain in the French Army; taken prisoner and imprisoned in Germany, 1940–45. Associate, Institut National d'Etudes Démographiques, 1946–91. Died Paris, 30 December 1991.

Principal Writings

Fécondité des mariages: nouvelle méthode de mesure, 1953; in English as *Fertility of Marriage: A New Method of Measurement*, 1980
Anciennes familles genevoises: étude démographique: XVIe–XXe siècle (Old Genevan Families: Demographic Studies from the 16th to the 20th Centuries), 1956
With Etienne Gautier, *La Population de Crulai, paroisse normande* (The Population of Crulai, a Norman Parish), 1958
Perspectives démographiques (Demographic Perspectives), 1964
Démographie: analyse et modèles, 1972, revised 1984; in English as *Population: Analysis and Models*, 1976
"Historical Demography," in D.V. Glass and Roger Revelle, eds., *Population and Social Change*, 1972
On the Measurement of Human Fertility: Selected Writings of Louis Henry, 1972

Techniques d'analyse en démographie historique (Analytical Techniques in Historical Demography), 1980
Multilingual Demographic Dictionary: English Section, 1982

Further Reading

"La Mesure des phénomènes démographiques: hommage à Louis Henry," *Population* (September 1977) [includes bibliography]

Herder, J.G. 1744–1803
German historical theorist

One of the major German thinkers of the late 18th century, J.G. Herder is sometimes viewed as an important founder of modern historical theory. In an age when universal history was popular, and one in which the traditional idea of the plan of God was no longer dominant, he laid the foundation for the modern approach to the history of mankind. Herder incorporated much of the science of the Enlightenment into his worldview. An early Romantic, he gave renewed emphasis to the importance of the spirit of the people (*Volk*) as it was expressed in literature and in history.

Herder was able to develop his ideas of national difference from his encounter with the diverse cultures of the Baltic region, France, Italy, and Germany. His fame was assured when he won the prize of the Berlin Academy of Sciences for his *Abhandlung über den Ursprung der Sprache*, (1772; *On the Origin of Language*, 1827). In it he argued that human reason made it possible for the human species to develop language and history. In his first work on the subject, *Auch eine Philosophie der Geschichte zur Bildung der Menschheit* (1774; *Yet Another Philosophy of History for the Education of Humanity*, 1968), he rejected the notion that only some ages were meant to be great. Accepting this theory meant that all the generations preceding such an age had existed merely to prepare for the one great age.

Once he was appointed general superintendent of the Lutheran church in the tiny duchy of Weimar in 1776, Herder was able to work with the poet Johann Wolfgang Goethe to create the literary image of classical Weimar, later so important for German culture. Opposed to autocratic government and the servile spirit it had produced in Germany, Herder argued for a faith in the ability of individuals to develop the full capacities of the human species. Each nation that emerged had to fulfill its own unique mission in history.

Herder was one of the first modern historians to celebrate cultural diversity. In his 2-volume work, *Ideen zur Philosophie der Geschichte der Menschheit* (1785–91; abridged as *Reflections on the Philosophy of the History of Mankind*, 1968), Herder elaborated upon an earlier conception of the relation of man to his culture. Freedom, reason, and language were integral to modern individualism. That human culture was influenced by climate was not a new idea, but Herder greatly modified the earlier theories when he argued that mankind forms a single species and is destined to expand over the entire surface of the earth. The human individual was a creature endowed with language. His biology, taken together with his consciousness and his reflective mind, made it possible for him to develop culture in the broadest sense. Herder's belief that the world's entire population formed a single species, may be contrasted with the early race theories of the 18th century, which he rejected.

Modern as Herder's work on *Reflections* was, the first volume cannot be treated as a primer of knowledge. No one any longer believes that planet earth is a star. Yet there is a wide area of agreement on the importance of reason for the development of technology. The scope of his arguments makes it possible to consider Herder as the first modern cultural historian. His keen interest in Hellenistic culture was turned to good advantage in the second volume of the *Reflections*. Having toured Italy in 1789, he was able to devote considerable attention to questions of Roman history. His survey of the migrations of peoples in Asia and Europe, and of their founding mythologies, foreshadows the 20th-century study of comparative mythology. The 17th-century notion of an original state of nature was rejected in favor of a more dynamic belief in a uniform organization of mankind for freedom through reason. Man was believed to be in a constant state of development towards goals of humanity and happiness.

The general influence of Herder's ideas on history contributed to shaping the traditions of historical thought in Germany and Europe during the next two centuries. His belief in the uniqueness of national culture made his work popular in many of the emerging nations of Europe during the 19th century. Herder rejected natural law theories but did express basic assumptions about human nature. Man was organized for reason. He was constituted for humanity and religion. Herder's notion of development seems to have fallen short of a theory of evolution, yet he did acknowledge a forward movement toward a higher level of civilization which he called "humanity." Herder's optimistic philosophy led him to predict a future in which the destructive forces would diminish as the use of reason improved. He looked forward to a new culture for Europe based on science and widespread education.

Without having an organic view of society, Herder believed that the human race was destined to pass through several stages of cultural development. It was his religious faith that shaped the belief that reason and a sense of fairness would increase. As it did so, the forces of reason would give impetus to a permanent sense of humanity. The key factors to observe in any study of human history were time, place, and circumstances. The human species did not appear to have only one form. Its culture was grounded in the multitude and diversity of nations that existed within the wider context of a recognizable unity of human characteristics.

Herder's work as a cultural historian remains at the optimistic level of the Enlightenment. The Romantic political conservatives of the post-Napoleonic era were in part influenced by his organic approach to history; yet they did not accept his anthropology or his egalitarian conceptions of human nature. The development of modern social science makes it possible to view Herder's work as a connecting link between Enlightenment optimism and contemporary historical science.

HELEN LIEBEL-WECKOWICZ

See also Agrarian; Berlin; Karamzin; Lecky; Meinecke; Nationalism; Philosophy of History; Religion; Schlözer; Treitschke; Wellhausen; Wilamovitz-Möllendorff

Biography

Johann Gottfried Herder. Born Mohrungen (now Morag), East Prussia, 25 August 1744, to a poor family. Educated locally, then at the University of Königsberg, 1762–64. Taught and preached at Riga, 1764–69; traveled and was royal tutor, 1769–71; held high religious posts in Bückeberg, 1771–76, and Weimar, 1776–1803. Married Caroline Flachsland, 1773 (7 sons, 1 daughter). Ennobled 1802. Died Weimar, 18 December 1803.

Principal Writings

Abhandlung über den Ursprung der Sprache, 1772; in English as *On the Origin of Language*, 1827

Auch eine Philosophie der Geschichte zur Bildung der Menschheit, 1774; in English as *Yet Another Philosophy of History for the Education of Humanity*, 1968

Ideen zur Philosophie der Geschichte der Menschheit, 4 vols., 1785–91; in English as *Outlines of a Philosophy of the History of Man*, 1800; abridged as *Reflections on the Philosophy of the History of Mankind*, 1968

Briefe zur Beförderung der Humanität (Letters on the Promotion of Humanity), 10 collections, 1793–97

Sämtliche Werke (Collected Works), 33 vols., 1877–1913

Further Reading

Barnard, Frederick M., ed., *Herder's Social and Political Thought: From Enlightenment to Nationalism*, Oxford: Clarendon Press, 1965

Barnard, Frederick M., ed., *J.G. Herder on Society and Political Culture*, Cambridge: Cambridge University Press, 1969

Berlin, Isaiah, *Vico and Herder: Two Studies in the History of Ideas*, London: Hogarth Press, and New York: Viking, 1976

Clark, Robert Thomas, *Herder: His Life and Thought*, Berkeley: University of California Press, 1955

Gillies, Alexander, *Herder*, Oxford: Blackwell, 1945

Lewis, Samuel Mark, *Modes of Historical Discourse in J.G. Herder and N.M. Karamzin*, New York: Lang, 1995

Herodotus *c.*484–after 424 BCE
Greek historian

Herodotus, the first great prose writer of classical Greece, was hailed as the "Father of History" by Cicero. He lived in Athens in the 440s and 430s, but after the Peace of Callias in 449 ended hostilities between Greece and Persia, he traveled to Egypt, Babylonia, and later Scythia (the present-day Ukraine). At the end of his life, he participated in the colonization of Thurii in southern Italy, where he died.

Herodotus published his famous Histories around 445. He wished to describe the great event of the 5th century, Greece's amazing defeat of the vast army and navy of the Persian king, Xerxes. For his readers to appreciate fully the enormity of that achievement, he described Persia's prior expansion over Babylonia, Lydia, Scythia, and Egypt.

Herodotus was an indefatigable investigator, but he was dependent at times upon dubious sources, especially in his travels abroad. He did try to check his sources, and often acknowledged that information was lacking. He loved to tell a good story, even when he did not believe it to be true, such as the circumnavigation of Africa. He recorded with wonder, but with respect, customs of foreigners that seemed bizarre to Greeks. In fact, Herodotus' generous treatment of the Persians later earned the scorn of Plutarch, who in his *On the Malignity of Herodotus* accused Herodotus of being a *philobarbaros*, or lover of barbarians.

Debate as to whether Herodotus should be viewed as the "Father of History" or the "Father of Lies" has persisted to the present day. The latter reputation prevailed from the Middle Ages to the Renaissance. In the 16th century Henri Estienne came to Herodotus' defence. But Herodotus was severely attacked in the 18th century by J.-B. Bonnaud and in the 19th century by A.H. Sayce. His severest critics today are Detlev Fehling and O. Kimball Armayor. Fehling has accused Herodotus of making up his sources, and Armayor has claimed that his description of the Labyrinth and Lake Moeris was not based on his observations in Egypt, but was patterned after literary models from Homer.

No one, however, can doubt that Herodotus did visit Egypt. His account of early Egyptian history is a grab-bag of folklore, although he correctly identified the first pharaoh as Min (Menes), and the builders of the three great pyramids at Giza as Cheops (Khufu), Chephren (Khafre), and Mycerinus (Menkaure). His account of the Saite era (XXVIth Dynasty), that is of the 7th–6th centuries, is quite accurate.

In 1883 Sayce questioned whether Herodotus had ever gone to Babylon. But the excavations of Robert Koldewey from 1899 to 1913 vindicated Herodotus, although he had exaggerated certain dimensions of the city. However, Herodotus shared very little useful information about Babylonian history and his promise of a separate Assyrian account was never written.

Herodotus did provide us with invaluable information about the Scythians, Medes, and Persians. His account of such savage Scythian customs as scalping and inhaling hemp fumes has been dramatically confirmed by the frozen burials of Pazyryk. Herodotus accurately described the overthrow of the Medes in 550 by the first great Persian king Cyrus, an account confirmed by a Babylonian chronicle. He preserved accurately a great number of Median and Persian names. Most impressively he rendered correctly six of the seven names of Darius' co-conspirators as recorded in the Behistun inscription. There are, however, some scholars (for example, Jack Balcer), who think that Darius made up the story of the murder of the usurper Gaumata (Smerdis), and that Herodotus was gullible in accepting the royal propaganda. But despite some difficulties, others (e.g., Richard Frye) believe that the official version remains more credible than revisionist theories. Herodotus remains our chief source for the Persian invasions of Greece in 490 and in 480–479. Despite his exaggeration of the Persian numbers, archaeology and topographical surveys have confirmed the credibility of his accounts.

Though Herodotus has been attacked by critics ancient and modern for his flaws, few writers in antiquity observed as widely and as dispassionately as he did, or wrote in such an arresting manner. Alan Lloyd concluded: "It is extremely doubtful whether any historian before modern times could have significantly improved on Herodotus' performance when faced with similar material and well-nigh certain that none would have made of it so consummate a literary masterpiece."

EDWIN M. YAMAUCHI

See also Africa: North; Archaeology; Bernal; Byzantium; Christianity; Greece: Ancient; Memory; Military; Momigliano; Near East; Plutarch; Popular; Procopius; Religion; Rhetoric; Schama; Thucydides; Universal; World; Xenophon

Biography
Born Halicaranassus, in Caria (now Bodrum, Turkey), traditionally *c.*484 BCE, of distinguished family. Moved to Samos during civil strife, *c.*460; traveled extensively, 455–447; helped found Athenian colony of Thurii in south Italy, 444/3. Died Thurii, after 424.

Principal Writings
Works (Loeb edition), translated by A.D. Godley, 4 vols., 1921–24
The Histories, translated by Aubrey de Sélincourt, 2nd edition 1972
The History, translated by David Grene, 1987

Further Reading
Armayor, O. Kimball, *Herodotus' Autopsy of the Fayoum: Lake Moeris and the Labyrinth of Egypt*, Amsterdam: Gieben, 1985
Balcer, Jack M., *Herodotus and Bisitun: Problems in Ancient Persian Historiography*, Stuttgart: Steiner, 1987
Burkert, Walter *et al.*, *Hérodote et les peuples non grecs* (Herodotus and non-Greek Peoples), Geneva: Hart, 1990
Dewald, Carolyn, and John Marincola, "A Selective Introduction to Herodotean Studies," *Arethusa* 20 (1987), 9–40
Drews, Robert, *The Greek Accounts of Eastern History*, Cambridge, MA: Harvard University Press, 1973
Evans, James Allan Stewart, *Herodotus, Explorer of the Past: Three Essays*, Princeton: Princeton University Press, 1991
Fehling, Detlev, *Die Quellenangaben bei Herodot: Studien zur Erzählkunst Herodots*, Berlin: de Gruyter, 1971; in English as *Herodotus and His "Sources": Citation, Invention and Narrative Art*, Leeds: Cairns, 1989
Fornara, Charles W., *Herodotus: An Interpretive Essay*, Oxford: Oxford University Press, 1971
Frye, Richard N., *The History of Ancient Iran*, Munich: Beck, 1984
Hart, John, *Herodotus and Greek History*, New York: St. Martin's Press, and London: Croom Helm, 1982
Hignett, Charles, *Xerxes' Invasion of Greece*, Oxford: Clarendon Press, 1963
Hunter, Virginia, *Past and Process in Herodotus and Thucydides*, Princeton: Princeton University Press, 1982
Immerwahr, Henry R., *Form and Thought in Herodotus*, Cleveland: Press of Western Reserve University, 1966
Lateiner, Donald, *The Historical Method of Herodotus*, Toronto: University of Toronto Press, 1989
Lloyd, Alan B., *Herodotus, Book II: Introduction*, Leiden: Brill, 1975
Lloyd, Alan B., "Herodotus' Account of Pharaonic History," *Historia* 37 (1988), 22–53
MacGinnis, John, "Herodotus' Description of Babylon," *Bulletin of the Institute of Classical Studies* 33 (1986), 67–86
Myres, John Linton, *Herodotus: Father of History*, Oxford: Oxford University Press, 1953
Pohlenz, Max, *Herodot: Der erste Geschichtsschreiber des Abendlandes* (Herodotus: The First Historian of the West), Leipzig: Teubner, 1937, 1961
Pritchett, W. Kendrick, *Studies in Ancient Greek Topography*, vol. 2: *Battlefields*, Berkeley: University of California Press, 1969
Pritchett, W. Kendrick, *The Liar School of Herodotos*, Amsterdam: Gieben, 1993
Yamauchi, Edwin M., *Foes from the Northern Frontier: Invading Hordes from the Russian Steppes*, Grand Rapids, MI: Baker, 1982
Yamauchi, Edwin M., *Persia and the Bible*, Grand Rapids, MI: Baker, 1990

Hexter, J.H. 1910–1996

US historian of early modern Britain

J.H. Hexter is one of the best-known 20th-century American historians to work in the field of Tudor-Stuart history. During an active career that began in the 1930s, he produced numerous carefully researched studies of early modern England and fostered debate over the methods of "doing history" through his critical appraisals of theory and method. Despite his stern admonitions against presentist interpretations of the past in his work on the historical profession, in recent years Hexter became a focal point for a heated methodological dispute in which charges of "Neo-Whiggism" were levelled at him. These charges of "Whiggery" result from Hexter's continuing interest in the political and constitutional history of early modern England and from his particular interest in the development of an opposition in the House of Commons in the early Stuart period.

Perhaps as a result of his concern for politics, Hexter is primarily a narrative historian who believes that the form of his writing serves as a vehicle of explanation since "the story itself becomes the explanation of the series of events that it recounts." His adversaries, and critics of narrative history in general, suggest that such a belief in a narrative structure is by its very nature "Whiggish." The flow of the narrative imputes a sense of inevitability that is only compounded by the process of making causal connections from later events to earlier ones, and from earlier events forward to suggest their future significance. In this matter, Hexter's interpretation of the causes of the English Civil War is especially suggestive. For Hexter, "revisionist" views of the Civil War as a great historical accident are fundamentally flawed and overlook a rising tide of Parliamentary opposition in defense of modern English liberty during the 17th century. For evidence of this discontent in early Stuart England, Hexter turned to the "Apology of the House of Commons" which raised a challenge to the royal prerogative in 1604. Parliament, however, never presented the "Apology" to James I. Thus, Hexter stands accused of fixing his eye firmly on the end result and then seeking out mile-markers on the high road to the Civil War that would explain the ultimate breakdown of the Elizabethan constitution.

Hexter's supporters claim that he was not "Whiggish" in his approach to history and assert that he was not guilty of falling into the linear progression, anachronism, or "the agony of anticipation" that characterize the abuses of the Whig interpretation of history. Rather, they claim that he was an astute observer of political characters and institutions, and the ways in which power and authority are wielded. His research interests and his preference for narrative do not necessarily imply a teleology in history, of course, and there is something to the claim that Hexter's focus on Parliamentary opposition accurately reflects the problems of political discourse in early modern England.

It is, in fact, difficult to believe that Hexter was not aware of the problems inherent in his approach to historical research and writing. First and foremost, he was an astute critic of the historical profession. His own work and his reflections in *The History Primer* and *Doing History* (both 1971) reflect his commitment to a practical understanding of the historian's craft. In particular, he embraced a practical ideal based on a belief that historians have an obligation to tell the truest, and

most complete, story possible. He thus did not subject historical writing to conformity with scientific rule or abandon it to utter relativism. These views on narrative history and on the meaning of historical knowledge reflect, in part, his concern with the fragmentation of the historical profession and the trend toward social and cultural history ("history with the politics left out"). Although the profession may not come full-circle and experience a total revitalization of interest in politics and in the narrative form, there is mounting evidence that Hexter was right to suggest that his style of history is moving out of a period of relative eclipse.

J.S.W. HELT

See also Gardiner; Hill; Mattingly; Stone

Biography

Jack H. Hexter. Born Memphis, Tennessee, 25 May 1910. Received BA, University of Cincinnati, 1931; MA, Harvard University 1933, PhD 1937. Taught at University of Cincinnati, 1936–37; Harvard University 1937–38; Massachusetts Institute of Technology, 1938–39; Queens College, New York, 1939–57; Washington University, St Louis, 1957–64; Yale University 1964–78; and Washington University, 1978–90 (emeritus). Married Ruth Mullin, 1942 (2 sons, 2 daughters). Died St. Louis, 8 December 1996.

Principal Writings

The Reign of King Pym, 1941
More's Utopia: The Biography of an Idea, 1952
Reappraisals in History, 1962
The Judeo-Christian Tradition, 1966
Doing History, 1971
The History Primer, 1971
"Parliament under the Lens," *British Studies Monitor* 7 (1972), 4–15.
The Vision of Politics on the Eve of the Reformation: More, Machiavelli, and Seyssel, 1973
"Power Struggle, Parliament, and Liberty in Early Stuart England," *Journal of Modern History* 50 (1978), 1–50
On Historians: Reappraisals of Some of the Makers of Modern History, 1979
"The Early Stuarts and Parliament: Old Hat and the *Nouvelle Vague*," *Parliamentary History* 1 (1982), 181–215
"Call Me Ishmael," *American Scholar* 52 (1983), 339–53
"Carl Becker, Professor Novick, and Me; or, Cheer up, Professor N!," *American Historical Review* 96 (1991), 675–82
Editor, *Parliament and Liberty from the Reign of Elizabeth to the English Civil War*, 1992

Further Reading

Dray, W.H., "J.H. Hexter, Neo-Whiggism, and Early Stuart Historiography," *History and Theory* 26 (1987), 133–49
Malamount, Barbara C., ed., *After the Reformation: Essays in Honor of J.H. Hexter*, Manchester: Manchester University Press, and Philadelphia: University of Pennsylvania, 1980 [includes bibliography]

Hilberg, Raul 1926–

US (Austrian-born) historian of the Holocaust

Raul Hilberg is recognized as the dean of Holocaust historiography and his book, *The Destruction of European Jews*

(1961; revised 1985), is viewed as the single most important work ever written on the subject. Prior to the publication of Hilberg's study in 1961, historians who examined the events that culminated in the systematic murder of six million Jews often focused on anti-Semitism as the "single key" to explain the grisly realities of twelve years of Nazi dictatorship. Léon Poliakov's *Bréviaire de la haine* (1951; *Harvest of Hate*, 1954) and Gerald Reitlinger's *The Final Solution* (1953) are representative of this genre of Holocaust historiography. Whereas Poliakov and Reitlinger were primarily concerned with tracing the historical sequence of events, Hilberg's work examines how they occurred.

The Destruction of European Jews analyzes the Final Solution, the term employed by the Nazis to indicate their plans for the genocidal elimination of the Jews of Europe, by describing the process of destruction as it unfolded across the European continent. Hilberg's study was the first systematically to comb the German materials on the Holocaust and examine the extensive bureaucracy that implemented the Final Solution. As Hilberg states in the preface to his work

> I wanted to explore the sheer mechanism of the destruction, and as I delved into the problem I saw that I was studying an administrative process carried out by bureaucrats in a network of offices spanning a continent. Understanding the components of this apparatus, with all the facets of its activities, became the principal task of my life.

Hilberg's training as a political scientist and the influence of his mentor, Franz Neumann, each contributed to the interpretive model on which his analysis is based – "the machinery of destruction."

According to Hilberg, the murder of European Jewry proceeded in stages, "sequential steps" initiated by bureaucrats involved in the machinery of destruction. Jews were defined according to Nazi racial ideology, had their property expropriated, they were concentrated in ghettos and other holding centers until they were deported and finally murdered. Ultimately it was the machinery of destruction itself, the system as opposed to individual decision makers, that was the driving force behind the genocidal policies of the Nazis. Hilberg argued that the human machine of the Nazis generated its own momentum: "With an unfailing sense of direction and with an uncanny pathfinding ability, the German bureaucracy found the shortest path to the final goal."

The impact of Hilberg's work within the field of Holocaust historiography was both immediate and long-lasting. Hannah Arendt's *Eichmann in Jerusalem: A Report on the Banality of Evil* (1963), a book that was based on her coverage of Adolf Eichmann's war-crimes trial in Jerusalem, seemingly reaffirmed Hilberg's assessment of the Final Solution as the product of non-ideological bureaucrats operating within a huge bureaucratic structure. This view, coupled with Arendt's charge that Jewish leaders willingly helped implement the policies of the Nazis, and Hilberg's argument that "two thousand years of historical conditioning" prevented Jews from opposing the machinery of death, set off a fire storm of debate concerning the actions of Jews during the Holocaust. In the wake of this debate, Holocaust historiography has become increasingly nuanced and methodologically sophisticated as historians continue to wrestle with the dilemma of explaining a historical event that resulted in the deaths of six million human beings. Although Hilberg's sensitivity to the question of Jewish resistance has increased since the initial publication of his work and his most recent book, *Perpetrators, Victims, Bystanders* (1992), offers a personal approach to the subject as opposed to a bureaucratic one, he continues to judge severely the leadership of European Jewry during the Holocaust and diminish the significance of Jewish resistance within the overall scheme of the destruction process.

KEITH H. PICKUS

See also Holocaust

Biography

Born Vienna, 1926. Went to the US via Cuba. Served in US Army, 1944–46. Received BA, Brooklyn College; PhD in public law and government, Columbia University, 1955. Taught at University of Vermont (rising to professor of political science), 1956–91 (emeritus).

Principal Writings

The Destruction of European Jews, 1961; revised in 3 vols., 1985
Perpetrators, Victims, Bystanders: The Jewish Catastrophe, 1933–1945, 1992

Further Reading

Bauer, Yehuda, *The Holocaust in Historical Perspective*, Seattle: University of Washington Press, 1978
Eley, Geoff, "Holocaust History," *London Review of Books*, (3–17 March 1982), 6–9
"The Historiography of the Holocaust," *Proceedings from the Fifth Yad Vashem International Historical Conference*, Jerusalem, 1983
Kulka, Otto Dov, "Major Trends and Tendencies in German Historiography on National Socialism and the 'Jewish Question' (1924–1984)," *Leo Baeck Institute Yearbook* 30 (1985), 215–42
Marrus, Michael R., *The Holocaust in History*, Hanover, NH: University Press of New England, 1987
Marrus, Michael R., "Reflections on the Historiography of the Holocaust," *Journal of Modern History* 66 (1994), 92–116
Pacy, James, and Alan P. Wertheimer, *Perspectives on the Holocaust: Essays in Honor of Raul Hilberg*, Boulder, CO: Westview Press, 1995

Hill, Christopher 1912–

British historian of early modern England

A prolific historian of 17th-century England, Christopher Hill has produced work that converges around one central proposition: that the great conflict of the mid-17th-century, which he conceives as a bourgeois revolution, was pivotal in shaping England's historical development and heritage. Hill's scholarship is remarkably wide-ranging. Drawing on a mastery of printed sources and prodigious work habits, he has produced essential work on the Anglican church, seminal studies of puritanism, and important scholarship on the history of ideas in their social context. A pioneer of history "from the bottom up," Hill has a particular interest in the radical and democratic ideologies that emerged during the 17th-century revolution.

Hill embraced Marxism as a university student in the 1930s when the reigning interpretation of the mid-17th-century political upheaval derived from the Whig historian, S.R. Gardiner.

For Gardiner, the English Civil War, which he termed the Puritan Revolution, was a conflict over religious and constitutional liberty, narrowly defined. Hill's earliest work advanced an essentialist class analysis of the Civil War. In a polemical essay of 1940, "The English Revolution," he argued that Parliament's victory swept away the feudal order of the Stuart monarchy, insuring bourgeois rule and the triumph of capitalism.

Hill produced relatively little scholarship during the ten years after his World War II military service. Nevertheless, that period proved crucial to his intellectual development as he gradually abandoned a narrow economic determinism and the reductionist base–superstructure model for a more complex materialist examination of culture, ideology, and politics. Much of the ferment took place within the Historians' Group of the Communist party, an extraordinary collection of scholars including Rodney Hilton, Eric Hobsbawm, and E.P. Thompson. In 1952 Hill and others from the HGCP founded *Past and Present* as an outlet for innovative scholarship. His close association with this prestigious journal has continued until the present day.

In 1956 Hill left the Communist party and also produced his first monograph, *Economic Problems of the Church*, considered the definitive treatment of the subject by many specialists. This study presented the Anglican church as an economically depleted institution, a problem dating to the Reformation. Unable to accommodate the demands of Elizabethan Protestants and estranged from key groups in the House of Commons, the church hierarchy drew increasingly close to the crown, a fatal dependence that contributed to the origins of the Civil War.

In successive works Hill further developed his analysis of the interrelation of the social, cultural, and ideological, addressing the connections of Puritanism to capitalism and the English Revolution. "Protestantism and the Rise of Capitalism" is Hill's contribution to the Weber-Tawney debate. In Hill's estimation, the characteristic Protestant values such as frugality and industry were not the inherent by-product of Protestant theology but a consequence of "the religion of the heart" in an already capitalist society. In contrast to his earlier essays which tended to reduce religiously defined groups to economic classes, *Society and Puritanism* (1964) began the project of developing a sociology of religious belief. According to Hill, Puritanism found its most ardent support from "the industrious sort," chiefly merchants, yeomen, and artisans. Richly detailed essays identify essential religious doctrines and beliefs as codes of social practice that fostered self-discipline and the desire for a more orderly society. As 17th-century events unfolded, Puritans found their vision of the good society at odds with the Stuart monarchy and Laudian church. They thus emerged as a critical base of support for Parliamentary forces in the Civil War. Several historians have questioned the imprecision in Hill's definition of Puritanism. Other have challenged his close identification of Puritanism with a narrow strata of the emerging middle class, an affinity that may have been far from consistent. In subsequent work Hill's analysis of the puritan role in the Revolution continued to evolve. He conceded that Puritans never intended to usher in a capitalist order. Hill insists, however, that guided by specific values and aspirations, they pushed events in that direction, turning the Civil War into a revolution.

One of Hill's most important contributions has been in exploring the social basis of ideas, an interest he developed in "The Norman Yoke" (1940), *Antichrist in Seventeenth-Century England* (1971), and with particular success in *Intellectual Origins of the English Revolution* (1965). There, Hill identified three sources of thought that prepared the ground for the 17th-century political convulsions: Ralegh's New History, Coke's elevation of the Common Law, and Bacon's empiricism. These thinkers gave voice to the ideas and aspirations of "the middling sort" and provided a direct challenge to the forces of traditional authority.

Much of Hill's attention has focused on the democratic and egalitarian currents of the Interregnum. He has written at length on Gerrard Winstanley, leader-theorist of the communist Diggers. In *The World Turned Upside Down* (1972), perhaps Hill's most popular work, he joined his interest in *mentalité* with history from the bottom up. Examining a spectrum of radical groups and individuals ignored by previous historians, including Seekers, Ranters, and early Quakers, Hill interpreted their activities as an expression of the radical and democratic sentiments of the common people, voices still worthy of our attention. Their presence, Hill argued, pushed the Revolution leftward, prompting an increasingly anxious elite to restore the Stuarts.

In 1975 the conservative American historian J.H. Hexter unleashed a scathing attack on Hill, challenging his integrity as a scholar. Hill's many defenders weighed in, but the subsequent growth of revisionism in 17th-century studies, much of it informed by an unimaginative and rigid empiricism, largely refused engagement with Hill's oeuvre. However, with revisionism's subsequent intellectual exhaustion, Hill's challenging scholarship, insistent on the links of past to present, commands renewed interest and respect. As Geoff Eley, a perceptive critic, has noted, Hill's breaching of narrow specialism has allowed for the exploration of the interrelationships of politics, economics, social structure, religion, and culture in historical process.

RICHARD J. SODERLUND

See also Britain: 1485–1750; Economic; Gardiner; History from Below; History Workshop; Hobsbawm; Jones, G.; Kiernan; Marxist Interpretation; Social; Thomas, K.; Thompson, E.

Biography

John Edward Christopher Hill. Born 6 February 1912. Educated at St. Peter's School, York; Balliol College, Oxford, BA 1931. Served in the British Army, then seconded to Foreign Office, 1943–45. Fellow, All Souls College, Oxford, 1934; taught at University College, Cardiff, 1936; fellow/tutor, Balliol College from 1938 (with interruption for war service), master, 1965–78. Married 1) Inez Waugh (1 daughter deceased); 2) Bridget Irene Sutton, 1956 (1 son, 1 daughter and 1 daughter deceased).

Principal Writings

Editor, *The English Revolution, 1640: Three Essays*, 1940 (includes his essay "The Norman Yoke")
Economic Problems of the Church: From Archbishop Whitgift to the Long Parliament, 1956
Puritanism and Revolution: Studies in Interpretation of the English Revolution of the 17th Century, 1958
The Century of Revolution, 1603–1714, 1961; revised 1972
Society and Puritanism in pre-Revolutionary England, 1964
Intellectual Origins of the English Revolution, 1965

Reformation to Industrial Revolution: 1530–1780, 1969
God's Englishman: Oliver Cromwell and the English Revolution, 1970
Antichrist in Seventeenth-Century England, 1971
The World Turned Upside Down: Radical Ideas during the English Revolution, 1972
Change and Continuity in Seventeenth-Century England, 1974
Milton and the English Revolution, 1977
The Experience of Defeat: Milton and Some Contemporaries, 1984
The Collected Essays of Christopher Hill, 3 vols., 1985–86
A Turbulent, Seditious, and Factious People: John Bunyan and His Church, 1628–1688, 1989; US edition as *A Tinker and a Poor Man: John Bunyan and His Church, 1628–1688*, 1989
A Nation of Change and Novelty: Politics, Religion and Literature in Seventeenth-Century England, 1990
The English Bible and the Seventeenth-Century Revolution, 1993

Further Reading

Adamo, Pietro, "Christopher Hill e la rivoluzione inglese: itinerario di uno storico" (Christopher Hill and the English Revolution: A Historian's Journey), *Società e Storia* 13 (1990), 129–58

Clark, J.C.D., *Revolution and Rebellion: State and Society in England in the Seventeenth and Eighteenth Centuries*, Cambridge and New York: Cambridge University Press, 1986

Davis, J.C., *Fear, Myth and History: The Ranters and Historians*, Cambridge and New York: Cambridge University Press, 1986

Eley, Geoff, and William Hunt, *Reviving the English Revolution: Reflections and Elaborations on the Work of Christopher Hill*, London and New York: Verso, 1988

Fulbrook, Mary, "The English Revolution and the Revisionist Revolt," *Social History*, 7 (1982), 249–64

Hexter, J.H., "The Burden of Proof," *Times Literary Supplement* (24 October 1975)

Hobsbawm, Eric J., "The Historians' Group of the Communist Party," in Maurice Cornforth, ed., *Rebels and Their Causes: Essays in Honor of A.L. Morton*, London: Lawrence and Wishart, 1978; Atlantic Highlands, NJ: Humanities Press, 1979

Kaye, Harvey J., *The British Marxist Historians: An Introductory Analysis*, Cambridge: Polity Press, 1984; New York: St. Martin's Press, 1995

Pennington, Donald, and Keith Thomas, eds., *Puritans and Revolutionaries*, Oxford and New York: Oxford University Press, 1978

Richardson, R.C., *The Debate on the English Revolution Revisited*, London: Methuen, and New York: St. Martin's Press, 1977

Samuel, Raphael, "British Marxist Historians, 1880–1980," *New Left Review*, 120 (March–April 1980), 21–96

Schwarz, Bill, "'The People' in History: The Communist Party Historians' Group, 1946–56," in Richard Johnson *et al.*, eds., *Making Histories: Studies in History-Writing and Politics*, London: Hutchinson, and Minneapolis: University of Minnesota Press, 1982

Underdown, David, "Radicals in Defeat," *New York Review of Books* (28 March 1985)

Hillgruber, Andreas 1925–1989

German political historian

During his 35-year-long career, Andreas Hillgruber occupied himself with the history of the German empire as it was founded by Bismarck and destroyed by Hitler, paying special attention to the collapse. Hillgruber's focus was on the empire's changing perception of its interests as a great power, his emphasis, overall, on continuity rather than discontinuity,

while his personal sympathies lay with the benign side of Germany's promise as the dominating power on the European continent.

The Germany that emerges from Hillgruber's work is a state that, tragically, never managed to come to grips with the new and difficult challenges it faced after unification. Hillgruber has no trouble finding faults with a great many policies this German empire pursued, but at the same time refuses to lose sight of the co-responsibility of others for some of the failures or disasters. Perhaps most important of all, Hillgruber does not believe the empire should have ended in the catastrophic way it did; in his eyes, Germany's leading presence in Central and Eastern Europe had many positive aspects, and not just for Germans.

Among his colleagues in the Federal Republic Hillgruber stood out, though not alone, because of his sympathy for the Prussian-German nation-state. He was, by his own admission, a conservative, one whose roots lay in the lost *Heimat* of East Prussia. Born in Angerburg, near Köningsberg, Hillgruber studied in Göttingen under Percy Ernst Schramm, a historian who, in the words of a former student, discussed World War II as "a conventional war in which the Nazis only appeared as unfortunately not having been as competent as the military experts" (Eberhard Jäckel in *Deutschland in Europa* [Germany in Europe], 1990). It would go too far to say that, at the time, Hillgruber viewed the war in entirely similar terms, but in light of his later work one can say that when he completed his dissertation (published as *Hitler, König Carol und Marschall Antonescu* [Hitler, King Carol, and Marshal Antonescu], 1954) he had not yet come to grips with the special nature of the regime under which he had grown up. His 1954 exchange (together with Hans-Günther Seraphim) with Gerhard L. Weinberg regarding the timing of and reasons for Hitler's decision to invade the Soviet Union suggests the same.

In subsequent years, however, Hillgruber lost this personal blind spot by examining the growing body of historical evidence, as his *Habilitationsschrift* of 1965 (published as *Hitlers Strategie* [Hitler's Strategy]) amply demonstrates. The book emphasizes that World War II was the opposite of a conventional second round of 1914–18; that it was instead a war Hitler wanted in order to realize his racist, imperial concept.

But while in his answers Hillgruber changed, he remained rather unchanged in the questions he asked, and in the topics he was personally most disposed to investigate. This was the case in his continuing and trend-setting pleas for the study of the "Bismarck" empire as an integral period – up to 1945. Such a plea was the topic of his inaugural address as professor of history in Freiburg in 1969. His own work in this regard, for example, *Deutsche Grossmacht- und Weltpolitik im 19. und 20. Jahrhundert* (German Great- and Global-Power Policy during the 19th and 20th Centuries, 1977) made a significant contribution to the argument.

Hillgruber's unchanging personal preferences (or independence) emerge most clearly when the issue concerns the more benign aspects of Germany's great power status after 1870. As he pointed out repeatedly, in light of the policy options that the new, and in many ways unevenly constituted empire had available to maintain itself as a great power in a rapidly changing world, the effort to strive independently for domination in Central and Eastern Europe was in itself a noble one. It was a policy that could have had – indeed, did have – positive results, both for Germans and other peoples in the region. That things went awry so disastrously after 1933 with the Germans finally being driven out of their homes in East Prussia, Silesia, and elsewhere in "the German East" was, in his eyes, a true tragedy (for Germany) as well as a missed opportunity (for Europe).

It was this argument that in 1987 caused Hillgruber to come under attack in the so-called German *Historikerstreit* (battle of the historians). In a 1986 essay, "Der Zusammenbruch im Osten 1944/45" (The Collapse in the East, 1944/45), in *Zweierlei Untergang* (Two Kinds of Ruin), he unapologetically took the perspective of the Germans who in 1944/45 had been forced to flee their homes ahead of the advancing Red Army, and he highlighted the efforts of the army and members of the Nazi party to facilitate a full and timely exodus. In the essay and the ensuing polemic, Hillgruber insisted that his objective was strictly scholarly: to call attention to a relatively underdeveloped area of research. But he also created the impression (not least because of the way he addressed some of the larger themes connected with this "collapse") that he preferred to see the German expulsion primarily as a tragedy for Germany and the Germans involved, rather than as the ultimately inevitable consequence of the aggressive policies of Hitler's Germany – policies few Germans had questioned early on.

There was merit in both Hillgruber's approach and the more reasonable attacks on this essay. More importantly, however, "Der Zusammenbruch im Osten" confirmed once more that Hillgruber, like any historian, was informed – indeed driven – by some very personal motivations taken from his background and personal experience. At the same time, the essay shows, and his entire body of work confirms, that he was a true scholar who made a valuable contribution to the historiography of his field.

RUUD VAN DIJK

See also Broszat; Germany: 1800–1945; Wehler

Biography

Andreas Fritz Hillgruber. Born Angerburg, Germany [now Wegorzewo, Poland], 18 January 1925, son of a teacher. Served in German Army, 1943–45; prisoner of war in France, 1945–48. Received PhD, University of Göttingen, 1952. Taught at schools in Wiesbaden, 1954–58; Darmstadt, 1958–61; Marburg, 1961–64; taught (rising to professor), University of Marburg, 1965–68; University of Freiburg/Breisgau, 1968–72; University of Cologne, 1972–89. Married Karin Zieran, 1960 (3 sons). Died Cologne, 8 May 1989.

Principal Writings

Hitler, König Carol und Marschall Antonescu: die deutschrumänischen Beziehungen, 1938–1944 (Hitler, King Carol, and Marshal Antonescu), 1954

With Hans-Günther Seraphim, "Hitlers Entschluss zum Angriff auf Russland. (Eine Entgegnung)" (Hitler's Decision for the Attack on Russia: A Reply) *Vierteljahrshefte für Zeitgeschichte* 2 (1954), 240–54

Hitlers Strategie: Politik und Kriegsführung, 1940–1941 (Hitler's Strategy), 1965

Deutschlands Rolle in der Vorgeschichte der beiden Weltkriege, 1967; in English as *Germany and the Two World Wars*, 1981

Kontinuität und Diskontinuität in der deutschen Aussenpolitik von Bismarck bis Hitler (Continuity and Discontinuity in German Foreign Policy from Bismarck to Hitler), 1969

Bismarcks Aussenpolitik (Bismarck's Foreign Policy), 1972

"Die 'Endlösung' und das deutsche Ostimperium als Kernstück des rassenideologischen Programms des Nationalsozialismus" (The 'Final Solution' and the German Empire in the East as the Core of National Socialism's Race-based Ideological Program), *Vierteljahrshefte für Zeitgeschichte* 20 (1972), 133–53

Deutsche Geschichte, 1945–1972: Die "deutsche Frage" in der Weltpolitik (German History, 1945–1972: The "German Question" in World Politics), 1974

Deutsche Grossmacht- und Weltpolitik im 19. und 20. Jahrhundert (German Great- and Global-Power Policy during the 19th and 20th Centuries), 1977

Otto von Bismarck: Gründer der europäischen Grossmacht Deutsches Reich (Otto von Bismarck: Founder of the European Great Power, the German Reich), 1978

Europa in der Weltpolitik der Nachkriegszeit (1945–1963) (Europe in World Politics during the Postwar Period, 1945–63), 1979

Sowjetische Aussenpolitik im Zweiten Weltkrieg (Soviet Foreign Policy in the Second World War), 1979

Die Gescheiterte Grossmacht: Eine Skizze des Deutschen Reiches, 1871–1945 (The Failed Great Power: A Sketch of the German Empire, 1871–1945), 1980

Der Zweite Weltkrieg, 1939–1945: Kriegsziele und Strategie der grossen Mächte (The Second World War, 1939–1945: War Aims and Strategy of the Great Powers), 1982

Die Last der Nation: Fünf Beiträge über Deutschland und die Deutschen (The Burden of the Nation: Five Contributions about Germany and the Germans), 1984

Zweierlei Untergang: Die Zerschlagung des Deutschen Reiches und das Ende des europäischen Judentums (Two Kinds of Ruin: The Fall of the German Empire and the End of European Jewry), 1986

Die Zerstörung Europas: Beiträge zur Weltkriegsepoche 1914 bis 1945 (The Destruction of Europe: Contributions on the Epoch of World Wars, 1914 to 1945), 1988

Further Reading

Dülffer, Jost *et al.* eds., *Deutschland in Europa: Kontinuität und Bruch: Gedenkschrift für Andreas Hillgruber* (Germany in Europe: Continuity and Break: Commemorative Volume for Andreas Hillgruber), Frankfurt: Propyläen, 1990

"Historikerstreit": Die Dokumentation der Kontroverse um die Einzigartigkeit der nationalsozialistischen Judenvernichtung, Munich: Piper, 1987; in English as *Forever in the Shadow of Hitler? The Dispute about the Germans' Understanding of History, Original Documents of the Historikerstreit, the Controversy Concerning the Singularity of the Holocaust*, Atlantic Highlands, NJ: Humanities Press, 1993

Hilton, Rodney 1916–
British medievalist

Rodney Hilton is among this century's most significant medieval historians. He has increased understanding of the medieval peasantry and their dynamic role in shaping Western European culture, through the application of Marxist theory.

He joined the Communist party as a student, prior to wartime service in the armed forces. Later his work evolved through membership of the influential Communist Party Historians' Group, under the guidance of Donna Torr, and after 1956, in the context of the New Left. His name is associated with the University of Birmingham, where he taught for most of his long career. Although concerned with the application of theoretical approaches to historical studies, his work has always been characterized by the meticulous use of evidence. His sources were manorial records, which survive in large quantities from the late 12th century. The manor was the basic administrative unit of much of medieval western Europe and landlords were concerned to document their legal and financial relations with the peasantry.

In *A Medieval Society* (1967), Hilton was inspired by the French historians of the Annales school, notably Marc Bloch and Georges Duby, to write "total history." He also shared their aim of defining feudalism more exactly. He argued that the peasant economy could not be studied in isolation from relations with feudal overlords and that there was always an element of class tension when lords appropriated the surplus of agricultural production from peasants through various forms of taxation. He was therefore a critic of J. Ambrose Raftis and the Toronto school of historians, who emphasized autonomous peasant activity in their reconstruction of village communities. Hilton's work brought him into contact with scholars of contemporary peasant societies. His theoretical approach was influential in shaping the new comparative and interdisciplinary field of Peasant studies, which evolved in the 1970s.

Hilton argued against the position taken by Michael Postan, that the profound social changes that occurred after the Black Death were the result of abstract economic and demographic laws. Hilton believed that collectively the peasants had been able to resist harsher exactions by landlords through class struggle. In *Bond Men Made Free* (1973) and other writings, he focused on the English Peasants' Revolt of 1381 and its antecedents. In this respect he stands in the English radical tradition, which interpreted the Peasants' Revolt and the English Civil War as the precursors of 19th-century working-class movements.

Hilton made a significant contribution to the debate on the transition from feudalism to capitalism, which grew up in response to the work of Maurice Dobb. Hilton maintained that capitalism was not a distinct phase of development arising out of feudal society, but that it had existed in parallel in urban culture throughout the Middle Ages. More recently Hilton has continued to explore this theme in his work on small commodity producers in the market towns of the West Midlands. Here too he has found tensions between landlords and craftsmen.

Hilton's work tends to emphasize the collective and radical aspects of peasant activity, rather than the social differentiation and innate conservatism that characterize other aspects of their lives. His focus on landlord-peasant relations must be redressed by reading other authors who emphasize their autonomous activities.

Nevertheless, Hilton's work has immeasurably enriched our knowledge of the lives of the vast majority of medieval people. His application of theoretical approaches has been subtle and genuinely illuminating. His writings, his participation in major intellectual debate, and his joint foundation and editorship of the journal *Past and Present* amount to a significant contribution to the new social history, history from the bottom up.

VIRGINIA R. BAINBRIDGE

See also Britain: 1066–1485; Economic; Hill; History from Below; Hobsbawm; Kiernan; Marx; Marxist Interpretation; Postan; Social

Biography

Rodney Howard Hilton. Born Middleton, Manchester, 17 November 1916. Educated at Manchester Grammar School; Balliol College, Oxford, BA 1938; Merton College, Oxford, PhD 1940. Served in British and Indian Army, 1940–46. Taught at University of Birmingham (rising to professor), 1946–82 (emeritus); director, Institute for Advanced Research in the Humanities, 1984–87. Married (2 sons, 1 daughter).

Principal Writings

The Economic Development of Some Leicestershire Estates in the 14th and 15th Centuries, 1947
With Hyman Fagan, *The English Rising of 1381*, 1950
A Medieval Society: The West Midlands at the End of the Thirteenth Century, 1967
The Decline of Serfdom in Medieval England, 1969
Bond Men Made Free: Medieval Peasant Movements and the English Rising of 1381, 1973
The English Peasantry in the Later Middle Ages: The Ford Lectures for 1973, and Related Studies, 1975
Class Conflict and the Crisis of Feudalism: Essays in Medieval Social History, 1985; revised 1990
English and French Towns in Feudal Society: A Comparative Study, 1992

Further Reading

Aston, Trevor *et al.*, eds., *Social Relations and Ideas: Essays in Honour of R.H. Hilton*, Cambridge and New York: Cambridge University Press, 1983 [includes bibliography]
Kaye, Harvey J., *The British Marxist Historians: An Introductory Analysis*, Cambridge: Polity Press, 1984; New York: St. Martin's Press, 1995

Hine, Darlene Clark 1947–

US women's historian

The name of Darlene Clark Hine is synonymous with black women's history in America. Part of the second wave of feminist historians, Hine bears much responsibility for the increasing prominence of the history of African American women as a field of study. Her archival activities, pursued to change the writing of history by making abundant sources accessible, have greatly facilitated the research and study of African American women. By devoting her life's work to a focus on people at the perimeters of society, she has enhanced our understanding of the theoretical underpinnings and practical applications of black women's history.

When she went off to graduate school in 1968, Hine's mother said that she would soon return home to Chicago, since "there can't be that much black history to study." Hine has yet to return home. She studied with August Meier, a founder of the field of African American men's history, and produced an examination of the white primary in Texas under his direction. Her subsequent writings focus almost exclusively upon women.

Influenced by the radicalism of the 1960s to study the past of blacks, Hine's work is notable for its class consciousness. In essay after essay, she shows how differences of race, class, and gender within and outside of the black community have produced changes in American society. Awareness of class has also influenced Hine's research methodology. Determined to give those at the bottom rung of society a voice, she has included oral histories in many of her writings in an attempt to avoid privileging the stories of the middle class.

Much more than chronicles of victimization, Hine's work shows how black women have struggled for power and agency. Trapped in the dual bind of being both black and female in a racist and sexist society, the subjects of Hine's work battle to uplift themselves and their neighbors. Her most influential work, the 2-volume reference book, *Black Women in America* (1993) marks her effort to lift the veil on black women's history. By discussing the impact of rape, in an essay on a culture of dissemblance within the black community, Hine prompted researchers to examine the unspoken as well as the spoken.

An incredibly prolific writer, Hine has worked to establish a foundation that others may build upon. *Black Women in the Middle West Project: A Comprehensive Resource Guide, Illinois and Indiana* touches on only part of the material collected by her Black Women in the Middle West project.

Hine's early writings focus on the efforts of black women to resist racism and to achieve greater respectability and power. Her first essay in black women's history, a 1979 piece entitled "Female Slave Resistance: The Economics of Sex," is representative of this work. After revealing the activism of African American women in *When the Truth Is Told* (1981), Hine shifted her research interests to the question of gender. Her work on the history of women in the medical and nursing fields falls into this area. Much of her effort in the 1990s has been devoted to creating the field of comparative black studies. By persuading specialists in African, African-Latino/a, African-Canadian, and African-American to find common ground, Hine is additionally becoming a pioneer in world women's history.

Hine once lamented that the historical experiences of African American women had been neglected, obscured, distorted, or relegated to the back pages of our collective consciousness. By analyzing the intersections of race, class, and gender, she has done much to bring the past of black women into the present.

CARYN E. NEUMANN

See also Women's History: African American

Biography

Born Morley, Missouri, 7 February 1947, daughter of a truckdriver and a homemaker. Received BA, Roosevelt University, 1968; MA, Kent State University, 1970, PhD 1975. Taught at South Carolina State College, 1972–74; Purdue University (rising to professor), 1974–87; and Michigan State University, from 1987. Married 1) William C. Hine, 1970 (marriage dissolved 1974), 2) Johnny E. Brown, 1981 (marriage dissolved 1986), 1 son.

Principal Writings

Black Victory: The Rise and Fall of the White Primary in Texas, 1979
When the Truth Is Told: A History of Black Women's Culture and Community in Indiana, 1875–1950, 1981
Editor with Patrick K. Bidelman, *The Black Women in the Middle West Project: Comprehensive Resource Guide, Illinois and Indiana*, 1985

Editor, *Black Women in the Nursing Profession: A Documentary History*, 1985
Editor, *The State of Afro-American History: Past, Present, and Future*, 1986
Black Women in White: Racial Conflict and Cooperation in the Nursing Profession, 1890–1950, 1989
Editor, *Black Women in United States History*, 16 vols., 1990
Editor, *Black Women in America: An Historical Encyclopedia*, 2 vols., 1993
Hine Sight: Black Women and the Re-Construction of American History, 1994
Editor with D. Barry Gaspar, *More than Chattel: Black Women and Slavery in the Americas*, 1996
Speak Truth to Power: Black Professional Class in United States History, 1996

Hintze, Otto 1861–1940

German historian

To many, Otto Hintze is primarily known as one of the foremost historians of Prussia. His reputation was established in the long collaboration with the *Acta Borussica*, some pathbreaking articles on administrative and constitutional history in Prussia, and culminated in the book *Die Hohenzollern und ihr Werk* (The Hohenzollerns and Their Work, 1915), which Hintze was commissioned to write to commemorate the 500th anniversary of the rule of the house of Hohenzollern in Brandenburg. But Hintze's contributions to historiography transcend the parochial limits of national or Prussian history. He contributed significantly to the development of historiographical methodology and broke ground in a field he described in 1914 as the "universal comparative constitutional and administrative history of the West."

J.G. Droysen, one of the main exponents of the Prussian historical school, and Gustav Schmoller were among Hintze's academic teachers. Schmoller invited Hintze to participate in the publication of the *Acta Borussica* in 1888. Hintze wrote introductions to the corresponding volumes on the Prussian silk industry (1892) and, more notably, on the Prussian bureaucratic structure at the time of the accession of Frederick the Great (1901), which emphasized the role of bureaucracies in the process of state building in Prussia and also took social and economic perspectives into account. A series of analyses over time on aspects of Prussian institutional and constitutional history established Hintze's reputation as the leading specialist in Prussian history. His book on the Hohenzollerns, which is widely distributed, still sets standards in its thorough, well-sourced, and balanced analysis of Prussian history.

Hintze's focus increasingly shifted to the comparative history of institutions, using Prussia as a paradigm. His plan to write a European administrative history exploring the common roots of European institutions and constitutions as well as their individuality and institutional variations materialized in several major articles. A manuscript on comparative administrative history, completed around 1930, has been lost. One of his main arguments was that a European core existed, mainly those areas that had been under Frankish rule. Over the centuries this core developed a military bureaucratic government, while on the European periphery institutions of self-government had been more likely to develop. Hintze transcended a static view of the state and came to a broad, sociological interpretation of the state that took developmental processes into account as well as the interdependence between domestic and external circumstances.

Hintze remained convinced of the existence of historical laws, of structures that influenced human action. He emphasized the explanatory task of history rather than the German tradition of historical understanding. He was one of the first German historians to incorporate sociological approaches into his analysis, and Max Weber's writings exerted a lasting influence on him. Hintze's writings also reflect the ruptures of German political history in the first third of the 20th century. A defender of the constitutional monarchy prior to World War I, he later argued that parliamentarism and representative government were the only recent achievements in European constitutional development.

Hintze's immediate influence remained limited. Because of illness he retired from his university chair at the University of Berlin in 1922 and remained secluded, cutting himself completely off in the years after 1933. His writings were not easily accessible and were collected only after his death. With the emergence of social and economic history, the writings of Hintze were rediscovered and his contributions to historiography re-evaluated. His broad theoretical sweep and his universal approach combined with a mastery of detail continue to offer historians and political scientists valuable insights in the development of the modern state in Europe.

MATTHIAS ZIMMER

See also Gilbert; Hartung; Rosenberg, H.; State

Biography
Born Pyritz, Hinterpommern [now Poland], 27 August 1861. Studied briefly at University of Greifswald, then moved to University of Berlin. Professor, University of Berlin, 1899–1922. Married historian Hedwig Guggenheimer Hintze, 1912. Died Berlin, 25 April 1940.

Principal Writings
Die Preussische Seidenindustrie im 18. Jahrhundert und ihre Begründung durch Friedrich den Grossen (The Prussian Silk Industry in the 18th Century and Its Foundation under Frederick the Great), 3 vols., 1892
Einleitende Darstellung der Behördenorganisation und allgemeinen Verwaltung in Preussen beim Regierungsamt Friedrichs II (A Preliminary Investigation into Early Organizational and Administrative Structures in Frederick II's Prussia), 1901
Die Hohenzollern und ihr Werk (The Hohenzollerns and Their Work), 1915
Staat und Verfassung: Gesammelte Abhandlungen zur Allgemeinen Verfassungsgeschichte (State and Constitution: Collected Treatises on Constitutional History), 1941
Zur Theorie der Geschichte (On the Theory of History), 1942; reprinted as *Soziologie und Geschichte: Gesammelte Abhandlungen zur Soziologie, Politik und Theorie der Geschichte* (Sociology and History: Collected Treatises on Sociology, Politics, and Theory of History), 1964
Geist und Epochen der preussischen Geschichte (Spirit and Epochs of Prussian History), 1943; reprinted as *Regierung und Verwaltung: Gesammelte Abhandlungen zur Staats-, Rechts- und Sozialgeschichte Preussens* (Government and Bureaucracy: Collected Treatises on State, Legal and Social History), 1967
The Historical Essays of Otto Hintze, edited by Felix Gilbert, 1975

Further Reading
Büsch, Otto, and Michael Erbe, eds., *Otto Hintze und die moderne Geschichtswissenschaft: Ein Tagungsbericht* (Otto Hintze and the Modern Science of History: A Conference Report), Berlin: Colloquium, 1983
DiCostanzo, Giuseppe, "Tra comparativismo e storia universale: il progetto di Otto Hintze" (Between Comparative and Universal History: The Progress of Otto Hintze), *Società e Storia* 13 (1990), 337–62
Gerhard, Dietrich, "Otto Hintze: His Work and His Significance in Historiography," *Central European History* 3 (1970), 17–48
Kocka, Jürgen, "Otto Hintze," Hans Ulrich Wehler, ed., *Deutsche Historiker*, vol. 3, Göttingen: Vandenhoeck & Ruprecht, 1971–72
Oestreich, Brigitta, "Hedwig und Otto Hintze: Eine biographische Skizze" (Hedwig and Otto Hintze: A Biographical Sketch), *Geschichte und Gesellschaft* 11 (1985), 397–419
Page, Edward C., "The Political Origins of Self Government and Bureaucracy: Otto Hintze's Conceptual Map of Europe," *Political Studies* 38 (1990), 39–55
Schira, Pierangelo, *Otto Hintze*, Naples: Guida, 1974
Simon, W.M., "Power and Responsibility: Otto Hintze's Place in German Historiography," in Leonard Krieger and Fritz Stern, eds., *The Responsibility of Power: Historical Essays in Honour of Hajo Holborn*, Garden City, NY: Doubleday, 1967; London: Macmillan, 1968

Historical Geography

The study of past geographical relationships has a long history, with Greek writers, such as Strabo and Hippocrates, and Enlightenment intellectuals, particularly Montesquieu, being interested in the impact of environment on social development and discussing the relationship, at least in part, in spatial terms. Eighteenth-century concerns lay behind the modern development of historical geography. The Enlightenment proposition that humans live in a universe governed by natural laws proclaimed, among other things, the existence of "nations" defined through a mixture of geography, language, culture, and physical features. The "interests of nations" were defined in terms of protecting their geographical, cultural, and physical integrity. Many of these ideas were fully expressed during the revolutionary period, especially by Anacharsis Kloots (1755–94), a German-born activist in the French Revolution who emphasized "natural frontiers." The 19th-century geopolitical school associated with Friedrich Ratzel (1844–1904) and his disciples continued this tradition, which became closely associated with nationalism.

Ratzel's emphasis on the interaction of environment and humanity greatly influenced historical geography, leading to differing analyses of the relationship. Ellen Churchill Semple's *American History and Its Geographic Conditions* (1903) adopted an environmental determinism, while the influential French geographer Paul Vidal de la Blache stressed "possibilism": mediation of environmental influences by cultural factors. The latter approach became more influential than that of Semple and was adopted by American scholars from the 1910s.

The weight to be placed on environmental constraints, the nature of cultural-historical factors, and the identity and identification of regions have all been major themes in subsequent historical geography. The subject has responded to developments in other disciplines, particularly anthropology and archaeology, and has shown increasing sophistication in its determination to analyze as well as describe the past.

Historical geography has attracted particular attention in Britain, France and the United States. In France the Annales school emphasized regions and environmental constraints, the two combining to produce in a structuralist interpretation the notion of a *pays*, a region given long-term unity, coherence, and identity by its environmental character.

In Britain and the United States there has recently been a greater emphasis on the sociocultural dimension, on humanity as playing an active role in molding the environment and creating regions, and doing so in response to ideas and theories of space and spatial organization, as well as the more traditional economic interests. Thus in place of positivism, structuralism, and functionalist interpretations there has been a stress on multiple and nuanced relationships that often reflect ideologies of power. The landscape as the product of power relationships is a major theme of the 1990s.

The theoretical agenda of much modern work is openly receptive to debates and developments in other disciplines and, in turn, seeks to apply geographical perspectives to them. This is true both of those historical geographers who emphasize environmental relationships and of those who focus on spatial relationships either at the geopolitical or at the regional level. The geopolitical approach looked back to Halford Mackinder (1861–1947) and his concern with the political causes, contexts, and consequences of spatial relationships. As with other branches of historical geography it is one that has been increasingly open to cultural readings and interpretations in the last decade.

Historical geography has expanded greatly from the 1960s, becoming in the Anglo-American world an increasingly important branch of geography, although making surprisingly little impact on history there, unlike in France where the two are more closely aligned. The subject has become increasingly institutionalized and the foundation of a journal, *Journal of Historical Geography* in 1975, was of great importance in providing a constant focus for debate and cohesion. Historians would be well advised to pay more attention to developments in the field.

JEREMY BLACK

See also Balkans; Computing; Environmental; Frontiers; Semple

Further Reading

Baker, Alan R.H., ed., *Progress on Historical Geography*, Newton Abbot, Devon: David and Charles, and New York: Willey, 1972

Baker, Alan R.H., and Mark Billinge, eds., *Period and Place: Research Methods in Historical Geography*, Cambridge and New York: Cambridge University Press, 1982

Baker, Alan R.H., and Derek Gregory, eds., *Explorations in Historical Geography: Interpretative Essays*, Cambridge and New York: Cambridge University Press, 1984

Baker, Alan R.H., *Place, Practice and Structure*, Cambridge: Cambridge University Press, 1988

Baker, Alan R.H., "Historical Geography: An Essay on its Basic Characteristics," *Deccan Geographer* 30 (1993)

Charlesworth, Andrew, "Towards a Geography of the Shoah," *Journal of Historical Geography* 18 (1992), 464–69

Cosgrove, Dennis, and P. Jackson, "New Directions in Cultural Geography," *Area*, 19 (1987), 95–101

Duncan, James, and David Ley, eds., *Place/Culture/Representation*, London: Routledge, 1993

Harley, J. Brian, "Historical Geography and the Cartographic Illusion," *Journal of Historical Geography* 15 (1989), 80–91

Humbert, André, "Géographie historique; ou, la dérive des systèmes géographiques" (Historical Geography; or, The derivation of Geographical Systems), *Hérodote* 74/75 (1994), 95–110

Jordan, Terry G., *North American Cattle-Ranching Frontiers: Origins, Diffusion, and Differentiation*, Albuquerque: University of New Mexico Press, 1993

Pitte, Jean-Robert, "De la géographie historique" (On Historical Geography), *Hérodote* 74/75 (1994), 14–21

Semple, Ellen Churchill, *American History and Its Geographic Conditions*, Boston: Houghton Mifflin, 1903; revised 1933

Turner, Frederick Jackson, *The Significance of the Frontier in American History*, Madison: State Historical Society of Wisconsin, 1894 [as lecture 1893]

Vidal de la Blache, Paul, *Principes de géographie humaines*, Paris: Colin, 1922; in English as *Principles of Human Geography*, New York: Holt, and London: Constable, 1926

Historical Maps and Atlases

Historical maps and atlases depict earlier eras, as opposed to historic maps and atlases which show the then-contemporary world. The early history of the genre was a long and varied one, for it included in Europe maps depicting the Holy Land at the time of Jesus or the classical world, such as the map of ancient Greece produced by the Venetian cartographer Ferdinando Bertelli in 1563. There was an independent and probably older tradition in China that depicted the history of the country. For example the 12th-century *Lidai dili zhi zhang tu* by Shui Anli reinforced ideas about the "natural" boundaries of China by displaying where the northern frontier of China had once been, and thus forever should be. Such an atlas showed, literally through graphic illustration, what had been and what had been taken away, seeding dreams of what might be again. It was a reminder of past glories and of humiliations one day to be avenged. The first known European historical atlas, the *Parergon* of Abraham Örtell (Ortelius), was published in Antwerp in 1579, initially as part of his general atlas, but from 1624 as a separate work. Like other works of the 16th and 17th centuries, the *Parergon* centered on the world of the Bible and the classics, which was seen as a crucial aspect and sphere of knowledge. The sense that a cartographic perspective was important to this process reflected in part the expansion of cartographical knowledge about the contemporary world which both made it possible to create more accurate maps and increased interest in the presentation of such a perspective. Thus the past could and should be explored and charted in the same manner as the present.

In the 18th century there was a growing interest in the post-classical world. Works appeared that included maps of medieval Europe, although the classical world remained the dominant theme and many historical atlases sought to go no further. The *Atlas Historique* (Historical Atlas, Amsterdam 1705) referred both to the public desire for knowledge and to the inseparable nature of geography and history. It contained much text and many genealogical charts and wrongly included Persia and Poland in the Roman empire, but the atlas was not restricted to the ancient world: there were maps of the Spanish empire, France, and the Low Countries, the last locating battles from the 16th century onwards.

The 19th century witnessed the great development of the historical atlas and wall map, with a growing concentration on post-classical maps. German historical atlases were especially important in the development. With a large and literate population, a strong sense of national identity that earlier disunity accentuated, a good cartographic tradition, and active publishers, Germany produced a series of major works that influenced developments elsewhere. The development of states and empires was the major theme of 19th-century works; these were political and Eurocentric in their focus.

In the 20th century the agenda became broader as efforts were made to incorporate advances in social, economic, and cultural history. A less Eurocentric approach has been adopted in works produced by European publishers and an expanding number of historical atlases have been produced outside Europe, principally in North America, but also in South America, Australasia, and, increasingly, the Orient. Very few historical atlases and maps have been published in Africa, but modern treatments of Africa pay much greater attention both to its precolonial history and to resistance to European imperialism.

The marketing strategies of publishers tend to be forgotten in historiographical studies, but they are of major consequence. Historical atlases have been attractive to publishers as they enjoy both academic and general, reference and personal sales, have long shelf lives and can be readily translated for foreign sale. Publishing economics are crucial: a serious atlas needs a very large investment that will be recovered very slowly. This clearly will affect the adoption of new technologies for the analysis and depiction of spatial information. Computers can construct spatial information systems and it is probable that eventually many atlases and maps will be generated and stored digitally and scanned in a different fashion (for example at various scales) by individual users. However, while this approach is already adopted for particular research programs, the nature of publishing economics ensures that a wider adoption is likely to be slower, especially in less affluent countries.

There has been a general neglect of the visual aspect of history. Illustrations in books are an important field for consideration and maps are another. Historical atlases provide both a series of maps and an implicit commentary on ways of seeing as exemplified in maps. Maps are texts. Their creation, use, and analysis offer opportunities for unlocking the past, for understanding past scholarship and the scholarship of the past.

JEREMY BLACK

Further Reading
Black, Jeremy, "Historical Atlases," *Historical Journal* 37 (1994), 643–67

Black, Jeremy, *Maps and History*, New Haven: Yale University Press, 1997

Dörflinger, Johannes, "Geschichtskarte, Geschichtsatlas" (Historical Maps, Historical Atlas), in Ingrid Kretschmer *et al.*, eds., *Lexikon zur Geschichte der Kartographie von den Anfängen bis zum ersten Weltkrieg* (A Dictionary of the History of Cartography from its Origins to the First World War), Vienna: Deuticke, 1986

Goffart, Walter, "The Map of the Barbarian Invasions: A Preliminary Report," *Nottingham Medieval Studies* 32 (1988), 49–64

Harris, C., "Reality, Bias and the Making of an Atlas," *Mapping History* 1 (1980)

Harvey, P.D.A., "The Medievalist's Atlas," *Nottingham Medieval Studies*, 30 (1986), 116–25

Petchenik, Barbara, "Cartography and the Making of an Historical Atlas: A Memoir," *American Cartographer* 4 (1977), 11–28

Smith, Catherine Delano, "Maps as Art and Science: Maps in Sixteenth Century Bibles," *Imago Mundi* 42 (1990), 65–83

Historiology/Philosophy of Historical Writing

The search for a theoretical understanding of historical thinking and writing has often been called "philosophy of history" – specifically, "analytic," "formal," or "critical" philosophy of history. But it is probably better to reserve the term "philosophy of history" for attempts to understand the general shape of history itself (discussed in the article Philosophy of History). The topic of the present article will be called "historiology," because use of a separate word helps to keep us from confusing two different, although not unconnected, projects. Historiology is a metahistorical discourse concerned with the work done by historians. At the end of the 20th century there exists a rich tradition of historiology, embracing four strands or orientations: analytic, hermeneutic, idealist, and narrative-linguistic. The first three strands arose from a late 19th- and early 20th-century controversy, carried out primarily in Germany, concerning the character of the human sciences; narrative-linguistic historiology, for its part, took on recognizable shape only in the 1970s.

Before the late 19th century history-writing had been discussed in various contexts. A 19th-century observer would have been aware of the discussion of historical style in the rhetorical tradition from Cicero and Quintilian onward. Some discussion of history-writing occurred in 19th-century philosophy of history: for example, G.W.F. Hegel began his lectures on philosophy of history with an account of "the varieties of historical writing." Historiology was also foreshadowed in the radical critique of 19th-century professional historiography offered by Friedrich Nietzsche in "Vom Nutzen und Nachteil der Historie für das Leben" ("On the Uses and Disadvantage of History for Life," 1874). Finally, and most importantly, historians themselves produced a large literature on the character and methodology of history: Ernst Bernheim's *Lehrbuch der historischen Methode* (Handbook of Historical Method, 1889) and Charles Langlois and Charles Seignobos' *Introduction to the Study of History* (1898) are two important examples. This reflective and methodological tendency was particularly strong in German universities, where, beginning with J.M. Chladenius (1710–59) in 1749–50, lecture courses were commonly given on *Historik*, or the principles of history. One should also note the older tradition of humanistic reflection on history, to which Jean Bodin (1530–96) was an important contributor, the theoretical reflections of Giambattista Vico (1688–1744), and the long tradition of historical and textual criticism represented by Jean Mabillon (1623–1707), Ludovico Muratori (1672–1750), and others.

Historiology as we know it now was a product of the rise in the 19th century of a professional discipline of history, one that claimed to be a science. Yet historiology was not an *immediate* product of that development, for its emergence required the further idea that the historian's enterprise is in some general way problematic (although not so problematic as to defy coherent discussion). Neither the rhetoricians, concerned with style in history, nor the reflective historians, concerned mostly with its method, found anything problematic in the historian's task. The rhetoricians and the reflective historians articulated the consciousness of historians themselves: the rhetoricians, the consciousness of those who saw their enterprise as mainly literary; the reflective historians, the consciousness of those who saw it as mainly professional. As for philosophers of history, they had little interest in the doings of mere historians, and the same is true of Nietzsche, the anti-philosopher of history. The reflective historians came closest to historiology, but they rarely went beyond method to more general questions of epistemology and cultural justification, although (as Blanke, Fleischer, and Rüsen have shown) J.G. Droysen (1808–84) was an important exception. Another exception, although not widely noticed, was the English philosopher F.H. Bradley (1846–1924), whose *The Presuppositions of Critical History* (1874) anticipated idealist historiology.

In sum, until late in the century in which the discipline of history emerged, little attention was devoted to the theory of historical investigation and writing. This fact is unsurprising: preoccupation with the theoretical underpinnings of an enterprise is not necessarily compatible with its enthusiastic pursuit. Even in the late 20th century, most historians are largely unconcerned with the theory of their discipline. Still, such unconcern is not universal. From the late 19th century onward some philosophers have been interested in the subject. From the 1960s onward the philosophers were joined by an eclectic group of theoretically-oriented social scientists, historians, and literary scholars. The journal *History and Theory* (1960–) provides a forum for work in the field, although such work appeared in many other places as well. By the 1980s there were indications that historiological reflection was having a significant impact on the practice of some historians.

Historiology began with a worry. The worry arose, in the second half of the 19th century, from the tension between history's claim to be a science and the growing cultural influence of natural science and of positivism. Positivism, which was systematized in mid-century in the work of Auguste Comte (1798–1857), was defined by three tenets: 1) *phenomenalism*, or the view that only things that can be perceived by our senses, or by scientific instruments extending our senses, are relevant to knowledge; 2) *correlationism*, or the view that the essential task of science is to articulate correlations among phenomena; and 3) *physicism*, or the view that physics is the highest science and ought to be emulated by all other sciences: thus it was thought that the really important correlations should have the form of universal laws, as in physics. The claim of positivists to possess *the* correct scientific method contradicted the claim of history to be a science, since historians did not see themselves as articulating universal laws, and since they characteristically held that history involved ethical and spiritual considerations as well as material ones. An early attempt to promote positivist history was *History of Civilization in England* (2 vols., 1857–61), by the English writer Henry Thomas Buckle (1821–62). Buckle's insistence

that historians ought to search for regularities in human action directly challenged traditional ways of doing history. In a famous review of Buckle, in repeated lecture courses on the principles of history, and in his *Grundriss der Historik* (1868; *Outlines of the Principles of History*, 1893), J.G. Droysen offered an answer to positivism, maintaining that history concerns itself with an ethical world not reducible either to the world of ideals or to the material world. The *Grundriss* can be regarded as the first systematic historiological treatise. However, its influence at the time was not great. It was a course outline rather than a fully argued treatise, and in any case Droysen was too rooted in early 19th-century German idealism for late 19th-century tastes.

A sustained and widely noticed controversy over the human sciences arose only in the 1890s. Three contributors to the discussion had a particularly strong impact on historiological thought. In an influential 1894 lecture, the philosopher Wilhelm Windelband (1848–1915) distinguished between nomothetic sciences, which seek to establish universal laws, and idiographic sciences, which describe particular realities, and he placed history firmly in the second category. Although Windelband did not seek to elevate one type of science over the other, there existed a widely held view that knowledge of universals is more meritorious than knowledge of mere particulars, and in consequence the nomothetic/idiographic distinction was seen in some quarters as confirming that historical knowledge is inferior to universalizing, natural scientific knowledge. In a number of writings, of which the most ambitious is *Einleitung in die Geisteswissenschaften* (1883; *Introduction to the Human Sciences*, 1989), the philosopher and intellectual historian Wilhelm Dilthey (1833–1911) offered an influential counter to this dismissive view. According to Dilthey, the natural sciences follow the method of detached *Erklären* (explanation), whereas the human sciences follow the method of *Verstehen* (understanding), in which the investigator, through the exercise of reflective judgment, grasps the intentions behind and the spirit embodied in cultural products and historical events. Finally, in a series of monographs published 1904–07, the sociologist Max Weber (1864–1920) argued that historical inquiry has both explanatory and interpretive dimensions.

Analytic historiology, which played the most important role in establishing historiology as a recognized field of research, emerged from the positivist side of the controversy. Fundamental was a 1942 article, "The Function of General Laws in History," by the philosopher Carl G. Hempel. Hempel began with Windelband's contrast between generalizing and particularizing investigation, but unlike Windelband he refused to give particularizing investigation the name and honor of science. Hempel's concern was to show how history might be accommodated, at least after a fashion, to the universalizing model. The centerpiece of his article was an account of the cracking of a car's radiator, for which Hempel offered an explanation in acceptable universalizing form, involving statements a) of determining conditions (e.g., the temperature fell below freezing), and b) of general laws (e.g., when water freezes, it expands). Explanations that do not follow this form, Hempel states, are mere "explanation sketches," and not proper explanations at all. Thus history is not properly a science: at most, it is an application of science.

Hempel's real interest was in philosophy of science and philosophy of explanation, not in history. Moreover, almost all historians who encountered his "covering law model" (CLM) of explanation, and many philosophers, found Hempel's treatment of history inadequate. Yet the CLM, and Hempel's article in particular, gave rise to a vigorous and sustained discussion, continuing well into the 1960s, that all but defined the field of analytic historiology. The discussion can be followed in *History and Theory* and in three anthologies: Patrick Gardiner's *Theories of History* (1959), Sidney Hook's *Philosophy and History: A Symposium* (1963), and W.H. Dray's *Philosophical Analysis and History* (1966). Books of some note that emerged from the tradition include Gardiner, *The Nature of Historical Explanation* (1952), Dray, *Laws and Explanation in History* (1957), Arthur C. Danto, *Analytical Philosophy of History* (1965), W.B. Gallie, *Philosophy and the Historical Understanding* (1964), and Morton White, *The Foundations of Historical Knowledge* (1965). Gardiner (1952) defended the CLM in a slightly modified form. Dray (1957), Gallie, and Danto each put forward narrativist conceptions of history that were soon to make the CLM obsolete, even as Morton White continued to defend it. Dray (1957), who offered a still useful account of the CLM discussion, emphasized agents' motives and meanings, a concern that also lent itself, subsequently, to a focus on narrative.

Hermeneutic historiology arose from the antipositivistic side of the controversy. Like analytic historiology, the hermeneutic strand was initially concerned with a much broader territory than simply the work of historians. Rather, its aim was to discern what was distinctive about the human sciences in general, and thereby to defend them – and humanistic values generally – against the threat posed by a positivism that was seen as insensitive to human culture and creativity. Unlike analytic philosophy of explanation, hermeneutics (philosophy of interpretation) was not hostile to history-writing in its extant forms. Dilthey was both a philosopher and an intellectual historian, and Weber's work was as much historical as sociological. In the hands of Martin Heidegger (*Sein und Zeit* [1927; *Being and Time*, 1962]) and Hans-Georg Gadamer (*Wahrheit und Methode* [1960; *Truth and Method*, 1989]), hermeneutics diverged from historiology, but remained persistently available to be brought back to the historical field.

One of the first to do so was the French philosopher and intellectual Raymond Aron, who in 1938 presented a remarkable doctoral dissertation, *Introduction à la philosophie de l'histoire: essai sur les limites de l'objectivité historique* (*Introduction to the Philosophy of History: An Essay on the Limits of Historical Objectivity*, 1961). Informed above all by Weber's work, Aron launched a devastating attack on the positivist view that historical reality exists prior to its reconstruction by the historian. At the same time, Weber's sociological aspect helped Aron to remain sensitive to the social-scientific dimension in history. Also within the tradition of hermeneutic historiology is *De la connaissance historique* (1954; *The Meaning of History*, 1966), by the French historian of early Christianity, Henri-Irénée Marrou. More influenced by Dilthey than by Weber, Marrou was correspondingly less attuned to the role of such non-intentional factors in history as social structure. Marrou, and especially Aron, are still worth reading. More recently, a Weberian inspiration is visible in Paul Veyne's *Comment on écrit l'histoire: essai d'épistémologie* (1971; *Writing History: Essay on Epistemology*, 1984), while much of the first volume of *Temps et récit* (1983; *Time and Narrative*, 1984), by Paul Ricoeur, a phenomenological philosopher deeply influenced by hermeneutics, is devoted to historiology. In fact, Ricoeur summarizes a large part of the historiological literature up to 1980, and thus offers a convenient, although slightly tendentious, introduction to the subject. It is significant that both Veyne and Ricoeur are interested in narrative: hermeneutic historiology tended, over time, to move in a narrativist direction.

Like hermeneutic historiology, idealist historiology arose as a reaction against positivism. Important contributions include Benedetto Croce's *Teoria et storia della storiografia* (1917; *History: Its Theory and Practice*, 1921) and *La storia come pensiero e come azione* (1938; *History as the Story of Liberty*, 1941), Michael Oakeshott's *Experience and Its Modes* (1933), and above all R.G. Collingwood's *The Idea of History* (1946). The publication of this last book was almost as important as the CLM in prompting the emergence of historiology as a recognized field. A characteristic later example of the idealist strand is Leon J. Goldstein's *Historical Knowing* (1976).

Idealist historiology shares many features with the hermeneutic strand. Both strands insist that the methods of the natural sciences are inadequate for understanding the human world. Both focus on human beings' intentional thought or action, tending to leave aside those aspects of human life that might be seen as determined by the unconscious, by social structure, or by other nonintentional factors (one should reiterate, however, that Weber and his followers allow room for both intentional and nonintentional factors in history). Finally, whereas analytic historiology is *analytic*, and in consequence tends to focus on specific descriptive or explanatory statements appearing in historical works, hermeneutic and idealist historiology are concerned, in two ways, with wholes. They are concerned with the attempt of the historian to make particular facts fit together in a coherent overall picture or conception, and they are concerned with defining the character of history-writing *as a project*, distinct from other ways of encountering the world, especially natural science.

Yet, although hermeneutic and idealist historiology have sometimes been confused with each other, the idealist variety differs from the hermeneutic in two important respects. First, idealist historiology focuses on past action. It is concerned with thought only insofar as it is embedded in action: thus Croce considered history "as thought and action," and Collingwood saw historical investigation as involving "re-enactment" of past experience. Its model for history generally is political history. In contrast, hermeneutic historiology, in Dilthey, Marrou, and others, is rooted in the project of understanding past texts, and it takes intellectual history as its model for history generally. Second, whereas hermeneutic historiology tends to see historical investigation as a matter of *reconstructing* the past (albeit from a particular perspective in the present), idealist historiology tends to see historical investigation as a matter of *constructing* the past (out of intellectual resources available in the present). Hence Croce held that all history, being a construct in the present, is contemporary history, while Collingwood's "re-enactment" is a re-enactment by us, now. In Oakeshott's words, "the historian's business is not to discover, to recapture, or even to interpret; it is to create and to construct." For hermeneuticists, such a view is too subjectivist: hermeneuticists hold that the historian's vocation is not to construct the past, but either to find and describe it or to engage in a dialogue with it.

Narrative-linguistic historiology is the most recent strand to emerge. Its founding figures were the literary critic and theorist Roland Barthes, the philosopher Louis Mink, and the historian and cultural critic Hayden White. White's work was particularly important in giving presence to narrative-linguistic historiology. His ungainly but immensely thought-provoking *Metahistory* (1973) and various of his essays, especially several collected in *The Content of the Form* (1987), were deeply influential. Additional works along a narrative-linguistic line include Stephen Bann's *The Clothing of Clio* (1984), Hans Kellner's *Language and Historical Representation* (1989), Lionel Gossmann's *Between History and Literature* (1990), Philippe Carrard's *Poetics of the New History* (1992), and Frank Ankersmit's *History and Tropology* (1994). *A New Philosophy of History*, edited by Ankersmit and Kellner (1995), includes a useful bibliographical essay by Ankersmit, and essays addressing the emergence of narrative-linguistic historiology by Kellner, Danto, and Richard T. Vann.

The defining feature of narrative-linguistic historiology is its insistence on seeing the work of history as, in two senses, a *linguistic* construct. The work of history is held to be a linguistic construct in the sense that it is constructed out of language in complex ways that can be understood only if one analyzes it as literary scholars and critics analyze works of literature. Additionally, it is held to be a linguistic construct in the sense that, through its use of literary resources, it constructs what we take to be the past. Within the general framework of narrative-linguistic historiology a variety of approaches are possible. One can emphasize the constructive role of the work's arrangement (its "disposition," whether narrative or otherwise). One can emphasize the role within the work of its tropes, or literary devices (stylistics). One can attend to the work's implied author, focusing on its "enunciation," or to its implied audience, focusing on the work as an effort at persuasion.

In part, narrative-linguistic historiology developed out of the other three strands. As already noted, analytic historiology's discussion of the covering law model led such writers as Dray and Danto to attend to the role of narrative in history-writing. The holistic bent of hermeneutic historiology pointed even more directly toward narrative, as Ricoeur's work suggests. Idealist historiology's insistence that the historical account is a construct opened the way to the insistence by narrative-linguistic historiology that it is a linguistic construct (it is no accident that Mink wrote a book on Collingwood and that White studied Croce early in his career). But narrative-linguistic historiology also had sources outside historiology. These include the immense ferment in the fields of poetics and literary criticism in the period after World War II, renewed interest in the ancient tradition of rhetoric, "poststructuralist" philosophy, and post-1970 science studies. Science studies in particular has tended to undermine the assumption (fundamental to hermeneutic and idealist historiology) that there is a sharp division between the natural and the human sciences. Also not to be forgotten are the changing conditions under which the discipline of history operates. In a social and intellectual order much less homogeneous than before, it is hard to avoid the epistemological, stylistic, interpretive, and rhetorical issues that narrative-linguistic historiology addresses.

More than at any time since its professionalization in the 19th century, historical writing at the end of the 20th century seems marked by a multiplicity of subject matters and approaches. As a result, historians find themselves confronted by choices that previously they did not need to think about. In such a situation it seems clear that analytic, hermeneutic, idealist, and narrative-linguistic historiology all have things (although slightly different things in each case) to contribute to historical practice. Further, in the face of multiplicity a theoretical perspective seems to offer one of the few ways of coming to grips with the historian's project as a whole.

ALLAN MEGILL

See also Bodin; Buckle; Collingwood; Comte; Croce; Dilthey; Droysen; Hegel; Mabillon; Muratori; Nietzsche; Seignobos; Vico; Weber, M.; White, H.

Further Reading

Ankersmit, F.R., *History and Tropology: The Rise and Fall of Metaphor*, Berkeley: University of California Press, 1994

Ankersmit, F.R., and Hans Kellner, eds., *A New Philosophy of History*, Chicago: University of Chicago Press, and London: Reaktion, 1995

Aron, Raymond, *Introduction à la philosophie de l'histoire: essai sur les limites de l'objectivité historique* (1938), Paris: Gallimard, 1938; in English as *Introduction to the Philosophy of History: An Essay on the Limits of Historical Objectivity*, Boston: Beacon Press, and London: Weidenfeld and Nicolson, 1961

Bann, Stephen, *The Clothing of Clio: A Study of the Representation of History in Nineteenth-Century Britain and France*, Cambridge: Cambridge University Press, 1984

Barthes, Roland, *Le Bruissement de la langue*, Paris: Seuil, 1984; in English as *The Rustle of Language*, New York: Hill and Wang, and Oxford: Blackwell, 1986 [includes "The Discourse of History" (1967) and "The Reality Effect" (1968)]

Bernheim, Ernst, *Lehrbuch der historischen Methode und der Geschichtsphilosophie, mit Nachweis der wichtigsten Quellen und Hilfsmittel zum Studium der Geschichte* (Handbook of Historical Method), Leipzig: Drucker & Humblot, 1889; revised 1914; reprinted New York: Burt Franklin, 1970

Blanke, Horst Walter, Dirk Fleischer, and Jörn Rüsen, "Theory of History in Historical Lectures: The German Tradition of *Historik*, 1750–1900," *History and Theory* 23 (1984), 331–56

Bodin, Jean, *Methodus ad facilem historiarum cognitionem*, 1566; in English as *Method for the Easy Comprehension of History*, New York: Columbia University Press, 1945

Bradley, Francis Herbert, *The Presuppositions of Critical History*, Oxford: Parker, 1874; reprinted Chicago: Quadrangle, 1968

Buckle, Henry Thomas, *History of Civilization in England*, 2 vols., London: Parker, and New York: Appleton, 1857–61

Carrard, Philippe, *Poetics of the New History: French Historical Discourse from Braudel to Chartier*, Baltimore, Johns Hopkins University Press, 1992

Collingwood, R.G., *The Idea of History*, edited by T.M. Knox, Oxford: Oxford University Press, 1946, New York: Oxford University Press, 1956; revised edition, with *Lectures 1926–1928*, edited by Jan van der Dussen, Oxford: Clarendon Press, 1993, New York: Oxford University Press, 1994

Croce, Benedetto, *Teoria e storia della storiografia*, Bari: Laterza, 1917; in English as *Theory and History of Historiography*, London: Harrap, 1921, and as *History: Its Theory and Practice*, New York: Harcourt Brace, 1921

Croce, Benedetto, *La storia come pensiero e come azione*, Bari: Laterza, 1938; in English as *History as the Story of Liberty*, London: Allen and Unwin, and New York: Norton, 1941

Danto, Arthur C., *Narration and Knowledge*, including the integral text of *Analytical Philosophy of History* (1965), New York: Columbia University Press, 1985

Dilthey, Wilhelm, *Einleitung in die Geisteswissenschaften*, Leipzig: Duncker & Humblot, 1883; in English as *Introduction to the Human Sciences*, Princeton: Princeton University Press, 1989

Domanska, Ewa, ed., *Encounters: Philosophy of History After Postmodernism*, Charlottesville: University Press of Virginia, 1998

Dray, W.H., *Laws and Explanation in History*, Oxford: Oxford University Press, 1957

Dray, W.H., ed., *Philosophical Analysis and History*, New York: Harper, 1966

Dray, W.H., *History as Re-enactment: R.G. Collingwood's Idea of History*, Oxford: Oxford University Press, 1995

Droysen, J.G., *Grundriss der Historik*, Leipzig: Veit, 1868, revised 1882; abridged in English as *Outline of the Principles of History*, Boston: Ginn, 1893; reprinted 1967

Gadamer, Hans-Georg, *Wahrheit und Methode*, Tübingen: Mohr, 1960; in English as *Truth and Method*, New York: Crossroads, and London: Sheed and Ward, 1989

Gallie, W.B., *Philosophy and the Historical Understanding*, New York: Schocken, and London: Chatto and Windus, 1964

Gardiner, Patrick, *The Nature of Historical Explanation*. Oxford: Oxford University Press, 1952

Gardiner, Patrick, ed., *Theories of History: Readings from Classical and Contemporary Sources*, New York: Free Press, and London: Collier Macmillan, 1959

Goldstein, Leon J., *Historical Knowing*, Austin: University of Texas Press, 1976

Gossman, Lionel, *Between History and Literature*, Cambridge, MA: Harvard University Press, 1990

Hegel, G.W.F., *Vorlesungen über die Philosophie der Geschichte*, Berlin: Humblot, 1837; in English as *Lectures on the Philosophy of World History: Introduction: Reason in History*, Cambridge and New York: Cambridge University Press, 1975

Heidegger, Martin, *Sein und Zeit*, Halle: Niemeyer, 1927; in English as *Being and Time*, New York: Harper, and London: SCM Press, 1962

Hempel, Carl G., "The Function of General Laws in History," *Journal of Philosophy* 39 (1942), 35–47; reprinted in Patrick Gardiner, ed., *Theories of History: Readings from Classical and Contemporary Sources*, New York: Free Press, and London: Collier/Macmillan, 1959

History and Theory, Middletown, CT, 1960–

Hook, Sidney, ed., *Philosophy and History: A Symposium*, New York: New York University Press, 1963

Kellner, Hans, *Language and Historical Representation: Getting the Story Crooked*, Madison: University of Wisconsin Press, 1989

Langlois, Charles Victor, and Charles Seignobos, *Introduction aux études historiques*, Paris: Hachette, 1898; in English as *Introduction to the Study of History*, London: Duckworth, 1898; New York: Holt, 1913

Marrou, Henri-Irénée, *De la connaissance historique*, Paris: Seuil, 1954; in English as *The Meaning of History*, Baltimore: Helicon, 1966

Mink, Louis O., *Historical Understanding*, edited by Brian Fay, Eugene O. Golob, and Richard T. Vann, Ithaca, NY: Cornell University Press, 1987

Nietzsche, Friedrich, "Vom Nutzen und Nachtheil der Historie für das Leben," in *Unzeitgemässe Betrachtungen*, vol. 2, Leipzig: Fritzsch, 1874; in English as "On the Use and Disadvantage of History," in *Complete Works*, edited by Oscar Levy, vol. 5, New York: Macmillan, and Edinburgh: Foulis, 1909, and as "On the Uses and Disadvantage of History for Life," in *Untimely Meditations*, edited by R.J. Hollindale, Cambridge: Cambridge University Press, 1983

Oakeshott, Michael, *Experience and Its Modes*, Cambridge: Cambridge University Press, 1933; reprinted 1966

Ricoeur, Paul, *Temps et récit*, 3 vols., Paris: Seuil, 1983–85; in English as *Time and Narrative*, 3 vols., Chicago: University of Chicago Press, 1984–88

Veyne, Paul, *Comment on écrit l'histoire: essai d'épistémologie*, Paris: Seuil, 1971; in English as *Writing History: Essay on Epistemology* Middleton, CT: Wesleyan University Press, and Manchester: Manchester University Press, 1984

Weber, Max, *The Methodology of the Social Sciences*, Glencoe, IL: Free Press, 1949

White, Hayden V., *Metahistory: The Historical Imagination in Nineteenth-Century Europe*, Baltimore: Johns Hopkins University Press, 1973

White, Hayden V., *The Content of the Form: Narrative Discourse and Historical Representation*, Baltimore: Johns Hopkins University Press, 1987

White, Morton, *The Foundations of Historical Knowledge*, New York: Harper, 1965

Windelband, Wilhelm, "History and Natural Science," *History and Theory* 19 (1980), 165–85 [originally published 1894]

History from Below

"Grass roots history, history seen from below, or the history of the common people," as E.J. Hobsbawm put it, gained prominence in the 1950s and 1960s. It is a historical perspective that rejects traditional history's political narrative, or the notion that, in Disraeli's words, "History is but the biography of great men." History from below was not alone in this rejection: consider, for example, the Annales school. But this historical school gained its distinctiveness from its concern to write the experience of the many into history as the subjects, rather than passive invisible recipients, of history. It was preoccupied with revolutions, popular protest, popular culture, and crime. As such it rejected also the old labor history of the Webbs which focused on the organizations of the working class.

The perspective was, not unsurprisingly, inspired by Marxism. This trend emerged out of the Communist Party Historians' Group and figures such as Christopher Hill, Rodney Hilton, E.J. Hobsbawm, George Rudé, John Saville, and E.P. Thompson. Their work was the driving force behind *Past and Present* which started life as a Marxist journal. From 1966, it also found organizational focus in the History Workshop at Ruskin College, Oxford.

One of the key concerns of history from below was to establish the centrality of great revolutions to historical change. In this respect the work of Christopher Hill on the English Civil War was pioneering. He has argued that the English Civil War was a bourgeois revolution fundamental to modernization of the English state and the development of capitalism. The revolutionary Puritanism of Cromwell and the Levellers demonstrated the complex and dynamic character of human agency in the emergence of capitalism in England. Again with the case of the French Revolution, historians such as Rudé persuaded us of the necessity to move beyond notions of the crowd as a manipulated animalistic mob or sentimentalized revolutionary masses and to examine the way in which revolution transformed the horizons of the French population, bringing together an amalgam of "perceptions, values, felt needs, experimental patterns and goals."

A more sensitive and imaginative approach also developed to popular protest and culture outside the major revolutions, for example Rudé and Hobsbawm's examination of the Captain Swing riots in 1830, the discussion of Robin Hood in *Past and Present*, or Geoffrey de Ste. Croix's *Class Struggle in the Ancient*

Greek World (1981). But at its most ambitious history from below posed questions about the very nature of class, consciousness, and agency; this is most clearly and successfully demonstrated in E.P. Thompson's *Making of the English Working Class* (1963) which sought to rescue Britain's early industrial workers and their allies from the organizational obsession of the old labor history or their statistical objectification in contemporary social and economic history.

The concern of history from below to see the "faces in the crowd" posed important methodological problems. First, the subjects of the historian's quest were almost entirely excluded from the range of sources that were typically used by historians. Historians of this school were therefore forced to find new material or ask new questions of old material. "There is generally no material until our questions have revealed it" (Hobsbawm). Hence criminal, police, judicial, and demographic sources were trawled in new ways. These sources are problematic. Historians have strained over police records that exaggerated the scale of subversive activities for motives of self-interest, and puzzled over occupational and class categories fundamentally at odds with our own. Second, the perspective of history from below was key to the development of oral history and the methodological problems posed by memory, where interviewees remember selectively, reconstruct events to make sense of them, and even conceal the truth. Third, history from below has posed grander theoretical question about popular consciousness. In general this has brought these historians into conflict with the static culturally constructed *mentalité* (Le Roy Ladurie, Robert Mandrou) or the deterministic ideological domination favored by structuralist historians (Louis Althusser). Indeed this tension developed into open public polemic in E.P. Thompson's *The Poverty of Theory* (1978) and in the pages of the *History Workshop Journal* between the Althusserians and those subscribing to history from below.

As history from below gained ground with the voluminous literature that emerged in the course of the 1960s and 1970s it underwent a transformation as it broke out of its Marxist origins with the development of the History Workshop, women's history, and oral history. By the 1980s history from below had been accused of being at an impasse. It was criticized by Floud for its lack of concern for theory and quantitative analysis, while Zeitlin argued that the rank and file perspective of history from below ignored the way in which workers' activity was shaped primarily by institutional arrangements of industrial relations. The impact on the discipline of history from below has been considerable, but it has not displaced traditional history. Indeed, of late we have seen a partial retrenchment of old orthodoxies with the changing political and educational climate.

MATT PERRY

See also Brazil; Burke; Cobb; Economic; Europe: Modern; Guha; History Workshop; Hufton; Mason; Memory; Rudé; Russia: Russian Revolution; Sport; Thompson, E.; Walkowitz

Further Reading

Coss, P.R., "Aspects of Cultural Diffusion in Medieval England: The Early Romance, Local Society, and Robin Hood," *Past and Present* 108 (1985), 35–79

de Ste. Croix, G.E.M., *The Class Struggle in the Ancient Greek World: From the Archaic Age to the Arab Conquests*, London: Duckworth, and Ithaca, NY: Cornell University Press, 1981

Floud, Roderick, "Quantitative History and People's History," *History Workshop Journal* 17 (1984), 113–214

Hobsbawm, Eric J., *Primitive Rebels: Studies in Archaic Forms of Social Movement in the Nineteenth and Twentieth Centuries*, Manchester: Manchester University Press, 1959; as *Social Bandits and Primitive Rebels*, Glencoe, IL: Free Press, 1960

Keen, Maurice, "Robin Hood: Peasant or Gentleman?" *Past and Present* 19 (1961), 7–15

Krantz, Frederick, ed., *History from Below: Studies in Popular Protest and Popular Ideology in Honour of George Rudé*, Montreal: Concordia University Press, 1985; Oxford: Blackwell, 1988

Rudé, George, *The Crowd in the French Revolution*, London: Oxford University Press, 1959

Rudé, George, *The Crowd in History: A Study of Popular Disturbances in France and England, 1730–1848*, New York: Wiley, 1964

Samuel, Raphael, ed., *People's History and Socialist Theory*, London and Boston: Routledge, 1981

Thompson, E.P., *The Making of the English Working Class*, London: Gollancz, 1963; New York: Pantheon, 1964

Thompson, E.P., *The Poverty of Theory and Other Essays*, London: Merlin Press, and New York: Monthly Review Press, 1978

Zeitlin, Jonathan, "From Labour History to the History of Industrial Relations," *Economic History Review* 40 (1987), 159–84

History Workshop

The History Workshop movement in Britain has been an active force in promoting the field known variously as history from below, the history of everyday life, or just people's history. It has sponsored research, books, pamphlets, conferences, a highly successful journal, and even television documentaries to promote histories alternative to those offered by the academy. Drawn from the political left, it was founded at Ruskin College, Oxford (the trade union college for mature students) in 1966 and was intended to bring academics together with workers, teachers and amateur historians. The movement's main founder, Raphael Samuel (1934–96), later defined the basic philosophy of History Workshop as "the belief that history is or ought to be a collaborative enterprise, one in which the researcher, the archivist, the curator and the teacher, the 'do-it-yourself' enthusiast and the local historian, the family history societies and the industrial archaeologists, should all be regarded as equally engaged." In practice, this involved the creation of a space in which research could be shared and dignity restored to everyday life.

History Workshop proved to be a non-sectarian forum for the propagation of socialist history. The leading figures were much influenced by the political events of 1968. Their style was engaged and partisan, linking history to the political struggles of the present. They cherished autobiography and the confessional response. The name was derived from Joan Littlewood's left-wing Theatre Workshop and indeed the movement took art and culture seriously. Important founder members included Tim Mason, Gareth Stedman Jones, Alun Howkins, and Anna Davin. All of these were very much under the influence of the older generation of socialist historians, particularly Eric Hobsbawm, E.P. Thompson, Christopher Hill, and John Saville, each of whom assisted in the movement by giving talks, writing articles, and providing critiques. The earliest Workshop publications were pamphlets by Ruskin students based on original research on sources that proved it was possible to write a history of working-class experience. Among these were Sally Alexander's *St. Giles's Fair* (1970), Stan Shipley's *Club Life and Socialism in mid-Victorian London* (1972), and Alun Howkins' *Whitsun in 19th Century Oxfordshire* (1974).

A central preoccupation was popular resistance and protest. The first History Workshop conference in 1967 was titled "A Day with the Chartists," but later Workshops featured strands on diverse topics linked only by the attempt to establish the possibilities of people's history. These annual conferences had a festival-like character, jamborees of history free from normal academic piety. Starting at Ruskin, they were eventually held around Britain and were well-attended by diverse groups of people. The most well-known Workshop session took place in 1979 when E.P. Thompson furiously confronted critics of *The Poverty of Theory* (1978), his assault on Althusserian structuralism. At the same time, the conferences provided a space in which women's history could be discussed and explored. Indeed the first Women's Liberation conference in Britain grew indirectly out of History Workshop. There were also themed conferences such as those devoted to religion in 1983 and patriotism in 1984, which in turn generated books. Volumes in the History Workshop series (especially *People's History and Socialist Theory*, 1981) were often intended to provide a feeling of the Workshop; hence the summaries of debates and the tentative nature of many articles in which ideas were floated for the first time. Key Workshop publications included Jerry White's *Rothschild Buildings* (1980) and *The Worst Street in North London* (1986), oral histories intended to provide a voice for popular experiences, then often neglected by conventional historians.

The movement inspired satellite organizations dedicated to documenting local working-class history not just in Britain but around the world. Similar groups sprang up in Germany and the United States. In the same spirit, Television History Workshop pioneered the production of oral histories devoted to Brixton residents and Cowley car workers. At its height in the 1970s and early 1980s, the movement was propelled by a formidable energy, although it was also characterized by a spirit of self-questioning about its methods and aims.

History Workshop Journal was founded in 1976 by a collective made up mainly of academics. Subtitled "a journal of socialist historians," it was inspired by the journal *Past and Present*, which in turn had been influenced by *Annales*. Hence the values of the journal were rather different from those of the movement at large, always opting for scholarly rigor and caution in approaching sources. Key articles included Stephen Yeo's "A New Life: The Religion of Socialism" (no.4), Anna Davin's "Imperialism and Motherhood" (no.5), Tim Mason's "Women in Nazi Germany" (nos.1–2), and Hugh Cunningham's "The Language of Patriotism" (no.12), as well as Tony Judt's critique of social history, "A Clown in Regal Purple" (no.7). Whereas the movement had tended to concentrate on British history, the journal also featured non-British topics. Furthermore, it began to focus less on class and the struggles of the labor movement and more on the home and particularly on gender issues. The importance of this shift was underlined in 1981 when the subtitle was changed to "a journal of socialist and feminist historians" after a lengthy debate. Both the journal and the wider movement remained highly political. Editorials were devoted to commenting on contemporary politics. In 1983, when Margaret Thatcher appropriated Victorian values as part of her ideology, History Workshop contested her interpretation of the past in a special supplement of the *New Statesman*. The debate on the future of the study of history in the National Curriculum led to a conference, "History, the Nation and the Schools" (1990), the proceedings of which were published in the journal (nos. 29 and 30).

In recent years, History Workshop has explored new areas, particularly psychoanalysis, where the influence of Barbara Taylor and Sally Alexander has been important, and postcolonial narratives. There has also been a concern with popular history and heritage, exemplified by the journal's "History at Large" column, examining history outside the academy. However, in the later 1980s, History Workshop as a movement went into decline. The annual workshops were discontinued and many local activities abandoned. This was partly a reflection of the general crisis of the left with the fall of communism in 1989. In 1995, the editorial collective made the symbolic decision to abandon the journal's subtitle. The decline of the movement also reflected the poor state of adult education which had so informed its ethos. However, the journal continues to thrive as a vehicle in which new approaches can be explored. Ironically, History Workshop may have been the victim of its own success. Many of its themes (for example, race, gender, and the history of sexuality) have now become the common sense of academic history. In the last thirty years, History Workshop has transformed the discipline in Britain and elsewhere and expanded the range of historical inquiry.

Rohan McWilliam

See also History from Below; Koselleck; Lüdtke; Mason; Oral; Quantitative; Rowbotham; Samuel; Scribner; Thompson, E.; Walkowitz

Further Reading

Alexander, Sally, *St. Giles's Fair, 1830–1914: Popular Culture and the Industrial Revolution in Nineteenth-Century Oxford*, Oxford: History Workshop, 1970

History Workshop Journal, 1976–

Howkins, Alun, *Whitsun in 19th Century Oxfordshire*, Oxford: History Workshop, 1974

New Statesman, 27 May 1983 [special supplement on Victorian values]

Samuel, Raphael, ed., *People's History and Socialist Theory*, London and Boston: Routledge, 1981

Samuel, Raphael, ed., *History Workshop: A Collectanea, 1967–1991*, Oxford: History Workshop, 1991

Shipley, Stan, *Club Life and Socialism in mid-Victorian London*, Oxford: History Workshop, 1972; West Nyack: NY: Journeyman, 1983

White, Jerry, *Rothschild Buildings: Life in an East End Tenement Block, 1887–1920*, London and Boston: Routledge, 1980

White, Jerry, *The Worst Street in North London: A Social History of Campbell Bunk, Islington, Between the Wars*, London: Routledge, 1986

Hobsbawm, E.J. 1917–

British historian of modern Europe

E.J. Hobsbawm was one of the influential group of British Marxist historians which formed the Communist Party Historians' Group (which also included E.P. Thompson, Christopher Hill, Victor Kiernan, Rodney Hilton, Royden Harrison, and Raphael Samuel). However, whereas many of these historians left the British Communist party in the wake of the suppression of the Hungarian uprising in 1956, Hobsbawm remained. As a result, the whole of his historical corpus has been written from this standpoint, something which perhaps explains his reluctance, until recently, to extend his historical scholarship into the 20th century.

Both the volume and range of Hobsbawm's historical output have been immense, and these themselves form only a part of a larger corpus that includes voluminous journalistic writings, and a long stint (under the pseudonym Francis Newman) as a jazz critic. He has remained firmly committed to dialogue within history between Marxists and non-Marxists (via, for example, the journal *Past and Present*, of whose first editorial board he was a member). He has been similarly wedded to the idea that academic historians need to write also for the wider reading public, not least because, as Hobsbawm himself put it, he has "increasingly com[e] back to the old-fashioned opinion that it is useful in politics to have a historical perspective if you want to know what is new in a situation."

It is this impetus that underpins Hobsbawm's widely-acclaimed 4-volume history of the world in the modern era, written over a 30-year span, and comprising *The Age of Revolution* (1962), *The Age of Capital* (1975), *The Age of Empire* (1987), and *The Age of Extremes*, (1994). These exercises in "haute vulgarization" provide the general reader with a masterful portrayal of the two centuries from 1789, displaying the range of Hobsbawm's knowledge, and the lightness of touch of his Marxism. Taken together they have been described as establishing a pattern of total or world history more rounded than those of either Braudel or Wallerstein. Not that the works are in any sense untheorized; Hobsbawm's Marxism comes through in the unifying theme of the volumes (and indeed of Hobsbawm's entire corpus), a study of the process of transition from precapitalist to capitalist society, under the influence of what Hobsbawm calls the "dual revolutions," the French Revolution and the Industrial Revolution.

Examining the working through of these two revolutions allowed Hobsbawm to develop an aspect of his historical approach which has been the hallmark of his work, and was clearly apparent in his early labor history. Hobsbawm never wrote the kind of *magnum opus* which established the reputation of E.P. Thompson; his characteristic medium was the article. Nevertheless, in the two volumes of his collected essays, *Labouring Men* (1964), and *Worlds of Labour* (1984), Hobsbawm did almost as much to set the parameters of British labor history as Thompson. Taking elements of the old Webbian emphasis on institutional trade union history, and marrying it to the broader social focus of the Hammonds, he created a broader discipline which sought to examine the full experience and agency of the common people. While apparently remaining more theoretically orthodox than those of Thompson,

Hobsbawm's studies, for example his re-examination of the concept of the labor aristocracy, often quietly turned established Marxist orthodoxies on their head.

Hobsbawm did not romanticize working-class culture. Without ever underestimating the hardships of industrialization, he also accepted that as a result of these hardships the working classes could develop some unattractive, self-destructive, and socially dangerous tendencies. He also stressed that the cultural triumphs of the working class were futile unless they led into political action. Nevertheless, his work crucially extended the boundaries of what had normally been encompassed by the notion of politics. This is especially apparent in his studies of *Primitive Rebels* (1959) and of *Bandits* (1969), in which Hobsbawm sought to rescue various kinds of protest or anti-establishment activity from the condescension of orthodox Marxism. The social bandit, secret societies such as the Mafia, or peasant millenarian movements, rather than mere aberrations, are significant popular responses to the upheavals of the transition from precapitalist to capitalist society; they may themselves be prepolitical movements which do not aspire to political power, but they can promote political consciousness and revolution. Hobsbawm's seminal scholarly contributions were characteristically supplemented by organization work, as one of the founding editorial team of the *Journal of Peasant Studies*.

In his studies of both urban working class and rural peasant societies, Hobsbawm had always shown himself interested in cultures and their development. This interest underpinned a shift from the 1970s towards a greater emphasis on the genesis and meanings of cultural practices. In a ground-breaking collection of essays edited with T.O. Ranger, *The Invention of Tradition* (1983), Hobsbawm drew attention to the extent to which many of the seemingly immutable traditions of modern societies are in fact of relatively recent origin, and often creations of states or governing elites seeking ways of securing legitimacy and allegiance. His own chapter on the production of European traditions in the later 19th century was subsequently expanded into an influential book-length essay on the rise and apparent decline of nationalism as a historical dynamic in the last two centuries, *Nations and Nationalism since 1780* (1992).

Hobsbawm established no personal school. In part this is because, as Eugene Genovese pointed out in his tribute to Hobsbawm, "to be 'Hobsbawmian' means to be Marxist." In part it is because Hobsbawm, despite his position as the editor of the journal *History of Marxism*, and the prescience of his commentary on Marx in *The Age of Revolution*, generally eschewed detailed theoretical interventions of his own in the debates over Marxism and history, contenting himself with tributes to the insights of Marx's preface to the *Introduction to the Critique of Political Economy*, with its base-superstructure model, reinvigorating Marxist history instead with his empirical studies. Nevertheless, the way in which individual instances of his work, such as his papers on the labor aristocracy thesis, became the foundational texts of whole historical sub-disciplines suggests an enduring, if unobtrusive influence.

MARTIN HEWITT

See also Althusser; Anthropology; Brazil; Brenner; Britain: since 1750; Central Europe; Cuba; Economic; Europe: Modern; France: French Revolution; Hill; History from Below; History Workshop;

Ileto; Jones, G.; Kiernan; Kula; Labor; Marks; Marx; Marxist
Interpretation; Nationalism; Polanyi; Procacci; Rudé; Samuel;
Social; Stone; Subaltern; Thompson, E.; Tilly, C.; World

Biography

Eric John Ernest Hobsbawm. Born Alexandria, Egypt, 9 June 1917.
Educated in Vienna and Berlin; at St. Marylebone Grammar School;
Cambridge University, BA, PhD. Taught (rising to professor),
Birkbeck College, University of London, 1948–82 (emeritus); fellow,
King's College, Cambridge, 1949–55. Married Marlene Schwarz,
1962 (1 son, 1 daughter).

Principal Writings

*Primitive Rebels: Studies in Archaic Forms of Social Movement in
    the Nineteenth and Twentieth Centuries*, 1959; in US as *Social
    Bandits and Primitive Rebels*, 1960
The Age of Revolution, 1789–1848, 1962
Labouring Men: Studies in the History of Labour, 1964
With George Rudé, *Captain Swing: A Social History of the Great
    English Agricultural Uprising of 1830*, 1968
Industry and Empire: An Economic History of Britain since 1750,
    1968
Bandits, 1969
The Age of Capital, 1848–1875, 1975
Editor with Terence O. Ranger, *The Invention of Tradition*, 1983
Worlds of Labour: Further Studies in the History of Labour, 1984;
    in US as *Workers: Worlds of Labor*, 1984
The Age of Empire, 1875–1914, 1987
*Echoes of the Marseillaise: Two Centuries Look Back on the French
    Revolution*, 1990
Nations and Nationalism since 1780: Programme, Myth, Reality, 1992
The Age of Extremes: The Short Twentieth Century, 1914–1991,
    1994 in US as *The Age of Extremes: A History of the World,
    1914–1991*, 1994
On History, 1997

Further Reading

Genovese, Eugene D., "The Politics of Class Struggle in the History
    of Society: An Appraisal of the Work of Eric Hobsbawm," in Pat
    Thane, Geoffrey Crossick, and Roderick Floud, eds., *The Power
    of the Past: Essays for Eric Hobsbawm*, Cambridge: Cambridge
    University Press, 1984
"Interview with Eric J. Hobsbawm," *Radical History Review* 19
    (1978–79), 111–32
Kaye, Harvey J., and Keith McClelland, "Bibliography of the
    Writings of Eric Hobsbawm," in Raphael Samuel and Gareth
    Stedman Jones, eds., *Culture, Ideology and Politics: Essays for
    Eric Hobsbawm*, London and Boston: Routledge, 1982
Samuel, Raphael, "British Marxist Historians, 1880–1980," *New
    Left Review*, 120 (March–April 1980), 21–96
Schwarz, Bill, "'The People' in History: The Communist Party
    Historians' Group, 1946–56," in Richard Johnson *et al.*, eds.,
    Making Histories: Studies in History-Writing and Politics, London:
    Hutchinson, and Minneapolis: University of Minnesota Press, 1982

Hodgson, Marshall G.S. 1922–1968

US Islamicist

Marshall Hodgson, an Islamicist and Quaker, is rightly seen as
one of the greatest Islamic historians of the 20th century. His
innovative methodological and conceptual approach to the
study of Islamic civilization provided new perspectives on the
place of Islam in world history, as it also inspired alternative

approaches to the study of history in general. Hodgson's views
on Islamic history were directly linked with his inclusive and
global vision of world history. For Hodgson, a meaningful
historical inquiry was possible only inasmuch as it related to
both the specifics as well as totalities of an all-encompassing
human history – a history shaped by the cumulative effects and
interactions of "natural and cultural ecology," "group interests
and calculations," and "individual vision and imagination." But
most importantly, it was necessary that this inquiry escape the
Eurocentric and essentialist approach of mainstream historiography which places the experience of Western Europe at the
center of the history of the modern world.

Hodgson's alternative historical perspective rejected the
exceptionalism of the Western historical experience, questioned
the validity of the predominant perception of its moral and cultural superiority, and ultimately, resituated both Islamic and
European civilizations in the global context of a united and interconnected human history. In *Rethinking World History* (1993),
a collection of his essays edited and introduced by Edmund
Burke III, Hodgson meticulously identified the historical ways in
which the destinies of the various sections of mankind began to
be intertwined, and the consequential interrelations between the
study of the Islamic societies on the one hand, and of Western
societies on the other. As Burke explains in his introductory essay
"Marshall Hodgson clearly saw that Islamic history was a strategic point from which to undertake a critique of the discourse on
Western civilization. As he notes, Islamic civilization is the sister
of our own. Its roots lie in the same basic Irano-Semitic religious
and cultural values, crossed with the ambiguous legacy of West
Asian imperium. [For Hodgson], the study of Islamic civilization
thus almost by necessity invites a re-examination of European
history in which its development can be placed in world historical context, and in the process, de-exceptionalized." In this context, Hodgson argued that the history of human civilization is
"necessarily an Asia-centered history." He noted that the inter-
connecting band of agrarian cited societies which spanned the
entire Afro-Eurasian landmass from China to Western Europe
(an ensemble of civilizations which he calls, after Toynbee, the
Oikoumene) is "predominantly Asian." Accordingly, Hodgson
contended that an "interregional" approach to world history
logically overrides the applicability and validity of the predominant Western-centred approach. He equally questioned (and
rejected) the validity of the map of the world (namely the
Mercator projection map which he calls "the Jim Crow projection") and European world atlases for their distorted images of
the southern hemisphere, especially Africa, and exaggeration of
the size of Europe and its geographical centrality. Furthermore,
and to avoid the distorted effects of misconstrued terminology
shaped by the Western experience, Hodgson developed a
whole array of more precise new terms and words – such
as "Islamicate," "Islamdom," "technicalism," "agrarianate" –
each reflecting an accurate meaning which commonly-used and
popular words do not communicate as clearly.

Hodgson's vigorous approach to the study of history was
best exemplified in his monumental 3-volume study, *The
Venture of Islam* (1974), which traced the development of
Islamic civilization and the whole Afro-Eurasian historical
complex from the beginning of recorded history to the middle
of the 20th century. The study grew out of Hodgson's famous
course on Islamic civilization at the University of Chicago, and

was assembled by his colleague Reuben Smith following Hodgson's sudden death, at the age of 47, in 1968. In this comprehensive study of the place of Islamdom in world history, Hodgson challenged conventional scholarships which typically emphasized the decline of Islamicate societies after 945 CE. Instead, he demonstrated with much accuracy and detail that, until the 18th century, Islamicate civilization dominated the greater part of "citied" mankind and enjoyed a remarkable level of superiority both in the quality of its high culture and artistic creation and in the strength of its legal system and bureaucratic agrarianate empires. In the same process, Hodgson re-examined and accentuated the centrality of the non-Arabic element of Islamdom, especially the Persianate culture and its major role in the elaboration of a powerful cosmopolitan Islamic civilization. The deterioration of this culture resulted, according to Hodgson, not from the ascendancy of traditional Western culture, but under the effects of what he called the "Great Western Transmutation" and its accompanying "technicalism" which stemmed from a global and long process of change rooted elsewhere (the Near East, India, or China) and diffused subsequently to Europe.

Hodgson's scholarship on the history of Islam and world history – at the time of his death he was at work on a world history manuscript – has provided new frameworks for understanding global history and civilizations. And despite many challenges to some of its general basis of explanation, and some pointed criticism of its marginalization of African history, *The Venture of Islam* has been a standard reference since first publication. It has been credited with a unique grasp of the complex impact of Islamic civilization, innovative modes of tracing large-scale history and comparing societies involved in it, and informative insights on current developments and future direction of Islamic societies.

SAMIRA ALI ATALLAH

See also Comparative; Massignon; Middle East; World

Biography
Marshall Goodwin Simms Hodgson. Born Richmond, Indiana, 11 April 1922. Received BA, University of Colorado, 1943; BA, Earlham College, 1943; PhD, University of Chicago, 1951. Taught (rising to professor), University of Chicago, 1953–68. Married Phyllis Eleanor Walker, 1958 (3 daughters). Died 10 June 1968.

Principal Writings
The Order of the Assassins: The Struggle of the Early Nizari Ismailis Against the Islamic World, 1955
Introduction to Islamic Civilization: Course Syllabus and Selected Readings, 3 vols., 1958–59
The Venture of Islam: Conscience and History in a World Civilization, 3 vols., 1974
Rethinking World History: Essays on Europe, Islam and World History, edited by Edmund Burke III, 1993

Hofstadter, Richard 1916–1970
US political historian

Richard Hofstadter ranks as perhaps the leading historian of the generation of scholars who came of age after World War

II. In his methodology and interpretations, Hofstadter effectively changed the way historians thought about both the substance and the contours of the American past.

Hofstadter's impact as a synthesizer and interpreter of the main lines of American history stemmed first from his book *The American Political Tradition* (1948). This work, a collection of portraits of American political leaders from the Founding Fathers to Franklin Roosevelt, explicitly challenged the regnant school of American historiography known as the "Progressive" school. This line of thought, exemplified by the various works of Frederick Jackson Turner, Charles Beard, and Vernon Parrington, emphasized the centrality of manifold areas of conflict in American life: geographic, economic and political, and cultural. These figures shared a belief in the idea that progress in history arose from the dynamic clash of interests.

Hofstadter rejected what he considered to be the crude, schematic Progressive emphasis upon conflict, regarding it as reductionist in its evaluation of the force of ideas in American politics, and overly binary in its understanding of American life. Rather, in *The American Political Tradition* he argued that American political culture rested upon "common, bourgeois entrepreneurial assumptions," with most of society tending to be grouped "ideologically around a Whiggish center rather than to be polarized in sharp ideological struggles."

Hofstadter by no means penned his analysis of what came to be known as the "Consensus" approach to American history in a mood of celebration of that ideological uniformity. To the contrary, he wrote out of an ongoing, presentist concern with the blandness and shallowness of American political ideas and culture. A former Depression-era leftist, Hofstadter throughout his life remained outside of and alienated from the dominant liberalism of American politics and thought. He experienced disillusionment as he reflected upon the intellectual shallowness and opportunism that marked American political rhetoric at the highest levels of power.

In his hands some of the epic figures of American political lore such as Jefferson, Jackson, and Roosevelt were pragmatists far more than intellectuals, opportunists more than visionaries. Thus Jackson, for example, appears merely as a liberal capitalist manipulating populist rhetoric to obfuscate his goal of economic upward mobility. This ignores the extent – argued by recent scholars – of a distinctive artisanal or working-class culture existing prior to and distinct from emerging middle-class society and mores. Hofstadter's only admiring portrait – of a committed visionary – is that of Wendell Phillips, the Brahmin abolitionist, the one non-officeholder portrayed. Only he committed himself unswervingly to an idea, and acted politically – as an agitator – to actualize that idea. Typical political conflicts were not about ideas, because politicians tended to lack them in the first place. Written in the early phase of the Cold War, this work reflected Hofstadter's unease with popular politics as a medium for the manipulation of the masses by unprincipled politicians. Similarly parties were merely engines of this political consensus concerning the beneficence of liberal capitalism.

Hofstadter's next work, the prize-winning *The Age of Reform* (1955), set out to apply interdisciplinary methodologies to two powerful reform movements in American history: Populism and Progressivism. Borrowing from his Columbia colleagues C. Wright Mills and Robert Merton, as well as from Freud and Karl Mannheim, Hofstadter explored the realm of political culture, taking into account the notion of politics as symbolic culture, the non-rational, non-economically based source of ideas, and the phenomenon of social "status." Rather than seeing these reform movements solely in terms of clashing group interests, Hofstadter attempted to plumb the depths of the identity and ideology of these reformers.

The Populists fared poorly in Hofstadter's hands: described as victims of their inability to perceive their true interests in a rapidly expanding global agricultural marketplace. They rejected this new world order, concocting instead an "agrarian myth." Hofstadter maintained that they chose "to believe that they were not themselves an organic part of the whole order of business enterprise and speculation that flourished in the city ... but rather the innocent pastoral victims of a conspiracy hatched in the distance." In this portrait Hofstadter betrayed his fundamental unease with what he termed the "village mind" – that is the worldview of small-town America. Throughout his writing, including his later works *Anti-Intellectualism in American Life* (1964) and *The Paranoid Style in American Politics and Other Essays* (1965), he considered this world to be the source of much of the anti-intellectualism in American life that he lamented. Later scholars, in response to this unflattering portrait of Populism, have pointed to the real trauma economic modernization caused in the world of American agriculture, as well as to the distinctive subcultures of American rural life that did not give way so easily to the putative liberal capitalist ethos that Hofstadter assumed.

The Populists harbored a real grievance with American capitalism; they could not deal with it rationally, according to Hofstadter. The Progressives, like the Populists, also mistrusted the growing "bigness" of American life: political urban machines, large corporations, managerial organizations. But these reformers, unlike the Populists, were not suffering materially from these trends. Hofstadter, using tools borrowed from sociology, argued that these declining social elites suffered from status anxiety: the fear that their stewardship of American society was being usurped by a new breed of leaders – robber barons, bureaucrats, ethnic pols. As he wrote, "Progressivism, in short, was to a very considerable extent led by men who suffered from the events of their time not through a shrinkage in their means but through the changed pattern in the distribution of deference and power." Like the Populists, they hearkened back to a more broadly based American society, in which power was widely dispersed, as was wealth and status. The individual citizen felt empowered in such a world. This imaginatively remembered tableau was being ineradicably altered by the looming power of the corporation and the political machine, reducing the citizen to a meaningless cipher in industrial America.

Like his portrait of Populism, this analysis of Progressivism demanded, and received, tremendous scrutiny among other scholars. Fundamental issues – who were the Progressives, did they represent old elites or emerging new ones, was there one Progressive group or were there manifold segments collectively that comprised the Progressives – these and other lines of inquiry all emerged from Hofstadter's scholarly interlocutors. What seems clear is that Hofstadter's distinction between "status" and "interest" politics perpetuated, rather than eliminated, the Beardian notion of rational politics as economically motivated. Status politics were "irrational" to Hofstadter,

representing the inability or unwillingness to act politically based upon one's rational economic interest. This assumed rather than demonstrated the reality of an all-encompassing liberal capitalist social ethos and marketplace. Subsequent scholars challenged this binary notion of political behavior altogether, arguing rather that status, power, and economic interest do not enjoy a constant, fixed relationship to one another, rather they vary depending upon context.

Hofstadter did not relish his standing as a founding father of the "Consensus" school, since he recognized its limited value as what he regarded as merely a historical commonplace: that every society possesses a framework enabling it to function civilly. Yet by the 1960s, in the midst of domestic turmoil, including student revolts on his own Columbia campus, Hofstadter judged Consensus more favorably, even as he increasingly sought to refocus on the conflicts of American life within the broader consensus. Thus he analyzed the positive role of political parties as forces for social cohesion, in *The Idea of a Party System* (1969). Hofstadter's final, unfinished project, cut short by his early death, was a social history of America, suggesting his interest in a reality, perhaps untouched by political rhetoric, politicians, and political culture. At the end of his life he seemed to recognize more fully than ever the limits of consensus, in the face of deep-seated conflicts such as race and ethnicity, if not always of economic class, and he understood that any political consensus, however necessary for the promotion of common moral and constitutional values, often did not address the reality of a nonconsensual society. People, and collectivities, were left behind in the course of the American quest for a political or social consensus.

DAVID B. STARR

See also Curti; Elkins; Hartz; Levine; Nash; Pessen; Political; Potter; United States: 19th Century; United States: 20th Century; United States: Historical Writing, 20th Century; Wiebe

Biography

Born Buffalo, New York, 6 August 1916, son of a furrier. Received BA, University of Buffalo, 1937; MA, Columbia University, 1938; PhD 1942. Taught at University of Maryland, 1942–46; rose to professor, Columbia University, 1946–70. Married 1) Felice Swados, 1936 (died 1945; 1 son); 2) Beatrice Kevitt, 1947 (1 daughter). Died New York City, 24 October 1970.

Principal Writings

Social Darwinism in American Thought, 1860–1915, 1944, revised 1955
The American Political Tradition and the Men Who Made It, 1948
The Age of Reform: From Bryan to FDR, 1955
Anti-Intellectualism in American Life, 1964
The Paranoid Style in American Politics and Other Essays, 1965
The Progressive Historians: Turner, Beard, Parrington, 1968
The Idea of a Party System: The Rise of Legitimate Opposition in the United States, 1780–1840, 1969
America at 1750: A Social Portrait, 1971

Further Reading

Baker, Susan Stout, *Radical Beginnings: Richard Hofstadter and the 1930s*, Westport, CT: Greenwood Press, 1985
Brinkley, Alan, "Richard Hofstadter's *The Age of Reform*: A Reconsideration," *Reviews in American History* 13 (1985), 462–80

Elkins, Stanley, and Eric McKitrick, eds., *The Hofstadter Aegis: A Memorial*, New York: Knopf, 1974 [includes bibliography]

Fass, Paula S., "Richard Hofstadter," in Clyde N. Wilson, ed., *Twentieth-Century American Historians*, Detroit: Gale, 1983 [*Dictionary of Literary Biography*, vol. 17]

Schlesinger, Arthur M., Jr., "Richard Hofstadter," in Marcus Cunliffe and Robin Winks, eds., *Pastmasters: Some Essays on American Historians*, New York: Harper, 1969

Singal, Daniel J., "Beyond Consensus: Richard Hofstadter and American Historiography," *American Historical Review* 89 (1984), 976–1004

Holanda, S.B. de 1902–1982

Brazilian social historian

Sérgio Buarque de Holanda is well-known in Brazilian historiography, as well as in Brazilian 20th-century thought. A distinguished scholar, he combined accurate empirical work with erudite scholarship, giving rise to a new approach to and style of writing about the history of the country, and going far beyond the positivist (in a large sense) tradition, still widespread at the time. His works, written in an "essay style" pointed towards the history of culture and of mentality, as based upon both material objects and serious psychosocial analysis. His basic theoretical background was derived from his study of law and complemented by his experience in Germany. Working from 1929 to 1931 as a correspondent of the newspaper *O Jornal*, he settled in Berlin, covering the news in Poland and the former Soviet Union, as well as in Germany. This stay in the Weimar republic during such a rich and crucial moment was of paramount importance in Holanda's intellectual life, encouraging him to plunge deeply into anthropology, sociology, and social studies, and the theory and philosophy of history. German authors, especially Max Weber, would strongly influence Holanda's works, along with the new French social history represented by the Annales school.

His first book, *Raízes do Brasil* (Roots of Brazil, 1936), is undoubtedly Holanda's most important and well-known work despite the fact that he considered *Do império à república* (From the Empire to the Republic, 1972) to be more complete. *Raízes* was first published in 1936, and had gone through 22 editions by 1995. The book became a "classic" from the very beginning and provoked distinct and passionate reactions. Along with Gilberto Freyre's *Casa Grande e Senzala* (1933) and Caio Prado Junior's *Formação do Brasil contemporâneo* (1942; *The Colonial Background of Modern Brazil*, 1967), Holanda's book is integrated into a set of key works which appeared after the Revolution of 1930. These studies deeply influenced Brazilian social and political thought with an influx of radical and innovative ideas. The importance and impact of *Raízes* is also confirmed by its translation into Italian, Spanish, and Japanese. The central focus of Holanda's analysis was an understanding of why and how European culture flourished in a large, peculiar, tropical environment, totally foreign to its traditions, and the manners and consequences of this development. The book is structured according to a methodology of oppositions that leads to a nondogmatic, dialectical construction of historical discourse. Holanda used a modified version of Weber's typological criteria to establish pairs of ideals to stress particular characteristics, while trying to understand/explain the local historical process: "work" and "adventure," "methodic" versus "capricious" action, "rural" and "urban," and "bureaucracy" versus "caudillismo" permeate the text.

In a strong criticism of the authoritarian and hierarchic structure of Brazilian society, Holanda employed the Weberian concepts of "patrimonialism" and "bureaucracy" for the first time in Brazilian studies. The message of *Raízes* is clearly that the future development of Brazil depends on the death of its roots, which were already in the process of transformation through the movement from a rural to an urban society. Since this first book, Holanda's understanding that history must be linked to current questions has been crystal clear, an unequivocal reflection of his personal political position: in 1945 he helped to found the Democratic Left (later to become the Brazilian Socialistic party), and in 1980, shortly before his death, he was one of the founding fathers of the Workers' Party.

His attempt to clarify national identity was a constant throughout his academic life and pursuits. The seeds of this interest were already evident during the 1920s, when he became involved in the Modernist movement, and even co-founded and co-edited the magazine *Estética* (Aesthetics) in 1924. Literary criticism was Holanda's original calling, and he would never abandon it but rather use it to enrich his historical research.

Holanda was invited to join the University of the Federal District (in Rio de Janeiro) when it was founded in 1936. There, he was an assistant professor of economic history and comparative literature until 1939, when the institution was closed after conflicts with the dictator Getúlio Vargas. Immediately afterwards he was hired at the Instituto Nacional do Livro (National Book Institute), where he remained until 1943. During 1943–46 he worked in the Biblioteca Nacional (National Library), returning to São Paulo (his birthplace) in 1946 to become director of the Museu Paulista (São Paulo Museum of History). In this same year, his second book, *Monções* (Monsoons), was published. It dealt with the history of the "Bandeirantes" and the conquest of the western hinterlands by families of Portuguese origin who settled in São Paulo. Holanda directed the museum for a decade, which included the two years he spent at the University of Rome (1953–55) occupying the chair of Brazilian studies. In 1957 he left the museum for the University of São Paulo, and, to obtain the chair of history of civilizations. He defended in 1959 the thesis entitled *Visão do paraíso: os motivos edênicos no descobrimento e colonização do Brasil* (Vision of Paradise: "Utopian" Motivations in the Discovery and Colonization of Brazil), which was a masterpiece in the combination of erudite scholarship and analytical density, within a sophisticated theoretical framework. Holanda remained in the Department of History of the University of São Paulo until 1969, when he retired as part of an act of solidarity with his colleagues who were forced to compulsory retirement by the military government. Nevertheless, he continued to work intensively, publishing in newspapers as well as editing important reference collections, such as *História Geral da civilização brasileira* (General History of Brazilian Civilization), *História do Brasil* (Brazilian History) and *História da Civilização* (History of Civilization). His personal book collection was donated to the University of

Campinas (UNICAMP) in the state of São Paulo, and is now available for public consultation.

SILVIA FIGUEIRÔA

Biography

Sérgio Buarque de Holanda. Born São Paulo, 11 July 1902. Graduated law school in Rio de Janeiro, 1925. Founder/director, with Prudente de Moraes Neto, modernist magazine *Estética* (Aesthetics), 1924; European correspondent, *O Jornal* newspaper, Berlin, 1929–31; assistant professor, University of the Federal District, 1936–39; employed by the National Books Institute, 1939–43, and the National Library, 1943–46; director, Museu Paulista, 1946–57; full professor of the history of civilization, University of São Paulo, 1957–69; director, Institute of Brazilian Studies, 1958–68. Founder member, Brazilian Socialist party, 1945, and Workers' party, 1980. Married Maria Amélia Alvim Buarque, 1936 (4 daughters, and 3 sons including the musician, Chico Buarque). Died São Paulo, 24 April 1982.

Principal Writings

Raízes do Brasil (Roots of Brazil), 1936
Cobra de Vidro (Glass Snake), 1944
Monções (Monsoons), 1945
Caminhos e fronteiras (Paths and Frontiers), 1957
Visão do paraíso: os motivos edênicos no descobrimento e colonização do Brasil (Vision of Paradise: Utopian Motivations in the Discovery and Colonization of Brazil), 1959
General editor, *História Geral da civilização brasileira* (General History of Brazilian Civilization), 1960–77
Do império à república (From the Empire to the Republic), 1972
Tentativas de mitologia (Attempts at Mythology), 1979
O extremo oeste (The Far West), 1986

Further Reading

Cândido, Antonio, "O significado de *Raízes do Brasil*" (The Significance of *Raízes do Brasil*), in Sérgio B. de Holanda, *Raízes do Brasil*, Rio de Janeiro: Olympio, 1967 (preface to the 5th edition)
Capelato, Maria Helena R., Raquel Glezer, Vera L. do A. Ferlini, "A escola uspiana de história" (The Historical School of the University of São Paulo), in Maria Helena R. Capelato, ed., *Produção histórica no Brasil (1985–1994)*, São Paulo: Xamã, 1995
Coloquio UERJ, *Sérgio Buarque de Holanda*, Rio de Janeiro: Imago, 1992
Eulálio, Alexandre, "Sérgio Buarque de Holanda escritor," in Sérgio Buarque de Holanda, *Raízes do Brasil*, Rio de Janeiro: Olympio, 1986 (18th edition)
Graham, Richard, "An Interview with Sérgio Buarque de Holanda," *Hispanic American Historical Review* 62 (1982), 3–17

Holdsworth, W.S. 1871–1944

British legal historian

Holdsworth is one of the most well-known English legal historians of this century; indeed he is the only legal historian so far to have been awarded the Order of Merit by the British crown. His reputation rests largely on his *magnum opus*, *A History of English Law* (1903–66), in which he intended to provide a comprehensive picture of English law from the time of the Norman Conquest to 1875, as "Pollock and Maitland's

classic volumes only carry the history of English law down to the reign of Edward I." This project was published eventually in 16 volumes, 12 of them during his own lifetime, and the remainder under the hand of his literary executors, Arthur L. Goodhart and Harold G. Hanbury. Holdsworth's wish was that the book would demonstrate "the impossibility of gaining a complete grasp of the principles of English law without a study of their history." Almost a century later, this hope has, sadly, not been realized; no law school in England requires the mandatory study of English legal history and the subject has been consigned to the list of optional subjects offered by most law schools.

Assessments of Holdsworth's endeavors in his *History*, almost a century after the publication of the first volume (1903), are less generous than they were at the time of publication. Although recognized as a formidable achievement and a unique contribution to the literature of English law for its time – in Plucknett's view, without which no other short history of English law could be written with any degree of confidence – it can no longer be regarded as the definitive exposition that it perhaps once was. The main reason is that Holdsworth's assessment was based on extensive reading of secondary materials available to him during the period when he was engaged in its writing. Holdsworth did not have an intimate knowledge of the primary materials available to the contemporary legal historian in the Public Record Office. Thus the more recent scholarship of legal historians on both sides of the Atlantic, based on extensive study of these materials, now requires Holdsworth's *History* to be read with caution, especially in his treatment of law during the medieval period and, increasingly, that also of the post-medieval period.

The astonishing volume of work embodied in the *History* sometimes eclipses Holdsworth's quite extraordinary range of publications falling outside it. This is a pity, for there is much of interest here, both in his books and in his writings in scholarly journals, notably the *Law Quarterly Review*. Works like *Sources and Literature of English Law* (1925), *An historical Introduction to Land Law* (1927) and *The Historians of Anglo-American Law* (1928), have inevitably been superseded by modern treatises. Still useful, however, are his Storrs lectures at Yale in 1928, *Charles Dickens as a Legal Historian* (1928), recently reprinted in the USA and *Some Makers of English Law* (1938), the text of his Tagore lectures in Calcutta in 1937–38.

It is sometimes forgotten that Holdsworth was, towards the end of his life, a joint literary director of the Selden Society, although this distinguished body regarded him as "emphatically *primus inter pares*." As literary director, he was primarily responsible for the direction of the society's work together with his two colleagues, but he was also directly responsible, with M.D. Legge and J.P. Collas, for volumes 52 (1934), 54 (1935) and 61 (1942) in the Society's Year Books series, the *Year Book 10 Edward II (1316–17)* and *Year Book 11 Edward II (1317–18)*.

Not all of Holdsworth's formidable energies were channelled into legal historical endeavor, reflecting his equally well-known reputation as one of Oxford's great law teachers during the period when he was a fellow at St. John's College. His contributions on contemporary law, including "Case Law," "Constitutional Position of the Judges," "Reform of Land Law" and

"A Chapter of Accidents in the Law of Libel," are to be found in the *Law Quarterly Review*. Some of these were later gathered and published as *Essays in Law and History* (1946) by his literary executors.

Sir Percy Winfield, in his 1924 *Cambridge Law Journal* review of Holdsworth's *Sources* remarked that "[he] has the gift of putting the reader on a height from which he can get a bird's-eye view of the external causes which have shaped the growth of English law." Much the same could be said of all his writing, the result, perhaps, of his training both as historian and as lawyer.

STEPHEN D. GIRVIN

See also Legal; Milsom; Simpson

Biography
Born Elmer's End, Kent, 7 May 1871. Educated at Dulwich College; New College, Oxford, BA in history 1893, BA in law 1894, MA, BCL 1897, DCL 1904. Called to the Bar, 1895; lecturer, New College, 1895; vice-president, St. John's College, Oxford 1902-03; professor of constitutional law, University College, London, 1903-08; fellow, St. John's College, 1897-1922; All Souls' reader in English law, 1910-22; Vinerian professor in English law, 1922-44; reader in constitutional law, Inns of Court, 1937-44. Married Jessie Annie Amelia Gilbert Wood, 1903 (1 son). Knighted 1929; Order of Merit 1943. Died Oxford, 2 January 1944.

Principal Writings
A History of English Law, 16 vols., 1903-66 [5 revised editions]
Sources and Literature of English Law, 1925
An Historical Introduction to the Land Law, 1927
The Historians of Anglo-American Law, 1928
Charles Dickens as a Legal Historian, 1928
Some Lessons from Our Legal History, 1928
Some Makers of English Law, 1938
Essays in Law and History, edited by A.L. Goodhart and H.G. Hanbury, 1946

Further Reading
Baker, J.H., "Sir William Searle Holdsworth" in A.W.B. Simpson, *A Biographical Dictionary of the Common Law*, London: Butterworth, and St. Paul, MN: Mason, 1984
Goff, Robert, *A Voyage round Holdsworth*, Birmingham: Holdsworth Club, 1988
Goodhart, Arthur L., *Sir William Searle Holdsworth, O.M. (1871-1944)*, London: Quaritch, 1954
Hanbury, Harold G., *The Vinerian Chair and Legal Education*, Oxford: Blackwell, 1958
"In Memoriam Sir William Searle Holdsworth," *Law Quarterly Review* 60 (1944), 138-59
Lawson, Frederick H., *The Oxford Law School, 1850-1965*, Oxford: Clarendon Press, 1968
Plucknett, T.F.T., *A Concise History of the Common Law*, London: Butterworth, 1929; 5th edition 1956

Holinshed, Raphael *fl.*1560-1580

English chronicler

As a historian, Raphael Holinshed is known for the English chronicles that bear his name. However, while Holinshed is listed as the author, the chronicles were actually by a group of authors. Holinshed himself is thought to have been the son of Ralph Holinshed of Cheshire and may have served as steward to Thomas Burdet of Bromcote, Warwickshire. He was educated, probably at Cambridge, and had taken orders. The original instigator of the project was Reginald Wolfe, a printer originally from Strasbourg. The idea was to produce a universal history and cosmography, somewhat on the lines of medieval encyclopedias and chronicles. Wolfe had hired Holinshed as an assistant, but Holinshed came to dominate the project after Wolfe's death in 1573. The final product was not a universal history but a history of England, Ireland, and Scotland. The first edition was published in 1577. Other contributors to the work included William Harrison who wrote the *Description of England*, and Richard Stanyhurst who wrote the *Description of Ireland* and the history of Ireland that had been outlined by Edmund Campion.

The chronicle was so popular that a new edition was planned soon after the publication of the first, and at Holinshed's death in 1580, the group of publishers and historians expanded to include Ralph Newberie, Henry Denham, Thomas Woodcock, John Hooker (Vowell), Abraham Fleming, Francis Boteville (Thynne), and John Stow. Who was considered most responsible for the edition of 1587 has been a subject of disagreement, with some agreeing with the *Dictionary of National Biography* that Hooker was in charge, while others support the claim of Abraham Fleming.

The chronicles themselves are still used as a source by historians of medieval and early modern English history, but they are best known as one of Shakespeare's main sources for the history plays. Annabel Patterson discusses the main historiographical arguments about the chronicles. Besides the above-stated contention that they are important only as a source for Shakespeare, they have been criticized on the grounds of not presenting history as a grand design, as they are unanalytical, random, and disorderly, yet, conversely, of having a grand design – that of bolstering the status quo. Patterson's own view is that Holinshed and his collaborators, by making every reader his own historian, were demonstrating the complexity and danger of life in post-Reformation England and that their goals were to preserve endangered records as well as to be a multivocal expression of national history that represented both the Protestants and the Catholics as well as being a better representation of various classes of society.

While the primary use of the chronicles has been as an adjunct for Shakespearean scholars, historians are also finding that the inclusion of many documents and the multivocal nature of the work have value in elucidating the social and political realities and tensions of the time.

SHARON D. MICHALOVE

See also Britain: 1066-1485

Principal Writings
The Chronicles of England, Scotland and Ireland, 1577

Further Reading
Clegg, Cyndia Susan, "Which Holinshed? Holinshed's *Chronicles* at the Huntington Library," *Huntington Library Quarterly* 55 (1994), 559-77

Donno, Elizabeth Story, "Some Aspects of Shakespeare's Holinshed," *Huntington Library Quarterly* 50 (1987), 229–48

Parry, G.J.R., "William Harrison and Holinshed's Chronicles," *Historical Journal* 27 (1984), 789–810

Patterson, Annabel, *Reading Holinshed's Chronicles*, Chicago: University of Chicago Press, 1994

Holocaust

For an event as convulsive as the Holocaust, it is not surprising that so much has been written about it. Its incredible scale of human destruction demands explanation. Excellent studies explain Nazism's rise to power, the popular support the movement received for its apocalyptic version of national reconstruction, its quest for a new racial world order, and the culture and ecology of survival. In spite of contrary opinion, they prove that the Holocaust is comprehensible.

Some writers, motivated by an intention to avenge evil or apportion blame – or, conversely, to commemorate victims and survivors – have sought a different kind of explanation, as in the question, "Exactly how do you explain yourself?" It is important to distinguish, therefore between two ways of recalling and explaining the Holocaust era: history and memory. The latter is a communal response: to hold on to entire lost communities, literally an act of remembrance, or to compensate, however inadequately, for the brutal, relentless assault by seeking justice or by venting understandable anger. Many memoirs, naturally (but certainly not all; notable exceptions are cited below), a legion of curriculum guides (unfortunately), and more than a few early monographs appeal primarily to this limited audience.

History, which deserves our attention here, offers answers to such questions as, What led Germany, and eventually all of Europe, into total war? Why did so few abstain from common racial anti-Semitism, let alone resist its destructive impulses? Why were Jews eventually singled out for extinction? How did Jews manage to endure under dreadful circumstances? (There are surely other questions, and other countries than Germany that have commanded attention, but for the most part these are not the subject of this brief essay.)

Not all these questions preoccupied writers at the same time. Before the explosion of popular interest in the subject in the late 1970s, most writers and the general public wanted to know more about the Nazi tyranny that the free world, by mobilizing considerable resources at significant cost, had recently defeated. William L. Shirer's *The Rise and Fall of the Third Reich* (1960) and Alan Bullock's *Hitler* (1952) were two studies that examined the seeds of political destruction in the personalities of its main perpetrators. Other studies, such as Hans Kohn's *The Mind of Germany* (1962) and Hajo Holborn's *A History of Modern Germany, 1840–1945* (1969) cut a wider swathe to explain how Germany, of all places, charted so disastrous a course, exemplifying an almost irresistible scholarly temptation to rewrite German history in Hitler's shadow. In addition, already in the early 1950s, two important studies delineated the scope of the Nazi assault on Jews: *Bréviaire de la haine* (1951; *Harvest of Hate*, 1954) by Léon Poliakov, and *The Final Solution* (1953) by Gerald Reitlinger.

At the time of the intensely observed Eichmann trial in 1961 two seminal works appeared that have left a lasting impression of the lethal if antiseptic mind at work in the Nazi regime. In *Eichmann in Jerusalem* (1963) Hannah Arendt proposed the still-astonishing thesis that Nazi technocrats committed murder, indeed mass murder (that may be part of the explanation), routinely and remorselessly: their "normality was much more terrifying than all the atrocities put together." Raul Hilberg, in *The Destruction of the European Jews* (1961), soberly and exhaustively examined the bureaucratic network that set the "machinery of destruction" (Hilberg's memorable phrase) in motion.

More recently, scholars have exposed wider circles of complicity beyond the regime itself. Christopher Browning, in *Ordinary Men* (1992), has shown convincingly how middle-ranking field officers, trained to fight and win wars, became ruthless, continuous killers of innocent men and women. Most, given a choice by their commanders, elected to participate in the killings. In *Death and Deliverance* (1994), Michael Burleigh provided important context for how euthanasia became acceptable practice in dealing with people deemed dubious and superfluous. The deadly ramifications of state-sponsored eugenics programs were explored in Henry Friedlander's *The Origins of Nazi Genocide* (1995). He argued that these programs effectively honed both skills and disposition of individuals, such as Franz Stangl and Christian Wirth, who eventually became death camp supervisors.

But perhaps the most fertile area of research for showing just how thoroughly Germans rejected or callously neglected Nazi victims is the complicity of professionals – attorneys, doctors and scientists, students and teachers, and theologians. In this area scholars have recently shattered two assumptions: that an advanced civilization is equipped with the necessary means to resist barbarous behavior, and that a society's cultural and literate elite is determined to make sure such a civilization remains civil.

In *Psychotherapy in the Third Reich* (1985), Geoffrey Cocks showed this profession's mistreatment of the mentally ill. In *Theologians under Hitler* (1985), Robert P. Ericksen discussed three internationally prominent Protestant leaders who welcomed Hitler's ascendancy and championed the notorious "stab-in-the-back" interpretation of Germany's defeat in World War I. Even though leading physicists, exploring the feasibility of obtaining fission for making atomic weapons, regarded Hitler with contempt, David Cassidy's *Uncertainty* (1992) raised disquieting questions about Heisenberg's willingness to conduct such ominous research at Nazi officials' behest.

At least five key studies since the mid-1980s demonstrated persuasively that many more than a handful of physicians, implicated in medical crimes in the late 1940s, regarded killing innocent "undesirables" as the most thorough means of healing the German nation: Robert Jay Lifton's *The Nazi Doctors* (1986), Benno Müller-Hill's *Tödliche Wissenschaft* (1984; *Murderous Science*, 1988), Robert N. Proctor's *Racial Hygiene* (1988), Michael H. Kater's *Doctors under Hitler* (1989), and Arthur L. Caplan's *When Medicine Went Mad* (1992).

Then there are studies of everyday life that suggest universal German support for Nazi evil. Gordon J. Horwitz's *In the Shadow of Death* (1990) scrutinized the behavior and rationalizations of Mauthausen death camp's nearby townspeople. More condemning, and more controversial, was Daniel Jonah

Goldhagen's *Hitler's Willing Executioners* (1996). Goldhagen argued that "eliminationist" anti-Semitism was entrenched in German society; Germans, believing annihilation of Jews was not merely defensible, but also necessary and just, were zealous killers.

How did Jews respond? What hope existed for them, real or imagined (under hopeless circumstances, the latter was more critical than the former)? Here, too, perspectives and emphases have changed over time. Take the Anne Frank story, for example. When *The Diary of a Young Girl* was published in America in 1952, few read it as anything more than a sensitive story of Anne's adolescent struggle to grow into a woman. The Holocaust and her Jewishness remained in the background, virtually invisible. (This is especially true for the 1955 play and 1959 film versions.)

The story received a new reading in 1987 when Miep Gies published *Anne Frank Remembered*. The point of view shifted from the young girl in hiding to the woman (and her husband Jan, "Henk" in the *Diary*) who ran the risk of hiding Anne and her family. It shifted again shortly afterward with the release of the film *The Last Seven Months of Anne Frank* and the publication in 1989 of the Anti-Defamation League (ADL) course of study by Karen Shawn, *The End of Innocence: Anne Frank and the Holocaust*. Both restored ambient terror to the foreground of her life, where, in spite of Anne's inner as well as physical flight from it, it surely belongs. Along the same lines, Lawrence Graver, in *An Obsession with Anne Frank* (1995), recounted Meyer Levin's futile efforts to preserve Anne's Jewishness in the story.

In similar fashion, firsthand renderings of day-to-day struggles to survive Nazi terror have grown in scope, taking into consideration new dimensions of Jewish life in extreme circumstances. The first postwar accounts were largely survivors' memoirs. Alexander Donat's *The Holocaust Kingdom* (1965), Elie Wiesel's *Un di velt hot geshvign* (1956; *Night* 1960) and Primo Levi's *Se questo e un uomo* (1958; *If This Is a Man*, 1959) remain among the most poignant recollections of the death camps. There are literally thousands of personal accounts, each its own story, on tape or in published or manuscript form. Diaries, too, have surfaced. Among the most enduring are insights into the Warsaw ghetto: Emmanuel Ringelblum's *Notes from the Warsaw Ghetto* (1952, translated 1958), *The Warsaw Diary of Chaim A. Kaplan* (1966, translated 1973), Janusz Korczak's *Ghetto Diary* (1978), Vladka Meed's *On Both Sides of the Wall* (1948, translated 1979), *The Warsaw Diary of Adam Czerniakow* (1979), and Yitzhak Zuckerman's *A Surplus of Memory* (1990, translated 1993).

Eventually, in the 1980s and 1990s, two dimensions of survivors' experiences became distinct subjects of personal testimonies: Jews and their rescuers, and Jews as "hidden children." Interestingly, the most memorable rescue stories to date are profiled in secondary sources, such as *The Moses of Rovno* (1985) by Douglas Huneke, *When Light Pierced the Darkness* (1986) by Nechama Tec, *The Altruistic Personality* (1988) by Samuel P. Oliner and Pearl M. Oliner, *Rescuers* (1992) – an arresting photographic essay by Gay Block and Malka Drucker – *The Path of the Righteous* (1993) by Mordecai Paldiel, and *Conscience and Courage* (1994) by Eva Fogelman.

Two books examined the extraordinary phenomenon of collective rescue: Leo Goldberger's *The Rescue of the Danish Jews* (1987) and Philip Hallie's *Lest Innocent Blood Be Shed* (1979), the story of some 5000 French villagers who sheltered about 5000 Jewish refugees.

Even though Anne Frank's ordeal is a story of a child in hiding, the hidden experience of Jewish child survivors – a natural counterpart to rescuer portraits – became a special subject of survivors' self-discovery and public fascination only in the early 1990s. This is not to say there weren't isolated but significant accounts before then. Anne Frank's journal is the obvious example. *Quand vient le souvenir* (1978; *When Memory Comes*, 1979), Saul Friedlander's account of his childhood life under the protection of a Catholic family, is still one of the most significant accounts of young Jews passing, and surviving, as Christians (he discovered that he was Jewish in 1946, just after he decided to enter a Jesuit seminary to prepare for the priesthood.) So is Nechama Tec's compassionately rendered *Dry Tears* (1982). But the hidden-child genre acquired momentum in 1991 with an article on the subject in *New York* magazine by Jane Marks (the basis of her book two years later called *The Hidden Children*, 1993) and the ADL's 1991 First International Gathering of Children Hidden during World War II. Two especially noteworthy memoirs appearing at the time were *Memory Fields* (1993) by Shlomo Breznitz ("People whom I loved kept disappearing") and *Wartime Lies* (1991) by Louis Begley.

What surprises many observers is the unabated publication of new books more that 50 years after the event. But the Holocaust refers to something more than its central, unavoidable horror. Each year new accounts broaden understanding and challenge presuppositions – studies of the German medical profession's unsuspected widespread involvement in genocide, observations on the "banality of evil," and reflections on exceptional rescuers, to name a few such major inquiries. Occasionally even a single book generates considerable public discussion. Jane Marks' *The Hidden Children*, Daniel Goldhagen's *Hitler's Willing Executioners*, Thomas Keneally's *Schindler's List* (1982) – the subject of Steven Spielberg's 1994 film – and Raul Hilberg's *The Destruction of the European Jews* stand out as examples of the Holocaust's unexpected currency. Some have noted that, when the survivor generations are gone, as they soon will be, few will remain to fuel interest and provide a sense of immediacy. Indeed these generations' formative influence on the field will be a thing of the past, but all signs point to sustained study of these themes.

DENNIS B. KLEIN

See also Braham; Broszat; Documentary; Dubnov; Elkins; Ethnicity; Germany: 1450–1800; Germany: 1800–1945; Hilberg; Jewish; Koonz; Marrus; Mayer; Memory; Mommsen, H.; Mosse; Oral; Poland: since the 18th Century; Poliakov; Russia: Modern

Further Reading

Arendt, Hannah, *Eichmann in Jerusalem: A Report on the Banality of Evil*, New York: Viking, 1963; Harmondsworth, Middlesex: Penguin, 1964; revised 1965

Begley, Louis, *Wartime Lies*, New York: Knopf, 1991; London: Picador, 1992

Block, Gay, and Malka Drucker, *Rescuers: Portraits of Moral Courage in the Holocaust*, New York: Holmes and Meier, 1992

Breznitz, Shlomo, *Sedot ha-zikaron*, Tel Aviv: 'Am 'oved, 1993; in English as *Memory Fields*, New York: Knopf, 1993

Browning, Christopher, *Ordinary Men: Reserve Police Battalion 101 and the Final Solution in Poland*, New York: HarperCollins, 1992

Bullock, Alan, *Hitler: A Study in Tyranny*, London: Odhams, and New York: Harper, 1952; revised 1958

Burleigh, Michael, *Death and Deliverance: "Euthanasia" in Germany, 1900–1945*, Cambridge and New York: Cambridge University Press, 1994

Caplan, Arthur L., *When Medicine Went Mad: Bioethics and the Holocaust*, Totowa, NJ: Humana, 1992

Cassidy, David, *Uncertainty: The Life and Science of Werner Heisenberg*, New York: Freeman, 1992

Cocks, Geoffrey, *Psychotherapy in the Third Reich: The Göring Institute*, New York: Oxford University Press, 1985

Czerniakow, Adam, *Dziennik getta warszawskiego*; in English as *The Warsaw Diary of Adam Czerniakow: Prelude to Doom*, New York: Stein and Day, 1979

Dawidowicz, Lucy, *The War Against the Jews, 1933–1945*, New York: Holt Rinehart, and London: Weidenfeld and Nicolson, 1975

Des Pres, Terrence, *The Survivor: An Anatomy of the Life in the Death Camps*, Oxford and New York: Oxford University Press, 1976

Dimensions: A Journal of Holocaust Studies, edited by Dennis B. Klein, 1985–

Donat, Alexander, *The Holocaust Kingdom: A Memoir*, New York: Holt Rinehart, and London: Secker and Warburg, 1965

Erickson, Robert P., *Theologians under Hitler: Gerhard Kittel, Paul Althaus, and Emanuel Hirsch*, New Haven: Yale University Press, 1985

Fogelman, Eva, *Conscience and Courage: Rescuers of Jews During the Holocaust*, New York: Anchor, 1994

Frank, Anne, *Het achterhuis: dagboekbrieven 12 juni 1942–1 augustus 1944*, Amsterdam: Contact, 1947; in English as *The Diary of a Young Girl*, New York: Doubleday, and London: Constellation, 1952

Friedlander, Henry, *The Origins of Nazi Genocide: From Euthanasia to the Final Solution*, Chapel Hill: University of North Carolina Press, 1995

Friedlander, Saul, *Quand vient le souvenir*, Paris: Seuil, 1978; in English as *When Memory Comes*, New York: Farrar Straus, 1979

Gies, Miep, *Anne Frank Remembered: The Story of the Woman Who Helped to Hide the Frank Family*, New York: Simon and Schuster, 1987; London: Corgi, 1988

Goldberger, Leo, *The Rescue of the Danish Jews: Moral Courage under Stress*, New York: New York University Press, 1987

Goldhagen, Daniel, *Hitler's Willing Executioners: Ordinary Germans and the Holocaust*, New York: Knopf, and London: Little Brown, 1996

Graver, Lawrence, *An Obsession with Anne Frank: Meyer Levin and the Diary*, Berkeley: University of California Press, 1995

Hallie, Philip, *Lest Innocent Blood Be Shed*, New York: Harper, 1979

Hilberg, Raul, *The Destruction of the European Jews*, Chicago: Quandrangle, and London: W.H. Allen, 1961; revised in 3 vols., 1985

Holborn, Hajo, *A History of Modern Germany*, vol. 3: *1840–1945*, New York: Knopf, and London: Eyre and Spottiswoode, 1969

Horwitz, Gordon J., *In the Shadow of Death: Living Outside the Gates of Mauthausen*, New York: Free Press, 1990

Huneke, Douglas, *The Moses of Rovno: The Stirring Story of Fritz Graebe Who Risked his Life to Lead Hundreds of Jews to Safety during the Holocaust*, New York: Dodd Mead, 1985

Kaplan, Chaim A., *Megilat yisurin*, Tel Aviv: 'Am 'oved, 1966; in English as *The Warsaw Diary of Chaim A. Kaplan*, New York: Collier, 1973

Kater, Michael H., *Doctors under Hitler*, Chapel Hill: University of North Carolina Press, 1989

Katz, Steven T., *The Holocaust in Historical Context: The Holocaust and Mass Death before the Modern Age*, New York: Oxford University Press, 1994

Keneally, Thomas, *Schindler's Ark*, London: Hodder and Stoughton 1982; as *Schindler's List*, New York: Simon and Schuster, 1982

Kohn, Hans, *The Mind of Germany*, London: Macmillan, 1962; New York: Scribner, 1963

Korczak, Janusz, *Pamietnik z getta*; in English as *Ghetto Diary*, New York: Holocaust Library, 1978

Levi, Primo, *Se questo e un uomo*, Turin: Einaudi, 1958; in English as *If This Is a Man*, New York: Orion Press, 1959; London: Bodley Head, 1966

Lifton, Robert Jay, *The Nazi Doctors: Medical Killing and the Psychology of Genocide*, New York: Basic Books, and London: Macmillan, 1986

Marks, Jane, *The Hidden Children: The Secret Survivors of the Holocaust*, New York: Fawcett Columbine, 1993

Marrus, Michael R., *The Holocaust in History*, Hanover, NH: University Press of New England, 1987

Marrus, Michael R., ed., *The Nazi Holocaust: Historical Articles on the Destruction of European Jews*, 9 vols., Westport, CT: Meckler, 1989

Meed, Vladka [Feygele Peltel Myendzizshetski], *Fun beyde zayt geto-moyer*, New York, 1948; in English as *On Both Sides of the Wall: Memoirs of the Warsaw Ghetto*, New York: Holocaust Library, 1979

Müller-Hill, Benno, *Tödliche Wissenschaft: die Aussonderung von Juden, Zigeunern und Geisteskranken, 1933–1945*, Hamburg: Rowohlt, 1984; in English as *Murderous Science: Elimination by Scientific Selection of Jews, Gypsies, and Others, 1933–1945*, New York and Oxford: Oxford University Press, 1988

Oliner, Samuel P., and Pearl M. Oliner, *The Altruistic Personality: Rescuers of Jews in Nazi Europe*, New York, Free Press, and London: Collier Macmillan, 1988

Paldiel, Mordecai, *The Path of the Righteous: Gentile Rescuers of Jews during the Holocaust*, Hoboken NJ: Ktav, 1993

Poliakov, Léon, *Bréviaire de la haine: le IIIe Reich et les Juifs*, Paris: Calmann Lévy, 1951; in English as *Harvest of Hate: The Nazi Program for the Destruction of the Jews of Europe*, Syracuse, NY: Syracuse University Press, 1954; London: Elek, 1956

Proctor, Robert N., *Racial Hygiene: Medicine under the Nazis*, Cambridge, MA: Harvard University Press, 1988

Reitlinger, Gerald, *The Final Solution: The Attempt to Exterminate the Jews of Europe, 1939–1945*, London: Vallentine Mitchell, and New York: Beechhurst, 1953; revised 1968

Ringelblum, Emmanuel, *Notitsn fun varshever geto*, Warsaw: Yiddish Book, 1952; in English as *Notes from the Warsaw Ghetto*, New York: McGraw Hill, 1958

Shirer, William L., *The Rise and Fall of the Third Reich: A History of Nazi Germany*, New York: Simon and Schuster, and London: Secker and Warburg, 1960

Tec, Nechama, *Dry Tears: The Story of a Lost Childhood*, Westport CT: Wildcat, 1982

Tec, Nechama, *When Light Pierced the Darkness: Christian Rescue of Jews in Nazi-Occupied Poland*, New York: Oxford University Press, 1986

Wiesel, Elie, *Un di velt hot geshvign*, Buenos Aires: Tsantral-fahrbund fun Poulishe Yedn in Argentina, 1956; in English as *Night*, New York: Hill and Wang, and London: MacGibbon and Kee, 1960

Young, James, *Writing and Rewriting the Holocaust: Narrative of the Consequences of Interpretation*, Bloomington: University of Indiana Press, 1988

Zuckerman, Yitzhak, *Shev' ha-shanim ha-hen, 1939–46*, Tel Aviv: ha-Kibuts ha-me'uhad, 1990; in English as *A Surplus of Memory: Chronicle of the Warsaw Ghetto Uprising*, Berkeley: University of California Press, 1993

Holy Roman Empire

In the English-speaking world, study of the series of institutions and ideas known collectively as the "Holy Roman empire" (from the late 15th century sometimes the "Holy Roman Empire of the German Nation" [Heiliges Römisches Reich deutscher Nation]) has been decisively influenced by two works: James Bryce's *The Holy Roman Empire* (1864), and Geoffrey Barraclough's *The Origins of Modern Germany* (1946). The two works are synthesizing and broad. Each represents a significantly different image of the empire: Bryce tied its history closely to that of Rome, beginning the story with Augustus; Barraclough tied its history (as his title implies) to the late 19th-century nation-state of Germany.

The term "Holy Roman empire" refers to a constitutional tradition particularly tied to various central European sites, including Aachen, Frankfurt am Main, Regensburg, and Rome. The emperors and empresses who claimed ties to this tradition also at times claimed rights and privileges over a "Kingdom of Italy" (often tied to Milan or Pavia) and one of Burgundy, often tied to Arles. The political unit connected with this term and these places shifted significantly in compass, claims, and cohesion over the course of European history. In the 19th century, claims to these imperial traditions were advanced by politicians from a variety of European political units, including the nation-states of France and Germany. Twentieth-century claims to connections with Holy Roman imperial traditions by leading members of the National Socialist party in Germany and their supporters, have largely led to the rejection of the term's explicit usage in late 20th-century political parlance.

Bryce, trained in law and eventually a member of Parliament in Great Britain and British ambassador to the United States, wrote the original essay on which his book is based in 1862. Following a semester in Heidelberg in 1863, he published the work in 1864 in a 176-page edition. In the years to come this work would be oft-published and revised. The paperback edition available today contains over 530 pages. It has been reissued or reprinted at least 36 times.

Influenced by Italian nationalism (Bryce reportedly almost volunteered to join the Italian nationalist leader Garibaldi's forces), Bryce sought to describe the empire "as an institution or system." He connected the empire to classical antiquity, an antiquity about which he was thoroughly trained, writing: "The Empire . . . was the same which the crafty nephew of Julius had won for himself . . . and which had preserved almost unaltered through 18 centuries of time."

This work, influenced by German nationalists eager to discredit the Habsburg dynasty's universalizing claims, set the tone for seeing the empire as an institution whose days were past. The picture painted was one of decline, and the Habsburg emperors had ruled over an empire that "was to Germany a mere clog and incumbrance, which the unhappy nation bore because she knew not how to rid herself of it."

Bryce's emphasis on the empire's "decay" or "decline" was echoed in the English-language literature. This literature built on north German nationalist conceptions of "Germany" in the late 19th and early 20th centuries. Edwin Zeydel's work *The Holy Roman Empire in German Literature* (1918) can stand for a variety of works whose authors chose to describe the empire in negative terms, as holding Germany back from its destiny. Zeydel wrote that, from the mid-11th century, the "torpid, retrogressive Empire continued to exist for nearly five and a half centuries, decaying gradually at the core, until it became a mass of putridity, one of the most colossal jokes and striking paradoxes in all history." But, "as soon as the musty imperial organisms had been buried, the country rapidly advanced toward political unity."

Synthesizing such ideas, Geoffrey Barraclough produced an essay in the mid-1940s which remains one of the standard English-language works on the subject of the Holy Roman empire. Trying to understand the political developments in Germany in the early 20th century, developments which had contributed to a major war and tremendous human, political, and social destruction, Barraclough took a clinical stance and posited in his *The Origins of Modern Germany* that "German history . . . is a story of discontinuity, of development cut short, of incompleteness and retardation" but "accurate diagnosis is the first step towards care, and accurate diagnosis of the causes of maladies in the body politic is an essential function of the historian." The problem with Germany's history had been that progress toward national unity and representative institutions had been postponed. This postponement could be traced to the Holy Roman empire and back to the 11th century.

Barraclough and Bryce, with their emphases on the retarding or regressive nature of the antinational institutional arrangements of the Holy Roman empire, do not represent the only interpretations of these imperial traditions. For example, there is a French school, represented by historians such as Jean Henri Dunant, who sought to tie imperial pretensions to the Holy Roman empire and then the Napoleonic dynasty. Presenting an alternative view of the European past, some French historiography has challenged German claims to the imperial legacy. (These modern German claims have even gone so far as to take aspects of Holy Roman imperial symbolism such as the eagle and the colors black and gold and associate them with the Federal Republic of Germany.)

Friedrich Heer has also presented a different image of the empire, one that points toward recent developments in the direction of European political and economic integration. Heer offered another alternative to simply seeing the Holy Roman empire as a check on "natural" German nationalist development. In his *Das Heilige Römische Reich* (1967; *The Holy Roman Empire*, 1968) Heer argued that the Holy Roman empire "eludes the categories of political theorizers who think in terms of the nation state." He preferred to sketch broadly, tying the empire not simply to Augustus and conquest, as Bryce chose to, but to Mesopotamia, Sumeria, Babylon, and Assyria, an "age-old sacral-political order." To Heer, the empire was more an idea, an idea tied to insignia and symbols, not to places or people speaking a particular language.

Since Heer, a slight revision of the image of the Holy Roman empire has been taking place. This empire's multinational, multi-ethnic traditions have come more to the fore. Historians have worked to understand not how the empire failed, but how it managed to survive. As the 20th century ends, the creation of structures of political authority that can survive seems to be increasingly of interest.

JOSEPH F. PATROUCH

See also Counter-Reformation; Ecclesiastical; Germany: 1450–1800; Hartung; Reformation; Rörig; Spain: Imperial; Srbik

Further Reading

Barraclough, Geoffrey, *The Origins of Modern Germany*, Oxford: Blackwell, 1946, revised 1947; New York: Capricorn, 1963

Birot, Jean, *Le Saint Empire du couronnement de Charlemagne au sacre de Napoléon* (The Holy Empire from the Coronation of Charlemagne until the Anointing of Napoleon), Paris: Lecoffre, 1903

Bryce, James, *The Holy Roman Empire*, Oxford: Shrimpton, 1864, revised 1866; reprinted New York: Schocken, 1966

Butler, Charles, *A Connected Series of Notes on the Chief Revolutions of the Principle States Which Composed the Empire of Charlemagne from His Coronation in 814 to Its Dissolution in 1806*, London: White, 1807

Comyn, Robert Buckley, *The History of the Western Empire: From Its Restoration by Charlemagne to the Accession of Charles V*, London: Allen, 1851

Dunant, Jean Henri, *L'Empire de Charlemagne rétabli; ou, Le Saint-Empire romain reconstitué par Sa Majesté l'empereur Napoléon III* (The Empire of Charlemagne Re-established; or, The Holy Roman Empire Reconstituted by His Majesty the Emperor Napoleon III), Geneva: Fick, 1859

Dunham, Samuel Astley, *History of the Germanic Empire*, 3 vols., London: Longman, 1834–35

Heiss, Johann von, *The History of the German Empire from Charlemagne, Down to the Present Emperor Charles VI, Being a Continuation of Mr. Echard's Roman History*, 2 vols., London: Gulliver, 1731

Heer, Friedrich, *Das Heilige Römische Reich*, Bern: Scherz, 1967; in English as *The Holy Roman Empire*, New York: Praeger, 1968

Jacob, Ernest Fraser, *Holy Roman Empire*, London: Benn, 1928

"Politics and Society in the Holy Roman Empire, 1500–1806" [supplementary issue], *Journal of Modern History* 58 (1986)

Reinhardt, Kurt F., *Germany 2000 Years*, vol. 1: *The Rise and Fall of the "Holy Empire,"* Milwaukee: Bruce, 1950; revised 1962

Strauss, Gerald, "The Holy Roman Empire Revisited," *Central European History* 11 (1978), 290–301

Zeydel, Edwin Hermann, *The Holy Roman Empire in German Literature*, New York: Columbia University Press, 1918; reprinted New York: AMS, 1966

Zophy, Jonathan W., *The Holy Roman Empire: A Dictionary Handbook*, Westport, CT: Greenwood Press, 1980

Zophy, Jonathan W., *An Annotated Bibliography of the Holy Roman Empire*, New York: Greenwood Press, 1986

Homosexuality

The history of same-sex erotic activity, of homosexuality, "queer history," the study of gays and lesbians in the past: this variety of names together outline a field of vigorous scholarly production. They hint as well at the centrality of theoretical and political questions in this relatively new area of historical research. Rooted in women's history, the new social history, and the Gay Liberation movement of the 1960s and 1970s, the "history of homosexuality" has been part of an interdisciplinary wave of gay/lesbian and queer studies. Historians have brought a range of different methods and approaches to their exploration of the queer past. An increasing number of current scholars, however, place their work in a broader history of sex (cross-sex, intergenerational, onanistic, ritualistic, etc.) and sexuality framework. They insist that these concerns are critical to any understanding of how people interacted in the past.

While some current historians occasionally mine the seminal work of British writers Edward Carpenter and John Addington Symonds or the Germans Magnus Hirschfeld or Karl Heinrich Ulrichs, most current works in this field have a more recent genealogy, in which the first volume of Michel Foucault's *Histoire de la sexualité* (1976; *History of Sexuality*, 1978), must be given pride of place. Foucault's articulation of the construction of a homosexual identity has superseded the somewhat earlier discussions of the topic by sociologist Mary McIntosh or historians Jeffrey Weeks and Jonathan Ned Katz. Foucault described the emergence of a species of human subject in the 19th century whose personal development and very being would lead her or him to lust after or love others of the same gender. He distinguished this development from a pre-existing cultural discourse in the West in which acts of sodomy, prohibited and on occasion actively punished, were assumed to be universal temptations.

Studies by Kenneth J. Dover and John Boswell were critical to professional historians' (still tentative) acceptance of the historical exploration of same-sex sexuality. Dover's *Greek Homosexuality* (1978), the work of one of the pre-eminent scholars of the classical world, gave a disciplinary imprimateur to a usually disdained academic focus. John Boswell's *Christianity, Social Tolerance, and Homosexuality* (1980) received wide attention and also helped establish the study of what Boswell called "gay persons" in the past. Boswell maintained a distinction between homosexual acts and homosexual identity, yet contrary to Foucault and others he argued that both have always existed. Some critics of Boswell raised important methodological and ideological questions regarding the ahistoricity of Boswell's claims about the universality of "gay people" and gay communities. Although Foucault himself praised the book as "groundbreaking," the concerns of American social constructionists about the work highlight one of the central debates among historians of homosexualities.

Boswell is not the only scholar to reject the social construction thesis as it relates to sexual identity. Some historians of female homosexuality and lesbianism further attenuate the relation of acts to identity. Lillian Faderman and Carroll Smith-Rosenberg depended on arguments associated with American cultural feminism to re-evaluate past emotional bonds between women. Faderman's *Surpassing the Love of Men* (1981) and Smith-Rosenberg's more compelling *Disorderly Conduct* (1985) proclaimed an understanding of identity informed by female/female love that rejects a coital determinism. Biographers, such as Blanche Wiesen Cook in her study of Eleanor Roosevelt, have pursued these insights with great vigor. Yet Martha Vicinus reminded readers that besides "neglecting both the element of sexual object-choice and of marginal status that was (and continues to be) so important in lesbian relations" the "female friendship" model ignored the different histories of women not of the middle class.

Biography has proven one of the most contested as well as popular forms of research into past homosexual lives. Biographers, such as Cook on Eleanor Roosevelt, too often reduced their subjects' thoughts and actions to expressions of a putative gay or lesbian identity. Many have ignored the troubling challenges to the very concepts of the coherent subject, identity, and the definitions of sex, desire, and pleasure contained in the theories of Foucault, Gayle Rubin, and Joan W. Scott, or in recent histories by George Chauncey, Laura Engelstein, Randolph Trumbach, or Lisa Duggan.

In foregrounding the particularities of same-sex sexual activity in the past, both as activity and as it was represented, some recent endeavors have unsettled assumptions about history as well as homosexuality. John D'Emilio in "Capitalism and Gay Identity" (1983) used Marxist insights to explain the concurrent emergence of homosexuality and industrial capitalism. His study carefully elaborated the different chronologies of male and female homosexual identity, and in describing the formation of homosexual subjects he insisted on the cultural repercussions of industrial capitalism's growth. Henry Abelove's "Freud, Male Homosexuality, and the Americans" (1986) explored the shifts in the American psychoanalytic profession's approach to, even obsession with, the treatment of the disease of homosexuality in men. Arguing from this research, he revealed how the national particularities of American psychoanalysis have entailed a rejection of Freud's most radical insights on human sexuality.

Attention to national differences has been of course critical to exploring configurations of sexuality while more recently a number of important studies have focused on specific urban cultures. Scholars have interrogated how cities became destinations of what Gayle Rubin terms "sexual migrations" as well as how sex and urbanity mutually informed city-dwellers' lives. Trumbach's studies of 17th- and 18th-century London suggest that this context allowed for the establishment of "molly-houses." In these taverns, effeminate men who recognized their lives as structured by sex with other men began to appear in a culture where "rakes," aristocrats who had sex with both women and boys, were well known. Madeline Davis and Elizabeth Lapovsky Kennedy in *Boots of Leather, Slippers of Gold* (1993) investigated the lesbian community of 1950s Buffalo, black and white groups united by the dynamics of butch/femme.

Chauncey's *Gay New York* (1994) is a landmark study of New York City and its "gay male world" from 1890 to 1940. He rejected as historically inapt the currently fashionable metaphor of "the closet." He mapped lively neighborhoods and widely-known institutions and recaptured the city-wide "pansy craze" which drew New Yorkers of all classes, black as well as white, to shows and speakeasies where "fairies" were the main attraction. He depended on diaries, mass-audience – particularly African American – tabloids, and court records to reveal a lost world yet also to taxonomize a historically-specific constellation of identities around same-sex eroticism. These identities were shaped both by person-to-person contact in the bars, bathhouses, and restaurants of the Bowery, Greenwich Village, Times Square, and Harlem, and the more widely visible media representations of this "gay world." Chauncey showed that among both black and white working-class New Yorkers there were no homosexual or heterosexual men; instead there were "fairies," effeminate men who wanted sex with men, and "normal men," who could and sometimes did have sex with "fairies" with little public or personal significance for their identity.

While for many periods and topics in the European and North American past historians have begun to explore how same-sex sexual acts and loves were understood and were

important, other areas of the globe have been less well served. Bret Hinsch's *Passions of the Cut Sleeve* (1990) and Tsuneo Watanabe, Iwata Jun'ichi, and Ihara Saikaku writing on "male love" and homosexuality in Japan represent a regional exception. *Defiant Desire* edited by Mark Gevisser and Edwin Cameron (1994) is an exciting collection of articles, histories, and documents hinting at the diversity of same-sex sex and sexualities in South Africa under apartheid. Still, the Eurocentric bias of the field has been criticized. Yet more recently "queer" historians have argued against another form of cultural imperialism: the presumption that concepts such as homosexuality, emerging from a specific recent Western context, should be employed to analyze other traditions and times. Even in surveying the modern West, queer historians demand scholarly hesitation and argument before deploying terms such as "gays," "lesbians," or "heterosexuals" to describe subjects in history. They instead seek to detail how sexual acts, emotions, and identities have been variously conceived in particular pasts. They ask how these terms relate to necessarily hierarchical definitions of communities, individuals, the "normal," gender, morality, or the body in history? As the field moves away from an obsession with isolated, invisible, and miserably victimized lives to an interrogation of how gendered sex and power intersected in the past, its insights should have wide implications for all historians.

TODD DAVID SHEPARD

See also Body; Foucault; Greece: Ancient; Miller, P.; Musicology; Sexuality; United States: Historical Writing, 20th Century; Women: North America

Further Reading

Abelove, Henry, "Freud, Male Homosexuality, and the Americans," *Dissent* 33 (1986), 59–69
Abelove, Henry, Michèle A. Barale, and David M. Halperin, eds., *The Lesbian and Gay Studies Reader*, New York: Routledge, 1993
Altman, Dennis, Carole Vance, Martha Vicinus and Jeffrey Weeks, eds., *Homosexuality, Which Homosexuality?*, Amsterdam: An Dekker, and London: GMP, 1989
Boswell, John, *Christianity, Social Tolerance, and Homosexuality: Gay People in Western Europe from the Beginning of the Christian Era to the Fourteenth Century*, Chicago: University of Chicago Press, 1980
Butler, Judith, *Gender Trouble: Feminism and the Subversion of Identity*, London and New York: Routledge, 1990
Butler, Judith, *Bodies That Matter: On the Discursive Limits of "Sex,"* New York: Routledge, 1993
Chauncey, George, Jr., *Gay New York: Gender, Urban Culture, and the Makings of the Gay World, 1890–1940*, New York: Basic Books, 1994
Cook, Blanche Wiesen, *Eleanor Roosevelt*, vol. 1: *1884–1933*, New York: Viking, and Harmondsworth: Penguin, 1993
Davis, Madeline, and Elizabeth Lapovsky Kennedy, *Boots of Leather, Slippers of Gold: The History of a Lesbian Community*, New York: Routledge, 1993
D'Emilio, John, "Not a Simple Matter: Gay History and Gay Historians," *Journal of American History* 76 (1989), 435–42
Derbyshire, Philip, "A Measure of Queer," *Critical Quarterly* 36 (1994), 39–45
Dover, Kenneth J., *Greek Homosexuality*, London: Duckworth, and Cambridge, MA: Harvard University Press, 1978
Duberman, Martin B., "Reclaiming the Gay Past," *Reviews in American History* 16 (1988), 515–25

Duberman, Martin B., Martha Vicinus, and George Chauncey, Jr., eds., *Hidden from History: Reclaiming the Gay and Lesbian Past*, New York: New American Library, 1989; London: Penguin, 1991

Duggan, Lisa, "The Discipline Problem: Queer Theory Meets Lesbian and Gay History," *GLQ: A Journal of Lesbian and Gay Studies* 2 (1995), 179–91

Faderman, Lillian, *Surpassing the Love of Men: Romantic Friendship and Love Between Women from the Renaissance to the Present*, New York: Morrow, 1981; London: Women's Press, 1985

Foucault, Michel, *Histoire de la sexualité*, vol. 1: *La Volonté de savoir*, Paris: Gallimard, 1976; in English as *The History of Sexuality*, vol. 1: *An Introduction*, New York: Pantheon, 1978, London: Allen Lane, 1979

Gevisser, Mark, and Edwin Cameron, *Defiant Desire: Gay and Lesbian Lives in South Africa*, New York: Routledge, 1994

Halperin, David M., *One Hundred Years of Homosexuality, and Other Essays on Greek Love*, New York: Routledge, 1990

Hinsch, Bret, *Passions of the Cut Sleeve: The Male Homosexual Tradition in China*, Berkeley: University of California Press, 1990

Ihara Saikaku, *Nanshoku okagami*, 1687; in English as *The Great Mirror of Male Love*, Stanford, CA: Stanford University Press, 1990

Penn, D., "Queer: Theorizing Politics and History," *Radical History Review* 62 (1995), 24–42

Schwarz, Judith, "The Archivist's Balancing Act: Helping Researchers While Protecting Individual Privacy," *Journal of American History* 79 (1992), 179–89

Sedgwick, Eve Kosofsky, *Epistemology of the Closet*, Berkeley: University of California Press, 1990; London: Harvester, 1991

Siegel, Jerrold, "Avoiding the Subject: A Foucaultian Itinerary," *Journal of the History of Ideas* 51 (1990), 273–99

Smith-Rosenberg, Carroll, *Disorderly Conduct: Visions of Gender in Victorian America*, New York: Knopf, 1985

Trumbach, Randolph, "The Origin and Development of the Modern Lesbian Role in the Western Gender System: Northwestern Europe and the United States, 1750–1990," *Historical Reflections/Reflexions historiques* 20 (1994), 287–320

Warner, Michael, ed., *Fear of a Queer Planet: Queer Politics and Social Theory*, Minneapolis: University of Minnesota Press, 1983

Watanabe, Tsuneo, Iwata Jun'ichi, and Ihara Saikaku, *The Love of the Samurai: A Thousand Years of Japanese Homosexuality*, London: Gay Men's Press, and Boston: Alyson, 1989

Weeks, Jeffrey, *Coming Out: Homosexual Politics in Britain from the Nineteenth Century to the Present*, London: Quartet, 1977; revised 1990

Horwitz, Morton J. 1938–

US legal historian

The Charles Warren professor of American legal history at Harvard Law School, Morton Horwitz has played a substantial role in energizing the field of American legal history. One of the heirs to the social history revolution of the 1960s, Horwitz, along with Mark Tushnet, David Trubek, Duncan Kennedy, Roberto Unger, and Richard Abel, helped bring the insights of Neo-Marxist and New Left intellectuals into legal scholarship by establishing the Critical Legal Studies (CLS) movement. As a result, Horwitz's scholarship has analyzed stark inequities of wealth, prestige and power behind the American legal tradition. Deeply concerned with "consensus" histories of uniformity and unanimity in the American legal system, Horwitz has argued that the study of law and its history is about the struggle for the nation's finite economic, political, and social resources. Through focusing on class struggle, fundamental biases, and change in American law, Horwitz's insights have challenged legal historians to re-evaluate the fundamental tenets driving legal scholarship.

Horwitz emerged as a highly controversial force with his 1973 article "The Conservative Tradition in the Writing of American Legal History." In it, he censured legal historians as "conservative" and "consciously anti-democratic" for failing to discuss obvious class tensions in American society while dismissing as inconsequential important democratic trends and movements (such as the codification movement during the Jacksonian era). Moreover, he criticized legal historians for limiting the bulk of their analyses to colonial America or constitutional history. Arguing that one could not analyze fundamental transformations in American law with such a limited focus, Horwitz urged legal historians to utilize non-constitutional and non-legal sources to broaden their analyses. Moreover, Horwitz rejected the belief that American law and jurisprudence was (and continues to be) an ageless system of continuity, conformity, professionalism, and reason. Rather, he has argued that law was (and continues to be) distinctly political and value-laden. Through critically evaluating the interrelated historical development of politics and economics in shaping the American legal tradition, Horwitz offered a profoundly new model for analyzing fundamental change in America's legal and social past.

A long-awaited articulation of Horwitz's model for legal historians arrived with the prize-winning *The Transformation of American Law, 1780–1860* (1977). As Horwitz's most influential and criticized piece of work, *The Transformation of American Law* represented the potential of CLS scholarship for redefining "conservative" legal histories. In his book, Horwitz argued that fundamental shifts in American private law during the 19th century facilitated the entrenchment and development of a modern capitalist economy in the United States. Dividing his analysis into instrumental and formal periods, Horwitz claimed that during the first half of the century, sympathetic American jurists molded legal rules and principles to the benefit of capitalist development. In contrast, after capitalism had been thoroughly established and legitimized in the latter decades of the 19th century, lawyers and jurists worked to formalize their positions as friends of capitalists within the stratified market order. At the expense of diminishing the potential of law as a beneficial agent of social change, Horwitz contended that the formalism of law and jurisprudence interjected uniformity, predictability, and social control for the captains of wealth in 19th-century America. At once, these distinctions became the most provocative and controversial elements of the book, as they inspired intense debates around the underlying and conflicting beliefs, values, ideas, attitudes, and struggles connecting law with the rest of American society.

Horwitz's work has significantly informed the insights of legal historians and legal scholarship. Inspired both by Horwitz and CLS criticisms of law and jurisprudence, minority scholars have worked to include gender and race in legal analyses, for example in Feminist Jurisprudence and in Critical Race Theory. Moreover, the development of Horwitz's own scholarship can be seen in *The Transformation of American Law, 1870–1960* (1992). Shifting his analysis from the 19th to the 20th century,

Horwitz delved into the struggle of ideas driving legal development and social change. Less concerned about substantive transformations in American law than with seismic shifts in jurisprudence and ideology, the second volume of *Transformation* analyzed the intense assault on "classical legal thought" waged by "progressive legal" scholars and the acrimonious debates they fostered about law as ideology. This second volume explained the historical foundation and tradition of Horwitz's own criticism of law and jurisprudence. Importantly, this placed law squarely within the contours of political, economic, and class struggle.

Not surprisingly, Horwitz's piercing criticisms of tenured legal scholars as well as his vocal support of CLS have generated rancorous reactions to his scholarship and to his political beliefs. His most vocal detractors have criticized his scholarship for ignoring or dismissing evidence in favor of propagating a model based on Marxist ideology. Indeed, for every piece of evidence Horwitz used to support his claim of a collusion of legal and socioeconomic elites, his detractors pointed to decisions or writings that arrived at the opposite conclusion. Moreover, criticism has not come exclusively from "conservative" legal scholarship. Feminist and Critical Race Theory scholars have criticized Horwitz's failure to discuss the importance of gender and race in the American legal tradition. Despite these criticisms, his detractors have conceded that Horwitz redefined the parameters and importance of law in American history. Writing in light of Horwitz's formidable assertions, not only legal historians, but historians in general have begun more thoroughly to re-evaluate the intense interplay of societal struggle and legal transformation.

TOM I. ROMERO II

See also Legal

Biography

Born 1938. Received BA, City College of New York, 1959; PhD, Harvard University, 1964, LLB 1967. Clerked for Judge Spottswood W. Robinson, III, US Court of Appeals, Washington, DC, 1967–68. Taught (rising to professor), Harvard University, from 1968.

Principal Writings

"The Conservative Tradition in the Writing of American Legal History," *American Journal of Legal History* 17 (1973), 275–94
American Legal History, 1975
The Transformation of American Law, 1780–1860, 1977
The Transformation of American Law, 1870–1960: The Crisis of Legal Orthodoxy, 1992
Editor with William W. Fisher III and Thomas Reed, *American Legal Realism*, 1993

Further Reading

Duxbury, Neil, "The Theory and History of American Law and Politics," *Oxford Journal of Legal Studies* 13 (Summer 1993), 249–70
Gilmore, Grant, "From Tort to Contract: Industrialization and the Law," *Yale Law Journal* 86 (March 1977), 788–97
Hall, Kermit, *The Magic Mirror: Law in American History*, Oxford and New York: Oxford University Press, 1989
Holt, Wythe, "Morton Horwitz and the Transformation of American Legal History," *William and Mary Law Review* 23 (Summer 1982), 663–723

Martin, John S., "Water Law and Economic Power: A Reinterpretation of Morton Horwitz's Subsidy Thesis," *Virginia Law Review* 77 (March 1991), 397–426
Presser, Stephen B., "Confessions of a Rogue Legal Historian: Killing the Fathers and Finding the Future of the Law's Past," *Benchmark* 4 (Summer 1990), 217–26
Schwartz, Gary, "Tort Law and the Economy in 19th-Century America: A Reinterpretation," *Yale Law Journal* (July 1981), 1717–75
Simpson, A.W.B., "The Horwitz Thesis and the Theory of Contracts," *University of Chicago Law Review* 46 (Spring 1979), 533–601
Sugarman, David, "Horwitz, Simpson, Atiyah and the Transformation of Anglo-American Law," in Gerry R. Rubin and David Sugarman, eds., *Law, Economy and Society, 1750–1914: Essays in the History of English Law*, Abingdon: Professional, 1984
Tushnet, Mark V., "Critical Legal Studies: An Introduction to Its Origins and Underpinnings," *Journal of Legal Education* 36 (1986), 505–17
White, G. Edward, "The Studied Ambiguity of Horwitz's Legal History," *William and Mary Law Review* 29 (Fall 1987), p 101–12
Williams, Patricia, *The Alchemy of Race and Rights: Diary of a Law Professor*, Cambridge, MA: Harvard University Press, 1991

Hourani, Albert 1915–1993

British historian of the modern Middle East

Albert Hourani was born in Manchester, England to a family of Syrian-Lebanese origin and Arab cultural background. While growing up, he was never interested in the Middle East or the Arab world. Ironically, his background and a series of historical events and circumstances transformed him into nothing less than the leading historian of the Arab world. This environment helped Hourani gain special insight into several aspects of Arab culture. Conversations with their family visitors, such as Philip Hitti, author of *History of the Arabs*, introduced Hourani to Arab history, others introduced him to Ibn Khaldun, the great Arab historian and sociologist.

Hourani, however, was educated in British schools where he studied European literature and philosophy. Consequently, he became fascinated by Western thought and developed a love for the English language. He possessed a great mastery of English, and a distinguished writing style that enabled him to express the most complex ideas with great ease and fluency. This was reflected later in his historical writing and enhanced its special appeal to readers. In 1933 he entered Magdalen College at Oxford University, reading for a degree in philosophy, politics, and economics. In college, he enjoyed reading Hegel and learning about modern German writing on the nature of historical thought, in particular that of Wilhelm Dilthey. In addition he was impressed by Max Weber's theory of "ideal types." Later he worked at the British Foreign Office with Sir Hamilton Gibb and Arnold Toynbee who each left a strong impression on his work. Other works also influenced Hourani, especially *Seven Pillars of Wisdom* (1935) by T.E. Lawrence, and *The Arab Awakening* (1938) by George Antonius.

The unfolding of the Palestinian tragedy and a trip to Lebanon made 1936 a turning point in Hourani's life. Hourani taught for two and a half years at the American University of

Beirut, at that time a hotbed of Arab nationalism. During these years, Hourani also met a number of Syrian and Arab nationalists including Qustantin Zurayq, and Charles Malik. At the beginning of World War II, he left the university to accept a position at the British research department of the Royal Institute of International Affairs. Through this position and other related appointments Hourani travelled and visited many Arab cities: Cairo, Beirut, Damascus, Baghdad, and Jerusalem. He met important leaders of the time, such as Glubb Pasha and David Ben Gurion, and interacted with young Arab nationalists and intellectuals. In 1945, he left the Royal Institute to help establish Arab offices to advocate the Palestinian cause. In 1946 he presented the Anglo-American Committee with persuasive testimony in support of the Palestinian case.

These experiences and contacts gave Hourani a greater understanding and a deep insight into Arab frustrations and aspirations, and motivated him to begin looking for his real identity. Through this soul-searching and his personal mission to reconcile his bicultural identity, he opted to study, analyze, criticize, revise, fill in the blanks, and reconstruct the history of the Middle East in many books and articles on various topics.

Hourani was a pioneer of modern Middle Eastern history. He revolutionized its writing by proposing and practicing new methods of looking at the Middle East in a rational, systematic, and analytic way. In addition to writing political history, he had a great influence, through his work and the work of his students, on establishing the socioeconomic field in Middle Eastern history. He was the author of two influential works, *Arabic Thought in the Liberal Age* (1962) and *A History of the Arab Peoples* (1991), and a significant essay on "Ottoman Reform and the Politics of the Notables" (1968).

Arabic Thought introduced Western scholars to Arab intellectuals and their ideas. It also presented Arab scholars with a systematic analysis of their own intellectual history. In this book Hourani focused on Arab intellectuals who were influenced by the West, and discussed their critique of Western thought and their attempts to reconcile and adapt their views to those of the West. However, Hourani became dissatisfied with this book and very critical of his exclusion of and failure to discuss Arab intellectuals who remained uninfluenced by the West. This was a reflection of a development in Hourani's approach to writing history which led him away from traditional methods, to become more interested in history's social and anthropological aspects. This sociohistorical approach is evident even in his earlier essays in the late 1960s on the Ottoman empire, in which Hourani refuted widespread notions about the stagnant status of Middle East society, or the static Ottoman era. In fact Hourani was the first historian to observe the role that the Notables played in influencing Ottoman politics. This sociohistorical analysis marked a milestone and led to new directions in writing Ottoman history.

Hourani's later work, *A History of the Arab Peoples*, which became a bestseller, was the culmination and application of this sociohistorical approach. In this work Hourani emphasized the cultural continuity of Arab communities regardless of the apparent differences manifested in their governments and rulers at different historical periods. Eventually this socioeconomic and anthropological perspective in writing history influenced many Middle Eastern historians who contributed, and continue to contribute, to a new understanding and interpretation of Middle Eastern history.

Hourani also enriched modern Middle Eastern history with the wide scope of his writings. The topics he dealt with ranged from historical issues to modern and developing topics. His writings reflect what he witnessed and was involved with during his stays in Beirut, Cairo and other cities, and were concerned with the emergence of a new Middle East.

Hourani discussed the policies of Russia and Western countries (Britain, the United States, France) in the Arab world. He especially focused on France and its mandate over Syria and Lebanon. Hourani also discussed Ottoman Lebanon and its feudal system, and the political society and social problems of modern Lebanon, including Lebanese emigration and its consequences. In addition, he addressed the Palestinian issue and discussed the Palestinian refugees' problem, and the future of Zionism and Israel. He also studied the Islamic city and discussed race relations in the Middle East, and shed light on the development process taking place in the Arab world and its impact on modernization and social change in the region. He examined the issue of diversity, and the history and the status of minorities in the Arab world. Finally, he discussed Arab unity and Arab nationalism in its ideology, motives and aspirations.

Hourani's main interest however was always in the history of ideas. He was especially interested in investigating intellectual and cultural exchange between Arab civilization, Islamic civilization, and the West. His bicultural background and his exceptional talent for analysis and detachment resulted in outstanding articles on the cultural relationship between the West and the Arab and Muslim worlds that conveyed rare insights into both worlds.

Hourani's contribution to the field of the modern Middle East went beyond his academic contributions to the active work of building the infrastructure of the field. Hourani was instrumental in establishing and developing modern Middle East studies in Britain and connecting it with Middle East centers in the US. He was one of the founding members of St. Antony's College and the Middle East Centre at Oxford and was instrumental in establishing its Centre for Lebanese Studies.

Above all, Hourani was the teacher for several generations of Middle Eastern historians. He advocated a detached scholarship seeking the truth when writing history. "Albert's Children," as his students chose to call themselves, have been instrumental in expanding and developing Middle Eastern studies in the West.

Hourani is widely considered one of the greatest modern Arab historians who lived in the West. His approach to history was that of a detached scholar in search for the truth. Hourani's approach, work, and character helped to establish and develop new fields in Middle Eastern studies. His legacy remains in his instrumental role in promoting new ways of thinking about the Middle East.

GLORIA IBRAHIM SALIBA

See also Eaton; Islamic; Middle East; Zāydan

Biography

Albert Habib Hourani. Born Manchester, England, 31 March 1915, to a Lebanese family which had emigrated to Britain. Educated at

Magdalen College, Oxford, BA and MA; then fellow, 1948–58. Taught at American University of Beirut; then worked at Royal Institute of International Affairs during World War II. Taught modern Middle Eastern history, Oxford University, 1958–80 (emeritus); director, Middle East Centre, St. Antony's College, Oxford, 1958–71. Died Oxford, 17 January 1993.

Principal Writings

Syria and Lebanon: A Political Essay, 1946
A Vision of History: Near East and Other Essays, 1961
Arabic Thought in the Liberal Age, 1798–1939, 1962
"Ottoman Reform and the Politics of the Notables," in William R. Polk and Richard L. Chambers, eds., *Beginning of Modernization in the Middle East: The Nineteenth Century*, 1968
Editor with S.M. Stern, *The Islamic City: A Colloquium*, 1970
The Ottoman Background of the Modern Middle East [pamphlet], 1970
Europe and the Middle East, 1980
The Emergence of the Modern Middle East, 1981
Advisory editor, *The Cambridge Encyclopedia of the Middle East and North Africa*, 1988
A History of the Arab Peoples, 1991
"How Should We Write the History of the Middle East?" *International Journal of Middle East Studies* 23 (1991), 125–36
Islam in European Thought, 1991
Editor with Nadim Shehadi, *The Lebanese in the World: A Century of Emigration*, 1992
Editor with Philip S. Khoury and Mary C. Wilson, *The Modern Middle East: A Reader*, 1993
"Patterns of the Past," in Thomas Naff, ed., *Paths to the Middle East: Ten Scholars Look Back*, 1993 [autobiography]

Further Reading

Fawaz, Leila, "In Memoriam: Albert Hourani (1915–1993)," *International Journal of Middle East Studies* 25 (May, 1993), i–iv
Gallagher, Nancy, ed., *Approaches to the History of the Middle East: Interviews with Leading Middle East Historians*, Reading, Berkshire: Ithaca Press, 1994
Hourani, Cecil, *An Unfinished Odyssey: Lebanon and Beirut*, London: Weidenfeld and Nicolson, 1984
Khoury, Philip, "Albert Hourani at Harvard," *Harvard Middle Eastern and Islamic Review* 1 (1994), vii–x
Reid, Donald M., "Arabic Thought in the Liberal Age, Twenty Years After," *International Journal of Middle East Studies* 14 (1982), 541–57
Schad, Geoffrey D., "From Orientalism to Social History: Albert Hourani and Anglo-American Historiography of the Middle East" (unpublished article)
Spagnolo, John P., "Albert Hourani: An Appreciation," in John Spagnolo, ed., *Problems of the Modern Middle East in Historical Perspective: Essays in Honour of Albert Hourani*, Reading: Ithaca Press, 1992
Sudairi, Abdulaziz A. al-, *The Making of Modern Arab Societies: An Intellectual Biography of Albert Hourani*, Ann Arbor: UMI Dissertation Services, 1994
Wilson, Mary, "A Bibliography of Albert Hourani's Published Works," in John Spagnolo, ed., *Problems of the Modern Middle East in Historical Perspective*, Reading, Berkshire: Ithaca Press, 1992

Howard, Michael 1922–
British military historian

Currently one of the world's leading military historians, Michael Howard is well known for his studies of German and British strategy and tactics as well as military theory, but his greatest contributions have undoubtedly been in the field of civil-military relations and peace studies.

Howard is one of a group of post-World War II military historians, most of them ex-combatants, including Gunther E. Rothenberg and Peter Paret, who have helped to improve the image of military history and emphasize its importance within the historical community. Howard's work concentrates almost exclusively on European military history. His first book, written in cooperation with John Sparrow, was a unit history, *The Coldstream Guards, 1920–1946* (1951), based on research and his own military service in the Mediterranean Theatre of Operations as an officer in the 2nd and 3rd Battalions of the Coldstream Guards.

Howard's first work to receive critical acclaim was his brief 92-page *Disengagement in Europe* (1958) in which he traced US and Soviet involvement in continental European affairs. This book established his reputation as a military historian and military theorist. Three years after the publication of this treatise, Howard's ground-breaking study *The Franco-Prussian War* (1961) appeared. In this, he examined German strategy and motives for the invasion of France in 1870 which made possible the unification of the various German states under the leadership of the Prussian statesman and later German chancellor Otto von Bismarck. It was at this point that Howard's reputation rapidly began to rise. In 1965, he published *The Theory and Practice of War* in which he traced the development of war and examined the role of military thought in history. Through his examination of military thought, Howard has forced a re-evaluation of the military's role in history and proved the need for studying military thinking in order better to understand political, diplomatic, and social history. This work, like much of Howard's later writing, has become a standard text for students of military history.

In the 1970s, Howard was involved in various publication projects. With *Studies in War and Peace* (1970), he was able to improve the traditionally negative reputation of military historians as militarists in the historical community and secure a place for that often misinterpreted and misunderstood discipline in the United Kingdom. By showing that the study of military history reveals a great deal about how nations can live together in peace and how wars can be avoided, Howard blazed new trails not only in military-historical circles, but also among social and political historians. His views, although not widely known, have promoted the integration of military history into other historical disciplines and helped broaden our understanding of events far distant from the battlefield. This revision of the role of military historians and military history surely has been his greatest service to the historical community.

In addition to this ground-breaking work, Howard has set the agenda for future military-historical research with his ideas about civil-military relations. The interaction between democratic civil governments and military leaders is presently a hotly debated topic which revolves around the question how much influence civil leaders actually have in making decisions about their armed forces. Howard believes that this interaction between civil and military authority is the key to integrating military history into the study of other areas of history. His views on this subject have earned him widespread international praise.

Following these projects, Howard produced a string of military histories that secured him a permanent place among the great military historians. His *War and the Liberal Conscience* (1978), *Restraints on War* (as editor, 1979), and *The Causes of War* (1983) in conjunction with his vice-presidency of the Council on Christian Approaches to Defense and Disarmament signaled Howard's own personal commitment to the preservation of peace through the study of military history and theory. In this period, Howard also wrote perhaps the best known biography of the German military thinker Carl von Clausewitz (1983). Through his tact, skill, and knowledge, Howard has established not only his own place as a first-rate military historian but also helped to improve the standing of military history as a historical discipline.

GREGORY WEEKS

See also Military; Vagts

Biography

Michael Eliot Howard. Born London, 29 November 1922. Educated at Wellington College, 1936–40; Christ Church, Oxford, BA 1946, MA 1948. Served in the Coldstream Guards, 1942–45. Taught at King's College, London (rising to professor), 1947–68; Oxford University, 1968–89: Regius professor of modern history, 1980–89 (emeritus); fellow, All Souls College, 1968–80; Oriel College, 1980–89; professor of military and naval history, Yale University, 1989–93. Knighted 1986.

Principal Writings

With John Sparrow, *The Coldstream Guards, 1920–1946*, 1951
Disengagement in Europe, 1958
The Franco-Prussian War: The German Invasion of France, 1870–1871, 1961
The Theory and Practice of War, 1965
Lord Haldane and the Territorial Army, 1967
The Mediterranean Strategy in the Second World War, 1967
Studies in War and Peace, 1970
The Continental Commitment: The Dilemma of British Defence Policy in the Era of the Two World Wars, 1972
War in European History, 1976
Clausewitz on War, 1977
Soldiers and Governments: Nine Studies in Civil Military Relations, 1978
War and the Liberal Conscience, 1978
Editor, *Restraints on War: Studies in the Limitation of Armed Conflict*, 1979
The Causes of War, and Other Essays, 1983; revised 1984
Clausewitz, 1983
British Intelligence in the Second World War, 1990
Strategic Deception in World War II, 1990
The Lessons of History, 1991
Editor with George J. Andreopoulous and Mark R. Schulman, *The Laws of War: Constraints on Warfare in the Western World*, 1995

Further Reading

Freedman, Lawrence, Paul Hayes, and Robert O'Neil, eds., *War, Strategy and International Politics: Essays in Honour of Sir Michael Howard*, Oxford and New York: Oxford University Press, 1992
Skaggs, David Curtis, "Michael Howard and the Dimensions of Military History," *Military Affairs* 49 (1985), 179–83

Hufton, Olwen H. 1938–

British historian of France

From the 1970s onwards, Olwen Hufton established herself as one of the foremost social historians of poverty and of women in the early modern period. Having taught in Britain (at the universities of Reading and, from 1997, Oxford), the United States (at Harvard University) and Italy (at the European University Institute in Florence), her influence on a generation of younger scholars has been profound.

The core of Hufton's research interests lies in French history in the late 18th century, including the Revolution. She received her training at a time when French Revolutionary historiography was particularly conflicted, as the "Jacobin-Marxist" model of Jaurès, Mathiez, Georges Lefebvre, and Albert Soboul was under vigorous attack from a number of "Anglo-Saxon" scholars, most prominent among whom was her doctoral supervisor, Alfred Cobban of the University of London. Her doctoral dissertation (and subsequently her first book), *Bayeux in the Late Eighteenth Century* (1967), showed the sleepy Norman town coming to grips with political changes that were shaded into relative insignificance by more apparently mundane realities such as poverty, the economic situation, religion, and personal ambitions and hatreds.

The wish to delve beneath overarching political narratives and to uncover social and psychological motivations brought her close to the work of Richard Cobb, at one stage an outspoken defender of Lefebvre and Soboul and polemical opponent of Cobban, but increasingly an acerbic critic of the French school. Her work was much praised by Cobb for its humane scholarship, and Hufton began to be viewed as one of his disciples. Remarkably then both a Cobbanite and a Cobbian, she was the only scholar to contribute essays to *Festschrift* volumes for both men (in 1973 and 1983).

Her next book, the hugely praised and widely influential *The Poor of Eighteenth-Century France* (1974), won the Wolfson prize for history and established her as a major scholar in her own right. Exemplifying a thoroughgoing commitment to "history from below," the work was in tune with the times and set an agenda for later scholars. The volume was constructed around a key concept associated with her work, the idea that the household economy of the poor was an "economy of makeshifts," and she reviewed the range of stratagems and maneuvers available to pauper families – migration, begging, charity and welfare, prostitution and crime – drawing (a Cobbian touch) on a huge amount of primary archival materials scooped from large numbers of provincial depositories. The work was vividly and grippingly written, often evincing a touching pathos. Moreover, by portraying the problems of the poor in late 18th-century France as those of any preindustrial economy – dependence on the state of the harvest, under-employment, technological backwardness – she opened up the topic to comparative approaches in other social sciences. Hufton showed scant sympathy for the attempts of the French Revolutionary assemblies to reform the poor laws. As she had showed in her remarkable article, "Women in Revolution, 1789–96" (1971), the arguments of which were reprised in *Women and the Limits of Citizenship in the French Revolution* (1992), her sympathies went instead to the poor themselves and to those she held to be closest to them and who were most understanding of the nature of poverty, namely Catholic parish priests and religious nursing communities.

Following the success of the book on the poor, Hufton widened the geographical scope of her writing, publishing a general history of 18th-century Europe in 1980. She was also coming to focus on the history of women, joining the cohort of scholars fashioning a new women's history. *The Prospect before Her* (1995), awarded the Fawcett prize, was a triumph on the scale of her earlier work on poverty. Like that built around a simple but powerful vantage-point – the fate in life awaiting the child born a girl – Hufton displayed all her powers of imaginative reconstruction, this time in the European as well as the French context, and extending back to the 16th century. A second volume, on the 19th and 20th centuries, is anticipated. Though she parted company with many of her pioneering peers in women's history in rejecting a move towards a more culturally-determined gender history approach, *The Prospect before Her* is a powerful testimony to the enduring validity of an experientialist approach to the history of women and the lives of the poor.

COLIN JONES

See also Women's History: Europe

Biography

Born Oldham, 2 June 1938, daughter of a textile engineer. Attended Hulme Grammar School, Oldham; BA, University of London, 1959, PhD 1962. Taught at University of Leicester, 1963–66; Reading University (rising to professor), 1966–88; European University Institute, Florence, from 1991; and Oxford University from 1997. Married Brian Taunton Murphy, 1965 (2 daughters).

Principal Writings

Bayeux in the Late Eighteenth Century: A Social Study, 1967
"The Life of the Very Poor in the Eighteenth Century," in Alfred Cobban, ed., *The Eighteenth Century*, 1969
"Women in Revolution, 1789–96," *Past and Present* 53 (1971), 90–108
"Begging, Vagrancy, Vagabondage and the Law: An Aspect of the Problem of Poverty in Eighteenth-Century France," *European Studies Review* 2 (1972), 97–123
"Towards an Understanding of the Poor of Eighteenth-Century France," in J.F. Bosher, ed., *French Government and Society, 1500–1850: Essays in Memory of Alfred Cobban*, 1973
The Poor of Eighteenth-Century France, 1750–1789, 1974
"Women and the Family Economy in Eighteenth-Century France," *French Historical Studies* 9 (1975), 1–22
"Attitudes Towards Authority in Eighteenth-Century Languedoc," *Social History* 3 (1978), 281–302
Europe: Privilege and Protest, 1730–1789, 1980
"The Reconstruction of a Church, 1796–1801," in Gwynne Lewis and Colin Lucas, eds., *Beyond the Terror: Essays in French Social and Regional History, 1794–1815 (In Honour of Richard Cobb)*, 1983
"Women Without Men: Widows and Spinsters in Britain and France in the Eighteenth Century," *Journal of Family History* 9 (1984), 355–76
With Frank Tallett, "Communities of Women, the Religious Life and Public Service in Eighteenth-Century France," in Marilyn J. Boxer and Jean H. Quataert, eds., *Connecting Spheres: Women in the Western World from 1500 to the Present*, 1987
"Women and Violence in Early Modern Europe," in Fia Dieteren and Els Kloek, eds., *Writing Women into History*, 1990

Women and the Limits of Citizenship in the French Revolution, 1992
Editor, *Historical Change and Human Rights*, 1994
The Prospect before Her: A History of Women in Western Europe, vol. 1, 1995

Hughes, Kathleen 1926–1977
British medievalist

Kathleen Hughes was one of the more prominent historians of early medieval Ireland working this century. Educated first at the University of London, in 1955 she took up a fellowship at Newnham College, Cambridge and it was there, in association with the Department of Anglo-Saxon, Norse and Celtic, that she produced the work for which she is remembered. Her specialty, ecclesiastical history, was prominent from the first, as manifested by her PhD on St. Finnian of Clonnard. This research work, published in various journals in the 1950s, established the modern understanding of Finnian's monastery and of his cult. Furthermore, she broadened an analysis of the manuscript transmission of Finnian's *Vitae* into a ground-breaking study of the distribution of Irish *scriptoria*.

Early Ireland had perhaps been envisaged too much in isolation by many of its historians, but that is not an accusation that could be levelled at Hughes. She saw Ireland not only as an integral part of the British Isles, but of Europe as well. She saw that the Irish people had learned from the classical heritage and had contributed to the civilization of the Germanic peoples. Among her many works she produced studies of the contacts between the Irish church and the papacy before the Norman Conquest, of the Irish influence on private prayer in Anglo-Saxon England, and on the connections between the English and Irish churches from the Synod of Whitby to the Viking age. Toward the end of her life, her interests were taking her increasingly toward Scotland, as witnessed by her Jarrow lecture on Christianity and the Picts.

While Hughes reserved her specialist work for presentation in article form, her two main books were nevertheless more than good textbooks (although certainly they were that) in that they contained much that was original and unique to her analysis of early medieval documentation as evidence for Irish life. *The Church in Early Irish Society* (1966) reinterpreted the history of the early Irish church and ensured that it was seen in relation to the society in which it had grown. The Roman church, after all, was a creature that had originated from the urban life of the Roman empire. In Ireland the church had to operate not merely in a rural environment, but one in which there had never been any tradition of Roman social or religious structures. Hughes traced the rise to prominence, and then to primacy, in Ireland of the church, before showing the vitality with which it resisted the Viking incursions.

Hughes' great interest in the special challenges posed by original source material was displayed in her second major work, *Early Christian Ireland* (1972). In this book she provided a ground-breaking and much-needed introduction to the investigation of early Irish history through examining the full range of categories of source material: archaeology, aerial photography, coins, secular literature and laws, monastic literature and lives of the saints, canon law and penitentials, annals and genealogies, art and architecture. The last chapter assesses the evidence of 11th- and 12th-century histories and compilations. She admitted frankly that she was not an expert in all these areas and had sought advice from others where necessary. In all those areas in which she felt she could exercise an authoritative opinion she indicated how she thought that new research could most usefully be developed. Her contribution can thus be seen to have lain both in the minutiae of historical study, but also in her work of opening up the subject of early medieval Ireland to students and other potential researchers.

DOMINIC JANES

See also Britain: Anglo-Saxon

Biography

Kathleen Winifred Hughes. Born Middlesbrough, 8 September 1926. Studied at Bedford College, University of London, BA 1944, then took a teacher's diploma at the Institute of Education, before becoming a research student; PhD 1951. Taught at Royal Holloway College, University of London, 1951–55; moved to Cambridge University, where she was a fellow of Newnham College, and a university lecturer rising to a readership in Celtic Studies, 1976. Died 20 April 1977.

Principal Writings

The Church in Early Irish Society, 1966
Early Christian Ireland: Introduction to the Sources, 1972
Celtic Britain in the Early Middle Ages: Studies in Scottish and Welsh Sources, 1980
Church and Society in Ireland, AD 400–1200, 1987

Further Reading

Whitelock, Dorothy, Rosamond McKitterick and David Dumville, eds., Ireland in Early Medieval Europe: Studies in Memory of Kathleen Hughes, Cambridge: Cambridge University Press, 1982

Hughes, Thomas P. 1923–

US historian of technology

In exploring the evolution of large technological systems, and the social and cultural forces that shaped them, Thomas P. Hughes has forged a dominant historiography of modern technology.

As a young itinerant historian, Hughes gained extraordinary access to the papers of Elmer Sperry, inventor of gyroscopic control and founder of the Sperry Corporation. Hughes published a biography of Sperry in 1971 that described the subtle transition from heroic, independent invention to institutional engineering. It also exemplified the aspirations of those who sought to develop a contextualist historiography of technology – in contrast to the internalists, who placed discrete machines and inventors within a litany of progress, or the technological determinists, who assumed machines were most interesting in their impact upon society. Hughes' biography opened up Sperry's black boxes (by stunning use of the visual materials Sperry used to explain them himself) by showing how Sperry's choice of problems and solutions emerged from his ethics of invention, his concern with safety, and his philosophy of cybernetic control in battleships and other large technological systems.

Hughes then turned from an inventor to an industry – electrification in the United States, Britain, and Germany from 1880 to 1930. He published a series of articles that advanced key concepts – "reverse salients" of lagging components along the advancing front of a new system, "critical problems" around which radically inventive activity coalesces, "acquired characteristics" imparted by social cataclysms like war, and "regional style" that described why electrical systems look different in London, Berlin, Chicago, and California.

His research culminated in Networks of Power (1983), one of the most widely cited books in the history of technology. It proposed a loose model of systems evolution and technological change, through invention, transfer, systems growth, momentum, and managerial consolidation and problem solving. Networks is explicitly comparative history, and thus engaged historians in other Western societies. Networks, above all, brought to life a group of "system builders" who envisioned and built one great thing – such as Thomas Edison's interconnected light and power system, Samuel Insull's capacity-controlled regional electrical utility, Ford's vertically-integrated River Rouge plant, and Frederick Taylor's rationalized factory. In Hughes' historiography, systems are "evolving cultural artifacts" shaped by diverse people over long periods of time.

The roots of Hughes' systems thinking are found in his training as an engineer, in his boyhood excitement over the promise of the Tennessee Valley Authority in his native Virginia, and his deep respect for the insights of Lewis Mumford. Hughes and his wife, Agatha, who has been active partner in all his work, co-edited a book of essays on Mumford published in 1990. It portrayed Mumford as a progenitor of all who seek to warn the public about how technological systems evolve to have an impact upon society.

Hughes' work and life has legitimated the history of technology as a field. He spoke often at multinational and multidisciplinary fora, urging sensitivity to the history of technology. American Genesis (1989) synthesized his seminal ideas for a wider audience, served as the textbook the field lacked, and showed how the history of modern America is largely a history of its sociotechnological systems. His argument extended to European history, by showing how modernism in art and architecture reflected European understandings of American technological enthusiasm. American Genesis also introduced us to large meta-organizations – such as the Manhattan Project and Rickover's nuclear navy – that create ever more-encompassing sociotechnical systems in the postwar period. A new wave of system builders – mostly military officers such as Bernard Schreiver and academic scientists such as Jay Forrester and Norbert Weiner – are the subject of Hughes' continuing research.

Hughes was a founder of the Society for the History of Technology in the late 1950s, in a bold effort to assert the independence of the field from economic history and history of science. The Society twice awarded Hughes its Dexter prize for best book, as well as its da Vinci medal for lifetime contributions to the field. Hughes trained the next generation of historians of technology as professor at the University of Pennsylvania, then the most vibrant graduate program in the social history of science and technology, and at the Royal Institute of Technology in Stockholm.

This new generation increasingly construed Hughes as a transitional figure – who moved the history of technology from internalism and determinism to the stark contingency of the new social constructionism. In 1987, Hughes co-edited a book defining the essence of the new social construction of technology and, in his contribution, suggested that "technological momentum" might still clarify the effect of large systems that build constituencies and shape the material landscape in ways that cannot be simply negotiated away. His work shows that knowledge, machines, culture, and economics are woven into a "seamless web," and that historians must respect and engage the "messy complexity" of human activity in creating our built environment.

GLENN E. BUGOS

Biography
Thomas Parke Hughes. Born Richmond, Virginia, 13 September 1923, son of a lumber merchant. Received BME, University of Virginia, 1947, MA 1950, PhD 1953. Taught engineering, University of Virginia, 1951–54; taught European history at Sweet Briar College, 1954–56; Washington and Lee University, 1956–63; Massachusetts Institute of Technology, 1963–66; and Johns Hopkins University, 1966–69; professor of history of technology, Institute of Technology, Southern Methodist University, 1969–73; and University of Pennsylvania, from 1973. Married Agatha Chipley, 1948 (2 sons, 1 daughter).

Principal Writings
Elmer Sperry: Inventor and Engineer, 1971
Networks of Power: Electrification in Western Society, 1880–1930, 1983
Editor with W.H. Bjiker and Trevor Pinch, *The Social Construction of Technological Systems: New Directions in the Sociology and History of Technology*, 1987
American Genesis: A Century of Invention and Technological Enthusiasm, 1870–1970, 1989
Editor with Agatha C. Hughes, *Lewis Mumford: Public Intellectual*, 1990

Further Reading
"The Dexter Prize" and "The Leonardo da Vinci Medal," *Technology and Culture* 27 (1986), 565–76
Hounshell, David A., "Hughesian History of Technology and Chandlerian Business History: Parallels, Departures, and Critics," *History and Technology* 12 (1995), 205–24

Huizinga, Johan 1872–1945
Dutch medievalist

Johan Huizinga was a brilliant figure in the intellectual life of the first half of the 20th century. The originality of his work makes him hard to categorize, but the subtlety of his intuition is apparent to all who have read his masterpiece *Herfsttij der middeleeuwen* (1919; *The Waning of the Middle Ages*, 1924; *The Autumn of the Middle Ages*, 1996).

Huizinga came from a family of Mennonite pastors in Groningen in the north of Holland and his father was a professor at the university there. Although he had been inspired by Dutch history as a child, his academic education and early researches were in Indo-Aryan philology and Oriental studies. He had published no historical works when he was appointed to the new chair of medieval history at Groningen in 1905. In this respect his career illustrates the fluidity between different areas of knowledge, which was disappearing as distinct academic disciplines emerged at this time. Huizinga's work stands at the intersection of several different disciplines: anthropology, psychology, sociology, linguistics, literature, and cultural history. After studying in Germany, he returned to Holland and chose as his doctoral subject "The Expression of Light and Sound Sensations in the Indo-Germanic Languages." He found this unworkable and so submitted as his thesis *De Vidûsaka in het Indisch tooneel* (The Jester in Indian Theater) in 1897. He then took up a post as history master at a school in Haarlem, but continued his research into ancient Indian culture and religion, giving occasional lecture series.

The continuities between this phase of his career and his later writings on European history lie in his preoccupation with what is now called the history of mentalities. He sought to understand the spirit of an age, not through its events, but through social interaction, particularly through rituals, which revealed the underlying cultural values or collective fictions that motivated human action. A problem that concerned him was whether people were conscious of their motives: how seriously they took, for example, the pursuit of chivalric ideals, and how far it was play. This led him to the subject of his final book, *Homo ludens* (1938; *Homo Ludens*, 1949), which looked at men at play.

Huizinga also studied the lives and works of artists and writers to see what they revealed about life in their times. He himself was an accomplished artist and was drawn to the study of the Renaissance. He admired Jacob Burckhardt's *The Civilization of the Renaissance in Italy* (1860).

He conceived his own study *The Waning of the Middle Ages* at the time when the origins of the northern Renaissance were being discovered in the last flowering of medieval chivalry at the court of Burgundy in the southern Netherlands. Not only was Huizinga an artist, but a poet who painted pictures in words. The Dutch title *Herfsttij der middeleeuwen* (The Autumn of the Middle Ages), gives some idea of his vivid use of metaphor to convey the essence of a culture. Although he placed too much emphasis on cultural decay rather than continuity, this book is a great work of literature, which explains its translation into many languages and its continuing popularity today.

Huizinga's important essay "De taak der cultuurgeschiedenis" (1929; "The Task of Cultural History," 1959) demonstrated his acute awareness of the difficulty of truly understanding the past. It may be read as a critique of his own methodology and of contemporary theoretical debate. Huizinga was criticized for not engaging in the ideological debates of the 1930s and was likened to the subject of one of his studies, *Erasmus* (1924), an intellectual dilettante who refused to take sides. This is not an accurate comparison: Erasmus was dominated by his intellectual vanity and his craving for recognition. Huizinga was primarily a mystic who believed that only imagination could transcend the limitations of human understanding, for example of the past, to give us a glimpse of the truth. His spiritual preoccupations were reflected more strongly in his two later books, *In de schaduwen van morgen* (1935; *In the*

Shadow of Tomorrow, 1936) and *Homo Ludens*. During World War II, he was interned by the German occupying forces for his views and died shortly before the end of the war.

His charming autobiographical essay "Mijn weg tot de historie" (written 1943; first published 1947; "My Path to History," 1968) is self-effacing and deceptively simple. He stood aloof from his own time: he had few students and was part of no historical movement. His preoccupations, however, were paralleled by German cultural historians and the French historians of the Annales school. Huizinga's work contains much that is still relevant concerning mentalities, cultural history, and the integration of approaches from social sciences.

VIRGINIA R. BAINBRIDGE

See also Burke; Cantimori; Góngora; Intellectual; Low Countries; Reformation; Schnabel; Schorske

Biography

Born Groningen, 7 December 1872, to a Mennonite clerical and academic family. Studied with literary faculty, University of Groningen, degree in Dutch language and literature, 1895; MA in philology, University of Leipzig, 1897. Schoolmaster, Haarlem, 1897–1903; external lecturer in Indian literature and cultural history, University of Amsterdam, 1903–05; professor, University of Groningen, 1905–15; and University of Leiden, 1915–40; taken hostage by Germans, 1940; released, but forbidden to return to the western Netherlands, 1942. Died De Steeg, 1 February 1945.

Principal Writings

De Vidûsaka in het Indisch tooneel (The Jester in Indian Theater), 1897

Herfsttij der middeleeuwen, 1919; in English as *The Waning of the Middle Ages: A Study of the Forms of Life, Thought, and Art in France and the Netherlands in the XIVth and XVth Centuries*, 1924; new translation as *The Autumn of the Middle Ages*, 1996

Erasmus, 1924; in English as *Erasmus*, 1924

"De taak der cultuurgeschiedenis," in his *Cultuur-historische verkenningen*, 1929; in English as "The Task of Cultural History," in *Men and Ideas: History, the Middle Ages, the Renaissance*, 1959

In de schaduwen van morgen: een diagnose van het geestelijk lijden van onzen tijd, 1935; in English as *In the Shadow of Tomorrow: A Diagnosis of the Spiritual Distemper of Our Time*, 1936

Homo ludens: proeve eener bepaling van het spel-element der cultuur, 1938; in English as *Homo Ludens: A Study of the Play-Element in Culture*, 1949

"Mijn weg tot de historie," 1947; in English as "My Path to History," in *Dutch Civilization in the Seventeenth Century and Other Essays*, 1968

Further Reading

Colie, R.L., "Johan Huizinga and the Task of Cultural History," *American Historical Review* 69 (1964), 607–30

Geyl, Pieter, "Huizinga as an Accuser of His Age," in his *Encounters in History*, Cleveland: Meridien, 1961; London: Collins, 1963

Koops, Willem R.H., Ernst Heinrich Kassman, and Gees van der Plaat, eds., *Johan Huizinga 1872–1972*, The Hague: Nijhoff, 1973

Vale, Malcolm, *War and Chivalry: Warfare and Aristocratic Culture in England, France and Burgundy at the End of the Middle Ages*, London: Duckworth, and Athens: University of Georgia Press, 1981

Hume, David 1711–1776

Scottish historian

Central to the discussion of David Hume, "the Great Infidel," as a major figure in European historiography is the uncomfortable knowledge that his immense 20th-century reputation rests almost entirely upon the *Treatise of Human Nature* (1739–40), which in its own time fell, in its disappointed author's famous words, "dead-born from the press."

Hume's 18th-century contemporaries willingly acknowledged that they were in the presence of a truly great historian. Few appreciated, and even fewer fully understood, the nature of his philosophical endeavors. Indeed, his historical works, and chiefly the *History of England* (1754–62), made him, as he quipped, "very opulent," while his more profound revolution in epistemology went largely unnoticed. Such a paradox makes it all the more difficult for us fully to see Hume – the popular historian rather than the abstruse metaphysician – as his own contemporaries apparently saw him.

The reasons for this state of affairs are clear enough. In the 19th century the *History* was inevitably superseded as a standard work by the endeavors of Macaulay, Stubbs, and Green. In our own age its sententious tone and specifically moralistic purposes have placed yet further distance between its author and ourselves. Thus, to understand properly the significance of the *History* and the associated historical works, it is necessary to approach them in the now-unfamiliar context of the 18th-century British political and intellectual culture within which Hume worked and wrote.

The crucial formative phase of Hume's remarkable approach to history as a response to his own times may be traced with some success through the urbane pages of the *Essays Moral and Political* (1741–48). Here it was that Hume developed the distinctive critique of contemporary politics and constitutional theory which, when embodied in the *History*, would represent his greatest contribution to the understanding of Britain's past. It was in the *Essays* that Hume first advanced his trademark argument that the greatest threats to "civilization" were in fact "fanaticism," "faction," and "the rage of party." Here too he insisted that the hallowed political liberty of Britons, so far from being the intentional product of an ancient constitution (as Whig propagandists preferred to suggest), was actually a recent development that had emerged through the messy political compromises of the later 17th century; and that only by acquiring a practiced moderation and reasonableness, through exposure to polite literature and genteel conversation, would the public find it possible to escape the dissension and disorder that now threatened to curtail their vulnerable modern freedoms. From these salutary observations sprang Hume's determination that his purpose as an author, as a public moralist and as a historian, was first and foremost to "refute the speculative systems of politics advanced in this nation."

The *History of England*, of which the first two volumes, dealing with the 17th century, were published in 1754 and 1756 under the broader title *History of Great Britain*, was finally completed with the appearance of the sixth and last volume in 1762, which took the curious reader back to Julius Caesar's momentous invasion of the island. The continually extending chronological scope of the successive volumes, however, should not mislead us into thinking that Hume had been distracted from his original intention of laying bare the unedifying reality and grubby origins of Hanoverian politics. On the contrary, Hume's analysis of the more recent reigns of Elizabeth, the two James's and the two Charles's formed the very cornerstone of the work. All of his formidable powers of reasoning were bent to the task of showing how finally, by his own time, a new-found liberty had come to be threatened by faction and favor.

For his misguided contemporaries, deafened by the din of party strife and misled by the self-serving ideologies of the Whigs and Tories, Hume tried to provide nothing less than an alternative account of British history, a narrative cleansed of the cant and hypocrisy of the hired propagandists. It explained with precision how commerce and liberty, those preconditions of 18th-century civilization, had progressed through the ages. It revealed how they had often developed unintentionally rather than as a result of men's designs. It showed how, since the time of James I, the influence of religious prejudice had served to excite rampant factionalism within the political nation and to threaten the very liberties which commerce had at last promised to underwrite. All of this allowed Hume to cast the sacred cows of 18th-century politics in a less-than-complimentary light. Rather than returning Britain to an ancient liberty, the Glorious Revolution of 1688 had in Hume's interpretation merely made possible, almost by chance, the first true age of freedom, which was now itself being placed in jeopardy by ideological conflict and religious dispute.

Such topical broadsides, if they explain his singular success in speaking meaningfully to his contemporaries, do not, however, exhaust Hume's wider achievements as one of the most intelligent of 18th-century historians. His theoretical contributions to the discipline included pioneering attempts at socio-logical analysis, as for example in "The Natural History of Religion," published as one of the Four Dissertations in 1757, in which he drew attention to the striking similarities between religious traditions in very different times and places, arguing that the development of monotheistic belief-systems was evidence simply of "the natural progress of human thought."

In this and other writings, Hume showed that he was, in fact, a consummate exponent of the Enlightenment science of history. He blithely drew examples from a bewildering variety of ages and circumstances in order to illustrate more general arguments. He used historical evidence frequently to exemplify specific philosophical points concerning human nature. He displayed a fine appreciation of the differentiated stages of human progress, from "rudeness" to "refinement," a tendency that he shared with his Scottish friends Adam Smith, William Robertson, and Adam Ferguson. And he exhibited the age's characteristic concern for the recovery of economic, cultural, and intellectual history, which in the History of England he suggested underlay and shaped the otherwise baffling contingency of political and religious events.

This sweeping philosophical vision, allied with acute political topicality, brought the History instant fame: five complete editions had appeared by the time of its author's death in 1776, and fifty more emerged in as many posthumous years. For all these reasons and more, Hume deserves far better than to be remembered only for what he himself dubbed "the unfortunate Treatise."

DAVID ALLAN

See also Britain: 1066–1485; Enlightenment; Foxe; Gardiner; Gatterer; Gibbon; Montesquieu; Religion; Scotland; Whewell; Whig

Biography
Born Edinburgh, 26 April 1711. Educated at University of Edinburgh, 1722–1725/6; studied privately in France, 1734–37. Independent scholar and lecturer; appointed keeper, Advocates Library, Edinburgh, 1752; secretary to Lord Hertford, British embassy, Paris, 1763–67; senior civil servant, London, 1767–69; returned to Edinburgh, 1769. Died Edinburgh, 25 August 1776.

Principal Writings
A Treatise of Human Nature, 1739–40
Essays Moral and Political, 1741–48
History of England, 6 vols., 1754–62 [1st edition of vols. 1–2 as History of Great Britain]
Four Dissertations, 1757

Further Reading
Daiches, David, The Scottish Enlightenment, Edinburgh: Saltire Society, 1986
Forbes, Duncan, Hume's Philosophical Politics, Cambridge and New York: Cambridge University Press, 1975
Livingston, Donald W., Hume's Philosophy of Common Life, Chicago: University of Chicago Press, 1984
Miller, David, Philosophy and Ideology in Hume's Political Thought, Oxford: Clarendon Press, and New York: Oxford University Press, 1981
Mossner, Ernest Campbell, The Life of David Hume, London: Nelson, and Austin: University of Texas Press, 1954
Norton, David Fate, and Richard H. Popkin, eds., David Hume: Philosophical Historian, Indianapolis: Bobbs Merrill, 1965
Phillipson, Nicholas, Hume, London: Weidenfeld and Nicolson, and New York: St. Martin's Press, 1989
Pompa, Leon, Human Nature and Historical Knowledge: Hume, Hegel, Vico, New York: Cambridge University Press, 1990
Wexler, Victor G., David Hume and the History of England, Philadelphia: American Philosophical Society, 1979

Hunt, Lynn 1945–
US cultural and social historian of France

Lynn Hunt has contributed enormously to the fields of French revolutionary history and cultural studies. As a proponent of the New Cultural History, Hunt has advocated a historical model based on examining texts, symbols, and rituals to replace earlier social historical models, including Marxism and the Annales school.

With the publication of Politics, Culture, and Class in the French Revolution (1984), Hunt challenged traditional interpretations of the French Revolution (Marxist, Toquevillian and "modernizing" models) that saw revolutionary politics as a reflection of social conflict. Such works, according to Hunt, focus on origins and outcomes of the Revolution to the neglect of "the character of the experience itself." Instead of looking to long-term social structures to explain the Revolution, Hunt sees the processes of the revolutionary experience as decisive to an understanding of the Revolution.

Politics, Culture, and Class is one of the best examples of the New Cultural History. Emerging with full force in the

1980s, proponents of the New Cultural History sought to recast the history of culture in society. Instead of examining social structures and ideology, Hunt insists that the "common values and shared expectations of behavior" provide a logic to the revolutionary experience. In *Politics, Culture, and Class*, Hunt examined the symbols, language, and rituals of the Revolution, arguing that cultural symbols and rhetoric did not merely reflect the political sphere; rather, cultural symbols and debates constituted revolutionary politics. Hunt's analysis, thus, focuses on costumes, festivals, and oaths as emblems of allegiance to a revolutionary class. In contrast to Marxists, Hunt's "class" does not connote a relationship to the means of production; rather, class, according to Hunt, is based on shared conceptions about culture and values.

In *The Family Romance of the French Revolution* (1992) Hunt continued to advocate an interpretation of the French Revolution that privileged cultural analyses. Instead of examining symbols and rituals of the Revolution, Hunt proposed a psychological model to understand the Revolution. She employed Freud's notion of family romance, sketched in *Totem and Taboo* (1913), to show that changes in unconscious attitudes toward familial relations preceded and conditioned conscious political decisions during the Revolution. The execution of the king, the creation of a new order based on *fraternité*, and the exclusion of women from public political roles were all rooted in literary images in the decades prior to the Revolution.

Hunt's critics argue that in focusing on culture, she has neglected a great deal of decisive revolutionary political activity. Specifically, many scholars contend that although discussions of culture provide insight into the revolutionary process, an analysis of culture alone is insufficient to explain the Revolution. Yet, most critics agree that both *Politics, Culture, and Class* and *The Family Romance* are required reading for students of the French Revolution and cultural history, for despite their shortcomings, these book provides two of the most stimulating analyses of the Revolution to date.

In addition to her monographs, Hunt has edited important collections of provocative historical essays. In 1991 she edited *Eroticism and the Body Politic*, a book which contains a series of cross-disciplinary essays, examining eroticism in politics, art, literature, and psychology. In *The Invention of Pornography* (1993), Hunt considered the cultural and political origins of pornography, arguing that explicit sexual literature and images were defining features of modernity.

Most recently, Hunt collaborated with Joyce Oldham Appleby and Margaret C. Jacob to publish *Telling the Truth about History* (1994). Examining the history of historiography, this work attempts to recover the "Truth" in history which, according to the authors, has been abandoned by poststructuralists. While the authors assert that the critiques of traditional history have advanced the profession, they nonetheless contend that recent trends in history have led to relativism. Instead, they argue for a "coherent narrative of the past" based on objective explanations.

SARA ANN SEWELL

See also Anthropology; Europe: Modern; Sexuality; Social

Biography

Lynn Avery Hunt. Born Panama City, Panama, 16 November 1945 to American parents. Received BA, Carleton College, 1967; MA, Stanford University, 1968, PhD 1973. Junior research fellow, University of Michigan Society of Fellows, 1972–74; taught (rising to professor), University of California, Berkeley, 1974–87; and University of Pennsylvania, from 1987.

Principal Writings

Revolution and Urban Politics in Provincial France: Troyes and Reims, 1786–1790, 1978
Politics, Culture, and Class in the French Revolution, 1984
"French History in the Last Twenty Years: The Rise and Fall of the Annales Paradigm," *Journal of Contemporary History* 21 (1986), 209–24
Editor, *The New Cultural History*, 1989
Editor, *Eroticism and the Body Politic*, 1991
The Family Romance of the French Revolution, 1992
Editor, *The Invention of Pornography: Obscenity and the Origins of Modernity, 1500–1800*, 1993
"The Objects of History: A Reply to Philip Stewart," *Journal of Modern History* 66 (1994), 539–46
With Joyce Appleby and Margaret Jacob, *Telling the Truth about History*, New York: Norton, 1994
"The Virtues of Disciplinarity (History and the Study of the French Revolution)," *Eighteenth-Century Studies* 28 (1994), 1–7
"Forgetting and Remembering: The French Revolution Then and Now," *American Historical Review* 100 (1995), 1119–35
Editor, with Jacques Revel, *Histories: French Constructions of the Past*, 1995

I

Ibn al-Athīr, 'Izz al-Dīn 1160–1233

Arab historian

Ibn al-Athīr is rightly considered the culminating point in a line of historians who produced the chief examples of the annals-based universal history characteristic of medieval Arabic historiography. His chief and lasting fame among medieval and modern historians is as the author of the world history *al-Kāmil fī al-ta'rīkh* (The Perfect History). The work begins with an account of creation and continues, in yearly increments, to the year 1230–31.

Ibn al-Athīr's views on the importance of history reflect the popular philosophy of his time in which history found an important place in education and social development. Although history often occupied an ambiguous position among the hard sciences of the time, Ibn al-Athīr was not alone in defending history as a fount of political and social wisdom. In his opinion – expressed in a brief defense of history in the introduction to *al-Kāmil fī al-ta'rīkh* – the benefits of history lay primarily in connecting people with past ages, expanding their core of experiential knowledge and honing the rhetorical skills employed in intellectual gatherings. Another of its benefits (and here we see a possible relation to the "mirrors for princes" genre of medieval Arabic belles-lettres) lay in providing rulers with political acumen.

In the introduction, Ibn al-Athīr also provides us with a glimpse into his methodology. He is not reluctant to charge past historians with the limitations they placed on historical writing. His main contentions are that previous historians often "blackened their pages" with irrelevant data (e.g. minor price increases), that they limited the scope of history to specific geographic areas, and that their accounts of major events were often disjointed, distributed as they were across the course of the yearly record. Ibn al-Athīr undoubtedly conceived of *al-Kāmil fī al-ta'rīkh* as a remedy to those shortcomings and by all accounts he succeeded in these areas. He further tells us that he extracted the accounts of the most important events from Tabarī's history (*The History of Tabarī*, 1989–) and supplemented those accounts with others from reliable historians, weaving them all into a narrative whole. In the process, he removed the often cumbersome list of transmitters attached to the discrete historical account, a decision which followed a new direction in Arab historiography. Sources for the period not covered by Tabarī (after 915) are rarely named, though modern scholarship has managed to identify the majority. It is

also known that he drew on histories from a variety of regions as his work includes information, if unevenly distributed, from all parts of the Islamic empire. Less important events and information he grouped at the end of the yearly account, along with necrologies of rulers, scholars, and notables. For those later years which coincided with his career as an intellectual and occasional diplomat at the Zangid court in northern Iraq (c.1180–1231), Ibn al-Athīr was either witness to or participated in significant political events and he duly recorded his accounts in his history. Other sources included official archives in Mosul, Baghdad, and perhaps Damascus, as well as accounts of traveling merchants, diplomats, and scholars.

Criticism has been leveled against Ibn al-Athīr by modern scholars, particularly with regard to his use of his sources. Though he notes his primary dependence on Tabarī for the years covered by the latter in his own universal history, he generally neglected to name his other sources. When those other sources have been identified, it has been found that in his attempt to combine a variety of accounts into a fluid narrative Ibn al-Athīr often misquoted or rearranged information. This also resulted in errors of fact, especially with regard to dates. Other criticism focuses on a perceived bias in his treatment of facts. His relations with the Zangid dynasty occasionally led him to skew the narrative of events in its favor; this is most evident in his treatment of Saladin's campaigns against the Crusader states. Such bias is perhaps less palpable in *al-Kāmil fī al-ta'rīkh* than in his dynastic history *al-Tārīkh al-bāhir fī al-dawla al-Atābakiyya* (The Resplendent History of the Atābak Dynasty). Ibn al-Athīr tells us that the latter work was written as a source of personal edification for one of the newly crowned Zangid rulers.

The difficulties modern scholars have encountered in consulting *al-Kāmil fī al-ta'rīkh* as a source for unequivocal data are largely balanced by the skill and insight Ibn al-Athīr brings to his job as a historian. Though generally restricted by the annals format, Ibn al-Athīr approached history in a refreshing, original manner. His choice of material from the great mass of information at his disposal proved a discerning one. His combining of discrete historical accounts into a larger narrative exemplifies his skill as a stylist and reflects a new method in Arabic historiography. He does not hesitate to draw larger conclusions about causal relations between historical events and, for example, in his discussion of the Crusades and the Christian conquest of Spain, is prepared to attempt a comparative approach to history. He is critical of his sources, challenging their conclusions, facts, and figures. In recording the actions of earlier rulers, he will on occasion assess and criticize their decisions. In his lively approach to history, he often employed the common technique, one perhaps contrived to the modern ear, of presenting the course of important events by means of an artificial dialogue between the antagonists. His tone could be personal; his anguish at the aftermath of the Mongol invasion of Iraq, for instance, was expressed in a way undoubtedly appreciated by his contemporaries.

While modern scholars must exercise caution when relying on Ibn al-Athīr, it is generally recognized that his work reflects an innovative and original approach to the annals-based history so popular in medieval Arabic historiography.

DAVID REISMAN

Biography

Born Jazīrat ibn 'Umar (now Cezre, Turkey), 12 May 1160. Educated privately. Spent most of his life in Mosul as a private scholar and diplomat; with Saladin's army against the Crusaders, 1188; lived at the Atābak court in Aleppo, 1228–31. Died Mosul, May or June 1233.

Principal Writings

al-Tārīkh al-bāhir fī al-dawla al-Atābakiyya (The Resplendent History of the Atābak Dynasty), 1211

al-Kāmil fī al-ta'rīkh (The Perfect History); c.1230; partial French translation in Recueil des historiens des Croisades: Historiens Orientaux, 1876; partial English translation in Franz Rosenthal, History of Muslim Historiography, revised edition, Leiden: Brill, 1968

Further Reading

Brockelmann, Carl, Das Verhältnis von Ibn-el-Athīrs Kāmil Fit-Ta'rih zu Tabaris Ahbār Errusul wal Mulūk (The Relationship of Ibn-al-Athīr's Kāmil fī al-ta'rīkh to Tabarī's Ahbār Errusul wal Mulūk), Strasbourg: Trübner, 1890

Cahen, Claude, "Editing Arabic Chronicles: A Few Suggestions," Islamic Studies 1 (1962), 1–25

Cahen, Claude, "History and Historians," in M.J.L. Young et al., eds., Religion, Learning, and Science in the 'Abbasid Period, Cambridge and New York: Cambridge University Press, 1990

Gabrieli, Francesco, "Arabic Historiography of the Crusades," in Bernard Lewis and Peter Malcolm Holt, eds., Historians of the Middle East, London and New York: Oxford University Press, 1962

Gibb, H.A.R., "Notes on the Arabic Material for the History of the Early Crusades," Bulletin of the School of Oriental and African Studies 7 (1933–35), 739–54

Gibb, H.A.R., "The Arabic Sources for the Life of Saladin," Speculum 25 (1950), 58–72

Hilwy, Muhammad, "Some Notes on Arabic Historiography during the Zangid and Ayyubid Periods," in Bernard Lewis and Peter Malcolm Holt, eds., Historians of the Middle East, London and New York: Oxford University Press, 1962

Richards, D. S., "Ibn al-Athīr and the Later Parts of the Kāmil," in D.O. Morgan, ed., Medieval Historical Writing in the Christian and Islamic Worlds, London: School of Oriental and African Studies, 1982

Rosenthal, Franz, A History of Muslim Historiography, Leiden: Brill, 1952; revised 1968

Rosenthal, Franz, "Ibn al-Athīr," Encyclopaedia of Islam, new edition, Leiden: Brill, 1960–, vol. 3, 723–25

Ibn Khaldūn 1332–1406

Arab historian

Ibn Khaldūn is known for two monumental works, the Muqaddima, a kind of encyclopedic prolegomena to Arab history, and the Kitāb al-'Ibar, a history of Arab and Berber dynasties to which the Muqaddima was the introduction.

Ibn Khaldūn's analysis of social behavior rests on a contrast between desert and urban environments and the associated lifestyles of nomadic and sedentary peoples. The harsh life of the desert Bedouin fosters a strong sense of 'asabiyya or group feeling, the feeling one has for one's agnates (paternal kinsmen): it thrives in the harshness of the desert, becomes weakened under the corrupting influence of cities. On this environmental antimony, Ibn Khaldūn constructs a model of dynastic growth, decline, and succession.

He gave a number of different versions of the model. In its simplest form it is a simple heuristic model of political behavior. The ruler who establishes the dynasty does so by riding group feeling to power, generally under the influence of some reinforcing religious stimulus. The second ruler begins to exclude his kinsmen, thus reducing the utility to the dynasty of those sharing the same 'asabiyya. In the reign of the third ruler, rigidity begins to set in: he relies on dynastic tradition rather than on support of his kinsmen. With the fourth ruler, incompetent and impoverished, the dynasty is fully senile and ripe for the picking by a new group of Bedouins, fresh from the desert and displaying strong group solidarity.

Somewhat later in his narrative he revisited the cycle, giving it an economic spin and converting it into a positive feedback loop. Thus the founding generation's policies are informed by the frugal and prudent habits of the desert. The second ruler adopts the luxurious habits of sedentary people, as a result of which the regime's expenses grow, especially those of the ruler who requires a large entourage. Taxes fail to meet the ruler's needs; he must rely on mercenary troops since his kinsmen have long since deserted him. The rulers of the next two generations increase taxes but are too weak to enforce their collection. Revenues decrease even as the dynasty's need for cash increases. Ibn Khaldūn goes on to elaborate on the economic problems of senile dynasties. When taxes are high, peasants will refrain from cultivating, giving rise to famine. Grain prices rise accordingly and so there is no incentive to store grain for future need. Famine brings epidemic disease to the overcrowded cities, and a weakened population is all too eager to embrace a new ruler, especially one promising an end to corruption. Ibn Khaldūn also believed that economic prosperity was the result of a high degree of specialization and division of labor.

Models of course, are as good as the data they are based on; therefore Ibn Khaldūn's model, while it cannot be generalized to all areas of the Islamic world, was fairly accurate for North Africa where the life-cycle of dynasties like Almoravids, Almohades and their successors conformed roughly to his patterns. He also applied elements of the model to Al-Andalus (Islamic Spain), his family's ancestral home. The Umayyad caliphate had failed because Arab 'asabiyya had been destroyed and Spain was no longer the abode of groups and tribes. The last rulers displayed the economic policies characteristic of senile dynasties by appropriating, through taxation, an ever larger share of decreasing income. The Taifa kingdoms in turn were defeated by the Almoravids, who were riding the crest of Lamtūnah Berber 'asabiyya. Both the Almoravids and the successor Almohade dynasty illustrated an ancillary point, that religious fervor provided a new dynasty with additional momentum that further mobilized group feeling.

The last 24 years of his life were spent in Cairo, where he was a chief qādi and served the Mamluks in various capacities. In 1400, in Damascus with an Egyptian army, he met Tamurlane, recited from memory the passages in the Kitāb al-'Ibar dealing with his exploits, and asked the Mongol emperor to correct any errors he noted.

Ibn Khaldūn was unknown in the West until the early 19th century; before that time, however, his work had been translated into Turkish and he influenced Turkish historians such as Hājjī Khalīfa (1609–57) and Mustafā Naima (1655–1716), who analyzed the weakness of the Ottoman state in the context of Ibn Khaldūn's theory of political growth and decline, believing that the solution to the empire's woes would be a reconstitution of Ibn Khaldūn's third stage, characterized by institutional stability. The recent history of his influence dates to 19th-century French Arabists such as Antoine Isaac Silvestre de Sacy (1758–1838), who produced the first western biographical notice of Ibn Khaldūn, Etienne Quatremère, who edited the Arabic text (1858), and William MacGuckin de Slane, who was responsible for the first translation of the Muqaddima in a western language (1862–68).

THOMAS F. GLICK

See also Africa: North; Hourani; Islamic; Issawi; Middle East; Naima; Near East; Universal; World

Biography

Born Tunis, 27 May 1332. Studied the Koran, Muslim traditions, Islamic jurisprudence, and philosophy before entering into a career in court politics during a turbulent period of North African history; served various chieftains, 1350–75; withdrew from politics to write, 1375; settled in Cairo, 1382; appointed professor at al-Azhar, and grand Maliki judge. Died Cairo, 1406.

Principal Writings

Muqaddima, written 1375–78; in English as The Muqaddimah: An Introduction to History, 2nd edition, 1967
Kitāb al-'Ibar (Book of Instructive Example)

Further Reading

al-Azmeh, Aziz, Ibn Khaldūn in Modern Scholarship: A Study in Orientalism, London: Third World Centre, 1981
al-Azmeh, Aziz, Ibn Khaldūn: An Essay in Reinterpretation, London: Cass, 1982
Fleischer, Cornell, "Royal Authority, Dynastic Cyclism, and 'Ibn Khaldūnism' in Sixteenth-Century Ottoman Letters," Journal of Asian and African Studies, 18 (1983), 198–220
Mahdi, Muhsin, Ibn Khaldūn's Philosophy of History: A Study in the Philosophic Foundation of the Science of Culture, London: Allen and Unwin, 1957; Chicago: University of Chicago Press, 1964
Toynbee, Arnold J., A Study of History, 12 vols., Oxford and New York: Oxford University Press, 1934–61, vol. 3

Ileto, Reynaldo Clemeña 1946–

Philippine historian

On the strength of his first major work, the provocative Pasyon and Revolution (1979), Rey Clemeña Ileto counts among the most influential of contemporary historians of Southeast Asia. His attempt to write history "from below," an endeavor of appeal to historians and social scientists throughout the world, has offered an alternative to more conventional research that subscribes to "post-Renaissance" Western notions of "objective historiography" and "historical progress."

In his first publication, Magindanao (1971; based on his Cornell MA thesis), Ileto had already touched on themes of his later work, taking as his subject the Magindanao, one of the Muslim ethnic groups ("Moros") of the southern Philippines, and their resistance to the inroads of Spanish colonial power. Challenging the myth of Magindanao unity, the book highlighted the tension between the upstream and downstream components of the polity, and, although a conventional patron-client analysis, it did suggest that Datu Uto's followers were not "passive receptors" but pursued a logic of participation (the ideology of "Holy War") which potentially justified political divergence from traditional patrons.

Pasyon and Revolution (1979) explored more deeply the paradoxical character of religious ideology as a means to undermine as well as uphold an oppressive social order. Examining a series of popular movements ranging from an anti-Spanish millenarian uprising to armed resistance to the imposition of American rule, Ileto contended that their protagonists all shared the conceptual world of the pasyon, versified retellings of Christ's Passion in Filipino vernaculars (derived from Spanish originals). Ileto argued that the pasyon, hitherto regarded as merely part of the ideological apparatus with which the "friarocracy" kept the native in his place, in fact provided the Filipino masses with the language through which to articulate their sense of social injustice and their call for a radical overturning of the status quo, which went far beyond the expulsion of foreign colonizers and the establishment of a sovereign republic, the aims professed by the Filipino elite, especially the Enlightenment-inspired intelligentsia. Identifying a body of folk religious literature as the key motor behind the mobilization of the masses in the anti-colonial struggle flew in the face of more conventional readings of the revolution – that the intelligentsia's Enlightenment ideals did penetrate to and inspire the masses, or that the masses participated only inasmuch as they were following their traditional patrons, local notables who wanted to replace the Spanish as masters. Pasyon and Revolution also challenged the teleological framework pioneered by Hobsbawm (and already applied to the Philippines by Sturtevant and others), which evaluated peasant movements according to where they fell along a progression from traditional/religious to modern/secular.

In a 1982 review, David Wurfel, a political scientist and Filipinist, declared Pasyon "one of the finest pieces of social science research to come out of Southeast Asia in the last decade," a judgment echoed by many others. The work's interdisciplinary approach impressed many; it was categorized as a work of "interpretative anthropology" to rank with such books as James Boon's Anthropological Romance of Bali. Pasyon epitomized "post-nationalist" (but hardly "anti-nationalist") Third World historiography which interrogated those narratives of the independence struggles that concentrated on the elite. The Latin Americanist Patricia Seed, in a 1991 review of the peasant movement literature, considered that Ileto had gone beyond Edward Said's injunction to "let the native speak" and on to a critical examination of the "internal politics of anti-colonialism."

For the most part, substantial criticisms of *Pasyon* have come from certain of Ileto's fellow Filipinist historians, largely within the context of academic politics at the University of the Philippines. In a 1981 review published in *Philippine Studies*, Milagros Guerrero questioned the extent to which the *pasyon* had indeed functioned as a "master text" (and motive force) for Filipino society, while there were regions, even within the Tagalog area, that had no popular tradition of *pasyon* recitation. At the same time, she attacked the distinction between an elite inspired by Enlightenment ideals and masses informed solely by the *pasyon* worldview, pointing out that the "patrician" Aguinaldo employed *pasyon* tropes and that "plebeian" Bonifacio was actually well-read in Western liberal literature (in a published rebuttal, Ileto denies that he ever drew the dichotomy so sharply). In a 1980 review, Jim Richardson found that the "*pasyon* prism" through which Ileto viewed so many disparate historical phenomena was distorting; he judged that it had led the author to make obsessive and forced connections.

Since *Pasyon*, Ileto has continued to explore the same territory. His contribution to *The Cambridge History of Southeast Asia* (1992) introduced general readers as well as scholars to his particular perspective on Southeast Asian social history. "Cholera and the Origins of the American Sanitary Regime" (1988), however, represented a new line of attack that addressed assumptions about the benefits for indigenous societies of colonialism and postcolonial development.

Wherever the quest for a "non-linear emplotment" of history takes Ileto, *Pasyon* has become a Filipino classic, known to the university-educated (a disproportionately high percentage of that country's population – the rest, if Ileto is right, *live* his book and do not need to read it). In a political environment where nuns can stop tanks and scapular-wearing vigilantes can be recruited against communist guerrillas, even the Philippine Left has recognized the need to take the masses' religious orientation seriously. In the world of scholarship, Ileto's lasting contribution will be an alternative way to view popular movements from that (in the words of Africanist anthropologist Jean Comaroff) of "social scientists unable to think of society in other than equilibrium terms [who] see popular movements as aberrations or the handiwork of crazed minds, alienated individuals, or external agitators." *Pasyon* will inspire historians who prefer to work less toward a reconstruction of events than toward a "description of unfamiliar modes of historical awareness."

ANDREW J. ABALAHIN

See also Southeast Asia

Biography

Born Manila, 3 October 1946. Attended Ateno de Manila; received BA, University of Manila, 1967; MA, Cornell University, 1970, PhD 1975. Taught at University of the Philippines, 1977–85; James Cook University, Australia, 1985–95; and Australian National University, from 1995. Married Maria Consuelo B. Carandang, 1967 (4 children).

Principal Writings

Magindanao, 1860–1888: The Career of Datu Uto of Buayan, 1971
"Tagalog Poetry and Image of the Past during the War Against Spain," in Anthony Reid and David Marr, eds., *Perceptions of the Past in Southeast Asia,* 1979
Pasyon and Revolution: Popular Movements in the Philippines, 1840–1910, 1979
"Rizal and the Underside of Philippine History," in David Wyatt and Alexander Woodside, eds., *Moral Order and the Question of Change,* 1983
"Orators. . .," in Peter W. Stanley, ed., *Reappraising an Empire: New Perspectives on Philippine–American History,* 1984
"The Past in the Present Crisis," in Ronald Jones May and Francisco Nemenzo, eds., *The Philippines after Marcos,* 1985
Critical Questions on Nationalism: A Historian's View, 1986
"Cholera and the Origins of the American Sanitary Regime," in David Arnold, ed., *Imperial Medicine and Indigenous Societies,* 1988
"Outlines of a Non-Linear Emplotment of Philippine History," in Lim Teck Ghee, ed., *Reflections on Development in Southeast Asia,* 1988
"Religion and Anti-Colonial Movements," in Nicholas Tarling, ed., *The Cambridge History of Southeast Asia,* vol. 2: *The Nineteenth and Twentieth Centuries,* 1992
"The Unfinished Revolution in Philippine Political Discourse," *Southeast Asian Studies* 31 (1993), 62–82
Editor with Rodney Sullivan, *Discovering Australasia: Essays on Philippine–Australian Interactions,* 1993
With Rodney J. Sullivan, "Americanism and the Politics of Health in the Philippines, 1902–1913," in Soma Hewa and Philo Hove, eds., *Philanthropy and Cultural Context: Western Philanthropy in South, East, and Southeast Asia in the Twentieth Century,* 1997
"Rural Life in a Time of Revolution," in Lorna Kalaw-Tirol, ed., *The World of 1896,* 1998

Further Reading

Guerrero, Milagros C., "Understanding Philippine Revolutionary Mentality," *Philippine Studies* 29 (1981), 240–56

Iliffe, John 1939–
British historian of Africa

Following his education at Cambridge, John Iliffe began fairly modestly as a scholar of Tanganyikan history. While teaching at the University of Dar-es-Salaam in the early years following Tanganyikan and Zanzibari unification, he produced five works. Two were papers and one a book published through the Historical Association of Tanzania. His first major work was *Tanganyika under German Rule* (1969). As with other scholarship of the late 1960s, it described the atrocities of colonial rule. As German "pacification" was particularly brutal, Iliffe had no shortage of material for discussion. The work also discussed the resistance of Africans, and in particular it analyzed the history of the Maji Maji resistance movement of 1905–07. While *Tanganyika under German Rule* did not have a huge influence upon scholarship outside East African studies, it was an important contribution to the developing literature of African resistance to colonialism.

Iliffe's second major work, *A Modern History of Tanganyika* (1979), investigated the history of Tanganyika since 1800. However, the colonial period received greater consideration than the early 19th century or the postcolonial era. A major focus of the work dealt with indigenous adaptation to the colonial experience including economic, cultural, religious, and intellectual manifestations. Again, resistance to the Germans, and later to the British, was also discussed. While the book was criticized for giving undue attention to the colonial epoch, it was innovative in its method of examining indigenous life. Traditionally, resistance and adaptation to colonialism had been viewed as a simple initiative (Europeans) and response (Africans). Iliffe problematized this dichotomy by awarding greater agency to Tanganyikans themselves and arguing against Europe as the diffusionist center of Tanganyikan culture.

The Emergence of African Capitalism (1983), a series of lectures given by Iliffe, continued to investigate themes that he examined in Tanganyikan history, but now applied to the entire continent. Iliffe began by investigating capitalism in precolonial Africa. The capitalism of Adam Smith has little relevance to Africa, and Iliffe had to redefine capitalism to make it applicable to African economic reality. He then examined the relationship capitalism had to the African peasantry, religious leaders, and politicians. The work was received as an incredibly erudite and yet accessible book. It was ground-breaking in the extent of its coverage and its readability. The breadth of its scholarship served as an important launching point for the work of many other scholars of African capitalism. As one would expect with a topic of this nature released in the early/mid-1980s, some found the book to be too critical of capitalism and thought it drew too much on Marxist theory. To the contrary, however, Iliffe tried to illustrate that the nature of African capitalism could not be sufficiently analyzed through either a strictly capitalist or a socialist model. African economic development bore characteristics of each, but was a unique economic system.

No other work of Iliffe's has come under as much scrutiny as *The African Poor* (1987). In it, Iliffe examined the roots and nature of poverty in Africa, beginning with 13th-century Ethiopia and concluding with 1980s South Africa. He distinguished two types of poverty, structural (long-term) and conjunctural (temporary). The book examined the individuals in the first group: those who have not only experienced hunger, but are never free from it. This method of investigation is one of two reasons Iliffe has been criticized for this work. Some scholars have claimed that the sources cannot support a differentiation between the poor and the extremely poor. Others have asserted that his separation of the poor follows a model of investigation in European history that is not applicable to Africa. Despite these critiques, there was also much praise for the book, even from his critics. He was applauded for his original research, his eye for detail, and for his imaginative use of sources such as travelogues, administrative accounts, and religious correspondence. The work also investigated charitable organizations and was innovative in that regard as well.

Iliffe has recently published a textbook on African history entitled *Africans: The History of a Continent* (1995); as was the case in *The African Poor*, he reported the history of the common person. The book was innovative in its focus upon Africa's population history as the organizing principle for the text. The themes of population movement, adaptation to the environment, the construction of enduring societies and cultures, and African defense against aggression from more ecologically favored regions were themes that can be traced throughout the book. His use of demography for a continent where demographic evidence is scanty has been questioned. At the same time, he has been praised for writing a history of the continent that puts the average African at the forefront. Iliffe has consistently pushed African history in new directions and his continued focus upon the African commoner has had profound influence upon the field of African history.

TOYIN FALOLA and JOEL E. TISHKEN

See also Africa: Eastern; Marks

Biography

Born 1 May 1939. Educated at Framlingham College; Peterhouse, Cambridge, BA 1961, MA, PhD 1965. Taught at University of Dar-es-Salaam, 1965–71; and Cambridge University (rising to professor) from 1971: fellow, St. John's College, from 1971.

Principal Writings

Tanganyika under German Rule, 1905–1912, 1969
Modern Tanzanians: A Volume of Biographies, 1973
A Modern History of Tanganyika, 1979
The Emergence of African Capitalism: The Anstey Memorial Lectures in the University of Kent at Canterbury, 10–13 May, 1982, 1983
"Poverty in Nineteenth-Century Yorubaland," *Journal of African History* 25 (1984), 43–57
The African Poor: A History, 1987
Famine in Zimbabwe, 1990
Africans: The History of a Continent, 1995

Further Reading

Peel, J.D.Y., "Poverty and Sacrifice in Nineteenth-Century Yorubaland: A Critique of Iliffe's Thesis," *Journal of African History* 31 (1990), 465–84
Spear, Thomas, "Africa's Population History" [review article], *Journal of African History* 37 (1996), 479–85

Imperial History

Doing imperial history is easier than defining it; unlike national histories, imperial history is not marked out by clear-cut geographical or chronological boundaries, nor do imperial historians subscribe to a common analytical framework, perspective, or methodology. What unites imperial historians is that they study empires, and a process (or more likely a set of processes) – imperialism – which produces and sustains empires. But what is an empire? Classical scholars speak of the Roman empire, whose most obvious characteristic, a political system in which authority is vested in an emperor, bears some similarity with other state formations in India, China, and the Americas. It is more common, though, to employ empire to refer to the lands that were brought under the control of various European powers after 1500, which is the emphasis of this article. Yet this definition, with its emphasis on formal political control over a fixed area, has also been found wanting, for it fails to address those instances where one state controls another without necessarily claiming sovereignty. Hence, we can speak of informal imperialism and cultural imperialism, neither of which requires overt political domination. Moreover, by limiting ourselves to formally constituted empires, it becomes difficult to address what Walter Rodney, André Gunder Frank and others have labelled neocolonialism, or the perpetuation of imperial influences in nominally independent countries.

It is therefore not surprising that the current trend in defining empires and imperialism is to leave them as broad as possible at the outset, and allow them to be refined by the particular context within which they are situated. Consequently, these terms can now be seen as umbrellas sheltering a variety of structures and processes. Imperialism then can be said to refer to the control and influence exercised by a strong state over a weaker state, with such controls and influences being applied in ways different from those that the dominant state would employ within its own metropolitan territories. Such a definition makes allowance for the great number of avenues through which authority can be exercised, and does not require power to be politically formalized and applied to a clearly demarcated territory. But such flexibility is not without its costs. Critics have pointed out that all types of power relationship could be included within such an elastic definition.

If historians have generally favored a looser definition of imperialism, they nevertheless have often found it convenient to partition the period after 1500 into several discrete phases. The first phase, sometimes referred to as the age of exploration, witnessed the establishment of Portuguese and Spanish bridgeheads in Asia, Africa, and the Americas from the late 15th century. Iberian ascendancy was then eclipsed in the mid-17th century with the breakout of the more commercially advanced states of northern Europe, particularly the Netherlands, Britain, and France. This ushered in what many have called the age of mercantilism, an era marked by the rise of trading empires (such as those of the Dutch East India Company and the British East India Company) that were established on the principle that a state's wealth could be enhanced if such chartered corporations were given a trade monopoly over particularly lucrative commodities. The period between 1500 and 1850 also witnessed the growth of settler colonies in lands which were not only well suited to European agricultural colonization, but were ones in which the indigenous inhabitants could easily be displaced, such as North America, South Africa, and Australia/New Zealand.

The next obvious era of imperialism was that which took place after 1880, often referred to as the New Imperialism. It has been primarily associated with the scramble for Africa which in twenty years left most of that continent partitioned out among participating European states. Traditional players like France and Britain were joined by new arrivals like Germany, Italy, and Belgium (in the person of king Leopold). Even Spain and Portugal reasserted themselves. For historians as well as contemporary observers, the very rapid and enthusiastic extension of European overseas control has been taken as indicative of a new phase in European imperialism.

Between the end of the age of mercantilist empires, situated somewhere in the early 19th century, and the New Imperialism of the 1880s, lay a rather confusing period that cannot be easily summarized. On an intellectual level, mercantilism was yielding to the doctrines of free trade, while politically most European powers were preoccupied with their own domestic troubles. This is not to say that imperialism was in retreat. While Britain's settler colonies in North America, Australia, and South Africa were granted more autonomy, British imperial frontiers in Asia were rolling forward. And France, despite political turmoil at home, commenced its occupation of Algeria. It has not been easy to reconcile territorial expansion with the apparent lack of a clearly articulated economic or political agenda. In what has become a watershed in imperial historiography, Ronald Robinson and John Gallagher published "The Imperialism of Free Trade" in the *Economic History Review* (1953). They downplayed what they saw as the superficial changes in British imperialism of the 19th century, and argued for a basic continuum across the century on the grounds that wherever possible the British sought to protect their interests by indirect means, and turned to outright annexation only when circumstances required. W.R. Louis in *Imperialism* (1976) provides an excellent sampling of the debates that their work triggered.

Decolonization, the final stage of imperialism, began in the immediate aftermath of World War II with independence being granted, often only grudgingly after prolonged periods of unrest and violent confrontations, to Europe's colonies in South and Southeast Asia. Decolonization then switched to Africa with most colonies gaining their independence by the mid-1960s, the exceptions being the white-dominated areas of Zimbabwe and South Africa and the Portuguese colonies of Mozambique and Angola. The history of decolonization, although still very young, is a burgeoning field as historians wrestle with a range of possible explanations. Some like Robert Holland and Peter Cain and Anthony Hopkins favor locating the impetus to imperial withdrawal in the changing political and economic situations in Europe, as well as the outbreak of the Cold War. Others, however, including D.A. Low, J.D. Hargreaves and John Darwin, account for decolonization by looking to the growing support that nationalist movements mobilized, and the subsequent difficulties that imperial powers faced in retaining their colonies.

Historians, political scientists, and economists have tried on many occasions to construct explanatory models which could account for the origin, consolidation, and fall of empires. Most of these have focused on the most visible manifestation of imperialism, that which came after 1880, and a good number of these have sought their answers in the economic conditions then gripping Europe. J.A. Hobson argued at the turn of the 20th century that imperialism was driven by the needs of capitalists who, coping with domestic underconsumption, looked overseas for investment opportunities. To reduce their risks, they manipulated their respective governments to provide them with political and military backing. Hobson's work was shortly to be taken up and modified by V.I. Lenin. By stressing that imperialism was driven by the capitalists' need for raw materials and secure markets, Lenin provided in 1916 the classic Marxist statement of imperialism, namely that imperialism was the highest stage of capitalism.

Not all historians were willing to subscribe to an economic explanation. There were those, especially in the 19th century, who saw humanitarian concerns as the driving force behind imperialism. By emphasizing the campaigns to stamp out the slave trade and the need to educate and uplift the "heathen" (the civilizing mission), imperialism could be presented in a more noble light. Today, however, while the importance of humanitarian lobby groups is acknowledged, and missionaries are seen as important if paternalistic agents in the dissemination of Western ideas and practices, few historians would recognize humanitarian agendas as being anything more than a contributing force. Many would go even further and insist that humanitarian rhetoric was little more than a mask covering over the baser motives that drove imperial expansion.

Ecological and technological explanations for imperialism have been pioneered by Alfred Crosby, Philip Curtin, and Daniel Headrick. They have shown clearly just how important ecological and technological factors were in facilitating or impeding imperial expansion, and have also helped us better understand the timing of imperial expansion. But critics have pointed out that ecological and technological models do not have much to add to the debate over why imperial expansion began in the first place, or why it continued.

Political and strategic explanations have also been employed to explain the origins and timing of imperial expansion. Robinson and Gallagher in *Africa and the Victorians* (1961) examined Britain's participation in the scramble for Africa, and concluded that Britain acted primarily to protect its strategic routes to India. Almost simultaneously, the French historian Henri Brunschwig launched a devastating critique of those who applied economic explanations to account for French imperialism. He argued instead that the roots of French imperialism lay in domestic politics, more particularly in the fragile nature of party politics and the need to restore prestige after embarrassing losses in the Franco-Prussian War. Economic arguments were also found wanting when German motives were explored. Bismarck, it has been suggested, was willing to promote German claims in Africa largely because he realized that he could use them to drive a wedge between France and Britain.

There were others who explained imperialism in terms of its value as a safety-valve, a vent for pent-up tensions at home. Imperial events and themes could be manipulated to play on the patriotism of the working classes and thereby distract them from their immediate grievances. Disraeli's Crystal Palace speech is often cited as an example of this, as are the appeals made to French voters in the aftermath of the Prussian War. Another example of a socially-rooted explanation for imperialism was that developed by Joseph Schumpeter. He saw imperialism as an atavistic reaction orchestrated by Europe's aristocracy and gentry who, faced with a world transformed by industry and commerce, sought refuge in empires where they could hopefully replicate the hierarchies that were so essential to their status and identity.

Efforts to explain particular episodes of imperial expansion, or the acts taken by a specific individual or group, on the grounds of strategic imperatives, social conditions, or political opportunism have made some headway. But such approaches do not work so well when it comes to providing an overarching interpretation of imperialism, for it can be argued that political and strategic decision-making and the pressures produced by social dynamics are in themselves only reflective of deeper processes. Consequently, many historians still look

to economics, though they have carefully steered clear of the over-determining nature of early theories of economic imperialism. Immanuel Wallerstein, for example, has ambitiously constructed a model to account for the origins and characteristics of European expansion from the 15th century to the present. His world-system analysis integrates the economic histories of diverse parts of the world to show how the world came to be dominated by a capitalist economy emanating from Europe. Other historians, including David Fieldhouse and W.G. Hynes, have reaffirmed the importance of economic motives in imperial expansion. More recently, Peter Cain and Anthony Hopkins have reasserted that imperialism was rooted in capitalism in their 2-volume account of British imperialism from the 17th century to the present. But their work has a novel twist, for capital to them was not the industrial capital favored by earlier generations of economic historians. Instead, imperialism was driven by the needs of "gentlemanly capitalists," a coalition of interests including those in the banking and trading sectors, service industries, and the rising professional classes, all of whom tended to cluster around London and who aspired to a "gentlemanly" lifestyle. Their work has produced a very lively debate which can be tracked in the pages of the *Economic History Review*, *Past and Present*, and *Journal of Imperial and Commonwealth History*.

While many imperial historians have aligned themselves with one of the above schools of interpretation, there remain many others who have expressed dissatisfaction with these approaches on the grounds that they are all firmly implanted in Europe. One of the earliest signs of dissatisfaction with the Eurocentric nature of much scholarship can be glimpsed in the writings of J.C. van Leur, a Dutch historian working on European traders in Southeast Asia. His work anticipated much of what has been written since the 1960s, which stresses that we cannot fully appreciate what actually happened in Europe's empires unless we cease treating the world outside Europe as an inert mass molded by decisions taken in Europe's capitals or by Europe's capitalists. The proliferation of area studies programs in the US, Britain, and France, which was accompanied by a growing recognition that African, Latin American, and Asian histories were all legitimate fields of inquiry, helped forge an important alternative to metropolitan readings of imperial history. It has since been demonstrated that imperial expansion often depended upon local intermediaries who provided the cash, the local expertise, and access to resources that colonial regimes needed. This dependency would outlast the initial period of conquest as colonial states came to rely upon intermediaries to assist in the consolidation of their authority. C.A. Bayly in *Imperial Meridian* (1989) framed his analysis of the development of British imperial regimes in Africa and Asia in the 18th and early 19th centuries within such a perspective. While few would deny that imperial history needed to balance metropolitan perspectives with what was happening on the periphery, there are those who warn that too much emphasis on indigenous agents and initiatives means that we risk losing sight of the fact that imperialism after all did emanate from Europe, and was intended to serve Europe's interests.

While debates over the origins and policies of imperialism show no signs of easing off, they have been joined by exciting work intended to unpack the cultural and social meanings of imperialism for colonizer and subject alike. Interest in the extent to which imperialism contributed to the fashioning of racist beliefs continues, and has expanded to consider questions first raised in postcolonial and postoriental studies. As Frantz Fanon noted, imperial regimes were not only guilty of economically and politically exploiting their colonial subjects, but also of stripping them of their identity and leaving them more vulnerable to their new masters. This raises important questions concerning the extent to which the systematic acquisition of knowledge about subject peoples strengthened imperial control, and what the legacy of such representations are today. This has led to many innovative works by among others David Arnold, Megan Vaughan, Richard Grove, Mark Harrison, Kristin Mann, and Ramachandra Guha which look at how imperial discourses were produced in such areas as health, gender, law, and nature, and what effects they had upon the functioning and impact of colonial power.

Other historians are asking what imprint imperialism left on European societies. Hitherto, it was largely assumed that with the exception of the occasional outburst of imperial patriotism, for example during the Boer War or at the outbreak of World War I, the working classes were largely apathetic and the middle classes only slightly less so. Imperialism was thought of as something that engaged only Europe's political, economic, and military elite. Although operating from different sets of assumptions, and disagreeing strongly on some points, Edward Said and John MacKenzie have written compelling studies which show that imperialism left very tangible impressions on both the high culture and popular culture of Europe in the 19th and 20th centuries. This has led to a proliferation of books and articles which show how imperialism helped to configure social structures and identities, primarily in the late 19th and 20th centuries. Important works have emerged which detail the ways in which imperialism helped define gender roles (e.g., Margaret Strobel, Antoinette Burton, Mrinalini Sinha, Graham Dawson), how imperialism helped to shape our understanding of sexuality (e.g., Ann Stoler, Ronald Hyam, Philippa Levine), and how citizenship and nationalism were intertwined with imperialism (eg. J.M. MacKenzie, J.A. Mangan).

By adopting a flexible definition of imperialism, and by taking advantage of insights and methods developed in other disciplines (literature, cultural studies, etc.) as well as in other fields of history (African, Asian, social, economic, etc.), imperial history has extended its reach into new and exciting areas. This has not been to everyone's liking, and there are many who feel imperial history needs to redefine itself more rigorously. But then again, imperial history has always struggled with its self-definition and perhaps therein lies its strength and vitality.

DOUGLAS PEERS

See also British Empire; Crosby; Curtin; Gallagher; Hargreaves; Rodney; Said; Spain: Imperial

Further Reading

Arnold, David, *Colonizing the Body: State Medicine and Epidemic Disease in Nineteenth-Century India*, Berkeley: University of California Press, 1993

Baumgart, Winfried, *Der Imperialismus: Idee und Wirklichkeit der englischen und französischen Kolonialexpansion, 1880-1914*, Wiesbad: Steiner, 1975; in English as *Imperialism: The Idea and Reality of British and French Colonial Expansion, 1880-1914*, Oxford: Oxford University Press, 1982

Bayly, C.A., *Imperial Meridian: The British Empire and the World, 1780-1830*, London and New York: Longman, 1989

Brunschwig, Henri, *Mythes et réalités de l'impérialisme colonial français, 1871-1914*, Paris: Colin, 1960; in English as *French Colonialism, 1871-1914: Myths and Realities*, New York: Praeger, 1964, revised London: Pall Mall Press, 1966

Cain, Peter J., and Anthony G. Hopkins, *British Imperialism: Innovation and Expansion, 1688-1914* and *Crisis and Deconstruction, 1914-1990*, 2 vols., London and New York: Longman, 1993

Crosby, Alfred W., Jr., *Ecological Imperialism: The Biological Expansion of Europe, 900-1900*, Cambridge and New York: Cambridge University Press, 1986

Curtin, Philip D., "The Environment Beyond Europe and the European Theory of Empire," *Journal of World History* 1 (1990), 131-50

Darwin, John, *Britain and Decolonisation: The Retreat from Empire in the Post-Colonial World*, Basingstoke: Macmillan, and New York: St. Martin's Press, 1988

Dawson, Graham, *Soldier Heroes: British Adventure, Empire, and the Imagining of Masculinities*, London and New York: Routledge, 1994

Emmer, P.C., and H.L. Wesseling, eds., *Reappraisals in Overseas History: Essays on Post-War Historiography about European Expansion*, Leiden: Leiden University Press, 1979

Fieldhouse, D.K., *Economics and Empire, 1830-1914*, London: Weidenfeld and Nicolson, and Ithaca, NY: Cornell University Press, 1973

Grove, Richard, *Green Imperialism: Colonial Experience, Tropical Island Edens and the Origins of Environmentalism, 1600-1800*, Cambridge and New York: Cambridge University Press, 1995

Guha, Ramachandra, *The Unquiet Woods: Ecological Change and Peasant Resistance in the Himalaya*, Delhi and Oxford: Oxford University Press, 1989; Berkeley: University of California Press, 1990

Hargreaves, John D., *Decolonization in Africa*, London and New York: Longman, 1988; 2nd edition, 1996

Harrison, Mark, "'The Tender Frame of Man': Disease, Climate, and Racial Difference in India and the West Indies, 1760-1860," *Bulletin of the History of Medicine* 70 (1986), 68-93

Headrick, Daniel R., *The Tools of Empire: Technology and European Imperialism in the Nineteenth Century*, New York: Oxford University Press, 1981

Hobson, J.A., *Imperialism: A Study*, London: Nisbet, 1902, revised 1938; 3rd edition, London: Unwin Hyman, 1988

Holland, Robert F., *European Decolonization, 1918-1981: An Introductory Survey*, London: Macmillan, and New York: St. Martins Press, 1985

Hyam, Ronald, *Empire and Sexuality: The British Experience*, Manchester and New York: Manchester University Press, 1990

Hynes, W.G., *The Economics of Empire: Britain, Africa and the New Imperialism*, London: Longman, 1979

Kennedy, Dore, "Imperial History and Postcolonial Theory," *Journal of Imperial and Commonwealth History* 24 (1996), 345-63

Kennedy, Paul M., *The Rise and Fall of the Great Powers: Economic Change and Military Conflict from 1500 to 2000*, New York: Random House, 1987; London: Unwin Hyman, 1988

Koebner, Richard, and Helmut D. Schmidt, *Imperialism: The Story and Significance of a Political Word, 1840-1960*, Cambridge: Cambridge University Press, 1964

Lenin, V.I., *Imperializm: kak noveishii etap kapitalizma*, 1917; in English as *Imperialism, The Highest Stage of Capitalism: A Popular Outline*, London: Lawrence, 1929; New York: International Publishers, 1933

Leur, J.C. van, *Indonesian Trade and Society: Essays in Asian Social and Economic History*, The Hague: Van Hoeve, 1955

Levine, Philippa, "Rereading the 1890s: Venereal Disease as 'Constitutional Crisis' in Britain and British India," *Journal of Asian Studies* 55 (1996), 585-612

Louis, William Roger, ed., *Imperialism: The Robinson and Gallagher Controversy*, New York: New Viewpoints, 1976

Louis, William Roger, general editor, *The Oxford History of the British Empire*, Oxford: Oxford University Press, 1998–

Low, Donald Anthony, *Eclipse of Empire*, Cambridge and New York: Cambridge University Press, 1991

MacKenzie, John M., *Propaganda and Empire: The Manipulation of British Public Opinion, 1880–1960*, Manchester: Manchester University Press, 1984

Mangan, J.A., *The Games Ethic and Imperialism: Aspects of the Diffusion of an Ideal*, New York and London: Viking, 1986

Mann, Kristin, and Richard Roberts, eds., *Law in Colonial Africa*, London: Currey, 1991

Marshall, P.J., and Glyndwr Williams, *The Great Map of Mankind: British Perceptions of the World in the Age of the Enlightenment*, London: Dent, and Cambridge, MA: Harvard University Press, 1982

Marshall, P.J., ed., *The Cambridge Illustrated History of the British Empire*, Cambridge and New York: Cambridge University Press, 1996

Owen, Roger, and Bob Sutcliffe, eds., *Studies in the Theory of Imperialism*, London: Longman, 1972

Porter, Bernard, *The Lion's Share: A Short History of British Imperialism, 1850–1970*, London and New York: Longman, 1975; 3rd edition [with dates 1850–1995], 1996

Robinson, Ronald, and John Gallagher, "The Imperialism of Free Trade," *Economic History Review* 6 (1953), 1–15

Robinson, Ronald, and John Gallagher with Alice Denny, *Africa and the Victorians: The Official Mind of Imperialism*, London: Macmillan, and New York: St. Martin's Press, 1961; revised 1981

Rodney, Walter, *How Europe Underdeveloped Africa*, London: Bogle-L'Ouverture, 1972; Washington, DC: Howard University Press, 1974, revised 1981

Said, Edward W., *Orientalism*, New York: Pantheon, and London: Routledge, 1978

Said, Edward W., *Culture and Imperialism*, New York: Knopf, and London: Chatto and Windus, 1993

Scammell, G.V., *The First Imperial Age: European Overseas Expansion, c.1400–1715*, London and Boston: Unwin Hyman, 1989

Schumpeter, Joseph Alois, "Zur Soziologie der Imperialismen," *Archiv für Sozialwissenschaft und Sozialpolitik* 46 (1919), and "Die sozialen Klassen im ethnisch homogenen Milieu," in *Archiv für Sozialwissenschaft und Sozialpolitik* 57 (1926); in English as *Imperialism and Social Classes*, Oxford: Blackwell, 1951

Sinha, Mrinalini, *Colonial Masculinity: The "Manly Englishman" and the "Effeminate Bengali" in the Late Nineteenth Century*, Manchester: Manchester University Press, and New York: St. Martin's Press, 1995

Stoler, Ann, "Rethinking Colonial Categories: European Communities and the Boundaries of Rule," *Comparative Studies in Society and History* 31 (1989), 134–61

Strobel, Margaret, *European Women and the Second British Empire*, Bloomington: Indiana University Press, 1991

Vaughan, Megan, *Curing Their Ills: Colonial Power and African Illness*, Stanford, CA: Stanford University Press, and Cambridge: Polity Press, 1991

Wallerstein, Immanuel, *The Modern World-System*, 3 vols., New York and London: Academic Press, 1974–89

Ware, Vron, *Beyond the Pale: White Women, Racism and History*, London: Verso, 1992

Inalcık, Halil 1916–

Turkish social and economic historian

Halil Inalcık is the doyen of historians of the Ottoman empire. His primary education in Ataturk's Turkey instilled in him an intense sense of national purpose. His works are infused with a strong desire to correct the negative views of Ottoman and Turkish civilization that can be found in Western historical accounts.

He first studied diplomatic history, especially the events surrounding the 19th-century. "Eastern Question," but soon shifted to social and economic history. His doctoral thesis, *Tanzimat and the Bulgarian Question* (1943), concentrated on conflicts over agricultural land in northern Bulgaria. He found the broad historical forces shaping the background of historical events to be more useful than diplomatic history in understanding the Ottoman past.

Inalcık consistently urged students to be prudent in interpreting the available source materials. He cautioned against strictly following theoretical models while neglecting the primary sources. He acknowledged that the historian could never hope to reach absolute objectivity, but should be prudent in his or her interpretations. He worried that comparative history often amounted to comparing an incomplete account of one region with an incomplete account of another. He was always careful, even conservative, in his historical assessments. For example, while some historians considered the *celali* (rebel) uprisings to be peasant rebellions, he insisted that they were merely raids by armed unemployed former soldiers over whom the state had no control and who had no revolutionary consciousness.

He wrote his book, *The Ottoman Empire: The Classical Age* (1973) at Princeton. This book, which Norman Itzkowitz and Colin Imber translated from Turkish into English, remains the authoritative text in the field of Ottoman history. Inalcık considered the Ottoman empire to have been a commonwealth founded by Turks, but built by Arabs, Greeks, Slavs, and Albanians along with its Turkish founders. On the much-discussed question of Ottoman decline, Inalcık believed that certain institutions changed their original forms and were maintained long after they had served their original purpose. The wider developments historians often describe as a decline, however, were to Inalcık adaptations and transformations to new conditions necessitated by advances in the West. Nevertheless, despite its attempts to adapt, the empire did not catch up to the West. The Ottomans reformed the army, the bureaucracy, and the fiscal system, but the culture, basically Islamic, could not adjust, and so Ataturk made a radical decision and opted for Western cultural models believing it was the only way the Turkish nation could survive.

After many years researching the Ottoman archival sources, Inalcık concluded that over 90 per cent of the Ottoman population worked in small peasant family production. He believed that this *çift-hane* (land worked by a peasant household, *hane*, on a certain amount of land workable by a pair of oxen) system was the basis of the Ottoman social and economic structure.

In recent years, world historians, influenced principally by Inalcık and other Ottoman historians, have stressed the importance of the Ottoman empire in European, Middle Eastern, African, and Asian history. Inalcık often argued that the historian could not study the history of Byzantium, the Arab world, and the Balkans without making extensive use of the Ottoman archives in order to gain a more "objective" approach. For the history of the modern Middle East, Inalcık noted that Ottoman newspapers, first published in the 1860s, were indispensable. He also endorsed the Annales school approach and periphery-center theorists such as Immanuel Wallerstein, who studied the place of the Ottoman empire within the "capitalist World economy" unlike those who treated the Ottoman empire as a marginal entity.

Throughout his career, Inalcık endeavored to make the Ottoman archival materials more accessible to scholars from around the world. He is currently translating and editing about 1,000 documents from the *qadi* court records of Bursa, an important trading center in the Ottoman empire. These records date from the 1460s and are an invaluable source for Ottoman economic and social history.

NANCY GALLAGHER

See also Barkan; Middle East; Ottoman

Biography

Born Istanbul, 25 May 1916. Studied at the Ghazi Enstitüsü and Dil-Tarih-Cografya Facültesi (Faculty of Geography, History, and Language) of Ankara University, MA 1940, PhD 1942; attended seminars at the School of Oriental and African Studies, London. Served in the Turkish Army in Ankara, 1943–45. Taught (rising to professor of Ottoman history) at Ankara University, 1942–72; and University of Chicago, 1972–86; after retirement in 1986 returned to Turkey to organize a history department at Bilkent University. Married Sevkeye Isil, 1945 (1 daughter).

Principal Writings

The Ottoman Empire: The Classical Age, 1300–1600, 1973
Translator, *The History of Mehmed the Conqueror,* by Tursun Beg, 1978
The Ottoman Empire: Conquest, Organization, and Economy [essays], 1978
Studies in Ottoman Social and Economic History [essays], 1985
The Middle East and the Balkans under the Ottoman Empire: Essays on Economy and Society, 1993
"The Ottoman State: Economy and Society, 1300–1600," in Halil Inalcik with Donald Quataert, *An Economic and Social History of the Ottoman Empire, 1300–1914,* 1994
From Empire to Republic: Essays on Ottoman and Turkish Social History, 1995
Sources and Studies on the Ottoman Black Sea: The Customs Register of Caffa, 1487–1490, 1995

Further Reading

Davison, Roderic H., "Westernized Education in Ottoman Turkey," in his *Essays in Ottoman and Turkish History, 1772–1923: The Impact of the West,* Austin: University of Texas Press, 1990
Gallagher, Nancy, ed., *Approaches to the History of the Middle East: Interviews with Leading Middle East Historians,* Reading, Berkshire: Ithaca Press, 1994
Naff, Thomas, ed., *Paths to the Middle East: Ten Scholars Look Back,* Albany: State University of New York Press, 1993

India: since 1750

The peoples of South Asia who came under British colonial rule from the middle of the 18th century had various traditions of history writing. Most accessible from the point of view of the conquerors were the narrative histories written in Persian that chronicled the reigns of Mughal emperors or other rulers. Eighteenth-century British scholars eagerly translated such

works and indeed commissioned a by no means uncritical history of the transition to British rule in eastern India by Ghulam Husain Khan, published in translation in 1789 as *View of Modern Times* (modern reprints available). British people also began to write histories to chronicle their own doings in India, Robert Orme's *History of the Military Transactions of the British Nation in Indostan* (1763–78) being the first of such books.

Indigenous traditions of writing about the past in the languages of the subcontinent never died out, but under colonial rule and with a colonial education system committed to a European view of what constituted subjects such as history, the dominant interpretations of the history of modern India in the 19th and early 20th centuries were inevitably written in English, usually by British people. In Britain they were often closely associated with the education of future Indian civil servants. With the notable exception of the highly "philosophical" *History of British India* (1817 and numerous subsequent editions) by James Mill, it has to be said that this body of writing does not now make very exciting reading. It is strongly narrative and much concerned with the doings of great men, usually the governors general. Its values are implicitly if not explicitly imperial. This tradition survived essentially intact until after World War II. *The Oxford History of India,* first published under the authorship of Vincent Smith in 1919 and still in print as revised by Percival Spear, is representative of this tradition in its later stages.

If, at least until the 1960s, the historiography of modern South Asia had little to offer other historians, this is most emphatically no longer the case. There has been an explosion of writing, much of it of high quality and in some cases setting trends that historians of other parts of the world have found it worthwhile to follow.

There are a number of obvious reasons for this transformation. In the subcontinent, above all in India, history writing in English has broken out of the old framework of imperial narratives. Since 1945, scholars in the United States have begun to interest themselves in modern South Asia, often applying social science approaches, especially anthropological ones. British scholars have also broken comprehensively with the old framework and the study of the history of modern India has spread throughout Europe and Australasia. As is inevitable, given the disparity between the facilities for conducting research in South Asian countries and in the West, many scholars from India, Pakistan, and Bangladesh have been attracted to western universities, where they have played a very notable part in the development of the subject. Since the 1960s historians have engaged with a wide range of problems in modern South Asian history, varying chronologically from the fall of the Mughals to the end of British rule. In almost every case debate has been lively and often sharply contentious.

In the 18th century the British saw themselves as creating a new empire out of the anarchic conditions left by the fall of the great Mughals. This interpretation became a historical orthodoxy that has been challenged only recently by historians who argue that, far from the 18th century being India's black century, economic growth enabled a process of political decentralization to create relatively stable regional states. The British were able to insinuate themselves into the thriving commercial economies of some of these states and to take over their military and tax-raising systems on which the new colonial order was to be based. This interpretation can be found in the work of C.A. Bayly, in the early chapters of both *Indian Society and the Making of the British Empire* (1987) and *Rulers, Townsmen and Bazaars* (1983), and in such articles as "Progress and Problems" (1988) by David Washbrook. Although generally endorsed by scholars working in India, others reject such interpretations and reassert the starkness of Mughal collapse and the decisive nature of the British conquest.

Those who see the rise of British power in India as built on Indian foundations tend to interpret the early years of British rule as a slow process of adaptation rather than as a sharp break with the past leading to the forced imposition of "modernity." What in the past was taken to have been the forces leading to modernity – the needs of British industrial capitalism, the ideals of the secular modernizers, such as the utilitarians, notably analyzed in Eric Stokes' *English Utilitarians and India* (1959), or those of the Christian missionaries – look relatively ineffective in this context. It is even argued by Washbrook in "Economic Depression and the Making of a 'Traditional' Society in Colonial India," that early British rule damped down the vibrant economic and social developments of the 18th century, helping to create what had long been seen as elements of an ancient traditional India: a predominantly peasant society and the dominance of Brahminical orthodoxy.

Significant change, it is often argued, came late, not until the 1870s or even later, when steamships, the Suez Canal, and the huge railway program linked India to the world economy and when there was a wider diffusion of new kinds of education. The economic effects of such developments have been the subject of vigorous debate since the 1960s. Those like Morris D. Morris, who argued that although the mass of the population were clearly in no sense enriched, enough people were able to take advantage of the opportunities created by the colonial system to ensure that it brought a modest overall improvement in living standards, were dubbed apologists for imperialism by their critics, who insisted that the lack of industrial development, unequal commercial relations between Britain and India, crippling taxation, support for exploitative landlords, and the "drain of wealth" from India to pay obligations in Britain, all meant that the British actually created poverty. These debates can be followed in a collection of some of the most important articles of the 1960s in *The Indian Economy in the Nineteenth Century: A Symposium* (1969), edited by Morris. Volume 2 of *The Cambridge Economic History of India* (edited by Kumar and Desai, 1983) set off another round of much the same debate. B.R. Tomlinson's *The Economy of Modern India, 1860–1950* (1993) is a so far uncontested statement of the current state of research.

Much writing about the political history of modern South Asia has been in the old tradition of "high politics" and the doings of great men. This is particularly true of the last phase of British rule. Biographies for this period proliferate: notable ones include Judith M. Brown's *Gandhi, Prisoner of Hope* (1989), Sarvepalli Gopal's 3-volume *Jawaharlal Nehru* (1975–84), and Philip Ziegler's *Mountbatten: The Official Biography* (1985). R.J. Moore's *Escape from Empire* (1983) is a shrewd assessment of British policies.

Another new development of the 1960s was studies of the workings of Indian politics from the later 19th century, when the British began to devolve power to representative bodies and overtly political Indian organizations emerged. The first wave of such studies largely emanated from Cambridge, following the appearance of Anil Seal's *The Emergence of Indian Nationalism* (1968). Other works on the same period included Francis Robinson's *Separatism among Indian Muslims* (1974) and C.A. Bayly's *The Local Roots of Indian Politics* (1975). Essays on the interwar years have been edited by D.A. Low as *Congress and the Raj* (1977). Among studies of the politics of partition, there is a contentious account of *The Sole Spokesman: Jinnah, the Muslim League and the Demand for Pakistan* (1985) by Ayesha Jalal. Such books have often proved controversial. The main criticism directed against them is that their approach to politics is excessively mechanistic, stressing the rivalries among nationalists and the degree of "collaboration" (as in the subtitle of Seal's book) as well as conflict with the Raj. Such an approach is sometimes alleged to show an imperial bias because it devalued nationalism by stressing its divisions and ignored the mass appeal of nationalism's message.

To many historians writing at present, there seems to be a less urgent need to vindicate the cause of nationalism and to expose "imperialist" interpretations. The nationalist achievement in both India and Pakistan, seen from the end of the 20th century, looks less imposing than it did in the heady days of the 1960s. Continuities with the Raj (a matter of satisfaction to some British people) look all too evident. For the idealistic of the present day, the conflicts of the British and the nationalists seem distinctly hollow. In a real sense they seem to have been allies beneath the surface in striving to contain the extent to which a transfer of power would have produced revolutionary social and political change. Even Gandhi's willingness fundamentally to change society has been called in question.

Scholars who hold these views tend to shift their perspective from the politics of the British and the nationalists to attempts to reconstruct the aspirations of the mass of the people of the subcontinent. It is generally assumed that far from the masses being quiescent under the Raj until aroused by nationalist ideology, there is a continuous history of popular resistance and commotions that eventually made India ungovernable by the British. This is the view put forward in the comprehensive general account in Sumit Sarkar's *Modern India, 1885–1947* (1983). The theme of rural disorder throughout the period of colonial rule is explored in Ranajit Guha's *Elementary Aspects of Peasant Insurgency in Colonial India* (1983).

The richest field for analysis of popular resistance is of course the great uprising of 1857. The most thorough examination of mass participation is in the studies of Eric Stokes, who sadly died before he could work them up into a full-scale book. His *The Peasant and the Raj* (1978) and *The Peasant Armed* (1986) reveal a very complex pattern of active rebellion and apparent quiescence even within the areas where the incidence of revolt was widespread.

The most ambitious attempt to write the history of the masses is that by the *Subaltern Studies* group under the initial direction of Ranajit Guha, the first volume of their series appearing in 1982. The "subalterns" are described as "the mass of the labouring population and the intermediate strata in town and country." *Subaltern Studies* attempts to free the history of such people from the perspectives of either the colonial rulers or the nationalist elite.

The writing of modern South Asian history is now a global activity. The rigid divide between "imperialist" western interpretations and "nationalist" South Asian ones has largely broken down. This is in part because of increasing recognition of the uncertainties and ambiguities of the imperial role and of the high degree of Indian involvement in it. In part, too, it arises from the awareness of historians that, powerful as the imperial presence was, South Asian people, subalterns and others, still made their own histories under colonial rule.

P.J. MARSHALL

See also Body; British Empire; Gopal; Guha; Subaltern

Further Reading

Bayly, C.A., *The Local Roots of Indian Politics: Allahabad, 1880–1920*, Oxford and New York: Oxford University Press, 1975

Bayly, C.A, *Rulers, Townsmen and Bazaars: North Indian Society in the Age of British Expansion, 1770–1870*, Cambridge and New York: Cambridge University Press, 1983

Bayly, C.A, *Indian Society and the Making of the British Empire*, Cambridge and New York: Cambridge University Press, 1987

Bayly, C.A., *Empire and Information: Intelligence Gathering and Social Communication in India, 1780–1870*, Cambridge and New York: Cambridge University Press, 1996

Brown, Judith M., *Modern India: The Origins of an Asian Democracy*, Delhi, Oxford, and New York: Oxford University Press, 1985; 2nd edition 1994

Brown, Judith M., *Gandhi, Prisoner of Hope*, New Haven: Yale University Press, 1989

Gopal, Sarvepalli, *Jawaharlal Nehru: A Biography*, 3 vols., London: Cape, 1975–84; Cambridge, MA: Harvard University Press, 1976–84

Guha, Ranajit *et al.*, eds., *Subaltern Studies: Writings on South Asian History and Society*, Delhi and Oxford: Oxford University Press, 1982–

Guha, Ranajit, *Elementary Aspects of Peasant Insurgency in Colonial India*, New Delhi and Oxford: Oxford University Press, 1983

Jalal, Ayesha, *The Sole Spokesman: Jinnah, the Muslim League and the Demand for Pakistan*, Cambridge and New York: Cambridge University Press, 1985

Khan, Ghulam Husain, *View of Modern Times*, 1789

Kumar, Dharma, and Meghnad Desai, eds., *The Cambridge Economic History of India*, vol. 2: *1757–c.1970*, Cambridge: Cambridge University Press, 1983

Low, Donald Anthony, ed., *Congress and the Raj: Facets of the Indian Struggle*, London: Heinemann, and Columbia, MO: South Asian Books, 1977

Metcalf, Thomas R., *Ideologies of the Raj*, Cambridge and New York: Cambridge University Press, 1994

Mill, James, *History of British India*, 3 vols., London: Baldwin Cradock and Joy, 1817

Moore, R.J., *Escape from Empire: The Attlee Government and the Indian Problem*, Oxford: Oxford University Press, 1983

Morris, Morris D., ed., *The Indian Economy in the Nineteenth Century: A Symposium*, New Delhi: Indian Economic and Historical Society, 1969

Orme, Robert, *History of the Military Transactions of the British Nation in Indostan*, 3 vols. in 2, London: Nourse, 1763–78

Robinson, Francis, *Separatism among Indian Muslims: The Politics of the United Provinces' Muslims, 1860–1920*, Cambridge: Cambridge University Press, 1974

Sarkar, Sumit, *Modern India, 1885–1947*, Delhi: Macmillan, 1983; Basingstoke: Macmillan, and New York: St. Martin's Press, 1989

Seal, Anil, *The Emergence of Indian Nationalism: Competition and Collaboration in the Later Nineteenth Century*, Cambridge: Cambridge University Press, 1968

Smith, Vincent, *The Oxford History of India*, Oxford: Oxford University Press, 1919; 4th edition, most recently revised by Percival Spear, 1981

Stokes, Eric, *English Utilitarians and India*, Oxford and New York: Oxford University Press, 1959

Stokes, Eric, *The Peasant and the Raj: Studies in Agrarian Society and Peasant Rebellion in Colonial India*, Cambridge: Cambridge University Press, 1978

Stokes, Eric, *The Peasant Armed: The Indian Rebellion of 1857*, Oxford: Oxford University Press, 1986

Tomlinson, B.R., *The Political Economy of the Raj, 1914–1947: The Economics of Decolonization in India*, London: Macmillan, 1979

Tomlinson, B.R., *The Economy of Modern India, 1860–1950*, Cambridge: Cambridge University Press, 1993

Washbrook, David, "Progress and Problems: South Asian Economic and Social History, c.1720–1860," *Modern Asian Studies* 22 (February 1988), 57–96

Washbrook, David, "Economic Depression and the Making of a 'Traditional' Society in Colonial India," *Transactions of the Royal Historical Society*, 6th series, 3 (1993), 237–63

Ziegler, Philip, *Mountbatten: The Official Biography*, London: Collins, and New York: Knopf, 1985

Indian Ocean Region

Although the Indian Ocean region has been an arena of intensive human economic and cultural interaction for the last 4,000 years, it has received little attention from historians. Indeed, until recently historians have concentrated upon the history of individual countries within the region – Australia, India, South Africa, Thailand – or of subregional areas – Southeast Asia, South Asia, the Middle East and East Africa.

Since the 1970s, however, there has been an increase in regionalism as a political and economic concept around the globe: in Europe the European Union (EU); in the Americas the North American Free Trade Association (NAFTA); and in the Asia-Pacific region the Association of Southeast Asian Nations (ASEAN) and the Asia Pacific Economic Council (APEC). This trend has both reflected and encouraged the emergence of a new type of historical writing that focuses on a much larger human canvas in the search for an understanding of how different societies have interacted, and continue to interact.

Within the Indian Ocean region, the lead in writing history from a regional perspective was taken between the 1930s and 1950s by several historians with a fascination for ships and maritime history.

In 1932 an Australian, Stanley Rogers, published *The Indian Ocean*, a popular work on the history of ships in the Indian Ocean region from the advent of the Portuguese in the late 15th century. The work had no pretensions to detailed historical or technical knowledge, but it did provide a broad backdrop to the history of navigation across the ocean in the last three centuries.

In the 1940s and 1950s this theme attracted several more historians. Alan Villiers, an Australian, produced *Sons of Sinbad* (1940); an Anglo-Australian, F.B. Eldridge, wrote *The*

Background of Eastern Sea Power (1945), and in 1953 the Indian historian K.M. Panikkar published *Asia and Western Dominance*.

Villiers' work was a mixture of disciplines. In part it was a description of Arab shipping and seafarers as they existed in his lifetime, and in part a brief excursion into the history of Arab shipping. In contrast, Eldridge was fascinated by the naval confrontations in the Pacific and Indian oceans during World War II, and his work reflected this preoccupation. He examined briefly, but more comprehensively than any previous author, the history of maritime power in both the Indian and Pacific oceans over a 2,000-year time span. But it was Panikkar, who produced the first substantial account of the history of maritime enterprise in the region. Panikkar was an unashamed Indian nationalist and his work covered an area from the Indian Ocean to East Asia. His central thesis was that the possession of superior maritime power enabled Europeans to overwhelm and colonize Asia, and he was a forthright supporter of Asia reclaiming its maritime heritage.

It was not until the late 1960s, however, that the historiography of the Indian Ocean region took on more substantial form. In 1966 a Mauritian historian, Auguste Toussaint, published *A History of the Indian Ocean*. Toussaint was fascinated by the many cultures and historical forces, both from within the region and from Europe and the Americas, that had given shape to Mauritian society. His work, while briefly attempting to analyze the main themes of regional history before the coming of the Portuguese, centered mainly on the period from the 16th century. Nevertheless, it explored new and more broadly based ideas than previous works, covering maritime trade, the movement of peoples, cultural interaction, and the ascent of Europe. In approach, Toussaint was not overly concerned with the pre-European period or with any in-depth economic or social analysis of the forces which had given the region its human geography.

In the 1980s, Toussaint's work was supplanted by the historian K.N. Chaudhuri with the publication of *Trade and Civilization in the Indian Ocean* (1985) and *Asia before Europe* (1990). In both works Chaudhuri attempted to apply sophisticated economic models to analyze the economic and social history of the littoral civilizations of the Indian Ocean. Chaudhuri's focus was on a detailed analysis of shipping and trade data and on discrete accountings of the various societies that existed on the Asian shore of the ocean. Africa was barely taken into account, nor was the 2,000-year period of human interaction with the sea prior to the rise of Islam.

In the 1980s and 1990s other historians began to take an interest in the history of the region. Some, such as Ashin Das Gupta, Michael Pearson, and Sanjay Subrahmanyam worked from particular perspectives, while Kenneth McPherson attempted a more broadly based approach in writing a history of the region that covered a span of several millennia to the present and included Africa, Asia, and Australia. Das Gupta and Pearson were primarily interested in the history of South Asian interaction with the ocean from the 15th century; Subrahmanyam was concerned with the history of Portuguese enterprise in the region both from a maritime and terrestrial perspective. McPherson, in contrast, followed on from Toussaint and Chaudhuri in attempting to locate a regional history through a maritime prism. McPherson's work, *The*

Indian Ocean (1993), contained elements of both Toussaint and Chaudhuri but aimed to locate a regional history by drawing together the commonalities of experience and contact of its component parts, from eastern and southern Africa to Australasia, from the earliest days of human interaction with the sea to the present.

By the 1990s an increasing number of historians were beginning to locate their specific subregional interests in a broader context, and a working consensus has been achieved that now recognizes the role of the Indian Ocean as a factor in shaping the history of the various peoples who inhabit its islands and shores.

KEN MCPHERSON

See also Australia; Southeast Asia

Further Reading

Broeze, Frank, ed., *Brides of the Sea: Port Cities of Asia from the 16th–20th Centuries*, Kensington: New South Wales University Press, and Honolulu: University of Hawaii Press, 1989

Chaudhuri, K.N., *Trade and Civilisation in the Indian Ocean: An Economic History from the Rise of Islam to 1750*, Cambridge and New York: Cambridge University Press, 1985

Chaudhuri, K.N. *Asia before Europe: Economy and Civilisation of the Indian Ocean from the Rise of Islam to 1750*, Cambridge and New York: Cambridge University Press, 1990

Das Gupta, Ashin, and Michael Pearson, eds., *India and the Indian Ocean 1500–1800*, Calcutta and New York: Oxford University Press, 1987

Eldridge, Frank Burgess, *The Background of Eastern Sea Power*, Melbourne: Georgian House, 1945; London: Phoenix, 1948

McPherson, Kenneth, *The Indian Ocean: A History of People and the Sea*, New Delhi and New York: Oxford University Press, 1993

Panikkar, Kavalam M., *Asia and Western Dominance: A Survey of the Vasco da Gama Epoch of Asian History, 1498–1945*, London: Allen and Unwin, 1953; New York: Day, 1954

Rogers, Stanley, *The Indian Ocean*, London: Harrap, and New York: Crowell, 1932

Subrahmanyam, Sanjay, *The Portuguese Empire in Asia 1500–1700*, London and New York: Longman, 1993

Subrahmanyam, Sanjay, *The Career and Legend of Vasco da Gama*, Cambridge: Cambridge University Press, 1997

Toussaint, Auguste, *Histoire de l'Océan Indien*, Paris: Presses Universitaires de France, 1961; in English as *A History of the Indian Ocean*, Chicago: University of Chicago Press, and London: Routledge and Kegan Paul, 1966

Villiers, Alan, *Sons of Sinbad*, New York: Scribner, 1940; as *Sons of Sindbad*, London: Hodder and Stoughton, 1940

Indigenous Peoples

Historical study of indigenous peoples has evolved in close conjunction with the development of Europeans' conceptions of Western culture and its relationship to non-Western peoples. Since World War II, European and American historians increasingly have abandoned the 19th-century colonialist view of Asian, African, and Native American societies, predicated as that view was on an assumption of European cultural superiority. Historians have favored instead more balanced, "multicultural" interpretations which recognize the cultural achievements of indigenous peoples, and the role of Europeans, through disease, violence, and colonial rule, in weakening or destroying indigenous civilizations.

Nineteenth- and early 20th-century historians tended to neglect the history of indigenous peoples, not only due to racist or ethnocentric assumptions regarding the inferiority of indigenous civilizations, but also as a consequence of the established assumptions regarding the nature of historical inquiry. As historical study became professionalized in the university system, historians insisted that scholarly studies be legitimized by strict documentation of sources. This reinforced the prevailing tendency among historians to define history as primarily the study of literate past societies based on examination of written sources. As a consequence, preliterate societies, among them many indigenous civilizations, tended to be relegated to the status of what Eric Wolf has called "the people without history." Historians and anthropologists thus divided the world between themselves, with historians appropriating Western civilizations and, to a lesser extent, literate non-Western societies, and anthropologists focusing on the rest.

Since World War II, the historical study of indigenous peoples has changed radically. As Europe shed its colonies, former colonies coalesced into nations eager to recover their own histories, and burgeoning world trade forced Europeans and Americans to reassess their role in an evolving global economy, historians began to grapple with the problem of studying preliterate societies.

Historians faced both methodological and theoretical obstacles in understanding indigenous peoples. On the methodological level, the problem of sources loomed the largest. How does a historian, trained primarily in the use of written documents, find the sources to study preliterate societies, many of which either have vanished or exist only in a form greatly altered from that of the period which the historian seeks to examine? If using texts written by Western travellers, traders, or conquerors, how can the historian correct for the inevitable biases and misinterpretations distorting the image of the indigenous civilization? Theoretical and interpretive difficulties were equally daunting. Could historians shed their own ethnocentric biases when viewing non-Western societies? How did the economic and cultural dominance of the West in the 20th century evolve? Was the evolution of that dominance inevitable? If not, was the rise of the West preordained, or even desirable? Finally, what does the term "indigenous people" mean, and does the use of the term itself connote a relationship of colonial dominance?

Historians adapted methodologies and insights from economics, anthropology, and literary theory as tools to aid them in their efforts to understand indigenous civilizations. One of the earliest and most important works challenging the dominant Eurocentric interpretation of the rise of the West and its successful colonization of the rest of the world was Immanuel Wallerstein's The Modern World-System (1974). World Systems Theory, as Wallerstein's interpretation is now called, is based upon an essentially Marxist conception of economic development. Wallerstein explained how Europe arose as the powerful capitalist "core" economy by feeding off the labor and primary resources of peripheral territories and their indigenous peoples. Thus the relationship between indigenous peoples and Europeans mirrored that between the bourgeoisie and the proletariat within capitalist economies.

Subsequent studies by Eric Wolf and James M. Blaut, among others, suggested that Europeans intellectually justified their empires by appropriating the histories, as well as the resources and labor, of the peoples they conquered. In Europe and the People Without History (1982), Wolf asserted that European dominance was based on the incorporation of indigenous peoples into a capitalist system that modified the indigenous societies forced to adapt to it. Yet historians and anthropologists alike have erroneously insisted on viewing indigenous cultures as essentially passive and static, outside of time and history. In fact, indigenous peoples had histories of economic adaptation and cultural development before the arrival of Europeans, and also during the period of European dominance. Blaut, in The Colonizer's Model of the World (1993) went even further, arguing that Europeans purposely created a "colonizer's" history that magnified the unique achievements of European culture and minimized those of competing cultures in order to justify European world dominance.

Wallerstein was not the only historian to look for parallels between class relations within European society and the relationship between Europeans and indigenous peoples. Historians reading the works of anthropologists such as Clifford Geertz, Jack Goody, and Victor Turner began to redefine the concept of indigenous peoples to include pre- or semiliterate subgroups in European civilization. Carlo Ginzburg and Emmanuel Le Roy Ladurie, for example, applied an anthropological approach to the study of European peasant societies. Historians interested in indigenous peoples and, especially, the problems of the frontier and contacts between natives and Europeans in North and South America also began to mine the works of anthropologists, thus giving rise to the field of ethnohistory. Ethnohistorians such as Olive Dickason, Bruce Trigger, and Ann M. Wightman have produced some of the finest recent works on indigenous peoples.

Finally, historians turned to textual analysis, semiotics, and literary theories such as deconstruction to cope with the problems of textual sources describing indigenous peoples. Postcolonial studies, such as Edward Said's precedent-setting Orientalism (1978), challenged the supposition that any objective, literal interpretation of documents relating to Europe's view of non-Western cultures was possible. In recent years, most historical studies of indigenous peoples have focused on provocative and at times controversial readings of European texts discussing indigenous peoples, for example Richard Trexler's Sex and Conquest: Gendered Violence, Political Order, and the European Conquest of the Americas (1995).

GAYLE K. BRUNELLE

See also Geertz; Postcolonialism; Said; Turner, V.; Wallerstein

Further Reading
Axtell, James, The Invasion Within: The Contest of Cultures in Colonial North America, New York: Oxford University Press, 1985
Blaut, James M., The Colonizer's Model of the World: Geographical Diffusionism and Eurocentric History, New York: Guilford Press, 1993
Campbell, Mary B., The Witness and the Other World: Exotic European Travel Writing, 400–1600, Ithaca, NY: Cornell University Press, 1988
Curtin, Philip D., The Rise and Fall of the Plantation Complex: Essays in Atlantic History, Cambridge and New York: Cambridge University Press, 1990

Dickason, Olive, *The Myth of the Savage and the Beginnings of French Colonialism in the Americas*, Edmonton: University of Alberta Press, 1984

Geertz, Clifford, *The Interpretation of Cultures: Selected Essays*, New York: Basic Books, 1973; London: Hutchinson, 1975

Ginzburg, Carlo, *Il formaggio e i vermi: il cosmo di un mugnaio del '500*, Turin: Einaudi, 1976; in English as *The Cheese and the Worms: The Cosmos of a Sixteenth-Century Miller*, Baltimore: Johns Hopkins University Press, and London: Routledge, 1980

Greenblatt, Stephen, *Marvelous Possessions: The Wonder of the New World*, Chicago: University of Chicago Press, and Oxford: Oxford University Press, 1991

Karttunen, Frances E., *Between Worlds: Interpreters, Guides, and Survivors*, New Brunswick, NJ: Rutgers University Press, 1994

Maalouf, Amin, *Les Croisades vues par les Arabes*, Paris: J'ai Lu, 1983; in English as *The Crusades through Arab Eyes*, London: Al Saqi, 1984; New York: Schocken, 1985

Mignolo, Walter D., *The Darker Side of the Renaissance: Literacy, Territoriality, and Colonization*, Ann Arbor: University of Michigan Press, 1995

Padden, R.C., *The Hummingbird and the Hawk: Conquest and Sovereignty in the Valley of Mexico, 1503–1541*, Columbus: Ohio State University Press, 1967

Said, Edward W., *Orientalism*, New York: Pantheon, and London: Routledge, 1978

Schwartz, Stuart B., ed., *Implicit Understandings: Observing, Reporting, and Reflecting on the Encounters between Europeans and Other Peoples in the Early Modern Era*, Cambridge: Cambridge University Press, 1994

Tiffin, Chris, and Alan Lawson, eds., *De-scribing Empire: Post-colonialism and Textuality*, London and New York: Routledge, 1994

Trexler, Richard C., *Sex and Conquest: Gendered Violence, Political Order, and the European Conquest of the Americas*, Ithaca, NY: Cornell University Press, and Cambridge: Polity Press, 1995

Trigger, Bruce G., *Natives and Newcomers: Canada's "Heroic Age" Reconsidered*, Montreal: McGill–Queen's University Press, 1985; Manchester: Manchester University Press, 1986

Wachtel, Nathan, *La Vision des vaincus: les Indiens du Pérou devant la conquête espagnole, 1530–1570*, Paris: Gallimard, 1971; in English as *The Vision of the Vanquished: The Spanish Conquest of Peru Through Indian Eyes, 1530–1570*, New York: Barnes and Noble, and Hassocks, Sussex: Harvester, 1977

Wallerstein, Immanuel, *The Modern World-System*, 3 vols., New York and London: Academic Press, 1974–89

White, Richard, *The Middle Ground: Indians, Empires, and Republics in the Great Lakes Region, 1650–1815*, Cambridge and New York: Cambridge University Press, 1991

Wightman, Ann M., *Indigenous Migration and Social Change: The Forasteros of Cuzco, 1570–1720*, Durham, NC: Duke University Press, 1990

Wolf, Eric R., *Europe and the People Without History*, Berkeley: University of California Press, 1982

Industrial Revolution

The term "Industrial Revolution" has had a mixed fortune. One historian, Rondo Cameron, has flatly characterized it as a "misnomer," for its implication of a sudden, abrupt change. Much debate has also accompanied its timing. Conventionally the term refers to the changes that took place in Britain between 1760 and 1830, with the mechanization of cotton and iron production, the introduction of steam engines, and the advent of the factory system. In an influential pamphlet *The Industrial Revolution, 1760–1830* (1948), Ashton widened its terms of reference to include "a revolution in ideas" marked by the beginnings of a new attitude to the "problems of human society."

Over time, other revolutions, whose nature is even more debatable, have been identified: a transport, an agricultural, a commercial revolution. In this way the topic overlaps with British economic history over one century or more. Even more contentious is the term's use to characterize the economic experience of continental Europe, or elsewhere. The notion of discontinuity, of a "take-off" (Rostow), or of a "spurt" (Gerschenkron), after enjoying some success in the 1950s and 1960s, is today well out of fashion, replaced by ideas of long-term development, gradual accumulation, and continuity.

Cannadine's article "The Present and the Past in the English Industrial Revolution, 1880–1980" (1984) reviewed the historiography of the British Industrial Revolution dividing it into four main stages, each influenced by prevailing contemporary concerns. The first stage was dominated by the "social reformers," such as Arnold Toynbee (1852–83) who, in his posthumously published *Lectures on the Industrial Revolution in England* (1884), decried the grave social illnesses begot by industrialization. The reformers saw the Industrial Revolution as abrupt and horrid. They blamed the capitalist ethos of laissez-faire and called for government intervention and social reform. In his 3-volume study, *An Economic History of Modern Britain* (1926–38), Clapham disagreed: he pointed to the gradual character of industrialization, and to its positive effects on wage levels.

A second generation of historians, working mainly in the interwar period, concentrated on the cyclical fluctuations of the capitalist economy. The Industrial Revolution, in their eyes, became an upswing of the capitalist business cycle, albeit perhaps the first one. William Beveridge's "The Trade Cycle in Britain before 1850" (1940) looked for an explanation for the shocks and unemployment that affected modern economies. Another good example of this literature is Gayer, Rostow and Schwartz's *The Growth and Fluctuations of the British Economy* (1953).

In the 1950s and 1960s, economic thought was dominated by assumptions of growth and by imperatives of development. The Industrial Revolution was seen as a laboratory out of which certain universal patterns could be extracted. Rostow's *The Stages of Economic Growth* (1960) pointed to the rise in investment and to the emergence of leading sectors as the crucial determinants. Gerschenkron's *Economic Backwardness in Historical Perspective* (1962) considered the specific requirements of industrialization in conditions of "relative backwardness" in countries of the European periphery which lacked the preconditions that he thought existed in Britain. Such countries, he argued, had to rely on the state and on large German-style investment banks to achieve the breakthrough towards industrialization.

The most recent historiographical stage has been characterized by a gradualist view, in the Clapham mold, underpinned by a reassessment of previous indexes of economic performance (GNP, investment ratios, per capita income). Crafts' *British Economic Growth during the Industrial Revolution* (1985) underplayed the performance of the British economy during the period 1760–1830, although still highlighting significant structural change. Technological innovation which, according to Landes' *The Unbound Prometheus* (1969), was the crucial factor in the Industrial Revolution, was also played down by revealing its piecemeal and patchy nature, especially by Von Tunzelmann's *Steam Power and British Industrialization to 1860* (1978). Confidence in patterns of development has waned, and the achievements of the British economy have been challenged as fragile and shortlived, in particular in many of the pieces in the collective work *The Economic History of Britain since 1700* (1981; revised 1994), edited by Floud and McCloskey.

Hudson's *The Industrial Revolution* (1992) reviewed a wide spectrum of interpretations, both general and thematic: about the importance of the state, agricultural performance, regional differences, commerce and consumption, class and gender. It is an attempt to return to a broader qualitative understanding, restoring to the term its radical significance. Its broad scope places it in the line of influential textbooks following Mantoux's *The Industrial Revolution in the Eighteenth Century* (1906, translated 1927); Deane's *The First Industrial Revolution* (1965); and Mathias's *The First Industrial Nation* (1969).

Wrigley's *People, Cities and Wealth* (1987) and *Continuity, Chance and Change* (1988) stemmed from a revisitation of the classical economists whose thinking, wedded to the theme of diminishing returns, reflected a modernized and commercial system, an "advanced organic economy," unable, however, to accommodate a sustained rise in per capita incomes. The key factor was the shift to a mineral-based energy economy, a shift that was long drawn out, but still revolutionary in its implications, for it generated sustained productivity gains that allowed output to outpace population growth. The fact that Britain had developed a very advanced modern economy, according to Wrigley, is not the explanation of its leadership in the new mineral-based technologies. Chance, in the form of the existence of large accessible coal stocks, had a larger role to play, and the Dutch republic, an even more advanced economy than England, failed to experience the Industrial Revolution until much later.

In "A new view of European Industrialization," (1985), Cameron agreed with the importance of coal as the prime mover toward industrialization. Belgium – with a similar mix of resources – followed the British pattern and was the first country on the continent to industrialize. Harris in "Movements of Technology Between Britain and Europe in the Eighteenth Century" (1991) pointed to the decisive advantage acquired by Britain over France in mineral-based technology of a kind that was very difficult to copy or transmit.

Most scholars, however, have tended to demur at monocausal explanations for Britain's forging ahead, and point to a unique combination of factors, built up over a long period of time. They insist on a link between modernization of the economy and society and the Industrial Revolution. Expressions of this view are, among others, Hartwell in "The Causes of the Industrial Revolution: An Essay in Methodology" (1965) and Mathias in "British Industrialization: Unique or Not?" (1972).

Differences in development between countries in northwestern Europe were not, however, very profound in the 18th century as Crouzet's *De la supériorité de l'Angleterre sur la France* (1985; *Britain Ascendant*, 1990) has convincingly shown. O'Brien and Keyder's *Economic Growth in Britain and France, 1780–1914* (1978) claimed that labor productivity in manufacturing was higher in France than in Britain. Industrialization was speeding up in certain parts of the continent, better endowed with skills and raw materials. According to Pollard's *Peaceful Conquest* (1981) the regional framework is more appropriate than the national one for the understanding of the Industrial Revolution.

Much research and controversy has been prompted by the concept of proto-industrialization, as a separate economic stage in the industrialization process, first introduced by Mendels in 1972. Proto-industrial regions are identified as those in which widespread specialized cottage industry production was commercially organized and oriented towards export markets. Some of these built on their acquired advantages to become centers of mechanized factory production; others deindustrialized. Some set in motion a different pattern, that of flexible, small-scale production which, according to Sabel and Zeitlin's "Historical Alternatives to Mass Production" (1985), may provide the distinctive long-term feature of European industrial development, as opposed to mass production in large factories.

Recent work has moved away from narrower spatial and chronological definitions to embrace a wider variety of patterns and configurations. Old myths have been questioned: according to O'Brien's "The Political Economy of British Taxation 1660–1815" (1988) it appears that the state was an important agent not only, as Gerschenkron believed, in backward countries, but also in Britain, helping industrialization by protectionism, warfare, and taxation. The old drama of the satanic mills has not been replayed while gradual change and modest growth have received a facelift. Many questions about this greatest of all transformations, however, still remain unanswered.

RUGGERO RANIERI

See also Beard; Cipolla; Clapham; Cole; Habakkuk; Hobsbawm; Rostow; Wrigley

Further Reading

Ashton, T.S., *The Industrial Revolution, 1760–1830*, London: Oxford University Press 1948

Ashworth, William, "Typologies and Evidence: Has Nineteenth-Century Europe a Guide to Economic Growth?," *Economic History Review* 30 (1977), 140–58

Bairoch, P., "Europe's Gross National Product, 1800–1975," *Journal of European Economic History* 5 (1976), 273–340

Bairoch, P., "International Industrialization Levels from 1750 to 1980," *Journal of European Economic History* 11 (1982), 269–333

Berg, Maxine, *The Age of Manufactures: Industry, Innovation and Work in Britain, 1700–1820*, Oxford: Blackwell, 1985, New York: Oxford University Press, 1986; 2nd edition London and New York: Routledge, 1994

Beveridge, William, "The Trade Cycle in Britain before 1850," *Oxford Economic Papers* 3 (1940), 47–109

Cameron, Rondo, ed., *Banking in the Early Stages of Industrialization: A Study in Comparative Economic History*, London and New York: Oxford University Press 1967

Cameron, Rondo, "The Industrial Revolution: A Misnomer" in J. Schneider, ed., *Wirtschaftskrafte und Wirstschaftswege: Festschrift für Hermann Kellenbenz*, Stuttgart, 1981

Cameron, Rondo "A New View of European Industrialization," *Economic History Review* 38 (1985), 1–23

Cannadine, David, "The Present and the Past in the English Industrial Revolution, 1880–1980," *Past and Present* 103 (1984), 114–31

Cipolla, Carlo M., *Storia economica dell'Europa pre-industriale*, Bologna: Mulino, 1974; in English as *Before the Industrial Revolution: European Society and Economy, 1000–1700*, New York: Norton, 1976, London: Methuen, 1981

Clapham, John Harold, *The Economic Development of France and Germany, 1815–1914*, Cambridge: Cambridge University Press, 1921

Clapham, John Harold, *An Economic History of Modern Britain*, 3 vols., Cambridge: Cambridge University Press, 1926–38

Clarkson, L.A., *Proto-Industrialization: The First Phase of Industrialization?*, Basingstoke: Macmillan 1985

Coleman, D.C., "Proto-industrialization: A Concept Too Many?" *Economic History Review* 36 (1983), 435–48

Crafts, N.F.R., *British Economic Growth during the Industrial Revolution*, Oxford: Clarendon Press, 1985

Crouzet, François, *De la supériorité de l'Angleterre sur la France: l'économie et l'imaginaire, XVIIe–XXe siècles*, Paris: Perrin, 1985; in English as *Britain Ascendant: Comparative Studies in Franco-British Economic History*, Cambridge and New York: Cambridge University Press, 1990

Cunningham, William, *The Growth of English Industry and Commerce*, 2 vols., Cambridge: Cambridge University Press, 1882; 4th edition 1905–07

Deane, Phyllis, and William Alan Cole, *British Economic Growth, 1688–1959: Trends and Structure*, Cambridge: Cambridge University Press, 1962

Deane, Phyllis, *The First Industrial Revolution*, Cambridge: Cambridge University Press, 1965

Earle, Peter, ed., *Essays in European Economic History, 1500–1800*, Oxford: Clarendon Press, 1974

Feinstein, Charles H., and Sidney Pollard, *Studies in Capital Formation in the United Kingdom, 1750–1920*, Oxford and New York: Oxford University Press, 1988

Floud, Roderick, and Donald McCloskey, eds., *The Economic History of Britain since 1700*, vol. 1: *1700–1860*, 2nd edition, Cambridge: Cambridge University Press, 1994

Gayer, Arthur D., W.W. Rostow and Anna Jacobson Schwartz, *The Growth and Fluctuation of the British Economy, 1790–1850*, 2 vols., Oxford University Press, 1953; reprinted New York: Barnes and Noble, and Hassocks, Sussex: Harvester, 1975

Gerschenkron, Alexander, *Economic Backwardness in Historical Perspective: A Book of Essays*, Cambridge, MA: Harvard University Press, and London: Oxford University Press, 1962

Goodman, Jordan, and Katrina Honeyman, *Gainful Pursuits: The Making of Industrial Europe, 1600–1914*, London: Arnold, and New York: Routledge, 1988

Griffiths, Richard T., *The Industrial Retardation in the Netherlands, 1830–1850*, The Hague: Nijhoff, 1979

Habakkuk, H.J., *American and British Technology in the Nineteenth Century*, Cambridge: Cambridge University Press, 1962

Hammond, J.L., and Barbara Hammond, *The Town Labourer, 1760–1832: The New Civilisation*, London and New York: Longman, 1917

Hammond, J.L., and Barbara Hammond, *The Rise of Modern Industry*, London: Methuen, 1925, New York: Harcourt Brace, 1926; revised 1937

Harris, J., "Movements of Technology Between Britain and Europe in the Eighteenth Century" in David J. Jeremy, ed., *International Technology Transfer: Europe, Japan and the U.S.A, 1700–1914*, Aldershot: Elgar, 1991

Hartwell, R.M., "The Causes of the Industrial Revolution: An Essay in Methodology," *Economic History Review* 18 (1965), 164–82

Hartwell, R.M., ed., *The Causes of the Industrial Revolution in England*, London: Methuen, 1967

Henderson, William Otto, *Britain and Industrial Europe 1750–1870: Studies in British Influence on the Industrial Revolution in Western Europe*, Liverpool: Liverpool University Press, 1954

Hobsbawm, Eric J., *Industry and Empire: An Economic History of Britain since 1750*, London: Weidenfeld and Nicolson, and New York: Pantheon, 1968

Hudson, Pat, *The Industrial Revolution*, London: Arnold, 1992

Jones, E.L., *The European Miracle: Environments, Economics and Geopolitics in the History of Europe and Asia*, Cambridge and New York: Cambridge University Press, 1981

Jones, E.L., *Growth Recurring: Economic Change in World History*, Oxford and New York: Oxford University Press, 1981

Kemp, Tom, *Industrialization in Nineteenth Century Europe*, London and New York: Longman, 1969

Kriedte, Peter, Hans Medick, Jürgen Schlumbohm, with contributions from Herbert Kisch and Franklin F. Mendels, *Industrialisierung vor der Industrialisierung: gewerbliche Warenproduktion auf dem Land in der Formationsperiode des Kapitalismus*, Göttingen: Vandenhoeck & Ruprecht, 1977; in English as *Industrialization before Industrialization: Rural Industry in the Genesis of Capitalism*, Cambridge and New York: Cambridge University Press, 1981

Landes, David S., *The Unbound Prometheus: Technological Change and Industrial Development in Western Europe from 1750 to the Present*, Cambridge: Cambridge University Press, 1969

Lieberman, Sima, ed., *Europe and the Industrial Revolution*, Cambridge: Schenkman, 1972

Mantoux, Paul, *La Révolution industrielle au XVIIIe siècle: essai sur les commencements de la grande industrie moderne en Angleterre*, Paris: Bellais, 1906; in English as *The Industrial Revolution in the Eighteenth Century: An Outline of the Modern Factory System in England*, New York: Harcourt Brace, 1927, London: Cape, 1928

Mathias, Peter, *The First Industrial Nation: An Economic History of Britain, 1700–1914*, London: Methuen, 1969

Mathias, Peter, "British Industrialization: Unique or Not?," in Pierre Leon, François Crouzet, and Richard Gascon, eds., *L'Industrialisation en Europe au XIXe siècle: cartographie et typologie*, Paris: CNRS, 1972

Mendels, Franklin F,. "Protoindustrialization: The First Phase of the Industrialization Process," *Journal of Economic History* 33 (1972), 241–61

Milward, Alan S., and S. B. Saul, *The Economic Development of Continental Europe, 1780–1870*, London: Allen and Unwin, and Totowa, NJ: Rowman and Littlefield, 1973

Mokyr, Joel, *Industrialization in the Low Countries, 1795–1850*, New Haven: Yale University Press, 1976

Mokyr, Joel, ed., *The British Industrial Revolution: An Economic Perspective*, Boulder, CO: Westview Press, 1993

Musson, A.E., *The Growth of British Industry*, London: Batsford, and New York: Holmes and Meier, 1978

North, Douglas Cecil, and Robert Paul Thomas, *The Rise of the Western World: A New Economic History*, Cambridge: Cambridge University Press, 1973

O'Brien, Patrick K., and Caglar Keyder, *Economic Growth in Britain and France, 1780–1914: Two Paths to the Twentieth Century*, London and Boston: Allen and Unwin 1978

O'Brien, Patrick K., "Do We Have a Typology for the Study of European Industrialization in the Nineteenth Century?," *Journal of European Economic History*, 15 (1986), 291–333

O'Brien, Patrick K., "The Political Economy of British Taxation, 1660–1815," *Economic History Review* 41 (1988), 1–32

O'Brien, Patrick K., and Roland Quinault, eds., *The Industrial Revolution and British Society*, Cambridge and New York: Cambridge University Press, 1993

Pollard, Sidney, "Industrialization and the European Economy," *Economic History Review* 26 (1973), 636–40

Pollard, Sidney, *Peaceful Conquest: The Industrialization of Europe, 1760–1970*, Oxford and New York: Oxford University Press, 1981

Rosenberg, Nathan, "Factors Affecting the Diffusion of Technology," *Explorations in Economic History* 10 (1972), 3–34

Rosenberg, Nathan, and Luther Earle Birdzell, *How the West Grew Rich: The Economic Transformation of the Industrial World*, New York: Basic Books, 1986

Rostow, W.W., *British Economy in the Nineteenth Century*, Oxford: Oxford University Press, 1948

Rostow, W.W., *The Stages of Economic Growth: A Non-Communist Manifesto*, Cambridge: Cambridge University Press, 1960, New York: Cambridge University Press, 1965; 3rd edition 1990

Sabel, Charles, and Jonathan Zeitlin, "Historical Alternatives to Mass Production: Politics, Markets and Technology in Nineteenth-Century Industrialization," *Past and Present* 108 (1985), 133–76

Schumpeter, Joseph Alois, *Theorie der wirtschaftlichen Entwicklung*, Leipzig: Duncker & Humblot, 1912; in English as *The Theory of Economic Development: An Inquiry into Profits, Capital, Credit, Interest, and the Business Cycle*, Cambridge, MA: Harvard University Press, 1936

Sylla, Richard, and Gianni Toniolo, eds., *Patterns of European Industrialization: The Nineteenth Century*, London and New York: Routledge, 1991

Toynbee, Arnold, *Lectures on the Industrial Revolution in England*, London: Rivington, 1884; as *Lectures on the Industrial Revolution of the Eighteenth Century in England*, New York: Humboldt, 1884

Trebilcock, Clive, *The Industrialization of the Continental Powers, 1780–1914*, London and New York: Longman, 1981

Von Tunzelmann, G.N., *Steam Power and British Industrialization to 1860*, Oxford: Clarendon Press, and New York: Oxford University Press, 1978

Wrigley, E.A., *People, Cities and Wealth: The Transformation of Traditional Society*, Oxford and New York: Blackwell, 1987

Wrigley, E.A., *Continuity, Chance and Change: The Character of the Industrial Revolution in England*, Cambridge and New York: Cambridge University Press, 1988

Youngson, A.J., ed., *Economic Development in the Long Run*, London: Allen and Unwin, and New York: St. Martin's Press, 1972

Innis, Harold A. 1894–1952

Canadian historian

Harold Adams Innis has been called the least readable of Canadian historians, yet he may well have been the most influential, in large part because of his most enduring contribution to Canadian history: the staples thesis. Many of Innis' contemporaries and successors adopted his notion that the country's institutional, cultural, and political development was shaped by the exploitation of a series of staples, but he was a much broader thinker than his work in economic history might suggest. In a career shortened by premature death, Innis turned his attention to religion, the press, labor relations, and communications, in addition to his voluminous writings on political economy.

Innis' first major work, his doctoral dissertation on the history of the Canadian Pacific Railway (1923), laid the groundwork for his later studies, but it took travels through European universities in the early 1920s to convince him that the precepts of European economic history were inadequate to explain the development of new economies like Canada's. For the rest of the decade, while Innis was teaching at the University of Toronto, he threw himself into the study of Canadian economic history. In 1929 he finished compiling *Select Documents in Canadian Economic History, 1497–1783*, the first attempt to assemble documents from Canada's formative years into a coherent and easy to use whole (a volume covering the next

century, edited with A.R.M. Lower, appeared in 1933). Much of Innis' motive for these compilations stemmed from a desire to rectify what he perceived as serious shortcomings in his dissertation. Specifically, he endeavored to demonstrate that Canada had a unity that predated the railroads: a unity conferred by the river and lake systems that penetrated the northern half of North America. In 1930 Innis published the fruits of his labor in the ground-breaking *The Fur Trade in Canada: An Introduction to Canadian Economic History*.

"The present Dominion emerged not in spite of geography but because of it," he wrote, neatly summing up the entire book in a pleasing aphorism. Settlement in North America depended upon supplying European markets with goods for which there was a strong demand. One of those products was the beaver pelt. According to Innis, the shape of, and indeed the justification for, the European presence in North America rested upon the structures necessary to move the valuable pelts from the interior of the continent to European markets. With this, the linkage between Innis' railway history and *The Fur Trade* became clear: wheat and the railway system were 19th-century heirs to the beaver pelt and the St. Lawrence River system.

Over the next decade, Innis applied his staples thesis to other commodities in books like *Settlement and the Mining Frontier* (1936) and *The Cod Fisheries* (1940). There was a fundamental difference with these studies, however. Instead of the staple providing a unifying element to draw together the regions of Canada into a single purpose, as had been the case with the beaver pelt, the mineral and cod staples affected different regions in different ways. In both instances, Innis identified features of the staples trade that tended to magnify the differences between regions. He had not altogether abandoned his notion of a staple providing unity, however. These studies merely asserted that different forms of communication had affected Canadian history in different ways: rivers and railways tended towards centralization, while ships, canals, and automobiles encouraged decentralization.

Research for his later staples books led Innis deeper into the role of social critic, a progression that affirmed his refusal as a historian to confine his thinking in any way; for example, an examination of the pulp and paper staple caused him to study the export of newsprint, and from there he went on to consider the changing role of communication in the broadest sense. Two of his last works, *Empire and Communications* (1950) and *The Bias of Communication* (1951), reflect this interest in the transmission of ideas as a determinant of historical events. In his last years, Innis also cultivated a reputation for good-natured gloominess, his pessimistic pronouncements (such as "each civilization has its own method of suicide") tempered by an engaging wit.

Perhaps Innis' greatest strength was his willingness to expand the purview of the economic historian. He wrote in 1929 that a student of Canadian economic history should possess a detailed knowledge of French, British, and American economic history, a fluency in French, German, and Latin, and a familiarity with the natural sciences. He truly practiced what he preached. To appreciate the impact of geology and geography on the fur trade, he travelled the Canadian northwest by canoe. As background to *The Cod Fisheries*, he mastered the fine points of water temperature and salinity in the Grand Banks, and the specific gravity of cods' eggs. For Innis, studying economic history demanded more than just an interest in economics. It demanded an enquiring mind that could range over a broad variety of subjects and reach beyond traditional determinants of economic, and therefore political and social, activity. In possessing such a mind, Innis stood above most of his peers in Canada.

JONATHAN F. VANCE

See also Burns; Canada; Creighton; Eccles; Lower; McLuhan; Trigger

Biography

Harold Adams Innis. Born South Norwich Township, Ontario, 5 November 1894. Received BA, McMaster University; PhD, University of Chicago, 1920. Served with Canadian Expeditionary Force, 1916–17. Taught, rising to professor, department of political economy, University of Toronto, 1919–52. Married Mary E. Quayle, 1921 (2 sons, 2 daughters). Died Toronto, 8 November 1952.

Principal Writings

A History of the Canadian Pacific Railway, 1923
Editor, Select Documents in Canadian Economic History, 1497–1783, 1929
The Fur Trade in Canada: An Introduction to Canadian Economic History, 1930; revised 1956
Editor with A.R.M. Lower, Select Documents in Canadian Economic History, 1783–1885, 1933
Settlement and the Mining Frontier, 1936
The Cod Fisheries: The History of an International Economy, 1940
Political Economy in the Modern State, 1946
Empire and Communications, 1950
The Bias of Communication, 1951
Changing Concepts of Time, 1952

Further Reading

Berger, Carl, The Writing of Canadian History: Aspects of English-Canadian Historical Writing, 1900–1970, Toronto: Oxford University Press, 1976; 2nd edition Toronto: University of Toronto Press, 1986
Brebner, J.B., "Harold Adams Innis as Historian," Canadian Historical Association Report (1953)
Christian, William, ed., The Idea File of Harold Adams Innis, Toronto: University of Toronto Press, 1980
Creighton, Donald Grant, Harold Adams Innis: Portrait of a Scholar, Toronto: University of Toronto Press, 1957
"Harold Innis, 1894–1952: Twenty-Five Years On" [special issue on Harold Innis], Journal of Canadian Studies 12 (1977)
Mackenzie, Ken L., "Harold A. Innis: A Study of Creative Intellect," MA thesis, Simon Fraser University, 1971
Melody, William H., Liora Salter, and Paul Heyer, eds., Culture, Communication and Dependency: The Tradition of H.A. Innis, Norwood, NJ: Ablex, 1981
Neill, Robin, A New Theory of Value: The Canadian Economics of H.A. Innis, Toronto: University of Toronto Press, 1972
Patterson, Graham H., History and Communications: Harold Innis, Marshall McLuhan and the Interpretations of History, Toronto: University of Toronto Press, 1990

Intellectual History/History of Ideas

The development of intellectual history and the history of ideas was largely a result of intellectual and cultural changes during the late 18th and early 19th centuries. Both disciplines are rooted in the rise of modern philosophical selfconsciousness seen perhaps most clearly in Kantian idealism and in Romanticism. Both approaches have consistently resisted theories of historical determinism. Nevertheless, despite common origins, intellectual history and the history of ideas differ considerably in their scope and in methodology.

Intellectual history has tended to focus on thinkers and their ideas, carrying a line of inquiry that began perhaps as early as Vasari in his 1550 Le vite de' più eccellenti architetti, pittori et scultori italani (Lives of the Most Eminent Painters, Sculptors and Architects, 1912–15). Vasari's attempt to categorize artists by artistic styles, relying heavily upon biographical and anecdotal information, can be seen in much of modern intellectual history. Intellectual history accepts the selfconscious nature of the thinker, the relevance of his/her experience to the development of ideas, and the importance of intellectual "movements" in history. Intellectual historians have thus tended to categorize thinkers and ideas, embedding the latter within intellectual systems that have lineages and maintain continuity over time. This has usually meant an attempt to reconstruct the mentalité of a certain period. It has also tended to privilege "serious thought," that is, the thought produced in the culture of an educated intellectual elite. Vasari helped form the basis of what was to become the history of men and ideas, but Romanticism, with its development of an intellectual class which was acutely self-aware, has probably had the greatest influence on the practices and prejudices of intellectual history. The key figure in the emergence of 19th-century intellectual history was Jacob Burckhardt and his Die Cultur der Renaissance in Italien (1860; The Civilization of the Renaissance in Italy, 1904). As a history of men and ideas Burckhardt's work partook of intellectual apprehension at materialist histories such as Marx's, and the tide of democratization in western politics and culture. This line of inquiry continued with Johan Huizinga, and later with 20th-century historians such as Crane Brinton, Jacques Barzun, and H. Stuart Hughes.

In the late 19th and early 20th centuries a number of German historians began to suggest that ideas had their own histories. This development arose out of unease with historicism and the positivist tendency to characterize human agency as subject to mechanistic forces and historical laws, absorbing history within the natural sciences. Perhaps the central figure here was Wilhelm Dilthey who, in a wide-ranging set of philosophical works, argued for an approach to history that would allow for the complex and often irrational processes through which human beings acted. Such an approach would provide Verstehen (understanding) through empathy with those who have acted in the past. Our understanding allows us to comprehend the Weltanschauung, that is, the picture of reality or the interpretation of the world, which characterized thought in a given time. Dilthey, along with Max Weber, suggested a wider, more philosophically oriented intellectual history, a history that gave primacy to ideas over thinkers and offered a history of the ideas themselves. Friedrich Meinecke followed this with his own movement away from political history toward what came to be known as Ideengeschichte, in which ideas now took the central role in politics.

It is rare to be able to say that a discipline developed because of the work of one individual, but the history of ideas came to life largely because of the work of one historian. While it was foreshadowed as early as Aristotle's work on the pre-Socratics in *Metaphysics*, the history of ideas was fathered by A.O. Lovejoy, and in the process greatly changed the practice of intellectual history. As a professor of philosophy at Johns Hopkins University, Lovejoy, along with the anthropologist George Boas, founded a "History of Ideas Club" at the university in 1922. He had already been exploring his concept of the "unit-idea" for some time when he presented it in a series of lectures at Harvard in 1933. The result of this was his truly seminal work *The Great Chain of Being: A Study of the History of an Idea* (1936). Tracing the "doctrine of plenitude" from Plato to the early 19th century, Lovejoy posited the notion of the "unit-idea," that is, "persistent dynamic factors, the ideas that produce effects in the history of thought." These are not abstractions but are "cases" embedded in human thought, manifesting themselves in a variety of areas and in different periods. Their continuity and persistence make them important objects for study and historians can consider the ways in which these unit-ideas change as well as how they influence those thinkers who contribute to them. As they constitute elements within systems of thought, or within various ideologies, unit-ideas are part of the traditional areas of interest for intellectual historians and philosophers of history.

Lovejoy suggested an almost endlessly broad and interdisciplinary endeavor that favored continuity over innovation and discontinuity. He later indicated that the historian of ideas needed to take into account the dozen fields which consider human thought, fields as diverse as political science and art history, if the unit-idea was to be understood in all of its various permutations through the ages. Inevitably, the anatomical nature of this endeavor required etymological awareness.

It would be difficult to underestimate Lovejoy's influence. In the 1920s and 1930s his work revolutionized the practice of intellectual history, especially in the English-speaking world. *The Great Chain of Being* and Lovejoy's *Essays in the History of Ideas* (1948) have both been in print for more than 50 years. Lovejoy was the major figure in the founding of the *Journal of the History of Ideas* (1940) which rapidly became the most important journal of intellectual history. Johns Hopkins University Press emerged as the leading publisher of monographs in the history of ideas.

As a discipline, the history of ideas clearly participates in the idealist tradition in history. It holds that history is in fact the history of human consciousness, resisting any notion that history shares "scientific" values, or that the human record is reducible to what Hayden White has called "the fiction of factual representation." Thus it shares a philosophical position akin to R.G. Collingwood's idea that "all history is the history of thought." In the end, the discipline resides firmly within the humanist volitional tradition, set against materialist and determinist interpretations of the past.

The history of ideas has been challenged almost from the outset (an accounting of the various debates about Lovejoy's *magnum opus* can be found in Daniel Wilson's "Lovejoy's *The Great Chain of Being* after Fifty Years" (1987). It has been challenged by historians eager to see history as a social science indebted to the natural sciences, and its idealism has been seen as problematic by a number of critics. In addition, the sometimes Olympian gaze of the historian of ideas has led to pointed criticism from various specialists in other disciplines (such as

the philosophers Anton Pegis and Henry Veatch who found Lovejoy's reading of Aquinas in *The Great Chain* to be philosophically deficient). At the same time, formalist literary critics have been consistently impressed and troubled by Lovejoy. But the heaviest criticism has been methodological in nature, usually coming from those challenging the concept of the unit-idea.

The major complaint of the unit-idea is that it treats ideas as if they are abstract realities. Lovejoy's language lent itself to this interpretation as he resorted to metaphorical terms borrowed from analytical chemistry. The seeming concreteness of unit-ideas led Leo Spitzer, in his "*Geistesgeschichte* vs. History of Ideas as Applied to Hitlerism" (1944), to state that "the assumption that an idea in history is a completely separate element is inconceivable to me." A host of similar criticisms have followed, criticizing the reification of unit-ideas and generally finding fault with the tendency of the history of ideas to remove thought from its historical context. In 1968, Louis Mink found logical inconsistency in Lovejoy's treatment of unit-ideas as unchanging things when he continued to treat his "doctrine of forces" as agents of change. He claimed that Lovejoy never provided a clear definition of the unit-idea. Quentin Skinner maintained that any history that reified doctrines and sought after persistent ideas was doomed to fail. Maurice Mandelbaum wrote more sympathetically, but he found that Lovejoy's stress on continuity ignored or destroyed any notion of authorial originality. Mandelbaum further proposed a history of ideas that took into account those ideas that "recurred" in history.

The methodological concerns have led to outright rejection of the history of ideas in the last thirty years by hermeneutical and deconstructionist critics. What has emerged to challenge the history of ideas is yet another "wing" in the practice of intellectual history – the interpretation of texts. Heavily influenced by developments in linguistics and semiotics, textual analysts hold that it is impossible to separate men and ideas in the way suggested by the history of ideas. Similarly, these textualists find intellectual history's embrace of an intellectual elite troubling. It also rejects the categorization by intellectual history of movements and "isms." In both of these cases textualists believe that historians rely on the use of historical narrative which presumes a linguistic unity, a position that the poststructuralist philosopher Jacques Derrida and the semiotician Roland Barthes believed to be a fiction. Perhaps the strongest critic of the history of ideas has been Michel Foucault who held that there were no "events in thought" which could be categorized or concretized. Any attempt to do so invariably subjects ideas to "rules of practice" imposed by the historian. He advocated a history of discourse that denied the independent and self-sustaining idea as well as "what you might call the creativity of individuals." Overall, "textualists" believe that the philosophy of language has discredited the foundations of history. The historian's hope to describe adequately historical context is groundless.

The work of Hayden White has proven to be critical in the attempt by the textualist historians to unite history and literary criticism. White's essay "The Burden of History," which first appeared in *History and Theory* in 1965, accused historians of "willful methodological naivete," ignoring developments in thought, and continuing to practice a form of history rooted in 19th-century positivism. Historians consistently refuse to acknowledge the moral and aesthetic values that determine the way history is pursued and written. This negative view of historical practice provided the foundation of Dominick LaCapra's *Rethinking Intellectual History* (1983), which argued that the historian must recognize the ways in which history is primarily a literary form. By the 1980s intellectual historians were grappling with the "return of literature" to history, feeling that the poststructuralist history of discourse has greater implications for their field than for other historians. As David Harlan has indicated, Skinner and others, most notably J.G.A. Pocock, have attempted to salvage intellectual history through "radical contextualization," but this has done little to halt the sense of doubt about language's "referential and representational categories."

At the end of the 20th century intellectual history and the history of ideas are caught in a widely recognized "crisis." Much of intellectual history has merged into other fields such as literary criticism and cultural history and the lines of demarcation between it and other fields are less and less clear. But the most recent debates have concerned questions as fundamental as the nature of the subject and the task before these historians. The textualists have questioned the foundations of historical practice and found particular fault with those who have studied human thought and consciousness. In a sense this criticism is just, as these discplines should be acutely aware of the ways in which thought and language have evolved and reflect the times, knowing how dependent human consciousness is and how it succumbs to forces that it cannot control. The tendency to hypostatize concepts, to reify ideas, and to deny the slippery nature of language/narrative, has laid both disciplines open to intense criticism. Nevertheless, this debate is a rich and ongoing one and notable for the ways in which historians of human consciousness are willing to grapple with fundamental issues in order to pursue their art.

SEÁN FARRELL MORAN

See also Berlin; Dilthey; Foucault; Lovejoy; Meinecke; Pocock; Skinner; Weber, M.; White, H.

Further Reading

Barthes, Roland, *Le Degré zéro de l'écriture*, Paris: Seuil, 1953; in English as *Writing Degree Zero*, London: Cape, 1967, New York: Hill and Wang, 1968
Barthes, Roland, *Michelet par lui-même*, Paris: Seuil, 1954; in English as *Michelet*, New York: Hill and Wang, and Oxford: Blackwell, 1987
Barzun, Jacques, *Darwin, Marx, and Wagner: Critique of a Heritage*, Boston: Little Brown, 1941, London: Secker and Warburg, 1942; revised 1958
Barzun, Jacques, *Romanticism and the Modern Ego*, Boston: Little Brown, and London: Secker and Warburg, 1943; revised as *Classic, Romantic, and Modern*, Little Brown, 1961, Secker and Warburg, 1962
Brinton, Crane, *Ideas and Men: The Story of Western Thought*, New York: Prentice Hall, 1950; London: Cape, 1951
Burckhardt, Jacob, *Die Cultur der Renaissance in Italien*, 2 vols., Basel: Schweighauss, 1860; in English as *The Civilization of the Renaissance in Italy*, 2 vols., New York: Macmillan, and London: Swan Sonnenschein, 1904
Derrida, Jacques, *De la grammatologie*, Paris: Minuit, 1967; in English as *Of Grammatology*, Baltimore: Johns Hopkins University Press, 1976

Dilthey, Wilhelm, *Texte zur Kritik der historischen Vernunft*, edited by Hans-Ulrich Lessing, Göttingen: Vandenhoeck & Ruprecht, 1983
Dilthey, Wilhelm, *Hermeneutics and the Study of History*, edited by Rudolf A. Makkreel and Frithjof Rodi, Princeton: Princeton University Press, 1996 [*Selected Works*, vol. 4]
Foucault, Michel, *L'Archéologie du savoir*, Paris: Gallimard, 1969; in English as *The Archaeology of Knowledge*, New York: Pantheon, and London: Tavistock, 1972
Foucault, Michel, *Histoire de la sexualité*, 3 vols., Paris: Gallimard, 1976–84; in English as *The History of Sexuality*, 3 vols., New York: Pantheon, 1978–86, London: Allen Lane, 1979–88
Harlan, David, "Intellectual History and the Return of Literature," *American Historical Review* 94 (1989), 581–609
Hughes, H. Stuart, *Consciousness and Society: The Reorientation of European Social Thought, 1890–1930*, New York: Knopf, 1958, London: MacGibbon and Kee, 1959; revised New York: Vintage, 1977
Hughes, H. Stuart, *The Sea Change: The Migration of Social Thought, 1930–1965*, New York: Harper, 1975
LaCapra, Dominick, and Steven L. Kaplan, eds., *Modern European Intellectual History: Reappraisals and New Perspectives*, Ithaca, NY: Cornell University Press, 1982
LaCapra, Dominick, *Rethinking Intellectual History: Texts, Contexts, and Language*, Ithaca, NY: Cornell University Press, 1983
Lovejoy, Arthur O., and George Boas, eds., *Primitivism and Related Ideas in Antiquity*, Baltimore: Johns Hopkins University Press, 1935
Lovejoy, Arthur O., *The Great Chain of Being: A Study of the History of an Idea*, Cambridge, MA: Harvard University Press, 1936
Lovejoy, Arthur O., *Essays in the History of Ideas*, Baltimore: Johns Hopkins University Press, 1948
Mandelbaum, Maurice, "The History of Ideas, Intellectual History, and the History of Philosophy," *History and Theory* 5 (1965), Beiheft 35–41
Meinecke, Friedrich, *Die Idee der Staatsräson in der neueren Geschichte*, Munich: Oldenbourg, 1924; in English as *Machiavellism: The Doctrine of Raison d'Etat and Its Place in Modern History*, New Haven: Yale University Press, and London: Routledge, 1957
Meinecke, Friedrich, *Die Entstehung des Historismus*, 2 vols., Munich: Oldenbourg, 1936; in English as *Historism: The Rise of a New Historical Outlook*, London and New York: Routledge, 1972
Mink, Louis O., "Change and Causality in the History of Ideas," *Eighteenth Century Studies* 2 (1968), 7–11
Pocock, J.G.A., *Politics, Language, and Time: Essays on Political Thought and History*, New York: Atheneum, 1971; London: Methuen, 1972
Pocock, J.G.A., *Virtue, Commerce, and History: Essays on Political Thought and History, Chiefly in the Eighteenth Century*, Cambridge and New York: Cambridge University Press, 1985
Skinner, Quentin, "Meaning and Understanding in the History of Ideas," *History and Theory* 8 (1969)
Spitzer, Leo, "*Geistesgeschichte* vs. History of Ideas as Applied to Hitlerism," *Journal of the History of Ideas* 5 (1944), 194–203
Vasari, Giorgio, *Le vite de' più eccellenti architetti, pittori et scultori italani*, 3 vols., Florence: H. Torrentino, 1550, revised 1568; in English as *Lives of the Most Eminent Painters, Sculptors and Architects*, 10 vols., London: Macmillan–Medici Society, 1912–15, reprinted New York: AMS, 1976
Weber, Max, "Die protestantische Ethik und der Geist des Kapitalismus," *Archiv für Sozialwissenschaft und Sozialpolitik* 20–21 (1904–05) revised in *Gesammelte Aufsätze zur Religionssoziologie*, Tübingen: Mohr, 1920; in English as *The Protestant Ethic and the Spirit of Capitalism*, London: Allen and Unwin, 1930, New York: Scribner, 1958
Weber, Max, *Wirtschaft und Gesellschaft*, Tübingen: Mohr, 1922, revised 1925, 1956; in English as *Economy and Society: An Outline of Interpretive Sociology*, 3 vols., New York: Bedminster Press, 1968

White, Hayden V., *Metahistory: The Historical Imagination in Nineteenth-Century Europe*, Baltimore: Johns Hopkins University Press, 1973

White, Hayden V., *Tropics of Discourse: Essays in Cultural Criticism*, Baltimore: Johns Hopkins University Press, 1978

White, Hayden V., *The Content of the Form: Narrative Discourse and Historical Representation*, Baltimore: Johns Hopkins University Press, 1987

Wiener, Philip, ed., *Dictionary of the History of Ideas: Studies of Selected Pivotal Ideas*, 5 vols., New York: Scribner, 1973–74

Wilson, Daniel J., "Lovejoy's *The Great Chain of Being* after Fifty Years," *Journal of the History of Ideas* 48 (1987), 187–206

Intelligence and Espionage

This is a comparatively young literature, the bulk of which has, until recently, concentrated on the contribution of intelligence to the conduct and outcome of wars, World War II in particular. However there have also been some impressive texts on earlier uses of intelligence, for example in ancient Greece and the American War of Independence, that possess a resonance in the modern context for both intelligence specialists and period historians. There are two primary limitations to the field. First, it is dependent to a considerable degree on government openness, without which, by necessity, it is reliant upon quite tenuous – often unverifiable – sources. Second, prior to the subject gaining a foothold in universities, which is only a recent phenomenon, the majority of authors were ex-intelligence staff. In some cases, this could be a unique advantage to the reliability and/or credibility of a text. But in other cases, institutional allegiance, self-aggrandizement, and uncritical analysis could undermine the veracity of the literature. While an understanding of bureaucratic structures and intelligence techniques is necessary to negotiate the field, many texts concentrate on these at the expense of the broader domestic and international political issues surrounding intelligence. How decisions are made, rather than their consequences – a concentration on means rather than ends – can mar intelligence texts. With those caveats in mind, the following will be a necessarily partial review of some of the best works in this large and rapidly expanding field.

The practice of spying, codebreaking, and covert intervention has existed for a far longer period than the literature that seeks to recount its history. In a brief but interesting account, Chester Starr told of espionage, subversion, and military intelligence in antiquity. Richard Wilmer Rowan's lengthy account encompassed a greater historical period yet concentrated perhaps too much on World War I given his broad historical remit. Secret British support of French royalists at the time of the French Revolution has been expertly discussed by Harvey Mitchell, and more recently by Lucien Bely, who provides a French perspective on intelligence of the period. Helen Augur contributed a memorable account, among many, of the secret machinations surrounding the American Revolution. Charles D. Ameringer and Nathan Miller have provided several well-researched and essentially accurate general works on American intelligence between 1776 and 1945.

There have been a number of excellent texts on premodern diplomatic intelligence including John Bossy, Charles Howard Carter, and much of Keith Neilson and B.J.C. McKerner's collection. While dated, James Westfall Thompson and Saul K. Padover's *Secret Diplomacy* (1963) is an engaging work that merits attention; however, David Kahn's *The Codebreakers* (1967) surpassed it as the definitive historical account of cryptography. As Kahn's strength is pre-World War II, one must turn to Harry Hinsley, Ralph Bennett, and Edward Drea for more precise discussions of the period after 1939.

M.R.D. Foot was the first scholar to write an official history of intelligence in World War II, and for many, *SOE in France* (1966) remains a classic. However, it was not until publication of Hinsley's unsurpassed *British Intelligence in the Second World War* (1979–90) that a full account of the important role of intelligence in that conflict was written. Hinsley was an intelligence analyst turned scholar, and his multivolume history has been described by the intelligence bibliophile Walter Pforzheimer as "the single greatest work on intelligence ever produced." Hinsley's historical acumen, exceptionally detailed research, clarity of expression, and unprecedented access to government files, set the benchmark by which all other works must be judged.

Other notable contributions to the extensive literature on World War II include H.J. Giskes' *London Calling North Pole* (1953), an account of successful German counterespionage operations against the British and Dutch by an Abwehr participant; David Kahn's classic *Hitler's Spies* (1978), an encyclopedic account of German intelligence which unfortunately lacked a well-formed notion of counterintelligence, and thus a discussion of German weaknesses in this area; John C. Masterman's *The Double Cross System* (1972), an outstanding work on double agents and deception written by the head of the XX Committee in MI5 immediately after the end of the war; and Bradley Smith's *The Shadow Warriors* (1983), a superb history of American intelligence in World War II and a crucial text for understanding the origins of the Central Intelligence Agency (CIA).

The contribution of intelligence to the Cold War has recently started to flourish as a field of historical research. For example, the emergence of the modern British intelligence community is well documented by Christopher Andrew in *Secret Service* (1985). Both the CIA and the KGB have attracted considerable attention. Some of the best accounts of the former include Anne Karalekas' study for the Church Committee, and William Blum's and John Parados' provocative critical histories. While little existed on the KGB until recently, Gordon Brook-Shepherd made a significant initial contribution, drawing attention to the importance of early defectors, including Stalin's secretary Boris Bajanov. While Andrew and Oleg Gordievsky were able to put many outstanding Cold War questions to rest with their astonishing work based on secret papers smuggled out of the USSR, Andrew has also recently authored an expansive account of US intelligence since 1776, *For the President's Eyes Only* (1995). Both Edward J. Epstein and Evgeniia Al'bats contributed interesting and well-researched analyses of both Cold War intelligence systems, the former from an American and the latter from a Russian perspective. The misdeeds and failure of postwar intelligence has also been well documented, for example on the Iran-Contra affair by Theodore Draper and Jonathan Marshall, and by Lawrence Freedman and by Parados separately on the inaccurate Western assessments of Soviet capabilities.

One of the first diplomatic historians to include intelligence sources as a matter of course in his thorough and penetrating examination of the Truman administration was Melvyn Leffler. Aside from Hinsley's authoritative account, Leffler's *A Preponderance of Power* (1992) is perhaps the best example of the contribution well-executed intelligence history, combined with other supporting sources, can make to an understanding of international history writ large. It may well presage the decline of the somewhat isolated history of intelligence and the emergence of a better informed diplomatic history where the contribution of intelligence is assessed as a routine step in the research process.

ADAM COBB

Further Reading

Al'bats, Evgeniia, *The State within a State: The KGB and Its Hold on Russia – Past, Present, and Future*, New York: Farrar Strauss, 1994

Ameringer, Charles D., *US Foreign Intelligence: The Secret Side of American History*, Lexington, MA: Lexington Press, 1990

Andrew, Christopher, *Secret Service: The Making of the British Intelligence Community*, London: Heinemann, 1985

Andrew, Christopher, and Oleg Gordievsky, *KGB: The Inside Story of Its Foreign Operations from Lenin to Gorbachev*, London: Hodder and Stoughton, and New York: HarperCollins, 1990

Andrew, Christopher, *For the President's Eyes Only: Secret Intelligence and the American Presidency from Washington to Bush*, New York: HarperCollins, 1995

Augur, Helen, *The Secret War of Independence*, New York: Duell Sloan and Pearce, 1955

Bely, Lucien, *Espions et ambassadeurs au temps de Louis XIV* (Spies and Ambassadors in the Time of Louis XIV), Paris: Fayard, 1990

Bennett, Ralph Francis, *Ultra in the West: The Normandy Campaign, 1944–45*, London: Hutchinson, 1979; New York: Scribner, 1980

Blum, William, *The CIA: A Forgotten History: US Global Interventions since World War Two*, Atlantic Highlands, NJ, and London: Zed, 1986

Bossy, John, *Giordano Bruno and the Embassy Affair*, New Haven: Yale University Press, 1991

Brook-Shepherd, Gordon, *The Storm Petrels: The First Soviet Defectors, 1928–1938*, London: Collins, 1977; New York: Harcourt Brace, 1978

Carter, Charles Howard, *The Secret Diplomacy of the Hapsburgs, 1598–1625*, New York: Columbia University Press, 1964

Draper, Theodore, *A Very Thin Line: The Iran-Contra Affairs*, New York: Hill and Wang, 1991

Drea, Edward J., *MacArthur's ULTRA: Codebreaking and the War Against Japan, 1942–1945*, Lawrence: University of Kansas Press, 1992

Epstein, Edward Jay, *Deception: The Invisible War Between the KGB and the CIA*, London: W.H. Allen, and New York: Simon and Schuster, 1989

Foot, M.R.D., *SOE in France: An Account of the Work of British Special Operations Executive in France 1940–44*, London: HMSO, 1966

Freedman, Lawrence, *US Intelligence and the Soviet Strategic Threat*, Boulder, CO: Westview Press, 1977

Giskes, H.J., *London Calling North Pole*, London: Kimber, 1953

Hinsley, Francis Harry, ed., *British Intelligence in the Second World War*, 5 vols., London: HMSO, and New York: Cambridge University Press, 1979–90

Kahn, David, *The Codebreakers: The Story of Secret Writing*, London: Weidenfeld and Nicolson, and New York: Macmillan, 1967

Kahn, David, *Hitler's Spies: German Military Intelligence in World War II*, London: Hodder and Stoughton, and New York: Macmillan, 1978

Karalekas, Anne, *History of the Central Intelligence Agency*, Laguna Hills, CA: Augean Park Press, 1977

Leffler, Melvyn P., *A Preponderance of Power: National Security, the Truman Administration, and the Cold War*, Stanford, CA: Stanford University Press, 1992

Marshall, Jonathan, Peter Dale Scott, and Jane Hunter, *The Iran-Contra Connection: Secret Teams and Covert Operations in the Reagan Era*, Boston: South End Press, 1987

Masterman, John Cecil, *The Double Cross System in the War of 1939 to 1945*, London and New Haven: Yale University Press, 1972

Miller, Nathan, *Spying for America: The Hidden History of US Intelligence*, New York: Paragon, 1989

Mitchell, Harvey, *The Underground War Against Revolutionary France: The Missions of William Wickham, 1794–1800*, Oxford: Clarendon Press, 1965

Neilson, Keith, and B.J.C. McKerner, eds., *Go Spy the Land: Military Intelligence in History*, Westport, CT: Praeger, 1992

Parados, John, *The Soviet Estimate: US Intelligence Analysis and Russian Military Strength*, New York: Dial Press, 1982

Parados, John, *Presidents' Secret Wars: CIA and Pentagon Covert Operations since World War II*, New York: Morrow, 1986

Rowan, Richard Wilmer, *The Story of Secret Service*, New York: Literary Guild of America, 1937

Smith, Bradley F., *The Shadow Warriors: OSS and the Origins of the CIA*, New York: Basic Books, and London: Deutsch 1983

Starr, Chester G., *Political Intelligence in Classical Greece*, Leiden: Brill, 1974

Thompson, James Westfall, and Saul K. Padover, *Secret Diplomacy: Espionage and Cryptography, 1500–1815*, New York: Ungar, 1963

Treverton, Gregory F., *Covert Action: The Limits of Intervention in the Postwar World*, New York: Basic Books, 1987

Iran: since 1500

Since 1950 the historical study of Iran has expanded and scholars trained in history have overtaken amateurs and those with philological training. It has also diversified from primarily political and cultural to economic, social, and intellectual history, though the number of works and debates remain fewer than those in Western history. Recent issues include the socio-economic nature of Iran (feudal, tribal-feudal, Oriental despotism, or tripartite nomadic-urban-rural), social classes, women, and the relations of religion and the state since Shi'i Islam became the state religion in 1501. This article and bibliography stress English-language books, but important work has also been done in Persian and several Western languages.

Recently, the very concept of Iran as a nation has been debated. Like those of many other nations, Iran's borders result from historical circumstances and do not conform to ethnicity. Iran does, however, comprise mainly Persian speakers and Shi'ite Muslims, and so has more cohesion than many countries. Like most nations, Iran is often treated as a unit even when it had little cohesion, as between 641 and 1501. This construction of unity often accompanies a glorification of Iran. In the 19th century writers like the Gobineau, Renan, and E.G. Browne glorified Iran above non-"Aryans," and this influenced Iranian nationalists. Iranocentrism has been challenged in an extreme way by Vaziri (1993), who sees it as a harmful import from the

West, and by less categorical scholars who stress the role of non-Persian peoples. One issue is the use of "Iran," and "Iranian," comprising various language groups, rather than "Persia," which emphasizes Persian-speakers.

Iran's unification under the Safavid dynasty after centuries of disunity was of enduring importance. Although few now accept an earlier characterization of Safavid Iran as a national state, the creation of a strong, unified state and the gradual, though sometimes forcible, conversion of most Iranians to Shi'ite Islam, were significant. Works that cover Iran since Safavid times include those by Foran (1993) and the multi-volume *Cambridge History of Iran*.

Much studied is how the 15th-century tribal-based and religiously radical Safavids became, after taking power, conservative rulers who encouraged an "orthodox" clergy with strong ties to the state, and how part of this clergy later became autonomously powerful. Relevant are Mazzaoui's study of the rise of Safavid Shi'ism (1972) showing the peculiarities of the original movement, the sociological history of Safavid and later Shi'ism by Arjomand (1984), and the historical work of Babayan. Safavid Shi'ism is also treated in overviews of Shi'ism by Momen (1985) and Richard (1995). Other topics studied are administration, by Minorsky and Savory (1980), and material culture and trade especially by Matthee. Safavid decline, dealt with in a personalist way by Lockhart, is interpreted in socio-economic terms including the impact of European trade by Foran. There has also been extensive writing on Safavid art history.

The fall of the dynasty in 1722 to Sunni Afghan conquerors, after internal disruption, was followed by decades of disorder, punctuated by the rule of the conqueror, Nader Shah. These events are discussed especially in the *Cambridge History of Iran*, but the 18th century, with its complex history of tribal warfare, has had few historians, with Perry a happy exception.

The Qajar Dynasty (1796–1925), which emerged from this warfare, restored Iran's unity. Its early years saw growing Western influence, especially in the Napoleonic Wars. This influence developed into substantial economic and political control by the later Qajar period. Western envoys and travellers wrote works on Iran, among which several, like the history of Iran by the British envoy John Malcolm (1769–1833), remain useful for their contemporary information. Such Western works often contain outmoded remarks on Iranian national character, disparaging or laudatory.

The first modern Orientalist Iran specialist, Browne, laid the basis for the history of Iranian literature, and of the revolution of 1905–11, though his work is not error-free. Minorsky was a more careful scholar whose historical work is still important. Ann K.S. Lambton is the most recent wide-ranging Iran scholar, whose scholarship is significant in a number of fields, including agrarian relations and administration.

Work on the Qajar period has stressed its middle and later stages. The first major event to interest Western scholars was the rise of the Babi religious movement in the 1840s, which made many converts and rebelled against the government. Most Babis later converted to the new Baha'i religion. Studied by Browne, the Babis are covered in later works, especially that of Amanat.

Scholars stress the reformist and oppositional thought and policies in the later Qajar period, the subject of books by both Bayat and Bakhash. The successful tobacco revolt of 1891–92 and the influential radical Jamal ad-Din "al-Afghani" are treated by Keddie. Work on the constitutional revolution of 1905–11 includes Afary, Martin, and Bayat. Browne and many Iranians stress the popular character of the revolution, Algar saw its clerical leaders as central and positive, while later writers viewed the clergy as self-interested and divided, and instead highlight merchants, the common people, socialists, and women.

On Qajar economic and social history, important work has been done in the edited book of Issawi and in articles by Floor, Gilbar, and others. Kazemzadeh and Atkin each shed light on relations with Russia and Great Britain.

Less thorough has been the treatment of the Pahlavi period (1925–79). Good books include Abrahamian's history covering the Pahlavi period, stressing the Tudeh party, Lambton's on rural conditions, and Akhavi on the clergy.

Banani's positive assessment of Reza Shah's reforms may be supplemented by the fine articles in *Iranian Studies* (1993). Land reform has been studied by both Hooglund and Lambton, who give alternative critical views. On Iran's international relations bill, Ramazani, Cottam, and Gasiorowski each said much of interest to the historian, especially on the roles of Russia, Great Britain, and later the United States, in influencing Iranian politics and economics.

The "Islamic revolution" of 1978–79 is central to many books, including those of Bakhash and of Arjomand, the comparative work of Munson, and a 1979 overview by Halliday. Excellent monographs are by Chehabi on the Islamic liberals, and Abrahamian on the Mojahedin. Authors disagree about the revolution's causes and nature, although the English-language literature generally stresses the disparity between the shah's modernization and his growing autocracy, the destabilizing effect of large oil revenues, and the unique autonomous role of the Iranian Shi'i clergy.

The burgeoning field of women's studies has produced books by Sanasarian, Nashat, Paidar, Moghadam, and Moghissi, concentrating on the 20th century. Several articles in Beck and Keddie's collection discussed Iranian women. Recently the partial restoration of many women's rights since the 1980s has been stressed.

Debates have been rather few, but one may mention the differences, with Algar at one end and Arjomand and Bayat at the other, on the role of the clergy in 20th-century politics; Gilbar's view that peasant conditions improved in the 19th century while Floor and Keddie say they did not; or the favorable view of Reza Shah by Banani versus the less favorable views of others.

NIKKI R. KEDDIE

See also Browne

Further Reading

Abrahamian, Ervand, *Iran Between Two Revolutions*, Princeton: Princeton University Press, 1982

Abrahamian, Ervand, *The Iranian Mojahedin*, New Haven: Yale University Press, 1989

Abrahamian, Ervand, *Khomeinism: Essays on the Islamic Republic*, Berkeley: University of California Press, and London: Tauris, 1993

Afary, Janet, *The Iranian Constitutional Revolution, 1906–1911: Grassroots Democracy, Social Democracy, and the Origins of Feminism*, New York: Columbia University Press, 1996

Akhavi, Shahrough, *Religion and Politics in Contemporary Iran: Clergy-State Relations in the Pahlavi Period*, Albany: State University of New York Press, 1980

Algar, Hamid, *Religion and State in Iran, 1785-1906: The Role of the Ulama in the Qajar Period*, Berkeley: University of California Press, 1969

Amanat, Abbas, *Resurrection and Renewal: The Making of the Babi Movement, 1844-1850*, Ithaca, NY: Cornell University Press, 1989

Amanat, Abbas, *Pivot of the Universe: Nasir al-Din Shah Qajar and the Iranian Monarchy, 1831-1896*, Berkeley: University of California Press, and London: Tauris, 1997

Arjomand, Said Amir, *The Shadow of God and the Hidden Imam: Religion, Political Order, and Societal Change in Shi'ite Iran from the Beginning to 1890*, Chicago: University of Chicago Press, 1984

Arjomand, Said Amir, *The Turban for the Crown: The Islamic Revolution in Iran*, Oxford: Oxford University Press, 1988

Ashraf, Ahmad, and Banuazizi, Ali, "The State, Classes, and Modes of Mobilization in the Iranian Revolution," *State, Culture, and Society* 1/3 (1985), 3-40

Atkin, Muriel, *Russia and Iran, 1780-1828*, Minneapolis: University of Minnesota Press, 1980

Azimi, Fakhreddin, *Iran: The Crisis of Democracy*, London: Tauris, and New York: St. Martin's Press, 1989

Bakhash, Shaul, *Iran: Monarchy, Bureaucracy, and Reform under the Qajars, 1858-1896*, London: Ithaca Press, 1978

Bakhash, Shaul, *The Reign of the Ayatollahs: Iran and the Islamic Revolution*, New York: Basic Books, 1984; London: Tauris, 1985

Banani, Amin, *The Modernization of Iran, 1921-1941*, Stanford, CA: Stanford University Press, 1961

Bayat, Mangol, *Mysticism and Dissent: Socioreligious Thought in Qajar Iran*, Syracuse, NY: Syracuse University Press, 1982

Bayat, Assef, *Workers and Revolution in Iran: A Third World Experience in Workers' Control*, London: Zed Press, 1987

Bayat, Mangol, *Iran's First Revolution: Shi'ism and the Constitutional Revolution of 1905-1909*, New York: Oxford University Press, 1991

Beck, Lois, and Nikki R. Keddie, eds., *Women in the Muslim World*, Cambridge, MA: Harvard University Press, 1978

Beck, Lois, *The Qashqa'i of Iran*, New Haven: Yale University Press, 1986

Bill, James A., *The Eagle and the Lion: The Tragedy of American-Iranian Relations*, New Haven: Yale University Press, 1988

Bill, James A., and William Roger Louis, *Musaddiq, Iranian Nationalism, and Oil*, Austin: University of Texas Press, and London: Tauris, 1988

Bosworth, Clifford Edmund, and Carole Hillenbrand, *Qajar Iran: Political, Social and Cultural Change, 1800-1925*, Edinburgh: Edinburgh University Press, 1983

Browne, Edward G., *The Persian Revolution of 1905-1909*, Cambridge: Cambridge University Press, 1910; reprinted with notes 1995

The Cambridge History of Iran, vols. 6-7, Cambridge: Cambridge University Press, 1986-91

Chehabi, Houchang, *Iranian Politics and Religious Modernism: The Liberation Movement of Iran under the Shah and Khomeini*, Ithaca, NY: Cornell University Press, 1990

Cole, Juan Ricardo I., *Modernity and the Millennium: The Genesis of the Baha'i Faith in the Nineteenth Century Middle East*, New York: Columbia University Press, 1998

Cottam, Richard, *Nationalism in Iran*, Pittsburgh: University of Pittsburgh Press, 1964; revised 1979

Curzon, George Nathaniel, *Persia and the Persian Question*, 2 vols., London and New York: Longman, 1892; reprinted as *Curzon's Persia*, London: Sidgwick and Jackson, 1986

Dabashi, Hamid, *Theology of Discontent: The Ideological Foundations of the Islamic Revolution*, New York: New York University Press, 1993

Floor, Willem M., "Traditional Crafts and Modern Industry in Qajar Iran," *Zeitschrift der Deutschen Morgenländischen Gesellschaft* 141 (1991), 317-52

Foran, John, *Fragile Resistance: Social Transformation in Iran from 1500 to the Revolution*, Boulder, CO: Westview Press, 1993

Garthwaite, Gene R., *Khans and Shahs: A Documentary Analysis of the Bakhtiaris in Iran*, Cambridge and New York: Cambridge University Press, 1983

Gasiorowski, Mark, *US Foreign Policy and the Shah: Building a Client State in Iran*, Ithaca, NY: Cornell University Press, 1991

Gilbar, Gad G., "The Opening of Qajar Iran: Some Economic and Social Aspects," *Bulletin of the School of Oriental and African Studies* 49 (1986), 76-89

Gobineau, Comte de, *Essai sur l'inégalité des races humaines*, 4 vols., Paris: Firmin Didot, 1853-55; in English as *The Inequality of the Human Races*, New York: Putnam, and London: Heinemann, 1915

Halliday, Fred, *Iran: Dictatorship and Development*, Harmondsworth: Penguin, 1979

Hooglund, Eric, *Land and Revolution in Iran, 1960-1980*, Austin: University of Texas Press, 1982

Iranian Studies, Chestnut Hills, MA: Society for Iranian Studies, 1967–

Issawi, Charles, ed., *The Economic History of Iran, 1800-1914*, Chicago: University of Chicago Press, 1971

Katouzian, Homa, *The Political Economy of Modern Iran: Despotism and Pseudo-Modernism, 1926-1979*, New York: New York University Press, and London: Macmillan, 1981

Kazemzadeh, Firuz, *Russia and Britain in Persia, 1864-1914: A Study in Imperialism*, New Haven: Yale University Press, 1968

Keddie, Nikki R., *Religion and Rebellion in Iran: The Tobacco Protest of 1891-92*, London: Cass, 1966

Keddie, Nikki R., *Roots of Revolution: An Interpretive History of Modern Iran*, New Haven: Yale University Press, 1981

Keddie, Nikki R., *Iran and the Muslim World: Resistance and Revolution*, London: Macmillan, and New York: New York University Press, 1995

Ladjevardi, Habibi, *Labor Unions and Autocracy in Iran*, Syracuse: Syracuse University Press, 1988

Lambton, Ann K.S., *Landlord and Peasant in Persia: A Study of Land Tenure and Land Revenue Administration*, London and New York: Oxford University Press, 1953

Lambton, Ann K.S., *The Persian Land Reform, 1962-1966*, Oxford: Clarendon Press, 1969

Lambton, Ann K.S. *Qajar Persia: Eleven Studies*, London: Tauris, 1987; Austin: University of Texas Press, 1988

Lockhart, Laurence, *Nadir Shah: A Critical Study Based Mainly upon Contemporary Sources*, London: Luzac, 1938; reprinted New York: AMS, 1973

Lockhart, Laurence, *The Fall of the Safavei Dynasty and the Afghan Occupation of Persia*, Cambridge: Cambridge University Press, 1958

Malcolm, John, *A History of Persia*, 2 vols., London: Murray, 1815

Martin, Vanessa, *Islam and Modernism: The Iranian Revolution of 1906*, Syracuse, NY: Syracuse University Press, 1989

Matthee, Rudolph P., "Politics and Trade in Late Safavid Iran: Commercial Crisis and Political Reaction under Shah Solayman (1666-1694)," doctoral dissertation, University of California, Los Angeles, 1991

Matthee, Rudolph P., "Anti-Ottoman Politics and Transit Rights: The Seventeenth-Century Trade in Silk Between Safavid Iran and Muscovy," *Cahiers du Monde Russe* 35 (1994), 739-61

Matthee, Rudolph P., "From Coffee to Tea: Shifting Patterns of Consumption in Qajar Iran," *Journal of World History* 7 (1996), 199-230

Mazzaoui, Michel M., *The Origins of the Safawids: Si'ism, Sufism, and the Gulat*, Wiesbaden: Steiner, 1972

Menashri, David, *Education and the Making of Modern Iran*, Ithaca, NY: Cornell University Press, 1992

Minorsky, Vladimir, *Studies in Caucasian History*, London: Taylor's Foreign Press, 1953

Minorsky, Vladimir, *Iranica: Twenty Articles*, Tehran: University of Tehran, and Hertford, England: Austin, 1964

Minorsky, Vladimir, *Medieval Iran and Its Neighbours*, London: Variorum, 1982

Moghadam, Valentine, *Modernizing Women: Gender and Social Change in the Middle East*, Boulder, CO: Rienner, 1993

Moghissi, Haideh, *Populism and Feminism in Iran: Women's Struggle in a Male-defined Revolutionary Movement*, New York: St. Martin's Press, and London: Macmillan, 1994

Momen, Moojan, *An Introduction to Shi'i Islam: The History and Doctrines of Twelver Shi'ism*, New Haven: Yale University Press, and London: Ronald, 1985

Munson, Henry, *Islam and Revolution in the Middle East*, New Haven: Yale University Press, 1989

Nashat, Guity, ed., *Women and Revolution in Iran*, Boulder, CO: Westview Press, 1983

Paidar, Parvin, *Women and the Political Process in Twentieth-Century Iran*, Cambridge: Cambridge University Press, 1995

Perry, John R., *Karim Khan Zand: A History of Iran, 1747–1779*, Chicago: University of Chicago Press, 1979

Ramazani, Rouhollah, *Iran's Foreign Policy, 1941–1973*, Charlottesville: University Press of Virginia, 1975

Renan, Ernest, *L'Islamisme et la science* (Islam and Science), Paris: Lévy, 1883

Richard, Yann, *Le Shi'isme en Iran: Iman et révolution*, Paris: Librairie d'Amérique et d'Orient, 1980; in English as *Shi'ite Islam: Polity, Ideology, and Creed*, Oxford and Cambridge, MA: Blackwell, 1995

Rubin, Barry, *Paved with Good Intentions: The American Experience and Iran*, New York and Oxford: Oxford University Press, 1980

Sanasarian, Eliz, *The Women's Rights Movement in Iran: Mutiny, Appeasement, and Repression from 1900 to Khomeini*, New York: Praeger, 1982

Savory, Roger, *Iran under the Safavids*, Cambridge and New York: Cambridge University Press, 1980

Shuster, W. Morgan, *The Strangling of Persia: A Record of European Diplomacy and Oriental Intrigue that Resulted in the Denationalization of Twelve Million Mohammedans, A Personal Narrative*, New York: Century, and London: Unwin, 1912; reprinted 1987

Sick, Gary, *All Fall Down: America's Tragic Encounter with Iran*, New York: Random House, and London: Tauris, 1985

Taj al-Saltana, *Crowning Anguish: The Memoirs of a Persian Princess from the Harem to Modernity, 1884-1914*, Washington, DC: Mage, 1993

Vaziri, Mostafa, *Iran as Imagined Nation: The Construction of National Identity*, New York: Paragon House, 1993

Zubaida, Sami, *Islam: The People and the State: Essays on Political Ideas and Movements in the Middle East*, London and New York: Routledge, 1989

Ireland

Historical writing in Ireland has been bound up with problems of national identity since its inception. At its most basic, Irish history has been viewed as the 800-year-old struggle of a Gaelic, Catholic people against the British oppressor. From the 1960s, a reaction against the Anglophobia of earlier writers set in, and a steady stream of research questioned the received image of a monolithic people united in their hostility to Britain and all its works. Until recently, Irish scholars have not been troubled by philosophical or methodological issues: the broader perspectives afforded by theories of class and language have often been reduced to glosses on the central theme of Anglo-Irish relations. Over the last five years, however, the underlying assumptions of the profession have been subjected to interrogation, bringing into sharper focus the peculiar problems presented by the Irish past.

The Irish tend to see their historical experience as wholly unique, by which they usually mean different from the English. The comparison is an instructive one, however. English history derives an overriding unity from a remarkable continuity of political frontiers and institutions; Irish history, in comparison, seems turbulent and disjointed. Following the arrival of the Anglo-Normans in the 12th century, Ireland ceased to exist as a separate entity: English rule was consolidated by conquest during the reign of Elizabeth I and by plantation in the 17th century, and in 1801 Ireland was incorporated into the United Kingdom under the Act of Union. Since political institutions were controlled by British colonists, many nationalist historians have concluded that the real Ireland must lie elsewhere – in popular culture, agrarian unrest, revolutionary movements, and the Roman Catholic church.

The nationalist interpretation has its origins in the Irish response to conquest and colonization. Against English apologists who had portrayed the subjection of Ireland as the triumph of civilization over barbarism, the pioneering *Foras Feasa ar Éirinn* by Geoffrey Keating (1570?-1644?) reconstructed an Irish golden age, a land of saints and scholars, whose cultural achievements overshadowed England and the rest of Europe. Some commentators have posited a direct line of descent from Keating, through the patriotic antiquarians of the 18th century and the romanticism of Young Ireland, to the full-blown Gaelic separatism of the 1916 generation. It has been argued that Irish historiography took a wrong turn in the 18th century: while the English and Scots constructed progressive or developmental models of the past, Irish historians retained their tribal role as keepers of the national conscience until the 1930s.

Not all early scholarship can be dismissed in this way, of course. The nationalist historians Eoin MacNeill (1867-1945) and Edmund Curtis (1881-1943) laid the foundations for the study of early and medieval Ireland respectively. Richard Bagwell's (1840-1918) books on Ireland under the Tudors and Stuarts remained standard works until the 1960s, while W.E.H. Lecky (1838-1903) is still a felt presence for scholars of the 18th century. By European or North American standards, however, the separation of history from hagiography has been relatively recent.

Modern Irish historiography can be dated from the launch of the periodical *Irish Historical Studies* (IHS) in 1938 by Theodore William Moody and Robin Dudley Edwards. This forum for the first generation of professional Irish historians united Protestants, Catholics, and Dissenters in a common commitment to "scientific" research; not the least of their achievements was the creation of a single community of scholars in an island now formally divided into two hostile states. *IHS* aimed to raise historical inquiry to a purer, more objective level by setting new standards of scholarship, archival research, and criticism. For Moody, in particular, the academic historian was also engaged in a moral crusade against the dangerous and divisive myths of loyalism and republicanism.

The work of the 1930s generation culminated in *A New History of Ireland*, an authoritative, multivolume project begun in the 1960s (published from 1976). Although some volumes have worn less well than others – and some were already considered out of date on their publication – they have provided a vital starting point for subsequent research. This liberal, optimistic school also produced two lasting monuments in the shape of J.C. Beckett's, *The Making of Modern Ireland, 1603–1923* (1966) and *Ireland since the Famine* (1971) by F.S.L. Lyons.

Inevitably, recent research has exposed some of the limitations of the "New History" group. A self-denying ordinance adopted by *IHS* long deterred research into Irish politics after 1900, and it was not until Joseph Lee's brilliant and impassioned critique of 20th-century economic and social structures, *Ireland 1912–1985*, that the republic received the full treatment which it deserves.

More generally, the New Historians concentrated on political and ecclesiastical institutions rather than on social and cultural change. The appearance of the journal *Irish Economic and Social History* in 1974 has gone some way to redress this imbalance, but work in this field remains uneven. While agrarian and population history have thrived, industry, urbanization, the labor market, and capital formation have received scant attention. The 18th century has been dominated by the revisionist scholarship of Louis Cullen, who has stressed the modernity and complexity of social and economic life. For the 19th century some pioneering work has been produced by Cormac Ó Gráda, whose *Ireland: A New Economic History 1780–1939* (1994) provides the best survey of the modern Irish economy. Social historians have mapped out the rural underworld of the Whiteboys, Defenders, Ribbonmen, and other resistance movements: *Irish Peasants: Violence and Political Unrest, 1780–1914* (1983), edited by Samuel Clark and James Donnelly, demonstrates the liveliness of the field.

During the boom years of the 1960s, as the Irish republic experienced increasing prosperity and security, the New Historians gave way to a second, more provocative wave of revisionists, whose disillusionment with the narrow intellectual ethos of independent Ireland was often made plain. Inevitably, existing interpretations were examined in the light of new evidence, methodologies, and perspectives. As in Britain, long-term structural explanations fell out of favor as emphasis was placed on ambiguity, contingency, and the survival of localism and provincialism. But "revisionism" was also to acquire a specific Irish meaning, as the reaction against nationalism intensified, a process accelerated by the eruption of violence in Northern Ireland in 1969.

Irish historians and Irish gunmen had crossed each other's paths before, most spectacularly when the IRA blew up the Public Record Office during the Civil War of 1921–22. But the emergence of the armed struggle in the north called for a complete reassessment of the cult of violence that had been central to Irish republicanism. Northern Ireland is now thought to be the most heavily researched area on the planet in proportion to its size; John Whyte's *Interpreting Northern Ireland* (1990) offers an indispensable guide to the thousands of articles and books which have appeared during the last 25 years. But "the troubles" also redirected historical inquiry in the south. The assault on traditional nationalism was most explicit in Conor Cruise O'Brien's influential *States of Ireland* (1972), which argued that revolutionary separatism, far from being central to Irish history, had always been confined to an extreme minority.

A vast body of work in the 1970s brought into question a whole range of assumptions about the impact of the 18th-century penal code, the evils of landlordism, and the origins and nature of the 1916 rebellion. The full diversity of Irish society was explored, as class conflicts *within* Catholic Ireland were laid bare. Northern Protestantism, too, was broken down into its component parts, as Paul Bew, Henry Patterson, and Peter Gibbon drew attention to the internal dynamics of Ulster Unionism. While it should be stressed that there was no single revisionist school, few historians now treated nationality as a fixed element, merely transmitted from father to son. Indeed, as Tom Garvin demonstrated in his analysis of the revolutionary generation of 1916–23, the origins of independent Ireland lay in the rebellion of one generation against another.

One complaint made about this growing literature was that it failed to replace older interpretations with new organizing principles. The need for a new synthesis was answered with the publication of Roy Foster's magisterial *Modern Ireland* (1988). To some extent Foster's concern with "varieties of Irishness" reflected a shift toward the recovery of collective identities and mentalities pioneered in F.S.L. Lyons' *Culture and Anarchy in Ireland, 1890–1939* (1979) and Oliver MacDonagh's *States of Mind* (1983), and evident too in the work of Nicholas Canny and others on earlier periods. Although *Modern Ireland* did not ignore the Anglo-Irish relationship, in both its constructive and destructive forms, it avoided an Anglocentric approach by concentrating on the evolution and interaction of the different cultures which have shared the island. Foster's latitudinarian approach coincided with the advance of more flexible definitions of Irishness, guaranteeing it a popular reception. At the same time, however, his attentiveness to the ironies, paradoxes, and subcultures of Irish history has upset the defenders of orthodoxy in both nationalist and unionist camps.

Reservations about the abandonment of traditional nationalism, first voiced in media circles, have lately found their way into the universities. For Brendan Bradshaw and others, the development of scientific research techniques has marginalized the traumatic dimensions of the Irish experience – conquest, colonization, and famine – making the modern Irish aliens in their own land. Recent interventions in the revisionist controversy, collected together by Ciaran Brady in *Interpreting Irish History* (1994), echo the partisanship of the early 20th century, an indication of the social and cultural divisions that still divide the Irish, north, south, and abroad. But they also raise important questions concerning the public role of the historian, the pursuit of objectivity, and the rights of ownership over historical memories.

Calls for a return to the old story of liberation have met with hostility. As yet, no attempt has been made to compile a general survey along counter-revisionist lines. More fruitful, perhaps, are the efforts of younger scholars to move the debate beyond revisionism, turning to hitherto neglected subjects such as local history and women's history. It seems likely, too, that future work will illuminate the loss of Gaelic language and culture, as postcolonial theorists offer more critical perspectives on both imperialism and nationalism.

At present the New Historians' goal of a history that satisfies all cultural traditions remains a distant one. But differences over method and ideology should be taken as a testimony to the vitality of the discipline, and to the cultural diversity of a small island whose export of people has guaranteed its historians a wide audience in Britain, North America, and many other parts of the world.

IAN McBRIDE

See also Lecky; Moody

Further Reading

Bagwell, Richard, *Ireland under the Tudors*, 3 vols., London: Longman, 1885–90

Bagwell, Richard, *Ireland under the Stuarts*, 3 vols., London: Longman, 1909–16

Bartlett, Thomas, *The Fall and Rise of the Irish Nation: The Catholic Question 1690–1830*, Dublin: Gill and Macmillan, and Savage, MD: Barnes and Noble, 1992

Beckett, J.C., *The Making of Modern Ireland, 1603–1923*, London: Faber, and New York: Knopf, 1966

Bew, Paul, Peter Gibbon, and Henry Patterson, *The State in Northern Ireland: Political Forces and Social Classes*, Manchester: Manchester University Press, and New York: St. Martin's Press, 1979; revised as *Northern Ireland, 1921–1994*, London: Serif, 1995

Boyce, David George, *Nationalism in Ireland*, London: Croom Helm, and Baltimore: Johns Hopkins University Press, 1982

Bradshaw, Brendan, "Nationalist Historical Scholarship in Modern Ireland," *Irish Historical Studies* 26 (1989), 239–351

Brady, Ciaran, ed., *Interpreting Irish History: The Debate on Historical Revisionism, 1938–1994*, Dublin: Irish Academic Press, 1994

Canny, Nicholas P., *Kingdom and Colony: Ireland in the Atlantic World, 1560–1800*, Baltimore: Johns Hopkins University Press, 1988

Clark, Samuel, *Social Origins of the Irish Land War*, Princeton: Princeton University Press, 1979

Clark, Samuel, and James S. Donnelly, Jr., eds., *Irish Peasants: Violence and Political Unrest, 1780–1914*, Manchester: Manchester University Press, and Madison: University of Wisconsin Press, 1983

Clarkson, L.A., "The Writing of Irish Economic and Social History since 1968," *Economic History Review*, 33 (1980), 100–11

Connolly, James, *Labor in Irish History*, Dublin: Maunsell, 1910; New York: Donnelly, 1919; frequently reprinted

Connolly, Sean, *Religion, Law and Power: The Making of Protestant Ireland, 1660–1760*, Oxford and New York: Oxford University Press, 1992

Connolly, Sean, ed., *The Oxford Companion to Irish History*, Oxford: Oxford University Press, 1998

Cosgrove, Art, "The Writing of Irish Medieval History," *Irish Historical Studies*, 27 (1990), 97–111

Cullen, Louis M., *An Economic History of Ireland since 1660*, London: Batsford, 1972

Cullen, Louis M., *The Emergence of Modern Ireland, 1600–1900*, London: Batsford, 1981

Curtis, Edmund, *A History of Medieval Ireland*, London: Macmillan, 1923

Dunne, Tom, "New Histories: Beyond Revisionism," *Irish Review*, 12 (Spring/Summer 1992), 1–12

Edwards, Ruth Dudley, *Patrick Pearse: The Triumph of Failure*, London: Gollancz, 1977

Ellis, Steven G., *Tudor Ireland: Crown, Community, and the Clash of Cultures, 1470–1603*, London and New York: Longman, 1985

Fanning, Ronan, *Independent Ireland*, Dublin: Helicon, 1983

Fitzpatrick, David, *Irish Emigration, 1801–1921*, Dundalk: Economic and Social History Society, 1984

Fitzpatrick, David, "Women, Gender and the Writing of Irish History," *Irish Historical Studies* 27 (1991), 267–73

Foster, Roy, *Modern Ireland, 1600–1972*, London: Allen Lane, and New York: Penguin, 1988

Frame, Robin, *Colonial Ireland, 1169–1369*, Dublin: Helicon, 1981

Garvin, Tom, *The Evolution of Irish Nationalist Politics*, Dublin: Gill and Macmillan, 1981

Garvin, Tom, *Nationalist Revolutionaries in Ireland, 1858–1928*, Oxford and New York: Oxford University Press, 1987

Gibbon, Peter, *The Origins of Ulster Unionism: The Formation of Popular Protestant Politics and Ideology in Nineteenth-Century Ireland*, Manchester: Manchester University Press, 1975

Graham, Colin, "'Liminal Spaces': Post-Colonial Theories and Irish Culture," *Irish Review* 16 (Autumn/Winter, 1994), 29–43

Hoppen, K. Theodore, *Ireland since 1800: Conflict and Conformity*, London: Longman, 1989

Keating, Geoffrey, *Foras Feasa ar Éirinn*, written c.1634; in English as *The General History of Ireland*, 1723; edited by David Comyn and P.S. Dinneen, 4 vols., London: Irish Texts Society, 1902–14

Kennedy, Liam, and Philip Ollerenshaw, editors, *An Economic History of Ulster, 1820–1940*, Manchester: Manchester University Press, 1985

Kinealy, Christine, *The Great Calamity: The Irish Famine, 1845–52*, Dublin: Gill and Macmillan, 1994

Lecky, W.E.H., *A History of Ireland in the Eighteenth Century*, 5 vols., London: Longman, and New York: Appleton, 1892–93

Lee, J.J., *The Modernisation of Irish Society, 1848–1918*, Dublin: Gill and Macmillan, 1973

Lee, J.J., ed., *Irish Historiography, 1970–79*, Cork: Cork University Press, 1981

Lee, J.J., *Ireland, 1912–1985: Politics and Society*, Cambridge and New York: Cambridge University Press, 1989

Lydon, James, ed., *England and Ireland in the Later Middle Ages: Essays in Honour of Jocelyn Otway-Ruthven*, Dublin: Irish Academic Press, 1981

Lydon, James, ed., *The English in Medieval Ireland: Proceedings of the First Joint Meeting of the Royal Irish Academy and the British Academy*, Dublin: Royal Irish Academy, 1984

Lyons, F.S.L., *Ireland since the Famine*, London: Weidenfeld and Nicolson, and New York: Scribner, 1971; revised 1973

Lyons, F.S.L., *Culture and Anarchy in Ireland, 1890–1939*, Oxford and New York: Oxford University Press, 1979

MacCurtain, Margaret, Mary O'Dowd, and Maria Luddy, "An Agenda for Women's History in Ireland, 1500–1900," *Irish Historical Studies* 28 (1992), 1–37

MacDonagh, Oliver, *States of Mind: A Study of Anglo-Irish Conflict, 1780–1980*, London and Boston: Allen and Unwin, 1983

MacNeill, Eoin, *Phases of Irish History*, Dublin: Gill, 1920; reprinted Port Washington, NY: Kennikat, 1970

Miller, David, *Queen's Rebels: Ulster Loyalism in Historical Perspective*, Dublin: Gill and Macmillan, and New York: Barnes and Noble, 1978

Moody, T.W., ed., *Irish Historiography, 1936–1970*, Dublin: Irish Committee of Historical Sciences, 1971

Moody, T.W., Francis X. Martin, Francis John Byrne, William Edward Vaughan, Art Cosgrove, and J.R. Hill, eds., *A New History of Ireland*, 9 vols., Oxford, Clarendon Press, 1976–

Morgan, Austen, *James Connolly: A Political Biography*, Manchester: Manchester University Press, and New York: St. Martin's Press, 1988

Ní Dhonnchadha, Máirín, and Theo Dorgan, eds., *Revising the Rising*, Derry: Field Day, 1991

O'Brien, Conor Cruise, *States of Ireland*, London: Hutchinson, and New York: Pantheon, 1972

Ó Gráda, Cormac, *The Great Irish Famine*, Dublin: Gill and Macmillan, and Basingstoke: Macmillan, 1989

Ó Gráda, Cormac, *Ireland: A New Economic History, 1780–1939*, Oxford and New York: Oxford University Press, 1994

Otway-Ruthven, Annette J., *A History of Medieval Ireland*, London: Benn, and New York: Barnes and Noble, 1968

Patterson, Henry, *Class Conflict and Sectarianism: The Protestant Working Class and the Belfast Labour Movement, 1868–1920*, Belfast: Blackstaff Press, 1980

Solow, Barbara, *The Land Question and the Irish Economy, 1870–1903*, Cambridge, MA: Harvard University Press, 1971

Townshend, Charles, *Political Violence in Ireland: Government and Resistance since 1848*, Oxford and New York: Oxford University Press, 1983

Vaughan, William Edward, *Landlords and Tenants in Ireland, 1848–1904*, Dundalk: Economic and Social History Society, 1984

Ward, Margaret, *Unmanageable Revolutionaries: Women and Irish Nationalism*, London: Pluto Press, 1983

Whyte, John, *Interpreting Northern Ireland*, Oxford and New York: Oxford University Press, 1990

Islamic Nations and Cultures

In the preface to his important study of Islamic history first published in 1931, the German historian Carl Brockelmann wrote that "it is still a very risky undertaking to write a history of the Islamic peoples and states from the beginnings down to the present, since the sources for such an account are far from having been made accessible, to say nothing of having been subjected to critical analysis." While the availability of sources and their analysis has made great advances during the last 65 years, a study of historical writings about Islamic societies still poses great challenges.

The nations and cultures which can be considered as falling within the Islamic world represent a vast geographical and ethnic spread. Indeed, it is because of this diversity that the scope of historical studies in the past has been varied in terms of breadth, depth, particular ideological orientations of the historians undertaking the research, and various other factors. Many historians have chosen to focus upon the broad history of Islamic societies per se, while others have devoted their research to specific Islamic nations and cultures in particular geographical areas. Moreover, the approach to historiography by the various scholars involved has been influenced by a range of other academic disciplines: anthropology, sociology, theology, missiology (from Christianity to Islam and from Islam to the outside), as well as linguistics and various other fields.

It is possible to discern certain stages in the development of historical writing focusing on the Islamic world. Among such stages one should include Muslim historiography during the period of classical Islam under the Caliphate; the European colonial era, which saw a significant number of historical and theological analyses of Islam undertaken by Western scholars, often conducting their research through a Christian mission filter; and since World War II a period that has witnessed a range of new phenomena. These include the independence of former European colonies which allowed Islam to come into its own, to some degree, in the eyes of Western scholarship, as well as the immigration of Muslim communities to form significant minorities in Western countries, which has led to a pluralist and somewhat relativist influence upon Western scholarship concerned with the history of Islamic nations and cultures.

In embarking on this subject, it is useful to start with those historical writings that took a broad focus, addressing the issue of the history of the worldwide Islamic community or *ummah*. This present study requires a principal focus on English-language scholarship, but one must not forget the important contributions made in other languages, especially Arabic and French. A selection of works in those languages is listed below.

Mention must be made of the important contribution made to the field of historiography by early Muslim historians. The work of writers such as al-Tabari (d. 923) and Ibn Khaldūn (1332–1406) was crucial not only in terms of laying the groundwork of modern historical method, but also in terms of providing tools for later scholars focusing on the histories of Islamic nations and cultures. These two historians represented very different styles of history writing. Al-Tabari, a traditionalist, chose to base himself upon the established Islamic sources of the Qur'an and the Traditions, believing that the authority of these sources negated a need rationally to examine and criticize them. As a result, his *History of Prophets and Kings* represented a vast array of assembled accounts from the Traditions concerning the history of mankind, which provided vast volumes of valuable historical information yet without being subjected to the rigor of detailed rationalist analysis. In contrast, Ibn Khaldūn, in his history of the world entitled *Kitāb al-'Ibar*, was not satisfied with providing an account of events and unquestioningly using scriptural sources, but rather based himself upon an analytical, rational, and rigorous approach, subjecting his sources to close examination. In his methodology even the authoritative Islamic Traditions were not beyond reproach, and in laying down the guidelines for modern historical writing he called for the use of "numerous sources and much varied knowledge . . . a good speculative mind and thoroughness."

With groundwork laid and historical methods established, a vast range of other Muslim historians were to write many works about the history of the various Islamic peoples. Mention should be made of Ibn Battuta (1304–*c*.1377), broadly contemporaneous with Ibn Khaldūn, who travelled widely and left detailed accounts of the various Islamic societies he visited throughout the Islamic world. Another Muslim theologian and historian, Nur ud-Din ar-Raniri (d. 1658), wrote extensively about his sojourns in the Indian subcontinent and Southeast Asia, and his voluminous work *Bustan us-Salatin* included a lengthy analysis of the history of the world; he was heavily influenced by the historiographical style of his predecessors al-Tabari and ash-Shahrastani (d. 1153). Nevertheless, although such Muslim historians developed a range of methodological approaches, criticism of sources, such as it was, was directed at their reliability rather than at the reliability of Islamic dogma presented therein. Thus, more recent Islamic thinkers such as Ameer Ali, writing at the turn of the 20th century, depended at times upon an essentially pastoral style, and in recording the life history of the prophet Muhammad, he included eulogies which seemed to be more legendary than historical, such as the following description: "sometimes gently sauntering, sometimes hurrying along, heedless of the passers-by, heedless of the gay scenes around him, deeply absorbed in his own thoughts." This essentially tendentious approach to historical record was to be mirrored, though in an opposite direction, in many of the works of Christian scholars writing about the history of the Islamic world.

The rapid expansion of Western colonial activity during the 18th and 19th centuries among many predominantly Muslim lands led to increasing attention being devoted by Western scholars to the history and thought of Islam and its various people groups. These works of scholarship were most commonly produced by Christian missionaries whose access to Muslim communities was facilitated by Western colonization. Characteristic of these new works was an interest in the historical interface between Islam and Christianity, with particular attention being devoted to the Judeo-Christian roots of Islam. Historians such as Mills, Forster, Taylor, and Pool often drew parallels that grew out of Christian frameworks, such as the use of the term "Muhammedanism" (which Muslims dislike) or variations on it, to reflect a view that Muhammad was the center of the Muslim religion as Christ was the center of Christianity. Many of these works were clearly absolutist rather than relativist in their ideological orientations, and sought to identify rights and wrongs, truths and falsehoods in a way that was to become unfashionable in the West in the late 20th century. Nevertheless, Bennett's recent study of Victorian images of Islam and Islamic history has shown that Western scholarship focusing on Islam during the colonial period was by no means uniform. Some Christian scholars tended to see Islam as having got the biblical message wrong and Islamic history as an aberration, while other Christian writers followed what Bennett termed a more "conciliatory" approach. The principal name in connection with the former approach was Sir William Muir, while the pioneer of the latter approach was Charles Forster. Although these two approaches can readily be distinguished by a modern retrospective study of documentary evidence, it is important to note that the view of Muir and his colleagues, perceiving Islam as essentially false, represented the mainstream view in the West during the colonial period.

Brockelmann's *Geschichte der Islamischen Völker und Staaten* (1939; *History of the Islamic Peoples*, 1947) represented an important stage in the rehabilitation of Islam and its history among mainstream Western scholarship. The work was essentially based on research conducted by Western rather than Muslim scholars, and it included a broad study of the chronology and history of Islam in various regions of the world. Largely absent from the work was any suggestion of Islam as a religion lacking in value, or the history of Islam being grounded in error, as was the case with mainstream Western scholarship prior to Brockelmann. Nevertheless, Brockelmann maintained the interest of his predecessors in the contribution of Judaism and Christianity to the history of Islam and at times the work undermined the revelatory claims of Islam by questioning the historicity of Muhammad's experiences. However, the work served as an indication that the conciliatory approach of the Forster school was gaining the ascendancy over the approach of the Muir school.

World War II was to have a profound effect on scholarship into the history of the Islamic peoples conducted by Westerners. The end of the colonial era after the war coincided with rapid expansion in the use of mass communications which had the effect of bringing hitherto distant and mysterious communities into clearer view for the West. Moreover, the migration of Muslims to form sizeable minorities in Western countries meant that for the first time Western masses found themselves regularly interacting with Islam in its various forms.

Scholarship on Islamic history in the West burgeoned, and became increasingly based upon a new-found respect for, and at times admiration for, the achievements of Islamic nations and cultures. The appearance of works such as Bosworth's *The Islamic Dynasties* in 1967 represents an important indicator of

this growth in interest. It summarized Islamic dynasties and rulers, providing brief comments and bibliographical suggestions, and represented a useful study tool for students of the Islamic world whose numbers were growing in the rapidly expanding academic discipline of Islamic Studies. The decade of the 1970s witnessed a rapid increase in output of works by Western scholarship focusing upon the history of Islamic societies. Studies such as *The Cambridge History of Islam* edited by Peter Holt and others (1970), Bernard Lewis' 2-volume edition (1974) of English translations of original Muslim sources, and Schacht and Bosworth's 2nd edition of *The Legacy of Islam* (1974) represented further evidence that Islam was enjoying a new-found respectability in Western scholarly circles. Such studies were characteristically chronological in their treatment of the history of Islamic peoples, they often represented edited works with multiple authors, and they tended to reinforce the pervasive notion of the Islamic world consisting of a center and a periphery, with the central lands of Islam being those located in the Middle East, and the periphery chiefly consisting of Islamic groups in Asia and Africa. But these works also represented an important step in that they made available to an increasingly large student body in Western universities the writings of Muslim scholars, both classical and modern. Thus Lewis' work presented writings by such prominent Muslim writers as al-Bukhari, al-Ghazali, Ibn Battuta, Ibn Taymiyya, and al-Tabari.

In a sense, Schacht and Bosworth's second edition of *The Legacy of Islam* is a useful yardstick for evaluating evolving interests among Western scholars when compared to the first edition of this work produced by Arnold and Guillaume more than forty years earlier. The first edition had created the impression of the outside world looking in at Islam, whereas the second edition devoted itself more to a view from the Muslim perspective looking out at the world around. The second edition included Muslim authorship, and also presented a greater focus on the interface between Islam and religions other than Christianity, especially those in Asia. Overall, newer scholarly methods were employed in the second edition, drawing upon advances in the historical and social sciences.

Lapidus' *A History of Islamic Societies* (1988) in a sense represents the apogee of contemporary trends among Western scholars studying the history of Islamic societies. It provides a fairly orthodox chronological presentation of the history of Islam in its various locations, is respectful, and avoids any dramatic challenges of any basic theological or historical dogmas of Islam. Nevertheless, the author carefully inserts terms such as "in the Muslim view" at strategic points in his study to specify his frame of reference without appearing to challenge these Muslim views. Lapidus is careful to distance himself from arguing for a strong and direct influence of Judaism and Christianity upon Islam in its early formative years, which had attracted such interest from Western scholars of Islamic history during the colonial period.

It is a fact of history that ideologies and trends operate in waves, and those that dominate at a particular point in time tend to marginalize alternative viewpoints and ideologies. Thus, the approach of the Muir school during the colonial era had tended to push aside, although not silence, that of the school led by Forster which had a more sympathetic attitude towards the claims of Islam. Likewise, the predominant approach by Western scholars researching Islamic history since

World War II has been to withdraw from making value judgments as a basic premise of research, and to allow Islam to have its voice on the stage of historical research. This has been more in tune with contemporary developments in historiographical method, but it has been at the expense of subjecting some of the dogmas and assumptions of the standard Islamic historical accounts to the sort of rigorous analysis that is a necessary ingredient of modern historical research.

In this context, the work of a group of British-based historians, principally Wansbrough, Crone, Cook, Hinds, and Hawting, supplemented by the Canadian Andrew Rippin, has been crucial in challenging some of the dogmas and assumptions about Islamic history and the sources of Islam. The research by this particular school of historians of Islam is as important to contemporary historical scholarship as was the alternative approach of the Forster school during the colonial era. This school is posing fundamental and serious challenges to standard history writing about Islam and is also employing methods that are no longer in fashion, such as drawing on early non-Muslim sources, long discarded by Western scholars as politically incorrect and rarely consulted by Muslim scholars. Thus, Crone and Cook in their preface to *Hagarism* (1977) describe it as "a pioneering expedition through some very rough country, not just a guided tour." Their research is of great value for many reasons, but principally for raising important questions at a time when asking difficult questions about other faiths is no longer fashionable. In short, the work of Crone and others represents an important stage in subjecting the dogma of Islamic history to the same rigorous tests of historical-critical methodology as Christianity underwent in the 19th century.

The stages evident in the development of Western historical scholarship focusing upon the Islamic world as a whole also apply to historical studies written about specific Islamic nations and cultures. It should be noted that most works concerned with Islamic world history *per se* also include chapters or sections relevant to specific Islamic communities. Thus *The Cambridge History of Islam* includes valuable studies focusing upon Islam in the Far East, Islam in Africa, and so forth. But other specialist studies focusing upon individual Islamic communities tend to adhere to a discernible system of regional distinction, based upon a five-fold categorization at the macro level, namely the Middle East, Africa, West and Central Asia, South Asia, and Southeast Asia. Within each of these broad regions are various subregions that attract the attention of specific historical studies. Research conducted covers wide-ranging themes including oral history and traditions, cultural change, art evolution and variations, pilgrimage, conversion to Islam, the history of revivalism, and Islamic historiography.

Studies of Islamic communities in the Middle East are many and varied. Hitti's *History of the Arabs*, which first appeared in 1937, represented a watershed in this field, and it has appeared in many subsequent editions. It served to provide an Arab window onto Islamic history for a Western audience, with a broad scope covering the Arab peoples from prehistory to the 20th century. It has served as an invaluable tool for several generations of students, and its greatest contribution is arguably in increasing interest among Western students in the Arab and Islamic world. One of the most recent contributions of Western scholarship to the history of Middle Eastern Islam is Hourani's

A History of the Arab Peoples (1991). In a sense it represents a refreshing change, as it is no longer bound by a purely chronological framework, but takes a thematic focus as its basis, while still adhering to a broad chronological flow. But as seen with the broader studies from the time of Brockelmann to Lapidus, the development of studies into the history of Arab Islam during the 20th century has demonstrated an increasing degree of rigor in historiographical method. At the same time, the enthusiasm of Western scholars to give voice to the formerly colonized communities has often failed to challenge many of the assumptions of the history of these peoples.

Studies of Islam in Africa and Asia have been copious in number and voluminous in size in recent decades. One of the greatest names in 20th-century historical writing on Islam in Africa is that of Trimingham, whose research covered a vast range of Islamic communities from West to East Africa, and whose work has provided crucial foundations for a subsequent generation of both Muslim and Western historians of Islam in the African continent. Research into Islam in Asia has been characterized by edited works, which is to be expected given the breadth of scope of Asia and the diversity of Islam in the region. Thus volumes edited by Israeli and Johns (1984), Esposito (1987) and Hooker (1988) provide students with the perceptions of a number of historians grouped into individual volumes. Although such edited works are often by nature uneven in focus, they nevertheless serve an important function in stimulating interest among the Western university sector in Islam on the periphery of the Muslim world. Nevertheless, there is an urgent need for more focused, single-author histories of Islamic nations and cultures, especially in Asia.

PETER G. RIDDELL

See also Hodgson; Hourani; Ibn Khaldūn; Issawi; Lewis, B.; ar-Raniri; Rashīd al-Dīn; Southeast Asia

Further Reading

Ahmed, Akbar S., *Discovering Islam: Making Sense of Muslim History and Society*, New York and London: Routledge, 1988

Ali, Ameer, *The Spirit of Islam: A History of the Evolution and Ideals of Islam*, Calcutta: Lahiri: 1902, revised and expanded 1922; reprinted 1974

Arnold, Thomas, and Alfred Guillaume, eds., *The Legacy of Islam*, Oxford: Oxford University Press, 1931

Babalola, E.O., *The Advent and Growth of Islam in West Africa*, Ado-Ekiti, Nigeria: Bamgboye, 1982

Balta, Paul, *Islam: civilisation et sociétés* (Islam: Civilization and Society), Monaco: Rocher, 1991

Bennett, Clinton, *Victorian Images of Islam*, London: Grey Seal, 1992

Bosworth, Clifford Edmund, *The Islamic Dynasties: A Chronological and Genealogical Handbook*, Edinburgh: Edinburgh University Press, 1967; revised 1980

Bravmann, René A., *African Islam*, Washington DC: Smithsonian Institution Press, and London: Ethnographica, 1983

Brockelmann, Carl, *Geschichte der Islamischen Völker und Staaten*, Munich: Oldenbourg, 1939; in English as *History of the Islamic Peoples*, New York: Putnam, 1947; London: Routledge, 1948

Bulliet, Richard W., *Conversion to Islam in the Medieval Period: An Essay in Quantitative History*, Cambridge, MA: Harvard University Press, 1979

Crone, Patricia, and Michael Cook, *Hagarism: The Making of the Islamic World*, Cambridge and New York: Cambridge University Press, 1977

Crone, Patricia, and Martin Hinds, *God's Caliph: Religious Authority in the First Centuries of Islam*, Cambridge and New York: Cambridge University Press, 1986

Crone, Patricia, *Meccan Trade and the Rise of Islam*, Princeton: Princeton University Press, 1987

Delanoue, Gilbert, *Moralistes et politiques musulmans dans l'Egypte du XIXe siècle, 1798–1882* (Muslim Moralists and Politicians in 19th-Century Egypt), Cairo: Institut Français d'Archéologie Orientale du Caire, 1982

Dia, Mamadou, *Islam et civilisations négro-africaines* (Islam and Black African Civilization), Dakar: Nouvelles Editions Africaines, 1980

Engineer, Asghar Ali, ed., *Islam in South and South-east Asia*, Delhi: Ajanta, 1985

Esposito, John L., ed., *Islam in Asia: Religion, Politics and Society*, New York: Oxford University Press, 1987

Esposito, John L., *Islam: The Straight Path*, New York and Oxford: Oxford University Press, 1988; revised 1991

Ferhat, Halima, *Le Maghreb aux XIIème et XIIIème siècles: les siècles de la foi* (The Maghreb in the 12th and 13th Centuries: The Centuries of Faith), Casablanca: Wallada, 1993

Fisher, Humphrey J., *The Mecca Pilgrimage in Black African History: Counting the Demographic Cost*, London: Dar es Salaam, 1986

Fletcher, Joseph F., *Studies on Chinese and Islamic Inner Asia*, Aldershot: Variorum, 1995

Forster, Charles, *Mahometanism Unveiled: An Inquiry, in Which that Arch-Heresy, Its Diffusion and Continuities, are Examined on a New Principle, Tending to Confirm the Evidences, and Aid the Propagation, of the Christian Faith*, London: Duncan and Cochran, 1829

Grunebaum, Gustave E. von, *Der Islam*, Ullstein: Propyläen, 1963; in English as *Classical Islam: A History 600–1258*, London: Allen and Unwin, and Chicago: Aldine, 1970

Hawting, Gerald R., *The First Dynasty of Islam: The Umayyad Caliphate AD 661–750*, London: Croom Helm, 1986

Hiskett, Mervyn, *The Development of Islam in West Africa*, London and New York: Longman, 1984

Hiskett, Mervyn, *The Course of Islam in Africa*, Edinburgh: Edinburgh University Press, 1994

Hitti, Philip Khuri, *History of the Arabs*, London and New York: Macmillan, 1937

Hodgson, Marshall G.S., *Rethinking World History: Essays on Europe, Islam and World History*, edited by Edmund Burke III, Cambridge and New York: Cambridge University Press, 1993

Holt, Peter Malcolm, Ann K.S. Lambton, and Bernard Lewis, eds., *The Cambridge History of Islam*, 2 vols., Cambridge: Cambridge University Press, 1970; revised in 4 vols., 1978

Hooker, M.B., ed., *Islam in South-East Asia*, Leiden: Brill, 1988

Hourani, Albert, *A History of the Arab Peoples*, Cambridge, MA: Harvard University Press, and London: Faber, 1991

Ibn Khaldūn, *Muqaddima*, written 1375–78; in English as *The Muqaddimah: An Introduction to History*, 2nd edition, Princeton: Princeton University Press, 1967, London: Routledge / Secker and Warburg, 1978

Israeli, Raphael, *Muslims in China: A Study in Cultural Confrontations*, London: Curzon, and Atlantic Highlands, NJ: Humanities Press, 1980

Israeli, Raphael, ed., *The Crescent in the East: Islam in Asia Major*, London: Curzon, and Atlantic Highlands, NJ: Humanities Press, 1982

Israeli, Raphael, and Anthony H. Johns, eds., *Islam in Asia, vol. 2: Southeast and East Asia*, Jerusalem: Magnes Press, and Boulder, CO: Westview Press, 1984

Kane, Moustapha, and David Robinson, *The Islamic Regime of Fuuta Tooro: An Anthology of Oral Tradition*, East Lansing: Michigan State University Press, 1984

Khalil, 'Imad al-Din, *Fi al-tarikh al-Islami* (On Islamic History), Beirut: al-Maktab al-Islami, 1981

Lapidus, Ira M., *A History of Islamic Societies*, Cambridge and New York: Cambridge University Press, 1988

Levtzion, Nehemia, and John Voll, eds., *Eighteenth-Century Renewal and Reform in Islam*, Syracuse, NY: Syracuse University Press, 1987

Levtzion, Nehemia, *Islam in West Africa: Religion, Society and Politics to 1800*, Aldershot: Variorum, 1994

Lewis, Bernard, ed. and trans., *Islam: From the Prophet Muhammad to the Capture of Constantinople*, 2 vols., New York: Harper, 1974

Mills, Charles, *An History of Muhammedanism*, London: Black Parbury and Allen, 1817

Miquel, André, *L'Islam et sa civilisation: VIIe–XXe siècle* (Islam and Its Civilization: 7th–20th Centuries), Paris: Colin, 1968

Muir, William, *The Life of Mahomet and History of Islam to the Era of the Hegira*, 4 vols., London: Smith Elder, 1858; reprinted Osnabrück: Biblio-Verlag, 1988

Naqar, Umar al-, *The Pilgrimage Tradition in West Africa: An Historical Study with Special Reference to the Nineteenth Century*, Khartoum: Khartoum University Press, 1972

Norris, H.T., *Islam in the Balkans: Religion and Society Between Europe and the Arab World*, London: Hurst, and Columbia: University of South Carolina Press, 1993

Peyronnet, Georges, *L'Islam et la civilisation islamique, VIIe–XIIIe siècle* (Islam and Islamic Civilization, 7th–13th Centuries), Paris: Colin, 1992

Pool, John J., *Studies in Mohammedanism, Historical and Doctrinal: with a Chapter on Islam in England*, Westminster: Archibald Constable, 1892

Pouwels, Randall L., *Horn and Crescent: Cultural Change and Traditional Islam on the East African Coast, 800–1900*, Cambridge: Cambridge University Press, 1987

Rosenthal, Franz, *A History of Muslim Historiography*, Leiden: Brill, 1952; revised 1968

Samatar, Said S., ed., *In the Shadow of Conquest: Islam in Colonial Northeast Africa*, Trenton, NJ: Red Sea Press, 1992

Schacht, Joseph, and Clifford Edmund Bosworth, eds., *The Legacy of Islam*, 2nd edition, Oxford: Oxford University Press, 1974

Sénac, Philippe, *Musulmans et sarrasins dans le sud de la Gaule VIIIe–XIe siècle* (Muslims and Saracens in Southern France, 8th–11th Centuries), Paris: Sycomore, 1980

Tabarī, Muhammad ibn Jarir al-, *The History of al-Tabarī*, vol. 1, edited by Ehsan Yar-Shater, Albany: State University of New York Press, 1989

Taylor, William Cooke, *The History of Mohammedanism, and Its Secrets: Derived Chiefly from Oriental Sources*, London: Parker, 1834

Trimingham, J. Spencer, *Islam in the Sudan*, London: Cass, 1949

Trimingham, J. Spencer, *Islam in Ethiopia*, London: Cass, 1952

Trimingham, J. Spencer, *Islam in West Africa*, London: Oxford University Press, 1959

Trimingham, J. Spencer, *A History of Islam in West Africa*, London and New York: Oxford University Press, 1962

Trimingham, J. Spencer, *Islam in East Africa*, Oxford: Clarendon Press, 1964; New York: Books for Libraries, 1980

Trimingham, J. Spencer, *The Influence of Islam upon Africa*, New York: Praeger, and London: Longman, 1968

Issawi, Charles P. 1916–

US (Egyptian-born) economic historian of the Middle East

Charles Issawi is a leading scholar in the field of Middle Eastern economic history. After working as an economist for the United Nations he joined the Economics department and the Middle East Institute at Columbia University. While there, he combined his interest in history with his training in economics and produced a series of books that have been enormously influential in shaping the field of economic history. His *An Economic History of the Middle East and North Africa* (1982) is an authoritative general work that is essential reading for students of Middle Eastern history.

Issawi's work seeks to understand patterns of underdevelopment and development in the Middle East. Using standard economic categories such as rent, marginal productivity, and comparative advantage, he isolates points of strength and weakness in Middle Eastern economies. In his historical work he is greatly influenced by Ibn Khaldūn, the 14th-century Muslim scholar who detected cycles in which nomads, inspired by religious leaders, swept into ruling cities to conquer and replace corrupt governors and re-establish good government, only to become corrupt in turn, and again be conquered by religiously inspired nomads. Issawi believes that there was a similar pattern in the "gunpowder empires" such as the Ottoman empire in which governors, notables, and the urban populace fought and replaced one another with no long-lasting or meaningful reforms. He observes that historians can detect specific trends in early Islamic civilization: the establishment of an imperial state, the elaboration of religious law and theology, and the incorporation of Greek, Persian, and Indian knowledge. However, Issawi argues that the Middle East from the period from 1400 to about 1800 saw a period of stagnation before re-entering the world economy on unequal terms, and that this imbalance still shapes the history of the region. He does not find in the region the kind of development he discerns in English and European history; fundamentally, he asks how and why Europe overtook the Middle East from about the 14th century, despite the region's many previous scientific, technological, and economic advances.

Issawi compares aspects of Middle Eastern economies and societies with those of Western Europe, Russia, Latin America, the Balkans, Japan, and China. Nevertheless, he argues that the Middle East should be studied on its own terms, not on those of other regions. The historian should, however, ask questions arising from the study of other cultures. In this way, the historian can better understand the course of Middle Eastern history and its place in world history.

Issawi's training as an economist makes him rather suspicious of historical methodologies such as "Deconstruction" and he is somewhat skeptical of the ideas of Foucault, Derrida, and other philosophers. He believes the historian should stay close to the original sources and pay careful attention to detail. In short, he believes that history is grounded in fact, but that historical interpretations of the meaning of the facts vary greatly from year to year and from generation to generation. He does not believe that, generally speaking, "great men" can change the course of history, but rather that history is determined by underlying demographic, economic, technological, and cultural developments information about which can be gleaned from the primary sources.

NANCY GALLAGHER

See also Egypt: since the 7th Century; Iran

Biography

Charles Philippe Elias Issawi. Born Cairo, 15 March 1916. Studied at Victoria College (a British boarding school for boys), Alexandria; Magdalen College, Oxford, BA 1937, MA 1944. Staff member, Egyptian Ministry of Finance, 1937–38; chief of research, National Bank of Egypt, 1938–43; taught political science, American University in Beirut, 1943–47; emigrated to US, 1947 (naturalized 1957); worked at the Arab Office, Washington, DC, 1947–48; and at the Middle East section of the Department of Economic Affairs, United Nations, 1948–55; taught in the Department of Economics and the School of International Affairs, Columbia University, 1951–75; professor of Near Eastern studies, Princeton University, 1975–86 (emeritus); visiting professor, New York University, 1987–91. Married Janina Maria Haftke, 1946.

Principal Writings

Egypt: An Economic and Social Analysis, 1947; revised 1954
An Arab Philosophy of History, 1950
With Mohammed Yeganeh, *The Economics of Middle Eastern Oil*, 1962
Egypt in Revolution: An Economic Analysis, 1963
Editor, *The Economic History of the Middle East, 1800–1914*, 1966
Editor, *The Economic History of Iran, 1800–1914*, 1971
Editor, *The Economic History of Turkey, 1800–1914*, 1980
The Arab World's Legacy: Essays, 1981
An Economic History of the Middle East and North Africa, 1982
Editor, *The Fertile Crescent, 1800–1914: A Documentary Economic History*, 1988
"The Middle East in the World Context: A Historical View" in Georges Sabagh, ed., *The Modern Economic and Social History of the Middle East in Its World Context*, 1989
"Technology, Energy, and Civilization: Some Historical Observations," *International Journal of Middle Eastern Studies* 23 (1991), 281–89
The Middle East Economy: Decline and Recovery, 1995

Further Reading

Gallagher, Nancy, ed., *Approaches to the History of the Middle East: Interviews with Leading Middle East Historians*, Reading, Berkshire: Ithaca Press, 1994
Owen, Roger, *The Middle East in the World Economy, 1800–1914*, London and New York: Methuen, 1981
Owen, Roger, "A Set of Accidents?," in Thomas Naff, ed., *Paths to the Middle East: Ten Scholars Look Back*, Albany: State University of New York Press, 1993

Italy: Renaissance

Two general problems face historians of the Italian Renaissance: first, defining "renaissance," and second, justifying study specific to Italy. Despite the long-standing acceptance of the concept of a particular cultural, literary, artistic, and geographical era based first in Florence and spreading out from that center through Italy and, with the help of both printing and the Reformation, to northern Europe, some medieval and modern historians reject this characterization. Regardless of this, there are many reasons for calling the period from about the 1340s to about 1527 as "the Italian Renaissance."

The "birthplace" of this Renaissance, and its cultural, artistic, literary, and political center, was Florence. The majority of the Italian intellectual leaders of the Renaissance lived and worked in that city, although not all were born there. Defining the intellectual trends of the period is more difficult than locating its center; the term "humanism," which is generally defined more as a method or an intellectual program than a philosophy, remains controversial. Studies of Renaissance humanism fall into several broad categories: defining humanism, either by itself or in relation to its antithesis, scholasticism (for example in the work of Paul Oskar Kristeller, Wallace K. Ferguson, Charles Trinkaus, and Erika Rummel); tracing humanism's effects (in the curriculum by Robert Black, Eugenio Garin, Paul Grendler, Paul Gehl; in politics by Hans Baron, Jerrold Siegel, Tommaso Bozza; in literature by Peter and Julia Bondanella, Benedetto Croce, Ernst Cassirer; in art and architecture by Millard Meiss, John Pope-Hennessy, Rudolf Wittkower; in music by Howard Mayer Brown, Nino Pirrotta, and Edward Lowinsky); by studying prominent humanists (Harold Bloom and Giuseppe Mazzotta on Petrarch, Vittore Branca on Boccaccio, Paolo Viti on Leonardo Bruni, Jasper Hopkins and Arnulf Vagenes on Nicholas of Cusa, Jacques Queron on Pico della Mirandola, and Julia Bolton Holloway on Latini); and by discussing humanist history and historiography (Eric Cochrane on historians and historiography in the Renaissance; Felix Gilbert on Machiavelli and Guicciardini; and William Bouwsma on Venetian humanism).

In fact, the modern discipline of professional historical writing and the analytical text-based methodology in use by most modern historians are products of the Renaissance. Renaissance humanist history, practiced by such diverse figures as Bruni (c.1370–1444), Niccolò Machiavelli (1469–1527), and Giorgio Vasari (1511–74), was secular, practical, and the product of human action. This viewpoint is directly based on the assumption, derived from humanism, that to understand the past one must return to the sources. History was part of the Renaissance *studia humanitatis*, alongside the disciplines of rhetoric, grammar, and poetry – studies designed to persuade as well as educate. In addition many Renaissance historians, including Bruni and Machiavelli, stressed the idea of history as a teacher of prudence and political wisdom. Machiavelli believed that humans, because they were always the same and always evil, were predictable; history was therefore circular, and the study of history would enable an individual to control it. Vasari's *Lives of the Artists* (1550) clearly espoused a "Great Individuals" theory of cultural history: Giotto, Brunelleschi, and other luminaries revived the ancient glories of art and architecture.

However, the Renaissance was a good deal more than humanism. Historians have also studied this time period in terms of art, architecture, economic development, religion, social change, technological advances, and theater. The Renaissance has received much laudatory attention from historians through the centuries. Most have, to a greater or lesser extent, accepted the humanists' own claims of rebirth and renewal after the "dark ages." The Renaissance, thus, is viewed as a high point in history, a period of enviable, if not unequalled, development. Enlightenment historians and philosophers such as Voltaire, lauded the rejection of the Middle Ages in favor of the classical heritage. They appreciated the focus on progress in history and reliance on reason characteristic of the Renaissance, and embraced the break with superstition that this made possible. Separating the Renaissance in Italy from the rest of Europe intellectually as well as geographically was a 19th-century phenomenon.

Despite many challenges to their interpretations, and many changes in the subjects of study, Jules Michelet and Jakob Burckhardt continue to define modern interpretations of the Renaissance. Their recognition of the importance the Renaissance granted to the individual – in Burckhardt's words, the "discovery of the world and of man" – remains current, but their insistence that the Renaissance was a completely amoral episode because of this excessive individualism does not. Increasingly historians focus on both the religious history of the centers of the Renaissance (although in this area, Florence remains relatively neglected) and on the functioning of corporate bodies in the political and social spheres. Studies by Richard Trexler, George Dameron, Peter Partner, and Nicholas Terpstra have shown not only religious vitality in the Renaissance, but the extent to which everyday life depended on religion: on festivals and saints' days as well as on participation in less spectacular ways, such as confraternities, charitable organizations, and hospitals. Confraternities are only one aspect of Renaissance corporate behavior; one should also consult the literature on guilds, revolts, family corporations, and civic organization. One noticeable trend in Renaissance historiography has been the shift away from a Marxist interpretation of the *causes* of peasant unrest in the 14th century, particularly the Ciompi Revolt, which was seen as a proto-bourgeois revolution due to its demands for better working conditions and greater guild representation. Niccolò Rodolico and his followers instead focused on the *results* of this unrest, which were conservative.

Burckhardt's focus on politics and culture also remains definitive. Italian 19th-century historians were less sympathetic to the Renaissance than their Italian predecessors and their foreign contemporaries; the patriotic agenda was that of the *Risorgimento* which in the early 20th century necessitated a rejection by Italians of the separation of cultural and political history. Machiavelli's support of tyrants was forgotten and he was glorified as the founder of political philosophy, for example by Benedetto Croce. Later 20th-century historians of the Renaissance searched for the "historical roots" of the Renaissance. They stressed that although Renaissance thinkers believed themselves to be "reviving" the ancient norms, for both historical and political reasons, in effect they were creative individuals as well. Using diverse sources such as census records, private letters and diaries, criminal records, and sumptuary legislation, modern historians can construct a far more complete and complex picture of Renaissance society.

The economic and political histories of the Renaissance have been granted equal prominence with the cultural history through the work of Hans Baron, Peter Burke, Carlo Cipolla, Samuel Cohn, Richard Goldthwaite, Robert Lopez, Lauro Martines, Harry Miskimin, Antony Molho, J.G.A. Pocock, and M.M. Postan, among others. The study of Renaissance "philosophy" remains strong, however, and has been dominated by Ernst Cassirer, Marcia Colish, Paul Oskar Kristeller, and Charles Trinkaus. Since the mid-20th century, the largest growth area in Italian Renaissance studies has been in the field of social history. Work on women as religious, social, and cultural figures, as well as on gender and the family is of particular interest, and among the most prominent historians in those fields are David Herlihy, Christiane Klapisch-Zuber, Stanley Chojnacki, Patricia Simons, and Guido Ruggiero. Recent studies of Jewish history in the Renaissance have focused on Jews by themselves, not merely as part of Christian rulers' economic, social, and religious policies; see, for example, Roberto Bonfil's *Gli Ebrei in Italia nell'epoca del Rinascimento* (1991; *Jewish Life in Renaissance Italy*, 1994).

Modern Renaissance historiography also seeks to shift the focus from Florence as the birthplace and center of the Renaissance and to consider other cities, in Italy as well as elsewhere in Europe. Among many examples of this scholarship are the work of John D'Amico and John O'Malley on Rome; William Bouwsma, Melissa M. Bullard, Frederick C. Lane, Carlo Ossola, Brian Pullan, Donald Queller, and Cesare Vasoli on Venice; and Maureen Mazzaoui, Maureen Miller, and Thomas Blomquist on Tuscany outside of Florence. The study of Renaissance science, technology, and medicine is of continued interest; recent work by Marie Boas Hall, Nancy Siriasi, and Silvana Seidel Menchi in this field increasingly undermines the long-held thesis that little of scientific importance took place in the Renaissance.

Finally, the art and architectural history of the Renaissance will continue to attract attention, particularly with the new historiographical appreciation of ways in which design represented not only artistic interest, but also power. A recent example is Richard Goldthwaite's *Wealth and the Demand for Art in Italy, 1300–1600* (1993). As historians of architecture begin to discard the notion that Renaissance Italy's rejection of the Gothic idioms of northern Europe does not represent a "failure" of Italian architectural achievement, they are led to new appreciations of native architectural designs. Wolfgang Lotz's *Architecture in Italy, 1500–1600* (1995) is a new standard text for the time period. In the sphere of art, interest in perspective, color, choice of subject, and patronage remain strong, although the recent restoration of the Michelangelo *Doni Tondo* after the 1993 bombing of the Uffizi, and the long-term project for the Sistine Chapel frescos have generated controversy over the transition from Renaissance to Mannerism. Among the more recent studies of this artist/architect are Giulio Carlo Argan and Bruno Contardi's *Michelangelo architetto* (1990; *Michelangelo Architect*, 1993). In addition, there is increasing attention focused on women artists, for example by Fredrika H. Jacobs.

KATHLEEN COMERFORD

See also Art; Baron, H.; Body; Burckhardt; Burke; Cantimori; Chabod; Christianity; Cipolla; Ecclesiastical; European Expansion; Feminism; Foucault; Garin; Giannone; Gilbert; Gombrich; Guicciardini; Huizinga; Intellectual; Kelly-Gadol; Kristeller; Machiavelli; Maravall; Martines; Mattingly; Panofsky; Pieri; Reformation; Renaissance Historical Writing; Sexuality; Skinner; Trevor-Roper; Ullman; Villari; White, H.; Women's History: Europe; Yates

Further Reading

Abulafia, David, "Southern Italy and the Florentine Economy, 1265–1370," *Economic History Review*, 34 (1981), 377–88

Argan, Giulio Carlo, and Bruno Contardi, *Michelangelo architetto*, Milan: Electa, 1990; in English as *Michelangelo Architect*, New York: Abrams, and London: Thames and Hudson, 1993

Baron, Hans, *The Crisis of the Early Italian Renaissance: Civic Humanism and Republican Life in an Age of Classicism and Tyranny*, 2 vols., Princeton: Princeton University Press, 1955; revised 1966

Becker, Marvin B., "Church and State in Florence on the Eve of the Renaissance (1343–1382)," *Speculum* 37 (1962), 509–27

Benson, Pamela, *The Invention of the Renaissance Woman: The Challenge of Female Independence in the Literature and Thought of Italy and England*, University Park: Pennsylvania State University Press, 1992

Bietenholz, Peter G., ed., *Contemporaries of Erasmus: A Biographical Register of the Renaissance and Reformation*, 3 vols., Toronto: University of Toronto Press, 1985–87

Black, Robert, "Humanism and Education in Renaissance Arezzo," *I Tatti Studies: Essays in the Renaissance* 2 (1987), 171–237

Blomquist, Thomas W., and Maureen Fennell Mazzaoui, eds., *The "Other Tuscany": Essays in the History of Lucca, Pisa, and Siena during the Thirteenth, Fourteenth, and Fifteenth Centuries*, Kalamazoo, MI: Medieval Institute Publications, Western Michigan University Press, 1994

Bondanella, Peter, and Mark Musa, eds., *The Portable Machiavelli*, New York: Penguin, 1979

Bonfil, Roberto, *Gli Ebrei in Italia nell'epoca del Rinascimento*, Florence: Sansoni, 1991; in English as *Jewish Life in Renaissance Italy*, Berkeley: University of California Press, 1994

Bouwsma, William J., *Venice and the Defense of Republican Liberty: Renaissance Values in the Age of the Counter Reformation*, Berkeley: University of California Press, 1968

Bowsky, William, *A Medieval Commune: Siena under the Nine, 1287–1355*, Berkeley: University of California Press, 1981

Brucker, Gene A., *Renaissance Florence*, Berkeley: University of California Press, 1969

Bullard, Melissa Meriam, *Lorenzo il Magnifico: Image and Anxiety, Politics and Finance*, Florence: Olschki, 1994

Burckhardt, Jacob, *Die Cultur der Renaissance in Italien*, 2 vols., Basel: Schweighauss, 1860; in English as *The Civilization of the Renaissance in Italy*, 2 vols., New York: Macmillan, and London: Swan Sonnenschein, 1904

Burke, Peter, *Culture and Society in Renaissance Italy, 1420–1540*, London: Batsford, and New York: Scribner, 1972; revised as *Tradition and Innovation in Renaissance Italy: A Sociological Approach*, London: Fontana, 1974, and as *The Italian Renaissance: Culture and Society in Italy*, Princeton: Princeton University Press, and Cambridge: Polity Press, 1987

Cassirer, Ernst, Paul Oskar Kristeller, and John Herman Randall, Jr., eds., *The Renaissance Philosophy of Man*, Chicago: University of Chicago Press, 1948

Cereta, Laura, *Collected Letters of a Renaissance Feminist*, edited by Diana Maury Robin, Chicago: Chicago University Press, 1997

Chabod, Federico, "The Concept of the Renaissance," in his *Machiavelli and the Renaissance*, London: Bowes and Bowes, and Cambridge, MA: Harvard University Press, 1958

Chambers, David, Brian Pullan, and Jennifer Fletcher, eds., *Venice: A Documentary History, 1450–1630*, Oxford: Blackwell, 1992

Chojnacki, Stanley, "Patrician Women in Early Renaissance Venice," *Studies in the Renaissance* 21 (1974), 176–203

Cipolla, Carlo M., "The Trends in Italian Economic History in the Later Middle Ages," *Economic History Review* 2 (1949), 181–84

Cipolla, Carlo M., *Storia economica dell'Europa pre-industriale*, Bologna: Mulino, 1974; in English as *Before the Industrial Revolution: European Society and Economy, 1000–1700*, New York: Norton, 1976, London: Methuen, 1981

Cochrane, Eric, *Historians and Historiography in the Italian Renaissance*, Chicago: University of Chicago Press, 1981

Croce, Benedetto, *Elementi di politica* (Elements of Politics), Bari: Laterza, 1925

Croce, Benedetto, *Storia dell'età barocca in Italia* (The Story of the Baroque Era in Italy), Bari: Laterza, 1929; reprinted 1993

D'Amico, John, *Renaissance Humanism in Papal Rome: Humanists and Churchmen on the Eve of the Reformation*, Baltimore: Johns Hopkins University Press, 1983

D'Entreves, A.P., "Introduction," in Federico Chabod, *Machiavelli and the Renaissance*, London: Bowes and Bowes, and Cambridge, MA: Harvard University Press, 1958

Ferguson, Wallace K., *The Renaissance in Historical Thought: Five Centuries of Interpretation*, Boston: Houghton Mifflin, 1948

Garin, Eugenio, *Il tumulto dei Ciompi: un momento di storia fiorentina ed europea* (The Ciompi Revolt: A Moment in Florentine and European History), Florence: Olschki, 1981

Gilbert, Felix, *Machiavelli and Guicciardini: Politics and History in Sixteenth-Century Florence*, Princeton: Princeton University Press, 1965

Goldthwaite, Richard, *Private Wealth in Renaissance Florence: A Study of Four Families*, Princeton: Princeton University Press, 1968

Goldthwaite, Richard, *Wealth and the Demand for Art in Italy, 1300–1600*, Baltimore: Johns Hopkins University Press, 1993

Grendler, Paul, *Schooling in Renaissance Italy: Literacy and Learning, 1300–1600*, Baltimore: Johns Hopkins University Press, 1989

Hall, Marie Boas, *The Scientific Renaissance, 1450–1630*, London: Collins, and New York: Harper, 1962

Hay, Denys, *The Italian Renaissance in Its Historical Background*, Cambridge: Cambridge University Press, 1961

Jacobs, Fredrika H., *Defining the Renaissance Virtuosa: Women Artists and the Language of Art History and Criticism*, Cambridge and New York: Cambridge University Press, 1997

Kent, Dale V., and Frances W. Kent, *Neighbours and Neighbourhood in Renaissance Florence: The district of the Red Lion in the Fifteenth Century*, Locust Valley, NY: Augustin, 1982

Klapisch-Zuber, Christiane, *Women, Family, and Ritual in Renaissance Italy*, Chicago: University of Chicago Press, 1985

Kristeller, Paul Oskar, *The Classics and Renaissance Thought*, Cambridge, MA: Harvard University Press, 1955; revised as *Renaissance Thought 1: The Classic, Scholastic, and Humanistic Strains*, New York: Harper, 1961

Lane, Frederic C., *Venice: A Maritime Republic*, Baltimore: Johns Hopkins University Press, 1973

Lopez, Robert S., and Harry A. Miskimin, "The Economic Depression of the Renaissance," *Economic History Review*, 2nd series 14 (1961–62), 400–26

Lotz, Wolfgang, *Architecture in Italy, 1500–1600*, New Haven: Yale University Press, 1995

Martines, Lauro, *The Social World of the Florentine Humanists, 1390–1460*, Princeton: Princeton University Press, and London: Routledge, 1963

Martines, Lauro, *Power and Imagination: City-States in Renaissance Italy*, New York: Knopf, 1979; London: Allen Lane, 1980

Matter, E. Ann, and John Coakley, eds., *Creative Women in Medieval and Early Modern Italy: A Religious and Artistic Renaissance*, Philadelphia: University of Pennsylvania Press, 1994

Miller, Maureen C., *The Formation of a Medieval Church: Ecclesiastical Change in Verona, 950–1150*, Ithaca, NY: Cornell University Press, 1993

Miskimin, Harry A., *The Economy of Early Renaissance Europe, 1300–1460*, Englewood Cliffs, NJ: Prentice Hall, 1969; Cambridge: Cambridge University Press, 1975

Molho, Anthony, *Florentine Public Finances in the Early Renaissance, 1400–1433*, Cambridge, MA: Harvard University Press, 1971

O'Malley, John W., *Praise and Blame in Renaissance Rome: Rhetoric, Doctrine, and Reform in the Sacred Orators of the Papal Court, c.1450–1521*, Durham, NC: Duke University Press, 1979

Ossola, Carlo, *Dal "cortegiano" all' "uomo di mondo": storia di un libro e di un modello sociale* (From "Courtier" to "Man of the World": The History of a Book and of a Social Type), Turin: Einaudi, 1987

Partner, Peter, "Florence and the Papacy, 1300–1375," in John R. Hale, J.R.L. Highfield, and Beryl Smalley, eds., *Europe in the Late Middle Ages*, Evanston, IL: Northwestern University Press, 1965

Peters, Edward, ed., *Heresy and Authority in Medieval Europe: Documents in Translation*, Philadelphia: University of Pennsylvania Press, 1980

Pullan, Brian, *Rich and Poor in Renaissance Venice: The Social Institutions of a Catholic State, to 1620*, Oxford: Blackwell, and Cambridge, MA: Harvard University Press, 1971

Queller, Donald, *The Venetian Patriciate: Reality versus Myth*, Urbana: University of Illinois Press, 1986

Rubinstein, Nicolai, ed., *Florentine Studies: Politics and Society in Renaissance Florence*, Evanston, IL: Northwestern University Press, 1968

Ruggiero, Guido, *The Boundaries of Eros: Sex Crime and Sexuality in Renaissance Venice*, Oxford and New York: Oxford University Press, 1989

Seidel Menchi, Silvana, *Erasmo in Italia, 1520–1580* (Erasmus in Italy), Turin: Bolatti Boringhieri, 1987

Simons, Patricia, "Lesbian (In)visibility in Italian Renaissance Culture: Diana and Other Cases of *donna con donna*," *Journal of Homosexuality* 27 (1994), 81–122

Siraisi, Nancy, *Medieval and Early Renaissance Medicine: An Introduction to Knowledge and Practice*, Chicago: University of Chicago Press, 1990

Stephens, John N., *The Fall of the Florentine Republic, 1512–1530*, Oxford and New York: Oxford University Press, 1983

Trexler, Richard C., *The Spiritual Power: Republican Florence under Interdict*, Leiden: Brill, 1974

Trinkaus, Charles, *The Scope of Renaissance Humanism*, Ann Arbor: University of Michigan Press, 1983

Vasari, Giorgio, *Le vite de' più eccellenti architetti, pittori et scultori italani*, 3 vols., Florence: H. Torrentino, 1550, revised 1568; in English as *Lives of the Most Eminent Painters, Sculptors and Architects*, 10 vols., London: Macmillan–Medici Society, 1912–15, reprinted New York: AMS, 1976

Vasoli, Cesare, *Civitas mundi: studi sulla cultura del Cinquecento* ("Civitas Mundi": Studies in the Culture of the Sixteenth Century), Rome: Edizioni di storia e letteratura, 1996

Vespasiano da Bisticci, *Viti di uomini illustri del secolo*, Rome, 1839; in English as *The Vespasiano Memoirs: Lives of the Illustrious Men of the XVth Century*, London: Routledge, and New York: Dial Press, 1926; reprinted as *Renaissance Princes, Popes, and Prelates*, New York: Harper, 1963

Waley, Daniel, *The Papal State in the Thirteenth Century*, London: Macmillan, and New York: St. Martin's Press, 1961

Waley, Daniel, *The Italian City-Republics*, New York: McGraw Hill, and London: Weidenfeld and Nicolson, 1969

Italy: since the Renaissance

Historians of both the Renaissance and the next period of Italian glory, the *Risorgimento*, have tended to see the 16th and 17th centuries as a period of crisis and decline, evident in economic difficulties, plagues, cooler temperatures, diminishing harvests, international conflicts and domestic rebellions, the secondhand impact of the Thirty Years' War (1618–48), the loss of the dominant position in the trade with the East, and a general sinking into poverty, coupled with an increasingly intolerant Counter-Reformation church, which smothered intellectual life. These problems continued to plague Italy during the 18th century, when, in the words of Edward Tannenbaum and Emiliana Noether, economic modernization lagged behind other European nations due to "mutually reinforcing handicaps inherited from the past," including disunity, foreign domination, antiquated agriculture, limited natural resources, and the continuing dominance of the Catholic church over society. This crisis perspective has been revised in the later 20th century through the work of historians such as Carlo Cipolla and Theodore Rabb, who suggested that the causes of Italy's problems were not foreign but internal, including the collapse of urban economies, the inability to meet increasing foreign competition, and the high cost of labor; and by both H.G. Koenigsberger and Domenico Sella, who independently contended that the evidence of cultural decline is incomplete and misleading. Instead the 17th century was a "golden age" of science, a period of architectural innovation, and a continuing tradition in music, in which sectors of economic strength remained. The revisionist view is that in the 17th century Italy's decline was not absolute but, compared to the rest of Europe, only relative.

Historians of the 18th century shifted their attention from economic to intellectual life. With some notable exceptions, however, they frequently ignored Italian contributions to the Enlightenment. To correct this Francophone bias, Franco Venturi focused not only on the Italian Enlightenment as a separate phenomenon, with a strong intellectual tradition in its own right (for example, Vico and Muratori), but also on the pan-European Enlightenment, of which Italy was an integral part. This viewpoint is particularly relevant when one considers, as have Maeve Edith Albano, Gustavo Costa, and Leon Pompa, that Vico himself entered a debate over the relative merits of Italian versus French intellectuals. Venturi also criticized Enlightenment historians for focusing on the abstract ideas of the movement, rather than on the realities behind the ideologies. A telling example is the case of Cesare Beccaria. His *Dei delitti e delle pene* (1764; *Essay on Crimes and Punishments*, 1767) called for more "reasonable" laws, condemned the existing justice system's reliance on torture and its presumption of guilt, and denounced capital punishment except in times of war or armed rebellion. The response of "Enlightened Despots" to this treatise has frequently been studied, but often in an idealized manner; for a corrective, see Cesare Mozzarelli's *Sovrano società e amministrazione locale nella Lombardia teresiana, 1749–1758* (Sovereign Society and Local Administration in the Lombardy of Maria Teresa, 1749–1758), which noted that although the response to Beccaria was widespread and positive, and included praise from Maria Teresa and Voltaire, the implementation of his suggested reforms was hardly immediate and did face opposition.

The era of Napoleon (1796–1815) was very traumatic in Italy; most historians agree that in the end, there were some benefits, but at a great cost. If nothing else, Napoleon stirred up widespread feelings of nationalism, which in some ways, as Noether discussed, contributed to the growing desire for unification. Frequently, Italian historians focus on Napoleon only inasmuch as he contributed to the *Risorgimento*, because of the harmful influences the dictator had on the peninsula. Despite his modernizing influence, however, Italian industrialization still lagged behind Europe as a whole. Alexander Gerschenkron studied the 19th-century economic development of Italy and concluded that the peninsula represented a special case in history because, despite many handicaps, there was a "Great Spurt" approximately 50 years after the beginning of the Industrial Revolution on a widespread scale. In a recent reassessment of that thesis, Alfredo Esposto upheld the pattern, but mainly for the northwest regions of Italy.

For most of the 19th century, nationalism commanded center stage. The unification, called the *Risorgimento* (1848–70), was both revolutionary and part of long-term trends. The heroes of the *Risorgimento*, Cavour, Garibaldi, and Mazzini, have been the subject of numerous monographs, articles, and collected studies; among the more comprehensive biographies of the three are those written by Denis Mack Smith and Harry Hearder. Christopher Hibbert's selfconsciously revisionist study of Garibaldi is very sympathetic to Garibaldi as a romantic, emotional figure, and places the glory of victory – ultimate unification – squarely on his shoulders. The local rebellions of the 19th century had previously been viewed by historians as expressions of national unity; Hibbert characterized them as discrete movements expressing local problems, thus emphasizing Garibaldi's integral role in coordinating a central movement.

As much as the Renaissance, the *Risorgimento* dominates Italian history and historical writing, and has as many controversial interpretations. Part of the controversy over the *Risorgimento* lies in the changes that followed it; after unification, the political leadership of Italy moved toward the left, under premier Francesco Crispi and prime minister Giovanni Giolitti. However, parliamentary government collapsed between 1919 and 1922 due to World War I and the unfavorable concluding peace treaty. By 1922 the fascists were firmly in power, with Mussolini as prime minister. This historiographical inquiry, then, explores the role of the *Risorgimento* in the development of fascism.

Early fascist policies have not been the subject of many monographs. In particular, the question of international relations has suffered from a paucity of studies. Alan Cassels' *Mussolini's Early Diplomacy* (1970) included a critical bibliography on the subject; he characterized earlier books as fragmentary, topical, and even superficial because of their neglect of what he saw as continuities in fascist foreign policy. This controversial revisionist viewpoint is also found in Renzo De Felice, author of a multivolume bibliography of Mussolini, and A. James Gregor, author of *Young Mussolini and the Intellectual Origins of Fascism* (1979). Both clearly sympathized with Mussolini and characterized him as original and consistent. This perspective remains unpopular; most historians see Mussolini's diplomacy as somewhat unpredictable. The fascist period has led to reinterpretation of aspects of *Risorgimento* historiography; the traditional method of tracing the development of political fascism through an unbroken line of Italian ideology, for example in G.M. Trevelyan, is seen since Gaetano Salvemini as inappropriate. Historians have struggled with the fascist period on several levels, including Mack Smith's intriguing question of why the triumph of liberalism characteristic of the *Risorgimento* was eclipsed by the fascist dictatorship in such a short time. In one of the most influential 20th-century histories of Italy in the English language, he identified the *Risorgimento* as an end in itself, rather than as a starting point: *Italy: A Modern History* (1959; revised 1969).

Postwar Italian historiography has largely been revisionist in one form or another: the attempt to redefine the place of the *Risorgimento*, new methods of interpreting the Renaissance, the inclusion of women and minorities into all periods, urbanization, and attempts to understand the path Italy took toward fascism. Most recently, studies of the latter also include statements on the 1990s trend of neofascism and the right-wing coalition government of 1994, under Silvio Berlusconi. The quickly changing governments and party alliances have left their mark, notably in the 1994 reorganization of the university system and the governmental focus on stamping out "corruption" which has, inevitably, turned attention towards the role of organized crime in Italian politics. The European Parliament elections and the new government that followed the collapse of the Berlusconi coalition demonstrate that Italy still lacks a unified ideology; factionalism and regionalism are more important indications of voting behavior than nationalism. Issues of taxation in support of the Catholic church, the protection of the environment, widening the female workforce, postmodernism, and Italy's role in both the Mediterranean and the European Union will be at the forefront in the 21st century.

KATHLEEN COMERFORD

See also Cipolla; Counter-Reformation; De Felice; Mack Smith; Muratori; Portelli; Romeo; Trevelyan; Vico

Further Reading

Albano, Maeve Edith, *Vico and Providence*, New York: Lang, 1986

Alpers, Svetlana, "The Glory of Venice: Art in the Eighteenth Century," *Art in America* 83 (1995), 62–69

Azzi, Stephen Corrado, "The Historiography of Fascist Foreign Policy," *Historical Journal* 36 (1993), 187–203

Baasner, Frank, "'L'uomo che domino due generazioni': Die öffentlichen Reaktionen auf den Tod Benedetto Croces 1952 und ihre Hintergrunde" ("The Man Who Dominated Two Generations": The Official Reaction, and That of the Underground, to the Death of Benedetto Croce, 1952), *Italienisch: Zeitschrift für Italienische Sprache und Literatur* 22 (1989), 62–72

Baranski, Zygmunt G., and Shirley W. Vinall, *Women and Italy: Essays on Gender, Culture and History*, London: Macmillan, and New York: St. Martin's Press, 1991

Beccaria, Cesare, *Dei delitti e delle pene*, 1764; in English as *Essay on Crimes and Punishments*, London: Almon, 1767; reprinted 1983

Bellamy, Richard, and Darrow Schecter, *Gramsci and the Italian State*, Manchester: Manchester University Press, 1993

Berdes, Jane L. Baldauf, *Women Musicians of Venice: Musical Foundations, 1525–1855*, Oxford and New York: Oxford University Press, 1993

Biagioli, Mario, *Galileo, Courtier: The Practice of Science in the Culture of Absolutism*, Chicago: University of Chicago Press, 1993

Blackwell, Richard J., *Galileo, Bellarmine, and the Bible*, Notre Dame, IN: University of Notre Dame Press, 1991

Boime, Albert, *The Art of the Macchia and the Risorgimento: Representing Culture and Nationalism in Nineteenth-Century Italy*, Chicago: University of Chicago Press, 1993

Bono, Paola, and Sandra Kemp, eds., *Italian Feminist Thought: A Reader*, Oxford and Boston: Blackwell, 1991

Bosworth, Richard J.B., and Sergio Romano, eds., *La politica estera italiana, 1860–1985* (Italian Foreign Policy, 1860–1985), Bologna: Mulino, 1991

Bucciantini, Massimo, and Maurizio Torrini, eds., *Geometria e atomismo nella scuola galileiana* (Geometry and Atomism in the School of Galileo), Florence: Olschki, 1992

Cannistraro, Philip V., ed., *Historical Dictionary of Fascist Italy*, Westport, CT: Greenwood Press, 1982

Carroll, Michael P., *Madonnas That Maim: Popular Catholicism in Italy since the Fifteenth Century*, Baltimore: Johns Hopkins University Press, 1992

Cassels, Alan, *Mussolini's Early Diplomacy*, Princeton: Princeton University Press, 1970

Cipolla, Carlo M., *Storia economica dell'Europa pre-industriale*, Bologna: Mulino, 1974; in English as *Before the Industrial Revolution: European Society and Economy, 1000–1700*, New York: Norton, 1976; London: Methuen, 1981

Clark, Martin, *Modern Italy, 1871–1995*, London and New York: Longman, 1984; revised 1996

Clough, Shepard B., and Salvatore Saladino, *A History of Modern Italy: Documents, Readings and Commentary*, New York: Columbia University Press, 1968

Cohen, Sherrill, *The Evolution of Women's Asylums since 1500: From Refuges for ex-Prostitutes to Shelters for Battered Women*, New York: Oxford University Press, 1992

Coppa, Frank J., ed., *Dictionary of Modern Italian History*, Westport, CT: Greenwood Press, 1985

Coppa, Frank J., and William Roberts, eds., *Modern Italian History: An Annotated Bibliography*, New York: Greenwood Press, 1990

Costa, Gustavo, *La leggenda de secoli d'oro nella letteratura italiana* (The Legend of the Golden Age in Italian Literature), Bari: Laterza, 1972

Croce, Benedetto, *A History of Italy, 1871–1915*, Oxford: Clarendon Press, 1929; New York: Russell and Russell, 1963

De Felice, Renzo, "D'Annunzio nella vita politica italiana" (D'Annunzio in Italian Political Life), *Il Veltro: rivista della civiltà italiana* 32 (1988), 169–78

De Grazia, Victoria, *How Fascism Rules Women: Italy, 1922–1945*, Berkeley: University of California Press, 1992

Delzell, Charles F., *Italy in Modern Times: An Introduction to the Historical Literature in English*, American Historical Association Service Center for Teachers of History pamphlet no.60, Washington, DC: AHA, 1964

Drake, Stillman, *Galileo: Pioneer Scientist*, Toronto: University of Toronto Press, 1990

Esposto, Alfredo G., "Italian Industrialization and the Gerschenkronian 'Great Spurt': A Regional Analysis," *Journal of Economic History* 52 (1992), 353–62

Federico, Giovanni, ed., *The Economic Development of Italy since 1870*, Aldershot and Brookfield, VT: Elgar, 1994

Gerschenkron, Alexander, *Economic Backwardness in Historical Perspective: A Book of Essays*, Cambridge, MA: Harvard University Press, and London: Oxford University Press, 1962

Ginsborg, Paul, *A History of Contemporary Italy: Society and Politics, 1943–1988*, Harmondsworth: Penguin, 1990

Gregor, A. James, *Young Mussolini and the Intellectual Origins of Fascism*, Berkeley: University of California Press, 1979

Hagopian, Viola Luther, *Italian Ars Nova Music: A Bibliographic Guide to Modern Editions and Related Literature*, Berkeley: University of California Press, 1964; revised and expanded 1973

Hearder, Harry, and Daniel Waley, eds., *A Short History of Italy: From Classical Times to the Present Day*, Cambridge: Cambridge University Press, 1963

Hearder, Harry, *Cavour*, London and New York: Longman, 1994

Hibbert, Christopher, *Garibaldi and His Enemies: The Clash of Arms and Personalities in the Making of Italy*, Boston: Little Brown, and London: Longman, 1965

Kertzer, David I., *Sacrificed for Honor: Italian Infant Abandonment and the Politics of Reproductive Control*, Boston: Beacon Press, 1993

Koenigsberger, H.G. "Decadence or Shift? Changes in the Civilization of Italy and Europe in the Sixteenth and Seventeenth Centuries," *Transactions of the Royal Historical Society* 5th series 10 (1960), 1–18

Larebo, Haile M., *The Building of an Empire: Italian Land Policy and Practice in Ethiopia, 1935–1941*, Oxford: Oxford University Press, 1994

Mack Smith, Denis, *Italy: A Modern History*, Ann Arbor: University of Michigan Press, 1959; revised 1969

Mack Smith, Denis, *Italy and Its Monarchy*, New Haven: Yale University Press, 1989

Mack Smith, Denis, *Mazzini*, New Haven: Yale University Press, 1994

Martineau, Jane, and Andrew Robison, eds., *The Glory of Venice: Art in the Eighteenth Century*, New Haven and London: Yale University Press, 1994

Mozzarelli, Cesare, *Sovrano società e amministrazione locale nella Lombardia teresiana, 1749–1758* (Sovereign Society and Local Administration in the Lombardy of Maria Teresa, 1749–1758), Bologna: Mulino, 1982

Musgrave, Peter, *Land and Economy in Baroque Italy: Valpolicella, 1630–1797*, Leicester: Leicester University Press, and New York: St. Martin's Press, 1992

Pernicone, Nunzio, *Italian Anarchism, 1864–1892*, Princeton: Princeton University Press, 1993

Pompa, Leon, *Vico: A Study of the New Science*, Cambridge and New York: Cambridge University Press, 1975

Pozzani, Silvio, "Cospirazione, insurrezione e bande repubblicane nella corrispodenza mazziniana del 1869–70" (Conspiracy, Insurrection, and Republican Groups in Mazzini's Correspondence, 1869–70), *Bollettino della Domus Mazziniana* 32 (1986), 15–53

Pullan, Brian, ed., *Crisis and Change in the Venetian Economy in the Sixteenth and Seventeenth Centuries*, London: Methuen, 1968

Putnam, Robert D., with Robert Leonardi and Raffaella Nanetti, *Making Democracy Work: Civic Traditions in Modern Italy*, Princeton: Princeton University Press, 1993

Rabb, Theodore K., and Robert I. Rotberg, eds., *Industrialization and Urbanization: Studies in Interdisciplinary History*, Princeton: Princeton University Press, 1981

Redondi, Pietro, *Galileo eretico*, Torino: Einaudi, 1983; in English as *Galileo Heretic*, Princeton: Princeton University Press, 1987

Reidy, Denis, ed., *The Italian Book, 1465–1800: Studies Presented to Dennis E. Rhodes on his 70th birthday*, London: British Library, 1993

Reinerman, Alan J., "The Failure of Popular Counter-Revolution in Risorgimento Italy: The Case of the Centurions, 1831–1847," *Historical Journal* 34 (1991), 21–41

Romani, Marzio A., "Regions in Italian History (XVth–XVIIIth Centuries)," *Journal of European Economic History* 23 (1994), 177–93

Sella, Domenico, *Crisis and Continuity: The Economy of Spanish Lombardy in the 17th Century*, Cambridge, MA: Harvard University Press, 1979

Setton, Kenneth M., *Venice, Austria, and the Turks in the Seventeenth Century*, Philadelphia: American Philosophical Society, 1991

Sidoti, Francesco, "The Significance of the Italian Elections," *Government and Opposition* 29 (1994), 332–47

Stille, Alexander, *Excellent Cadavers: The Mafia and the Death of the First Italian Republic*, New York: Pantheon, and London: Cape, 1995

Sznajder, Mario, "Italy's Right-wing Government: Legitimacy and Criticism," *International Affairs* 71 (1995), 83–102

Tannenbaum, Edward R., and Emiliana P. Noether, eds., *Modern Italy: A Topical History since 1861*, New York: New York University Press, 1974

Trevelyan, G.M., *Garibaldi and the Making of Italy: June–November, 1860*, New York and London: Nelson, 1911

Tyler, M.A., "Vincenzo Gioberti's Primato and the Unification of Italy," *Italian Studies* 13 (1988), 95–103

Venturi, Franco, *Italy and the Enlightenment: Studies in a Cosmopolitan Century*, New York: New York University Press, and London: Longman, 1972

Vigezzi, Brunello, *Politica estera e opinione pubblica in Italia dall'unita ai giorni nostri: orientamenti degli studi e prospective della ricerca* (Foreign Policy and Public Opinion in Italy from Unification to Our Time: Orientations for Study and Prospectives for Research), Milan: Jaca, 1991

Wittkower, Rudolf, *Art and Architecture in Italy, 1600 to 1750*, Harmondsworth: Penguin, 1958; revised 1980

Woodhouse, J.R., "D'Annunzio's Election Victory of 1897: New Documents, New Perspectives," *Italian Studies* 10 (1985), 63–81

Zamagni, Vera, *Dalla periferia al centro: la seconda riniscita economica dell'Italia, 1861–1981*, Bologna: Mulino, 1990; in English as *The Economic History of Italy, 1860–1990: From the Periphery to the Centre*, Oxford and New York: Oxford University Press, 1993

Zapponi, Niccolo, "Fascism in Italian Historiography, 1986–93: A Fading National Identity," *Journal of Contemporary History* 29 (1994), 547–68

J

James, C.L.R. 1901–1989

Trinidadian political historian

One of the two fathers of modern black history (with W.E.B. Du Bois), C.L.R. James wrote widely on politics and culture, the Caribbean, Britain, the US, and, to a lesser degree, Africa and the Soviet Union. Like his friend E.P. Thompson the model of an engaged scholar, James wrote most of his work while on the move politically. A leading participant in Pan-Africanist, Trotskyist, and Caribbean independence movements of the 1930s–50s, he emerged in late life an *éminence grise* on the lecture circuit, using his own historical theses to explain current political points and vice-versa. At least two of his works, *The Black Jacobins* (1938) and *Beyond a Boundary* (1963), have become classics in their respective historical fields of slavery and sport.

James himself can hardly be said to be part of any scholarly cohort, whether national, ethnic, or generational. A schoolteacher and novelist in his native Trinidad, he wrote as his first historical study a biographical pamphlet, *The Life of Captain Cipriani* (1933). It gained publication in Britain, where he quickly became known as a cricket reporter (for the Manchester *Guardian*) and an anticolonialist.

Soon, he turned from playwriting to a history of his chosen subject, the New World's only successful slave revolt. *Black Jacobins*, the first work to trace independence to slaves' economic socialization and to the interaction of European and Caribbean events, immediately gained wide recognition. *A History of Negro Revolt* (1938), a brief sequel of sorts, traced subsequent events across the US, the Caribbean, and Africa, with careful attention to "irrational" forms of protest and uprising, such as the Back to Africa movement and crypto-political revolts espousing religious syncretism.

James had meanwhile turned some of his political attention to Marxism and specifically to the anti-Stalin "Left Opposition." His *World Revolution, 1917–1936: The Rise and Fall of the Communist International* (1937) was regarded as the "Bible of Trotskyism," although the least originally researched of his major works. (He also translated Boris Souvarine's polemical history, *Stalin*, from the French.) Trotskyism brought him to the US in 1939 and there he remained until his expulsion in 1953, a victim of McCarthyism. For the most part, during these years, history became a backdrop for questions of political theory. His *State Capitalism and World Revolution* (1950) and *Notes on Dialectics* (written in 1950, but not published in book form until

1980) both concerned themselves with tracing Stalinism and its Western bureaucratic counterparts to the long history of the working-class movement.

Only on the eve of his expulsion did James begin to publish his version of a partial antidote to bureaucratic supersession of the socialist project, via the historic possibilities of popular culture. *Mariners, Renegades, and Castaways* (1953), reaching print as the author was incarcerated on Ellis Island, put forward novelist Herman Melville as a philosopher of American life. *American Civilization* (written 1953, published 1993) argued that the 19th- and 20th-century quest by the masses for self-recognition contained within it the seed for overcoming the fetters of consumerist class society. *Beyond a Boundary* (1963) was the finest fruit of the larger investigation into popular life. Rehearsing the rise of organized sport in 19th-century England and considering its perfection in the 20th-century colonies of nonwhites, James saw in cricket the promise of masses taking history into their own hands.

Unlike his other works after *Black Jacobins*, *Beyond a Boundary* reached a wide and sympathetic audience, many of them not at all concerned with politics as such. *Black Jacobins* returned to print in 1963, and as a paperback became a favored textbook for the emerging academic fields of US black history and Pan-African history. By this time, James had abandoned Trinidad after being removed from the leadership of Trinidad's independence movement by his own former pupil, Dr. Eric Williams (whose monumental volume, *Capitalism and Slavery*, had been inspired and guided by James' work). After a few years in London, he returned to the US as a peripatetic lecturer and historical personage.

And it was in the US that his effect could be felt most directly, on several younger generations of historians and other scholars. Black history notables, including Vincent Harding, Eugene Genovese, George Rawick, Manning Marable, and Robin D.G. Kelley, and history-minded cultural scholars such as Edward Said, Stuart Hall, Sylvia Wynter, and George Lipsitz among a field of others have variously testified to James' significant influence on their work. Within Caribbean historical studies, his books remain a foundation stone for nearly all further scholarship.

None of his admirers could, however, have interpreted his scholarly trajectory or his influence either simply or comprehensively. As a self-trained writer with what one scholar calls a "floating center," he had variously emphasized the socialization of labor, slave (or peasant), and proletarian self-guided activity, cultural forms of mass self-assertion, and a historical (but also distinctly poetic) view of theater and literature. Close scholarly attention to the human possibility, and to its rooting in the lives of ordinary people, was perhaps the philosophical kernel of his scholarly legacy.

PAUL BUHLE

See also Williams, E.

Biography

Cyril Lionel Robert James. Born Tunapuna, Trinidad, 4 January 1901. Attended school at Queen's Royal College, Port of Spain, Trinidad, teacher's certificate, 1919. Lived in: Trinidad 1901–32, 1958–59, and 1981–82; UK 1932–39, 1953–58, 1960–68, and 1982–89; US 1939–53 and 1969–81. Lecturer, Northwestern University, 1969; and Federal City College, Washington, DC, 1972–80; resident scholar, Institute for the Black World, Atlanta, 1970–72. Married 1) Juanita James, 1930 (divorced; 1 son); 2) Constance Webb, 1950 (divorced); 3) Selma Weinstein, 1955. Died London, 31 May 1989.

Principal Writings

World Revolution, 1917–1936: The Rise and Fall of the Communist International, 1937

A History of Negro Revolt, 1938; revised as *A History of Pan-African Revolt*, 1969

The Black Jacobins: Toussaint L'Ouverture and the San Domingo Revolution, 1938; revised 1963

State Capitalism and World Revolution, 1950; 3rd edition 1969

Mariners, Renegades, and Castaways: The Story of Herman Melville and the World We Live In, 1953

Beyond a Boundary, 1963

The Hegelian Dialectic and Modern Politics, 1970; revised as *Notes on Dialectics: Hegel, Marx, Lenin*, 1980

The Future in the Present, 1977

Spheres of Existence, 1980

At the Rendezvous of Victory, 1984

The C.L.R. James Reader, edited by Anna Grimshaw and Keith Hart 1992

American Civilization, edited by Anna Grimshaw and Keith Hart, 1993

Further Reading

Buhle, Paul, ed., *C.L.R. James: His Life and Work*, London: Allison and Busby, 1986

Buhle, Paul, *C.L.R. James: The Artist as Revolutionary*, London: Verso, 1989

Cudjoe, Selwyn, and William Cain, eds., *C.L.R. James: His Intellectual Legacies*, Amherst: University of Massachusetts Press, 1995

Henry, Paget, and Paul Buhle, eds., *C.L.R. James's Caribbean*, Durham, NC: Duke University Press, 1992

James, C.L.R., *C.L.R. James*, Madison, WI: Radical America, 1970

Ragoonath, Bishnu, ed., *Tribute to a Scholar: Appreciating C.L.R. James*, Kingston, Jamaica: Consortium Graduate School of Social Sciences, 1990

Janssen, Johannes 1829–1891
German church historian

After a varied educational experience in Münster, Bonn, Berlin, and in Louvain, Belgium, Johannes Janssen was to spend the greater part of his academic career as professor of history at Frankfurt am Main. He published numerous works on aspects of German history, but is chiefly remembered for his 8-volume study of late medieval and early modern Germany, *Geschichte des deutschen Volkes seit dem Ausgang des Mittelalters* (1876–94; 17 vols., *History of the German People at the Close of the Middle Ages*, 1896–1910). This work enjoyed phenomenal success, running to 15 editions between 1876 and 1890.

Janssen undertook a prodigious amount of archival research, and between 1863 and 1875 published extensive sources from the archives of Frankfurt, and of other German and Swiss cities. He remained strongly committed to the ideal of unbiased historical research based on authentic records.

From as early as 1854 he had resolved to make a "History of the German People" the principal work of his life. Within that broad field he expressed a preference for concentrating on "civil and intellectual development" (*Kulturgeschichte*) rather than political history in the narrower sense. In the preface to the 15th edition of his work he described his aims as "not to give marked preference to so-called state events, campaigns and battles but to depict the German national life in all its varying conditions, and stages, and phases of destiny." His abiding preoccupation was neither institutions nor individuals, but the German people in their manifold activities.

The *History of the German People* is most widely known on account of its highly distinctive interpretation of the Protestant Reformation. Janssen was "ultramontanist" in his sympathies and enjoyed a consistently harmonious relationship with Roman ecclesiastical authority. Notwithstanding his sincere commitment to fair and unbiased historical research, his very one-sided view of 15th- and 16th-century Germany amounted to an apologia for medieval Catholicism and provided the dominant historical framework for Roman Catholic interpretation of the Reformation during subsequent generations.

Given his focus on the history of the German people, Janssen was able to avoid the obsessive preoccupation with Luther the individual that marked most Roman Catholic polemic of the time, and approached his subject from the point of view of an assessment of the quality of late medieval church life. He refuted the common Protestant judgment that the 15th and early 16th century in Germany was a period of religious degeneration, asserting rather that the late medieval church was fundamentally healthy and flourishing.

He did not gloss over altogether the existence of serious clerical abuses and the pervasiveness of confusion and unrest that preceded Luther's emergence. Moreover, he recognized and paid tribute to Luther's profound religious gifts, his sublimity of language, and the depth of his religious grasp recalling the heyday of German mysticism – all of which he attributed to the "rich stream of influence from the Catholic past."

He argued, nevertheless, that the Catholic church of the time possessed all the necessary resources for cleansing from within – resources which were already being used – and that mid-15th-century Germany witnessed the beginnings of a great period of reform in all levels of society expressed in a prodigious output of sermons, scriptural translations, and devotional writings and a blossoming of religious art.

Given this assessment of a healthy and vigorous church, Janssen inevitably cast Luther in the role of the destroyer, responding to a degree of genuine confusion and unrest, but unable to see that the necessary means for reform were at hand

and already at work. Accordingly Luther's impact was to undo past achievements and nip new reform in the bud, like a sledgehammer destroying everything hitherto held sacred and venerable. He was pulled down by his arrogance and the reckless violence with which he attacked church traditions – violence born of attempts at self-justification in the face of a disquieted conscience.

At no stage, however, did Janssen adopt a simplistic or reductionist view of the causality of the Reformation. Among the contextual factors that he explored as contributing to the climate of revolutionary change were the political weakness of the empire, which had undermined the strong and harmonious relationship between empire and papacy which Germany had enjoyed during the Middle Ages, the introduction of Roman law which had fostered princely despotism, and the pernicious effects of capitalist commerce.

While Janssen's distinctive and one-sided judgment on the Reformation has aroused most scholarly interest in his work, his broader achievement should not be forgotten. Despite his tendency towards polemical selectivity, his work provides a rich source of unfamiliar detail on the social and religious life of all classes in Germany from the early 15th century to the Thirty Years' War.

JOHN TONKIN

Biography

Born Xanten, Lower Rhine, 11 April 1829, son of a wicker worker. Studied at Münster, Louvain, Bonn, and Berlin before receiving PhD, University of Bonn, 1853. Taught at University of Münster, 1854, then became Catholic priest and theologian, 1860. Professor of history for Catholic pupils, Frankfurt Gymnasium. Died Frankfurt, 24 December 1891.

Principal Writings

Geschichte des deutschen Volkes seit dem Ausgang des Mittelalters, 8 vols., 1876–94; in English as *History of the German People at the Close of the Middle Ages*, 17 vols., 1896–1910

Further Reading

Dickens, A.G., and John Tonkin, *The Reformation in Historical Thought*, Cambridge, MA: Harvard University Press, and Oxford: Blackwell, 1985, chapter 8

Japan

The tradition of historical writing in Japan dates back to the late 6th century, when ruler-lists were first compiled, and native myths standardized. These texts do not survive, but the *Kojiki* (Record of Ancient Matters, 712) and *Nihon shoki* (or *Nihongi: Chronicle of Japan*, 720), prepared for a courtly audience, have remained extremely influential. They reveal strong Chinese influence; the very idea of written, official accounts of the past, designed to legitimize existing political authority, was a continental import – part of the package of Korean and Chinese ideas and institutions embraced by the Yamato court with the introduction of Buddhism from the mid-6th century.

The *Nihongi* in particular followed a Chinese-style format.

Organized according to (real or mythical) imperial reigns, it listed events as seen from court on a year-to-year basis. Five additional works of this genre constitute, with the *Nihongi*, the "Six National Histories" (*Rikkokushi*), covering events until 887. Thereafter, the decline of imperial power *vis-à-vis* that of the Fujiwara noble family is reflected in the quasi-historical works *Eiga monogatari* (*A Tale of Flowering Fortunes*, 11th century) and *Ōkagami* (*c.*1119), which glorify this family, and particularly the powerful court minister Fujiwara Michinaga (966–1027) under whom it reached its peak.

While written in classical Chinese, the early chronicles display uniquely Japanese features, such as an overriding concern with establishing the lineage (often divine or imperial) of the leading courtly families. The Mandate of Heaven notion, while not entirely absent, is not applied in such a way as to challenge the eternal legitimacy of the ruling line, regarded as virtuous by definition.

The *Eiga monogatari* and *Ōkagami* constitute a major break with this tradition. Written in Japanese, they show the influence of courtly fiction, especially novels such as *Genji Monogatari* (*The Tale of Genji*), by Murasaki Shikibu (b. *c.*978). But fictional elements, such as the implausibly aged narrators of *Ōkagami*, do not detract from the historical value of these works, which seem accurately to recount key events at court during the 11th century, while providing invaluable information as well about many aspects of contemporary culture.

Such works in turn influenced the *gunki monogatari*, or warrior tales, which describe not only events at court but in the society of the samurai class. Here again the style is narrative, rather than merely chronological; the usually anonymous authors were concerned with interpreting major shifts in power, and the rise and decline of martial families. Examples of this genre include the *Heike monogatari* and *Taiheiki*. The former recounted the events surrounding the establishment of the first military government or shogunate in the 1180s; the latter dealt with a brief effort at imperial restoration in the 1330s and subsequent imposition of a second military regime. These works, which circulated as texts chanted by itinerant monks, are filled with fictitious elements, but are important sources of information about general political and military events, and reliable in their descriptions of costume, battle tactics, religious practices, and other things.

The first truly interpretive history produced in Japan is probably *Gukanshō* by the monk Jien (*c.*1220). Written by a member of the Fujiwara family, who was also a high-ranking prelate of the Tendai Buddhist sect and intimate of the imperial family, the work is largely concerned with the interrelationship between these three institutions. Although organized as a chronicle, divided into imperial reigns, it emphasizes the determining role of "principles" (*dōri*) in history. These are both destructive (the present age, according to Hindu and Buddhist conceptions, inevitably headed towards ruin), and constructive (Buddhism and Shinto both providing methods of at least temporary amelioration of social decay). This history, advocating a proper empowerment of Jien's branch of the Fujiwara, and of the Tendai establishment, also justifies a political role for the warrior or samurai class. It is an effort to explain the emergence of the shogunate or military government which, having been established in 1185, was at the time Jien wrote encountering significant (but ultimately futile) opposition from the imperial court.

Jinnō shōtōki (c.1339; *A Chronicle of Gods and Sovereigns*, 1980) was also written during a period of confrontation between a military government and the imperial court, and its author, Kitabatake Chikafusa (1293–1354), was also anxious to promote and examine the appropriate relations among a trio of historical institutions: the imperial family, the Fujiwara, and the Ise sect of the indigenous Shinto faith. Far more influential than Jien's work, upon which it drew, the *Jinnō shōtōki* rejects any notion of predestined decline and emphasizes the inherent virtues of Japan as "the country of the gods" and those of its hereditary rulers. Chikafusa also, however, stressed the importance of the proper handling of imperial succession, arguing that in the past, the mishandling of this had always produced disorder. So, also, had direct involvement of emperors in politics produced negative results; hence, emperors should remain aloof from administration, entrusting affairs to capable ministers of aristocratic families (such as the Kitabatake, and most importantly, the Fujiwara).

With a few exceptions, such as Zuikei Shūhō's *Zenrinkoku hōki* (Precious Record of Friendly Relations with Neighbor Countries, 1470), which traced the history of Japan's foreign relations, late medieval historical works focused on political and military affairs, and generally revealed a mounting neo-Confucian influence. During the Tokugawa period (1603–1868) this influence grew, reflecting in part the decline of Buddhist institutions, but also the desire of the newly-established Tokugawa shogunate to lend philosophical justification for the rigid class divisions it sought to enforce. Neo-Confucian thought, which depicted such class division as the appropriate reflection of a hierarchically-organized cosmic order, attained quasi-official status during this era.

The Hayashi school of historians, intimately associated with the Tokugawa regime, compiled a massive national history, the *Honchō tsugan* (Comprehensive Mirror of the Japanese Court) between 1644 and 1670, then followed up with other projects characterized by a basic humanism, rationalism, antipathy towards Buddhism and supernatural explanations of events, and nationalistic sentiment. Such works stressed the moral uprightness of the military or samurai class, justifying its ascent to power, and naturally extoled the virtues of the Tokugawa administration which had brought enduring peace to the country.

Rival historical schools also flourished; the Mito school, based in the barony (*han*) of that name, produced more critical historical writing than the Hayashi, delivering bolder moral verdicts on historical subjects. A branch of the Tokugawa family, related to the shoguns, ruled this *han* and sponsored the Mito school, so the latter not surprisingly emphasized the historical necessity for the samurai rise to power. It employed the Mandate of Heaven concept to suggest that the emperors of the past had lost favor with Heaven, while the military had inherited this approval from the days of the Kamakura shogunate. At the same time, by stressing the divine origins of the imperial line, Mito school historians contributed to the revival of pro-imperial sentiment which, along with mounting dissatisfaction with aspects of shogunal rule, intensified from the 18th century.

Meanwhile the *Kokugaku* (National-Learning or Native Studies) school of religious, literary, and historical thought revived interest in the *Kojiki* and other classical texts, and

schools associated with heterodox Confucian philosophers such as Ogyu Sorai (1666–1728) promoted new standards of critical textual analysis.

Following the Meiji restoration of 1868, Japanese scholars inspired by Western historical thought built upon some of the late Tokugawa trends to produce not only vast compilations of historical documents with accompanying textual criticism, but also general histories emphasizing economic change. This was a new development, as was the appearance of historical scholarship linking indigenous religious beliefs – vital to the legitimatization of the imperial institution – to traditions widely observed throughout East Asia. Such avenues of inquiry were strongly discouraged by the government, which promoted state Shinto and the cult of the emperor for political purposes.

Continuing earlier tradition, the Meiji regime commissioned historians, including Shigeno Yasutsugu (1827–1910), to produce a new official history in 1881, but fourteen years later the project was abandoned, reflecting the regime's concern that purely objective historical writing might undermine aspects of state ideology. However, historians at the Historiographical Institute (*Shiryō hensanjo*) at Tokyo Imperial University (now Tokyo University) devoted great effort to the collection and publication of an enormous number of primary materials, which remain indispensable to the study of premodern and early modern Japanese history.

During the 1920s and 1930s, Marxism made a tremendous impact on many fields of Japanese scholarship, including history. Historians in, or in association with, the Japanese Communist party felt obliged to define the historical situation of Japan as a quasi-feudal or fully capitalistic society, and in connection with debates on this topic, they produced various assessments of the significance of the Meiji restoration, and of economic trends in late Tokugawa society. The former was generally cast as an "imperfect bourgeois revolution" whose flaws hampered Japan's subsequent development as a modern industrial society, although some scholars argued that by the early 20th century Japan had essentially shed its feudal heritage and emerged as a fully capitalistic nation.

Among the various schools of Marxists, discussion of Tokugawa society focused on the "manufacture" issue, with some (associated with the *Rōnō* or "Labor-Farmer" faction) contending that by the early 19th century, manufacture in the Marxist sense had become a significant and rising mode of production. Others (linked to the *Kōza* or "Lectures" faction) downplayed the importance of this phenomenon, but most came to agree that significant elements of capitalism had appeared in Japan, quite independently of developments in Europe, prior to Japan's incorporation into the world economy after 1859. Hattori Shisō (1901–56) and Noro Eitarō (1900–34), among others, made important contributions to these debates.

Meanwhile Japanese historical scholarship was reaching the Western world through translations of works by Takekoshi Yosaburō (1865–1950), Honjō Eijiro, and other scholars. Asakawa Kan'ichi (1873–1948), who taught at Yale University from 1910 to 1942, was the first Japanese scholar systematically to compare Japanese and European feudalism.

Objective historical inquiry became increasingly difficult during the 1930s, as militaristic governments suppressed any scholarship shedding doubt on the basis of the emperor cult or Shinto mythology. In 1940 Tsuda Sōkichi (1873–1961) was convicted on the charge of *lèse majesté* for questioning the historicity of the earliest emperors mentioned in the Japanese chronicles. On the other hand, Takamure Itsue (1894–1964) published her *Bokeisei no kenkyū* (Studies in Matriarchy), a pioneering work of feminist scholarship focusing on matrilineal practices in ancient Japan, in 1938.

Following Japan's defeat in World War II, the intellectual climate liberalized and an extraordinarily rich field of historical scholarship has emerged, encouraged by an exceptionally strong public interest in the national history. The Marxist tradition remains strong, dogmatic approaches having largely given way to detailed analyses of specific questions. Historians of all schools have devoted new attention to demographic history and methods of quantitative analysis, using such sources as population registers (*ninbetsuchō*). *Minshūshi* ("the history of the masses"), women's history, and the history of *burakumin* (communities traditionally subjected to discrimination) have also made great strides.

The study of Japanese history has become internationalized in the postwar period. The first work in the field by a foreigner to make an impact in Japan was perhaps *Japan's Emergence as a Modern State* (1940) by the Canadian scholar-diplomat E.H. Norman (1909–57). General textbooks of Japanese history by Western scholars such as George B. Sansom (1883–1965) and Edwin O. Reischauer (1910–90) have now been augmented by countless monographs, many of high standard, by non-Japanese historians, and frequent conferences and scholarly exchange would seem to guarantee continued cross-fertilization.

GARY P. LEUPP

See also Arai; Boxer; Diplomatic; Gunki; Hayashi; Homosexuality; Japanese Chronicles; Kitabatake; Korea; Maritime; Maruyama; Mito; Niida; Otsuka; Shigeno; Shiratori; Vietnam; Women's History: Asia; World War II

Further Reading

Arai Hakuseki, *Lessons from History: Arai Hakuseki's Tokushi Yoron*, St. Lucia: University of Queensland Press, 1982

Asakawa Kan'ichi, *The Russo-Japanese Conflict: Its Causes and Issues*, London: Constable, and Boston: Houghton Mifflin, 1904; reprinted 1972

Blacker, Carmen, "Japanese Historical Writing in the Tokugawa Period," in William G. Beasley and Edwin G. Pulleyblank, eds., *Historians of China and Japan*, London: Oxford University Press, 1961

Eiga monogatari, 11th century; in English as *A Tale of Flowing Fortunes: Annals of Japanese Aristocratic Life in the Heian Period*, 2 vols., Stanford, CA: Stanford University Press, 1980

Hall, John W., and Marius B. Jansen, eds., *Studies in the Institutional History of Early Modern Japan*, Princeton: Princeton University Press, 1968

Hall, John W., *Japan: From Prehistory to Modern Times*, New York: Delacorte Press, and London: Weidenfeld and Nicolson, 1970; reprinted Ann Arbor: Center for Japanese Studies, University of Michigan, 1991

Hall, John W. et al., eds., *The Cambridge History of Japan*, 6 vols., Cambridge and New York: Cambridge University Press, 1988–93

Heike monogatari; in English as *The Heike Mongatari*, 2 vols., Tokyo: Asiatic Society of Japan, 1918–21; and as *The Tale of the Heike*, Stanford, CA: Stanford University Press, 1988

Honjō Eijirō, *The Social and Economic History of Japan*, Kyoto: Institute for Research in Japanese History, 1935; New York: Russell and Russell, 1965

Honjō Eijirō, *A Bibliography of Japanese Economic History, 1796-1935*, Kyoto: Nihon keizaishi Kenkyusho, 1936

Honjō Eijirō, *Economic Theory and History of Japan in the Tokugawa Period*, Tokyo: Marazan, 1943; reprinted New York: Russell and Russell, 1965

Hoston, Germaine A., *Marxism and the Crisis of Development in Prewar Japan*, Princeton: Princeton University Press, 1986

Jien, *Gukanshō*, c.1220; in English as *The Future and the Past*, Berkeley: University of California Press, 1979

Kitabatake Chikafusa, *Jinnō shōtōki*, revised 1343; in English as *A Chronicle of Gods and Sovereigns*, New York: Columbia University Press, 1980

Kojiki, 712; in English as *Kojiki*, Tokyo: Tokyo University Press, 1968; Princeton: Princeton University Press, 1969; and in *The Sacred Scriptures of the Japanese*, New York: Schuman, 1952

Kuroda Toshio, "Gukanshō and Jinnō Shōtōki," in John A. Harrison, ed., *New Light on Early and Medieval Japanese Historiography*, Gainesville: University of Florida Press, 1960

Nakai, Kate Wildman, "Tokugawa Confucian Historiography: The Hayashi, the Early Mito School, and Arai Hakuseki," in Peter Nosco, ed., *Confucianism and Tokugawa Culture*, Princeton: Princeton University Press, 1984

Nihon shoki [or *Nihongi*], 720; in English as *Nihongi: Chronicles of Japan from the Earliest Times to AD 697*, London: Routledge, 1896; reprinted London: Allen and Unwin, 1956, Rutland, VT: Tuttle, 1972; and in *The Sacred Scriptures of the Japanese*, New York: Schuman, 1952

Norman, E.H., *Japan's Emergence as a Modern State: Political and Economic Problems of the Meiji Period*, New York: Institute of Pacific Relations, 1940

Norman, E.H., *Origins of the Modern Japanese State: Selected Writings of E.H. Norman*, New York: Random House, 1974

Ōkagami, c.1119; in English as *The Ōkagami: A Japanese Historical Tale*, Rutland, VT: Tuttle, 1977

Reischauer, Edwin O., *Japan: Past and Present*, New York: Knopf, 1946; London: Duckworth, 1947; 4th edition as *Japan: The Story of a Nation*, New York: McGraw Hill, 1990

Rikkokushi, 9th century; in English as *The Six National Histories of Japan*, Vancouver: University of British Columbia Press, and Tokyo: University of Tokyo Press, 1991

Robinson, G.W., "Early Japanese Chronicles: The Six National Histories," in William G. Beasley and Edwin G. Pulleyblank, eds., *Historians of China and Japan*, London: Oxford University Press, 1961

Sansom, George Bailey, *Japan: A Short Cultural History*, New York: Century, 1931, revised 1943; reprinted Stanford, CA: Stanford University Press, 1978, London: Century, 1987

Taiheiki, 14th century; in English as *Taiheiki: A Chronicle of Medieval Japan*, New York: Columbia University Press, 1959

Takamure Itsue, *Bokeisei no kenkyū* (Studies in Matriarchy), Tokyo: Kōseikaku, 1938

Takekoshi Yosaburō, *The Economic Aspects of the of the History of the Civilization of Japan*, 3 vols., London: Allen and Unwin, and New York: Macmillan, 1930; reprinted 1967

Tsuda Sōkichi, *Bungaku ni arawaretaru waga kokumin shisō no kenkyū*, 4 vols., Tokyo: Rakúyodo, 1916-21; volume 3 translated as *An Inquiry into the Japanese Mind as Mirrored in Literature: The Flowering Period of Common People Literature*, Tokyo: Japan Society for the Promotion of Science, 1970; New York: Greenwood, 1988

Varley, H. Paul, "The Place of Gukanshō in Japanese Intellectual History," *Monumenta Nipponica* 34/4 (1979)

Webb, Herschel, "What Is the *Dai Nihon Shi*?" *Journal of Asian Studies* 19 (1960), 135–50

Wray, Harry, and Hilary Conroy, eds., *Japan Examined: Perspectives on Modern Japanese History*, Honolulu: University of Hawaii Press, 1983

Zuikei Shūhō, *Zenrinkoku hōki* (Precious Record of Friendly Relations with Neighbor Countries), 1470; reprinted Tokyo: Kokusho Kankōkai, 1975

Japanese Chronicles

Japanese chronicles is the collective term for the official chronicles of the Japanese imperial court, beginning with the *Nihongi* or *Nihon shoki* (Chronicle of Japan, 720 CE). This work, along with five successive works covering the period to 887, are known as the "six national histories" (*Rikkokushi*). A surviving earlier work, the *Kojiki* (Chronicle of Ancient Matters, 712) is also of considerable importance.

The earliest compilation of national histories in Japan clearly resulted from heightened contact with China and Korea, and the influx of foreign monks well trained in the Chinese literary tradition following the introduction of Buddhism to the Yamato (Japanese) court in the mid-6th century. The authors of these works, however, were Japanese, who only gradually came to understand and apply Chinese historiographical principles to their material.

As early as the 6th century, leading figures at the court are thought to have sponsored the compilation of genealogies and anecdotal histories. In 620, Prince Shōtoku, regent to the female emperor Suiko, commissioned three works, described in the *Nihongi* as *Tennōki* (The Record of the Emperors), *Kokki* (The National Record), and *Hongi* (The Fundamental Records). The last dealt primarily with titled families. These were subsequently destroyed during political upheavals in 645 and 672. At least two important sources survived: a genealogical document, referred to as *Teiki* (Imperial Chronicle), and an anecdotal source document called *Honji* (Fundamental Dicta) or *Kuji* (Ancient Dicta).

Serious efforts at historical writing were revived by emperor Tenmu (reigned 673–86), who according to the *Kojiki*, determined that the records "handed down by the various houses have come to differ from the truth and that many falsehoods have been added to them." They were to be corrected, primarily, it is thought, to establish the genealogies of the various courtly families, and their hierarchical relationships with one another.

A 28-year-old court attendant named Hieda no Are, who may have been a woman, and a scribe named Ō no Yasumaro, played the key roles in the production of a new history, the *Kojiki*. Hieda no Are's precise contribution is the subject of some controversy; he/she was ordered to "learn" or "recite" the above-named documents, perhaps because in a still largely preliterate court society, oral recitation was more useful than text. Hieda no Are also probably memorized a considerable oral tradition, organizing all these materials in his or her mind. Many years later (711) the female emperor Genmei commanded Ō no Yasumaro to transcribe and probably rearrange Hieda's memorized material. He did so using Chinese characters in their conventional ideographic meanings, as well as for their purely phonetic value (for writing Japanese names, replicating poems, etc.) The resulting text is extremely difficult, but provides invaluable insight into the ancient Japanese language.

The *Kojiki* is divided into three books. The first is almost entirely mythological, dealing with the age of the gods, describing the descent to earth (Japan) of the grandson of the sun goddess, Amaterasu, and the deeds of his divine descendants up to the birth of Jinmu, the first emperor. The second describes how Jinmu marched from Kyushu to central Japan, conquering various foes and establishing the empire. It covers

the reigns of the first 15 emperors, most of whom appear to be purely mythological, up to Ōjin. The latter is thought to be a historical ruler who reigned in the early 5th century. Book 3 recorded events up to the reign of Suiko (the 33rd ruler according to the traditional account) in the early 7th century. This third book appears to have general historical credibility; unfortunately, in the last ten chapters, covering the late 5th to early 7th centuries, narrative elements disappear and attention is focused mostly on the question of imperial succession.

Soon joined by the more polished and substantial *Nihongi*, the *Kojiki* received little scholarly attention until the Edo or Tokugawa period, when adherents of the Nativist or *Kokugaku* school subjected it to detailed philological examination. The 18th-century historian Motoori Norinaga's *Kojiki den* (Study of the Kojiki) enthused about its comparative lack of Chinese influence, and pronounced it "the classic of classics." It remains a strangely moving work of mythology and religion, as well as history.

The *Nihongi* covers much of the same ground as the *Kojiki*, but is written in classical Chinese. Compiled by many people, including a son of emperor Tenmu (reigned 673–86), it constitutes 30 volumes, plus one volume of genealogical charts. Unlike the *Kojiki*, it draws on several Chinese sources, including the *Wei chih*, and on a number of Korean historical accounts. Like the *Kojiki*, it begins with the creation of the world and the establishment of the empire of Japan by Jinmu, but it provides much more useful information about historical reigns, beginning with that of the late 5th-century ruler Yūryaku (covered in volume 14), and continuing through the reign of the female emperor Jitō (reigned 686–97). In contrast to the *Kojiki*, it often provided several conflicting accounts of the same historical event, suggesting an effort at historical objectivity.

On the other hand, the *Nihongi* editors were willing to indulge in outright falsification. Emulating Chinese attention to chronological detail, they appended specific dates, according to the Chinese lunar calendar, to reigns and events which are clearly wholly contrived. The chronology of the *Nihongi* placed the foundation of the empire under Jinmu at what in the Western calendar would be 660 BCE. The date was apparently chosen with reference to Chinese astrological principles, and perhaps to assert greater antiquity for the Japanese court than the Chinese. But the use of named eras, rather than a serial chronological system, would have reduced the weight of such a claim.

Since the ruling Yamato clan had probably ruled only from the 4th century, it was necessary to posit a number of past rulers – some of whom were accorded implausibly long life spans – to bring the list of emperors up to date. Thus while Jinmu probably has a historical prototype, the second through 14th emperors, supposedly reigning from 581 BCE to 201 CE, are probably fictitious.

The *Nihongi* editors also falsified the past by projecting material borrowed from the Chinese official histories into the remote Japanese past. We find reference to battle-axes, for example, before such weapons had appeared in Japan, and a speech attributed to the emperor Yūryaku turns out to be lifted from an official history of the Sui dynasty. Yet despite such distortions of the past, which sophisticated foreign visitors might have discerned, a major function of the *Nihongi* seems to have been to impress outsiders, and to indicate that Japan, like China, had a carefully documented historical record establishing the legitimacy of the ruling family.

The *Nihongi* was followed by five other officially-sponsored, Chinese-language histories: *Shoku Nihongi* (Chronicle of Japan, Continued), covering the period from 697 to 791; *Nihon kōki* (Later Chronicle of Japan), covering the period 792–833 (only part of this survives); *Shoku Nihon kōki* (Later Chronicle of Japan, Continued), covering 834 to 850; *Montoku Tennō jitsuroku* (Veritable Records of the emperor Montoku [reigned 851–58]); and the *Nihon sandai jitsuroku* (Veritable Records of Three Reigns of Japan) dealing with the period from 859 to 887. A later history, *Shin Kokushi* (New National History) brought the record up to 930, but this text does not survive.

All these histories follow the Chinese-style annalistic form (*hennentai*); that is, each section covers a reign, and begins with genealogical and biographical information about the emperor. They are written strictly from the point of view of the court, and record official actions in response to such events as famine or disease in the provinces. Beginning with the *Nihon shoki*, they reflect the Chinese notion that history should serve a didactic purpose. According to the *Nihon Kōki*, "it is the function of history to ensure that no fault be concealed, which might serve as a warning, and that every excellence be published, which might illuminate the path of virtue." Unlike the Chinese official histories, however, the Japanese chronicles assume the legitimacy and moral worth of each sovereign in an unbroken line of rulers; the Mandate of Heaven concept, if present, is never employed to condemn an emperor.

With the ascendence of the Fujiwara regency from the mid-9th century, and consequent decline of the authority of the imperial bureaucracy, the practice of compiling official chronicles died out. From this point the historian must rely on such sources as historical tales (*rekishi monogatari*), such as the *Eiga monogatari* (Tale of Splendor, 11th century) and *Ōkagami* (The Great Mirror, late 11th or early 12th century), both of which deal primarily with the Fujiwara; the *gunki* (warrior tales), such as *Heike monogatari* (Tale of the Heike, early 13th century); and privately produced comprehensive histories, such as Chikafusa Kitabatake's *Jinnō Shōtoki*.

GARY P. LEUPP

See also Japan

Further Reading

Aston, W.G., trans., *Nihongi: Chronicles of Japan from the Earliest Times to AD 697*, Tokyo: Tuttle, 1972
Chamberlain, Basil Hall, trans., *The Kojiki: Records of Ancient Matters*, Tokyo: Tuttle, 1981
Konishi Jin'ichi, *A History of Japanese Literature*, vol. 1: *The Archaic and Ancient Ages*, Princeton: Princeton University Press, 1984
Philippi, Donald L., trans., *Kojiki*, Tokyo: Tokyo University Press, and Princeton: Princeton University Press, 1969
Robinson, G.W., "Early Japanese Chronicles: The Six National Histories," in William G. Beasley and Edwin G. Pulleyblank, eds., *Historians of China and Japan*, London: Oxford University Press, 1961

Jelavich, Barbara 1923–1995 and Charles Jelavich 1922–

US historians of Eastern Europe

In many respects, Western historians "discovered" Eastern Europe in the years following World War II. Although politicians and the public saw the region through the prism of the Cold War, scholars in greater numbers began to look at the region as a distinct, vital entity. Among the pioneers in the field were Barbara and Charles Jelavich, who together paved the way for future generations of historians of Eastern Europe.

The Jelaviches' research, collaboratively as well as independently, spanned five decades. Avoiding the polemics that often plagued scholarship concerning, and emanating from, the region, they examined Eastern Europe, especially the Balkans, as an integral part of European history, not separate from it. At the same time, the rich – and unique – mosaic nature of the region was not lost. Their publications fall into a number of major categories: the Balkans, the Habsburg empire and Austria, Ottoman and Russian/Soviet diplomacy, nationalism, and specialized studies in Romanian and Yugoslav history. In twenty books and more than one hundred published articles, the Jelaviches brought East European studies to a wider audience than merely specialists.

The core of the Jelaviches' research concerned the Balkans. Although a short work, *The Balkans* (1965) presented a general thematic introduction to the region. Their seminal treatises on southeastern Europe came in the form of two later, more exhaustive studies, *The Establishment of the Balkan National States, 1804–1920* (1977), written jointly, and Barbara's 2-volume *History of the Balkans* (1983). The former centered on the problems of the emerging states in terms of both their own nationalism as well as their positions within the geopolitical framework of Europe. The latter represented the first major treatment of the region as the whole in a quarter century. What emerged was a picture that balanced the legacy of the Balkan peoples' distinct histories with the experience of centuries of Ottoman and Habsburg rule. Those two forces converged to shape a region in which nationalism, economic backwardness, and great power politics posed insurmountable barriers to the solution of common problems. The dislocations of the 1990s seem to add one more chapter to Barbara's portrayal of a region that after World War I never could resolve the fundamental economic and political issues that constantly threatened internal disruption. The Balkans remained in a state of tension; once the shackles of communist rule had been removed, those explosive forces, which she had analyzed nearly a decade prior to the collapse of the "bloc," re-emerged.

Apart from these broad syntheses of Balkan history, both Jelaviches published widely in their own special areas of interest. Charles often focused on the impact of nationalism upon Eastern Europe, especially in Serbia/Yugoslavia. His examination of the dynamics of nationalism led to an analysis of the clash between the ideal of Yugoslavism and the reality of ethnic divisions. He found the conflict mirrored in the schools and textbooks which seemed to stress a Yugoslav ideal, but in reality served to promote the nationalistic instincts of the various ethnic groups within the state. The publication in 1990 of *South Slav Nationalisms*, in fact, was as timely as any work of history might be, for it laid bare the deeply entrenched heritage of groups that defined themselves very differently from the thinly-rooted sense of Yugoslav unity. At the same time, Charles also worked on numerous projects devoted to developing resource opportunities and materials, endeavors that proved to be invaluable to other scholars.

Barbara meanwhile was pursuing her myriad interests, researching and writing numerous broadly analytical studies as well as more narrowly-focused monographs. The title of her first book, *Russia and the Rumanian National Cause, 1858–1859* (1959) reflected two of her principal research areas: diplomacy and the development of the Romanian state. She constantly returned to the theme of Russia's intrusion into the complex world of the Balkans, first expanding her earlier study into the comprehensive *Russia and the Formation of the Romanian National State, 1821–1878* (1984) and later writing *Russia's Balkan Entanglements, 1806–1914* (1991); both chronicled St. Petersburg's emotional and geopolitical attachment to a region that led Russia into disaster in 1854 and again in 1914. This interest in the pitfalls of the Eastern Question for the great powers also led her to publish four other major works on diplomatic history: *A Century of Russian Foreign Policy, 1814–1914* (1964) [later expanded into *St. Petersburg and Moscow*], *The Ottoman Empire, the Great Powers, and the Straits Question, 1870–1887* (1973), and *The Habsburg Empire in European Affairs, 1814–1918* (1969). The last was an especially thought-provoking account of a great power whose traditional pillars of support could not confront its realities as a multinational state. Paralleling these analyses of the various great powers was her research in 19th- and 20th-century Romanian history, a lifetime of work which led to her election to the Romanian Academy of Sciences, a singular tribute to a historian who pointed the way for future Romanian scholars, and did so with the same writing style that had marked all her work, one which was as readable as it was precise.

Even considered separately, the contributions of Charles and Barbara Jelavich to historical writing would be remarkable. Taken together, they serve as the standard against which others will be judged for decades to come. No discussion of Eastern Europe's past can take place without taking their work into account.

RICHARD FRUCHT

See also Austro-Hungarian; Balkans; East Central Europe; Ottoman

Biography
Barbara Brightfield Jelavich. Born Belleville, Illinois, 12 April 1923. Received BA, University of California, 1943, MA 1944, PhD 1948. Taught at Mills College and University of California, Berkeley, then at University of Indiana, Bloomington, 1962–92. Married Charles Jelavich (2 children). Died Bloomington, Indiana, 14 January 1995. **Charles Jelavich.** Born Mount View, California, 15 November 1922. Received BA, University of California, 1944, MA 1947, PhD 1949. Taught at University of California, 1959–62; and University of Indiana, Bloomington, from 1962. Married Barbara Brightfield Jelavich (died 1995; 2 children).

Principal Writings

Barbara Jelavich
Russia and the Rumanian National Cause, 1858–1859, 1959

Russia and Greece during the Regency of King Othon, 1832–1835, 1962
Editor, *Russland, 1852–1871: Aus den Berichten der Bayerischen Gesandtschaft in St Petersburg* (Russia 1852–1871: From the Reports of the Bavarian Legation in St. Petersburg), 1963
A Century of Russian Foreign Policy, 1814–1914, 1964
Russia and the Greek Revolution of 1843, 1966
The Habsburg Empire in European Affairs, 1814–1918, 1969
The Ottoman Empire, the Great Powers, and the Straits Question, 1870–1887, 1973
St. Petersburg and Moscow: Tsarist and Soviet Foreign Policy, 1814–1974, 1974 [expanded edition of *A Century of Russian Foreign Policy*]
History of the Balkans, 2 vols., 1983
Russia and the Formation of the Romanian National State, 1821–1878, 1984
Modern Austria: Empire and Republic, 1815–1986, 1987
Russia's Balkan Entanglements, 1806–1914, 1991

Charles Jelavich
Russian Influence in Serbia and Bulgaria, 1881–1897, 1949
Tsarist Russia and Balkan Nationalism: Russian Influence in the Internal Affairs of Bulgaria and Serbia, 1879–1886, 1958
Editor, *Language and Area Studies: East Central Europe and Southeastern Europe: A Survey*, 1969
South Slav Nationalisms: Textbooks and Yugoslav Union before 1914, 1990

Joint Publications
Editors, *Russia in the East, 1876–1880: The Russo-Turkish War and the Kuldja Crisis as Seen Through the Letters of A.G. Jomini to N.K. Giers*, 1959
The Habsburg Empire: Toward a Multinational Empire or National States?, 1959
Editors, *The Education of a Russian Statesman: The Memoirs of Nicholas Karlovich Giers*, 1962
Editors, *The Balkans in Transition: Essays on the Development of Balkan Life and Politics since the Eighteenth Century*, 1963
The Balkans, 1965
The Establishment of the Balkan National States, 1804–1920, 1977

Further Reading

Bodea, Cornelia, "Barbara Jelavich and Eastern European Historiography," *Revue Romaine d'Histoire* 4 (1985), 267–76
Michelson, Paul E., and Jean T. Michelson, "Charles and Barbara Jelavich: A Bibliographical Appreciation," in Richard Frucht, ed., *Labyrinth of Nationalism, Complexities of Diplomacy: Essays in Honor of Charles and Barbara Jelavich*, Columbus, OH: Slavica, 1989
Vinogradov, Vladlen Nikolaevich, "Rossiia i Balkany v trudakh Barbary i Charl'za Elavichii" (Russia and the Balkans in the Works of Barbara and Charles Jelavich), *Sovetskoe Slavianovedenic* 3 (1989), 27–41

Jensen, Merrill 1905–1980
US historian

Merrill Jensen has often been characterized as the last of the Progressive historians. Although he did not readily accept such labels, he closely followed the Progressive historical interpretations initially forwarded by Charles Beard and Carl Becker. By applying this approach to historiography to the decades surrounding the birth of the United States, Jensen successfully delineated the tensions and conflicts that marked American political life between 1763 and 1789. He did not portray the Revolution as the victory of a united people marching forward to a harmonious future. Instead, Jensen's American Revolution was a story of citizens from different backgrounds and social groups interacting with each other and trying to solve basic issues of government and society.

Jensen's first foray into the study of the revolutionary era appeared in 1940. With the publication of *The Articles of Confederation: An Interpretation of the Social-Constitutional History of the American Revolution, 1774–1781*, he immediately established his reputation as a leading historian of the period. He described a Revolution fought on grounds that were material rather than ideological, internal rather than international. He argued that the Revolution was essentially a democratic movement within the 13 colonies. The significance of this movement lay in its tendency to elevate the political and economic status of the majority of the people. This newfound status for many Americans was preserved through the Articles of Confederation, which were the embodiment of the Declaration of Independence in governmental form.

Jensen's second book, *The New Nation* (1950), continued on the interpretive path set forth in his initial scholarship. Broader in scope, this volume covered the economic, political, social, and cultural history of the period. These years were marked by a continuing conflict between the true "federalists" who supported the Confederation and nationalists who desired a strong central government. Jensen concluded that the Revolution transformed the nation in two ways: by the unleashing of democracy, which was exemplified by the revolutionary state constitutions, and by the elimination of an imperial government. Therefore, it was the "federalists," frequently misnamed Antifederalists, who worked to continue the essence of the Revolution. The Confederation era emerged as a time of popular democracy and governmental achievement.

In 1968, Jensen completed *The Founding of a Nation*. This work, in conjunction with the two previously mentioned publications, constituted an informal trilogy of his thoughts and conclusions on the period from 1763 to 1789. Once again, Jensen stressed the political factionalism that existed in the colonies. He described how the various parliamentary acts instituted after 1763 worked to increase bitter political struggles. Arising out of these struggles were "popular leaders" who attempted to unite opposition to the "enemies of America." In distinct opposition to these popular leaders, many members of the American aristocracy thought the masses would seize too much control in revolution and plunge the society into chaos. The truly revolutionary act was the eventual union of these differing factions into a new nation. It was this thrashing out of differences that Jensen argued gave form and character to the Revolution before and after 1776.

The scholarship of Jensen provides a vivid and detailed look into the early struggles for independence and the prolonged battle for governmental control. Following the lead of Beard and Becker, Jensen's story is one of ever-increasing factionalism and conflict. The Revolution brought about an increase in status for a majority of Americans. In addition, the Articles of Confederation embodied democratic principles that allowed these citizens a voice in the government. Not all Americans, however, were happy with these developments. Great numbers of the social elite feared that rule by the masses would lead the nation down a path toward chaos. For this reason, the internal revolution that followed America's victory over Britain was checked by the formation and ratification of the Constitution. Jensen does not try to hide his sympathies when relating the path of the fledgling nation in his scholarship. He sees the ultimate decisions of the leaders of this new nation as a repudiation of the principles for which the Revolution was fought and a lost opportunity for the common man.

MATTHEW A. MINICHILLO

See also LaFeber; United States: Colonial

Biography
Born Elkhorn, Iowa, 16 July 1905, to a farming family. After finishing high school, briefly taught at a local school; studied at University of Washington, BA 1929, MA 1931; University of Wisconsin, PhD 1934. Taught at University of Washington, 1935–44; and University of Wisconsin, Madison, 1944–76 (emeritus). Died Madison, 30 January 1980.

Principal Writings
The Articles of Confederation: An Interpretation of the Social-Constitutional History of the American Revolution, 1774–1781, 1940
The New Nation: A History of the United States during the Confederation, 1781–1789, 1950
Editor, *Regionalism in America*, 1952
The Making of the American Constitution, 1964
The Founding of a Nation: A History of the American Revolution, 1763–1776, 1968
The American Revolution within America, 1974

Further Reading
Ferguson, E. James, "Merrill Jensen: A Personal Comment" in James Kirby Martin, ed., *The Human Dimensions of Nation Making: Essays on Colonial and Revolutionary America*, Madison: State Historical Society of Wisconsin, 1976
Martin, James Kirby, "The Human Dimensions of Nation Making: Merrill Jensen's Scholarship and the American Revolution," in James Kirby Martin, ed., *The Human Dimensions of Nation Making: Essays on Colonial and Revolutionary America*, Madison: The State Historical Society of Wisconsin, 1976

Jewish History

The histories that Jews lived created special problems for the histories Jewish historians wrote. Thus, both Greco-Roman and much later Christian historiography was political and military history that was *narrativo res gestarum*, the narration of great deeds. It was difficult, if not actually impossible, to write that kind of history after Jewish sovereignty was extinguished with the destruction of the Second Commonwealth in 70 CE. Moreover, the diaspora – the scattering of the Jews among the nations that rabbinic tradition termed the "exile" (*galut*) – made it hard to locate the subject of Jewish history: the rabbis maintained that Jews everywhere formed a single community (*clal Yisrael*), but did the large Babylonian community really share the same history as the remaining Palestinian community, not to mention the larger communities in Greek-speaking Alexandria or at Rome itself? Could a people in exile have a history in pre-messianic times? The really important things had either happened long before or had yet to occur.

Furthermore, the Jewish legal system – the central subject for study and reverence – was everlasting. Why, then, study the record of changes? That is why Moses Maimonides (1135–1204) thought history was a waste of time and energy.

Under these conditions, political narrative held little attraction for Jews. The chief exception to this rule, Flavius Josephus, in fact proves it. A product of the Greek-speaking Alexandrian Jewish community, he participated in the Great Rebellion (66–70 CE) on both sides, and narrated the war in his highly readable *Jewish War*. In this and his other historical works, *Contra Apionem* (*Against Apion* – a refutation of Apion's anti-Jewish history) and *Antiquitates Judaicae* (*The Jewish Antiquities*), the classically educated Josephus borrowed heavily from Hellenistic models. His Jewish rebels made speeches that would be entirely in place in Thucydides. This political classicism was incongruous under diaspora conditions. In consequence, Josephus had almost no intellectual heirs, if we except the anonymous 9th-or 10th-century Italian book that circulated under the the name Yosippon or Josippon. Its author(s) drew heavily on Josephus and other sources for what became the standard medieval account of the Second Temple period. Its popularity, however, suggests that some Jewish demand for history existed, though the *Book of Josippon* is more a collection of stories and memories than a history in any precise sense of the term.

There were several special senses, however, in which rabbinic interest in history was intense, although the results were more historical arguments than narrative histories. Certainly their authors did not view themselves as historians. First, rabbis passionately read the historical books of scripture. Strictly speaking, of course, this did not mean reading texts like Samuel I and II as narrative history because, in the rabbinic scheme, these were not books of history but of prophecy. Nevertheless, rabbis knew that these were also accounts of Israel's glorious past, a past also remembered in such festivals as *pesach* (passover) celebrating the escape from Egypt or *tishe b'av*, bewailing the fall of the first and second Temples. Second, the rabbinic genres of *parshanut* (biblical commentary), *midrash* (intertextual biblical commentary), and *talmud* (legal disquisition and commentary on the *mishnah*, the record of the oral law) were all rich in historical materials. That is, the rabbinic classics have two components, *halakhah* and *aggadah*. The former is the law, and the latter the illustrative and supplementary anecdote that is often very beautiful and occasionally rich in historical data. These are chiefly the means to nonhistorical ends, and in any case are presented without criticism or system. The hardships of exile also provoked interest in the shape of future history, and *aggadah* readily offered two schemes, first the traditional four kingdoms based on the *Book of Daniel* and, second, the notion of 2,000 years of chaos followed by 2,000 years of Torah, followed by 2,000 years of the messianic reign written of in the Babylonian *Talmud* (*Sanhedrin* 97a).

Rabbis were also deeply interested in historical matters in yet a third way. The text of the Babylonian Talmud (*Bavli*) was closed in the late 6th century, but in the following centuries those Jews who argued solely from written scripture, the Karaites, questioned the authority of this magisterial rabbinic text. Some rabbis responded by defensively researching the history of the Talmud. The results were such works as the *Seder Tannaim ve-Amoraim* (Order of the Tannaim and Amoraim) from the late 9th century and the much grander *Sefer ha-Qabbalah* (Book of Tradition) by Abraham Ibn Daud (c.1110–80). There are many later specimens of this genre, as late as the *Yad-Malakhi* (Hand of Malachi) by Malakhi ha-Kohen of Livorno in the early 18th century, at the threshold of the *haskala*, the Jewish Enlightenment, and the emancipation of the 19th century. The common goal of these works, evidently derived from comparable Muslim studies of Islamic traditions (*isnad*), was to validate textual authority by establishing its line of transmission. These are historical demonstrations conducted for the ahistorical purpose of reinforcing the authority of timeless texts.

In time painful events also turned Jews to historical writing. Medieval Jews in northern Europe, the *Ashkenazim*, and the Jews from Spain, the *Sephardim*, experienced catastrophes at Christian hands that provoked historical writings of a different sort. For example, the launching of the First Crusade in 1096 provoked violent attacks on Jews in the Rhenish cities of Mainz, Speyer, Worms, and Cologne. These attacks, evidently, provoked many Jews to commit suicide as an escape from forced conversion. Jews in the next generation wrote now much debated chronicles of these events, for both commemorative and didactic purposes. The longest and most detailed of these was written by Solomon bar Simeon. The final expulsion of Jews from Spain in 1492 similarly created an intense historical interest that found expression in such works as the *Shevet Yehuda* (Staff of Yehuda) written by Solomon ibn Verga and published by his son in 1554 and the *Consolacam as tribulacoens de Israel* (Tribulations of Israel) written in Portuguese rather than Hebrew, by Samuel Usque and published in 1553. These works had some novel features. Their authors were sephardic Jews who escaped Spain for Portugal and there underwent forced conversion. Usque resorted to the traditional Jewish explanation for calamity: Yes, it was the work of evil men, but it was also a just punishment "for our sins" (*mipnei hattatenu*). Ibn Verga, by contrast, explained the expulsion as a specific consequence of Jewish/Christian relations in Spain – that is a result of largely secular causes condoned by a still active deity.

Rather different in shape is the 1522 *Seder Eliyahu Zuta* (Lesser Order of Eliahu) by Elijah Capsali. Capsali's text is a study of the Ottoman Turkish empire that also pays close attention to the frightful events in Christian Spain that led to the stream of sephardic refugees into the more tolerant Turkish polity. Capsali's *Divrey yamim le-malkhey Tsarefat u-beth Ottomon ha-Togar* (Deeds of the Kingdoms of France and the House of Ottomon), like the later 16th-century Prague Jew David Ganz's *Zemach David* (The Sprout of David), is history in the sense of being a narrative of actions. In contrast, the brilliant and provocative *Meor Eynaim* (Light of the Eyes), which was published in 1573 and is often cited as evidence of a Renaissance in Jewish historiography – and whose historically-based essays anticipate modern historicism and inspired Salo Baron – is not. Nevertheless, Azariah expressed the need for an understanding of history appropriate to the special circumstances of the Jewish people, and he neither dismissed history as unworthy of serious study nor tried to justify its study through utilitarian religious arguments.

However one regards these 16th-century efforts, it is at least clear that Jewish historiography was indisputably central to the scholarly and ideological movement that termed itself *Wissenschaft des Judenthums*. Its appearance can be precisely dated to foundation in Berlin in 1819 of the *Verein für Cultur and Wissenschaft des Judenthums* (Union for Culture and Study of Judaism). The Jewish students and the older followers of Moses Mendelssohn who founded it acted in shocked response to attacks on the limited emancipation legislation already in place and to the recent *Hep! Hep!* riots in southern Germany. The German term *Wissenschaft* is significant. It means "science," but it also means reasoned, verified research and disquisition in the widest sense. Its chief founders were Eduard Gans (1798–1839), Immanuel Wolf (1799–1829), Joel Abraham List (1780–c.1848), and Leopld Zunz (1794–1886). Their immediate purposes were to correct the defamatory misinformation published by German judaeophobes and to undergird their recent and tenuous emancipation by revealing the proud prior history of Judaism. They also regretted that much writing on the Jewish past was by Christian scholars and, therefore, warped if not openly hostile in perspective. Their efforts, however, easily transcended these purely defensive and apologetic aims and had a longer prehistory in the Enlightenment and partial Emancipation of the preceding decades. The founders sought nothing less than what Gans termed the "unbiased and completely independent study of the Science of Judaism" which they then sought to integrate into "the whole of human knowledge."

This was, in fact, a campaign for self-knowledge according to the canons the new scholarship practiced and taught in the German universities, and its effects on Jews were profound. On the one hand, this new "scholarship" relativized Jewish past and present by making them mere objects of study. On the other hand, of course, the purpose of study was to defend and validate Judaism, although by novel means and according to unfamiliar standards. The writing of Jewish history was an important plank in the program of this Jewish scholarship, although it had an independent beginning as well in the mind of its first 19th-century practitioner, I.M. Jost (1793–1860) at Göttingen, who began gathering materials for the first of several synthetic Jewish histories, the *Geschichte der Israeliten* (A History of the Israelites, 1820–29), as early as 1814. It progressed in tandem with the rapid development of historical study in German academe. Its appearance, that is, was exactly contemporaneous with the professionalization and systematization of history associated with Leopold von Ranke, just as its prizing of Jewish selfconsciousness borrowed heavily from the then intellectually popular philosophy of G.W.F. Hegel. The singularity of the Jewish historical experience, however, assured that Jewish historiography would differ significantly from its gentile equivalents. The new Jewish historians were aware of this difference.

Jost, for example, insisted that Jews were unlike all other peoples because they had survived so long and through such adversity. Historians had somehow to show that difference, and he mused whether one could easily write the history of slaves. In his later works, such as his 1832 *Allgemeine Geschichte des israelitischen Volkes* (General History of the Israelite People), he included the new, essentially Hegelian notion of a Jewish destiny in world history: events that had once seemed calamitous now appeared in their true light as necessary to purify and improve the Jewish understanding of the true and the good.

History, then, was spiritual at its core, and a theodicy in its long run. Historically-minded proponents of Reform Judaism, notably Abraham Geiger in his later *Das Judenthum und seine Geschichte* (Judaism and Its History, 1865–71), elaborated the "mission" theory more fully by emphasizing Judaism's evolving quality as a universal religion. This supposed Jewish universalism, in turn, undergirded Geiger's Reform theology.

Heinrich Graetz (1817–1891) continued the work of writing synthetic Jewish history, and accepted elements of the "mission theory," but his understanding of Jewish history and its historical significance was original and sharply opposed to Jost's and Geiger's. Although Graetz had abandoned the talmudic traditionalism of his youth in Prussian Posen, he remained, as an ally of Zacharias Frankel at the Jewish Theological Seminary in Breslau, far more traditional in Jewish thought and practice than Geiger or Jost. His outlook in his history was diffusely rationalist and often moralizing, and he remained convinced – as most German academic historians of his age also did – that God works in the furtherance of a kind of progress. Graetz also believed, however, that Jewish history resisted formulaic definition, that it could be understood only through the narration of events. To that end, he wrote between 1853 and 1875 the volumes of his very readable *Geschichte der Juden* (History of the Jews, 1891–98). Graetz also theorized, however, as when he argued in his essay *Die Konstruktion der jüdischen Geschichte* (written 1846; in *The Structure of Jewish History*, 1975), that Jewish history is historically significant because it is unique, not because it has a universal content. He could not, therefore, deplore the rabbinism of earlier times or celebrate the modernization of Judaism in which he nevertheless took part. In part influenced by the Jewish historical philosopher Nachman Krochmal, he envisioned Jewish history as alternating through periods of growth and decay that, over the long term, constituted a progressive evolution that served a purpose in world history. His outlook was optimistic about the Jewish future, although the renewal of German anti-Semitism in 1881 discouraged him personally and led him to question the self-sufficient beneficence of the historical process.

Anti-Semitism in emancipated Germany, not to mention the pogroms in Russia in and after 1880 and the *fin de siècle* Dreyfus affair in Third Republic France all threw into question the optimistic "mission" theory of the 19th-century German Jewish historians. In any case, they had followed the logic of emancipation and the intellectualizing bent of German historiography in general to conceive of historical Judaism primarily as a belief system. That let them link the experiences of far-flung diaspora communities and kept them from seeming to be a state within the Prusso-German state. This spiritual definition made less sense when Jews were attacked for being Jewish people rather than Jewish believers, nor did it accord with the historical experience of Jews in Eastern Europe who plainly lived as a separate nationality in the lands of mixed nationalities. A more ethnographic historiography was required, and Simon Dubnov (1860–1941) was the most successful and prestigious of those who supplied it.

Dubnov began writing history fairly late in his long career. In an essay from 1893 he already parted company with Graetz inasmuch as he equated Jewish nationhood in the diaspora as something sustained by Jewish historical awareness. Jewish history was about Jewish nationality and it was also a means to Jewish nationality. Unlike Graetz, Dubnov had already begun to treat Jewish writings less for their own sake than as evidence of Jewish national awareness. This idea is most fully developed in his 10-volume *Weltgeschichte des jüdischen Volkes* (1925–30; *History of the Jews*, 1967–73), written in Russian by Dubnov who now, after the Russian Revolution, lived in Berlin. The history is of a people that has lasted scattered through time, and its focus, though narrative, is typically more social than religious. His scholarship was rigorous, but his history was also a work of advocacy in behalf of autonomism, his belief – of course undercut by the Holocaust – that Jews could live well in diaspora if granted cultural autonomy and other legal rights in the lands where they lived. Although events tragically outpaced the idea of autonomism, after Dubnov Jewish history was fully a national narrative. Zionism, with its insistence that Jews should live in *eretz Israel*, was seemingly quite the opposite of autonomism, and so it is in programmatic political terms, but the nationalist historiography of classic Zionist historians such as Benzion Dinur, in what David N. Myers termed "the Zionist return to history," presuppose the nationalism of Dubnov.

Most modern Jewish historiography is also greatly in the debt of Salo Baron (1895–1989). Baron published voluminously, although he is most famous for his *A Social and Religious History of the Jews*, published in three volumes in 1937, and then in a greatly lengthened and never completed revised edition that stopped with his account of the 17th century. Baron argued against the "lachrymose conception" of Jewish history by showing that Jews were not mere victims in medieval Europe and often acted for their own benefit. More generally, he directed historical attention to hitherto little discussed matters such as demography within a conception of Jewish history that valued equally Jewish life in diaspora and in Israel. Like Dubnov, he preceded and shaped the great expansion of Jewish historical studies in recent decades which has resulted in a literature too large and variegated to be captured in any simple formula. It is fair to say, however, that the study of Jewish history became normalized, as one among many national narratives, and has followed other histories into such new areas of inquiry such as women's history.

ROBERT FAIRBAIRN SOUTHARD

See also Argentina; Baron, S.; Braham; Broszat; Crusades; Dubnov; Goitein; Graetz; Hegel; Hilberg; Holocaust; Josephus; Katz; Marrus; Memory

Further Reading

Baron, Salo Wittmayer, *A Social and Religious History of the Jews*, 3 vols., New York: Columbia University Press, 1937; revised in 18 vols., 1952–83

Dawidowicz, Lucy S. *What Is the Use of Jewish History? Essays*, New York: Schocken, 1992

Dubnov, Simon, *Die Weltgeschichte des jüdischen Volkes*, 10 vols., Berlin: Jüdischer Verlag, 1925–30; in English as *History of the Jews*, 5 vols., South Brunswick, NJ: Yoseloff, 1967–73

Frankel, Jonathan, ed., *Reshaping the Past: Jewish History and the Historians*, New York and Oxford: Oxford University Press, 1994

Funkenstein, Amos, *Perceptions of Jewish History*, Berkeley: University of California Press, 1993

Geiger, Abraham, *Das Judenthum und seine Geschichte* (Judaism and Its History), 3 vols., Breslau: Skutch, 1865–71

Graetz, Heinrich, *Geschichte der Juden von den ältesten Zeiten bis auf die Gegenwart*, 11 vols., Leipzig: Leiner, 1853–75; in English as *History of the Jews*, 6 vols., Philadelphia: Jewish Publication Society of America, 1891–98

Graetz, Heinrich, *Die Konstruktion der jüdischen Geschichte* (1846), Berlin: Schocken, 1936; in English as *The Structure of Jewish History, and Other Essays*, New York: Jewish Theological Seminary of America, 1975

Jost, Isaak Markus, *Geschichte der Israeliten seit der Zeit der Maccabaer bis auf unsere Tage* (A History of the Israelites from the Time of Maccabbeas to Our Day), 9 vols., Berlin: Schlesinger, 1820–29

Jost, Isaak Markus, *Allgemeine Geschichte des israelitischen Volkes* (General History of the Israelite People), 2 vols., Berlin: Amelang, 1832

Meyer, Michael A., ed., *Ideas of Jewish History*, New York: Behram House, 1974

Michael, Reuven, *Ha-ketivah ha-historit ha-Yehudit mi-ha-Renasens* (Jewish Writing since the Renaissance), Jerusalem: Mosad Byalik, 1993

Myers, David N., *Reinventing the Jewish Past: European Jewish Intellectuals and the Zionist Return to History*, New York and Oxford: Oxford University Press, 1995

Rapoport-Albert, Ada, ed., "Essays in Jewish Historiography," in *History and Theory Beiheft* 27 (1988)

Yerushalmi, Yosef Haim, *Zakhor: Jewish History and Jewish Memory*, Seattle: University of Washington Press, 1982

Yosippon [Josippon], *The Compendious and Most Marvellous History of the Latter Times of the Jews*, 1558; as *The Wonderful and Most Deplorable History of the Latter Times of the Jews*, 1652

Joll, James 1918–1994
British historian of modern Europe

James Joll was a leading historian of Western Europe since the French Revolution, and author of several influential textbooks. His publications included studies of aspects of modern German, French, Italian, Spanish, and British history, as well as the interrelations between European states, social groups, and individuals. Joll rejected the cult of success as the basis for the selection of historical topics, arguing in *The Anarchists* (1964) that "if the aim of the historian, like that of the artist, is to enlarge our picture of the world, to give us a new way of looking at things, then the study of failure can often be as instructive and rewarding as the study of success." This expansive view of the role of the historian led Joll to study both conventional and radical subjects in European history, from conservative European politicians to their anarchist and syndicalist opponents. Joll's historical span was exceptional, including a special sympathy for outsiders and the dispossessed, which in part explains his continuing influence since the 1950s in a number of different historical fields. Further, his books and essays were models of lucid expression and thoughtful analysis.

In a *Festschrift* by his former students (*Ideas into Politics*, 1984), a "triple interest" was perceived in Joll's work: "an interest in the achievements of states and societies and of the evolution of state systems; a determination to uncover and explain the impact of ideas upon society; (and) a marked preoccupation with the role of the individual in history . . . (each) part of the larger whole of international history." These interests were evident from the early stages of his career as a professional university historian in Oxford and London, with a perspective based on, in Joll's words, "the comparative safety and detachment of an English middle-class life." Joll's initial research was undertaken in the aftermath of World War II, as an editor-in-chief for the important series *Documents on German Foreign Policy 1918–1945* (1949–), and as editor of a volume of documents on *Britain and Europe* (1950). Joll emphasized the historian's responsibility to return to the original sources in the original languages, and to seek out new evidence, including oral history. In *Britain and Europe* he underlined psychological attitudes and traditional beliefs as sources for understanding British policy towards Europe, a psychological theme that recurred throughout his work. Joll's first monograph, *The Second International, 1889–1914* (1955), elegantly synthesized the complex individual, ideological, national, and international currents evident in the congresses and other activities of the Second International, as socialism became a major intellectual and political force, especially in Germany and France. This outstanding capacity to integrate a vast range of international historical data in a clear and interesting narrative pattern was a characteristic feature of Joll's work.

In the 1960s Joll published two important books on intellectuals and European politics, *Intellectuals in Politics* (1960) and *The Anarchists*. The three essays on Blum, Rathenau, and Marinetti were subtle and probing studies of very different French, German, and Italian intellectuals, two of whom were Jews, and all of whom were men of ideas attempting to influence European politics. There was an underlying pessimism in Joll's book as to "whether the intellectual in politics is not always going to be doomed to failure because of the nature of his own virtues"; this was especially evident in his sympathetic analysis of Léon Blum, the great interwar hope for French socialism. Joll later added a short volume on the Italian Marxist Antonio Gramsci to his case studies of intellectuals in politics and argued for Gramsci as "a possible bridge between Marxist and non-Marxist thought" – a characteristic attempt at reconciliation. Joll's book on *The Anarchists* was immediately recognized as a benchmark study, and remains the best 1-volume synthesis on European anarchism. Joll emphasized the importance of individual temperament as a stimulus for anarchist ideas, and his analysis of the anarchist as heretic gave new insights into complex intellectuals such as Proudhon in France and movements such as Spanish anarchism.

In the 1960s Joll also introduced English readers to the controversial German historian Fritz Fischer and his revisionist work, *Germany's Aims in the First World War* (1961, translated 1967). Joll pioneered a reassessment by English historians, including his graduate research students, of the origins of World War I. His influential and invigorating inaugural lecture at the London School of Economics, "1914: The Unspoken Assumptions" (1968), highlighted the "ideological furniture" of European political and military leaders in 1914, especially the pernicious influences of "pseudo-Darwinism" and Nietzsche. He concluded that "it is only by studying the minds of men that we shall understand the causes of anything." Joll's last book, *The Origins of the First World War* (1984), explored the major interpretations of the war from an international and comparative perspective, and was immediately recognized as a masterful account of our historical understanding of World War I. Joll rejected any claims for an economic determinism at work in the war or elsewhere, and

was always skeptical about any monocausal models of history. His essential thesis remained unchanged: "To understand the men of 1914 we have to understand the values of 1914; and it is by these values that their actions must be measured."

Europe since 1870 (1973) was arguably Joll's most influential and widely read book, acknowledged for its remarkable synthesis of a century of political, diplomatic, ideological, and cultural history. Generations of students have been raised on the Pelican edition of *Europe since 1870*, rediscovering the great ideological battles, the world wars, and their aftermaths, and the revolutionary changes in industrial society and culture in Europe. In characteristic fashion the last section of Joll's *Europe* featured questions rather than judgments, and a balance between hope and pessimism. Joll created outstanding international and comparative history, essential if we are to understand "the cloudy residues of discarded beliefs" that still prevail.

JOHN HOOPER

See also World War I

Biography

James Bysse Joll. Born 21 June 1918. Educated at Winchester School; University of Bordeaux; New College, Oxford. Served in Devonshire Regiment and Special Operations Executive, 1939–45. Fellow/tutor in politics, New College, Oxford, 1946–50, fellow, 1951–67; fellow and subwarden, St. Antony's College, Oxford, 1951–67 (emeritus); Stevenson professor of international history, London School of Economics, 1967–81. Died 12 July 1994.

Principal Writings

Editor, *Britain and Europe: Pitt to Churchill, 1793–1940*, 1950
The Second International, 1889–1914, 1955
Editor, *The Decline of the Third Republic*, 1959
Intellectuals in Politics: Three Biographical Essays, 1960
The Anarchists, 1964
"The 1914 Debate Continues: Fritz Fischer and His Critics," (1966), and "1914: The Unspoken Assumptions," (1968), in Hannsjoachim Wolfgang Koch, ed., *The Origins of the First World War: Great Power Rivalry and German War Aims*, 1972
Editor with David E. Apter, *Anarchism Today*, 1971
Europe since 1870: An International History, 1973
Antonio Gramsci, 1977
The Origins of the First World War, 1984

Further Reading

Bullen, R.J., Hartmut Pogge von Strandmann, and Antony Polonsky, eds., *Ideas into Politics: Aspects of European History, 1880–1950* London: Croom Helm, and Totowa, NJ: Barnes and Noble, 1984 [includes bibliography]

Jones, A.H.M. 1904–1970
British ancient historian

A.H.M. Jones worked at a prodigious pace and his energy gained him an almost unparalleled knowledge of the original literary sources, especially documentary and epigraphic, for the classical world. Educated at Oxford in the 1920s, he was confronted by an academic establishment that had neglected the study of considerable periods and regions of antiquity. After a fellowship at All Souls College, Oxford, Jones left to work on excavations at Jerash and Constantinople, but these experiences failed to distract him from his primary interest in a comprehensive knowledge of texts. His tenure, from 1929 to 1934, of the readership in ancient history at Cairo encouraged his work on the East and it was shortly afterward that he published his first major work, *The Cities of the Eastern Roman Provinces* (1937). This was the first work to discuss the diffusion of Greek cities during the age following Alexander and it stands in striking contrast to the comparative neglect of Hellenistic studies at Oxford at this time. Proceeding in great detail from the region to region, this work made pioneering use of the immense mass of literary and epigraphic materials pertinent to the inner workings and official organization of these towns. This study was followed by *The Greek City from Alexander to Justinian* (1940), which sought to build on the earlier work by charting developments through to the end of the Roman period.

In 1946, after the end of his wartime service, Jones was appointed to the chair of ancient history at University College, London. He signalled his concern with understanding the mechanisms of the ancient world through the topic of his inaugural lecture (published as *Ancient Economic History*, 1948). This, however, may have disturbed certain members of the audience with its uncompromising emphasis on what *cannot* be known about antiquity, most especially matters that would require reliable figures for their explication. Jones was always concerned with establishing facts from ancient sources and we can here sense his frank acknowledgment of the limitations of his own personal science.

In 1951 he moved to Cambridge and it was there that he brought his two most influential projects to fruition. The first was his initiation of the multivolume *Prosopography of the Later Roman Empire* project, of which he lived to complete the first volume. The second great contribution was the appearance of his masterwork, *The Later Roman Empire, 284–602*. It is in two parts, the first being a clear yet detailed narrative. But it is for the second section, a structural survey of the empire, that this work is justly famed. Jones had made it his business to acquaint himself with all the pieces of textual evidence available, and his work is distinctive in that it was written almost entirely on the basis of that material. Although he read modern writers, he tried, as far as possible, to keep their thoughts from his mind when he constructed his own analyses. The result, it must be said, is more remarked upon than imitated, yet it is difficult to see how, in its own terms, it could easily be bettered. While Jones fails to evoke the mental world of late antiquity, his survey provides one of the most detailed compendia of factual detail that has ever been collected on organizational structures of government and society in the period. This vast mass of information is presented in Jones' characteristically and refreshingly clear style, and if the subject matter is dry the exposition is not.

Jones was still hard at work in his last years. He produced *The Decline of the Ancient World* (1966), which is essentially a textbook version of *The Later Roman Empire*, together with a variety of other surveys and collections of source material. His articles number around fifty and they show how Jones brought his expertise in social order and structure to bear on a wide variety of problems in ancient history, on topics ranging from the nature of documents to the social processes of Christian heresies. In all his major works he set a grand and austere example of scholarly perfection in the knowledge of primary sources, which few could rival then or can now.

DOMINIC JANES

See also Brown; Cameron; Roman; Syme

Biography
Arnold Hugh Martin Jones. Born Birkenhead, 9 March 1904. Educated at Cheltenham College; New College, Oxford, 1922–26, BA. Fellow, All Souls College, Oxford, 1926–46; worked on excavations in Constantinople and Jerash, 1927–29; reader in ancient history, Egyptian University, Cairo, 1929–34; lecturer in ancient history, Wadham College, Oxford, 1939–46; professor of ancient history, University College, London, 1946–51; fellow, Jesus College, Cambridge, 1951–70; professor of ancient history, Cambridge University, 1951–70. During World War II, posted to Ministry of Labour, then to intelligence at War Office. Married medievalist Freda Katherine Mackrell, 1927 (2 sons, 1 daughter). Died 9 April 1970.

Principal Writings
The Cities of the Eastern Roman Provinces, 1937
The Herods of Judaea, 1938
The Greek City from Alexander to Justinian, 1940
Ancient Economic History, 1948
Constantine and the Conversion of Europe, 1948
Athenian Democracy, 1957
Studies in Roman Government and Law, 1960
The Later Roman Empire, 284–602: A Social, Economic and Administrative Survey, 3 vols., 1964
The Decline of the Ancient World, 1966
Prosopography of the Later Roman Empire, vol. 1, 1971
The Criminal Courts of the Roman Republic and Principate, 1972
The Roman Economy: Studies in Ancient Economic and Administrative History, 1973

Jones, Gareth Stedman 1942–
British historian

Gareth Stedman Jones defies easy classification or summary. In part this is because at the time of writing so much of his recent work remains in progress and unpublished; in part it is the result of an idiosyncratic combination of engagement in the debates of social history while using the methodologies and insights of the history of ideas. Perhaps most importantly it derives from his increasingly explicit project not so much to contribute to the long tradition of Marxist exegesis, but instead to dismantle many of the fundamental tenets of Marxist theory.

From the outset, Jones occupied a position critical of the dominant trends of British social history. In the deep divisions of English Marxism of the 1960s, Jones was aligned with Perry Anderson and the *New Left Review* group, impatient (as his 1967 article, "The Pathology of English History" showed) with what he saw as the inadequate empiricism of Hobsbawm, Hill, and Thompson. His early aspiration to write an account of the late 19th-century triumph of liberal ideas and assumptions among the masses ultimately resulted in an empirically rich engagement with the "social problem" presented by the poor of East London and the various responses to them, published in 1971 as *Outcast London*. Jones explored the inherently casualized nature of the London labor market, demonstrating that this had concentrated population in the central districts, so that slum clearing programs after mid-century only intensified the threat of the "rookeries." He further demonstrated that the response of the middle classes to the intensified segregation of rich and poor, and their belief in the "deformation of the gift" (the severing of the link between charity and obligation), was not an evolving policy of welfare reforms, but rather various increasingly illiberal and punitive attempts to moralize the masses.

On the surface, *Outcast London* displayed little theoretical originality, and most comment focused on its lack of direct engagement with the culture of the London working class, rectified in an article published in 1974. It was only when this essay was collected with several other studies published over the ensuing decade in a volume entitled *Languages of Class* (1983), and prefaced with an introduction that drew out the theoretical implications of this work, that the extent of Jones' originality became apparent. Two themes dominated. The first was the rejection of explanations of social stability associated with the concept of social control: the roots of late 19th-century working-class conservatism, Jones argued, lay not in the impact of the kinds of middle-class moralization noted in *Outcast London*, but in the self-creation of a distinct, but defensive, "culture of consolation." The second, developed especially in the reworking of his earlier essay on "The Language of Chartism," was that Chartism as a movement, and especially as an ideology, was not the product of some materially-situated "working-class" condition, but arose from a much more complicated relationship between social processes and political and linguistic processes. Despite occasionally hazy theoretical underpinnings, its uncertainty about the status of the "social," its questioning of class as the fundamental constituent of social identity, and its emphasis on the constitutive role of language, coupled with its obvious familiarity with the historical sources, effected a decisive break with the hitherto dominant influence of Thompsonian historical materialism. In effect, Jones produced the founding British text of the "linguistic turn" in social history.

Since 1983, Jones has written nothing to rival *Languages of Class*, although his essay "The Cockney and the Nation," which appeared in the collection of essays he edited with David Feldman, *Metropolis London* (1989), provided an intriguing example of the trend in British social history that he was championing – to disengage identities and representations from any rootedness in (and hence reflection of) prior social change, and instead to present such changes as part of a relatively autonomous process of cultural construction. In various unpublished lectures and conference papers, this approach has been directed at the basic building blocks of the bulk of postwar social history, not merely identities such as "the middle class," but also at the foundational texts of the Marxist theory of history. The eventual product of this period is a projected study, *Visions of Prometheus*, a critical examination of the uses of languages of class in the later 18th and early 19th centuries, disputing the "teleological" accounts of the development of language presented by Raymond Williams and others, and exploring more fully the contingencies between the poles of

linguistic and material determinism, and in the process rejecting as misguided much of the contemporary analysis on which Marx's thought was based. In the interim, Jones has shaped the development of British social history through his influence on the generation of research students and young scholars who have come within his orbit.

MARTIN HEWITT

See also Britain: since 1750; Burke; Europe: Modern; Habakkuk; History Workshop; Labor; Political; Scott, Joan; Sociology; Thompson, E.

Biography
Born London, 17 December 1942. Studied at Lincoln College, Oxford, BA 1964; PhD, Nuffield College, Oxford, 1970. Taught at King's College, Cambridge, from 1976; university lecturer from 1979.

Principal Writings
"The Pathology of English History," *New Left Review* 46 (1967), 29–44
Outcast London: A Study in the Relationship Between Classes in Victorian Society, 1971
Editor with Raphael Samuel, *Culture, Ideology and Politics: Essays for Eric Hobsbawm*, 1982
Languages of Class: Studies in English Working-Class History, 1832–1982, 1983
Editor with David Feldman, *Metropolis London: Histories and Representations since 1800*, 1989

Further Reading
Cronin, J.E., "Language, Politics and the Critique of Social History," *Journal of Social History* 20 (1986), 177–83
Mayfield, David, and Susan Thorne, "Social History and Its Discontents: Gareth Stedman Jones and the Politics of Language," *Social History* 17 (1992), 165–88; and reply: Jon Lawrence and Miles Taylor, "The Poverty of Protest," *Social History* 18 (1993), 1–15

Jordan, Winthrop D. 1931–
US historian of African Americans

In 1968 Winthrop Jordan published his massive study *White Over Black*, perhaps the single most important book ever written on the development of racial thought in America. Jordan hoped to identify how Africans came to be "treated as somehow deserving a life and status radically different from English and other European settlers." Earlier studies had attempted to resolve this vexing historical problem by examining the causal relationship, chicken and egg fashion, between racism and slavery. Jordan rejected the premise of this approach. To argue that racism resulted from the debased condition of the African, or that Africans were enslaved because of racist beliefs, he argued was too simple. Slavery and racism, Jordan found, were interrelated forces, "continuously reacting upon each other, dynamically joining hands to hustle the Negro down the road to complete degradation." The enslavement of Africans, then, was an "unthinking decision" with slavery and racism reinforcing each other.

Critics have pointed out that Jordan paid little attention to the economic forces that provided an important justification for the enslavement of Africans. Others have criticized the implicit American exceptionalism in *White Over Black*. As J.H. Plumb noted in the most thoughtful review of Jordan's book, the expression of deeply-felt racial antipathies by no means was limited to Tudor and Stuart Englishmen. Indeed, Plumb pointed out, the literature of 16th- and 17th-century western expansion was "full of savagely expressed racism directed not only to the negro but to the Hindu, the Hottentot, the Welsh, Scots, Irish, French against English, English against Dutch."

Still, Jordan provided a powerfully and charismatically argued case for understanding the concomitant development of race hatred and slavery in the North American colonies. No fuller explication of the nature and origin of Anglo-American racial attitudes exists, attitudes which combined a deeply rooted antipathy to "blackness" and an equation in the English mind of Africans with a potent, bestial sexuality. From first contact with the African continent, Jordan found, English explorers and writers tended to compare themselves to the people they found, stressing "what they conceived to be radically contrasting qualities of color, religion, and style of life, as well as animality and a particularly potent sexuality."

Jordan also analyzed in *White Over Black* the saliency of "slavery" in the rhetoric of the American Revolution. The rebellious colonists, he noted, were faced with a powerful contradiction: justifying rebellion in the face of British attempts to enslave them while at the same time holding Africans in bondage. "A revolution carried forward in the name of liberty and equality," Jordan argued, "was bound to intensify and reshape the thinking of Americans concerning men who were not free, and, perhaps, not equal with white men." Given the extent to which slavery "mocked the ideals upon which the new republic was founded," Jordan argued, the failure to eradicate it in the late 18th century was the greatest failure of the revolutionary period.

Jordan noted that antislavery did make some gains during the revolutionary period. Most of the northern states passed gradual emancipation acts, made possible largely because slavery had declined in economic importance in these states. Still, for several reasons, antislavery failed to make progress where the institution was most firmly entrenched. First of all, dramatic changes had occurred in patterns of American thought after the Revolution. Environmentalism, a vital element in the ideology of the independence movement, weakened in the last decades of the 18th century. Environmentalist thought assumed that man was improvable, that all human beings were born essentially equal, and that whatever differences existed could be attributed to differences in environment. As environmentalism declined, a more scientific study of human diversity developed. The idea of a "Great Chain of Being," and the organizing systems developed by Linnaeus, Blumenbach, and later, Samuel Stanhope Smith, reflected a style of thought that placed unprecedented emphasis on hierarchy. As interest in the physical structure of God's creation grew, faith in man's plasticity diminished, and any argument stressing the improvability of the African could increasingly be countered by a "scientific" explanation for his inferiority.

Also important in the decline of revolutionary antislavery, Jordan argued, was the rise of sentimental humanitarianism in the postwar years. Humanitarianism found its origins in the increased secularization that followed the Revolution. A decline in religiosity made it "less possible to shrug off suffering as inherent in the God-ordained social order." Since slavery was viewed as an institution that stimulated cruelty, it became an object of sentimental humanitarian reform. While humanitarianism did have limited success in making slavery less brutal, Jordan maintained, "this happy development left the real enemy more firmly entrenched than ever. As slavery became less brutal there was less reason why it should be abolished."

Most important, in Jordan's view, for the failure of antislavery was the inability of Americans to overcome their deep-seated fear of miscegenation and race war. The belief that emancipation would lead to widespread race-mixing was "nearly universal" in the young republic, resting on a contorted and deeply irrational interpretation of the American sense of mission. "A darkened nation," Jordan argued, "would present incontrovertible evidence that sheer animal sex was governing the American destiny and that the great experiment in the wilderness had failed to maintain the social and personal restraints which were the hallmarks and the very best stuff of civilization."

The black uprising at Santo Domingo and Gabriel's Plot in Virginia in 1801 delivered the final blows to American revolutionary antislavery. Haiti provided a living example of the South's worst nightmare, a world turned upside down. Gabriel's abortive assault on Richmond taught many slaveholders that they could never again count on the tranquil submission of their slaves. The two events, Jordan found, also signalled the abandonment of the idealism of the Revolution, which "had entailed upon the institution of slavery a gigantic question mark and upon Americans the necessity of facing up to the prospect of what it would be like actually to have Negroes free." Faced with the example of Santo Domingo and the potential of Richmond, "they backed off from its inherent implications."

Jordan's perceptive grasp of the nature of Anglo American racial attitudes has cast a long shadow, influencing scores of studies in American southern and African American history. There can be no disputing that *White Over Black* has been one of the most important books ever written on the early history of the United States, and Jordan deserves credit for giving energy to the study of race relations in the colonial period, and African American history in general.

MICHAEL L. OBERG

See also African American; Elkins; United States: Colonial

Biography

Winthrop Donaldson Jordan. Born Worcester, Massachusetts, 11 November 1931. Received BA, Harvard University, 1953; MA, Clark University, 1957; PhD, Brown University, 1960. Taught at Phillips Exeter Academy, 1955–56; and Brown University, 1959–61; fellow, Institute of Early American History and Culture, Williamsburg, Virginia, 1961–63; taught (rising to professor), University of California, Berkeley, 1963–81; and University of Mississippi from 1982. Married 1) Phyllis Henry, 1952 (marriage dissolved 1979; 3 sons); 2) Cora Miner Reilly, 1982.

Principal Writings

White over Black: American Attitudes toward the Negro, 1550–1812, 1968; abridged as *The White Man's Burden: Historical Origins of Racism in the United States*, 1974

With Kenneth Goode, *From Africa to the United States and then . . .:
A Concise Afro-American History*, 1969
*Tumult and Silence at Second Creek: An Inquiry into a Civil War
Slave Conspiracy*, 1993

Josephus 37/38–c.94 CE
Jewish historian

Josephus is the most valuable historical source for the events
that took place in Judea in the 1st century. His father was
Matthias, one of the best known priests in Jerusalem. His
mother was descended from the royal Hasmonean family.
Josephus investigated the ways of the Sadducees, the Pharisees,
and the Essenes and after spending three years with an ascetic
hermit, became a Pharisee at the age of 18. At the age of 26
in 64 CE, Josephus traveled to Italy to obtain the release of
Jewish priests who were his friends. After surviving a ship-
wreck, he reached Rome where he obtained an audience with
Nero's empress, Poppaea. In 66, soon after his return to
Palestine, the Jews rebelled against Rome. In spite of the fact
that Josephus was a priest without any military background,
he was made the commander of Galilee. In 67 Josephus was
besieged by Vespasian at Jotapata. Instead of committing
suicide as many others did, Josephus surrendered to the
Romans – an action that his enemies attributed to cowardice
but which Josephus ascribed to Providence. Josephus blamed
the outbreak of the war on the "zealots," whom he labeled
"brigands." He tried in vain to persuade the Jews in the
besieged city of Jerusalem to surrender. He depicted Titus as
a courageous general and compassionate conqueror, and tried
to absolve him of the responsibility for the destruction of the
temple in the year 70.

By predicting the elevation of Vespasian as the future
emperor, Josephus gained the favor of the Flavian family, that
is, Vespasian and his sons Titus and Domitian, who were to
rule as emperors from 69 to 96. He also received the name
"Flavius," Roman citizenship, and a residence in Rome.
Josephus was honored in Rome, but was vilified by his compatriots as a turncoat. He attempted in his writings to defend
himself and the actions of his Roman patrons, but he also
championed the Jews and their religion.

Josephus' native language was Aramaic, but he wrote his
four works in Greek. *Bellum Judaicum (The Jewish War)*
is his masterpiece, a riveting, eyewitness account of the First
Jewish Revolt against the Romans (66–74), which was
published before the death of Vespasian in 79. The first edition
of the work was written in Aramaic and sent to the Jews of
Mesopotamia to dissuade them from revolting against the
Romans.

The Life of Josephus was an appendix to *Jewish Antiquities*.
This apologia was called forth by the account of a Justus of
Tiberias, who blamed Josephus as the instigator of the revolt
against the Romans in Galilee. In *The Jewish War* Josephus
had depicted himself as a valiant general; in *The Life* he transformed himself into a man of peace, who reluctantly accepted
the command of Galilee. Josephus' *Against Apion* is a refutation of slanderous attacks upon the Jews and is a brilliant
defence of Judaism.

Antiquitates Judaicae (Jewish Antiquities) is his *magnum
opus*, which was evidently completed around 94. It contains
some divergent accounts of the same incidents recounted in
The Jewish War. The first ten books parallel the Old Testament,
books 11 to 13 cover the Intertestamental era, books 15 to
17 describe the events of the reign of Herod the Great, and
books 18 to 20 continue the narrative to the end of the war.
In paraphrasing scriptures, Josephus omitted disreputable incidents, and reinterpreted the stories to appeal to his Roman
audience. Josephus explicated the prophecy of Daniel 8 as
being fulfilled by the capture of Jerusalem by the Romans.

Josephus has important references to John the Baptist and
to the martyrdom of James, the brother of Jesus. His most
celebrated passage is the "Testimonium Flavianum," which has
laudatory references to Jesus. This was cited by both Origen
in the 3rd century and by Eusebius in the 4th. The Testimonium
Flavianum has been rejected as a total fabrication by some
scholars, but the consensus of Jewish and Christian scholars
today is that the core of the passage is authentic, although
clearly Christian interpolations have been added.

It is ironic that Josephus was for centuries neglected by the
Jews. It was only in the 10th century that a Hebrew version
attributed to Yosippon (or Josippon) came into circulation
among them. On the other hand, Josephus was cherished by
Christians, especially for the Testimonium Flavianum and
for his account of the destruction of Jerusalem, which was
held to be God's ratification of Judaism's replacement by
Christianity. Many Crusaders carried copies of Josephus with
them to the Holy Land. Recent developments such as the
discovery of the Dead Sea Scrolls, and excavations in Israel
have enhanced Josephus' reputation as they confirm his account
of the Essenes and his description of various sites such as
Jerusalem and Masada.

EDWIN M. YAMAUCHI

See also Cassiodorus; Eusebius; Jewish; Roman; Wellhausen

Biography
Flavius Josephus. Born Jerusalem, 37/38 CE, to a noble family,
descended from priests and royalty. Studied at a rabbinic school,
with training from Pharisees, Sadducees, and Essenes. Emissary to
Rome, 64; military commander in Jewish revolt against Rome,
66–67: besieged at Jotapata and captured, but pardoned by
Vespasian; settled in Rome and became citizen. Died, probably in
Rome, c.94.

Principal Writings
Bellum Judaicum, c.75/79
Antiquitates Judaicae, c.93/94
Works (Loeb edition; includes *The Life*, *Against Apion*, *The Jewish
War*, *Jewish Antiquities*), translated by H. St.J. Thackeray, Ralph
Marcus, A.P. Wikgren, and L.H. Feldman, 10 vols., 1926–81

Further Reading
Attridge, Harold W., *The Presentation of Biblical History in the
"Antiquitates Judaicae" of Flavius Josephus*, Missoula, MT:
Scholars Press, 1976
Attridge, Harold W., "Josephus and His Works," in Michael E.
Stone, ed., *Jewish Writings of the Second Temple Period:
Apocrypha, Pseudepigrapha, Qumran*, Aasen, Netherlands: Van
Gorcum, and Philadelphia: Fortress Press, 1984

Bilde, Per, *Flavius Josephus Between Jerusalem and Rome: His Life, His Works, and Their Importance*, Sheffield: Sheffield Academic Press, 1988

Cohen, Shaye, *Josephus in Galilee and Rome: His Vita and Development as a Historian*, Leiden: Brill, 1979

Feldman, Louis, and Gohei Hata, eds., *Josephus, Judaism and Christianity*, Detroit: Wayne State University Press, 1987

Feldman, Louis, and Gohei Hata, eds., *Josephus, the Bible, and History*, Detroit: Wayne State University Press, 1989

Maier, Paul, *Josephus: The Essential Writings: A Condensation of Jewish Antiquities and the Jewish War*, Grand Rapids, MI: Kregel, 1988

Mason, Steve, *Josephus and the New Testament*, Peabody, MA: Hendrickson, 1992

Meier, John P., "Jesus in Josephus: A Modest Proposal," *Catholic Biblical Quarterly* 52 (1990), 76–103

Parente, Fausto, and Joseph Sievers, eds., *Josephus and the History of the Greco-Roman Period: Essays in Memory of Morton Smith*, Leiden: Brill, 1995

Rajak, Tessa, *Josephus: The Historian and His Society*, London: Duckworth, 1983; Philadelphia: Fortress Press, 1984

Schreckenberg, Heinz, and Karl Schubert, *Jewish Historiography and Iconography in Early and Medieval Christianity*, Assen: Van Gorcum, and Minneapolis: Fortress Press, 1992

Yamauchi, Edwin M., "Josephus and the Scriptures," *Fides et Historia* 13 (1980), 42–63

Julien, Charles-André 1891–1989

French Africanist

Charles-André Julien was born in 1891, and went to Algeria at the age of 15. For many years a schoolmaster, he finally retired as professor of the history of colonization at the Sorbonne, before spending a further five years as dean of the Faculty of Letters at Rabat. Meanwhile, as a left-wing intellectual he was enlisted by the Popular Front government of Léon Blum in 1936 to coordinate policy on North Africa, and as a distinguished academic he was honored by the Fourth Republic as a counsellor of the French Union. As a writer with a firm political aim, however, his career continued far longer. It began with the publication of the first edition of *Histoire de l'Afrique du Nord* (1931; *History of North Africa*, 1970), in the midst of the celebrations of a hundred years of French rule in Algeria. Against the colonial view of North Africa as a region created by the Romans, ruined by the Arabs, and recreated by the French, he offered a well-balanced account of its history which supported the current demand of North African nationalists for reform within the French system. As such, the work came as a revelation to many brought up on the colonial literature, and went on to serve as a bible for North African nationalism. At the same time it earned him the hostility of colonial opinion and the colonial administration, which twenty years later stopped the sale in North Africa of his second book, *L'Afrique du Nord en marche* (North Africa on the March, 1952). This was a straightforward account of the progressive rise of North African demands since the beginning of the century, at first for reform and then for independence. The case it presented on behalf of "the right of people to manage their own affairs," and against the postwar policy of repression, was unanswerable at the time simply on the evidence it offered for the growing strength and popularity of

the various nationalist movements, and was certainly so in retrospect.

The book was written with passion, and total familiarity with the subject, and in the space of two months, its polemical attack on what Julien called the French "policy of lost opportunities," embroiled him in controversy not only with government, but with his peers in academia as well. That controversy was pugnaciously recalled by Julien in the critical bibliography he added to the third edition in 1972, providing a masterly survey of the whole literature of the subject. At the time it involved a quarrel with Christian Courtois and especially Roger Le Tourneau, responsible for the first two volumes of the revised second edition of *Histoire de l'Afrique du Nord*, which appeared in 1952–53. Julien's own volume, on North Africa since 1830, was further complicated by the Algerian war, and was finally abandoned for a large *Histoire de l'Algérie contemporaine* (History of Contemporary Algeria), of which Julien published the first volume in 1964. Whereas the first two works had effectively defined the whole subject for his successors, this was a more conventional account of a particular period, a scholarly work beautifully written, with a splendid bibliography. In contrast, *Le Maroc face aux impérialismes* (Morocco's Confrontation with Imperialism, 1978) is an entertainingly hostile, blow-by-blow account (written from inside knowledge) of the French attempt to unseat the sultan in the 1950s. It was followed in 1985 by a similar work on Tunisia. It is a pity – but in keeping with Julien's life's work – that these works of extreme but lively old age should be all that remains of the final volume of *Histoire de l'Afrique du Nord*, and projected accounts of the end of the two Protectorates and of the Algerian war. A considered overview of the controversial modern history of North Africa eluded him as it has eluded his successors in France, until the appearance of a work of which he would not have approved, Jean Ganiage's *Histoire contemporaine du Maghreb* (Contemporary History of the Maghreb, 1994), and it is ironic that the English-language *A History of the Maghrib in the Islamic Period*, by Jamil M. Abun-Nasr (1987) should take the place of his original study of 1931 as the standard history of the region. Julien's status as a champion of the native peoples of North Africa, extending to those of Africa as a whole, is best represented by his responsibility as editor-in-chief for *Les Africains* (1977–), 12 volumes of long and scholarly biographies of notable Africans over the centuries. The inspiration of that championship, however, is to be found in the collection of his articles and interviews selected and presented to him by Magaly Morsy in 1979. Written or given as contributions to the ongoing argument over colonial policy, these are the credo of the historian as participant in the events he describes.

MICHAEL BRETT

See also Africa: North; Middle East

Biography

Charles-André Delorme Julien. Born Caen, 2 September 1891, son of a professor. Educated at the Sorbonne. Taught in Algeria and France, 1912–36; secretary general, Mediterranean and North African High Commissions, 1936–39; taught at University of Paris, 1939–47; professor, the Sorbonne, 1947–61 (emeritus). Married Lucie Momy, 1921 (1 daughter). Died 1989.

Principal Writings

Histoire de l'Afrique du Nord: Tunisie, Algérie, Maroc, 1931; in English as *History of North Africa: From the Arab Conquest to 1830*, 1970

Histoire de l'Afrique (History of Africa), 1941

L'Afrique du Nord en marche: nationalismes musulmans et souveraineté française (North Africa on the March: Muslim Nationalism and French Sovreignty), 1952; revised 1972

Histoire de l'Algérie contemporaine, vol. 1: *La Conquête et les débuts de la colonisation (1827–1871)* (A History of Contemporary Algeria, vol. 1: Conquest and the Beginnings of Colonization, 1827–1871), 1964

Histoire de l'Afrique blanche, des origines à 1945 (A History of White Africa from its Origins to 1945), 1966

General editor, *Les Africains* (The Africans), 12 vols., 1977–

Le Maroc face aux impérialismes (1415–1956) (Morocco's Confrontation with Imperialism from 1415 to 1956), 1978

Une Pensée anti-coloniale: positions, 1914–1979 (Anti-colonialist Positions: From 1914 to 1979), edited by Magali Morsy, 1979

Et la Tunisie devint indépendante, 1951–1957 (And Tunisia Became Independent, 1951–57), 1985

K

Kantorowicz, Ernst H. 1895–1963

US (German-born) medievalist

Ernst H. Kantorowicz's standing as a historian began with the publication in Berlin of his monumental monograph on the emperor Frederick II, the text volume appearing in 1927, and that with sources in 1931. His *"Laudes Regiae"* (1946), written in collaboration with the musicologist Manfred F. Bukofzer, proved to be an introduction to his *The King's Two Bodies* (1957). In this latter book Kantorowicz explained the significance of an important Tudor political theory. That theory solved the problem of political legitimacy by locating political authority in a fiction of the king's two bodies – the body natural, which is mortal, and the body politic, which is not subject to death. Throughout Kantorowicz's specialty remained western medieval history, but over the years his interests broadened to encompass the Byzantine empire as well as the Near and the Middle East, while his chronological range extended in both directions. Consistently at the heart of his research was the elucidation of ideas that in their day had been paramount, but which had become either obscure or forgotten. This emphasis was apparent in his Heidelberg dissertation of 1921, *Das Wesen der muslimischen Handwerkerverbände* (The Islamic Artisan Guild System), a study fostered by his four years as a German cavalry officer stationed in Turkey during World War I. In this, as in his subsequent monographs and forty or so articles (published as pamphlets and in periodicals and recondite publications), his attempt to trace the origins and development of ideas necessitated a breadth of research that included archaeology, art history, numismatics, literature, and legal and theological study. His exceptional intellectual breadth was based on his capacity to read in Latin, Greek, Turkish, Polish, and the Romance languages, while his English was to become fluent.

Born to an affluent Jewish family of the Germany city of Posen (it became Polish in 1918), Kantorowicz remained committed to Judaism throughout his life; the rise of German Nazism in the 1930s meant that he became a wandering Jew. At the University of California, Berkeley, in 1950 he refused the loyalty oath, deeming it a threat to academic freedom, and he justified himself with a privately printed pamphlet entitled: *The Fundamental Issue: Documents and Marginal Notes on the University of California's Loyalty Oath* (1950). This for him was yet another of life's little ironies; a previous one had been that his monograph on Frederick II was originally published in a series with the swastika impressed into its covers.

From his days in Heidelberg in the early 1920s Kantorowicz belonged to the so-called "circle" of the poet-philosopher Stefan George, whose photograph was to have the place of honor on Kantorowicz's desk throughout the rest of his life. George was a Romantic with a poetic vision of early German history, as well as a considerable knowledge of Romance culture. He believed that Frederick II was the keystone bonding Germanic and Italian cultures, and this was the determining factor in Kantorowicz's researches on the emperor. Kantorowicz's monumental new-style biography, where Frederick was virtually lost to sight amidst the determining factors of his life, can be seen as the one extensive tangible outcome of George's circle. The work appealed to the ethos then current in Germany, when interest in Frederick II was at its zenith. Von der Steinen's *Staatsbriefe Friedrichs II* had appeared in 1923, and the following year commemorated the 700th charter day of the founding by the emperor of the University of Naples, when some of George's followers placed a wreath on the emperor's tomb in Palermo.

Kantorowicz's 1927 volume on Frederick II brought together a vast amount of disparate information, much of it related to individuals and subjects associated with Romance culture rather than with the subject of the biography directly. German contemporary scholars appreciated the originality, but its methodology was criticized in reviews written by Baethgen and by Brackmann, published early in 1930. The heart of the criticism was that literature, on which Kantorowicz drew heavily, was factually unreliable and that in effect Kantorowicz had merely accepted the literary myth of Frederick II, mistaking rhetoric for action, and pretence and wishful thinking for reality. Kantorowicz's counterblast appeared in the right-wing Berlin daily *Deutsche Allgemeine Zeitung* of 25 April 1930, which five days later printed a reply from the critics. The *Ergänzungsband* of the following year was Kantorowicz's attempt to meet the core criticism by providing sources (his text volume had none at all), but his problem remained that by and large archival documents are not usually a rewarding source for the history of ideas.

Kantorowicz's achievement in his historical writing was in forging an attractive synthesis of history, literature, art, and religion, which while stimulating, even challenging, is an approach now out of favor, and impossible to follow without exceptional knowledge. Indeed critics have been wont to claim that Kantorowicz was misled by his own erudition. His friend Leonardo Olschki once commented that the basic flaw of *"Laudes Regiae"* was the failure to recognize the Hebrew prototype of the relevant models, a relationship that should have been obvious to anyone aware of orthodox Jewish liturgy, as Kantorowicz, of course, was.

CECIL H. CLOUGH

See also Body; France: 1450–1789; Germany: to 1450

Biography

Ernst Hartwig Kantorowicz. Born Posen, Germany (now Posnań, Poland), 1895, to a Jewish merchant family. Attended universities of Berlin, Munich, and Heidelberg, 1918–21; PhD, Heidelberg, 1921. Served in the German cavalry in Turkey during World War I. Taught (rising to professor), University of Heidelberg, 1922–30; and University of Frankfurt, 1930–34; after rise of Nazism accepted a year's post as research fellow, New College, Oxford, 1933–34; compulsory retirement from Frankfurt, 1934; emigrated to US, 1938 (later naturalized); obtained non-tenured post in history at the University of California, Berkeley, 1939: full professor, 1945; refused to take the University of California's loyalty oath and resigned, 1950; visiting scholar, Dumbarton Oaks Foundation, 1951; professor, School of Historical Studies, Institute for Advanced Study, Princeton, 1951–63. Died Princeton, 9 September 1963.

Principal Writings

Das Wesen der muslimischen Handwerkerverbände (The Islamic Artisan Guild System), 1921
Kaiser Friedrich der Zweite, 1927, revised 1931; vol. 1 in English as Frederick the Second, 1194–1250, 1931
With Manfred F. Bukofzer, "Laudes Regiae": A Study in Liturgical Acclamations and Medieval Ruler Worship, 1946
The King's Two Bodies: A Study in Mediaeval Political Theology, 1957
Selected Studies, 1965

Further Reading

Abulafia, David, "Kantorowicz and Frederick II," in his Italy, Sicily and the Mediterranean, 1050–1400, London: Variorum, 1987
Boureau, Alain, Histoires d'un historien: Kantorowicz, Paris: Gallimard, 1990
Cantor, Norman F., Inventing the Middle Ages: The Lives, Works, and Ideas of the Great Medievalists of the Twentieth Century, New York: Morrow, 1991; Cambridge: Lutterworth Press, 1992
Davis, Natalie Zemon, "History's Two Bodies," American Historical Review 93 (1988)
Epstein, Catherine, "E.H. Kantorowicz," in her Civiltà italiana e studiosi stranieri, Pisa: Pubblicazione del Venticiquennale, 1986; in English as A Past Renewed: A Catalog of German-Speaking Refugee Historians in the United States after 1933, Cambridge and New York: Cambridge University Press, 1993
Giesey, Ralph E., "Ernst H. Kantorowicz: Scholarly Triumphs and Academic Travails in Weimar Germany and the United States," Leo Baeck Institute Yearbook 30 (1985), 191–202
Malkiel, Y., "E.H. Kantorowicz," in A.R. Evans, ed., On Four Modern Humanists: Hofmannsthal, Gundolf, Curtius, Kantorowicz, Princeton: Princeton University Press, 1970
Wolf, Gunther, ed., Stupor Mundi: Zur Geschichte Friedrichs II von Hohenstaufen (Stupor Mundi: On the History of Frederick II), Darmstadt: Wissenschaftliche Buchgesellschaft, 1966

Karamzin, N.M. 1766–1826
Russian historian, statesman, and novelist

A celebrated founder of the state school of Russian historians, N.M. Karamzin was early attracted to the mystical element of the Moscow Masonic society of N.I. Novikov, who first instilled in him an interest in Russian history. Freemasonry also enabled Karamzin to develop an openness toward the European Enlightenment, including its faith in the promise of education, its humanitarianism, and its rejection of religious and ethnic intolerance. From May 1789 until September 1790 he toured France, Germany, Switzerland, and England; a few years after his return he wrote Pis'ma russkogo puteshestvennika (1797; Letters of a Russian Traveler, 1957). By that time he had fashioned a reputation as a romantic novelist seeking to free the Russian language from its dependence on Church Slavonic and Latin, and to use Lomonosov's French style in Russian letters.

The Letters reveal a strong attraction to the German J.G. Herder, whose writings helped him to reconcile a love of one's homeland with the notion of the universal brotherhood of all men. Karamzin wrote that "All that is national is nothing compared to that which is common to humanity. The chief thing is to be people, not Slavs." Hence in his historical works Karamzin followed the approach of Herder by stressing the importance of the "volk" or "narod," although the latter could only be identified by association with the growth of the state. Both the state and the people grew from an organic foundation in which every society contained the seed of its future development, which explains why Karamzin grew to dislike Peter the Great, who strove to alter the nation's natural development by forcing vital psychological changes in society within one generation. Karamzin was not opposed to cultural associations, even borrowings, but he thought that only gradual accommodations were possible. His belief in inevitable growth and progress placed him within the mainstream of the European Enlightenment.

Finding no barrier to universalism and nationalism, he announced in Vestnik Evropy (Messenger of Europe), which he edited from 1802–03, his desire to explore the nation's archives and write the history of Russia, a work that he supposed would have both a literary and patriotic character, and thus show Russians how their history could provide inspiration. His models, he wrote in 1790, were Tacitus, Hume, and Gibbon, and the Scot, Robertson. What was not interesting would be abbreviated (princely genealogy, internecine wars among princes, the raids of the Steppe nomads, and so forth); the attainments of heroes would be central (Vladimir the Saint, Dmitrii Donskoi, and Ivan III).

The work was enormously successful, and Karamzin was correct that the reading public craved a serious, yet attractive narration of Russia's past. Almost every historian of Russia in the 19th century and after complimented the author's contribution. The first eight volumes of Istoriia gosudarstva rossiiskogo (History of the Russian State) were published in 1818. The 12th would be published posthumously (1829) since it was left unfinished when Karamzin died in 1826, bringing his account only to 1611, just before the end of the "Troubles."

Like many Russian historians of the 18th century, Karamzin held that a successful history must appeal to national pride, stimulate good citizenship, be thorough and based on the latest documentation (evident in his extensive annotation), and be written in a style designed to elicit warmth and emotion. Even his detractors admit that he accomplished these ends. As a state-appointed archivist, he was the first to examine closely many of the chronicles, bishops registers, and even the accounts of foreign travelers. His annotations from the *Troitskii letopis'* (*Troitsky Chronicle*) is all that remains of that document, destroyed in the Napoleonic fires of Moscow.

Criticism centered on Karamzin's open advocacy of autocracy and on his interpretation of the sources. Karamzin was a product of the 18th-century infatuation with enlightened despotism, and concluded that the people identified with their monarchs, who were the only vehicles for national progress. His *O drevnei novoi Russii* (1811; *Memoir on Ancient and Modern Russia*, 1959) was a criticism of Aleksandr I's early promotion of liberal reforms. He was not a Slavophile, but he pleased that movement by his insistence that Russians were unique in forming a state without the need for conquest; he pleased the Pan-Slavists by his insistence that Poland and Lithuania must remain part of the Russian empire; he pleased the Westerners by his continued attachment to western principles of justice and adherence to the belief that Russia's history, like that of other nations, was subject to an organic process of progressive development (although he was criticized for excessive attention to the personality of Ivan III).

Yet he was most remembered for his contribution to the state school of historiography. It is argued that Karamzin was preceded in this matter by the German historian of Russia, A.L. von Schlözer. Nevertheless, it was Karamzin's *History* that most avowedly claimed the proposition that the state was historically responsible for most of Russia's history, whether for good or for ill. Where Westerners deplored the influence of the state in opposition to Karamzin's espousal of that principle, they agreed on the state's primary role in fashioning the Russian nation. In his triumphal last volume on the Time of Troubles the author's conclusion about how the classes united to preserve the state was a premonition of later lectures by Vasilii O. Kliuchevskii.

Despite his unabashed national attachments, Karamzin continued to explain the similarity between Russians and other peoples, and despite his belief in the organic evolution of societies, he continued to believe that "the destiny of peoples is decided by the secret hand of Providence via chosen, sovereign-heroes." Russia, he argued, was fashioned and supported by one-man rule, a wise autocrat who saved the nation from ruin at the hands of competing interests.

JOHN D. WINDHAUSEN

See also Europe: Modern; Russia: Medieval; Russia: Early Modern; Russia: Modern; Solov'ev

Biography

Nikolai Mikhailovich Karamzin. Born Mikhailovka Village, Samara Province (present-day Buzuluk Raion, Orenburg Oblast'), 12 December 1766, to a noble family. Educated at a Moscow private school; then took Grand Tour, 1789–90. Appointed official Russian imperial historiographer, 1803. Died St. Petersburg, 3 June 1826.

Principal Writings

Pis'ma russkogo puteshestvennika, 6 vols., 1797–1801; abridged in English as *Letters of a Russian Traveler, 1789–1790: An Account of a Young Russian Gentleman's Tour Through Germany, Switzerland, France, and England*, 1957
Istoričeskõe pokhval'noe slovo Ekaterine (Historical Eulogy to Catherine II), 1802

"O liubvi k otechestvu i narodnoi gordosti," *Vestnik Evropy*, 4 (1802); in English as "Love of Country and National Pride," in Mark Raeff, *Russian Intellectual History: An Anthology*, 1966
O drevnei i novoi Rossii, 1811; in English as *Memoir on Ancient and Modern Russia*, 1959
Istoriia gosudarstva rossiiskogo (History of the Russian State), 12 vols. (to 1611), 1818–29

Further Reading

Black, Joseph Laurence, *Essays on Karamzin: Russian Man of Letters, Political Thinker, Historian, 1766–1826*, The Hague: Mouton, 1974
Black, Joseph Laurence, *Nicholas Karamzin and Russian Society in the Nineteenth Century: A Study in Russian Political and Historical Thought*, Toronto: University of Toronto Press, 1975
Cross, Anthony Glenn, *N.M. Karamzin: A Study of His Literary Career (1783–1803)*, Carbondale: Southern Illinois University Press, 1971
Kliuchevskii, V.O., "N.M. Karamzin" in his *Istoricheskie portrety* (Historical Portraits), Moscow: Pravda, 1990
Kochetkova, Natalya, *Nikolay Karamzin*, Boston: Twayne, 1975
Lewis, Samuel Mark, *Modes of Historical Discourse in J.G. Herder and N.M. Karamzin*, New York: Lang, 1995
Mazour, Anatole G., *An Outline of Russian Historiography*, Berkeley: University of California Press, 1939; revised as *Modern Russian Historiography*, Princeton, NJ: Van Nostrand, 1958; revised Westport, CT: Greenwood Press, 1975
Pipes, Richard, *Karamzin's Memoir on Ancient and Modern Russia: A Translation and Analysis*, Cambridge, MA: Harvard University Press, 1959
Thaden, Eduard C., "Karamzin, Nikolai Mikhailovich," in Joseph L. Wieczynski, ed., *Modern Encyclopedia of Russian and Soviet History*, vol. 11, Gulf Breeze, FL: Academic International Press, 1980

Kasravi, Ahmad 1890–1946

Iranian historian, language scholar, jurist, and social thinker

Ahmad Kasravi's interest in developing a detailed theory of historiography resulted from his dissatisfaction with traditional Persian histories and from his familiarity with western histories, including those of pre-Islamic Iran. He considered Plutarch's *Lives* an example of good history, translated twelve of these lives (from English) into Persian, and used the introduction to discuss his own views on history for the first time.

Kasravi believed that "history for a nation is like root to a tree." It can make citizens more durable, more firm, enabling them in difficult times to see how their ancestors had united and overcome their problems. The purpose of reading history, however, should be to learn from the past, not to become obsessed with it. He found most Iranians at the time ignorant of their national history, each religious or ethnic group interested only in its own history.

Kasravi recognized several types of history. The first consisted of a mere recounting of events, read for pleasure. Reading such history may have had no benefit, but writing it would prevent events from being forgotten, contributing data for better, more knowledgeable writers. The second type supplied role models – good and bad – enabling writers and readers to follow the good examples among historical individuals, and to avoid their mistakes. The writers of such histories needed to be honest about historical persons, and to avoid exaggeration. The third type gave information about the way of life and the behavior of rulers. Such histories evaluated past events, looking for connections among them, and drawing conclusions, since what happens today is the result of what happened yesterday. As for individuals, attention should be paid only to those few who brought about great changes in the world or their own country. Kasravi considered this kind of history very difficult to write, and thought that very few of the historians who had tried it had succeeded.

These types of history were for the general reader. There were other types, Kasravi noted, including political-diplomatic history. This type of history, dealing as it does with secret activities, could be done only by someone personally involved, or who had access to extensive written sources. He rejected resorting to guesswork or outright fabrication. Instead, Kasravi argued, an alert historian may be able, by comparing various events, and using careful judgment, to figure out what lay behind some secrets, but if so he should not go too far and exaggerate. Furthermore, such historians should inform readers of their methods. Writing history, Kasravi said, may seem easy, but it is very hard – especially writing contemporary history, where the historian's judgment may be affected by considerations of friendship or expectation of favors, or by feelings of jealousy and competition. He pointed out that he himself had sometimes had to change what he had written several times, even redoing what had already been printed.

Kasravi acknowledged that few had the special talent for writing history. Historians had to be truthful, but that did not mean that they should only report events, with no interpretation. As a good example, Kasravi used Plutarch, who wrote to describe the progress of his own nation, Greece, and the value of that nation's historical figures, comparing them with those of Rome. Plutarch was after the truth: he did not praise or reproach anyone without good reason, and in this he made no distinction among Greeks, Romans, and Persians. Iranian historians, however, according to Kasravi, had centuries ago stopped making judgments about events and persons. A historian, in his view, should be objective in reporting facts, but should also make judgments.

Kasravi's own historical research has been recognized by other scholars. The Orientalist Vladimir Minorsky believed that "Kasravi possessed the spirit of a true historian. He was accurate in detail and clear in presentation." Furthermore, Kasravi refused to accept without question even universal assumptions. Thus, when Pan-Turkists claimed that the natives of the province of Azarbaijan were ethnically Turks, since they speak Turkish, Kasravi undertook extensive research using not only Persian and Arabic sources but also classical Greek ones. He concluded that they were Iranians ethnically, originally spoke an Iranian language called Azari, that the use of Turkish began there after the Turkish invasions, that it took several centuries before its use became universal, and that traces of Azari were still to be found there. Azari has recently come to be used to refer to the Turkish dialect used in that province, a mistake found even in the new edition of the *Encyclopaedia of Islam*. Kasravi's research also revealed the inaccuracy of three major assumptions about the Safavi dynasty (1501–1722), employing some of the very sources cited in support of those assumptions. He discovered that their ancestor Shaykh Safi was not a direct descendant of the prophet Mohammad as they claimed; that he

was a Sunni Muslim, but his descendants had switched to the Shia sect; and that his language was Azari (not Persian), while his descendants had adopted Turkish, as had others in the province. Another of Kasravi's research projects involved the southwestern province of Khuzistan, which because of the presence of some Arabs there, its common border with Iraq, and the fact that it was at the time called "Arabistan," was claimed to be part of the Arab world. Kasravi's research showed that the name was quite new, that the revived name "Khuzistan" had a long history, and that the province had been part of Iran since ancient times.

His most important and most widely used work is *Tārikh-e Mashrūte-e Irān* (1940–42), on the history of the Iranian Constitutional Revolution (1905–11), which he witnessed as a teenager. The work was written about 30 years after the Revolution, and its publication marked a major event in Iranian historiography. "Here for the first time," according to the historian Farmayan, "one feels that there is a philosophy behind the writings of a Persian historian." Farmayan, in fact, considered Kasravi as one of the two men responsible for "a sudden awakening of interest in Persian historiography." To the historian Adamiyat, it represented "the most methodical" and "most reliable" research on the Revolution. Based in part on Kasravi's personal observations and interviews as well as the published sources (very few at the time), it is rich in detail and often disagrees with other versions and interpretations of events. It also reflects his views on the writing of history. His objectivity is perhaps best seen in his giving of credit to some clergymen among the leaders of the Revolution, since in his extensive writings on Iran's social problems, he is on the whole very critical of the clergy. The major reason for writing his history of the Revolution, he explained, was the failure of others to give credit to the many brave ordinary people, some of whom lost their lives for the Revolution. Other writers had praised the enemies of the Revolution, some of whom were even responsible for the killing of revolutionaries, but once the Revolution had succeeded over despotism, they joined the new regime and for years occupied high positions in it. No one else had made this point, and this in itself is enough to justify Kasravi's prominent place among Iranian historians.

M.A. JAZAYERY

Biography

Born 29 September 1890. Educated as a clergyman, but he left the clergy because he found their ideas and behavior harmful to the country. Entered the Ministry of Justice, 1919; forced to resign when, as a judge, he returned a verdict against the royal court in favor of a group of peasants; thereafter practiced as a lawyer. Briefly taught history at the University of Tehran, which he left in 1934 because he refused to retract his criticism of much of classical Persian literature. Editor of the journals *Paymān* and *Parcham* (first a newspaper, later a journal). The Āzādegān party was established to promote his ideology. At the instigation of the Speaker of Parliament, and the Ministries of Education and Justice, he was charged with "slandering Islam": during the preliminary hearings in the Palace of Justice in Tehran, assassinated by two members of the Fedā'iyān-e Eslām ("Devotees of Islam"), 11 March 1946.

Principal Writings

Āzārīyā zabān-e bāstān-e Āzarbāijān (Azari or the Ancient Language of Azarbaijan), 1925

Shahriyārān-e gumnām (The Forgotten Rulers), 3 vols., 1928–31

Tārikhche-ye shir-o-Khvurshid (History of "The Lion and Sun"), 1930

Tārikh-e pānsad sālah-i Khuzistān (The Five Hundred Years of the History of Khuzistan), 1933

Tārikh-i hijdah sālah-'i Āzarbāyjān (The History of Eighteen Years in Azarbaijan), 6 vols., 1934–40 [supplements to the journal *Paymān*, vols. 2–7]

Translator, *Golchini az ketāb-e Pelutārkh* (Selections from Plutarch), 2 vols., 1937

Tārikh-e Mashrūte-e Irān (The History of the Constitutional Revolution of Iran), 3 vols., 1940–42 [revised version of vols. 1 and 2 of *Tarikh-e hijdah-sāle-ye Āzarbāyjān*]

Shaykh Safi va tabārash (Shaykh Safi and His Ancestry), 1944

Dādgāh (Court of Justice), 1944

Mosha'sha'iyān (The Mosha'sha'is), 1945 [revised version of the first part of *Tārikh-e pānsad*]

Dar pirāmun-i Islam, 1978; in English as *On Islam, and Shi'ism*, 1990

Further Reading

Ādamiyat, Faridun, *Fekr-e āzādi va Moqaddame-ye nehzat-e Mashautiyyat-e Irān* (The Idea of Freedom and the Constitutional Movement in Iran), Tehran, 1961

Farmayan, Hafez F., "Observations on Sources for the Study of Nineteenth- and Twentieth-Century Iranian History," *International Journal of Middle East Studies* 5 (1974), 32–49

Fasihi, Simin, *Jarayānhā-ye asli-ye Tārikhnegāri dar dowre-ye Pahlavi* (Main Currents in Historiography in the Pahlavi Era), Mashhad: Nashr-i Navand, 1372/1993

Jazayery, Mohammad Ali, "Kasravi Tabrīzī, Sayyid Ahmad," *The Enclopaedia of Islam*, new edition, Leiden: Brill, 1960–, vol. 4, 732–33

Jazayery, Mohammad Ali, "Kasravi, Iconoclastic Thinker of Twentieth-Century Iran," introductory essay in Ahmad Kasravi, *On Islam and Shi'ism*, Costa Mesa, CA: Mazda, 1990

Jung, Edeltrud, *Ahmad Kasrawī: ein Beitrag zur Ideengeschichte Persiens im 20. Jahrhundert* (Ahmad Kasravi: A Contribution to Persian Intellectual History in the 20th Century), Freiburg im Breisgau: Albert Ludwigs University, 1976

Katirai, Mahmud, "Ketābshenāsi-ye Kasravi: Tarh-e besyār Moqaddamāti" (Bibliography of Kasravi: A Very Introductory Project), *Farhang-e Irān-Zamin* 18 (1351/1972), 361–98

Staley, William C., Jr., *The Intellectual Development of Ahmad Kasravī*, PhD dissertation, Princeton University, 1966

Katz, Jacob 1904–

Hungarian-born Jewish historian

Jacob Katz is one of the foremost scholars in the field of Jewish history; his methodology, choice of subject matter, and interpretive conclusions have influenced the contours and content of large areas of Jewish historical scholarship. This essay treats the following: Katz's application of sociological categories to Jewish legal texts for the writing of legal and social history; the process in which Jews encountered and entered into modernity; and Katz's coining of phrases and concepts ("traditional society," and "[semi-]neutral society") which he utilized in his interpretive model connecting premodern and modern Jewry. This list omits other areas of Jewish history on which Katz has also written, such as Orthodox Judaism, Zionism, and anti-Semitism.

Arguably Katz's most influential and enduring work has been *Masoret u-mashber, ha-hevrah ha-Yehudit be-motsa'e*

Yeme-ha-Benayim (1958; *Tradition and Crisis*, 1958). Its importance lay in its description and analysis of categories of Jewish social and communal life, from family life to education to communal leadership. What had heretofore been characterized merely as the "end of the Middle Ages" in Jewish history, that is, the 16th to 18th centuries, later became seen as the "early modern period," largely owing to Katz's portrait of a society with a rich life of institutions and culture, expressed in new forms of literary creativity and spiritual dynamism. Owing to his training in both classical rabbinic texts as well as in the academic disciplines of sociology and history, Katz was able to make innovative use of rabbinic texts as documents of the reality of Jewish life in the Middle Ages. Katz employed the concept of the "traditional society" to describe a society of shared ideals and institutions, in which all "assume that all the practical and theoretical knowledge that they require has been inherited by them from their forefathers, and that it is man's duty to act in accordance with ancient customs." According to Katz, the world of Ashkenazic Jewry, from Alsace to Poland, while living under different external political regimes, and thus comprising discrete geographical centers of Jewish life, was unified in its maintenance of Jewish self-government, organized around the corpus of Talmudic and post-Talmudic legal and ethical texts. By employing sociological methodology to categorize various institutions that defined Jewish society, Katz hoped to reveal the intellectual and ideological underpinnings of Jewish society in the Middle Ages, both in its internal workings as well as in its response to external conditions and attitudes. He thereby synthesized the fields of intellectual and social history, arguing that ideas underlay social practice and structure.

The notion of Jewish life constituting a "traditional society" included a relatively high degree of separation from its Christian counterparts. In *Exclusiveness and Tolerance* (1961), Katz attempted to understand the social relationships between Jews and Christians through analysis of Jewish legal texts governing a variety of contexts of interactions between the two groups: commercial, social, domestic, and the like. In *Be-mo 'enai* (1989; *With My Own Eyes*, 1995), he concluded "that traditional Judaism upheld neither absolute religious tolerance nor a universalist code of morality."

Katz coined the term "neutral society," in *Tradition and Crisis* (and later the less affirmative "semi-neutral society," in *Out of the Ghetto*, 1973), to describe the "process of the absorption of Jews in modern state and society." This involved the creation of an intellectual and cultural milieu in Christian society within which select Jews were accepted as equals. Harking back to his work on Jewish hostility to Christianity first developed in *Exclusiveness and Tolerance*, Katz argued that the process of modernization involved the creation of a more neutral sphere in which such definitions and perceptions were supplanted by more integrative visions of Jewish identity within European society and culture, on the part of Jew and Gentile alike. This heralded the massive changes both in the external reality of the advent of the centralized, absolutist nation-state, and its demolition of the *Ancien Régime*, including the "traditional society" of the Jewish community.

Central to Katz's work, and intimately related to his work on traditional society, has been his study of the development of Jewish law. This followed logically from his understanding of traditional society as being defined and articulated with reference to both a textual and customary body of legal doctrines and practices. The historical study of Jewish law revealed both the inner dynamic of the ways in which law and behavioral norms developed over time, and the manner in which such changes reflected sociohistorical reality. In so doing, Katz thereby argued that the history of law was crucial not merely for its centrality in Jewish religious and intellectual life, but because studied historically, it furnished the scholar with the tools for the description and analysis of Jewish society and social change. This assumed that rabbinic norms were actually the constitutive element in the construction of Jewish society, sometimes prescribing social reality *a priori*, or ratifying – *a posteriori* – social practice. Katz's work also raised the issue of whether such religious thought structures were merely ideal types that bore little resemblance to actual Jewish norms. This begs the question of whether social history may be written from such "elite" sources as rabbinic texts, or whether these slight expressions of popular religion that may have been fundamentally different from, rather than merely popularized expressions, of "high" culture. Social history of this sort depends on archival sources of a different type than legal documents, which have been put to use by scholars attempting to reconstruct the social and economic world of European Jewry in the early modern period.

Traditional society experienced – according to Katz – twin crises: the response to the emerging nation-state, and to those forces within Jewish society that undermined Jewish communal institutions, and gave rise to new movements such as *Hasidism* in Eastern Europe and *Haskalah* (Jewish Enlightenment) in Central and Western Europe. First in *Tradition and Crisis*, then in *Out of the Ghetto*, Katz articulated this dual dynamic. He termed the *Maskilim*, the advocates of Jewish Enlightenment, a "New Social Type" – advocating mastery of gentile languages and general education, and greater participation in gentile society and culture. The deeper significance of the *Maskilim* lay not just in their cultural goals, but in their drive to challenge the traditional assumptions and hierarchy of Jewish communal leadership, as embodied in the rabbinate, replacing the traditional masters of Jewish text with themselves, and their re-visioning of what Jewish culture and Jewish identity should be.

DAVID B. STARR

Biography

Born Magyargencs, Hungary, 15 November 1904. Received PhD, University of Frankfurt. Teacher and principal in high schools and teachers colleges in Israel, 1936–50; taught at Hebrew University from 1950: rector, 1969–72. Married Gerti Birnbaum (3 sons).

Principal Writings

Bonim hofshim vi-Yehudim: kishrehem ha-amitiyim veha-medumim, 1938; in English as *Jews and Freemasons in Europe, 1723–1939*, 1970
Masoret u-mashber, ha-hevrah ha-Yehudit be-motsa'e Yeme-ha-Benayim, 1958; in English as *Tradition and Crisis: Jewish Society at the End of the Middle Ages*, 1958
Exclusiveness and Tolerance: Studies in Jewish-Gentile Relations in Medieval and Modern Times, 1961

Emancipation and Assimilation: Studies in Modern Jewish History, 1972
Out of the Ghetto: The Social Background of Jewish Emancipation, 1770–1870, 1973
From Prejudice to Destruction: Anti-Semitism, 1700–1933, 1980
"Traditional Society and Modern Society," in Shlomo Deshen and Walter P. Zenner, eds., *Jewish Societies in the Middle East: Community, Culture and Authority*, 1982
Halakha ve-Kabala: Mehkarim be-Toldot dat Yisra'el 'al Medoreha ve-Zikatah ha-Hevratit (Halakha and Kabbalah: Studies in the History of Jewish Religion, Its Various Faces and Social Relevance), 1984
Richard Wagner: Vorbote des Antisemitismus, 1985; in English as *The Darker Side of Genius: Richard Wagner's Anti-Semitism*, 1986
Jewish Emancipation and Self-Emancipation, 1986
Be-mo 'enai: otobiyografyah shel historyon, 1989; in English as *With My Own Eyes: The Autobiography of an Historian*, 1995
Ha-Halakha Be-Metsar: Michsholim 'al Derech Ha-Ortodoksia Be-Hithavutah (Halacha in Straits: Obstacles to Orthodoxy at Its Inception), 1992

Kazhdan, A.P. 1922–1997
Russian historian of Byzantium

A.P. Kazhdan was one of the most influential and prolific Byzantine scholars of the 20th century, with more than 600 articles and books to his credit. Writing on numerous subjects, Kazhdan had an immense impact on modern Byzantine studies, and his views and ideas have influenced the modern conception of the Byzantine empire. Unlike previous scholars, Kazhdan saw Byzantium not as a static and unchanging remnant of the Roman empire, but as a dynamic and constantly changing society filled with new, creative artists and unique personalities. For him, a historian's goal was to comprehend the interaction between individual psychology and surrounding social processes.

Kazhdan was born in Moscow in 1922 into the first fully Soviet generation under Stalin. Participation in this new Soviet experience caused him to view the ultimate origins of Stalinist oppression in Byzantium. Problems with his eyesight kept him out of the army and he was able to complete his university training after World War II. An intense nationalism swept through Russia immediately after the war and this included public and state interest in Byzantium and its history. Kazhdan was to experience anti-Semitism throughout his scholarly career in Russia, finding and then losing positions at small institutions far from the capital.

The subject of Kazhdan's early work, dictated by the Soviet historical model that emphasized peasants and artisans, was agrarian history and the interaction between cities and the surrounding countryside. In *Agrarnye otnosheniia v Vizantii XIII–XIV vv* (Agrarian Relations in 13th- and 14th-Century Byzantium, 1952), he examined feudalism in the Byzantine empire. In 1954 he published an article that attacked the accepted view that ancient cities continued an unchanged existence into the Middle Ages. Kazhdan, basing his theory in part on the archaeological data, suggested that the cities went through a period of discontinuity that severed their ties to the ancient world. While he was sharply criticized for this hypothesis at the time, his opening of the discussion resulted in academic debate and archaeological investigation of the subject that has over time largely substantiated his position.

With the 1960s in Russia came the thaw under Khrushchev and an easing of controls. Kazhdan was able to explore other topics in Byzantine history, such as Christianity. Kazhdan and other revisionists saw Christianity not as the religion of the rulers who exploited the masses, but as a major factor in the development of civilization. He then published several articles in the liberal periodical *Novyi mir*. This publication proved to be a forum that he could use to address delicate issues such as tyranny, bureaucracy, and the effect revolution had on both current and past culture and morality.

In 1976, Kazhdan's son David emigrated to the United States and immediately pressure was brought to bear upon Kazhdan that eventually forced him to leave academia in Russia and seek a new venue for his work. In 1978 Kazhdan emigrated to the United States and began an association with Dumbarton Oaks in Washington, DC that was to have a major impact on Byzantine studies in America. Soon after his arrival, Kazhdan was struck by the solitary nature of American scholars and scholarship. He, by contrast, was more interested in creating associations and partnerships in order to exchange ideas and theories. To help encourage collaboration, he published *People and Power in Byzantium* with Giles Constable in 1982 and *Change in Byzantine Culture* with Ann Wharton Epstein in 1985. These works succeeded in helping to foster an interest in collaboration among scholars in Byzantine history that is continuing to grow.

Kazhdan's most influential work was undoubtedly *The Oxford Dictionary of Byzantium*, which he initiated and edited. This mammoth project of 2,232 pages, published in three volumes in 1991, covers a broad array of subjects. While considered a major breakthrough by many scholars, the work was criticized by some for its inclusion of minor topics at the expense of more important ones. Kazhdan's influence is clear throughout the work, both in the many entries he wrote (often in collaboration with others) and in its general spirit.

R. SCOTT MOORE

See also Byzantium

Biography

Aleksandr Petrovich Kazhdan. Born Moscow, 3 September 1922, son of an engineer. Graduated from the Teachers' College, Ufa, 1942; studied at Institute for Universal History, Moscow, PhD 1946. Taught at provincial universities in Ivanovo, 1947–49; Tula, 1950–52; and Velikie Luki, 1953–56; senior research associate in Byzantine studies, Institute for Universal History, 1956–78; emigrated to US, 1979; senior researcher, Dumbarton Oaks, Washington, DC, 1979–97. Married Rimma (Musia) A. Ivanskaia, 1944 (1 son). Died Washington, DC, 29 May 1997.

Principal Writings

Agrarnye otnosheniia v Vizantii XIII–XIV vv (Agrarian Relations in 13th- and 14th-Century Byzantium), 1952

Sotsial'nyi sostav gospodstvuiushchego klassa Vizantii XI–XIIvv (Social Composition of the Ruling Class in 11th- and 12th-Century Byzantium), 1974

With Anthony Cutler, "Continuity and Discontinuity in Byzantine History," *Byzantion* 52 (1982), 429–78

With Giles Constable, *People and Power in Byzantium: An Introduction to Modern Byzantine Studies*, 1982

With Simon Franklin, *Studies on Byzantine Literature of the Eleventh and Twelfth Centuries*, 1984

With Ann Wharton Epstein, *Change in Byzantine Culture in the Eleventh and Twelfth Centuries*, 1985

"Do We Need a New History of Byzantine Law?", *Jahrbuch für österreichische Byzantinistik* 39 (1989), 1–28

Editor, *The Oxford Dictionary of Byzantium*, 3 vols., 1991

Further Reading

Cutler, Anthony, and Simon Franklin, eds., *Homo Byzantinus: Papers in Honor of Alexander Kazhdan*, Washington, DC: Dumbarton Oaks, 1992

Kedourie, Elie 1926–1992
British historian of the modern Middle East

For forty years Elie Kedourie was the most formidable practitioner of a dissident historiography of the Middle East, one who rejected the postcolonial dichotomy between Western guilt and Eastern innocence. In detailed studies of British diplomatic history, he attributed the failure of British imperial will in the Middle East to romantic illusions about the Arab-Muslim world. In his studies of Middle Eastern politics, he documented the importation of radical nationalism that ultimately transformed the Middle East into what he called "a wilderness of tigers." A deep conservatism, born of a disbelief in the redemptive power of ideological politics, suffused all of Kedourie's writings. Armed with a potent and lucid style, he waged a determined defense against the siege of Middle Eastern history by leftist theory, the social sciences, and fashionable Third Worldism. Kedourie's iconoclastic work forms the foundation of a diffuse school that views the post-Ottoman history of the Middle East not as an "awakening," but as a resurgence of its own despotic tradition, exacerbated by Western dissemination of the doctrine of self-determination.

Kedourie made his first systematic critique of British policy in his Oxford thesis, later published as *England and the Middle East* (1956). The thesis constituted a closely documented indictment of the British for their encouragement of Arab nationalism during and after World War I, especially in Kedourie's native Iraq, where Britain had imposed a militantly Arab nationalist regime on a diverse society. It also included a devastating account of the adventurism of T.E. Lawrence, at a time when Lawrence was still an unassailable hero. (Richard Aldington's debunking biography would not appear until two years later.) Kedourie's thesis enraged one of his examiners, the Oxford Orientalist Sir Hamilton Gibb, who insisted that Kedourie alter his conclusions. In a decision that demonstrated the depth of his convictions, the 28-year-old candidate refused, withdrawing the thesis and forgoing the doctorate. By then, the conservative political philosopher Michael Oakeshott had extended a hand to Kedourie, bringing him back to the London School of Economics (LSE) in 1953, where he remained for his entire career.

Kedourie's criticism of Britain's indulgence of Arab nationalism animated much of his later work. This reached its culmination in his monumental study of the correspondence exchanged during World War I between the British high commissioner in Egypt, Sir Henry McMahon, and the leader of the Arab Revolt, the Sharif Hussein. *In the Anglo-Arab Labyrinth* (1976) demonstrated how later British officials, motivated by a mixture of self-doubt and self-interest, accepted the Arab nationalist claim that Britain had promised the Sharif a vast Arab kingdom including Palestine. Kedourie argued that Britain had made no such promise, and that British self-reproach over "defrauding" the Arabs rested on a myth of Britain's own making.

In an earlier essay, his most famous, Kedourie traced the intellectual origins of this British loss of confidence. "The Chatham House Version" (1970), a reference to the influential Royal Institute of International Affairs in London, constituted a sharp critique of its guiding spirit, Arnold J. Toynbee. Kedourie regarded Toynbee's theory of civilizational decline, built on improbable analogies, as an exercise in moral self-flagellation that denied the civilizing role of empires, Britain's included. For Kedourie, the end of empires – of Hapburgs, Ottomans, British – tended to bring not national liberation but misgovernment, frequently followed by lawlessness and oppression. The failure of the Middle East to find political equilibrium figured as the theme of his last book, *Politics in the Middle East* (1992).

In his critique of modern nationalism, Kedourie ranged beyond the Middle East, as did much of his teaching at the LSE. In his book *Nationalism* (1960), he emphasized the fluid character of national identity, which rendered national self-determination "a principle of disorder." For Kedourie, nationalism represented an ideological temptation, which spread across the world in no discernible pattern, but largely in parallel with European influence. Ernest Gellner later criticized Kedourie for failing to explain the spread of nationalism in sociological terms, particularly as a feature of the early stages of industrialization. Kedourie pointed to many obvious exceptions to this postulate, and rejected any sociological explanation as a form of reductionist "economism."

In this as in many other debates, Kedourie vigorously resisted the penetration of the social sciences into history, maintaining the primacy of evidence over all theory. In his many general writings on historiography, he criticized Marxist determinism, the structuralism of the French Annales school, and psychohistory of any kind. Kedourie maintained that "history has no depths to be plumbed or main lines to be traced out," and that "history does not need explanatory principles, but only words to tell how things were." These views, combined with his conservative politics, made him an adversary of mainstream trends in Middle Eastern studies. Kedourie's own preferences governed *Middle Eastern Studies*, the quarterly he founded in 1964.

In his later years Kedourie became a well-known public intellectual in the United States, warning Americans against the same flagging of will that had diminished Britain. While his influence among conservative American intellectuals grew, he became disillusioned by the declining standards of British universities, including his own. He retired from the LSE in 1990, and was about to take up a new chair in modern Middle Eastern history at Brandeis University, when he died at the age of 66.

MARTIN KRAMER

Biography
Born Baghdad, 25 January 1926. Attended Collège A-D Sasson and Shamash School, Baghdad; BSc, London School of Economics, 1951; graduate work, St. Antony's College, Oxford, 1951–53. Taught (rising to professor) at London School of Economics, 1953–90. Married Sylvia Haim in 1950 (2 sons, 1 daughter). Died 29 June 1992.

Principal Writings
England and the Middle East: The Destruction of the Ottoman Empire, 1914–1921, 1956
Nationalism, 1960; revised 1993
Afghani and Abduh: An Essay on Religious Unbelief and Political Activism in Islam, 1966
The Chatham House Version and Other Middle Eastern Studies, 1970
Editor, *Nationalism in Asia and Africa*, 1970
Arabic Political Memoirs and Other Studies, 1974
In the Anglo-Arab Labyrinth: The McMahon-Husayn Correspondence and Its Interpretations, 1914–1939, 1976
Islam in the Modern World and Other Studies, 1980
The Crossman Confessions and Other Essays in Politics, History and Religion, 1984
Politics in the Middle East, 1992
Hegel and Marx: Introductory Lectures, edited by Sylvia Kedourie and Helen Kedourie, 1995

Further Reading
Cowling, Maurice, *Religion and Public Doctrine in Modern England*, 2 vols., Cambridge: Cambridge University Press, 1980–85

Keegan, John 1934–
British military historian

As the advocate of a new approach to military history, John Keegan has written academic works accessible to an interested but non-academic audience. He has written both general reference works and in-depth monographs. All of his works are united by the desire to discover what in history is applicable to our own circumstances and to apply such lessons to the way modern societies conceive and conduct armed conflict. Unlike many traditional military histories, which tend toward accounts of battles and campaigns and the decisions of great captains, Keegan's writings focus on what might be termed the culture or anthropology of war. Some of the issues Keegan has explored are why and how people become soldiers, what the experience of battle means to soldiers, and the way different societies conceive and conduct warfare.

Perhaps Keegan's most influential work was *The Face of Battle* (1976), which bridged the gap that often exists between academic and lay audiences. In the book's first chapter, Keegan situated himself within the sub-discipline of military history, offering a critique of his chosen field. He cited military history as a useful means for training officers but felt that this history too often fails to answer the main question of student officers: what is battle really like? Keegan felt that this shortcoming was inherent to the ways traditional military history has been written, focusing on generals, institutions, the mechanics of war (logistics, organization, etc.), and what he refers to as "the battle piece," which tends toward rationalized abstraction (or, worse, myth-making). In order to get behind abstractions, Keegan posed a simple question: what is it like to be in the thick of a battle? Whereas traditional battle accounts tended to emphasize heroic bravery, Keegan placed fear at the center of the combat experience. This allowed him to draw the conclusion, not original to him but made more convincing by his approach, that battle is an inherently frightening occurrence. It follows that it is not the leader's role to exhort his men to acts of courage so much as it is his responsibility to keep men from succumbing to the natural instinct to flee.

The body of *The Face of Battle* focused on Agincourt, Waterloo, and the Somme. In order to capture accurately the experience of these battles, Keegan was compelled to weaken or demolish some of the long-accepted constructions used in the writing of the "battle piece." For example, in his accounts of Agincourt and Waterloo, Keegan used modern knowledge of animal, specifically equine, behavior to lend greater realism to the cavalry charge, which is generally romanticized. He also demonstrated how the battlefield has changed over time, including the amount of ground involved, and related problems of communications, changes in weaponry, casualty procedures, and how all of these relate to one another. Keegan concluded that while many factors of battle are unlikely to change, the dominant trend is toward "a greater alienation of the soldier from anything recognizably human or natural on the field of battle."

Keegan views past battles as grounded historically in their own eras. This is indicated further by his conclusion in *Six Armies in Normandy* (1982) that the Allied build-up and conduct of the Normandy invasion would be impossible in an era of satellites and long-range weapons. The dual themes of the experience of the soldier and of the changing face of battle were also the major focus of a general reference work, co-authored with Richard Holmes, *Soldiers: A History of Men in Battle* (1987). This was followed by *The Mask of Command* (1987), in which Keegan analyzed four historic types of leadership. He concluded that in a modern age dominated by weapons of mass, indiscriminate destruction, military leadership had to eschew emotional appeals to national glory. In *A History of Warfare* (1993) the themes Keegan introduced in *The Face of Battle* – the culture of warfare, the historicity of battle linked to the metahistorical theme of armed conflict, and the experience of the soldier – come to fruition. Rather than presenting an account of warfare's evolution, *A History of Warfare* is a collection of essays organized around an examination of dominant levels of technology. In these essays, Keegan endeavored to demonstrate that individual cultures have particular ways of waging war, which are influenced but not dominated by technology and resources. Keegan's primary point is that warfare has always been rooted in culture. For example, he points out that certain modes of warfare, such as that based on heavily-mounted, heavily-armored cavalry (i.e., knights), were often dependent on a mutual willingness, even desire, on the part of the combatants to abide by common rules. In such an instance, neither side could deploy on unsuitable terrain or employ effective missile weapons for knightly combat to remain viable. Expanding on his theory of war's link with culture, Keegan examines Carl von Clausewitz's analysis of war, arguing that it did not produce a universal theory but was firmly rooted in its historical context of modern Western societies and mass armies, dating from the French Revolution. The Clausewitzean dictum of war being a means of state policy is too easily transformable to state policy becoming war. Given that Clausewitz's theories have served as a foundation of modern military thought, Keegan's critique has far-reaching implications for the present era.

What Keegan does see as metahistorical, however, is humankind's propensity for violence, a propensity that does not seem to have abated following the Cold War and has taken on an even more ominous tone with recent nuclear proliferation. While he views the modern West's approach to warfare as historically specific, Keegan also points out that Western ideas have spread widely through non-Western cultures, overwhelming traditional restraints on mass killing without effectively introducing new means of containing violence. For Keegan, the spread of Western culture in the wake of Western imperialism is a source of great concern. He notes that, while Western modes of warfare were effective in conquering non-Western peoples, these modes have proven to be even more effective as a means of self-destruction for the West. This said, for Keegan "a world without armies – disciplined, obedient, law-abiding armies – would be uninhabitable." Without such armies, there would be no protection from the violence Keegan sees inherent to human beings.

Some of Keegan's fellow military historians have given his works mixed reviews. Criticism tends to be directed not at his conclusions but at his approach, which is seen by some as too subjective or too given to fashionable trends within the historical profession, such as newer approaches to cultural history. It should be pointed out that such criticism is often leveled at historians who take new scholarly approaches. A few critics have claimed to detect a sense of cultural determinism in Keegan's work. However, most critics acknowledge that he has introduced an important new facet to the study of military history and an understanding of contemporary affairs.

JAMES E. FRANKLIN

See also Europe: Modern; Military; Napoleonic Wars; World

Biography

John Desmond Patrick Keegan. Born 15 May 1934. Educated at King's College, Taunton; Wimbledon College; Balliol College, Oxford, BA 1957, MA 1962. Political analyst, US embassy, London, 1958–60; taught at Royal Military Academy, Sandhurst, 1960–86. Defense editor, London *Daily Telegraph*, from 1986.

Principal Writings

Barbarossa: Invasion of Russia, 1941, 1971
The Face of Battle, 1976
With Andrew Wheatcroft, *Who's Who in Military History: From 1453 to the Present Day,* 1976
Editor, *Who Was Who in World War II,* 1978
With Joseph Darracott, *The Nature of War,* 1981
Six Armies in Normandy: From D-Day to the Liberation of Paris, 1982
The Mask of Command, 1987
With Richard Holmes, *Soldiers: A History of Men in Battle,* 1987
The Price of Admiralty: The Evolution of Naval Warfare, 1988
The Second World War, 1990
A History of Warfare, 1993
Warpaths: Travels of a Military Historian in North America, 1995

Kehr, Eckart 1902–1933

German historian

Eckart Kehr was Weimar Germany's most creative and original young historian. But his death from a heart attack in 1933 at the age of 31 cut short his enormous scholarly potential while the advent of Hitler and the deepseated preferences of German political historians for foreign policy, great personalities, and ideas delayed the influence on German historiography of the substantial work he had done until the 1960s. At that time Kehr's influence over both historical method and substance was renewed with scholarly vigor when West German historians led by Hans Ulrich Wehler formulated and developed the manipulative elite school of modern German social history which became the dominant orthodoxy of the 1970s and 1980s.

Kehr's published scholarly achievement, upon which his reputation rests, consisted of a monograph, *Schlachtflottenbau und Parteipolitik* (1930; *Battleship Building and Party Politics in Germany, 1894–1901*, 1973), commonly regarded as one of the best books ever written on Wilhelmine Germany, and some 16 essays exploring themes ranging from the evolution of bureaucratic authority in Prussia and foreign and military policy during the imperial era to idealistic political historiography. By employing Marxist and Weberian categories of analysis, he uncovered several processes subsequently considered crucial to an understanding of modern German history, such as the primacy of domestic policy over foreign policy, the feudalization of the bourgeoisie, and the role of materialistic and economic interests in the formulation of state policies of an allegedly nonpartisan national nature. His ultimate achievement was to show that class structures and economic interests underpinned and drove the political development of imperial Germany to its fateful and unfortunate end. Specifically, his provocative thesis argued that plutocratic industrialists and agrarian Junkers forged at times during the 19th or early 20th centuries either an anachronistic alliance or a simple compromise in opposition to radical democratic forces, in order to generate a special interest which official policymakers, whether bureaucrats or statesmen, could not ignore in formulating state policies. By this development, wherein the national interest was in effect betrayed, imperial Germany went to its ruin isolated on the world stage, bitterly divided on the home front, and destined to leave a legacy that threatened the stability of the new Weimar democracy. By discrediting through scholarship social classes and arrangements he disliked, Kehr also believed that he was fulfilling his political role as a scholar who wished both to understand and to change the world.

Kehr brilliantly revealed his interpretation of German history in his studies of the naval policies of Emperor Wilhelm II and the personnel policies of the imperial government, particularly of the Puttkamer ministry after about 1886. Concerning his naval studies, he showed that the move to create a world-class navy began in the 1890s when the National Liberal minister, Johannes von Miquel, advocated the association of all the state supporting forces against the socialist movement. As implemented by the Bulow government, this union of the possessor classes led to a Reichstag majority created by the Naval League, which promised profits to the industrialists and high grain tariffs to the agrarians, and firm opposition to the Social Democratic party. This marriage of interests enabled the bureaucrats and even the emperor to overcome their sensible aversion to policies alienating both Russia and England at the same time. Thus Kehr neatly tied the growth of the navy to major developments within Germany rather than to the national-interest argument used to justify the naval legislation. The capacity of the upper bourgeoisie and the aristocracy to collaborate was itself also the result of a process known as the feudalization of the bourgeoisie, which Kehr illustrated in his study of the Puttkamer ministry and Prussian bureaucracy. Kehr showed that Puttkamer had purged the bureaucracy of independent elements at the same time as the bureaucracy promoted a series of neofeudal values, including anti-Semitism, which called attention to its role as preserver of the status quo and defender of property against atheistic socialism. The role of the reserve officer corps in militarizing the bourgeoisie was most vividly described in his analysis when he showed how the bourgeoisie aped the Junker aristocrat.

Strongly aware that his perspectives were controversial, Kehr also attacked the dominant views of the historical profession of his day. He argued that *Geistesgeschichte* (History of Ideas), as then practiced even by his doctoral professor, the great Friedrich Meinecke, was essentially escapist in nature. He suggested that intellectualized history constituted a kind of compensation for the loss of political power experienced by the bourgeoisie, which now justified itself through the importance of its intellectual achievements. In the meanwhile, German history, Kehr lamented, lacked a social history which made a serious attempt to deal with real problems of class conflict and economic interest. He scolded professionals for letting their fear of the proletariat cause them stupidly to confuse social history with socialist history and to exaggerate the importance of personality as a force in history.

Mistaken in many of his judgments and awakening hostility by an irreverent polemical style of writing, Kehr was justly criticized in his day and by subsequent scholarship which has refined or overturned much of his work, particularly in regard to the solidity of the infamous bourgeois-noble alliance. However, as the great scholarly works of Western historians from the 1960s and 1970s still demonstrate, Kehr deserves to be remembered for what he tried to do and the questions he asked. He showed how German historians could boldly use Marxist categories to achieve penetrating insights concerning the connection between social structure and political developments, and how important it was for historians to criticize the German nation's desire for self-idealization. His work ultimately reminds German social historians that the most important question for them remains the impact of industrialization upon society.

JOHN F. FLYNN

See also Germany: 1800–1945; Gilbert; Koselleck; Wehler

Biography

Born Brandenburg an der Havel, 1902, son of the director of the Ritterakademie in Brandenburg an der Havel, and nephew of medievalist Paul Kehr, who became director of Prussian State Archives. Studied history, philosophy, economics, and sociology with Friedrich Meinecke, Ernst Troeltsch, Adolf von Harnack and others,

University of Berlin, PhD 1927. Awarded Rockefeller fellowship, 1932. Died while on a research trip, Washington, DC, 1933.

Principal Writings

Schlachtflottenbau und Parteipolitik, 1894–1901, 1930; in English as *Battleship Building and Party Politics in Germany, 1894-1901: A Cross-Section of the Political, Social, and Ideological Preconditions of German Imperialism*, 1973

Der Primat der Innenpolitik: Gesammelte Aufsätze zur preussisch-deutschen Sozialgeschichte im 19 und 20. Jahrhundert, 1965; in English as *Economic Interest, Militarism, and Foreign Policy: Essays on German History*, 1977

Preussische Finanzpolitik, 1806–1810: Quellen zur Verwaltung der Ministerien Stein und Altenstein (Prussian Economic Politics, 1806–1810: Sources for Administration in the Ministries of Stein and Altenstein), 1984

Further Reading

Craig, Gordon, Introduction, to Kehr, *Economic Interest, Militarism, and Foreign Policy*, Berkeley: University of California Press, 1977

Epstein, Klaus, "The Socioeconomic History of the Second German Empire," *Review of Politics* 29 (1967), 100–12

Sheehan, James J., "The Primacy of Domestic Politics: Eckart Kehr's Essays on Modern German History," *Journal of Central European History*, 1/2 (June, 1968), 166–74

Wehler, Hans-Ulrich, Introduction, to Kehr, *Der Primat der Innenpolitik*, Berlin: de Gruyter, 1965

Kelly-Gadol, Joan 1928–1982

US feminist historian

One of the early founders of the women's history movement, Joan Kelly played a formative role in the innovation, development, and consolidation of feminist theoretical approaches. Her notion of women's "vantage point" has forced historians to question previously accepted schemes of periodization, categories of social analysis, and theories of social change.

Kelly began her career as an Italian Renaissance scholar; her study of the work of Leon Battista Alberti linked the development of painter's perspective to wider changes in the intellectual perception of the world during the 15th and 16th centuries. Having played an active role in the women's liberation movement of the late 1960s, she went on to examine how her political convictions could be followed through in academic life. Influenced by another pioneer of women's history, Gerda Lerner, she began to develop women's history and women's studies courses for students from 1971 onwards. Her work on Alberti had drawn her attention to the importance of perspectives; her next project was to consider how history could be perceived very differently from the perspective of women instead of men.

In her influential essay "Did Women Have a Renaissance?" (1974 – collected with her other essays in *Women, History, and Theory*, 1984) Kelly questioned the whole set of premises upon which previous historians had based their demarcation of historical periods. She argued that, if history is surveyed from the "vantage point" of the emancipation of women, then major trends become very different in appearance. Those periods usually seen as times of progress – the French Revolution or the Renaissance – did in fact result in a contraction of women's social and personal options. Kelly's proposal that the status of women declined substantially during the Renaissance opened up considerable debate, leading to intensive research as historians focused on (re)discovering women of the Renaissance. While new research has created a more complex picture of Renaissance women, Kelly's theoretical questioning of traditional perspectives and periodization retains its cogency.

Kelly clarified and developed a solid theoretical basis for women's history. She argued that any analysis of historical change must include an examination of the relations between the sexes, relations which were not "natural" but socially and historically constructed. Sex, as a social category, must be "fundamental to our analysis of the social order as other classifications, such as class and race." The specificity of women's experience was, she added, produced through the interaction of class, sex, and race. In her 1979 essay "The Doubled Vision of Feminist Theory" she attempted a thorough synthesis of Marxist-Feminist and Radical-Feminist thought. Where Marxists had focused on economic structures as the basis of women's oppression, radical feminists had pointed to male control of women's bodies which was maintained through "sexual and ideological structures." Kelly argued that both approaches had an element of commonality: they both stressed the "centrality of reproduction" in organizing women's lives. The two separate visions needed to be superimposed so that sex and class could be depicted as social categories operating simultaneously. Kelly linked the separation of sex and class to notions of distinctive private and public spheres that had dominated political theory from the 19th century onwards. She argued that it was impossible to separate public and private, just as it was impossible to separate production and reproduction or the family and society.

At the time of her death in 1982 Kelly was working on a major project on the history and development of feminist thought; although the book she planned was never completed, her ground-breaking essay "Early Feminist Theory and the *Querelle des Femmes*" provided the first systematic analysis of women's involvement in debates on sexual politics from the 15th to the 18th centuries. Kelly argued that, although histories of feminism usually looked back no further than the French Revolution, its origins could be traced to the work of Christine de Pizan who began writing in defence of women in 1399. Kelly provided an extremely useful working definition of feminism which was historically valid whether applied to the 18th century or the later Middle Ages. She argued that feminism implied the taking of a conscious oppositional stance to the subjection and mistreatment of women, as well as an awareness that sexual difference was culturally constructed.

Throughout her work, Kelly was keen to deconstruct ideologies and to explain their operation in society. In her essay "Did Women Have a Renaissance?" she analyzed the ideals of courtly love and sought to explain the apparent paradox that beliefs that appeared to condone adultery could still function so as to uphold the institution of marriage. Her discussion of the "doubled vision" of sex and work was clearly structured to demonstrate the connections between ideological and economic systems. Kelly was particularly interested in the relationship between ideology and opposition, agency and resistance. In her study of early feminism, Kelly set herself the task of explaining the process of "coming into consciousness." What factors made a feminist consciousness possible? She sought to uncover how early feminists had been able to shift their perspective from one shaped by traditional ideologies to an alternative view that foregrounded women.

Perhaps Kelly's most significant contribution to women's history lay in her skills of communication and her ability to articulate theoretical arguments in lucid and fluent prose. While feminist historians have continued to develop theories of gender in a multitude of different ways, Kelly's collection of essays *Women, History, and Theory* remains a classic text and a powerful statement of the aims and methods of women's history.

LOUISE AINSLEY JACKSON

See also Feminism; Pieroni-Bortolotti; Scott, Joan

Biography

Joan Kelly. Born New York City, 29 March 1928. Received BA, St. John's University, New York, 1953; MA, Columbia University, 1954; PhD 1963. Taught at City College of New York, 1956–82. Died New York City, 15 August 1982.

Principal Writings

Leon Battista Alberti: Universal Man of the Early Renaissance, 1969

Women, History, and Theory: The Essays of Joan Kelly, 1984

Further Reading

Cook, Blanche Wiesen, Clare Coss, Alice Kessler-Harris, Rosalind P. Petchesky and Amy Swerdlow, Introduction, to *Women, History, and Theory: The Essays of Joan Kelly*, Chicago: University of Chicago Press, 1984

Herlihy, David, "Did Women Have a Renaissance? A Reconsideration," *Medievalia et Humanistica* 13 (1985), 1–22

Stuard, Susan Mosher, ed., *Women in Medieval Society*, Philadelphia: University of Pennsylvania Press, 1976

Kennedy, Paul M. 1945–

British international historian

Paul Kennedy is certainly one of the most well-known and innovative historians of modern international relations. His recent scholarship has exhibited an exceptional willingness to bridge the gap between academic history and the lay public, as well as to inform contemporary political and strategic debates with rigorous historical insights. In the field of international history, Kennedy's work has come to exemplify the structuralist approach to the discipline.

The formation of Kennedy's methodology must be seen against the backdrop of developments since the 1960s in German historiography and parallel shifts in English-language scholarship. Largely under the influence of Fritz Fischer and his followers, who asserted that domestic-political incentives took primacy over international ones in Germany's decision for war in 1914, a reappraisal of the methods and presuppositions of orthodox diplomatic history was initiated. Although Fischer's one-sided approach was in most cases rejected, it was nonetheless widely admitted by foreign policy historians that the study of the decisions of statesmen, diplomatic activity, and military competition had to take into account what Kennedy has himself dubbed the "background influences" of socio-economic, cultural, ideological, and domestic-political factors. Kennedy's *The Rise of the Anglo-German Antagonism, 1860–1914* (1980) pioneered this trend by employing a novel analytical format. The progress of chronological diplomatic narrative is twice suspended to supply lengthy "structural examinations" of themes such as lobby groups, liberalism, trade links, and armaments competition.

Antecedents of Kennedy's celebrated thesis on the long-term patterns of national ascendancy and decay can be found in his early writings. In his study of Anglo-German relations before 1914, he asserted that the most profound cause of the antagonism was economic. Specifically, he argued that the astonishing rise in German financial and industrial capacity, which produced a relative decline in Britain's competitive ranking, reinforced the geographical, ideological, and other factors that influenced key policymakers in both capitals and turned them to mutual enmity. Kennedy had also stressed the significance of shifting geo-strategic and geo-economic patterns for armed strength in his acclaimed *The Rise and Fall of British Naval Mastery* (1976). He showed that the rise and fall of Britain's seapower since the Tudors was closely bound up with its economic prosperity. Britain was suitably placed to benefit disproportionately in the accumulation of wealth and power from the revolutions in sea warfare and overseas trade of the 17th and 18th centuries, and it held naval and commercial standing by exploiting its early industrial lead in the 19th century. But the relative eclipse of Britain's productive potential in the late 19th and early 20th centuries, and the coming dominance of the large continental powers through industrialization and technological advance (the railway and later powered flight), doomed British seapower.

Unquestionably, Kennedy's boldest work is *The Rise and Fall of the Great Powers* (1987). It seeks to explain and to forecast the interactions between economic change and military conflict in the world-power system from 1500 to 2000. After examining the fates of the Habsburg, the French, and the British empires, as well as the arrival of the bipolar post-1945 order, Kennedy argues that in the long run there is a correlation between a power's economic capacity and its military or imperial power potential. Slowly, fluctuations in the pattern of global economic growth, plus technological and organizational breakthroughs, spur the expansion of some powers and work to undermine others. Kennedy detects a "lag time" between when a power attains its elevated economic rank and its military one: rising powers usually desire to become richer rather than spend on armaments. Great power status, however, entails external obligations – reliance on overseas markets and raw materials and military alliances – that demand more armed strength. Yet, inevitably, with the uneven distribution of economic change, the defence burden becomes difficult to sustain since the relative productive edge that made economic ascent possible in the first place has eroded. Consequently "imperial overstretch" sets in, while rivals on the upswing lurk ominously offstage. Ultimately, though, conclusive adjustments to the international balance are the result of prolonged wars between blocs of the leading powers, since victory is the reward of those belligerents with an overpowering productive and revenue-raising capacity.

The Rise and Fall of the Great Powers became a bestseller in the United States because it resonated with widespread public fears about American decline. While some historians greeted the book with glowing references to Toynbee, Gibbon, and Ranke, others denounced the rise-and-fall cycle as crude economic determinism. Perceptive reviewers have criticized Kennedy for turning the story of the British empire into a model for the rise and decline of all the great powers. International historians find his materialist view of power wanting. It interprets power as a commodity, open to quantification, and ready to be graphed. Instead, critics assert, power should be seen as a process of interaction and thus context-dependent: the means to influence a state to do what it would not do otherwise may be employable in one case, but not in another (for example, the failure of American armed might in Vietnam). The treadmill-like advance of Kennedy's thesis, which discounts as he puts it "the vagaries of personality" and the "week-by-week shifts in diplomacy," overlooks the intangible elements of power, such as diplomatic skill, leadership quality, national unity, and the ability of the abstract framework of the international system to regulate inter-state action.

Nevertheless, the debate sparked by *The Rise and Fall of the Great Powers* is an indication of the influence Kennedy has had on the historiography of the world-power system. Although international historians have declined to embrace an entirely structuralist or cyclical outlook, no one disputes that Kennedy's exploration of the "background influences" on diplomacy has helped to enrich the discipline as a whole.

JOSEPH MAIOLO

See also Britain: to 1750; Europe: Modern; Military; Naval; World

Biography

Paul Michael Kennedy. Born Wallsend near Newcastle-on-Tyne, 17 June 1945. Received BA, University of Newcastle, 1966; PhD, University of Oxford, 1970. Taught (rising to professor), University of East Anglia, 1970–83; and Yale University, from 1983. Married Catherine Urwin, 1967 (3 sons).

Principal Writings

"The Decline of Nationalistic History in the West, 1900–1970," *Journal of Contemporary History* 8 (1973), 77–100
The Samoan Tangle: A Study in Anglo-German Relations, 1878–1900, 1974
The Rise and Fall of British Naval Mastery, 1976
The Rise of the Anglo-German Antagonism, 1860–1914, 1980
The Realities behind Diplomacy: Background Influences on British External Policy, 1865–1980, 1981
Strategy and Diplomacy, 1870–1945: Eight Studies, 1983
The Rise and Fall of the Great Powers: Economic Change and Military Conflict from 1500 to 2000, 1987
Preparing for the Twenty-First Century, 1993

Further Reading

Berridge, G.R., and J. W. Young, "What Is a 'Great Power'?" *Political Studies* 36 (1988), 224–34
Kennedy, Paul M., and Edward N. Luttwak, "The Rise and Fall of the Great Powers: An Exchange," *American Scholar* 59 (1990), 283–99
Martel, G., "The Meaning of Power: Rethinking the Decline and Fall of Great Britain," *International History Review* 13 (1991), 662–94
Moore, J.T., "Paul Kennedy's *The Rise and Fall of the Great Powers*: A Summary and Reactions," *Midwest Quarterly* 31 (1989), 93–105
Reynolds, David, "Power and Wealth in the Modern World," *Historical Journal* 32 (1989), 475–87

Kerber, Linda K. 1940–
US women's historian

Linda Kerber is among the vanguard of American women's history. She received her doctorate from Columbia University where she was a student of Richard Hofstadter, and her career has been marked by success, as a writer, researcher, and educator. Her success is a reflection of the variety of ways Kerber has woven often overlooked data into portraits of American life during one of its most tumultuous periods, the Early Republic. Her work crosses the boundaries of history, Women's Studies, and American Studies and provided a template for multidisciplinary studies long before it became fashionable.

Kerber's early career was well situated in the Early Republic period. "Politics and Literature: The Adams Family and 'The Port Folio'" (1966) marked the beginning of her interest in ideas. Kerber's keen attention to the uses of language in law, letters, and speeches showed both the subtle and not so subtle ways men situated themselves in this new country. By borrowing from the growing toolbox of the "new social history," Kerber applied the notions of history from the bottom up to intellectual explorations of the Early Republic. The result was a series of articles that documented race riots in New York City and conversations on the best way to deal with the Indian question.

In 1970, Kerber published her doctoral work as *Federalists in Dissent* (1970), using the writings of articulate New England Federalists to illustrate that the differences between the Federalists and the Republicans went deeper than partisan issues. The Federalists perceived their world to be in disarray. As proof, Kerber cited changes in arts, science, law, and education. Unlike the Republicans, the Federalists felt that the culture of the republic was disintegrating. This was just the beginning for Kerber. By focusing on the Early Republic period and citizens' simultaneous struggles to define themselves and their country, her research pool seemed bottomless.

In 1976, inspired by the burgeoning field of women's history, Kerber refocused her interests on women's experiences. What started as an attempt to find American reactions to Mary Wollstonecraft's *A Vindication of the Rights of Woman* (1792) turned into the beginning of a very successful career. Kerber became a pre-eminent historian of women's thoughts and experiences during the Revolutionary War and the Early Republic periods. She started with the ideal of the Republican mother, tracing the archetype back to the Enlightenment. Political theorists seldom considered women's role in civic culture, and when they thought of women, it was only in relation to their domestic contributions as wives and mothers. The "Republican mother" was devised as a means to combine domesticity and politics, to provide a prototype for women to raise sons devoted to their country and remind husbands to be virtuous citizens. In practice it meant that American women, primarily illiterate and lacking any connection to the public sphere, needed to politicize the domestic sphere and agree that actions such as boycotting British tea and clothing were their patriotic contribution to the Revolution. Women could further contribute to the patriotic movement by making homespun clothing for the troops and housing prisoners of war. For Kerber, "the shape of American women's patriotism has been thought to be different from men's precisely because it has to be conditioned on the maintenance of the domestic world while fighting for political objectives."

Women of the Republic (1980) eloquently synthesized these ideas. Rather than seeing these women as victims of a patriarchal ideology, Kerber recognized their involvement in creating a place for themselves in this chaotic period. "They devised their own interpretations of what the Revolution meant to them as women, and they began to invent an ideology of citizenship that merged the domestic domain of the preindustrial woman with the new public ideology of individual responsibility and civic virtue." Women of the Republic challenged conventional historians' perceptions of the American revolutionary experience and established Kerber as a leading historian of women's experiences.

Women of the Republic also marked a methodological turn for Kerber. Her work, while clearly still within history's boundaries, began to reflect changes in the growing field of American Studies. American Studies combined a diversity of academic disciplines, topics, interpretations, and historical periods to present a variety of portraits of American life. In addition, American Studies was among the first to welcome feminists and feminist ideas, and to recognize the importance of race and ethnicity to American culture. Race, class, and gender – themes Kerber was already exploring – were right at home in American Studies.

In more recent years, Kerber has worked with other women's historians of note to test the boundaries of women's history. She joined Nancy Cott, Carroll Smith-Rosenberg, and Christine Stansell in a forum on gender in the Early Republic. They argued that women's history affords a better understanding, not only of gender, but also of institutional, social, and intellectual development overall. Kerber worked with Jane De Hart Mathews in editing Women's America: Refocusing the Past (1982), a text that surveyed American women's history from 1600 to 1980, and most recently she teamed up with Alice Kessler-Harris and Kathryn Kish Sklar to edit US History as Women's History (1995) which covered 1770 to 1994. As a historian, Kerber never fell prey to the "add women and stir" line of inquiry. She remains as aware today as when she began that men and women are simultaneously controlled by law and society, although the means and results may be different. Her task has been to illuminate those differences.

AMY STEVENS

See also Lerner; Painter; United States: American Revolution; Women's History: North America

Biography

Linda Kaufman Kerber. Born New York City, 23 January 1940. Received BA, Barnard College, 1960; MA, New York University, 1961; PhD, Columbia University, 1968. Taught at Stern College for Women of Yeshiva University, 1963–68; San José State College (now University), 1969–70; Stanford University, 1970–71; and University of Iowa, (rising to professor) from 1971. Married Richard Kerber, 1960 (2 sons).

Principal Writings

With Walter John Harris, "Politics and Literature: The Adams Family and 'The Port Folio,'" William and Mary Quarterly 23 (1966), 450–76

Federalists in Dissent: Imagery and Ideology in Jeffersonian America, 1970

"The Republican Mother: Women and the Enlightenment, The American Perspective," American Quarterly 28 (1976), 187–205

Women of the Republic: Intellect and Ideology in Revolutionary America, 1980

Editor with Jane De Hart Mathews, Women's America: Refocusing the Past, 1982

"Separate Spheres, Female Worlds, Woman's Place: The Rhetoric of Women's History," Journal of American History 75 (1988), 9–39

"Diversity and the Transformation of American Studies: A History," American Quarterly 41 (1989), 415–31

"Women, Mothers, and the Law of Fright," Michigan Law Review 88 (1990), 814–86

"The Paradox of Women's Citizenship in the Early Republic: The Case of Martin v. Massachusetts, 1805," American Historical Review 97 (1992), 349–78

"A Right to be Treated Like. . .Ladies: Women, Citizenship, and Military Obligation," University of Chicago Law School Roundtable 1 (1993), 95–128

Editor with Alice Kessler-Harris and Kathryn Kish Sklar, US History as Women's History: New Feminist Essays, 1995

Towards an Intellectual History of Women: Essays, 1997

Kessler-Harris, Alice 1941–

US (British-born) historian of women and labor

The scholarship of Alice Kessler-Harris serves as a guide to the approaches, debates, and research emphases in US labor and women's history in the past twenty years. While her work has evolved, from the compensatory view of women's history in the 1970s, to the use of gender as a historical category of analysis in the 1980s and 1990s, Kessler-Harris has remained committed to a social feminist perspective that views working women's lives in a class- and gender-based context.

The title of Kessler-Harris's first major essay, "Where Are the Organized Women Workers?" (1975), was both an indictment of New Labor History's dismal treatment of women and a challenge to women's historians to widen their focus beyond that of elite women. Kessler-Harris and other scholars answered her question by producing abundant research on such topics as women's labor force participation, family relations and paid work, and women in unions. She demonstrated that women's marginalization in the industrial workforce was a result not only of employers' actions, but male workers excluding them from high-paying jobs and union membership. Nevertheless, she found that women workers were militant in both traditional and non-traditional ways.

Kessler-Harris presented a synthesis of her findings in Out to Work (1982). She offered two new interpretations of working women. First, she argued that sex differences were crucial in identifying men's and women's experiences: the ideology of separate spheres, which idealized women's domestic role, was interdependent with the dynamics of the masculine-privileged marketplace. The outcome – a gender-segregated workplace – forced women to toil at jobs while not really being acknowledged as workers, and to complete household chores masked by the cheery, elite-dominated ideology of domesticity. Second, Kessler-Harris took the long view of working women's history. Instead of focusing on women's short-term, cyclical participation in paid work, she looked to their long-term tendency to enter the workforce in greater numbers through the course of this century as a result of the changing formation of the household and the growing expectation of self-fulfillment that made employment central to women's lives.

Ironically, Kessler-Harris found herself in the midst of a legal firestorm in the mid-1980s in which *Out to Work* was used for decidedly antifeminist ends in court. The case, filed by the US Equal Employment Opportunity Commission (EEOC) against Sears, Roebuck, & Co. for sex discrimination against women with respect to commission sales jobs, pointed to the limitations of using feminist scholarship in non-academic settings. Kessler-Harris served as an expert witness for the EEOC in the Sears case (as it became known); historian Rosalind Rosenberg testified for Sears. On the stand Rosenberg was required only to show that women's values and attitudes played some role in job choices. This she did, drawing on Kessler-Harris's work. Kessler-Harris faced a more difficult task: appearing as part of a poorly presented EEOC case based largely on questionable statistical evidence, she had to demonstrate that such factors played no role.

The proceedings and the court's decision in favor of Sears prompted Kessler-Harris to regret her participation. "History should never have been in that courtroom," she later commented. The problem, she claimed, was that "subtlety and nuance were omitted . . . complexities and exceptions vanished from sight" in a forum designed to identify clear guilt. The court was not friendly to Kessler-Harris' argument that Sears had not provided enough incentive or opportunity for women to take advantage of commission-sales positions. The feminist community (and, indeed, Sears' women employees) were left bruised by the proceedings. It gave rise to personal and political clashes within scholars' ranks, and left feminist attorneys and historians with little sense of how best to proceed in future class-action suits.

By the late 1980s Kessler-Harris joined others in answering Joan Scott's challenge to historians to consider gender as a tool of historical analysis. Kessler-Harris engaged in a systematic reassessment of E.P. Thompson's definition of class popularized by labor historians. She insisted that historians "pull class apart" and reconceptualize it as a process and ideology constructed in a gendered context. She has called on scholars to combine the Foucauldian approach to observing power in widely dispersed sites with a state-centered consideration of how state mechanisms control and regulate ideology.

Kessler-Harris continued to examine the economic, social, and familial forces embodied in women's changing ideological stance to paid work. In *A Woman's Wage* (1990) she posited how the "wage" was a lens in which to observe the fluid and contingent nature of gender relations. In particular, she pointed out that the close relationship between family and workplace helped construct a changing public policy ideal of what should constitute a woman's wage. Subjective and political forces –

more than the traditional "individual choice" explanation economists put forth – created the slogans and objectives that appeared to describe what jobs women should hold and what they should be paid: a living wage, a minimum wage for women, luxury wage, necessity wage, equal pay for equal work, and comparable worth.

Kessler-Harris has provided labor historians with conceptually creative syntheses of women's experiences. Her influence comes in part as a result of her ability to incorporate the approaches of others into her own innovative research. In her recent writings on US social security legislation of the 1930s, for example, she draws on the approach of historians of race relations by incorporating an explanation of how New Deal legislation excluded minority women and how those state policies, in turn, had long-range implications for the construction of racialized gender relations.

As a member of the generation of activists-scholars associated with the emerging fields of social, labor, and women's history of the 1960s and 1970s, Kessler-Harris has served as editor, teacher, and adviser to a new group of historians, urging them to engage in comparative scholarship, across cultures and national boundaries.

DENNIS A. DESLIPPE

See also Kerber; Lerner; United States: 19th Century; United States: 20th Century; United States: Historical Writing, 20th Century; Women's History: North America

Biography

Born Leicester, England, 2 June 1941. Studied at Goucher College, BA 1961; Rutgers University, MA 1962, PhD 1968. Taught in Baltimore public schools, 1961–66; at Douglass College, 1964–65; Hofstra University, 1968–73; and Sarah Lawrence College, 1974–76; professor, Hofstra University, 1977–88; Temple University, 1988–90; and Rutgers University, from 1990. Married 1) Jay Evans Harris, 1960 (marriage dissolved 1974; 1 daughter); 2) Bertram Silverman, 1982.

Principal Writings

Editor with Blanche Wiesen Cook and Ronald Radosh, *Past Imperfect: Alternative Essays in American History*, 1973

"Where Are the Organized Women Workers?" *Feminist Studies* 3 (1975), 92–110

Women Have Always Worked: A Historical Overview, 1981

Out to Work: A History of Wage-Earning Women in the United States, 1982

Editor with J. Carroll Moody, *Perspectives on American Labor History: The Problems of Synthesis*, 1989

A Woman's Wage: Historical Meanings and Social Consequences, 1990

Editor with Ulla Wikander and Jane Lewis, *Protecting Women: Labor Legislation in Europe, the United States, and Australia, 1880–1920*, 1995

Editor with Linda K. Kerber and Kathryn Kish Sklar, *US History as Women's History: New Feminist Essays*, 1995

Further Reading

Blewett, Mary, "Review of *A Woman's Wage: Historical Meanings and Social Consequences*," *Labor History* 32 (1991), 443–44

"Interview with Alice Kessler-Harris," *New Perspectives* 18 (1986)

Milkman, Ruth, "Women's History and the Sears Case," *Feminist Studies* 12 (1986), 375–400

Kiernan, V.G. 1913–

British historian of imperialism

A historian of wide interests, encyclopedic learning, and vast erudition, V.G. Kiernan has written on an impressive range of fields from the early modern period to contemporary times. He has also published widely on literary history and translated two volumes of Urdu poetry, but is best known as a historian of modern imperialism.

Kiernan's life played an important role in the development of his scholarly approach and interests. He joined the Communist party of Great Britain in 1934, the year he took his degree at Cambridge. Thereafter, his intellectual pursuits were always closely linked to political involvements. From 1939 to 1946 Kiernan taught in India. Time abroad nurtured a continuing fascination with the subcontinent, widened his intellectual horizons, and strengthened a commitment to examine Europe in its relationship to the wider world. On returning to Britain in 1946 he became an active member of the Historians' Group of the Communist party, a remarkable collection of scholars that included Christopher Hill, Rodney Hilton, Eric Hobsbawm, and E.P. Thompson. The ensuing period of intellectual ferment led Kiernan to subjects that he would pursue for the next half-century: absolutism, nation-state formation, and the place of class struggle in history.

Kiernan's wider reputation rests on his work as a historian of European imperialism. Approaching the subject with little patience for dogma, he has attempted, as he explains in *Marxism and Imperialism* (1974), to stake out "an independent Marxist standpoint." In that volume Kiernan enters into a penetrating discussion of the corpus of work by Marxist historians of imperialism. He criticizes Lenin's detractors on the grounds that they "have found no better interpretation," but takes issue with the Marxists' reliance on economic determinism. For Kiernan, Lenin's work, however formidable, did more to restrain than to foster future research. Especially regrettable, in his view, was the subsequent marginalization of important theorists like Luxemburg and Bukharin.

In subsequent monographs Kiernan acted on that admonition, exploring the noneconomic dimensions of imperialism. *The Lords of Human Kind* (1969), his most original work, is a pioneering study of the historical psychology of race in the colonial experience. Global in scope, his main interest is in examining the impressions and opinions of western colonialists about the peoples they sought to "civilize" in the century before World War I. The colonizers were engaged in conduct that often violated their own moral precepts, and their attitudes were typically shaped by sheer psychological necessity: "By thinking the worst of their subjects they avoided having to think badly of themselves." However, if Europeans came to the task of conquest with elaborate racist and ethnocentric preconceptions, their views were far from static. Kiernan scrutinized the interaction between conqueror and conquered, drawing out the ways in which the relationship altered European views of race, and in rare cases, of their own culture. *European Empires from Conquest to Collapse* (1982) can be read as a companion volume that attends to the military side of 19th- and 20th-century imperialism. This study offers a detailed account of the violence that Europeans unleashed as they mastered the non-European world, and the manner in which military technology and tactics of conquest shaped ideologies of colonialism. Kiernan's broader concern, however, is the relationship of imperialism to society. Expansion had serious consequences for European domestic political culture. If imperial adventure could serve as an outlet for the internal class frictions that plagued industrial society, violence engaged in abroad often rebounded, leading to new types of brutality at home. With huge moral reservations, Kiernan granted that western imperialism sometimes furthered the development of remote and backward societies. Yet imperialism also tended to reinforce existing patterns of class power, securing the authority both of comprador clients in colonial societies, and of plutocratic rule in Europe.

Kiernan is an accomplished historian of early modern Europe, a field where he has made extensive use of class analysis. Unlike other prominent Marxist historians of his generation, who pioneered the study of social history "from the bottom up," Kiernan has retained an interest in Europe's traditional rulers, the aristocracy. *The Duel in History* (1988), a product of this interest, considered a politically and culturally charged aristocratic practice. Kiernan argued that if aristocratic origins were closely linked to violence, duelling helped to limit intra-class conflicts to ritualized contests between individuals. Duelling also performed key ideological and moral objectives, distinguishing an exclusive caste in a time of change and buttressing the *esprit de corps* of an increasingly embattled but still privileged order.

In *State and Society in Europe, 1550–1650* (1980), Kiernan examined the relationship of the absolutist state to the evolving European social structure on the threshold of modernity. Elaborating an analysis that Marx first put forward, Kiernan insisted on the class basis of absolutism, seeing the origins of the New Monarchs in the late medieval crisis of feudalism. Kiernan characterized absolutism as an essentially feudal formation that consolidated seignorial rule. For that reason he conceived of absolutism as the triumph of the "aristocratic state." Crucial for Kiernan, since absolutism was vital in forging modernity, it also insured the survival of feudal elements. In the short term, this helps account for the notably warlike character of absolutism itself, a subject examined in his classic essay "Foreign Mercenaries and Absolute Monarchy." The endurance of a powerful feudal stratum would also prove a stubborn obstacle to progress in the modern age. Thus Kiernan's *The Revolution of 1854 in Spanish History* (1966) located the origins of Spain's ruinous 20th-century civil war in the earlier defeat of an anemic liberalism by a declining but tenacious aristocratic-dominated regime.

Harvey J. Kaye has observed that Kiernan's Marxist history is distinguished by his sense of the tragic nature of the human experience. Even-handed in approach and refusing neat moral dichotomies, Kiernan's work is suffused with sympathy for the downtrodden, but also a deep respect for the human values and qualities of elites. His greatest legacy is a lifelong devotion to the primacy of history for an understanding of the world.

RICHARD J. SODERLUND

See also Brenner; Hobsbawn; Marxist Interpretation

Biography

Victor Gordon Kiernan. Born Manchester, 4 September 1913. Educated at Trinity College, Cambridge, BA 1934. Fellow, Trinity College, Cambridge, 1937–39, 1946–48; taught in India, 1939–46; taught (rising to professor), University of Edinburgh, from 1948 (emeritus).

Principal Writings

British Diplomacy in China, 1880 to 1885, 1939
The Revolution of 1854 in Spanish History, 1966
The Lords of Human Kind: European Attitudes Towards the Outside World in the Imperial Age, 1969; in US as *The Lords of Human Kind: Black Man, Yellow Man, and White Man in an Age of Empire*, 1969
Marxism and Imperialism: Studies, 1974
America, the New Imperialism: From White Settlement to World Hegemony, 1978
State and Society in Europe, 1550–1650, 1980
European Empires from Conquest to Collapse, 1815–1960, 1982; in US as *From Conquest to Collapse: European Empires from 1815 to 1960*, 1982
The Duel in History: Honour and the Reign of Aristocracy, 1988
History, Classes and Nation-States: Selected Writings of V.G. Kiernan, edited by Harvey J. Kaye, 1988
Poets, Politics and the People, edited by Harvey J. Kaye, 1989
Tobacco: A History, 1991
Imperialism and Its Contradictions [collected essays], 1995

Further Reading

Edwards, Owen Dudley, "History and Humanism: Essays in Honor of V.G. Kiernan," *New Edinburgh Review* 38–39 (1977)
Hobsbawm, Eric J., "The Historians' Group of the Communist Party," in Maurice Cornforth, ed., *Rebels and Their Causes: Essays in Honor of A.L. Morton*, London: Lawrence and Wishart, 1978; Atlantic Highlands, NJ: Humanities Press, 1979
Kiernan, V.G., "The Communist Party of India and the Second World War: Some Reminiscences," *South Asia* 10 (1987), 61–73
Samuel, Raphael, "British Marxist Historians, 1880–1980," *New Left Review* 120 (March–April 1980), 21–96
Schwarz, Bill, "'The People' in History: The Communist Party Historians' Group, 1946–56," in Richard Johnson *et al.*, eds, *Making Histories: Studies in History-Writing and Politics*, London: Hutchinson, and Minneapolis: University of Minnesota Press, 1982

Kitabatake Chikafusa 1293–1354

Japanese historian

Kitabatake Chikafusa was a Japanese political figure, poet, and author of one of the first interpretive national histories of Japan, the *Jinnō shōtōki* (*A Chronicle of Gods and Sovereigns*). Kitabatake occupied high posts at court during the reign of emperor Go-Daigo from 1318 to 1330, and after the fall of the Kamakura shogunate, in the Kenmu Restoration of 1333, returned to Go-Daigo's service. A split between Go-Daigo and the warlord Ashikaga Takauji occurred in 1335; the latter established a new military regime (the Muromachi shogunate), headquartered in the imperial capital of Kyoto, and declared the accession of a new emperor from a collateral branch of the imperial family. Meanwhile Go-Daigo fled Kyoto to establish a rival regime in Yoshino. Thus began the period of Northern and Southern courts (1336–92), during which warlords throughout Japan backed rival claimants to imperial legitimacy.

Kitabatake attempted to raise support for the Southern (Yoshino) cause in the eastern provinces from 1338 to 1343. His authorship of *Jinnō shōtōki* during this period reflects his effort to establish the legitimacy of the Go-Daigo line, and persuade powerful court and military figures of the advantages of aligning themselves with Go-Daigo (d.1339) and his successor Go-Murakami. Failing in his effort to win over eastern chieftains, Kitabatake returned to Yoshino in 1344, where he became the principal civil and military leader until his death. While negotiating a peace settlement with Takauji and the Northern court, Kitabatake refused to accept the proposed compromise of alternately enthroning emperors from each court, insisting instead upon the primacy of the Southern line. Breaking a truce agreement in 1352, he sent troops against the shogunate, capturing Kyoto and formally enthroning Go-Murakami. Repulsed by Ashikaga forces, the adherents of the Southern court returned to Yoshino. Four decades later the North-South division was mended by the shogun Ashikaga Yoshimitsu, whose solution to the succession problem (alternate rule by members of the two imperial lineage groups) would have never received Kitabatake's approval.

In addition to the *Jinnō shōtōki*, Kitabatake, who took holy orders in 1329, also authored a work on Shingon Buddhist doctrine, *Shingon naigōgi* (Inner Meaning of Shingon, 1345); a historical study of official posts in Japan, *Shokugenshō* (Origins of Office, 1339); an 8-volume account of Japan's origins, according to Shinto teaching, *Gengenshō*; and *waka* poetry.

Kitabatake's historical thought combines elements of Shinto, Buddhism, and Chinese thought, and expresses the concerns of the Kyoto nobility confronted with the dramatic rise of the military after 1185. In these features it resembles the earlier thought of Jien, abbot of the Tendai Buddhist sect, as reflected in the historico-religious work *Gukanshō* (c.1219); but it places greater emphasis on Shinto themes, and contains a more complex and sophisticated theoretical framework.

At the core of Kitabatake's thought is the conviction that Japan is "the country of the Gods" (*shinkoku*), superior to all others. The sacred character of Japan, as described in the *Nihongi* and other chronicles, has been historically demonstrated by the fact that its imperial line, established by the great-great-grandson of the Sun Goddess Amaterasu, has continued through unbroken succession from the empire's founding in 660 BCE. While drawing on Indian and Chinese thought, and seeking to reconcile foreign creation stories with the Shinto account, Kitabatake thus privileges Shinto.

Drawing particularly upon the doctrines of the Ise sect of Shinto, Kitabatake links the durability of the imperial house with the divine will, and with the mystical properties of the sacred imperial Regalia (a sword, mirror, and jewel) which have been enshrined in Japan for over one million years. The moral values inhering within them (strength, honesty, and gentleness) have preserved the imperial house. Thus Kitabatake links the imperial succession to divine favor and moral worth.

Not all emperors, however, have been upright; some indeed have committed acts against the will of Heaven (as conceived of by Chinese thinkers). To prevent imperial government from falling into error, Kitabatake stresses 1) the proper handling of the imperial succession; and 2) emperors' avoidance of personal rule and delegation of authority to capable ministers. Power should appropriately pass from reigning emperor to a designated son; when it is passed collaterally, and does not soon return to the original line, misrule eventually occurs. Even if the succession is properly arranged, the emperor himself should serve as a moral symbol rather than active ruler.

Clearly Kitabatake's emphasis upon the first point reflects his adherence to the cause of the Southern court, and opposition to its rival. By "capable ministers" Kitabatake means members of the Kyoto aristocracy (including his own family, but most importantly, the Fujiwara, who had administered Japan from 884 to 1185). Kitabatake regards this "middle period" (chūko) as a golden age of emperors who remained aloof from the real exercise of power, relying upon the Fujiwara regents.

The emergence of military rule after 1185 had produced disaster. The warriors (bushi) had become self-seeking, trampling on imperial prerogatives. Jien had employed the Buddhist concept of mappō, or "decline of the Buddhist law," to suggest that further degeneration was inevitable. Kitabatake, however, rejected any notion of predestined decline, insisting that the divine will and imperial Regalia still protect Japan. The failure of the Mongol invasions of the previous century had demonstrated their continuing efficacy.

Kitabatake's arguments are designed to promote the causes of the Southern court, for which he fought; the aristocratic class, of whom he was a member; and Ise Shinto, to which his family adhered. His narrative, sparse in historical detail, reflects religious dogmatism and personal political commitment rather than objective historical inquiry. Yet the Jinnō shōtōki offers a path-breaking general theory of Japanese history as a divinely governed process, subject to periods of decadence stemming from improper handling of the succession, and from the usurpation of imperial power by corrupt agents. Its doctrine of shinkoku and treatment of imperial supremacy remained influential into the mid-20th century.

GARY P. LEUPP

See also Arai; Japan; Japanese Chronicles

Biography

Born 1293, to a noble family. Entered service of emperor Go-Daigo whom he aided in an unsuccessful struggle to retain power and reassert direct imperial rule. Died Yamato Province, now Nara Prefecture, 1354.

Principal Writings

Jinnō shōtōki, c.1339; in English as A Chronicle of Gods and Sovereigns: Jinnō Shōtōki of Kitabatake Chikafusa, 1980
Shokugenshō (Origins of Office), 1339
Shingon naigōgi (Inner Meaning of Shingon), 1345
Gengenshō (Shinto Accounts of Japan's Origins), 8 vols.

Further Reading

Beasley, William G., "Japanese Historical Writing in the Eleventh to Fourteenth Centuries," in Beasley and Edwin G. Pulleyblank, eds., Historians of China and Japan, London: Oxford University Press, 1961
Kuroda Toshio,"Gukanshō and Jinnō Shōtōki," in John A. Harrison, New Light on Early and Medieval Japanese Historiography, Gainesville: University of Florida Press, 1960

Ryusaku Tsunoda, William Theodore de Bary and Donald Keene, eds., Sources of Japanese Tradition, vol. 1, New York: Columbia University Press, 1958
Varley, H. Paul, Imperial Restoration in Medieval Japan, New York: Columbia University Press, 1971

Kliuchevskii, V.O. 1841–1911

Russian social historian

One of the founders of the liberal tendency in Russian historiography, V.O. Kliuchevskii began his research with the scientific examination of historical sources. Early works explored sources never before used as historical documents in Russia: foreign travellers' accounts of Muscovy and early Russian hagiographies. Kliuchevskii demonstrated that both were more than literary or religious accounts, and merited historical analysis.

Kliuchevskii's doctoral work deepened this analysis as he turned to a rigorous study of early modern Russian society in the shape of the boyar duma (council of nobility). Again he employed scientific principles in his attempt to illustrate the relationships and preoccupations of different social strata through the study of the structure, role, and evolution of a key institution of early modern Russia.

In his best-known work, Kurs russkoi istorii (1904–21; A History of Russia, 1911–31), Kliuchevskii pulled together strands to create a survey of Russian history from the 7th to the 19th centuries. A History of Russia was based on his lectures at Moscow University; they were steeped in the positivist historical tradition, relying on documentary sources and presenting historical debates rather than adhering to the earlier Russian tradition of focusing solely on the state to understand the nation's history. Thus Kliuchevskii's history presented a new interpretation of the development of Russia, rather than offering a simple narrative. He combined the social, political, and economic factors generally favored by his fellow historians with an understanding of the influence of geography, psychology, and culture to present a more nuanced vision of the Russian past. He found geography to be a critical factor in Russian development, and this was amplified in his discussion of the colonization of nearby lands as the state grew. For Kliuchevskii, the study of historical process was central to the science of history. Historical processes embraced all of a society, not just its rulers, and he sought to understand the national character as well as the structures of the state.

Kliuchevskii rejected historoigraphical trends that examined only small segments of Russian history, preferring to recognize the continuity between different areas, and he reconceptualized the divisions accordingly. The Dnepr or Kievan period from the 7th to the 13th centuries was followed by a stagnant period until the central state was organized in the 15th and 16th centuries. Then came an era of noble monarchy (17th–19th centuries), which entered a period of capitalist development in the 1860s. Kliuchevskii's periodization continues to dominate Russian historiography to the present.

Kliuchevskii also recognized that Russian history was affected by events and movements within Europe; indeed that it was guided by the same factors and general historical laws at work in its geographical neighbors. He thus rejected the ideal of Russian particularity and sought to situate it within broader movements.

Kliuchevskii's historical synthesis was instrumental in shaping the intellectual atmosphere in the decades preceding the Russian Revolution. His use of primary documents, his ability to interpret them, and his skill at synthesizing them for presentation at his enormously popular public lectures, and then in his books, meant that Kliuchevskii's ideas helped to shape the way Russian society conceptualized itself. In this way he played a role far greater than most historians in shaping the destiny of the people he studied.

DMITRY A. GOUTNOV

See also Karamzin; Miliukov; Platonov; Russia: Medieval; Russia: Early Modern; Russia: Modern; Vernadsky

Biography

Vasilii Osipovich Kliuchevskii. Born Voskresenskoe Village, Penza Uezd, 16 October 1841, son of a village priest. Studied at Penza parish theological school; Uezd theological school, and seminary, 1851–60; with Buslaev, Eshevskii, Soloviev, and Shchahpov at Moscow University, 1861–65, BA 1865 and postgraduate work leading to PhD, 1882. Lecturer in various academies, 1867–79; taught at Moscow University, 1879–1911. Died Moscow, 12 May 1911.

Principal Works

Skazanii inostrantsev o moskovskom gosudarstve (Foreigners' Accounts of Muscovy), 1865

Drevnerusskie zhitiia sviatykh kak istoricheskii istochnik (Old Russian Saints' Lives as Historical Sources), 1871; reprinted 1988

Boiarskaia duma drevnei Rusi (The Boyar Duma in Old Rus), 1882

Kurs russkoi istorii, 5 vols., 1904–21; in English as *A History of Russia*, 5 vols., 1911–31, selections as *Peter the Great*, 1958, *A Course in Russian History: The Seventeenth Century*, 1968, and *The Rise of the Romanovs*, 1970

Kharakteristiki i vospominaniia (Descriptions and Memoirs), 1912

Pis'ma, dnevniki, aforizmy i mysli ob istorii (Letters, Diaries, Aphorisms, and Ideas about Russian History), 1968

Neopublikovannye proizvedeniia (Unpublished Works), 1983

Sochineniia (Works), 9 vols. to date, 1987–

Istoricheskie portrety (Historical Portraits), 1990

Further Reading

Byrnes, Robert F., "Nechkina's Kliuchevskii," *Russian Review* 37 (1978), 68–81

Chumachenko, Erika Georgievna, *V.O. Kliuchevskii: istochnikoved* (Kliuchevskii and Source Studies), Moscow: Nauka, 1970

Dukes, Paul, "Klyuchevsky and the Course of Russian History," *History Today* 37 (July 1987), 51–54

Karagodin, Anatolii Ivanovich, *"Filosofiia istorii" V.O. Kliuchevskogo* (Kliuchevskii's Philosophy of History), Saratov: Izd-vo Saratovskogo, 1976

Kireeva, Raisa Aleksandrovna, *V.O. Kliuchevskii kak istorik russkoi istoricheskoi nauki* (Klyuchevsky as a Russian Historiographer), Moscow: Nauka, 1966

Mazour, Anatole G., *An Outline of Russian Historiography*, Berkeley: University of California Press, 1939; revised as *Modern Russian Historiography*, Princeton, NJ: Van Nostrand, 1958; revised Westport, CT: Greenwood Press, 1975

Mazour, Anatole G., "V.O. Kliuchevsky: The Making of a Historian," *Russian Review* 31 (1972), 345–59 and 32 (1973), 15–27

Nechkina, Militsa V., *Vasilii Osipovich Kliuchevskii: istoriia zhizni i tvorchestva* (Kliuchevskii: His Life and Work), Moscow: Nauka, 1974

Parry, A., "Vasily Osipovich Kliuchevsky," in Bernadotte E. Schmitt, ed., *Some Historians of Modern Europe: Essays in Historiography*, Chicago: University of Chicago Press, 1942; revised 1966

Vernadsky, George, *Russian Historiography: A History*, Belmont, MA: Nordland, 1978

Knowles, David 1896–1974

British medievalist

David Knowles is one of Britain's most important church historians. He was a Benedictine monk who wrote extensively on ecclesiastical history, concentrating on monasticism.

Knowles came from a prosperous manufacturing family in Birmingham, the only child of parents who were Catholic converts, and was educated at Downside Abbey. He remained in the abbey and took his final vows in 1918. From 1919 to 1922 he studied classics at Cambridge and then theology for a year at Rome. Thereafter he returned to Downside as a teacher.

As a young man Knowles had wide intellectual interests, and especially enjoyed reading literature, a pleasure he renounced as his spiritual life deepened. Aside from his first book, *The American Civil War* (1926), he confined himself to writing on three main subjects: mysticism, medieval monastic life, and Catholic historiography. During the interwar period there was a general readership of books on mysticism, or the development of the soul's inner relationship with God. Knowles' understanding centered on his reading of the Spanish mystical poet St. John of the Cross (1542–91). Knowles' *The English Mystics* (1927) explored the lives of medieval writers on this subject. It was a theme that informed his life's work on the monastic life, and one to which he returned in *The English Mystical Tradition* (1960) with a more analytical perspective. During the 1930s Knowles became spiritual director to Elizabeth Kornerup, a Swedish medical doctor and psychiatrist, with an intense mystical life: Knowles believed she was a saint and they retained a complex relationship until the end of their lives. It seems it was partly this relationship and partly the tension between Knowles' life under the monastic rule and his intellectual exertions, that precipitated him into some form of nervous breakdown in the late 1930s, for which he was treated by Dr. Kornerup. After the publication of his masterpiece *The Monastic Order in England* (1940), he found a new niche teaching history at Peterhouse, Cambridge. In 1946 he gained a papal dispensation to live apart from his monastic community in order to hold a professorship at Cambridge, but experienced a similar tension with his new community at Peterhouse, and was dispensed from academic residence requirements and lived in London with Dr. Kornerup, his spiritual companion. *The Monastic Order in England* concentrated on monks, but contained little information on canons, friars, or nuns. Eileen Power's *Medieval English Nunneries* (1922) was the authority on this subject, so Knowles avoided this area. *The Religious Orders in England* (1948–59) redressed the other imbalances and took the story up to the dissolution of the monasteries in the 16th century. These four books are

Knowles' greatest contribution to historical literature. In addition he and Neville Hadcock, a historical geographer, produced a gazetteer, *Medieval Religious Houses: England and Wales* (1953), which covered all the known houses. *Great Historical Enterprises* (1963) and *The Historian and Character* (1963) contain Knowles' main writings on historiography. Knowles himself continued a tradition of Benedictine historians, which reached back to St. Bede and Jean Mabillon and included Edmund Bishop and Abbot Cuthbert Butler, whom Knowles had known in his youth at Downside.

Knowles' prolific authorship was fostered by the creative tension between his vocation and his intellect. As is often the case with complex personalities, his life contained paradoxes, such as his attachment to Dr. Kornerup, which caused his community at Downside great pain. However he was a deeply spiritual man with a quiet strength, who inspired admiration and friendship among colleagues and deep affection and loyalty among his students. It remained to later scholars to assess the contribution of the laity to the medieval church, but Knowles produced unparalleled insights into the monastic life.

VIRGINIA R. BAINBRIDGE

See also Britain: 1066–1485; Reformation; Ullmann

Biography

Michael Clive Knowles; in religion: Dom David Knowles. Born Studley, Warwickshire, 29 September 1896, son of a manufacturer. Educated at Downside Abbey School, 1910–14; Christ's College, Cambridge, BA 1922; Collegio Sant' Anselmo, Rome, 1922–23. Entered novitiate at Downside, 1914; priest, 1922; taught at Downside Abbey; editor, *Downside Review*, 1930–34; lived at Ealing Priory, 1933–39; fellow, Peterhouse, Cambridge, 1944–63; taught at Cambridge University (rising to professor), 1946–63. Died in Sussex, 21 November 1974.

Principal Writings

The American Civil War: A Brief Sketch, 1926
The English Mystics, 1927
The Monastic Order in England: A History of Its Development from the Times of St. Dunstan to the Fourth Lateran Council, 943–1216, 1940; 2nd edition [with dates 940–1216], 1963
The Religious Orders in England, 3 vols., 1948–59; vol. 3 abridged as *Bare Ruined Choirs: The Dissolution of the English Monasteries*, 1976
With R. Neville Hadcock, *Medieval Religious Houses: England and Wales*, 1953; revised 1971
The English Mystical Tradition, 1960
The Evolution of Medieval Thought, 1962
Great Historical Enterprises [and] *Problems in Monastic History*, 1963
The Historian and Character, and Other Essays, 1963
With Dimitri Obolensky, *The Middle Ages*, 1968 [*The Christian Centuries*, vol. 2]
Christian Monasticism, 1969

Further Reading

Brooke, C.N.L., ed., *David Knowles Remembered*, Cambridge: Cambridge University Press, 1991
Cowling, Maurice, *Religion and Public Doctrine in Modern England*, Cambridge: Cambridge University Press, 2 vols., 1980–85
Morey, Adrian, *David Knowles: A Memoir*, London: Darton Longman and Todd, 1979

Pantin, William Abel, "Curriculum Vitae" in Knowles, *The Historian and Character, and Other Essays*, Cambridge: Cambridge University Press, 1963
Stacpole, A., "The Making of a Monastic Historian," *Ampleforth Journal* 80 (1975) 71–91

Kocka, Jürgen 1941–
German social historian

Jürgen Kocka has been one of the leading German social historians since the 1970s. Together with Hans-Ulrich Wehler, with whom he collaborated closely at the newly founded University of Bielefeld between 1973 and 1988, he developed and defended a concept and program of social history, known under such labels as *Gesellschaftsgeschichte*, *Sozialgeschichte*, or *Geschichte als (kritische) historische Sozialwissenschaft*. This conception of history was formulated in the late 1960s and 1970s primarily in a conscious opposition to traditional history. In *Sozialgeschichte* (Social History, 1977) Kocka outlined its characteristics: in contrast to traditional history, social history stressed the importance of social and economic factors, while simultaneously striving to connect the social, political, and cultural spheres. In contrast to traditional history, social history also emphasized the importance of collective factors in history and downplayed the role of the individual. In the same vein it stressed, in contrast to traditional narrative history, the necessity of social science methods and theories in the study of history, especially comparative approaches. Kocka demonstrated the potential of this approach in his dissertation on the history of the Siemens company, and then in his social history of Germany during World War I: *Klassengesellschaft im Krieg* (1973; *Facing Total War*, 1984). In the Siemens book – at the same time a pioneer work in the emerging field of entrepreneurial history – he used Max Weber's typology of formal bureaucracy for modern capitalistic enterprises; in *Klassengesellschaft* he used a model inspired by Marxist theories of class and state.

Although in many respects the *Gesellschaftsgeschichte* was part of a broad international movement of historiographical renewal in Europe and North America, at the same time it bore important historiographical characteristics peculiar to post-1945 (West) Germany. This is borne out by the fact that, in an indirect way, most studies by Kocka (and by Wehler) tried to answer the question of how it was possible that Germany started two world wars within three decades and how it had organized a mass murder without precedent in history. This so-called problem of the German *Sonderweg* structured the research agenda and the debates of the *Gesellschaftsgeschichte* from the 1960s until the 1990s. Paradoxically, the *Sonderweg* thesis itself has been seriously modified – and to some extent undermined – along the way.

Kocka's first major area of interest was the rise and the political role of the middle classes (*Mittelstand*) in German history from 1850 to 1940. The new middle class of white collar workers (*Angestellten*) especially drew his attention because Nazi voters had been disproportionately recruited from these social groups. In his *Habilitationsschrift: Angestellte zwischen Faschismus und Demokratie* (1977; *White Collar Workers in America*, 1980) and in *Die Angestellten in der deutschen Geschichte* (White Collar Workers in German History, 1981) he analyzed the characteristics of the new middle classes in Germany in comparison with the United States, England, and France. According to Kocka it was their identification with the state and with the civil servant as "role model" and normative "reference group" that distinguished German employees from their counterparts elsewhere. The orientation in Germany of the new middle classes toward the state created a deeper social and political cleavage between them and the working class than, for instance, in France and the US, and was promoted by the state and the employers for exactly this reason – with fatal consequences in 1933. Only after the disastrous experience with the Nazi state did the employees in Germany lose their traditional *Privatbeamte* orientation toward the state and develop a consciousness as salaried workers or *angestellte Arbeitnehmer*.

After his studies of the new German middle classes Kocka devoted his attention to the "making" of the German working class. In *Lohnarbeit und Klassenbildung* (1983; "Problems of Working-Class Formation in Germany," 1986), *Weder Stand noch Klasse* (Neither Estate nor Class, 1990), and *Arbeitsverhältnisse und Arbeiterexistenzen* (Labor Relations and Labor Lives, 1990), he traced in a detailed way the experiences of the different groups belonging to the working class.

These experiences were interpreted in the general framework Kocka had developed earlier and in which the particular role of the Prussian-German bureaucratic state was emphasized in comparison with France. The state in Prussia/Germany represented a stronger disciplining power with regard to the working class than in Western Europe by identifying itself more intensively and for a longer period with the interests of the trades and employers. As a consequence the tension between the classes in Germany was more intense than in Western Europe and the ideological and political orientation of the working class more radical: the political party of the German working class was the only one in the West that officially adopted Marxism as its ideology and political program. Consequently, the liberals in Germany were faced with an independent political party of the working class much earlier than elsewhere and were in a worse position *vis-à-vis* the conservatives. Under the leadership of the "white revolutionary" Bismarck the conservatives were even able to tap the forces of nationalism – traditionally linked to liberalism – for their rightist policies. After the German unification of 1871, made possible by a victorious Prussian army, they therefore could exploit democratic means – the introduction of universal male suffrage – to reach undemocratic political ends – the conservation of political power by a small, predominantly aristocratic elite.

Because of these events the German liberals were not equal to the tasks their Western European counterparts had fulfilled under more favorable circumstances: the introduction of a democratic parliamentary system. According to Kocka, the conjunction of three major problems in Germany between 1848 and 1870 – the problems of creating a constitution and a national state, and of solving the "social problem" caused by 19th-century industrialization – problems that could be solved one at a time elsewhere in Western Europe – was simply too much for the German liberals to handle. In the Weimar period the resulting illiberal legacy of the German empire could be exploited by the old and new Right in politics – with the Nazi takeover in 1933 the fatal result.

The alleged particularity of German liberalism and its social support, the German bourgeoisie, became the focus of a major research project for Kocka in the 1980s and early 1990s. Remarkably for social history, the defining characteristics of the bourgeoisie came from a distinctive culture and lifestyle and not a distinctive social position. In the 3-volume *Bürgertum im 19. Jahrhundert* (1988; *Bourgeois Society in Nineteenth-Century Europe*, 1993), the comparison of the German bourgeoisie was extended to Eastern Europe and put into a new perspective. The German bourgeoisie was more modern and liberal than that of Eastern Europe. However, the bourgeois orientation towards the state – and the relative importance of the state-employed *Bildungsbürgertum* – remained a major distinctive feature of Germany in contrast to the West.

This focus on an east-west comparison and on the role of culture – including nationalism – also characterizes Kocka's latest project, which is the successor of the *Bürgertums* project: a comparative history of the rise of civil society in Europe. His work on the history of the former German Democratic Republic and its integration in the new Federal Republic, begun after his move from Bielefeld to Berlin in 1988, already exemplified his interest in Eastern Europe following the collapse of the Soviet empire. The central role in this project of the idea of civil society as both a cultural and a political force will illustrate how social history integrates cultural history into its conception.

CHRIS LORENZ

See also Conze; Europe: Modern; Germany: 1800–1945; Quantitative; Wehler

Biography

Born Haindorf, Germany, 19 April 1941, son of an engineer. Attended University of Marburg, 1960–61; MA, University of North Carolina, Chapel Hill, 1965; PhD, Free University of Berlin, 1968. Taught at University of Münster, 1968–73; University of Bielefeld, 1973–88: director, Center for Interdisciplinary Research, 1984–88; and Free University of Berlin, from 1988. Married Ute Schild, teacher, 1967.

Principal Writings

Unternehmensverwaltung und Angestelltenschaft am Beispiel Siemens, 1847–1914: Zum Verhältnis von Kapitalismus und Bürokratie in der deutschen Industrialisierung (Firm Management and the Employee: Siemens, 1847–1914: The Relationship Between Capitalism and Bureaucracy in German Industrialization), 1969

Klassengesellschaft im Krieg: Deutsche Sozialgeschichte, 1914–1918, 1973; in English as *Facing Total War: German Society, 1914–1918*, 1984

Editor, with Gerhard Albert Ritter, *Statistische Arbeitsbucher zur neueren deutschen Geschichte* (Statistical Workbooks on Contemporary German History), 9 vols. to date, 1975–

Unternehmer in der deutschen Industrialisierung (Industrialists of German Industrialization), 1975

Angestellte zwischen Faschismus und Demokratie: Zur politischen Sozialgeschichte der Angestellten: USA 1890–1940 im internationalen Vergleich, 1977; in English as *White Collar Workers in America, 1890–1950: A Social-Political History in International Perspective*, 1980

Sozialgeschichte: Begriff, Entwicklung, Probleme (Social History: Concept, Development, Problems), 1977

Editor with Thomas Nipperdey, *Theorie und Erzählung in der Geschichte* (Theory and Narrative in History), 1979

Die Angestellten in der deutschen Geschichte, 1850–1980: Vom Privatbeamten zum angestellten Arbeitnehmer (White Collar Workers in German History, 1850–1980: From the Private "Civil Servant" to the White Collar Worker), 1981

Lohnarbeit und Klassenbildung: Arbeiter und Arbeiterbewegung in Deutschland, 1800–1875, 1983; in English as "Problems of Working-Class Formation in Germany: The Early Years," in Ira Katznelson and Aristide R. Zolberg, eds., *Working-Class Formation: Nineteenth Century Patterns in Western Europe and the United States*, 1986

Bürgertum im 19. Jahrhundert: Deutschland im europäischen Vergleich, 3 vols., 1988; revised 1995; editor with Allan Mitchell in English as *Bourgeois Society in Nineteenth-Century Europe*, 1993

Arbeitsverhältnisse und Arbeiterexistenzen: Grundlagen der Klassenbildung im 19. Jahrhundert (Labor Relations and Labor Lives: Foundations of Class Formation in the 19th Century), 1990

Weder Stand noch Klasse: Unterschichten um 1800 (Neither Estate nor Class: The Lower Estates around 1800), 1990

Vereinigungskrise: Zur Geschichte der Gegenwart (The Crises of Unification: The Present as History), 1995

Editor with Heinz-Gerhard Haupt, *Geschichte und Vergleich: Ansätze und Ergebnisse international vergleichender Geschichtsschreibung* (History and Comparison: Approaches and Results of International Comparative History), 1996

"The Difficult Rise of a Civil Society: Societal History of Modern Germany," in Mary Fulbrook, ed., *German History since 1800*, 1997

Further Reading

Mergel, Thomas, and Thomas Welskopp, eds., *Geschichte zwischen Kultur und Gesellschaft: Beiträge zur Theoriedebatte* (History between Culture and Society: Contributions to the Debate on Historical Theory), 1997

Kołakowski, Leszek 1927–
Polish historian of philosophy and religion

Few intellectual historians can match the range of Leszek Kołakowski's contributions to the history of philosophy and religion. In a career that now spans over forty years, he has produced dazzling studies of such major figures as Augustine, Spinoza, Pascal, Bergson, and Husserl; a first-rate history and critique of the positivist strand in modern philosophy; and a series of penetrating essays on the themes of myth, religion, and the quest for the Absolute. But the work for which he is best known is a 3-volume history of Marxism, *Glowne nurty marksizmu* (1976–78). This magisterial survey, which appeared as *Main Currents of Marxism* in 1978, weighed in at 1500 pages, and analyzed over a hundred significant figures in the Marxist tradition.

Before Kołakowski, perhaps only George Lichtheim had written on the whole history of Marxist thought with comparable breadth and insight. But Lichtheim had tended to view the history of Marxism through social democratic lenses: for him, Marx's legacy was damaged first by Engels' crude positivism, then by Lenin's elitism, Stalin's barbarism, and Mao's

populism. For Kołakowski, in contrast, the later catastrophes to which the Marxist tradition was prone were already implicit in Marx's own theorizing, and Marx was no social democrat. To be sure, Kołakowski had once been a leading advocate of a revisionist Marxist humanism in Poland, but by the mid-1970s, writing in exile, he had repudiated that perspective. *Main Currents of Marxism* is a long and rigorous critique of a tradition Kołakowski regarded as hopelessly flawed by the dream of perfect unity that he traced all the way back to Neoplatonism.

Kołakowski's interpretation of Marx owed a great deal to the work of the Hungarian philosopher Georgy Lukács. Lukács had been one of the first commentators to emphasize the Hegelian roots of Marxism. Before Lukács, in the "golden age" of the Second International, Marxists tended to divide into two warring camps: the orthodox (Kautsky, Plekhanov) who regarded Marxism as a science and who took a determinist view of allegedly immanent laws of historical development; and neo-Kantian revisionists (Bernstein, Jaurès) who sought to inject a medley of ethical notions into Marxist thought. Lukács, according to Kołakowski, was the first to show that neither side fully comprehended the dialectical role of the proletariat in Marx's thought: theory and practice, freedom and necessity, existence and essence, normative values and historical realities, subjective experience and objective laws – all arrive at identity in the consciousness of the working class as it suffers and overcomes the alienation of labor in history. "It is an essential feature of Marx's thought," Kołakowski wrote in his first volume, "that he avoided both the normative and the purely deterministic approach, and it is in this that he shows himself to be a Hegelian and not a member of the utopian school."

But Kołakowski found a concealed utopianism in Marx's thought after all: to overcome alienation and the division of labor, to put an end to class conflict, to the division of life into public and private spheres – these are utopian goals, however much Marx may have claimed to have found them grounded in the objective movement of historical events. But since the proletariat cannot in fact spontaneously fulfill these messianic functions, the Marxist program for the unification of civil and political society can be accomplished only by coercion from above, the recipe for which was supplied by Lenin. Kołakowski's third volume traced "the breakdown" of the Marxist tradition: on the one hand, the ossification of Marxism in the party-states of the east; on the other, the development of what Kołakowski regarded as a variety of fraudulent and academic versions of Marxism in the west.

In the brilliant essays ("semiphilosophical sermons," as he called them) on contemporary dilemmas of politics and religion collected in *Modernity on Endless Trial* (1990), Kołakowski emerges as a powerful anti-utopian thinker. Here he was "trying to point out a number of unpleasant and insoluble dilemmas that loom up every time we attempt to be perfectly consistent when we think about our culture, our politics, and our religious life." Kołakowski has been faithful to Kant, committed to that philosopher's belief in the progression of rationality, but also persuaded that "the crooked timber" of humanity can never be fully straightened, that human recalcitrance subverts the dream of perfectibility. His most recent book, *God Owes Us Nothing*, analyzed Christian questions of sin and grace from the perspectives of Augustine and Pascal;

like them, he is resolutely anti-Pelagian. For Kołakowski, philosophy's original sin is monism, the aspiration toward perfect unity; religion is the corrective, the perpetual reminder of human imperfection. With another great historian of ideas, Isaiah Berlin, Kołakowski has been one of the most eloquent and erudite advocates of pluralism in the second half of the 20th century.

BRUCE THOMPSON

See also Thompson, E.

Biography

Born Radom, 23 October 1927. Educated at University of Lodz, 1945–50, MA 1950; PhD, University of Warsaw, 1953. Taught philosophy, University of Lodz, 1947–49; and (rising to professor) University of Warsaw, 1950–68: expelled from Poland for political reasons, 1968; senior research fellow, All Souls College, Oxford, 1970–95. Married Tamara Dynenson, psychiatrist, 1949 (1 daughter).

Principal Writings

Klucz niebieski: albo, Opowieści budujace z historii świętej zebrane ku pouczeniu i przestrodge, 1964; in English as *The Devil and Scripture*, 1973

Filozofia pozytywistyczna; od Hume'a do Koła Wiedeńskiego, 1966; in English as *The Alienation of Reason: A History of Positivist Thought*, 1968; and as *Positivist Philosophy from Hume to the Vienna Circle*, 1972

Marxism and Beyond: On Historical Understanding and Individual Responsibility, 1969

Główne nurty marksizmu: powstanie, rozwój, rozkład, 3 vols., 1976–78; in English as *Main Currents of Marxism: Its Rise, Growth, and Dissolution*, 3 vols., 1978

Religion, If There Is No God – : On God, the Devil, Sin, and Other Worries of the So-Called Philosophy of Religion, 1982

Modernity on Endless Trial, 1990

God Owes Us Nothing: A Brief Remark on Pascal's Religion and on the Spirit of Jansenism, 1995

Further Reading

Hook, Sidney, "Spectral Marxism," *American Scholar* 49 (Spring 1980), 250–71

Kline, George L., "Beyond Revisionism: Leszek Kołakowski's Recent Philosophical Development," *TriQuarterly* 22 (Fall 1971), 13–47

Siegel, Jerrold, "Consciousness and Practice in the History of Marxism," *Comparative Studies in Society and History* 24 (1982), 164–77

Thompson, E.P., "An Open Letter to Leszek Kołakowski," *The Socialist Register 1973*, edited by Ralph Miliband and John Saville, London: Merlin, 1974, 1–100

Kolko, Gabriel 1932–

US historian

A neo-Marxist and economic determinist, Gabriel Kolko is arguably the most "left" of the New Left historians who emerged in the 1960s. Kolko was a founding member of this radical group of relatively young historians, and his unremitting and relentless attack on American foreign policy has never strayed from his belief that the American capitalist system is fundamentally flawed. Kolko maintains that from a historic commitment to ever-expanding markets and easy access to raw materials, the United States has formulated an aggressive foreign policy that is innately exploitative, immoral, and imperialistic. As Joseph Siracusa notes in his *New Left Diplomatic Histories and Historians* (1993), New Left historians believed that effective foreign policy could be achieved only by throwing off the capitalist political economy and establishing a non-expanding democratic socialist state.

Disillusioned by the Vietnam War and convinced that the simplistic good versus evil approach to the Cold War was a fabrication of American foreign policymakers, the New Left embarked on an economic interpretation of American foreign policy. Dennis Smith, in his review of *Empire and Revolution* by David Horowitz (1970), called the New Left a "historiography of protest," challenging both the Orthodox school and the Realist school. The former was dismissed by the New Left for its belief that the USSR was an aggressive state and thus responsible for the Cold War. The latter was faulted for misinterpreting the guiding principles of American foreign policy. Foreign policy was not based on what George Kennan called "the legalistic-moralistic approach to international problems" (*American Diplomacy, 1900–1950*, 1951) but rather on America's pro-active commitment to establishing a capitalist world order dominated by the United States. There is no doubt that, just like the schools they criticized, New Left historians let their political agenda influence their assessment of history. However, their approach and the questions they raised cannot be dismissed as irrelevant.

Gabriel Kolko's most important works are *The Politics of War* (1968) and *The Limits of Power* (1972), which he wrote with his wife Joyce Kolko. In *The Politics of War*, Kolko argues that the foundation of postwar American foreign policy was rooted in a history of aggressive expansionism. In the years 1943–45, America was committed to a dual policy of winning the war through military prowess and laying the foundation for a postwar world in which America's economic needs were met by an easy access to raw materials and the continual expansion of markets for surplus American goods. This second component was promoted by secretary of state Cordell Hull, who, according to Kolko, was the primary American policy-maker during the war.

Postwar American foreign policy, according to Kolko, was active imperialism, not a reaction to perceived aggressive Soviet moves. Kolko, in fact, broke from other members of the New Left by insisting that the atomic bomb was not utilized to intimidate the Soviets, but rather it was primarily used as a means to end the war. Anti-Soviet policy actually preceded the use of the bombs. American foreign policy was based on a commitment to exert American economic power worldwide, dominate the newly established United Nations, International Monetary Fund, and World Bank, suppress leftist movements, as they were seen as inherently threatening to worldwide stability, break down the British empire and its preferential trade practices, and check the expansion of the USSR.

Most New Left historians concede some responsibility of the USSR for the Cold War, but they place primary blame on the United States. The Kolkos, however, in *The Limits of Power*, argued that the United States was solely responsible. Building on *The Politics of War*, *The Limits of Power* analyzed American foreign policy in the years 1945–54. "Conflict and violence," the Kolkos stated, "are inevitable consequences" of America's postwar objective to dominate a worldwide open door policy of unencumbered access to trade and investment and perpetually expanding markets. American business needed stable, capitalist trading partners. To protect its interests and secure such states, the United States was willing to flex its military and economic muscle to obstruct leftist revolutionary nationalist movements abroad. Rhetoric by policymakers that espoused the importance of self-determination or America's concern with aiding nations in their postwar recovery could be easily dismissed as disingenuous. The bottom line for all American foreign policy decisions, according to Kolko, "was not the containment of communism, but rather more directly the extension and expansion of American capitalism according to its new economic power and needs."

Fearing another depression, American policymakers wore blinkers when it came to the Left and the Soviet Union. Both business and government leaders saw the Left and the Soviets as synonymous, and they mistakenly concluded that leftist movements were orchestrated by Moscow. Stalin was wrongly seen as an ideologue bent on world revolution. In fact, according to Kolko, Stalin was conservative, the consummate pragmatist whose actions were dictated by a realistic assessment of Soviet strengths and weaknesses in postwar Europe.

Kolko has been accused of projecting the disillusionment he felt with America in the 1960s back onto his interpretation of American history. There is merit to the charge that Kolko at least minimized, if not discounted, non-economic factors in his assessment of American foreign policy. In addition, his focus of faulting only American foreign policy, overlooking even egregious Soviet actions, gives fuel to his critics. But any student of American foreign policy would be wrong to dismiss Kolko as a mere polemicist. Certainly his Marxist revisionism took the arguments of the New Left to the extreme. But while other New Left historians have softened their view of America's responsibility for the Cold War, Kolko remains an unrepentant and unyielding New Left historian, condemning the United States for its imperialist foreign policy. Kolko's penetrating look at the historical continuity of an American foreign policy based on economic interests and an open door policy, which he sees as inherently imperialist, must be recognized, even if it is not embraced.

ELIZABETH B. ELLIOT-MEISEL

See also LaFeber; United States: 20th Century; United States: Historical Writing, 20th Century; Vietnam

Biography
Born Paterson, New Jersey, 17 August 1932. Received BA, Kent State University, 1954; MS, University of Wisconsin, 1955; PhD, Harvard University, 1962. Fellow, Social Science Research Council, 1963–64; taught at University of Pennsylvania, 1964–68; rose to professor, State University of New York, Buffalo, 1968–70; and York University, 1970–92 (emeritus). Married Joyce Manning, historian, 1955.

Principal Writings
"American Business and Germany, 1930–1941," *Western Political Quarterly* 15 (1962), 713–28
Wealth and Power in America: An Analysis of Social Class and Income Distribution, 1962

The Triumph of Conservatism: A Reinterpretation of American History, 1900–1916, 1963
Railroads and Regulation, 1877–1916, 1965
The Politics of War: The World and United States Foreign Policy, 1943–1945, 1968
The Roots of American Foreign Policy: An Analysis of Power and Purpose, 1969
With Joyce Kolko, *The Limits of Power: The World and United States Foreign Policy, 1945–1954*, 1972
Main Currents in Modern American History, 1976
Anatomy of a War: Vietnam, the United States, and the Modern Historical Experience, 1985; in UK as *Vietnam: Anatomy of a War, 1940–1975*, 1987
Confronting the Third World: United States Foreign Policy, 1945–1980, 1988
Vietnam: Anatomy of a Peace, 1997

Further Reading
Cohen, Warren I., *The American Revisionists: The Lessons of Intervention in World War I*, Chicago: University of Chicago Press, 1967
Paterson, Thomas G., and Robert J. McMahon, eds., *The Origins of the Cold War*, 3rd edition, Lexington, MA: Heath, 1991.
Siracusa, Joseph M., *New Left Diplomatic Histories and Historians: The American Revisionists*, Port Washington, NY: Kennikat Press, 1973; revised edition Claremont, CA: Regina, 1993

Komnene, Anna 1083–c.1153/4
Byzantine princess and Greek historian

One of the few female historians of any importance until modern times, Anna Komnene came of a society that did not totally deny education to women, especially to those who enjoyed her status as a princess of the reigning dynasty. She was understandably proud of her learning, which seems to have given her a solid command of the ancient Greek traditions of literature, philosophy, science, and medicine. A surviving eulogy of her by the 12th-century writer George Tornikios confirms her own professions of delight in scholarship.

Born early in the reign of her father, Alexios I Komnenos (1081–1118), she observed through youthful eyes the momentous events of that epoch, while her status would have given her, for much of her life, access to its important personalities and documents. Her only surviving literary work is one of the crown-jewels of Byzantine historical writing, and one of the most important histories written between ancient and modern times, both as a source and as a work of literature. This is her *Alexías*, or *Alexiad*, her laudatory history of her father's life and reign, a prose history in Greek whose title consciously evokes that of the *Ilías* or *Iliad* by her favorite poet, Homer, casting her father thereby as a veritably epic character. It is not known when she began to write it, but the bulk of the work, and certainly the latter portions, clearly date from the 1140s, some three decades after her father's death, and reflect her resentments toward her brother, emperor John II, and the bitter frustrations of her later years; it has been suggested that she also meant to praise her father's glories as a critique of her nephew, emperor Manuel I (reigned 1143–80).

One motivation was certainly in line with the traditions of Byzantine historical writing, the convention of one writer picking up where a predecessor had left off. Komnene's husband, a cultivated man, had written, some time after Alexios' death, a memoir of the years 1070–79, describing the struggles among leading aristocratic families for the throne. Anna felt an obligation to pick up the thread of narrative from her husband, though his possible covert hints of criticism of the young Alexios may have prompted her the more to create a glowing picture of her father, while a nostalgic return to the years of her youth would have provided an escape from the sorrows of her old age.

Despite her personal agenda, Komnene understood the responsibilities of serious and "professional" historical writing, to which she paid eloquent tribute in her prologue. She cast her work in 15 books, the first two of which traced her father's career up to his accession, the remainder covering his reign until his death. Komnene's chronology is sometimes less than strict or clear, and she sometimes omitted information or treatments that had to be taken from other sources of the time. Nevertheless, she was remarkably thorough and conscientious in what she covered. Her account of the First Crusade and its passage through Byzantium – which she would have observed as a teenage girl – is one of the most important we have. She was particularly fascinated by military operations, and gave some invaluable descriptions of weapons and tactics. She had a strong feeling for personalities and offered some remarkably perceptive and subtle portraits of leading characters (such as her grandmother Anna Dalassena, the Norman leaders Robert Guiscard and Bohemond, and the heterodox philosopher John Italos).

Conservative in her viewpoint, Komnene displayed strong biases. Although her learning tempered her own religious beliefs with some rationalism, she detested heresy and expressed unseemly exultation in the martyrdom of Basil the Bogomil. In her characteristically Byzantine ethnic pride, she was contemptuous of all things foreign, especially regarding the Western Europeans and the Roman church. She exhibited ostentatious horror at foreign names, doing her best to retain archaizing nomenclature. Beyond this, her Greek style displayed all the foibles of classicizing artificiality favored by Byzantium's intellectuals.

Whatever her faults and deficiencies, however, Komnene remains a writer and historian of remarkable stature, whose work still has the capacity to bring alive the personalities and events of a dramatic era.

JOHN W. BARKER

See also Byzantium; Eastern Orthodoxy

Biography

Born Constantinople, 2 December 1083, first child of emperor Alexios I Komnenos, and betrothed early to Constantine Doukas, initial heir-presumptive. Received a broad and thorough classical education. With the demotion and death of Constantine, wed in 1097 to the important noble Nikephoros Bryennios (4 children). Despite great family controversy, she was denied succession rights at Alexios' death in 1118, in favor of her younger brother John II (1118–43); failed in attempted coup on husband's behalf against John; after husband's death in 1137 kept in semi-confinement at Kecharitomene convent; in her last years, deep in nostalgia, bitterness, and self-pity, composed the *Alexiad* in praise of her father. Alive during reign of her nephew Manuel I (1143–80) at least until 1148; exact date of death disputed, *c.*1153/4.

Principal Writings

Alexiad, written 1138–48; as *The Alexiad of Anna Comnena*, translated by E.R.A. Sewter, 1969

Further Reading

Angold, Michael, *The Byzantine Empire, 1025–1204: A Political History*, London and New York: Longman, 1984
Buckler, Georgina, *Anna Comnena: A Study*, Oxford: Oxford University Press, 1929
Chalandon, Ferdinand, *Les Comnène*, vol. 1: *Essai sur le règne d'Alexis 1er Comnène (1081–1118)* (The Comnenas, vol. 1: Essay on the Reign of Alexios I Comnena), Paris: Picard, 1900; reprinted New York: B. Franklin, 1960
Dalven, Rae, *Anna Comnena*, New York: Twayne, 1972
Diehl, Charles, "Anne Comnène," in his *Figures byzantines*, vol. 2, Paris: Colin, 1927
Foakes-Jackson, F.J., "Anna Comnena," *Hibbert Journal* 33 (1935), 430–42
Hunger, Herbert, "Stilstufen in der byzantinischen Geschichtsschreibung des 12. Jahrhunderts: Anna Komnena und Michael Glykas" (Styles in Byzantine Historical Writing of the 12th Century), *Byzantine Studies/Etudes Byzantines* 5 (1978), 139–70
Kurtz, E., "Das Testament der Anna Komnena" (The Testament of Anna Komnene), *Byzantinische Zeitschrift* 16 (1907), 93–101
Miller, William, "A Byzantine Blue Stocking: Anna Comnena," in his *Essays on the Latin Orient*, Cambridge: Cambridge University Press, 1921, 533–50
Mitchison, Naomi, *Anna Comnena*, London: Howe, 1928

Kong-zi [Confucius] 551–479 BCE
Chinese philosopher-historian

Universally renowned as China's first teacher and first self-conscious philosopher, Kong-zi (better known by the 16th-century Latinization of Kong Fu-zi, Confucius) has exerted greater influence on the intellectual heritage of China than any other single individual. Kong-zi claimed always to be a "transmitter" rather than a "creator" of tradition, and his legacy largely rests on his reputation as an enthusiastic guardian of an idealized past. Committed to the values that he most closely associated with the early or Western Zhou dynasty (c.1100–771 BCE), Kong-zi dedicated his life to an attempt to recreate the early Zhou world in his own time. Most notably, he desired to restore the harmonious sociopolitical order that the Zhou forebears had reputedly enjoyed. In this effort, he considered himself ultimately to have failed.

Kong-zi subscribed to the values of the ancient *shi* (knight) class, originally the lowest tier of the Zhou aristocracy without the benefits of hereditary privilege. Several centuries before Kong-zi's birth, this class had already begun to become increasingly merged with the class of *ru* (weaklings) – whose members, by virtue of their role as custodians of the revered past literary tradition, had been the original authorities on the performance of rites and ceremonies. This progressive merging of classes led to a blending of functions that finally resulted in the appearance of a new type of ministerial *shi* – a class skilled in the arts of diplomacy and knowledgeable in the use of classical texts and proper etiquette, but also often unscrupulous and cruel in its pragmatism. Kong-zi distinguished himself within this emerging class by his unwavering beliefs that the lost moral equilibrium of a much earlier age could be recaptured and that this could be facilitated only by a unique political actor called the *junzi* (superior man or gentleman).

Despite desiring to establish himself as an expert on the inheritance of Chinese cultural tradition up to his time, Kong-zi left behind no written work expressing his own views. For all reliable information on his life and thought, we are dependent on a short collection of miscellaneous sayings assembled by at least two generations of his disciples called the *Lunyu* (*The Analects*). Thus, the source that best informs our own understanding of Kong-zi's ideas and aspirations is entirely indirect. Nevertheless, despite its removed authorship and its almost random and jumbled flavor, the *Analects* does supply us with a legitimate – albeit sole – means of penetrating and making intelligible Kong-zi's thinking.

In the *Analects*, the term *junzi* – which originally meant merely "ruler" – becomes transformed into Kong-zi's image of the most humanistically accomplished of individuals. Kong-zi defined *junzi* status as a product of education rather than birthright. Consequently, becoming a *junzi* was now within the reach of anyone because it first and foremost involved deeply educating oneself in the *li*, or rites appropriate to one's station, which itself naturally changed throughout the course of life. "Let the ruler be a ruler, the minister a minister, the father a father, the son a son," said Kong-zi. This, after all, constituted the essence of government, since governing well meant nothing more than extending the same protocol regulating the family to the venue of the state.

A further aim of Kong-zi and the men hardly younger than himself who clustered around him as students was to establish the *junzi* as a model purveyor of what was called the "kingly" Dao, or Way. The *junzi* led others along this Way and this itself was facilitated by his example, which was always forthright, loyal, tolerant, and refined but, most of all, *ren* – "benevolent" or "humane." *Ren* is the all-embracing altruism that became the most central virtue Kong-zi esteemed, and it was to be demonstrated in his time as it had been in the early Zhou – by cherishing antiquity, following the rites, and doing nothing to anyone that one would not wish visited upon oneself. For Kong-zi, *ren* represented the core of humanity and it was not only a defining but an irresistible state. Said Kong-zi, "Of neighborhoods, benevolence is the most beautiful. How can the man be considered wise who, given the choice, does not settle in benevolence?"

Nevertheless, despite the exalted and almost transcendental qualities he attributed to the *junzi* and to the virtue *ren*, we cannot find much in Kong-zi's outlook that readily resembles conventional religion. Preoccupied with affairs of the present moment, Kong-zi consciously focused on man's concerns and commented little on the gods and spirits that had so obsessed the generations of the pre-Zhou world. Even his position on the existence of the supernatural was suggestively agnostic and he posited absolutely no belief in an afterlife. "While according respect to supernatural beings," he said, "one should keep them at a distance."

History was obviously important to Kong-zi but, aside from mention of the fabled Duke of Zhou – his consummate *junzi* archetype – he made only scant references to past personages. Kong-zi instead provides much information on his many aristocratic contemporaries both within and beyond his small home state of Lu, and especially on their unreceptive attitudes.

His familiarity with the views of these feudal dukes stemmed directly from his frustrating search to find one of them willing to put his perhaps overly idealistic system into practice. Thirteen years of wandering near the end of his life produced no discernible results. But, even in this failure, Kong-zi established the role of itinerant counselor to the powerful that has characterized all *shi* who have succeeded him.

Although he lamented in the end being "known by Heaven but not at all by men," Kong-zi left behind an imprint on his civilization that is indelible and that belies his claims of having had nothing original to contribute. His dignity amidst turmoil and his opposition to the destructive trends of his era against which he was overmatched make his many insights appear all the more noble and fresh today. For his principled defense of traditional mores and the learned life, Kong-zi's reward after death was the eventual adoption of his beloved values by an entire culture.

DON J. WYATT

See also China: Ancient; China: Historical Writing, Ancient; China: Historical Writing, Late Imperial; Rhetoric

Biography

Kong-zi or Confucius. Born Zou (now in Shandong Province), 551 BCE. Studied in Lu. Died 479 BCE.

Principal Writings

Lunyu; in English as *The Analects*

Further Reading

Creel, H.G., *Confucius: The Man and the Myth*, New York: Day, 1949; London: Routledge, 1951

Dawson, Raymond, *Confucius*, Oxford: Oxford University Press, and New York: Hill and Wang, 1981

Do-Dinh, Pierre, *Confucius and Chinese Humanism*, New York: Funk and Wagnalls, 1969

Eber, Irene, *Confucianism: The Dynamics of Tradition*, New York: Macmillan, 1986

Fingarette, Herbert, *Confucius: The Secular as Sacred*, New York: Harper & Row, 1972

Hall, David L., *Thinking Through Confucius*, Albany: State University of New York Press, 1987

Jensen, Lionel M., *Manufacturing Confucianism: Chinese Traditions and Universal Civilization*, Durham, NC: Duke University Press, 1997

Kaizuka, Shigeki, *Confucius*, London: Allen and Unwin, and New York, Macmillan, 1956

Liu Wu-chi, *Confucius: His Life and Times*, New York: Philosophical Library, 1955

Mote, Frederick W., *Intellectual Foundations of China*, New York: Knopf, 1971

Munro, Donald J., *The Concept of Man in Early China*, Stanford, CA: Stanford University Press, 1969

Rubin, Vitalii A., *Ideologia i kul'tura Drevnego Kitaia*, Moscow: Nauka, 1970; in English as *Individual and State in Ancient China: Essays on Four Chinese Philosophers*, New York: Columbia University Press, 1976

Schwartz, Benjamin I., *The World of Thought in Ancient China*, Cambridge, MA: Harvard University Press, 1985

Smith, D. Howard, *Confucius*, London: Temple Smith, and New York: Scribner, 1973

Wills, John E., Jr., *Mountain of Fame: Portraits in Chinese History*, Princeton: Princeton University Press, 1994

Koonz, Claudia

US historian of Germany

In 1969 Claudia Koonz began her academic career with an unpublished dissertation on Walther Rathenau's vision for the future of Germany. In addition to his service as a leader of industry and as a government official, Rathenau was also a prolific essayist who believed Germany required a radical redistribution of wealth and a reorganization of its economy. While serving as foreign minister in 1921–22, he was killed by right-wing extremists. Although this interesting figure still requires more study, in the 1970s, Koonz began to make a name for herself as a scholar of modern German women's history. In 1976, she produced several articles on the role of women during the Weimar years, and a year later, with Renate Bridenthal she co-edited *Becoming Visible: Women in European History* (1977).

In 1986, Koonz published her most important work, *Mothers in the Fatherland*, since translated into French, German, and Japanese. With this work, she gained prominence as an authority on the subject of women and national socialism. More important than Koonz's own research results, which were relatively predictable, are the questions she has raised about the role of feminism in preparing the way for genocide.

Koonz has forced historians of gender issues and of German history to acknowledge that national socialism cannot be identified as strictly masculine, without real appeal to women. She has shown that women's involvement in national socialism was not limited to a fascination with Hitler's charisma, but that women eagerly participated in the activities of the regime. The leaders of women's organizations were as eager to accomplish self-imposed *Gleichschaltung* (political coordination) as were the leaders of traditionally male organizations. According to Koonz, the elimination of working-class women's organizations tied to political parties facilitated the subordination of the remaining bourgeois German women's organizations to the national socialist leadership. Koonz notes with regret that women attracted to national socialism accepted the division of masculine from feminine spheres. Man's realm was the political and entrepreneurial, while women were to establish their separate sphere, the original *Lebensraum* – living space – for men's recreation and procreation. Here Koonz's work becomes problematic for feminists. On the one hand, she criticized the subordination of women to men and the establishment of this illusory feminine sphere, on the other hand she noted that women could be more successful than men as members of the resistance since women escaped notice in a society dominated by a cult of masculinity. Koonz also noted that those women who most clearly broke down the gender barriers surrounding them were those who also most clearly transgressed against the norms of civilized society: the concentration camp guards such as Ilse Koch, wife of the commandant at Buchenwald. Because the questions which Koonz has raised about feminism and civilization are important, her *Mothers in the Fatherland* will remain the standard reference point for both the study of women in national socialism and for work on broader gender issues.

With *Mothers in the Fatherland*, Koonz sparked a lively debate. For one, it has been noted that her work does not address the experience of working-class women. More significantly, Koonz has been criticized because she did not pursue the most important question of her book, the relationship of women and the Holocaust, to any firm conclusions.

Since publishing *Mothers in the Fatherland*, Koonz has pursued the contradictions between feminism and femininity in the Third Reich. In "Ethical Dilemmas and Nazi Eugenics" Koonz raised the issue of how religious women could oppose the regime's sterilization and euthanasia programs while turning a blind eye to the persecution of the Jews. She arrives at the conclusion that rejection of a particular policy did not imply a rejection of the regime as a whole. Thus, single-issue dissent could not be considered resistance.

MARTIN R. MENKE

See also Bock; Germany: 1800–1945

Biography

Claudia Ann Koonz. Received PhD, Rutgers University, 1970. Taught (rising to professor), College of the Holy Cross, Worcester, Massachusetts; and Duke University, from 1988.

Principal Writings

With Renate Bridenthal, "Beyond Kinder, Küche, Kirche: Weimar Women in Politics and Work," in Berenice Carroll, ed., *Liberating Women's History: Theoretical and Critical Essays*, 1976
"Conflicting Allegiances: Political Ideology and Women Legislators in Weimar Germany," *Signs: Journal of Women in Culture and Society* 1 (1976), 663–83
Editor with Renate Bridenthal, *Becoming Visible: Women in European History*, 1977; revised edition, with Bridenthal and Susan Stuard, 1987
Mothers in the Fatherland: Women, the Family, and Nazi Politics, 1986
"Ethical Dilemmas and Nazi Eugenics: Single-Issue Dissent in Religious Contexts," *Journal of Modern History* 64 (1992), S8–S31

Further Reading

Gordon, Linda, "Review of *Mothers in the Fatherland*," *Feminist Review* 27 (1987), 97–105

Köprülü, M.F. 1890–1966

Turkish literary and cultural historian

The most outstanding and widely recognized Turkish historian of the 20th century, Köprülü produced a body of historical writing that includes works on cultural, social, religious, legal, economic, and political history. His forte was literary, religious and cultural history. He is recognized internationally as the first Turkish scholar to employ European techniques, such as comparative textual criticism and critical methodology in his scholarly work. He had a superb mastery of Ottoman Turkish, Persian, and French and he knew German, English, and Arabic. He also had access to many unpublished manuscripts in the public and private libraries of Istanbul which greatly facilitated his work.

Köprülü was influenced in his early twenties by Ziya Gökalp, the Turkish nationalist ideologist, thinker, and exponent of the Turkism movement. He was an ardent Turkish nationalist and became active in politics at a young age, published poetry in his late teens, and by the age of 28 had already published one of his masterpieces, *Türk edebiyatında ilk mutasavvıflar* (Early Mystics in Turkish Literature, 1918). This work focused on the great Turkic poets Ahmet Yesevi and Yunus Emre. Köprülü situated the two poets into a broad historical context, illuminating many aspects of the ways and means by which much of Central Asia and Turkey was turkized and islamized. Both of these developments are at the core of contemporary Ottoman, Turkic, and Islamic studies. His early work on comparative texts provided the foundation of the epochal study of the origins of the Ottoman empire 12 years later.

In 1920–21 Köprülü published *Türk edebiyatı tarihi* (The History of Turkish Literature) which was the first attempt by any scholar to write a comprehensive history of Turkic literature up to the 15th century. This endeavor necessitated wide research into the early religious and cultural history of all of the Turkic peoples, and especially the role of the Muslim mystical brotherhood (*tarikats*). This work, as well as most of his subsequent work, demonstrated the fundamental contribution of the beliefs, feelings, and practices of the pre-Islamic Turkic peoples of Central Asia to Islamic Turkic and Ottoman literature. This work far surpassed that of European Orientalists Joseph von Hammer and E.J.W. Gibb. These early publications demonstrated that the Turkic peoples had a history, a culture, and a "national spirit" prior to their islamization, and that the Turkic peoples were not dominated by Iranian literary and cultural forms. His ideas on these topics are still widely influential.

Starting in the 1930s, Köprülü had to struggle with extreme Turkish nationalist ideology and theories, strongly supported and advocated by the government, that postulated that Turks were the first people to inhabit the earth and that Turkish was the original language (*güneş lisanı*) spoken by mankind. The desire and need to combat such nonsensical theories played a role in Köprülü's publication of *Les Origines de l'Empire Ottoman* (1935; *The Origins of the Ottoman Empire*, 1992), which was the result of three lectures he delivered at the Sorbonne in 1934. This epochal work laid the foundations for the modern study of the origins of the empire, and it still influences strongly contemporary research. His scholarly explanations of the origins of the Ottoman empire were not appreciated in Turkey and the work was not published in Turkish until 1959. *Origins* is an original and brilliant history. It demolished H.A. Gibbons' theory that the first Ottomans were a "tribe of 400 tents" and that most of the first Ottomans were converted Greeks. Gibbons, reflecting the racism of European scholars of the time, suggested that Muslims, let alone Turks, would not have the genius to establish a great empire: only Christians could accomplish such a feat. Although Köprülü's emphasis on the tribal origins of the empire is no longer accepted, many of his ideas still obtain.

One of Köprülü's major works, "Bizans müesseselerinin Osmanlı müesselerine tesiri hakkında bâzı mülâhazalar" (Some Observations on the Influence of Byzantine Institutions on Ottoman Institutions), first published in article form in 1931, made a major contribution in establishing that most of the religious, cultural, legal, and financial institutions of the Ottoman empire were of Seljuk provenance and not mere imitations of Byzantine institutions as European Byzantinists emphatically stated. In this article Köprülü not only demonstrated the inadequacy of the scholarship of his European colleagues, but revealed the cultural bias and racism in which it was ensconced.

He was an able defender of the "other" long before it became a popular focus of scholarship in the 1980s and 1990s.

After 1940 Köprülü did not produce any major scholarly works. The reason for this was his active participation in politics. He became a member of parliament in 1935 and an active member of the leadership of the Republican Peoples' party (RPP). He helped lead the fight to keep Turkey neutral in World War II, and joined the opposition Democratic party (DP) in 1946, which, contrary to all expectations, came into power in 1950. Köprülü was appointed foreign minister (a position he held until 1955). After the DP was overthrown by a military coup in 1960, he was arrested on charges of treason, but was acquitted. Köprülü subsequently engaged in scholarly pursuits, but produced no more major studies. He died in 1966 as a result of injuries he sustained after he was struck by an automobile while walking back to his home from a meeting of his beloved Turkish History Society.

ROBERT OLSON

See also Ottoman

Biography

Mehmed[t] Fuad[t] Köprülü. Born 4 December 1890, a descendant of the famous Köprülü Ottoman imperial family. Attended Istanbul Law School, 1908–10, but did not graduate. Appointed instructor (rising to professor) in the history of Turkish literature, Istanbul University, 1913: director, Faculty of Letters in 1923. Member of parliament, 1935–45. One of three founding members of the Democratic party, which he served as foreign minister, 1950–55; arrested after the military coup in 1960, but acquitted of all charges. Married (1 daughter). Died 28 June 1966.

Principal Writings

Türk edebiyatında ilk mutasavvıflar (Early Mystics in Turkish Literature), 1918, revised, 1966
Türk edebiyatı tarihi (The History of Turkish Literature), 2 vols., 1920–21, reprinted 1980
Türkiye tarihi (The History of Turkey), 1923
Bizans müesseselerinin Osmanlı müesseselerine tesiri hakkında bâzı mülâhazalar, originally published 1931; reprinted in book form, 1981; in English as *Some Observations on the Influence of Byzantine Institutions on Ottoman Institutions*, 1996
Eski şairlerimiz: Dîvân edebiyatı antolojisi (Our Early Poets: An Anthology of Dîvân Literature), 1934
Türk dili ve edebiyatı hakkında araştırmalar (Research on Turkish Language and Literature), 1934
Les Origines de l'Empire Ottoman, 1935; in English as *The Origins of the Ottoman Empire*, 1992

Further Reading

Ahmad, Feroz, *The Turkish Experiment in Democracy, 1950–1975*, London: Hurst, and Boulder, CO: Westview Press, 1977
Berktay, Halil, *Cumhuriyet ideolojisi ve Fuat Köprülü* (The Ideology of the Republic and Fuat Köprülü), Istanbul: Kaynak Yayınları, 1983
Bisbee, Eleanor, *The New Turks: Pioneers of the Republic, 1920–1950*, Philadelphia: University of Pennsylvania Press, 1951
The Encyclopaedia of Islam, new edition, Leiden: Brill, 1960–, vol. 5
Köprülü, Orhan R., ed., *Fuad Köprülü*, Ankara: Kültür ve Turizm Bakanlığı, 1987
Park, George, *The Life and Writings of Mehmed Fuad Köprülü: The Intellectual and Turkish Modernization*, doctoral dissertation, Baltimore: Johns Hopkins University, 1975

Tamkoç, Metin, *The Warrior Diplomats: Guardians of the National Security and Modernization of Turkey*, Salt Lake City: University of Utah Press, 1976

Tansel, F.A., "Memleketimizin acı kayı, Prof. Dr. Fuad Köprülü (Our Country's Great Loss, Prof. Dr. Fuad Köprülü), *Belleten*, 30 (1966)

Turan, Osman, ed., *60. dogum yili munasebetiyle: Fuad Köprülü Armağanı* (*Festschrift* for Fuad Köprülü), Istanbul: Osman Yalcin Matbaasi, 1953

Korea

The long Confucian tradition of historical writing in Korea came under severe challenge in the last decades of the 19th century with the arrival of Western influence. Japan's forcible annexation and occupation of Korea in 1910, before Korea was able to adjust to the new realities, set much of the tone of Korea's historiography in the 20th century. Adapting quickly to Western practices, Japanese scholars were the first to apply the modern methodology of the West to the study of Korean history. Although their pioneering studies made significant contributions, Japanese scholarship on Korean history was often marred by the prejudices and biases that many Japanese carried toward Korea, resulting in negative images of Korean history. With the end of Japanese rule in 1945, Korean scholars tried to "rediscover" their history by rectifying the damage done by Japanese historians. Frustrated by the division of their country, historians in both North and South Korea were strongly influenced by nationalism in their effort to assert their ethos. One interesting phenomenon in South Korea is the near universal recognition of the importance of historical scholarship, so that important historical findings are closely watched even by the general public. Scholarship in English on Korean history, on the other hand, is still relatively underdeveloped, especially in comparison with that on China or Japan. Historical writings in English deal mostly with the modern period, leaving a large vacuum in the traditional period. Recently, however, there have been some important publications shedding significant new light on our understanding of Korean history.

The relationship between Korea and Japan in the ancient period is one of the most controversial topics in the historiography of the two countries. Perhaps the most significant contribution to this topic was the famous thesis first presented by Namio Egami in 1949 (and translated into English in 1964), based largely on archaeological evidence, that horseriders from the Asian continent may have conquered Japan, founding the first state of Yamato. Providing a sounder historical basis to the Egami thesis, Gari Ledyard, in his "Galloping along with the Horseriders" (1975) argued that it was the Puyŏ warriors from the present-day Manchuria region who conquered Japan, forming a "thalassocracy", which extended from the southern shore of Korea to Japan. Whether Japan had maintained a foothold in southern Korea in ancient times remains a subject of bitter contention among scholars in both Korea and Japan. In "Japan's Relations with the Asian Continent and the Korean Peninsula," (1958), Yasukazu Suematsu insisted that Japan extended its dominance in southern Korea through the intermediary of Mimana (Imna in Korean). This view, however, is vehemently rejected by Korean scholars. In *The Early History of Korea* (1969), K.H.J. Gardiner gave a succinct account of the earliest period of Korean history with emphasis on interactions with China and Japan. Gardiner, however, has been criticized for his ready acceptance of Japanese interpretations of controversial issues, such as Mimana, that are being disputed by Korean scholars.

For the study of Buddhism under Silla rule (57 BCE–935 CE), Robert Buswell, Jr., in his *The Formation of Ch'an Ideology in China and Korea* (1989), advanced a startling new thesis that the text of *Vajrasamadhi-sutra*, which had an enormous influence in the rise of Zen Buddhism in Asia, was authored by a Korean Buddhist named Pŏmnang, c.680 CE, and did not have a Chinese origin as earlier believed. The transition from the Unified Silla to the Koryŏ dynasty (918–1392), especially with regard to the alignment of power, is the subject of an important study by Hugh H.W. Kang in his "The First Succession Struggle of Koryŏ in 945" (1977). According to Kang, in 945, two opposing forces – one representing the former Silla aristocrats and the other embodying the upstart maritime interest group – collided head-on, and the triumph of the former narrowed the power base of the ruling structure of Koryŏ. The military rule under Koryŏ from 1170 to 1258 is the subject of several studies by Edward J. Shultz. In "Military Revolt in Koryŏ" (1979), Shultz disputed the traditional interpretation and contended that the military coup was the result of a power struggle between the king and his followers on one hand and the central aristocratic clans on the other. William E. Henthorn gave a narrative account of the Mongol invasion and an analysis of the Mongol demands made upon the Korean court in his *Korea: The Mongol Invasions* (1963). In Korea there were lively discussions on many issues about this period, such as whether the Koryŏ state can be characterized as aristocratic or bureaucratic.

The Chosŏn dynasty (1392–1910), also known as the Yi dynasty, was once much maligned historiographically in Korea for its inability, in the end, to resist Japanese imperialism. In addition, Japanese scholars before 1945 tried to cast the Neo-Confucian dynasty in a negative image in their efforts to justify the Japanese domination of Korea. Today, however, Korean scholars tend to view the Chosŏn dynasty more positively, and Western scholarship has also made some important contributions toward better understanding of the last Korean dynasty.

In *The Confucian Transformation of Korea* (1992), Martina Deuchler traced how Chosŏn society was transformed into a Neo-Confucian state with the implementation of the rigid Confucian rituals that emphasized patrilineality at the expense of women's social and economic positions. A masterly combination of historical and socio-anthropological study, this work made a seminal contribution toward understanding Korean society. The political conflict in the form of literati purges in the late 15th and the 16th centuries is generally interpreted by Korean scholars in terms of conflict between the entrenched meritorious elites (*hun'gu*) and the upstart Neo-Confucian literati (*sarim*). In *The Literati Purges* (1974), however, Edward W. Wagner sees the conflict more as an institutional power struggle between the monarchy on one hand and the censors on the other. Although those who upheld the principle of freedom of remonstrance became the victims of the purges, their cause nevertheless prevailed in the end, allowing the censors to exercise virtual veto power within the government, according to Wagner. The Chosŏn dynasty is generally known for its rigid class structure, whereby the *yangban* elites maintained their privileged status based on birth. Yŏng-ho Choe, however, argued in his *The Civil Examinations and the Social Structure in Early Yi Dynasty Korea* (1987) that the recruitment examinations for the all-important officialdom were based on merit, not birth, allowing men with talent, but of more common birth, to rise through the examination system in the early period of the dynasty. After the devastating foreign invasions by Japan (1592–98) and the Manchus (1636), a number of individual scholars, collectively known as the *Sirhak* (School of Practical Learning), proposed a series of drastic reform measures to remedy the political, social, and economic ills of the time. One of the most important scholars of this *Sirhak* school, Yu Hyŏngwŏn is the subject of a massive study by James B. Palais. In *Confucian Statecraft and Korean Institutions* (1996), Palais gave a scholarly analysis of Yu's reform ideas on society, land, military, government organization, finance, economy, and statecraft, tracing Yu's scholarly endeavors to classical and historical Chinese sources as well as to Korean sources. In *Chŏng Yagyong* (1997), Mark Setton studied the worldview of Chŏng Yagyong, another important *Sirhak* scholar, analyzing his Confucian and Catholic background. Donald L. Baker has also written several important articles on the *Sirhak*. Politics in the 17th and 18th centuries were largely dominated by factional struggle, and the recent scholarship in Korea is inclined to view the factionalism more in terms of partisan politics, in which different groups of like-minded people competed for power. King Yŏngjo (1724–76) was one ruler who staked his monarchical authority with considerable success on alleviating the ills of partisan politics and on instituting various reforms designed to lessen the crushing burdens of the general population. In her *A Heritage of Kings* (1988) JaHyun Kim Haboush portrayed how King Yŏngjo astutely utilized the rhetoric of a Confucian sage ruler to overcome formidable opposition and to realize his reform goals. The rule of the Taewŏngun as a de facto regent from 1864 to 1873 continues to remain controversial, as the assessments of him range from regarding him as a reactionary xenophobe to a forerunner of modernization. In *The Rule of the Taeŏn'gun* (1972), Ching Young Choe sees the Taewŏngun as a strong leader who, continuing the *Sirhak* tradition, tried to restore the vitality of the country that had once flourished at the beginning of the dynasty. James B. Palais on the other hand treated him in his *Politics and Policy in Traditional Korea* (1975) as a pragmatic reformer who was determined to revive the diminished royal prestige and authority, and to have the central government regain its control over the population and resources. In this important study, Palais characterized the Taewŏngun as a conservative reformer who, although willing to step on the toes of the *yangban* opposition, nevertheless failed to tackle more fundamental problems, such as landownership, military tax, and grain loans, that had plagued the country.

The arrival of the Western powers on Korean shores in the 19th century posed an unprecedented challenge, which the Confucian traditionalists regarded as a direct threat to their whole *Weltanschauung*. In *A Korean Confucian Encounter with the Modern World* (1995), Chai-sik Chung examined the intellectual tradition of Korean Confucian orthodoxy that led to the total rejection of the West, while Key-Hiuk Kim offered a provocative study of the diplomatic maneuvering among Korea, China, and Japan in *The Last Phase of the East Asian World Order* (1980), examining how the traditional China-centered East Asian world order gave way to the new West-oriented order. In Vipan Chandra's *Imperialism, Resistance, and Reform in Late Nineteenth-Century Korea* (1988), one can get a good picture of how the Korean reformers rallied around the Independence Club to assert Korea's independence through internal reforms, though without success.

The Japanese colonial rule from 1910 to 1945 still remains a sensitive and controversial subject and has so far eluded a comprehensive study in English, except perhaps Andrew J. Grajdanzev's *Modern Korea*, (1944). Using the official statistics given by the Japanese, Grajdanzev in this still very useful book interpreted the Japanese policy as detrimental to the well-being of the Koreans. In *Landownership under Colonial Rule* (1994), Edwin H. Gragert insisted that, contrary to the claims made by many Korean scholars, the cadastral survey by the Japanese in 1910–18 did not bring any significant change in landownership and that instead the depression in the 1930s was responsible for depriving many Korean farmers of land. In the thought-provoking *Offspring of Empire* (1991), Carter J. Eckert argued that Korea's modern industrial capitalism had its genesis under the Japanese colonial rule as selected Korean enterprises were nurtured by the Japanese in an attempt to wean the Korean bourgeoisie away from their nationalistic compatriots. Through a case study of one important Korean enterprise under Japan, Eckert presented how the Korean capitalists came to depend on the government for financial as well as political support. Michael E. Robinson's *Cultural Nationalism in Colonial Korea* (1988) is a study of the rise of "cultural nationalism" in the 1920s, which was championed largely by moderate Koreans, who, increasingly impelled to accommodate to colonial rule, advocated long-term gradual solutions to Korea's independence problem. *The Politics of Korean Nationalism* (1963) by Chong-Sik Lee is a classic study of the many phases of modern Korean nationalism, ranging from the simple outbursts in defence of the old order to the bitter struggles waged against Japan by many different groups of nationalists for the common purpose of regaining Korea's independence.

The Japanese colonization and the transition from traditional to modern society provided, or so it seemed, a fertile ground for the rise of communism in Korea. In *The Korean Communist Movement* (1967), Dae-Sook Suh presented a detailed account and analysis of the communist attempts to implant their ideology in Korea up to the rise of Kim Il-sung in North Korea. Among many difficulties that dogged the Korean communists were constant pursuit by the Japanese police, internal factional feuds, inconsistent Comintern instructions, and the issue of whether to fight for class struggle or for national liberation. In the first volume of *Communism in Korea* (1972), Robert A. Scalapino and Chong-Sik Lee provide a comprehensive study of communism in Korea from its beginning until 1972. Among the many interesting assessments Scalapino and Lee made is that the American occupation, and the mistakes committed by the communists themselves, such as blindly following Soviet instructions and resorting readily to violence, deprived them of a good opportunity to gain strength in South Korea in the 1940s.

The liberation and division of the country after 1945 plunged Korea into intense ideological rivalry. Gregory Henderson contended in *Korea: The Politics of the Vortex* (1968) that Korea, with its unusually homogeneous population, is a mass society and that in its politics there has been a constant pull toward the capital city, as if by a vortex. In the first volume of the monumental study *The Origins of the Korean War* (1981), Bruce Cumings argued for the civil and revolutionary nature of the Korean War, asserting that South Korea was ripe for revolutionary changes following the end of the Japanese colonial rule, but that the American occupation, with the resurgence of the reactionary forces they supported, suppressed the momentum for a revolution.

YŎNG-HO CHOE

See also Arai; Eberhard; Shiratori; Women's History: Asia

Further Reading

Baker, Donald L., "Sirhak Medicine: Measles, Smallpox and Chŏng Tasan," *Korean Studies* 14 (1990), 135–66

Buswell, Robert, Jr., *The Formation of Ch'an Ideology in China and Korea: The "Vajrasamadhi-Sutra," a Buddhist Apocryphon*, Princeton: Princeton University Press, 1989

Chandra, Vipan, *Imperialism, Resistance, and Reform in Late Nineteenth-Century Korea: Enlightenment and the Independence Club*, Berkeley: Institute of East Asian Studies, University of California, 1988

Choe, Ching Young, *The Rule of the Taewŏn'gun, 1864–1873: Restoration in Yi Korea*, Cambridge, MA: East Asia Research Center, Harvard University, 1972

Choe, Yŏng-ho, "An Outline History of Korean Historiography," *Korean Studies* 4 (1980), 1–27

Choe, Yŏng-ho, "Reinterpreting Traditional History in North Korea," *Journal of Asian Studies* 40 (1981), 503–23

Choe, Yŏng-ho, *The Civil Examinations and the Social Structure in Early Yi Korea, 1392–1600*, Seoul: Korea Research Center, 1987

Chung, Chai-sik, *A Korean Confucian Encounter with the Modern World: Yi Hang-no and the West*, Berkeley: Institute of East Asian Studies, University of California, 1995

Cumings, Bruce, *The Origins of the Korean War*, 2 vols., Princeton: Princeton University Press, 1981–90

Deuchler, Martina, *Confucian Gentlemen and Barbarian Envoys: The Opening of Korea, 1875–1885*, Seattle: University of Washington Press, 1977

Deuchler, Martina, *The Confucian Transformation of Korea: A Study of Society and Ideology*, Cambridge, MA: Council of East Asian Studies, Harvard University, 1992

Duus, Peter, *The Abacus and the Sword: The Japanese Penetration of Korea, 1895–1910*, Berkeley: University of California Press, 1995

Eckert, Carter J., *Offspring of Empire: The Koch'ang Kims and the Colonial Origins of Korean Capitalism*, Seattle: University of Washington Press, 1991

Egami, Namio, "The Formation of the People and the Origin of the State in Japan," *Memoirs of the Toyo Bunko* 23 (1964), 35–70

Gardiner, Kenneth Herbert James, *The Early History of Korea: The Historical Development of the Peninsula up to the Introduction of Buddhism in the 4th Century*, Canberra: Australian National University Press, and Honolulu: University of Hawaii Press, 1969

Gragert, Edwin H., *Landownership under Colonial Rule: Korea's Japanese Experience, 1900–1935*, Honolulu: University of Hawaii Press, 1994

Grajdanzev, Andrew J., *Modern Korea*, New York: Institute of Pacific Relations, 1944; reprinted, New York: Octagon, 1978

Haboush, JaHyun Kim, *A Heritage of Kings: One Man's Monarchy in the Confucian World*, New York: Columbia University Press, 1988

Han, Sungjoo, *The Failure of Democracy in South Korea*, Berkeley: University of California Press, 1974

Henderson, Gregory, *Korea: The Politics of the Vortex*, Cambridge, MA: Harvard University Press, 1968

Henthorn, William E., *Korea: The Mongol Invasions*, Leiden: Brill, 1963

Kang, Hugh H.W., "Images of Korean History," Andrew C. Nahm, ed., *Traditional Korea: Theory and Practice*, Kalamazoo: Western Michigan University, 1974

Kang, Hugh H.W., "The First Succession Struggle of Koryŏ in 945: A Reinterpretation," *Journal of Asian Studies* 36 (1977), 411–28

Kawashima, Fujiya, "Historiographic Development in South Korea: State and Society from the mid-Koryŏ to mid-Yi Dynasty," *Korean Studies* 2 (1978), 29–56

Kawashima, Fujiya, "A Study of the *Hyangan*: Kin Groups and Aristocratic Localism in the 17th- and 18th-Century Korean Countryside," *Journal of Korean Studies* 5 (1984), 3–38

Kim, C.I. Eugene, and Han-Kyo Kim, *Korea and the Politics of Imperialism, 1876–1910*, Berkeley: University of California Press, 1967

Kim, Key-Hiuk, *The Last Phase of the East Asian World Order: Korea, Japan, and the Chinese Empire, 1860–1882*, Berkeley: University of California Press, 1980

Ledyard, Gari, "Galloping along with the Horseriders: Looking for the Founders of Japan," *Journal of Japanese Studies* 1 (1975), 217–54

Lee, Chong-Sik, *The Politics of Korean Nationalism*, Berkeley: University of California Press, 1963

Lee, Hoon K., *Land Utilization and Rural Economy in Korea*, Chicago: University of Chicago Press, 1936; reprint, New York: Greenwood Press, 1969

Lee, Peter H. *et al.*, eds., *Sourcebook of Korean Civilization*, 2 vols., New York: Columbia University Press, 1993–96

McNamara, Dennis L., *The Colonial Origins of Korean Enterprise, 1910–1945*, Cambridge and New York: Cambridge University Press, 1990

Nelson, M. Frederick, *Korea and the Old Orders in Eastern Asia*, Baton Rouge: Louisiana State University Press, 1945; reprinted 1967

Palais, James B., *Politics and Policy in Traditional Korea*, Cambridge, MA: Harvard University Press, 1975

Palais, James B., *Confucian Statecraft and Korean Institutions: Yu Hyŏngwŏn and the Late Chŏson Dynasty*, Seattle: University of Washington Press, 1996

Robinson, Michael E., *Cultural Nationalism in Colonial Korea, 1920–1925*, Seattle: University of Washington Press, 1988

Scalapino, Robert A., and Chong-Sik Lee, *Communism in Korea*, 2 vols., Berkeley: University of California Press, 1972

Setton, Mark, *Chŏng Yagyong: Korea's Challenge to Orthodox Neo-Confucianism*, Albany: State University of New York Press, 1997

Shultz, Edward J., "Military Revolt in Koryŏ: The 1170 Military Coup d'Etat," *Korean Studies* 3 (1979), 19–48

Suematsu, Yasukazu, "Japan's Relations with the Asian Continent and the Korean Peninsula," *Cahiers d'Histoire Mondiale* 4 (1958), 671–87

Suh, Chang Chul, *Growth and Structural Changes in the Korean Economy, 1910–1940*, Cambridge: Council on East Asian Studies, Harvard University, 1978

Suh, Dae-Sook, *The Korean Communist Movement, 1918–1948*, Princeton: Princeton University Press, 1967

Wagner, Edward W., *The Literati Purges: Political Conflict in Early Yi Korea*, Cambridge, MA: East Asia Research Center, Harvard University, 1974

Kosambi, D.D. 1907–1966

Indian mathematician, numismatist, and historian

D.D. Kosambi was one of the first Indians to grasp the modern transformation of science and its implications, particularly for India. Through his writings on Indian history, mythology, religion, literature, and sociology he not only applied scientific methods in these areas but showed that new explanations to age-old beliefs were desirable and possible. His formula for chromosome distance occupies a central place in classical genetics. His work on coins makes the numismatics of hoards into an exact science. An unrivalled collection of microliths, the discovery of a Brahmin inscription at Karle, and of a remarkable number of megaliths with rock engraving, form a substantial contribution to archaeology. His editions of the poetry of Bhartrhari and of the oldest known Sanskrit anthology are landmarks in Indian text criticism.

All this was achieved through an insatiable spirit of enquiry, a love of wondering, and a sharp versatile intellect, which gave his views a rare sense of originality. Kosambi used his abstract methods for obtaining new results in various fields. Although Kosambi was a mathematician by profession, his first book, *An Introduction to the Study of Indian History* (1956), broke new ground as he presented history not as a chronological narrative of the various dynasties, but as a chronology of successive developments in the means and relations of production. He argued that due to the absence of reliable historical records, Indian history would have to use the comparative method. The comparative method required historians to be interdisciplinary in their use of investigative techniques. Kosambi had the firm conviction that historians in India were in a happy position, since so much of the past had survived to the present. This according to him amply made up for the absence of reliable historical records.

In the 1930s most of Kosambi's work was related to various aspects of mathematics; in the 1940s his interest shifted to Indian history and culture, and to Marxism; from the 1950s until his death in 1966 he focused on these, although his interest in mathematics remained constant. Kosambi first examined Indian sources by making a critical assessment of the classical text Bhartrhari and then later edited (with V.V. Gokhale) the Vidyakara's anthology *Subhasitaratnakosa* for the Harvard Oriental series. The latter is testimony to his versatile genius and quick mastery of the latest advances in literary criticism. He placed these texts in a historical context not merely through a chronological analysis, but by reference to the society from which they emerged. He argued that from the 1st millennium CE Sanskrit replaced Prakrit in the royal court and that this is evident in the change from Prakrit to Sanskrit in the language of royal inscriptions between the Mauryan and Gupta period.

Kosambi also attempted to analyze the *Bhagavad-Gita* as a document of class conflict. He drew a parallel between feudalism and the devotion stated in the *Gita*. To him the concept of Bhakti as propounded in the *Gita* emphasized an unquestioning faith in a personal deity and loyalty that corresponded to the "Chains of personal loyalty which binds retainer to chief, tenant to lord and baron to king or emperor." In the text's emphasis on the requirement to do one's ordained duty as a member of a particular caste, he saw the reinforcement of caste society, propounded by the upper castes to keep the rest of the society passive. He uncovered a contradiction between the single-minded devotion in the *Gita* to the universal ethics of the later Bhakti movement, which enabled it to become a powerful mobilizer of various social groups as the social context of the two changed.

Under Kosambi, numismatics became a science rather than a branch of epigraphy and archaeology. In his study of punch-marked coins that were in circulation between 500 and 100 CE, he demonstrated the applications of scientific method to obtain information on numismatic evidence. He worked on a statistical analysis of the distribution of the coins by meticulously weighing each coin and carefully analyzing its fabric and alloy. Through this method he arranged in definite chronological order the punch mark coins of the Texila hoard.

Kosambi also made use of archaeology to reconstruct the prehistorical period. On the basis of his work on microlithic sites and through his typology of microlithic artifacts he was able to trace the routes that herders, pastoralists, and early traders would have taken across western Deccan in the prehistoric period. His assessment of the historical importance of a site was based on the logic of geography. He contended that in the western Deccan region geographical considerations were partially responsible for the location of urban centers and Buddhist monasteries in the 1st millennium CE with a continuity of Maratha forts and British railway links in the 2nd millennium.

According to Kosambi, at a broad anthropological level the clue to understanding India's past was the basic factor of the transition from tribe to caste, from small localized groups to a generalized society. This was mainly due to the introduction of plough agriculture in various regions which changed the system of production, broke the structure of the tribes, and made caste an alternative form of social organization.

Kosambi used Marxist methodology to investigate a possible pattern and suggest a new framework. He felt that one thing common to all human societies was the need to find the means of living. So Kosambi suggested that society was held together by bonds of production. Far from destroying human values, materialism revealed how they were related to contemporary social conditions and to the prevalent concept of value. Kosambi attempted to analyze Indian myth, religion, philosophy, and early history within this framework with much success. To him the Indus valley civilization was a culture without the plough, and the river bank was cultivated with seasonal flood water controlled by dams and embankments dams and embankments. He regarded technological changes and migrations as responsible for the domination of the Aryans. The plough agriculture and iron technology in the Ganges valley led to the growth of urban centers and caste forms. To him the Mauryan monarchy became a feasible political system because there was an expansion of the village economy through the use of prisoners of war and of low-caste Sudras for agriculture. He attributed the rise of Buddhism and Jainism to major technological changes and urbanization.

Kosambi did not blindly accept this as the Marxist Asiatic mode of production. He questioned the notion of self-sufficiency because the very dependence of villages on salt and metals precluded it. However, he agreed that from the end of the Gupta period there was a relative increase in self-sufficiency and that this produced a static mode of production. Kosambi divided the feudal mode of production into two distinct aspects: feudalism from above and feudalism from below. Feudalism from above could be characterized as the changes that came after the Gupta period. These changes included an increase in the granting of land, with a quick transition from tribe to caste through the introduction of plough agriculture, a decline in trade and commodity production which saw a decline in urban centers, the decentralization of the army, and a concentration of wealth at local courts.

Feudalism from below was characterized by political decentralization accompanied by a low level of technology, by production for the household and village and not for a market, and by the holding of land on a service tenure. The lord also had a judicial or quasi-judicial function in relation to a dependent population. Kosambi found much difference between European feudalism and Indian feudalism. In India he noted the absence of demesne farming and of an organized religion.

Kosambi recast the writing of Indian history. To him history was not a sequence of haphazard events narrated in a chronological way, but was made by human beings for the satisfaction of their daily needs. History had to reflect man's progress in meeting his needs in cooperation with all his fellow men, not the success of a few at satisfying themselves at the expense of their fellows. To Kosambi the proper study of history in a class society meant the analysis of the difference between the interest of the classes at the top and the rest of the people. It demanded a consideration of the extent to which an emergent class had something new to contribute during its rise to power, and of the stage where it turned to reaction in order to preserve its interests. This was indeed a new kind of scientific history which emphasized not kinship relations but the production and mutual exchange of commodities.

REKHA PANDE

See also Thapar; Women's History: India

Biography

Damodar Dharmanand Kosambi. Born Kostben in Goa, 31 July 1907, son of a renowned Buddhist scholar. Educated initially in India, then at Cambridge Latin school; BA in mathematics from Harvard University. Returned to India and taught at Banaras Hindu University and Aligarh Muslim University; professor in mathematics, Fergusson College, 1932–46; chair of mathematics, Tata Institute of Fundamental Research, 1946–60. Died Poona, 29 June 1966.

Principal Writings

Editor, *The Epigrams Attributed to Bhartrhari*, 1948
An Introduction to the Study of Indian History, 1956
Editor with V.V. Gokhale, *The Subhasitaratnakosa*, 1957
Exasperating Essays: Exercise in the Dialectical Method, 1957
Myth and Reality: Studies in the Formation of Indian Culture, 1962
The Culture and Civilisation of Ancient India in Historical Outline, 1965
Indian Numismatics, 1981

Further Reading

Sharma, Ramesh Chandra *et al.*, eds., *History and Historians in India since Independence*, Agra: MG Publishers, 1991

Sharma, R.S., ed., *Indian Society: Historical Probings in Memory of D.D. Kosambi*, New Delhi: People's Publishing House, 1974
Syed, A.J., ed., *D.D. Kosambi on History and Society*, Bombay: University of Bombay, 1985
Thapar, Romila, *Interpreting Early India*, Delhi and New York: Oxford University Press, 1992

Koselleck, Reinhart 1923–
German social and conceptual historian

Reinhart Koselleck is one of the most important contemporary German historians. He made critical contributions to the history of the European Enlightenment and the Prussian Reform era. He also contributed to the development of theory through his many essays on the problem of modernity, and is one of the chief architects of an important field in German theoretical history: conceptual history (*Begriffsgeschichte*). Most recently he has concentrated on visual depictions of the past in paintings and monuments. The overarching theme in his monographs, theoretical writings, and iconography is the genesis of modernity. Through his participation in the Social History Workshop project (*Arbeitskreise für moderne Sozialgeschichte*) and his role in the founding of the University of Bielefeld, where he taught modern and theoretical history, Koselleck made fundamental contributions to the fields of social and conceptual history in modern Germany.

The 18th-century Enlightenment formed the subject of his first work. Written in the shadow of 1945 and at the height of the Cold War the book examined the roots of the crisis in the modern world. In *Kritik und Krise* (1959; *Critique and Crisis*, 1988), Koselleck argued that absolutism, which had ended decades of destructive religious wars, was also responsible for the emergence of the de-politicized critical Enlightenment discourses whose chief protagonists, barred from political participation, detached their discussion of morality from the constraints of practical politics. The Utopian, highly moralistic and, according to Koselleck, even hypocritical critique eventually subverted the authority of the absolute system which collapsed in 1789. However, criticism of the old regime alone was not enough to create a new social and political cohesion. Since then, according to Koselleck, the separation of morality and politics has been at the root of an ongoing civil war and the reconciliation of the two themes remains unresolved. Thus, he presented the reign of Terror, the totalitarian state, and the dictatorship of ideologies as one of the unintended consequences of the critical attitude originating in the Enlightenment. At the same time, Enlightenment rationalism initiated a new concept of time and place, of past and future. Traditional cyclical structures and their eschatological teleologies were replaced by the idea of an openended and unknowable future that, nevertheless, held out hope for the realization of Utopian ideals. This new understanding of past and future forms, one of the more important legacies of the 18th century, characterizes the historical outlook of the "modern era." Often misinterpreted as a negative interpretation of the Enlightenment and its legacy, *Critique and Crisis* demonstrated Koselleck's erudition, his interest in metahistorical questions, and his originality. The central thesis of his work, a crisis generated by the Utopian expectations of the future, has lost little of its cogency.

Koselleck's second major study, *Preussen zwischen Reform und Revolution* (Prussia Between Reform and Revolution, 1967), focused on Prussia from 1791 (the beginning of Prussian legal code reform) to the failed Revolution of 1848. Through his discussion of the Prussian Landrecht, the role of the administration, and the influence of social movements Koselleck portrayed the socio-structural transformation of a state from an estates-based monarchy to a developing society, a transformation from the old era to modernity. In this massive and extensively researched work Koselleck traced the efforts of Prussian administrators to implement "reform from above" as a conscientious choice "for Adam Smith against Napoleon." It was an attempt to achieve the political and economic goals of the French and Industrial revolutions without the political dislocation that occurred in France. Koselleck described how, after the initial success of the reform phase in the wake of the Napoleonic defeat, the administrators encountered growing opposition from the landed elite and had to abandon their efforts to achieve political reform and a constitutional monarchy in order to implement their social and economic reforms. In the absence of a strong bourgeoisie and of mounting opposition from the nobility, especially in the eastern regions, the political reform efforts were doomed to fail.

The failure of the reforms in Prussia and the absence of a successful revolution in Germany have long been held responsible for the "peculiarity" of German history. The reform period has been presented as a "defensive modernization" by Hans-Ulrich Wehler in *Deutsche Gesellschaftsgeschichte* (German Society in History, 1987); it was intended to introduce liberal economics without challenging the authority of crown, army, and nobility. Earlier, Hans Rosenberg in *Bureaucracy, Aristocracy, and Autocracy* (1958) and Eckart Kehr in *Der Primat der Innenpolitik* (1965; *Economic Interest, Militarism, and Foreign Policy: Essays on German History*, 1977) questioned the sincerity of the reformers and criticized the hagiographical historiography of the older "Borussian" school of historians. More recently scholars such as Herbert Obenaus in *Anfänge des Parlamentarismus in Preussen bis 1848* (The Beginnings of Parliamentarianism in Prussia before 1848, 1984) and Robert Berdahl in *The Politics of the Prussian Nobility* (1988) have again emphasized the interest of reformers in genuine political reform, although these reforms were never meant to restrict the power of the monarchy. Thirty years after its initial publication, and despite the reservations of critics about the homogeneity of the administration as presented by Koselleck or the sincerity and significance of their actions, his study remains an invaluable contributions to the historiography of Prussia and a splendid example of the successful merging of political and social history.

Since the 1960s Koselleck has been involved in the development of a new field in German social and theoretical history both through his theoretical essays and his work as editor, together with Otto Brunner and Werner Conze, of a historical lexicon. The premise for this project is that between approximately 1770 and 1850 the semantic content of key concepts, for instance labor, property, state, society, and law experienced a fundamental transformation from their classical meaning to their modern definition. This semantic change reflected the social, political, and economic change during the genesis of the modern age, but the changing content of these terms also shaped the perception of this process. Koselleck intended *Begriffsgeschichte* as an auxiliary science to social history because the "semantic struggle for the definition of political or social position" illuminates the structural economic and social developments addressed by the social historian. In seven volumes the changing value of more than a 150 key concepts have been analyzed by a host of experts whose contributions range from short essays to monograph-length articles. The lexicon is an invaluable source for anyone interested in the semantic reflection and contested nature of historical change.

In *Vergangene Zukunft* (1979; *Futures Past: On the Semantics of Historical Time*, 1985), a collection of essays, Koselleck addressed the theoretical aspects of *Begriffsgeschichte* and provided important observations on the notions of past and future, time and place, "experience and expectation." Reflecting the influence of Gadamer, Schmitt, and Heidegger Koselleck's rich and complex oeuvre has focused not on antiquarian detail, but emphasized structural processes and the meta-historical aspects of the themes he has addressed. His command of literature and sources is impressive, but his lasting contribution will be through the originality of his work, which challenges historians to think outside the narrow confines of their specialization.

FRANK SCHUURMANS

See also Begriffsgeschichte; Conze

Biography

Born Görlitz, 23 April 1923. Received doctorate 1954; Habilitation, 1965. Taught at University of Bochum, 1966–68; University of Heidelberg, 1968–73; and University of Bielefeld, from 1973.

Principal Writings

Kritik und Krise: Ein Beitrag zur Pathogenese der bürgerlichen Welt, 1959; in English as *Critique and Crisis: Enlightenment and the Parthogenesis of Modern Society*, 1988

Preussen zwischen Reform und Revolution: allgemeines Landrecht, Verwaltung und soziale Bewegung von 1791 bis 1848 (Prussia Between Reform and Revolution: General Land Rights, Administration, and Social Movement from 1791 to 1848), 1967; 2nd edition 1989

Editor with Otto Brunner and Werner Conze, *Geschichtliche Grundbegriffe: historisches Lexikon zur politisch-sozialen Sprache in Deutschland* (Historical Concepts: A Historical Dictionary of Political-Social Language in Germany), 1972–

Historische Semantik und Begriffsgeschichte (The Semantics of History and Begriffsgeschichte), 1979

Vergangene Zukunft: zur Semantik geschichtlicher Zeiten, 1979; in English as *Futures Past: On the Semantics of Historical Time*, 1985

Further Reading

Goodman, Dena, "Public Sphere and Private Life: Toward a Synthesis of Current Historiographical Approaches to the Old Regime," *History and Theory*, 31 (1992), 1–20

Richter, Melvin, "Zur Rekonstruktion der Geschichte der Politischen Sprachen: Pocock, Skinner und die Geschichtlichen Grundbegriffe," in Hans Erich Bödeker and Ernst Hinrichs, eds., *Alteuropa – Ancien Régime – Frühe Neuzeit: Probleme und Methoden der Forschung*, Stuttgart: Frommann Holzboog, 1991

Sperber, Jonathan, "State and Civil Society in Prussia: Thoughts on a New Edition of Reinhart Koselleck's *Preussen zwischen Reform und Revolution*," *Journal of Modern History* 57 (1985), 278–96

Kristeller, Paul Oskar 1905–

US (German-born) historian of philosophy

Paul Oskar Kristeller's writings testify to perception, to lucidity of style, and to exceptional intellectual energy: some 200 major publications over 70 years are his remarkable contribution to scholarship, marked by no less than six individual homage volumes. The history of philosophy in the Italian Renaissance has become synonymous with the name Kristeller. As a boy he received a firm grounding in the classics, that is Latin and Greek texts in their original languages. Philosophy, notably that of classical Greece, fired his interest, resulting in his doctoral thesis, published in 1929, on the concept of the "soul" in the ethics of Plotinus. Kristeller continued to study philosophy, and its history and associated disciplines, for some years; from 1939 throughout his academic career at Columbia University he lectured almost annually on Greek philosophy, which bore fruit as *Greek Philosophers of the Hellenistic Age* (1993). Here he analyzed the thought of eleven important thinkers from Epicurus to Antiochus of Ascalon on the basis of primary evidence comprising their often fragmentary texts.

The early 1930s marked the broadening of Kristeller's interests, with a focus on the Italian Renaissance. He began research on Marsilio Ficino (1433–99), the most distinguished Neoplatonist of the Medici circle. First he collected Ficino's unpublished and rarely printed writings, *Supplementum Ficinianum* (A Supplement to Ficino's Writings, 1937), which remains the standard work on the subject. He examined Ficino's thought in *The Philosophy of Marsilio Ficino* (1943). In articles published in the following years Kristeller provided new evidence about Ficino in consequence of his discoveries, culminating in his *Marsilio Ficino and His Work after Five Hundred Years* (1987). Like Petrarch, Kristeller proselytized with lectures; the publication of these as papers followed, and they often matured as substantial books, which in subsequent editions were further elaborated. Over the years Kristeller brought together some 110 of his previously published articles as *Studies in Renaissance Thought and Letters* (1956–96), each volume with detailed indexes. A number of studies, too, are in various other collections of his writings, and these sometimes have been reprinted with identical, or almost identical, titles, but somewhat different contents. This proliferation, while splendid for its accessibility, can make for problems in locating a particular reference. The articles in periodicals and collections of all kinds furnish detailed information on the life, thought, and times of Italian Renaissance scholars in particular, and are neglected at a researcher's peril.

Kristeller himself provided a synthesis of some of the new material that he discovered in his *Eight Philosophers of the Italian Renaissance* (1964). Its approach was that adopted in his later book on the Greek philosophers. A chapter each is dedicated to Petrarch, Lorenzo Valla, Ficino, Giovanni Pico, Pomponazzi, Telesio, Patrizi, Bruno. For each individual there is the pertinent background of thought, followed by a biographical sketch; thereafter are details of the philosopher's concepts as revealed by his writings, while in conclusion the influence of his ideas is examined. The book, typically, is a model of lucidity, and can be read easily by anyone interested in the period, and no command of specialist terminology is needed. The documentation is precise and supported by a detailed bibliography, consistent features of Kristeller's publications. Kristeller catered for philosophy-trained readers, with *Renaissance Thought and Its Sources* (1979), based on his annual lecture course at Columbia University, "Philosophical Literature and the Renaissance."

In an appendix to *Eight Philosophers of the Italian Renaissance* was printed Kristeller's lecture "The Medieval Antecedents of Renaissance Humanism," exceptionally lacking any references. The case made had appeared in earlier writings, notably *The Classics and Renaissance Thought* (1955; revised as *Renaissance Thought*, 1961), and was to be further elaborated and even more fully documented in *Renaissance Philosophy and the Mediaeval Tradition* (1966). A related strand was picked out for particular investigation in 1965 in three lectures on Albertus Magnus's importance for Italian Renaissance thought, *Medieval Aspects of Renaissance Learning* (1974). Kristeller categorically opposed the then prevailing view that Italian Renaissance ideas were in essence a reiteration of classical thought, and here his profound knowledge of classical thought was crucial. He also convincingly demonstrated that medieval ideas and values were inextricably enmeshed in Renaissance concepts. Accordingly Kristeller could dismiss the assumption that a new Italian Renaissance philosophy emerged in response to the scholasticism of the Middle Ages. He saw Italian Renaissance ideas as very different, as will emerge below.

In his *The Classics and Renaissance Thought*, as in his *Eight Philosophers of the Italian Renaissance* and elsewhere, Kristeller considered the portmanteau term "humanism" in relation to "humanist" and "humanities." He evaluated the former as most misleading, and so to be avoided (though he himself did not always do so). It originated in the mid-19th century and was popularized by the German historian Georg Voigt. "Humanist," as used in the late 15th century, was applied to those who taught the humanities, and by extension could be applied to individuals who received such instruction and sought to promote it, often as patrons. The phrase *studia humanitatis* (the study of the humanities) appears in 1368, meaning a course comprising the study through lectures, reading, and interpretation, of standard classical authors in Latin, eventually even in Greek, in the disciplines of grammar, rhetoric, history, poetry, and moral philosophy. Kristeller's original contribution was to stress that the creativity of the humanists was not mainly philosophical, but rather literary and artistic. In *Eight Philosophers* he wrote: "Their common denominator is to be found in an educational, scholarly and stylistic ideal, and in the range of their problems and interests, rather than in their allegiance to any given set of philosophical or theological views." His broader conclusion was that the Italian Renaissance consciously involved "a tremendous expansion" of secular culture. Classical texts were influential in rejuvenating prognostications, and fomenting discussion on free will; moreover, inevitably humanists placed new emphasis on the dignity of man, and esteemed individualism more highly than had their scholastic predecessors, points forcefully made in Kristeller's *Renaissance Concepts of Man and Other Essays* (1972), providing a vindication, if with a somewhat different emphasis, of Burckhardt's writing on the subject a century earlier.

Kristeller's publications are all based on primary sources, usually literary, occasionally archival, most exceptionally artistic.

His awareness of difficulties inherent in locating such material stimulated him to produce two remarkable bibliographic tools, which resulted in the award of the Bibliographical Society of London's Gold Medal. These are *Latin Manuscript Books before 1600* (1948) and *Iter Italicum* (1963–93). Today any scholar in the field contemplating research must begin by consulting these. The *Iter Italicum*, in particular, will remain Kristeller's lasting memorial.

CECIL H. CLOUGH

See also Italy: Renaissance; Ullman

Biography
Born Berlin, 22 May 1905, to a Jewish middle-class family; his father died the day of his birth, and he was raised by his mother. Studied at the universities of Heidelberg, Berlin, Freiburg, and Marburg, 1923–28; PhD, University of Heidelberg, 1928; continued the study of philosophy at Berlin, 1928–31; and Freiburg, 1931–33. Left Germany because of the rise of Nazism, 1933; taught Latin and Greek in Florence, 1934–35; taught German, University of Pisa and Scuola Normale Superiore, Pisa, 1935–38; emigrated to US, 1939 (naturalized, 1945); taught philosophy, Yale University, 1939; rose to professor, Columbia University, 1939–73. Married Edith Lewinnek, 1940 (died 1992).

Principal Writings
Der Begriff der Seele in der Ethik des Plotin (The Concept of Soul in Plotinus' Moral Philosophy), 1929
Editor, *Supplementum Ficinianum* (A Supplement to Ficino's Writings), 2 vols., 1937
The Philosophy of Marsilio Ficino, 1943
"Latin Manuscript Books before 1600: A Bibliography of the Printed Catalogue of Extant Collections," *Traditio* 6 (1948), 227–317, and part 2: "A Tentative List of Unpublished Inventories of Imperfectly Catalogued Extant Collections," *Traditio* 9 (1953), 393–418; revised as *Latin Manuscript Books before 1600*, 1960, 1965, and revised by Sigrid Kramer, 1993
The Classics and Renaissance Thought, 1955; revised as *Renaissance Thought 1: The Classic, Scholastic, and Humanistic Strains*, 1961
Studies in Renaissance Thought and Letters, 4 vols., 1956–96
Iter Italicum: A Finding List of Uncatalogued or Incompletely Catalogued Humanistic Manuscripts of the Renaissance in Italian and Other Libraries, 6 vols., 1963–93; cumulative index, 1997; CD ROM version, 1995
Eight Philosophers of the Italian Renaissance, 1964
Renaissance Thought 2, 1965; reprinted as *Renaissance Thought and the Arts: Collected Essays*, 1980
Renaissance Philosophy and the Mediaeval Tradition, 1966
Renaissance Concepts of Man and Other Essays, 1972
Medieval Aspects of Renaissance Learning: Three Essays, edited by Edward P. Mahoney, 1974
Renaissance Thought and Its Sources, edited by Michael Mooney, 1979
Marsilio Ficino and His Work after Five Hundred Years, 1987
A Life of Learning, 1990
Greek Philosophers of the Hellenistic Age, 1993
With M.L. King, "*Iter Kristellerianum*: The European Journey (1905–1939)," *Renaissance Quarterly* 47 (1994), 907–29

Further Reading
Bolelli, Tristano, "Speech on Occasion of [P.O. Kristeller] Winning the 1968 International Galileo Galilei Prize," in Tristano Bolelli, ed., *Italian Civilization and Non-Italian Scholars*, Pisa: Giardini, 1987

Epstein, Catherine, "P.O. Kristeller," in her *Civiltà italiana e studiosi stranieri*, Pisa: Pubblicazione del Venticiquennale, 1986; in English as *A Past Renewed: A Catalog of German-Speaking Refugee Historians in the United States after 1933*, Cambridge and New York: Cambridge University Press, 1993
"Paul Oskar Kristeller and His Contribution to Scholarship," in Edward P. Mahoney, ed., *Philosophy and Humanism: Renaissance Essays in Honor of Paul Oskar Kristeller*, New York: Columbia University Press, 1976

Krusch, Bruno 1857–1940
German archivist and early medievalist

Bruno Krusch was a professional archivist, and simultaneously worked at the *Monumenta Germaniae Historica* (MGH) – a state-supported project to identify and publish manuscript sources relevant to the early history of "Germany" – where he served, from 1903 onwards, on the *Zentraldirektion* (Board of Directors). The MGH published critical editions, that is, editions based on the comparison of multiple manuscript witnesses of a given text, and Krusch was instrumental in developing the conventions of this new scholarly genre. Furthermore, he was a pioneer among medieval historians in the type of source he selected for publication: he valorized as historical sources a variety of narrative texts from the normally-ignored Merovingian period, including the biographies of saints, the passion accounts of martyrs, and other materials that historians had tended to avoid. Krusch also discovered two previously completely unknown yet extremely important sources: the *Chronicle* of pseudo-Fredegar and the *Liber Historiae Francorum* (Book of the History of the Franks). While Krusch was the pioneering spirit behind many of the MGH editions, much of the actual work on the later volumes was executed with the help of Wilhelm Levison, Krusch's younger protégé and friend. Levison was a mild-mannered and masterful avoider of controversy, which enabled him to work for decades with the irascible Krusch; Levison even neglected his own projects to work with Krusch when the latter's failing eyesight rendered a collaborator essential. The products of their collaboration, namely the multivolume source collection Scriptores Rerum Merovingicarum (SRM, Writers of Merovingian Affairs) are used regularly by historians as canonical sources for the early Middle Ages.

To have worked at the MGH for decades on end, and to have published so many essential sources in that series, would normally place a historian among the most influential in the age of academic historiography. However, Krusch's personality has prevented his legacy from being taken completely seriously, even where his contribution was solid. Krusch loved controversy. As a student of the eminent paleographer Wilhelm Arndt and as an archivist by profession, Krusch consistently positioned himself as the ultimate expert on codicological matters, rarely accepting any other scholar as a peer when it came to dating, localizing, and otherwise assessing the value of manuscript materials. Krusch's self-conception was not a result of empty pride; he was recognized as a sort of manuscript specialist in three different departments of the MGH (Scriptores, Auctores Antiquissimi, and Scriptores Rerum Merovingicarum) before becoming the head of the SRM department. Nevertheless, it is generally agreed that he often went too far in his attacks on the judgments of other scholars. The most famous example of Krusch's scholarly hubris was his insistence that Mario Krammer's completed edition of the Lex Salica (Laws of the Salian Franks) be consigned to the pulp-mill rather than printed in the MGH series, on the grounds that Krusch alone, and not Krammer, truly understood the manuscript tradition of the text. Krusch's opinion turned out to be erroneous, and the fiasco has discredited all of his other critiques of Frankish legal materials as well. Krusch later attempted to demonstrate in numerous diatribes, largely unread, that he alone among active scholars – including his colleagues at the MGH – had mastered the techniques of textual scholarship, but to no avail.

Krusch's own approach was always hypercritical: either he would date the genesis of a given source to the latest possible year, or he would dismiss the source completely as a forgery. No other volume in the entire MGH series ever came close to provoking the polemical storm that greeted the publication of volumes 3 and 4 of the MGH SRM department, volumes that appeared in 1896 and 1898 respectively. Krusch ruthlessly slashed the knife of his "philological-historical method" through the entire corpus of known Merovingian texts until hardly a one remained that he was willing to recognize as an authentic source. Many of those same texts have since been rehabilitated, for Krusch's hypercritical method was rigorously logical in appearance only. For instance, having assumed that Merovingian-era Latinity was particularly decrepit, Krusch proceeded to date to the early Middle Ages – and to label therefore as reliable – whichever manuscripts had the largest number of grammatical infelicities; such linguistic characteristics have more recently been seen as marks of a late version of a text, deformed through scribal errors.

Krusch did not reserve his extreme stands for technical matters of codicology per se, but entered into historical controversies on the basis of his hypercritical interpretation of the codices. Perhaps the most famous controversy in which Krusch became embroiled was over the date of composition of the biography of Genovefa (Geneviève), patron saint of Paris, a text which Krusch dated to the 8th century, but which previous scholars had placed in the 5th century. The multiple salvos in the decades-long scholarly battle that ensued between Krusch and the Belgian historian Godefroid Kurth (1847–1916) were analyzed – and Krusch exposed as in error – in a book-length study by Martin Heinzelmann and Joseph-Claude Poulin. Krusch did not shrink from using extreme, often abusive, rhetorical strategies in pursuing his controversial theses, and as a result he left behind him few allies in the historical profession. As an archivist, rather than a university professor, he had no students.

FELICE LIFSHITZ

See also France: to 1000; Germany: to 1450; Levison

Biography
Born Görlitz, 8 July 1857. Studied in Leipzig and Munich. Joined staff of *Monumenta Germaniae Historica*, 1879, eventually joining its board of directors. Married Johanna Bramer, 1888 (6 children). Died Hannover, 26 June 1940.

Critical Editions
With Wilhelm Arndt, *Gregorii Turonensis Opera* (The Works of Gregory of Tours), 1884–85

Opera Apollinaris Sidonii (The Works of Sidonius Apollinaris), 1886
With Friedrich Leo, *Venantii Fortunati Opera* (The Works of Venantius Fortunatus), 1886
Fredegarii et Aliorum Chronica: Vitae Sanctorum (Chronicles of Fredegar and of Others: Biographies of Saints), 1888
With Wilhelm Levison, *Passionaes vitaeque sanctorum aevi Merovingici et antiquiorum aliquot* (Passion-Accounts and Biographies of Saints of the Merovingian Age and Earlier), 5 vols., 1896–1920
With Wilhelm Levison, *Ionae Vitae sanctorum Columbani, Vedastis, Iohannis* (Jonas' Biographies of Saints Columbanus, Vedast, John), 1905
Vitae Emmerami et Corbiniani (Biographies of Emmeramus and Corbinianus), 1920
Die Lex Bajuvariorum: Textgeschichte, Handschriftenkritik und Entstehung: mit zwei Anhängen, Lex Alamannorum und Lex Ribuaria (The "Laws of the Bavarians": Textual History, Manuscript Criticism, and Development; with Two Appendices, Laws of the Alamanni and Laws of the Ripuarian Franks), 1924

Further Reading
Bresslau, Harry, *Geschichte der Monumenta Germaniae Historica* (History of the *Monumenta Germaniae Historica*), Hannover: Hahnsche, 1921
Heinzelmann, Martin, and Joseph-Claude Poulin, *Les Vies anciennes de Sainte Geneviève de Paris: études Critiques* (Ancient Biographies of St. Genevieve of Paris: Critical Studies), Paris: Champion, 1986
Schieffer, Theodor *et al.*, *In memoriam: Wilhelm Levison (1876–1947)*, Cologne: Hanstein, 1977

Kuczynski, Jürgen 1904–1977
German economic historian

Amidst the dreary background and dogmatic excesses of historical scholarship in the former German Democratic Republic, Jürgen Kuczynski stood out as one of the more notable figures in East German historiography; indeed, it is fair to describe him as the Nestor of East German historical writing and its internationally most well-known representative. After studying philosophy, finance economics, and statistics in Berlin, Heidelberg, and Erlangen, Kuczynski received his doctorate in Erlangen in 1925 for a study of economic value. In the mid-1920s, Kuczynski studied in the US and then worked as a researcher for the American Federation of Labor. From 1936 to 1945, he lived in Britain, where he worked for the German Communist party (KPD), wrote for the *Labour Monthly*, and ended his second sojourn to the West as a colonel in the US Army attached to the Strategic Bombing Survey. Together with a handful of other prominent historians such as Ernst Engelberg and Walter Markov who, like Kuczynski himself, had been active in the Weimar KPD, after 1945 Kuczynski opted for the then-Soviet Zone of Occupation and, subsequently, participated actively in the scholarly life of the East German communist state. From 1946 to 1956, Kuczynski served as a professor at the Humboldt University in Berlin. From 1956 to 1968, he was director of the department of economic history in the German Academy of Sciences and then of the Institute for Economic History, which developed a reputation for relative independence in the increasingly straitjacketed world of East German humanistic scholarship.

A member of the Socialist Unity party, Kuczynski served as Erich Honecker's international economics adviser, and, in this capacity, he wrote those segments of Honecker's long-winded annual reports to the Central Committee that discussed developments in the capitalist world. Kuczynski, however, scrupulously avoided taking public stances on the creeping economic and political malaise in the GDR during the Honecker years. His career thus exemplified the relative weakness of the critical intelligentsia in the "first peasants' and workers' state on German soil," where – in stark contrast to Poland, for example – the continuing hegemony of Marxism within the academic world served to reinforce the regime's claim to legitimacy while simultaneously inhibiting the formation of an independent, critical academic elite willing and able to transmit an understanding of the opportunities offered by non-Marxist historical analysis. Whereas the stance taken by Kuczynski and the other members of his cohort immediately after the defeat of Nazi Germany was very much in keeping with a left-wing intellectual tradition rooted in the Weimar period, their later compromises and self-imposed silence helped render the GDR one the most conformist members the Soviet bloc.

At the center of Kuczynski's scholarly career stand three mammoth works: the 38-volume *Geschichte der Lage der Arbeiter unter dem Kapitalismus* (History of the Worker under Capitalism, 1947–72); the 10-volume *Studien zu einer Geschichte der Gesellschaftswissenschaften* (Studies on the History of the Social Sciences, 1975–78); and the 6-volume *Geschichte des Alltags des deutschen Volkes* (History of Daily Life in the German Nation, 1980–85). For an English-language introduction to his work, see *The Rise of the Working Class* (1967). Those interested in tracing Kuczynski's evolution as a Marxist scholar within the East German context should consult his two volumes of memoirs, published in 1973 and 1992. The publication of his autobiographical *Dialog mit meinem Urenkel* (Dialogue with My Great-Grandchild, 1983) unleashed an unusual, though controlled public debate in the GDR about German communism in general and the nature of the GDR in particular. Finally, those wishing to verify that Kuczynski remained a committed Marxist-Leninist after 1989 should read his *Ein Leben in der Wissenschaft der DDR* (A Life in East German Scholarship, 1994).

LEE BLACKWOOD

See also Labor

Biography

Born Elberfeld, 19 September 1904, son of a banker and economist. Studied philosophy, finance, and statistics, universities of Berlin, Heidelberg and Erlangen, PhD in economics, 1925; postgraduate study in the US, where he worked at the Brookings Institute, and in the economic department, American Federation of Labor. Joined Communist party of Germany, 1930; left Germany and lived in Britain, 1936–45; returned to Germany, 1945. Professor, Humboldt University, 1946–56; director, department of economic history, German Academy of Sciences, 1956–68; director, Institute of Economic History. Married Marguerite Steinfeld (2 sons, 1 daughter). Died 6 August 1997.

Principal Writings

Die Geschichte der Lage der Arbeiter unter dem Kapitalismus (History of the Worker under Capitalism), 38 vols., 1947–72

Das Entstehen der Arbeiterklasse, 1967; in English as *The Rise of the Working Class*, 1967

Memoiren: die Erziehung des Jürgen Kuczynski zum Kommunisten und Wissenschaftler (Memoirs: Jürgen Kuczynski's Education as a Communist and Scholar), 1973

Studien zu einer Geschichte der Gesellschaftswissenschaften (Studies on the History of the Social Sciences), 10 vols., 1975–78

Geschichte des Alltags des deutschen Volkes (History of Daily Life in the German Nation), 6 vols., 1980–85

Dialog mit meinem Urenkel (Dialogue with My Great-Grandchild), 1983

"Ein linientreuer Dissident," Memoiren 1945–1989 ("A Local Dissident": Memoirs), 1992

Ein Leben in der Wissenschaft der DDR (A Life in East German Scholarship), 1994

Further Reading

Jahrbuch für Wirtschaftsgeschichte (1974), 133–241; (1979), 39–85; (1984), 215–49; and (1989), 107–37 [includes bibliography]

Kuhn, Thomas S. 1922–1996

US historian of science

Since the Enlightenment, science has generally been viewed as a steady, cumulative acquisition of knowledge and a model of rationality. It was Thomas S. Kuhn who, with the publication of his *The Structure of Scientific Revolutions* (1962), presented the most radical challenge to this view. Rejecting the notion that science is its own best, because most dispassionate, judge, Kuhn took a thoroughly historical approach to his subject. This approach was also a departure from that of the Whiggish historians who in the spirit of the Enlightenment tended to look at the "defeated" past from the perspective of the "victorious " present. Against them, he maintained that it was a mistake to regard the scientific theories of previous generations as incompletely constructed versions of our own. Historical works erected on this false foundation have been attempts at a rational reconstruction of science, whereas, Kuhn insisted, only a historical reconstruction of it was possible. The reason for this is that science, contrary to the received view, can never look at objective phenomena directly but always only through the contingent historical context of the observing scientist. In this sense, observation is always "theory laden."

Scientists were previously thought of as free thinkers and skeptics, but in fact, Kuhn argued in his book, they are rather conservative individuals who readily accept what they are taught and apply their knowledge to solving problems that come before them. This patient problem-solving activity performed within the boundaries of a commonly accepted conceptual framework is characteristic of what Kuhn called "normal science." The shared conceptual framework constitutes a "paradigm," that is, a consensus among a community of practicing scientists about certain concrete problem-solution patterns. The scientists' commitment to the paradigm, a commitment that ensures the consensus, is derived from their training, and *not* from a critical testing of the paradigm.

Kuhn saw the history of science as a series of peaceful interludes (normal science) punctuated by intellectually violent revolutions (paradigm shifts). Revolutions in science pivoted around an accumulated cluster of recalcitrant anomalies, that is, around an increasing number of problems incapable of solution within the conceptual fabric of the old paradigm. Kuhn had two important points to make about the nature of paradigm shifts, and these two points formed the radical core of his thesis. First, just as there is, ultimately, no rational justification for commitment to a particular paradigm, there is none for its replacement by another. The victory of a new paradigm (say, Einstein's relativity theory) over an old one (Newtonian physics) is a cultural, social, and thus historical, not intellectual, scientific, and rational feat. Second, because no rationality independent of historical context is available to link or measure successive paradigms, they remain fundamentally incommensurable and, as a consequence, they cannot be objectively ranked. So, the claim that relativity theory mirrors reality more clearly and thus it is intrinsically better than Newtonian physics lacks any rational ground for support. Instead of correct and incorrect paradigms it is more appropriate to talk of alternative forms of scientific life. Those committed to different paradigms carry out their research in different worlds.

Kuhn did not seek to develop a sociological theory, or to understand knowledge and culture in the most general possible terms. He wanted to discover what was peculiarly distinctive and efficacious in scientific research. Although he tended to discourage the extension of his ideas beyond the scope of the natural sciences, his concentrated attack on traditional epistemology, his treatment of rationality and convention, science and history sparked great interest and had considerable influence among sociologists, psychologists, and historians.

There are many, however, especially scientists and philosophers of science, who find Kuhn's arguments less than impressive. Some complain about what they take to be his distorted picture of science: long periods of dreary conformity (normal science) interrupted by brief periods of irrational deviance (revolution). Others doubt if the distinction between normal and revolutionary science can be drawn adequately, or if normal science actually occurs. But the most serious charges brought against him are those of irrationalism and idealism. If, as Kuhn claimed, every paradigm produces its own criterion of rationality then every one of them will be inevitably self-justifying; the distinction between reason and unreason is blurred, and nothing stands in the way of fanatics and religious maniacs justifying their own brand of irrationalism. And, if all observations are indeed tainted by theory so that scientists laboring in different paradigms see things differently because they inhabit different worlds, then all of us observers, scientific or not, are hopelessly shut up in the universe of our own individual ideas. This spells plain anti-empirical idealism.

Kuhn's controversial book as well as his other works do indeed supply enough evidence to substantiate these charges, but whether they amount to a "crime" or a "virtue," these ideas are certainly not out of step with the intellectual climate of our age. While some add relativism to the list of charges, this undeniable implication of his doctrines finds plenty of supporters among postmodern social scientists. Historians of this creed, for instance, welcome the dethronement of context-independent absolute reason. Now, they say, we no longer have to measure the worth of our histories against the invisible authority of objective truth, and our suspicion that every history is interpretation is justified after all.

The direct intellectual origin of Kuhn's thesis, and especially of his discussion of paradigms, is Wittgenstein. Other influences, acknowledged by Kuhn himself, are Quine, Whorf, and Piaget. The controversy created by *The Structure of Scientific Revolutions* is alive and well long after the book's first publication. Some find its central thesis liberating and convincing while others find this very fact depressing, and dream of sunnier intellectual climates where ideas such as these evaporate in the natural light of reason.

JANOS SALAMON

See also Bernal; Collingwood; Fleck; Garin; Heilbron; Medicine; Merchant; Science

Biography

Thomas Samuel Kuhn. Born Cincinnati, 18 July 1922, son of an industrial engineer. Received BS in physics, Harvard University, 1943, MA 1946, PhD 1949. Civilian employee, US Office of Scientific Research and Development, Harvard University, 1943–44; and in Europe, 1944–45. Junior fellow, Harvard University, 1948–51, instructor, 1951–52, and assistant professor of general education and history of science, 1952–56; taught history and philosophy (rising to professor of history of science), University of California, Berkeley, 1956–64; professor of history of science, Princeton University, 1964–79; professor of philosophy and history of science, Massachusetts Institute of Technology, 1979–91. Married 1) Kathryn Louise Muhs, 1948 (marriage dissolved 1978; 2 daughters, 1 son); 2) Jehane Robin Burns, 1982. Died Cambridge, Massachusetts, 17 June 1996.

Principal Writings

The Copernican Revolution: Planetary Astronomy in the Development of Western Thought, 1957
The Structure of Scientific Revolutions, 1962; revised 1970
The Essential Tension: Selected Studies in Scientific Tradition and Change, 1977
Black-body Theory and the Quantum Discontinuity, 1894–1912, 1978

Further Reading

Barnes, Barry, *T.S. Kuhn and Social Science,* New York: Columbia University Press, and London: Macmillan, 1982
Cedarbaum, Daniel G.,"Paradigms," *Studies in History and Philosophy of Science* 14 (1983), 173–213
Cohen, Bernard I., *Revolution in Science,* Cambridge, MA: Harvard University Press, 1985
Geertz, Clifford, "The Legacy of Thomas Kuhn: The Right Text at the Right Time," *Common Knowledge* 6 (1997), 1–5
Gutting, Gary, ed., *Paradigms and Revolutions: Appraisals and Applications of Thomas Kuhn's Philosophy of Science,* Notre Dame, IN: University of Notre Dame Press, 1980
Hacking, Ian, ed., *Scientific Revolutions,* Oxford: Oxford University Press, 1981
Horwich, Paul, ed., *World Changes: Thomas Kuhn and the Nature of Science,* Cambridge, MA: MIT Press, 1993
Hoyningen-Huene, Paul, *Die Wissenschaftsphilosophie Thomas S. Kuhns: Rekonstruktion und Grundlagen probleme,* Braunschweig: Vieweg, 1989; in English as *Reconstructing Scientific Revolutions: Thomas S. Kuhn's Philosophy of Science,* Chicago: University of Chicago Press, 1993
Lakatos, Imre, and Alan Musgrave, eds., *Criticism and the Growth of Knowledge,* Cambridge: Cambridge University Press, 1970
Musser, Joseph F., "The Perils of Relying on Thomas Kuhn: Alternative Paradigms for the Interpretation of the Physiological Assumptions of Eighteenth-Century Picturesque Theorists," *Eighteenth-Century Studies* 18 (Winter 1984/85), 215–26

Kula, Witold 1916–1988
Polish economic historian

The best known Polish economic historian of the 20th century, Witold Kula received his PhD in 1939 from the University of Warsaw. Kula belonged to a cohort of Warsaw historians that included Tadeusz Manteuffel, Stefan Kieniewicz, and Aleksander Gieysztor, all of whom studied with Stanisław Arnold and Marceli Handelsman, two of the most eminent professors of history in the Polish Second Republic. During the German occupation of Poland, Kula participated in the pro-London resistance movement, serving in the Home Army's Information and Propaganda Office and then as a radio reporter during the Warsaw uprising of 1944.

His prewar pedigree and his wartime activities, however, did not prevent Kula, together with his Warsaw comrades and other historians in Kraków and Poznan with similar backgrounds, from entering the top ranks of the scholarly community in People's Poland. In 1953, Kula acted as co-founder of the Polish Academy of Science's Institute of History, where he served as scientific secretary until 1963. Kula and others like him thus embodied the continuity between pre- and postwar Poland that was a distinguishing characteristic of scholarship in post-1945 Poland.

Into the Stalinist 1950s, the communists relied on Kula to give lectures on Marxist methodology, and, as one might suspect, his collaboration with the authorities later give rise to recriminations. Kula, to be sure, openly admitted his intellectual indebtedness to Marxism; however, the roots of this methodological orientation lay in the 1930s and the wartime period, when Kula was confronted with what he believed was incontrovertible evidence of capitalism's failure. Although his wartime diary (*Dziennik czasu okupacji* [An Occupation Diary], 1994) does contain some pro-Soviet musings that were not at all uncommon among elements of the Polish intelligentsia at the time, Kula never joined the Polish Workers party or, after 1948, the Polish United Workers' party. Yet he never recanted his Marxist identity, nor did he cease to criticize conventional "bourgeois" historiography for its failure to ascribe a proper place to the struggle of common people against exploitation and oppression. Published in the wake of the Polish October of 1956, Kula's popular book *Rozwazania o historii* (Reflections on History, 1958) documented both his rejection of communist dogmatism as well as the spiritual and intellectual dangers confronting even Marxist thinkers within the communist system.

Kula's scholarship benefited from a combination of original archival research and theoretical erudition that attracted an audience well beyond Poland. His most well-known book, *Teoria ekonomiczna ustroju feudalnego* (1962; *An Economic Theory of the Feudal System*, 1976) was translated into English, Italian, Spanish, Portuguese, French, and Hungarian, which makes it one of the most widely read and cited works by a Polish historian. Kula established noteworthy and useful parameters for the study of economic and social development across time. Looking at the Polish-Lithuanian Commonwealth, he investigated, for example, the coexistence of small and large landholdings and the resulting dualism in social and economic development, in the process elucidating what could be described as mechanisms likely to produce backwardness. The systemic aspects of Kula's work appealed to historians who detected certain parallels between backwardness and civilizational lag in Eastern Europe and other parts of the world, for example, the Iberian peninsula and Latin America.

Polish scholarship also benefited from Kula's contacts with the French Annales school. He was instrumental in bringing to Poland the research methods popularized by Fernand Braudel, who, it should be noted, wrote the introduction to the English and French editions of *An Economic Theory of the Feudal System*. Kula helped to sustain lively contact between the French and Polish historical communities at the height of the Cold War. In 1970, he published *Miary i ludzie* (*Measures and Men*, 1986), a study of the history of weights and measures in Europe that drew above all on research in France and Poland. This work drew inspiration from Kula's ability to combine the methodology of economic history with the insights of cultural anthropology.

Kula's thinking and writing undoubtedly had a major impact on his western colleagues. As such, his career is evidence of the high standards maintained by Polish scholarship during the communist period. Of course, it is not coincidental that Kula – like all other Polish historians who attained international prominence during the communist period – specialized in the more distant past, and not in contemporary history. At the same time, he remained an intellectual who identified with the left. In this respect, he shared not only methodological similarities but also ideological affinities with such western historians as Eric Hobsbawm and Immanuel Wallerstein.

LEE BLACKWOOD

See also Marxist Interpretation; Poland: to the 18th Century

Biography
Born Warsaw, 18 April 1916. Received degree from the University of Warsaw, 1937, PhD 1939, Habilitation 1947. Spent World War II in Polish underground. Taught at Lódź, 1945–49; rose to professor, University of Warsaw, 1949–88. Died Warsaw, 12 February 1988.

Principal Writings
Rozwazania o historii (Reflections on History), 1958
Teoria ekonomiczna ustroju feudalnego, 1962, revised 1983; in English as *An Economic Theory of the Feudal System: Towards a Model of the Polish Economy, 1500–1800*, 1976
Miary i ludzie, 1970; in English as *Measures and Men*, 1986
Dziennik czasu okupacji (An Occupation Diary), 1994

Further Reading
Dziedzictwo Witolda Kuli, Warsaw, 1990 [includes bibliography]

L

Labor History

The origins of labor history lie in the late 19th century when journalists, union organizers, and reformers tried to use the history of labor to sway contemporary public opinion away from support for unbridled capitalism. Beatrice and Sidney Webb's *History of Trade Unionism* (1894; revised 1920), Emile Levasseur's *Histoire des classes ouvrières en France* (A History of the Working Classes in France, 1859), and Richard Ely's *The Labor Movement in America* (1886) were simultaneously pioneering contributions in labor history and contemporary commentary. These and similar writers argued that the problems of workers under industrialization were part of a long history that could be remedied only through trade unions, labor legislation, and social welfare measures. Because German writers were so concerned with the rise of socialism and because German historians were so conservative, labor history in Germany was much less developed. Sociologists, not historians, often were most influential. German labor history began and for a long time remained more narrowly political in focus despite some contributions such as Werner Sombart's *Sozialismus und Soziale Bewegung im 19. Jahrhundert* (1897; *Socialism and the Social Movement*, 1898) and Robert Michels' classic study of the socialists translated into English as *Political Parties* (1911). Ironically, Sombart helped start one of the largest debates in American labor history with the publication of his work, *Warum gibt es in den Vereinigten Staaten keinen Sozialismus?* (1906; *Why Is There No Socialism in the United States?*). Although his work was not translated fully into English until 1976, excerpts and references to the question which he raised helped inspire a large literature. Much of mid-20th-century American labor scholarship, as exemplified by Selig Perlman's *A Theory of the Labor Movement* (1928), contrasted the supposedly pragmatic, reformist labor movements of the English-speaking world to the more ideological socialist, Catholic, or communist movements of continental Europe.

From approximately the 1920s to the 1950s, the history of labor unions, labor law and legislation, and working-class political parties became an established sub-discipline in most of the western world. The major focus of the field in this period was what might be termed institutional history. The publications of the "Wisconsin school" in the United States such as J.R. Commons' *History of Labour in the United States* (1918–35), British scholarship such as Henry Pelling's *A History of British Trade Unionism* (1963) and H.A. Turner's *Trade Union Growth* (1962), Georges Lefranc's *Histoire du mouvement ouvrier en France des origines à nos jours* (A History of the Labor Movement in France from Its Origins to the Present, 1946), and James Coleman, Martin A. Trow, and S.M. Lipset's classic social scientific study of the typographical union, *Union Democracy* (1956), all focused primarily on organized trade unions and working-class political parties as the crucial factors in understanding workers' relationships to the rest of society. This focus developed in part because domestic politics in almost all modern states involved satisfying the claims made by workers' organizations. Through legislation and judicial decisions, most governments granted workers' claims to collective bargaining, insurance and pensions, and health and safety on the job. Thus, studying how organized groups of workers arose was not only a key to the past, but a critical contribution to present politics. The disadvantage of the institutional approach was that workers not heavily represented in formal organizations were much less studied.

The institutional bias of this school is clear in the articles in the international *Encyclopedia of the Social Sciences* (edited by Seligmann, 1930–35) on labor banks, labor contract, labor law, and labor parties, with little attention paid to workers' lives outside law or formal institutions. Important contributions to labor history in this genre continued to come from outside the ranks of professional historians. Labor historians sometimes taught in workers' education programs as well as in training schools for labor or industrial relations specialists. An important writer such as the American Lewis Lorwin (Louis Levine) served as an official with the International Labour Office. Histories of trade unions also formed a major contribution to scholarship, done both by veterans of the labor movement and professional scholars. One important reason for the success of this kind of institutional history was the accessibility of sources: party and union newspapers, congress proceedings, and official publications, in addition to government documents, were the most available sources. In a sense, much of what labor historians did in this period was to borrow the techniques of diplomatic, constitutional, and political historians and to apply them to working-class institutions.

The only major alternative approach was Marxist. Both Marxist and non-Marxist scholars tested Marx and Engels' argument that workers suffered materially from the rise of capitalism. In Britain, this debate became what was known as the "standard-of-living" question. Historians and economists debated the extent to which industrialization in the first half of the 19th century was accompanied by a decline in workers' economic situation. In the same tradition, the Marxist historian Jürgen Kuczynski's multivolume *Geschichte der Lage der Arbeiter unter dem Kapitalismus* (History of the Condition of the Worker under Capitalism, 1947–72) was a major contribution to the study of living conditions for the lower classes all over Europe. Many, however, had argued that oppression, which began in the work-place, could only be solved through control of the state. Thus most Marxist historians in the mid-20th century also tended to study organizations of workers in order to write labor history. Wolfgang Abendroth's widely-read *Sozialgeschichte der europäischen Arbeiterbewegung* (1965; *A Short History of the European Working Class*, 1972) virtually equated labor unions and parties with the working class, as did much of Philip Foner's pioneering multivolume *History of the Labor Movement in the United States* (1947–92). The major difference between non-Marxist and Marxist labor historians was that non-Marxists saw the gradual integration of workers' organizations into society as a natural development, while Marxists saw it as an unfortunate deflection of revolutionary potential. The focus on trade unions and parties did not always result in studies devoted to domestic politics. The German socialist refugee Adolf Sturmthal analyzed the failure of socialists to meet the challenge of communism and fascism during the era of the world wars in his classic work, *The Tragedy of European Labor* (1944).

With the waning of the post-World War II political consensus and a new interest in Marxism by the New Left, many historians in the 1960s and 1970s turned toward the social history of labor and working people as a new way to connect the past to contemporary political activism. The founding of the Society for the Study of Labour History in London in 1960, with its own *Bulletin* (now *Labour History Review*), was a major first step. The publication of E.P. Thompson's *The Making of the English Working Class* (1963) marks the clearest broadening of labor history to include the lives of workers outside organized institutions, although the essays by E.J. Hobsbawm collected in his *Labouring Men* (1964) were also influential. Well before factories or trade unions, Thompson argued, workers in 19th-century England evolved a strong sense of class consciousness in reaction to capitalist practices and political oppression. Thompson's scholarship suggested that historians could uncover a rich tradition of activism that went beyond the limits of the institutional labor movement. Traditional labor history had focused on work and politics as the defining characteristics of labor and neglected the rest of workers' lives as simply leisure. Following Thompson, historians instead studied workers' lives on and off the job, in and out of politics. Workers in all parts of their lives were members of communities and the working class. Moving beyond the categories of traditional labor history, American, British, and French scholars studied resistance to work discipline, the culture of the shopfloor, and wildcat strikes. To explain workers' relation to work, however, also meant looking at neighborhoods, family life, and popular culture. Labor historians vastly widened their range of sources. Much like Thompson, historians such as Herbert Gutman read pamphlets, broadsides, letters, and workers' literature to reconstruct the attitudes and beliefs of ordinary people. To investigate workers' actions beyond the scope of unions and parties, historians relied on unpublished sources such as police reports on strikes, business records on workplace conditions, and personal writings of ordinary workers and activists.

To criticize the previous institutional school, social historians drew on the insights of earlier 20th-century writers. Sombart's question about the absence of American socialism helped spark a search by scholars such as David Montgomery and Sean Wilentz for a radical working-class consciousness outside the organized labor movement in the United States. James Hinton, writing on the shop stewards in Britain after World War I, and Michelle Perrot writing on French strikes in the late 19th century explored Rosa Luxemburg's argument that the organization of unions curtailed the genuine radicalism of workers. Drawing on Lenin's argument that an elite of well-paid skilled workers had undermined the radicalism of British labor, Hobsbawm formulated an influential theory of the "labour aristocracy" as a crucial element in the working class. Erhard Lucas, for example, applied Hobsbawm's theory to Germany, while André Mommen did so in Belgium. Marxist theory also inspired new attempts to understand how employers actually controlled workers. Building in part on Paul Sweezy and Paul Baran's expositions of Marxist theory, both historians and social scientists such as Harry Braverman, Michael Burrawoy, and Stephen Marglin examined the process by which workers were compelled to accept discipline and hindered from acting collectively.

German labor history as a whole still followed a somewhat different path. During the period when historians elsewhere greatly expanded the field using institutional approaches, labor history in Germany suffered because of years of suppression by Nazism and domination by a narrowly ideological Marxism. German historians still tended overwhelmingly to do political history. Given the pioneering contributions of sociologists such as Sombart and Michels, it is appropriate that the work with the greatest impact was that of a sociologist influenced by American social scientific models. Günther Roth in his *The Social Democrats in Imperial Germany* (1963) portrayed socialist workers as trapped in an isolated subculture by dogmatic Marxism and upper-class repression. Subsequent work such as Dieter Groh's *Negative Integration und revolutionärer Attentismus* (Negative Integration and Revolutionary Expectations, 1973) made Roth's argument into a crucial reason for socialism's failure to stop the outbreak of World War I. The other trend in Germany has been an extreme reaction to political history and politicized labor history: *Alltagsgeschichte*, or the history of everyday life, as seen, for example, in Jürgen Reulecke and Wolfhard Weber's *Fabrik, Familie, Feierabend* (Factory, Family, and After Work, 1978).

Nonetheless, in most of Europe and North America, labor history by the 1990s had become an established sub-discipline with an impressive set of institutional supports. During the 1970s and 1980s, journals such as the *International Review of Social History*, *Labor History*, and *Le Mouvement Social* were rejuvenated by a flood of articles on the social history of labor, while labor history has been the primary or a major focus of a number of newer journals: *History Workshop*, *International Labor and Working Class History*, *Labour/Le Travail*, the *Journal of Social History*, and *Social History*. Meanwhile, the biannual North American Labor History Conference in Detroit, and special conferences sponsored by the International Institute for Social History in Amsterdam regularly draw large audiences. Archives and research institutions in the field have formed the International Association of

Labour History Institutes, or IALHI, whose website and Labour History List help to connect the discipline. Thanks to the tireless efforts of scholars such as Jean Maitron, Joyce Bellamy and John Saville, and Franco Andreucci and Tommaso Detti, important reference works have provided a solid foundation for research, for example, the *Dictionnaire biographique du mouvement ouvrier français* (A Biographical Dictionary of the French Labor Movement, 1963–), the *Dictionary of Labour Biography* (1972–), and *Il movimento operaio italiano* (The Italian Labor Movement, 1975–79).

The very vitality and broadening of labor history has encouraged scholars to expand the field beyond its traditional boundaries and even question its implicit assumptions. Much of labor history has always focused on factory workers or at least on workers in modern industry. These were primarily male, and usually the members of the dominant ethnic or racial group in each society. Workers outside factories or mines, women, immigrants, and workers of other racial or ethnic groups were studied far less often. Beginning in the 1970s, historians such as Agulhon, Hanagan, Prothero, Scott, and Wilentz showed that artisans, skilled craftsmen often working in small shops, rather than factory workers were usually the instigators of working-class action in the 19th century. Tilly and Scott argued that low pay, discrimination, and the demands of families created a radically different set of experiences for women workers during the Industrial Revolution from that of men. Benson, Kwolek-Folland, and others have since argued that employers of white collar workers could structure the entire workplace and even whole industries around a gendered view of labor and society.

The more historians explored the world of workers beyond the boundaries of organized movements the more varied and diverse the working class appeared. In many societies, immigrants and ethnic or racial minorities have formed a disproportionate part of the labor force. A vigorous debate has emerged over whether or not workers identified themselves more by ethnicity and race or by class and occupation. Historians such as Gutman, Roediger, and Tabili found that religious, ethnic, or racial identity virtually acted as a substitute for class for many American and British workers. Social scientists in the Marxist tradition such as Gordon, Reich, and Edwards argued that the ethnic divisions among American workers had been used by employers to create a distinctively weak and divided working class. Hoerder, Kulczycki, and Montgomery, by contrast, argued that American, German, and Polish workers could often still work together even when deeply divided by race or ethnicity.

The large debate over whether class, in the sense of a body of people defined by a particular set of economic conditions, is still a viable concept has been more vigorous among labor specialists than any other group of historians. Patrick Joyce has argued that British workers simply did not think or act collectively along class lines. Instead, various kinds of "populism" and paternalism often united many workers and members of other classes, while status distinctions, which did not run along class lines, frequently divided people. To find other explanations for workers' actions, some labor historians turned to linguistic analysis. Gareth Stedman Jones argued that Chartism was not fueled by class consciousness but by the political discourse of British radicalism. Jacques Rancière virtually turned traditional labor history on its head by asserting that Parisian craftsmen longed to escape from the working class and that later scholars had woven a whole set of schemes to reinterpret workers' lives. Joan Scott criticized Thompson and the vast bulk of labor history by arguing that the very marginalization of women workers and the silence about male-female relations revealed the tremendous role of gender in shaping both the world of work and scholarship about labor.

At the same time, labor historians have expanded into a variety of new areas of research. Thanks to the work of a large number of scholars such as Burnett, Vincent, and Maynes, workers' autobiographies have proved much more abundant and more susceptible of analysis than earlier scholars had imagined. Following the lead of anthropologists and sociologists, historians such as Paul Thompson have used oral histories to enrich our knowledge of workers' lives. Both institutional labor history and the social history of labor since the 1960s had workers in the 19th century as their major subject and their implicit model for workers as a type. Some historians of periods before industrialization have helped recapture the old emphasis of late 19th-century reformers who saw modern workers as part of a long tradition. Alain Lottin's subtle reading of the autobiography of a 17th-century French wool weaver demonstrated that historians can hope to recreate some of the everyday life of ordinary people even in earlier centuries. Historians of medieval and early modern Europe had long documented the existence of guilds, corporate bodies with legal privileges which controlled wages and working conditions in many trades. The concern of labor historians of these periods has been to investigate how guilds affected workers outside them and how workers inside and outside guilds interacted with each other. Historians such as Cynthia Truant have also uncovered more about groups such as the French *compagnonages*, journeymen's associations whose members banded together for recreation, education, and defence.

Expanding the subject area of labor history also has meant exploring the vast numbers of servants, migratory laborers, and domestic industry workers. Traditional labor history had emphasized the factory as the crucial gateway to modern labor, that is, earning wages and accepting the supervision of owners of capital. Recently, historians such as Maxine Berg have argued that the transition from pre-industrial to industrial work went through several stages, with the factory as only one, and perhaps not always the most important one. Rural industry, also known as "proto-industrialization," in which people mixed farming with simple manufacturing tasks, probably introduced large parts of the European and North American population to wages and work discipline. All these kinds of work – especially domestic service and rural industry – are vital to understanding the experience of women. Often confined to these tasks by family pressures and the gendered division of labor, women did these kinds of work in disproportionate numbers long before and long after the coming of industrialization.

The role of the state was a key concern for late 19th-century labor reformers, but it is an area into which labor historians are still expanding their research. In dealing with workers in the Industrial Revolution, historians often could treat workers and the state as opponents or as having minimal connections. Dealing with workers in the 20th century, when the state has closely regulated them, guaranteed their welfare, or even employed them, has raised many new issues. Workers in the French aircraft industry, for example, unionized more to pressure the state than their own employers. Over the last century, mining in all countries moved from being one of the most capitalist of industries to one of the most statist, as shown by Feldman and Tenfelde's *Workers, Owners, and Politics in Coal Mining* (1990).

Labor history has been overwhelmingly devoted to North America and Western Europe, and even most of this writing has focused on one country, industry, or community. Much of the labor history on Africa, Asia, and Latin America naturally focuses on agricultural labor, a topic which European and North American historians usually deal with as part of the history of agriculture rather than labor. The founding of the Labour History Association of India in 1997 indicates that labor historians are increasingly studying industrial work outside Europe and North America. International migration is the area where labor historians have come the closest to integrating different continents, as seen in the work of Hoerder, and Marks and Richardson. The vast majority of migrants in modern history have been workers prior to migration or have been forced to seek wage labor even if they had not been workers before. In the late 19th century, the movement of Mexican agricultural workers to the southwest United States, of Chinese coolies to Malaya, of Polish miners to the Ruhr, and of Italian laborers to Argentina were all part of the vast expansion of the world economy. The movement of these people, along with the spread of industrialization itself, provided a way to compare and connect the story of labor in diverse countries. The nationalism of the period of the world wars and the concentration of labor movements on domestic politics curtailed many of the connections between countries during the mid-20th century, a narrowing of vision reflected in the largely nationalist focus of most labor history until recently. With the globalization of the world economy in the late 20th century, labor historians have the opportunity to begin to write a truly global history of labor.

CARL STRIKWERDA

See also Business; Commons; Conze; Economic; Foner, P.; Gutman; Hobsbawm; Kuczynski; Marks; Marx; Marxist Interpretation; Montgomery; Thompson, E.; Tilly, C.; Tilly, L.; Urban; Webb

Further Reading

Abendroth, Wolfgang, *Sozialgeschichte der europäischen Arbeiterbewegung*, Frankfurt: Suhrkamp, 1965; in English as *A Short History of the European Working Class*, New York: Monthly Review Press, and London: NLB, 1972

Agulhon, Maurice, *Une Ville ouvrière au temps du socialisme utopique: Toulon de 1815 à 1851* (A Village of Workers during the Period of Utopian Socialism: Toulon, 1815–51), The Hague: Mouton, 1970

Amdur, Kathryn, *Syndicalist Legacy: Trade Unions and Politics in Two French Cities in the Era of World War I*, Urbana: University of Illinois Press, 1986

Baron, Ava, ed., *Work Engendered: Toward a New History of American Labor*, Ithaca, NY: Cornell University Press, 1991

Berg, Maxine, *The Age of Manufactures: Industry, Innovation and Work in Britain, 1700–1820*, Oxford: Blackwell, 1985, New York: Oxford University Press, 1986; 2nd edition London and New York: Routledge, 1994

Berlanstein, Lenard R., ed., *Rethinking Labor History: Essays on Discourse and Class Analysis*, Urbana: University of Illinois Press, 1993

Benson, Susan Porter, *Counter Cultures: Saleswomen, Managers, and Customers in American Department Stores, 1890–1940*, Urbana: University of Illinois Press, 1986

Bodnar, John, *Anthracite People: Families, Unions, and Work, 1900–1940*, Harrisburg: Pennsylvania Historical and Museum Commission, 1983

Bonnell, Victoria E., *Roots of Rebellion: Workers' Politics and Organizations in St. Petersburg and Moscow, 1900–1914*, Berkeley: University of California Press, 1983

Braverman, Harry, *Labor and Monopoly Capital*, New York: Monthly Review Press, 1974

Brody, David, *Steelworkers in America: The Nonunion Era*, Cambridge, MA: Harvard University Press, 1960

Burawoy, Michael, *The Politics of Production: Factory Regimes under Capitalism and Socialism*, London: Verso, 1985

Burnett, John, David Vincent, and David Mayne, eds., *The Autobiography of the Working Class: An Annotated Critical Bibliography*, 3 vols., Brighton: Harvester, and New York: New York University Press, 1984–89

Chapman, Herrick, *State Capitalism and Working Class Radicalism in the French Aircraft Industry*, Berkeley: University of California Press, 1991

Chesneaux, Jean, *The Chinese Labor Movement, 1919–1927*, Stanford, CA: Stanford University Press, 1968

Cohn, Samuel Kline, *The Laboring Classes in Renaissance Florence*, New York: Academic Press, 1980

Coleman, James, Martin A. Trow, and Seymour Martin Lipset, *Union Democracy: The Internal Politics of the International Typographical Union*, Glencoe, IL: Free Press, 1956

Commons, John R. *et al.*, *History of Labour in the United States*, 4 vols., New York: Macmillan, 1918–35

Cooper, Frederick, *On the African Waterfront: Urban Disorder and the Transformation of Work in Colonial Mombasa*, New Haven: Yale University Press, 1987

Crew, David F., *Town in the Ruhr: A Social History of Bochum, 1860–1914*, New York: Columbia University Press, 1979

Dawley, Alan, *Class and Community: The Industrial Revolution in Lynn*, Cambridge, MA: Harvard University Press, 1976

Ely, Richard, *The Labor Movement in America*, New York: Crowell, 1886

Epstein, Steven, *Wage Labor and Guilds in Medieval Europe*, Chapel Hill: University of North Carolina Press, 1991

Evans, Richard J., ed., *The German Working Class, 1888–1933: The Politics of Everyday Life*, London: Croom Helm, and Totowa, NJ: Barnes and Noble, 1982

Farr, James R., *Hands of Honor: Artisans and Their World in Dijon, 1550–1650*, Ithaca, NY: Cornell University Press, 1988

Feldman, Gerald, and Klaus Tenfelde, eds., *Workers, Owners, and Politics in Coal Mining: An International Comparison of Industrial Relations*, New York: St. Martin's, and London: Berg, 1990

Foner, Philip S., *History of the Labor Movement in the United States*, 10 vols., New York: International Publishers, 1947–92

Foster, John, *Class Struggle and the Industrial Revolution: Early Industrial Capitalism in Three English Towns*, London: Weidenfeld and Nicolson, and New York: St. Martin's Press, 1974

Gordon, David M., Richard Edwards, and Michael Reich, *Segmented Work, Divided Workers: The Historical Transformation of Labor in the United States*, Cambridge and New York: Cambridge University Press, 1982

Groh, Dieter, *Negative Integration und revolutionärer Attentismus: Die deutsche Sozialdemokratie am Vorabend des Ersten Weltkrieges* (Negative Integration and Revolutionary Expectations: German Social Democracy on the Eve of World War I), Frankfurt: Propyläen, 1973

Guerin-Gonzales, Camille, and Carl Strikwerda, eds., *The Politics of Immigrant Workers: Labor Activism and Migration in the World Economy since 1830*, New York: Holmes and Meier, 1993

Gullickson, Gay, *Spinners and Weavers of Auffay: Rural Industry and the Sexual Division of Labor in a French Village, 1750–1850*, Cambridge and New York: Cambridge University Press, 1986

Gutman, Herbert G., *Work, Culture, and Society in Industrializing America: Essays in American Working-Class and Social History*, New York: Knopf, 1976; Oxford, Blackwell, 1977

Hanagan, Michael, *The Logic of Solidarity: Artisans and Industrial Workers in Three French Towns, 1871–1914*, Urbana: University of Illinois Press, 1980

Hareven, Tamara, *Family Time and Industrial Time: The Relationship Between the Family and Work in a New England Industrial Community*, Cambridge and New York: Cambridge University Press, 1982

Hershatter, Gail, *The Workers of Tianjin, 1900–1949*, Stanford, CA: Stanford University Press, 1986

Higginson, John, *A Working Class in the Making: Belgian Colonial Labor Policy, Private Enterprise, and the African Mineworker, 1907–1951*, Madison: University of Wisconsin Press, 1989

Hobsbawm, Eric J., *Labouring Men: Studies in the History of Labour*, London: Weidenfeld and Nicolson, 1964; New York: Basic Books, 1965

Hobsbawm, Eric J., *Worlds of Labour: Further Studies in the History of Labour*, London: Weidenfeld and Nicolson, 1984; in US as *Workers: Worlds of Labor*, New York: Pantheon, 1984

Hoerder, Dirk, ed., *Labor Migration in the Atlantic Economies: The European and North American Working Classes during the Period of Industrialization*, Westport, CT: Greenwood Press, 1985

Hoerder, Dirk, ed., *"Struggle a Hard Battle": Essays on Working-Class Immigrants*, DeKalb: Northern Illinois University Press, 1986

Honig, Emily, *Sisters and Strangers: Women in the Shanghai Cotton Mills, 1919–1949*, Stanford, CA: Stanford University Press, 1986

Jones, Gareth Stedman, *Languages of Class: Studies in English Working-Class History, 1832–1982*, Cambridge and New York: Cambridge University Press, 1983

Jones, Jaqueline, *Labor of Love, Labor of Sorrow: Black Women, Work, and the Family from Slavery to the Present*, New York: Basic Books, 1985

Joyce, Patrick, *Work, Society, and Politics: The Culture of the Factory in Later Victorian England*, New Brunswick, NJ: Rutgers University Press, and Hassocks, Sussex: Harvester, 1980

Joyce, Patrick, *Visions of the People: Industrial England and the Question of Class, 1840–1914*, Cambridge and New York: Cambridge University Press, 1991

Katzman, David, *Seven Days a Week: Women and Domestic Service in Industrializing America*, New York: Oxford University Press, 1978

Katznelson Ira, and Aristide R. Zolberg, eds., *Working-Class Formation: Nineteenth-Century Patterns in Western Europe and the United States*, Princeton: Princeton University Press, 1986

Koditschek, Theodore, *Class Formation and Urban-Industrial Society: Bradford, 1750–1850*, Cambridge and New York: Cambridge University Press, 1992

Kuczynski, Jürgen, *Die Geschichte der Lage der Arbeiter unter dem Kapitalismus* (History of the Worker under Capitalism), 38 vols., Berlin: various publishers, 1947–72

Kulczycki, John J., *The Foreign Worker and the German Labor Movement: Xenophobia and Solidarity in the Coal Fields of the Ruhr, 1871–1914*, Oxford: Berg, 1994

Kwolek-Folland, Angel, *Engendering Business: Men and Women in the Corporate Office, 1870–1930*, Baltimore: Johns Hopkins University Press, 1994

Laslett, John, and Seymour Martin Lipset, eds., *Failure of a Dream? Essays in the History of American Socialism*, Berkeley: University of California Press, 1974

Laurie, Bruce, *Artisans into Workers: Labor in Nineteenth-Century America*, New York: Hill and Wang, 1989

Lefranc, Georges, *Histoire du mouvement ouvrier en France des origines à nos jours* (A History of the Labor Movement in France from Its Origins to the Present), Paris: Aubier, 1946

Lequin, Yves, *Les ouvriers de la région lyonnaise (1848–1914)* (Workers from the Lyon Region, 1848–1914), 2 vols., Lyon: Presses Universitaires de Lyon, 1977

Levasseur, Emile, *Histoire des classes ouvrières en France* (A History of the Working Classes in France), 2 vols., Paris, 1859; revised 1901

Lottin, Alain, *Chavatte, ouvrier lillois: un contemporain de Louis XIV* (Chavatte, a Worker of Lille: A Contemporary of Louis XIV), Paris: Flammarion, 1979

Lucas-Busemann, Erhard, *Zwei Formen von Radikalismus in der deutschen Arbeiterbewegung* (Two Forms of Radicalism in the German Workers' Movement), Frankfurt: Stern, 1976

Marglin, Stephen, "What Do Bosses Do? The Origins and Functions of Hierarchy in Capitalist Production," *Review of Radical Political Economics*, 6 (1974), 60–112

Marks, Shula, and Peter Richardson, editors, *International Labour Migration: Historical Perspectives*, London: Temple Smith, 1984

Maynes, Mary Jo, *Taking the Hard Road: Life Course in French and German Workers' Autobiographies in the Era of Industrialization*, Chapel Hill: University of North Carolina Press, 1995

Merriman, John M., *The Red City: Limoges and the French Nineteenth Century*, New York: Oxford University Press, 1985

Michel, Robert, *Zur Soziologie des Parteiwesens in der modernen Demokratie: Untersuchungen über die oligarchischen Tendenzen des Gruppenlebens*, Leipzig: Klinkhardt, 1911; in English as *Political Parties: A Sociological Study of the Oligarchical Tendencies of Modern Democracy*, New York: Hearst, and London: Jarrold, 1915

Mommen, André, *De Belgische Werkliedenpartij, 1880–1914* (The Belgian Workers' Party, 1800–1914), Ghent: Masereelfonds, 1980

Mommsen, Wolfgang J., and Hans-Gerhard Husung, eds., *The Development of Trade Unionism in Great Britain and Germany, 1880–1914*, London: Allen and Unwin, 1985

Montgomery, David, *The Fall of the House of Labor: The Workplace, the State, and American Labor Activism, 1865–1925*, Cambridge and New York: Cambridge University Press, 1987

Mörner, Magnus, *Aventureros y proletarios: los emigrantes en hispanoamerica*, Madrid: MAPFRE, 1992; in English as *Adventurers and Proletarians: The Story of Migrants in Latin America*, Pittsburgh: University of Pittsburgh Press, 1985

Palmer, Bryan D., *The Descent into Discourse: The Reification of Language and the Writing of Social History*, Philadelphia: Temple University Press, 1990

Pelling, Henry, *A History of British Trade Unionism*, London: Macmillan, 1963; 5th edition 1992

Perlman, Selig, *A Theory of the Labor Movement*, New York: Macmillan, 1928

Perrot, Michelle, *Les Ouvriers en grève: France, 1871–1890*, The Hague: Mouton, 1974; abridged in English as *Workers on Strike: France, 1871–1890*, New Haven: Yale University Press, 1987

Prothero, I.J., *Artisans and Politics in Early Nineteenth-Century London: John Gast and His Times*, Baton Rouge: Louisiana State University Press, 1979

Rancière, Jacques, *La Nuit des prolétaires*, Paris: Fayard, 1981; in English as *The Nights of Labor: The Worker's Dream in Nineteenth-Century France*, Philadelphia: Temple University Press, 1989

Reid, Donald, *Paris Sewers and Sewermen: Realities and Representations*, Cambridge, MA: Harvard University Press, 1991

Reulecke, Jürgen, and Wolfhard Weber, eds., *Fabrik, Familie, Feierabend: Beiträge zur Sozialgeschichte des Alltags im Industriezeitalter* (Factory, Family, and After Work: Contributions to the Social History of Everyday Life in the Age of Industrialization), Wuppertal: Hammer, 1978

Rodney, Walter, *A History of the Guyanese Working People, 1881–1905*, Baltimore: Johns Hopkins University Press, and Kingston, Jamaica: Heinemann, 1981

Roediger, David R., *The Wages of Whiteness: Race and the Making of the American Working Class*, London and New York: Verso, 1991

Roth, Günther, *The Social Democrats in Imperial Germany: A Study in Working-Class Isolation and National Integration*, Totowa, NJ: Bedminster, 1963

Sandbrook, Richard, and Robin Cohen, eds., *The Development of an African Working Class: Studies in Class Formation and Action*, Toronto: University of Toronto Press, and London: Longman, 1975

Schofer, Lawrence, *The Formation of a Modern Labor Force: Upper Silesia, 1865–1914*, Berkeley: University of California Press, 1975

Scott, Joan Wallach, *The Glassworkers of Carmaux: French Craftsmen and Political Action in a Nineteenth-Century City*, Cambridge, MA: Harvard University Press, 1974

Scott, Joan Wallach, *Gender and the Politics of History*, New York: Columbia University Press, 1988

Seligmann, Edwin R.A., ed., *Encyclopedia of the Social Sciences*, 15 vols., New York: Macmillan, 1930–35

Sewell, William H., Jr., *Work and Revolution in France: The Language of Labor from the Old Regime to 1848*, Cambridge and New York: Cambridge University Press, 1988

Sombart, Werner, *Sozialismus und Soziale Bewegung im 19. Jahrhundert*, Jena: Fischer, 1897; in English as *Socialism and the Social Movement*, London and New York: Putnam, 1898

Sombart, Werner, *Warum gibt es in den Vereinigten Staaten keinen Sozialismus?*, Tübingen: Mohr, 1906; in English as *Why Is There No Socialism in the United States?*, White Plains, NY: International Arts and Sciences Press, and London: Macmillan, 1976

Sturmthal, Adolf, *The Tragedy of European Labor, 1918–1939*, New York: Columbia University Press, and London: Gollancz, 1944

Tabili, Laura, *We Ask for British Justice: Workers and Racial Difference in Late Imperial Britain*, Ithaca, NY: Cornell University Press, 1994

Thompson, E.P., *The Making of the English Working Class*, London: Gollancz, 1963; New York: Pantheon, 1964

Thompson, Paul, *The Voice of the Past: Oral History*, Oxford and New York: Oxford University Press, 1978

Tilly, Louise A., and Joan Wallach Scott, *Women, Work, and Family*, New York: Holt Rinehart, 1978; London: Methuen, 1987

Tilly, Louise A., *Politics and Class in Milan, 1881–1901*, New York: Oxford University Press, 1992

Truant, Cynthia, *The Rites of Labor: Brotherhoods of Compagnonage in Old and New Regime France*, Ithaca, NY: Cornell University Press, 1994

Turner, H.A., *Trade Union Growth: Structure and Policy, A Comparative Study of the Cotton Unions in England*, Toronto: University of Toronto Press, 1962

Vincent, David, *Bread, Knowledge and Freedom: A Study of Nineteenth-Century Working-Class Autobiography*, London: Europa, 1981; New York: Methuen, 1982

Webb, Sidney and Beatrice, *The History of Trade Unionism*, London and New York: Longman, 1894; revised 1920

Wilentz, Sean, *Chants Democratic: New York City and the Rise of the American Working Class, 1788–1850*, New York: Oxford University Press, 1984

Winn, Peter, *Weavers of Revolution: The Yarut Workers and Chile's Road to Socialism*, Oxford and New York: Oxford University Press, 1986

Labrousse, Ernest 1895–1988

French historian

In 1955, Ernest Labrousse presented a paper entitled "How Revolutions are Born" which remains a seminal reference for social and economic historians alike. The paper provided a comparative approach to the understanding of the 1789, 1830 and 1848 revolutions in France. It revolved around two key ideas that are central to Labrousse's contributions to historical writing: that economic realities are essential to the understanding of history, and that social structures are significant.

The study of prices, Labrousse insisted, was essential if one wished to comprehend economic realities. This would help the historian to understand the depth of misery people faced at certain times. It would also explain governmental reactions to a crisis. This approach implied a long term as well as a short term analysis. It followed the broad division of time elaborated by François Simiand in his attempt to give history an economic base. Labrousse identified cyclical changes, crises, and seasonal fluctuations within the course of fifty years or more, referring at times to secular trends. Thus the crisis of 1788–89 was the culmination of a long period of price rises over the 18th century, combined with a short-term harvest failure which led to a considerable increase in the price of bread. Labrousse emphasized that not all people in society were hit in the same way by such developments. His analysis implied different consequences for various social groups, leading to differing levels of class consciousness.

Labrousse's attempt at assessing the depth of the social problems besetting 18th-century French society was developed on local and regional lines. A series of thirty monographs were written by Labrousse's students, designed to build up a broader, national picture. Based on the departmental archives, these monographs do not provide overall results, but they emphasize the differences, geographically as well as socially. It would be easy at this stage to classify Labrousse as an economic historian whose impact on historical writing is best illustrated by the use of long series of statistical evidence as reflected in his two famous works: *Esquisse du Mouvement des prix et des revenus en France au 18ème siècle* (Sketch of the Movement of Prices and Revenues in France in the 18th Century, 1933) and *La Crise de l'économie française à la fin de l'Ancien Régime* (The Crisis of the French Economy at the End of the *Ancien Régime*, 1944). Not so. To Labrousse, economic analysis was vital because "people spend a lot of time working in order to eat," but prices and wages were only one part of the overall story. Labrousse, like Lefebvre, was hoping to write *Histoire totale* (Total History).

This is particularly clear when he wrote about agricultural issues. He placed an emphasis on the relationship between production for self consumption (as opposed to production for sale) and for profit. He was aware of profits gained from new modes of cultivation and breeding, he stressed the importance of the cost of production, and he related agricultural prices to wages and taxes. He was therefore able to define different models of exploitation as well as budgets of consumption. In doing so, Labrousse developed a thorough method of investigation including an analysis of seigneurial accounts, series of land leases, notarial archives, wedding contracts, wills, and inventories of properties after death. He also covered all official documents dealing with taxation. The complexity of his findings are contained in his *Histoire économique et sociale de la France* (Economic and Social History of France, begun 1970). In it, Labrousse combined the long-term economic findings which illustrate his contribution to the Annales school – he worked with Febvre and Braudel in the Sixth Section of the Ecole des Hautes Etudes – with a refined and complex analysis of class realities in France. It can be argued that, in bringing together economic analysis and social realities, Labrousse was following in the footsteps of Jaurès who believed that history could not be divided because it had a single subject: society.

It would be tempting to classify Labrousse as one of the Annales writers with debts to Jaurès and Lefebvre in his desire to write the ultimate social picture of France in the 18th century. In the present circumstances, Labrousse may appear somewhat anachronistic. This is because history is divided up into numerous specialist areas, and because economic history is under attack for being deterministic. It is also because the anti-Marxist/revisionist outcry is dominant among a majority of historians of the French Revolution (at least in the English-speaking world). This would be to ignore his scholarly contribution to the study of 18th-century France and the Revolution. It would be to distort his overwhelming concern with social realities, and it would be ignoring his understanding of myths and memory, symbols and language in history.

Labrousse had opportunities to add another dimension to the writing of history as director of one other publication, *Le Dictionnaire biographique du monde ouvrier français* (Biographical Dictionary of the French Working Class). In it, a great deal of concern is shown for the meaning of revolutionary words and symbols. In fact, Labrousse had already pointed the way towards such an approach during the celebrations of the centenary of the Paris Commune, which led him to conclude that various memories reveal different mentalities and cultures. These in turn take different shapes depending on classes, groups, and nations. Such conclusions should not be altogether surprising given Labrousse's work alongside Braudel and Febvre at the Ecole Pratique des Hautes Etudes.

Labrousse stands out as a complex historian who combined long-term economic analysis with social and cultural awareness. For Labrousse, this was the only way to understand society and history, for according to him "there could be no History if it were not for Social History."

MARTINE BONDOIS MORRIS

See also Annales School; France: since the Revolution; Le Roy Ladurie; Simiand; Soboul; Vovelle

Biography

Ernest Camille Labrousse. Born Barbezieux, 16 March 1895, son of a merchant. Educated at the Collège de Barbezieux; then in the faculty of arts and law, Paris, receiving his doctorate, 1943. Taught at Rodez and Cognac; at the 6th section, Ecole Pratique des Hautes Etudes, 1934–35; succeeded Marc Bloch at the chair of economic history at the Sorbonne, 1945. Married Anne-Marie Ramaroni, 1918 (1 daughter). Died Paris, 24 May 1988.

Principal Writings

Esquisse du Mouvement des prix et des revenus en France au 18ème siècle (Sketch of the Movement of Prices and Revenues in France in the 18th Century), 1933

La Crise de l'économie française à la fin de l'Ancien Régime et au début de la Révolution (The Crisis of the French Economy at the End of the *Ancien Régime* and at the Beginning of the Revolution), 1944

Le Mouvement ouvrier et les théories sociales en France de 1815 à 1948 (The Worker's Movement and Social Theories in France, 1815–1948), 1961

Histoire économique et sociale de la France (Economic and Social History of France), 4 vols. in 8, 1970–82

Further Reading

Burke, Peter, *The French Historical Revolution: The Annales School, 1929–89*, Cambridge: Polity Press, and Stanford, CA: Stanford University Press, 1990

Caron, François, "Ernest Labrousse et l'Histoire Economique" (Ernest Labrousse and Economic History), *Histoire, Economie et Société* 9 (1990), 423–40

Cullen, Louis M., "History, Economic Crises and Revolution: Understanding Eighteenth-Century France," *Economic History Review* 46 (1993), 635–57

Grenier, Jean-Yves, and Bernard Lepetit, "L'Expérience historique: A propos de C.-E. Labrousse" (Historical Experience: According to Labrousse), *Annales ESC* 44 (1989), 1337–60

Iggers, Georg G., *New Directions in European Historiography*, Middletown, CT: Wesleyan University Press, 1975, revised 1985; London: Methuen, 1985

Renouvin, Pierre, "Ernest Labrousse," in Hans A. Schmitt, ed., *Historians of Modern Europe*, Baton Rouge: Louisiana University Press, 1971

Saly, Pierre, "Réflexions sur un héritage: Ernest Labrousse et le marxisme" (Reflections on a Heritage: Ernest Labrousse and Marxism), *Cahiers d'Histoire de l'Institut de Recherches Marxistes* 39 (1989), 3–34

Vovelle, Michelle, Pierre Vilar, Jean-René Suratteau, Maurice Agulhon, Guy Lemarchand, Madeleine Rebérioux, special issue, *Annales Historiques de la Révolution Française* 276 (April-June 1989)

LaFeber, Walter 1933–

US diplomatic historian

Walter LaFeber is one of the most prominent members of the group of historians known as the New Left or the Wisconsin school. Most of these individuals studied at the University of Wisconsin under William Appleman Williams, Fred Harvey Harrington, and Merrill Jensen. Following their mentors' lead, from the early 1960s onwards such historians as LaFeber, Lloyd Gardner, Thomas J. McCormick, and Gabriel Kolko began to challenge the consensus and often celebratory liberal interpretation of US history popular in the 1940s and 1950s. Drawing both upon radical Marxist critiques of the United States and upon the earlier Progressive tradition exemplified by Charles Beard and Vernon Parrington, they put forward a radical revisionist, dissenting analysis of the US, particularly its role in foreign affairs, one highly critical of their country and its effects upon the world. One of this school's most notable features was a renewed emphasis upon the economic roots of the growth of US international power. Whereas the Realist school of diplomatic history dominant in the 1940s and 1950s stressed what it perceived as the strategic, national security reasons for American expansionism, the New Left ascribed this development to a sustained attempt on the part of US policymakers to expand their country's economy and overseas markets. Some went so far as to suggest that American leaders did so because they feared that, without such foreign commercial outlets, the existing American political and economic system would collapse. This approach also argued that, in order to create a world safe for American business, the US government adopted a policy of opposing revolutionary movements elsewhere in the world, thereby becoming a conservative force in international affairs. Adherents of the Wisconsin school suggested that, ever since the foundation of the United States, such goals had governed the making of its foreign policies. The New Left school was strongly influenced by the 1960s climate of radical questioning of and dissent from contemporary US foreign policies precipitated by American involvement in the Vietnam War and the consequent protest movement. As the further reading listed suggests, this essentially pejorative interpretation gave rise to bitter debate between its proponents and more orthodox historians who stressed the role of national security, ideology, or a sense of mission, and suggested that US expansionism was in many ways beneficial.

LaFeber is one of the foremost exponents of the New Left school. His first, well-received book, *The New Empire* (1963), concentrated upon the role of US business interests in American intervention in the Spanish-American War of 1898 and the consequent decision to retain the Philippine Islands as a colony. LaFeber contended that the McKinley administration entered the war only after leading American business groups finally determined that war was the most economical and effective way of ending the ongoing turmoil in Cuba and thereby protecting their commercial interests. Likewise, while other forces were involved, economic considerations, including hopes for expanded US trade throughout the Pacific region, were crucial in the ensuing annexation of the Philippines.

LaFeber continues to write prolifically on US diplomacy. His survey textbooks, *America, Russia, and the Cold War* (1967) and *The American Age* (1989), applied the Open Door interpretation to other periods. In both, he argued that the furtherance of US economic interests, the creation and defense of a stable, free-market international order conducive to liberal capitalism and American trade and investment, was the fundamental aim of post World War II US policymakers. As US involvement in Central America became a burning political issue during the 1980s, LaFeber published *Inevitable Revolutions* (1983), a scathing critique of what he saw as the errors of American policy in that region, and the manner in which the economic interests of the Central American countries had been subordinated to the diplomatic and commercial aims of their larger neighbor.

By the early 1990s the worst of the acidulous heat had dissipated from the debates between revisionists and more orthodox diplomatic historians. Aspects of the New Left interpretation, particularly its emphasis upon the domestic roots of many American foreign policies, and the need to bear in mind the role of economic interests, had been incorporated into more general accounts of US diplomacy. The brash young men of the 1960s had become revered senior figures in their profession. It was symptomatic of this metamorphosis that LaFeber was asked to write a volume of The Cambridge History of American Foreign Relations covering the years 1865 to 1913. In *The American Search for Opportunity* (1993) he drew attention, not only to the American search for commercial opportunities overseas, an

aspect of the country's growing industrialization, but also to the fact that US economic involvement in less developed nations in the Caribbean, Latin America, and Asia had helped to create revolutionary situations in those areas. He also focused upon the effects the search for overseas influence had upon the US itself, among them the enhancement of the power of its military forces due to demands for the development of naval forces and the acquisition of bases and the army's role in the acquisition and of overseas colonies, and the beginning of the growth of an imperial presidency bolstered by the country's increased foreign interventions. By no means all historians agree with every aspect of LaFeber's interpretation, but most would admit that he has produced some of the most challenging and provocative work on US international expansion in the past 150 years, with which they must at least engage.

PRISCILLA M. ROBERTS

See also United States: 20th Century; United States: Historical Writing, 20th Century; Williams, W.

Biography
Born Walkerton, Indiana, 30 August 1933. Received BA, Hanover College, 1955; MA, Stanford University, 1956; PhD, University of Wisconsin, 1959. Taught at Cornell University, from 1956. Married 1955 (2 children).

Principal Writings
The New Empire: An Interpretation of American Expansion, 1860–1898, 1963
America, Russia, and the Cold War, 1945–1966, 1967; 7th edition [with dates 1945–1992], 1993
America in the Cold War: Twenty Years of Revolutions and Response, 1947–1967, 1969
The Panama Canal: The Crisis in Historical Perspective, 1978
Inevitable Revolutions: The United States in Central America, 1983; revised 1993
The American Age: United States Foreign Policy at Home and Abroad since 1750, 1989; 2nd edition 1994
The American Search for Opportunity, 1865–1913, 1993
Editor with Thomas J. McCormick, *Behind the Throne: Servants of Power to Imperial Presidents, 1898–1968*, 1993
The Clash: A History of US–Japan Relations, 1997

Further Reading
Blaser, Kent, "What Happened to New Left History?" *South Atlantic Quarterly* 85 (1986), 283–96; and 86 (1987), 209–28
Buhle, Paul, *History and the New Left: Madison, Wisconsin, 1950–1970*, Philadelphia: Temple University Press, 1990
Combs, Jerald A., *American Diplomatic History: Two Centuries of Changing Interpretations*, Berkeley: University of California Press, 1983
Evans, Richard William, "In Search of a Useable Past: Young Leftist Historians in the 1960s," PhD thesis, Cleveland: Case Western University, 1979
Kraus, Michael, and Davis D. Joyce, *The Writing of American History*, revised edition, Norman: University of Oklahoma Press, 1985
Maddox, Robert James, *The New Left and the Origins of the Cold War*, Princeton: Princeton University Press, 1973
Novick, Peter, *That Noble Dream: The "Objectivity Question" and the American Historical Profession*, Cambridge and New York: Cambridge University Press, 1988
Perkins, Bradford, "The Tragedy of American Diplomacy: Twenty-Five Years After," *Reviews in American History* 12 (1984), 1–18

Sharp, Edward Frank, "The Cold War Revisionists and their Critics," PhD thesis, University of North Carolina at Chapel Hill, 1979

Siracusa, Joseph M., *New Left Diplomatic Histories and Historians: The American Revisionists*, Port Washington, NY: Kennikat Press, 1973; revised edition Claremont, CA: Regina, 1993

Sternsher, Bernard, *Consensus, Conflict, and American Historians*, Bloomington: Indiana University Press, 1975

Thelen, David P., Jonathan Wiener, John D'Emilio, Herbert Aptheker, Gerda Lerner, Christopher Lasch, John Higham, Carl Degler, and David Levering Lewis, "A Round Table: What Has Changed and Not Changed in American Historical Practice?" *Journal of American History* 76 (1989), 393–478

Thompson, J.A., "William Appleman Williams and the `American Empire,'" *Journal of American Studies* 7 (1973), 91–104

Tucker, Robert W., *The Radical Left and American Foreign Policy*, Baltimore: Johns Hopkins Press, 1971

Tyrrell, Ian, *The Absent Marx: Class Analysis and Liberal History in Twentieth-Century America*, Westport, CT: Greenwood Press, 1986

Wise, Gene, *American Historical Explanations: A Strategy for Grounded Inquiry*, Homewood, IL: Dorsey Press, 1973; revised Minneapolis: University of Minnesota Press, 1980

Lake, Marilyn 1949–

Australian historian

One of Australia's most important historians and its leading practitioner of feminist history, Marilyn Lake has contributed to the transformation of historical inquiry in Australia since the 1970s. Her particular achievement has been the application of feminist perspectives to a diversity of topics in Australian history.

Emerging in the 1970s primarily in the fields of labor history, and in war and society studies, Lake fostered a new interpretation of the Australian homefront during World War I with her first book, *A Divided Society* (1975). Her entry into feminist history occurred with her critical review in 1976 of Miriam Dixson's path-breaking Australian feminist study, *The Real Matilda* (1976). Lake has subsequently examined women's roles in rural families, investigated both men's and women's experiences of the soldier settlement scheme in the state of Victoria, contributed to the study of the history of work in Australia, and undertaken research on citizenship.

Adopting a feminist framework, she has reinterpreted such dominant themes in Australian historiography as the significance of Anzac and the nature of Australian socialism. Lake has even applied feminist insights to a study of historical homes in Australia, a topic that had been largely untouched by feminist theory. In addition to her contribution to the broadening of Australian historiography through her own research, Lake has facilitated new interpretations of Australian experiences of war through her co-editorship with Joy Damousi of *Gender and War* (1995), the first book to explore the relationship in Australia between these two subjects.

Lake has also applied her skills of reinterpretation to the history of Australian feminism itself, exploring its racial dimensions and the status of its proponents as both colonized and colonizers. Her analysis draws on and contributes to a growing international literature which interrogates feminism itself. Her work on women's sexuality during World War II has challenged the previous characterization of the effects of this period on Australian women through her argument that femininity itself changed at this time.

Alongside other major Australian historians including Jill Julius Matthews, Kay Saunders, and Raymond Evans, Lake has been prominent in urging the transformation of women's history into a history of gender relations. She has urged that gendered analyses should be applied to all areas of history, rather than concentrating exclusively on "women's sphere," and has recognized the importance of exploring the specificities and gendered dimensions of men's as well as women's experiences. Her enthusiasm for such gendered analysis has been tempered, however, by a concern, shared with some other feminist historians, that a shift to the concept of gender may weaken the feminist project. She therefore advocates and practices a dual approach for feminist history which both deconstructs universal categories and constructs the history of women.

Lake's significance in Australian history extends beyond her own prolific output to include the debates which her work has generated. In her 1986 article, "The Politics of Respectability," she called for historical explorations of "manhood," "manliness," and "masculinity." Her arguments concerning masculinist culture and first wave feminism prompted responses, both supportive and critical, from other historians. Lake has also contributed to historiographical debates through her critiques of developments in particular areas, notably her claim in 1992 that labor history, one of the most important strands of Australian historiography, had adopted an assimilationist approach by which women "have been incorporated and rendered similar to the male subjects of labor history."

The diversity of topics on which Lake has written reflects her determination to address "the problem of how to reconstitute history so that women are integral to it." In conjunction with three other leading Australian feminist historians, she co-authored a major contribution to this project with the 1994 book, *Creating a Nation*, an attempt to produce a general history of Australia that emphasizes women's lives. Most general histories of this country have remained resistant to the insights of feminism. Lake and her co-authors have thus seized and hopefully transformed one of the most conservative fields of Australian history. Like much of Lake's other work, *Creating a Nation* has engendered widespread academic interest and debate.

JOANNE SCOTT

See also Australia; Women's History: Australia

Biography

Marilyn Calvert Lake. Born Hobart, Tasmania, 5 January 1949. Received BA and MA, University of Tasmania; PhD, Monash University. Taught history and social theory, University of Melbourne; taught (rising to professor), La Trobe University, from 1988. Married Philip Spencer Lake, 1968 (2 daughters).

Principal Writings

A Divided Society: Tasmania during World War I, 1975

"'To be Denied a Sense of Past Generations': A Review of Miriam Dixson, *The Real Matilda: Women and Identity in Australia, 1788–1975*," *Hecate*, 2 (1976), 68–73

"'Building Themselves Up with Aspros': Pioneer Women Re-assessed," *Hecate*, 7 (1981), 7–19

Editor with Farley Kelly, *Double Time: Women in Victoria, 150 Years*, 1985

"Helpmeet, Slave, Housewife: Women in Rural Families, 1870–1930" in Patricia Grimshaw, Chris McConville and Ellen McKewen, eds., *Families in Colonial Australia*, 1985, 173–85

"The Politics of Respectability: Identifying the Masculinist Context," *Historical Studies* 22 (1986), 116–31

"Socialism and Manhood: The Case of William Lane," *Labor History* 50 (1986), 54–62

The Limits of Hope: Soldier Settlement in Victoria, 1915–38, 1987

"Intimate Strangers" in Verity Burgmann and Jenny Lee, eds., *Making a Life: A People's History of Australia since 1788*, 1988, 152–65

"The Power of Anzac," in Michael McKernan and Margaret Browne, eds., *Australia: Two Centuries of War and Peace*, 1988, 194–222

Editor with Charles Fox, *Australians at Work: Commentaries and Sources*, 1990

"Female Desires: The Meaning of World War II," *Australian Historical Studies* 24 (1990), 267–84

"Historical Homes" in John Rickard and Peter Spearritt, eds., *Packaging the Past? Public Histories*, special issue of *Australian Historical Studies* 24 (1991), 46–54

"The Desire for a Yank: Sexual Relations Between Australian Women and American Servicemen during World War II," *Journal of the History of Sexuality* 2 (1992), 621–37

"The Independence of Women and the Brotherhood of Man: Debates in the Labor Movement over Equal Pay and Motherhood Endowment in the 1920s," *Labor History* 63 (1992), 1–24

"Mission Impossible: How Men Gave Birth to the Australian Nation: Nationalism, Gender, and Other Seminal Acts," *Gender and History* 4 (1992), 305–22

"Between Old World 'Barbarism' and Stone Age 'Primitivism': The Double Difference of the White Australian Feminist" in Norma Grieve and Ailsa Burns, eds., *Australian Women: Contemporary Feminist Thought*, 1994, 80–91

With Patricia Grimshaw, Ann McGrath, and Marian Quartly, *Creating a Nation*, 1994

"Personality, Individuality, Nationality: Feminist Conceptions of Citizenship 1902–1940," *Australian Feminist Studies* 19 (1994), 25–38

Editor with Katie Holmes, *Freedom Bound 2: Documents on Women in Modern Australia*, 1995

Editor with Joy Damousi, *Gender and War: Australians at War in the Twentieth Century*, 1995

Lamprecht, Karl 1856–1915

German cultural and social historian

Most famous historians owe their place in the historiographical tradition to a seminal work, a far-reaching historical concept, or an academic school founded by them. Karl Lamprecht, by contrast, is still remembered mainly in connection with a methodological dispute that concerned German historians around the turn of the century. The question at the heart of this dispute can be stated, in simplified terms, as "Traditional event- and character-based history or economic, social and cultural history?"; Lamprecht fought vehemently for the latter alternative and lost the debate within Germany. After the controversy was over, traditional German historicism reaffirmed its dominant position, isolated the challenger, and treated him thereafter with incomprehension. With Lamprecht's early death it seemed at first that the matter was closed, and yet it soon became clear that his influence would continue and that he would not be simply consigned to oblivion.

Lamprecht was born in 1856 in a Protestant vicarage in Jessen, in the province of Saxony. Tutoring from his father and his subsequent education in distinguished establishments, including the famous Fürstenschule (royal academy) at Schulpforta, left a lasting imprint on his character, contributing to the development of an individual and often controversial personality. After taking his Abitur in 1874, Lamprecht began his historical studies: from the very beginning it seems that he regarded the historical tradition as being in need of revision. A number of academic teachers, notably Ernst Bernheim, encouraged his critical views and guided the thoughts they provoked.

Far-reaching social changes in Germany in the late 19th century, together with the rapid rise of science, confronted historians with the challenge of how history should be written in the future. However, a number of special factors affected developments in Germany, among them the strong influence of Ranke and the restrictive scope of contemporary cultural history writing, which limited itself purely to the history of ideas. These factors meant that in Germany the tension between existing historiographical practice and the search for innovation was much more pronounced than in other European countries.

Lamprecht's research interests quickly focused on economic history. After studying in Bonn, Leipzig, and Munich he submitted his dissertation in 1877; it was immediately published by Gustav Schmoller, as the third volume of his newly-founded series on social and political science.

It is no surprise that from this time onward Lamprecht was influenced by the new German school of political economy with which Schmoller was closely connected and took an increasingly psychohistorical approach to the past. The foundations of his later work were already laid when he took up a post as a private tutor in Cologne in 1879, thus becoming economically self-sufficient for the first time.

Soon after this, thanks to financial support from his Rhineland patron Gustav Mevissen, Lamprecht was able to spend a number of years continuing his studies on the economic history of the Rhineland; he presented his postdoctoral thesis on this subject in Bonn in 1880. He pursued his research into the history of this region tenaciously, despite receiving no support from other historians, taking on substantial administrative duties in order to extend his knowledge of the subject. Eventually he did achieve recognition in the German academic world, principally for his 3-volume work from this period, *Deutsches Wirtschaftsleben im Mittelalter* (The Economic Life of Germany in the Middle Ages, 1885–86).

Lamprecht held an associate professorship in Bonn from 1889 to 1890, and during this time he drew up the outline of a history of Germany, the aim of which was to encompass social, economic, political, and intellectual phenomena – in short to present the material and intellectual development of German civilization, to uncover reciprocal effects and influences, and to delineate successive states of historical development on this basis of cultural totality.

After a brief stay in Marburg in 1890, Lamprecht was offered a professorship in Leipzig, which he took up in 1891; he remained on the teaching staff of this university until his death. At this time Leipzig had developed a very distinctive intellectual climate. Academics from far afield were attracted to the university, adding to its reputation as an unusually productive and innovative intellectual center that was open to new ideas. Lamprecht joined Wilhelm Ostwald, Wilhelm Wundt, Karl Bücher, Friedrich Ratzel, and other professors who met for weekly discussions in the famous "postivists' circle." This group was an additional source of inspiration to Lamprecht: along with his own plans and his wide-ranging awareness of contemporary academic developments it spurred him on to develop his ideas further and to present them to the public in his *Deutsche Geschichte* (History of Germany), whose 12 volumes appeared in quick succession between 1891 and 1909.

By contrast, Lamprecht's colleagues in the history department treated him with restraint at best, and in some cases with outright disapproval. The methodological dispute, which started as early as 1891, erupted fully when Georg von Below wrote a damning review of the first volumes of the *Deutsche Geschichte* in 1893; it intensified when subsequent volumes received an equally comprehensive dismissal from the same source in 1895. Germany's leading contemporary historians had pronounced a judgment on Lamprecht that was regarded as conclusive throughout his lifetime. His thoughts, reflections, suggestions, and proposals were rejected by the historical establishment, a situation that was exacerbated by the overemphasis on psychological phenomena that characterized his later works. A renewal of interest in Lamprecht came only much later, when traditional historicism in Germany had lost its long-standing and more or less unchallenged dominance, and when new historical approaches were being sought: then he came to be seen as a forerunner in the search for a history of social psychology and of research into the pyschology of peoples.

None of these troubles prevented Lamprecht completing his *Deutsche Geschichte*, which was a striking success with the public right through to the last volume, in spite of the methodological dispute. Alongside this he published a series of other works, was highly active in academic administration (and from time to time in cultural and educational politics), undertook a reformation of the history curriculum, and battled for university reform (notably during his period as rector of the University of Leipzig). During the last years of his life he planned a world history, which he was not able to complete. He drew considerable inspiration for his many activities from his travels abroad: a visit to the US in 1904 stands out in this respect. His experience there spurred him on, and he was extremely grateful for the assurance of sympathy for his work outside Germany.

The most enduring product of Lamprecht's efforts in these years was the Königlich-Sächsisches Institut für Kultur- und Universalgeschichte bei der Universität Leipzig, which was founded in 1909. Lamprecht's considerable skill in attracting private funding for the establishment enabled him effectively to split from the university's history department. Although the new institute further exacerbated the tensions between Lamprecht and his colleagues, it also provided a multifaceted teaching and research facility that was fully geared to its founder's ideas of cultural and world history. Lamprecht's extension of his theories to the idea of world history, and his use of comparison as a methodological principle connecting

states and continents attracted many academics and students from Germany and abroad, creating an international academic center that was unique in Germany at the time.

When Lamprecht died suddenly in 1915, the first era of this institute came to an abrupt end. Nonetheless it continued to exist as part of the University of Leipzig for the next eight decades, although it saw changes of name and direction, as well as some departures from its founder's intentions, during this time. In 1992 the Institute was separated from the university and today it operates independently, in association with the Karl Lamprecht Society of Leipzig.

Although he published prolifically, Lamprecht did not leave a rounded oeuvre behind him. Despite the huge range of material he dealt with, all his work displays the exploratory, investigative approach that sometimes led him to pursue false trails. Lamprecht has often been critized, doubtless rightly, for a lack of historical accuracy in detail, and his complex personality often colored the disputes in which he was involved. Although Lamprecht cannot be said to have founded a school of history, nonetheless he was an inspiring researcher and teacher who constantly encouraged others to tackle new questions and problems.

GERALD DIESENER

See also *See also* Germany: 1800–1945; Pirenne; Schnabel; Social; World

Biography

Born Jessen, Saxony, 25 February 1856, son of a Protestant minister. Taught at University of Bonn, 1885–90; University of Marburg, 1890–91; University of Leipzig, 1891–1915. Married Mathilde Mühle, 1887 (2 daughters). Died Leipzig, 10 May 1915.

Principal Writings

Deutsches Wirtschaftsleben im Mittelalter (The Economic Life of Germany in the Middle Ages), 3 vols., 1885–86
Deutsche Geschichte (History of Germany), 12 vols. and 2 supplementary vols., 1891–1909
Alte und neue Richtungen in der Geschichtswissenschaft (Old and New Directions in History), 1896
"Was ist Kulturgeschichte? Beitrag zu einer empirischen Historik" (What is Cultural History? Toward an Empirical History), *Deutsche Zeitschrift für Geschichtswissenschaft*, new series 1 (1896/97)
Die kulturhistorische Methode (The Methodology of Cultural History), 1900
"Zur universalgeschichtlichen Methodenbildung" (Toward a Methodological Basis for World History), *Abhandlungen der philologisch-historischen Klasse der Königlich-Sächsischen Gesellschaft der Wissenschaften*, vol. 27, 1909

Further Reading

Chickering, Roger, *Karl Lamprecht: A German Academic Life (1856–1915)*, Atlantic Highlands, NJ: Humanities Press, 1993
Diesener, Gerald, ed., *Karl Lamprecht weiterdenken* (A Continuation of Karl Lamprecht's Ideas), Leipzig: Leipziger Universität Verlag, 1993
Schleier, Hans, ed., *Karl Lamprecht: Alternative zu Ranke* (Karl Lamprecht: Alternative to Ranke), Leipzig: Reclam, 1988
Schorn-Schütte, Louise, *Karl Lamprecht: Kulturgeschichtsschreibung zwischen Wissenschaft und Politik* (Karl Lamprecht: Cultural History Writing Between Science and Politics), Göttingen: Vandenhoeck & Ruprecht, 1984

Landes, David S. 1924–

US economic historian

David Landes has been one of the leading postwar figures in the development of the study of European economic history. Having held appointments in both economics and history, he has long encouraged the interdisciplinary exchange of ideas. Landes' importance goes beyond his published work, as significant as it is: over several decades, he helped create or inspire a number of large research projects and journals, some of which continue today. He has particularly influenced scholarship in four broad areas: entrepreneurship and business history; banking; technology and the process of industrialization; and the culture of capitalism, that is, attitudes and beliefs that encourage capitalist activity.

Beginning with his earliest articles around 1950, Landes helped spark a long-running debate by arguing that many French industrialists had hindered their country's industrialization in the 19th century. These French businessmen, he argued, formed a distinctive type of cautious entrepreneur who resisted capital investment, expansion, and innovation and who tried thereby to maintain their enterprises as family firms. Whereas much of business history remained rather narrowly focused on the development of firms, Landes broadened the field to include a study of how cultural attitudes shaped business and how entrepreneurship, or the lack thereof, in turn shaped society. Although subsequent scholarship has modified Landes' original picture of French business, his ideas inspired numerous works in French business history as well as comparative studies of entrepreneurship in other countries. To further this kind of comparative research, Landes was one of the most active participants of the Research Center in Entrepreneurial History at Harvard University (1948–58) as well as an influential editor of the journal *Explorations in Entrepreneurial History* (presently *Explorations in Economic History*). The Center and *Explorations* helped inspire other efforts, for example, the German business history journal *Tradition*, presently *Zeitschrift für Unternehmengeschichte*.

Second, Landes defined for both historians and economists what was new about 19th-century banking and how it arose. The great change, he argued, was from family-owned, merchant banking houses such as the Rothschilds to incorporated, joint stock bank companies such as the French *Crédit Mobilier* in the 1860s. Landes pointed out, however, that merchant bankers themselves often brought about the "banking revolution" by helping form new banking companies and by pioneering the kinds of investments which their successors would exploit more fully. Not only did Landes' own publications helped define the field of banking history, but he assisted in the research of one of the works which brought banking history into the mainstream of historical writing, Fritz Stern's *Gold and Iron: Bismarck, Bleichröder and the Building of the German Empire* (1977) which detailed the vital financial support Bleichröder, the "German Rothschild," provided to Bismarck.

Third, in the area of technology and industrialization, Landes' most widely-known work is also probably the most frequently cited scholarly work on European economic history: *The Unbound Prometheus* (1969), an expansion of his enormous chapter on industrialization in the 6th volume of *The Cambridge Economic History of Europe*. Almost all previous attempts to deal with the history of industrialization had focused either on Britain or on one or two countries as imitators of the British. Using an impressive range of sources in French and German, Landes covered a much vaster scope, giving special treatment to how industrialization spread from Britain to the Continent, the role of smaller countries such as Belgium and Switzerland, and competition between Britain and Germany in the late 19th century. Drawing on his earlier work, he argued that both the original impetus of the Industrial Revolution in Britain and the later "closing of the gap" with Britain by Germany were deeply dependent both on cultural habits and innovations such as modern banking as well as on technological breakthroughs. He was also one of the first historians to use the concept of a "Second Industrial Revolution," the group of innovations beginning in the late 19th century and centered around electricity, fuel oil, refrigeration, the internal combustion engine, and synthetic dyes which shaped industrialization in the 20th century.

A fourth area to which Landes devoted a great deal of study was the cultural attributes that underlie economic development, a concern that has run through much of his career in various forms. Landes approached the question of why Western Europe pioneered the industrial revolution in the broadest of contexts, comparing Europe to other great centers of civilizations such as East Asia and the Middle East. This comparative focus grew in part out of his earliest research on French banking interests in 19th-century Egypt, work that allowed him to see how two cultures could engage in economic relations from widely different perceptions and expectations. In *Unbound Prometheus*, Landes suggested that Western merchants had – through law, religious sanction, and associations – gradually won a freedom that non-Western merchants lacked. Similarly, in his *Revolution in Time*, he argued that Europe, rather than China, perfected clocks because time itself had a different meaning in Europe while, within Europe, Protestantism and openness to markets helped a small part of Switzerland become the world leader in timepieces for centuries.

CARL STRIKWERDA

See also Habakkuk; Industrial Revolution

Biography

David Saul Landes. Born New York, 29 April 1924. Educated at City College, New York; Harvard University, PhD. Served in the US Army signal corps, 1943–46. Research fellow, Harvard University, 1950–53; taught in the economics department, Columbia University, 1952–58; fellow, Center for Advanced Study in Behavioral Sciences, Stanford University, 1957–58; professor of history and economics, University of California, Berkeley, 1958–64; various professorships in history and economics, Harvard University, from 1964. Married Sonia Tarnopol, 1943 (1 son, 2 daughters).

Principal Writings

"French Entrepreneurship and Industrial Growth in the Nineteenth Century," *Journal of Economic History*, 9 (1949), 45–61
"French Business and the Businessman: A Social and Cultural Analysis," in Edward Mead Earle, ed., *Modern France: Problems of the Third and Fourth Republic*, 1951
"Social Attitudes, Entrepreneurship, and Economic Development: A Comment," *Explorations in Entrepreneurial History*, 6 (1953–54), 245–72

"Vieille banque et banque nouvelle: la révolution financière du dix-neuvième siècle," *Revue d'histoire moderne et contemporaine*, 3 (1956), 204–22; in English as "The Old Bank and the New: The Financial Revolution of the Nineteenth Century," in François Crouzet, William Henry Chaloner, and Walter M. Stern, eds., *Essays in European Economic History, 1789–1914*, 1969
Bankers and Pashas: International Finance and Economic Imperialism in Egypt, 1958
"Some Thoughts on the Nature of Economic Imperialism," *Journal of Economic History*, 21 (1961), 496–512
"Japan and Europe: Contrasts in Industrialization," in William W. Lockwood, ed., *The State and Economic Enterprise in Japan: Essays in the Political Economy of Growth*, 1965
"Technological Change and Economic Development in Western Europe, 1750–1914," in H.J. Habakkuk and M.M. Postan, eds., *The Cambridge Economic History of Europe*, chapter 5 of vol. 6, *The Industrial Revolutions and After: Incomes, Population and Technological Change*, 1965
Editor, *The Rise of Capitalism*, 1966
The Unbound Prometheus: Technological Change and Industrial Development in Western Europe from 1750 to the Present, 1969
Editor with Charles Tilly, *History as Social Science*, 1971
"Religion and Enterprise: The Case of the French Textile Industry," Edward C. Carter, Robert Forster, and Joseph N. Moody, eds., *Enterprise and Entrepreneurs in Nineteenth and Twentieth-Century France*, 1976
Revolution in Time: Clocks and the Making of the Modern World, 1983
"What Do Bosses Really Do?" *Journal of Economic History*, 46 (1986), 585–623
"Introduction: On Technology and Growth," Patrice Higonnet, David S. Landes, and Henry Rosovsky, eds., *Favorites of Fortune: Technology, Growth, and Economic Development since the Industrial Revolution*, 1991
"The Fable of the Dead Horse; or, The Industrial Revolution Revisited," in Joel Mokyr, ed., *The British Industrial Revolution: An Economic Perspective*, 1993

Further Reading

Mokyr, Joel, ed., *The Economics of the Industrial Revolution*, Totowa, NJ: Rowman and Allanheld, and London: Allen and Unwin, 1985

Laroui, Abdallah ['Abd Allāh al-'Arawī]

1933–
Moroccan historian

Abdallah Laroui is a Moroccan Arab historian whose credo was set out in *La Crise des intellectuels arabes* (1974; *The Crisis of the Arab Intellectual*, 1976). Drawing on Ranke and Meinecke, he employed the terms positivism and historicism to set out a view of history as a chain of cause and effect, in which societies and their values progressively change according to circumstance, but also according to action. This philosophy of history was adopted by the Arab world as a political philosophy in its historical confrontation with the West, one that condemned traditionalism and the appeal to the values of the past. The result was a dangerous delusion that prevented the Arabs from coming to terms with the reality of their predicament, made all the worse for its equation with nationalism, a selective and divisive approach to the problems of society. Laroui felt it was essential that Arabs understand

precisely how the present situation had come about, including the way in which their traditions had evolved, otherwise they would remain the victims of events over which they had no control. Such an understanding of the past, which postulated that truth was not given, or possessed by some authority, but was needed to be worked at by everyone, was the foundation of democracy, a system in which the ideal was progressively established by continuous debate and choice. It was, for that matter, the principle of scientific inquiry. The crisis of the Arab intellectual was that it fell to him to be the prophet who dared to denounce the cherishing of tradition, to proclaim the need for history as the road to democracy, and to stand against the forces of tyranny across the Arab world. To do so, he had to work inside the territorial state of which he was a citizen, while using the freedom conferred on him by his wider Arabism to criticize the government of which he disapproved.

This program of political opposition translated into Laroui's practice as a historian of Morocco and the Maghrib as a whole. His doctoral thesis, published as *Les Origines sociales et culturelles du nationalisme marocain, 1830–1912* (The Social and Cultural Origins of Moroccan Nationalism, 1830–1912) (1977) proposed that the traditionalism admired and cultivated by the French Protectorate (1912–56) for its own political purposes, had been established only in the 18th century because of the isolation of the country from the rest of the Arab-Muslim world. It had then served the purpose of the Moroccans in the 19th century as a means of resisting the European penetration which culminated in the loss of independence in 1912. Out of that resistance, however, had grown Moroccan nationalism, which, as circumstances changed, had willingly embraced Western rationalism as the key to the future. In *L'Histoire du Maghrib* (1970; *The History of the Maghrib*, 1977), the thesis had been extended to the rest of North Africa and back to classical antiquity, to provide a comprehensive interpretation of the region's history. Here Laroui took exception, not only to the colonial view of the population's inherent backwardness (variously ascribed to Islam, the Arabs, and the Turks), but also to the "decolonization of history" by nationalist historians concerned to praise everything previously denigrated by colonialism. Instead, Laroui argued that continual outside pressure – military, political, and economic – applied over the past two or three thousand years in a progressive chain of cause and effect, had inhibited the independent development of the Maghrib into a prosperous economy, society, and state. National independence at last offered the hope of a new departure.

The *Histoire du Maghreb* therefore concluded in 1930–32, with North African nationalism variously engaged in repudiating the colonial power and its values, in cooperating with it for tactical advantage, and in preparing to overtake it on its own rational, scientific grounds, at the beginning of the countdown to independence. Reviewing the outcome of independence, however, Laroui offered a pessimistic conclusion, arguing that "the real problem is cultural": the peoples of North Africa have so long been accustomed to dictatorship that government is still left to those only too anxious to cling to power. Only when those governments take positive steps to involve their peoples in the decisions that affect their future will true independence be achieved in the form of participatory, pluralist democracy. Only in that democracy will the necessary rationalism come into play, and then only if people thoroughly understand the historical process which has defined their collective identity. If it is the task of the state to establish the practice, it is very much the task of the historian to establish the principle.

MICHAEL BRETT

Biography
Born Azemmour (Azmur), Morocco, 7 November 1933. Educated at Lycée Moulay Youssef, Rabat; the Sorbonne; Institute of Political Studies, Paris, PhD. Counsellor of foreign affairs, Rabat, 1960–63. Professor, University of Rabat from 1964; taught at University of California, Los Angeles, 1967–70.

Principal Writings
L'Histoire du Maghreb: un essai de synthèse, 1970; in English as The History of the Maghrib: An Interpretive Essay, 1977
La Crise des intellectuels arabes: traditionalisme ou historicisme?, 1974; in English as The Crisis of the Arab Intellectual: Traditionalism or Historicism?, 1976
L'Algérie et le sahara marocain (Algeria and the Moroccan Sahara), 1976
Les Origines sociales et culturelles du nationalisme marocain, 1830–1912 (The Social and Cultural Origins of Moroccan Nationalism, 1830–1912), 1977

Las Casas, Bartolomé de 1474–1566
Spanish historian and Dominican missionary in the Americas

Bartolomé de Las Casas was the first to expose the oppression of Latin American Indians by Europeans, and to call for the abolition of Indian slavery. Even though in his later years Las Casas became an influential figure of the Spanish court, he failed to stave off enslavement of the indigenous people in Latin America. Las Casas was a prolific writer and his written works are a fundamental source for the early history of the Spanish dominions in America.

Las Casas left Spain for the West Indies in 1502. As a reward for his participation in various expeditions, he was given an encomienda (a royal land grant including its Indian inhabitants). He soon began to evangelize the Indians, teaching them the catechism; Las Casas was ordained a priest in 1512 or 1513. In a famous sermon on 15 August 1514, Las Casas announced that he was returning his Indian serfs to the governor, and in 1515 returned to Spain to plead for their better treatment. In addition to studying the juridical problems of the Indies, Las Casas began to work out a plan for peaceful colonization of the Indians. Upon his return to Santo Domingo, his attempt to carry out colonization plans by peaceful means failed. Soon after, Las Casas abandoned his reformist activities and took refuge in religious life. In 1523 he joined the Dominican order. At a convent of Puerto de Plata in Santo Domingo he began to write the introduction to his masterpiece Historia de las Indias (History of the Indies), finished in 1562.

Las Casas' long works were interspersed with letters and petitions which he sent to the Council of the Indies in Madrid accusing Spaniards and the colonial institutions of the sin of oppressing the Indians, particularly through the encomienda system. After various attempts at founding Indian settlements in Central America free of the encomenderos (holders of encomiendas), Las Casas' ideas brought him into conflict with the Spanish authorities. In 1537 Las Casas wrote Del único modo de atraer a todos los pueblos a la verdadera religión (The Only Way, 1992), in which he set forth the doctrine of peaceful evangelization of the Indians.

Las Casas' following work, Brevísima relación de la destrucción de las Indias (The Tears of the Indians, 1656) was written in 1542 and is an indictment of the Spanish colonizers' greed for gold, which lay at the heart of their cruelty toward the Indians. In contrast, Las Casas portrayed the Indians as naturally good human beings. The same year, Las Casas' work bore fruit as King Charles signed the so-called New Laws, according to which the encomienda was not to be considered a hereditary grant. Instead, the owners had to set free their Indians after the span of a single generation. To ensure enforcement of these laws, Las Casas was named bishop of Chiapas, then part of the captaincy general of Guatemala. Upon his arrival there in January 1545, he issued Avisos y reglas para los confesores de españoles (Admonitions and Regulations for the Confessors of Spaniards), in which he forbade that absolution be given to the encomenderos. Las Casas' uncompromising pro-Indian position alienated not only the Spanish faithful but also his colleagues. In 1547, Las Casas returned to Spain.

An influential figure at the court and the Council of the Indies, Las Casas came into direct confrontation with the learned Juan Ginés de Sepúlveda, the author of a treatise "Concerning the Just Cause of the War Against the Indians." Ginés de Sepúlveda alleged that in accordance with Aristotelian principles the Indians were inferior to the Spaniards as children were to adults, women to men and apes to humans. At the Council of Valladolid Las Casas publicly disputed with Ginés de Sepúlveda, but the debate did not lead to the abolishment of Indian servitude. Las Casas continued to write books, tracts, and petitions in order to leave in written form his arguments in defense of the American Indians.

In 1562 Las Casas finished the Historia de las Indias. As well as a chronicle, Historia was meant to be a prophetic interpretation of the events as Las Casas had seen them or heard of them. The purpose of all the facts he sets forth is the exposure of the "sin" of domination, oppression, and injustice that the Europeans were inflicting upon the colonized people. Las Casas intended to reveal to Spain the reason for the misfortune that would inevitably befall her when she became the object of God's punishment. Las Casas left a written instruction that the work itself should be published only "after forty years have passed, so that, if God determines to destroy Spain, it may be seen that it is because of the destruction that we have wrought in the Indies and His just reason for it may be clearly evident." In fact, Historia de las Indias remained unpublished until 1875.

Las Casas had an enduring influence on latter-day liberators like the 19th-century Simón Bolívar and the protagonists of Mexico's struggle for independence from Spain. Las Casas' adversaries charged him with propagating the Black Legend of Spanish cruelty inflicted on the subject populations in her colonies. His modern significance lies in the fact that he was the first European to perceive the economic, political, and cultural injustice of the colonial system maintained by the North Atlantic powers when in control of Latin America and its people. His eye-witness account remains a powerful source for the study of the European conquest of the New World.

DANIELA SPENSER

See also Borah; European Expansion; Hanke; Latin America: Colonial; Spain: Imperial

Biography

Born Seville, August 1474, son of Pedro de las Casas of Tarifa (Cadiz), who accompanied Columbus on his second voyage to the New World, and Isabel de Sosa of Seville. Educated at the cathedral school, Seville. Fought Moorish inhabitants of Granada as member of Sevillian militia. Went to New World with Nicolás de Ovando, 1502; helped suppress Indian uprising, Santo Domingo, receiving Indians and land as reward. Entered priesthood and later Dominican order; became bishop of Chiapas, 1544; lived in Latin America where he was known as a champion of Indian rights; returned to Spain, 1547. Died Madrid, 18 July 1566.

Principal Writings

Del único modo de atraer a todos los pueblos a la verdadera religión, in Latin as *De unico vocationis*, 1537; in English as *The Only Way*, 1992
Avisos y reglas para los confesores de españoles (Admonitions and Regulations for the Confessors of Spaniards), 1545
Brevísima relación de la destrucción de las Indias, 1552; in English as *The Tears of the Indians*, 1656; and *The Devastation of the Indies: A Brief Account*, 1974
Apologética historia sumaria (Summary of the Historical Defense), written 1550s, published 2 vols., 1967
Historia de las Indias, completed 1562, first published, 1875; in English as *History of the Indies*, 1971

Further Reading

Florescano, Enrique, and Ricardo Pérez Montfort, eds., *Historiadores de México en el siglo XX* (Mexican Historians of the 20th Century), Mexico City: FCE & CONACULTA, 1995
Friede, Juan, and Benjamin Keen, eds., *Bartolomé de las Casas in History: Toward an Understanding of the Man and his Work*, DeKalb: Northern Illinois University Press, 1971
Hanke, Lewis, *The Spanish Struggle for Justice in the Conquest of America*, Philadelphia: University of Pennsylvania Press, 1949
Hanke, Lewis, *Bartolomé de las Casas, Historian: An Essay in Spanish Historiography*, Gainesville: University of Florida Press, 1952
Hanke, Lewis, and Manuel Giménez Fernández, *Bartolomé de Las Casas, 1474–1566: bibliografía crítica* (Bartolomé de Las Casas, 1474–1566: A Critical Bibliography), Santiago de Chile: Fondo Histórico y Bibliográfico José Toribio Medina, 1954
Sanderlin, George, ed. and trans., *Bartolomé de las Casas: A Selection of His Writings*, New York: Knopf, 1967

Lasch, Christopher 1932–1994

US social historian

Christopher Lasch was one of the most expansive historians and critical public intellectuals of the entire postwar period. His legacy was an often brilliant corpus of work that, perhaps ironically, combined intense moralism and deep politicization with the idea that intellectuals always have a calling higher than politics.

Lasch was above all an intellectual historian, but his was an extremely broad vision of the range of the intellect. His first book, *The American Liberals and the Russian Revolution* (1962), was methodologically and politically rather traditional. His critique there, though, of intellectuals who glorified the Bolshevik revolution instead of examining its antidemocratic outcomes served to foreshadow the book that brought him critical acclaim among historians, *The New Radicalism in America* (1965).

The New Radicalism in America had a deep influence, particularly among young scholars, because of Lasch's castigation of intellectuals' worship of the "real world" when their true vocation should be speaking truth to power. Lasch's didacticism, however, was relatively restrained in *The New Radicalism* as he explored the psyches of thinkers ranging from Jane Addams to Norman Mailer.

As the 1960s wore on Lasch increasingly chose to play the role of the public intellectual attempting to maintain his autonomy while being engaged in highly politicized times. His essays, particularly those in collaboration with Eugene Genovese, on issues ranging from the betrayal of the life of the mind by Cold War intellectuals as well as New Left activists to the rise of the Black Power movement, were some of the most important to appear in the *New York Review of Books* during the Vietnam War era. The best examples of this kind of writing appear in *The Agony of the American Left* (1969) and *The World of Nations* (1973).

During the 1960s Lasch had become quite radicalized and was consistently critical of bureaucratic power and capitalist domination. Yet as the New Left self-immolated, and the left as a whole fell apart, Lasch turned his attention to blending the Marxism that simultaneously attracted and repelled him with Freudian models of psychological analysis. Here he followed in the footsteps of the Frankfurt school of disillusioned cultural critics. The key works from this middle period of Lasch's intellectual career are *Haven in a Heartless World* (1977), *The Culture of Narcissism* (1978), and *The Minimal Self* (1984). Here Lasch's concerns with traditional historical method became fairly tenuous. His main purpose became the castigation of the hegemony of capitalist consumer culture, the "helping professions" of the welfare state, and the quest for self-realization, all of which he felt were a dreadful substitute for genuine political and communal participation. In particular, *The Culture of Narcissism* generated significant debate, and at least indirectly president Jimmy Carter used the book to frame his famous "malaise" speech.

In the last phase of his life Lasch returned to a serious consideration of history, interested not only in a critical attack on the American present, but equally significantly in some grounds for hope from the past. Lasch's *magnum opus*, *The True and Only Heaven* (1991), was a *tour de force* that, even if flawed by an insufficient appreciation of the complexities of social life, brought together the intellectual lives of Jonathan Edwards and 19th-century labor organizers, Ralph Waldo Emerson and antibusing activists of the 1970s. Above all, Lasch here argued that real alternatives have indeed existed to the predominant Anglo-American addiction to secular material progress. In particular, Lasch maintained that Americans must take seriously and help to rehabilitate the petit bourgeois populism that has inspired the most democratic (and anticapitalist) movements and ideas in the American past. Lasch explored such themes, often in even more of the fashion of the jeremiad, in the posthumously published *The Revolt of the Elites* (1995).

Lasch relished controversy, and many intellectuals were more than happy to engage him in contention. Such debates often turned vituperative, and in some circles Lasch acquired a reputation for meanness. Yet at the heart of his critical mind was a recognition that intellectual respect came most fully out of constructive disagreement. It is then indeed in his naysaying, born curiously out of generosity, that Lasch continues to serve as a model for the reconstruction of intellectual (and perhaps even civic) life in an age of far too uncritical acceptance of the ideas of one's friends and far too harsh dismissal of one's supposed enemies.

ROBERT D. JOHNSTON

See also Family; Mentalities

Biography

Robert Christopher Lasch. Born Omaha, Nebraska, 1 June 1932, son of a journalist and a professor. Received BA, Harvard University, 1954; MA, Columbia University, 1955, PhD 1961. Taught at Williams College, 1957–59; Roosevelt University, 1960–61; University of Iowa, 1961–66; Northwestern University, 1966–70; and University of Rochester, 1970–94. Married Nell Commager, daughter of the historian Henry Steele Commager, 1956 (2 sons, 2 daughters). Died Pittsford, New York, 14 February 1994.

Principal Writings

The American Liberals and the Russian Revolution, 1962
The New Radicalism in America, 1889–1963: The Intellectual as a Social Type, 1965
The Agony of the American Left, 1969
The World of Nations: Reflections on American History, Politics, and Culture, 1973
Haven in a Heartless World: The Family Besieged, 1977
The Culture of Narcissism: American Life in an Age of Diminishing Expectations, 1978
The Minimal Self: Psychic Survival in Troubled Times, 1984
The True and Only Heaven: Progress and Its Critics, 1991
The Revolt of the Elites and the Betrayal of Democracy, 1995

Further Reading

Blake, Casey, and Christopher Phelps, "History of Social Criticism: Conversations with Christopher Lasch," *Journal of American History* 80 (1994), 1310–32
Lears, T.J. Jackson, "The Man Who Knew Too Much," *New Republic* (2 October 1995), 43–50
Watts, Steven, "Sinners in the Hands of an Angry Critic: Christopher Lasch's Struggle with Progressive America," *American Studies* 33 (1992), 113–20
Westbrook, Robert B., "Christopher Lasch, the New Radicalism, and the Vocation of Intellectuals," *Reviews in American History* 23 (1995), 176–91

Latin America: Colonial

Latin America's historiography has been organized around the large-scale, and dramatic, themes of its history. For the colonial period these have been the meaning and substance of its pre-Columbian Indian civilizations; the Iberian discovery and conquest of America; Spain's imperial supremacy based on its New World empire, and its subsequent decline; the rise of other European powers and their empires; and the hope of recovery as expressed in the 18th-century Bourbon and Pombaline reforms. For the National Period the dominant themes have been the Wars of Independence; how the individual nation-states of Latin America should be constituted and developed given the lead and dominant position of the industrialized nations of Western Europe and the United States; the region's unequal social order; and what modernity holds for Latin America.

The historians have been not only Latin Americans but English, French, Germans, North Americans, and others. They frequently have been burdened with a world or national view that they sought to confirm or deny in the lessons they thought they saw in the drama of Latin American history. For some the "rise and fall" of Spain validated the "correctness" of the English way, while the underdevelopment of Latin America provided grist for the theory-mills of neo-Liberal, Marxist, and other historians.

The conquest, the demographic disaster, the mixing of the different races, the slavery and exploitation, the skewed development wrought by precious metals, sugar, oil, tin, copper, bananas, coffee, wheat, beef, and other primary products, and the unequal social order left an ambiguous historical legacy as to how Latin America should understand its past, face its future, and transform itself. This ambiguity in the historiography metaphorically reflects an implicit fall from grace and the stain of many original sins. How redemption can be achieved has long been at the heart of the historiographical debate. Those historians who have looked beyond the minutiae for organizing principles from other disciplines – demography, philosophy, theology, economics, anthropology, political science, sociology – have played a larger role in the historiography.

More than a few historians have been seduced by the monumental legacy of the pre-Columbian Indian civilizations and the epic quality of the discovery and conquest. Hernando Cortés' secretary Francisco López de Gómara transformed Mexico's destroyer and creator into a Renaissance hero in *La historia general de las Indias* (1552; *Cortés*, 1964), while Christopher Columbus' 20th-century counterpart Samuel Eliot Morison remade the *Admiral of the Ocean Sea* (1942) into the sailor of all sailors. The romantic traditions of the first half of the 19th century brought the possibilities of this genre to a full flowering in William H. Prescott's novelistic and entertaining *History of the Conquest of Mexico* (1843) and *History of the Conquest of Peru* (1847). But there is a larger intellectual, even metaphysical and ontological, meaning to the discovery of America that has been explored by J.H. Elliott in *The Old World and the New* (1970) and Edmundo O'Gorman in *La invención de América* (1958; *The Invention of America*, 1961).

From the time of the discovery and conquest there were conquistadors, clerics, and official historians of the Spanish court who wrote histories of what had been achieved and its larger meaning. Cortés in his self-serving *Cartas* (written 1519–26; *Letters from Mexico*, 1986) to the Emperor Charles V had a Renaissance vision of what the new world order could be for Europe's potentially greatest monarch, while Cortés' foot soldier Bernal Díaz del Castillo had a more accurate but earthbound account in *Historia verdadera de la conquista de la Nueva España* (written 1568; *The Discovery and Conquest of Mexico*, 1928). But both were from the conquerors' point of view.

Early on there were those who sought to temper the Euro-centrism by describing indigenous achievements in America before the arrival of the Europeans. Fray Bernardino de Sahagún's encyclopedic presentation of Aztec civilization in *Historia general de las cosas de Nueva España* (written 1540s–1560s; *General History of the Things of New Spain: Florentine Codex*, 1950–82) was a remarkable recording and understanding of Aztec culture by Indians in Nahuatl, while the Peruvian mestizo Garcilaso de la Vega [El Inca] praised his conquered ancestors in *Los comentarios reales de los Incas* (1609–17; *Royal Commentaries of the Yncas*, 1869–71). The Peruvian Indian Felipe Guamán Poma de Ayala wrote a 1,200 page "letter" to the King of Spain as *Nueva crónica y buen gobierno* (New History and Good Government, 1615), describing the "real" pre-Columbian and colonial life of the Indians, so that Spaniards would not forget and the king would reform bad Spanish government.

The most remarkable defender of the Indians, however, was the Dominican Bartolomé de Las Casas, whose life was a campaign against Spanish mistreatment and in favor of Indian rationality. More influential than his massive *Historia de las Indias* (written 1520–62; *History of the Indies*, 1971) and *Apologética historia sumaria* (Summary of the Historical Defense, written 1550s) was the widely reprinted propagandistic *Brevísima relación de la destrucción de las Indias* (1552; *The Devastation of the Indies*, 1974). Las Casas' arguments brought the Spanish court to a standstill, gave form and substance to the Spanish theory of government and international law, and supplied ample ammunition for those fomenting the "Black Legend" of Spanish wrongdoing. The ensuing historiographical debate has now been ongoing for almost half a millennium. Its most famous 20th-century devotee has been Lewis Hanke. In *The Spanish Struggle for Justice in the Conquest of America* (1949) and *Aristotle and the American Indians* (1959) he breathed new fire into an old debate.

In recent times there has been a flowering of ethnohistorical research on Mesoamerica and the Andes. The publication and analysis of 16th- and 17th-century indigenous writings and documents in Nahuatl, Maya, Quiche, Mixtec, Quechua, and Aymara have been especially helpful in recovering some of what had been lost. Miguel León-Portilla's anthologies such as *Visión de los vencidos* (1959; *The Broken Spears*, 1962) and Nathan Wachtel's *La vision des vaincus* (1971; *The Vision of the Vanquished*, 1977) offered an entirely new viewpoint on the native reaction to the European invasion. But without a doubt the most important work on native Americans has been Charles Gibson's *The Aztecs under Spanish Rule* (1964). It became the standard against which others measured their own analysis of individual Indian societies. Gibson's examination of indigenous social structures, demographic decline, and evolution of native and Spanish forced labor institutions, land tenure systems, and internal economy had many imitators but few equals, although Nancy Farriss in *Maya Society under Colonial Rule* (1984) approached it in scope. Like Farriss others had to struggle with the distinct nature of each Indian society and differentiate it and its evolution under Spanish rule, especially the nature and chronology of forced-labor institutions, from Gibson's study of the Aztecs.

Historians have also been concerned with the indigenous response to foreign rule. William B. Taylor in *Drinking, Homicide, and Rebellion in Colonial Mexican Villages* (1979) has explored what for the Spanish were specific Indian vices.

Steve J. Stern in *Peru's Indian Peoples and the Challenge of Spanish Conquest* (1982) had a less than benign view of colonial rule where a once proud and vigorous people in time became an "inferior caste of Indians" yoked to a world economy and the Spanish system of rule.

The Iberian world's complex history and enormous treasure house of rich but virtually untapped documentation have often led historians to dedicate a lifetime to a single subject in the hope of achieving a structural breakthrough in understanding that past. Earl J. Hamilton in *American Treasure and the Price Revolution in Spain, 1501–1650* (1934) gave scholars a graph of precious metals production that seemed to mirror the rise and fall of Spain. Until challenged by Michel Morineau's *Incroyables gazettes et fabuleux métaux* (Unbelievable Newspapers and Mythical Metals, 1985), Hamilton's graph reigned supreme for half a century. It also implicitly anchored a series of other monocausal efforts whose preliminary findings were set out by Woodrow Borah in *New Spain's Century of Depression* (1951) where demographic trends seemed to correlate with other structural changes and downturns in the 17th century.

The Berkeley "school" of historical demography of Borah, Sherburne F. Cook, and Carl O. Sauer in a series of works, most notably *The Aboriginal Population of Central Mexico on the Eve of the Spanish Conquest* (1963) and *Essays In Population History* (1971–79), concluded that Mexico's indigenous population declined more than 95 per cent from 20–25,000,000 on the eve of the conquest to less than 1,000,000 by 1600. Other historians followed, using the same techniques, and counted Indians elsewhere in the New World generally with the same results. For South America the most rigorous was Noble David Cook in *Demographic Collapse: Indian Peru, 1520–1620* (1981). But the collapse manifested itself in the historiography in other ways. François Chevalier in *La formation des grands domaines au Mexique* (1952; *Land and Society in Colonial Mexico*, 1963) had the giant hacienda filling up the "vacant" Mexican countryside as the Indian communities disappeared just as the feudal estates had appeared in Europe with the fall of the Roman empire. Another 17th-century reversal was the dramatic fall in transatlantic shipping between Spain and America as demonstrated by Pierre and Huguette Chaunu in *Séville et l'Atlantique, 1504–1650* (Seville and the Atlantic, 1955–60). Macroeconomic trends of decline elsewhere were demonstrated by Murdo J. MacLeod in *Spanish Central America* (1973).

With the success of Chevalier's work haciendas became a favorite subject of research, with the Jesuit estates drawing much of the attention, since an unusually rich body of hacienda records were generated by the order's expulsion in 1759 and 1767. Inevitably in-depth studies of haciendas led to an emphasis on the regional economy and with it came the basis for a new kind of regional history. The overall picture that emerged was of a changing, growing, and expanding society and economy that was at variance with the depression thesis advanced by Borah. William Taylor's *Landlord and Peasant in Colonial Oaxaca* (1972) found that the indigenous population had resisted Spanish rule much better in southern Mexico, and Keith A. Davies in *Landowners in Colonial Peru* (1984) like Taylor showed that the emergence of the hacienda did not mean the disappearance of Indian communities and other forms of land holding. David A. Brading in *Haciendas and Ranchos in the Mexican Bajío* (1978) detailed the role of the middling-size *ranchos* that filled the interstices between the haciendas. These regional studies provided a better understanding of the role and function of regions as well as how they changed over time. Taylor's Oaxaca had resisted and adapted yet still remained very Indian, while Brading's Querétaro-Guadalajara-Zacatecas triangle appeared dynamic and very mestizo, in short, fundamentally different from Oaxaca.

Since precious metals had played such an important role in structuring the historiography, historians began to examine the mining industry more closely. Peter J. Bakewell gave us more rigorous silver-production figures and a more exact chronology for when production peaked, bottomed out, and began to recover in the 17th century in both Mexico and Peru in *Silver Mining and Society in Colonial Mexico* (1971) and *Miners of the Red Mountain* (1984). He also showed that mining labor in Mexico was free and that it was moving in that direction in Peru. In neither case did the demographic curve of the Berkeley "school" or the transatlantic shipping patterns of the Chaunus coincide with the mining figures. They were out of synchronization. Other historians have suggested, but not thoroughly documented, that the mining downturn probably had more to do with shortages of capital, credit, and mercury, and the general imperial implosion for the period 1630–60 than anything else.

James Lockhart in *Spanish Peru, 1532–1560* (1968) radically changed the direction of Latin American social history with his innovative use of notarial archives which allowed him to follow the day-to-day activities of different social groups. The result was an unusually informed panoramic view of Spanish society where conquistadors, *encomenderos* (holders of an *encomienda*, a royal land grant, including its Indian inhabitants), landowners, bureaucrats, judges, clergymen, merchants, artisans, sailors, women, blacks, and Indians revealed themselves as real, flesh-and-blood figures. The extent and limits of human action of the different groups allowed a much more exacting characterization of their role and function. Some of Lockhart's techniques and work had been foreshadowed by Mario Góngora in *Los grupos de conquistadores en Tierra Firme, 1509–1530* (Conquistador Groups on the Spanish Main, 1509–1530, 1962). A plethora of studies on different groups – *encomenderos*, bureaucrats, merchants, artisans, clerics, women, slaves, and Indians – began to appear. Louisa Schell Hoberman in *Mexico's Merchant Elite, 1590–1660* (1991) provided one of the best portraits of any group for any time period. Her picture of the merchants' extraordinary power and range has significantly revised the importance assigned to their role in Mexico.

The 18th century and the new Bourbon monarchy saw a revival of Spain's imperial fortunes and significant administrative, political, economic, and social changes in its American colonies. Historians have been concerned with what the Bourbon reforms were and any possible causal relationship between them and the new-found growth and dynamism of the late colonial period. Also considered important in the historiography is what role the reforms may have played in the final break as expressed in the wars of independence as well as in any carryover in the formation of the new nation-states of Latin America. For the introduction of the intendancy system in Latin America, John Lynch in *Spanish Colonial Administration, 1782–1810* (1958), Luis Navarro García in *Intendencias en*

Indias (Intendancies of the Indies, 1959), and John R. Fisher in *Government and Society in Colonial Peru* (1970) analyzed the nature and impact of this crucial reform. Horst Pietschmann in "Consideraciones en torno al protoliberalismo (Reflections on the Beginnings of Liberalism)," (1991) suggested that the institutional basis for 19th-century federalism rested on the administrative structures of the intendancy system, while Nettie Lee Benson in *La diputación provincial y el federalismo mexicano* (1955; *The Provincial Deputation in Mexico*, 1992) showed just how dynamic this local government had become by the time of the wars of independence. Covering the military aspects of the Bourbon reforms were Christon I. Archer in *The Army in Bourbon Mexico* (1977), Leon G. Campbell in *The Military and Society in Colonial Peru* (1978), and Allan J. Kuethe in *Military Reform and Society in New Granada, 1773–1808* (1978). Juan Marchena Fernández in *Ejército y milicias en el mundo colonial americano* (Army and Militias in the Colonial American World, 1992) has documented the increasing Americanization of the military as the colonial period came to a close. All four studies showed evidence of the fault line between the army and local militias that after independence divided centralists from federalists. Nancy M. Farriss in *Crown and Clergy in Colonial Mexico* (1968) followed the erosion of the clerical position under the Bourbon reforms and the church's reaction to the beginnings of liberalism. Mark A. Burkholder and D.S. Chandler in *From Impotence to Authority* (1977) showed how Spain reasserted control over its New World bureaucracy in the second half of the 18th century by replacing American-born Creoles with peninsular-born Spaniards. Many historians have assumed that the resulting Creole resentment was the crucial factor in the final break.

The inevitable reaction to the reforms and new taxes produced rebellion, but not, initially, independence. Brian Hamnett in *Roots of Insurgency* (1986) identified the sources of conflict in the different regions of Mexico, and Scarlett O'Phelan Godoy in *Rebellions and Revolts in Eighteenth-Century Peru and Upper Peru* (1985) traced the great uprising of Tupac Amaru while John Leddy Phelan did the same for the Comunero revolt in Colombia in *The People and the King* (1978). Enrique Florescano in *Precios del maíz y crisis agrícolas en México* (Corn Prices and Agrarian Crises in Mexico, 1969) elaborated a price series for corn that is unique in the historiography, but whose conclusions about famine and imminent collapse do not appear to be generalizable or applicable as a cause for the break with Spain. Much of the stimulus for independence came from events in Europe and the constitutional crisis over who would rule when Napoleon sequestered the king of Spain in 1808. Nettie Lee Benson and her students in *Mexico and the Spanish Cortes, 1810–1822* (1966) documented the profound impact the Spanish Constitution of 1812 had in the New World as the source of a radical set of ground rules for the newly emerging nation-states. John Lynch has written the best synthesis of the wars of independence in *The Spanish American Revolutions* (1973). David Brading in *Los orígenes del nacionalismo mexicano* (1973; *The Origins of Mexican Nationalism*, 1985) and *The First America* (1991) has begun the task of searching for incipient nationalism, Creole identity, and the protoliberal state which became the constituent parts of the new order in Latin America in the national period.

MAURICE P. BRUNGARDT

See also Chevalier; Díaz; Elliott; European Expansion; Gibson; Góngora; Hanke; Las Casas; Léon-Portilla; Mexico; Morison; Prescott; Sauer; Spain: Imperial

Further Reading

Archer, Christon I., *The Army in Bourbon Mexico, 1760–1810*, Albuquerque: University of New Mexico Press, 1977

Bakewell, Peter J., *Silver Mining and Society in Colonial Mexico: Zacatecas, 1546–1700*, Cambridge: Cambridge University Press, 1971

Bakewell, Peter J., *Miners of the Red Mountain: Indian Labor in Potosí, 1545–1650*, Albuquerque: University of New Mexico Press, 1984

Benson, Nettie Lee, *La diputación provincial y el federalismo mexicano*, Mexico: Colegio de México, 1955; in English as *The Provincial Deputation in Mexico: Harbinger of Provincial Autonomy, Independence, and Federalism*, Austin: University of Texas Press, 1992

Benson, Nettie Lee, ed., *Mexico and the Spanish Cortes, 1810–1822*, Austin: University of Texas Press, 1966

Bethell, Leslie, ed., *The Cambridge History of Latin America*, 11 vols., Cambridge: Cambridge University Press, 1984–95

Borah, Woodrow, *New Spain's Century of Depression*, Berkeley: University of California Press, 1951

Borah, Woodrow, and Sherburne F. Cook, *The Aboriginal Population of Central Mexico on the Eve of the Spanish Conquest*, Berkeley: University of California Press, 1963

Brading, David A., *Los orígenes del nacionalismo mexicano*, Mexico City: Secretaría de Educación Pública, 1973; in English as *The Origins of Mexican Nationalism*, Cambridge: Cambridge University Press, 1985

Brading, David. A., *Haciendas and Ranchos in the Mexican Bajío: Léon, 1700–1860*, Cambridge: Cambridge University Press, 1978

Brading, David. A., *The First America: The Spanish Monarchy, Creole Patriots, and the Liberal State, 1492–1867*, Cambridge and New York: Cambridge University Press, 1991

Burkholder, Mark A., and D.S. Chandler, *From Impotence to Authority: The Spanish Crown and the American Audiencias, 1687–1808*, Columbia: University of Missouri Press, 1977

Campbell, Leon G., *The Military and Society in Colonial Peru, 1750–1810*, Philadelphia: American Philosophical Society, 1978

Chaunu, Huguette, and Pierre Chaunu, *Séville et l'Atlantique, 1504–1650*, (Seville and the Atlantic), 8 vols., Paris: Colin, 1955–60

Chevalier, François, *La Formation des grands domaines au Mexique: terre et société aux XVI–XVII siècles*, Paris: Institut d'Ethnologie, 1952; in English as *Land and Society in Colonial Mexico: The Great Hacienda*, Berkeley: University of California Press, 1963

Cook, Noble David, *Demographic Collapse: Indian Peru, 1520–1620*, Cambridge and New York: Cambridge University Press, 1981

Cook, Sherburne F., and Woodrow Borah, *Essays in Population History: Mexico and the Caribbean*, 3 vols., Berkeley: University of California Press, 1971–79

Cortés, Hernando, *Cartas y documentos*, Mario Hernández Sánchez-Barba ed., Mexico City: Porrua, 1963; in English as *Letters from Mexico*, New Haven: Yale University Press, 1986 [written 1519–26]

Davies, Keith A., *Landowners in Colonial Peru*, Austin: University of Texas Press, 1984

Díaz del Castillo, Bernal, *Historia verdadera de la conquista de la Nueva España*, written 1568, published *c.*1575; in English as *The Discovery and Conquest of Mexico, 1517–1521*, New York: Harper, and London: Routledge, 1928, and as *The Conquest of New Spain*, London: Penguin, 1963

Elliott, J.H., *The Old World and the New, 1492–1650*, Cambridge: Cambridge University Press, 1970

Farriss, Nancy M., *Crown and Clergy in Colonial Mexico, 1759–1821: The Crisis of Ecclesiastical Privilege*, London: Athlone Press, 1968

Farriss, Nancy M., *Maya Society under Colonial Rule: The Collective Enterprise of Survival*, Princeton: Princeton University Press, 1984

Fisher, John R., *Government and Society in Colonial Peru: The Intendant System, 1784–1814*, London: Athlone Press, 1970

Florescano, Enrique, *Precios del maíz y crisis agrícolas en México (1708–1810): ensayo sobre el movimiento de los precios y sus consecuencias económicas y sociales* (Corn Prices and Agrarian Crises in Mexico), Mexico City: El Colegio de México, 1969; revised 1986

Garcilaso de la Vega, *Comentarios reales de los Incas*, Lisbon, 1609 (*Primera parte* [First Part]); in English as *First Part of the Royal Commentaries of the Yncas*, 2 vols., London: Hakluyt Society, 1869–71

Gibson, Charles, *The Aztecs under Spanish Rule: A History of the Indians of the Valley of Mexico, 1519–1810*, Stanford, CA: Stanford University Press, 1964

Góngora, Mario, *Los grupos de conquistadores en Tierra Firme, 1509–1530: fisonomía histórico-social de un tipo de conquesta* (Conquistador Groups on the Spanish Main, 1509–1530: Historical and Social Physiognomy of a Style of Conquest), Santiago: Universidad de Chile, 1962

Guamán Poma de Ayala, Felipe, *Nueva crónica y buen gobierno* (New History and Good Government), written 1615; edited by John V. Murra and Rolena Adorno, 3 vols., Lima: Tallers, 1955–66

Hamilton, Earl J., *American Treasure and the Price Revolution in Spain, 1501–1650*, Cambridge, MA: Harvard University Press, 1934

Hamnett, Brian, *Roots of Insurgency: Mexican Regions, 1750–1824*, Cambridge: Cambridge University Press, 1986

Hanke, Lewis, *The Spanish Struggle for Justice in the Conquest of America*, Philadelphia: University of Pennsylvania Press, 1949

Hanke, Lewis, *Aristotle and the American Indians*, Chicago: Regnery, and London: Hollis and Carter, 1959

Hoberman, Louisa Schell, *Mexico's Merchant Elite, 1590–1660: Silver, State, and Society*, Durham, NC: Duke University Press, 1991

Kuethe, Allan J., *Military Reform and Society in New Granada, 1773–1808*, Gainesville: University of Florida Press, 1978

Las Casas, Bartolomé de, *Apologética historia sumaria* (Summary of the Historical Defense), 2 vols., México: UNAM, 1967 [written 1550s]

Las Casas, Bartolomé de, *Brevísima relación de la destrucción de las Indias*, 1552; in English as *The Tears of the Indians*, 1656, and *The Devastation of the Indies: A Brief Account*, New York: Seabury Press 1974

Las Casas, Bartolomé de, *Historia de las Indias*, completed 1562; first published, 5 vols., Madrid: Ginesta, 1875; in English as *History of the Indies*, New York: Harper, 1971

León-Portilla, Miguel, ed., *Visión de los vencidos: relaciones indígenas de la conquista*, México City: UNAM, 1959; in English as *The Broken Spears: The Aztec Account of the Conquest of Mexico*, Boston: Beacon Press, 1962

Lockhart, James, *Spanish Peru, 1532–1560: A Colonial Society*, Madison: University of Wisconsin Press, 1968

López de Gómara, Francisco, *La historia general de las Indias*, Zaragoza: Millán, 1552; partially translated as *Cortés: The Life of the Conqueror by his Secretary*, edited by Lesley Byrd Simpson, Berkeley: University of California Press, 1964

Lynch, John, *Spanish Colonial Administration, 1782–1810: The Intendant System in the Viceroyalty of Rio de la Plata*, London: Athlone Press, 1958; New York: Greenwood Press, 1969

Lynch, John, *The Spanish American Revolutions, 1808–1826*, New York: Norton, and London:Weidenfeld and Nicolson, 1973

MacLeod, Murdo J., *Spanish Central America: A Socioeconomic History, 1520–1720*, Berkeley: University of California Press, 1973

Marchena Fernández, Juan, *Ejército y milicias en el mundo colonial americano* (Army and Militias in the Colonial American World), Madrid: MAPFRE, 1992

Morineau, Michel, *Incroyables gazettes et fabuleux métaux: les retours des trésors américains d'après les gazettes hollandaises (XVIe–XVIIIe siècles)* (Unbelievable Newspapers and Mythical Metals), Paris: Maison des Sciences de l'homme, and Cambridge: Cambridge University Press, 1985

Morison, Samuel Eliot, *Admiral of the Ocean Sea: A Life of Christopher Columbus*, 2 vols., Boston: Little Brown, 1942; as *Christopher Columbus: Admiral of the Ocean Sea*, Oxford: Oxford University Press, 1942

Navarro García, Luis, *Intendencias en Indias* (Intendancies of the Indies), Sevilla: Escuela de Estudios Hispano-Americanos, 1959

O'Gorman, Edmundo, *La invención de América: el universalismo de la cultura de Occidente*, Mexico City: Fondo de Cultura, 1958; in English as *The Invention of America: An Inquiry into the Historical Nature of the New World and the Meaning of Its History*, Bloomington: Indiana University Press, 1961

O'Phelan Godoy, Scarlett, *Rebellions and Revolts in Eighteenth Century Peru and Upper Peru*, Cologne: Böhlau, 1985

Phelan, John L., *The People and the King: The Comunero Revolution in Colombia, 1781*, Madison: University of Wisconsin Press, 1978

Pietschmann, Horst, "Consideraciones en torno al protoliberalismo, reformas borbónicas y revolución: la Nueva España en el último tercio del siglo XVIII" (Reflections on the Beginnings of Liberalism, the Bourbon Reforms, and Revolution: New Spain in the Last Third of the 18th Century), *Historia mexicana* 41 (1991), 167–206

Prescott, William H., *The History of the Conquest of Mexico*, 3 vols., New York: Harper, 1843

Prescott, William H., *The History of the Conquest of Peru*, 2 vols., Philadelphia: Lippincott, 1847

Sahagún, Bernardino de, *General History of the Things of New Spain: Florentine Codex*, combined Spanish, English, and Nahuatl edition in parallel columns, 12 vols., Santa Fe, NM: School of American Research, 1950–82 [written 1540s–1560s]

Stern, Steve J., *Peru's Indian Peoples and the Challenge of Spanish Conquest: Huamanga to 1640*, Madison: University of Wisconsin Press, 1982

Taylor, William B., *Landlord and Peasant in Colonial Oaxaca*, Stanford, CA: Stanford University Press, 1972

Taylor, William B., *Drinking, Homicide, and Rebellion in Colonial Mexican Villages*, Stanford, CA: Stanford University Press, 1979

Wachtel, Nathan, *La Vision des vaincus: les Indiens du Pérou devant la conquête espagnole, 1530–1570*, Paris: Gallimard, 1971; in English as *The Vision of the Vanquished: The Spanish Conquest of Peru Through Indian Eyes, 1530–1570*, New York: Barnes and Noble, and Hassocks, Sussex: Harvester, 1977

Latin America: National (since 1810)

Latin America's break with Spain and Portugal inevitably shifted the historiographical focus away from the panoramic perspective characteristic of much of the work on the colonial period that came from operating within the larger imperial context. The viewpoint now was the individual histories of the separate nation-states, and much of the work on Latin America in the national period never transcended this narrower starting point. The exceptions were related to issues of development and modernization. Competing theories – liberalism, conservatism, structuralism, and dependency – of how best to transform Latin America underlay most of the debate. The oldest and most enduring is liberalism toward which most of the newly independent countries began to move as they organized their systems of government and their development policies.

This involved liquidating the corporate legacy of the church and the state of the colonial past that restricted the political, economic, intellectual, and social liberties of individuals. The story is best told by Bushnell and Macaulay in *The Emergence of Latin America in the Nineteenth Century* (1988). While all Latin American countries moved in the direction of liberalism, none ever instituted the complete package of reforms, especially in the area of civil and political rights, and many a regime was liberal only in its anticlericalism. Conservatives at first fought a mainly rearguard action, but they found enough in their Iberian past to formulate alternative approaches emphasizing authoritarian solutions and the role of the church and the state. The liberal failure to bring sufficient progress and incorporate enough of the masses into the national enterprise led to a periodic rejection of its theory and program when more radical and/or authoritarian formulae pushed liberalism off center stage. Nevertheless, by the 1990s it had once again reasserted itself and become the prevailing force in theory and practice, and in the historiography.

No one more than Domingo F. Sarmiento in *Civilización i barbarie* (1845; *Life in the Argentine Republic in the Days of the Tyrants*, 1960) ever formulated the choice for liberalism in Latin America in such a paradigmatic fashion. Sarmiento's vision of building the emerging Latin American nation-states on the ideals of European liberalism has remained a haunting reference point in the historiography of Latin America. For Sarmiento, to choose otherwise spelled dictatorship, authoritarianism, stagnation, and slavery – in short barbarism. The supposed evils of the caudillos (political bosses) against whom Sarmiento fought are explored by Lynch in *Argentine Dictator: Juan Manuel de Rosas, 1829–1852* (1981) and by Woodward in *Rafael Carrera and the Emergence of the Republic of Guatemala, 1821–1871* (1993). In the Central American case Woodward demonstrated that the caudillo was a popular reaction to the real-life inadequacies and excesses of liberalism. In the Argentine case the same was true and Rosas served as a model for some of the authoritarian approaches of the 20th century, where, as Rock showed in *Politics in Argentina, 1890–1930* (1975), the liberal politicians of the Argentine middle class failed to bring the lower orders into the political process and set the stage for the rise Juan Perón.

Other less visionary and more practical 19th-century contemporaries of Sarmiento looked to the past for the national essence and tried to find the indispensable components around which to construct their new nation-states. In the process they frequently used and abused history and helped create many of the early myths and stereotypes associated with their country's specific historiography. While they did insist on and root out essential documentation and did establish the basic chronology, they also tended to do only political history and to glorify or denigrate their country's conquistadors, clerics, missionaries, founding fathers, and rulers uncritically.

Among early conservatives the most able was Alamán who skillfully defended the Spanish past in *Historia de Méjico* (History of Mexico, 1849–1852) and warned of the dangers lurking in the new freedoms especially from the Indian masses. Among liberals Barros Arana in *Historia general de Chile* (General History of Chile, 1884–1902) seemed to supply complete documentation and ample evidence for the church's role in the decadence of Spain. He also created the myth of the Chilean yeoman farmer as the distinguishing national characteristic that allowed Chile its early successes against neighboring nation-states. Góngora and Borde called the myth into question in *Evolución de la propiedad rural en el Valle del Puangue* (Evolution of Rural Property in the Valley of Puangue, 1956) and Góngora himself effectively destroyed it in *Origen de los 'inquilinos' de Chile central* (Origin of the Sharecroppers of Central Chile, 1960) and *Encomenderos y estancieros* (Encomenderos and Landowners, 1970).

In Argentina, Brazil, and Peru, Mitre, Varnhagen, and Basadre, like Barros Arana, insisted on the necessity of primary documents and helped focus and establish the canons of historiography in their respective countries. Mitre in *Historia de Belgrano* (History of Belgrano, 1859) and *Historia de San Martín* (1887–90; *Emancipation of South America*, 1893) explored the independence movement in Argentina and South America through the lives of two of its leaders. Varnhagen's nationalism was more restrained but his implicit goal, as he wrote in *História geral do Brasil* (General History of Brazil, 1854–57), was in "forming or improving the general national spirit." He did this more directly in *História das lutas com os holandêses* (History of the Struggles Against the Dutch, 1871) and *História da independência do Brasil* (History of the Independence of Brazil, 1917). Basadre, their 20th-century counterpart, documented in *Historia de la República del Péru* (History of the Republic of Peru, 1939–) an optimistic vision of Peru's progress and development that in retrospect seems at variance with its history.

Toward the end of the 19th century, under the influence of positivism and new social and economic forces, Latin American historians began to turn their attention away from great men and the actions of individuals and to consider natural, political, and social phenomena that had a more enduring affect on the formation of a nation. Leading this change in Mexico was Justo Sierra in *Mexico, su evolución social* (1900–1902; *Mexico: Its Social Evolution*, 1900–04). In Brazil Capistrano de Abreu moved well beyond positivism and the German historians he read in the original with a range and style in *Capítulos de história colonial* (Chapters in Colonial History, 1907) that oriented and molded modern Brazilian historiography. In *Caminhos antigos e povoamento* (Ancient Roads and Settlement, 1930), which dates from the 1880s, Capistrano anticipated Frederick Jackson Turner's *The Significance of the Frontier in American History* (1894) and reoriented Brazilian history away from the coast to the hinterland and the Brazilian drama of expansion and incorporation. His present-day counterpart is Rodrigues who established the parameters of modern Brazilian historiography in *Teoria da história do Brasil* (Theory of the History of Brazil, revised 1957) and *Aspirações nacionais* (1963; *The Brazilians*, 1967).

The growing interest in social and economic factors at the turn of the century led historians to believe that they had found the roots of modern Latin America. Each in turn searched for the obvious problems or features of the contemporary landscape whose resolution or study might provide a way out of their country's perceived backwardness. In Mexico the corrupt political system and unequal land tenure provided Molina Enríquez with an appropriate target in *Los grandes problemas nacionales* (The Great National Problems, 1909) which inspired similar studies in other Latin American countries. The

Mexican Revolution itself, the first great social revolution of the 20th century, furnished one model of what could be done. Knight in *The Mexican Revolution* (1986) followed the overall popular thrust of the destruction, while Womack rode the singular wave of the Zapatista movement in *Zapata and the Mexican Revolution* (1969). After demolition came the rebuilding and mythmaking. In the process, however flawed, Mexico emerged with the strongest state in Latin America, perhaps as a counterweight to the power of its continental neighbor to the north and as a mechanism to control internal forces. Historians are only beginning to understand the meaning and consequence of the Mexican Revolution although Aguilar Camín and Meyer illustrated some of the possibilities in *A la sombra de la revolución mexicana* (1989; *In the Shadow of the Mexican Revolution*, 1993), and González Casanova offered a sober assessment of political life in *La democracia en México* (1965; *Democracy in Mexico*, 1970).

One important contribution to Latin American historiography as a result of the Mexican Revolution came from Cosío Villegas, probably Mexico's greatest historian and certainly the most innovative in Latin America. As founder of the graduate school El Colegio de México and its scholarly journals and as president of El Colegio from 1958 to 1963 Cosío succeeded in creating institutional support unparalleled in Latin America for the study of history. Today El Colegio has the finest graduate program in history and the social sciences in the region. The outcome parallels the super state that has been the defining feature of the Mexican Revolution. Cosío oversaw the team production of *Historia moderna de México* (Modern History of Mexico, 1955–74) and authored several of the volumes. His dating of Mexico's modern history as beginning prior to the Revolution with the restored republic in 1867 influenced the choice of 1870 as an appropriate date for closing and beginning a major period in Latin America's history. His assignment of separate volumes to the political, economic, social, and diplomatic life of the country, while not attempted elsewhere, did stimulate the study of railroads, export commodities, urbanization, and US-Latin American relations.

In Cuba and Brazil the problem of national identity got caught up in the issue of race and the legacy of slavery. Ortiz pioneered Black Studies in Latin America with his investigations of African cultural survivals in Cuba, most notably in *La africanía de la música folklórica de Cuba* (The Africanness of the Folkloric Music of Cuba, 1950). His earlier works like *Hampa afro-cubana* (Afro-Cuban Criminality, 1906) had a racist thrust that agonized over how Cuba could develop given its African heritage. In Brazil Freyre looked at the social relations of the plantation house and recast the negative perceptions of blackness and African heritage and asserted in *Casa grande e senzala* (1933; *The Masters and the Slaves*, 1946) that Brazil's racial mixing had produced a racial democracy. This hopeful assessment infused with nationalist sentiments was seen as a uniquely Brazilian achievement and a contribution to the rest of the world, especially when contrasted with the legal segregation practiced in the United States. Tannenbaum was so struck by Freyre's work that he formulated in *Slave and Citizen* (1946) the notion that slavery had been more benign in Latin America and that its race relations offered important lessons for the United States. The "Tannenbaum thesis," as labeled in the historiography, generated an intense interest in and numerous studies on not only slavery but the related topics of manumission, abolition, and race relations. Stanley J. Stein in *Vassouras* (1957) and Warren Dean in *Rio Claro* (1976) suggested that on the coffee plantations Freyre's positive view of master-slave relations was a myth. Curtin in *The Atlantic Slave Trade* (1969) certified the numbers for those transported to the New World, while Degler in *Neither Black nor White* (1971) argued that the answer to why the race relations of Brazil and the United States were different could be found in the role played by the mulatto. Wade in *Blackness and Race Mixture* (1993) offered a more comprehensive explanation by contrasting the dynamics of racial identity in Colombia and placing that country's experience within the wider framework of national ideologies and the pressures of how a country develops and modernizes.

It was this preoccupation with development and modernization that gave birth to Latin America's two original contributions to historiography – structuralism and dependency theory. The birthplace was Santiago, Chile where the United Nations' Economic Commission for Latin America (ECLA) had its headquarters and met for the first time in June 1948, and where most of the theorists worked at one time or another. As head of ECLA the Argentine Raúl Prebisch was in charge of producing a plan for Latin America's development. In *El desarrollo económico de América Latina y sus principales problemas* (1949; *The Economic Development of Latin America and Its Principal Problems*, 1950) he formulated the initial premises of structuralism when he noted the unequal exchange between the Periphery and the Center, a relationship and terminology articulated in public lectures as early as 1944. The inequality came from Latin America supplying primary products when the long-term trends of trade favored the finished goods produced by industrialized countries. For Prebisch Latin America's continued backwardness relative to developed countries showed that growth dependent on traditional exports was incapable of transforming the region. He urged government-induced industrialization through a policy of import substitution which it was hoped would bring about the necessary structural changes. In the *Economic Survey of Latin America: 1949* (1950) Prebisch reviewed the economic history of Latin America from the 1880s to 1950 with special emphasis on Argentina, Brazil, Chile, and Mexico. This survey served as a model for the study carried out by Furtado in *Formação econômica do Brasil* (1959; *The Economic Growth of Brazil*, 1963) and *Formação econômica da América Latina* (1969; *Economic Development of Latin America* 1970). In these works Furtado offered a clearer and tighter structuralist analysis of the economic history of Brazil and Latin America. His typology of the different commodities that Latin America exported and how they had changed the economy and society as well as his arguments that the economic disengagement and dislocation occasioned by World War I and II and the 1930s Depression had speeded up industrialization suggested that governments could structure and force much of the desired development.

The move from structuralism to dependency theory took place when doubts grew over whether import substitution could bring the promised development. Structuralism was not only challenged by neoclassical liberals but by heterodox leftists as well. Furtado himself created the initial categories for the theory in *Desenvolvimento e subdesenvolvimento* (1961; *Development and Underdevelopment*, 1964) where he argued that the two processes were linked, and, therefore, underdevelopment could not be a stage on the road to development. Cardoso turned the debate toward an analysis of social relations in *Empresário industrial e desenvolvimento econômico no Brasil* (Industrial Entrepreneurs and Economic Underdevelopment in Brazil, 1964), *Política e desenvolvimento em sociedades dependentes* (Politics and Underdevelopment in Dependent Societies, 1971), and (along with Enzo Faletto) *Dependencia y desarrollo en América Latina* (1969; *Dependency and Development in Latin America*, 1979). For Cardoso Latin America lacked a conquering bourgeoisie and an independent working class, and they could not therefore be counted upon to transform the region as had been the case elsewhere.

As structuralism and dependency theory were making their appearance, other historians were producing case studies that threw further light on the subject without necessarily committing their authors to either school. Coatsworth in *Growth against Development* (1981) studied the impact of railroads in Mexico before the Revolution. Dean in *The Industrialization of São Paulo* (1969) contradicted one of the tenets of structuralism when he showed that industrialization increased directly and not inversely with exports. Scobie in *Revolution on the Pampas* (1964) and *Argentina* (1964) showed how far commodity exports could transform an individual country. The transformation involved a process of immigration and urbanization unequaled anywhere else in the world, and Scobie continued to follow this in his pioneering *Buenos Aires* (1974) and *Secondary Cities of Argentina* (1988). Also with a primary focus on Argentina, Germani in *Sociología de la modernización* (1969; *The Sociology of Modernization*, 1981) and *Authoritarianism, Fascism, and National Populism* (1978) showed that modernization did not necessarily produce democracy.

For those not so well grounded in or wedded to classical economic theory, the very term "dependency" suggested the relationship could be broken, and Latin America's Marxist tradition provided an ample supply of authors with a more radical approach such as Prado Júnior in *A revolução brasileira* (The Brazilian Revolution, 1966). But it was Frank in *Capitalism and Underdevelopment in Latin America* (1969) who borrowed, synthesized, and popularized what had been done and who pushed for a breakout from the limitations imposed internally and externally. For Frank Latin America's impasse had come from four centuries of "underdeveloping," and the "development of underdevelopment" was the predicament of all the Third World. The way out of this dead-end was a revolutionary struggle on the pattern of the Cuban Revolution.

The Cuban was the other great social revolution in Latin America, and its meaning, like its Mexican counterpart, also has defied explanation. However, Thomas and and Pérez in their books on Cuba have identified the overweening role of the United States and the necessity for a reordering of property relations as keys to that understanding. Fidel Castro, as a Marxist caudillo without equal in Latin America, never has been properly placed within the region's extensive caudillo tradition, but Quirk's negative assessment in *Fidel Castro* (1993) is a powerful indictment of the man, and has yet to be answered satisfactorily.

Under the impact of dependency theory many historians reformulated their analysis of Latin American history so as to reflect what they saw as foreign and elite control over the course and direction of the region's history. Stanley J. and Barbara H. Stein, probably the most notable examples, produced a lucid synthesis in *The Colonial Heritage of Latin America* (1970). Contrarians like Platt in *Latin America and British Trade* (1972) insisted on a neoliberal interpretation in which they saw Latin Americans freely choosing the direction they wanted to pursue without any overall control and direction from abroad.

By the 1990s liberalism had come full circle and was once again back in the driver's seat. Symptomatic was how many mass-based, formerly authoritarian political movements such as Mexico's PRI, Argentina's Peronism, and Peru's APRA tried to gain respectability by transforming themselves into something akin to liberal parties. The election of Cardoso, one of the original dependency theorists, as president of Brazil and his embrace of some of the principles of neoliberalism suggested that many of the theorists had never strayed that far. Cardoso himself in "On the Characterization of Authoritarian Regimes in Latin America" (1979) had suggested that Latin America's problem and its turn toward military rule had come from an anachronistic relationship between traditional elites and "backward" workers willing to accept clientelistic roles. Clearly he hoped to see international capitalism and multinational corporations transform the region and sweep away the old order. Whether liberalism would fail once again and bring renewed populist and authoritarian solutions remained to be seen. Góngora's *Ensayo histórico sobre la noción de estado en Chile en los siglos XIX y XX* (Historical Essay on the Idea of the State in Chile in the 19th and 20th Centuries, 1981) was a painful remainder that even one of Latin America's most democratic countries had a reservoir of choices other than Sarmiento's liberal democracy.

MAURICE P. BRUNGARDT

See also Argentina; Brazil; Cardoso; Cosío Villegas; Cuba; Curtin; Degler; Freyre; Góngora; Mexico; Prado Junior; Scobie; Stein; Tannenbaum

Further Reading

Abreu, João Capistrano de, *Capítulos de história colonial, 1500–1800* (Chapters in Colonial History), Rio de Janeiro: Orosco, 1907; 7th edition 1988

Abreu, João Capistrano de, *Caminhos antigos e povoamento do Brasil* (Ancient Roads and Settlement), Rio de Janeiro: Briguiet, 1930

Aguilar Camín, Héctor, and Lorenzo Meyer, *A la sombra de la revolución mexicana*, Mexico: Cal y Arena, 1989; in English as *In the Shadow of the Mexican Revolution: Contemporary Mexican History, 1910–1989*, Austin: University of Texas Press, 1993

Alamán, Lucas, *Historia de Méjico desde los primeros movimientos que prepararon su independencia en el año de 1808, hasta la época presente* (History of Mexico from 1808), 5 vols., Mexico City: Lara, 1849–52

Barros Arana, Diego, *Historia general de Chile* (General History of Chile), 16 vols., Santiago: Jover, 1884–1902

Basadre, Jorge, *Historia de la República del Perú* (A History of the Republic of Peru), 2 vols., Lima: Gil, 1939; 7th edition, 17 vols., 1983

Bethell, Leslie, ed., *The Cambridge History of Latin America*, 11 vols., Cambridge: Cambridge University Press, 1984–95

Bushnell, David, and Neill Macaulay, *The Emergence of Latin America in the Nineteenth Century*, New York: Oxford University Press, 1988

Cardoso, Fernando Henrique, *Empresário industrial e desenvolvimento econômico no Brasil* (Industrial Entrepreneurs and Economic Underdevelopment in Brazil), São Paulo: Difusão Européia do Livro, 1964

Cardoso, Fernando Henrique, and Enzo Faletto, *Dependencia y desarrollo en América Latina: ensayo de interpretación sociológica*, Mexico City: Cultura, 1969; in English as *Dependency and Development in Latin America*, Berkeley: University of California Press, 1979

Cardoso, Fernando Henrique, *Política e desenvolvimento em sociedades dependentes: ideologias do empresariado industrial argentino e brasileiro* (Politics and Underdevelopment in Dependent Societies), Rio de Janeiro: Zahar, 1971

Cardoso, Fernando Henrique, "On the Characterization of Authoritarian Regimes in Latin America," in David Collier, ed., *The New Authoritarianism in Latin America*, Princeton: Princeton University Press, 1979

Coatsworth, John H., *Growth Against Development: The Economic Impact of Railroads in Porfirian Mexico*, DeKalb: Northern Illinois University Press, 1981

Cosío Villegas, Daniel, ed., *Historia moderna de México* (Modern History of Mexico), 10 vols., Mexico City: Hermes, 1955–74

Curtin, Philip D., *The Atlantic Slave Trade: A Census*, Madison: University of Wisconsin Press, 1969

Dean, Warren, *The Industrialization of São Paulo, 1880–1945*, Austin: University of Texas Press, 1969

Dean, Warren, *Rio Claro: A Brazilian Plantation System, 1820–1920*, Stanford, CA: Stanford University Press, 1976

Degler, Carl N., *Neither Black nor White: Slavery and Race Relations in Brazil and the United States*, New York: Macmillan, 1971

Frank, Andre Gunder, *Capitalism and Underdevelopment in Latin America: Historical Studies of Chile and Brazil*, New York: Monthly Review Press, 1969

Freyre, Gilberto, *Casa-grande e senzala: formação da família brasileira sob o regime de economia patriarcal*, 2 vols., Rio de Janeiro: Maia & Schmidt, 1933; in English as *The Masters and the Slaves: A Study in the Development of Brazilian Civilization*, New York: Knopf, 1946, London: Secker and Warburg, 1947

Furtado, Celso, *Formação econômica do Brasil*, Rio de Janeiro: Cultura, 1959, 17th edition, 1980; in English as *The Economic Growth of Brazil: A Survey from Colonial to Modern Times*, Berkeley: University of California Press, 1963

Furtado, Celso, *Desenvolvimento e subdesenvolvimento*, Rio de Janeiro: Cultura, 1961; in English as *Development and Underdevelopment*, Berkeley: University of California Press, 1964

Furtado, Celso, *Formação econômica da América Latina*, Rio de Janeiro: Lia, 1969; in English as *Economic Development of Latin America: A Survey from Colonial Times to the Cuban Revolution*, Cambridge: Cambridge University Press, 1970

Germani, Gino, *Sociología de la modernización: estudios teóricos, metodológicos, y aplicados a América Latina*, Buenos Aires: Paidos, 1969; in English as *The Sociology of Modernization: Studies on Its Historical and Theoretical Aspects with Special Regards to the Latin American Case*, New Brunswick, NJ: Transaction, 1981

Germani, Gino, *Autoritarismo, fascismo e classi sociali*, Bologna: Mulino, 1975; in English as *Authoritarianism, Fascism, and National Populism*, New Brunswick, NJ: Transaction, 1978

Góngora, Mario, and Jean Borde, *Evolución de la propiedad rural en el Valle del Puangue* (Evolution of Rural Property in the Valley of Puangue), 2 vols., Santiago: Universitaria, 1956

Góngora, Mario, *Origen de los 'inquilinos' de Chile central* (Origin of the Sharecroppers of Central Chile), Santiago: Universidad de Chile, 1960

Góngora, Mario, *Encomenderos y estancieros: Estudios acerca de la constitución social aristocrática de Chile después de la conquista, 1580–1660* (Encomenderos and Landowners: Studies in the Aristocratic Social Composition of Chile since the Conquest), Santiago: Universitaria, 1970

Góngora, Mario, *Ensayo histórico sobre la noción de estado en Chile en los siglos XIX y XX* (Historical Essay on the Idea of the State in Chile in the 19th and 20th Centuries), Santiago: Ciudad, 1981

González Casanova, Pablo, *La democracia en México*, Mexico City: ERA, 1965; in English as *Democracy in Mexico*, New York: Oxford University Press, 1970

Knight, Alan, *The Mexican Revolution*, 2 vols., Cambridge and New York: Cambridge University Press, 1986

Lynch, John, *Argentine Dictator: Juan Manuel de Rosas, 1829–1852*, Oxford and New York: Oxford University Press, 1981

Mitre, Bartolomé, *Historia de Belgrano y de la independencia argentina* (History of Belgrano and of Argentine Independence), Buenos Aires: Mayo, 1859

Mitre, Bartolomé, *Historia de San Martín y de la emancipación sudamericana*, 3 vols., Buenos Aires: Nación, 1887–90; abridged in English as *The Emancipation of South America*, London: Chapman and Hall, 1893, New York: Cooper Square, 1969

Molina Enríquez, Andrés, *Los grandes problemas nacionales* (The Great National Problems), México: Carranza, 1909

Ortiz, Fernando, *Hampa afro-cubana: los negros brujos (apuntes para un estudio de etnología criminal)* (Afro-Cuban Criminality), Madrid: Fe, 1906

Ortiz, Fernando, *La africanía de la música folklórica de Cuba* (The Africanness of the Folkloric Music of Cuba), Havana: Cárdenas, 1950

Pérez, Louis A., Jr., *Cuba: Between Reform and Revolution*, Oxford and New York: Oxford University Press, 1988

Platt, Desmond Christopher Martin, *Latin America and British Trade, 1806–1914*, London: A. & C. Black, 1972; New York: Barnes and Noble, 1973

Prado Júnior, Caio, *A revolução brasileira* (The Brazilian Revolution), São Paulo: Editôra Brasiliense, 1966

Prebisch, Raúl, for United Nations Economic Commission for Latin America, *El desarrollo económico de América Latina y sus principales problemas*, Santiago: ECLA, 1949; in English as *The Economic Development of Latin America and Its Principal Problems*, Lake Success: UN Department of Economic Affairs, 1950

Prebisch, Raúl, for United Nations Economic Commission for Latin America, *Economic Survey of Latin America: 1949*, Lake Success: UN Department of Economic Affairs, 1951 [Spanish edition 1950]

Quirk, Robert E., *Fidel Castro*, New York: Norton, 1993

Rock, David, *Politics in Argentina, 1890–1930: The Rise and Fall of Radicalism*, Cambridge and New York: Cambridge University Press, 1975

Rodrigues, José Honório, *Teoria da história do Brasil: introdução metodológica* (Theory of the History of Brazil), 2 vols., São Paulo: Instituto Progresso, 1949; revised 1957

Rodrigues, José Honório, *Aspirações nacionais: interpretação histórico-político*, São Paulo: Fulgor, 1963; in English as *The Brazilians: Their Character and Aspirations*, Austin: University of Texas Press, 1967

Sarmiento, Domingo F., *Civilización i barbarie: vida de Juan Facundo Quiroga, aspecto físco, costumbres, i abitos de la República Argentina*, Santiago: Progreso, 1845; in English as *Life in the Argentine Republic in the Days of the Tyrants; or, Civilization and Barbarism*, New York: Hurd and Houghton, 1868, reprinted 1960

Scobie, James R., *Argentina: A City and a Nation*, New York: Oxford University Press, 1964

Scobie, James R., *Revolution on the Pampas: A Social History of Argentine Wheat, 1860–1910*, Austin: University of Texas Press, 1964

Scobie, James R., *Buenos Aires: Plaza to Suburb, 1870–1910*, New York: Oxford University Press, 1974

Scobie, James R., *Secondary Cities of Argentina: The Social History of Corrientes, Salta, and Mendoza, 1850–1910*, Stanford, CA: Stanford University Press, 1988

Sierra, Justo, *México, su evolución social*, 2 in 3 vols., Mexico [Barcelona]: Ballescá, 1900–02; in English as *Mexico: Its Social Evolution*, 2 in 3 vols., Ballescá, 1900–04

Stein, Stanley J., *Vassouras: A Brazilian Coffee County, 1850–1900: The Roles of Planter and Slave in a Plantation Society*, Cambridge, MA: Harvard University Press, 1957

Stein, Stanley J., and Barbara H. Stein, *The Colonial Heritage of Latin America: Essays on Economic Dependence in Perspective*, New York: Oxford University Press, 1970

Tannenbaum, Frank, *Slave and Citizen: The Negro in the Americas*, New York: Knopf, 1946

Thomas, Hugh, *Cuba: The Pursuit of Freedom*, New York: Harper, and London: Eyre and Spottiswoode, 1971; abridged as *The Cuban Revolution*, Harper, 1977

Varnhagen, Francisco Adolfo de, *História geral do Brasil* (General History of Brazil), 6 vols., 1854–57; 10th edition, 1981

Varnhagen, Francisco Adolfo de, *História das lutas com os holandêses no Brasil desde 1624 a 1654* (History of the Conflicts with the Dutch in Brazil from 1624 to 1654), Vienna: Finsterbeck, 1871; reprinted São Paulo: Cultura, 1943

Varnhagen, Francisco Adolfo de, *História da independência do Brasil* (History of the Independence of Brazil), Rio: Nacional, 1917; 6th edition, 1972

Wade, Peter, *Blackness and Race Mixture: The Dynamics of Racial Identity in Colombia*, Baltimore: Johns Hopkins University Press, 1993

Womack, John, *Zapata and the Mexican Revolution*, New York: Knopf, and London: Thames and Hudson, 1969

Woodward, Ralph Lee, Jr., *Rafael Carrera and the Emergence of the Republic of Guatemala, 1821–1871*, Athens: University of Georgia Press, 1993

Lavisse, Ernest 1842–1922
French historian

In Third Republic France, where the figure of the teacher was at the center of wide-ranging institutional and ideological efforts to make France republican, Ernest Lavisse was the pre-eminent teacher. As an author and public figure, he was central to the emergence of history as a professional discipline in France, particularly in the intertwining of research and pedagogy as inseparably foundational for the historian. In his work, he pursued three directions: history, teaching, and civic responsibility. His endeavors in each of these fields shaped his own undertaking of the others, as well as what these activities came to mean in France.

Lavisse was one of the most well-known of France's so-called positivist historians, along with Charles Seignobos and Charles Victor Langlois. Trained in Prussia, Lavisse promoted the study of history as a positivist science, marked by the careful scrutiny of documents to establish veracity (through methods more rigorously articulated in the seminal work of Langlois and Seignobos, *L'Introduction aux études historiques* [Introduction to the Study of History], 1898) and a refusal of subjectivism, by which he meant that the historian should attempt to present the facts neutrally and avoid explicit political engagement. With both of these guidelines, his approach was neither philosophically sophisticated nor particularly well-defined.

Lavisse wrote history in order to detail the exemplary, the singular events and individuals of the past which, when described, explained how the present came to be. In his biographies of Louis XIV of France and Frederick II of Prussia, he provided abundant details and precise accounts. In these tomes, as in all of his writings, the past is available to present scrutiny; nothing is exotic or unknowable. His refusal of any opacity to the past helps explain how his exhaustive biographies of reference became so popular among the general public. Lavisse laid out a vision of history in which current political debates and questions were always prefigured if not already in play. He isolated the key actors in the past and showed how their behavior had been heroic, as in the case of Colbert, who had sought to advance rational and scientific approaches to politics and economics, or blameworthy, such as Louis XIV, whose absolutism had stymied the efforts of reformers and thus the progress of France. Such examples offered clear lessons for contemporary Frenchmen.

Lavisse's histories were widely taught at every level of the French education system; his pedagogical guidebooks helped form how teaching itself took place. As Pierre Benoît proclaimed in homage: "for university teaching, for secondary teaching, for primary teaching: to invert the Trinity, there were three gods in one person, Ernest Lavisse." Lavisse himself played a key role in the expansion of history's importance in French education under the Third Republic. He held numerous positions in governmental and professional organizations where he was instrumental in reshaping university training and teaching. These activities were reinforced in articles and speeches, collected in Questions d'enseignement national (Issues of National Education, 1885), Etudes et étudiants (Studies and Students, 1890), and À propos de nos écoles (About Our Schools, 1895). One of the hallmarks of his approach to pedagogy was his insistence that there were no contradictions or significant differences between the needs of teachers at varying levels, from schoolteachers to university professors. The research of this last group guided the efforts of the former.

The research Lavisse deployed in his monographs, exemplars to generations of historians in training, informed the giant collective works that he directed, such as the Histoire générale du IVe siècle à nos jours (A General History from the 4th Century until Today, 1892–1901) or the Histoire de France contemporaine (History of Contemporary France, 1921–22). His most celebrated effort was "le petit Lavisse." This collection of "thin manuals with blue covers," first widely available in 1884, were carefully prepared and repeatedly revised by Lavisse. The five guides were for decades read and memorized by French primary students, from ages seven to fourteen.

Strictly chronological, presenting political and military events while mostly excluding discussions of philosophy, religion, or social conditions, Lavisse's manuals surveyed and codified what was history for most French of the Third Republic. In Lavisse's evocation of the past the nation-state, la patrie, was at the center. His work on Prussia makes this insistence clear, yet it is in his writings about France that his analysis is most fully developed. While both states have always had specific identities which developed and evolved over time, Lavisse insisted that through the Revolution, the mission of the French Republic was now linked to human destiny. His active public engagement in a variety of civic activities reinforced his role as a teacher of French nationalism. He was particularly active in efforts to bring attention to the cause of German-occupied Alsace-Lorraine.

Today, Lavisse has become more a historical figure – an exemplary citizen of late 19th- and early 20th-century France – than historiographically important. In France, his role as one of the positivist fathers metaphorically killed by their Annaliste offspring has further alienated him from current debates among historians. However, the methods he practiced, the institutions and disciplinary yardsticks he founded or reformed, and the bond of research and pedagogy he forged for historical practice, all remain issues of current importance and necessary interrogation.

TODD DAVID SHEPARD

See also France: 1000–1450; France: 1450–1789; Seignobos; Social

Biography

Born Le Nouvion-en-Thiérache, Aisne, 1842. Educated at the Ecole Normale Supérieure, 1862–65. Tutor of the imperial prince (Napoleon III's son), 1867–69; secretary to minister, Victor Duruy, 1867–69; professor of modern history, Sorbonne, 1888–1919; director, Ecole Normale Supérieure, 1904–19. Elected to Académie Française, 1892. Died Paris, 1922.

Principal Writings

Etudes sur l'histoire de Prusse (Studies on the History of Prussia), 1879
Questions d'enseignement national (Issues of National Education), 1885
Etudes et étudiants (Studies and Students), 1890
La Jeunesse du grand Frédéric, 1891; in English as The Youth of Frederick the Great, 1892
Editor with Alfred Rambaud, Histoire générale du IVe siècle à nos jours (A General History from the 4th Century until Today), 12 vols., 1892–1901
Le Grand Frédéric avant l'Avènement (Frederick the Great before His Accession), 1893
À propos de nos écoles (About Our Schools), 1895
General editor, Histoire de France depuis les origines jusqu'à la révolution (A History of France from Its Origins to the Revolution), 9 vols., 1900–11
Souvenirs (Memoirs), 1912
General editor, Histoire de France contemporaine depuis la révolution jusqu'à la paix de 1919 (History of Contemporary France, from the Revolution until the Peace of 1919), 10 vols., 1921–22

Further Reading

Carbonell, Charles-Olivier, Histoire et historiens: une mutation idéologique des historiens français, 1865–1885 (History and Historians: The Ideological Changes within the French Historical Profession, 1865–1885), Toulouse: Privat, 1976
Crubellier, Maurice, L'Ecole républicaine 1870–1940 (Republican Schooling, 1870–1940), Paris: Christian, 1993
Fitou, Jean-François, "Comment on récrit l'histoire: Louis XIV de Lavisse à Gaxotte" (How to Rewrite History: Louis XIV According to Lavisse or Gaxotte), Annales 44 (1989), 479–97
Furet, François, L'Atelier de l'histoire, Paris: Flammarion, 1982; in English as In the Workshop of History, Chicago: University of Chicago Press, 1984
Keylor, William R., Academy and Community: The Foundation of the French Historical Profession, Cambridge, MA: Harvard University Press, 1975

Lavrin, Asunción

Cuban-born historian of Latin American women

The doyenne of Latin American women's history, Asunción Lavrin has shown that the manner in which women have become politically visible is one of the most important subjects of concern for the contemporary historian. A strong proponent of history written to raise awareness as well as to achieve knowledge, Lavrin broke new ground by studying Latin American feminism. Setting Latina feminism in comparative context with European and North American philosophies, she has demonstrated that, while the progress of feminism in Latin America has been influenced by feminism in the First World, it is an ideology that sprouted from native soil and not one imposed by foreigners.

Lavrin, a Cuban immigrant to the United States, completed her dissertation on women's religious life in 18th-century Mexico. It served as a starting point for a career devoted to research in women's history. Her publications have focused on women, women in the church, ecclesiastical history and, most recently, 20th-century feminism in Latin America. An explicit aim of Lavrin's principal writings is to stress that feminism is an ideology indigenous to Latin America.

No general histories of women in any of the countries of the Southern Cone (Chile, Argentina, and Uruguay) as yet exist. The field of Latin American women's history itself is quite young and still quite small, although beginning to boom. Lavrin found in a 1978 survey that little of the available literature in English on Latin American women followed the historical method or dealt with issues in a historical fashion. She has supported historical scholarship over the years by raising theoretical questions for feminist historians to consider. Many of her essays discuss emerging key themes in Latin American women's history, specifically in labor, politics, and the family. Other essays focus on encouraging a multicultural understanding of feminist ideologies. By studying the development of feminism in the Southern Cone, she has demonstrated that little common ground of understanding for the study of feminism exists.

The manner in which women have become "visible" throughout history is one of the most important subjects of concern for the contemporary historian. In the usual histories of Latin American nations, the manner in which sociopolitical changes affected the female half of the population, or the activities generated by women themselves are mostly neglected. Lavrin addresses this oversight. *The Ideology of Feminism in the Southern Cone, 1900–1940* (1985) argued that feminism accelerated the educational and material transition of women from the 19th into the 20th century. Lavrin's magnum opus *Women, Feminism, and Social Change in Argentina, Chile, and Uruguay, 1890–1940* (1996) addressed politics as an activity beyond either party alignments or the exercise of sheer power. Lavrin analyzed gender relations in these nations by following a socialist feminist philosophy that focuses on the particular qualities traditionally attributed to women, such as compassion and nurturing ability. She moved from the first discussions of feminist ideas in the Southern Cone to the organization of women's parties and the full participation of women in national politics.

The study of women in Latin America, as Lavrin has noted, is methodologically complex and the fact that most Latin American nations are in several stages of historical and economic development does not make it easier. Scholars also face the fragmentation resulting from the limited communication among women of several countries, which has contributed to considerable ignorance of each other's problems. Lavrin has been tremendously influential in the broad arena of women's history by arguing that our reconstruction of the feminist experience should take into consideration the very real confines created by legislation, family ties, education, and the economic means of those involved. By pushing scholars to look at cross-cultural communication, she has also blurred the boundaries between North American and South American history, between an "Anglo" and an "Hispanic" past.

CARYN E. NEUMANN

See also Spain: Imperial; Women's History: Latin America

Biography

Asunción Irigoyen Lavrin. Born Havana. Received BA, University of Havana; MA, Radcliffe College; PhD, Harvard University, 1963. Taught at Columbia University; Bryn Mawr College; Princeton University; Georgetown University; rose to professor, Howard University, 1977–88; professor, Arizona State University, from 1988. Married David H. Lavrin (1 son, 1 daughter).

Principal Writings

Editor, *Latin American Women: Historical Perspectives*, 1978
The Ideology of Feminism in the Southern Cone, 1900–1940, 1985
"Female Religious," in Louisa Schell Hoberman and Susan Migden Socolow, eds., *Cities and Society in Colonial Latin America*, 1986
"Women, the Family, and Social Change in Latin America," *World Affairs* 150 (1987), 109–28
"Anthologies," in K. Lynn Stoner, ed., *Latinas of the Americas*, New York: Garland, 1989, 3–22
"El segundo sexo en México: experiencia, estudio e introspección (The Second Sex in Mexico: Experience, Study and Introspection)," *Mexican Studies/Estudios mexicanos* 5 (1989), 297–312
"Sexuality in Colonial Mexico: A Church Dilemma," in Asunción Lavrin, ed., *Sexuality and Marriage in Colonial Latin America*, 1989
"Women, Labor, and the Left: Argentina and Chile, 1900–1925," *Journal of Women's History* 1 (1989), 87–113
"La mujer en México: veinte años de estudio, 1968–1988" (The Woman in Mexico: Twenty Years of Study), in *Simposio de historiografía mexicanista* (Symposium on Mexican Historiography) Mexico City: UNAM, 1990
Women, Feminism, and Social Change in Argentina, Chile, and Uruguay, 1890–1940, 1995

Lea, Henry Charles 1825–1909

US medievalist and religious historian

Henry Charles Lea was one of the most influential historians to work in America during the 19th century. His work epitomizes the liberal tradition, with all its strengths and weaknesses, and today remains an important resource for medieval and early modern ecclesiastical history. Best known for his work on the medieval and Spanish Inquisitions, Lea brought institutional history to a new level of sophistication and demonstrated the centrality of this approach to the scientific model of historical inquiry.

Lea was born in Philadelphia on 19 September 1825, the son of a noted publisher and scientist. As a young man, he was trained as a scientist and his first publication was a monograph on fossils found in a formation close to Petersburg, Virginia. He entered the family publishing firm at the age of eighteen, but an emotional breakdown led to his leaving the business and starting the study of history. A member of the upper echelons of Americas elite society he adopted the role, in a manner very similar to W.H. Prescott a generation before, of the gentleman intellectual who used his social position and material wealth to foster the growth of scholarship in the United States.

Lea came to the study of the Inquisition through the pursuit of several controlling interests that formed the underlying themes of his life's work. He believed that his task as a historian was to chronicle the manner in which the human spirit has struggled to overcome its corruption by superstition and coercive institutions. The Inquisition, in both its medieval and Spanish incarnations, called out to him as the perfect laboratory in which to observe how institutions had the capacity to pervert positive social patterns (e.g., the belief in God and the authority of the church) into tools of repression and persecution. In addition, this investigation, by its contrast with Lea's positive understanding of American institutions and his belief in their efficacy and justice, highlighted his confidence in the progress made by 19th-century society. The study of the Inquisition provided a vehicle for articulating the manner in which institutions affect the possibilities of social and moral expression – for good or for ill – and implicitly placed the American experience within a developmental context in which it was understood to be the culmination of historical progress.

Lea began his study of the Inquisition in 1867 and worked on it for the rest of his life. He published his 3-volume work *The Inquisition of the Middle Ages*, in 1887 and 1888; *A History of the Inquisition of Spain* (four volumes) came out in 1906–07; and *The Inquisition in the Spanish Dependencies* came out just before his death in 1908. In addition to his work on the Inquisition he also published a book on the Moriscos (Muslim converts to Christianity) of Spain, and produced various studies on the medieval church. At his death he left unfinished an investigation into the history of witchcraft – a work that was published posthumously.

Lea's research into the history of the Inquisition was made possible by the opening and reorganization of the archives of the Inquisition in the early part of the 19th century. Prior to this, the vast documentation produced by this institution had been hidden from all but its own members, with the consequence that its image rested primarily on rumor and hearsay. One of Lea's most important contributions to the history of the church and to western civilization in general, was to establish a consistent and thorough documentary basis for interpreting the historical impact of this influential but inscrutable institution; he was one of the first scholars to integrate ecclesiastical institutions into the framework of scientific history. Congruent with this spirit he also incorporated into his studies a strong conviction in the necessity of limiting historical judgments to assessments compatible with the spirit of the age under consideration. Despite his Protestant background, Lea's work does not exhibit the blatant anti-Catholic or anti-Spanish bias that was typical of many of his contemporaries. He attempted to found his judgments on a well-documented argument and eschewed the practice of imposing moral judgments that presupposed an ethical continuity among all historical periods.

This is not to say that he was not critical of the impact of the Inquisition. One of his motives for studying this institution was to elucidate the process of persecution in the modern world. He clearly understood the Inquisition to be an agent of repression – one that had fortunately been transcended by modern institutions – that demonstrated how the spirit of man could betray its best intentions and produce a social environment causing misery and despair. In *The Inquisition of the Middle Ages*, he writes, "The judgment of impartial history must be that the Inquisition was the monstrous offspring of mistaken zeal, utilized by selfish greed and lust of power to smother the higher aspirations of humanity and stimulate its baser appetites."

While Lea consciously advocated the importance of writing an objective historical account, he was still a product of his time. His conviction in the progressive development of history predisposed him to see in the Inquisition a typology of superstition and obscurantism that contemporary society had, for the most part, successfully transcended. Such a confidence in the forward movement of history does not resonate with today's relativistic approach to historical interpretation. Yet Lea's work cannot be dismissed on that account. The solidity of his documentary research and the keenness of his institutional analysis retain their relevance to the modern student of the subject. His works stand as classics and rank H.C. Lea as one of the most significant historians produced by America.

LINCOLN A. DRAPER

Biography

Born Philadelphia, 19 September 1825. Privately tutored. Entered family publishing firm, M. Carey & Sons, 1843; after a breakdown in 1847, traveled and wrote; returned to publishing, 1860: manager, 1865–80, special partner (after firm became Henry C. Lea's Son & Co.), 1880–85; repeated breakdown, 1880. Married Anna Caroline Jaudon, 1850. Died Philadelphia, 1909.

Principal Writings

Superstition and Force: Essays on the Wager of Law, the Wager of Battle, the Ordeal-Torture, 1866

An Historical Sketch of Sacerdotal Celibacy in the Christian Church, 1867

Studies in Church History, 1869

The Inquisition of the Middle Ages, 3 vols., 1887–88

Chapters from the Religious History of Spain Connected with the Inquisition, 1890

A History of Auricular Confession and Indulgences in the Latin Church, 3 vols., 1896

The Moriscos of Spain: Their Conversion and Expulsion, 1901

A History of the Inquisition of Spain, 4 vols., 1906–07

The Inquisition in the Spanish Dependencies: Sicily, Naples, Sardinia, Milan, the Canaries, Mexico, Peru, New Granada, 1908

Materials Toward a History of Witchcraft, edited by Arthur C. Howland, 1939

Further Reading

Krieger, Leonard, "European History in America," in *History: The Development of Historical Studies in the United States*, by John Higham, Leonard Krieger, and Felix Gilbert, Englewood Cliffs, NJ: Prentice Hall, 1965

Peters, Edward, "Henry Charles Lea and the Abode of Monsters," in Angel Alcalá, ed., *The Spanish Inquisition and the Inquisitorial Mind*, Boulder, CO: Social Science Monographs, 1987

Tedeschi, John, "The Dispersed Archives of the Roman Inquisition," in Gustav Henningsen, John Tedeschi, and Charles Amiel, eds., *The Inquisition in Early Modern Europe: Studies on Sources and Methods*, DeKalb: Northern Illinois University Press, 1986

Trevor-Roper, Hugh, "The European Witch-Craze of the Sixteenth and Seventeenth Centuries," in his *Religion, the Reformation and Social Change*, London: Macmillan 1967, 3rd edition, London: Secker and Warburg, 1984; as *The Crisis of the Seventeenth Century*, New York: Harper, 1968

Lecky, W.E.H. 1838–1903

Anglo-Irish historian

W.E.H. Lecky is Ireland's most famous and popular 19th-century historian. In his time he exerted considerable influence both through his historiographical judgment and his political criticism. His late and rather short political career as a member of Parliament for Trinity College, Dublin was the climax of his personal ambition, but also the consequence of his intellectual achievements. One of Lecky's major questions concerned the relevance of Ireland's history for current political discussions. Therefore the history of the 18th century and especially that of the Protestant Ascendancy and its political outcome in Grattan's Parliament of 1782 played a central role in his historical thinking and in his political assessment of Irish nationalism and the Home Rule movement of his own time. From a landlord background himself, Lecky naturally sympathized with the Anglo-Irish upper-class. The (non-Celtic) nationalism of his youth became the unionism of his old age.

Nonetheless Lecky tried to avoid any clear political affiliation. He attempted to follow his own maxim that the historian's task was to remain impartial and primarily to enable complex historical questions to be understood before any judgment was taken. Accordingly, Lecky did not belong to any particular school of historians. He claimed intellectual sympathy for and was strongly influenced by some philosophers of the Enlightenment. But probably the greatest influence came from Henry T. Buckle, Thomas Carlyle, and the so-called liberal Anglican historians such as, for example, Henry Hart Milman and Thomas Arnold. At a later stage he freed himself from his predecessors and formulated his own philosophy and methodology of history. This became an amalgamation of Buckle's ideas on the universal laws of civilization and of Carlyle's ideas on the role of the individual in history.

Lecky was a typical Victorian man of letters, a "public moralist" who thought the intellectual's destiny was not only to be in constant dialogue with public opinion, but also to influence it, especially on matters such as what was regarded as morally acceptable and politically correct behavior. Lecky produced a considerable number of historical publications most of which were widely reviewed in Britain, the US, and in Europe. His books were predominantly devoted to political, cultural, intellectual, social, and economic history of the 18th century in England and Ireland, but he also sought to include aspects of Scottish, imperial, and continental history.

Two of Lecky's best known works are his cultural and philosophical studies *History of the Rise and Influence of the Spirit of Rationalism in Europe* (1865) and *History of European Morals from Augustus to Charlemagne* (1869). As he explained in a letter written in 1870, both books were closely connected in their attempt to show how theological and philosophical opinions can arise and succeed (*Morals*), and how they can subsequently decay (*Rationalism*). Here Lecky built on the historical writings of Vico, Condorcet, Herder, and Hegel, and particularly on what he regarded as one of Buckle's main achievements, namely looking at history as an organic entity that is compounded by historical laws. According to Lecky, who put forward his theoretical concept of history in these two books, civilization was a process of continued and uninterrupted development, and progress was best achieved by evolutionary reform. Thus ideas could not be put into practice until the appropriate stage of civilization had been reached. This Whiggish concept of cultural development could well be translated into a contemporary political context showing how Lecky defined the Home Rule movement as a revolution that did not positively comply with Irish history or with imperial needs.

Lecky's concept of morphological laws laid the basis for his model of a history of rationalism. According to this model a civilization could be receptive to new ideas only if it had attained a certain cultural and social level. As far as this qualification was concerned he stated that the "believing age" as described in his *History of European Morals* was over, and that the time for a "reforming age" had come. The secularization of social life followed the rationalization of politics. While in the one book Lecky studied the history of progress, the subject of the other was the history of retrogression. History was thus seen as a linear process of perfection, governed by universal laws but nevertheless influenced by what he called "accidents," that is, the role of individuals.

In his book *The Leaders of Public Opinion in Ireland* (1861) Lecky examined the role of individuals (Swift, Flood, Grattan, O'Connell) who had been of crucial significance for the course of Irish history between Swift's "Drapier's Letters" and O'Connell's Catholic emancipation movement. This history of the rise and fall of the Anglo-Irish Ascendancy in Ireland showed the shift in power from the Protestant-oriented patriotism of the 18th century to the Catholic-dominated nationalism of the 19th century. Lecky described these intellectuals in order to demonstrate the importance of the development of a lay public opinion in producing what he termed a "healthy national feeling" that would prevent further sectarianism. Thus Lecky tried to combine his ideas of history as a process driven by laws and the inherent and irresistible forces of history, with his belief that the individual could under certain circumstances direct this process.

Lecky elaborated on his historiographical thinking much more comprehensively in his 8-volume masterpiece *History of England in the Eighteenth Century* (1878–90). As he explained in the introduction, Lecky did not wish to write a year-by-year history. Rather he was attempting to show the permanent forces of his chosen period, and to analyze those features that his method of ordering by subject rather than by chronology had revealed as characteristic. Thus he described the history (to give only a few examples) of the monarchy, aristocracy, church and dissent; of the parliament, press, political ideas; the history of agricultural and commercial interests; of art, manners, fashion; of the colonies, the American and the French revolutions. Consequently, he paid much less attention to aspects of mainly biographical or party interest.

Lecky's passionate examination of J.A. Froude's polemical study *The English in Ireland* (1872–74) preceded these books. While Froude defended his historiographical and anti-Irish opinions against Lecky's criticism, Lecky later felt he had to clarify his standpoint in a debate with Gladstone. The British prime minister interpreted Lecky's *History of England* and especially his description of the Grattan Parliament of 1782 as historical justification for his commitment to Irish Home Rule. Lecky's *History of England* is a good example of how an intellectual could become engaged in a political discussion in which history was relevant to politics, and politics to historiography.

Lecky did not really produce any historical school of writing in Ireland. However, in the context of Irish historiography in general, it is one of his main achievements to have attempted to write an impartial history that primarily called for a better understanding between England and Ireland.

BENEDIKT STUCHTEY

See also Froude; Ireland; Trevelyan

Biography

William Edward Hartpole Lecky. Born Newton Park, County Dublin, Ireland, 26 March 1838. Attended Cheltenham College, 1852–55; Trinity College, Dublin, BA 1859. Settled in London, 1866. Married Elisabeth, Baroness von Dedem, 1871. Member of Parliament for Dublin University, 1896–1902. Died London, 22 October 1903.

Principal Writings

The Religious Tendencies of the Age, 1860
The Leaders of Public Opinion in Ireland, 1861, 1871, 1903
History of the Rise and Influence of the Spirit of Rationalism in Europe, 2 vols., 1865
History of European Morals from Augustus to Charlemagne, 2 vols., 1869
A History of England in the Eighteenth Century, 8 vols., 1878–90
A History of Ireland in the Eighteenth Century, 5 vols., 1892–93
Democracy and Liberty, 2 vols., 1896
The Map of Life: Conduct and Character, 1899
Historical and Political Essays, edited by Elisabeth Lecky, 1908
A Victorian Historian: Private Letters of W.E.H. Lecky, 1859–1878, edited by H. Montgomery Hyde, 1947

Further Reading

Auchmuty, James Johnston, *Lecky: A Biographical and Critical Essay*, London and New York: Longman, 1945
McCartney, Donal, *W.E.H. Lecky: Historian and Politician, 1838–1903*, Dublin: Lilliput Press, 1994
Stuchtey, Benedikt, "The Lecky Papers in Trinity College, Dublin," *European Review of History* 1 (1994), 257–61
Stuchtey, Benedikt, "Die irische Historiographie im 19. Jahrhundert und Lecky's Geschichtskonzeption" (19th-Century Irish Historiography and Lecky's Conception of History) *Comparativ* 5/3 (1995), 83–98
Stuchtey, Benedikt, *W.E.H. Lecky (1838–1903): Historisches Denken und politisches Urteilen im Werk eines anglo-irischen Gelehrten*, (Historical Thinking and Political Judgment of an Anglo-Irish Intellectual), Göttingen: Vandenhoeck & Ruprecht, 1997
von Arx, Jeffrey Paul, *Progress and Pessimism: Religion, Politics, and History in Late Nineteenth-Century Britain*, Cambridge, MA: Harvard University Press, 1985, 64–123
Wyatt, Anne, "Froude, Lecky and the 'Humblest Irishman'," *Irish Historical Studies* 19 (1975), 261–85

Lefebvre, Georges 1874–1959
French historian of the French Revolution

Quatre-vingt-neuf (1939; *The Coming of the French Revolution*, 1947) is Georges Lefebvre's best known work in English and provides a synthesis of the Marxist interpretation of the French Revolution. The Revolution is seen as a bourgeois one, ushered in by the unwillingness of the nobility to accept reforms in 1787–88. Lefebvre characterized it as a "revolution aristocratique" (an aristocratic revolution), a somewhat misleading expression. The book remains required reading for all students of the period.

Yet, to summarize Lefebvre's work and thinking on the French Revolution in this way is to distort grossly his scholarly contribution to the history of the Revolution. Above all, Lefebvre was the historian of the French peasantry. Indeed, he argued that the Revolution was in great part a peasant revolution. In his unsurpassed doctoral thesis, published as *Les Paysans du Nord pendant la Révolution française* (The Peasants of Northern France during the French Revolution, 1924), Lefebvre developed his theories in a very sophisticated way. By examining the distinct geographical region of northern France, he outlined specific methodological problems and sought to understand social structures on the eve of the Revolution. This led him first to a detailed statistical examination of peasant life, which covered 200 pages appended to the end of his thesis. He left no archival material untouched. Sources relating to feudal dues, taxation, sale of church lands, implementation of the "maximum" policy, and practice of Terror, changes in religious practices, all were tapped in an attempt to grasp the realities of peasant society in northern France. Lefebvre's conclusions were complex. Broadly speaking, he outlined differences between various groups of peasants. The peasants who were already well off before 1789 were satisfied with the revolutionary settlement. It allowed them to buy church lands and expand their holdings. Others, less fortunate, benefited from the abolition of seigneurial dues but failed to buy more land. They too tended to accept the revolutionary settlement which turned them into peasant owners, albeit small ones. This broad division excluded the group of landless peasants, difficult to track down in the archives because they did not pay taxes or leave wills. In his conclusion, Lefebvre pointed out that the first category of peasants was particularly strong in the north of France. But Lefebvre went further, bringing into the picture a political dimension, relating the impact of the distribution of land to the myth of equality. Admittedly, few peasants benefited from the distribution of émigré lands as conceived by Saint-Just in March 1794. But the notion that small property for all could be achieved lay at the very foundation of the concept of equality handed down by the Revolution. This is a point taken up by P.M. Jones in his *The Peasantry in the French Revolution* (1988). Lefebvre did more than count the peasants and divide them into various categories, he sought to understand the motives behind their actions.

In so doing, there is little doubt that Lefebvre was influenced by Emile Durkheim who introduced a psychological dimension to the study of history. Equally significant was Lefebvre's connection with Marc Bloch, his colleague at the University of Strasbourg. Although not a major figure among Annales historians, Lefebvre has nevertheless a place in the movement. This is best illustrated in his *Etudes sur la Révolution française* (Studies on the French Revolution, 1954). Under the heading "Social History," Lefebvre displayed his concern over "mentalities" in two remarkable articles: "Foules revolutionnaires" (Revolutionary Crowds) and "Le meurtre du comte de Dampierre" (The Murder of the Count of Dampierre). Indeed the latter remains to this day a brilliant example of storytelling used as an exercise in *Histoire des mentalités*. The scene is set near Varenne in June 1791. As the royal coach was being driven back to Paris, the count, a local nobleman, came to pay his respects to the king and his family. The next day, he was found dead, having been killed by local peasants who had clearly associated his gesture with a sign of betrayal of the Revolution. Lefebvre used the story as a springboard for an analysis of the peasant mentality in 1791, at a time when lords were still trying to levy feudal dues. This practice had resulted from the legislation put in place after 4 August 1789. In a similar way, Lefebvre analyzed the motives behind the Great Fear of 1789, and showed how peasants acted for themselves with their own agenda. These works show the influence of sociological thinking on Lefebvre.

It is clear that to reduce Lefebvre's writings to social and economic history is inadequate. He himself often referred to his attempts at "histoire totale" (total history). In this, he expressed his desire to place human beings in all their complexities and activities at the center of historical writing. A historian influenced by sociological discoveries and scientific aspirations as they occurred in the 19th century, Lefebvre has left behind a marvelously complex body of work that combines the best of scholarly output with brilliant insights into mythmaking and cultural behavior.

MARTINE BONDOIS MORRIS

See also Bloch; Duby; Europe: Modern; France: French Revolution; France: since the Revolution; Hufton; Labrousse; Marxist Interpretation; Rudé; Soboul; Social

Biography

Born Lille, 6 August 1874, to a working-class family. Educated in the best republican tradition; received various grants for secondary and university education. Taught in secondary schools at Boulogne sur Mer, Cherbourg, Tourcoing, Lille, Saint-Omer, and Orléans; after World War I, taught in prestigious Paris schools (Pasteur, Montaigne, and Henri IV); submitted his doctoral thesis, and moved to universities of Clermont-Ferrand, 1924–28; Strasbourg, 1928–35 (where he met Marc Bloch, one of the founder of the Annales school); and the Sorbonne from 1935: held chair of the French Revolution, 1937–45. Director, *Annales Historiques de la Révolution Française*, 1932–59. Died Boulogne-Billancourt, 28 August 1959.

Principal Writings

Les Paysans du Nord pendant la Révolution française (The Peasants of Northern France during the French Revolution), 1924

La Révolution française, 1930; in English as *The French Revolution*, 2 vols., 1962–64
La Grande peur de 1789, 1932; in English as *The Great Fear of 1789: Rural Panic in Revolutionary France*, 1973
Questions agraires au temps de la Terreur (Agrarian Issues during the Terror), 1932
Napoléon, 1935, revised 1965; in English, 1969
Les Thermidoriens, 1937; in English as *The Thermidorians and The Directory: Two Phases of the French Revolution*, 1964
Quatre-vingt-neuf, 1939; In English as *The Coming of the French Revolution*, 1947
Le Directoire, 1946; in English as *The Directory*, 1964
Etudes sur la Révolution française (Studies on the French Revolution), 1954

Further Reading

Burke, Peter, *The French Historical Revolution: The Annales School, 1929–89*, Cambridge: Polity Press, and Stanford, CA: Stanford University Press, 1990
"Hommage à Lefebvre" *Annales Historiques de la Révolution Française* 185 (1946); and 188 (1947)
Iggers, Georg G., *New Directions in European Historiography*, Middletown, CT: Wesleyan University Press, 1975, revised 1985; London: Methuen, 1985
Jones, Peter M., *The Peasantry in the French Revolution*, Cambridge and New York: Cambridge University Press, 1988

Legal History

The history of law has been a core field of history since its inception as a professional discipline in the late 19th century. In fact, its first practitioners were lawyers, ranging in England from Thomas More, William Lambarde, John Selden, and Henry Spelman as the amateur historians of the 16th and early 17th centuries, to Henry Maine, F.W. Maitland, and Paul Vinogradoff in the rise of the academic historians of the late 19th and early 20th centuries. Similar parallels exist in continental Europe, with Alberto Gentili, Joachim Hopper, and Jean Bodin in the early modern era, and Max Weber, A.H. Post, Felix Liebermann, and S.J. Fockema Andreae at the turn of the 20th century.

The increasing specialization of the historical profession, however, has not been kind to the history of the law. Major mainstream legal historians in the Maitland tradition, such as S.F.C. Milsom and John Baker in England, and Heinrich Brunner and Andre Groulx in Europe, are not often read beyond the confines of their sub-discipline. The same point could be made with increasing relevance for more specialized historians of the law who write for an ever-decreasing readership. The mainstream, however, is changing in the 1990s, as both older and younger legal historians enrich their research and writing from new developments in the social sciences and a greater exposure to comparative history.

A fundamental distinction has occurred in the research and writing of legal history in Europe and North America. In Europe, the focus has been primarily factual, and increasingly localized, with an emphasis on historical facts and sociocultural context that emerged from the Annales school of French historiography. In North America, however, it is primarily doctrinal, pinned to the rise of the modern state, with an emphasis on theory that has developed from the "critical studies" movement. Thus a major work in European legal history, such as Paul Brand's *The Origins of the English Legal Profession* (1992), which assessed in rich detail the complex origins of common lawyers, reads in sharp contrast to a major North American work such as Morton Horwitz's *Transformation of American Law* (1977), which was written to demonstrate a thesis about *how* lawyers, judges, and the courts expanded legal concepts to enable the modern corporation to develop over the rights of individuals. Occasionally, some of the best legal historical writing on Europe has this "North American" perspective, whether it is written from Lancaster by Gerry Rubin and David Sugarman, Paris by Nicole and Yves Castan, or Houston by Robert C. Palmer. Likewise, some of the best North American legal history, such as that of Lawrence Friedman and Gordon Morris Bakken, still follows the classical European tradition.

One of the major differences between legal historical writing on the two continents stems from the nature of the sources and the discipline. In Europe, for example, such excellent original legal records survive from the medieval era that historians of law have nearly ten centuries of history to discover and illuminate what happened. Thus European historians have been able to learn the history of the law in individual communities in terms of structure (the long *durée*), conjuncture (the era), and event (the moment), as well as in the rise of the modern state. Only recently have European legal-historical research and writing turned to what used to be called the "margins" of history in a serious manner: children, women, immigrants, unskilled workers, and the poor.

In North America the documentary legal record is much shorter, no more than three centuries, more often two. Moreover, since most North American jurisdictions began life as colonies, their history has been perceived in linear terms: an evolution from colonies to nation-states. Thus many North American historians are more interested in the history of law *vis-à-vis* the nation-state and its ideological roots. For example, some of the best North American legal history, from James Hurst's *Law and the Conditions of Freedom in the Nineteenth-Century United States* (1956) to Allen Steinberg's *The Transformation of Criminal Justice* (1989), has been concerned primarily with legal history on the ground (facts), rather than in the air (theory), and sees the law in political, social, and economic constructs.

The difference methodologically has been the rise of the "critical legal studies" school in the United States in the 1980s. Its influence has been profound. The issues were made prominent in articles in American law journals that developed a history of their own, beginning with Robert Gordon's classic statement, "Critical Legal Histories" (1984), and its rebuttal by G. Edward White, "From Realism to Critical Legal Studies" (1986). This school, which takes a more pessimistic view of the law, has given rise in the 1990s to the school of "legal realism." Building on the rich texture of cases that revealed epic stories, as in A.W.B. Simpson's *Cannibalism and the Common Law* (1984), legal realism attempts to see the operation of the law in its broader construct and to understand how it resonates with its constituencies. Good examples include *American Legal Realism* (1993) edited by William Fisher III, Morton Horwitz, and Thomas Reed; Laura Kalman's *The*

Strange Career of Legal Liberalism (1996); and *Canadian State Trials* (1996) edited by F. Murray Greenwood and Barry Wright. It also points to other subjects that were previously seldom examined. Two prominent examples are recent works in medical legal history, Ruth Harris' *Murders and Madness* (1989) and Michael Clark and Catherine Crawford's *Legal Medicine in History* (1994), and in wartime legal history, A.W.B. Simpson's *In the Highest Degree Odious* (1992) and Jean-Claude Farcy's *Les Camps de concentration français de la première guerre mondiale* (French Concentration Camps of World War I, 1995).

Perhaps some of the best of both the traditional and the ideological worlds can be observed in non-European and non-North American legal history. In Africa, legal anthropologists have redefined the field of legal-historical scholarship by going behind the state to groups of people, and focusing on what they call "law-makers" (communal governors), "law-ways" (courts), and "law-finders" (judges). Conceptualizing institutions by what they do instead of by what they are named, scholars have created a typology by function. Distinguishing between state, quasi-state, and non-statal law, they have opened up the parameters of legal historical writing in such a way that brings together ideas of law in ancient and pre-industrial societies with law in modern ones, as in *Law, Society, and the State* (1995) edited by Louis Knafla and Susan Binnie. Sally Moore's *Law as Process* (1978) and Sally Merry's *Getting Justice and Getting Even* (1990) are the basic theoretical works of the new field of "legal pluralism," and the achievements have been spectacular given the scarcity of recorded evidence. Masaji Chiba's *Legal Pluralism* (1989) also pushed the field beyond Africa to Japan, while other non-Western as well as Western societies were examined in M.B. Hooker's *Legal Pluralism* (1975) and Antony Allott and Gordon Woodman's *People's Law and State Law* (1985).

Such scholarship has exercised an influence in writing on legal-historical topics concerning Native American and African American peoples in North America, and in English- and French-speaking societies in the Far East and South Pacific. The origins lay in the pioneering work and foundation studies of the legal culture of the Plains Indians by E. Adamson Hoebel, both alone – *The Law of Primitive Man* (1954) – and with Karl Nickerson Llewellyn – *The Cheyenne Way* (1941). They have been followed in a more highly textured manner by scholars such as Sidney Harring and Ronald Wright. Some of the best current work in this field of law, which is often called "law and society" in North America, has also spilled over to Southeast Asia, Australia, New Zealand, and Canada. Thus the study of non-European law and legal systems continues to have an important impact upon the legal histories of the European and North American continents.

Specialization may well advance the relevance of legal history to other subject areas. Economic, social, cultural, political, religious, and gender historians are increasingly using the law and legal records in their work. The law has always been central to individuals, groups, communities, and the state, as well as to mores, values, and ideas. Since the academic community has seen "national" historians replaced by "subject" ones, studying how law *works* in persons, groups, and institutions may bring it back into focus as a tool to understand the rich tapestry of history, rather than as a subject unto itself. What is needed?

More theoretical work on the sociocultural and intellectual side of the law, such as *Legal Theory and the Common Law* (1986) edited by William Twining, Donald R. Kelley's *The Human Measure* (1990), and William O'Barr's *Rules versus Relationships* (1990); more interdisciplinary thought such as *Hong Kong, China and 1997* (1993) edited by Raymond Wacks, and Mark Tushnet's "Interdisciplinary Legal Scholarship" (1996); more comparative perspectives such as William Nelson's *Americanization of the Common Law* (1975); collections of what has been written, as in the multivolume *Major Historical Interpretations* (1987) edited by Kermit Hall; and critical surveys of the literature and sources as in William Nelson and John Phillip Reid's *The Literature of American Legal History* (1985) and *American Legal History* (1991) edited by Paul Finkelman, Kermit Hall, and William Wiecek.

Topically, legal-historical studies can be divided among three general areas: constitutional, legal, and social. While this is not the place to identify the major works in all subjects of these areas, a few of what may be called the leading works will be mentioned. While it would be difficult to survey the field worldwide, this survey is based largely on the common law world, with reference to relevant civil law and non-Western countries. Since regional studies in the field have developed prolifically in recent decades, only a few of those major authors will be included here.

Constitutional history, comprising the history of states, their governments, and legislatures, both central and local, has not been very fashionable. In Britain and continental Europe, it is generally no longer written, although an exception is David Lieberman's *The Province of Legislation Determined* (1989). But it has had a long and strong tradition in the United States, and has developed in Africa in Claire Palley's *The Constitutional History and Law of Southern Rhodesia* (1966) and in Yash Ghai and J.P.W.B. McAuslan's *Public Law and Political Change in Kenya* (1970). The United States has benefited from a critical perspective in *American Law and the Constitutional Order* (1978) edited by Harry Scheiber and Lawrence Friedman, and in Mark Tushnet's *Red, White, and Blue* (1988), and excellent synthetic histories are to be found in John Phillip Reid's *Constitutional History of the American Revolution* (1986–93) and Michael Benedict's *The Blessings of Liberty* (1996). This work has led a major European scholar to write a survey for the Western world: R.C. van Caenegem's *An Historical Introduction to Western Constitutional Law* (1995). Perhaps a future subject that will receive more study is the informal law that lives in government, business, and community forums, although H.W. Arthurs' *"Without the Law"* (1985) and Robert Ellickson's *Order Without Law* (1991) have already made a good start in the field.

Legal history *per se* is the study of the law in civil and criminal actions, courts, judges, lawyers, juries, and legal process. It has been by far the largest and most extensive sector of the field, and in recent years it has become controversial. The legal historical profession had its modern birth with the work of Henry Maine, Frederick Pollock, and F.W. Maitland. The first sweeping history was William Searle Holdsworth's *A History of English Law* (1903–66). This "English" brand of legal history had developed traditionally as law from within, case law as judicial precedent and the interaction of courts, judges, and legislatures. It has not only been written by reign and by era, but also in doctrinal and terse histories, as in S.F.C. Milsom's *Historical Foundations of the Common Law* (1969) and J.H. Baker's *An Introduction to English Legal History* (revised 1990), with the single exception for the modern era being A.H. Manchester's *A Modern Legal History of England and Wales* (1980). This brand has been continued in a more conceptual manner in Australia in Alex Castles' *An Introduction to Australian Legal History* (1982) and in Southeast Asia by M.B. Hooker's *A Concise Legal History of South-East Asia* (1978). The conceptual model also has been written for Europe in R.C. van Caenegem's *Legal History* (1991) and the United States in Kermit Hall's *The Magic Mirror* (1989). Moving the history of the law to incorporate the history of society in England was attempted in W.R. Cornish and G.N. Clark's *Law and Society in England* (1989); more grand and successful was Lawrence M. Friedman's *Total Justice* (1985) on the United States.

The history of the courts has been at the forefront of legal historical scholarship. Curiously, however, Americans have been more active in this field than the British or Europeans. The English courts that have been examined by original research, apart from the Selden Society volumes of records for the medieval era, were largely excavated by North American authors: see, for example, W.J. Jones' *The Elizabethan Court of Chancery* (1967); J.S. Cockburn's *A History of English Assizes* (1972); John Beattie's *Crime and the Courts in England* (1986); and Louis Knafla's *Kent at Law 1602* (1994–98). There has been a strong tradition of court histories in the United States at the local level, as in Robert Silverman's *Law and Urban Growth* (1981), the private level, as in Edwin Firmage and Richard Mangrum's *Zion in the Courts* (1988), and at the national level, as in G. Edward White's *The Marshall Court and Cultural Change* (1988). In Canada only the national level can be seen in Ian Bushnell's *The Captive Court* (1992) and *The Federal Court of Canada* (1997). Court histories have, however, been rare in Europe, even though there is extensive records evidence. The interest there has been chiefly with the criminal courts, prosecutions, and crime as in Nicole Castan and Yves Castan's *Vivre ensemble* (Living Together, 1981).

The biographical side of the law has been quite rich in its literature, and most prolific in North America. For judges, the biographical tradition in Britain has been strong throughout the century, and recently a new manuscript tradition for biographical study has arisen with the publication of James Oldham's *The Mansfield Manuscripts* (1992). In the United States, studies of Supreme Court judges have been prominent and of a very high literary standard; for example, Leonard Levy's *The Law of the Commonwealth and Chief Justice Shaw* (1957), G. Edward White's *Justice Oliver Wendell Holmes* (1993), and Gerald Gunther's *Learned Hand* (1994). In Canada, David Williams' *The Man for a New Country* (1977) and Patrick Brode's *Sir John Beverley Robinson* (1984) were similarly successful. At the lower level of Justices of the Peace there have been many regional studies, but the major survey, Thomas Skyrme's *History of the Justices of the Peace* (1991), is problematic, especially at the comparative level. Studies of lawyers and law firms have been a sudden growth industry in North America in this decade. The British led the subject with Jerold S. Auerbach's *Unequal Justice* (1976), Wilfrid Prest's *The Rise of the Barristers* (1986), and Brian Abel Smith and

Robert Stephens' *Lawyers and the Courts* (1967) until the 1990s. Then the history of lawyers, and especially of law firms, took off in the United States with the publication of Gerard Gawalt's *The New High Priests* (1984), Marc Galanter and Thomas Palay's *Tournament of Lawyers* (1991), and Kenneth Lipartito and Joseph Pratt's *Baker & Botts in the Development of Modern Houston* (1991), and in Canada with Curtis Cole's *Osler, Hoskin & Harcourt* (1995), and *Beyond the Law* (1990) and *Inside the Law* (1996) both edited by Carol Wilton. Perhaps the problem of researching law firms in Britain has been the extreme privacy of the profession, as noted in David Sugarman's *A Brief History of the Law Society* (1995), as it has been with Europe and Australasia.

While criminal law has been discussed in this volume under "Crime and Deviance," and is a principal side of the law's history still to be written, civil actions have had prominent studies even though few scholars are engaged in their research. Civil actions begin with the land law, the chief branch of the law in the pre-industrial world when rights stemmed from land rather than from birth or commerce. While the history of land law was fully developed in England, it came later to the United States with Paul Wallace Gates' *History of Public Land Law Development* (1968) and remains unwritten in much of the common law world. Personal actions and contracts, therefore, have been prominent in the civil field, with some incisive treatises written for England in A.W.B. Simpson's *A History of the Common Law of Contract* (1975) and P.S. Atiyah's *The Rise and Fall of Freedom of Contract* (1979), for Europe in R.C. van Caenegem's *An Historical Introduction to Private Law* (translated 1992), for the United States in Lawrence M. Friedman's *Contract Law in America* (1965), and across national boundaries in James Steven Rogers' *The Early History of the Law of Bills and Notes* (1995). The law of tort has received some outstanding writing in G. Edward White's *Tort Law in America* (1980), and in *Major Historical Interpretations* (1987) edited by Kermit Hall. Within contracts, labor has been studied, notably in the United States in Christopher Tomlins' *The State and the Unions* (1985), William Forbath's *Law and the Shaping of the American Labor Movement* (1991), and Robert Steinfeld's *The Invention of Free Labor* (1991). In the law and economy sector, industry has been examined widely in England in *Law, Economy, and Society* (1984) edited by Gerry Rubin and David Sugarman, in Africa in Francis Snyder's *Capitalism and Legal Change* (1981), and in the United States in James Willard Hurst's *Law and Economic Growth* (1964); this field should have a rich future.

The social side of legal history has been the main growth industry of the late 20th century. It comprises a wide range of subjects, including in particular poverty, crime, class, race, ethnicity, and gender. Poverty and crime have been discussed elsewhere. But these other subjects have been at the cutting edge of legal-historical research. The study of class has had a long European history, stemming from the Marxist tradition, itself a concern of both the Annales and the Warwick schools of historical research exhibited in the work of the Castans and of E.P. Thompson. Race has been more of a concern in North America, and splendid studies exist on Native Americans in John Phillip Reid's *A Better Kind of Hatchet* (1976), Yasuhide Kawashima's *Puritan Justice and the Indian* (1986), Ronald Wright's *Stolen Continents* (1992), and Sidney Harring's *Crow*

Dog's Law (1994), and for Native Canadians in Thomas Berger's *A Long and Terrible Shadow* (1991). It comprises some of the most stimulating work in legal history. Gender and family history have also been the subject of legal-historical work in Mary Jane Mossman's "Feminism and Legal Method" (1986). Significant studies can be seen in Britain in R.H. Helmholz's *Canon Law and the Law of England* (1987), Lawrence Stone's *Road to Divorce* (1990), and Eileen Spring's *Law, Land, and Family* (1993), in the United States in Michael Grossberg's *Governing the Hearth* (1985) and Carol Smart's *Regulating Womanhood* (1992), in Canada in Constance Backhouse's *Petticoats and Prejudice* (1991) and James Snell's *In the Shadow of the Law* (1991), and in the Neo-European colonies in Stephanie Daly's *The Developing Legal Status of Women in Trinidad and Tobago* (1982).

Whether class, race, or gender, the social side of legal history has always been there with the study of human rights in pre- as well as post-industrial societies. The classic work of James Willard Hurst, *Law and the Conditions of Freedom in the Nineteenth-Century United States* (1956), marked the contribution of American legal history in examining provocatively the intersection of personal rights with those of the nation-state. It stemmed from Revolution, from 17th-century England and 18th-century France, and has been portrayed in James MacGregor Burns and Stewart Burns' *A People's Charter* (1991) and by a group of stimulating essays, *A Culture of Rights* edited by Michael Lacey and Knud Haakonssen (1991). The upheavals in legal-historical writing over the past two decades bear testimony that the field is not dead, but in the midst of being reborn.

LOUIS A. KNAFLA

See also Crime; Horwitz; Maitland; Milsom; Niida; Political; Selden; Simpson; Stone; Thompson, E.

Further Reading

Abel Smith, Brian, and Robert Stephens, *Lawyers and the Courts: A Sociological Study of the English Legal System, 1750–1965*, London: Heinemann, 1967

Allott, Antony, and Gordon R. Woodman, eds., *People's Law and State Law: The Bellagio Papers*, Dordrecht: Foris, 1985

Arthurs, Harry William, *"Without the Law": Administrative Justice and Legal Pluralism in Nineteenth-Century England*, Toronto and Buffalo: University of Toronto Press, 1985

Atiyah, P.S., *The Rise and Fall of Freedom of Contract*, Oxford and New York: Oxford University Press, 1979

Auerbach, Jerold S., *Unequal Justice: Lawyers and Social Change in Modern America*, London and New York: Oxford University Press, 1976

Backhouse, Constance, *Petticoats and Prejudice: Women and Law in Nineteenth-Century Canada*, Toronto: Osgoode Society/Women's Press, 1991

Baker, J.H., *An Introduction to English Legal History*, London: Butterworth, 1971; revised 1990

Bakken, Gordon Morris, *The Development of Law on the Rocky Mountain Frontier: Civil Law and Society, 1850–1912*, Westport, CT: Greenwood Press, 1983

Beattie, John Maurice, *Crime and the Courts in England, 1660–1800*, Princeton: Princeton University Press, and Oxford: Oxford University Press, 1986

Benedict, Michael Les, *The Blessings of Liberty: A Concise History of the Constitution of the United States*, Lexington, MA: Heath, 1996

Berger, Thomas R., *A Long and Terrible Shadow: White Values, Native Rights in the Americas, 1492–1992*, Vancouver: Douglas and McIntyre, 1991; Seattle: University of Washington Press, 1992

Brand, Paul, *The Origins of the English Legal Profession*, Oxford and Cambridge, MA: Blackwell, 1992

Brode, Patrick, *Sir John Beverley Robinson: Bone and Sinew of the Compact*, Toronto and Buffalo: University of Toronto Press, 1984

Burns, James MacGregor and Stewart Burns, *A People's Charter: The Pursuit of Rights in America*, New York: Knopf, 1991

Bushnell, Ian, *The Captive Court: A Study of the Supreme Court of Canada*, Montreal: McGill–Queen's University Press, 1992

Bushnell, Ian, *The Federal Court of Canada: A History, 1875–1992*, Toronto: Osgoode Society, 1997

Caenegem, R.C. van, *Introduction historique au droit privé*, Brussels: Story-Scientia, 1988; in English as *An Historical Introduction to Private Law*, Cambridge and New York: Cambridge University Press, 1992

Caenegem, R.C. van, *Legal History: A European Perspective*, London and Rio Grande, OH: Hambledon Press, 1991

Caenegem, R.C. van, *An Historical Introduction to Western Constitutional Law*, Cambridge and New York: Cambridge University Press, 1995

Castan, Nicole, and Yves Castan, *Vivre ensemble: ordre et désordre en Languedoc, XVIIe–XVIIIe siècles* (Living Together: Order and Disorder in 17th- and 18th-century Languedoc), Paris: Gallimard/Julliard, 1981

Castles, Alex C., *An Introduction to Australian Legal History*, Sydney: Law Book, 1982

Chiba, Masaji, *Legal Pluralism: Toward a General Theory Through Japanese Legal Culture*, Tokyo: Tokai University Press, 1989

Clark, Michael, and Catherine Crawford, eds., *Legal Medicine in History*, Cambridge and New York: Cambridge University Press, 1994

Cockburn, J.S., *A History of English Assizes, 1558–1714*, Cambridge: Cambridge University Press, 1972

Cole, Curtis, *Osler, Hoskin & Harcourt: Portrait of a Partnership*, Toronto and New York: McGraw Hill Ryerson, 1995

Cornish, William Rodolph, and G.N. Clark, *Law and Society in England, 1750–1950*, London: Sweet and Maxwell, 1989

Daly, Stephanie, *The Developing Legal Status of Women in Trinidad and Tobago*, Trinidad: National Commission on the Status of Women, 1982

Ellickson, Robert C., *Order Without Law: How Neighbors Settle Disputes*, Cambridge, MA: Harvard University Press, 1991

Farcy, Jean-Claude, *Les Camps de concentration français de la première guerre mondiale, 1914–1920* (French Concentration Camps of World War I, 1914–1920), Paris: Economica, 1995

Finkelman, Paul, Kermit L. Hall, and William M. Wiecek, eds., *American Legal History: Cases and Materials*, New York: Oxford University Press, 1991; revised 1996

Firmage, Edwin Brown, and Richard Collin Mangrum, *Zion in the Courts: A Legal History of the Church of Jesus Christ of Latter-day Saints, 1830–1900*, Urbana: University of Illinois Press, 1988

Fisher, William W. III, Morton J. Horwitz, and Thomas Reed, eds., *American Legal Realism*, Oxford and New York: Oxford University Press, 1993

Forbath, William E., *Law and the Shaping of the American Labor Movement*, Cambridge, MA: Harvard University Press, 1991

Friedman, Lawrence M., *Contract Law in America: A Social and Economic Case Study*, Madison: University of Wisconsin Press, 1965

Friedman, Lawrence M., *A History of American Law*, New York: Simon and Schuster, 1973; revised 1985

Friedman, Lawrence M., *Total Justice*, New York: Russell Sage Foundation, 1985

Galanter, Marc, and Thomas Palay, *Tournament of Lawyers: The Transformation of the Big Law Firm*, Chicago: University of Chicago Press, 1991

Gates, Paul Wallace, *History of Public Land Law Development*, Washington, DC: United States Government Printing Office, 1968

Gawalt, Gerard W., ed., *The New High Priests: Lawyers in Post-Civil War America*, Westport, CT: Greenwood Press, 1984

Ghai, Yash P., and J. Patrick W.B. McAuslan, *Public Law and Political Change in Kenya: A Study of the Legal Framework of Government from Colonial Times to the Present*, Nairobi, Oxford, and New York: Oxford University Press, 1970

Gordon, Robert W., "Critical Legal Histories," *Stanford Law Review* 36 (1984), 57–125

Greenwood, F. Murray, and Barry Wright, eds., *Canadian State Trials*, vol. 1: *Law, Politics, and Security Measures, 1608–1837*, Toronto and Buffalo: University of Toronto Press, 1996

Grossberg, Michael, *Governing the Hearth: Law and Family in Nineteenth-Century America*, Chapel Hill: University of North Carolina Press, 1985

Gunther, Gerald, *Learned Hand: The Man and the Judge*, New York: Knopf, 1994

Hall, Kermit, ed., *Major Historical Interpretations*, 10 vols., New York: Garland, 1987

Hall, Kermit, *The Magic Mirror: Law in American History*, Oxford and New York: Oxford University Press, 1989

Harring, Sidney L., *Crow Dog's Law: American Indian Sovereignty, Tribal Law, and United States Law in the Nineteenth Century*, Cambridge and New York: Cambridge University Press, 1994

Harris, Ruth, *Murders and Madness: Medicine, Law, and Society in the Fin de Siècle*, Oxford and New York: Oxford University Press, 1989

Helmholz, R.H., *Canon Law and the Law of England*, London and Ronceverte, WV: Hambledon Press, 1987

Hoebel, E. Adamson, *The Law of Primitive Man: A Study in Comparative Legal Dynamics*, Cambridge, MA: Harvard University Press, and Oxford: Oxford University Press, 1954

Holdsworth, W.S., *A History of English Law*, 16 vols., London: Methuen, and Boston: Little Brown, 1903–66 [5 revised editions]

Hooker, M.B., *Legal Pluralism: An Introduction to Colonial and Neo-Colonial Laws*, Oxford: Oxford University Press, 1975

Hooker, M.B., *A Concise Legal History of South-East Asia*, Oxford and New York: Oxford University Press, 1978

Horwitz, Morton J., *The Transformation of American Law, 1780–1860*, Cambridge, MA: Harvard University Press, 1977

Hurst, James Willard, *Law and the Conditions of Freedom in the Nineteenth-Century United States*, Madison: University of Wisconsin Press, 1956

Hurst, James Willard, *Law and Economic Growth: The Legal History of the Lumber Industry in Wisconsin, 1836–1915*, Cambridge, MA: Harvard University Press, 1964

Jones, W.J., *The Elizabethan Court of Chancery*, Oxford: Oxford University Press, 1967

Kalman, Laura, *The Strange Career of Legal Liberalism*, New Haven and London: Yale University Press, 1996

Kawashima, Yasuhide, *Puritan Justice and the Indian: White Man's Law in Massachusetts, 1630–1763*, Middletown, CT: Wesleyan University Press, 1986

Kelley, Donald R., *The Human Measure: Social Thought in the Western Legal Tradition*, Cambridge, MA: Harvard University Press, 1990

Knafla, Louis A., *Kent at Law 1602*, vols. 1–2, London: HMSO, 1994–98

Knafla, Louis A., and Susan Binnie, eds., *Law, Society, and the State: Essays in Modern Legal History*, Toronto and Buffalo: University of Toronto Press, 1995

Lacey, Michael J., and Knud Haakonssen, eds., *A Culture of Rights: The Bill of Rights in Philosophy, Politics and Law, 1791 and 1991*, Cambridge and New York: Cambridge University Press, 1991

Levy, Leonard W., *The Law of the Commonwealth and Chief Justice Shaw: The Evolution of American Law, 1830–1860*, Cambridge, MA: Harvard University Press, 1957; Oxford: Oxford University Press, 1988

Lieberman, David, *The Province of Legislation Determined*, Cambridge and New York: Cambridge University Press, 1989

Lipartito, Kenneth J., and Joseph A. Pratt, *Baker & Botts in the Development of Modern Houston*, Austin: University of Texas Press, 1991

Llewellyn, Karl Nickerson, and E. Adamson Hoebel, *The Cheyenne Way: Conflict and Case Law in Primitive Jurisprudence*, Norman: University of Oklahoma Press, 1941

McLaren, John, Hamar Foster, and Chet Orloff, eds., *Law for the Elephant, Law for the Beaver: Essays in the Legal History of the North American West*, Regina, Saskatchewan: Canadian Plains Research Center, University of Regina, and Pasadena, CA: Ninth Judicial Circuit Historical Society, 1992

Maine, Henry Sumner, *Ancient Law: Its Connection with the Early History of Society*, London: Murray, 1861; New York: Scribner, 1864

Manchester, A.H., *A Modern Legal History of England and Wales, 1750–1950*, London: Butterworth, 1980

Merry, Sally Engle, *Getting Justice and Getting Even: Legal Consciousness among Working-Class Americans*, Chicago: University of Chicago Press, 1990

Milsom, S.F.C., *Historical Foundations of the Common Law*, London: Butterworth, 1969; 2nd edition 1981

Moore, Sally Falk, *Law as Process: An Anthropological Approach*, London: Routledge, 1978

Mossman, Mary Jane, "Feminism and Legal Method: The Difference It Makes," *Australian Journal of Law and Society* 30 (1986), 30–52

Nelson, William E., *Americanization of the Common Law: The Impact of Legal Change on Massachusetts Society, 1760–1830*, Cambridge, MA: Harvard University Press, 1975

Nelson, William E., and John Phillip Reid, *The Literature of American Legal History*, New York and London: Oceana, 1985

O'Barr, William M., *Rules versus Relationships: The Ethnography of Legal Discourse*, Chicago: University of Chicago Press, 1990

Oldham, James, *The Mansfield Manuscripts and the Growth of English Law in the Eighteenth Century*, 2 vols., Chapel Hill: University of North Carolina Press, 1992

Palley, Claire, *The Constitutional History and Law of Southern Rhodesia, 1888–1965, with Special Reference to Imperial Control*, Oxford: Oxford University Press, 1966

Palmer, Robert C., *English Law in the Age of the Black Death, 1348–1381*, Chapel Hill: University of North Carolina Press, 1993

Pollock, Frederick, and F. W. Maitland, *The History of English Law before the Time of Edward I*, 2 vols., Cambridge: Cambridge University Press, and Boston: Little Brown, 1895; revised 1898

Prest, Wilfrid R., *The Rise of the Barristers: A Social History of the English Bar, 1590–1740*, Oxford and New York: Oxford University Press, 1986

Reid, John Phillip, *A Better Kind of Hatchet: Law, Trade, and Diplomacy in the Cherokee Nation during the Early Years of European Contact*, University Park: Pennsylvania State University Press, 1976

Reid, John Phillip, *Constitutional History of the American Revolution*, 4 vols., Madison: University of Wisconsin Press, 1986–93

Rogers, James Steven, *The Early History of the Law of Bills and Notes: A Study of the Origins of Anglo-American Commercial Law*, Cambridge and New York: Cambridge University Press, 1995

Rubin, Gerry R., and David Sugarman, eds., *Law, Economy and Society, 1750–1914: Essays in the History of English Law*, Abingdon: Professional, 1984

Scheiber, Harry N., and Lawrence M. Friedman, eds., *American Law and the Constitutional Order: Historical Perspectives*, Cambridge, MA: Harvard University Press, 1978; revised 1988

Silverman, Robert A., *Law and Urban Growth: Civil Litigation in Boston Trial Courts, 1800–1900*, Princeton: Princeton University Press, 1981

Simpson, A.W.B., *A History of the Common Law of Contract: The Rise of the Action of Assumpsit*, Oxford: Oxford University Press, 1975

Simpson, A.W.B., *Cannibalism and the Common Law: The Story of the Tragic Last Voyage of the Mignonette and the Strange Legal Proceedings to Which It Gave Rise*, Chicago: University of Chicago Press, 1984

Simpson, A.W.B., *In the Highest Degree Odious: Detention Without Trial in Wartime Britain*, Oxford and New York: Oxford University Press, 1992

Skyrme, Thomas, *History of the Justices of the Peace*, 3 vols., Chichester: Barry Rose, 1991

Smart, Carol, ed., *Regulating Womanhood: Historical Essays on Marriage, Motherhood, and Sexuality*, London and New York: Routledge, 1992

Snell, James G., *In the Shadow of the Law: Divorce in Canada, 1900–1939*, Toronto and Buffalo: University of Toronto Press, 1991

Snyder, Francis G., *Capitalism and Legal Change: An African Transformation*, New York and London: Academic Press, 1981

Spring, Eileen, *Law, Land, and Family: Aristocratic Inheritance in England, 1300–1800*, Chapel Hill: University of North Carolina Press, 1993

Steinberg, Allen, *The Transformation of Criminal Justice: Philadelphia, 1800–1880*, Chapel Hill: University of North Carolina Press, 1989

Steinfeld, Robert J., *The Invention of Free Labor: The Employment Relation in English and American Law and Culture, 1350–1870*, Chapel Hill: University of North Carolina Press, 1991

Stone, Lawrence, *Road to Divorce: England, 1530–1987*, Oxford and New York: Oxford University Press, 1990

Sugarman, David, *A Brief History of the Law Society*, London: Law Society, 1995

Thompson, E.P., *Customs in Common*, London: Merlin Press, and New York: New Press, 1991

Tomlins, Christopher L., *The State and the Unions: Labor Relations, Law and the Organized Labor Movement in America, 1880–1960*, Cambridge and New York: Cambridge University Press, 1985

Tushnet, Mark V., *Red, White, and Blue: A Critical Analysis of Constitutional Law*, Cambridge, MA: Harvard University Press, 1988

Tushnet, Mark V., "Interdisciplinary Legal Scholarship: The Use of History in Law," *Chicago-Kent Law Review*, 71:3 (1996)

Twining, William, ed., *Legal Theory and the Common Law*, Oxford and Cambridge, MA: Blackwell, 1986

Wacks, Raymond, ed., *Hong Kong, China and 1997: Essays on Legal Theory*, Hong Kong: Hong Kong University Press, 1993

White, G. Edward, *Tort Law in America: An Intellectual History*, Oxford and New York: Oxford University Press, 1980

White, G. Edward, "From Realism to Critical Legal Studies: A Truncated Intellectual History," *Southwestern Law Journal* 40 (1986), 819–43

White, G. Edward, *The Marshall Court and Cultural Change, 1815–35*, New York: Macmillan, 1988; abridged New York: Oxford University Press, 1991

White, G. Edward, *Justice Oliver Wendell Holmes: Law and the Inner Self*, Oxford and New York: Oxford University Press, 1993

Williams, David Ricardo, *The Man for a New Country: Sir Matthew Baillie Begbie*, Sidney, BC: Gray's, 1977

Wilton, Carol, ed., *Beyond the Law: Lawyers and Business in Canada, 1830 to 1930*, Toronto: Osgoode Society, 1990

Wilton, Carol, ed., *Inside the Law: Canadian Law Firms in Historical Perspective*, Toronto: University of Toronto Press, 1996

Wright, Ronald, *Stolen Continents: The America Through Indian Eyes since 1492*, Boston: Houghton Mifflin, 1992; as *Stolen Continents: The Indian Story*, London: Murray, 1992

Leisure

The concept of leisure was well established in ancient Greece. To the Greeks, leisure referred to a time for contemplation. The goal of leisure was neither amusement nor recreation; instead, leisure was dedicated to personal enhancement. Since the late 19th century, leisure has come to mean the opposite of work. Leisure is non-work time, or "free time." For most historians, this definition predominates in their research. Leisure connotes renewal from work, or recreation.

As contemporaries became aware of the growth and changing nature of non-work time in the late 19th century, they began to study leisure. In the 1899 classic, *The Theory of the Leisure Class*, American economist Thorstein Veblen asserted that social classes accept "as their ideal of decency" the behaviors of the next higher class. Leisure was not only an indicator of class, but it also became linked to conspicuous consumption. Today it seems obvious that leisure is a commodity – a ticket to a baseball game, a drink at the local pub, a television. But the significance of the commodification of leisure is a topic that historians debate. In one early study (1929), Robert and Helen Lynd argued that in modern society traditional leisure has been displaced by modern commercial forms. As workers attained higher wages and shorter work hours, leisure consumption blossomed, and so too did the profits of those who provided commercial leisure.

Recently, historians have presented a more complex story of leisure in modern capitalist society. Influenced by post-structuralism, these scholars have stressed that consumption and recreation are based on a dynamic relationship between the producer and the consumer, and that each has brought their own values and goals to this exchange. In a study on women's leisure in New York City, Kathy Peiss showed that working-class women rejected attempts by bourgeois reformers to control their leisure time. Instead, women, in an alliance with entrepreneurs, turned to dance halls as a source of recreational activity. Working-class women, thus, were not the pawns of capitalists; rather, they appropriated leisure activities and public spaces for their own entertainment and sociability.

With modernization, leisure has become democratized. Although it is doubtful that we have more free time today than in previous eras, individuals living in the Western world have accumulated numerous leisure products and participate in a plethora of leisure activities. Yet, leisure choices are limited. Even though mass markets and mass culture have brought into existence a vast array of leisure alternatives, capitalism has mediated leisure time and leisure forms. Entrepreneurs, guided by profits, defined the leisure of modern society. From baseballs to compact discs, leisure was standardized in order to be profitable. However, capitalists' control over individual consumers is not total. As Richard Butsch argues, "resistance and class expression not only persist but are important sources for the innovations on which consumer industries depend."

Nations have also played pivotal roles in defining leisure activities, as they have recognized leisure as an important sphere in which national identity could be invoked. The creation of national holidays, for example, became a critical means of sublimating regional, ethnic, and class loyalties. National sporting teams have also provided rallying points.

The Olympic Games furnish an opportunity to display national prowess, while simultaneously concealing social conflict, creating what Steven Pope has referred to as "a factitious national communal identity."

Class analysis has been instrumental in the study of leisure. Early scholarship focused on workers' leisure from the standpoint of political organizations. From sport clubs, to singing groups, to libraries, workers' political parties and trade unions played a significant role in defining the leisure activities of workers. While the study of organized labor culture has grown immensely, sometimes this research conceals much, for beneath organized labor was a vast array of autonomous workers' culture. Historians like Vernon Lidtke have begun to shift their purview from organized leisure to workers' informal recreational activities. The local pub, the neighborhood, and the home have accordingly become important sites in the study of workers' leisure.

Some historians, however, contend that class analysis is inadequate in the study of leisure because it is intrinsically linked to the world of white men. In the United States, class analysis ignored the many ethnicities and their unique leisure forms. As Lizabeth Cohen has shown, ethnic groups integrated supermarkets, radio, and movies into their worlds while simultaneously maintaining their cultural identities. They negotiated the meanings and practices of leisure in such a way that their ethnic culture was reinforced and renewed.

A number of scholars also argue that women have been excluded from the world of public leisure. Christine Stansell, for example, contends that the predominance of patriarchal social relations in Western society ensured that women not only had less disposable income, but also less leisure time. Furthermore, society placed stricter limits of propriety on women's leisure. Beginning in the 19th century, however, women entered the world of public consumption and recreation. From the promenade, to dance halls, to department stores, the late 19th century marked a significant transformation in the world of women's leisure – one in which safe, respectable public spaces were created for women.

The study of leisure shows, as David Nasaw and Steven Riess have asserted, how societal power relationships are reproduced in the cultural realm. Power dynamics has become a central theme in the study of leisure, particularly workers' leisure. Peter Bailey, for example, has argued, that industrial society "required the building of a new social conformity – a play discipline to complement the work discipline." Focusing on questions of domination, historians such as Susan Davis, have examined how governments, fearing the outbreak of working-class political disturbances, regulated workers' leisure, especially the use of public spaces. Other historians have studied the attempts of bourgeois reform movements to control workers' behavior. But as Suzanne Waserman has shown, many workers were actually quite resistant to such endeavors.

Influenced by Raymond Williams and Antonio Gramsci, in the last decade some historians have modified their conceptions of domination and resistance, offering a more complex picture of power relations in leisure practices. Steven Pope has contended that social conflicts are embedded in social structures, and these conflicts are negotiated continuously in cultural practices, including leisure. Power (or hegemony) is not constant; rather, it is a complex and contradictory process which, as Raymond Williams has articulated, "must be continually renewed, recreated, defended and modified."

SARA ANN SEWELL

See also Consumerism; Film; Media

Further Reading

Bailey, Peter, *Leisure and Class in Victorian England: Rational Recreation and the Contest for Control, 1830–1885*, Toronto and Buffalo: University of Toronto Press, and London: Routledge, 1978; revised London and New York: Methuen, 1987

Butsch, Richard, ed., *For Fun and Profit: The Transformation of Leisure into Consumption*, Philadelphia: Temple University Press, 1990

Cohen, Lizabeth, "Encountering Mass Culture at the Grassroots: The Experience of Chicago Workers in the 1920s," *American Quarterly* 41 (1989), 6–33

Cross, Gary S., *Time and Money: The Making of Consumer Culture*, London and New York: Routledge, 1993

Dare, Byron et al., *Concepts of Leisure in Western Thought: A Critical and Historical Analysis*, Dubuque, IA: Kendall Hunt, 1987

Davies, Andrew, *Leisure, Gender and Poverty: Working-Class Culture in Salford and Manchester, 1900–1939*, Milton Keynes: Open University Press, 1992

Davis, Susan G., *Parades and Power: Street Theatre in Nineteenth-Century Philadelphia*, Philadelphia: Temple University Press, 1986

De Grazia, Victoria, *The Culture of Consent: Mass Organization of Leisure in Fascist Italy*, Cambridge and New York: Cambridge University Press, 1981

Evans, Richard J., ed., *The German Working Class, 1888–1933: The Politics of Everyday Life*, London: Croom Helm, and Totowa, NJ: Barnes and Noble, 1982

Jones, Stephen, *Workers at Play: A Social and Economic History of Leisure, 1918–1939*, London: Routledge, 1986

Lidtke, Vernon L., *The Alternative Culture: Socialist Labor in Imperial Germany*, New York: Oxford University Press, 1985

Lynd, Robert, and Helen Merrell Lynd, *Middletown: A Study in Contemporary American Culture*, New York: Harcourt Brace, 1929

McCrone, Kathleen, *Playing the Games: Sport and the Physical Emancipation of English Women, 1870–1914*, Lexington: University Press of Kentucky, 1988; as *Sport and the Physical Emancipation of English Women, 1870–1914*, London: Routledge, 1988

Nasaw, David, *Children of the City: At Work and at Play*, Garden City, NY: Anchor Press, 1985

Peiss, Kathy, *Cheap Amusements: Working Women and Leisure in Turn-of-the-Century New York City*, Philadelphia: Temple University Press, 1986

Pope, Steven W, "American Muscles and Minds: Public Discourse and the Shaping of National Identity during Early Olympiads, 1896–1920," *Journal of American Culture* 15 (1992), 83–94

Riess, Steven A., *City Games: The Evolution of American Urban Society and the Rise of Sports*, Urbana: University of Illinois Press, 1989

Rosenzweig, Roy, *Eight Hours for What We Will: Workers and Leisure in an Industrial City, 1870–1920*, Cambridge and New York: Cambridge University Press, 1983

Smith, Bonnie G., *Ladies of the Leisure Class: The Bourgeoises of Northern France in the Nineteenth Century*, Princeton: Princeton University Press, 1981

Stansell, Christine, *City of Women: Sex and Class in New York, 1789–1860*, New York: Knopf, 1986

Veblen, Thorstein, *The Theory of the Leisure Class: An Economic Study in the Evolution of Institutions*, New York: Macmillan, 1899; London: Allen and Unwin, 1924

Waserman, Suzanne, "Cafes, Clubs, Corners, and Candy Stores: Youth Leisure-Culture in New York City's Lower East Side during the 1930s," *Journal of American Culture* 14 (Winter 1990), 43–48

Williams, Raymond, *Marxism and Literature*, Oxford and New York: Oxford University Press, 1977

Williams, Rosalind, *Dream Worlds: Mass Consumption in Late Nineteenth Century France*, Berkeley: University of California Press, 1982

Lelewel, Joachim 1786–1861

Polish historian

Joachim Lelewel, one of Poland's foremost historians and political thinkers, has been called a founding father of modern historical studies. He was an expert in Polish and world history, historical thought, library science, genealogy, heraldry, printing, and paleology. His works of medieval geography and numismatics are still considered outstanding today.

Lelewel was as influential on the development of modern historical method as were two of his contemporaries, Leopold von Ranke (1795–1886), and Jules Michelet (1798–1874). The philosophy of idealism current in early 19th-century Europe influenced all three scholars. But Lelewel, facing political exigencies neither Ranke nor Michelet confronted, transformed idealism into a political philosophy to justify insurrection against the three states that partitioned Poland at the end of the 18th century, Russia, Prussia, and Austria. Loss of the their state forced Poles into an intense national self-examination. Historians and other intellectuals looked to the past to determine why the state fell and to find evidence of Poland's "true" political traditions on which a new state could be built. Virtually all Polish historians of the 19th century used scholarship to justify one or another liberation plan. Lelewel idealized primitive democracy, which he offered as a blueprint for reconstructing all of human society.

In Polish historiography, Lelewel, following on the work of Polish historian Adam Naruszewicz (1733–96), called for a broadening of the scope of historical research to include consideration of geographical, cultural, economic, and social factors. He also developed the comparative approach to history, writing a work on the parallels between early modern Spain and Poland.

His major work of historical thought was *Historyka* (The Art of History, 1815). In that book, Lelewel divided the historian's work into three areas: criticism, which is a discovery of what happened in the past through a critical analysis of primary sources; etiology, a determination of causes and effects of events and of the importance of geography, climate, anthropology, politics, and statistics in understanding the past; and historiography, the clear and truthful writing of history.

In his discussion of Poland's origins, geography and politics were especially important. Lelewel drew sharp distinctions between the political development of the peoples who fell under Roman rule and the peoples of northeast Europe. Rome spread a despotic autocracy, he said, from which arose medieval feudal states based on rigid social systems. Outside Rome's influence, that is, among the ancient Slavs, primitive but free social and political traditions flowered. Lelewel endowed the ancient Slavs with the qualities of *wolność* (freedom) and *obywatelstwo* ("citizenship," a sense of belonging to a community), the fundamental elements of *gminowładztwo*, a form of communal self-rule that was, he thought, the basis of any successful, dynamic society.

Lelewel believed that through the course of its history Poland alternated between freedom and servitude. Feudalism and Catholicism undermined traditional Slavic principles, forcing the peasantry eventually to give up its ancient rights. "Gentry Democracy," which lasted from the 15th to the 17th century, promised to restore those rights and to expand them to all social classes, Lelewel argued. But the selfishness of Poland's kings and powerful magnates distorted the egalitarian principles of the gentry and blocked the full democratization of the Polish commonwealth. The peasantry struggled for its rights, but the kings and magnates refused to adopt liberal government reforms. An internal crisis ensued, and by the end of the 18th century Poland was too weak to fend off pressure from Russia, Prussia, and Austria. Lelewel blamed both the ruling elite and Poland's neighbors for the loss of the state, and felt that Poland's republican institutions were basically sound.

Lelewel's interpretation of the partitions became the basis for armed action against the partitioning powers. In his *Trzy konstitucje polskie: 1791, 1807, 1815* (Three Polish Constitutions: 1791, 1803, 1815, [1832]), he wrote that Poland's freedom could be regained only by restoring the *gminowładztwo*, which meant establishing "the self-rule of the people, political equality, representative leaders, and the responsibility of officials directly to the nation, from the lowest to the highest office holders." But before Poland could enjoy the fruits of *gminowładztwo*, it had to be independent. The people had to assert natural rights over the state, which, in this case, meant overthrowing the three foreign states that ruled Poland.

After the Russian government expelled Lelewel from the University of Wilno in 1824, he went to Warsaw and became involved in insurrectionary politics. As a member of the National government, Lelewel helped organize the November Insurrection (1830–31). After its failure, he spent the rest of his life in exile, first in Paris, later in Brussels. He participated in revolutionary politics until after the Springtime of Nations (1848), and spent the rest of his life devoted to scholarship.

Although his scholarship was highly regarded and influenced many leading historians of his day, it was based on limited access to primary documents. Indeed, his demand for the critical analysis of primary sources, one of his most important contributions to historical thought, went unfulfilled until after his death. The chance to apply modern methods to primary sources of Polish history came only after 1867 in Galicia, where Austria granted the Poles autonomy. In 1873, the Academy of Learning was established and began publishing archival documents. Polish history chairs eventually were established at the universities in Kraków and Lwów.

An intense critique of Lelewel's romantic views of Poland's history followed. The Kraków school of historians, particularly its most ardent representative, Michał Bobrzyński (1849–1935), made a strong case against Gentry Democracy, arguing that its own idealization of freedom and equality masked inherent weaknesses in the social and political order that spawned anarchy in pre-partition Poland. Furthermore, subsequent

archaeological and historical research has disproved the existence of a communal Slavic society as Lelewel envisioned it.

Despite these later findings, Lelewel still is considered a national treasure for his contributions to historical literature. Beyond all else, he is remembered for giving his country a heroic past that inspired Poland during its time of servitude over the last two centuries and guides it yet today in its struggle to create a sovereign, stable political society.

GENE GEORGE

See also Europe: Modern; Poland: to the 18th Century

Biography

Joachim Lelewel. Born Warsaw, 22 March 1786. Educated at University of Wilno. Taught school at Krzemieniec in Volhynia, 1807–14; taught at University of Wilno, 1814–18; professor, University of Warsaw, 1818–21; and University of Wilno, 1821–24, but was removed from his professorship for political reasons; settled in Warsaw, 1824, and combined political and research work; exiled 1831; then lived mostly in Brussels. Died Paris, 29 May 1861.

Principal Writings

Historyka (The Art of History), 1815
Dzieje starożytne Indji ze szczególnem zastanowieniem się nad wpływem jaki mieć mogła na strony zachodnie (History of Ancient India with Special Attention to the Influence it May Have Had on Western Countries), 1820
Dzieje Polski potocznym sposobem opowiedziane (Poland's Past Retold in a Familiar way), 1829
Historyczna parallela Hiszpanii z Polską w wieku XVI, XVII, XVIII (Spain's Historical Parallel with Poland during the 16th, 17th, and 18th Centuries), 1831
Trzy konstitucje polskie: 1791, 1807, 1815 (Three Polish Constitutions: 1791, 1807, 1815), 1832
Numismatique du Moyen Age (Medieval Numismatics), 2 vols., 1835
Géographie du Moyen Age (Medieval Geography), 4 vols., 1850–52
Polska, dzieje i rzeczy jej (Poland, Her History and Everything about Her), 13 vols., 1853–64
Wybór pism politycznych (Selected Political Writings), 1954
Dzieła (Works), 10 vols. 1957–

Further Reading

Bronowski, Franciszek, "Idea gminowładztwa w historii powszechnej Lelewela" (The Idea of Communal Self-Rule in Lelewel's World History), *Kwartalnik Historyczne* (Historical Quarterly) 67 (1961), 879–86
Bronowski, Franciszek, *Idea gminowładztwa w Polskiej historiografii: geneza i formowania się syntezy republikanskiej J. Lelewela* (The Concept of Communal Self-Rule in Polish Historiography: The Genesis and Formulation of J. Lelewel's Republican Synthesis), Lódź, 1969
Rose, William J., "Polish Historical Writing," *Journal of Modern History* 2 (1930), 569–85
Rose, William J., "Lelewel as Historian," *Slavonic and East European Review* 15 (1936), 649–62
Serejski, Marian Henryk, *Historycy o historii: od Adam Naruszewicza do Stanisława Ketrzyńskiego* (Historians on history), Warsaw: Państwowe Wydawn, 1963
Skurnowicz, Joan, *Romantic Nationalism and Liberalism: Joachim Lelewel and the Polish National Idea*, Boulder, CO: East European Monographs, 1981
Trzeciakowski, Lech, "Idea Państwa w historiografii Polskiej XIX w na przykładzie Joachima Lelewela, Michała Bobrzyńskiego, i Bolesława Limanoskiego" (The Idea of the State in Nineteenth-

Century Polish Historiography in the Case of Joachim Lelewel, Michał Bobrzyński, and Bolesław Limanoski), in Wojchiech Wrzesiński, ed. *Państwo w polskiej myśli politycznej* (The State in Polish Political Thought), Wrocław: Zaklad Narodowy im Ossolinskich, 1988

Walicki, Andrzej, *Philosophy and Romantic Nationalism: The Case of Poland*, Oxford and New York: Oxford University Press, 1982

Walicki, Andrzej, "National Messianism and the Historical Controversies in the Polish Thought of 1831–1848," in Roland Sussex and J.C. Eade, eds., *Culture and Nationalism in Nineteenth-Century Eastern Europe*, Columbus, OH: Slavica, 1983

Wandycz, Piotr S., "Historiography of the Countries of Eastern Europe: Poland," *American Historical Review* 97 (1992), 1011–25

Wereszycki, Henryk, "Polish Insurrections as a Controversial Problem in Polish Historiography," *Canadian Slavonic Papers* 9 (1967), 107–21

Wierbicka, Maria, "Joachim Lelewel," in *Historycy warszawascy ostatnich dwóch stuleci* (Warsaw Historians of the Last Two Centuries), Warsaw, 1986

Ziffer, Bernard, *Poland: History and Historians: Three Bibliographical Essays*, New York: Mid-European Studies Center, 1952

León-Portilla, Miguel 1926–

Mexican historian

Miguel León-Portilla has dedicated his life to the study of pre-Hispanic manuscripts, in addition to codices, accounts, chronicles, and histories written during the colonial period which recorded the social and cultural life of the pre-conquest, Náhuatl-speaking Aztec population.

León-Portilla's works began to appear in the 1950s and include *Ritos, sacerdotes y atavíos de los dioses* (Rituals, Priests, and Gods' Attire, 1958) and *La filosofía náhuatl estudiada en sus fuentes* (1956; *Aztec Thought and Culture*, 1963), a ground-breaking analysis of Náhuatl materials in which the author reconstructed Aztec cosmology, theology, metaphysics, and views of humankind and nature. In this work, León-Portilla also purported to show that Aztec philosophy was comparable to the most complex systems of thought in ancient Greece.

In 1959 León-Portilla published *Visión de los vencidos* (*The Broken Spears*, 1962) which contained selections from Aztec texts describing the Spanish conquest of Mexico from the Indian point of view, including their graphic commentaries on the conquistadors' behavior and lamentations over the loss of the native civilization.

In 1964 León-Portilla edited *El reverso de la conquista* (The Obverse Side of the Conquest). Like the previous book, León-Portilla presented the "vision of the vanquished," the native views of the conquest and pacification, but this time adding the experience also of the Maya of Mexico and Central America and the Inca population of Peru. With this volume León-Portilla also initiated an editorial series, "The Legacy of Indigenous America," with the aim of incorporating into the mainstream modern culture the traditions that the pre-Hispanic civilizations bequeathed to present-day Mexico in terms of ideas and works of art, and in order to awaken an appreciation of the contemporary Indian cultures. León-Portilla believed that a better understanding of the traumatic experience of the conquest suffered by the native populations could help to overcome the ensuing shock from the encounter of the indigenous and the European civilizations, and eventually help present-day populations to be better able to find their roots.

As the preparations of the celebration of the 500 years of Mexico's conquest by Spain began in 1985, León-Portilla suggested that the word "discovery" of the New World be replaced by the phrase "encounter of two worlds." His argument in favor of an "encounter" instead of a "discovery" was that both the New and the Old worlds were equally revolutionized as a result. The word "encounter" better reflected the influence that the New World had on the Old as well as the profound impact the Old had on the New. Furthermore, to insist on using the concept of discovery was to keep on using European, or Eurocentric, historical categories. León-Portilla's position was challenged publicly by Edmundo O'Gorman. Even though León-Portilla never answered his opponent, a debate ensued on the meaning of the event and the process that the discovery of America had provoked.

DANIELA SPENSER

See also European Expansion; Latin America: Colonial; Mexico; O'Gorman

Biography

Born Mexico City, 22 February 1926. Received BA, Loyola University, Los Angeles (now Loyola Marymount University), 1948, MA 1951; PhD, National Autonomous University of Mexico, 1956. Taught ancient history and anthropology, Mexico City College (now University of the Americas), 1954–57; rose to professor of Nahuatl culture, National Autonomous University of Mexico, from 1957; director, Institute of Historical Research, from 1973. Married Ascensión Hernández Treviño, historian, 1965.

Principal Writings

La filosofía náhuatl estudiada en sus fuentes, 1956, revised 1993; in English as *Aztec Thought and Culture: A Study of the Ancient Nahuatl Mind*, 1963

Ritos, sacerdotes y atavíos de los dioses (Rituals, Priests, and Gods' Attire), 1958

Editor, *Visión de los vencidos: relaciones indígenas de la conquista*, 1959; in English as *The Broken Spears: The Aztec Account of the Conquest of Mexico*, 1962

Los antiguos mexicanos a través de sus crónicas y cantares, 1961; in English as *The Aztec Image of Self and Society: An Introduction to Nahua Culture*, 1992

Las literaturas precolumbinas de México, 1964; in English as *Pre-Columbian Literatures of Mexico*, 1969

Editor, *El reverso de la conquista: relaciones aztecas, mayas e incas* (The Obverse Side of the Conquest: Aztec, Maya, and Inca Accounts), 1964

Trece poetas del mundo azteca (13 Poets from the Aztec World), 1967

Tiempo y realidad en el pensamiento maya, 1968; in English as *Time and Reality in the Thought of the Maya*, 1973

Culturas en peligro, 1976; in English as *Endangered Cultures*, 1990

Toltecáyotl, aspectos de la cultura náhuatl (Toltecayotl: Aspects of the Nahuatl Culture), 1980

Further Reading

Florescano, Enrique, and Ricardo Pérez Montfort, eds., *Historiadores de México en el siglo XX* (Mexican Historians of the 20th Century), Mexico City: FCE & CONACULTA, 1995

Homenaje a Miguel León-Portilla (Homage to Miguel León-Portilla), Guadalajara: Secretaría de Educación y Cultura, Programas de Estudios Jaliscienses, 1990

Miguel León-Portilla: imagen y otra escogida (Miguel León-Portilla: Image and Another Selection), Mexico City: UNAM, 1984

Le Quy Don *c.1726–c.1784*

Vietnamese historian

Le Quy Don was born into a scholarly family in the Duyen Ha district of today's Thai Binh province of the Red River Delta. He passed the traditional civil examination in 1752 and later held many governmental posts, including head of the Historical Board of the kingdom in 1781.

Among his most important works was *Le Trieu Thong Su* (Complete History of the Le Dynasty), also known as *Dai Viet Thong Su* (Complete History of Dai Viet). Since Le Quy Don finished this work before passing the examination in 1752 and becoming a mandarin, he had been less restrained by the orthodox thought and style of historical writing. This work represents a completely new form of Vietnamese historiography, one not in chronicle form. *Le Trieu Thong Su* presented a century of Le history in a series of biographies of 10 kings, 28 queens and concubines, 9 dukes, 19 loyal high mandarins, and 21 rebellious mandarins. Moreover, Le Quy Don added "Nghe Van Chi," a chapter listing Vietnamese classic texts written – in order to preserve the valuable heritage of the nation – by Vietnamese kings and scholars since the Ly and Tran dynasties. They were divided into four categories: *hien chuong* (law and constitution), *tho van* (literature), *truyen ky* (biography), and *phuong ky* (religion and geography). *Le Trieu Thong Su* was, more importantly, a vehicle for Le Quy Don's own views on Vietnamese history. His introduction to the book systematically articulated his views and is an important contribution to Vietnamese historiography in its own right. Rejecting a rigid method of choosing sources, he pointed out that historical writing should consult as wide a range as possible, including unofficial records, tablet rubbings, family genealogies, and journals on Vietnam written by Chinese scholars. While he praised earlier historians such as Le Van Huu, Phan Phu Tien, and Ngo Si Lien, he criticized the writing of the *Dai Viet Su Ky Toan Thu* of the late Le period for its lack of sources and unrefined style. Consequently, according to him, some crucially important plots and events of this period were not properly recorded in the chronicles and even hidden from future generations. *Le Trieu Thong Su* is thus a masterpiece created by a well-educated young Vietnamese scholar full of national consciousness, and a milestone marking a new era of Vietnamese historiography. Its influence on 19th-century historical writing was profound. Phan Huy Chu's *Lich Trieu Hien Chuong Loai Chi* was directly influenced, and another important chronicle compiled in the 19th century, *Viet Su Thong Giam Cuong Muc*, adopted many materials from *Le Trieu Thong Su*.

Le Quy Don's other historical works included two of encyclopedic scope, *Van Dai Loai Ngu* (The Classified Discourse of the Library) and *Kien Van Tieu Luc* (Small Chronicle of Things Seen and Heard). Another historical work by Le Quy

Don was *Phu Bien Tap Luc* (Miscellaneous Records of Pacification in the Border Area), providing many details personally obtained from the documents of the Nguyen southern regime in the 18th century. It is therefore the major source for studying southern Vietnam of this period. Le Quy Don is remembered as one of the most prominent scholars in Vietnamese history.

LI TANA

See also Vietnamese Chronicles

Biography
Born *c.*1726. Academic child prodigy, placed first in civil service examination, 1752; traveled to China as envoy of Vietnamese court. Died *c.*1784

Principal Writings
Le Trieu Thong Su (Complete History of the Le Dynasty); also known as *Dai Viet Thong Su* (Complete History of Dai Viet), 50 vols., 1749
Van Dai Loai Ngu (The Classified Discourse of the Library), 1773
Kien Van Tieu Luc (Small Chronicle of Things Seen and Heard), 1777
Phu Bien Tap Luc (Miscellaneous Records of Pacification in the Border Area)
Le Quy Don Toan Tap (A Complete Collection of Le Quy Don's Works), 3 vols., 1977

Further Reading
Duiker, William J., "Le Quy Don," in his *Historical Dictionary of Vietnam*, Metuchen, NJ: Scarecrow Press, 1989
Gaspardone, Emile, "Bibliographie annamite," *Bulletin de Ecole Française d'Extrême Orient* 34 (1934), 18–31
Nguyen Huyen Anh, "Le Quy Don," in his *Viet Nam Danh Nhan Tu Dien* (A Dictionary of the Famous People in Vietnam), Saigon: Khai Tri, 1967
Tran Van Giap, "Le Trieu Thong Su," and "Phu Bien Tap Luc," in *Tim Hieu Kho Sach Han-Nom* (Understanding the Chinese and Nom collections), 2 vols., Hanoi: Van Hoa, 1984
Woodside, Alexander B., "Conceptions of Change and of Human Responsibility for Change in Late Traditional Vietnam," in David Wyatt and Alexander Woodside, eds., *Moral Order and the Question of Change: Essays on Southeast Asian Thought*, New Haven: Yale University Press, 1982

Lerner, Gerda 1920–

US (Austrian-born) women's historian

Gerda Lerner, a founder of women's history as an academic field, was born in 1920 in Vienna, Austria. Her formal education there ended in 1938 with Hitler's rise to power. She emigrated to America, learned English, married Carl Lerner, raised two children, and earned her living "at every variety of women's jobs." These experiences were, as she related it, "as good an education as any for becoming a specialist in the history of women." In *The Majority Finds Its Past* (1979), she described the birth of her commitment to recording women's history. The experience of the women she had met during those years, most of whom worked "quietly and without public recognition," was entirely missing from the writings of contemporary historians.

Lerner was an active political organizer for social justice and women's equality in the 1940s and 1950s, and wrote short stories and a novel. In 1955, she and Eve Merriam wrote a musical, later performed off-Broadway, entitled *Singing of Women*, to bring to public attention heroic American women. As she prepared to write a fictionalized biography of the abolitionist Grimké sisters, Lerner realized that she lacked sufficient formal knowledge of American history.

In 1959 she enrolled in the New School for Social Research for her BA. "While there," she recalls, "without any planning or conscious effort on my part, it turned out that every paper I did on any subject related to women . . . Now I realize that I ran my own little Women's Studies major, only there was no such thing in existence then." While still an undergraduate she offered the first course in Women's History at an American college, in the autumn of 1962, but it was cancelled when fewer than ten students enrolled. She taught it successfully in the spring of 1963.

Lerner entered Columbia to work for her doctorate in 1963 at the age of 43. "In those days women my age did not generally attend graduate school and I was somewhat apprehensive, and so, I think, were some of my professors . . . In a way, my three years of graduate study were the happiest years of my life. Mostly, it was the first time in my life I had time and space for thinking and learning." Her supportive family relieved her of many domestic responsibilities. Her dissertation became her first historical publication, *The Grimké Sisters from South Carolina* (1967), a crucial restoration of the role of European-American women in the abolitionist movement, and a crucial exploration of the origins of American feminism.

Lerner was inspired by historian Mary Beard's insight that women have been subordinate, yet central; victimized, yet active. Her announcement to her advisers that she intended "to complete the work begun by Mary Beard" was "greeted by astonished silence." Lerner persevered, ignoring the advice that "women's history" would not advance her career. "What I brought as a person to history," she writes, "was inseparable from my intellectual approach to the subject; I never accepted the need for a separation of theory and practice."

Lerner's awareness of the impact of race shaped the screenplay for *Black like Me*, a film produced with her husband Carl in 1964. Her subsequent travels throughout the South, visiting churches, schools, and families, produced *Black Women in White America* (1972), which confirmed her thesis that generalizations about oppression of women are inadequate unless qualified by race and class. Lerner's classic article "The Lady and the Mill Girl" (1969) demonstrated how differences in class altered women's relationships to each other and to technology.

Lerner founded the MA program in women's history at Sarah Lawrence College in 1972, which became a model for graduate education in the field. She also organized programs for secondary school teachers, and for scholars of African American women's history. In her 1975 essay "Placing Women in History" (in *The Majority Finds Its Past*), she accurately predicted the general outlines of the future historiography of the field. Critical of the traditional narrative framework, her documentary history *The Female Experience* (1977), reorganized history around life-cycle categories, with new possibilities for analysis. By the end of the 1970s, she had concluded that studying American history alone was insufficient. Working

with religious artifacts, literature, and archaeology, she historicized the construction of patriarchy and of feminism in *The Creation of Patriarchy* (1986) and *The Creation of Feminist Consciousness* (1993).

Lerner has accomplished the goals for women's history that she developed in 1963. She has done so by her research and writing; by proving the existence of sources; by upgrading the status of women in the profession; and by creating student interest and designing courses and graduate programs. Lerner nurtured and made possible the next generation of feminist historians. In *US History as Women's History* (1995), Kerber, Kessler-Harris and Sklar wrote: "At a time when many American academics insisted that good historical practice required that historians distance themselves from the political passions of their time, Lerner taught that one wrote history to save one's own life, indeed one's own sanity." They also note that before Lerner, women figured in history only "for their ritual status, as wives . . . for their role as spoilers . . . or for their sacrificial caregiving." Her scholarly work has "stretched the boundaries of our knowledge about women's lives and encouraged historians to ask questions previously considered impossible," making the study of history immeasurably more inclusive.

LAUREN COODLEY

See also Feminism; Kelly-Gadol; Women's History: North America

Biography

Gerda Kronstein Lerner. Born Vienna, 30 April 1920. Emigrated to US, 1939; naturalized 1943. Professional writer/translator, 1941–60. Received BA, New School of Social Research, 1963; MA, Columbia University, 1965, PhD 1966. Taught at New School, 1963–65; Long Island University, 1965–68; Sarah Lawrence College, 1968–80; and University of Wisconsin, Madison, from 1980 (emeritus). Married Carl Lerner, filmmaker, 1941 (died 1973; 1 son, 1 daughter).

Principal Writings

The Grimké Sisters from South Carolina: Rebels Against Slavery, 1967
The Woman in American History, 1971
Editor, *Black Women in White America: A Documentary History*, 1972
Editor, *The Female Experience: An American Documentary*, 1977
The Majority Finds Its Past: Placing Women in History, 1979
The Creation of Patriarchy, 1986
The Creation of Feminist Consciousness: From the Middle Ages to Eighteen-Seventy, 1993
Why History Matters: Life and Thought, 1997
The Feminist Thought of Sarah Grimké, 1998

Le Roy Ladurie, Emmanuel 1929–
French social historian

Emmanuel Le Roy Ladurie has not only a good claim to be the most wide-ranging and prolific of the Annales historians, but the development of his career is also paradigmatic of the triumph and subsequent atrophy of the Annales school. The publication of his doctoral thesis *Les Paysans de Languedoc* (1966; *The Peasants of Languedoc*, 1974) established his reputation as the leading member of the second generation of Annales scholars. Le Roy Ladurie was indebted to his mentor Braudel, whom he succeeded as professor at the Collège de France in 1973, for the methodological innovations in the structure of his thesis. This work attempted to construct the "total history" (social, economic, and cultural) of one region over the long term, stressing the constraints imposed by the physical environment on the individual. He was also indebted to the work of Labrousse who argued for a scientific and quantitative approach to history in order to uncover long-term structural and demographic patterns. Le Roy Ladurie demonstrated how the level of subsistence of the peasants of Languedoc was determined by the Malthusian-Ricardian model of population growth. He distinguished three phases in the agrarian cycle between the 15th and 18th centuries. Between the Black Death and the early 16th century the low population level ensured that resources and consumption were in equilibrium: there was an abundance of land, a low level of rents, and high wages. During the 16th century population growth continued to fuel economic expansion, but population began to outstrip agricultural production. After 1600 Languedoc became locked in the Malthusian cycle of economic and demographic stagnation. Population outstripped resources as inheritances were subdivided and lords were able to increase rents, consequently subsistence crises became more acute. War and adverse climatic conditions contributed to the abject condition of the peasantry. In contrast to many of the Annales historians, Le Roy Ladurie did not neglect cultural and religious history. However, he argued for the primacy of the underlying demographic and economic structures in determining change. The superstructure of ideas, politics, and belief (vie culturelle) was influenced and often conditioned by imperceptible long-term changes in the base (vie matérielle). Le Roy Ladurie's continuing interest in long-term ecological change was developed in L'Histoire du climat depuis l'an mil (1967; Times of Feast, Times of Famine, 1971). His methodological approach had a profound impact in the 1960s, causing him to remark that "the quantitative model has completely transformed the craft of the historian in France."

By the 1970s a number of historians were beginning to question the validity of the demographic model as the prime cause of historical change (see, for example, Brenner, 1976). Few would now accept that cultural and political change are largely the products of long-term developments in the economic and demographic base. Indeed, Le Roy Ladurie's next major work, Montaillou (1975), demonstrated how far he himself had moved away from quantitative history over the long term to an interest in the developing field of social anthropology. Montaillou was a radical departure. Ladurie used the trial records left by the early 13th-century repression of Catharism in Languedoc both to reconstruct the material existence of Pyrenean mountain villagers and to explore their mental world. Using this microhistorical approach he aspired to a wider understanding of medieval mentalités (mentalities), to see "the ocean through a drop of liquid." His evocation of the lives of ordinary villagers and his reconstruction of their mental horizons earned him the plaudits of professional historians, as well as making him a household name in France. Critics of Montaillou have questioned both Montaillou's typicality and Ladurie's rudimentary understanding of the Inquisition registers, which are not, as he claimed, unmediated texts. His move

away from the Annales paradigm was confirmed by Le Carnaval de Romans (1979; Carnival in Romans, 1979). Although the Annalistes had previously rejected event history in favor of long-term structural change, Le Roy Ladurie analyzed the events of the uprising of 1580 in Romans as a social drama that provided an example of "the mental and social layers which made up the Old Regime." It attempted to explore the nature of social conflict in early modern France and to demonstrate the manner in which conflicts were structured. In recent years Le Roy Ladurie has concentrated on the types of history that thirty years previously he and his colleagues had rejected as outdated. L'Etat royal (1987; The Royal French State, 1994) and Le Siècle des Platter (The Century of the Platter Family, 1995) displayed signs of the positivist event history and biography that he claimed in 1973 in Le Territoire de l'historien (The Territory of the Historian, 1979) had been replaced by the primacy of quantitative methods and the analysis of long-term structural change. As professor at the Collège de France, co-editor of Annales, and more recently as director of the Bibliothèque Nationale, Le Roy Ladurie has had a profound impact on the development of the historical profession in France and beyond. In particular, his interest in developments in other disciplines and his commitment to an interdisciplinary approach to historical analysis will be an enduring legacy.

STUART CARROLL

See also Agrarian; Annales School; Anthropology; Burke; Computing; Consumerism; Environmental; France: 1000–1450; France: 1450–1789; History from Below; Indigenous; Mentalities

Biography

Emmanuel Bernard Le Roy Ladurie. Born Moutiers-en-Cinglais, 19 July 1929. Received agrégation, Sorbonne, DèsL, 1952. Taught at Lycée de Montpellier, 1953–57; research assistant, Centre National de la Recherche Scientifique (CNRS), 1957–60; assistant, Faculté des Lettres de Montpellier, 1960–63; assistant lecturer, 1963, Ecole Pratique des Hautes Etudes, director of studies, from 1965; professor of the history of modern civilization, Collège de France, from 1973; general administrator, Bibliothèque Nationale, from 1987. Married Madeleine Pupponi, 1955 (1 son, 1 daughter).

Principal Writings

Les Paysans de Languedoc, 2 vols., 1966; in English as The Peasants of Languedoc, 1974
L'Histoire du climat depuis l'an mil, 1967; in English as Times of Feast, Times of Famine: A History of Climate since the Year 1000, 1971
Le Territoire de l'historien, 2 vols. 1973–78; selections in English as The Territory of the Historian, 1979; and The Mind and Method of the Historian, 1981
Montaillou, village occitan de 1294 à 1324, 1975; in English as Montaillou: Cathars and Catholics in a French Village, 1294–1324 and as Montaillou: The Promised Land of Error, 1978
"Symposium: Agrarian Class Structure and Economic Development in Pre-Industrial Europe: A Reply," Past and Present 79 (1978), 55–59
Le Carnaval de Romans: de la chandeleur au mercredi des cendres, 1579–1580, 1979; in English as Carnival in Romans, 1979
L'Argent, l'amour et la mort en pays d'Oc, 1980; in English as Love, Death, and Money in the Pays d'Oc, 1982
Paris-Montpellier: PC-PSU, 1945–63, 1982

Parmi les historiens: articles et comptes rendus (Collected Book Reviews), 2 vols. to date, 1983–94

La Sorcière de Jasmin, 1983; in English as *Jasmin's Witch*, 1987

L'Etat royal: de Louis XI à Henri IV, 1460–1610, 1987; in English as *The Royal French State, 1460–1610*, 1994

The French Peasantry, 1450–1660, 1987

L'Ancien Régime de Louis XIII à Louis XV, 1610–1774, 2 vols., 1991; in English as *The Ancien Régime: A History of France, 1610–1774*, 1996

Le Siècle des Platter, 1499–1628 (The Century of the Platter family), vol.1, 1995; in English as *The Beggar and the Professor*, 1997

Further Reading

Brenner, Robert, "Agrarian Class Structure and Economic Development in Pre-Industrial Europe," *Past and Present* 70 (February 1976), 30–74

Burke, Peter, *The French Historical Revolution*, Stanford, CA: University of Stanford Press, and Cambridge: Polity Press, 1990

Carrard, Philippe, *Poetics of the New History: French Historical Discourse from Braudel to Chartier*, Baltimore: Johns Hopkins University Press, 1992

Peters, Jan, "Das Angebot der Annales und das Beispiel Le Roy Ladurie: Nachdenkenswertes über französische Sozialgeschichtse-forschung" (The Offering of the Annales School and the Example of Le Roy Ladurie: Reflections on French Social History Research), *Jahrbuch für Wirtschaftsgeschichte* 1 (1989), 139–59

Leuchtenburg, William E. 1922–

US political historian

As one reviewer of William E. Leuchtenburg's *The Supreme Court Reborn* (1995) noted, Leuchtenburg has occupied a unique position in the historiography of Franklin D. Roosevelt's New Deal and, more broadly, in 20th-century American political historiography. Leuchtenburg's generation (including, most famously, Arthur M. Schlesinger, Jr., John Morton Blum, and Frank Freidel), which lived through the 1930s Depression, has been more likely than a succeeding generation of historians to judge the New Deal in terms of the creative solutions it generated to address a host of weaknesses in American socio-economic institutions. That generation's students, who were themselves either born after the Depression or are too young to remember it, have been more critical of FDR's programs, choosing to view them in the light of problems that the New Deal either could not solve or positively ignored – problems such as gross economic inequality and the political subjugation of African Americans.

The body of Leuchtenburg's work has provided an ideological balance and an intellectual bridge between these two camps. The author of *The Perils of Prosperity, 1914–1932* (1958), one of the first scholarly syntheses of the period between World War I and the Depression, Leuchtenburg was uniquely qualified to comment later on the New Deal as an answer to problems that the Depression exposed, but did not create, in American society. Weaving together cultural, political, and social history, he covered the range of events from the US entrance into a world war through internal debates over the League of Nations, Red Scares, the decline of progressivism, the resurgence of the Ku Klux Klan and immigration restriction, Prohibition, and, finally, the collapse of the stock market in 1929. Leuchtenburg saw these conflicts, by themselves and in total, as reflections of the conflict between rural and urban values in a society that was urbanizing, centralizing political power, and industrializing. Seen from this perspective, the economic collapse of 1929 and the social catastrophe of the Depression were more the natural result of wrenching internal divides than unexplainable aberrations.

Leuchtenburg established himself as the pre-eminent political historian of the decade of the 1930s with his landmark book, *Franklin D. Roosevelt and the New Deal, 1932–1940*. First published in 1963, the book won the Bancroft and Parkman prizes and framed debates over Roosevelt's responses to the Depression that have yet to be satisfactorily transcended. Unlike some of the historians and Roosevelt biographers who had come to be associated with Leuchtenburg and who had been accused of fawning over FDR, their political hero, Leuchtenburg applied a passionate but critical analysis to the New Deal. *Franklin D. Roosevelt and the New Deal* addressed the dominant historiographical questions of its time, but it also opened the door for a more critical interpretation of Roosevelt's programs, an interpretation that has dominated the great majority of work on the New Deal that followed. It also showcased a fluent writing style that wove together material from oral histories, memoirs, contemporary journal and newspaper articles, and an astonishing array of documents from manuscript collections. If any one thing has characterized Leuchtenburg's writing style, it is his use of anecdotal evidence that would at times seem to border on the fictional, and which has served to "bring history alive" for countless numbers of undergraduates. As an example, Leuchtenburg illustrated the depth of feeling – negative as well as positive – that FDR generated as the first modern president, with the following vignette culled from the Naomi Achenbach Benson manuscript collection: "In Kansas, a man went down into his cyclone cellar and announced he would not emerge until Roosevelt was out of office. (While he was there, his wife ran off with a traveling salesman.)"

The vast majority of Leuchtenburg's work has focused on Roosevelt and his legacy. Subsequent books and scores of articles have assessed Roosevelt's influence on the presidents who succeeded him. He has also tried to make sense of the ill-fated "court-packing" scheme of 1937, by which – Leuchtenburg concludes – FDR doomed his own New Deal by overreaching his own political possibilities. Among his students are many of the most important political and cultural historians of 20th-century America: William H. Chafe, Robert Dallek, Jacquelyn Dowd Hall, Alonzo Hamby, Steven F. Lawson, Harvard Sitkoff, and Howard Zinn.

Leuchtenburg has also been active in the "popular history" movement, contributing articles to the magazine *American Heritage* and serving as a consultant to Ken Burns, the creator of *The Civil War* and *Baseball*, the documentaries that won immense popular success by way of America's Public Broadcasting System. In this way the historian has improved the quality and depth of public debate on issues of historical importance. Among historians, however, Leuchtenburg will be remembered for the way he has shaped debates over the Depression and the New Deal, arguably the most important event and transformative government program in American history since the Civil War.

J. TODD MOYE

See also Political; United States: 20th Century

Biography
William Edward Leuchtenburg. Born Ridgewood, New York, 28 September 1922. Received BA, Cornell University, 1943; MA, Columbia University, 1944, PhD 1951. Taught at New York University, 1947; Smith College 1949–51; Harvard University, 1951–52; Columbia University, 1952–82; and University of North Carolina from 1983. Married 1948 (second marriage; 3 children from first marriage).

Principal Writings
Flood Control Politics: The Connecticut River Valley Problem, 1927–1950, 1953
The Perils of Prosperity, 1914–1932, 1958
Franklin D. Roosevelt and the New Deal, 1932–1940, 1963
Editor, *Franklin D. Roosevelt: A Profile*, 1967
A Troubled Feast: American Society since 1945, 1973; revised 1979, 1983
In the Shadow of FDR: From Harry Truman to Ronald Reagan, 1983; revised [with subtitle *From Harry Truman to Bill Clinton*], 1993
The Supreme Court Reborn: The Constitutional Revolution in the Age of Roosevelt, 1995
The FDR Years: On Roosevelt and His Legacy, 1995

Further Reading
Garraty, John A., *Interpreting American History: Conversations with Historians*, 2 vols., New York: Macmillan, 1970

Levene, Ricardo 1885–1959
Argentinian historian

Ricardo Levene took some of the tendencies of 19th-century Argentine and Latin American historiography and carried them into the 20th century. He wrote a 2-volume textbook on Argentine history, *Lecciones de historia Argentina* (1913; *A History of Argentina*, 1937), which became the standard textbook in Argentine schools for many years, going through 23 editions. In addition he edited a well-received 10-volume national history. But these were not his only, nor his major contributions. Levene was interested in the history of all of Latin America and he contrasted the history of his native Argentina with the histories of other Latin American countries, thereby introducing the concept of comparative history at a time when most Latin American historians confined themselves to studying their own past. Beyond that he wrote on Argentine law and he researched the economic and judicial history of Argentina's independence period. Still another of his works examined the role of Bartolomé Mitre in Argentine historiography in the 19th century through an examination of Mitre's *Historia del Belgrano de la independencia Argentina* (History of Belgrano and of Argentine Independence, 1859) in which Levene concluded that Mitre had, in that study and in the subsequent historiographic polemics with other historians, charted the historiographic field for his contemporaries and for later historians. Levene also wrote social and cultural histories moving away from the typical political studies written by his Latin American contemporaries.

Levene not only introduced new areas for historical study in Argentina, he also moved the study of history chronologically forward from a concentration on colonial and independence themes to the contemporary period. Even more significant, however, was his participation in a debate among historians concerning the proper method for carrying out research. Some of his peers after 1930 announced that a "New" school of Argentine historians was then advancing historiography far beyond the so-called "Erudite" school of the early historians such as Bartolomé Mitre, Pablo Groussac, and others. This "New" school presumably was influenced by French historians and by the German Leopold von Ranke. Ever the committed nationalist, Levene leaped into this polemic and insisted that the "New" school was not new at all and certainly was not inspired by European historians, but was merely a continuation of Mitre's research ideas along with an acceptance of Mitre's work in social and intellectual history. Levene argued that the same emphasis on documentary research on which Mitre had insisted and the same determination to test documentary evidence was accepted by the "New" school historians. Consequently, the "New" school was nothing more than an extension of the "Erudite" school.

If Mitre was the leading Argentine historian of the 19th century, Levene was the outstanding historian of the 20th century. Not only did he influence historical method by his forays into historiographic debates, but his own works served as models for younger historians. Additionally, he founded and directed the Instituto de Historia del Derecho (Institute of Legal History) which produced more than fifty publications under his direction. He also founded in 1926 the Archivo Histórico de la Provincia de Buenos Aires (Buenos Aires Provincial Historical Archive) in which he could carry out his historiographic commitment on the need for documentary evidence for historiographic study. This archive not only enabled historians to research a wide range of topics, but it published a large number of histories written from its materials.

Levene assisted young historians in their research, and, by providing the opportunity for young scholars to follow his concepts, he left a distinct imprint on Argentine historiography. At the same time his interest in other nations led him to provide information on Argentine history for scholars from other countries with whom he corresponded extensively. Beyond these many activities he was a prolific writer in his own right, publishing more than twenty books between 1911 and 1958.

JACK RAY THOMAS

Biography
Born Buenos Aires, 7 February 1885. Studied at Buenos Aires National College; graduated in law, University of Buenos Aires, 1906. Taught history, National College, 1906–11; professor of sociology, University of Buenos Aires, 1911–14, professor of judicial and social sciences, 1914–19; professor of history, later dean, then president, University of La Plata, from 1919. Founder/director, Institute of Legal History. Founder, Buenos Aires Provincial Historical Archive, 1926. Married Amelia Rosa Peylonbet (1 son). Died Buenos Aires, 13 March 1959.

Principal Writings
Lecciones de historia Argentina, 2 vols., 1913; later retitled *Historia argentina y americana*; in English as *A History of Argentina*, 1937

Introducción a la historia del derecho indiano (Introduction to the History of Indian Law), 1924

Investigaciones acerca de la historia económica del Virreinato (Research on the Economic History of the La Plata Viceroyalty), 2 vols., 1927–29

La anarquía de 1820 en Buenos Aires (1820 Anarchy in Buenos Aires), 1933

General editor, *Historia de la nación argentina* (History of the Argentine Nation), 10 vols., 1936–42

La Academia de Jurisprudencia y la vida de su fundador, Manuel Antonio de Castro: con apendice documental (The Academy of Jurisprudence and the Life of Its Founder, Manuel Antonio Castro: with a Documental Appendix), 1941

La cultura historica y el sentimiento de la nacionalidad (Historical Culture and the Perception of Nationality), 1942

Mitre y los estudios historicós en la Argentina (Mitre and Historical Studies in Argentina), 1944

Historia del derecho argentino (History of Argentine Law), 11 vols., 1945–57

Las Indias no eran colonias (The Indies were Not Colonies), 1951

Manual de historia del derecho Argentino (Historical Manual of Argentine Law), 1952

El mundo de las ideas y la revolución hispanoamericana de 1810 (The World of Ideas and the Hispanic American Revolution of 1810), 1956

Obras (Works), 1961–

Further Reading

Barager, Joseph R., "The Historiography of the Rio de la Plata Area since 1830," *Hispanic American Historical Review* 39 (1959), 587–642

Instituto Panamericano de Geografía e Historia, *Guía de personas que cultivan la historia de América* (Guide to Scholars of American History), Mexico City, 1951

Mariluz Urquijo, José M., "Ricardo Levene, 1885–1959," *Hispanic American Historical Review* 39 (1959), 643–46

Parker, William Belmont, *Argentines of Today*, New York: Hispanic Society of America, 1920

Pla, Alberto J., *Ideología y método en la historiografía argentina* (Ideology and Method in Argentine Historiography), Buenos Aires: Nueva Vision, 1972

Wright, Ione S., and Lisa M. Nekhom, *Historical Dictionary of Argentina*, Metuchen, NJ: Scarecrow Press, 1978

Levine, Lawrence W. 1933–

US social historian

Lawrence Levine has played an important role in shaping the fields of African American and US social history. By employing sources which previously had been bypassed or ignored, Levine has added great complexity to our understanding of the mental world of African Americans before and after emancipation. He has consistently emphasized the value of popular culture as a means for understanding American society, and has played an important role in redefining intellectual history, in Joseph Levenson's words, as "the history not of thought, but of men thinking."

Levine's first book, *Defender of the Faith* (1965), a biography of William Jennings Bryan, grew out of the doctoral dissertation he wrote at Columbia University under the supervision of Richard Hofstadter. Where earlier studies had traced Bryan's transformation from reform to reaction in the years after he resigned from Wilson's cabinet, Levine contended that Bryan's

involvement in fundamentalist and anti-evolution crusades late in life was consistent with his earlier reform activities. Throughout his career, Levine argued, Bryan had always fought to preserve and strengthen the values and beliefs of the rural West and South which formed the core of his constituency, and with which he had always been closely identified.

In the process of completing his study of Bryan, Levine became, as he wrote in 1989, increasingly troubled by the assumption in *Defender of the Faith* "that one necessarily can derive the consciousness of people from the goals and aspirations of their leaders." Thereafter, he turned increasingly to folk sources, historical materials produced by ordinary people, which shed light on their mental universe. The result was his important study, *Black Culture and Black Consciousness* (1977).

By scrutinizing folk sources – the humor, songs, dance, speech patterns, tales, games, folk beliefs, and aphorisms of African Americans – Levine was able to contribute to a number of long-running debates about the nature of slavery, the origins and development of slave culture, and the effects of slavery on post-emancipation African American society.

Scholars as diverse as the black sociologist E. Franklin Frazier and the historian Stanley Elkins had argued that the brutality of slavery had destroyed all vestiges of African culture, leaving the slave a *tabula rasa*, ready to receive either the imprint of white American values, or a dysfunctional slave culture. Levine strongly disagreed. African Americans successfully kept alive important elements of African consciousness in their folk culture, and they were able to do so because these cultural forms proved both resistant to, and a means of resisting, white influences. Whites tended not to interfere with black folk practices, because these practices often supported white assumptions about black inferiority. In other areas there existed important cultural parallels that provided wide room for the syncretic coexistence of African and European beliefs. The important point was that these African cultural forms were more than merely an accommodation to slavery or a strategy for survival. "Slave music, slave religion, slave folk beliefs – the entire sacred world of the black slaves," Levine argued, "created the necessary space between the slaves and their owners and were the means of preventing legal slavery from becoming spiritual slavery." Slavery was a brutal institution, but within it slaves were able to forge cultural bonds that enabled them to develop a greater sense of group pride than the system of slavery ever intended them to have.

While Levine showed that the strong traces of African consciousness preserved in the folk life of the slave helped African Americans survive the horrors and degradation of slavery, he also pointed out that African cultural forms helped shape the contours of black life after emancipation. African Americans refashioned slave tales, humor, and music to reflect the new realities of a world free from slavery, but not of the power and force of white racism. As African Americans adapted to freedom, so did their folk culture. There was little room in Levine's account for what Daniel Patrick Moynihan described as the "tangle of pathologies" that left the African American male emasculated, and the black family deeply dysfunctional. The story of African Americans, Levine recognized, was not one solely of brutalization and victimization. In the face of adversity African Americans forged cultural institutions that helped them to cope with the pain of slavery and resist the burden of white racism.

After the publication of *Black Culture and Black Consciousness*, Levine continued to research American folk and popular culture. Both as a historian and as president of the Organization of American Historians, Levine has consistently defended a multicultural approach to American history on scholarly grounds. No history, he has argued, can be complete unless it embraces the diversity of the ethnic, class, gender, racial, regional, and occupational groups which for so long had been ignored by American historians, yet which have contributed fundamentally to the development of American culture. Many historians in recent years have joined Levine in broadening the range of historical inquiry, and in recognizing the multifaceted complexity of the American past.

MICHAEL L. OBERG

See also African American; Elkins; Slavery: Modern

Biography

Lawrence William Levine. Born New York City, 27 February 1933. Received BA, City College, New York, 1948; University of Pennsylvania, MA, PhD 1954. Taught at City College of New York, 1959–61; Princeton University, 1961–62; University of California, Berkeley, from 1962; and George Mason University from mid-1980s.

Principal Writings

Defender of the Faith: William Jennings Bryan, The Last Decade, 1915–1925, 1965
Black Culture and Black Consciousness: Afro-American Folk Thought from Slavery to Freedom, 1977
Highbrow/Lowbrow: The Emergence of Cultural Hierarchy in America, 1988
The Unpredictable Past: Explorations in American Cultural History, 1993

Lévi-Provençal, Evariste 1894–1956

French medievalist, Arabist, and Hispanist

Born in Algiers, Evariste Lévi-Provençal was a member of the great school of French Arabists associated with the Institute of Higher Moroccan Studies in Rabat, along with Georges S. Colin and Henri Terrasse, and was director of the Institute after the death of Henri Basset in 1926. He was thus in the right place to take advantage of the opening of a sealed chamber of the Qarawiyin mosque in Fez which revealed numerous important new sources of the history of Islamic Spain, including many of the early chapters of Ibn Hayyān's *al-Muqtabas*, which allowed him to give a much more complete narrative of the Umayyad period of the history of Islamic Spain than had been possible before. Moreover, his Moroccan perspective led him to promote a view of a unified "Western Islamic" culture that still carries considerable influence.

Lévi-Provençal defined for his and all succeeding generations the narrative structure of the history of the Umayyads of Islamic Spain, or al-Andalus. It is his narrative of Umayyad emirate and caliphate that has determined the particular emphases of all subsequent narratives, because he was the first historian of Islamic Spain who dominated the historical sources of Umayyad times.

Lévi-Provençal criticized Reinhart Dozy (whose history of Islamic Spain he revised in 1932) for overemphasizing the role of tribal in-fighting in the political history of the emirate. But in downplaying the role of tribalism, he exaggerated both the nature and speed of the cultural fusion that took place among the conquering Muslims and the indigenous Hispano-Roman population. First, he overestimated the rapidity of the conversion process, and, second, he mistook the massive conversion of Christians in the 8th and 9th centuries for a process of fusion with their Arab overlords, a process better described in terms of acculturation and assimilation. He believed that the process of conversion was quite rapid, more so in cities than in rural areas, and that it was pushed by "matrimonial alliances and a communality of material interests" among all ethnic groups, whether Arab, Berber, or indigenous. These groups eventually were able to form a distinctive and unified Andalusi ethnic group, in part characterized by somatic diversity unknown elsewhere in the Arab world and by the residual use of Romance dialect, which combined to present the Eastern traveler with an impression of an exotic society. His account of the social history, particularly of the emirate, is vitiated by his lack of understanding of tribal social structure as well as by his tendency to revert to analogies with Morocco in order to explain events in al-Andalus.

The institutions of the Umayyad state, however, were almost wholly of Eastern inspiration, both Umayyad and 'Abbasid. Nothing remained of Visigothic institutions except for certain elements of the regime of land tenure. Lévi-Provençal's account of the fall of Caliphate consisted simply of a minute description of the political events of 1010–23, concluding with an expression of the historian's inability to comprehend the suddenness of the phenomenon.

Among Lévi-Provençal's important editions of Arabic texts was al-Himyari's geography of al-Andalus, containing detailed descriptions of the great cities of Islamic Spain. This text served as the basis for his numerous articles on Andalusi cities in the first and second editions of the *Encyclopaedia of Islam*. Lévi-Provençal also stimulated interest in the institution known as *hisba* in al-Andalus by his translation of the treatise of Ibn 'Abdūn and his insistence on the genre's importance for understanding the fine texture of urban life. *Hisba* manuals were chapbooks for the guidance of the *muhtasib*, an urban magistrate who oversaw the daily life of the city: as market inspector, overseer of building codes, and as censor of public morality. Lévi-Provençal also edited the Arabic texts of the treatises of Ibn 'Abdūn, Abd 'al-Ra'ūf, and al-Jarsifi.

THOMAS F. GLICK

See also Guichard; Middle East; Sánchez-Albornoz; Spain: Islamic; Spain: to 1450

Biography

Born Algiers, 4 January 1894. Took a degree in Arabic, University of Algiers, 1913. Served in French army and was wounded in Dardanelles during World War I. Worked in Office of Native Affairs, Morocco, 1919. Taught Arabic, Institut des Hautes Etudes Marocaines, Rabat, 1919–35, where he also earned his PhD. Chair of history, University of Algiers, 1935: dismissed under Vichy because he was Jewish; chair in Islam, the Sorbonne, 1945–56; director, Institut des Etudes Islamiques, 1950–56. Died 1956.

Principal Writings

Contributor, *The Encyclopaedia of Islam: A Dictionary of the Geography, Ethnography and Biography of the Muhammadan Peoples*, 4 vols., 1913–36

L'Espagne musulmane au Xème siècle: institutions et vie sociale (Muslim Spain in the 10th century), 1932

Editor of new edition, *Histoire des Musulmans d'Espagne jusqu'à la conquête de l'Andalousie par les Almoravides (711–1110)* (History of the Muslims of Spain) by Reinhart Dozy, 3 vols., 1932

Editor/translator, *La Péninsule ibérique au Moyen Age d'après le Kitab al-Rawd al-mi'tar' d'Ibn 'Abd al-Muncim al-Himyari* (The Iberian Peninsula in the Middle Ages), 1938

Editor/translator, *Séville musulmane au début du XIIe siècle: le traité d'Ibn 'Abdun sur la vie urbaine et les corps de métiers* (Muslim Seville in the 12th Century), 1947

Islam d'Occident: études d'histoire médiévale (Islam in the West: Studies in Medieval History), 1948

Histoire de l'Espagne musulmane (A History of Muslim Spain), 3 vols., 1950–67 [vol. 1 originally published 1945]

Further Reading

"Bibliografie analytique de l'oeuvre d'E. Lévi-Provençal" (Analytic Bibliography of the work of E. Lévi-Provençal), in *Etudes d'orientalisme dédiées à la mémoire de Lévi-Provençal*, 2 vols., Paris: Maisonneuve et Larose, 1962

Levison, Wilhelm 1876–1947
German medievalist

Wilhelm Levison's list of his publications bore this quotation from Bede: "I have always found it delightful to learn and to teach and to write." Levison was a consistently popular, indeed venerated, teacher-scholar. He devoted significant energy simply to making relevant information available to the historical community, typically asserting his intention to put future debates on a more secure evidentiary footing. Levison's 1898 discussion of the sources relevant to the (still-debated) date of the Christian baptism of Clovis brought him to the attention of Bruno Krusch. Krusch brought Levison to work at the *Monumenta Germaniae Historica* (MGH), a collaborative scholarly effort dedicated to identifying sources for the early history of "Germany" and publishing them in critical editions. Critical editions, based on the comparison of numerous manuscripts, were a relatively new development in 1899, and the MGH project was central to creating the conventions of the genre; Levison, due to his meticulous approach to texts and his dedication to his scholarly calling, contributed broadly to the new era of professional medieval Geschichtswissenschaft (historical science) by undertaking to compile indices, check proofs, and fulfill other ancillary but essential tasks even for departments of the MGH outside his own specialization. Levison himself worked primarily (although not exclusively) on early medieval saints' biographies, attempting to establish their relative degrees of "source-worthiness" (*Quellenwert*), then publishing (in the MGH and elsewhere) all or part of those texts that he determined to possess value. At the time, these sources were relatively little known or used, and Levison – following his mentor Krusch – was a pioneer among nonclerical historians. Levison's expertise in the field was so respected that he was called on to train new members of the (Jesuit) Society of Bollandists, the clerical group which had inaugurated, centuries earlier, the critical analysis of the legends of the saints. Through his editorial work at the MGH, Levison became tremendously influential: the products of his labor are owned in multiple copies by every serious research library in Europe and North America, are regularly consulted by almost every active medievalist, and effectively constitute a canon of essential sources for medieval history. Not only the sources which Levison made available, but also his posthumous *Deutschlands Geschichtsquellen im Mittelalter* (Germany's Historical Sources of the Middle Ages 1952–73), remain fundamental for medieval historical scholarship. He published hundreds of contributions of varying length in scholarly journals – including a constant flow of short notices concerning manuscripts and sources which appeared in the journal of the MGH, the *Neues Archiv* – and was the primary mentor of dozens of prominent German medievalists. Levison must be reckoned as one of the most influential medieval historians of the 20th century.

Levison eschewed outright controversy. Instead, he gave meaning to historical evidence in more subtle ways, for example, through providing each edited text with an elaborate apparatus, which itself would determine how future users would interpret the evidence. Levison sifted through saints' biographies with the intention of labelling some narratives as more reliable than others, and sifted through the narratives themselves searching for nuggets of "data" among the disposable filler. Rooted in the 19th-century German philological approach to history, Levison dated and localized the genesis of each text largely on the basis of linguistic evidence, to which other considerations were added: codicological evidence; textual references to dateable events and personages; comparisons with liturgical, calendrical, documentary, and similar ancillary materials; and the identification of prior sources used and posterior narratives influenced by the text in question. Through decades of low-key source-critical work dedicated to distinguishing reliable "historical" evidence from unreliable "legendary" accretions, Levison constructed a picture of the process of the Christianization of the British Isles and of continental Europe north of the Alps. Despite all his sophisticated source-critical methods, Levison rarely controlled for bias in narrative sources; as a result, the picture he painted effectively repeated the historiographic views of whatever sources he had judged to be reliable. Nor did his vision of the past remain unaffected by contemporary events. Levison was forced to flee his beloved ancestral Rhineland *Heimat* (homeland) as a result of Nazi racial laws, and produced his only full-fledged monograph, *England and the Continent in the Eighth Century* (1946), while in England; the work, written during World War II, is a synthetic statement of the salvific influence of insular pilgrims on a decrepit continental religious culture.

Levison – himself named in honor of a German emperor – was a victim of the so-called "fatal embrace" of the liberal state by European-Jewish intellectuals, who saw in the secular, bureaucratic authority of the nation-state a sort of latter-day savior. Levison worked assiduously, along with a large number of other Jewish Germans, on the MGH project, serving from 1925 onwards on the Board of Directors (*Zentraldirektion*) of that state-supported scholarly effort. The nationalism Levison worked to promote in Germany was not without effect on the popularity of anti-Semitic, *Blut-und-Boden* ("Blood-and-Soil") Nazism. Furthermore, as medieval literary scholars have increasingly questioned the validity of "editions" of texts whose manuscript witnesses diverge from one another, the very ideal of creating monumental textual editions – a project to which Levison contributed so much – has been criticized as politically motivated. A provocative analysis of Levison's editorial work can be found in David Townsend's 1993 article. The role of Levison and other Jewish intellectuals in the creation of a German nationalist consciousness is one of the tragic ironies of the modern historical profession, an example of the unintended consequences that can result from historical representations.

FELICE LIFSHITZ

See also Britain: Anglo-Saxon; France: to 1000; Krusch

Biography

Born Düsseldorf, 25 May 1876, to an assimilated Jewish family. Studied history and classical languages in Bonn and Berlin, 1894–95. Editor on the *Monumenta Germaniae Historica* from 1898; taught at the University of Bonn, from 1909; because of Nazi racial laws, dismissed from his post, 1933; settled in Durham, England, 1939, where he was connected to the university. Married Elsa Freundlich, 1917. Died Durham, 17 January 1947.

Principal Writings

"Zur Geschichte des Frankenkönigs Chlodowech" (On the History of Clovis, King of the Franks), *Bonner Jahrbücher* 103 (1898), 42–86

"Bischof Germanus von Auxerre und die Quellen zu seiner Geschichte" (Bishop Germanus of Auxerre and the Sources for His History), *Neues Archiv* 29 (1903), 95–175

"Die Iren und die Fränkische Kirche" (The Irish and the Frankish Church), *Historische Zeitschrift* 109 (1912), 1–22

"Konstantinische Schenkung und Silvester-Legende" (The Donation of Constantine and the Legend of Silvester), *Miscellanea Francesco Erle II* (Rome, 1924), 159–247

Das Werden der Ursula-Legende (The Making of the Ursula Legend), 1928

"Die Anfänge rheinischer Bistümer in der Legende" (The Beginning of Rhenish Bishoprics in Legend), *Annalen des Historischen Vereins für den Niederrhein* 116 (1930), 5–28

"St. Willibrord and His Place in History" *Durham University Journal* new series 1 (1940), 23–41

England and the Continent in the Eighth Century, 1946

Aus rheinischer und fränkischer Frühzeit: Ausgewählte Aufsätze (Rhenish and Frankish Early Middle Ages: Selected Essays), edited by Walther Holtzmann, 1948 [collected articles and bibliography]

Critical Editions

With Bruno Krusch, *Passionaes vitaeque sanctorum aevi Merovingici et antiquiorum aliquot* (Passion-Accounts and Biographies of Saints of the Merovingian Age and Earlier), 5 vols., 1896–1920

With Bruno Krusch, *Ionae Vitae sanctorum Columbani, Vedastis, Iohannis* (Jonas' Biographies of Saints Columbanus, Vedast, John), 1905

Vitae sancti Bonifatii archiepiscopi moguntini (Biographies of St. Boniface, Archbishop of Mainz), 1905

Gregorii Turonensis Opera (The Works of Gregory of Tours), revised edition, 1951

With Heinz Löwe, *Deutschlands Geschichtsquellen im Mittelalter: Vorzeit und Karolinger* (Germany's Historical Sources of the Middle Ages: Antiquity and the Carolingians), 1952–73 [revision of Wilhelm Wattenbach's edition]

Further Reading

Schieffer, Theodor *et al.*, *In memoriam, Wilhelm Levison (1876–1947)*, Cologne: Hanstein, 1977
Townsend, David, "Alcuin's Willibrod, Wilhelm Levison and the *Monumenta Germaniae Historica*," in Roberta Frank, ed., *The Politics of Editing Medieval Texts*, New York: AMS Press, 1993

Lewin, Moshe 1921–

Polish-born historian of Russia

Moshe Lewin came late to the world of professional history but soon established a reputation as the most influential social historian of 20-century Russia. He was born into left-wing Zionist circles in Poland in 1921, fled to the East in 1941 where he saw Stalin's Russia at first hand, and worked on a kolkhoz and in industry before joining the Red Army. He returned to Poland after the war, and after staying in France, spent most of the 1950s in Israel. In 1961 he obtained a research scholarship at the Sorbonne which led to his pioneering thesis on the collectivization of the Russian peasantry, published as *Russian Peasants and Soviet Power* (1968), and described by one commentator as "a manifesto for social history." He then taught in France, Britain, and the US, playing a central role in each country in helping to define the agenda of a new concern with Russian social history.

Lewin rejected the then prevailing totalitarian model of the USSR, arguing that it was "useless as a conceptual category . . . the term was . . . itself 'totalitarian' in its empty self-sufficiency; it did not recognize any mechanism of change in the Soviet Union and had no use for even a shadow of some historical process." In its place Lewin emphasized, first, the importance of alternatives in modern Russian history. This can be seen in his sympathy with many of the aims of the 1917 Revolution but his rejection of many of its eventual outcomes. He made a pioneering study of *Lenin's Last Struggle* (1967, translated 1968) to document Lenin's own deathbed resistance to the bureaucratization of the Revolution. He went on to stress later policies, arguing that modern Russia emerged more from the era of collectivization and industrialization than the Revolution, although recognizing that Stalin's power depended on pressures evident earlier.

Lewin emphasized, second, the centrality of social change to Soviet and Russian history. Although his early work focused on the 1930s, he was unusual in stressing the scale of change after 1945. This was reflected, for instance, in the growing urban share from 18 per cent of the population in 1926 to 32 per cent in 1939, to 49 per cent in 1960 and 70 per cent in 1980. For Lewin the true urban-industrial revolution in Russia was occurring from the 1950s to the 1970s when many political commentators were emphasizing relative immobility in the system, and it was this social change, he argued, that eventually allowed Gorbachev to appear with his reform program.

Lewin emphasized, third, the role of Russian society, arguing for the need to break down "the usual antithesis of 'state' versus 'society.'" *Russian Peasants and Soviet Power* offered an initial analysis of collectivization that he later extended backward and forward into a discussion of what he called "the rural nexus" in Russian life – the dominance of peasant mores across society well into the 1950s. Collectivization and industrialization only partly broke this rural nexus but helped in the short run to establish a "quicksand society" in the 1930s. Both the working class and bureaucratic professional groups were in constant turmoil without completely losing all possibility of resisting those above. For Lewin, however, "Stalinism turned out to be a passing phenomenon." He argued that the main theme of post-1945 Soviet history was the re-emergence of civil society. In *Political Undercurrents in Soviet Economic Debates* (1974) he looked at the coded debates about economic reform in the 1960s revealing their concern with alternative pasts, presents, and futures as well as showing how they had spilled over into a wider concern with law, culture, and democratization. He later argued that the reformers of the 1960s, although defeated in the short run, prefigured perestroika under Gorbachev. In 1988 he published *The Gorbachev Phenomenon: An Historical Interpretation*, one of the first attempts to explore the social preconditions of the rise of perestroika and glasnost'.

Like growing numbers on the left from the 1960s, Lewin rejected the view that the USSR was socialist but he never offered a clear analysis of an alternative categorization. He was an optimistic supporter of Gorbachev's reforms and therefore disappointed with their eventual outcome. Ironically, with hindsight, he could be criticized for failing to extend his own analysis to an appreciation of the social contours of power and the way that these might condition eventual political and economic choices. But his rejection of "one-dimensional analysis" of Russia's past continues to be a powerful inspiration for those following in the footsteps of his pioneering analysis of Russian social history.

MICHAEL HAYNES

See also Davies, N.; Russia: Modern

Biography

Born Wilno, Poland, 6 November 1921. Grew up in Poland, but fled to Russia in 1941, working and eventually joining the Red Army. Returned to Poland after the war, but left, first for France, then for Israel. Received BA, Tel Aviv University, 1961; PhD, the Sorbonne, 1964. Taught at Ecole des Hautes Etudes, Paris, 1965–66; Columbia University, 1967–68; University of Birmingham, England, 1968–78; and University of Pennsylvania, from 1978.

Principal Writings

La Paysannerie et le pouvoir soviétique, 1928–1930, 1966; in English as *Russian Peasants and Soviet Power: A Study of Collectivization*, 1968
Le Dernier Combat de Lénine, 1967; in English as *Lenin's Last Struggle*, 1968
Political Undercurrents in Soviet Economic Debates: From Bukharin to the Modern Reformers, 1974; reprinted with new introduction as *Stalinism and the Seeds of Soviet Reform: The Debates of the 1960s*, 1991
The Making of the Soviet System: Essays in the Social History of Interwar Russia, 1985
The Gorbachev Phenomenon: An Historical Interpretation, 1988
Russia–U.S.S.R.–Russia: The Drive and Drift of a Superstate, 1995

Further Reading

Abelove, Henry *et al.*, eds., *Visions of History*, by MARHO: The Radical Historians Organisation, Manchester: Manchester University Press, and New York: Pantheon, 1983

Andrle, Vladimir, *A Social History of Twentieth-Century Russia*, London and New York: Arnold, 1994
Lampert, Nick, and Gabor T. Rittersporn, eds., *Stalinism: Its Nature and Aftermath: Essays in Honour of Moshe Lewin*, London: Macmillan, and Armonk, NY: Sharpe, 1992
Lew, R., "Grappling with Soviet Realities: Moshe Lewin and the Making of Social History," in Nick Lampert and Gabor T. Rittersporn, eds., *Stalinism: Its Nature and Aftermath: Essays in Honour of Moshe Lewin*, London: Macmillan, and Armonk, NY: Sharpe, 1992

Lewis, Bernard 1916–

US (British-born) historian of Islam, the Ottoman Empire, and the modern Middle East

Over a 60-year career, Bernard Lewis emerged as the most influential postwar historian of Islam and the Middle East. His elegant syntheses made Islamic history accessible to a broad public in Europe and America. In his more specialized studies, he pioneered social and economic history and the use of the vast Ottoman archives. His work on the premodern Muslim world conveyed both its splendid richness and its smug self-satisfaction. His studies in modern history rendered intelligible the inner dialogues of Muslim peoples in their encounter with the values and power of the West. While Lewis' work demonstrated a remarkable capacity for empathy across time and place, he stood firm against the Third Worldism that came to exercise a broad influence over the historiography of the Middle East. In Lewis' work, the liberal tradition in Islamic historical studies reached its apex.

Lewis drew upon the reservoir of Orientalism, with its emphasis on philology, culture, and religion. But while Lewis possessed all the tools of Orientalist scholarship – his work displayed an astonishing mastery of languages – he was a historian by training and discipline, intimately familiar with new trends in historical writing. He was one of the very first historians (along with the Frenchman Claude Cahen) to apply new approaches in economic and social history to the Islamic world. While a student in Paris, Lewis had a brief encounter with the Annales school, which inspired an early and influential article on guilds in Islamic history. A youthful Marxism colored his first book, *The Origins of Isma'ilism* (1940: his doctorate for the University of London, where he taught for thirty years). He subsequently jettisoned this approach, refusing the straitjacket of any overarching theory. But his studies of dissident Muslim sects, slaves, and Jews in Muslim societies broke new ground by expanding the scope of history beyond the palace and the mosque.

Lewis' early work centered on medieval Arab-Islamic history, especially in what is now Syria. However, after the creation of Israel, it became impossible for scholars of Jewish origin to conduct archival and field research in most Arab countries. Lewis turned his efforts to the study of Arab lands through Ottoman archives available in Istanbul, and to the study of the Ottoman empire itself. *The Emergence of Modern Turkey* (1961) examined the history of modernizing reform not through the European lens of the "Eastern Question," but through the eyes of the Ottoman reformers themselves. Lewis relied almost entirely on Turkish sources, and his history from within became a model for many other studies of 19th-century reform in the Middle East. It also signaled his own deepening interest in the history of ideas and attitudes in Islam's relationship to the West.

Lewis regarded the "challenge" or "impact" of the West as the watershed between the premodern and modern Middle East. Over the last two decades, some historians have sought to establish that the Ottoman empire remained vital through the 18th century and even began to regenerate – a process nipped in the bud by Europe's economic and military expansion. Lewis, however, insisted that Ottoman decline was both real and self-inflicted. It resulted not only from the West's material superiority, but from a Muslim attitude of cultural superiority, which impeded borrowing. The importance of creative borrowing, and the costs of Muslim insularity, were major themes in *The Muslim Discovery of Europe* (1982).

Twentieth-century Turkey's eagerness to belong to the West accorded it a privileged place in Lewis's vision of the Middle East. From the early 1950s, Lewis became alarmed by the expansion of Soviet influence in the region, and he consistently advocated close Western ties with Turkey. Soviet support for the Arabs from the 1960s likewise led him to emphasize the importance of Western relations with Israel. In 1974, Lewis relocated from London to Princeton, where he became a public intellectual. His long-standing critique of the Soviet Union was reinforced by his revulsion at the combined Soviet and Arab effort to delegitimize Israel as racist. He expressed his views in several articles, and later in a book, *Semites and Anti-Semites* (1986).

His engagement in these controversies set the scene for his confrontation with the Palestinian-American literary critic Edward Said. In 1978, Said published *Orientalism*, which argued that the modern study of Islam in the West had evolved as a tool of imperialist domination, and that the West's pursuit of knowledge had conspired with its pursuit of power. Orientalism, effectively a form of racism, had misrepresented Islam as static, irrational, and in permanent opposition to the West.

Lewis maintained that the development of Orientalism was a facet of Europe's humanism, which arose independently of, and sometimes in opposition to, imperial interests. Islamic studies, after neutralizing the medieval religious prejudice against Islam, had been an important arena of discovery and achievement. Lewis rejected the view that only Muslims, Arabs, or their political sympathizers could write the region's history: he called this "intellectual protectionism." A combination of curiosity, empathy, competence, and self-awareness was the only prerequisite for the writing of "other people's history."

The Said-Lewis exchange prompted a charged debate about the representation of Islam and the Arabs in Western academe. It created a new awareness among Western historians that their readers included Arabs and Muslims. It also exposed ethnic and political differences among historians in their rawest form.

Lewis's influence extended far beyond academe. He wrote three major syntheses for general audiences: *The Arabs in History* (1950), *The Middle East and the West* (1964), and *The Middle East* (1995). These books were translated into more than 20 languages, and made his name synonymous with Islamic history for educated publics in the West. Leading newspapers often interviewed him on past and present issues. (One such interview, granted to *Le Monde* in 1993, resulted in a controversial suit against him by opponents of his interpretation of the Armenian tragedy of 1915–16.) Lewis has had an active retirement and his views carry weight in Western capitals, and are sought by prime ministers, presidents, and monarchs in Israel, Turkey, and Jordan.

MARTIN KRAMER

See also Islamic; Middle East; Orientalism; Ottoman

Biography

Born London, 31 May 1916. Attended Wilson College and The Polytechnic; received BA, University of London, 1936; Diplôme des Etudes Sémitiques, University of Paris, 1937; PhD, University of London, 1939. Served in Royal Armoured Corps and Intelligence Corps, 1940–41; attached to Foreign Office, 1941–45. Taught (rising to professor), School of Oriental and African Studies, University of London, 1938–39, 1945–74; Princeton University, 1974–86 (also member, Institute for Advanced Study, Princeton); and Cornell University, 1986–90. Naturalized US citizen, 1982. Married Ruth Hélène Oppenhejm, 1947 (marriage dissolved 1974; 1 daughter, 1 son).

Principal Writings

The Origins of Isma'ilism: A Study of the Historical Background of the Fatimid Caliphate, 1940
The Arabs in History, 1950, revised 1958; 6th edition, 1993
The Emergence of Modern Turkey, 1961; revised 1968
Editor, with Peter Malcolm Holt, *Historians of the Middle East*, 1962
Istanbul and the Civilization of the Ottoman Empire, 1963
The Middle East and the West, 1964; revised as *The Shaping of the Middle East*, 1994
The Assassins: A Radical Sect in Islam, 1967
Editor, with Peter Malcolm Holt and Ann K.S. Lambton, *The Cambridge History of Islam*, 2 vols., 1970; revised in 4 vols., 1978
Race and Color in Islam, 1971; revised and expanded as *Race and Slavery in the Middle East: An Historical Enquiry*, 1990
Islam in History: Ideas, Men and Events in the Middle East, 1973; revised, 1993
Editor, *Islam: From the Prophet Muhammad to the Capture of Constantinople*, 2 vols., 1974
History – Remembered, Recovered, Invented, 1975
Editor, with Benjamin Braude, *Christians and Jews in the Ottoman Empire: The Functioning of a Plural Society*, 2 vols., 1982
The Muslim Discovery of Europe, 1982
The Jews of Islam, 1984
Semites and Anti-Semites: An Inquiry into Conflict and Prejudice, 1986
The Political Language of Islam, 1988
Islam and the West, 1994
The Middle East: A Brief History of the Last 2,000 Years, 1995; in UK as *The Middle East: 2,000 Years of History from the Rise of Christianity to the Present Day*, 1995

Further Reading

Humphreys, R. Stephen, "Bernard Lewis: An Appreciation," *Humanities* 11/3 (May/June 1990), 17–20

Lewis, David Levering 1936–
US intellectual historian

Currently the holder of the Martin Luther King, Jr. chair in history at Rutgers University, David Levering Lewis has made his mark as a historian by producing significant monographs in the fields of Afro-American, European, and African history. Concern with interactions as well as similarities and differences between European, African, and American social, political, and cultural history has led Lewis to merge his dominant interest in European history with African American and African history. His 1993 Pulitzer Prize-winning biography, *W.E.B. Du Bois: Biography of a Race, 1868–1919*, aptly demonstrates this point. Lewis' biography places the life of W.E.B. Du Bois, the first African American to receive the PhD from Harvard University (1895) within the larger context of the Gilded Age and the Progressive Era. But the study is also informed by a keen awareness of the international milieu in which Du Bois' life was formed. Issues such as European imperialism in Africa, the intensification of scientific racism, and larger trends of modernization command Lewis' attention.

The biography also makes a dramatic break with the earlier historiography on Du Bois' life. Lewis, through a combination of prodigious research and extensive knowledge of American and European history, moves away from constructing Du Bois as simply a petit bourgeois intellectual or as a consistent advocate of one position or another throughout his lifetime. Instead, Lewis utilizes a more multifaceted and complex approach to reconstruct Du Bois' life. First, he explores the centrality of race in the development Du Bois' personality and lifework. Second, he uncovers the importance of intellectual pursuits and engagement. Finally, he examines the significance of Du Bois' organizational affiliations in the actualization of his goals and achievements.

Lewis' other work in African American history has also been significant. *King* (1970) was one of the earliest biographical assessments of Martin Luther King's contribution to civil rights in America. *When Harlem Was in Vogue* (1981) was an intellectual history of the black literati during the Harlem Renaissance of the 1920s. Focusing on writers and academics such as Claude McKay, Countee Cullen, W.E.B Du Bois, Alain Locke, and Walter Thurman, Lewis recreated the dynamism of post-World War I Harlem. However, Lewis' focus on the literati leads to a stilted portrait of the Harlem Renaissance. While correcting the image of Harlem as a tragic slum in the 1920s, Lewis failed to engage with the role of music and religion in the creation of its culture.

His engaging style and considerable literary skills have also been brought to bear on seminal events in European history. With the publication of *Prisoner of Honor* (1973), Lewis renewed his interest in modern French history. The Dreyfus affair, possibly the most infamous legal case in modern European history, involved a French artillery captain of Jewish faith, Alfred Dreyfus (c.1859–1935). Dreyfus, who was assigned to the general staff in Paris, was accused of having written a *bordereau* ("schedule") for delivery to the German embassy in Paris. Dreyfus was charged with treason and in 1894, found guilty and transported to Devil's Island to serve out a sentence of lifelong imprisonment. Lewis constructs his text against the backdrop of the larger implications of the Dreyfus affair. Issues of national security, religious intolerance, institutional corruption, and minority rights dominate his account. The recurring theme of the intersection between national experiences also finds its way into Lewis' work on African history.

The Race to Fashoda (1987) identified the linkages between national characters and interactions between nations as a means of drawing larger meanings. Lewis used Fashoda not to re-examine the tensions between European imperial powers, but to investigate African resistance and twenty years of earlier negotiations. Lewis' treatment of the Fashoda incident (1898), which brought France and Britain to the brink of war in the Sudan, represents a balanced portrait of both European imperialism and African resistance.

As an African American historian, Lewis continues to set high standards for African American and American history. His emphasis on research, contextualization, the examination of a multiplicity of causal factors, and an advanced understanding of the influence of European history on the development of African American history, makes him an important contributor to the historical debate.

STEPHEN GILROY HALL

Biography

Born Little Rock, Arkansas, 25 May 1936. Received BA, Fisk University, 1956; MA, Columbia University, 1959; PhD, London School of Economics, 1962. Taught at University of Ghana, Legon, 1963–64; Howard University, 1964–65; Morgan State University, 1966–70; rose to professor, University of the District of Columbia, 1970–80; University of California, San Diego, 1981–85; and Rutgers University, from 1985. Married 1) Sharon Lynn Siskind, 1965 (divorced 1988; 2 sons, 1 daughter); 2) Ruth Ann Stewart, 1994 (1 daughter).

Principal Writings

King: A Critical Biography, 1970
Prisoner of Honor: The Dreyfus Affair, 1973
When Harlem Was in Vogue, 1981
The Race to Fashoda: Colonialism and African Resistance, 1987
W.E.B. Du Bois: Biography of a Race, 1868–1919, 1993

Leyser, Karl 1920–1992
British (German-born) medieval historian

Karl Leyser was the son of a prosperous Jewish mercantile family from Düsseldorf, who came to England as a refugee in 1937 and studied history at St. Paul's School and Magdalen College, Oxford, where he was particularly influenced by the medievalist Bruce McFarlane. During the war he served in the Pioneer Corps and then the Black Watch, rising to the rank of captain, before returning to complete his degree at Oxford and then to take up a teaching fellowship at his college; except for brief visiting professorships in the US at the end of his life he spent his entire scholarly career in Oxford, becoming professor of medieval history in 1984. A heavy teaching load meant that he published virtually nothing before the age of 45, and it took the shock of a near-fatal car accident in 1977 to propel him into publishing ideas that had already inspired generations of undergraduates, and latterly also postgraduates. Once *Rule and Conflict in an Early Medieval Society* (1979) had appeared, he became a more prolific writer, producing some thirty articles between then and his death in 1992.

Rule and Conflict was a work of startling originality, which has had considerable impact on the way in which many medievalists have come to view the archaic polities of the early Middle Ages. Leyser stressed the alterity of the 10th-century world: it could not be understood by mere intuitive empathy or by the unthinking application of modern notions of political behavior. Its rulers and magnates were not locked in a permanent structural conflict with each other, but they were involved in some conflicts, and in particular 10th-century rulers "did not stand outside the circle of feud and revenge." Equally novel was his stress on the significance of the women of the Saxon aristocracy and their religious life, and his interpretation of the Ottonians' "sacral kingship" as a means of allowing magnates and rulers to end conflicts in ways that the harsh rules of feud and honor might otherwise not have allowed.

This ability to take an apparently well-studied topic and view it from an angle throwing unusual highlights and shadows was found in most of Leyser's published work. He was particularly sensitive to the insights that we can gain from close reading of narrative sources, at a time when many medievalists had come to dismiss these as inherently "unreliable" and not to be used if "record evidence" was available. His writing was at its most characteristic when he lingered over a strange or inconsequential detail in a narrative and used it to reveal a whole set of contemporary attitudes and beliefs that we had forgotten or ignored. Saints, for example, showed themselves to be aristocratic in their behavior by not visiting kings and bishops directly; they sent their messages via servants, who were almost as terrified of interrupting their masters as they were of the saints who had appeared to them in visions, and usually needed reminding and even the application of physical violence before they would act.

Leyser's own life history was more closely linked with his historical work than it has usually been for later generations of historians growing up in a more sheltered and untroubled world. His early experiences of persecution and exile gave him, as with many other émigré Central European intellectuals, a deep sense of the fragility of human society and institutions; his war service offered profound insights into the problems presented by the raising, feeding, and leading of armies; and his early historical training under McFarlane, who remained a mentor and powerful influence even after his death in 1966, drew him to the study of medieval aristocracies. In historical outlook he was in many ways an English empiricist, eschewing wide-ranging theories and model-based interpretations; yet his very wide reading and his fluent German – a highly unusual accomplishment for a medievalist of his generation, even though he had little contact with German medievalists for the first two decades of his scholarly career – made it impossible for him to accept the kind of historical stance that he would denounce as "bloody British pragmatism." He had few pupils and founded no "school," but few medievalists since World War II have been more influential.

TIMOTHY REUTER

See also Germany: to 1450; Widukind

Biography

Born Düsseldorf, Germany, 24 October 1920, son of a manufacturer and a musician. Educated at Hindenburg Gymnasium, Düsseldorf, before emigrating to England, where he attended St. Paul's School, London. Served in Pioneer Corps, 1940–43; the Black Watch,

1943–45: received command, 1944; officer, Territorial Army, 1945–63. Studied at Magdalen College, Oxford, BA 1947; graduate study, 1947–48. Taught at Oxford University (rising to professor) 1948–88 (emeritus); fellow: Magdalen College, 1948–84; All Souls College, 1984–88. Married Henrietta Bateman, historian, 1962 (2 sons, 2 daughters). Died 27 May 1992.

Principal Writings

Rule and Conflict in an Early Medieval Society: Ottonian Saxony, 1979
Medieval Germany and Its Neighbours, 900–1250, 1982
Communications and Power in Medieval Europe, vol 1: *The Carolingian and Ottonian Centuries*; vol. 2: *The Gregorian Revolution and Beyond*, edited by Timothy Reuter, 2 vols., 1994

Further Reading

Campbell, James, "Review of *Communications and Power*," *Bulletin of the German Historical Institute, London* 17 (1995)
Harriss, Gerald, "Karl Leyser as a Teacher" in Timothy Reuter, ed., *Warriors and Churchmen in the High Middle Ages: Essays Presented to Karl Leyser*, London and Rio Grande, OH: Hambledon Press, 1992
Leyser, Karl, "Kenneth Bruce McFarlane, 1903–1966," *Proceedings of the British Academy* 62 (1976), 485–506
Mayr-Harting, Henry, "Karl Leyser, 1920–1992," *Proceedings of the British Academy* 94 (1996)
Reuter, Timothy, "Karl Leyser the Historian," in Leyser, *Communications and Power in Medieval Europe*, vol. 2: *The Gregorian Revolution and Beyond*, London and Rio Grande, OH: Hambledon Press, 1994

Liang Qichao [Liang Ch'i-ch'ao]

1873–1929
Chinese political activist, journalist, and historian

The intellectual history of modern China cannot be adequately understood without reference to Liang Qichao. His keen mind and prolific writings addressed the problem of what to do about the declining fortunes of China and its imperial Confucian order, and once it collapsed in 1912, what to substitute for it. This involved not only consideration of political institutions but of social and economic thought and behavior, since Confucianism articulated a worldview for both elite and multitude. In this undertaking, Liang occasionally became an active participant in politics, usually to little effect. More substantive are the accomplishments of Liang the journalist or historian, for his essays and books not only influenced his generation but raised questions about the future of China that are still being debated.

Born near Canton [Guangzhou] in 1873, the precocious Liang took the traditional path that young boys of intellectual promise pursued, namely a study of the Confucian classics (such as the *Analects*) and commentaries on them, which served as the bases of civil service examination testing. Since the classics and questions about them emphasized rule by moral example and tended to neglect more pragmatic subject matter, and because the examination system served as the "ladder of success" to government office, China's elite comprised a Confucian elite equipped with agile minds, knowledge of general principles, and explanations for social and natural phenomena.

By the time Liang became a member of that elite by passing county and provincial examinations in the 1890s, however, chronic domestic rebellion and successful foreign assaults called into question the efficacy of Confucianism. China's lopsided defeat in the First Sino-Japanese War (1894–95) generated heated debate that divided intellectuals into three broad positions: conservatives who wanted no substantive change; various assortments of reformers; and revolutionaries. Liang became a radical reformer determined to accommodate the Confucian system to modern ways (just as Meiji Japan had successfully adapted its tradition) so that it could protect China from the hostile international environment of the late 19th and early 20th centuries. Liang became part of an activist triumvirate which convinced the young Guangxu [Kuang-hsu] emperor to launch a major modernization program in the spring of 1898. Crushed by the empress dowager Cixi [Tz'u-hsi] on 21 September, this Hundred Days of Reform resulted in the emperor being placed under house arrest, the execution of triumvirate member Tan Sitong [T'an Ssu-t'ung], and the escape of leader Kang Youwei [K'ang Yu-wei] and Liang to foreign legations. Until the collapse of the Qing [Ch'ing] dynasty in 1912, Liang travelled through Asia and America, raising funds and organizing overseas Chinese for Kang's Protect the Emperor Society, and resided in Japan, where he edited and wrote for several newspapers and journals. The founding of the Republic of China in 1912 did not solve China's political problems, and although Liang worked for president Yuan Shikai [Yuan Shih-k'ai] and a successor warlord government, his political activism all but ended by 1919. Thereafter until his death in 1929 he turned to a life of writing and teaching, hoping to develop an intellectual consensus about what would replace the imperial order.

Liang's historical vision was both controversial and stimulating. Thus he did not attempt to justify modernization in the late 19th century in the typical way, by claiming that the Confucian tradition would continue to form the moral foundation of China while Western innovations would serve as mere subsidiary techniques. Instead he insisted that Confucius had always been a reformer whose approach to proper governing had been obscured and obfuscated by generations of Confucian literati interpreting counterfeit classics. His biographer Joseph Levenson has argued that "Liang's constant concern is to protect Chinese culture from the imputation of failure. Therefore, borrowings must be converted into natural elements of the native tradition." Moving further away from orthodox Confucianism, Liang turned to nationalism as the device that would revive China's fortunes. By the turn of the century, in exile in Japan editing the fortnightly journal *New People*, he apparently looked to the common man (or "new citizen") and not earlier moral exemplars as the key to progress. As Liang put it, "Morality cannot remain absolutely unchanged. It is not something that could be put into a fixed formula by the ancients several thousand years ago, to be followed by all generations to come. Hence, we who live in the present group should observe the main trends of the world, study what will suit our nation, and create a new morality in order to solidify, benefit, and develop our group" (*Sources of Chinese Tradition*).

How far Liang departed from the Confucian heritage is the issue most debated among historians. Levenson's view that the divergence was psychologically intense and intellectually sweeping has been challenged by more recent assessments. Philip Huang asserts that although Liang's liberalism and nationalism represented a break with China's tradition, it "had not been total; his Confucian ideas had continued to influence and interact with his new ideas." Chang Hao likewise contends that the "inner dimensions" of Chinese culture continued to affect profoundly Liang's thinking. Thus his "new citizen" who operates within a modern constitutional political framework seems to be the model of classical liberalism in action. But instead of liberalism's goals of freedom from government that we might associate with Adam Smith and Thomas Jefferson, Liang's notion of liberalism more closely mirrored the political and social arrangements in Bismarck's Germany or in Meiji Japan: authoritarian rule, statist economics, and collectivist goals. Individual "citizen" input was valued only to the extent that it benefited the nation; rights and freedoms were viewed as collective, not individual. Perhaps Liang's radicalism did not depart substantially from China's Confucian past.

However one chooses to interpret Liang before World War I, there is little disagreement that after the war the allure of the West diminished considerably in his eyes. Upon his return to China from Versailles in January 1920, Liang taught at Qinghua [Tsinghua] University in Beijing and Nankai University in Tianjin [Tientsin], and devoted himself to serious scholarship, most of it surveys of ideas. And although he did not ignore Western thought, its most radical manifestations such as Marxism were rejected, as he returned to China's patrimony for guidance. *Qingdai xueshu gailun* (Intellectual Trends in the Qing Period, 1920) examined the movement away from the more abstract notions of Ming times (1368–1644) and the beginnings of a more practical analysis that, alas, itself became pedantic even as the clash between China and the West commenced and generated a revitalization of pensive discourse. *A History of Pre-Qin Political Thought* (1930) not only outlined the Confucian, Daoist [Taoist], Moist, and Legalist schools of thought, but pondered various other issues, ancient and modern (e.g., disarmament, democracy, the class system). Other writings included a study of Chinese historical research methods (1921–22) and a history of 300 years of Chinese scholarship (1924), and Liang was working on a world history, a history of China, and a cultural history of China when he died of kidney disease in 1929.

Liang Qichao's impact on modern China has been immense. He has animated several generations of intellectuals and political leaders, beginning with Confucian scholars in the late Qing, New Culture and May Fourth radicals and revolutionaries such as Hu Shi [Hu Shih] and Ch'en Tu-hsiu [Chen Duxiu], communists such as Mao Zedong [Mao Tse-tung], and concerned Chinese today. His questions about how past and present, native and foreign, and citizen and government interact are just as vital today as they were a century ago, owing to China's continuing quest for an acceptable modern political and social order.

THOMAS D. REINS

See also China: Modern; World

Biography

Born Zinhui, Guangdong, 23 February 1873. Classical Chinese education; passed provincial examination, *ju ren* degree, 1889.

Influenced by Kang Yuwei, took part in failed 1890s reform movement, then took refuge in Japan; returned to China after revolution of 1911; served in various ministries, and as adviser to China delegation to Versailles peace conference, 1919. Taught at Qinghua [Tsinghua] University, Beijing; and Nankai University, Tianjin [Tientsin], 1923–29. Died Beijing, 19 January 1929.

Principal Writings

Zhongguo tongshi (A General History of China)
Zhongguoshi xulun (Discussion of Chinese History), 1901
Xinshixue (The New Historiography), 1902
Lun Zhongguo xueshu sixiang biangian zhi dashi (Major Trends in Chinese Scholarly Thought), 1902
Qingdai xueshu gailun (Intellectual Trends in the Qing Period, 1644–1911), 1920
Zhongguo lijiufa (Methodology of Chinese Historical Research), 1921–22
Zhongguo jin sanbainian xueshushi (A History of Chinese Scholarship over the Past 300 Years), 1924
Zhongguo lishi yanjiufa bubian (Supplement to Methodology of Chinese Historical Research), 1926–27
Yinbingshi heji, wenji (Collected Essays from the Ice-drinker's Studio), 1936
Yinbingshi heji, zhuanji (Collected Works from the Ice-drinker's Studio), 1936

In translation
History of Chinese Political Thought in the Early Tsin Period (better rendered as *A History of Pre-Qin Political Thought*), translated by L. T. Chen, London: Kegan Paul, 1930
Ssu-yu Teng and John K. Fairbank, eds., *China's Response to the West: A Documentary Survey, 1839–1923*, Cambridge, MA: Harvard University Press, 1954
Intellectual Trends of the Ch'ing Period (*Qingdai xueshu gailun*), translated by Immanuel C. Y. Hsu, Cambridge, MA: Harvard University Press, 1959
Contributor to William T. de Bary, Wing-tsit Chan, and Burton Watson, eds., *Sources of Chinese Tradition*, 2 vols., New York: Columbia University Press, 1960

Further Reading

Beasley, William G., and Edwin G. Pulleyblank, eds., *Historians of China and Japan*, London: Oxford University Press, 1961
Chang Hao, *Liang Ch'i-ch'ao and Intellectual Transition in China, 1890–1907*, Cambridge, MA: Harvard University Press, 1971
Hsiao Kung-ch'uan [Xiao Gungquan], *Zhongguo zhengzhi sixiang shi*, 6 vols., Taipei: Commercial Press, 1960; in English as *A History of Chinese Political Thought*, vol. 1, Princeton: Princeton University Press, 1979
Huang, Philip C.C., *Liang Ch'i-ch'ao and Modern Chinese Liberalism*, Seattle: University of Washington Press, 1972
Levenson, Joseph R., *Liang Ch'i-ch'ao and the Mind of Modern China*, Cambridge, MA: Harvard University Press, 1953; revised 1959
Nathan, Andrew J., *Chinese Democracy: An Investigation into the Nature and Meaning of "Democracy" in China Today*, New York: Knopf, 1985
Schwartz, Benjamin I., *In Search of Wealth and Power: Yen Fu and the West*, Cambridge, MA: Harvard University Press, 1964
Wills, John E., Jr., *Mountain of Fame: Portraits in Chinese History*, Princeton: Princeton University Press, 1994
Young, Ernest P., "The Reformer as Conspirator: Liang Ch'i-ch'ao and the 1911 Revolution," in Albert Feuerwerker, ed., *Approaches to Modern Chinese History*, Berkeley: University of California Press, 1967

Link, Arthur S. 1920–1998

US political historian, biographer, and editor

Arthur S. Link was the unquestioned *primus inter pares* among scholars of president Woodrow Wilson, all of whom acknowledged his unrivaled pre-eminence. Since the late 1940s, Link has devoted his life to the study of Wilson: his works include a 5-volume biography, which takes Wilson up to April 1917; the 69 volumes of *The Papers of Woodrow Wilson*, a project on which Link served as editor-in-chief for over thirty years; three shorter, interpretive volumes on Wilson; numerous articles; and several edited volumes of essays by other scholars. A highly productive scholar in the tradition of Allan Nevins and Henry Steele Commager, in the late 20th century Link stands alone among American historians, a monumental figure, *sui generis*.

Link's doctoral research carried the seeds of his lifelong interest in Wilson; by the time he had completed his doctoral dissertation, "The South and the Democratic Campaign of 1910–1912," he had already decided to undertake a full-scale, multivolume Wilson biography. Over the next fifteen years, first as an instructor in history at Princeton University (1945–49), then as an increasingly senior professor at Northwestern University (1949–60), Link produced the first three volumes of this biography, together with a volume in the New American Nation series, *Woodrow Wilson and the Progressive Era, 1910–1917* (1954), and *Wilson the Diplomatist: A Look at His Major Foreign Policies* (1957), an overview of Wilsonian diplomacy.

In the late 1950s, Link was offered the position of chief editor of a massive project, supported by Princeton University and the Ford, Rockefeller, and Woodrow Wilson foundations, to produce a full documentary version of the papers of Woodrow Wilson. Despite justified misgivings that this would prevent the completion of his biography of Wilson – two further volumes appeared in 1964 and 1965, but they took the story only up to 1917 – Link accepted this offer, and would devote the next thirty years of his life to the publication of this series. The series is a tribute to Link's awesome industry, energy, and scholarship, as he scoured scores of archives for all materials relating to its subject. It is universally admired as a model of historical editing, a project that was brought to completion relatively speedily, and which has made the character and attainments of Wilson far more accessible to both the general public and the scholar. Link also continued to publish articles and essays on Wilson, and encouraged other scholars' work in this area; several of the resulting monographs were published as supplementary volumes to the Wilson papers, and he also edited collections of essays on Wilson. Overall, Link did more than anyone to further the study of Wilson, and to focus scholarly attention upon the president's achievements, particularly in the field of foreign affairs. (Link's own monumental work on Wilson's earlier years has perhaps inhibited his successors from tackling the domestic field to the same extent.)

In his own essay of 1962, "The Higher Realism of Woodrow Wilson," Link suggested that, far from being an ineffectual idealist, Wilson "was in fact the supreme realist," who was percipient enough to know that only a peace of justice, reconciliation, and mercy would endure, and whose international aims were rooted in a sophisticated understanding of the world. By no means all those who have studied Wilson have accepted Link's interpretation, but the accessibility of materials on Wilson has undoubtedly enhanced both the quantity of historical writing on his presidency and the president's general stature in the eyes of historians.

Link's concentration upon the 28th president has perhaps been enhanced by certain parallels between the two men's careers. Both southerners, who received their high school education in that region, and went on to distinguished academic careers in the Northwest, the two were also devout Presbyterians, sons of the manse whose faith informed their entire outlook on life. Indeed, in his entry in *Who's Who in America*, Link states: "I have no thoughts on life that do not stem from my Christian faith. I believe that God created me to be a loving, caring person to do His work in the world. I also believe that He called me to my vocation of teacher and scholar." Link bears a pronounced physical resemblance to Wilson, and in later years has done his editorial work at the former President's desk. In his works published in the 1950s, Link was sometimes critical of the president – to the extent that Wilson's daughter, Margaret Wilson McAdoo, expressed serious misgivings when he was appointed editor-in-chief of her father's papers – but over time he came to take an extremely sympathetic view of Wilson. Some historians have suggested that in his later years Link identified himself so strongly with Wilson that he was unwilling to admit that his subject had any flaws, though others defend Link's impartiality.

Beside his work on Wilson, Link influenced generations of undergraduates through several textbooks, collections of readings, and short works on particular historical problems. He supervised numerous doctoral dissertations, and was known for his close attention to detail when dealing with graduate students' work. He also served on many professional committees of the National Historical Publications Commission, the Organization of American Historians, the Southern Historical Association, and the American Historical Association. He frequently received academic awards and honors, including two Bancroft prizes for different volumes of his biography of Wilson. Undoubtedly, though, he will be best remembered for his work as biographer and editor of Woodrow Wilson, which has set many of the terms of the historical debate on the 28th president.

PRISCILLA M. ROBERTS

See also United States: 20th Century

Biography
Born New Market, Virginia, 8 August 1920. Received BA, University of North Carolina, 1941, MA 1942, PhD 1945. Taught at North Carolina State College, 1943–44; Princeton University, 1945–49; and Northwestern University, 1949–60; returned to Princeton in 1960 to serve as director of the Woodrow Wilson Papers. Married Margaret McDowell Douglas, 1945 (4 children). Died Bermuda Village, North Carolina, 26 March 1998.

Principal Writings
Wilson, 5 vols., 1947–65
Woodrow Wilson and the Progressive Era, 1910–1917, 1954
Wilson the Diplomatist: A Look at His Major Foreign Policies, 1957

General editor, *The Papers of Woodrow Wilson*, 69 vols., 1966–94
The Higher Realism of Woodrow Wilson, and Other Essays, 1971
Woodrow Wilson: Revolution, War, and Peace, 1979

Further Reading
Accinelli, Robert D., "Confronting the Modern World: Woodrow Wilson and Harry S. Truman: Link's Case for Wilson the Diplomatist," *Reviews in American History* 9 (1981), 285–94
Cooper, John Milton, Jr., and Charles E. Neu, eds., *The Wilson Era: Essays in Honor of Arthur S. Link*, Arlington Heights, IL: Harlan Davidson, 1991.
Grantham, Dewey S., Foreword, in Arthur S. Link, *The Higher Realism of Woodrow Wilson, and Other Essays*, Nashville: Vanderbilt University Press, 1971
Link, Arthur S., Thomas D. Clark, Brooks D. Simpson, and John Milton Cooper, Jr., "Round Table: The Papers of Woodrow Wilson," *OAH Newsletter* (November 1993), 4–5
Smith, Daniel M., "National Interest and American Intervention, 1917: An Historiographical Appraisal," *Journal of American History* 52 (1965), 5–24
Synnott, Marcia G., "Arthur S. Link," in Clyde N. Wilson, ed., *Twentieth-Century American Historians*, Detroit: Gale, 1983 [*Dictionary of Literary Biography*, vol. 17]
Watson, Richard L., Jr, "Woodrow Wilson and His Interpreters, 1947–1957," *Mississippi Valley Historical Review* 44 (1957), 207–36

Literature and History

The topic "Literature and History" immediately raises the question of how we are to define two extremely broad terms. We shall here take "history" to mean not the past, but historians' texts dealing with the past. As for the even more amorphous term, "literature," the most obvious approach in the present context is to define it as writing that is not literally true, but is instead fictional, imaginative, creative. But this will not do: there is much fact in works of literature and much fiction in works of history (for example, every explanatory statement that a historian makes presupposes a contrary-to-fact conditional: the claim that imperialism caused World War I presupposes our imagining a fictive world in which there was no imperialism and hence no World War I). Another approach, proposed by the French critic Roland Barthes, is to focus not on the content but on the form of the text, and specifically on authorial voice. Thus Barthes claimed that whereas fictional discourse is characterized by authorial presence, in "the discourse of history" a neutral voice prevails. But as Philippe Carrard has shown, Barthes' claim is false: historians are not, in fact, absent from their texts. Moreover, Carrard, Lionel Gossman, and others have established that history is a heterogeneous field, and consequently that there is no such thing as *one* historical discourse. In short, uncertainty of definition arises on both sides of the literature/history divide.

Until the 19th century an encyclopedia entry on "Literature and History" would have been all but inconceivable. One complication is that, as Raymond Williams has noted, the concept of literature became fully developed only in that century, as a specialization of what was earlier known as rhetoric and grammar. Until the 19th century, history was generally seen as a species of the genus "rhetoric." Commentators saw no problem in the rhetoric/history relation and hence paid little attention to it. Rhetoricians, from Cicero and Quintilian in Roman antiquity to Hugh Blair in the 18th century, devoted some minor attention to the matter of style in history, but said little of theoretical interest. The general claim was that historians ought to write truthfully and for the instruction of mankind. "Truth" did not imply an obsessive concern with conformity to particular fact; on the contrary, moral edification was just as important a consideration.

But the French Revolution and its aftermath led people to think differently about their world and about the task of making sense of that world. In the wake of Leopold von Ranke (1795–1886) and his successors, the very meaning of history changed. In Ranke's view, the historian should not seek to derive moral lessons from the past, as many earlier, rhetorically-oriented historians held, but should seek only to "show" or "tell" the past *wie es eigentlich gewesen ist* – as it actually was. Furthermore, history in this new conception was a collective enterprise, aimed at a convergence of historians on a single, not yet told universal history of mankind that would reveal the meaning of historical change (see the article Universal History). In brief, the impulse of Ranke and of countless disciplinary historians after him was to remove history from the rubric of rhetoric and to classify it as, fundamentally, a scientific pursuit (as Bonnie Smith has shown, the pursuit was also defined as essentially male). Meanwhile, with the advent of what we now think of as pre-Romanticism and Romanticism, literature came to be seen in many quarters as having a special concern with the subjective and personal, a shift that tended to put it at a greater distance from history in the Rankean, disciplinary tradition, which was concerned with the public and political.

To be sure, the story is more complicated than this, since, on the one hand, many 19th-century historians (e.g., Thomas Carlyle, Jules Michelet, Jacob Burckhardt) insisted on seeing history as essentially a rhetorical, literary, or aesthetic project, while, on the other hand, many creative writers (e.g., Walter Scott, Honoré de Balzac, Emile Zola) insisted on seeing literature as historical, sociological, and even scientific. But our concern is with the history/literature relation viewed as a *problem*. It was the *Verwissenschaftlichung* (scientization) of history championed by partisans of the newly emergent historical discipline, combined with a certain subjectivization of literature, that allowed the problem to emerge. The problem was often encapsulated in the question: is history an art or a science? A minor literature canvassing the question arose: interested readers can consult excerpts on the subject from Thomas Babington Macaulay (1800–59), J. B. Bury (1861–1927), and G. M. Trevelyan (1876–1962) in Fritz Stern's collection *The Varieties of History from Voltaire to the Present* (1973), as well as H. Stuart Hughes' *History as Art and as Science* (1964). Until the 1960s, answers to the question were utterly predictable. Famously, Bury insisted that "history is a science, no less and no more." Other commentators held that it ought to be a combination of art (imagination) and science (reason). One widely held view among professional historians was that history is moving *from* literature *to* science. For example, in *Apologie pour l'histoire* (1949; *The Historian's Craft*, 1953), Marc Bloch, holding that history is a "science in its infancy," expressed the hope that it would outgrow the embryonic form

of "mere narrative," would reject "legend and rhetoric," and would become a "reasoned enterprise of analysis." Left unexamined by Bloch was the question of how such analysis was to be made interesting, intelligible, and persuasive to its presumed audience.

Historians' attempts to address the literature/history, art/science relation are interesting mainly as manifestations of the hopes and anxieties occasioned by history's scientization. On a theoretical plane, however, they are banal, as the maverick American historian Hayden White pointed out in 1966 in a controversial article, "The Burden of History." The problem first became *theoretically* interesting as a result of discussions in "historiology," or philosophy of historical writing (see the article Historiology). Much early work in historiology addressed the so-called "covering law model" (CLM) of historical explanation. By the 1960s, problems with the CLM led some theorists of history to examine the role of narrative in history. In addition, R.G. Collingwood in *The Idea of History* (1946), and some other theorists, argued that the historian *constructs* the past, a view that opened the way for some later theorists to ask what role the historian's language might play in this construction.

The three theorists who did the most to animate discussion of the literature/history relation were Hayden White and the American philosopher Louis Mink, both of whom were deeply influenced by historiological discussion, and the French literary critic Roland Barthes, who was not. An important book on the subject was White's *Metahistory* (1973). Also worthy of note are Mink's "Narrative Form as a Cognitive Instrument" (1978) and Barthes' "The Discourse of History" (1967) and "The Reality Effect" (1968) – although the Barthes essays need to be read in the light of Carrard's criticisms in his *Poetics of the New History* (1992). In "History and Literature: Reproduction or Signification" (1978), Lionel Gossman offers a valuable survey of treatments of the literature/history relation to that date. Carrard's *Poetics of the New History* is perhaps the most illuminating recent discussion. There is also a useful anthology, with many references, edited by Frank Ankersmit and Hans Kellner (1995).

An important question is why, beyond the internal dynamics of theoretical discussion, there has been something of a "return to literature" in some parts of the historical discipline since the 1970s. In *The Idea of History* Collingwood noted three points of distinction between history and fiction: 1) the historian, unlike the novelist or artist, must localize his account in time and space; 2) all history must be consistent with itself; and 3) the historical imagination has to take account of "something called evidence." As Gossman has observed, point (1) is really an aspect of point (2), since localization in time and space means localization to a single time and space determined by historians generally. Underlying the two points is the assumption that the historical world is ultimately unified (whereas there exist a multiplicity of fictional worlds). However, since Collingwood's time a great diversification in the perspectives and interests of historians has occurred.

The greater multiplicity of history's possible objects brings the discipline closer to literature than it was when disciplinary historians defined history as more or less exclusively European, male, and political. Multiplicity of object implies some multiplicity of approach. Issues of arrangement, enunciation, rhetoric, and stylistics (as discussed by Carrard and others) now begin to appear as choices made by the historian, rather than as the fully predetermined consequences of disciplinary rules. Diversification in the objects of historical interest makes history more "literary," in the sense that, with more choices in matters of presentation available to historians, a more intelligent assessment of the various options becomes necessary; and rhetoric and literary criticism offer resources for such an assessment. A further, quite unpredictable element is the possibility of a shift "from book to screen" associated with improving computer and video technology (see Lanham), which would also require a rethinking of modes of presentation.

However, the fact that literature has something to contribute to history does not mean that there is any strong possibility of a unification of history and literature into some sort of historical-literary metafield. Even a unification of history and literary *studies* is highly unlikely. The myriad differences between the conventions of the historical discipline on the one hand and the conventions of literature (as a body of texts) and of literary studies (as a way of thinking about these texts) on the other cannot be canvassed here. Instead, consider a matter that is both highly relevant and of great interest to historians, namely, evidence. Issues of evidence are only one part of the larger problem of the history/literature relation, but from the point of view of historians it is perhaps the most important part.

It seems clear that talk of the "literary" dimension of history, vague though that talk sometimes is, has to do with history's interpretive task. "Interpretation" is here taken to mean the task of making a historical account appear meaningful (significant, important) to an audience in the present – to an identity or subjectivity, whether collective or individual, that the author intends to be affected by the account (on "interpretation" in this sense, see Megill). Historians "interpret," that is, they attempt to connect their statements about the past to a present subjectivity, just as we expect literary artists to do. In this task, literature and history are in close conjunction. But another task of historiography is the evidential or justificatory one of establishing that the statements the historian makes about the past are true. In the view of most historians, history differs from literature in its adherence to standards of evidence that are sharply different from the evaluative standards that prevail in literature. It is in their evidential or justificatory aspects that history and literature, it appears, stand furthest apart.

From time to time commentators have reflected on the evidential status, for history, of literary texts or literary approaches. As noted above, Collingwood held that the historical imagination is constrained by evidence whereas the literary imagination is not. The difference persists, it seems, even when greater multiplicity brings history closer to literature in others respects. In two articles published in the late 1940s the historian William O. Aydelotte commented on the limits of literature as a historical source. Further, both Benedetto Croce in *Teoria e storia della storiografia* (1917; *History: Its Theory and Practice*, 1921) and Siegfried Kracauer in *History: The Last Things Before the Last* (1969) commented on the limits of an aesthetic *approach* to history. Croce referred to "the new erroneous form," which he called "*poetical* history," in which "*aesthetic* coherence" is allowed to substitute for "logical coherence." Kracauer referred to the "sham transitions" and the "harmonizing tendency" involved in "the aesthetic approach."

In many ways a more appropriate parallel to the work of historians is not literature but the study of literature, for literary scholars need to cite evidence for their views, just as historians do. In this respect, an interesting test case is provided by the movement in literary scholarship known as "the new historicism," associated with Stephen Greenblatt and other literary scholars, which emerged in the 1980s (two anthologies edited by H. Aram Veeser offer a sampling of their work). Characteristically, "new historicists" sought to engage in at least a partial contextualization of literary texts, usually by juxtaposing one set of literary or nonliterary texts to some other set. This project of juxtaposition was not in principle different from what disciplinary historians often do, and indeed there has been productive collaboration between new historicists and disciplinary historians (manifested in, for example, the journal *Representations*).

But there are also differences, two of which seem interesting here. First, new historicists characteristically paid more attention to works that could be seen as part of the literary canon (albeit a canon that they were eager to expand), and less attention to the almost always humdrum contents of past archives and libraries, than do historians. In other words, sharing in the axiological, or value-oriented, perspective that is prominent in literary studies, new historicists were attracted to sources that appeared to have some inherent interest or value as texts, whereas historians tend to look at sources only for the information about the past that they convey. Second, new historicists were often more "abductive" in their use of evidence than historians tend to be. That is, new historicists were more inclined to make claims that were possibly true, but that in the eyes of most historians would require a wider canvassing of sources before being raised to probability. For example, they were often willing to suggest, or at least imply, broad conclusions on the basis of some striking detail or anecdote. However, one should not overestimate these differences. The second difference, especially, is a matter of degree, for the "perhapses" and "maybes" of the past are an important aspect of historical study.

In sum, literature and literary studies seem to offer historians two things. First, they alert historians to the importance of rhetoric, style, and the literary dimension of history generally, and to the importance of making intelligent choices in these domains; they also offer an instructive repertoire of different modes of presentation. Modes of presentation are not merely decorative, but on the contrary are intimately connected to the historical enterprise, especially in its interpretive aspect. Second, literature and literary studies cultivate an awareness of aspects of human experience, particularly those related to subjectivity and to identity, that risk being missed by historians not aware of and sensitive to modern literature, and to aesthetically creative work generally. Indeed, in its recent questioning (in postcolonial criticism and elsewhere) of the very notions of subjectivity and identity, literary studies promotes a salutary skepticism concerning any simple use of history for identity-promoting purposes. Having made these points, one must also note that the changeableness of the two categories – but especially of the category "literature" – makes it hard to be definitive about the relations between them.

ALLAN MEGILL

See also Bloch; Burckhardt; Bury; Carlyle; Collingwood; Croce; Macaulay; Michelet; Ranke; Trevelyan; Universal; White, H.

Further Reading

Ankersmit, F.R., and Hans Kellner, eds., *A New Philosophy of History*, Chicago: University of Chicago Press, and London: Reaktion, 1995

Aydelotte, William O., "The England of Marx and Mill as Reflected in Fiction," *Journal of Economic History* 8 (1948), supplement: 42–58

Aydelotte, William O., "The Detective Story as a Historical Source," *Yale Review* 39 (1949), 76–95

Barthes, Roland, "The Discourse of History" (1967) and "The Reality Effect" (1968), in Barthes, *The Rustle of Language*, New York: Hill and Wang, and Oxford: Blackwell, 1986

Bloch, Marc, *Apologie pour l'histoire, ou, métier d'historien*, Paris: Colin, 1949; in English as *The Historian's Craft*, New York: Knopf, 1953, Manchester: Manchester University Press, 1954

Britain, Ian, "The Empiricist's New Clothes: Some Personal Reflections on the 'State of the Art' in Literature and History," *Critical Review* (Melbourne) 32 (1992), 174–94

Carrard, Philippe, *Poetics of the New History: French Historical Discourse from Braudel to Chartier*, Baltimore: Johns Hopkins University Press, 1992

Collingwood, R.G., *The Idea of History*, edited by T.M. Knox, Oxford: Oxford University Press, 1946, New York: Oxford University Press, 1956; revised edition, with *Lectures 1926–1928*, edited by Jan van der Dussen, Oxford: Clarendon Press, 1993, New York: Oxford University Press, 1994

Croce, Benedetto, *Teoria e storia della storiografia*, Bari: Laterza, 1917; in English as *Theory and History of Historiography*, London: Harrap, 1921, and as *History: Its Theory and Practice*, New York: Harcourt Brace, 1921

Gossman, Lionel, "History and Literature: Reproduction or Signification" (1978), in his *Between History and Literature*, Cambridge, MA: Harvard University Press, 1990

Hughes, H. Stuart, *History as Art and as Science: Twin Vistas on the Past*, New York: Harper, 1964

Kracauer, Siegfried, *History: The Last Things before the Last*, New York: Oxford University Press, 1969; reprinted 1995

Lanham, Richard A., *The Electronic Word: Democracy, Technology, and the Arts*, Chicago: University of Chicago Press, 1993

Megill, Allan, "Recounting the Past: 'Description,' Explanation, and Narrative in Historiography," *American Historical Review* 94 (1989), 627–53

Mink, Louis O., *Historical Understanding*, edited by Brian Fay, Eugene O. Golob, and Richard T. Vann, Ithaca, NY: Cornell University Press, 1987

Nadel, George H., "Philosophy of History before Historicism," *History and Theory* 3 (1963), 291–315

Representations, Berkeley: University of California Press, 1983–

Smith, Bonnie G., "Gender and the Practices of Scientific History: The Seminar and Archival Research in the Nineteenth Century," *American Historical Review* 100 (1995), 1150–76

Stern, Fritz, ed., *The Varieties of History from Voltaire to the Present*, 2nd edition, New York: Random House, 1973

Unger, Rudolf, "The Problem of Historical Objectivity: A Sketch of Its Development to the Time of Hegel" (1923), *History and Theory*, *Beiheft* 11 (1971), 60–68

Veeser, H. Aram, ed., *The New Historicism*, New York: Routledge, 1989

Veeser, H. Aram, ed., *The New Historicism Reader*, New York: Routledge, 1994

White, Hayden V., "The Burden of History," *History and Theory* 5 (1966), 111–34; reprinted in White, *Tropics of Discourse: Essays in Cultural Criticism*, Baltimore: Johns Hopkins University Press, 1978

White, Hayden V., *Metahistory: The Historical Imagination in Nineteenth-Century Europe*, Baltimore: Johns Hopkins University Press, 1973

White, Hayden V., "The Historical Text as Literary Artifact," *Clio* 3 (1974), 277–303; reprinted in Robert H. Canary and Henry Kozicki, eds., *The Writing of History: Literary Form and Historical Understanding*, Madison: University of Wisconsin Press, 1978

Williams, Raymond, *Marxism and Literature*, Oxford and New York: Oxford University Press, 1977

Litwack, Leon F. 1929–

US historian of African American and labor history

A widely respected authority on 19th-century African American history, Leon Litwack reached intellectual maturity as a historian during the turbulent period of change ushered in by the black civil rights movement in the United States from 1955 to 1968. Like other historians of his generation, Litwack was inspired to research into the history of race relations in America, but with a more critical, radical perspective than had been displayed in most existing studies.

This approach was reflected in his first major work, *North of Slavery* (1961). Examining northern white attitudes towards African Americans during the antebellum period, Litwack demonstrated that racial intolerance was not an exclusively southern problem. *North of Slavery* was a key work in highlighting the political, legal, and social injustices suffered by free blacks in the northern states before the Civil War.

Litwack's research has been guided by a belief in the need to study history from the "bottom up" – to focus on the historical experience of poor and oppressed groups in society rather than the political and socioeconomic elites. This commitment was evident in his next significant publication, *The American Labor Movement* (1962), a collection of edited primary sources on the struggle for trade union recognition in 19th- and 20th-century America.

However, Litwack's main area of work continued to be the study of 19th-century African American history, specifically the black experience in the South during the Reconstruction era, 1865–77, that followed the American Civil War. In this research Litwack was guided and influenced by his colleague and mentor Kenneth M. Stampp, with whom he jointly edited a collection of essays, *Reconstruction* (1969).

By the 1950s changing racial attitudes in America had led some revisionist historians, such as Stampp and John Hope Franklin, to engage in a fundamental reappraisal of existing standard accounts on the Civil War and Reconstruction. These earlier works, many published in the first years of the 20th century, by historians such as William A. Dunning and James Ford Rhodes, were now seen to be seriously marred by their racial conservatism. Dunning, and scholars influenced by him, had viewed Reconstruction as a decade when the southern states had been subjected to a period of wholesale corruption, financial mismanagement and abuse, at the hands of northern "Carpetbagger" politicians, their renegade southern white allies, the "Scalawags," and newly enfranchised but ignorant ex-slaves. Stampp and other revisionists challenged this interpretation.

They showed conservative critiques to be exaggerated, and pointed to the positive achievements of Reconstruction, for example the introduction of state public education systems in the South.

Building on the work of Stampp, Litwack's own research culminated in *Been in the Storm So Long* (1979), his single most important publication, for which he was awarded the Pulitzer prize in history. *Been in the Storm So Long* confirmed Litwack's individual reputation as a writer on Reconstruction. It also marked him out as one of the leading influences of the newly emerging historiographical school of radical revisionism or post-revisionism.

Post-revisionists, such as Litwack and Eric Foner, went further than previous revisionist writers, dismissing as all but irrelevant the now badly dated accounts of Dunning and others. Concentrating on the experiences of African Americans, rather than southern whites, *Been in the Storm So Long*, like other post-revisionist works, tended to criticize Republican politicians during Reconstruction for being insufficiently radical in advancing the interests of southern blacks. Attention was paid to the failure to provide effective means for emancipated slaves to achieve landownership, and to the inability of politicians to bring about any widespread redistribution of socio-economic power in the South after the Civil War.

Although sometimes criticized for not taking full account of the deeply laissez-faire values of 19th-century America, post-revisionism has emerged as the new dominant school in Reconstruction historiography.

KEVERN J. VERNEY

See also African American

Biography

Leon Frank Litwack. Born Santa Barbara, California, 2 December 1929. Received BA, University of California, 1951, MA 1952, PhD 1958. Taught at University of Wisconsin, Madison, 1958–65; University of California, Berkeley (rising to professor), from 1965. Married Rhoda Lee Goldberg, 1952 (2 children).

Principal Writings

North of Slavery: The Negro in the Free States, 1790–1860, 1961
Editor, *The American Labor Movement*, 1962
Editor with Kenneth M. Stampp, *Reconstruction: An Anthology of Revisionist Writings*, 1969
Been in the Storm So Long: The Aftermath of Slavery, 1979

Liu Zhiji [Liu Chih-chi] 661–721
Chinese historian

Based upon his creation of one of the first works in Chinese historical criticism, Liu Zhiji has been lauded by some as the one of the few true historians produced by China before the modern period. At the same time, others have argued that his understanding of historical method was not accompanied by an equal ability to draw meaning from history. The difference of opinion stems from Liu's relationship with traditional Chinese historiography as practiced up to his lifetime and, with little alteration, after his death. Liu lived during a crucial juncture in the writing of Chinese history. During the early years of the Tang dynasty, a state-sponsored Bureau of Historiography was established, recognizing history as a discipline separate from literary writing, while maintaining state control over the production of the historical record.

In 705 Liu was called upon to serve as one of the historians working on the official record of the reign of the recently deceased empress Wu. The task was politically charged, since the empress had usurped the throne, and although she was gone, many of those who had supported her, or at least acquiesced to her actions, were still alive. For Liu this context underscored many of his criticisms of official historiography. In general, Chinese official historiography has been characterized as strongly didactic. The role of the historian was to dole out praise and blame, in order to give readers models of action. The political climate during Liu's period in office created an atmosphere in which such moralizing statements could be dangerous, especially since the late empress's nephew oversaw Liu's official work. Liu found this unacceptable and resigned in 708. In 710 he completed his *magnum opus*, *Shitong* (Study of Historiography).

Shitong can arguably be considered the first work of historical criticism in China. Twitchett has gone so far to call it "the most important single book on the craft of the historian in Chinese." Liu discussed the history of Chinese historiography, its strengths and weaknesses, and provided examples from previous texts. He was particularly adamant about independent, individual scholars writing objective history. Objectivity was to be based on proper selection and presentation of evidence, stressing the need for honesty and truth in forming the record.

Liu recognized two sources for writing history: documents (or "records of words") and records of events. Liu argued that greater trust could be put into documentary history, since the historian had the words in front of him; whereas records of events could never capture the full story. Furthermore, if one did not know the author recording the event, Liu questioned whether the record itself could be fully understood. In particular, he was wary of accounts that tried to rewrite history in order to please the powerful by creating images of imperial courts brimming with totally moral or totally immoral figures, depending on the historian's audience. Liu also objected to ascribing events to supernatural rather than to human causes. This is a particularly important point, because writing history is also critiquing past human action. His penchant for accurate accounts even led Liu to question passages in the hitherto sacrosanct classical historical records. His chapters in *Shitong* entitled "Yigu" (Suspicions about the Past) and "Huo jing" (Doubting the Classics) drew strong disapproval from later readers, since Liu cast doubts upon classical events based either on conflicting reports, or on his sense of plausibility.

In sum, Liu Zhiji was the first historian in China to create a guide focusing on the craft of historical writing. As such, *Shitong* presents the reader with the means to write history, but not the means to analyze it. Liu maintained the centrality of history as a moral record, but demanded accuracy in compiling it.

ROBERT WALLACE FOSTER

See also China: Historical Writing, Early and Middle

Biography

Born Pencheng, Xuzhou in the Tang, now Xuzhou, 661. Arrived Changan, 669; passed civil service exam, 680, and received *jin-shi* degree. Provincial civil servant, then returned to Changan, 699; appointed to staff of history office, 701, resigned 708. Died Anzhou, now Anlu, Hubei, 721.

Principal Writings

Shitong (Study of Historiography), 710

Further Reading

Byongik Koh, "Zur Werttheorie in der chinesischen Historiographie auf Grund der Shih-t'ung des Liu Chih-chi (661–721)" (Toward a Value-Theory in Chinese Historiography, Based on Liu Zhiji's *Study of Historiography*), *Oriens Extremus* 4 (1957), 5–51, 125–81

Fu Zhenlun, *Liu Zhiji nianpu* (Chronological Biography of Liu Zhiji), Beijing, 1963

Gagnon, Guy, *Concordance combinée du Shitong et du Shitong xiaofan* (Combined Concordance of *Study of Historiography* and the *Revised Study of Historiography*), 2 vols., Paris: Maisonneuve, 1977

Hung, William, "A T'ang Historiographer's Letter of Resignation," *Harvard Journal of Asiatic Studies* 29 (1969), 5–52

Masui, Tsuneo, "Liu Chih-chi and the *Shih-t'ung*," *Memoirs of the Toyo Bunko* 34 (1976), 113–62

Qilong, Fu, *Shitong tongshi* (A Comprehensive Explanation of the *Study of Historiography*), Taibei: Yiwen yinshu guan, 1978

Pulleyblank, E.G., "Chinese Historical Criticism: Liu Chih-chi and Ssu-ma Kuang," in William G. Beasley and Edwin G. Pulleyblank, eds., *Historians of China and Japan*, London: Oxford University Press, 1961

Twitchett, Denis, *The Writing of Official History under the T'ang*. Cambridge and New York: Cambridge University Press, 1992

Yin Da, ed., *Zhongguo shixue fazhanshi* (History of the Development of Chinese Historiography), Henan, China, 1985

Livy 59 BCE–*c*.17 CE
Roman historian

Livy is considered the foremost Latin historian, approached only by Sallust and Tacitus. He is the author of *Ab urbe condita* (From the Founding of the City or *The History*). The scope of *The History* was vast. Composed of 142 ancient books or scrolls equal to some 25 modern books of approximately 300 pages each, Livy's *History* told Rome's story. It is reckoned he produced the equivalent of about 900 modern pages per year. The enormity of Livy's project alone made him a celebrity in the ancient world. The *History* began with the founding of Rome in 753 BCE continuing to 9 BCE and the death of Drusus the Elder, son of Livia, Augustus's wife, and brother of Tiberius the future emperor. The last portion of the work on the reign of Augustus avoided controversy and may not have been published in the emperor's lifetime. Only 35 books survive, covering the period 753–243 and 210–167. The other 107 books are lost or survive only in fragments, extracts, or epitomes. In the 16th century rumors circulated that a complete copy of Livy existed, but the rumors were never proven.

Livy used the traditional theme of the decline of Rome. This decline was usually ascribed by the historian Sallust and most educated Romans to the loss of virtues in Roman life such as propriety, courage, self-restraint, discipline, frugality, and respect for authority. While Sallust had ascribed this change in morality to Rome's lack of an external enemy, after the destruction of Carthage, Livy also saw the influence of Eastern cultures as changing the nature of Roman morality. In agreement with Augustus and the giants of the Augustan literary world, Livy saw not the end of Rome but the end of Old Rome in history. New Rome would continue the promise of Eternal Rome as found in Virgil's epic *The Aeneid*. Livy and Virgil both reflect the Augustan age and it moral seriousness. Although he was influenced by the Augustan spirit, Livy should not be taken to be a court historian. His work was not done for the court of Augustus.

Like Virgil, Livy gave public readings from his *History*, although the work was never meant to be taken as a prose poem. Critics who have faulted Livy as a bad poet seem to be missing the point. His popularity in the ancient world attests to the entertaining nature of his work, but his ability to dramatize events and characters should not be seen as a lack of concern for accuracy. He claimed to be aiming for a style between the informality of conversation and the formality of writing. Therefore, Livy abandoned Sallust's pointed abruptness in favor of a rhetorical Ciceronian rotundity. He structured his stories dramatically and probed his characters whom he portrayed not as representives of partisan politics but as individuals. Bringing the emotional conflicts and desperations of historical figures to his readers, Livy had the ability to recreate atmosphere and convey the feelings of those involved in stirring events.

Livy believed that a lively narrative of Roman history would rekindle Roman patriotism. Having drawn his material from a wide range of sources, his personal moralizing holds together his *History*. Quintilian said that in Livy's inclination to dramatize stories he wished to emphasize and abbreviate to abruptness matters of lesser concern in order to produce a "milky richness." Through dramatic writing he drew attention to certain characters, and was a great influence on Tacitus.

Livy devoted himself to his *History* in his youth. He moved to Rome after the Battle of Actium in 27 BCE to be near his sources. Livy was never a Roman official or priest. He never served in the military nor does it seem that he ever traveled. This lack of experience contributed to errors within his work and bookish naivety about the functioning of Roman institutions.

Some modern critics have seen Livy as a compiler rather than a composer of history. There is internal evidence that Livy did compare sources and noted that the credibility of one source over another is sometimes impossible to discern. He admitted that much of what had been passed down to the Romans as their history before the Second Punic War was probably legend not fact. Still, critics have accused him of being a novelist rather than a historian.

The scientific methods of modern historians were not known to Livy. The process of writing a history of Rome in Livy's time was much less complex than today when literary sources are scrutinized with archaeologic, numismatic, and other sources. The physical process of rolling, unrolling, and comparing passages in the scrolls that contained Livy's sources must have presented a different sort of complexity over the many years of labor on the *History*. Livy's popularity among his contemporaries in Augustan Rome should tell us that his work offered something more than they could expect to glean from reading various histories for themselves. For later readers Livy is the only historian in whose work we can find how Romans evaluated their own history.

Critics of Livy's *History* should bear in mind the author's philosophy of history: "What chiefly makes the study of history wholesome and profitable is this, that in history you have a record of the infinite variety of human experience plainly set out for all to see, and in that record you can find for yourself and your country both examples and warnings."

NANCY PIPPEN ECKERMAN

See also Dionysius; Machiavelli; Niebuhr; Roman; Sallust

Biography
Titus Livius. Born Patavium [now Padua, Italy], 59 BCE, to a prominent but not aristocratic family which probably suffered during the civil wars of the 40s. Moved to Rome, where from about 27 he began writing his *History*, which seems to have been his sole occupation throughout his adult life; literary adviser to the future emperor Claudius. Had a daughter and a son. Died Patavium, *c*.17 CE.

Principal Works
Ab urbe condita (From the Founding of the City), 31 BCE–*c*.17 BCE
Works (Loeb edition), translated by B.O. Foster, F.G. Moore, E.T. Sage, and A.C. Schlesinger, 14 vols., 1919–59

Further Reading
Breisach, Ernst, *Historiography: Ancient, Medieval, and Modern*, Chicago: University of Chicago Press, 1983; revised 1994
Dorey, Thomas Alan, ed., *Latin Historians*, New York: Basic Books, and London: Routledge, 1966
Dorey, Thomas Alan, ed., *Livy*, London: Routledge, 1971
Grant, Michael, ed., *Readings in the Classical Historians*, New York: Scribner, and London: Maxwell Macmillan, 1992
Laistner, Max Ludwig Wolfram, *The Greater Roman Historians*, Berkeley: University of California Press, 1947
Lipovsky, James P., "Livy" in T. James Luce, ed., *Ancient Writers: Greece and Rome*, 2 vols., New York: Scribner, 1982
Luce, T. James, *Livy: The Composition of His Histories*, Princeton: Princeton University Press, 1977
Miles, Gary B., *Livy: Reconstructing Early Rome*, Ithaca, NY: Cornell University Press, 1995
Ogilivie, Robert M., *A Commentary on Livy, Books 1–5*, Oxford: Clarendon Press, 1965
Walsh, P.G., "The Negligent Historian: 'Howlers' in Livy," *Greece and Rome* new series 5 (1958), 83–88
Walsh, P.G., *Livy: His Historical Aims and Methods*, Cambridge: Cambridge University Press, 1961

Local History

Local history most often describes a range of historical writings focusing on specific, geographically small areas, frequently produced by non-professional historians for a non-academic audience. Yet, since the advent of the "new social history" in the 1960s and 1970s, professional historians – increasingly specialized – have also conducted intensive studies on urban neighborhoods and rural villages in an attempt to reveal the "undersides" of history. Although this has resulted in a great deal of in-depth information about certain areas, it has usually not been classified as "local history." Thus, the term "local history" continues to be associated, unfairly or not, with antiquarianism and amateur historians.

The first systematic local studies were undertaken in the 18th and early 19th centuries by talented local elites, particularly in Britain, France, and the United States. In England, the creation of survey maps showing local areas in great detail, helped spur the process on. Influenced by the ideals of the Enlightenment, many amateur scholars developed a distinctly scientific bent. In a process described by Peter Burke as "the discovery of the people," these individuals, including, for example, Thomas Jefferson, conducted archaeological digs, studied local flora and fauna, recorded regional folklore and customs, and surveyed the local past. Despite the fact that amateur archaeological digs, in particular, caused severe problems for later scholars, such work revealed a wealth of information.

The United States experienced a boom in the creation of local studies during the late 19th century. Usually commissioned by native-born local elites with a view toward enshrining their social status, these local histories combined a narrative of the founding of a particular region, lists of early local political officials, and short biographies of area leaders. These studies were undertaken consciously to promote the locale as a matter of civic pride. Thus, the process of writing local history often began while the area was still being settled, and state and county historical societies were formed quite early on. In Minnesota, for example, the state historical society came into being before the state was incorporated. Many counties boasted large, multivolume histories within half a century of their founding. Although such works have proved of somewhat limited value for later scholars, they are storehouses of detailed factual information.

Since World War II there has been a increasing interest in local history by professional historians. Part of this results from simply having more historians, in the United States and Western Europe as well as in traditionally understudied areas such as Eastern and Central Europe. Part also results from the influence of new methodologies such as the Annales school in France. Local history has found especially fertile ground in France, with the work of historians such as Guy Thuillier, whose work has in turn influenced such prominent scholars as Eugen Weber.

In the United States local history was encouraged by the celebration of the national bicentennial in 1976, as well as by increasing interest in genealogy in a nation long the victim of poor history teaching in primary and secondary schools. Most local histories remain largely exercises in antiquarianism, but with greater emphasis on ethnicity, women, religion, crime, and other previously ignored topics. New approaches to local and regional history are in evidence, with the work of scholars such as Joseph Amato, who has used the approach of the Annales school in the American Midwest, as well as in the greater professionalization in state and local historical societies. Although professionalization and the interest of the new social historians has provided a cure for excessive antiquarianism, it is still unclear whether such historians will retain the interest of non-academics who have long been the primary audience for local history.

JOHN RADZILOWSKI

See also Burke; Le Roy Ladurie

Further Reading

Amato, Joseph A., *Servants of the Land: God, Family, and Farm: A Trinity of Belgian Economic Folkways in Southwestern Minnesota*, Marshall, MN: Crossings Press, 1990

Amato, Joseph A., *The Great Jerusalem Artichoke Circus: The Buying and Selling of the Rural American Dream*, Minneapolis: University of Minnesota Press, 1993

Amato, Joseph A., "Guy Thuillier: 'Paris Will Save Nothing,'" *Journal of Social History* 27 (1993), 375–80

Burke, Peter, *Popular Culture in Early Modern Europe*, London: Temple Smith, and New York: New York University Press, 1978

Kostash, Myrna, *All of Baba's Children*, Edmonton: Hurtig, 1977

Le Roy Ladurie, Emmanuel, *Montaillou, village occitan de 1294 à 1324*, Paris: Gallimard, 1975; in English as *Montaillou: The Promised Land of Error*, New York: Braziller, 1978, and as *Montaillou: Cathars and Catholics in a French Village, 1294–1324*, London: Scolar Press, 1978

Thuillier, Guy, *Les Ecoles historiques* (Schools of History), Paris: Presses Universitaires de France, 1990

Thuillier, Guy, and Jean Tulard, *Le Métier d'historien* (The Historian's Profession), Paris: Presses Universitaires de France, 1991

Thuillier, Guy, and Jean Tulard, *Histoire locale et régionale* (Local and Regional History), Paris: Presses Universitaires de France, 1992

Lopez, Robert S. 1910–1986

Italian medieval economic historian

Roberto Lopez began his career as an archivally-based specialist on the late medieval economic history of his native Genoa, publishing three monographs and over three times as many articles on that subject between 1933 and 1938. Even as a "local" historian, Lopez was required to range from the Sea of Azov to the Straits of Gibraltar, from Flanders to Egypt, for "the history of Genoa was made more from without than from within; her inhabitants lived, struggled, distinguished themselves more outside the walls." Thus, along with narratives of Genoese merchants, the young Lopez produced a thoroughly documented picture of the interconnected workings of the late medieval Mediterranean and beyond. Lopez's ability to combine methodological rigor with a broad view of the Mediterranean world enabled him to distinguish himself, like his predecessors, far outside the walls of his native town. Like many other Jewish medievalists, Lopez emigrated to the United States where he helped to transform US medieval historiography. More than any of his fellow exiles, Lopez was himself influenced by US academic structures. He turned his attention to the general economic history of Europe; his shift to the early Middle Ages and to the evidence of printed sources and of coinage enabled him to keep working despite reduced access to archives.

Lopez was, in effect, a historian of the relations among Europeans, Asians, and Africans, seen particularly from an economic perspective. Such issues had been of special interest in Italy during the 1930s (when the fascist government sought historical precedents for more recent activities) and continued to preoccupy European and North American analysts throughout the widespread decolonization movements of succeeding decades. Despite the clear political importance, during the 1940s, 1950s, and 1960s, of global economic relations, Lopez was almost alone among medievalists in pursuing continuous active research in the field; in his final synthetic work, *The Commercial Revolution of the Middle Ages* (1971), Lopez situated his research within the "Development Paradigm" (now under attack as a "Eurocentric Masterplot") which has in fact determined relations with the "Third World" for decades. Furthermore, throughout the early Cold War, which pitted against one another communist and capitalist visions of the ideal economy, Lopez was the leading US specialist on European economic growth and commercial development along capitalist lines, the origins of which he traced to the Italian Middle Ages, that "outstanding anticipation of the European future." Lopez became one of the most eminent US medievalists of the 20th century, and attracted large numbers of graduate students.

Beginning in 1942 with "Byzantine Law in the Seventh Century and its Reception by the Germans and the Arabs," Lopez produced a string of classic articles. By taking a bird's-eye view, he was able to demonstrate the equivalent of biology's "Butterfly Effect," wherein a butterfly beating its wings on one side of the globe eventually influences events on the other side. One of his most famous works, "Mohammed and Charlemagne: A Revision" (1943), constituted a specific refutation of the work of the still-influential Belgian historian, Henri Pirenne, and his vision of an isolated medieval West. For Lopez, when the use of gold coinage declined – not disappeared – in Latin Europe in the early Middle Ages, it was a result of Byzantine legal policies concerning state monopolies and of Carolingian political decisions, not of simple isolation and economic depression; when the importation of papyrus ceased in Latin Europe in the 10th century, it was a result of specific Caliphal industrial developments and monopolistic trade policies, not of the general absence of trade contacts between Europe and the rest of Eurasia. In another essential work, "Settecento anni fa: il ritorno all'oro nell'occidente duecentesco" (1953; "Back to Gold," 1956), Lopez focused on the continuous circulation of gold coins, of Byzantine or Islamic manufacture, in the complex economy of medieval Europe and (again in opposition to Pirenne and the French medievalist Marc Bloch) ascribed the mid-13th-century striking of gold currency by Genoa and Florence to a complex series of largely political motivations and to changes in the African gold and European silver industries, rather than to some simple and sudden return to prosperity in Europe after centuries of depression. Another essential article, published in the same year ("An Aristocracy of Money in the Early Middle Ages," 1953), posed an equally stunning challenge to the Francophone-influenced vision of medieval Europe which has nevertheless tended to dominate Anglophone scholarship. Lopez demonstrated once more – with characteristically exhaustive documentation – the continuous, sophisticated innovations of medieval economic actors, analyzing "a bourgeois aristocracy founded on money at a time when the survival of money and of the bourgeoisie has been doubted."

Lopez did much to create, during the 1940s and 1950s, the new fields of social and economic history. He asserted in 1971 that "the main achievement of [his] generation has been to shift the emphasis from prominent individuals to ordinary people, and from a small number to entire collectivities." He was among the first to exploit the numerous contracts and other commercial documents preserved in Italian archives, many of which have since been used (including by his own students) to illuminate the lives of ordinary women and men. In 1955, at the height of his path-breaking career, he produced a sourcebook (*Medieval Trade in the Mediterranean World* – still in print) so that students, normally shown a world of cathedrals and castles, could be introduced to medieval Italian business, a "gift of that gifted nation to the modern world . . . the prototype of the modern commercial economy."

FELICE LIFSHITZ

See also Cipolla; Italy: Renaissance

Biography
Roberto Sabatini Lopez. Born Genoa, Italy, 8 October 1910. Received DLitt, University of Milan, 1932; PhD, University of Wisconsin, 1952. Taught at teachers colleges in Cagliari, Pavia, and Genoa, 1933–36; University of Genoa, 1936–38; emigrated to US, 1938; research assistant, University of Wisconsin, 1939–42. Script editor, Italian section, Office of War Information, 1942–43; foreign news editor, CBS, 1944–45. Taught at Brooklyn College, 1943–44; Columbia University, 1945–46; and (rising to professor), Yale University, 1946–81 (emeritus). Married Claudia Kirschen, 1946 (2 sons). Died New Haven, 6 July 1986.

Principal Writings
Storia delle colonie genovesi nel Mediterraneo (History of Genoese Colonies in the Mediterranean), 1938
"Byzantine Law in the Seventh Century and Its Reception by the Germans and Arabs," *Byzantion* 16 (1942–43), 445–61
"European Merchants in the Medieval Indies: The Evidence of Commercial Documents," *Journal of Economic History* 3 (1943), 164–84
"Mohammed and Charlemagne: A Revision," *Speculum* 18 (1943), 14–38
"Silk Industry in the Byzantine Empire," *Speculum* 20 (1945), 1–42
"The Dollar of the Middle Ages," *Journal of Economic History* 11 (1951), 209–34
"Still Another Renaissance?" *American Historical Review* 57 (1951–52), 1–21
"An Aristocracy of Money in the Early Middle Ages," *Speculum* 28 (1953), 1–43
"Settecento anni fa: il ritorno all'oro nell'occidente duecentesco" (700 Years Ago: The Return of Gold in the 13th-Century West) *Rivista storica Italiana* 65 (1953), 19–55 and 161–98; partially summarized and simplified in "Back to Gold, 1252," *Economic History Review* 2nd series, 9 (1956), 219–40
"La città dell'Europa post-carolingia: il commercio dell'Europa post-carolingia" (The City in Post-Carolingian Europe) *Settimane di studio del centro italiano di studi sull'alto medioevo* 2 (1955), 547–99
"East and West in the Early Middle Ages: Economic Relations," *Relazioni del X Congresso internazionale di scienze storiche*, Roma 1955, vol. 3, 1955
With Irving W. Raymond, *Medieval Trade in the Mediterranean World: Illustrative Documents Translated*, 1955
"The Evolution of Land Transport in the Middle Ages," *Past and Present* 9 (1956), 17–29
"Il medioevo negli Stati Uniti" (The Middle Ages in the United States), *Studi medievali* 3 (1962), 677–82
Naissance de l'Europe, 1962; in English as *The Birth of Europe*, 1967
The Three Ages of the Italian Renaissance, 1970
The Commercial Revolution of the Middle Ages, 950–1350, 1971
"Medieval and Renaissance Economy and Society," in Norman F. Cantor, ed., *Perspectives on the European Past: Conversations with Historians*, 1971

Byzantium and the World Around It: Economic and Institutional Relations, 1978 [collected essays]
The Shape of Medieval Monetary History, 1986 [collected essays]

Further Reading
Miskimin, Harry A., David Herlihy, and A.L. Udovitch, eds., *The Medieval City*, New Haven: Yale University Press, 1977 [includes bibliography]

Lovejoy, Arthur O. 1873–1962
US philosopher and historian of ideas

Few individuals can be said to have created a discipline, but Arthur O. Lovejoy, on top of his considerable influence as an important early 20th-century American epistemologist, was the virtual father of the history of ideas. He is responsible for the reinvigoration of the practice of intellectual history in the United States, significant not only for his extensive and influential writings, but also for his establishment in 1940 of perhaps what is the dominant journal in intellectual history, the *Journal of the History of Ideas*. Additionally, Lovejoy is notable for his role in promoting scientific standards to foster the development of philosophy as an American academic profession through his participation in the American Philosophical Society. He played a pivotal role, as well, in the establishment of the Association of American University Professors.

Born in Berlin, Lovejoy went on to study at Berkeley and then Harvard before teaching at a number of American universities. Most of his academic career was spent at Johns Hopkins University where he retired in 1938. His early career was dominated by the writing of articles, mostly of a philosophical nature, where his work took a critical realist position against pragmatism, absolute idealism in the work of thinkers such as Josiah Royce, and against what Lovejoy perceived to be "anti-intellectualism" not only in philosophy, but generally within western intellectual life. His major philosophical work was *The Revolt Against Dualism* (1930), a philosophical defense of dualism against monist forms of epistemology.

Lovejoy's philosophical position was to be the foundation of his view of intellectual history. His earliest work in history was in religious thought and it was there that he began to formulate his notion of "unit-ideas," that is, ideas that have continued over time, manifesting themselves in a variety of guises and espoused by major and minor thinkers alike. The study of these unit-ideas focused on considerations of their presence in the tacitly held assumptions of a particular time or group. Critical in this endeavor is a consideration of etymology and morphology, the meaning of words in these ideas, and the recurrent use of certain terms or phrases over time. The clearest exposition of Lovejoy's purpose and methodology can be seen in his preface to *Essays in the History of Ideas* (1948) and demonstrated in his most celebrated work, *The Great Chain of Being* (1936).

The Great Chain of Being traced the history of the doctrine of plenitude in western thought from Plato's *Timaeus* to its decline in the late 18th and early 19th centuries. The doctrine of plenitude had led to the idea of a "Great Chain of Being" linking all forms of being in a single chain from highest to lowest. In the modern period evolutionary ideas effectively replaced this idea as the dominant explanation of diversity, gradations of being, and continuity. Nevertheless, throughout its history this unit-idea manifested itself in all western conceptions of being as the organizing assumption on which religious, metaphysical, and ethical ideas were based.

Lovejoy's scholarly interests were wide-ranging and included important work on romanticism, religion, ethics, and naturalism. He was greatly interested in primitivism, and with George Boas embarked on a multivolume project to produce a documentary history of it even though only one volume was to be realized. Lovejoy was a noted defender of academic freedom and helped write the American Association of University Professors' statements on it in the 1910s. While his work on epistemology has been largely eclipsed, the history of ideas has sustained itself as a discipline even while it has been increasingly challenged by the history of discourses as well as by alternative approaches to intellectual history.

SEÁN FARRELL MORAN

See also Curti; Gilbert; Intellectual; Miller; Science; Skinner

Biography

Arthur Oncken Lovejoy. Born Berlin, 10 October 1873, where his American father was studying medicine. After his mother's death from an accidental drug overdose, his father became a clergyman. Graduated from Germantown Academy, 1891; studied philosophy with George Holmes Howison, University of California, Berkeley, BA 1895; then with Josiah Royce and William James, Harvard University, MA 1897; studied comparative religions, the Sorbonne, 1898–99. Taught philosophy at Stanford University, 1899–1901: resigned over issues of academic freedom; Washington University, St. Louis, 1901–07; Columbia University, 1907–08; University of Missouri, 1908–10; and Johns Hopkins University, 1910–38. Died Baltimore, 30 December 1962.

Principal Writings

"Reflections of a Temporalist on the New Realism," *Journal of Philosophy* 8 (1911), 589–99

"Some Antecedents of the Philosophy of Bergson," *Mind* 22 (1913), 465–83

"On Some Conditions of Progress in Philosophical Inquiry," *Philosophical Review* 26 (1917), 123–63

"The Paradox of the Thinking Behaviorist," *Philosophical Review* 31 (1922), 135–47

The Revolt Against Dualism: An Inquiry into the Existence of Ideas, 1930

Editor with Gilbert Chinaud, George Boas, and Ronald S. Crane, *Documentary History of Primitivism and Related Ideas*, 1935

Editor with George Boas, *Primitivism and Related Ideas in Antiquity*, 1935

The Great Chain of Being: A Study of the History of an Idea, 1936

Essays in the History of Ideas, 1948

The Reason, the Understanding, and Time, 1961

Reflections on Human Nature, 1961

The Thirteen Pragmatisms, and Other Essays, 1963

Further Reading

Boas, George, "A.O. Lovejoy as Historian of Philosophy," *Journal of the History of Ideas*, 9 (1948), 404–11

Kelley, Donald R., "Historians of Intellectual History: Retrospect, Circumspect, Prospect," *Journal of the History of Ideas* 48 (1987), 143–70

Mahoney, Edward P., "Lovejoy and the Hierarchy of Being," *Journal of the History of Education* 48 (1987), 211–31

Mandelbaum, Maurice, "Arthur O. Lovejoy and the Theory of Historiography," *Journal of the History of Ideas* 9 (1948), 412–23

Murphy, Arthur, "Mr. Lovejoy's Counter-Revolution," *Journal of Philosophy* 28 (1931), 29–42, 57–71

Oakley, Francis, "Lovejoy's Unexplored Option," *Journal of the History of Ideas* 48 (1987), 231–47

Taylor, Harold A., "Further Reflections on the History of Ideas: An Examination of A.O. Lovejoy's Program," *Journal of Philosophy* 40 (1943), 281–99

Wiener, Philip, "Lovejoy's Role in American Philosophy," in *Studies in Intellectual History*, Baltimore: Johns Hopkins Press, 1953

Wilson, Daniel J., *Arthur O. Lovejoy and the Quest for Intelligibility*, Chapel Hill: University of North Carolina Press, 1980

Wilson, Daniel J., *Arthur O. Lovejoy: An Annotated Bibliography*, New York: Garland, 1982

Wilson, Daniel J., "Lovejoy's Great Chain of Being after Fifty Years," *Journal of the History of Ideas* 48 (1987), 187–207

Lovejoy, Paul E. 1943–
US historian of Africa

Paul E. Lovejoy perceives himself not as an Africanist historian but rather as a social and economic historian who studies African topics. He rejects any schema that treats African history as a sub-discipline, seeing it rather, as part of mainstream history which uses the same methodology and theories as other aspects of history.

Lovejoy has focused on the colonial context of West African history, concentrating on northern Nigerian history, as well as on the impact of the slave trade. He has produced outstanding works discussing the internal consequences of the slave trade, its abolition, and overseas repercussions. In "Revolutionary Mahdism and Resistance to Colonial Rule in the Sokoto Caliphate, 1905–06" (1990), he examined the connection between Mahdism and the colonial conquest. Fierce Mahdist resistance met the spread of British rule in northern Nigeria and, as Lovejoy argued, can only be understood in context. This careful attention to context that has marked all of Lovejoy's work. His studies of slavery, for example, reveal his meticulous attention to detail. In his 1989 review of the literature on the Atlantic slave trade, he argued that not only did Africa suffer an enormous net loss of population, but also that there was a significant increase in the enslaved population within Africa itself. Thus Lovejoy rejected earlier notions that downplayed the amount of indigenous slavery within Africa, and contended that the amount of slavery within West Africa was proportionately higher than in the Americas.

In *Slow Death for Slavery* (1993) Lovejoy traced the abolition of slavery in one significant area of West Africa, among the Hausa-Fulani emirates. Large internal raids were carried out by the Fulani and the elimination of slavery among these people was difficult and long-drawn-out. As the Fulani emir and slaver Ngawase was reputed to have said, "I can no more give up slaving than a cat can give up mousing. I shall die with a slave in my mouth!" Furthermore, in his 1995 article on British abolition, Lovejoy suggested that long-held views regarding the drop in slave prices in Africa after Britain's 1807 abolition of the slave trade along the Atlantic coast of Africa were incorrect. Careful and detailed analysis of prices before and after abolition demonstrate that rather than dropping, the prices had, in fact, increased.

This careful attention to detail and willingness to go against accepted and popular wisdom marks Lovejoy's writings. He often embraces unpopular positions, risking attack from those who would use history as a means of ethnic cheerleading to counter past distortions. Lovejoy has clung to a more old-fashioned perspective that holds to empirical evidence and to the possibility of good and evil in all peoples. His use of economic records is impeccable and has proved useful in bringing rationality back into many debates on the slave trade.

FRANK A. SALAMONE

See also Africa: West

Biography

Paul Ellsworth Lovejoy. Born Girard, Pennsylvania, 6 May 1943. Received BA, Clarkson University, 1965; MS, University of Wisconsin, 1967, PhD 1973. Taught at York University, Ontario, (rising to professor) from 1971. Editor, Sage Series on African Modernization and Development. Married Elspeth Cameron, 1977.

Principal Writings

Caravans of Kola: The Hausa Kola Trade, 1700–1900, 1980
Editor, *The Ideology of Slavery in Africa*, 1981
Transformations in Slavery: A History of Slavery in Africa, 1983
Editor with Catherine Coquery-Vidrovitch, *The Workers of African Trade*, 1985
Editor, *Africans in Bondage: Studies in Slavery and the Slave Trade: Essays in Honor of Philip D. Curtin on the Occasion of the Twenty-Fifth Anniversary of African Studies at the University of Wisconsin*, 1986
Salt of the Desert Sun: A History of Salt Production and Trade in the Central Sudan, 1986
"The Impact of the Atlantic Slave Trade on Africa: A Review of the Literature," *Journal of African History* 30 (1989), 365–94
"Revolutionary Mahdism and Resistance to Colonial Rule in the Sokoto Caliphate, 1905–06," *Journal of African History* 31 (1990), 217–44
With Jan S. Hogendorn, *Slow Death for Slavery: The Course for Abolition in Northern Nigeria, 1897–1936*, 1993
Editor with Toyin Falola, *Pawnship in Africa: Debt Bondage in Historical Perspective*, 1994
Editor with A.S. Kanya-Forstner, *The Sokoto Caliphate and the European Powers, 1890–1907*, 1994
Editor with Nicholas Rogers, *Unfree Labour in the Development of the Atlantic World*, 1994
With David Richardson, "British Abolition and Its Impact on Slave Prices along the Atlantic Coast of Africa, 1783–1850," *Journal of Economic History* 55 (1995), 98–119
Editor with Jordan Goodman and Andrew Sherratt, *Consuming Habits: Drugs in History and Anthropology*, 1995

Low Countries

Sharp religious divisions in Dutch society and linguistic divisions in Belgium determined the approaches to history in the Low Countries up to World War II, while strongly nationalist

perspectives inhibited any research into variations in regional or social experience. In the Netherlands, more resources were provided to national and local archives than in Belgium; public access was assured from the mid-19th century, while strict Belgian privacy laws prevented historians' access to many documents, so that the history of the Dutch has been studied in much greater volume than that of the Belgians. After the war, some broadening began to appear, which is reflected in Houtte's 12-volume *Algemene Geschiedenis der Nederlanden* (General History of the Low Countries), produced between 1949 and 1958. But only since the 1960s, when the social segmentation began to break down, greater attention began to be given to social and cultural history, and the archival situation in Belgium improved, did an ever more complex picture of the Low Countries' past emerge. This made necessary a new *Algemene Geschiedenis der Nederlanden* (15 volumes edited by Blok), published between 1977 and 1983.

The revolt of the Netherlands against Spain during the 16th and 17th centuries has been the most studied topic in Low Countries history since the 19th century, when historians sought to find the roots of the Dutch and Belgian nations in the revolt. The standard Protestant interpretation held that the revolt was the work of Calvinists seeking to throw off the persecution they suffered under the Catholic rulers of Spain. In contrast, Robert Fruin argued in *Het voorspel van den Tachtigjarigen Oorlog* (The Prologue of the Eighty Years' War, 1859–60) and other works that the revolt was a rebellion against foreign rule that linked Calvinist and Catholic, burgher and noble in a war for independence. Meanwhile, a growing Catholic historiography, best represented by L.J. Rogier's *Geschiedenis van het katholicisme in Noord Nederland in de XVIe en XVIIe eeuw* (History of Catholicism in the Northern Netherlands in the 16th and 17th Centuries, 1945–47) began to dispute the Protestant interpretation. Pieter Geyl shifted the focus away from religious conflict, convinced that an undivided Great Netherlands nation was coming into existence during the 16th century, one which was split into two nations only because the Spanish army could not operate effectively in the north. More recently, the secularization of Dutch intellectual life has permitted development of a more nuanced understanding of religious ideas in the 16th century, particularly in the work of Alastair Duke and J.J. Woltjer. Other works, including James Tracy's *A Financial Revolution in the Habsburg Netherlands* (1985) and his *Holland under Habsburg Rule, 1506–1566* (1990), focused on highly detailed analyses of the centralization process under the Habsburgs, since local elites were rebelling to protect local privilege against this centralization. These strands have been brought together by Jonathan Israel in his synthesis, *The Dutch Republic* (1995), which covers not only the revolt, but the entire history of the Republic.

Politics in the 17th-century Dutch Republic were dominated by the conflict between the urban oligarchies or regents and the stadholders of the House of Orange-Nassau. While 19th-century histories of the period were critical of the stadholders, 20th-century scholars tended to view the regents as defenders of liberty. D.J. Roorda has led a school of historians in shifting the emphasis to prosopographical analyses of local urban elites and especially of the factions within those groups in *Partij en factie* (Party and Faction, 1978) and, with Hendrik van Dijk, *Het Patriciaat in Zierikzee tijdens de Republiek* (The Patriciate in Zierikzee during the Republic, 1980).

Until recently, the 18th century, seen as an age of decline and ending with invasion and occupation by foreign armies, attracted much less attention from historians than the Golden Age. Typical of this attitude was H.T. Colenbrander's *De Patriottentijd* (The Patriots' Time, 1897–99), which denied that the conflicts of the period (the Patriotic and Batavian revolutions) were anything more than a by-product of international diplomacy. Geyl, however, pointed out similarities between the Patriots' ideas and those of earlier Dutch reformers in the last volume of *De geschiedenis van de Nederlandsche Stam* (1930–59) and in his *De Patriottenbeweging, 1780–1787* (The Patriot Movement, 1947), bringing the revolution into the mainstream of Dutch history. In the 1960s, C.H.E. de Wit provided the "social interpretation" of the Patriot Revolution in *De Strijd tussen aristocratie en democratie in Nederland, 1780–1848* (The Struggle between Aristocracy and Democracy in the Netherlands, 1965), making it the beginning of a long struggle between aristocrats (i.e., the regents) and burghers seeking political emancipation, a struggle that ended only when the latter won a democratic constitution in 1848. Wit is generally faulted for over-simplifying the picture, and Simon Schama, whose *Patriots and Liberators* (1977) is largely a synthesis of all three interpretations, has been likewise criticized for accepting Wit's categories too uncritically. Subsequently, historians have taken a much closer look at the ways in which the Dutch Enlightenment created the political culture that framed the conflict. A good introduction to this research is *The Dutch Republic in the Eighteenth Century*, edited by Margaret C. Jacob and Wijnand W. Mijnhardt (1992).

E.H. Kossmann's *The Low Countries, 1780–1940* (1978) is a comprehensive survey of the history of the Netherlands and of Belgium in the modern period and contains a useful bibliographic essay. When it appeared in Dutch as *De Lage Landen, 1780–1980* in 1986, several chapters on the years from 1940 to 1980 were added.

The Dutch experience of German occupation during World War II is probably the most fertile area of 20th-century history in the Netherlands. The central study of the period is Louis de Jong's 14-volume *Het Koninkrijk der Nederlanden in de Tweede Wereldoorlog* (The Kingdom of the Netherlands in World War II, 1969–91). Werner Warmbrunn's *The Dutch under German Occupation, 1940–45* is a good English-language survey. More recently, scholars such as Gerhard Hirschfeld in his *Fremdherrschaft und Kollaboration* (1984; revised as *Nazi Rule and Dutch Collaboration*, 1988) have tended to veer away from Jong's simple categorization of the population into either collaborators or resistance fighters. No synthesis of the Belgian experience on the scale of Jong's exists, but Jules Gérard-Libois, *L'an 40* (The Year '40, 1971) and A. de Jonghe's, *Hitler en het politieke lot van Belgie, 1940–1944* (Hitler and the Political Destiny of Belgium, 1972) were seminal.

Significant work in the economic and social history of the Low Countries during the early modern period is usually thought to have begun only in the 1960s, but the important work of N.W. Posthumus, *De Geschiedenis van de Leidsche lakenindustrie* (The History of the Leiden Cloth Industry, 1908–39) and J.G. van Dillen's synthesis, *Van rijkdom en regenten* (Of Wealth and Regents, 1970) should not be overlooked. The real breakthrough in this area, however, came with the publication of B. Slicher van Bath's *Een samenleving onder spanning* (A

Society under Stress, 1957). Slicher van Bath's book, which presented a great deal of quantitative data regarding the province of Overijssel's rural population, economy, and social structure between 1600 and 1800, was the model for a whole series of case studies of the Dutch countryside published by scholars associated with the Department of Rural History at the University of Wageningen, usually in the journal, *A.A.G. Bijdragen*.

One of the major debates in Dutch history has been on the reasons for Holland's economic growth in the early modern period. One school emphasizes the contributions of skilled immigrants (and their capital) fleeing north from Flanders and Brabant during the revolt. Another credits the absence of any feudal system in Holland, thus permitting the early development of a free market economy. A third school argues that various favorable conditions outside Holland were the decisive factors. The articles in *The Dutch Economy in the Golden Age*, edited by Karel Davids and Leo Noordegraaf (1993), provide a good overview of these viewpoints.

Economic historians have also focused on explaining the end of the era of strong economic growth, beginning sometime in the middle of the 1600s. Research into this topic began with Johannes de Vries' *De economische achteruitgang der Republiek in de achttiende eeuw* (The Economic Decline of the Republic in the 18th Century, 1959). Vries denied that there had been any real overall economic decline until around 1780, suggesting instead that certain sectors of the Dutch economy stood still while the economies of other nations grew, resulting in a relative decline only. He has been repeatedly attacked by historians whose research into demography, agriculture, and export industries give them a more pessimistic view. These include the Wageningen group, especially A.M. van der Woude, Jan de Vries in *Barges and Capitalism* (1981), and J.L. van Zanden in *The Rise and Decline of Holland's Economy* (1993). But James C. Riley in *International Government Finance and the Amsterdam Capital Market* (1980) pointed to the financial sector to suggest that the Republic's economy remained buoyant until the last decades of the century. Related to this debate is the attempt to explain the late industrialization of the Netherlands. Notable here are Richard T. Griffiths' *Industrial Retardation in the Netherlands, 1830–1850* (1979) and Joel Mokyr's *Industrialization in the Low Countries, 1795–1850* (1976).

Meanwhile, the image of Belgium as a backward and stagnant society in the 18th century has been revised. Recent interpretations, such as those of Mokyr, of Franklin Mendels in his 1972 article, and of Pierre Lebrun and others, in *Essai sur la révolution industrielle en Belgique* (Essay on the Industrial Revolution in Belgium, 1979), have demonstrated that the roots of Belgium's position as the "second industrial nation" are apparent in the 18th century.

While significant individual works in women's history in the Low Countries have been produced for many decades, this area truly began to flourish from the 1970s onward. Various topics have received attention, including working women, education, witchcraft. A number of theoretical debates also have been central to this historiography. A good introduction to this literature can be found in José Eijt's 1992 essay on women's history.

Postcolonial work on the colonial past of the Netherlands has been marked by attempts to place the Dutch East India Company and later government officials into a more Asian context. This trend began with J.C. van Leur in *Eenige beschouwingen betreffende den ouden Aziatischen handel* (1934; included in *Indonesian Trade and Society: Essays in Asian Social and Economic History*, 1955). His influence can be seen in much current research, notably Meilink-Roelofsz's *Asian Trade and European Influence in the Indonesian Archipelago Between 1500 and about 1640* (1962).

MARYBETH CARLSON

See also de Vries; Geyl; Huizinga; Schama

Further Reading

Blok, D.P., general editor, *Algemene Geschiedenis der Nederlanden* (General History of the Low Countries), 15 vols., Haarlem: Fibula Van Dishoeck, 1977–83

Blok, Petrus Johannes, *Geschiedenis van het Nederlandsche volk*, 8 vols., Groningen: Wolters, 1892–1908; in English as *The History of the People of the Netherlands*, 5 vols., New York: Putnam, 1898–1912

Boogman, J.C., *Rondom 1848: de politieke ontwikkeling van Nederland, 1840–1858* (Around 1848: The Political Development of the Netherlands, 1840–1858), Amsterdam: Fibula Van Dishoeck, 1978

Bosch, Mineke, with Annemarie Kloosterman, eds., *Lieve Dr Jacobs: Breven uit de wereldbond voor Vrouwenkiesrecht, 1902–1942*, Amsterdam: Sava, 1985; in English as *Politics and Friendship: Letters from the International Woman Suffrage Alliance, 1902–1942*, Columbus: Ohio State University Press, 1990

Brugmans, I.J., *Paardenkracht en mensenmacht: sociaal-economische geschiedenis van Nederland 1795–1940* (Horsepower and Human Power: Social-Economic History of the Netherlands, 1795–1940), The Hague: Nijhoff, 1961

Buck, Hendrik de, *Bibliografie der geschiedenis van Nederland* (Bibliography on the History of the Netherlands), Leiden: Brill, 1968

Bulletin critique d'histoire de Belgique (Critical Bulletin on the History of Belgium), Ghent: Université de Gand, 1967–75

Carter, Alice C., "Bibliographical Surveys," *Acta Historiae Neerlandicae* 6–8 (1973–75)

Carter, Alice C. et al., eds., *Historical Research in the Low Countries, 1970–1975: A Critical Survey*, The Hague: Nijhoff, 1981

Colenbrander, H.T., *De Patriottentijd: Hoofdzakelijk naar buitenlandse beschieden* (The Patriots' Time: Chiefly from Foreign Documents), 3 vols., The Hague: M. Nijhoff, 1897–99

Coolhaas, Willem Phillipus, *A Critical Survey of Studies on Dutch Colonial History*, The Hague: Nijhoff, 1960; revised by G.J. Schutte, 1980

Davids, Karel, and Leo Noordegraaf, eds., *The Dutch Economy in the Golden Age: Nine Studies*, Amsterdam: Nederlandsch Economisch-Historisch Archief, 1993

Davids, Karel, "Honderd jaar beachtzaamheid: denken over sociale en economische geschiedenis in Nederland, 1894–1994 (One Hundred Years of Caution: Social and Economic History in the Netherlands, 1894–1994), *Tijdschrift voor Sociale Geschiedenis* 20 (1994), 251–62

Dekker, Rudolf, *Holland in beroering: oproeren in de 17de en 18de eeuw* (Holland in Turmoil: Uprisings in the 17th and 18th Centuries), Baarn: Ambo, 1982

Deursen, Arie Theodorus van, *Het kopergeld van de Gouden Eeuw*, 4 vols., Assen: Van Gorcum, 1978–81; in English as *Plain Lives in a Golden Age*, Cambridge: Cambridge University Press, 1991

de Vries, Jan, *Barges and Capitalism: Passenger Transportation in the Dutch Economy, 1632–1839*, Utrecht: HES, 1981

Dijk, Hendrik van, and D.J. Roorda, "Sociale mobiliteit onder regenten van de Republiek" (Social Mobility under the Regents of the Republic), *Tijdschrift voor geschiedenis* 84 (1971), 306–28

Dijk, Hendrik van, and D.J. Roorda, *Het Patriciaat in Zierikzee tijdens de Republiek* (The Patriciate in Zierikzee during the Republic), 1980

Dillen, Johannes Gerard van, *Van rijkdom en regenten* (Of Wealth and Regents), The Hague: Nijhoff, 1970

Duke, A.C., and C.A. Tamse, *Clio's Mirror: Historiography in Britain and the Netherlands*, Zutphen: De Walburg Pers, 1985

Duke, A.C., *Reformation and Revolt in the Low Countries*, London: Hambledon Press, 1990

Dumont, Sylvia et al., eds., *In haar verleden ingewijd: de ontwikkeling van vrouwengeschiedenis in Nederland* (Initiated into Her History: The Development of Women's History in the Netherlands), Zutphen: Walburg Pers, 1991

Dumoulin, M., "Historiens étrangers et historiographie de l'expansion belge aux XIXe et XX siècles" (Foreign Historians and Historiography Concerning Belgian Expansion in the 19th and 20th centuries), *Bijdragen en Mededelingen betreffende de Geschiedenis der Nederlanden* 100 (1985), 685–99

Eijt, José, "Women's History: The 'Take-Off' of an Important Discipline: Developments in the Netherlands and Belgium since 1985," N.C.F. van Sas and Els Witte, eds., *Historical Research in the Low Countries*, The Hague: Nederlands Historisch Genootschap, 1992

Essen, Mineke van, *Opvoeden met een dubbel doel: twee eeuwen meisjesonderwijs in Nederland* (Education with a Double Goal: Two Centuries of Girls' Schooling in the Netherlands), Amsterdam: SUA, 1990

Faber, J.A. et al., "Population Changes and Economic Developments in the Netherlands: A Historical Survey," *A.A.G. Bijdragen* 12 (1965), 47–113

Fruin, Robert, *Het voorspel van den Tachtigjarigen Oorlog* (The Prologue of the Eighty Years' War), Utrecht: Spektrum, 1859–60

Genicot, Léopold, ed., *Vingt Ans de recherche historique en Belgique, 1969–1988* (Twenty Years of Historical Research in Belgium), Brussels: Credit Communal, 1990

Gérard-Libois, Jules, *L'an 40: la Belgique occupée* (The Year '40: Occupied Belgium), Brussels: CRISP, 1971

Geyl, Pieter, *De geschiedenis van de Nederlandsche Stam*, 3 vols., Amsterdam: Wereldbibliothek, 1930–59; partially translated as *The Revolt of the Netherlands, 1555–1609*, and *The Netherlands Divided, 1609–1648*, London: Williams and Norgate, 1932–36; revised and expanded as *The Netherlands in the Seventeenth Century*, London: Benn, and New York: Barnes and Noble, 1961–64

Geyl, Pieter, *De Patriottenbeweging, 1780–1787* (The Patriot Movement), Amsterdam: van Kampen, 1947

Grever, Maria, "Het verborgen continent: een historiografische verkenning van vrouwengeschiedenis" (The Hidden Continent: A Historiographical Explanation of Women's History), *Tijdschrift voor Sociale Geschiedenis* 12 (1986), 221–68

Griffiths, Richard T., *Industrial Retardation in the Netherlands, 1830–1850*, The Hague: Nijhoff, 1979

Haan, Francisca de, "Women's History behind the Dykes: Reflections on the Situation in the Netherlands," in Karen Offen, Ruth Roach Pierson, and Jane Rendall, eds., *Writing Women's History: International Persepectives*, Bloomington: Indiana University Press, 1991

Hirschfeld, Gerhard, *Fremdherrschaft und Kollaboration: die Niederlande unter deutscher Besatzung, 1940–1945*, Stuttgart: Deutsche Verlags-Anstalt, 1984; revised and expanded in English as *Nazi Rule and Dutch Collaboration: The Netherlands under German Occupation, 1940–1945*, Oxford and New York: Berg, 1988

Houtte, J.A. van, ed., *Un quart de siècle de recherche historique en Belgique, 1944–1968* (A Quarter of a Century's Historical Research in Belgium), 1944–1968, Louvain: Nauwelaerts, 1970

Houtte, J.A. van, general editor, *Algemene Geschiedenis der Nederlanden* (General History of the Low Countries), 12 vols., Utrecht: De Haan, 1949–58

Huizinga, Johan, *Dutch Civilization in the Seventeenth Century and Other Essays*, London: Collins, and New York: Ungar, 1968

Israel, Jonathan, *The Dutch Republic: Its Rise, Greatness, and Fall, 1477–1806*, Oxford and New York: Oxford University Press, 1995

Jacob, Margaret, and W.W. Mijnhardt, eds., *The Dutch Republic in the Eighteenth Century: Decline, Enlightenment, and Revolution*, Ithaca, NY: Cornell University Press, 1992

Jong, Louis de, *Het Koninkrijk der Nederlanden in de Tweede Wereldoorlog* (The Kingdom of the Netherlands in World War II), 14 vols., The Hague: Staatsdruukerij en uitgeverijbedrijt, 1969–91

Jonghe, A. de, *Hitler en het politieke lot van Belgie, 1940–1944* (Hitler and the Political Destiny of Belgium), Antwerp: Uitgeverij de Nederlandsche Boehke, 1972

Keymolen, Denise, *Vrowenarbied in Belgie van c.1860 tot 1914* (Women's Work in Belgium from c.1860 to 1914), Leuven: Acco, 1977

Keymolen, Denise, *De geschiedenis geweld aangedaan: de strijd voor het vrouwenstemrecht, 1886–1948* (History Done Violence: The Fight for Women's Suffrage, 1886–1948), Brussels: Instituut voor Politieke Vorming, 1981

Kossmann, E.H., and J. Kossmann, "Bulletin critique de l'historiographie néerlandaise" (Critical Bulletin of Dutch History), *Revue du Nord* 36–43, 46–47 (1954–61, 1964–65)

Kossmann, E.H., *The Low Countries, 1780–1940*, Oxford and New York: Oxford University Press, 1978; revised and expanded in Dutch as *De Lage Landen, 1780–1980: twee eeuwen Nederland en Belgie*, 2 vols., Amsterdam: Elsevier, 1986

Kossmann-Putto, J., and Els Witte, eds., *Historical Research in the Low Countries, 1981–1983: A Critical Survey*, Leiden: Brill, 1985

Kossmann-Putto, J., Els Witte, and C.R. Emery, eds., *Historical Research in the Low Countries, 1983–1985: A Critical Survey*, The Hague: Nederlands Historisch Genootschap, 1990

Lebrun, Pierre *et al.*, *Essai sur la révolution industrielle en Belgique* (Essay on the Industrial Revolution in Belgium), Brussels: Palais des Akademies, 1979

Leur, J.C. van, *Indonesian Trade and Society: Essays in Asian Social and Economic History*, The Hague: Van Hoeve, 1955

Lijphart, Arend, *The Politics of Accommodation: Pluralism and Democracy in the Netherlands*, Berkeley: University of California Press, 1968

Lucassen, Jan, and Rinus Penninx, *Nieuwkomers, nakomelingen, Nederlanders: immigranten in Nederland, 1550–1993* (Newcomers, Descendants, Dutch People: Immigrants in the Netherlands, 1550–1993), Amsterdam: Spinhuis, 1994

Meilink-Roelofsz, Marie Antoinette Petronella, *Asian Trade and European Influence in the Indonesian Archipelago Between 1500 and about 1640*, The Hague: Nijhoff, 1962

Mendels, Franklin F., "Proto-industrialization," *Journal of Economic History* 32 (1972), 241–61

Mijnhardt, W.W., ed., *Kantelend geschiedbeeld: nederlandse historiografie sinds 1945* (History Upended: Dutch Historiography since 1945), Utrecht: Spectrum, 1983

Mokyr, Joel, *Industrialization in the Low Countries, 1795–1850*, New Haven: Yale University Press, 1976

Pirenne, Henri, *Histoire de Belgique* (History of Belgium), 7 vols., 1899–1932

Posthumus, N.W., *De Geschiedenis van de Leidsche lakenindustrie* (The History of the Leiden Cloth Industry), 3 vols., The Hague: Nijhoff, 1908–39

Prak, Maarten, "De nieuwe sociale geschiedschrijving in Nederland" (The New Social History in the Netherlands), *Tijdschrift voor Social Geschiedenis* 20 (1994), 121–48

Raxhon, Philippe, *La Révolution liégeoise de 1789 vue par les historiens belges de 1805 à nos jours* (The 1789 Revolution of Liège Seen by Belgian Historians from 1805 to Our Time), Brussels: Editions de l'Université de Bruxelles, 1989

Riley, James C., *International Government Finance and the Amsterdam Capital Market, 1740–1815*, Cambridge and New York: Cambridge University Press, 1980

Rogier, L.J., *Geschiedenis van het katholicisme in Noord Nederland in de XVIe en XVIIe eeuw* (History of Catholicism in the Northern Netherlands in the 16th and 17th Centuries), 3 vols., Amsterdam: Urbi et Orbi, 1945–47

Roorda, D.J., *Partij en factie: de oproeren van 1672 in de steden van Holland en Zeeland, een Krachtmeting tussen partijen en facties* (Party and Faction: The Riots of 1672 in the Towns of Holland and Zeeland, A Trial of Strength Between Parties and Factions), Groningen: Wolters, 1978

Sas, N.C.F. van, and Els Witte, eds., *Historical Research in the Low Countries*, The Hague: Nederlands Historisch Genootschap, 1992

Schama, Simon, *Patriots and Liberators: Revolution in the Netherlands, 1780–1813*, New York: Knopf, and London: Collins, 1977

Schama, Simon, *The Embarrassment of Riches: An Interpretation of Dutch Culture in the Golden Age*, New York: Knopf, 1987; London: Collins, 1988

Slicher van Bath, B., *Een samenleving onder spanning: geschiedenis van het platteland van Overijssel* (A Society under Stress: A History of the Countryside of Overijssel), Assen: Van Gorcum, 1957

Smits, A., *1830: Scheuring in de Nederlanden* (1830: A Split in the Low Countries), 2 vols., Heule: UGA, 1983

Tollebeek, Jo, *De toga van Fruin: denken over geschiedenis in Nederland sinds 1860* (Fruin's Toga: Thinking about History in the Netherlands since 1860), Amsterdam: Wereldbibliotheek, 1990

Tracy, James D., *A Financial Revolution in the Habsburg Netherlands: Renten and Renteniers in the County of Holland, 1515–1565*, Berkeley: University of California Press, 1985

Tracy, James D., *Holland under Habsburg Rule, 1506–1566: The Formation of a Body Politic*, Berkeley: University of California Press, 1990

Verhaegen, Paul, *La Belgique sous la domination française, 1792–1814* (Belgium under French Domination), 5 vols., Brussels: Goemaere, 1922–29

Vries, Johannes de, *De economische achteruitgang der Republiek in de achttiende eeuw* (The Economic Decline of the Republic in the 18th Century), Amsterdam: Harms, 1959

Warmbrunn, Werner, *The Dutch under German Occupation, 1940–45*, Stanford, CA: Stanford University Press, 1963

Warmbrunn, Werner, *The German Occupation of Belgium, 1940–1944*, New York: Lang, 1993

Wee, Herman van der, *The Growth of the Antwerp Market and the European Economy*, 3 vols., The Hague: Nijhoff, 1963

Weerdt, Denise de, *En de vrouwen: vrouw, vrouwenbegweging en feminisme in Belgie 1830–1960* (And the Women: Women, Women's Movement, and Feminism in Belgium, 1830–1960), Ghent: Masereelfonds, 1980

Wesseling, H.L., *Onder historici: opstellen over geschiedenis en geschiedschrijving* (Among Historians: Essays on History and Historical Writing), Amsterdam: Bakker, 1995

Wils, Lode, *Honderd jaar vlaamse beweging* (One Hundred Years of the Flemish Movement), 3 vols., Leuven: Davidsfonds, 1977–89

Wit, C.H.E. de, *De Strijd tussen aristocratie en democratie in Nederland, 1780–1848* (The Struggle Between Aristocracy and Democracy in the Netherlands), Heerlen: Winants, 1965

Woltjer, J.J., *Friesland in hervormingstijd* (Friesland during the Time of the Reformation), Leiden: Universitaire Pers, 1962

Woude, A.M. van der, "The A.A.G Bijdragen and the Study of Dutch Rural History," *Journal of European Economic History* 4 (1975), 215–42

Zanden, J.L. van, *The Rise and Decline of Holland's Economy: Merchant Capitalism and the Labour Market*, Manchester: Manchester University Press, 1993

Lower, A.R.M. 1889-1988

Canadian historian

It is possible to divide A.R.M. Lower's work into two types: analytical, research-based monographs on the timber industry in Canada; and polemical ruminations on the nature of the Canadian nation. Yet to do so is to minimize the linkages between the two, for in Lower's work they were simply different ways to come to terms with the same fundamental problem: the need to give Canada a deeper appreciation of its own nationhood. From his earliest formative years, Lower was determined to search out and interpret the historical facts that underlay Canadian national identity.

That search led him to write four penetrating accounts of the North American forestry industry. These dense, detailed studies (Lower himself called them arid) reflected his interest in metropolitanism, and examined through the lens of the lumber industry the relationship between the European commercial metropolis and the resource hinterland it exploited.

In this sense, Lower's timber books placed his work squarely in the staples thesis of Harold Innis. But Lower brought a different dimension to the theory. In the first place, he demonstrated a well-developed environmental conscience (born of his youth spent in the wilds of northern Canada) that led him to deplore the commercial plunder of North America's forests. More importantly, Lower lacked Innis' fondness for the more technical aspects of the staples trades. Instead, he was interested in the human side of the timber industry, and his books are underpinned by a fascination with the way the wilderness shaped the character and outlook of Canadians.

It was this interest in the relationship between a community and its environment that informed most of Lower's work. The frontier thesis of Frederick Jackson Turner stimulated Lower intellectually, but he found it profoundly unsatisfying when applied to Canada. Above all, he believed the thesis was too parochial, and took no account of the conflict between French- and English-Canadian ways of life. As one of the few English-Canadian academics to attempt to understand French-Canadian society in the interwar years, he married the two nations theory with his metropolitanism and concluded that Canada could only be understood in terms of two dialectics: between the French and English faces of the country; and between colony and metropolis.

Lower's fullest discussion of these dialectics appeared in Colony to Nation (1946), his greatest contribution to Canadian history. It combines impressive evidence, impassioned arguments, and no mean literary flair into a plea for Canadians to realize the importance of national feeling, not only in their past but also in their future. Where other academics turned to collectivism as a way for Canada to realize its destiny, Lower turned to nationalism, and Colony to Nation stood as his prescription for the nation's ills.

Lower wrote considerably more broadly than this brief synopsis suggests. With Canada and the Far East (1940), he became one of the first observers to consider Canada as a Pacific nation. His judgmental and provocative Canadians in the Making (1958) was an early attempt at cultural and intellectual history which emphasized piety as a force that shaped Canada in its formative years. Historical theory, political philosophy, religion, educational policy – all were tackled by Lower's keen eye and sometimes acerbic pen. In his later years, Lower devoted himself primarily to thought-pieces on his earlier work, polemical essays, and tributes to his contemporaries, most of whom he outlived. Indeed, with Colony to Nation, his historical thought was essentially complete. He refined his ideas but never substantially revised them.

Although Lower tried to assume the mantle of both social scientist and humanist, he was never entirely happy about considering himself in the former role. The timber books, his most assiduous attempts at being a social scientist, struck Lower as having "no epoch-making significance." Damning them with faint praise, he considered them to be merely "useful in the sense that snow shovels or cars are useful." Much like Donald Creighton, Lower conceived of the historian in more than utilitarian terms: the historian should be an artist. The role of the historian demanded more than a facility for facts; it also demanded imagination, literary ability, and above all the willingness to combine reality and perception into a story of the past. For this reason he saw his later works, particularly Colony to Nation and Canadians in the Making as being greater achievements than his more empirical works. Few people who have read Lower's entire corpus would disagree with him.

JONATHAN F. VANCE

See also Canada; Innis; Morton

Biography

Arthur Reginald Marsden Lower. Born Barrie, Ontario, 12 August 1889. Educated at University of Toronto, BA 1914, MA 1923; Harvard University, MA 1926, PhD 1929. Briefly a country school teacher, then taught language and history, University of Toronto, 1914–16. Served in Royal Naval Volunteer Reserve, 1916–19. Assistant chairman, Board of Historical Publications, Canadian Archives, 1919–25. Taught at Tufts College, 1926–27; Harvard University, 1927, while working on doctorate; professor, United College, University of Manitoba, 1929–47; professor of Canadian history, Queen's University, Kingston, Ontario, 1947–59. Married Evelyn Marion Smith, 1920 (1 daughter). Died 7 January 1988.

Principal Works

The Square Timber Trade in Canada, 1932
Settlement and the Forest Frontier in Eastern Canada, 1936
The North American Assault on the Canadian Forest: A History of the Lumber Trade Between Canada and the United States, 1938
Canada and the Far East, 1940
Colony to Nation: A History of Canada, 1946
Canadians in the Making: A Social History of Canada, 1958
Great Britain's Woodyard: British America and the Timber Trade, 1763–1867, 1973
Ocean of Destiny: A Concise History of the North Pacific, 1500–1978, 1978
A Pattern for History, 1978

Further Reading

Berger, Carl, The Writing of Canadian History: Aspects of English-Canadian Historical Writing, 1900–1970, Toronto: Oxford University Press, 1976; 2nd edition Toronto: University of Toronto Press, 1986
Cook, Ramsay, The Craft of History, Toronto: Canadian Broadcasting Corporation, 1973

Heick, Welf H., ed., *His Own Man: Essays in Honour of Arthur Reginald Marsden Lower*, Montreal: McGill-Queen's University Press, 1974

Heick, Welf H., ed., *History and Myth: Arthur Lower and the Making of Canadian Nationalism*, Vancouver: University of British Columbia Press, 1975

Levitt, Joseph, *A Vision beyond Reach: A Century of Images of Canadian Destiny*, Ottawa: Deneau, 1982

Lower, A.R.M., *My First Seventy-Five Years*, Toronto: Macmillan, 1967

Lüdtke, Alf 1943–

German anthropological and political historian

A pioneer in developing both the theory and practice of *Alltagsgeschichte* (the history of everyday life), Alf Lüdtke is a fellow of the Max-Planck-Institut for History, currently the only major center for work on *Alltagsgeschichte*, anthropological history, and "microhistory." Lüdtke has also been central in supporting and showcasing this work as produced by other professional historians, as well as within a wider community of practitioners of history, the latter particularly through his active role in the German history workshop movement.

Lüdtke has written widely in historical theory, drawing on an array of historical traditions and on methods outside the discipline, and considering forms of historical practice and expression that reach outside its traditional purview. He has focused on *Alltagsgeschichte*, a method that emphasizes the lives of "ordinary" people, by examining their experiences, their webs of relationships with others and with the material world, and their individual and collective agency. This approach leads Lüdtke to redefine politics and political activism, viewing the latter as a subset of available "survival tactics" by which people negotiate their lives through the endless contradictions in which they find themselves. Lüdtke has emphasized the virtues of a "microhistorical" site of study, permitting familiarity with a dense network of interactions and "fields of force" that highlight specificity and contingency, enriching and revising studies that identify broad and apparently general historical trends.

This theoretical work has earned Lüdtke a high international profile; his most difficult task, perhaps, has been to assert *Alltagsgeschichte*'s value in his native Germany – a setting in which structural history has been for several decades the dominant paradigm, and whose practitioners have criticized *Alltagsgeschichte* as "unscientific" and lacking "objectivity." In his own development of the method Lüdtke notes rather *Alltagsgeschichte*'s emphasis on the necessity of the historian's critical self-examination and distancing from the object of study. This methodological rancor is traced in part to a subtext of the political implications of different historical practices, related most specifically to how Germans should best understand the Third Reich. Lüdtke's own historical studies have taken on some of the most difficult and contentious themes relating to this period, including workers' lack of resistance to the Nazi regime, despite their general lack of interest in and even antipathy to the party. This work emphasizes individual and collective choice and agency, such as it was, precisely as a counter to a "romanticization" of the role of ordinary Germans in this period.

Lüdtke has as a practitioner of *Alltagsgeschichte* written voluminously on a broad range of subjects; these topics seem to reflect a postwar West German experience of confronting widespread political complacency, German state deference to Western military interests, and state willingness to curtail civil liberties, especially in response to the threat of terrorism. His subjects may be generally clustered into two areas, both of which span the modern era: the first is state violence and bureaucratic domination; the second is worker experience and politics, industrial work processes, and images of work and workers. Lüdtke spelled out his findings on the former in most sustained fashion in his work on the development of a "police state" in early 19th-century Prussia. He found that the Prussian state commanded police and military forces to counteract all perceived potential unrest through "short shrift": sure, rapid, and preemptive physical violence, which created a climate of fear and repression. Lüdtke concluded by observing the potential dangers of bureaucratic state structures that purport to operate for the "common good," but which through "citadel practices" exercise both physical violence and invasive symbolic authority on individual state subjects. His work considers such practices, among others, under the GDR regime as well.

Lüdtke has also done considerable work on the German working class, between 1860 and 1945, and again in East Germany in the 1980s. It is through this work that he has developed his central concept of *Eigensinn*, or, "sense of self." Through numerous articles Lüdtke examines laborers at work; with great concreteness and attention to detail, he recreates the repetitive motion and loud noises of factory work, linking this experience to workers' relationships with workmates, bosses, and even with the state. He consistently identifies workers' practice of *Eigensinn*: spontaneous efforts to create and take charge of their own domain, and to assert themselves in it, on the job, and in the broader world. Lüdtke carefully connects such quotidian practices with prevailing political processes. He finds, for example, that, during the Third Reich, workers practiced their "opposition" to the regime primarily through horseplay and pranks, through extended coffee breaks, and through other means that caused little actual damage to the regime. Through such painstaking study, Lüdtke helps explain what has been little understood: how the Nazis maintained their power despite the large segments of society from whom they had little support. As part of a broader social critique, crossing academic boundaries, the impact of this work has been considerable, just as Lüdtke's theoretical writings continue to provoke widespread discussion.

BELINDA DAVIS

See also Anthropology; Crime

Biography

Born 18 October 1943. Received doctorate, University of Konstanz, 1981; Habilitation, University of Hannover, 1988. Affiliated faculty member, University of Hannover. Married Helga Mueller (1 daughter).

Principal Writings

"The Role of State Violence in the Period of Transition to Industrial Capitalism: The Example of Prussia from 1815 to 1848," *Social History* 4 (1979), 175–222

"Gemeinwohl," Polizei und "Festungspraxis": staatliche
Gewaltsamkeit und innere Verwaltung in Preussen, 1815–1850,
1982; in English as Police and State in Prussia, 1815–1850, 1989

"The Historiography of Everyday Life: The Personal and the
Political," in Raphael Samuel and Gareth Stedman Jones, eds.,
Culture, Ideology and Politics: Essays for Eric Hobsbawm, 1982

"Organizational Order or 'Eigensinn'? Workers' Privacy and
Workers' Politics in Imperial Germany," in Sean Wilentz, ed.,
Rites of Power, 1985

"Cash, Coffee-breaks, Horseplay: Eigensinn and Politics among
Factory Workers in Germany circa 1900," in Michael Hanagan
and Charles Stephenson, eds., Confrontation, Class
Consciousness, and the Labor Process: Studies in Proletarian
Class Formation, 1986

"Hunger in der grossen Depression" (Hunger in the Great
Depression), Archiv für Sozialgeschichte 27 (1987), 145–76

Editor, Alltagsgeschichte: zur Rekonstruktion historischer
Erfahrungen und Lebensweisen, 1989; in English as The History
of Everyday Life: Reconstructing Historical Experiences and Ways
of Life, 1995

Editor, Herrschaft als soziale Praxis: historische und sozialanthro-
pologische Studien (Domination as Social Practice: Historical and
Social-Anthropological Studies), 1991

"The Appeal of Exterminating 'Others': German Workers and the
Limits of Resistance," Journal of Modern History 64 (1992),
supplement: 46–67

Editor, "Sicherheit" und "Wohlfahrt": Polizei, Gesellschaft und
Herrschaft im 19. und 20. Jahrhundert ("Security" and
"Welfare": Police, Society, and Domination in the 19th and 20th
Centuries), 1992

"'Coming to Terms with the Past': Illusions of Remembering, Ways
of Forgetting Nazism in West Germany," Journal of Modern
History 65 (1993), 542–72

Eigen-Sinn: Fabrikalltag, Arbeitererfahrungen und Politik vom
Kaiserreich bis in den Faschismus ("Sense of Self": Everyday
Factory Life, Worker Experience and Politics from the Second
Empire to Fascism), 1993

"Polymorphous Synchrony: German Industrial Workers and the
Politics of Everyday Life," International Review of Social History
38 (1993), 39–84

"Geschichte und Eigensinn" (History and Sense of Self), in Berliner
Geschichtswerkstatt, ed., Alltagsgeschichte, Subjektivität und
Geschichte: zur Theorie und Praxis von Alltagsgeschichte, 1994

"'Helden der Arbeit': Mühen beim Arbeiten, Zur missmutigen
Loyalität von Industriearbeitern in der DDR" ("Heroes of
Work": Labors of Work: On the Discontented Loyalty of
Industrial Workers in the GDR), in Hartmut Kaelble, Jürgen
Kocka, and Hartmut Zwahr, eds., Sozialgeschichte der DDR,
1994

Editor with Thomas Lindenberger, Physische Gewalt: Studien zur
Geschichte der Neuzeit (Physical violence: Studies in Modern
History), 1995

Editor with Inge Marssolek and Adelheid von Saldern,
Amerikanisierung: Traum und Alptraum im Deutschland des
20. Jahrhunderts (Americanization: Dreams and Nightmares in
Germany in the 20th Century), 1996

"Der Bann der Wörter: 'Todesfabriken,'" (The Banishment of
Words: "Death Factories") Werkstatt Geschichte 13 (1996)

Further Reading

Crew, David F., "Alltagsgeschichte: A New Social History from
Below?," Central European History 22 (1989), 394–407

Eley, Geoff, "Labor History, Social History, Alltagsgeschichte:
Experience, Culture, and the Politics of the Everyday – A New
Direction for German Social History?" Journal of Modern
History 61 (1989), 297–343

Rosenhaft, Eve, "History, Anthropology, and the Study of Everyday
Life: A Review Article," Comparative Studies in History and
Society 29 (1987), 99–105

Lyons, F.S.L. 1923–1983

Irish historian

In divided societies history can be an explosive commodity. As one Irish historian, A.T.Q. Stewart, once remarked, "to the Irish all history is applied history, and the past is simply a convenient quarry which provides ammunition to use against enemies in the present." Leland Lyons' aim was to write history which would convert that quarry back to its legitimate purpose. In temperament a private man, he took on an increasingly public role; he had few research students, yet he influenced the method and approach of a generation of Irish historians. Birth and family linked him to the north of Ireland, but in outlook he was very much a southern Irish Protestant of the post-independence era; his work was described on occasion as unsympathetic towards Ulster Unionism, or even as neo-republican, yet he was as much at home in England as in Ireland, while in later years he spoke and wrote against the stifling of the southern Protestant identity by the majority Catholic tradition in the Republic.

Lyons published seven books, three of them blockbusters, and at the time of his death had just embarked on the official biography of W.B. Yeats. His third book, Internationalism in Europe, 1815–1914 (1963), was a commissioned study for the Council of Europe and is not well known, though its conception reflected his inclusive and pluralist approach to the problem of national conflict. His reputation as the leading Irish historian of the postwar generation is based on the remaining six books, and on twenty or so published articles, which all deal with the history of Ireland since the mid-19th century. His work was characterized by a fine style and balanced judgments. His approach was cool and analytical, and his ideological underpinnings liberal, integrationist, and inclusive.

Lyons' method was based on scrupulous examination of archival evidence, mainly private correspondence, in a way that is taken for granted by later generations of historians, but which had not been much applied in Irish history prior to the work of his teacher and friend T.W. Moody (1907–84) and others who founded the journal Irish Historical Studies in 1938. Although his PhD thesis and, interestingly, to a lesser degree, his related first book, drew quite markedly on political science methods, he did not subsequently use social-scientific or theoretical approaches. He adhered to the classic historian's virtues of evidential rigor and a striving for objectivity, tending to regard theory almost as the articulation of prejudice. In the Moody Festschrift (1980) Lyons acknowledged a debt to his mentor for "a training in how to define one's subject, how to locate one's sources, how to evaluate different kinds of evidence, how to progress from description to analysis, how to handle footnotes and bibliographies, and at the end how to set out one's conclusions clearly, reasonably and, if all went well, even with some degree of style." The historian, Lyons observed in The Burden of Our History (1979), while being "imaginatively committed to his subject . . . must use all the disciplines of his training to distance himself from that subject. He deals in explanations, not solutions." Likewise he thought that historical revisionism "is proper revisionism if it is a response to new evidence which, after being duly tested, brings us nearer to a truth independent of the wishes and aspirations of those for whom truth consists solely of what happens to coincide with those wishes and aspirations."

For much of his career Lyons was closely wedded to the study of high politics and, in four books, effectively wrote the history of the constitutional nationalist movement from its origins in the 1870s to its demise at the hands of Sinn Fein in the general election of 1918. But in his later work he branched out – encouraged, perhaps, by his successful handling of a wider gamut of historical themes in *Ireland since the Famine* (1971) where, though confessing to feeling something like an "ancient Israelite condemned to make bricks without straw," he managed to transcend both the textbook format and the lack of research on many topics to produce a major piece of total history, which is still a standard work. First came his acceptance of the sadly unfulfilled Yeats commission, then his Ford lectures at Oxford, *Culture and Anarchy in Ireland, 1890–1939* (1979), which opened up debate on the cultural and social history of the period in the way that his earliest work had done for high politics a generation earlier. A private comment made during the final year of his life, that biography was "the last refuge of a disillusioned historian," was probably no more than modest self-deprecation on the part of the author of two acclaimed biographies who was in process of embarking on a third. The remark did, however, accord with his continued preoccupation with epistolary sources and with questions of personality and relationships in public life, as well as reflecting that recurring sense of fatalism that must have struck a chord with him in the personality of John Dillon.

Lyons' main achievement was to rescue Dillon's reputation as the leading figure in constitutional nationalism after Parnell. Dillon published nothing himself: he was cast as villain of the piece in the recriminatory and voluminous memoirs of his rivals William O'Brien and Tim Healy; while Denis Gwynn's 1932 study of John Redmond, though solidly researched, is uncritical in praise of its subject. In Lyons' accounts Dillon is the lynchpin of the movement, first seeing more clearly than Parnell the future direction for party strategy, and later making his Dublin home the real interface between the Irish grassroots and Westminster politics. Redmond by contrast is seen as more of a figurehead, Healy a vituperative spoiler, and O'Brien as increasingly raving and demented. This view still holds the field, although two impressive books by Paul Bew have presented subtle and rather different slants both on Parnell and on the roles of Redmond and O'Brien, while also providing insights into the connections between nationalist politics and rural society at a more intimate level than Lyons in his time could have hoped to achieve. But Lyons' work continues to set the terms for debate in many areas, not only in the study of the parliamentary party, but also through the general text which still competes with Roy Foster's excellent study, and in his late work on the clash of cultures.

A.C. HEPBURN

See also Ireland

Biography

Francis Stewart Leland Lyons. Born Londonderry, Northern Ireland, 11 November 1923, but spent most of his childhood in the Irish Republic, in County Roscommon and in Dublin. Educated at Dover College; in England; and at Trinity College, University of Dublin, BA in modern history and political science, 1945, PhD 1948. Taught at University of Hull, 1947–51; fellow, Trinity College, Dublin, 1951–64; rose to professor, University of Kent at Canterbury, 1964–74; returned to Trinity College, Dublin: provost [i.e., president], 1974–81: professor, 1981–83. Married Jennifer Ann McAlister, 1954 (2 sons). Died Dublin, 21 September 1983.

Principal Writings

The Irish Parliamentary Party, 1890–1910, 1951
The Fall of Parnell, 1890–91, 1960
Internationalism in Europe, 1815–1914, 1963
John Dillon: A Biography, 1968
Ireland since the Famine, 1971; revised 1973
Charles Stewart Parnell, 1977
The Burden of Our History, 1979
Culture and Anarchy in Ireland, 1890–1939, 1979
Editor with R.A.J. Hawkins, *Ireland under the Union: Varieties of Tension: Essays in Honour of T.W. Moody*, 1980
Editor, *The Bank of Ireland, 1783–1983: Bicentenary Essays*, 1983

Further Reading

Bew, Paul, *C.S. Parnell*, Dublin: Gill and Macmillan, 1980
Bew, Paul, *Conflict and Conciliation in Ireland, 1890–1910*, Oxford and New York: Oxford University Press, 1987
Boyce, David George, and Alan O'Day, eds., *The Making of Modern Irish History: Revisionism and the Revisionist Controversy*, London and New York: Routledge, 1996
Brady, Ciaran, ed., *Interpreting Irish History: The Debate on Historical Revisionism, 1938–1994*, Dublin: Irish Academic Press, 1994
Foster, Roy, "Francis Stewart Leland Lyons, 1923–1983," *Proceedings of the British Academy* 70 (1985), 463–79
Foster, Roy, *Modern Ireland, 1600–1972*, London: Allen Lane, and New York: Penguin, 1988
O'Day, Alan, "F.S.L. Lyons: Historian of Modern Ireland," in Walter L. Arnstein, ed., *Recent Historians of Great Britain: Essays on the post-1945 Generation*, Ames: Iowa State University Press, 1990